2007 ESPN
SPORTS ALMANAC

With Exclusive Year in Review Commentary from ESPN Anchors and Analysts, Writers from ESPN The Magazine and ESPN.com

Chris Berman

Stuart Scott

Dan Patrick

10TH
ANNIVERSARY
EDITION
★ ★ ★

Dick Vitale

Scott Van Pelt

Lee Corso   **Chris Fowler**   Rey Wingo

ALSO CONTRIBUT

The Champions of 2006

Auto Racing
For all the statistics, see the Auto Racing section.

NASCAR Circuit
Daytona 500 . . . . .Jimmie Johnson
Coca-Cola 600 . . . . Kasey Kahne
Allstate 400 at the Brickyard . . . . .Jimmie Johnson
UAW-Ford 500. . . . . .Brian Vickers
Nextel Cup Points Leader . . . . . . Matt Kenseth, 6008 pts
. . . . (through Oct. 29)

Champ Car World Series Circuit
Points Championship . . . . . . Sebastien Bourdais, 353 pts
. . . . (through Oct. 29)

Indy Racing League Circuit
Indianapolis 500 . . . . Sam Hornish Jr.
IndyCar Championship. . . . . . . Sam Hornish Jr., 475 pts

Formula One Circuit
U.S. Grand Prix. . . . . Michael Schumacher
World Driving Champion . . . . Fernando Alonso, 134 pts

Baseball
For all the statistics, see the Baseball section.

World Series . . . . . . St. Louis def. Detroit, 4 games to 1
MVP . . . . David Eckstein, St. Louis, SS
ALCS . . . . Detroit def. Oakland, 4 games to 0
NLCS . . . . St. Louis def. N.Y. Mets, 4 games to 2
All-Star Game . . American League 3, National League 2
MVP . . . . Michael Young, AL (Texas), 2B
Coll. World Series. Oregon St. def. UNC, 2 games to 1
MVP . . . . Jonah Nickerson, Oregon St., P

College Basketball
For all the statistics, see the College Basketball section.

Men's NCAA Tournament
Championship . . . . Florida 73, UCLA 57
MVP . . . . .Joakim Noah, Florida, C

Women's NCAA Tournament
Championship . . . . Maryland 78, Duke 75 OT
MVP . . . . Laura Harper, Maryland, F

Pro Basketball
For all the statistics, see the Pro Basketball section.

NBA Finals . . . . Miami def. Dallas, 4 games to 2
MVP . . . . Dwyane Wade, Miami, G
Eastern Final . . . . Miami def. Detroit, 4 games to 2
Western Final . . . . . Dallas def. Phoenix, 4 games to 2
All-Star Game . . . . East 122, West 120
MVP . . . . LeBron James, East (Cleveland), F
Regular Season MVP . . . . Steve Nash, Phoenix, G
FIBA World Championships . . . . Spain 70, Greece 47

College Football (2005)
For all the statistics, see the College Football section.

National Champions
AP . . . . Texas (13-0)
USA Today Coaches' . . . . Texas (13-0)
Major Bowls
Rose . . . . Texas 41, USC 38
Orange . . . . Penn St. 26, Florida St. 23 3OT
Fiesta . . . . Ohio St. 34, Notre Dame 20
Sugar. . . . . West Virginia 38, Georgia 35
Heisman Trophy. . . . . Reggie Bush, USC, RB

Pro Football (2005)
For all the statistics, see the Pro Football section.

Super Bowl XL . . . . Pittsburgh 21, Seattle 10
MVP . . . . Hines Ward, Pittsburgh, WR
AFC Championship . . . . Pittsburgh 34, Denver 17
NFC Championship . . . . Seattle 34, Carolina 14
Pro Bowl . . . . NFC 23, AFC 17
MVP . . . . Derrick Brooks, Tampa Bay, LB
CFL Grey Cup Final . . . . Edmonton 38, Montreal 35
MVP . . . . Ricky Ray, Edmonton, QB

Golf
For all the statistics, see the Golf section.

Men's Major Championships
Masters . . . . Phil Mickelson
U.S. Open . . . . Geoff Ogilvy
British Open . . . . Tiger Woods
PGA Championship. . . . . Tiger Woods

Champions (Seniors) Major Championships
The Tradition . . . . Eduardo Romero
Senior PGA Championship . . . . Jay Haas
U.S. Senior Open . . . . Allen Doyle
Senior Players Championship . . . . Bobby Wadkins
Senior British Open . . . . Loren Roberts

Women's Major Championships
Kraft Nabisco Championship . . . . Karrie Webb
LPGA Championship . . . . Se Ri Pak
U.S. Women's Open . . . . Annika Sorenstam
Women's British Open. . . . . Sherri Steinhauer

National Team Competition
Ryder Cup. . . . . Europe 18½, United States 9½

Hockey
For all the statistics, see the Hockey section.

Stanley Cup. . . . . Carolina def. Edmonton, 4 games to 3
MVP. . . . . Cam Ward, Carolina, G
Eastern Final . . . . . . Carolina def. Buffalo, 4 games to 3
Western Final . . . Edmonton def. Anaheim, 4 games to 1
All-Star Game . . . . not held
MVP . . . . not awarded
Winter Olympics Gold Medal . . Sweden 3, Finland 2

Horse Racing
For all the statistics, see the Horse Racing section.

Triple Crown Champions
Kentucky Derby . . . . Barbaro (Edgar Prado)
Preakness Stakes . . . . Bernardini (Javier Castellano)
Belmont Stakes . . . . Jazil (Fernando Jara)

Harness Racing
Hambletonian . . . . Glidemaster (John Campbell)
Little Brown Jug . . . . . . Mr. Feelgood (Mark MacDonald)

Soccer
For all the statistics, see the Soccer section.

FIFA World Cup 2006 . . . . Italy 1, France 1
. . . . Italy won shootout, 5-3
FIFA Club Championship 2005 . .Sao Paulo 1, Liverpool 0
MLS Cup 2005. . . . . L.A. Galaxy 1, New England 0
MVP . . . . Guillermo Ramirez, Los Angeles, F

Tennis
For all the statistics, see the Tennis section.

Men's Grand Slam Championships
Australian Open . . . . Roger Federer
French Open . . . . Rafael Nadal
Wimbledon . . . . Roger Federer
U.S. Open . . . . Roger Federer

Women's Grand Slam Championships
Australian Open . . . . Amelie Mauresmo
French Open . . . . Justine Henin-Hardenne
Wimbledon. . . . . Amelie Mauresmo
U.S. Open . . . . : . . . . Maria Sharapova

Miscellaneous Champions
For more, see the Miscellaneous & Int'l Sports sections.

PBA Bowler of the Year . . . . Tommy Jones
Little League World Series . . . . Columbus, Ga.
Tour de France . . . . Floyd Landis (USA)
Iditarod . . . . Jeff King
World Series of Poker . . . . Jamie Gold
Boston Marathon . . . . Robert Cheruiyot (Kenya)
Bassmasters Classic . . . . Luke Clausen
Ironman Triathlon . . . . Normann Stadler (Men)
Michellie Jones (Women)

2007
ESPN®
SPORTS
ALMANAC

Gerry Brown
Michael Morrison
EDITORS

ESPN®
BOOKS

Editors

Gerry Brown

Michael Morrison

Contributing Writers

Pat Forde	Chris Broussard
Jerry Crasnick	E.J. Hradek
Mike Hall	Gene Wojciechowski
Dan Rafael	Eric Adelson
Jeff Bradley	Mary Fenton
Russell Baxter	Mark Ashenfelter

Copyright © 2006 by Sports Almanac, Inc.

All rights reserved worldwide. No part of this book may be used or reproduced in any manner whatsoever without prior written permission. For information about permission to reproduce selections from this book in print form address: ESPN Books, 19 East 34th St., New York, New York 10016.

Printed in the United States of America.

Comments and suggestions from readers are invited. Because of the many letters received, however, it is not possible to respond personally to every correspondent. Nevertheless, all letters are welcome and each will be carefully considered. The **ESPN Sports Almanac** does not rule on bets or wagers. Address all correspondence to: Sports Almanac, Inc., P.O. Box 542281, Lake Worth, FL 33454-2281. Email: info@espnalmanac.com.

ISBN13: 978-1-933060-16-3

ISBN: 1-933060-16-6

FIRST EDITION

10 9 8 7 6 5 4 3 2 1

CONTENTS 5

CONTENTS

EDITORS' NOTE

10TH
ANNIVERSARY
EDITION
★ ★ ★

A LOT CAN HAPPEN IN 10 YEARS.

Just a decade ago there was no such thing as an iPod. The Internet was a curiosity for most of us and the ESPN Sports Almanac was in its rookie year. Tiger Woods had yet to win a major. Roger Maris was the single-season home run champ. There was no BCS. Michael Jordan still owned the NBA (he still might, see the SportsNation poll on page 22).

The NHL still mattered. NASCAR didn't.

Barry Bonds had 374 career homers. The Arizona Diamondbacks and Tampa Bay Devil Rays didn't exist. Roger Federer and the Williams sisters had yet to win a Grand Slam event.

Nowadays the Almanac is a seasoned veteran with a track record and tales to tell. With all the great moments and broken records, we've added a ton of stats, records and results to these pages over the past 10 years. In fact it was getting so jam-packed with information that we had a tough decision to make: either shrink the type size even further and include a free magnifying glass with every book or add a bunch of pages to hold the overflow. We went with the latter. Your eyes will thank us.

We'd never be able to do this expanded 10th anniversary edition of the Almanac without the assistance and support of the following folks...

ESPN director of research Craig Winston was an invaluable resource in more ways than we can count. Craig's team, including Anna Clemmons, Simon Brennan, Mary Fenton, Adesina Koiki, Gueorgui Milkov and Michael Woods, is a true all-star lineup.

Chris Raymond, our main man at ESPN Books, continues to believe and we thank him for that. Big thanks also to production manager John Glenn and designer Henry Lee.

Former editor John Hassan is embedded in Bristol and is quicker than Steve Nash with an assist. Thanks also to Russell Baxter, Mark Ashenfelter and John Broder for scaring up some key information right when we needed it. Also we owe a debt to Jim Loftus at Scouts, Inc., and Andy and John Buchanan at Wise Guides, and Daniel Dodd at SportsNation.

Thank you as well to Elvis Brathwaite at AP/Wide World, Barbara Zidovsky at Nielsen Media Research, Rick Sommers at Command Web and Rob Conte at SCI for answering all the calls and emails.

Editor emeritus Mike Meserole continues to care and his influence is still felt throughout the book.

Thanks also to our wives, Lisa and Lori for taking the kids all those nights and weekends during deadline season. We owe you dinner and a movie, times infinity.

Finally, God bless you Nelson de la Rosa, wherever you are.

Gerry Brown
Michael Morrison

October 28, 2006

Major League Cities & Teams

As of Oct. 30, 2006, there were 134 major league teams playing or scheduled to play baseball, men's basketball, NFL football, hockey and soccer in 53 cities in the United States and Canada. Listed below are the cities and the teams that play there.

Anaheim
AL   Los Angeles Angels of Anaheim
NHL   Ducks

Atlanta
NL   Braves   NFL   Falcons
NBA   Hawks   NHL   Thrashers

Baltimore
AL   Orioles   NFL   Ravens

Boston
AL   Red Sox
NBA   Celtics
NFL   N.E. Patriots (Foxboro)
NHL   Bruins
MLS   N.E. Revolution (Foxboro)

Buffalo
NFL   Bills (Orchard Park)
NHL   Sabres

Calgary
NHL   Flames

Charlotte
NBA   Bobcats
NFL   Carolina Panthers

Chicago
AL   White Sox
NL   Cubs
NBA   Bulls
NFL   Bears
NHL   Blackhawks
MLS   Fire

Cincinnati
NL   Reds   NFL   Bengals

Cleveland
AL   Indians   NBA   Cavaliers
NFL   Browns

Columbus
NHL   Blue Jackets
MLS   Crew

Dallas
AL   Texas Rangers (Arlington)
NBA   Mavericks
NFL   Cowboys (Irving)
NHL   Stars
MLS   FC Dallas

Denver
NL   Colorado Rockies
NBA   Nuggets
NFL   Broncos
NHL   Colorado Avalanche
MLS   Colorado Rapids

Detroit
AL   Tigers
NBA   Pistons (Auburn Hills)
NFL   Lions
NHL   Red Wings

East Rutherford
NBA   New Jersey Nets
NFL   New York Giants
NFL   New York Jets
NHL   New Jersey Devils
MLS   Red Bull New York

Edmonton
NHL   Oilers

Green Bay
NFL   Packers

Houston
NL   Astros
NBA   Rockets
NFL   Texans
MLS   Dynamo

Indianapolis
NBA   Indiana Pacers
NFL   Colts

Jacksonville
NFL   Jaguars

Kansas City
AL   Royals
NFL   Chiefs
MLS   Wizards

Los Angeles
NL   Dodgers
NBA   Clippers
NBA   Lakers
NHL   Kings
MLS   Galaxy (Carson)
MLS   Club Chivas USA (Carson)

Memphis
NBA   Grizzlies

Miami
NL   Florida Marlins
NBA   Heat
NFL   Dolphins
NHL   Florida Panthers (Sunrise)

Milwaukee
NL   Brewers
NBA   Bucks

Minneapolis
AL   Minnesota Twins
NBA   Minnesota Timberwolves
NFL   Minnesota Vikings

Montreal
NHL   Canadiens

Nashville
NFL   Tennessee Titans
NHL   Predators

New Orleans
NBA   New Orleans Hornets
NFL   New Orleans Saints

New York
AL   Yankees
NL   Mets (Flushing)
NBA   Knicks
NHL   Rangers
NHL   Islanders (Uniondale)

Oakland
AL   Athletics
NBA   Golden St. Warriors
NFL   Raiders

Oklahoma City
NBA   New Orleans Hornets

Orlando
NBA   Magic

Ottawa
NHL   Senators (Kanata)

Philadelphia
NL   Phillies
NBA   76ers
NFL   Eagles
NHL   Flyers

Phoenix
NL   Arizona Diamondbacks
NBA   Suns
NFL   Arizona Cardinals (Glendale)
NHL   Coyotes (Glendale)

Pittsburgh
NL   Pirates
NFL   Steelers
NHL   Penguins

Portland
NBA   Trail Blazers

Raleigh
NHL   Carolina Hurricanes

Sacramento
NBA   Kings

St. Louis
NL   Cardinals
NFL   Rams
NHL   Blues

St. Paul
NHL   Minnesota Wild

Salt Lake City
NBA   Utah Jazz
MLS   Real Salt Lake

San Antonio
NBA   Spurs
NFL   New Orleans Saints

San Diego
NL   Padres
NFL   Chargers

San Francisco
NL   Giants
NFL   49ers

San Jose
NHL   Sharks

Seattle
AL   Mariners
NBA   SuperSonics
NFL   Seahawks

Tampa
AL   T.B. Devil Rays (St. Petersburg)
NFL   T.B. Buccaneers
NHL   T.B. Lightning

Toronto
AL   Blue Jays
NBA   Raptors
NHL   Maple Leafs
MLS   Toronto FC (2007)

Vancouver
NHL   Canucks

Washington
NL   Nationals
NBA   Wizards
NFL   Redskins (Raljon, Md.)
NHL   Capitals
MLS   D.C. United

YEAR IN REVIEW

2005 / 2006

Swiss tennis star **Roger Federer,** who won three Grand Slam events, had plenty to celebrate in 2006.

THE YEAR IN REVIEW

We sat down with ESPN Radio's Mike Golic & Mike Greenberg to get their takes on the biggest stories and most memorable moments of the year in sports.

Almanac: It was another year filled with plenty of memorable stories. Let's go over the biggest ones rapid fire style...

VINCE YOUNG AND TEXAS WIN THRILLING ROSE BOWL

Almanac: Texas ended USC's win streak and won their first national championship since 1970 in one of the most exciting games in the 100-plus years of the Rose Bowl, thanks in most part to the amazing performance of their junior quarterback...

Greenie: "Vince Young had the greatest individual performance in a championship game in football history."

Golic: "I agree. And in football, one of the more team-concept sports there is, it was one of the best individual efforts I have ever seen."

Greenie: "It doesn't necessarily mean it will translate to the NFL, but for one game—college football basis—it was the best I ever saw."

STEELERS WIN SUPER BOWL

Almanac: Pittsburgh, a wil card team, makes history and win three playoff games on the roac including a huge upset over Peyto and the Colts at Indianapolis, the wins Super Bowl XL over Seattle...

Golic: "Just an incredible ru through the playoffs. They said couldn't be done on the road a much as it was. And what an incred ible defense! I was impressed wit that side of the ball most."

Greenie: "That said, the Supe Bowl itself was marred by horrer dous officiating that isn't the Steeler fault, but the officials took that gam away from Seattle."

Mike Golic & Mike Greenberg can be heard weekday mornings from 6 A.M. to 10 A.M. ET on ESPN Radio's *Mike & Mike in the Morning*.

➤ Longtime Steelers running back **Jerome Bettis** retired as a champion in 2006. Super Bowl MVP **Hines Ward** apparently likes really big foam rubber hats.

LINDSEY JACOBELLIS HOT-DOGS HER WAY OUT OF A CERTAIN GOLD MEDAL AT TURIN

Almanac: American snowboarder Lindsey Jacobellis seemed to have the gold medal sewn up but a bit of showboating backfired when she fell down just before the finish line when trying to land a trick...

Golic: "It's amazing how instead of owning up to the fact of what really happened, she made excuses to justify it. She had a chance at the gold medal and she blew it. That's the bottom line."

Greenie: "It was especially bad because they created these events in the Olympics just so we could get some gold medals. So she really didn't follow the script."

SHAUN WHITE TAKES X GAMES TO TURIN AND WINS GOLD IN HALFPIPE

Almanac: Teenage X Gamer and Gen Y pitchman Shaun White fulfilled his mandate and won the gold medal in Halfpipe at Turin...

Mike & MIKE
in the morning

Bode Miller couldn't bear to watch his results at the 2006 Winter Olympics in Turin, Italy.

BODE MILLER FLAME OUT

Almanac: Skier Bode Miller, who made comment on 60 Minutes about skiing drunk, seemed to be every where before the Winte Olympics and then, during the Games in Turin, he barely showed up and he failed to win a single medal of any type after some expected him to have a great chance at multi ple gold medals...

Golic: "He's an embarrass ment and I'm not talking abou what he did on the slopes. You can have bad days in any sport, but the way that he car ries himself was embarrass ing."

Greenie: "The notion tha anyone would in anyway give the impression that drinking and skiing is an acceptable thing to do when it is ridicu lously dangerous. Forget the people around you, it is so irresponsible That I don't even have words to describe it."

GEORGE MASON'S FINAL FOUR MIRACLE

Almanac: The 11th-seeded George Mason Patriots, out of the mid-major Colonial Athletic Assoc iation, knocks off some of college basketball's giants and makes a memorable run to the 2006 Fina Four...

Golic: "Again events created for America to do well, but I like the kid. He was personable, I'm not sure how well he is doing market ing, but I hope he does well for him self. He looked like a kid who likes to have fun."

Greenie: "I don't know that there is a better nickname in all of sports than 'The Flying Tomato'."

Greenie: "The best! That's what makes that tournament so great. That was Cinderella and the slipper fitting. That was probably my favorite story of the year."

Golic: "That's March Madness! That's what it's all about and why we do what we do."

JOAKIM NOAH AND FLORIDA WIN NATIONAL CHAMPIONSHIP

Almanac: *Billy Donovan's Gators win their first basketball national championship behind Tournament MVP Joakim Noah's outstanding play...*

Greenie: "The football school wins the basketball national championship. Right now there is no greater 1-2 punch in college sports as far as the two big programs than at Florida. That's the number one school for the football/basketball combo."

Golic: "They were a great story, because everyone thought it was going to be UConn and then they get dumped by Mason. Then Florida became a fun team to follow. And Greenie is right, football and basketball wise they sure are a heck of a 1-2 punch."

Greenie: "Golic just doesn't want to give any credit to Urban Meyer. That's why he almost overlooked my comments."

AP/Wide World Photos

George Mason made the slipper fit in 2006 and was the biggest Cinderella of the year.

BARBARO INJURED IN PREAKNESS

Almanac: *Triple Crown threat Barbaro dominated at the Kentucky Derby and was a heavy favorite at the Preakness Stakes before breaking down early in the race...*

Greenie: "This was horrible! That horse was going to win the Triple Crown. I'm not an expert, but that horse was going to win the Triple Crown and this was really tough to watch."

It's good to be **Shaun White**. The young snowboarder won gold medals at the Winter Olympics and Winter X Games in 2006. Now close your mouth Shaun.

AP/Wide World Photos

Golic: "It *was* tough to watch, but you could just see it in the horse and to see it end that way really was a shame."

NHL BACK IN BUSINESS

Almanac: After a year's hiatus the National Hockey League finally settled its labor dispute with the players and returned to action with a slew of rules changes designed to improve the offensive flow of the game...

Greenie: "When did that happen?"

Golic: "Yeah, listen I love hockey and I always have, but it's certainly a better sport to watch live than to see on TV or talk about much. I'm glad its back, I'm glad to see that both sides agreed there was a problem and tried to fix it. Attendance went up; scoring went up, not to say that scoring going up is going to help every sport. However hockey needed its stars to be a little freer in this game and they are now."

Greenie: "Unfortunately no one in America has any idea who any of them are."

FLOYD LANDIS HAS MIRACLE COMEBACK AT TOUR DE FRANCE THEN FAILS DRUG TEST

Almanac: *American cyclist Floyd Landis picked up where the retired Lance Armstrong left off and won the Tour de France with an amazing comeback in the Alps. It was later announced that he flunked a drug test. His appeals are still pending...*

Golic: "To be determined. I don't know what to think of this. He is so vehemently denying this and saying something went wrong. Though our process of innocent until proven guilty is so out of wack now. These tests coming back positive say he's guilty. I don't know what to say about that one."

Greenie: "I throw up my hands at this point on the whole drug thing. I'm beginning to lose hope. I'm beginning to think there is nothing we can do."

Golic: "If people want to cheat they are going to cheat. Simply put, they are going to find a way."

Greenie: "I'm starting to question whether we'll ever be able to believe that anything is fully real in any sport."

AP/Wide World Photos

American **Floyd Landis** was the toast of Paris after his amazing comeback at the Tour de France but was grilled by charges of drug use after a positive test.

taken off and has put himself in another class in the eyes of the rest of the NBA."

Greenie: "It was a throw-back to the days that I consider the golden era of the NBA. To see Pat Riley back at the top of the mountain with his hair still slicked back and holding the trophy. I enjoyed watching that."

DUKE LACROSSE SCANDAL

Almanac: *Scandal struck one of the schools you'd least expect when rape allegations surfaced surrounding a party held by some members of the Duke University Lacrosse Team...*

Greenie: "To be determined. My suspicion is there are multiple twists and turns left to that story."

Dwyane Wade rose to a whole new level in 2006 and took Miami to the NBA title.

DWYANE WADE, SHAQ AND RILES BRING A TITLE TO MIAMI

Almanac: *Dwyane Wade seemed to take it to another level this season, Shaquille O'Neal got a ring without Kobe and Pat Riley stepped from the front office and back to the sidelines to get his fifth title...*

Golic: "It was great to watch and there was that whole Shaq vs. Kobe thing as to who would get one by themselves first. Dwyane Wade has

Golic: "If and when the case goes to trial it's again going to be splashed across the front of the newspaper. It's all behind the scenes right now. Who knows if it will ever get to court? But I think it was ridiculous that they cancelled the season. I thought it was completely wrong and one of the worst things they did, punishing the other guys for that."

Greenie: "I disagree with that completely. If they had taken scholarships away I would have been against that. They didn't deprive anyone of anything except the ability to play lacrosse. Which is not a right, it's a privilege."

KOBE BRYANT'S 81-POINT NIGHT

Almanac: *Kobe Bryant didn't win a title without Shaq but he did have a huge game against Toronto, scoring 81 points, the second most in NBA history and the most since Wilt Chamberlain's 100-point night in 1962...*

Greenie: "It's a team sport at the end of the day. But that's a great individual performance."

Golic: "I guess if you want to focus on one person getting all the points. 'Eh ya know."

ZINEDINE ZIDANE'S HEAD BUTT IN WORLD CUP FINAL

Almanac: *French soccer legend Zinedine Zidane lost his head in the World Cup Final when he used his head to attack an Italian opponent in response to a verbal taunt. He was ejected and his team went on to lose the game in a shootout...*

Golic: "Absolutely ridiculous! To give the excuses that he gave is just a joke. There is no excuse for him doing that at all in that situation. He's been playing the game long enough. To be baited out on the field is ridiculous."

Greenie: "People say nastier

France's **Zinedine Zidane** was sent off at the World Cup Final for headbutting.

AP/Wide World Photos

things than that to me everyday and I've never head-butted anyone in my life."

ANOTHER LOSS FOR THE USA IN THE RYDER CUP

Almanac: *The United States lost to Europe once again in the Ryder Cup. After years and years of dominating the competition the U.S. has now lost five of the last six tournaments despite having most of the world's best players...*

Golic: "I wonder what we we're

the best at in the world in sports. The list keeps shrinking at what we are the best at."

Greenie: "Making money. We're the best at making money of any country in sports. There is no country where sports are as big of an industry as it is here."

ANDRE AGASSI'S RETIREMENT

Almanac: Tennis legend Andre Agassi hung up his racquet after a long successful career in which he became only one of five men in history to win the career Grand Slam...

Greenie: "One of the greats. His image sometimes overshadowed what a great player he was. You could make an argument that historically he's a better player than Sampras, because he won on all surfaces. It's like winning the British Open and the Masters."

Golic: "I loved his transformation from the rebel to what we saw at the end. Most people go through that, but he went though it in the public eye. He wasn't afraid to admit 'I don't dig the person that much with the long hair and everything.' I like Andre's transformation."

Golic   **Greenie**

FEDERER HAS ANOTHER AMAZING YEAR

Almanac: The world's top-ranked tennis player Roger Federer of Switzerland continues to crush the competition, winning three more Grand Slam events in 2006...

Golic: "We talk about this all the time. Who is the most dominant in all of professional sports, Roger or Tiger Woods? Until someone beats this guy, he belongs in the mix with Tiger as far as domination."

Greenie: "I've been a tennis fan all my life and Roger Federer the past three years has been the best player I've ever seen."

TIGER DOMINATES

Almanac: Tiger Woods won two more majors in 2006 at the British Open and PGA Championship despite the loss of his father, his first coach and biggest influence, Woods continues to be the best player in the world, by far...

Greenberg: "When it's all said and done, there will be no discussion of the greatest athletes of all time that does not include his name."

Golic: "The most clutch and focused player in all of sports at this time, his domination usually leads to other players changing their games to try and catch him."

YANKEES POST SEASON FAILURE

Almanac: *Despite their record payroll and intimidating lineup, the New York Yankees failed again to win the World Series...*

Greenie: "I guess $200 million doesn't buy you what it use to."

Golic: "Are you in it to draw 4 million fans or to win a World Series? It goes to show you that if you get a bunch of superstars and put them together it doesn't guarantee you a thing."

DETROIT TIGERS TURN IT AROUND UNDER JIM LEYLAND

Almanac: *The Tigers have been league also-rans since the mid 1980s but hired veteran manager Jim Leyland and shot to the top of the standings...*

Greenie: "Jim Leyland does the greatest managerial job in recent baseball memory."

Golic: "We haven't seen anything like this since last year with the White Sox. Great story and young players who have played consistently throughout the year."

NIKOLAI VALUEV BECOMES THE BIGGEST HEAVYWEIGHT CHAMP EVER

Russia's **Nikolai Valuev** is the biggest man in history to win a heavyweight title.

Almanac: *Russian giant Nikolai Valuev, nicknamed "the Beast from the East" beats John Ruiz and at 7-feet-tall and well over 300 pounds, becomes the largest heavyweight champion in history...*

Golic: "It puts a new meaning to the word *heavyweight*. You see smaller guys fighting and this guy truly is a giant. Boxing is just awful now. You don't have the freak show in Tyson anymore; Holyfield is trying to make a comeback. So now this is the next ring in the three-ring circus."

Greenie: "It's going to take Rocky to kick his ass."

Overheard in Bristol...

Original takes from ESPN's best and brightest on some of the year's biggest stories

"This year won't be looked at in the same awe as the 2000 season was for **Tiger Woods**, but perhaps it should be. History just might tell us when it's all said and done that this was the year we realized just how much better Tiger is than not only every golfer currently playing, but everyone who has ever tried to take a crooked stick and put a dimpled ball in a hole 18 times.

The year started slowly with Tiger taking some early events, then pushing too hard to win one final major for his dying father at Augusta in the Masters. The subsequent nine-week layoff after that, including his father's death, finally brought Tiger back at the U.S. Open, where he missed the cut in a major for the first time in his professsional career. How did Tiger respond? Well a second place finish at the Western Open, was followed up by a six tournament winning streak, including the year's final two majors, and two more World Golf Championships. And while the wins weren't blowouts like his 15-stroke victory at the 2000 U.S. Open, they were masterful nonetheless.

A win at the British where he used his driver exactly once, out thinking the field in a surgical win at Hoylake, a win at the PGA where he putted brilliantly and sucked the life out of playing partner Luke Donald, a win at Firestone where his approach in a driving rain storm ended Stewart Cink's chance at stopping him in a playoff, a win at the Deutsche Bank where he made up a final round three-stroke deficit in the first seven holes to Vijay Singh, and a win at the American Express Championships in London where he eagled the 18th hole three straight days. These things only happen in comic books!

So now with 12 majors on his resume, the chase to 18 is officially underway, the record currently held by Jack Nicklaus. And lest we think someone out there will stop him, chew on this for a while: in the last two years, he's won four majors. That's more than any other active golfer has won *in their entire career*. The man to challenge Tiger Woods, isn't even playing on a regular basis yet."

—Trey Wingo

"First of all, he doesn't even look real. He looks more like a 1980s cartoonist's version of what some menacing giant Russian should look like. I always thought Ivan Drago was too plastic...all clean cut, handsome...no body hair...fake, really.

Nikolai Valuev is the realistic version of what a make-believe Russian bad guy would look like: elongated face, rigid eyebrows that jut out over cold looking eyes.

I can hear them in central casting now 'Let's make him 6-8, 290 pounds—but wait—if we're really gonna scare the kids with this behemoth of a man, lets just make it so overboard...make him seven feet tall...325 pounds....make him Shaq with boxing gloves. Then, cover his arms and back with hair. Lots of hair. Make him seem like he's 20 years overdue for his back/arm/face waxing. And make him undefeated, 45-0 with 33 knockouts.'

In the ring he paws at opponents. That is, until he actually hits one of them. When a giant fist from a giant man comes screaming *down* at you from an absurd angle, it hurts. Make him heavyweight champion (at least, one of four). Then try and figure out, what American hero can beat him. Keep thinking because at the end of 2006 the only possibility never actually existed. Still, if Rocky Balboa can make a comeback in theatres around Christmas, perhaps our best bet is that the fictional Balboa can knock out the fictional giant again. Hold up, there's only one small problem. Nikolai Valuev is real. Hair and all."

–Stuart Scott

"The **George Mason** run was one of the more amazing things I've seen since I have been at ESPN.

This just doesn't happen. You don't beat Michigan State and Tom Izzo, North Carolina and Roy Williams and Connecticut and Jim Calhoun if you are Colonial Athletic Association champs...but Mason did.

The UConn game seemed the ultimate in impossible dreams. When Denham Brown's reverse layup at the buzzer bounced forever before dropping for the Huskies you just assumed overtime would favor the better team.

I guess it did.

The newsroom was electric as the three-pointer, again from Denham Brown, that would've won it for the #1 seed was in the air. Given what they had done the previous Friday night against Washington, I was sure it would drop. When it didn't, you had to enjoy the moment for Jim Laranaga and Jai Lewis and every other coach and player who dreamed the dream that they were living.

–Scott Van Pelt

"The television ratings were down for the World Series. But is anybody surprised? I'm not. Still, there were plenty of storylines: Kenny Rogers, the fact that the **St. Louis Cardinals** could be one of the most unsung teams in baseball history to win the World Series, the whole resurgence and rebirth of baseball in Detroit, all the young arms, Jim Leyland as a reclamation project, is Tony La Russa a genius or not?, Albert Pujols. To me it's intruging but I'm not shocked that nobody else was watching this year outside of St. Louis and Detriot.

I think there was sloppy play and the weather was a factor but give the Cardinals credit. They did what nobody thought—or very few of us thought—they could do. It's a good story.

I just think these two teams lacked a little pizzazz for the average viewer."

–Dan Patrick

ESPN STi
sportsnation

As part of the 10th Anniversary of the ESPN Sports Almanac, SportsNation asked you to rank the top athletes of the past decade.

And here is how you voted...

1 Michael Jordan.
2 Tiger Woods.
3 Lance Armstrong
4 Shaquille O'Neal
5 Pete Sampras
6 Tom Brady
7 Kobe Bryant
8 Andre Agassi
9 Barry Bonds
10 Mia Hamm
11 Roy Jones Jr.
12 Tony Hawk
13 David Beckham
14 Dale Earnhardt
15 Serena Williams

AP/Wide World Photos

Michael Jordan topped the list.

EXTRA POINTS

2005 / 2006 YEAR IN REVIEW

Six-foot-eight, 13-year-old Aaron Durley towered over the competition at the Little League World Series.

EXTRA POINTS

A look back at some of the more offbeat sports moments, quotes and personalities from the past year.

Just Drop It!

This year's edition of Extra Points features...well...an actual extra point. With 6:10 remaining in the fourth quarter of the Patriots' fairly meaningless final regular-season game against the Dolphins, 43-year-old Doug Flutie came onto the field for what seemed to be a two-point conversion attempt. Instead he took the snap, let the ball hit the grass and booted it straight through the uprights. The last successful NFL dropkick occurred on Dec. 21, 1941 – two weeks after the bombing of Pearl Harbor.

"Flutie might have been there the last time it happened," placekicker Adam Vinatieri joked.

Is there anything this man can't do? We're still a little jealous (and maybe a little annoyed) that he's been to four Major League Baseball games and has caught four foul balls. And speaking of strange foul ball coincidences...

Love Hurts

On September 23, Orioles outfielder Jay Gibbons fouled a ball that went straight back over the screen at Camden Yards...and right into the rib cage of his wife, Laura. She was a little bruised, but otherwise unhurt. Attendance for the game was only 21,980, but the odds were still pretty slim.

Stay 'Tooned

On February 10, 2006, NBC acquired the rights to announcer Al Michaels from ABC/ESPN for its new Sunday Night Football team. In return, ESPN received the rights to (among other things) Ryder Cup matches, expanded Olympic highlights...and Oswald the Lucky Rabbit. Apparently Walt Disney produced 26 Oswald cartoons in 1927, but then lost rights to Universal. Now after 80 years, Oswald is back where he belongs. "Having Oswald around again is going to be a lot of fun," said Walt Disney's daughter Diane Disney Miller.

American **Joey Chestnut** (52 dogs) gave it a valiant effort, but in the end couldn't unseat the masterful **Kobayashi** ($53\frac{3}{4}$) at the annual Nathan's Famous Hot Dog Eating Contest on July 4 at Coney Island.

AP/Wide World Photos

Daytona 500..the Cologne?

Go ahead and make your jokes about the Daytona 500's new fragrance smelling like exhaust fumes and burnt rubber. But hey, why can't NASCAR fans smell nice too? According to Scott Beattie, CEO of Elizabeth Arden, the scent's producer, "It's a fresh, masculine and modern fragrance." The cologne comes in a bottle that resembles a tire and includes touches of tarragon, sage, mandarin, nutmeg and cardamom. But you can't get it just anywhere. Beginning in April 2006, the fragrant Eau de Toilette was available in only these select boutiques: Sears and J.C. Penney.

One for Baseball fans too...

Not to be outdone, Derek Jeter announced his new line of fragrances and grooming products, called Driven, "reflecting the unique personality of one of the most driven men in America." Scheduled release was for November, 2006. The fragrance is a blend of crushed leaves, black pepper, chilled grapefruit, rhubarb, lavender, spearmint, bamboo, driftwood and oak moss. Sure, why not?

2006 Names of the Year
1. Will Power, Champ Car rookie
2. Jim Bob Cooter, U. of Tennessee reserve quarterback

AP/Wide World Photos

You probably thought you'd never have to see a picture of **Barry Bonds** dressed up as Paula Abdul for the rest of your lives, right? Sorry.

Having a Ball

When Red Sox slugger David Ortiz swatted home run number 50, tying Jimmie Foxx's team record, it was caught by a lucky fan from Rhode Island sitting in the Fenway bleachers. The fan had no problem turning the ball over to Big Papi, as long as the Red Sox met just a few small demands. Namely:

- A signed David Ortiz jersey
- A signed Curt Schilling jersey
- A jersey signed by the entire team
- A game-used first base signed by Ortiz
- A bat signed by Ortiz
- Ten tickets for games in the 2006-07 season
- The opportunity to hit batting practice before a game
- An invitation to throw out the first pitch before a game
- Permission to have his wedding at Fenway Park.

Well it doesn't hurt to ask right? The Red Sox did end up acquiring the ball, which was auctioned off for charity. It wasn't disclosed which of the demands were met.

Big Papi Part Two

On May 4, investment manager Drew Sawyer and two of his friends from Harvard Business School were the winning bidders at an auction for a game of Whiffle Ball with David Ortiz. The price? $30,000. "I evaluated it as being priceless," Sawyer said. "So we got a steal."

Don't Hassle the 'Hoff

So now we know. After hitting two clutch free throws to lead the Mavericks to a playoff win in May, star Dirk Nowitzki, a career 86 percent free throw shooter, revealed the key to his success.

"You just try to relax," he said. "I try to sing sometimes to kind of take the pressure off."

And what exactly does he sing? *Looking for Freedom* by David Hasselhoff, a smash hit when Nowitzki was growing up in Germany. When Miami Heat forward Udonis Haslem heard, he responded, "I like Knight Rider. Michael Knight and all that. I didn't know he had a music video. That was one thing I did not know." You're not alone, Udonis.

David Ortiz **Dirk Nowitzki**

High School Football Performances of the Year

1) In late September, Paul McCoy of Matewan in West Virginia rushed for 658 yards on 29 carries and scored 10 touchdowns in a 64-0 win over rival Burch. He scored on runs of 69, 1, 52, 56, 52, 20, 31, 84, 87 and 25 yards, and had a 77-yard TD run called back due to a penalty.

2) In early October, Kendric Smith of Hughes High School in Arkansas rushed for nine touchdowns and 424 yards...and his team LOST, 73-72, to East Poinsett County and their quarterback Brett Hardin, who had 835 all-purpose yards.

Brotherly Love

Tank Carter, brother of Steelers safety Tyrone Carter, was scheduled to report to prison on January 6 for driving with a revoked license. The problem was...his brother's team was in the NFL playoffs and he couldn't miss a possible chance to see him get a Super Bowl ring. So Carter saw his brother win, then reported to prison...for five years, instead of the six months he would have received had he reported on time! "Even knowing what I know now, I would do it again," Carter said. "It was the greatest game in my life."

Nickname of the Year

"The Shrub"

Kyle Busch, NASCAR driver and younger brother of Kurt Busch

Fantasy Meets Reality

In December, 2005, the Washington Redskins pounded the Dallas Cowboys, 35-7, behind a three-touchdown performance from tight end Chris Cooley.

The win was bittersweet for Cooley, however, as his performance actually caused him to lose his fantasy football game.

"I had four teams last year," Cooley told the Washington Post, "and I made the playoffs with one and honestly lost because I beat myself against Dallas. The guy on the other team had me, and I scored three touchdowns against Dallas, and I lost to myself on fantasy points."

> "These fantasy people — they have to be stopped. They're turning sports into Geek-arama."
>
> — Emmy-award winning sports announcer **Bob Costas**

The Next Tiger

Colorado golfer Brayden Bozak calmly steps up to the practice tee and methodically sends 50-to-60-yard drives straight down the fairway. Now this may not seem like a major accomplishment until you realize this: Brayden is two years old!

"It's amazing because he is still in diapers," said Brayden's father, Reid. Brayden has no intentions of jumping into life on Tour too soon. He reportedly has no plans to turn pro until he turns seven.

Hole-in-One for Alex

As if being one of the world's best hockey players isn't enough, Washington Capitals star Alexander Ovechkin appears to have a knack for golf as well. At a charity tournament in early October, he aced the par-3, 160-yard hole...and what makes this a truly amazing accomplishment is that it was the first day he'd ever swung a club! After just a few minutes of instruction that included several swings and misses, he finally got a hold of one that ended up in the cup after three bounces.

Let's just call it beginner's luck.

...And on the flip side...

Mitsuhiro Tateyama narrowly missed a hole-in-one on a par-3 hole at the Japan Tour's Acom International in late September. OK maybe narrowly isn't the right choice of words. He shot a 19. Doing his best John Daly/Tin Cup impression, Tateyama found the rough with his second shot, hit the bushes with his third, and then took 14 shots to hack his way out. He then two-putted for the 19. No word on whether any of the bushes survived.

Chris Cooley   **Alex Ovechkin**

 And the 2006 award for Best 70's Mustache goes to? You decide...Denver Broncos quarterback **Jake Plummer**, left, or former Gonzaga star and current Charlotte Bobcats forward **Adam Morrison**.

Get Married Or Else!

Ivelin Popov, a 19-year-old Bulgarian soccer player known for his wild behavior and numerous girlfriends, was ordered to get married in the upcoming year to curtail his unacceptable lifestyle. "My bosses are right to want such a thing from me because they know my temper," he said. "I know I'm a very bad boy and I want to meet my 20th birthday as a married man." As a bonus, Popov will also soon be eligible to participate in this...

Wife Carrying Championships

Former Olympic cross-country skier John Farra won the seventh North American Wife Carrying Championship at Sunday River in Maine on October 7. He made it through the 278-yard course with his wife Tess in one minute, four seconds. The couple won her weight in beer (110 pounds, but don't tell anyone), plus $550, five times her weight in cash.

'Til Death to Us Part

You may think you're a pretty big fan of your favorite team, but this is a true test to see whether you're really a die-hard fan. Eternal image, Inc. now sells urns and caskets emblazed with the logo of all 30 major league baseball teams. Prices range from $600 to $3,500. Naming rights for other sports leagues are currently in the works.

AP/Wide World Photos

Here we have a photo of Carolina Hurricanes defenseman **Mike Commodore** getting his hair cut by Ronald McDonald with an oversized plastic comb and scissors. Does anything else need to be said?

When Fans Attack

Fans of Italian soccer team Inter Milan, some of them masked, attacked team members at the Malpensa Airport because they were upset about their team's early elimination from the Champions League.

In less violent instances of fans striking back...

Royal Headache

Chad Carroll, a lifetime Kansas City Royals fan, finally became fed up with his team's lack of spending and losing ways, and started an eBay auction to sell "My loyalty to the Kansas City Royals (jersey included)." The price of a man's loyalty, at least in Carroll's case, was $278.47.

Free Birds

On September 21, during a game against the Tigers, nearly a thousand Orioles fans stood up en masse and walked out of Oriole Park at Camden Yards as a show of protest towards ineffective team owner Peter Angelos. The walkout occurred at precisely 5:08, in honor of Brooks Robinson (No. 5) and Cal Ripken (No. 8).

Lesson Learned?

In January, high school student Joshua Vannoy had the gall to wear a Denver Broncos jersey to his school...which is just outside of Pittsburgh. Reportedly his teacher John Kelly, a die-hard Steelers fan, told Vannoy to sit on the floor, then instructed his other students to throw paper at the "stinking Denver fan."

Jerk Hotline

Cincinnati Bengals fans that are tired of dealing with unruly patrons at Paul Brown Stadium now have a number they can call — (513) 381-JERK. Security officials will then make use of the stadium's video cameras, and offending fans could have their season tickets revoked...or possibly be arrested.

Police Blotter

Tonya-Nancy Revisited

University of Northern Colorado backup punter Mitch Cozad was arrested for allegedly stabbing starting punter Rafael Mendoza in his kicking leg. Mendoza beat out Cozad and another punter for the starting job in preseason. Cozad is charged with attempted first-degree murder and second-degree assault and faces the possibility of 48 years behind bars if convicted. The case is still ongoing.

What Are You Thinking?

A French father, Christophe Fauviau was sentenced to eight years in prison for drugging his children's tennis opponents. He was accused of spiking their water bottles with the anti-anxiety drug Temesta.

Bennie the Bull

Not to be confused with mafia turncoat Sammy the Bull, Bennie the Bull is the Chicago Bulls mascot who was charged with attacking an off-duty police officer at an outdoor festival in Chicago. Apparently Bennie (or technically, Barry Anderson, the actual human being inside the red, fluffy bull suit) rode a motorcycle through the festival without a permit. When the officer chased after him and caught him, Bennie punched him with his big, red hand, knocking off his glasses and breaking his watch.

When mascot **Bennie the Bull** wasn't attacking police officers in 2006, he was busy doing what he does best — entertaining fans at Chicago Bulls games. **Disclaimer:** The man or woman in the suit may or may not be the individual that slapped the officer. Please hold all lawsuits. Thank you.

Sharp Sense of Humor

A 15-year-old high school football player from Utah was kicked off his team and faced assault charges for putting a thumbtack in his glove as a prank, before shaking hands with players from a rival school.

AP/Wide World Photos

On July 27, **"El Picante," the chorizo** (middle, No. 5) signed a deal with Brewers general manager Doug Melvin to become the fifth pork product to take part in the sausage races at Milwaukee's Miller Park. He joined the Bratwurst, Polish Sausage, Italian Sausage and Hot Dog for a Brewers-Reds game (he finished third), then was "optioned out to the minor leagues for more seasoning." Melvin said, "I had been out looking for a fifth starter, and realized that was very difficult. As important as a fifth starter is to a franchise, a fifth sausage is important, too."

'Atta Boy

Smokey IX, Tennessee's bluetick coonhound mascot was accused of biting an Alabama player before a game at Neyland Stadium (for the record, Smokey is an actual dog, not a person in a dog suit). Crimson Tide wide receiver Mike McCoy leapt for a pass during warmups, missed it and came down squarely on poor Smokey. The dog's handlers deny that anyone was bitten, but McCoy reportedly played the game with a hole in his pants.

Worst Quote By An Announcer In 2006

Keith Hernandez:

"Who is the girl in the dugout, with the long hair? You have got to be kidding me. Only player personnel in the dugout."
[Hernandez later learned the woman was Kelly Calabrese, a Padres trainer, but continued]
"I won't say that women belong in the kitchen, but they don't belong in the dugout."

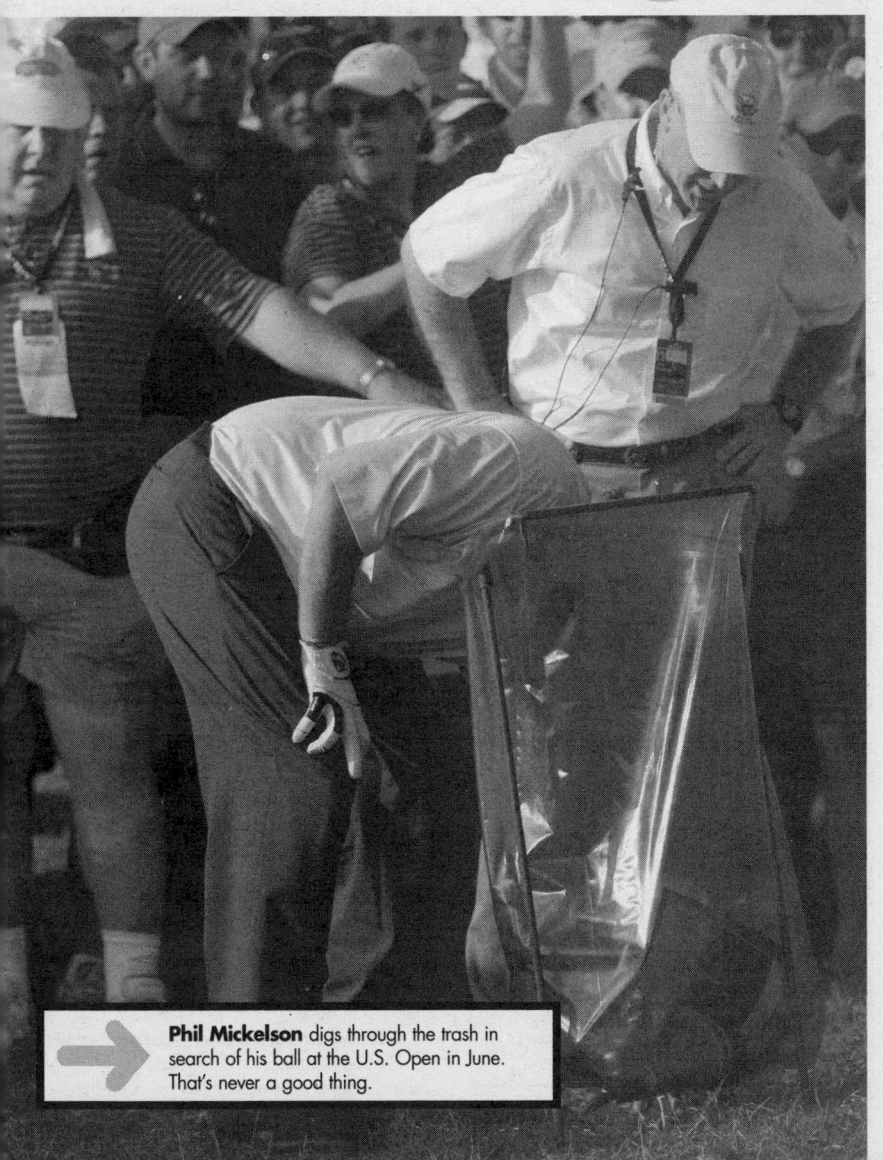

Phil Mickelson digs through the trash in search of his ball at the U.S. Open in June. That's never a good thing.

November 2005

Sun	Mon	Tue	Wed	Thu	Fri	Sat
		1	2	3	4	5
6	7	8	9	10	11	12
13	14	15	16	17	18	19
20	21	22	23	24	25	26
27	28	29	30			

Baseball Postseason Awards

A-Rod or Big Papi for AL MVP was a major source of contention in November 2005. Turns out the baseball writers did their job pretty well. Here's how SportsNation voted (top 2 and vote totals listed), Actual winners are in *italics*.

Who is your pick for AL MVP?

47.1% — *Alex Rodriguez, Yankees*
36.9% — David Ortiz, Red Sox

Who is your pick for NL MVP?

49.2% — *Albert Pujols, Cardinals*
27.8% — Andruw Jones, Braves

Who is your pick for AL Cy Young?

39.6% — *Bartolo Colon, Angels*
27.1% — Mariano Rivera, Yankees

Who is your pick for NL Cy Young?

41.9% — *Chris Carpenter, Cardinals*
30.0% — Dontrelle Willis, Marlins

Who is your pick for AL Manager of the Year?

80.8% — *Ozzie Guillen, White Sox*
9.8% — Eric Wedge, Indians

Who is your pick for NL Manager of the Year?

41.9% — *Bobby Cox, Braves*
27.5% — Phil Garner, Astros

Total Votes: 54,312

1 **The 2005-06 NBA season tips off** with the defending champion San Antonio Spurs raising their third championship banner, then picking up right where they left off, beating the Denver Nuggets, 102-91.

2 **PGA commissioner Tim Finchem**, evidently a big NASCAR fan, announces the creation of a new four-tournament playoff system beginning in 2007, to be called the FedEx Cup. A $10 million check will be handed to the series' winner.

3 **Receiver Terrell Owens** blasts the Philadelphia Eagles for not publicly recognizing his 100th career touchdown catch in late October. He also takes shots at his quarterback, Donovan McNabb, claiming the Eagles might be better off if Packers' quarterback Brett Favre were leading the offense.

5 **And now it's the Eagles' turn.** The team suspends Terrell Owens indefinitely "for conduct detrimental to the team." Aside from the inflammatory comments, details also emerge about a locker room altercation with Eagles' defensive end Hugh Douglas.

Kansas routs Nebraska, 40-15, to snap its 36-game losing streak to the Cornhuskers. Chaos ensues and goalposts are torn down.

6 **Former Boston Bruins' tough guy**, goal-scorer extraordinaire and fan-favorite Cam Neely leads a class of three to be inducted into the Hockey Hall of Fame.

Kenya's Paul Tergat surges at the finish line to beat defending champ Hendrick Ramaala by a mere third of a second at the New York City Marathon. It is the closest finish in the race's history. Latvia's Jelena Prokopcuka takes the women's division.

Two Carolina Panthers cheerleaders, Renee Thomas and Angela Keathley, are arrested after allegedly having sex in a bathroom stall at a Florida club. They are subsequently booted from the Panthers' squad.

7 **Phillies slugger Ryan Howard** and A's reliever Huston Street are named the NL and AL rookies of the year.

8 **We now return to T.O.** The soap opera continues as Terrell Owens apologizes to the Eagles, a couple of days too late, and asks to be back on the team. Agent Drew Rosenhaus gets involved with his now-famous, "Next Question" press conference.

10 **Cardinals hurler Chris Carpenter** wins the NL Cy Young award. The Angels' Bartolo Colon took the AL award three days earlier.

AP/Wide World Photos

Agent **Drew Rosenhaus** had Terrell Owens' back when the wide receiver was finally kicked to the curb by the Eagles after a number of off-field incidents.

11 **American Lindsay Davenport** clinches the WTA No. 1 ranking for 2005, despite losing to Maria Sharapova at the Tour Championships.

13 **Bears cornerback Nathan Vasher** catches a missed field goal attempt and runs it back 108 yards for a touchdown against the 49ers in what is the longest play in NFL history. "I felt like I was running the 400 meters out there," he said.

14 **Alex Rodriguez edges** Red Sox designated hitter David Ortiz to win his second AL MVP award in the past three seasons. On the following day, Cardinals slugger Albert Pujols wins his first NL award.

15 **Major League Baseball** players and owners reach an agreement on a tougher steroid policy, that includes a 50-game suspension for a first offense, 100 games for a second offense and lifetime ban for a third.

19 **On Rivalry Saturday** in NCAA football, Ohio State beats Michigan in Ann Arbor,

25-21, Harvard defeats Yale, Auburn gets past Alabama, and Oregon, Washington St. and California are all winners. Elsewhere USC star Reggie Bush puts up 513 all purpose yards to lead the Trojans to a win over Fresno St.

20 **Tony Stewart finishes** in 15th in the season-ending Nextel Cup race at Homestead, but that's good enough for him to clinch his second overall points championship.

23 **The Florida Marlins'** mass payroll dump continues as Carlos Delgado is shipped to the Mets just days after Josh Beckett and Mike Lowell are traded to the Red Sox.

24 **Denver nips Dallas** in overtime, 24-21, and the Falcons pound the Lions, 27-7, in annual Thanksgiving Day NFL football.

25 **Chelsea Memmel and Nastia Liukin** give the U.S. women a Gold-Silver finish in the all-around competition at the World Gymnastics Championships.

26 **Steve Mariucci is fired** as coach of the Detroit Lions and replaced by Dick Jauron.

December 2005

Sun	Mon	Tue	Wed	Thu	Fri	Sat
				1	2	3
4	5	6	7	8	9	10
11	12	13	14	15	16	17
18	19	20	21	22	23	24
25	26	27	28	29	30	31

Bush for President?

USC's Reggie Bush won the Heisman Trophy in a landslide, and judging by your responses below, you'd agree.

Who is the most exciting college football player in the ESPN era (since 1979)?

42.3% —	Reggie Bush
36.6% —	Marcus Allen
8.9% —	Ricky Williams
6.4% —	Terrell Davis
4.7% —	Junior Seau
0.4% —	Rashaan Salaam
0.4% —	Akili Smith
0.4% —	Mark Malone

If Bush enters the 2006 NFL draft, where will he be picked?

64.3% —	No. 1, no matter who has the pick.
25.3% —	No. 1, only if he fills a team's specific need.
8.6% —	Top 5
1.2% —	First round
0.7% —	Top 10

Total Votes: 44,975

3 **Texas destroys Colorado,** 70-3, in the Big 12 Championship Game, while.Reggie Bush piles up another 260 yards rushing to lead USC over UCLA, 66-19.

Jermain Taylor wins a unanimous decision over 40-year-old Bernard Hopkins in a rematch from their controversial split decision five months earlier. Taylor retains his WBO, WBA and WBC middleweight belts.

6 **Surprise, surprise.** Tiger Woods wins the PGA Tour Player of the Year for the seventh time in his nine full seasons on the tour. Sean O'Hair is voted tour Rookie of the Year.

7 **NASCAR finalizes** its television deal with ABC, ESPN, FOX and Turner, worth an estimated $4.5 billion to run from 2007-2014.

Hall of famer Mario Lemieux is sidelined and hospitalized for an irregular heartbeat.

10 **USC running back Reggie Bush** is a landslide winner of the 2005 Heisman Trophy.

12 **Stan Van Gundy** steps down as head coach of the Miami Heat (11-10), and team president Pat Riley takes over.

13 **American sprinter Tim Montgomery** is handed a two-year ban from competition, despite never testing positive for a banned substance. The decision is based on evidence uncovered in the BALCO investigation, as well as testimony from banned sprinter Kelli White.

15 **Four Minnesota Vikings,** Daunte Culpepper, Bryant McKinnie, Moe Williams and Fred Smoot, are charged with misdemeanor offenses in connection with the infamous "sex cruise" incident back in October, 2005.

16 **Appalachian St. beats** Northern Iowa, 21-16, for its first I-AA football national championship.

17. **Russian Nikolai Valuev,** all seven feet, 323 pounds of him, earns a split decision over "The Quiet Man," John Ruiz to win the WBA heavyweight title. He becomes the tallest and heaviest champion of all time. Ruiz, as expected is none too happy: "Boxing is the only sport where you can get robbed without a gun."

18 **The 1972 Miami Dolphins** can breathe easier and sip their champagne, after the San Diego Chargers take down the Indianapolis Colts, 26-17, to drop the Colts to 13-1. For at least another year, the '72 Dolphins will remain the only perfect team in NFL history.

19 **Brazilian soccer star Ronaldinho** wins his second consecutive FIFA Player of the Year award. Germany's Birgit Prinz wins the woman's award for the third straight year.

AP/Wide World Photos

→ Rockstar centerfielder **Johnny Damon** greets his new fans in New York City after inking a four-year deal with the Yankees on December 20.

20 Long-haired centerfielder Johnny Damon, the face of the Red Sox in their 2004 world championship season, agrees to a four-year, $52 million deal to patrol center field for the rival New York Yankees.

Kobe Bryant nets 62 points in just three quarters of action to lead the Lakers to a 112-90 win over the Dallas Mavericks.

22 James Dungy, the 18-year-old son of Colts coach Tony Dungy, is found dead in his Tampa-area apartment of an apparent suicide.

25 The Heat get the better of the Lakers, 97-92, in what seems like the annual Kobe-Shaq matchup on Christmas Day. Bryant pours in 37 in the loss.

26 *Monday Night Football* comes to a close on ABC, strangely similar to the way it began in 1970, with the Jets on the losing end of a 31-21 contest. It was the Browns beating them in the series opener, and the Patriots beating them in the finale. The series switches to ESPN beginning with the 2006 season.

28 Cyclist Lance Armstrong and golfer Annika Sorenstam are named the AP male and female athletes of the year. It is Sorenstam's third straight year winning the prestigious award, and Armstrong's fourth.

Nebraska comes from behind to beat Michigan, 32-28, in the Alamo Bowl.

30 LSU pounds Miami, 40-3, in the Peach Bowl to give the Hurricanes their worst defeat since their 66-13 loss to Syracuse in 1998. There is also a nasty brawl in the tunnel following the game that sees two players knocked unconscious, reportedly by players swinging helmets.

In other Bowl action, UCLA takes care of Northwestern, 50-38, in a wild Sun Bowl, Missouri downs South Carolina, 38-31 in the Independence Bowl, and Virginia edges Minnesota, 34-31, in the Music City Bowl.

31 Maurice Clarett is accused of robbing two people at gunpoint in an alley behind a Columbus, Ohio bar.

January 2006

Sun	Mon	Tue	Wed	Thu	Fri	Sat
1	2	3	4	5	6	7
8	9	10	11	12	13	14
15	16	17	18	19	20	21
22	23	24	25	26	27	28
29	30	31				

Kobe pours in 81

Which of the following facts about Bryant's performance is most impressive?

38.4% —	55 points in second half equals Kareem Abdul-Jabbar's high for an entire game.
31.3% —	Scoring 66% of team's points (81 of 122) on 61% shooting (28-for-46)
30.3% —	99 times this season, a team has scored fewer than 81 points in a game

Which active player other than Kobe Bryant has the best chance to reach the 70-point mark in a game?

39.3% —	LeBron James
27.9% —	Allen Iverson
18.3% —	No active player will do it
11.9% —	Tracy McGrady
1.8% —	Vince Carter
0.8% —	Ray Allen

Which individual sports accomplishment would you most like to see in person?

51.8% —	Hoops player with 70 pts or more
25.5% —	Pitcher throw a perfect game
9.0% —	Football player score or throw for 6 touchdowns or more
7.3% —	Batter hit 4 home runs
3.5% —	Golfer shoot 60 or under
2.9% —	Hockey player score 6 goals or more

Total Votes: 42,197

1 On the final day of the NFL regular season, Seattle running back Shaun Alexander scores his 28th touchdown to set a new single-season mark. Elsewhere, Minnesota coach Mike Tice is fired after the Vikings' 34-10 win over the Bears, and the Patriots' Doug Flutie executes the league's first drop kick since the 1941 championship game, in a 28-26 loss to Miami.

Martina Hingis makes a triumphant return to the court after a three-year hiatus, with a 6-1, 6-1 victory over Nicole Pratt in Australia. She would advance all the way to the semifinals before finally bowing out.

2 It's "Black Monday" in the NFL as four more head coaches are fired. Green Bay's Mike Sherman, New Orleans' Jim Haslett, St. Louis' Mike Martz and Houston's Dom Capers are all relieved of their duties.

Quarterback Troy Smith outduels Brady Quinn as No. 4 Ohio State takes care of No. 5 Notre Dame, 34-20, in the Fiesta Bowl.

3 Penn State beats Florida State, 26-23, on Kevin Kelly's 29-yard field goal in the third overtime at the Orange Bowl. Also, No. 11 West Virginia impresses with a 38-35 win over No. 8 Georgia in the Sugar Bowl.

4 Vince Young scores on an eight-yard, fourth-down scramble with 19 seconds left to boost No. 2 Texas over top-ranked USC, 41-38, in the Rose Bowl. The win gives the Longhorns their first national football championship since 1970, and snaps the Trojans' 34-game winning streak. Young connects on 30 of 40 pass attempts, and rushes 19 times for 200 yards.

5 Seahawks running back Shaun Alexander runs away with the Associated Press Most Valuable Player award.

7 The NFL playoffs kick off as the Redskins defeat Tampa Bay, 17-10, and the Patriots rout the Jaguars, 28-3, for their tenth straight postseason win.

8 Olympic skier Bode Miller causes a stir when he goes on *60 Minutes* and discusses his partying ways and his experiences while skiing drunk. "If you ever tried to ski when you're wasted, it's not easy," he says.

The Steelers win their opening-round playoff matchup with the Bengals, 31-17, after Cincinnati quarterback Carson Palmer suffers a major knee injury on his first pass of the game.

10 Closer Bruce Sutter, who helped popularize the split-fingered fastball, becomes the fourth reliever to be inducted into the Baseball Hall of Fame.

AP/Wide World Photos

> **Kobe Bryant** was unstoppable on January 22, scoring every which way...on his way to an 81-point night, the second-highest single-game total in NBA history..

12 USC star and Heisman Trophy winner Reggie Bush announces his intentions to declare for the 2006 NFL Draft in April.

13 The New York Knicks win their sixth consecutive game (yes, it's true) with a 105-94 victory in Atlanta to give head coach Larry Brown his 1,000th career win. He joins Lenny Wilkens, Don Nelson and Pat Riley in that club.

14 The Broncos handle the Patriots, 27-13, and the Seahawks get past the Redskins, 20-10, to advance to their respective conference championship games.

15 Ben Roethlisberger makes a game-saving tackle and Colts kicker Mike Vanderjagt misses a 46-yard field goal with 21 seconds left, as the Steelers advance, 21-18 over Indianapolis. Also, Steve Smith leads the Panthers to a 29-21 win over the Bears.

19 Knicks forward Antonio Davis is given a five-game suspension for entering the stands in Chicago to confront a fan that he believed was threatening his wife.

20 The U.S. government reverses its controversial decision and will now allow Cuba to participate in the upcoming World Baseball Classic on U.S. soil.

22 81! Kobe Bryant scores an amazing 81 points in a 122-104 Lakers win over the Toronto Raptors. It is the second highest total (behind Wilt Chamberlain's 100) in league history. He goes 28-of-46 from the floor and 18-of-20 from the free throw line.

The Steelers and Seahawks each win their conference title games with ease — the Steelers with a 34-17 win over Denver, and the Seahawks with a 34-14 win over Carolina — to advance to Super Bowl XL.

24 "This is it," says hall of famer Mario Lemieux. The longtime Penguins star retires for the final time due to an irregular heartbeat.

28 Roger Federer defeats Marcos Baghdatis to win the Australian Open, two days after Amelie Mauresmo won the women's title with her victory over Justine Henin-Hardenne.

February 2006

Sun	Mon	Tue	Wed	Thu	Fri	Sat
			1	2	3	4
5	6	7	8	9	10	11
12	13	14	15	16	17	18
19	20	21	22	23	24	25
26	27	28				

Top Stories at Turin

Which was the biggest U.S. story of the 2006 Winter Olympics?

1. Snowboarders
2. Bode Miller
3. Apolo Anton Ohno
4. Hedrick vs. Davis
5. Shani Davis
6. Sasha Cohen
7. Joey Cheek
8. Lindsey Jacobellis
9. Michelle Kwan
10. Ben Agosto/Tanith Belbin

Who do you think is more at fault in the feud between U.S. skaters?

55.3% —	Chad Hedrick
44.7% —	Shani Davis

Do you consider athletes in individual events who are from the same country to be teammates?

71.3% —	Yes
28.7% —	No

How extensive do you think is the prejudice, whether intentional or unintentional, encountered by African-American athletes participating in what have been predominantly white sports?

34.3% —	Not very extensive
30.7% —	Somewhat extensive
17.7% —	Very extensive
17.3% —	No such prejudice exists

Total Votes: 206,997

1 **The Kentucky Derby** announces its five-year deal with Yum Brands, the fast food restaurant company that owns KFC, Taco Bell and Pizza Hut. The race's official name will be the *Kentucky Derby, presented by Yum Brands.* Yuck.

4 **Troy Aikman, Reggie White,** Rayfield Wright, Warren Moon, Harry Carson and coach and longtime announcer John Madden are all voted into the Pro Football Hall of Fame in Canton, Ohio.

5 **Steelers win one for the thumb.** The Pittsburgh Steelers defeat the Seattle Seahawks, 21-10, in Super Bowl XL for their fifth all-time Super Bowl title. Wide receiver Hines Ward catches five balls for 123 yards, including a 43-yard touchdown from Antwaan Randle El, and is named the game's most valuable player. Jerome Bettis follows John Elway's lead by rolling into retirement as an NFL champion.

7 **A betting scandal,** known as "Operation Slap Shot," strikes the NHL when former player and current assistant coach Rick Tocchet is one of three people arrested on charges of operating a multi-million dollar bookmaking operation. Wayne Gretzky's wife, Janet Jones, is fingered as someone who placed bets with the ring, but Gretzky himself is not accused of any wrongdoing.

8 **Tony Kornheiser joins** the new ESPN Monday Night Football broadcasting team (joining Mike Tirico and Joe Theisman in the booth) and Al Michaels teams with John Madden on Sunday Night Football.

10 **Dazzling opening ceremonies** take place in Turin, Italy, signifying the beginning of the 2006 Winter Olympic Games.

11 **Speedskater Chad Hedrick,** who came to Turin with hopes of winning five gold medals, gets his first with a win in the 5,000-meters.

12 **Decorated American figure skater** Michelle Kwan announces her decision to withdraw from the Turin Games due to a nagging groin injury. Her position will be filled by Emily Hughes, sister of reigning gold-medalist Sarah.

Shaun White, a.k.a. The Flying Tomato, wins a gold medal in the halfpipe competition. He immediately sets his sights on a higher, and probably elusive, prize. "I'm hoping Sasha Cohen digs gold medals," he says.

14 **American skier Ted Ligety** takes the men's Olympic combined competition after Bode Miller is disqualified for straddling a gate during his first slalom run.

AP/Wide World Photos

➡ Who says they don't like each other? American speed-skaters **Shani Davis** and **Chad Hedrick** share a flight out of Turin after the 2006 Olympics.

Duke All-American J.J. Redick becomes the NCAA's all-time leading three-point shooter when he nails his 414th in Duke's 93-70 win over Wake Forest.

15 The Darko Milicic era is over in Detroit as the Pistons deal the former No. 2 overall pick in the NBA draft to the Orlando Magic. He was drafted in 2003 after LeBron James, but before such stars as Carmelo Anthony, Chris Bosh and Dwyane Wade.

"The five medals isn't a big thing," said speedskater Chad Hedrick, moments after the Americans were eliminated in the team pursuit.

16 Russian Evgeni Plushenko wins gold in the men's Olympic figure skating competition. The U.S. is shut out after Johnny Weir misses the bus to the competition, then finishes in fifth.

18 Speedskater Shani Davis wins gold in the men's 1,000-meter race to become the first African-American individual winter gold medalist.

19 Jimmie Johnson holds off Casey Mears and Ryan Newman to win the Daytona 500 just days after his crew chief, Chad Knauss, was suspended for an infraction.

MVP LeBron James and Dwyane Wade lead the Eastern Conference to a come-from-behind 122-120 win over the West at the NBA All-Star Game.

20 Curt Gowdy, longtime sports broadcaster and hall of famer, dies of leukemia at the age of 86.

23 Sasha Cohen slips and still comes away with the silver medal, while Japan's Shizuka Arakawa skates beautifully to win the gold medal at the women's figure skating competition in Turin. Russian Irina Slutskaya takes the bronze.

25 Apolo Anton Ohno leads from start to finish to win the 500-meter short track speed-skating gold in Turin.

26 Sweden defeats Finland, 3-2, to win the Olympic men's hockey gold. Nicklas Lidstrom nets the game winner early in the third.

March 2006

Sun	Mon	Tue	Wed	Thu	Fri	Sat
			1	2	3	4
5	6	7	8	9	10	11
12	13	14	15	16	17	18
19	20	21	22	23	24	25
26	27	28	29	30	31	

Cinderella's Ball

SportsNation ranked its favorite Cinderellas since the NCAA mens basketball tournament expanded to 64 teams in 1985.

Note: this poll was taken before the tournament began and therefore *before* George Mason made its stunning run. Where do you think they belong?

	Team	Seed	Year
1.	Villanova	8	1985
2.	Gonzaga	10	1999
3.	Valparaiso	13	1998
4.	UNC	8	2000
5.	Kent St.	10	2002
6.	Wisconsin	8	2000
7.	LSU	11	1986
8.	Loyola Mary.	11	1990
9.	Temple	11	2001
10.	Hampton	15	2001

Buzzer Beaters

SportsNation ranked the top NCAA tournament buzzer beaters of all time. The top 5 are listed.

68.0%	—	Christian Laettner, '92 Duke vs Kentucky
42.4%	—	Lorenzo Charles, '83, NC State vs Houston
38.5%	—	Bryce Drew, '98, Valparaiso vs Ole Miss
36.1%	—	Christian Laettner, '90, Duke vs UConn
26.6%	—	Keith Smart, '87, Indiana vs Syracuse

4 **No. 2 Rafael Nadal** beats top-ranked Roger Federer, 2-6, 6-4, 6-4, in the finals of the Dubai Open, ending Federer's 56-match hard-court winning streak and his three-year dominance at the event.

Cameron Crazies need consoling as their beloved Duke Blue Devils fall to rival North Carolina, 83-76, on Senior Night.

6 **Kirby Puckett,** baseball hall of famer, World Series hero and fan favorite for the Minnesota Twins, dies at the age of 45, a day after suffering a massive stroke. Puckett batted .318 over his 12-year career, won six Gold Gloves and two World Series titles (1987, 1991).

7 **An excerpt from *Game of Shadows*,** a new book which details steroid use by Barry Bonds, is printed in an upcoming issue of *Sports Illustrated,* throwing Bonds and baseball's steroid issue back into the spotlight as the World Baseball Classic gets underway. The book, written by *San Francisco Chronicle* reporters Lance Williams and Mark Fainaru-Wada, uses research and supposedly secret grand jury testimony to chronicle Bonds' specific steroid regimen as well as his obsession with bettering former single-season home run champ Mark McGwire.

The United States wins its opening game at the World Baseball Classic, 2-0, over Mexico on strong pitching by Jake Peavy and solo homers by Derrek Lee and Chipper Jones.

8 **The NFL and its players union** reach a new six-year extension on its collective bargaining agreement that, among other things, eliminates the threat of an NFL work stoppage and increases the salary cap from $94.5 million to $102 million for the 2006 season The owners vote 30-2 to accept the deal, with only Buffalo and Cincinnati dissenting.

Canada shocks the U.S., 8-6, to hand the Americans their first loss at the World Baseball Classic.

9 **Energy drink manufacturer** Red Bull Co. Ltd. purchases Major League Soccer's MetroStars, as well as a part of their stadium, and renames the team Red Bull New York.

10 **The NCAA men's hoops tournament** field is set on Selection Sunday, with Duke, Connecticut, Villanova and Memphis being awarded the top seeds.

Edgerrin James bolts the Colts, inking a four-year, $30 million contract with the Arizona Cardinals after playing his first seven seasons with Indianapolis.

AP/Wide World Photos

> **Jeff King and his dogs** mushed 1,100 miles in just over nine days and 11 hours to win the annual Iditarod sled dog race in Alaska.

13 Temple coach John Chaney retires after an inspiring, albeit occasionally controversial, career than spanned 34 seasons — 24 with the Owls.

15 Jeff King wins his fourth Iditarod, completing the annual 1,100-mile trek from Anchorage to Nome in nine days, 11 hours and 11 minutes — more than three hours ahead of runner-up Doug Swingley.

16 The 2006 NCAA men's basketball tournament tips off, as Duke rolls and Tennessee needs a last-second jumper to beat No. 15 Winthrop.

The loaded U.S. team is eliminated from the World Baseball Classic after a 2-0 loss to Mexico, despite a strong outing from Roger Clemens.

17 14-seed Northwestern State takes down #3 Iowa, 64-63, in the first major upset of the NCAA tournament. Elsewhere, lightly regarded George Mason (an 11-seed) is off and rolling as it stuns six-seed and heavily favored Michigan State, 75-65.

18 He's baaaack! The Dallas Cowboys and owner Jerry Jones decide to dance with the devil, signing talented yet disruptive receiver Terrell Owens to a three-year, $25 million contract.

19 George Mason advance to the Sweet 16 with a 65-60 shocker over North Carolina.

Tennessee's Candace Parker, a 6-foot-3 freshman, becomes the first player to dunk in an NCAA women's tournament game, in a 102-54 win over Army.

20 Japan defeats Cuba, 10-6, in the championship game to win the inaugural World Baseball Classic. Ichiro Suzuki goes 2-for-4 and scores three runs.

24 Holy Cross stuns Minnesota, 4-3, in OT at the NCAA Division I men's hockey tourney in perhaps the biggest upset in college hockey history.

26 Cinderella George Mason does it again, beating Connecticut, 86-84, in overtime to join Florida, UCLA and LSU in the 2006 men's Final Four.

April 2006

Sun	Mon	Tue	Wed	Thu	Fri	Sat
						1
2	3	4	5	6	7	8
9	10	11	12	13	14	15
16	17	18	19	20	21	22
23/30	24	25	26	27	28	29

Potential Draft Busts

SportsNation took the top 20 prospects in the 2006 NFL draft and gave its opinion on who is most likely to be the next Ryan Leaf, Blair Thomas, Tony Mandarich...or worse!

15.8%	—	Vince Young, QB, Texas
12.2%	—	Jay Cutler, QB, Vanderbilt
7.9%	—	Mario Williams, DE, NC State
7.7%	—	Matt Leinart, QB, USC
5.6%	—	Santonio Holmes, WR, Ohio St.
5.3%	—	Chad Jackson, WR, Florida
4.8%	—	Kamerion Wimbley, DE, Fla. St.
4.7%	—	Reggie Bush, RB, USC
4.0%	—	Chad Greenway, LB, Iowa
4.0%	—	Tye Hill, CB, Clemson
3.9%	—	Jimmy Williams, CB, Va. Tech
3.9%	—	Brodrick Bunkley, DT, Florida St.
3.8%	—	Haloti Ngata, DT, Oregon
3.3%	—	DeAngelo Williams, RB, Memphis
3.2%	—	Ernie Sims, LB, Florida St.
2.4%	—	A.J. Hawk, LB, Ohio St.
2.3%	—	Winston Justice, OT, USC
1.8%	—	Vernon Davis, TE, Maryland
1.8%	—	D'Brickashaw Ferguson, OT, UVA
1.5%	—	Michael Huff, DB, Texas

Total Votes: 115,326

1 **Cinderella's slipper** is finally removed as Florida ends George Mason's amazing run through the NCAA tournament with a convincing 73-58 win. UCLA beats LSU, 59-45, in the other semifinal matchup to set up Monday night's championship game.

2 **The 2006 Major League baseball season** is underway as the defending champion Chicago White Sox pound the Cleveland Indians, 10-4.

3 **The Florida Gators romp** to a dominating 73-57 victory over UCLA in the men's basketball championship game. The Gators built up an 11-point, first-half lead and never relented. Forward Joakim Noah scores 16 points, grabs nine boards and blocks six shots and his named the most outstanding player of the Final Four. It is the first NCAA men's hoops title for Florida, and for head coach Billy Donovan.

Charles Barkley, Dominique Wilkens and Joe Dumars are among six newly named inductees into the Basketball Hall of Fame.

4 **Maryland edges Duke,** 78-75, in overtime to win its first NCAA women's basketball national championship. After freshman Marissa Coleman nailed two free throws with 13 seconds remaining, Duke's last second three-point bid wouldn't fall.

5 **Duke president Richard Brodhead officially cancels** the remainder of his school's men's lacrosse season, and 16-year head coach Mike Pressler resigns. The program has been embroiled in scandal after a dancer hired to perform at a party thrown by the lacrosse team claimed she was sexually assaulted by three players.

LSU's Seimone Augustus is taken first overall by the Minnesota Lynx at the WNBA draft.

6 **Phillies shortstop Jimmy Rollins** goes 0 for 4 in a 4-2 loss to the St. Louis Cardinals, putting an end to his 38-game hit streak (dating back to the 2005 season).

7 **Maggie Dixon,** head coach of the Army women's basketball team, dies of a heart arrhythmia at the age of 28.

8 **Wisconsin beats Boston College,** 2-1, to win its sixth NCAA hockey national championship and first since 1990.

Floyd Mayweather earns a unanimous decision over Zab Judah in their IBF welterweight title. The fight is highlighted, or perhaps lowlighted, by a nasty 10th-round brawl between the fighters' camps that eventually has trainer Roger Mayweather fined $200,000 and suspended.

AP/Wide World Photos

→ The Houston Texans selected defensive end **Mario Williams**, center, with the top pick in the 2006 draft. Here he is with commissioner Paul Tagliabue and Texans owner Bob McNair.

9 Phil Mickelson claims a two-shot victory over Tim Clark for his second consecutive Masters title and second straight major victory (2005 PGA Championship). He cards a 3-under-par 69 in the final round to cruise to the victory.

17 Albert Pujols ties a major league record with home runs in four consecutive at bats. He had hit three homers the night before in an 8-7 win over Cincinnati then lead off the following game with one against the Pirates.

Robert Cheruiyot sets a new course record, winning the Boston Marathon in 2:07:14. He breaks Cosmas Ndeti's 12-year-old mark by one second. Fellow Kenyan Rita Jeptoo wins the women's division in 2:23:38.

20 Cubs slugger Derrek Lee breaks two bones in his wrist in a collision with Dodgers shortstop Rafael Furcal, sidelining him for much of the season.

Longtime coach Pat Quinn is fired by the Toronto Maple Leafs after failing to reach the postseason.

23 Deena Kastor wins the London Marathon in 2:19:35 to break the American women's marathon record.

24 The Pac-10 Conference begins an investigation into whether any NCAA rules were violated surrounding the living arrangement for Reggie Bush's family while the running back was at USC. The family lived in the home owned by Michael Michaels, who reportedly was trying to steer Bush towards signing with agent David Caravantes.

22 Finally! Barry Bonds hits his first home run, No. 709 overall, in the Giants' 17th game of the season.

25 Dolphins RB Ricky Williams is suspended for the entire season after his fourth failed drug test.

29 The Houston Texans surprise pretty much everyone by passing on Heisman Trophy winner Reggie Bush to select N.C. State defensive end Mario Williams with the top pick in the NFL draft. Bush goes second to the Saints and Vince Young goes third to the Titans.

May 2006

Sun	Mon	Tue	Wed	Thu	Fri	Sat
	1	2	3	4	5	6
7	8	9	10	11	12	13
14	15	16	17	18	19	20
21	22	23	24	25	26	27
28	29	30	31			

Sports Gambling

With the revelations of John Daly (see May 1 entry) and Charles Barkley, and the scandal surrounding Rick Tocchet, sports gambling was thrust into the spotlight in 2006. Here are some of your thoughts...

Should sports gambling be legal nationwide?

70.9% —	Yes
29.1% —	No

Have you bet illegally on sports in the last 12 months?

42.3% —	Yes
57.7% —	No

What percentage of professional athletes do you think gamble, legally or illegally, on pro sports other than their own?

35.7% —	25-49
26.9% —	50-74
19.8% —	Less than 25
17.5% —	75 or more

Do you think a game in any of the four major sports (NBA, NFL, NHL or MLB) has been fixed in the last 20 years?

74.4% —	Yes
25.6% —	No

Total Votes: 7,442

1 **Excerpts from John Daly's** autobiography, *John Daly: My Life In and Out of the Rough,* are released, claiming the troubled PGA golfer has lost between $50 and $60 million during 12 years of heavy gambling. He mentions that if he can't get his addiction under control, it could "flat out ruin me."

2 **Phoenix guard Raja Bell** throws Kobe Bryant to the ground during the Suns' 114-97 win over the Lakers, drawing a one-game suspension. "I think he's a pompous, arrogant individual," said Bell. Bryant joked that maybe Bell wasn't hugged enough as a child.

3 **Earl Woods,** Tiger's father, friend and mentor, dies at the age of 74 after a lengthy battle with cancer.

6 **Barbaro, under jockey Edgar Prado,** cruises to a 6½-length win at the 132nd Kentucky Derby. It is the largest margin of victory at the Derby since Assault's 8-length victory in 1946. Bluegrass Cat and Steppenwolfer finish in second and third, respectively.

Oscar De La Hoya returns from a 20-month layoff to pound Ricardo Mayorga and earn a sixth-round technical knockout to claim the WBC junior middleweight (154-pound) title.

7 **Phoenix point guard Steve Nash** wins his second consecutive NBA Most Valuable Player award, outdistancing Cavaliers phenom LeBron James by a comfortable margin (924-688). He is the 11th player to have multiple NBA MVP awards.

8 **Zab Judah** is fined $250,000 and stripped of his Nevada boxing license for his role in the mid-fight fight last month against Floyd Mayweather. His father and trainer, Yoel, was also fined $100,000.

Hornets guard Chris Paul is voted the NBA's Rookie of the Year, while Pistons forward Ben Wallace wins the Defensive Player of Year award for the fourth time.

9 **Delmon Young,** the 2003 top overall selection by the Tampa Bay Devil Rays, is suspended 50 games for throwing a bat at an umpire during a minor league game.

11 **Floyd Patterson,** the former heavyweight champ, and first to lose then regain the title, dies at the age of 71.

12 **American sprinter Justin Gatlin** blazes to what is thought to be a new world record in the 100-meters when he runs a 9.76 in Qatar. Days later, however, the IAAF announces that his actual time was 9.766 and should have been rounded up to 9.77, thus tying the record.

AP/Wide World Photos

Giants slugger **Barry Bonds** tied, then passed legend Babe Ruth on the all-time home run list in May, and now has only Hank Aaron in front of him.

France's Laure Manaudou breaks Janet Evans' 18-year-old record in the 400-meter freestyle when she swims a 4:03.03 at the French national championships.

14 This barely qualifies as news but Pistons' forward Rasheed Wallace makes another guarantee, this time claiming Detroit will win Game 4 of its series with Cleveland.

15 Guarantee shmarantee. LeBron James scores 22 to lead the Cavs to a series-tying 74-72 victory over the Pistons.

16 Down 9-0 in the second inning, the New York Yankees storm back to win their slugfest with the Texas Rangers, 14-13.

Florida State coach Bobby Bowden and Penn State's Joe Paterno headline a class of 15 voted into the College Football Hall of Fame.

20 Barry Bonds hits homer #714, tying Babe Ruth for second place on the all-time home run list. The shot is off Oakland starter Brad Halsey. He had gone 29 at-bats since hitting #713.

Bernardini wins the Preakness by 5¼ lengths, but all thoughts are with Barbaro, the Kentucky Derby winner and pre-race favorite who takes a bad step 100 yards into the race and pulls up lame with a severely broken right hind leg. His injury is considered life-threatening.

Cubs catcher Michael Barrett slugs cross-town counterpart A.J. Pierzynski in a White Sox 7-0 victory. Days later he is handed a 10-game suspension.

21 The Pistons beat the Cavaliers in Game 7, setting up an Eastern Conference showdown with the Miami Heat.

28 Barry Bonds passes Babe Ruth with the 715th home run of his career in a 6-3 loss to the Colorado Rockies. The count was 3-and-2, the pitcher was Byung-Hyun Kim and the ball landed an estimated 445 feet from home plate, over the right centerfield wall.

Penske's Sam Hornish Jr. wins his first Indy 500 as Marco Andretti and father Michael finish second and third, respectively.

June 2006

Sun	Mon	Tue	Wed	Thu	Fri	Sat
				1	2	3
4	5	6	7	8	9	10
11	12	13	14	15	16	17
18	19	20	21	22	23	24
25	26	27	28	29	30	

Trade Robberies

On June 22, San Jose Sharks center Joe Thornton not only won the Art Ross Trophy as the NHL's top scorer, but also won the Hart Trophy as league MVP. What in the world were the Boston Bruins thinking when they traded him back in late November? Listed are what you think are the **worst** trades of all time.

58.5% — **Brett Favre** to Packers (from Falcons for 17th pick in '92 draft)

50.3% — **Kareem Abdul-Jabbar** to Lakers (from Bucks for Junior Bridgeman, Dave Meyers, Elmore Smith and Brian Winters

47.5% — **Jerry Rice** to 49ers (traded up with New England to 16th overall pick in 1985 draft)

46.1% — **Kobe Bryant** to Lakers (from Hornets on 1996 draft day, for Vlade Divac)

41.0% — **Herschel Walker** to Vikings (from the Cowboys for five players and six future draft picks that turned out to include Emmitt Smith, Russell Maryland and Darren Woodson)

27.3% — **Wilt Chamberlain** to Warriors (Not so much a trade, but the Warriors got the NBA to agree that, since Chamberlain grew up in Philadelphia, the Warriors held his territorial rights.

26.4% — **Nolan Ryan** to Angels (from the Mets for infielder Jim Fregosi)

Also mentioned: Pedro Martinez to the Expos, Jeff Bagwell to the Astros, Ryne Sandberg to the Cubs

Total Votes: 14,210

1 **Dirk Nowitzki scores 50** points to lead the Dallas Mavericks to a 117-101 win and a 3-2 series lead over the Suns in the Western Conference finals.

2 **The Miami Heat** advance to the NBA Finals for the first time in the club's 18-year history as they trounce the Detroit Pistons, 95-78, in Game 6 to win their series four games to two.

Free-spirited Ricky Williams, serving a year-long suspension from the NFL, gains seven yards on four carries in his debut with the CFL's Toronto Argonauts.

3 **The Dallas Mavericks earn** their ticket to the big dance as they rally from an 18-point deficit to beat Phoenix, 102-93, and win their series four games to two.

5 **Edmonton goaltender** Dwayne Roloson is injured in the Oilers' last-second 5-4 loss to the Carolina Hurricanes in Game 1 of the Stanley Cup finals. Roloson had been instrumental in leading the eight-seeded Oilers to the finals.

Bowler Kelly Kulick becomes the first woman to be a full-time member of the Professional Bowlers Association. She averages 224 to finish sixth at the Tour Trials to earn her season-long exemption.

6 **The Kansas City Royals** select righthanded pitcher Luke Hochevar with the first pick in the Major League Baseball draft. Hochevar was a first-round compensatory choice (40th overall) of the Los Angeles Dodgers but couldn't come to terms.

Arizona Diamondbacks pitcher Jason Grimsley's home is searched by 13 federal agents and details are released about Grimsley's use of human growth hormone, steroids and amphetamines. In April, Grimsley had identified several other major league players who had either used or supplied the drugs to him, but the names were blacked out in court documents.

9 **The 2006 World Cup kicks off** as host Germany rolls over Costa Rica, 4-2, in opening round Group A pool play.

10 **Justine Henin-Hardenne** beats Svetlana Kuznetsova, 6-4, 6-4, to become the first woman since Steffi Graf in 1995-96 to win back-to-back French Open titles.

Jazil, ridden by 18-year-old jockey Fernando Jara, wins the Belmont Stakes (the third leg of thoroughbred racing's Triple Crown) by 1¼ lengths. Bluegrass Cat and Sunriver finish in second and third, respectively. Jara is the youngest jockey to saddle a Triple Crown winner since 18-year-old Steve Cauthen in 1978.

AP/Wide World Photos

> Pittsburgh police officers examine what's left of Steelers quarterback **Ben Roethlisberger's** motorcycle after his horrific accident on June 12.

10 **Rafael Nadal tops** Roger Federer on clay once again, 1-6, 6-1, 6-4, 7-6, to win his second consecutive French Open.

Bernard Hopkins, 41, scores a unanimous decision over Antonio Tarver to win the light heavyweight title in Atlantic City.

12 **Ben Roethlisberger** is severely injured in a motorcycle accident in downtown Pittsburgh. The 24-year-old, who was not wearing a helmet, undergoes several hours of surgery to repair a broken jaw, broken nose and several deep lacerations.

The United States has a poor showing in their opening World Cup match, as they're blanked by the Czech Republic, 3-0.

14 **White Sox manager Ozzie Guillen** is seen screaming at his rookie pitcher Sean Tracey in the dugout, presumably for not plunking Rangers batter Hank Blalock in retaliation for A.J. Pierzynski being hit earlier.

16 **Tiger Woods misses the cut** at the U.S. Open, his first major since the death of his father, Earl.

18 **"I can't believe I just did that."** Phil Mickelson hits a hospitality tent, then a tree on the 18th hole at the U.S. Open at Winged Foot, blowing what appeared to be a rock-solid lead. Geoff Ogilvy takes advantage of Phil's gaffes to win his first major.

19 **The Carolina Hurricanes** hoist the Stanley Cup after beating Edmonton, 3-1, in Game 7. Rookie goaltender Cam Ward wins the Conn Smythe Award as playoff MVP.

20 **The Miami Heat rally to beat** the Dallas Mavericks, 95-92, in Game 6 of the NBA Finals to win their first championship. Dwyane Wade is named finals MVP as coach Pat Riley wins his fifth title.

22 **It's all over for the U.S.** as Bruce Arena's squad loses to Ghana, 2-1, and is eliminated from World Cup play.

27 **Brazilian Ronaldo scores his 15th** career World Cup goal to become the tournament's all-time leading goal scorer.

28 **The Toronto Raptors** make Italian Andrea Bargnani the top pick in the NBA draft.

July 2006

Sun	Mon	Tue	Wed	Thu	Fri	Sat
						1
2	3	4	5	6	7	8
9	10	11	12	13	14	15
16	17	18	19	20	21	22
23/30	24/31	25	26	27	28	29

This again?

With the Zinedine Zidane headbutt being shown on every television station and Internet site across the world, SportsNation thought it was the perfect time to rank the most overplayed sports moments of all-time. Note: list does not include the Zidane headbutt.

56.4%	—	Bill Buckner's error
39.0%	—	Steve Bartman's foul ball
38.9%	—	Janet Jackson's wardrobe malfunction
34.0%	—	Terrell Owens' Sharpie
32.8%	—	Dennis Rodman's wedding dress
32.3%	—	Cal-Stanford's band finale
30.8%	—	Nancy Kerrigan's "Why me?"
28.3%	—	Bob Knight's chair fling
24.5%	—	Brandi Chastain's bra
24.3%	—	Michael Jordan's shrug
20.8%	—	Chris Webber's timeout
15.2%	—	George Brett's pine-tarred bat
14.9%	—	Roger Clemens throwing bat towards Mike Piazza
13.9%	—	Mike Tyson's freakout
13.2%	—	Joe Namath's index finger
13.1%	—	John McEnroe's, "You can't be serious!"
12.2%	—	Jose Canseco's header home run
7.6%	—	Kellen Winslow being carried off field by teammates
6.2%	—	Bobby Thomson's shot off Branca
4.5%	—	Bobby Orr's flyover

Total Votes: 6,979

1 Shocker! Perennial World Cup favorite and five-time champ Brazil is ousted by France and Zinedine Zidane, 1-0, in the quarterfinals. England is also dealt a blow, as it is eliminated in a penalty shootout to Portugal. David Beckham gives up his captainship the following day.

3 Annika Sorenstam wins the U.S. Women's Open in an 18-hole playoff with Pat Hurst for her 10th career major championship. She ties Babe Zaharias for fourth on the LPGA's all-time list.

Classy Steve Yzerman retires from the NHL after 22 brilliant seasons with the Detroit Red Wings.

4 Italy scores two goals in overtime to beat host Germany, 2-0, and advance to the World Cup final.

Big Ben Wallace, a four-time NBA defensive player of the year, signs a four-year, $60 million deal with the Chicago Bulls, after seven seasons with the Detroit Pistons.

5 Zinedine Zidane scores on a controversial penalty kick (aren't they all?) to lift France to a 1-0 win over Portugal, setting up a World Cup final showdown with Italy.

7 Indians slugger Travis Hafner becomes the first player in major league history to hit five grand slams before the all-star break.

8 No. 1-ranked Amelie Mauresmo beats Justine Henin-Hardenne, 2-6, 6-3, 6-4, in the finals at Wimbledon for her second grand slam title of the year.

9 Italy wins its fourth World Cup title and first since 1982, beating France, 5-3 in penalty kicks after a 1-1 tie in two hours of regulation and overtime. The win is perhaps overshadowed by the violent and surprising head butt leveled by French star Zinedine Zidane into the chest of Italian defender Marco Materazzi in the 110th minute. It was first reported that Materazzi called Zidane a terrorist, then the story was changed, claiming simply that he said derogatory things about Zidane's mother and sister. Either way, Zidane earns an immediate ejection, removing him from the penalty kick shootout.

Roger Federer takes care of business, as usual, beating Rafael Nadal, 6-0, 7-5, 6-7, 6-3, for his eighth grand slam victory and fourth straight Wimbledon title.

Formula One star Juan Pablo Montoya announces his intentions to switch to NASCAR, beginning with the 2007 season. A day later, McLaren-Mercedes replaces him for the final eight races of the Formula One season.

France's **Zinedine Zidane** is forced to do the walk of shame, past the World Cup trophy, after being sent off for his infamous headbutt of Marco Materazzi.

11 Michael Young lines a two-out, two-run triple of National League closer Trevor Hoffman to give the American League a 3-2 win in the 77th Major League All-Star Game. It is the AL's ninth consecutive victory (not including the infamous tie in 2002). Young wins the games most valuable player award.

13 Kentucky Derby winning horse Barbaro's condition is downgraded after he develops an acute form of laminitis, a painful, often fatal condition in his "non-injured" foot. His doctor says the horse is a "long shot" to survive.

14 Bruce Arena is fired as the coach of the U.S. national soccer team after a disappointing performance in the World Cup.

16 Strangely enough, it is the first day since Sept. 15, 1978 that no save is recorded in major league baseball during a full slate of games. Six saves are blown, however.

Mariano Rivera records his 400th save, the fourth pitcher to reach that milestone, in a 6-4 Yankees win over the White Sox.

17 ESPN analyst Peter Gammons is released from the hospital, where he's been since suffering a brain aneurysm on June 27.

20 American cyclist Floyd Landis makes up close to eight minutes on the leader to finish the day in third place after a sensational Stage 17 ride at the Tour de France.

23 Landis picks up right where Lance Armstrong left off, cruising down the Champs-Eylsees for his surprising Tour de France win.

Tiger Woods' 11th major title is an emotional one as he breaks down after winning the British Open by two strokes over Chris DiMarco. It is his third British Open title and first major win since the death of his father.

27 Let the firestorm, and the excuses, begin. Reports emerge that Floyd Landis failed a drug test after his outstanding Stage 17 performance at the Tour de France. Officials now await the results of his backup "B" sample.

29 American sprinter Justin Gatlin is the latest high-profile athlete to test positive for performance-enhancing drugs.

AP/Wide World Photos

August 2006

Sun	Mon	Tue	Wed	Thu	Fri	Sat
		1	2	3	4	5
6	7	8	9	10	11	12
13	14	15	16	17	18	19
20	21	22	23	24	25	26
27	28	29	30	31		

NFL Free Agents

With the NFL preseason in full swing, SportsNation gave its opinion on the best and worst free agent signings of the year.

Which team made the best free-agent addition on offense?

53.6%	—	Cardinals sign RB Edgerrin James
16.7%	—	Browns sign C LeCharles Bentley
16.4%	—	Saints sign QB Drew Brees
6.4%	—	Colts sign K Adam Vinatieri
5.9%	—	Redskins sign WR A. Randle El

Which team made the best free-agent addition on defense?

38.7%	—	Browns sign LB Willie McGinest
35.5%	—	Seahawks sign LB Julian Peterson
9.6%	—	Rams sign LB Will Witherspoon
8.8%	—	Redskins sign S Adam Archuleta
4.1%	—	Panthers sign DT Maake Kemoeatu

Who would have been the best choice at QB for the New Orleans Saints?

50.3%	—	Drew Brees
29.7%	—	Matt Leinart
13.2%	—	Vince Young
6.8%	—	Jay Cutler

Total Votes: 87,058

3 **Irish jockey Paul O'Neill** is given a one-day ban by The Horseracing Regulatory Authority for headbutting his horse, City Affair, before a race in England.

Champ Car driver Cristiano da Matta undergoes surgery to remove a ruptured blood vessel in his head after his car collides with a deer that had wandered onto the track during a practice run in Elkhart Lake, Wisconsin.

4 **Phillies 2B Chase Utley** goes 0 for 5 against the Mets to snap his consecutive-game hitting streak at 35 games.

5 **Floyd Landis' backup sample** tests positive for having an illegal ratio of testosterone in his blood. He continues to deny any wrongdoing, and searches for an explanation. Landis is subsequently fired from Team Phonak (who would eventually disband) and his Tour de France win is in serious jeopardy. The case is currently under appeal, but if it goes against Landis, he would be the first cyclist in the Tour's 103-year history to be stripped of a title for doping. Runner-up Oscar Pereira of Spain would be declared the race's winner.

Terrell Owens misses his third straight day of training camp with a bad hamstring, and the situation has already become a media circus, as we all wonder what Owens will do next and how head coach Bill Parcells will react.

6 **Jimmie Johnson,** winner of the 2006 Daytona 500, adds the prestigious Allstate 400 at the Brickyard to his growing resume as he overcomes a blown tire for the victory.

Tiger Woods becomes the seventh golfer in PGA Tour history to win 50 events, with his three-stroke victory at the Buick Open.

Travis Pastrana flies high, landing an unprecedented double backflip on his motorcycle in Moto X Best Trick to win his third gold medal at the Summer X Games.

8 **Former NFL intern Roger Goodell** is selected by the league's 32 owners to succeed Paul Tagliabue as the NFL Commissioner. Tagliabue had announced his intention to retire earlier in the year.

A U.S. District Court judge rules that Major League Baseball names and statistics are not copyrightable, and therefore fantasy baseball leagues are allowed to use them without securing licensing agreements. Whew!

9 **Maurice Clarett is arrested** again after a high-speed chase, and found with four loaded guns in his SUV, as well as a partially full bottle of vodka. He is also wearing a bullet-proof vest.

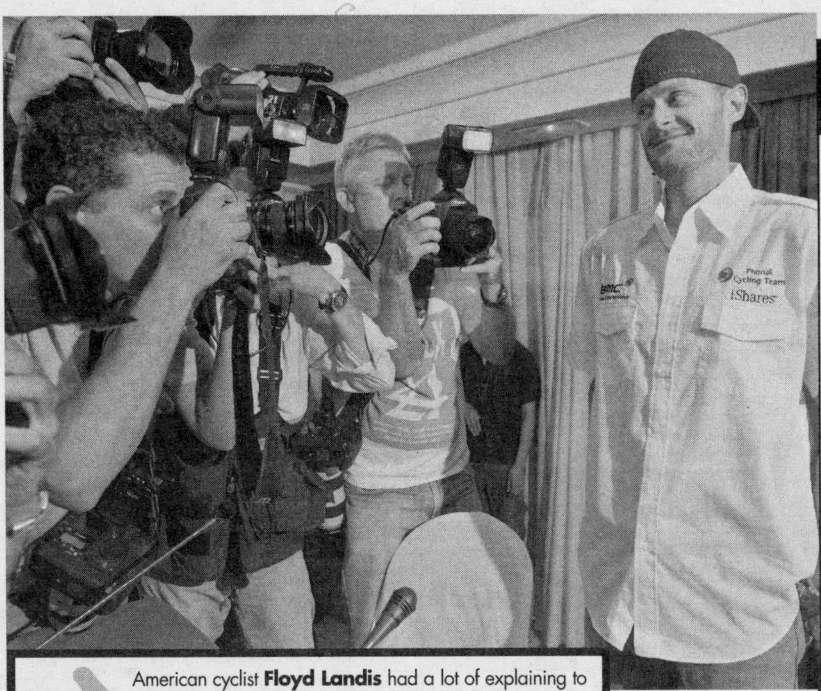

AP/Wide World Photos

American cyclist **Floyd Landis** had a lot of explaining to after two of his samples taken during his Tour de France win tested positive for an illegal ratio of testosterone.

11 Jamie Gold, 36, defeats Paul Wasicka to become the World Series of Poker champion in Las Vegas, and take home the accompanying $12 million prize. He outlasts more than 8,700 other poker players.

12 Russian Evgeni Malkin, the highly touted Pittsburgh Penguins prospect considered the best player outside of the NHL, bolts his team's training camp in Finland, presumably to join the NHL earlier than expected.

In the first week of NFL preseason action, Clinton Portis dislocates his shoulder making a tackle, Reggie Bush dazzles for the Saints and Ben Roethlisberger is back on the field, just weeks after his life-threatening motorcycle accident.

16 Teenager Andy Murray beats the world's top player Roger Federer in straight sets, 7-5, 6-4, in Cincinnati, ending Federer's 55-match win streak in North America.

20 Legend Ricky Carmichael clinches his 10th consecutive AMA Motocross championship with his win in Binghamton, N.Y.

Tiger Woods makes it look easy, winning his second consecutive major and 12th overall, with his 18-under-par, five-stroke victory at the PGA Championship. Shaun Micheel places second.

21 The New York Yankees all but wrap up the AL East title as they complete a five-game sweep of the Red Sox in Fenway Park.

22 Justin Gatlin is given an eight-year ban from Track & Field, and must forfeit his share of the 100-meter record due to his positive drug test.

24 Jerry Rice signs with the San Francisco 49ers, then officially retires from the NFL.

27 Despite an errant shot that bounces off the roof of the clubhouse, Tiger Woods wins his fourth straight tourney with a playoff win over Stewart Cink at the Bridgestone Invitational.

28 Columbus, GA beats Japan, 2-1, on Cody Walker's two-run homer and Kyle Carter's stellar pitching to win the Little League World Series championship.

September 2006

Sun	Mon	Tue	Wed	Thu	Fri	Sat
					1	2
3	4	5	6	7	8	9
10	11	12	13	14	15	16
17	18	19	20	21	22	23
24	25	26	27	28	29	30

Should writers reveal sources?

San Francisco Chronicle reporters Mark Fainaru-Wada and Lance Williams were sentenced to a maximum of 18 months in prison (pending appeal) for refusing to testify about who leaked secret grand jury testimony in the BALCO case investigating Barry Bonds and other elite athletes. What would you do?

Should Mark Fainaru-Wada and Lance Williams give up their source or sources?

51.0% —	Yes
49.0% —	No

Should the justice system be allowed to punish journalists for not revealing their sources?

30.9% —	No
27.8% —	Yes, with lengthy prison time
21.5% —	Yes, with minor incarceration
19.8% —	Yes, with a fine

What do you make of the maximum 18-month sentence?

52.7% —	Too long
25.5% —	That's about right
21.9% —	Not long enough

Do you believe Barry Bonds committed perjury when he testified to a grand jury that he did not knowingly take steroids?

79.8% —	Yes
20.2% —	No

Total Votes: 9,037

2 **Dwyane Wade scores 32** and LeBron James adds 19 points, nine rebounds and seven assists to lead the U.S. past Argentina, 96-81, in the bronze medal game of the World Basketball Championships.

3 **Andre Agassi delivers** a tearful farewell speech after losing to Benjamin Becker, 7-5, 6-7, 6-4, 7-5, in the third round of the U.S. Open. He receives a lengthy standing ovation by the 23,000-plus at Arthur Ashe Stadium, and retires with eight grand slam titles and 60 career wins.

Spain, playing without its top player Pau Gasol, trounces Greece, 70-47, to win the gold at the World Basketball Championships. Gasol, sidelined by a foot fracture in the semifinals, still wins the tournament MVP award.

4 **Tiger Woods cards** a final-round 63 to overtake Vijay Singh and win his fifth consecutive PGA event at the Deutcshe Bank Championship outside of Boston.

5 **Wunderkind Evgeni Malkin** signs an NHL contract with the Penguins, weeks after slipping away from his Russian team in Finland.

6 **Marlins rookie Anibal Sanchez** fires Major League Baseball's first no-hitter in over two years, with a 2-0 win over the Arizona Diamondbacks. Sanchez, 22, walks four and strikes out six to improve to 7-2.

Marion Jones' "B" sample comes back clean, clearing her of allegations that she used performance-enhancing drugs at the U.S. Track and Field Championships in June. Her "A" sample had tested positive for EPO, but Jones and her lawyer vehemently denied any wrongdoing.

7 **The 2006 NFL season** kicks off with the defending champion Pittsburgh Steelers whipping the Miami Dolphins, 28-17. Charlie Batch fills in for injured quarterback Ben Roethlisberger, who is sidelined with appendicitis.

9 **Smooth 19-year-old Russian Maria Sharapova** defeats Justine Henin-Hardenne, 6-4, 6-4, to win the U.S. Open women's title, the second major championship (Wimbledon 2004) of her career.

The Detroit Shock, coached by Bill Laimbeer, wins its second WNBA title in the last four years with a 80-75 victory over the defending champion Sacramento Monarchs.

Kasey Kahne finishes third at the Chevy Rock & Roll 400, which is enough to vault him into the Chase for the Nextel Cup playoff series, and knock defending champ Tony Stewart out.

10 **Peyton Manning outduels** brother Eli as the Colts defeat the Giants, 26-21.

AP/Wide World Photos

Oh what a difference a year makes. New Orleans still has a long road to recovery, but on September 25, a big step was taken when the Saints returned to the **Superdome**.

Roger Federer tops Andy Roddick, 6-2, 4-6, 7-5, 6-1, in the finals of the U.S. open for his third straight Open championship and ninth grand slam title. Also, 49-year-old living legend Martina Navratilova retires, but not before winning the mixed doubles title with teammate Bob Bryan for her 59th overall grand slam title.

Sam Hornish Jr. places third at the Indy 300 in Joliet to clinch his third IRL IndyCar season points championship.

11 Two of Lance Armstrong's former teammates admit to using the endurance-boosting EPO in preparation for the 1999 Tour de France, Armstrong's first Tour victory.

12 The New York Islanders sign goaltender Rick DiPietro to a record 15-year deal that will pay him $67.5 million and lock up the former top overall pick until he's nearly 40.

19 The Los Angeles Dodgers hit four consecutive home runs in the bottom of the ninth to tie the Padres, then win, 11-10, on Nomar Garciaparra's two-run shot in the 10th.

21 *San Francisco Chronicle* reporters Lance Williams and Mark Fainaru-Wada are sentenced to a maximum 18 months in jail for refusing to divulge sources surrounding Barry Bonds' alleged drug use.

24 Europe gives the U.S. team yet another lesson in team golf play, whipping the Americans, 18½-9½, at the Ryder Cup.

Tampa Bay quarterback Chris Simms is rushed to the hospital and has his spleen removed after the Bucs' loss to Carolina.

Padres closer Trevor Hoffman earns his 479th career save, breaking Lee Smith's all-time major league record.

25 The Saints march back in to the Superdome for the first time since Hurricane Katrina and rock the Falcons, 23-3.

26 Terrell Owens is taken to a hospital after his publicist called 911, claiming the star receiver may have overdosed on pain medication. The police report includes the word "suicide" but Owens vehemently denies that, insisting he simply had an allergic reaction.

October 2006

Sun	Mon	Tue	Wed	Thu	Fri	Sat
1	2	3	4	5	6	7
8	9	10	11	12	13	14
15	16	17	18	19	20	21
22	23	24	25	26	27	28
29	30	31				

College vs. Pro Football
Which do you prefer?

Postseason: BCS championship game vs. Super Bowl

65.1%	—	Pro football
34.9%	—	College Football

Legendary coaches: Joe Paterno vs. Bill Parcells

81.4%	—	College football
18.6%	—	Pro Football

Cheerleaders: USC Trojans vs Dallas Cowboys

57.7%	—	Pro football
42.3%	—	College Football

Rivalries: Michigan-Ohio St. vs. Cowboys-Redskins

90.7%	—	College football
9.3%	—	Pro Football

Traditions: Dotting the "I" in Columbus vs. Lambeau Leap

61.1%	—	College football
38.9%	—	Pro Football

Holiday viewing: New Year's Day vs. Thanksgiving

69.3%	—	College football
30.7%	—	Pro Football

Total Votes: 112,028

1 Dangerous, malicious and reckless" is what pitcher Roger Clemens calls a document by former teammate Jason Grimsley, claiming Clemens used performance-enhancing drugs. Clemens' name, along with four others, was originally blacked out when the document was originally released. The other four exposed names on the list were Andy Pettitte, Miguel Tejada, Brian Roberts and Jay Gibbons. All five strongly deny the claim.

Tiger Woods goes wire-to-wire in winning his sixth straight PGA Tour event, an eight-stroke victory over Ian Poulter and Adam Scott at the American Express Championship.

2 Albert Haynesworth, a defensive end for the Tennessee Titans, is suspended for five games for kicking and scraping his cleats across the forehead of helmetless Dallas center Andre Gurode. Gurode reportedly needed 30 stitches to close seven lacerations. He declined to press criminal charges.

4 The Carolina Hurricanes raise their championship banner to the rafters, then lose to the Sabres in a shootout, as the 2006-07 NHL season gets underway.

5 The Pittsburgh Penguins are sold by Mario Lemieux to Research in Motion (RIM) co-CEO Jim Balsillie. RIM is the Canadian company that produces the ubiquitous BlackBerry wireless handheld.

6 Buck O'Neil, the former Negro League star and beloved baseball ambassador, dies at the age of 94.

7 The wild card champion Detroit Tigers take down the mighty New York Yankees in four games (3-1) and advance to the ALCS. The Big Apple isn't completely shut out of the LCS as the Mets complete their sweep of the Dodgers.

8 Brian Vickers wins the UAW-Ford 500 after accidentally spinning out Chase contenders Dale Earnhardt Jr. and Jimmie Johnson on the final lap.

Terrell Owens is a non-factor in his return to Philadelphia, as Donovan McNabb leads the Eagles over the Cowboys, 38-24. Owens has three catches for 45 yards.

11 Yankees pitcher Cory Lidle, 34, and his flight instructor are killed when the small plane Lidle is piloting crashes into a high-rise apartment building in Manhattan.

13 Arnold Palmer withdraws from a Champions Tour event early in the opening round and announces he's done playing competitive golf.

AP/Wide World Photos

It was a surreal scene in Manhattan on October 11, when it was learned that the plane that hit a 50-story apartment building was piloted by Yankees pitcher **Cory Lidle**.

14 Miami-FL and Florida International engage in a nasty on-field brawl, complete with stomping and helmet-swinging. The Sun Belt Conference suspends 18 players from FIU while the ACC sits down 13 Miami players.

Magglio Ordonez hits a three-run, walk-off home run to push the Detroit Tigers past the Oakland A's in Game 4 of the ALCS, 6-3, and into the World Series.

16 Lou Piniella is hired to replace the recently fired Dusty Baker as manager of the Chicago Cubs.

Down 20-0 at halftime, the Chicago Bears record a stirring come-from-behind 24-23 win over the Arizona Cardinals on Monday Night Football.

18 Giants running back Tiki Barber announces his intentions to retire from the NFL after the season, sending fantasy football keeper league owners into a frenzy.

19 The St. Louis Cardinals beat the New York Mets in Game 7 of the NLCS, 3-1, on catcher Yadier Molina's ninth-inning home run.

21 Michigan St. overcomes a 38-3 second half deficit to beat Northwestern, 41-38, while Notre Dame beats UCLA, 20-17, on a last-minute Brady Quinn touchdown pass.

22 The Tigers beat the Cardinals, 3-1, to even the World Series at a game apiece, but all eyes are on the dirt, pine tar, shmutz, or whatever it is that has to be removed from Kenny Rogers' pitching hand.

Fernando Alonso wins the Formula One World Drivers Championship, while seven-time champ Michael Schumacher, possibly F-1's best all-time driver, retires.

24 MLB and its players union avoid any potential work stoppage by inking a new 5-year labor agreement, good through 2011.

27 It's all over! The St. Louis Cardinals are World Series champions for the first time since 1982 after their 4-2 win over the Tigers in Game 5. David Eckstein is named series MVP.

28 Red Auerbach, the former coach and architect of the Boston Celtics' dynasties dating back to the 1950's, dies of a heart attack at 89.

W2W4: What To Watch For in 2007

AP/Wide World Photos

Tiger Woods, *who trails only Jack Nicklaus in major titles, looks to close the gap even further.*

AP/Wide World Photos

*The 32nd **America's Cup** sets sail on June 23 in Valencia, Spain.*

AP/Wide World Photos

Troy Smith *and Ohio State hope to be in the BCS Championship Game in Glendale, Ariz.*

AP/Wide World Photos

Barry Bonds *needs 22 homers to pass Hank Aaron and become the all-time home run king.*

2005 / 2006 YEAR IN REVIEW

Jovial Phillies slugger **Ryan Howard** broke out in 2006, swatting 58 homers and driving in 149 runs.

CARDINAL RULE

Despite only 83 wins in the regular season, the St. Louis Cardinals catch lightning in the postseason for their tenth title.

AFTER YEARS OF TRYING, MAJOR LEAGUE BASEBALL FOUND THAT ELUSIVE, NFL-LIKE STATE OF PARITY IN 2006.

Whether it was a welcome development depends more upon your interest in high Nielsen ratings or what commissioner Bud Selig likes to call the "hope and faith" factor.

The most unpredictable season in recent memory reached a topsy-turvy conclusion when the St. Louis Cardinals beat the Detroit Tigers for their first title since 1982. It was the first time in history that two teams with losing records after the All- Star break met in a World Series, and the lack of star power (Albert Pujols aside) and all-around ragged play put a damper on television viewing and a crimp in company cafeteria buzz.

The most compelling early storyline of the Series came when Detroit starter Kenny Rogers was caught with a brown substance on his left hand that might have been: a) dirt, b) pine tar or c) leftover chocolate cake. The incident led to several days of controversy and gave Rogers yet another reason to dislike TV cameramen — as if he really needed one.

While Detroit batted .199 as a team and played shoddy defense, St. Louis rode strong starting pitching and the inspired play of shortstop David Eckstein to a 4-1 Series victory. The Cardinals became the seventh different club to win a title since 2000, further debunking the notion that the Yankees' $200 million payroll makes them invincible.

The American League Central, derided as a baseball wasteland a few years ago, emerged as the game's power center in 2006. The Tigers, fueled by an array of strong young arms and the leadership of new manager Jim Leyland, got off to a 76-36 start before slumping in August and September and settling for the wild card. Still, it was a major step forward for a franchise that went 43-119 just three years earlier.

 Jerry Crasnick covers baseball for ESPN Insider and is the author of *License To Deal.*

> **Scott Rolen** and **Albert Pujols** celebrate with the rest of St. Louis after the Cardinals beat the Tigers, 4-2, in Game 5 for their first World Series title since 1982.

The Minnesota Twins, behind batting champion Joe Mauer, MVP candidate Justin Morneau and the game's top pitcher Johan Santana, posted a 69-32 record after mid-June and overtook Detroit on the final day of the season to capture their fourth division title in five years.

That left no room for the Cleveland Indians, who finished with a 78-84 record despite scoring 88 more runs than they allowed, or the defending champion Chicago White Sox. By the end of the season, even the perpetually chatty Ozzie Guillen had relatively little to say about his team's disappointing performance.

In the National League, general manager Omar Minaya's offseason moves worked out well for the Mets, who established themselves as the class of the league. The two Carloses — Delgado and Beltran — had big seasons, and Tom Glavine won 15 games to pull within 10 of the 300 mark. But Pedro Martinez's injury problems proved fatal for the Mets, who lost to St. Louis in the playoffs after beating the Dodgers in the Division Series.

The American League had ample reason to regard itself as the varsity, holding an overwhelming 154-98 advantage in interleague play. Boston (16-2), Minnesota (16-2), Detroit (15-3), Chicago (14-4) and Seattle (14-4) all cleaned up against inferior NL competition.

Mets left fielder **Endy Chavez** made one of the best catches in postseason history in the NLCS. Unfortunately for the Mets, it was in a losing effort.

AP/Wide World Photos

There were plenty of exceptional individual performances in 2006 as well. Santana led the American League in wins, ERA and strikeouts — the so-called pitcher's "Triple Crown." Boston's David Ortiz hit 54 homers and drove in 137 runs even as the Red Sox pulled a late-season fade. And Cleveland's Travis Hafner hit five grand slams...before the all-star break.

In the National League, 28-year-old Pirates overachiever Freddy Sanchez fended off Miguel Cabrera to win the batting title. Not bad for a guy who was behind Joe Randa on the depth chart in April.

After a spring of speculation over whether he would be willing to shift to left field — and several months of summer trade rumors — Washington's Alfonso Soriano busted out with 46 home runs and 41 stolen bases, joining Jose Canseco, Barry Bonds and Alex Rodriguez as the fourth player in the 40-40 club.

The Phillies failed to make the postseason for the 13th consecutive season, but contributed some impressive individual performances. Jimmy Rollins hit safely in his first two games of 2006 to extend his hitting streak to 38, then later in the season, second baseman Chase Utley hit in 35 straight games. The city fell in love with Ryan Howard, the game's most dynamic young slugger, as he passed Mike Schmidt's franchise record of 48 home runs on the way to 58. The six-foot-four first baseman also threw in a win in the Home Run Derby for good measure.

In hindsight, 2006 will go down as one of the strongest rookie crops in history. Pitchers Justin Verlander, Jonathan Papelbon, Francisco Liriano, Jered Weaver and Joel Zumaya wowed opponents in the American League, while Washington's Ryan Zimmerman and Florida's middle infield combination of shortstop Hanley Ramirez and second baseman Dan Uggla were among a slew of National Leaguers to make an impression.

JERRY CRASNICK'S

10 ↓

Biggest Stories of the Year in **Baseball**

10 Death of Kirby.

Baseball took a big emotional hit in March with the news that Kirby Puckett, the effervescent Minnesota Twins center fielder, died of a stroke at age 45. Puckett, a 10-time All-Star and six-time Gold Glover, was the second youngest person to die after being enshrined in Cooperstown – behind only Lou Gehrig, who passed away at age 37. "He was revered throughout the country and will be remembered wherever the game is played," said commissioner Bud Selig.

09 Finally a No-No.

Anibal Sanchez, acquired by Florida from Boston in an off-season trade for Josh Beckett, beat the Diamondbacks 2-0 on Sept. 6 for Major League Baseball's first no-hitter since Randy Johnson's perfect game against the Braves on May 18, 2004. Sanchez went 10-3 to become one of four rookie pitchers to post double-figure wins for the surprising Marlins.

08 Job security...or not.

For the first time since 2000 and only the second time since 1942, no big-league managers were fired during the season. But teams made up for it in October. Texas' Buck Showalter, Oakland's Ken Macha, the Cubs' Dusty Baker, San Francisco's Felipe Alou, Florida's Joe Girardi and Washington's Frank Robinson all got the heave-ho after the final game.

07 New saves leader.

Trevor Hoffman, so quietly efficient over 14 seasons in San Diego, blew a save as the National League lost another All-Star Game. But he was old reliable when it mattered most, converting 46 of 51 opportunities and finishing the year with 482 saves — four more than Lee Smith's career record.

06 New NL East champ.

One of the most impressive team accomplishments in sports came to an end when the Atlanta Braves, plagued by mediocre starting pitching and season-long bullpen issues, failed to win a division title in a full season for the first time since 1990. Bobby Cox's team went 79-83 to finish third in the National League East, 18 games behind the first-place New York Mets.

05 Japan wins Classic

Ichiro Suzuki and friends made a statement on the international stage when Japan beat Cuba, 10-6, to win the first World

Baseball Classic. The tournament featured three weeks of the sublime (Korea's snappy infield defense and the artistry of Japanese pitcher Daisuke Matsuzaka) to the ridiculous (Roger Clemens shutting out South Africa, 17-0). When a Canadian squad with eight left-handed hitters beat the all-star laden U.S. team, 8-6, it was fondly referred to as the "Miracle on Grass."

04 Bronx Tale.
The Yankees won their ninth straight American League East title, but it didn't help the team avoid a turbulent summer. Alex Rodriguez hit 35 homers and drove in 121 runs, but he also tied career highs for strikeouts (139) and errors (24) and batted .071 against Detroit in the playoffs. After the Yankees lost to the Tigers, owner George Steinbrenner flirted with firing manager Joe Torre before the organization decided to bring him back for 2007.

03 Barry passes the Babe.
Barry Bonds hit his 715th homer to move past Babe Ruth into second place on baseball's career list, but didn't hear many cheers. After the best-seller *Game of Shadows* shed light on Bonds' use of performance-enhancing drugs, the Giants star was the focus of animosity and/or apathy as he crept closer to Hank Aaron's

career mark of 755. Selig appointed former United States Senator George Mitchell to head a committee to investigate steroid use in the 1990s. But the Mitchell group made little headway in finding answers.

02 Labor Peace.
Baseball's owners and the Players Association negotiated a new five-year collective bargaining agreement, ensuring labor peace through the 2011 season. The labor deal was forged nearly two months before the old one expired, thanks to a new spirit of cooperation in a game awash with money. Major League Baseball produced $5.2 billion in revenue, quadrupling the total from 1992.

01 Cards are Champs
The Cardinals, who nearly blew an 8½-game lead over the Houston Astros in the final 10 days of the regular season, regroup to beat the San Diego Padres, New York Mets and Detroit Tigers in October to capture the franchise's tenth World Series championship. Tony La Russa (A's, Cardinals) joins Sparky Anderson (Reds, Tigers) as the second manager to win titles in both leagues. Stellar starting pitching and the inspired play of scrappy shortstop and series MVP David Eckstein carry the club to the title. As Jack Buck might say, "go crazy," St. Louis.

2006
Season in Review

SPORTS ALMANAC

Final Major League Standings

Division champions (*) and Wild Card (†) winners are noted. Number of seasons listed after each manager refers to current tenure with club.

American League
East Division

	W	L	Pct	GB	Home	Road
*New York	97	65	.599	—	50-31	47-34
Toronto	87	75	.537	10	50-31	37-44
Boston	86	76	.531	11	48-33	38-43
Baltimore.....	70	92	.432	27	40-41	30-51
Tampa Bay ...	61	101	.377	36	41-40	20-61

2006 Managers: NY–Joe Torre (11th season); **Tor**–John Gibbons (3rd); **Bos**–Terry Francona (3rd); **Bal**–Sam Perlozzo (2nd); **TB**–Joe Maddon (1st).
2005 Standings: 1. New York (95-67); 2. Boston (95-67); 3. Toronto (80-82); 4. Baltimore (74-88); 5. Tampa Bay (67-95).

Central Division

	W	L	Pct	GB	Home	Road
*Minnesota....	96	66	.593	—	54-27	42-39
†Detroit......	95	67	.586	1	46-35	49-32
Chicago	90	72	.556	6	49-32	41-40
Cleveland	78	84	.481	18	44-37	34-47
Kansas City ...	62	100	.383	34	34-47	28-53

2006 Managers: Min–Ron Gardenhire (5th season); **Det**–Jim Leyland (1st); **Chi**–Ozzie Guillen (3rd); **Cle**–Eric Wedge (4th); **KC**–Buddy Bell (2nd).
2005 Standings: 1. Chicago (99-63); 2. Cleveland (93-69); 3. Minnesota (83-79); 4. Detroit (71-91); 5. Kansas City (56-106).

West Division

	W	L	Pct	GB	Home	Road
*Oakland.....	93	69	.574	—	49-32	44-37
Los Angeles...	89	73	.549	4	45-36	44-37
Texas	80	82	.494	13	39-42	41-40
Seattle	78	84	.481	15	44-37	34-47

2006 Managers: Oak–Ken Macha (4th season); **LAA**–Mike Scioscia (7th); **Tex**–Buck Showalter (4th); **Sea**–Mike Hargrove (2nd).
2005 Standings: 1. Los Angeles (95-67); 2. Oakland (88-74); 3. Texas (79-83); 4. Seattle (69-93).

National League
East Division

	W	L	Pct	GB	Home	Road
*New York	97	65	.599	—	50-31	47-34
Philadelphia ..	85	77	.525	12	41-40	44-37
Atlanta	79	83	.488	18	40-41	39-42
Florida	78	84	.481	19	42-39	36-45
Washington...	71	91	.438	26	41-40	30-51

2006 Managers: NY–Willie Randolph (2nd season); **Phi**–Charlie Manuel (2nd); **Atl**–Bobby Cox (17th); **Fla**–Joe Girardi (1st); **Wash**–Frank Robinson (5th).
2005 Standings: 1. Atlanta (90-72); 2. Philadelphia (88-74); 3. Florida (83-79); 4. New York (83-79); 5. Washington (81-81).

Central Division

	W	L	Pct	GB	Home	Road
*St. Louis	83	78	.516	—	49-31	34-47
Houston	82	80	.506	1½	44-37	38-43
Cincinnati	80	82	.494	3½	42-39	38-43
Milwaukee ...	75	87	.463	8½	48-33	27-54
Pittsburgh	67	95	.414	16½	43-38	24-57
Chicago	66	96	.407	17½	36-45	30-51

2006 Managers: St.L–Tony La Russa (11th season); **Hou**–Phil Garner (3rd); **Cin**–Jerry Narron (2nd); **Mil**–Ned Yost (4th); **Pit**–Jim Tracy (1st); **Chi**–Dusty Baker (4th).
2005 Standings: 1. St. Louis (100-62); 2. Houston (89-73); 3. Milwaukee (81-81); 4. Chicago (79-83); 5. Cincinnati (73-89); 6. Pittsburgh (67-95).

West Division

	W	L	Pct	GB	Home	Road
*San Diego ...	88	74	.543	—	43-38	45-36
†Los Angeles..	88	74	.543	—	49-32	39-42
San Francisco .	76	85	.472	11½	43-38	33-47
Arizona	76	86	.469	12	39-42	37-44
Colorado	76	86	.469	12	44-37	32-49

2006 Managers: SD–Bruce Bochy (12th season); **LA**–Grady Little (1st); **SF**–Felipe Alou (4th); **Ari**–Bob Melvin (2nd); **Col**–Clint Hurdle (5th).
2005 Standings: 1. San Diego (82-80); 2. Arizona (77-85); 3. San Francisco (75-87); 4. Los Angeles (71-91); 5. Colorado (67-95).
Note: San Diego won the division due to a better head-to-head record (13-5) against Los Angeles.

Interleague Play Standings

American League

	W-L	Pct		W-L	Pct
Boston.....	16-2	.889	Baltimore	9-9	.500
Minnesota..	16-2	.889	Toronto	9-9	.500
Detroit.....	15-3	.833	Cleveland	8-10	.444
Chicago ...	14-4	.778	Oakland	8-10	.444
Seattle	14-4	.778	Los Angeles ...	7-11	.389
Tampa Bay .	10-8	.556	Texas........	7-11	.389
Kansas City .	10-8	.556	**Totals**	**154-98**	**.611**
New York ..	10-8	.556			

National League

	W-L	Pct		W-L	Pct
Colorado ...	11-4	.733	Atlanta	5-10	.333
San Francisco	8-7	.533	Los Angeles ..	5-10	.333
Florida	9-9	.500	St. Louis	5-10	.333
San Diego ..	7-8	.467	Philadelphia ..	5-13	.278
Cincinnati ...	6-9	.400	Arizona	4-11	.267
Milwaukee ..	6-9	.400	Chicago......	4-11	.267
New York ...	6-9	.400	Pittsburgh.....	3-12	.200
Washington.	7-11	.389	**Totals**	**98-154**	**.389**
Houston ...	7-11	.389			

Minnesota Twins
Joe Mauer
Batting Avg.

Cleveland Indians
Grady Sizemore
Doubles, Runs

Boston Red Sox
David Ortiz
RBI

Minnesota Twins
Johan Santana
ERA, W, K, IP, WHIP

American League Leaders

(*) indicates rookie.

Batting

	Bat	Gm	AB	R	H	Avg	TB	2B	3B	HR	RBI	BB	SO	SB	Slg Pct	OBP
Joe Mauer, Min.	L	140	521	86	181	**.347**	264	36	4	13	84	79	54	8	.507	.429
Derek Jeter, NY	R	154	623	118	214	**.343**	301	39	3	14	97	69	102	34	.483	.417
Robinson Cano, NY	L	122	482	62	165	**.342**	253	41	1	15	78	18	54	5	.525	.365
Miguel Tejada, Bal	R	162	648	99	214	**.330**	323	37	0	24	100	46	79	6	.498	.379
Vladimir Guerrero, LA	R	156	607	92	200	**.329**	335	34	1	33	116	50	68	15	.552	.382
Ichiro Suzuki, Sea	L	161	695	110	224	**.322**	289	20	9	9	49	49	71	45	.416	.370
Justin Morneau, Min.	L	157	592	97	190	**.321**	331	37	1	34	130	53	93	3	.559	.375
Manny Ramirez, Bos	R	130	449	79	144	**.321**	278	27	1	35	102	100	102	0	.619	.439
Carlos Guillen, Det	S	153	543	100	174	**.320**	282	41	5	19	85	71	87	20	.519	.400
Reed Johnson, Tor	R	134	461	86	147	**.319**	221	34	2	12	49	33	81	8	.479	.390
Victor Martinez, Cle	S	153	572	82	181	**.316**	266	37	0	16	93	71	78	0	.465	.391
Jermaine Dye, Chi	R	146	539	103	170	**.315**	335	27	3	44	120	59	118	7	.622	.385
Michael Young, Tex	R	162	691	93	217	**.314**	317	52	3	14	103	48	96	7	.459	.356
Gary Matthews Jr., Tex	S	147	620	102	194	**.313**	307	44	6	19	79	58	99	10	.495	.371
Paul Konerko, Chi	R	152	566	97	177	**.313**	312	30	0	35	113	60	104	1	.551	.381

Note: Batters must have 3.1 plate appearances per their team's games played to qualify.

Home Runs

Ortiz, Bos	54
Dye, Chi	44
Thome, Chi	42
Hafner, Cle	42
Thomas, Oak	39
Glaus, Tor	38
Giambi, NY	37
Ramirez, Bos	35
Rodriguez, NY	35
Konerko, Chi	35
Swisher, Oak	35

Triples

Crawford, TB	16
Sizemore, Cle	11
Suzuki, Sea	9
Granderson, Det	9
Figgins, LA	8
Lopez, Sea	8

On Base Pct.

Ramirez, Bos	.439
Hafner, Cle	.439
Mauer, Min	.429
Jeter, NY	.417
Thome, Chi	.416
Giambi, NY	.413
Ortiz, Bos	.413
Guillen, Det	.400

Runs Batted In

Ortiz, Bos	137
Morneau, Min	130
Ibanez, Sea	123
Rodriguez, NY	121
Dye, Chi	120
Hafner, Cle	117
Guerrero, LA	116
Thomas, Oak	114
Giambi, NY	113
Konerko, Chi	113

Doubles

Sizemore, Cle	53
Young, Tex	52
Lowell, Bos	47
Overbay, Tor	46
Cabrera, LA	45
Teixeira, Tex.	45
Matthews Jr., Tex	44

Slugging Pct.

Hafner, Cle	.659
Ortiz, Bos	.636
Dye, Chi	.622
Ramirez, Bos	.619
Thome, Chi	.598
Morneau, Min	.559
Giambi, NY	.558
Guerrero, LA	.552

Hits

Suzuki, Sea	224
Young, Tex.	217
Jeter, NY	214
Tejada, Bal	214
Guerrero, LA	200
Matthews Jr., Tex	194
Morneau, Min	190
Sizemore, Cle	190
Wells, Tor	185
Crawford, TB	183

Runs

Sizemore, Cle	134
Jeter, NY	118
Damon, NY	115
Ortiz, Bos	115
Rodriguez, NY	113
Suzuki, Sea	110
Thome, Chi	108
Swisher, Oak	106
Glaus, Tor	105

Walks

Ortiz, Bos	119
Giambi, NY	110
Thome, Chi	107
Ramirez, Bos	100
Hafner, Cle	100
Swisher, Oak	97

Stolen Bases

	SB	CS
Crawford, TB	.58	9
Figgins, LA	.52	16
Suzuki, Sea	.45	2
Podsednik, Chi . . .	.40	19
Roberts, Bal	.36	7
Jeter, NY	.34	5
Cabrera, LA	.27	3
Damon, NY	.25	10
Castillo, Min	.25	11

Total Bases

Ortiz, Bos	355
Sizemore, Cle	349
Dye, Chi	335
Guerrero, LA	335
Morneau, Min	331
Wells, Tor	331
Ibanez, Sea.	323
Teixeira, Tex.	323
Tejada, Bal	323

Strikeouts

Granderson, Det	174
Sexson, Sea.	154
Sizemore, Cle	153
Peralta, Cle	152
Swisher, Oak.	152

Pitching

	Arm	W	L	ERA	Gm	GS	CG	ShO	Sv	IP	H	R	ER	HR	HB	BB	SO	WP
Johan Santana, Min	L	19	6	**2.77**	34	34	1	0	0	233.2	186	79	72	24	4	47	245	4
Roy Halladay, Tor	R	16	5	**3.19**	32	32	4	0	0	220.0	208	82	78	19	5	34	132	3
C.C. Sabathia, Cle	L	12	11	**3.22**	28	28	6	2	0	192.2	182	83	69	17	7	44	172	3
Mike Mussina, NY	R	15	7	**3.51**	32	32	1	0	0	197.1	184	88	77	22	5	35	172	3
John Lackey, LA	R	13	11	**3.56**	33	33	3	0	0	217.2	203	98	86	14	9	72	190	16
Kelvim Escobar, LA	R	11	14	**3.61**	30	30	1	0	0	189.1	192	93	76	17	4	50	147	7
Justin Verlander*, Det	R	17	9	**3.63**	30	30	1	1	0	186.0	187	78	75	21	6	60	124	5
Chien-Ming Wang, NY . . .	R	19	6	**3.63**	34	33	2	1	1	218.0	233	92	88	12	2	52	76	6
Erik Bedard, Bal	L	15	11	**3.76**	33	33	0	0	0	196.1	196	92	82	16	5	69	171	6
Barry Zito, Oak	L	16	10	**3.83**	34	34	0	0	0	221.0	211	99	94	27	13	99	151	4
Kenny Rogers, Det	L	17	8	**3.84**	34	33	0	0	0	204.0	195	97	87	23	9	62	99	5
Nate Robertson, Det	L	13	13	**3.84**	32	32	1	0	0	208.2	206	98	89	29	8	67	137	6
Curt Schilling, Bos	R	15	7	**3.97**	31	31	0	0	0	204.0	220	90	90	28	3	28	183	1
Jeremy Bonderman, Det . .	R	14	8	**4.08**	34	34	0	0	0	214.0	214	104	97	18	3	64	202	3
Dan Haren, Oak	R	14	13	**4.12**	34	34	2	0	0	223.0	224	109	102	31	10	45	176	10

Note: Pitchers must have one inning pitched per their team's games played to qualify.

Wins

Santana, Min 19-6
Wang, NY 19-6
Garland, Chi 18-7
Rogers, Det 17-8
Johnson, NY . . . 17-11
Garcia, Chi 17-9
Verlander*, Det . . . 17-9
Six tied with 15 each.

Appearances

Proctor, NY 83
Rincon, Min 75
Camp, TB 75
Shields, LA 74
Farnsworth, NY . . . 72
Putz, Sea 72
Sherrill, Sea 72

Complete Games

Sabathia, Cle 6
Halladay, Tor 4
Benson, Bal 3
Westbrook, Cle 3
Lackey, LA 3
Johnson, NY 2
Millwood, Tex 2
Redman, KC 2
Haren, Oak 2
Hernandez, Sea 2
Wang, NY 2

Shutouts

Westbrook, Cle 2
Sabathia, Cle 2
Lackey, LA 2
Seven tied with 1 each.

Losses

Lopez, Bal 9-18
Silva, Min 11-15
Washburn, Sea 8-14
Escobar, LA 11-14
Hernandez, Sea . . . 12-14
Five tied with 13 each.

Innings

Santana, Min 233.2
Haren, Oak 223.0
Zito, Oak 221.0
Halladay, Tor 220.0
Wang, NY 218.0
Lackey, LA 217.2
Garcia, Chi 216.1
Millwood, Tex 215.0
Bonderman, Det . . . 214.0
Garland, Chi 211.1
Westbrook, Cle . . . 211.1

Saves

	SV	BS
Rodriguez, LAA . . .47		4
Jenks, Chi 41		4
Ryan, Tor 38		4
Jones, Det 37		6
Street, Oak 37		11
Nathan, Min 36		2
Putz, Sea 36		7
Papelbon*, Bos . .35		6
Rivera, NY 34		3
Ray, Bal 33		5
Otsuka, Tex 32		4

Walks

Zito, Oak 99
Meche, Sea 84
Lilly, Tor 81
Beckett, Bos 74
Lackey, LA 72
Padilla, Tex 70
Santana, LA 70
Bedard, Bal 69

HRs Allowed

Silva, Min 38
Beckett, Bos 36
Buehrle, Chi 36
Benson, Bal 33
Garcia, Chi 32
Lopez, Bal 32
Haren, Oak 31

Wild Pitches

Lackey, LA 16
Contreras, Chi 16
Redman, KC 12
Beckett, Bos 11
Hernandez, Sea 11
Haren, Oak 10
Santana, LA 10

Hit Batters

Padilla, Tex 17
Vazquez, Chi 15
Zito, Oak 13
Santana, LA 11
Five tied with 10 each.

Strikeouts

Santana, Min 245
Bonderman, Det 202
Lackey, LA 190
Vazquez, Chi 184
Schilling, Bos 183
Haren, Oak 176
Hernandez, Sea 176
Johnson, NY 172
Mussina, NY 172
Sabathia, Cle 172

Opp. Batting Average

Santana, Min 216
Santana, LA 241
Mussina, NY 241
Beckett, Bos 245
Lackey, LA 246
Sabathia, Cle 247
Johnson, NY 250
Halladay, Tor 251
Rogers, Det 253
Lilly, Tor 254

WHIP

(Walks + Hits/IP)
Santana, Min 1.00
Halladay, Tor 1.10
Mussina, NY 1.11
Sabathia, Cle 1.17
Haren, Oak 1.21
Schilling, Bos 1.22
Santana, LA 1.23
Johnson, NY 1.24
Rogers, Det 1.26
Lackey, LA 1.26

Fielding

Put Outs

Texeira, Tex 1480
Overbay, Tor 1357
Morneau, Min 1297
Sexson, Sea 1235
Konerko, Chi 1173
Youkilis, Bos 1035
Shelton, Det 1003
Kendall, Oak 924
Johjima*, Sea 882
Mauer, Min 866

Assists

Young, Tex 492
Peralta, Cle 459
Betancourt, Sea 430
Guillen, Det 428
Tejada, Bal 418
Lopez, Sea 417
Inge, Det 398
Kinsler*, Tex 393
Loretta, Bos 389
Jeter, NY 381

OF Assists

Rivera, LA 13
Monroe, Det 12
Johnson, Tor 12
DeJesus, KC 12
Cabrera*, NY 12
Ibanez, Sea 11
Cuddyer, Min 11
Crawford, TB 10
Catalanotto, Tor 10
Brown, KC 10

Errors

Guillen, Det 28
Rodriguez, NY 24
Inge, Det 22
Betancourt, Sea 20
Tejada, Bal 19
Berroa, KC 18
Kinsler*, Tex 18
Mora, Bal 17
Three tied with 16 each.

Pittsburgh Pirates
Freddy Sanchez
Batting Average

Philadelphia Phillies
Ryan Howard
Home Runs, RBI, TB

New York Mets
Jose Reyes
Stolen Bases, Triples

San Diego Padres
Trevor Hoffman
Saves

National League Leaders

(*) indicates rookie.

Batting

	Bat	Gm	AB	R	H	Avg	TB	2B	3B	HR	RBI	BB	SO	SB	Slg Pct	OBP
Freddy Sanchez, Pit	R	157	582	85	200	**.344**	275	53	2	6	85	31	52	3	.473	.378
Miguel Cabrera, Fla	R	158	576	112	195	**.339**	327	50	2	26	114	86	108	9	.568	.430
Albert Pujols, St.L.	R	143	535	119	177	**.331**	359	33	1	49	137	92	50	7	.671	.431
Garrett Atkins, Col.	R	157	602	117	198	**.329**	335	48	1	29	120	79	76	4	.556	.409
Matt Holliday, Col.	R	155	602	119	196	**.326**	353	45	5	34	114	47	110	10	.586	.387
Paul Lo Duca, NY	R	124	512	80	163	**.318**	219	39	1	5	49	24	38	3	.428	.355
Lance Berkman, Hou	S	152	536	95	169	**.315**	333	29	0	45	136	98	106	3	.621	.420
Ryan Howard, Phi	L	159	581	104	182	**.313**	383	25	1	58	149	108	181	0	.659	.425
David Wright, NY	R	154	582	96	181	**.311**	309	40	5	26	116	66	113	20	.531	.381
Chase Utley, Phi.	L	160	658	131	203	**.309**	347	40	4	32	102	63	132	15	.527	.379
Adrian Gonzalez, SD	L	156	570	83	173	**.304**	285	38	1	24	82	52	113	0	.500	.362
Nomar Garciaparra, LA	R	122	469	82	142	**.303**	237	31	2	20	93	42	30	3	.505	.367
Todd Helton, Col	L	145	546	94	165	**.302**	260	40	5	15	81	91	64	3	.476	.404
Kenny Lofton, LA	L	129	469	79	141	**.301**	189	15	12	3	41	45	42	32	.403	.360
Jamey Carroll, Col.	R	136	463	84	139	**.300**	187	23	5	5	36	56	66	10	.404	.377

Note: Batters must have 3.1 plate appearances per their team's games played to qualify.

Home Runs

Howard, Phi	58
Pujols, St.L.	49
Soriano, Wash.	46
Berkman, Hou	45
A. Jones, Atl	41
Beltran, NY	41
Dunn, Cin	40
Delgado, NY	38
Ramirez, Chi	38
Hall, Mil	35
Bay, Pit	35

Runs Batted In

Howard, Phi	149
Pujols, St.L.	137
Berkman, Hou	136
A. Jones, Atl	129
Atkins, Col.	120
Ramirez, Chi	119
Beltran, NY	116
Wright, NY	116
Delgado, NY	114
Cabrera. Fla	114
Holliday, Col	114

Hits

Pierre, Chi	204
Utley, Phi.	203
Sanchez, Pit.	200
Atkins, Col.	198
Furcal, LA	196
Holliday, Col	196
Cabrera, Fla	195
Reyes, NY	194
Rollins, Phi.	191

Runs

Utley, Phi.	131
Beltran, NY	127
Rollins, Phi.	127
Reyes, NY	122
Soriano, Wash.	119
Pujols, St.L.	119
Holliday, Col	119
Ramirez*, Fla	119

Stolen Bases

	SB	CS
Reyes, NY	64	17
Pierre, Chi	58	20
Ramirez*, Fla	51	15
Roberts, SD	49	6
Lopez, Cin-Wash	44	12
Soriano, Wash	41	17
Furcal, LA	37	13
Freel, Cin	37	11
Rollins, Phi.	36	4

Triples

Reyes, NY	17
Roberts, SD	13
Pierre, Chi	13
Finley, SF.	12
Lofton, LA	12
Ramirez*, Fla	11

Doubles

Sanchez, Pit.	53
Gonzalez, Ari	52
Cabrera, Fla	50
Rolen, St.L.	48
Atkins, Col.	48
Zimmerman, Wash.	47

Total Bases

Howard, Phi	383
Soriano, Wash.	362
Pujols, St.L.	359
Holliday, Col	353
Utley, Phi.	347
Atkins, Col.	335
Ramirez, Chi	333
Berkman, Hou	333

On Base Pct.

Pujols, St.L.	.431
Cabrera, Fla	.430
Johnson, Wash.	.428
Howard, Phi	.425
Berkman, Hou	.420
Atkins, Col	.409
Helton, Col	.404

Slugging Pct.

Pujols, St.L.	.671
Howard, Phi	.659
Berkman, Hou	.621
Beltran, NY	.594
Holliday, Col	.586
Cabrera, Fla	.568
LaRoche, Atl	.561

Walks

Dunn, Cin	112
Johnson, Wash.	110
Howard, Phi	108
Giles, SD	104
Bay, Pit	102
Berkman, Hou	98
Burrell, Phi.	98

Strikeouts

Dunn, Cin	194
Howard, Phi	181
Hall, Mil	162
Soriano, Wash.	160
Bay, Pit	156
Cameron, SD	142

Pitching

	Arm	W	L	ERA	Gm	GS	CG	ShO	Sv	IP	H	R	ER	HR	HB	BB	SO	WP
Roy Oswalt, Hou	R	15	8	**2.98**	33	32	2	0	0	220.2	220	76	73	18	6	38	166	1
Chris Carpenter, St.L	R	15	8	**3.09**	32	32	5	3	0	221.2	194	81	76	21	10	43	184	3
Brandon Webb, Ari	R	16	8	**3.10**	33	33	5	3	0	235.0	216	91	81	15	6	50	178	5
Bronson Arroyo, Cin	R	14	11	**3.29**	35	35	3	1	0	240.2	222	98	88	31	5	64	184	6
Carlos Zambrano, Chi	R	16	7	**3.41**	33	33	0	0	0	214.0	162	91	81	20	9	115	210	9
Chris Young, SD	R	11	5	**3.46**	31	31	0	0	0	179.1	134	72	69	28	6	69	164	6
John Smoltz, Atl	R	16	9	**3.49**	35	35	3	1	0	232.0	221	93	90	23	9	55	211	5
Jason Schmidt, SF	R	11	9	**3.59**	32	32	3	1	0	213.1	189	94	85	21	6	80	180	11
Derek Lowe, LA	R	16	8	**3.63**	35	34	1	0	0	218.0	221	97	88	14	5	55	123	3
Clay Hensley, SD	R	11	12	**3.71**	37	29	1	1	0	187.0	174	82	77	15	3	76	122	3
Aaron Harang, Cin	R	16	11	**3.76**	36	35	6	2	0	234.1	242	109	98	28	8	56	216	6
Jason Jennings, Col	R	9	13	**3.78**	32	32	3	2	0	212.0	206	94	89	17	3	85	142	10
Tom Glavine, NY	L	15	7	**3.82**	32	32	0	0	0	198.0	202	94	84	22	6	62	131	1
Dontrelle Willis, Fla	L	12	12	**3.87**	34	34	4	1	0	223.1	234	106	96	21	19	83	160	6
Brett Myers, Phi	R	12	7	**3.91**	31	31	1	0	0	198.0	194	93	86	29	3	63	189	3

Note: Pitchers must have one inning pitched per their team's games played to qualify.

Wins

Zambrano, Chi 16-7
Lowe, LA 16-8
Webb, Ari 16-8
Smoltz, Atl 16-9
Penny, LA 16-9
Harang, Cin 16-11
Glavine, NY 15-7
Carpenter, St.L 15-8
Oswalt, Hou 15-8
Maddux, Chi-LA . . . 15-14

Appearances

Torres, Pit 94
Rauch, Wash 85
Capps*, Pit 85
Howry, Chi 84
Stanton, Wash-SF 82
Geary, Phi 81
Qualls, Hou 81
Coffey, Cin 81

Complete Games

Harang, Cin 6
Carpenter, St.L 5
Webb, Ari 5
Willis, Fla 4
Seven tied with 3 each.

Shutouts

Carpenter, St.L 3
Webb, Ari 3
Jennings, Col 2
Harang, Cin 2
Capuano, Mil 2
Bush, Mil 2

Losses

Ortiz, Wash 11-16
Marquis, St.L 14-16
Cook, Col 9-15
Morris, SF 10-15
Duke, Pit 10-15
Peavy, SD 11-14
Maddux, Chi-LA . . . 15-14

Innings

Arroyo, Cin 240.2
Webb, Ari 235.0
Harang, Cin 234.1
Smoltz, Atl 232.0
Willis, Fla 223.1
Carpenter, St.L 221.2
Capuano, Mil 221.1
Oswalt, Hou 220.2
Hudson, Atl 218.1
Lowe, LA 218.0

Saves

	SV	BS
Hoffman, SD	.46	5
Wagner, NY	.40	5
Borowski, Fla	.36	7
Gordon, Phi	.34	5
Isringhausen, St.L	.33	10
Lidge, Hou	.32	6
Fuentes, Col	.30	6
Cordero, Wash	.29	4
Dempster, Chi	.24	9
Turnbow, Mil	.24	8
Gonzalez, Pit	.24	0
Saito*, LA	.24	2

Walks

Zambrano, Chi 115
Davis, Mil 102
Cain*, SF 87
Jennings, Col 85
Batista, Ari 84
Willis, Fla 83
Maholm*, Pit 81
Schmidt, SF 80

HR Allowed

Marquis, St.L 35
Ortiz, Wash 31
Arroyo, Cin 31
Hernandez, Wash 29
Myers, Phi 29
Capuano, Mil 29
Snell, Pit 29

Wild Pitches

Batista, Ari 14
Schmidt, SF 11
Jennings, Col 10
Zambrano, Chi 9
Vargas, Ari 9
Cain*, SF 9
Four tied with 8 each.

Hit Batters

Willis, Fla 19
Ortiz, Wash 18
Bush, Mil 18
Marquis, St.L 16
Morris, SF 14
Francis, Col 13

Strikeouts

Harang, Cin 216
Peavy, SD 215
Smoltz, Atl 211
Zambrano, Chi 210
Myers, Phi 189
Carpenter, St.L 184
Arroyo, Cin 184
Schmidt, SF 180
Cain*, SF 179
Pettitte, Hou 178
Webb, Ari 178

Opp. Batting Average

Young, SD 206
Zambrano, Chi 208
Cain*, SF 222
Carpenter, St.L 235
Schmidt, SF 238
Olsen*, Fla 239
Peavy, SD 242
Arroyo, Cin 243
Webb, Ari 246

WHIP
(Walks + Hits/IP)

Carpenter, St.L 1.07
Webb, Ari 1.13
Young, SD 1.13
Bush, Mil 1.14
Oswalt, Mil 1.17
Arroyo, Cin 1.19
Smoltz, Atl 1.19
Maddux, Chi-LA 1.22

Fielding

Put Outs

Howard, Phi 1373
Helton, Col 1366
Pujols, St.L 1348
Fielder*, Mil 1260
Gonzalez, SD 1242
Delgado, NY 1199
Johnson, Wash 1165
LaRoche, Atl 1117
Jackson*, Ari 1110
Garciaparra, LA 1059

Assists

Hudson, Ari 510
Furcal, LA 493
Everett, Hou 479
Rollins, Phi 446
J. Wilson, Pit 426
Utley, Phi 425
Uggla*, Fla 423
Ramirez*, Fla 411
Renteria, St.L 399
Carroll, Col 397

OF Assists

Soriano, Wash 22
Hawpe, Col 16
Francoeur, Atl 13
Beltran, NY 13
Freel, Cin 12
Victorino, Phi 11
Bay, Pit 10
Taveras, Hou 9
Chavez, NY 9
Six tied with 8 each.

Errors

Lopez, Cin-Wash 28
Furcal, LA 27
Ramirez*, Fla 26
Tracy, Ari 25
Encarnacion, Cin 25
Cedeno, Chi 23
Weeks, Mil 22
Feliz, SF 21
Three tied with 19 each.

Team Batting Statistics

American League

Team	Avg	AB	R	H	HR	RBI	SB
Minnesota . . .	.287	5602	801	1608	143	754	101
New York . . .	.285	5651	930	1608	210	902	139
Toronto	.284	5596	809	1591	199	778	65
Cleveland . . .	.280	5619	870	1576	196	839	55
Chicago	.280	5657	868	1586	236	839	93
Texas	.278	5659	835	1571	183	799	53
Baltimore. . .	.277	5610	768	1556	164	727	121
Los Angeles .	.274	5609	766	1539	159	737	148
Detroit.	.274	5642	822	1548	203	785	60
Seattle.	.272	5670	756	1540	172	703	106
Kansas City .	.271	5589	757	1515	124	718	65
Boston.	.269	5619	820	1510	192	777	51
Oakland	.260	5500	771	1429	175	735	61
Tampa Bay . .	.255	5474	689	1395	190	650	134

National League

Team	Avg	AB	R	H	HR	RBI	SB
Los Angeles .	.276	5628	820	1552	153	787	128
Atlanta	.270	5583	849	1510	222	818	52
Colorado. . . .	.270	5562	813	1504	157	761	85
St. Louis	.269	5522	781	1484	184	745	59
Chicago	.268	5587	716	1496	166	677	121
Philadelphia. .	.267	5687	865	1518	216	823	92
Arizona.	.267	5645	773	1506	160	743	76
New York . . .	.264	5558	834	1469	200	800	146
Florida	.264	5502	758	1454	182	713	110
Pittsburgh . . .	.263	5558	691	1462	141	656	68
San Diego . . .	.263	5576	731	1465	161	698	123
Washington . .	.262	5495	746	1437	164	695	123
San Francisco .	.259	5472	746	1418	163	711	58
Milwaukee . . .	.258	5433	730	1400	180	695	71
Cincinnati . . .	.257	5515	749	1419	217	718	124
Houston.	.255	5521	735	1407	174	708	79

Team Pitching Statistics

American League

Team	ERA	W	Sv	CG	ShO	HR	BB	SO
Detroit	3.84	95	46	3	16	160	489	1003
Minnesota . . .	3.95	96	40	1	6	182	356	1164
Los Angeles . .	4.04	89	50	5	12	158	471	1164
Oakland.	4.21	93	54	5	11	162	529	1003
Toronto.	4.37	87	42	6	6	185	504	1076
Cleveland	4.41	78	24	13	13	166	429	948
New York	4.41	97	43	5	8	170	496	1019
Texas	4.60	80	42	3	8	162	496	972
Seattle	4.60	78	47	6	6	183	560	1067
Chicago	4.61	90	46	5	11	200	433	1012
Boston	4.83	86	46	3	6	181	509	1070
Tampa Bay . . .	4.96	61	33	3	7	180	606	979
Baltimore	5.35	70	35	5	9	216	613	1016
Kansas City . .	5.65	62	35	3	5	213	637	904

National League

Team	ERA	W	Sv	CG	ShO	HR	BB	SO
San Diego . . .	3.87	88	50	4	11	176	468	1097
Houston	4.08	82	42	5	12	182	480	1160
New York	4.14	97	43	5	12	180	527	1161
Los Angeles . .	4.23	88	40	1	10	152	492	1068
Florida	4.37	78	41	6	6	166	622	1088
Arizona	4.48	76	34	8	9	168	536	1115
Cincinnati . . .	4.51	80	36	9	10	213	464	1053
Pittsburgh . . .	4.52	67	39	2	10	156	620	1060
St. Louis	4.54	83	38	6	9	193	504	970
Atlanta	4.60	79	38	6	6	183	572	1049
Philadelphia . .	4.60	85	42	4	6	211	512	1138
San Francisco .	4.63	76	37	7	9	153	584	992
Colorado	4.66	76	34	5	8	155	553	952
Chicago.	4.74	66	29	2	7	210	687	1250
Milwaukee . . .	4.82	75	43	7	8	177	514	1145
Washington . .	5.03	71	32	1	3	193	584	960

Team Fielding Statistics

American League

Team	Pct	TC	E	PO	A	DP	TP
Boston.	.989	6053	66	4324	1663	174	0
Oakland.	.986	6065	84	4355	1626	173	0
Minnesota . . .	.986	6049	84	4318	1647	135	1
Seattle.	.985	6058	88	4340	1630	150	0
Chicago	.985	6092	90	4347	1655	145	2
Texas	.984	6140	98	4294	1748	174	0
Kansas City . .	.984	6035	98	4279	1658	189	1
Toronto.	.984	6096	99	4285	1712	157	0
Detroit.	.983	6230	106	4344	1780	162	0
Baltimore. . . .	.983	5967	102	4257	1608	156	0
New York	.983	6028	104	4331	1593	145	0
Tampa Bay . .	.981	5971	116	4261	1594	156	1
Cleveland	.981	6057	118	4270	1669	165	0
Los Angeles . .	.979	6027	124	4358	1545	154	0

National League

Team	Pct	TC	E	PO	A	DP	TP
Houston.	.987	6239	80	4406	1753	164	0
Colorado. . . .	.985	6249	91	4342	1816	190	0
San Diego . . .	.985	6079	92	4391	1596	138	0
San Francisco .	.985	5961	91	4289	1581	132	0
St. Louis	.984	6169	98	4289	1782	170	0
Atlanta	.984	6031	99	4324	1608	146	0
Arizona.	.983	6259	104	4379	1776	172	0
Pittsburgh . . .	.983	6199	104	4305	1790	168	0
Philadelphia. .	.983	6170	104	4381	1685	153	0
New York . . .\.	.983	6126	104	4384	1638	131	0
Chicago	.982	5903	106	4317	1480	122	0
Los Angeles . .	.982	6293	115	4381	1797	174	0
Milwaukee . . .	.980	5976	117	4277	1582	126	0
Florida	.979	6014	126	4300	1588	166	0
Cincinnati . . .	.979	6064	128	4337	1599	139	0
Washington. .	.979	5941	131	4309	1501	123	0

Pct—Fielding Percentage; **TC**—Total Chances; **E**—Errors; **PO**—Put Outs; **A**—Assists; **DP**—Double Plays; **TP**—Triple Plays.

2006 All-Star Game

77th Baseball All-Star Game. **Date:** July 11 at PNC Park, Pittsburgh, Pa.; **Managers:** Ozzie Guillen, Chicago (AL) and Phil Garner, Houston (NL); **Ted Williams MVP Award:** Michael Young (AL) 1-for-2 with 2 RBI and a game-winning triple.

Note: The league that wins the All-Star Game also secures home-field advantage for the World Series.

American League

	AB	R	H	BI	BB	SO	Avg
Ichiro Suzuki, Sea, rf	3	0	0	0	0	1	.000
Jermaine Dye, Chi, rf	1	0	0	0	0	0	.000
Derek Jeter, NY, ss	3	0	0	0	0	2	.000
Miguel Tejada, Bal, ss	1	0	0	0	0	0	.000
David Ortiz, Bos, 1b	2*	0	0	0	0	1	.000
Paul Konerko, Chi, 1b	2	0	2	0	0	0	1.000
Jose Lopez, Sea, pr-3b	1	0	0	0	0	0	—
Alex Rodriguez, NY, 3b	2	0	0	0	0	0	.000
Troy Glaus, Tor, 3b-1b	2	1	1	0	0	0	.500
Vladimir Guerrero, LA, lf	2	1	1	1	0	0	.500
Michael Young, Tex, 2b	2	0	1	2	0	0	.500
Ivan Rodriguez, Det, c	2	0	0	0	0	0	.000
Joe Mauer, Min, c	2	0	0	0	0	1	.000
Vernon Wells, Tor, cf	2	0	1	0	0	0	.500
Gary Matthews Jr., Tex, lf	1	0	1	0	0	0	1.000
Mark Loretta, Bos, 2b	2	0	0	0	0	0	.000
Jim Thome, Chi, ph	1	0	0	0	0	0	.000
Magglio Ordonez, Det, ph	1	0	0	0	0	1	.000
Grady Sizemore, Cle, cf	2	0	0	0	0	1	.000
TOTALS	33	3	7	3	0	7	.212

National League

	AB	R	H	BI	BB	SO	Avg
Alfonso Soriano, Wash, lf	2	0	1	0	0	0	.500
Freddy Sanchez, Pit, ss-2b	2	0	0	0	0	0	.000
Carlos Beltran, NY, cf	4	1	2	0	0	0	.500
Albert Pujols, St.L, 1b	3	0	0	0	0	1	.000
Ryan Howard, Phi, 1b	1	0	0	0	0	0	.000
Jason Bay, Pit, rf-lf	3	0	1	0	0	2	.333
Carlos Lee, Mil, lf	1	0	0	0	0	0	.000
Edgar Renteria, St.L, ss	2	0	0	0	0	0	.000
Lance Berkman, Hou, ph	0	0	0	0	1	0	—
David Wright, NY, 3b	3	1	1	1	0	0	.333
Chase Utley, Phi, 2b	2	0	1	0	0	0	.500
Brian McCann, Atl, c	1	0	0	0	0	0	.000
Paul Lo Duca, NY, c	2	0	0	0	0	0	.000
David Eckstein, St.L, ss	1	0	0	0	0	1	.000
Matt Holliday, Col, ph-rf	3	0	0	0	0	0	.000
TOTALS	30	2	6	1	1	4	.200

	1	2	3	4	5	6	7	8	9		R	H	E
American League	0	1	0	0	0	0	0	0	2	–	3	7	1
National League	0	1	1	0	0	0	0	0	0	–	2	6	0

E—Lopez (AL). **LOB**—American 3, National 2. **2B**—Glaus (AL); Beltran (NL). **3B**—Young (AL). **HR**—Guerrero (AL, off Penny, 0 on); Wright (NL, off Rogers, 0 on). **SB**—Soriano and Beltran (NL). **SF**—none. **GIDP**—Glaus (AL); Renteria, Wright, Lo Duca (NL). **DP**—American 3, National 1.

AL Pitching	IP	H	R	ER	BB	SO
Kenny Rogers, Det	2	3	1	1	0	1
Roy Halladay, Tor	2	3	1	1	0	1
Barry Zito, Oak	1	0	0	0	0	0
Scott Kazmir, TB	1	0	0	0	0	0
Johan Santana, Min	1	0	0	0	1	1
B.J. Ryan, Tor (W, 1-0)	1	0	0	0	0	1
Mariano Rivera, NY (S, 1)	1	0	0	0	0	0
TOTALS	9	6	2	2	1	4

NL Pitching	IP	H	R	ER	BB	SO
Brad Penny, LA	2	1	1	1	0	3
Roy Oswalt, Hou	1	0	0	0	0	1
Brandon Webb, Ari	1	0	0	0	0	1
Bronson Arroyo, Cin	1	1	0	0	0	0
Brian Fuentes, Col	1	0	0	0	0	1
Derrick Turnbow, Mil	1	1	0	0	0	0
Tom Gordon, Phi	1	1	0	0	0	1
Trevor Hoffman (L, 0-1)	1	3	2	2	0	0
TOTALS	9	7	3	3	0	7

WP—Halladay (AL). **Umpires**—Jerry Crawford (plate); Randy Marsh (1b); Fieldin Culbreth (2b); Jeff Nelson (3b); Mike Everitt (lf); Alfonso Marquez (rf). **Attendance**—38,904 (38,496 capacity). **Time**—2:33. **TV Rating**—9.3/16 share (FOX).

Home Run Derby

Results of the 2006 All-Star Home Run Derby held at PNC Park in Pittsburgh, Pa. on July 10. After last year's experiment that had players representing their native countries, the contest returned to its long-time format that includes four sluggers from the American League and four from the National League. Note that length of home runs listed below is in feet.

First Round

	HR	Long
David Wright, New York (NL)	16	476
David Ortiz, Boston	10	488
Miguel Canrera, Florida	9	471
Ryan Howard, Philadelphia	9	471
Jermaine Dye, Chicago (AL)	7	476
Miguel Tejada, Baltimore	3	461
Lance Berkman, Houston	3	456
Troy Glaus, Toronto	1	450

(Top four advance to second round)

Second Round

	2R	HR	Long
Ryan Howard, Philadelphia	10	18	461
David Wright, New York (NL)	2	18	438
Miguel Cabrera, Florida	6	15	455
David Ortiz, Boston	3	13	472

HR from first round are carried over to second.
(Top two advance to Finals)

Finals

	HR	Long
Ryan Howard, Philadelphia	5	463
David Wright, New York (NL)	4	453

AL Team by Team Statistics

At least 135 at bats or 40 innings pitched during the regular season, unless otherwise indicated. Players who competed for more than one AL team are listed with their final club. Players traded from the NL are listed with AL team only if they have 135 AB or 40 IP. Note that (*) indicates rookie and PTBN indicates player to be named.

Baltimore Orioles

Batting (135 AB)	Avg	AB	R	H	HR	RBI	SB
Miguel Tejada	.330	648	99	214	24	100	6
Nick Markakis*	.291	491	72	143	16	62	2
Brian Roberts	.286	563	85	161	10	55	36
Jay Gibbons	.277	343	34	95	13	46	0
Corey Patterson	.276	463	75	128	16	53	45
Ramon Hernandez	.275	501	66	138	23	91	1
Melvin Mora	.274	624	96	171	16	83	11
Kevin Millar	.272	430	64	117	15	64	1
Jeff Conine	.265	389	43	103	9	49	3
Brandon Fahey*	.235	251	36	59	2	23	3

Traded: OF Conine and cash to Phi. for IF Angel Chavez (Aug. 28). **Signed:** P Ortiz (June 26).

Pitching (40 IP)	ERA	W-L	Gm	IP	BB	SO
Chris Ray	2.73	4-4	61	66.0	27	51
Chris Britton*	3.35	0-2	52	53.2	17	41
Erik Bedard	3.76	15-11	33	196.1	69	171
Sendy Rleal*	4.44	1-1	42	46.2	23	19
LaTroy Hawkins	4.48	3-2	60	60.1	15	27
Todd Williams	4.74	2-4	62	57.0	19	24
Daniel Cabrera	4.74	9-10	26	148.0	104	157
Kris Benson	4.82	11-12	30	183.0	58	88
Adam Loewen	5.37	6-6	22	112.1	62	98
Rodrigo Lopez	5.90	9-18	36	189.0	59	136
Bruce Chen	6.93	0-7	40	98.2	35	70
Russ Ortiz	8.48	0-3	20	40.1	18	23

Saves: Ray (33); Britton and Williams (1). **Complete games:** Benson (3); Cabrera (2). **Shutouts:** Cabrera (1).

Boston Red Sox

Batting (165 AB)	Avg	AB	R	H	HR	RBI	SB
Manny Ramirez	.321	449	79	144	35	102	0
Wily Mo Pena	.301	276	36	83	11	42	0
David Ortiz	.287	558	115	160	54	137	1
Mark Loretta	.285	635	75	181	5	59	4
Mike Lowell	.284	573	79	163	20	80	2
Kevin Youkilis	.279	569	100	159	13	72	5
Eric Hinske	.271	277	43	75	13	34	2
Trot Nixon	.268	381	59	102	8	52	0
Coco Crisp	.264	413	58	109	8	36	22
Alex Gonzalez	.255	388	48	99	9	50	1
Javy Lopez	.251	342	36	86	8	35	0
Alex Cora	.238	235	31	56	1	18	6

Acquired: P Johnson from Cle. for PTBN (June 22); C Lopez from Bal. for PTBN (Aug. 5); IF Hinske from Tor. for PTBN (Aug. 18). **Traded:** P Wells to SD for PTBN (Sept. 1). **Designated:** P Johnson (Aug. 19). **Released:** Lopez (Sept. 9). **Claimed:** P Snyder off waivers from KC (June 17).

Pitching (47 IP)	ERA	W-L	Gm	IP	BB	SO
Jonathan Papelbon*	0.92	4-2	59	68.1	13	75
Curt Schilling	3.97	15-7	31	204.0	28	183
Keith Foulke	4.35	3-1	44	49.2	7	36
Mike Timlin	4.36	6-6	68	64.0	16	30
Julian Tavarez	4.47	5-4	58	98.2	44	56
Tim Wakefield	4.63	7-11	23	140.1	51	90
Jon Lester*	4.76	7-2	15	81.1	43	60
David Wells	4.98	2-3	8	47.0	8	24
Josh Beckett	5.01	16-11	33	204.2	74	158
Manny Delcarmen*	5.06	2-0	50	53.1	17	45
Jason Johnson	6.35	3-12	20	106.1	35	50
Kyle Snyder	6.56	4-5	17	60.1	20	57
Matt Clement	6.61	5-5	12	65.1	38	43

Saves: Papelbon (35); Timlin (9); Tavarez and Javier Lopez (1). **Complete games:** Tavarez, Wakefield and Devern Hansack (1). **Shutouts:** Hansack (1).

Chicago White Sox

Batting (135 AB)	Avg	AB	R	H	HR	RBI	SB
Pablo Ozuna	.328	189	25	62	2	17	6
Ross Gload	.327	156	22	51	3	18	6
Jermaine Dye	.315	539	103	170	44	120	7
Paul Konerko	.313	566	97	177	35	113	1
A.J. Pierzynski	.295	509	65	150	16	64	1
Rob Mackowiak	.290	255	31	74	5	23	5
Jim Thome	.288	490	108	141	42	109	0
Alex Cintron	.285	288	35	82	5	41	10
Joe Crede	.283	544	76	154	30	94	0
Tadahito Iguchi	.281	555	97	156	18	67	11
Scott Podsednik	.261	524	86	137	3	45	40
Juan Uribe	.235	463	53	109	21	71	1
Brian Anderson*	.225	365	46	82	8	33	4

Acquired: P Riske from Bos. for P Javier Lopez (June 16).

Pitching (40 IP)	ERA	W-L	Gm	IP	BB	SO
Matt Thornton	3.33	5-3	63	54.0	21	49
David Riske	3.89	1-2	41	44.0	17	28
Bobby Jenks	4.00	3-4	67	69.2	31	80
Jose Contreras	4.27	13-9	30	196.0	55	134
Jon Garland	4.51	18-7	33	211.1	41	112
Freddy Garcia	4.53	17-9	33	216.1	48	135
Brandon McCarthy	4.68	4-7	53	84.2	33	69
Javier Vazquez	4.84	11-12	33	202.2	56	184
Mark Buehrle	4.99	12-13	32	204.0	48	98
Neal Cotts	5.17	1-2	70	54.0	24	43

Saves: Jenks (41); Thornton (2); Cotts, Boone Logan, Charlie Haeger and Mike MacDougal (1). **Complete games:** Contreras, Garland, Garcia, Vazquez and Buehrle (1). **Shutouts:** Contreras and Garland (1).

Cleveland Indians

Batting (160 AB)	Avg	AB	R	H	HR	RBI	SB
Victor Martinez	.316	572	82	181	16	93	0
Travis Hafner	.308	454	100	140	42	117	0
Ryan Garko*	.292	185	28	54	7	45	0
Ronnie Belliard	.291	350	43	102	8	44	2
Grady Sizemore	.290	655	134	190	28	76	22
Joe Inglett*	.284	201	26	57	2	21	5
Casey Blake	.282	401	63	113	19	68	6
Shin-Soo Choo*	.280	157	23	44	3	22	5
Franklin Gutierrez*	.272	136	21	37	1	8	0
Jason Michaels	.267	494	77	132	9	55	9
Jhonny Peralta	.257	569	84	146	13	68	0
Aaron Boone	.251	354	50	89	7	46	5
Andy Marte*	.226	164	20	37	5	20	0

Acquired: OF Choo and PTBN from Sea. for IF Ben Broussard (July 27). **Traded:** P Wickman to Atl. for C Max Ramirez (July 21); IF Belliard to St.L for IF Hector Luna (July 31); P Mota to NYM for PTBN (Aug. 21).

Pitching (35 IP)	ERA	W-L	Gm	IP	BB	SO
C.C. Sabathia	3.22	12-11	28	192.2	44	172
Jeremy Sowers*	3.57	7-4	14	88.1	20	37
Jason Davis	3.74	3-2	59	55.1	14	37
Rafael Betancourt	3.81	3-4	50	56.2	11	48
Jake Westbrook	4.17	15-10	32	211.1	55	109
Cliff Lee	4.40	14-11	33	200.2	58	129
Paul Byrd	4.88	10-9	31	179.0	38	88
Fernando Cabrera	5.19	3-3	51	60.2	32	71
Fausto Carmona	5.42	1-10	38	74.2	31	58
Guillermo Mota	6.21	1-3	34	37.2	19	27

Saves: Bob Wickman (15); Tom Mastny (5); Betancourt (3); Davis (1). **Complete games:** Sabathia (6); Westbrook (3); Sowers (2); Lee and Byrd (1). **Shutouts:** Sabathia, Sowers and Westbrook (2).

Detroit Tigers

Batting (135 AB)	Avg	AB	R	H	HR	RBI	SB
Carlos Guillen	.320	543	100	174	19	85	20
Ivan Rodriguez	.300	547	74	164	13	69	8
Magglio Ordonez	.298	593	82	177	24	104	1
Placido Polanco	.295	461	58	136	4	52	1
Vance Wilson	.283	152	18	43	5	18	0
Omar Infante	.277	224	35	62	4	25	3
Chris Shelton	.273	373	50	102	16	47	1
Curtis Granderson	.260	596	90	155	19	68	8
Marcus Thames	.256	348	61	89	26	60	1
Craig Monroe	.255	541	89	138	28	92	2
Brandon Inge	.253	542	83	137	27	83	7
Dmitri Young	.250	172	19	43	7	23	1
Matt Stairs	.247	348	42	86	13	51	0
Sean Casey	.245	184	17	45	5	30	0

Acquired: IF Casey from Pit. for P Brian Rogers (July 31);
Claimed: OF Stairs off waivers from Tex. (Sept. 15)).

Pitching (40 IP)	ERA	W-L	Gm	IP	BB	SO
Joel Zumaya*	1.94	6-3	62	83.1	42	97
Jamie Walker	2.81	0-1	56	48.0	8	37
Fernando Rodney	3.52	7-4	63	71.2	34	65
Wilfredo Ledezma	3.58	3-3	24	60.1	23	39
Justin Verlander*	3.63	17-9	30	186.0	60	124
Kenny Rogers	3.84	17-8	34	204.0	62	99
Nate Robertson	3.84	13-13	32	208.2	67	137
Todd Jones	3.94	2-6	62	64.0	11	28
Jeremy Bonderman	4.08	14-8	34	214.0	64	202
Mike Maroth	4.19	5-2	13	53.2	16	24
Jason Grilli	4.21	2-3	51	62.0	25	31
Zach Miner*	4.84	7-6	27	93.0	32	59

Saves: Jones (37); Rodney (7); Zumaya and Roman Colon
(1). **Complete games:** Verlander, Robertson and Miner
(1). **Shutouts:** Verlander (1).

Kansas City Royals

Batting (200 AB)	Avg	AB	R	H	HR	RBI	SB
Esteban German	.326	279	44	91	3	34	7
Mark Grudzielanek	.297	548	85	163	7	52	3
David DeJesus	.295	491	83	145	8	56	6
Mark Teahen	.290	393	70	114	18	69	10
Emil Brown	.287	527	77	151	15	81	6
Doug Mientkiewicz	.283	314	37	89	4	43	3
Shane Costa	.274	237	23	65	3	23	2
Tony Graffanino	.268	220	34	59	5	32	3
Mike Sweeney	.258	217	23	56	8	33	2
Reggie Sanders	.246	325	45	80	11	49	7
John Buck	.245	371	37	91	11	50	0
Joey Gathright	.238	383	59	91	1	42	22
Angel Berroa	.234	474	45	111	9	54	3

Acquired: OF Gathright and IF Fernando Cortez from TB
for P J.P. Howell (June 21); P De La Rosa from Mil. for IF
Graffanino (July 26). **Claimed:** P Wellemeyer off waivers
from Fla. (June 10).

Pitching (45 IP)	ERA	W-L	Gm	IP	BB	SO
Todd Wellemeyer	3.63	1-2	28	57.0	37	37
Joel Peralta	4.40	1-3	64	73.2	17	57
Elmer Dessens	4.50	5-7	43	54.0	13	36
Luke Hudson	5.12	7-6	26	102.0	38	64
Jimmy Gobble	5.14	4-6	60	84.0	29	80
Jorge De La Rosa	5.18	3-4	10	48.2	32	36
Scott Elarton	5.34	4-9	20	114.2	52	49
Ambiorix Burgos	5.52	4-5	68	73.1	37	72
Odalis Perez	5.64	2-4	12	67.0	18	48
Mike Wood	5.71	3-3	23	64.2	23	29
Mark Redman	5.71	11-10	29	167.0	63	76
Brandon Duckworth	6.11	1-5	10	45.2	24	27
Runelvys Hernandez	6.48	6-10	21	109.2	48	50
Andrew Sisco	7.10	1-3	65	58.1	40	52

Saves: Burgos (18); Nelson (9); Gobble (2); Wellemeyer,
Peralta and Sisco (1). **Complete games:** Redman (2),
Hernandez (1). **Shutouts:** Redman and Hernandez (1).

Los Angeles Angels

Batting (135 AB)	Avg	AB	R	H	HR	RBI	SB
Vladimir Guerrero	.329	607	92	200	33	116	15
Robb Quinlan	.321	234	28	75	9	32	2
Juan Rivera	.310	448	65	139	23	85	0
Maicer Izturis	.293	352	64	103	5	44	14
Howie Kendrick*	.285	267	25	76	4	30	6
Orlando Cabrera	.282	607	95	171	9	72	27
Garret Anderson	.280	543	63	152	17	85	1
Adam Kennedy	.273	451	50	123	4	55	16
Chone Figgins	.267	604	93	161	9	62	52
Tim Salmon	.265	211	30	56	9	27	0
Jose Molina	.240	225	18	54	4	22	4
Kendry Morales*	.234	197	21	46	5	22	1
Mike Napoli*	.228	268	47	61	16	42	2

Traded: P Jeff Weaver to St.L for OF Terry Evans (July 6).

Pitching (40 IP)	ERA	W-L	Gm	IP	BB	SO
Francisco Rodriguez	1.73	3-3	69	73.0	28	98
Jered Weaver*	2.56	11-2	19	123.0	33	105
Scot Shields	2.87	7-7	74	87.2	24	84
Hector Carrasco	3.41	7-3	56	100.1	27	72
John Lackey	3.56	13-11	33	217.2	72	190
Kelvin Escobar	3.61	11-14	30	189.1	50	147
Brendan Donnelly	3.94	6-0	62	64.0	28	53
Kevin Gregg	4.14	3-4	32	78.1	21	71
Ervin Santana	4.28	16-8	33	204.0	70	141
Joe Saunders*	4.71	7-3	13	70.2	29	51
Bartolo Colon	5.11	1-5	10	56.1	11	31
Jeff Weaver	6.29	3-10	16	88.2	21	62
J.C. Romero	6.70	1-2	65	48.1	28	31

Saves: Rodriguez (47); Shields (3); Carrasco (1).
Complete games: Lackey (3); Escobar and Colon (1).
Shutouts: Lackey (2); Colon (1).

Minnesota Twins

Batting (135 AB)	Avg	AB	R	H	HR	RBI	SB
Joe Mauer	.347	521	86	181	13	84	8
Mike Redmond	.341	179	20	61	0	23	0
Justin Morneau	.321	592	97	190	34	130	3
Jason Tyner	.312	218	29	68	0	18	4
Jason Bartlett	.309	333	44	103	2	32	10
Luis Castillo	.296	584	84	173	3	49	25
Shannon Stewart	.293	174	21	51	2	21	3
Nick Punto	.290	459	73	133	1	45	17
Michael Cuddyer	.284	557	102	158	24	109	6
Torii Hunter	.278	557	86	155	31	98	12
Rondell White	.246	337	32	83	7	38	1
Jason Kubel*	.241	220	23	53	8	26	2
Tony Batista	.236	178	24	42	5	21	0
Lew Ford	.226	234	40	53	4	18	9
Phil Nevin	.211	218	28	46	10	35	0

Acquired: IF Nevin from ChC for PTBN (Sept. 1). **Traded:**
P Lohse to Cin. for P Zach Ward (July 31).

Pitching (40 IP)	ERA	W-L	Gm	IP	BB	SO
Dennys Reyes	0.89	5-0	66	50.2	15	49
Joe Nathan	1.58	7-0	64	68.1	16	95
Francisco Liriano*	2.16	12-3	28	121.0	32	144
Johan Santana	2.77	19-6	34	233.2	47	245
Juan Rincon	2.91	3-1	75	74.1	24	65
Matt Guerrier	3.36	1-0	39	69.2	21	37
Jesse Crain	3.52	4-5	68	76.2	18	60
Boof Bonser*	4.22	7-6	18	100.1	24	84
Brad Radke	4.32	12-9	28	162.1	32	83
Willie Eyre*	5.31	1-0	42	59.1	22	26
Matt Garza	5.76	3-6	10	50.0	23	38
Carlos Silva	5.94	11-15	36	180.1	32	70
Scott Baker	6.37	5-8	16	83.1	16	62
Kyle Lohse	7.07	2-5	22	63.2	25	46

Saves: Nathan (36), Liriano, Rincon, Guerrier and Crain
(1). **Complete games:** Santana (1). **Shutouts:** none.

New York Yankees

Batting (135 AB)	Avg	AB	R	H	HR	RBI	SB
Derek Jeter	.344	623	118	214	14	97	34
Robinson Cano	.342	482	62	165	15	78	-5
Bobby Abreu	.330	209	37	69	7	42	10
Hideki Matsui	.302	172	32	52	8	29	1
Gary Sheffield	.298	151	22	45	6	25	5
Alex Rodriguez	.290	572	113	166	35	121	15
Johnny Damon	.285	593	115	169	24	80	25
Bernie Williams	.281	420	65	118	12	61	0
Melky Cabrera*	.280	460	75	129	7	50	12
Jorge Posada	.277	465	65	129	23	93	3
Jason Giambi	.253	446	92	113	37	113	2
Andy Phillips	.240	246	30	59	7	29	1
Miguel Cairo	.239	222	28	53	0	30	13

Acquired: OF Abreu and P Lidle from Phi. for IF C.J. Henry, P Matt Smith and Carlos Monasterios and C Jesus Sanchez (July 31). **Traded:** P Chacon to Pit. for IF Craig Wilson (July 31).

Pitching (40 IP)	ERA	W-L	Gm	IP	BB	SO
Mariano Rivera	1.80	5-5	63	75.0	11	55
Mike Mussina	3.51	15-7	32	197.1	35	172
Scott Proctor	3.52	6-4	83	102.1	33	89
Chien-Ming Wang	3.63	19-6	34	218.0	52	76
Jeff Karstens*	3.80	2-1	8	42.2	11	16
Kyle Farnsworth	4.36	3-6	72	66.0	28	75
Jaret Wright	4.49	11-7	30	140.1	57	84
Randy Johnson	5.00	17-11	33	205.0	60	172
Ron Villone	5.04	3-3	70	80.1	51	72
Cory Lidle	5.16	4-3	10	45.1	19	32
Shawn Chacon	7.00	5-3	17	63.0	36	35

Saves: Rivera (34), Farnsworth (6); Proctor, Wang and Jose Veras (1). **Complete games:** Wang and Johnson (2); Mussina (1). **Shutouts:** Wang (1).

Oakland Athletics

Batting (135 AB)	Avg	AB	R	H	HR	RBI	SB
Jay Payton	.296	557	78	165	10	59	8
Jason Kendall	.295	552	76	163	1	50	11
Milton Bradley	.276	351	53	97	14	52	10
Mark Kotsay	.275	502	57	138	7	59	6
Frank Thomas	.270	466	77	126	39	114	0
Bobby Kielty	.270	270	35	73	8	36	2
Marco Scutaro	.266	365	52	97	5	41	5
Nick Swisher	.254	556	106	141	35	95	1
Mark Ellis	.249	441	64	110	11	52	4
Eric Chavez	.241	485	74	117	22	72	3
Dan Johnson	.234	286	30	67	9	37	0
Bobby Crosby	.229	358	42	82	9	40	8

Pitching (40 IP)	ERA	W-L	Gm	IP	BB	SO
Justin Duchscherer	2.91	2-1	53	55.2	9	51
Chad Gaudin	3.09	4-2	55	64.0	42	36
Huston Street	3.31	4-4	69	70.2	13	67
Kiko Calero	3.41	3-2	70	58.0	24	67
Barry Zito	3.83	16-10	34	221.0	99	151
Dan Haren	4.12	14-13	34	223.0	45	176
Rich Harden	4.24	4-0	9	46.2	26	49
Brad Halsey	4.67	5-4	52	94.1	46	53
Kirk Saarloos	4.75	7-7	35	121.1	53	52
Joe Blanton	4.82	16-12	32	194.1	58	107
Esteban Loaiza	4.89	11-9	26	154.2	40	97

Saves: Street (37); Duchscherer (9); Gaudin (2); Calero, Saarloos, Joe Kennedy and Ron Flores (1). **Complete games:** Haren and Loaiza (2); Blanton (1). **Shutouts:** Blanton and Loaiza (1).

Seattle Mariners

Batting (190 AB)	Avg	AB	R	H	HR	RBI	SB
Ichiro Suzuki	.322	695	110	224	9	49	45
Kenji Johjima*	.291	506	61	147	18	76	3
Ben Broussard	.289	432	61	125	21	63	2
Raul Ibanez	.289	626	103	181	33	123	2
Yuniesky Betancourt	.289	558	68	161	8	47	11
Jose Lopez	.282	603	78	170	10	79	5
Adrian Beltre	.268	620	88	166	25	89	11
Richie Sexson	.264	591	75	156	34	107	1
Willie Bloomquist	.247	251	36	62	1	15	16
Carl Everett	.227	308	37	70	11	33	1
Jeremy Reed	.217	212	27	46	6	17	2

Acquired: IF Broussard from Cle. for OF Shin-Soo Choo and PTBN (July 27). **Traded:** P Eddie Guardado to Cin. for P Travis Chick (July 7); P Moyer to Phi. for P Andrew Barb and Andrew Baldwin (Aug. 19).

Pitching (40 IP)	ERA	W-L	Gm	IP	BB	SO
Rafael Soriano	2.25	1-2	53	60.0	21	65
J.J. Putz	2.30	4-1	72	78.1	13	104
Julio Mateo	4.19	9-4	48	53.2	22	31
Jake Woods	4.20	7-4	37	105.0	53	66
George Sherrill	4.28	2-4	72	40.0	27	42
Jamie Moyer	4.39	6-12	25	160.0	44	82
Gil Meche	4.48	11-8	32	186.2	84	156
Felix Hernandez	4.52	12-14	31	191.0	60	176
Jarrod Washburn	4.67	8-14	31	187.0	55	103
Joel Pineiro	6.36	8-13	40	165.2	64	87

Saves: Putz (36); Guardado (5); Soriano (2); Woods, Sherrill, Pineiro and Emiliano Fruto (1). **Complete games:** Hernandez and Moyer (2); Meche and Pineiro (1). **Shutouts:** Hernandez and Moyer (1).

Tampa Bay Devil Rays

Batting (170 AB)	Avg	AB	R	H	HR	RBI	SB
Julio Lugo	.308	289	53	89	12	27	18
Carl Crawford	.305	600	89	183	18	77	58
Rocco Baldelli	.302	364	59	110	16	57	10
Greg Norton	.296	294	47	87	17	45	1
Aubrey Huff	.283	230	26	65	8	28	0
Ty Wigginton	.275	444	55	122	24	79	4
Jorge Cantu	.249	413	40	103	14	62	1
B.J. Upton	.246	175	20	43	1	10	11
Dioner Navarro	.244	193	23	47	4	20	1
Toby Hall	.231	221	15	51	8	23	0
Damon Hollins	.228	333	37	76	15	33	3
Travis Lee	.224	343	35	77	11	31	5
Ben Zobrist*	.224	183	10	41	2	18	2
Jonny Gomes	.216	385	53	83	20	59	1
Tomas Perez	.212	241	31	51	2	16	1

Acquired: P Seo and C Navarro from LAD for P Hendrickson and C Hall (June 28); IF Zobrist and P Mitch Talbot from Hou. for OF Huff (July 13). **Traded:** IF Lugo to LAD for IF Joel Guzman and Sergio Pedroza (July 31).

Pitching (45 IP)	ERA	W-L	Gm	IP	BB	SO
Scott Kazmir	3.24	10-8	24	144.2	52	163
Ruddy Lugo*	3.81	2-4	64	85.0	37	48
Mark Hendrickson	3.81	4-8	13	89.2	34	51
Tim Corcoran*	4.38	5-9	21	90.1	48	59
Shawn Camp	4.68	7-4	75	75.0	19	53
James Shields*	4.84	6-8	21	124.2	38	104
Travis Harper	4.93	2-0	30	42.0	13	32
Jae Seo	5.00	1-8	17	90.0	31	39
Brian Meadows	5.17	3-6	53	69.2	15	35
Casey Fossum	5.33	6-6	25	130.0	63	88
Seth McClung	6.29	6-12	39	103.0	68	107
Doug Waechter	6.62	1-4	11	53.0	19	25

Saves: Meadows (8); Tyler Walker (10); McClung (6); Camp and Dan Miceli (4); Harville (1). **Complete games:** Kazmir, Hendrickson and Shields (1). **Shutouts:** Kazmir and Hendrickson.

Texas Rangers

Batting (100 AB)

	Avg	AB	R	H	HR	RBI	SB
Carlos Lee	.322	236	42	76	9	35	7
Michael Young	.314	691	93	217	14	103	7
Gary Matthews Jr.	.313	620	102	194	19	79	10
Gerald Laird	.296	243	46	72	7	22	3
Mark DeRosa	.296	520	78	154	13	74	4
Ian Kinsler*	.286	423	65	121	14	55	11
Kevin Mench	.284	320	36	91	12	50	1
Mark Teixeira	.282	628	99	177	33	110	2
Hank Blalock	.266	591	76	157	16	89	1
Rod Barajas	.256	344	49	88	11	41	0
Nelson Cruz*	.223	130	15	29	6	22	1
Brad Wilkerson	.222	320	56	71	15	44	3

Acquired: OF Lee and OF Cruz from Mil. for OF Mench and Laynce Nix and P Cordero and Julian Cordero (July 28).

Pitching (35 IP)

	ERA	W-L	Gm	IP	BB	SO
Wes Littleton*	1.73	2-1	33	36.1	13	17
Akinori Otsuka	2.11	2-4	63	59.2	11	47
Rick Bauer	3.55	3-1	58	71.0	25	35
Scott Feldman*	3.92	0-2	36	41.1	10	30
Ron Mahay	3.95	1-3	62	57.0	28	56
C.J. Wilson	4.06	2-4	44	44.1	18	43
Robinson Tejeda	4.28	5-5	14	73.2	32	40
Vicente Padilla	4.50	15-10	33	200.0	70	156
Kevin Millwood	4.52	16-12	34	215.0	53	157
Francisco Cordero	4.81	7-4	49	48.2	16	54
Joaquin Benoit	4.86	1-1	56	79.2	38	85
Adam Eaton	5.12	7-4	13	65.0	24	43
John Koronka*	5.69	7-7	23	125.0	47	61
John Rheinecker*	5.86	4-6	21	70.2	19	28
Kameron Loe	5.86	3-6	15	78.1	22	34

Saves: Otsuka (32); Cordero (6); Bauer (2); Littleton and Wilson (1). **Complete games:** Millwood (2); Loe (1). **Shutouts:** Loe (1).

Toronto Blue Jays

Batting (135 AB)

	Avg	AB	R	H	HR	RBI	SB
Reed Johnson	.319	461	86	147	12	49	8
Lyle Overbay	.312	581	82	181	22	92	5
Vernon Wells	.303	611	91	185	32	106	17
Alex Rios	.302	450	68	136	17	82	15
Shea Hillenbrand	.301	296	40	89	12	39	1
Frank Catalanotto	.300	437	56	131	7	56	1
Aaron Hill	.291	546	70	159	6	50	5
Bengie Molina	.284	433	44	123	19	57	1
Gregg Zaun	.272	290	39	79	12	40	0
Troy Glaus	.252	540	105	136	38	104	3
John McDonald	.223	260	35	58	3	23	7
Russ Adams	.219	251	31	55	3	28	1

Acquired: P Accardo from SF for IF Hillenbrand and P Vinnie Chulk (July 22). **Traded:** P Schoeneweis to Cin. for PTBN (Aug. 17).

Pitching (30 IP)

	ERA	W-L	Gm	IP	BB	SO
B.J. Ryan	1.37	2-2	65	72.1	20	86
Brandon League	2.53	1-2	33	42.2	9	29
Justin Speier	2.98	2-0	58	51.1	21	55
Roy Halladay	3.19	16-5	32	220.0	34	132
Brian Tallet	3.81	3-0	44	54.1	31	37
A.J. Burnett	3.98	10-8	21	135.2	39	118
Scott Downs	4.09	6-2	59	77.0	30	61
Ted Lilly	4.31	15-13	32	181.2	81	160
Jason Frasor	4.32	3-2	51	50.0	17	51
Ty Taubenheim*	4.89	1-5	12	35.0	18	26
Gustavo Chacin	5.05	9-4	17	87.1	38	47
Shaun Marcum*	5.06	3-4	21	78.1	38	65
Casey Janssen*	5.07	6-10	19	94.0	21	44
Pete Walker	5.40	1-1	23	30.0	13	27
Jeremy Accardo*	5.97	1-1	27	28.2	9	14
Scott Schoeneweis	6.51	2-2	55	37.1	16	18
Josh Towers	8.42	2-10	15	62.0	17	35

Saves: Ryan (38); League, Downs, Walker and Schoeneweis (1). **Complete games:** Halladay (4), Burnett (2). **Shutouts:** Burnett (1).

Home Attendance

Overall 2006 Major League Baseball regular season attendance (based on tickets sold) was 76,043,902, the highest total in history. It is the third consecutive season that the attendance record has been broken. The average per game crowd was 31,423. Numbers in parentheses indicate ranking in 2005. HD indicates home dates.

American League

		Attendance	HD	Average
1	New York (1)	4,248,067	81	52,445
2	Los Angeles (2)	3,406,790	81	42,059
3	Chicago (7)	2,957,414	81	36,511
4	Boston (3)	2,930,588	81	36,180
5	Detroit (9)	2,595,937	81	32,048
6	Seattle (4)	2,481,165	81	30,632
7	Texas (6)	2,388,757	81	29,490
8	Toronto (11)	2,302,212	81	28,422
9	Minnesota (10)	2,285,018	81	28,210
10	Baltimore (5)	2,153,139	81	26,582
11	Cleveland (12)	1,997,995	81	24,667
12	Oakland (8)	1,976,625	81	24,403
13	Kansas City (13)	1,372,638	80	17,158
14	Tampa Bay (14)	1,368,950	81	16,901
	TOTALS	34,465,295	1133	30,420

National League

		Attendance	HD	Average
1	Los Angeles (1)	3,758,545	81	46,402
2	St. Louis (2)	3,407,104	80	42,589
3	New York (6)	3,379,535	78	43,327
4	San Francisco (3)	3,130,313	81	38,646
5	Chicago (4)	3,123,215	80	39,040
6	Houston (7)	3,022,763	81	37,318
7	Philadelphia (9)	2,701,815	79	34,200
8	San Diego (5)	2,659,757	81	32,837
9	Atlanta (10)	2,550,524	80	31,882
10	Milwaukee (11)	2,335,643	81	28,835
11	Washington (8)	2,153,056	81	26,581
12	Cincinnati (13)	2,134,607	81	26,353
13	Colorado (14)	2,104,362	81	25,980
14	Arizona (12)	2,091,685	81	25,823
15	Pittsburgh (15)	1,861,549	80	23,269
16	Florida (16)	1,164,134	81	14,372
	TOTALS	41,578,607	1287	32,307

NL Team by Team Statistics

At least 135 at bats or 40 innings pitched during the regular season unless otherwise indicated. Players who competed for more than one NL team are listed with their final club. Players traded from the AL are listed with NL team only if they have 135 AB or 40 IP. Note that (*) indicates rookie and PTBN indicates player to be named.

Arizona Diamondbacks

Batting (135 AB)	Avg	AB	R	H	HR	RBI	SB
Stephen Drew*	.316	209	27	66	5	23	2
Johnny Estrada	.302	414	43	125	11	71	0
Conor Jackson*	.291	485	75	141	15	79	1
Jeff DaVanon	.290	221	38	64	5	35	10
Orlando Hudson	.287	579	87	166	15	67	9
Chad Tracy	.281	597	91	168	20	80	5
Chris Snyder	.277	184	19	51	6	32	0
Luis Gonzalez	.271	586	93	159	15	73	0
Eric Byrnes	.267	562	82	150	26	79	25
Craig Counsell	.255	372	56	95	4	30	15
Carlos Quentin*	.253	166	23	42	9	32	1
Damion Easley	.233	189	24	44	9	28	1

Acquired: P Julio from NYM for P Orlando Hernandez (May 24); P Hernandez from Wash. for P Garrett Mock and Matt Chico (Aug. 7).

Pitching (40 IP)	ERA	W-L	Gm	IP	BB	SO
Brandon Webb	3.10	16-8	33	235.0	50	178
Luis Vizcaino	3.58	4-6	70	65.1	29	72
Brandon Medders	3.64	5-3	60	71.2	28	47
Brandon Lyon	3.89	2-4	68	69.1	22	46
Juan Cruz	4.18	5-6	31	94.2	47	88
Edgar Gonzalez	4.22	3-4	11	42.2	9	28
Jorge Julio	4.23	2-4	62	66.0	35	88
Greg Aquino	4.47	2-0	42	48.1	24	51
Miguel Batista	4.58*	11-8	34	206.1	84	110
Claudio Vargas	4.83	12-10	31	167.2	52	123
Livan Hernandez	4.83	13-13	34	216.0	78	128
Enrique Gonzalez*	5.67	3-7	22	106.1	34	66
Jose Valverde	5.84	2-3	44	49.1	22	69

Saves: Valverde (18); Julio (16); Tony Pena (1). **Complete games:** Webb (5); Batista (3). **Shutouts:** Webb (3); Batista (1).

Atlanta Braves

Batting (140 AB)	Avg	AB	R	H	HR	RBI	SB
Brian McCann	.333	442	61	147	24	93	2
Matt Diaz	.327	297	37	97	7	32	5
Chipper Jones	.324	411	87	133	26	86	6
Edgar Renteria	.293	598	100	175	14	70	17
Adam LaRoche	.285	492	89	140	32	90	0
Willy Aybar*	.280	243	32	68	4	30	1
Andruw Jones	.262	565	107	148	41	129	4
Marcus Giles	.262	550	87	144	11	60	10
Jeff Francoeur	.260	651	83	169	29	103	1
Pete Orr	.253	154	22	39	1	8	2
Ryan Langerhans	.241	315	46	76	7	28	1

Acquired: P Wickman to from Cle for C Max Ramirez (July 21); IF Aybar and P Baez from LAD for IF Wilson Betemit (July 28).

Pitching (40 IP)	ERA	W-L	Gm	IP	BB	SO
Chad Paronto	3.18	2-3	65	56.2	19	41
John Smoltz	3.49	16-9	35	232.0	55	211
Oscar Villarreal	3.61	9-1	58	92.1	27	55
Macay McBride*	3.65	4-1	71	56.2	32	46
Chuck James*	3.78	11-4	25	119.0	47	91
Tyler Yates	3.96	2-5	50	31	46	
Horacio Ramirez	4.48	5-5	14	76.1	31	37
Ken Ray*	4.52	1-1	69	67.2	38	50
Danys Baez	4.53	5-6	57	59.2	17	39
John Thomson	4.82	2-7	18	80.1	32	46
Tim Hudson	4.86	13-12	35	218.1	79	141
Lance Cormier	4.89	4-5	29	73.2	39	43
Kyle Davies	8.38	3-7	14	63.1	33	51

Saves: Bob Wickman (18); Baez (9); Chris Reitsma (8); Ray (5); Mike Remlinger (2); McBride and Yates (1). **Complete games:** Smoltz (3), Hudson (2), Davies (1). **Shutouts:** Smoltz and Hudson (1).

Chicago Cubs

Batting (175 AB)	Avg	AB	R	H	HR	RBI	SB
Michael Barrett	.307	375	54	115	16	53	0
Matt Murton	.297	455	70	135	13	62	5
Juan Pierre	.292	699	87	204	3	40	58
Aramis Ramirez	.291	594	93	173	38	119	2
Derrek Lee	.286	175	30	50	8	30	8
Jacque Jones	.285	533	73	152	27	81	9
Phil Nevin	.274	179	26	49	12	33	0
Henry Blanco	.266	241	23	64	6	37	0
Freddie Bynum*	.257	136	20	35	4	12	8
Neifi Perez	.254	236	27	60	2	24	0
Ronny Cedeno	.245	534	51	131	6	41	8
Cesar Izturis	.245	192	14	47	1	18	1
John Mabry	.205	210	16	43	5	25	0

Acqured: IF Nevin from Tex. for IF Jerry Hairston Jr. (May 31); IF Izturis from LAD for P Greg Maddux (July 31). **Traded:** IF Perez to Det. for C Chris Robinson (Aug. 20); IF Nevin to Min. for PTBN (Sept. 1).

Pitching (60 IP)	ERA	W-L	Gm	IP	BB	SO
Bob Howry	3.17	4-5	84	76.2	17	71
Scott Eyre	3.38	1-3	74	61.1	30	73
Carlos Zambrano	3.41	16-7	33	214.0	115	210
David Aardsma*	4.08	3-0	45	53.0	28	49
Will Ohman	4.13	1-1	78	65.1	34	74
Rich Hill*	4.17	6-7	17	99.1	39	90
Roberto Novoa	4.26	2-1	66	76.0	32	53
Ryan Dempster	4.80	1-9	75	75.0	36	67
Sean Marshall*	5.59	6-9	24	125.2	59	77
Carlos Marmol*	6.08	5-7	19	77.0	59	59
Glendon Rusch	7.46	3-8	25	66.1	33	59

Saves: Dempster (24); Howry (5). **Complete games:** Hill (2). **Shutouts:** Hill (1).

Cincinnati Reds

Batting (190 AB)	Avg	AB	R	H	HR	RBI	SB
Rich Aurilia	.300	440	61	132	23	70	3
Scott Hatteberg	.289	456	62	132	13	51	2
Brandon Phillips	.276	536	65	148	17	75	25
Edwin Encarnacion	.276	406	60	112	15	72	6
Ryan Freel	.271	454	67	123	8	27	37
Royce Clayton	.258	454	49	117	2	40	14
David Ross	.255	247	37	63	21	52	0
Ken Griffey Jr.	.252	428	62	108	27	72	0
Adam Dunn	.234	561	99	131	40	92	7
Jason LaRue	.194	191	22	37	8	21	0

Acquired: P Eddie Guardado from Sea. for P Travis Chick (July 7); IF Clayton, IF Brendan Harris, P Bray, Majewski and Daryl Thompson from Wash. for OF Austin Kearns, IF Felipe Lopez and P Ryan Wagner (July 13); P Lohse from Cin. for P Zach Ward (July 31); P Franklin from Phi. for PTBN (Aug. 7).

Pitching (50 IP)	ERA	W-L	Gm	IP	BB	SO
Bronson Arroyo	3.29	14-11	35	240.2	64	184
David Weathers	3.54	4-4	67	73.2	34	50
Todd Coffey	3.58	6-7	81	78.0	27	60
Aaron Harang	3.76	16-11	36	234.1	56	216
Bill Bray	4.09	3-2	48	50.2	18	39
Ryan Franklin	4.54	6-7	66	77.1	33	43
Kyle Lohse	4.57	3-5	12	63.0	19	51
Gary Majewski	4.61	4-4	65	70.1	29	43
Eric Milton	5.19	8-8	26	152.2	42	90
Elizardo Ramirez	5.37	4-9	21	104.0	29	69
Brandon Claussen	6.19	3-8	14	77.0	28	57

Saves: Weathers (12); Coffey and Guardado (8); Scott Schoeneweis (3); Bray (2); Kent Mercker and Esteban Yan (1). **Complete games:** Harang (6); Arroyo (3). **Shutouts:** Harang (2); Arroyo (1).

Colorado Rockies

Batting (135 AB)

	Avg	AB	R	H	HR	RBI	SB
Garrett Atkins.	.329	602	117	198	29	120	4
Matt Holliday.	.326	602	119	196	34	114	10
Todd Helton	.302	546	94	165	15	81	3
Jamey Carroll.	.300	463	84	139	5	36	10
Brad Hawpe	.293	499	67	146	22	84	5
Ryan Spilborghs*	.287	167	26	48	4	21	5
Kazuo Matsui.	.267	243	32	65	3	26	10
Yorvit Torrealba	.247	223	23	55	7	43	4
Luis A. Gonzalez	.242	149	7	36	2	14	1
Choo Freeman*	.237	173	24	41	2	18	5
Vinny Castilla	.229	275	26	63	5	27	0
Clint Barmes	.220	478	57	105	7	56	5

Acquired: IF Matsui from NYM for IF Eli Marrero (June 9). **Signed:** IF Castilla (Aug. 15).

Pitching (40 IP)

	ERA	W-L	Gm	IP	BB	SO
Brian Fuentes	3.44	3-4	66	65.1	26	73
Ramon Ramirez*	3.46	4-3	61	67.2	27	61
Jason Jennings	3.78	9-13	32	212.0	85	142
Jose Mesa	3.86	1-5	79	72.1	36	39
Jeff Francis	4.16	13-11	32	199.0	69	117
Aaron Cook	4.23	9-15	32	212.2	55	92
Ray King	4.43	1-4	67	44.2	20	23
Tom Martin	5.07	2-0	68	60.1	25	46
Josh Fogg	5.49	11-9	31	172.0	60	93
Byung-Hyun Kim	5.57	8-12	27	155.0	61	129

Saves: Fuentes (30), Mesa, King, Jeremy Affeldt and Scott Dohmann (1). **Complete games:** Jennings (3), Francis and Fogg (1). **Shutouts:** Jennings (2), Francis and Fogg (1).

Florida Marlins

Batting (135 AB)

	Avg	AB	R	H	HR	RBI	SB
Miguel Cabrera*	.339	576	112	195	26	114	9
Wes Helms	.329	240	30	79	10	47	0
Hanley Ramirez*	.292	633	119	185	17	59	51
Dan Uggla*	.282	611	105	172	27	90	6
Josh Willingham* . . .	.277	502	62	139	26	74	2
Miguel Olivo	.263	430	52	113	16	58	2
Mike Jacobs*	.262	469	54	123	20	77	3
Alfredo Amezaga . . .	.260	334	42	87	3	19	20
Jeremy Hermida	.251	307	37	77	5	28	4
Joe Borchard	.230	230	30	53	10	28	0
Matt Treanor	.229	157	12	36	2	14	0
Cody Ross*	.227	269	34	61	13	46	1
Reggie Abercrombie* .	.212	255	39	54	5	24	6

Acquired: OF Ross from Cin. for PTBN (May 27); **Claimed:** OF Borchard off waivers from Sea. (May 4).

Pitching (40 IP)

	ERA	W-L	Gm	IP	BB	SO
Anibal Sanchez* . . .	2.83	10-3	18	114.1	46	72
Taylor Tankersley* . .	2.85	2-1	49	41.0	26	46
Josh Johnson*	3.10	12-7	31	157.0	68	133
Joe Borowski	3.75	3-3	72	69.2	33	64
Dontrelle Willis* . . .	3.87	12-12	34	223.1	83	160
Scott Olsen*	4.04	12-10	31	180.2	75	166
Matt Herges	4.31	2-3	66	71.0	28	36
Logan Kensing*	4.54	1-3	37	37.2	19	45
Ricky Nolasco	4.82	11-11	35	140.0	41	99
Randy Messenger . . .	5.67	2-7	59	60.1	24	45
Sergio Mitre	5.71	1-5	15	41.0	20	31
Brian Moehler.	6.57	7-11	29	122.0	38	58
Jason Vargas	7.33	1-2	12	43.0	30	25

Saves: Borowski (36); Tankersley (3); Kensing and Renyel Pinto (1). **Complete games:** Willis (4); Sanchez (2). **Shutouts:** Willis and Sanchez (1).

Houston Astros

Batting (135 AB)

	Avg	AB	R	H	HR	RBI	SB
Luke Scott	.336	214	31	72	10	37	2
Lance Berkman	.315	536	95	169	45	136	3
Mike Lamb.	.307	381	70	117	12	45	2
Willy Taveras	.278	529	83	147	1	30	33
Chris Burke	.276	366	58	101	9	40	11
Aubrey Huff	.250	224	31	56	13	38	0
Craig Biggio	.246	548	79	135	21	62	3
Adam Everett	.239	514	52	123	6	59	9
Morgan Ensberg . . .	.235	387	67	91	23	58	1
Brad Ausmus	.230	439	37	101	2	39	3
Jason Lane.	.201	288	44	58	15	45	1
Eric Munson.	.199	141	18	28	5	19	0

Acquired: OF Huff from TB for IF Ben Zobrist and P Mitch Talbot (July 13).

Pitchers (45 IP)

	ERA	W-L	Gm	IP	BB	SO
Roger Clemens	2.30	7-6	19	113.1	29	102
Dan Wheeler	2.52	3-5	75	71.1	24	68
Roy Oswalt	2.98	15-8	33	220.2	38	166
Trever Miller	3.02	2-3	70	50.2	13	56
Russ Springer	3.47	1-1	72	59.2	16	64
Chad Qualls.	3.76	7-3	81	88.2	28	56
Andy Pettitte	4.20	14-13	36	214.1	70	178
Fernando Nieve*	4.20	3-3	40	96.1	41	70
Dave Borkowski	4.69	3-2	40	71.0	23	52
Brad Lidge	5.28	1-5	78	75.0	36	104
Wandy Rodriguez . . .	5.64	9-10	30	135.2	63	98
Taylor Buchholz.	5.89	6-10	22	113.0	34	77

Saves: Lidge (32), Wheeler (9); Miller (1). **Complete games:** Oswalt and Pettitte (2); Buchholz (1). **Shutouts:** Pettitte and Buchholz (1).

Los Angeles Dodgers

Batting (135 AB)

	Avg	AB	R	H	HR	RBI	SB
Andre Ethier*	.308	396	50	122	11	55	5
Nomar Garciaparra . .	.303	469	82	142	20	93	3
Kenny Lofton	.301	469	79	141	3	41	32
Rafael Furcal	.300	654	113	196	15	63	37
Marlon Anderson . . .	.297	279	43	83	12	38	4
Olmedo Saenz.	.296	179	30	53	11	48	0
Jeff Kent	.292	407	61	119	14	68	1
J.D. Drew	.283	494	84	140	20	100	2
Russell Martin*	.282	415	65	117	10	65	10
Ramon Martinez	.278	176	20	49	2	24	0
Wilson Betemit	.263	373	49	98	18	53	3
Matt Kemp*	.253	154	30	39	7	23	6
Jose Cruz Jr.	.233	223	34	52	5	17	5
Julio Lugo	.219	146	16	32	0	10	6

Acquired: IF Betemit from Atl. for IF Willy Aybar and P Danys Baez (July 28); P Hendrickson and C Toby Hall from TB for P Seo and C Dioner Navarro (June 28); IF Lugo from TB for IF Joel Guzman and Sergio Pedroza (July 31); P Maddux from ChC for IF Cesar Izturis (July 31); IF Anderson from Wash. for P Jhonny Nunez (Sept. 1).

Pitching (40 IP)

	ERA	W-L	Gm	IP	BB	SO
Takashi Saito*	2.07	6-2	72	78.1	23	107
Jonathan Broxton . . .	2.59	4-1	68	76.1	33	97
Joe Beimel	2.96	2-1	62	70.0	21	30
Derek Lowe	3.63	16-8	35	218.0	55	123
Chad Billingsley* . . .	3.80	7-4	18	90.0	58	59
Greg Maddux	4.20	15-14	34	210.0	37	117
Hong-Chih Kuo*	4.22	1-5	28	59.2	33	71
Brad Penny	4.33	16-9	34	189.0	54	148
Aaron Sele	4.53	8-6	28	103.1	30	57
Mark Hendrickson . . .	4.68	2-7	18	75.0	28	48
Brett Tomko	4.73	8-7	44	112.1	29	76
Jae Seo	5.78	2-4	19	67.0	25	49
Odalis Perez	6.83	4-4	20	59.1	13	33

Saves: Saito (24), Broxton (3); Beimel (2); Eric Gagne and Giovanni Carrara (1). **Complete games:** Lowe (1). **Shutouts:** none.

Milwaukee Brewers

Batting (145 AB)	Avg	AB	R	H	HR	RBI	SB
Jeff Cirillo	.319	263	33	84	3	23	1
Carlos Lee	.286	388	60	111	28	81	12
Corey Hart*	.283	237	32	67	9	33	5
Tony Graffanino	.280	236	34	66	2	27	2
Rickie Weeks	.279	359	73	100	8	34	19
Gabe Gross	.274	208	42	57	9	38	1
Geoff Jenkins	.271	484	62	131	17	70	4
Prince Fielder*	.271	569	82	154	28	81	7
Bill Hall	.270	537	101	145	35	85	8
David Bell	.270	504	60	136	10	63	3
Brady Clark	.263	415	51	109	4	29	3
Corey Koskie	.261	257	29	67	12	33	1
Damian Miller	.251	331	34	83	6	38	0

Acquired: P Gonzalez from NYM for P Mike Adams (May 26); IF Graffanino from KC for P Jorge De La Rosa (July 26); OF Kevin Mench, OF Laynce Nix, P Francisco Cordero and P Julian Cordero from Tex. for OF Lee and OF Nelson Cruz (July 28); IF Bell from Phi. for P Wilfido Laureano (July 28).

Pitching (45 IP)	ERA	W-L	Gm	IP	BB	SO
Carlos Villanueva*	3.69	2-2	10	53.2	11	39
Ben Sheets	3.82	6-7	17	106.0	11	116
Chris Capuano	4.03	11-12	34	221.1	47	174
Jose Capellan*	4.40	4-2	61	71.2	31	58
Dave Bush	4.41	12-11	34	210.0	38	166
Tomo Ohka	4.82	4-5	18	97.0	35	50
Dan Kolb	4.84	2-2	53	48.1	20	26
Doug Davis	4.91	11-11	34	203.1	102	159
Geremi Gonzalez	5.79	4-2	24	56.0	23	44
Derrick Turnbow	6.87	4-9	64	56.1	39	69

Saves: Turnbow (24); Francisco Cordero (16); Brian Shouse (2); Kolb (1). **Complete games:** Capuano and Bush (3); Davis (1). **Shutouts:** Capuano and Bush (2); Davis (1).

New York Mets

Batting (135 AB)	Avg	AB	R	H	HR	RBI	SB
Paul Lo Duca	.318	512	80	163	5	49	3
David Wright	.311	582	96	181	26	116	20
Endy Chavez	.306	353	48	108	4	42	12
Jose Reyes	.300	647	122	194	19	81	64
Shawn Green	.277	530	73	147	15	66	4
Carlos Beltran	.275	510	127	140	41	116	18
Julio Franco	.273	165	14	45	2	26	6
Jose Valentin	.271	384	56	104	18	62	6
Carlos Delgado	.265	524	89	139	38	114	0
Cliff Floyd	.244	332	45	81	11	44	6
Lastings Milledge*	.241	166	14	40	4	22	1
Chris Woodward	.216	222	25	48	3	25	1

Acquired: P O. Hernandez from Ari. for P Jorge Julio (May 24); P Williams from Cin. for P Robert Manuel (May 25); P R. Hernandez and Perez from Pit. for OF Xavier Nady (July 31); OF Green from Ari. for P Evan MacLane (Aug. 23).

Pitching (40 IP)	ERA	W-L	Gm	IP	BB	SO
Pedro Feliciano	2.09	7-2	64	60.1	20	54
Billy Wagner	2.24	3-2	70	72.1	21	94
Duaner Sanchez	2.60	5-1	49	55.1	24	44
Chad Bradford	2.90	4-2	70	62.0	13	45
Roberto Hernandez	3.11	0-3	68	63.2	32	48
Darren Oliver	3.44	4-1	45	81.0	21	60
John Maine*	3.60	6-5	16	90.0	33	71
Aaron Heilman	3.62	4-5	74	87.0	28	73
Tom Glavine	3.82	15-7	32	198.0	62	131
Pedro Martinez	4.48	9-8	23	132.2	39	137
Orlando Hernandez	4.66	11-11	29	162.1	61	164
Steve Trachsel	4.97	15-8	30	164.2	78	79
Alay Soler*	6.00	2-3	8	45.0	21	23
Dave Williams	6.52	5-4	14	69.0	20	32
Oliver Perez	6.55	3-13	22	112.2	68	102

Saves: Wagner (40); Bradford and Hernandez (2). **Complete games:** Maine, O. Hernandez, Trachsel, Soler and Perez (1). **Shutouts:** Maine, Soler and Perez (1).

Philadelphia Phillies

Batting (135 AB)	Avg	AB	R	H	HR	RBI	SB
Chris Coste*	.328	198	25	65	7	32	0
Ryan Howard	.313	581	104	182	58	149	0
Chase Utley	.309	658	131	203	32	102	15
David Dellucci	.292	264	41	77	13	39	1
Shane Victorino	.287	415	70	119	6	46	4
Bobby Abreu	.277	339	61	94	8	65	20
Jimmy Rollins	.277	689	127	191	25	83	36
Mike Lieberthal	.273	209	22	57	9	36	0
Jose Hernandez	.263	152	12	40	3	19	0
Aaron Rowand	.262	405	59	106	12	47	10
Pat Burrell	.258	462	80	119	29	95	0
Sal Fasano	.243	140	9	34	4	10	0
Abraham Nunez	.211	322	42	68	2	32	1

Acuired: P Moyer from Sea. for P Andrew Barb and Andrew Baldwin (Aug. 19); IF Hernandez from Pit. for cash (Aug. 23). **Traded:** C Fasano to NYY for IF Hector Made (July 27); OF Abreu and P Lidle to NYY for IF C.J. Henry, P Matt Smith and Carlos Monasterios and C Jesus Sanchez (July 31). **Claimed:** P White off waivers from Cin. (June 23).

Pitchers (40 IP)	ERA	W-L	Gm	IP	BB	SO
Geoff Geary	2.96	7-1	81	91.1	20	60
Tom Gordon	3.34	3-4	59	59.1	22	68
Brett Myers	3.91	12-7	31	198.0	63	189
Jamie Moyer	4.03	5-2	8	51.1	7	26
Cole Hamels*	4.08	9-8	23	132.1	48	145
Aaron Fultz	4.54	3-1	66	71.1	28	62
Cory Lidle	4.74	8-7	21	125.1	39	98
Jon Lieber	4.93	9-11	27	168.0	24	100
Rick White	5.15	4-1	64	64.2	20	40
Randy Wolf	5.56	4-0	12	56.2	33	44
Ryan Madson	5.69	11-9	50	134.1	50	99
Gavin Floyd	7.29	4-3	11	54.1	32	34

Saves: Gordon (34); Arthur Rhodes (4); Madson (2); Geary, White and Fabio Castro (1). **Complete games:** Lieber (2); Myers and Floyd (1). **Shutouts:** Lieber and Floyd (1).

Pittsburgh Pirates

Batting (135 AB)	Avg	AB	R	H	HR	RBI	SB
Freddy Sanchez	.344	582	85	200	6	85	3
Ronny Paulino*	.310	442	37	137	6	55	0
Sean Casey	.296	213	30	63	3	29	0
Jason Bay	.286	570	101	163	35	109	11
Xavier Nady	.280	468	57	131	17	63	3
Jack Wilson	.273	543	70	148	8	35	4
Joe Randa	.267	206	23	55	4	28	0
Craig Wilson	.267	255	38	68	13	41	1
Chris Duffy	.255	314	46	80	2	18	26
Jose Castillo	.253	518	54	131	14	65	6
Jose Bautista	.235	400	58	94	16	51	2
Nate McLouth*	.233	270	50	63	7	16	10
Jeromy Burnitz	.230	313	35	72	16	49	1
Ryan Doumit	.208	149	15	31	6	17	0

Acquired: P Chacon from NYY for IF C. Wilson (July 31); OF Nady from NYM for P Roberto Hernandez and P Oliver Perez (July 31). **Traded:** IF Casey to Det. for P Brian Rogers (July 31).

Pitching (40 IP)	ERA	W-L	Gm	IP	BB	SO
Mike Gonzalez	2.17	3-4	54	54.0	31	64
Salomon Torres	3.28	3-6	94	93.1	38	72
Damaso Marte	3.70	1-7	75	58.1	31	63
Matt Capps*	3.79	9-1	85	80.2	12	56
Tom Gorzelanny*	3.79	2-5	11	61.2	31	40
John Grabow	4.13	4-2	72	69.2	30	60
Zach Duke	4.47	10-15	34	215.1	68	117
Ian Snell	4.74	14-11	32	186.0	74	169
Paul Maholm*	4.76	8-10	30	176.0	81	117
Shawn Chacon	5.48	2-3	9	46.0	27	27
Victor Santos	5.70	5-9	25	115.1	42	81

Saves: Gonzalez (24); Torres (12); Capps (1). **Complete games:** Duke (2). **Shutouts:** Duke (1).

St. Louis Cardinals

Batting (145 AB)	Avg	AB	R	H	HR	RBI	SB
Albert Pujols	.331	535	119	177	49	137	7
John Rodriguez	.301	183	31	55	2	19	0
Scott Rolen.	.296	521	94	154	22	95	7
Chris Duncan*	.293	280	60	82	22	43	0
David Eckstein	.292	500	68	146	2	23	7
Hector Luna	.291	223	27	65	4	21	5
Juan Encarnacion . . .	.278	557	74	155	19	79	6
Scott Spiezio	.272	276	44	75	13	52	1
So Taguchi.	.266	316	46	84	2	31	11
Preston Wilson	.263	501	58	132	17	72	12
Aaron Miles.	.263	426	48	112	2	30	2
Jim Edmonds	.257	350	52	90	19	70	4
Ronnie Belliard	.237	194	20	46	5	23	0
Gary Bennett	.223	157	13	35	4	22	0
Yadier Molina	.216	417	29	90	6	49	1

Acquired: P Weaver from LAA for OF Terry Evans (July 6); IF Belliard from Cle. for IF Luna (July 31); P Sosa from Atl. for P Rich Scalamandre (July 31). **Released:** P Ponson (July 13). **Signed:** OF Wilson (Aug. 19)).

Pitching (45 IP)	ERA	W-L	Gm	IP	BB	SO
Chris Carpenter	3.09	15-8	32	221.2	43	184
Adam Wainwright* . .	3.12	2-1	61	75.0	22	72
Brad Thompson	3.34	1-2	43	56.2	20	32
Jason Isringhausen . .	3.55	4-8	59	58.1	38	52
Braden Looper	3.56	9-3	69	73.1	20	41
Josh Hancock	4.09	3-3	62	77.0	23	50
Jeff Suppan	4.12	12-7	32	190.0	69	104
Anthony Reyes*	5.06	5-8	17	85.1	34	72
Jeff Weaver	5.18	5-4	15	83.1	26	45
Sidney Ponson	5.24	4-4	14	68.2	29	33
Jorge Sosa	5.42	3-11	45	118.0	40	75
Jason Marquis	6.02	14-16	33	194.1	75	96
Mark Mulder	7.14	6-7	17	93.1	35	50

Saves: Isringhausen (33); Sosa (4); Wainwright (3); Hancock (1). **Complete games:** Carpenter (5); Reyes (1). **Shutouts:** Carpenter (3).

San Diego Padres

Batting (135 AB)	Avg	AB	R	H	HR	RBI	SB
Josh Bard	.338	231	28	78	9	40	1
Adrian Gonzalez . . .	.304	570	83	173	24	82	0
Dave Roberts	.293	499	80	146	2	44	49
Mike Piazza	.283	399	39	113	22	68	0
Josh Barfield*	.280	539	72	151	13	58	21
Todd Walker	.278	442	56	123	9	53	2
Mike Cameron	.268	552	88	148	22	83	25
Brian Giles	.263	604	87	159	14	83	9
Geoff Blum	.254	276	27	70	4	34	0
Khalil Greene	.245	412	56	101	15	55	5
Mark Bellhorn	.190	253	26	48	8	27	0

Acquired: C Bard, P Meredith and PTBN from Bos. for C Doug Mirabelli (May 2); IF Walker from ChC for P Jose Ceda (July 31).

Pitching (40 IP)	ERA	W-L	Gm	IP	BB	SO
Cla Meredith*	1.07	5-1	45	50.2	6	37
Trevor Hoffman	2.14	0-2	65	63.0	13	50
Scott Cassidy	2.53	6-4	42	42.2	19	49
Brian Sweeney*	3.20	2-0	37	56.1	16	23
Alan Embree	3.27	4-3	73	52.1	15	53
Chris Young	3.46	11-5	31	179.1	69	164
Scott Linebrink	3.57	7-4	73	75.2	22	68
Woody Williams	3.65	12-5	25	145.1	35	72
Clay Hensley	3.71	11-12	37	187.0	76	122
Jon Adkins	3.98	2-1	55	54.1	20	30
Jake Peavy	4.09	11-14	32	202.1	62	215
Chan Ho Park	4.81	7-7	24	136.2	44	96
Mike Thompson*	4.99	4-5	19	92.0	30	53

Saves: Hoffman (46); Sweeney and Linebrink (2). **Complete games:** Peavy (2); Hensley and Park (1). **Shutouts:** Hensley and Park (1).

San Francisco Giants

Batting (135 AB)	Avg	AB	R	H	HR	RBI	SB
Moises Alou.	.301	345	52	104	22	74	2
Omar Vizquel	.295	579	88	171	4	58	24
Ray Durham.	.293	498	79	146	26	93	7
Todd Greene	.289	159	16	46	2	17	0
Barry Bonds	.270	367	74	99	26	77	3
Eliezer Alfonso*	.266	286	27	76	12	39	1
Randy Winn	.262	573	82	150	11	56	10
Mark Sweeney	.251	259	32	65	5	37	0
Shea Hillenbrand . . .	.248	234	33	58	9	29	0
Steve Finley	.246	426	66	105	6	40	7
Lance Niekro	.246	199	27	49	5	31	0
Pedro Feliz	.244	603	75	147	22	98	1
Mike Matheny	.231	160	10	37	3	18	0

Acquired: IF Hillenbrand and P Vinnie Chulk from Tor. for P Accardo (July 22); P Stanton from Wash. for P Shairon Martis (July 28).

Pitching (40 IP)	ERA	W-L	Gm	IP	BB	SO
Kevin Correia	3.49	2-0	48	69.2	22	57
Jason Schmidt	3.59	11-9	32	213.1	80	180
Steve Kline	3.66	4-3	72	51.2	26	33
Mike Stanton	3.99	7-7	82	67.2	27	48
Matt Cain*	4.15	13-12	32	190.2	87	179
Brad Hennessey	4.26	5-6	34	99.1	42	42
Noah Lowry	4.74	7-10	27	159.1	56	84
Jeremy Accardo	4.91	1-3	38	40.1	11	40
Jonathan Sanchez* . .	4.95	3-1	27	40.0	23	33
Matt Morris	4.98	10-15	33	207.2	63	117
Jamey Wright	5.19	6-10	34	156.0	64	79

Saves: Armando Benitez (17); Stanton (8); Tim Worrell (6); Accardo (3); Kline, Hennessey and Brian Wilson (1). **Complete games:** Schmidt (3); Morris (2); Cain and Lowry (1). **Shutouts:** Schmidt, Cain and Lowry (1).

Washington Nationals

Batting (135 AB)	Avg	AB	R	H	HR	RBI	SB
Nick Johnson	.290	500	100	145	23	77	10
Jose Vidro	.289	463	52	134	7	47	1
Ryan Zimmerman* . . .	.287	614	84	176	20	110	11
Alfonso Soriano	.277	647	119	179	46	95	41
Ryan Church	.276	196	22	54	10	35	6
Felipe Lopez	.274	617	98	169	11	52	44
Austin Kearns	.264	537	86	142	24	86	9
Brian Schneider	.256	410	30	105	4	55	2
Marlon Byrd	.223	197	28	44	5	18	3
Jose Guillen	.216	241	28	52	9	40	1

Acquired: OF Kearns, IF Lopez and P Ryan Wagner from Cin. for IF Royce Clayton, IF Brendan Harris, P Bill Bray, Gary Majewski and Daryl Thompson (July 13). **Claimed:** P Day off waivers from Col. (April 27).

Pitching (35 IP)	ERA	W-L	Gm	IP	BB	SO
Chad Cordero	3.19	7-4	68	73.1	22	69
Jon Rauch	3.35	4-5	85	91.1	36	86
Saul Rivera*	3.43	3-0	54	60.1	32	41
John Patterson	4.43	1-2	8	40.2	9	42
Shawn Hill*	4.66	1-3	6	36.2	12	16
Mike O'Connor*	4.80	3-8	21	105.0	45	59
Tony Armas	5.03	9-12	30	154.0	64	97
Ramon Ortiz	5.57	11-16	33	190.2	64	104
Pedro Astacio	5.98	5-5	17	90.1	31	42
Billy Traber	6.44	4-3	15	43.1	14	25
Jason Bergmann* . . .	6.68	0-2	29	64.2	27	54
Zach Day	6.75	2-5	8	40.0	21	19

Saves: Cordero (29); Rauch (2); Rivera (1). **Complete games:** Astacio (1). **Shutouts:** Astacio (1).

BASEBALL PLAYOFFS

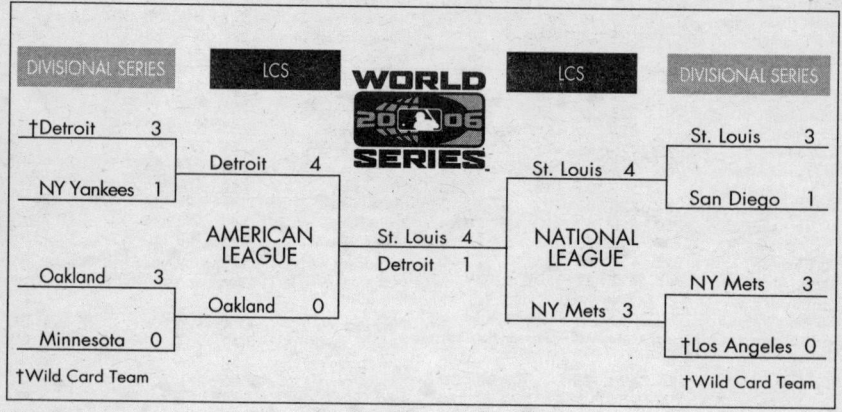

Divisional Series Summaries
AMERICAN LEAGUE
Tigers, 3-1

Date	Winner	Home Field
Oct. 3	Yankees, 8-4	at New York
Oct. 5	Tigers, 4-3	at New York
Oct. 6	Tigers, 6-0	at Detroit
Oct. 7	Tigers, 8-3	at Detroit

Game 1
Tuesday, Oct. 3, at New York

	1 2 3	4 5 6	7 8 9	R H E
Detroit	0 0 0	0 3 0	1 0 0 -	4 12 1
New York	0 0 5	0 0 2	0 1 x -	8 14 0

Win: Wang, NY (1-0). **Loss:** Robertson, Det. (0-1).

2B: Detroit—Polanco (1), Casey (1), Ordonez (1), Guillen (1), Thames (1); New York—Jeter 2 (2), Abreu (1). **HR:** Detroit—Monroe (1, off Wang, 0 on), Granderson (1, off Myers, 0 on); New York—Giambi (1, off Robertson, 1 on), Jeter (1, off Walker, 0 on). **RBI:** Detroit—Granderson (1), Polanco (1), Casey (1), Monroe (1); New York—Jeter (1), Abreu 4 (4), Sheffield (1), Giambi 2 (2). **SB:** New York—Giambi (1). **CS:** Detroit—Guillen (1); New York—Jeter (1). **E:** Detroit—Grilli (1).

Attendance: 56,291 (56,937). **Time:** 3:14.

Game 2
Thursday, Oct. 5, at New York

	1 2 3	4 5 6	7 8 9	R H E
Detroit	0 1 0	0 1 1	1 0 0 -	4 8 0
New York	0 0 0	3 0 0	0 0 0 -	3 8 1

Win: Walker, Det. (1-0). **Loss:** Mussina, NY (0-1). **Save:** Jones, Det. (1).

2B: Detroit—Guillen (2), Monroe (1), Thames (2); New York—Jeter (3). **3B:** Detroit—Granderson (1). **HR:** Detroit—Guillen (1, off Mussina, 0 on); New York—Damon (1, off Verlander, 2 on). **RBI:** Detroit—Granderson 2 (3), Guillen (1), Thames (1); New York—Damon 3 (3). **E:** New York—Jeter (1).

Attendance: 56,252 (56,937). **Time:** 3:15.

Game 3
Friday, Oct. 6, at Detroit

	1 2 3	4 5 6	7 8 9	R H E
New York	0 0 0	0 0 0	0 0 0 -	0 5 0
Detroit	0 3 0	0 0 2	1 0 x -	6 10 0

Win: Rogers, Det. (1-0). **Loss:** Johnson, NY (0-1).

2B: New York—Jeter (4), Posada (1), Matsui (1); Detroit—Rodriguez (1), Casey (2). **HR:** Detroit—Granderson (2, off Bruney, 0 on). **RBI:** Detroit—Polanco (2), Rodriguez (1), Casey 2 (3), Granderson 2 (5). **SB:** Detroit—Granderson (1). **CS:** Detroit—Polanco (1).

Attendance: 43,440 (41,070). **Time:** 3:05.

Game 4
Saturday, Oct. 7, at Detroit

	1 2 3	4 5 6	7 8 9	R H E
New York	0 0 0	0 0 0	1 0 2 -	3 6 2
Detroit	0 3 1	0 3 1	0 0 x -	8 13 0

Win: Bonderman, Det. (1-0). **Loss:** Wright, NY (0-1).

2B: Detroit—Casey (3), Guillen (3). **HR:** New York—Posada (1, off Walker, 1 on); Detroit—Ordonez (1, off Wright, 0 on), Monroe (2, off Wright, 1 on). **RBI:** New York—Matsui (1), Posada 2 (2); Detroit—Casey (4), Ordonez 2 (2), Guillen (2), Rodriguez 2 (3), Monroe 2 (3). **E:** New York—Sheffield (1), Rodriguez (1).

Attendance: 43,126 (41,070). **Time:** 2:54.

Athletics, 3-0

Date	Winner	Home Field
Oct. 3.	Athletics, 3-2	at Minnesota
Oct. 4.	Athletics, 5-2	at Minnesota
Oct. 6.	Athletics, 8-3	at Oakland

Game 1

Tuesday, Oct. 3, at Minnesota

	1 2 3	4 5 6	7 8 9	R H E
Oakland	0 2 0	0 0 0	0 0 1	- 3 7 0
Minnesota	0 0 0	0 0 0	1 0 1	- 2 5 2

Win: Zito, Oak (1-0). **Loss:** Santana, Min. (0-1). **Save:** Street, Oak (1).

2B: Oakland—Scutaro (1); Minnesota—White (1), Bartlett (1). **3B:** Minnesota—Cuddyer (1). **HR:** Oakland—Thomas 2 (2, off Santana, 0 on; off Crain, 0 on); Minnesota—White (1, off Zito, 0 on). **RBI:** Oakland—Thomas 2 (2), Scutaro (1); Minnesota—Hunter (1), White (1). **CS:** Minnesota—Castillo (1). **E:** Minnesota—Cuddyer (1), Bartlett (1).

Attendance: 55,542 (46,564). **Time:** 2:19.

Game 2

Wednesday, Oct. 4, at Minnesota

	1 2 3	4 5 6	7 8 9	R H E
Oakland	0 0 0	0 2 0	2 0 1	- 5 11 0
Minnesota	0 0 0	0 0 2	0 0 0	- 2 9 0

Win: Calero, Oak (1-0). **Loss:** Neshek, Min. (0-1). **Save:** Street, Oak (2).

2B: Oakland—Kendall (1), Thomas (1), Swisher 2 (2), Scutaro (2). **HR:** Oakland—Kotsay (1, off Reyes, 1 on); Minnesota—Cuddyer (1, off Loaiza, 0 on), Morneau (1, off Loaiza, 0 on). **RBI:** Oakland—Kendall (1), Kotsay 2 (2), Scutaro (2); Minnesota—Cuddyer (1), Morneau (1). **SB:** Minnesota—Tyner (1).

Attendance: 55,710 (46,564). **Time:** 3:02.

Game 3

Friday, Oct. 6, at Oakland

	1 2 3	4 5 6	7 8 9	R H E
Minnesota	0 0 0	1 0 1	0 1 0	- 3 12 3
Oakland	0 2 2	0 0 0	4 0 x	- 8 8 1

Win: Haren, Oak (1-0). **Loss:** Radke, Min. (0-1).

2B: Minnesota—Morneau (1), Hunter (1); Oakland—Scutaro 2 (4), Chavez (1). **HR:** Minnesota—Hunter (1, off Haren, 0 on), Morneau (2, off Duchscherer, 0 on); Oakland—Chavez (1, off Radke, 0 on), Bradley (1, off Radke, 1 on). **RBI:** Minnesota—Hunter (2), White (2), Morneau (2); Oakland—Bradley 2 (2), Chavez (1), Scutaro 4 (6), Swisher (1). **E:** Minnesota—Morneau (1), Bartlett (2), Radke (1); Oakland—Kendall (1).

Attendance: 35,694 (34,077). **Time:** 2:55.

NATIONAL LEAGUE

Mets, 3-0

Date	Winner	Home Field
Oct. 4.	Mets, 6-5	at New York
Oct. 5.	Mets, 4-1	at New York
Oct. 7.	Mets, 9-5	at Los Angeles

Game 1

Wednesday, Oct. 4, at New York

	1 2 3	4 5 6	7 8 9	R H E
Los Angeles	0 1 0	0 0 0	3 0 1	- 5 11 1
New York	0 0 0	2 0 2	2 0 x	- 6 9 1

Win: Mota, NY (1-0). **Loss:** Penny, LA (0-1). **Save:** Wagner, NY (1).

2B: Los Angeles—Anderson (1), Garciaparra (1), Betemit (1), Martinez (1); New York—Wright 2 (2). **HR:** New York—Delgado (1, off Lowe, 0 on), Floyd (1, off Lowe, 0 on). **RBI:** Los Angeles—Furcal (1), Martinez (1), Garciaparra 2 (2), Anderson (1); New York—Delgado 2 (2), Floyd (1), Wright 3 (3). **SB:** Los Angeles—Furcal (1); New York—Reyes (1). **E:** Los Angeles—Kent (1); New York—Valentin (1).

Attendance: 56,979 (57,333). **Time:** 3:05.

Game 2

Thursday, Oct. 5, at New York

	1 2 3	4 5 6	7 8 9	R H E
Los Angeles	0 0 0	0 0 0	0 1 0	- 1 5 1
New York	0 0 1	0 1 2	0 x	- 4 7 0

Win: Glavine, NY (1-0). **Loss:** Kuo, LA (0-1). **Save:** Wagner, NY (2).

2B: Los Angeles—Lugo (1); New York—Lo Duca (1). **HR:** Los Angeles—Betemit (1, off Heilman, 0 on). **RBI:** Los Angeles—Betemit (1); New York—Reyes 2 (2), Lo Duca (1), Franco (1). **E:** Los Angeles—Tomko (1).

Attendance: 57,029 (57,333). **Time:** 2:57.

Game 3

Saturday, Oct. 7, at Los Angeles

	1 2 3	4 5 6	7 8 9	R H E
New York	3 0 1	0 0 3	0 2 0	- 9 14 2
Los Angeles	0 0 0	2 3 0	0 0 0	- 5 16 2

Win: Feliciano, NY (1-0). **Loss:** Broxton, LA (0-1).

2B: New York—Green 2 (2), Woodward (1); Los Angeles—Kent (1). **HR:** Los Angeles—Kent (1, off Oliver, 1 on). **RBI:** New York—Wright (4), Floyd (2), Green 2 (2), Reyes (3), Lo Duca 2 (3), Beltran (1); Los Angeles—Loney 3 (3), Kent 2 (2). **SB:** New York—Beltran (1); Los Angeles—Furcal (2). **CS:** New York—Reyes (1). **E:** New York—Beltran (1), Wright (1); Los Angeles—Loney (1), Betemit (1).

Attendance: 56,293 (56,000). **Time:** 3:51.

N.L. Divisional Series Summaries (Cont.)

Cardinals, 3-1

Date	Winner	Home Field
Oct. 3	Cardinals, 5-1	at San Diego
Oct. 5	Cardinals, 2-0	at San Diego
Oct. 7	Padres, 3-1	at St. Louis
Oct. 8	Cardinals, 6-2	at St. Louis

Game 1
Tuesday, Oct. 3, at San Diego

	1 2 3	4 5 6	7 8 9	R H E
St. Louis	0 0 0	3 1 1	0 0 0	5 12 0
San Diego	0 0 0	0 0 1	0 0 0	1 6 0

Win: Carpenter, St.L (1-0). **Loss:** Peavy, SD (0-1).
2B: St. Louis—Rolen (1); San Diego—Giles (1). **3B:** San Diego—Roberts (1), Branyan (1). **HR:** St. Louis—Pujols (1, off Peavy, 1 on). **RBI:** St. Louis—Pujols 2 (2), Encarnacion (1), Edmonds (1), Molina (1); San Diego—Giles (1). **SB:** St. Louis—Belliard (1). **CS:** St. Louis—Encarnacion (1).
Attendance: 43,107 (42,445). **Time:** 2:54.

Game 2
Thursday, Oct. 5, at San Diego

	1 2 3	4 5 6	7 8 9	R H E
St. Louis	0 0 0	2 0 0	0 0 0	2 10 0
San Diego	0 0 0	0 0 0	0 0 0	0 4 0

Win: Weaver, St.L (1-0). **Loss:** Wells, SD (0-1). **Save:** Wainwright, St.L (1).
2B: St. Louis—Wilson (1), Pujols (1); San Diego—Barfield (1). **RBI:** St. Louis—Pujols (3), Edmonds (2). **CS:** St. Louis—Molina (1).
Attendance: 46,463 (42,445). **Time:** 2:54.

Game 3
Saturday, Oct. 7, at St. Louis

	1 2 3	4 5 6	7 8 9	R H E
San Diego	0 0 0	3 0 0	0 0 0	3 10 0
St. Louis	0 0 0	0 0 0	0 1 0	1 5 2

Win: Young, SD (1-0). **Loss:** Suppan, St.L (0-1). **Save:** Hoffman, SD (1).
2B: San Diego—Cameron (1), Branyan (1), Blum (1), Piazza (1); St. Louis—Belliard (1). **HR:** St. Louis—Taguchi (1, off Linebrink, 0 on). **RBI:** San Diego—Branyan 2 (2), Blum (1); St. Louis—Taguchi (1). **SB:** San Diego—Roberts (1); St. Louis—Eckstein (1). **E:** St. Louis—Duncan (1), Molina (1).
Attendance: 46,634 (43,975). **Time:** 3:33.

Game 4
Sunday, Oct. 8, at St. Louis

	1 2 3	4 5 6	7 8 9	R H E
San Diego	2 0 0	0 0 0	0 0 0	2 9 1
St. Louis	2 0 0	0 0 4	0 0 x	6 7 0

Win: Carpenter, St.L (2-0). **Loss:** Williams, SD (0-1).
2B: San Diego—Klesko (1); St. Louis—Molina (1). **3B:** St. Louis—Encarnacion (1). **RBI:** San Diego—Branyan (3), Cameron (1); St. Louis—Belliard 2 (2), Encarnacion (2), Spiezio (1), Eckstein (1). **SB:** San Diego—Cameron (1). **CS:** San Diego—Roberts (1). **E:** San Diego—Branyan (1).
Attendance: 46,476 (43,975). **Time:** 2:44.

American League Championship Series

Tigers, 4-0

Date	Winner	Home Field
Oct. 10	Tigers, 5-1	at Oakland
Oct. 11	Tigers, 8-5	at Oakland
Oct. 13	Tigers, 3-0	at Detroit
Oct. 14	Tigers, 6-3	at Detroit

Most Valuable Player						
Placido Polanco, Detroit, 2B						
AVG	AB	R	H	HR	RBI	BB
.529	17	2	9	0	2	2

Game 1
Tuesday, Oct. 10, at Oakland

	1 2 3	4 5 6	7 8 9	R H E
Detroit	0 0 2	3 0 0	0 0 0	5 11 1
Oakland	0 0 0	0 0 0	0 1 0	1 8 1

Win: Robertson, Det. (1-0). **Loss:** Zito, Oak. (0-1).
2B: Detroit—Granderson (1), Inge (1); Oakland—Payton 2 (2), Bradley (1). **HR:** Detroit—Inge (1, off Zito, 0 on), Rodriguez (1, off Zito, 0 on). **RBI:** Detroit—Inge 2 (2), Ordonez (1), Rodriguez (1), Polanco (1); Oakland—Payton (1). **E:** Detroit—Guillen (1); Oakland—Jimenez (1).
Attendance: 35,655 (34,077). **Time:** 3:20.

Game 2
Wednesday, Oct. 11, at Oakland

	1 2 3	4 5 6	7 8 9	R H E
Detroit	0 1 0	4 0 2	0 0 1	8 11 0
Oakland	1 0 2	0 0 1	1 0 0	5 11 1

Win: Verlander, Det. (1-0). **Loss:** Loaiza, Oak. (0-1). **Save:** Jones, Det. (1).
2B: Detroit—Guillen (1), Monroe (1); Oakland—Kotsay 2 (2). **HR:** Detroit—Gomez (1, off Loaiza, 1 on), Granderson (1, off Street, 0 on); Oakland—Bradley 2 (2, off Verlander, 1 on; off Ledezma, 0 on), Chavez (1, off Verlander, 0 on). **RBI:** Detroit—Monroe 2 (2), Gomez 4 (4), Inge (3), Granderson (1); Oakland—Bradley 4 (4), Chavez (1). **E:** Oakland—Jimenez (2).
Attendance: 36,168 (34,077). **Time:** 3:06.

Game 3
Friday, Oct. 13, at Detroit

	1 2 3	4 5 6	7 8 9	R	H	E
Oakland	0 0 0	0 0 0	0 0 0	0	2	0
Detroit	2 0 0	0 1 0	0 0 x	3	6	0

Win: Rogers, Det. (1-0). **Loss:** Harden, Oak. (0-1). **Save:** Jones (2).

2B: Detroit—Polanco (1). **HR:** Detroit—Monroe (1, off Harden, 0 on). **RBI:** Detroit—Polanco (2), Ordonez (2), Monroe (3). **SB:** Detroit—Granderson (1), Infante (1). **Attendance:** 41,669 (41,070). **Time:** 2:57.

Game 4
Saturday, Oct. 14, at Detroit

	1 2 3	4 5 6	7 8 9	R	H	E
Oakland	2 0 0	1 0 0	0 0 0	3	8	1
Detroit	0 0 0	0 2 1	0 0 3	6	11	0

Win: Ledezma, Det. (1-0). **Loss:** Street, Oak. (0-1).

2B: Oakland—Bradley (2), Chavez (1); Detroit—Granderson (2), Monroe (3). **HR:** Oakland—Payton (1, off Bonderman, 0 on); Detroit—Ordonez (2, off Haren, 0 on; off Street, 2 on). **RBI:** Oakland—Bradley (5), Chavez (2), Payton (2); Detroit—Granderson (2), Monroe (4), Ordonez 4 (6). **E:** Oakland—Chavez (1).
Attendance: 42,967 (41,070). **Time:** 3:23.

ALCS Composite Box Score

Detroit Tigers

Batting	LCS vs. Oakland								Overall AL Playoffs							
	Avg	AB	R	H	HR	RBI	BB	SO	Avg	AB	R	H	HR	RBI	BB	SO
Placido Polanco	.529	17	2	9	0	2	2	1	.471	34	5	16	0	4	3	2
Omar Infante	.500	2	0	1	0	0	1	1	.500	2	0	1	0	0	1	1
Alexis Gomez	.444	9	1	4	1	4	0	2	.444	9	1	4	1	4	0	2
Craig Monroe	.429	14	5	6	1	4	3	4	.300	30	8	9	3	7	3	7
Sean Casey	.333	3	0	1	0	0	1	0	.350	20	1	7	0	4	1	0
Brandon Inge	.333	12	3	4	1	3	3	3	.222	27	4	6	1	3	3	9
Curtis Granderson	.333	15	4	5	1	2	4	2	.313	32	7	10	3	7	4	3
Magglio Ordonez	.235	17	3	4	2	6	2	2	.250	32	6	8	3	8	3	4
Carlos Guillen	.188	16	1	3	0	0	1	4	.367	30	4	11	1	2	3	5
Ivan Rodriguez	.125	16	2	2	1	1	1	4	.172	29	5	5	1	4	3	7
Neifi Perez	.000	4	0	0	0	0	0	1	.000	4	0	0	0	0	0	1
Ramon Santiago	.000	7	0	0	0	0	1	0	.000	7	0	0	0	0	1	0
Marcus Thames	.000	5	1	0	0	0	0	1	.250	20	3	5	0	1	1	6
TOTALS	.285	137	22	39	7	22	19	25	.297	276	44	82	13	44	26	47

Pitching	ERA	W-L	Sv	Gm	IP	H	BB	SO	ERA	W-L	Sv	Gm	IP	H	BB	SO
Kenny Rogers	0.00	1-0	0	1	7.1	2	2	6	0.00	2-0	0	2	15.0	7	4	14
Todd Jones	0.00	0-0	2	3	3.0	3	1	2	0.00	0-0	3	5	5.0	4	1	4
Jamie Walker	0.00	0-0	0	1	0.1	0	0	1	4.50	1-0	0	4	4.0	3	1	2
Jason Grilli	0.00	0-0	0	2	1.0	1	3	1	0.00	0-0	0	3	1.1	1	3	1
Fernando Rodney	0.00	0-0	0	3	3.2	1	1	4	0.00	0-0	0	3	3.2	1	1	4
Nate Robertson	0.00	1-0	0	1	5.0	6	3	4	5.91	1-1	0	2	10.2	18	3	5
Wilfredo Ledezma	3.38	1-0	0	2	2.2	2	1	1	3.38	1-0	0	2	2.2	2	1	1
Jeremy Bonderman	4.05	0-0	0	1	6.2	6	2	3	3.00	1-0	0	2	15.0	11	3	7
Justin Verlander	6.75	1-0	0	1	5.1	7	1	6	5.91	1-0	0	2	10.2	14	5	11
Joel Zumaya	9.00	0-0	0	1	1.0	1	0	0	3.00	0-0	0	3	3.0	1	0	3
TOTALS	2.25	4-0	2	4	36.0	29	14	28	2.92	7-1	3	8	71.0	62	22	52

Oakland Athletics

Batting	LCS vs. Detroit								Overall AL Playoffs							
	Avg	AB	R	H	HR	RBI	BB	SO	Avg	AB	R	H	HR	RBI	BB	SO
Milton Bradley	.500	18	4	9	2	5	0	2	.323	31	5	10	3	7	0	3
Jason Kendall	.294	17	0	5	0	0	2	2	.258	31	1	8	0	1	2	6
Jay Payton	.286	14	1	4	1	2	1	2	.308	26	4	8	1	2	1	3
Mark Kotsay	.250	16	3	4	0	0	2	3	.200	30	5	6	1	2	2	5
Eric Chavez	.231	13	1	3	1	2	4	2	.217	23	3	5	2	3	4	8
D'Angelo Jimenez	.167	12	0	2	0	0	0	2	.125	16	0	2	0	0	0	3
Nick Swisher	.100	10	0	1	0	0	5	5	.200	20	3	4	0	1	7	7
Marco Scutaro	.067	15	0	1	0	0	0	3	.185	27	1	5	0	6	0	4
Frank Thomas	.000	13	0	0	0	0	2	4	.217	23	3	5	2	2	4	5
Adam Melhuse	.000	1	0	0	0	0	0	1	.000	1	0	0	0	0	0	1
Bobby Kielty	.000	2	0	0	0	0	0	0	.000	2	0	0	0	0	0	0
Mark Ellis	—	0	0	0	0	0	0	0	.286	7	0	2	0	0	0	2
TOTALS	.221	131	9	29	4	9	14	28	.232	237	25	55	9	24	20	47

ALCS Composite Box Score (Cont.)

Oakland Athletics (Cont.)

Pitching	LCS vs. Detroit								Overall AL Playoffs							
	ERA	W-L	Sv	Gm	IP	H	BB	SO	ERA	W-L	Sv	Gm	IP	H	BB	SO
Joe Kennedy	0.00	0-0	0	4	3.2	2	2	2	0.00	0-0	0	4	3.2	2	2	2
Kiko Calero	0.00	0-0	0	3	2.0	3	1	1	0.00	1-0	0	4	3.0	3	2	2
Chad Gaudin	0.00	0-0	0	3	3.1	2	3	1	0.00	0-0	0	3	3.1	2	3	1
Joe Blanton	0.00	0-0	0	1	2.0	0	2	2	0.00	0-0	0	1	2.0	0	2	2
Rich Harden	4.76	0-1	0	1	5.2	5	5	4	4.76	0-1	0	1	5.2	5	5	4
Dan Haren	5.40	0-0	0	1	5.0	7	2	7	4.09	1-0	0	2	11.0	16	3	9
Esteban Loaiza	10.50	0-1	0	1	6.0	9	1	5	7.36	0-1	0	2	11.0	17	1	7
Huston Street	10.80	0-1	0	2	3.1	4	0	3	7.11	0-1	0	5	6.1	8	1	4
Barry Zito	12.27	0-1	0	1	3.2	7	3	0	4.63	1-1	0	2	11.2	11	6	1
Justin Duchscherer	—	0-0	0	0	0.0	0	0	0	2.25	0-0	0	2	4.0	1	0	4
TOTALS	5.71	0-4	0	4	34.2	39	19	25	4.23	3-4	2	7	61.2	65	25	36

Score by Innings

	1	2	3	4	5	6	7	8	9		R	H	E
Detroit	2	1	2	7	3	3	0	0	4	–	22	39	1
Oakland	3	0	2	1	0	1	1	1	0	–	9	29	3

E: Detroit—Guillen; Oakland—Jimenez 2, Chavez. **2B:** Detroit—Monroe 2, Granderson 2, Polanco, Inge, Guillen; Oakland—Bradley 2, Payton 2, Kotsay 2, Chavez. **HR:** Detroit—Ordonez 2, Gomez, Monroe, Inge, Granderson, Rodriguez; Oakland—Bradley 2, Payton, Chavez. **SB:** Detroit—Infante, Granderson. **S:** Detroit—Perez. **SF:** Detroit—Inge, Monroe. **HBP:** by Rogers (Thomas). **WP:** Detroit—Verlander, Bonderman; Oakland—Haren 2, Kennedy. **Balk:** Detroit—Verlander. **DP:** Detroit—7; Oakland—4. **LOB:** Detroit—33; Oakland—29.
Umpires: Derryl Cousins, Chuck Meriwether, Gary Cederstrom, Mike Reilly, Jerry Crawford, Hunter Wendelstedt.

National League Championship Series

Cardinals, 4-3

Date	Winner	Home Field
Oct. 12	Mets, 2-0	at New York
Oct. 13	Cardinals, 9-6	at New York
Oct. 14	Cardinals, 5-0	at St. Louis
Oct. 15	Mets, 12-5	at St. Louis
Oct. 17	Cardinals, 4-2	at St. Louis
Oct. 18	Mets, 4-2	at New York
Oct. 19	Cardinals, 3-1	at New York

Game 1
Thursday, Oct. 12, at New York

	1 2 3	4 5 6	7 8 9	R H E
St. Louis	0 0 0	0 0 0	0 0 0	- 0 4 0
New York	0 0 0	0 0 2	0 0 x	- 2 6 0

Win: Glavine, NY (1-0). **Loss:** Weaver, St.L (0-1). **Save:** Wagner, NY (1).
2B: New York—Delgado 2 (2). **HR:** New York—Beltran (1, off Weaver, 1 on). **RBI:** New York—Beltran 2 (2). **SB:** New York—Green (1).
Attendance: 56,311 (57,333). **Time:** 2:52.

Game 2
Friday, Oct. 13, at New York

	1 2 3	4 5 6	7 8 9	R H E
St. Louis	0 2 2	0 0 0	2 0 3	- 9 10 1
New York	3 1 0	0 1 1	0 0 0	- 6 9 2

Win: Kinney, St.L (1-0). **Loss:** Wagner, NY (0-1).
2B: St. Louis—Molina (1), Pujols (1), Spiezio (1); New York—Reyes (1), Chavez (1), Lo Duca (1). **HR:** St. Louis—Edmonds (1, off Maine (1), Taguchi (1, off Wagner, 0 on); New York—Delgado 2 (2, off Carpenter, 2 on; off Carpenter, 0 on). **RBI:** St. Louis—Molina 2 (2), Edmonds 2 (2), Spiezio 3 (3), Taguchi (1), Encarnacion (1); New York—Delgado 4 (4), Reyes (1), Lo Duca (1). **SB:** St. Louis—Eckstein (1). **E:** St. Louis—Belliard (1); New York—Delgado (1), Lo Duca (1).
Attendance: 56,349 (57,333). **Time:** 3:58.

Game 3
Saturday, Oct. 14, at St. Louis

	1 2 3	4 5 6	7 8 9	R H E
New York	0 0 0	0 0 0	0 0 0	- 0 3 0
St. Louis	2 3 0	0 0 0	0 0 x	- 5 8 0

Win: Suppan, St.L (1-0). **Loss:** Trachsel, NY (0-1).
3B: New York—Reyes (1); St. Louis—Spiezio (1). **HR:** St. Louis—Suppan (1, off Trachsel, 0 on). **RBI:** St. Louis—Spiezio 2 (5), Suppan (1), Edmonds (3). **SB:** New York—Beltran (1).
Attendance: 47,053 (43,975). **Time:** 2:53.

Game 4
Sunday, Oct. 15, at St. Louis

	1 2 3	4 5 6	7 8 9	R H E
New York	0 0 2	0 3 6	1 0 0	- 12 14 1
St. Louis	0 1 1	0 1 2	0 0 0	- 5 11 1

Win: Perez, NY (1-0). **Loss:** Thompson, St.L (0-1).
2B: New York—Delgado (3), Valentin (1). **3B:** St. Louis—Encarnaion (1). **HR:** New York—Beltran 2 (2, off Reyes, 0 on; off Looper, 1 on), Wright (1, off Reyes, 0 on), Delgado (3, off Thompson, 2 on); St. Louis—Eckstein (1, off Perez, 0 on), Edmonds (2, off Perez, 0 on); Molina (1, off Perez, 0 on). **RBI:** New York—Beltran 2 (4), Wright (1), Delgado 5 (9), Green (1), Valentin 3 (3); St. Louis—Molina 2 (4), Encarnacion (2), Eckstein (1), Edmonds (4). **SB:** St. Louis—Belliard (1). **E:** New York—Delgado (2); St. Louis—Belliard (2). **Attendance:** 46,600 (43,975). **Time:** 3:31.

Game 5
Tuesday, Oct. 17, at St. Louis

	1 2 3	4 5 6	7 8 9	R H E
New York	0 0 0	2 0 0	0 0 0	- 2 8 0
St. Louis	0 0 0	2 1 1	0 0 x	- 4 10 0

Win: Weaver, St.L (1-1). **Loss:** Glavine, NY (1-1). **Save:** Wainwright, St.L (1).
2B: New York—Chavez (2), Green (1), Valentin (2), Wright (1); St. Louis—Wilson (1). **3B:** St. Louis—Miles (1). **HR:** St. Louis—Pujols (1, off Glavine, 0 on), Duncan (1, off Feliciano, 0 on). **RBI:** New York—Valentin 2 (5); St. Louis—Pujols (1), Belliard (1), Wilson (1), Duncan (1). **SB:** St. Louis—Eckstein (2). **CS:** St. Louis—Rolen (1).
Attendance: 46,496 (43,975). **Time:** 3:26.

Game 6
Wednesday, Oct. 18, at New York

	1 2 3	4 5 6	7 8 9	R H E
St. Louis	0 0 0	0 0 0	0 0 2	- 2 7 1
New York	1 0 0	1 0 0	2 0 x	- 4 10 0

Win: Maine, NY (1-0). **Loss:** Carpenter (0-1).
2B: St. Louis—Rolen (1), Taguchi (1). **HR:** New York—Reyes (1, off Carpenter, 0 on). **RBI:** St. Louis—Taguchi 2 (3); New York—Reyes (2), Green (2), Lo Duca 2 (3). **SB:** St. Louis—Eckstein (3); New York—Reyes 2 (2), Tucker (1). **E:** St. Louis—Rolen (1).
Attendance: 56,334 (57,333). **Time:** 2:56.

Game 7
Thursday, Oct. 19, at New York

	1 2 3	4 5 6	7 8 9	R H E
St. Louis	0 1 0	0 0 0	0 0 2	- 3 6 1
New York	1 0 0	0 0 0	0 0 0	- 1 4 1

Win: Flores, St.L (1-0). **Loss:** Heilman, NY (0-1). **Save:** Wainwright (2)
2B: St. Louis—Eckstein (1); New York—Beltran (1). **HR:** St. Louis—Molina (2, off Heilman, 1 on). **RBI:** St. Louis—Belliard (2), Molina 2 (6); New York—Wright (2). **E:** St. Louis—Rolen (2); New York—Delgado (3).
Attendance: 56,357 (57,333). **Time:** 3:23.

Most Valuable Player
Jeff Suppan, St. Louis, P

G	W-L	IP	H	BB	K	ERA
2	1-0	15.0	5	6	6	0.60

NLCS Composite Box Score

St. Louis Cardinals

Batting	Avg	AB	R	H	HR	RBI	BB	SO	Avg	AB	R	H	HR	RBI	BB	SO
		LCS vs. New York								Overall NL Playoffs						
So Taguchi	1.000	3	1	3	1	3	0	0	1.000	4	2	4	2	4	0	0
Aaron Miles	.667	3	0	2	0	0	0	0	.600	5	0	3	0	0	0	0
Yadier Molina	.348	23	2	8	2	6	3	2	.333	36	2	12	2	7	3	4
Jeff Suppan	.333	3	1	1	1	1	0	1	.250	4	1	1	1	1	0	2
Albert Pujols	.318	22	5	7	1	1	7	3	.324	37	8	12	2	4	8	7
Jeff Weaver	.250	4	0	1	0	0	0	1	.333	6	0	2	0	0	0	2
Ronnie Belliard	.240	25	0	6	0	2	2	3	.316	38	2	12	0	4	3	3
Scott Rolen	.238	21	4	5	0	0	3	1	.188	32	4	6	0	0	3	3
Scott Spiezio	.235	17	3	4	0	5	2	5	.227	22	4	5	0	6	2	6
David Eckstein	.231	26	3	6	1	1	4	0	.195	41	4	8	1	2	4	0
Jim Edmonds	.227	22	5	5	2	4	5	5	.257	35	7	9	2	6	7	8
Juan Encarnacion	.182	22	1	4	0	2	2	3	.222	36	2	8	0	4	3	5
Preston Wilson	.176	17	2	3	0	1	1	4	.200	25	4	5	0	1	1	5
Chris Duncan	.125	8	1	1	1	1	0	2	.143	14	2	2	1	1	2	4
Gary Bennett	.000	1	0	0	0	0	0	1	.000	1	0	0	0	0	0	1
Chris Carpenter	.000	4	0	0	0	0	0	1	.111	9	0	1	0	0	0	3
Anthony Reyes	.000	1	0	0	0	0	0	0	.000	1	0	0	0	0	0	0
John Rodriguez	.000	4	0	0	0	0	0	1	.000	5	0	0	0	0	0	1
TOTALS	.248	226	28	56	9	27	29	33	.256	351	42	90	11	40	36	54

Pitching	ERA	W-L	Sv	Gm	IP	H	BB	SO	ERA	W-L	Sv	Gm	IP	H	BB	SO
Randy Flores	0.00	1-0	0	4	3.2	2	0	3	0.00	1-0	0	6	4.2	4	1	4
Adam Wainwright	0.00	0-0	2	3	3.0	2	1	4	0.00	0-0	3	6	6.2	5	1	10
Josh Kinney	0.00	1-0	0	3	3.1	3	1	4	0.00	1-0	0	5	5.1	3	2	5
Jeff Suppan	0.60	1-0	0	2	15.0	5	6	6	1.86	1-1	0	3	19.1	11	9	9
Tyler Johnson	2.45	0-0	0	4	3.2	2	1	5	1.42	0-0	0	8	6.1	4	2	11
Jeff Weaver	3.09	1-1	0	2	11.2	10	4	2	2.16	2-1	0	3	16.2	12	7	5
Anthony Reyes	4.50	0-0	0	1	4.0	3	4	4	4.50	0-0	0	1	4.0	3	4	4
Chris Carpenter	5.73	0-1	0	2	11.0	13	4	5	3.70	2-1	0	4	24.1	25	8	17
Braden Looper	5.79	0-0	0	3	4.2	7	0	1	4.26	0-0	0	4	6.1	8	0	1
Brad Thompson	27.00	0-1	0	2	0.2	3	0	1	13.50	0-1	0	3	1.1	3	1	2
Josh Hancock	162.00	0-0	0	2	0.1	4	3	1	27.00	0-0	0	3	2.0	5	5	2
TOTALS	3.84	4-3	2	7	61.0	54	24	36	2.97	7-4	3	11	97.0	83	40	70

NLCS Composite Box Score (Cont.)

New York Mets

Batting	LCS vs. St. Louis								Overall NL Playoffs							
	Avg	AB	R	H	HR	RBI	BB	SO	Avg	AB	R	H	HR	RBI	BB	SO
Michael Tucker	.400	5	1	2	0	0	0	1	.333	6	2	2	0	0	1	1
Carlos Delgado	.304	23	5	7	3	9	6	3	.351	37	8	13	4	11	6	6
Shawn Green	.304	23	2	7	0	2	4	3	.313	32	3	10	0	4	4	5
Carlos Beltran	.296	27	8	8	3	4	4	3	.278	36	10	10	3	5	9	5
Jose Reyes	.281	32	5	9	1	2	1	3	.250	44	7	11	1	5	3	5
Jose Valentin	.250	24	0	6	0	5	2	5	.182	33	2	6	0	5	4	9
Paul Lo Duca	.207	29	3	6	0	3	2	2	.275	40	5	11	0	6	3	3
Endy Chavez	.185	27	1	5	0	0	0	1	.229	35	2	8	0	0	0	1
David Wright	.160	25	2	4	1	2	4	4	.216	37	3	8	1	6	5	8
Julio Franco	.000	2	0	0	0	0	0	2	.000	4	0	0	0	1	0	3
Tom Glavine	.000	4	0	0	0	0	0	2	.000	5	0	0	0	0	0	3
Darren Oliver	.000	2	0	0	0	0	0	2	.000	2	0	0	0	0	0	2
Cliff Floyd	.000	3	0	0	0	0	0	1	.333	12	3	4	1	2	1	3
Oliver Perez	.000	5	0	0	0	0	1	3	.000	5	0	0	0	0	1	3
John Maine	.000	2	0	0	0	0	0	2	.000	3	0	0	0	0	0	3
Anderson Hernandez	.000	1	0	0	0	0	0	1	.000	1	0	0	0	0	0	1
Steve Trachsel	—	0	0	0	0	0	0	0	.000	2	0	0	0	0	0	0
Guillermo Mota	—	0	0	0	0	0	0	0	.000	1	0	0	0	0	0	0
Chris Woodward	—	0	0	0	0	0	0	0	1.000	1	0	1	0	0	0	0
TOTALS	.231	234	27	54	8	27	24	36	.250	336	46	84	10	45	37	58

Pitching	ERA	W-L	Sv	Gm	IP	H	BB	SO	ERA	W-L	Sv	Gm	IP	H	BB	SO
Roberto Hernandez	0.00	0-0	0	3	2.1	0	2	0	0.00	0-0	0	3	2.1	0	2	0
Darren Oliver	0.00	0-0	0	1	6.0	3	1	3	3.68	0-0	0	2	7.1	6	1	3
Chad Bradford	0.00	0-0	0	5	5.1	3	0	2	0.00	0-0	0	7	5.2	4	1	2
Tom Glavine	2.45	1-1	0	2	11.0	11	5	4	1.59	2-1	0	3	17.0	15	7	6
John Maine	2.89	1-0	0	2	9.1	4	9	8	2.63	1-0	0	3	13.2	10	11	13
Pedro Feliciano	3.00	0-0	0	3	3.0	2	0	1	1.93	1-0	0	6	4.2	2	2	3
Guillermo Mota	4.15	0-0	0	5	4.1	4	2	2	5.40	1-0	0	7	8.1	10	2	7
Aaron Heilman	4.15	0-1	0	3	4.1	4	1	5	4.63	0-1	0	6	7.1	7	1	6
Oliver Perez	4.63	1-0	0	2	11.2	13	3	7	4.63	1-0	0	2	11.2	13	3	7
Billy Wagner	16.88	0-1	1	3	2.2	7	1	0	9.53	0-1	3	6	5.2	10	1	4
Steve Trachsel	45.00	0-1	0	1	1.0	5	5	1	14.54	0-1	0	2	4.1	11	6	3
TOTALS	3.98	3-4	0	7	61.0	56	29	33	3.89	6-4	3	10	88.0	88	37	54

Score by Innings

	1	2	3	4	5	6	7	8	9		R	H	E
St. Louis	2	7	3	2	2	3	2	0	7	–	28	56	4
New York	5	1	2	3	4	9	3	0	0	–	27	54	4

E: St. Louis—Belliard 2, Rolen 2; New York—Delgado 3, Lo Duca 2. **2B:** St. Louis—Taguchi, Molina, Pujols, Rolen, Spiezio, Eckstein, Wilson; New York—Reyes. **HR:** St. Louis—Molina 2, Edmonds 2, Taguchi, Suppan, Pujols, Eckstein, Duncan; New York—Delgado 3, Beltran 3, Reyes, Wright. **SB:** St. Louis—Eckstein 3, Belliard; New York—Reyes 2, Tucker, Green, Beltran. **CS:** St. Louis—Rolen. **S:** St. Louis—Suppan 3, Belliard; New York—Lo Duca, Maine. **HBP:** by Carpenter (Tucker), by Bradford (Eckstein), by Johnson (Green), by Maine (Encarnacion), by Perez (Eckstein), by Suppan (Valentin). **WP:** New York—Heilman, Oliver, Feliciano, R. Hernandez. **Balk:** none. **DP:** St. Louis—4; New York—10. **LOB:** St. Louis—51; New York—53.

Umpires: Tim Welke, Jim Joyce, Jerry Layne, Fieldin Culbreth, Gary Darling, Jeff Kellogg.

WORLD SERIES

Cardinals, 4-1

Date	Winner	Home Field
Oct. 21	Cardinals, 7-2	at Detroit
Oct. 22	Tigers, 3-1	at Detroit
Oct. 24	Cardinals, 5-0	at St. Louis
Oct. 26	Cardinals, 5-4	at St. Louis
Oct. 27	Cardinals, 4-2	at St. Louis

Game 1
Saturday, Oct. 21, at Detroit

St. Louis	AB	R	H	RBI	Detroit	AB	R	H	RBI
Eckstein, ss	5	0	0	0	Granderson, cf	4	0	0	0
Duncan, dh	4	1	1	1	Monroe, lf	4	2	2	1
Wilson, ph-dh	1	0	0	0	Polanco, 2b	4	0	0	0
Pujols, 1b	3	2	1	2	Ordonez, rf	3	0	0	0
Edmonds, cf	4	1	2	1	Guillen, 1b	4	0	2	0
Rolen, 3b	4	2	2	1	Rodriguez, c	4	0	0	0
Encarnacion, rf	3	0	0	1	Casey, dh	3	0	0	0
Belliard, 2b	4	0	0	0	Inge, 3b	3	0	0	0
Molina, c	4	1	1	0	Santiago, ss	2	0	0	0
Taguchi, lf	4	0	1	0	Thames, ph	1	0	0	0
					Perez, ss	0	0	0	0
Totals	37	7	8	6	**Totals**	32	2	4	2

			R	H	E
St. Louis	013	003	000	—	7 8 2
Detroit	100	000	001	—	2 4 3

E: St. Louis—Encarnacion (1), Rolen (1); Detroit—Inge 2 (2), Verlander (1). **2B:** St. Louis—Duncan (1), Rolen (1); Detroit—Monroe (1). **HR:** St. Louis—Rolen (1, off Verlander, 0 on), Pujols (2, off Verlander, 1 on); Detroit—Monroe (1, off Reyes, 0 on). **BB:** St. Louis—Pujols, Encarnacion; Detroit—Ordonez.

St. Louis	IP	H	R	ER	BB	SO	P	ERA
Reyes (W, 1-0)	8	4	2	2	1	4	92	2.25
Looper	1	0	0	0	0	1	22	0.00

Detroit	IP	H	R	ER	BB	SO	P	ERA
Verlander (L, 0-1)	5	6	7	6	2	8	96	10.80
Grilli	1	0	0	0	0	0	11	0.00
Rodney	1	0	0	0	0	1	12	0.00
Ledezma	1	1	0	0	0	0	15	0.00
Jones	⅔	1	0	0	0	0	8	0.00
Walker	⅓	0	0	0	0	1	7	0.00

WP: Detroit—Walker.
Attendance: 42,479 (41,070). **Time:** 2:54.

Game 2
Sunday, Oct. 22, at Detroit

St. Louis	AB	R	H	RBI	Detroit	AB	R	H	RBI
Eckstein, ss	4	0	0	0	Granderson, cf	5	0	0	0
Spiezio, dh	3	0	0	0	Monroe, lf	3	1	1	1
Pujols, 1b	3	0	0	0	Polanco, 2b	3	0	0	0
Rolen, 3b	4	1	2	0	Ordonez, rf	4	1	2	0
Encarnacion, rf	4	0	0	0	Guillen, 1b	3	1	3	1
Edmonds, cf	3	0	1	1	Rodriguez, c	4	0	0	0
Wilson, lf	3	0	0	0	Casey, dh	3	0	1	0
Molina, c	4	0	1	0	Inge, 3b	4	0	2	0
Miles, 2b	3	0	0	0	Santiago, ss	3	0	1	0
Totals	31	1	4	1	**Totals**	32	3	10	3

			R	H	E
St. Louis	000	000	001	—	1 4 1
Detroit	200	010	00x	—	3 10 3

E: St. Louis—Pujols (1); Detroit—Jones (1). **2B:** St. Louis—Edmonds (1); Detroit—Guillen (1). **3B:** Detroit—Guillen (1). **HR:** Detroit—Monroe (2, off Weaver, 0 on). **BB:** St. Louis—Spiezio, Pujols, Edmonds; Detroit—Monroe, Guillen. **S:** Detroit—Santiago.

St. Louis	IP	H	R	ER	BB	SO	P	ERA
Weaver (L, 0-1)	5	9	3	3	1	5	85	5.40
Johnson	⅔	0	0	0	0	0	9	0.00
Kinney	⅓	0	0	0	1	0	8	0.00
Flores	1	1	0	0	0	0	12	0.00
Thompson	⅔	0	0	0	0	1	8	0.00
Wainwright	⅓	0	0	0	0	1	5	0.00

Detroit	IP	H	R	ER	BB	SO	P	ERA
Rogers (W, 1-0)	8	2	0	0	3	5	99	0.00
Jones (S, 1)	1	2	1	0	0	0	15	0.00

HBP: by Jones (Wilson); by Kinney (Polanco); by Weaver (Casey).
Attendance: 42,533 (41,070). **Time:** 2:55.

Game 3
Tuesday, Oct. 24, at St. Louis

Detroit	AB	R	H	RBI	St. Louis	AB	R	H	RBI
Granderson, cf	4	0	0	0	Eckstein, 2b	4	1	2	0
Monroe, lf	4	0	0	0	Wilson, lf	3	1	1	0
Polanco, 2b	3	0	0	0	Pujols, 1b	4	1	1	0
Ordonez, rf	3	0	0	0	Rolen, 3b	4	1	1	0
Guillen, ss	3	0	0	0	Belliard, 2b	4	0	0	0
Rodriguez, c	3	0	0	0	Edmonds, cf	2	0	1	2
Casey, 1b	3	0	2	0	Molina, c	3	0	1	0
Inge, 3b	3	0	1	0	Taguchi, rf	3	1	0	0
Robertson, p	0	0	0	0	Carpenter, p	3	0	0	0
Gomez, ph	1	0	0	0					
Infante, ph	1	0	0	0					
Totals	28	0	3	0	**Totals**	30	5	7	2

			R	H	E
Detroit	000	000	000	—	0 3 1
St. Louis	000	200	21x	—	5 7 0

E: Detroit—Zumaya (1). **2B:** St. Louis—Pujols (1), Edmonds (2), Molina (1). **BB:** St. Louis—Wilson 2, Edmonds 2, Eckstein, Rolen, Molina, Taguchi. **S:** Detroit—Robertson; St. Louis—Carpenter.

Detroit	IP	H	R	ER	BB	SO	P	ERA
Robertson (L, 0-1)	5	5	2	2	3	3	93	3.60
Ledezma	⅓	1	0	0	0	1	10	0.00
Zumaya	1	0	2	0	2	1	24	0.00
Grilli	⅔	0	0	0	1	0	11	0.00
Rodney	⅓	1	1	1	2	0	17	6.75
Miner	⅔	0	0	0	0	0	8	0.00

St. Louis	IP	H	R	ER	BB	SO	P	ERA
Carpenter (W, 1-0)	8	3	0	0	0	6	82	0.00
Looper	1	0	0	0	0	0		

HBP: by Miner (Pujols). **IBB:** by Grilli (Edmonds), by Robertson (Molina). **WP:** Detroit—Miner; St. Louis—Carpenter.
Attendance: 46,513 (43,975). **Time:** 3:03.

Most Valuable Player
David Eckstein, St. Louis, SS

AVG	AB	R	H	HR	RBI	BB
.364	22	3	8	0	4	1

World Series Box Scores (Cont.)

Game 4
Thursday, Oct. 26, at St. Louis

Detroit	AB	R	H	RBI	St. Louis	AB	R	H	RBI
Granderson, cf	5	1	1	0	Eckstein, ss	5	1	4	2
Monroe, lf	5	0	0	0	Duncan, rf	2	0	0	0
Guillen, ss	3	1	1	0	Taguchi, ph,rf,lf	1	1	0	0
Ordonez, rf	5	0	0	0	Pujols, 1b	2	0	0	0
Casey, 1b	4	1	3	2	Edmonds, cf	4	0	0	0
Rodriguez, c	4	1	3	1	Rolen, 3b	4	1	2	0
Polanco, 2b	4	0	0	0	Wilson, lf	3	0	1	1
Inge, 3b	3	0	2	1	Molina, c	2	0	1	1
Bonderman, p	2	0	0	0	Miles, 2b	3	2	1	0
Gomez, ph	1	0	0	0	Suppan, p	2	0	0	0
					Rodriguez, ph	1	0	0	0
					Encarnacion, rf	1	0	0	0
Totals	**36**	**4**	**10**	**4**	**Totals**	**30**	**5**	**9**	**4**

					R	H	E
Detroit	012	000	010	—	4	10	1
St. Louis	001	100	21x	—	5	9	0

E: Detroit—Rodney (1). **2B:** Detroit—Granderson (1), Rodriguez (1), Inge (1); St. Louis—Eckstein 3 (3), Rolen 2 (3), Molina (2). **HR:** Detroit—Casey (1, off Suppan, 0 on). **SB:** Detroit—Guillen (1); St. Louis—Miles (1). **BB:** Detroit—Guillen, Inge; St. Louis—Pujols 2, Molina 2, Duncan, Miles. **S:** Detroit—Bonderman, Suppan; St. Louis—Taguchi, Wilson.

Detroit	IP	H	R	ER	BB	SO	P	ERA
Bonderman	5⅓	6	2	2	4	4	92	3.38
Rodney	1⅔	2	2	0	1	4	30	3.00
Zumaya (L, 0-1)	1	1	1	1	1	1	19	4.50
St. Louis	**IP**	**H**	**R**	**ER**	**BB**	**SO**	**P**	**ERA**
Suppan	6	8	3	3	2	4	87	4.50
Kinney	⅔	0	0	0	1	1	13	0.00
Johnson	⅓	0	0	0	0	0	1	0.00
Looper	⅓	1	1	1	0	0	6	3.86
Wainwright (W, 1-0)	1⅔	0	0	0	3	23	0.00

IBB: by Rodney (Pujols), by Bonderman (Miles), by Suppan (Inge). **WP:** Detroit—Zumaya.

Attendance: 46,470 (43,975). **Time:** 3:35.

Game 5
Friday, Oct. 27, at St. Louis

Detroit	AB	R	H	RBI	St. Louis	AB	R	H	RBI
Granderson, cf	3	0	1	0	Eckstein, ss	4	1	2	2
Monroe, lf	4	0	0	0	Duncan, rf	2	0	0	0
Guillen, ss	4	0	0	0	Pujols, 1b	3	0	1	0
Ordonez, rf	4	1	0	0	Edmonds, cf	3	0	0	0
Casey, 1b	4	1	3	2	Rolen, 3b	3	0	1	1
Rodriguez, c	4	0	0	0	Belliard, 2b	2	0	0	0
Polanco, 2b	3	0	0	0	Molina, c	4	2	3	0
Inge, 3b	4	0	1	0	Taguchi, lf-rf	3	1	1	0
Verlander, p	2	0	0	0	Weaver, p	3	0	0	0
Gomez, ph	1	0	0	0	Spiezio, ph	1	0	0	0
Totals	**33**	**2**	**5**	**2**	**Totals**	**31**	**4**	**8**	**3**

					R	H	E
Detroit	000	200	000	—	2	5	2
St. Louis	010	200	10x	—	4	8	1

E: Detroit—Inge (3), Verlander (2); St. Louis—Duncan (1). **2B:** Detroit—Casey 2 (2), Inge (2). **HR:** Detroit—Casey (2, off Weaver, 1 on). **CS:** St. Louis—Pujols (1). **BB:** Detroit—Granderson, Polanco; St. Louis—Duncan, Wilson, Pujols, Rolen. **S:** St. Louis—Taguchi.

Detroit	IP	H	R	ER	BB	SO	P	ERA
Verlander (L, 0-2)	6	6	3	1	3	4	101	5.73
Rodney	1	2	1	1	1	0	25	4.50
Zumaya	1	0	0	0	0	1	6	3.00
St. Louis	**IP**	**H**	**R**	**ER**	**BB**	**SO**	**P**	**ERA**
Weaver (W, 1-1)	8	4	2	1	1	9	99	2.77
Wainwright (S, 1)	1	1	0	0	1	1	26	0.00

WP: Detroit—Verlander 2; St. Louis—Wainwright.

Attendance: 46,638 (43,975). **Time:** 2:54.

World Series Composite Box Score

St. Louis Cardinals

Batting	WS vs. Detroit								Overall Playoffs							
	Avg	AB	R	H	HR	RBI	BB	SO	Avg	AB	R	H	HR	RBI	BB	SO
Scott Rolen	.421	19	5	8	1	2	2	4	.275	51	9	14	1	2	5	7
Yadier Molina	.412	17	3	7	0	1	3	1	.358	53	5	19	2	8	6	5
David Eckstein	.364	22	3	8	0	4	1	1	.254	63	7	16	1	6	5	1
Jim Edmonds	.235	17	1	4	0	4	3	8	.250	52	8	13	2	10	10	16
Preston Wilson	.200	10	1	2	0	1	3	2	.200	35	5	7	0	2	4	7
Albert Pujols	.200	15	3	3	1	2	5	3	.288	52	11	15	3	6	13	10
So Taguchi	.182	11	3	2	0	0	1	2	.400	15	5	6	2	4	1	2
Aaron Miles	.167	6	2	1	0	0	1	2	.364	11	2	4	0	0	1	2
Chris Duncan	.125	8	1	1	0	1	2	3	.136	22	3	3	1	2	4	7
Jeff Suppan	.000	2	0	0	0	0	0	0	.167	6	1	1	1	1	0	3
Scott Spiezio	.000	4	0	0	0	0	0	1	.192	26	4	5	0	6	3	7
Ronnie Belliard	.000	12	0	0	0	0	0	3	.240	50	2	12	0	4	3	6
Chris Carpenter	.000	3	0	0	0	0	0	0	.083	12	0	1	0	0	0	3
Juan Encarnacion	.000	8	0	0	0	1	1	2	.182	44	2	8	0	5	4	7
Jeff Weaver	.000	3	0	0	0	0	0	2	.222	9	0	2	0	0	0	2
John Rodriguez	.000	1	0	0	0	0	0	1	.000	6	0	0	0	0	0	2
Gary Bennett	—	0	0	0	0	0	0	0	.000	0	0	0	0	0	0	1
Anthony Reyes	—	0	0	0	0	0	0	0	.000	1	0	0	0	0	0	0
TOTALS	.228	158	22	36	2	16	23	34	.248	509	64	126	13	56	59	88

WS vs. Detroit / Overall Playoffs

Pitching	ERA	W-L	Sv	Gm	IP	H	BB	SO	ERA	W-L	Sv	Gm	IP	H	BB	SO
Chris Carpenter	0.00	1-0	0	1	8.0	3	0	6	2.78	3-1	0	5	32.1	28	8	23
Randy Flores	0.00	0-0	0	0	1.0	1	0	0	0.00	1-0	0	7	5.2	5	1	4
Adam Wainwright	0.00	1-0	1	0	3.0	2	1	5	0.00	1-0	4	9	9.2	7	2	15
Tyler Johnson	0.00	0-0	0	0	1.0	0	0	1	1.23	0-0	0	10	7.1	4	2	12
Brad Thompson	0.00	0-0	0	0	0.2	0	0	1	9.00	0-1	0	4	2.0	3	1	3
Josh Kinney	0.00	0-0	0	0	1.0	0	2	1	0.00	1-0	0	7	6.1	3	4	6
Anthony Reyes	2.25	1-0	0	1	8.0	4	1	4	3.00	1-0	0	2	12.0	7	5	8
Jeff Weaver	2.77	1-1	0	2	13.0	13	2	14	2.43	3-2	0	5	29.2	25	9	19
Braden Looper	3.86	0-0	0	0	2.1	1	0	1	4.15	0-0	0	7	8.2	9	0	2
Jeff Suppan	4.50	0-0	0	1	6.0	8	2	4	2.49	1-1	0	4	25.1	19	11	13
Josh Hancock	—	0-0	0	0	0.0	0	0	0	27.00	0-0	0	3	2.0	5	5	2
TOTALS	2.05	4-1	1	5	44.0	32	8	37	2.68	11-5	4	16	141.0	115	48	107

Detroit Tigers

WS vs. St. Louis / Overall Playoffs

Batting	Avg	AB	R	H	HR	RBI	BB	SO	Avg	AB	R	H	HR	RBI	BB	SO
Sean Casey	.529	17	2	9	2	5	0	2	.432	37	3	16	2	9	1	2
Carlos Guillen	.353	17	2	6	0	2	3	4	.362	47	6	17	1	4	6	9
Brandon Inge	.353	17	0	6	0	1	1	6	.273	44	4	12	1	4	4	15
Ramon Santiago	.200	5	0	1	0	0	0	2	.083	12	0	1	0	0	1	2
Ivan Rodriguez	.158	19	1	3	0	1	0	3	.167	48	6	8	1	5	3	10
Craig Monroe	.150	20	3	3	2	2	1	5	.240	50	11	12	5	9	4	12
Magglio Ordonez	.105	19	2	2	0	0	1	4	.196	51	8	10	3	8	4	8
Curtis Granderson	.095	21	1	2	0	0	1	7	.226	53	8	12	3	7	5	10
Placido Polanco	.000	17	0	0	0	0	1	1	.314	51	5	16	0	4	4	3
Marcus Thames	.000	1	0	0	0	0	0	0	.238	21	3	5	0	1	1	6
Alexis Gomez	.000	3	0	0	0	0	0	1	.333	12	1	4	1	4	0	3
Omar Infante	.000	1	0	0	0	0	0	0	.333	3	0	1	0	0	1	1
Jeremy Bonderman	.000	2	0	0	0	0	0	1	.000	2	0	0	0	0	0	1
Justin Verlander	.000	2	0	0	0	0	0	1	.000	2	0	0	0	0	0	1
Neifi Perez	—	0	0	0	0	0	0	0	.000	4	0	0	0	0	0	1
TOTALS	.199	161	11	32	4	11	8	37	.261	437	55	114	17	55	34	84

Pitching	ERA	W-L	Sv	Gm	IP	H	BB	SO	ERA	W-L	Sv	Gm	IP	H	BB	SO
Kenny Rogers	0.00	1-0	0	1	8.0	2	3	5	0.00	3-0	0	3	23.0	9	7	19
Todd Jones	0.00	0-0	1	2	1.2	3	0	0	0.00	0-0	4	7	6.2	7	1	4
Jamie Walker	0.00	0-0	0	1	0.1	0	0	1	4.15	1-0	0	5	4.1	3	1	3
Jason Grilli	0.00	0-0	0	2	1.2	0	1	0	0.00	0-0	0	5	3.0	1	4	1
Wilfredo Ledezma	0.00	0-0	0	2	1.1	2	0	1	2.25	1-0	0	4	4.0	4	1	2
Zach Miner	0.00	0-0	0	1	0.2	0	0	0	0.00	0-0	0	1	0.2	0	0	0
Joel Zumaya	3.00	0-1	0	3	3.0	1	3	3	3.00	0-1	0	6	6.0	2	3	6
Jeremy Bonderman	3.38	0-0	0	1	5.1	6	4	4	3.10	1-0	0	3	20.1	17	7	11
Nate Robertson	3.60	0-1	0	1	5.0	5	3	3	5.17	1-2	0	3	15.2	23	6	8
Fernando Rodney	4.50	0-0	0	4	4.0	5	4	5	2.35	0-0	0	7	7.2	6	5	9
Justin Verlander	5.73	0-2	0	2	11.0	12	5	12	5.82	1-2	0	4	21.2	26	10	23
TOTALS	3.00	1-4	1	5	42.0	36	23	34	2.95	8-5	4	13	113.0	98	45	86

Score by Innings

	1	2	3	4	5	6	7	8	9		R	H	E
St. Louis	0	2	4	5	0	3	5	2	1	–	22	36	4
Detroit	3	1	2	2	1	0	0	1	1	–	11	32	8

E: St. Louis—Duncan, Encarnacion, Pujols; Detroit—Inge 3, Verlander 2, Jones, Rodney, Zumaya. **2B:** St. Louis—Rolen 3, Eckstein 3, Molina 2, Edmonds 2, Pujols, Duncan; Detroit—Casey 2, Inge 2, Guillen, Rodriguez, Monroe, Granderson. **3B:** Detroit—Guillen. **HR:** St. Louis—Rolen, Pujols; Detroit—Casey 2, Monroe 2. **SB:** St. Louis—Miles; Detroit—Inge. **CS:** St. Louis—Pujols. **S:** St. Louis—Taguchi 2, Carpenter, Wilson; Detroit—Bonderman, Robertson. **HBP:** by Jones (Wilson), by Kinney (Polanco), by Weaver (Casey), by Miner (Pujols). **WP:** St. Louis—Carpenter, Wainwright; Detroit—Verlander 2, Miner, Walker, Zumaya. **Balk:** none. **DP:** St. Louis—3; Detroit—4. **LOB:** St. Louis—39; Detroit—31.

Umpires: John Hirschbeck, Tim Mcclelland, Randy Marsh, Alfonso Marquez, Mike Winters, Wally Bell.

2006 WORLD BASEBALL CLASSIC

The inaugural **World Baseball Classic** was played from March 3-20 in Anaheim, Orlando, Phoenix, San Juan and Tokyo. The 16-nation tournament was sanctioned by the International Baseball Federation (IBAF), and featured arguably the best players in the World competing for their home countries for the first time.

Teams were divided into four pools. Rounds 1 and 2 were based on a standard round robin format with the top two teams (*) advancing. The Semifinals and the Final were both single elimination.

Official rules of Major League Baseball were used, including the use of the designated hitter.

Note: the current plan is for the next World Baseball Classic to be played in 2009, with subsequent tournaments taking place once every four years thereafter.

Also note that **RA/9** denotes runs allowed per nine innings, while **Avg** is the team's total batting average for that round. After head-to-head records, RA/9 was the first tiebreaker used to determine which team advanced to the next round.

Final Round Robin Standings

Round 1

Pool A	W-L-T	RA/9	Avg
*Korea	3-0-0	1.00	.313
*Japan	2-1-0	3.00	.356
Chinese Taipei	1-2-0	6.84	.265
China	0-3-0	14.40	.185

Pool B	W-L-T	RA/9	Avg
*Mexico	2-1-0	2.42	.297
*United States	2-1-0	3.13	.337
Canada	2-1-0	7.67	.279
South Africa	0-3-0	15.55	.253

Pool C	W-L-T	RA/9	Avg
*Puerto Rico	3-0-0	2.16	.302
*Cuba	2-1-0	6.67	.314
Netherlands	1-2-0	6.84	.265
Panama	0-3-0	6.92	.165

Pool D	W-L-T	RA/9	Avg
*Dominican Republic	3-0-0	4.00	.314
*Venezuela	2-1-0	3.67	.235
Italy	1-2-0	5.48	.200
Australia	0-3-0	6.85	.113

Round 2

Pool 1	W-L-T	RA/9	Avg
*Korea	3-0-0	1.67	.205
*Japan	1-2-0	2.36	.274
Mexico	1-2-0	3.12	.159
United States	1-2-0	4.32	.242

Pool 2	W-L-T	RA/9	Avg
*Dominican Republic	2-1-0	3.67	.216
*Cuba	2-1-0	4.00	.226
Venezuela	1-2-0	3.12	.133
Puerto Rico	1-2-0	3.67	.271

Semifinals

Japan 6 . . . . .Korea 0

Cuba 3 . . . . .Dominican Republic 1

Championship Game

Japan 10 . . . . .Cuba 6

Batting Leaders

	Avg	AB	R	H	HR	RBI	SB
Adam Stern, CAN	.667	9	3	6	1	5	1
Ken Griffey Jr., USA	.524	21	4	11	3	10	0
Brett Willemburg, RSA	.500	10	2	5	0	3	0
Yoandy Garlobo, CUB	.480	25	4	12	1	4	0
Sidney de Jong, NED	.455	11	2	5	0	0	0
Jason Bay, CAN	.455	11	5	5	0	0	0
N. Dempsey, RSA	.455	11	0	5	0	0	0
Derek Jeter, USA	.450	20	5	9	0	1	0
N. Matsunaka, JPN	.433	30	11	13	0	2	0
Yi Feng, CHN	.429	7	0	3	0	0	0
Chin-lung Hu, TPE	.417	12	2	5	0	1	2

Pitching Leaders

(Min. 8 IP)	ERA	W-L	Gm	IP	BB	SO
Yadel Marti, CUB	0.00	1-0	4	12.2	4	11
Chan Ho Park, KOR	0.00	0-0	4	10.0	0	8
Bartolo Colon, DOM	0.64	1-0	3	14.0	2	7
Jae Seo, KOR	0.64	2-0	3	14.0	3	8
Jose Santiago, PR	1.13	1-0	5	8.0	1	4
Dae-Sung Koo, KOR	1.13	1-0	5	8.0	1	3
D. Matsuzaka. JPN	1.38	3-0	3	13.0	3	10
Koji Uehara, JPN	1.59	2-0	3	17.0	0	16
S. Watanabe, JPN	1.98	0-0	3	13.2	2	6
Joel Pineiro, PR	2.08	0-1	2	8.2	4	5
Roger Clemens, USA	2.08	1-1	2	8.2	0	10
Johan Santana, VEN	2.16	0-2	2	8.1	3	10

Tournament MVP

Daisuke Matsuzaka, P, Japan

All-Tournament Team

C	Tomoya Satozaki	Japan
1B	Seung Yeop Lee	Korea
2B	Yuliesky Gourriel	Cuba
SS	Derek Jeter	United States
3B	Adrian Beltre	Dominican Rep.
OF	Ken Griffey Jr.	United States
OF	Ichiro Suzuki	Japan
OF	Jong Beom Lee	Korea
DH	Yoandy Garlobo	Cuba
P	Daisuke Matsuzaka	Japan
P	Chan Ho Park	Korea
P	Yadel Marti	Cuba

COLLEGE

Final *Baseball America* Top 25

Final 2006 Division I Top 25, voted on by the editors of *Baseball America* and released after the NCAA CollegeWorld Series. Given are final records (excluding ties) and winning percentage (including all postseason games); records in College World Series and team eliminated by (DNP indicates team did not play in tourney); head coach (career years and four-year college record including 2006 postseason); preseason ranking and rank before start of CWS.

	Record	Pct	CWS Recap	Head Coach	Preseason Rank	Rank before CWS
1 Oregon St.	50-16	.758	6-2	Pat Casey (12 yrs: 386-250-4)	8	4
2 North Carolina	54-15	.783	4-2 (Oregon St.)	Mike Fox (23 yrs: 881-01-5)	6	5
3 CS-Fullerton	50-15	.769	2-2 (N. Carolina)	George Horton (10 yrs: 452-187-1)	5	2
4 Rice	57-13	.814	2-2 (Oregon St.)	Wayne Graham (15 yrs: 684-270)	7	1
5 Clemson	53-16	.768	1-2 (CS-Fullerton)	Jack Leggett (27 yrs: 985-549)	2	3
6 Georgia	47-23	.671	0-2 (Oregon St.)	David Perno (5 yrs: 183-126)	NR	6
7 Georgia Tech	50-18	.735	0-2 (CS-Fullerton)	Danny Hall (19 yrs: 787-365)	4	7
8 Miami-FL	42-24	.636	1-2 (Oregon St.)	Jim Morris (25 yrs: 1109-465-3)	NR	8
9 Oklahoma	45-22	.672		Sunny Golloway (10 yrs: 392-184)	NR	9
10 Alabama	44-21	.677		Jim Wells (16 yrs: 714-335)	NR	10
11 Mississippi	44-22	.667		Mike Bianco (9 yrs: 342-203-1)	23	11
12 Texas	41-21	.661		Augie Garrido (38 yrs: 1583-738-8)	1	12
13 South Carolina	41-25	.621		Ray Tanner (19 yrs: 849-373-3)	14	13
14 Coll. of Charleston	46-17	.730		John Pawlowski (7 yrs: 260-153-1)	NR	14
15 Nebraska	40-23	.635		Mike Anderson (4 yrs: 180-79)	NR	15
16 Virginia	47-15	.758		Brian O'Connor (3 yrs: 132-50)	NR	16
17 Oral Roberts	41-16	.719		Rob Walton (9 yrs: 133-47)	NR	17
18 Missouri	36-25	.590		Tim Jamieson (12 yrs: 425-300-9)	10	18
19 Stanford	33-27	.550		Mark Marquess (30 yrs: 1235-597-5)	NR	19
20 Kentucky	43-17	.717		John Cohen (7 yrs: 243-158)	NR	20
21 Pepperdine	42-21	.667		Steve Rodriguez (3 yrs: 113-76)	11	21
22 Fresno St.	45-18	.714		Mike Batesole (11 yrs: 390-263-1)	21	22
23 Oklahoma St.	40-21	.656		Frank Anderson (3 yrs: 112-70)	NR	23
24 Houston	39-22	.639		Rayner Noble (12 yrs: 429-305)	NR	24
25 Wichita St.	46-22	.676		Gene Stephenson (29 yrs: 1552-511-3)	NR	25

College World Series

CWS participants: CS-Fullerton (48-13); Clemson (52-14); Georgia (47-21); Georgia Tech (50-16); Miami-FL (41-22); North Carolina (50-13); Oregon St. (44-14); Rice (55-11).

Bracket One

June 16—Clemson 8 . . . . Georgia Tech 4
June 16—North Carolina 7 . . . 13 inn. . . CS-Fullerton 5
June 18—CS-Fullerton 7 . . . . Georgia Tech 5 (out)
June 18—North Carolina 2 . . . . Clemson 0
June 20—CS-Fullerton 7 . . . . Clemson 6 (out)
June 21—North Carolina 6 . . . . CS-Fullerton 5 (out)

Bracket Two

June 17—Rice 6 . . . . Georgia 4
June 17—Miami-FL 11 . . . . Oregon St. 1
June 19—Oregon St. 5 . . . . Georgia 3 (out)
June 19—Rice 3 . . . . Miami-FL 2
June 20—Oregon St. 8 . . . . Miami-FL 1 (out)
June 21—Oregon St. 5 . . . . Rice 0
June 22—Oregon St. 2 . . . . Rice 0 (out)

Championship Series

June 24—North Carolina 4 . . . . Oregon St. 3
June 25—Oregon St. 11 . . . . North Carolina 7
June 26—Oregon St. 3 . . . . North Carolina 2 (out)

Most Outstanding Player

Jonah Nickerson, Oregon St., P

W-L	IP	H	ER	BB	K	ERA
2-0	21.3	12	2	4	19	0.84

All-Tournament Team

C—Tim Federowicz, UNC; **1B**—Bill Rowe, Oregon St.; **2B**—Justin Turner, CS-Fullerton; **3B**—Shea McFeely, Oregon St.; **SS**—Josh Horton, UNC; **OF**—Danny Dorn, CS-Fullerton; Cole Gillespie, Oregon St.; Jay Cox, UNC; **DH**—David Cooper, CS-Fullerton; **P**—Jonah Nickerson, Oregon St. and Kevin Gunderson, Oregon St.

Annual Awards

Chosen by *Baseball America, Collegiate Baseball,* National Collegiate Baseball Writers Association, American Baseball Coaches Association and USA Baseball.

Players of the Year

Andrew Miller, North Carolina, P . . . . .BA
Brad Lincoln, Houston, P/UT . . . . .ABCA, Dick Howser (NCBWA)
Tim Lincecum, Washington, P . . . . .Golden Spikes (USA Baseball)

Wes Roemer, CS-Fullerton, P . . . . .CB
& Kellen Kulbacki, James Madison

Coach of the Year

Pat Casey, Oregon St. . . . . .BA, ABCA, CB

BASEBALL

Baseball America All-America Team

NCAA Division I All-Americans. Holdover from 2005 First Team in **bold**.

First Team

Pos		Cl	Avg	HR	RBI
C	Matt Wieters, Georgia Tech	So.	.355	15	71
1B	Mark Hamilton, Tulane	Jr.	.336	20	69
2B	**Jim Negrych**, Pittsburgh	Jr.	.396	11	60
3B	Pedro Alvarez, Vanderbilt	Fr.	.329	22	64
SS	Brian Friday, Rice	So.	.353	9	57
OF	Kellen Kulbacki, JMU	So.	.464	24	75
OF	Cole Gillespie, Oregon St.	Jr.	.374	13	57
OF	Tyler Colvin, Clemson	Jr.	.356	13	70
DH	Ryan Strieby, Kentucky	Jr.	.343	20	77
UT	Brad Lincoln, Houston	Jr.	.295	14	53

Pos		Cl	W-L	Sv	ERA
SP	Andrew Miller, North Carolina	Jr.	13-2	1	2.48
SP	Tim Lincecum, Washington	Jr.	12-4	3	1.94
SP	Eddie Degerman, Rice	Sr.	13-2	0	2.00
SP	Wes Roemer, CS-Fullerton	So.	13-2	1	2.38
RP	Cole St. Clair, Rice	So.	7-2	11	1.82

Second Team

Pos		Cl	Avg	HR	RBI
C	Kode Valverde, Alabama	Sr.	.347	12	59
1B	Craig Cooper, Notre Dame	Sr.	.425	9	41
2B	Justin Turner, CS-Fullerton	Jr.	.355	4	43
SS	Emmanuel Burris, Kent St.	Jr.	.360	4	28
3B	Evan Longoria, Long Beach St.	Jr.	.353	11	43
OF	Jacob Dempsey, Winthrop	Sr.	.403	17	78
OF	Jon Jay, Miami-FL	Jr.	.361	6	46
OF	Drew Stubbs. Texas	Jr.	.342	12	58
DH	Josh Horton, North Carolina	So.	.395	7	59
UT	Sean Doolittle, Virginia	So.	.324	4	57

Pos		Cl	W-L	Sv	ERA
SP	Jake Arrieta, TCU	So.	14-4	1	2.35
SP	Jonah Nickerson, Oregon St.	Jr.	13-4	0	2.24
SP	Nick Schmidt, Arkansas	So.	9-3	0	3.01
SP	Stephen Wright, Hawaii	Jr.	11-2	1	2.30
RP	Don Czyz, Kansas	Sr.	6-0	19	1.56

NCAA Division I Leaders

Batting

Average

(At least 100 AB & 2.5/Gm)	Cl	Gm	AB	H	Avg
Mike Goetz, Wis.-Milwaukee	Sr.	57	225	111	.493
Kellen Kulbacki, James Madison	So.	53	194	90	.464
Joaquin Rodriguez, Jackson St.	Jr.	39	140	64	.457
Shundell Russaw, Jackson St.	Sr.	38	141	62	.440
Ryan Khoury, Utah	Sr.	56	224	98	.438
Craig Cooper, Notre Dame	Sr.	57	228	97	.425
Marcus Davis, Alcorn St.	Jr.	43	170	72	.424
Nate Schill, James Madison	Sr.	58	227	95	.419
Matt McBride, Lehigh	Jr.	56	211	88	.417
Bradley Hubbert, Alcorn St.	Jr.	47	166	69	.416

Home Runs (per game)

(At least 15 HR)	Cl	Gm	HR	Avg
Kellen Kulbacki, James Madison	So.	53	24	0.45
Shawn Scobee, Nevada	Sr.	53	22	0.42
Patrick Nichols, Old Dominion	Sr.	44	18	0.41
Michael Cowgill, James Madison	Sr.	59	23	0.39
Quinn Stewart, LSU	Sr.	59	23	0.39
Luke Hopkins, New Mexico St.	So.	44	16	0.36
Drew Holder, Dallas Baptist	Sr.	56	20	0.36
Mark Shorey, High Point	Sr.	56	20	0.36
Chris Carlson, New Mexico	Jr.	59	21	0.36
Ben Saylor, Brigham Young	Sr.	59	21	0.36

Runs Batted In (per game)

(At least 50 RBI)	Cl	Gm	RBI	Avg
Marcus Davis, Alcorn St.	Jr.	43	64	1.49
Luke Hopkins, New Mexico St.	So.	44	65	1.48
Kellen Kulbacki, James Madison	So.	53	75	1.42
Joaquin Rodriguez, Jackson St.	Jr.	39	54	1.38
Drew Holder, Dallas Baptist	Sr.	56	75	1.34
Chris Carlson, New Mexico	Jr.	59	79	1.34
Shawn Taylor, Alcorn St.	Jr.	47	61	1.30
Cody Montgomery, Dallas Baptist	Sr.	54	70	1.30
Brendan Murphy, Marshall	Sr.	54	70	1.30
Ben Humphrey, Central Michigan	Jr.	56	72	1.29

Stolen Bases (per game)

(At least 25)	Cl	Gm	SB	CS	Avg
Calvin Lester, Prairie View	Jr.	54	56	9	1.04
Zach Penprase, Miss. Valley St.	Jr.	55	56	7	1.02
Mike Epping, New Orleans	Jr.	55	42	7	0.76
Emmannuel Burriss, Kent St.	Jr.	56	42	2	0.75
Michael Richard, Prairie View	Jr.	55	41	12	0.75
Nate Parks, Virginia Tech	Jr.	43	30	6	0.70
Jimmy Miles, Old Dominion	Jr.	56	39	6	0.70
Corey Littleton, Miss. Valley St.	Jr.	46	32	3	0.70
Eric Nieto, Manhattan	So.	57	39	4	0.68
Ryan Keena, IPFW	Sr.	48	32	6	0.67
John Raynor, UNC Wilmington	Sr.	63	42	4	0.67

Pitching

Earned Run Avg.

(At least 55 inn.)	Cl	Gm	IP	ERA
Jonathan Hovis. North Carolina	Sr.	38	69.1	1.17
Steve Holmes, Rhode Island	Jr.	14	104.0	1.30
Nick Chigges, Coll. of Charleston	Jr.	17	115.2	1.40
Chris Cody, Manhattan	Sr.	14	108.0	1.42
Ben Hunter, Wake Forest	So.	33	55.0	1.47
Derrik Lutz, George Washington	Jr.	14	99.2	1.53
Justin Pigott, Mississippi St.	So.	19	65.0	1.66
Brad Lincoln, Houston	Jr.	17	127.2	1.69
Mitch Harris, Navy	So.	13	82.2	1.74
Cole St. Clair, Rice	So.	37	74.1	1.82

Wins

	Cl	Gm	IP	W-L
Jake Arrieta, TCU	So.	19	111.0	14-4
Lauren Gagnier, CS-Fullerton	Jr.	21	131.2	14-5
Eddie Degerman, Rice	Sr.	20	130.2	13-2
Barry Enright, Pepperdine	So.	21	124.1	13-2
Andrew Miller, North Carolina	Jr.	20	123.1	13-2
Wes Roemer, CS-Fullerton	So.	21	155.0	13-2
Eddie Romero, Fresno St.	Jr.	21	125.2	13-2
Dallas Buck, Oregon St.	Jr.	21	128.1	13-3
Alex Wilson, Winthrop	Fr.	20	138.0	13-3
Jonah Nickerson, Oregon St.	Jr.	20	136.2	13-4
Heath Rollins, Winthrop	Jr.	22	123.0	13-4

Strikeouts (per 9 inn.)

(At least 55 inn.)	Cl	IP	SO	Avg
Tim Lincecum, Washington	Jr.	125.1	199	14.3
Christian Friedrich, Eastern Ky.	Fr.	82.0	118	13.0
David Price, Vanderbilt	So.	110.1	155	12.6
Mitch Harris, Navy	So.	82.2	113	12.3
Cole St. Clair, Rice	So.	74.1	100	12.1
Mike Felix, Troy	Jr.	101.2	134	11.9
Eddie Degerman, Rice	Sr.	130.2	172	11.8
Ryan Reid, James Madison	So.	94.1	124	11.8
Adam Ottavino, Northeastern	Jr.	93.2	120	11.5
Ben Hunter, Wake Forest	So.	55.0	70	11.5

Saves

	Cl	Gm	IP	Sv
Kevin Gunderson, Oregon St.	Jr.	37	53.1	20
Don Czyz, Kansas	Sr.	37	63.1	19
Kyle Weiland, Notre Dame	Fr.	30	49.1	16
Andrew Urena, Mercer	Sr.	30	48.1	15
Josh McLaughlin, C of Charleston	Jr.	31	56.2	15
Andrew Carignan, North Carolina.	So.	32	33.2	15
Link Saunders, Citadel	Jr.	33	47.2	15
Joshua Fields, Georgia	So.	35	50.0	15
Four tied with 14 each.				

Other College World Series
Participants' final records in parentheses.

NCAA Div. II
at Montgomery, Ala. (May 27-June 3)

Participants: Ashland (47-17); Cal State-Chico (46-21); Emporia St. (48-13); Francis Marion (41-18); Franklin Pierce (46-13); Montevallo (43-18); Tampa (54-6); West Chester (39-20); .

Championship: Tampa def. CS-Chico, 3-2 (10 inn.).

NCAA Div. III
at Appleton, Wis. (May 26-30)

Participants: Aurora (34-14); Chapman (33-13); Eastern Conn. St. (36-20); Marietta (43-11); Montclair St. (35-19-2); N.C. Wesleyan (31-19); Wheaton, Mass. (42-10); Wis.-Stevens Point (35-18).

Championship: Marietta def. Wheaton, Mass., 7-2.

2006 MLB First-Year Player Draft

First round selections at the 42nd First-Year Player Draft held June 6-7, 2006 in New York. Clubs select in reverse order of their standing from the preceding season. In 2006 the Kansas City Royals chose 22-year-old pitcher Luke Hochevar with the top overall pick. Hochevar was originally drafted by the Los Angeles Dodgers with the 40th pick in the 2005 draft, but re-entered the draft after failing to come to financial terms. The former U. of Tennessee pitcher had been pitching for the independent Fort Worth Cats. Note that picks 31-44 are supplemental compensatory selections.

First Round

No		Pos
1	Kansas City . . Luke Hochevar, Ft. Worth (indep.)	RHP
2	Colorado . . . . Greg Reynolds, Stanford	RHP
3	Tampa Bay . . . . Evan Longoria, Long Beach St.	3B
4	Pittsburgh . . . . Brad Lincoln, Houston	RHP
5	Seattle . . . . Brandon Morrow, California	RHP
6	Detroit . . . . Andrew Miller, North Carolina	LHP
7	LA Dodgers . . . Clayton Kershaw, Highland Park HS, Dallas, Texas	LHP
8	Cincinnati . . . . Drew Stubbs, Texas	OF
9	Baltimore . . . . . William Rowell, Bishop Eustace Prep, Pennsauken, N.J.	3B
10	San Francisco . . . . . Tim Lincecum, Washington	RHP
11	Arizona . . . . Max Scherzer, Missouri	RHP
12	Texas . . . . Kasey Kiker, Russell County HS Phenix City, Ala.	LHP
13	Chicago-NL . . . . Tyler Colvin, Clemson	OF
14	Toronto . . . . Travis Snider, Jackson HS Everett, Wash.	OF
15	Washington . . . Chris Marrero, Monsignor Pace HS, Opa Locka, Fla.	OF
16	Milwaukee . . . . Jeremy Jeffress, Halifax County Sr. HS, South Boston, Va.	RHP
17	San Diego . . . . Matthew Antonelli, Wake Forest	3B
18	**a-**Philadelphia . . . Kyle Drabek, The Woodlands (Tex.) HS	RHP
19	Florida . . . . Brett Sinkbeil, Missouri St.	RHP
20	Minnesota . . . . Chris Parmelee, Chino Hills (Calif.) HS	OF
21	**b-**NY Yankees . . . . Ian Kennedy, USC	RHP
22	**c-**Washington . . . . Colton Willems, John Carroll HS, Fort Pierce, Fla.	RHP
23	Houston . . . . Max Sapp, Bishop Moore HS Windermere, Fla.	C
24	Atlanta . . . . John Johnson, Crawford Mosley HS Panama City, Fla.	OF
25	**d-**LA Angels . . Hank Conger, Huntington Beach (Calif.) HS	C
26	**e-**LA Dodgers . . . Avery Morris, Motlow St. CC	RHP
27	Boston . . . . Jason Place, Wren (S.C.) HS	OF
28	**f-**Boston . . . . Daniel Bard, North Carolina	RHP
29	Chicago-AL . . . . Kyle McCulloch, Texas	RHP
30	St. Louis . . . . Adam Ottavino, Northeastern	RHP
31	**g-**LA Dodgers . . . . Preston Mattingly, Evansville Central HS (Indiana)	SS
32	**h-**Baltimore . . . . Pedro Beato, St. Petersburg JC	RHP
33	**i-**San Francisco . . . . Emmanuel Burriss, Kent St.	SS
34	**j-**Arizona . . . . Brooks Brown, Georgia	RHP
35	**k-**San Diego . . Kyler Burke, Ooltewah (Ten.) HS	OF
36	**l-**Florida . . . . . Christopher Coghlan, Mississippi	3B
37	**m-**Philadelphia . . Adrian Cardenas, Monsignor Edward Pace HS (Florida)	SS
38	**n-**Atlanta . . . . Cory Rasmus, Russell County (Ala.) HS	RHP
39	**o-**Cleveland . . . . David Huff, UCLA	LHP
40	**p-**Boston . . . . Kristofer Johnson, Wichita St.	LHP
41	**q-**NY Yankees . . Joba Chamberlain, Nebraska	RHP
42	**r-**St. Louis . . . . Christopher Perez, Miami-FL	RHP
43	**s-**Atlanta . . . . Steven Evarts, Robinson (Fla.) HS	LHP
44	**t-**Boston . . . . Caleb Clay, Cullman (Ala.) HS	RHP

a-from NYM for Billy Wagner; **b-**from Phi. for Tom Gordon; **c-**from Oak. for Esteban Loaiza; **d-**from Cle. for Paul Byrd; **e-**from LAA for Jeff Weaver; **f-**from NYY for Johnny Damon; **g-**for Jeff Weaver; **h-**for B.J. Ryan; **i-**for Scott Eyre; **j-**for Tim Worrell; **k-**for Ramon Hernandez; **l-**for A.J. Burnett; **m-**for Billy Wagner; **n-**for Kyle Farnsworth; **o-**for Bobby Howry; **p-**for Johnny Damon; **q-**for Tom Gordon; **r-**for Matt Morris; **s-**for Rafael Furcal; **t-**for Bill Mueller.

Minor League Triple-A Final Standings
Playoff qualifiers (*) are noted.

International League

North Division	W	L	Pct	GB
*Scranton-Wilkes Barre (Phillies) . . .	84	58	.592	—
*Rochester (Twins)	79	64	.552	5½
Buffalo (Indians)	73	68	.518	10½
Ottawa (Orioles)	74	69	.517	10½
Pawtucket (Red Sox)	69	75	.479	16
Syracuse (Blue Jays)	64	79	.448	20½

South Division	W	L	Pct	GB
*Charlotte (White Sox)	79	62	.560	—
Durham (Devil Rays)	64	78	.451	15½
Norfolk (Mets)	57	84	.404	22
Richmond (Braves)	57	86	.399	23

West Division	W	L	Pct	GB
*Toledo (Tigers)	76	66	.535	—
Indianapolis (Pirates)	76	66	.535	—
Louisville (Reds)	75	68	.524	1½
Columbus (Yankees)	69	73	.486	7

Playoffs
First Round (Best-of-Five)

Toledo 3 . . . . Charlotte 1
Rochester 3 . . . . Scranton-Wilkes Barre 1

Championship (Best-of-Five)
Toledo vs. Rochester

Sept. 12	Toledo, 6-3	at Rochester
Sept. 13	Rochester, 6-1	at Rochester
Sept. 14	Rochester, 10-4	at Toledo
Sept. 15	Toledo, 6-0	at Toledo
Sept. 16	Toledo, 10-1	at Toledo

Toledo wins Governors' Cup, 3-2

Pacific Coast League

American Conference

Northern Division	W	L	Pct	GB
*Nashville (Brewers)	76	68	.528	—
Iowa (Cubs)	76	68	.528	—
Memphis (Cardinals)	58	86	.403	18
Omaha (Royals)	53	91	.368	23

Southern Division	W	L	Pct	GB
*Round Rock (Astros)	85	59	.590	—
Oklahoma (Rangers)	74	70	.514	11
New Orleans (Nationals)	72	71	.503	12½
Albuquerque (Marlins)	70	72	.493	14

Pacific Conference

Northern Division	W	L	Pct	GB
*Salt Lake (Angels)	81	63	.563	—
Tacoma (Mariners)	74	70	.514	7
Portland (Padres)	68	76	.472	13
Colorado Springs (Rockies)	66	77	.462	14½

Southern Division	W	L	Pct	GB
*Tucson (Diamondbacks)	91	53	.632	—
Sacramento (A's)	78	66	.542	13
Las Vegas (Dodgers)	67	77	.465	24
Fresno (Giants)	61	83	.424	30

Playoffs
Conference Finals (Best-of-Five)

Tucson 3 . . . . Salt Lake 1
Round Rock 3 . . . . Nashville 2

Championship (Best-of-Five)
Tucson vs. Round Rock

Sept. 12	Tucson, 3-1	at Tucson
Sept. 13	Tucson, 6-3	at Tucson
Sept. 15	Tucson, 6-3	at Round Rock

Tucson wins PCL Championship, 3-0

2006 International League All-Star Team
As selected by IL managers, coaches and media.

Pos	Name/Team
C	Carlos Ruiz, Scranton/WB
1B	Kevin Witt, Durham
2B	Joe Thurston, Scranton/WB
SS	Jorge Velandia, Charlotte
3B	Josh Fields, Charlotte
DH	Josh Phelps, Toledo
OF	Jason Dubois, Buffalo
OF	Norris Hopper, Louisville
OF	Darnell McDonald, Durham
UT	Dustin Pedroia, Pawtucket
SP	Heath Phillips, Charlotte
REL	Pat Neshek, Rochester

2006 Pacific Coast League All-Star Team
As selected by PCL managers and media representatives.

Pos	Name/Team
C	Jeff Mathis, Salt Lake
1B	James Loney, Las Vegas
2B	Alberto Callaspo, Tucson
SS	Stephen Drew, Tucson
3B	Scott McClain, Sacramento
DH	Jon Knott, Portland
OF	Scott Hairston, Tucson
OF	Jeff Baker, Colorado Springs
OF	Reggie Willits, Salt Lake
RHP	Jason Hirsh, Round Rock
LHP	Rich Hill, Iowa
REL	Nate Field, Colorado Springs

1876-2006
Through the Years

SPORTS ALMANAC

The World Series

The World Series began in 1903 when Pittsburgh of the older National League (founded in 1876) invited Boston of the American League (founded in 1901) to play a best-of-9 game series to determine which of the two league champions was the best. Boston was the surprise winner, 5 games to 3. The 1904 NL champion New York Giants refused to play Boston the following year, so there was no Series. Giants' owner John T. Brush and his manager John McGraw both despised AL president Ban Johnson and considered the junior circuit to be a minor league. By the following year, however, Brush and Johnson had smoothed out their differences and the Giants agreed to play Philadelphia in a best-of-7 game series. Since then the World Series has been a best-of-7 format, except from 1919-21 when it returned to best-of-9.

In the chart below, the National League teams are listed in CAPITAL letters. Also, each World Series champion's wins and losses are noted in parentheses after the Series score in games.

Multiple champions: New York Yankees (26); St. Louis Cardinals (10); Philadelphia-Oakland A's (9); Boston Red Sox and Brooklyn-Los Angeles Dodgers (6); Cincinnati Reds, New York-San Francisco Giants and Pittsburgh Pirates (5); Detroit Tigers (4); Baltimore Orioles, Boston-Milwaukee-Atlanta Braves, Chicago White Sox and Washington Senators-Minnesota Twins (3); Chicago Cubs, Cleveland Indians, Florida Marlins, New York Mets and Toronto Blue Jays (2).

Year	Winner	Manager	Series	Loser	Manager
1903	Boston Red Sox	Jimmy Collins	5-3 (LWLLWWWW)	PITTSBURGH	Fred Clarke
1904	Not held				
1905	NY GIANTS	John McGraw	4-1 (WLWWW)	Philadelphia A's	Connie Mack
1906	Chicago White Sox	Fielder Jones	4-2 (WLWLWW)	CHICAGO CUBS	Frank Chance
1907	CHICAGO CUBS	Frank Chance	4-0-1 (TWWWW)	Detroit	Hughie Jennings
1908	CHICAGO CUBS	Frank Chance	4-1 (WWLWW)	Detroit	Hughie Jennings
1909	PITTSBURGH	Fred Clarke	4-3 (WLWLWLW)	Detroit	Hughie Jennings
1910	Philadelphia A's	Connie Mack	4-1 (WWWLW)	CHICAGO CUBS	Frank Chance
1911	Philadelphia A's	Connie Mack	4-2 (LWWWLW)	NY GIANTS	John McGraw
1912	Boston Red Sox	Jake Stahl	4-3-1 (WTLWWLLW)	NY GIANTS	John McGraw
1913	Philadelphia A's	Connie Mack	4-1 (WLWWW)	NY GIANTS	John McGraw
1914	BOSTON BRAVES	George Stallings	4-0	Philadelphia A's	Connie Mack
1915	Boston Red Sox	Bill Carrigan	4-1 (LWWWW)	PHILA. PHILLIES	Pat Moran
1916	Boston Red Sox	Bill Carrigan	4-1 (WWLWW)	BROOKLYN	Wilbert Robinson
1917	Chicago White Sox	Pants Rowland	4-2 (WWLLWW)	NY GIANTS	John McGraw
1918	Boston Red Sox	Ed Barrow	4-2 (WLWWLW)	CHICAGO CUBS	Fred Mitchell
1919	CINCINNATI	Pat Moran	5-3 (WWLWWLLW)	Chicago White Sox	Kid Gleason
1920	Cleveland	Tris Speaker	5-2 (LLWWWWW)	BROOKLYN	Wilbert Robinson
1921	NY GIANTS	John McGraw	5-3 (LLWWLWWW)	NY Yankees	Miller Huggins
1922	NY GIANTS	John McGraw	4-0-1 (WTWWW)	NY Yankees	Miller Huggins
1923	NY Yankees	Miller Huggins	4-2 (LWLWWW)	NY GIANTS	John McGraw
1924	Washington	Bucky Harris	4-3 (LWLWLWW)	NY GIANTS	John McGraw
1925	PITTSBURGH	Bill McKechnie	4-3 (LWLLWWW)	Washington	Bucky Harris
1926	ST.L. CARDINALS	Rogers Hornsby	4-3 (LWWLLWW)	NY Yankees	Miller Huggins
1927	NY Yankees	Miller Huggins	4-0	PITTSBURGH	Donie Bush
1928	NY Yankees	Miller Huggins	4-0	ST.L. CARDINALS	Bill McKechnie
1929	Philadelphia A's	Connie Mack	4-1 (WWLWW)	CHICAGO CUBS	Joe McCarthy
1930	Philadelphia A's	Connie Mack	4-2 (WWLLWW)	ST.L. CARDINALS	Gabby Street
1931	ST.L. CARDINALS	Gabby Street	4-3 (LWWLWLW)	Philadelphia A's	Connie Mack
1932	NY Yankees	Joe McCarthy	4-0	CHICAGO CUBS	Charlie Grimm
1933	NY GIANTS	Bill Terry	4-1 (WWLWW)	Washington	Joe Cronin
1934	ST.L. CARDINALS	Frankie Frisch	4-3 (WLWLLWW)	Detroit	Mickey Cochrane
1935	Detroit	Mickey Cochrane	4-2 (LWWWLW)	CHICAGO CUBS	Charlie Grimm
1936	NY Yankees	Joe McCarthy	4-2 (WLWWLW)	NY GIANTS	Bill Terry
1937	NY Yankees	Joe McCarthy	4-1 (WWWLW)	NY GIANTS	Bill Terry
1938	NY Yankees	Joe McCarthy	4-0	CHICAGO CUBS	Gabby Hartnett
1939	NY Yankees	Joe McCarthy	4-0	CINCINNATI	Bill McKechnie
1940	CINCINNATI	Bill McKechnie	4-3 (LWLWLWW)	Detroit	Del Baker
1941	NY Yankees	Joe McCarthy	4-1 (WLWWW)	BKLN. DODGERS	Leo Durocher
1942	ST.L. CARDINALS	Billy Southworth	4-1 (LWWWW)	NY Yankees	Joe McCarthy
1943	NY Yankees	Joe McCarthy	4-1 (WLWWW)	ST.L. CARDINALS	Billy Southworth
1944	ST.L. CARDINALS	Billy Southworth	4-2 (LWLWWW)	St. Louis Browns	Luke Sewell
1945	Detroit	Steve O'Neill	4-3 (LWLWLWW)	CHICAGO CUBS	Charlie Grimm

The World Series (Cont.)

Year	Winner	Manager	Series	Loser	Manager
1946	ST.L. CARDINALS	Eddie Dyer	4-3 (LWLWLWW)	Boston Red Sox	Joe Cronin
1947	NY Yankees	Bucky Harris	4-3 (WWLLWLW)	BKLN. DODGERS	Burt Shotton
1948	Cleveland	Lou Boudreau	4-2 (LWWWLW)	BOSTON BRAVES	Billy Southworth
1949	NY Yankees	Casey Stengel	4-1 (WLWWW)	BKLN. DODGERS	Burt Shotton
1950	NY Yankees	Casey Stengel	4-0	PHILA. PHILLIES	Eddie Sawyer
1951	NY Yankees	Casey Stengel	4-2 (LWLWWW)	NY GIANTS	Leo Durocher
1952	NY Yankees	Casey Stengel	4-3 (LWLWLWW)	BKLN. DODGERS	Charlie Dressen
1953	NY Yankees	Casey Stengel	4-2 (WWLLWW)	BKLN. DODGERS	Charlie Dressen
1954	NY GIANTS	Leo Durocher	4-0	Cleveland	Al Lopez
1955	BKLN. DODGERS	Walter Alston	4-3 (LLWWWLW)	NY Yankees	Casey Stengel
1956	NY Yankees	Casey Stengel	4-3 (LLWWWLW)	BKLN. DODGERS	Walter Alston
1957	MILW. BRAVES	Fred Haney	4-3 (LWLWWLW)	NY Yankees	Casey Stengel
1958	NY Yankees	Casey Stengel	4-3 (LLWLWWW)	MILW. BRAVES	Fred Haney
1959	LA DODGERS	Walter Alston	4-2 (LWWWLW)	Chicago White Sox	Al Lopez
1960	PITTSBURGH	Danny Murtaugh	4-3 (LWLWLWW)	NY Yankees	Casey Stengel
1961	NY Yankees	Ralph Houk	4-1 (WLWWW)	CINCINNATI	Fred Hutchinson
1962	NY Yankees	Ralph Houk	4-3 (WLWLWLW)	SF GIANTS	Alvin Dark
1963	LA DODGERS	Walter Alston	4-0	NY Yankees	Ralph Houk
1964	ST.L. CARDINALS	Johnny Keane	4-3 (WLLWWLW)	NY Yankees	Yogi Berra
1965	LA DODGERS	Walter Alston	4-3 (LLWWWLW)	Minnesota	Sam Mele
1966	Baltimore	Hank Bauer	4-0	LA DODGERS	Walter Alston
1967	ST.L. CARDINALS	Red Schoendienst	4-3 (WLWWLLW)	Boston Red Sox	Dick Williams
1968	Detroit	Mayo Smith	4-3 (LWLLWWW)	ST.L. CARDINALS	Red Schoendienst
1969	NY METS	Gil Hodges	4-1 (LWWWW)	Baltimore	Earl Weaver
1970	Baltimore	Earl Weaver	4-1 (WWWLW)	CINCINNATI	Sparky Anderson
1971	PITTSBURGH	Danny Murtaugh	4-3 (LLWWWLW)	Baltimore	Earl Weaver
1972	Oakland A's	Dick Williams	4-3 (WWLWLLW)	CINCINNATI	Sparky Anderson
1973	Oakland A's	Dick Williams	4-3 (WLWLWLW)	NY METS	Yogi Berra
1974	Oakland A's	Alvin Dark	4-1 (WLWWW)	LA DODGERS	Walter Alston
1975	CINCINNATI	Sparky Anderson	4-3 (LWWLWLW)	Boston Red Sox	Darrell Johnson
1976	CINCINNATI	Sparky Anderson	4-0	NY Yankees	Billy Martin
1977	NY Yankees	Billy Martin	4-2 (WLWWLW)	LA DODGERS	Tommy Lasorda
1978	NY Yankees	Bob Lemon	4-2 (LLWWWW)	LA DODGERS	Tommy Lasorda
1979	PITTSBURGH	Chuck Tanner	4-3 (LWLLWWW)	Baltimore	Earl Weaver
1980	PHILA. PHILLIES	Dallas Green	4-2 (WWLLWW)	Kansas City	Jim Frey
1981	LA DODGERS	Tommy Lasorda	4-2 (LLWWWW)	NY Yankees	Bob Lemon
1982	ST.L. CARDINALS	Whitey Herzog	4-3 (LWWLLWW)	Milwaukee Brewers	Harvey Kuenn
1983	Baltimore	Joe Altobelli	4-1 (LWWWW)	PHILA. PHILLIES	Paul Owens
1984	Detroit	Sparky Anderson	4-1 (WLWWW)	SAN DIEGO	Dick Williams
1985	Kansas City	Dick Howser	4-3 (LLWLWWW)	ST.L. CARDINALS	Whitey Herzog
1986	NY METS	Davey Johnson	4-3 (LLWWLWW)	Boston Red Sox	John McNamara
1987	Minnesota	Tom Kelly	4-3 (WWLLLWW)	ST.L. CARDINALS	Whitey Herzog
1988	LA DODGERS	Tommy Lasorda	4-1 (WWLWW)	Oakland A's	Tony La Russa
1989	Oakland A's	Tony La Russa	4-0	SF GIANTS	Roger Craig
1990	CINCINNATI	Lou Piniella	4-0	Oakland A's	Tony La Russa
1991	Minnesota	Tom Kelly	4-3 (WWLLLWW)	ATLANTA BRAVES	Bobby Cox
1992	Toronto	Cito Gaston	4-2 (LWWWLW)	ATLANTA BRAVES	Bobby Cox
1993	Toronto	Cito Gaston	4-2 (WLWWLW)	PHILA. PHILLIES	Jim Fregosi
1994	Not held				
1995	ATLANTA BRAVES	Bobby Cox	4-2 (WWLWLW)	Cleveland	Mike Hargrove
1996	NY Yankees	Joe Torre	4-2 (LLWWWW)	ATLANTA BRAVES	Bobby Cox
1997	FLORIDA	Jim Leyland	4-3 (WLWLWLW)	Cleveland	Mike Hargrove
1998	NY Yankees	Joe Torre	4-0	SAN DIEGO	Bruce Bochy
1999	NY Yankees	Joe Torre	4-0	ATLANTA BRAVES	Bobby Cox
2000	NY Yankees	Joe Torre	4-1 (WWLWW)	NY METS	Bobby Valentine
2001	ARIZONA	Bob Brenly	4-3 (WWLLLWW)	NY Yankees	Joe Torre
2002	Anaheim	Mike Scioscia	4-3 (LWWLLWW)	SF GIANTS	Dusty Baker
2003	FLORIDA	Jack McKeon	4-2 (WLLWWW)	NY Yankees	Joe Torre
2004	Boston	Terry Francona	4-0	ST. LOUIS	Tony La Russa
2005	Chicago White Sox	Ozzie Guillen	4-0	HOUSTON	Phil Garner
2006	ST. LOUIS	Tony La Russa	4-1 (WLWWW)	Detroit	Jim Leyland

Most Valuable Players

Currently selected by media panel and World Series official scorers. Presented by *Sport* magazine from 1955-88 and by Major League Baseball since 1989. Winner who did not play for World Series champions is in **bold** type.

Multiple winners: Bob Gibson, Reggie Jackson and Sandy Koufax (2).

Year
1955 Johnny Podres, Bklyn, P
1956 Don Larsen, NY, P
1957 Lew Burdette, Mil., P
1958 Bob Turley, NY, P
1959 Larry Sherry, LA, P
1960 **Bobby Richardson**, NY, 2B
1961 Whitey Ford, NY, P
1962 Ralph Terry, NY, P
1963 Sandy Koufax, LA, P
1964 Bob Gibson, St.L., P
1965 Sandy Koufax, LA, P
1966 Frank Robinson, Bal., OF
1967 Bob Gibson, St.L., P
1968 Mickey Lolich, Det., P
1969 Donn Clendenon, NY, 1B
1970 Brooks Robinson, Bal., 3B
1971 Roberto Clemente, Pit., OF
1972 Gene Tenace, Oak., C
1973 Reggie Jackson, Oak., OF

Year
1974 Rollie Fingers, Oak., P
1975 Pete Rose, Cin., 3B
1976 Johnny Bench, Cin., C
1977 Reggie Jackson, NY, OF
1978 Bucky Dent, NY, SS
1979 Willie Stargell, Pit., 1B
1980 Mike Schmidt, Phi., 3B
1981 Pedro Guerrero, LA, OF;
    Ron Cey, LA, 3B;
    & Steve Yeager, LA, C
1982 Darrell Porter, St.L., C
1983 Rick Dempsey, Bal., C
1984 Alan Trammell, Det., SS
1985 Bret Saberhagen, KC, P
1986 Ray Knight, NY, 3B
1987 Frank Viola, Min., P
1988 Orel Hershiser, LA, P
1989 Dave Stewart, Oak., P
1990 Jose Rijo, Cin., P

Year
1991 Jack Morris, Min., P
1992 Pat Borders, Tor., C
1993 Paul Molitor, Tor., DH/1B/3B
1994 Series not held.
1995 Tom Glavine, Atl., P
1996 John Wetteland, NY, P
1997 Livan Hernandez, Fla., P
1998 Scott Brosius, NY, 3B
1999 Mariano Rivera, NY, P
2000 Derek Jeter, NY, SS
2001 Curt Schilling, Ari., P
    & Randy Johnson, Ari., P
2002 Troy Glaus, Ana., 3B
2003 Josh Beckett, Fla., P
2004 Manny Ramirez, Bos., OF
2005 Jermaine Dye, Chi., OF
2006 David Eckstein, St.L, SS

All-Time World Series Leaders

CAREER

World Series leaders through 2006. Years listed indicate number of World Series appearances.

Hitting

Games

	Yrs	Gm
Yogi Berra, NY Yankees	14	75
Mickey Mantle, NY Yankees	12	65
Elston Howard, NY Yankees—Boston	10	54
Hank Bauer, NY Yankees	9	53
Gil McDougald, NY Yankees	8	53

At Bats

	Yrs	AB
Yogi Berra, NY Yankees	14	259
Mickey Mantle, NY Yankees	12	230
Joe DiMaggio, NY Yankees	10	199
Frankie Frisch, NY Giants-St.L. Cards	8	197
Gil McDougald, NY Yankees	8	190

Batting Avg. (minimum 50 AB)

	AB	H	Avg
Pepper Martin, St.L. Cards	55	23	.418
Paul Molitor, Mil. Brewers-Tor. Blue Jays	55	23	.418
Lou Brock, St. Louis	87	34	.391
Marquis Grissom, Atl-Cle	77	30	.390
Thurman Munson, NY Yankees	67	25	.373
George Brett, Kansas City	51	19	.373
Hank Aaron, Milw. Braves	55	20	.364

Hits

	AB	H	Avg
Yogi Berra, NY Yankees	259	71	.274
Mickey Mantle, NY Yankees	230	59	.257
Frankie Frisch, NYG-St.L. Cards	197	58	.294
Joe DiMaggio, NY Yankees	199	54	.271
Hank Bauer, NY Yankees	188	46	.245
Pee Wee Reese, Brooklyn	169	46	.272

Runs

	Gm	R
Mickey Mantle, NY Yankees	65	42
Yogi Berra, NY Yankees	75	41
Babe Ruth, Boston Red Sox-NY Yankees	41	37
Lou Gehrig, NY Yankees	34	30
Joe DiMaggio, NY Yankees	51	27
Derek Jeter, NY Yankees	32	27

Home Runs

	AB	HR
Mickey Mantle, NY Yankees	230	18
Babe Ruth, Boston Red Sox-NY Yankees	129	15
Yogi Berra, NY Yankees	259	12
Duke Snider, Brooklyn-LA	133	11
Lou Gehrig, NY Yankees	119	10
Reggie Jackson, Oakland-NY Yankees	98	10

Runs Batted In

	Gm	RBI
Mickey Mantle, NY Yankees	65	40
Yogi Berra, NY Yankees	75	39
Lou Gehrig, NY Yankees	34	35
Babe Ruth, Boston Red Sox-NY Yankees	41	33
Joe DiMaggio, NY Yankees	51	30

Stolen Bases

	Gm	SB
Lou Brock, St. Louis	21	14
Eddie Collins, Phi. A's-Chisox	34	14
Frank Chance, Chi. Cubs	20	10
Davey Lopes, Los Angeles	23	10
Phil Rizzuto, NY Yankees	52	10

All-Time World Series Leaders (Cont.)

Total Bases

	Gm	TB
Mickey Mantle, NY Yankees	.65	123
Yogi Berra, NY Yankees	.75	117
Babe Ruth, Boston Red Sox-NY Yankees	.41	96
Lou Gehrig, NY Yankees	.34	87
Joe DiMaggio, NY Yankees	.51	84

Slugging Pct. (minimum 50 AB)

	AB	Pct
Reggie Jackson, Oakland-NY Yankees	.98	.755
Babe Ruth, Boston Red Sox-NY Yankees	.129	.744
Lou Gehrig, NY Yankees	.119	.731
Al Simmons, Phi. A's-Cincinnati	.73	.658
Lou Brock, St. Louis	.87	.655

Pitching

Games

	Yrs	Gm
Whitey Ford, NY Yankees	.11	22
Mike Stanton, Atlanta-NY Yankees	.6	20
Mariano Rivera, NY Yankees	.6	20
Rollie Fingers, Oakland	.3	16
Jeff Nelson, NY Yankees	.5	16
Allie Reynolds, NY Yankees	.6	15
Bob Turley, NY Yankees	.5	15

Shutouts

	GS	CG	ShO
Christy Mathewson, NY Giants	.11	10	4
Three Finger Brown, Chi. Cubs	.7	5	3
Whitey Ford, NY Yankees	.22	7	3
Seven pitchers tied with 2 each.			

Wins

	Gm	W-L
Whitey Ford, NY Yankees	.22	10-8
Bob Gibson, St. Louis	.9	7-2
Allie Reynolds, NY Yankees	.15	7-2
Red Ruffing, NY Yankees	.10	7-2
Lefty Gomez, NY Yankees	.7	6-0
Chief Bender, Philadelphia A's	.10	6-4
Waite Hoyt, NY Yankees-Phi. A's	.12	6-4

Innings Pitched

	Gm	IP
Whitey Ford, NY Yankees	.22	146.0
Christy Mathewson, NY Giants	.11	101.2
Red Ruffing, NY Yankees	.10	85.2
Chief Bender, Philadelphia A's	.10	85.0
Waite Hoyt, NY Yankees-Phi. A's	.12	83.2

Complete Games

	GS	CG	W-L
Christy Mathewson, NY Giants	.11	10	5-5
Chief Bender, Philadelphia A's	.10	9	6-4
Bob Gibson, St. Louis	.9	8	7-2
Whitey Ford, NY Yankees	.22	7	10-8
Red Ruffing, NY Yankees	.10	7	7-2

ERA (minimum 25 IP)

	Gm	IP	ERA
Jack Billingham, Cincinnati	.7	25.1	0.36
Harry Brecheen, St. Louis	.7	32.2	0.83
Babe Ruth, Boston Red Sox	.3	31.0	0.87
Sherry Smith, Brooklyn	.3	30.1	0.89
Sandy Koufax, Los Angeles	.8	57.0	0.95

Strikeouts

	Gm	IP	SO
Whitey Ford, NY Yankees	.22	146.0	94
Bob Gibson, St. Louis	.9	81.0	92
Allie Reynolds, NY Yankees	.15	77.1	62
Sandy Koufax, Los Angeles	.8	57.0	61
Red Ruffing, NY Yankees	.10	85.2	61

Saves

	Gm	IP	Sv
Mariano Rivera, NY Yankees	.20	31.0	9
Rollie Fingers, Oakland	.16	33.1	6
Allie Reynolds, NY Yankees	.15	77.1	4
Johnny Murphy, NY Yankees	.8	16.1	4
John Wetteland, NY Yankees	.5	4.1	4
Robb Nen, Florida-SF	.7	7.2	4
Nine pitchers tied with 3 each.			

Losses

	Gm	W-L
Whitey Ford, NY Yankees	.22	10-8
Christy Mathewson, NY Giants	.11	5-5
Joe Bush, Phi. A's-Bosox-NY Yankees	.9	2-5
Rube Marquard, NY Giants-Brooklyn	.11	2-5
Eddie Plank, Philadelphia A's	.7	2-5
Schoolboy Rowe, Detroit	.8	2-5

World Series Appearances

In the 102 years that the World Series has been contested, American League teams have won 60 championships while National League teams have won 42. Note that the Brewers, now in the NL, were in the AL when they won their title. The following teams are ranked by number of appearances through the 2006 World Series; (*) indicates AL teams.

	App	W	L	Pct.	Last Series	Last Title
NY Yankees*	.39	26	13	.667	2003	2000
Bklyn/LA Dodgers	.18	6	12	.333	1988	1988
St.L. Cardinals	.17	10	7	.588	2006	2006
NY/SF Giants	.17	5	12	.294	2002	1954
Phi/KC/Oak.A's*	.14	9	5	.643	1990	1989
Boston Red Sox*	.10	6	4	.600	2004	2004
Detroit Tigers*	.10	4	6	.400	2006	1984
Chicago Cubs	.10	2	8	.200	1945	1908
Cincinnati Reds	.9	5	4	.556	1990	1990
Bos/Mil/Atl.Braves	.9	3	6	.333	1999	1995
Pittsburgh Pirates	.7	5	2	.714	1979	1979
St.L/Bal.Orioles*	.7	3	4	.429	1983	1983
Wash/Min.Twins*	.6	3	3	.500	1991	1991

	App	W	L	Pct.	Last Series	Last Title
Chi. White Sox*	.5	3	2	.600	2005	2005
Cle. Indians*	.5	2	3	.400	1997	1948
Phi. Phillies	.5	1	4	.200	1993	1980
NY Mets	.4	2	2	.500	2000	1986
Fla. Marlins	.2	2	0	1.000	2003	2003
Tor. Blue Jays*	.2	2	0	1.000	1993	1993
KC Royals*	.2	1	1	.500	1985	1985
SD Padres	.2	0	2	.000	1998	—
LA Angels of Anaheim*	1	1	0	1.000	2002	2002
Ari. Diamondbacks	.1	1	0	1.000	2001	2001
Sea/Mil.Brewers*	.1	0	1	.000	1982	—
Houston Astros	.1	0	1	.000	2005	—

League Championship Series

Division play came to the major leagues in 1969 when both the American and National Leagues expanded to 12 teams. With an East and West Division in each league, League Championship Series (LCS) became necessary to determine the NL and AL pennant winners. In 1994, teams were realigned into three divisions, the East, Central, and West with division winners and one wildcard team playing a best-of-5 League Divisional Series (see following pages for LDS results) to determine the LCS competitors.

In the tables below, the East Division champions are noted by the letter E, the Central division champions by C and the West Division champions by W. Wildcard winners are noted by WC. Also, each playoff winner's wins and losses are noted in parentheses after the series score. The LCS changed from best-of-5 to best-of-7 in 1985. Each league's LCS was canceled in 1994 due to the players' strike.

National League

Multiple champions: Atlanta, Cincinnati, LA Dodgers and St. Louis (5); NY Mets (4); Philadelphia (3); Florida, Pittsburgh, San Diego and San Francisco (2).

Year	Winner	Manager	Series	Loser	Manager
1969	E–New York	Gil Hodges	3-0	W–Atlanta	Lum Harris
1970	W–Cincinnati	Sparky Anderson	3-0	E–Pittsburgh	Danny Murtaugh
1971	E–Pittsburgh	Danny Murtaugh	3-1 (LWWW)	W–San Francisco	Charlie Fox
1972	W–Cincinnati	Sparky Anderson	3-2 (LWLWW)	E–Pittsburgh	Bill Virdon
1973	E–New York	Yogi Berra	3-2 (LWWLW)	W–Cincinnati	Sparky Anderson
1974	W–Los Angeles	Walter Alston	3-1 (WWLW)	E–Pittsburgh	Danny Murtaugh
1975	W–Cincinnati	Sparky Anderson	3-0	E–Pittsburgh	Danny Murtaugh
1976	W–Cincinnati	Sparky Anderson	3-0	E–Philadelphia	Danny Ozark
1977	W–Los Angeles	Tommy Lasorda	3-1 (LWWW)	E–Philadelphia	Danny Ozark
1978	W–Los Angeles	Tommy Lasorda	3-1 (WWLW)	E–Philadelphia	Danny Ozark
1979	E–Pittsburgh	Chuck Tanner	3-0	W–Cincinnati	John McNamara
1980	E–Philadelphia	Dallas Green	3-2 (WLLWW)	W–Houston	Bill Virdon
1981	W–Los Angeles	Tommy Lasorda	3-2 (WLLWW)	E–Montreal	Jim Fanning
1982	E–St. Louis	Whitey Herzog	3-0	W–Atlanta	Joe Torre
1983	E–Philadelphia	Paul Owens	3-1 (WLWW)	W–Los Angeles	Tommy Lasorda
1984	W–San Diego	Dick Williams	3-2 (LLWWW)	E–Chicago	Jim Frey
1985	E–St. Louis	Whitey Herzog	4-2 (LLWWWW)	W–Los Angeles	Tommy Lasorda
1986	E–New York	Davey Johnson	4-2 (LWWWLW)	W–Houston	Hal Lanier
1987	E–St. Louis	Whitey Herzog	4-3 (WLWLLWW)	W–San Francisco	Roger Craig
1988	W–Los Angeles	Tommy Lasorda	4-3 (LWLWWLW)	E–New York	Davey Johnson
1989	W–San Francisco	Roger Craig	4-1 (WLWWW)	E–Chicago	Don Zimmer
1990	W–Cincinnati	Lou Piniella	4-2 (WWWLW)	E–Pittsburgh	Jim Leyland
1991	W–Atlanta	Bobby Cox	4-3 (LWWLLWW)	E–Pittsburgh	Jim Leyland
1992	W–Atlanta	Bobby Cox	4-3 (WWWLWLLW)	E–Pittsburgh	Jim Leyland
1993	E–Philadelphia	Jim Fregosi	4-2 (WLLWWW)	W–Atlanta	Bobby Cox
1994	Not held				
1995	E–Atlanta	Bobby Cox	4-0	C–Cincinnati	Davey Johnson
1996	E–Atlanta	Bobby Cox	4-3 (WLLLWWW)	C–St. Louis	Tony La Russa
1997	WC–Florida	Jim Leyland	4-2 (WLWLWW)	E–Atlanta	Bobby Cox
1998	W–San Diego	Bruce Bochy	4-2 (WWWLLW)	E–Atlanta	Bobby Cox
1999	E–Atlanta	Bobby Cox	4-2 (WWWLLW)	WC–New York	Bobby Valentine
2000	WC–New York	Bobby Valentine	4-1 (WWLWW)	C–St. Louis	Tony La Russa
2001	W–Arizona	Bob Brenly	4-1 (WLWW)	E–Atlanta	Bobby Cox
2002	WC–San Francisco	Dusty Baker	4-1 (WWLWW)	C–St. Louis	Tony La Russa
2003	WC–Florida	Jack McKeon	4-3 (WLLLWWW)	C–Chicago	Dusty Baker
2004	C–St. Louis	Tony La Russa	4-3 (WWWLLLWW)	WC–Houston	Phil Garner
2005	WC–Houston	Phil Garner	4-2 (LWWWLW)	C–St. Louis	Tony La Russa
2006	C–St. Louis	Tony La Russa	4-3 (LWWLWLW)	E–New York	Willie Randolph

NLCS Most Valuable Players

Winners who did not play for NLCS champions are in **bold** type.

Multiple winner: Steve Garvey (2).

Year	Year	Year
1977 Dusty Baker, LA, OF	1988 Orel Hershiser, LA, P	1998 Sterling Hitchcock, SD, P
1978 Steve Garvey, LA, 1B	1989 Will Clark, SF, 1B	1999 Eddie Perez, Atl., C
1979 Willie Stargell, Pit., 1B	1990 Rob Dibble, Cin., P	2000 Mike Hampton, NY, P
1980 Manny Trillo, Phi., 2B	& Randy Myers, Cin., P	2001 Craig Counsell, Ari., 2B
1981 Burt Hooton, LA, P	1991 Steve Avery, Atl., P	2002 Benito Santiago, SF, C
1982 Darrell Porter, St.L., P	1992 John Smoltz, Atl., P	2003 Ivan Rodriguez, Fla., C
1983 Gary Matthews, Phi., OF	1993 Curt Schilling, Phi., P	2004 Albert Pujols, St.L., 1B
1984 Steve Garvey, SD, 1B	1994 LCS not held.	2005 Roy Oswalt, Hou., P
1985 Ozzie Smith, St.L., SS	1995 Mike Devereaux, Atl., OF	2006 Jeff Suppan, St.L, P
1986 **Mike Scott**, Hou., P	1996 Javy Lopez, Atl., C	
1987 **Jeff Leonard**, SF, OF	1997 Livan Hernandez, Fla., P	

League Championship Series (Cont.)
American League

Multiple champions: NY Yankees (10); Oakland (6); Baltimore (5); Boston (3); Cleveland, Detroit, Kansas City, Minnesota and Toronto (2).

Year	Winner	Manager	Series	Loser	Manager
1969	E–Baltimore	Earl Weaver	3-0	W–Minnesota	Billy Martin
1970	E–Baltimore	Earl Weaver	3-0	W–Minnesota	Bill Rigney
1971	E–Baltimore	Earl Weaver	3-0	W–Oakland	Dick Williams
1972	W–Oakland	Dick Williams	3-2 (WWLLW)	E–Detroit	Billy Martin
1973	W–Oakland	Dick Williams	3-2 (LWWLW)	E–Baltimore	Earl Weaver
1974	W–Oakland	Alvin Dark	3-1 (LWWW)	E–Baltimore	Earl Weaver
1975	E–Boston	Darrell Johnson	3-0	W–Oakland	Alvin Dark
1976	E–New York	Billy Martin	3-2 (WLWLW)	W–Kansas City	Whitey Herzog
1977	E–New York	Billy Martin	3-2 (LWLWW)	W–Kansas City	Whitey Herzog
1978	E–New York	Bob Lemon	3-1 (WLWW)	W–Kansas City	Whitey Herzog
1979	E–Baltimore	Earl Weaver	3-1 (WWLW)	W–California	Jim Fregosi
1980	W–Kansas City	Jim Frey	3-0	E–New York	Dick Howser
1981	E–New York	Bob Lemon	3-0	W–Oakland	Billy Martin
1982	E–Milwaukee	Harvey Kuenn	3-2 (LLWWW)	W–California	Gene Mauch
1983	E–Baltimore	Joe Altobelli	3-1 (LWWW)	W–Chicago	Tony La Russa
1984	E–Detroit	Sparky Anderson	3-0	W–Kansas City	Dick Howser
1985	W–Kansas City	Dick Howser	4-3 (LLWLWWW)	E–Toronto	Bobby Cox
1986	E–Boston	John McNamara	4-3 (LWLLWWW)	W–California	Gene Mauch
1987	W–Minnesota	Tom Kelly	4-1 (WWLWW)	E–Detroit	Sparky Anderson
1988	W–Oakland	Tony La Russa	4-0	E–Boston	Joe Morgan
1989	W–Oakland	Tony La Russa	4-1 (WWLWW)	E–Toronto	Cito Gaston
1990	W–Oakland	Tony La Russa	4-0	E–Boston	Joe Morgan
1991	W–Minnesota	Tom Kelly	4-1 (WLWWW)	E–Toronto	Cito Gaston
1992	E–Toronto	Cito Gaston	4-2 (LWWWLW)	W–Oakland	Tony La Russa
1993	E–Toronto	Cito Gaston	4-2 (WWWLLWW)	W–Chicago	Gene Lamont
1994	Not held				
1995	C–Cleveland	Mike Hargrove	4-2 (LWLWWW)	W–Seattle	Lou Piniella
1996	E–New York	Joe Torre	4-1 (WLWWW)	WC–Baltimore	Davey Johnson
1997	C–Cleveland	Mike Hargrove	4-2 (LWWWLW)	E–Baltimore	Davey Johnson
1998	E–New York	Joe Torre	4-2 (WLLWWW)	C–Cleveland	Mike Hargrove
1999	E–New York	Joe Torre	4-1 (WWLWW)	WC–Boston	Jimy Williams
2000	E–New York	Joe Torre	4-2 (LWWWLW)	WC–Seattle	Lou Piniella
2001	E–New York	Joe Torre	4-1 (WWLWW)	W–Seattle	Lou Piniella
2002	WC–Anaheim	Mike Scioscia	4-1 (LWWWW)	C–Minnesota	Ron Gardenhire
2003	E–New York	Joe Torre	4-3 (LWWLWLW)	WC–Boston	Grady Little
2004	WC–Boston	Terry Francona	4-3 (LLLWWWW)	E–New York	Joe Torre
2005	C–Chicago	Ozzie Guillen	4-1 (LWWWW)	W–Los Angeles	Mike Scioscia
2006	WC–Detroit	Jim Leyland	4-0	W–Oakland	Ken Macha

ALCS Most Valuable Players

Winner who did not play for ALCS champions is in **bold** type.

Year		Year		Year	
1980	Frank White, KC, 2B	1989	Rickey Henderson, Oak., OF	1998	David Wells, NY, P
1981	Graig Nettles, NY, 3B	1990	Dave Stewart, Oak., P	1999	Orlando Hernandez, NY, P
1982	**Fred Lynn,** Cal., OF	1991	Kirby Puckett, Min., OF	2000	Dave Justice, NY, OF
1983	Mike Boddicker, Bal., P	1992	Roberto Alomar, Tor., 2B	2001	Andy Pettitte, NY, P
1984	Kirk Gibson, Det., OF	1993	Dave Stewart, Tor., P	2002	Adam Kennedy, Ana., 2B
1985	George Brett, KC, 3B	1994	LCS not held.	2003	Mariano Rivera, NY, P
1986	Marty Barrett, Bos., 2B	1995	Orel Hershiser, Cle., P	2004	David Ortiz, Bos., DH
1987	Gary Gaetti, Min., 3B	1996	Bernie Williams, NY, OF	2005	Paul Konerko, Chi., 1B
1988	Dennis Eckersley, Oak., P	1997	Marquis Grissom, Cle., OF	2006	Placido Polanco, Det., 2B

Multiple winner: Dave Stewart (2).

Walk-off HR to Win a Postseason Series

Year	Player	Team	Series, Game	Opponent	Final Score
2006	Magglio Ordonez	Detroit	ALCS, Game 4	Oakland	6-3
2005	Chris Burke	Houston	NLDS Game 4	Atlanta	7-6 (18 inn.)
2004	David Ortiz	Boston	ALDS Game 3	Anaheim	8-6 (10 inn.)
2003	Aaron Boone	NY Yankees	ALCS Game 7	Boston	6-5 (11 inn.)
1999	Todd Pratt	NY Mets	NLDS Game 4	Arizona	4-3 (10 inn.)
1993	Joe Carter	Toronto	WS, Game 6	Philadelphia	8-6
1976	Chris Chambliss	NY Yankees	ALCS, Game 5	Kansas City	7-6
1960	Bill Mazeroski	Pittsburgh	WS, Game 7	NY Yankees	10-9

League Divisional Series

In 1994, leagues were realigned into three divisions, the East, Central, and West with division winners and one wildcard team playing a best-of-5 League Divisional Series to determine the LCS competitors. In the tables below, the East Division champions are noted by the letter E, the Central division champions by C and the West Division champions by W. Wildcard winners are noted by WC. Also, each playoff winner's wins and losses are noted in parentheses after the series score. Each league's LDS was cancelled in 1994 due to the players' strike.

National League

Multiple champions: Atlanta and St. Louis (6); NY Mets (3); Florida and Houston (2).

Year	Winner	Manager	Series	Loser	Manager
1995	E–Atlanta	Bobby Cox	3-1 (WWLW)	WC–Colorado	Don Baylor
	C–Cincinnati	Davey Johnson	3-0	W–Los Angeles	Tommy Lasorda
1996	E–Atlanta	Bobby Cox	3-0	WC–Los Angeles	Bill Russell
	C–St. Louis	Tony La Russa	3-0	W–San Diego	Bruce Bochy
1997	E–Atlanta	Bobby Cox	3-0	C–Houston	Larry Dierker
	WC–Florida	Jim Leyland	3-0	W–San Francisco	Dusty Baker
1998	E–Atlanta	Bobby Cox	3-0	WC–Chicago	Jim Riggleman
	W–San Diego	Bruce Bochy	3-1 (WLWW)	C–Houston	Larry Dierker
1999	E–Atlanta	Bobby Cox	3-1 (LWWW)	C–Houston	Larry Dierker
	WC–New York	Bobby Valentine	3-1 (WLWW)	W–Arizona	Buck Showalter
2000	C–St. Louis	Tony La Russa	3-0	E–Atlanta	Bobby Cox
	WC–New York	Bobby Valentine	3-1 (LWWW)	W–San Francisco	Dusty Baker
2001	E–Atlanta	Bobby Cox	3-0	C–Houston	Larry Dierker
	W–Arizona	Bob Brenly	3-2 (WLWLW)	WC–St. Louis	Tony La Russa
2002	WC–San Francisco	Dusty Baker	3-2 (WLLWW)	E–Atlanta	Bobby Cox
	C–St. Louis	Tony La Russa	3-0	W–Arizona	Bob Brenly
2003	C–Chicago	Dusty Baker	3-2 (WLWLW)	E–Atlanta	Bobby Cox
	WC–Florida	Jack McKeon	3-1 (LWWW)	W–San Francisco	Felipe Alou
2004	C–St. Louis	Tony La Russa	3-1 (WWLW)	W–Los Angeles	Jim Tracy
	WC–Houston	Phil Garner	3-2 (WLWLW)	E–Atlanta	Bobby Cox
2005	C–St. Louis	Tony La Russa	3-0	W–San Diego	Bruce Bochy
	WC–Houston	Phil Garner	3-1 (WLWW)	E–Atlanta	Bobby Cox
2006	C–St. Louis	Tony La Russa	3-1 (WWLW)	W–San Diego	Bruce Bochy
	E–New York	Willie Randolph	3-0	WC–Los Angeles	Grady Little

American League

Multiple champions: NY Yankees (7); Boston, Cleveland and Seattle (3); Anaheim-Los Angeles Angels, Baltimore (2).

Year	Winner	Manager	Series	Loser	Manager
1995	C–Cleveland	Mike Hargrove	3-0	E–Boston	Kevin Kennedy
	W–Seattle	Lou Piniella	3-2 (LLWWW)	WC–New York	Buck Showalter
1996	E–New York	Joe Torre	3-1 (LWWW)	W–Texas	Johnny Oates
	WC–Baltimore	Davey Johnson	3-1 (WWLW)	C–Cleveland	Mike Hargrove
1997	E–Baltimore	Davey Johnson	3-1 (WWLW)	W–Seattle	Lou Piniella
	C–Cleveland	Mike Hargrove	3-2 (LWLWW)	WC–New York	Joe Torre
1998	E–New York	Joe Torre	3-0	W–Texas	Johnny Oates
	C–Cleveland	Mike Hargrove	3-1 (LWWW)	WC–Boston	Jimy Williams
1999	E–New York	Joe Torre	3-0	W–Texas	Johnny Oates
	WC–Boston	Jimy Williams	3-2 (LLWWW)	C–Cleveland	Mike Hargrove
2000	E–New York	Joe Torre	3-2 (LWWLW)	W–Oakland	Art Howe
	WC–Seattle	Lou Piniella	3-0	C–Chicago	Jerry Manuel
2001	E–New York	Joe Torre	3-2 (LLWWW)	WC–Oakland	Art Howe
	W–Seattle	Lou Piniella	3-2 (LWLWW)	C–Cleveland	Charlie Manuel
2002	WC–Anaheim	Mike Scioscia	3-1 (LWWW)	E–New York	Joe Torre
	C–Minnesota	Ron Gardenhire	3-2 (WLLWW)	W–Oakland	Art Howe
2003	E–New York	Joe Torre	3-1 (LWWW)	C–Minnesota	Ron Gardenhire
	WC–Boston	Grady Little	3-2 (LLWWW)	W–Oakland	Ken Macha
2004	E–New York	Joe Torre	3-1 (LWWW)	C–Minnesota	Ron Gardenhire
	WC–Boston	Terry Francona	3-0	W–Anaheim	Mike Scioscia
2005	W–Los Angeles	Mike Scioscia	3-2 (LWWLW)	E–New York	Joe Torre
	C–Chicago	Ozzie Guillen	3-0	WC–Boston	Terry Francona
2006	W–Oakland	Ken Macha	3-0	C–Minnesota	Ron Gardenhire
	WC–Detroit	Jim Leyland	3-1 (LWWW)	E–New York	Joe Torre

Other Playoffs

Ten times since 1946, playoffs have been necessary to decide league or division championships or wild card berths when two teams were tied at the end of the regular season. Additionally, in the strike year of 1981 there were playoffs between the first and second half-season champions in both leagues.

National League

Year	NL	W	L	Manager
1946	Brooklyn	96	58	Leo Durocher
	St. Louis	96	58	Eddie Dyer
	Playoff: (Best-of-3) St. Louis, 2-0			

Year	NL	W	L	Manager
1951	Brooklyn	96	58	Charlie Dressen
	New York	96	58	Leo Durocher
	Playoff: (Best-of-3) New York, 2-1 (WLW)			

Year	NL	W	L	Manager
1959	Milwaukee	86	68	Fred Haney
	Los Angeles	86	68	Walter Alston
	Playoff: (Best-of-3) Los Angeles, 2-0			

Year	NL	W	L	Manager
1962	Los Angeles	101	61	Walter Alston
	San Francisco	101	61	Alvin Dark
	Playoff: (Best-of-3) San Francisco, 2-1 (WLW)			

Year	NL West	W	L	Manager
1980	Houston	92	70	Bill Virdon
	Los Angeles	92	70	Tommy Lasorda
	Playoff: (1 game) Houston, 7-1 (at LA)			

Year	NL East	W	L	Manager
1981	(1st Half) Philadelphia	34	21	Dallas Green
	(2nd Half) Montreal	30	23	Jim Fanning
	Playoff: (Best-of-5) Montreal, 3-2 (WWLLW)			

Year	NL West	W	L	Manager
1981	(1st Half) Los Angeles	36	21	Tommy Lasorda
	(2nd Half) Houston	33	20	Bill Virdon
	Playoff: (Best-of-5) Los Angeles, 3-2 (LLWWW)			

Year	NL Wild Card	W	L	Manager
1998	Chicago	89	73	Jim Riggleman
	San Francisco	89	73	Dusty Baker
	Playoff: (1 game) Chicago, 5-3 (at Chicago)			

Year	NL Wild Card	W	L	Manager
1999	Cincinnati	96	66	Jack McKeon
	New York	96	66	Bobby Valentine
	Playoff: (1 game) New York, 5-0 (at Cincinnati)			

American League

Year	AL	W	L	Manager
1948	Boston	96	58	Joe McCarthy
	Cleveland	96	58	Lou Boudreau
	Playoff: (1 game) Cleveland, 8-3 (at Boston)			

Year	AL East	W	L	Manager
1978	Boston	99	63	Don Zimmer
	New York	99	63	Bob Lemon
	Playoff: (1 game) New York, 5-4 (at Boston)			

Year	AL East	W	L	Manager
1981	(1st Half) N.Y.	34	22	Bob Lemon
	(2nd Half) Milw	31	22	Buck Rodgers
	Playoff: (Best-of-5) New York, 3-2 (WWLLW)			

Year	AL West	W	L	Manager
1981	(1st Half) Oakland	37	23	Billy Martin
	(2nd Half) Kan. City	30	23	Jim Frey
	Playoff: (Best-of-5), Oakland, 3-0			

Year	AL West	W	L	Manager
1995	Seattle	78	66	Lou Piniella
	California	78	66	M. Lachemann
	Playoff: (1 game) Seattle, 9-1 (at Seattle)			

Regular Season League & Division Winners

Regular season National and American League pennant winners from 1900-68, as well as West and East divisional champions from 1969-93. In 1994, both leagues went to three divisions, West, Central and East, and each league also sent a wild card (WC) team to the playoffs. Note that (*) indicates 1994 divisional champion is unofficial (due to the players' strike). Note that **GA** column indicates games ahead of the second place club.

National League

Year		W	L	Pct	GA	Year		W	L	Pct	GA
1900	Brooklyn	82	54	.603	4½	1920	Brooklyn	93	61	.604	7
1901	Pittsburgh	90	49	.647	7½	1921	New York	94	59	.614	4
1902	Pittsburgh	103	36	.741	27½	1922	New York	93	61	.604	7
1903	Pittsburgh	91	49	.650	6½	1923	New York	95	58	.621	4½
1904	New York	106	47	.693	13	1924	New York	93	60	.608	1½
1905	New York	105	48	.686	9	1925	Pittsburgh	95	58	.621	8½
1906	Chicago	116	36	.763	20	1926	St. Louis	89	65	.578	2
1907	Chicago	107	45	.704	17	1927	Pittsburgh	94	60	.610	1½
1908	Chicago	99	55	.643	1	1928	St. Louis	95	59	.617	2
1909	Pittsburgh	110	42	.724	6½	1929	Chicago	98	54	.645	10½
1910	Chicago	104	50	.675	13	1930	St. Louis	92	62	.597	2
1911	New York	99	54	.647	7½	1931	St. Louis	101	53	.656	13
1912	New York	103	48	.682	10	1932	Chicago	90	64	.584	4
1913	New York	101	51	.664	12½	1933	New York	91	61	.599	5
1914	Boston	94	59	.614	10½	1934	St. Louis	95	58	.621	2
1915	Philadelphia	90	62	.592	7	1935	Chicago	100	54	.649	4
1916	Brooklyn	94	60	.610	2½	1936	New York	92	62	.597	5
1917	New York	98	56	.636	10	1937	New York	95	57	.625	3
1918	Chicago	84	45	.651	10½	1938	Chicago	89	63	.586	2
1919	Cincinnati	96	44	.686	9	1939	Cincinnati	97	57	.630	4½

Year		W	L	Pct	GA	Year		W	L	Pct	GA
1940	Cincinnati	100	53	.654	12	1987	West—San Francisco	90	72	.556	6
1941	Brooklyn	100	54	.649	2½		East—St. Louis	95	67	.586	3
1942	St. Louis	106	48	.688	2	1988	West—Los Angeles	94	67	.584	7
1943	St. Louis	105	49	.682	18		East—N.Y. Mets	100	60	.625	15
1944	St. Louis	105	49	.682	14½	1989	West—San Francisco	92	70	.568	3
1945	Chicago	98	56	.636	3		East—Chicago	93	69	.574	6
1946	St. Louis†	98	58	.628	2	1990	West—Cincinnati	91	71	.562	5
1947	Brooklyn	94	60	.610	5		East—Pittsburgh	95	67	.586	4
1948	Boston	91	62	.595	6½	1991	West—Atlanta	94	68	.580	1
1949	Brooklyn	97	57	.630	1		East—Pittsburgh	98	64	.605	14
1950	Philadelphia	91	63	.591	2	1992	West—Atlanta	98	64	.605	8
1951	New York†	98	59	.624	1		East—Pittsburgh	96	66	.593	9
1952	Brooklyn	96	57	.627	4½	1993	West—Atlanta	104	58	.642	1
1953	Brooklyn	105	49	.682	13		East—Philadelphia	97	65	.599	3
1954	New York	97	57	.630	5	1994	West—Los Angeles*	58	56	.509	3½
1955	Brooklyn	98	55	.641	13½		Central—Cincinnati*	66	48	.579	½
1956	Brooklyn	93	61	.604	1		East—Montreal*	74	40	.649	6
1957	Milwaukee	95	59	.617	8	1995	West—Los Angeles	78	66	.542	1
1958	Milwaukee	92	62	.597	8		Central—Cincinnati	85	59	.590	9
1959	Los Angeles†	88	68	.564	2		East—Atlanta	90	54	.625	21
							WC—Colorado	77	67	.535	—
1960	Pittsburgh	95	59	.617	7	1996	West—San Diego	91	71	.562	1
1961	Cincinnati	93	61	.604	4		Central—St. Louis	88	74	.543	6
1962	San Francisco†	103	62	.624	1		East—Atlanta	96	66	.593	8
1963	Los Angeles	99	63	.611	6		WC—Los Angeles	90	72	.556	—
1964	St. Louis	93	69	.574	1	1997	West—San Francisco	90	72	.556	2
1965	Los Angeles	97	65	.599	2		Central—Houston	84	78	.519	5
1966	Los Angeles	95	67	.586	1½		East—Atlanta	101	61	.623	9
1967	St. Louis	101	60	.627	10½		WC—Florida	92	70	.568	—
1968	St. Louis	97	65	.599	9	1998	West—San Diego	98	64	.605	9½
1969	West—Atlanta	93	69	.574	3		Central—Houston	102	60	.630	12½
	East—N.Y. Mets	100	62	.617	8		East—Atlanta	106	56	.654	18
							WC—Chicago†	90	73	.552	—
1970	West—Cincinnati	102	60	.630	14½	1999	West—Arizona	100	62	.617	14
	East—Pittsburgh	89	73	.549	5		Central—Houston	97	65	.599	1½
1971	West—San Francisco	90	72	.556	1		East—Atlanta	103	59	.636	6½
	East—Pittsburgh	97	65	.599	7		WC—N.Y. Mets†	97	66	.595	—
1972	West—Cincinnati	95	59	.617	10½	2000	West—San Francisco	97	65	.599	11
	East—Pittsburgh	96	59	.619	11		Central—St. Louis	95	67	.586	10
1973	West—Cincinnati	99	63	.611	3½		East—Atlanta	95	67	.586	1
	East—N.Y. Mets	82	79	.509	1½		WC—N.Y. Mets	94	68	.580	—
1974	West—Los Angeles	102	60	.630	4	2001	West—Arizona	92	70	.568	2
	East—Pittsburgh	88	74	.543	1½		Central—Houston@	93	69	.574	—
1975	West—Cincinnati	108	54	.667	20		East—Atlanta	88	74	.543	2
	East—Pittsburgh	92	69	.571	6½		WC—St. Louis	93	69	.574	—
1976	West—Cincinnati	102	60	.630	10	2002	West—Arizona	98	64	.605	2½
	East—Philadelphia	101	61	.623	9		Central—St. Louis	97	65	.599	13
1977	West—Los Angeles	98	64	.605	10		East—Atlanta	101	59	.631	19
	East—Philadelphia	101	61	.623	5		WC—San Francisco	95	66	.590	—
1978	West—Los Angeles	95	67	.586	2½	2003	West—San Francisco	100	61	.621	15½
	East—Philadelphia	90	72	.556	1½		Central—Chicago	88	74	.543	1
1979	West—Cincinnati	90	71	.559	1½		East—Atlanta	101	61	.623	10
	East—Pittsburgh	98	64	.605	2		WC—Florida	91	71	.562	—
1980	West—Houston†	93	70	.571	1	2004	West—Los Angeles	93	69	.574	2
	East—Philadelphia	91	71	.562	1		Central—St. Louis	105	57	.648	13
1981	West—Los Angeles$	63	47	.573	—		East—Atlanta	96	66	.593	10
	East—Montreal$	60	48	.556	—		WC—Houston	92	70	.568	—
1982	West—Atlanta	89	73	.549	1	2005	West—San Diego	82	80	.506	5
	East—St. Louis	92	70	.568	3		Central—St. Louis	100	62	.617	11
1983	West—Los Angeles	91	71	.562	3		East—Atlanta	90	72	.556	2
	East—Philadelphia	90	72	.556	6		WC—Houston	89	73	.549	—
1984	West—San Diego	92	70	.568	12	2006	West—San Diego@	88	74	.543	—
	East—Chicago	96	65	.596	6½		Central—St. Louis	83	78	.516	1½
1985	West—Los Angeles	95	67	.586	5½		East—N.Y. Mets	97	65	.599	12
	East—St. Louis	101	61	.623	3		WC—Los Angeles	88	74	543	—
1986	West—Houston	96	66	.593	10						
	East—N.Y. Mets	108	54	.667	21½						

†**Regular season playoffs:** See "Other Playoffs" on page 102 for details.
$**Divisional playoffs:** See "Other Playoffs" on page 102 for details.
@In 2001, Houston (93-69) won the Central over St. Louis (93-69) due to a better head-to-head record. In 2006, San Diego (88-74) won the West over Los Angeles (88-74) due to a better head-to-head record.

Regular Season League & Division Winners (Cont.)

American League

Year	Team	W	L	Pct	GA
1901	Chicago	83	53	.610	4
1902	Philadelphia	83	53	.610	5
1903	Boston	91	47	.659	14½
1904	Boston	95	59	.617	1½
1905	Philadelphia	92	56	.622	2
1906	Chicago	93	58	.616	3
1907	Detroit	92	58	.613	1½
1908	Detroit	90	63	.588	½
1909	Detroit	98	54	.645	3½
1910	Philadelphia	102	48	.680	14½
1911	Philadelphia	101	50	.669	13½
1912	Boston	105	47	.691	14
1913	Philadelphia	96	57	.627	6½
1914	Philadelphia	99	53	.651	8½
1915	Boston	101	50	.669	2½
1916	Boston	91	63	.591	2
1917	Chicago	100	54	.649	9
1918	Boston	75	51	.595	2½
1919	Chicago	88	52	.629	3½
1920	Cleveland	98	56	.636	2
1921	New York	98	55	.641	4½
1922	New York	94	60	.610	1
1923	New York	98	54	.645	16
1924	Washington	92	62	.597	2
1925	Washington	96	55	.636	8½
1926	New York	91	63	.591	3
1927	New York	110	44	.714	19
1928	New York	101	53	.656	2½
1929	Philadelphia	104	46	.693	18
1930	Philadelphia	102	52	.662	8
1931	Philadelphia	107	45	.704	13½
1932	New York	107	47	.695	13
1933	Washington	99	53	.651	7
1934	Detroit	101	53	.656	7
1935	Detroit	93	58	.616	3
1936	New York	102	51	.667	19½
1937	New York	102	52	.662	13
1938	New York	99	53	.651	9½
1939	New York	106	45	.702	17
1940	Detroit	90	64	.584	1
1941	New York	101	53	.656	17
1942	New York	103	51	.669	9
1943	New York	98	56	.636	13½
1944	St. Louis	89	65	.578	1
1945	Detroit	88	65	.575	1½
1946	Boston	104	50	.675	12
1947	New York	97	57	.630	12
1948	Cleveland†	97	58	.626	1
1949	New York	97	57	.630	1
1950	New York	98	56	.636	3
1951	New York	98	56	.636	5
1952	New York	95	59	.617	2
1953	New York	99	52	.656	8½
1954	Cleveland	111	43	.721	8
1955	New York	96	58	.623	3
1956	New York	97	57	.630	9
1957	New York	98	56	.636	8
1958	New York	92	62	.597	10
1959	Chicago	94	60	.610	5
1960	New York	97	57	.630	8
1961	New York	109	53	.673	8
1962	New York	96	66	.593	5
1963	New York	104	57	.646	10½
1964	New York	99	63	.611	1
1965	Minnesota	102	60	.630	7
1966	Baltimore	97	63	.606	9
1967	Boston	92	70	.568	1
1968	Detroit	103	59	.636	12
1969	West—Minnesota	97	65	.599	9
	East—Baltimore	109	53	.673	19
1970	West—Minnesota	98	64	.605	9
	East—Baltimore	108	54	.667	15
1971	West—Oakland	101	60	.627	16
	East—Baltimore	101	57	.639	12
1972	West—Oakland	93	62	.600	5½
	East—Detroit	86	70	.551	½
1973	West—Oakland	94	68	.580	6
	East—Baltimore	97	65	.599	8
1974	West—Oakland	90	72	.556	5
	East—Baltimore	91	71	.562	2
1975	West—Oakland	98	64	.605	7
	East—Boston	95	65	.594	4½
1976	West—KansasCity	90	72	.556	2½
	East—New York	97	62	.610	10½
1977	West—Kansas City	102	60	.630	8
	East—New York	100	62	.617	2½
1978	West—Kansas City	92	70	.568	5
	East—New York†	100	63	.613	1
1979	West—California	88	74	.543	3
	East—Baltimore	102	57	.642	8
1980	West—Kansas City	97	65	.599	14
	East—New York	103	59	.636	3
1981	West—Oakland$	64	45	.587	—
	East—New York$	59	48	.551	—
1982	West—California	93	69	.574	3
	East—Milwaukee	95	67	.586	1
1983	West—Chicago	99	63	.611	20
	East—Baltimore	98	64	.605	6
1984	West—Kansas City	84	78	.519	3
	East—Detroit	104	58	.642	15
1985	West—Kansas City	91	71	.562	1
	East—Toronto	99	62	.615	2
1986	West—California	92	70	.568	5
	East—Boston	95	66	.590	5½
1987	West—Minnesota	85	77	.525	2
	East—Detroit	98	64	.605	2
1988	West—Oakland	104	58	.642	13
	East—Boston	89	73	.549	1
1989	West—Oakland	99	63	.611	7
	East—Toronto	89	73	.549	2
1990	West—Oakland	103	59	.636	9
	East—Boston	88	74	.543	2
1991	West—Minnesota	95	67	.586	8
	East—Toronto	91	71	.562	7
1992	West—Oakland	96	66	.593	6
	East—Toronto	96	66	.593	4
1993	West—Chicago	94	68	.580	8
	East—Toronto	95	67	.586	7
1994	West—Texas*	52	62	.456	1
	Central—Chicago*	67	46	.593	1
	East—New York*	70	43	.619	6½
1995	West—Seattle†	79	66	.545	1
	Central—Cleveland	100	44	.694	30
	East—Boston	86	58	.597	7
	WC—New York	79	65	.549	—
1996	West—Texas	90	72	.556	4½
	Central—Cleveland	99	62	.615	14½
	East—New York	92	70	.568	4
	WC—Baltimore	88	74	.543	—
1997	West—Seattle	90	72	.556	6
	Central—Cleveland	86	75	.534	6
	East—Baltimore	98	64	.605	2
	WC—New York	96	66	.593	—

Year		W	L	Pct	GA	Year		W	L	Pct	GA
1998	West—Texas	88	74	.543	3	2003	West—Oakland	96	66	.593	3
	Central—Cleveland	89	73	.549	9		Central—Minnesota	90	72	.556	4
	East—New York	114	48	.704	22		East—New York	101	61	.623	6
	WC—Boston	92	70	.568	—		WC—Boston	95	67	.586	—
1999	West—Texas	95	67	.586	8	2004	West—Anaheim	92	70	.568	1
	Central—Cleveland	97	65	.599	21½		Central—Minnesota	92	70	.568	9
	East—New York	98	64	.605	4		East—New York	101	61	.623	3
	WC—Boston	94	68	.580	—		WC—Boston	98	64	.605	—
2000	West—Oakland	91	70	.565	½	2005	West—Los Angeles	95	67	.586	7
	Central—Chicago	95	67	.586	5		Central—Chicago	99	63	.611	6
	East—New York	87	74	.540	2½		East—New York@	95	67	.586	—
	WC—Seattle	91	71	.562	—		WC—Boston	95	67	.586	—
2001	West—Seattle	116	46	.716	14	2006	West—Oakland	93	69	.574	4
	Central—Cleveland	91	71	.562	6		Central—Minnesota	96	66	.593	1
	East—New York	95	65	.594	13½		East—New York	97	65	.599	10
	WC—Oakland	102	60	.630	—		WC—Detroit	95	67	.586	—
2002	West—Oakland	103	59	.636	4						
	Central—Minnesota	94	67	.584	13½						
	East—New York	103	58	.640	10½						
	WC—Anaheim	99	63	.611	—						

†**Regular season playoffs:** See "Other Playoffs" on page 102 for details.
$**Divisional playoffs:** See "Other Playoffs" on page 102 for details.
@In 2005, New York (95-67) won the East over Boston (95-67) due to a better head-to-head record.

The All-Star Game

Baseball's first All-Star Game was held on July 6, 1933, before 47,595 at Comiskey Park in Chicago. From that year on, the All-Star Game has matched the best players in the American League against the best in the National. From 1959-62, two All-Star Games were played. The only year an All-Star Game wasn't played was 1945, when World War II travel restrictions made it necessary to cancel the meeting. The NL leads the series, 40-35-2. In the chart below, the American League is listed in **bold** type.

Since 2002, the game's MVP award has been named the Ted Williams Award, after the Red Sox Hall of Famer. The actual trophy is the Arch Ward Trophy, named after the Chicago Tribune sports editor who founded the game in 1933. First given at the two All-Star Games in 1962, the name of the award was changed to the Commissioner's Trophy in 1970 and back to the Arch Ward Memorial Trophy in 1985.

Beginning in 2003, the league that won the All-Star Game received home-field advantage in that season's World Series.

MVP Multiple winners: Gary Carter, Steve Garvey, Willie Mays and Cal Ripken Jr. (2).

Year	Host		AL Manager	NL Manager	MVP
1933	**American,** 4-2	Chicago (AL)	Connie Mack	John McGraw	No award
1934	**American,** 9-7	New York (NL)	Joe Cronin	Bill Terry	No award
1935	**American,** 4-1	Cleveland	Mickey Cochrane	Frankie Frisch	No award
1936	National, 4-3	Boston (NL)	Joe McCarthy	Charlie Grimm	No award
1937	**American,** 8-3	Washington	Joe McCarthy	Bill Terry	No award
1938	National, 4-1	Cincinnati	Joe McCarthy	Bill Terry	No award
1939	**American,** 3-1	New York (AL)	Joe McCarthy	Gabby Hartnett	No award
1940	National, 4-0	St. Louis (NL)	Joe Cronin	Bill McKechnie	No award
1941	**American,** 7-5	Detroit	Del Baker	Bill McKechnie	No award
1942	**American,** 3-1	New York (NL)	Joe McCarthy	Leo Durocher	No award
1943	**American,** 5-3	Philadelphia (AL)	Joe McCarthy	Billy Southworth	No award
1944	National, 7-1	Pittsburgh	Joe McCarthy	Billy Southworth	No award
1945	Not held				
1946	**American,** 12-0	Boston (AL)	Steve O'Neill	Charlie Grimm	No award
1947	**American,** 2-1	Chicago (NL)	Joe Cronin	Eddie Dyer	No award
1948	**American,** 5-2	St. Louis (AL)	Bucky Harris	Leo Durocher	No award
1949	**American,** 11-7	Brooklyn	Lou Boudreau	Billy Southworth	No award
1950	National, 4-3 (14)	Chicago (AL)	Casey Stengel	Burt Shotton	No award
1951	National, 8-3	Detroit	Casey Stengel	Eddie Sawyer	No award
1952	National, 3-2 (5, rain)	Philadelphia (NL)	Casey Stengel	Leo Durocher	No award
1953	National, 5-1	Cincinnati	Casey Stengel	Charlie Dressen	No award
1954	**American,** 11-9	Cleveland	Casey Stengel	Walter Alston	No award
1955	National, 6-5 (12)	Milwaukee	Al Lopez	Leo Durocher	No award
1956	National, 7-3	Washington	Casey Stengel	Walter Alston	No award
1957	**American,** 6-5	St. Louis	Casey Stengel	Walter Alston	No award
1958	**American,** 4-3	Baltimore	Casey Stengel	Fred Haney	No award
1959-a	National, 5-4	Pittsburgh	Casey Stengel	Fred Haney	No award
1959-b	**American,** 5-3	Los Angeles	Casey Stengel	Fred Haney	No award
1960-a	National, 5-3	Kansas City	Al Lopez	Walter Alston	No award
1960-b	National, 6-0	New York	Al Lopez	Walter Alston	No award

The All-Star Game (Cont.)

Year		Host	AL Manager	NL Manager	MVP
1961-a	National, 5-4 (10)	San Francisco	Paul Richards	Danny Murtaugh	No award
1961-b	TIE, 1-1 (9, rain)	Boston	Paul Richards	Danny Murtaugh	No award
1962-a	National, 3-1	Washington	Ralph Houk	Fred Hutchinson	Maury Wills, LA (NL), SS
1962-b	**American,** 9-4	Chicago (NL)	Ralph Houk	Fred Hutchinson	Leon Wagner, LA (AL), OF
1963	National, 5-3	Cleveland	Ralph Houk	Alvin Dark	Willie Mays, SF, OF
1964	National, 7-4	New York (NL)	Al Lopez	Walter Alston	Johnny Callison, Phi., OF
1965	National, 6-5	Minnesota	Al Lopez	Gene Mauch	Juan Marichal, SF, OF
1966	National, 2-1 (10)	St. Louis	Sam Mele	Walter Alston	Brooks Robinson, Bal., 3B
1967	National, 2-1 (15)	California	Hank Bauer	Walter Alston	Tony Perez, Cin., 3B
1968	National, 1-0	Houston	Dick Williams	Red Schoendienst	Willie Mays, SF, OF
1969	National, 9-3	Washington	Mayo Smith	Red Schoendienst	Willie McCovey, SF, 1B
1970	National, 5-4 (12)	Cincinnati	Earl Weaver	Gil Hodges	Carl Yastrzemski, Bos., OF-1B
1971	**American,** 6-4	Detroit	Earl Weaver	Sparky Anderson	Frank Robinson, Bal., OF
1972	National, 4-3 (10)	Atlanta	Earl Weaver	Danny Murtaugh	Joe Morgan, Cin., 2B
1973	National, 7-1	Kansas	Dick Williams	Sparky Anderson	Bobby Bonds, SF, OF
1974	National, 7-2	Pittsburgh	Dick Williams	Yogi Berra	Steve Garvey, LA, 1B
1975	National, 6-3	Milwaukee	Alvin Dark	Walter Alston	Bill Madlock, Chi. (NL), 3B & Jon Matlack, NY (NL), P
1976	National, 7-1	Philadelphia	Darrell Johnson	Sparky Anderson	George Foster, Cin., OF
1977	National, 7-5	New York (AL)	Billy Martin	Sparky Anderson	Don Sutton, LA, P
1978	National, 7-3	San Diego	Billy Martin	Tommy Lasorda	Steve Garvey, LA, 1B
1979	National, 7-6	Seattle	Bob Lemon	Tommy Lasorda	Dave Parker, Pit., OF
1980	National, 4-2	Los Angeles	Earl Weaver	Chuck Tanner	Ken Griffey, Cin., OF
1981	National, 5-4	Cleveland	Jim Frey	Dallas Green	Gary Carter, Mon., C
1982	National, 4-1	Montreal	Billy Martin	Tommy Lasorda	Dave Concepcion, Cin., SS
1983	**American,** 13-3	Chicago (AL)	Harvey Kuenn	Whitey Herzog	Fred Lynn, Cal., OF
1984	National, 3-1	San Francisco	Joe Altobelli	Paul Owens	Gary Carter, Mon., C
1985	National, 6-1	Minnesota	Sparky Anderson	Dick Williams	LaMarr Hoyt, SD, P
1986	**American,** 3-2	Houston	Dick Howser	Whitey Herzog	Roger Clemens, Bos., P
1987	National, 2-0 (13)	Oakland	John McNamara	Davey Johnson	Tim Raines, Mon., OF
1988	**American,** 2-1	Cincinnati	Tom Kelly	Whitey Herzog	Terry Steinbach, Oak., C
1989	**American,** 5-3	California	Tony La Russa	Tommy Lasorda	Bo Jackson, KC, OF
1990	**American,** 2-0	Chicago (NL)	Tony La Russa	Roger Craig	Julio Franco, Tex., 2B
1991	**American,** 4-2	Toronto	Tony La Russa	Lou Piniella	Cal Ripken Jr., Bal., SS
1992	**American,** 13-6	San Diego	Tom Kelly	Bobby Cox	Ken Griffey Jr., Sea., OF
1993	**American,** 9-3	Baltimore	Cito Gaston	Bobby Cox	Kirby Puckett, Min., OF
1994	National, 8-7 (10)	Pittsburgh	Cito Gaston	Jim Fregosi	Fred McGriff, Atl., 1B
1995	National, 3-2	Texas	Buck Showalter	Felipe Alou	Jeff Conine, Fla., PH
1996	National, 6-0	Philadelphia	Mike Hargrove	Bobby Cox	Mike Piazza, LA, C
1997	**American,** 3-1	Cleveland	Joe Torre	Bobby Cox	Sandy Alomar Jr., Cle., C
1998	**American,** 13-8	Colorado	Mike Hargrove	Jim Leyland	Roberto Alomar, Bal., 2B
1999	**American,** 4-1	Boston	Joe Torre	Bruce Bochy	Pedro Martinez, Bos., P
2000	**American,** 6-3	Atlanta	Joe Torre	Bobby Cox	Derek Jeter, NY (AL), SS
2001	**American,** 4-1	Seattle	Joe Torre	Bobby Valentine	Cal Ripken Jr., Bal., SS-3B
2002	TIE, 7-7 (11 inn.) *	Milwaukee	Joe Torre	Bob Brenly	No award
2003	**American,** 7-6	Chicago (AL)	Mike Scioscia	Dusty Baker	Garret Anderson, Ana., OF
2004	**American,** 9-4	Houston	Joe Torre	Jack McKeon	Alfonso Soriano, Tex., 2B
2005	**American,** 7-5	Detroit	Terry Francona	Tony La Russa	Miguel Tejada, Bal., SS
2006	**American,** 3-2	Pittsburgh	Ozzie Guillen	Phil Garner	Michael Young, Tex., 2B

* Due to the depletion of both the AL and NL rosters, the 2002 game was called a tie after 11 innings.

Like Father, Like Son

When Texas Rangers outfielder Gary Matthews, Jr. made his first All-Star appearance in 2006, he and his father, Gary Matthews, Sr., became the 14th father-son All-Star combination. **Source:** MLB.com.

Family	Father	Son(s)
Alomar	Sandy Sr. (1970)	Sandy Jr. (1990, 91, 92, 96-98), Roberto (1990-2001)
Alou	Felipe (1962, 66, 68)	Moises (1994, 97, 98, 2001, 04, 05)
Bell	Gus (1953, 54, 56, 57)	Buddy (1973, 80, 81, 82, 84)
Bonds	Bobby (1971, 73, 75)	Barry (1990, 92-98, 2000, 01, 02, 03, 04)
Boone	Ray (1954, 56)	Bob (1976, 78, 79, 83)
	Bob (1976, 78, 79, 83)	Aaron (2003), Bret (1998, 2001, 03)
Coleman	Joe Sr. (1948)	Joe Jr. (1972)
Griffey	Ken Sr. (1976, 77, 80)	Ken Jr. (1990-99, 2000, 04)
Hegan	Jim (1947, 49-52)	Mike (1969)
Hundley	Randy (1969)	Todd (1996)
Law	Vern (1960)	Vance (1988)
Matthews	Gary Sr. (1979)	Gary Jr. (2006)

Major League Franchise Origins

Here is what the current 30 teams in Major League Baseball have to show for the years they have put in as members of the National League (NL) and American League (AL). Pennants and World Series championships are since 1901.

National League

	1st Year	Pennants & World Series	Franchise Stops
Arizona Diamondbacks	1998	1 NL (2001) 1 WS (2001)	• Phoenix (1998–)

Atlanta Braves	1876	9 NL (1914,48,57-58,91-92,95,96,99)
		3 WS (1914,57,95)
			• Boston (1876–1952)
			  Milwaukee (1953–65)
			  Atlanta (1966–)

Chicago Cubs	1876	10 NL (1906-08,10,18,29,32,35,38,45) 2 WS (1907-08)	• Chicago (1876–)
Cincinnati Reds	1876	9 NL (1919,39-40,61,70,72,75-76,90) 5 WS (1919,40,75-76,90)	• Cincinnati (1876–80) Cincinnati (1890–)
Colorado Rockies	1993	None	• Denver (1993–)
Florida Marlins	1993	2 NL (1997, 2003) 2 WS (1997, 2003)	• Miami (1993–)
Houston Astros	1962	1 NL (2005)	• Houston (1962–)
Los Angeles Dodgers	1890	18 NL (1916,20,41,47,49,52-53,55-56, 59,63, 65-66,74,77-78, 81,88) 6 WS (1955,59,63,65,81,88)	• Brooklyn (1890-1957) Los Angeles (1958–)
Milwaukee Brewers	1969	1 AL (1982)	• Seattle (1969) Milwaukee (1970–)
New York Mets	1962	4 NL (1969,73,86,00) 2 WS (1969,86)	• New York (1962–)
Philadelphia Phillies	1883	5 NL (1915,50,80,83,93) 1 WS (1980)	• Philadelphia (1883–)
Pittsburgh Pirates	1887	7 NL (1903,09,25,27,60,71,79) 5 WS (1909,25,60,71,79)	• Pittsburgh (1887–)
St. Louis Cardinals	1892	17 NL (1926,28,30-31,34,42-44,46,64, 67-68,82,85,87,2004,06) 10 WS (1926,31,34,42,44,46,64,67,82,2006)	• St. Louis (1892–)
San Diego Padres	1969	2 NL (1984,98)	• San Diego (1969–)
San Francisco Giants	1883	17 NL (1905,11-13,17,21-24,33,36-37,51, 54,62,89,2002) 5 WS (1905,21-22,33,54)	• New York (1883–1957) San Francisco (1958–)
Washington Nationals	1969	None	• Montreal (1969–2004) Washington, DC (2005–)

American League

	1st Year	Pennants & World Series	Franchise Stops

Baltimore Orioles	1901	7 AL (1944,66,69-71,79,83)
		3 WS (1966,70,83)
			• Milwaukee (1901)
			  St. Louis (1902–53)
			  Baltimore (1954–)

Boston Red Sox	1901	10 AL (1903,12,15-16,18,46,67,75,86,2004) 6 WS (1903,12,15-16,18,2004)	• Boston (1901–)
Chicago White Sox	1901	5 AL (1906,17,19,59,2005) 3 WS (1906,17,2005)	• Chicago (1901–)
Cleveland Indians	1901	5 AL (1920,48,54,95,97) 2 WS (1920,48)	• Cleveland (1901–)
Detroit Tigers	1901	10 AL (1907-09,34-35,40,45,68,84,2006) 4 WS (1935,45,68,84)	• Detroit (1901–)
Kansas City Royals	1969	2 AL (1980,85) 1 WS (1985)	• Kansas City (1969–)
Los Angeles Angels of Anaheim	1961	1 AL (2002) 1 WS (2002)	• Los Angeles (1961–65) Anaheim, CA (1966–)

Minnesota Twins	1901	6 AL (1924-25,33,65,87,91)
		3 WS (1924,87,91)
			• Washington, DC (1901–60)
			  Bloomington, MN (1961–81)
			  Minneapolis (1982–)

New York Yankees	1901	39 AL (1921-23,26-28,32,36-39,41-43,47, 49-53,55-58,60-64,76-78,81,96,98-01,03) 26 WS (1923,27-28,32,36-39,41,43,47, 49-53,56,58,61-62,77-78,96,98-00)	• Baltimore (1901–02) New York (1903–)

Oakland Athletics	1901	14 AL (1905,10-11,13-14,29-31,72-74,
		88-90)
		9 WS (1910-11,13,29-30,72-74,89)
			• Philadelphia (1901-54)
			  Kansas City (1955–67)
			  Oakland (1968–)

Seattle Mariners	1977	None	• Seattle (1977–)
Tampa Bay Devil Rays	1998	None	• Tampa Bay (1998–)
Texas Rangers	1961	None	• Washington, DC (1961–71) Arlington, TX (1972–)
Toronto Blue Jays	1977	2 AL (1992-93) 2 WS (1992-93)	• Toronto (1977–)

The Growth of Major League Baseball

The National League (founded in 1876) and the American League (founded in 1901) were both eight-team circuits at the turn of the century and remained that way until expansion finally came to Major League Baseball in the 1960s. The AL added two teams in 1961 and the NL did the same a year later. Both leagues went to 12 teams and split into two divisions in 1969. The AL then grew by two more teams to 14 in 1977, but the NL didn't follow suit until adding its 13th and 14th clubs in 1993. The NL added two teams (making it 16) in 1998 when the expansion Arizona Diamondbacks entered the league and the Milwaukee Brewers moved over from the AL. The Tampa Bay Devil Rays joined the AL in 1998, keeping the AL at 14 teams.

Expansion Timetable (Since 1901)

1961—Los Angeles Angels and Washington Senators (now Texas Rangers) join AL; **1962**—Houston Colt .45s (now Astros) and New York Mets join NL; **1969**—Kansas City Royals and Seattle Pilots (now Milwaukee Brewers) join AL, while Montreal Expos (now Washington Nationals) and San Diego Padres join NL; **1977**—Seattle Mariners and Toronto Blue Jays join AL; **1993**—Colorado Rockies and Florida Marlins join NL; **1998**—Arizona Diamondbacks join NL and Tampa Bay Devil Rays join AL.

City and Nickname Changes
National League

1953—Boston Braves move to Milwaukee; **1958**—Brooklyn Dodgers move to Los Angeles and New York Giants move to San Francisco; **1965**—Houston Colt .45s renamed Astros; **1966**—Milwaukee Braves move to Atlanta; **2004**—Montreal Expos move to Washington, D.C. and become Washington Nationals.

Other nicknames: Boston (Beaneaters and Doves through 1908, and Bees from 1936-40); **Brooklyn** (Superbas through 1926, then Robins from 1927-31; then Dodgers from 1932-57); **Cincinnati** (Red Legs from 1944-45, then Redlegs from 1954-60, then Reds since 1961); **Philadelphia** (Blue Jays from 1943-44).

American League

1902—Milwaukee Brewers move to St. Louis and become Browns; **1903**—Baltimore Orioles move to New York and become Highlanders; **1913**—NY Highlanders renamed Yankees; **1954**—St. Louis Browns move to Baltimore and become Orioles; **1955**—Philadelphia Athletics move to Kansas City; **1961**—Washington Senators move to Bloomington, Minn., and become Minnesota Twins; **1965**—LA Angels renamed California Angels; **1966**—California Angels move to Anaheim; **1968**—KC Athletics move to Oakland and become A's; **1970**—Seattle Pilots move to Milwaukee and become Brewers; **1972**—Washington Senators move to Arlington, Texas, and become Rangers; **1982**—Minnesota Twins move to Minneapolis; **1987**—Oakland A's renamed Athletics; **1997**—California Angels renamed Anaheim Angels; **2005**—Anaheim Angels renamed Los Angeles Angels of Anaheim.

Other nicknames: Boston (Pilgrims, Puritans, Plymouth Rocks and Somersets through 1906); **Cleveland** (Bronchos, Blues, Naps and Molly McGuires through 1914); **Washington** (Senators through 1904, then Nationals from 1905-44, then Senators again from 1945-60).

National League Pennant Winners from 1876-99

Founded in 1876, the National League played 24 seasons before the turn of the century and its eventual rivalry with the younger American League.

Multiple winners: Boston (8); Chicago (6); Baltimore (3); Brooklyn, New York and Providence (2).

Year		Year		Year		Year	
1876	Chicago	1882	Chicago	1888	New York	1894	Baltimore
1877	Boston	1883	Boston	1889	New York	1895	Baltimore
1878	Boston	1884	Providence	1890	Brooklyn	1896	Baltimore
1879	Providence	1885	Chicago	1891	Boston	1897	Boston
1880	Chicago	1886	Chicago	1892	Boston	1898	Boston
1881	Chicago	1887	Detroit	1893	Boston	1899	Brooklyn

Champions of Leagues That No Longer Exist

A Special Baseball Records Committee appointed by the commissioner found in 1968 that four extinct leagues qualified for major league status—the American Association (1882-91), the Union Association (1884), the Players' League (1890) and the Federal League (1914-15). The first years of the American League (1900) and Federal League (1913) were not recognized.

American Association

Year	Champion	Manager	Year	Champion	Manager	Year	Champion	Manager
1882	Cincinnati	Pop Snyder	1886	St. Louis	Charlie Comiskey	1890	Louisville	Jack Chapman
1883	Philadelphia	Lew Simmons	1887	St. Louis	Charlie Comiskey	1891	Boston	Arthur Irwin
1884	New York	Jim Mutrie	1888	St. Louis	Charlie Comiskey			
1885	St. Louis	Charlie Comiskey	1889	Brooklyn	Bill McGunnigle			

Union Association

Year	Champion	Manager
1884	St. Louis	Henry Lucas

Players' League

Year	Champion	Manager
1890	Boston	King Kelly

Federal League

Year	Champion	Manager
1914	Indianapolis	Bill Phillips
1915	Chicago	Joe Tinker

Annual Batting Leaders (since 1900)

Batting Average

National League

Multiple winners: Tony Gwynn and Honus Wagner (8); Rogers Hornsby and Stan Musial (7); Roberto Clemente and Bill Madlock (4); Pete Rose, Larry Walker and Paul Waner (3); Hank Aaron, Richie Ashburn, Barry Bonds, Jake Daubert, Tommy Davis, Ernie Lombardi, Willie McGee, Lefty O'Doul, Dave Parker and Edd Roush (2).

Year		Avg	Year		Avg	Year		Avg
1900	Honus Wagner, Pit	.381	1936	Paul Waner, Pit.	.373	1972	Billy Williams, Chi	.333
1901	Jesse Burkett, St.L	.382	1937	Joe Medwick, St.L	.374	1973	Pete Rose, Cin	.338
1902	Ginger Beaumont, Pit	.357	1938	Ernie Lombardi, Cin	.342	1974	Ralph Garr, Atl	.353
1903	Honus Wagner, Pit	.355	1939	Johnny Mize, St.L	.349	1975	Bill Madlock, Chi	.354
1904	Honus Wagner, Pit	.349	1940	Debs Garms, Pit	.355	1976	Bill Madlock, Chi	.339
1905	Cy Seymour, Cin	.377	1941	Pete Reiser, Bklyn	.343	1977	Dave Parker, Pit	.338
1906	George Stone, St.L	.339	1942	Ernie Lombardi, Bos	.330	1978	Dave Parker, Pit	.334
1907	Honus Wagner, Pit	.350	1943	Stan Musial, St.L	.357	1979	Keith Hernandez, St.L	.344
1908	Honus Wagner, Pit	.354	1944	Dixie Walker, Bklyn	.357	1980	Bill Buckner, Chi	.324
1909	Honus Wagner, Pit	.339	1945	Phil Cavarretta, Chi.	.355	1981	Bill Madlock, Pit	.341
1910	Sherry Magee, Phi	.331	1946	Stan Musial, St.L	.365	1982	Al Oliver, Mon	.331
1911	Honus Wagner, Pit	.334	1947	Harry Walker, St.L-Phi	.363	1983	Bill Madlock, Pit	.323
1912	Heinie Zimmerman, Chi.	.372	1948	Stan Musial, St.L	.376	1984	Tony Gwynn, SD	.351
1913	Jake Daubert, Bklyn	.350	1949	Jackie Robinson, Bklyn	.342	1985	Willie McGee, St.L	.353
1914	Jake Daubert, Bklyn	.329	1950	Stan Musial, St.L	.346	1986	Tim Raines, Mon	.334
1915	Larry Doyle, NY	.320	1951	Stan Musial, St.L	.355	1987	Tony Gwynn, SD	.370
1916	Hal Chase, Cin	.339	1952	Stan Musial, St.L	.336	1988	Tony Gwynn, SD	.313
1917	Edd Roush, Cin	.341	1953	Carl Furillo, Bklyn	.344	1989	Tony Gwynn, SD	.336
1918	Zack Wheat, Bklyn	.335	1954	Willie Mays, NY	.345	1990	Willie McGee, St.L	.335
1919	Edd Roush, Cin	.321	1955	Richie Ashburn, Phi	.338	1991	Terry Pendleton, Atl	.319
1920	Rogers Hornsby, St.L	.370	1956	Hank Aaron, Mil	.328	1992	Gary Sheffield, SD	.330
1921	Rogers Hornsby, St.L	397	1957	Stan Musial, St.L	.351	1993	Andres Galarraga, Col	.370
1922	Rogers Hornsby, St.L	.401	1958	Richie Ashburn, Phi	.350	1994	Tony Gwynn, SD	.394
1923	Rogers Hornsby, St.L	.384	1959	Hank Aaron, Mil	.355	1995	Tony Gwynn, SD	.368
1924	Rogers Hornsby, St.L	.424	1960	Dick Groat, Pit	.325	1996	Tony Gwynn, SD	.353
1925	Rogers Hornsby, St.L	.403	1961	Roberto Clemente, Pit	.351	1997	Tony Gwynn, SD	.372
1926	Bubbles Hargrave, Cin	.353	1962	Tommy Davis, LA	.346	1998	Larry Walker, Col	.363
1927	Paul Waner, Pit.	.380	1963	Tommy Davis, LA	.326	1999	Larry Walker, Col	.379
1928	Rogers Hornsby, Bos	.387	1964	Roberto Clemente, Pit	.339	2000	Todd Helton, Col	.372
1929	Lefty O'Doul, Phi	.398	1965	Roberto Clemente, Pit	.329	2001	Larry Walker, Col	.350
1930	Bill Terry, NY	.401	1966	Matty Alou, Pit	.342	2002	Barry Bonds, SF	.370
1931	Chick Hafey, St.L	.349	1967	Roberto Clemente, Pit	.357	2003	Albert Pujols, St.L	.359
1932	Lefty O'Doul, Bklyn	.368	1968	Pete Rose, Cin	.335	2004	Barry Bonds, SF	.362
1933	Chuck Klein, Phi	.368	1969	Pete Rose, Cin	.348	2005	Derrek Lee, Chi.	.335
1934	Paul Waner, Pit.	.362	1970	Rico Carty, Atl	.366	2006	Freddy Sanchez, Pit.	.344
1935	Arky Vaughan, Pit	.385	1971	Joe Torre, St.L	.363			

American League

Multiple winners: Ty Cobb (12); Rod Carew (7); Ted Williams (6); Wade Boggs (5); Harry Heilmann (4); George Brett, Nap Lajoie, Tony Oliva and Carl Yastrzemski (3); Luke Appling, Joe DiMaggio, Ferris Fain, Jimmie Foxx, Nomar Garciaparra, Edgar Martinez, Pete Runnels, Al Simmons, George Sisler, Ichiro Suzuki and Mickey Vernon (2).

Year		Avg	Year		Avg	Year		Avg
1901	Nap Lajoie, Phi.	.422	1925	Harry Heilmann, Det	.393	1949	George Kell, Det.	.343
1902	Ed Delahanty, Wash.	.376	1926	Heinie Manush, Det	.378	1950	Billy Goodman, Bos	.354
1903	Nap Lajoie, Cle	.355	1927	Harry Heilmann, Det	.398	1951	Ferris Fain, Phi	.344
1904	Nap Lajoie, Cle	.381	1928	Goose Goslin, Wash.	.379	1952	Ferris Fain, Phi	.327
1905	Elmer Flick, Cle.	.306	1929	Lew Fonseca, Cle	.369	1953	Mickey Vernon, Wash.	.337
1906	George Stone, St.L	.358	1930	Al Simmons, Phi	.381	1954	Bobby Avila, Clev.	.341
1907	Ty Cobb, Det	.350	1931	Al Simmons, Phi	.390	1955	Al Kaline, Det.	.340
1908	Ty Cobb, Det	.324	1932	Dale Alexander, Det-Bos	.367	1956	Mickey Mantle, NY	.353
1909	Ty Cobb, Det	.377	1933	Jimmie Foxx, Phi	.356	1957	Ted Williams, Bos	.388
1910	Ty Cobb, Det	.383	1934	Lou Gehrig, NY	.363	1958	Ted Williams, Bos	.328
1911	Ty Cobb, Det	.420	1935	Buddy Myer, Wash.	.349	1959	Harvey Kuenn, Det	.353
1912	Ty Cobb, Det	.409	1936	Luke Appling, Chi.	.388	1960	Pete Runnels, Bos	.320
1913	Ty Cobb, Det	.390	1937	Charlie Gehringer, Det	.371	1961	Norm Cash, Det	.361*
1914	Ty Cobb, Det	.368	1938	Jimmie Foxx, Bos.	.349	1962	Pete Runnels, Bos	.326
1915	Ty Cobb, Det	.369	1939	Joe DiMaggio, NY	.381	1963	Carl Yastrzemski, Bos.	.321
1916	Tris Speaker, Cle.	.386	1940	Joe DiMaggio, NY	.352	1964	Tony Oliva, Min	.323
1917	Ty Cobb, Det	.383	1941	Ted Williams, Bos	.406	1965	Tony Oliva, Min	.321
1918	Ty Cobb, Det	.382	1942	Ted Williams, Bos.	.356	1966	Frank Robinson, Bal	.316
1919	Ty Cobb, Det	.384	1943	Luke Appling, Chi.	.328	1967	Carl Yastrzemski, Bos.	.326
1920	George Sisler, St.L	.407	1944	Lou Boudreau, Clev.	.327	1968	Carl Yastrzemski, Bos.	.301
1921	Harry Heilmann, Det	.394	1945	Snuffy Stirnweiss, NY.	.309	1969	Rod Carew, Min	.332
1922	George Sisler, St.L	.420	1946	Mickey Vernon, Wash.	.353	1970	Alex Johnson, Cal.	.329
1923	Harry Heilmann, Det	.403	1947	Ted Williams, Bos	.343	1971	Tony Oliva, Min	.337
1924	Babe Ruth, NY	.378	1948	Ted Williams, Bos	.369	1972	Rod Carew, Min	.318

Batting Average (Cont.)

Year		Avg	Year		Avg	Year		Avg
1973	Rod Carew, Min	.350	1985	Wade Boggs, Bos.	.368	1997	Frank Thomas, Chi	.347
1974	Rod Carew, Min	.364	1986	Wade Boggs, Bos.	.357	1998	Bernie Williams, NY.	.339
1975	Rod Carew, Min	.359	1987	Wade Boggs, Bos.	.363	1999	Nomar Garciaparra, Bos.	.357
1976	George Brett, KC	.333	1988	Wade Boggs, Bos.	.366	2000	Nomar Garciaparra, Bos.	.372
1977	Rod Carew, Min	.388	1989	Kirby Puckett, Min.	.339	2001	Ichiro Suzuki, Sea.	.350
1978	Rod Carew, Min	.333	1990	George Brett, KC	.329	2002	Manny Ramirez, Bos.	.349
1979	Fred Lynn, Bos	.333	1991	Julio Franco, Tex	.341	2003	Bill Mueller, Bos.	.326
1980	George Brett, KC	.390	1992	Edgar Martinez, Sea.	.343	2004	Ichiro Suzuki, Sea.	.372
1981	Carney Lansford, Bos.	.336	1993	John Olerud, Tor	.363	2005	Michael Young, Tex.	.331
1982	Willie Wilson, KC.	.332	1994	Paul O'Neill, NY	.359	2006	Joe Mauer, Min.	.347
1983	Wade Boggs, Bos.	.361	1995	Edgar Martinez, Sea.	.356			
1984	Don Mattingly, NY	.343	1996	Alex Rodriguez, Sea.	.358			

*Norm Cash later admitted to using a corked bat the entire season. He played 16 other seasons and never hit better than .286.

Home Runs
National League

Multiple winners: Mike Schmidt (8); Ralph Kiner (7); Gavvy Cravath and Mel Ott (6); Hank Aaron, Chuck Klein, Willie Mays, Johnny Mize, Cy Williams and Hack Wilson (4); Willie McCovey (3); Ernie Banks, Johnny Bench, Barry Bonds, George Foster, Rogers Hornsby, Tim Jordan, Dave Kingman, Eddie Mathews, Mark McGwire, Dale Murphy, Bill Nicholson, Dave Robertson, Wildfire Schulte, Sammy Sosa and Willie Stargell (2).

Year		HR	Year		HR	Year		HR
1900	Herman Long, Bos	12	1934	Rip Collins, St.L	35	1968	Willie McCovey, SF	36
1901	Sam Crawford, Cin.	16		& Mel Ott, NY.	35	1969	Willie McCovey, SF	45
1902	Tommy Leach, Pit	6	1935	Wally Berger, Bos.	34	1970	Johnny Bench, Cin	45
1903	Jimmy Sheckard, Bklyn	9	1936	Mel Ott, NY.	33	1971	Willie Stargell, Pit.	48
1904	Harry Lumley, Bklyn	9	1937	Joe Medwick, St.L.	31	1972	Johnny Bench, Cin	40
1905	Fred Odwell, Cin.	9		& Mel Ott, NY.	31	1973	Willie Stargell, Pit.	44
1906	Tim Jordan, Bklyn	12	1938	Mel Ott, NY.	36	1974	Mike Schmidt, Phi.	36
1907	Dave Brain, Bos	10	1939	Johnny Mize, St.L	28	1975	Mike Schmidt, Phi.	38
1908	Tim Jordan, Bklyn	12	1940	Johnny Mize, St.L	43	1976	Mike Schmidt, Phi.	38
1909	Red Murray, NY	7	1941	Dolph Camilli, Bklyn.	34	1977	George Foster, Cin	52
1910	Fred Beck, Bos.	10	1942	Mel Ott, NY.	30	1978	George Foster, Cin	40
	& Wildfire Schulte, Chi	10	1943	Bill Nicholson, Chi	29	1979	Dave Kingman, Chi	48
1911	Wildfire Schulte, Chi	21	1944	Bill Nicholson, Chi	33	1980	Mike Schmidt, Phi.	48
1912	Heinie Zimmerman, Chi.	14	1945	Tommy Holmes, Bos	28	1981	Mike Schmidt, Phi.	31
1913	Gavvy Cravath, Phi.	19	1946	Ralph Kiner, Pit.	23	1982	Dave Kingman, NY.	37
1914	Gavvy Cravath, Phi.	19	1947	Ralph Kiner, Pit.	51	1983	Mike Schmidt, Phi.	40
1915	Gavvy Cravath, Phi.	24		& Johnny Mize, NY	51	1984	Dale Murphy, Atl.	36
1916	Cy Williams, Chi	12	1948	Ralph Kiner, Pit.	40		& Mike Schmidt, Phi.	36
	& Dave Robertson, NY.	12		& Johnny Mize, NY	40	1985	Dale Murphy, Atl.	37
1917	Gavvy Cravath, Phi.	12	1949	Ralph Kiner, Pit.	54	1986	Mike Schmidt, Phi.	37
	& Dave Robertson, NY.	12	1950	Ralph Kiner, Pit.	47	1987	Andre Dawson, Chi	49
1918	Gavvy Cravath, Phi.	8	1951	Ralph Kiner, Pit.	42	1988	Darryl Strawberry, NY.	39
1919	Gavvy Cravath, Phi.	12	1952	Ralph Kiner, Pit.	37	1989	Kevin Mitchell, SF	47
1920	Cy Williams, Phi.	15		& Hank Sauer, Chi	37	1990	Ryne Sandberg, Chi	40
1921	George Kelly, NY	23	1953	Eddie Mathews, Mil	47	1991	Howard Johnson, NY.	38
1922	Rogers Hornsby, St.L.	42	1954	Ted Kluszewski, Cin	49	1992	Fred McGriff, SD	35
1923	Cy Williams, Phi.	41	1955	Willie Mays, NY.	51	1993	Barry Bonds, SF	46
1924	Jack Fournier, Bklyn	27	1956	Duke Snider, Bklyn	43	1994	Matt Williams, SF	43
1925	Rogers Hornsby, St.L.	39	1957	Hank Aaron, Mil.	44	1995	Dante Bichette, Col.	40
1926	Hack Wilson, Chi	21	1958	Ernie Banks, Chi.	47	1996	Andres Galarraga, Col	47
1927	Cy Williams, Phi.	30	1959	Eddie Mathews, Mil	46	1997	Larry Walker, Col	49
	& Hack Wilson, Chi	30	1960	Ernie Banks, Chi.	41	1998	Mark McGwire, St.L	70
1928	Jim Bottomley, St.L.	31	1961	Orlando Cepeda, SF.	46	1999	Mark McGwire, St.L.	65
	& Hack Wilson, Chi	31	1962	Willie Mays, SF	49	2000	Sammy Sosa, Chi	50
1929	Chuck Klein, Phi	43	1963	Hank Aaron, Mil.	44	2001	Barry Bonds, SF	73
1930	Hack Wilson, Chi	56		& Willie McCovey, SF.	44	2002	Sammy Sosa, Chi	49
1931	Chuck Klein, Phi.	31	1964	Willie Mays, SF	47	2003	Jim Thome, Phi	47
1932	Chuck Klein, Phi.	38	1965	Willie Mays, SF	52	2004	Adrian Beltre, LA	48
	& Mel Ott, NY.	38	1966	Hank Aaron, Atl	44	2005	Andruw Jones, Atl.	51
1933	Chuck Klein, Phi.	28	1967	Hank Aaron, Atl	39	2006	Ryan Howard, Phi.	58

Note: In 1997 Mark McGwire hit 58 home runs but hit 34 of them in the AL with Oakland before his trade to St. Louis.

American League

Multiple winners: Babe Ruth (12); Harmon Killebrew (6); Home Run Baker, Harry Davis, Jimmie Foxx, Hank Greenberg, Ken Griffey Jr., Reggie Jackson, Mickey Mantle, Alex Rodriguez and Ted Williams (4); Lou Gehrig and Jim Rice (3); Dick Allen, Tony Armas, Jose Canseco, Joe DiMaggio, Larry Doby, Cecil Fielder, Juan Gonzalez, Mark McGwire, Wally Pipp, Al Rosen and Gorman Thomas (2).

Year		HR	Year		HR	Year		HR
1901	Nap Lajoie, Phi	14	1904	Harry Davis, Phi	10	1907	Harry Davis, Phi.	8
1902	Socks Seybold, Phi	16	1905	Harry Davis, Phi.	8	1908	Sam Crawford, Det.	7
1903	Buck Freeman, Bos	13	1906	Harry Davis, Phi.	12	1909	Ty Cobb, Det	9

Year	HR
1910	Jake Stahl, Bos 10
1911	Home Run Baker, Phi. 11
1912	Home Run Baker, Phi 10
	& Tris Speaker, Bos. 10
1913	Home Run Baker, Phi. . . .12
1914	Home Run Baker, Phi. 9
1915	Braggo Roth, Chi-Cle 7
1916	Wally Pipp, NY. 12
1917	Wally Pipp, NY 9
1918	Babe Ruth, Bos. 11
	& Tilly Walker, Phi 11
1919	Babe Ruth, Bos. 29
1920	Babe Ruth, NY 54
1921	Babe Ruth, NY 59
1922	Ken Williams, St.L. 39
1923	Babe Ruth, NY 41
1924	Babe Ruth, NY 46
1925	Bob Meusel, NY. 33
1926	Babe Ruth, NY 47
1927	Babe Ruth, NY 60
1928	Babe Ruth, NY 54
1929	Babe Ruth, NY 46
1930	Babe Ruth, NY 49
1931	Lou Gehrig, NY. 46
	& Babe Ruth, NY 46
1932	Jimmie Foxx, Phi 58
1933	Jimmie Foxx, Phi. 48
1934	Lou Gehrig, NY. 49
1935	Jimmie Foxx, Phi. 36
	& Hank Greenberg, Det. . . 36
1936	Lou Gehrig, NY. 49
1937	Joe DiMaggio, NY 46
1938	Hank Greenberg, Det. . . . 58
1939	Jimmie Foxx, Bos. 35
1940	Hank Greenberg, Det. . . . 41
1941	Ted Williams, Bos 37
1942	Ted Williams, Bos 36

Year	HR
1943	Rudy York, Det. 34
1944	Nick Etten, NY 22
1945	Vern Stephens, St.L 24
1946	Hank Greenberg, Det. . . . 44
1947	Ted Williams, Bos. 32
1948	Joe DiMaggio, NY 39
1949	Ted Williams, Bos 43
1950	Al Rosen, Cle. 37
1951	Gus Zernial, Chi-Phi 33
1952	Larry Doby, Cle. 32
1953	Al Rosen, Cle. 43
1954	Larry Doby, Cle. 32
1955	Mickey Mantle, NY. 37
1956	Mickey Mantle, NY. 52
1957	Roy Sievers, Wash 42
1958	Mickey Mantle, NY. 42
1959	Rocky Colavito, Cle 42
	& Harmon Killebrew, Wash .42
1960	Mickey Mantle, NY. 40
1961	Roger Maris, NY. 61
1962	Harmon Killebrew, Min. . . 48
1963	Harmon Killebrew, Min. . . 45
1964	Harmon Killebrew, Min. . . 49
1965	Tony Conigliaro, Bos. 32
1966	Frank Robinson, Bal 49
1967	Harmon Killebrew, Min . . . 44
	& Carl Yastrzemski, Bos. . . 44
1968	Frank Howard, Wash. 44
1969	Harmon Killebrew, Min . . . 49
1970	Frank Howard, Wash. 44
1971	Bill Melton, Chi 33
1972	Dick Allen, Chi. 37
1973	Reggie Jackson, Oak 32
1974	Dick Allen, Chi. 32
1975	Reggie Jackson, Oak 36
	& George Scott, Mil 36

Year	HR
1976	Graig Nettles, NY 32
1977	Jim Rice, Bos 39
1978	Jim Rice, Bos 46
1979	Gorman Thomas, Mil 45
1980	Reggie Jackson, NY 41
	& Ben Oglivie, Mil 41
1981	Tony Armas, Oak 22
	Dwight Evans, Bos 22
	Bobby Grich, Cal 22
	& Eddie Murray, Bal. 22
1982	Reggie Jackson, Cal. 39
	& Gorman Thomas, Mil. . . 39
1983	Jim Rice, Bos 39
1984	Tony Armas, Bos. 43
1985	Darrell Evans, Det. 40
1986	Jesse Barfield, Tor 40
1987	Mark McGwire, Oak 49
1988	Jose Canseco, Oak. 42
1989	Fred McGriff, Tor 36
1990	Cecil Fielder, Det 51
1991	Jose Canseco, Oak. 44
	& Cecil Fielder, Det. 44
1992	Juan Gonzalez, Tex. 43
1993	Juan Gonzalez, Tex. 46
1994	Ken Griffey Jr., Sea. 40
1995	Albert Belle, Cle 50
1996	Mark McGwire, Oak 52
1997	Ken Griffey Jr., Sea. 56
1998	Ken Griffey Jr., Sea. 56
1999	Ken Griffey Jr., Sea. 48
2000	Troy Glaus, Ana 47
2001	Alex Rodriguez, Tex 52
2002	Alex Rodriguez, Tex 57
2003	Alex Rodriguez, Tex 47
2004	Manny Ramirez, Bos. 43
2005	Alex Rodriguez, NY 48
2006	David Ortiz, Bos. 54

Runs Batted In
National League

Multiple winners: Hank Aaron, Rogers Hornsby, Sherry Magee, Mike Schmidt and Honus Wagner (4); Johnny Bench, George Foster, Joe Medwick, Johnny Mize and Heinie Zimmerman (3); Ernie Banks, Jim Bottomley, Orlando Cepeda, Gavvy Cravath, Andres Galarraga, George Kelly, Chuck Klein, Willie McCovey, Dale Murphy, Stan Musial, Bill Nicholson, Sammy Sosa and Hack Wilson (2).

Year	RBI
1900	Elmer Flick, Phi 110
1901	Honus Wagner, Pit 126
1902	Honus Wagner, Pit 91
1903	Sam Mertes, NY. 104
1904	Bill Dahlen, NY 80
1905	Cy Seymour, Cin 121
1906	Jim Nealon, Pit. 83
	& Harry Steinfeldt, Chi. . . 83
1907	Sherry Magee, Phi 85
1908	Honus Wagner, Pit 109
1909	Honus Wagner, Pit 100
1910	Sherry Magee, Phi 123
1911	Wildfire Schulte, Chi. . . . 121
1912	Heinie Zimmerman, Chi. . . 103
1913	Gavvy Cravath, Phi. 128
1914	Sherry Magee, Phi 103
1915	Gavvy Cravath, Phi. 115
1916	Heinie Zimmerman, Chi-NY .83
1917	Heinie Zimmerman, NY. . . 102
1918	Sherry Magee, Cin. 76
1919	Hy Myers, Bklyn 73
1920	Rogers Hornsby, St.L. . . . 94
	& George Kelly, NY 94
1921	Rogers Hornsby, St.L . . . 126
1922	Rogers Hornsby, St.L . . . 152
1923	Irish Meusel, NY. 125
1924	George Kelly, NY. 136
1925	Rogers Hornsby, St.L . . . 143

Year	RBI
1926	Jim Bottomley, St.L. 120
1927	Paul Waner, Pit. 131
1928	Jim Bottomley, St.L. 136
1929	Hack Wilson, Chi. 159
1930	Hack Wilson, Chi. 191
1931	Chuck Klein, Phi 121
1932	Don Hurst, Phi. 143
1933	Chuck Klein, Phi 120
1934	Mel Ott, NY. 135
1935	Wally Berger, Bos 130
1936	Joe Medwick, St.L. 138
1937	Joe Medwick, St.L. 154
1938	Joe Medwick, St.L. 122
1939	Frank McCormick, Cin . . . 128
1940	Johnny Mize, St.L 137
1941	Dolph Camilli, Bklyn 120
1942	Johnny Mize, NY 110
1943	Bill Nicholson, Chi 128
1944	Bill Nicholson, Chi 122
1945	Dixie Walker, Bklyn 124
1946	Enos Slaughter, St.L. 130
1947	Johnny Mize, NY 138
1948	Stan Musial, St.L 131
1949	Ralph Kiner, Pit. 127
1950	Del Ennis, Phi 126
1951	Monte Irvin, NY 121
1952	Hank Sauer, Chi. 121
1953	Roy Campanella, Bklyn . . 142

Year	RBI
1954	Ted Kluszewski, Cin 141
1955	Duke Snider, Bklyn 136
1956	Stan Musial, St.L. 109
1957	Hank Aaron, Mil 132
1958	Ernie Banks, Chi. 129
1959	Ernie Banks, Chi. 143
1960	Hank Aaron, Mil 126
1961	Orlando Cepeda, SF. 142
1962	Tommy Davis, LA 153
1963	Hank Aaron, Mil 130
1964	Ken Boyer, St.L. 119
1965	Deron Johnson, Cin. 130
1966	Hank Aaron, Atl 127
1967	Orlando Cepeda, St.L. . . . 111
1968	Willie McCovey, SF 105
1969	Willie McCovey, SF 126
1970	Johnny Bench, Cin 148
1971	Joe Torre, St.L. 137
1972	Johnny Bench, Cin 125
1973	Willie Stargell, Pit. 119
1974	Johnny Bench, Cin 129
1975	Greg Luzinski, Phi. 120
1976	George Foster, Cin. 121
1977	George Foster, Cin. 149
1978	George Foster, Cin. 120
1979	Dave Winfield, SD 118
1980	Mike Schmidt, Phi. 121
1981	Mike Schmidt, Phi. 91

Runs Batted In (Cont.)

Year		RBI
1982	Dale Murphy, Atl	109
	& Al Oliver, Mon	109
1983	Dale Murphy, Atl	121
1984	Gary Carter, Mon.	106
	& Mike Schmidt, Phi.	106
1985	Dave Parker, Cin	125
1986	Mike Schmidt, Phi.	119
1987	Andre Dawson, Chi	137
1988	Will Clark, SF	109

Year		RBI
1989	Kevin Mitchell, SF.	125
1990	Matt Williams, SF.	122
1991	Howard Johnson, NY	117
1992	Darren Daulton, Phi.	109
1993	Barry Bonds, SF	123
1994	Jeff Bagwell, Hou	116
1995	Dante Bichette, Col	128
1996	Andres Galarraga, Col.	150
1997	Andres Galarraga, Col.	140

Year		RBI
1998	Sammy Sosa, Chi.	158
1999	Mark McGwire, St.L.	147
2000	Todd Helton, Col	147
2001	Sammy Sosa, Chi.	160
2002	Lance Berkman, Hou	128
2003	Preston Wilson, Col	141
2004	Vinny Castilla, Col	131
2005	Andruw Jones, Atl.	128
2006	Ryan Howard, Phi.	149

Multiple winners: Babe Ruth (6); Lou Gehrig (5); Ty Cobb, Hank Greenberg and Ted Williams (4); Albert Belle, Sam Crawford, Cecil Fielder, Jimmie Foxx, Jackie Jensen, Harmon Killebrew, Vern Stephens and Bobby Veach (3); Home Run Baker, Cecil Cooper, Harry Davis, Joe DiMaggio, Buck Freeman, Nap Lajoie, Roger Maris, David Ortiz, Jim Rice, Al Rosen and Bobby Veach (2).

American League

Year		RBI
1901	Nap Lajoie, Phi.	125
1902	Buck Freeman, Bos.	121
1903	Buck Freeman, Bos.	104
1904	Nap Lajoie, Cle	102
1905	Harry Davis, Phi.	83
1906	Harry Davis, Phi.	96
1907	Ty Cobb, Det.	116
1908	Ty Cobb, Det.	108
1909	Ty Cobb, Det.	107
1910	Sam Crawford, Det.	120
1911	Ty Cobb, Det.	144
1912	Home Run Baker, Phi.	133
1913	Home Run Baker, Phi.	126
1914	Sam Crawford, Det.	104
1915	Sam Crawford, Det.	112
	& Bobby Veach, Det	112
1916	Del Pratt, St.L.	103
1917	Bobby Veach, Det.	103
1918	Bobby Veach, Det.	78
1919	Babe Ruth, Bos.	114
1920	Babe Ruth, NY	137
1921	Babe Ruth, NY	171
1922	Ken Williams, St.L.	155
1923	Babe Ruth, NY	131
1924	Goose Goslin, Wash.	129
1925	Bob Meusel, NY.	138
1926	Babe Ruth, NY.	145
1927	Lou Gehrig, NY	175
1928	Lou Gehrig, NY	142
	& Babe Ruth, NY	142
1929	Al Simmons, Phi	157
1930	Lou Gehrig, NY	174
1931	Lou Gehrig, NY	184
1932	Jimmie Foxx, Phi.	169
1933	Jimmie Foxx, Phi.	163
1934	Lou Gehrig, NY	165
1935	Hank Greenberg, Det	170
1936	Hal Trosky, Cle.	162

Year		RBI
1937	Hank Greenberg, Det	183
1938	Jimmie Foxx, Bos	175
1939	Ted Williams, Bos.	145
1940	Hank Greenberg, Det	150
1941	Joe DiMaggio, NY.	125
1942	Ted Williams, Bos.	137
1943	Rudy York, Det	118
1944	Vern Stephens, St.L.	109
1945	Nick Etten, NY	111
1946	Hank Greenberg, Det	127
1947	Ted Williams, Bos.	114
1948	Joe DiMaggio, NY.	155
1949	Ted Williams, Bos.	159
	& Vern Stephens, Bos.	159
1950	Walt Dropo, Bos.	144
	& Vern Stephens, Bos.	144
1951	Gus Zernial, Chi-Phi.	129
1952	Al Rosen, Cle.	105
1953	Al Rosen, Cle.	145
1954	Larry Doby, Cle.	126
1955	Ray Boone, Det.	116
	& Jackie Jensen, Bos.	116
1956	Mickey Mantle, NY.	130
1957	Roy Sievers, Wash.	114
1958	Jackie Jensen, Bos.	122
1959	Jackie Jensen, Bos.	112
1960	Roger Maris, NY	112
1961	Roger Maris, NY	142
1962	Harmon Killebrew, Min	126
1963	Dick Stuart, Bos	118
1964	Brooks Robinson, Bal	118
1965	Rocky Colavito, Cle	108
1966	Frank Robinson, Bal	122
1967	Carl Yastrzemski, Bos	121
1968	Ken Harrelson, Bos	109
1969	Harmon Killebrew, Min	140
1970	Frank Howard, Wash	126
1971	Harmon Killebrew, Min	119

Year		RBI
1972	Dick Allen, Chi.	113
1973	Reggie Jackson, Oak.	117
1974	Jeff Burroughs, Tex	118
1975	George Scott, Mil.	109
1976	Lee May, Bal	109
1977	Larry Hisle, Min	119
1978	Jim Rice, Bos	139
1979	Don Baylor, Cal	139
1980	Cecil Cooper, Mil.	122
1981	Eddie Murray, Bal.	78
1982	Hal McRae, KC.	133
1983	Cecil Cooper, Mil.	126
	& Jim Rice, Bos.	126
1984	Tony Armas, Bos.	123
1985	Don Mattingly, NY	145
1986	Joe Carter, Cle.	121
1987	George Bell, Tor	134
1988	Jose Canseco, Oak.	124
1989	Ruben Sierra, Tex	119
1990	Cecil Fielder, Det	132
1991	Cecil Fielder, Det	133
1992	Cecil Fielder, Det	124
1993	Albert Belle, Cle.	129
1994	Kirby Puckett, Min.	112
1995	Albert Belle, Cle.	126
	& Mo Vaughn, Bos.	126
1996	Albert Belle, Cle.	148
1997	Ken Griffey Jr., Sea.	147
1998	Juan Gonzalez, Tex.	157
1999	Manny Ramirez, Cle.	165
2000	Edgar Martinez, Sea.	145
2001	Bret Boone, Sea	141
2002	Alex Rodriguez, Tex.	142
2003	Carlos Delgado, Tor	145
2004	Miguel Tejada, Bal	150
2005	David Ortiz, Bos.	148
2006	David Ortiz, Bos.	137

Batting Triple Crown Winners

Players who led either league in Batting Average, Home Runs and Runs Batted In over a single season.

National League

	Year	Avg	HR	RBI
Paul Hines, Providence	1878	.358	4	50
Hugh Duffy, Boston.	1894	.438	18	145
Heinie Zimmerman, Chicago.	1912	.372	14	103
Rogers Hornsby, St. Louis	1922	.401	42	152
Rogers Hornsby, St. Louis	1925	.403	39	143
Chuck Klein, Philadelphia	1933	.368	28	120
Joe Medwick, St. Louis	1937	.374	31*	154

*Tied for league lead in HRs with Mel Ott, NY.

American League

	Year	Avg	HR	RBI
Nap Lajoie, Philadelphia.	1901	.422	14	125
Ty Cobb, Detroit.	1909	.377	9	115
Jimmie Foxx, Philadelphia	1933	.356	48	163
Lou Gehrig, New York	1934	.363	49	165
Ted Williams, Boston	1942	.356	36	137
Ted Williams, Boston	1947	.343	32	114
Mickey Mantle, New York.	1956	.353	52	130
Frank Robinson, Baltimore.	1966	.316	49	122
Carl Yastrzemski, Boston	1967	.326	44*	121

*Tied for league lead in HRs with Harmon Killebrew, Min.

Stolen Bases
National League

Multiple winners: Max Carey (10); Lou Brock (8); Vince Coleman and Maury Wills (6); Honus Wagner (5); Bob Bescher, Kiki Cuyler, Willie Mays and Tim Raines (4); Bill Bruton, Frankie Frisch, Pepper Martin and Tony Womack (3); George Burns, Luis Castillo, Frank Chance, Augie Galan, Marquis Grissom, Stan Hack, Sam Jethroe, Davey Lopes, Omar Moreno, Pete Reiser, Jose Reyes and Jackie Robinson (2).

Year		SB	Year		SB	Year		SB
1900	Patsy Donovan, St.L	45	1935	Augie Galan, Chi	22	1972	Lou Brock, St.L	63
	& George Van Haltren, NY.	45	1936	Pepper Martin, St.L	23	1973	Lou Brock, St.L	70
1901	Honus Wagner, Pit	49	1937	Augie Galan, Chi	23	1974	Lou Brock, St.L	118
1902	Honus Wagner, Pit	42	1938	Stan Hack, Chi	16	1975	Davey Lopes, LA	77
1903	Frank Chance, Chi	67	1939	Stan Hack, Chi	17	1976	Davey Lopes, LA	63
	& Jimmy Sheckard, Bklyn.	67		& Lee Handley, Pit	17	1977	Frank Taveras, Pit	70
1904	Honus Wagner, Pit	53	1940	Lonny Frey, Cin	22	1978	Omar Moreno, Pit.	71
1905	Art Devlin, NY.	59	1941	Danny Murtaugh, Phi	18	1979	Omar Moreno, Pit.	77
	& Billy Maloney, Chi.	59	1942	Pete Reiser, Bklyn	20	1980	Ron LeFlore, Mon	97
1906	Frank Chance, Chi	57	1943	Arky Vaughan, Bklyn.	20	1981	Tim Raines, Mon.	71
1907	Honus Wagner, Pit	61	1944	Johnny Barrett, Pit	28	1982	Tim Raines, Mon.	78
1908	Honus Wagner, Pit	53	1945	Red Schoendienst, St.L.	26	1983	Tim Raines, Mon.	90
1909	Bob Bescher, Cin	54	1946	Pete Reiser, Bklyn	34	1984	Tim Raines, Mon.	75
1910	Bob Bescher, Cin	70	1947	Jackie Robinson, Bklyn.	29	1985	Vince Coleman, St.L.	110
1911	Bob Bescher, Cin	81	1948	Richie Ashburn, Phi.	32	1986	Vince Coleman, St.L.	107
1912	Bob Bescher, Cin	67	1949	Jackie Robinson, Bklyn.	37	1987	Vince Coleman, St.L.	109
1913	Max Carey, Pit	61	1950	Sam Jethroe, Bos.	35	1988	Vince Coleman, St.L	81
1914	George Burns, NY	62	1951	Sam Jethroe, Bos.	35	1989	Vince Coleman, St.L	65
1915	Max Carey, Pit	36	1952	Pee Wee Reese, Bklyn.	30	1990	Vince Coleman, St.L	77
1916	Max Carey, Pit	63	1953	Bill Bruton, Mil.	26	1991	Marquis Grissom, Mon	76
1917	Max Carey, Pit	46	1954	Bill Bruton, Mil.	34	1992	Marquis Grissom, Mon	78
1918	Max Carey, Pit	58	1955	Bill Bruton, Mil.	25	1993	Chuck Carr, Fla.	58
1919	George Burns, NY	40	1956	Willie Mays, NY	40	1994	Craig Biggio, Hou	39
1920	Max Carey, Pit	52	1957	Willie Mays, NY	38	1995	Quilvio Veras, Fla.	56
1921	Frankie Frisch, NY	49	1958	Willie Mays, SF	31	1996	Eric Young, Col	53
1922	Max Carey, Pit	51	1959	Willie Mays, SF	27	1997	Tony Womack, Pit.	60
1923	Max Carey, Pit	51	1960	Maury Wills, LA	50	1998	Tony Womack, Pit.	58
1924	Max Carey, Pit	49	1961	Maury Wills, LA	35	1999	Tony Womack, Ari	72
1925	Max Carey, Pit	46	1962	Maury Wills, LA	104	2000	Luis Castillo, Fla	62
1926	Kiki Cuyler, Pit.	35	1963	Maury Wills, LA	40	2001	Juan Pierre, Col.	46
1927	Frankie Frisch, St.L	48	1964	Maury Wills, LA	53		& Jimmy Rollins, Phi	46
1928	Kiki Cuyler, Chi.	37	1965	Maury Wills, LA	94	2002	Luis Castillo, Fla	48
1929	Kiki Cuyler, Chi.	43	1966	Lou Brock, St.L	74	2003	Juan Pierre, Fla.	65
1930	Kiki Cuyler, Chi.	37	1967	Lou Brock, St.L	52	2004	Scott Podsednik, Mil	70
1931	Frankie Frisch, St.L	28	1968	Lou Brock, St.L	62	2005	Jose Reyes, NY.	60
1932	Chuck Klein, Phi	20	1969	Lou Brock, St.L	53	2006	Jose Reyes, NY.	64
1933	Pepper Martin, St.L.	26	1970	Bobby Tolan, Cin	57			
1934	Pepper Martin, St.L.	23	1971	Lou Brock, St.L	64			

30 Homers & 30 Stolen Bases in One Season

National League

	Year	Gm	HR	SB
Willie Mays, NY Giants	1956	152	36	40
Willie Mays, NY Giants	1957	152	35	38
Hank Aaron, Milwaukee	1963	161	44	31
Bobby Bonds, San Francisco	1969	158	32	45
Bobby Bonds, San Francisco	1973	160	39	43
Dale Murphy, Atlanta	1983	162	36	30
Eric Davis, Cincinnati	1987	129	37	50
Howard Johnson, NY Mets.	1987	157	36	32
Darryl Strawberry, NY Mets	1987	154	39	36
Howard Johnson, NY Mets.	1989	153	36	41
Ron Gant, Atlanta	1990	152	32	33
Barry Bonds, Pittsburgh	1990	151	33	52
Ron Gant, Atlanta	1991	154	32	34
Howard Johnson, NY Mets.	1991	156	38	30
Barry Bonds, Pittsburgh	1992	140	34	39
Sammy Sosa, Chicago	1993	159	33	36
Barry Bonds, San Francisco	1995	144	33	31
Sammy Sosa, Chicago	1995	144	36	34
Barry Bonds, San Francisco	1996	158	42	40
Ellis Burks, Colorado	1996	156	40	32
Dante Bichette, Colorado	1996	159	31	31
Barry Larkin, Cincinnati.	1996	152	33	36
Larry Walker, Colorado	1997	153	49	33
Barry Bonds, San Francisco	1997	159	40	37

	Year	Gm	HR	SB
Raul Mondesi, Los Angeles.	1997	159	30	32
Jeff Bagwell, Houston	1997	162	43	31
Jeff Bagwell, Houston	1999	162	42	30
Raul Mondesi, Los Angeles.	1999	159	33	36
Preston Wilson, Florida	2000	161	31	36
Vladimir Guerrero, Montreal	2001	159	34	37
Bobby Abreu, Philadelphia.	2001	162	31	36
Vladimir Guerrero, Montreal	2002	161	39	40
Bobby Abreu, Philadelphia.	2004	159	30	40
Alfonso Soriano, Washington	2006	159	46	41

American League

	Year	Gm	HR	SB
Kenny Williams, St. Louis	1922	153	39	37
Tommy Harper, Milwaukee.	1970	154	31	38
Bobby Bonds, New York.	1975	145	32	30
Bobby Bonds, California.	1977	158	37	41
Bobby Bonds, Chicago-Texas.	1978	156	31	43
Joe Carter, Cleveland	1987	149	32	31
Jose Canseco, Oakland	1988	158	42	40
Alex Rodriguez, Seattle.	1998	161	42	46
Shawn Green, Toronto	1998	158	35	35
Jose Cruz Jr., Toronto.	2001	146	34	32
Alfonso Soriano, New York	2002	156	39	41
Alfonso Soriano, New York	2003	156	38	35
Alfonso Soriano, Texas.	2005	156	36	30

Note: In 2004, Carlos Beltran switched leagues mid-season. Combining his AL and NL totals, he hit 38 HR and stole 42 bases.

Stolen Bases (Cont.)
American League

Multiple winners: Rickey Henderson (12); Luis Aparicio (9); Bert Campaneris, George Case and Ty Cobb (6); Kenny Lofton (5); Ben Chapman, Eddie Collins and George Sisler (4); Carl Crawford, Bob Dillinger, Minnie Minoso and Bill Werber (3); Elmer Flick, Tommy Harper, Brian Hunter, Clyde Milan, Johnny Mostil, Bill North and Snuffy Stirnweiss (2).

Year		SB	Year		SB	Year		SB
1901	Frank Isbell, Chi	52	1936	Lyn Lary, St.L	37	1971	Amos Otis, KC	52
1902	Topsy Hartsel, Phi	47	1937	Ben Chapman, Wash-Bos	35	1972	Bert Campaneris, Oak.	52
1903	Harry Bay, Cle	45		& Bill Werber, Phi	35	1973	Tommy Harper, Bos	54
1904	Elmer Flick, Cle	42	1938	Frank Crosetti, NY	27	1974	Bill North, Oak.	54
1905	Danny Hoffman, Phi	46	1939	George Case, Wash	51	1975	Mickey Rivers, CA	70
1906	John Anderson, Wash	39	1940	George Case, Wash	35	1976	Bill North, Oak.	75
	& Elmer Flick, Cle	39	1941	George Case, Wash	33	1977	Freddie Patek, KC.	53
1907	Ty Cobb, Det	49	1942	George Case, Wash	44	1978	Ron LeFlore, Det	68
1908	Patsy Dougherty, Chi	47	1943	George Case, Wash	61	1979	Willie Wilson, KC.	83
1909	Ty Cobb, Det	76	1944	Snuffy Stirnweiss, NY.	55	1980	Rickey Henderson, Oak.	100
1910	Eddie Collins, Phi	81	1945	Snuffy Stirnweiss, NY.	33	1981	Rickey Henderson, Oak.	56
1911	Ty Cobb, Det	83	1946	George Case, Cle	28	1982	Rickey Henderson, Oak.	130
1912	Clyde Milan, Wash.	88	1947	Bob Dillinger, St.L	34	1983	Rickey Henderson, Oak.	108
1913	Clyde Milan, Wash.	75	1948	Bob Dillinger, St.L	28	1984	Rickey Henderson, Oak.	66
1914	Fritz Maisel, NY	74	1949	Bob Dillinger, St.L	20	1985	Rickey Henderson, NY.	80
1915	Ty Cobb, Det	96	1950	Dom DiMaggio, Bos.	15	1986	Rickey Henderson, NY.	87
1916	Ty Cobb, Det	68	1951	Minnie Minoso, Cle-Chi.	31	1987	Harold Reynolds, Sea	60
1917	Ty Cobb, Det	55	1952	Minnie Minoso, Chi	22	1988	Rickey Henderson, NY.	93
1918	George Sisler, St.L	45	1953	Minnie Minoso, Chi	25	1989	R. Henderson, NY-Oak	77
1919	Eddie Collins, Chi.	33	1954	Jackie Jensen, Bos.	22	1990	Rickey Henderson, Oak.	65
1920	Sam Rice, Wash.	63	1955	Jim Rivera, Chi.	25	1991	Rickey Henderson, Oak.	58
1921	George Sisler, St.L	35	1956	Luis Aparicio, Chi.	21	1992	Kenny Lofton, Cle	66
1922	George Sisler, St.L	51	1957	Luis Aparicio, Chi.	28	1993	Kenny Lofton, Cle	70
1923	Eddie Collins, Chi.	47	1958	Luis Aparicio, Chi.	29	1994	Kenny Lofton, Cle	60
1924	Eddie Collins, Chi.	42	1959	Luis Aparicio, Chi.	56	1995	Kenny Lofton, Cle	54
1925	Johnny Mostil, Chi	43	1960	Luis Aparicio, Chi.	51	1996	Kenny Lofton, Cle	75
1926	Johnny Mostil, Chi	35	1961	Luis Aparicio, Chi.	53	1997	Brian Hunter, Det	74
1927	George Sisler, St.L	27	1962	Luis Aparicio, Chi.	31	1998	Rickey Henderson, Oak.	66
1928	Buddy Myer, Bos.	30	1963	Luis Aparicio, Bal	40	1999	Brian Hunter, Det-Sea.	44
1929	Charlie Gehringer, Det.	28	1964	Luis Aparicio, Bal	57	2000	Johnny Damon, KC.	46
1930	Marty McManus, Det	23	1965	Bert Campaneris, KC	51	2001	Ichiro Suzuki, Sea.	56
1931	Ben Chapman, NY.	61	1966	Bert Campaneris, KC	52	2002	Alfonso Soriano, NY	41
1932	Ben Chapman, NY.	38	1967	Bert Campaneris, KC	55	2003	Carl Crawford, TB	55
1933	Ben Chapman, NY.	27	1968	Bert Campaneris, Oak.	62	2004	Carl Crawford, TB	59
1934	Bill Werber, Bos	40	1969	Tommy Harper, Sea	73	2005	Chone Figgins, LAA	62
1935	Bill Werber, Bos	29	1970	Bert Campaneris, Oak.	42	2006	Carl Crawford, TB	58

Consecutive Game Streaks
(Regular season games through 2006)

Games Played

Gm		Dates of Streak
2632	Cal Ripken Jr., Bal	5/30/82 to 9/19/98
2130	Lou Gehrig, NY	6/1/25 to 4/30/39
1307	Everett Scott, Bos-NY	6/20/16 to 5/5/25
1207	Steve Garvey, LA-SD.	9/3/75 to 7/29/83
1117	Billy Williams, Cubs	9/22/63 to 9/2/70
1103	Joe Sewell, Cle	9/13/22 to 4/30/30
1080	Miguel Tejada, Oak-Bal	6/1/00 to present
895	Stan Musial, St.L	4/15/52 to 8/23/57
829	Eddie Yost, Wash	4/30/49 to 5/11/55
822	Gus Suhr, Pit	9/11/31 to 6/4/37
798	Nellie Fox, Chisox.	8/8/55 to 9/3/60
745	Pete Rose, Cin-Phi	9/2/78 to 8/23/83
740	Dale Murphy, Atl.	9/26/81 to 7/8/86
730	Richie Ashburn, Phi	6/7/50 to 4/13/55
717	Ernie Banks, Cubs.	8/28/56 to 6/22/61
678	Pete Rose, Cin	9/28/73 to 5/7/78

Others

Gm		Gm	
673	Earl Averill	577	George Pinckney
652	Frank McCormick	574	Steve Brodie
648	Sandy Alomar Sr.	565	Aaron Ward
618	Eddie Brown	546	Alex Rodriguez
585	Roy McMillan	540	Candy LaChance

Hitting

	Gm	Year
Joe DiMaggio, New York (AL)	56	1941
Willie Keeler, Baltimore (NL).	44	1897
Pete Rose, Cincinnati (NL)	44	1978
Bill Dahlen, Chicago (NL)	42	1894
George Sisler, St. Louis (AL)	41	1922
Ty Cobb, Detroit (AL)	40	1911
Paul Molitor, Milwaukee (AL)	39	1987
Jimmy Rollins, Philadelphia (NL)	38	2005-06
Tommy Holmes, Boston (NL)	37	1945
Billy Hamilton, Philadelphia (NL)	36	1894
Fred Clarke, Louisville (NL)	35	1895
Ty Cobb, Detroit (AL)	35	1917
Luis Castillo, Florida (NL).	35	2002
Chase Utley, Philadelphia (NL)	35	2006
Ty Cobb, Detroit (AL)	34	1912
George Sisler, St. Louis (AL)	34	1925
George McQuinn, St. Louis (AL).	34	1938
Dom DiMaggio, Boston (AL)	34	1949
Benito Santiago, San Diego (NL)	34	1987
George Davis, New York (NL)	33	1893
Hal Chase, New York (AL)	33	1907
Rogers Hornsby, St. Louis (NL)	33	1922
Heinie Manush, Washington (AL).	33	1933

Note: Rollins had a 36-game streak at the end of 2005.

Annual Pitching Leaders (since 1900)
Winning Percentage
At least 15 wins, except in strike years of 1981 and 1994 (when the minimum was 10).

National League

Multiple winners: Ed Reulbach and Tom Seaver (3); Larry Benton, Harry Brecheen, Jack Chesbro, Paul Derringer, Freddie Fitzsimmons, Don Gullett, Claude Hendrix, Carl Hubbell, Randy Johnson, Sandy Koufax, Bill Lee, Greg Maddux, Christy Mathewson, Don Newcombe, Preacher Roe and John Smoltz (2).

Year		W-L	Pct	Year		W-L	Pct
1900	Jesse Tannehill, Pittsburgh	20-6	.769	1956	Don Newcombe, Brooklyn	27-7	.794
1901	Jack Chesbro, Pittsburgh	21-10	.677	1957	Bob Buhl, Milwaukee	18-7	.720
1902	Jack Chesbro, Pittsburgh	28-6	.824	1958	Warren Spahn, Milwaukee	22-11	.667
1903	Sam Leever, Pittsburgh	25-7	.781		& Lew Burdette, Milwaukee	20-10	.667
1904	Joe McGinnity, New York	35-8	.814	1959	Roy Face, Pittsburgh	18-1	.947
1905	Christy Mathewson, New York	31-8	.795				
1906	Ed Reulbach, Chicago	19-4	.826	1960	Ernie Broglio, St. Louis	21-9	.700
1907	Ed Reulbach, Chicago	17-4	.810	1961	Johnny Podres, Los Angeles	18-5	.783
1908	Ed Reulbach, Chicago	24-7	.774	1962	Bob Purkey, Cincinnati	23-5	.821
1909	Howie Camnitz, Pittsburgh	25-6	.806	1963	Ron Perranoski, Los Angeles	16-3	.842
	& Christy Mathewson, New York	25-6	.806	1964	Sandy Koufax, Los Angeles	19-5	.792
				1965	Sandy Koufax, Los Angeles	26-8	.765
1910	King Cole, Chicago	20-4	.833	1966	Juan Marichal, San Francisco	25-6	.806
1911	Rube Marquard, New York	24-7	.774	1967	Dick Hughes, St. Louis	16-6	.727
1912	Claude Hendrix, Pittsburgh	24-9	.727	1968	Steve Blass, Pittsburgh	18-6	.750
1913	Bert Humphries, Chicago	16-4	.800	1969	Tom Seaver, New York	25-7	.781
1914	Bill James, Boston	26-7	.788				
1915	Grover Alexander, Phila.	31-10	.756	1970	Bob Gibson, St. Louis	23-7	.767
1916	Tom Hughes, Boston	16-3	.842	1971	Don Gullett, Cincinnati	16-6	.727
1917	Ferdie Schupp, New York	21-7	.750	1972	Gary Nolan, Cincinnati	15-5	.750
1918	Claude Hendrix, Chicago	19-7	.731	1973	Tommy John, Los Angeles	16-7	.696
1919	Dutch Ruether, Cincinnati	19-6	.760	1974	Andy Messersmith, Los Angeles	20-6	.769
				1975	Don Gullett, Cincinnati	15-4	.789
1920	Burleigh Grimes, Brooklyn	23-11	.676	1976	Steve Carlton, Philadelphia	20-7	.741
1921	Bill Doak, St. Louis	15-6	.714	1977	John Candelaria, Pittsburgh	20-5	.800
1922	Pete Donohue, Cincinnati	18-9	.667	1978	Gaylord Perry, San Diego	21-6	.778
1923	Dolf Luque, Cincinnati	27-8	.771	1979	Tom Seaver, Cincinnati	16-6	.727
1924	Emil Yde, Pittsburgh	16-3	.842				
1925	Bill Sherdel, St. Louis	15-6	.714	1980	Jim Bibby, Pittsburgh	19-6	.760
1926	Ray Kremer, Pittsburgh	20-6	.769	1981	Tom Seaver, Cincinnati	14-2	.875
1927	Larry Benton, Boston-NY	17-7	.708	1982	Phil Niekro, Atlanta	17-4	.810
1928	Larry Benton, New York	25-9	.735	1983	John Denny, Philadelphia	19-6	.760
1929	Charlie Root, Chicago	19-6	.760	1984	Rick Sutcliffe, Chicago	16-1	.941
				1985	Orel Hershiser, Los Angeles	19-3	.864
1930	Freddie Fitzsimmons, NY	19-7	.731	1986	Bob Ojeda, New York	18-5	.783
1931	Paul Derringer, St. Louis	18-8	.692	1987	Dwight Gooden, New York	15-7	.682
1932	Lon Warneke, Chicago	22-6	.786	1988	David Cone, New York	20-3	.870
1933	Ben Cantwell, Boston	20-10	.667	1989	Mike Bielecki, Chicago	18-7	.720
1934	Dizzy Dean, St. Louis	30-7	.811				
1935	Bill Lee, Chicago	20-6	.769	1990	Doug Drabek, Pittsburgh	22-6	.786
1936	Carl Hubbell, New York	26-6	.813	1991	John Smiley, Pittsburgh	20-8	.714
1937	Carl Hubbell, New York	22-8	.733		& Jose Rijo, Cincinnati	15-6	.714
1938	Bill Lee, Chicago	22-9	.710	1992	Bob Tewksbury, St. Louis	16-5	.762
1939	Paul Derringer, Cincinnati	25-7	.781	1993	Mark Portugal, Houston	18-4	.818
				1994	Marvin Freeman, Colorado	10-2	.833
1940	Freddie Fitzsimmons, Bklyn	16-2	.889	1995	Greg Maddux, Atlanta	19-2	.905
1941	Elmer Riddle, Cincinnati	19-4	.826	1996	John Smoltz, Atlanta	24-8	.750
1942	Larry French, Brooklyn	15-4	.789	1997	Greg Maddux, Atlanta	19-4	.826
1943	Mort Cooper, St. Louis	21-8	.724	1998	John Smoltz, Atlanta	17-3	.850
1944	Ted Wilks, St. Louis	17-4	.810	1999	Mike Hampton, Houston	22-4	.846
1945	Harry Brecheen, St. Louis	14-4	.778				
1946	Murray Dickson, St. Louis	15-6	.714	2000	Randy Johnson, Arizona	19-7	.731
1947	Larry Jansen, New York	21-5	.808	2001	Curt Schilling, Arizona	22-6	.786
1948	Harry Brecheen, St. Louis	20-7	.741	2002	Randy Johnson, Arizona	24-5	.828
1949	Preacher Roe, Brooklyn	15-6	.714	2003	Jason Schmidt, San Francisco	17-5	.773
				2004	Roger Clemens, Houston	18-4	.818
1950	Sal Maglie, New York	18-4	.818	2005	Chris Carpenter, St. Louis	21-5	.808
1951	Preacher Roe, Brooklyn	22-3	.880	2006	Carlos Zambrano, Chicago	16-7	.696
1952	Hoyt Wilhelm, New York	15-3	.833				
1953	Carl Erskine, Brooklyn	20-6	.769				
1954	Johnny Antonelli, New York	21-7	.750				
1955	Don Newcombe, Brooklyn	20-5	.800				

Note: In 1984, Sutcliffe was also 4-5 with Cleveland for a combined AL-NL record of 20-6 (.769).

Winning Percentage (Cont.)

American League

Multiple winners: Lefty Grove (5); Chief Bender, Roger Clemens and Whitey Ford (3); Johnny Allen, Eddie Cicotte, Mike Cuellar, Lefty Gomez, Ron Guidry, Roy Halladay, Catfish Hunter, Randy Johnson, Walter Johnson, Pedro Martinez, Jim Palmer, Pete Vuckovich and Smokey Joe Wood (2).

Year		W-L	Pct	Year		W-L	Pct
1901	Clark Griffith, Chicago	24-7	.774	1957	Dick Donovan, Chicago	16-6	.727
1902	Bill Bernhard, Phila-Cleve	18-5	.783		& Tom Sturdivant, New York	16-6	.727
1903	Cy Young, Boston	28-9	.757	ˋ1958	Bob Turley, New York	21-7	.750
1904	Jack Chesbro, New York	41-12	.774	1959	Bob Shaw, Chicago	18-6	.750
1905	Andy Coakley, Philadelphia	20-7	.741				
1906	Eddie Plank, Philadelphia	19-6	.760	1960	Jim Perry, Cleveland	18-10	.643
1907	Wild Bill Donovan, Detroit	25-4	.862	1961	Whitey Ford, New York	25-4	.862
1908	Ed Walsh, Chicago	40-15	.727	1962	Ray Herbert, Chicago	20-9	.690
1909	George Mullin, Detroit	29-8	.784	1963	Whitey Ford, New York	24-7	.774
				1964	Wally Bunker, Baltimore	19-5	.792
1910	Chief Bender, Philadelphia	23-5	.821	1965	Mudcat Grant, Minnesota	21-7	.750
1911	Chief Bender, Philadelphia	17-5	.773	1966	Sonny Siebert, Cleveland	16-8	.667
1912	Smokey Joe Wood, Boston	34-5	.872	1967	Joe Horlen, Chicago	19-7	.731
1913	Walter Johnson, Washington	36-7	.837	1968	Denny McLain, Detroit	31-6	.838
1914	Chief Bender, Philadelphia	17-3	.850	1969	Jim Palmer, Baltimore	16-4	.800
1915	Smokey Joe Wood, Boston	15-5	.750				
1916	Eddie Cicotte, Chicago	15-7	.682	1970	Mike Cuellar, Baltimore	24-8	.750
1917	Reb Russell, Chicago	15-5	.750	1971	Dave McNally, Baltimore	21-5	.808
1918	Sad Sam Jones, Boston	16-5	.762	1972	Catfish Hunter, Oakland	21-7	.750
1919	Eddie Cicotte, Chicago	29-7	.806	1973	Catfish Hunter, Oakland	21-5	.808
				1974	Mike Cuellar, Baltimore	22-10	.688
1920	Jim Bagby, Cleveland	31-12	.721	1975	Mike Torrez, Baltimore	20-9	.690
1921	Carl Mays, New York	27-9	.750	1976	Bill Campbell, Minnesota	17-5	.773
1922	Joe Bush, New York	26-7	.788	1977	Paul Splittorff, Kansas City	16-6	.727
1923	Herb Pennock, New York	19-6	.760	1978	Ron Guidry, New York	25-3	.893
1924	Walter Johnson, Washington	23-7	.767	1979	Mike Caldwell, Milwaukee	16-6	.727
1925	Stan Coveleski, Washington	20-5	.800				
1926	George Uhle, Cleveland	27-11	.711	1980	Steve Stone, Baltimore	25-7	.781
1927	Waite Hoyt, New York	22-7	.759	1981	Pete Vuckovich, Milwaukee	14-4	.778
1928	General Crowder, St. Louis	21-5	.808	1982	Pete Vuckovich, Milwaukee	18-6	.750
1929	Lefty Grove, Philadelphia	20-6	.769		& Jim Palmer, Baltimore	15-5	.750
				1983	Rich Dotson, Chicago	22-7	.759
1930	Lefty Grove, Philadelphia	28-5	.848	1984	Doyle Alexander, Toronto	17-6	.739
1931	Lefty Grove, Philadelphia	31-4	.886	1985	Ron Guidry, New York	22-6	.786
1932	Johnny Allen, New York	17-4	.810	1986	Roger Clemens, Boston	24-4	.857
1933	Lefty Grove, Philadelphia	24-8	.750	1987	Roger Clemens, Boston	20-9	.690
1934	Lefty Gomez, New York	26-5	.839	1988	Frank Viola, Minnesota	24-7	.774
1935	Eldon Auker, Detroit	18-7	.720	1989	Bret Saberhagen, Kansas City	23-6	.793
1936	Monte Pearson, New York	19-7	.731				
1937	Johnny Allen, Cleveland	15-1	.938	1990	Bob Welch, Oakland	27-6	.818
1938	Red Ruffing, New York	21-7	.750	1991	Scott Erickson, Minnesota	20-8	.714
1939	Lefty Grove, Boston	15-4	.789	1992	Mike Mussina, Baltimore	18-5	.783
				1993	Jimmy Key, New York	18-6	.750
1940	Schoolboy Rowe, Detroit	16-3	.842	1994	Jason Bere, Chicago	12-2	.857
1941	Lefty Gomez, New York	15-5	.750	1995	Randy Johnson, Seattle	18-2	.900
1942	Ernie Bonham, New York	21-5	.808	1996	Charles Nagy, Cleveland	17-5	.773
1943	Spud Chandler, New York	20-4	.833	1997	Randy Johnson, Seattle	20-4	.833
1944	Tex Hughson, Boston	18-5	.783	1998	David Wells, New York	18-4	.818
1945	Hal Newhouser, Detroit	25-9	.735	1999	Pedro Martinez, Boston	23-4	.852
1946	Boo Ferriss, Boston	25-6	.806				
1947	Allie Reynolds, New York	19-8	.704	2000	Tim Hudson, Oakland	20-6	.769
1948	Jack Kramer, Boston	18-5	.783	2001	Roger Clemens, New York	20-3	.870
1949	Ellis Kinder, Boston	23-6	.793	2002	Pedro Martinez, Boston	20-4	.833
				2003	Roy Halladay, Toronto	22-7	.759
1950	Vic Raschi, New York	21-8	.724	2004	Curt Schilling, Boston	21-6	.778
1951	Bob Feller, Cleveland	22-8	.733	2005	Cliff Lee, Cleveland	18-5	.783
1952	Bobby Shantz, Philadelphia	24-7	.774	2006	Roy Halladay, Toronto	16-5	.762
1953	Ed Lopat, New York	16-4	.800				
1954	Sandy Consuegra, Chicago	16-3	.842				
1955	Tommy Byrne, New York	16-5	.762				
1956	Whitey Ford, New York	19-6	.760				

Earned Run Average

Earned Run Averages were based on at least 10 complete games pitched (1900-49), at least 154 innings pitched (1950-60), and at least 162 innings pitched since 1961 in the AL and 1962 in the NL. In the strike years of 1981, '94 and '95, qualifiers had to pitch at least as many innings as the total number of games their team played that season.

National League

Multiple winners: Grover Alexander, Sandy Koufax and Christy Mathewson (5); Greg Maddux (4); Carl Hubbell, Randy Johnson, Tom Seaver, Warren Spahn and Dazzy Vance (3); Kevin Brown, Bill Doak, Ray Kremer, Dolf Luque, Howie Pollet, Nolan Ryan, Bill Walker and Bucky Walters (2).

Year		ERA	Year		ERA	Year		ERA
1900	Rube Waddell, Pit	2.37	1936	Carl Hubbell, NY	2.31	1972	Steve Carlton, Phi	1.97
1901	Jesse Tannehill, Pit	2.18	1937	Jim Turner, Bos	2.38	1973	Tom Seaver, NY	2.08
1902	Jack Taylor, Chi	1.33	1938	Bill Lee, Chi	2.66	1974	Buzz Capra, Atl	2.28
1903	Sam Leever, Pit	2.06	1939	Bucky Walters, Cin	2.29	1975	Randy Jones, SD	2.24
1904	Joe McGinnity, NY	1.61	1940	Bucky Walters, Cin	2.48	1976	John Denny, St.L	2.52
1905	Christy Mathewson, NY	1.27	1941	Elmer Riddle, Cin	2.24	1977	John Candelaria, Pit	2.34
1906	Three Finger Brown, Chi	1.04	1942	Mort Cooper, St.L	1.78	1978	Craig Swan, NY	2.43
1907	Jack Pfiester, Chi	1.15	1943	Howie Pollet, St.L	1.75	1979	J.R. Richard, Hou	2.71
1908	Christy Mathewson, NY	1.43	1944	Ed Heusser, Cin	2.38	1980	Don Sutton, LA	2.21
1909	Christy Mathewson, NY	1.14	1945	Hank Borowy, Chi	2.13	1981	Nolan Ryan, Hou	1.69
1910	George McQuillan, Phi	1.60	1946	Howie Pollet, St.L	2.10	1982	Steve Rogers, Mon	2.40
1911	Christy Mathewson, NY	1.99	1947	Warren Spahn, Bos	2.33	1983	Atlee Hammaker, SF	2.25
1912	Jeff Tesreau, NY	1.96	1948	Harry Brecheen, St.L	2.24	1984	Alejandro Peña, LA	2.48
1913	Christy Mathewson, NY	2.06	1949	Dave Koslo, NY	2.50	1985	Dwight Gooden, NY	1.53
1914	Bill Doak, St.L	1.72	1950	Jim Hearn, St.L-NY	2.49	1986	Mike Scott, Hou	2.22
1915	Grover Alexander, Phi	1.22	1951	Chet Nichols, Bos	2.88	1987	Nolan Ryan, Hou	2.76
1916	Grover Alexander, Phi	1.55	1952	Hoyt Wilhelm, NY	2.43	1988	Joe Magrane, St.L	2.18
1917	Grover Alexander, Phi	1.86	1953	Warren Spahn, Mil	2.10	1989	Scott Garrelts, SF	2.28
1918	Hippo Vaughn, Chi	1.74	1954	Johnny Antonelli, NY	2.30	1990	Danny Darwin, Hou	2.21
1919	Grover Alexander, Chi	1.72	1955	Bob Friend, Pit	2.83	1991	Dennis Martinez, Mon	2.39
1920	Grover Alexander, Chi	1.91	1956	Lew Burdette, Mil	2.70	1992	Bill Swift, SF	2.08
1921	Bill Doak, St.L	2.59	1957	Johnny Podres, Bklyn	2.66	1993	Greg Maddux, Atl	2.36
1922	Rosy Ryan, NY	3.01	1958	Stu Miller, SF	2.47	1994	Greg Maddux, Atl	1.56
1923	Dolf Luque, Cin	1.93	1959	Sam Jones, SF	2.83	1995	Greg Maddux, Atl	1.63
1924	Dazzy Vance, Bklyn	2.16	1960	Mike McCormick, SF	2.70	1996	Kevin Brown, Fla.	1.89
1925	Dolf Luque, Cin	2.63	1961	Warren Spahn, Mil	3.02	1997	Pedro Martinez, Mon	1.90
1926	Ray Kremer, Pit	2.61	1962	Sandy Koufax, LA	2.54	1998	Greg Maddux, Atl	2.22
1927	Ray Kremer, Pit	2.47	1963	Sandy Koufax, LA	1.88	1999	Randy Johnson, Ari.	2.48
1928	Dazzy Vance, Bklyn	2.09	1964	Sandy Koufax, LA	1.74	2000	Kevin Brown, LA	2.58
1929	Bill Walker, NY	3.09	1965	Sandy Koufax, LA	2.04	2001	Randy Johnson, Ari.	2.49
1930	Dazzy Vance, Bklyn	2.61	1966	Sandy Koufax, LA	1.73	2002	Randy Johnson, Ari.	2.32
1931	Bill Walker, NY	2.26	1967	Phil Niekro, Atl	1.87	2003	Jason Schmidt, SF	2.34
1932	Lon Warneke, Chi	2.37	1968	Bob Gibson, St.L	1.12	2004	Jake Peavy, SD	2.27
1933	Carl Hubbell, NY	1.66	1969	Juan Marichal, SF	2.10	2005	Roger Clemens, Hou	1.87
1934	Carl Hubbell, NY	2.30	1970	Tom Seaver, NY	2.81	2006	Roy Oswalt, Hou	2.98
1935	Cy Blanton, Pit	2.58	1971	Tom Seaver, NY	1.76			

Note: In 1945, Borowy had a 3.13 ERA in 18 games with New York (AL) for a combined ERA of 2.65.

American League

Multiple winners: Lefty Grove (9); Roger Clemens (6); Walter Johnson (5); Pedro Martinez (4); Spud Chandler, Stan Coveleski, Red Faber, Whitey Ford, Lefty Gomez, Ron Guidry, Addie Joss, Hal Newhouser, Jim Palmer, Gary Peters, Johan Santana, Luis Tiant and Ed Walsh (2).

Year		ERA	Year		ERA	Year		ERA
1901	Cy Young, Bos	1.62	1918	Walter Johnson, Wash	1.27	1934	Lefty Gomez, NY	2.33
1902	Ed Siever, Det	1.91	1919	Walter Johnson, Wash	1.49	1935	Lefty Grove, Bos	2.70
1903	Earl Moore, Cle	1.77	1920	Bob Shawkey, NY	2.45	1936	Lefty Grove, Bos	2.81
1904	Addie Joss, Cle	1.59	1921	Red Faber, Chi	2.48	1937	Lefty Gomez, NY	2.33
1905	Rube Waddell, Phi	1.48	1922	Red Faber, Chi	2.80	1938	Lefty Grove, Bos	3.08
1906	Doc White, Chi	1.52	1923	Stan Coveleski, Cle	2.76	1939	Lefty Grove, Bos	2.54
1907	Ed Walsh, Chi	1.60	1924	Walter Johnson, Wash	2.72	1940	Ernie Bonham, NY	1.90
1908	Addie Joss, Cle	1.16	1925	Stan Coveleski, Wash	2.84	1941	Thornton Lee, Chi	2.37
1909	Harry Krause, Phi	1.39	1926	Lefty Grove, Phi	2.51	1942	Ted Lyons, Chi	2.10
1910	Ed Walsh, Chi	1.27	1927	Wilcy Moore, NY	2.28	1943	Spud Chandler, NY	1.64
1911	Vean Gregg, Cle	1.81	1928	Garland Braxton, Wash	2.51	1944	Dizzy Trout, Det.	2.12
1912	Walter Johnson, Wash	1.39	1929	Lefty Grove, Phi	2.81	1945	Hal Newhouser, Det	1.81
1913	Walter Johnson, Wash	1.09	1930	Lefty Grove, Phi	2.54	1946	Hal Newhouser, Det	1.94
1914	Dutch Leonard, Bos	1.01	1931	Lefty Grove, Phi	2.06	1947	Spud Chandler, NY	2.46
1915	Smokey Joe Wood, Bos	1.49	1932	Lefty Grove, Phi	2.84	1948	Gene Bearden, Cle	2.43
1916	Babe Ruth, Bos	1.75	1933	Monte Pearson, Cle	2.33	1949	Mel Parnell, Bos	2.77
1917	Eddie Cicotte, Chi	1.53						

Earned Run Average (Cont.)

Year		ERA
1950	Early Wynn, Cle	3.20
1951	Saul Rogovin, Det-Chi	2.78
1952	Allie Reynolds, NY	2.06
1953	Ed Lopat, NY	2.42
1954	Mike Garcia, Cle	2.64
1955	Billy Pierce, Chi	1.97
1956	Whitey Ford, NY	2.47
1957	Bobby Shantz, NY	2.45
1958	Whitey Ford, NY	2.01
1959	Hoyt Wilhelm, Bal.	2.19
1960	Frank Baumann, Chi	2.67
1961	Dick Donovan, Wash	2.40
1962	Hank Aguirre, Det.	2.21
1963	Gary Peters, Chi	2.33
1964	Dean Chance, LA	1.65
1965	Sam McDowell, Cle	2.18
1966	Gary Peters, Chi	1.98
1967	Joe Horlen, Chi	2.06
1968	Luis Tiant, Cle	1.60
1969	Dick Bosman, Wash	2.19

Year		ERA
1970	Diego Segui, Oak.	2.56
1971	Vida Blue, Oak	1.82
1972	Luis Tiant, Bos	1.91
1973	Jim Palmer, Bal	2.40
1974	Catfish Hunter, Oak	2.49
1975	Jim Palmer, Bal	2.09
1976	Mark Fidrych, Det.	2.34
1977	Frank Tanana, Cal	2.54
1978	Ron Guidry, NY	1.74
1979	Ron Guidry, NY	2.78
1980	Rudy May, NY	2.47
1981	Steve McCatty, Oak	2.32
1982	Rick Sutcliffe, Cle	2.96
1983	Rick Honeycutt, Tex	2.42
1984	Mike Boddicker, Bal	2.79
1985	Dave Stieb, Tor	2.48
1986	Roger Clemens, Bos	2.48
1987	Jimmy Key, Tor	2.76
1988	Allan Anderson, Min	2.45
1989	Bret Saberhagen, KC	2.16

Year		ERA
1990	Roger Clemens, Bos	1.93
1991	Roger Clemens, Bos	2.62
1992	Roger Clemens, Bos	2.41
1993	Kevin Appier, KC	2.56
1994	Steve Ontiveros, Oak	2.65
1995	Randy Johnson, Sea	2.48
1996	Juan Guzman, Tor.	2.93
1997	Roger Clemens, Tor	2.05
1998	Roger Clemens, Tor	2.65
1999	Pedro Martinez, Bos	2.07
2000	Pedro Martinez, Bos	1.74
2001	Freddy Garcia, Sea	3.05
2002	Pedro Martinez, Bos	2.26
2003	Pedro Martinez, Bos	2.22
2004	Johan Santana, Min	2.61
2005	Kevin Millwood, Cle	2.86
2006	Johan Santana, Min	2.77

Strikeouts

National League

Multiple winners: Dazzy Vance (7); Grover Alexander (6); Steve Carlton, Randy Johnson, Christy Mathewson and Tom Seaver (5); Dizzy Dean, Sandy Koufax and Warren Spahn (4); Don Drysdale, Sam Jones and Johnny Vander Meer (3); David Cone, Dwight Gooden, Bill Hallahan, J.R. Richard, Robin Roberts, Nolan Ryan, Curt Schilling, John Smoltz and Hippo Vaughn (2).

Year		SO
1900	Rube Waddell, Pit	130
1901	Noodles Hahn, Cin	239
1902	Vic Willis, Bos	225
1903	Christy Mathewson, NY	267
1904	Christy Mathewson, NY	212
1905	Christy Mathewson, NY	206
1906	Fred Beebe, Chi-St.L.	171
1907	Christy Mathewson, NY	178
1908	Christy Mathewson, NY	259
1909	Orval Overall, Chi	205
1910	Earl Moore, Phi	185
1911	Rube Marquard, NY	237
1912	Grover Alexander, Phi	195
1913	Tom Seaton, Phi	168
1914	Grover Alexander, Phi	214
1915	Grover Alexander, Phi	241
1916	Grover Alexander, Phi	167
1917	Grover Alexander, Phi	201
1918	Hippo Vaughn, Chi	148
1919	Hippo Vaughn, Chi	141
1920	Grover Alexander, Chi	173
1921	Burleigh Grimes, Bklyn	136
1922	Dazzy Vance, Bklyn	134
1923	Dazzy Vance, Bklyn	197
1924	Dazzy Vance, Bklyn	262
1925	Dazzy Vance, Bklyn	221
1926	Dazzy Vance, Bklyn	140
1927	Dazzy Vance, Bklyn	184
1928	Dazzy Vance, Bklyn	200
1929	Pat Malone, Chi	166
1930	Bill Hallahan, St.L	177
1931	Bill Hallahan, St.L	159
1932	Dizzy Dean, St.L	191
1933	Dizzy Dean, St.L	199
1934	Dizzy Dean, St.L	195
1935	Dizzy Dean, St.L	190
1936	Van Lingle Mungo, Bklyn	238

Year		SO
1937	Carl Hubbell, NY	159
1938	Clay Bryant, Chi	135
1939	Claude Passeau, Phi-Chi	137
	& Bucky Walters, Cin	137
1940	Kirby Higbe, Phi	137
1941	John Vander Meer, Cin	202
1942	John Vander Meer, Cin	186
1943	John Vander Meer, Cin	174
1944	Bill Voiselle, NY	161
1945	Preacher Roe, Pit	148
1946	Johnny Schmitz, Chi.	135
1947	Ewell Blackwell, Cin.	193
1948	Harry Brecheen, St.L	149
1949	Warren Spahn, Bos	151
1950	Warren Spahn, Bos	191
1951	Don Newcombe, Bklyn	164
	& Warren Spahn, Bos	164
1952	Warren Spahn, Bos	183
1953	Robin Roberts, Phi	198
1954	Robin Roberts, Phi	185
1955	Sam Jones, Chi	198
1956	Sam Jones, Chi	176
1957	Jack Sanford, Phi	188
1958	Sam Jones, St.L	225
1959	Don Drysdale, LA	242
1960	Don Drysdale, LA	246
1961	Sandy Koufax, LA	269
1962	Don Drysdale, LA	232
1963	Sandy Koufax, LA	306
1964	Bob Veale, Pit	250
1965	Sandy Koufax, LA	382
1966	Sandy Koufax, LA	317
1967	Jim Bunning, Phi	253
1968	Bob Gibson, St.L	268
1969	Ferguson Jenkins, Chi	273
1970	Tom Seaver, NY	283
1971	Tom Seaver, NY	289

Year		SO
1972	Steve Carlton, Phi	310
1973	Tom Seaver, NY	251
1974	Steve Carlton, Phi	240
1975	Tom Seaver, NY	243
1976	Tom Seaver, NY	235
1977	Phil Niekro, Atl	262
1978	J.R. Richard, Hou	303
1979	J.R. Richard, Hou	313
1980	Steve Carlton, Phi	286
1981	F. Valenzuela, LA	180
1982	Steve Carlton, Phi	286
1983	Steve Carlton, Phi	275
1984	Dwight Gooden, NY	276
1985	Dwight Gooden, NY	268
1986	Mike Scott, Hou	306
1987	Nolan Ryan, Hou	270
1988	Nolan Ryan, Hou	228
1989	Jose DeLeon, St.L	201
1990	David Cone, NY	233
1991	David Cone, NY	241
1992	John Smoltz, Atl.	215
1993	Jose Rijo, Cin	227
1994	Andy Benes, SD	189
1995	Hideo Nomo, LA	236
1996	John Smoltz, Atl	276
1997	Curt Schilling, Phi	319
1998	Curt Schilling, Phi	300
1999	Randy Johnson, Ari	364
2000	Randy Johnson, Ari	347
2001	Randy Johnson, Ari	372
2002	Randy Johnson, Ari	334
2003	Kerry Wood, Chi	266
2004	Randy Johnson, Ari	290
2005	Jake Peavy, SD	216
2006	Aaron Harang, Cin.	216

Note: In 1998, Randy Johnson struck out 329 batters — 213 in the AL with Seattle, then 116 in the NL with Houston.

American League

Multiple winners: Walter Johnson (12); Nolan Ryan (9); Bob Feller and Lefty Grove (7); Rube Waddell (6); Roger Clemens and Sam McDowell (5); Randy Johnson (4); Lefty Gomez, Mark Langston, Pedro Martinez, Johan Santana and Camilo Pascual (3); Len Barker, Tommy Bridges, Jim Bunning, Hal Newhouser, Allie Reynolds, Herb Score, Ed Walsh and Early Wynn (2).

Year		SO	Year		SO	Year		SO
1901	Cy Young, Bos	158	1937	Lefty Gomez, NY	194	1972	Nolan Ryan, Cal	329
1902	Rube Waddell, Phi	210	1938	Bob Feller, Cle	240	1973	Nolan Ryan, Cal	383
1903	Rube Waddell, Phi	302	1939	Bob Feller, Cle	246	1974	Nolan Ryan, Cal	367
1904	Rube Waddell, Phi	349				1975	Frank Tanana, Cal	269
1905	Rube Waddell, Phi	287	1940	Bob Feller, Cle	261	1976	Nolan Ryan, Cal	327
1906	Rube Waddell, Phi	196	1941	Bob Feller, Cle	260	1977	Nolan Ryan, Cal	341
1907	Rube Waddell, Phi	232	1942	Tex Hughson, Bos	113	1978	Nolan Ryan, Cal	260
1908	Ed Walsh, Chi	269		& Bobo Newsom, Wash	113	1979	Nolan Ryan, Cal	223
1909	Frank Smith, Chi.	177	1943	Allie Reynolds, Cle	151			
1910	Walter Johnson, Wash	313	1944	Hal Newhouser, Det	187	1980	Len Barker, Cle	187
1911	Ed Walsh, Chi	255	1945	Hal Newhouser, Det	212	1981	Len Barker, Cle	127
1912	Walter Johnson, Wash	303	1946	Bob Feller, Cle	348	1982	Floyd Bannister, Sea	209
1913	Walter Johnson, Wash	243	1947	Bob Feller, Cle	196	1983	Jack Morris, Det	232
1914	Walter Johnson, Wash	225	1948	Bob Feller, Cle	164	1984	Mark Langston, Sea	204
1915	Walter Johnson, Wash	203	1949	Virgil Trucks, Det	153	1985	Bert Blyleven, Cle-Min	206
1916	Walter Johnson, Wash	228	1950	Bob Lemon, Cle	170	1986	Mark Langston, Sea	245
1917	Walter Johnson, Wash	188	1951	Vic Raschi, NY	164	1987	Mark Langston, Sea	262
1918	Walter Johnson, Wash	162	1952	Allie Reynolds, NY	160	1988	Roger Clemens, Bos	291
1919	Walter Johnson, Wash	147	1953	Billy Pierce, Chi	186	1989	Nolan Ryan, Tex	301
1920	Stan Coveleski, Cle	133	1954	Bob Turley, Bal	185	1990	Nolan Ryan, Tex	232
1921	Walter Johnson, Wash	143	1955	Herb Score, Cle	245	1991	Roger Clemens, Bos	241
1922	Urban Shocker, St.L	149	1956	Herb Score, Cle	263	1992	Randy Johnson, Sea	241
1923	Walter Johnson, Wash	130	1957	Early Wynn, Cle.	184	1993	Randy Johnson, Sea	308
1924	Walter Johnson, Wash	158	1958	Early Wynn, Chi.	179	1994	Randy Johnson, Sea	204
1925	Lefty Grove, Phi	116	1959	Jim Bunning, Det	201	1995	Randy Johnson, Sea	294
1926	Lefty Grove, Phi	194	1960	Jim Bunning, Det	201	1996	Roger Clemens, Bos	257
1927	Lefty Grove, Phi	174	1961	Camilo Pascual, Min	221	1997	Roger Clemens, Tor	292
1928	Lefty Grove, Phi	183	1962	Camilo Pascual, Min	206	1998	Roger Clemens, Tor	271
1929	Lefty Grove, Phi	170	1963	Camilo Pascual, Min	202	1999	Pedro Martinez, Bos	313
1930	Lefty Grove, Phi	209	1964	Al Downing, NY	217	2000	Pedro Martinez, Bos	284
1931	Lefty Grove, Phi	175	1965	Sam McDowell, Cle	325	2001	Hideo Nomo, Bos	220
1932	Red Ruffing, NY	190	1966	Sam McDowell, Cle	225	2002	Pedro Martinez, Bos	239
1933	Lefty Gomez, NY	163	1967	Jim Lonborg, Bos	246	2003	Esteban Loaiza, Chi	207
1934	Lefty Gomez, NY	158	1968	Sam McDowell, Cle	283	2004	Johan Santana, Min	265
1935	Tommy Bridges, Det	163	1969	Sam McDowell, Cle	279	2005	Johan Santana, Min	238
1936	Tommy Bridges, Det	175	1970	Sam McDowell, Cle	304	2006	Johan Santana, Min	245
			1971	Mickey Lolich, Det	308			

Pitching Triple Crown Winners

Pitchers who led either league in Earned Run Average, Wins and Strikeouts over a single season.

National League

	Year	ERA	W-L	SO
Tommy Bond, Bos	1877	2.11	40-17	170
Hoss Radbourn, Prov	1884	1.38	60-12	441
Tim Keefe, NY	1888	1.74	35-12	333
John Clarkson, Bos	1889	2.73	49-19	284
Amos Rusie, NY.	1894	2.78	36-13	195
Christy Mathewson, NY	1905	1.27	31-8	206
Christy Mathewson, NY	1908	1.43	37-11	259
Grover Alexander, Phi	1915	1.22	31-10	241
Grover Alexander, Phi	1916	1.55	33-12	167
Grover Alexander, Phi	1917	1.86	30-13	201
Hippo Vaughn, Chi	1918	1.74	22-10	148
Grover Alexander, Chi	1920	1.91	27-14	173
Dazzy Vance, Bklyn	1924	2.16	28-6	262
Bucky Walters, Cin	1939	2.29	27-11	137
Sandy Koufax, LA	1963	1.88	25-5	306
Sandy Koufax, LA	1965	2.04	26-8	382
Sandy Koufax, LA	1966	1.73	27-9	317
Steve Carlton, Phi	1972	1.97	27-10	310
Dwight Gooden, NY	1985	1.53	24-4	268
Randy Johnson, Ari	2002	2.32	24-5	334

Ties: In 1894, Rusie tied for league lead in wins with Jouett Meekin, NY (36-10); in 1939, Walters tied for league lead in strikeouts with Claude Passeau, Phi-Chi; in 1963, Koufax tied for the league lead in wins with Juan Marichal, SF.

American League

	Year	ERA	W-L	SO
Cy Young, Bos	1901	1.62	33-10	158
Rube Waddell, Phi.	1905	1.48	26-11	287
Walter Johnson, Wash	1913	1.09	36-7	243
Walter Johnson, Wash	1918	1.27	23-13	162
Walter Johnson, Wash	1924	2.72	23-7	158
Lefty Grove, Phi	1930	2.54	28-5	209
Lefty Grove, Phi	1931	2.06	31-4	175
Lefty Gomez, NY	1934	2.33	26-5	158
Lefty Gomez, NY	1937	2.33	21-11	194
Hal Newhouser, Det	1945	1.81	25-9	212
Roger Clemens, Tor	1997	2.05	21-7	292
Roger Clemens, Tor	1998	2.65	20-6	271
Pedro Martinez, Bos	1999	2.07	23-4	313
Johan Santana, Min	2006	2.77	19-6	245

Ties: In 1998, Clemens tied for league lead in wins with David Cone, NY (20-7) and Rick Helling, Tex (20-7); in 2006, Santana tied for league lead in wins with Chien-Ming Wang, NY (19-6).

Saves

The "save" was created by Chicago baseball writer Jerome Holtzman in the 1960's and accepted as an official statistic by the Official Rules Committee of Major League Baseball in 1969. From 1969-72, a save was credited to a pitcher who finished a game his team won. From 1973-74, a save was credited to a pitcher who finished a game his team won with the tying or winning run on base or at bat. Since 1975 a pitcher has been credited with a save when he meets all three of the following conditions:

(1) He is the finishing pitcher in a game won by his club; (2) He is not the winning pitcher; (3) He qualifies under one of the following conditions: (a) He enters the game with a lead of no more than three runs and pitches for at least one inning; (b) He enters the game with the potential tying run either on base, or at bat, or on deck; (c) He pitches effectively for at least three innings. No more than one save may be credited in each game.

National League

Multiple winners: Bruce Sutter (5); John Franco and Lee Smith (3); Rawly Eastwick, Rollie Fingers, Trevor Hoffman, Mike Marshall, Randy Myers and Todd Worrell (2).

Year		Svs	Year		Svs	Year		Svs
1969	Fred Gladding, Hou	.29	1982	Bruce Sutter, St.L	.36	1996	Jeff Brantley, Cin	.44
1970	Wayne Granger, Cin	.35	1983	Lee Smith, Chi	.29		& Todd Worrell, LA	.44
1971	Dave Giusti, Pit	.30	1984	Bruce Sutter, St.L	.45	1997	Jeff Shaw, Cin	.42
1972	Clay Carroll, Cin.	.37	1985	Jeff Reardon, Mon	.41	1998	Trevor Hoffman, SD	.53
1973	Mike Marshall, Mon.	.31	1986	Todd Worrell, St.L	.36	1999	Ugueth Urbina, Mon	.41
1974	Mike Marshall, LA	.21	1987	Steve Bedrosian, Phi.	.40	2000	Antonio Alfonseca, Fla	.45
1975	Rawly Eastwick, Cin	.22	1988	John Franco, Cin	.39	2001	Robb Nen, SF	.45
	& Al Hrabosky, St.L	.22	1989	Mark Davis, SD.	.44	2002	John Smoltz, Atl	.55
1976	Rawly Eastwick, Cin	.26	1990	John Franco, NY	.33	2003	Eric Gagne, LA	.55
1977	Rollie Fingers, SD	.35	1991	Lee Smith, St.L	.47	2004	Armando Benitez, Fla	.47
1978	Rollie Fingers, SD	.37	1992	Lee Smith, St.L	.43		& Jason Isringhausen, St.L	.47
1979	Bruce Sutter, Chi	.37	1993	Randy Myers, Chi	.53	2005	Chad Cordero, Wash	.47
1980	Bruce Sutter, Chi	.28	1994	John Franco, NY	.30	2006	Trevor Hoffman, SD	.46
1981	Bruce Sutter, St.L	.25	1995	Randy Myers, Chi	.38			

American League

Multiple winners: Dan Quisenberry (5); Rich Gossage and Mariano Rivera (3); Dennis Eckersley, Sparky Lyle, Ron Perranoski and Francisco Rodriguez (2).

Year		Svs	Year		Svs	Year		Svs
1969	Ron Perranoski, Min	.31	1982	Dan Quisenberry, KC	.35	1995	Jose Mesa, Cle	.46
1970	Ron Perranoski, Min	.34	1983	Dan Quisenberry, KC	.45	1996	John Wetteland, NY	.43
1971	Ken Sanders, Mil.	.31	1984	Dan Quisenberry, KC	.44	1997	Randy Myers, Bal	.45
1972	Sparky Lyle, NY.	.35	1985	Dan Quisenberry, KC	.37	1998	Tom Gordon, Bos	.46
1973	John Hiller, Det	.38	1986	Dave Righetti, NY	.46	1999	Mariano Rivera, NY	.45
1974	Terry Forster, Chi	.24	1987	Tom Henke, Tor	.34	2000	Todd Jones, Det.	.42
1975	Rich Gossage, Chi	.26	1988	Dennis Eckersley, Oak	.45		& Derek Lowe, Bos	.42
1976	Sparky Lyle, NY.	.23	1989	Jeff Russell, Tex	.38	2001	Mariano Rivera, NY.	.50
1977	Bill Campbell, Bos	.31	1990	Bobby Thigpen, Chi	.57	2002	Eddie Guardado, Min	.45
1978	Rich Gossage, NY	.27	1991	Bryan Harvey, Cal	.46	2003	Keith Foulke, Oak	.43
1979	Mike Marshall, Min	.32	1992	Dennis Eckersley, Oak	.51	2004	Mariano Rivera, NY	.53
1980	Rich Gossage, NY	.33	1993	Jeff Montgomery, KC	.45	2005	Francisco Rodriguez, LA	.45
	& Dan Quisenberry, KC	.33		& Duane Ward, Tor	.45		& Bob Wickman, Cle	.45
1981	Rollie Fingers, Mil	.28	1994	Lee Smith, Bal	.33	2006	Francisco Rodriguez, LA	.47

Perfect Games

Eighteen pitchers have thrown perfect games (27 up, 27 down) in major league history. However, the game pitched by Ernie Shore is not considered to be official.

National League

	Game	Date	Score
Lee Richmond	Wor. vs Cle.	6/12/1880	1-0
Monte Ward	Prov. vs Buf.	6/17/1880	5-0
Jim Bunning	Phi. at NY	6/21/1964	6-0
Sandy Koufax	LA vs Chi.	9/9/1965	1-0
Tom Browning	Cin. vs LA	9/16/1988	1-0
Dennis Martinez	Mon. at LA	7/28/1991	2-0
Randy Johnson	Ari. at Atl.	5/18/2004	2-0

Note: Pittsburgh's Harvey Haddix pitched 12 perfect innings against the Milwaukee Braves on May 26, 1959 before losing, 1-0, in the 13th. Braves' lead-off batter Felix Mantilla reached on a throwing error by Pirates 3B Don Hoak, Eddie Mathews sacrificed Mantilla to 2nd, Hank Aaron was walked intentionally, and Joe Adcock hit a 3-run HR. Adcock, however, passed Aaron on the bases and was only credited with a 1-run double.

Note: Montreal's Pedro Martinez pitched nine perfect innings against the San Diego Padres on June 3, 1995 before surrendering a leadoff double to Bip Roberts in the 10th. He was then relieved by Mel Rojas, who finished the game, which Montreal won, 1-0.

American League

	Game	Date	Score
Cy Young	Bos. vs Phi.	5/5/1904	3-0
Addie Joss	Cle. vs Chi.	10/2/1908	1-0
Ernie Shore	Bos. vs Wash.	6/23/1917	4-0*
Charlie Robertson	Chi. at Det.	4/30/1922	2-0
Catfish Hunter	Oak. vs Min.	5/8/1968	4-0
Len Barker	Cle. vs Tor.	5/15/1981	3-0
Mike Witt	Cal. at Tex.	9/30/1984	1-0
Kenny Rogers	Tex. vs Cal.	7/28/1994	4-0
David Wells	NY vs Min.	5/17/1998	4-0
David Cone	NY vs Mon.	7/18/1999	6-0

*Babe Ruth started for Boston, walking Senators' lead-off batter Ray Morgan, then was thrown out of game by umpire Brick Owens for arguing the call. Shore came on in relief. Morgan was caught stealing and Shore retired the next 26 batters in a row. While technically not a perfect game—since he didn't start—Shore gets credit anyway.

World Series

Pitcher	Game	Date	Score
Don Larsen	NY vs Bklyn	10/8/1956	2-0

No-Hit Games

Nine innings or more, including perfect games, since 1876. Losing pitchers in **bold** type. **Multiple no-hitters:** Nolan Ryan (7); Sandy Koufax (4); Larry Corcoran, Bob Feller and Cy Young (3); Jim Bunning, Steve Busby, Carl Erskine, Bob Forsch, Pud Galvin, Ken Holtzman, Randy Johnson, Addie Joss, Hub (Dutch) Leonard, Jim Maloney, Christy Mathewson, Hideo Nomo, Allie Reynolds, Warren Spahn, Bill Stoneman, Virgil Trucks, Johnny Vander Meer and Don Wilson (2).

National League

Year	Date	Pitcher	Result
1876	7/15	George Bradley	St.L vs Har, 2-0
1880	6/12	Lee Richmond	Wor vs Cle, 1-0 (perfect game)
	6/17	Monte Ward	Prov vs Buf, 5-0 (perfect game)
	8/19	Larry Corcoran	Chi vs Bos, 6-0
	8/20	Pud Galvin	Buf at Wor, 1-0
1882	9/20	Larry Corcoran	Chi vs Wor, 5-0
1883	7/25	Old Hoss Radbourn	Prov at Cle, 8-0
	9/13	Hugh Daily	Cle at Phi, 1-0
1884	6/27	Larry Corcoran	Chi vs Prov, 6-0
	8/4	Pud Galvin	Buf at Det, 18-0
1885	7/27	John Clarkson	Chi vs Prov, 6-0
	8/29	Charlie Ferguson	Phi vs Prov, 1-0
1891	6/22	Tom Lovett	Bklyn vs NY, 4-0
	7/31	Amos Rusie	NY vs Bklyn, 6-0
1892	8/6	John Stivetts	Bos vs Bklyn, 11-0
	8/22	Ben Sanders	Lou vs Bal, 6-2
	10/15	Bumpus Jones	Cin vs Pit, 7-1 (1st major league game)
1893	8/16	Bill Hawke	Bal vs Wash, 5-0
1897	9/18	Cy Young	Cle vs Cin, 6-0
1898	4/22	Ted Breitenstein	Cin vs Pit, 11-0
	4/22	Jim Hughes	Bal vs Bos, 8-0
	7/8	Red Donahue	Phi vs Bos, 5-0
	8/21	Walter Thornton	Chi vs Bklyn, 2-0
1899	5/25	Deacon Phillippe	Lou vs NY, 7-0
1900	7/12	Noodles Hahn	Cin vs Phi, 4-0
1901	7/15	Christy Mathewson	NY at St.L, 5-0
1903	9/18	Chick Fraser	Phi at Chi, 10-0
1905	6/13	Christy Mathewson	NY at Chi, 1-0
1906	5/1	John Lush	Phi at Bklyn, 6-0
	7/20	Mal Eason	Bklyn at St.L, 2-0
1907	5/8	Frank Pfeffer	Bos vs Cin, 6-0
	9/20	Nick Maddox	Pit vs Bkn, 2-1
1908	7/4	Hooks Wiltse	NY vs Phi, 1-0 (10)
	9/5	Nap Rucker	Bklyn vs Bos, 6-0
1912	9/6	Jeff Tesreau	NY at Phi, 3-0
1914	9/9	George Davis	Bos vs Pht, 7-0
1915	4/15	Rube Marquard	NY vs Bklyn, 2-0
	8/31	Jimmy Lavender	Chi at N.Y, 2-0
1916	6/16	Tom Hughes	Bos vs. Pit, 2-0
1917	5/2	Fred Toney	Cin at Chi, 1-0 (10)
1919	5/11	Hod Eller	Cin at St.L, 6-0
1922	5/7	Jesse Barnes	NY vs Phi, 6-0
1924	7/17	Jesse Haines	St.L vs Bos, 5-0
1925	9/13	Dazzy Vance	Bklyn vs Phi, 10-1
1929	5/8	Carl Hubbell	NY vs Pit, 11-0
1934	9/21	Paul Dean	St.L at Bklyn, 3-0
1938	6/11	Johnny Vander Meer	Cin vs Bos, 3-0
	6/15	Johnny Vander Meer	Cin at Bklyn, 6-0 (consecutive starts)
1940	4/30	Tex Carleton	Bklyn at Cin, 3-0
1941	8/30	Lon Warneke	St.L at Cin, 2-0
1944	4/27	Jim Tobin	Bos vs Bklyn, 2-0
	5/15	Clyde Shoun	Cin vs Bos, 1-0
1946	4/23	Ed Head	Bklyn vs Bos, 5-0
1947	6/18	Ewell Blackwell	Cin vs Bos, 6-0
1948	9/9	Rex Barney	Bklyn at NY, 2-0
1950	8/11	Vern Bickford	Bos vs Bklyn, 7-0
1951	5/6	Cliff Chambers	Pit at Bos, 3-0
1952	6/19	Carl Erskine	Bklyn vs Chi, 5-0
1954	6/12	Jim Wilson	Mil vs Phi, 2-0
1955	5/12	Sam Jones	Chi vs Pit, 4-0
1956	5/12	Carl Erskine	Bklyn vs NY, 3-0
	9/25	Sal Maglie	Bklyn vs Phi, 5-0
1960	5/15	Don Cardwell	Chi vs St.L, 4-0
	8/18	Lew Burdette	Mil vs Phi, 1-0
	9/16	Warren Spahn	Mil vs Phi, 4-0
1961	4/28	Warren Spahn	Mil vs SF, 1-0
1962	6/30	Sandy Koufax	LA vs NY, 5-0
1963	5/11	Sandy Koufax	LA vs SF, 8-0
	5/17	Don Nottebart	Hou vs Phi, 4-1
	6/15	Juan Marichal	SF vs Hou, 1-0
1964	4/23	**Ken Johnson**	Hou vs Cin, 0-1
	6/4	Sandy Koufax	LA at Phi, 3-0
	6/21	Jim Bunning	Phi at NY, 6-0 (perfect game)
1965	8/19	Jim Maloney	Cin at Chi, 1-0 (10)
	9/9	Sandy Koufax	LA vs Chi, 1-0 (perfect game)
1967	6/18	Don Wilson	Hou vs Atl, 2-0
1968	7/29	George Culver	Cin at Phi, 6-1
	9/17	Gaylord Perry	SF vs St.L, 1-0
	9/18	Ray Washburn	St.L at SF, 2-0 (next day, same park)
1969	4/17	Bill Stoneman	Mon at Phi, 7-0
	4/30	Jim Maloney	Cin vs Hou, 10-0
	5/1	Don Wilson	Hou at Cin, 4-0
	8/19	Ken Holtzman	Chi vs Atl, 3-0
	9/20	Bob Moose	Pit at NY, 4-0
1970	6/12	Dock Ellis	Pit vs SD, 2-0
	7/20	Bill Singer	LA vs Phi, 5-0
1971	6/3	Ken Holtzman	Chi at Cin, 1-0
	6/23	Rick Wise	Phi at Cin, 4-0
	8/14	Bob Gibson	St.L at Pit, 11-0
1972	4/16	Burt Hooton	Chi vs Phi, 4-0
	9/2	Milt Pappas	Chi vs SD, 8-0
	10/2	Bill Stoneman	Mon vs NY, 7-0
1973	8/5	Phil Niekro	Atl vs SD, 9-0
1975	8/24	Ed Halicki	SF vs NY, 6-0
1976	7/9	Larry Dierker	Hou vs Mon, 6-0
	8/9	John Candelaria	Pit vs LA, 2-0
	9/29	John Montefusco	SF vs Atl, 9-0
1978	4/16	Bob Forsch	St.L vs Phi, 5-0
	6/16	Tom Seaver	Cin vs St.L, 4-0
1979	4/7	Ken Forsch	Hou vs Atl, 6-0
1980	6/27	Jerry Reuss	LA at SF, 8-0
1981	5/10	Charlie Lea	Mon vs SF, 4-0
	9/26	Nolan Ryan	Hou vs LA, 5-0
1983	9/26	Bob Forsch	St.L vs Mon, 3-0
1986	9/25	Mike Scott	Hou vs SF, 2-0
1988	9/16	Tom Browning	Cin vs LA, 1-0 (perfect game)
1990	6/29	Fernando Valenzuela	LA vs St.L, 6-0
	8/15	Terry Mulholland	Phi vs SF, 6-0
1991	5/23	Tommy Greene	Phi at Mon, 2-0
	7/28	Dennis Martinez	Mon at LA, 2-0 (perfect game)
	9/11	Mercker (6), Wohlers (2) & Peña (1)	Atl vs SD, 1-0 (combined no-hitter)
1992	8/17	Kevin Gross	LA vs SF, 2-0
1993	9/8	Darryl Kile	Hou vs NY, 7-1
1994	4/8	Kent Mercker	Atl at LA, 6-0
1995	7/14	Ramon Martinez	LA vs Fla, 7-0
1996	5/11	Al Leiter	Fla vs Col, 11-0
	9/17	Hideo Nomo	LA at Col, 9-0
1997	6/10	Kevin Brown	Fla at SF, 9-0
	7/12	Francisco Cordova (9) Ricardo Rincon (1)	Pit vs. Hou, 3-0 (10 inn.) (combined no-hitter)
1999	6/25	Jose Jimenez	St.L vs Ari, 1-0
2001	5/12	A.J. Burnett	Fla at SD, 3-0
	9/3	Bud Smith	St.L at SD, 4-0
2003	4/27	Kevin Millwood	Phi vs SF, 1-0
	6/11	Oswalt (2.2), Munro (2.2) Saarloos (1.1), Lidge (2), Dotel (1) & Wagner (1)	Hou at NY-AL, 8-0 (combined no-hitter)
2004	5/18	Randy Johnson	Ari at Atl, 2-0 (perfect game)
2006	9/6	Anibal Sanchez	Ari at Fla, 2-0

No-Hit Games (Cont.)
American League

Year	Date	Pitcher	Result
1902	9/20	Jimmy Callahan	Chi vs Det, 3-0
1904	5/5	Cy Young	Bos vs Phi, 3-0
			(perfect game)
	8/17	Jesse Tannehill	Bos at Chi, 6-0
1905	7/22	Weldon Henley	Phi at St. L, 6-0
	9/6	Frank Smith	Chi at Det, 15-0
	9/27	Bill Dinneen	Bos vs Chi, 2-0
1908	6/30	Cy Young	Bos at NY, 8-0
	9/18	Dusty Rhoades	Cle vs Bos, 2-1
	9/20	Frank Smith	Chi vs Phi, 1-0
	10/2	Addie Joss	Cle vs Chi, 1-0
			(perfect game)
1910	4/20	Addie Joss	Cle at Chi, 1-0
	5/12	Chief Bender	Phi vs Cle, 4-0
1911	7/29	Smokey Joe Wood	Bos vs St. L, 5-0
	8/27	Ed Walsh	Chi vs Bos, 5-0
1912	7/4	George Mullin	Det vs St. L, 7-0
	8/30	Earl Hamilton	St. L at Det, 5-1
1914	5/31	Joe Benz	Chi vs Cle, 6-1
1916	6/16	Rube Foster	Bos vs NY, 2-0
	8/26	Joe Bush	Phi vs Cle, 5-0
	8/30	Hub (Dutch) Leonard	Bos vs St. L, 4-0
1917	4/14	Ed Cicotte	Chi at St. L, 11-0
	4/24	George Mogridge	NY at Bos, 2-1
	5/5	Ernie Koob	St. L vs Chi, 1-0
	5/6	Bob Groom	St. L vs Chi, 3-0
			(next day, same park)
	6/23	Babe Ruth (0) & Ernie Shore (9)	Bos vs Wash, 4-0 (combined no-hitter)
1918	6/3	Hub (Dutch) Leonard	Bos at Det, 5-0
1919	9/10	Ray Caldwell	Cle at NY, 3-0
1920	7/1	Walter Johnson	Wash at Bos, 1-0
1922	4/30	Charlie Robertson	Chi at Det, 2-0
			(perfect game)
1923	9/4	Sam Jones	NY at Phi, 2-0
	9/7	Howard Ehmke	Bos at Phi, 4-0
1926	8/21	Ted Lyons	Chi at Bos, 6-0
1931	4/29	Wes Ferrell	Cle vs St. L, 9-0
	8/8	Bob Burke	Wash vs Bos, 5-0
1935	8/31	Vern Kennedy	Chi vs Cle, 5-0
1937	6/1	Bill Dietrich	Chi vs St. L, 8-0
1938	8/27	Monte Pearson	NY vs Cle, 13-0
1940	4/16	Bob Feller	Cle at Chi, 1-0
			(Opening Day)
1945	9/9	Dick Fowler	Phi vs St. L, 1-0
1946	4/30	Bob Feller	Cle at NY, 1-0
1947	7/10	Don Black	Cle vs Phi, 3-0
	9/3	Bill McCahan	Phi vs Wash, 3-0
1948	6/30	Bob Lemon	Cle at Det, 2-0
1951	7/1	Bob Feller	Cle vs Det, 2-1
	7/12	Allie Reynolds	NY at Cle, 1-0
	9/28	Allie Reynolds	NY vs Bos, 8-0
1952	5/15	Virgil Trucks	Det vs Wash, 1-0
	8/25	Virgil Trucks	Det at NY, 1-0
1953	5/6	Bobo Holloman	St. L vs Phi, 6-0
			(first major league start)
1956	7/14	Mel Parnell	Bos vs Chi, 4-0
	10/8	Don Larsen	NY vs Bklyn, 2-0
			(perfect W. Series game)
1957	8/20	Bob Keegan	Chi vs Wash, 6-0
1958	7/20	Jim Bunning	Det at Bos, 3-0
	9/20	Hoyt Wilhelm	Bal vs NY, 1-0
1962	5/5	Bo Belinsky	LA vs Bal, 2-0
	6/26	Earl Wilson	Bos vs LA, 2-0
	8/1	Bill Monbouquette	Bos at Chi, 1-0
	8/26	Jack Kralick	Min vs KC, 1-0

Year	Date	Pitcher	Result
1965	9/16	Dave Morehead	Bos vs Cle, 2-0
1966	6/10	Sonny Siebert	Cle vs Wash, 2-0
1967	4/30	**Steve Barber** (8⅔) & **Stu Miller** (⅓)	Bal vs Det, 1-2 (combined no-hitter)
	8/25	Dean Chance	Min at Cle, 2-1
	9/10	Joel Horlen	Chi vs Det, 6-0
1968	4/27	Tom Phoebus	Bal vs Bos, 6-0
	5/8	Catfish Hunter	Oak vs Min, 4-0 (perfect game)
1969	8/13	Jim Palmer	Bal vs Oak, 8-0
1970	7/3	Clyde Wright	Cal vs Oak, 4-0
	9/21	Vida Blue	Oak vs Min, 6-0
1973	4/27	Steve Busby	KC at Det, 3-0
	5/15	Nolan Ryan	Cal at KC, 3-0
	7/15	Nolan Ryan	Cal at Det, 6-0
	7/30	Jim Bibby	Tex at Oak, 6-0
1974	6/19	Steve Busby	KC at Mil, 2-0
	7/19	Dick Bosman	Cle vs Oak, 4-0
	9/28	Nolan Ryan	Cal vs Min, 4-0
1975	6/1	Nolan Ryan	Cal vs Bal, 1-0
	9/28	Vida Blue (5), Glenn Abbott (1), Paul Lindblad (1), & Rollie Fingers (2)	Oak vs Cal, 5-0 (combined no-hitter)
1976	7/28	John Odom (5) & Francisco Barrios (4)	Chi at Oak, 2-1 (combined no-hitter)
1977	5/14	Jim Colborn	KC vs Tex, 6-0
	5/30	Dennis Eckersley	Cle vs Cal, 1-0
	9/22	Bert Blyleven	Tex at Cal, 6-0
1981	5/15	Len Barker	Cle vs Tor, 3-0 (perfect game)
1983	7/4	Dave Righetti	NY vs Bos, 4-0
	9/29	Mike Warren	Oak vs Chi, 3-0
1984	4/7	Jack Morris	Det at Chi, 4-0
	9/30	Mike Witt	Cal at Tex, 1-0 (perfect game)
1986	9/19	Joe Cowley	Chi at Cal, 7-1
1987	4/15	Juan Nieves	Mil at Bal, 7-0
1990	4/11	Mark Langston (7) & Mike Witt (2)	Cal vs Sea, 1-0 (combined no-hitter)
	6/2	Randy Johnson	Sea vs Det, 2-0
	6/11	Nolan Ryan	Tex at Oak, 5-0
	6/29	Dave Stewart	Oak at Tor, 5-0
	9/2	Dave Stieb	Tor at Cle, 3-0
1991	5/1	Nolan Ryan	Tex vs Tor, 3-0
	7/13	Bob Milacki (6), Mike Flanagan (1), Mark Williamson (1) & Gregg Olson (1)	Bal at Oak, 2-0 (combined no-hitter)
	8/11	Wilson Alvarez	Chi at Bal, 7-0
	8/26	Bret Saberhagen	KC vs Chi, 7-0
1993	4/22	Chris Bosio	Sea vs Bos, 7-0
	9/4	Jim Abbott	NY vs Cle, 4-0
1994	4/27	Scott Erickson	Min vs Mil, 6-0
	7/28	Kenny Rogers	Tex vs Cal, 4-0 (perfect game)
1996	5/14	Dwight Gooden	NY vs Sea, 2-0
1998	5/17	David Wells	NY vs Min, 4-0 (perfect game)
1999	7/18	David Cone	NY vs Mon, 6-0 (perfect game)
	9/11	Eric Milton	Min vs Ana, 7-0
2001	4/4	Hideo Nomo	Bos at Bal, 3-0
2002	4/27	Derek Lowe	Bos vs TB, 10-0

All-Time Major League Leaders
Through the 2006 regular season.
CAREER
Players active in 2006 in **bold** type.
Batting
Note that (*) indicates left-handed hitter and (†) indicates switch-hitter.

Batting Average
(Minimum 3,000 AB)

		Yrs	AB	H	Avg
1	Ty Cobb*	24	11,434	4189	.366
2	Rogers Hornsby	23	8,173	2930	.358
3	Joe Jackson*	13	4,981	1772	.356
4	Ed Delahanty*	16	7,505	2596	.346
5	Tris Speaker*	22	10,195	3514	.345
6	Ted Williams*	19	7,706	2654	.344
7	Billy Hamilton*	14	6,269	2159	.344
8	Dan Brouthers*	19	6,711	2296	.342
9	Babe Ruth*	22	8,399	2873	.342
10	Harry Heilmann	17	7,787	2660	.342
11	Pete Browning	13	4,820	1646	.341
12	Willie Keeler*	19	8,591	2932	.341
13	Bill Terry*	14	6,428	2193	.341
14	George Sisler*	15	8,267	2812	.340
15	Lou Gehrig*	17	8,001	2721	.340
16	Jesse Burkett*	16	8,421	2850	.338
17	Tony Gwynn*	20	9,288	3141	.338
18	Nap Lajoie	21	9,589	3242	.338
19	Riggs Stephenson	14	4,508	1515	.336
20	Al Simmons	20	8,759	2927	.334
21	Paul Waner*	20	9,459	3152	.333
22	Eddie Collins*	25	9,949	3315	.333
23	**Todd Helton***	10	5,106	1700	.333
24	**Albert Pujols**	6	3,489	1159	.332
25	Stan Musial*	22	10,972	3630	.331

Players Active in 2006

		Yrs	AB	H	Avg
1	Todd Helton*	10	5,106	1700	.333
2	Albert Pujols	6	3,489	1159	.332
3	Ichiro Suzuki*	6	4,096	1354	.331
4	Vladimir Guerrero	11	5,502	1786	.325
5	Nomar Garciaparra	11	4,832	1537	.318
6	Derek Jeter	12	6,790	2150	.317
7	Manny Ramirez	14	6,575	2066	.314
8	Mike Piazza	15	6,602	2042	.309
9	Alex Rodriguez	13	6,767	2067	.305
10	Magglio Ordonez	10	4,705	1436	.305
11	Frank Thomas	17	7,422	2262	.305
12	Chipper Jones†	13	6,385	1944	.304

Hits

		Yrs	AB	H	Avg
1	Pete Rose†	24	14,053	**4256**	.303
2	Ty Cobb*	24	11,434	**4189**	.366
3	Hank Aaron	23	12,364	**3771**	.305
4	Stan Musial*	22	10,972	**3630**	.331
5	Tris Speaker*	22	10,195	**3514**	.345
6	Carl Yastrzemski*	23	11,988	**3419**	.285
7	Honus Wagner	21	10,430	**3415**	.327
8	Paul Molitor	21	10,835	**3319**	.306
9	Eddie Collins*	25	9,949	**3315**	.333
10	Willie Mays	22	10,881	**3283**	.302
11	Eddie Murray†	21	11,336	**3255**	.287
12	Nap Lajoie	21	9,589	**3242**	.338
13	Cal Ripken Jr	21	11,551	**3184**	.276
14	George Brett*	21	10,349	**3154**	.305
15	Paul Waner*	20	9,459	**3152**	.333
16	Robin Yount	20	11,008	**3142**	.285
17	Tony Gwynn*	20	9,288	**3141**	.338
18	Dave Winfield	22	11,003	**3110**	.283
19	Rickey Henderson	25	10,961	**3055**	.279
20	Rod Carew*	19	9,315	**3053**	.328
21	Lou Brock*	19	10,332	**3023**	.293
22	Rafael Palmeiro*	20	10,472	**3020**	.288
23	Wade Boggs*	18	9,180	**3010**	.328
24	Al Kaline	22	10,116	**3007**	.297
25	Cap Anson	22	9,108	**3000**	.329
	Roberto Clemente	18	9,454	**3000**	.317

Players Active in 2006

		Yrs	AB	H	Avg
1	Craig Biggio	19	10,359	**2930**	.283
2	Barry Bonds*	21	9,507	**2841**	.299
3	Julio Franco	22	8,587	**2566**	.299
4	Steve Finley*	18	9,303	**2531**	.272
5	Omar Vizquel†	18	8,966	**2472**	.276
6	Ken Griffey Jr.*	18	8,298	**2412**	.291
7	Gary Sheffield	19	8,037	**2390**	.297
8	Luis Gonzalez*	17	8,352	**2373**	.284
9	Ivan Rodriguez	16	7,745	**2354**	.304
10	Bernie Williams†	16	7,869	**2336**	.297
11	Kenny Lofton*	16	7,630	**2283**	.299
12	Frank Thomas	17	7,422	**2262**	.305

Games Played

1	Pete Rose	3562
2	Carl Yastrzemski	3308
3	Hank Aaron	3298
4	Rickey Henderson	3081
5	Ty Cobb	3035
6	Stan Musial	3026
	Eddie Murray	3026
8	Cal Ripken Jr.	3001
9	Willie Mays	2992
10	Dave Winfield	2973
11	Rusty Staub	2951
12	Brooks Robinson	2896
13	**Barry Bonds**	2860
14	Robin Yount	2856
15	Al Kaline	2834
16	Rafael Palmeiro	2831
17	Harold Baines	2830
18	Eddie Collins	2826
19	Reggie Jackson	2820
20	Frank Robinson	2808

At Bats

1	Pete Rose	14,053
2	Hank Aaron	12,364
3	Carl Yastrzemski	11,988
4	Cal Ripken Jr.	11,551
5	Ty Cobb	11,434
6	Eddie Murray	11,336
7	Robin Yount	11,008
8	Dave Winfield	11,003
9	Stan Musial	10,972
10	Rickey Henderson	10,961
11	Willie Mays	10,881
12	Paul Molitor	10,835
13	Brooks Robinson	10,654
14	Rafael Palmeiro	10,472
15	Honus Wagner	10,430
16	**Craig Biggio**	10,359
17	George Brett	10,349
18	Lou Brock	10,332
19	Luis Aparicio	10,230
20	Tris Speaker	10,195

Total Bases

1	Hank Aaron	6856
2	Stan Musial	6134
3	Willie Mays	6066
4	Ty Cobb	5854
5	Babe Ruth	5793
6	**Barry Bonds**	5784
7	Pete Rose	5752
8	Carl Yastrzemski	5539
9	Eddie Murray	5397
10	Rafael Palmeiro	5388
11	Frank Robinson	5373
12	Dave Winfield	5221
13	Cal Ripken Jr.	5168
14	Tris Speaker	5101
15	Lou Gehrig	5060
16	George Brett	5044
17	Mel Ott	5041
18	Jimmie Foxx	4956
19	Ted Williams	4884
20	Honus Wagner	4862

Home Runs

		Yrs	AB	HR	AB/HR
1	Hank Aaron	23	12,364	755	16.4
2	Barry Bonds*	21	9,507	734	13.0
3	Babe Ruth*	22	8,399	714	11.8
4	Willie Mays	22	10,881	660	16.5
5	Sammy Sosa	17	8,401	588	14.3
6	Frank Robinson	21	10,006	586	17.1
7	Mark McGwire	16	6,187	583	10.6
8	Harmon Killebrew	22	8,147	573	14.2
9	Rafael Palmeiro*	20	10,472	569	18.4
10	Reggie Jackson*	21	9,864	563	17.5
	Ken Griffey Jr.*	18	8,298	563	14.7
12	Mike Schmidt	18	8,352	548	15.2
13	Mickey Mantle†	18	8,102	536	15.1
14	Jimmie Foxx	20	8,134	534	15.2
15	Ted Williams*	19	7,706	521	14.8
	Willie McCovey*	22	8,197	521	15.7
17	Eddie Mathews*	17	8,537	512	16.7
	Ernie Banks	19	9,421	512	18.4
19	Mel Ott*	22	9,456	511	18.5
20	Eddie Murray†	21	11,336	504	22.5
21	Lou Gehrig*	17	8,001	493	16.2
	Fred McGriff*	22	8,757	493	17.8
23	Frank Thomas	17	7,422	487	15.2
24	Willie Stargell*	21	7,927	475	16.7
	Stan Musial*	22	10,972	475	23.1

Runs Batted In

		Yrs	Gm	RBI	P/G
1	Hank Aaron	23	3298	2297	.70
2	Babe Ruth*	22	2503	2213	.88
3	Lou Gehrig*	17	2164	1995	.92
4	Stan Musial*	22	3026	1951	.64
5	Ty Cobb	24	3034	1938	.64
6	Barry Bonds*	21	2860	1930	.67
7	Jimmie Foxx	20	2317	1922	.83
8	Eddie Murray†	21	2980	1917	.64
9	Willie Mays	22	2992	1903	.64
10	Mel Ott*	22	2730	1860	.68
11	Carl Yastrzemski*	23	3308	1844	.56
12	Ted Williams*	19	2292	1839	.80
13	Rafael Palmeiro*	20	2831	1835	.65
14	Dave Winfield	22	2973	1833	.62
15	Al Simmons	20	2215	1827	.82
16	Frank Robinson	21	2808	1812	.65
17	Honus Wagner	21	2792	1732	.62
18	Cap Anson	22	2276	1715	.75
19	Reggie Jackson*	21	2820	1702	.60
20	Cal Ripken Jr.	21	3001	1695	.56
21	Tony Perez	23	2777	1652	.59
22	Ernie Banks	19	2528	1636	.65
23	Harold Baines*	22	2830	1628	.58
24	Goose Goslin*	18	2287	1609	.70
25	Ken Griffey Jr.*	18	2234	1608	.72

Players Active in 2006

		Yrs	AB	HR	AB/HR
1	Barry Bonds*	21	9,507	734	13.0
2	Ken Griffey Jr.*	18	8,298	563	14.7
3	Frank Thomas	17	7,422	487	15.2
4	Jim Thome*	16	6,409	472	13.6
5	Manny Ramirez	14	6,575	470	14.0
6	Alex Rodriguez	13	6,767	464	14.6
7	Gary Sheffield	19	8,037	455	17.7
8	Mike Piazza	15	6,602	419	15.8
9	Carlos Delgado*	14	6,053	407	14.9
10	Chipper Jones†	13	6,385	357	17.9
11	Jim Edmonds*	14	5,907	350	16.9
	Jason Giambi*	12	5,620	350	16.1
13	Jeff Kent	15	7,564	345	21.9
14	Andruw Jones	11	5,836	342	17.1
15	Vladimir Guerrero	11	5,502	338	16.3

Players Active in 2006

		Yrs	Gm	RBI	P/G
1	Barry Bonds*	21	2860	1930	.67
2	Ken Griffey Jr.*	18	2234	1608	.72
3	Frank Thomas	17	2096	1579	.75
4	Manny Ramirez	14	1817	1516	.83
5	Gary Sheffield	19	2229	1501	.67
6	Jeff Kent	16	2041	1380	.68
7	Alex Rodriguez	13	1746	1347	.77
8	Luis Gonzalez*	17	2316	1324	.57
9	Ruben Sierra†	20	2186	1322	.60
10	Jim Thome*	16	1881	1302	.69
11	Mike Piazza	15	1829	1291	.71
12	Carlos Delgado*	14	1711	1287	.75
13	Bernie Williams†	16	2076	1257	.61
14	Moises Alou	15	1840	1229	.67
15	Chipper Jones†	13	1761	1197	.68

Runs

1	Rickey Henderson	2295
2	Ty Cobb	2246
3	Babe Ruth	2174
	Hank Aaron	2174
5	Pete Rose	2165
6	Barry Bonds	2152
7	Willie Mays	2062
8	Stan Musial	1949
9	Lou Gehrig	1888
10	Tris Speaker	1882
11	Mel Ott	1859
12	Frank Robinson	1829
13	Eddie Collins	1821
14	Carl Yastrzemski	1816
15	Ted Williams	1798
16	Paul Molitor	1782
17	Craig Biggio	1776
18	Charlie Gehringer	1774
19	Jimmie Foxx	1751
20	Honus Wagner	1736

Extra Base Hits

1	Hank Aaron	1477
2	Barry Bonds	1398
3	Stan Musial	1377
4	Babe Ruth	1356
5	Willie Mays	1323
6	Rafael Palmeiro	1192
7	Lou Gehrig	1190
8	Frank Robinson	1186
9	Carl Yastrzemski	1157
10	Ty Cobb	1136
11	Tris Speaker	1131
12	George Brett	1119
13	Ted Williams	1117
	Jimmie Foxx	1117
15	Eddie Murray	1099
16	Dave Winfield	1093
17	Cal Ripken Jr.	1078
18	Reggie Jackson	1075
19	Mel Ott	1071
20	Ken Griffey Jr.	1048

Slugging Percentage
(Minimum 3,000 AB)

1	Babe Ruth	.690
2	Ted Williams	.634
3	Lou Gehrig	.632
4	Albert Pujols	.629
5	Jimmie Foxx	.609
6	Barry Bonds	.608
7	Hank Greenberg	.605
8	Manny Ramirez	.600
9	Todd Helton	.593
10	Mark McGwire	.588
11	Vladimir Guerrero	.583
12	Joe DiMaggio	.579
13	Rogers Hornsby	.577
14	Alex Rodriguez	.573
15	Lance Berkman	.567
16	Frank Thomas	.566
17	Larry Walker	.565
18	Jim Thome	.565
19	Albert Belle	.564
20	Johnny Mize	.562

Stolen Bases

1 Rickey Henderson 1406
2 Lou Brock 938
3 Billy Hamilton 912
4 Ty Cobb 892
5 Tim Raines 808
6 Vince Coleman 752
7 Eddie Collins 745
8 Max Carey 738
9 Honus Wagner 722
10 Joe Morgan 689
11 Arlie Latham 679
12 Willie Wilson 668
13 Bert Campaneris 649
14 Tom Brown 627
15 Otis Nixon 620
16 George Davis 616
17 **Kenny Lofton** 599
18 Dummy Hoy 594
19 Maury Wills 586
20 George Van Haltren 583

Walks

1 **Barry Bonds** 2426
2 Rickey Henderson 2190
3 Babe Ruth 2062
4 Ted Williams 2019
5 Joe Morgan 1865
6 Carl Yastrzemski 1845
7 Mickey Mantle 1733
8 Mel Ott 1708
9 Eddie Yost 1614
10 Darrell Evans 1605
11 Stan Musial 1599
12 Pete Rose 1566
13 Harmon Killebrew 1559
14 **Frank Thomas** 1547
15 Lou Gehrig 1508
16 Mike Schmidt 1507
17 Eddie Collins 1499
18 Willie Mays 1464
19 Jimmie Foxx 1452
20 Eddie Mathews 1444

Strikeouts

1 Reggie Jackson 2597
2 Sammy Sosa 2194
3 Andres Galarraga 2003
4 Jose Canseco 1942
5 Willie Stargell 1936
6 **Jim Thome** 1909
7 Mike Schmidt 1883
8 Fred McGriff 1882
9 Tony Perez 1867
10 Dave Kingman 1816
11 Bobby Bonds 1757
12 Dale Murphy 1748
13 Lou Brock 1730
14 Mickey Mantle 1710
15 Harmon Killebrew 1699
16 Chili Davis 1698
17 Dwight Evans 1697
18 Rickey Henderson 1694
19 Dave Winfield 1686
20 **Craig Biggio** 1641

Pitching

Note that (*) indicates left-handed pitcher. Active pitching leaders are listed for wins and strikeouts.

Wins

		Yrs	GS	W	L	Pct
1	Cy Young	22	815	511	316	.618
2	Walter Johnson	21	666	417	279	.599
3	Christy Mathewson	17	551	373	188	.665
	Grover Alexander	20	598	373	208	.642
5	Pud Galvin	15	688	365	310	.541
6	Warren Spahn*	21	665	363	245	.597
7	Kid Nichols	15	561	361	208	.634
8	**Roger Clemens**	22	690	348	178	.662
9	Tim Keefe	14	594	342	225	.603
10	Greg Maddux	21	677	333	203	.621
11	Steve Carlton*	24	709	329	244	.574
12	John Clarkson	12	518	328	178	.648
13	Eddie Plank*	17	529	326	194	.627
14	Don Sutton	23	756	324	256	.559
	Nolan Ryan	27	773	324	292	.526
16	Phil Niekro	24	716	318	274	.537
17	Gaylord Perry	22	690	314	265	.542
18	Tom Seaver	20	647	311	205	.603
19	Old Hoss Radbourn	12	503	309	195	.613
20	Mickey Welch	13	549	307	210	.594
21	Lefty Grove*	17	456	300	141	.680
	Early Wynn	23	612	300	244	.551
23	Bobby Mathews	15	568	297	248	.545
24	**Tom Glavine***	20	635	290	191	.603
25	Tommy John*	26	700	288	231	.555
26	Bert Blyleven	22	685	287	250	.534
27	Robin Roberts	19	609	286	245	.539
28	Tony Mullane	13	504	284	220	.563
	Ferguson Jenkins	19	594	284	226	.557
30	Jim Kaat*	25	625	283	237	.544

Strikeouts

		Yrs	IP	SO	P/9
1	Nolan Ryan	27	5386.0	5714	9.55
2	**Roger Clemens**	23	4817.2	4604	8.60
3	**Randy Johnson***	19	3798.2	4544	10.77
4	Steve Carlton*	24	5217.1	4136	7.13
5	Bert Blyleven	22	4970.0	3701	6.70
6	Tom Seaver	20	4782.2	3640	6.85
7	Don Sutton	23	5282.1	3574	6.09
8	Gaylord Perry	22	5350.1	3534	5.94
9	Walter Johnson	21	5914.1	3508	5.34
10	Phil Niekro	24	5404.1	3342	5.57
11	Ferguson Jenkins	19	4500.2	3192	6.38
12	**Greg Maddux**	21	4616.1	3169	6.18
13	Bob Gibson	17	3884.1	3117	7.22
14	**Curt Schilling**	19	3110.0	3015	8.73
15	**Pedro Martinez**	15	2645.2	2998	10.20
16	Jim Bunning	17	3760.1	2855	6.83
17	Mickey Lolich*	16	3638.1	2832	7.01
18	Cy Young	22	7356.0	2803	3.43
19	**John Smoltz**	19	3161.1	2778	7.91
20	Frank Tanana*	21	4186.2	2773	5.96
21	David Cone	17	2898.2	2668	8.28
22	Chuck Finley*	17	3197.1	2610	7.35
23	Warren Spahn*	21	5243.2	2583	4.43
24	Bob Feller	18	3827.0	2581	6.07
25	**Mike Mussina**	16	3210.1	2572	7.21
26	Tim Keefe	14	5049.2	2564	4.57
27	Jerry Koosman*	19	3839.1	2556	5.99
28	Christy Mathewson	17	4781.0	2502	4.71
29	Don Drysdale	14	3432.0	2486	6.52
30	**Tom Glavine***	20	4149.2	2481	5.38

Pitchers Active in 2006

		Yrs	GS	W	L	Pct
1	Roger Clemens	22	690	348	178	.662
2	Greg Maddux	21	677	333	203	.621
3	Tom Glavine*	20	635	290	191	.603
4	Randy Johnson*	19	546	280	147	.656
5	Mike Mussina	16	475	239	134	.641
6	David Wells*	20	460	230	148	.608
7	Jamie Moyer*	20	518	216	166	.565
8	Curt Schilling	19	412	207	138	.600
	Kenny Rogers*	18	433	207	139	.598
10	Pedro Martinez	15	375	206	92	.691

Pitchers Active in 2006

		Yrs	IP	SO	P/9
1	Roger Clemens	23	4817.2	4604	8.60
2	Randy Johnson*	19	3798.2	4544	10.77
3	Greg Maddux	21	4616.1	3169	6.18
4	Curt Schilling	19	3110.0	3015	8.73
5	Pedro Martinez	15	2645.2	2998	10.20
6	John Smoltz	19	3161.1	2778	7.91
7	Mike Mussina	16	3210.1	2572	7.21
8	Tom Glavine*	20	4149.2	2481	5.38
9	David Wells*	20	3281.2	2119	5.81
10	Jamie Moyer*	20	3351.0	1992	5.35

Winning Pct.
(Minimum 100 wins)

		Yrs	W-L	Pct
1	Al Spalding	.7	252-65	.795
2	Spud Chandler	.11	109-43	.717
3	**Pedro Martinez**	.15	206-92	.691
4	Dave Foutz	.11	147-66	.690
5	Whitey Ford*	.16	236-106	.690
6	Bob Caruthers	.9	218-99	.688
7	Don Gullett*	.9	109-50	.686
8	Lefty Grove*	.17	300-141	.680
9	Smokey Joe Wood	.11	117-57	.672
10	Vic Raschi	.10	132-66	.667
11	Larry Corcoran	.8	177-89	.665
12	Christy Mathewson	.17	373-188	.665
13	**Tim Hudson**	.8	119-60	.665
14	**Roger Clemens**	.23	348-178	.662
15	Sam Leever	.13	194-100	.660

Losses

		Yrs	GS	W	L	Pct
1	Cy Young	.22	815	511	**316**	.618
2	Pud Galvin	.15	688	365	**310**	.541
3	Nolan Ryan	.27	773	324	**292**	.526
4	Walter Johnson	.21	666	417	**279**	.599
5	Phil Niekro	.24	716	318	**274**	.537
6	Gaylord Perry	.22	690	314	**265**	.542
7	Don Sutton	.23	756	324	**256**	.559
8	Jack Powell	.16	516	245	**254**	.491
9	Eppa Rixey*	.21	552	266	**251**	.515
10	Bert Blyleven	.22	685	287	**250**	.534
11	Bobby Mathews	.15	568	297	**248**	.545
12	Robin Roberts	.19	609	286	**245**	.539
	Warren Spahn*	.21	665	363	**245**	.597
14	Early Wynn	.23	612	300	**244**	.551
	Steve Carlton*	.24	709	329	**244**	.574

Appearances

1	Jesse Orosco	.1252
2	John Franco	.1119
3	**Mike Stanton**	.1109
4	Dennis Eckersley	.1071
5	Hoyt Wilhelm	.1070
6	Dan Plesac	.1064
7	Kent Tekulve	.1050
8	Lee Smith	.1022
9	Mike Jackson	.1005
10	Rich Gossage	.1002
11	Lindy McDaniel	.987
12	**Jose Mesa**	.966
13	**Mike Timlin**	.961
14	**Roberto Hernandez**	.960
15	Rollie Fingers	.944

Innings Pitched

1	Cy Young	.7356.0
2	Pud Galvin	.6003.1
3	Walter Johnson	.5914.1
4	Phil Niekro	.5404.1
5	Nolan Ryan	.5386.0
6	Gaylord Perry	.5350.1
7	Don Sutton	.5282.1
8	Warren Spahn	.5243.2
9	Steve Carlton	.5217.1
10	Grover Alexander	.5190.0
11	Kid Nichols	.5056.1
12	Tim Keefe	.5049.2
13	Bert Blyleven	.4970.0
14	Bobby Mathews	.4956.0
15	**Roger Clemens**	.4817.2

Earned Run Avg.
(Minimum 1500 IP)

1	Ed Walsh	.1.82
2	Addie Joss	.1.89
3	Al Spalding	.2.04
4	Three Finger Brown	.2.06
5	Monte Ward	.2.10
6	Christy Mathewson	.2.13
7	Rube Waddell	.2.16
8	Walter Johnson	.2.17
9	Orval Overall	.2.23
10	Tommy Bond	.2.25
11	Will White	.2.28
12	Ed Reulbach	.2.28
13	Jim Scott	.2.30
14	Eddie Plank	.2.35
15	Larry Corcoran	.2.36

Shutouts

1	Walter Johnson	.110
2	Grover Alexander	.90
3	Christy Mathewson	.79
4	Cy Young	.76
5	Eddie Plank	.69
6	Warren Spahn	.63
7	Nolan Ryan	.61
	Tom Seaver	.61
9	Bert Blyleven	.60
10	Don Sutton	.58
11	Pud Galvin	.57
	Ed Walsh	.57
13	Bob Gibson	.56
14	Three Finger Brown	.55
	Steve Carlton	.55

Walks Allowed

1	Nolan Ryan	.2795
2	Steve Carlton	.1833
3	Phil Niekro	.1809
4	Early Wynn	.1775
5	Bob Feller	.1764
6	Bobo Newsom	.1732
7	Amos Rusie	.1704
8	Charlie Hough	.1665
9	Gus Weyhing	.1566
10	**Roger Clemens**	.1549
11	Red Ruffing	.1541
12	Bump Hadley	.1442
13	Warren Spahn	.1434
14	Earl Whitehill	.1431
15	**Randy Johnson**	.1409

HRs Allowed

1	Robin Roberts	.505
2	Ferguson Jenkins	.484
3	Phil Niekro	.482
4	Don Sutton	.472
5	Frank Tanana	.448
6	Warren Spahn	.434
7	Bert Blyleven	.430
8	Steve Carlton	.414
	Jamie Moyer	.414
10	Gaylord Perry	.399
11	Jim Kaat	.395
12	Jack Morris	.389
13	**David Wells**	.385
14	Charlie Hough	.383
15	Tom Seaver	.380

Saves

1	**Trevor Hoffman**	.482
2	Lee Smith	.478
3	John Franco	.424
4	**Mariano Rivera**	.413
5	Dennis Eckersley	.390
6	Jeff Reardon	.367
7	Randy Myers	.347
8	Rollie Fingers	.341
9	John Wetteland	.330
10	**Roberto Hernandez**	.326
11	**Billy Wagner**	.324
	Troy Percival	.324
13	**Jose Mesa**	.320
14	Rick Aguilera	.318
15	Robb Nen	.314
16	Tom Henke	.311
17	Rich Gossage	.310
18	Jeff Montgomery	.304
19	Doug Jones	.303
20	Bruce Sutter	.300
21	Rod Beck	.286
22	**Armando Benitez**	.280
23	**Todd Jones**	.263
24	Todd Worrell	.256
25	Dave Righetti	.252
26	**Jason Isringhausen**	.249
27	**Bob Wickman**	.247
28	Dan Quisenberry	.244
29	Sparky Lyle	.238
30	Ugueth Urbina	.237

SINGLE SEASON

Through 2006 regular season.

Batting

Home Runs

		Year	Gm	AB	HR
1	Barry Bonds, SF	2001	153	476	73
2	Mark McGwire, St.L	1998	155	509	70
3	Sammy Sosa, Chi-NL	1998	159	643	66
4	Mark McGwire, St.L	1999	153	521	65
5	Sammy Sosa, Chi-NL	2001	160	577	64
6	Sammy Sosa, Chi-NL	1999	162	625	63
7	Roger Maris, NY-AL	1961	162	590	61
8	Babe Ruth, NY-AL	1927	151	540	60
9	Babe Ruth, NY-AL	1921	152	540	59
10	Mark McGwire, Oak-St.L	1997	156	540	58
	Hank Greenberg, Det	1938	155	556	58
	Ryan Howard, Phi	2006	159	581	58
	Jimmie Foxx, Phi-AL	1932	154	585	58
14	Alex Rodriguez, Tex	2002	162	624	57
	Luis Gonzalez, Ari	2001	162	609	57
16	Hack Wilson, Chi-NL	1930	155	585	56
	Ken Griffey Jr., Sea	1997	157	608	56
	Ken Griffey Jr., Sea	1998	161	633	56
19	Babe Ruth, NY-AL	1920	142	458	54
	Mickey Mantle, NY-AL	1961	153	514	54
	Babe Ruth, NY-AL	1928	154	536	54
	David Ortiz, Bos	2006	151	558	54
	Ralph Kiner, Pit	1949	152	549	54

Hits

		Year	AB	H	Avg
1	Ichiro Suzuki, Sea.	2004	704	**262**	.372
2	George Sisler, StL-AL	1920	631	**257**	.407
3	Bill Terry, NY-NL	1930	633	**254**	.401
	Lefty O'Doul, Phi-NL	1929	638	**254**	.398
5	Al Simmons, Phi-AL	1925	658	**253**	.384
6	Rogers Hornsby, StL-NL	1922	623	**250**	.401
	Chuck Klein, Phi-NL	1930	648	**250**	.386
8	Ty Cobb, Det	1911	591	**248**	.420
9	George Sisler, StL-AL	1922	586	**246**	.420
10	Ichiro Suzuki, Sea	2001	692	**242**	.350
11	Babe Herman, Bklyn	1930	614	**241**	.393
	Heinie Manush, StL-AL	1928	638	**241**	.378
13	Wade Boggs, Bos	1985	653	**240**	.368
	Darin Erstad, Ana	2000	676	**240**	.355
15	Rod Carew, Min	1977	616	**239**	.388
16	Don Mattingly, NY-AL	1986	677	**238**	.352
17	Harry Heilmann, Det	1921	602	**237**	.394
	Paul Waner, Pit	1927	623	**237**	.380
	Joe Medwick, StL-NL	1937	633	**237**	.374
20	Jack Tobin, StL-AL	1921	671	**236**	.352

Batting Average

From 1900-49

		Year	AB	H	Avg
1	Rogers Hornsby, Stl-NL	1924	536	227	.424
2	Nap Lajoie, Phi-AL	1901	543	229	.422
3	George Sisler, StL-AL	1922	586	246	.420
4	Ty Cobb, Det	1911	591	248	.420
5	Ty Cobb, Det	1912	533	227	.410
6	Joe Jackson, Cle	1911	571	233	.408
7	George Sisler, StL-AL	1920	631	257	.407
8	Ted Williams, Bos-AL	1941	456	185	.406
9	Rogers Hornsby, StL-NL	1925	504	203	.403
10	Harry Heilmann, Det	1923	524	211	.403

Since 1950

		Year	AB	H	Avg
1	Tony Gwynn, SD	1994	419	175	.394
2	George Brett, KC	1980	449	175	.390
3	Ted Williams, Bos	1957	420	163	.388
4	Rod Carew, Min	1977	616	239	.388
5	Larry Walker, Col	1999	438	166	.379
6	Todd Helton, Col	2000	580	216	.372
7	Nomar Garciaparra, Bos	2000	529	197	.372
8	Ichiro Suzuki, Sea	2004	704	262	.372
9	Tony Gwynn, SD	1997	592	220	.372
10	Andres Galarraga, Col	1993	470	174	.370

Total Bases

From 1900-49

		Year	TB
1	Babe Ruth, New York-AL	1921	457
2	Rogers Hornsby, St. Louis-NL	1922	450
3	Lou Gehrig, New York-AL	1927	447
4	Chuck Klein, Philadelphia-NL	1930	445
5	Jimmie Foxx, Philadelphia-AL	1932	438
6	Stan Musial, St. Louis-NL	1948	429
7	Hack Wilson, Chicago-NL	1930	423
8	Chuck Klein, Philadelphia-NL	1932	420
9	Lou Gehrig, New York-AL	1930	419
10	Joe DiMaggio, New York-AL	1937	418

Since 1950

		Year	TB
1	Sammy Sosa, Chicago-NL	2001	425
2	Luis Gonzalez, Arizona	2001	419
3	Sammy Sosa, Chicago-NL	1998	416
4	Barry Bonds, San Francisco	2001	411
5	Larry Walker, Colorado	1997	409
6	Jim Rice, Boston	1978	406
7	Todd Helton, Colorado	2000	405
8	Todd Helton, Colorado	2001	402
9	Hank Aaron, Milwaukee	1959	400
10	Albert Belle, Chicago-AL	1998	399

Runs Batted In

From 1900-49

		Year	Avg	HR	RBI
1	Hack Wilson, Chi-NL	1930	.356	56	191
2	Lou Gehrig, NY-AL	1931	.341	46	184
3	Hank Greenberg, Det	1937	.337	40	183
4	Lou Gehrig, NY-AL	1927	.373	47	175
	Jimmie Foxx, Bos-AL	1938	.349	50	175
6	Lou Gehrig, NY-AL	1930	.379	41	174
7	Babe Ruth, NY-AL	1921	.378	59	171
8	Chuck Klein, Phi-NL	1930	.386	40	170
	Hank Greenberg, Det	1935	.328	36	170
10	Jimmie Foxx, Phi-AL	1932	.364	58	169

Since 1950

		Year	Avg	HR	RBI
1	Manny Ramirez, Cle	1999	.333	44	165
2	Sammy Sosa, Chi-NL	2001	.328	64	160
3	Sammy Sosa, Chi-NL	1998	.308	66	158
4	Juan Gonzalez, Tex	1998	.318	45	157
5	Tommy Davis, LA-NL	1962	.346	27	153
6	Albert Belle, Chi-AL	1998	.328	49	152
7	Andres Galarraga, Col	1996	.304	47	150
	Miguel Tejada, Bal	2004	.311	34	150
9	George Foster, Cin	1977	.320	52	149
	Ryan Howard, Phi	2006	.313	58	149

Runs

		Year	Runs
1	Babe Ruth, New York-AL	1921	177
2	Lou Gehrig, New York-AL	1936	167
3	Babe Ruth, New York-AL	1928	163
	Lou Gehrig, New York-AL	1931	163
5	Babe Ruth, New York-AL	1920	158
	Babe Ruth, New York-AL	1927	158
	Chuck Klein, Philadelphia-NL	1930	158
8	Rogers Hornsby, Chicago-NL	1929	156
9	Kiki Cuyler, Chicago-NL	1930	155
10	Lefty O'Doul, Philadelphia-NL	1929	152
	Woody English, Chicago-NL	1930	152
	Al Simmons, Philadelphia-AL	1930	152
	Chuck Klein, Philadelphia-NL	1932	152
	Jeff Bagwell, Houston	2000	152
15	Babe Ruth, New York-AL	1923	151
	Jimmie Foxx, Philadelphia-AL	1932	151
	Joe DiMaggio, New York-AL	1937	151
18	Babe Ruth, New York-AL	1930	150
	Ted Williams, Boston-AL	1949	150
20	Lou Gehrig, New York-AL	1927	149
	Babe Ruth, New York-AL	1931	149

Walks

		Year	BB
1	Barry Bonds, San Francisco	2004	232
2	Barry Bonds, San Francisco	2002	198
3	Barry Bonds, San Francisco	2001	177
4	Babe Ruth, New York-AL	1923	170
5	Ted Williams, Boston-AL	1947	162
	Ted Williams, Boston-AL	1949	162
	Mark McGwire, St. Louis	1998	162
8	Ted Williams, Boston-AL	1946	156
9	Barry Bonds, San Francisco	1996	151
	Eddie Yost, Washington	1956	151

Extra Base Hits

		Year	EBH
1	Babe Ruth, New York-AL	1921	119
2	Lou Gehrig, New York-AL	1927	117
3	Chuck Klein, Philadelphia-NL	1930	107
	Barry Bonds, San Francisco	2001	107
5	Todd Helton, Colorado	2001	105
6	Chuck Klein, Philadelphia-NL	1932	103
	Hank Greenberg, Detroit	1937	103
	Stan Musial, St. Louis-NL	1948	103
	Albert Belle, Cleveland	1995	103
	Todd Helton, Colorado	2000	103
	Sammy Sosa, Chicago-NL	2001	103

Slugging Percentage
From 1900-49

		Year	Pct
1	Babe Ruth, New York-AL	1920	.847
2	Babe Ruth, New York-AL	1921	.846
3	Babe Ruth, New York-AL	1927	.772
4	Lou Gehrig, New York-AL	1927	.765
5	Babe Ruth, New York-AL	1923	.764
6	Rogers Hornsby, St. Louis-NL	1925	.756
7	Jimmie Foxx, Philadelphia-AL	1932	.749
8	Babe Ruth, New York-AL	1924	.739
9	Babe Ruth, New York-AL	1926	.737
10	Ted Williams, Boston-AL	1941	.735

Since 1950

		Year	Pct
1	Barry Bonds, San Francisco	2001	.863
2	Barry Bonds, San Francisco	2004	.812
3	Barry Bonds, San Francisco	2002	.799
4	Mark McGwire, St. Louis	1998	.752
5	Jeff Bagwell, Houston	1994	.750
6	Barry Bonds, San Francisco	2003	.749
7	Sammy Sosa, Chicago-NL	2001	.737
8	Ted Williams, Boston	1957	.731
9	Mark McGwire, Oakland	1996	.730
10	Frank Thomas, Chicago-AL	1994	.729

Doubles

		Year	2B
1	Earl Webb, Boston-AL	1931	67
2	George Burns, Cleveland	1926	64
	Joe Medwick, St. Louis-NL	1936	64
4	Hank Greenberg, Detroit	1934	63
5	Paul Waner, Pittsburgh	1932	62
6	Charlie Gehringer, Detroit	1936	60
7	Tris Speaker, Cleveland	1923	59
	Chuck Klein, Philadelphia-NL	1930	59
	Todd Helton, Colorado	2000	· 59
10	Three tied with 57 each.		

Triples
From 1900-49

		Year	3B
1	Chief Wilson, Pittsburgh	1912	36
2	Joe Jackson, Cleveland	1912	26
3	Sam Crawford, Detroit	1914	26
4	Kiki Cuyler, Pittsburgh	1925	26
5	Three tied with 25 each.		

Since 1950

		Year	3B
1	Willie Wilson, Kansas City	1985	21
	Lance Johnson, New York-NL	1996	21
3	Willie Mays, New York-NL	1957	20
	George Brett, Kansas City	1979	20
	Cristian Guzman, Minnesota	2000	20

Stolen Bases

		Year	SB
1	Rickey Henderson, Oakland	1982	130
2	Lou Brock, St. Louis	1974	118
3	Vince Coleman, St. Louis	1985	110
4	Vince Coleman, St. Louis	1987	109
5	Rickey Henderson, Oakland	1983	108
6	Vince Coleman, St. Louis	1986	107
7	Maury Wills, Los Angeles-NL	1962	104
8	Rickey Henderson, Oakland	1980	100
9	Ron LeFlore, Montreal	1980	97
10	Ty Cobb, Detroit	1915	96
	Omar Moreno, Pittsburgh	1980	96
12	Maury Wills, Los Angeles	1965	94
13	Rickey Henderson, New York-AL	1988	93
14	Tim Raines, Montreal	1983	90
15	Clyde Milan, Washington	1912	88

Strikeouts

		Year	SO
1	Adam Dunn, Cincinnati	2004	195
2	**Adam Dunn**, Cincinnati	2006	194
3	Bobby Bonds, San Francisco	1970	189
4	Jose Hernandez, Milwaukee	2002	188
5	Bobby Bonds, San Francisco	1969	187
	Preston Wilson, Florida	2000	187
7	Rob Deer, Milwaukee	1987	186
8	Pete Incaviglia, Texas	1986	185
	Jose Hernandez, Milwaukee	2001	185
	Jim Thome, Cleveland	2001	185
11	Cecil Fielder, Detroit	1990	182
	Jim Thome, Philadelphia	2003	182

Pinch Hits
Career pinch hits in parentheses.

		Year	PH	
1	John Vander Wal, Colorado	1995	28	(129)
2	Lenny Harris, Col-Ari	1999	26	(212)
3	Jose Morales, Montreal	1976	25	(123)
4	Dave Philley, Baltimore	1961	24	(93)
	Vic Davalillo, St. Louis	1970	24	(95)
	Rusty Staub, New York-NL	1983	24	(100)
	Gerald Perry, St. Louis	1993	24	(95)

Note: Harris (212) is the career leader.

Pitching
Wins

From 1900-49

		Year	W	L	Pct
1	Jack Chesbro, NY-AL	1904	41	12	.774
2	Ed Walsh, Chi-AL	1908	40	15	.727
3	Christy Mathewson, NY-NL	1908	37	11	.771
4	Walter Johnson, Wash	1913	36	7	.837
5	Joe McGinnity, NY-NL	1904	35	8	.814
6	Smokey Joe Wood, Bos-AL	1912	34	5	.872
7	Cy Young, Bos-AL	1901	33	10	.767
	Grover Alexander, Phi-NL	1916	33	12	.733
	Christy Mathewson, NY-NL	1904	33	12	.733
10	Cy Young, Bos-AL	1902	32	11	.744

Since 1950

		Year	W	L	Pct
1	Denny McLain, Det	1968	31	6	.838
2	Robin Roberts, Phi-NL	1952	28	7	.800
3	Bob Welch, Oak	1990	27	6	.818
	Don Newcombe, Bklyn	1956	27	7	.794
	Sandy Koufax, LA	1966	27	9	.750
	Steve Carlton, Phi	1972	27	10	.730
7	Sandy Koufax, LA	1965	26	8	.765
	Juan Marichal, SF	1968	26	9	.743

Note: 11 pitchers tied with 25 wins, including Marichal twice.

Earned Run Average

From 1900-49

		Year	ShO	ERA
1	Dutch Leonard, Bos-AL	1914	7	1.01
2	Three Finger Brown, Chi-NL	1906	10	1.04
3	Walter Johnson, Wash	1913	11	1.09
4	Christy Mathewson, NY-NL	1909	8	1.14
5	Jack Pfiester, Chi-NL	1907	3	1.15
6	Addie Joss, Cle	1908	9	1.16
7	Carl Lundgren, Chi-NL	1907	7	1.17
8	Grover Alexander, Phi-NL	1915	12	1.22
9	Cy Young, Bos-AL	1908	3	1.26
10	Three pitchers tied at 1.27			

Since 1950

		Year	ShO	ERA
1	Bob Gibson, St.L	1968	13	1.12
2	Dwight Gooden, NY-NL	1985	8	1.53
3	Greg Maddux, Atl	1994	3	1.56
4	Luis Tiant, Cle	1968	9	1.60
5	Greg Maddux, Atl	1995	3	1.63
6	Dean Chance, LA-AL	1964	11	1.65
7	Nolan Ryan, Cal	1981	3	1.69
8	Sandy Koufax, LA	1966	5	1.73
9	Sandy Koufax, LA	1964	7	1.74
10	Pedro Martinez, Bos	2000	4	1.74

Note: Koufax's ERA in 1964 was 1.735. Martinez' ERA in 2000 was 1.742. The Yankees' Ron Guidry narrowly missed the top 10 list with an ERA of 1.743 in 1978.

Winning Pct.

		Year	W-L	Pct
1	Roy Face, Pit	1959	18-1	.947
2	Rick Sutcliffe, Chi-NL*	1984	16-1	.941
3	Johnny Allen, Cle	1937	15-1	.938
4	Greg Maddux, Atl	1995	19-2	.904
5	Randy Johnson, Sea	1995	18-2	.900
6	Ron Guidry, NY-AL	1978	25-3	.893
7	Freddie Fitzsimmons, Bklyn	1940	16-2	.889
8	Lefty Grove, Phi-AL	1931	31-4	.886
9	Bob Stanley, Bos	1978	15-2	.882
10	Preacher Roe, Bklyn	1951	22-3	.880

*Sutcliffe began 1984 with Cleveland and was 4-5 before being traded to the Cubs; his overall winning pct. was .769 (20-6).

Strikeouts

		Year	SO	P/9
1	Nolan Ryan, Cal	1973	383	10.57
2	Sandy Koufax, LA	1965	382	10.24
3	Randy Johnson, Ari	2001	372	13.41
4	Nolan Ryan, Cal	1974	367	9.93
5	Randy Johnson, Ari	1999	364	12.06
6	Rube Waddell, Phi-AL	1904	349	8.20
7	Bob Feller, Cle	1946	348	8.43
8	Randy Johnson, Ari	2000	347	12.56
9	Nolan Ryan, Cal	1977	341	10.26
10	Randy Johnson, Ari	2002	334	11.56

Appearances

		Year	App	Sv
1	Mike Marshall, LA	1974	106	21
2	Kent Tekulve, Pit	1979	94	31
	Salomon Torres, Pit	2006	94	12
4	Mike Marshall, LA	1973	92	31
5	Kent Tekulve, Pit	1978	91	31
6	Wayne Granger, Cin	1969	90	27
	Mike Marshall, Min	1979	90	32
	Kent Tekulve, Phi	1987	90	3

Saves

		Year	App	Sv
1	Bobby Thigpen, Chi-AL	1990	77	57
2	John Smoltz, Atl	2002	75	55
	Eric Gagne, LA	2003	77	55
4	Randy Myers, Chi-NL	1993	73	53
	Trevor Hoffman, SD	1998	66	53
	Mariano Rivera, NY-AL	2004	74	53
7	Eric Gagne, LA	2002	77	52
8	Dennis Eckersley, Oak	1992	69	51
	Rod Beck, Chi-NL	1998	81	51
10	Mariano Rivera, NY-AL	2001	71	50

Innings Pitched *(since 1920)*

		Year	IP	W-L
1	Wilbur Wood, Chi-AL	1972	376.2	24-17
2	Mickey Lolich, Det	1971	376.0	25-14
3	Bob Feller, Cle	1946	371.1	26-15
4	Grover Alexander, Chi-NL	1920	363.1	27-14
5	Wilbur Wood, Chi-AL	1973	359.1	24-20

Shutouts

		Year	ShO	ERA
1	Grover Alexander, Phi-NL	1916	16	1.55
2	Jack Coombs, Phi-AL	1910	13	1.30
	Bob Gibson, St.L	1968	13	1.12
4	Christy Mathewson, NY-NL	1908	12	1.43
	Grover Alexander, Phi-NL	1915	12	1.22

Walks Allowed *(since 1920)*

		Year	BB	SO
1	Bob Feller, Cle	1938	208	240
2	Nolan Ryan, Cal	1977	204	341
3	Nolan Ryan, Cal	1974	202	367
4	Bob Feller, Cle	1941	194	260
5	Bobo Newsom, St.L-AL	1938	192	226

Home Runs Allowed

		Year	HRs
1	Bert Blyleven, Minnesota	1986	50
2	Jose Lima, Houston	2000	48
3	Robin Roberts, Philadelphia	1956	46
	Bert Blyleven, Minnesota	1987	46
5	Jamie Moyer, Seattle	2004	44

SINGLE GAME
Through 2006 regular season.

Batting

Home Runs

No		Date	Inn
4	Bobby Lowe, Boston-NL 5/30/1894		9
	Ed Delahanty, Philadelphia-NL . .7/13/1896		9
	Lou Gehrig, New York-AL 6/3/1932		9
	Chuck Klein, Philadelphia-NL . . .7/10/1936		10
	Pat Seerey, Chicago-AL 7/18/1948		11
	Gil Hodges, Brooklyn 8/31/1950		9
	Joe Adcock, Milwaukee 7/31/1954		9
	Rocky Colavito, Cleveland 6/10/1959		9
	Willie Mays, San Francisco 4/30/1961		9
	Mike Schmidt, Philadelphia 4/17/1976		10
	Bob Horner, Atlanta 7/6/1986		9
	Mark Whiten, St. Louis 9/7/1993		9
	Mike Cameron, Seattle 5/2/2002		9
	Shawn Green, Los Angeles 5/23/2002		9
	Carlos Delgado, Toronto 9/25/2003		9

Runs

No		Date	Inn
7	Guy Hecker, Louisville 8/15/1886		9

Hits

No		Date	Inn
9	Johnny Burnett, Cleveland (9-for-11) 7/10/1932		18
7	Wilbert Robinson, Baltimore 3 (7-for-7) 6/10/1892		9
	Rennie Stennett, Pittsburgh (7-for-7) 9/16/1975		9
	Cesar Gutierrez, Detroit (7-for-7) 6/21/1970		12
	Rocky Colavito, Detroit (7-for-10) 6/24/1962		22

Runs Batted In

No		Date	Inn
12	Jim Bottomley, St. Louis-NL 9/16/1924		9
	Mark Whiten, St. Louis 9/7/1993		9

Pitching

Strikeouts

No		Date	Inn
21	Tom Cheney, Washington 9/12/1962		16
20	Roger Clemens, Boston 4/29/1986		9
	Roger Clemens, Boston 9/18/1996		9
	Kerry Wood, Chicago-NL 5/6/1998		9
	Randy Johnson, Arizona 5/8/2001		9*

Innings Pitched

No		Date
26	Leon Cadore, Brooklyn (tie, 1-1) 5/1/1920	
	Joe Oeschger, Boston-NL (tie, 1-1) 5/1/1920	

*Johnson struck out 20 in nine innings and was removed with the game tied, 1-1. Arizona beat Cincinnati, 4-3, in 11 innings.

Unassisted Triple Plays

One of the rarest feats in baseball, the unassisted triple play has been accomplished only 13 times in major league history. Ironically, in what can only be described as a statistic anomaly, the trick was turned twice in two days in May of 1927.

Player, Position, Team	Date	Opponent
Paul Hines, OF, Providence . . . . .May 8, 1878		Boston-NL
Neal Ball, SS, Cleveland . . . . .July 19, 1909		Boston-AL
Bill Wambganss, 2B, Cleveland* . . . . .Oct. 10, 1920		Brooklyn
George Burns, 1B, Boston-AL . . . . .Sept. 14, 1923		Cleveland
Ernie Padgett, SS, Boston-NL . . . . .Oct. 6, 1923		Philadelphia
Glenn Wright, SS, Pittsburgh . . . . .May 7, 1925		St.Louis-NL
Jimmy Cooney, SS, Chicago-NL . . . . .May 30, 1927		Pittsburgh
Johnny Neun, 1B, Detroit . . . . .May 31, 1927		Cleveland
Ron Hansen, SS, Washington . . . . .July 30, 1968		Cleveland
Mickey Morandini, 2B, Philadelphia . . . . .Sept. 20, 1992		Pittsburgh
John Valentin, SS, Boston . . . . .July 8, 1994		Seattle
Randy Velarde, 2B, Oakland . . . . .May 29, 2000		NY Yankees
Rafael Furcal, SS, Atlanta . . . . .Aug. 10, 2003		St. Louis

* World Series game

Most Gold Gloves (by position)

Gold Gloves have been awarded since the 1957 season by Rawlings Sporting Goods to superior major league fielders at each position in both leagues. Voting has been conducted by a panel of sportswriters appointed by *The Sporting News* publisher J.G. Taylor Spink (1957), major league players (1958-1964) and managers and coaches (1965-present). Top 5 in each position are listed, through the 2006 season.

Pitchers	No	Catchers	No	First Basemen	No	Second Basemen	No
1 Jim Kaat	.16	1 Ivan Rodriguez	.11	1 Keith Hernandez	.11	1 Roberto Alomar	.10
2 Greg Maddux	.15	2 Johnny Bench	.10	2 Don Mattingly	.9	2 Ryne Sandberg	.9
3 Bob Gibson	.9	3 Bob Boone	.7	3 George Scott	.8	3 Bill Mazeroski	.8
4 Bobby Shantz	.8	4 Jim Sundberg	.6	4 Vic Power	.7	Frank White	.8
5 Mark Langston	.7	5 Bill Freehan	.5	Bill White	.7	5 Joe Morgan	.5
						Bobby Richardson	.5

Third Basemen	No	Shortstops	No	Outfielders	No		
1 Brooks Robinson	.16	1 Ozzie Smith	.13	1 Roberto Clemente	.12		
2 Mike Schmidt	.10	2 Omar Vizquel	.10	Willie Mays	.12		
3 Buddy Bell	.6	3 Luis Aparicio	.9	3 Ken Griffey Jr.	.10		
Robin Ventura	.6	4 Mark Belanger	.8	Al Kaline	.10		
Scott Rolen	.6	5 Dave Concepcion	.5	5 Seven tied with 8 each			

All-Time Winningest Managers

Top 20 Major League career victories through the 2006 season. Career, regular season and postseason (playoffs and World Series) records are noted along with AL and NL pennants and World Series titles won. Managers active during 2006 season in **bold** type.

		Career			Regular Season			Postseason			
		Yrs	W	L	Pct	W	L	Pct	W	L	Pct	Titles
1	Connie Mack	.53	**3755**	3967	.486	3731	3948	.486	24	19	.558	9 AL, 5 WS
2	John McGraw	.33	**2866**	2012	.588	2840	1984	.589	26	28	.482	10 NL, 3 WS
3	**Tony La Russa**	.28	**2356**	2034	.537	2297	1986	.536	59	48	.551	3 AL, 2 NL, 2 WS
4	**Bobby Cox**	.25	**2237**	1752	.561	2171	1686	.563	66	66	.500	5 NL, 1 WS
5	Sparky Anderson	.26	**2228**	1855	.547	2194	1834	.545	34	21	.618	4 NL, 1 AL, 3 WS
6	Bucky Harris	.29	**2168**	2228	.493	2157	2218	.493	11	10	.524	3 AL, 2 WS
7	Joe McCarthy	.24	**2155**	1346	.616	2125	1333	.615	30	13	.698	1 NL, 8 AL, 7 WS
8	Walter Alston	.23	**2063**	1634	.558	2040	1613	.558	23	21	.523	7 NL, 4 WS
9	Leo Durocher	.24	**2015**	1717	.540	2008	1709	.540	7	8	.467	3 NL, 1 WS
10	**Joe Torre**	.25	**2048**	1749	.539	1973	1702	.537	75	47	.615	6 AL, 4 WS
11	Casey Stengel	.25	**1942**	1868	.510	1905	1842	.508	37	26	.587	10 AL, 7 WS
12	Gene Mauch	.26	**1907**	2044	.483	1902	2037	.483	5	7	.417	—None—
13	Bill McKechnie	.25	**1904**	1737	.523	1896	1723	.524	8	14	.364	4 NL, 2 WS
14	Tommy Lasorda	.21	**1630**	1469	.526	1599	1439	.526	31	30	.508	4 NL, 2 WS
15	Ralph Houk	.20	**1627**	1539	.514	1619	1531	.514	8	8	.500	3 AL, 2 WS
16	Fred Clarke	.19	**1609**	1189	.575	1602	1181	.576	7	8	.467	4 NL, 1 WS
17	Dick Williams	.21	**1592**	1474	.519	1571	1451	.520	21	23	.477	3 AL, 1 NL, 2 WS
18	Lou Piniella	.19	**1542**	1441	.517	1519	1420	.517	23	21	.523	1 NL, 1 WS
19	Earl Weaver	.17	**1506**	1080	.582	1480	1060	.583	26	20	.565	4 AL, 1 WS
20	Clark Griffith	.20	**1491**	1367	.522	1491	1367	.522	0	0	.000	1 AL (1901)

Notes: John McGraw's postseason record also includes two World Series tie games (1912, '22).

Where They Managed

Alston—Brooklyn/Los Angeles NL (1954-76); **Anderson**—Cincinnati NL (1970-78), Detroit AL (1979-95); **Clarke**—Louisville NL (1897-99), Pittsburgh NL (1900-15); **Cox**—Atlanta (1978-81, 1990-), Toronto (1982-85); **Durocher**—Brooklyn NL (1939-46,48), New York NL (1948-55), Chicago NL (1966-72), Houston NL (1972-73); **Griffith**—Chicago AL (1901-02), New York AL (1903-08), Cincinnati NL (1909-11), Washington AL (1912-20); **Harris**—Washington AL (1924- 28,35-42,50-54), Detroit AL (1929-33,55-56), Boston AL (1934), Philadelphia NL (1943), New York AL (1947-48); **Houk**—New York AL (1961-63,66-73), Detroit AL (1974-78), Boston AL (1981-84); **La Russa**—Chicago AL (1979-86), Oakland (1986-95); St. Louis (1996-) **Lasorda**—Los Angeles NL (1976-96); **Mack**—Pittsburgh NL (1894-96), Philadelphia AL (1901-50).

Mauch—Philadelphia NL (1960-68), Montreal NL (1969-75), Minnesota NL (1976-80), California AL (1981-82,85-87); **McCarthy**—Chicago NL (1926-30), New York AL (1931-46), Boston AL (1948-50); **McGraw**—Baltimore NL (1899), Baltimore AL (1901-02), New York NL (1902-32); **McKechnie**—Newark FL (1915), Pittsburgh NL (1922-26), St. Louis NL (1928-29), Boston NL (1930-37), Cincinnati NL (1938-46); **Piniella**—New York AL (1986-88), Cincinnati (1990-92), Seattle (1993-2002), Tampa Bay (2003-05), Chicago NL (2007-); **Stengel**—Brooklyn NL (1934-36), Boston NL (1938-43), New York AL (1949-60), New York NL (1962-65); **Torre**—New York NL (1977-81), Atlanta (1982-84), St. Louis (1990-95), New York AL (1996-); **Weaver**—Baltimore AL (1968-82,85-86); **Williams**—Boston AL (1967-69), Oakland AL (1971-73), California AL (1974-76), Montreal NL (1977-81), San Diego NL (1982-85), Seattle AL (1986-88).

Regular Season Winning Pct.

Minimum of 750 victories.

		Yrs	W	L	Pct	Pen
1	Joe McCarthy	.24	2125	1333	**.615**	9
2	Charlie Comiskey	.12	838	541	**.608**	4
3	Frank Selee	.16	1284	862	**.598**	5
4	Billy Southworth	.13	1044	704	**.597**	4
5	Frank Chance	.11	946	648	**.593**	4
6	John McGraw	.33	2840	1984	**.589**	10
7	Al Lopez	.17	1410	1004	**.584**	2
8	Earl Weaver	.17	1480	1060	**.583**	4
9	Cap Anson	.20	1296	947	**.578**	5
10	Fred Clarke	.19	1602	1181	**.576**	4
11	Davey Johnson	.14	1148	888	**.564**	1
12	**Bobby Cox**	.25	2171	1686	**.563**	5
13	Steve O'Neill	.14	1040	821	**.559**	1
14	Walter Alston	.23	2040	1613	**.558**	7
15	Bill Terry	.10	823	661	**.555**	3
16	Miller Huggins	.17	1413	1134	**.555**	6
17	Billy Martin	.16	1253	1013	**.553**	2
18	Harry Wright	.18	1000	825	**.548**	3
19	Charlie Grimm	.19	1287	1067	**.547**	3
20	Sparky Anderson	.26	2194	1834	**.545**	5

World Series Victories

		App	W	L	T	Pct	WS
1	Casey Stengel	.10	**37**	26	0	.587	7
2	Joe McCarthy	.9	**30**	13	0	.698	7
3	John McGraw	.9	**26**	28	2	.482	3
4	Connie Mack	.8	**24**	19	0	.558	5
5	**Joe Torre**	.6	**21**	11	0	.656	4
6	Walter Alston	.7	**20**	20	0	.500	4
7	Miller Huggins	.6	**18**	15	1	.544	3
8	Sparky Anderson	.5	**16**	12	0	.571	3
9	Tommy Lasorda	.4	**12**	11	0	.522	2
	Dick Williams	.4	**12**	14	0	.462	2
11	Frank Chance	.4	**11**	9	1	.548	2
	Bucky Harris	.3	**11**	10	0	.524	2
	Billy Southworth	.4	**11**	11	0	.500	2
	Earl Weaver	.4	**11**	13	0	.458	1
	Bobby Cox	.5	**11**	18	0	.379	1
16	Whitey Herzog	.3	**10**	11	0	.476	1
17	**Tony La Russa**	.5	**9**	13	0	.409	2
18	Bill Carrigan	.2	**8**	2	0	.800	2
	Danny Murtaugh	.2	**8**	6	0	.571	2
	Cito Gaston	.2	**8**	6	0	.571	2
	Tom Kelly	.2	**8**	6	0	.571	2
	Ralph Houk	.3	**8**	8	0	.500	2
	Bill McKechnie	.4	**8**	14	0	.364	2

Active Managers' Records

Regular season games only; through 2006 (updated as of Oct. 20).

National League

		Yrs	W	L	Pct
1	Tony La Russa, St.L	28	**2297**	1986	.536
2	Bobby Cox, Atl.	25	**2171**	1686	.563
3	Lou Piniella, Chi	19	**1519**	1420	.517
4	Bruce Bochy, SD	12	**951**	975	.494
5	Phil Garner, Hou.	14	**927**	981	.486
6	Jim Tracy, Pit.	6	**494**	478	.508
7	Charlie Manuel, Phi	5	**393**	342	.535
8	Clint Hurdle, Col	5	**352**	436	.447
9	Bob Melvin, Ari	4	**309**	339	.477
10	Ned Yost, Mil	4	**291**	356	.450
11	Grady Little, LA	3	**276**	210	.568
12	Jerry Narron, Cin	4	**260**	290	.473
13	Willie Randolph, NY	2	**180**	144	.556
14	Fredi Gonzalez, Fla.	0	**0**	0	.000
	Washington				
	San Francisco				

American League

		Yrs	W	L	Pct
1	Joe Torre, NY	25	**1973**	1702	.537
2	Jim Leyland, Det.	15	**1164**	1198	.493
3	Mike Hargrove, Sea	15	**1143**	1140	.501
4	Mike Scioscia, Ana.	7	**609**	525	.537
5	Terry Francona, Bos.	7	**564**	570	.497
6	Ron Gardenhire, Min.	5	**455**	354	.562
7	Buddy Bell, KC	8	**450**	631	.416
8	Eric Wedge, Cle.	4	**319**	330	.492
9	Ozzie Guillen, Chi	3	**272**	214	.560
10	John Gibbons, Tor.	3	**187**	187	.500
11	Joe Maddon, TB	4	**94**	127	.425
12	Sam Perlozzo, Bal	2	**93**	124	.429
	Oakland				
	Texas				

Annual Awards

MOST VALUABLE PLAYER

There have been three different Most Valuable Player awards in baseball since 1911—the Chalmers Award (1911-14), presented by the Detroit-based automobile company; the League Award (1922-29), presented by the National and American Leagues; and the Baseball Writers' Award (since 1931), presented by the Baseball Writers' Association of America. Statistics for winning players are provided below. Stats for winning pitchers before advent of Cy Young Award are in MVP Pitchers' Statistics table.

Multiple winners: NL—Barry Bonds (7); Roy Campanella, Stan Musial and Mike Schmidt (3); Ernie Banks, Johnny Bench, Rogers Hornsby, Carl Hubbell, Willie Mays, Joe Morgan and Dale Murphy (2). **AL**—Yogi Berra, Joe DiMaggio, Jimmie Foxx and Mickey Mantle (3); Mickey Cochrane, Lou Gehrig, Juan Gonzalez, Hank Greenberg, Walter Johnson, Roger Maris, Hal Newhouser, Cal Ripken Jr., Alex Rodriguez, Frank Thomas, Ted Williams and Robin Yount (2). **NL & AL**—Frank Robinson (2, one in each).

Chalmers Award

National League

Year		Pos	HR	RBI	Avg
1911	Wildfire Schulte, Chi	OF	21	121	.300
1912	Larry Doyle, NY	2B	10	90	.330
1913	Jake Daubert, Bklyn	1B	2	52	.350
1914	Johnny Evers, Bos	2B	1	40	.279

American League

Year		Pos	HR	RBI	Avg
1911	Ty Cobb, Det	OF	8	144	.420
1912	Tris Speaker, Bos	OF	10	98	.383
1913	Walter Johnson, Wash	P	—	—	—
1914	Eddie Collins, Phi	2B	2	85	.344

League Award

National League

Year		Pos	HR	RBI	Avg
1922	No selection				
1923	No selection				
1924	Dazzy Vance, Bklyn	P	—	—	—
1925	Rogers Hornsby, St.L	2B-Mgr	39	143	.403
1926	Bob O'Farrell, St.L	C	7	68	.293
1927	Paul Waner, Pit	OF	9	131	.380
1928	Jim Bottomley, St.L	1B	31	136	.325
1929	Rogers Hornsby, Chi	2B	39	149	.380

American League

Year		Pos	HR	RBI	Avg
1922	George Sisler, St.L	1B	8	105	.420
1923	Babe Ruth, NY	OF	41	131	.393
1924	Walter Johnson, Wash	P	—	—	—
1925	Roger Peckinpaugh, Wash	SS	4	64	.294
1926	George Burns, Cle	1B	4	114	.358
1927	Lou Gehrig, NY	1B	47	175	.373
1928	Mickey Cochrane, Phi	C	10	57	.293
1929	No selection				

Most Valuable Player

National League

Year		Pos	HR	RBI	Avg	Year		Pos	HR	RBI	Avg
1931	Frankie Frisch, St.L	2B	4	82	.311	1950	Jim Konstanty, Phi	P	—	—	—
1932	Chuck Klein, Phi	OF	38	137	.348	1951	Roy Campanella, Bklyn	C	33	108	.325
1933	Carl Hubbell, NY	P	—	—	—	1952	Hank Sauer, Chi	OF	37	121	.270
1934	Dizzy Dean, St.L	P	—	—	—	1953	Roy Campanella, Bklyn	C	41	142	.312
1935	Gabby Hartnett, Chi	C	13	91	.344	1954	Willie Mays, NY	OF	41	110	.345
1936	Carl Hubbell, NY	P	—	—	—	1955	Roy Campanella, Bklyn	C	32	107	.318
1937	Joe Medwick, St.L	OF	31	154	.374	1956	Don Newcombe, Bklyn	P	—	—	—
1938	Ernie Lombardi, Cin	C	19	95	.342	1957	Hank Aaron, Mil	OF	44	132	.322
1939	Bucky Walters, Cin	P	—	—	—	1958	Ernie Banks, Chi	SS	47	129	.313
1940	Frank McCormick, Cin	1B	19	127	.309	1959	Ernie Banks, Chi	SS	45	143	.304
1941	Dolf Camilli, Bklyn	1B	34	120	.285	1960	Dick Groat, Pit	SS	2	50	.325
1942	Mort Cooper, St.L	P	—	—	—	1961	Frank Robinson, Cin	OF	37	124	.323
1943	Stan Musial, St.L	OF	13	81	.357	1962	Maury Wills, LA	SS	6	48	.299
1944	Marty Marion, St.L	SS	6	63	.267	1963	Sandy Koufax, LA	P	—	—	—
1945	Phil Cavarretta, Chi	1B	6	97	.355	1964	Ken Boyer, St.L	3B	24	119	.295
1946	Stan Musial, St.L	1B-OF	16	103	.365	1965	Willie Mays, SF	OF	52	112	.317
1947	Bob Elliott, Bos	3B	22	113	.317	1966	Roberto Clemente, Pit	OF	29	119	.317
1948	Stan Musial, St.L	OF	39	131	.376	1967	Orlando Cepeda, St.L	1B	25	111	.325
1949	Jackie Robinson, Bklyn	2B	16	124	.342	1968	Bob Gibson, St.L	P	—	—	—

Year		Pos	HR	RBI	Avg	Year		Pos	HR	RBI	Avg
1969	Willie McCovey, SF	1B	45	126	.320	1987	Andre Dawson, Chi	OF	49	137	.287
1970	Johnny Bench, Cin	C	45	148	.293	1988	Kirk Gibson, LA	OF	25	76	.290
1971	Joe Torre, St.L	3B	24	137	.363	1989	Kevin Mitchell, SF	OF	47	125	.291
1972	Johnny Bench, Cin	C	40	125	.270	1990	Barry Bonds, Pit	OF	33	114	.301
1973	Pete Rose, Cin	OF	5	64	.338	1991	Terry Pendleton, Atl	3B	22	86	.319
1974	Steve Garvey, LA	1B	21	111	.312	1992	Barry Bonds, Pit	OF	34	103	.311
1975	Joe Morgan, Cin	2B	17	94	.327	1993	Barry Bonds, SF	OF	46	123	.336
1976	Joe Morgan, Cin	2B	27	111	.320	1994	Jeff Bagwell, Hou	1B	39	116	.368
1977	George Foster, Cin	OF	52	149	.320	1995	Barry Larkin, Cin	SS	15	66	.319
1978	Dave Parker, Pit	OF	30	117	.334	1996	Ken Caminiti, SD	3B	40	130	.326
1979	Keith Hernandez, St.L	1B	11	105	.344	1997	Larry Walker, Col	OF	49	130	.366
	Willie Stargell, Pit	1B	32	82	.281	1998	Sammy Sosa, Chi	OF	66	158	.308
1980	Mike Schmidt, Phi	3B	48	121	.286	1999	Chipper Jones, Atl	3B	45	110	.319
1981	Mike Schmidt, Phi	3B	31	91	.316	2000	Jeff Kent, SF	2B	33	125	.334
1982	Dale Murphy, Atl	OF	36	109	.281	2001	Barry Bonds, SF	OF	73	137	.328
1983	Dale Murphy, Atl	OF	36	121	.302	2002	Barry Bonds, SF	OF	46	110	.370
1984	Ryne Sandberg, Chi	2B	19	84	.314	2003	Barry Bonds, SF	OF	45	90	.341
1985	Willie McGee, St.L	OF	10	82	.353	2004	Barry Bonds, SF	OF	45	101	.362
1986	Mike Schmidt, Phi	3B	37	119	.290	2005	Albert Pujols, St.L	1B	41	117	.330

American League

Year		Pos	HR	RBI	Avg	Year		Pos	HR	RBI	Avg
1931	Lefty Grove, Phi	P	—	—	—	1969	Harmon Killebrew, Min	3B-1B	49	140	.276
1932	Jimmie Foxx, Phi	1B	58	169	.364	1970	Boog Powell, Bal	1B	35	114	.297
1933	Jimmie Foxx, Phi	1B	48	163	.356	1971	Vida Blue, Oak	P	—	—	—
1934	Mickey Cochrane, Det	C-Mgr	2	76	.320	1972	Dick Allen, Chi	1B	37	113	.308
1935	Hank Greenberg, Det	1B	36	170	.328	1973	Reggie Jackson, Oak	OF	32	117	.293
1936	Lou Gehrig, NY	1B	49	152	.354	1974	Jeff Burroughs, Tex	OF	25	118	.301
1937	Charlie Gehringer, Det	2B	14	96	.371	1975	Fred Lynn, Bos	OF	21	105	.331
1938	Jimmie Foxx, Bos	1B	50	175	.349	1976	Thurman Munson, NY	C	17	105	.302
1939	Joe DiMaggio, NY	OF	30	126	.381	1977	Rod Carew, Min	1B	14	100	.388
1940	Hank Greenberg, Det	OF	41	150	.340	1978	Jim Rice, Bos	OF-DH	46	139	.315
1941	Joe DiMaggio, NY	OF	30	125	.357	1979	Don Baylor, Cal	OF-DH	36	139	.296
1942	Joe Gordon, NY	2B	18	103	.322	1980	George Brett, KC	3B	24	118	.390
1943	Spud Chandler, NY	P	—	—	—	1981	Rollie Fingers, Mil	P	—	—	—
1944	Hal Newhouser, Det	P	—	—	—	1982	Robin Yount, Mil	SS	29	114	.331
1945	Hal Newhouser, Det	P	—	—	—	1983	Cal Ripken Jr., Bal	SS	27	102	.318
1946	Ted Williams, Bos	OF	38	123	.342	1984	Willie Hernandez, Det	P	—	—	—
1947	Joe DiMaggio, NY	OF	20	97	.315	1985	Don Mattingly, NY	1B	35	145	.324
1948	Lou Boudreau, Cle	SS-Mgr	18	106	.355	1986	Roger Clemens, Bos	P	—	—	—
1949	Ted Williams, Bos	OF	43	159	.343	1987	George Bell, Tor	OF	47	134	.308
1950	Phil Rizzuto, NY	SS	7	66	.324	1988	Jose Canseco, Oak	OF	42	124	.307
1951	Yogi Berra, NY	C	27	88	.294	1989	Robin Yount, Mil	OF	21	103	.318
1952	Bobby Shantz, Phi	P	—	—	—	1990	Rickey Henderson, Oak	OF	28	61	.325
1953	Al Rosen, Cle	3B	43	145	.336	1991	Cal Ripken Jr., Bal	SS	34	114	.323
1954	Yogi Berra, NY	C	22	125	.307	1992	Dennis Eckersley, Oak	P	—	—	—
1955	Yogi Berra, NY	C	27	108	.272	1993	Frank Thomas, Chi	1B	41	128	.317
1956	Mickey Mantle, NY	OF	52	130	.353	1994	Frank Thomas, Chi	1B	38	101	.353
1957	Mickey Mantle, NY	OF	34	94	.365	1995	Mo Vaughn, Bos	1B	39	126	.300
1958	Jackie Jensen, Bos	OF	35	122	.286	1996	Juan Gonzalez, Tex	OF-DH	47	144	.314
1959	Nellie Fox, Chi	2B	2	70	.306	1997	Ken Griffey Jr., Sea	OF	56	147	.304
1960	Roger Maris, NY	OF	39	112	.283	1998	Juan Gonzalez, Tex	OF	45	157	.318
1961	Roger Maris, NY	OF	61	142	.269	1999	Ivan Rodriguez, Tex	C	35	113	.332
1962	Mickey Mantle, NY	OF	30	89	.321	2000	Jason Giambi, Oak	1B	43	137	.333
1963	Elston Howard, NY	C	28	85	.287	2001	Ichiro Suzuki, Sea	OF	8	69	.350
1964	Brooks Robinson, Bal	3B	28	118	.317	2002	Miguel Tejada, Oak	SS	34	131	.308
1965	Zoilo Versalles, Min	SS	19	77	.273	2003	Alex Rodriguez, Tex	SS	47	118	.298
1966	Frank Robinson, Bal	OF	49	122	.316	2004	Vladimir Guerrero, Ana	OF	39	126	.337
1967	Carl Yastrzemski, Bos	OF	44	121	.326	2005	Alex Rodriguez, NY	3B	48	130	.321
1968	Denny McLain, Det	P									

MVP Pitchers' Statistics

Pitchers have been named Most Valuable Player on 23 occasions, 10 times in the NL and 13 in the AL. Four have been relief pitchers—Jim Konstanty, Rollie Fingers, Willie Hernandez and Dennis Eckersley. For statistics of MVP pitchers since 1956, see Cy Young Award tables on following page.

National League

Year		Gm	W-L	SV	ERA
1924	Dazzy Vance, Bklyn	35	28-6	0	2.16
1933	Carl Hubbell, NY	45	23-12	5	1.66
1934	Dizzy Dean, St.L	50	30-7	7	2.66
1936	Carl Hubbell, NY	42	26-6	3	2.31
1939	Bucky Walters, Cin	39	27-11	0	2.29
1942	Mort Cooper, St.L	37	22-7	0	1.78
1950	Jim Konstanty, Phi	74	16-7	22	2.66

American League

Year		Gm	W-L	SV	ERA
1913	Walter Johnson, Wash	47	36-7	2	1.09
1924	Walter Johnson, Wash	38	23-7	0	2.72
1931	Lefty Grove, Phi	41	31-4	5	2.06
1943	Spud Chandler, NY	30	20-4	0	1.64
1944	Hal Newhouser, Det	47	29-9	2	2.22
1945	Hal Newhouser, Det	40	25-9	2	1.81
1952	Bobby Shantz, Phi	33	24-7	0	2.48

CY YOUNG AWARD

Voted on by the Baseball Writers Association of America. One award was presented from 1956-66, two since 1967. Pitchers who won the MVP and Cy Young awards in the same season are in **bold** type.

Multiple winners: NL—Steve Carlton, Greg Maddux and Randy Johnson (4); Sandy Koufax and Tom Seaver (3); Bob Gibson and Tom Glavine (2). **AL**—Roger Clemens (6); Jim Palmer (3); Pedro Martinez and Denny McLain (2). **NL & AL**—Roger Clemens (7, six in AL, one in NL); Randy Johnson (5, four in NL, one in AL), Pedro Martinez (3, two in AL, one in NL) and Gaylord Perry (2, one in each).

NL and AL Combined

Year	National League	Gm	W-L	SV	ERA	Year	American League	Gm	W-L	SV	ERA
1956	**Don Newcombe**, Bklyn	38	27-7	0	3.06	1958	Bob Turley, NY	33	21-7	1	2.97
1957	Warren Spahn, Mil	39	21-11	3	2.69	1959	Early Wynn, Chi	37	22-10	0	3.17
1960	Vernon Law, Pit	35	20-9	0	3.08	1961	Whitey Ford, NY	39	25-4	0	3.21
1962	Don Drysdale, LA	43	25-9	1	2.83	1964	Dean Chance, LA	46	20-9	4	1.65
1963	**Sandy Koufax**, LA	40	25-5	0	1.88						
1965	Sandy Koufax, LA	43	26-8	2	2.04						
1966	Sandy Koufax, LA	41	27-9	0	1.73						

Separate League Awards

National League					American League				
Year		Gm	W-L	SV	ERA	Year		Gm	W-L	SV	ERA
1967	Mike McCormick, SF	40	22-10	0	2.85	1967	Jim Lonborg, Bos	39	22-9	0	3.16
1968	**Bob Gibson**, St.L	34	22-9	0	1.12	1968	**Denny McLain**, Det	41	31-6	0	1.96
1969	Tom Seaver, NY	36	25-7	0	2.21	1969	Denny McLain, Det	42	24-9	0	2.80
1970	Bob Gibson, St.L	34	23-7	0	3.12		Mike Cuellar, Bal	39	23-11	0	2.38
1971	Ferguson Jenkins, Chi	39	24-13	0	2.77	1970	Jim Perry, Min	40	24-12	0	3.03
1972	Steve Carlton, Phi	41	27-10	0	1.97	1971	**Vida Blue**, Oak	39	24-8	0	1.82
1973	Tom Seaver, NY	36	19-10	0	2.08	1972	Gaylord Perry, Cle	41	24-16	1	1.92
1974	Mike Marshall, LA	106	15-12	21	2.42	1973	Jim Palmer, Bal	38	22-9	1	2.40
1975	Tom Seaver, NY	36	22-9	0	2.38	1974	Catfish Hunter, Oak	41	25-12	0	2.49
1976	Randy Jones, SD	40	22-14	0	2.74	1975	Jim Palmer, Bal	39	23-11	1	2.09
1977	Steve Carlton, Phi	36	23-10	0	2.64	1976	Jim Palmer, Bal	40	22-13	0	2.51
1978	Gaylord Perry, SD	37	21-6	0	2.72	1977	Sparky Lyle, NY	72	13-5	26	2.17
1979	Bruce Sutter, Chi	62	6-6	37	2.23	1978	Ron Guidry, NY	35	25-3	0	1.74
1980	Steve Carlton, Phi	38	24-9	0	2.34	1979	Mike Flanagan, Bal	39	23-9	0	3.08
1981	Fernando Valenzuela, LA	25	13-7	0	2.48	1980	Steve Stone, Bal	37	25-7	0	3.23
1982	Steve Carlton, Phi	38	23-11	0	3.10	1981	**Rollie Fingers**, Mil	47	6-3	28	1.04
1983	John Denny, Phi	36	19-6	0	2.37	1982	Pete Vuckovich, Mil	30	18-6	0	3.34
1984	Rick Sutcliffe, Chi	20*	16-1	0	2.69	1983	LaMarr Hoyt, Chi	36	24-10	0	3.66
1985	Dwight Gooden, NY	35	24-4	0	1.53	1984	**Willie Hernandez**, Det	80	9-3	32	1.92
1986	Mike Scott, Hou	37	18-10	0	2.22	1985	Bret Saberhagen, KC	32	20-6	0	2.87
1987	Steve Bedrosian, Phi	65	5-3	40	2.83	1986	**Roger Clemens**, Bos	33	24-4	0	2.48
1988	Orel Hershiser, LA	35	23-8	1	2.26	1987	Roger Clemens, Bos	36	20-9	0	2.97
1989	Mark Davis, SD	70	4-3	44	1.85	1988	Frank Viola, Min	35	24-7	0	2.64
1990	Doug Drabek, Pit	33	22-6	0	2.76	1989	Bret Saberhagen, KC	36	23-6	0	2.16
1991	Tom Glavine, Atl	34	20-11	0	2.55	1990	Bob Welch, Oak	35	27-6	0	2.95
1992	Greg Maddux, Chi	35	20-11	0	2.18	1991	Roger Clemens, Bos	35	18-10	0	2.62
1993	Greg Maddux, Atl	36	20-10	0	2.36	1992	**Dennis Eckersley**, Oak	69	7-1	51	1.91
1994	Greg Maddux, Atl	25	16-6	0	1.56	1993	Jack McDowell, Chi	34	22-10	0	3.37
1995	Greg Maddux, Atl	28	19-2	0	1.63	1994	David Cone, KC	23	16-5	0	2.94
1996	John Smoltz, Atl	35	24-8	0	2.94	1995	Randy Johnson, Sea	30	18-2	0	2.48
1997	Pedro Martinez, Mon	31	17-8	0	1.90	1996	Pat Hentgen, Tor	35	20-10	0	3.22
1998	Tom Glavine, Atl	33	20-6	0	2.47	1997	Roger Clemens, Tor	34	21-7	0	2.05
1999	Randy Johnson, Ari	35	17-9	0	2.48	1998	Roger Clemens, Tor	33	20-6	0	2.65
2000	Randy Johnson, Ari	35	19-7	0	2.64	1999	Pedro Martinez, Bos	31	23-4	0	2.07
2001	Randy Johnson, Ari	35	21-6	0	2.49	2000	Pedro Martinez, Bos	29	18-6	0	1.74
2002	Randy Johnson, Ari	35	24-5	0	2.32	2001	Roger Clemens, NY	33	20-3	0	3.51
2003	Eric Gagne, LA	77	2-3	55	1.20	2002	Barry Zito, Oak	35	23-5	0	2.75
2004	Roger Clemens, Hou	33	18-4	0	2.98	2003	Roy Halladay, Tor	36	22-7	0	3.25
2005	Chris Carpenter, St.L	33	21-5	0	2.83	2004	Johan Santana, Min	34	20-6	0	2.61
						2005	Bartolo Colon, LA	33	21-8	0	3.48

*NL games only, Sutcliffe pitched 15 games with Cleveland before being traded to the Cubs.

ROOKIE OF THE YEAR

Voted on by the Baseball Writers Assn. of America. One award was presented from 1947-48. Two awards (one for each league) have been presented since 1949. Winners who were also named MVP in the same season are in **bold** type.

NL and AL Combined

Year		Pos	Year		Pos
1947	Jackie Robinson, Brooklyn	1B	1948	Alvin Dark, Boston-NL	SS

National League

Year		Pos	Year		Pos	Year		Pos
1949	Don Newcombe, Bklyn	P	1951	Willie Mays, NY	OF	1953	Jim Gilliam, Bklyn	2B
1950	Sam Jethroe, Bos	OF	1952	Joe Black, Bklyn	P	1954	Wally Moon, St.L	OF

Year		Pos	Year		Pos	Year		Pos
1955	Bill Virdon, St.L	OF	1973	Gary Matthews, SF	OF	1989	Jerome Walton, Chi	OF
1956	Frank Robinson, Cin	OF	1974	Bake McBride, St.L	OF	1990	David Justice, Atl	OF
1957	Jack Sanford, Phi	P	1975	John Montefusco, SF	P	1991	Jeff Bagwell, Hou	1B
1958	Orlando Cepeda, SF	1B	1976	Butch Metzger, SD	P	1992	Eric Karros, LA	1B
1959	Willie McCovey, SF	1B		& Pat Zachry, Cin	P	1993	Mike Piazza, LA	C
1960	Frank Howard, LA	OF	1977	Andre Dawson, Mon	OF	1994	Raul Mondesi, LA	OF
1961	Billy Williams, Chi	OF	1978	Bob Horner, Atl	3B	1995	Hideo Nomo, LA	P
1962	Ken Hubbs, Chi	2B	1979	Rick Sutcliffe, LA	P	1996	Todd Hollandsworth, LA	OF
1963	Pete Rose, Cin	2B	1980	Steve Howe, LA	P	1997	Scott Rolen, Phi	3B
1964	Richie Allen, Phi	3B	1981	Fernando Valenzuela, LA	P	1998	Kerry Wood, Chi	P
1965	Jim Lefebvre, LA	2B	1982	Steve Sax, LA	2B	1999	Scott Williamson, Cin	P
1966	Tommy Helms, Cin	3B	1983	Darryl Strawberry, NY	OF	2000	Rafael Furcal, Atl	SS
1967	Tom Seaver, NY	P	1984	Dwight Gooden, NY	P	2001	Albert Pujols, St.L	OF-3B
1968	Johnny Bench, Cin	C	1985	Vince Coleman, St.L	OF	2002	Jason Jennings, Col	P
1969	Ted Sizemore, LA	2B	1986	Todd Worrell, St.L	P	2003	Dontrelle Willis, Fla	P
1970	Carl Morton, Mon	P	1987	Benito Santiago, SD	C	2004	Jason Bay, Pit	OF
1971	Earl Williams, Atl	C	1988	Chris Sabo, Cin	3B	2005	Ryan Howard, Phi	1B
1972	Jon Matlack, NY	P						

American League

Year		Pos	Year		Pos	Year		Pos
1949	Roy Sievers, St.L	OF	1969	Lou Piniella, KC	OF	1987	Mark McGwire, Oak	1B
1950	Walt Dropo, Bos	1B	1970	Thurman Munson, NY	C	1988	Walt Weiss, Oak	SS
1951	Gil McDougald, NY	3B	1971	Chris Chambliss, Cle	1B	1989	Gregg Olson, Bal	P
1952	Harry Byrd, Phi	P	1972	Carlton Fisk, Bos	C	1990	Sandy Alomar Jr., Cle	C
1953	Harvey Kuenn, Det	SS	1973	Al Bumbry, Bal	OF	1991	Chuck Knoblauch, Min	2B
1954	Bob Grim, NY	P	1974	Mike Hargrove, Tex	1B	1992	Pat Listach, Mil	SS
1955	Herb Score, Cle	P	1975	**Fred Lynn**, Bos	OF	1993	Tim Salmon, Cal	OF
1956	Luis Aparicio, Chi	SS	1976	Mark Fidrych, Det	P	1994	Bob Hamelin, KC	DH
1957	Tony Kubek, NY	INF-OF	1977	Eddie Murray, Bal	DH-1B	1995	Marty Cordova, Min	OF
1958	Albie Pearson, Wash	OF	1978	Lou Whitaker, Det	2B	1996	Derek Jeter, NY	SS
1959	Bob Allison, Wash	OF	1979	John Castino, Min	3B	1997	Nomar Garciaparra, Bos	SS
1960	Ron Hansen, Bal	SS		& Alfredo Griffin, Tor	SS	1998	Ben Grieve, Oak	OF
1961	Don Schwall, Bos	P	1980	Joe Charboneau, Cle	OF-DH	1999	Carlos Beltran, KC	OF
1962	Tom Tresh, NY	SS-OF	1981	Dave Righetti, NY	P	2000	Kazuhiro Sasaki, Sea	P
1963	Gary Peters, Chi	P	1982	Cal Ripken Jr., Bal	SS-3B	2001	**Ichiro Suzuki**, Sea	OF
1964	Tony Oliva, Min	OF	1983	Ron Kittle, Chi	OF	2002	Eric Hinske, Tor	3B
1965	Curt Blefary, Bal	OF	1984	Alvin Davis, Sea	1B	2003	Angel Berroa, KC	SS
1966	Tommie Agee, Chi	OF	1985	Ozzie Guillen, Chi	SS	2004	Bobby Crosby, Oak	SS
1967	Rod Carew, Min	2B	1986	Jose Canseco, Oak	OF	2005	Huston Street, Oak	P
1968	Stan Bahnsen, NY	P						

MANAGER OF THE YEAR

Voted on by the Baseball Writers Association of America. Two awards (one for each league) presented since 1983. Note that (*) indicates manager's team won division championship and (†) indicates unofficial division won in 1994.

Multiple winners: Bobby Cox and Tony La Russa (4); Dusty Baker (3); Sparky Anderson, Tommy Lasorda, Jim Leyland, Jack McKeon, Lou Piniella, Buck Showalter and Joe Torre (2).

National League

Year		Diff. from previous year
1983	Tommy Lasorda, LA	88-74 to 91-71*
1984	Jim Frey, Chi	71-91 to 96-75*
1985	Whitey Herzog, St. L	84-78 to 101-61*
1986	Hal Lanier, Hou	83-79 to 96-66*
1987	Buck Rodgers, Mon	78-83 to 91-71
1988	Tommy Lasorda, LA	73-89 to 94-67*
1989	Don Zimmer, Chi	77-85 to 93-69*
1990	Jim Leyland, Pit	74-88 to 95-67*
1991	Bobby Cox, Atl	65-97 to 94-68*
1992	Jim Leyland, Pit	98-64* to 96-66*
1993	Dusty Baker, SF	72-90 to 103-59
1994	Felipe Alou, Mon	94-68 to 74-40†
1995	Don Baylor, Col	53-64 to 77-67
1996	Bruce Bochy, SD	70-74 to 91-71
1997	Dusty Baker, SF	68-94 to 90-72
1998	Larry Dierker, Hou	84-78 to 102-60*
1999	Jack McKeon, Cin	77-85 to 96-67
2000	Dusty Baker, SF	86-76 to 97-65*
2001	Larry Bowa, Phi	65-97 to 86-76
2002	Tony La Russa, St.L	93-69 to 97-65*
2003	Jack McKeon, Fla	79-83 to 91-71
2004	Bobby Cox	101-61 to 96-66*
2005	Bobby Cox	96-66* to 90-72*

American League

Year		Diff. from previous year
1983	Tony La Russa, Chi	87-75 to 99-63*
1984	Sparky Anderson, Det	92-70 to 104-58*
1985	Bobby Cox, Tor	89-73 to 99-62*
1986	John McNamara, Bos	81-81 to 95-66*
1987	Sparky Anderson, Det	87-75 to 98-64*
1988	Tony La Russa, Oak	81-81 to 104-58*
1989	Frank Robinson, Bal	54-107 to 87-75
1990	Jeff Torborg, Chi	69-92 to 94-68
1991	Tom Kelly, Min	74-88 to 95-67*
1992	Tony La Russa, Oak	84-78 to 96-66*
1993	Gene Lamont, Chi	86-76 to 94-68*
1994	Buck Showalter, NY	88-74 to 70-43†
1995	Lou Piniella, Sea	49-63 to 79-66*
1996	Joe Torre, NY	79-65 to 92-70
	& Johnny Oates, Tex	74-70 to 90-72
1997	Davey Johnson, Bal	88-74 to 98-64
1998	Joe Torre, NY	96-66 to 114-48*
1999	Jimy Williams, Bos	92-70 to 94-68
2000	Jerry Manuel, Chi	75-86 to 95-67*
2001	Lou Piniella, Sea	91-71 to 116-46*
2002	Mike Scioscia, Ana	75-87 to 99-63
2003	Tony Pena, KC	62-100 to 83-79
2004	Buck Showalter, Tex	71-91 to 89-73
2005	Ozzie Guillen, Chi	83-79 to 99-63*

COLLEGE BASEBALL

College World Series

The NCAA Division I College World Series has been held in Kalamazoo, Mich. (1947-48), Wichita, Kan. (1949) and Omaha, Neb. (since 1950). Beginning in 2003, the championship series has been best-of-three series.

Multiple winners: USC (12); Texas (6); Arizona St. and LSU (5); CS-Fullerton and Miami-FL (4); Arizona and Minnesota (3); California, Michigan, Oklahoma and Stanford (2).

Year	Winner	Coach	Score	Runner-up
1947	California	Clint Evans	8-7	Yale
1948	USC	Sam Barry	9-2	Yale
1949	Texas	Bibb Falk	10-3	W. Forest
1950	Texas	Bibb Falk	3-0	Wash. St.
1951	Oklahoma	Jack Baer	3-2	Tennessee
1952	Holy Cross	Jack Barry	8-4	Missouri
1953	Michigan	Ray Fisher	7-5	Texas
1954	Missouri	Hi Simmons	4-1	Rollins
1955	Wake Forest	Taylor Sanford	7-6	W. Mich.
1956	Minnesota	Dick Siebert	12-1	Arizona
1957	California	Geo. Wolfman	1-0	Penn St.
1958	USC	Rod Dedeaux	8-7	Missouri
1959	Oklahoma St.	Toby Greene	5-3	Arizona
1960	Minnesota	Dick Siebert	2-1	USC
1961	USC	Rod Dedeaux	1-0	Okla. St.
1962	Michigan	Don Lund	5-4	S. Clara
1963	USC	Rod Dedeaux	5-2	Arizona
1964	Minnesota	Dick Siebert	5-1	Missouri
1965	Arizona St.	Bobby Winkles	2-1	Ohio St.
1966	Ohio St.	Marty Karow	8-2	Okla. St.
1967	Arizona St.	Bobby Winkles	11-2	Houston
1968	USC	Rod Dedeaux	4-3	So. Ill.
1969	Arizona St.	Bobby Winkles	10-1	Tulsa
1970	USC	Rod Dedeaux	2-1	Fla. St.
1971	USC	Rod Dedeaux	7-2	So. Ill.
1972	USC	Rod Dedeaux	1-0	Ariz. St.
1973	USC	Rod Dedeaux	4-3	Ariz. St.
1974	USC	Rod Dedeaux	7-3	Miami-FL
1975	Texas	Cliff Gustafson	5-1	S. Carolina
1976	Arizona	Jerry Kindall	7-1	E. Michigan
1977	Arizona St.	Jim Brock	2-1	S. Carolina
1978	USC	Rod Dedeaux	10-3	Ariz. St.
1979	CS-Fullerton	Augie Garrido	2-1	Arkansas
1980	Arizona	Jerry Kindall	5-3	Hawaii
1981	Arizona St.	Jim Brock	7-4	Okla. St.
1982	Miami-FL	Ron Fraser	9-3	Wichita St.
1983	Texas	Cliff Gustafson	4-3	Alabama
1984	CS-Fullerton	Augie Garrido	3-1	Texas
1985	Miami-FL	Ron Fraser	10-6	Texas
1986	Arizona	Jerry Kindall	10-2	Fla. St.
1987	Stanford	M. Marquess	9-5	Okla. St.
1988	Stanford	M. Marquess	9-4	Ariz. St.
1989	Wichita St.	G. Stephenson	5-3	Texas
1990	Georgia	Steve Webber	2-1	Okla. St.
1991	LSU	Skip Bertman	6-3	Wichita St.
1992	Pepperdine	Andy Lopez	3-2	CS-Fullerton
1993	LSU	Skip Bertman	8-0	Wichita St.
1994	Oklahoma	Larry Cochell	13-5	Ga. Tech
1995	CS-Fullerton	Augie Garrido	11-5	USC
1996	LSU	Skip Bertman	9-8	Miami-FL
1997	LSU	Skip Bertman	13-6	Alabama
1998	USC	Mike Gillespie	21-14	Arizona St.
1999	Miami-FL	Jim Morris	6-5	Fla. St.
2000	LSU	Skip Bertman	6-5	Stanford
2001	Miami-FL	Jim Morris	12-1	Stanford
2002	Texas	Augie Garrido	12-6	S. Carolina
2003	Rice	Wayne Graham	4-3	Stanford
			3-8	
			14-2	
2004	CS-Fullerton	George Horton	6-4	Texas
			3-2	
2005	Texas	Augie Garrido	4-2	Florida
			6-2	
2006	Oregon St.	Pat Casey	3-4	N. Carolina
			11-7	
			3-2	

Most Outstanding Player

The Most Outstanding Player has been selected every year of the College World Series since 1949. Winners who did not play for the CWS champion are listed in **bold** type. No player has won the award more than once.

Year		
1949 **Charles Teague,** W. Forest, 2B	1970 **Gene Ammann,** Fla. St., P	1991 Gary Hymel, LSU, C
1950 **Ray VanCleef,** Rutgers, CF	1971 **Jerry Tabb,** Tulsa, 1B	1992 **Phil Nevin,** CS-Fullerton, 3B
1951 **Sidney Hatfield,** Tenn., P-1B	1972 Russ McQueen, USC, P	1993 Todd Walker, LSU, 2B
1952 James O'Neill, Holy Cross, P	1973 **Dave Winfield,** Minn., P-OF	1994 Chip Glass, Oklahoma, OF
1953 **J.L. Smith,** Texas, P	1974 George Milke, USC, P	1995 Mark Kotsay, CS-Fullerton, OF
1954 **Tom Yewcic,** Mich. St., C	1975 Mickey Reichenbach, Texas, 1B	1996 **Pat Burrell,** Miami-FL, 3B
1955 **Tom Borland,** Okla. St., P	1976 Steve Powers, Arizona, P-DH	1997 Brandon Larson, LSU, SS
1956 Jerry Thomas, Minn., P	1977 Bob Horner, Ariz. St., 3B	1998 Wes Rachels, USC, 2B
1957 **Cal Emery,** Penn St., P-1B	1978 Rod Boxberger, USC, P	1999 **Marshall McDougall,** Fla. St., 2B
1958 Bill Thom, USC, P	1979 Tony Hudson, CS-Fullerton, P	
1959 Jim Dobson, Okla. St., 3B	1980 Terry Francona, Arizona, LF	2000 Trey Hodges, LSU, P
	1981 Stan Holmes, Ariz. St., LF	2001 Charlton Jimerson, Miami-FL, CF
1960 John Erickson, Minn., 2B	1982 Dan Smith, Miami-FL, P	2002 Huston Street, Texas, P
1961 **Littleton Fowler,** Okla. St., P	1983 Calvin Schiraldi, Texas, P	2003 **John Hudgins,** Stanford, P
1962 **Bob Garibaldi,** Santa Clara, P	1984 John Fishel, CS-Fullerton, LF	2004 Jason Windsor, CS-Fullerton, P
1963 Bud Hollowell, USC, C	1985 Greg Ellena, Miami-FL, LF	2005 David Maroul, Texas, 3B
1964 **Joe Ferris,** Maine, P	1986 Mike Senne, Arizona, DH	2006 Jonah Nickerson, Oregon St., P
1965 Sal Bando, Ariz. St., 3B	1987 Paul Carey, Stanford, RF	
1966 Steve Arlin, Ohio St., P	1988 Lee Plemel, Stanford, P	
1967 Ron Davini, Ariz. St., C	1989 Greg Brummett, Wich. St., P	
1968 Bill Seinsoth, USC, 1B	1990 Mike Rebhan, Georgia, P	
1969 John Dolinsek, Ariz. St., LF		

Annual Awards
Golden Spikes Award

First presented in 1978 by USA Baseball, honoring the nation's best amateur player; sponsored by the Major League Baseball Players Association. Alex Fernandez, the 1990 winner, has been the only junior college player chosen.

Year		Year		Year	
1978	Bob Horner, Ariz. St, 2B	1988	Robin Ventura, Okla. St., 3B	1998	Pat Burrell, Miami-FL, 3B
1979	Tim Wallach, CS-Fullerton, 1B	1989	Ben McDonald, LSU, P	1999	Jason Jennings, Baylor, DH/P
1980	Terry Francona, Arizona, OF	1990	Alex Fernandez, Miami-Dade, P	2000	Kip Bouknight, South Carolina, P
1981	Mike Fuentes, Fla. St., OF	1991	Mike Kelly, Ariz. St., OF	2001	Mark Prior, USC, P
1982	Augie Schmidt, N. Orleans, SS	1992	Phil Nevin, CS-Fullerton, 3B	2002	Khalil Greene, Clemson, SS
1983	Dave Magadan, Alabama, 1B	1993	Darren Dreifort, Wichita St., P	2003	Rickie Weeks, Southern, 2B
1984	Oddibe McDowell, Ariz. St., OF	1994	Jason Varitek, Ga. Tech, C	2004	Jered Weaver, Long Beach St., P
1985	Will Clark, Miss. St., 1B	1995	Mark Kotsay, CS-Fullerton, OF	2005	Alex Gordon, Nebraska, IF
1986	Mike Loynd, Fla. St., P	1996	Travis Lee, San Diego St., 1B	2006	Tim Lincecum, Washington, P
1987	Jim Abbott, Michigan, P	1997	J.D. Drew, Florida St., OF		

Baseball America Player of the Year

Presented to the College Player of the Year since 1981 by *Baseball America*.

Year		Year		Year	
1981	Mike Sodders, Ariz. St., 3B	1990	Mike Kelly, Ariz. St., OF	1999	Jason Jennings, Baylor, DH/P
1982	Jeff Ledbetter, Fla. St., OF/P	1991	David McCarty, Stanford, 1B	2000	Mark Teixeira, Ga. Tech, 3B
1983	Dave Magadan, Alabama, 1B	1992	Phil Nevin, CS-Fullerton, 3B	2001	Mark Prior, USC, P
1984	Oddibe McDowell, Ariz. St., OF	1993	Brooks Kieschnick, Texas, DH/P	2002	Khalil Greene, Clemson, SS
1985	Pete Incaviglia, Okla. St., OF	1994	Jason Varitek, Ga. Tech, C	2003	Rickie Weeks, Southern, 2B
1986	Casey Close, Michigan, OF	1995	Todd Helton, Tenn., 1B/P	2004	Jered Weaver, Long Beach St., P
1987	Robin Ventura, Okla. St., 3B	1996	Kris Benson, Clemson, P	2005	Alex Gordon, Nebraska, IF
1988	John Olerud, Wash. St., 1B/P	1997	J.D. Drew, Florida St., OF	2006	Andrew Miller, N. Carolina, P
1989	Ben McDonald, LSU, P	1998	Jeff Austin, Stanford, P		

Dick Howser Trophy

Presented to the College Player of the Year since 1987, by the American Baseball Coaches Association (ABCA) from 1987-98 and the National Collegiate Baseball Writers Association (NCBWA) beginning in 1999. Founded and owned by the St. Petersburg (Fla.) Area Chamber of Commerce. Named after the late two-time All-America shortstop and college coach at Florida State. Howser was also a major league manager with Kansas City and the New York Yankees.

Multiple winner: Brooks Kieschnick (2).

Year		Year		Year	
1987	Mike Fiore, Miami-FL, OF	1994	Jason Varitek, Ga. Tech, C	2001	Mark Prior, USC, P
1988	Robin Ventura, Okla. St., 3B	1995	Todd Helton, Tenn., 1B/P	2002	Khalil Greene, Clemson, SS
1989	Scott Bryant, Texas, DH	1996	Kris Benson, Clemson, P	2003	Rickie Weeks, Southern, 2B
1990	Paul Ellis, UCLA, C	1997	J.D. Drew, Florida St., OF	2004	Jered Weaver, Long Beach St., P
1991	Bobby Jones, Fresno St., P	1998	Eddie Furniss, LSU, 1B	2005	Alex Gordon, Nebraska, IF
1992	Brooks Kieschnick, Texas, DH/P	1999	Jason Jennings, Baylor, DH/P	2006	Brad Lincoln, Houston, P/UT
1993	Brooks Kieschnick, Texas, DH/P	2000	Mark Teixeira, Ga. Tech, 3B		

Baseball America Coach of the Year

Presented to the College Coach of the Year since 1981 by *Baseball America*.

Multiple winners: Skip Bertman, Augie Garrido, Dave Snow and Gene Stephenson (2).

Year		Year		Year	
1981	Ron Fraser, Miami-FL	1989	Dave Snow, Long Beach St.	1998	Pat Murphy, Arizona St.
1982	Gene Stephenson, Wichita St.	1990	Steve Webber, Georgia	1999	Wayne Graham, Rice
1983	Barry Shollenberger, Alabama	1991	Jim Hendry, Creighton	2000	Ray Tanner, S. Carolina
1984	Augie Garrido, CS-Fullerton	1992	Andy Lopez, Pepperdine	2001	Dave Van Horn, Nebraska
1985	Ron Polk, Mississippi St.	1993	Gene Stephenson, Wichita St.	2002	Augie Garrido, Texas
1986	Skip Bertman, LSU & Dave Snow, Loyola-CA	1994	Jim Morris, Miami-FL	2003	George Horton, CS-Fullerton
		1995	Rod Delmonico, Tennessee	2004	Dave Perno, Georgia
1987	Mark Marquess, Stanford	1996	Skip Bertman, LSU	2005	Rick Jones, Tulane
1988	Jim Brock, Arizona St.	1997	Jim Wells, Alabama	2006	Pat Casey, Oregon St.

All-Time Winningest Division I Coaches

Coaches active in 2006 are in **bold** type. Records given are for four-year colleges only. For winning percentage, a minimum 10 years in Division I is required.

Top 10 Winning Percentage

		Yrs	W	L	T	Pct
1	John Barry	.40	619	146	5	.807
2	Cliff Gustafson	.29	1427	373	2	.792
3	Harry Carlson	.17	143	41	0	.777
4	**Gene Stephenson**	.29	1552	511	3	.752
5	Bobby Winkles	.13	524	173	0	.752
6	Frank Sancet	.23	831	283	8	.744
7	**Mike Martin**	.27	1435	493	4	.744
8	Bob Wren	.23	464	160	4	.742
9	George Jacobs	.11	106	37	0	.741
10	Ron Fraser	.30	1267	440	9	.741

Top 10 Victories

		Yrs	W	L	T	Pct
1	**Augie Garrido**	.38	**1583**	738	8	.681
2	**Gene Stephenson**	.29	**1552**	511	3	.752
3	**Larry Hays**	.36	**1455**	803	3	.644
4	**Chuck Hartman**	.47	**1444**	816	8	.638
5	**Mike Martin**	.27	**1435**	493	4	.744
6	Cliff Gustafson	.29	**1427**	373	2	.792
7	Rod Dedeaux	.44	**1342**	597	16	.691
8	Larry Cochell	.39	**1330**	814	3	.620
9	**Ron Polk**	.33	**1313**	647	2	.670
10	Bob Bennett	.34	**1300**	757	8	.631

Other NCAA Champions

Division II

Multiple winners: Florida Southern (9); Tampa (4); Cal Poly Pomona (3); Central Missouri St., CS-Chico, CS-Northridge, Jacksonville St., Troy St., UC-Irvine and UC-Riverside (2).

Year		Year		Year		Year	
1968	Chapman, CA	1978	Florida Southern	1988	Florida Southern	1998	Tampa
1969	Illinois St.	1979	Valdosta St., GA	1989	Cal Poly SLO	1999	CS-Chico
1970	CS-Northridge	1980	Cal Poly Pomona	1990	Jacksonville St., AL	2000	Southeastern Okla.
1971	Florida Southern	1981	Florida Southern	1991	Jacksonville St., AL	2001	St. Mary's, TX
1972	Florida Southern	1982	UC-Riverside	1992	Tampa	2002	Columbus St., GA
1973	UC-Irvine	1983	Cal Poly Pomona	1993	Tampa	2003	Central Missouri St.
1974	UC-Irvine	1984	CS-Northridge	1994	Central Missouri St.	2004	Delta St., MS
1975	Florida Southern	1985	Florida Southern	1995	Florida Southern	2005	Florida Southern
1976	Cal Poly Pomona	1986	Troy St., AL	1996	Kennesaw St., GA	2006	Tampa
1977	UC-Riverside	1987	Troy St., AL	1997	CS-Chico		

Division III

Multiple winners: Eastern Conn. St. and Marietta (4); Montclair St. (3); CS-Stanislaus, Glassboro St., Ithaca, NC-Wesleyan, Southern Maine and Wm. Paterson, NJ (2).

Year		Year		Year		Year	
1976	CS-Stanislaus	1984	Ramapo, NJ	1992	Wm. Paterson, NJ	2000	Montclair St., NJ
1977	CS-Stanislaus	1985	Wisconsin-Oshkosh	1993	Montclair St., NJ	2001	St. Thomas, MN
1978	Glassboro St., NJ	1986	Marietta, OH	1994	Wisconsin-Oshkosh	2002	Eastern Conn. St.
1979	Glassboro St., NJ	1987	Monclair St., NJ	1995	La Verne, CA	2003	Chapman, CA
1980	Ithaca, NY	1988	Ithaca, NY	1996	Wm. Paterson, NJ	2004	George Fox, OR
1981	Marietta, OH	1989	NC-Wesleyan	1997	Southern Maine	2005	Wis.-Whitewater
1982	Eastern Conn. St.	1990	Eastern Conn. St.	1998	Eastern Conn. St.	2006	Marietta, OH
1983	Marietta, OH	1991	Southern Maine	1999	NC-Wesleyan		

Major League Number One Draft Picks

The Major League First-Year Player Draft has been held every year since 1965. Clubs select in reverse order of their won-loss records from the previous regular season. Until 2005, the National League and American League teams alternated, with AL teams selecting first in odd-numbered years and NL teams going first in even-numbered years. Now, league affiliation does not come into play. Listed are the top selections from each draft.

Year		Pos	Team	Year		Pos	Team
1965	Rick Monday	OF	Kansas City Athletics	1986	Jeff King	IF	Pittsburgh Pirates
1966	Steve Chilcott	C	New York Mets	1987	Ken Griffey Jr.	OF	Seattle Mariners
1967	Rom Blomberg	1B	New York Yankees	1988	Andy Benes	P	San Diego Padres
1968	Tim Foli	IF	New York Mets	1989	Ben McDonald	P	Baltimore Orioles
1969	Jeff Burroughs	OF	Washington Senators	1990	Chipper Jones	SS	Atlanta Braves
1970	Mike Ivie	C	San Diego Padres	1991	Brien Taylor	P	New York Yankees
1971	Danny Goodwin	C	Chicago White Sox	1992	Phil Nevin	3B	Houston Astros
1972	Dave Roberts	IF	San Diego Padres	1993	Alex Rodriguez	SS	Seattle Mariners
1973	David Clyde	P	Texas Rangers	1994	Paul Wilson	P	New York Mets
1974	Bill Almon	IF	San Diego Padres	1995	Darin Erstad	OF/P	California Angels
1975	Danny Goodwin	C	California Angels	1996	Kris Benson	P	Pittsburgh Pirates
1976	Floyd Bannister	P	Houston Astros	1997	Matt Anderson	P	Detroit Tigers
1977	Harold Baines	OF	Chicago White Sox	1998	Pat Burrell	3B	Philadelphia Phillies
1978	Bob Horner	3B	Atlanta Braves	1999	Josh Hamilton	OF	T.B. Devil Rays
1979	Al Chambers	OF	Seattle Mariners	2000	Adrian Gonzalez	1B	Florida Marlins
1980	Darryl Strawberry	OF	New York Mets	2001	Joe Mauer	C	Minnesota Twins
1981	Mike Moore	P	Seattle Mariners	2002	Bryan Bullington	P	Pittsburgh Pirates
1982	Shawon Dunston	SS	Chicago Cubs	2003	Delmon Young	OF	T.B. Devil Rays
1983	Tim Belcher	P	Minnesota Twins	2004	Matt Bush	SS	San Diego Padres
1984	Shawn Abner	OF	New York Mets	2005	Justin Upton	SS	Ariz. Diamondbacks
1985	B.J. Surhoff	C	Milwaukee Brewers	2006	Luke Hochevar	P	Kansas City Royals

COLLEGE FOOTBALL

2005 / 2006 YEAR IN REVIEW

Texas quarterback **Vince Young** made the Trojans miss all night long at the Rose Bowl.

TEXAS
HOLD 'EM

Vince Young ends the Trojan dynasty and quarterbacks Texas to a national title with a thrilling win in the Rose Bowl.

WAS ANYBODY BREATHING?

The most thrilling championship game in college football history would be decided on a single snap.

One play to decide the title, deliver one team's dream ending, and break hearts on the opposite sideline. One play to define the legacies of a quarterback and his coach. One play to change the course of a dynasty, to snap one long winning streak, and prolong another.

More than 94,000 hearts in the Rose Bowl were thumping. Each pair of eyes seemed to find the same focal point: the tall man striding slowly from his huddle to his spot at the center of the backfield. The tall man in the white jersey with a burnt orange number 10 and the hopes of the entire Longhorn Nation.

In the end it all distilled down to Vince Young versus the entire USC defense. There, feeling helpless on the Trojans' sideline, was Matt Leinart. Young's counterpart and comrade in mutual respect knew well the full meaning of carrying his team's dreams on his shoulders, and the thrill of coming through.

Leinart had twice tasted national championship glory and even delayed a multi-million dollar payday to hunt for a third. A few months earlier it was Leinart wandering with glazed eyes outside Notre Dame stadium, in numb disbelief over the chaotic finish that had propelled USC toward this potential rendezvous with history.

Standing a few feet away from him was the man who had literally pushed Leinart over the line that day. Reggie Bush pushed, then took the Heisman baton from his teammate.

Aggressively targeted by the Texas defense, he had still far exceeded his season average in all-purpose yards, with 279. But in the final game of his brilliant USC career he might be best remembered for a brain cramp—Bush's attempted lateral, while slicing through open field in the first half, that fell into Texas hands and instantly reversed momentum. His farewell was punctuated by a play he took no part in: the

Chris Fowler is the host of ESPN's College GameDay

AP/Wide World Photos

Texas head coach **Mack Brown** celebrates the Longhorns' national championship following his team's win over USC at the Rose Bowl.

fourth-and-two call from the Texas 45 with 2:13 remaining.

It was perfect Pete Carroll—a gamble founded in unflinching belief in his team. Simple: make two yards, deny number 10 the football, win a third straight championship. Bush was a spectator, but Texas hadn't stopped the 240-pound LenDale White all night. So, there was no mystery.

Muscle would win this moment.

Texas read the off-tackle run, flooded the point of attack, and stoned Troy's short-yardage bid inches from the final link in the chain. This was a defense that had limped off the field looking totally defeated a short time ago, after Leinart's laser to Dwayne Jarrett had put USC up by 12 in the final minutes.

The Longhorns would later say they never lost belief, but this was a bunch that sure appeared beaten.

Young's heroics were still not at an end. To stop him, Carroll tried everything his brilliant defensive mind could conjure—sending blitzers like guided missiles from all angles.

Nothing worked. Schemes were being beaten by sandlot.

Young passed and scrambled until the Rose Bowl's chewed-up lawn shrank away. Just eight yards separated Texas from a title. It was fourth and five with 19 seconds left.

Did everyone know they were watching a moment that would be part of sports history? Did anyone doubt the football would stay in Young's hands?

USC's **Reggie Bush** ran away from the competition and won the Heisman, keeping it in the Trojan family for the third time in four seasons.

cannons kicked in, there was Young, right next to our set, waving at the jubilant Texas fans.

His celebration was aggressive, defiant in the new millennium mode. Young was snapping his arms into the pose known to fans everywhere—one arm cradling an imaginary football, the other aimed straight out. He was shouting over and over to all within earshot, "Who's da Heisman?"

You couldn't blame him, I guess. In producing perhaps the greatest championship game effort ever, Young had clearly outperformed Bush. He'd silenced all who said he was playing out of position and would never get to the top under center.

A few minutes later, there was Leinart and Bush showing class by visiting the Texas locker room and offering congratulations. In the months that followed, Young and the two Trojans would become closer, sharing the pressure of the NFL draft circus, and toasting each other at the ESPY awards.

The moment was eerie... surprisingly quiet. From my vantage point near the pylon, it all seemed to play out in slow motion. There was the USC defense flowing to the left side of the formation, and Young galloping back to the right corner...a large man moving quickly, but with so little visible effort. Young glided untouched into immortality, to be quickly swallowed by the swarm.

In the moments after the final gun sounded and just before the confetti

The rest of us should raise a glass, too. We may never see the perfect storm of circumstances that created a championship game to remember: the perfect Pasadena setting for a controversy-free collision of two powers, stocked with such star power, locked in a game that actually surpassed the heap of hype. I left the field buoyed by the night's thrills, but tugged by a tinge of sadness.

Would we ever have it so good again?

AP/Wide World Photos

LEE CORSO'S

10 ⬇

Greatest Stories of the Year in College Football

10 Tennessee Collapse. Annual SEC and national title contender Tennessee had their rockiest season in a long time. Fueled by off-the-field problems, injuries and a QB controversy, the Vols missed a bowl for the first time since 1988 and lost at home to Vanderbilt for the first time since 1975.

09 LSU's Surreal Season. I can't even begin to imagine what Les Miles and the LSU community went through in the Hurricane Katrina aftermath, but the Tigers served as an inspiration to the state of Louisiana. They won their season opener in dramatic fashion in a "home" game at Arizona State and captured the SEC Western Division title before finishing the season with their best game, a 40-3 rout of Miami in the Peach Bowl.

08 Reggie Bush. If it seemed like every week Reggie Bush was making highlight play after highlight play, it was because he was. But one performance stood out over all others. Bush's performance in the comeback win against Fresno State on Nov. 19 was one for the ages. Bush tallied

TD runs of 45 and 50 yards and finished with 514 all-purpose yards —a total that stands as the second-highest single-game total by an individual in Division 1-A history. It was the highlight of a marvelous Heisman-winning campaign for Bush.

07 USC. From the three-peat quest, to the streak, to the consecutive Heisman Trophies, to the comebacks at Arizona State and Notre Dame, USC was front and center every week in the college football world. Hard for them not to be with players like Reggie Bush, Matt Leinart, Dwayne Jarrett, etc. The way USC went out each week and executed their offense was a thing of beauty and a joy to watch. They just fell short of a third straight title, but that shouldn't diminish anything the Trojans accomplished on the field.

06 Steve Spurrier. It was a welcome sight to see Steve Spurrier back on the college sidelines, coaching at South Carolina. And it didn't take long for Spurrier to have success in Columbia, as the Gamecocks knocked off Tennessee in Knoxville and beat his former team, Florida, en route to a bowl berth. Don't be surprised if the Gamecocks become a contender in the SEC— sooner than later.

05 Mack Brown. The cries were all too familiar. Mack Brown couldn't win the big game. So the Longhorns went into Columbus at night and beat Ohio State. Mack Brown couldn't beat Oklahoma—all the Longhorns did was rout the Sooners 45-12. Mack Brown can't win the Big 12 title. Then Texas dismantles Colorado in the Big 12 title game. The final monkey was taken off Brown's back when Texas beat USC in the Rose Bowl for the national title. And it couldn't have happened any better for a terrific man.

04 Notre Dame. We saw it first hand week one in Pittsburgh when Charlie Weis' Irish dominated the Panthers. And that was only the beginning. Behind star quarterback Brady Quinn, the Irish knocked off Michigan and nearly ended USC's winning streak in South Bend in October. The Irish finished in the top ten for the first time since 1993 and are poised for bigger and better things in 2006 and beyond.

03 Joe Paterno. Some thought the game had passed him by, but Paterno proved his critics wrong with one of the best seasons in school history. The Nittany Lions won the Big Ten title and finished the season 11-1 and ranked number three in the nation after an Orange Bowl win over Florida State less than two weeks after his 80th birthday.

02 Vince Young in the Rose Bowl. In what was the best individual performance I have ever seen, Vince Young single-handedly snapped USC's 34-game winning streak with his 467-yard, three touchdown performance in the Rose Bowl, giving Texas their first national championship since 1970. Young did it with his arm and his legs, proving all the skeptics wrong.

01 BCS passed with flying colors. It was the best set of BCS games that we have seen so far. The Rose Bowl will certainly be remembered forever. But don't forget that the Orange Bowl went to overtime, the Sugar Bowl shootout wasn't decided until a fake punt on fourth down, and the Fiesta Bowl pitted two of the most historic programs (Ohio State and Notre Dame) in college football against one another. It couldn't have worked out much better for the BCS.

 Lee Corso is the host of ESPN's College GameDay

>> **Joe Paterno and Bobby Bowden entered** their 41st seasons pacing the college sidelines in 2006. Paterno has spent his entire career at Happy Valley >> **Did you know the only other** major college coach to have served 40 years as head coach at a single institution was **coaching legend Amos Alonzo Stagg**? JoePa's got a ways to go to match Stagg who was a head coach for 57 years, including 41 at the University of Chicago (1892-1932).

2005-2006 Season in Review

ESPN SPORTS ALMANAC

Final AP Top 25 Poll

Voted on by panel of 65 sportswriters & broadcasters and released on Jan. 6, 2006, following the Rose Bowl: winning team receives the Bear Bryant Trophy, given since 1983; first place votes in parentheses, records, total points (based on 25 for 1st, 24 for 2nd, etc.) bowl game result, head coach and career record, preseason rank (released Aug. 20, 2005) and final regular season rank (released Dec. 6, 2005).

		Final Record	Points	Bowl Game	Head Coach	Aug. 20 Rank	Dec. 6 Rank
1	Texas (65)	13-0	1,625	won Rose	Mack Brown (22 yrs: 169-93-1)	2	2
2	USC	12-1	1,560	lost Rose	Pete Carroll (5 yrs: 54-10)	1	1
3	Penn St.	11-1	1,484	won Orange	Joe Paterno (40 yrs: 354-117-3)	NR	3
4	Ohio St.	10-2	1,428	won Fiesta	Jim Tressel (20 yrs: 185-70-1)	6	4
5	West Virginia	11-1	1,325	won Sugar	Rich Rodriguez (13 yrs: 84-58-2)	NR	11
6	LSU	11-2	1,314	won Peach	Les Miles (5 yrs: 39-23)	5	10
7	Virginia Tech	11-2	1,197	won Gator	Frank Beamer (25 yrs: 188-102-4)	8	12
8	Alabama	10-2	1,081	won Cotton	Mike Shula (3 yrs: 20-17)	NR	13
9	Notre Dame	9-3	1,019	lost Fiesta	Charlie Weis (1 yr: 9-3)	NR	5
10	Georgia	10-3	994	lost Sugar	Mark Richt (5 yrs: 52-13)	13	8
11	TCU	11-1	937	won Houston	Gary Patterson (6 yrs: 43-18)	NR	14
12	Florida	9-3	817	won Outback	Urban Meyer (5 yrs: 48-11)	10	16
	Oregon	10-2	817	lost Holiday	Mike Bellotti (16 yrs: 111-67-2)	NR	6
14	Auburn	9-3	799	lost Capital One	Tommy Tuberville (11 yrs: 85-47)	16	7
15	Wisconsin	10-3	786	won Capital One	Barry Alvarez (16 yrs: 118-73-4)	NR	21
16	UCLA	10-2	778	won Sun	Karl Dorrell (3 yrs: 22-15)	NR	17
17	Miami-FL	9-3	589	lost Peach	Larry Coker (5 yrs: 53-9)	9	9
18	Boston College	9-3	545	won MPC	Tom O'Brien (9 yrs: 66-42)	22	19
19	Louisville	9-3	410	lost Gator	Bobby Petrino (3 yrs: 29-8)	12	15
20	Texas Tech	9-3	359	lost Cotton	Mike Leach (6 yrs: 48-28)	21	18
21	Clemson	8-4	339	won Champs Sports	Tommy Bowden (9 yrs: 70-37)	NR	23
22	Oklahoma	8-4	329	won Holiday	Bob Stoops (7 yrs: 75-16)	7	NR
23	Florida St.	8-5	232	lost Orange	Bobby Bowden (40 yrs: 359-107-4)	14	22
24	Nebraska	8-4	128	won Alamo	Bill Callahan (2 yrs: 13-10)	NR	NR
25	California	8-4	45	won Las Vegas	Jeff Tedford (4 yrs: 33-17)	19	NR

Other teams receiving votes: 26. **Toledo** (9-3, won GMAC, 35 pts); 27. **Tulsa** (9-4, won Liberty, 34 pts); 28. **Michigan** (7-5, lost Alamo, 26 pts); 29. **Nevada** (9-3, won Hawaii, 25 pts); 30. **Navy** (8-4, won Poinsettia, 20 pts); 31. **Iowa** (7-5, lost Outback, 19 pts); 32. **Fresno St.** (8-5, lost Liberty, 8 pts); 34. **Virginia** (7-5, won Music City, 7 pts); 35. **Boise St.** (9-4, lost MPC Computers, 3 pts); 36. **Kansas** (7-5, won Fort Worth), **N.C. State** (7-5, won Meineke) and **Northwestern** (7-5, lost Sun, 2 pts); 39. **South Carolina** (7-5, lost Independence), **Utah** (7-5, won Emerald), **Missouri** (7-5, won Independence), **Arizona St.** (7-5, won Insight), **Georgia Tech** (7-5, lost Emerald, 1 pt).

AP Preseason and Final Regular Season Polls

First place votes in parentheses.

Top 25
(Aug. 20, 2005)

		Pts			Pts
1	USC (60)	1,619	14	Florida St.	764
2	Texas (4)	1,500	15	Purdue	711
3	Tennessee	1,376	16	Auburn	650
4	Michigan	1,329	17	Texas A&M	576
5	LSU	1,291	18	Boise St.	375
6	Ohio St.	1,205	19	California	358
7	Oklahoma	1,204	20	Arizona St.	313
8	Virginia Tech	1,184	21	Texas Tech	256
9	Miami-FL	1,142	22	Boston College	232
10	Florida	1,080	23	Pittsburgh	211
11	Iowa	1,011	24	Fresno St.	196
12	Louisville (1)	892	25	Virginia	153
13	Georgia	869			

Top 25
(Dec. 6, 2005)

		Pts			Pts
1	USC (56)	1,616	14	TCU	790
2	Texas (9)	1,569	15	Louisville	644
3	Penn St.	1,483	16	Florida	588
4	Ohio St.	1,375	17	UCLA	542
5	Notre Dame	1,327	18	Texas Tech	533
6	Oregon	1,241	19	Boston College	410
7	Auburn	1,221	20	Michigan	377
8	Georgia	1,202	21	Wisconsin	325
9	Miami-FL	1,098	22	Florida St.	296
10	LSU	1,028	23	Clemson	240
11	West Virginia	991	24	Georgia Tech	189
12	Virginia Tech	943	25	Iowa	86
13	Alabama	813			

2005-2006 Bowl Games

Listed by bowls matching highest-ranked teams as of final regular season AP poll (released Dec. 6, 2005). Attendance figures indicate tickets sold.

Bowl		Winner	Regular Season		Loser	Regular Season	Score	Date	Attendance
Rose	#2	Texas	12-0	#1	USC	12-0	41-38	Jan. 4	93,986
Orange	#3	Penn St.	11-0	#22	Florida St.	8-4	26-23 3OT	Jan. 3	77.773
Fiesta	#4	Ohio St.	10-2	#5	Notre Dame	9-2	34-20	Jan. 2	76,196
Holiday		Oklahoma	7-4	#6	Oregon	10-1	17-14	Dec. 29	65,416
Capital One	#21	Wisconsin	10-2	#7	Auburn	8-3-	24-10	Jan. 2	57,221
Sugar	#11	West Virginia	10-1	#8	Georgia	10-2	38-35	Jan. 2	74,458
Peach	#10	LSU	10-2	#9	Miami-FL	9-2	40-3	Dec. 30	65,620
Gator	#12	Virginia Tech	10-2	#15	Louisville	9-2	35-24	Jan. 2	63,780
Cotton	#13	Alabama	9-2	#18	Texas Tech	9-2	13-10	Jan. 2	74,222
Houston	#14	TCU	10-1		Iowa St.	7-4	27-24	Dec. 31	37,286
Outback	#16	Florida	8-3	#25	Iowa	7-4	31-24	Jan. 2	65,881
Sun	#17	UCLA	9-2		Northwestern	7-4	50-38	Dec. 30	50,426
MPC Computers	#19	Boston College	8-3		Boise St.	9-3	27-21	Dec. 28	30,493
Alamo		Nebraska	7-4	#20	Michigan	7-4	32-28	Dec. 28	62,000
Champs Sports	#23	Clemson	7-4		Colorado	7-5	19-10	Dec. 27	31,470
Emerald		Utah	6-5	#24	Georgia Tech	7-4	38-10	Dec. 29	25,742
Liberty		Tulsa	8-4		Fresno St.	8-4	31-24	Dec. 31	54,894
Meineke Car Care		N.C. State	6-5		South Florida	6-5	14-0	Dec. 31	57,937
Independence		Missouri	6-5		South Carolina	7-4	38-31	Dec. 30	41,332
Music City		Virginia	6-5		Minnesota	7-4	34-31	Dec. 30	40,519
Insight		Arizona St.	6-5		Rutgers	7-4	45-40	Dec. 27	43,536
Motor City		Memphis	6-5		Akron	7-5	38-31	Dec. 26	50,616
Hawaii		Nevada	8-3		Central Florida	8-4	49-48 OT	Dec. 24	26,254
Fort Worth		Kansas	6-5		Houston	6-5	42-13	Dec. 23	33,505
Las Vegas		California	7-4		BYU	6-5	35-28	Dec. 22	40,053
Poinsettia		Navy	7-4		Colorado St.	6-5	51-30	Dec. 22	36,842
GMAC		Toledo	8-3		UTEP	8-3	45-13	Dec. 21	35,422
New Orleans		Southern Miss.	6-5		Arkansas St.	6-5	31-19	Dec. 20	18,338

2005 Final BCS Rankings

The Bowl Championship Series rankings were used for the first time during the 1998 season to determine BCS bowl match-ups and revised slightly for the 1999, 2001, 2002, 2004 and 2005 seasons. The final rankings were released Dec. 4, 2005.

		Polls					Computer Rankings								BCS
	Harris	Pts	%	USA	Pts	%	A&H	RB	CM	KM	JS	PW	%	Avg	Avg
1 USC	1	2811	.9950	1	1543	.9955	25	25	24	24	24	24	.970	2	.9868
2 Texas	2	2726	.9650	2	1543	.9645	24	24	25	25	25	25	.990	1	.9732
3 Penn St.	3	2592	.9175	3	1424	.9187	23	23	23	23	23	23	.920	3	.9187
4 Ohio St.	4	2398	.8488	4	1300	.8387	22	17	22	22	22	22	.880	4	.8559
5 Oregon	6	2205	.7805	5	1234	.7961	21	15	21	19	21	21	.820	5	.7989
6 Notre Dame	5	2295	.8124	6	1219	.7865	17	12	16	12	18	15	.600	10	.7329
7 Georgia	8	2053	.7267	8	1097	.7077	20	22	18	16	14	18	.720	8	.7182
8 Miami-FL	9	1942	.6874	9	1075	.6935	18	19	17	20	19	17	.730	7	.7037
9 Auburn	7	2085	.7381	7	1141	.7361	12	21	14	15	11	14	.550	12	.6747
10 Virginia Tech	11	1719	.6085	12	955	.6161	19	16	20	21	20	20	.790	6	.6715
11 West Virginia	12	1673	.5922	11	959	.6187	14	18	19	18	16	19	.710	9	.6403
12 LSU	10	1812	.6414	10	1002	.6465	16	20	15	11	13	16	.600	10	.6293
13 Alabama	13	1451	.5136	13	787	.5077	8	13	10	7	6	9	.340	18	.4538
14 TCU	14	1328	.4701	14	734	.4735	13	14	13	0	1	12	.390	17	.4445
15 Texas Tech	15	1147	.4060	15	636	.4103	10	9	12	14	12	13	.470	13	.4288
16 UCLA	17	1004	.3554	17	531	.3426	15	11	11	2	8	11	.410	14	.3693
17 Florida	17	1004	.3554	18	530	.3419	6	6	7	3	2	7	.220	21	.3058
18 Wisconsin	20	675	.2389	20	399	.2574	9	3	9	13	15	10	.410	14	.3021
19 Louisville	16	1016	.3596	16	585	.3774	1	10	3	0	0	1	.050	NR	.2624
20 Michigan	21	556	.1968	21	274	.1768	7	4	8	17	17	8	.400	16	.2579
21 Boston College	19	763	.2701	19	427	.2755	4	8	6	5	4	3	.190	22	.2452
22 Florida St.	22	474	.1678	22	256	.1652	0	0	0	1	0	0	.000	NR	.1110
23 Oklahoma	26	87	.0308	26	45	.0290	11	0	5	8	5	6	.240	19	.0999
24 Georgia Tech	24	282	.0998	24	114	.0735	2	5	1	4	3	2	.110	25	.0945
25 Northwestern	29	30	.0106	28	24	.0155	5	1	4	10	10	5	.240	19	.0887

Note: Team percentages are derived by dividing a team's actual voting points by a maximum 2850 possible points in the Harris Interactive Poll and 1550 in the USA Today Coaches Poll. Six computer rankings calculated in inverse points order (25 for #1, 24 for #2, etc.) are used to determine the overall computer component. The best and worst ranking for each team is dropped, and the remaining four are added and divided by 100 (the maximum possible points) to produce a Computer Rankings Percentage. Each computer ranking accounts for schedule strength and home/away performance in its formula. The BCS Average is calculated by averaging the percent totals of the Harris, USA Today Coaches, and Computer polls. Computer Rankings—A&H = Anderson & Hester, RB = Richard Billingsley, CM = Colley Matrix, KM = Kenneth Massey, JS = Jeff Sagarin, PW = Peter Wolfe, Avg. refers to the teams average position in the computer rankings.

BCS Championship Game

Undefeated USC and Texas were ranked first and second, respectively, in the final Bowl Championship Series standings (as well as the AP and *USA Today* Coaches polls) and met in the Rose Bowl to decide Div. 1 college football's national championship. Opponents' records and AP rank listed below are day of game. Final statistics listed below include the bowl games.

USC Trojans (12-1)

Date	AP Rank	Opponent	Result
Sept. 3	#1	at Hawaii (0-0)	W, 63-17
Sept. 17	#1	Arkansas (1-1)	W, 70-17
Sept. 24	#1	at #24 Oregon (3-0)	W, 45-13
Oct. 1	#1	at #14 Arizona St. (3-1)	W, 38-28
Oct. 8	#1	Arizona (2-2)	W, 42-21
Oct. 15	#1	at #9 Notre Dame (4-1)	W, 34-31
Oct. 29	#1	Washington St. (4-3)	W, 55-13
Nov. 5	#1	Stanford (4-3)	W, 51-21
Nov. 12	#1	at California (6-3)	W, 35-10
Nov. 19	#1	#16 Fresno St. (8-1)	W, 50-42
Dec. 3	#1	#11 UCLA (9-1)	W, 66-19
Jan. 4	#1	#2 Texas (12-0)†	L, 38-41

†Rose Bowl

Final Individual Statistics

Passing (5 Att)	Att	Cmp	Pct.	Yds	TD	Rate
Matt Leinart	431	283	65.7	3815	28	157.7
J.D. Booty	42	27	64.3	327	3	143.7

Interceptions: Leinart 8, Booty 2.

Top Receivers	No	Yds	Avg	Long	TD
Dwayne Jarrett	91	1274	14.0	61	16
Steve Smith	60	957	15.9	67	5
Reggie Bush	37	478	12.9	43	2
Dominique Byrd	29	306	10.6	52	0
David Kirtman	22	281	12.8	42	1
Chris McFoy	17	172	10.1	16	0
LenDale White	14	219	15.6	49	2
Fred Davis	13	145	11.2	24	2

Top Rushers	Car	Yds	Avg	Long	TD
Reggie Bush	200	1740	8.7	76	16
LenDale White	197	1302	6.6	46	24
Desmond Reed	19	137	7.2	43	1
M. Coleman	20	95	4.8	16	1

Most Touchdowns	TD	Run	Rec	Ret	Pts
LenDale White	26	24	2	0	156
Reggie Bush	19	16	2	1	114
Dwayne Jarrett	16	0	16	0	96
Matt Leinart	6	6	0	0	36
Steve Smith	5	0	5	0	30

2-Pt. Conversions: none.

Kicking	FG/Att	Lg	PAT/Att	Pts
Mario Danelo	11/12	43	83/86	116

Punting	No	Yds	Long	Blkd	Avg
Tom Malone	32	1335	62	0	41.7
Taylor Odegard	1	38	38	0	38.0

Most Interceptions		Most Sacks	
Darnell Bing	4	Lawrence Jackson	10
Josh Pinkard	2	Frostee Rucker	6.5
John Walker	2	Sedrick Ellis	4.5
Ryan Ting	2		

Texas Longhorns (13-0)

Date	AP Rank	Opponent	Result
Sept. 3	#2	LA-Lafayette (0-0)	W, 60-3
Sept. 10	#2	at #4 Ohio St. (1-0)	W, 25-22
Sept. 17	#2	Rice (0-1)	W, 51-10
Oct. 1	#2	at Missouri (2-1)	W, 51-20
Oct. 8	#2	Oklahoma* (2-2)	W, 45-12
Oct. 15	#2	#24 Colorado (4-2)	W, 42-17
Oct. 22	#2	#10 Texas Tech (6-0)	W, 52-17
Oct. 29	#2	at Oklahoma St. (3-4)	W, 47-28
Nov. 5	#2	at Baylor (4-4)	W, 62-0
Nov. 12	#2	Kansas (5-4)	W, 66-14
Nov. 25	#2	at Texas A&M (5-5)	W, 40-29
Dec. 3	#2	# Colorado† (7-4)	W, 70-3
Jan. 4	#2	#1 USC‡ (12-0)	W, 41-38

*at Dallas
†Big 12 Championship at Houston, Texas.
‡Rose Bowl

Final Individual Statistics

Passing (5 Att)	Att	Cmp	Pct.	Yds	TD	Rate
Vince Young	325	212	65.2	3036	26	164.0
Matt Nordgren	11	6	54.4	47	0	72.3

Interceptions: Young 10, Nordgren 1.

Top Receivers	No	Yds	Avg	Long	TD
David Thomas	50	613	12.3	32	5
Limas Sweed	36	545	15.1	45	5
Billy Pittman	34	750	22.1	75	5
Romance Taylor	27	265	9.8	42	3
Brian Carter	18	263	14.6	40	0
Quan Cosby	15	270	18.0	64	2
Jamaal Charles	14	157	11.2	36	2

Top Rushers	Car	Yds	Avg	Long	TD
Vince Young	155	1050	6.8	80	12
Jamaal Charles	119	878	7.4	80	11
Romance Taylor	76	513	6.8	57	12
Selvin Young	96	461	4.8	28	8
Henry Melton	87	432	5.0	27	10

Most Touchdowns	TD	Run	Rec	Ret	Pts
Romance Taylor	15	12	3	0	90
Jamaal Charles	13	11	2	0	78
Vince Young	12	12	0	0	74
Henry Melton	10	10	0	0	60
Selvin Young	8	8	0	0	48

2-Pt. Conversions: Young (2).

Kicking	FG/Att	Lg	PAT/Att	Pts
David Pino	14/18	46	71/77	113

Punting	No	Yds	Long	Blkd	Avg
Richmond McGee	35	1325	56	0	37.9

Most Interceptions		Most Sacks	
Michael Griffin	3	Brian Robison	7.0
Aaron Ross	3	Rodrique Wright	4.5
		Aaron Harris	4.0
		Robert Killebrew	4.0

USC's 34-game win streak, that ended with their loss to Texas at the Rose Bowl was the third-longest streak since World War I and tied for sixth all-time (see page 205). **Did you know**, *Texas enters the 2006 season with a 20-game win streak of its own?*

Rose Bowl

Wednesday, Jan. 4, 2006 at The Rose Bowl, Pasadena, Calif.

Texas 41, USC 38

	1	2	3	4	F
#1 USC (Pac 10)	7	3	14	14	38
#2 Texas (Big 12)	0	16	7	18	41

Favorite: USC by 7
Field: Grass
Time: 3:59
Attendance: 93,986
Weather: hazy
TV Rating: 21.7/35 (ABC)

Scoring Summary

1st: 12:27; **USC**—LenDale White 4-yd run (Mario Danelo kick), 5 plays, 46 yards, 1:12.

2nd: 10:38; **UT**—David Pino 46-yd field goal, 9 plays, 52 yards, 4:02.
04:57; **UT**—Selvin Young 12-yd run (Pino kick), 7 plays, 80 yards, 1:53.
02:34; **UT**—Romance Taylor 30-yd run (Pino kick), 4 plays, 51 yards, 1:12.
00:02; **UT**—Danelo 43-yd field goal, 11 plays, 53 yards, 0:49.

3rd: 10:36; **USC**—White 3-yd run (Danelo kick), 7 plays, 62 yards, 3:27.
08:34; **UT**—Vince Young 14-yd run (Pino kick), 7 plays, 80 yards, 2:02.

3rd: 04:07; **USC**—White 12-yd run (Danelo kick), 9 plays, 74 yards, 4:27.

4th: 11:19; **USC**—Reggie Bush 26-yd run (Danelo kick), 9 plays, 80 yards, 3:36.
08:46; **UT**—David Pino 34-yd field goal, 9 plays, 52 yards, 2:33.
06:42; **USC**—Dwayne Jarrett 22-yd pass from Matt Leinart (Danelo kick), 4 plays, 80 yards, 2:04.
04:03; **UT**—V. Young 17-yd run (Pino kick), 8 plays, 69 yards, 2:39
00:19; **UT**—V. Young 8-yd run (V. Young rush), 10 plays, 56 yards, 1:50

Team Statistics

	UT	USC
First downs	30	30
Total Plays	76	82
Total Net Yards	556	574
Carries/yards (includ. sacks)	36/289	41/209
Passing yards	267	365
Completions/attempts	30/40	29/41
Had intercepted	0	1
Fumbles/lost	0/0	0/0

	UT	USC
Penalties/yards	4/34	5/30
Punts/average	2/34.0	2/41.5
3rd down conversions	3/11	8/14
4th down conversions	1/2	1/3
Red-Zone scores/chances	5/6	4/5
Sacks by/yards	3/15	0/0
Time of possession	28:00	32:00

Individual Statistics

Texas Longhorns

Passing	Att	Cmp	Int	Yds	TD	Sack
Vince Young	40	30	0	267	0	0

Receivers	No	Yds	Avg	Long	TD
David Thomas	10	88	8.8	18	0
Limas Sweed	8	65	8.1	14	0
Billy Pittman	4	53	13.3	23	0
Brian Carter	3	52	17.3	26	0
Quan Cosby	2	16	8.0	9	0
Romance Taylor	1	-3	-3.0	0	0
Selvin Young	1	-4	-4.0	0	0
TOTALS	30	267	8.9	26	0

Rushers	Car	Yds	Avg	Long	TD
Vince Young	19	200	10.5	45	3
Selvin Young	7	45	6.4	8	1
Jamaal Charles	5	34	6.8	15	0
Romance Taylor	4	12	3.0	30	1
TOTALS	36	289	8.0	45	5

Field Goals	20-29	30-39	40-49	50-59	Total
David Pino	0-0	1-2	1-1	0-0	2-3

Punting	No	Yds	Long	Blkd	Avg
Richmond McGee	2	68	39	0	34.0

Punt Returns	No	Yds	Long	Avg	TD
Aaron Ross	2	19	15	9.5	0

Kickoff Returns	No	Yds	Long	Avg	TD
Romance Taylor	1	29	29	29.0	0

USC Trojans

Passing	Att	Cmp	Int	Yds	TD	Sack
Matt Leinart	40	29	1	365	1	3
Dwayne Jarrett	1	0	0	0	0	0
TOTALS	41	29	1	365	1	3

Receivers	No	Yds	Avg	Long	TD
Dwayne Jarrett	10	121	12.1	24	1
Reggie Bush	6	95	15.8	37	0
Dominique Byrd	4	32	8.0	12	0
David Kirtman	3	61	20.3	33	0
Steve Smith	3	29	9.7	15	0
Fred Davis	2	19	9.5	12	0
B. Hancock	1	8	8.0	8	0
TOTALS	29	365	12.6	37	1

Rushers	Car	Yds	Avg	Long	TD
LenDale White	20	124	6.2	15	3
Reggie Bush	13	82	6.3	26	1
Dwayne Jarrett	1	5	5.0	5	0
Matt Leinart	6	2	0.3	14	0
Chris McFoy	1	-4	-4.0	0	0
TOTALS	41	209	5.1	26	4

Field Goals	20-29	30-39	40-49	50-59	Total
Mario Danelo	0-0	0-0	1-1	0-0	1-1

Punting	No	Yds	Long	Blkd	Avg
Tom Malone	2	83	43	0	41.5

Punt Returns	No	Yds	Long	Avg	TD
none					

Kickoff Returns	No	Yds	Long	Avg	TD
Reggie Bush	5	102	30	20.4	0
Darnell Bing	1	21	21	21.0	0
Rey Maualuga	1	7	7	7.0	0
TOTALS	7	130	30	18.6	0

Young wins second Rose Bowl MVP

Texas QB Vince Young (2005-06) is one of only four two-time winners of the Rose Bowl MVP award. Young joined Bob Schloredt (Washington, 1960-61), Charles White (USC, 1979-80), Ron Dayne (Wisconsin, 1999-2000).

Other Final Division I-A Polls
USA Today Coaches Poll

Voted on by panel of 62 Division I-A head coaches; winning team receives the Sears Trophy (originally the McDonald's Trophy, 1991-93); first place votes in parentheses with total points (based on 25 for 1st, 24 for 2nd, etc.).

	Rec	Pts	Pvs		Rec	Pts	Pvs
1 Texas (62)	13-0	1550	2	14 Auburn	9-3	760	7
2 USC	12-1	1483	1	15 Wisconsin	10-3	739	20
3 Penn St.	11-1	1421	3	16 Florida	9-3	718	18
4 Ohio St.	10-2	1357	4	17 Boston College	9-3	584	19
5 LSU	11-2	1281	10	18 Miami-FL	9-3	558	9
6 West Virginia	11-1	1235	11	19 Texas Tech	9-3	422	15
7 Virginia Tech	11-2	1176	12	20 Louisville	9-3	342	16
8 Alabama	10-2	1066	13	21 Clemson	8-4	310	23
9 TCU	11-1	914	14	22 Oklahoma	8-4	274	NR
10 Georgia	10-3	900	8	23 Florida St.	8-5	209	22
11 Notre Dame	9-3	866	6	24 Nebraska	8-4	109	NR
12 Oregon	10-2	837	5	25 California	8-4	68	NR
13 UCLA	10-2	774	17				

Other teams receiving votes: 26. Tulsa (52 points), 27. Nevada (35), 28. Michigan (32), 29. Toledo (18), 30. Navy (17), 31. Iowa (15), 32. Boise St. and South Carolina (7), 34. Georgia Tech (5), 35. Arizona St., Northwestern and Rutgers (2), 38. N.C. State, Utah and Virginia (1).

AP Weekly Rankings

The Associated Press Top 25 college football polls on a weekly basis are listed below. The table starts with the preseason and progresses through the season.

	Pre	Sept 4	Sept 11	Sept 18	Sept 25	Oct 2	Oct 9	Oct 16	Oct 23	Oct 30	Nov 6	Nov 13	Nov 20	Nov 27	Dec 4	Jan 8
USC	1	1	1	1	1	1	1	1	1	1	1	1	1	1	1	2
Texas	2	2	2	2	2	2	2	2	2	2	2	2	2	2	2	1
Tennessee	3	6	5	10	10	8	17	17	23	-	-	-	-	-	-	-
Michigan	4	3	14	14	-	21	-	-	25	22	21	17	22	20	20	-
LSU	5	5	3	3	4	11	10	7	7	6	5	4	3	3	10	6
Ohio St.	6	4	9	8	8	6	15	14	12	12	10	9	7	6	4	4
Oklahoma	7	18	21	-	-	-	-	-	-	-	-	-	-	-	-	22
Virginia Tech	8	7	4	4	3	3	3	3	3	3	8	7	5	5	12	7
Miami-FL	9	4	9	12	9	9	7	6	6	5	3	3	10	10	9	17
Florida	10	10	6	5	5	13	11	18	16	13	12	20	19	17	16	12
Iowa	11	8	22	21	-	-	-	-	-	-	-	-	-	25	25	-
Louisville	12	12	11	9	24	23	19	-	-	24	23	18	17	16	15	19
Georgia	13	9	7	7	7	5	5	4	4	11	9	14	13	13	8	10
Florida St.	14	11	8	6	6	4	4	11	10	9	17	22	23	-	22	23
Purdue	15	13	12	11	22	-	-	-	-	-	-	-	-	-	-	-
Auburn	16	-	-	-	-	22	21	16	19	17	15	11	9	9	7	14
Texas A&M	17	-	-	-	-	-	-	-	-	-	-	-	-	-	-	-
Boise St.	18	-	-	-	-	-	-	-	-	-	-	-	-	-	-	-
California	19	16	15	13	12	10	18	25	24	23	-	-	-	-	-	25
Arizona St.	20	15	18	18	14	17	-	-	-	-	-	-	-	-	-	-
Texas Tech	21	21	19	19	16	15	13	10	17	16	13	21	18	18	18	20
Boston College	22	19	17	-	21	18	14	13	13	19	-	23	21	19	19	18
Pittsburgh	23	-	-	-	-	-	-	-	-	-	-	-	-	-	-	-
Fresno St.	24	24	23	-	-	-	24	22	21	-	20	16	16	23	-	-
Virginia	25	23	25	23	19	-	23	-	-	-	-	-	-	-	-	-
Georgia Tech	-	17	16	15	25	24	-	-	-	-	24	-	20	24	24	-
Notre Dame	-	20	10	16	13	12	9	9	9	8	7	6	6	7	5	9
TCU	-	22	-	-	-	25	21	20	20	-	18	15	15	15	14	11
Clemson	-	25	20	-	-	-	-	-	-	-	-	-	25	22	23	21
Iowa St.	-	-	24	22	23	-	-	-	-	-	-	-	-	-	-	-
Michigan St.	-	-	-	17	11	19	16	22	-	-	-	-	-	-	-	-
Alabama	-	-	-	20	15	7	6	5	5	4	8	14	14	13	13	8
Oregon	-	-	-	24	-	25	20	15	14	15	11	10	8	8	6	12
UCLA	-	-	-	25	20	20	12	8	8	7	14	12	11	11	17	16
Wisconsin	-	-	-	-	17	14	23	19	15	14	19	25	24	21	21	15
Minnesota	-	-	-	-	18	22	-	-	-	-	-	-	-	-	-	-
Penn St.	-	-	-	-	16	8	12	11	10	-	6	5	4	4	3	3
Colorado	-	-	-	-	-	24	-	-	25	22	-	-	-	-	-	-
West Virginia	-	-	-	-	-	-	20	18	18	16	13	12	12	11	-	5
Northwestern	-	-	-	-	-	-	21	-	25	-	-	-	-	-	-	-
South Carolina	-	-	-	-	-	-	-	-	-	-	19	-	-	-	-	-
UTEP	-	-	-	-	-	-	-	-	-	-	-	24	-	-	-	-
Nebraska	-	-	-	-	-	-	-	-	-	-	-	-	-	-	-	24

NCAA Division I-A Final Standings

Standings based on conference games only; overall records include postseason games.

Atlantic Coast Conference

Atlantic	W	L	PF	PA	W	L	PF	PA
*Florida St.	5	3	219	180	8	5	376	286
*Boston College	5	3	181	160	9	3	310	191
*Clemson	4	4	222	161	8	4	316	211
*N.C. State	3	5	136	182	7	5	249	212
Maryland	3	5	190	217	5	6	270	275
Wake Forest	3	5	202	227	4	7	269	316

Coastal	W	L	PF	PA	W	L	PF	PA
*Virginia Tech	7	1	263	86	11	2	440	168
*Miami-FL	6	2	238	118	9	3	325	171
*Georgia Tech	5	3	154	162	7	5	222	241
North Carolina	4	4	148	188	5	6	198	288
*Virginia	3	5	177	202	7	5	320	279
Duke	0	8	95	342	1	10	177	408

ACC championship game: Florida St. 27, Virginia Tech 22 (Dec. 3, 2005).

Bowls (5-3): Florida St. (lost Orange); Virginia Tech (won Gator); Miami-FL (lost Peach); Boston College (won MPC Computers); Clemson (won Champs Sports); N.C. State (won Meineke Car Care); Georgia Tech (lost Emerald); Virginia (won Music City).

Big East Conference

	W	L	PF	PA	W	L	PF	PA
*West Virginia	7	0	244	104	11	7	385	214
*Louisville	5	2	273	175	9	3	521	284
*Rutgers	4	3	188	199	7	5	344	298
*South Florida	4	3	188	135	6	6	276	216
Pittsburgh	4	3	189	178	5	6	267	243
Connecticut	2	5	115	170	5	6	272	211
Cincinnati	2	5	117	230	4	7	192	345
Syracuse	0	7	73	196	1	10	152	295

Bowls (1-3): West Virginia (won Sugar); Louisville (lost Gator) Rutgers (lost Insight); South Florida (lost Meineke Car Care).

Big Ten Conference

	W	L	PF	PA	W	L	PF	PA
*Penn St.	7	1	282	141	11	1	413	204
*Ohio St.	7	1	275	118	10	2	392	183
*Wisconsin	5	3	246	228	10	3	446	309
*Iowa	5	3	232	165	7	5	360	240
*Michigan	5	3	219	178	7	5	345	244
*Northwestern	5	3	253	254	7	5	388	407
*Minnesota	4	4	255	273	7	5	429	348
Purdue	3	5	222	212	5	6	330	309
Michigan St.	2	6	237	247	5	6	372	316
Indiana	1	7	155	303	4	7	248	361
Illinois	0	8	94	351	2	9	187	435

Bowls (3-4): Penn St. (won Orange); Ohio St. (won Fiesta); Wisconsin (won Capital One); Iowa (lost Outback); Michigan (lost Alamo); Northwestern (lost Sun); Minnesota (lost Music City).

I-A Independents

	W	L	PF	PA
*Notre Dame	9	3	440	294
*Navy	8	4	410	313
Army	4	7	220	294
Temple	0	11	107	497

Bowls (1-1): Navy (won Poinsettia); Notre Dame (lost Fiesta).

Big 12 Conference

North	W	L	PF	PA	W	L	PF	PA
*Colorado	5	3	219	167	7	6	305	307
*Iowa St.	4	4	232	158	7	5	339	230
*Nebraska	4	4	201	208	8	4	296	252
*Missouri	4	4	200	236	7	5	369	350
*Kansas	3	5	127	210	7	5	269	264
Kansas St.	2	6	179	258	5	6	289	305

South	W	L	PF	PA	W	L	PF	PA
*Texas	8	0	405	137	13	0	652	213
*Texas Tech	6	2	264	183	9	3	473	226
*Oklahoma	6	2	241	190	8	4	323	277
Texas A&M	3	5	218	279	5	6	352	343
Baylor	2	6	140	240	5	6	236	291
Oklahoma St.	1	7	164	321	4	7	222	344

Big 12 championship game: Texas 70, Colorado 3 (Dec. 3, 2005).

Bowls (5-3): Texas (won Rose); Texas Tech (lost Cotton); Iowa St. (lost Houston); Missouri (won Independence); Oklahoma (won Holiday); Nebraska (won Alamo), Colorado (lost Champs Sports), Kansas (won Fort Worth).

Conference USA

East	W	L	PF	PA	W	L	PF	PA
*UCF	7	1	245	204	8	5	373	373
*Memphis	5	3	207	201	7	5	326	276
*Southern Miss	5	3	238	182	7	5	355	272
East Carolina	4	4	194	232	5	6	267	317
UAB	3	5	235	212	5	6	307	264
Marshall	3	5	135	199	4	7	204	285

West	W	L	PF	PA	W	L	PF	PA
*Tulsa	6	2	276	180	9	4	430	305
*UTEP	5	3	269	236	8	4	382	311
*Houston	4	4	241	218	6	6	337	324
SMU	4	4	177	176	5	6	229	280
Tulane	1	7	171	257	2	9	234	348
Rice	1	7	201	292	1	10	241	447

Conference USA championship game: Tulsa 44, UCF 27 (Dec. 3, 2005).

Bowls (3-3): UCF (lost Hawaii); Memphis (won Motor City); Southern Miss (won New Orleans); Tulsa (won Liberty); UTEP (lost GMAC); Houston (lost Fort Worth).

Mid-American Conference

East	W	L	PF	PA	W	L	PF	PA
*Akron	5	3	204	174	7	6	307	318
Miami-OH	5	3	272	194	7	4	371	258
Bowling Green	5	3	240	193	6	5	372	304
Ohio	3	5	162	243	4	7	192	336
Buffalo	1	7	107	241	1	10	110	327
Kent St.	0	8	102	236	1	10	180	331

West	W	L	PF	PA	W	L	PF	PA
Northern Illinois	6	2	263	169	7	5	389	274
*Toledo	6	2	266	173	9	3	429	261
Western Michigan	3	5	282	267	7	4	354	342
Central Michigan	5	3	230	190	6	5	260	260
Ball St.	4	4	230	259	4	7	233	416
Eastern Michigan	3	5	183	202	4	7	240	295

MAC championship game: Akron 31, Northern Illinois 30 (Dec. 1, 2005).

Bowls (1-1): Akron (lost Motor City); Toledo (won GMAC).

Mountain West Conference

	Conference				Overall			
	W	L	PF	PA	W	L	PF	PA
*TCU	.8	0	306	151	11	1	371	199
*BYU	.5	3	297	237	6	6	368	316
*Colorado State	.5	3	197	210	6	6	291	318
New Mexico	.4	4	230	250	6	5	326	327
*Utah	.4	4	247	217	7	5	322	279
San Diego St.	.4	4	206	184	5	7	323	325
Air Force	.3	5	262	278	4	7	330	349
Wyoming	.2	6	195	251	4	7	271	297
UNLV	.1	7	135	297	2	9	207	381

Bowls (2-2): TCU (won Houston); Utah (won Emerald); Colorado St. (lost Poinsettia); BYU (lost Las Vegas).

Pacific-10 Conference

	Conference				Overall			
	W	L	PF	PA	W	L	PF	PA
*USC	.8	0	383	149	12	1	638	297
*Oregon	.7	1	278	189	10	2	414	268
*UCLA	.6	2	271	306	10	2	469	410
*California	.4	4	243	190	8	4	295	254
*Arizona St.	.4	4	251	247	7	5	442	359
Stanford	.4	4	180	241	5	6	269	237
Oregon St.	.3	5	195	261	5	6	293	365
Arizona	.2	6	173	220	3	8	252	290
Washington St.	.1	7	227	292	4	7	368	346
Washington	.1	7	169	275	2	9	237	337

Bowls (3-2): USC (lost Rose); Oregon (lost Holiday); UCLA (won Sun); California (won Las Vegas), Arizona St. (won Insight).

Sun Belt Conference

	Conference				Overall			
	W	L	PF	PA	W	L	PF	PA
*Arkansas St.	.5	2	182	163	6	6	294	303
LA-Lafayette	.5	2	203	161	6	5	286	304
LA-Monroe	.5	2	194	186	5	6	239	339
Florida Int'l	.3	4	172	191	5	6	257	323
Middle Tenn.	.3	4	176	124	4	7	210	206
Troy	.3	4	100	121	4	7	175	255
Florida Atlantic	.2	5	109	179	2	9	148	339
North Texas	.2	5	131	142	2	9	157	346

Bowls (0-1): Arkansas St. (lost New Orleans).

Southeastern Conference

	Conference				Overall			
	W	L	PF	PA	W	L	PF	PA
*Georgia	.6	2	209	134	10	3	384	213
*South Carolina	.5	3	175	193	7	5	284	279
*Florida	.5	3	205	178	9	3	343	226
Vanderbilt	.3	5	223	271	5	6	299	321
Tennessee	.3	5	147	138	5	6	205	205
Kentucky	.2	6	160	277	3	8	239	375

	Conference				Overall			
Western	W	L	PF	PA	W	L	PF	PA
*LSU	.7	1	214	114	.11	2	383	185
*Auburn	.7	1	262	122	9	3	386	186
*Alabama	.6	2	159	87	10	2	263	128
Arkansas	.2	6	173	169	4	7	283	271
Mississippi St.	.1	7	78	211	3	8	153	259
Mississippi	.1	7	97	208	3	8	148	245

SEC championship game: Georgia 34, LSU 14 (Dec. 3, 2005).

Bowls (3-3): Georgia (lost Sugar); Auburn (lost Capital One); Alabama (won Cotton); Florida (won Outback); LSU (won Peach); South Carolina (lost Independence).

Western Athletic Conference

	Conference				Overall			
	W	L	PF	PA	W	L	PF	PA
*Nevada	.7	1	297	224	9	3	410	383
*Boise St.	.7	1	339	178	9	4	469	317
La. Tech	.6	2	259	192	7	4	316	281
*Fresno St.	.6	2	292	143	8	5	491	292
Hawaii	.4	4	264	244	5	7	368	428
San Jose St.	.2	6	173	241	3	8	248	357
Utah St.	.2	6	167	270	3	8	208	360
Idaho	.2	6	180	313	2	9	243	419
New Mexico St.	.0	8	147	313	0	12	198	465

Bowls (1-2): Nevada (won Hawaii); Boise St. (lost MPC Computers); Fresno St. (lost Liberty).

> **Owls to join MAC ranks in '07**
> Temple, currently playing as an independent, will join the Mid-American Conference for the 2007 season and will play in the East Division.

NCAA Division I-A Individual Leaders

Total Offense

		Rushing				Passing			Total Offense		
	Cl	Car	Gain	Loss	Net	Att	Yds	Plays	Yds	YdsPP	YdsPG
Colt Brennan, Hawaii	So.	99	371	217	154	515	4301	614	4455	7.26	371.3
Cody Hodges, Texas Tech	Sr.	109	496	305	191	531	4238	640	4429	6.92	369.1
Brett Basanez, Northwestern	Sr.	113	550	127	423	497	3622	610	4045	6.63	337.1
Brian Johnson, Utah	So.	152	690	212	478	330	2892	482	3370	6.99	337.0
Brady Quinn, Notre Dame	Jr.	70	245	155	90	450	3919	520	4009	7.71	334.1
Vince Young, Texas	Jr.	155	1186	136	1050	325	3036	480	4086	8.51	314.3
John Beck, BYU	Sr.	73	242	181	61	513	3709	586	3770	6.43	314.2
Drew Stanton, Michigan St.	Jr.	121	520	182	338	354	3077	475	3415	7.19	310.5
Brad Smith, Missouri	Sr.	229	1457	156	1301	399	2304	628	3605	5.74	300.4
Jay Cutler, Vanderbilt	Sr.	106	443	228	215	462	3073	568	3288	5.79	298.9

All-Purpose Yards

	Cl	Gm	Rush	Rec	PR	KOR	Total Yds	YdsPG
Reggie Bush, USC	Jr.	13	1740	478	179	493	2890	222.31
Gattett Wolfe, Northern Illinois	Jr.	9	1580	222	0	0	1802	200.22
Jerome Harrison, Washington St.	Sr.	11	1900	206	0	7	2113	192.09
DeAngelo Williams, Memphis	Sr.	11	1964	78	0	33	2075	188.64
Rafael Little, Kentucky	So.	11	1045	449	355	133	1982	180.18
Brian Calhoun, Wisconsin	Jr.	13	1636	571	0	0	2207	169.77
Domenik Hixon, Akron	Sr.	13	24	1210	200	705	2139	164.54
Brandon Williams, Wisconsin	Sr.	13	47	1095	380	616	2138	164.46
Marshawn Lynch, California	So.	10	1246	125	0	271	1642	164.20

Arizona St.
Rudy Carpenter
Passing Efficiency

Memphis
DeAngelo Williams
Rushing

Louisville
Elvis Dumervil
Sacks

Western Mich.
Greg Jennings
Receptions

Passing Efficiency

(Minimum 15 attempts per game)

	Cl	Gm	Att	Cmp	Cmp Pct	Int	Int Pct	Yds	Yds/Att	TD	TD Pct	Rating Points
Rudy Carpenter, Arizona St.	Fr.	9	228	156	68.42	2	0.88	2273	9.97	17	7.46	175.0
Brian Brohm, Louisville	So.	10	301	207	68.77	5	1.66	2883	9.58	19	6.31	166.7
Vince Young, Texas	Jr.	13	325	212	65.23	10	3.08	3036	9.34	26	8.00	163.9
Troy Smith, Ohio St.	Sr.	11	237	149	62.87	4	1.69	2282	9.63	16	6.75	162.7
Drew Olson, UCLA	Sr.	12	378	242	64.02	6	1.59	3198	8.46	34	8.99	161.6
Phil Horvath, Northern Ill.	Jr.	9	238	168	70.59	8	3.36	2001	8.41	18	7.56	159.4
Brady Quinn, Notre Dame	Jr.	12	450	292	64.89	7	1.56	3919	8.71	32	7.11	158.4
Matt Leinart, USC	Sr.	13	431	283	65.66	8	1.86	3815	8.85	28	6.50	157.7
Colt Brennan, Hawaii	So.	12	515	350	67.96	13	2.52	4301	8.35	35	6.80	155.5
Drew Stanton, Michigan St.	Jr.	11	354	236	66.67	12	3.39	3077	8.69	22	6.21	153.4
Brian Johnson, Utah	So.	10	330	210	63.64	7	2.12	2892	8.76	18	5.45	151.0
Omar Jacobs, Bowling Green	Jr.	9	321	195	60.75	7	2.18	2590	8.07	26	8.10	150.9
John Stocco, Wisconsin	Jr.	13	328	197	60.06	9	2.74	2920	8.90	21	6.40	150.5
Justin Holland, Colorado St.	Sr.	12	369	235	63.69	15	4.07	3185	8.63	23	6.23	148.6
Cody Hodges, Texas Tech	Sr.	12	531	353	66.48	12	2.26	4238	7.98	31	5.84	148.3

Rushing

	Cl	Car	Yds	TD	YdsPG
DeAngelo Williams, Memphis	Sr.	310	1964	18	178.55
Garrett Wolfe, Northern Ill.	Jr.	242	1580	16	175.56
Jerome Harrison, Wash. St.	Sr.	308	1988	16	172.73
Reggie Bush, USC	Jr.	200	1740	16	133.85
Laurence Maroney, Minn.	Jr.	281	1464	10	133.09
Brian Calhoun, Wisconsin	Jr.	348	1636	22	125.85
Marshawn Lynch, California	Jr.	196	1246	10	124.60
Tyrell Sutton, Northwestern	Fr.	250	1474	16	122.83
Yvenson Bernard, Oregon St.	So.	299	1321	13	120.09
DonTrell Moore, New Mex.	Sr.	275	1298	14	118.00
B.J. Mitchell, Nevada	Sr.	261	1399	12	116.58
Andre Hall, South Florida	Sr.	270	1374	13	114.50

Games: All played 11, except Wolfe (9), Bush and Calhoun (13), Lynch (10), and Mitchell, Sutton and Hall (12).

Receptions

	Cl	No	Yds	TD	P/Gm
Greg Jennings, West. Mich.	Sr.	98	1259	14	8.91
Mike Hass, Oregon St.	Sr.	90	1532	6	8.18
Jeffrey Webb, San Diego St.	Sr.	92	1109	10	7.67
Aundrae Allison, East Caro.	Sr.	83	1024	7	7.55
Davone Bess, Hawaii	Fr.	89	1124	14	7.42
Martin Nance, Miami-OH	Jr.	81	1107	14	7.36
Chad Jackson, Florida	Jr.	88	900	9	7.33
Dorien Bryant, Purdue	So.	80	960	4	7.27
Earl Bennett, Vanderbilt	Fr.	79	876	9	7.18
David Anderson, Colo. St.	Sr.	86	1221	8	7.17
Ryan Grice-Mullen, Hawaii	Sr.	85	1228	12	7.08
Jovon Bouknight, Wyoming	Fr.	77	1116	12	7.00

Games: All played 11, except Webb, Bess, Jackson, Anderson and Grice-Mullen (12).

Field Goals

	Cl	FG/Att	Pct	P/Gm
Paul Martinez, Oregon	Jr.	19/24	.792	2.11
Alexis Serna, Oregon St.	So.	23/28	.821	2.09
Jad Dean, Clemson	Jr.	24/31	.774	2.00
Darren McCaleb, So. Miss.	Jr.	23/28	.821	1.92
Josh Huston, Ohio St.	Sr.	22/28	.786	1.83
Stephen Gostkowski, Memphis	Sr.	22/25	.880	1.83
Brandon Coutu, Georgia	So.	23/29	.793	1.77
Connor Hughes, Virginia	Jr.	21/24	.875	1.75
Sam Swank, Wake Forest	Fr.	19/24	.792	1.73
Todd Soderquist, Miami-OH	Sr.	19/27	.704	1.73

Games: All played 12, except Martinez (9), Serna, Swank and Soderquist (11) and Coutu (13).

Interceptions

	Cl	No	Yds	TD	P/Gm
Aaron Gipson, Oregon	Sr.	7	117	1	0.58
Anthony Smith, Syracuse	Sr.	6	78	0	0.55
Dion Byrum, Ohio	Sr.	6	153	2	0.55
Jelani Jordan, Bowling Green	Sr.	6	66	0	0.55
Chaz Williams, LA-Monroe	So.	5	138	1	0.50
Marcus Hamilton, Virginia	Jr.	6	28	0	0.50
Alan Zemaitis, Penn St.	Sr.	6	35	0	0.50
Nick Graham, Tulsa	Jr.	6	66	0	0.46

Seven tied at 0.45 per game.

Games: All played 11, except Gipson, Hamilton and Zemaitis (12), Williams (10) and Graham (13).

Scoring

Non-Kickers

	Cl	TD	Pts	P/Gm
Michael Bush, Louisville	Jr.	24	144	14.40
LenDale White, USC	Jr.	26	156	12.00
Steve Slaton, W. Virginia	Fr.	19	114	11.40
Garrett Wolfe, Northern Ill.	Jr.	17	102	11.33
Brian Calhoun, Wisconsin	Jr.	24	144	11.08
Taurean Henderson, Tex. Tech	Sr.	22	132	11.00
DeAngelo Williams, Memphis	Sr.	19	114	10.36
Maurice Drew, UCLA	Jr.	20	120	10.00
Gary Russell, Minnesota	So.	19	116	9.67
DonTrell Moore, N. Mexico	Sr.	17	104	9.45

Games: All played 12, except Bush and Slaton (10), White and Calhoun (13), Wolfe (9), Williams and Moore (11).

Kickers

	FG/Att	PAT/Att	Pts	P/Gm
Paul Martinez, Oregon	19/24	26/30	83	9.22
Alexis Serna, Oregon St.	23/28	32/32	101	9.18
Josh Huston, Ohio St.	22/28	44/45	110	9.17
Todd Soderquist, Miami-OH	19/27	43/44	100	9.09
Mario Danelo, USC	11/12	83/86	116	8.92
Darren McCaleb, So. Miss.	23/28	38/39	107	8.92
Jad Dean, Clemson	24/31	34/35	106	8.83
Brandon Coutu, Georgia	23/29	45/45	114	8.77
Arthur Carmody, Louisville	14/16	63/65	105	8.75
David Pino, Texas	14/18	71/77	113	8.69
Stephen Gostkowski, Mem.	22/25	35/35	101	8.42

Games: All played 12, Wellock (11), Killeen and Pace (13).

Sacks

	Cl	No	Yds	P/Gm
Elvis Dumervil, Louisville	Sr.	20	151	1.67
Dan Bazuin, Central Mich.	Jr.	16	147	1.45
Willie Evans, Mississippi St.	Sr.	15	96	1.36
Mario Williams, N.C. State	Jr.	14½	80	1.21
John Chick, Utah St.	Sr.	12½	89	1.14

Punting

(Minimum of 3.6 per game)

	Cl	No	Yds	Avg
Ryan Plackemeier, Wake Forest	Sr.	67	3165	47.24
Sam Koch, Nebraska	Sr.	71	3302	46.51
Daniel Sepulveda, Baylor	Jr.	62	2863	46.18
Jim Kaylor, Colorado St.	So.	53	2400	45.28
John Torp, Colorado	Sr.	80	3613	45.16
Kody Bliss, Auburn	Jr.	44	1975	44.89
Luke Johnson, So. Miss.	Sr.	53	2378	44.87
Kenneth DeBauche, Wisconsin	So.	57	2555	44.82
Michael Hughes, San Diego St.	So.	67	3003	44.82
Joel Stelly, LA-Monroe	Sr.	59	2634	44.64

Punt Returns

(Minimum of 1.2 per game)

	Cl	No	Yds	TD	Avg
Maurice Drew, UCLA	Jr.	15	427	3	28.47
Quinton Jones, Boise St.	Jr.	22	459	3	20.86
Terrence Nunn, Nebraska	So.	16	293	0	18.31
Willie Reid, Florida St.	Sr.	31	541	3	17.45
Rafael Little, Kentucky	So.	21	355	0	16.90
Joe Burnett, UCF	Jr.	28	463	2	16.54
Terry Richardson, Ariz. St.	Jr.	22	337	2	15.32
Cory Rodgers, TCU	Jr.	19	290	0	15.26
Tim Mixon, California	Jr.	24	357	1	14.88
Aaron Ross, Texas	Jr.	34	500	2	14.71

Kickoff Returns

(Minimum of 1.2 per game)

	Cl	No	Yds	TD	Avg
Jonathan Stewart, Oregon	Fr.	12	404	2	33.67
Felix Jones, Arkansas	Fr.	17	543	1	31.94
Cory Rodgers, TCU	Jr.	17	515	2	30.29
Ted Ginn Jr., Ohio St.	So.	18	532	1	29.56
Tony Pennyman, Utah St.	Jr.	23	675	2	29.35
Darrell Blackman, N.C. State	So.	20	582	0	29.10
Adam Jennings, Fresno St.	Sr.	20	580	0	29.00
Steve Breaston, Michigan	Sr.	23	646	1	28.09
Brandon Williams, Wisconsin	Sr.	22	616	0	28.00
Lee Marks, Boise St.	Sr.	17	474	1	27.88

NCAA Division I-A Team Leaders

Scoring Offense

	Gm	Record	Pts	Avg
Texas	13	13-0	652	50.2
USC	13	12-1	638	49.1
Louisville	12	9-3	521	43.4
Texas Tech	12	9-3	473	39.4
UCLA	12	10-2	469	39.1
Fresno St.	13	8-5	491	37.8
Arizona St.	12	7-5	442	36.8
Notre Dame	12	9-3	440	36.7
Boise St.	13	9-4	469	36.1
Minnesota	12	7-5	429	35.8
Toledo	12	9-3	429	35.8

Scoring Defense

	Gm	Record	Pts	Avg
Alabama	12	10-2	128	10.7
Virginia Tech	13	11-2	168	12.9
LSU	13	11-2	185	14.2
Miami-FL	12	9-3	171	14.3
Ohio St.	12	10-2	183	15.3
Auburn	12	9-3	186	15.5
Boston College	12	9-3	191	15.9
Georgia	13	10-3	213	16.4
Texas	13	13-0	213	16.4
Penn St.	12	11-1	204	17.0

Total Offense

	Gm	Plays	Yds	Avg	TD	YdsPG
USC	13	1006	7537	7.49	87	579.8
Arizona St.	12	940	6229	6.63	59	519.1
Texas	13	941	6657	7.07	88	512.1
Northwestern	12	974	6004	6.16	51	500.3
Michigan St.	11	834	5470	6.56	50	497.3
Texas Tech	12	896	5950	6.64	62	495.8
Minnesota	12	933	5937	6.36	56	494.8
Washington St.	11	821	5382	6.56	47	489.3
Louisville	12	848	5785	6.82	69	482.1
Notre Dame	12	945	5728	6.06	58	477.3

Note: Touchdowns scored by rushing and passing only.

Total Defense

	Gm	Plays	Yds	Avg	TD	YdsPG
Virginia Tech	13	789	3219	4.08	19	247.6
Alabama	12	713	3061	4.29	15	255.1
LSU	13	833	3469	4.16	21	266.9
Miami-FL	12	828	3241	3.91	19	270.1
Ohio St.	12	780	3376	4.33	21	281.3
Connecticut	11	732	3269	4.47	28	297.2
Tennessee	11	720	3280	4.56	21	298.2
N.C. State	12	841	3584	4.26	23	298.7
Florida	12	748	3598	4.81	30	299.8
Texas	13	897	3938	4.39	25	302.9

Note: Opponents' TDs scored by rushing and passing only.

Single Game Highs

INDIVIDUAL

Rushing Yards

Yds
294	Reggie Bush, USC vs. Fresno St. (Nov. 19)
277	Garrett Wolfe, Northern Ill. vs. W. Mich. (Nov. 23)
270	Garrett Wolfe, Northern Ill. vs. Akron (Dec. 1)
267	Vince Young, Texas vs. Oklahoma St. (Oct. 29)

Total Offense

Yds
604	Cody Hodges, Texas Tech vs. Kansas St. (Oct. 15)
561	Colt Brennan, Hawaii vs. New Mexico St. (Oct. 15)
515	Alex Brink, Wash. St. vs. Oregon St. (Oct. 1)

Passing Yards

Yds
643	Cody Hodges, Texas Tech vs. Kansas St. (Oct. 15)
531	Alex Brink, Washington St. vs. Oregon St. (Oct. 1)
517	John Beck, BYU vs. TCU (Sept. 24)

Passes Completed

No
46	Kent Smith, Central Mich. vs. West. Mich. (Nov. 12)
44	Cody Hodges, Texas Tech vs. Kansas St. (Oct. 15)
42	Cody Hodges, Texas Tech vs. Texas (Oct. 22)

Receptions

No
16	Five players tied.

Receiving Yards

Yds
269	Daniel Smith, Idaho vs. New Mexico St. (Oct. 29)
266	Sam Hurd, Northern Ill. vs. Central Mich. (Nov. 5)
255	Joel Filani, Texas Tech vs. Kansas St. (Oct. 15)

Touchdowns

No
6	Steve Slaton, West Virginia vs. Louisville (Oct. 15)

TEAM

Total Offense Yards Gained

Yds
773	Arizona St. vs. Northwestern (Sept. 17)
770	Texas Tech vs. Sam Houston St. (Sept. 17)

Total Defense Yards Allowed

Yds
35	Virginia Tech vs. Duke (Sept. 10)
45	Wisconsin vs. Temple (Sept. 10)

Annual Awards

Players of the Year

Reggie Bush, USC, RB . . . . .Camp, Heisman
Vince Young, Texas, QB . . . . .Maxwell

Payton Award (I-AA) . . . . .Erik Meyer, E. Washington, QB
Hill Trophy (Div. II) . . Jimmy Terwilliger, E. Stroudsburg, QB
Gagliardi Trophy (Div. III) . . . . . . .Brett Elliott, Linfield, QB

Position Players of the Year

O'Brien Award (Quarterback) . . . . . . .Vince Young, Texas
Walker Award (Running Back) . . . . .Reggie Bush, USC
Biletnikoff Award (Receiver) . . . . . .Mike Hass, Oregon St.
Outland Trophy (Int. Lineman) . . .Greg Eslinger, Minnesota
Lombardi Award (Lineman) . . . . .A.J. Hawk, Ohio St.
Butkus Award (Linebacker) . . . . . . .Paul Posluszny, Penn St.
Thorpe Award (Def. Back) . . . . .Michael Huff, Texas
Nagurski Award (Def. Player) . . .Elvis Dumervile, Louisville
Bednarik Award (Def. Player) . . . .Paul Posluszny, Penn St.
Groza Award (Kicker) . . . . .Alexis Serna, Oregon St.
Ray Guy Award (Punter) . . .Ryan Plackemeier, Wake Forest
Mackey Award (Tight End) . . . . . . .Marcedes Lewis, UCLA

Coaches of the Year

Joe Paterno, Penn St. . . . . .AFCA, AP, Camp, Dodd
Charlie Weis, Notre Dame . . . . FWAA

Heisman Trophy Vote

Presented since 1935 by the Downtown Athletic Club of New York City and named after former college coach and DAC athletic director John W. Heisman. Voting done by national media and former Heisman winners. Each ballot allows for three names (points based on 3 for 1st, 2 for 2nd and 1 for 3rd).

Top 10 Vote-Getters

	Pos	1st	2nd	3rd	Pts
Reggie Bush, USC . . . . .RB		784	89	11	2541
Vince Young, Texas . . . . . . .QB		79	613	145	1608
Matt Leinart, USC . . . . .QB		18	147	449	797
Brady Quinn, Notre Dame . .QB		7	21	128	191
Michael Robinson, Penn St. . .QB		2	7	29	49
A.J. Hawk, Ohio St. . . . . .LB		0	3	23	29
DeAngelo Williams, Memphis RB		1	2	19	26
Drew Olson, UCLA . . . . . . .QB		1	2	14	21
Jerome Harrison, Wash. St. . .RB		0	4	12	20
Elivs Dumervil, Louisville . . . .DE		0	0	9	9

Consensus All-America Team

NCAA Division I-A players cited most frequently by the following selectors: AFCA, AP, and Walter Camp Foundation. (*) indicates unanimous selection. Holdovers from the 2004 team is in **bold** type.

Offense

	Player	Class	Ht	Wt
WR	Dwayne Jarrett*, USC . . . . .So.		6-5	210
WR	Mike Hass, Oregon St. . . . . . . .Sr.		6-1	210
TE	Vernon Davis, Maryland . . . . . .Jr.		6-3	253
C	Greg Eslinger*, Minnesota . . . . .Sr.		6-3	285
OL	Jonathan Scott*, Texas . . . . . . .Sr.		6-7	310
OL	Max Jean-Giles*, Georgia . . . . .Sr.		6-4	340
OL	Marcus McNeil, Auburn . . . . . . .Sr.		6-8	335
OL	Eric Winston, Miami-FL . . . . . . .Sr.		6-6	311
QB	**Matt Leinart**, USC . . . . .Sr.		6-5	225
RB	Reggie Bush*, USC . . . . .Jr.		6-0	200
RB	DeAngelo Williams, Memphis . . .Sr.		5-9	207
K	Mason Crosby, Colorado . . . . . .Jr.		6-2	210

Defense

	Player	Class	Ht	Wt
DL	Elvis Dumervil*, Louisville . . . . . .Sr.		5-11	257
DL	Tamba Hali*, Penn St. . . . . .Sr.		6-3	273
DL	Rodrique Wright, Texas . . . . . . .Sr.		6-5	315
DL	Haloti Ngata, Oregon . . . . .Jr.		6-5	338
LB	DeMeco Ryans*, Alabama . . . . .Sr.		6-1	236
LB	Paul Posluszny, Penn St. . . . . . . .Jr.		6-2	229
LB	**A.J. Hawk**, Ohio St. . . . . .Sr.		6-2	238
DB	Jimmy Williams, Virginia Tech . . .Sr.		6-3	216
DB	Greg Blue, Georgia . . . . .Sr.		6-2	214
DB	Michael Huff, Texas . . . . .Sr.		6-0	204
DB	Tye Hill, Clemson . . . . .Sr.		5-9	186
P	Ryan Plackemeier*, Wake Forest .Sr.		6-3	252

Underclassmen who declared for the 2006 draft

Forty-eight players forfeited the remainder of their college eligibility and declared for the NFL draft in 2006. NFL teams drafted 33 underclassmen. Players listed in alphabetical order; first round selections in **bold** type.

	Pos	Drafted by	Overall Pick
Darnell Bing, USC	S	Oakland	101
Cornell Brockington, UConn	RB	not drafted	-
Reggie Bush, USC	RB	New Orleans	2
Brian Calhoun, Wisconsin	RB	Detroit	74
Antonio Cromartie, Fla. St.	CB	San Diego	19
Vernon Davis, Maryland	TE	San Francisco	6
Maurice Drew, UCLA	RB	Jacksonville	60
Ray Edwards, Purdue	DE	Minnesota	127
Anthony Fasano, Notre Dame	TE	Dallas	53
Charles Gordon, Kansas	CB	not drafted	-
Willie Hall, Mid. Tenn. St.	OT	not drafted	-
Devin Hester, Miami-FL	CB	Chicago	57
Santonio Holmes, Ohio St.	WR	Pittsburgh	25
Chad Jackson, Florida	WR	New England	36
Omar Jacobs, Bowling Green	QB	Pittsburgh	164
Cornell Johnson, Indiana St.	RB	not drafted	-
Marquis Johnson, Texas Tech	WR	not drafted	-
Johnathan Joseph, So. Car.	CB	Cincinnati	24
Winston Justice, USC	OT	Philadelphia	39
Brandon Kirsch, Purdue	QB	not drafted	-
Greg Lee, Pittsburgh	WR	not drafted	-
Laurence Maroney, Minn.	RB	New England	21
Richard Marshall, Fresno St.	CB	Carolina	58
Derrick Martin, Wyoming	CB	Baltimore	208
Fred Matua, USC	G	Detroit	217
John McCargo, N.C. State	DT	N.C. State	26
Stanley McClover, Auburn	DE	Carolina	237
Tony McDaniel, Tennessee	DT	not drafted	-
Derek Morris, N.C. State	OT	not drafted	-
Haloti Ngata, Oregon	DT	Baltimore	12
Kai Parham, Virginia	LB	not drafted	-
Bobby Payne, Mid. Tenn. St.	DE	not drafted	-
Bernard Pollard, Purdue	S	Kansas City	54
Leonard Pope, Georgia	TE	Arizona	72
Drouzon Quillen, LA-Monroe	WR	not drafted	-
Cory Rodgers, TCU	WR	Green Bay	104
Ko Simpson, S. Carolina	S	Buffalo	105
Ernie Sims, Florida St.	LB	Detroit	9
D.J. Smith, Idaho	WR	not drafted	-
Rob Smith, Tennessee	G	not drafted	-
Stephen Tulloch, N.C. State	LB	N.C. State	116
Marcus Vick, Va. Tech	QB	not drafted	-
Dee Webb, Florida	CB	Jacksonville	236
LenDale White, USC	RB	Tennessee	45
Donte Whitner, Ohio St.	S	Buffalo	8
Mario Williams, N.C. State	DE	Houston	1
Ashton Youboty, Ohio St.	CB	Buffalo	70
Vince Young, Texas	QB	Tennessee	3

NCAA Division I-AA Final Standings

Standings based on conference games only; overall records include postseason games.

Atlantic 10 Conference

North	Conference W	L	PF	PA	Overall W	L	PF	PA
*New Hampshire	.7	1	344	211	11	2	542	289
Massachusetts	.6	2	178	95	7	4	259	146
Hofstra	.5	3	206	171	7	4	338	222
Maine	.3	5	150	251	5	6	216	283
Northeastern	.2	6	182	250	2	9	248	340
Rhode Island	.2	6	187	231	4	7	312	306

South	Conference W	L	PF	PA	Overall W	L	PF	PA
*Richmond	.7	1	240	150	9	4	349	231
James Madison	.5	3	243	130	7	4	391	168
Delaware	.3	5	163	187	6	5	274	264
Towson	.3	5	208	329	6	5	345	372
William & Mary	.3	5	237	240	5	6	358	283
Villanova	.2	6	185	278	4	7	257	350

*Playoffs (2-2): New Hampshire (1-1), Richmond (1-1).

Big Sky Conference

	Conference W	L	PF	PA	Overall W	L	PF	PA
*Eastern Wash.	.5	2	251	151	7	5	423	278
Montana St.	.5	2	194	175	7	4	276	251
*Montana	.5	2	173	109	8	4	306	218
Portland St.	.4	3	230	182	6	5	313	273
Weber St.	.4	3	172	171	6	5	277	277
Idaho St.	.3	4	184	215	5	6	298	304
Sacramento St.	.1	6	128	236	2	9	192	352
Northern Arizona	.1	6	125	236	3	8	233	328

*Playoffs (0-2): Montana (0-1), Eastern Wash. (0-1).

Big South Conference

	Conference W	L	PF	PA	Overall W	L	PF	PA
Coastal Carolina	.3	1	126	100	9	2	338	220
Charleston So.	.3	1	115	98	4	313	303	
Gardner-Webb	.2	2	114	140	5	6	386	367
VMI	.2	2	110	112	3	8	230	319
Liberty	.0	4	74	89	1	10	146	348

Playoffs: No teams invited.

Gateway Football Conference

	Conference W	L	PF	PA	Overall W	L	PF	PA
*Northern Iowa	.5	2	165	147	11	4	449	357
Youngstown St.	.5	2	185	107	8	3	306	178
*Southern Ill.	.5	2	227	190	9	4	449	298
Illinois St.	.4	3	285	177	7	4	431	234
Western Ky.	.4	3	204	193	6	5	339	292
Western Ill.	.3	4	204	216	5	6	352	371
SW Missouri St.	.2	5	160	228	4	6	273	312
Indiana St.	.0	7	148	320	0	11	193	476

*Playoffs (0-2): Northern Iowa (2-1), Southern Ill. (0-1).

Great West Football Conference

	Conference W	L	PF	PA	Overall W	L	PF	PA
*Cal Poly	.4	1	125	66	9	4	354	232
UC Davis	.4	1	111	78	6	5	217	184
North Dakota St.	.3	2	142	95	7	4	320	151
South Dakota St.	.3	2	134	100	6	5	363	251
Southern Utah	.1	4	79	162	1	9	126	328
No. Colorado	.0	5	59	149	4	7	255	285

*Playoffs (1-1): Cal Poly (1-1).

Ivy League

	Conference W	L	PF	PA	Overall W	L	PF	PA
Brown	.6	1	252	166	9	1	368	218
Harvard	.5	2	231	137	7	3	310	221
Princeton	.5	2	192	109	7	3	245	163
Cornell	.4	3	167	132	6	4	268	180
Yale	.4	3	174	140	4	6	228	214
Pennsylvania	.3	4	151	155	5	5	269	194
Dartmouth	.1	6	64	162	2	8	126	260
Columbia	.0	7	63	293	2	8	117	337

Playoffs: League does not play postseason games.

NCAA Division I-AA Final Standings (Cont.)

Metro Atlantic Athletic Conference

	Conference				Overall		
	W	L	PF	PA	W	L	PF	PA
Duquesne	4	0	133	45	7	3	264	161
Marist	3	1	121	83	7	4	305	283
La Salle	2	2	83	129	4	7	266	373
Iona	1	3	103	124	3	7	171	280
St. Peter's	0	4	74	133	1	9	200	379

Playoffs: No teams invited.

Mid-Eastern Athletic Conference

	Conference				Overall		
	W	L	PF	PA	W	L	PF	PA
*Hampton	8	0	250	96	11	1	376	168
S. Carolina St.	7	1	276	116	9	2	378	166
Delaware St.	6	2	174	118	7	4	225	213
Florida A&M	5	3	175	194	6	5	196	261
Bethune-Cookman	4	4	263	214	7	4	384	251
Norfolk St.	2	6	194	266	4	7	292	346
N. Carolina A&T	2	6	141	238	3	8	188	276
Howard	1	7	87	179	4	7	173	228
Morgan St.	1	7	146	285	2	9	248	375

*Playoffs (1-1): Hampton (1-1).

Northeast Conference

	Conference				Overall		
	W	L	PF	PA	W	L	PF	PA
Central Conn. St.	5	2	161	145	7	4	273	274
Stony Brook	5	2	164	157	6	5	220	270
Monmouth (N.J.)	4	3	159	94	6	4	266	190
Albany	4	3	133	87	5	6	188	194
Wagner	3	4	159	204	6	5	287	294
Sacred Heart	3	4	160	195	4	6	239	287
St. Francis (Pa.)	3	4	196	219	4	8	287	343
Robert Morris	1	6	154	185	2	8	243	256

Playoffs: No teams invited.

Ohio Valley Conference

	Conference				Overall		
	W	L	PF	PA	W	L	PF	PA
*Eastern Illinois	8	0	273	124	9	3	319	230
Eastern Ky.	7	1	299	132	7	4	346	233
Jacksonville St.	6	2	211	131	6	5	292	224
Tenn.-Martin	4	4	224	201	6	5	297	319
Samford	4	4	182	222	6	5	279	322
Tennessee Tech	3	5	191	269	4	7	269	351
SE Missouri St.	2	6	212	238	2	9	268	374
Tennessee St.	1	6	92	234	2	9	136	303
Murray St.	0	7	143	276	2	9	218	377

*Playoffs (0-1): Eastern Illinois (0-1).

Patriot League

	Conference				Overall		
	W	L	PF	PA	W	L	PF	PA
*Colgate	5	1	152	96	8	4	283	245
*Lafayette	5	1	151	95	8	4	273	204
Lehigh	4	2	207	97	8	3	399	228
Holy Cross	3	3	167	141	6	5	317	263
Georgetown	2	4	77	177	4	7	116	292
Fordham	2	4	86	155	2	9	150	326
Bucknell	0	6	110	189	1	10	179	332

*Playoffs (0-2): Colgate (0-1), Lafayette (0-1).

NCAA I-AA Independent

	W	L	PF	PA
Savannah St.	0	11	215	480

Playoffs: No teams invited.

Pioneer Football League

North	Conference				Overall		
	W	L	PF	PA	W	L	PF	PA
San Diego	4	0	191	78	11	1	511	205
Dayton	3	1	142	79	9	1	403	141
Drake	2	2	148	90	6	4	376	229
Valparaiso	1	3	86	185	3	8	187	424
Butler	0	4	45	180	0	11	154	468

South	Conference				Overall		
	W	L	PF	PA	W	L	PF	PA
Morehead St.	3	0	106	37	8	4	407	336
Jacksonville	2	1	66	70	4	4	236	211
Davidson	1	2	70	58	4	6	201	237
Austin Peay	0	3	44	121	2	9	140	412

PFL Championship Game: San Diego 47, Morehead St. 40.

Playoffs: No teams invited.

Southern Conference

	Conference				Overall		
	W	L	PF	PA	W	L	PF	PA
*Appalachian St.	6	1	271	117	12	3	455	282
*Furman	5	2	253	192	11	3	488	383
*Ga. Southern	5	2	242	107	8	4	456	277
W. Carolina	4	3	155	164	5	4	179	178
Wofford	3	4	114	168	6	5	249	292
Chattanooga	3	4	156	218	6	5	245	339
The Citadel	2	5	127	199	4	7	194	316
Elon	0	7	69	222	3	8	173	281

*Playoffs (6-2): Appalachian St. (4-0), Furman (2-1), Georgia Southern (0-1).

Southland Conference

	Conference				Overall		
	W	L	PF	PA	W	L	PF	PA
*Texas St.	5	1	203	114	11	3	518	284
*Nicholls St.	5	1	198	151	6	4	308	226
McNeese St.	3	3	132	191	5	4	221	287
Northwestern St.	3	3	139	121	5	5	215	240
SE Louisiana	2	4	153	170	4	6	279	275
Sam Houston St.	2	4	159	146	3	7	270	288
Stephen F. Austin	1	5	139	230	5	6	324	380

*Playoffs (2-2): Texas St. (2-1), Nicholls St. (0-1).

Southwestern Athletic Conference

Eastern	Conference				Overall		
	W	L	PF	PA	W	L	PF	PA
Alabama A&M	7	2	224	165	9	3	299	224
Alabama St.	6	3	317	200	6	5	358	255
Alcorn St.	5	4	208	227	6	5	253	282
Miss. Valley St.	5	4	277	254	6	5	360	292
Jackson St.	2	7	180	325	2	9	201	365

Western	Conference				Overall		
	W	L	PF	PA	W	L	PF	PA
Grambling St.	9	0	395	175	11	1	529	236
Southern	4	5	250	239	4	5	250	239
Prairie View A&M	3	6	150	276	5	6	229	296
Ark.-Pine Bluff	3	6	212	252	3	8	238	296
Texas Southern	1	8	194	294	1	10	222	385

SWAC Champ. Game: Grambling 45, Alabama A&M 6.
Playoffs: No teams invited.

Gridiron Classic Debuts in '06

The **Northeast Conference** and **Pioneer Football League**, traditionally left out of the NCAA 1-AA playoff field, announced a two-year deal to stage an exempted postseason game matching the champions of the two leagues. The NEC champion will host the optimistically titled game on Nov. 18, 2006.

NCAA Division I-AA Leaders
INDIVIDUAL
Passing Efficiency

	Cl	Gm	Att	Cmp	Cmp Pct	Int	Int Pct	Yds	Yds/ Att	TD	TD Pct	Rating Points
Bruce Eugene, Grambling	Sr.	12	456	254	55.70	6	1.32	4360	9.56	56	12.28	173.9
Josh Johnson, San Diego	So.	12	371	260	70.08	8	2.16	3256	8.78	34	9.70	171.5
Ricky Santos, New Hampshire . . .	So.	13	429	301	70.16	9	2.10	3797	8.85	39	9.09	170.3
Erik Meyer, Eastern Wash.	Sr.	12	410	269	65.61	5	1.22	4003	9.76	30	7.32	169.3
Eric Sanders, Northern Iowa	So.	13	312	213	68.27	5	1.60	2929	9.39	23	7.37	168.2
Tarvaris Jackson, Alabama St. . . .	Sr.	11	320	195	60.94	5	1.56	2940	9.19	29	9.06	164.9
Kevin Hoyng, Dayton	Jr.	10	193	114	59.07	5	2.59	1989	10.31	14	7.25	164.4
Justin Rascati, James Madison . .	Jr.	11	214	149	69.63	5	2.34	1822	8.51	17	7.94	162.7
Connor Jostes, Drake	Sr.	10	186	111	59.68	5	2.69	1580	8.49	19	10.22	159.4
Steve LaFalce, Western Ill.	Jr.	11	298	201	67.45	8	2.68	2586	8.68	19	6.38	156.0
Luke Drone, Illinois St.	So.	11	332	214	64.46	12	3.61	2930	8.83	22	6.63	153.2
Richie Williams, Appalachian St. .	Sr.	15	338	211	62.43	4	1.18	2809	8.31	20	5.92	149.4
Joel Sambursky, Southern Ill. . . .	Sr.	13	330	210	63.64	9	2.73	2695	8.17	22	6.67	148.8

Total Offense

	Cl	Rush	Pass	Yds	YdsPG
Bruce Eugene, Grambling . . .	Sr.	157	4360	4517	376.4
Erik Meyer, Eastern Wash. . .	Sr.	221	4003	4224	352.0
Ricky Santos, N. Hampshire .	So.	499	3797	4296	330.5
Trey Willie, SE Louisiana . . .	Sr.	449	2777	3226	322.6
Josh Johnson, San Diego . . .	So.	379	3256	3635	302.9
John Sciarra, Wagner	Sr.	-19	3321	3302	300.2
Anton Clarkson, Hofstra . . .	Sr.	-53	3020	2967	296.7
Travis Lulay, Montana St. . . .	Sr.	611	2629	3240	294.5
Tarvaris Jackson, Ala. St. . .	Sr.	285	2940	3225	293.2
Aries Nelson, Miss. Valley .	Jr.	254	2942	3196	290.5

Games: All played 11, except Eugene and Meyer (12), Santos (13) Willie and Clarkson (10).

Rushing

	Cl	Car	Yds	TD	YdsPG
Nick Hartigan, Brown	Sr.	314	1727	20	172.70
Scott Phaydavong, Drake . . .	So.	204	1550	8	155.00
Joe Rubin, Portland St.	Sr.	345	1702	17	154.73
James Noble, Cal Poly	Fr.	223	1578	16	143.45
Jermaine Austin, Ga. Southern	Sr.	233	1546	14	128.83
Donald Chpman, Tenn-Martin	So.	302	1396	16	126.91
Jeremy McCoy, Alcorn St. . .	Jr.	185	1129	5	125.44
Jordan Scott, Colgate	Fr.	320	1364	10	124.00
Jeff Horton, Valparaiso	Jr.	257	1358	10	123.45
Jayson Foster, Ga. Southern . .	So.	239	1481	21	123.42

Games: All played 11, except McCoy (9), Hartigan, Phaydavong (10), Austin and Foster (12).

Field Goals

	Cl	FG/Att	Pct	P/Gm
Steve Morgan, Brown	So.	18/23	.783	1.80
Blake Bercegeay, McNeese St.	Fr.	16/19	.842	1.78
Andrew Paterini, Hampton .	Jr.	20/30	.667	1.67
Derek Javarone, Princeton . .	Sr.	16/18	.889	1.60
Peter Gaertner, Delaware St. .	Jr.	16/21	.762	1.60
Rob Zarrilli, Hofstra	So.	17/19	.895	1.55
Jaret Johnson, Idaho St.	Sr.	17/19	.895	1.55
Joseph Fore, Richmond	Jr.	16/20	.800	1.45
Jeff Hastings, Montana St. .	Jr.	16/21	.762	1.45

Games: All played 11, except Morgan, Javarone, Gaertner (10), Bercegeay (9) and Paterini (12).

Receptions

	Cl	No	Yds	TD	P/Gm
Michael Caputo, St. Francis (Pa.)	Jr.	92	1433	12	8.36
Laurnt Robinson, Illinois St.	Jr.	86	1465	12	7.82
Luke Palko, St. Francis (Pa.) . . .	Jr.	85	812	7	7.73
J.J. Outlaw, Villanova	Jr.	83	878	7	7.55
Eric Kimble, Eastern Wash.	Sr.	87	1419	12	7.25
Shaun Grover, Wagner	Sr.	78	1051	8	7.09
Sam Logan, Indiana St.	Jr.	77	849	5	7.00
Devale Ellis, Hofstra	Sr.	74	943	5	6.73
David Ball, New Hampshire . . .	Jr.	87	1551	24	6.69
Marques Colston, Hofstra	Sr.	70	975	5	6.36
Arel Gordon, Maine	Jr.	70	484	1	6.36

Games: All played 11, except Kimble (12) and Ball (13).

Interceptions

	Cl	No	Yds	TD	Int/Gm
Jay McCareins, Princeton . . .	Sr.	9	236	2	0.90
James Gasparella, Brown	Sr.	7	42	0	0.70
Bobbie Williams, Beth-Cookman	So.	6	80	0	0.60
Casey Klaus, Dayton	Jr.	6	146	1	0.60
Brian Ford, Wofford	So.	6	5	0	0.55
Keldrick Holman, S.F. Austin .	Jr.	6	112	0	0.55
Codera Jackson, Youngstown St.	Jr.	6	103	1	0.55
Courtney Brown, Cal Poly . . .	Jr.	7	54	1	0.54

Six players tied at 0.50 INTs per game

Games: All played 10, except Ford, Holman, Jackson (11), and Brown (13).

Punt/Kickoff Leaders

Punting

	Cl	No	Yds	Avg
Wesley Taylor, Florida A&M . .	So.	59	2707	45.88
Erik Contos, Delaware St.	Sr.	65	2876	44.25
Christian Koegel, Massachusetts	Jr.	49	2108	43.02

Punt Returns

	Cl	No	Yds	TD	Avg
Nick Feldman, Morehead St. .	So.	27	512	2	18.96
James Vernon, Southern U. . .	Sr.	19	355	1	18.68
Steve Silva, Holy Cross	Sr.	22	395	2	17.95

Kickoff Returns

	Cl	No	Yds	TD	Avg
Ricky Williams, Beth-Cookman	Sr.	21	659	2	31.38
Mike Malone, W. Carolina .	So.	17	532	1	31.29
Tyjuan Massey, Robert Morris	Sr.	20	615	0	30.75

NCAA Division I-AA Leaders (Cont.)

Scoring
(ranked by points per game)

Non-Kickers

	Cl	TD	XPt	Pts	P/Gm
Nick Hartigan, Brown	Sr.	21	0	126	12.60
David Ball, New Hampshire	Jr.	24	0	144	11.08
Jayson Foster, Ga. Southern	So.	21	0	126	10.50
Henry Tolbert, Grambling	Jr.	20	0	120	10.00
Omar Cuff, Delaware	So.	18	0	108	9.82
Eric Rath, Lehigh	Sr.	18	0	108	9.82
Alonzo Coleman, Hampton	Jr.	19	0	114	9.50
Obozua Ehikioya, Marist	So.	17	0	102	9.27
Joe Rubin, Portland St.	Sr.	17	0	102	9.27

Games: All played 11, except Foster, Tolbert, Coleman (12) and Hartigan (10) and Ball (13).

Kickers

	FG/Att	PAT/Att	Pts	P/Gm
Steve Morgan, Brown	18/23	44/45	98	9.80
Andrew Paterini, Hampton	20/30	44/45	104	8.67
Chris James, Western Ky.	15/17	42/42	87	7.91
Joseph Fore, Richmond	16/20	36/39	84	7.64
Rob Zarrilli, Hofstra	17/19	33/36	84	7.64
Kevin Mazur, Illinois St.	9/13	49/53	76	7.60
Greg Kuehn, Wm. & Mary	13/22	43/44	82	7.42

Games: All played 11 except Morgan, Mazur (10), and Paterini (12).

TEAM

Scoring Offense

	Gm	Record	Pts	Avg
Grambling	12	11-1	529	44.08
San Diego	12	11-1	511	42.58
New Hampshire	13	11-2	542	41.69
Dayton	10	9-1	403	40.30
Illinois St.	11	7-4	431	39.18
Ga. Southern	12	8-4	456	38.00
Drake	10	6-4	376	37.60
Texas St.	14	11-3	518	37.00
Brown	10	9-1	368	36.80
Lehigh	11	8-3	399	36.27
James Madison	11	7-4	391	35.55
Gardner-Webb	11	5-6	386	35.09
Eastern Wash.	12	7-5	420	35.00
Bethune-Cookman	11	7-4	384	34.91
Furman	14	11-3	488	34.86

Scoring Defense

	Gm	Record	Pts	Avg
Massachusetts	11	7-4	146	13.3
Hampton	12	11-1	168	14.0
Dayton	10	9-1	141	14.1
South Carolina St.	11	9-2	166	15.1
James Madison	11	7-4	168	15.3
Duquesne	10	7-3	161	16.1
Youngstown St.	11	8-3	178	16.2
Princeton	10	7-3	163	16.3
Lafayette	12	8-4	204	17.0
San Diego	12	11-1	205	17.1
Albany	11	5-6	194	17.6
Richmond	13	9-4	231	17.8
Cal Poly	13	9-4	232	17.8
Cornell	10	6-4	180	18.0
Montana	12	8-4	218	18.2

Total Offense

	Record	Plays	Yds	Avg
Grambling	11-1	845	5947	495.58
New Hampshire	11-2	980	6415	493.46
San Diego	11-1	914	5823	485.25
Eastern Washington	7-5	898	5734	477.83
Illinois St.	7-4	835	5253	477.55
Dayton	9-1	710	4707	470.70
Furman	11-3	1060	6578	469.86
Ga. Southern	8-4	860	5637	469.75
Alabama St.	6-5	759	5073	461.18
Gardner-Webb	5-6	870	4851	441.00
Texas St.	11-3	1037	6147	439.07
Morehead St.	8-4	885	5195	432.92
Drake	6-4	656	4303	430.30
Hofstra	7-4	781	4728	429.82
Rhode Island	4-7	841	4681	425.55
Mississippi Valley St.	6-5	756	4657	423.36

Total Defense

	Record	Plays	Yds	Avg
Duquesne	7-3	674	2059	205.90
Howard	4-7	659	2813	255.73
Massachusetts	7-4	684	2873	261.18
Cornell	6-4	611	2613	261.30
Delaware St.	7-4	713	2966	269.64
Hampton	11-1	812	3251	270.92
South Carolina St.	9-2	703	3162	287.45
James Madison	7-4	718	3166	287.82
Dayton	9-1	617	2945	294.50
San Diego	11-1	745	3535	296.92
Lafayette	8-4	835	3563	296.92
Princeton	7-3	652	2976	297.60
Alabama A&M	9-3	748	3627	302.25
Pennsylvania	5-5	687	3030	303.00
Albany	5-6	751	3359	305.36
Colgate	8-4	767	3706	308.83

Home Attendance Leaders

	Gm	Total	Average
Montana	7	157,355	22,479
Delaware	6	133,060	22,177
Yale	5	108,333	21,667
Southern U.	4	79,552	19,888
Appalachian St.	7	125,417	17,917
Georgia Southern	6	97,443	16,241
Florida A&M	4	60,706	15,177
Tennessee St.	4	60,092	15,023
N.C. A&T	4	58,438	14,610
Jackson St.	5	72,986	14,597

Division I-AA, II and III Awards
Players of the Year

NCAA I-AA	Erik Meyer, E. Washington, QB
NCAA II	Jimmy Terwilliger, E. Stroudsburg, QB
NCAA III	Brett Elliott, Linfield, QB
NAIA	Tyler Emmert, Carroll College, QB

I-AA Coaches of the Year

FWAA	Sean McDonnell, New Hampshire
AFCA	Jerry Moore, Appalachian

NCAA Playoffs

Division I-AA

First Round (Nov. 26)

at New Hampshire 55 . . . . .Colgate 21
at Northern Iowa 41 . . . . .Eastern Washington 38
Cal Poly 35 . . . . .at Montana 21
at Texas St. 50 . . . . .Georgia Southern 35
Richmond 38 . . . . .at Hampton 10
at Furman 14 . . . . .Nicholls St. 12
Southern Ill. 21 . . . . .at Eastern Ill. 6
at Appalachian St. 34 . . . . .Lafayette 23

Quarterfinals (Dec. 3)

Northern Iowa 24 . . . . .at New Hampshire 21
at Texas St. 14 . . . . .Cal Poly 7
Furman 24 .at Richmond 20
at Appalachian St. 38 . . . . .Southern Ill. 24

Semifinals (Dec. 9-10)

Northern Iowa 40 . . . . .OT . . . . . .at Texas St. 37
at Appalachian St. 29 . . . . .Furman 23

Championship Game

Dec. 16 at Chattanooga, Tenn. (Att: 20,236)
Appalachian St. 21 . . . . Northern Iowa 16
(12-3)   (11-4)

Division II

First Round (Nov. 12)

Central Arkansas 28 . . . . .at Albany St. (Ga.) 20
North Alabama 40 . . . . .at Valdosta 13
Pittsburg St. 49 . . . . .at Nebraska-Kearney 20
NW Missouri St. 45 . . . . .at Angelo St. 14
at C.W. Post 24 . . . . .West Chester 20
at East Stroudsburg 55 . . . . .Southern Conn. St. 33
at North Dakota 23 . . . . .Minnesota Duluth 16
at Saginaw Valley 31 . . . . .Northwood 16

Second Round (Nov. 19)

Central Arkansas 52 . . . . .at Presbyterian 28
North Alabama 24 . . . . .at N.C. Central 21
Pittsburg St. 41 . . . . .at West Texas A&M 3
NW Missouri St. 42 . . . . .at Washburn 32
C.W. Post 28 . . . . .at Shepherd 21
East Stroudsburg 52 . . . . .at Bloomsburg 39
at Grand Valley St. 17 . . . . .North Dakota 3
Saginaw Valley 24 . . . . .at Nebraska-Omaha 21

Quarterfinals (Nov. 26)

North Alabama 41 . . . . .OT . .Central Arkansas 38
NW Missouri St. 21 . . . . .at Pittsburg St. 10
at East Stroursburg 55 . . . . .C.W. Post 28
at Grand Valley St. 24 . . . . .Saginaw Valley 17

Semifinals (Dec. 3)

NW Missouri St. 25 . . . . .at North Alabama 24
at Grand Valley St. 55 . . . . .East Stroursburg 20

Championship Game

Dec. 10 at Florence, Ala. (Att: 6,837)
Grand Valley St. 21 . . . . .NW Missouri St. 17
(13-0)   (11-4)

Division III

First Round (Nov. 19)

at Linfield 63 . . . . .Occidental 21
at Concordia Morehead 27 . . . . .Coe 14
at St. John's (Minn.) 62 . . . . .Monmouth (Ill.) 3
at WI-Whitewater 34 . . . . .Central (Iowa) 14
Mary Hardin-Baylor 35 . . . . .at Trinity (Tex.) 6
at Wesley 59 . . . . .Ferrum 14
at Bridgewater (Va.) 30 . . . . . .Washington &Jefferson 21
at Thiel 28 . . . . .Johns Hopkins 3
at Wabash 38 . . . . .Albion 20
Capital 21 . . . . .North Central (Ill.) 19
at Augustana (Ill.) 49 . . . . .Lakeland 22
at Mount Union 49 . . . . .Mt. St. Joseph 6
at Delaware Valley 37 . . . . .Curry 22
at Hobart 23 . . . . .Cortland St. 22
at Rowan 42 . . . . .Wilkes 3
at Union (N.Y.) 55 . . . . .Ithaca 41

Second Round (Nov. 26)

at Linfield 28 . . . . .Concordia Morehead 14
at WI-Whitewater 34 . . . . .St. John's 7
Wesley 46 . . . . .at Mary Hardin-Baylor 36
Bridgewater (Va.) 24 . . . . .at Thiel 13
Capital 14 . . . . .at Wabash 11
at Mount Union 44 . . . . .Augustana 7
at Delaware Valley 21 . . . . .Hobart 14
Rowan 28 . . . . .at Union 24

Quarterfinals (Dec. 3)

WI-Whitewater 44 . . . . .at Linfield 41
at Wesley 46 . . . . .Bridgewater (Va.) 7
at Mount Union 34 . . . . .Capital 31
Rowan 27 . . . . .at Delaware Valley 21

Semifinals (Dec. 10)

at WI-Whitewater 58 . . . . .Wesley 6
at Mount Union 19 . . . . .Rowan 7

Amos Alonzo Stagg Bowl

Dec. 17 at Salem, Va. (Att: 4,619)
Mount Union 35 . . . . .WI-Whitewater 28
(14-1)   (13-1)

NAIA Playoffs

Division I

First Round (Nov. 20)

St. Francis (Ind.) 41 . . . . .Pikeville (Ky.) 7
Sioux Falls (S.D.) 31 . . . . .St. Xavier (Ill.) 28
Georgetown (Ky.) 36 . . . . .Geneva (Pa.) 35
Evangel (Mo.) 34 . . . . .McKendree (Ill.) 31
Morningside (Iowa) 58 . . . . .St. Ambrose (Iowa) 7
Carroll (Mont.) 23 . . . . .Dickinson St. (N.D.) 13
Tabor (Kan.) 17 . . . . .Graceland (Iowa) 14
Montana Tech 24 . . . . .Azusa Pacific (Calif.) 17

Quarterfinals (Nov. 26)

St. Francis 44 . . . . .Georgetown 14
Sioux Falls 48 . . . . .Tabor 13
Morningshide 54 . . . . .Evangel 14
Carroll 24 . . . . .Montana Tech 0

Semifinals (Dec. 3)

St. Francis 42 . . . . .Morningside 14
Carroll 55 .Sioux Falls 0

Championship

Dec. 17 at Savannah, Tenn. (Att: 6,313)
Carroll 27 . . . . .St. Francis 10
(14-0)   (13-1)

1869-2006
Through the Years

ESPN SPORTS ALMANAC

National Champions

Over the last 132 years, there have been 25 major selectors of national champions by way of polls (11), mathematical rating systems (10) and historical research (4). The best-known and most widely circulated of these surveys, the Associated Press poll of sportswriters and broadcasters, first appeared during the 1936 season. Champions prior to 1936 have been determined by retro polls, ratings and historical research.

The Early Years (1869-1935)

National champions based on the Dickinson mathematical system (DS) and three historical retro polls taken by the College Football Researchers Association (CFRA), the National Championship Foundation (NCF) and the Helms Athletic Foundation (HF). The CFRA and NCF polls start in 1869, college football's inaugural year, while the Helms poll begins in 1883, the first season the game adopted a point system for scoring. Frank Dickinson, an economics professor at Illinois, introduced his system in 1926 and retro-picked winners in 1924 and '25. Bowl game results were counted in the Helms selections, but not in the other three.

Multiple champions: Yale (18); Princeton (17); Harvard (9); Michigan (7); Notre Dame and Penn (4); Alabama, California, Cornell, Illinois, Pittsburgh and USC (3); Georgia Tech, Minnesota and Penn St. (2).

Year		Record
1869	**Princeton**	.1-1-0
1870	**Princeton**	.1-0-0
1871	No games played	
1872	**Princeton**	.1-0-0
1873	**Princeton**	.1-0-0
1874	**Yale**	.3-0-0
1875	**Princeton** (CFRA)	.2-0-0
	& **Harvard** (NCF)	.4-0-0
1876	**Yale**	.3-0-0
1877	**Yale**	.3-0-1
1878	**Princeton**	.6-0-0
1879	**Princeton**	.4-0-1

Year		Record
1880	**Yale** (CFRA)	.4-0-1
	& **Princeton** (NCF)	.4-0-1
1881	**Yale**	.5-0-1
1882	**Yale**	.8-0-0
1883	**Yale**	.8-0-0
1884	**Yale**	.8-0-1
1885	**Princeton**	.9-0-0
1886	**Yale**	.9-0-1
1887	**Yale**	.9-0-0
1888	**Yale**	.13-0-0
1889	**Princeton**	.10-0-0
1890	**Harvard**	.11-0-0

Year		Record
1891	**Yale**	.13-0-0
1892	**Yale**	.13-0-0
1893	**Princeton**	.11-0-0
1894	**Yale**	.16-0-0
1895	**Penn**	.14-0-0
1896	**Princeton** (CFRA)	.10-0-1
	& **Lafayette** (NCF)	.11-0-1
1897	**Penn**	.15-0-0
1898	**Harvard**	.11-0-0
1899	**Princeton** (CFRA)	.12-1-0
	& **Harvard** (NCF, HF)	10-0-1

Year		Record	Bowl Game	Head Coach	Outstanding Player
1900	**Yale**	.12-0-0	No bowl	Malcolm McBride	Perry Hale, HB
1901	**Harvard** (CFRA)	.12-0-0	No bowl	Bill Reid	Bob Kernan, HB
	& **Michigan** (NCF, HF)	.11-0-0	Won Rose	Hurry Up Yost	Neil Snow, E
1902	**Michigan**	.11-0-0	No bowl	Hurry Up Yost	Boss Weeks, QB
1903	**Princeton**	.11-0-0	No bowl	Art Hillebrand	John DeWitt, G
1904	**Penn** (CFRA, HF)	.12-0-0	No bowl	Carl Williams	Andy Smith, FB
	& **Michigan** (NCF)	.10-0-0	No bowl	Hurry Up Yost	Willie Heston, HB
1905	**Chicago**	.10-0-0	No bowl	Amos Alonzo Stagg	Walter Eckersall, QB
1906	**Princeton**	.9-0-1	No bowl	Bill Roper	Cap Wister, E
1907	**Yale**	.9-0-1	No bowl	Bill Knox	Tad Jones, HB
1908	**Penn** (CFRA, HF)	.11-0-1	No bowl	Sol Metzger	Hunter Scarlett, E
	& **LSU** (NCF)	.10-0-0	No bowl	Edgar Wingard	Doc Fenton, QB
1909	**Yale**	.12-1-0	No bowl	Howard Jones	Ted Coy, FB
1910	**Harvard** (CFRA, HF)	.8-0-1	No bowl	Percy Haughton	Percy Wendell, HB
	& **Pittsburgh** (NCF)	.9-0-0	No bowl	Joe Thompson	Ralph Galvin, C
1911	**Princeton** (CFRA, HF)	.8-0-2	No bowl	Bill Roper	Sam White, E
	& **Penn St.** (NCF)	.8-0-1	No bowl	Bill Hollenback	Dexter Very, E
1912	**Harvard** (CFRA, HF)	.9-0-0	No bowl	Percy Haughton	Charley Brickley, HB
	& **Penn St.** (NCF)	.8-0-0	No bowl	Bill Hollenback	Dexter Very, E
1913	**Harvard**	.9-0-0	No bowl	Percy Haughton	Eddie Mahan, FB
1914	**Army**	.9-0-0	No bowl	Charley Daly	John McEwan, C
1915	**Cornell**	.9-0-0	No bowl	Al Sharpe	Charley Barrett, QB
1916	**Pittsburgh**	.8-0-0	No bowl	Pop Warner	Bob Peck, C
1917	**Georgia Tech**	.9-0-0	No bowl	John Heisman	Ev Strupper, HB
1918	**Pittsburgh** (CFRA, HF)	.4-1-0	No bowl	Pop Warner	Tom Davies, HB
	& **Michigan** (NCF)	.5-0-0	No bowl	Hurry Up Yost	Frank Steketee, FB
1919	**Harvard**-tie (CFRA, HF)	.9-0-1	Won Rose	Bob Fisher	Eddie Casey, HB
	Illinois (CFRA-tie)	.6-1-0	No bowl	Bob Zuppke	Chuck Carney, E
	& **Notre Dame** (NCF)	.9-0-0	No bowl	Knute Rockne	George Gipp, HB
1920	**California**	.9-0-0	Won Rose	Andy Smith	Dan McMillan, T
1921	**California** (CFRA)	.9-0-1	Tied Rose	Andy Smith	Brick Muller, E
	& **Cornell** (NCF, HF)	.8-0-0	No bowl	Gil Dobie	Eddie Kaw, HB
1922	**Princeton** (CFRA)	.8-0-0	No bowl	Bill Roper	Herb Treat, T
	California (NCF)	.9-0-0	No bowl	Andy Smith	Brick Muller, E
	& **Cornell** (HF)	.8-0-0	No bowl	Gil Dobie	Eddie Kaw, HB

Year		Record	Bowl Game	Head Coach	Outstanding Player
1923	**Illinois** (CFRA, HF)	8-0-0	No bowl	Bob Zuppke	Red Grange, HB
	& **Michigan** (NCF)	8-0-0	No bowl	Hurry Up Yost	Jack Blott, C
1924	**Notre Dame**	10-0-0	Won Rose	Knute Rockne	"The Four Horsemen"*
1925	**Alabama** (CFRA, HF)	10-0-0	Won Rose	Wallace Wade	Johnny Mack Brown, HB
	& **Dartmouth** (DS)	8-0-0	No bowl	Jesse Hawley	Swede Oberlander, HB
1926	**Alabama** (CFRA, HF)	9-0-1	Tied Rose	Wallace Wade	Hoyt Winslett, E
	& **Stanford** (DS)	10-0-1	Tied Rose	Pop Warner	Ted Shipkey, E
1927	**Yale** (CFRA)	7-1-0	No bowl	Tad Jones	Bill Webster, G
	& **Illinois** (NCF, HF, DS)	7-0-1	No bowl	Bob Zuppke	Bob Reitsch, C
1928	**Georgia Tech** (CFRA, NCF, DS)	10-0-0	Won Rose	Bill Alexander	Pete Pund, C
	& **USC** (DS)	9-0-1	No bowl	Howard Jones	Jesse Hibbs, T
1929	**Notre Dame**	9-0-0	No bowl	Knute Rockne	Frank Carideo, QB
1930	**Alabama** (CFRA)	10-0-0	Won Rose	Wallace Wade	Fred Sington, T
	& **Notre Dame** (NCF, HF, DS)	10-0-0	No bowl	Knute Rockne	Marchy Schwartz, HB
1931	**USC**	10-1-0	Won Rose	Howard Jones	John Baker, G
1932	**USC** (CFRA, NCF, HF)	10-0-0	Won Rose	Howard Jones	Ernie Smith, T
	& **Michigan** (DS)	8-0-0	No bowl	Harry Kipke	Harry Newman, QB
1933	**Michigan**	8-0-0	No bowl	Harry Kipke	Chuck Bernard, C
1934	**Minnesota**	8-0-0	No bowl	Bernie Bierman	Pug Lund, HB
1935	**Minnesota** (CFRA, NCF, HF)	8-0-0	No bowl	Bernie Bierman	Dick Smith, T
	& **SMU** (DS)	12-1-0	Lost Rose	Matty Bell	Bobby Wilson, HB

*Notre Dame's Four Horsemen were Harry Stuhldreher (QB), Jim Crowley (HB), Don Miller (HB-P) and Elmer Layden (FB).

The Media Poll Years (since 1936)

National champions according to seven media and coaches' polls: Associated Press (since 1936), United Press (1950-57), International News Service (1952-57), United Press International (1958-92), Football Writers Association of America (since 1954), National Football Foundation and Hall of Fame (since 1959) and USA Today/CNN (since 1991). In 1991, the American Football Coaches Association switched outlets for its poll from UPI to USA Today/CNN and then to USA Today/ESPN in 1997.

After 29 years of releasing its final Top 20 poll in early December, AP named its 1965 national champion following that season's bowl games. AP returned to a pre-bowls final vote in 1966 and '67, but has polled its writers and broadcasters after the bowl games since the 1968 season. The FWAA has selected its champion after the bowl games since the 1955 season, the NFF-Hall of Fame since 1971, UPI after 1974, USA Today/CNN 1991-96, and USA Today/ESPN since 1997.

The Associated Press changed the name of its national championship award from the AP trophy to the Bear Bryant Trophy after the legendary Alabama coach's death in 1983. The FootballWriters' trophy is called the Grantland Rice Award (after the celebrated sportswriter) and the NFF-Hall of Fame trophy is called the MacArthur Bowl (in honor of Gen. Douglas MacArthur).

Multiple champions: Notre Dame (9); Alabama, Ohio St., Oklahoma and USC (7); Miami-FL and Nebraska (5); Minnesota and Texas (4); Michigan St. (3); Army, Florida St., Georgia Tech, LSU, Michigan, Penn St., Pittsburgh and Tennessee (2).

Year		Record	Bowl Game	Head Coach	Outstanding Player
1936	**Minnesota**	7-1-0	No bowl	Bernie Bierman	Ed Widseth, T
1937	**Pittsburgh**	9-0-1	No bowl	Jock Sutherland	Marshall Goldberg, HB
1938	**TCU**	11-0-0	Won Sugar	Dutch Meyer	Davey O'Brien, QB
1939	**Texas A&M**	11-0-0	Won Sugar	Homer Norton	John Kimbrough, FB
1940	**Minnesota**	8-0-0	No Bowl	Bernie Bierman	George Franck, HB
1941	**Minnesota**	8-0-0	No bowl	Bernie Bierman	Bruce Smith, HB
1942	**Ohio St.**	9-1-0	No bowl	Paul Brown	Gene Fekete, FB
1943	**Notre Dame**	9-1-0	No bowl	Frank Leahy	Angelo Bertelli, QB
1944	**Army**	9-0-0	No bowl	Red Blaik	Glenn Davis, HB
1945	**Army**	9-0-0	No bowl	Red Blaik	Doc Blanchard, FB
1946	**Notre Dame**	8-0-1	No bowl	Frank Leahy	Johnny Lujack, QB
1947	**Notre Dame**	9-0-0	No bowl	Frank Leahy	Johnny Lujack, QB
1948	**Michigan**	9-0-0	No bowl	Bennie Oosterbaan	Dick Rifenburg, E
1949	**Notre Dame**	10-0-0	No bowl	Frank Leahy	Leon Hart, E
1950	**Oklahoma**	10-1-0	Lost Sugar	Bud Wilkinson	Leon Heath, FB
1951	**Tennessee**	10-0-0	Lost Sugar	Bob Neyland	Hank Lauricella, TB
1952	**Michigan St.** (AP, UP)	9-0-0	No bowl	Biggie Munn	Don McAuliffe, HB
	& **Georgia Tech** (INS)	12-0-0	Won Sugar	Bobby Dodd	Hal Miller, T
1953	**Maryland**	10-1-0	Lost Orange	Jim Tatum	Bernie Faloney, QB
1954	**Ohio St.** (AP, INS)	10-0-0	Won Rose	Woody Hayes	Howard Cassady, HB
	& **UCLA** (UP, FW)	9-0-0	No bowl	Red Sanders	Jack Ellena, T
1955	**Oklahoma**	11-0-0	Won Orange	Bud Wilkinson	Jerry Tubbs, C
1956	**Oklahoma**	10-0-0	No bowl	Bud Wilkinson	Tommy McDonald, HB
1957	**Auburn** (AP)	10-0-0	No bowl	Shug Jordan	Jimmy Phillips, E
	& **Ohio St.** (UP, FW, INS)	9-1-0	Won Rose	Woody Hayes	Bob White, FB
1958	**LSU** (AP, UPI)	11-0-0	Won Sugar	Paul Dietzel	Billy Cannon, HB
	& **Iowa** (FW)	8-1-1	Won Rose	Forest Evashevski	Randy Duncan, QB
1959	**Syracuse**	11-0-0	Won Cotton	Ben Schwartzwalder	Ernie Davis, HB
1960	**Minnesota** (AP, UPI, NFF)	8-2-0	Lost Rose	Murray Warmath	Tom Brown, G
	& **Mississippi** (FW)	10-0-1	Won Sugar	Johnny Vaught	Jake Gibbs, QB
1961	**Alabama** (AP, UPI, NFF)	11-0-0	Won Sugar	Bear Bryant	Billy Neighbors, T
	& **Ohio St.** (FW)	8-0-1	No bowl	Woody Hayes	Bob Ferguson, HB
1962	**USC**	11-0-0	Won Rose	John McKay	Hal Bedsole, E
1963	**Texas**	11-0-0	Won Cotton	Darrell Royal	Scott Appleton, T

National Champions (Cont.)

Year	Champion	Record	Bowl Game	Head Coach	Outstanding Player
1964	**Alabama** (AP, UPI),	.10-1-0	Lost Orange	Bear Bryant	Joe Namath, QB
	Arkansas (FW)	.11-0-0	Won Cotton	Frank Broyles	Ronnie Caveness, LB
	& **Notre Dame** (NFF)	.9-1-0	No bowl	Ara Parseghian	John Huarte, QB
1965	**Alabama** (AP, FW-tie)	.9-1-1	Won Orange	Bear Bryant	Paul Crane, C
	& **Michigan St.** (UPI, NFF, FW-tie)	.10-1-0	Lost Rose	Duffy Daugherty	George Webster, LB
1966	**Notre Dame** (AP, UPI, FW, NFF-tie)	.9-0-1	No bowl	Ara Parseghian	Jim Lynch, LB
	& **Michigan St.** (NFF-tie)	.9-0-1	No bowl	Duffy Daugherty	Bubba Smith, DE
1967	**USC**	.10-1-0	Won Rose	John McKay	O.J. Simpson, HB
1968	**Ohio St.**	.10-0-0	Won Rose	Woody Hayes	Rex Kern, QB
1969	**Texas**	.11-0-0	Won Cotton	Darrell Royal	James Street, QB
1970	**Nebraska** (AP, FW)	.11-0-1	Won Orange	Bob Devaney	Jerry Tagge, QB
	Texas (UPI, NFF-tie),	.10-1-0	Lost Cotton	Darrell Royal	Steve Worster, RB
	& **Ohio St.** (NFF-tie)	.9-1-0	Lost Rose	Woody Hayes	Jim Stillwagon, MG
1971	**Nebraska**	.13-0-0	Won Orange	Bob Devaney	Johnny Rodgers, WR
1972	**USC**	.12-0-0	Won Rose	John McKay	Charles Young, TE
1973	**Notre Dame** (AP, FW, NFF)	.11-0-0	Won Sugar	Ara Parseghian	Mike Townsend, DB
	& **Alabama** (UPI)	.11-1-0	Lost Sugar	Bear Bryant	Buddy Brown, OT
1974	**Oklahoma** (AP)	.11-0-0	No bowl	Barry Switzer	Joe Washington, RB
	& **USC** (UPI, FW, NFF)	.10-1-1	Won Rose	John McKay	Anthony Davis, RB
1975	**Oklahoma**	.11-1-0	Won Orange	Barry Switzer	Lee Roy Selmon, DT
1976	**Pittsburgh**	.12-0-0	Won Sugar	Johnny Majors	Tony Dorsett, RB
1977	**Notre Dame**	.11-1-0	Won Cotton	Dan Devine	Ross Browner, DE
1978	**Alabama** (AP, FW, NFF)	.11-1-0	Won Sugar	Bear Bryant	Marty Lyons, DT
	& **USC** (UPI)	.12-1-0	Won Rose	John Robinson	Charles White, RB
1979	**Alabama**	.12-0-0	Won Sugar	Bear Bryant	Jim Bunch, OT
1980	**Georgia**	.12-0-0	Won Sugar	Vince Dooley	Herschel Walker, RB
1981	**Clemson**	.12-0-0	Won Orange	Danny Ford	Jeff Davis, LB
1982	**Penn St.**	.11-1-0	Won Sugar	Joe Paterno	Todd Blackledge, QB
1983	**Miami-FL**	.11-1-0	Won Orange	H. Schnellenberger	Bernie Kosar, QB
1984	**BYU**	.13-0-0	Won Holiday	LaVell Edwards	Robbie Bosco, QB
1985	**Oklahoma**	.11-1-0	Won Orange	Barry Switzer	Brian Bosworth, LB
1986	**Penn St.**	.12-0-0	Won Fiesta	Joe Paterno	D.J. Dozier, RB
1987	**Miami-FL**	.12-0-0	Won Orange	Jimmy Johnson	Steve Walsh, QB
1988	**Notre Dame**	.12-0-0	Won Fiesta	Lou Holtz	Tony Rice, QB
1989	**Miami-FL**	.11-1-0	Won Sugar	Dennis Erickson	Craig Erickson, QB
1990	**Colorado** (AP, FW, NFF)	.11-1-1	Won Orange	Bill McCartney	Eric Bieniemy, RB
	& **Georgia Tech** (UP)	.11-0-1	Won Citrus	Bobby Ross	Shawn Jones, QB
1991	**Miami-FL** (AP)	.12-0-0	Won Orange	Dennis Erickson	Gino Torretta, QB
	& **Washington** (USA, FW, NFF)	.12-0-0	Won Rose	Don James	Steve Emtman, DT
1992	**Alabama**	.13-0-0	Won Sugar	Gene Stallings	Eric Curry, DE
1993	**Florida St.**	.12-1-0	Won Orange	Bobby Bowden	Charlie Ward, QB
1994	**Nebraska**	.13-0-0	Won Orange	Tom Osborne	Zach Wiegert, OT
1995	**Nebraska**	.12-0-0	Won Fiesta	Tom Osborne	Tommie Frazier, QB
1996	**Florida**	.12-1*	Won Sugar	Steve Spurrier	Danny Wuerffel, QB
1997	**Michigan** (AP, FW, NFF)	.12-0	Won Rose	Lloyd Carr	Charles Woodson, DB
	& **Nebraska** (ESPN/USA)	.13-0	Won Orange	Tom Osborne	Ahman Green, RB
1998	**Tennessee**	.13-0	Won Fiesta	Phillip Fulmer	Peerless Price, WR
1999	**Florida St.**	.13-0	Won Sugar	Bobby Bowden	Peter Warrick, WR
2000	**Oklahoma**	.13-0	Won Orange	Bob Stoops	Josh Heupel, QB
2001	**Miami-FL**	.12-0	Won Rose	Larry Coker	Ken Dorsey, QB
2002	**Ohio St.**	.14-0	Won Fiesta	Jim Tressel	Craig Krenzel, QB
2003	**USC** (AP)	.12-1	Won Rose	Pete Carroll	Matt Leinart, QB
	& **LSU** (ESPN/USA)	.13-1	Won Sugar	Nick Saban	Matt Mauck, QB
2004	**USC**	.13-0	Won Orange	Pete Carroll	Matt Leinart, QB
2005	**Texas**	.13-0	Won Rose	Mack Brown	Vince Young, QB

*The NCAA instituted overtime for regular season games in 1996.

Number 1 vs. Number 2

Since the Associated Press writers poll started keeping track of such things in 1936, the No. 1 and No. 2 ranked teams in the country have met 35 times; 20 during the regular season and 15 in bowl games. Since the first showdown in 1943, the No. 1 team has beaten the No. 2 team 22 times, lost 11 and there have been two ties. Each showdown is listed below with the date, the match-up, each team's record going into the game, the final score, the stadium and site.

Date		Match-up	Stadium	Date		Match-up	Stadium
Oct. 9	#1	Notre Dame (2-0) ...35	Michigan	Nov. 10	#1	Army (6-0) 48	Yankee
1943	#2	Michigan (3-0) 12	(Ann Arbor)	1945	#2	Notre Dame (5-0-1) ..0	(New York)
Nov. 20	#1	Notre Dame (8-0) ...14	Notre Dame	Dec. 1	#1	Army (8-0) 32	Municipal
1943	#2	Iowa Pre-Flight (8-0) .13	(South Bend)	1945	#2	Navy (7-0-1) 13	(Philadelphia)
Dec. 2	#1	Army (8-0) 23	Municipal	Nov. 9	#1	Army (7-0) 0	Yankee
1944	#2	Navy (6-2) 7	(Baltimore)	1946	#2	Notre Dame (5-0) 0	(New York)

Date		Match-up	Stadium
Jan. 1 1963	#1	USC (10-0) 42	ROSE BOWL
	#2	Wisconsin (8-1) 37	(Pasadena)
Oct. 12 1963	#1	Texas (3-0) 28	Cotton Bowl
	#2	Oklahoma (2-0) 7	(Dallas)
Jan. 1 1964	#1	Texas (10-0) 28	COTTON BOWL
	#2	Navy (9-1) 6	(Dallas)
Nov. 19 1966	#1	Notre Dame (8-0) ..10	Spartan
	#2	Michigan St. (9-0) ..10	(East Lansing)
Sept. 28 1968	#1	Purdue (1-0) 37	Notre Dame
	#2	Notre Dame (1-0) ...22	(South Bend)
Jan. 1 1969	#1	Ohio St. (9-0) 27	ROSE BOWL
	#2	USC (9-0-1) 16	(Pasadena)
Dec. 6 1969	#1	Texas (9-0) 15	Razorback
	#2	Arkansas (9-0) 14	(Fayetteville)
Nov. 25 1971	#1	Nebraska (10-0) ...35	Owen Field
	#2	Oklahoma (9-0) 31	(Norman)
Jan. 1 1972	#1	Nebraska (12-0) ...38	ORANGE BOWL
	#2	Alabama (11-0) 6	(Miami)
Jan. 1 1979	#1	Alabama (10-1) 14	SUGAR BOWL
	#2	Penn St. (11-0) 7	(New Orleans)
Sept. 26 1981	#1	USC (2-0) 28	Coliseum
	#2	Oklahoma (1-0) 24	(Los Angeles)
Jan. 1 1983	#1	Penn St. (10-1) 27	SUGAR BOWL
	#2	Georgia (11-0) 23	(New Orleans)
Oct. 19 1985	#1	Iowa (5-0) 12	Kinnick
	#2	Michigan (5-0) 10	(Iowa City)
Sept. 27 1986	#1	Miami-FL (3-0) 28	Orange Bowl
	#2	Oklahoma (2-0) 16	(Miami)
Jan. 2 1987	#1	Penn St. (11-0) 14	FIESTA BOWL
	#2	Miami-FL (11-0) 10	(Tempe)
Nov. 21 1987	#2	Oklahoma (10-0) ...17	Memorial
	#1	Nebraska (10-0) 7	(Lincoln)
Jan. 1 1988	#2	Miami-FL (11-0) 20	ORANGE BOWL
	#1	Oklahoma (11-0) ...14	(Miami)
Nov. 26 1988	#1	Notre Dame (10-0) ...27	Coliseum
	#2	USC (10-0) 10	(Los Angeles)
Sept. 16 1989	#1	Notre Dame (1-0) ...24	Michigan
	#2	Michigan (0-0) 19	(Ann Arbor)
Nov. 16 1991	#2	Miami-FL (8-0) 17	Doak Campbell
	#1	Florida St. (10-0) ...16	(Tallahassee)
Jan. 1 1993	#2	Alabama (12-0) 34	SUGAR BOWL
	#1	Miami-FL (11-0) 13	(New Orleans)
Nov. 13 1993	#2	Notre Dame (9-0) ...31	Notre Dame
	#1	Florida St. (9-0) ...24	(South Bend)
Jan. 1 1994	#1	Florida St. (11-1) ...18	ORANGE BOWL
	#2	Nebraska (11-0) ...16	(Miami)
Jan. 2 1996	#1	Nebraska (11-0) ...62	FIESTA BOWL
	#2	Florida (12-0) 24	(Tempe)
Nov. 30 1996	#2	Florida St. (10-0) ...24	Doak Campbell
	#1	Florida (10-1) 21	(Tallahassee)
Jan. 4 1999	#1	Tennessee (12-0) ...23	FIESTA BOWL
	#2	Florida St. (11-1) ...16	(Tempe)
Jan. 4 2000	#1	Florida St. (11-0) ...46	SUGAR BOWL
	#2	Virginia Tech (11-0) .29	(New Orleans)
Jan. 3 2003	#1	Ohio St. (13-0) ...31	FIESTA BOWL
	#2	Miami-FL (12-0) .2OT 24	(Tempe)
Jan. 4 2005	#1	USC (12-0) 55	ORANGE BOWL
	#2	Oklahoma (12-0) ...19	(Miami)
Jan. 4 2006	#2	Texas (12-0) 41	ROSE BOWL
	#1	USC (12-0) 38	(Pasadena)

Note: Bowl games are listed in CAPITAL letters.

Top 50 Rivalries

Top Division I-A and I-AA series records, including games through the 2005 season. All rivalries listed below are renewed annually with the following exception. **Nebraska-Oklahoma** now play only when matched up as part of the rotating Big 12 schedule.

RECENTLY DISCONTINUED SERIES: **LSU vs Tulane** in 2002 after 94 games (LSU ahead 65-22-7)*; **Penn State vs Pitt** in 2001 after 96 games (Penn State ahead 50-42-4)

	Gm	Series Leader		Gm	Series Leader
Air Force-Army	40	Air Force (26-13-1)	**Michigan-Michigan St.**	98	Michigan (65-28-5)
Air Force-Navy	38	Air Force (25-13-0)	**Michigan-Notre Dame**	33	Michigan (18-14-1)
Alabama-Auburn	70	Alabama (38-31-1)	**Michigan-Ohio St.**	102	Michigan (57-39-6)
Alabama-Tennessee	88	Alabama (44-37-7)	**Minnesota-Wisconsin**	114	Minnesota (58-48-8)
Arizona-Arizona St.	79	Arizona (44-34-1)	**Mississippi-Miss. St.**	102	Ole Miss (58-38-6)
Army-Navy	106	Navy (50-49-7)	**Missouri-Kansas**	114	Kansas (53-52-9)
Auburn-Georgia	109	Auburn (53-48-8)	**Nebraska-Oklahoma**	82	Oklahoma (41-38-3)
California-Stanford	108	Stanford (54-43-11)	**N. Mexico-N. Mexico St.**	95	New Mexico (62-28-5)
The Citadel-VMI	64	The Citadel (32-30-2)	**N. Carolina-N.C. State**	95	N. Carolina (62-27-6)
Clemson-S. Carolina	103	Clemson (63-36-4)	**Notre Dame-Purdue**	77	Notre Dame (51-24-2)
Colorado-Nebraska	64	Nebraska (45-17-2)	**Notre Dame-USC**	77	Notre Dame (42-30-5)
Colo. St.-Wyoming	95	Colorado St. (51-39-5)	**Oklahoma-Okla. St.**	100	Oklahoma (77-16-7)
Duke-N. Carolina	91	N. Carolina (52-36-4)*	**Oregon-Oregon St.**	109	Oregon (55-44-10)
Florida-Florida St.	50	Florida (29-19-2)	**Penn-Cornell**	112	Penn (65-42-5)
Florida-Georgia	84	Georgia (47-35-2)	**Pittsburgh-West Va**	98	Pitt (58-37-3)
Florida St.-Miami,FL	50	Miami (29-21-0)	**Princeton-Yale**	128	Yale (69-49-10)
Georgia-Georgia Tech	100	Georgia (57-38-5)*	**Purdue-Indiana**	108	Purdue (67-35-6)
Grambling-Southern	54	Southern (28-26-0)	**Richmond-Wm. & Mary**	115	Wm. & Mary (58-52-5)
Harvard-Yale	122	Yale (64-50-8)	**Tennessee-Vanderbilt**	99	Tennessee (67-27-5)
Iowa-Iowa St.	53	Iowa (35-18-0)	**Texas-Oklahoma**	100	Texas (57-38-5)
Kansas-Kansas St.	103	Kansas (62-36-5)	**Texas-Texas A&M**	112	Texas (73-34-5)
Kentucky-Tennessee	101	Tennessee (69-23-9)	**UCLA-USC**	75	USC (40-28-7)
Lafayette-Lehigh	141	Lafayette (74-62-5)	**Utah-BYU**	81	Utah (49-28-4)*
LSU-Mississippi	94	LSU (53-37-4)	**Utah-Utah St.**	103	Utah (70-29-4)
Miami,OH-Cincinnati	110	Miami (59-44-7)	**Washington-Wash. St.**	98	Washington (64-28-6)

*Disputed series records: UNC claims lead of 53-35-4; Georgia claims lead of 57-36-5; Tulane claims LSU leads 62-23-7; Utah claims lead of 52-31-4

Associated Press Final Polls

The Associated Press introduced its weekly college football poll of sportswriters (later, sportswriters and broadcasters) in 1936. The final AP poll was released at the end of the regular season until 1965, when bowl results were included for one year. After a two-year return to regular season games only, the final poll has come out after the bowls since 1968. Starting in 1989, the AP Poll has ranked 25 teams.

1936

Final poll released Nov. 30. Top 20 regular season results after that: **Dec. 5**–#8 Notre Dame tied USC, 13-13; #17 Tennessee tied Ole Miss, 0-0; #18 Arkansas over Texas, 6-0. **Dec. 12**–#16 TCU over #6 Santa Clara, 9-0.

		As of Nov. 30	Head Coach	After Bowls
1	Minnesota	7-1-0	Bernie Bierman	same
2	LSU	9-0-1	Bernie Moore	9-1-1
3	Pittsburgh	7-1-1	Jock Sutherland	8-1-1
4	Alabama	8-0-1	Frank Thomas	same
5	Washington	7-1-1	Jimmy Phelan	7-2-1
6	Santa Clara	7-0-0	Buck Shaw	8-1-0
7	Northwestern	7-1-0	Pappy Waldorf	same
8	Notre Dame	6-2-0	Elmer Layden	6-2-1
9	Nebraska	7-2-0	Dana X. Bible	same
10	Penn	7-1-0	Harvey Harman	same
11	Duke	9-1-0	Wallace Wade	same
12	Yale	7-1-0	Ducky Pond	same
13	Dartmouth	7-1-1	Red Blaik	same
14	Duquesne	7-2-0	John Smith	8-2-0
15	Fordham	5-1-2	Jim Crowley	same
16	TCU	7-2-2	Dutch Meyer	9-2-2
17	Tennessee	6-2-1	Bob Neyland	6-2-2
18	Arkansas	6-3-0	Fred Thomsen	7-3-0
	Navy	6-3-0	Tom Hamilton	same
20	Marquette	7-1-0	Frank Murray	7-2-0

Key Bowl Games

Sugar–#6 Santa Clara over #2 LSU, 21-14; **Rose**–#3 Pitt over #5 Washington, 21-0; **Orange**–#14 Duquesne over Mississippi St., 13-12; **Cotton**–#16 TCU over #20 Marquette, 16-6.

1937

Final poll released Nov. 29. Top 20 regular season results after that: **Dec. 4**–#18 Rice over SMU, 15-7.

		As of Nov. 29	Head Coach	After Bowls
1	Pittsburgh	9-0-1	Jock Sutherland	same
2	California	9-0-1	Stub Allison	10-0-1
3	Fordham	7-0-1	Jim Crowley	same
4	Alabama	9-0-0	Frank Thomas	9-1-0
5	Minnesota	6-2-0	Bernie Bierman	same
6	Villanova	8-0-1	Clipper Smith	same
7	Dartmouth	7-0-2	Red Blaik	same
8	LSU	9-1-0	Bernie Moore	9-2-0
9	Notre Dame	6-2-1	Elmer Layden	same
	Santa Clara	8-0-0	Buck Shaw	9-0-0
11	Nebraska	6-1-2	Biff Jones	same
12	Yale	6-1-1	Ducky Pond	same
13	Ohio St.	6-2-0	Francis Schmidt	same
14	Holy Cross	8-0-2	Eddie Anderson	same
	Arkansas	6-2-2	Fred Thomsen	same
16	TCU	4-2-2	Dutch Meyer	same
17	Colorado	8-0-0	Bunnie Oakes	8-1-0
18	Rice	4-3-2	Jimmy Kitts	6-3-2
19	North Carolina	7-1-1	Ray Wolf	same
20	Duke	7-2-1	Wallace Wade	same

Key Bowl Games

Rose–#2 Cal over #4 Alabama, 13-0; **Sugar**–#9 Santa Clara over #8 LSU, 6-0; **Cotton**–#18 Rice over #17 Colorado, 28-14; **Orange**–Auburn over Michigan St., 6-0.

1938

Final poll released Dec. 5. Top 20 regular season results after that: **Dec. 26**–#14 Cal over Georgia Tech, 13-7.

		As of Dec. 5	Head Coach	After Bowls
1	TCU	10-0-0	Dutch Meyer	11-0-0
2	Tennessee	10-0-0	Bob Neyland	11-0-0
3	Duke	9-0-0	Wallace Wade	9-1-0
4	Oklahoma	10-0-0	Tom Stidham	10-1-0
5	Notre Dame	8-1-0	Elmer Layden	same
6	Carnegie Tech	7-1-0	Bill Kern	7-2-0
7	USC	8-2-0	Howard Jones	9-2-0
8	Pittsburgh	8-2-0	Jock Sutherland	same
9	Holy Cross	8-1-0	Eddie Anderson	same
10	Minnesota	6-2-0	Bernie Bierman	same
11	Texas Tech	10-0-0	Pete Cawthon	10-1-0
12	Cornell	5-1-1	Carl Snavely	same
13	Alabama	7-1-1	Frank Thomas	same
14	California	9-1-0	Stub Allison	10-1-0
15	Fordham	6-1-2	Jim Crowley	same
16	Michigan	6-1-1	Fritz Crisler	same
17	Northwestern	4-2-2	Pappy Waldorf	same
18	Villanova	8-0-1	Clipper Smith	same
19	Tulane	7-2-1	Red Dawson	same
20	Dartmouth	7-2-0	Red Blaik	same

Key Bowl Games

Sugar–#1 TCU over #6 Carnegie Tech, 15-7; **Orange**–#2 Tennessee over #4 Oklahoma, 17-0; **Rose**–#7 USC over #3 Duke, 7-3; **Cotton**–St. Mary's over #11 Texas Tech 20-13.

1939

Final poll released Dec. 11. Top 20 regular season results after that: None.

		As of Dec. 11	Head Coach	After Bowls
1	Texas A&M	10-0-0	Homer Norton	11-0-0
2	Tennessee	10-0-0	Bob Neyland	10-1-0
3	USC	7-0-2	Howard Jones	8-0-2
4	Cornell	8-0-0	Carl Snavely	same
5	Tulane	8-0-1	Red Dawson	8-1-1
6	Missouri	8-1-0	Don Faurot	8-2-0
7	UCLA	6-0-4	Babe Horrell	same
8	Duke	8-1-0	Wallace Wade	same
9	Iowa	6-1-1	Eddie Anderson	same
10	Duquesne	8-0-1	Buff Donelli	same
11	Boston College	9-1-0	Frank Leahy	9-2-0
12	Clemson	8-1-0	Jess Neely	9-1-0
13	Notre Dame	7-2-0	Elmer Layden	same
14	Santa Clara	5-1-3	Buck Shaw	same
15	Ohio St.	6-2-0	Francis Schmidt	same
16	Georgia Tech	7-2-0	Bill Alexander	8-2-0
17	Fordham	6-2-0	Jim Crowley	same
18	Nebraska	7-1-1	Biff Jones	same
19	Oklahoma	6-2-1	Tom Stidham	same
20	Michigan	6-2-0	Fritz Crisler	same

Key Bowl Games

Sugar–#1 Texas A&M over #5 Tulane, 14-13; **Rose**–#3 USC over #2 Tennessee, 14-0; **Orange**–#16 Georgia Tech over #6 Missouri, 21-7; **Cotton**–#12 Clemson over #11 Boston College, 6-3.

1940

Final poll released Dec. 2. Top 20 regular season results after that: **Dec. 7**–#16 SMU over Rice, 7-6.

	As of Dec. 2	Head Coach	After Bowls
1	Minnesota 8-0-0	Bernie Bierman	same
2	Stanford 9-0-0	Clark Shaughnessy	10-0-0
3	Michigan 7-1-0	Fritz Crisler	same
4	Tennessee 10-0-0	Bob Neyland	10-1-0
5	Boston College . .10-0-0	Frank Leahy	11-0-0
6	Texas A&M 8-1-0	Homer Norton	9-1-0
7	Nebraska 8-1-0	Biff Jones	8-2-0
8	Northwestern 6-2-0	Pappy Waldorf	same
9	Mississippi St. 9-0-1	Allyn McKeen	10-0-1
10	Washington 7-2-0	Jimmy Phelan	same
11	Santa Clara 6-1-0	Buck Shaw	same
12	Fordham 7-1-0	Jim Crowley	7-2-0
13	Georgetown 8-1-0	Jack Hagerty	8-2-0
14	Penn 6-1-0	George Munger	same
15	Cornell 6-2-0	Carl Snavely	same
16	SMU 7-1-1	Matty Bell	8-1-1
17	Hardin-Simmons . .9-0-0	Warren Woodson	same
18	Duke 7-2-0	Wallace Wade	same
19	Lafayette 9-0-0	Hooks Mylin	same
20	–		

Note: Only 19 teams ranked.

Key Bowl Games

Rose–#2 Stanford over #7 Nebraska, 21-13; **Sugar**– #5 Boston College over #4 Tennessee, 19-13; **Cotton**–#6 Texas A&M over #12 Fordham, 13-12; **Orange**–#9 Mississippi St. over #13 Georgetown, 14-7.

1941

Final poll released Dec. 1. Top 20 regular season results after that: **Dec. 6**–#4 Texas over Oregon, 71-7; #9 Texas A&M over #19 Washington St., 7-0; #16 Mississippi St. over San Francisco, 26-13-14.

	As of Dec. 1	Head Coach	After Bowls
1	Minnesota 8-0-0	Bernie Bierman	same
2	Duke 9-0-0	Wallace Wade	9-1-0
3	Notre Dame 8-0-1	Frank Leahy	same
4	Texas 7-1-1	Dana X. Bible	8-1-1
5	Michigan 6-1-1	Fritz Crisler	same
6	Fordham 7-1-0	Jim Crowley	8-1-0
7	Missouri 8-1-0	Don Faurot	8-2-0
8	Duquesne 8-0-0	Buff Donelli	same
9	Texas A&M 8-1-0	Homer Norton	9-2-0
10	Navy 7-1-1	Swede Larson	same
11	Northwestern 5-3-0	Pappy Waldorf ·	same
12	Oregon St. 7-2-0	Lon Stiner	8-2-0
13	Ohio St. 6-1-1	Paul Brown	same
14	Georgia 8-1-1	Wally Butts	9-1-1
15	Penn 7-1-1	George Munger	same
16	Mississippi St. 7-1-1	Allyn McKeen	8-1-1
17	Mississippi 6-2-1	Harry Mehre	same
18	Tennessee 8-2-0	John Barnhill	same
19	Washington St. . . .6-3-0	Babe Hollingbery	6-4-0
20	Alabama 8-2-0	Frank Thomas	9-2-0

Note: 1942 Rose Bowl moved to Durham, N.C., for one year after outbreak of World War II.

Key Bowl Games

Rose–#12 Oregon St. over #2 Duke, 20-16; **Sugar**–#6 Fordham over #7 Missouri, 2-0; **Cotton**–#20 Alabama over #9 Texas A&M, 29-21; **Orange**–#14 Georgia over TCU, 40-26.

1942

Final poll released Nov. 30. Top 20 regular season results after that: **Dec. 5**–#6 Notre Dame tied Great Lakes Naval Station, 13-13; #13 UCLA over Idaho, 40-13; #14 William & Mary over Oklahoma, 14-7; #17 Washington St. lost to Texas A&M, 21-0; #18 Mississippi St. over San Francisco, 19-7. **Dec. 12**–#13 UCLA over USC, 14-7.

	As of Nov. 30	Head Coach	After Bowls
1	Ohio St. 9-1-0	Paul Brown	same
2	Georgia 10-1-0	Wally Butts	11-1-0
3	Wisconsin 8-1-1	Harry Stuhldreher	same
4	Tulsa 10-0-0	Henry Frnka	10-1-0
5	Georgia Tech 9-1-0	Bill Alexander	9-2-0
6	Notre Dame 7-2-1	Frank Leahy	7-2-2
7	Tennessee 8-1-1	John Barnhill	9-1-1
8	Boston College 8-1-0	Denny Myers	8-2-0
9	Michigan 7-3-0	Fritz Crisler	same
10	Alabama 7-3-0	Frank Thomas	8-3-0
11	Texas 8-2-0	Dana X. Bible	9-2-0
12	Stanford 6-4-0	Marchy Schwartz	same
13	UCLA 5-3-0	Babe Horrell	7-4-0
14	William & Mary . .8-1-1	Carl Voyles	9-1-1
15	Santa Clara 7-2-0	Buck Shaw	same
16	Auburn 6-4-1	Jack Meagher	same
17	Washington St. 6-1-2	Babe Hollingbery	6-2-2
18	Mississippi St. 7-2-0	Allyn McKeen	8-2-0
19	Minnesota 5-4-0	George Hauser	same
	Holy Cross 5-4-1	Ank Scanlon	same
	Penn St. 6-1-1	Bob Higgins	same

Key Bowl Games

Rose–#2 Georgia over #13 UCLA, 9-0; **Sugar**–#7 Tennessee over #4 Tulsa, 14-7; **Cotton**–#11 Texas over #5 Georgia Tech, 14-7; **Orange**–#10 Alabama over #8 Boston College, 37-21.

1943

Final poll released Nov. 29. Top 20 regular season results after that: **Dec.11**–#10 March Field over #19 Pacific, 19-0.

	As of Nov. 29	Head Coach	After Bowls
1	Notre Dame 9-1-0	Frank Leahy	same
2	Iowa Pre-Flight 9-1-0	Don Faurot	same
3	Michigan 8-1-0	Fritz Crisler	same
4	Navy 8-1-0	Billick Whelchel	same
5	Purdue 9-0-0	Elmer Burnham	same
6	Great Lakes Naval Station . . .10-2-0	Tony Hinkle	same
7	Duke 8-1-0	Eddie Cameron	same
8	DelMonte Pre-Flight 7-1-0	Bill Kern	same
9	Northwestern 6-2-0	Pappy Waldorf	same
10	March Field 8-1-0	Paul Schissler	9-1-0
11	Army 7-2-1	Red Blaik	same
12	Washington 4-0-0	Ralph Welch	4-1-0
13	Georgia Tech 7-3-0	Bill Alexander	8-3-0
14	Texas 7-1-0	Dana X. Bible	7-1-1
15	Tulsa 6-0-1	Henry Frnka	6-1-1
16	Dartmouth 6-1-0	Earl Brown	same
17	Bainbridge Navy Training School . . .7-0-0	Joe Maniaci	same
18	Colorado College . .7-0-0	Hal White	same
19	Pacific 7-1-0	Amos A. Stagg	7-2-0
20	Penn 6-2-1	George Munger	same

Key Bowl Games

Rose–USC over #12Washington, 29-0; **Sugar**–#13 Georgia Tech over #15 Tulsa, 20-18; **Cotton**–#14 Texas tied Randolph Field, 7-7; **Orange**–LSU over Texas A&M, 19-14.

Associated Press Final Polls (Cont.)

1944

Final poll released Dec. 4. Top 20 regular season results after that: **Dec. 10**–#3 Randolph Field over #10 March Field, 20-7; #18 Fort Pierce over Kessler Field, 34-7; Morris Field over #20 Second Air Force, 14-7.

		As of Dec. 4	Head Coach	After Bowls
1	Army	9-0-0	Red Blaik	same
2	Ohio St.	9-0-0	Carroll Widdoes	same
3	Randolph Field	10-0-0	Frank Tritico	12-0-0
4	Navy	6-3-0	Oscar Hagberg	same
5	Bainbridge Navy Training School	10-0-0	Joe Maniaci	same
6	Iowa Pre-Flight	10-1-0	Jack Meagher	same
7	USC	7-0-2	Jeff Cravath	8-0-2
8	Michigan	8-2-0	Fritz Crisler	same
9	Notre Dame	8-2-0	Ed McKeever	same
10	March Field	7-0-2	Paul Schissler	7-1-2
11	Duke	5-4-0	Eddie Cameron	6-4-0
12	Tennessee	7-0-1	John Barnhill	7-1-1
13	Georgia Tech	8-2-0	Bill Alexander	8-3-0
14	Norman Pre-Flight	6-0-0	John Gregg	same
15	Illinois	5-4-1	Ray Eliot	same
16	El Toro Marines	8-1-0	Dick Hanley	same
17	Great Lakes Naval Station	9-2-1	Paul Brown	same
18	Fort Pierce	8-0-0	Hamp Pool	9-0-0
19	St. Mary's Pre-Flight	4-4-0	Jules Sikes	same
20	Second Air Force	10-2-1	Bill Reese	10-4-1

Key Bowl Games
Treasury–#3 Randolph Field over #20 Second Air Force, 13-6; **Rose**–#7 USC over #12 Tennessee, 25-0; **Sugar**–#11 Duke over Alabama, 29-26; **Orange**–Tulsa over #13 Georgia Tech, 26-12; **Cotton**–Oklahoma A&M over TCU, 34-0.

1945

Final poll released Dec. 3. Top 20 regular season results after that: None.

		As of Dec. 3	Head Coach	After Bowls
1	Army	9-0-0	Red Blaik	same
2	Alabama	9-0-0	Frank Thomas	10-0-0
3	Navy	7-1-1	Oscar Hagberg	same
4	Indiana	9-0-1	Bo McMillan	same
5	Oklahoma A&M	8-0-0	Jim Lookabaugh	9-0-0
6	Michigan	7-3-0	Fritz Crisler	same
7	St. Mary's-CA	7-1-0	Jimmy Phelan	7-2-0
8	Penn	6-2-0	George Munger	same
9	Notre Dame	7-2-1	Hugh Devore	same
10	Texas	9-1-0	Dana X. Bible	10-1-0
11	USC	7-3-0	Jeff Cravath	7-4-0
12	Ohio St.	7-2-0	Carroll Widdoes	same
13	Duke	6-2-0	Eddie Cameron	same
14	Tennessee	8-1-0	John Barnhill	same
15	LSU	7-2-0	Bernie Moore	same
16	Holy Cross	8-1-0	John DeGrosa	8-2-0
17	Tulsa	8-2-0	Henry Frnka	8-3-0
18	Georgia	8-2-0	Wally Butts	9-2-0
19	Wake Forest	4-3-1	Peahead Walker	5-3-1
20	Columbia	8-1-0	Lou Little	same

Key Bowl Games
Rose–#2 Alabama over #11 USC, 34-14; **Sugar**–#5 Oklahoma A&M over #7 St. Mary's, 33-13; **Cotton**–#10 Texas over Missouri, 40-27; **Orange**–Miami-FL over #16 Holy Cross, 13-6.

1946

Final poll released Dec. 2. Top 20 regular season results after that: None.

		As of Dec. 2	Head Coach	After Bowls
1	Notre Dame	8-0-1	Frank Leahy	same
2	Army	9-0-1	Red Blaik	same
3	Georgia	10-0-0	Wally Butts	11-0-0
4	UCLA	10-0-0	Bert LaBrucherie	10-1-0
5	Illinois	7-2-0	Ray Eliot	8-2-0
6	Michigan	6-2-1	Fritz Crisler	same
7	Tennessee	9-1-0	Bob Neyland	9-2-0
8	LSU	9-1-0	Bernie Moore	9-1-1
9	North Carolina	8-1-1	Carl Snavely	8-2-1
10	Rice	8-2-0	Jess Neely	9-2-0
11	Georgia Tech	8-2-0	Bobby Dodd	9-2-0
12	Yale	7-1-1	Howard Odell	same
13	Penn	6-2-0	George Munger	same
14	Oklahoma	7-3-0	Jim Tatum	8-3-0
15	Texas	8-2-0	Dana X. Bible	same
16	Arkansas	6-3-1	John Barnhill	6-3-2
17	Tulsa	9-1-0	J.O. Brothers	same
18	N.C. State	8-2-0	Beattie Feathers	8-3-0
19	Delaware	9-0-0	Bill Murray	10-0-0
20	Indiana	6-3-0	Bo McMillan	same

Key Bowl Games
Sugar–#3 Georgia over #9 N. Carolina, 20-10; **Rose**–#5 Illinois over #4 UCLA, 45-14; **Orange**–#10 Rice over #7 Tennessee, 8-0; **Cotton**–#8 LSU tied #16 Arkansas, 0-0.

1947

Final poll released Dec. 8. Top 20 regular season results after that: None.

		As of Dec. 8	Head Coach	After Bowls
1	Notre Dame	9-0-0	Frank Leahy	same
2	Michigan	9-0-0	Fritz Crisler	10-0-0
3	SMU	9-0-1	Matty Bell	9-0-2
4	Penn St.	9-0-0	Bob Higgins	9-0-1
5	Texas	9-1-0	Blair Cherry	10-1-0
6	Alabama	8-2-0	Red Drew	8-3-0
7	Penn	7-0-1	George Munger	same
8	USC	7-1-1	Jeff Cravath	7-2-1
9	North Carolina	8-2-0	Carl Snavely	same
10	Georgia Tech	9-1-0	Bobby Dodd	10-1-0
11	Army	5-2-2	Red Blaik	same
12	Kansas	8-0-2	George Sauer	8-1-2
13	Mississippi	8-2-0	Johnny Vaught	9-2-0
14	William & Mary	9-1-0	Rube McCray	9-2-0
15	California	9-1-0	Pappy Waldorf	same
16	Oklahoma	7-2-1	Bud Wilkinson	same
17	N.C. State	5-3-1	Beattie Feathers	same
18	Rice	6-3-1	Jess Neely	same
19	Duke	4-3-2	Wallace Wade	same
20	Columbia	7-2-0	Lou Little	same

Key Bowl Games
Rose–#2 Michigan over #8 USC, 49-0; **Cotton**–#3 SMU tied #4 Penn St., 13-13; **Sugar**–#5 Texas over #6 Alabama, 27-7; **Orange**–#10 Georgia Tech over #12 Kansas, 20-14.
Note: An unprecedented "Who's No. 1?" poll was conducted by AP after the Rose Bowl game, pitting Notre Dame against Michigan. The Wolverines won the vote, 226-119, but AP ruled that the Irish would be the No. 1 team of record.

1948

Final poll released Nov. 29. Top 20 regular season results after that: **Dec. 3**–#12 Vanderbilt over Miami-FL, 33-6. **Dec. 4**–#2 Notre Dame tied USC, 14-14; #11 Clemson over The Citadel, 20-0.

		As of Nov. 29	Head Coach	After Bowls
1	Michigan	9-0-0	Bennie Oosterbaan	same
2	Notre Dame	9-0-0	Frank Leahy	9-0-1
3	North Carolina	9-0-1	Carl Snavely	9-1-1
4	California	10-0-0	Pappy Waldorf	10-1-0
5	Oklahoma	9-1-0	Bud Wilkinson	10-1-0
6	Army	8-0-1	Red Blaik	same
7	Northwestern	7-2-0	Bob Voigts	8-2-0
8	Georgia	9-1-0	Wally Butts	9-2-0
9	Oregon	9-1-0	Jim Aiken	9-2-0
10	SMU	8-1-1	Matty Bell	9-1-1
11	Clemson	9-0-0	Frank Howard	11-0-0
12	Vanderbilt	7-2-1	Red Sanders	8-2-1
13	Tulane	9-1-0	Henry Frnka	same
14	Michigan St.	6-2-2	Biggie Munn	same
15	Mississippi	8-1-0	Johnny Vaught	same
16	Minnesota	7-2-0	Bernie Bierman	same
17	William & Mary	6-2-2	Rube McCray	7-2-2
18	Penn St.	7-1-1	Bob Higgins	same
19	Cornell	8-1-0	Lefty James	same
20	Wake Forest	6-3-0	Peahead Walker	6-4-0

Note: Big Nine "no-repeat" rule kept Michigan from Rose Bowl.

Key Bowl Games

Sugar–#5 Oklahoma over #3 North Carolina, 14-6; **Rose**–#7 Northwestern over #4 Cal, 20-14; **Orange**–Texas over #8 Georgia, 41-28; **Cotton**–#10 SMU over #9 Oregon, 21-13.

1949

Final poll released Nov. 28. Top 20 regular season results after that: **Dec. 2**–#14 Maryland over Miami-FL, 13-0. **Dec. 3**–#1 Notre Dame over SMU, 27-20; #10 Pacific over Hawaii, 75-0.

		As of Nov. 28	Head Coach	After Bowls
1	Notre Dame	9-0-0	Frank Leahy	10-0-0
2	Oklahoma	10-0-0	Bud Wilkinson	11-0-0
3	California	10-0-0	Pappy Waldorf	10-1-0
4	Army	9-0-0	Red Blaik	same
5	Rice	9-1-0	Jess Neely	10-1-0
6	Ohio St.	6-1-2	Wes Fesler	7-1-2
7	Michigan	6-2-1	Bennie Oosterbaan	same
8	Minnesota	7-2-0	Bernie Bierman	same
9	LSU	8-2-0	Gaynell Tinsley	8-3-0
10	Pacific	10-0-0	Larry Siemering	11-0-0
11	Kentucky	9-2-0	Bear Bryant	9-3-0
12	Cornell	8-1-0	Lefty James	same
13	Villanova	8-1-0	Jim Leonard	same
14	Maryland	7-1-0	Jim Tatum	9-1-0
15	Santa Clara	7-2-1	Len Casanova	8-2-1
16	North Carolina	7-3-0	Carl Snavely	7-4-0
17	Tennessee	7-2-1	Bob Neyland	same
18	Princeton	6-3-0	Charlie Caldwell	same
19	Michigan St.	6-3-0	Biggie Munn	same
20	Missouri	7-3-0	Don Faurot	7-4-0
	Baylor	8-2-0	Bob Woodruff	same

Key Bowl Games

Sugar–#2 Oklahoma over #9 LSU, 35-0; **Rose**–#6 Ohio St. over #3 Cal, 17-14; **Cotton**–#5 Rice over #16 North Carolina, 27-13; **Orange**–#15 Santa Clara over #11 Kentucky, 21-13.

1950

Final poll released Nov. 27. Top 20 regular season results after that: **Nov. 30**–#3 Texas over Texas A&M, 17-0. **Dec. 1**–#15 Miami-FL over Missouri, 27–9. **Dec. 2**–#1 Oklahoma over Okla. A&M, 41-14; Navy over #2 Army, 14-2; #4 Tennessee over Vanderbilt, 43-0; #16 Alabama over Auburn, 34-0; #19 Tulsa over Houston, 28-21; #20 Tulane tied LSU, 14-14. **Dec. 9**–#3 Texas over LSU, 21-6.

		As of Nov. 27	Head Coach	After Bowls
1	Oklahoma	9-0-0	Bud Wilkinson	10-1-0
2	Army	8-0-0	Red Blaik	8-1-0
3	Texas	7-1-0	Blair Cherry	9-2-0
4	Tennessee	9-1-0	Bob Neyland	11-1-0
5	California	9-0-1	Pappy Waldorf	9-1-1
6	Princeton	9-0-0	Charlie Caldwell	same
7	Kentucky	10-1-0	Bear Bryant	11-1-0
8	Michigan St.	8-1-0	Biggie Munn	same
9	Michigan	5-3-1	Bennie Oosterbaan	6-3-1
10	Clemson	8-0-1	Frank Howard	9-0-1
11	Washington	8-2-0	Howard Odell	same
12	Wyoming	9-0-0	Bowden Wyatt	10-0-0
13	Illinois	7-2-0	Ray Eliot	same
14	Ohio St.	6-3-0	Wes Fesler	same
15	Miami-FL	8-0-1	Andy Gustafson	9-1-1
16	Alabama	8-2-0	Red Drew	9-2-0
17	Nebraska	6-2-1	Bill Glassford	same
18	Wash. & Lee	8-2-0	George Barclay	8-3-0
19	Tulsa	8-1-1	J.O. Brothers	9-1-1
20	Tulane	6-2-0	Henry Frnka	6-2-1

Key Bowl Games

Sugar–#7 Kentucky over #1 Oklahoma, 13-7; **Cotton**–#4 Tennessee over #3 Texas, 20-14; **Rose**–#9 Michigan over #5 Cal, 14-6; **Orange**–#10 Clemson over #15 Miami-FL, 15-14.

1951

Final poll released Dec. 3. Top 20 regular season results after that: None.

		As of Dec. 3	Head Coach	After Bowls
1	Tennessee	10-0-0	Bob Neyland	10-1-0
2	Michigan St.	9-0-0	Biggie Munn	same
3	Maryland	9-0-0	Jim Tatum	10-0-0
4	Illinois	8-0-1	Ray Eliot	9-0-1
5	Georgia Tech	10-0-1	Bobby Dodd	11-0-1
6	Princeton	9-0-0	Charlie Caldwell	same
7	Stanford	9-1-0	Chuck Taylor	9-2-0
8	Wisconsin	7-1-1	Ivy Williamson	same
9	Baylor	8-1-1	George Sauer	8-2-1
10	Oklahoma	8-2-0	Bud Wilkinson	same
11	TCU	6-4-0	Dutch Meyer	6-5-0
12	California	8-2-0	Pappy Waldorf	same
13	Virginia	8-1-0	Art Guepe	same
14	San Francisco	9-0-0	Joe Kuharich	same
15	Kentucky	7-4-0	Bear Bryant	8-4-0
16	Boston Univ.	6-4-0	Buff Donelli	same
17	UCLA	5-3-1	Red Sanders	same
18	Washington St.	7-3-0	Forest Evashevski	same
19	Holy Cross	8-2-0	Eddie Anderson	same
20	Clemson	7-2-0	Frank Howard	7-3-0

Key Bowl Games

Sugar–#3 Maryland over #1 Tennessee, 28-13; **Rose**–#4 Illinois over #7 Stanford, 40-7; **Orange**–#5 Georgia Tech over #9 Baylor, 17-14; **Cotton**–#15 Kentucky over #11 TCU, 20-7.

The Special Election That Didn't Count

There was a No. 1 vs. No. 2 battle not noted in the table on pages 162-163. It came in a special election or re-vote of AP selectors following the 1948 Rose Bowl. Here's what happened: Unbeaten Notre Dame was declared 1947 national champion by the AP on Dec. 1, two days after ending their undefeated season with a 38-7 rout of then third-ranked USC in Los Angeles. A day later, however, unbeaten Michigan, AP's final No. 2 team, clobbered now 8th-ranked USC, 49-0, in the Rose Bowl. An cry went up for an unprecedented two-team "Who's No. 1?" ballot and the AP gave in. Michigan won the election 226-119, with 12 voters calling it even. However, AP ruled that the Dec. 8 final poll vote won by Notre Dame would be the poll of record.

Associated Press Final Polls (Cont.)

1952

Final poll released Dec. 1. Top 20 regular season results after that: **Dec. 6**–#15 Florida over #20 Kentucky, 27-20.

		As of Dec. 1	Head Coach	After Bowls
1	Michigan St.	.9-0-0	Biggie Munn	same
2	Georgia Tech	.11-0-0	Bobby Dodd	12-0-0
3	Notre Dame	.7-2-1	Frank Leahy	same
4	Oklahoma	.8-1-0	Bud Wilkinson	same
5	USC	.9-1-0	Jess Hill	10-1-0
6	UCLA	.8-1-0	Red Sanders	same
7	Mississippi	.8-0-2	Johnny Vaught	8-1-2
8	Tennessee	.8-1-1	Bob Neyland	8-2-1
9	Alabama	.9-2-0	Red Drew	10-2-0
10	Texas	.8-2-0	Ed Price	9-2-0
11	Wisconsin	.6-2-1	Ivy Williamson	6-3-1
12	Tulsa	.8-1-1	J.O. Brothers	8-2-1
13	Maryland	.7-2-0	Jim Tatum	same
14	Syracuse	.7-2-0	Ben Schwartzwalder	7-3-0
15	Florida	.6-3-0	Bob Woodruff	8-3-0
16	Duke	.8-2-0	Bill Murray	same
17	Ohio St.	.6-3-0	Woody Hayes	same
18	Purdue	.4-3-2	Stu Holcomb	same
19	Princeton	.8-1-0	Charlie Caldwell	same
20	Kentucky	.5-3-2	Bear Bryant	5-4-2

Note: Michigan St. would officially join Big Ten in 1953.

Key Bowl Games

Sugar–#2 Georgia Tech over #7 Ole Miss, 24-7; **Rose**–#5 USC over #11 Wisconsin, 7-0; **Cotton**–#10 Texas over #8 Tennessee, 16-0; **Orange**–#9 Alabama over #14 Syracuse, 61-6.

1953

Final poll released Nov. 30. Top 20 regular season results after that: **Dec. 5**–#2 Notre Dame over SMU, 40-14.

		As of Nov. 30	Head Coach	After Bowls
1	Maryland	.10-0-0	Jim Tatum	10-1-0
2	Notre Dame	.8-0-1	Frank Leahy	9-0-1
3	Michigan St.	.8-1-0	Biggie Munn	9-1-0
4	Oklahoma	.8-1-1	Bud Wilkinson	9-1-1
5	UCLA	.8-1-0	Red Sanders	8-2-0
6	Rice	.8-2-0	Jess Neely	9-2-0
7	Illinois	.7-1-1	Ray Eliot	same
8	Georgia Tech	.8-2-1	Bobby Dodd	9-2-1
9	Iowa	.5-3-1	Forest Evashevski	same
10	West Virginia	.8-1-0	Art Lewis	8-2-0
11	Texas	.7-3-0	Ed Price	same
12	Texas Tech	.10-1-0	DeWitt Weaver	11-1-0
13	Alabama	.6-2-3	Red Drew	6-3-3
14	Army	.7-1-1	Red Blaik	same
15	Wisconsin	.6-2-1	Ivy Williamson	same
16	Kentucky	.7-2-1	Bear Bryant	same
17	Auburn	.7-2-1	Shug Jordan	7-3-1
18	Duke	.7-2-1	Bill Murray	same
19	Stanford	.6-3-1	Chuck Taylor	same
20	Michigan	.6-3-0	Bennie Oosterbaan	same

Key Bowl Games

Orange–#4 Oklahoma over #1 Maryland, 7-0; **Rose**–#3 Michigan St. over #5 UCLA, 28-20; **Cotton**–#6 Rice over #13 Alabama, 28-6; **Sugar**–#8 Georgia Tech over #10 West Virginia, 42-19.

1954

Final poll released Nov. 29. Top 20 regular season results after that: **Dec. 4**–#4 Notre Dame over SMU, 26-14.

		As of Nov. 29	Head Coach	After Bowls
1	Ohio St.	.9-0-0	Woody Hayes	10-0-0
2	UCLA	.9-0-0	Red Sanders	same
3	Oklahoma	.10-0-0	Bud Wilkinson	same
4	Notre Dame	.8-1-0	Terry Brennan	9-1-0
5	Navy	.7-2-0	Eddie Erdelatz	8-2-0
6	Mississippi	.9-1-0	Johnny Vaught	9-2-0
7	Army	.7-2-0	Red Blaik	same
8	Maryland	.7-2-1	Jim Tatum	same
9	Wisconsin	.7-2-0	Ivy Williamson	same
10	Arkansas	.8-2-0	Bowden Wyatt	8-3-0
11	Miami-FL	.8-1-0	Andy Gustafson	same
12	West Virginia	.8-1-0	Art Lewis	same
13	Auburn	.7-3-0	Shug Jordan	8-3-0
14	Duke	.7-2-1	Bill Murray	8-2-1
15	Michigan	.6-3-0	Bennie Oosterbaan	same
16	Virginia Tech	.8-0-1	Frank Moseley	same
17	USC	.8-3-0	Jess Hill	8-4-0
18	Baylor	.7-3-0	George Sauer	7-4-0
19	Rice	.7-3-0	Jess Neely	same
20	Penn St.	.7-2-0	Rip Engle	same

Note: PCC and Big Seven "no-repeat" rules kept UCLA and Oklahoma from Rose and Orange bowls, respectively.

Key Bowl Games

Rose–#1 Ohio St. over #17 USC, 20-7; **Sugar**–#5 Navy over #6 Ole Miss, 21-0; **Cotton**–Georgia Tech over #10 Arkansas, 14-6; **Orange**–#14 Duke over Nebraska, 34-7.

1955

Final poll released Nov. 28. Top 20 regular season results after that: None.

		As of Nov. 28	Head Coach	After Bowls
1	Oklahoma	.10-0-0	Bud Wilkinson	11-0-0
2	Michigan St.	.8-1-0	Duffy Daugherty	9-1-0
3	Maryland	.10-0-0	Jim Tatum	10-1-0
4	UCLA	.9-1-0	Red Sanders	9-2-0
5	Ohio St.	.7-2-0	Woody Hayes	same
6	TCU	.9-1-0	Abe Martin	9-2-0
7	Georgia Tech	.8-1-1	Bobby Dodd	9-1-1
8	Auburn	.8-1-1	Shug Jordan	8-2-1
9	Notre Dame	.8-2-0	Terry Brennan	same
10	Mississippi	.9-1-0	Johnny Vaught	10-1-0
11	Pittsburgh	.7-3-0	John Michelosen	7-4-0
12	Michigan	.7-2-0	Bennie Oosterbaan	same
13	USC	.6-4-0	Jess Hill	same
14	Miami-FL	.6-3-0	Andy Gustafson	same
15	Miami-OH	.9-0-0	Ara Parseghian	same
16	Stanford	.6-3-1	Chuck Taylor	same
17	Texas A&M	.7-2-1	Bear Bryant	same
18	Navy	.6-2-1	Eddie Erdelatz	same
19	West Virginia	.8-2-0	Art Lewis	same
20	Army	.6-3-0	Red Blaik	same

Note: Big Ten "no-repeat" rule kept Ohio St. from Rose Bowl.

Key Bowl Games

Orange–#1 Oklahoma over #3 Maryland, 20-6; **Rose**–#2 Michigan St. over #4 UCLA, 17-14; **Cotton**–#10 Ole Miss over #6 TCU, 14-13; **Sugar**–#7 Georgia Tech over #11 Pitt, 7-0; **Gator**–Vanderbilt over #8 Auburn, 25-13.

1956

Final poll released Dec. 3. Top 20 regular season results after that: **Dec. 8**–#13 Pitt over #6 Miami-FL, 14-7.

		As of Dec. 3	Head Coach	After Bowls
1	Oklahoma	10-0-0	Bud Wilkinson	same
2	Tennessee	10-0-0	Bowden Wyatt	10-1-0
3	Iowa	8-1-0	Forest Evashevski	9-1-0
4	Georgia Tech	9-1-0	Bobby Dodd	10-1-0
5	Texas A&M	9-0-1	Bear Bryant	same
6	Miami-FL	8-0-1	Andy Gustafson	8-1-1
7	Michigan	7-2-0	Bennie Oosterbaan	same
8	Syracuse	7-1-0	Ben Schwartzwalder	7-2-0
9	Michigan St.	7-2-0	Duffy Daugherty	same
10	Oregon St.	7-2-1	Tommy Prothro	7-3-1
11	Baylor	8-2-0	Sam Boyd	9-2-0
12	Minnesota	6-1-2	Murray Warmath	same
13	Pittsburgh	6-2-1	John Michelosen	7-3-1
14	TCU	7-3-0	Abe Martin	8-3-0
15	Ohio St.	6-3-0	Woody Hayes	same
16	Navy	6-1-2	Eddie Erdelatz	same
17	G. Washington	7-1-1	Gene Sherman	8-1-1
18	USC	8-2-0	Jess Hill	same
19	Clemson	7-1-2	Frank Howard	7-2-2
20	Colorado	7-2-1	Dallas Ward	8-2-1

Note: Big Seven "no-repeat" rule kept Oklahoma from Orange Bowl and Texas A&M was on probation.

Key Bowl Games

Sugar–#11 Baylor over #2 Tennessee, 13-7; **Rose**–#3 Iowa over #10 Oregon St., 35-19; **Gator**–#4 Georgia Tech over #13 Pitt, 21-14; **Cotton**–#14 TCU over #8 Syracuse, 28-27; **Orange**–#20 Colorado over #19 Clemson, 27-21.

1957

Final poll released Dec. 2. Top 20 regular season results after that: **Dec. 7**–#10 Notre Dame over SMU, 54-21.

		As of Dec. 2	Head Coach	After Bowls
1	Auburn	10-0-0	Shug Jordan	same
2	Ohio St.	8-1-0	Woody Hayes	9-1-0
3	Michigan St.	8-1-0	Duffy Daugherty	same
4	Oklahoma	9-1-0	Bud Wilkinson	10-1-0
5	Navy	8-1-1	Eddie Erdelatz	9-1-1
6	Iowa	7-1-1	Forest Evashevski	same
7	Mississippi	8-1-1	Johnny Vaught	9-1-1
8	Rice	7-3-0	Jess Neely	7-4-0
9	Texas A&M	8-2-0	Bear Bryant	8-3-0
10	Notre Dame	6-3-0	Terry Brennan	7-3-0
11	Texas	6-3-1	Darrell Royal	6-4-1
12	Arizona St.	10-0-0	Dan Devine	same
13	Tennessee	7-3-0	Bowden Wyatt	8-3-0
14	Mississippi St.	6-2-1	Wade Walker	same
15	N.C. State	7-1-2	Earle Edwards	same
16	Duke	6-2-2	Bill Murray	6-3-2
17	Florida	6-2-1	Bob Woodruff	same
18	Army	7-2-0	Red Blaik	same
19	Wisconsin	6-3-0	Milt Bruhn	same
20	VMI	9-0-1	John McKenna	same

Note: Auburn on probation, ineligible for bowl game.

Key Bowl Games

Rose–#2 Ohio St. over Oregon, 10-7; **Orange**–#4 Oklahoma over #16 Duke, 48-21; **Cotton**–#5 Navy over #8 Rice, 20-7; **Sugar**–#7 Ole Miss over #11 Texas, 39-7; **Gator**–#13 Tennessee over #9 Texas A&M, 3-0.

1958

Final poll released Dec. 1. Top 20 regular season results after that: None.

		As of Dec. 1	Head Coach	After Bowls
1	LSU	10-0-0	Paul Dietzel	11-0-0
2	Iowa	7-1-1	Forest Evashevski	8-1-1
3	Army	8-0-1	Red Blaik	same
4	Auburn	9-0-1	Shug Jordan	same
5	Oklahoma	9-1-0	Bud Wilkinson	10-1-0
6	Air Force	9-0-1	Ben Martin	9-0-2
7	Wisconsin	7-1-1	Milt Bruhn	same
8	Ohio St.	6-1-2	Woody Hayes	same
9	Syracuse	8-1-0	Ben Schwartzwalder	8-2-0
10	TCU	8-2-0	Abe Martin	8-2-1
11	Mississippi	8-2-0	Johnny Vaught	9-2-0
12	Clemson	8-2-0	Frank Howard	8-3-0
13	Purdue	6-1-2	Jack Mollenkopf	same
14	Florida	6-3-1	Bob Woodruff	6-4-1
15	South Carolina	7-3-0	Warren Giese	same
16	California	7-3-0	Pete Elliott	7-4-0
17	Notre Dame	6-4-0	Terry Brennan	same
18	SMU	6-4-0	Bill Meek	same
19	Oklahoma St.	7-3-0	Cliff Speegle	8-3-0
20	Rutgers	8-1-0	John Stiegman	same

Key Bowl Games

Sugar–#1 LSU over #12 Clemson, 7-0; **Rose**–#2 Iowa over #16 Cal, 38-12; **Orange**–#5 Oklahoma over #9 Syracuse, 21-6; **Cotton**–#6 Air Force tied #10 TCU, 0-0.

1959

Final poll released Dec. 7. Top 20 regular season results after that: None.

		As of Dec. 7	Head Coach	After Bowls
1	Syracuse	10-0-0	Ben Schwartzwalder	11-0-0
2	Mississippi	9-1-0	Johnny Vaught	10-1-0
3	LSU	9-1-0	Paul Dietzel	9-2-0
4	Texas	9-1-0	Darrell Royal	9-2-0
5	Georgia	9-1-0	Wally Butts	10-1-0
6	Wisconsin	7-2-0	Milt Bruhn	7-3-0
7	TCU	8-2-0	Abe Martin	8-3-0
8	Washington	9-1-0	Jim Owens	10-1-0
9	Arkansas	8-2-0	Frank Broyles	9-2-0
10	Alabama	7-1-2	Bear Bryant	7-2-2
11	Clemson	8-2-0	Frank Howard	9-2-0
12	Penn St.	8-2-0	Rip Engle	9-2-0
13	Illinois	5-3-1	Ray Eliot	same
14	USC	8-2-0	Don Clark	same
15	Oklahoma	7-3-0	Bud Wilkinson	same
16	Wyoming	9-1-0	Bob Devaney	same
17	Notre Dame	5-5-0	Joe Kuharich	same
18	Missouri	6-4-0	Dan Devine	6-5-0
19	Florida	5-4-1	Bob Woodruff	same
20	Pittsburgh	6-4-0	John Michelosen	same

Note: Big Seven "no-repeat" rule kept Oklahoma from Orange Bowl.

Key Bowl Games

Cotton–#1 Syracuse over #4 Texas, 23-14; **Sugar**–#2 Ole Miss over #3 LSU, 21-0; **Orange**–#5 Georgia over #18 Missouri, 14-0; **Rose**–#8 Washington over #6 Wisconsin, 44-8; **Bluebonnet**–#11 Clemson over #7 TCU, 23-7; **Gator**–#9 Arkansas over Georgia Tech, 14-7; **Liberty**–#12 Penn St. over #10 Alabama, 7-0.

Associated Press Final Polls (Cont.)

1960

Final poll released Nov. 28. Top 20 regular season results after that: **Dec. 3**–UCLA over #10 Duke, 27-6.

		As of Nov. 28	Head Coach	After Bowls
1	Minnesota	8-1-0	Murray Warmath	8-2-0
2	Mississippi	9-0-1	Johnny Vaught	10-0-1
3	Iowa	8-1-0	Forest Evashevski	same
4	Navy	9-1-0	Wayne Hardin	9-2-0
5	Missouri	9-1-0	Dan Devine	10-1-0
6	Washington	9-1-0	Jim Owens	10-1-0
7	Arkansas	8-2-0	Frank Broyles	8-3-0
8	Ohio St.	7-2-0	Woody Hayes	same
9	Alabama	8-1-1	Bear Bryant	8-1-2
10	Duke	7-2-0	Bill Murray	8-3-0
11	Kansas	7-2-1	Jack Mitchell	same
12	Baylor	8-2-0	John Bridgers	8-3-0
13	Auburn	8-2-0	Shug Jordan	same
14	Yale	9-0-0	Jordan Olivar	same
15	Michigan St.	6-2-1	Duffy Daugherty	same
16	Penn St.	6-3-0	Rip Engle	7-3-0
17	New Mexico St.	10-0-0	Warren Woodson	11-0-0
18	Florida	8-2-0	Ray Graves	9-2-0
19	Syracuse	7-2-0	Ben Schwartzwalder	same
	Purdue	4-4-1	Jack Mollenkopf	same

Key Bowl Games

Rose–#6 Washington over #1 Minnesota, 17-7; **Sugar**–#2 Ole Miss over Rice, 14-6; **Orange**–#5 Missouri over #4 Navy, 21-14; **Cotton**–#10 Duke over #7 Arkansas, 7-6; **Bluebonnet**–#9 Alabama tied Texas, 3-3.

1961

Final poll released Dec. 4. Top 20 regular season results after that: None.

		As of Dec. 4	Head Coach	After Bowls
1	Alabama	10-0-0	Bear Bryant	11-0-0
2	Ohio St.	8-0-1	Woody Hayes	same
3	Texas	9-1-0	Darrell Royal	10-1-0
4	LSU	9-1-0	Paul Dietzel	10-1-0
5	Mississippi	9-1-0	Johnny Vaught	9-2-0
6	Minnesota	7-2-0	Murray Warmath	8-2-0
7	Colorado	9-1-0	Sonny Grandelius	9-2-0
8	Michigan St.	7-2-0	Duffy Daugherty	same
9	Arkansas	8-2-0	Frank Broyles	8-3-0
10	Utah St.	9-0-1	John Ralston	9-1-1
11	Missouri	7-2-1	Dan Devine	same
12	Purdue	6-3-0	Jack Mollenkopf	same
13	Georgia Tech	7-3-0	Bobby Dodd	7-4-0
14	Syracuse	7-3-0	Ben Schwartzwalder	8-3-0
15	Rutgers	9-0-0	John Bateman	same
16	UCLA	7-3-0	Bill Barnes	7-4-0
17	Rice	7-3-0	Jess Neely	7-4-0
	Penn St.	7-3-0	Rip Engle	8-3-0
	Arizona	8-1-1	Jim LaRue	same
20	Duke	7-3-0	Bill Murray	same

Note: Ohio St. faculty council turned down Rose Bowl invitation citing concern with OSU's overemphasis on sports.

Key Bowl Games

Sugar–#1 Alabama over #9 Arkansas, 10-3; **Cotton**–#3 Texas over #5 Ole Miss, 12-7; **Orange**–#4 LSU over #7 Colorado, 25-7; **Rose**–#6 Minnesota over #16 UCLA, 21-3; **Gotham**–Baylor over #10 Utah St., 24-9.

1962

Final poll released Dec. 3. Top 10 regular season results after that: None.

		As of Dec. 3	Head Coach	After Bowls
1	USC	10-0-0	John McKay	11-0-0
2	Wisconsin	8-1-0	Milt Bruhn	8-2-0
3	Mississippi	9-0-0	Johnny Vaught	10-0-0
4	Texas	9-0-1	Darrell Royal	9-1-1
5	Alabama	9-1-0	Bear Bryant	10-1-0
6	Arkansas	9-1-0	Frank Broyles	9-2-0
7	LSU	8-1-1	Charlie McClendon	9-1-1
8	Oklahoma	8-2-0	Bud Wilkinson	8-3-0
9	Penn St.	9-1-0	Rip Engle	9-2-0
10	Minnesota	6-2-1	Murray Warmath	same

Key Bowl Games

Rose–#1 USC over #2 Wisconsin, 42-37; **Sugar**–#3 Ole Miss over #6 Arkansas, 17-13; **Cotton**–#7 LSU over #4 Texas, 13-0; **Orange**–#5 Alabama over #8 Oklahoma, 17-0; **Gator**–Florida over #9 Penn St.,17-7.

1963

Final poll released Dec. 9. Top 10 regular season results after that: **Dec.14**–#8 Alabama over Miami-FL, 17-12.

		As of Dec. 9	Head Coach	After Bowls
1	Texas	10-0-0	Darrell Royal	11-0-0
2	Navy	9-1-0	Wayne Hardin	9-2-0
3	Illinois	7-1-1	Pete Elliott	8-1-1
4	Pittsburgh	9-1-0	John Michelosen	same
5	Auburn	9-1-0	Shug Jordan	9-2-0
6	Nebraska	9-1-0	Bob Devaney	10-1-0
7	Mississippi	7-0-2	Johnny Vaught	7-1-2
8	Alabama	7-2-0	Bear Bryant	9-2-0
9	Michigan St.	6-2-1	Duffy Daugherty	same
10	Oklahoma	8-2-0	Bud Wilkinson	same

Key Bowl Games

Cotton–#1 Texas over #2 Navy, 28-6; **Rose**–#3 Illinois over Washington, 17-7; **Orange**–#6 Nebraska over #5 Auburn, 13-7; **Sugar**–#8 Alabama over #7 Ole Miss, 12-7.

1964

Final poll released Nov. 30. Top 10 regular season results after that: **Dec. 5**–Florida over #7 LSU, 20-6.

		As of Nov. 30	Head Coach	After Bowls
1	Alabama	10-0-0	Bear Bryant	10-1-0
2	Arkansas	10-0-0	Frank Broyles	11-0-0
3	Notre Dame	9-1-0	Ara Parseghian	same
4	Michigan	8-1-0	Bump Elliott	9-1-0
5	Texas	9-1-0	Darrell Royal	10-1-0
6	Nebraska	9-1-0	Bob Devaney	9-2-0
7	LSU	7-1-1	Charlie McClendon	8-2-1
8	Oregon St.	8-2-0	Tommy Prothro	8-3-0
9	Ohio St.	7-2-0	Woody Hayes	same
10	USC	7-3-0	John McKay	same

Key Bowl Games

Orange–#5 Texas over #1 Alabama, 21-17; **Cotton**–#2 Arkansas over #6 Nebraska, 10-7; **Rose**–#4 Michigan over #8 Oregon St., 34-7; **Sugar**–#7 LSU over Syracuse, 13-10.

1965

Final poll taken after bowl games for the first time.

		Head Coach	Regular Season
	After Bowls		
1	Alabama 9-1-1	Bear Bryant	8-1-1
2	Michigan St 10-1-0	Duffy Daugherty	10-0-0
3	Arkansas 10-1-0	Frank Broyles	10-0-0
4	UCLA 8-2-1	Tommy Prothro	7-1-1
5	Nebraska 10-1-0	Bob Devaney	10-0-0
6	Missouri 8-2-1	Dan Devine	7-2-1
7	Tennessee 8-1-2	Doug Dickey	6-1-2
8	LSU 8-3-0	Charlie McClendon	7-3-0
9	Notre Dame . . .7-2-1	Ara Parseghian	same
10	USC 7-2-1	John McKay	same

Key Bowl Games

Rankings below reflect final regular season poll, released Nov. 29. No bowls for then #8 USC or #9 Notre Dame. **Rose**–#5 UCLA over #1 Michigan St., 14-12; **Cotton**–LSU over #2 Arkansas, 14-7; **Orange**–#4 Alabama over #3 Nebraska, 39-28; **Sugar**–#6 Missouri over Florida, 20-18; **Bluebonnet**–#7 Tennessee over Tulsa, 27-6; **Gator**–Georgia Tech over #10 Texas Tech, 31-21.

1966

Final poll released Dec. 5, returning to pre-bowl status. Top 10 regular season results after that: None.

	As of Dec. 5	Head Coach	After Bowls
1	Notre Dame . . .9-0-1	Ara Parseghian	same
2	Michigan St . . .9-0-1	Duffy Daugherty	same
3	Alabama 10-0-0	Bear Bryant	11-0-0
4	Georgia 9-1-0	Vince Dooley	10-1-0
5	UCLA 9-1-0	Tommy Prothro	same
6	Nebraska 9-1-0	Bob Devaney	9-2-0
7	Purdue 8-2-0	Jack Mollenkopf	9-2-0
8	Georgia Tech . . .9-1-0	Bobby Dodd	9-2-0
9	Miami-FL 7-2-1	Charlie Tate	8-2-1
10	SMU 8-2-0	Hayden Fry	8-3-0

Key Bowl Games

Sugar–#3 Alabama over #6 Nebraska, 34-7; **Cotton**–#4 Georgia over #10 SMU, 24-9; **Rose**–#7 Purdue over USC, 14-13; **Orange**–Florida over #8 Georgia Tech, 27-12; **Liberty**–#9 Miami-FL over Virginia Tech, 14-7.

1967

Final poll released Nov. 27. Top 10 regular season results after that: **Dec. 2**–#2 Tennessee over Vanderbilt, 41-14; #3 Oklahoma over Oklahoma St., 38-14; #8 Alabama over Auburn, 7-3.

	As of Nov. 27	Head Coach	After Bowls
1	USC 9-1-0	John McKay	10-1-0
2	Tennessee 8-1-0	Doug Dickey	9-2-0
3	Oklahoma 8-1-0	Chuck Fairbanks	10-1-0
4	Indiana 9-1-0	John Pont	9-2-0
5	Notre Dame 8-2-0	Ara Parseghian	same
6	Wyoming 10-0-0	Lloyd Eaton	10-1-0
7	Oregon St. 7-2-1	Dee Andros	same
8	Alabama 7-1-1	Bear Bryant	8-2-1
9	Purdue 8-2-0	Jack Mollenkopf	same
10	Penn St. 8-2-0	Joe Paterno	8-2-1

Key Bowl Games

Rose–#1 USC over #4 Indiana, 14-3; **Orange**–#3 Oklahoma over #2 Tennessee, 26-24; **Sugar**–LSU over #6 Wyoming, 20-13; **Cotton**–Texas A&M over #8 Alabama, 20-16; **Gator**–#10 Penn St. tied Florida St. 17-17.

1968

Final poll taken after bowl games for first time since close of 1965 season.

	After Bowls	Head Coach	Regular Season
1	Ohio St. 10-0-0	Woody Hayes	9-0-0
2	Penn St. 11-0-0	Joe Paterno	10-0-0
3	Texas 9-1-1	Darrell Royal	8-1-1
4	USC 9-1-1	John McKay	9-0-1
5	Notre Dame 7-2-1	Ara Parseghian	same
6	Arkansas 10-1-0	Frank Broyles	9-1-0
7	Kansas 9-2-0	Pepper Rodgers	9-1-0
8	Georgia 8-1-2	Vince Dooley	8-0-2
9	Missouri 8-3-0	Dan Devine	7-3-0
10	Purdue 8-2-0	Jack Mollenkopf	same
11	Oklahoma 7-4-0	Chuck Fairbanks	7-3-0
12	Missouri 8-2-0	Bump Elliott	same
13	Tennessee 8-2-1	Doug Dickey	8-1-1
14	SMU 8-3-0	Hayden Fry	7-3-0
15	Oregon St. 7-3-0	Dee Andros	same
16	Auburn 7-4-0	Shug Jordan	6-4-0
17	Alabama 8-3-0	Bear Bryant	8-2-0
18	Houston 6-2-2	Bill Yeoman	same
19	LSU 8-3-0	Charlie McClendon	7-3-0
20	Ohio Univ 10-1-0	Bill Hess	10-0-0

Key Bowl Games

Rankings below reflect final regular season poll, released Dec. 2. No bowls for then #7 Notre Dame and #11 Pudue. **Rose**–#1 Ohio St. over #2 USC, 27-16; **Orange**–#3 Penn St. over #6 Kansas, 15-14; **Sugar**–#9 Arkansas over #4 Georgia, 16-2; **Cotton**–#5 Texas over #8 Tennessee, 36-13; **Bluebonnet**–#20 SMU over #10 Oklahoma, 28-27; **Gator**–#16 Missouri over #12 Alabama, 35-10.

1969

Final poll taken after bowl games.

	After Bowls	Head Coach	Regular Season
1	Texas 11-0-0	Darrell Royal	10-0-0
2	Penn St 11-0-0	Joe Paterno	10-0-0
3	USC 10-0-1	John McKay	9-0-1
4	Ohio St. 8-1-0	Woody Hayes	same
5	Notre Dame 8-2-1	Ara Parseghian	8-1-1
6	Missouri 9-2-0	Dan Devine	9-1-0
7	Arkansas 9-2-0	Frank Broyles	9-1-0
8	Mississippi 8-3-0	Johnny Vaught	7-3-0
9	Michigan 8-3-0	Bo Schembechler	8-2-0
10	LSU 9-1-0	Charlie McClendon	same
11	Nebraska 9-2-0	Bob Devaney	8-2-0
12	Houston 9-2-0	Bill Yeoman	8-2-0
13	UCLA 8-1-1	Tommy Prothro	same
14	Florida 9-1-1	Ray Graves	8-1-1
15	Tennessee 9-2-0	Doug Dickey	9-1-0
16	Colorado 8-3-0	Eddie Crowder	7-3-0
17	West Virginia . .10-1-0	Jim Carlen	9-1-0
18	Purdue 8-2-0	Jack Mollenkopf	same
19	Stanford 7-2-1	John Ralston	same
20	Auburn 8-3-0	Shug Jordan	8-2-0

Key Bowl Games

Rankings below reflect final regular season poll, released Dec. 8. No bowls for then #4 Ohio St., #8 LSU and #10 UCLA.

Cotton–#1 Texas over #9 Notre Dame, 21-17; **Orange**–#2 Penn St. over #6 Missouri, 10-3; **Sugar**–#13 Ole Miss over #3 Arkansas, 27-22; **Rose**–#5 USC over #7 Michigan, 10-3.

Associated Press Final Polls (Cont.)

1970

		After Bowls	Head Coach	Regular Season
1	Nebraska	11-0-1	Bob Devaney	10-0-1
2	Notre Dame	10-1-0	Ara Parseghian	9-0-1
3	Texas	10-1-0	Darrell Royal	10-0-0
4	Tennessee	11-1-0	Bill Battle	10-1-0
5	Ohio St.	9-1-0	Woody Hayes	9-0-0
6	Arizona St.	11-0-0	Frank Kush	10-0-0
7	LSU	9-3-0	Charlie McClendon	9-2-0
8	Stanford	9-3-0	John Ralston	8-3-0
9	Michigan	9-1-0	Bo Schembechler	same
10	Auburn	9-2-0	Shug Jordan	8-2-0
11	Arkansas	9-2-0	Frank Broyles	same
12	Toledo	12-0-0	Frank Lauterbur	11-0-0
13	Georgia Tech	9-3-0	Bud Carson	8-3-0
14	Dartmouth	9-0-0	Bob Blackman	same
15	USC	6-4-1	John McKay	6-3-1
16	Air Force	9-3-0	Ben Martin	9-2-0
17	Tulane	8-4-0	Jim Pittman	7-4-0
18	Penn St.	7-3-0	Joe Paterno	7-3-0
19	Houston	8-3-0	Bill Yeoman	same
20	Oklahoma	7-4-1	Chuck Fairbanks	7-4-0
	Mississippi	7-4-0	Johnny Vaught	7-3-0

Key Bowl Games

Rankings below reflect final regular season poll, released Dec. 7. No bowls for then #4 Arkansas and #7 Michigan.
Cotton—#6 Notre Dame over #1 Texas, 24-11; **Rose**—#12 Stanford over #2 Ohio St., 27-17; **Orange**—#3 Nebraska over #8 LSU, 17-12; **Sugar**—#5 Tennessee over #11 Air Force, 34-13; **Peach**—#9 Ariz. St. over N. Carolina, 48-26.

1971

		After Bowls	Head Coach	Regular Season
1	Nebraska	13-0-0	Bob Devaney	12-0-0
2	Oklahoma	11-1-0	Chuck Fairbanks	10-1-0
3	Colorado	10-2-0	Eddie Crowder	9-2-0
4	Alabama	11-1-0	Bear Bryant	11-0-0
5	Penn St.	11-1-0	Joe Paterno	10-1-0
6	Michigan	11-1-0	Bo Schembechler	11-0-0
7	Georgia	11-1-0	Vince Dooley	10-1-0
8	Arizona St.	11-1-0	Frank Kush	10-1-0
9	Tennessee	10-2-0	Bill Battle	9-2-0
10	Stanford	9-3-0	John Ralston	8-3-0
11	LSU	9-3-0	Charlie McClendon	8-3-0
12	Auburn	9-2-0	Shug Jordan	9-1-0
13	Notre Dame	8-2-0	Ara Parseghian	same
14	Toledo	12-0-0	John Murphy	11-0-0
15	Mississippi	10-2-0	Billy Kinard	9-2-0
16	Arkansas	8-3-1	Frank Broyles	8-2-1
17	Houston	9-3-0	Bill Yeoman	9-2-0
18	Texas	8-3-0	Darrell Royal	8-2-0
19	Washington	8-3-0	Jim Owens	same
20	USC	6-4-1	John McKay	same

Key Bowl Games

Rankings below reflect final regular season poll, released Dec. 6.
Orange—#1 Nebraska over #2 Alabama, 38-6; **Sugar**—#3 Oklahoma over #5 Auburn, 40-22; **Rose**—#16 Stanford over #4 Michigan, 13-12; **Gator**—#6 Georgia over N. Carolina, 7-3; **Bluebonnet**—#7 Colorado over #15 Houston, 29-17; **Fiesta**—#8 Ariz. St. over Florida St., 45-38; **Cotton**—#10 Penn St. over #12 Texas, 30-6.

1972

		After Bowls	Head Coach	Regular Season
1	USC	12-0-0	John McKay	11-0-0
2	Oklahoma	11-1-0	Chuck Fairbanks	10-1-0
3	Texas	10-1-0	Darrell Royal	9-1-0
4	Nebraska	9-2-1	Bob Devaney	8-2-1
5	Auburn	10-1-0	Shug Jordan	9-1-0
6	Michigan	10-1-0	Bo Schembechler	same
7	Alabama	10-2-0	Bear Bryant	10-1-0
8	Tennessee	10-2-0	Bill Battle	9-2-0
9	Ohio St.	9-2-0	Woody Hayes	9-1-0
10	Penn St.	10-2-0	Joe Paterno	10-1-0
11	LSU	9-2-1	Charlie McClendon	9-1-1
12	North Carolina	11-1-0	Bill Dooley	10-1-0
13	Arizona St.	10-2-0	Frank Kush	9-2-0
14	Notre Dame	8-3-0	Ara Parseghian	8-2-0
15	UCLA	8-3-0	Pepper Rodgers	same
16	Colorado	8-4-0	Eddie Crowder	8-3-0
17	N.C. State	8-3-1	Lou Holtz	7-3-1
18	Louisville	9-1-0	Lee Corso	same
19	Washington St.	7-4-0	Jim Sweeney	same
20	Georgia Tech	7-4-1	Bill Fulcher	6-4-1

Key Bowl Games

Rankings below reflect final regular season poll, released Dec. 4. No bowl for then #8 Michigan.
Rose—#1 USC over #3 Ohio St., 42-17; **Sugar**—#2 Oklahoma over #5 Penn St., 14-0; **Cotton**—#7 Texas over #4 Alabama, 17-13; **Orange**—#9 Nebraska over #12 Notre Dame, 40-6; **Gator**—#6 Auburn over #13 Colorado, 24-3; **Bluebonnet**—#11 Tennessee over #10 LSU, 24-17.

1973

		After Bowls	Head Coach	Regular Season
1	Notre Dame	11-0-0	Ara Parseghian	10-0-0
2	Ohio St.	10-0-1	Woody Hayes	9-0-1
3	Oklahoma	10-0-1	Barry Switzer	same
4	Alabama	11-1-0	Bear Bryant	11-0-0
5	Penn St.	12-0-0	Joe Paterno	11-0-0
6	Michigan	10-0-1	Bo Schembechler	same
7	Nebraska	9-2-1	Tom Osborne	8-2-1
8	USC	9-2-1	John McKay	9-1-1
9	Arizona St.	11-1-0	Frank Kush	10-1-0
	Houston	11-1-0	Bill Yeoman	10-1-0
11	Texas Tech	11-1-0	Jim Carlen	10-1-0
12	UCLA	9-2-0	Pepper Rodgers	same
13	LSU	9-3-0	Charlie McClendon	9-2-0
14	Texas	8-3-0	Darrell Royal	8-2-0
15	Miami-OH	11-0-0	Bill Mallory	10-0-0
16	N.C. State	9-3-0	Lou Holtz	8-3-0
17	Missouri	8-4-0	Al Onofrio	7-4-0
18	Kansas	7-4-1	Don Fambrough	7-3-1
19	Tennessee	8-4-0	Bill Battle	8-3-0
20	Maryland	8-4-0	Jerry Claiborne	8-3-0
	Tulane	9-3-0	Bennie Ellender	9-2-0

Key Bowl Games

Rankings below reflect final regular season poll, released Dec. 3. No bowls for then #2 Oklahoma (probation), #5 Michigan and #9 UCLA.
Sugar—#3 Notre Dame over #1 Alabama, 24-23; **Rose**—#4 Ohio St. over #7 USC, 42-21; **Orange**—#6 Penn St. over #13 LSU, 16-9; **Cotton**—#12 Nebraska over #8 Texas, 19-3; **Fiesta**—#10 Ariz. St. over Pitt, 28-7; **Bluebonnet**—#14 Houston over #17 Tulane, 47-7.

1974

	After Bowls	Head Coach	Regular Season
1	Oklahoma 11-0-0	Barry Switzer	same
2	USC 10-1-1	John McKay	9-1-1
3	Michigan 10-1-0	Bo Schembechler	same
4	Ohio St. 10-2-0	Woody Hayes	10-1-0
5	Alabama 11-1-0	Bear Bryant	11-0-0
6	Notre Dame . .10-2-0	Ara Parseghian	9-2-0
7	Penn St. 10-2-0	Joe Paterno	9-2-0
8	Auburn 10-2-0	Shug Jordan	9-2-0
9	Nebraska 9-3-0	Tom Osborne	8-3-0
10	Miami-OH 10-0-1	Dick Crum	9-0-1
11	N.C. State 9-2-1	Lou Holtz	9-2-0
12	Michigan St. 7-3-1	Denny Stolz	same
13	Maryland 8-4-0	Jerry Claiborne	8-3-0
14	Baylor 8-4-0	Grant Teaff	8-3-0
15	Florida 8-4-0	Doug Dickey	8-3-0
16	Texas A&M 8-3-0	Emory Ballard	same
17	Mississippi St. . . .9-3-0	Bob Tyler	8-3-0
	Texas 8-4-0	Darrell Royal	8-3-0
19	Houston 8-3-1	Bill Yeoman	8-3-0
20	Tennessee 7-3-2	Bill Battle	6-3-2

Key Bowl Games

Rankings below reflect final regular season poll, released Dec. 2. No bowls for #1 Oklahoma (probation) and then #4 Michigan.

Orange–#9 Notre Dame over #2 Alabama, 13-11; **Rose**–#5 USC over #3 Ohio St., 18-17; **Gator**–#6 Auburn over #11 Texas, 27-3; **Cotton**–#7 Penn St. over #12 Baylor, 41-20; **Sugar**–#8 Nebraska over #18 Florida, 13-10; **Liberty**–Tennessee over #10 Maryland, 7-3.

1975

	After Bowls	Head Coach	Regular Season
1	Oklahoma 11-1-0	Barry Switzer	10-1-0
2	Arizona St. 12-0-0	Frank Kush	11-0-0
3	Alabama 11-1-0	Bear Bryant	10-1-0
4	Ohio St. 11-1-0	Woody Hayes	11-0-0
5	UCLA 9-2-1	Dick Vermeil	8-2-1
6	Texas 10-2-0	Darrell Royal	9-2-0
7	Arkansas 10-2-0	Frank Broyles	9-2-0
8	Michigan 8-2-2	Bo Schembechler	8-1-2
9	Nebraska 10-2-0	Tom Osborne	10-1-0
10	Penn St. 9-3-0	Joe Paterno	9-2-0
11	Texas A&M . . .10-2-0	Emory Ballard	10-1-0
12	Miami-OH 11-1-0	Dick Crum	10-1-0
13	Maryland 9-2-1	Jerry Claiborne	8-2-1
14	California 8-3-0	Mike White	same
15	Pittsburgh 8-4-0	Johnny Majors	7-4-0
16	Colorado 9-3-0	Bill Mallory	9-2-0
17	USC 8-4-0	John McKay	7-4-0
18	Arizona 9-2-0	Jim Young	same
19	Georgia 9-3-0	Vince Dooley	9-2-0
20	West Virginia 9-3-0	Bobby Bowden	8-3-0

Key Bowl Games

Rankings below reflect final regular season poll, released Dec. 1. Texas A&M was unbeaten and ranked 2nd in that poll, but lost to #18 Arkansas, 31-6, in its final regular season game on Dec.6.

Rose–#11 UCLA over #1 Ohio St., 23-10; **Liberty**–#17 USC over #2 Texas A&M, 20-0; **Orange**–#3 Oklahoma over #5 Michigan, 14-6; **Sugar**–#4 Alabama over #8 Penn St., 13-6; **Fiesta**–#7 Ariz. St. over #6 Nebraska, 17-14; **Bluebonnet**–#9 Texas over #10 Colorado, 38-21; **Cotton**–#18 Arkansas over #12 Georgia, 31-10.

1976

	After Bowls	Head Coach	Regular Season
1	Pittsburgh 12-0-0	Johnny Majors	11-0-0
2	USC 11-1-0	John Robinson	10-1-0
3	Michigan 10-2-0	Bo Schembechler	10-1-0
4	Houston 10-2-0	Bill Yeoman	9-2-0
5	Oklahoma 9-2-1	Barry Switzer	8-2-1
6	Ohio St. 9-2-1	Woody Hayes	8-2-1
7	Texas A&M . . .10-2-0	Emory Bellard	9-2-0
8	Maryland 11-1-0	Jerry Claiborne	11-0-0
9	Nebraska 9-3-1	Tom Osborne	8-3-1
10	Georgia 10-2-0	Vince Dooley	10-1-0
11	Alabama 9-3-0	Bear Bryant	8-3-0
12	Notre Dame 9-3-0	Dan Devine	8-3-0
13	Texas Tech 10-2-0	Steve Sloan	10-1-0
14	Oklahoma St. . . .9-3-0	Jim Stanley	8-3-0
15	UCLA 9-2-1	Terry Donahue	9-1-1
16	Colorado 8-4-0	Bill Mallory	8-3-0
17	Rutgers 11-0-0	Frank Burns	same
18	Kentucky 8-4-0	Fran Curci	7-4-0
19	Iowa St. 8-3-0	Earle Bruce	same
20	Mississippi St. . . .9-2-0	Bob Tyler	same

Key Bowl Games

Rankings below reflect final regular season poll, released Nov. 29. No bowl for then #20 Miss. St. (probation).

Sugar–#1 Pitt over #5 Georgia, 27-3; **Rose**–#3 USC over #2 Michigan, 14-6; **Cotton**–#6 Houston over #4 Maryland, 30-21; **Liberty**–#16 Alabama over #7 UCLA, 36-6; **Fiesta**–#8 Oklahoma over Wyoming, 41-7; **Bluebonnet**–#13 Nebraska over #9 Texas Tech, 27-24; **Sun**–#10 Texas A&M over Florida, 37-14; **Orange**–#11 Ohio St. over #12 Colorado, 27-10.

1977

	After Bowls	Head Coach	Regular Season
1	Notre Dame 11-1-0	Dan Devine	10-1-0
2	Alabama 11-1-0	Bear Bryant	10-1-0
3	Arkansas 11-1-0	Lou Holtz	10-1-0.
4	Texas 11-1-0	Fred Akers	11-0-0
5	Penn St. 11-1-0	Joe Paterno	10-1-0
6	Kentucky 10-1-0	Fran Curci	same
7	Oklahoma 10-2-0	Barry Switzer	10-1-0
8	Pittsburgh 9-2-1	Jackie Sherrill	8-2-1
9	Michigan 10-2-0	Bo Schembechler	10-1-0
10	Washington 8-4-0	Don James	7-4-0
11	Ohio St. 9-3-0	Woody Hayes	9-2-0
12	Nebraska 9-3-0	Tom Osborne	8-3-0
13	USC 8-4-0	John Robinson	7-4-0
14	Florida St. 10-2-0	Bobby Bowden	9-2-0
15	Stanford 9-3-0	Bill Walsh	8-3-0
16	San Diego St. . . .10-1-0	Claude Gilbert	same
17	North Carolina . . .8-3-1	Bill Dooley	8-2-1
18	Arizona St. 9-3-0	Frank Kush	9-2-0
19	Clemson 8-3-1	Charley Pell	8-2-1
20	BYU 9-2-0	LaVell Edwards	same

Key Bowl Games

Rankings below reflect final regular season poll, released Nov. 28. No bowl for then #7 Kentucky (probation).

Cotton–#5 Notre Dame over #1 Texas, 38-10; **Orange**–#6 Arkansas over #2 Oklahoma, 31-6; **Sugar**–#3 Alabama over #9 Ohio St., 35-6; **Rose**–#13 Washington over #4 Michigan, 27-20; **Fiesta**–#8 Penn St. over #15 Ariz. St., 42-30; **Gator**–#10 Pitt over #11 Clemson, 34-3.

Associated Press Final Polls (Cont.)

1978

		After Bowls	Head Coach	Regular Season
1	Alabama	11-1-0	Bear Bryant	10-1-0
2	USC	12-1-0	John Robinson	11-1-0
3	Oklahoma	11-1-0	Barry Switzer	10-1-0
4	Penn St.	11-1-0	Joe Paterno	11-0-0
5	Michigan	10-2-0	Bo Schembechler	10-1-0
6	Clemson	11-1-0	Charley Pell	10-1-0
7	Notre Dame	9-3-0	Dan Devine	8-3-0
8	Nebraska	9-3-0	Tom Osborne	9-2-0
9	Texas	9-3-0	Fred Akers	8-3-0
10	Houston	9-3-0	Bill Yeoman	9-2-0
11	Arkansas	9-2-1	Lou Holtz	9-2-0
12	Michigan St.	8-3-0	Darryl Rogers	same
13	Purdue	9-2-1	Jim Young	8-2-1
14	UCLA	8-3-1	Terry Donahue	8-3-0
15	Missouri	8-4-0	Warren Powers	7-4-0
16	Georgia	9-2-1	Vince Dooley	9-1-1
17	Stanford	8-4-0	Bill Walsh	7-4-0
18	N.C. State	9-3-0	Bo Rein	8-3-0
19	Texas A&M	8-4-0	Emory Bellard (4-2) & Tom Wilson (4-2)	7-4-0
20	Maryland	9-3-0	Jerry Claiborne	9-2-0

Key Bowl Games

Rankings below reflect final regular season poll, released Dec. 4. No bowl for then #12 Michigan St. (probation).

Sugar–#2 Alabama over #1 Penn St., 14-7; **Rose**–#3 USC over #5 Michigan, 17-10; **Orange**–#4 Oklahoma over #6 Nebraska, 31-24; **Gator**–#7 Clemson over #20 Ohio St., 17-15; **Fiesta**–#8 Arkansas tied #15 UCLA, 10-10; **Cotton**–#10 Notre Dame over #9 Houston, 35-34.

1979

		After Bowls	Head Coach	Regular Season
1	Alabama	12-0-0	Bear Bryant	11-0-0
2	USC	11-0-1	John Robinson	10-0-1
3	Oklahoma	11-1-0	Barry Switzer	10-1-0
4	Ohio St.	11-1-0	Earle Bruce	11-0-0
5	Houston	11-1-0	Bill Yeoman	10-1-0
6	Florida St.	11-1-0	Bobby Bowden	11-0-0
7	Pittsburgh	11-1-0	Jackie Sherrill	10-1-0
8	Arkansas	10-2-0	Lou Holtz	10-1-0
9	Nebraska	10-2-0	Tom Osborne	10-1-0
10	Purdue	10-2-0	Jim Young	9-2-0
11	Washington	9-3-0	Don James	8-3-0
12	Texas	9-3-0	Fred Akers	9-2-0
13	BYU	11-1-0	LaVell Edwards	11-0-0
14	Baylor	8-4-0	Grant Teaff	7-4-0
15	North Carolina	8-3-1	Dick Crum	7-3-1
16	Auburn	8-3-0	Doug Barfield	same
17	Temple	10-2-0	Wayne Hardin	9-2-0
18	Michigan	8-4-0	Bo Schembechler	8-3-0
19	Indiana	8-4-0	Lee Corso	7-4-0
20	Penn St.	8-4-0	Joe Paterno	7-4-0

Key Bowl Games

Rankings below reflect final regular season poll, released Dec. 3. No bowl for then #17 Auburn (probation).

Sugar–#2 Alabama over #6 Arkansas, 24-9; **Rose**–#3 USC over #1 Ohio St., 17-16; **Orange**–#5 Oklahoma over #4 Florida St., 24-7; **Sun**–#13 Washington over #11 Texas, 14-7; **Cotton**–#8 Houston over #7 Nebraska, 17-14; **Fiesta**–#10 Pitt over Arizona, 16-10.

1980

		After Bowls	Head Coach	Regular Season
1	Georgia	12-0-0	Vince Dooley	11-0-0
2	Pittsburgh	11-1-0	Jackie Sherrill	10-1-0
3	Oklahoma	10-2-0	Barry Switzer	9-2-0
4	Michigan	10-2-0	Bo Schembechler	9-2-0
5	Florida St.	10-2-0	Bobby Bowden	10-1-0
6	Alabama	10-2-0	Bear Bryant	9-2-0
7	Nebraska	10-2-0	Tom Osborne	9-2-0
8	Penn St.	10-2-0	Joe Paterno	9-2-0
9	Notre Dame	9-2-1	Dan Devine	9-1-1
10	North Carolina	11-1-0	Dick Crum	10-1-0
11	USC	8-2-1	John Robinson	same
12	BYU	12-1-0	LaVell Edwards	11-1-0
13	UCLA	9-2-0	Terry Donahue	same
14	Baylor	10-2-0	Grant Teaff	10-1-0
15	Ohio St.	9-3-0	Earle Bruce	9-2-0
16	Washington	9-3-0	Don James	9-2-0
17	Purdue	9-3-0	Jim Young	8-3-0
18	Miami-FL	9-3-0	H. Schnellenberger	8-3-0
19	Mississippi St.	9-3-0	Emory Bellard	9-2-0
20	SMU	8-4-0	Ron Meyer	8-3-0

Key Bowl Games

Rankings below reflect final regular season poll, released Dec. 8.

Sugar–#1 Georgia over #7 Notre Dame, 17-10; **Orange**–#4 Oklahoma over #2 Florida St., 18-17; **Gator**–#3 Pitt over #18 S. Carolina, 37-9; **Rose**–#5 Michigan over #16 Washington, 23-6; **Cotton**–#9 Alabama over #6 Baylor, 30-2; **Sun**–#8 Nebraska over #17 Miss. St., 31-17; **Fiesta**–#10 Penn St. over #11 Ohio St., 31-19; **Bluebonnet**–#13 N. Carolina over Texas, 16-7.

1981

		After Bowls	Head Coach	Regular Season
1	Clemson	12-0-0	Danny Ford	11-0-0
2	Texas	10-1-1	Fred Akers	9-1-1
3	Penn St.	10-2-0	Joe Paterno	9-2-0
4	Pittsburgh	11-1-0	Jackie Sherrill	10-1-0
5	SMU	10-1-0	Ron Meyer	same
6	Georgia	10-2-0	Vince Dooley	10-1-0
7	Alabama	9-2-1	Bear Bryant	9-1-1
8	Miami-FL	9-2-0	H. Schnellenberger	same
9	North Carolina	10-2-0	Dick Crum	9-2-0
10	Washington	10-2-0	Don James	9-2-0
11	Nebraska	9-3-0	Tom Osborne	9-2-0
12	Michigan	9-3-0	Bo Schembechler	8-3-0
13	BYU	11-2-0	LaVell Edwards	10-2-0
14	USC	9-3-0	John Robinson	9-2-0
15	Ohio St.	9-3-0	Earle Bruce	8-3-0
16	Arizona St.	9-2-0	Darryl Rogers	same
17	West Virginia	9-3-0	Don Nehlen	8-3-0
18	Iowa	8-4-0	Hayden Fry	8-3-0
19	Missouri	8-4-0	Warren Powers	7-4-0
20	Oklahoma	7-4-1	Barry Switzer	6-4-1

Key Bowl Games

Rankings below reflect final regular season poll, released Nov. 30. No bowl for then #5 SMU (probation), #9 Miami-FL (probation), and #17 Ariz. St. (probation).

Orange–#1 Clemson over #4 Nebraska, 22-15; **Sugar**–#10 Pitt over #2 Georgia, 24-20; **Cotton**–#6 Texas over #3 Alabama, 14-12; **Fiesta**–#7 Penn St. over #8 USC, 26-10; **Gator**–#11 N. Carolina over Arkansas, 31-27; **Rose**–#12 Washington over #13 Iowa, 28-0.

1982

		After Bowls	Head Coach	Regular Season
1	Penn St.	11-1-0	Joe Paterno	10-1-0
2	SMU	11-0-1	Bobby Collins	10-0-1
3	Nebraska	12-1-0	Tom Osborne	11-1-0
4	Georgia	11-1-0	Vince Dooley	11-0-0
5	UCLA	10-1-1	Terry Donahue	9-1-1
6	Arizona St.	10-2-0	Darryl Rogers	9-2-0
7	Washington	10-2-0	Don James	9-2-0
8	Clemson	9-1-1	Danny Ford	same
9	Arkansas	9-2-1	Lou Holtz	8-2-1
10	Pittsburgh	9-3-0	Foge Fazio	9-2-0
11	LSU	8-3-1	Jerry Stovall	8-2-1
12	Ohio St.	9-3-0	Earle Bruce	8-3-0
13	Florida St.	9-3-0	Bobby Bowden	8-3-0
14	Auburn	9-3-0	Pat Dye	8-3-0
15	USC	8-3-0	John Robinson	same
16	Oklahoma	8-4-0	Barry Switzer	8-3-0
17	Texas	9-3-0	Fred Akers	9-2-0
18	North Carolina	8-4-0	Dick Crum	7-4-0
19	West Virginia	9-3-0	Don Nehlen	9-2-0
20	Maryland	8-4-0	Bobby Ross	8-3-0

Key Bowl Games

Rankings below reflect final regular season poll, released Dec. 6. No bowl for then #7 Clemson (probation) and #15 USC (probation).

Sugar–#2 Penn St. over #1 Georgia, 27-23; **Orange**–#3 Nebraska over #13 LSU, 21-20; **Cotton**–#4 SMU over #6 Pitt, 7-3; **Rose**–#5 UCLA over #19 Michigan, 24-14; **Aloha**–#9 Washington over #16 Maryland, 21-20; **Fiesta**–#11 Ariz. St. over #12 Oklahoma, 32-21; **Bluebonnet**–#14 Arkansas over Florida, 28-24.

1983

		After Bowls	Head Coach	Regular Season
1	Miami-FL	11-1-0	H. Schnellenberger	10-1-0
2	Nebraska	12-1-0	Tom Osborne	12-0-0
3	Auburn	11-1-0	Pat Dye	10-1-0
4	Georgia	10-1-1	Vince Dooley	9-1-1
5	Texas	11-1-0	Fred Akers	11-0-0
6	Florida	9-2-1	Charley Pell	8-2-1
7	BYU	11-1-0	LaVell Edwards	10-1-0
8	Michigan	9-3-0	Bo Schembechler	9-2-0
9	Ohio St.	9-3-0	Earle Bruce	8-3-0
10	Illinois	10-2-0	Mike White	10-1-0
11	Clemson	9-1-1	Danny Ford	same
12	SMU	10-2-0	Bobby Collins	10-1-0
13	Air Force	10-2-0	Ken Hatfield	9-2-0
14	Iowa	9-3-0	Hayden Fry	9-2-0
15	Alabama	8-4-0	Ray Perkins	7-4-0
16	West Virginia	9-3-0	Don Nehlen	8-3-0
17	UCLA	7-4-1	Terry Donahue	6-4-1
18	Pittsburgh	8-3-1	Foge Fazio	8-2-1
19	Boston College	9-3-0	Jack Bicknell	9-2-0
20	East Carolina	8-3-0	Ed Emory	same

Key Bowl Games

Rankings below reflect final regular season poll, released Dec. 5. No bowl for then #12 Clemson (probation).

Orange–#5 Miami-FL over #1 Nebraska, 31-30; **Cotton**–#7 Georgia over #2 Texas, 10-9; **Sugar**–#3 Auburn over #8 Michigan, 9-7; **Rose**–UCLA over #4 Illinois, 45-9; **Holiday**–#9 BYU over Missouri, 21-17; **Gator**–#11 Florida over #10 Iowa, 14-6; **Fiesta**–#14 Ohio St. over #15 Pitt, 28-23.

1984

		After Bowls	Head Coach	Regular Season
1	BYU	13-0-0	LaVell Edwards	12-0-0
2	Washington	11-1-0	Don James	10-1-0
3	Florida	9-1-1	Charley Pell (0-1-1) & Galen Hall (9-0)	same
4	Nebraska	10-2-0	Tom Osborne	9-2-0
5	Boston College	10-2-0	Jack Bicknell	9-2-0
6	Oklahoma	9-2-1	Barry Switzer	9-1-1
7	Oklahoma St.	10-2-0	Pat Jones	9-2-0
8	SMU	10-2-0	Bobby Collins	9-2-0
9	UCLA	9-3-0	Terry Donahue	8-3-0
10	USC	9-3-0	Ted Tollner	8-3-0
11	South Carolina	10-2-0	Joe Morrison	10-1-0
12	Maryland	9-3-0	Bobby Ross	8-3-0
13	Ohio St.	9-3-0	Earle Bruce	9-2-0
14	Auburn	9-4-0	Pat Dye	8-4-0
15	LSU	8-3-1	Bill Arnsparger	8-2-1
16	Iowa	8-4-1	Hayden Fry	7-4-1
17	Florida St.	7-3-2	Bobby Bowden	7-3-1
18	Miami-FL	8-5-0	Jimmy Johnson	8-4-0
19	Kentucky	9-3-0	Jerry Claiborne	8-3-0
20	Virginia	8-2-2	George Welsh	7-2-2

Key Bowl Games

Rankings below reflect final regular season poll, released Dec. 3. No bowl for then #3 Florida (probation).

Holiday–#1 BYU over Michigan, 24-17; **Orange**–#4 Washington over #2 Oklahoma, 28-17; **Sugar**–#5 Nebraska over #11 LSU, 28-10; **Rose**–#18 USC over #6 Ohio St., 20-17; **Gator**–#9 Okla. St. over #7 S. Carolina, 21-14; **Cotton**–#8 BC over Houston, 45-28; **Aloha**–#10 SMU over #17 Notre Dame, 27-20.

1985

		After Bowls	Head Coach	Regular Season
1	Oklahoma	11-1-0	Barry Switzer	10-1-0
2	Michigan	10-1-1	Bo Schembechler	9-1-1
3	Penn St.	11-1-0	Joe Paterno	11-0-0
4	Tennessee	9-1-2	Johnny Majors	8-1-2
5	Florida	9-1-1	Galen Hall	same
6	Texas A&M	10-2-0	Jackie Sherrill	9-2-0
7	UCLA	9-2-1	Terry Donahue	8-2-1
8	Air Force	12-1-0	Fisher DeBerry	11-1-0
9	Miami-FL	10-2-0	Jimmy Johnson	10-1-0
10	Iowa	10-2-0	Hayden Fry	10-1-0
11	Nebraska	9-3-0	Tom Osborne	9-2-0
12	Arkansas	10-2-0	Ken Hatfield	9-2-0
13	Alabama	9-2-1	Ray Perkins	8-2-1
14	Ohio St.	9-3-0	Earle Bruce	8-3-0
15	Florida St.	9-3-0	Bobby Bowden	8-3-0
16	BYU	11-3-0	LaVell Edwards	11-2-0
17	Baylor	9-3-0	Grant Teaff	8-3-0
18	Maryland	9-3-0	Bobby Ross	8-3-0
19	Georgia Tech	9-2-1	Bill Curry	8-2-1
20	LSU	9-2-1	Bill Arnsparger	9-1-1

Key Bowl Games

Rankings below reflect final regular season poll, released Dec. 9. No bowl for then #6 Florida (probation).

Orange–#3 Oklahoma over #1 Penn St., 25-10; **Sugar**–#8 Tennessee over #2 Miami-FL, 35-7; **Rose**–#13 UCLA over #4 Iowa, 45-28; **Fiesta**–#5 Michigan over #7 Nebraska, 27-23; **Bluebonnet**–#10 Air Force over Texas, 24-16; **Cotton**–#11 Texas A&M over #16 Auburn, 36-16.

Associated Press Final Polls (Cont.)

1986

		After Bowls	Head Coach	Regular Season
1	Penn St.	12-0-0	Joe Paterno	11-0-0
2	Miami-FL	11-1-0	Jimmy Johnson	11-0-0
3	Oklahoma	11-1-0	Barry Switzer	10-1-0
4	Arizona St.	10-1-1	John Cooper	9-1-1
5	Nebraska	10-2-0	Tom Osborne	9-2-0
6	Auburn	10-2-0	Pat Dye	9-2-0
7	Ohio St.	10-3-0	Earle Bruce	9-3-0
8	Michigan	11-2-0	Bo Schembechler	11-1-0
9	Alabama	10-3-0	Ray Perkins	9-3-0
10	LSU	9-3-0	Bill Arnsparger	9-2-0
11	Arizona	9-3-0	Larry Smith	8-3-0
12	Baylor	9-3-0	Grant Teaff	8-3-0
13	Texas A&M	9-3-0	Jackie Sherrill	9-2-0
14	UCLA	8-3-1	Terry Donahue	7-3-1
15	Arkansas	9-3-0	Ken Hatfield	9-2-0
16	Iowa	9-3-0	Hayden Fry	8-3-0
17	Clemson	8-2-2	Danny Ford	7-2-2
18	Washington	8-3-1	Don James	8-2-1
19	Boston College	9-3-0	Jack Bicknell	8-3-0
20	Virginia Tech	9-2-1	Bill Dooley	8-2-1

Key Bowl Games

Rankings below reflect final regular season poll, released Dec. 1.

Fiesta—#2 Penn St. over #1 Miami-FL, 14-10; **Orange**—#3 Oklahoma over #9 Arkansas, 42-8; **Rose**—#7 Ariz. St. over #4 Michigan, 22-15; **Sugar**—#6 Nebraska over #5 LSU, 30-15; **Cotton**—#11 Ohio St. over #8 Texas A&M, 28-12; **Citrus**—#10 Auburn over USC, 16-7; **Sun**—#13 Alabama over #12 Washington, 28-6.

1988

		After Bowls	Head Coach	Regular Season
1	Notre Dame	12-0-0	Lou Holtz	11-0-0
2	Miami-FL	11-1-0	Jimmy Johnson	10-1-0
3	Florida St.	11-1-0	Bobby Bowden	10-1-0
4	Michigan	9-2-1	Bo Schembechler	8-2-1
5	West Virginia	11-1-0	Don Nehlen	11-0-0
6	UCLA	10-2-0	Terry Donahue	9-2-0
7	USC	10-2-0	Larry Smith	10-1-0
8	Auburn	10-2-0	Pat Dye	10-1-0
9	Clemson	10-2-0	Danny Ford	9-2-0
10	Nebraska	11-2-0	Tom Osborne	11-1-0
11	Oklahoma St.	10-2-0	Pat Jones	9-2-0
12	Arkansas	10-2-0	Ken Hatfield	10-1-0
13	Syracuse	10-2-0	Dick MacPherson	9-2-0
14	Oklahoma	9-3-0	Barry Switzer	9-2-0
15	Georgia	9-3-0	Vince Dooley	8-3-0
16	Washington St.	9-3-0	Dennis Erickson	8-3-0
17	Alabama	9-3-0	Bill Curry	8-3-0
18	Houston	9-3-0	Jack Pardee	9-2-0
19	LSU	8-4-0	Mike Archer	8-3-0
20	Indiana	8-3-1	Bill Mallory	7-3-1

Key Bowl Games

Rankings below reflect final regular season poll, released Dec. 5.

Fiesta—#1 Notre Dame over #3 West Va., 34-21; **Orange**—#2 Miami-FL over #6 Nebraska, 23-3; **Sugar**—#4 Florida St. over #7 Auburn, 13-7; **Rose**—#11 Michigan over #5 USC, 22-14; **Cotton**—#9 UCLA over #8 Arkansas, 17-3; **Citrus**—#13 Clemson over #10 Oklahoma, 13-6.

1987

		After Bowls	Head Coach	Regular Season
1	Miami-FL	12-0-0	Jimmy Johnson	11-0-0
2	Florida St.	11-1-0	Bobby Bowden	10-1-0
3	Oklahoma	11-1-0	Barry Switzer	11-0-0
4	Syracuse	11-0-1	Dick MacPherson	11-0-0
5	LSU	10-1-1	Mike Archer	9-1-1
6	Nebraska	10-2-0	Tom Osborne	10-1-0
7	Auburn	9-1-2	Pat Dye	9-1-1
8	Michigan St.	9-2-1	George Perles	8-2-1
9	UCLA	10-2-0	Terry Donahue	9-2-0
10	Texas A&M	10-2-0	Jackie Sherrill	9-2-0
11	Oklahoma St.	10-2-0	Pat Jones	9-2-0
12	Clemson	10-2-0	Danny Ford	9-2-0
13	Georgia	9-3-0	Vince Dooley	8-3-0
14	Tennessee	10-2-1	Johnny Majors	9-2-1
15	South Carolina	8-4-0	Joe Morrison	8-3-0
16	Iowa	10-3-0	Hayden Fry	9-3-0
17	Notre Dame	8-4-0	Lou Holtz	8-3-0
18	USC	8-4-0	Larry Smith	8-3-0
19	Michigan	8-4-0	Bo Schembechler	7-4-0
20	Arizona St.	7-4-1	John Cooper	6-4-1

Key Bowl Games

Rankings below reflect final regular season poll, released Dec. 7.

Orange—#2 Miami-FL over #1 Oklahoma, 20-14; **Fiesta**—#3 Florida St. over #5 Nebraska, 31-28; **Sugar**—#4 Syracuse tied #6 Auburn, 16-16; **Gator**—#7 LSU over #9 S. Carolina, 30-13; **Rose**—#8 Mich. St. over #16 USC, 20-17; **Aloha**—#10 UCLA over Florida, 20-16; **Cotton**—#13 Texas A&M over #12 Notre Dame, 35-10.

1989

		After Bowls	Head Coach	Regular Season
1	Miami-FL	11-1-0	Dennis Erickson	10-1-0
2	Notre Dame	12-1-0	Lou Holtz	11-1-0
3	Florida St.	10-2-0	Bobby Bowden	9-2-0
4	Colorado	11-1-0	Bill McCartney	11-0-0
5	Tennessee	11-1-0	Johnny Majors	10-1-0
6	Auburn	10-2-0	Pat Dye	9-2-0
7	Michigan	10-2-0	Bo Schembechler	10-1-0
8	USC	9-2-1	Larry Smith	8-2-1
9	Alabama	10-2-0	Bill Curry	10-1-0
10	Illinois	10-2-0	John Mackovic	9-2-0
11	Nebraska	10-2-0	Tom Osborne	10-1-0
12	Clemson	10-2-0	Danny Ford	9-2-0
13	Arkansas	10-2-0	Ken Hatfield	10-1-0
14	Houston	9-2-0	Jack Pardee	same
15	Penn St.	8-3-1	Joe Paterno	7-3-1
16	Michigan St.	8-4-0	George Perles	7-4-0
17	Pittsburgh	8-3-1	Mike Gottfried (7-3-1) & Paul Hackett (1-0)	7-3-1
18	Virginia	10-3-0	George Welsh	10-2-0
19	Texas Tech	9-3-0	Spike Dykes	8-3-0
20	Texas A&M	8-4-0	R.C. Slocum	8-3-0
21	West Virginia	8-3-1	Don Nehlen	8-2-1
22	BYU	10-3-0	LaVell Edwards	10-2-0
23	Washington	8-4-0	Don James	7-4-0
24	Ohio St.	8-4-0	John Cooper	8-3-0
25	Arizona	8-4-0	Dick Tomey	7-4-0

Key Bowl Games

Rankings below reflect final regular season poll, released Dec. 11. No bowl for then #13 Houston (probation).

Orange—#4 Notre Dame over #1 Colorado, 21-6; **Sugar**—#2 Miami-FL over #7 Alabama, 33-25; **Rose**—#12 USC over #3 Michigan, 17-10; **Fiesta**—#5 Florida St. over #6 Nebraska, 41-17; **Cotton**—#8 Tennessee over #10 Arkansas, 31-27; **Hall of Fame**—#9 Auburn over #21 Ohio St., 31-14; **Citrus**—#11 Illinois over #15 Virginia, 31-21.

1990

		After Bowls	Head Coach	Regular Season
1	Colorado	11-1-1	Bill McCartney	10-1-1
2	Georgia Tech	11-0-1	Bobby Ross	10-0-1
3	Miami-FL	10-2-0	Dennis Erickson	9-2-0
4	Florida St.	10-2-0	Bobby Bowden	9-2-0
5	Washington	10-2-0	Don James	9-2-0
6	Notre Dame	9-3-0	Lou Holtz	9-2-0
7	Michigan	9-3-0	Gary Moeller	8-3-0
8	Tennessee	9-2-2	Johnny Majors	8-2-2
9	Clemson	10-2-0	Ken Hatfield	9-2-0
10	Houston	10-1-0	John Jenkins	same
11	Penn St.	9-3-0	Joe Paterno	9-2-0
12	Texas	10-2-0	David McWilliams	10-1-0
13	Florida	9-2-0	Steve Spurrier	same
14	Louisville	10-1-1	H. Schnellenberger	9-1-1
15	Texas A&M	9-3-1	R.C. Slocum	8-3-1
16	Michigan St.	8-3-1	George Perles	7-3-1
17	Oklahoma	8-3-0	Gary Gibbs	same
18	Iowa	8-4-0	Hayden Fry	8-3-0
19	Auburn	8-3-1	Pat Dye	7-3-1
20	USC	8-4-1	Larry Smith	8-3-1
21	Mississippi	9-3-0	Billy Brewer	9-2-0
22	BYU	10-3-0	LaVell Edwards	10-2-0
23	Virginia	8-4-0	George Welsh	8-3-0
24	Nebraska	9-3-0	Tom Osborne	9-2-0
25	Illinois	8-4-0	John Mackovic	8-3-0

Key Bowl Games

Rankings below reflect final regular season poll, released Dec. 3. No bowl for then #9 Houston (probation), #11 Florida (probation) and #20 Oklahoma (probation).
Orange—#1 Colorado over #5 Notre Dame, 10-9; **Citrus**—#2 Ga. Tech over #19 Nebraska, 45-21; **Cotton** —#4 Miami-FL over #3 Texas, 46-3; **Blockbuster**—#6 Florida St. over #7 Penn St., 24-17; **Rose**—#8 Washington over #17 Iowa, 46-34; **Sugar**—#10 Tennessee over Virginia, 23-22; **Gator**—#12 Michigan over #15 Ole Miss, 35-3.

1991

		After Bowls	Head Coach	Regular Season
1	Miami-FL	12-0-0	Dennis Erickson	11-0-0
2	Washington	12-0-0	Don James	11-0-0
3	Penn St.	11-2-0	Joe Paterno	10-2-0
4	Florida St.	11-2-0	Bobby Bowden	10-2-0
5	Alabama	11-1-0	Gene Stallings	10-1-0
6	Michigan	10-2-0	Gary Moeller	10-1-0
7	Florida	10-2-0	Steve Spurrier	10-1-0
8	California	10-2-0	Bruce Snyder	9-2-0
9	East Carolina	11-1-0	Bill Lewis	10-1-0
10	Iowa	10-1-1	Hayden Fry	10-1-0
11	Syracuse	10-2-0	Paul Pasqualoni	9-2-0
12	Texas A&M	10-2-0	R.C. Slocum	10-1-0
13	Notre Dame	10-3-0	Lou Holtz	9-3-0
14	Tennessee	9-3-0	Johnny Majors	9-2-0
15	Nebraska	9-2-1	Tom Osborne	9-1-1
16	Oklahoma	9-3-0	Gary Gibbs	8-3-0
17	Georgia	9-3-0	Ray Goff	8-3-0
18	Clemson	9-2-1	Ken Hatfield	9-1-1
19	UCLA	9-3-0	Terry Donahue	8-3-0
20	Colorado	8-3-1	Bill McCartney	8-2-1
21	Tulsa	10-2-0	David Rader	9-2-0
22	Stanford	8-4-0	Dennis Green	8-3-0
23	BYU	8-3-2	LaVell Edwards	8-3-1
24	N.C. State	9-3-0	Dick Sheridan	9-2-0
25	Air Force	10-3-0	Fisher DeBerry	9-3-0

Key Bowl Games

Rankings below reflect final regular season poll, taken Dec. 2. **Orange**—#1 Miami-FL over #11 Nebraska, 22-0; **Rose**—#2 Washington over #4 Michigan, 34-14; **Sugar**—#18 Notre Dame over #3 Florida, 39-28; **Cotton**—#5 Florida St. over #9 Texas A&M, 10-2; **Fiesta**—#6 Penn St. over #10 Tennessee, 42-17; **Holiday**—#7 Iowa tied BYU, 13-13; **Blockbuster**—#8 Alabama over #15 Colorado, 30-25; **Citrus**—#14 California over #13 Clemson, 37-13.

1992

		After Bowls	Head Coach	Regular Season
1	Alabama	13-0-0	Gene Stallings	12-0-0
2	Florida St.	11-1-0	Bobby Bowden	10-1-0
3	Miami-FL	11-1-0	Dennis Erickson	11-0-0
4	Notre Dame	10-1-1	Lou Holtz	9-1-1
5	Michigan	9-0-3	Gary Moeller	8-0-3
6	Syracuse	10-2-0	Paul Pasqualoni	9-2-0
7	Texas A&M	12-1-0	R.C. Slocum	12-0-0
8	Georgia	10-2-0	Ray Goff	9-2-0
9	Stanford	10-3-0	Bill Walsh	9-3-0
10	Florida	9-4-0	Steve Spurrier	8-4-0
11	Washington	9-3-0	Don James	9-2-0
12	Tennessee	9-3-0	Johnny Majors (5-3) & Phillip Fulmer (4-0)	8-3-0
13	Colorado	9-2-1	Bill McCartney	9-1-1
14	Nebraska	9-3-0	Tom Osborne	9-2-0
15	Washington St.	9-3-0	Mike Price	8-3-0
16	Mississippi	9-3-0	Billy Brewer	8-3-0
17	N.C. State	9-3-1	Dick Sheridan	9-2-1
18	Ohio St.	8-3-1	John Cooper	8-2-1
19	North Carolina	9-3-0	Mack Brown	8-3-0
20	Hawaii	11-2-0	Bob Wagner	10-2-0
21	Boston College	8-3-1	Tom Coughlin	8-2-1
22	Kansas	8-4-0	Glen Mason	7-4-0
23	Mississippi St.	7-5-0	Jackie Sherrill	7-4-0
24	Fresno St.	9-4-0	Jim Sweeney	9-3-0
25	Wake Forest	8-4-0	Bill Dooley	7-4-0

Key Bowl Games

Rankings below reflect final regular season poll, taken Dec. 5. **Sugar**—#2 Alabama over #1 Miami-FL, 34-13; **Orange**—#3 Florida St. over #11 Nebraska, 27-14; **Cotton**—#5 Notre Dame over #4 Texas A&M, 28-3; **Fiesta**—#6 Syracuse over #10 Colorado, 26-22; **Rose**—#7 Michigan over #9 Washington, 38-31; **Citrus**—#8 Georgia over #15 Ohio St., 21-14.

1993

		After Bowls	Head Coach	Regular Season
1	Florida St	12-1-0	Bobby Bowden	11-1-0
2	Notre Dame	11-1-0	Lou Holtz	10-1-0
3	Nebraska	11-1-0	Tom Osborne	11-0-0
4	Auburn	11-0-0	Terry Bowden	11-0-0
5	Florida	11-2-0	Steve Spurrier	10-2-0
6	Wisconsin	10-1-1	Barry Alvarez	9-1-1
7	West Virginia	11-1-0	Don Nehlen	11-0-0
8	Penn St	10-2-0	Joe Paterno	9-2-0
9	Texas A&M	10-2-0	R.C. Slocum	10-1-0
10	Arizona	10-2-0	Dick Tomey	9-2-0
11	Ohio St	10-1-1	John Cooper	9-1-1
12	Tennessee	9-2-1	Phillip Fulmer	9-1-1
13	Boston College	9-3-0	Tom Coughlin	8-3-0
14	Alabama	9-3-1	Gene Stallings	8-3-1
15	Miami-FL	9-3-0	Dennis Erickson	9-2-0
16	Colorado	8-3-1	Bill McCartney	7-3-1
17	Oklahoma	9-3-0	Gary Gibbs	8-3-0
18	UCLA	8-4-0	Terry Donahue	8-3-0
19	North Carolina	10-3-0	Mack Brown	10-2-0
20	Kansas St	9-2-1	Bill Snyder	8-2-1
21	Michigan	8-4-0	Gary Moeller	7-4-0
22	Va. Tech	9-3-0	Frank Beamer	9-2-0
23	Clemson	9-3-0	Ken Hatfield (8-3) & Tommy West (1-0)	8-3-0
24	Louisville	9-3-0	H. Schnellenberger	8-3-0
25	California	9-4-0	Keith Gilbertson	8-4-0

Key Bowl Games

Rankings below reflect final regular season poll, taken Dec. 5. No bowl for then #5 Auburn (probation). **Orange**—#1 Florida St. over #2 Nebraska, 18-16; **Sugar**—#8 Florida over #3 West Virginia, 41-7; **Cotton**—#4 Notre Dame over #7 Texas A&M, 24-21; **Citrus**—#13 Penn St. over #6 Tennessee, 31-13; **Rose**—#9 Wisconsin over #14 UCLA, 21-16; **Fiesta**—#16 Arizona over #10 Miami-FL, 29-0;

Associated Press Final Polls (Cont.)

1994

		After Bowls	Head Coach	Regular Season
1	Nebraska	13-0-0	Tom Osborne	12-0-0
2	Penn St	12-0-0	Joe Paterno	11-0-0
3	Colorado	11-1-0	Bill McCartney	10-1-0
4	Florida St	10-1-1	Bobby Bowden	9-1-1
5	Alabama	12-1-0	Gene Stallings	11-1-0
6	Miami-FL	10-2-0	Dennis Erickson	10-1-0
7	Florida	10-2-1	Steve Spurrier	10-1-1
8	Texas A&M	10-0-1	R.C. Slocum	same
9	Auburn	9-1-1	Terry Bowden	same
10	Utah	10-2-0	Ron McBride	9-2-0
11	Oregon	9-4-0	Rich Brooks	9-3-0
12	Michigan	8-4-0	Gary Moeller	7-4-0
13	USC	8-3-1	John Robinson	7-3-1
14	Ohio St	9-4-0	John Cooper	9-3-0
15	Virginia	9-3-0	George Welsh	8-3-0
16	Colorado St	10-2-0	Sonny Lubick	10-1-0
17	N.C. State	9-3-0	Mike O'Cain	8-3-0
18	BYU	10-3-0	LaVell Edwards	9-3-0
19	Kansas St	9-3-0	Bill Snyder	9-2-0
20	Arizona	8-4-0	Dick Tomey	8-3-0
21	Washington St	8-4-0	Mike Price	7-4-0
22	Tennessee	8-4-0	Phillip Fulmer	7-4-0
23	Boston College	7-4-1	Dan Henning	6-4-1
24	Mississippi St	8-4-0	Jackie Sherrill	8-3-0
25	Texas	8-4-0	John Mackovic	7-4-0

Key Bowl Games

Rankings below reflect final regular season poll, taken Dec. 4. No bowls for then #8 Texas A&M (probation) and #9 Auburn (probation). **Orange**–#1 Nebraska over #3 Miami-FL, 24-17; **Rose**–#2 Penn St. over #12 Oregon, 38-20; **Fiesta**–#4 Colorado over Notre Dame, 41-24; **Sugar**–#7 Florida St. over #5 Florida, 23-17; **Citrus**–#6 Alabama over #13 Ohio St., 24-17; **Freedom**–#14 Utah over #15 Arizona, 16-13.

1995

		After Bowls	Head Coach	Regular Season
1	Nebraska	12-0-0	Tom Osborne	11-0-0
2	Florida	12-1-0	Steve Spurrier	12-0-0
3	Tennessee	11-1-0	Phillip Fulmer	10-1-0
4	Florida St	10-2-0	Bobby Bowden	9-2-0
5	Colorado	10-2-0	Rick Neuheisel	9-2-0
6	Ohio St	11-2-0	John Cooper	11-1-0
7	Kansas St	10-2-0	Bill Snyder	9-2-0
8	Northwestern	10-2-0	Gary Barnett	10-1-0
9	Kansas	10-2-0	Glen Mason	9-2-0
10	Va. Tech	10-2-0	Frank Beamer	9-2-0
11	Notre Dame	9-3-0	Lou Holtz	9-2-0
12	USC	9-2-1	John Robinson	8-2-1
13	Penn St	9-3-0	Joe Paterno	8-3-0
14	Texas	10-2-1	John Mackovic	10-1-1
15	Texas A&M	9-3-0	R.C. Slocum	8-3-0
16	Virginia	9-4-0	George Welsh	8-4-0
17	Michigan	9-4-0	Lloyd Carr	9-3-0
18	Oregon	9-3-0	Mike Bellotti	9-2-0
19	Syracuse	9-3-0	Paul Pasqualoni	8-3-0
20	Miami-FL	8-3-0	Butch Davis	same
21	Alabama	8-3-0	Gene Stallings	same
22	Auburn	8-4-0	Terry Bowden	8-3-0
23	Texas Tech	9-3-0	Spike Dykes	8-3-0
24	Toledo	11-0-1	Gary Pinkel	10-0-1
25	Iowa	8-4-0	Hayden Fry	7-4-0

Key Bowl Games

Rankings below reflect final regular season poll, taken Dec. 3. No bowl for then #21 Ala. (probation) and #22 Miami-FL (probation). **Fiesta**–#1 Neb. over #2 Fla., 62-24; **Rose**–#17 USC over #3 Northwestern, 41-32; **Citrus**–#4t Tenn. over #4t Ohio St., 20-14; **Orange**–#8 Fla. St. over #6 N. Dame, 31-26; **Cotton**–#7 Colo. over #12 Oregon, 38-6; **Sugar**–#13 Va. Tech over #9 Texas, 28-10.

1996

		After Bowls	Head Coach	Regular Season
1	Florida	12-1	Steve Spurrier	11-1
2	Ohio St	11-1	John Cooper	10-1
3	Florida St	11-1	Bobby Bowden	11-0
4	Arizona St	11-1	Bruce Snyder	11-0
5	BYU	14-1	LaVell Edwards	13-1
6	Nebraska	11-2	Tom Osborne	10-2
7	Penn St	11-2	Joe Paterno	10-2
8	Colorado	10-2	Rick Neuheisel	9-2
9	Tennessee	10-2	Phillip Fulmer	9-2
10	North Carolina	10-2	Mack Brown	9-2
11	Alabama	10-3	Gene Stallings	9-3
12	LSU	10-2	Gerry DiNardo	9-2
13	Virginia Tech	10-2	Frank Beamer	10-1
14	Miami-FL	9-3	Butch Davis	8-3
15	Northwestern	9-3	Gary Barnett	9-2
16	Washington	9-3	Jim Lambright	9-2
17	Kansas St.	9-3	Bill Snyder	9-2
18	Iowa	9-3	Hayden Fry	8-3
19	Notre Dame	8-3	Lou Holtz	same
20	Michigan	8-4	Lloyd Carr	8-3
21	Syracuse	9-3	Paul Pasqualoni	8-3
22	Wyoming	10-2	Joe Tiller	same
23	Texas	8-5	John Mackovic	8-4
24	Auburn	8-4	Terry Bowden	7-4
25	Army	10-2	Bob Sutton	10-1

Key Bowl Games

Rankings below reflect final regular season poll, taken Dec. 8. No bowl for then #18 N. Dame and #22 Wyoming. **Sugar**–#3 Fla. over #1 Fla. St., 52-20; **Rose**–#4 Ohio St. over #2 Ariz. St., 20-17; **Fiesta**–#7 Penn St. over #20 Texas, 38-15; **Cotton**–#5 BYU over #14 Kansas St., 19-15; **Citrus**–#9 Tenn. over #11 Northwestern, 48-28; **Orange**–#6 Neb. over #10 Va. Tech, 41-21.

1997

		After Bowls	Head Coach	Regular Season
1	Michigan	12-0	Lloyd Carr	11-0
2	Nebraska	13-0	Tom Osborne	12-0
3	Florida St	11-1	Bobby Bowden	10-1
4	Florida	10-2	Steve Spurrier	9-2
5	UCLA	10-2	Bob Toledo	9-2
6	North Carolina	11-1	Mack Brown (10-1) & Carl Torbush (1-0)	10-1 (1-0)
7	Tennessee	11-2	Phillip Fulmer	11-1
8	Kansas St	11-1	Bill Snyder	10-1
9	Washington St.	10-2	Mike Price	10-1
10	Georgia	10-2	Jim Donnan	9-2
11	Auburn	10-3	Terry Bowden	9-3
12	Ohio St.	10-3	John Cooper	10-2
13	LSU	9-3	Gerry DiNardo	8-3
14	Arizona St.	9-3	Bruce Snyder	7-3
15	Purdue	9-3	Joe Tiller	8-3
16	Penn St.	9-3	Joe Paterno	9-2
17	Colorado St.	11-2	Sonny Lubick	10-2
18	Washington	8-4	Jim Lambright	7-4
19	So. Mississippi	9-3	Jeff Bower	8-3
20	Texas A&M	9-4	R.C. Slocum	9-3
21	Syracuse	9-4	Paul Pasqualoni	9-3
22	Mississippi	8-4	Tommy Tuberville	7-4
23	Missouri	7-5	Larry Smith	6-5
24	Oklahoma St.	8-4	Bobby Simmons	8-3
25	Georgia Tech	7-5	George O'Leary	6-5

Key Bowl Games

Rankings below reflect final regular season poll, taken Dec. 7. **Rose**–#1 Michigan over #7 Washington St., 21-16; **Orange**–#2 Nebraska over #3 Tennessee, 42-17; **Sugar**–#4 Florida St. over #10 Ohio St., 31-14; **Gator**–#5 North Carolina over Virginia Tech, 42-3; **Cotton**–#6 UCLA over #19 Texas A&M, 29-23; **Citrus**–#8 Florida over #12 Penn St., 21-6; **Fiesta**–#9 Kansas St. over #14 Syracuse, 35-18.

1998

	Team	After Bowls	Head Coach	Regular Season
1	Tennessee	13-0	Phillip Fulmer	12-0
2	Ohio St.	11-1	John Cooper	10-1
3	Florida St.	11-2	Bobby Bowden	11-1
4	Arizona	12-1	Dick Tomey	11-1
5	Florida	10-2	Steve Spurrier	9-2
6	Wisconsin	11-1	Barry Alvarez	10-1
7	Tulane	12-0	Tommy Bowden	11-0
8	UCLA	10-2	Bob Toledo	10-1
9	Georgia Tech	10-2	George O'Leary	9-2
10	Kansas St.	11-2	Bill Snyder	11-1
11	Texas A&M	11-3	R.C. Slocum	11-2
12	Michigan	10-3	Lloyd Carr	9-3
13	Air Force	12-1	Fisher DeBerry	11-1
14	Georgia	9-3	Jim Donnan	8-3
15	Texas	9-3	Mack Brown	8-3
16	Arkansas	9-3	Houston Nutt	9-2
17	Penn St.	9-3	Joe Paterno	8-3
18	Virginia	9-3	George Welsh	9-2
19	Nebraska	9-4	Frank Solich	9-3
20	Miami-FL	9-3	Butch Davis	8-3
21	Missouri	8-4	Larry Smith	7-4
22	Notre Dame	9-3	Bob Davie	9-2
23	Va. Tech	9-3	Frank Beamer	8-3
24	Purdue	9-4	Joe Tiller	8-4
25	Syracuse	8-4	Paul Pasqualoni	8-3

Key Bowl Games

Rankings below reflect final regular season poll, taken Dec. 6. **Fiesta**– #1 Tennessee over #2 Florida St., 23-16; **Sugar**–#3 Ohio St. over #8 Texas A&M, 24-14; **Orange**–#7 Florida over #18 Syracuse, 31-10; **Rose**–#9 Wisconsin over #6 UCLA, 38-31; **Holiday**–#5 Arizona over #14 Nebraska, 23-20; **Alamo**–Purdue over #4 Kansas St., 37-34.

2000

	Team	After Bowls	Head Coach	Regular Season
1	Oklahoma	13-0	Bob Stoops	12-0
2	Miami-FL	11-1	Butch Davis	10-1
3	Washington	11-1	Rick Neuheisel	10-1
4	Oregon St.	11-1	Dennis Erickson	10-1
5	Florida St.	11-2	Bobby Bowden	11-1
6	Va. Tech	11-1	Frank Beamer	10-1
7	Oregon	10-2	Mike Bellotti	9-2
8	Nebraska	10-2	Frank Solich	9-2
9	Kansas St.	11-3	Bill Snyder	10-3
10	Florida	10-3	Steve Spurrier	10-2
11	Michigan	9-3	Lloyd Carr	8-3
12	Texas	9-3	Mack Brown	9-2
13	Purdue	8-4	Joe Tiller	8-3
14	Colorado St.	10-2	Sonny Lubick	9-2
15	Notre Dame	9-3	Bob Davie	9-2
16	Clemson	9-3	Tommy Bowden	9-2
17	Georgia Tech	9-3	George O'Leary	9-2
18	Auburn	9-4	Tommy Tuberville	9-3
19	South Carolina	8-4	Lou Holtz	7-4
20	Georgia	8-4	Jim Donnan	7-4
21	TCU	10-2	D. Franchione (10-1) & G. Patterson (0-1)	10-1
22	LSU	8-4	Nick Saban	7-4
23	Wisconsin	9-4	Barry Alvarez	8-4
24	Mississippi St.	8-4	Jackie Sherrill	7-4
25	Iowa St.	9-3	Dan McCarney	8-3

Key Bowl Games

Rankings below reflect final regular season poll, taken Dec. 4. **Orange**–#1 Oklahoma over #8 Florida St., 13-2; **Sugar**–#2 Miami-FL over #7 Florida, 37-20; **Rose**–#4 Washington over #14 Purdue, 34-24; **Fiesta**–#5 Oregon St. over #10 Notre Dame, 41-9; **Gator**–#6 Virginia Tech over #16 Clemson, 41-20; **Holiday**–#8 Oregon over #12 Texas, 35-30; **Alamo**–#9 Nebraska over #18 Northwestern, 66-17.

1999

	Team	After Bowls	Head Coach	Regular Season
1	Florida St.	12-0	Bobby Bowden	11-0
2	Va. Tech	11-1	Frank Beamer	11-0
3	Nebraska	12-1	Frank Solich	11-1
4	Wisconsin	10-2	Barry Alvarez	9-2
5	Michigan	10-2	Lloyd Carr	9-2
6	Kansas St.	11-1	Bill Snyder	10-1
7	Michigan St.	10-2	Nick Saban (9-2) & B. Williams (1-0)	9-2
8	Alabama	10-3	Mike DuBose	10-2
9	Tennessee	9-3	Phillip Fulmer	8-3
10	Marshall	13-0	Bob Pruett	12-0
11	Penn St.	10-3	Joe Paterno	9-3
12	Florida	9-4	Steve Spurrier	9-3
13	Mississippi St.	10-2	Jackie Sherrill	9-2
14	Southern Miss.	9-3	Jeff Bower	8-3
15	Miami-FL	9-4	Butch Davis	8-4
16	Georgia	8-4	Jim Donnan	7-4
17	Arkansas	8-4	Houston Nutt	7-4
18	Minnesota	8-4	Glen Mason	8-3
19	Oregon	9-3	Mike Bellotti	8-3
20	Georgia Tech	8-4	George O'Leary	8-3
21	Texas	9-5	Mack Brown	9-4
22	Mississippi	8-4	David Cutcliffe	7-4
23	Texas A&M	8-4	R.C. Slocum	8-3
24	Illinois	8-4	Ron Turner	7-4
25	Purdue	7-5	Joe Tiller	7-4

Key Bowl Games

Rankings below reflect final regular season poll, taken Dec. 5. **Sugar**–#1 Florida St. over #2 Va. Tech, 46-29; **Fiesta**–#3 Nebraska over #6 Tennessee, 31-21; **Rose**–#4 Wisconsin over #22 Stanford, 17-9; **Orange**–#8 Michigan over #5 Alabama, 35-34; **Holiday**–#7 Kansas St. over Washington, 24-20; **Citrus**–#9 Michigan St. over #10 Florida, 37-34.

2001

	Team	After Bowls	Head Coach	Regular Season
1	Miami-FL	12-0	Larry Coker	11-0
2	Oregon	11-1	Mike Bellotti	10-1
3	Florida	10-2	Steve Spurrier	9-2
4	Tennessee	11-2	Phillip Fulmer	10-2
5	Texas	11-2	Mack Brown	10-2
6	Oklahoma	11-2	Bob Stoops	10-2
7	LSU	10-3	Nick Saban	9-3
8	Nebraska	11-2	Frank Solich	11-1
9	Colorado	10-3	Gary Barnett	10-2
10	Washington St.	10-2	Mike Price	9-2
11	Maryland	10-2	Ralph Friedgen	10-1
12	Illinois	10-2	Ron Turner	10-1
13	South Carolina	9-3	Lou Holtz	8-3
14	Syracuse	10-3	Paul Pasqualoni	9-3
15	Florida St.	8-4	Bobby Bowden	7-4
16	Stanford	9-3	Tyrone Willingham	9-2
17	Louisville	11-2	John L. Smith	10-2
18	Va. Tech	8-4	Frank Beamer	8-3
19	Washington	8-4	Rick Neuheisel	8-3
20	Michigan	8-4	Lloyd Carr	8-3
21	Boston College	8-4	Tom O'Brien	7-4
22	Georgia	8-4	Mark Richt	8-3
23	Toledo	10-2	Tom Amstutz	9-2
24	Georgia Tech	8-5	George O'Leary (7-5) & Mac McWhorter (1-0)	7-5
25	BYU	12-2	Gary Crowton	12-1

Key Bowl Games

Rankings below reflect final regular season poll, taken Dec. 9. **Rose**–#1 Miami-FL over #4 Nebraska, 37-14; **Fiesta**–#2 Oregon over #3 Colorado, 38-16; **Orange**–#5 Florida over #6 Maryland, 56-23; **Sugar**–#12 LSU over #7 Illinois 47-34; **Citrus**–#8 Tennessee over #17 Michigan, 45-17; **Holiday**–#9 Texas over #21 Washington, 47-43; **Cotton**–#10 Oklahoma over Arkansas, 10-3;

Associated Press Final Polls (Cont.)

2002

		Head Coach	Regular Season
1	Ohio St. 14-0	Jim Tressel	13-0
2	Miami-FL 12-1	Larry Coker	12-0
3	Georgia 13-1	Mark Richt	12-1
4	USC 11-2	Pete Carroll	10-2
5	Oklahoma 12-2	Bob Stoops	11-2
6	Texas 11-2	Mack Brown	10-2
7	Kansas St. 11-2	Bill Snyder	10-2
8	Iowa 11-2	Kirk Ferentz	11-1
9	Michigan 10-3	Lloyd Carr	9-3
10	Washington St. ..10-3	Mike Price	10-2
11	Alabama 10-3	Dennis Franchione	10-3
12	N.C. State 11-3	Chuck Amato	10-3
13	Maryland 11-3	Ralph Friedgen	10-3
14	Auburn 9-4	Tommy Tuberville	8-4
15	Boise St. 12-1	Dan Hawkins	11-1
16	Penn St. 9-4	Joe Paterno	9-2
17	Notre Dame 10-3	Tyrone Willingham	10-2
18	Va. Tech 10-4	Frank Beamer	9-4
19	Pittsburgh 9-4	Walt Harris	8-4
20	Colorado 9-5	Gary Barnett	9-4
21	Florida St. 9-5	Bobby Bowden	9-4
22	Virginia 9-5	Al Groh	8-5
23	TCU 10-2	Gary Patterson	9-2
24	Marshall 11-2	Bob Pruett	10-2
25	West Virginia ...9-4	Rich Rodriguez	9-3

Key Bowl Games

Rankings below reflect final regular season poll, taken Dec. 8. No bowl for then #13 Alabama (probation). **Fiesta**–#2 Ohio St. over #1 Miami-FL, 31-24 (2OT); **Orange**–#5 USC over #3 Iowa, 38-17; **Sugar**–#4 Georgia over #16 Florida St. 26-13; **Holiday**–#6 Kansas St. over Arizona St., 34-27; **Rose**–#8 Oklahoma over #7 Washington St., 34-14; **Cotton**–#9 Texas over LSU, 35-20; **Capital One**–#19 Auburn over #10 Penn St., 13-9;

2004

		Head Coach	Regular Season
1	USC 13-0	Pete Carroll	12-0
2	Auburn 13-0	Tommy Tuberville	12-0
3	Oklahoma 12-1	Bob Stoops	12-0
4	Utah 12-0	Urban Meyer	11-0
5	Texas 11-1	Mack Brown	10-1
6	Louisville 11-1	Bobby Petrino	10-1
7	Georgia 10-2	Mark Richt	9-2
8	Iowa 10-2	Kirk Ferentz	9-2
9	California 10-2	Jeff Tedford	10-1
10	Virginia Tech ...10-3	Frank Beamer	12-1
11	Miami-FL 9-3	Larry Coker	8-3
12	Boise St. 11-1	Dan Hawkins	11-0
13	Tennessee 10-3	Philip Fullmer	9-3
14	Michigan 9-3	Lloyd Carr	8-3
15	Florida St. 9-3	Bobby Bowden	8-3
16	LSU 9-3	Nick Saban	9-2
17	Wisconsin 9-3	Barry Alvarez	9-2
18	Texas Tech 8-4	Mike Leach	7-4
19	Arizona St. 9-3	Dirk Koetter	8-3
20	Ohio St. 8-4	Jim Tressel	7-4
21	Boston College ..9-3	Tom O'Brien	8-3
22	Fresno St. 9-3	Pat Hill	8-3
23	Virginia 8-4	Al Groh	8-3
24	Navy 10-2	Paul Johnson	9-2
25	Pittsburgh 8-4	Walt Harris	8-3

Key Bowl Games

Rankings below reflect final regular season poll, taken Dec. 5. **Orange**–#1 USC over #2 Oklahoma, 55-19; **Sugar**–#3 Auburn over #9 Virginia Tech, 16-13; **Holiday**–#23 Texas Tech over #4 California, 45-31; **Fiesta**–#5 Utah over #19 Pittsburgh, 35-7; **Rose**–#6 Texas over #13 Michigan, 38-37; **Liberty**–#7 Louisville over #10 Boise St., 44-40; **Outback**–#8 Georgia over #16 Wisconsin, 24-21.

2003

		Head Coach	Regular Season
1	USC 12-1	Pete Carroll	11-1
2	LSU 13-1	Nick Saban	12-1
3	Oklahoma 12-2	Bob Stoops	12-1
4	Ohio State 11-2	Jim Tressel	10-2
5	Miami-FL 11-2	Larry Coker	10-2
6	Michigan 11-2	Lloyd Carr	11-1
7	Georiga 11-3	Mark Richt	10-3
8	Iowa 10-3	Kirk Ferentz	9-3
9	Washington St. ..10-3	Bill Doba	9-3
10	Miami-OH 13-1	Terry Hoeppner	12-1
11	Florida St. 10-3	Bobby Bowden	10-2
12	Texas 10-3	Mack Brown	10-2
13	Mississippi 10-3	David Cutliffe	9-3
14	Kansas St. 11-4	Bill Snyder	11-3
15	Tennessee 10-3	Phillip Fulmer	10-2
16	Boise St. 13-1	Dan Hawkins	12-1
17	Maryland 10-3	Ralph Friedgen	9-3
18	Purdue 9-4	Joe Tiller	9-3
19	Nebraska 10-3	Frank Solich (9-3) & Bo Pelini (1-0)	9-3
20	Minnesota 10-3	Glen Mason	9-3
21	Utah 10-2	Urban Meyer	9-2
22	Clemson 9-4	Tommy Bowden	8-4
23	Bowling Green ..11-3	Gregg Brandon	10-3
24	Florida 8-5	Ron Zook	8-4
25	TCU 11-2	Gary Patterson	11-1

Key Bowl Games

Rankings below reflect final regular season poll, taken Dec. 7. **Rose**–#1 USC over #4 Michigan, 28-14; **Sugar**–#2 LSU over #3 Oklahoma, 21-14; **Holiday**–#14 Washington St. over #5 Texas, 28-20; **Fiesta**–#6 Ohio St. over #10 Kansas St., 35-28; **Peach**–Clemson over #7 Tennessee, 27-14; **Orange**–#9 Miami-FL over #8 Florida St., 16-14.

2005

		Head Coach	Regular Season
1	Texas 13-0	Mack Brown	12-0
2	USC 12-1	Pete Carroll	12-0
3	Penn St. 11-1	Joe Paterno	10-1
4	Ohio St. 10-2	Jim Tressel	9-2
5	West Virginia ...11-1	Rich Rodriguez	10-1
6	LSU 11-2	Les Miles	10-2
7	Virginia Tech ...11-2	Frank Beamer	10-2
8	Alabama 10-2	Mike Shula	9-2
9	Notre Dame 9-3	Charlie Weis	9-2
10	Georgia 10-3	Mark Richt	9-3
11	TCU 11-1	Gary Patterson	10-1
12	Florida 9-3	Urban Meyer	8-3
	Oregon 10-2	Mike Bellotti	10-1
14	Auburn 9-3	Tommy Tuberville	9-2
15	Wisconsin 10-3	Barry Alvarez	9-3
16	UCLA 10-2	Karl Dorrell	9-2
17	Miami-FL 9-3	Larry Coker	9-2
18	Boston College ..9-3	Tom O'Brien	8-3
19	Louisville 9-3	Bobby Petrino	9-2
20	Texas Tech 9-3	Mike Leach	9-2
21	Clemson 8-4	Tommy Bowden	7-4
22	Oklahoma 8-4	Bob Stoops	7-4
23	Florida St. 8-5	Bobby Bowden	8-4
24	Nebraska 8-4	Bill Callahan	7-4
25	California 8-4	Jeff Tedford	7-4

Key Bowl Games

Rankings below reflect final regular season poll, taken Dec. 6. **Rose**–#2 Texas over #1 USC over 41-38; **Orange**–#3 Penn St. over #22 Florida St., 26-23 3OT; **Fiesta**–#4 Ohio St. over #5 Notre Dame, 34-20; **Holiday**– Oklahoma over #6 Oregon, 17-14; **Capital One**–#21 Wisconsin over #7 Auburn, 24-10; **Sugar**–#11 West Virginia over #8 Georgia, 38-35; **Peach**–#10 LSU over #9 Miami-FL, 40-3.

The Bowl Championship Series: a Convoluted History

Division I-A football remains the only NCAA sport on any level that does not have a sanctioned national champion. In an effort to clear up the confusion more than a decade ago, the Bowl Coalition was formed in 1992. The 1992 Coalition, which lasted three seasons, consolidated the resources of four major bowl games (the Cotton, Fiesta, Orange and Sugar), the champions of five major conferences (the ACC, Big East, Big Eight, Southeastern and Southwest) and the national following of independent Notre Dame. It worked two out of three years with #1 vs. #2 showdowns in the 1993 Sugar Bowl (#2 Alabama over #1 Miami-FL) and 1994 Orange Bowl (#1 Florida St. over #2 Nebraska). The 1995 Orange Bowl had to settle for #1 Nebraska beating #3 Miami-FL because #2 Penn St., the Big Ten champion, was obligated to play in the Rose Bowl.

It was updated and redubbed the Bowl Alliance in 1995 in an attempt to keep the bowl system intact while forcing an annual championship game between the regular season's two top-ranked teams. The Bowl Alliance ended a three-year run after the 1997 season.

Organized in 1998, the Bowl Championship Series is the organizers' latest attempt to finally guarantee that the teams ranked #1 and #2 will play each other in a "national title game" come January. The key difference from the 1992-97 Bowl Coalition/Bowl Alliance is that the Bowl Championship Series includes the Big 10 and Pac-10 champions. These teams, which were originally locked into playing in the Rose Bowl, were allowed under the new system to move to another bowl game in order to create a match-up featuring the #1 and #2 teams.

The bowls (the Fiesta, Orange, and Sugar) which made up the old Bowl Alliance kept their spots when the Rose Bowl joined this new four-bowl alliance. The Fiesta Bowl held the first national championship (#1 vs. #2) game under the Bowl Championship Series contract (Jan. 4, 1999 and then again in Jan. 3, 2003), it was followed by the Sugar (Jan. 4, 2000 and Jan. 4, 2004) the Orange (Jan. 3, 2001 and Jan. 4, 2005) and the Rose Bowl (Jan. 3, 2002 and Jan. 4, 2006). The BCS, using a complex and frequently evolving rankings system, has successfully matched the top two teams in the country (according to the AP Poll) in five of the last eight years.

Oklahoma played Florida St. in the BCS title game on Jan. 3, 2001 despite the fact that Miami-FL was #2 in the AP poll. FSU was the second-ranked team in the BCS rankings and therefore met Oklahoma, the top-ranked team, even though the Seminoles lost to Miami during the regular season. Controversy was averted when Oklahoma beat FSU 13-2 in the Orange Bowl. The following season, top-ranked Miami met BCS #2 Nebraska instead of Oregon, which was ranked second in both polls, at the Rose Bowl. Once again, total anarchy was avoided when Miami beat the Cornhuskers in the BCS title game to remain unbeaten.

The BCS's luck ran out following the 2003 season. The final BCS rankings matched the AP's #2 LSU (12-1) and #3 Oklahoma (12-1) in the Sugar Bowl but USC (11-1) sat atop the AP Poll but were third in the BCS rankings and met Michigan in the Rose Bowl. Both LSU and USC won their bowl games and the AP and Coaches polls split the national championship for the first time in the BCS era.

Originally, ABC paid the BCS members $525 million over seven years in rights fees for the four "title" games, with a three year option clause. The option was exercised in January 2000 and ABC and the BCS agreed on an additional eighth year as well.

With the 2006-07 season a separate BCS championship game will be added to be held one week following the four BCS bowls and therefore two more at-large teams will be added to the pool. The future schedule/locations for the BCS championship game: Jan. 8, 2007 (Glendale, Arizona); Jan. 8, 2008 (New Orleans, Louisiana); Jan. 8, 2009 (Miami, Florida); Jan. 8, 2010 (Pasadena, California).

All-Time BCS Top 20

The composite BCS Top 20 from the 1998 season through the 2005 season, based on the final rankings of each year. The original BCS rankings listed 15 teams from 1998-2002 before expanding the rankings to a Top 25 in 2003. Team point totals are based on 20 points for all 1st place finishes, 19 for each 2nd, etc. Also listed are the number of times each team has been ranked first, in the final Top 10 and Top 20.

		Pts	No.1	Top 10	Top 20
1	Texas	91	0	5	7
2	Miami-FL	90	2	5	6
3	Florida St	84	1	4	6
4	Oklahoma	83	2	4	5
5	USC	75	2	4	4
6	Tennessee	70	1	4	5
7	Ohio St	69	0	4	4
	Kansas St.	69	0	5	5
9	Florida	64	0	4	6
10	Nebraska	61	0	3	5
11	Virginia Tech	59	0	4	4
12	Georgia	55	0	3	4
13	Michigan	49	0	2	5
14	LSU	46	0	1	4
15	Oregon	44	0	3	3
16	Notre Dame	37	0	2	3
	Penn St	37	0	1	3
18	Wisconsin	33	0	2	4
	Iowa	33	0	1	3
20	Auburn	30	0	2	2

Bowl Games

From Jan. 1, 1902 through Jan. 4, 2005. Please note that the Bowl selection process is now dominated by the Bowl Championship Series (which includes the Fiesta, Orange, Rose and Sugar bowls) and the following non-BCS bowls' so called "automatic berths" are contingent upon several factors, including the leftovers from the BCS, Notre Dame's record and the record of their designated choices.

Rose Bowl

City: Pasadena, Calif. **Stadium:** Rose Bowl. **Capacity:** 102,083. **Playing surface:** Grass. **First game:** Jan. 1, 1902. **Playing sites:** Tournament Park (1902, 1916-22), Rose Bowl (1923-41 and since 1943) and Duke Stadium in Durham, N.C. (1942, due to wartime restrictions following Japan's attack at Pearl Harbor on Dec. 7, 1941). **Corporate sponsors:** AT&T (1998-2002), Sony Playstation 2 (2003) and Citi (2004).

Automatic berths: Pacific Coast Conference champion vs. opponent selected by PCC (1924-45 seasons); Big Ten champion vs. Pac-10 champion (1946-97); Bowl Championship Series: Big Ten champion vs. Pac-10 champion, if available (1998-2000, 2002-05 seasons) and #1 vs. #2 in Jan. 2002 and Jan. 2006.

Multiple wins: USC (21); Michigan (8); Washington (7); Ohio St. (6); Stanford and UCLA (5); Alabama (4); Illinois, Michigan St. and Wisconsin (3); California, Iowa and Texas (2).

Year		Year		Year	
1902*	Michigan 49, Stanford 0	1946	Alabama 34, USC 14	1977	USC 14, Michigan 6
1916	Washington St. 14, Brown 0	1947	Illinois 45, UCLA 14	1978	Washington 27, Michigan 20
1917	Oregon 14, Penn 0	1948	Michigan 49, USC 0	1979	USC 17, Michigan 10
1918	Mare Island 19, Camp Lewis 7	1949	Northwestern 20, California 14	1980	USC 17, Ohio St. 16
1919	Great Lakes 17, Mare Island 0	1950	Ohio St. 17, California 14	1981	Michigan 23, Washington 6
1920	Harvard 7, Oregon 6	1951	Michigan 14, California 6	1982	Washington 28, Iowa 0
1921	California 28, Ohio St. 0	1952	Illinois 40, Stanford 7	1983	UCLA 24, Michigan 14
1922	0-0, California vs Wash. & Jeff.	1953	USC 7, Wisconsin 0	1984	UCLA 45, Illinois 9
1923	USC 14, Penn St. 3	1954	Michigan St. 28, UCLA 20	1985	USC 20, Ohio St. 17
1924	14-14, Navy vs Washington	1955	Ohio St. 20, USC 7	1986	UCLA 45, Iowa 28
1925	Notre Dame 27, Stanford 10	1956	Michigan St. 17, UCLA 14	1987	Arizona St. 22, Michigan 15
1926	Alabama 20, Washington 19	1957	Iowa 35, Oregon St. 19	1988	Michigan St. 20, USC 17
1927	7-7, Alabama vs Stanford	1958	Ohio St. 10, Oregon 7	1989	Michigan 22, USC 14
1928	Stanford 7, Pittsburgh 6	1959	Iowa 38, California 12		
1929	Georgia Tech 8, California 7	1960	Washington 44, Wisconsin 8	1990	USC 17, Michigan 10
1930	USC 47, Pittsburgh 14	1961	Washington 17, Minnesota 7	1991	Washington 46, Iowa 34
1931	Alabama 24, Washington St. 0	1962	Minnesota 21, UCLA 3	1992	Washington 34, Michigan 14
1932	USC 21, Tulane 12	1963	USC 42, Wisconsin 37	1993	Michigan 38, Washington 31
1933	USC 35, Pittsburgh 0	1964	Illinois 17, Washington 7	1994	Wisconsin 21, UCLA 16
1934	Columbia 7, Stanford 0	1965	Michigan 34, Oregon St. 7	1995	Penn St. 38, Oregon 20
1935	Alabama 29, Stanford 13	1966	UCLA 14, Michigan St. 12	1996	USC 41, Northwestern 32
1936	Stanford 7, SMU 0	1967	Purdue 14, USC 13	1997	Ohio St. 20, Arizona St. 17
1937	Pittsburgh 21, Washington 0	1968	USC 14, Indiana 3	1998	Michigan 21, Washington St. 16
1938	California 13, Alabama 0	1969	Ohio St. 27, USC 16	1999	Wisconsin 38, UCLA 31
1939	USC 7, Duke 3	1970	USC 10, Michigan 3	2000	Wisconsin 17, Stanford 9
1940	USC 14, Tennessee 0	1971	Stanford 27, Ohio St. 17	2001	Washington 34, Purdue 24
1941	Stanford 21, Nebraska 13	1972	Stanford 13, Michigan 12	2002	Miami-FL 37, Nebraska 14
1942	Oregon St. 20, Duke 16	1973	USC 42, Ohio St. 17	2003	Oklahoma 34, Washington St. 14
1943	Georgia 9, UCLA 0	1974	Ohio St. 42, USC 21	2004	USC 28, Michigan 14
1944	USC 29, Washington 0	1975	USC 18, Ohio St. 17	2005	Texas 38, Michigan 37
1945	USC 25, Tennessee 0	1976	UCLA 23, Ohio St. 10	2006	Texas 41, USC 38
					* January game since 1902.

Fiesta Bowl

City: Glendale, Ariz. **Stadium:** Cardinals. **Capacity:** 73,000. **Playing surface:** Grass. **First game:** Dec. 27, 1971. **Playing site:** Sun Devil Stadium (since 1971). **Corporate title sponsors:** Sunkist Citrus Growers (1986-91), IBM OS/2 (1993-95) and Frito-Lay Tostitos chips (since 1996).

Automatic berths: Western Athletic Conference champion vs. at-large opponent (1971-79 seasons); Two of first five picks from 8-team Bowl Coalition pool (1992-94). Bowl Alliance (#1 vs. #2 on Jan. 2, 1996; #3 vs. #5 on Jan. 1, 1997; and #4 vs. #6 on Dec. 31, 1997); Big 12 champion vs. next best team in pool (New Bowl Alliance 1995-1997 seasons); Bowl Championship Series: #1 vs. #2 on Jan. 4, 1999, Jan., 2003 and Jan 2007 and Big 12 champion, if available, vs. at-large (1999-2001 and 2003-05 seasons).

Multiple wins: Penn St. (6); Arizona St. (5); Ohio St. (4); Florida St. and Nebraska (2).

Year		Year		Year	
1971†	Arizona St. 45, Florida St. 38	1985	UCLA 39, Miami-FL 37	1997†	Kansas St. 35, Syracuse 18
1972	Arizona St. 49, Missouri 35	1986	Michigan 27, Nebraska 23	1999	Tennessee 23, Florida St. 16
1973	Arizona St. 28, Pittsburgh 7	1987	Penn St. 14, Miami-FL 10	2000	Nebraska 31, Tennessee 21
1974	Oklahoma 16, BYU 6	1988	Florida St. 31, Nebraska 28	2001	Oregon St. 41, Notre Dame 9
1975	Arizona St. 17, Nebraska 14	1989	Notre Dame 34, West Va. 21	2002	Oregon 38, Colorado 16
1976	Oklahoma 41, Wyoming 7	1990	Florida St. 41, Nebraska 17	2003	Ohio St. 31, Miami-FL 24 (2OT)
1977	Penn St. 42, Arizona St. 30	1991	Louisville 34, Alabama 7	2004	Ohio St. 35, Kansas St. 28
1978	10-10, Arkansas vs UCLA	1992	Penn St. 42, Tennessee 17	2005	Utah 35, Pittsburgh 7
1979	Pittsburgh 16, Arizona 10	1993	Syracuse 26, Colorado 22	2006	Ohio St. 34, Notre Dame 20
1980	Penn St. 31, Ohio St. 19	1994	Arizona 29, Miami-FL 0	†December game from 1971-80 and in
1982*	Penn St. 26, USC 10	1995	Colorado 41, Notre Dame 24	'97.
1983	Arizona St. 32, Oklahoma 21	1996	Nebraska 62, Florida 24	*January game since 1982.
1984	Ohio St. 28, Pittsburgh 23	1997	Penn St. 38, Texas 15		

Sugar Bowl

City: Atlanta, Ga. **Stadium:** Georgia Dome. **Capacity:** 71,228. **Playing surface:** Turf. **First game:** Jan. 1, 1935. **Playing sites:** Tulane Stadium (1935-74), Louisiana Superdome (1975-2005), Georgia Dome (2006). **Corporate title sponsors:** USF&G Financial Services (1987-95) and Nokia (starting in 1995).

Automatic berths: SEC champion vs. at-large opponent (1976-91 seasons); SEC champion vs. one of first five picks from 8-team Bowl Coalition pool (1992-94 seasons); #4 vs. #6 on Dec. 31, 1995; #1 vs. #2 on Jan. 2, 1997; and #3 vs. #5 on Jan. 1, 1998; Bowl Championship Series: SEC champion, if available, vs. at-large (1998-99, 2000-02, 2004-05 seasons) and #1 vs. #2 on Jan. 4, 2000 and Jan. 2004.

Multiple wins: Alabama (8); Mississippi (5); Florida St., Georgia Tech, LSU, Oklahoma and Tennessee (4); Georgia and Nebraska (3); Auburn, Florida, Miami-FL, Notre Dame, Pittsburgh, Santa Clara and TCU (2).

Year		Year		Year	
1935*	Tulane 20, Temple 14	1960	Mississippi 21, LSU 0	1985	Nebraska 28, LSU 10
1936	TCU 3, LSU 2	1961	Mississippi 14, Rice 6	1986	Tennessee 35, Miami-FL 7
1937	Santa Clara 21, LSU 14	1962	Alabama 10, Arkansas 3	1987	Nebraska 30, LSU 15
1938	Santa Clara 6, LSU 0	1963	Mississippi 17, Arkansas 13	1988	16-16, Syracuse vs Auburn
1939	TCU 15, Carnegie Tech 7	1964	Alabama 12, Mississippi 7	1989	Florida St. 13, Auburn 7
		1965	LSU 13, Syracuse 10		
1940	Texas A&M 14, Tulane 13	1966	Missouri 20, Florida 18	1990	Miami-FL 33, Alabama 25
1941	Boston College 19, Tennessee 13	1967	Alabama 34, Nebraska 7	1991	Tennessee 23, Virginia 22
1942	Fordham 2, Missouri 0	1968	LSU 20, Wyoming 13	1992	Notre Dame 39, Florida 28
1943	Tennessee 14, Tulsa 7	1969	Arkansas 16, Georgia 2	1993	Alabama 34, Miami-FL 13
1944	Georgia Tech 20, Tulsa 18			1994	Florida 41, West Va. 7
1945	Duke 29, Alabama 26	1970	Mississippi 27, Arkansas 22	1995	Florida St. 23, Florida 17
1946	Okla. A&M 33, St. Mary's 13	1971	Tennessee 34, Air Force 13	1995†	Va. Tech 28, Texas 10
1947	Georgia 20, N. Carolina 10	1972	Oklahoma 40, Auburn 22	1997	Florida 52, Florida St. 20
1948	Texas 27, Alabama 7	1972†	Oklahoma 14, Penn St. 0	1998	Florida St. 31, Ohio St. 14
1949	Oklahoma 14, N. Carolina 6	1973	Notre Dame 24, Alabama 23	1999	Ohio St. 24, Texas A&M 14
		1974	Nebraska 13, Florida 10	2000	Florida St. 46, Va. Tech 29
1950	Oklahoma 35, LSU 0	1975	Alabama 13, Penn St. 6	2001	Miami-FL 37, Florida 20
1951	Kentucky 13, Oklahoma 7	1977*	Pittsburgh 27, Georgia 3	2002	LSU 47, Illinois 34
1952	Maryland 28, Tennessee 13	1978	Alabama 35, Ohio St. 6	2003	Georgia 26, Florida St. 13
1953	Georgia Tech 24, Mississippi 7	1979	Alabama 14, Penn St. 7	2004	LSU 21, Oklahoma 14
1954	Georgia Tech 42, West Va. 19			2005	Auburn 16, Va. Tech 13
1955	Navy 21, Mississippi 0	1980	Alabama 24, Arkansas 9	2006	West Virginia 38, Georgia 35
1956	Georgia Tech 7, Pittsburgh 0	1981	Georgia 17, Notre Dame 10		* January game from 1935-72 and
1957	Baylor 13, Tennessee 7	1982	Pittsburgh 24, Georgia 20		since 1977 (except in 1995).
1958	Mississippi 39, Texas 7	1983	Penn St. 27, Georgia 23		† Game played on Dec. 31 from
1959	LSU 7, Clemson 0	1984	Auburn 9, Michigan 7		1972-75 and in 1995.

Orange Bowl

City: Miami, Fla. **Stadium:** Dolphin. **Capacity:** 74,916. **Playing surface:** Grass. **First game:** Jan. 1, 1935. **Playing sites:** Orange Bowl (1935-95); Dolphin Stadium (since 1996). Dolphin Stadium was originally named Joe Robbie Stadium then was named Pro Player Stadium (1996-2004). **Corporate title sponsor:** Federal Express (since 1989).

Automatic berths: Big 8 champion vs. Atlantic Coast Conference champion (1953-57 seasons); Big 8 champion vs. at-large opponent (1958-63 seasons and 1975-91 seasons); Big 8 champion vs. one of first five picks from 8-team Bowl Coalition pool (1992-94 seasons); #3 vs. #5 on Jan. 1, 1996; #4 vs. #6 on Dec. 31, 1996; and #1 vs. #2 on Jan. 2, 1998 (New Bowl Alliance 1995-97 seasons); Bowl Championship Series: Big East or ACC champion, if available, vs. at-large (1998-99, 2001-03, 2005 seasons) and #1 vs. #2 Jan. 3, 2001 and Jan. 2005.

Multiple wins: Oklahoma (12); Nebraska (8); Miami-FL (6); Alabama and Penn St. (4); Florida, Florida State and Georgia Tech (3); Clemson, Colorado, Georgia, LSU, Notre Dame, Texas and USC (2).

Year		Year		Year	
1935*	Bucknell 26, Miami-FL 0	1955	Duke 34, Nebraska 7	1975	Notre Dame 13, Alabama 11
1936	Catholic U. 20, Mississippi 19	1956	Oklahoma 20, Maryland 6	1976	Oklahoma 14, Michigan 6
1937	Duquesne 13, Mississippi St. 12	1957	Colorado 27, Clemson 21	1977	Ohio St. 27, Colorado 10
1938	Auburn 6, Michigan St. 0	1958	Oklahoma 48, Duke 21	1978	Arkansas 31, Oklahoma 6
1939	Tennessee 17, Oklahoma 0	1959	Oklahoma 21, Syracuse 6	1979	Oklahoma 31, Nebraska 24
1940	Georgia Tech 21, Missouri 7	1960	Georgia 14, Missouri 0	1980	Oklahoma 24, Florida St. 7
1941	Mississippi St. 14, Georgetown 7	1961	Missouri 21, Navy 14	1981	Oklahoma 18, Florida St. 17
1942	Georgia 40, TCU 26	1962	LSU 25, Colorado 7	1982	Clemson 22, Nebraska 15
1943	Alabama 37, Boston College 21	1963	Alabama 17, Oklahoma 0	1983	Nebraska 21, LSU 20
1944	LSU 19, Texas A&M 14	1964	Nebraska 13, Auburn 7	1984	Miami-FL 31, Nebraska 30
1945	Tulsa 26, Georgia Tech 12	1965†	Texas 21, Alabama 17	1985	Washington 28, Oklahoma 17
1946	Miami-FL 13, Holy Cross 6	1966	Alabama 39, Nebraska 28	1986	Oklahoma 25, Penn St. 10
1947	Rice 8, Tennessee 0	1967	Florida 27, Georgia Tech 12	1987	Oklahoma 42, Arkansas 8
1948	Georgia Tech 20, Kansas 14	1968	Oklahoma 26, Tennessee 24	1988	Miami-FL 20, Oklahoma 14
1949	Texas 41, Georgia 28	1969	Penn St. 15, Kansas 14	1989	Miami-FL 23, Nebraska 3
1950	Santa Clara 21, Kentucky 13	1970	Penn St. 10, Missouri 3	1990	Notre Dame 21, Colorado 6
1951	Clemson 15, Miami-FL 14	1971	Nebraska 17, LSU 12	1991	Colorado 10, Notre Dame 9
1952	Georgia Tech 17, Baylor 14	1972	Nebraska 38, Alabama 6	1992	Miami-FL 22, Nebraska 0
1953	Alabama 61, Syracuse 6	1973	Nebraska 40, Notre Dame 6	1993	Florida St. 27, Nebraska 14
1954	Oklahoma 7, Maryland 0	1974	Penn St. 16, LSU 9	1994	Florida St. 18, Nebraska 16

Bowl Games (Cont.)
Orange Bowl (Cont.)

Year		Year		Year	
1995	Nebraska 24, Miami-FL 17	2001	Oklahoma 13, Florida St. 2	2006	Penn St. 26, Florida St. 23 3OT
1996	Florida St. 31, Notre Dame 26	2002	Florida 56, Maryland 23	* January game 1935-1996 and since	
1996**	Nebraska 41, Virginia Tech 21	2003	USC 38, Iowa 17	'98.	
1998*	Nebraska 42, Tennessee 17	2004	Miami-FL 16, Florida St. 14	** December game in 1996	
1999	Florida 31, Syracuse 10	2005	USC 55, Oklahoma 19	† Night game since 1965.	
2000	Michigan 35, Alabama 34				

Cotton Bowl

City: Dallas, Tex. **Stadium:** Cotton Bowl. **Capacity:** 68,252. **Playing surface:** Grass. **First game:** Jan 1, 1937. **Playing sites:** Fair Park Stadium (1937) and Cotton Bowl (since 1938). **Corporate title sponsor:** Mobil Corporation (1988-95), SBC Communications Inc., previously Southwestern Bell, (since 1997).

Automatic berths: SWC champion vs. at-large opponent (1941-91 seasons); SWC champion vs. one of first five picks from 8-team Bowl Coalition pool (1992-1994 seasons); second pick from Big 12 vs. first choice of WAC champion or second pick from Pac-10 (1995-97 seasons); Big 12 vs. SEC (since 1998).

Multiple wins: Texas (11); Notre Dame (5); Texas A&M (4); Alabama, Arkansas, Rice and Tennessee (3); Georgia, Houston, LSU, Mississippi, Penn St., SMU, TCU and UCLA (2).

Year		Year		Year	
1937*	TCU 16, Marquette 6	1962	Texas 12, Mississippi 7	1987	Ohio St. 28, Texas A&M 12
1938	Rice 28, Colorado 14	1963	LSU 13, Texas 0	1988	Texas A&M 35, Notre Dame 10
1939	St. Mary's 20, Texas Tech 13	1964	Texas 28, Navy 6	1989	UCLA 17, Arkansas 3
1940	Clemson 6, Boston College 3	1965	Arkansas 10, Nebraska 7	1990	Tennessee 31, Arkansas 27
1941	Texas A&M 13, Fordham 12	1966	LSU 14, Arkansas 7	1991	Miami-FL 46, Texas 3
1942	Alabama 29, Texas A&M 21	1966†	Georgia 24, SMU 9	1992	Florida St. 10, Texas A&M 2
1943	Texas 14, Georgia Tech 7	1968*	Texas A&M 20, Alabama 16	1993	Notre Dame 28, Texas A&M 3
1944	7-7, Texas vs Randolph Field	1969	Texas 36, Tennessee 13	1994	Notre Dame 24, Texas A&M 21
1945	Oklahoma A&M 34, TCU 0	1970	Texas 21, Notre Dame 17	1995	USC 55, Texas Tech 14
1946	Texas 40, Missouri 27	1971	Notre Dame 24, Texas 11	1996	Colorado 38, Oregon 6
1947	0-0, Arkansas vs LSU	1972	Penn St. 30, Texas 6	1997	BYU 19, Kansas St. 15
1948	13-13, SMU vs Penn St.	1973	Texas 17, Alabama 13	1998	UCLA 29, Texas A&M 23
1949	SMU 21, Oregon 13	1974	Nebraska 19, Texas 3	1999	Texas 38, Mississippi St. 11
1950	Rice 27, N. Carolina 13	1975	Penn St. 41, Baylor 20	2000	Arkansas 27, Texas 6
1951	Tennessee 20, Texas 14	1976	Arkansas 31, Georgia 10	2001	Kansas St. 35, Tennessee 21
1952	Kentucky 20, TCU 7	1977	Houston 30, Maryland 21	2002	Oklahoma 10, Arkansas 3
1953	Texas 16, Tennessee 0	1978	Notre Dame 38, Texas 10	2003	Texas 35, LSU 20
1954	Rice 28, Alabama 6	1979	Notre Dame 35, Houston 34	2004	Mississippi 31, Oklahoma St. 28
1955	Georgia Tech 14, Arkansas 6	1980	Houston 17, Nebraska 14	2005	Tennessee 38, Texas A&M 7
1956	Mississippi 14, TCU 13	1981	Alabama 30, Baylor 2	2006	Alabama 13, Texas Tech 10
1957	TCU 28, Syracuse 27	1982	Texas 14, Alabama 12	* January game from 1937-66 and
1958	Navy 20, Rice 7	1983	SMU 7, Pittsburgh 3	since 1968.
1959	0-0, TCU vs Air Force	1984	Georgia 10, Texas 9	† Game played on Dec. 31, 1966.
1960	Syracuse 23, Texas 14	1985	Boston College 45, Houston 28		
1961	Duke 7, Arkansas 6	1986	Texas A&M 36, Auburn 16		

Capital One Bowl

City: Orlando, Fla. **Stadium:** Florida Citrus Bowl. **Capacity:** 70,188. **Playing surface:** Grass. **First game:** Jan. 1, 1947. **Name change:** Tangerine Bowl (1947-82), Florida Citrus Bowl (1983-2002) and Capital One Bowl (since 2003). **Playing sites:** Tangerine Bowl (1947-72, 1974-82), Florida Field in Gainesville (1973), Orlando Stadium (1983-85) and Florida Citrus Bowl (since 1986). The Tangerine Bowl, Orlando Stadium and Florida Citrus Bowl are all the same stadium. **Corporate title sponsors:** Florida Department of Citrus (1983-2002), CompUSA (1992-99), Ourhouse.com (2000) and Capital One (since 2001).

Automatic berths: Championship game of Atlantic Coast Regional Conference (1964-67 seasons); Mid-American Conference champion vs. Southern Conference champion (1968-71 seasons); ACC champion vs. at-large opponent (1988-91 seasons); second pick from SEC, if available, vs. second pick from Big 10, if available (since 1992 season).

Multiple wins: Tennessee (4); Auburn, East Texas St., Miami-OH and Toledo (3); Catawba, Clemson, East Carolina, Florida, Georgia and Michigan (2).

Year		Year		Year	
1947*	Catawba 31, Maryville 6	1958†	E. Texas St. 26, Mo. Valley 7	1970	Toledo 40, Wm. & Mary 12
1948	Catawba 7, Marshall 0	1960*	Mid. Tenn. 21, Presbyterian 12	1971	Toledo 28, Richmond 3
1949	21-21, Murray St. vs Sul Ross St.	1960†	Citadel 27, Tenn. Tech 0	1972	Tampa 21, Kent St. 18
1950	St. Vincent 7, Emory & Henry 6	1961	Lamar 21, Middle Tenn. 14	1973	Miami-OH 16, Florida 7
1951	M. Harvey 35, Emory & Henry 14	1962	Houston 49, Miami-OH 21	1974	Miami-OH 21, Georgia 10
1952	Stetson 35, Arkansas St. 20	1963	Western Ky. 27, Coast Guard 0	1975	Miami-OH 20, S. Carolina 7
1953	E. Texas St. 33, Tenn. Tech 0	1964	E. Carolina 14, Massachusetts 13	1976	Oklahoma 49, BYU 21
1954	7-7, E. Texas St. vs Arkansas St.	1965	E. Carolina 31, Maine 0	1977	Florida St. 40, Texas Tech 17
1955	Neb.-Omaha 7, Eastern Ky. 6	1966	Morgan St. 14, West Chester 6	1978	N.C. State 30, Pittsburgh 17
1956	6-6, Juniata vs Missouri Valley	1967	Tenn-Martin 25, West Chester 8	1979	LSU 34, Wake Forest 10
1957	W. Texas St. 20, So. Miss. 13	1968	Richmond 49, Ohio U. 42	1980	Florida 35, Maryland 20
1958	E. Texas St. 10, So. Miss. 9	1969	Toledo 56, Davidson 33	1981	Missouri 19, Southern Miss. 17

Year		Year		Year	
1982	Auburn 33, Boston College 26	1993	Georgia 21, Ohio St. 14	2003	Auburn 13, Penn St. 9
1983	Tennessee 30, Maryland 23	1994	Penn St. 31, Tennessee 13	2004	Georiga 34, Purdue 27 OT
1984	17-17, Florida St. vs Georgia	1995	Alabama 24, Ohio St. 17	2005	Iowa 30, LSU 25
1985	Ohio St. 10, BYU 7	1996	Tennessee 20, Ohio St. 14	2006	Wisconsin 24, Auburn 10
1987*	Auburn 16, USC 7	1997	Tennessee 48, Northwestern 28		
1988	Clemson 35, Penn St. 10	1998	Florida 21, Penn St. 6	*January game from 1947-58, in	
1989	Clemson 13, Oklahoma 6	1999	Michigan 45, Arkansas 31	1960 and since 1987.	
1990	Illinois 31, Virginia 21	2000	Michigan St. 37, Florida 34	†December game in 1958, 1960-85.	
1991	Georgia Tech 45, Nebraska 21	2001	Michigan 31, Auburn 28		
1992	California 37, Clemson 13	2002	Tennessee 45, Michigan 17		

Gator Bowl

City: Jacksonville, Fla. **Stadium:** ALLTEL Stadium. **Capacity:** 73,000. **Playing surface:** Grass. **First game:** Jan. 1, 1946. **Playing sites:** Gator Bowl (1946-93), Florida Field in Gainesville (1994) and New Gator Bowl (since 1995). Name was changed to ALLTEL Stadium in 1997. **Corporate title sponsors:** Mazda Motors of America, Inc. (1986-91), Outback Steakhouse, Inc. (1992-94) and Toyota Motor Co. (since 1995).

Automatic berths: Third pick from SEC vs. sixth pick from 8-team Bowl Coalition pool (1992-94 seasons); second pick from ACC, if available, vs. second pick from Big East or Notre Dame, if available (since 1995 season).

Multiple wins: Florida (6); Florida St. and North Carolina (5); Auburn, Clemson (4); Georgia Tech, Maryland and Tennessee (3); Georgia, Miami-FL, Oklahoma, Pittsburgh, Texas Tech and Virginia Tech (2).

Year		Year		Year	
1946*	Wake Forest 26, S. Carolina 14	1968	Missouri 35, Alabama 10	1991†	Oklahoma 48, Virginia 14
1947	Oklahoma 34, N.C. State 13	1969	Florida 14, Tennessee 13	1992	Florida 27, N.C. State 10
1948	20-20, Maryland vs Georgia	1971*	Auburn 35, Mississippi 28	1993	Alabama 24, N. Carolina 10
1949	Clemson 24, Missouri 23	1971†	Georgia 7, N. Carolina 3	1994	Tennessee 45, Va. Tech 23
1950	Maryland 20, Missouri 7	1972	Auburn 24, Colorado 3	1996*	Syracuse 41, Clemson 0
1951	Wyoming 20, Wash. & Lee 7	1973	Texas Tech 28, Tennessee 19	1997	N. Carolina 20, West Va. 13
1952	Miami-FL 14, Clemson 0	1974	Auburn 27, Texas 3	1998	N. Carolina 42, Va. Tech 3
1953	Florida 14, Tulsa 13	1975	Maryland 13, Florida 0	1999	Ga. Tech 35, Notre Dame 28
1954	Texas Tech 35, Auburn 13	1976	Notre Dame 20, Penn St. 9	2000	Miami-FL 28, Ga. Tech 13
1954†	Auburn 33, Baylor 13	1977	Pittsburgh 34, Clemson 3	2001	Va. Tech 41, Clemson 20
1955	Vanderbilt 25, Auburn 13	1978	Clemson 17, Ohio St. 15	2002	Florida St. 30, Va. Tech 17
1956	Georgia Tech 21, Pittsburgh 14	1979	N. Carolina 17, Michigan 15	2003	N.C. State 28, Notre Dame 6
1957	Tennessee 3, Texas A&M 0	1980	Pittsburgh 37, S. Carolina 9	2004	Maryland 41, West Va. 7
1958	Mississippi 7, Florida 3	1981	N. Carolina 31, Arkansas 27	2005	Florida St. 30, West Va. 18
1960*	Arkansas 14, Georgia Tech 7	1982	Florida St. 31, West Va. 12	2006	Va. Tech 35, Louisville 24
1960†	Florida 13, Baylor 12	1983	Florida 14, Iowa 6	* January game from 1946-54, 1960,	
1961	Penn St. 30, Georgia Tech 15	1984	Oklahoma St. 21, S. Carolina 14	1965, 1971, 1989, 1991 and since	
1962	Florida 17, Penn St. 7	1985	Florida St. 34, Oklahoma St. 23	1996.	
1963	N. Carolina 35, Air Force 0	1986	Clemson 27, Stanford 21	† December game from 1954-58, 1960-	
1965*	Florida St. 36, Oklahoma 19	1987	LSU 30, S. Carolina 13	63, 1965-69, 1971-87, 1989 and	
1965†	Georgia Tech 31, Texas Tech 21	1989*	Georgia 34, Michigan St. 27	1991-94.	
1966	Tennessee 18, Syracuse 12	1989†	Clemson 27, West Va. 7		
1967	17-17, Florida St. vs Penn St.	1991*	Michigan 35, Mississippi 3		

Holiday Bowl

City: San Diego, Calif. **Stadium:** Qualcomm. **Capacity:** 71,000. **Playing surface:** Grass. **First game:** Dec. 22, 1978. **Playing site:** San Diego/Jack Murphy Stadium (since 1978). Name changed to Qualcomm Stadium in 1997. **Corporate title sponsors:** SeaWorld (1986-90), Thrifty Car Rental (1991-94), Chrysler-Plymouth Division of Chrysler Corp. (1995-97), U.S. Filter/Culligan Water Tech. (1998-2001) and Pacific Life Insurance Co. (since 2002).

Automatic berths: WAC champion vs. at-large opponent (1978-84, 1986-90 seasons); WAC champ vs. second pick from Big 10 (1991 season); WAC champ vs. third pick from Big 10 (1992-94 seasons); choice of WAC champion, if available, or second pick from Pac-10, if available vs. third pick from Big 12, if available (1995-99); second pick from Pac-10 vs. third pick from Big 12 (since 2000).

Multiple wins: BYU (4); Kansas St. (3) Iowa and Ohio St. (2).

Year		Year		Year	
1978†	Navy 23, BYU 16	1988	Oklahoma St. 62, Wyoming 14	1998	Arizona 23, Nebraska 20
1979	Indiana 38, BYU 37	1989	Penn St. 50, BYU 39	1999	Kansas St. 24, Washington 20
1980	BYU 46, SMU 45	1990	Texas A&M 65, BYU 14	2000	Oregon 35, Texas 30
1981	BYU 38, Washington St. 36	1991	13-13, Iowa vs BYU	2001	Texas 47, Washington 43
1982	Ohio St. 47, BYU 17	1992	Hawaii 27, Illinois 17	2002	Kansas St. 34, Arizona St. 27
1983	BYU 21, Missouri 17	1993	Ohio St. 28, BYU 21	2003	Washington St. 28, Texas 20
1984	BYU 24, Michigan 17	1994	Michigan 24, Colo. St. 14	2004	Texas Tech 45, California 31
1985	Arkansas 18, Arizona St. 17	1995	Kansas St. 54, Colorado St. 21	2005	Oklahoma 17, Oregon 14
1986	Iowa 39, San Diego St. 38	1996	Colorado 33, Washington 21		
1987	Iowa 20, Wyoming 19	1997	Colorado St. 35, Missouri 24	†December game since 1978.	

Bowl Games (Cont.)
Peach Bowl

City: Atlanta, Ga. **Stadium:** Georgia Dome. **Capacity:** 71,228. **Playing surface:** Turf. **First game:** Dec. 30, 1968. **Playing sites:** Grant Field (1968-70), Atlanta-Fulton County Stadium (1971-92) and Georgia Dome (since 1993). **Corporate title sponsor:** Chick-fil-A (since 1998).

Automatic berths: Third pick from ACC vs. at-large opponent (1992 season); third pick from ACC vs. fourth pick from SEC (1993-94 seasons); third pick from ACC, if available, vs. fourth pick from SEC, if available (since 1995 season).

Multiple wins: N.C. State (4); LSU and West Virginia (3); Auburn, Georgia, Miami-FL, North Carolina and Virginia (2).

Year		Year		Year	
1968†	LSU 31, Florida St. 27	1983	Florida St. 28, N. Carolina 3	1998*	Auburn 21, Clemson 17
1969	West Va. 14, S. Carolina 3	1984	Virginia 27, Purdue 24	1998†	Georgia 35, Virginia 33
1970	Arizona St. 48, N. Carolina 26	1985	Army 31, Illinois 29	1999	Mississippi St. 17, Clemson 7
1971	Mississippi 41, Georgia Tech 18	1986	Va. Tech 25, N.C. State 24	2000	LSU 28, Ga. Tech 14
1972	N.C. State 49, West Va. 13	1988*	Tennessee 27, Indiana 22	2001	N. Carolina 16, Auburn 10
1973	Georgia 17, Maryland 16	1988†	N.C. State 28, Iowa 23	2002	Maryland 30, Tennessee 3
1974	6-6, Vanderbilt vs Texas Tech	1989	Syracuse 19, Georgia 18	2004*	Clemson 27, Tennessee 14
1975	West Va. 13, N.C. State 10	1990	Auburn 27, Indiana 23	2004†	Miami-FL 27, Florida 10
1976	Kentucky 21, N. Carolina 0	1992*	E. Carolina 37, N.C. State 34	2005	LSU 40, Miami-FL 3
1977	N.C. State 24, Iowa St. 14	1993	N. Carolina 21, Miss. St. 17		†December game from 1968-79,
1978	Purdue 41, Georgia Tech 21	1993†	Clemson 14, Kentucky 13		1981-86, 1988-90, 1993, 1995,
1979	Baylor 24, Clemson 18	1995*	N.C. State 28, Miss. St. 24		1996, 1998, 1999-2002 and 2004.
1981*	Miami-FL 20, Va. Tech 10	1995†	Virginia 34, Georgia 27		*January game in 1981, 1988, 1992-
1981†	West Va. 26, Florida 6	1996	LSU 10, Clemson 7		93, 1995 and 1998 and 2004.
1982	Iowa 28, Tennessee 22				

Sun Bowl

City: El Paso, Tex. **Stadium:** Sun Bowl. **Capacity:** 52,000. **Playing surface:** Turf. **First game:** Jan. 1, 1936. **Name changes:** Sun Bowl (1936-85), John Hancock Sun Bowl (1986-88), John Hancock Bowl (1989-93) and Sun Bowl (since 1994). **Playing sites:** Kidd Field (1936-62) and Sun Bowl (since 1963). **Corporate title sponsors:** John Hancock Financial Services (1986-93), Norwest Bank (1996-98), Wells Fargo (1999-2003) and Vitalis (since 2004).

Automatic berths: Eighth pick from 8-team Bowl Coalition pool vs. at-large opponent (1992); Seventh and eighth picks from 8-team Bowl Coalition pool (1993-94 seasons); third pick from Pac-10, if available, vs. fifth pick from Big 10, if available (since 1995 season).

Multiple wins: Texas Western/UTEP (5); Alabama and Wyoming (3); Arizona St., Nebraska, New Mexico St., North Carolina, Oklahoma, Oregon, Pittsburgh, Southwestern, Stanford, Texas, UCLA, West Texas St. and West Virginia (2).

Year		Year		Year	
1936*	14-14, Hardin-Simmons vs New Mexico St.	1958†	Wyoming 14, Hardin-Simmons 6	1983	Alabama 28, SMU 7
1937	Hardin-Simmons 34, Texas Mines 6	1959	New Mexico St. 28, N. Texas 8	1984	Maryland 28, Tennessee 27
1938	West Va. 7, Texas Tech 6	1960	New Mexico St. 20, Utah St. 13	1985	13-13, Georgia vs Arizona
1939	Utah 26, New Mexico 0	1961	Villanova 17, Wichita St. 9	1986	Alabama 28, Washington 6
1940	0-0, Catholic U. vs Arizona St.	1962	West Texas 15, Ohio U. 14	1987	Oklahoma St. 35, West Va. 33
1941	W. Reserve 26, Arizona St. 13	1963	Oregon 21, SMU 14	1988	Alabama 29, Army 28
1942	Tulsa 6, Texas Tech 0	1964	Georgia 7, Texas Tech 0	1989	Pittsburgh 31, Texas A&M 28
1943	Second Air Force 13, Hardin-Simmons 7	1965	Texas Western 13, TCU 12	1990	Michigan St. 17, USC 16
1944	Southwestern 7, New Mexico 0	1966	Wyoming 28, Florida St. 20	1991	UCLA 6, Illinois 3
1945	Southwestern 35, U. of Mexico 0	1967	UTEP 14, Mississippi 7	1992	Baylor 20, Arizona 15
1946	New Mexico 34, Denver 24	1968	Auburn 34, Arizona 10	1993	Oklahoma 41, Texas Tech 10
1947	Cincinnati 18, Va. Tech 6	1969	Nebraska 45, Georgia 6	1994	Texas 35, N. Carolina 31
1948	Miami-OH 13, Texas Tech 12	1970	Georgia Tech 17, Texas Tech 9	1995	Iowa 38, Washington 18
1949	West Va. 21, Texas Mines 12	1971	LSU 33, Iowa St. 15	1996	Stanford 38, Michigan St. 0
1950	Tex. Western 33, Georgetown 20	1972	N. Carolina 32, Texas Tech 28	1997	Arizona St. 17, Iowa 7
1951	West Texas 14, Cincinnati 13	1973	Missouri 34, Auburn 17	1998	TCU 28, USC 19
1952	Texas Tech 25, Pacific 14	1974	Miss. St. 26, N. Carolina 24	1999	Oregon 24, Minnesota 20
1953	Pacific 26, Southern Miss. 7	1975	Pittsburgh 33, Kansas 19	2000	Wisconsin 21, UCLA 20
1954	Tex. Western 37, So. Miss. 14	1977*	Texas A&M 37, Florida 14	2001	Washington St. 33, Purdue 27
1955	Tex. Western 47, Florida St. 20	1977†	Stanford 24, LSU 14	2002	Purdue 34, Washington 24
1956	Wyoming 21, Texas Tech 14	1978	Texas 42, Maryland 0	2003	Minnesota 31, Oregon 30
1957	Geo. Wash. 13, Tex. Western 0	1979	Washington 14, Texas 7	2004	Arizona St. 27, Purdue 23
1958*	Louisville 34, Drake 20	1980	Nebraska 31, Miss. St. 17	2005	UCLA 50, Northwestern 38
		1981	Oklahoma 40, Houston 14		*January game from 1936-58 and in
		1982	N. Carolina 26, Texas 10		1977.
					†December game from 1958-75 and since 1977.

Outback Bowl

City: Tampa, Fla. **Stadium:** Raymond James. **Capacity:** 66,005. **Playing surface:** Grass. **First game:** Dec. 23, 1986. **Name change:** Hall of Fame Bowl (1986-95) and Outback Bowl (since 1995). **Playing sites:** Tampa/Houlihan's Stadium (1986-98) and Raymond James Stadium (since 1999). **Corporate title sponsor:** Outback Steakhouse, Inc. (since 1995).

Automatic berths: Fourth pick from ACC vs. fourth pick from Big 10 (1993-94 seasons); third pick from Big 10, if available, vs. third pick from SEC, if available (1995-99); fourth pick from Big 10 vs. third pick from SEC (2000 season).

Multiple wins: Georgia and Michigan (3); Penn St., South Carolina and Syracuse (2).

Year		Year		Year	
1986†	Boston College 27, Georgia 24	1995	Wisconsin 34, Duke 20	2003	Michigan 38, Florida 30
1988*	Michigan 28, Alabama 24	1996	Penn St. 43, Auburn 14	2004	Iowa 37, Florida 17
1989	Syracuse 23, LSU 10	1997	Alabama 17, Michigan 14	2005	Georgia 24, Wisconsin 21
1990	Auburn 31, Ohio St. 14	1998	Georgia 33, Wisconsin 6	2006	Florida 31, Iowa 24
1991	Clemson 30, Illinois 0	1999	Penn St. 26, Kentucky 14		
1992	Syracuse 24, Ohio St. 17	2000	Georgia 28, Purdue 25 OT	†December game in 1986.	
1993	Tennessee 38, Boston Col. 23	2001	S. Carolina 24, Ohio St. 7	*January game since 1988.	
1994	Michigan 42, N.C. State 7	2002	S. Carolina 31, Ohio St. 28		

Liberty Bowl

City: Memphis, Tenn. **Stadium:** Liberty Bowl Memorial. **Capacity:** 62,380. **Playing surface:** Grass. **First game:** Dec. 19, 1959. **Playing sites:** Municipal Stadium in Philadelphia (1959-63), Convention Hall in Atlantic City, N.J. (1964), Memphis Memorial Stadium (1965-75) and Liberty Bowl Memorial Stadium (since 1976). Memphis Memorial Stadium renamed Liberty Bowl Memorial in 1976. **Corporate title sponsors:** St. Jude's Hospital (since 1993), AXA/Equitable (since 1997).

Automatic berths: Commander-in-Chief's Trophy winner (Army, Navy or Air Force) vs. at-large opponent (1989-92 seasons); none (1993 season); first pick from independent group of Cincinnati, East Carolina, Memphis, Southern Miss. and Tulane vs. at-large opponent (for 1994 and '95 seasons); Conference USA champion vs. fourth pick from the Big East (1996-97 seasons); Conference USA champion, if available, vs. fifth, sixth or seventh pick or at-large from SEC (1998-99 seasons); Mountain West champion vs. Conference USA champion, if available (2000-05); SEC vs. Conference USA champ (since 2006).

Multiple wins: Mississippi (4); Penn St. and Tennessee (3); Air Force, Alabama, Louisville, N.C. State, Southern Miss., Syracuse and Tulane (2).

Year		Year		Year	
1959†	Penn St. 7, Alabama 0	1975	USC 20, Texas A&M 0	1991	Air Force 38, Mississippi St. 15
1960	Penn St. 41, Oregon 12	1976	Alabama 36, UCLA 6	1992	Mississippi 13, Air Force 0
1961	Syracuse 15, Miami-FL 14	1977	Nebraska 21, N. Carolina 17	1993	Louisville 18, Michigan St. 7
1962	Oregon St. 6, Villanova 0	1978	Missouri 20, LSU 15	1994	Illinois 30, E. Carolina 0
1963	Mississippi St. 16, N.C. State 12	1979	Penn St. 9, Tulane 6	1995	E. Carolina 19, Stanford 13
1964	Utah 32, West Virginia 6	1980	Purdue 28, Missouri 25	1996	Syracuse 30, Houston 17
1965	Mississippi 13, Auburn 7	1981	Ohio St. 31, Navy 28	1997	Southern Miss. 41, Pittsburgh 7
1966	Miami-FL 14, Virginia Tech 7	1982	Alabama 21, Illinois 15	1998	Tulane 41, BYU 27
1967	N.C. State 14, Georgia 7	1983	Notre Dame 19, Boston Col. 18	1999	Southern Miss. 23, Colorado St. 17
1968	Mississippi 34, Virginia Tech 17	1984	Auburn 21, Arkansas 15	2000	Colorado St. 22, Louisville 17
1969	Colorado 47, Alabama 33	1985	Baylor 21, LSU 7	2001	Louisville 28, BYU 10
1970	Tulane 17, Colorado 3	1986	Tennessee 21, Minnesota 14	2002	TCU 17, Colorado St. 3
1971	Tennessee 14, Arkansas 13	1987	Georgia 20, Arkansas 17	2003	Utah 17, Southern Miss. 0
1972	Georgia Tech 31, Iowa St. 30	1988	Indiana 34, S. Carolina 10	2004	Louisville 44, Boise St. 40
1973	N.C. State 31, Kansas 18	1989	Mississippi 42, Air Force 29	2005	Tulsa 31, Fresno St. 24
1974	Tennessee 7, Maryland 3	1990	Air Force 23, Ohio St. 11	† December game since 1959.	

Champs Sports Bowl

City: Orlando, Fla. **Stadium:** Florida Citrus Bowl. **Capacity:** 70,188. **Playing surface:** Grass. **First game:** Dec. 28, 1990. **Name change:** Blockbuster Bowl (1990-93), Carquest Bowl (1994-97), Micron PC Bowl (1998), MicronPC.com Bowl (1999-2000) and Tangerine Bowl (2001-03). The game was called the Sunshine Football Classic for a short time in the offseason after Carquest Auto Parts dropped its sponsorship and before Micron signed on. Also, this game should not be confused with the Tangerine Bowl that became the Citrus Bowl in 1982. **Playing sites:** Joe Robbie Stadium (1990-2000). Name changed to Pro Player Stadium in 1996; Florida Citrus Bowl (since 2001). ∂**Corporate title sponsors:** Blockbuster Video (1990-93), Carquest Auto Parts (1993-97), Micron Electronics (1998-2000), Mazda (2002-04) and Champs Sports (since 2005).

Automatic berths: Penn St. vs. seventh pick from 8-team Bowl Coalition pool (1992 season); third pick from Big East vs. fifth pick from SEC (1993-94 seasons); third pick from Big East vs. fifth pick from SEC (1995 season); third pick from Big East vs. fourth pick from ACC (1996-97 seasons); sixth pick from Big Ten, if available, vs. fourth pick from ACC, if available (1998-2000 seasons); fifth pick from ACC vs. third pick from Big East (2001).

Multiple wins: Georgia Tech, Miami-FL and N.C. State (2).

Year		Year		Year	
1990†	Florida St. 24, Penn St. 17	1997	Ga. Tech 35, W. Virginia 30	2003	N.C. State 56, Kansas 26
1991	Alabama 30, Colorado 25	1998	Miami-FL 46, N.C. State 23	2004	Ga. Tech 51, Syracuse 14
1993*	Stanford 24, Penn St. 3	1999	Illinois 63, Virginia 21	2005	Clemson 19, Colorado 10
1994	Boston College 31, Virginia 13	2000	N.C. State 38, Minnesota 30		
1995	S. Carolina 24, West Va. 21	2001	Pittsburgh 34, N.C. State 19	†December game from 1990-91 and	
1995†	N. Carolina 20, Arkansas 10	2002	Texas Tech 55, Clemson 15	since 1995.	
1996	Miami-FL 31, Virginia 21			*January game 1993-95.	

Bowl Games (Cont.)
Insight Bowl

City: Tempe, Ariz. **Stadium:** Sun Devil. **Capacity:** 73,379. **Playing surface:** Grass. **First game:** Dec. 31, 1989. **Name change:** Copper Bowl (1989-1996), Insight.com Bowl (1997-2001) and Insight Bowl (since 2002). **Playing sites:** Arizona Stadium (1989-2000), Chase Field (formerly Bank One Ballpark) (2000-05) and Sun Devil Stadium (2006–). **Corporate title sponsors:** Domino's Pizza (1990-91), Weiser Lock (1992-1996) and Insight Enterprises (since 1997).

Automatic berths: Third pick from WAC vs. at-large opponent (1992 season); third pick from WAC vs. fourth pick from Big Eight (1993-94 seasons); second pick from WAC vs. sixth pick from Big 12 (1995-97); third pick from Big East or Notre Dame, if available vs. fifth pick from Big 12, if available (1998-2001); third pick from Big East or Notre Dame, if available vs. fourth pick from Big East (since 2002).

Multiple wins: Arizona and California (2).

Year		Year		Year	
1989†	Arizona 17, N.C. State 10	1995	Texas Tech 55, Air Force 41	2001	Syracuse 26, Kansas St. 3
1990	California 17, Wyoming 15	1996	Wisconsin 38, Utah 10	2002	Pittsburgh 38, Oregon St. 13
1991	Indiana 24, Baylor 0	1997	Arizona 20, New Mexico 14	2003	California 52, Virginia Tech 49
1992	Washington St. 31, Utah 28	1998	Missouri 34, W. Virginia 31	2004	Oregon St. 38, Notre Dame 21
1993	Kansas St. 52, Wyoming 17	1999	Colorado 62, Boston College 28	2005	Arizona St. 45, Rutgers 40
1994	BYU 31, Oklahoma 6	2000	Iowa St. 37, Pittsburgh 29		

†December game since 1989.

MPC Computers Bowl

City: Boise, Idaho. **Stadium:** Bronco. **Capacity:** 30,000. **Playing surface:** Turf. **First game:** Dec. 29, 1997. **Playing sites:** Bronco Stadium (since 1997). **Corporate title sponsors:** World Sports Humanitarian Hall of Fame (since 1997) and Crucial.com (1999-2002), MPC Computers (since 2004).

Automatic berths: Big West champion, if available, vs. at-large (1997-2002) WAC vs. ACC (since 2004).

Multiple wins: Boise St. (3).

Year		Year		Year	
1997†	Cincinnati 35, Utah St. 19	2001	Clemson 49, La. Tech 24	2005	Boston College 27, Boise St. 21
1998	Idaho 42, Southern Miss. 35	2002	Boise St. 34, Iowa St. 16		
1999	Boise St. 34, Louisville 31	2004*	Georgia Tech 52, Tulsa 10	†December game 1997-2002 and '04.
2000	Boise St. 38, UTEP 23	2004†	Fresno St. 37, Virginia 34 OT	*January game in 2004

Las Vegas Bowl

City: Las Vegas, Nev. **Stadium:** Sam Boyd. **Capacity:** 40,000. **Playing surface:** Turf. **First game:** Dec. 18, 1992. **Playing site:** Sam Boyd Stadium (since 1992). **Corporate title sponsors:** EA Sports (1999-2000) Sega Sports (2001-02).

Automatic berths: Mid-American champion vs. Big West champion (1992-96 season); none (1997 season); second or third pick from WAC, if available vs. at-large (1998-2000), second pick from Mountain West vs. fifth pick from Pac-10 (since 2001).

Multiple wins: Fresno St. (4); UNLV (3); Bowling Green, San Jose St., Toledo and Utah (2).

Year		Year		Year	
1981†	Toledo 27, San Jose St. 25	1991	Bowling Green 28, Fresno St. 21	2001	Utah 10, USC 6
1982	Fresno St. 29, Bowling Green 28	1992	Bowling Green 35, Nevada 34	2002	UCLA 27, New Mexico 13
1983	Northern Ill. 20, CS-Fullerton 13	1993	Utah St. 42, Ball St. 33	2003	Oregon St. 55, New Mexico 14
1984*	UNLV 30, Toledo 13	1994	UNLV 52, C. Michigan 24	2004	Wyoming 24, UCLA 21
1985	Fresno St. 51, Bowling Green 7	1995	Toledo 40, Nevada 37 (OT)	2005	California 35, BYU 28
1986	San Jose St. 18, Miami-OH 7	1996	Nevada 18, Ball St. 15	†December game since 1981.
1987	E. Michigan 30, San Jose St. 27	1997	Oregon 41, Air Force 13	*Toledo later ruled winner of 1984
1988	Fresno St. 35, W. Michigan 30	1998	N. Carolina 20, San Diego St. 13	game by forfeit because UNLV used
1989	Fresno St. 27, Ball St. 6	1999	Utah 17, Fresno St. 16	ineligible players.
1990	San Jose St. 48, C. Michigan 24	2000	UNLV 31, Arkansas 14	

Note: The MAC and Big West champs met in a bowl game from 1981 to 1996, originally in Fresno at the California Bowl (1981-88, 1992) and California Raisin Bowl (1989-91). The results from 1981-91 are included above.

Independence Bowl

City: Shreveport, La. **Stadium:** Independence. **Capacity:** 50,832. **Playing surface:** Grass. **First game:** Dec. 13, 1976. **Playing site:** Independence Stadium (since 1976). **Corporate title sponsors:** Poulan/Weed Eater (1990-97), Sanford (1998-2000) and MainStay (since 2001). **Automatic berths:** Southland Conference champion vs. at-large opponent (1976-81 seasons); none (1982-95 seasons); fifth pick from SEC, if available, vs. at-large (1995-97 season); fifth, sixth or seventh pick from SEC, if available, vs. at-large (1998-99 season); sixth pick from Big 12 vs. SEC (since 2000 season).

Multiple wins: Mississippi (4); Air Force, LSU and Southern Miss (2).

Year		Year		Year	
1976†	McNeese St. 20, Tulsa 16	1987	Washington 24, Tulane 12	1998	Mississippi 35, Texas Tech 18
1977	La. Tech 24, Louisville 14	1988	Southern Miss 38, UTEP 18	1999	Mississippi 27, Oklahoma 25
1978	E. Carolina 35, La. Tech 13	1989	Oregon 27, Tulsa 24	2000	Mississippi St. 43, Texas A&M 41
1979	Syracuse 31, McNeese St. 7	1990	34-34, La. Tech vs Maryland	2001	Alabama 14, Iowa St. 13
1980	Southern Miss 16, McNeese St. 14	1991	Georgia 24, Arkansas 15	2002	Mississippi 27, Nebraska 23
1981	Texas A&M 33, Oklahoma St. 16	1992	Wake Forest 39, Oregon 35	2003	Arkansas 27, Missouri 14
1982	Wisconsin 14, Kansas St. 3	1993	Va. Tech 45, Indiana 20	2004	Iowa St. 17, Miami-OH 13
1983	Air Force 9, Mississippi 3	1994	Virginia 20, TCU 10	2005	Missouri 38, South Carolina 31
1984	Air Force 23, Va. Tech 7	1995	LSU 45, Michigan St. 26	†December game since 1976.
1985	Minnesota 20, Clemson 13	1996	Auburn 32, Army 29	
1986	Mississippi 20, Texas Tech 17	1997	LSU 27, Notre Dame 9	

Alamo Bowl

City: San Antonio, Tex. **Stadium:** Alamodome. **Capacity:** 65,000. **Playing surface:** Turf. **First game:** Dec. 31, 1993.
Playing site: Alamodome (since 1993). **Corporate title sponsor:** Builders Square (1993-98), Sylvania (1999-2001) and Mastercard (2004).
  Automatic berths: third pick from SWC vs. fourth pick from Pac-10 (1993-94 seasons); fourth pick from Big 10, if available vs. fourth pick from Big 12, if available (1995-99 seasons); fourth pick from Big 12 vs. third pick from Big 10 (2000 season).
  Multiple wins: Nebraska (3), Iowa and Purdue (2).

Year		Year		Year	
1993†	California 37, Iowa 3	1998	Purdue 37, Kansas St. 34	2003	Nebraska 17, Michigan St. 3
1994	Washington St. 10, Baylor 3	1999	Penn St. 24, Texas A&M 0	2004	Ohio St. 33, Oklahoma St. 7
1995	Texas A&M 22, Michigan 20	2000	Nebraska 66, Northwestern 17	2005	Nebraska 32, Michigan 28
1996	Iowa 27, Texas Tech 0	2001	Iowa 19, Texas Tech 16	†December game since 1993.	
1997	Purdue 33, Oklahoma St. 20	2002	Wisconsin 31, Colorado 28 (OT)		

Motor City Bowl

City: Detroit, Mich. **Stadium:** Ford Field. **Capacity:** 65,000. **Playing surface:** Turf. **First game:** Dec. 26, 1997. **Playing site:** Pontiac Silverdome (1997-2001) and Ford Field (since 2002). **Corporate title sponsor:** Ford Division of Ford Motor Company (since 1997), Daimler Chrysler and General Motors (since 2002). **Automatic berths:** Mid-American champions vs at-large (1997-99 season); Mid-American champions vs. fourth pick from Conference USA (2000 season).
  Multiple wins: Marshall (3).

Year		Year		Year	
1997†	Mississippi 34, Marshall 31	2001	Toledo 23, Cincinnati 16	2005	Memphis 38, Akron 31
1998	Marshall 48, Louisville 29	2002	Boston College 51, Toledo 25	†December game since 1997.	
1999	Marshall 21, BYU 3	2003	Bowling Green 28, N'western 24		
2000	Marshall 25, Cincinnati 14	2004	Connecticut 39, Toledo 10		

Music City Bowl

City: Nashville, Tenn. **Stadium:** LP Field. **Capacity:** 67,000. **Playing surface:** Grass. **First game:** Dec. 29, 1998.
Playing sites: Vanderbilt Stadium (1998) and Adelphia Coliseum (since 1999). **Corporate title sponsors:** American General (1998), HomePoint.com (1999-2000) and Gaylord Hotels (since 2002). **Automatic berths:** sixth choice from the SEC, if available, vs. at-large (1998-99 season); fourth pick from Big East, if available vs. SEC (2000-01).
  Multiple wins: Minnesota (2).

Year		Year		Year	
1998†	Va. Tech 38, Alabama 7	2001	Boston College 20, Georgia 16	2004	Minnesota 20, Alabama 16
1999	Syracuse 20, Kentucky 13	2002	Minnesota 29, Arkansas 14	2005	Virginia 34, Minnesota 31
2000	West Va. 49, Mississippi 38	2003	Auburn 28, Wisconsin 14	†December game since 1998.	

GMAC Bowl

City: Mobile, Ala. **Stadium:** Ladd-Peebles. **Capacity:** 40,646. **Playing surface:** Grass. **First game:** Dec. 22, 1999.
Name change: Mobile Bowl (1999-2000), GMAC Bowl (since 2001). **Playing sites:** Ladd-Peebles Stadium (since 1999).
Corporate title sponsors: GMAC Financial Services (since 2001). **Automatic berths:** WAC champions (if team is from the east) or second pick from WAC vs. second pick from Conference USA, if available (2000 season).
Multiple wins: Marshall (2).

Year		Year		Year	
1999†	TCU 28, E. Carolina 14	2002	Marshall 38, Louisville 15	2005	Toledo 45, UTEP 13
2000	So. Miss 28, TCU 21	2003	Miami-OH 49, Louisville 28	†December game since 1999.	
2001	Marshall 64, East Carolina 61	2004	Bowling Green 52, Memphis 35		

Houston Bowl

City: Houston, Tex. **Stadium:** Reliant. **Capacity:** 69,500. **Playing surface:** Turf. **First game:** Dec. 27, 2000. **Name change:** GalleryFurniture.com Bowl (2000-01), Houston Bowl (2002) and EV1.net Houston Bowl (since 2003). **Playing sites:** Astrodome (2000-2002), Reliant Stadium (since 2003). **Corporate title sponsors:** GalleryFurniture.com (2000-2002) and EV1 (since 2003). **Automatic berths:** Big 12 vs. Conference USA.

Year		Year		Year	
2000†	E. Carolina 40, Tex. Tech 27	2002	Oklahoma St. 33, So. Miss. 23	2004	Colorado 33, UTEP 28
2001	Texas A&M 28, TCU 9	2003	Texas Tech 38, Navy 14	2005	TCU 27, Iowa St. 24
				†December game since 2000.	

New Orleans Bowl

City: Lafayette, La. **Stadium:** Cajun Field. **Capacity:** 31,000. **Playing surface:** Grass. **First game:** Dec. 18, 2001.
Playing sites: Louisiana Superdome (2001-04), Cajun Field (2005). **Corporate title sponsors:** Wyndam Hotels (since 2004). **Automatic berths:** Sun Belt champion vs. Conference USA (since 2002).
Multiple wins: Southern Mississippi (2).

Year		Year		Year	
2001†	Colorado St. 45, North Texas 20	2003	Memphis 27, North Texas 17	2005	So. Miss. 31, Arkansas St. 19
2002	North Texas 24, Cincinnati 19	2004	So. Miss. 31, North Texas 10	†December game since 2001.	

Bowl Games (Cont.)

Emerald Bowl

City: San Francisco, Calif. **Stadium:** SBC Park. **Capacity:** 37,000. **Playing surface:** Grass. **First game:** Dec. 31, 2002. **Name change:** Diamond Walnut San Francisco Bowl (2002-03), Emerald Bowl (since 2004). **Playing sites:** SBC (formerly known as Pacific Bell) Park (since 2002). **Corporate title sponsors:** Diamond Walnut (2002-03), Emerald Nuts (since 2004). **Automatic berths:** Mountain West vs. Big East or Notre Dame (2002-03).

Year		Year		Year	
2002†	Virginia Tech 20, Air Force 13	2004	Navy 34, New Mexico 19	2005	Utah 38, Georgia Tech 10
2003	Boston Col. 35, Colorado St. 21				

†December game since 2002.

Meineke Car Care Bowl

City: Charlotte, N.C. **Stadium:** Bank of America. **Capacity:** 73,367. **Playing surface:** Grass. **First game:** Dec. 28, 2002. **Name change:** Continental Tire Bowl (2002-04), Meineke Car Care Bowl (starting in Dec. 2005). **Playing sites:** Bank of America (formerly known as Ericsson) Stadium (since 2002). **Corporate title sponsors:** Continental Tire North America (2002-04), Meineke Car Care (since 2005). **Automatic berths:** ACC vs. Big East or Notre Dame (since 2002).

Year		Year		
2002†	Virginia 48, West Va. 22	2004	Boston Col. 37, N. Carolina 24	†December game since 2002.
2003	Virginia 23, Pittsburgh 16	2005	N.C. State 14, So. Florida 0	

Hawaii Bowl

City: Honolulu, Hi. **Stadium:** Aloha Bowl. **Capacity:** 50,000. **Playing surface:** Turf. **First game:** Dec. 25, 2002. **Playing sites:** Aloha Bowl (since 2002). **Corporate title sponsors:** ConAgra Foods (2002) and Sheraton Hotels & Resorts (since 2003). **Automatic berths:** Hawaii (if bowl eligible) otherwise another WAC school vs. Conference USA (since 2002). **Multiple wins:** Hawaii (2).

Year		Year		
2002†	Tulane 36, Hawaii 28	2004	Hawaii 59, UAB 40	
2003	Hawaii 54, Houston 48 (3OT)	2005	Nevada 49, C. Florida 48 OT	†December game since 2002.

Fort Worth Bowl

City: Fort Worth, Tex. **Stadium:** Amon Carter. **Capacity:** 46,000. **Playing surface:** Grass **First game:** Dec. 23, 2003. **Playing sites:** Amon Carter Stadium (since 2003). **Corporate title sponsors:** PlainsCapital Corp. (since 2003). **Automatic berths:** Big 12 vs. Conference USA (since 2003).

Year		Year		
2003†	Bosie St. 34, TCU 31	2005	Kansas 42, Houston 13	
2004	Cincinnati 32, Marshall 14			†December game since 2003.

Poinsettia Bowl

City: San Diego, Calif. **Stadium:** Qualcomm Stadium. **Capacity:** 71,500. **Playing surface:** Grass **First game:** Dec. 22, 2005. **Playing sites:** Qualcomm Stadium (since 2005). **Corporate title sponsors:** San Diego County Credit Union. (since 2005). **Automatic berths:** Mountain West vs. at-large (since 2005).

Year		
2005†	Navy 51, Colorado St. 30	†December game since 2005.

NCAA certifies 31 Bowl Games for 2006-07

Among those certified were the newly established **Birmingham Bowl** to be played Dec. 23, 2006 in Birmingham, Alabama between a team from Conference USA and one from either the Big East or MAC, the **New Mexico Bowl** to be played Dec. 23, 2006 in Albuquerque, New Mexico between a team from the Mountain West and the WAC and the **International Bowl** to be played Jan. 6, 2007 in Toronto, Canada between a team from the MAC and the Big East. Also new for the 2006-07 Bowl season will be the **BCS Championship Game** set for Jan. 8, 2007 at the University of Phoenix Stadium in Glendale, Arizona, matching the two top ranked teams following the four BCS bowls.

The NCAA will adopt a 12- game regular season and the board of directors passed legislation to allow teams that finish with a record of 6-6 to qualify for a bowl game. However, a team with a 6-6 record can only play in a bowl game that is not contracted with its conference after all teams with records better than 6-6 have gotten bowl bids.

Division I-A Teams

Schools classified as Division I-A for at least 10 years; through 2005 season (including bowl games).

Top 25 Winning Percentage

		Yrs	Gm	W	L	T	Pct	Bowls App	Record	2005 Season Bowl	Record
1	Michigan	126	1165	849	280	36	.7442	37	18-19-0	lost Alamo	7-5
2	Notre Dame	117	1119	811	266	42	.7435	27	13-14-0	lost Fiesta	9-3
3	Texas	113	1143	800	313	33	.714	45	22-21-2	won Rose	13-0
4	Oklahoma	111	1099	757	289	53	.713	39	24-14-1	won Holiday	8-4
5	Alabama*	111	1118	774	301	43	.712	53	30-20-3	won Cotton	10-2
6	Ohio St.	116	1127	774	300	53	.710	37	18-19-0	won Sugar	10-2
7	Nebraska	116	1155	794	321	40	.705	43	22-21-0	won Alamo	8-4
8	USC	113	1084	732	298	54	.700	44	28-16-0	lost Rose	12-1
9	Tennessee*	109	1114	751	311	52	.697	45	24-21-0	none	5-6
10	Penn St.	119	1151	771	339	41	.688	38	24-12-2	won Orange	11-1
11	Boise St.	38	446	304	140	2	.684	6	4-2-0	lost MPC Computers	9-4
12	Florida St.*	59	658	436	205	17	.676	34	19-13-2	lost Orange	8-5
13	Georgia	112	1122	693	375	54	.642	41	22-16-3	lost Sugar	10-3
14	Miami-OH*	117	1035	639	352	44	.639	9	6-3-0	none	7-4
15	Miami-FL	79	835	525	291	19	.638	30	17-13-0	lost Peach	9-3
16	LSU*	112	1090	669	374	47	.635	37	18-18-1	won Peach	11-2
17	Washington*	116	1063	641	372	50	.627	29	14-14-1	none	2-9
18	Auburn*	113	1085	656	382	47	.626	32	17-13-2	lost Capital One	9-3
19	Arizona St.	93	865	523	318	24	.618	22	12-9-1	won Insight	7-5
20	Florida	99	1013	606	367	40	.618	33	14-19-0	lost Outback	9-3
21	Colorado*	116	1088	650	402	36	.614	27	12-15-0	lost Champs Sports	7-6
22	Central Michigan	105	906	532	338	36	.607	2	0-2-0	none	4-7
23	UCLA	87	896	521	338	37	.602	27	13-13-1	won Sun	10-2
24	Texas A&M	111	1102	639	415	48	.602	28	13-15-0	none	5-6
25	Bowling Green	87	820	465	303	52	.599	7	4-3-0	none	6-5

*Includes games forfeited following rulings by the NCAA Executive Council and/or the Committee on Infractions.

Top 50 Victories

		Wins			Wins			Wins
1	Michigan	.849	19	Miami-OH	.639	37	Rutgers	.569
2	Notre Dame	.811	20	Georgia Tech	.637		Missouri	.569
3	Texas	.800	21	Pittsburgh	.633	39	Utah	.566
4	Nebraska	.794	22	Army	.628	40	Purdue	.550
5	Alabama	.774		Arkansas	.628	41	Illinois	.547
	Ohio St	.774	24	Virginia Tech	.626	42	Iowa	.546
7	Penn St	.771	25	North Carolina	.624	43	Kentucky	.542
8	Oklahoma	.757	26	Minnesota	.623		Stanford	.542
9	Tennessee	.751	27	Clemson	.608	45	Vanderbilt	.538
10	USC	.732	28	Navy	.607	46	Kansas	.537
11	Georgia	.693	29	Florida	.606	47	Central Michigan	.532
12	LSU	.669	30	Virginia	.593		Oregon	.532
13	Syracuse	.665	31	California	.592	49	Arizona	.525
14	Auburn	.656	32	Mississippi	.590	50	Miami-FL	.525
15	Colorado	.650		Michigan St	.590			
16	West Virginia	.642	34	Boston College	.579			
17	Washington	.641	35	Maryland	.576			
18	Texas A&M	.639	36	Wisconsin	.575			

Top 30 Bowl Appearances

		App	Record			App	Record			App	Record
1	Alabama	53	30-20-3	12	Arkansas	34	11-20-3	23	Notre Dame	27	13-14-0
2	Tennessee	45	24-21-0		Georgia Tech	34	22-12-0		Colorado	27	12-15-0
	Texas	45	22-21-2		Florida St	34	19-13-2		UCLA	27	13-13-1
4	USC	44	28-16-0	15	Florida	33	15-18-0	26	North Carolina	25	12-13-0
5	Nebraska	43	22-21-0	16	Auburn	32	17-13-2		West Virginia	25	10-15-0
6	Georgia	41	22-16-3	17	Mississippi	31	19-12-0	28	Pittsburgh	24	10-13-0
7	Oklahoma	39	24-14-1	18	Miami-FL	30	17-13-0		BYU	24	7-16-1
8	Penn St	38	24-12-2	19	Washington	29	14-14-1	30	Missouri	23	10-13-0
9	LSU	37	18-18-1		Texas Tech	29	8-20-1		N.C. State	23	12-10-1
	Ohio St	37	18-19-0	21	Texas A&M	28	13-15-0				
	Michigan	37	18-19-0		Clemson	28	15-13-0				

Major Conference Champions
Atlantic Coast Conference

Founded in 1953 when charter members all left Southern Conference to form ACC. **Charter members** (7): Clemson, Duke, Maryland, North Carolina, N.C. State, South Carolina and Wake Forest. **Admitted later** (6): Virginia in 1953 (began play in '54), Georgia Tech in 1979 (began play in '83), Florida St. in 1990 (began play in '92), Boston College, Virginia Tech and Miami-FL in 2003 (Virginia Tech and Miami began play in '04, Boston College in '05). **Withdrew later** (1): South Carolina in 1971 (became an independent after '70 season). **2006 playing membership** (12): ATLANTIC—Boston College, Clemson, Florida St., Maryland, N.C. State and Wake Forest; COASTAL—Duke, Georgia Tech, Miami-FL, North Carolina, Virginia and Virginia Tech.

Multiple titles: Clemson (13); Florida St. (11); Maryland (9); Duke and N.C. State (7); North Carolina (5); Georgia Tech & Virginia (2).

Year		Year		Year		Year	
1953	Duke (4-0) & Maryland (3-0)	1965	Clemson (5-2) & N.C. State (5-2)	1980	North Carolina (6-0)	1994	Florida St. (8-0)
1954	Duke (4-0)	1966	Clemson (6-1)	1981	Clemson (6-0)	1995	Virginia (7-1) & Florida St. (7-1)
1955	Maryland (4-0) & Duke (4-0)	1967	Clemson (6-0)	1982	Clemson (6-0)	1996	Florida St. (8-0)
1956	Clemson (4-0-1)	1968	N.C. State (6-1)	1983	Clemson (7-0) † & Maryland (5-0)	1997	Florida St. (8-0)
1957	N.C. State (5-0-1)	1969	South Carolina (6-0)	1984	Maryland (5-0)	1998	Florida St. (7-1) & Georgia Tech (7-1)
1958	Clemson (5-1)	1970	Wake Forest (5-1)	1985	Maryland (6-0)	1999	Florida St. (8-0)
1959	Clemson (6-1)	1971	North Carolina (6-0)	1986	Clemson (5-1-1)	2000	Florida St. (8-0)
1960	Duke (5-1)	1972	North Carolina (6-0)	1987	Clemson (6-1)	2001	Maryland (7-1)
1961	Duke (5-1)	1973	N.C. State (6-0)	1988	Clemson (6-1)	2002	Florida St. (7-1)
1962	Duke (6-0)	1974	Maryland (6-0)	1989	Virginia (6-1) & Duke (6-1)	2003	Florida St. (7-1)
1963	North Carolina (6-1) & N.C. State (6-1)	1975	Maryland (5-0)	1990	Georgia Tech (6-0-1)	2004	Virginia Tech (7-1)
1964	N.C. State (5-2)	1976	Maryland (5-0)	1991	Clemson (6-0)		
		1977	North Carolina (5-0-1)	1992	Florida St. (8-0)	†On probation, ineligible for championship.	
		1978	Clemson (6-0)	1993	Florida St. (8-0)		
		1979	N.C. State (5-1)				

ACC Championship Game

After expanding to 12 teams and splitting into two divisions in 2005, the ACC began staging a conference championship game between the two division winners on the first Saturday in December. The inaugural game was played at Alltel Stadium in Jacksonville, Fla. and the 2006 game was to be played there as well.

Year
2005   Florida St. 27, Va. Tech 22

Big East Conference

Founded in 1991 when charter members gave up independent football status to form Big East. **Charter members** (8): Boston College, Miami-FL, Pittsburgh, Rutgers, Syracuse, Temple, Virginia Tech and West Virginia. **Admitted later** (4): Connecticut (a charter member in all other sports) in 2004; Cincinnati, Louisville and South Florida in 2003 (to begin play in '05). **Withdrew later** (4): Boston College, Miami-FL and Virginia Tech in 2003 (Miami and Va. Tech joined ACC for 2004 season, Boston College joined ACC in 2005). Temple became an independent following 2004 season.

2006 playing membership (8): Cincinnati, Connecticut, Louisville, Pittsburgh, Rutgers, South Florida, Syracuse and West Virginia. **Conference champion:** Member schools needed two years to adjust their regular season schedules in order to begin round-robin conference play in 1993. In the meantime, the 1991 and '92 Big East titles went to the highest-ranked member in the final regular season USA Today/CNN coaches' poll.

Multiple titles: Miami-FL (9); Syracuse (5); West Virginia (4); Virginia Tech (3).

Year		Year		Year		Year	
1991	Miami-FL (2-0, #1) & Syracuse (5-0, #16)	1996	Virginia Tech (6-1), Miami-FL (6-1) & Syracuse (6-1)	2000	Miami-FL (7-0)	2004	Boston College (4-2), Pittsburgh (4-2), Syracuse (4-2) & West Virginia (4-2)
1992	Miami-FL (4-0, #1)			2001	Miami-FL (7-0)		
1993	West Virginia (7-0)	1997	Syracuse (6-1)	2002	Miami-FL (7-0)		
1994	Miami-FL (7-0)	1998	Syracuse (6-1)	2003	Miami-FL (6-1) & West Virginia (6-1)	2005	West Virginia (7-0)
1995	Virginia Tech (6-1) & Miami-FL (6-1)	1999	Virginia Tech (7-0)				

Big Ten Conference

Originally founded in 1895 as the Intercollegiate Conference of Faculty Representatives, better known as the Western Conference. **Charter members** (7): Chicago, Illinois, Michigan, Minnesota, Northwestern, Purdue and Wisconsin. **Admitted later** (5): Indiana and Iowa in 1899; Ohio St. in 1912; Michigan St. in 1950 (began play in '53); Penn St. in 1990 (began play in '93). **Withdrew later** (2): Michigan in 1907 (rejoined in '17); Chicago in 1940 (dropped football after '39 season). **Note:** Iowa belonged to both the Western and Missouri Valley conferences from 1907-10.

Unofficially called the **Big Ten** from 1912 until Chicago's withdrawal in 1939, then the **Big Nine** from 1940 until Michigan St. began conference play in 1953. Formally named the **Big Ten** in 1984 and has kept the name even after adding Penn St. as its 11th member in 1990.

2006 playing membership (11): Illinois, Indiana, Iowa, Michigan, Michigan St., Minnesota, Northwestern, Ohio St., Penn St., Purdue and Wisconsin.

Multiple titles: Michigan (42); Ohio St. (30); Minnesota (18); Illinois (15); Iowa and Wisconsin (11); Purdue and Northwestern (8); Chicago and Michigan St. (6); Indiana and Penn St. (2).

Year		Year		Year		Year	
1896	Wisconsin (2-0-1)	1901	Michigan (4-0) & Wisconsin (2-0)	1904	Minnesota (3-0) & Michigan (2-0)	1907	Chicago (4-0)
1897	Wisconsin (3-0)					1908	Chicago (5-0)
1898	Michigan (3-0)	1902	Michigan (5-0)	1905	Chicago (7-0)	1909	Minnesota (3-0)
1899	Chicago (4-0)	1903	Michigan (3-0-1), Minnesota (3-0-1) & Northwestern (1-0-2)	1906	Wisconsin (3-0), Minnesota (2-0) & Michigan (1-0)	1910	Illinois (4-0) & Minnesota (2-0)
1900	Iowa (3-0-1) & Minnesota (3-0-1)					1911	Minnesota (3-0-1)

Year		Year		Year		Year	
1912	Wisconsin (6-0)	1934	Minnesota (5-0)	1962	Wisconsin (6-1)	1985	Iowa (7-1)
1913	Chicago (7-0)	1935	Minnesota (5-0)	1963	Illinois (5-1-1)	1986	Michigan (7-1)
1914	Illinois (6-0)		& Ohio St. (5-0)	1964	Michigan (6-1)		& Ohio St. (7-1)
1915	Minnesota (3-0-1)	1936	Northwestern (6-0)	1965	Michigan St. (7-0)	1987	Michigan St. (7-0-1)
	& Illinois (3-0-2)	1937	Minnesota (5-0)	1966	Michigan St. (7-0)	1988	Michigan (7-0-1)
1916	Ohio St. (4-0)	1938	Minnesota (4-1)	1967	Indiana (6-1),	1989	Michigan (8-0)
1917	Ohio St. (4-0)	1939	Ohio St. (5-1)		Purdue (6-1)	1990	Iowa (6-2),
1918	Illinois (4-0),	1940	Minnesota (6-0)		& Minnesota (6-1)		Michigan (6-2),
	Michigan (2-0)	1941	Minnesota (5-0)	1968	Ohio St. (7-0)		Michigan St. (6-2)
	& Purdue (1-0)	1942	Ohio St. (5-1)	1969	Ohio St. (6-1)		& Illinois (6-2)
1919	Illinois (6-1)	1943	Purdue (6-0)		& Michigan (6-1)	1991	Michigan (8-0)
1920	Ohio St. (5-0)		& Michigan (6-0)	1970	Ohio St. (7-0)	1992	Michigan (6-0-2)
1921	Iowa (5-0)	1944	Ohio St. (6-0)	1971	Michigan (8-0)	1993	Wisconsin (6-1-1)
1922	Iowa (5-0)	1945	Indiana (5-0-1)	1972	Ohio St. (7-1)		& Ohio St. (6-1-1)
	& Michigan (4-0)	1946	Illinois (6-1)		& Michigan (7-1)	1994	Penn St. (8-0)
1923	Illinois (5-0)	1947	Michigan (6-0)	1973	Ohio St. (7-0-1)	1995	Northwestern (8-0)
	& Michigan (4-0)	1948	Michigan (6-0)		& Michigan (7-0-1)	1996	Ohio St. (7-1)
1924	Chicago (3-0-3)	1949	Ohio St. (4-1-1)	1974	Ohio St. (7-1)		& Northwestern (7-1)
1925	Michigan (5-1)		& Michigan (4-1-1)		& Michigan (7-1)	1997	Michigan (8-0)
1926	Michigan (5-0)	1950	Michigan (4-1-1)	1975	Ohio St. (8-0)	1998	Ohio St. (7-1),
	& Northwestern (5-0)	1951	Illinois (5-0-1)	1976	Michigan (7-1)		Wisconsin (7-1)
1927	Illinois (5-0)	1952	Wisconsin (4-1-1)		& Ohio St. (7-1)		& Michigan (7-1)
	& Minnesota (3-0-1)		& Purdue (4-1-1)	1977	Michigan (7-1)	1999	Wisconsin (7-1)
1928	Illinois (4-1)	1953	Michigan St. (5-1)		& Ohio St. (7-1)	2000	Purdue (6-2),
1929	Purdue (5-0)		& Illinois (5-1)	1978	Michigan (7-1)		Michigan (6-2)
1930	Michigan (5-0)	1954	Ohio St. (7-0)		& Michigan St. (7-1)		& Northwestern (6-2)
	& Northwestern (5-0)	1955	Ohio St. (6-0)	1979	Ohio St. (8-0)	2001	Illinois (7-1)
1931	Purdue (5-1),	1956	Iowa (5-1)	1980	Michigan (8-0)	2002	Ohio St. (8-0)
	Michigan (5-1)	1957	Ohio St. (7-0)	1981	Iowa (6-2)		& Iowa (8-0)
	& Northwestern (5-1)	1958	Iowa (5-1)		& Ohio St. (6-2)	2003	Michigan (7-1)
1932	Michigan (6-0)	1959	Wisconsin (5-2)	1982	Michigan (8-1)	2004	Iowa (7-1)
	& Purdue (5-0-1)	1960	Minnesota (5-1)	1983	Illinois (9-0)		& Michigan (7-1)
1933	Michigan (5-0-1)		& Iowa (5-1)	1984	Ohio St. (7-2)	2005	Ohio St. (7-1)
	& Minnesota (2-0-4)	1961	Ohio St. (6-0)				& Penn St. (7-1)

Big 12 Conference

Originally founded in 1996 by the former teams of the Big Eight and four schools from the Southwest Conference. The league stages a conference championship game between the two division winners on the first Saturday in December. **Playing sites:** Trans World Dome in St. Louis (1996, 1998), the Alamodome in San Antonio (1997, 1999), Arrowhead Stadium in Kansas City, Mo. (2000, 2003, 2004), Texas Stadium in Irving, Texas (2001) and Reliant Stadium in Houston, Texas (2002.)
   2006 playing membership: (12) NORTH—Colorado, Iowa St., Kansas, Kansas St., Missouri and Nebraska; SOUTH—Baylor, Oklahoma, Oklahoma St., Texas, Texas A&M and Texas Tech.
   Multiple titles: Oklahoma (3), Nebraska and Texas (2).

Year		Year		Year	
1996	Texas 37, Nebraska 27	2000	Oklahoma 27, Kansas St. 24	2004	Oklahoma 42, Colorado 3
1997	Nebraska 54, Texas A&M 15	2001	Colorado 39, Texas 37	2005	Texas 70, Colorado 3
1998	Texas A&M 36, Kansas St. 33	2002	Oklahoma 29, Colorado 7		
1999	Nebraska 22, Texas 6	2003	Kansas St. 35, Oklahoma 7		

Big West Conference (1969-2000)

Originally founded in 1969 as Pacific Coast Athletic Assn. **Charter members** (7): CS-Los Angeles, Fresno St., Long Beach St., Pacific, San Diego St., San Jose St. and UC-Santa Barbara. **Admitted later** (12): CS-Fullerton in 1974; Utah St. in 1977 (began play in '78); UNLV in 1982; New Mexico St. in 1983 (began play in '84); Nevada in 1991 (began play in '92); Arkansas St., Louisiana Tech, Northern Illinois and SW Louisiana in 1992 (all four began play in football only in '93); Boise St., Idaho and North Texas in 1994 (all three began play in '96); Arkansas St. rejoined in 1999 (in football only). **Withdrew later** (14): CS-Los Angeles and UC-Santa Barbara in 1972 (both dropped football after '71 season); San Diego St. in 1975 (became an independent after '75 season); Fresno St. in 1991 (left for WAC after '91 season); Long Beach St. in 1991 (dropped football after '91 season); CS-Fullerton in 1992 (dropped football after '92 season); San Jose St. and UNLV in 1994 (left for WAC after '94 season); Pacific in 1995 (dropped football after '95 season); Arkansas St., Louisiana Tech, Northern Illinois and SW Louisiana in 1995 (all four returned to independent football status after '95 season); Nevada in 2000 (left for WAC after '99 season). **Conference renamed** Big West in 1988.
   Multiple titles: San Jose St. (8); Fresno St. (6); Nevada, San Diego St. and Utah St. (5); Long Beach St. (3); Boise St., CS-Fullerton and SW Louisiana (2).

Year		Year		Year		Year	
1969	San Diego St. (6-0)	1979	Utah St. (4-0-1)*	1991	Fresno St. (6-1)	1997	Utah St. (4-1)
1970	Long Beach St. (5-1)	1980	Long Beach St. (5-0)		& San Jose St. (6-1)		& Nevada (4-1)
	& San Diego St. (5-1)	1981	San Jose St. (5-0)	1992	Nevada (5-1)	1998	Idaho (4-1)
1971	Long Beach St. (5-1)	1982	Fresno St. (6-0)	1993	Utah St. (5-1)	1999	Boise St. (5-1)
1972	San Diego St. (4-0)	1983	CS-Fullerton (5-1)		& SW Louisiana (5-1)	2000	Boise St. (5-0)
1973	San Diego St. (3-0-1)	1984	CS-Fullerton (6-1)†	1994	UNLV (5-1),		
1974	San Diego St. (4-0)	1985	Fresno St. (7-0)		Nevada (5-1),	*San Jose St. (4-0-1) forfeit-
1975	San Jose St. (5-0)	1986	San Jose St. (7-0)		& SW Louisiana (5-1)	ed share of 1979 title for
1976	San Jose St. (4-0)	1987	San Jose St. (7-0)	1995	Nevada (6-0)	using ineligible player.
1977	Fresno St. (4-0)	1988	Fresno St. (7-0)	1996	Nevada (4-1)	†UNLV (7-0) forfeited title in
1978	San Jose St. (4-1)	1989	Fresno St. (7-0)		& Utah St. (4-1)	1984 for use of ineligible
	& Utah St. (4-1)	1990	San Jose St. (7-0)			players.

Big Eight Conference (1907-1996)

Originally founded in 1907 as the Missouri Valley Intercollegiate Athletic Assn. **Charter members** (5): Iowa, Kansas, Missouri, Nebraska and Washington University of St. Louis. **Admitted later** (11): Drake and Iowa St. (then Ames College) in 1908; Kansas St. (then Kansas College of Applied Science and Agriculture) in 1913; Grinnell (Iowa) College in 1919; Oklahoma in 1920; Oklahoma A&M (now Oklahoma St.) in 1925; Colorado in 1947 (began play in '48).

Withdrew later (9): Iowa in 1911 (left for Big Ten after 1910 season), Colorado, Iowa St., Kansas, Kansas St. Missouri, Nebraska, Oklahoma and Oklahoma St. in 1996 (left for Big 12 after 1995 season); **Excluded later** (4): Drake, Grinnell, Oklahoma A&M and Washington-MO (left out when MVIAA cut membership to six teams in 1928).

Streamlined MVIAA unofficially called **Big Six** from 1928-47 with surviving members Iowa St., Kansas, Kansas St., Missouri, Nebraska and Oklahoma. Became the **Big Seven** after 1947 season when Colorado came over from the Skyline Conference, and then the **Big Eight** with the return of Oklahoma A&M in 1957. A&M, which resumed conference play in '60, became Oklahoma St. on July 10, 1957. The MVIAA was officially renamed the Big Eight in 1964. The league folded in 1996 when the existing members formed the newly created Big 12 along with four schools from the Southwest Conference.

Multiple titles: Nebraska (43); Oklahoma (34); Missouri (12); Colorado and Kansas (5); Iowa St. and Oklahoma St. (2).

Year		Year		Year		Year	
1907	Iowa (1-0) & Nebraska (1-0)	1928	Nebraska (4-0)	1952	Oklahoma (5-0-1)	1976	Colorado (5-2), Oklahoma (5-2) & Oklahoma St. (5-2)
1908	Kansas (4-0)	1929	Nebraska (3-0-2)	1953	Oklahoma (6-0)		
1909	Missouri (4-0-1)	1930	Kansas (4-1)	1954	Oklahoma (6-0)		
1910	Nebraska (2-0)	1931	Nebraska (5-0)	1955	Oklahoma (6-0)		
1911	Iowa St. (2-0-1) & Nebraska (2-0-1)	1932	Nebraska (5-0)	1956	Oklahoma (6-0)	1977	Oklahoma (7-0)
		1933	Nebraska (5-0)	1957	Oklahoma (6-0)	1978	Nebraska (6-1) & Oklahoma (6-1)
1912	Iowa St. (2-0) & Nebraska (2-0)	1934	Kansas St. (5-0)	1958	Oklahoma (6-0)		
		1935	Nebraska (4-0-1)	1959	Oklahoma (5-1)	1979	Oklahoma (7-0)
1913	Missouri (4-0) & Nebraska (3-0)	1936	Nebraska (5-0)	1960	Missouri (7-0)	1980	Oklahoma (7-0)
		1937	Nebraska (3-0-2)	1961	Colorado (7-0)	1981	Nebraska (7-0)
1914	Nebraska (3-0)	1938	Oklahoma (5-0)	1962	Oklahoma (7-0)	1982	Nebraska (7-0)
1915	Nebraska (4-0)	1939	Missouri (5-0)	1963	Nebraska (7-0)	1983	Nebraska (7-0)
1916	Nebraska (3-1)	1940	Nebraska (5-0)	1964	Nebraska (6-1)	1984	Oklahoma (6-1) & Nebraska (6-1)
1917	Nebraska (2-0)	1941	Missouri (5-0)	1965	Nebraska (7-0)		
1918	Vacant (WW I)	1942	Missouri (4-0-1)	1966	Nebraska (6-1)	1985	Oklahoma (7-0)
1919	Missouri (4-0)	1943	Oklahoma (4-0-1)	1967	Oklahoma (7-0)	1986	Oklahoma (7-0)
1920	Oklahoma (4-0-1)	1944	Oklahoma (4-0-1)	1968	Kansas (6-1) & Oklahoma (6-1)	1987	Oklahoma (7-0)
1921	Nebraska (3-0)	1945	Missouri (5-0)			1988	Nebraska (7-0)
1922	Nebraska (5-0)	1946	Oklahoma (4-1) & Kansas (4-1)	1969	Missouri (6-1) & Nebraska (6-1)	1989	Colorado (7-0)
1923	Nebraska (3-0-2) & Kansas (3-0-3)	1947	Kansas (4-0-1) & Oklahoma (4-0-1)			1990	Colorado (7-0)
				1970	Nebraska (7-0)	1991	Nebraska (6-0-1) & Colorado (6-0-1)
1924	Missouri (5-1)	1948	Oklahoma (5-0)	1971	Nebraska (7-0)		
1925	Missouri (5-1)	1949	Oklahoma (6-0)	1972	Nebraska (5-1-1)*	1992	Nebraska (6-1)
1926	Okla. A&M (3-0-1)	1950	Oklahoma (6-0)	1973	Oklahoma (7-0)	1993	Nebraska (7-0)
1927	Missouri (5-1)	1951	Oklahoma (6-0)	1974	Oklahoma (7-0)	1994	Nebraska (7-0)
				1975	Nebraska (6-1) & Oklahoma (6-1)	1995	Nebraska (7-0)

*Oklahoma (6-1) forfeited title in 1972 after a player was ruled ineligible.

Conference USA

Founded in 1994 by six independent football schools which began play as a conference in 1996. **Charter members** (6): Cincinnati, Houston, Louisville, Memphis, Southern Mississippi and Tulane. **Admitted later** (11): East Carolina in 1997, Army in 1998, Univ. of Alabama-Birmingham in 1999, Texas Christian Univ. in 2001, South Florida in 2003, Central Florida, Marshall, Rice, SMU, Tulsa and UTEP in 2005. **Withdrew later** (5): Cincinnati, Louisville and South Florida are set to leave for the Big East in 2005; Army is going back to independent and TCU is going to the Mountain West in 2005.

2006 playing members (12): EAST—Alabama-Birmingham, Central Florida, East Carolina, Marshall, Memphis and Southern Mississippi, WEST—Houston, Rice, SMU, Tulane, Tulsa and UTEP.

Multiple titles: Southern Mississippi (4), Louisville (3).

Year		Year		Year	
1996	Southern Mississippi (4-1) & Houston (4-1)	1999	Southern Mississippi (6-0)	2002	TCU (6-2) & Cincinnati (6-2)
1997	Southern Mississippi (6-0)	2000	Louisville (6-1)	2003	Southern Mississippi (8-0)
1998	Tulane (6-0)	2001	Louisville (6-1)	2004	Louisville (8-0)

Conference USA Championship Game

After expanding to 12 teams and splitting into two divisions in 2005, Conference USA began staging a conference championship game between the two division winners on the first Saturday in December. The inaugural game was held Dec. 3, 2005 at the Florida Citrus Bowl in Orlando, Fla.

Year
2005 Tulsa 44, Central Florida 27

Mid-American Conference

Founded in 1946. **Charter members** (6): Butler, Cincinnati, Miami-OH, Ohio University, Western Michigan and Western Reserve (Miami and WMU began play in '48). **Admitted later** (12): Kent St. (now Kent) and Toledo in 1951 (Toledo began play in '52); Bowling Green in 1952; Marshall in 1954; Central Michigan and Eastern Michigan in 1972 (CMU began play in '75 and EMU in '76); Ball St. and Northern Illinois in 1973 (both began play in '75); Akron in 1991 (began play in '92); Marshall and Northern Illinois in 1995 (both resumed play in '97); Buffalo in 1995 (resumed play in '99); Central Florida in 2002; Temple in 2007.

Withdrew later (5): Butler in 1950 (left for the Indiana Collegiate Conference); Cincinnati in 1953 (went independent); Western Reserve (now Case Western) in 1955 (left for President's Athletic Conference); Marshall in 1969 (went independent) and again in 2005 (left for Conference USA); Northern Illinois in 1986 (went independent); Central Florida in 2005 (left. for Conference USA). **2006 playing membership** (12): EAST—Akron, Bowling Green, Buffalo, Kent St., Miami-OH and Ohio University; WEST—Ball St., Central Michigan, Eastern Michigan, Northern Illinois, Toledo and Western Michigan. Note: Independent Temple is set to join the Mid-American Conference for the 2007 season and play in the East division.

Multiple titles: Miami-OH (14); Bowling Green (10); Toledo (9); Ball St., Marshall and Ohio University (5); Central Michigan, Cincinnati (4); Western Michigan (2).

Year		Year		Year		Year	
1947	Cincinnati (3-1)	1959	Bowling Green (6-0)	1970	Toledo (5-0)	1985	Bowling Green (9-0)
1948	Miami-OH (4-0)	1960	Ohio Univ. (6-0)	1971	Toledo (5-0)	1986	Miami-OH (6-2)
1949	Cincinnati (4-0)	1961	Bowling Green (5-1)	1972	Kent St. (4-1)	1987	Eastern Mich. (7-1)
		1962	Bowling Green (5-0-1)	1973	Miami-OH (5-0)	1988	Western Mich. (7-1)
1950	Miami-OH (4-0)	1963	Ohio Univ. (5-1)	1974	Miami-OH (5-0)	1989	Ball St. (6-1-1)
1951	Cincinnati (3-0)	1964	Bowling Green (5-1)	1975	Miami-OH (6-0)		
1952	Cincinnati (3-0)	1965	Bowling Green (5-1)	1976	Ball St. (4-1)	1990	Central Mich. (7-1)
1953	Ohio Univ. (5-0-1)		& Miami-OH (5-1)	1977	Miami-OH (5-0)		& Toledo (7-1)
	& Miami-OH (3-0-1)	1966	Miami-OH (5-1)	1978	Ball St. (8-0)	1991	Bowling Green (8-0)
1954	Miami-OH (4-0)		& Western Mich: (5-1)	1979	Central Mich. (8-0-1)	1992	Bowling Green (8-0)
1955	Miami-OH (5-0)	1967	Toledo (5-1)			1993	Ball St. (7-0-1)
1956	Bowling Green (5-0-1)		& Ohio Univ. (5-1)	1980	Central Mich. (7-2)	1994	Central Mich. (8-1)
	& Miami-OH (4-0-1)	1968	Ohio Univ. (6-0)	1981	Toledo (8-1)	1995	Toledo (7-0-1)
1957	Miami-OH (5-0)	1969	Toledo (5-0)	1982	Bowling Green (7-2)	1996	Ball St. (7-1)
1958	Miami-OH (5-0)			1983	Northern Ill. (8-1)		
				1984	Toledo (7-1-1)		

MAC Championship Game

After expanding to 12 teams and splitting into two divisions in 1997, the MAC began staging a conference championship game between the two division winners on the first Saturday in December. The game has been played at Marshall Stadium in Huntington, W.V. (1997-2000, 2002), Glass Bowl Stadium in Toledo, Ohio (2001), Doyt Perry Stadium in Bowling Green, Ohio (2003) and Ford Field in Detroit (2004-06).

Year		Year		Year	
1997	Marshall 34, Toledo 13	2000	Marshall 19, W. Michigan 14	2003	Miami-OH 49, Bowl. Green 27
1998	Marshall 23, Toledo 17	2001	Toledo 41, Marshall 36	2004	Toledo 35, Miami-OH 27
1999	Marshall 34, W. Michigan 30	2002	Marshall 49, Toledo 45	2005	Akron 31, Northern Illinois 30

Mountain West Conference

Founded in 1999. **Charter members** (8): Air Force, Brigham Young, Colorado St., New Mexico, Nevada-Las Vegas, San Diego St., Utah and Wyoming. **Admitted later** (1): TCU (from Conference USA) is set to join in 2005.

2006 playing membership (9): Air Force, Brigham Young, Colorado St., New Mexico, Nevada-Las Vegas, San Diego St., TCU, Utah and Wyoming.

Multiple titles: Colorado St. and Utah (3), BYU (2).

Year		Year		Year	
1999	BYU (5-2),	2000	Colorado St. (6-1)	2003	Utah (6-1)
	Colorado St. (5-2)	2001	BYU (7-0)	2004	Utah (7-0)
	& Utah (5-2)	2002	Colorado St. (6-1)	2005	TCU (8-0)

Pacific-10 Conference

Originally founded in 1915 as Pacific Coast Conference. **Charter members** (4): California, Oregon, Oregon St. and Washington. **Admitted later** (6): Washington St. in 1917; Stanford in 1918; Idaho and USC (Southern Cal) in 1922; Montana in 1924; and UCLA in 1928. **Withdrew later** (1): Montana in 1950 (left for the Mountain States Conf.).

The **PCC** dissolved in 1959 and the **AAWU** (Athletic Assn. of Western Universities) was founded. **Charter members** (5): California, Stanford, UCLA, USC and Washington. **Admitted later** (5):Washington St. in 1962; Oregon and Oregon St. in 1964; Arizona and Arizona St. in 1978. **Conference renamed** Pacific-8 in 1968 and Pacific-10 in 1978.

2006 playing membership (10): Arizona, Arizona St., California, Oregon, Oregon St., Stanford, UCLA, USC, Washington and Washington St.

Multiple titles: USC (35); UCLA (17); Washington (15); California (13); Stanford (12); Oregon (7); Oregon St. (5); Washington (4); Arizona St. (2).

Year		Year		Year		Year	
1916	Washington (3-0-1)	1933	Oregon (4-1)	1947	USC (6-0)	1962	USC (4-0)
1917	Washington St. (3-0)		& Stanford (4-1)	1948	California (6-0)	1963	Washington (4-1)
1918	California (3-0)	1934	Stanford (5-0)		& Oregon (6-0)	1964	Oregon St. (3-1)
1919	Oregon (2-1)	1935	California (4-1),	1949	California (7-0)		& USC (3-1)
	& Washington (2-1)		Stanford (4-1)	1950	California (5-0-1)	1965	UCLA (4-0)
1920	California (3-0)		& UCLA (4-1)	1951	Stanford (6-1)	1966	USC (4-1)
1921	California (5-0)	1936	Washington (6-0-1)	1952	USC (6-0)	1967	USC (6-1)
1922	California (3-0)	1937	California (6-0-1)	1953	UCLA (6-1)	1968	USC (6-0)
1923	California (5-0)	1938	USC (6-1)	1954	UCLA (6-0)	1969	USC (6-0)
1924	Stanford (3-0-1)		& California (6-1)	1955	UCLA (6-0)	1970	Stanford (6-1)
1925	Washington (5-0)	1939	USC (5-0-2)	1956	Oregon St. (6-1-1)	1971	Stanford (6-1)
1926	Stanford (4-0)		& UCLA (5-0-3)	1957	Oregon (6-2)	1972	USC (7-0)
1927	USC (4-0-1)	1940	Stanford (7-0)		& Oregon St. (6-2)	1973	USC (7-0)
	& Stanford (4-0-1)	1941	Oregon St. (7-2)	1958	California (6-1)	1974	USC (6-0-1)
1928	USC (4-0-1)	1942	UCLA (6-1)	1959	Washington (3-1),	1975	UCLA (6-1)
1929	USC (6-1)	1943	USC (4-0)		USC (3-1)		& California (6-1)
1930	Washington St. (6-0)	1944	USC (3-0-2)		& UCLA (3-1)	1976	USC (7-0)
1931	USC (7-0)	1945	USC (5-1)	1960	Washington (4-0)	1977	Washington (6-1)
1932	USC (6-0)	1946	UCLA (7-0)	1961	UCLA (3-1)	1978	USC (6-1)

Major Conference Champions (Cont.)
Pacific-10 Conference (Cont.)

Year		Year		Year		Year	
1979	USC (6-0-1)	1988	USC (8-0)	1995	USC (6-1-1)	2001	Oregon (7-1)
1980	Washington (6-1)	1989	USC (6-0-1)		& Washington (6-1-1)	2002	Washington St. (7-1)
1981	Washington (6-2)	1990	Washington (7-1)	1996	Arizona St. (8-0)		& USC (7-1)
1982	UCLA (5-1-1)	1991	Washington (8-0)	1997	Washington St. (7-1)	2003	USC (7-1)
1983	UCLA (6-1-1)	1992	Washington (6-2)		& UCLA (7-1)	2004	USC (8-0)
1984	USC (7-1)		& Stanford (6-2)	1998	UCLA (8-0)	2005	USC (8-0)
1985	UCLA (6-2)	1993	UCLA (6-2),	1999	Stanford (7-1)		
1986	Arizona St. (5-1-1)		Arizona (6-2)	2000	Washington (7-1),		
1987	USC (7-1)		& USC (6-2)		Oregon St. (7-1)		
	& UCLA (7-1)	1994	Oregon (7-1)		& Oregon (7-1)		

Southwest Conference (1914-95)

Founded in 1914 as Southwest Intercollegiate Athletic Conference to form SWC. **Charter members** (8): Arkansas, Baylor, Oklahoma, Oklahoma A&M (now Oklahoma St.), Rice, Southwestern, Texas and Texas A&M. **Admitted later** (5): SMU (Southern Methodist) in 1918; Phillips University in 1920; TCU (Texas Christian) in 1923; Texas Tech in 1956 (began play in '60); Houston in 1971 (began play in '76). **Withdrew later** (13): Southwestern in 1917 (went independent); Oklahoma in 1920 (left for Missouri Valley after '19 season); Phillips in 1921; Oklahoma A&M (now Oklahoma St.) in 1925 (left for Big Six); Arkansas in 1990 (left for SEC after '91 season); Baylor, Texas, Texas A&M and Texas Tech in 1994 (all four left for Big 12 after '95 season); Rice, SMU and TCU in 1994 (all three left for WAC after '95 season); Houston in 1994 (left for Conference USA after '95 season). Conference folded on June 30, 1996.

Multiple titles: Texas (25); Texas A&M (17); Arkansas (13); SMU (9); TCU (9); Rice (7); Baylor (5); Houston (4); Texas Tech (2).

Year		Year		Year		Year	
1914	No champion	1940	Texas A&M (5-1)	1961	Texas (6-1)	1981	SMU (7-1)
1915	Oklahoma (3-0)	1941	Texas A&M (5-1)		& Arkansas (6-1)	1982	SMU (7-0-1)
1916	No champion	1942	Texas (5-1)	1962	Texas (6-0-1)	1983	Texas (8-0)
1917	Texas A&M (2-0)	1943	Texas (5-0)	1963	Texas (7-0)	1984	SMU (6-2)
1918	No champion	1944	TCU (3-1-1)	1964	Arkansas (7-0)		& Houston (6-2)
1919	Texas A&M (4-0)	1945	Texas (5-1)	1965	Arkansas (7-0)	1985	Texas A&M (7-1)
1920	Texas (5-0)	1946	Rice (5-1)	1966	SMU (6-1)	1986	Texas A&M (7-1)
1921	Texas A&M (3-0-2)		& Arkansas (5-1)	1967	Texas A&M (6-1)	1987	Texas A&M (6-1)
1922	Baylor (5-0)	1947	SMU (5-0-1)	1968	Arkansas (6-1)	1988	Arkansas (7-0)
1923	SMU (5-0)	1948	SMU (5-0-1)		& Texas (6-1)	1989	Arkansas (7-1)
1924	Baylor (4-0-1)	1949	Rice (6-0)	1969	Texas (7-0)	1990	Texas (8-0)
1925	Texas A&M (4-1)	1950	Texas (6-0)	1970	Texas (7-0)	1991	Texas A&M (8-0)
1926	SMU (5-0)	1951	TCU (5-1)	1971	Texas (6-1)	1992	Texas A&M (7-0)
1927	Texas A&M (4-0-1)	1952	Texas (6-0)	1972	Texas (7-0)	1993	Texas A&M (7-0)
1928	Texas (5-1)	1953	Rice (5-1)	1973	Texas (7-0)	1994	Baylor, Rice, TCU,
1929	TCU (4-0-1)		& Texas (5-1)	1974	Baylor (6-1)		Texas and Texas Tech†
1930	Texas (4-1)	1954	Arkansas (5-1)	1975	Arkansas (6-1),		(4-3)
1931	SMU (5-0-1)	1955	TCU (5-1)		Texas (6-1)	1995	Texas (7-0)
1932	TCU (6-0)	1956	Texas A&M (6-0)		& Texas A&M (6-1)	*Arkansas (4-1) forced to
1933	Arkansas (4-1)*	1957	Rice (5-1)	1976	Houston (7-1)	vacate 1933 title for use of
1934	Rice (5-1)	1958	TCU (5-1)		& Texas Tech (7-1)	ineligible player.
1935	SMU (6-0)	1959	Texas (5-1),	1977	Texas (8-0)	†Texas A&M had the best
1936	Arkansas (5-1)		TCU (5-1)	1978	Houston (7-1)	record (6-0-1) in 1994 but
1937	Rice (4-1-1)		& Arkansas (5-1)	1979	Houston (7-1)	was on probation and
1938	TCU (6-0)	1960	Arkansas (6-1)		& Arkansas (7-1)	therefore ineligible for the
1939	Texas A&M (6-0)			1980	Baylor (8-0)	Southwest championship.

Southeastern Conference

Founded in 1933 when charter members all left Southern Conference to form SEC. **Charter members** (13): Alabama, Auburn, Florida, Georgia, Georgia Tech, Kentucky, LSU (Louisiana St.), Mississippi, Mississippi St., Sewanee, Tennessee, Tulane and Vanderbilt. **Admitted later** (2): Arkansas and South Carolina in 1990 (both began play in '92). **Withdrew later** (3): Sewanee in 1940; Georgia Tech in 1964; and Tulane in 1966.

2006 playing membership (12): Alabama, Arkansas, Auburn, Florida, Georgia, Kentucky, LSU, Mississippi, Mississippi St., South Carolina, Tennessee and Vanderbilt. **Note:** Conference title decided by championship game between Western and Eastern division winners since 1992.

Multiple titles: Alabama (21); Tennessee (13); Georgia (12); Florida and LSU (9); Auburn and Mississippi (6); Georgia Tech (5); Kentucky and Tulane (3).

Year		Year		Year		Year	
1933	Alabama (5-0-1)	1940	Tennessee (5-0)	1948	Georgia (6-0)	1957	Auburn (7-0)
1934	Tulane (8-0)	1941	Mississippi St. (4-0-1)	1949	Tulane (5-1)	1958	LSU (6-0)
	& Alabama (7-0)	1942	Georgia (6-1)	1950	Kentucky (5-1)	1959	Georgia (7-0)
1935	LSU (5-0)	1943	Georgia Tech (3-0)	1951	Georgia Tech (7-0)	1960	Mississippi (5-0-1)
1936	LSU (6-0)	1944	Georgia Tech (4-0)		& Tennessee (5-0)	1961	Alabama (7-0)
1937	Alabama (6-0)	1945	Alabama (6-0)	1952	Georgia Tech (6-0)		& LSU (6-0)
1938	Tennessee (7-0)	1946	Georgia (5-0)	1953	Alabama (4-0-3)	1962	Mississippi (6-0)
1939	Tennessee (6-0),		& Tennessee (5-0)	1954	Mississippi (5-1)	1963	Mississippi (5-0-1)
	Georgia Tech (6-0)	1947	Mississippi (6-1)	1955	Mississippi (5-1)	1964	Alabama (8-0)
	& Tulane (5-0)			1956	Tennessee (6-0)		

Year		Year		Year		Year	
1965	Alabama (6-1-1)	1974	Alabama (6-0)	1981	Georgia (6-0)	1988	Auburn (6-1)
1966	Alabama (6-0)	1975	Alabama (6-0)		& Alabama (6-0)		& LSU (6-1)
	& Georgia (6-0)	1976	Georgia (5-1)	1982	Georgia (6-0)	1989	Alabama (6-1),
1967	Tennessee (6-0)		& Kentucky (5-1)	1983	Auburn (6-0)		Tennessee (6-1)
1968	Georgia (5-0-1)	1977	Alabama (7-0)	1984	Florida (5-0-1)*		& Auburn (6-1)
1969	Tennessee (5-1)		& Kentucky (6-0)	1985	Florida (5-1)†	1990	Florida (6-1)†
1970	LSU (5-0)	1978	Alabama (6-0)		& Tennessee (5-1)		& Tennessee (5-1-1)
1971	Alabama (7-0)	1979	Alabama (6-0)	1986	LSU (5-1)	1991	Florida (7-0)
1972	Alabama (7-1)	1980	Georgia (6-0)	1987	Auburn (5-0-1)		*Title vacated.
1973	Alabama (8-0)						†On probation, ineligible
							for championship.

SEC Championship Game

Since expanding to 12 teams and splitting into two divisions in 1992, the SEC has staged a conference championship game between the two division winners on the first Saturday in December. The game has been played at Legion Field in Birmingham, Ala., (1992-93) and the Georgia Dome in Atlanta (since 1994). The divisions: EAST— Florida, Georgia, Kentucky, South Carolina, Tennessee and Vanderbilt; WEST— Alabama, Arkansas, Auburn, LSU, Mississippi and Mississippi St.

Year		Year		Year	
1992	Alabama 28, Florida 21	1997	Tennessee 30, Auburn 29	2002	Georgia 30, Arkansas 3
1993	Florida 28, Alabama 23	1998	Tennessee 24, Miss. St. 14	2003	LSU 34, Georgia 13
1994	Florida 24, Alabama 23	1999	Alabama 34, Florida 7	2004	Auburn 38, Tennessee 28
1995	Florida 34, Arkansas 3	2000	Florida 28, Auburn 6	2005	Georgia 34, LSU 14
1996	Florida 45, Alabama 30	2001	LSU 31, Tennessee 20		

Sun Belt Conference

Founded in 2001 when the Sun Belt Conference sponsored football for the first time. **Charter members** (7): Arkansas State, Idaho, Louisiana-Lafayette, Louisiana-Monroe, Middle Tennessee State, New Mexico State and North Texas. **Admitted later** (4): Utah St. in 2003, Troy St. in 2004, Florida Atlantic and Florida International in 2005. **Withdrew later** (3): Idaho, New Mexico St. and Utah St. in 2005 (left for WAC). **2006 playing membership** (8): Arkansas State, Florida Atlantic, Florida International, Louisiana-Lafayette, Louisiana-Monroe, Middle Tennessee, North Texas and Troy

Multiple titles: North Texas (4)

Year		Year		Year	
2001	North Texas (5-1)	2003	North Texas (7-0)	2005	Arkansas St. (5-2),
	& Mid. Tenn. St. (5-1)	2004	North Texas (7-0)		LA-Lafayette (5-2),
2002	North Texas (6-0)				LA-Monroe (5-2)

Western Athletic Conference

Founded in 1962 when charter members left the Skyline and Border conferences to form the WAC. **Charter members** (6): Arizona and Arizona St. from Border; BYU (Brigham Young), New Mexico, Utah and Wyoming from Skyline. **Admitted later** (18): Colorado St. and UTEP (Texas-El Paso) in 1967 (both began play in '68); San Diego St. in 1978; Hawaii in 1979; Air Force in 1980; Fresno St. in 1991 (began play in '92); Rice, San Jose St., SMU, TCU , Tulsa and UNLV in 1994 (all began play in '96); Nevada in 2000; Boise St. and Louisiana Tech in 2001; Idaho, New Mexico St. and Utah St. in 2005. **Withdrew later** (13): Arizona and Arizona St. in 1978 (left for Pac-10 after '77 season); Air Force, BYU, Colorado St., New Mexico, San Diego St., UNLV, Utah and Wyoming (left to form Mountain West conference in '99); TCU in 2000 (left for Conference USA after 2000 season); Rice, SMU, Tulsa and UTEP in 2005 (left for Conference USA).

2006 playing membership (9): Boise St., Fresno St., Hawaii, Idaho, Louisiana Tech, Nevada, New Mexico St., San Jose St. and Utah St.

Multiple titles: BYU (19); Arizona St. and Wyoming (7); Boise St. (4); Air Force, Fresno St., New Mexico and Colorado St. (3); Arizona, Hawaii, TCU and Utah (2).

Year		Year		Year		Year	
1962	New Mexico (2-1-1)	1975	Arizona St. (7-0)	1988	Wyoming (8-0)	1999	Fresno St. (5-2),
1963	New Mexico (3-1)	1976	BYU (6-1)	1989	BYU (7-1)		Hawaii (7-2)
1964	Utah (3-1),		& Wyoming (6-1)	1990	BYU (7-1)		& TCU (7-2)
	New Mexico (3-1)	1977	Arizona St. (6-1)	1991	BYU (7-0-1)	2000	TCU (7-1)
	& Arizona (3-1)		& BYU (6-1)	1992	Hawaii (6-2),		& UTEP (7-1)
1965	BYU (4-1)	1978	BYU (5-1)		BYU (6-2)	2001	La. Tech (7-1)
1966	Wyoming (5-0)	1979	BYU (7-0)		& Fresno St. (6-2)	2002	Boise St. (8-0)
1967	Wyoming (5-0)	1980	BYU (6-1)	1993	BYU (6-2),	2003	Boise St. (8-0)
1968	Wyoming (6-1)	1981	BYU (7-1)		Fresno St. (6-2)	2004	Boise St. (8-0)
1969	Arizona St. (6-1)	1982	BYU (7-1		& Wyoming (6-2)	2005	Nevada (7-1)
1970	Arizona St. (7-0)	1983	BYU (7-0)	1994	Colorado St. (7-1)		& Boise St. (7-1)
1971	Arizona St. (7-0)	1984	BYU (8-0)	1995	Colorado St. (6-2),		
1972	Arizona St. (5-1)	1985	Air Force (7-1)		Air Force (6-2),		
1973	Arizona St. (6-1)		& BYU (7-1)		BYU (6-2)		
	& Arizona (6-1)	1986	San Diego St. (7-1)		& Utah (6-2)		
1974	BYU (6-0-1)	1987	Wyoming (8-0)	1996-98	See below		

WAC Championship Game (1996-98)

In addition to expanding to 16 teams and splitting into two divisions in 1996, the WAC staged a conference championship game between the two division winners on the first Saturday in December at Sam Boyd Stadium in Las Vegas until eight teams split off and formed the Mountain West Conference in 1999. The divisions: PACIFIC—BYU, Fresno St., Hawaii, New Mexico, San Diego St., San Jose St., UTEP, Utah; MOUNTAIN—Air Force, Colorado St., Rice, SMU, TCU, Tulsa, UNLV, Wyoming.

Year		Year		Year	
1996	BYU 28, Wyoming 25 (OT)	1997	Colorado St. 41, New Mexico 13	1998	Air Force 20, BYU 13

Annual NCAA Division I-A Leaders

Rushing

Individual championship decided on Rushing Yards (1937-69), and on Yards Per Game (since 1970).

Multiple winners: Troy Davis, Marshall Faulk, Art Luppino, Ed Marinaro, Rudy Mobley, Jim Pilot, O.J. Simpson, LaDainian Tomlinson and Ricky Williams (2).

Year		Car	Yards	Year		Car	Yards	P/Gm
1937	Byron (Whizzer) White, Colorado	181	1121	1970	Ed Marinaro, Cornell	285	1425	158.3
1938	Len Eshmont, Fordham	132	831	1971	Ed Marinaro, Cornell	356	1881	209.0
1939	John Polanski, Wake Forest	137	882	1972	Pete VanValkenburg, BYU	232	1386	138.6
1940	Al Ghesquiere, Detroit	146	957	1973	Mark Kellar, Northern Ill	291	1719	156.3
1941	Frank Sinkwich, Georgia	209	1103	1974	Louie Giammona, Utah St.	329	1534	153.4
1942	Rudy Mobley, Hardin-Simmons	187	1281	1975	Ricky Bell, USC	357	1875	170.5
1943	Creighton Miller, Notre Dame	151	911	1976	Tony Dorsett, Pittsburgh	338	1948	177.1
1944	Red Williams, Minnesota	136	911	1977	Earl Campbell, Texas	267	1744	158.5
1945	Bob Fenimore, Oklahoma A&M	142	1048	1978	Billy Sims, Oklahoma	231	1762	160.2
1946	Rudy Mobley, Hardin-Simmons	227	1262	1979	Charles White, USC	293	1803	180.3
1947	Wilton Davis, Hardin-Simmons	193	1173	1980	George Rogers, S. Carolina	297	1781	161.9
1948	Fred Wendt, Texas Mines	184	1570	1981	Marcus Allen, USC	403	2342	212.9
1949	John Dottley, Ole Miss	208	1312	1982	Ernest Anderson, Okla. St.	353	1877	170.6
1950	Wilford White, Arizona St	199	1502	1983	Mike Rozier, Nebraska	275	2148	179.0
1951	Ollie Matson, San Francisco	245	1566	1984	Keith Byars, Ohio St.	313	1655	150.5
1952	Howie Waugh, Tulsa	164	1372	1985	Lorenzo White, Mich. St.	386	1908	173.5
1953	J.C. Caroline, Illinois	194	1256	1986	Paul Palmer, Temple	346	1866	169.6
1954	Art Luppino, Arizona	179	1359	1987	Ickey Woods, UNLV	259	1658	150.7
1955	Art Luppino, Arizona	209	1313	1988	Barry Sanders, Okla. St.	344	2628	238.9
1956	Jim Crawford, Wyoming	200	1104	1989	Anthony Thompson, Ind	358	1793	163.0
1957	Leon Burton, Arizona St	117	1126	1990	Gerald Hudson, Okla. St.	279	1642	149.3
1958	Dick Bass, Pacific	205	1361	1991	Marshall Faulk, S. Diego St.	201	1429	158.8
1959	Pervis Atkins, New Mexico St	130	971	1992	Marshall Faulk, S. Diego St.	265	1630	163.0
1960	Bob Gaiters, New Mexico St	197	1338	1993	LeShon Johnson, No. Ill.	327	1976	179.6
1961	Jim Pilot, New Mexico St	191	1278	1994	Rashaan Salaam, Colorado	298	2055	186.8
1962	Jim Pilot, New Mexico St	208	1247	1995	Troy Davis, Iowa St.	345	2010	182.7
1963	Dave Casinelli, Memphis St	219	1016	1996	Troy Davis, Iowa St.	402	2185	198.6
1964	Brian Piccolo, Wake Forest	252	1044	1997	Ricky Williams, Texas.	279	1893	172.1
1965	Mike Garrett, USC	267	1440	1998	Ricky Williams, Texas.	361	2124	193.1
1966	Ray McDonald, Idaho	259	1329	1999	LaDainian Tomlinson, TCU	268	1850	168.2
1967	O.J. Simpson, USC.	266	1415	2000	LaDainian Tomlinson, TCU	369	2158	196.2
1968	O.J. Simpson, USC.	355	1709	2001	Chance Kretschmer, Nevada	302	1732	157.5
1969	Steve Owens, Oklahoma	358	1523	2002	Larry Johnson, Penn St.	271	2087	160.5
				2003	Patrick Cobbs, No. Texas	307	1680	152.7
				2004	Jamario Thomas, No. Texas	285	1801	180.1
				2005	DeAngelo Williams, Memphis	310	1964	178.6

All-Purpose Yardage

Multiple winners: Marcus Allen, Pervis Atkins, Ryan Benjamin, Troy Davis, Troy Edwards, Louie Giammona, Tom Harmon, Art Luppino, Napolean McCallum, O.J. Simpson, Charles White and Gary Wood (2).

Year		Yards	P/Gm	Year		Yards	P/Gm
1937	Byron (Whizzer) White, Colorado	1970	246.3	1957	Overton Curtis, Utah St	1608	160.8
1938	Parker Hall, Ole Miss	1420	129.1	1958	Dick Bass, Pacific	1878	187.8
1939	Tom Harmon, Michigan	1208	151.0	1959	Pervis Atkins, New Mexico St	1800	180.0
1940	Tom Harmon, Michigan.	1312	164.0	1960	Pervis Atkins, New Mexico St	1613	161.3
1941	Bill Dudley, Virginia	1674	186.0	1961	Jim Pilot, New Mexico St	1606	160.6
1942	Complete records not available			1962	Gary Wood, Cornell	1395	155.0
1943	Stan Koslowski, Holy Cross	1411	176.4	1963	Gary Wood, Cornell	1508	167.6
1944	Red Williams, Minnesota	1467	163.0	1964	Donny Anderson, Texas Tech	1710	171.0
1945	Bob Fenimore, Oklahoma A&M	1577	197.1	1965	Floyd Little, Syracuse	1990	199.0
1946	Rudy Mobley, Hardin-Simmons	1765	176.5	1966	Frank Quayle, Virginia	1616	161.6
1947	Wilton Davis, Hardin-Simmons	1798	179.8	1967	O.J. Simpson, USC	1700	188.9
1948	Lou Kusserow, Columbia	1737	193.0	1968	O.J. Simpson, USC.	1966	196.6
1949	Johnny Papit, Virginia	1611	179.0	1969	Lynn Moore, Army	1795	179.5
1950	Wilford White, Arizona St.	2065	206.5	1970	Don McCauley, North Carolina	2021	183.7
1951	Ollie Matson, San Francisco	2037	226.3	1971	Ed Marinaro, Cornell	1932	214.7
1952	Billy Vessels, Oklahoma	1512	151.2	1972	Howard Stevens, Louisville.	2132	213.2
1953	J.C. Caroline, Illinois	1470	163.3	1973	Willard Harrell, Pacific	1777	177.7
1954	Art Luppino, Arizona	2193	219.3	1974	Louie Giammona, Utah St	1984	198.4
1955	Jim Swink, TCU	1702	170.2	1975	Louie Giammona, Utah St	2045	185.9
	& Art Luppino, Arizona	1702	170.2	1976	Tony Dorsett, Pittsburgh	2021	183.7
1956	Jack Hill, Utah St	1691	169.1	1977	Earl Campbell, Texas	1855	168.6
				1978	Charles White, USC.	2096	174.7

Year		Yards	P/Gm
1979	Charles White, USC.	1941	194.1
1980	Marcus Allen, USC.	1794	179.4
1981	Marcus Allen, USC.	2559	232.6
1982	Carl Monroe, Utah	2036	185.1
1983	Napoleon McCallum, Navy	2385	216.8
1984	Keith Byars, Ohio St	2284	207.6
1985	Napoleon McCallum, Navy	2330	211.8
1986	Paul Palmer, Temple	2633	239.4
1987	Eric Wilkerson, Kent St.	2074	188.6
1988	Barry Sanders, Oklahoma St.	3250	295.5
1989	Mike Pringle, CS-Fullerton	2690	244.6
1990	Glyn Milburn, Stanford	2222	202.0
1991	Ryan Benjamin, Pacific.	2995	249.6
1992	Ryan Benjamin, Pacific.	2597	236.1
1993	LeShon Johnson, Northern Ill.	2082	189.3

Year		Yards	P/Gm
1994	Rashaan Salaam, Colorado	2349	213.5
1995	Troy Davis, Iowa St.	2466	224.2
1996	Troy Davis, Iowa St.	2364	214.9
1997	Troy Edwards, La. Tech	2144	194.9
1998	Troy Edwards, La. Tech	2784	232.0
1999	Trevor Insley, Nevada	2176	197.8
2000	Emmett White, Utah St.	2628	238.9
2001	Levron Williams, Indiana	2201	200.1
2002	Larry Johnson, Penn St.	2655	204.2
2003	DeAngelo Williams, Memphis	2113	192.1
2004	Darren Sproles, Kansas St.	2067	187.9
2005	Reggie Bush, USC	2890	222.3

Total Offense

Individual championship decided on Total Yards (1937-69) and on Yards Per Game (since 1970).

Multiple winners: Tim Rattay (3); Johnny Bright, Bob Fenimore, Mike Maxwell and Jim McMahon (2).

Year		Plays	Yards
1937	Byron (Whizzer) White, Colorado.	224	1596
1938	Davey O'Brien, TCU	291	1847
1939	Kenny Washington, UCLA	259	1370
1940	Johnny Knolla, Creighton	298	1420
1941	Bud Schwenk, Washington-MO	354	1928
1942	Frank Sinkwich, Georgia.	341	2187
1943	Bob Hoernschemeyer, Indiana	355	1648
1944	Bob Fenimore, Oklahoma A&M.	241	1758
1945	Bob Fenimore, Oklahoma A&M.	203	1641
1946	Travis Tidwell, Auburn	339	1715
1947	Fred Enke, Arizona	329	1941
1948	Stan Heath, Nevada-Reno.	233	1992
1949	Johnny Bright, Drake	275	1950
1950	Johnny Bright, Drake	320	2400
1951	Dick Kazmaier, Princeton	272	1827
1952	Ted Marchibroda, Detroit	305	1813
1953	Paul Larson, California.	262	1572
1954	George Shaw, Oregon	276	1536
1955	George Welsh, Navy.	203	1348
1956	John Brodie, Stanford.	295	1642
1957	Bob Newman, Washington St	263	1444
1958	Dick Bass, Pacific	218	1440
1959	Dick Norman, Stanford	319	2018
1960	Billy Kilmer, UCLA.	292	1889
1961	Dave Hoppmann, Iowa St.	320	1638
1962	Terry Baker, Oregon St	318	2276
1963	George Mira, Miami-FL	394	2318
1964	Jerry Rhome, Tulsa	470	3128
1965	Bill Anderson, Tulsa	580	3343
1966	Virgil Carter, BYU.	388	2545
1967	Sal Olivas, New Mexico St.	368	2184
1968	Greg Cook, Cincinnati	507	3210
1969	Dennis Shaw, San Diego St	388	3197

Year		Plays	Yards	P/Gm
1970	Pat Sullivan, Auburn.	333	2856	285.6
1971	Gary Huff, Florida St.	386	2653	241.2
1972	Don Strock, Va. Tech	480	3170	288.2
1973	Jesse Freitas, San Diego St.	410	2901	263.7
1974	Steve Joachim, Temple	331	2227	222.7
1975	Gene Swick, Toledo	490	2706	246.0
1976	Tommy Kramer, Rice	562	3272	297.5
1977	Doug Williams, Grambling	377	3229	293.5
1978	Mike Ford, SMU	459	2957	268.8
1979	Marc Wilson, BYU	488	3580	325.5
1980	Jim McMahon, BYU	540	4627	385.6
1981	Jim McMahon, BYU	487	3458	345.8
1982	Todd Dillon, Long Beach St	585	3587	326.1
1983	Steve Young, BYU.	531	4346	395.1
1984	Robbie Bosco, BYU	543	3932	327.7
1985	Jim Everett, Purdue	518	3589	326.3
1986	Mike Perez, San Jose St.	425	2969	329.9
1987	Todd Santos, San Diego St.	562	3688	307.3
1988	Scott Mitchell, Utah	589	4299	390.8
1989	Andre Ware, Houston	628	4661	423.7
1990	David Klingler, Houston	704	5221	474.6
1991	Ty Detmer, BYU	478	4001	333.4
1992	Jimmy Klingler, Houston	544	3768	342.6
1993	Chris Vargas, Nevada	535	4332	393.8
1994	Mike Maxwell, Nevada	477	3498	318.0
1995	Mike Maxwell, Nevada	443	3623	402.6
1996	Josh Wallwork, Wyoming	525	4209	350.8
1997	Tim Rattay, La. Tech	541	3968	360.7
1998	Tim Rattay, La. Tech	602	4840	403.3
1999	Tim Rattay, La. Tech	562	3810	381.0
2000	Drew Brees, Purdue	564	3939	358.1
2001	Rex Grossman, Florida	429	3904	354.9
2002	Byron Leftwich, Marshall	528	4267	355.6
2003	B.J. Symons, Texas Tech	798	5976	459.7
2004	Sonny Cumbie, Texas Tech	694	4575	381.3
2005	Colt Brennan, Hawaii	614	4455	371.3

Sacks

Pass sacks have only been compiled by the NCAA since the 2000 season.

Year		Gms	Total
2000	Michael Josiah, Louisville	91	12½
2001	Dwight Freeney, Syracuse	12	17½
2002	Terrell Suggs, Arizona St.	14	24
2003	Dave Ball, UCLA	13	16½
	Kenechi Udeze, USC	13	16½
	& D.D. Acholonu, Wash. St.	13	16½

Year		Gms	Total
2004	Jonathan Goddard, Marshall	12	16
2005	Elvis Dumervil, Louisville	12	20

Annual NCAA Division I-A Leaders (Cont.)

Passing

Individual championship decided on Completions (1937-69), on Completions Per Game (1970-78) and on Passing Efficiency rating points (since 1979).

Multiple winners: Elvis Grbac, Don Heinrich, Jim McMahon, Davey O'Brien and Don Trull (2).

Year		Cmp	Pct	TD	Yds
1937	Davey O'Brien, TCU	.94	.402	–	969
1938	Davey O'Brien, TCU	.93	.557	–	1457
1939	Kay Eakin, Arkansas	.78	.404	–	962
1940	Billy Sewell, Wash. St	.86	.494	–	1023
1941	Bud Schwenk, Wash.-MO	.114	.487	–	1457
1942	Ray Evans, Kansas	.101	.505	–	1117
1943	Johnny Cook, Georgia	.73	.465	–	1007
1944	Paul Rickards, Pittsburgh	.84	.472	–	997
1945	Al Dekdebrun, Cornell	.90	.464	–	1227
1946	Travis Tidwell, Auburn	.79	.500	5	943
1947	Charlie Conerly, Ole Miss	.133	.571	18	1367
1948	Stan Heath, Nev-Reno	.126	.568	22	2005
1949	Adrian Burk, Baylor	.110	.576	14	1428
1950	Don Heinrich, Washington	.134	.606	14	1846
1951	Don Klosterman, Loyola-CA	.159	.505	9	1843
1952	Don Heinrich, Washington	.137	.507	13	1647
1953	Bob Garrett, Stanford	.118	.576	17	1637
1954	Paul Larson, California	.125	.641	10	1537
1955	George Welsh, Navy	.94	.627	8	1319
1956	John Brodie, Stanford	.139	.579	12	1633
1957	Ken Ford, H-Simmons	.115	.561	14	1254
1958	Buddy Humphrey, Baylor	.112	.574	7	1316
1959	Dick Norman, Stanford	.152	.578	11	1963
1960	Harold Stephens, H-Simm	.145	.566	3	1254
1961	Chon Gallegos, S. Jose St	.117	.594	14	1480
1962	Don Trull, Baylor	.125	.546	11	1627
1963	Don Trull, Baylor	.174	.565	12	2157
1964	Jerry Rhome, Tulsa	.224	.687	32	2870
1965	Bill Anderson, Tulsa	.296	.582	30	3464
1966	John Eckman, Wichita St	.195	.426	7	2339
1967	Terry Stone, N. Mexico	.160	.476	9	1946
1968	Chuck Hixson, SMU	.265	.566	21	3103
1969	John Reaves, Florida	.222	.561	24	2896

Year		Cmp	P/Gm	TD	Yds
1970	Sonny Sixkiller, Wash	.186	18.6	15	2303
1971	Brian Sipe, S. Diego St	.196	17.8	17	2532
1972	Don Strock, Va. Tech	.228	20.7	16	3243
1973	Jesse Freitas, S. Diego St.	.227	20.6	21	2993
1974	Steve Bartkowski, Cal	.182	16.5	12	2580
1975	Craig Penrose, S. Diego St.	.198	18.0	15	2660
1976	Tommy Kramer, Rice	.269	24.5	21	3317
1977	Guy Benjamin, Stanford	.208	20.8	19	2521
1978	Steve Dils, Stanford	.247	22.5	22	2943

Year		Cmp	TD	Yds	Rating
1979	Turk Schonert, Stanford	.148	19	1922	163.0
1980	Jim McMahon, BYU	.284	47	4571	176.9
1981	Jim McMahon, BYU	.272	30	3555	155.0
1982	Tom Ramsey, UCLA	.191	21	2824	153.5
1983	Steve Young, BYU	.306	33	3902	168.5
1984	Doug Flutie, BC	.233	27	3454	152.9
1985	Jim Harbaugh, Michigan	.139	18	1913	163.7
1986	Vinny Testaverde, Miami-FL	.175	26	2557	165.8
1987	Don McPherson, Syracuse	.129	22	2341	164.3
1988	Timm Rosenbach, Wash. St.	199	23	2791	162.0
1989	Ty Detmer, BYU	.265	32	4560	175.6
1990	Shawn Moore, Virginia	.144	21	2262	160.7
1991	Elvis Grbac, Michigan	.152	24	1955	169.0
1992	Elvis Grbac, Michigan	.112	15	1465	154.2
1993	Trent Dilfer, Fresno St.	.217	28	3276	173.1
1994	Kerry Collins, Penn St.	.176	21	2679	172.9
1995	Danny Wuerffel, Florida	.210	35	3266	178.4
1996	Steve Sarkisian, BYU	.278	33	4027	173.6
1997	Cade McNown, UCLA	.173	22	2877	168.6
1998	Shaun King, Tulane	.223	36	3232	183.3
1999	Michael Vick, Va. Tech	.90	12	1840	180.4
2000	Bart Hendricks, Boise St	.210	35	3364	170.6
2001	Rex Grossman, Florida	.259	34	3896	170.8
2002	Brad Banks, Iowa	.170	26	2573	157.1
2003	Philip Rivers, N.C. State	.348	34	4491	170.5
2004	Stefan Lefors, Louisville	.189	20	2596	181.7
2005	Rudy Carpenter, Arizona St.	156	17	2273	175.0

Receptions

Championship decided on Passes Caught (1937-69) and on Catches Per Game (since 1970). Touchdown totals unavailable in 1939 and 1941-45.

Multiple winners: Neil Armstrong, Hugh Campell, Manny Hazard, Reid Moseley, Jason Phillips, Howard Twilley and Alex Van Dyke (2).

Year		No	TD	Yds
1937	Jim Benton, Arkansas	.47	7	754
1938	Sam Boyd, Baylor	.32	5	537
1939	Ken Kavanaugh, LSU	.30	–	467
1940	Eddie Bryant, Virginia	.30	2	222
1941	Hank Stanton, Arizona	.50	–	820
1942	Bill Rogers, Texas A&M	.39	–	432
1943	Neil Armstrong, Okla. A&M	.39	–	317
1944	Reid Moseley, Georgia	.32	–	506
1945	Reid Moseley, Georgia	.31	–	662
1946	Neil Armstrong, Okla. A&M	.32	1	479
1947	Barney Poole, Ole Miss	.52	8	513
1948	Red O'Quinn, Wake Forest	.39	7	605
1949	Art Weiner, N. Carolina	.52	7	762
1950	Gordon Cooper, Denver	.46	8	569
1951	Dewey McConnell, Wyoming	.47	9	725
1952	Ed Brown, Fordham	.57	6	774
1953	John Carson, Georgia	.45	4	663
1954	Jim Hanifan, California	.44	7	569
1955	Hank Burnine, Missouri	.44	2	594
1956	Art Powell, San Jose St	.40	5	583
1957	Stuart Vaughan, Utah	.53	5	756

Year		No	TD	Yds
1958	Dave Hibbert, Arizona	.61	4	606
1959	Chris Burford, Stanford	.61	6	756
1960	Hugh Campbell, Wash. St	.66	10	881
1961	Hugh Campbell, Wash. St	.53	5	723
1962	Vern Burke, Oregon St	.69	10	1007
1963	Lawrence Elkins, Baylor	.70	8	873
1964	Howard Twilley, Tulsa	.95	13	1178
1965	Howard Twilley, Tulsa	.134	16	1779
1966	Glenn Meltzer, Wichita St	.91	4	1115
1967	Bob Goodridge, Vanderbilt	.79	6	1114
1968	Ron Sellers, Florida St	.86	12	1496
1969	Jerry Hendren, Idaho	.95	12	1452

Year		No	P/Gm	TD	Yds
1970	Mike Mikolayunas, Davidson	87	8.7	8	1128
1971	Tom Reynolds, San Diego St	.67	6.7	7	1070
1972	Tom Forzani, Utah St	.85	7.7	8	1169
1973	Jay Miller, BYU	.100	9.1	8	1181
1974	D. McDonald, San Diego St	.86	7.8	7	1157
1975	Bob Farnham, Brown	.56	6.2	2	701
1976	Billy Ryckman, La. Tech	.77	7.0	10	1382
1977	W. Tolleson, W. Carolina	.73	6.6	7	1101

Year		No	P/Gm	TD	Yds	Year		No	P/Gm	TD	Yds
1978	Dave Petzke, Northern Ill	91	8.3	11	1217	1994	Alex Van Dyke, Nevada	98	8.9	10	1246
1979	Rick Beasley, Appalach. St	74	6.7	12	1205	1995	Alex Van Dyke, Nevada	129	11.7	16	1854
1980	Dave Young, Purdue	67	6.1	8	917	1996	Damond Wilkins, Nevada	114	10.4	4	1121
1981	Pete Harvey, N. Texas St	57	6.3	3	743	1997	Eugene Baker, Kent	103	9.4	18	1549
1982	Vincent White, Stanford	68	6.8	8	677	1998	Troy Edwards, La. Tech	140	11.7	27	1996
1983	Keith Edwards, Vanderbilt	97	8.8	8	909	1999	Trevor Insley, Nevada	134	12.2	13	2060
1984	David Williams, Illinois	101	9.2	8	1278	2000	James Jordan, La. Tech	109	9.1	4	1003
1985	Rodney Carter, Purdue	98	8.9	4	1099	2001	Kevin Curtis, Utah St.	100	9.1	10	1531
1986	Mark Templeton, L. Beach St	99	9.0	2	688	2002	Nate Burleson, Nevada	138	11.5	12	1629
1987	Jason Phillips, Houston	99	9.0	3	875	2003	Lance Moore, Toledo	103	8.6	9	1194
1988	Jason Phillips, Houston	108	9.8	15	1444	2004	Dante Ridgeway, Ball St.	105	9.6	8	1399
1989	Manny Hazard, Houston	142	12.9	22	1689	2005	Greg Jennings, W. Mich.	98	8.9	14	1259
1990	Manny Hazard, Houston	78	7.8	9	946						
1991	Fred Gilbert, Houston	106	9.6	7	957						
1992	Sherman Smith, Houston	103	9.4	6	923						
1993	Chris Penn, Tulsa	105	9.6	12	1578						

Scoring

Championship decided on Total Points (1937-69) and on Points Per Game (since 1970).

Multiple winners: Tom Harmon and Billy Sims (2).

Year		TD	XP	FG	Pts	Year		TD	XP	FG	Pts	P/Gm
1937	Byron (Whizzer) White, Colo	16	23	1	122	1970	Brian Bream, Air Force	20	0	0	120	12.0
							& Gary Kosins, Dayton	18	0	0	108	12.0
1938	Parker Hall, Ole Miss	11	7	0	73	1971	Ed Marinaro, Cornell	24	4	0	148	16.4
1939	Tom Harmon, Michigan	14	15	1	102	1972	Harold Henson, Ohio St	20	0	0	120	12.0
1940	Tom Harmon, Michigan	16	18	1	117	1973	Jim Jennings, Rutgers	21	2	0	128	11.6
1941	Bill Dudley, Virginia	18	23	1	134	1974	Bill Marek, Wisconsin	19	0	0	114	12.7
1942	Bob Steuber, Missouri	18	13	0	121	1975	Pete Johnson, Ohio St	25	0	0	150	13.6
1943	Steve Van Buren, LSU	14	14	0	98	1976	Tony Dorsett, Pitt	22	2	0	134	12.2
1944	Glenn Davis, Army	20	0	0	120	1977	Earl Campbell, Texas	19	0	0	114	10.4
1945	Doc Blanchard, Army	19	1	0	115	1978	Billy Sims, Oklahoma	20	0	0	120	10.9
1946	Gene Roberts, Tenn-Chatt	18	9	0	117	1979	Billy Sims, Oklahoma	22	0	0	132	12.0
1947	Lou Gambino, Maryland	16	0	0	96	1980	Sammy Winder, So. Miss	20	0	0	120	10.9
1948	Fred Wendt, Texas Mines	20	32	0	152	1981	Marcus Allen, USC	23	0	0	138	12.5
1949	George Thomas, Oklahoma	19	3	0	117	1982	Greg Allen, Fla. St	21	0	0	126	11.5
1950	Bobby Reynolds, Nebraska	22	25	0	157	1983	Mike Rozier, Nebraska	29	0	0	174	14.5
1951	Ollie Matson, San Francisco	21	0	0	126	1984	Keith Byars, Ohio St	24	0	0	144	13.1
1952	Jackie Parker, Miss. St.	16	24	0	120	1985	Bernard White, B. Green.	19	0	0	114	10.4
1953	Earl Lindley, Utah St.	13	3	0	81	1986	Steve Bartalo, Colo. St.	19	0	0	114	10.4
1954	Art Luppino, Arizona	24	22	0	166	1987	Paul Hewitt, S. Diego St.	24	0	0	144	12.0
1955	Jim Swink, TCU	20	5	0	125	1988	Barry Sanders, Okla.St.	39	0	0	234	21.3
1956	Clendon Thomas, Oklahoma	18	0	0	108	1989	Anthony Thompson, Ind	25	4	0	154	14.0
1957	Leon Burton, Ariz. St.	16	0	0	96	1990	Stacey Robinson, No. Ill.	19	6	0	120	10.9
1958	Dick Bass, Pacific	18	8	0	116	1991	Marshall Faulk, S.D. St.	23	2	0	140	15.6
1959	Pervis Atkins, N. Mexico St.	17	5	0	107	1992	Garrison Hearst, Georgia	21	0	0	126	11.5
1960	Bob Gaiters, N. Mexico St.	23	7	0	145	1993	Bam Morris, Texas Tech	22	2	0	134	12.2
1961	Jim Pilot, N. Mexico St.	21	12	0	138	1994	Rashaan Salaam, Colo	24	0	0	144	13.1
1962	Jerry Logan, W. Texas St.	13	32	0	110	1995	Eddie George, Ohio St.	24	0	0	144	12.0
1963	Cosmo Iacavazzi, Princeton	14	0	0	84	1996	Corey Dillon, Washington	23	0	0	138	12.6
	& Dave Casinelli, Memphis St.	14	0	0	84	1997	Ricky Williams, Texas	25	2	0	152	13.8
1964	Brian Piccolo, Wake Forest	17	9	0	111	1998	Troy Edwards, La. Tech	31	2	0	188	15.7
1965	Howard Twilley, Tulsa	16	31	0	127	1999	Shaun Alexander, Alabama	24	0	0	144	13.1
1966	Ken Hebert, Houston	11	41	2	113	2000	Lee Suggs, Va. Tech	28	0	0	168	15.3
1967	Leroy Keyes, Purdue	19	0	0	114	2001	Luke Staley, BYU	28	2	0	170	15.5
1968	Jim O'Brien, Cincinnati	12	31	13	142	2002	Brock Forsey, Boise St.	32	0	0	192	14.8
1969	Steve Owens, Oklahoma	23	0	0	138	2003	Patrick Cobbs, No. Texas	21	0	0	126	11.5
						2004	Tyler Jones, Boise St.	0	69	24	141	11.8
						2005	Michael Bush, Louisville	24	0	0	144	14.4

All-Time Best Records by a Starting Quarterback

(Minimum 25 starts) Source: NCAA Record Book

	Years	W-L-T	Win Pct.
Chuck Ealey, Toledo	1969-71	35-0-0	1.000
Jimmy Harris, Oklahoma	1954-56	25-0-0	1.000
Steve Davis, Oklahoma	1973-75	32-1-1*	.956
Ken Dorsey, Miami-FL	1999-2002	38-2-0	.950
Matt Leinart, USC	2002-05	37-2-0	.949
Jerry Tagge, Nebraska	1969-71	24-1-1	.942
Vince Young, Texas	2003-05	30-2-0	.938

All-Time NCAA Division I-A Leaders

Through the 2005 regular season. The NCAA does not recognize active players among career Per Game leaders.

CAREER

Passing
(Minimum 500 Completions)

Passing Efficiency	Years	Rating
1 Ryan Dinwiddie, Boise St.	2000-03	168.4
2 Danny Wuerffel, Florida	1993-96	163.6
3 Ty Detmer, BYU.	1988-91	162.7
4 Steve Sarkisian, BYU	1995-96	162.0
5 Matt Leinart, USC	2002-05	159.5

Yards Gained	Years	Yards
1 Timmy Chang, Hawaii	2000-04	17,072
2 Ty Detmer, BYU.	1988-91	15,031
3 Philip Rivers, N.C. State	2000-03	13,484
4 Tim Rattay, La. Tech	1997-99	12,746
5 Luke McCown, La. Tech	2000-03	12,666

Completions	Years	No
1 Timmy Chang, Hawaii	2000-04	1388
2 Kliff Kingsbury, Texas Tech	1999-02	1231
3 Philip Rivers, N.C. State	2000-03	1147
4 Chris Redman, Louisville	1996-99	1031
5 Tim Rattay, La. Tech	1997-99	1015

Receptions

Catches	Years	No
1 Taylor Stubblefield, Purdue	2001-04	316
2 Josh Davis, Marshall	2001-04	306
3 Taurean Henderson, Texas Tech	2002-05	303
4 Arnold Jackson, Louisville	1997-00	300
5 Trevor Insley, Nevada	1996-99	298

Catches Per Game	Years	No	P/Gm
1 Manny Hazard, Houston.	1989-90	220	10.5
2 Alex Van Dyke, Nevada	1994-95	227	10.3
3 Howard Twilley, Tulsa	1963-65	261	10.0
4 Jason Phillips, Houston	1987-88	207	9.4
5 Troy Edwards, La. Tech	1996-98	280	8.2

Yards Gained	Years	No	Yards
1 Trevor Insley, Nevada	1996-99	298	5005
2 Marcus Harris, Wyoming	1993-96	259	4518
3 Rashaun Woods, Oklahoma St.	2000-03	293	4412
4 Ryan Yarborough, Wyoming	1990-93	229	4357
5 Troy Edwards, La. Tech	1996-98	280	4352

Rushing

Yards Gained	Years	Yards
1 Ron Dayne, Wisconsin	1996-99	6397
2 Ricky Williams, Texas	1995-98	6279
3 Tony Dorsett, Pittsburgh	1973-76	6082
4 DeAngelo Williams, Memphis	2002-05	6026
5 Charles White, USC	1976-79	5598

Yards Per Game	Years	Yards	P/Gm
1 Ed Marinaro, Cornell.	1969-71	4715	174.6
2 O.J. Simpson, USC	1967-68	3124	164.4
3 Herschel Walker, Georgia	1980-82	5259	159.4
4 LeShon Johnson, No. Ill.	1992-93	3314	150.6
5 Ron Dayne, Wisconsin	1996-99	6397	148.8

Total Offense

Yards Gained	Years	Yards
1 Timmy Chang, Hawaii	2000-04	16,910
2 Ty Detmer, BYU.	1988-91	14,665
3 Philip Rivers, N.C. State	2000-03	13,582
4 Brad Smith, Missouri	2002-05	13,088
5 Luke McCown, La. Tech	2000-03	12,731
6 Tim Rattay, La. Tech	1997-99	12,618

Yards Per Game	Years	Yards	P/Gm
1 Tim Rattay, La. Tech	1997-99	12,689	382.4
2 Chris Vargas, Nevada	1992-93	6,417	320.9
3 Timmy Chang, Hawaii	2000-04	16,910	319.1
4 Ty Detmer, BYU.	1988-91	14,665	318.8
5 Daunte Culpepper*, C. Fla.	1996-98	10,344	313.5

*Culpepper played I-AA with Central Florida in 1995.

All-Purpose Yardage

Yards Gained	Years	Yards
1 DeAngelo Williams, Memphis	2002-05	7573
2 Ricky Williams, Texas	1995-98	7206
3 Napoleon McCallum, Navy	1981-85	7172
4 Darrin Nelson, Stanford	1977-78, 80-81	6885
5 Kevin Faulk, LSU.	1995-98	6833

Yards Per Game	Years	Yards	P/Gm
1 Ryan Benjamin, Pacific	1990-92	5706	237.8
2 Sheldon Canley, S. Jose St.	1988-90	5146	205.8
3 Howard Stevens, Louisville	1971-72	3873	193.7
4 O.J. Simpson, USC	1967-68	3666	192.9
5 Alex Van Dyke, Nevada	1994-95	4146	188.5

Miscellaneous

Punting Average*	Years	Avg
1 Shane Lechler, Texas A&M	1996-99	44.7
2 Bill Smith, Mississippi	1983-86	44.3
3 Jim Arnold, Vanderbilt	1979-82	43.9
4 Ralf Mojsiejenko, Michigan St.	1981-84	43.6
5 Jim Miller, Mississippi	1976-79	43.4

*Minimum 250 punts.

Punting Return Average*	Years	Avg
1 Jack Mitchell, Oklahoma.	1946-48	23.6
2 Gene Gibson, Cincinnati	1949-50	20.5
3 Eddie Macon, Pacific.	1949-51	18.9
4 Jackie Robinson, UCLA	1939-40	18.8
5 Dan Shelton, N. Illinois	2001-04	17.9

*Minimum 1.2 punt returns per game and 30 career returns.

Kickoff Return Average*	Years	Avg
1 Anthony Davis, USC	1972-74	35.1
2 Eric Booth, So. Miss.	1994-97	32.4
3 Overton Curtis, Utah St	1957-58	31.0
4 Fred Montgomery, New Mexico St.	1991-92	30.5
5 Altie Taylor, Utah St.	1966-68	29.3

*Minimum 1.2 kickoff returns per game and 30 career returns.

Interceptions	Years	No
1 Al Brosky, Illinois	1950-52	29
2 John Provost, Holy Cross	1972-74	27
Martin Bayless, Bowling Green	1980-83	27
4 Tom Curtis, Michigan	1967-69	25
Tony Thurman, Boston College	1981-84	25
Tracy Saul, Texas Tech.	1989-92	25

Blocked Kicks	Years	FG	XP	P	Tot
1 James Ferebee, N. Mexico St.	1978-81	8	6	5	19
2 Max McGeary, Baylor	1977-80	6	4	6	16
3 James King, C. Michigan	2001-04	1	2	10	13
4 Terrence Holt, N.C. State	1999-02	8	0	4	12
5 Matt Harding, Hawaii	1992-95	5	1	6	12

Note: The blocked kicks category is a combined total of blocked field goals (FG), extra points (XP) and punts (P).

> **Editor's Note:** The keeping of complete defensive statistics, except for blocked kicks (see above), had been inconsistent until recently. As a result the NCAA only tracks most defensive stats back to 2000 and due to the lack of historical context, those records have been omitted here.

Scoring
Non-kickers

Points	Years	TD	Xpt	FG	Pts
1 Travis Prentice, Miami-OH	1996-99	78	0	0	468
2 Ricky Williams, Texas	1995-98	75	2	0	452
3 Taurean Henderson, Tex. Tech	2002-05	69	0	0	414
3 Brock Forsey, Boise St.	1999-02	68	0	0	408
4 Cedric Benson, Texas	2001-04	67	1	0	404

Points Per Game	Years	Pts	P/Gm
1 Marshall Faulk, S. Diego St.	1991-93	376	12.1
2 Ed Marinaro, Cornell.	1969-71	318	11.8
3 Bill Burnett, Arkansas	1968-70	294	11.3
4 Steve Owens, Oklahoma	1967-69	336	11.2
5 Eddie Talboom, Wyoming	1948-50	303	10.8

Touchdowns Rushing	Years	No
1 Travis Prentice, Miami-OH	1996-99	73
2 Ricky Williams, Texas	1995-98	72
3 Anthony Thompson, Indiana	1986-89	64
Cedric Benson, Texas	2001-04	64
5 Ron Dayne, Wisconsin	1996-99	63

Touchdowns Passing	Years	No
1 Ty Detmer, BYU	1988-91	121
2 Timmy Chang, Hawaii	2000-04	117
3 Tim Rattay, La. Tech	1997-99	115
4 Danny Wuerffel, Florida	1993-96	114
5 Chad Pennington, Marshall	1997-99	100

Touchdowns Catches	Years	No
1 Troy Edwards, La. Tech	1996-98	50
2 Darius Watts, Marshall	2000-03	47
3 Aaron Turner, Pacific	1989-92	43
4 Ryan Yarborough, Wyoming	1990-93	42
Rashaun Woods, Oklahoma St.	2000-03	42

Kickers

Points	Years	FG	XP	Pts
1 Roman Anderson, Hou	1988-91	70	213	423
2 Billy Bennett, Georgia	2000-03	87	110	409
3 Carlos Huerta, Mia-FL	1988-91	73	178	397
4 Jason Elam, Hawaii	1988-89, 91-92	79	158	395
5 Nick Novak, Maryland	2001-04	80	153	393
Derek Schmidt, Florida St.	1984-87	73	174	393

Field Goals	Years	No
1 Billy Bennett, Georgia	2000-03	87
2 Jeff Jaeger, Washington	1983-86	80
Nick Novak, Maryland	2001-04	80
4 John Lee, UCLA	1982-85	79
Jason Elam, Hawaii	1988-89, 91-92	79

SINGLE SEASON

Note that starting with the 2002 season postseason and bowl games are included in single season records

Rushing

Yards Gained	Year	Gm	Car	Yards
Barry Sanders, Okla. St	1988	11	344	2628
Marcus Allen, USC	1981	11	403	2342
Troy Davis, Iowa St.	1996	11	402	2185
LaDainian Tomlinson, TCU	2000	11	369	2158
Mike Rozier, Nebraska	1983	12	275	2148

Yards Per Game	Year	Gm	Yards	P/Gm
Barry Sanders, Okla. St	1988	11	2628	238.9
Marcus Allen, USC	1981	11	2342	212.9
Ed Marinaro, Cornell.	1971	9	1881	209.0
Troy Davis, Iowa St.	1996	11	2185	198.6
LaDainian Tomlinson, TCU	2000	11	2158	196.2

Passing
(Minimum 15 Attempts Per Game)

Passing Efficiency	Year	Rating
Shaun King, Tulane	1998	183.3
Stefan Lefors, Louisville	2004	181.7
Michael Vick, Va. Tech	1999	180.4
Danny Wuerffel, Florida	1995	178.4
Jim McMahon, BYU	1980	176.9

Yards Gained	Year	Yards
B.J. Symons, Texas Tech	2003	5833
Ty Detmer, BYU.	1990	5188
David Klingler, Houston.	1990	5140
Kliff Kingsbury, Texas Tech	2002	5017
Tim Rattay, La. Tech	1998	4943

Completions	Year	Att	No
Kliff Kingsbury, Texas Tech	2002	712	479
B.J. Symons, Texas Tech	2003	719	470
Tim Rattay, La. Tech	1998	559	380
David Klingler, Houston.	1990	643	374
Andre Ware, Houston	1989	578	365

Receptions

Catches	Year	Gm	No
Manny Hazard, Houston	1989	11	142
Troy Edwards, La. Tech	1998	12	140
Nate Burleson, Nevada	2002	12	138
Howard Twilley, Tulsa	1965	10	134
Trevor Insley, Nevada	1999	11	134

Catches Per Game	Year	No	P/Gm
Howard Twilley, Tulsa	1965	134	13.4
Manny Hazard, Houston	1989	142	12.9
Trevor Insley, Nevada	1999	134	12.2
Alex Van Dyke, Nevada	1995	129	11.7
Troy Edwards, La. Tech	1998	140	11.7

Yards Gained	Year	No	Yards
Trevor Insley, Nevada	1999	134	2060
Troy Edwards, La. Tech	1998	140	1996
Alex Van Dyke, Nevada	1995	129	1854
J.R. Tolver, San Diego St.	2002	128	1785
Howard Twilley, Tulsa	1965	134	1779
Josh Reed, LSU	2001	94	1740

Total Offense

Yards Gained	Year	Gm	Plays	Yards
B.J. Symons, Texas Tech	2003	13	798	5976
David Klingler, Houston.	1990	11	704	5221
Ty Detmer, BYU.	1990	12	635	5022
Kliff Kingsbury, Texas Tech	2002	14	814	4903
Tim Rattay, La. Tech	1998	12	602	4840

Yards Per Game	Year	Gm	Yards	P/Gm
David Klingler, Houston.	1990	11	5221	474.6
B.J. Symons, Texas Tech	2003	13	5976	459.7
Andre Ware, Houston	1989	11	4661	423.7
Ty Detmer, BYU.	1990	12	5022	418.5
Tim Rattay, La. Tech	1998	12	4840	403.3

All-Purpose Yardage

Yards Gained	Year	Yards
Barry Sanders, Okla. St	1988	3250
Ryan Benjamin, Pacific	1991	2995
Reggie Bush, USC	2005	2890
Troy Edwards, La. Tech	1998	2784
Darren Sproles, Kansas St.	2003	2735

Yards Per Game	Year	Yards	P/Gm
Barry Sanders, Okla. St	1988	3250	295.5
Ryan Benjamin, Pacific	1991	2995	249.6
Byron (Whizzer) White, Colo	1937	1970	246.3
Mike Pringle, CS-Fullerton	1989	2690	244.6
Paul Palmer, Temple	1986	2633	239.4

All-Time NCAA Division I-A Leaders (Cont.)
SINGLE SEASON
Scoring

Points	Year	TD	Xpt	FG	Pts
Barry Sanders, Okla. St	1988	39	0	0	234
Brock Forsey, Boise St.	2002	32	0	0	192
Troy Edwards, La. Tech	1998	31	2	0	188
Mike Rozier, Nebraska	1983	29	0	0	174
Lydell Mitchell, Penn St	1971	29	0	0	174

Points Per Game	Year	Pts	P/Gm
Barry Sanders, Okla. St	1988	234	21.3
Bobby Reynolds, Nebraska	1950	157	17.4
Art Luppino, Arizona	1954	166	16.6
Ed Marinaro, Cornell	1971	148	16.4
Lydell Mitchell, Penn St	1971	174	15.8

Touchdowns Rushing	Year	No
Barry Sanders, Okla. St	1988	37
Mike Rozier, Nebraska	1983	29
Willis McGahee, Miami-FL	2002	28
Ricky Williams, Texas	1998	27
Lee Suggs, Va. Tech	2000	27
Brock Forsey, Boise St.	2002	26

Touchdowns Passing	Year	No
David Klingler, Houston	1990	54
B.J. Symons, Texas Tech	2003	52
Jim McMahon, BYU	1980	47
Andre Ware, Houston	1989	46
Tim Rattay, La. Tech	1998	46

Touchdown Catches	Year	No
Troy Edwards, La. Tech	1998	27
Randy Moss, Marshall	1997	25
Manny Hazard, Houston	1989	22
Larry Fitzgerald, Pittsburgh	2003	22
Desmond Howard, Michigan	1991	19
Ashley Lelie, Hawaii	2001	19

Field Goals	Year	No
Billy Bennett, Georgia	2003	31
John Lee, UCLA	1984	29
Paul Woodside, West Virginia	1982	28
Luis Zendejas, Arizona St	1983	28
Nick Browne, TCU	2003	28

Miscellaneous

Interceptions	Year	No
Al Worley, Washington	1968	14
George Shaw, Oregon	1951	13
Eight tied with 12 each.		

Punting Average*	Year	Avg
Chad Kessler, LSU	1997	50.3
Reggie Roby, Iowa	1981	49.8
Kirk Wilson, UCLA	1956	49.3
Todd Sauerbrun, West Virginia	1994	48.4
Travis Dorsch, Purdue	2001	48.4

*Qualifiers for championship.

Punt Return Average*	Year	Avg
Maurice Drew, UCLA	2005	28.5
Bill Blackstock, Tennessee	1951	25.9
Ted Ginn Jr., Ohio St.	2004	25.6
George Sims, Baylor	1948	25.0
*At least 1.2 punt returns per game.		

Kickoff Return Average*	Year	Avg
Paul Allen, BYU	1961	40.1
Tremain Mack, Miami-FL	1996	39.5
Leeland McElroy, Texas A&M	1993	39.3
Forrest Hall, San Francisco	1946	38.2
*At least 1.2 kickoff returns per game.		

SINGLE GAME
Rushing

Yards Gained	Opponent	Year	Yds
LaDainian Tomlinson, TCU	UTEP	1999	406
Tony Sands, Kansas	Missouri	1991	396
Marshall Faulk, San Diego St	Pacific	1991	386
Troy Davis, Iowa St.	Missouri	1996	378
Anthony Thompson, Indiana	Wisconsin	1989	377
Robbie Mixon, C. Michigan	E. Michigan	2002	377

Passing

Yards Gained	Opponent	Year	Yds
David Klingler, Houston	Arizona St.	1990	716
Matt Vogler, TCU	Houston	1990	690
B.J. Symons, Texas Tech	Mississippi	2003	661
Cody Hodges, Texas Tech	Kansas St.	2005	643
Brian Lindgren, Idaho	Mid. Tenn. St.	2001	637

Completions	Opponent	Year	No
Drew Brees, Purdue	Wisconsin	1998	55
Rusty LaRue, Wake Forest	Duke	1995	55
Rusty LaRue, Wake Forest	N.C. St.	1995	50

Four tied with 49 each (including twice by Kliff Kingsbury).

Total Offense

Yards Gained	Opponent	Year	Yds
David Klingler, Houston	Arizona St.	1990	732
Matt Vogler, TCU	Houston	1990	696
B.J. Symons, Texas Tech	Mississippi	2003	681
David Klingler, Houston	TCU	1990	625
Scott Mitchell, Utah	Air Force	1988	625

Receiving

Catches	Opponent	Year	No
Randy Gatewood, UNLV.	Idaho	1994	23
Jay Miller, BYU	New Mexico	1973	22
Troy Edwards, La. Tech	Nebraska	1998	21
Chris Daniels, Purdue	Mich. St.	1999	21
Two tied with 20 each.			

Yards Gained	Opponent	Year	Yds
Troy Edwards, La. Tech	Nebraska	1998	405
Randy Gatewood, UNLV.	Idaho	1994	363
Chuck Hughes, UTEP*	N. Texas St.	1965	349
Nate Burleson, Nevada	San Jose St.	2001	326
Rick Eber, Tulsa	Idaho St.	1967	322

*UTEP was Texas Western in 1965.

Scoring

Points	Opponent	Year	Pts
Howard Griffith, Illinois	So. Ill.	1990	48
Marshall Faulk, S. Diego St	Pacific	1991	44
Jim Brown, Syracuse	Colgate	1956	43
Showboat Boykin, Ole Miss	Miss. St.	1951	42
Fred Wendt, UTEP*	N. Mex. St.	1948	42
Rashaun Woods, Oklahoma St.	SMU	2003	42
*UTEP was Texas Mines in 1948.

Touchdowns Rushing	Opponent	Year	No
Howard Griffith, Illinois	So. Ill	1990	8
Showboat Boykin, Ole Miss	Miss. St.	1951	7
Note: Griffith's TD runs (5-51-7-41-5-18-5-3).

Touchdown Catches	Opponent	Year	No
Rashaun Woods, Oklahoma St.	SMU	2003	7
Tim Delaney, S. Diego St	N. Mex. St.	1969	6
Note: Woods's TD catches (2-10-34-32-25-5-11).

Touchdowns Passing	Opponent	Year	No
David Klingler, Houston	E.Wash.	1990	11
Dennis Shaw, San Diego St	N. Mex. St.	1969	9
Note: Klingler's TD passes (5-48-29-7-3-7-40-8-7-8-51).

Field Goals	Opponent	Year	No
Dale Klein, Nebraska	Missouri	1985	7
Mike Prindle, W. Michigan	Marshall	1984	7
Note: Klein's FGs (32-22-43-44-29-43-43); Prindle's FGs (32-44-42-23-48-41-27).

Extra Points (Kick)	Opponent	Year	No
Terry Leiweke, Houston	Tulsa	1968	13
Derek Mahoney, Fresno St	New Mexico	1991	13

Longest Plays (since 1941)

Rushing	Opponent	Year	Yds
Gale Sayers, Kansas	Nebraska	1963	99
Max Anderson, Ariz. St	Wyoming	1967	99
Ralph Thompson, W. Texas St	Wich. St.	1970	99
Kelsey Finch, Tennessee	Florida	1977	99
Eric Vann, Kansas	Oklahoma	1997	99
Eleven tied at 98 each.

Passing	Opponent	Year	Yds
Fred Owens to Jack Ford, Portland	St. Mary's	1947	99
Bo Burris to Warren McVea, Houston	Wash. St.	1966	99
Colin Clapton to Eddie Jenkins, Holy Cross	Boston U.	1970	99
Terry Peel to Robert Ford, Houston	Syracuse	1970	99
Terry Peel to Robert Ford, Houston	S. Diego St.	1972	99
Cris Collinsworth to Derrick Gaffney, Florida	Rice	1977	99
Scott Ankrom to James Maness, TCU	Rice	1984	99
Gino Torretta to Horace Copeland, Miami-FL	Ark.	1991	99

Passing (cont.)	Opponent	Year	Yds
John Paci to Thomas Lewis, Indiana	Penn St.	1993	99
Troy DeGar to Wes Caswell, Tulsa	Oklahoma	1996	99
Drew Brees to Vinny Sutherland, Purdue	N'western	1999	99
Dan Urban to Justin McCariens, N. Ill	Ball St.	2000	99
Jason Johnson to Brandon Marshall, Ariz.	Idaho	2001	99
Jim Sorgi to Lee Evans, Wisconsin	Akron	2003	99
Dondrial Pinkins to Troy Williamson, South Carolina	Virginia	2003	99

Field Goals	Opponent	Year	Yds
Steve Little, Arkansas	Texas	1977	67
Russell Erxleben, Texas	Rice	1977	67
Joe Williams, Wichita St	So. Ill.	1978	67
Tony Franklin, Tex. A&M	Baylor	1976	65
Martin Gramatica, Kan. St.	No. Ill.	1998	65
Note: Gramatica's FG is the only one listed above that was not off a tee and through the narrower (18'6") goal posts.

Longest Division I Streaks

Winning Streaks
(Including bowl games)

No		Seasons	Spoiler	Score
47	Oklahoma	1953-57	Notre Dame	7-0
39	Washington	1908-14	Oregon St.	0-0
37	Yale	1890-93	Princeton	6-0
37	Yale	1887-89	Princeton	10-0
35	Toledo	1969-71	Tampa	21-0
34	USC	2003-05	Texas	41-38*
34	Miami-FL	2000-02	Ohio St.	31-24*
34	Penn	1894-96	Lafayette	6-4
31	Oklahoma	1948-50	Kentucky	13-7*
31	Pittsburgh	1914-18	Cleve. Naval	10-9
31	Penn	1896-98	Harvard	10-0
30	Texas	1968-70	Notre Dame	24-11*
29	Miami-FL	1990-93	Alabama	34-13
29	Michigan	1901-03	Minnesota	6-6

*Texas beat USC in 2006 Rose Bowl; Ohio St. beat Miami in 2003 Fiesta Bowl in double overtime; Kentucky beat Oklahoma in 1951 Sugar Bowl and Notre Dame beat Texas in 1971 Cotton Bowl.

Unbeaten Streaks
(Including bowl games)

No	W-T		Seasons	Spoiler	Score
63	59-4	Washington	1907-17	California	27-0
56	55-1	Michigan	1901-05	Chicago	2-0
50	46-4	California	1920-25	Olympic Club	15-0
48	47-1	Oklahoma	1953-57	N. Dame	7-0
48	47-1	Yale	1885-89	Princeton	10-0
47	42-5	Yale	1879-85	Princeton	6-5
44	42-2	Yale	1894-96	Princeton	24-6
42	39-3	Yale	1904-08	Harvard	4-0
39	37-2	N. Dame	1946-50	Purdue	28-14

Losing Streaks

No		Seasons	Victim	Score
80	Prairie View	1989-98	Langston	14-12
44	Columbia	1983-88	Princeton	16-14
34	Northwestern	1979-82	No. Illinois	31-6
28	Virginia	1958-60	Wm. & Mary	21-6
28	Kansas St	1944-48	Arkansas St.	37-6

Note: Virginia ended its losing streak in the opening game of the 1961 season.

Annual Awards
Heisman Trophy

Originally presented in 1935 as the DAC Trophy by the Downtown Athletic Club of New York City to the best college football player east of the Mississippi. In 1936, players across the country were eligible and the award was renamed the Heisman Trophy following the death of former college coach and DAC athletic director John W. Heisman.

Multiple winner: Archie Griffin (2).

Winners in junior year (16): Doc Blanchard (1945), Reggie Bush (2005), Ty Detmer (1990); Archie Griffin (1974), Desmond Howard (1991), Vic Janowicz (1950), Matt Leinart (2004), Rashaan Salaam (1994), Barry Sanders (1988), Billy Sims (1978), Roger Staubach (1963), Doak Walker (1948), Herschel Walker (1982), Andre Ware (1989), Jason White (2003) and Charles Woodson (1997)

Winners on AP national champions (11): Angelo Bertelli (Notre Dame, 1943); Doc Blanchard (Army, 1945); Tony Dorsett (Pittsburgh, 1976); Leon Hart (Notre Dame, 1949); Matt Leinart (USC, 2004); Johnny Lujack (Notre Dame, 1947); Davey O'Brien (TCU, 1938); Bruce Smith (Minnesota, 1941); Charlie Ward (Florida St., 1993); Danny Wuerffel (Florida, 1996); Charles Woodson (Michigan, 1997).

Year		Points
1935	**Jay Berwanger,** Chicago, HB	.84
	2nd–Monk Meyer, Army, HB	.29
	3rd–Bill Shakespeare, Notre Dame, HB	.23
	4th–Pepper Constable, Princeton, FB	.20
1936	**Larry Kelley,** Yale, E	.219
	2nd–Sam Francis, Nebraska, FB	.47
	3rd–Ray Buivid, Marquette, HB	.43
	4th–Sammy Baugh, TCU, HB	.39
1937	**Clint Frank,** Yale, HB	.524
	2nd–Byron (Whizzer) White, Colo., HB	.264
	3rd–Marshall Goldberg, Pitt, HB	.211
	4th–Alex Wojciechowicz, Fordham, C	.85
1938	**Davey O'Brien,** TCU, QB	.519
	2nd–Marshall Goldberg, Pitt, HB	.294
	3rd–Sid Luckman, Columbia, QB	.154
	4th–Bob MacLeod, Dartmouth, HB	.78
1939	**Nile Kinnick,** Iowa, HB	.651
	2nd–Tom Harmon, Michigan, HB	.405
	3rd–Paul Christman, Missouri, QB	.391
	4th–George Cafego, Tennessee, QB	.296
1940	**Tom Harmon,** Michigan, HB	.1303
	2nd–John Kimbrough, Texas A&M, FB	.841
	3rd–George Franck, Minnesota, HB	.102
	4th–Frankie Albert, Stanford, QB	.90
1941	**Bruce Smith,** Minnesota, HB	.554
	2nd–Angelo Bertelli, Notre Dame, QB	.345
	3rd–Frankie Albert, Stanford, QB	.336
	4th–Frank Sinkwich, Georgia, HB	.249
1942	**Frank Sinkwich,** Georgia, TB	.1059
	2nd–Paul Governali, Columbia, QB	.218
	3rd–Clint Castleberry, Ga. Tech, HB	.99
	4th–Mike Holovak, Boston College, FB	.95
1943	**Angelo Bertelli,** Notre Dame, QB	.648
	2nd–Bob Odell, Penn, HB	.177
	3rd–Otto Graham, Northwestern, QB	.140
	4th–Creighton Miller, Notre Dame, HB	.134
1944	**Les Horvath,** Ohio St., TB-QB	.412
	2nd–Glenn Davis, Army, HB	.287
	3rd–Doc Blanchard, Army, FB	.237
	4th–Don Whitmire, Navy, T	.115
1945	**Doc Blanchard,** Army, FB	.860
	2nd–Glenn Davis, Army, HB	.638
	3rd–Bob Fenimore, Oklahoma A&M, HB	.187
	4th–Herman Wedemeyer, St. Mary's, HB	.152
1946	**Glenn Davis,** Army, HB	.792
	2nd–Charlie Trippi, Georgia, HB	.435
	3rd–Johnny Lujack, Notre Dame, QB	.379
	4th–Doc Blanchard, Army, FB	.267
1947	**Johnny Lujack,** Notre Dame, QB	.742
	2nd–Bob Chappuis, Michigan, HB	.555
	3rd–Doak Walker, SMU, HB	.196
	4th–Charlie Conerly, Mississippi, QB	.186
1948	**Doak Walker,** SMU, HB	.778
	2nd–Charlie Justice, N. Carolina, HB	.443
	3rd–Chuck Bednarik, Penn, C	.336
	4th–Jackie Jensen, California, HB	.143
1949	**Leon Hart,** Notre Dame, E	.995
	2nd–Charlie Justice, N. Carolina, HB	.272
	3rd–Doak Walker, SMU, HB	.229
	4th–Arnold Galiffa, Army, QB	.196

Year		Points
1950	**Vic Janowicz,** Ohio St., HB	.633
	2nd–Kyle Rote, SMU, HB	.280
	3rd–Reds Bagnell, Penn, HB	.231
	4th–Babe Parilli, Kentucky, QB	.214
1951	**Dick Kazmaier,** Princeton, TB	.1777
	2nd–Hank Lauricella, Tennessee, HB	.424
	3rd–Babe Parilli, Kentucky, QB	.344
	4th–Bill McColl, Stanford, E	.313
1952	**Billy Vessels,** Oklahoma, HB	.525
	2nd–Jack Scarbath, Maryland, QB	.367
	3rd–Paul Giel, Minnesota, HB	.329
	4th–Donn Moomaw, UCLA, C	.257
1953	**Johnny Lattner,** Notre Dame, HB	.1850
	2nd–Paul Giel, Minnesota, HB	.1794
	3rd–Paul Cameron, UCLA, HB	.444
	4th–Bernie Faloney, Maryland, QB	.258
1954	**Alan Ameche,** Wisconsin, FB	.1068
	2nd–Kurt Burris, Oklahoma, C	.838
	3rd–Howard Cassady, Ohio St., HB	.810
	4th–Ralph Guglielmi, Notre Dame, QB	.691
1955	**Howard Cassady,** Ohio St., HB	.2219
	2nd–Jim Swink, TCU, HB	.742
	3rd–George Welsh, Navy, QB	.383
	4th–Earl Morrall, Michigan St., QB	.323
1956	**Paul Hornung,** Notre Dame, QB	.1066
	2nd–Johnny Majors, Tennessee, HB	.994
	3rd–Tommy McDonald, Oklahoma, HB	.973
	4th–Jerry Tubbs, Oklahoma, C	.724
1957	**John David Crow,** Texas A&M, HB	.1183
	2nd–Alex Karras, Iowa, T	.693
	3rd–Walt Kowalczyk, Mich. St., HB	.630
	4th–Lou Michaels, Kentucky, T	.330
1958	**Pete Dawkins,** Army, HB	.1394
	2nd–Randy Duncan, Iowa, QB	.1021
	3rd–Billy Cannon, LSU, HB	.975
	4th–Bob White, Ohio St., FB	.365
1959	**Billy Cannon,** LSU, HB	.1929
	2nd–Richie Lucas, Penn St., QB	.613
	3rd–Don Meredith, SMU, QB	.286
	4th–Bill Burrell, Illinois, G	.196
1960	**Joe Bellino,** Navy, HB	.1793
	2nd–Tom Brown, Minnesota, G	.731
	3rd–Jake Gibbs, Mississippi, QB	.453
	4th–Ed Dyas, Auburn, HB	.319
1961	**Ernie Davis,** Syracuse, HB	.824
	2nd–Bob Ferguson, Ohio St., HB	.771
	3rd–Jimmy Saxton, Texas, HB	.551
	4th–Sandy Stephens, Minnesota, QB	.543
1962	**Terry Baker,** Oregon St., QB	.707
	2nd–Jerry Stovall, LSU, HB	.618
	3rd–Bobby Bell, Minnesota, T	.429
	4th–Lee Roy Jordan, Alabama, C	.321
1963	**Roger Staubach,** Navy, QB	.1860
	2nd–Billy Lothridge, Ga. Tech, QB	.504
	3rd–Sherman Lewis, Mich. St., HB	.369
	4th–Don Trull, Baylor, QB	.253
1964	**John Huarte,** Notre Dame, QB	.1026
	2nd–Jerry Rhome, Tulsa, QB	.952
	3rd–Dick Butkus, Illinois, C	.505
	4th–Bob Timberlake, Michigan, QB	.361

Year		Points
1965	**Mike Garrett,** USC, HB	.926
	2nd–Howard Twilley, Tulsa, E	.528
	3rd–Jim Grabowski, Illinois, FB	.481
	4th–Donny Anderson, Texas Tech, HB	.408
1966	**Steve Spurrier,** Florida, QB	.1679
	2nd–Bob Griese, Purdue, QB	.816
	3rd–Nick Eddy, Notre Dame, HB	.456
	4th–Gary Beban, UCLA, QB	.318
1967	**Gary Beban,** UCLA, QB	.1968
	2nd–O.J. Simpson, USC, HB	.1722
	3rd–Leroy Keyes, Purdue, HB	.1366
	4th–Larry Csonka, Syracuse, FB	.136
1968	**O.J. Simpson,** USC, HB	.2853
	2nd–Leroy Keyes, Purdue, HB	.1103
	3rd–Terry Hanratty, Notre Dame, QB	.387
	4th–Ted Kwalick, Penn St., TE	.254
1969	**Steve Owens,** Oklahoma, HB	.1488
	2nd–Mike Phipps, Purdue, QB	.1344
	3rd–Rex Kern, Ohio St., QB	.856
	4th–Archie Manning, Mississippi, QB.	.582
1970	**Jim Plunkett,** Stanford, QB	.2229
	2nd–Joe Theismann, Notre Dame, QB	.1410
	3rd–Archie Manning, Mississippi, QB	.849
	4th–Steve Worster, Texas, RB	398
1971	**Pat Sullivan,** Auburn, QB	.1597
	2nd–Ed Marinaro, Cornell, RB	.1445
	3rd–Greg Pruitt, Oklahoma, RB	.586
	4th–Johnny Musso, Alabama, RB	.365
1972	**Johnny Rodgers,** Nebraska, FL.	.1310
	2nd–Greg Pruitt, Oklahoma, RB.	.966
	3rd–Rich Glover, Nebraska, MG.	.652
	4th–Bert Jones, LSU, QB.	.351
1973	**John Cappelletti,** Penn St., RB.	.1057
	2nd–John Hicks, Ohio St., OT	.524
	3rd–Roosevelt Leaks, Texas, RB	.482
	4th–David Jaynes, Kansas, QB.	.394
1974	**Archie Griffin,** Ohio St., RB	.1920
	2nd–Anthony Davis, USC, RB.	.819
	3rd–Joe Washington, Oklahoma, RB.	.661
	4th–Tom Clements, Notre Dame, QB.	.244
1975	**Archie Griffin,** Ohio St., RB	.1800
	2nd–Chuck Muncie, California, RB	.730
	3rd–Ricky Bell, USC, RB	.708
	4th–Tony Dorsett, Pitt, RB	.616
1976	**Tony Dorsett,** Pittsburgh, RB	.2357
	2nd–Ricky Bell, USC, RB	.1346
	3rd–Rob Lytle, Michigan, RB	.413
	4th–Terry Miller, Oklahoma St., RB	.197
1977	**Earl Campbell,** Texas, RB	.1547
	2nd–Terry Miller, Oklahoma St., RB.	.812
	3rd–Ken MacAfee, Notre Dame, TE	.343
	4th–Doug Williams, Grambling, QB	.266
1978	**Billy Sims,** Oklahoma, RB	.827
	2nd–Chuck Fusina, Penn St., QB	.750
	3rd–Rick Leach, Michigan, QB.	.435
	4th–Charles White, USC, RB	.354
1979	**Charles White,** USC, RB	.1695
	2nd–Billy Sims, Oklahoma, RB	.773
	3rd–Marc Wilson, BYU, QB	.589
	4th–Art Schlichter, Ohio St., QB.	.251
1980	**George Rogers,** South Carolina, RB	.1128
	2nd–Hugh Green, Pittsburgh, DE	.861
	3rd–Herschel Walker, Georgia, RB	.683
	4th–Mark Herrmann, Purdue, QB.	.405
1981	**Marcus Allen,** USC, RB	.1797
	2nd–Herschel Walker, Georgia, RB	.1199
	3rd–Jim McMahon, BYU, QB	.706
	4th–Dan Marino, Pitt, QB	.256
1982	**Herschel Walker,** Georgia, RB	.1926
	2nd–John Elway, Stanford, QB	.1231
	3rd–Eric Dickerson, SMU, RB	.465
	4th–Anthony Carter, Michigan, WR	.142
1983	**Mike Rozier,** Nebraska, RB.	.1801
	2nd–Steve Young, BYU, QB	.1172
	3rd–Doug Flutie, Boston College, QB	.253
	4th–Turner Gill, Nebraska, QB.	.190

Year		Points
1984	**Doug Flutie,** Boston College, QB	.2240
	2nd–Keith Byars, Ohio St., RB	.1251
	3rd–Robbie Bosco, BYU, QB	.443
	4th–Bernie Kosar, Miami-FL, QB.	.320
1985	**Bo Jackson,** Auburn, RB	.1509
	2nd–Chuck Long, Iowa, QB	.1464
	3rd–Robbie Bosco, BYU, QB	.459
	4th–Lorenzo White, Michigan St., RB	.391
1986	**Vinny Testaverde,** Miami-FL, QB	.2213
	2nd–Paul Palmer, Temple, RB	.672
	3rd–Jim Harbaugh, Michigan, QB.	.458
	4th–Brian Bosworth, Oklahoma, LB	.395
1987	**Tim Brown,** Notre Dame, WR.	.1442
	2nd–Don McPherson, Syracuse, QB	.831
	3rd–Gordie Lockbaum, Holy Cross, WR-DB.	.657
	4th–Lorenzo White, Michigan St., RB	.632
1988	**Barry Sanders,** Oklahoma St., RB	.1878
	2nd–Rodney Peete, USC, QB	.912
	3rd–Troy Aikman, UCLA, QB	.582
	4th–Steve Walsh, Miami-FL, QB	.341
1989	**Andre Ware,** Houston, QB	.1073
	2nd–Anthony Thompson, Ind., RB	.1003
	3rd–Major Harris, West Va., QB	.709
	4th–Tony Rice, Notre Dame, QB	.523
1990	**Ty Detmer,** BYU, QB.	.1482
	2nd–Rocket Ismail, Notre Dame, FL.	.1177
	3rd–Eric Bieniemy, Colorado, RB	.798
	4th–Shawn Moore, Virginia, QB	.465
1991	**Desmond Howard,** Michigan, WR	.2077
	2nd–Casey Weldon, Florida St., QB	.503
	3rd–Ty Detmer, BYU, QB.	.445
	4th–Steve Emtman, Washington, DT	.357
1992	**Gino Torretta,** Miami-FL, QB	.1400
	2nd–Marshall Faulk, San Diego St., RB	.1080
	3rd–Garrison Hearst, Georgia, RB	.982
	4th–Marvin Jones, Florida St., LB	.392
1993	**Charlie Ward,** Florida St., QB	.2310
	2nd–Heath Shuler, Tennessee, QB	.688
	3rd–David Palmer, Alabama, RB	.292
	4th–Marshall Faulk, S. Diego St., RB	.250
1994	**Rashaan Salaam,** Colorado, RB	.1743
	2nd–Ki-Jana Carter, Penn St., RB	.901
	3rd–Steve McNair, Alcorn St., QB.	.655
	4th–Kerry Collins, Penn St., QB	.639
1995	**Eddie George,** Ohio St., RB	.1460
	2nd–Tommie Frazier, Nebraska, QB.	.1196
	3rd–Danny Wuerffel, Florida, QB	.987
	4th–Darnell Autry, Northwestern, RB	.535
1996	**Danny Wuerffel,** Florida, QB	.1363
	2nd–Troy Davis, Iowa St., RB	.1174
	3rd–Jake Plummer, Arizona St., QB.	.685
	4th–Orlando Pace, Ohio St., OT	.599
1997	**Charles Woodson,** Michigan, DB-WR	.1815
	2nd–Peyton Manning, Tennessee, QB.	.1543
	3rd–Ryan Leaf, Washington St., QB	.861
	4th–Randy Moss, Marshall, WR.	.253
1998	**Ricky Williams,** Texas, RB	.2355
	2nd–Michael Bishop, Kansas St., QB	.792
	3rd–Cade McNown, UCLA, QB	.696
	4th–Tim Couch, Kentucky, QB.	.527
1999	**Ron Dayne,** Wisconsin, RB	.2042
	2nd–Joe Hamilton, Ga. Tech, QB.	.994
	3rd–Michael Vick, Va. Tech, QB	.319
	4th–Drew Brees, Purdue, QB.	.308
2000	**Chris Weinke,** Florida St., QB	.1628
	2nd–Josh Heupel, Oklahoma, QB.	.1552
	3rd–Drew Brees, Purdue, QB	.619
	4th–LaDainian Tomlinson, TCU, RB	.566
2001	**Eric Crouch,** Nebraska, QB	.770
	2nd–Rex Grossman, Florida, QB	.708
	3rd–Ken Dorsey, Miami-FL, QB	.638
	4th–Joey Harrington, Oregon, QB.	.364
2002	**Carson Palmer,** USC, QB	.1328
	2nd–Brad Banks, Iowa, QB	.1095
	3rd–Larry Johnson, Penn St., RB	.726
	4th–Willis McGahee, Miami-FL, RB	.660

Annual Awards (Cont.)

2003	**Jason White**, Oklahoma, QB 1481		2005	**Reggie Bush**, USC, RB 2541
	2nd-Larry Fitzgerald, Pittsburgh, WR 1353			2nd-Vince Young, Texas, QB 1608
	3rd-Eli Manning, Mississippi, QB 710			3rd-Matt Leinart, USC, QB 797
	4th-Chris Perry, Michigan, RB 341			4th-Brady Quinn, Notre Dame, QB 191
2004	**Matt Leinart**, USC, QB 1325			
	2nd-Adrian Peterson, Oklahoma, RB 997			
	3rd-Jason White, Oklahoma, QB 957			
	4th-Alex Smith, Utah, QB 635			

Maxwell Award

First presented in 1937 by the Maxwell Memorial Football Club of Philadelphia, the award is named after Robert (Tiny) Maxwell, a Philadelphia native who was a standout lineman at the University of Chicago at the turn of the century. Like the Heisman, the Maxwell is given to the outstanding college player in the nation. Both awards have gone to the same player in the same season 34 times. Those players are preceded by (#). Glenn Davis of Army and Doak Walker of SMU won both but in different years.

Multiple winner: Johnny Lattner (2).

Year		Year		Year	
1937	#Clint Frank, Yale, HB	1960	#Joe Bellino, Navy, HB	1983	#Mike Rozier, Nebraska, RB
1938	#Davey O'Brien, TCU, QB	1961	Bob Ferguson, Ohio St., HB	1984	#Doug Flutie, Boston Col., QB
1939	#Nile Kinnick, Iowa, HB	1962	#Terry Baker, Oregon St., QB	1985	Chuck Long, Iowa, QB
1940	#Tom Harmon, Michigan, HB	1963	#Roger Staubach, Navy, QB	1986	#V. Testaverde, Miami-FL, QB
1941	Bill Dudley, Virginia, HB	1964	Glenn Ressler, Penn St., G	1987	Don McPherson, Syracuse, QB
1942	Paul Governali, Columbia, QB	1965	Tommy Nobis, Texas, LB	1988	#Barry Sanders, Okla. St., RB
1943	Bob Odell, Penn, HB	1966	Jim Lynch, Notre Dame, LB	1989	Anthony Thompson, Indiana, RB
1944	Glenn Davis, Army, HB	1967	#Gary Beban, UCLA, QB	1990	#Ty Detmer, BYU, QB
1945	#Doc Blanchard, Army, FB	1968	#O.J. Simpson, USC, HB	1991	#Desmond Howard, Mich., WR
1946	Charley Trippi, Georgia, HB	1969	Mike Reid, Penn St., DT	1992	#Gino Torretta, Miami-FL, QB
1947	Doak Walker, SMU, HB	1970	#Jim Plunkett, Stanford, QB	1993	#Charlie Ward, Florida St., QB
1948	Chuck Bednarik, Penn, C	1971	Ed Marinaro, Cornell, RB	1994	Kerry Collins, Penn St., QB
1949	#Leon Hart, Notre Dame, E	1972	Brad Van Pelt, Michigan St., DB	1995	#Eddie George, Ohio St., RB
1950	Reds Bagnell, Penn, HB	1973	#John Cappelletti, Penn St., RB	1996	#Danny Wuerffel, Florida, QB
1951	#Dick Kazmaier, Princeton, TB	1974	Steve Joachim, Temple, QB	1997	Peyton Manning, Tennessee, QB
1952	Johnny Lattner, Notre Dame, HB	1975	#Archie Griffin, Ohio St., RB	1998	#Ricky Williams, Texas, RB
1953	#Johnny Lattner, N. Dame, HB	1976	#Tony Dorsett, Pitt, RB	1999	#Ron Dayne, Wisconsin, RB
1954	Ron Beagle, Navy, E	1977	Ross Browner, Notre Dame, DE	2000	Drew Brees, Purdue, QB
1955	#Howard Cassady, Ohio St., HB	1978	Chuck Fusina, Penn St., QB	2001	Ken Dorsey, Miami-FL, QB
1956	Tommy McDonald, Okla., HB	1979	#Charles White, USC, RB	2002	Larry Johnson, Penn St., RB
1957	Bob Reifsnyder, Navy, T	1980	Hugh Green, Pitt, DE	2003	Eli Manning, Mississippi, QB
1958	#Pete Dawkins, Army, HB	1981	#Marcus Allen, USC, RB	2004	Jason White, Oklahoma, QB
1959	Rich Lucas, Penn St., QB	1982	#Herschel Walker, Georgia, RB	2005	Vince Young, Texas, QB

Outland Trophy

First presented in 1946 by the Football Writers Association of America, honoring the nation's outstanding interior lineman. The award is named after its benefactor, Dr. John H. Outland (Kansas, Class of 1898). Players listed in **bold** type helped lead their team to a national championship (according to AP).

Multiple winner: Dave Rimington (2). **Winners in junior year:** Ross Browner (1976), Steve Emtman (1991), Rien Long (2002), Orlando Pace (1996) and Rimington (1981).

Year		Year		Year	
1946	**George Connor,** N. Dame, T	1966	Loyd Phillips, Arkansas, T	1986	Jason Buck, BYU, DT
1947	Joe Steffy, Army, G	1967	**Ron Yary,** USC, T	1987	Chad Hennings, Air Force, DT
1948	Bill Fischer, Notre Dame, G	1968	Bill Stanfill, Georgia, T	1988	Tracy Rocker, Auburn, DT
1949	Ed Bagdon, Michigan St., G	1969	Mike Reid, Penn St., DT	1989	Mohammed Elewonibi, BYU, G
1950	Bob Gain, Kentucky, T	1970	Jim Stillwagon, Ohio St., MG	1990	Russell Maryland, Miami-FL, NT
1951	Jim Weatherall, Oklahoma, T	1971	**Larry Jacobson,** Neb., DT	1991	Steve Emtman, Washington, DT
1952	Dick Modzelewski, Maryland, T	1972	Rich Glover, Nebraska, MG	1992	Will Shields, Nebraska, G
1953	J.D. Roberts, Oklahoma, G	1973	John Hicks, Ohio St., OT	1993	Rob Waldrop, Arizona, NG
1954	Bill Brooks, Arkansas, G	1974	Randy White, Maryland, DT	1994	**Zach Wiegert,** Nebraska, OT
1955	Calvin Jones, Iowa, G	1975	**Lee Roy Selmon,** Okla., DT	1995	Jonathan Ogden, UCLA, OT
1956	Jim Parker, Ohio St., G	1976	Ross Browner, Notre Dame, DE	1996	Orlando Pace, Ohio St., OT
1957	Alex Karras, Iowa, T	1977	Brad Shearer, Texas, DT	1997	Aaron Taylor, Nebraska, G
1958	Zeke Smith, Auburn, G	1978	Greg Roberts, Oklahoma, G	1998	Kris Farris, UCLA, OT
1959	Mike McGee, Duke, T	1979	Jim Richter, N.C. State, C	1999	Chris Samuels, Alabama, OT
1960	**Tom Brown,** Minnesota, G	1980	Mark May, Pittsburgh, OT	2000	John Henderson, Tennessee, DT
1961	Merlin Olsen, Utah St., T	1981	Dave Rimington, Nebraska, C	2001	**Bryant McKinnie,** Miami-FL, OT
1962	Bobby Bell, Minnesota, T	1982	Dave Rimington, Nebraska, C	2002	Rien Long, Washington St., DT
1963	**Scott Appleton,** Texas, T	1983	Dean Steinkuhler, Nebraska, G	2003	Robert Gallery, Iowa, OT
1964	Steve DeLong, Tennessee, T	1984	Bruce Smith, Virginia Tech, DT	2004	Jammal Brown, Oklahoma, OT
1965	Tommy Nobis, Texas, G	1985	Mike Ruth, Boston College, NG	2005	Greg Eslinger, Minnesota, C

Butkus Award

First presented in 1985 by the Downtown Athletic Club of Orlando, Fla., to honor the nation's outstanding linebacker. The award is named after Dick Butkus, two-time consensus All-America at Illinois and six-time All-Pro with the Chicago Bears.

Multiple winner: Brian Bosworth (2).

Year		Year		Year	
1985	Brian Bosworth, Oklahoma	1992	Marvin Jones, Florida St.	1999	LaVar Arrington, Penn St.
1986	Brian Bosworth, Oklahoma	1993	Trev Alberts, Nebraska	2000	Dan Morgan, Miami-FL
1987	Paul McGowan, Florida St.	1994	Dana Howard, Illinois	2001	Rocky Calmus, Oklahoma
1988	Derrick Thomas, Alabama	1995	Kevin Hardy, Illinois	2002	E.J. Henderson, Maryland
1989	Percy Snow, Michigan St.	1996	Matt Russell, Colorado	2003	Teddy Lehman, Oklahoma
1990	Alfred Williams, Colorado	1997	Andy Katzenmoyer, Ohio St.	2004	Derrick Johnson, Texas
1991	Erick Anderson, Michigan	1998	Chris Claiborne, USC	2005	Paul Posluszny, Penn St.

Lombardi Award

First presented in 1970 by the Rotary Club of Houston, honoring the nation's best lineman. The award is named after pro football coach Vince Lombardi, who, as a guard, was a member of the famous "Seven Blocks of Granite" at Fordham in the 1930s. The Lombardi and Outland awards have gone to the same player in the same year ten times. Those players are preceded by (#). Ross Browner of Notre Dame won both, but in different years.

Multiple winner: Orlando Pace (2).

Year		Year		Year	
1970	#Jim Stillwagon, Ohio St., MG	1982	#Dave Rimington, Neb., C	1994	Warren Sapp, Miami-FL, DT
1971	Walt Patulski, Notre Dame, DE	1983	#Dean Steinkuhler, Neb., G	1995	Orlando Pace, Ohio St., OT
1972	#Rich Glover, Nebraska, MG	1984	Tony Degrate, Texas, DT	1996	#Orlando Pace, Ohio St., OT
1973	#John Hicks, Ohio St., OT	1985	Tony Casillas, Oklahoma, NG	1997	Grant Wistrom, Nebraska, DE
1974	#Randy White, Maryland, DT	1986	Cornelius Bennett, Alabama, LB	1998	Dat Nguyen, Tex. A&M, LB
1975	#Lee Roy Selmon, Okla., DT	1987	Chris Spielman, Ohio St., LB	1999	Corey Moore, Va. Tech, DE
1976	Wilson Whitley, Houston, DT	1988	#Tracy Rocker, Auburn, DT	2000	Jamal Reynolds, Florida St., DE
1977	Ross Browner, Notre Dame, DE	1989	Percy Snow, Michigan St., LB	2001	Julius Peppers, N. Carolina, DE
1978	Bruce Clark, Penn St., DT	1990	Chris Zorich, Notre Dame, NT	2002	Terrell Suggs, Arizona St., DE
1979	Brad Budde, USC, G	1991	#Steve Emtman, Wash., DT	2003	Tommie Harris, Oklahoma, DT
1980	Hugh Green, Pitt, DE	1992	Marvin Jones, Florida St., LB	2004	David Pollack, Georgia, DE
1981	Kenneth Sims, Texas, DT	1993	Aaron Taylor, Notre Dame, OT	2005	A.J. Hawk, Ohio St., LB

O'Brien Quarterback Award

First presented in 1977 as the O'Brien Memorial Trophy, the award went to the outstanding player in the Southwest. In 1981, however, the Davey O'Brien Educational and Charitable Trust of Ft. Worth renamed the prize the O'Brien National Quarterback Award and now honors the nation's best quarterback. The award is named after 1938 Heisman Trophy-winning QB Davey O'Brien of Texas Christian.

Multiple winners: Ty Detmer, Mike Singletary, Jason White and Danny Wuerffel (2).

Memorial Trophy

Year		Year		Year	
1977	Earl Campbell, Texas, RB	1979	Mike Singletary, Baylor, LB	1980	Mike Singletary, Baylor, LB
1978	Billy Sims, Oklahoma, RB				

National QB Award

Year		Year		Year	
1981	Jim McMahon, BYU	1990	Ty Detmer, BYU	1999	Joe Hamilton, Ga. Tech
1982	Todd Blackledge, Penn St.	1991	Ty Detmer, BYU	2000	Chris Weinke, Florida St.
1983	Steve Young, BYU	1992	Gino Torretta, Miami-FL	2001	Eric Crouch, Nebraska
1984	Doug Flutie, Boston College	1993	Charlie Ward, Florida St.	2002	Brad Banks, Iowa
1985	Chuck Long, Iowa	1994	Kerry Collins, Penn St.	2003	Jason White, Oklahoma
1986	Vinny Testaverde, Miami, FL	1995	Danny Wuerffel, Florida	2004	Jason White, Oklahoma
1987	Don McPherson, Syracuse	1996	Danny Wuerffel, Florida	2005	Vince Young, Texas
1988	Troy Aikman, UCLA	1997	Peyton Manning, Tennessee		
1989	Andre Ware, Houston	1998	Michael Bishop, Kansas St.		

Thorpe Award

First presented in 1986 by the Jim Thorpe Athletic Club of Oklahoma City to honor the nation's outstanding defensive back. The award is named after Jim Thorpe–Olympic champion and two-time consensus All-America halfback at Carlisle.

Year		Year		Year	
1986	Thomas Everett, Baylor	1992	Deon Figures, Colorado	1999	Tyrone Carter, Minnesota
1987	Bennie Blades, Miami-FL	1993	Antonio Langham, Alabama	2000	Jamar Fletcher, Wisconsin
	& Rickey Dixon, Oklahoma	1994	Chris Hudson, Colorado	2001	Roy Williams, Oklahoma
1988	Deion Sanders, Florida St.	1995	Greg Myers, Colorado St.	2002	Terence Newman, Kansas St.
1989	Mike Carrier, USC	1996	Lawrence Wright, Florida	2003	Derrick Strait, Oklahoma
1990	Darryl Lewis, Arizona	1997	Charles Woodson, Michigan	2004	Carlos Rogers, Auburn
1991	Terrell Buckley, Florida St.	1998	Antoine Winfield, Ohio St.	2005	Michael Huff, Texas

All-Time Winningest Division I-A Coaches

Minimum of 10 years in Division I-A through 2005 season. Regular season and bowl games included. Coaches active in 2004 in **bold** type.

Top 25 Winning Percentage

		Yrs	W	L	T	Pct
1	Knute Rockne	13	105	12	5	.881
2	Frank Leahy	13	107	13	9	.864
3	George Woodruff	12	142	25	2	.846
4	Barry Switzer	16	157	29	4	.837
5	Tom Osborne	25	255	49	3	.836
6	Percy Haughton	13	96	17	6	.832
7	Bob Neyland	21	173	31	12	.829
8	Hurry Up Yost	29	196	36	12	.828
9	Bud Wilkinson	17	145	29	4	.826
10	Jock Sutherland	20	144	28	14	.812
11	Bob Devaney	16	136	30	7	.806
12	Frank Thomas	19	141	33	9	.795
13	Henry Williams	23	141	34	12	.786
14	Gil Dobie	33	180	45	15	.781
15	Bear Bryant	38	323	85	17	.780
16	Fred Folsom	19	106	28	6	.779
17	**Phillip Fulmer**	14	128	37	0	.776
18	Bo Schembechler	27	234	65	8	.775
19	**Bobby Bowden**	40	359	105	4	.771
20	Fritz Crisler	18	116	32	9	.768
21	Charley Moran	18	122	33	12	.766
22	**Steve Spurrier**	16	149	45	2	.765
23	Wallace Wade	24	171	49	10	.765
24	Frank Kush	22	176	54	1	.764
25	Dan McGugin	30	197	55	19	.762

Top 25 Victories

		Yrs	W	L	T	Pct
1	**Bobby Bowden**	40	359	105	4	.771
2	**Joe Paterno**	40	354	117	3	.750
3	Bear Bryant	38	323	85	17	.780
4	Pop Warner	44	319	106	32	.733
5	Amos Alonzo Stagg	57	314	199	35	.605
6	LaVell Edwards	29	257	101	3	.722
7	Tom Osborne	25	255	49	3	.836
8	Lou Holtz	33	249	132	7	.651
9	Woody Hayes	33	238	72	10	.759
10	Bo Schembechler	27	234	65	8	.775
11	Hayden Fry	37	232	178	10	.564
12	Jess Neely	40	207	176	19	.539
13	Warren Woodson	31	203	95	14	.673
14	Don Nehlen	30	202	128	8	.609
15	Vince Dooley	25	201	77	10	.715
	Eddie Anderson	39	201	128	15	.606
17	Jim Sweeney	32	200	154	4	.564
18	Dana X. Bible	33	198	72	23	.715
19	Dan McGugin	30	197	55	19	.762
20	Hurry Up Yost	29	196	36	12	.828
21	Howard Jones	29	194	64	21	.733
22	John Cooper	24	192	84	6	.691
23	Johnny Vaught	25	190	61	12	.745
24	George Welsh	28	189	132	4	.588
25	**Frank Beamer**	25	188	102	4	.646

Note: John Gagliardi of Division III St. John's (Minn.) became the all-time leader in college football coaching wins in 2003 (passing Grambling's Eddie Robinson at 408 wins), finishing the year with a career record of 414-114-11 over 52 seasons at St. John's and three seasons at Montana's Carroll College.

Where They Coached

Anderson–Loras (1922-24), DePaul (1925-31), Holy Cross (1933-38), Iowa (1939-42), Holy Cross (1950-64); **Beamer**–Murray St. (1981-86), Virginia Tech (1987–); **Bible**– Mississippi College (1913-15), LSU (1916), Texas A&M (1917,1919-28), Nebraska (1929-36), Texas (1937-46); **Bowden**– Samford (1959-62), West Virginia (1970-75), Florida St. (1976–); **Bryant**–Maryland (1945), Kentucky (1946-53), Texas A&M (1954-57), Alabama (1958-82); **Cooper**– Tulsa (1977-84), Arizona St. (1985-87), Ohio St. (1988-2000); **Crisler**– Minnesota (1930-31), Princeton (1932-37), Michigan (1938-47); **Devaney**–Wyoming (1957-61), Nebraska (1962-72); **Dobie**–North Dakota St. (1906-07), Washington (1908-16), Navy (1917-19), Cornell (1920-35), Boston College (1936- 38); **V. Dooley**–Georgia (1964-88); **Edwards**–BYU (1972-2000); **Folsom**–Colorado (1895-99, 1901-02), Dartmouth (1903-06), Colorado (1908-15); **Fry**–SMU (1962-72), North Texas (1973-78), Iowa (1979-98); **Fulmer**–Tennessee (1992–).

Haughton–Cornell (1899-1900), Harvard (1908-16), Columbia (1923-24); **Hayes**–Denison (1946-48), Miami-OH (1949-50), Ohio St. (1951-78); **Holtz**–William & Mary (1969-71), N.C. State (1972-75), Arkansas (1977-83), Minnesota (1984-85), Notre Dame (1986-96), South Carolina (1999-2004); **Jones**–Syracuse (1908), Yale (1909), Ohio St. (1910), Yale (1913), Iowa (1916-23), Duke (1924), USC (1925- 40); **Kush**–Arizona St. (1958-79); **Leahy**–Boston College (1939-40), Notre Dame (1941-43, 1946-53); **Moran**–Texas A&M (1909-14), Centre (1919-23), Bucknell (1924-26), Catawba (1930-33).

Neely–Rhodes (1924-27), Clemson (1931-39), Rice (1940-66); **Nehlen**–Bowling Green (1968-76), West Virginia (1980-2000); **Neyland**–Tennessee (1926-34, 1936-40, 1946-52); **Osborne**–Nebraska (1973-97); **Paterno**–Penn St. (1966–); Rockne–Notre Dame (1918-30); **Schembechler**–Miami-OH (1963-68), Michigan (1969-89); **Spurrier**–Duke (1987-89), Florida (1990-2001); **Stagg**–Springfield College (1890-91), Chicago (1892-1932), Pacific (1933-46); **Sutherland**–Lafayette (1919-23), Pittsburgh (1924-38); **Sweeney**–Montana St. (1963-67), Washington St. (1968-75), Fresno St. (1976-96); **Switzer**–Oklahoma (1973-88).

Thomas–Chattanooga (1925-28), Alabama (1931-42, 1944-46); **Vaught**–Mississippi (1947-70); **Wade**–Alabama (1923-30), Duke (1931-41, 1946-50); **Warner**–Georgia (1895-96), Cornell (1897-98), Carlisle (1899-1903), Cornell (1904-06), Carlisle (1907-13), Pittsburgh (1915-23), Stanford (1924-32), Temple (1933-38); **Welsh**–Navy (1973-81), Virginia (1982-2000); **Wilkinson**–Oklahoma (1947-63); **Williams**–Army (1891), Minnesota (1900-21); **Woodruff**–Penn (1892-1901), Illinois (1903), Carlisle (1905); **Woodson**–Central Arkansas (1935-39), Hardin-Simmons (1941-42, 1946-51), Arizona (1952-56), New Mexico St. (1958-67), Trinity-TX (1972-73); **Yost**–Ohio Wesleyan (1897), Nebraska (1898), Kansas (1899), Stanford (1900), Michigan (1901-23, 1925-26).

All-Time Bowl Appearances
Coaches active in 2005 in **bold** type.

		App	W	L	T
1	**Joe Paterno**	32	21	10	1
2	Bear Bryant	29	15	12	2
	Bobby Bowden	29	19	9	1
4	Tom Osborne	25	12	13	0
5	LaVell Edwards	22	7	14	1
	Lou Holtz	22	12	8	2
7	Vince Dooley	20	8	10	2
8	Johnny Vaught	18	10	8	0
9	Hayden Fry	17	7	9	1
	Bo Schembechler	17	5	12	0
11	Johnny Majors	16	9	7	0
	Darrell Royal	16	8	7	1
13	Don James	15	10	5	0
	George Welsh	15	5	10	0
15	Jackie Sherrill	14	8	6	0
	Mack Brown	14	8	6	0
	John Cooper	14	5	9	0
18	Eight coaches tied at 13.				

Active Coaches' Victories
(Minimum 5 years in Division I-A.)

		Yrs	W	L	T	Pct
1	Bobby Bowden, Fla. St	40	**359**	105	4	.771
2	Joe Paterno, Penn St	40	**354**	117	3	.750
3	Frank Beamer, Va. Tech	25	**188**	102	4	.646
4	Dennis Franchione, Tex. A&M	22	**171**	93	2	.647
5	Mack Brown, Texas	22	**169**	93	1	.644
6	Fisher DeBerry, Air Force	22	**165**	101	1	.620
7	Dick Tomey, San Jose St.	25	**161**	118	7	.575
8	Steve Spurrier, So. Carolina	16	**149**	45	2	.765
9	Mike Price, UTEP	24	**145**	130	0	.527
10	John L. Smith, Michigan St.	17	**128**	78	0	.621
	Phillip Fulmer, Tennessee	14	**128**	37	0	.776
12	Sonny Lubick, Colorado St.	17	**122**	76	0	.616
13	Glen Mason, Minnesota	20	**117**	114	1	.506
14	Mike Bellotti, Oregon	16	**111**	67	2	.622
15	Joe Tiller, Purdue	15	**106**	73	1	.592
16	Jeff Bower, So. Mississippi	16	**103**	72	1	.588
17	Lloyd Carr, Michigan	11	**102**	34	0	.750
	Gary Pinkel, Missouri	15	**102**	67	3	.612
19	Rich Brooks, Kentucky	21	**100**	134	0	.427
	Bobby Ross, Army	17	**100**	92	2	.521

AFCA Coach of the Year
First presented in 1935 by the American Football Coaches Association.

Multiple winners: Joe Paterno (5), Bear Bryant (3), John McKay and Darrell Royal (2).

Year		Year		Year	
1935	Pappy Waldorf, Northwestern	1960	Murray Warmath, Minnesota	1983	Ken Hatfield, Air Force
1936	Dick Harlow, Harvard	1961	Bear Bryant, Alabama	1984	LaVell Edwards, BYU
1937	Hooks Mylin, Lafayette	1962	John McKay, USC	1985	Fisher DeBerry, Air Force
1938	Bill Kern, Carnegie Tech	1963	Darrell Royal, Texas	1986	Joe Paterno, Penn St.
1939	Eddie Anderson, Iowa	1964	Frank Broyles, Arkansas	1987	Dick MacPherson, Syracuse
1940	Clark Shaughnessy, Stanford		& Ara Parseghian, Notre Dame	1988	Don Nehlen, West Virginia
1941	Frank Leahy, Notre Dame	1965	Tommy Prothro, UCLA	1989	Bill McCartney, Colorado
1942	Bill Alexander, Georgia Tech	1966	Tom Cahill, Army	1990	Bobby Ross, Georgia Tech
1943	Amos Alonzo Stagg, Pacific	1967	John Pont, Indiana	1991	Bill Lewis, East Carolina
1944	Carroll Widdoes, Ohio St.	1968	Joe Paterno, Penn St.	1992	Gene Stallings, Alabama
1945	Bo McMillin, Indiana	1969	Bo Schembechler, Michigan	1993	Barry Alvarez, Wisconsin
1946	Red Blaik, Army	1970	Charlie McClendon, LSU	1994	Tom Osborne, Nebraska
1947	Fritz Crisler, Michigan		& Darrell Royal, Texas	1995	Gary Barnett, Northwestern
1948	Bennie Oosterbaan, Michigan	1971	Bear Bryant, Alabama	1996	Bruce Snyder, Arizona St.
1949	Bud Wilkinson, Oklahoma	1972	John McKay, USC	1997	Lloyd Carr, Michigan
1950	Charlie Caldwell, Princeton	1973	Bear Bryant, Alabama	1998	Phillip Fulmer, Tennessee
1951	Chuck Taylor, Stanford	1974	Grant Teaff, Baylor	1999	Frank Beamer, Va. Tech
1952	Biggie Munn, Michigan St.	1975	Frank Kush, Arizona St.	2000	Bob Stoops, Oklahoma
1953	Jim Tatum, Maryland	1976	Johnny Majors, Pittsburgh	2001	Ralph Friedgen, Maryland
1954	Red Sanders, UCLA	1977	Don James, Washington		& Larry Coker, Miami-FL
1955	Duffy Daugherty, Michigan St.	1978	Joe Paterno, Penn St.	2002	Jim Tressel, Ohio St.
1956	Bowden Wyatt, Tennessee	1979	Earle Bruce, Ohio St.	2003	Pete Carrol, USC
1957	Woody Hayes, Ohio St.	1980	Vince Dooley, Georgia	2004	Tommy Tuberville, Auburn
1958	Paul Dietzel, LSU	1981	Danny Ford, Clemson	2005	Joe Paterno, Penn St.
1959	Ben Schwartzwalder, Syracuse	1982	Joe Paterno, Penn St.		

FWAA Coach of the Year
First presented in 1957 by the Football Writers Association of America. The FWAA and AFCA awards have both gone to the same coach in the same season 32 times. Those double winners are preceded by (#).

Multiple winners: Woody Hayes and Joe Paterno (3); Lou Holtz, Johnny Majors and John McKay (2).

Year		Year		Year	
1957	#Woody Hayes, Ohio St.	1970	Alex Agase, Northwestern	1983	Howard Schnellenberger, Miami-FL
1958	#Paul Dietzel, LSU	1971	Bob Devaney, Nebraska	1984	#LaVell Edwards, BYU
1959	#Ben Schwartzwalder, Syracuse	1972	#John McKay, USC	1985	#Fisher DeBerry, Air Force
1960	#Murray Warmath, Minnesota	1973	Johnny Majors, Pitt	1986	#Joe Paterno, Penn St.
1961	Darrell Royal, Texas	1974	#Grant Teaff, Baylor	1987	#Dick MacPherson, Syracuse
1962	#John McKay, USC	1975	Woody Hayes, Ohio St.	1988	Lou Holtz, Notre Dame
1963	#Darrell Royal, Texas	1976	#Johnny Majors, Pitt	1989	#Bill McCartney, Colorado
1964	#Ara Parseghian, Notre Dame	1977	Lou Holtz, Arkansas	1990	#Bobby Ross, Georgia Tech
1965	Duffy Daugherty, Michigan St.	1978	#Joe Paterno, Penn St.	1991	Don James, Washington
1966	#Tom Cahill, Army	1979	#Earle Bruce, Ohio St.	1992	#Gene Stallings, Alabama
1967	#John Pont, Indiana	1980	#Vince Dooley, Georgia	1993	Terry Bowden, Auburn
1968	Woody Hayes, Ohio St.	1981	#Danny Ford, Clemson	1994	Rich Brooks, Oregon
1969	#Bo Schembechler, Michigan	1982	#Joe Paterno, Penn St.	1995	#Gary Barnett, Northwestern

FWAA Coach of the Year (Cont.)

Year		Year		Year	
1996	#Bruce Snyder, Arizona St.	2000	#Bob Stoops, Oklahoma	2004	Urban Meyer, Utah
1997	Mike Price, Washington St.	2001	#Ralph Friedgen, Maryland	2005	Charlie Weis, Notre Dame
1998	#Phillip Fulmer, Tennessee	2002	#Jim Tressel, Ohio St.		
1999	#Frank Beamer, Va. Tech	2003	Nick Saban, LSU		

All-Time NCAA Division I-AA Leaders
CAREER

Total Offense

	Yards Gained	Years	Yards
1	Steve McNair, Alcorn St.	1991-94	16,823
2	Bruce Eugene, Grambling	2002-05	14,023
3	Marcus Brady, CS-Northridge	1998-01	13,095
4	Willie Totten, Miss. Valley	1982-85	13,007
5	Robert Kent, Jackson St.	2000-03	12,538

	Yards per Game	Years	Yards	P/Gm
1	Steve McNair, Alcorn St.	1991-94	16,823	400.5
2	Neil Lomax, Portland St.	1978-80	11,647	352.9
3	Bruce Eugene, Grambling	2002-05	14,023	350.6
4	Aaron Flowers, CS-N'ridge	1996-97	6,754	337.7
5	David Macchi, Valparaiso	2002-03	7,628	331.7

Passing
(Minimum 300 Completions)

	Passing Efficiency	Years	Rating
1	Shawn Knight, William & Mary	1991-94	170.8
2	Erik Meyer, E. Washington	2002-05	166.5
3	Dave Dickenson, Montana	1992-95	166.3
4	Drew Miller, Montana	1999-00	160.5
5	Eric Rasmussen, San Diego	2001-03	160.1

	Yards Gained	Years	Yards
1	Steve McNair, Alcorn St.	1991-94	14,496
2	Bruce Eugene, Grambling	2002-05	12,820
3	Willie Totten, Miss. Valley	1982-85	12,711
4	Marcus Brady, CS-Northridge	1998-01	12,479
5	Jamie Martin, Weber St.	1989-92	12,207

Receiving

	Catches	Years	No
1	Jacquay Nunnally, Fla. A&M	1997-00	317
2	Stephen Campbell, Brown	1997-00	305
3	Jerry Rice, Miss. Valley	1981-84	301
4	Javarus Dudley, Fordham	2000-03	295
5	Chas Gessner, Brown	1999-02	292

	Yards Gained	Years	No	Yards
1	Jerry Rice, Miss. Valley	1981-84	301	4693
2	Jacquay Nunnally, Fla. A&M	1997-00	317	4239
3	Javarus Dudley, Fordham	2000-03	295	4197
4	Eric Kimble, E. Washington	2002-05	253	4140
5	Fred Amey, Sacramento St.	2001-04	248	4049

All-Purpose Yardage

	Yards per Game	Years	Yards	P/Gm
1	B. Westbrook, Villanova	1997-98,00-01	9512	216.2
2	Jerry Azumah, N. Hampshire	1995-98	9376	204.3
3	Arnold Mickens, Butler	1994-95	3947	197.4
4	Tim Hall, Robert Morris	1994-95	3701	194.8
5	Reggie Greene, Siena	1994-97	6959	193.3

Rushing

	Yards Gained	Years	Yards
1	Adrian Peterson, Ga. So.	1998-01	6559
2	Charles Roberts, CS-Sac.	1997-00	6553
3	Jerry Azumah, N. Hampshire	1995-98	6193
4	Matt Cannon, S. Utah	1997-00	5489
5	Reggie Greene, Siena	1994-97	5415

	Yards per Game	Years	Yards	P/Gm
1	Arnold Mickens, Butler	1994-95	3813	190.7
2	Adrian Peterson, Ga. So.	1998-01	6559	156.2
3	Aaron Stecker, W. Ill.	1997-98	3081	154.1
4	Tim Hall, Robert Morris	1994-95	2908	153.1
5	Jerry Azumah, N. Hampshire	1995-98	6193	151.0

Miscellaneous

	Interceptions	Years	No
1	Rashean Mathis, Bethune-Cookman	1999-02	31
2	Dave Murphy, Holy Cross	1986-89	28
	Leigh Bodde, Duquesne	1999-02	28
4	Cedric Walker, S.F. Austin	1990-93	25
5	Three tied at 24.		

	Punting Average (min. 150 punts)	Years	Avg
1	Mark Gould, Northern Ariz.	2000-03	44.8
2	Pumpy Tudors, Tenn.-Chatt.	1989-91	44.4
3	Case de Brujin, Idaho St.	1978-81	43.7
4	Mike Scifres, Western Illinois	1999-02	43.6
5	Terry Belden, Northern Ariz.	1990-93	43.4

Note: Northeastern's Tyler Grogan holds the I-AA record for longest punt with a 93-yarder against Villanova in 2001.

	Punt Return Average*	Years	Avg
1	Terrence McGee, Northwesern St.	1999-02	17.4
2	Willie Ware, Miss. Valley	1982-85	16.4
3	Buck Phillips, Western Ill.	1994-95	16.4
4	Tim Egerton, Delaware St.	1986-89	16.1
5	Mark Orlando, Towson St.	1991-94	15.7

	Kickoff Return Average*	Years	Avg
1	Lamont Brightful, E. Wash.	1998-01	30.0
2	Troy Brown, Marshall	1991-92	29.7
3	Cedric Bowen, Ark-Pine Bluff	2001-04	29.6
4	Charles Swann, Indiana St.	1989-91	29.3
5	Craig Richardson, Eastern Wash.	1983-86	28.5

*(Minimum 1.2 returns per game)

	Blocked Kicks	Years	FG	XP	P	Tot
1	Leonard Smith, McNeese St.	1980-82	10	4	3	17
2	Trey Woods, Sam Houston St.	1992-95	2	2	8	12
3	Ryan Crawford, Davidson	1997-00	5	0	7	12
4	Bryan Cox, W. Illinois	1987-90	4	5	1	10
5	Tim Hauck, Montana	1987-89	2	7	0	9

Note: The blocked kicks category is a combined total of blocked field goals (FG), extra points (XP) and punts (P).

Scoring
Non-Kickers

	Points	Years	TD	XP	Pts
1	B. Westbrook, Villanova	1997-98,00-01	89	10	544
2	Adrian Peterson, Ga. Southern	1998-01	87	2	524
3	Matt Cannon, S. Utah	1997-00	69	6	420
4	Jerry Azumah, New Hampshire	1995-98	69	4	418
5	David Dinkins, Morehead St.	1997-00	63	6	384

	Touchdowns Passing	Years	No
1	Willie Totten, Miss. Valley	1982-85	139
2	Steve McNair, Alcorn St.	1991-94	119
3	Marcus Brady, CS-Northridge	1998-01	109
4	Robert Kent, Jackson St.	2000-03	104
5	Niel Loebig, Duquesne	2001-04	103

	Touchdowns Rushing	Years	No
1	Adrian Peterson, Ga. Southern	1998-01	84
2	Matt Cannon, S. Utah	1997-00	69
3	David Dinkins, Morehead St.	1997-00	63
4	Chaz Willaims, Ga. Southern	2001-04	62
5	Jerry Azumah, New Hampshire	1995-98	60

	Touchdown Catches	Years	No
1	Jerry Rice, Miss. Valley	1981-84	50
2	Rennie Benn, Lehigh	1982-85	44
3	Dedric Ward, N. Iowa	1993-96	41
4	Rob Giancola, Valparaiso	2001-04	40
5	Sean Morey, Brown	1995-98	39
	Gharun Hester, Georgetown	1997-00	39

Kickers

	Points	Years	FG	XP	Pts
1	Chris Snyder, Montana	2000-03	70	182	394
2	Marty Zendejas, Nevada	1984-87	72	169	385
3	Justin Langan, W. Illinois	2001-04	53	174	335
4	Dave Ettinger, Hofstra	1994-97	62	140	326
5	Brian Morgan, Grambling	2001-04	50	174	324

Note: Chris Snyder's point total includes 1 2-point conversion. Scott Shields's point total includes 2 touchdowns.

	Field Goals	Years	FG	Att
1	Marty Zendejas, Nevada	1984-87	.72	90
2	Kirk Roach, Western Carolina	1984-87	.71	102
3	Tony Zendejas, Nevada	1981-83	.70	86
	Chris Snyder, Montana	2000-03	.70	105
5	Scott Shields, Weber St.	1995-98	.67	90

Note: South Florida's Bill Gramatica, Arkansas State's Scott Roper and Georgia Southern's Tim Foley share the 1-AA record for longest field goal at 63 yards.

Payton Award

First presented in 1987 by the Sports Network and Division I-AA sports information directors to honor the nation's outstanding Division I-AA player. The award is named after Walter Payton, the NFL's all-time leading rusher who was an All-America running back at Jackson St.

Year
1987 Kenny Gamble, Colgate, RB
1988 Dave Meggett, Towson St., RB
1989 John Friesz, Idaho, QB
1990 Walter Dean, Grambling, RB
1991 Jamie Martin, Weber St., QB
1992 Michael Payton, Marshall, QB
1993 Doug Nussmeier, Idaho, QB
1994 Steve McNair, Alcorn St., QB

Year
1995 Dave Dickenson, Montana, QB
1996 Archie Amerson, N. Arizona, RB
1997 Brian Finneran, Villanova, WR
1998 Jerry Azumah, N. Hampshire, RB
1999 Adrian Peterson,
        Ga. Southern, RB
2000 Louis Ivory, Furman, RB

Year
2001 Brian Westbrook, Villanova, RB
2002 Tony Romo, Eastern Illinois, QB
2003 Jamaal Branch, Colgate, RB
2004 Lang Campbell,
        Wm & Mary, QB
2005 Erik Meyer, E. Washington, QB

All-Time NCAA Division I-AA Winningest Programs

Includes record at a senior college only, minimum of 20 seasons of competition. Bowl and playoff games are included in the overall records but only 1-AA playoff games (since they began in 1978) are included in the W-L column under 1-AA playoffs.

Top 20 Winning Percentage

		Yrs	Gm	W	L	T	Pct.	1-AA Playoffs W-L	Titles
1	Georgia Southern	24	312	235	76	1	.755	38-10	6
2	Grambling St.	63	681	477	189	15	.711	9-7	0
3	Yale	133	1211	830	326	55	.708	0-0	0
4	Florida A&M	73	749	512	279	18	.696	5-6	1
5	Tennessee St.	78	740	484	226	30	.674	2-5	0
6	Princeton	136	1163	763	350	50	.678	0-0	0
7	Harvard	131	1192	774	368	50	.670	0-0	0
8	Pennsylvania	129	1263	781	440	42	.635	0-0	0
9	Southern	84	827	512	290	25	.634	0-0	0
10	Dayton	98	937	579	330	26	.632	0-0	0
11	Eastern Kentucky	82	823	506	290	27	.631	16-15	2
12	Jackson St.	60	622	384	225	13	.628	0-12	0
13	Fordham	107	1195	722	420	53	.626	1-1	0
14	Appalachian St.	76	810	490	291	29	.623	12-12	1
15	McNeese St.	55	600	366	220	14	.622	11-10	0
16	S. Carolina St.	78	734	440	267	27	.618	2-2	0
17	Hofstra	65	637	385	241	11	.613	2-5	0
18	Dartmouth	124	1079	638	395	46	.613	0-0	0
19	Delaware	115	1046	613	389	44	.607	16-12	1
20	Western Kentucky	87	843	495	317	31	.606	8-7	1

Top 50 Victories

		Wins
1	Yale	830
2	Pennsylvania	781
3	Harvard	774
4	Princeton	763
5	Fordham	722
6	Dartmouth	638
7	Lafayette	620
8	Delaware	613
9	Lehigh	609
10	Cornell	603
11	Dayton	579
12	Colgate	567
13	N. Iowa	564
14	Holy Cross	562
15	Brown	549
16	Bucknell	545
17	Drake	528

		Wins
18	Villanova	524
19	Furman	529
20	Butler	514
21	Southern	512
22	Florida A&M	512
23	William & Mary	509
	Massachusetts	509
25	E. Kentucky	506
26	Hampton	496
27	W. Kentucky	495
28	Appalachian St.	490
29	Tennessee St.	484
30	Montana	479
31	Northwestern St.	477
	Grambling St.	477
33	New Hampshire	475
34	Chattanooga	464

		Wins
35	Western Ill.	463
	Maine	463
37	Georgetown	457
38	Howard	453
	Texas St.	453
40	Richmond	449
41	VMI	446
42	Elon	441
	S. Carolina St.	440
44	Eastern Ill.	439
45	Idaho St.	436
46	The Citadel	435
	Wofford	435
48	E. Washington	430
49	Murray St.	429
50	Alabama St.	424

Top 10 Playoff Game Appearances

Ranked by NCAA Division 1-AA playoff games played from 1978-2005. CH refers to championships won.

		Years	Games	Record	CH			Years	Games	Record	CH
1	Georgia Southern	16	**48**	38-10	6		Youngstown St.	10	**29**	23-6	4
2	Montana	16	**36**	22-14	2	7	Delaware	13	**28**	16-12	1
3	Eastern Ky.	17	**31**	16-15	2	8	Northern Iowa	12	**27**	15-12	0
4	Furman	14	**30**	17-13	1	9	Appalachian St.	13	**24**	12-12	1
5	Marshall*	8	**29**	23-6	2	10	McNeese St.	11	**22**	11-11	0

*Marshall moved up to I-A in 1997.

All-Time Winningest Division I-AA Coaches

Minimum of 10 years as a Division I-A and/or Division I-AA through 2005 season. Coaches active in 1-AA in 2005 in **bold** type. Active coaches and former 1-AA coaches who coached at only one school are listed with current/sole school.

Top 15 Winning Percentage

		Yrs	W	L	T	Pct
1	**Mike Kelly**, Dayton	25	231	47	1	.830
2	**Al Bagnoli**, Penn	24	185	58	0	.761
3	Greg Gattuso, Duquesne	12	97	32	0	.752
4	W.C. Gorden, Jackson St.	11	89	30	5	.738
5	**Pete Richardson**, Southern	18	150	57	1	.724
6	Chris Ault*, Nevada	16	138	53	1	.721
7	**Joe Taylor**, Hampton	23	183	71	4	.717
8	Tubby Raymond, Delaware	36	300	119	3	.714
9	Roy Kidd, Eastern Ky.	39	313	124	8	.712
10	Eddie Robinson, Grambling	55	408	165	15	.707
11	Billy Joe	31	237	108	4	.685
12	**Dick Biddle**, Colgate	10	84	35	0	.706
13	Jim Tressel*, Youngstown St.	15	135	57	2	.701
14	**Walt Hameline**, Wagner	25	175	86	2	.669
15	Mark Whipple	16	120	60	0	.667

Top 15 Victories

		Yrs	W	L	T	Pct
1	Eddie Robinson, Grambling	55	**408**	165	15	.707
2	Roy Kidd, Eastern Ky.	39	**313**	124	8	.712
3	Tubby Raymond, Delaware	36	**300**	119	3	.714
4	Billy Joe	31	**237**	108	4	.685
5	**Mike Kelly**, Dayton	25	**231**	47	1	.830
6	Ron Randleman	36	**218**	167	6	.565
7	**Robert Ford**, Albany	37	**210**	154	1	.576
8	Bill Hayes	27	**196**	103	2	.654
9	**Al Bagnoli**, Penn	24	**185**	58	0	.761
10	**Joe Taylor**, Hampton	23	**183**	71	4	.717
11	Carmen Cozza, Yale	32	**179**	119	5	.599
12	**Walt Hameline**, Wagner	25	**175**	86	2	.669
	Jimmye Laycock, Wm. & Mary	26	**175**	119	2	.591
14	**Rob Ash**, Drake	26	**167**	97	5	.630
	Jerry Moore, Appalachian St.	24	**167**	115	2	.592

*Chris Ault (Nevada) and Jim Tressel (Ohio St.) are still active in 1-A. Only their 1-AA numbers are included above.

Division I-AA Coach of the Year

First presented in 1983 by the American Football Coaches Association.

Multiple winners: Mark Duffner, Paul Johnson and Erk Russell (2).

Year		Year		Year	
1983	Rey Dempsey, Southern Ill.	1991	Mark Duffner, Holy Cross	1999	Paul Johnson, Ga. Southern
1984	Dave Arnold, Montana St.	1992	Charlie Taaffe, Citadel	2000	Paul Johnson, Ga. Southern
1985	Dick Sheridan, Furman	1993	Dan Allen, Boston Univ.	2001	Bobby Johnson, Furman
1986	Erk Russell, Ga. Southern	1994	Jim Tressel, Youngstown St.	2002	Jack Harbaugh, E. Kentucky
1987	Mark Duffner, Holy Cross	1995	Don Read, Montana	2003	Dick Biddle, Colgate
1988	Jimmy Satterfield, Furman	1996	Ray Tellier, Columbia	2004	Mickey Matthews, James Madison
1989	Erk Russell, Ga. Southern	1997	Andy Talley, Villanova	2005	Jerry Moore, Appalachian St.
1990	Tim Stowers, Ga. Southern	1998	Mark Whipple, Massachusetts		

NCAA Playoffs

Division I-AA

Established in 1978 as a four-team playoff. Tournament field increased to eight teams in 1981, 12 teams in 1982 and 16 teams in 1986. Automatic berths are awarded to champions of the Big Sky, Gateway, Mid-Eastern Athletic, Ohio Valley, Patriot, Southern, Southland and Atlantic 10 conferences.

Multiple winners: Georgia Southern (6); Youngstown St. (4); Eastern Kentucky, Marshall and Montana (2).

Year	Winner	Score	Loser	Year	Winner	Score	Loser
1978	Florida A&M	35-28	Massachusetts	1992	Marshall	31-28	Youngstown St.
1979	Eastern Kentucky	30-7	Lehigh, PA	1993	Youngstown St.	17-5	Marshall
1980	Boise St., ID	31-29	Eastern Kentucky	1994	Youngstown St.	28-14	Boise St.
1981	Idaho St.	34-23	Eastern Kentucky	1995	Montana	22-20	Marshall
1982	Eastern Kentucky	17-14	Delaware	1996	Marshall	49-29	Montana
1983	Southern Illinois	43-7	Western Carolina	1997	Youngstown St.	10-9	McNeese St.
1984	Montana St.	19-6	Louisiana Tech	1998	Massachusetts	55-43	Georgia Southern
1985	Georgia Southern	44-42	Furman, SC	1999	Georgia Southern	59-24	Youngstown St.
1986	Georgia Southern	48-21	Arkansas St.	2000	Georgia Southern	27-25	Montana
1987	NE Louisiana	43-42	Marshall, WV	2001	Montana	13-6	Furman
1988	Furman, SC	17-12	Georgia Southern	2002	Western Kentucky	34-14	McNeese St.
1989	Georgia Southern	37-34	S.F. Austin St.	2003	Delaware	40-0	Colgate
1990	Georgia Southern	36-13	Nevada-Reno	2004	James Madison	31-21	Montana
1991	Youngstown St., OH	25-17	Marshall	2005	Appalachian St.	21-16	Northern Iowa

Division II

Established in 1973 as an eight-team playoff. Tournament field increased to 16 teams in 1988. From 1964-72, eight qualifying NCAA College Division member institutions competed in four regional bowl games, but there was no tournament and no national championship until 1973.

Multiple winners: North Dakota St. (5); Grand Valley St. and North Alabama (3); Northern Colorado, Northwest Missouri St., Southwest Texas St. and Troy St. (2).

Year	Winner	Score	Loser	Year	Winner	Score	Loser
1973	Louisiana Tech	34-0	Western Kentucky	1990	North Dakota St.	51-11	Indiana, PA
1974	Central Michigan	54-14	Delaware	1991	Pittsburg St., KS	23-6	Jacksonville St., AL
1975	Northern Michigan	16-14	Western Kentucky	1992	Jacksonville St., AL	17-13	Pittsburg St., KS
1976	Montana St.	24-13	Akron, OH	1993	North Alabama	41-34	Indiana, PA
1977	Lehigh, PA.	33-0	Jacksonville St., AL	1994	North Alabama	16-10	Tex. A&M (Kings.)
1978	Eastern Illinois	10-9	Delaware	1995	North Alabama	27-7	Pittsburg St., KS
1979	Delaware	38-21	Youngstown St., OH	1996	Northern Colorado	23-14	Carson-Newman
1980	Cal Poly-SLO	21-13	Eastern Illinois	1997	Northern Colorado	51-0	New Haven
1981	SW Texas St.	42-13	North Dakota St.	1998	NW Missouri St.	24-6	Carson-Newman
1982	SW Texas St.	34-9	UC-Davis	1999	NW Missouri St.	58-52*	Carson-Newman
1983	North Dakota St.	41-21	Central St., OH	2000	Delta St., MS	63-34	Bloomsburg, PA
1984	Troy St., AL	18-17	North Dakota St.	2001	North Dakota	17-14	Grand Valley St.
1985	North Dakota St.	35-7	North Alabama	2002	Grand Valley St., OH	31-24	Valdosta St., GA
1986	North Dakota St.	27-7	South Dakota	2003	Grand Valley St., OH	10-3	North Dakota
1987	Troy St., AL	31-17	Portland St., OR	2004	Valdosta St., GA	36-31	Pittsburg St., KS
1988	North Dakota St	35-21	Portland St., OR	2005	Grand Valley St., OH	21-17	NW Missouri St.
1989	Mississippi Col.	3-0	Jacksonville St., AL		*Four overtimes		

Hill Trophy

First presented in 1986 by the Harlon Hill Awards Committee in Florence, Ala., to honor the nation's outstanding Division II player. The award is named after three-time NFL All-Pro Harlon Hill, who played college ball at North Alabama.

Multiple winners: Johnny Bailey (3), Dusty Bonner (2).

Year		Year		Year	
1986	Jeff Bentrim, N. Dakota St., QB	1993	Roger Graham, New Haven, RB	2000	Dusty Bonner, Valdosta St., QB
1987	Johnny Bailey, Texas A&I, RB	1994	Chris Hatcher, Valdosta St., QB	2001	Dusty Bonner, Valdosta St., QB
1988	Johnny Bailey, Texas A&I, RB	1995	Ronald McKinnon, N. Ala., LB	2002	Curt Anes, Grand Valley St., QB
1989	Johnny Bailey, Texas A&I, RB	1996	Jarrett Anderson, Truman St., RB	2003	Will Hall, N. Alabama, QB
1990	Chris Simdorn, N. Dakota St., QB	1997	Irv Sigler, Bloomsburg, RB	2004	Chad Friehauf, Colo-Mines, QB
1991	Ronnie West, Pittsburg St., WR	1998	Brian Shay, Emporia St., RB	2005	Jimmy Terwilliger,
1992	Ronald Moore, Pittsburg St., RB	1999	Corte McGuffet, N. Colo., QB		E. Stroudsburg, QB

Division III

Established in 1973 as a four-team playoff. Tournament field increased to eight teams in 1975, 16 teams in 1985 and 28 teams in 1999. From 1969-72, four qualifying NCAA College Division member institutions competed in two regional bowl games, but there was no tournament and no national championship until 1973. (*) denotes overtime.

Multiple winners: Mt. Union (8); Augustana (4); Ithaca (3); Dayton, St. John's, Widener, WI-La Crosse and Wittenberg (2).

Year	Winner	Score	Loser	Year	Winner	Score	Loser
1973	Wittenberg, OH	41-0	Juniata, PA	1990	Allegheny, PA	21-14*	Lycoming, PA
1974	Central, IA	10-8	Ithaca, NY	1991	Ithaca, NY	34-20	Dayton, OH
1975	Wittenberg, OH	28-0	Ithaca, NY	1992	WI-La Crosse	16-12	Wash. & Jeff., PA
1976	St. John's, MN	31-28	Towson St., MD	1993	Mt. Union, OH	34-24	Rowan, NJ
1977	Widener, PA	39-36	Wabash, IN	1994	Albion, MI	38-15	Wash. & Jeff.
1978	Baldwin-Wallace	24-10	Wittenberg, OH	1995	WI-La Crosse	36-7	Rowan, NJ
1979	Ithaca, NY	14-10	Wittenberg, OH	1996	Mt. Union, OH	56-24	Rowan, NJ
1980	Dayton, OH	63-0	Ithaca, NY	1997	Mt. Union, OH	61-12	Lycoming
1981	Widener, PA	17-10	Dayton, OH	1998	Mt. Union, OH	44-24	Rowan, NJ
1982	West Georgia	14-0	Augustana, IL	1999	Pacific Lutheran	42-13	Rowan, NJ
1983	Augustana, IL	21-17	Union, NY	2000	Mt. Union, OH	10-7	St. John's, MN
1984	Augustana, IL	21-12	Central, IA	2001	Mt. Union, OH	30-27	Bridgewater, VA
1985	Augustana, IL	20-7	Ithaca	2002	Mt. Union, OH	48-7	Trinity, TX
1986	Augustana, IL	31-3	Salisbury St., MD	2003	St. John's, MN	24-6	Mt. Union, OH
1987	Wagner, NY	19-3	Dayton, OH	2004	Linfield	28-21	Mary Hardin-Baylor
1988	Ithaca, NY	39-24	Central, IA	2005	Mt. Union, OH	35-28	WI-Whitewater
1989	Dayton, OH	17-7	Union, NY				

Gagliardi Trophy

First presented in 1993 by the St. John's (Minn.) University J-Club, to honor the nation's outstanding Division III player. The award is named after John Gagliardi, St. John's legendary head coach, one of only two (Ediie Robinson) coaches in college football history with 400 wins.

Year		Year		Year	
1993	Jim Ballard, Mt. Union, QB	1998	Scott Hvistendahl,	2002	Dan Pugh, Mt. Union, RB
1994	Carey Bender, Coe, RB		Augsburg, WR/P	2003	Blake Elliott, St. John's, WR
1995	Chris Palmer, St. John's, WR	1999	Danny Ragsdale, Redlands, QB	2004	Rocky Myers, Wesley, S
1996	Lon Erickson, Ill. Wesleyan, QB	2000	Chad Johnson, Pac. Luth., QB	2005	Brett Elliott, Linfield, QB
1997	Bill Borchert, Mt. Union, QB	2001	Chuck Moore, Mt. Union, RB		

NAIA Playoffs

Division I

Established in 1956 as two-team playoff. Tournament field increased to four teams in 1958, eight teams in 1978 and 16 teams in 1987 before cutting back to eight teams in 1989. NAIA went back to a single division 16-team playoff in 1997. The title game has ended in a tie four times (1956, '64, '84 and '85). Note that Northeastern St., OK was called NE Oklahoma in 1958.

Multiple winners: Texas A&I (7); Carson-Newman (5); Carroll-MT (4); Central Arkansas and Central St-OH (3); Abilene Christian, Central St-OK, Elon, Georgetown-KY, Northeastern St-OK, Pittsburg St. and St. John's-MN (2).

Year	Winner	Score	Loser	Year	Winner	Score	Loser
1956	Montana St.	0-0	St. Joseph's, IN	1982	Central St., OK	14-11	Mesa, CO
1957	Pittsburg St., KS	27-26	Hillsdale, MI	1983	Car-Newman, TN	36-28	Mesa, CO
1958	NE Oklahoma	19-13	Northern Arizona	1984	Car-Newman, TN	19-19	Central Arkansas
1959	Texas A&I	20-7	Lenoir-Rhyne, NC	1985	Hillsdale, MI	10-10	Central Arkansas
1960	Lenoir-Rhyne, NC	15-14	Humboldt St., CA	1986	Car-Newman, TN	17-0	Cameron, OK
1961	Pittsburg St., KS	12-7	Linfield, OR	1987	Cameron, OK	30-2	Car-Newman, TN
1962	Central St., OK	28-13	Lenoir-Rhyne, NC	1988	Car-Newman, TN	56-21	Adams St., CO
1963	St. John's, MN	33-27	Prairie View A&M, TX	1989	Car-Newman, TN	34-20	Emporia St., KS
1964	Concordia, MN	7-7	Sam Houston St., TX	1990	Central St., OH	38-16	Mesa, CO
1965	St. John's, MN	33-0	Linfield, OR	1991	Central Arkansas	19-16	Central St., OH
1966	Waynesburg, PA	42-21	WI-Whitewater	1992	Central St., OH	19-16	Gardner-Webb, NC
1967	Fairmont St., WV	28-21	Eastern Wash.	1993	E. Central, OK	49-35	Glenville St., WV
1968	Troy St., AL	43-35	Texas A&I	1994	N'eastern St., OK	13-12	Ark-Pine Bluff
1969	Texas A&I	32-7	Concordia, MN	1995	Central St., OH	37-7	N'eastern St., OK
1970	Texas A&I	48-7	Wofford, SC	1996	SW Oklahoma St.	33-31	Montana Tech
1971	Livingston, AL	14-12	Arkansas Tech	1997	Findlay, OH	14-7	Willamette, OR
1972	East Texas St.	21-18	Car-Newman, TN	1998	Azusa Pacific, CA	17-14	Olivet Nazarene, IL
1973	Abilene Christian	42-14	Elon, NC	1999	NW Oklahoma St.	34-26	Georgetown, KY
1974	Texas A&I	34-23	Henderson St., AR	2000	Georgetown, KY	20-0	NW Oklahoma St.
1975	Texas A&I	37-0	Salem, WV	2001	Georgetown, KY	49-27	Sioux Falls, S.D.
1976	Texas A&I	26-0	Central Arkansas	2002	Carroll, MT	28-7	Georgetown, KY
1977	Abilene Christian	24-7	SW Oklahoma	2003	Carroll, MT	41-28	NW Oklahoma St.
1978	Angelo St., TX	34-14	Elon, NC	2004	Carroll, MT	15-13	St. Francis, IN
1979	Texas A&I	20-14	Central St., OK	2005	Carroll, MT	27-10	St. Francis, IN
1980	Elon, NC	17-10	NE Oklahoma				
1981	Elon, NC	3-0	Pittsburg St., KS				

Division II

Established in 1970 as four-team playoff. Tournament field increased to eight teams in 1978 and 16 teams in 1987. NAIA went back to a single division playoff in 1997. The title game has ended in a tie twice (1981 and '87).

Multiple winners: Westminster (6); Findlay, Linfield and Pacific Lutheran (3); Concordia-MN, Northwestern-IA and Texas Lutheran (2).

Year	Winner	Score	Loser	Year	Winner	Score	Loser
1970	Westminster, PA	21-16	Anderson, IN	1984	Linfield, OR	33-22	Northwestern, IA
1971	Calif. Lutheran	30-14	Westminster, PA	1985	WI-La Crosse	24-7	Pacific Lutheran
1972	Missouri Southern	21-14	Northwestern, IA	1986	Linfield, OR	17-0	Baker, KS
1973	Northwestern, IA	10-3	Glenville St., WV	1987	Pacific Lutheran	16-16	WI-Stevens Pt.*
1974	Texas Lutheran	42-0	Missouri Valley	1988	Westminster, PA	21-14	WI-La Crosse
1975	Texas Lutheran	34-8	Calif. Lutheran	1989	Westminster, PA	51-30	WI-La Crosse
1976	Westminster, PA	20-13	Redlands, CA	1990	Peru St., NE	17-7	Westminster, PA
1977	Westminster, PA	17-9	Calif. Lutheran	1991	Georgetown, KY	28-20	Pacific Lutheran
1978	Concordia, MN	7-0	Findlay, OH	1992	Findlay, OH	26-13	Linfield, OR
1979	Findlay, OH	51-6	Northwestern, IA	1993	Pacific Lutheran	50-20	Westminster, PA
1980	Pacific Lutheran	38-10	Wilmington, OH	1994	Westminster, PA	27-7	Pacific Lutheran
1981	Austin College, TX	24-24	Concordia, MN	1995	Findlay, OH	21-21	Central Wash.
1982	Linfield, OR	33-15	Wm. Jewell, MO	1996	Sioux Falls, S.D.	47-25	W. Washington
1983	Northwestern, IA	25-21	Pacific Lutheran				

*Wisconsin-Stevens Point forfeited its entire 1987 schedule due to its use of an ineligible player.

PRO FOOTBALL

2005 / 2006 YEAR IN REVIEW

Jerome Bettis and Super Bowl MVP **Hines Ward** celebrate the Steelers' 21-10 win over the Seahawks.

MOTOR CITY MIRACLE

Steelers finally get one for the thumb and let The Bus roll into retirement with a Super Bowl title.

GETTING "ONE FOR THE THUMB" TURNED OUT TO BE ONE FOR THE AGES.

The Pittsburgh Steelers went from the brink of elimination to making an unprecedented playoff run, winning three playoff games on the road, then capping it off with a 21-10 triumph over the Seattle Seahawks in Super Bowl XL at Detroit's Ford Field.

It was the third time in nine years that a wild card team had captured the Lombardi Trophy, and the seventh time in nine seasons that the team with the league's best record failed to win it all.

The Steelers opted to do it the hard way. With his team at 7-5 and riding a three-game losing streak, Bill Cowher rallied his troops to four straight wins, capturing a wild card berth as well as the sixth seed in the AFC. A 31-17 triumph at Cincinnati in the Wild Card Game was followed by a stunning 21-18 upset of the top-seeded Colts at Indianapolis, and a week later, a 34-17 drubbing of the Broncos in Denver in the AFC Championship Game. Then Cowher's road warriors made their way to Motown, where the tenacity of Super Bowl MVP Hines Ward, the versatility of wide receiver Antwaan Randle El, and the speed of running back Willie Parker were the difference.

The win was sweet for Cowher, who never again will be reminded that his marvelous 14-year run as Steelers' coach (after succeeding the legendary Chuck Noll) was dulled by four AFC Championship Game losses. It was also sweet for the legions of Steelers' fans across the country, many of whom made the trip to Detroit. It was perhaps the sweetest for veteran running back Jerome Bettis, a Motor City native who capped his 13-year career in his hometown.

And he owed a big part of that to Ben Roethlisberger, who at age 23 became the youngest quarterback to win a Super Bowl and whose biggest play in the postseason was an open

Chris Berman is the host of ESPN's *NFL Prime Time*.

AP/Wide World Photos

Quarterback **Ben Roethlisberger** made good on the promise he made to **Jerome Bettis** to get the future hall of fame running back to the Super Bowl in 2006.

field tackle in Indianapolis following a Bettis fumble at the goal line that protected the Steelers' shocker over the Colts, not to mention their Super Bowl drive.

Call it "The Immaculate Redemption."

Of course, Pittsburgh's unexpected championship was not the only story of a wild season. The Indianapolis Colts flirted with perfection, starting 13-0, until numerous circumstances derailed their title hopes. There was a long-awaited revival in Cincinnati as the Bengals captured a winning season, division title and playoff berth for the first time since 1990. Defense was alive and well in the Windy City as Defensive Player of the Year Brian Urlacher led the newest "Monsters of the Midway" to the NFC North title thanks to a six-game improvement. And Shaun Alexander earned MVP honors thanks to 1,880 yards rushing and an NFL record 28 touchdowns for the Seahawks and Mike Holmgren, who almost became the first head coach to win Super Bowls with two different teams.

It was also a season of disappointment for the previous Super Bowl teams. After winning three NFL titles in four years, the Patriots found themselves just short of becoming the first team to win three straight Lombardi Trophies as quarterback Tom Brady led the NFL in passing yards, but couldn't overcome a turnover-plagued

Seattle running back **Shaun Alexander** eluded tacklers quite a bit in 2005, as he set an NFL record for single-season touchdowns with 28.

AP/Wide World Photos

loss at Denver in the Divisional Playoffs.

But that was nothing compared to the goings on in Philadelphia as Andy Reid's team found itself in the middle of TOtal chaos as the Eagles went from perennial playoff participants and defending conference champion to the only team with a losing record in their division.

There were plenty of eye-opening performances all around the league. One season after breaking his leg in his season opener, Panthers' wide receiver Steve Smith was electrifying all season and got his team to within a game of the Super Bowl. Larry Johnson took over for an injured Priest Holmes in Kansas City and ran for an amazing 1,351 yards in his final nine games. The Cardinals' wideout tandem of Larry Fitzgerald and Anquan Boldin both hit the century mark in receptions. And Bears' cornerback Nathan Vasher put himself in the record books by returning a missed field goal 108 yards for a touchdown, the longest play in the league's 86-year history.

All in all, it proved to be another wild season in the NFL. And when the smoke finally cleared in the Motor City, The Bus and the Pittsburgh Steelers proved to be the wildest card of them all.

THE TOP

10 ⬇

Stories of the Year in Pro Football

10 Comeback Kids.

New England's Tedy Bruschi and Carolina's Steve Smith return to the field to lead their respective teams into the postseason. Bruschi returns from a stroke he suffered in February 2005 and bolsters the Pats defense to the tune of 7 wins over their last ten games. Smith fights back from a major knee injury to lead the NFC in receiving yards and touchdowns.

09 Lucky Man.

On June 12, a helmetless Ben Roethlisberger is involved in a motorcycle accident in a Pittsburgh intersection that leaves him lying on the street and close to death. He undergoes seven hours of surgery in which titanium plates and screws are inserted to repair a broken jaw and multiple facial fractures. Amazingly, he is back on the field for Steelers' first preseason game just two months later. He is snakebit once again, however, as just before the regular season opener, he has an emergency appendectomy and misses the first two weeks of the year.

08 Bears Lovin' Lovie.

When Lovie Smith was hired on January 14, 2004, he declared his No. 1 goal was beating the rival Green Bay Packers. He accomplished a lot more than that in 2005 as the Bears, the league's top defensive team, finish 11-5 and atop the NFC North Division. Incidentally, two of those 11 wins were against the Packers.

07 Carson City.

In his second season as the Bengals' starting quarterback, Carson Palmer throws a league-leading 32 touchdown passes to propel Cincinnati to the AFC North Division title. His season ends on a down note, however, as he suffers a major knee injury when Pittsburgh's 300-pound defensive end Kimo von Oelhoffen is blocked into him.

06 The Houston Texans select...

At the 2006 NFL Draft in April, the Texans take N.C. State defensive end Mario Williams with the top overall pick as opposed to running back Reggie Bush. Saints fans, searching for any glimmer of hope after Katrina destroyed their 2005 season and much more, are elated. Only time will tell if the Texans' bold move was the right one.

05 New TD record.

Seattle running back Shaun Alexander rushes for 1,880 yards and sets a new single-season touchdown record with 28. He carries the Seahawks to the best record in the NFC and their first Super Bowl berth.

04 **Season-saving tackle.**
Given all the hall of fame defensive players the Steelers have had in their illustrious history, it's ironic that the most prolific tackle may have been made by quarterback Ben Roethlisberger. Leading 21-18 in the waning moments of their playoff game with the Colts, Pittsburgh running back Jerome Bettis fumbled on the goal line. Colts cornerback Nick Harper scooped the ball up and looked like he was going to return it for a game-winning touchdown until Roethlisberger tripped him up at midfield for a game-saving tackle.

03 **Next Question!**
Enigmatic wide receiver Terrell Owens makes a spectacle of himself after not receiving the new contract he demanded from the Eagles in the offseason. He makes disparaging remarks about the organization, coach Andy Reid and in particular, quarterback Donovan McNabb. The tenuous relationship ends after Game 8, when the Eagles suspend him, deactivate him, then release him after the season. The Eagles were 4-3 at the time of the suspension and finish the season at 6-10. Owens later signs with Dallas.

02 **Quest for perfection.**
The Indianapolis Colts win the first 13 games of the season, the first team to do so since the 1998 Denver Broncos. The following week, however, members of the 1972 Dolphins could sip their champagne as the Chargers handed the Colts their first loss, 26-17. Things turned tragic for the organization later that week when head coach Tony Dungy's 18-year-old son, James, was found dead in a Tampa area apartment.

01 **One for the Thumb!**
The Pittsburgh Steelers end their 25-year championship drought by winning their fifth Super Bowl, 21-10, over the Seattle Seahawks. Running back Jerome Bettis returns home to Detroit and wins his first Super Bowl in the last game of his hall of fame career. Ben Roethlisberger, 23, becomes the youngest Super Bowl winning quarterback ever, while longtime coach Bill Cowher removes the monkey from his back in his 14th season with the club. Wide receiver Hines Ward wins the MVP award with 123 yards receiving and a 43-yard touchdown catch from Antwaan Randle-El.

The Arizona Cardinals' 31-14 victory over the San Francisco 49ers at Mexico City's Azteca Stadium on Oct. 2, 2005 was the first-ever regular-season NFL game played outside the United States. An NFL record 103,467 fans attended the game.

DID YOU KNOW?

2005-2006
Season in Review

Final NFL Standings

Division champions (*) and wild card playoff qualifiers (†) are noted; division champions with two best records received first round byes. Number of seasons listed after each head coach refers to latest tenure with club through 2005 season.

American Football Conference

East Division

	W	L	T	PF	PA	vs Div	vs AFC
*New England	10	6	0	379	338	5-1	7-5
Miami	9	7	0	318	317	3-3	7-5
Buffalo	5	11	0	271	367	2-4	5-7
NY Jets	4	12	0	240	355	2-4	3-9

2005 Head Coaches: NE—Bill Belichick (6th season); **Mia**—Nick Saban (1st); **Buf**—Mike Mularkey (2nd); **NY**—Herman Edwards (5th).

2004 Standings: 1. New England (14-2); 2. NY Jets (10-6); 3. Buffalo (9-7); 4. Miami (4-12).

North Division

	W	L	T	PF	PA	vs Div	vs AFC
*Cincinnati	11	5	0	421	350	5-1	7-5
†Pittsburgh	11	5	0	389	258	4-2	7-5
Baltimore	6	10	0	265	299	2-4	4-8
Cleveland	6	10	0	232	301	1-5	4-8

2005 Head Coaches: Cin—Marvin Lewis (3rd season); **Pit**—Bill Cowher (14th); **Bal**—Brian Billick (7th); **Cle**—Romeo Crennel (1st).

2004 Standings: 1. Pittsburgh (15-1); 2. Baltimore (9-7); 3. Cincinnati (8-8); 4. Cleveland (4-12).

Note: Cincinnati (11-5) won the AFC North over Pittsburgh (11-5) due to a better record within the division.

South Division

	W	L	T	PF	PA	vs Div	vs AFC
*Indianapolis	14	2	0	439	247	6-0	11-1
†Jacksonville	12	4	0	361	269	4-2	9-3
Tennessee	4	12	0	299	421	2-4	3-9
Houston	2	14	0	260	431	0-6	1-11

2005 Head Coaches: Ind—Tony Dungy (4th season); **Jax**—Jack Del Rio (3rd); **Ten**—Jeff Fisher (12th); **Hou**—Dom Capers (4th).

2004 Standings: 1. Indianapolis (12-4); 2. Jacksonville (9-7); 3. Houston (7-9); 4. Tennessee (5-11).

West Division

	W	L	T	PF	PA	vs Div	vs AFC
*Denver	13	3	0	395	258	5-1	10-2
Kansas City	10	6	0	403	325	4-2	9-3
San Diego	9	7	0	418	312	3-3	7-5
Oakland	4	12	0	290	383	0-6	2-10

2005 Head Coaches: Den—Mike Shanahan (11th season); **KC**—Dick Vermeil (5th); **SD**—Marty Schottenheimer (4th); **Oak**—Norv Turner (2nd).

2004 Standings: 1. San Diego (12-4); 2. Denver (10-6); 3. Kansas City (7-9); 4. Oakland (5-11).

National Football Conference

East Division

	W	L	T	PF	PA	vs Div	vs NFC
*NY Giants	11	5	0	422	314	4-2	8-4
†Washington	10	6	0	359	293	5-1	10-2
Dallas	9	7	0	325	308	3-3	7-5
Philadelphia	6	10	0	310	388	0-6	3-9

2005 Head Coaches: NY—Tom Coughlin (2nd season); **Wash**—Joe Gibbs (2nd); **Dal**—Bill Parcells (3rd); **Phi**—Andy Reid (7th).

2004 Standings: 1. Philadelphia (13-3); 2. NY Giants (6-10); 3. Dallas (6-10); 4. Washington (6-10).

North Division

	W	L	T	PF	PA	vs Div	vs NFC
*Chicago	11	5	0	260	202	5-1	10-2
Minnesota	9	7	0	306	344	5-1	8-4
Detroit	5	11	0	254	345	1-5	3-9
Green Bay	4	12	0	298	344	1-5	4-8

2005 Head Coaches: Chi—Lovie Smith (2nd season); **Min**—Mike Tice (5th); **Det**—Steve Mariucci (3rd, 4-7) was fired on Nov. 28, 2005 and replaced by def. coordinator Dick Jauron (1-4); **GB**—Mike Sherman (6th).

2004 Standings: 1. Green Bay (10-6); 2. Minnesota (8-8); 3. Detroit (6-10); 4. Chicago (5-11).

South Division

	W	L	T	PF	PA	vs Div	vs NFC
*Tampa Bay	11	5	0	300	274	5-1	9-3
†Carolina	11	5	0	391	259	4-2	8-4
Atlanta	8	8	0	351	341	2-4	5-7
New Orleans	3	13	0	235	398	1-5	1-11

2005 Head Coaches: TB—Jon Gruden (4th season); **Car**—John Fox (4th); **Atl**—Jim Mora Jr. (2nd); **NO**—Jim Haslett (6th).

2004 Standings: 1. Atlanta (11-5); 2. New Orleans (8-8); 3. Carolina (7-9); 4. Tampa Bay (5-11).

Note: Tampa Bay (11-5) won the NFC South over Carolina (11-5) due to a better record within the division.

West Division

	W	L	T	PF	PA	vs Div	vs NFC
*Seattle	13	3	0	452	271	6-0	10-2
†St. Louis	6	10	0	363	429	1-5	3-9
Arizona	5	11	0	311	387	3-3	4-8
San Francisco	4	12	0	239	428	2-4	3-9

2005 Head Coaches: Sea—Mike Holmgren (7th season); **St.L**—Mike Martz (6th; 2-3) was replaced by asst. Joe Vitt (4-7) on Oct. 17, 2005 due to health issues; **Ariz**—Dennis Green (2nd); **SF**—Mike Nolan (1st).

2004 Standings: 1. Seattle (9-7); 2. St. Louis (8-8); 3. Arizona (6-10); 4. San Francisco (2-14).

NFL Regular Season Individual Leaders
(* indicates rookies)

Passing Efficiency
(Minimum of 224 attempts)

AFC	Att	Cmp	Cmp Pct	Yds	Yds/ Att	TD	Long	Int	Sack/Lost	Rating Points
Peyton Manning, Ind	453	305	67.3	3747	8.27	28	80-td	10	17/81	104.1
Carson Palmer, Cin	509	345	67.8	3836	7.54	32	70-td	12	19/105	101.1
Ben Roethlisberger, Pit	268	168	62.7	2385	8.90	17	85-td	9	23/129	98.6
Tom Brady, NE	530	334	63.0	4110	7.75	26	71	14	26/188	92.3
Jake Plummer, Den	456	277	60.7	3366	7.38	18	72	7	22/135	90.2
Trent Green, KC	507	317	62.5	4014	7.92	17	60-td	10	32/204	90.1
Byron Leftwich, Jax	302	175	57.9	2123	7.03	15	45-td	5	23/110	89.3
Drew Brees, SD	500	323	64.6	3576	7.15	24	54	15	27/223	89.2
Kelly Holcomb, Buf	230	155	67.4	1509	6.56	10	65	8	17/140	85.6
Steve McNair, Ten	476	292	61.3	3161	6.64	16	57	11	20/134	82.4
Kerry Collins, Oak	565	302	53.5	3759	6.65	20	79	12	39/261	77.3
David Carr, Hou	423	256	60.5	2488	5.88	14	53-td	11	68/424	77.2
Trent Dilfer, Cle	333	199	59.8	2321	6.97	11	80-td	12	23/139	76.9
Brooks Bollinger, NYJ	266	150	56.4	1558	5.86	7	60-td	6	32/193	72.9
Gus Frerotte, Mia	494	257	52.0	2996	6.06	18	60-td	13	26/158	71.9

NFC	Att	Cmp	Cmp Pct	Yds	Yds/ Att	TD	Long	Int	Sack/Lost	Rating Points
Matt Hasselbeck, Sea	449	294	65.5	3459	7.70	24	56	9	24/154	98.2
Marc Bulger, St.L	287	192	66.9	2297	8.00	14	57-td	9	26/188	94.4
Brad Johnson, Min	294	184	62.6	1885	6.41	12	80-td	4	23/134	88.9
Jake Delhomme, Car	435	262	60.2	3421	7.86	24	80-td	16	28/214	88.1
Mark Brunell, Wash	454	262	57.7	3050	6.72	23	78-td	10	27/213	85.9
Kurt Warner, Ari	375	242	64.5	2713	7.23	11	63	9	23/158	85.8
Donovan McNabb, Phi	357	211	59.1	2507	7.02	16	91-td	9	19/112	85.0
Drew Bledsoe, Dal	499	300	60.1	3639	7.29	23	71-td	17	49/295	83.7
Chris Simms, TB	313	191	61.0	2035	6.50	10	78-td	7	29/205	81.4
Eli Manning, NYG	557	294	52.8	3762	6.75	24	78-td	17	28/184	75.9
Josh McCown, Ari	270	163	60.4	1836	6.80	9	49	11	18/101	74.9
Michael Vick, Atl	387	214	55.3	2412	6.23	15	58	13	33/201	73.1
Joey Harrington, Det	330	188	57.0	2021	6.12	12	86	12	24/136	72.0
Brett Favre, GB	607	372	61.3	3881	6.39	20	59	29	24/170	70.9
Aaron Brooks, NO	431	240	55.7	2882	6.69	13	66	17	33/202	70.0

Receptions

AFC	No	Yds	Avg	Long	TD
Chad Johnson, Cin	97	1432	14.8	70-td	9
Antonio Gates, SD	89	1101	12.4	38	10
Derrick Mason, Bal	86	1073	12.5	39-td	3
Rod Smith, Den	85	1105	13.0	72	6
Reggie Wayne, Ind	83	1055	12.7	66-td	5
Marvin Harrison, Ind	82	1146	14.0	80-td	12
Chris Chambers, Mia	82	1118	13.6	77-td	11
Eric Moulds, Buf	81	816	10.1	55-td	4
Deion Branch, NE	78	998	12.8	51	5
T.J. Houshmandzadeh, Cin	78	956	12.3	43-td	7
Tony Gonzalez, KC	78	905	11.6	39	2
Jerry Porter, Oak	76	942	12.4	49-td	5
Todd Heap, Bal	75	855	11.4	48	7
Laveranues Coles, NYJ	73	845	11.6	43	5

NFC	No	Yds	Avg	Long	TD
Steve Smith, Car	103	1563	15.2	80-td	12
Larry Fitzgerald, Ari	103	1409	13.7	47	10
Anquan Boldin, Ari	102	1402	13.7	54-td	7
Torry Holt, St.L	102	1331	13.0	44	9
Donald Driver, GB	86	1221	14.2	59	5
Santana Moss, Wash	84	1483	17.7	78-td	9
Joey Galloway, TB	83	1287	15.5	80-td	10
Plaxico Burress, NYG	76	1214	16.0	78-td	7
Keyshawn Johnson, Dal	71	839	11.8	34	6
Chris Cooley, Wash	71	774	10.9	32	7
Donte' Stallworth, NO	70	945	13.5	43	7
Jermaine Wiggins, Min	69	568	8.2	24	1
Bobby Engram, Sea	67	778	11.6	56	3
Jason Witten, Dal	66	757	11.5	34	6

Rushing Yards

AFC	Att	Yds	Avg	Long	TD
Larry Johnson, KC	336	1750	5.2	49-td	20
Edgerrin James, Ind	360	1506	4.2	33	13
LaDainian Tomlinson, SD	339	1462	4.3	62	18
Rudi Johnson, Cin	337	1458	4.3	33	12
Willis McGahee, Buf	325	1247	3.8	27	5
Reuben Droughns, Cle	309	1232	4.0	75-td	2
Willie Parker, Pit	255	1202	4.7	80-td	4
LaMont Jordan, Oak	272	1025	3.8	26	9
Mike Anderson, Den	239	1014	4.2	44-td	12
Domanick Davis, Hou	230	976	4.2	44	2
Tatum Bell, Den	173	921	5.3	68	8
Ronnie Brown*, Mia	207	907	4.4	65-td	4
Jamal Lewis, Bal	269	806	3.4	25	3
Chris Brown, Ten	224	851	3.8	38-td	5

NFC	Att	Yds	Avg	Long	TD
Shaun Alexander, Sea	370	1880	5.1	88-td	27
Tiki Barber, NYG	357	1860	5.2	95-td	9
Clinton Portis, Wash	352	1516	4.3	47-td	11
Warrick Dunn, Atl	280	1416	5.1	65	3
Thomas Jones, Chi	314	1335	4.3	42	9
Cadillac Williams*, TB	290	1178	4.1	71-td	6
Steven Jackson, St.L	254	1046	4.1	51	8
Julius Jones, Dal	257	993	3.9	51	5
DeShaun Foster, Car	205	879	4.3	70-td	2
Kevin Jones, Det	186	664	3.6	40	5
Mewelde Moore, Min	155	662	4.3	33	1
Antowain Smith, NO	166	659	4.0	42	3
Brian Westbrook, Phi	156	617	4.0	31	3
Frank Gore*, SF	127	608	4.8	72-td	3

Indianapolis Colts
Peyton Manning
Passing Efficiency

Carolina Panthers
Steve Smith
Receptions

Seattle Seahawks
Shaun Alexander
Rushing, Touchdowns

Buffalo Bills
Terrence McGee
Kickoff Returns

All-Purpose Yardage

AFC	Rush	Rec	Ret	Total	NFC	Rush	Rec	Ret	Total
Dante Hall, KC	11	436	1836	2283	Tiki Barber, NYG	1860	530	0	2390
Wes Welker, Mia	5	434	1769	2208	Shaun Alexander, Sea	1880	78	0	1958
Larry Johnson, KC	1750	343	0	2093	Steve Smith, Car	25	1563	347	1935
Chris Carr*, Oak	0	0	1938	1938	Reggie Swinton, Ari	0	0	1790	1790
Edgerrin James, Ind	1506	337	0	1843	Clinton Portis, Wash	1516	216	0	1732
LaDainian Tomlinson, SD	1462	370	0	1832	Warrick Dunn, Atl	1416	220	0	1636
Darren Sproles*, SD	50	10	1636	1696	Tyson Thompson*, Dal	182	16	1399	1597
Jerome Mathis*, Hou	0	65	1610	1675	Koren Robinson, Min	27	347	1221	1595
Reuben Droughns, Cle	1232	369	0	1601	Santana Moss, Wash	-3	1483	40	1520
Tab Perry*, Cin	9	21	1562	1592	Thomas Jones, Chi	1335	143	0	1478
LaMont Jordan, Oak	1025	563	0	1588	Larry Fitzgerald, Ari	41	1409	0	1450
Justin Miller*, NYJ	0	0	1586	1586	Anquan Boldin, Ari	45	1402	0	1447
Rudi Johnson, Cin	1458	90	0	1548	Steven Jackson, St.L	1046	320	0	1366
Terrence McGee, Buf	0	0	1488	1488	Torry Holt, St.L	2	1331	0	1333
Chad Johnson, Cin	33	1432	0	1465	Josh Scobey, Sea	0	0	1326	1326

Ret column indicates all kickoff, punt, fumble and interception returns.

Scoring

Touchdowns

AFC	TD	Rush	Rec	Ret	Pts
Larry Johnson, KC	21	20	1	0	126
LaDainian Tomlinson, SD	20	18	2	0	120
Edgerrin James, Ind	14	13	1	0	84
Mike Anderson, Den	13	12	1	0	78
Corey Dillon, NE	13	12	1	0	78
Marvin Harrison, Ind	12	0	12	0	72
Rudi Johnson, Cin	12	12	0	0	72
LaMont Jordan, Oak	11	9	2	0	68†
Chris Chambers, Mia	11	0	11	0	66
Hines Ward, Pit	11	0	11	0	66
Antonio Gates, SD	10	0	10	0	60

Three tied with 9 TD for 54 pts.
† Two-point conversions: Jordan (1).

NFC	TD	Rush	Rec	Ret	Pts
Shaun Alexander, Sea	28	27	1	0	168
Steve Smith, Car	13	1	12	0	78
Stephen Davis, Car	12	12	0	0	72
Tiki Barber, NYG	11	9	2	0	68†
Clinton Portis, Wash	11	11	0	0	68†
Larry Fitzgerald, Ari	10	0	10	0	60
Joey Galloway, TB	10	0	10	0	60
Steven Jackson, St.L	10	8	2	0	60
Joe Jurevicius, Sea	10	0	10	0	60
Torry Holt, St.L	9	0	9	0	54
Thomas Jones, Chi	9	9	0	0	54
Santana Moss, Wash	9	0	9	0	54

Four tied with 8 TD for 48 pts.
† Two-point conversions: Barber and Portis (1).

Kickers

AFC	PAT	FG	Long	Pts
Shayne Graham, Cin	47/47	28/32	49	131
Lawrence Tynes, KC	44/45	27/33	52	125
Mike Vanderjagt, Ind	52/52	23/25	48	121
Jeff Reed, Pit	45/45	24/29	44	117
Jason Elam, Den	42/43	24/32	51	114
Rian Lindell, Buf	26/26	29/35	53	113
Matt Stover, Bal	23/23	30/34	49	113
Nate Kaeding, SD	49/49	21/24	49	112
Olindo Mare, Mia	33/33	25/30	53	108
Josh Scobee, Jax	38/39	23/30	53	107
Kris Brown, Hou	24/24	26/34	53	102
Phil Dawson, Cle	19/21	27/29	44	100
Adam Vinatieri, NE	40/41	20/25	49	100

NFC	PAT	FG	Long	Pts
Jay Feely, NYG	43/43	35/42	52	148
Neil Rackers, Ari	20/20	40/42	54	140
John Kasay, Car	43/44	26/34	52	121
Jeff Wilkins, St.L	36/36	27/31	53	117
Josh Brown, Sea	56/57	18/25	55	110
Paul Edinger, Min	31/31	25/34	56	106
Todd Peterson, Atl	35/35	23/25	43	104
John Carney, NO	22/22	25/32	49	97
Joe Nedney, SF	19/19	26/28	56	97
Matt Bryant, TB	31/31	21/25	50	94
Ryan Longwell, GB	30/31	20/27	53	90
Jason Hanson, Det	27/27	19/24	52	84
Robbie Gould*, Chi	19/20	21/27	45	82

NFL Regular Season Individual Leaders (Cont.)

Sacks

AFC

	No
Derrick Burgess, Oak	16.0
Kyle Vanden Bosch, Ten	12.5
Aaron Schobel, Buf	12.0
Jason Taylor, Mia	12.0
Robert Mathis, Ind	11.5

NFC

	No
Osi Umenyiora, NYG	14.5
Simeon Rice, TB	14.0
Michael Strahan, NYG	11.5
Rod Coleman, Atl	10.5
Julius Peppers, Car	10.5

Interceptions

AFC

	No	Yds	Long	TD
Ty Law, NYJ	10	195	74-td	1
Deltha O'Neal, Cin	10	103	37	0
Champ Bailey, Den	8	139	65-td	2
Greg Wesley, KC	6	106	51	0
Six tied with 5 int's each.				

NFC

	No	Yds	Long	TD
Darren Sharper, Min	9	276	92-td	2
Nathan Vasher, Chi	8	145	46	1
Chris Gamble, Car	7	157	61-td	1
Three tied with 6 int's each.				

Punting

AFC

	No	Yds	Lg	Avg	In20
Brian Moorman, Buf	71	3242	68	45.7	22
Shane Lechler, Oak	82	3744	64	45.7	26
Josh Miller, NE	76	3431	59	45.1	22
Hunter Smith, Ind	52	2301	58	44.3	23
Todd Sauerbrun, Den	72	3157	66	43.8	24

NFC

	No	Yds	Lg	Avg	In20
Josh Bidwell, TB	90	4101	61	45.6	24
Chris Kluwe*, Min	71	3130	62	44.1	17
Scott Player, Ari	73	3206	60	43.9	18
Nick Harris, Det	84	3656	60	43.5	34
Jason Baker, Car	72	3118	59	43.3	23

Punt Returns
(Minimum of 20 returns)

AFC

	No	Yds	Avg	Long	TD
B.J. Sams, Bal	33	401	12.2	51	0
Dennis Northcutt, Cle	35	368	10.5	62-td	1
Antwaan Randle El, Pit	44	448	10.2	81-td	2
Bobby Wade, Chi-Ten	33	317	9.6	73-td	1
Pacman Jones*, Ten	29	272	9.4	52-td	1

NFC

	No	Yds	Avg	Long	TD
Reno Mahe, Phi	21	269	12.8	44	0
Mewelde Moore, Min	21	245	11.7	71-td	1
Steve Smith, Car	27	286	10.6	44	0
Mark Jones, TB	51	492	9.6	31	0
Chad Morton, NYG	47	453	9.6	58	1

Kickoff Returns
(Minimum of 20 returns)

AFC

	No	Yds	Avg	Long	TD
Terrence McGee, Buf	46	1391	30.2	99-td	1
Jerome Mathis*, Hou	54	1542	28.6	99-td	2
Justin Miller*, NYJ	60	1577	26.3	95-td	1
Pacman Jones*, Ten	43	1127	26.2	85	0
Quincy Morgan, Pit	23	583	25.3	74	0

NFC

	No	Yds	Avg	Long	TD
Koren Robinson, Min	47	1221	26.0	86-td	1
Ladell Betts, Wash	24	621	25.9	94-td	1
Willie Ponder, NYG	35	905	25.9	95-td	1
Tyson Thompson*, Dal	57	1399	24.5	49	0
Roderick Hood, Phi	38	900	23.7	53	0

Single Game Highs

Passing Yards

AFC

	Cmp/Att	Yds	TD
Ben Roethlisberger, Pit vs Cin (12/4)	29/41	386	3
Tom Brady, NE vs Pit (9/25)	31/41	372	0
Peyton Manning, Ind vs Cin (11/20)	24/40	365	3
Gus Frerotte, Mia vs NE (11/13)	25/47	360	2
Tom Brady, NE vs Atl (10/9)	22/27	350	3

NFC

	Cmp/Att	Yds	TD
Marc Bulger, St.L vs NYG (10/2)	40/62	442	2
Josh McCown, Ari vs Car (10/9)	29/46	398	2
Josh McCown, Ari vs SF (10/2)	32/46	385	2
Aaron Brooks, NO vs NYG (9/19)	27/45	375	1
Donovan McNabb, Phi vs KC (10/2)	33/48	369	3

Rushing Yards

AFC

	Car	Yds	TD
Larry Johnson, KC vs Hou (11/20)	36	211	2
Larry Johnson, KC vs Cin (1/1)	26	201	3
LaDainian Tomlinson, SD vs NYG (9/25)	21	192	3
LaDainian Tomlinson, SD vs Wash (11/27 OT)	25	184	3
Ricky Williams, Mia vs Ten (12/24)	26	172	1

NFC

	Car	Yds	TD
Tiki Barber, NYG vs KC (12/17)	29	220	2
Tiki Barber, NYG vs Wash (10/30)	24	206	1
Tiki Barber, NYG vs Oak (12/31)	28	203	1
Julius Jones, Dal vs Car (12/24)	34	194	2
Steven Jackson, St.L vs Jax (10/30)	25	179	0

Receiving Yards

AFC

	Ct	Yds	TD
Chris Chambers, Mia vs Buf (12/4)	15	238	1
Chad Johnson, Cin vs Ind (11/20)	8	189	1
Andre Johnson, Hou vs St.L (11/27 OT)	12	159	1
Eddie Kennison, KC vs Cin (1/1)	7	151	0
T.J. Houshmandzadeh, Cin vs Bal (11/27)	9	147	1

NFC

	Ct	Yds	TD
Plaxico Burress, NYG vs St.L (10/2)	10	204	2
Steve Smith, Car vs Min (10/30)	11	201	1
Santana Moss, Wash vs KC (10/16)	10	173	2
Terrell Owens, Phi vs KC (10/2)	11	171	1
Steve Smith, Car vs Mia (9/25)	11	170	3

NFL Bests

Longest Field Goal
58 yds . . . . Michael Koenen*, Atl vs NE (10/9)

Longest Run from Scrimmage
95 yds . . . . Tiki Barber, NYG vs Oak (12/31) TD

Longest Pass Play
91 yds . . D. McNabb to T. Owens, Phi vs. Den (10/30) TD

Longest Interception Return
95 yds . . . . Nick Barnett, GB vs NO (10/9) TD
Charles Tillman, Chi vs GB (12/4)

Longest Punt Return
85 yds . . . . Antonio Chatman, GB vs Chi (12/25) TD

Longest Kickoff Return
99 yds . . . . by three players

NFL Regular Season Team Leaders

Offense

AFC	Points		Yardage			
	For	Avg	Rush	Pass	Total	Avg
Kansas City	403	25.2	2382	3810	6192	387.0
Indianapolis	439	27.4	1703	4096	5799	362.4
Denver	395	24.7	2539	3227	5766	360.4
Cincinnati	421	26.3	1910	3820	5730	358.1
New England	379	23.7	1512	4120	5632	352.0
San Diego	418	26.1	2072	3495	5567	347.9
Miami	318	19.9	1898	3300	5198	324.9
Jacksonville	361	22.6	1959	3190	5149	321.8
Pittsburgh	389	24.3	2223	2926	5149	321.8
Tennessee	299	18.7	1525	3597	5122	320.1
Oakland	290	18.1	1369	3582	4951	309.4
Baltimore	265	16.6	1605	3088	4693	293.3
Cleveland	232	14.5	1503	3047	4550	284.4
Buffalo	271	16.9	1607	2515	4122	257.6
Houston	260	16.3	1816	2237	4053	253.3
NY Jets	240	15.0	1328	2642	3970	248.1

NFC	Points		Yardage			
	For	Avg	Rush	Pass	Total	Avg
Seattle	452	28.3	2457	3458	5915	369.7
NY Giants	422	26.4	2209	3578	5787	361.7
Arizona	311	19.4	1138	4437	5575	348.4
St. Louis	363	22.7	1535	4036	5571	348.2
Washington	359	22.4	2183	3106	5289	330.6
Atlanta	351	21.9	2546	2679	5225	326.6
Dallas	325	20.3	1861	3341	5202	325.1
Green Bay	298	18.6	1352	3766	5118	319.9
Philadelphia	310	19.4	1432	3677	5109	319.3
New Orleans	235	14.7	1688	3343	5031	314.4
Carolina	391	24.4	1679	3271	4950	309.4
Tampa Bay	300	18.8	1826	2890	4716	294.8
Minnesota	306	19.1	1467	3146	4613	288.3
Detroit	254	15.9	1471	2848	4319	269.9
Chicago	260	16.3	2099	2002	4101	256.3
San Francisco	239	14.9	1689	1898	3587	224.2

Defense

AFC	Points		Yardage			
	Opp	Avg	Rush	Pass	Total	Avg
Pittsburgh	258	16.1	1376	3168	4544	284.0
Baltimore	299	18.7	1591	2958	4549	284.3
Jacksonville	269	16.8	1709	2946	4655	290.9
Indianapolis	247	15.4	1762	3151	4913	307.1
NY Jets	355	22.2	2185	2755	4940	308.8
San Diego	312	19.5	1349	3599	4948	309.3
Denver	258	16.1	1363	3643	5006	312.9
Cleveland	301	18.8	2202	2867	5069	316.8
Miami	317	19.8	1771	3307	5078	317.4
Tennessee	421	26.3	1894	3216	5110	319.4
Kansas City	325	20.3	1570	3679	5249	328.1
New Orleans	338	21.1	1580	3703	5283	330.2
Oakland	383	23.9	2049	3243	5292	330.8
Cincinnati	350	21.9	1850	3569	5419	338.7
Buffalo	367	22.9	2205	3291	5496	343.5
Houston	431	26.9	2303	3521	5824	364.0

NFC	Points		Yardage			
	Opp	Avg	Rush	Pass	Total	Avg
Tampa Bay	274	17.1	1515	2929	4444	277.8
Chicago	202	12.6	1637	2872	4509	281.8
Carolina	259	16.2	1465	3057	4522	282.6
Green Bay	344	21.5	2010	2680	4690	293.1
Arizona	387	24.2	1632	3097	4729	295.6
Washington	293	18.3	1686	3081	4767	297.9
Dallas	308	19.3	1731	3083	4814	300.9
New Orleans	398	24.9	2145	2849	4994	312.1
Seattle	271	16.9	1510	3559	5069	316.8
Detroit	345	21.6	2040	3118	5158	322.4
Minnesota	344	21.5	1841	3332	5173	323.3
Atlanta	341	21.3	2063	3137	5200	325.0
Philadelphia	388	24.3	1883	3323	5206	325.4
NY Giants	314	19.6	1656	3584	5240	327.5
St. Louis	429	26.8	2178	3424	5602	350.1
San Francisco	428	26.8	1832	4427	6259	391.2

Overall Club Rankings

Combined AFC and NFC rankings by yards gained on offense and yards given up on defense. Teams are ranked alphabetically, with AFC teams in *italics*. (t) indicates tied for position.

	Offense			Defense		
	Rush	Pass	Rank	Rush	Pass	Rank
Arizona	32	1	8	10	12	8
Atlanta	1	27	12	26	14	22
Baltimore	21	22	24	9	8	5
Buffalo	20	29	28	31	19	29
Carolina	19	17	22	4	9	3
Chicago	8	31	29	11	5	2
Cincinnati	11	5	6	20	26	28
Cleveland	25	23	26	30	4	16t
Dallas	13	15	13	15	11	10
Denver	2	18	5	2	29	15
Detroit	26	26	27	24	13	20
Green Bay	30	7	18	23	1	7
Houston	15	30	30	32	24	31
Indianapolis	16	3	3	16	15	11
Jacksonville	10	19	15t	14	7	6
Kansas City	4	6	1	7	30	25

	Offense			Defense		
	Rush	Pass	Rank	Rush	Pass	Rank
Miami	12	16	14	17	20	18
Minnesota	27	20	25	19	22	21
New England	24	2	7	8	31	26
New Orleans	18	14	20	27	3	14
NY Giants	6	11	4	12	27	24
NY Jets	31	28	31	29	2	12
Oakland	29	10	21	25	18	27
Philadelphia	28	8	19	21	21	23
Pittsburgh	5	24	15t	3	16	4
St. Louis	22	4	9	28	23	30
San Diego	9	12	10	1	28	13
San Francisco	17	32	32	18	32	32
Seattle	3	13	2	5	25	16t
Tampa Bay	14	25	23	6	6	1
Tennessee	23	9	17	22	17	19
Washington	7	21	11	13	10	9

AFC Team by Team Results

(*) indicates overtime game.

Baltimore Ravens (6-10)

Indianapolis	L, 7-24
at Tennessee	L, 10-25
BYE	—
NY Jets	W, 13-3
at Detroit	L, 17-35
Cleveland	W, 16-3
at Chicago	L, 6-10
at Pittsburgh	L, 19-20
Cincinnati	L, 9-21
at Jacksonville	L, 3-30
Pittsburgh	W, 16-13*
at Cincinnati	L, 29-42
Houston	W, 16-15
at Denver	L, 10-12
Green Bay	W, 48-3
Minnesota	W, 30-23
at Cleveland	L, 16-20

Buffalo Bills (5-11)

Houston	W, 22-7
at Tampa Bay	L, 3-19
Atlanta	L, 16-24
at New Orleans	L, 7-19
Miami	W, 20-14
NY Jets	W, 27-17
at Oakland	L, 17-38
at New England	L 16-21
BYE	—
Kansas City	W, 14-3
at San Diego	L, 10-48
Carolina	L, 9-13
at Miami	L, 23-24
New England	L, 7-35
Denver	L, 17-28
at Cincinnati	W, 37-27
at NY Jets	L, 26-30

Cincinnati Bengals (11-5)

at Cleveland	W, 27-13
Minnesota	W, 37-8
at Chicago	W, 24-7
Houston	W, 16-10
at Jacksonville	L, 20-23
at Tennessee	W, 31-23
Pittsburgh	L, 13-27
Green Bay	W, 21-14
at Baltimore	W, 21-9
BYE	—
Indianapolis	L, 37-45
Baltimore	W, 42-29
at Pittsburgh	W, 38-31
Cleveland	W, 23-20
at Detroit	W, 41-17
Buffalo	L, 27-37
at Kansas City	L, 3-37

Cleveland Browns (6-10)

Cincinnati	L, 13-27
at Green Bay	W, 26-24
at Indianapolis	L, 6-13
BYE	—
Chicago	W, 20-10
at Baltimore	L, 3-16
Detroit	L, 10-13
at Houston	L, 16-19
Tennessee	W, 20-14
at Pittsburgh	L, 21-34
Miami	W, 22-0
at Minnesota	L, 12-24
Jacksonville	L, 14-20
at Cincinnati	L, 20-23
at Oakland	W, 9-7
Pittsburgh	L, 0-41
Baltimore	W, 20-16

Denver Broncos (13-3)

at Miami	L, 10-34
San Diego	W, 20-17
Kansas City	W, 30-10
at Jacksonville	W, 20-7
Washington	W, 21-19
New England	W, 28-20
at NY Giants	L, 23-24
Philadelphia	W, 49-21
BYE	—
at Oakland	W, 31-17
NY Jets	W, 27-0
at Dallas	W, 24-21*
at Kansas City	L, 27-31
Baltimore	W, 12-10
at Buffalo	W, 28-17
Oakland	W, 22-3
at San Diego	W, 23-7

Houston Texans (2-14)

at Buffalo	L, 7-22
Pittsburgh	L, 7-27
BYE	—
at Cincinnati	L, 10-16
Tennessee	L, 20-34
at Seattle	L, 10-42
Indianapolis	L, 20-38
Cleveland	W, 19-16
at Jacksonville	L, 14-21
at Indianapolis	L, 17-31
Kansas City	L, 17-45
St. Louis	L, 27-33*
at Baltimore	L, 15-16
at Tennessee	L, 10-13
Arizona	W, 30-19
Jacksonville	L, 20-38
at San Francisco	L, 17-20*

Indianapolis Colts (14-2)

at Baltimore	W, 24-7
Jacksonville	W, 10-3
Cleveland	W, 13-6
at Tennessee	W, 31-10
at San Francisco	W, 28-3
St. Louis	W, 45-28
at Houston	W, 38-20
BYE	—
at New England	W, 40-21
Houston	W, 31-17
at Cincinnati	W, 45-37
Pittsburgh	W, 26-7
Tennessee	W, 35-3
at Jacksonville	W, 26-18
San Diego	L, 17-26
at Seattle	L, 13-28
Arizona	W, 17-13

Jacksonville Jaguars (12-4)

Seattle	W, 26-14
at Indianapolis	L, 3-10
at NY Jets	W, 26-20*
Denver	L, 7-20
Cincinnati	W, 23-20
at Pittsburgh	W, 23-17*
BYE	—
at St. Louis	L, 21-24
Houston	W, 21-14
Baltimore	W, 30-3
at Tennessee	W, 31-28
at Arizona	W, 24-17
at Cleveland	W, 20-14
Indianapolis	L, 18-26
San Francisco	W, 10-9
at Houston	W, 38-20
Tennessee	W, 40-13

Kansas City Chiefs (10-6)

NY Jets	W, 27-7
at Oakland	W, 23-17
at Denver	L, 10-30
Philadelphia	L, 31-37
BYE	—
Washington	W, 28-21
at Miami	W, 30-20
at San Diego	L, 20-28
Oakland	W, 27-23
at Buffalo	L, 3-14
at Houston	W, 45-17
New England	W, 26-16
Denver	W, 31-27
at Dallas	L, 28-31
at NY Giants	L, 17-27
San Diego	W, 20-7
Cincinnati	W, 37-3

Miami Dolphins (9-7)

Denver	W, 34-10
at NY Jets	L, 7-17
Carolina	W, 27-24
BYE	—
at Buffalo	L, 14-20
at Tampa Bay	L, 13-27
Kansas City	L, 20-30
at New Orleans	W, 21-6
Atlanta	L, 10-17
New England	L, 16-23
at Cleveland	L, 0-22
at Oakland	W, 33-21
Buffalo	W, 24-23
at San Diego	W, 23-21
NY Jets	W, 24-20
Tennessee	W, 24-10
at New England	W, 28-26

New England Patriots (10-6)

Oakland	W, 30-20
at Carolina	L, 17-27
at Pittsburgh	W, 23-20
San Diego	L, 17-41
at Atlanta	W, 31-28
at Denver	L, 20-28
BYE	—
Buffalo	W, 21-16
Indianapolis	L, 21-40
at Miami	W, 23-16
New Orleans	W, 24-17
at Kansas City	L, 16-26
NY Jets	W, 16-3
at Buffalo	W, 35-7
Tampa Bay	W, 28-0
at NY Jets	W, 31-21
Miami	L, 26-28

New York Jets (4-12)

at Kansas City	L, 7-27
Miami	W, 17-7
Jacksonville	L 20-26*
at Baltimore	L, 3-13
Tampa Bay	W, 14-12
at Buffalo	L, 17-27
at Atlanta	L, 14-27
BYE	—
San Diego	L, 26-31
at Carolina	L, 3-30
at Denver	L, 0-27
New Orleans	L, 19-21
at New England	L, 3-16
Oakland	W, 26-10
at Miami	L, 20-24
New England	L, 21-31
Buffalo	W, 30-26

Oakland Raiders (4-12)

at New England	L, 20-30
Kansas City	L, 17-23
at Philadelphia	L, 20-23
Dallas	W, 19-13
BYE	—
San Diego	L, 14-27
Buffalo	W, 38-17
at Tennessee	W, 34-25
at Kansas City	L, 23-27
Denver	L, 17-31
at Washington	W, 16-13
Miami	L, 21-33
at San Diego	L, 10-34
at NY Jets	L, 10-26
Cleveland	L, 7-9
at Denver	L, 3-22
NY Giants	L, 21-30

Pittsburgh Steelers (11-5)

Tennessee	W, 34-7
at Houston	W, 27-7
New England	L, 20-23
BYE	—
at San Diego	W, 24-22
Jacksonville	L, 17-23*
at Cincinnati	W, 27-13
Baltimore	W, 20-19
at Green Bay	W, 20-10
Cleveland	W, 34-21
at Baltimore	L, 13-16*
at Indianapolis	L, 7-26
Cincinnati	L, 31-38
Chicago	W, 21-9
at Minnesota	W, 18-3
at Cleveland	W, 41-0
Detroit	W, 35-21

San Diego Chargers (9-7)

Dallas	L, 24-28
at Denver	L, 17-20
NY Giants	W, 45-23
at New England	W, 41-17
Pittsburgh	L, 22-24
at Oakland	W, 27-14
at Philadelphia	L, 17-20
Kansas City	W, 28-20
at NY Jets	W, 31-26
BYE	—
Buffalo	W, 48-10
at Washington	W, 23-17*
Oakland	W, 34-10
Miami	L, 21-23
at Indianapolis	W, 26-17
at Kansas City	L, 7-20
Denver	L, 7-23

Tennessee Titans (4-12)

at Pittsburgh	L, 7-34
Baltimore	W, 25-10
at St. Louis	L, 27-31
Indianapolis	L, 10-31
at Houston	W, 34-20
Cincinnati	L, 23-31
at Arizona	L, 10-20
Oakland	L, 25-34
at Cleveland	L, 14-20
BYE	—
Jacksonville	L, 28-31
San Francisco	W, 33-22
at Indianapolis	L, 3-35
Houston	W, 13-10
Seattle	L, 24-28
at Miami	L, 10-24
at Jacksonville	L, 13-40

NFC Team by Team Results
(*) indicates overtime game

Arizona Cardinals (5-11)

at NY Giants	L, 19-42
St. Louis	L, 12-17
at Seattle	L, 12-37
San Francisco	W, 31-14
Carolina	L, 20-24
BYE	—
Tennessee	W, 20-10
at Dallas	L, 13-34
Seattle	L, 19-33
at Detroit	L, 21-29
at St. Louis	W, 38-28
Jacksonville	L, 17-24
at San Francisco	W, 17-10
Washington	L, 13-17
at Houston	L, 19-30
Philadelphia	W, 27-21
at Indianapolis	L, 13-17

Atlanta Falcons (8-8)

Philadelphia	W, 14-10
at Seattle	L, 18-21
at Buffalo	W, 24-16
Minnesota	W, 30-10
New England	L, 28-31
at New Orleans	W, 34-31
NY Jets	W, 27-14
BYE	—
at Miami	W, 17-10
Green Bay	L, 25-33
Tampa Bay	L, 27-30
at Detroit	W, 27-7
at Carolina	L, 6-24
New Orleans	W, 36-17
at Chicago	L, 3-16
at Tampa Bay	L, 24-27
Carolina	L, 11-44

Carolina Panthers (11-5)

New Orleans	L, 20-23
New England	W, 27-17
at Miami	L, 24-27
Green Bay	W, 32-29
at Arizona	W, 24-20
at Detroit	W, 21-20
BYE	—
Minnesota	W, 38-13
at Tampa Bay	W, 34-14
NY Jets	W, 30-3
at Chicago	L, 3-13
at Buffalo	W, 13-9
Atlanta	W, 24-6
Tampa Bay	L, 10-20
at New Orleans	W, 27-10
Dallas	L, 20-24
at Atlanta	W, 44-11

Chicago Bears (11-5)

at Washington	L, 7-9
Detroit	W, 38-6
Cincinnati	L, 7-24
BYE	—
at Cleveland	L, 10-20
Minnesota	W, 28-3
Baltimore	W, 10-6
at Detroit	W, 19-13*
at New Orleans	W, 20-17
San Francisco	W, 17-9
Carolina	W, 13-3
at Tampa Bay	W, 13-10
Green Bay	W, 19-7
at Pittsburgh	L, 9-21
Atlanta	W, 16-3
at Green Bay	W, 24-17
at Minnesota	L, 10-34

Dallas Cowboys (9-7)

at San Diego	W, 28-24
Washington	L, 13-14
at San Francisco	W, 34-31
at Oakland	L, 13-19
Philadelphia	W, 33-10
NY Giants	W, 16-13*
at Seattle	L, 10-13
Arizona	W, 34-13
BYE	—
at Philadelphia	W, 21-20
Detroit	W, 20-7
Denver	L, 21-24*
at NY Giants	L, 10-17
Kansas City	W, 31-28
at Washington	L, 7-35
at Carolina	W, 24-20
St. Louis	L, 10-20

Detroit Lions (5-11)

Green Bay	W, 17-3
at Chicago	L, 6-38
BYE	—
at Tampa Bay	L, 13-17
Baltimore	W, 35-17
Carolina	L, 20-21
at Cleveland	W, 13-10
Chicago	L, 13-19*
at Minnesota	L, 14-27
Arizona	W, 29-21
at Dallas	L, 7-20
Atlanta	L, 7-27
Minnesota	L, 16-21
at Green Bay	L, 13-16*
Cincinnati	L, 17-41
at New Orleans	W, 13-12
at Pittsburgh	L, 21-35

Green Bay Packers (4-12)

at Detroit	L, 3-17
Cleveland	L, 24-26
Tampa Bay	L, 16-17
at Carolina	L, 29-32
New Orleans	W, 52-3
BYE	—
at Minnesota	L, 20-23
at Cincinnati	L, 14-21
Pittsburgh	L, 10-20
at Atlanta	W, 33-25
Minnesota	L, 17-20
at Philadelphia	L, 14-19
at Chicago	L, 7-19
Detroit	W, 16-13*
at Baltimore	L, 3-48
Chicago	L, 17-24
Seattle	W, 23-17

Minnesota Vikings (9-7)

Tampa Bay	L, 13-24
at Cincinnati	L, 8-37
New Orleans	W, 33-16
at Atlanta	L, 10-30
BYE	—
at Chicago	L, 3-28
Green Bay	W, 23-20
at Carolina	L, 13-38
Detroit	W, 27-14
at NY Giants	W, 24-21
at Green Bay	W, 20-17
Cleveland	W, 24-12
at Detroit	W, 21-16
St. Louis	W, 27-13
Pittsburgh	L, 3-18
at Baltimore	L, 23-30
Chicago	W, 34-10

NFC Team by Team Results (Cont.)

New Orleans Saints (3-13)

at Carolina	W, 23-20
NY Giants	L, 10-27
at Minnesota	L, 16-33
Buffalo	W, 19-7
at Green Bay	L, 3-52
Atlanta	L, 31-34
at St. Louis	L, 17-28
Miami	L, 6-21
Chicago	L, 17-20
BYE	—
at New England	L, 17-24
at NY Jets	W, 21-19
Tampa Bay	L, 3-10
at Atlanta	L, 17-36
Carolina	L, 10-27
Detroit	L, 12-13
at Tampa Bay	L, 13-27

New York Giants (11-5)

Arizona	W, 42-19
at New Orleans	W, 27-10
at San Diego	L, 23-45
St. Louis	W, 44-24
BYE	—
at Dallas	L, 13-16*
Denver	W, 24-23
Washington	W, 36-0
at San Francisco	W, 24-6
Minnesota	L, 21-24
Philadelphia	W, 27-17
at Seattle	L, 21-24*
Dallas	W, 17-10
at Philadelphia	W, 26-23*
Kansas City	W, 27-17
at Washington	L, 20-35
at Oakland	W, 30-21

Philadelphia Eagles (6-10)

at Atlanta	L, 10-14
San Francisco	W, 42-3
Oakland	W, 23-20
at Kansas City	W, 37-31
at Dallas	L, 10-33
BYE	—
San Diego	W, 20-17
at Denver	L, 21-49
at Washington	L, 10-17
Dallas	L, 20-21
at NY Giants	L, 17-27
Green Bay	W, 19-14
Seattle	L, 0-42
NY Giants	L, 23-26*
at St. Louis	W, 17-16
at Arizona	L, 21-27
Washington	L, 20-31

St. Louis Rams (6-10)

at San Francisco	L, 25-28
at Arizona	W, 17-12
Tennessee	W, 31-27
at NY Giants	L, 24-44
Seattle	L, 31-37
at Indianapolis	L, 28-45
New Orleans	W, 28-17
Jacksonville	W, 24-21
BYE	—
at Seattle	L, 16-31
Arizona	L, 28-38
at Houston	W, 33-27*
Washington	L, 9-24
at Minnesota	L, 13-27
Philadelphia	L, 16-17
San Francisco	L, 20-24
at Dallas	W, 20-10

San Francisco 49ers (4-12)

St. Louis	W, 28-25
at Philadelphia	L, 3-42
Dallas	L, 31-34
at Arizona	L, 14-31
Indianapolis	L, 3-28
BYE	—
at Washington	L, 17-52
Tampa Bay	W, 15-10
NY Giants	L, 6-24
at Chicago	L, 9-17
Seattle	L, 25-27
at Tennessee	L, 22-33
Arizona	L, 10-17
at Seattle	L, 3-41
at Jacksonville	L, 9-10
at St. Louis	W, 24-20
Houston	W, 20-17*

Seattle Seahawks (13-3)

at Jacksonville	L, 14-26
Atlanta	W, 21-18
Arizona	W, 37-12
at Washington	L, 17-20*
at St. Louis	W, 37-31
Houston	W, 42-10
Dallas	W, 13-10
BYE	—
at Arizona	W, 33-19
St. Louis	W, 31-16
at San Francisco	W, 27-25
NY Giants	W, 24-21*
at Philadelphia	W, 42-0
San Francisco	W, 41-3
at Tennessee	W, 28-24
Indianapolis	W, 28-13
at Green Bay	L, 17-23

Tampa Bay Buccaneers (11-5)

at Minnesota	W, 24-13
Buffalo	W, 19-3
at Green Bay	W, 17-16
Detroit	W, 17-13
at NY Jets	L, 12-14
Miami	W, 27-13
BYE	—
at San Francisco	L, 10-15
Carolina	L, 14-34
Washington	W, 36-35
at Atlanta	W, 30-27
Chicago	L, 10-13
at New Orleans	W, 10-3
at Carolina	W, 20-10
at New England	L, 0-28
Atlanta	W, 27-24*
New Orleans	W, 27-13

Washington Redskins (10-6)

Chicago	W, 9-7
at Dallas	W, 14-13
BYE	—
Seattle	W, 20-17*
at Denver	L, 19-21
at Kansas City	L, 21-28
San Francisco	W, 52-17
at NY Giants	L, 0-36
Philadelphia	W, 17-10
at Tampa Bay	L, 35-36
Oakland	L, 13-16
San Diego	L, 17-23*
at St. Louis	W, 24-9
at Arizona	W, 17-13
Dallas	W, 35-7
NY Giants	W, 35-20
at Philadelphia	W, 31-20

Takeaways/Giveaways

AFC	Takeaways Int	Fum	Total	Giveaways Int	Fum	Total	Net Diff	NFC	Takeaways Int	Fum	Total	Giveaways Int	Fum	Total	Net Diff
Cincinnati	31	13	44	14	6	20	+24	Carolina	23	19	42	16	10	26	+16
Denver	20	16	36	7	9	16	+20	NY Giants	17	20	37	17	8	25	+12
Indianapolis	18	13	31	11	8	19	+12	Seattle	16	11	27	10	7	17	+10
Jacksonville	19	9	28	6	11	17	+11	Tampa Bay	17	13	30	14	9	23	+7
Kansas City	16	15	31	10	13	23	+8	Chicago	24	10	34	15	13	28	+6
Pittsburgh	15	15	30	14	9	23	+7	Minnesota	24	11	35	16	14	30	+5
Buffalo	17	13	30	16	10	26	+4	Detroit	19	12	31	18	12	30	+1
Miami	14	17	31	16	14	30	+1	Washington	16	12	28	11	16	27	+1
Oakland	5	14	19	14	9	23	-4	Atlanta	16	13	29	13	16	29	0
New England	10	8	18	15	9	24	-6	Dallas	15	11	26	17	14	31	-5
NY Jets	21	7	28	15	19	34	-6	Philadelphia	17	10	27	20	14	34	-7
Tennessee	9	11	20	14	12	26	-6	San Francisco	16	10	26	21	14	35	-9
Cleveland	15	8	23	17	13	30	-7	St. Louis	13	14	27	24	13	37	-10
Houston	7	9	16	13	11	24	-8	Arizona	15	11	26	21	16	37	-11
San Diego	10	10	20	16	12	28	-8	Green Bay	10	11	21	30	15	45	-24
Baltimore	11	15	26	21	15	36	-10	New Orleans	10	9	19	24	19	43	-24
TOTALS	238	193	431	219	180	399	+32	TOTALS	268	197	465	287	210	497	-32

AFC Team by Team Statistics

Players with more than one team during the regular season are listed with club they ended season with; (*) indicates rookies.

Baltimore Ravens

Passing (5 Att)	Att	Cmp	Pct	Yds	TD	Rate
Kyle Boller 293	171	58.4	1799	11	71.8
Anthony Wright . . .266	164	61.7	1582	6	71.7

Interceptions: Boller 12, Wright 9.

Top Receivers	No	Yds	Avg	Long	TD
Derrick Mason 86	1073	12.5	39-td	3
Todd Heap 75	855	11.4	48	7
Mark Clayton* 44	471	10.7	47-td	2
Chester Taylor 41	292	7.1	20	1
Jamal Lewis 32	191	6.0	15-td	1
Daniel Wilcox 20	154	7.7	17-td	1
Randy Hymes 11	132	12.0	21	2

Top Rushers	Car	Yds	Avg	Long	TD
Jamal Lewis 269	906	3.4	25	3
Chester Taylor 117	487	4.2	52	0
Anthony Wright 18	68	3.8	22	0
Kyle Boller 23	66	2.9	9	1

Most Touchdowns	TD	Run	Rec	Ret	Pts
Todd Heap 7	0	7	0	42
Jamal Lewis 4	3	1	0	24
Mark Clayton* 3	1	2	0	18
Derrick Mason 3	0	3	0	18
Adalius Thomas 3	0	0	3	18

2-Pt. Conversions: (1-2) Justin Green.

Kicking	PAT/Att	FG/Att	Lg	Pts
Matt Stover 23/23	30/34	49	113
Aaron Elling 0/0	0/0	—	0

Punts (10 or more)	No	Yds	Long	Avg	In20
Dave Zastudil 84	3653	60	43.5	11

Most Interceptions		**Most Sacks**
Three tied with 2 each.		Adalius Thomas 9.0

Buffalo Bills

Passing (5 Att)	Att	Cmp	Pct	Yds	TD	Rate
Kelly Holcomb 230	155	67.4	1509	10	85.6
J.P. Losman 228	113	49.6	1340	8	64.9

Interceptions: Holcomb 8, Losman 8.

Top Receivers	No	Yds	Avg	Long	TD
Eric Moulds 81	816	10.1	55-td	4
Lee Evans 48	743	15.5	65	7
Josh Reed 32	449	14.0	51-td	2
Willis McGahee 28	178	6.4	19	0
Mark Campbell 19	139	7.3	27	0
Shaud Williams 17	118	6.9	23	0

Top Rushers	Car	Yds	Avg	Long	TD
Willis McGahee 325	1247	3.8	27	5
Shaud Williams 45	161	3.6	28	0
J.P. Losman 31	154	5.0	30	0
Lee Evans 4	38	9.5	39	0

Most Touchdowns	TD	Run	Rec	Ret	Pts
Lee Evans 7	0	7	0	42
Willis McGahee 5	5	0	0	30
Eric Moulds 4	0	4	0	24
Terrence McGee 2	0	0	2	12
Josh Reed 2	0	2	0	12

2-Pt. Conversions: (0-0).

Kicking	PAT/Att	FG/Att	Lg	Pts
Rian Lindell 26/26	29/35	53	113

Punts (10 or more)	No	Yds	Long	Avg	In20
Brian Moorman 71	3242	68	45.7	22

Most Interceptions		**Most Sacks**
Troy Vincent 4		Aaron Schobel 12.0
Terrence McGee 4	

Cincinnati Bengals

Passing (5 Att)	Att	Cmp	Pct	Yds	TD	Rate
Carson Palmer 509	345	67.8	3836	32	101.1
Jon Kitna 29	17	58.6	99	0	36.4

Interceptions: Palmer 12, Kitna 2.

Top Receivers	No	Yds	Avg	Long	TD
Chad Johnson 97	1432	14.8	70-td	9
T.J. Houshmandzadeh .78	956	12.3	43-td	7
Chris Perry 51	328	6.4	28	2
Chris Henry* 31	422	13.6	47	6
Rudi Johnson 23	90	3.9	15	0
Kevin Walter 19	211	11.1	33	1
Matt Schobel 18	193	10.7	28	1

Top Rushers	Car	Yds	Avg	Long	TD
Rudi Johnson 337	1458	4.3	33	12
Chris Perry 61	279	4.6	30	0
T.J. Houshmandzadeh .8	62	7.8	17	1
Carson Palmer 34	41	1.2	14	1

Most Touchdowns	TD	Run	Rec	Ret	Pts
Rudi Johnson 12	12	0	0	72
Chad Johnson 9	0	9	0	54
T.J. Houshmandzadeh 8	1	7	0	48
Chris Henry* 6	0	6	0	36
Jeremi Johnson 3	0	3	0	18

2-Pt. Conversions: (1-1) Schobel.

Kicking	PAT/Att	FG/Att	Lg	Pts
Shayne Graham 47/47	28/32	49	131

Punts (10 or more)	No	Yds	Long	Avg	In20
Kyle Larson 60	2591	75	43.2	13

Most Interceptions		**Most Sacks**
Deltha O'Neal 10		Justin Smith 6.0

Cleveland Browns

Passing (5 Att)	Att	Cmp	Pct	Yds	TD	Rate
Trent Dilfer 333	199	59.8	2321	11	76.9
Charlie Frye* 164	98	59.8	1002	4	72.8

Interceptions: Dilfer 12, Frye 5.

Top Receivers	No	Yds	Avg	Long	TD
Antonio Bryant 69	1009	14.6	54	4
Steve Heiden 43	401	9.3	62-td	3
Dennis Northcutt 42	441	10.5	58-td	2
Reuben Droughns . . .39	369	9.5	51	0
Braylon Edwards* . . .32	512	16.0	80-td	3
Frisman Jackson 24	287	12.0	68-td	1
Aaron Shea 18	153	8.5	27	1

Top Rushers	Car	Yds	Avg	Long	TD
Reuben Droughns . . .309	1232	4.0	75-td	2
William Green 20	78	3.9	17	0
Charlie Frye* 18	60	3.3	16	1
Trent Dilfer 20	46	2.3	12	0

Most Touchdowns	TD	Run	Rec	Ret	Pts
Antonio Bryant 4	0	4	0	24
Braylon Edwards* 3	0	3	0	18
Steve Heiden 3	0	3	0	18
Dennis Northcutt 3	0	2	1	18

2-Pt. Conversions: (0-1).

Kicking	PAT/Att	FG/Att	Lg	Pts
Phil Dawson 19/21	27/29	44	100

Punts (10 or more)	No	Yds	Long	Avg	In20
Kyle Richardson 78	3181	61	40.8	22

Most Interceptions		**Most Sacks**
Leigh Bodden 3		Chaun Thompson 5.0
Brian Russell 3		Alvin McKinley 5.0

Denver Broncos

Passing (5 Att)	Att	Cmp	Pct	Yds	TD	Rate
Jake Plummer	.456	277	60.7	3366	18	90.2
Bradlee Van Pelt*	.8	2	25.0	7	0	39.6

Interceptions: Plummer 7.

Top Receivers	No	Yds	Avg	Long	TD
Rod Smith	.85	1105	13.0	72	6
Ashley Lelie	.42	770	18.3	56	1
Jeb Putzier	.37	481	13.0	32	0
Charlie Adams	.21	203	9.7	21	0
Stephen Alexander	.21	170	8.1	15	1
Mike Anderson	.18	212	11.8	66-td	1
Tatum Bell	.18	104	5.8	14	0

Top Rushers	Car	Yds	Avg	Long	TD
Mike Anderson	.239	1014	4.2	44-td	12
Tatum Bell	.173	921	5.3	68	8
Ron Dayne	.53	270	5.1	55	1
Jake Plummer	.46	151	3.3	22	2
Ashley Lelie	.5	84	16.8	39	0

Most Touchdowns	TD	Run	Rec	Ret	Pts
Mike Anderson	.13	12	1	0	78
Tatum Bell	.8	8	0	0	48
Kyle Johnson	.6	1	5	0	36
Rod Smith	.6	0	6	0	36

Three tied with 2 TD each for 12 pts.

2-Pt. Conversions: (1-2) Putzier.

Kicking	PAT/Att	FG/Att	Lg	Pts
Jason Elam	.43/44	24/32	51	115

Punts (10 or more)	No	Yds	Long	Avg	In20
Todd Sauerbrun	.72	3157	66	43.8	24

Most Interceptions | | **Most Sacks** |
---|---|---|---
Champ Bailey | .8 | Ebenezer Ekuban | 4.0
 | | John Lynch | 4.0
 | | Trevor Pryce | 4.0

Houston Texans

Passing (5 Att)	Att	Cmp	Pct	Yds	TD	Rate
David Carr	.423	256	60.5	2488	14	77.2
Tony Banks	.25	14	56.0	173	1	57.6

Interceptions: Carr 11, Banks 2.

Top Receivers	No	Yds	Avg	Long	TD
Andre Johnson	.63	688	10.9	53-td	2
Jabar Gaffney	.55	492	8.9	29	2
Domanick Davis	.39	337	8.6	33	4
Corey Bradford	.34	436	12.8	50-td	5
Marcellus Rivers	.24	168	7.0	20	0
Jonathan Wells	.22	179	8.1	20	0
Vernand Morency*	.10	87	8.7	16	0

Top Rushers	Car	Yds	Avg	Long	TD
Domanick Davis	.230	976	4.2	44	2
Jonathan Wells	.90	325	3.6	14-td	4
David Carr	.56	308	5.5	20	1
Vernand Morency*	.46	184	4.0	25-td	2

Most Touchdowns	TD	Run	Rec	Ret	Pts
Domanick Davis	.6	2	4	0	36
Corey Bradford	.5	0	5	0	32
Jonathan Wells	.4	4	0	0	24
Jerome Mathis*	.3	0	1	2	18

Three tied with 2 TD each for 12 pts.

2-Pt. Conversions: (1-2) Bradford.

Kicking	PAT/Att	FG/Att	Lg	Pts
Kris Brown	.24/24	26/34	53	102

Punts (10 or more)	No	Yds	Long	Avg	In20
Chad Stanley	.77	2990	61	38.8	29

Most Interceptions | | **Most Sacks** |
---|---|---|---
Glenn Earl | .2 | Shantee Orr | 7.0

Indianapolis Colts

Passing (5 Att)	Att	Cmp	Pct	Yds	TD	Rate
Peyton Manning	.453	305	67.3	3747	28	104.1
Jim Sorgi	.61	42	68.9	444	3	99.4

Interceptions: Manning 10, Sorgi 1.

Top Receivers	No	Yds	Avg	Long	TD
Reggie Wayne	.83	1055	12.7	66-td	5
Marvin Harrison	.82	1146	14.0	80-td	12
Edgerrin James	.44	337	7.7	20	1
Brandon Stokley	.41	543	13.2	45	1
Dallas Clark	.37	488	13.2	56	4

Top Rushers	Car	Yds	Avg	Long	TD
Edgerrin James	.360	1506	4.2	33	13
Dominic Rhodes	.40	118	3.0	24	4
Peyton Manning	.33	45	1.4	12	0

Most Touchdowns	TD	Run	Rec	Ret	Pts
Edgerrin James	.14	13	1	0	84
Marvin Harrison	.12	0	12	0	72
Reggie Wayne	.5	0	5	0	30
Dallas Clark	.4	0	4	0	24
Dominic Rhodes	.4	4	0	0	24

2-Pt. Conversions: (0-1)

Kicking	PAT/Att	FG/Att	Lg	Pts
Mike Vanderjagt	.52/52	23/25	48	119
Jose Cortez	.18/19	12/17	45	54
DAL	.13/14	12/16	45	49
PHI	.3/3	0/0	—	3
SF	.2/2	0/1	—	2
IND	.0/0	0/0	—	0

Signed: Cortez (Dec. 25).

Punts (10 or more)	No	Yds	Long	Avg	In20
Hunter Smith	.52	2301	58	44.3	23

Most Interceptions | | **Most Sacks** |
---|---|---|---
Cato June | .5 | Robert Mathis | 11.5

Jacksonville Jaguars

Passing (15 Att)	Att	Cmp	Pct	Yds	TD	Rate
Byron Leftwich	.302	175	57.9	2123	15	89.3
David Garrard	.168	98	58.3	1117	4	83.9
Quinn Gray	.14	8	57.1	100	2	119.0

Interceptions: Leftwich 5, Garrard 1.

Top Receivers	No	Yds	Avg	Long	TD
Jimmy Smith	.70	1023	14.6	45-td	6
Ernest Wilford	.41	681	16.6	39	7
Matt Jones*	.36	432	12.0	42	5
Reggie Williams	.35	445	12.7	41	0
Alvin Pearman*	.32	240	7.5	19	0

Top Rushers	Car	Yds	Avg	Long	TD
Fred Taylor	.194	787	4.1	71-td	3
Greg Jones	.151	575	3.8	27	4
David Garrard	.31	172	5.5	28	3
Alvin Pearman*	.39	149	3.8	45	1
LaBrandon Toefield	.36	142	3.9	32-td	4

Most Touchdowns	TD	Run	Rec	Ret	Pts
Ernest Wilford	.7	0	7	0	42
Jimmy Smith	.6	0	6	0	36
Matt Jones*	.5	0	5	0	30
Greg Jones	.4	4	0	0	24
LaBrandon Toefield	.4	4	0	0	24

2-Pt. Conversions: (1-1) Garrard.

Kicking	PAT/Att	FG/Att	Lg	Pts
Josh Scobee	.38/39	23/30	53	107

Punts (10 or more)	No	Yds	Long	Avg	In20
Chris Hanson	.82	3517	74	42.9	33

Most Interceptions | | **Most Sacks** |
---|---|---|---
Rashean Mathis | .5 | Reggie Hayward | 8.5

Kansas City Chiefs

Passing (5 Att) **Att Cmp Pct Yds TD Rate**
Trent Green 507   317   62.5 4014   17   90.1
Interceptions: Green 10.

Top Receivers	No	Yds	Avg	Long	TD
Tony Gonzalez 78		905	11.6	39	2
Eddie Kennison 68		1102	16.2	55	5
Samie Parker 36		533	14.8	49	3
Dante Hall 34		436	12.8	52-td	3
Larry Johnson 33		343	10.4	36	1
Priest Holmes 21		197	9.4	60-td	1
Chris Horn 18		187	10.4	50	0
Tony Richardson 9		68	7.6	22	1

Top Rushers	Car	Yds	Avg	Long	TD
Larry Johnson 336		1750	5.2	49-td	20
Priest Holmes 119		451	3.8	35-td	6
Trent Green 35		82	2.3	13	0
Eddie Kennison 7		43	6.1	23	0

Most Touchdowns	TD	Run	Rec	Ret	Pts
Larry Johnson 21		20	1	0	126
Priest Holmes 7		6	1	0	42
Eddie Kennison 5		0	5	0	30
Dante Hall 4		0	3	1	24
Samie Parker 3		0	3	0	18
Tony Gonzalez 2		0	2	0	12

2-Pt. Conversions: (1-1) Marc Boerigter.

Kicking	PAT/Att	FG/Att	Lg	Pts
Lawrence Tynes 44/45	27/33	52	125

Punts (10 or more)	No	Yds	Long	Avg	In20
Dustin Colquitt* 65	2564	62	39.4	27

Most Interceptions   **Most Sacks**
Greg Wesley 6   Jared Allen 11.0

Miami Dolphins

Passing (5 Att) **Att Cmp Pct Yds TD Rate**
Gus Frerotte 494   257   52.0   2996   18   71.9
Sage Rosenfels 61   34   55.7   462   4   81.5
Interceptions: Frerotte 13, Rosenfels 3.

Top Receivers	No	Yds	Avg	Long	TD
Chris Chambers 82		1118	13.6	77-td	11
Randy McMichael . . .60		582	9.7	30-td	5
Marty Booker 39		686	17.6	60-td	3
Ronnie Brown* 32		232	7.3	38	1
Wes Welker 29		434	15.0	47	0
Ricky Williams 17		93	5.5	19	0

Top Rushers	Car	Yds	Avg	Long	TD
Ronnie Brown* 207		907	4.4	65-td	4
Ricky Williams 168		743	4.4	35	6
Chris Chambers 12		92	7.7	61	0
Gus Frerotte 27		61	2.3	14	0
Sammy Morris 16		58	3.6	9-td	1

Most Touchdowns	TD	Run	Rec	Ret	Pts
Chris Chambers 11		0	11	0	66
Ricky Williams 6		6	0	0	36
Ronnie Brown* 5		4	1	0	30
Randy McMichael 5		0	5	0	30
Marty Booker 3		0	3	0	18

2-Pt. Conversions: (0-1).

Kicking	PAT/Att	FG/Att	Lg	Pts
Olindo Mare . . . . . . : . .33/33	25/30	53	108

Punts (10 or more)	No	Yds	Long	Avg	In20
Donnie Jones 88	3827	63	43.5	31

Most Interceptions   **Most Sacks**
Lance Schulters 4   Jason Taylor 12.0

New England Patriots

Passing (5 Att) **Att Cmp Pct Yds TD Rate**
Tom Brady 530   334   63.0   4110   26   92.3
Matt Cassel 24   13   54.2   183   2   89.4
Doug Flutie 10   5   50.0   29   0   56.3
Interceptions: Brady 14, Cassel 1.

Top Receivers	No	Yds	Avg	Long	TD
Deion Branch 78		998	12.8	51	5
David Givens 59		738	12.5	40	2
Troy Brown 39		466	11.9	71	2
Ben Watson 29		441	15.2	35	4
Kevin Faulk 29		260	9.0	23	0

Top Rushers	Car	Yds	Avg	Long	TD
Corey Dillon 209		733	3.5	29	12
Patrick Pass 54		245	4.5	31	3
Heath Evans 52		192	3.7	21	0
MIA 1		0	0.0	0	0
NE 51		192	3.8	21	0
Kevin Faulk 51		145	2.8	13	0

Signed: Free agent Evans on Nov. 1.

Most Touchdowns	TD	Run	Rec	Ret	Pts
Corey Dillon 13		12	1	0	78
Deion Branch 5		0	5	0	30
Mike Vrabel 4		0	3	1	24
Ben Watson 4		0	4	0	24

Three tied with 2 TDs for 12 pts.
2-Pt. Conversions: (1-4) Evans.

Kicking	PAT/Att	FG/Att	Lg	Pts
Adam Vinatieri 40/41	20/25	49	100
Doug Flutie 1/1	0/0	—	1

Punts (10 or more)	No	Yds	Long	Avg	In20
Josh Miller 76	3431	59	45.1	22

Most Interceptions   **Most Sacks**
Asante Samuel 3   Rosevelt Colvin 7.0
Ellis Hobbs* 3

New York Jets

Passing (5 Att) **Att Cmp Pct Yds TD Rate**
Brooks Bollinger . . .266   150   56.4   1558   7   72.9
Vinny Testaverde . . .106   60   56.6   777   1   59.4
Chad Pennington . . .83   49   59.0   530   2   70.9
Jay Fiedler 13   8   61.5   107   1 113.3
Interceptions: Bollinger and Testaverde 6, Pennington 3.

Top Receivers	No	Yds	Avg	Long	TD
Laveranues Coles . . .73		845	11.6	43	5
Justin McCareins 43		713	16.6	45	2
Doug Jolley 29		324	11.2	60-td	1
Jerald Sowell 28		155	5.5	28	2
Curtis Martin 24		118	4.9	14	0
Jerricho Cotchery 19		251	13.2	45	0

Top Rushers	No	Yds	Avg	Long	TD
Curtis Martin 220		735	3.3	49	5
Cedric Houston 81		302	3.7	17	2
Brooks Bollinger 35		135	3.9	15	0

Most Touchdowns	TD	Run	Rec	Ret	Pts
Laveranues Coles 5		0	5	0	30
Curtis Martin 5		5	0	0	30
Jerald Sowell 3		1	2	0	18

Three tied with 2 TD each for 12 pts.
2-Pt. Conversions: (0-1).

Kicking	PAT/Att	FG/Att	Lg	Pts
Mike Nugent* 24/24	22/28	49	90

Punts (10 or more)	No	Yds	Long	Avg	In20
Ben Graham* 74	3233	59	43.7	18

Most Interceptions   **Most Sacks**
Ty Law 10   John Abraham 10.5

Oakland Raiders

Passing (5 Att)	Att	Cmp	Pct	Yds	TD	Rate
Kerry Collins 565	302	53.5	3759	20	77.3
Marques Tuiasosopo .26	14	53.8	124	1	47.6

Interceptions: Collins 12, Tuiasosopo 2.

Top Receivers	No	Yds	Avg	Long	TD
Jerry Porter 76	942	12.4	49-td	5
LaMont Jordan 70	563	8.0	28	2
Randy Moss 60	1005	16.8	79	8
Doug Gabriel 37	554	15.0	38	3
Courtney Anderson . .24	303	12.6	36	3
Alvis Whitted 14	183	13.1	26	0

Top Rushers	Car	Yds	Avg	Long	TD
LaMont Jordan 272	1025	3.8	26	9
Zack Crockett 60	208	3.5	24	1
Alvis Whitted 2	51	25.5	27	0
Kerry Collins 17	39	2.3	18-td	1

Most Touchdowns	TD	Run	Rec	Ret	Pts
LaMont Jordan 11	9	2	0	68
Randy Moss 8	0	8	0	48
Jerry Porter 5	0	5	0	30
Courtney Anderson 3	0	3	0	18
Doug Gabriel 3	0	3	0	18

2-Pt. Conversions: (1-3) Alvis Whitted.

Kicking	PAT/Att	FG/Att	Lg	Pts
Sebastian Janikowski 30/30	20/30	49	90

Punts (10 or more)	No	Yds	Long	Avg	In20
Shane Lechler 82	3744	64	45.7	26

Most Interceptions		Most Sacks	
Stuart Schweigert 2		Derrick Burgess 16.0	

Pittsburgh Steelers

Passing (5 Att)	Att	Cmp	Pct	Yds	TD	Rate
Ben Roethlisberger . .268	168	62.7	2385	17	98.6
Tommy Maddox 71	34	47.9	406	2	51.7
Charlie Batch 36	23	63.9	246	1	81.5

Interceptions: Roethlisberger 9, Maddox 4, Batch 1.

Top Receivers	No	Yds	Avg	Long	TD
Hines Ward 69	975	14.1	85-td	11
Heath Miller* 39	459	11.8	50	6
Antwaan Randle El . .35	558	15.9	63-td	1
Cedrick Wilson 26	451	17.3	46	0
Willie Parker 18	218	12.1	48	1
Verron Haynes 11	113	10.3	18	0
Quincy Morgan 9	150	16.7	31-td	2

Top Rushers	Car	Yds	Avg	Long	TD
Willie Parker 255	1202	4.7	80-td	4
Jerome Bettis 110	368	3.3	39	9
Verron Haynes 74	274	3.7	20	3
Duce Staley 38	148	3.9	17	1
Antwaan Randle El . .12	73	6.1	43	0
Ben Roethlisberger 31	69	2.2	13	3

Most Touchdowns	TD	Run	Rec	Ret	Pts
Hines Ward 11	0	11	0	66
Jerome Bettis 9	9	0	0	54
Heath Miller* 6	0	6	0	36
Willie Parker 5	4	1	0	30

Three tied with 3 TD each for 18 pts.

2-Pt. Conversions: (0-0).

Kicking	PAT/Att	FG/Att	Lg	Pts
Jeff Reed 45/45	24/29	44	117

Punts (10 or more)	No	Yds	Long	Avg	In20
Chris Gardocki 67	2803	65	41.8	22

Most Interceptions		Most Sacks	
Chris Hope 3		Joey Porter 10.5	

San Diego Chargers

Passing (5 Att)	Att	Cmp	Pct	Yds	TD	Rate
Drew Brees 500	323	64.6	3576	24	89.2
Philip Rivers 22	12	54.5	115	0	50.4

Interceptions: Brees 15, Rivers 1.

Top Receivers	No	Yds	Avg	Long	TD
Antonio Gates 89	1101	12.4	38	10
Keenan McCardell . . .70	917	13.1	54	9
Eric Parker 57	725	12.7	49	3
LaDainian Tomlinson .51	370	7.3	41	2
Reche Caldwell 28	352	12.6	43	1
Lorenzo Neal 24	145	6.0	21	1
Justin Peelle 11	38	3.5	11	1

Top Rushers	No	Yds	Avg	Long	TD
LaDainian Tomlinson . .339	1462	4.3	62	18
Michael Turner 57	335	5.9	83-td	3
Lorenzo Neal 29	98	3.4	9	0
Eric Parker 4	55	13.8	30	0

Most Touchdowns	TD	Run	Rec	Ret	Pts
LaDainian Tomlinson 20	18	2	0	120
Antonio Gates 10	0	10	0	60
Keenan McCardell 9	0	9	0	54
Eric Parker 3	0	3	0	18
Michael Turner 3	3	0	0	18

2-Pt. Conversions: (0-1).

Kicking	PAT/Att	FG/Att	Lg	Pts
Nate Kaeding 49/49	21/24	49	112

Punts (10 or more)	No	Yds	Long	Avg	In20
Mike Scifres 71	3104	71	43.7	25

Most Interceptions		Most Sacks	
Bhawoh Jue 3		Shawne Merriman . . .10.0	

Tennessee Titans

Passing (5 Att)	Att	Cmp	Pct	Yds	TD	Rate
Steve McNair 476	292	61.3	3161	16	82.4
Billy Volek 88	50	56.8	474	4	77.6
Matt Mauck 27	15	55.6	136	0	53.9

Interceptions: McNair 11, Volek 2, Mauck 2.

Top Receivers	No	Yds	Avg	Long	TD
Drew Bennett 58	738	12.7	55-td	4
Erron Kinney 55	543	9.9	27	2
Ben Troupe 55	530	9.6	35	4
Bo Scaife* 37	273	7.4	19	2
Chris Brown 25	327	13.1	57	2
Brandon Jones* 23	299	13.0	38-td	2
Tyrone Calico 22	191	8.7	18	0
Roydell Williams* . . .21	299	14.2	50-td	0
Courtney Roby* 21	289	13.8	32	1

Top Rushers	Car	Yds	Avg	Long	TD
Chris Brown 224	851	3.8	38-td	5
Travis Henry 88	335	3.8	29	0
Steve McNair* 32	139	4.3	19	1
Jarrett Payton* 33	105	3.2	15	2

Most Touchdowns	TD	Run	Rec	Ret	Pts
Chris Brown 7	5	2	0	42
Drew Bennett 4	0	4	0	24
Ben Troupe 4	0	4	0	24

Six tied with 2 TDs for 12 pts.

2-Pt. Conversions: (0-1).

Kicking	PAT/Att	FG/Att	Lg	Pts
Rob Bironas* 30/32	23/29	53	99

Punts (10 or more)	No	Yds	Long	Avg	In20
Craig Hentrich 78	3371	59	43.2	21

Most Interceptions		Most Sacks	
Reynaldo Hill 3		Kyle Vanden Bosch . .12.5	

NFC Team by Team Statistics

Players with more than one team during the regular season are listed with club they ended season with; (*) indicates rookies.

Arizona Cardinals

Passing (5 Att)

	Att	Cmp	Pct	Yds	TD	Rate
Kurt Warner	.375	242	64.5	2713	11	85.8
Josh McCown	.270	163	60.4	1836	9	74.9
John Navarre	.24	14	58.3	174	1	77.4

Interceptions: McCown 11, Warner 9, Navarre 1.

Top Receivers

	No	Yds	Avg	Long	TD
Larry Fitzgerald	.103	1409	13.7	47	10
Anquan Boldin	.102	1402	13.7	54-td	7
Bryant Johnson	.40	432	10.8	41	1
Marcel Shipp	.35	255	7.3	28	0
Obafemi Ayanbadejo	34	231	6.8	18	0

Top Rushers

	Car	Yds	Avg	Long	TD
Marcel Shipp	.157	451	2.9	19	0
J.J. Arrington*	.112	370	3.3	32	2
Josh McCown	.29	139	4.8	12	0
Obafemi Ayanbadejo	22	46	2.1	11	0

Most Touchdowns

	TD	Run	Rec	Ret	Pts
Larry Fitzgerald	.10	0	10	0	60
Anquan Boldin	.7	0	7	0	44
J.J. Arrington*	.2	2	0	0	12
Karlos Dansby	.2	0	0	2	12

2-Pt. Conversions: (3-6) Ayanbadejo 2, Boldin 1.

Kicking

	PAT/Att	FG/Att	Lg	Pts
Neil Rackers	.20/20	40/42	54	140
Nick Novak*	.15/15	8/10	40	39
WASH	.15/15	5/7	40	30
ARI	.0/0	3/3	35	9

Signed: Free agent Novak (Dec. 2).

Punts (10 or more)

	No	Yds	Long	Avg	In20
Scott Player	.73	3206	60	43.9	18

Most Interceptions
Karlos Dansby 3

Most Sacks
Adrian Wilson 8.0

Atlanta Falcons

Passing (5 Att)

	Att	Cmp	Pct	Yds	TD	Rate
Michael Vick	.387	214	55.3	2412	15	73.1
Matt Schaub	.64	33	51.6	495	4	98.1

Interceptions: Vick 13.

Top Receivers

	No	Yds	Avg	Long	TD
Alge Crumpler	.65	877	13.5	48	5
Brian Finneran	.50	611	12.2	53	2
Michael Jenkins	.36	508	14.1	58	3
Roddy White*	.29	446	15.4	54-td	3
Warrick Dunn	.29	220	7.6	24	1

Top Rushers

	Car	Yds	Avg	Long	TD
Warrick Dunn	.280	1416	5.1	65	3
Michael Vick	.102	597	5.9	32	6
T.J. Duckett	.121	380	3.1	25	8

Most Touchdowns

	TD	Run	Rec	Ret	Pts
T.J. Duckett	.8	8	0	0	48
Michael Vick	.6	6	0	0	36
Alge Crumpler	.5	0	5	0	32
Warrick Dunn	.4	3	1	0	24

Three tied with 3 TD each for 18 pts.

2-Pt. Conversions: (4-4) Finneran 3, Crumpler 1.

Kicking

	PAT/Att	FG/Att	Lg	Pts
Todd Peterson	.35/35	23/25	43	104
Michael Koenen*	.0/0	1/2	58	3

Punts (10 or more)

	No	Yds	Long	Avg	In20
Michael Koenen*	.78	3300	67	42.3	23

Most Interceptions
DeAngelo Hall 6

Most Sacks
Rod Coleman 10.5

Carolina Panthers

Passing (5 Att)

	Att	Cmp	Pct	Yds	TD	Rate
Jake Delhomme	.435	262	60.2	3421	24	88.1
Chris Weinke	.13	7	53.8	64	1	93.1

Interceptions: Delhomme 16.

Top Receivers

	No	Yds	Avg	Long	TD
Steve Smith	.103	1563	15.2	80-td	12
DeShaun Foster	.34	372	10.9	47	1
Ricky Proehl	.25	441	17.6	69	4
Keary Colbert	.25	282	11.3	42	2
Kris Mangum	.23	202	8.8	24	1

Top Rushers

	Car	Yds	Avg	Long	TD
DeShaun Foster	.205	879	4.3	70-td	2
Stephen Davis	.180	549	3.1	39	12
Nick Goings	.37	133	3.6	17	0
Jamal Robertson	.14	41	2.9	11	1

Most Touchdowns

	TD	Run	Rec	Ret	Pts
Steve Smith	.13	1	12	0	78
Stephen Davis	.12	12	0	0	72
Ricky Proehl	.4	0	4	0	24
DeShaun Foster	.3	2	1	0	18

Three tied with 2 TDs for 12 pts.

2-Pt. Conversions: (0-1).

Kicking

	PAT/Att	FG/Att	Lg	Pts
John Kasay	.43/44	26/34	52	121

Punts (10 or more)

	No	Yds	Long	Avg	In20
Jason Baker	.72	3118	59	43.3	23

Most Interceptions
Chris Gamble 7

Most Sacks
Julius Peppers 10.5

Chicago Bears

Passing (5 Att)

	Att	Cmp	Pct	Yds	TD	Rate
Kyle Orton*	.368	190	51.6	1869	9	59.7
Rex Grossman	.39	20	51.3	259	1	59.7
Jeff Blake	.9	8	88.9	55	1	129.2

Interceptions: Orton 13, Grossman 2.

Top Receivers

	No	Yds	Avg	Long	TD
Muhsin Muhammad	.64	750	11.7	33	4
Justin Gage	.31	346	11.2	25	2
Thomas Jones	.26	143	5.5	41	0
Desmond Clark	.24	229	9.5	31	2
Mark Bradley*	.18	230	12.8	54	0
Bernard Berrian	.13	246	18.9	54	0

Top Rushers

	Car	Yds	Avg	Long	TD
Thomas Jones	.314	1335	4.3	42	9
Adrian Peterson	.76	391	5.1	36	2
Cedric Benson*	.67	272	4.1	36	0
Kyle Orton	.24	44	1.8	15	0

Most Touchdowns

	TD	Run	Rec	Ret	Pts
Thomas Jones	.9	9	0	0	54
Muhsin Muhammad	.4	0	4	0	24

Five tied with 2 TD each.

2-Pt. Conversions: (0-0).

Kicking

	PAT/Att	FG/Att	Lg	Pts
Robbie Gould*	.19/20	21/27	45	82
Doug Brien	.7/7	1/4	48	10

Signed: Gould (Oct. 8).
Released: Brien (Oct. 12).

Punts (10 or more)

	No	Yds	Long	Avg	In20
Brad Maynard	.96	3937	63	41.0	24

Most Interceptions
Nathan Vasher 8

Most Sacks
Adewale Ogunleye . .10.0

Dallas Cowboys

Passing (5 Att)	Att	Cmp	Pct	Yds	TD	Rate
Drew Bledsoe	.499	300	60.1	3639	23	83.7

Interceptions: Bledsoe 17.

Top Receivers	No	Yds	Avg	Long	TD
Keyshawn Johnson	.71	839	11.8	34	6
Jason Witten	.66	757	11.5	34	6
Terry Glenn	.62	1136	18.3	71-td	7
Julius Jones	.35	218	6.2	26	0
Patrick Crayton	.22	341	15.5	63-td	2
Marion Barber*	.18	115	6.4	21	0

Top Rushers	Car	Yds	Avg	Long	TD
Julius Jones	.257	993	3.9	51	5
Marion Barber*	.138	538	3.9	28-td	5
Tyson Thompson	.46	182	4.0	16	0
Drew Bledsoe	.34	50	1.5	9	2

Most Touchdowns	TD	Run	Rec	Ret	Pts
Terry Glenn	.8	1	7	0	48
Keyshawn Johnson	.6	0	6	0	38
Jason Witten	.6	0	6	0	36
Marion Barber*	.5	5	0	0	30
Julius Jones	.5	5	0	0	30

2-Pt. Conversions: (1-2) Johnson.

Kicking	PAT/Att	FG/Att	Lg	Pts
Billy Cundiff	.14/14	5/8	56	29
Shaun Suisham*	.8/8	3/4	22	17

Signed: Suisham (Oct. 24); Suisham (Dec. 25). **Released:** Jose Cortez (Oct 24, see Ind.); Cundiff (Dec. 25).

Punts (10 or more)	No	Yds	Long	Avg	In20
Mat McBriar	.81	3439	63	42.5	28

Most Interceptions
Aaron Glenn 4

Most Sacks
Greg Ellis 8.0
DeMarcus Ware 8.0

Detroit Lions

Passing (5 Att)	Att	Cmp	Pct	Yds	TD	Rate
Joey Harrington	.330	188	57.0	2021	12	72.0
Jeff Garcia	.173	102	59.0	937	3	65.1
Dan Orlovsky*	.17	7	41.2	63	0	51.8

Interceptions: Harrington 12, Garcia 6.

Top Receivers	No	Yds	Avg	Long	TD
Marcus Pollard	.46	516	11.2	86	3
Roy Williams	.45	687	15.3	51-td	8
Scott Vines	.40	417	10.4	40	0
Shawn Bryson	.37	284	7.7	63	0
Mike Williams*	.29	350	12.1	49	1
Artose Pinner	.21	181	8.6	24	0

Top Rushers	Car	Yds	Avg	Long	TD
Kevin Jones	.186	664	3.6	40	5
Artose Pinner	.106	349	3.3	19	3
Shawn Bryson	.64	306	4.8	77-td	1
Joey Harrington	.24	80	3.3	15	0

Most Touchdowns	TD	Run	Rec	Ret	Pts
Roy Williams	.8	0	8	0	48
Kevin Jones	.5	5	0	0	30
Artose Pinner	.3	3	0	0	18
Marcus Pollard	.3	0	3	0	18

Nine tied with 1 TD for 6 pts.

2-Pt. Conversions: (0-0).

Kicking	PAT/Att	FG/Att	Lg	Pts
Jason Hanson	.27/27	19/24	52	84
Remy Hamilton*	.0/1	0/0	—	0

Punts (10 or more)	No	Yds	Long	Avg	In20
Nick Harris	.84	3656	60	43.5	34

Most Interceptions
Dre' Bly 6

Most Sacks
Kalimba Edwards 7.0

Green Bay Packers

Passing (5 Att)	Att	Cmp	Pct	Yds	TD	Rate
Brett Favre	.607	372	61.3	3881	20	70.9
Aaron Rodgers	.16	9	56.3	65	0	39.8

Interceptions: Favre 29, Rodgers 1.

Top Receivers	No	Yds	Avg	Long	TD
Donald Driver	.86	1221	14.2	59	5
Antonio Chatman	.49	549	11.2	25	4
Tony Fisher	.49	347	7.2	15	1
Donald Lee	.33	294	8.9	27	2
William Henderson	.30	264	8.8	32	0
Robert Ferguson	.27	366	13.6	51	3
David Martin	.27	224	8.3	21-td	3

Top Rushers	Car	Yds	Avg	Long	TD
Samkon Gado*	.143	582	4.1	64-td	6
Ahman Green	.77	255	3.3	13	0
Tony Fisher	.60	173	2.9	17	1

Most Touchdowns	TD	Run	Rec	Ret	Pts
Samkon Gado*	.7	6	1	0	42
Antonio Chatman	.5	0	4	1	30
Donald Driver	.5	0	5	0	30
Robert Ferguson	.3	0	3	0	20
David Martin	.3	0	3	0	20

Five tied with 2 TD for 12 pts.

2-Pt. Conversions: (2-3) Ferguson, Martin.

Kicking	PAT/Att	FG/Att	Lg	Pts
Ryan Longwell	.30/31	20/27	53	90

Punts (10 or more)	No	Yds	Long	Avg	In20
B.J. Sander	.64	2508	53	39.2	11

Most Interceptions
Al Harris 3

Most Sacks
Kabeer Gbaja-
Biamila 8.0

Minnesota Vikings

Passing (5 Att)	Att	Cmp	Pct	Yds	TD	Rate
Brad Johnson	.294	184	62.6	1885	12	88.9
Daunte Culpepper	.216	139	64.4	1564	6	72.0

Interceptions: Culpepper 12, Johnson 4.

Top Receivers	No	Yds	Avg	Long	TD
Jermaine Wiggins	.69	568	8.2	24	1
Travis Taylor	.50	604	12.1	31	4
Mewelde Moore	.37	339	9.2	29	2
Marcus Robinson	.31	515	16.6	68	5
Nate Burleson	.30	328	10.9	20	1
Michael Bennett	.27	124	4.6	20	0
Troy Williamson*	.24	372	15.5	56	2
Koren Robinson	.24	347	15.8	80-td	1

Top Rushers	Car	Yds	Avg	Long	TD
Mewelde Moore	.155	662	4.3	33	1
Michael Bennett	.126	473	3.8	61-td	3
Daunte Culpepper	.24	147	6.1	18	1
Ciatrick Fason*	.32	62	1.9	15	4

Most Touchdowns	TD	Run	Rec	Ret	Pts
Marcus Robinson	.5	0	5	0	32
Michael Bennett	.5	3	2	0	30
Ciatrick Fason*	.4	4	0	0	24
Mewelde Moore	.4	1	2	1	24
Travis Taylor	.4	0	4	0	24
Koren Robinson	.3	1	1	1	18

2-Pt. Conversions: (1-2) M. Robinson.

Kicking	PAT/Att	FG/Att	Lg	Pts
Paul Edinger	.31/31	25/34	56	106

Punts (10 or more)	No	Yds	Long	Avg	In20
Chris Kluwe*	.71	3130	62	44.1	17

Most Interceptions
Darren Sharper 9

Most Sacks
Lance Johnstone 7.5

New Orleans Saints

Passing (5 Att)	Att	Cmp	Pct	Yds	TD	Rate
Aaron Brooks	.431	240	55.7	2882	13	70.0
Todd Bouman	.122	68	55.7	722	2	54.7

Interceptions: Brooks 17, Bouman 7.

Top Receivers	No	Yds	Avg	Long	TD
Donte' Stallworth	.70	945	13.5	43	7
Joe Horn	.49	654	13.3	30	1
Zach Hilton	.35	396	11.3	29	1
Aaron Stecker	.35	281	8.0	41	0
Az-Zahir Hakim	.34	489	14.4	42	2
Devery Henderson	.22	343	15.6	66	3
Deuce McAllister	.17	117	6.9	22	0

Top Rushers	Car	Yds	Avg	Long	TD
Antowain Smith	.166	659	4.0	42	3
Aaron Stecker	.95	363	3.8	32	0
Deuce McAllister	.93	335	3.6	26	3
Aaron Brooks	.45	281	6.2	22	2

Most Touchdowns	TD	Run	Rec	Ret	Pts
Donte' Stallworth	.7	0	7	0	42
Devery Henderson	.3	0	3	0	18
Deuce McAllister	.3	3	0	0	18
Antowain Smith	.3	3	0	0	18
Aaron Brooks	.2	2	0	0	12
Az-Zahir Hakim	.2	0	2	0	12

2-Pt. Conversions: (0-1).

Kicking	PAT/Att	FG/Att	Lg	Pts
John Carney	.22/22	25/32	49	97

Punts (10 or more)	No	Yds	Long	Avg	In20
Mitch Berger	.71	3066	69	43.2	28

Most Interceptions
Jason Craft 3

Most Sacks
Will Smith 8.5

New York Giants

Passing (5 Att)	Att	Cmp	Pct	Yds	TD	Rate
Eli Manning	.557	294	52.8	3762	24	75.9

Interceptions: Manning 17.

Top Receivers	No	Yds	Avg	Long	TD
Plaxico Burress	.76	1214	16.0	78-td	7
Jeremy Shockey	.65	891	13.7	59	7
Amani Toomer	.60	684	11.4	37	7
Tiki Barber	.54	530	9.8	48	2
Jim Finn	.13	98	7.5	15	0
Tim Carter	.10	186	18.6	44	0
Visanthe Shiancoe	.8	91	11.4	17	0

Top Rushers	Car	Yds	Avg	Long	TD
Tiki Barber	.357	1860	5.2	95-td	9
Derrick Ward	.35	123	3.5	12	0
Brandon Jacobs*	.38	99	2.6	21	7
Eli Manning	.29	80	2.8	14	1

Most Touchdowns	TD	Run	Rec	Ret	Pts
Tiki Barber	.11	9	2	0	68
Jeremy Shockey	.7	0	7	0	44
Plaxico Burress	.7	0	7	0	42
Brandon Jacobs*	.7	7	0	0	42
Amani Toomer	.7	0	7	0	42

Six tied with 1 TD each.

2-Pt. Conversions: (2-2) Barber, Shockey.

Kicking	PAT/Att	FG/Att	Lg	Pts
Jay Feely	.43/43	35/42	52	148

Punts (10 or more)	No	Yds	Long	Avg	In20
Jeff Feagles	.73	3070	56	42.1	26

Most Interceptions
Brent Alexander 4

Most Sacks
Osi Umenyiora 14.5

Philadelphia Eagles

Passing (5 Att)	Att	Cmp	Pct	Yds	TD	Rate
Donovan McNabb	.357	211	59.1	2507	16	85.0
Mike McMahon	.207	94	45.4	1158	5	55.2
Koy Detmer	.56	32	57.1	238	0	45.1

Interceptions: McNabb 8, McMahon 8, Detmer 3.

Top Receivers	No	Yds	Avg	Long	TD
L.J. Smith	.61	682	11.2	48	3
Brian Westbrook	.61	616	10.1	62	4
Greg Lewis	.48	561	11.7	34	1
Terrell Owens	.47	763	16.2	91-td	6
Reggie Brown*	.43	571	13.3	56-td	4

Top Rushers	Car	Yds	Avg	Long	TD
Brian Westbrook	.156	617	4.0	31	3
Ryan Moats*	.55	278	5.1	59-td	3
Lamar Gordon	.54	182	3.4	11	1

Most Touchdowns	TD	Run	Rec	Ret	Pts
Brian Westbrook	.7	3	4	0	44
Terrell Owens	.6	0	6	0	36
Reggie Brown*	.4	0	4	0	24

2-Pt. Conversions: (1-2) Westbrook.

Kicking	PAT/Att	FG/Att	Lg	Pts
David Akers	.23/23	16/22	50	71

Signed: Todd France (Sept. 20); **Claimed:** Jose Cortez off waivers from Dal. (Oct. 25). **Released:** France (Oct. 25, see TB); Cortez (Nov. 22, see Ind.).

Punts (10 or more)	No	Yds	Long	Avg	In20
Reggie Hodges*	.41	1535	55	37.4	9
ST.L	.22	836	55	38.0	3
PHI	.19	699	51	36.8	6
Dirk Johnson	.39	1615	59	41.4	11
Sean Landeta	.34	1483	56	43.6	7

Signed: Hodges (Nov. 2); Landeta (Nov. 28).

Most Interceptions
Sheldon Brown 4

Most Sacks
Jevon Kearse 7.5

St. Louis Rams

Passing (5 Att)	Att	Cmp	Pct	Yds	TD	Rate
Marc Bulger	.287	192	66.9	2297	14	94.4
Jamie Martin	.177	124	70.1	1277	5	83.5
Ryan Fitzpatrick*	.135	76	56.3	777	4	58.2

Interceptions: Bulger 9, Fitzpatrick 8, Martin 7.

Top Receivers	No	Yds	Avg	Long	TD
Torry Holt	.102	1331	13.0	44	9
Kevin Curtis	.60	801	13.4	83-td	6
Shaun McDonald	.46	523	11.4	31	0
Marshall Faulk	.44	291	6.6	18	1
Steven Jackson	.43	320	7.4	27	2
Isaac Bruce	.36	525	14.6	46-td	3

Top Rushers	Car	Yds	Avg	Long	TD
Steven Jackson	.254	1046	4.1	51	8
Marshall Faulk	.65	292	4.5	20	0
Aveion Cason	.10	65	6.5	14	1

Most Touchdowns	TD	Run	Rec	Ret	Pts
Steven Jackson	.10	8	2	0	60
Torry Holt	.9	0	9	0	54
Kevin Curtis	.7	1	6	0	42
Isaac Bruce	.3	0	3	0	18

2-Pt. Conversions: (2-3) Faulk, Arlen Harris.

Kicking	PAT/Att	FG/Att	Lg	Pts
Jeff Wilkins	.36/36	27/31	53	117

Punts (10 or more)	No	Yds	Long	Avg	In20
Bryan Barker	.50	2137	54	42.7	13

Released: Reggie Hodges (Oct. 11, see Phi.).

Most Interceptions
Mike Furrey 4

Most Sacks
Leonard Little 9.5

San Francisco 49ers

Passing (5 Att)	Att	Cmp	Pct	Yds	TD	Rate
Alex Smith*	.165	84	50.9	875	1	40.8
Ken Dorsey	.90	48	53.3	481	2	66.9
Cody Pickett	.35	14	40.0	140	0	28.3

Interceptions: Smith 11, Dorsey and Pickett 2.
Traded: Tim Rattay to TB for '06 6th-round pick (Oct. 19).

Top Receivers	No	Yds	Avg	Long	TD
Brandon Lloyd	.48	733	15.3	89-td	5
Arnaz Battle	.32	363	11.3	39	3
Kevan Barlow	.31	241	7.8	24	0
Johnnie Morton	.21	288	13.7	30	0
Frank Gore*	.15	131	8.7	47	0

Top Rushers	Car	Yds	Avg	Long	TD
Frank Gore*	.127	608	4.8	72-td	3
Kevan Barlow	.176	581	3.3	29	3
Maurice Hicks	.59	308	5.2	73-td	3
Alex Smith*	.30	103	3.4	19	0

Most Touchdowns	TD	Run	Rec	Ret	Pts
Brandon Lloyd	.5	0	5	0	30
Kevan Barlow	.3	3	0	0	18
Arnaz Battle	.3	0	3	0	18
Frank Gore*	.3	3	0	0	18
Maurice Hicks	.3	3	0	0	18

2-Pt. Conversions: (1-2) Terry Jackson.

Kicking	PAT/Att	FG/Att	Lg	Pts
Joe Nedney	19/19	26/28	56	97

Punts (10 or more)	No	Yds	Long	Avg	In20
Andy Lee	.107	4447	58	41.6	15

Most Interceptions		Most Sacks	
Shawntae Spencer	.4	Bryant Young	.8.0
Mike Adams	.4		

Seattle Seahawks

Passing (5 Att)	Att	Cmp	Pct	Yds	TD	Rate
Matt Hasselbeck	..449	294	65.5	3459	24	98.2
Seneca Wallace	25	13	52.0	173	1	70.9

Interceptions: Hasselbeck 9, Wallace 1.

Top Receivers	No	Yds	Avg	Long	TD
Bobby Engram	.67	778	11.6	56	3
Joe Jurevicius	.55	694	12.6	52	10
Jerramy Stevens	.45	554	12.3	35-td	5
Darrell Jackson	.38	482	12.7	48	3
D.J. Hackett	.28	400	14.3	47	2
Mack Strong	.22	166	7.5	27	0

Top Rushers	Car	Yds	Avg	Long	TD
Shaun Alexander	...370	1880	5.1	88-td	27
Maurice Morris	.71	288	4.1	49	1
Matt Hasselbeck	.36	124	3.4	23	1
Leonard Weaver*	17	80	4.7	24	0
Mack Strong	.17	78	4.6	16	0

Most Touchdowns	TD	Run	Rec	Ret	Pts
Shaun Alexander	.28	27	1	0	168
Joe Jurevicius	.10	0	10	0	60
Jerramy Stevens	.5	0	5	0	30
Bobby Engram	.3	0	3	0	18
Darrell Jackson	.3	0	3	0	18

2-Pt. Conversions: (0-0).

Kicking	PAT/Att	FG/Att	Lg	Pts
Josh Brown	.56/57	18/25	55	110

Punts (10 or more)	No	Yds	Long	Avg	In20
Tom Rouen	.61	2359	62	41.6	20
Leo Araguz	.18	723	53	40.2	4

Signed: Rouen (Oct. 5). **Released:** Araguz (Oct. 5).

Most Interceptions		Most Sacks	
Michael Boulware	.4	Bryce Fisher	.9.0

Tampa Bay Buccaneers

Passing (5 Att)	Att	Cmp	Pct	Yds	TD	Rate
Chris Simms	313	191	61.0	2035	10	81.4
Brian Griese	174	112	64.4	1136	7	79.6
Tim Rattay	.97	56	57.7	667	5	70.3
SF	.97	56	57.7	667	5	70.3

Interceptions: Simms and Griese 7, Rattay 6.
Acquired: Rattay from SF for '06 6th-round pick (Oct. 19).

Top Receivers	No	Yds	Avg	Long	TD
Joey Galloway	.83	1287	15.5	80-td	10
Alex Smith*	.41	367	9.0	24	2
Michael Pittman	.36	300	8.3	41-td	1
Ike Hilliard	.35	282	8.1	22	1
Michael Clayton	.32	372	11.6	41	0

Top Rushers	Car	Yds	Avg	Long	TD
Cadillac Williams*	..290	1178	4.1	71-td	6
Michael Pittman	.70	436	6.2	64	1
Earnest Graham	.28	83	3.0	16	0
Mike Alstott	.34	80	2.4	9	6

Most Touchdowns	TD	Run	Rec	Ret	Pts
Joey Galloway	.10	0	10	0	60
Mike Alstott	.7	6	1	0	44
Cadillac Williams*	.6	6	0	0	36

Two tied with 2 TD for 12 pts.
2-Pt. Conversions: (1-1) Alstott.

Kicking	PAT/Att	FG/Att	Lg	Pts
Matt Bryant	.31/31	21/25	50	94
Todd France	.6/6	7/9	44	27
PHI	.5/5	6/7	44	23
TB	.1/1	1/2	28	4

Signed: France (Nov. 29). **Released:** France (Dec. 20).

Punts (10 or more)	No	Yds	Long	Avg	In20
Josh Bidwell	.90	4101	61	45.6	24

Most Interceptions		Most Sacks	
Ronde Barber	.5	Simeon Rice	.14.0

Washington Redskins

Passing (5 Att)	Att	Cmp	Pct	Yds	TD	Rate
Mark Brunell	454	262	57.7	3050	23	85.9
Patrick Ramsey	.25	15	60.0	279	1	95.3

Interceptions: Brunell 10, Ramsey 1.

Top Receivers	No	Yds	Avg	Long	TD
Santana Moss	.84	1483	17.7	78-td	9
Chris Cooley	.71	774	10.9	32	7
Clinton Portis	.30	216	7.2	23	0
David Patten	.22	217	9.9	32	0
Robert Royal	.18	131	7.3	29	1
James Thrash	.14	194	13.9	41	0

Top Rushers	Car	Yds	Avg	Long	TD
Clinton Portis	.352	1516	4.3	47-td	11
Ladell Betts	.89	338	3.8	22	1
Rock Cartwright	.27	199	7.4	52	2

Most Touchdowns	TD	Run	Rec	Ret	Pts
Clinton Portis	.11	11	0	0	68
Santana Moss	.9	0	9	0	54
Mike Sellers	.8	1	7	0	48
Chris Cooley	.7	0	7	0	42
Ladell Betts	.3	1	1	1	18

2-Pt. Conversions: (1-2) Portis.

Kicking	PAT/Att	FG/Att	Lg	Pts
John Hall	.27/27	12/14	45	63

Punts (10 or more)	No	Yds	Long	Avg	In20
Derrick Frost	.76	3074	55	40.4	23
Andy Groom*	.11	429	57	39.0	2

Most Interceptions		Most Sacks	
Lemar Marshall	.4	Phillip Daniels	.8.0

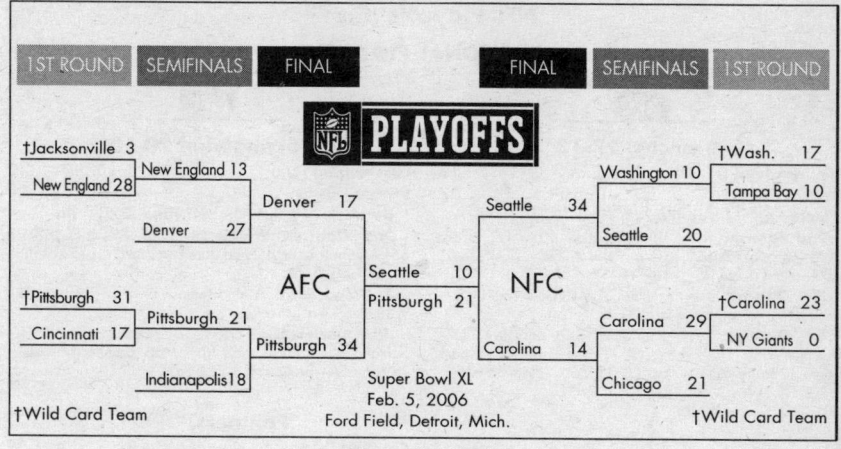

1ST ROUND | **SEMIFINALS** | **FINAL** | **FINAL** | **SEMIFINALS** | **1ST ROUND**

NFL PLAYOFFS

†Jacksonville 3
New England 13
New England 28
Denver 17
Denver 27

AFC

†Pittsburgh 31
Pittsburgh 21
Cincinnati 17
Pittsburgh 34
Indianapolis 18

Seattle 10
Pittsburgh 21

Super Bowl XL
Feb. 5, 2006
Ford Field, Detroit, Mich.

†Wash. 17
Washington 10
Tampa Bay 10
Seattle 34
Seattle 20

NFC

Carolina 14
Carolina 29
Chicago 21

†Carolina 23
NY Giants 0

†Wild Card Team

†Wild Card Team

Playoff Game Summaries
Team records listed in parentheses indicate records before game.

WILD CARD ROUND

AFC

Patriots, 28-3

Jacksonville (12-4)	0	3	0	0—	3
New England (10-6)	0	7	14	7—	28

Date—Jan. 7. **Att**—68,756. **Time**—2:55.

2nd Quarter: NE—Troy Brown 11-yd pass from Tom Brady (Adam Vinatieri kick), 12:08; JAX—Josh Scobee 36-yd FG, 1:05.

3rd Quarter: NE—David Givens 3-yd pass from Brady (Vinatieri kick), 7:13; NE—Ben Watson 63-yd pass from Brady (Vinatieri kick), 3:03.

4th Quarter: NE—Asante Samuel 73-yd interception return (Vinatieri kick), 14:46.

Steelers, 31-17

Pittsburgh (11-5)	0	14	14	3—	31
Cincinnati (11-5)	10	7	0	0—	17

Date—Jan. 8. **Att**—65,870. **Time**—3:03.

1st Quarter: CIN—Shayne Graham 23-yd FG, 6:54; CIN—Rudi Johnson 20-yd run (Graham kick), 1:09.

2nd Quarter: PIT—Willie Parker 19-yd pass from Ben Roethlisberger (Jeff Reed kick), 13:11; CIN—T.J. Houshmandzadeh 7-yd pass from Jon Kitna (Graham kick), 6:13; PIT—Hines Ward 5-yd pass from Roethlisberger (Reed kick), 3:48.

3rd Quarter: PIT—Jerome Bettis 5-yd run (Reed kick), 5:12; PIT—Cedrick Wilson 43-yd pass from Roethlisberger (Reed kick), 1:13.

4th Quarter: PIT—Reed 21-yd FG, 10:29.

NFC

Redskins, 17-10

Washington (10-6)	14	3	0	0—	17
Tampa Bay (11-5)	0	3	7	0—	10

Date—Jan. 7. **Att**—65,514. **Time**—3:01.

1st Quarter: WASH—Clinton Portis 6-yd run (John Hall kick), 8:40; WASH—Sean Taylor 51-yd fumble recovery (Hall kick), 4:15.

2nd Quarter: TB—Matt Bryant 43-yd FG, 10:02; WASH—Hall 47-yd FG, 5:34.

3rd Quarter: TB—Chris Simms 2-yd run (Bryant kick), 9:40.

Panthers, 23-0

Carolina (11-5)	0	10	7	6—	23
NY Giants (11-5)	0	0	0	0—	0

Date—Jan. 8. **Att**—79,378. **Time**—2:39.

2nd Quarter: CAR—Steve Smith 22-yd pass from Jake Delhomme (John Kasay kick), 9:41; CAR—Kasay 31-yd FG, 0:30.

3rd Quarter: CAR—Smith 12-yd run (Kasay kick), 6:57.

4th Quarter: CAR—Kasay 45-yd FG, 13:33; CAR—Kasay 18-yd FG, 2:40.

In The Money
2005 NFL player shares for all playoff games

Game/Round		Amount
Wild Card	(Division Winner)	$19,000
	(Wild Card Team)	17,000
Divisional Playoff		19,000
Conference Championship		37,000
Super Bowl XL	(Winning Team)	73,000
	(Losing Team)	38,000

Source: *NFL Media*

NFL Playoffs (Cont.)
DIVISIONAL PLAYOFFS

AFC

Broncos, 27-13

New England (11-6)	0	3	3	7—	**13**
Denver (13-3)	0	10	7	10—	**27**

Date—Jan. 14. **Att**—76,238. **Time**—3:15.

2nd Quarter: NE—Adam Vinatieri 40-yd FG, 3:48; DEN—Mike Anderson 1-yd run (Jason Elam kick), 1:42; DEN—Elam 50-yd FG, 0:43.

3rd Quarter: NE—Vinatieri 32-yd FG, 7:49; DEN—Anderson 1-yd run (Elam kick), 0:43.

4th Quarter: DEN—Rod Smith 4-yd pass from Jake Plummer (Elam kick), 8:38; NE—David Givens 4-yd pass from Tom Brady (Vinatieri kick), 8:05; DEN—Elam 34-yd FG, 3:20.

Steelers, 21-18

Pittsburgh (12-5)	14	0	7	0—	**21**
Indianapolis (14-2)	0	3	0	15—	**18**

Date—Jan. 15. **Att**—57,449. **Time**—3:18.

1st Quarter: PIT—Antwaan Randle-El 6-yd pass from Ben Roethlisberger (Jeff Reed kick), 9:25; PIT—Heath Miller 7-yd pass from Roethlisberger (Reed kick), 3:12.

2nd Quarter: IND—Mike Vanderjagt 20-yd FG, 1:20.

3rd Quarter: PIT—Bettis 1-yd run (Reed kick), 1:26.

4th Quarter: IND—Dallas Clark 50-yd pass from Peyton Manning (Vanderjagt kick), 14:09; IND—Edgerrin James 3-yd run (Reggie Wayne pass from Manning), 4:24.

NFC

Seahawks, 20-10

Washington (11-6)	0	3	0	7—	**10**
Seattle (13-3)	0	7	7	6—	**20**

Date—Jan. 14. **Att**—67,551. **Time**—3:01.

2nd Quarter: WASH—John Hall 26-yd FG, 8:59; SEA—Darrell Jackson 29-yd pass from Matt Hasselbeck (Josh Brown kick), 3:22.

3rd Quarter: SEA—Hasselbeck 6-yd run (Brown kick), 9:35.

4th Quarter: SEA—Brown 33-yd FG, 14:16; WASH—Santana Moss 20-yd pass from Mark Brunell (Hall kick), 11:59; SEA—Brown 31-yd FG, 2:54.

Panthers, 29-21

Carolina (12-5)	7	9	7	6—	**29**
Chicago (11-5)	0	7	7	7—	**21**

Date—Jan. 15. **Att**—62,209. **Time**—3:23.

1st Quarter: CAR—Steve Smith 58-yd pass from Jake Delhomme (John Kasay kick), 14:05.

2nd Quarter: CAR—Kasay 20-yd FG, 14:57; CAR—Kasay 38-yd FG, 6:26; CHI—Adrian Peterson 1-yd run (Robbie Gould kick), 1:57; CAR—Kasay 37-yd FG, 0:00.

3rd Quarter: CHI—Desmond Clark 1-yd pass from Rex Grossman (Gould kick), 11:21; CAR—Smith 39-yd pass from Delhomme (Kasay kick), 2:07.

4th Quarter: CHI—Jason McKie 3-yd run (Gould kick), 12:23; CAR—Kris Mangum 1-yd pass from Delhomme (kick failed), 8:04.

CONFERENCE CHAMPIONSHIPS

AFC

Steelers, 34-17

Pittsburgh (13-5)	3	21	0	10—	**34**
Denver (14-3)	0	3	7	7—	**17**

Date—Jan. 22. **Att**—76,775. **Time**—3:03.

1st Quarter: PIT—Jeff Reed 47-yd FG, 4:11.

2nd Quarter: PIT—Cedrick Wilson 12-yd pass from Ben Roethlisberger (Reed kick), 14:54; DEN—Elam 23-yd FG, 9:23; PIT—Jerome Bettis 3-yd run (Reed kick), 1:55; PIT—Hines Ward 17-yd pass from Roethlisberger (Reed kick), 0:07.

3rd Quarter: DEN—Ashley Lelie 30-yd pass from Jake Plummer (Jason Elam kick), 3:36.

4th Quarter: PIT—Reed 42-yd FG, 13:38; DEN—Mike Anderson 3-yd run (Elam kick), 7:52; PIT—Roethlisberger 4-yd run (Reed kick), 2:59.

NFC

Seahawks, 34-14

Carolina (13-5)	0	7	0	7—	**14**
Seattle (14-3)	10	10	7	7—	**34**

Date—Jan. 22. **Att**—67,837. **Time**—3:09.

1st Quarter: SEA—Jerramy Stevens 17-yd pass from Matt Hasselbeck (Josh Brown kick), 5:31; SEA—Brown 24-yd FG, 2:23.

2nd Quarter: SEA—Shaun Alexander 1-yd run (Brown kick), 14:53; CAR—Steve Smith 59-yd punt return (John Kasay kick), 4:03.

3rd Quarter: SEA—Darrell Jackson 20-yd pass from Hasselbeck (Brown kick), 11:09.

4th Quarter: SEA—Alexander 1-yd run (Brown kick), 6:00; CAR—Drew Carter 47-yd pass from Jake Delhomme (Kasay kick), 5:09.

Super Bowl XL

Sunday, Feb. 5, 2006 at Ford Field in Detroit, Michigan

Seattle (15-3)	3	0	7	0—	**10**
Pittsburgh (14-5)	0	7	7	7—	**21**

1st Quarter: SEA—Josh Brown 47-yd FG, 0:22. Drive: 22 yards in 7 plays. Key play: Darrell Jackson 20-yd pass from Matt Hasselbeck to PIT 27.

2nd Quarter: PIT—Ben Roethlisberger 1-yd run (Jeff Reed kick), 1:55. Drive: 59 yards in 11 plays. Key play: Hines Ward 37-yd pass from Roethlisberger on 3rd-and-28 to SEA 3.

3rd Quarter: PIT—Willie Parker 75-yd run (Reed kick), 14:38. Drive: 75 yards in 2 plays. **SEA**—Jerramy Stevens 16-yd pass from Hasselbeck (Brown kick), 6:45. Drive: 20 yards in 3 plays. Key play: Kelly Herndon 76-yd interception return of Roethlisberger pass from SEA 4 to PIT 20.

4th Quarter: PIT—Ward 43-yd pass from Antwaan Randle El (Reed kick), 8:56. Drive: 56 yards in 4 plays.

Favorite: Steelers by 3½ **Attendance:** 68,206
Field: Field Turf **Time:** 3:36
Weather: Indoors **TV Rating:** 41.5/62 share (ABC)

Officials: Bill Leavy (referee), Garth DeFelice (umpire), Mark Hittner (HL), Mark Perlman (LJ), Tom Hill (SJ), Steve Zimmer (FJ), Bob Waggoner (BJ), Bob Boylston (Replay).

Most Valuable Player

Hines Ward, Pittsburgh, WR
5 catches for 123 yards and 1 TD, 1 rush for 18 yards

Team Statistics

	Seahawks	Steelers
First downs	20	14
Rushing	5	6
Passing	15	8
Penalty	0	0
3rd down efficiency	5/17	8/15
4th down efficiency	1/2	0/0
Total offense (net yards)	396	339
Plays	77	56
Average gain	5.1	6.1
Rushes/yards	25/137	33/181
Yards per rush	5/5	5/5
Passing yards (net)	259	158
Times sacked/yards lost	3/14	1/8
Passing yards (gross)	273	166
Completions/attempts	26/49	10/22
Yards per pass play	5.0	6.9
Times intercepted	1	2
Return yardage	174	99
Punt returns/yards	4/27	2/32
Kickoff returns/yards	4/71	2/43
Interceptions/yards	2/76	1/24
Fumbles/lost	0/0	0/0
Penalties/yards	7/70	3/20
Punts/average	6/50.2	6/48.7
Punts blocked	0	0
Field Goals made/attempted	1/3	0/0
Time of possession	33:02	26:58

Individual Statistics

Seattle Seahawks

Passing	Att	Cmp	Pct.	Yds	TD	Int	Rate
M. Hasselbeck	49	26	53.1	273	1	1	67.8

Receiving	No	Yds	Avg	Long	TD
Bobby Engram	6	70	11.7	21	0
Joe Jurevicius	5	93	18.6	35	0
Darrell Jackson	5	50	10.0	20	0
Jerramy Stevens	3	25	8.3	16-td	1
Mack Strong	2	15	7.5	13	0
Ryan Hannam	2	12	6.0	9	0
Shaun Alexander	2	2	1.0	4	0
Maurice Morris	1	6	6.0	6	0
TOTAL	26	273	10.5	35	1

Rushing	Car	Yds	Avg	Long	TD
Shaun Alexander	20	95	4.8	21	0
Matt Hasselbeck	3	35	11.7	18	0
Mack Strong	2	7	3.5	7	0
TOTAL	25	137	5.5	21	0

Field Goals	20-29	30-39	40-49	50-59	Total
Josh Brown	0-0	0-0	1-1	0-2	1-3

Punting	No	Yds	Avg	Long	In20	Blk
Tom Rouen	6	301	50.2	57	0	0

Punt Returns	Ret	Yds	Avg	Long	FC	TD
Peter Warrick	4	27	6.8	15	0	0

Kickoff Returns	Ret	Yds	Avg	Long	FC	TD
Josh Scobey	3	55	18.3	25	0	0
Maurice Morris	1	16	16.0	16	0	0

Interceptions	No	Yds	Avg	Long	TD
Kelly Herndon	1	76	76.0	76	0
Michael Boulware	1	0	0.0	0	0

Sacks		Most Tackles (solo + asst)	
Grant Wistrom	1.0	Lofa Tatupu	9

Pittsburgh Steelers

Passing	Att	Cmp	Pct.	Yds	TD	Int	Rate
B. Roethlisberger	21	9	42.9	123	0	2	22.6
A. Randle El	1	1	100.0	43	1	0	158.3

Receiving	No	Yds	Avg	Long	TD
Hines Ward	5	123	24.6	43-td	1
Antwaan Randle El	3	22	7.3	8	0
Cedrick Wilson	1	20	20.0	20	0
Willie Parker	1	1	1.0	1	0
TOTAL	10	166	16.6	43-td	1

Rushing	Car	Yds	Avg	Long	TD
Willie Parker	10	93	9.3	75-td	1
Jerome Bettis	14	43	3.1	12	0
Ben Roethlisberger	7	25	3.6	10	1
Hines Ward	1	18	18.0	18	0
Verron Haynes	1	2	2.0	2	0
TOTAL	33	181	5.5	75-td	2

Field Goals	20-29	30-39	40-49	50-59	Total
none					

Punting	No	Yds	Avg	Long	In20	Blk
Chris Gardocki	6	292	48.7	60	1	0

Punt Returns	Ret	Yds	Avg	Long	FC	TD
Antwaan Randle El	2	32	16.0	20	0	0

Kickoff Returns	Ret	Yds	Avg	Long	FC	TD
Ricardo Colclough	2	43	21.5	22	0	0

Interceptions	No	Yds	Avg	Long	TD
Ike Taylor	1	24	24.0	24	0

Sacks		Most Tackles (solo + asst)	
Deshea Townsend	1.0	Ike Taylor	7
Clark Haggans	1.0	Deshea Townsend	6
Casey Hampton	1.0	James Farrior	6

Super Bowl Finalists' Playoff Statistics

Seattle Seahawks (2-1)

Passing (5 att)	Att	Cmp	Pct.	Yds	TD	Rating
Matt Hasselbeck	.103	62	60.2	707	4	89.7

Interceptions: Hasselbeck 1.

Top Receivers	No	Yds	Avg	Long	TD
Darrell Jackson	20	268	13.4	37	2
Bobby Engram	11	115	10.5	21	0
Jerramy Stevens	11	104	9.5	17-td	2
Joe Jurevicius	7	130	18.6	35	0
Ryan Hannam	4	20	5.0	9	0

Top Rushers	Car	Yds	Avg	Long	TD
Shaun Alexander	60	236	3.9	21	2
Matt Hasselbeck	15	83	5.5	18	1
Maurice Morris	25	73	2.9	10	0
Mack Strong	9	54	6.0	32	0

Most Touchdowns	TD	Run	Rec	Ret	Pts
Shaun Alexander	2	2	0	0	12
Darrell Jackson	2	0	2	0	12
Jerramy Stevens	2	0	2	0	12
Matt Hasselbeck	1	1	0	0	6

2-Pt. Conversions: (0-0).

Kicking	PAT/Att	FG/Att	Lg	Pts
Josh Brown	.7/7	5/8	47	22

Punts (5 or more)	No	Yds	Avg	Long	In20
Tom Rouen	.15	682	45.5	57	5

Interceptions		Most Sacks	
Michael Boulware	2	Rocky Bernard	2.0
Kelly Herndon	1	Bryce Fisher	1.0
Marquand Manuel	1	Grant Wistrom	1.0
Lofa Tatupu	1	Chartric Darby	1.0

Pittsburgh Steelers (4-0)

Passing (5 att)	Att	Cmp	Pct.	Yds	TD	Rating
Ben Roethlisberger	.93	58	62.4	803	7	101.7

Interceptions: Roethlisberger 3.

Top Receivers	No	Yds	Avg	Long	TD
Hines Ward	15	260	17.3	45	3
Antwaan Randle El	12	119	9.9	20	1
Willie Parker	10	81	8.1	19-td	1
Cedrick Wilson	9	216	24.0	54	2

Top Rushers	Car	Yds	Avg	Long	TD
Willie Parker	57	225	3.9	75-td	1
Jerome Bettis	56	180	3.2	25	3
Verron Haynes	6	56	9.3	26	0
Ben Roethlisberger	19	37	1.9	10	2

Most Touchdowns	TD	Run	Rec	Ret	Pts
Jerome Bettis	3	3	0	0	18
Hines Ward	3	0	3	0	18
Willie Parker	2	1	1	0	12
Ben Roethlisberger	2	2	0	0	12
Cedrick Wilson	2	0	2	0	12

2-Pt. Conversions: (0-0).

Kicking	PAT/Att	FG/Att	Lg	Pts
Jeff Reed	.14/14	3/3	47	23

Punts (5 or more)	No	Yds	Avg	Long	In20
Chris Gardocki	.18	789	43.8	60	7

Interceptions		Most Sacks	
Ike Taylor	2	Joey Porter	3.0
James Farrior	1	James Farrior	2.5
Larry Foote	1	Brett Keisel	2.0
Troy Polamalu	1	Clark Haggans	1.5

NFL Playoff Leaders

Passing Efficiency
(Minimum of 25 attempts)

	Gm	Att	Cmp	Cmp%	Yards	Avg Gain	TD	TD%	Int	Int%	Rating
Ben Roethlisberger, Pit	4	93	58	62.4	803	8.63	7	7.5	3	3.2	101.7
Tom Brady, NE	2	63	35	55.6	542	8.60	4	6.3	2	3.2	92.2
Peyton Manning, Ind	1	38	22	57.9	290	7.63	0	2.6	0	0.0	90.9
Matt Hasselbeck, Sea	3	103	62	60.2	707	6.86	4	3.9	1	1.0	89.7
Jake Delhomme, Car	3	90	54	60.0	655	7.28	5	5.6	4	4.4	82.4

Receptions

	No	Yds	Avg	Long	TD
Steve Smith, Car	27	335	12.4	58-td	3
Darrell Jackson, Sea	20	268	13.4	37	2
Hines Ward, Pit	15	260	17.3	45	3
Antwaan Randle El, Pit	12	119	9.9	20	1

Two tied with 11 receptions.

Kicking

	PAT	FG	Long	Pts
John Kasay, Car	.6/7	6/6	45	24
Jeff Reed, Pit	.14/14	3/3	47	23
Josh Brown, Sea	.7/7	5/8	47	22
Jason Elam, Den	.5/5	3/3	50	14
Adam Vinatieri, NE	.5/5	2/3	40	11

Rushing

	No	Yds	Avg	Long	TD
Shaun Alexander, Sea	60	236	3.9	21	2
Willie Parker, Pit	57	225	3.9	75-td	1
DeShaun Foster, Car	43	205	4.8	31	0
Jerome Bettis, Pit	56	180	3.2	25	3
Mike Anderson, Den	28	105	3.8	18	3

Interceptions

	No	Yds	Long	TD
Asante Samuel, NE	2	73	73-td	1
Ike Taylor, Pit	2	25	24	0
Ken Lucas, Car	2	15	14	0
Marlon McCree, Car	2	-9	0	0
Michael Boulware, Sea	2	14	14	0

Touchdowns

	TD	Rush	Rec	Ret	Pts
Steve Smith, Car	5	1	3	1	30
Jerome Bettis, Pit	3	3	0	0	18
Hines Ward, Pit	3	0	0	0	18
Mike Anderson, Den	3	3	0	0	18

Sacks

	No
Willie McGinest, NE	4.5
Joey Porter, Pit	3.0
James Farrior, Pit	2.5

Four tied with 2.0 each.

NFL Pro Bowl

56th NFL Pro Bowl Game and 36th AFC-NFC contest (Series is tied,18-18). **Date:** Feb. 12, 2006 at Aloha Stadium in Honolulu. **Coaches:** Mike Shanahan, Den. (AFC) and John Fox, Car. (AFC). **Most Valuable Player:** LB Derrick Brooks, TB (2 tackles, 1 interception for 59-yd TD). **Attendance:** 50,190. **TV Rating:** 3.7 (ESPN). **Time:** 3:38.

AFC	.7	3	0	7—	**17**
NFC	.0	10	7	6—	**23**

1st Quarter: AFC—Chris Chambers 16-yd pass from Peyton Manning (Shayne Graham kick), 5:09.

2nd Quarter: NFC—Neil Rackers 32-yd FG, 7:45; **AFC**—Shayne Graham 31-yd FG, 3:22; **NFC**—Alge Crumpler 14-yd pass from Michael Vick (Rackers kick), 0:02.

3rd Quarter: NFC—Derrick Brooks 59-yd interception return (Rackers kick), 5:01.

4th Quarter: AFC—Trent Green 1-yd run (Graham kick), 12:47; **NFC**—Rackers 22-yd FG, 6:29; **NFC**—Rackers 20-yd FG, 1:10.

Individual Offensive Statistics

AFC

Passing	Att	Cmp	Pct.	Yds	TD	Int	Rate
Peyton Manning	26	13	50.0	139	1	3	39.3
Trent Green	11	5	45.5	39	0	1	16.9
Steve McNair	8	2	25.0	25	0	0	40.1

Receiving	No	Yds	Avg	Long	TD
Tony Gonzalez	5	36	7.2	14	0
Marvin Harrison	4	74	18.5	33	0
Chris Chambers	2	34	17.0	18	1
LaDainian Tomlinson	2	18	9.0	11	0
Chad Johnson	2	15	7.5	11	0
Rod Smith	2	13	6.5	8	0
Antonio Gates	2	7	3.5	5	0
Lorenzo Neal	1	6	6.0	6	0

Rushing	Car	Yds	Avg	Long	TD
Larry Johnson	8	33	4.1	20	0
Edgerrin James	6	22	3.7	9	0
LaDainian Tomlinson	5	13	2.6	6	0
Trent Green	3	3	1.0	3	1
Steve McNair	2	0	0.0	0	0

NFC

Passing	Att	Cmp	Pct.	Yds	TD	Int	Rate
M. Hasselbeck	17	10	58.8	85	0	1	47.4
Michael Vick	12	4	33.3	69	1	1	46.9
Jake Delhomme	10	7	70.0	53	0	0	82.5

Receiving	No	Yds	Avg	Long	TD
Steve Smith	8	46	5.8	14	0
Santana Moss	3	39	13.0	19	0
Alge Crumpler	3	35	11.7	16	1
Torry Holt	2	18	9.0	11	0
Mack Strong	2	17	8.5	9	0
Larry Fitzgerald	1	32	32.0	32	0
Warrick Dunn	1	14	14.0	14	0
Tiki Barber	1	6	6.0	6	0

Rushing	Car	Yds	Avg	Long	TD
Tiki Barber	11	33	3.0	11	0
Santana Moss	1	18	18.0	18	0
Michael Vick	2	17	8.5	17	0
Warrick Dunn	7	12	1.7	6	0
Larry Fitzgerald	1	12	12.0	12	0
Steve Smith	1	6	6.0	6	0

Two tied with 1 rush for 0 yards.

2005 All-NFL Team

The 2005 All-NFL team combining the All-Pro selections of the Associated Press, *The Sporting News* (TSN) and the Pro Football Writers of America/*Pro Football Weekly* (PFWA). Holdovers from the 2004 All-NFL Team in **bold** type.

Offense

Pos		Selectors
WR—	Steve Smith, Carolina	AP, *TSN*, PFWA
WR—	Chad Johnson, Cincinnati	AP, *TSN*, PFWA
TE—	**Antonio Gates**, San Diego	AP, *TSN*, PFWA
T—	**Walter Jones**, Seattle	AP, *TSN*, PFWA
T—	**Willie Anderson**, Cincinnati	AP, PFWA
T—	**Willie Roaf**, Kansas City	*TSN*
G—	Steve Hutchinson, Seattle	AP, *TSN*, PFWA
G—	**Brian Waters**, Kansas City	AP
G—	**Alan Faneca**, Pittsburgh	AP, *TSN*, PFWA
C—	Jeff Saturday, Indianapolis	AP
C—	Olin Kreutz, Chicago	*TSN*, PFWA
QB—	**Peyton Manning**, Indianapolis	AP, *TSN*, PFWA
RB—	**Shaun Alexander**, Seattle	AP, *TSN*, PFWA
RB—	Tiki Barber, NY Giants	AP, PFWA
RB—	**LaDainian Tomlinson**, San Diego	*TSN*
FB—	Mack Strong, Seattle	AP

Defense

Pos		Selectors
DE—	**Dwight Freeney**, Indianapolis	AP, *TSN*, PFWA
DE—	Osi Umenyiora, NY Giants	AP, PFWA
DE—	Michael Strahan, NY Giants	*TSN*
DT—	Jamal Williams, San Diego	AP, *TSN*
DT—	**Richard Seymour**, New England	AP, PFWA
DT—	Marcus Stroud, Jacksonville	*TSN*
DT—	Rod Coleman, Atlanta	PFWA
LB—	Brian Urlacher, Chicago	AP, *TSN*, PFWA
LB—	Lance Briggs, Chicago	AP, PFWA
LB—	**Derrick Brooks**, Tampa Bay	AP
LB—	Al Wilson, Denver	AP, *TSN*
LB—	Shawne Merriman, San Diego	*TSN*
LB—	Cato June, Indianapolis	PFWA
CB—	**Champ Bailey**, Denver	AP, *TSN*, PFWA
CB—	**Ronde Barber**, Tampa Bay	AP
CB—	Deltha O'Neal, Cincinnati	*TSN*
S—	Bob Sanders, Indianapolis	AP
S—	Troy Polamalu, Pittsburgh	AP, *TSN*, PFWA
S—	Darren Sharper, Minnesota	*TSN*, PFWA

Specialists

Pos		Selectors	Pos		Selectors
K—	Neil Rackers, Arizona	AP, *TSN*, PFWA	KR—	Jerome Mathis, Houston	AP, *TSN*, PFWA
P—	Brian Moorman, Buffalo	AP, *TSN*, PFWA	PR—	B.J. Sams, Baltimore	*TSN*
ST—	David Tyree, NY Giants	PFWA	PR—	Antwaan Randle El, Pittsburgh	PFWA

Annual Awards

The NFL does not sanction any of the major postseason awards for players and coaches, but many are given out. Among the presenters for the 2005 regular season were AP, The Maxwell Football Club of Philadelphia (Bert Bell Award for player; Greasy Neale Award for coach), *The Sporting News* and the Pro Football Writers of America/*Pro Football Weekly*.

Most Valuable Player
Shaun Alexander, Seattle, RB . . . . . . AP, *TSN*, Bell, PFWA

Offensive Player of the Year
Shaun Alexander, Seattle, RB . . . . AP, PFWA

Defensive Player of the Year
Brian Urlacher, Chicago, LB . . . . AP, PFWA

Comeback Players of the Year
Tedy Bruschi, New England, LB . . . . AP
& Steve Smith, Carolina, WR . . . . AP, PFWA

Rookies of the Year
NFL	Shawne Merriman, San Diego, LB	*TSN*
Offense	Cadillac Williams, Tampa Bay, RB . .	AP, PFWA
Defense	Shawne Merriman, San Diego, LB . .	AP, PFWA

Coaches of the Year
Lovie Smith, Chicago . . . . AP, PFWA
Tony Dungy, Indianapolis . . . . *TSN*, Neale

---

2006 College Draft

First and second round selections at the 71st annual NFL College Draft held April 29-30, 2006, at Radio City Music Hall in New York City. Twenty-one underclassmen were among the first 64 players chosen and are listed in capital LETTERS.

First Round

No	Team		Pos
1	Houston	MARIO WILLIAMS, NC State	DE
2	New Orleans	REGGIE BUSH, USC	RB
3	Tennessee	VINCE YOUNG, Texas	QB
4	NY Jets	D'Brickashaw Ferguson, Virginia	OT
5	Green Bay	A.J. Hawk, Ohio St.	LB
6	San Francisco . . .	VERNON DAVIS, Maryland	TE
7	Oakland	Michael Huff, Texas	DB
8	Buffalo	DONTE' WHITNER, Ohio St.	DB
9	Detroit	ERNIE SIMS, Florida St.	LB
10	Arizona	Matt Leinart, USC	QB
11	**a**-Denver	Jay Cutler, Vanderbilt	QB
12	**b**-Baltimore	HALOTI NGATA, Oregon	DT
13	**c**-Cleveland	Kamerion Wimbley, Florida St.	DE
14	Philadelphia	Brodrick Bunkley, Florida St.	DT
15	**d**-St. Louis	Tye Hill, Clemson	DB
16	Miami	Jason Allen, Tennessee	DB
17	Minnesota	Chad Greenway, Iowa	LB
18	Dallas	Bobby Carpenter, Ohio St.	LB
19	San Diego .	ANTONIO CROMARTIE, Florida St.	DB
20	Kansas City	Tamba Hali, Penn St.	DE
21	New England	LAURENCE MARONEY, Minnesota	RB
22	**e**-San Francisco . . .	Manny Lawson, NC State	DE
23	Tampa Bay	Davin Joseph, Oklahoma	OG
24	Cincinnati	JOHNATHAN JOSEPH, South Carolina	DB
25	**f**-Pittsburgh . .	SANTONIO HOLMES, Ohio St.	WR
26	**g**-Buffalo	JOHN McCARGO, NC State	DT
27	Carolina	DeAngelo Williams, Memphis	RB
28	Jacksonville	Marcedes Lewis, UCLA	TE
29	**h**-NY Jets	Nick Mangold, Ohio St.	C
30	Indianapolis	Joesph Addai, LSU	RB
31	Seattle	Kelly Jennings, Miami-FL	DB
32	**i**-NY Giants	Mathias Kiwanuka, BC	DE

Second Round

No	Team		Pos
33	Houston	DeMeco Ryans, Alabama	LB
34	**j**-Cleveland	D'Qwell Jackson, Maryland	LB
35	**k**-Washington	Rocky McIntosh, Miami-FL	LB
36	**l**-New England	CHAD JACKSON, Florida	WR
37	**m**-Atlanta	Jimmy Williams, Virginia Tech	DB
38	Oakland	Thomas Howard, UTEP	LB
39	**n**-Philadelphia	WINSTON JUSTICE, USC	OT
40	Detroit	Daniel Bullocks, Nebraska	DB
41	Arizona	Deuce Lutui, USC	G
42	**o**-Chicago . .	DANIEAL MANNING, Abilene Chr.	DB
43	**p**-New Orleans	Roman Harper, Alabama	DB
44	**q**-NY Giants	Sinorice Moss, Miami-FL	WR
45	**r**-Tennessee	LENDALE WHITE, USC	RB
46	St. Louis	Joe Klopfenstein, Colorado	TE
47	**s**-Green Bay	Daryn Colledge, Boise St.	OT
48	Minnesota	Cedric Griffin, Texas	DB
49	**t**-NY Jets	Kellen Clemens, Oregon	QB
50	San Diego	Marcus McNeill, Auburn	OT
51	**u**-Minnesota	Ryan Cook, New Mexico	C
52	**v**-Green Bay . . .	Greg Jennings, Western Mich.	WR
53	**w**-Dallas . .	ANTHONY FASANO, Notre Dame	TE
54	Kansas City	BERNARD POLLARD, Purdue	DB
55	Cincinnati	Andrew Whitworth, LSU	OT
56	**x**-Baltimore	Chris Chester, Oklahoma	C
57	Chicago	DEVIN HESTER, Miami-FL	DB
58	Carolina	RICHARD MARSHALL, Fresno St.	DB
59	Tampa Bay	Jeremy Trueblood, BC	OT
60	Jacksonville	MAURICE DREW, UCLA	RB
61	Denver . . .	Tony Scheffler, Western Michigan	TE
62	Indianapolis	Tim Jennings, Georgia	DB
63	Seattle	Darryl Tapp, Virginia Tech	DE
64	**y**-Minnesota . . .	Tarvaris Jackson, Alabama St.	QB

a-from St.L; **b**-from Cle.; **c**-from Bal.; **d**-from Atl. via Den.; **e**-from Wash. via Den.; **f**-from NYG; **g**-from Chi.; **h**-from Den.; **i**-from Pit.; **j**-from NO; **k**-from NYJ; **l**-from GB; **m**-from SF via Den. and GB; **n**-from Ten.; **o**-from Buf.; **p**-from Cle.; **q**-from Bal.; **r**-from Phi.; **s**-from Atl.; **t**-from Dal.; **u**-from Mia.; **v**-from NE; **w**-from Wash. via NYJ; **x**-from NYG; **y**-from Pit.

2006 Draft By The Numbers
Through all seven rounds of the 2006 draft (255 players total).

By Conference — Top 5		By Position — Top 5	
1 Atlantic Coast Conference 51		1 Defensive Back 49	
2 Big Ten Conference 41		2 Linebacker .34	
3 Southeastern Conference 37		3 Wide Receiver 30	
4 Pacific-10 Conference 32		4 Offensive Tackle 25	
5 Big 12 Conference 29		5 Defensive End 21	

Canadian Football League
Final 2005 Standings

Division champions (*) and playoff qualifiers (†) are noted. Wins are worth two points in the standings, ties are worth one point.

East Division

	W	L	T	Pts	PF	PA
*Toronto	11	7	0	22	486	387
†Montreal	10	8	0	20	592	519
Ottawa	7	11	0	14	458	578
Hamilton	5	13	0	10	383	583

West Division

	W	L	T	Pts	PF	PA
*British Columbia	12	6	0	24	550	444
†Calgary	11	7	0	22	529	443
†Edmonton	11	7	0	22	453	421
†Saskatchewan	9	9	0	18	441	433
Winnipeg	5	13	0	10	474	558

Playoffs
Division Semifinals (Nov. 13)
East: at Montreal 30 . . . . .Saskatchewan 14
West: Edmonton 33 . . . . .at Calgary 26

Division Finals (Nov. 20)
East: Montreal 33 . . . . .at Toronto 17
West: Edmonton 28 . . . . .at British Columbia 23

93rd Grey Cup Championship
November 27, 2005
at B.C. Place Stadium in Vancouver
(Att: 59,157)

Edmonton	3	7	10	8	10—	**38**
Montreal	1	0	17	10	7—	**35**

MVP: Ricky Ray, Edmonton, QB (35 of 45 for 359 yards and 2 TD, plus 4 rushes for 18 yards and 1 TD)

Regular Season Individual Leaders
Passing Yards

	Att	Cmp	Cmp Pct	Yds	Yds/ Att	TD	TD Pct	Int	Int Pct	Rating
Anthony Calvillo, Mon	661	437	66.1	5556	8.4	34	5.1	19	2.9	97.4
Ricky Ray, Edm	715	479	67.0	5510	7.7	25	3.5	24	3.4	87.7
Damon Allen, Tor	549	352	64.1	5082	9.3	33	6.0	15	2.7	102.7
Kerry Joseph, Ott	527	331	62.8	4423	8.4	25	4.7	22	4.2	87.8
Henry Burris, Calg	435	265	60.9	4290	9.9	23	5.3	12	2.8	100.1

Scoring

Touchdowns	TD	Rus	Rec	Ret	Pts
Milt Stegall, Win	17	0	17	0	102
Antonio Warren, B.C.	16	13	3	0	96
Charles Roberts, Win	12	12	0	0	72
Arland Bruce III, Tor	11	0	11	0	66
Jason Tucker, Edm	11	0	11	0	66
Nikolas Lewis, Calg	11	0	9	2	66

Kicking	PAT	FG	S*	Pts
Damon Duval, Mon	60/60	38/52	17	191
Sandro DeAngelis, Calg	54/54	40/52	5	179
Noel Prefontaine, Tor	49/49	33/44	12	160
Paul McCallum, Sask	38/38	31/42	13	144
Troy Westwood, Win	49/49	28/40	8	141

*Singles (or Rouges)

Rushing

	Car	Yards	Avg	TD
Charles Roberts, Win	290	1624	5.6	12
Joffrey Reynolds, Calg	247	1453	5.9	8
Robert Edwards, Mon	183	1172	6.4	8
Troy Davis, Ham	240	1151	4.8	5
Josh Ranek, Ott	212	1135	5.4	5

Receptions

	No	Yards	Avg	TD
Kerry Watkins, Mon	97	1364	14.1	9
Derrell Mitchell, Edm	94	1207	12.8	5
Terry Vaughn, Mon	93	1113	12.0	8
Tony Miles, Tor	91	1275	14.0	8
Jason Tucker, Edm	89	1411	15.9	11
Geroy Simon, B.C.	89	1322	14.9	10
Jason Armstead, Ott	89	1307	14.7	5

All-CFL Team

Offense		Defense	
WR Kerry Watkins, Mon.		E Brent Johnson, B.C.	
WR Jason Armstead, Ott.		E Jonathan Brown, Tor.	
T Uzooma Okeke, Mon.		T Scott Schultz, Sask.	
T Gene Makowsky, Sask.		T Adriano Belli, Ham.	
G Scott Flory, Mon.		LB John Grace, Calg.	
G Andrew Greene, Sask.		LB Kevin Eiben, Tor.	
C Bryan Chiu, Mon.		LB Michael Fletcher, Tor.	
QB Damon Allen, Tor.		CB Omarr Morgan, Sask.	
RB Charles Roberts, Win.		CB Jordan Younger, Tor.	
RB Joffrey Reynolds, Calg.		DB Eddie Davis, Sask.	
SB Jason Tucker, Edm.		DB Korey Banks, Ott.	
SB Milt Stegall, Win.		S Richard Karikari, Mon.	

Specialists
PK Sandro DeAngelis, Calg.   P Jon Ryan, Win.
Special Teams Corey Holmes, Sask.

Most Outstanding Awards

Player . . . . .Damon Allen, Toronto, QB	Rookie . . . . .Gavin Walls, Winnipeg, DE
Canadian . . . . . . .Brent Johnson, British Columbia, DE	Special Teams . . . . . .Corey Holmes, Saskatchewan, RB
Lineman . . . . .Gene Makowsky, Saskatchewan, OT	Coach (Annis Stukus award) . . . . .Tom Higgins, Calgary
Defensive Player . . . . .John Grace, Calgary, LB	Tom Pate Award (Sportsmanship) . . . .Danny McManus, Hamilton, QB

NFL Europe

Final 2006 Standings

	W	L	T	Pct.	PF	PA
*Amsterdam	7	3	0	.700	259	234
*Frankfurt	7	3	0	.700	172	160
Rhein	6	4	0	.600	207	165
Cologne	4	6	0	.400	151	170
Hamburg	3	6	1	.350	194	193
Berlin	2	7	1	.250	180	241

*The teams with the top two records after the regular season advance directly to the World Bowl.

Individual Leaders

Touchdowns	Chad Lucas, Amsterdam (GB) 8
Kicking Points	Ryan Killeen, Amsterdam (Sea) 71
Passer Rating	Gibran Hamdan, Amsterdam (Sea) 113.4
Passing Yards	Gibran Hamdan, Amsterdam (Sea) 1629
Rushing Yards	Roger Robinson, Frankfurt (Ari.) 1087
Receptions	Skyler Fulton, Amsterdam (Sea.) 53
Receiving Yards	Skyler Fulton, Amsterdam (Sea.) 992
Sacks	Jerome Nichols, Frankfurt (GB) 7.0
Interceptions	Brandon Haw, Frankfurt (Sea.) 5
Punting Avg.	Glenn Pakulak, Amsterdam (Oak.) 42.1

Note: the team in parentheses is the player's NFL affiliation.

Annual Awards

Offensive MVP	Gibran Hamdan, Ams. (Sea.), QB
Defensive MVPs	Tony Brown, Ams. (Car.), DT & Philippe Gardent, Col., LB
Coach of the Year	Mike Jones, Frankfurt

World Bowl XIV

May 27, 2006 at LTU Arena, Dusseldorf, Germany (Att: 36,286)

Frankfurt (7-3)	2	0	10	10—	**22**
Amsterdam (7-3)	0	7	0	0—	**7**

MVP: Butchie Wallace, Frankfurt, RB (18 rushes for 143 yards and 1 TD)

All-NFL Europe League Team

The All-NFL Europe League Team as selected by NFL Europe coaches, media and fans.

	Offense		Defense
QB	Gibran Hamdan, Ams.	DE	Scott Scharff, Ham.
RB	Roger Robinson, Fra.	DT	Jerome Nichols, Fra.
WR	Skyler Fulton, Ams.	DT	Bryan Save, Col.
WR	Chad Lucas, Ams.	DE	Derrick Strong, Col.
WR	Aaron Hosack, Fra.	LB	Terrence Robinson, Rhe.
TE	Aaron Halterman, Rhe.	LB	Derrick Ballard, Ams.
T	Will Svitek, Fra.	LB	Philippe Gardent, Col.
G	Erik Pears, Col.	CB	Rayshun Reed, Ham.
C	Tyler Lenda, Ams.	S	Brandon Haw, Fra.
G	Chad Beasley, Ber.	S	Anthony Floyd, Ber.
T	Jeff Roehl, Ams.	CB	Ronyell Whitaker, Rhe.

	Special Teams
K	Ryan Killeen, Ams.
P	Gabe Lindstrom, Col.
ST	Noriaki Kinoshita, Ams.

Arena Football
Final 2006 Standings

Division champions (*) and playoff qualifiers (†) are noted; top eight teams advance to the playoffs.

American Conference
Central Division

	W	L	T	Pct.	PF	PA
*Colorado	11	5	0	.688	903	833
†Nashville	8	8	0	.500	818	799
†Chicago	7	9	0	.438	825	834
Grand Rapids	5	11	0	.312	722	875

Western Division

	W	L	T	Pct.	PF	PA
*San Jose	10	6	0	.625	898	849
†Arizona	8	8	0	.500	774	756
†Utah	7	9	0	.438	871	904
Los Angeles	5	11	0	.312	809	906
Las Vegas	5	11	0	.312	769	895

National Conference
Eastern Division

	W	L	T	Pct.	PF	PA
*Dallas	13	3	0	.812	929	710
†New York	10	6	0	.625	848	887
†Philadelphia	9	7	0	.562	777	747
Columbus	8	8	0	.500	724	717

Southern Division

	W	L	T	Pct.	PF	PA
*Orlando	10	6	0	.625	816	760
†Austin	10	6	0	.625	816	757
†Georgia	8	8	0	.500	855	735
Tampa Bay	7	9	0	.438	810	862
Kansas City	3	13	0	.188	704	842

Annual Awards

Ironman of the Year	Randy Gatewood, Ari., WR/DB
Offensive Player of the Year	Damian Harrell, Col., OS
Defensive Player of the Year	Jerald Brown, Clb., DS
Lineman of the Year	Colston Weatherington, Dal., OL/DL
Rookie of the Year	Ben Nelson, SJ, OS
Coach of the Year	Will McClay, Dallas
Al Lucas Hero Award	Kenny McEntyre, Orl., DS

ArenaBowl XX

June 11, 2006 at the Thomas & Mack Center, Las Vegas (Att: 13,476)

Chicago	10	24	14	21—	**69**
Orlando	0	28	6	27—	**61**

MVP: Off—Matt D'Orazio, Chi., QB (26 for 36 for 250 yds, 6 TD; 5 rushes for 12 yds, 2 TD)

Def—Dennison Robinson, Chi., DB (1 int. for 44 yds and a TD; 4 tackles; 1 forced fumble)

1920-2006
Through the Years

SPORTS ALMANAC

The Super Bowl

The first AFL-NFL World Championship Game, as it was originally called, was played seven months after the two leagues agreed to merge in June of 1966. It became the Super Bowl (complete with roman numerals) by the third game in 1969. The Super Bowl winner has been presented the Vince Lombardi Trophy since 1971. Lombardi, whose Green Bay teams won the first two title games, died in 1970. NFL champions (1966-69) and NFC champions (since 1970) are listed in CAPITAL letters.

Multiple winners: Dallas, Pittsburgh and San Francisco (5); Green Bay, New England, Oakland-LA Raiders and Washington (3); Denver, Miami and NY Giants (2).

Bowl	Date	Winner	Head Coach	Score	Loser	Head Coach	Site
I	1/15/67	GREEN BAY	Vince Lombardi	35-10	Kansas City	Hank Stram	Los Angeles
II	1/14/68	GREEN BAY	Vince Lombardi	33-14	Oakland	John Rauch	Miami
III	1/12/69	NY Jets	Weeb Ewbank	16-7	BALT. COLTS	Don Shula	Miami
IV	1/11/70	Kansas City	Hank Stram	23-7	MINNESOTA	Bud Grant	New Orleans
V	1/17/71	Balt. Colts	Don McCafferty	16-13	DALLAS	Tom Landry	Miami
VI	1/16/72	DALLAS	Tom Landry	24-3	Miami	Don Shula	New Orleans
VII	1/14/73	Miami	Don Shula	14-7	WASHINGTON	George Allen	Los Angeles
VIII	1/13/74	Miami	Don Shula	24-7	MINNESOTA	Bud Grant	Houston
IX	1/12/75	Pittsburgh	Chuck Noll	16-6	MINNESOTA	Bud Grant	New Orleans
X	1/18/76	Pittsburgh	Chuck Noll	21-17	DALLAS	Tom Landry	Miami
XI	1/9/77	Oakland	John Madden	32-14	MINNESOTA	Bud Grant	Pasadena
XII	1/15/78	DALLAS	Tom Landry	27-10	Denver	Red Miller	New Orleans
XIII	1/21/79	Pittsburgh	Chuck Noll	35-31	DALLAS	Tom Landry	Miami
XIV	1/20/80	Pittsburgh	Chuck Noll	31-19	LA RAMS	Ray Malavasi	Pasadena
XV	1/25/81	Oakland	Tom Flores	27-10	PHILADELPHIA	Dick Vermeil	New Orleans
XVI	1/24/82	SAN FRANCISCO	Bill Walsh	26-21	Cincinnati	Forrest Gregg	Pontiac, MI
XVII	1/30/83	WASHINGTON	Joe Gibbs	27-17	Miami	Don Shula	Pasadena
XVIII	1/22/84	LA Raiders	Tom Flores	38-9	WASHINGTON	Joe Gibbs	Tampa
XIX	1/20/85	SAN FRANCISCO	Bill Walsh	38-16	Miami	Don Shula	Stanford
XX	1/26/86	CHICAGO	Mike Ditka	46-10	New England	Raymond Berry	New Orleans
XXI	1/25/87	NY GIANTS	Bill Parcells	39-20	Denver	Dan Reeves	Pasadena
XXII	1/31/88	WASHINGTON	Joe Gibbs	42-10	Denver	Dan Reeves	San Diego
XXIII	1/22/89	SAN FRANCISCO	Bill Walsh	20-16	Cincinnati	Sam Wyche	Miami
XXIV	1/28/90	SAN FRANCISCO	George Seifert	55-10	Denver	Dan Reeves	New Orleans
XXV	1/27/91	NY GIANTS	Bill Parcells	20-19	Buffalo	Marv Levy	Tampa
XXVI	1/26/92	WASHINGTON	Joe Gibbs	37-24	Buffalo	Marv Levy	Minneapolis
XXVII	1/31/93	DALLAS	Jimmy Johnson	52-17	Buffalo	Marv Levy	Pasadena
XXVIII	1/30/94	DALLAS	Jimmy Johnson	30-13	Buffalo	Marv Levy	Atlanta
XXIX	1/29/95	SAN FRANCISCO	George Seifert	49-26	San Diego	Bobby Ross	Miami
XXX	1/28/96	DALLAS	Barry Switzer	27-17	Pittsburgh	Bill Cowher	Tempe, AZ
XXXI	1/26/97	GREEN BAY	Mike Holmgren	35-21	New England	Bill Parcells	New Orleans
XXXII	1/25/98	Denver	Mike Shanahan	31-24	GREEN BAY	Mike Holmgren	San Diego
XXXIII	1/31/99	Denver	Mike Shanahan	34-19	ATLANTA	Dan Reeves	Miami
XXXIV	1/30/00	ST.L RAMS	Dick Vermeil	23-16	Tennessee	Jeff Fisher	Atlanta
XXXV	1/28/01	Balt. Ravens	Brian Billick	34-7	NY GIANTS	Jim Fassel	Tampa
XXXVI	2/3/02	New England	Bill Belichick	20-17	ST.L RAMS	Mike Martz	New Orleans
XXXVII	1/26/03	TAMPA BAY	Jon Gruden	48-21	Oakland	Bill Callahan	San Diego
XXXVIII	2/1/04	New England	Bill Belichick	32-29	CAROLINA	John Fox	Houston
XXXIX	2/6/05	New England	Bill Belichick	24-21	PHILADELPHIA	Andy Reid	Jacksonville
XL	2/5/06	Pittsburgh	Bill Cowher	21-10	SEATTLE	Mike Holmgren	Detroit

While the Detroit Lions have never made it to the Super Bowl, their General Manager sure has. Did you know that Matt Millen is the only player to win the Super Bowl with three different teams? He was a member of the Raiders in Super Bowls XV and XVIII, the 49ers in Super Bowl XXIV, and the Redskins in XXVI.

Super Bowl Appearances

App		W	L	Pct	PF	PA	App		W	L	Pct	PF	PA
8	Dallas	5	3	.625	221	132	2	Baltimore Colts	1	1	.500	23	29
6	Pittsburgh	5	1	.833	141	110	2	Kansas City	1	1	.500	33	42
6	Denver	2	4	.333	115	206	2	Cincinnati	0	2	.000	37	46
5	San Francisco	5	0	1.000	188	89	2	Philadelphia	0	2	.000	31	51
5	New England	3	2	.600	107	148	1	Baltimore Ravens	1	0	1.000	34	7
5	Oak/LA Raiders	3	2	.600	132	114	1	Chicago	1	0	1.000	46	10
5	Washington	3	2	.600	122	103	1	NY Jets	1	0	1.000	16	7
5	Miami	2	3	.400	74	103	1	Tampa Bay	1	0	1.000	48	21
4	Green Bay	3	1	.750	127	76	1	Atlanta	0	1	.000	19	34
4	Buffalo	0	4	.000	73	139	1	Carolina	0	1	.000	29	32
4	Minnesota	0	4	.000	34	95	1	San Diego	0	1	.000	26	49
3	NY Giants	2	1	.667	66	73	1	Seattle	0	1	.000	10	21
3	LA/St.L Rams	1	2	.333	59	67	1	Tennessee	0	1	.000	16	23

Pete Rozelle Award (MVP)

The Most Valuable Player in the Super Bowl. Currently selected by a panel made up of national pro football writers and broadcasters chosen by the NFL (80 percent) and fans voting via the internet and text message (20 percent). Presented by *Sport* magazine from 1967-89 and by the NFL since 1990. Named after former NFL commissioner Pete Rozelle in 1990. Winner who did not play for Super Bowl champion is in **bold** type.

Multiple winners: Joe Montana (3); Terry Bradshaw, Tom Brady and Bart Starr (2).

Bowl		Bowl		Bowl	
I	Bart Starr, Green Bay, QB	XIV	Terry Bradshaw, Pittsburgh, QB	XXVIII	Emmitt Smith, Dallas, RB
II	Bart Starr, Green Bay, QB	XV	Jim Plunkett, Oakland, QB	XXIX	Steve Young, San Fran., QB
III	Joe Namath, NY Jets, QB	XVI	Joe Montana, San Francisco, QB	XXX	Larry Brown, Dallas, CB
IV	Len Dawson, Kansas City, QB	XVII	John Riggins, Washington, RB	XXXI	Desmond Howard, Gr. Bay, KR
V	Chuck Howley, Dallas, LB	XVIII	Marcus Allen, LA Raiders, RB	XXXII	Terrell Davis, Denver, RB
VI	Roger Staubach, Dallas, QB	XIX	Joe Montana, San Francisco, QB	XXXIII	John Elway, Denver, QB
VII	Jake Scott, Miami, S	XX	Richard Dent, Chicago, DE	XXXIV	Kurt Warner, St. Louis, QB
VIII	Larry Csonka, Miami, RB	XXI	Phil Simms, NY Giants, QB	XXXV	Ray Lewis, Baltimore, LB
IX	Franco Harris, Pittsburgh, RB	XXII	Doug Williams, Washington, QB	XXXVI	Tom Brady, New England, QB
X	Lynn Swann, Pittsburgh, WR	XXIII	Jerry Rice, San Francisco, WR	XXXVII	Dexter Jackson, Tampa Bay, S
XI	Fred Biletnikoff, Oakland, WR	XXIV	Joe Montana, San Francisco, QB	XXXVIII	Tom Brady, New England, QB
XII	Harvey Martin, Dallas, DE	XXV	Ottis Anderson, NY Giants, RB	XXXIX	Deion Branch, New England, WR
	& Randy White, Dallas, DT	XXVI	Mark Rypien, Washington, QB	XL	Hines Ward, Pittsburgh, WR
XIII	Terry Bradshaw, Pittsburgh, QB	XXVII	Troy Aikman, Dallas, QB		

All-Time Super Bowl Leaders

Through 2006; participants in Super Bowl XL in **bold** type.

CAREER

Passing Efficiency

	(Minimum 25 passing attempts)	Gm	Att	Cmp	Cmp%	Yards	Avg Gain	TD	TD%	Int	Int%	Rating
1	Phil Simms, NYG	1	25	22	88.0	268	10.72	3	12.0	0	0.0	150.9
2	Steve Young, SF	2	39	26	66.7	345	8.85	6	15.4	0	0.0	134.1
3	Doug Williams, Wash.	1	29	18	62.1	340	11.72	4	13.8	1	3.4	128.1
4	Joe Montana, SF	4	122	83	68.0	1142	9.36	11	9.0	0	0.0	127.8
5	Jim Plunkett, Raiders	2	46	29	63.0	433	9.41	4	8.7	0	0.0	122.8
6	Jake Delhomme, Car.	1	33	16	48.5	323	9.79	3	9.1	0	0.0	113.6
7	Terry Bradshaw, Pit.	4	84	49	58.3	932	11.10	9	10.7	4	4.8	112.8
8	Troy Aikman, Dal	3	80	56	70.0	689	8.61	5	6.3	1	1.3	111.9
9	Bart Starr, GB	2	47	29	61.7	452	9.62	3	6.4	1	2.1	106.0
10	Tom Brady, NE	3	108	71	65.7	735	6.81	6	5.6	1	0.9	99.9

Ratings based on performance standards established for completion percentage, average gain, touchdown percentage and interception percentage. Quarterbacks are allocated points according to how their statistics measure up to those standards.

Passing Yards

		Gm	Att	Cmp	Pct	Yds
1	Joe Montana, SF	4	122	83	68.0	1142
2	John Elway, Den	5	152	76	50.0	1128
3	Terry Bradshaw, Pit	4	84	49	58.3	932
4	Jim Kelly, Buf	4	145	81	55.9	829
5	Kurt Warner, St.L	2	89	52	58.4	779
6	Tom Brady, NE	3	108	71	65.7	735
7	Roger Staubach, Dal	4	98	61	62.2	734
8	Troy Aikman, Dal	3	80	56	70.0	689
9	Brett Favre, GB	2	69	39	56.5	502
10	Fran Tarkenton, Min	3	89	46	51.7	489

Receptions

		Gm	No	Yds	Avg	TD
1	Jerry Rice, SF-Oak	4	33	589	17.8	8
2	Andre Reed, Buf	4	27	323	12.0	0
3	Deion Branch, NE	2	21	276	13.1	1
4	Roger Craig, SF	3	20	212	10.6	2
	Thurman Thomas, Buf	4	20	144	7.2	0
6	Jay Novacek, Dal	3	17	148	8.7	0
7	Lynn Swann, Pit	4	16	364	22.8	3
	Michael Irvin, Dal	3	16	256	16.0	2
	Troy Brown, NE	3	16	182	11.4	0
10	Chuck Foreman, Min	3	15	139	9.3	0

Rushing

	Gm	Car	Yds	Avg	TD
1 Franco Harris, Pit	.4	101	354	3.5	4
2 Larry Csonka, Mia	.3	57	297	5.2	2
3 Emmitt Smith, Dal	.3	70	289	4.1	5
4 Terrell Davis, Den	.2	55	259	4.7	3
5 John Riggins, Wash	.2	64	230	3.6	2
6 Timmy Smith, Wash	.1	22	204	9.3	2
Thurman Thomas, Buf	.4	52	204	3.9	4
8 Roger Craig, SF	.3	52	201	3.9	2
9 Marcus Allen, Raiders	.1	20	191	9.5	2
10 Antowain Smith, NE	.2	44	175	4.0	1

Scoring
Points

	Gm	TD	FG	PAT	Pts
1 Jerry Rice, SF-Oak	.4	8	0	0	48
2 Emmitt Smith, Dal	.3	5	0	0	30
3 Roger Craig, SF	.3	4	0	0	24
Franco Harris, Pit	.4	4	0	0	24
Thurman Thomas, Buf	.4	4	0	0	24
John Elway, Den	.5	4	0	0	24
7 Adam Vinatieri, NE	.4	0	4	11	23
8 Ray Wersching, SF	.2	0	5	7	22
9 Don Chandler, GB	.2	0	4	8	20
10 Six tied with 18 pts. each.					

Touchdowns

	Gm	Rush	Rec	Ret	TD
1 Jerry Rice, SF-Oak	.4	0	8	0	8
2 Emmitt Smith, Dal	.3	5	0	0	5
3 Roger Craig, SF	.3	2	2	0	4
Franco Harris, Pit	.4	4	0	0	4
John Elway, Den	.5	4	0	0	4
Thurman Thomas, Buf	.4	4	0	0	4
7 Six tied with 3 TD each.					

Punting

	Gm	No	Yds	Avg.
(Minimum 10 Punts)				
1 Jerrel Wilson, KC	.2	11	511	46.5
2 **Tom Rouen**, Den-Sea	.3	11	482	43.8
3 Tom Tupa, NE-TB	.2	12	516	43.0
Kyle Richardson, Bal	.1	10	430	43.0
5 Ray Guy, Raiders	.3	14	587	41.9

All-Purpose Yards

	Gm	Rush	Rec	Ret	Total
1 Jerry Rice, SF-Oak	.4	15	589	0	604
2 Franco Harris, Pit	.4	354	114	0	468
3 Roger Craig, SF	.3	201	212	0	413
4 Lynn Swann, Pit	.4	-7	364	34	391
5 Thurman Thomas, Buf	.4	204	144	0	348

Punt Returns

	Gm	No	Yds	Avg.	TD
(Minimum 4 Returns)					
1 John Taylor, SF	.3	6	94	15.7	0
2 Desmond Howard, GB	.1	6	90	15.0	0
3 Dave Meggett, NYG-NE	.2	6	67	11.2	0
4 Neal Colzie, Raiders	.1	4	43	10.8	0
5 Dana McLemore, SF	.1	5	51	10.2	0

Kickoff Returns

	Gm	No	Yds	Avg.	TD
(Minimum 4 Returns)					
1 Tim Dwight, Atl	.1	5	210	42.0	1
2 Desmond Howard, GB	.1	4	154	38.5	1
3 Fulton Walker, Mia	.2	8	283	35.4	1
4 Andre Coleman, SD	.1	8	242	30.3	1
5 Larry Anderson, Pit	.2	8	207	25.9	0

Interceptions

	Gm	No	Yds	TD
1 Larry Brown, Dal	.3	3	77	0
Chuck Howley, Dal	.2	3	63	0
Rod Martin, Raiders	.2	3	44	0
4 Thirteen tied with 2 each.				

Sacks

	Gm	No
1 Charles Haley, SF-Dal	.5	4.5
2 Reggie White, GB	.2	3.0
Leonard Marshall, NYG	.2	3.0
Danny Stubbs, SF	.2	3.0
Mike Vrabel, NE	.3	3.0
Jeff Wright, Buf	.4	3.0
Tedy Bruschi, NE	.4	3.0
Willie McGinest, NE	.4	3.0

Note: The NFL did not begin officially compiling sacks until 1982.

SINGLE GAME
Passing

	Year	Att/Cmp	Yds
1 Kurt Warner, St.L vs Ten	.2000	45/24	414
2 Kurt Warner, St.L vs NE	.2002	44/28	365
3 Joe Montana, SF vs Cin	.1989	36/23	357
Donovan McNabb, Phi vs NE	.2005	51/30	357
5 Tom Brady, NE vs Car	.2004	48/32	354

Touchdown Passes	Year	TD	Int
1 Steve Young, SF vs SD	.1995	6	0
2 Joe Montana, SF vs Den	.1990	5	0
3 Terry Bradshaw, Pit vs Dal	.1979	4	1
Doug Williams, Wash vs Den	.1988	4	1
Troy Aikman, Dal vs Buf	.1993	4	0

Receiving

Catches	Year	No	Yds	TD
1 Dan Ross, Cin vs SF	.1982	11	104	2
Jerry Rice, SF vs Cin	.1989	11	215	1
Deion Branch, NE vs Phi	.2005	11	133	0
4 Tony Nathan, Mia vs SF	.1985	10	83	0
Jerry Rice, SF vs SD	.1995	10	149	3
Andre Hastings, Pit vs Dal	.1996	10	98	0
Deion Branch, NE vs Car	.2004	10	143	1

Yards Gained	Year	No	Yds	TD
1 Jerry Rice, SF vs Cin	.1989	11	215	1
2 Ricky Sanders, Wash vs Den	.1988	9	193	2
3 Isaac Bruce, St.L vs Ten	.2000	6	162	1
4 Lynn Swann, Pit vs Dal	.1976	4	161	1
5 Andre Reed, Buf vs Dal	.1993	8	152	0
Rod Smith, Den vs Atl	.1999	5	152	1

All-Time Super Bowl Leaders (Cont.)

Rushing

	Yards Gained	Year	Car	Yds	TD
1	Timmy Smith, Wash vs Den	.1988	22	204	2
2	Marcus Allen, Raiders vs Wash	.1984	20	191	2
3	John Riggins, Wash vs Mia	.1983	38	166	1
4	Franco Harris, Pit vs Min	.1975	34	158	1
5	Terrell Davis, Den vs GB	.1998	30	157	3

Scoring

	Points	Year	TD	FG	PAT	Pts
1	Roger Craig, SF vs Mia	.1985	3	0	0	18
	Jerry Rice, SF vs Den	.1990	3	0	0	18
	Jerry Rice, SF vs SD	.1995	3	0	0	18
	Ricky Watters, SF vs SD	.1995	3	0	0	18
	Terrell Davis, Den vs GB	.1998	3	0	0	18

	Touchdowns	Year	TD	Rush	Rec
1	Roger Craig, SF vs Mia	.1985	3	1	2
	Jerry Rice, SF vs Den	.1990	3	0	3
	Jerry Rice, SF vs SD	.1995	3	0	3
	Ricky Watters, SF vs SD	.1995	3	1	2
	Terrell Davis, Den vs GB	.1998	3	3	0

Punting

	(Minimum 4 punts)	Year	No	Yds	Avg
1	**Tom Rouen**, Sea vs Pit	.2006	6	301	50.2
2	Bryan Wagner, SD vs SF	.1995	4	195	48.8
3	**Chris Gardocki**, Pit vs Sea	.2006	6	292	48.7
4	Jerrel Wilson, KC vs Min	.1970	4	194	48.5
5	Jim Miller, SF vs Cin	.1982	4	185	46.3

All-Purpose Yards

	Yards Gained	Year	Run	Rec	Tot
1	Desmond Howard, GB vs NE	.1997	0	0	244
2	Andre Coleman, SD vs SF	.1995	0	0	242
3	Ricky Sanders, Wash vs Den	.1988	193	-4	235
4	Antonio Freeman, GB vs Den	.1998	0	126	230
5	Jerry Rice, SF vs Cin	.1989	5	215	220

Return Yardage: Howard 244, Coleman 242, Sanders 46, Freeman 104.

Punt Returns

	(Minimum 3 returns)	Year	No	Yds	Avg
1	John Taylor, SF vs Cin	.1989	3	56	18.7
2	Desmond Howard, GB vs NE	.1997	6	90	15.0
3	John Taylor, SF vs Den	.1990	3	38	12.7
4	Kelvin Martin, Dal vs Buf	.1993	3	35	11.7
5	Lynn Swann, Pit vs Min	.1975	3	34	11.3
	Jermaine Lewis, Bal vs NYG	.2001	3	34	11.3

Kickoff Returns

	(Minimum 3 returns)	Year	No	Yds	Avg
1	Fulton Walker, Mia vs Wash	.1983	4	190	47.5
2	Tim Dwight, Atl vs Den	.1999	5	210	42.0
3	Desmond Howard, GB vs NE	.1997	4	154	38.5
4	Larry Anderson, Pit vs Rams	.1980	5	162	32.4
5	Rick Upchurch, Den vs Dal	.1978	3	94	31.3

Interceptions

		Year	No	Yds	TD
1	Rod Martin, Raiders vs Phi	.1981	3	44	0

Eleven tied with 2 each.

Super Bowl Playoffs

The Super Bowl forced the NFL to set up pro football's first guaranteed multiple-game playoff format. Over the years, the NFL-AFL merger, the creation of two conferences comprised of four divisions each and the proliferation of wild card entries has seen the postseason field grow from four teams (1966), to six (1967-68), to eight (1969-77), to 10 (1978-81, 1983-89), to the present 12 (since1990). In 1968, there was a special playoff between Oakland and Kansas City which were both 12-2 and tied for first in the AFL's Western Division. In 1982, when a 57-day players' strike shortened the regular season to just nine games, playoff berths were extended to 16 teams (eight from each conference) and a 15-game tournament was played.

Note that in the following year-by-year summary, records of finalists include all games leading up to the Super Bowl; (*) indicates non-division winners or wild card teams.

1966 SEASON

AFL Playoffs

Championship . . . . .Kansas City 31, at Buffalo 7

NFL Playoffs

Championship . . . . .Green Bay 34, at Dallas 27

Super Bowl I

Jan. 15, 1967
Memorial Coliseum, Los Angeles
Favorite: Packers by 14—Attendance: 61,946

Kansas City (12-2-1) . . . . .0 10 0 0 — **10**
Green Bay (13-2) . . . . .7 7 14 7 — **35**
MVP: Green Bay QB Bart Starr (16 for 23, 250 yds, 2 TD)

1967 SEASON

AFL Playoffs

Championship . . . . .at Oakland 40, Houston 7

NFL Playoffs

Eastern Conference . . . . .at Dallas 52, Cleveland 14
Western Conference . . . . . . .at Green Bay 28, LA Rams 7
Championship . . . . .at Green Bay 21, Dallas 17

Super Bowl II

Jan. 14, 1968   Orange Bowl, Miami
Favorite: Packers by 13½—Attendance: 75,546

Green Bay (11-4-1) . . . . .3 13 10 7 — **33**
Oakland (14-1) . . . . .0 7 0 7 — **14**
MVP: Green Bay QB Bart Starr (13 for 24, 202 yds,1 TD)

1968 SEASON

AFL Playoffs

Western Div. Playoff . . . . . .at Oakland 41, Kansas City 6
AFL Championship . . . . .at NY Jets 27, Oakland 23

NFL Playoffs

Eastern Conference . . . . .at Cleveland 31, Dallas 20
Western Conference . . . . .at Baltimore 24, Minnesota 14
NFL Championship . . . . . . .Baltimore 34, at Cleveland 0

Super Bowl III

Jan. 12, 1969   Orange Bowl, Miami
Favorite: Colts by 18—Attendance: 75,389

NY Jets (12-3) . . . . .0 7 6 3 — **16**
Baltimore (15-1) . . . . .0 0 0 7 — **7**
MVP: NY Jets QB Joe Namath (17 for 28, 206 yds)

1969 SEASON

AFL Playoffs

Inter-Division . . . .*Kansas City 13, at NY Jets 6
at Oakland 56, *Houston 7
AFL Championship . . . . . . .Kansas City 17, at Oakland 7

NFL Playoffs

Eastern Conference . . . . .Cleveland 38, at Dallas 14
Western Conference . . . . . .at Minnesota 23, LA Rams 20
NFL Championship . . . . . . .at Minnesota 27, Cleveland 7

Super Bowl IV

Jan. 11, 1970   Tulane Stadium, New Orleans
Favorite: Vikings by 12—Attendance: 80,562

Minnesota (14-2) 0   0   7   0 — **7**
Kansas City (13-3) . . . . .3 13   7   0 — **23**
MVP: KC QB Len Dawson (12 for 17, 142 yds, 1 TD, 1Int)

1970 SEASON

AFC Playoffs

First Round . . . . .at Baltimore 17, Cincinnati 0
at Oakland 21,*Miami 14
Championship . . . . .at Baltimore 27, Oakland 17

NFC Playoffs

First Round. . . . . .at Dallas 5, *Detroit 0
San Francisco 17, at Minnesota 14
Championship . . . . .Dallas 17, at San Francisco 10

Super Bowl V

Jan. 17, 1971   Orange Bowl, Miami
Favorite: Cowboys by 2½—Attendance: 79,204

Baltimore (13-2-1) 0   6   0 10 — **16**
Dallas (12-4) . . . . .3 10   0   0 — **13**
MVP: Dallas LB Chuck Howley (2 interceptions for 22 yds)

1971 SEASON

AFC Playoffs

First Round . . . . .Miami 27, at Kansas City 24 (OT)
*Baltimore 20, at Cleveland 3
Championship . . . . .at Miami 21, Baltimore 0

NFC Playoffs

First Round . . . . .Dallas 20, at Minnesota 12
at San Francisco 24,*Washington 20
Championship . . . . .at Dallas 14, San Francisco 3

Super Bowl VI

Jan. 16, 1972   Tulane Stadium, New Orleans
Favorite: Cowboys by 6—Attendance: 81,023

Dallas (13-3) 3   7   7   7 — **24**
Miami (12-3-1) 0   3   0   0 — **3**
MVP: Dallas QB Roger Staubach (12 for 19, 119 yds, 2 TDs)

1972 SEASON

AFC Playoffs

First Round . . . . .at Pittsburgh 13, Oakland 7
at Miami 20, *Cleveland 14
Championship . . . . .Miami 21, at Pittsburgh 17

NFC Playoffs

First Round . . . .*Dallas 30, at San Francisco 28
at Washington 16, Green Bay 3
Championship . . . . .at Washington 26, Dallas 3

Super Bowl VII

Jan. 14, 1973
Memorial Coliseum, Los Angeles
Favorite: Redskins by 1½—Attendance: 90,182

Miami (16-0) 7   7   0   0 — **14**
Washington (13-3) 0   0   0   7 — **7**
MVP: Miami safety Jake Scott (2 Interceptions for 63 yds)

1973 SEASON

AFC Playoffs

First Round . . . . .at Oakland 33, *Pittsburgh 14
at Miami 34, Cincinnati 16
Championship . . . . .at Miami 27, Oakland 10

NFC Playoffs

First Round . . . . .at Minnesota 27, *Washington 20
at Dallas 27, LA Rams 16
Championship . . . . .Minnesota 27, at Dallas 10

Super Bowl VIII

Jan. 13, 1974
Rice Stadium, Houston
Favorite: Dolphins by 6½—Attendance: 71,882

Minnesota (14-2) 0   0   0   7 — **7**
Miami (12-4) 14   3   7   0 — **24**
MVP: Miami FB Larry Csonka (33 carries, 145 yds, 2 TD)

1974 SEASON

AFC Playoffs

First Round . . . . .at Oakland 28, Miami 26
at Pittsburgh 32, *Buffalo 14
Championship . . . . .Pittsburgh 24, at Oakland 13

NFC Playoffs

First Round . . . . .at Minnesota 30, St. Louis 14
at LA Rams 19, *Washington 10
Championship . . . . .at Minnesota 14, LA Rams 10

Super Bowl IX

Jan. 12, 1975
Tulane Stadium, New Orleans
Favorite: Steelers by 3—Attendance: 80,997

Pittsburgh (12-3-1) 0   2   7   7 — **16**
Minnesota (12-4) 0   0   0   6 — **6**
MVP: Pittsburgh RB Franco Harris (34 carries, 158 yds, 1 TD)

1975 SEASON

AFC Playoffs

First Round . . . . .at Pittsburgh 28, Baltimore 10
at Oakland 31, *Cincinnati 28
Championship . . . . .at Pittsburgh 16, Oakland 10

NFC Playoffs

First Round . . . . .at LA Rams 35, St. Louis 23
*Dallas 17, at Minnesota 14
Championship . . . . .Dallas 37, at LA Rams 7

Super Bowl X

Jan. 18, 1976   Orange Bowl, Miami
Favorite: Steelers by 6½—Attendance: 80,187

Dallas (12-4) 7   3   0   7 — **17**
Pittsburgh (14-2) 7   0   0 14 — **21**
MVP: Pittsburgh WR Lynn Swann (4 catches, 161 yds, 1 TD)

1976 SEASON

AFC Playoffs

First Round . . . . .at Oakland 24, *New England 21
Pittsburgh 40, at Baltimore 14
Championship . . . . .at Oakland 24, Pittsburgh 7

NFC Playoffs

First Round . . . . .at Minnesota 35, *Washington 20
LA Rams 14, at Dallas 12
Championship . . . . .at Minnesota 24, LA Rams 13

Super Bowl XI

Jan. 9, 1977   Rose Bowl, Pasadena
Favorite: Raiders by 4½—Attendance: 103,438

Oakland (15-1) . . . . .0' 16   3 13 **—32**
Minnesota (13-2-1) 0   0   7   7 **—14**
MVP: Oakland WR Fred Biletnikoff (4 catches, 79 yds)

1977 SEASON

AFC Playoffs

First Round . . . . .at Denver 34, Pittsburgh 21
*Oakland 37, at Baltimore 31 (OT)
Championship . . . . .at Denver 20, Oakland 17

NFC Playoffs

First Round . . . . .at Dallas 37, *Chicago 7
Minnesota 14, at LA Rams 7
Championship . . . . .at Dallas 23, Minnesota 6

Super Bowl XII

Jan. 15, 1978   Louisiana Superdome, New Orleans
Favorite: Cowboys by 6—Attendance: 75,583

Dallas (14-2) 10   3   7   7 **— 27**
Denver (14-2) 0   0 10   0 **— 10**
MVPs: Dallas DE Harvey Martin and DT Randy White
(Cowboys' defense forced 8 turnovers)

1978 SEASON

AFC Playoffs

First Round . . . .*Houston 17, at *Miami 9
Second Round . . . . .Houston 31, at New England 14
at Pittsburgh 33, Denver 10
Championship . . . . .at Pittsburgh 34, Houston 5

NFC Playoffs

First Round . . . . .at *Atlanta 14, *Philadelphia 13
Second Round . . . . .at Dallas 27, Atlanta 20
at LA Rams 34, Minnesota 10
Championship . . . . .Dallas 28, at LA Rams 0

Super Bowl XIII

Jan. 21, 1979   Orange Bowl, Miami
Favorite: Steelers by 4—Attendance: 79,484

Pittsburgh (16-2) . . . . .7 14   0 14 **— 35**
Dallas (14-4) 7   7   3 14 **— 31**
MVP: Pit. QB Terry Bradshaw (17 for 30, 318 yds, 4 TD)

1979 SEASON

AFC Playoffs

First Round . . . . .at *Houston 13, *Denver 7
Second Round . . . . .Houston 17, at San Diego 14
at Pittsburgh 34, Miami 14
Championship . . . . .at Pittsburgh 27, Houston 13

NFC Playoffs

First Round . . . . .at *Philadelphia 27, *Chicago 17
Second Round . . . . . . .at Tampa Bay 24, Philadelphia 17
LA Rams 21, at Dallas 19
Championship . . . . .LA Rams 9,at Tampa Bay 0

Super Bowl XIV

Jan. 20, 1980   Rose Bowl, Pasadena
Favorite: Steelers by 10½—Attendance: 103,985

LA Rams (11-7) 7   6   6   0 **— 19**
Pittsburgh (14-4) 3   7   7 14 **— 31**
MVP: Pit. QB Terry Bradshaw (14 for 21, 309 yds, 2 TD)

1980 SEASON

AFC Playoffs

First Round . . . . .at *Oakland 27, *Houston 7
Second Round . . . . .at San Diego 20, Buffalo 14
Oakland 14, at Cleveland 12
Championship . . . . .Oakland 34, at San Diego 27

NFC Playoffs

First Round . . . . .at *Dallas 34, *LA Rams 13
Second Round . . . . .at Philadelphia 31, Minnesota 16
Dallas 30, at Atlanta 27
Championship . . . . .at Philadelphia 20, Dallas 7

Super Bowl XV

Jan. 25, 1981   Louisiana Superdome, New Orleans
Favorite: Eagles by 3—Attendance: 76,135

Oakland (14-5) 14   0 10   3 **— 27**
Philadelphia (14-4) 0   3   0   7 **— 10**
MVP: Oakland QB Jim Plunkett (13 for 21, 261 yds, 3 TD)

1981 SEASON

AFC Playoffs

First Round . . . .*Buffalo 31, at *NY Jets 27
Second Round . . . . .San Diego 41, at Miami 38 (OT)
at Cincinnati 28, Buffalo 21
Championship . . . . .at Cincinnati 27, San Diego 7

NFC Playoffs

First Round . . . .*NY Giants 27, at *Philadelphia 21
Second Round . . . . .at Dallas 38, Tampa Bay 0
at San Francisco 38, NY Giants 24
Championship . . . . .at San Francisco 28, Dallas 27

Super Bowl XVI

Jan. 24, 1982   Pontiac Silverdome, Pontiac, Mich.
Favorite: Pick'em—Attendance: 81,270

San Francisco (15-3) . . . . .7 13   0   6 **— 26**
Cincinnati (14-4) 0   0   7 14 **— 21**
MVP: San Francisco QB Joe Montana (14 for 22, 157
yds, 1 TD; 6 carries, 18 yds, 1 TD)

1982 SEASON

*A 57-day players' strike shortened the regular season from
16 games to nine. The playoff format was changed to a
16-team tournament open to the top eight teams in each
conference.*

AFC Playoffs

First Round . . . . .at LA Raiders 27, Cleveland 10
at Miami 28, New England 3
NY Jets 44, at Cincinnati 17
San Diego 31, at Pittsburgh 28
Second Round . . . . .NY Jets 17, at LA Raiders 14
at Miami 34, San Diego 13
Championship . . . . .at Miami 14, NY Jets 0

NFC Playoffs

First Round . . . . .at Washington 31, Detroit 7
at Dallas 30, Tampa Bay 0
at Green Bay 41, St. Louis 16
at Minnesota 30, Atlanta 24
Second Round . . . . .at Washington 21, Minnesota 7
at Dallas 37, Green Bay 26
Championship . . . . .at Washington 31, Dallas 17

Super Bowl XVII
Jan. 30, 1983
Rose Bowl, Pasadena
Favorite: Dolphins by 3—Attendance: 103,667

Miami (10-2) . . . . .7 10 0   0 **—17**
Washington (11-1) . . . . .0 10 3 14 **—27**
MVP: Washington RB John Riggins (38 carries, 166 yds, 1 TD; 1 catch, 15 yds)

1983 SEASON

AFC Playoffs

First Round . . . . .at *Seattle 31, *Denver 7
Second Round . . . . .Seattle 27, at Miami 20
at LA Raiders 38, Pittsburgh 10
Championship . . . . .at LA Raiders 30, Seattle 14

NFC Playoffs

First Round . . . .*LA Rams 24, at *Dallas 17
Second Round . . . . .at San Francisco 24, Detroit 23
at Washington 51, LA Rams 7
Championship . . . . . .at Washington 24, San Francisco 21

Super Bowl XVIII
Jan. 22, 1984
Tampa Stadium, Tampa
Favorite: Redskins by 3—Attendance: 72,920

Washington (16-2) 0   3   6   0 **— 9**
LA Raiders (14-4) . . . . .7 14 14   3 **—38**
MVP: LA Raiders RB Marcus Allen (20 carries, 191 yds, 2 TD; 2 catches, 18 yds)

1984 SEASON

AFC Playoffs

First Round . . . . .at *Seattle 13, *LA Raiders 7
Second Round . . . . .at Miami 31, Seattle 10
Pittsburgh 24, at Denver 17
Championship . . . . .at Miami 45, Pittsburgh 28

NFC Playoffs

First Round . . . .*NY Giants 16, at *LA Rams 13
Second Round . . . . . . .at San Francisco 21, NY Giants 10
Chicago 23, at Washington 19
Championship . . . . .at San Francisco 23, Chicago 0

Super Bowl XIX
Jan. 20, 1985
Stanford Stadium, Stanford, Calif.
Favorite: 49ers by 3—Attendance: 84,059

Miami (16-2) 10   6   0   0 **— 16**
San Francisco (17-1) . . . . .7 21 10   0 **— 38**
MVP: San Francisco QB Joe Montana (24 for 35, 331 yds, 2 TD; 5 carries, 59 yards, 1 TD)

Most Popular Playing Sites
Stadiums hosting more than one Super Bowl.

No		Years
6	Superdome (N. Orleans)	1978, 81, 86, 90, 97, 2002
5	Orange Bowl (Miami)	1968-69, 71, 76, 79
5	Rose Bowl (Pasadena)	1977, 80, 83, 87, 93
3	Tulane Stadium (N. Orleans)	1970, 72, 75
3	Joe Robbie/Pro Player Stadium (Miami)	1989, 95, 99
3	Jack Murphy/Qualcomm Stadium (San Diego)	1988, 98, 2003
2	LA Memorial Coliseum	1967, 73
2	Tampa Stadium	1984, 91
2	Georgia Dome (Atlanta)	1994, 2000

1985 SEASON

AFC Playoffs

First Round . . . .*New England 26, at *NY Jets 14
Second Round . . . . .at Miami 24, Cleveland 21
New England 27, at LA Raiders 20
Championship . . . . .New England 31, at Miami 14

NFC Playoffs

First Round . . . . .at *NY Giants 17, *San Francisco 3
Second Round . . . . .at LA Rams 20, Dallas 0
at Chicago 21, NY Giants 0
Championship . . . . .at Chicago 24, LA Rams 0

Super Bowl XX
Jan. 26, 1986
Louisiana Superdome, New Orleans
Favorite: Bears by 10—Attendance: 73,818

Chicago Bears (17-1) . . . . .13 10 21   2 **— 46**
New England (14-5) 3   0   0   7 **— 10**
MVP: Chicago DE Richard Dent (Bears defense: 7 sacks, 6 turnovers, 1 safety and gave up just 123 total yards)

1986 SEASON

AFC Playoffs

First Round . . . . .at *NY Jets 35, *Kansas City 15
Second Round . . . . .at Cleveland 23, NY Jets 20 (OT)
at Denver 22, New England 17
Championship . . . . .Denver 23, at Cleveland 20 (OT)

NFC Playoffs

First Round . . . . .at *Washington 19, *LA Rams 7
Second Round . . . . .Washington 27, at Chicago 13
at NY Giants 49, San Francisco 3
Championship . . . . . . .at NY Giants 17, Washington 0

Super Bowl XXI
Jan. 25, 1987
Rose Bowl, Pasadena
Favorite: Giants by 9½—Attendance: 101,063

Denver (13-5) 10   0   0 10 **— 20**
NY Giants (16-2) 7   2 17 13 **— 39**
MVP: NY Giants QB Phil Simms (22 for 25, 268 yds, 3 TD; 3 carries, 25 yds)

1987 SEASON

A 24-day players' strike shortened the regular season to 15 games with replacement teams playing for three weeks.

AFC Playoffs

First Round . . . . .at *Houston 23, *Seattle 20 (OT)
Second Round . . . . .at Cleveland 38, Indianapolis 21
at Denver 34, Houston 10
Championship . . . . .at Denver 38, Cleveland 33

NFC Playoffs

First Round . . . .*Minnesota 44, at *New Orleans 10
Second Round . . . . . .Minnesota 36, at San Francisco 24
Washington 21, at Chicago 17
Championship . . . . . . .at Washington 17, Minnesota 10

Super Bowl XXII
Jan. 31, 1988
San Diego/Jack Murphy Stadium
Favorite: Broncos by 3½—Attendance: 73,302

Washington (13-4) . . . . .0 35   0   7 **—42**
Denver (12-4-1) 10   0   0   0 **—10**
MVP: Washington QB Doug Williams (18 for 29, 340 yds, 4 TD, 1 Int)

1988 SEASON

AFC Playoffs

First Round . . . .*Houston 24, at *Cleveland 23
Second Round . . . . .at Buffalo 17, Houston 10
at Cincinnati 21, Seattle 13
Championship . . . . .at Cincinnati 21, Buffalo 10

NFC Playoffs

First Round . . . . .at *Minnesota 28, *LA Rams 17
Second Round . . . . .at San Francisco 34, Minnesota 9
at Chicago 20, Philadelphia 12
Championship . . . . .San Francisco 28, at Chicago 3

Super Bowl XXIII

Jan. 22, 1989
Joe Robbie Stadium, Miami
Favorite: 49ers by 7—Attendance: 75,129

Cincinnati (14-4) 0   3 10   3 **— 16**
San Francisco (12-6) 3   0   3 14 **— 20**
MVP: San Francisco WR Jerry Rice (11 catches, 215 yds, 1 TD; 1 carry, 5 yds)

1989 SEASON

AFC Playoffs

First Round . . . .*Pittsburgh 26, at *Houston 23
Second Round . . . . .at Cleveland 34, Buffalo 30
at Denver 24, Pittsburgh 23
Championship . . . . .at Denver 37, Cleveland 21

NFC Playoffs

First Round . . . .*LA Rams 21, at *Philadelphia 7
Second Round . . . . .LA Rams 19, NY Giants 13 (OT)
at San Francisco 41, Minnesota 13
Championship . . . . .at San Francisco 30, LA Rams 3

Super Bowl XXIV

Jan. 28, 1990
Louisiana Superdome, New Orleans
Favorite: 49ers by 12½—Attendance: 72,919

San Francisco (17-2) . . . . .13 14 14 14 **— 55**
Denver (13-6) 3   0   7   0 **— 10**
MVP: San Francisco QB Joe Montana (22 for 29, 297 yds, 5 TD)

1990 SEASON

AFC Playoffs

First Round . . . . .at *Miami 17, *Kansas City 16
at Cincinnati 41, *Houston 14
Second Round . . . . .at Buffalo 44, Miami 34
at LA Raiders 20, Cincinnati 10
Championship . . . . .at Buffalo 51, LA Raiders 3

NFC Playoffs

First Round . . . .*Washington 20, at *Philadelphia 6
at Chicago 16, *New Orleans 6
Second Round . . . . . .at San Francisco 28, Washington 10
at NY Giants 31, Chicago 3
Championship . . . . . . .NY Giants 15, at San Francisco 13

Super Bowl XXV

Jan. 27, 1991
Tampa Stadium, Tampa
Favorite: Bills by 7—Attendance: 73,813

Buffalo (15-4) 3   9   0   7 **—19**
NY Giants (16-3) 3   7   7   3 **—20**
MVP: NY Giants RB Ottis Anderson (21 carries, 102 yds, 1 TD; 1 catch, 7 yds)

1991 SEASON

AFC Playoffs

First Round . . . . .at *Kansas City 10, *LA Raiders 6
at Houston 17, *NY Jets 10
Second Round . . . . .at Denver 26, Houston 24
at Buffalo 37, Kansas City 14
Championship . . . . .at Buffalo 10, Denver 7

NFC Playoffs

First Round . . . .*Atlanta 27, at New Orleans 20
*Dallas 17, at *Chicago 13
Second Round . . . . .at Washington 24, Atlanta 7
at Detroit 38, Dallas 6
Championship . . . . .at Washington 41, Detroit 10

Super Bowl XXVI

Jan. 26, 1992
Hubert Humphrey Metrodome, Minneapolis
Favorite: Redskins by 7—Attendance: 63,130

Washington (16-2) . . . . .0 17 14   6 **— 37**
Buffalo (15-3) 0   0 10 14 **— 24**
MVP: Washington QB Mark Rypien (18 for 33, 292 yds, 2 TD, 1 Int)

1992 SEASON

AFC Playoffs

First Round . . . . .at *Buffalo 41, *Houston 38 (OT)
at San Diego 17, *Kansas City 0
Second Round . . . . .Buffalo 24, at Pittsburgh 3
at Miami 31, San Diego 0
Championship . . . . .Buffalo 29, at Miami 10

NFC Playoffs

First Round . . . .*Washington 24, at Minnesota 7
*Philadelphia 36, at *New Orleans 20
Second Round . . . . . .at San Francisco 20, Washington 13
at Dallas 34, Philadelphia 10
Championship . . . . .Dallas 30, at San Francisco 20

Super Bowl XXVII

Jan. 31, 1993
Rose Bowl, Pasadena
Favorite: Cowboys by 7—Attendance: 98,374

Buffalo (14-5) 7   3   7   0 **— 17**
Dallas (15-3) . . . . .14 14   3 21 **— 52**
MVP: Dallas QB Troy Aikman (22 for 30, 273 yds, 4 TD)

1993 SEASON

AFC Playoffs

First Round . . . . . . .at Kansas City 27, *Pittsburgh 24 (OT)
at *LA Raiders 42, *Denver 24
Second Round . . . . .at Buffalo 29, LA Raiders 23
Kansas City 28, at Houston 20
Championship . . . . .at Buffalo 30, Kansas City 13

NFC Playoffs

First Round . . . .*Green Bay 28, at Detroit 24
at *NY Giants 17, *Minnesota 10
Second Round . . . . .at San Francisco 44, NY Giants 3
at Dallas 27, Green Bay 17
Championship . . . . .at Dallas 38, San Francisco 21

Super Bowl XXVIII

Jan. 30, 1994
Georgia Dome, Atlanta
Favorite: Cowboys by 10½—Attendance: 72,817

Dallas (15-4) 6   0 14 10 **— 30**
Buffalo (14-5) . . . . .3 10   0   0 **— 13**
MVP: Dallas RB Emmitt Smith (30 carries, 132 yds, 2 TDs; 4 catches, 26 yds)

1994 SEASON

AFC Playoffs

First Round . . . . .at Miami 27, *Kansas City 17
at *Cleveland 20, *New England 13
Second Round . . . . .at Pittsburgh 29, Cleveland 9
at San Diego 22, Miami 21
Championship . . . . .San Diego 17, at Pittsburgh 13

NFC Playoffs

First Round . . . . at *Green Bay 16, *Detroit 12
*Chicago 25, at Minnesota 18
Second Round . . . . .at San Francisco 44, Chicago 15
at Dallas 35, Green Bay 9
Championship . . . . .at San Francisco 38, Dallas 28

Super Bowl XXIX
Jan. 29, 1995
Joe Robbie Stadium, Miami
Favorite: 49ers by 18 —Attendance: 74,107

San Diego (13-5) . . . . .7 3 8 8 —**26**
San Francisco (15-3) . . . . .14 14 14 7 —**49**
MVP: San Francisco QB Steve Young (24 for 36, 325 yds, 6 TD)

1995 SEASON

AFC Playoffs

First Round . . . . .at Buffalo 37, *Miami 22
*Indianapolis 35, at *San Diego 20
Second Round . . . . .at Pittsburgh 40, Buffalo 21
Indianapolis 10, at Kansas City 7
Championship . . . . .at Pittsburgh 20, Indianapolis 16

NFC Playoffs

First Round . . . . at *Philadelphia 58, *Detroit 37
at Green Bay 37, *Atlanta 20
Second Round . . . . . . Green Bay 27, at San Francisco 17
at Dallas 30, Philadelphia 11
Championship . . . . .at Dallas 38, Green Bay 27

Super Bowl XXX
Jan. 28, 1996
Sun Devil Stadium, Tempe, Ariz.
Favorite: Cowboys by 13½—Attendance: 76,347

Dallas (14-4) . . . . .10 3 7 7 — **27**
Pittsburgh (13-5) . . . . .0 7 0 10 — **17**
MVP: Dallas CB Larry Brown (2 interceptions for 77 yds)

1996 SEASON

AFC Playoffs

First Round . . . . *Jacksonville 30, at *Buffalo 27
at Pittsburgh 42, *Indianapolis 14
Second Round . . . . Jacksonville 30, at Denver 27
at New England 28, Pittsburgh 3
Championship . . . . . . .at New England 20, Jacksonville 6

NFC Playoffs

First Round . . . . at Dallas 40, *Minnesota 15
at *San Francisco 14, *Philadelphia 0
Second Round . . . . . . at Green Bay 35, San Francisco 14
at Carolina 26, Dallas 17
Championship . . . . . . at Green Bay 30, Carolina 13

Super Bowl XXXI
Jan. 26, 1997
Louisiana Superdome, New Orleans
Favorite: Packers by 14—Attendance: 72,301

New England (13-5) . . . . .14 0 7 0 — **21**
Green Bay (15-3) . . . . .10 17 8 0 — **35**
MVP: Green Bay KR Desmond Howard (4 kickoff returns for 154 yds and 1 TD, also 6 punt returns for 90 yds)

1997 SEASON

AFC Playoffs

First Round . . . . .at *Denver 42, *Jacksonville 17
at New England 17, *Miami 3
Second Round . . . . .at Pittsburgh 7, New England 6
Denver 14, at Kansas City 10
Championship . . . . Denver 24, at Pittsburgh 21

NFC Playoffs

First Round . . . . *Minnesota 23, at NY Giants 22
at *Tampa Bay 20, *Detroit 10
Second Round . . . . . . .at San Francisco 38, Minnesota 22
at Green Bay 21, Tampa Bay 7
Championship . . . . . . .Green Bay 23, at San Francisco 10

Super Bowl XXXII
Jan. 25, 1998
Qualcomm Stadium, San Diego
Favorite: Packers by 11½—Attendance: 68,912

Green Bay (15-3) . . . . .7 7 3 7 —**24**
Denver (15-4) . . . . .7 10 7 7 —**31**
MVP: Denver RB Terrell Davis (30 carries, 157 yds, 3 TD)

1998 SEASON

AFC Playoffs

First Round . . . . .at *Miami 24, *Buffalo 17
at Jacksonville 25, *New England 10
Second Round . . . . .at NY Jets 34, Jacksonville 24
at Denver 38, Miami 3
Championship . . . . at Denver 23, NY Jets 10

NFC Playoffs

First Round . . . . . . .at *San Francisco 30, *Green Bay 27
*Arizona 20, at Dallas 7
Second Round . . . . .at Atlanta 20, San Francisco 18
at Minnesota 41, Arizona 21
Championship . . . . .Atlanta 30, at Minnesota 27 (OT)

Super Bowl XXXIII
Jan. 31, 1999
Pro Player Stadium, Miami
Favorite: Broncos by 7½—Attendance: 74,803

Denver (16-2) . . . . .7 10 0 17 — **34**
Atlanta (16-2) . . . . .3 3 0 13 — **19**
MVP: Denver QB John Elway (18 for 29, 336 yds, 1 TD, 1 Int and 1 rushing TD)

1999 SEASON

AFC Playoffs

First Round . . . . .at *Tennessee 22, *Buffalo 16
*Miami 20, at Seattle 17
Second Round . . . . .at Jacksonville 62, Miami 7
Tennessee 19, at Indianapolis 16
Championship . . . . . , . . .Tennessee 33, at Jacksonville 14

NFC Playoffs

First Round . . . . .at Washington 27, *Detroit 13
at *Minnesota 27, *Dallas 10
Second Round . . . . .at Tampa Bay 14, Washington 13
at St. Louis 49, Minnesota 37
Championship . . . . .at St. Louis 11, Tampa Bay 6

Super Bowl XXXIV
Jan. 30, 2000
Georgia Dome, Atlanta
Favorite: Rams by 7—Attendance: 72,625

St. Louis (15-3) . . . . .3 6 7 7 —**23**
Tennessee (16-3) . . . . .0 0 6 10 —**16**
MVP: St. Louis QB Kurt Warner (24 for 45, 414 yds, 2 TD)

2000 SEASON

AFC Playoffs

First Round . . . . .at Miami 23, *Indianapolis 17 (OT)
at *Baltimore 21, *Denver 3
Second Round . . . . .at Oakland 27, Miami 0
Baltimore 24, at Tennessee 10
Championship . . . . .Baltimore 16, at Oakland 3

NFC Playoffs

First Round . . . . .at New Orleans 31, *St. Louis 28
at *Philadelphia 21, *Tampa Bay 3
Second Round . . . . . . .at Minnesota 34, New Orleans 16
at NY Giants 20, Philadelphia 10
Championship . . . . .at NY Giants 41, Minnesota 0

Super Bowl XXXV

Jan. 28, 2001
Raymond James Stadium, Tampa
Favorite: Ravens by 3—Attendance: 71,921

Baltimore (15-4)		.7	3	14	10 — **34**
NY Giants (14-4)		.0	0	7	0 — **7**

MVP: Baltimore LB Ray Lewis (5 tackles, 4 passes defended)

2001 SEASON

AFC Playoffs

First Round . . . . .at Oakland 38, *NY Jets 24
*Baltimore 20, at *Miami 3
Second Round . . . .at New England 16, Oakland 13 (OT)
at Pittsburgh 27, Baltimore 10
Championship . . . . New England 24, at Pittsburgh 17

NFC Playoffs

First Round . . . . .at Philadelphia 31, *Tampa Bay 9
at *Green Bay 25, *San Francisco 15
Second Round . . . . .Philadelphia 33, at Chicago 19
at St. Louis 45, Green Bay 17
Championship . . . . .at St. Louis 29, Philadelphia 24

Super Bowl XXXVI

Feb. 3, 2002
Louisiana Superdome, New Orleans
Favorite: Rams by 14—Attendance: 72,922

St. Louis (16-2)		.3	0	14	— **17**
New England (13-5)		.0	14	3	3 — **20**

MVP: New England QB Tom Brady (16 for 27, 145 yds; 1 TD)

2002 SEASON

AFC Playoffs

First Round . . . . .at NY Jets 41, *Indianapolis 0
at Pittsburgh 36, *Cleveland 33
Second Round . . . . .at Tennessee 34, Pittsburgh 31 (OT)
at Oakland 30, NY Jets 10
Championship . . . . .at Oakland 41, Tennessee 24

NFC Playoffs

First Round . . . .*Atlanta 27, at Green Bay 7
at San Francisco 39, *NY Giants 38
Second Round . . . . .at Philadelphia 20, Atlanta 6
at Tampa Bay 31, San Francisco 6
Championship . . . . . . Tampa Bay 27, at Philadelphia 10

Super Bowl XXXVII

Jan. 26, 2003
Qualcomm Stadium, San Diego
Favorite: Raiders by 3½—Attendance: 67,603

Oakland (13-5)		.3	0	6	12 — **21**
Tampa Bay (14-4)		.3	17	14	14 — **48**

MVP: Tampa Bay S Dexter Jackson (2 interceptions for 34 yards)

2003 SEASON

AFC Playoffs

First Round . . . .*Tennessee 20, at Baltimore 17
at Indianapolis 41, *Denver 10
Second Round . . . . . .at New England 17, Tennessee 14
Indianapolis 38, at Kansas City 31
Championship . . . . at New England 24, Indianapolis 14

NFC Playoffs

First Round . . . . .at Carolina 29, *Dallas 10
at Green Bay 33, Seattle 27 (OT)
Second Round . . . . .Carolina 29, at St. Louis 23 (2OT)
at Philadelphia 20, Green Bay 17 (OT)
Championship . . . . .Carolina 14, at Philadelphia 3

Super Bowl XXXVIII

Feb. 1, 2004
Reliant Stadium, Houston
Favorite: Patriots by 7—Attendance: 71,525

Carolina (14-5)		.0	10	0	19 — **29**
New England (16-2)		.0	14	0	18 — **32**

MVP: New England QB Tom Brady (32 for 48, 354 yds, 3 TD, 1 Int)

2004 SEASON

AFC Playoffs

First Round . . . .*NY Jets 20, at San Diego 17 (OT)
at Indianapolis 49, *Denver 24
Second Round . . . . . . .at Pittsburgh 20, NY Jets 17 (OT)
at New England 20, Indianapolis 3
Championship . . . . . . New England 41, at Pittsburgh 27

NFC Playoffs

First Round . . . .*St. Louis 27, at Seattle 20
*Minnesota 31, at Green Bay 17
Second Round . . . . .at Atlanta 47, St. Louis 17
at Philadelphia 27, Minnesota 14
Championship . . . . .at Philadelphia 27, Atlanta 10

Super Bowl XXXIX

Feb. 6, 2005
ALLTEL Stadium, Jacksonville
Favorite: Patriots by 7—Attendance: 78,125

New England (16-2)		.0	7	7	10 — **24**
Philadelphia (15-3)		.0	7	7	7 — **21**

MVP: New England WR Deion Branch (11 catches, 133 yds)

2005 SEASON

AFC Playoffs

First Round . . . . . . .at New England 28, *Jacksonville 3
*Pittsburgh 31, at Cincinnati 17
Second Round . . . . . . .at Denver 27, New England 13
Pittsburgh 21, at Indianapolis 18
Championship . . . . Pittsburgh 34, at Denver 17

NFC Playoffs

First Round . . . .*Washington 17, at Tampa Bay 10
*Carolina 23, at NY Giants 0
Second Round . . . . .at Seattle 20, Washington 10
Carolina 29, at Chicago 21
Championship . . . . .at Seattle 34, Carolina 14

Super Bowl XL

Feb. 5, 2006
Ford Field, Detroit
Favorite: Steelers by 3½—Attendance: 68,206

Seattle (15-3)		.3	0	7	0 — **10**
Pittsburgh (14-5)		.0	7	7	7 — **21**

MVP: Pittsburgh WR Hines Ward (5 catches, 123 yds, 1 TD)

Before the Super Bowl

The first NFL champion was the Akron Pros in 1920, when the league was called the American Professional Football Association (APFA) and the title went to the team with the best regular season record. The APFA changed its name to the National Football League in 1922.

The first playoff game with the championship at stake came in 1932, when the Chicago Bears (6-1-6) and Portsmouth (Ohio) Spartans (6-1-4) ended the regular season tied for first place. The Bears won the subsequent playoff, 9-0. Due to a snowstorm and cold weather, the game was moved from Wrigley Field to an improvised 80-yard dirt field at Chicago Stadium, making it the first indoor title game as well.

The NFL Championship Game decided the league title until the NFL merged with the AFL and the first Super Bowl was played following the 1966 season.

NFL Champions, 1920-32

Winning player-coaches noted by position.

Multiple winners: Canton-Cleveland Bulldogs and Green Bay (3); Chicago Staleys/Bears (2).

Year	Champion	Head Coach	Year	Champion	Head Coach
1920	Akron Pros	Fritz Pollard, HB & Elgie Tobin, QB	1927	New York Giants	Earl Potteiger, QB
			1928	Providence Steam Roller	Jimmy Conzelman, HB
1921	Chicago Staleys	George Halas, E	1929	Green Bay Packers	Curly Lambeau, QB
1922	Canton Bulldogs	Guy Chamberlin, E	1930	Green Bay Packers	Curly Lambeau
1923	Canton Bulldogs	Guy Chamberlin, E	1931	Green Bay Packers	Curly Lambeau
1924	Cleveland Bulldogs	Guy Chamberlin, E	1932	Chicago Bears	Ralph Jones
1925	Chicago Cardinals	Norm Barry		(Bears beat Portsmouth-OH in playoff, 9-0)	
1926	Frankford Yellow Jackets	Guy Chamberlin, E			

NFL-NFC Championship Game

NFL Championship games from 1933-69 and NFC Championship games since the completion of the NFL-AFL merger following the 1969 season.

Multiple winners: Green Bay (10); Dallas (8); Chicago Bears and Washington (7); NY Giants (6); San Francisco, Cle-LA-St.L Rams and Philadelphia (5); Cleveland Browns, Detroit and Minnesota (4); Baltimore Colts (3).

Season	Winner	Head Coach	Score	Loser	Head Coach	Site
1933	Chicago Bears	George Halas	23-21	New York	Steve Owen	Chicago
1934	New York	Steve Owen	30-13	Chicago Bears	George Halas	New York
1935	Detroit	Potsy Clark	26-7	New York	Steve Owen	Detroit
1936	Green Bay	Curly Lambeau	21-6	Boston Redskins	Ray Flaherty	New York
1937	Washington Redskins	Ray Flaherty	28-21	Chicago Bears	George Halas	Chicago
1938	New York	Steve Owen	23-17	Green Bay	Curly Lambeau	New York
1939	Green Bay	Curly Lambeau	27-0	New York	Steve Owen	Milwaukee
1940	Chicago Bears	George Halas	73-0	Washington	Ray Flaherty	Washington
1941	Chicago Bears	George Halas	37-9	New York	Steve Owen	Chicago
1942	Washington	Ray Flaherty	14-6	Chicago Bears	Hunk Anderson & Luke Johnsos	Washington
1943	Chicago Bears	Hunk Anderson & Luke Johnsos	41-21	Washington	Arthur Bergman	Chicago
1944	Green Bay	Curly Lambeau	14-7	New York	Steve Owen	New York
1945	Cleveland Rams	Adam Walsh	15-14	Washington	Dudley DeGroot	Cleveland
1946	Chicago Bears	George Halas	24-14	New York	Steve Owen	New York
1947	Chicago Cardinals	Jimmy Conzelman	28-21	Philadelphia	Greasy Neale	Chicago
1948	Philadelphia	Greasy Neale	7-0	Chicago Cardinals	Jimmy Conzelman	Philadelphia
1949	Philadelphia	Greasy Neale	14-0	Los Angeles Rams	Clark Shaughnessy	Los Angeles
1950	Cleveland Browns	Paul Brown	30-28	Los Angeles	Joe Stydahar	Cleveland
1951	Los Angeles	Joe Stydahar	24-17	Cleveland	Paul Brown	Los Angeles
1952	Detroit	Buddy Parker	17-7	Cleveland	Paul Brown	Cleveland
1953	Detroit	Buddy Parker	17-16	Cleveland	Paul Brown	Detroit
1954	Cleveland	Paul Brown	56-10	Detroit	Buddy Parker	Cleveland
1955	Cleveland	Paul Brown	38-14	Los Angeles	Sid Gillman	Los Angeles
1956	New York	Jim Lee Howell	47-7	Chicago Bears	Paddy Driscoll	New York
1957	Detroit	George Wilson	59-14	Cleveland	Paul Brown	Detroit
1958	Balt. Colts	Weeb Ewbank	23-17*	New York	Jim Lee Howell	New York
1959	Balt. Colts	Weeb Ewbank	31-16	New York	Jim Lee Howell	Baltimore
1960	Philadelphia	Buck Shaw	17-13	Green Bay	Vince Lombardi	Philadelphia
1961	Green Bay	Vince Lombardi	37-0	New York	Allie Sherman	Green Bay
1962	Green Bay	Vince Lombardi	16-7	New York	Allie Sherman	New York
1963	Chicago	George Halas	14-10	New York	Allie Sherman	Chicago
1964	Cleveland	Blanton Collier	27-0	Balt. Colts	Don Shula	Cleveland
1965	Green Bay	Vince Lombardi	23-12	Cleveland	Blanton Collier	Green Bay
1966	Green Bay	Vince Lombardi	34-27	Dallas	Tom Landry	Dallas
1967	Green Bay	Vince Lombardi	21-17	Dallas	Tom Landry	Green Bay
1968	Balt. Colts	Don Shula	34-0	Cleveland	Blanton Collier	Cleveland

NFL-NFC Championship Game (Cont.)

Season	Winner	Head Coach	Score	Loser	Head Coach	Site
1969	Minnesota	Bud Grant	27-7	Cleveland	Blanton Collier	Minnesota
1970	Dallas	Tom Landry	17-10	San Francisco	Dick Nolan	San Francisco
1971	Dallas	Tom Landry	14-3	SanFrancisco	Dick Nolan	Dallas
1972	Washington	George Allen	26-3	Dallas	Tom Landry	Washington
1973	Minnesota	Bud Grant	27-10	Dallas	Tom Landry	Dallas
1974	Minnesota	Bud Grant	14-10	Los Angeles	Chuck Knox	Minnesota
1975	Dallas	Tom Landry	37-7	Los Angeles	Chuck Knox	Los Angeles
1976	Minnesota	Bud Grant	24-13	Los Angeles	Chuck Knox	Minnesota
1977	Dallas	Tom Landry	23-6	Minnesota	Bud Grant	Dallas
1978	Dallas	Tom Landry	28-0	Los Angeles	Ray Malavasi	Los Angele
1979	Los Angeles	Ray Malavasi	9-0	Tampa Bay	John McKay	Tampa Bay
1980	Philadelphia	Dick Vermeil	20-7	Dallas	Tom Landry	Philadelphia
1981	San Francisco	Bill Walsh	28-27	Dallas	Tom Landry	San Francisco
1982	Washington	Joe Gibbs	31-17	Dallas	Tom Landry	Washington
1983	Washington	Joe Gibbs	24-21	San Francisco	Bill Walsh	Washington
1984	San Francisco	Bill Walsh	23-0	Chicago	Mike Ditka	San Francisco
1985	Chicago	Mike Ditka	24-0	Los Angeles	John Robinson	Chicago
1986	New York	Bill Parcells	17-0	Washington	Joe Gibbs	New York
1987	Washington	Joe Gibbs	17-10	Minnesota	Jerry Burns	Washington
1988	San Francisco	Bill Walsh	28-3	Chicago	Mike Ditka	Chicago
1989	San Francisco	George Seifert	30-3	Los Angeles	John Robinson	San Francisco
1990	New York	Bill Parcells	15-13	San Francisco	George Seifert	San Francisco
1991	Washington	Joe Gibbs	41-10	Detroit	Wayne Fontes	Washington
1992	Dallas	Jimmy Johnson	30-20	San Francisco	George Seifert	San Francisco
1993	Dallas	Jimmy Johnson	38-21	San Francisco	George Seifert	Dallas
1994	San Francisco	George Seifert	38-28	Dallas	Barry Switzer	San Francisco
1995	Dallas	Barry Switzer	38-27	Green Bay	Mike Holmgren	Dallas
1996	Green Bay	Mike Holmgren	30-13	Carolina	Dom Capers	Green Bay
1997	Green Bay	Mike Holmgren	23-10	San Francisco	Steve Mariucci	San Francisco
1998	Atlanta	Dan Reeves	30-27*	Minnesota	Dennis Green	Minnesota
1999	St. Louis	Dick Vermeil	11-6	Tampa Bay	Tony Dungy	St. Louis
2000	New York	Jim Fassel	41-0	Minnesota	Dennis Green	New York
2001	St. Louis	Mike Martz	29-24	Philadelphia	Andy Reid	St. Louis
2002	Tampa Bay	Jon Gruden	27-10	Philadelphia	Andy Reid	Philadelphia
2003	Carolina	John Fox	14-3	Philadelphia	Andy Reid	Philadelphia
2004	Philadelphia	Andy Reid	27-10	Atlanta	Jim Mora Jr.	Philadelphia
2005	Seattle	Mike Holmgren	34-14	Carolina	John Fox	Seattle

*Sudden death overtime

NFL-NFC Championship Game Appearances

App		W	L	Pct	PF	PA	App		W	L	Pct	PF	PA
17	NY Giants	6	11	.353	281	322	8	Minnesota	4	4	.500	135	151
16	Dallas Cowboys	8	8	.500	361	319	6	Detroit	4	2	.667	139	141
14	Cle-LA-St.L Rams	5	9	.357	163	300	4	Baltimore Colts	3	1	.750	88	60
13	Green Bay Packers	10	3	.769	303	177	3	Tampa Bay	1	2	.333	33	30
13	Chicago Bears	7	6	.538	286	245	3	Carolina	1	2	.333	41	67
12	Boston-Wash. Redskins	7	5	.583	222	255	2	Chicago Cardinals	1	1	.500	28	28
12	San Francisco	5	7	.417	245	222	2	Atlanta	1	1	.500	40	54
11	Cleveland Browns	4	7	.364	224	253	1	Seattle	1	0	1.000	34	14
9	Philadelphia	5	4	.556	143	128							

AFL-AFC Championship Game

AFL Championship games from 1960-69 and AFC Championship games since the completion of the NFL-AFL merger following the 1969 season.

Multiple winners: Buffalo, Denver and Pittsburgh (6); Miami, Oakland-LA Raiders and New England (5); Dallas Texans-KC Chiefs and Houston Oilers-Tennessee Titans (3); Cincinnati and San Diego (2).

Season	Winner	Head Coach	Score	Loser	Head Coach	Site
1960	Houston	Lou Rymkus	24-16	LA Chargers	Sid Gillman	Houston
1961	Houston	Wally Lemm	10-3	SD Chargers	Sid Gillman	San Diego
1962	Dallas	Hank Stram	20-17*	Houston	Pop Ivy	Houston
1963	San Diego	Sid Gillman	51-10	Boston Patriots	Mike Holovak	San Diego
1964	Buffalo	Lou Saban	20-7	SanDiego	Sid Gillman	Buffalo
1965	Buffalo	Lou Saban	23-0	San Diego	Sid Gillman	San Diego
1966	Kansas City	Hank Stram	31-7	Buffalo	Joe Collier	Buffalo
1967	Oakland	John Rauch	40-7	Houston	Wally Lemm	Oakland
1968	NY Jets	Weeb Ewbank	27-23	Oakland	John Rauch	New York
1969	Kansas City	Hank Stram	17-7	Oakland	John Madden	Oakland
1970	Balt. Colts	Don McCafferty	27-17	Oakland	John Madden	Baltimore
1971	Miami	Don Shula	21-0	Balt. Colts	Don McCafferty	Miami

Season	Winner	Head Coach	Score	Loser	Head Coach	Site
1972	Miami	Don Shula	21-17	Pittsburgh	Chuck Noll	Pittsburgh
1973	Miami	Don Shula	27-10	Oakland	John Madden	Miami
1974	Pittsburgh	Chuck Noll	24-13	Oakland	John Madden	Oakland
1975	Pittsburgh	Chuck Noll	16-10	Oakland	John Madden	Pittsburgh
1976	Oakland	John Madden	24-7	Pittsburgh	Chuck Noll	Oakland
1977	Denver	Red Miller	20-17	Oakland	John Madden	Denver
1978	Pittsburgh	Chuck Noll	34-5	Houston	Bum Phillips	Pittsburgh
1979	Pittsburgh	Chuck Noll	27-13	Houston	Bum Phillips	Pittsburgh
1980	Oakland	Tom Flores	34-27	San Diego	Don Coryell	San Diego
1981	Cincinnati	Forrest Gregg	27-7	San Diego	Don Coryell	Cincinnati
1982	Miami	Don Shula	14-0	NYJets	Walt Michaels	Miami
1983	LA Raiders	Tom Flores	30-14	Seattle	Chuck Knox	Los Angeles
1984	Miami	Don Shula	45-28	Pittsburgh	Chuck Noll	Miami
1985	New England	Raymond Berry	31-14	Miami	Don Shula	Miami
1986	Denver	Dan Reeves	23-20*	Cleveland	Marty Schottenheimer	Cleveland
1987	Denver	Dan Reeves	38-33	Cleveland	Marty Schottenheimer	Denver
1988	Cincinnati	Sam Wyche	21-10	Buffalo	Marv Levy	Cincinnati
1989	Denver	Dan Reeves	37-21	Cleveland	Bud Carson	Denver
1990	Buffalo	Marv Levy	51-3	LA Raiders	Art Shell	Buffalo
1991	Buffalo	Marv Levy	10-7	Denver	Dan Reeves	Buffalo
1992	Buffalo	Marv Levy	29-10	Miami	Don Shula	Miami
1993	Buffalo	Marv Levy	30-13	Kansas City	Marty Schottenheimer	Buffalo
1994	San Diego	Bobby Ross	17-13	Pittsburgh	Bill Cowher	Pittsburgh
1995	Pittsburgh	Bill Cowher	20-16	Indianapolis	Ted Marchibroda	Pittsburgh
1996	New England	Bill Parcells	20-6	Jacksonville	Tom Coughlin	New England
1997	Denver	Mike Shanahan	24-21	Pittsburgh	Bill Cowher	Pittsburgh
1998	Denver	Mike Shanahan	23-10	NY Jets	Bill Parcells	Denver
1999	Tennessee	Jeff Fisher	33-14	Jacksonville	Tom Coughlin	Jacksonville
2000	Balt. Ravens	Brian Billick	16-3	Oakland	Jon Gruden	Oakland
2001	New England	Bill Belichick	24-17	Pittsburgh	Bill Cowher	Pittsburgh
2002	Oakland	Bill Callahan	41-24	Tennessee	Jeff Fisher	Oakland
2003	New England	Bill Belichick	24-14	Indianapolis	Tony Dungy	New England
2004	New England	Bill Belichick	41-27	Pittsburgh	Bill Cowher	Pittsburgh
2005	Pittsburgh	Bill Cowher	34-17	Denver	Mike Shanahan	Denver

*Sudden death overtime

AFL-AFC Championship Game Appearances

App		W	L	Pct	PF	PA	App		W	L	Pct	PF	PA
14	Oakland-LA Raiders	5	9	.357	272	304	4	Dallas Texans/KC Chiefs	3	1	.750	81	61
12	Pittsburgh	6	6	.500	258	229	4	Baltimore-Indy Colts	1	3	.250	57	82
8	Buffalo	6	2	.750	180	92	3	NY Jets	1	2	.333	37	60
8	Denver	6	2	.750	189	166	3	Cleveland	0	3	.000	74	98
8	Houston Oilers/Ten. Titans	3	5	.375	133	195	2	Cincinnati	2	0	1.000	48	17
5	LA-San Diego Chargers	2	6	.250	128	161	2	Jacksonville	0	2	.000	20	53
7	Miami	5	2	.714	152	115	1	Baltimore Ravens	1	0	1.000	16	3
6	Boston-NE Patriots	5	1	.833	150	129	1	Seattle	0	1	.000	14	30

NFL Divisional Champions

The NFL adopted divisional play for the first time in 1967, splitting both conferences into two four-team divisions—the Capitol and Century divisions in the East and the Central and Coastal divisions in the West. A merger with the AFL in 1970 increased NFL membership to 26 teams and made it necessary for realignment. Two 13-team conferences—the AFC and NFC—were formed by moving established NFL clubs in Baltimore, Cleveland and Pittsburgh to the AFC and rearranging both conferences into Eastern, Central and Western divisions. Expansion has since increased the league to 32 teams (beginning in 2002) with four NFC divisions and four AFC divisions, all with four teams each.

Division champions are listed below; teams that went on to win the Super Bowl are in **bold** type. Note that in the 1980 season, Oakland won the Super Bowl as a wild card team, as did Denver in 1997, Baltimore in 2000 and Pittsburgh in 2005; and in 1982, the players' strike shortened the regular season to nine games and eliminated divisional play for one season.

Multiple champions (since 1970): **AFC**–Pittsburgh (17); Miami and Oakland-LA Raiders (12); Denver (10); Baltimore-Indianapolis Colts (9); New England (8); Buffalo (7); Cincinnati, Cleveland and San Diego (6); Kansas City (5); Houston Oilers-Tennessee Titans (4); Jacksonville, NY Jets and Seattle (2). **NFC**–San Francisco (17); Dallas (15); Minnesota (14); LA-St. Louis Rams (11); Chicago (8); Green Bay (7); NY Giants, Philadelphia and Washington (6); Tampa Bay (5); Atlanta and Detroit (3); Carolina, New Orleans, Seattle and St. Louis Cardinals (2).

American Football League			National Football League		
Season	**East**	**West**	**Season**	**East**	**West**
1966	Buffalo	Kansas City	1966	Dallas	**Green Bay**

Season	**East**	**West**	**Season**	**Capitol**	**Century**	**Central**	**Coastal**
1967	Houston	Oakland	1967	Dallas	Cleveland	**Green Bay**	LA Rams
1968	**NY Jets**	Oakland	1968	Dallas	Cleveland	Minnesota	Baltimore
1969	NY Jets	Oakland	1969	Dallas	Cleveland	Minnesota	LA Rams

Note: Kansas City, an AFL second-place team, won the Super Bowl in the 1969 season.

NFL Divisional Champions (Cont.)

American Football Conference

Season	East	Central	West
1970	**Balt. Colts**	Cincinnati	Oakland
1971	Miami	Cleveland	Kansas City
1972	**Miami**	Pittsburgh	Oakland
1973	**Miami**	Cincinnati	Oakland
1974	Miami	**Pittsburgh**	Oakland
1975	Balt.Colts	**Pittsburgh**	Oakland
1976	Balt.Colts	Pittsburgh	**Oakland**
1977	Balt.Colts	Pittsburgh	Denver
1978	New England	**Pittsburgh**	Denver
1979	Miami	**Pittsburgh**	San Diego
1980	Buffalo	Cleveland	San Diego
1981	Miami	Cincinnati	San Diego
1982	—	—	—
1983	Miami	Pittsburgh	**LA Raiders**
1984	Miami	Pittsburgh	Denver
1985	Miami	Cleveland	LA Raiders
1986	New England	Cleveland	Denver
1987	Indianapolis	Cleveland	Denver
1988	Buffalo	Cincinnati	Seattle
1989	Buffalo	Cleveland	Denver
1990	Buffalo	Cincinnati	LA Raiders
1991	Buffalo	Houston	Denver
1992	Miami	Pittsburgh	San Diego
1993	Buffalo	Houston	Kansas City
1994	Miami	Pittsburgh	San Diego
1995	Buffalo	Pittsburgh	Kansas City
1996	New England	Pittsburgh	Denver
1997	New England	Pittsburgh	Kansas City
1998	NY Jets	Jacksonville	**Denver**
1999	Indianapolis	Jacksonville	Seattle
2000	Miami	Tennessee	Oakland
2001	**New England**	Pittsburgh	Oakland

Season	East	North	South	West
2002	NY Jets	Pittsburgh	Tennessee	Oakland
2003	**New Eng.**	Baltimore	Indianapolis	Kansas City
2004	**New Eng.**	Pittsburgh	Indianapolis	San Diego
2005	New Eng.	Cincinnati	Indianapolis	Denver

National Football Conference

Season	East	Central	West
1970	Dallas	Minnesota	San Francisco
1971	**Dallas**	Minnesota	San Francisco
1972	Washington	Green Bay	San Francisco
1973	Dallas	Minnesota	LA Rams
1974	St. Louis	Minnesota	LA Rams
1975	St. Louis	Minnesota	LA Rams
1976	Dallas	Minnesota	LA Rams
1977	**Dallas**	Minnesota	LA Rams
1978	Dallas	Minnesota	LA Rams
1979	Dallas	Tampa Bay	LA Rams
1980	Philadelphia	Minnesota	Atlanta
1981	Dallas	Tampa Bay	**San Francisco**
1982	—	—	—
1983	Washington	Detroit	San Francisco
1984	Washington	Chicago	**San Francisco**
1985	Dallas	**Chicago**	LA Rams
1986	**NY Giants**	Chicago	San Francisco
1987	**Washington**	Chicago	San Francisco
1988	Philadelphia	Chicago	**San Francisco**
1989	NY Giants	Minnesota	**San Francisco**
1990	**NY Giants**	Chicago	San Francisco
1991	**Washington**	Detroit	New Orleans
1992	**Dallas**	Minnesota	San Francisco
1993	**Dallas**	Detroit	San Francisco
1994	Dallas	Minnesota	**San Francisco**
1995	**Dallas**	Green Bay	San Francisco
1996	Dallas	**Green Bay**	Carolina
1997	NY Giants	Green Bay	San Francisco
1998	Dallas	Minnesota	Atlanta
1999	Washington	Tampa Bay	**St. Louis**
2000	NY Giants	Minnesota	New Orleans
2001	Philadelphia	Chicago	St. Louis

Season	East	North	South	West
2002	Philadelphia	Green Bay	**Tampa Bay**	San Fran.
2003	Philadelphia	Green Bay	Carolina	St. Louis
2004	Philadelphia	Green Bay	Atlanta	Seattle
2005	NY Giants	Chicago	Tampa Bay	Seattle

Overall Postseason Games

The postseason records of all NFL teams, ranked by number of playoff games participated in from 1933 through the 2005-06 postseason.

Gm		W	L	Pct	PF	PA
54	Dallas Cowboys	32	22	.593	1281	1008
46	Pittsburgh Steelers	28	18	.609	1066	928
43	Oakland-LA Raiders	25	18	.581	1028	797
43	Cle-LA-St.L Rams	19	24	.442	770	944
42	San Francisco 49ers	25	17	.595	1044	853
42	Minnesota Vikings	18	24	.429	824	957
39	Boston-Wash. Redskins	23	16	.590	805	672
39	Miami Dolphins	20	19	.513	780	848
38	Green Bay Packers	24	14	.632	888	723
38	New York Giants	16	22	.421	647	722
32	Denver Broncos	17	15	.531	694	794
32	Philadelphia Eagles	16	16	.500	606	561
31	Houston Oilers/Ten. Titans	14	17	.452	563	732
31	Cleveland Browns	11	20	.355	629	728
30	Chicago Bears	14	16	.467	619	614
29	Buffalo Bills	14	15	.483	681	658

Gm		W	L	Pct	PF	PA
29	Balt-Indianapolis Colts	13	16	.448	556	602
28	Boston-NE Patriots	17	11	.607	569	542
20	Dallas Texans/KC Chiefs	8	12	.400	332	422
19	LA-San Diego Chargers	7	12	.368	349	448
18	New York Jets	8	10	.444	372	352
17	Detroit Lions	7	10	.412	365	404
14	Atlanta Falcons	6	8	.429	298	331
14	Tampa Bay Buccaneers	6	8	.429	216	255
13	Cincinnati Bengals	5	8	.385	263	268
13	Seattle Seahawks	5	8	.385	256	264
9	Jacksonville Jaguars	4	5	.444	211	228
7	Baltimore Ravens	5	2	.714	142	73
7	Chi-St.L.-Ari. Cardinals	2	5	.286	122	182
9	Carolina Panthers	6	3	.667	206	170
6	New Orleans Saints	1	5	.167	103	185

Champions of Leagues That No Longer Exist

No professional league in American sports has had to contend with more pretenders to the throne than the NFL. Eight times in nine decades, a rival league has risen up to challenge the NFL and seven of them went under in less than five seasons. Only the fourth American Football League (1960-69) succeeded, forcing the older league to sue for peace and a full partnership in 1966.

Of the seven leagues that didn't make it, only the All-America Football Conference (1946-49) lives on—the Cleveland Browns and San Francisco 49ers joined the NFL after the AAFC folded in 1949. The champions of leagues past are listed below.

American Football League I

Year		Head Coach
1926	Philadelphia Quakers (8-2)	Bob Folwell

Note: Philadelphia was challenged to a postseason game by the 7th place New York Giants (8-4-1) of the NFL. The Giants won, 31-0, in a snowstorm.

American Football League II

Year		Head Coach
1936	Boston Shamrocks (8-3)	George Kenneally
1937	Los Angeles Bulldogs (9-0)	Gus Henderson

Note: Boston was scheduled to play 2nd place Cleveland (5-2-2) in the '36 championship game, but the Shamrock players refused to participate because they were owed pay for past games.

American Football League III

Year		Head Coach
1940	Columbus Bullies (8-1-1)	Phil Bucklew
1941	Columbus Bullies (5-1-2)	Phil Bucklew

All-America Football Conference

Year	Winner	Head Coach	Score	Loser	Head Coach	Site
1946	Cleveland Browns	Paul Brown	14-9	NY Yankees	Ray Flaherty	Cleveland
1947	Cleveland Browns	Paul Brown	14-3	NY Yankees	Ray Flaherty	New York
1948	Cleveland Browns	Paul Brown	49-7	Buffalo Bills	Red Dawson	Cleveland
1949	Cleveland Browns	Paul Brown	21-7	S.F. 49ers	Buck Shaw	Cleveland

World Football League

Year	Winner	Head Coach	Score	Loser	Head Coach	Site
1974	Birmingham Americans	Jack Gotta	22-21	Florida Blazers	Jack Pardee	Birmingham

United States Football League

Year	Winner	Head Coach	Score	Loser	Head Coach	Site
1983	Michigan Panthers	Jim Stanley	24-22	Philadelphia Stars	Jim Mora	Denver
1984	Philadelphia Stars	Jim Mora	23-3	Arizona Wranglers	George Allen	Tampa
1985	Baltimore Stars	Jim Mora	28-24	Oakland Invaders	Charlie Sumner	E. Rutherford

XFL

Year	Winner	Head Coach	Score	Loser	Head Coach	Site
2001	Los Angeles Xtreme	Al Luginbill	38-6	San Fran. Demons	Jim Skipper	Los Angeles

Defunct Leagues

AFL I (1926): Boston Bulldogs, Brooklyn Horseman, Chicago Bulls, Cleveland Panthers, Los Angeles Wildcats, New York Yankees, Newark Bears, Philadelphia Quakers, Rock Island Independents.

AFL II (1936-37): Boston Shamrocks (1936-37); Brooklyn Tigers (1936); Cincinnati Bengals (1937); Cleveland Rams (1936); Los Angeles Bulldogs (1937); New York Yankees (1936-37); Pittsburgh Americans (1936-37); Rochester Tigers (1936-37).

AFL III (1940-41): Boston Bears (1940); Buffalo Indians (1940-41); Cincinnati Bengals (1940-41); Columbus Bullies (1940-41); Milwaukee Chiefs (1940-41); New York Yankees (1940) renamed Americans (1941).

AAFC (1946-49): Brooklyn Dodgers (1946-48) merged to become Brooklyn-New York Yankees (1949); Buffalo Bisons (1946) renamed Bills (1947-49); Chicago Rockets (1946-48) renamed Hornets (1949); Cleveland Browns (1946-49); Los Angeles Dons (1946-49); Miami Seahawks (1946) became Baltimore Colts (1947-49); New York Yankees (1946-48) merged to become Brooklyn-New York Yankees (1949); San Francisco 49ers (1946-49).

WFL (1974-75): Birmingham Americans (1974) renamed Vulcans (1975); Chicago Fire (1974) renamed Winds (1975); Detroit Wheels (1974); Florida Blazers (1974) became San Antonio Wings (1975); The Hawaiians (1974-75); Houston Texans (1974) became Shreveport (La.) Steamer (1974-75); Jacksonville Sharks (1974) renamed Express (1975); Memphis Southmen (1974) also known as Grizzlies (1975); New York Stars (1974) became Charlotte Hornets (1974-75); Philadelphia Bell (1974-75); Portland Storm (1974) renamed Thunder (1975); Southern California Sun (1974-75).

USFL (1983-85): Arizona Wranglers (1983-84) merged with Oklahoma to become Arizona Outlaws (1985); Birmingham Stallions (1983-85); Boston Breakers (1983) became New Orleans Breakers (1984) and then Portland Breakers (1985); Chicago Blitz (1983-84); Denver Gold (1983-85); Houston Gamblers (1984-85); Jacksonville Bulls (1984-85); Los Angeles Express (1983-85); Memphis Showboats (1984-85).

Michigan Panthers (1983-84) merged with Oakland (1985); New Jersey Generals (1983-85); Oakland Invaders (1983-85); Oklahoma Outlaws (1984) merged with Arizona to become Arizona Outlaws (1985); Philadelphia Stars (1983-84) became Baltimore Stars (1985); Pittsburgh Maulers (1984); San Antonio Gunslingers (1984-85); Tampa Bay Bandits (1983-85); Washington Federals (1983-84) became Orlando Renegades (1985).

XFL (2001): Birmingham Thunderbolts, Chicago Enforcers, Las Vegas Outlaws, Los Angeles Xtreme, Memphis Maniax, New York New Jersey Hitmen, Orlando Rage, San Francisco Demons.

NFL Pro Bowl

A postseason All-Star game between the new league champion and a team of professional all-stars was added to the NFL schedule in 1939. In the first game at Wrigley Field in Los Angeles, the NY Giants beat a team made up of players from NFL teams and two independent clubs in Los Angeles (the LA Bulldogs and Hollywood Stars). An all-NFL All-Star team provided the opposition over the next four seasons, but the game was cancelled in 1943.

The Pro Bowl was revived in 1951 as a contest between conference all-star teams: American vs National (1951-53), Eastern vs Western (1954-70), and AFC vs NFC (since 1971). The current AFC-NFC series is tied, 18-18.

The MVP trophy was named the Dan McGuire Award in 1984 after the late SF 49ers publicist and *Honolulu Advertiser* sports columnist.

Year	Winner	Score	Loser
1939	NY Giants	13-10	All-Stars
1940	Green Bay	16- 7	All-Stars
1940	Chicago Bears	28-14	All-Stars
1942	Chicago Bears	35-24	All-Stars
1942	All-Stars	17-14	Washington
1943-50		No game	

Year	Winner	MVP
1951	American, 28-27	Otto Graham, Cle., QB
1952	National, 30-13	Dan Towler, LA Rams, HB
1953	National, 27-7	Don Doll, Det., DB
1954	East, 20-9	Chuck Bednarik, Phi., LB
1955	West, 26-19	Billy Wilson, SF, E
1956	East, 31-30	Ollie Matson, Cards, HB
1957	West, 19-10	Back—Bert Rechichar, Bal.
		Line—Ernie Stautner, Pit.
1958	West, 26-7	Back—Hugh McElhenny, SF
		Line—Gene Brito, Wash.
1959	East, 28-21	Back—Frank Gifford, NY
		Line—Doug Atkins, Chi.
1960	West, 38-21	Back—Johnny Unitas, Bal.
		Line—Big Daddy Lipscomb, Pit.
1961	West, 35-31	Back—Johnny Unitas, Bal.
		Line—Sam Huff, NY
1962	West, 31-30	Back—Jim Brown, Cle.
		Line—Henry Jordan, GB
1963	East, 30-20	Back—Jim Brown, Cle.
		Line—Big Daddy Lipscomb, Pit.
1964	West, 31-17	Back—Johnny Unitas, Bal.
		Line—Gino Marchetti, Bal.
1965	West, 34-14	Back—Fran Tarkenton, Min.
		Line—Terry Barr, Det.
1966	East, 36-7	Back—Jim Brown, Cle.
		Line—Dale Meinhart, St. L.
1967	East, 20-10	Back—Gale Sayers, Chi.
		Line—Floyd Peters, Phi.
1968	West, 38-20	Back—Gale Sayers, Chi.
		Line—Dave Robinson, GB
1969	West, 10-7	Back—Roman Gabriel, LA Rams
		Line—Merlin Olsen, LA Rams
1970	West, 16-13	Back—Gale Sayers, Chi.
		Line—George Andrie, Dal.

Year	Winner	MVP
1971	NFC, 27-6	Back—Mel Renfro, Dal.
		Line—Fred Carr, GB
1972	AFC, 26-13	Off—Jan Stenerud, KC
		Def—Willie Lanier, KC
1973	AFC, 33-28	O.J. Simpson, Buf., RB
1974	AFC, 15-13	Garo Yepremian, Mia., PK
1975	NFC, 17-10	James Harris, LA Rams, QB
1976	NFC, 23-20	Billy Johnson, Hou., KR
1977	AFC, 24-14	Mel Blount, Pit., CB
1978	NFC, 14-13	Walter Payton, Chi., RB
1979	NFC, 13-7	Ahmad Rashad, Min., WR
1980	NFC, 37-27	Chuck Muncie, NO, RB
1981	NFC, 21-7	Eddie Murray, Det., PK
1982	AFC, 16-13	Kellen Winslow, SD, WR
		& Lee Roy Selmon, TB, DE
1983	NFC, 20-19	Dan Fouts, SD, QB
		& John Jefferson, GB, WR
1984	NFC, 45-3	Joe Theismann, Wash., QB
1985	AFC, 22-14	Mark Gastineau, NYJ, DE
1986	NFC, 28-24	Phil Simms, NYG, QB
1987	AFC, 10-6	Reggie White, Phi., DE
1988	AFC, 15-6	Bruce Smith, Buf., DE
1989	NFC, 34-3	Randall Cunningham, Phi., QB
1990	NFC, 27-21	Jerry Gray, LA Rams, CB
1991	AFC, 23-21	Jim Kelly, Buf., QB
1992	AFC, 21-15	Michael Irvin, Dal., WR
1993	AFC, 23-20 (OT)	Steve Tasker, Buf., Sp. Teams
1994	NFC, 17-3	Andre Rison, Atl., WR
1995	AFC, 41-13	Marshall Faulk, Ind., RB
1996	NFC, 20-13	Jerry Rice, SF, WR
1997	AFC, 26-23 (OT)	Mark Brunell, Jax, QB
1998	AFC, 29-24	Warren Moon, Sea., QB
1999	AFC, 23-10	Ty Law, NE, CB
		& Keyshawn Johnson, NYJ, WR
2000	NFC, 51-31	Randy Moss, Min., WR
2001	AFC, 38-17	Rich Gannon, Oak., QB
2002	AFC, 38-30	Rich Gannon, Oak., QB
2003	AFC, 45-20	Ricky Williams, Mia., RB
2004	NFC, 55-52	Marc Bulger, St.L, QB
2005	AFC, 38-27	Peyton Manning, Ind., QB
2006	NFC, 23-17	Derrick Brooks, TB, LB

Playing sites: Wrigley Field in Los Angeles (1939); Gilmore Stadium in Los Angeles (1940–both games); Polo Grounds in New York (Jan., 1942); Shibe Park in Philadelphia (Dec., 1942); Memorial Coliseum in Los Angeles (1951-72 and 1979); Texas Stadium in Irving, TX (1973); Arrowhead Stadium in Kansas City (1974); Orange Bowl in Miami (1975); Superdome in New Orleans (1976); Kingdome in Seattle (1977); Tampa Stadium in Tampa (1978) and Aloha Stadium in Honolulu (since 1980).

AFL All-Star Game

The AFL did not play an All-Star game after its first season in 1960 but did stage All-Star games from 1962-70. All-Star teams from the Eastern and Western divisions played each other every year except 1966 with the West winning the series, 6-2. In 1966, the league champion Buffalo Bills met an elite squad made up of the best players from the league's other eight clubs and lost, 30-19.

Year	Winner	MVP	Year	Winner	MVP
1962	West, 47-27	Cotton Davidson, Oak., QB	1967	East, 30-23	Off—Babe Parilli, Bos.
1963	West, 21-14	Off—Curtis McClinton, Dal.			Def—Verlon Biggs, NY
		Def—Earl Faison, SD	1968	East, 25-24	Off—Joe Namath, NY
1964	West, 27-24	Off—Keith Lincoln, SD			& Don Maynard, NY
		Def—Archie Matsos, Oak.			Def—Speedy Duncan, SD
1965	West, 38-14	Off—Keith Lincoln, SD	1969	West, 38-25	Off—Len Dawson, KC
		Def—Willie Brown, Den.			Def—George Webster, Hou.
1966	All-Stars 30	Off—Joe Namath, NY	1970	West, 26-3	John Hadl, SD, QB
	Buffalo 19	Def—Frank Buncom, SD			

Playing sites: Balboa Stadium in San Diego (1962-64); Jeppesen Stadium in Houston (1965); Rice Stadium in Houston (1966); Oakland Coliseum (1967); Gator Bowl in Jacksonville (1968-69) and Astrodome in Houston (1970).

NFL Franchise Origins

Here is what the current 32 teams in the National Football League have to show for the years they have put in as members of the American Professional Football Association (APFA), the NFL, the All-America Football Conference (AAFC) and the American Football League (AFL). Years given for league titles indicate seasons championships were won.

American Football Conference

	First Season	League Titles	Franchise Stops
Baltimore Ravens	1996 (NFL)	1 Super Bowl (2000)	• Baltimore (1996—)
Buffalo Bills	1960 (AFL)	2 AFL (1964-65)	• Buffalo (1960-72) Orchard Park, NY (1973—)
Cincinnati Bengals	1968 (AFL)	None	• Cincinnati (1968—)
Cleveland Browns	1946 (AAFC)	4 AAFC (1946-49) 4 NFL (1950,54-55,64)	• Cleveland (1946-95, 99—)
Denver Broncos	1960 (AFL)	2 Super Bowls (1997-98)	• Denver (1960—)
Houston Texans	2002 (NFL)	None	• Houston (2002—)
Indianapolis Colts	1953 (NFL)	3 NFL (1958-59,68) 1 Super Bowl (1970)	• Baltimore (1953-83) Indianapolis (1984—)
Jacksonville Jaguars	1995 (NFL)	None	• Jacksonville, FL (1995—)
Kansas City Chiefs	1960 (AFL)	3 AFL (1962,66,69) 1 Super Bowl (1969)	• Dallas (1960-62) Kansas City (1963—)
Miami Dolphins	1966 (AFL)	2 Super Bowls (1972-73)	• Miami (1966—)
New England Patriots	1960 (AFL)	3 Super Bowls (2001,03-04)	• Boston (1960-70) Foxboro, MA (1971—)
New York Jets	1960 (AFL)	1 AFL (1968) 1 Super Bowl (1968)	• New York (1960-83) E. Rutherford, NJ (1984—)
Oakland Raiders	1960 (AFL)	1 AFL (1967) 3 Super Bowls (1976,80,83)	• Oakland (1960-81, 1995—) Los Angeles (1982-94)
Pittsburgh Steelers	1933 (NFL)	5 Super Bowls (1974-75,78-79, 2005)	• Pittsburgh (1933—)
San Diego Chargers	1960 (AFL)	1 AFL (1963)	• Los Angeles (1960) San Diego (1961—)
Tennessee Titans	1960 (AFL)	2 AFL (1960-61)	• Houston (1960-96) Memphis (1997) Nashville (1998—)

National Football Conference

	First Season	League Titles	Franchise Stops
Arizona Cardinals	1920 (APFA)	2 NFL (1925,47)	• Chicago (1920-59) St. Louis (1960-87) Tempe, AZ (1988-2005) Glendale, AZ (2006—)
Atlanta Falcons	1966 (NFL)	None	• Atlanta (1966—)
Carolina Panthers	1995 (NFL)	None	• Clemson, SC (1995) Charlotte, NC (1996—)
Chicago Bears	1920 (APFA)	8 NFL (1921, 32-33,40-41,43,46,63) 1 Super Bowl (1985)	• Decatur, IL (1920) Chicago (1921—)
Dallas Cowboys	1960 (NFL)	5 Super Bowls (1971,77,92-93,95)	• Dallas (1960-70) Irving, TX (1971—)
Detroit Lions	1930 (NFL)	4 NFL (1935,52-53,57)	• Portsmouth, OH (1930-33) Detroit (1934-74, 2002—) Pontiac, MI (1975-2001)
Green Bay Packers	1921 (APFA)	11 NFL (1929-31,36,39,44,61-62,65-67) 3 Super Bowls (1966-67,96)	• Green Bay (1921—)
Minnesota Vikings	1961 (NFL)	1 NFL (1969)	• Bloomington, MN (1961-81) Minneapolis, MN (1982—)
New Orleans Saints	1967 (NFL)	None	• New Orleans (1967—)
New York Giants	1925 (NFL)	4 NFL (1927,34,38,56) 2 Super Bowls (1986,90)	• New York (1925-73,75) New Haven, CT (1973-74) E. Rutherford, NJ (1976—)
Philadelphia Eagles	1933 (NFL)	3 NFL (1948-49,60)	• Philadelphia (1933—)
St. Louis Rams	1937 (NFL)	2 NFL (1945,51) 1 Super Bowl (1999)	• Cleveland (1937-45) Los Angeles (1946-79) Anaheim (1980-94) St. Louis (1995—)
San Francisco 49ers	1946 (AAFC)	5 Super Bowls (1981,84,88-89,94)	• San Francisco (1946—)
Seattle Seahawks	1976 (NFL)	None	• Seattle (1976—)
Tampa Bay Buccaneers	1976 (NFL)	1 Super Bowl (2002)	• Tampa, FL (1976—)
Washington Redskins	1932 (NFL)	2 NFL (1937,42) 3 Super Bowls (1982,87,91)	• Boston (1932-36) Washington, DC (1937-96) Raljon, MD (1997—)

The Growth of the NFL

Of the 14 franchises that comprised the American Professional Football Association in 1920, only two remain—the Arizona Cardinals (then the Chicago Cardinals) and the Chicago Bears (originally the Decatur-IL Staleys). Green Bay joined the APFC in 1921 and the league changed its name to the NFL in 1922. Since then, 54 NFL clubs have come and gone, six rival leagues have expired and two other leagues have been swallowed up.

The NFL merged with the **All-America Football Conference** (1946-49) following the 1949 season and adopted three of its seven clubs—the Baltimore Colts, Cleveland Browns and San Francisco 49ers. The four remaining AAFC teams—the Brooklyn/NY Yankees, Buffalo Bills, Chicago Hornets and Los Angeles Dons—did not survive. After the 1950 season, the financially troubled Colts were sold back to the NFL. The league folded the team and added its players to the 1951 college draft pool. A new Baltimore franchise, also named the Colts, joined the NFL in 1953.

The formation of the **American Football League** (1960-69) was announced in 1959 with ownership lined up in eight cities—Boston, Buffalo, Dallas, Denver, Houston, Los Angeles, Minneapolis and New York. Set to begin play in the autumn of 1960, the AFL was stunned early that year when Minneapolis withdrew to accept an offer to join the NFL as an expansion team in 1961. The new league responded by choosing Oakland to replace Minneapolis and inherit the departed team's draft picks. Since no AFL team actually played in Minneapolis, it is not considered the original home of the Oakland Raiders.

In 1966, the NFL and AFL agreed to a merger that resulted in the first Super Bowl (originally called the AFL-NFL World Championship Game) following the '66 league playoffs. In 1970, the now 10-member AFL officially joined the NFL, forming a 26-team league made up of two conferences of three divisions each. In 2002, the 32-team league was realigned into two conferences of four divisions each.

Expansion/Merger Timetable

For teams currently in NFL.

1921–Green Bay Packers; **1925**–New York Giants; **1930**–Portsmouth-OH Spartans (now Detroit Lions); **1932**–Boston Braves (now Washington Redskins); **1933**–Philadelphia Eagles and Pittsburgh Pirates (now Steelers); **1937**–Cleveland Rams (now St. Louis); **1950**–added AAFC's Cleveland Browns and San Francisco 49ers; **1953**–Baltimore Colts (now Indianapolis).

1960–Dallas Cowboys; **1961**–Minnesota Vikings; **1966**–Atlanta Falcons; **1967**–New Orleans Saints; **1970**–added AFL's Boston Patriots (now New England), Buffalo Bills, Cincinnati Bengals (1968 expansion team), Denver Broncos, Houston Oilers (now Tennessee Titans), Kansas City Chiefs, Miami Dolphins (1966 expansion team), New York Jets, Oakland Raiders and San Diego Chargers (the AFL-NFL merger divided the league into two 13-team conferences with old-line NFL clubs Baltimore, Cleveland and Pittsburgh moving to the AFC); **1976**–Seattle Seahawks and Tampa Bay Buccaneers (Seattle was originally in the NFC West and Tampa Bay in the AFC West, but were switched to AFC West and NFC Central, respectively, in 1977); **1995**–Carolina Panthers and Jacksonville Jaguars; **1996**–Cleveland Browns move to Baltimore and become Ravens. City of Cleveland retains rights to team name, colors and all memorabilia; **1999**–Cleveland Browns return to the NFL. **2002**–Houston Texans. Seattle moves back to the NFC West.

City and Nickname Changes

1921—Decatur Staleys move to Chicago; **1922**—Chicago Staleys renamed Bears; **1933**—Boston Braves renamed Redskins; **1937**—Boston Redskins move to Washington; **1934**—Portsmouth (Ohio) Spartans move to Detroit and become Lions; **1941**—Pittsburgh Pirates renamed Steelers; **1943**—Philadelphia and Pittsburgh merge for one season and become Phil-Pitt, or the "Steagles"; **1944**—Chicago Cardinals and Pittsburgh merge for one season and become Card-Pitt; **1946**—Cleveland Rams move to Los Angeles.

1960—Chicago Cardinals move to St. Louis; **1961**—Los Angeles Chargers (AFL) move to San Diego; **1963**—New York Titans (AFL) renamed Jets and Dallas Texans (AFL) move to Kansas City and become Chiefs; **1971**—Boston Patriots become New England Patriots; **1982**—Oakland Raiders move to Los Angeles; **1984**—Baltimore Colts move to Indianapolis; **1988**—St. Louis Cardinals move to Phoenix; **1994**—Phoenix Cardinals become Arizona Cardinals; **1995**—L.A. Rams move to St. Louis and L.A. Raiders move back to Oakland; **1996**—Cleveland Browns move to Baltimore and become Ravens. City of Cleveland retains rights to team name, colors and all memorabilia; **1997**—Houston Oilers move to Memphis and become Tennessee Oilers; **1998**—Tennessee Oilers move to Nashville; **1999**—Tennessee Oilers renamed Titans.

Defunct NFL Teams

Teams that once played in the APFA and NFL, but no longer exist.

Akron-OH–Pros (1920-25) and Indians (1926); **Baltimore**–Colts (1950); **Boston**–Bulldogs (1926) and Yanks (1944-48); **Brooklyn**–Lions (1926), Dodgers (1930-43) and Tigers (1944); **Buffalo**–All-Americans (1920-23), Bisons (1924-25), Rangers (1926), Bisons (1927,1929); **Canton-OH**–Bulldogs (1920-23,1925-26); **Chicago**–Tigers (1920); **Cincinnati**–Celts (1921) and Reds (1933-34); **Cleveland**–Tigers (1920), Indians (1921), Indians (1923), Bulldogs (1924-25,1927) and Indians (1931); **Columbus-OH**–Panhandles (1920-22) and Tigers (1923-26); **Dallas**–Texans (1952); **Dayton-OH**–Triangles (1920-29).

Detroit–Heralds (1920-21), Panthers (1925-26) and Wolverines (1928); **Duluth-MN**–Kelleys (1923-25) and Eskimos (1926-27); **Evansville-IN**–Crimson Giants (1921-22); **Frankford-PA**–Yellow Jackets (1924-31); **Hammond-IN**–Pros (1920-26); **Hartford**–Blues (1926); **Kansas City**–Blues (1924) and Cowboys (1925-26); **Kenosha-WI**–Maroons (1924); **Los Angeles**–Buccaneers (1926); **Louisville**–Brecks (1921-23) and Colonels (1926); **Marion-OH**–Oorang Indians (1922-23); **Milwaukee**–Badgers (1922-26); **Minneapolis**–Marines (1922-24) and Red Jackets (1929-30); **Muncie-IN**–Flyers (1920-21).

New York–Giants (1921), Yankees (1927-28), Bulldogs (1949) and Yankees (1950-51); **Newark-NJ**–Tornadoes (1930); **Orange-NJ**–Tornadoes (1929); **Pottsville-PA**–Maroons (1925-28); **Providence-RI**–Steam Roller (1925-31); **Racine-WI**–Legion (1922-24) and Tornadoes (1926); **Rochester-NY**–Jeffersons (1920-25); **Rock Island-IL**–Independents (1920-26); **Staten Island-NY**–Stapletons (1929-32); **St. Louis**–All-Stars (1923) and Gunners (1934); **Toledo-OH**–Maroons (1922-23); **Tonawanda-NY**–Kardex (1921), also called Lumbermen; **Washington**–Senators (1921).

Annual NFL Leaders

Individual leaders in NFL (1932-69), NFC (since 1970), AFL (1960-69) and AFC (since 1970).

Passing

Since 1932, the NFL has used several formulas to determine passing leadership, from Total Yards alone (1932-37), to the current rating system—adopted in 1973—that takes Completions, Completion Percentage, Yards Gained, TD Passes, Interceptions, Interception Percentage and other factors into account. The quarterbacks listed below all led the league according to the system in use at the time.

NFL-NFC

Multiple winners: Sammy Baugh and Steve Young (6); Joe Montana and Roger Staubach (5); Arnie Herber, Sonny Jurgensen, Bart Starr and Norm Van Brocklin (3); Daunte Culpepper, Ed Danowski, Otto Graham, Cecil Isbell, Milt Plum, Kurt Warner and Bob Waterfield (2).

Year		Att	Cmp	Yds	TD	Year		Att	Cmp	Yds	TD
1932	Arnie Herber, GB	101	37	639	9	1969	Sonny Jurgensen, Wash	442	274	3102	22
1933	Harry Newman, NY	136	53	973	11	1970	John Brodie, SF	378	223	2941	24
1934	Arnie Herber, GB	115	42	799	8	1971	Roger Staubach, Dal	211	126	1882	15
1935	Ed Danowski, NY	113	57	794	10	1972	Norm Snead, NY	325	196	2307	17
1936	Arnie Herber, GB	173	77	1239	11	1973	Roger Staubach, Dal	286	179	2428	23
1937	Sammy Baugh, Wash	171	81	1127	8	1974	Sonny Jurgensen, Wash	167	107	1185	11
1938	Ed Danowski, NY	129	70	848	7	1975	Fran Tarkenton, Min	425	273	2994	25
1939	Parker Hall, Cle. Rams	208	106	1227	9	1976	James Harris, LA	158	91	1460	8
1940	Sammy Baugh, Wash	177	111	1367	12	1977	Roger Staubach, Dal	361	210	2620	18
1941	Cecil Isbell, GB	206	117	1479	15	1978	Roger Staubach, Dal	413	231	3190	25
1942	Cecil Isbell, GB	268	146	2021	24	1979	Roger Staubach, Dal	461	267	3586	27
1943	Sammy Baugh, Wash	239	133	1754	23	1980	Ron Jaworski, Phi	451	257	3529	27
1944	Frank Filchock, Wash	147	84	1139	13	1981	Joe Montana, SF	488	311	3565	19
1945	Sammy Baugh, Wash	182	128	1669	11	1982	Joe Theismann, Wash	252	161	2033	13
	& Sid Luckman, Chi. Bears	217	117	1725	14	1983	Steve Bartkowski, Atl	432	274	3167	22
1946	Bob Waterfield, LA	251	127	1747	18	1984	Joe Montana, SF	432	279	3630	28
1947	Sammy Baugh, Wash	354	210	2938	25	1985	Joe Montana, SF	494	303	3653	27
1948	Tommy Thompson, Phi	246	141	1965	25	1986	Tommy Kramer, Min	372	208	3000	24
1949	Sammy Baugh, Wash	255	145	1903	18	1987	Joe Montana, SF	398	266	3054	31
1950	Norm Van Brocklin, LA	233	127	2061	18	1988	Wade Wilson, Min	332	204	2746	15
1951	Bob Waterfield, LA	176	88	1566	13	1989	Don Majkowski, GB	599	353	4318	27
1952	Norm Van Brocklin, LA	205	113	1736	14	1990	Joe Montana, SF	520	321	3944	26
1953	Otto Graham, Cle	258	167	2722	11	1991	Steve Young, SF	279	180	2517	17
1954	Norm Van Brocklin, LA	260	139	2637	13	1992	Steve Young, SF	402	268	3465	25
1955	Otto Graham, Cle	185	98	1721	15	1993	Steve Young, SF	462	314	4023	29
1956	Ed Brown, Chi. Bears	168	96	1667	11	1994	Steve Young, SF	461	324	3969	35
1957	Tommy O'Connell, Cle	110	63	1229	9	1995	Brett Favre, GB	570	359	4413	38
1958	Eddie LeBaron, Wash	145	79	1365	11	1996	Steve Young, SF	316	214	2410	14
1959	Charlie Conerly, NY	194	113	1706	14	1997	Steve Young, SF	356	241	3029	19
1960	Milt Plum, Cle	250	151	2297	21	1998	Randall Cunningham, Min	425	259	3704	34
1961	Milt Plum, Cle	302	177	2416	16	1999	Kurt Warner, St.L	499	325	4353	41
1962	Bart Starr, GB	285	178	2438	12	2000	Trent Green, St.L	240	145	2063	16
1963	Y.A. Tittle, NY	367	221	3145	36	2001	Kurt Warner, St.L	546	375	4830	36
1964	Bart Starr, GB	272	163	2144	15	2002	Brad Johnson, TB	451	281	3049	22
1965	Rudy Bukich, Chi	312	176	2641	20	2003	Daunte Culpepper, Min	454	295	3479	25
1966	Bart Starr, GB	251	156	2257	14	2004	Daunte Culpepper, Min	548	379	4717	39
1967	Sonny Jurgensen, Wash	508	288	3747	31	2005	Matt Hasselbeck, Sea	449	294	3459	24
1968	Earl Morrall, Bal	317	182	2909	26						

AFL-AFC

Multiple winners: Dan Marino (5); Ken Anderson and Len Dawson (4); Peyton Manning (3); Bob Griese, Daryle Lamonica, Warren Moon and Ken Stabler (2).

Year		Att	Cmp	Yds	TD	Year		Att	Cmp	Yds	TD
1960	Jack Kemp, LA	406	211	3018	20	1983	Dan Marino, Mia	296	173	2210	20
1961	George Blanda, Hou	362	187	3330	36	1984	Dan Marino, Mia	564	362	5084	48
1962	Len Dawson, Dal	310	189	2759	29	1985	Ken O'Brien, NY	488	297	3888	25
1963	Tobin Rote, SD	286	170	2510	20	1986	Dan Marino, Mia	623	378	4746	44
1964	Len Dawson, KC	354	199	2879	30	1987	Bernie Kosar, Cle	389	241	3033	22
1965	John Hadl, SD	348	174	2798	20	1988	Boomer Esiason, Cin	388	223	3572	28
1966	Len Dawson, KC	284	159	2527	26	1989	Dan Marino, Mia	550	308	3997	24
1967	Daryle Lamonica, Oak	425	220	3228	30	1990	Warren Moon, Hou	584	362	4689	33
1968	Len Dawson, KC	224	131	2109	17	1991	Jim Kelly, Buf	474	304	3844	33
1969	Greg Cook, Cin	197	106	1854	15	1992	Warren Moon, Hou	346	224	2521	18
1970	Daryle Lamonica, Oak	356	179	2516	22	1993	John Elway, Den	551	348	4030	25
1971	Bob Griese, Mia	263	145	2089	19	1994	Dan Marino, Mia	615	385	4453	30
1972	Earl Morrall, Mia	150	83	1360	11	1995	Jim Harbaugh, Ind	314	200	2575	17
1973	Ken Stabler, Oak	260	163	1997	14	1996	John Elway, Den	466	287	3328	26
1974	Ken Anderson, Cin	328	213	2667	18	1997	Mark Brunell, Jax	435	264	3281	18
1975	Ken Anderson, Cin	377	228	3169	21	1998	Vinny Testaverde, NYJ	421	259	3256	29
1976	Ken Stabler, Oak	291	194	2737	27	1999	Peyton Manning, Ind	533	331	4135	26
1977	Bob Griese, Mia	307	180	2252	22	2000	Brian Griese, Den	336	216	2688	19
1978	Terry Bradshaw, Pit	368	207	2915	28	2001	Rich Gannon, Oak	549	361	3828	27
1979	Dan Fouts, SD	530	332	4082	24	2002	Chad Pennington, NYJ	399	275	3120	22
1980	Brian Sipe, Cle	554	337	4132	30	2003	Steve McNair, Ten	400	250	3215	24
1981	Ken Anderson, Cin	479	300	3753	29	2004	Peyton Manning, Ind	497	336	4557	49
1982	Ken Anderson, Cin	309	218	2495	12	2005	Peyton Manning, Ind	453	305	3747	28

Receptions

NFL-NFC

Multiple winners: Don Hutson (8); Raymond Berry, Tom Fears, Pete Pihos, Jerry Rice, Sterling Sharpe and Billy Wilson (3); Dwight Clark, Torry Holt, Herman Moore, Muhsin Muhammad, Ahmad Rashad and Charley Taylor (2).

Year	Player	No	Yds	Avg	TD	Year	Player	No	Yds	Avg	TD
1932	Ray Flaherty, NY	21	350	16.7	3	1970	Dick Gordon, Chi	71	1026	14.5	13
1933	Shipwreck Kelly, Bklyn	22	246	11.2	3	1971	Bob Tucker, NY	59	791	13.4	4
1934	Joe Carter, Phi	16	238	14.9	4	1972	Harold Jackson, Phi	62	1048	16.9	4
	& Red Badgro, NY	16	206	12.9	1	1973	Harold Carmichael, Phi	67	1116	16.7	9
1935	Tod Goodwin, NY	26	432	16.6	4	1974	Charles Young, Phi	63	696	11.0	3
1936	Don Hutson, GB	34	536	15.8	8	1975	Chuck Foreman, Min	73	691	9.5	9
1937	Don Hutson, GB	41	552	13.5	7	1976	Drew Pearson, Dal	58	806	13.9	6
1938	Gaynell Tinsley, Chi. Cards	41	516	12.6	1	1977	Ahmad Rashad, Min	51	681	13.4	2
1939	Don Hutson, GB	34	846	24.9	6	1978	Rickey Young, Min	88	704	8.0	5
1940	Don Looney, Phi	58	707	12.2	4	1979	Ahmad Rashad, Min	80	1156	14.5	9
1941	Don Hutson, GB	58	739	12.7	10	1980	Earl Cooper, SF	83	567	6.8	4
1942	Don Hutson, GB	74	1211	16.4	17	1981	Dwight Clark, SF	85	1105	13.0	4
1943	Don Hutson, GB	47	776	16.5	11	1982	Dwight Clark, SF	60	913	12.2	5
1944	Don Hutson, GB	58	866	14.9	9	1983	Roy Green, St.L	78	1227	15.7	14
1945	Don Hutson, GB	47	834	17.7	9		Charlie Brown, Wash	78	1225	15.7	8
1946	Jim Benton, LA	63	981	15.6	6		& Earnest Gray, NY	78	1139	14.6	5
1947	Jim Keane, Chi. Bears	64	910	14.2	10	1984	Art Monk, Wash	106	1372	12.9	7
1948	Tom Fears, LA	51	698	13.7	4	1985	Roger Craig, SF	92	1016	11.0	6
1949	Tom Fears, LA	77	1013	13.2	9	1986	Jerry Rice, SF	86	1570	18.3	15
1950	Tom Fears, LA	84	1116	13.3	7	1987	J.T. Smith, St.L	91	1117	12.3	8
1951	Elroy Hirsch, LA	66	1495	22.7	17	1988	Henry Ellard, LA	86	1414	16.4	10
1952	Mac Speedie, Cle	62	911	14.7	5	1989	Sterling Sharpe, GB	90	1423	15.8	12
1953	Pete Pihos, Phi	63	1049	16.7	10	1990	Jerry Rice, SF	100	1502	15.0	13
1954	Pete Pihos, Phi	60	872	14.5	10	1991	Michael Irvin, Dal	93	1523	16.4	8
	& Billy Wilson, SF	60	830	13.8	5	1992	Sterling Sharpe, GB	108	1461	13.5	13
1955	Pete Pihos, Phi	62	864	13.9	7	1993	Sterling Sharpe, GB	112	1274	11.4	11
1956	Billy Wilson, SF	60	889	14.8	5	1994	Cris Carter, Min	122	1256	10.3	7
1957	Billy Wilson, SF	52	757	14.6	6	1995	Herman Moore, Det	123	1686	13.7	14
1958	Raymond Berry, Bal	56	794	14.2	9	1996	Jerry Rice, SF	108	1254	11.6	8
	& Pete Retzlaff, Phi	56	766	13.7	2	1997	Herman Moore, Det	104	1293	12.4	8
1959	Raymond Berry, Bal	66	959	14.5	14	1998	Frank Sanders, Ari	89	1145	12.9	3
1960	Raymond Berry, Bal	74	1298	17.5	10	1999	Muhsin Muhammad, Car	96	1253	13.1	8
1961	Red Phillips, LA	78	1092	14.0	5	2000	Muhsin Muhammad, Car	102	1183	11.6	6
1962	Bobby Mitchell, Wash	72	1384	19.2	11	2001	Keyshawn Johnson, TB	106	1266	11.9	1
1963	Bobby Joe Conrad, St.L	73	967	13.2	10	2002	Randy Moss, Min	106	1347	12.7	7
1964	Johnny Morris, Chi. Bears	93	1200	12.9	10	2003	Torry Holt, St.L	117	1696	14.5	12
1965	Dave Parks, SF	80	1344	16.8	12	2004	Joe Horn, NO	94	1399	14.9	11
1966	Charley Taylor, Wash	72	1119	15.5	12		& Torry Holt, St.L	94	1372	14.6	10
1967	Charley Taylor, Wash	70	990	14.1	9	2005	Steve Smith, Car	103	1563	15.2	12
1968	Clifton McNeil, SF	71	994	14.0	7		& Larry Fitzgerald, Ari	103	1409	13.7	10
1969	Dan Abramowicz, NO	73	1015	13.9	7						

AFL-AFC

Multiple winners: Lionel Taylor (5); Lance Alworth, Haywood Jeffires, Lydell Mitchell and Kellen Winslow (3); Fred Biletnikoff, Todd Christensen, Marvin Harrison, Carl Pickens and Al Toon (2).

Year	Player	No	Yds	Avg	TD	Year	Player	No	Yds	Avg	TD
1960	Lionel Taylor, Den	92	1235	13.4	12	1983	Todd Christensen, LA	92	1247	13.6	12
1961	Lionel Taylor, Den	100	1176	11.8	4	1984	Ozzie Newsome, Cle	89	1001	11.2	5
1962	Lionel Taylor, Den	77	908	11.8	4	1985	Lionel James, SD	86	1027	11.9	6
1963	Lionel Taylor, Den	78	1101	14.1	10	1986	Todd Christensen, LA	95	1153	12.1	8
1964	Charley Hennigan, Hou	101	1546	15.3	8	1987	Al Toon, NY	68	976	14.4	5
1965	Lionel Taylor, Den	85	1131	13.3	6	1988	Al Toon, NY	93	1067	11.5	5
1966	Lance Alworth, SD	73	1383	18.9	13	1989	Andre Reed, Buf	88	1312	14.9	9
1967	George Sauer, NY	75	1189	15.9	6	1990	Haywood Jeffires, Hou	74	1048	14.2	8
1968	Lance Alworth, SD	68	1312	19.3	10		& Drew Hill, Hou	74	1019	13.8	5
1969	Lance Alworth, SD	64	1003	15.7	4	1991	Haywood Jeffires, Hou	100	1181	11.8	7
1970	Marlin Briscoe, Buf	57	1036	18.2	8	1992	Haywood Jeffires, Hou	90	913	10.1	9
1971	Fred Biletnikoff, Oak	61	929	15.2	9	1993	Reggie Langhorne, Ind	85	1038	12.2	3
1972	Fred Biletnikoff, Oak	58	802	13.8	4	1994	Ben Coates, NE	96	1174	12.2	7
1973	Fred Willis, Hou	57	371	6.5	1	1995	Carl Pickens, Cin	99	1234	12.5	17
1974	Lydell Mitchell, Bal	72	544	7.6	2	1996	Carl Pickens, Cin	100	1180	11.8	12
1975	Reggie Rucker, Cle	60	770	12.8	3	1997	Tim Brown, Oak	104	1408	13.5	5
	& Lydell Mitchell, Bal	60	544	9.1	4	1998	O.J. McDuffie, Mia	90	1050	11.7	7
1976	MacArthur Lane, KC	66	686	10.4	1	1999	Jimmy Smith, Jax	116	1636	14.1	6
1977	Lydell Mitchell, Bal	71	620	8.7	4	2000	Marvin Harrison, Ind	102	1413	13.9	14
1978	Steve Largent, Sea	71	1168	16.5	8	2001	Rod Smith, Den	113	1343	11.9	11
1979	Joe Washington, Bal	82	750	9.1	3	2002	Marvin Harrison, Ind	143	1722	12.0	11
1980	Kellen Winslow, SD	89	1290	14.5	9	2003	LaDainian Tomlinson, SD	100	725	7.3	4
1981	Kellen Winslow, SD	88	1075	12.2	10	2004	Tony Gonzalez, KC	102	1258	12.3	7
1982	Kellen Winslow, SD	54	721	13.4	6	2005	Chad Johnson, Cin	97	1432	14.8	9

Rushing
NFL-NFC

Multiple winners: Jim Brown (8); Walter Payton and Barry Sanders (5); Emmitt Smith and Steve Van Buren (4); Eric Dickerson (3); Shaun Alexander, Cliff Battles, John Brockington, Larry Brown, Bill Dudley, Leroy Kelly, Bill Paschal, Joe Perry, Gale Sayers, Stephen Davis and Whizzer White (2).

Year		Car	Yds	Avg	TD	Year		Car	Yds	Avg	TD
1932	Cliff Battles, Bos	148	576	3.9	3	1969	Gale Sayers, Chi	236	1032	4.4	8
1933	Jim Musick, Bos	173	809	4.7	5	1970	Larry Brown, Wash	237	1125	4.7	5
1934	Beattie Feathers, Chi. Bears	119	1004	8.4	8	1971	John Brockington, GB	216	1105	5.1	4
1935	Doug Russell, Chi. Cards	140	499	3.6	0	1972	Larry Brown, Wash	285	1216	4.3	8
1936	Tuffy Leemans, NY	206	830	4.0	2	1973	John Brockington, GB	265	1144	4.3	3
1937	Cliff Battles, Wash	216	874	4.0	5	1974	Lawrence McCutcheon, LA	236	1109	4.7	3
1938	Whizzer White, Pit	152	567	3.7	4	1975	Jim Otis, St.l.	269	1076	4.0	5
1939	Bill Osmanski, Chi. Bears	121	699	5.8	7	1976	Walter Payton, Chi	311	1390	4.5	13
1940	Whizzer White, Det	146	514	3.5	5	1977	Walter Payton, Chi	339	1852	5.5	14
1941	Pug Manders, Bklyn	111	486	4.4	5	1978	Walter Payton, Chi	333	1395	4.2	11
1942	Bill Dudley, Pit	162	696	4.3	5	1979	Walter Payton, Chi	369	1610	4.4	14
1943	Bill Paschal, NY	147	572	3.9	10	1980	Walter Payton, Chi	317	1460	4.6	6
1944	Bill Paschal, NY	196	737	3.8	9	1981	George Rogers, NO	378	1674	4.4	13
1945	Steve Van Buren, Phi	143	832	5.8	15	1982	Tony Dorsett, Dal	177	745	4.2	5
1946	Bill Dudley, Pit	146	604	4.1	3	1983	Eric Dickerson, LA	390	1808	4.6	18
1947	Steve Van Buren, Phi	217	1008	4.6	13	1984	Eric Dickerson, LA	379	2105	5.6	14
1948	Steve Van Buren, Phi	201	945	4.7	10	1985	Gerald Riggs, Atl	397	1719	4.3	10
1949	Steve Van Buren, Phi	263	1146	4.4	11	1986	Eric Dickerson, LA	404	1821	4.5	11
1950	Marion Motley, Cle	140	810	5.8	3	1987	Charles White, LA	324	1374	4.2	11
1951	Eddie Price, NY Giants	271	971	3.6	7	1988	Herschel Walker, Dal	361	1514	4.2	5
1952	Dan Towler, LA	156	894	5.7	10	1989	Barry Sanders, Det	280	1470	5.3	14
1953	Joe Perry, SF	192	1018	5.3	10	1990	Barry Sanders, Det	255	1304	5.1	13
1954	Joe Perry, SF	173	1049	6.1	8	1991	Emmitt Smith, Dal	365	1563	4.3	12
1955	Alan Ameche, Bal	213	961	4.5	9	1992	Emmitt Smith, Dal	373	1713	4.6	18
1956	Rick Casares, Chi. Bears	234	1126	4.8	12	1993	Emmitt Smith, Dal	283	1486	5.3	9
1957	Jim Brown, Cle	202	942	4.7	9	1994	Barry Sanders, Det	331	1883	5.7	7
1958	Jim Brown, Cle	257	1527	5.9	17	1995	Emmitt Smith, Dal	377	1773	4.7	25
1959	Jim Brown, Cle	290	1329	4.6	14	1996	Barry Sanders, Det	307	1553	5.1	11
1960	Jim Brown, Cle	215	1257	5.8	9	1997	Barry Sanders, Det	335	2053	6.1	11
1961	Jim Brown, Cle	305	1408	4.6	8	1998	Jamal Anderson, Atl	410	1846	4.5	14
1962	Jim Taylor, GB	272	1474	5.4	19	1999	Stephen Davis, Wash	290	1405	4.8	17
1963	Jim Brown, Cle	291	1863	6.4	12	2000	Robert Smith, Min	295	1521	5.2	7
1964	Jim Brown, Cle	280	1446	5.2	7	2001	Stephen Davis, Wash	356	1432	4.0	5
1965	Jim Brown, Cle	289	1544	5.3	17	2002	Deuce McAllister, NO	325	1388	4.3	13
1966	Gale Sayers, Chi	229	1231	5.4	8	2003	Ahman Green, GB	355	1883	5.3	15
1967	Leroy Kelly, Cle	235	1205	5.1	11	2004	Shaun Alexander, Sea	353	1696	4.8	16
1968	Leroy Kelly, Cle	248	1239	5.0	16	2005	Shaun Alexander, Sea	370	1880	5.1	27

Note: Jim Brown led the NFL in rushing eight of his nine years in the league. The one season he didn't win (1962) he finished fourth (996 yds) behind Jim Taylor, John Henry Johnson of Pittsburgh (1,141 yds) and Dick Bass of the LA Rams (1,033 yds).

AFL-AFC

Multiple winners: Earl Campbell and O.J. Simpson (4); Terrell Davis and Thurman Thomas (3); Eric Dickerson, Cookie Gilchrist, Edgerrin James, Floyd Little, Curtis Martin, Jim Nance and Curt Warner (2).

Year		Car	Yds	Avg	TD	Year		Car	Yds	Avg	TD
1960	Abner Haynes, Dal	157	875	5.6	9	1983	Curt Warner, Sea	335	1449	4.3	13
1961	Billy Cannon, Hou	200	948	4.7	6	1984	Earnest Jackson, SD	296	1179	4.0	8
1962	Cookie Gilchrist, Buf	214	1096	5.1	13	1985	Marcus Allen, LA	380	1759	4.6	11
1963	Clem Daniels, Oak	215	1099	5.1	3	1986	Curt Warner, Sea	319	1481	4.6	13
1964	Cookie Gilchrist, Buf	230	981	4.3	6	1987	Eric Dickerson, Ind	223	1011	4.5	5
1965	Paul Lowe, SD	222	1121	5.0	7	1988	Eric Dickerson, Ind	388	1659	4.3	14
1966	Jim Nance, Bos	299	1458	4.9	11	1989	Christian Okoye, KC	370	1480	4.0	12
1967	Jim Nance, Bos	269	1216	4.5	7	1990	Thurman Thomas, Buf	271	1297	4.8	11
1968	Paul Robinson, Cin	238	1023	4.3	8	1991	Thurman Thomas, Buf	288	1407	4.9	7
1969	Dickie Post, SD	182	873	4.8	6	1992	Barry Foster, Pit	390	1690	4.3	11
1970	Floyd Little, Den	209	901	4.3	3	1993	Thurman Thomas, Buf	355	1315	3.7	6
1971	Floyd Little, Den	284	1133	4.0	6	1994	Chris Warren, Sea	333	1545	4.6	9
1972	O.J. Simpson, Buf	292	1251	4.3	6	1995	Curtis Martin, NE	368	1487	4.0	14
1973	O.J. Simpson, Buf	332	2003	6.0	12	1996	Terrell Davis, Den	345	1538	4.5	13
1974	Otis Armstrong, Den	263	1407	5.3	9	1997	Terrell Davis, Den	369	1750	4.7	15
1975	O.J. Simpson, Buf	329	1817	5.5	16	1998	Terrell Davis, Den	392	2008	5.1	21
1976	O.J. Simpson, Buf	290	1503	5.2	8	1999	Edgerrin James, Ind	369	1553	4.2	13
1977	Mark van Eeghen, Oak	324	1273	3.9	7	2000	Edgerrin James, Ind	387	1709	4.4	13
1978	Earl Campbell, Hou	302	1450	4.8	13	2001	Priest Holmes, KC	327	1555	4.8	8
1979	Earl Campbell, Hou	368	1697	4.6	19	2002	Ricky Williams, Mia	383	1853	4.8	16
1980	Earl Campbell, Hou	373	1934	5.2	13	2003	Jamal Lewis, Bal	387	2066	5.3	14
1981	Earl Campbell, Hou	361	1376	3.8	10	2004	Curtis Martin, NYJ	371	1697	4.6	12
1982	Freeman McNeil, NY	151	786	5.2	6	2005	Larry Johnson, KC	336	1750	5.2	20

Note: Eric Dickerson was traded to Indianapolis from the NFC's LA Rams during the 1987 season. In three games with the Rams, he carried the ball 60 times for 277 yds, a 4.6 avg and 1 TD. His official AFC statistics above came in nine games with the Colts.

Scoring

NFL-NFC

Multiple winners: Don Hutson (5); Dutch Clark, Pat Harder, Paul Hornung, Chip Lohmiller and Mark Moseley (3); Kevin Butler, Mike Cofer, Fred Cox, Marshall Faulk, Jack Manders, Chester Marcol, Eddie Murray, Emmitt Smith, Gordy Soltau, Jeff Wilkins and Doak Walker (2).

Year		TD	FG	PAT	Pts	Year		TD	FG	PAT	Pts
1932	Dutch Clark, Portsmouth	6	3	10	55	1969	Fred Cox, Min	0	26	43	121
1933	Glenn Presnell, Portsmouth	6	6	10	64	1970	Fred Cox, Min	0	30	35	125
	& Ken Strong, NY	6	5	13	64	1971	Curt Knight, Wash	0	29	27	114
1934	Jack Manders, Chi. Bears	3	10	31	79	1972	Chester Marcol, GB	0	33	29	128
1935	Dutch Clark, Det	6	1	16	55	1973	David Ray, LA	0	30	40	130
1936	Dutch Clark, Det	7	4	19	73	1974	Chester Marcol, GB	0	25	19	94
1937	Jack Manders, Chi. Bears	5	8	15	69	1975	Chuck Foreman, Min	22	0	0	132
1938	Clarke Hinkle, GB	7	3	7	58	1976	Mark Moseley, Wash	0	22	31	97
1939	Andy Farkas, Wash	11	0	2	68	1977	Walter Payton, Chi	16	0	0	96
1940	Don Hutson, GB	7	0	15	57	1978	Frank Corral, LA	0	29	31	118
1941	Don Hutson, GB	12	1	20	95	1979	Mark Moseley, Wash	0	25	39	114
1942	Don Hutson, GB	17	1	33	138	1980	Eddie Murray, Det	0	27	35	116
1943	Don Hutson, GB	12	3	26	117	1981	Rafael Septien, Dal	0	27	40	121
1944	Don Hutson, GB	9	0	31	85		& Eddie Murray, Det	0	25	46	121
1945	Steve Van Buren, Phi	18	0	2	110	1982	Wendell Tyler, LA	13	0	0	78
1946	Ted Fritsch, GB	10	9	13	100	1983	Mark Moseley, Wash	0	33	62	161
1947	Pat Harder, Chi. Cards	7	7	39	102	1984	Ray Wersching, SF	0	25	56	131
1948	Pat Harder, Chi. Cards	6	7	53	110	1985	Kevin Butler, Chi	0	31	51	144
1949	Gene Roberts, NY Giants	17	0	0	102	1986	Kevin Butler, Chi	0	28	36	120
	& Pat Harder, Chi. Cards	8	3	45	102	1987	Jerry Rice, SF	23	0	0	138
1950	Doak Walker, Det	11	8	38	128	1988	Mike Cofer, SF	0	27	40	121
1951	Elroy Hirsch, LA	17	0	0	102	1989	Mike Cofer, SF	0	29	49	136
1952	Gordy Soltau, SF	7	6	34	94	1990	Chip Lohmiller, Wash	0	30	41	131
1953	Gordy Soltau, SF	6	10	48	114	1991	Chip Lohmiller, Wash	0	31	56	149
1954	Bobby Walston, Phi	11	4	36	114	1992	Chip Lohmiller, Wash	0	30	30	120
1955	Doak Walker, Det	7	9	27	96		& Morten Andersen, NO	0	29	33	120
1956	Bobby Layne, Det	5	12	33	99	1993	Jason Hanson, Det	0	34	28	130
1957	Sam Baker, Wash	1	14	29	77	1994	Emmitt Smith, Dal	22	0	0	132
	& Lou Groza, Cle	0	15	32	77		& Fuad Reveiz, Min	0	34	30	132
1958	Jim Brown, Cle	18	0	0	108	1995	Emmitt Smith, Dal	25	0	0	150
1959	Paul Hornung, GB	7	7	31	94	1996	John Kasay, Car	0	37	34	145
1960	Paul Hornung, GB	15	15	41	176	1997	Richie Cunningham, Dal	0	34	24	126
1961	Paul Hornung, GB	10	15	41	146	1998	Gary Anderson, Min	0	35	59	164
1962	Jim Taylor, GB	19	0	0	114	1999	Jeff Wilkins, St.L	0	20	64	124
1963	Don Chandler, NY	0	18	52	106	2000	Marshall Faulk, St.L	26	0	4	160
1964	Lenny Moore, Bal	20	0	0	120	2001	Marshall Faulk, St.L	21	0	2	128
1965	Gale Sayers, Chi	22	0	0	132	2002	Jay Feely, Atl	0	32	42	138
1966	Bruce Gossett, LA	0	28	29	113	2003	Jeff Wilkins, St.L	0	39	46	163
1967	Jim Bakken, St.L	0	27	36	117	2004	David Akers, Phi	0	27	41	122
1968	Leroy Kelly, Cle	20	0	0	120	2005	Shaun Alexander, Sea	28	0	0	168

AFL-AFC

Multiple winners: Gino Cappelletti (5); Gary Anderson (3); Jim Breech, Roy Gerela, Priest Holmes, Gene Mingo, Nick Lowery, John Smith, Pete Stoyanovich, Jim Turner and Mike Vanderjagt (2).

Year		TD	FG	PAT	Pts	Year		TD	FG	PAT	Pts
1960	Gene Mingo, Den	6	18	33	123	1983	Gary Anderson, Pit	0	27	38	119
1961	Gino Cappelletti, Bos	8	17	48	147	1984	Gary Anderson, Pit	0	24	45	117
1962	Gene Mingo, Den	4	27	32	137	1985	Gary Anderson, Pit	0	33	40	139
1963	Gino Cappelletti, Bos	2	22	35	113	1986	Tony Franklin, NE	0	32	44	140
1964	Gino Cappelletti, Bos	7	25	36	155	1987	Jim Breech, Cin	0	24	25	97
1965	Gino Cappelletti, Bos	9	17	27	132	1988	Scott Norwood, Buf	0	32	33	129
1966	Gino Cappelletti, Bos	6	16	35	119	1989	David Treadwell, Den	0	27	39	120
1967	George Blanda, Oak	0	20	56	116	1990	Nick Lowery, KC	0	34	37	139
1968	Jim Turner, NY	0	34	43	145	1991	Pete Stoyanovich, Mia	0	31	28	121
1969	Jim Turner, NY	0	32	33	129	1992	Pete Stoyanovich, Mia	0	30	34	124
1970	Jan Stenerud, KC	0	30	26	116	1993	Jeff Jaeger, LA	0	35	27	132
1971	Garo Yepremian, Mia	0	28	33	117	1994	John Carney, SD	0	34	33	135
1972	Bobby Howfield, NY	0	27	40	121	1995	Norm Johnson, Pit	0	34	39	141
1973	Roy Gerela, Pit	0	29	36	123	1996	Cary Blanchard, Ind	0	36	27	135
1974	Roy Gerela, Pit	0	20	33	93	1997	Mike Hollis, Jax	0	31	41	134
1975	O.J. Simpson, Buf	23	0	0	138	1998	Steve Christie, Buf	0	33	41	140
1976	Toni Linhart, Bal	0	20	49	109	1999	Mike Vanderjagt, Ind	0	34	43	145
1977	Errol Mann, Oak	0	20	39	99	2000	Matt Stover, Bal	0	35	30	135
1978	Pat Leahy, NY	0	22	41	107	2001	Mike Vanderjagt, Ind	0	28	41	125
1979	John Smith, NE	0	23	46	115	2002	Priest Holmes, KC	24	0	0	144
1980	John Smith, NE	0	26	51	129	2003	Priest Holmes, KC	27	0	0	162
1981	Nick Lowery, KC	0	26	37	115	2004	Adam Vinatieri, NE	0	31	48	141
	& Jim Breech, Cin	0	22	49	115	2005	Shayne Graham, Cin	0	28	47	131
1982	Marcus Allen, LA	14	0	0	84						

All-Time NFL Leaders
Through 2005 regular season.

CAREER
Players active in 2005 in **bold** type.

Passing Efficiency
Ratings based on performance standards established for completion percentage, average gain, touchdown percentage and interception percentage. Quarterbacks are allocated points according to how their statistics measure up to those standards. Minimum 1500 passing attempts.

		Yrs	Att	Cmp	Cmp%	Yards	Avg Gain	TD	TD%	Int	Int%	Rating
1	Steve Young	.15	4149	2667	64.3	33,124	7.98	232	5.6	107	2.6	96.8
2	**Kurt Warner**	.8	2340	1537	65.7	19,214	8.21	119	5.1	78	3.3	94.1
3	**Peyton Manning**	.8	4333	2769	63.9	33,189	7.66	244	5.6	130	3.0	93.5
4	Joe Montana	.15	5391	3409	63.2	40,551	7.52	273	5.1	139	2.6	92.3
5	**Daunte Culpepper**	.7	2607	1678	64.4	20,162	7.73	135	5.2	86	3.3	91.5
6	**Marc Bulger**	.4	1518	987	65.0	11,932	7.86	71	4.7	51	3.4	90.6
7	**Tom Brady**	.6	2548	1577	61.9	18,035	7.08	123	4.8	66	2.6	88.5
8	**Trent Green**	.8	3329	2022	60.7	25,621	7.70	150	4.5	92	2.8	88.3
9	**Matt Hasselbeck**	.7	2205	1342	60.9	15,925	7.22	96	4.4	57	2.6	86.6
10	Dan Marino	.17	8358	4967	59.4	61,361	7.34	420	5.0	252	3.0	86.4
11	**Brett Favre**	.15	7610	4678	61.5	53,615	7.05	396	5.2	255	3.4	86.0
12	**Jeff Garcia**	.7	2785	1695	60.9	19,076	6.85	126	4.5	71	2.5	85.8
13	**Drew Brees**	.5	1809	1125	62.2	12,348	6.83	80	4.4	53	2.9	84.9
14	**Brian Griese**	.8	2318	1463	63.1	16,344	7.05	103	4.4	78	3.4	84.8
15	Rich Gannon	.16	4206	2533	60.2	28,743	6.83	180	4.3	104	2.5	84.7
16	**Jake Delhomme**	.5	1503	888	59.1	11,160	7.43	75	5.0	52	3.5	84.5
17	Jim Kelly	.11	4779	2874	60.1	35,467	7.42	237	5.0	175	3.7	84.4
18	**Brad Johnson**	.12	3798	2350	61.9	25,798	6.79	155	4.1	102	2.7	84.4
19	**Donovan McNabb**	.7	2943	1718	58.4	19,433	6.60	134	4.6	66	2.2	84.1
20	**Mark Brunell**	.12	4334	2576	59.4	30,037	6.93	174	4.0	102	2.4	84.1
21	Roger Staubach	.11	2958	1685	57.0	22,700	7.67	153	5.2	109	3.7	83.4
22	**Steve McNair**	.11	3871	2305	59.5	27,141	7.01	156	4.0	103	2.7	83.3
23	Neil Lomax	.8	3153	1817	57.6	22,771	7.22	136	4.3	90	2.9	82.7
24	Sonny Jurgensen	.18	4262	2433	57.1	32,224	7.56	255	6.0	189	4.4	82.6
25	Len Dawson	.19	3741	2136	57.1	28,711	7.67	239	6.4	183	4.9	82.6

Note: The NFL does not recognize records from the All-American Football Conference (1946-49). If it did, **Otto Graham** would rank 10th (after Hasselbeck) with the following stats: 10 Yrs; 2,626 Att; 1,464 Comp; 55.8 Comp Pct; 23,584 Yards; 8.98 Avg Gain; 174 TD; 6.6 TD Pct; 135 Int; 5.1 Int Pct; and 86.6 Rating Pts.

Touchdown Passes

		No
1	Dan Marino	420
2	**Brett Favre**	396
3	Fran Tarkenton	342
4	John Elway	300
5	Warren Moon	291
6	Johnny Unitas	290
7	Joe Montana	273
8	**Vinny Testaverde**	269
9	Dave Krieg	261
10	Sonny Jurgensen	255
11	Dan Fouts	254
12	Boomer Esiason	247
13	John Hadl	244
	Drew Bledsoe	244
	Peyton Manning	244

		No
16	Len Dawson	239
17	Jim Kelly	237
18	George Blanda	236
19	Steve Young	232
20	John Brodie	214
21	Terry Bradshaw	212
	Y.A. Tittle	212
23	Jim Hart	209
24	Randall Cunningham	207
25	Jim Everett	203
26	Roman Gabriel	201
27	Phil Simms	199
28	Ken Anderson	197
29	Joe Ferguson	196
	Bobby Layne	196

		No
	Norm Snead	196
	Steve DeBerg	196
33	Ken Stabler	194
34	Bob Griese	192
35	Sammy Baugh	187
36	Craig Morton	183
37	Steve Grogan	182
38	Rich Gannon	180
39	Ron Jaworski	179
40	Babe Parilli	178
41	**Mark Brunell**	174
42	Charlie Conerly	173
	Joe Namath	173
	Norm Van Brocklin	173
	Kerry Collins	173

Note: The NFL does not recognize records from the All-American Football Conference (1946-49). If it did, **Y.A. Tittle** would move up from 21st to 14th (after Hadl) with 242 TDs and **Otto Graham** would rank 41st (after Parilli) with 174 TDs.

Passes Intercepted

		No
1	George Blanda	277
2	John Hadl	268
3	Fran Tarkenton	266
4	**Vinny Testaverde**	261
5	Norm Snead	257
6	**Brett Favre**	255
7	Johnny Unitas	253
8	Dan Marino	252
9	Jim Hart	247

		No
10	Bobby Layne	245
11	Dan Fouts	242
12	Warren Moon	233
13	John Elway	226
14	John Brodie	224
15	Ken Stabler	222
16	Y.A. Tittle	221
17	Joe Namath	220
	Babe Parilli	220

		No
19	Terry Bradshaw	210
20	Joe Ferguson	209
21	Steve Grogan	208
22	Steve DeBerg	204
23	Sammy Baugh	203
24	Dave Krieg	199
25	Jim Plunkett	198
	Drew Bledsoe	198

All-Time NFL Leaders (Cont.)

Passing Yards

		Yrs	Att	Comp	Pct	Yards
1	Dan Marino	.17	8358	4967	59.4	61,361
2	**Brett Favre**	.15	7610	4678	61.5	53,615
3	John Elway	.16	7250	4123	56.9	51,475
4	Warren Moon	.17	6823	3988	58.5	49,325
5	Fran Tarkenton	.18	6467	3686	57.0	47,003
6	**Vinny Testaverde**	19	6526	3691	56.6	45,252
7	**Drew Bledsoe**	.13	6548	3749	57.3	43,447
8	Dan Fouts	.15	5604	3297	58.8	43,040
9	Joe Montana	.15	5391	3409	63.2	40,551
10	Johnny Unitas	.18	5186	2830	54.6	40,239
11	Dave Krieg	.15	5311	3105	58.5	38,147
12	Boomer Esiason	.14	5205	2969	57.0	37,920
13	Jim Kelly	.11	4779	2874	60.1	35,467
14	Jim Everett	.12	4923	2841	57.7	34,837
15	Jim Hart	.19	5076	2593	51.1	34,665
16	Steve DeBerg	.17	5024	2874	57.2	34,241
17	**Kerry Collins**	.11	5082	2826	55.6	33,637
18	John Hadl	.16	4687	2363	50.4	33,503
19	Phil Simms	.14	4647	2576	55.4	33,462
20	**Peyton Manning**	.8	4333	2769	63.9	33,189
21	Steve Young	.15	4149	2667	64.3	33,124
22	Troy Aikman	.12	4715	2898	61.5	32,942
23	Ken Anderson	.16	4475	2654	59.3	32,838
24	Sonny Jurgensen	.18	4262	2433	57.1	32,224
25	John Brodie	.17	4491	2469	55.0	31,548

Note: The NFL does not recognize records from the All-American Football Conference (1946-49). If it did, **Y.A. Tittle** would rank 22nd (after Young) with the following stats: 17 Yrs; 4,395 Att; 2,427 Comp; 55.2 Pct; and 33,070 Yards.

Receptions

		Yrs	No	Yards	Avg	TD
1	Jerry Rice	.20	1549	22,895	14.8	197
2	Cris Carter	.16	1101	13,899	12.6	130
3	Tim Brown	.17	1094	14,934	13.7	100
4	Andre Reed	.16	951	13,198	13.9	87
5	Art Monk	.16	940	12,721	13.5	68
6	**Marvin Harrison**	.10	927	12,331	13.3	110
7	**Jimmy Smith**	.12	862	12,287	14.3	67
8	Irving Fryar	.17	851	12,785	15.0	84
9	Larry Centers	.14	827	6,797	8.2	28
10	Keenan McCardell	.14	825	10,680	12.9	62
11	Steve Largent	.14	819	13,089	16.0	100
12	Shannon Sharpe	.14	815	10,060	12.3	62
13	Henry Ellard	.16	814	13,777	16.9	65
14	**Isaac Bruce**	.12	813	12,278	15.1	77
15	**Rod Smith**	.11	797	10,877	13.6	65
16	**Marshall Faulk**	.12	767	6,875	9.0	36
17	James Lofton	.16	764	14,004	18.3	75
18	Charlie Joiner	.18	750	12,146	16.2	65
	Michael Irvin	.12	750	11,904	15.9	65
20	**Keyshawn Johnson**	10	744	9,756	13.1	60
21	Andre Rison	.12	743	10,205	13.7	84
22	**Terrell Owens**	.10	716	10,535	14.7	101
23	Gary Clark	.11	699	10,856	15.5	65
24	Terance Mathis	.13	689	8,809	12.8	63
25	**Eric Moulds**	.9	675	9,096	13.5	48

Rushing Yards

		Yrs	Car	Yards	Avg	TD
1	Emmitt Smith	.15	4409	18,355	4.2	164
2	Walter Payton	.13	3838	16,726	4.4	110
3	Barry Sanders	.10	3062	15,269	5.0	99
4	**Curtis Martin**	.11	3518	14,101	4.0	90
5	**Jerome Bettis**	.13	3479	13,662	3.9	91
6	Eric Dickerson	.11	2996	13,259	4.4	90
7	Tony Dorsett	.12	2936	12,739	4.3	77
8	Jim Brown	.9	2359	12,312	5.2	106
9	**Marshall Faulk**	.12	2836	12,279	4.3	100
10	Marcus Allen	.16	3022	12,243	4.1	123
11	Franco Harris	.13	2949	12,120	4.1	91
12	Thurman Thomas	.13	2877	12,074	4.2	65
13	John Riggins	.14	2916	11,352	3.9	104
14	O.J. Simpson	.11	2404	11,236	4.7	61
15	Ricky Watters	.10	2622	10,643	4.1	78
16	Eddie George	.9	2865	10,441	3.6	68
17	**Corey Dillon**	.9	2419	10,429	4.3	69
18	Ottis Anderson	.14	2562	10,273	4.0	81
19	Earl Campbell	.8	2187	9,407	4.3	74
20	**Edgerrin James**	.9	2188	9,226	4.2	64
21	**Tiki Barber**	.9	1890	8,787	4.6	50
22	Terry Allen	.10	2152	8,614	4.0	73
23	Jim Taylor	.10	1941	8,597	4.4	83
24	Joe Perry	.14	1737	8,378	4.8	53
25	**Fred Taylor**	.8	1831	8,367	4.6	51

Note: The NFL does not recognize records from the All-American Football Conference (1946-49). If it did, **Joe Perry** would move up from 24th to 19th (after Anderson) with the following stats: 16 Yrs; 1,929 Att; 9,723 Yards; 5.0 Avg; and 71 TD.

All-Purpose Yards

		Rush	Rec	Ret	Total
1	Jerry Rice	.645	22,895	6	23,546
2	Brian Mitchell	.1,967	2,336	19,027	23,330
3	Walter Payton	.16,726	4,538	539	21,803
4	Emmitt Smith	.18,355	3,224	-15	21,564
5	Tim Brown	.190	14,934	4,558	19,682
6	**Marshall Faulk**	.12,279	6,875	36	19,190
7	Barry Sanders	.15,269	2,921	118	18,308
8	Herschel Walker	.8,225	4,859	5,084	18,168
9	Marcus Allen	.12,243	5,411	-6	17,648
10	**Curtis Martin**	.14,101	3,329	-9	17,421
11	Eric Metcalf	.2,392	5,572	9,266	17,230
12	Thurman Thomas	.12,074	4,458	0	16,532
13	Tony Dorsett	.12,739	3,554	33	16,326
14	Henry Ellard	.50	13,777	1,891	15,718
15	Irving Fryar	.242	12,785	2,567	15,594
16	Jim Brown	.12,312	2,499	648	15,459
17	Eric Dickerson	.13,259	2,137	15	15,411
18	**Tiki Barber**	.8,787	4,718	1,727	15,232
19	**Jerome Bettis**	.13,662	1,449	2	15,113
20	Glyn Milburn	.817	1,322	12,772	14,911
21	James Brooks	.7,962	3,621	3,327	14,910
22	Ricky Watters	.10,643	4,248	0	14,891
23	Franco Harris	.12,120	2,287	215	14,622
24	O.J. Simpson	.11,236	2,142	990	14,368
25	James Lofton	.246	14,004	27	14,277

Years played: Allen (16), Barber (9), Bettis (12), Brooks (12), J. Brown (9), T. Brown (17), Dickerson (11), Dorsett (12), Ellard (16), Faulk (11), Fryar (17), Harris (13), Lofton (16), Martin (10), Metcalf (13), Milburn (9), Mitchell (14), Payton (13), Rice (20), Sanders (10), Simpson (11), Smith (15), Thomas (13), Walker (12) and Watters (10).

Scoring

Points

		Yrs	TD	FG	PAT	Total
1	Gary Anderson	23	0	538	820	2434
2	Morten Andersen	23	0	520	798	2358
3	George Blanda	26	9	335	943	2002
4	Norm Johnson	18	0	366	638	1736
5	Nick Lowery	18	0	383	562	1711
6	Jan Stenerud	19	0	373	580	1699
7	**John Carney**	18	0	390	464	1634
8	Eddie Murray	19	0	352	538	1594
	Matt Stover	15	0	380	454	1594
10	Al Del Greco	17	0	347	543	1584
11	**Jason Elam**	13	0	341	534	1557
12	Steve Christie	15	0	336	468	1476
13	Pat Leahy	18	0	304	558	1470
14	Jim Turner	16	1	304	521	1439
	Matt Bahr	17	0	300	522	1422
16	**Jason Hanson**	14	0	327	439	1420
17	Mark Moseley	16	0	300	482	1382
18	Jim Bakken	17	0	282	534	1380
19	Fred Cox	15	0	282	519	1365
20	Lou Groza	17	1	234	641	1349
21	**John Kasay**	15	0	310	375	1305
22	Jerry Rice	20	208	0	0	1256†
23	Jim Breech	14	0	243	517	1246
24	Pete Stoyanovich	12	0	272	420	1236
25	Chris Bahr	14	0	241	490	1213

†Rice's total includes four 2-point conversions.

Note: The NFL does not recognize records from the All-American Football Conference (1946-49). If it did, **Lou Groza** would move up from 20th to 8th (after Carney) with the following stats: 21 Yrs; 1 TD; 264 FG, 810 PAT; 1,608 Pts.

Interceptions

		Yrs	No	Yards	TD
1	Paul Krause	16	81	1185	3
2	Emlen Tunnell	14	79	1282	4
3	Rod Woodson	17	71	1483	12
4	Dick (Night Train) Lane	14	68	1207	5
5	Ken Riley	15	65	596	5

Sacks

		Yrs	No
1	Bruce Smith	19	200.0
2	Reggie White	15	198.0
3	Kevin Greene	15	160.0
4	Chris Doleman	15	150.5
5	Richard Dent	15	137.5
	John Randle	14	137.5

Note: The NFL did not begin officially compiling sacks until 1982. Deacon Jones, who played with the Rams, Chargers and Redskins from 1961-74, is often credited with 173.5 sacks. Jack Youngblood and Alan Page are unofficially credited with 150.5 and 148, respectively. Also, Lawrence Taylor has 142 career sacks if you count his rookie year of 1981, the year before sacks became an official stat.

Safeties

		Yrs	No
1	Ted Hendricks	15	4
	Doug English	10	4
3	Seventeen players tied with 3 each.		

Touchdowns

		Yrs	Rush	Rec	Ret	Total
1	Jerry Rice	20	10	197	1	208
2	Emmitt Smith	15	164	11	0	175
3	Marcus Allen	16	123	21	1	145
4	**Marshall Faulk**	12	100	36	0	136
5	Cris Carter	16	0	130	1	131
6	Jim Brown	9	106	20	0	126
7	Walter Payton	13	110	15	0	125
8	John Riggins	14	104	12	0	116
9	Lenny Moore	12	63	48	2	113
10	**Marvin Harrison**	10	0	110	0	110
11	Barry Sanders	10	99	10	0	109
12	Don Hutson	11	3	99	3	105
	Tim Brown	17	1	100	4	105
14	**Terrell Owens**	10	2	101	0	103
15	Steve Largent	14	1	100	0	101
16	**Shaun Alexander**	6	89	11	0	100
	Franco Harris	13	91	9	0	100
	Curtis Martin	11	90	10	0	100
19	**Randy Moss**	8	0	98	1	99
20	Eric Dickerson	11	90	6	0	96
21	**Jerome Bettis**	13	91	3	0	94
	Priest Holmes	9	86	8	0	94
23	Jim Taylor	10	83	10	0	93
24	Tony Dorsett	12	77	13	1	91
	Bobby Mitchell	11	18	65	8	91
	Ricky Watters	10	78	13	0	91

Kickoff Returns

Minimum 75 returns.

		Yrs	No	Yards	Avg	TD
1	Gale Sayers	7	91	2781	30.6	6
2	Lynn Chandnois	7	92	2720	29.6	3
3	Abe Woodson	9	193	5538	28.7	5
4	Buddy Young	6	90	2514	27.9	2
5	**Terrence McGee**	3	106	2921	27.6	4

Punting

Minimum 300 punts.

		Yrs	No	Yards	Avg
1	**Shane Lechler**	6	442	20,266	45.9
2	Sammy Baugh	16	338	15,245	45.1
3	Tommy Davis	11	511	22,833	44.7
4	Yale Lary	11	503	22,279	44.3
5	**Todd Sauerbrun**	11	832	36,600	44.0

Punt Returns

Minimum 75 returns.

		Yrs	No	Yards	Avg	TD
1	George McAfee	8	112	1431	12.8	2
2	Jack Christiansen	8	85	1084	12.8	8
3	Claude Gibson	5	110	1381	12.6	3
4	Bill Dudley	9	124	1515	12.2	3
5	Rick Upchurch	9	248	3008	12.1	8

Long-Playing Records

Seasons

		No
1	George Blanda, QB-K	26
2	Gary Anderson, K	23
	Morten Andersen, K	23
4	**Sean Landeta**, P	21
	Earl Morrall, QB	21

Games

		No
1	Morten Andersen, K	354
2	Gary Anderson, K	353
3	George Blanda, QB-K	340
4	Jerry Rice, WR	303
5	Bruce Matthews, OL	296

Consecutive Games

		No
1	**Jeff Feagles**, P	288
2	Jim Marshall, DE	282
3	Morten Andersen, K	248
4	Bill Romanowski, LB	243
5	Mick Tingelhoff, C	240

All-Time NFL Leaders (Cont.)

SINGLE SEASON

Passing

Yards Gained	Year	Att	Cmp	Pct	Yds
Dan Marino, Mia	1984	564	362	64.2	5084
Kurt Warner, St.L	2001	546	375	68.7	4830
Dan Fouts, SD	1981	609	360	59.1	4802
Dan Marino, Mia	1986	623	378	60.7	4746
Daunte Culpepper, Min	2004	548	379	69.2	4717
Dan Fouts, SD	1980	589	348	59.1	4715
Warren Moon, Hou	1991	655	404	61.7	4690
Rich Gannon, Oak	2002	618	418	67.6	4689
Warren Moon, Hou	1990	584	362	62.0	4689
Neil Lomax, St.L	1984	560	345	61.6	4614

Efficiency	Year	Att/Cmp	TD	Rtg
Peyton Manning, Ind	2004	497/336	49	121.1
Steve Young, SF	1994	461/324	35	112.8
Joe Montana, SF	1989	386/271	26	112.4
Daunte Culpepper, Min	2004	548/379	39	110.9
Milt Plum, Cle	1960	250/151	21	110.4
Sammy Baugh, Wash	1945	182/128	11	109.9
Kurt Warner, St.L	1999	499/325	41	109.2
Dan Marino, Mia	1984	564/362	48	108.9
Sid Luckman, Chi. Bears	1943	202/110	28	107.5
Steve Young, SF	1992	402/268	25	107.0

Receptions

Catches	Year	No	Yds
Marvin Harrison, Ind	2002	143	1722
Herman Moore, Det	1995	123	1686
Jerry Rice, SF	1995	122	1848
Cris Carter, Min	1995	122	1371
Cris Carter, Min	1994	122	1256
Isaac Bruce, St.L	1995	119	1781
Torry Holt, St.L	2003	117	1696
Jimmy Smith, Jax	1999	116	1636
Marvin Harrison, Ind	1999	115	1663
Rod Smith, Den	2001	113	1343
Hines Ward, Pit	2002	112	1329
Jimmy Smith, Jax	2001	112	1373
Jerry Rice, SF	1994	112	1499
Sterling Sharpe, GB	1993	112	1274

Rushing

Yards Gained	Year	Car	Yds	Avg
Eric Dickerson, LA Rams	1984	379	2105	5.6
Jamal Lewis, Bal.	2003	387	2066	5.3
Barry Sanders, Det	1997	335	2053	6.1
Terrell Davis, Den	1998	392	2008	5.1
O.J. Simpson, Buf	1973	332	2003	6.0
Earl Campbell, Hou	1980	373	1934	5.2
Barry Sanders, Det	1994	331	1883	5.7
Ahman Green, GB	2003	355	1883	5.3
Shaun Alexander, Sea	2005	370	1880	5.1
Jim Brown, Cle	1963	291	1863	6.4
Tiki Barber, NYG	2005	357	1860	5.2
Ricky Williams, Mia	2002	383	1853	4.8
Walter Payton, Chi	1977	339	1852	5.5
Jamal Anderson, Atl	1998	410	1846	4.5

Scoring

Points

	Year	TD	PAT	FG	Pts
Paul Hornung, GB	1960	15	41	15	176
Shaun Alexander, Sea	2005	28	0	0	168
Gary Anderson, Min	1998	0	59	35	164
Jeff Wilkins, St.L	2003	0	46	39	163
Priest Holmes, KC	2003	27	0	0	162
Mark Moseley, Wash	1983	0	62	33	161
Marshall Faulk, St.L	2000	26	4	0	160
Mike Vanderjagt, Ind	2003	0	46	37	157
Gino Cappelletti, Bos	1964	7	38	25	155
Emmitt Smith, Dal	1995	25	0	0	150
Chip Lohmiller, Wash	1991	0	56	31	149
Jay Feely, NYG	2005	0	43	35	148

Touchdowns

	Year	Rush	Rec	Ret	Total
Shaun Alexander, Sea	2005	27	1	0	28
Priest Holmes, KC	2003	27	0	0	27
Marshall Faulk, St.L	2000	18	8	0	26
Emmitt Smith, Dal	1995	25	0	0	25
John Riggins, Wash	1983	24	0	0	24
Priest Holmes, KC	2002	21	3	0	24
Terrell Davis, Den	1998	21	2	0	23
O.J. Simpson, Buf	1975	16	7	0	23
Jerry Rice, SF	1987	1	22	0	23
Gale Sayers, Chi	1966	14	6	2	22
Chuck Foreman, Min	1975	13	9	0	22
Emmitt Smith, Dal	1994	21	1	0	22

Note: The NFL regular season schedule grew from 12 games (1947-60) to 14 (1961-77) to 16 (1978-present). The AFL regular season schedule was always 14 games (1960-69).

Touchdowns Passing

	Year	No
Peyton Manning, Indianapolis	2004	49
Dan Marino, Miami	1984	48
Dan Marino, Miami	1986	44
Kurt Warner, St. Louis	1999	41
Brett Favre, Green Bay	1996	39
Daunte Culpepper, Minnesota	2004	39
Brett Favre, Green Bay	1995	38
George Blanda, Houston	1961	36
Y.A. Tittle, NY Giants	1963	36
Steve Young, San Francisco	1998	36
Steve Beuerlein, Carolina	1999	36
Kurt Warner, St. Louis	2001	36
Brett Favre, Green Bay	1997	35
Steve Young, San Francisco	1994	35

Touchdowns Receiving

	Year	No
Jerry Rice, San Francisco	1987	22
Mark Clayton, Miami	1984	18
Sterling Sharpe, Green Bay	1994	18
Don Hutson, Green Bay	1942	17
Elroy (Crazylegs) Hirsch, LA Rams	1951	17
Bill Groman, Houston	1961	17
Jerry Rice, San Francisco	1989	17
Cris Carter, Minnesota	1995	17
Carl Pickens, Cincinnati	1995	17
Randy Moss, Minnesota	1998	17
Randy Moss, Minnesota	2003	17
Art Powell, Oakland	1963	16
Terrell Owens, SF	2001	16
Muhsin Muhammad, Carolina	2004	16

Touchdowns Rushing

	Year	No
Priest Holmes, Kansas City	2003	27
Shaun Alexander, Seattle	2005	27
Emmitt Smith, Dallas	1995	25
John Riggins, Washington	1983	24
Joe Morris, NY Giants	1985	21
Emmitt Smith, Dallas	1994	21
Terry Allen, Washington	1996	21
Terrell Davis, Denver	1998	21
Priest Holmes, Kansas City	2002	21
Larry Johnson, Kansas City	2005	20
Jim Taylor, Green Bay	1962	19
Earl Campbell, Houston	1979	19
Chuck Muncie, San Diego	1981	19

Field Goals

	Year	Att	No
Neil Rackers, Arizona	2005	42	40
Jeff Wilkins, St. Louis	2003	42	39
Olindo Mare, Miami	1999	46	39
Mike Vanderjagt, Indianapolis	2003	37	37
John Kasay, Carolina	1996	45	37
Cary Blanchard, Indianapolis	1996	40	36
Al Del Greco, Tennessee	1998	39	36
Ali Haji-Sheikh, NY Giants	1983	42	35
Jeff Jaeger, LA Raiders	1993	44	35
Gary Anderson, Minnesota	1998	35	35
Matt Stover, Baltimore	2000	39	35
Jay Feely, NY Giants	2005	42	35
Ten tied with 34 FG each.			

Interceptions

	Year	No
Dick (Night Train) Lane, Detroit	1952	14
Dan Sandifer, Washington	1948	13
Spec Sanders, NY Yanks	1950	13
Lester Hayes, Oakland	1980	13
Nine tied with 12 each.		

Punting

Qualifiers	Year	Avg
Sammy Baugh, Washington	1940	51.4
Yale Lary, Detroit	1963	48.9
Sammy Baugh, Washington	1941	48.7
Yale Lary, Detroit	1961	48.4
Sammy Baugh, Washington	1942	48.2

Kickoff Returns

	Year	Avg
Travis Williams, Green Bay	1967	41.1
Gale Sayers, Chicago Bears	1967	37.7
Ollie Matson, Chicago Cards	1958	35.5
Jim Duncan, Baltimore Colts	1970	35.4
Lynn Chandnois, Pittsburgh	1952	35.2

Punt Returns

	Year	Avg
Herb Rich, Baltimore	1950	23.0
Jack Christiansen, Detroit	1952	21.5
Dick Christy, NY Titans	1961	21.3
Bob Hayes, Dallas	1968	20.8
Claude Young, NY Yanks	1951	19.3

Sacks

	Year	No		Year	No
Michael Strahan, NY Giants	2001	22.5	Chris Doleman, Minnesota	1989	21
Mark Gastineau, NY Jets	1984	22	Lawrence Taylor, NY Giants	1986	20.5
Reggie White, Philadelphia	1987	21	Derrick Thomas, Kansas City	1990	20

Note: The NFL did not begin officially compiling sacks until 1982. Cincinnati's Coy Bacon is widely, although not officially, credited with 26 sacks during the 1976 season.

SINGLE GAME

Passing

Yards Gained	Date	Yds
Norm Van Brocklin, LA vs NY Yanks	9/28/51	554
Warren Moon, Hou vs KC	12/16/90	527
Boomer Esiason, Ariz vs Wash.	11/10/96	522
Dan Marino, Mia vs NYJ	10/23/88	521
Phil Simms, NYG vs Cin	10/13/85	513

Completions	Date	No
Drew Bledsoe, NE vs Min	11/13/94	45
Rich Gannon, Oak vs Pit	9/15/02	43
Richard Todd, NYJ vs SF	9/21/80	42
Vinny Testaverde, NYJ vs Sea	12/6/98	42
Warren Moon, Hou vs Dal	11/10/91	41
Five tied with 40 each.		

Receiving

Catches	Date	No
Terrell Owens, SF vs Chi	12/17/00	20
Tom Fears, LA vs GB	12/3/50	18
Clark Gaines, NYJ vs SF	9/21/80	17
Four tied with 16 each.		

Yards Gained	Date	Yds
Flipper Anderson, LA Rams vs NO	11/26/89	336
Stephone Paige, KC vs SD	12/22/85	309
Jim Benton, Cle vs Det	11/22/45	303
Cloyce Box, Det vs Bal	12/3/50	302
Jimmy Smith, Jax vs Bal	9/10/00	291
Jerry Rice, SF vs Det	9/25/95	289

Rushing

Yards Gained	Date	Yds
Jamal Lewis, Bal vs Cle	9/14/03	295
Corey Dillon, Cin vs Den	10/22/00	278
Walter Payton, Chi vs Min	11/20/77	275
O.J. Simpson, Buf vs Det	11/25/76	273
Shaun Alexander, Sea vs Oak	11/11/01	266
Mike Anderson, Den vs NO	12/3/00	251
O.J. Simpson, Buf vs NE	9/16/73	250
Willie Ellison, LA Rams vs NO	12/5/71	247

All-Purpose Yards

	Date	Yds
Glyn Milburn, Den vs Sea	12/10/95	404
Billy Cannon, Hou vs NY Titans	12/10/61	373
Michael Lewis, NO vs Wash	10/13/02	356
Tyrone Hughes, NO vs LA Rams	10/23/94	347
Lionel James, SD vs Raiders	11/10/85	345
Timmy Brown, Phi vs St.L	12/16/62	341
Gale Sayers, Chi vs Min	12/18/66	339
Gale Sayers, Chi vs SF	12/12/65	336
Flipper Anderson, LA Rams vs NO	11/26/89	336

All-Time Single Game NFL Leaders (Cont.)
Scoring

Points

	Date	Pts
Ernie Nevers, Chi. Cards vs Chi. Bears	11/28/29	40
Dub Jones, Cle vs Chi. Bears	11/25/51	36
Gale Sayers, Chi vs SF	12/12/65	36
Paul Hornung, GB vs Bal	10/8/61	33
Bob Shaw, Chi. Cards vs Bal	10/2/50	30
Jim Brown, Cle vs Bal	11/1/59	30
Abner Haynes, Dal. Texans vs Oak	11/26/61	30
Billy Cannon, Hou vs NY Titans	12/10/61	30
Cookie Gilchrist, Buf vs NY Jets	12/8/63	30
Kellen Winslow, SD vs Oak	11/22/81	30
Jerry Rice, SF vs Atl	10/14/90	30
James Stewart, Jax vs Phi.	10/12/97	30
Shaun Alexander, Sea vs Min.	9/29/02	30
Clinton Portis, Den vs KC	12/7/03	30

Note: Nevers celebrated Thanksgiving, 1929, by scoring all of the Chicago Cardinals' points on six rushing TDs and four PATs. The Cards beat Red Grange and the Chicago Bears, 40-6.

Touchdowns Passing

	Date	No
Sid Luckman, Chi. Bears vs NYG	11/14/43	7
Adrian Burk, Phi vs Wash	10/17/54	7
George Blanda, Hou vs NY Titans	11/19/61	7
Y.A. Tittle, NYG vs Wash	10/28/62	7
Joe Kapp, Min vs Bal	9/28/69	7

Touchdowns Receiving

	Date	No
Bob Shaw, Chi. Cards vs Bal	10/2/50	5
Kellen Winslow, SD vs Oak	11/22/81	5
Jerry Rice, SF vs Atl	10/14/90	5

Touchdowns Rushing

	Date	No
Ernie Nevers, Chi. Cards vs Chi. Bears	11/28/29	6
Jim Brown, Cle vs Bal	11/1/59	5
Cookie Gilchrist, Buf vs NY Jets	12/8/63	5
James Stewart, Jax vs Phi.	10/12/97	5
Clinton Portis, Den vs KC	12/7/03	5

Field Goals

	Date	No
Jim Bakken, St.L vs Pit	9/24/67	7
Rich Karlis, Min vs LA Rams	11/5/89	7
Chris Boniol, Dal vs GB	11/18/96	7
Billy Cundiff, Dal vs NYG	9/15/03	7

Note: Bakken was 7-for-9, Cundiff was 7-for-8, Boniol and Karlis were 7-for-7.

Extra Point Kicks

	Date	No
Pat Harder, Cards vs NYG	10/17/48	9
Bob Waterfield, LA Rams vs Bal	10/22/50	9
Charlie Gogolak, Wash vs NYG	11/27/66	9

Interceptions

	No
By 18 players	4

Sacks

	Date	No
Derrick Thomas, KC vs Sea	11/11/90	7.0
Fred Dean, SF vs NO	11/13/83	6.0
Derrick Thomas, KC vs Oak	9/6/98	6.0
William Gay, Det vs TB	9/4/83	5.5

Longest Plays

Passing (all for TDs)

	Date	Yds
Frank Filchock to Andy Farkas, Wash vs Pit	10/15/39	99
George Izo to Bobby Mitchell, Wash vs Cle	9/15/63	99
Karl Sweetan to Pat Studstill, Det vs Bal	10/16/66	99
Sonny Jurgensen to Gerry Allen, Wash vs Chi	9/15/68	99
Jim Plunkett to Cliff Branch, LA Raiders vs Wash	10/2/83	99
Ron Jaworski to Mike Quick, Phi vs Atl	11/10/85	99
Stan Humphries to Tony Martin, SD vs Sea	9/18/94	99
Brett Favre to Robert Brooks, GB vs Chi	9/11/95	99
Trent Green to Marc Boerigter, KC vs SD	12/22/02	99
Jeff Garcia to Andre Davis, Cle vs Cin	10/17/04	99

Runs from Scrimmage (all for TDs)

	Date	Yds
Tony Dorsett, Dal vs Min	1/3/83	99
Ahman Green, GB vs Den	12/28/03	98
Andy Uram, GB vs Chi. Cards	10/8/39	97
Bob Gage, Pit vs Bears	12/4/49	97

Four players tied with 96-yd rushes.

Punts

	Date	Yds
Steve O'Neal, NYJ vs Den	9/21/69	98
Joe Lintzenich, Chi. Bears vs NYG	11/15/31	94
Shawn McCarthy, NE vs Buf	11/3/91	93

Field Goals

	Date	Yds
Tom Dempsey, NO vs Det	11/8/70	63
Jason Elam, Den vs Jax	10/25/98	63
Steve Cox, Cle vs Cin	10/21/84	60
Morten Andersen, NO vs Chi	10/27/91	60
Tony Franklin, Phi vs Dal	11/12/79	59
Pete Stoyanovich, Mia vs NYJ	11/12/89	59
Steve Christie, Buf vs Mia	9/26/93	59
Morten Andersen, Atl vs SF	12/24/95	59

Punt Returns (all for TDs)

	Date	Yds
Robert Bailey, Rams vs NO	10/23/94	103
Gil Lefebvre, Cin vs Bklyn	12/3/33	98
Charlie West, Min vs Wash	11/3/68	98
Dennis Morgan, Dal vs St.L	10/13/74	98
Terance Mathis, NYJ vs Dal	11/4/90	98
Greg Pruitt, LA Raiders vs Wash.	10/2/83	97

Kickoff Returns (all for TDs)

	Date	Yds
Al Carmichael, GB vs Chi. Bears	10/7/56	106
Noland Smith, KC vs Den	12/17/67	106
Roy Green, St.L vs Dal	10/21/79	106

Interception Returns (all for TDs)

	Date	Yds
Ed Reed, Bal vs Cle	11/17/04	106
James Willis (14 yds) lateral to Troy Vincent (90 yds), Phi vs Dal	11/3/96	104
Vencie Glenn, SD vs Den	11/29/87	103
Louis Oliver, Mia vs Buf	10/4/92	103

Seven players tied with 102-yd returns.

Note: On 11/13/05 Chicago's Nathan Vasher returned a missed FG 108 yards, the longest play in NFL history.

Monday Night Football All-Time Leaders

The first episode of *Monday Night Football* aired on ABC on September 21,1970 with the Cleveland Browns defeating the New York Jets, 31-21, at Municipal Stadium in Cleveland. The series continued on ABC for 36 seasons, until ESPN bought the rights to Monday Night games beginning with the 2006 season. Listed are all-time *Monday Night Football* records, as compiled by *The ESPN Pro Football Encyclopedia* (1st Ed.). Records are through 2005 regular season.

Passing

Yards		Touchdowns		300-yd Games	
Dan Marino	9654	Dan Marino	74	Dan Marino	8
Brett Favre	7076	Brett Favre	54	Brett Favre	7
Joe Montana	5148	Steve Young	42	Joe Montana	6
John Elway	5012	Joe Montana	36	Randall Cunningham	6
Troy Aikman	4614	Jim Kelly	31	Steve Young	5
Steve Young	4608	Danny White	27	Dan Fouts	5
Jim Kelly	4348	Ken Stabler	27	Kurt Warner	4
Phil Simms	3760	John Elway	25	Phil Simms	4
Dan Fouts	3721	Troy Aikman	23	Joe Theismann	4
Danny White	3693	Dave Krieg	22	Peton Manning	4
				Ken Anderson	4

Rushing

Yards		Touchdowns		100-yd Games	
Emmitt Smith	2434	Emmitt Smith	23	Emmitt Smith	12
Tony Dorsett	1897	Marcus Allen	17	Jerome Bettis	8
Thurman Thomas	1769	Eric Dickerson	14	Franco Harris	7
Marcus Allen	1486	John Riggins	13	Eric Dickerson	7
Franco Harris	1435	Chuck Muncie	10	Thurman Thomas	6
Walter Payton	1391	Terrell Davis	10	Ahman Green	6
Jerome Bettis	1330	Nine tied with 9 TD each.		Tony Dorsett	6
Eric Dickerson	1326			Six tied with 5 games each.	
Ahman Green	1138				
Garrison Hearst	1112				

Receiving

Receptions		Yards		Touchdowns	
Jerry Rice	254	Jerry Rice	4029	Jerry Rice	34
Andre Reed	124	Andre Reed	1783	Terrell Owens	15
Cris Carter	123	Art Monk	1537	Mark Clayton	15
Tim Brown	121	Michael Irvin	1512	Andre Reed	13
Art Monk	114	Tony Hill	1480	Tony Hill	12
Rod Smith	102	Tim Brown	1479	Randy Moss	11
Torry Holt	96	Torry Holt	1443	Brent Jones	10
Michael Irvin	96	Cris Carter	1431	Cris Carter	10
Shannon Sharpe	93	Mark Clayton	1339	Rod Smith	9
Ed McCaffrey	93	Rod Smith	1333	John Taylor	9
				Nat Moore	9
				Cliff Branch	9

Interceptions

Everson Walls	11
Merton Hanks	9
Emmitt Thomas	8
Terrell Buckley	7
Michael Downs	7
Dick Anderson	7
18 tied with 6 int's each.	

Sacks

Bruce Smith	24.5
Richard Dent	20.0
Kevin Greene	18.0
Reggie White	16.5
Chris Doleman	16.5
Charles Haley	16.0
Lawrence Taylor	15.5
Kabeer Gbaja-Biamila	14.5
John Randal	14.0
Greg Townsnend	14.0

Source: *The ESPN Pro Football Encyclopedia* (1st Edition)

Chicago College All-Star Game

On Aug. 31, 1934, a year after sponsoring Major League Baseball's first All-Star Game, *Chicago Tribune* sports editor Arch Ward presented the first Chicago College All-Star Game at Soldier Field. A crowd of 79,432 turned out to see an all-star team of graduated college seniors battle the 1933 NFL champion Chicago Bears to a scoreless tie. The preseason game was played at Soldier Field and pitted the College All-Stars against the defending NFL champions (1933-1966) or Super Bowl champions (1967-75) every year except 1935 until it was cancelled in 1977. The NFL champs won the series, 31-9-1.

Year		Year		Year	
1934	Chi. Bears 0, All-Stars 0	1949	Philadelphia 38, All-Stars 0	1964	Chi. Bears 28, All-Stars 17
1935	Chi. Bears 5, All-Stars 0			1965	Cleveland 24, All-Stars 16
1936	Detroit 7, All-Stars 0	1950	All-Stars 17, Philadelphia 7	1966	Green Bay 38, All-Stars 0
1937	All-Stars 6, Green Bay 0	1951	Cleveland 33, All-Stars 0	1967	Green Bay 27, All-Stars 0
1938	All-Stars 28, Washington 16	1952	LA Rams 10, All-Stars 7	1968	Green Bay 34, All-Stars 17
1939	NY Giants 9, All-Stars 0	1953	Detroit 24, All-Stars 10	1969	NY Jets 26, All-Stars 24
		1954	Detroit 31, All-Stars 6		
1940	Green Bay 45, All-Stars 28	1955	All-Stars 30, Cleveland 27	1970	Kansas City 24, All-Stars 3
1941	Chi. Bears 37, All-Stars 13	1956	Cleveland 26, All-Stars 0	1971	Baltimore 24, All-Stars 17
1942	Chi. Bears 21, All-Stars 0	1957	NY Giants 22, All-Stars 12	1972	Dallas 20, All-Stars 7
1943	All-Stars 27, Washington 7	1958	All-Stars 35, Detroit 19	1973	Miami 14, All-Stars 3
1944	Chi. Bears 24, All-Stars 21	1959	Baltimore 29, All-Stars 0	1974	No Game (NFLPA Strike)
1945	Green Bay 19, All-Stars 7			1975	Pittsburgh 21, All-Stars 14
1946	All-Stars 16, LA Rams 0	1960	Baltimore 32, All-Stars 7	1976	Pittsburgh 24, All-Stars 0*
1947	All-Stars 16, Chi. Bears 0	1961	Philadelphia 28, All-Stars 14		
1948	Chi. Cards 28, All-Stars 0	1962	Green Bay 42, All-Stars 20	*Downpour flooded field, game called
		1963	All-Stars 20, Green Bay 17	with 1:22 left in 3rd quarter.

Number One Draft Choices

In an effort to blunt the dominance of the Chicago Bears and New York Giants in the 1930s and distribute talent more even-ly throughout the league, the NFL established the college draft in 1936. The first player chosen in the first draft was Jay Berwanger, who was also college football's first Heisman Trophy winner. In all, 17 Heisman winners have also been the NFL's No. 1 draft choice. They are noted in **bold** type. The American Football League (formed in 1960) held its own draft for six years before agreeing to merge with the NFL and select players in a common draft starting in 1967.

Year	Team		Year	Team	
1936	Philadelphia	**Jay Berwanger**, HB, Chicago	1968	Minnesota	Ron Yary, T, USC
1937	Philadelphia	Sam Francis, FB, Nebraska	1969	Buffalo	**O.J. Simpson**, RB, USC
1938	Cleveland Rams	Corbett Davis, FB, Indiana			
1939	Chicago Cards	Ki Aldrich, C, TCU	1970	Pittsburgh	Terry Bradshaw, QB, La.Tech
			1971	New England	**Jim Plunkett**, QB, Stanford
1940	Chicago Cards	George Cafego, HB, Tennessee	1972	Buffalo	Walt Patulski, DE, Notre Dame
1941	Chicago Bears	**Tom Harmon**, HB, Michigan	1973	Houston	John Matuszak, DE, Tampa
1942	Pittsburgh	Bill Dudley, HB, Virginia	1974	Dallas	Ed (Too Tall) Jones, DE, Tenn. St.
1943	Detroit	**Frank Sinkwich**, HB, Georgia	1975	Atlanta	Steve Bartkowski, QB, Calif.
1944	Boston Yanks	**Angelo Bertelli**, QB, N. Dame	1976	Tampa Bay	Lee Roy Selmon, DE, Oklahoma
1945	Chicago Cards	Charley Trippi, HB, Georgia	1977	Tampa Bay	Ricky Bell, RB, USC
1946	Boston Yanks	Frank Dancewicz, QB, N. Dame	1978	Houston	**Earl Campbell**, RB, Texas
1947	Chicago Bears	Bob Fenimore, HB, Okla. A&M	1979	Buffalo	Tom Cousineau, LB, Ohio St.
1948	Washington	Harry Gilmer, QB, Alabama			
1949	Philadelphia	Chuck Bednarik, C, Penn	1980	Detroit	**Billy Sims**, RB, Oklahoma
			1981	New Orleans	**George Rogers**, RB, S. Carolina
1950	Detroit	**Leon Hart**, E, Notre Dame	1982	New England	Kenneth Sims, DT, Texas
1951	NY Giants	Kyle Rote, HB, SMU	1983	Baltimore	John Elway, QB, Stanford
1952	LA Rams	Bill Wade, QB, Vanderbilt	1984	New England	Irving Fryar, WR, Nebraska
1953	San Francisco	Harry Babcock, E, Georgia	1985	Buffalo	Bruce Smith, DE, Va. Tech
1954	Cleveland	Bobby Garrett, QB, Stanford	1986	Tampa Bay	**Bo Jackson**, RB, Auburn
1955	Baltimore	George Shaw, QB, Oregon	1987	Tampa Bay	**V. Testaverde**, QB, Miami-FL
1956	Pittsburgh	Gary Glick, DB, Colo. A&M	1988	Atlanta	Aundray Bruce, LB, Auburn
1957	Green Bay	**Paul Hornung**, QB, N. Dame	1989	Dallas	Troy Aikman, QB, UCLA
1958	Chicago Cards	King Hill, QB, Rice			
1959	Green Bay	Randy Duncan, QB, Iowa	1990	Indianapolis	Jeff George, QB, Illinois
			1991	Dallas	Russell Maryland, DT, Miami-FL
1960	NFL–LA Rams	**Billy Cannon**, HB, LSU	1992	Indianapolis	Steve Emtman, DT, Washington
	AFL–No choice		1993	New England	Drew Bledsoe, QB, Washington St.
1961	NFL–Minnesota	Tommy Mason, HB, Tulane	1994	Cincinnati	Dan Wilkinson, DT, Ohio St.
	AFL–Buffalo	Ken Rice, G, Auburn	1995	Cincinnati	Ki-Jana Carter, RB, Penn St.
1962	NFL–Washington	**Ernie Davis**, HB, Syracuse	1996	NY Jets	Keyshawn Johnson, WR, USC
	AFL–Oakland	Roman Gabriel, QB, N.C. State	1997	St. Louis	Orlando Pace, OT, Ohio St.
1963	NFL–LA Rams	**Terry Baker**, QB, Oregon St.	1998	Indianapolis	Peyton Manning, QB, Tennessee
	AFL–Kan.City	Buck Buchanan, DT, Grambling	1999	Cleveland	Tim Couch, QB, Kentucky
1964	NFL–San Fran	Dave Parks, E, Texas Tech			
	AFL–Boston	Jack Concannon, QB, Boston Col.	2000	Cleveland	Courtney Brown, DE, Penn St.
1965	NFL–NY Giants	Tucker Frederickson, FB, Auburn	2001	Atlanta	Michael Vick, QB, Va. Tech
	AFL–Houston	Lawrence Elkins, E, Baylor	2002	Houston	David Carr, QB, Fresno St.
1966	NFL–Atlanta	Tommy Nobis, LB, Texas	2003	Cincinnati	**Carson Palmer**, QB, USC
	AFL–Miami	Jim Grabowski, FB, Illinois	2004	San Diego	Eli Manning, QB, Mississippi
1967	Baltimore	Bubba Smith, DT, Michigan St.	2005	San Francisco	Alex Smith, QB, Utah
			2006	Houston	Mario Williams, DE, NC State

AP/Wide World Photos
Don Shula

NFL Media
Marv Levy

NFL Media
Bill Cowher

NFL Media
Mike Shanahan

All-Time Winningest NFL Coaches

NFL career victories through the 2005 season. Career, regular season and playoff records are noted along with NFL, AFL and Super Bowl titles won. Coaches active during 2005 season in **bold** type.

			Career				Regular Season				Playoffs			
		Yrs	W	L	T	Pct	W	L	T	Pct	W	L	Pct.	League Titles
1	Don Shula	.33	**347**	173	6	.665	328	156	6	.676	19	17	.528	2 Super Bowls and 1 NFL
2	George Halas	.40	**324**	151	31	.671	318	148	31	.671	6	3	.667	5 NFL
3	Tom Landry	.29	**270**	178	6	.601	250	162	6	.605	20	16	.556	2 Super Bowls
4	Curly Lambeau	.33	**229**	134	22	.623	226	132	22	.624	3	2	.600	6 NFL
5	Chuck Noll	.23	**209**	156	1	.572	193	148	1	.566	16	8	.667	4 Super Bowls
6	Dan Reeves	.23	**201**	174	2	.536	190	165	2	.535	11	9	.550	—None—
7	Chuck Knox	.22	**193**	158	1	.550	186	147	1	.558	7	11	.389	—None—
8	**M. Schottenheimer**	.20	**191**	136	1	.584	186	124	1	.600	5	12	.294	—None—
9	**Bill Parcells**	.18	**174**	130	1	.572	163	123	1	.570	11	7	.611	2 Super Bowls
10	Paul Brown	.21	**170**	108	6	.609	166	100	6	.621	4	8	.333	3 NFL
11	Bud Grant	.18	**168**	108	5	.607	158	96	5	.620	10	12	.455	1 NFL
12	**Joe Gibbs**	.14	**157**	82	0	.657	140	76	0	.648	17	6	.739	3 Super Bowls
13	Marv Levy	.17	**154**	120	0	.562	143	112	0	.561	11	8	.579	—None—
14	**Bill Cowher**	.14	**153**	91	1	.627	141	82	1	.632	12	9	.571	1 Super Bowl
	Steve Owen	.23	**153**	108	17	.581	151	100	17	.595	2	8	.200	2 NFL
16	**Mike Holmgren**	.14	**149**	95	0	.611	138	86	0	.616	11	9	.550	1 Super Bowl
17	Hank Stram	.17	**136**	100	10	.573	131	97	10	.571	5	3	.625	1 Super Bowl and 3 AFL
18	Weeb Ewbank	.20	**134**	130	7	.507	130	129	7	.502	4	1	.800	1 Super Bowl, 2 NFL, and 1 AFL
19	**Mike Shanahan**	.13	**130**	79	0	.622	122	74	0	.622	8	5	.615	2 Super Bowls
20	Mike Ditka	.14	**127**	101	0	.557	121	95	0	.560	6	6	.500	1 Super Bowl
21	**Dick Vermeil**	.15	**126**	114	0	.525	120	109	0	.524	6	5	.545	1 Super Bowl
22	Jim Mora	.15	**125**	112	0	.527	125	106	0	.541	0	6	.000	—None—
23	George Seifert	.11	**124**	67	0	.649	114	62	0	.648	10	5	.667	2 Super Bowls
24	Sid Gillman	.18	**123**	104	7	.541	122	99	7	.550	1	5	.167	1 AFL
25	George Allen	.12	**118**	54	5	.681	116	47	5	.705	2	7	.222	—None—

Notes: The NFL does not recognize records from the All-American Football Conference (1946-49). If it did, **Paul Brown** (52-4-3 in four AAFC seasons) would move up from 10th to 5th on the all-time list with the following career stats— 25 Yrs; 222 Wins; 112 Losses; 9 Ties; .660 Pct; 9-8 playoff record; and 4 AAFC titles.

The NFL also considers the Playoff Bowl or "Runner-up Bowl" (officially: the Bert Bell Benefit Bowl) as a postseason exhibition game. The Playoff Bowl was contested every year from 1960-69 in Miami between Eastern and Western Conference second place teams. While the games did not count, six of the coaches above went to the Playoff Bowl at least once and came away with the following records— Allen (2-0), Brown (0-1), Grant (0-1), Landry (1-2) and Shula (2-0).

Where They Coached

Allen—LA Rams (1966-70), Washington (1971-77); **Brown**—Cleveland (1950-62), Cincinnati (1968-75); **Cowher**—Pittsburgh (1992—); **Ditka**— Chicago (1982-92), New Orleans (1997-99); **Ewbank**— Baltimore (1954-62), NY Jets (1963-73); **Gibbs**—Washington (1981-92, 2004—); **Gillman**—LA Rams (1955-59), LA-San Diego Chargers (1960-69), Houston (1973-74); **Grant**—Minnesota (1967-83,1985); **Halas**—Chicago Bears (1920-29,33-42,46-55,58-67).

Holmgren—Green Bay (1992-98), Seattle (1999—); **Knox**— LA Rams (1973-77, 1992-94); Buffalo (1978-82), Seattle (1983-91); **Lambeau**— Green Bay (1921-49), Chicago Cards (1950-51), Washington (1952-53); **Landry**—Dallas (1960-88); **Levy**— Kansas City (1978-82), Buffalo (1986-97); **Mora**—New Orleans (1986-1995), Indianapolis (1998-2001); **Noll**—Pittsburgh (1969-91).

Owen—NY Giants (1931-53); **Parcells**— NY Giants (1983-90), New England (1993-97), NY Jets (1997-99), Dallas (2003—); **Reeves**— Denver (1981-92), NY Giants (1993-96), Atlanta (1997-2003); **Schottenheimer**— Cleveland (1984-88), Kansas City (1989-98), Washington (2001), San Diego (2002—); **Seifert**—San Francisco (1989-96), Carolina (1999-2001); **Shanahan**—LA Raiders (1988-89), Denver (1995—); **Shula**—Baltimore (1963-69), Miami (1970-95); **Stram**—Dallas-Kansas City (1960-74), New Orleans (1976-77); **Vermeil**—Philadelphia (1976-82); St. Louis (1997-99); Kansas City (2001-05).

Top Winning Percentages

Minimum of 85 NFL victories, including playoffs.

		Yrs	W	L	T	Pct
1	Vince Lombardi	10	105	35	6	.740
2	John Madden	10	112	39	7	.731
3	George Allen	12	118	54	5	.681
4	George Halas	40	324	151	31	.671
5	Don Shula	33	347	173	6	.665
6	**Joe Gibbs**	14	157	82	0	.657
7	George Seifert	11	124	67	0	.649
8	**Bill Cowher**	14	153	91	1	.627
9	Curly Lambeau	33	229	134	22	.623
10	**Mike Shanahan**	13	130	79	0	.622
11	**Tony Dungy**	10	107	66	0	.618
12	Bill Walsh	10	102	63	1	.617
13	**Mike Holmgren**	14	149	95	0	.611
14	Paul Brown	21	170	108	6	.609
15	Bud Grant	18	168	108	5	.607
16	Tom Landry	29	270	178	6	.601
17	**Marty Schottenheimer**	20	191	136	1	.584
18	**Bill Belichick**	11	110	79	0	.582
19	Steve Owen	23	153	108	17	.581
20	Buddy Parker	15	107	76	9	.581
21	Hank Stram	17	136	100	10	.573
22	Chuck Noll	23	209	156	1	.572
23	**Bill Parcells**	18	174	130	1	.572
24	Jimmy Johnson	9	89	68	0	.567
25	Marv Levy	17	154	120	0	.562

Note: If AAFC records are included, **Paul Brown** moves from 14th to 6th with a percentage of .660 (25 yrs, 222-112-9) and **Buck Shaw** would be 12th at .619 (8 yrs, 91-55-5).

Active Coaches' Victories

Through 2005 season, including playoffs.

		Yrs	W	L	T	Pct
1	Marty Schottenheimer, SD	20	191	136	1	.584
2	Bill Parcells, Dallas	18	174	130	1	.572
3	Joe Gibbs, Washington	14	157	82	0	.657
4	Bill Cowher, Pittsburgh	14	153	91	1	.627
5	Mike Holmgren, Seattle	14	149	95	0	.611
6	Mike Shanahan, Denver	13	130	79	0	.622
7	Dennis Green, Arizona	12	112	91	0	.552
8	Bill Belichick, New England	11	110	79	0	.582
9	Tony Dungy, Indianapolis	10	107	66	0	.618
10	Jeff Fisher, Tennessee	12	102	89	0	.534
11	Tom Coughlin, NY Giants	10	89	80	0	.527
12	Jon Gruden, Tampa Bay	8	78	58	0	.574
13	Andy Reid, Philadelphia	7	77	47	0	.621
14	Brian Billick, Baltimore	7	67	52	0	.563
15	Art Shell, Oakland	6	56	41	0	.577
16	John Fox, Carolina	4	41	30	0	.577
	Herman Edwards, KC	5	41	44	0	.482
18	Dick Jauron, Buffalo	6	36	50	0	.419
19	Marvin Lewis, Cincinnati	3	27	22	0	.551
20	Jack Del Rio, Jacksonville	3	26	23	0	.531
21	Jim Mora Jr., Atlanta	2	20	14	0	.588
22	Lovie Smith, Chicago	2	16	17	0	.485
23	Nick Saban, Miami	1	9	7	0	.563
24	Romeo Crennel, Cleveland	1	6	10	0	.375
25	Mike Nolan, San Fran.	1	4	12	0	.250
26	Brad Childress, Minnesota	0	0	0	0	.000
	Gary Kubiak, Houston	0	0	0	0	.000
	Scott Linehan, St. Louis	0	0	0	0	.000
	Eric Mangini, NY Jets	0	0	0	0	.000
	Rod Marinelli, Detroit	0	0	0	0	.000
	Mike McCarthy, Green Bay	0	0	0	0	.000
	Sean Payton, New Orleans	0	0	0	0	.000

Annual Awards
Most Valuable Player

Currently, the NFL does not sanction an official MVP award. It awarded the Joe F. Carr Trophy (Carr was NFL president from 1921-39) to the league MVP from 1938 to 1946. Since then, four principal MVP awards have been given out throughout the years and are noted below: UPI (1953-69), AP (since 1957), the Maxwell Club of Philadelphia's Bert Bell Trophy (since 1959) and the Pro Football Writers Assn. (since 1976). UPI switched to AFC and NFC Player of the Year awards in 1970 and then discontinued its awards in 1997.

Multiple winners (more than one season): Jim Brown (4); Randall Cunningham, Brett Favre, Johnny Unitas and Y.A. Tittle (3); Earl Campbell, Marshall Faulk, Rich Gannon, Otto Graham, Don Hutson, Peyton Manning, Joe Montana, Walter Payton, Barry Sanders, Ken Stabler, Joe Theismann, Kurt Warner and Steve Young (2).

Year	Awards
1938 Mel Hein, NY Giants, C	Carr
1939 Parker Hall, Cleveland Rams, HB	Carr
1940 Ace Parker, Brooklyn, HB	Carr
1941 Don Hutson, Green Bay, E	Carr
1942 Don Hutson, Green Bay, E	Carr
1943 Sid Luckman, Chicago Bears, QB	Carr
1944 Frank Sinkwich, Detroit, HB	Carr
1945 Bob Waterfield, Cleveland Rams, QB	Carr
1946 Bill Dudley, Pittsburgh, HB	Carr
1947-52 No award	
1953 Otto Graham, Cleveland Browns, QB	UPI
1954 Joe Perry, San Francisco, FB	UPI
1955 Otto Graham, Cleveland, QB	UPI
1956 Frank Gifford, NY Giants, HB	UPI
1957 Y.A. Tittle, San Francisco, QB	UPI
& Jim Brown, Cleveland, FB	AP
1958 Jim Brown, Cleveland, FB	UPI
& Gino Marchetti, Baltimore, DE	AP
1959 Johnny Unitas, Baltimore, QB	UPI, Bell
& Charley Conerly, NY Giants, QB	AP
1960 Norm Van Brocklin, Phi., QB	UPI, AP (tie), Bell
& Joe Schmidt, Detroit, LB	AP (tie)
1961 Paul Hornung, Green Bay, HB	UPI, AP, Bell
1962 Y.A. Tittle, NY Giants, QB	UPI
Jim Taylor, Green Bay, FB	AP
& Andy Robustelli, NY Giants, DE	Bell
1963 Jim Brown, Cleveland, FB	UPI, Bell
& Y.A. Tittle, NY Giants, QB	AP

Year	Awards
1964 Johnny Unitas, Baltimore, QB	UPI, AP, Bell
1965 Jim Brown, Cleveland, FB	UPI, AP
& Pete Retzlaff, Philadelphia, TE	Bell
1966 Bart Starr, Green Bay, QB	UPI, AP
& Don Meredith, Dallas, QB	Bell
1967 Johnny Unitas, Baltimore, QB	UPI, AP, Bell
1968 Earl Morrall, Baltimore, QB	UPI, AP
& Leroy Kelly, Cleveland, RB	Bell
1969 Roman Gabriel, LA Rams, QB	UPI, AP, Bell
1970 John Brodie, San Francisco, QB	AP
& George Blanda, Oakland, QB-PK	Bell
1971 Alan Page, Minnesota, DT	AP
& Roger Staubach, Dallas, QB	Bell
1972 Larry Brown, Washington, RB	AP, Bell
1973 O.J. Simpson, Buffalo, RB	AP, Bell
1974 Ken Stabler, Oakland, QB	AP
& Merlin Olsen, LA Rams, DT	Bell
1975 Fran Tarkenton, Minnesota, QB	AP, Bell
1976 Bert Jones, Baltimore, QB	AP, PFWA
& Ken Stabler, Oakland, QB	Bell
1977 Walter Payton, Chicago, RB	AP, PFWA
& Bob Griese, Miami, QB	Bell
1978 Terry Bradshaw, Pittsburgh, QB	AP, Bell
& Earl Campbell, Houston, RB	PFWA
1979 Earl Campbell, Houston, RB	AP, Bell, PFWA
1980 Brian Sipe, Cleveland, QB	AP, PFWA
& Ron Jaworski, Philadelphia, QB	Bell
1981 Ken Anderson, Cincinnati, QB	AP, Bell, PFWA

Year	Awards	Year	Awards
1982 Mark Moseley, Washington, PK	AP	1993 Emmitt Smith, Dallas, RB	AP, Bell, PFWA
Joe Theismann, Washington, QB	Bell	1994 Steve Young, San Francisco, QB	AP, Bell, PFWA
& Dan Fouts, San Diego, QB	PFWA	1995 Brett Favre, Green Bay, QB	AP, Bell, PFWA
1983 Joe Theismann, Washington, QB	AP, PFWA	1996 Brett Favre, Green Bay, QB	AP, Bell, PFWA
& John Riggins, Washington, RB	Bell	1997 Barry Sanders, Detroit, RB	AP (tie), Bell, PFWA
1984 Dan Marino, Miami, QB	AP, Bell, PFWA	& Brett Favre, Green Bay, QB	AP (tie)
1985 Marcus Allen, LA Raiders, RB	AP, PFWA	1998 Terrell Davis, Denver, RB	AP, PFWA
& Walter Payton, Chicago, RB	Bell	& Randall Cunningham, Minnesota, QB	Bell
1986 Lawrence Taylor, NY Giants, LB	AP, Bell, PFWA	1999 Kurt Warner, St. Louis, QB	AP, Bell, PFWA
1987 Jerry Rice, San Francisco, WR	Bell, PFWA	2000 Marshall Faulk, St. Louis, RB	AP, PFWA
& John Elway, Denver, QB	AP	& Rich Gannon, Oakland, QB	Bell
1988 Boomer Esiason, Cincinnati, QB	AP, PFWA &	2001 Kurt Warner, St. Louis, QB	AP
Randall Cunningham, Phila., QB	Bell	& Marshall Faulk, St. Louis, RB	Bell, PFWA
1989 Joe Montana, San Francisco, QB	AP, Bell, PFWA	2002 Rich Gannon, Oakland, QB	AP, Bell, PFWA
1990 Randall Cunningham, Phila., QB	Bell, PFWA	2003 Peyton Manning, Indianapolis, QB	AP (tie), PFWA
& Joe Montana, San Francisco, QB	AP	Steve McNair, Tennessee, QB	AP (tie)
1991 Thurman Thomas, Buffalo, RB	AP, PFWA	& Jamal Lewis, Baltimore, RB	PFWA
& Barry Sanders, Detroit, RB	Bell	2004 Peyton Manning, Indianapolis, QB	AP, Bell, PFWA
1992 Steve Young, San Francisco, QB	AP, Bell, PFWA	2005 Shaun Alexander, Seattle, RB	AP, Bell, PFWA

AP Offensive Player of the Year

Selected by The Associated Press in balloting by a nationwide media panel. Given out since 1972. Rookie winners are in **bold** type.
Multiple winners: Earl Campbell and Marshall Faulk (3); Terrell Davis, Jerry Rice and Barry Sanders (2).

Year	Pos	Year	Pos	Year	Pos
1972 Larry Brown, Was	RB	1984 Dan Marino, Mia	QB	1996 Terrell Davis, Den	RB
1973 O.J. Simpson, Buf	RB	1985 Marcus Allen, Raiders	RB	1997 Barry Sanders, Det	RB
1974 Ken Stabler, Oak	QB	1986 Eric Dickerson, Rams	RB	1998 Terrell Davis, Den	RB
1975 Fran Tarkenton, Min	QB	1987 Jerry Rice, SF	WR	1999 Marshall Faulk, St.L	RB
1976 Bert Jones, Bal	QB	1988 Roger Craig, SF	RB	2000 Marshall Faulk, St.L	RB
1977 Walter Payton, Chi	RB	1989 Joe Montana, SF	QB	2001 Marshall Faulk, St.L	RB
1978 **Earl Campbell**, Hou	RB	1990 Warren Moon, Hou	QB	2002 Priest Holmes, KC	RB
1979 Earl Campbell, Hou	RB	1991 Thurman Thomas, Buf	RB	2003 Jamal Lewis, Bal	RB
1980 Earl Campbell, Hou	RB	1992 Steve Young, SF	QB	2004 Peyton Manning, Ind	QB
1981 Ken Anderson, Cin	QB	1993 Jerry Rice, SF	WR	2005 Shaun Alexander, Sea	RB
1982 Dan Fouts, SD	QB	1994 Barry Sanders, Det	RB		
1983 Joe Theismann, Was	QB	1995 Brett Favre, GB	QB		

AP Defensive Player of the Year

Selected by The Associated Press in balloting by a nationwide media panel. Given out since 1971. Rookie winners are in **bold** type.
Multiple winners: Lawrence Taylor (3); Joe Greene, Ray Lewis, Mike Singletary, Bruce Smith and Reggie White (2).

Year	Pos	Year	Pos	Year	Pos
1971 Alan Page, Min	DT	1983 Doug Betters, Mia	DE	1995 Bryce Paup, Buf	LB
1972 Joe Greene, Pit	DT	1984 Kenny Easley, Sea	S	1996 Bruce Smith, Buf	DE
1973 Dick Anderson, Mia	S	1985 Mike Singletary, Chi	LB	1997 Dana Stubblefield, SF	DT
1974 Joe Greene, Pit	DT	1986 Lawrence Taylor, NYG	LB	1998 Reggie White, GB	DE
1975 Mel Blount, Pit	CB	1987 Reggie White, Phi	DE	1999 Warren Sapp, TB	DT
1976 Jack Lambert, Pit	LB	1988 Mike Singletary, Chi	LB	2000 Ray Lewis, Bal	LB
1977 Harvey Martin, Dal	DE	1989 Keith Millard, Min	DT	2001 Michael Strahan, NYG	DE
1978 Randy Gradishar, Den	LB	1990 Bruce Smith, Buf	DE	2002 Derrick Brooks, TB	LB
1979 Lee Roy Selmon, TB	DE	1991 Pat Swilling, NO	LB	2003 Ray Lewis, Bal	LB
1980 Lester Hayes, Oak	CB	1992 Cortez Kennedy, Sea	DT	2004 Ed Reed, Bal	CB
1981 **Lawrence Taylor**, NYG	LB	1993 Rod Woodson, Pit	CB	2005 Brian Urlacher, Chi	LB
1982 Lawrence Taylor, NYG	LB	1994 Deion Sanders, SF	CB		

UPI NFC Player of the Year

Given out by UPI from 1970-96. Offensive and defensive players honored since 1983. Rookie winners are in **bold** type.
Multiple winners: Eric Dickerson, Reggie White and Mike Singletary (3); Brett Favre, Charles Haley, Walter Payton, Lawrence Taylor and Steve Young (2).

Year	Pos	Year	Pos	Year	Pos
1970 John Brodie, SF	QB	1984 Off–Eric Dickerson, Rams	RB	1991 Off–Mark Rypien, Was	QB
1971 Alan Page, Min	DT	Def–Mike Singletary, Chi	LB	Def–Reggie White, Phi	DE
1972 Larry Brown, Was	RB	1985 Off–Walter Payton, Chi	RB	1992 Off–Steve Young, SF	QB
1973 John Hadl, Rams	QB	Def–Mike Singletary, Chi	LB	Def–Chris Doleman, Min	DE
1974 Jim Hart, St.L	QB	1986 Off–Eric Dickerson, Rams	RB	1993 Off–Emmitt Smith, Dal	RB
1975 Fran Tarkenton, Min	QB	Def–Lawrence Taylor, NYG	LB	Def–Eric Allen, Phi	CB
1976 Chuck Foreman, Min	RB	1987 Off–Jerry Rice, SF	WR	1994 Off–Steve Young, SF	QB
1977 Walter Payton, Chi	RB	Def–Reggie White, Phi	DE	Def–Charles Haley, Dal	DE
1978 Archie Manning, NO	QB	1988 Off–Roger Craig, SF	RB	1995 Off–Brett Favre, GB	QB
1979 Ottis Anderson, St.L	RB	Def–Mike Singletary, Chi	LB	Def–Reggie White, GB	DE
1980 Ron Jaworski, Phi	QB	1989 Off–Joe Montana, SF	QB	1996 Off–Brett Favre, GB	QB
1981 Tony Dorsett, Dal	RB	Def–Keith Millard, Min	DT	Def–Kevin Greene, Car	LB
1982 Mark Moseley, Was	PK	1990 Off–Randall Cunningham, Phi.	QB	1997 Award discontinued.	
1983 Off–Eric Dickerson, Rams	RB	Def–Charles Haley, SF	LB		
Def–Lawrence Taylor, NYG	LB				

Annual Awards (Cont.)

UPI AFL-AFC Player of the Year

Presented by UPI to the top player in the AFL (1960-69) and AFC (1970-96). Offensive and defensive players have been honored since 1983. Rookie winners are in **bold** type.
  Multiple winners: Bruce Smith (4); O.J. Simpson (3); Cornelius Bennett, George Blanda, John Elway, Dan Fouts, Daryle Lamonica, Dan Marino and Curt Warner (2).

Year		Pos	Year		Pos	Year		Pos
1960	**Abner Haynes**, Dal	HB	1978	**Earl Campbell**, Hou	RB	1989	Off–Christian Okoye, KC	RB
1961	George Blanda, Hou	QB	1979	Dan Fouts, SD	QB		Def–Michael Dean Perry,Cle	NT
1962	Cookie Gilchrist, Buf	FB	1980	Brian Sipe, Cle	QB	1990	Off–Warren Moon, Hou	QB
1963	Lance Alworth, SD	FL	1981	Ken Anderson, Cin	QB		Def–Bruce Smith,Buf	DE
1964	Gino Cappelletti, Bos	FL-PK	1982	Dan Fouts, SD	QB	1991	Off–Thurman Thomas, Buf	RB
1965	Paul Lowe, SD	HB	1983	Off–**Curt Warner**, Sea	RB		Def–Cornelius Bennett, Buf	LB
1966	Jim Nance, Bos	FB		Def–Rod Martin, Raiders	LB	1992	Off–Barry Foster, Pit	RB
1967	Daryle Lamonica, Raiders	QB	1984	Off–Dan Marino, Mia	QB		Def–Junior Seau, SD	LB
1968	Joe Namath, NYJ	QB		Def–Mark Gastineau, NYJ	DE	1993	Off–John Elway, Den	QB
1969	Daryle Lamonica, Raiders	QB	1985	Off–Marcus Allen, Raiders	RB		Def–Rod Woodson, Pit	CB
1970	George Blanda, Raiders	QB-PK		Def–Andre Tippett, NE	LB	1994	Off–Dan Marino, Mia	QB
1971	Otis Taylor, KC	WR	1986	Off–Curt Warner, Sea	RB		Def–Greg Lloyd, Pit	LB
1972	O.J. Simpson, Buf	RB		Def–Rulon Jones, Den	DE	1995	Off–Jim Harbaugh, Ind	QB
1973	O.J. Simpson, Buf	RB	1987	Off–John Elway, Den	QB		Def–Bryce Paup, Buf	LB
1974	Ken Stabler, Raiders	QB		Def–Bruce Smith, Buf	DE	1996	Off–Terrell Davis, Den	RB
1975	O.J. Simpson, Buf	RB	1988	Off–Boomer Esiason, Cin	QB		Def–Bruce Smith, Buf	DE
1976	Bert Jones, Bal	QB		Def–Bruce Smith, Buf	DE	1997	Award discontinued.	
1977	Craig Morton, Den	QB		& Cornelius Bennett, Buf	LB			

UPI NFL-NFC Rookie of the Year

Presented by UPI to the top rookie in the NFL (1955-69) and NFC (1970-96). Players who were the overall first pick in the NFL draft are in **bold** type.

Year		Pos	Year		Pos	Year		Pos
1955	Alan Ameche, Bal	FB	1970	Bruce Taylor, SF	DB	1985	Jerry Rice, SF	WR
1956	Lenny Moore, Bal	HB	1971	John Brockington, GB	RB	1986	Reuben Mayes, NO	RB
1957	Jim Brown, Cle	FB	1972	Chester Marcol, GB	PK	1987	Robert Awalt, St.L	TE
1958	Jimmy Orr, Pit	FL	1973	Charle Young, Phi	TE	1988	Keith Jackson, Phi	TE
1959	Boyd Dowler, GB	FL	1974	John Hicks, NY	G	1989	Barry Sanders, Det	RB
1960	Gail Cogdill, Det	FL	1975	Mike Thomas, Wash	RB	1990	Mark Carrier, Chi	S
1961	Mike Ditka, Chi	TE	1976	Sammy White, Min	WR	1991	Lawrence Dawsey, TB	WR
1962	Ronnie Bull, Chi	FB	1977	Tony Dorsett, Dal	RB	1992	Robert Jones, Dal	LB
1963	Paul Flatley, Min	FL	1978	Bubba Baker, Det	DE	1993	Jerome Bettis, LA	RB
1964	Charley Taylor, Wash	HB	1979	Ottis Anderson, St.L	RB	1994	Bryant Young, SF	DT
1965	Gale Sayers, Chi	HB	1980	**Billy Sims**, Det	RB	1995	Rashaan Salaam, Chi	RB
1966	Johnny Roland, St.L	HB	1981	**George Rogers**, NO	RB	1996	Simeon Rice, Ari.	DE
1967	Mel Farr, Det	RB	1982	Jim McMahon, Chi	QB	1997	Award discontinued.	
1968	Earl McCullough, Det	FL	1983	Eric Dickerson, LA	RB			
1969	Calvin Hill, Dal	RB	1984	Paul McFadden, Phi	PK			

UPI AFL-AFC Rookie of the Year

Presented by UPI to the top rookie in the AFL (1960-69) and AFC (1970-96). Players who were the overall first pick in the AFL or NFL draft are in **bold** type.

Year		Pos	Year		Pos	Year		Pos
1960	Abner Haynes, Dal	HB	1973	Bobbie Clark, Cin	RB	1986	Leslie O'Neal, SD	DE
1961	Earl Faison, SD	DE	1974	Don Woods, SD	RB	1987	Shane Conlan, Buf	LB
1962	Curtis McClinton, Dal	FB	1975	Robert Brazile, Hou	LB	1988	John Stephens, NE	RB
1963	Billy Joe, Den	FB	1976	Mike Haynes, NE	DB	1989	Derrick Thomas, KC	LB
1964	Matt Snell, NY	FB	1977	A.J. Duhe, Mia	DE	1990	Richmond Webb, Mia	OT
1965	Joe Namath, NY	QB	1978	**Earl Campbell**, Hou	RB	1991	Mike Croel, Den	LB
1966	Bobby Burnett, Buf	HB	1979	Jerry Butler, Buf	WR	1992	Dale Carter, KC	CB
1967	George Webster, Hou	LB	1980	Joe Cribbs, Buf	RB	1993	Rick Mirer, Sea	QB
1968	Paul Robinson, Cin	RB	1981	Joe Delaney, KC	RB	1994	Marshall Faulk, Ind	RB
1969	Greg Cook, Cin	QB	1982	Marcus Allen, LA	RB	1995	Curtis Martin, NE	RB
1970	Dennis Shaw, Buf	QB	1983	Curt Warner, Sea	RB	1996	Terry Glenn, NE	WR
1971	**Jim Plunkett**, NE	QB	1984	Louis Lipps, Pit	WR	1997	Award discontinued.	
1972	Franco Harris, Pit	RB	1985	Kevin Mack, Cle	RB			

AP Offensive Rookie of the Year

Selected by The Associated Press in balloting by a nationwide media panel. Given out since 1967.

Year	Pos	Year	Pos	Year	Pos
1967 Mel Farr, Det	RB	1980 Billy Sims, Det	RB	1993 Jerome Bettis, Rams	RB
1968 Earl McCullouch, Det	OE	1981 George Rogers, NO	RB	1994 Marshall Faulk, Ind	RB
1969 Calvin Hill, Dal	RB	1982 Marcus Allen, Raiders	RB	1995 Curtis Martin, NE	RB
1970 Dennis Shaw, Buf	QB	1983 Eric Dickerson, Rams	RB	1996 Eddie George, Hou	RB
1971 John Brockington, GB	RB	1984 Louis Lipps, Pit	WR	1997 Warrick Dunn, TB	RB
1972 Franco Harris, Pit	RB	1985 Eddie Brown, Cin	WR	1998 Randy Moss, Min	WR
1973 Chuck Foreman, Min	RB	1986 Reuben Mayes, NO	RB	1999 Edgerrin James, Ind	RB
1974 Don Woods, SD	RB	1987 Troy Stradford, Mia	RB	2000 Mike Anderson, Den	RB
1975 Mike Thomas, Was	RB	1988 John Stephens, NE	RB	2001 Anthony Thomas, Chi	RB
1976 Sammy White, Min	WR	1989 Barry Sanders, Det	RB	2002 Clinton Portis, Den	RB
1977 Tony Dorsett, Dal	RB	1990 Emmitt Smith, Dal	RB	2003 Anquan Boldin, Ari	WR
1978 Earl Campbell, Hou	RB	1991 Leonard Russell, NE	RB	2004 Ben Roethlisberger, Pit	QB
1979 Ottis Anderson, St.L	RB	1992 Carl Pickens, Cin	WR	2005 Cadillac Williams, TB	RB

AP Defensive Rookie of the Year

Selected by The Associated Press in balloting by a nationwide media panel. Given out since 1967.

Year	Pos	Year	Pos	Year	Pos
1967 Lem Barney, Det	CB	1981 Lawrence Taylor, NYG	LB	1996 Simeon Rice, Ari	DE
1968 Claude Humphrey, Atl	DE	1982 Chip Banks, Cle	LB	1997 Peter Boulware, Bal	LB
1969 Joe Greene, Pit	DT	1983 Vernon Maxwell, Bal	LB	1998 Charles Woodson, Raiders	CB
1970 Bruce Taylor, SF	CB	1984 Bill Maas, KC	DT	1999 Jevon Kearse, Ten	DE
1971 Isiah Robertson, Rams	LB	1985 Duane Bickett, Ind	LB	2000 Brian Urlacher, Chi	LB
1972 Willie Buchanon, GB	CB	1986 Leslie O'Neal, SD	DE	2001 Kendrell Bell, Pit	LB
1973 Wally Chambers, Chi	DT	1987 Shane Conlan, Buf	LB	2002 Julius Peppers, Car	DE
1974 Jack Lambert, Pit	LB	1988 Erik McMillan, NYJ	S	2003 Terrell Suggs, Bal	LB
1975 Robert Brazile, Hou	LB	1989 Derrick Thomas, KC	LB	2004 Jonathan Vilma, NYJ	LB
1976 Mike Haynes, NE	CB	1990 Mark Carrier, Chi	S	2005 Shawne Merriman, SD	LB
1977 A.J. Duhe, Mia	DE	1991 Mike Croel, Den	LB		
1978 Al Baker, Det	DE	1992 Dale Carter, KC	CB		
1979 Jim Haslett, Buf	LB	1993 Dana Stubblefield, SF	DT		
1980 Buddy Curry, Atl	LB	1994 Tim Bowens, Mia	DT		
& Al Richardson, Atl	LB	1995 Hugh Douglas, NYJ	DE		

Coach of the Year

Presented by UPI to the top coach in the AFL-NFL (1955-69) and AFC-NFC (1970-96). In 1997, the UPI awards were discontinued. Awards beginning in 1997 are the consensus selections from presenters such as AP, The Maxwell Football Club of Philadelphia, The Sporting News and the Pro Football Writers Association. Records indicate the team's change in record from the previous season.

Multiple winners: Dan Reeves (4); Paul Brown, Chuck Knox, Marty Schottenheimer and Don Shula (3); George Allen, Leeman Bennett, Mike Ditka, George Halas, Tom Landry, Marv Levy, Bill Parcells, Jack Pardee, Sam Rutigliano, Lou Saban, Allie Sherman, Dick Vermeil and Bill Walsh (2).

Year	Improvement	Year	Improvement
1955 NFL–Joe Kuharich, Washington	3-9 to 8-4	1970 NFC–Alex Webster, New York	6-8 to 9-5
1956 NFL–Buddy Parker, Detroit	3-9 to 9-3	AFC–Paul Brown, Cincinnati	4-9-1 to 8-6
1957 NFL–Paul Brown, Cleveland	5-7 to 9-2-1	1971 NFC–George Allen, Washington	6-8 to 9-4-1
1958 NFL–Weeb Ewbank, Baltimore	7-5 to 9-3	AFC–Don Shula, Miami	10-4 to 10-3-1
1959 NFL–Vince Lombardi, Green Bay	1-10-1 to 7-5	1972 NFC–Dan Devine, Green Bay	4-8-2 to 10-4
1960 NFL–Buck Shaw, Philadelphia	7-5 to 10-2	AFC–Chuck Noll, Pittsburgh	6-8 to 11-3
AFL–Lou Rymkus, Houston	10-4	1973 NFC–Chuck Knox, Los Angeles	6-7-1 to 12-2
1961 NFL–Allie Sherman, New York	6-4-2 to 10-3-1	AFC–John Ralston, Denver	5-9 to 7-5-2
AFL–Wally Lemm, Houston	10-4 to 10-3-1	1974 NFC–Don Coryell, St. Louis	4-9-1 to 10-4
1962 NFL–Allie Sherman, New York	10-3-1 to 12-2	AFC–Sid Gillman, Houston	1-13 to 7-7
AFL–Jack Faulkner, Denver	3-11 to 7-7	1975 NFC–Tom Landry, Dallas	8-6 to 10-4
1963 NFL–George Halas, Chicago	9-5 to 11-1-2	AFC–Ted Marchibroda, Baltimore	2-12 to 10-4
AFL–Al Davis, Oakland	1-13 to 10-4	1976 NFC–Jack Pardee, Chicago	4-10 to 7-7
1964 NFL–Don Shula, Baltimore	8-6 to 12-2	AFC–Chuck Fairbanks, New England	3-11 to 11-3
AFL–Lou Saban, Buffalo	7-6-1 to 12-2	1977 NFC–Leeman Bennett, Atlanta	4-10 to 7-7
1965 NFL–George Halas, Chicago	5-9 to 9-5	AFC–Red Miller, Denver	9-5 to 12-2
AFL–Lou Saban, Buffalo	12-2 to 10-3-1	1978 NFC–Dick Vermeil, Philadelphia	5-9 to 9-7
1966 NFL–Tom Landry, Dallas	7-7 to 10-3-1	AFC–Walt Michaels, New York	3-11 to 8-8
AFL–Mike Holovak, Boston	4-8-2 to 8-4-2	1979 NFC–Jack Pardee, Washington	8-8 to 10-6
1967 NFL–George Allen, Los Angeles	8-6 to 11-1-2	AFC–Sam Rutigliano, Cleveland	8-8 to 9-7
AFL–John Rauch, Oakland	8-5-1 to 13-1	1980 NFC–Leeman Bennett, Atlanta	6-10 to 12-4
1968 NFL–Don Shula, Baltimore	11-1-2 to 13-1	AFC–Sam Rutigliano, Cleveland	9-7 to 11-5
AFL–Hank Stram, Kansas City	9-5 to 12-2	1981 NFC–Bill Walsh, San Francisco	6-10 to 13-3
1969 NFL–Bud Grant, Minnesota	8-6 to 12-2	AFC–Forrest Gregg, Cincinnati	6-10 to 12-4
AFL–Paul Brown, Cincinnati	3-11 to 4-9-1	1982 NFC–Joe Gibbs, Washington	8-8 to 8-1
		AFC–Tom Flores, Los Angeles	7-9 to 8-1

Annual Awards (Cont.)

Year		Improvement
1983	NFC–John Robinson, Los Angeles	2-7 to 9-7
	AFC–Chuck Knox, Seattle	4-5 to 9-7
1984	NFC–Bill Walsh, San Francisco	10-6 to 15-1
	AFC–Chuck Knox, Seattle	9-7 to 12-4
1985	NFC–Mike Ditka, Chicago	10-6 to 15-1
	AFC–Raymond Berry, New England	9-7 to 11-5
1986	NFC–Bill Parcells, New York	10-6 to 14-2
	AFC–Marty Schottenheimer, Cleveland	8-8 to 12-4
1987	NFC–Jim Mora, New Orleans	7-9 to 12-3
	AFC–Ron Meyer, Indianapolis	3-13 to 9-6
1988	NFC–Mike Ditka, Chicago	11-4 to 12-4
	AFC–Marv Levy, Buffalo	7-8 to 12-4
1989	NFC–Lindy Infante, Green Bay	4-12 to 10-6
	AFC–Dan Reeves, Denver	8-8 to 11-5
1990	NFC–Jimmy Johnson, Dallas	1-15 to 7-9
	AFC–Art Shell, Los Angeles	8-8 to 12-4
1991	NFC–Wayne Fontes, Detroit	6-10 to 12-4
	AFC–Dan Reeves, Denver	5-11 to 12-4
1992	NFC–Dennis Green, Minnesota	8-8 to 11-5
	AFC–Bobby Ross, San Diego	4-12 to 11-5

Year		Improvement
1993	NFC–Dan Reeves, New York	6-10 to 11-5
	AFC–Marv Levy, Buffalo	11-5 to 12-4
1994	NFC–Dave Wannstedt, Chicago	7-9 to 9-7
	AFC–Bill Parcells, New England	5-11 to 10-6
1995	NFC–Ray Rhodes, Philadelphia	7-9 to 10-6
	AFC–Marty Schottenheimer, Kansas City	9-7 to 13-3
1996	NFC–Dom Capers, Carolina	7-9 to 12-4
	AFC–Tom Coughlin, Jacksonville	4-12 to 9-7
1997	NFL–Jim Fassel, NY Giants	6-10 to 10-5-1
1998	NFL–Dan Reeves, Atlanta	7-9 to 14-2
1999	NFL–Dick Vermeil, St. Louis	4-12 to 13-3
2000	NFL–Jim Haslett, New Orleans	3-13 to 10-6
2001	NFL–Dick Jauron, Chicago	5-11 to 13-3
2002	NFL–Andy Reid, Philadelphia	11-5 to 12-4
2003	NFL–Bill Belichick, New England	9-7 to 14-2
2004	NFL–Marty Schottenheimer, San Diego	4-12 to 12-4
2005	NFL–Lovie Smith, Chicago	5-11 to 11-5

CANADIAN FOOTBALL

The Grey Cup

Earl Grey, the Governor-General of Canada (1904-11), donated a trophy in 1909 for the Rugby Football Championship of Canada. The trophy, which later became known as the Grey Cup, was originally open to competition for teams registered with the Canada Rugby Union. Since 1954, the Cup has gone to the champion of the Canadian Football League (CFL).

Overall multiple winners: Toronto Argonauts (15); Edmonton Eskimos (13); Winnipeg Blue Bombers (9); Hamilton Tiger-Cats (8); Ottawa Rough Riders (7); Calgary Stampeders, Hamilton Tigers and Montreal Alouettes (5); B.C. Lions and University of Toronto (4); Queen's University (3); Ottawa Senators, Sarnia Imperials, Saskatchewan Roughriders and Toronto Balmy Beach (2).

CFL multiple winners (since 1954): Edmonton (13); Hamilton and Winnipeg (7); Ottawa and Toronto (5); B.C. Lions, Calgary and Montreal (4); Saskatchewan (2).

Year Cup Final
1909 Univ. of Toronto 26, Toronto Parkdale 6
1910 Univ. of Toronto 16, Hamilton Tigers 7
1911 Univ. of Toronto 14, Toronto Argonauts 7
1912 Hamilton Alerts 11, Toronto Argonauts 4
1913 Hamilton Tigers 44, Toronto Parkdale 2
1914 Toronto Argonauts 14, Univ. of Toronto 2
1915 Hamilton Tigers 13, Toronto Rowing 7
1916-19 Not held (WWI)

1920 Univ. of Toronto 16, Toronto Argonauts 3
1921 Toronto Argonauts 23, Edmonton Eskimos 0
1922 Queens Univ. 13, Edmonton Elks 1
1923 Queens Univ. 54, Regina Roughriders 0
1924 Queens Univ. 11, Toronto Balmy Beach 3
1925 Ottawa Senators 24, Winnipeg Tigers 1
1926 Ottawa Senators 10, Univ. of Toronto 7
1927 Toronto Balmy Beach 9, Hamilton Tigers 6
1928 Hamilton Tigers 30, Regina Roughriders 0
1929 Hamilton Tigers 14, Regina Roughriders 3

1930 Toronto Balmy Beach 11, Regina Roughriders 6
1931 Montreal AAA 22, Regina Roughriders 0
1932 Hamilton Tigers 25, Regina Roughriders 6
1933 Toronto Argonauts 4, Sarnia Imperials 3

Year Cup Final
1934 Sarnia Imperials 20, Regina Roughriders 12
1935 Winnipeg 'Pegs 18, Hamilton Tigers 12
1936 Sarnia Imperials 26, Ottawa Rough Riders 20
1937 Toronto Argonauts 4, Winnipeg Blue Bombers 3
1938 Toronto Argonauts 30, Winnipeg Blue Bombers 7
1939 Winnipeg Blue Bombers 8, Ottawa Rough Riders 7

1940 Gm 1: Ottawa Rough Riders 8, Toronto B-Beach 2
      Gm 2: Toronto Rough Riders 12, Toronto B-Beach 5
1941 Winnipeg Blue Bombers 18, Ottawa Rough Riders 16
1942 Toronto RACF 8, Winnipeg RACF 5
1943 Hamilton Wildcats 23, Winnipeg RACF 14
1944 Montreal HMCS 7, Hamilton Wildcats 6
1945 Toronto Argonauts 35, Winnipeg Blue Bombers 0
1946 Toronto Argonauts 28, Winnipeg Blue Bombers 6
1947 Toronto Argonauts 10, Winnipeg Blue Bombers 9
1948 Calgary Stampeders 12, Ottawa Rough Riders 7
1949 Montreal Alouettes 28, Calgary Stampeders 15

1950 Toronto Argonauts 13, Winnipeg Blue Bombers 0
1951 Ottawa Rough Riders 21, Saskatch. Roughriders 14
1952 Toronto Argonauts 21, Edmonton Eskimos 11
1953 Hamilton Tiger-Cats 12, Winnipeg Blue Bombers 6

Year	Winner	Head Coach	Score	Loser	Head Coach	Site
1954	Edmonton	Frank (Pop) Ivy	26-25	Montreal	Doug Walker	Toronto
1955	Edmonton	Frank (Pop) Ivy	34-19	Montreal	Doug Walker	Vancouver
1956	Edmonton	Frank (Pop) Ivy	50-27	Montreal	Doug Walker	Toronto
1957	Hamilton	Jim Trimble	32-7	Winnipeg	Bud Grant	Toronto
1958	Winnipeg	Bud Grant	35-28	Hamilton	Jim Trimble	Vancouver
1959	Winnipeg	Bud Grant	21-7	Hamilton	Jim Trimble	Toronto
1960	Ottawa	Frank Clair	16-6	Edmonton	Eagle Keys	Vancouver
1961	Winnipeg	Bud Grant	21-14 (OT)	Hamilton	Jim Trimble	Toronto
1962	Winnipeg	Bud Grant	28-27*	Hamilton	Jim Trimble	Toronto

Year	Winner	Head Coach	Score	Loser	Head Coach	Site
1963	Hamilton	Ralph Sazio	21-10	B.C. Lions	Dave Skrien	Vancouver
1964	B.C. Lions	Dave Skrien	34-24	Hamilton	Ralph Sazio	Toronto
1965	Hamilton	Ralph Sazio	22-16	Winnipeg	Bud Grant	Toronto
1966	Saskatchewan	Eagle Keys	29-14	Ottawa	Frank Clair	Vancouver
1967	Hamilton	Ralph Sazio	24-1	Saskatchewan	Eagle Keys	Ottawa
1968	Ottawa	Frank Clair	24-21	Calgary	Jerry Williams	Toronto
1969	Ottawa	Frank Clair	29-11	Saskatchewan	Eagle Keys	Montreal
1970	Montreal	Sam Etcheverry	23-10	Calgary	Jim Duncan	Toronto
1971	Calgary	Jim Duncan	14-11	Toronto	Leo Cahill	Vancouver
1972	Hamilton	Jerry Williams	13-10	Saskatchewan	Dave Skrien	Hamilton
1973	Ottawa	Jack Gotta	22-18	Edmonton	Ray Jauch	Toronto
1974	Montreal	Marv Levy	20-7	Edmonton	Ray Jauch	Vancouver
1975	Edmonton	Ray Jauch	9-8	Montreal	Marv Levy	Calgary
1976	Ottawa	George Brancato	23-20	Saskatchewan	John Payne	Toronto
1977	Montreal	Marv Levy	41-6	Edmonton	Hugh Campbell	Montreal
1978	Edmonton	Hugh Campbell	20-13	Montreal	Joe Scannella	Toronto
1979	Edmonton	Hugh Campbell	17-9	Montreal	Joe Scannella	Montreal
1980	Edmonton	Hugh Campbell	48-10	Hamilton	John Payne	Toronto
1981	Edmonton	Hugh Campbell	26-23	Ottawa	George Brancato	Montreal
1982	Edmonton	Hugh Campbell	32-16	Toronto	Bob O'Billovich	Toronto
1983	Toronto	Bob O'Billovich	18-17	B.C. Lions	Don Matthews	Vancouver
1984	Winnipeg	Cal Murphy	47-17	Hamilton	Al Bruno	Edmonton
1985	B.C. Lions	Don Matthews	37-24	Hamilton	Al Bruno	Montreal
1986	Hamilton	Al Bruno	39-15	Edmonton	Jack Parker	Vancouver
1987	Edmonton	Joe Faragalli	38-36	Toronto	Bob O'Billovich	Vancouver
1988	Winnipeg	Mike Riley	22-21	B.C. Lions	Larry Donovan	Ottawa
1989	Saskatchewan	John Gregory	43-40	Hamilton	Al Bruno	Toronto
1990	Winnipeg	Mike Riley	50-11	Edmonton	Joe Faragalli	Vancouver
1991	Toronto	Adam Rita	36-21	Calgary	Wally Buono	Winnipeg
1992	Calgary	Wally Buono	24-10	Winnipeg	Urban Bowman	Toronto
1993	Edmonton	Ron Lancaster	33-23	Winnipeg	Cal Murphy	Calgary
1994	B.C. Lions	Dave Ritchie	26-23	Baltimore	Don Matthews	Vancouver
1995	Baltimore	Don Matthews	37-20	Calgary	Wally Buono	Regina
1996	Toronto	Don Matthews	43-37	Edmonton	Ron Lancaster	Hamilton
1997	Toronto	Don Matthews	47-23	Saskatchewan	Jim Daley	Edmonton
1998	Calgary	Wally Buono	26-24	Hamilton	Ron Lancaster	Winnipeg
1999	Hamilton	Ron Lancaster	32-21	Calgary	Wally Buono	Vancouver
2000	B.C. Lions	Steve Buratto	28-26	Montreal	Charlie Taaffe	Calgary
2001	Calgary	Wally Buono	27-19	Winnipeg	Dave Ritchie	Montreal
2002	Montreal	Don Matthews	25-16	Edmonton	Tom Higgins	Edmonton
2003	Edmonton	Tom Higgins	34-22	Montreal	Don Matthews	Regina
2004	Toronto	Mike Clemons	27-19	B.C. Lions	Wally Buono	Ottawa
2005	Edmonton	Danny Maciocia	38-35 (OT)	Montreal	Don Matthews	Vancouver

*Halted by fog in 4th quarter, final 9:29 played the following day.

CFL Most Outstanding Player

Regular season Player of the Year as selected by The Football Reporters of Canada since 1953.
Multiple winners: Doug Flutie (6); Russ Jackson and Jackie Parker (3); Dieter Brock, Ron Lancaster and Mike Pringle (2).

Year		
1953 Billy Vessels, Edmonton, RB	1971 Don Jonas, Winnipeg, QB	1989 Tracy Ham, Edmonton, QB
1954 Sam Etcheverry, Montreal, QB	1972 Garney Henley, Hamilton, WR	1990 Mike Clemons, Toronto, RB
1955 Pat Abbruzzi, Montreal, RB	1973 Geo. McGowan, Edmonton, WR	1991 Doug Flutie, B.C. Lions, QB
1956 Hal Patterson, Montreal, E-DB	1974 Tom Wilkinson, Edmonton, QB	1992 Doug Flutie, Calgary, QB
1957 Jackie Parker, Edmonton, RB	1975 Willie Burden, Calgary, RB	1993 Doug Flutie, Calgary, QB
1958 Jackie Parker, Edmonton, QB	1976 Ron Lancaster, Saskatch., QB	1994 Doug Flutie, Calgary, QB
1959 Johnny Bright, Edmonton, RB	1977 Jimmy Edwards, Hamilton, RB	1995 Mike Pringle, Baltimore, RB
1960 Jackie Parker, Edmonton, QB	1978 Tony Gabriel, Ottawa, TE	1996 Doug Flutie, Toronto, QB
1961 Bernie Faloney, Hamilton, QB	1979 David Green, Montreal, RB	1997 Doug Flutie, Toronto, QB
1962 George Dixon, Montreal, RB	1980 Dieter Brock, Winnipeg, QB	1998 Mike Pringle, Montreal, RB
1963 Russ Jackson, Ottawa, QB	1981 Dieter Brock, Winnipeg, QB	1999 Danny McManus, Hamilton, QB
1964 Lovell Coleman, Calgary, RB	1982 Condredge Holloway, Tor., QB	2000 Dave Dickenson, Calgary, QB
1965 George Reed, Saskatchewan, RB	1983 Warren Moon, Edmonton, QB	2001 Khari Jones, Winnipeg, QB
1966 Russ Jackson, Ottawa, QB	1984 Willard Reaves, Winnipeg, RB	2002 Milt Stegall, Winnipeg, SB
1967 Peter Liske, Calgary, QB	1985 Merv Fernandez, B.C. Lions, WR	2003 Anthony Calvillo, Montreal, QB
1968 Bill Symons, Toronto, RB	1986 James Murphy, Winnipeg, WR	2004 Casey Printers, B.C. Lions, QB
1969 Russ Jackson, Ottawa, QB	1987 Tom Clements, Winnipeg, QB	2005 Ricky Ray, Edmonton, QB
1970 Ron Lancaster, Saskatch., QB	1988 David Williams, B.C. Lions, WR	

NFL EUROPE

The World League of American Football was formed in 1991 and consisted of three European teams (London, Barcelona and Frankfurt), and seven North American teams (New York/New Jersey, Orlando, Montreal, Raleigh-Durham, Birmingham, Sacramento and San Antonio). In the fall of 1992, the NFL and WLAF Board of Directors voted to restructure the league to include more European teams. Play was subsequently suspended. In 1993, NFL clubs approved a six-team European-only league to resume play in 1995. In January 1998, the name of the league was changed to NFL Europe.

The World Bowl

Multiple Winners: Frankfurt (4); Berlin and Rhein (2).

Bowl	Year	Winner	Head Coach	Score	Loser	Head Coach	Site
I	1991	London	Larry Kennan	21-0	Barcelona	Jack Bicknell	London
II	1992	Sacramento	Kay Stephenson	21-17	Orlando	Galen Hall	Montreal
III	1995	Frankfurt	Ernie Stautner	26-22	Amsterdam	Al Luginbill	Amsterdam
IV	1996	Scotland	Jim Criner	32-27	Frankfurt	Ernie Stautner	Edinburgh, Scot.
V	1997	Barcelona	Jack Bicknell	38-24	Rhein	Galen Hall	Barcelona
VI	1998	Rhein	Galen Hall	34-10	Frankfurt	Dick Curl	Frankfurt
VII	1999	Frankfurt	Dick Curl	38-24	Barcelona	Jack Bicknell	Dusseldorf
VIII	2000	Rhein	Galen Hall	13-10	Scotland	Jim Criner	Frankfurt
IX	2001	Berlin	Peter Vaas	24-17	Barcelona	Jack Bicknell	Amsterdam
X	2002	Berlin	Peter Vaas	26-20	Rhein	Pete Kuharchek	Dusseldorf
XI	2003	Frankfurt	Doug Graber	35-16	Rhein	Pete Kuharchek	Glasgow
XII	2004	Berlin	Rick Lantz	30-24	Frankfurt	Mike Jones	Gelsenkirchen, Ger.
XIII	2005	Amsterdam	Bart Andrus	27-21	Berlin	Rick Lantz	Dusseldorf
XIV	2006	Frankfurt	Mike Jones	22-7	Amsterdam	Bart Andrus	Dusseldorf

World Bowl MVP

Year
1991 Dan Crossman, London, S
1992 Davis Archer, Sacramento, QB
1995 Paul Justin, Frankfort, QB
1996 Yo Murphy, Scotland, WR
1997 Jon Kitna, Barcelona, QB

Year
1998 Jim Arellanes, Rhein, QB
1999 Andy McCullough, Frankfort, WR
2000 Aaron Stecker, Scotland, RB
2001 Jonathan Quinn, Berlin, QB
2002 Dane Looker, Berlin, WR

Year
2003 Jonas Lewis, Frankfort, RB
2004 Eric McCoo, Berlin, RB
2005 Kurt Kittner, Amsterdam, QB
2006 Butchie Wallace, Frankfort, RB

ARENA FOOTBALL

The Arena Football League debuted in June of 1987 with four teams in Chicago, Denver, Pittsburgh and Washington D.C. Currently there are 18 teams in the league (including expansion Utah in 2006), divided into two conferences and four divisions.

ArenaBowl

Multiple Winners: Tampa Bay (5); Detroit (4); Arizona, Orlando and San Jose (2).

Bowl	Year	Winner	Head Coach	Score	Loser	Head Coach	Site
I	1987	Denver	Tim Marcum	45-16	Pittsburgh	Joe Haering	Pittsburgh
II	1988	Detroit	Tim Marcum	24-13	Chicago	Perry Moss	Chicago
III	1989	Detroit	Tim Marcum	39-26	Pittsburgh	Joe Haering	Detroit
IV	1990	Detroit	Perry Moss	51-27	Dallas	Ernie Stautner	Detroit
V	1991	Tampa Bay	Fran Curci	48-42	Detroit	Tim Marcum	Detroit
VI	1992	Detroit	Tim Marcum	56-38	Orlando	Perry Moss	Orlando
VII	1993	Tampa Bay	Lary Kuharich	51-31	Detroit	Tim Marcum	Detroit
VIII	1994	Arizona	Danny White	36-31	Orlando	Perry Moss	Orlando
IX	1995	Tampa Bay	Tim Marcum	48-35	Orlando	Perry Moss	St. Petersburg
X	1996	Tampa Bay	Tim Marcum	42-38	Iowa	John Gregory	Des Moines
XI	1997	Arizona	Danny White	55-33	Iowa	John Gregory	Phoenix
XII	1998	Orlando	Jay Gruden	62-31	Tampa Bay	Tim Marcum	Tampa
XIII	1999	Albany	Mike Dailey	59-48	Orlando	Jay Gruden	Albany
XIV	2000	Orlando	Jay Gruden	41-38	Nashville	Pat Sperduto	Orlando
XV	2001	Grand Rapids	Michael Trigg	64-42	Nashville	Pat Sperduto	Grand Rapids
XVI	2002	San Jose	Darren Arbet	52-14	Arizona	Danny White	San Jose
XVII	2003	Tampa Bay	Tim Marcum	43-29	Arizona	Danny White	Tampa
XVIII	2004	San Jose	Darren Arbet	69-62	Arizona	Danny White	Phoenix
XIX	2005	Colorado	Mike Dailey	51-48	Georgia	Doug Plank	Las Vegas
XX	2006	Chicago	Mike Hohensee	69-61	Orlando	Jay Gruden	Las Vegas

ArenaBowl MVP

Multiple Winners: George LaFrance (3); Stevie Thomas (2).

Year
1987 Gary Mullen, Denver, WR
1988 Steve Griffin, Detroit, WR/DB
1989 George LaFrance, Det., WR/DB
1990 Art Schlichter, Detroit, QB
1991 Stevie Thomas, TB, WR/LB
1992 George LaFrance, Detroit, OS
1993 Jay Gruden, Tampa Bay, QB
1994 Sherdrick Bonner, Arizona, QB

Year
1995 George LaFrance, Tampa Bay, OS
1996 Stevie Thomas, TB, WR/LB
1997 Donnie Davis, Arizona, QB
1998 Rick Hamilton, Orlando, FB/LB
1999 Eddie Brown, Albany, OS
2000 Connell Maynor, Orlando, QB
2001 Terrill Shaw, Grand Rapids, OS
2002 John Dutton, San Jose, QB

Year
2003 Lawrence Samuels, TB, WR/LB
2004 Off–Mark Grieb, San Jose, QB
　　　Def–Ricky Parker, Arizona, DB
2005 Off–Willis Marshall, Col., WR
　　　Def–Ahmad Hawkins, Col., DB
2006 Off–Matt D'Orazio, Chi. QB
　　　Def–Dennison Robinson, Chi., DB

COLLEGE BASKETBALL

2005 / 2006 YEAR IN REVIEW

George Mason's thrilling run ended against Joakim Noah and eventual national champions **Florida**.

GEORGE WHO?

Eleven-seed George Mason crashed the party in Indianapolis while Billy Donovan's Florida Gators took the title.

IT WAS THE YEAR OF THE PONY TAIL AND THE FAIRY TALE IN COLLEGE BASKETBALL.

The pony tail belonged to Joakim Noah, whose ball of fur on the back of his neck and ball-of-fury approach to the game made him the charismatic leading man of March.

The multicultural, multiracial, multi-skilled big man, son of former tennis star Yannick Noah, morphed into a monster late in the season to carry the Florida Gators to their first national championship.

But while record books like this almanac will record the Gators as the champions of 2006 (see page 310), the fairy tale team from George Mason will likely linger longer in our memories. The Patriots shattered the modern template for a national title contender and injected some badly needed romance into the Final Four, leading a stirring mid-major challenge to the college basketball establishment.

A record four teams (Southern Illinois, Bradley, Wichita State and Northern Iowa) from the Missouri Valley Conference made the NCAA Tournament. Two more joined from the Colonial Athletic Association (North Carolina-Wilmington and George Mason).

Critics howled that the selection committee went overboard in rewarding the little guys at the expense of presumably superior teams from major conferences. But when half of those little guys from the MVC and CAA reached the Sweet Sixteen, the little guys had the last laugh.

And George Mason re-affirmed our belief in the Cinderella story. It's always been part of the charm of March Madness, but Cinderella had fallen on hard times of late. The historic tournament run by GMU changed that, at least for one year.

 **Pat Forde** is a senior writer for ESPN.com

AP/Wide World Photos

➡ The **George Mason Patriots** were Super-Cinderellas in 2006, getting a controversial at-large bid from the mid major CAA then making the Final Four as an 11 seed.

The Patriots were a No. 11 seed, their bonafides questioned by many as unworthy of their at-large bid to the NCAA Tournament. After eliminating 2005 Final Four teams Michigan State and North Carolina in the tourney's first weekend, the nation stopped wondering whether Mason belonged.

After trouncing fellow mid-major Wichita State and stunning pre-tournament favorite Connecticut in the tourney's second week to reach the first Final Four in their league's history, the nation started wondering whether Mason could pull off the impossible and go all the way. By the time the Patriots reached Indianapolis as a modern-day Milan miracle, coach Jim Larranaga was everyone's favorite surrogate uncle. Center Jai Lewis, with at least 295 pounds packed into his 6-foot-7 body, was everyone's favorite fat guy.

Lamar Butler, Folarin Campbell, Will Thomas—even guard Tony Skinn, who began the NCAAs on the bad-boy list, suspended for punching Hofstra's Loren Stokes in the groin during the CAA tournament—became everyone's favorite band of brothers.

But Indy is where the pony tail ended the fairy tale. In the national semifinals Noah and his long, athletic, aggressive teammates dominated George Mason in a 15-point

Duke's **J.J. Redick** hit plenty of threes—457 of them to be exact—during his career with the Blue Devils, breaking the ACC scoring record.

3.2 assists and 1.3 steals. After hardly playing as a freshman, the sophomore's amazing breakout season established him as a top-five NBA draft pick.

Then he chose to stick around for another year with his classmates, roommates and close friends Al Horford, Corey Brewer and Taurean Green. That was the final unexpected twist in a surprising season that ended far from where it began.

By the time it was all over, we realized that we'd spent much of the season watching the wrong guys, the wrong teams, the wrong leagues. J.J. Redick and Adam Morrison captivated the nation with their East Coast-West Coast scoring duel, but neither would make it to the Final Four.

The newly expanded 16-team Big East was all the talk during the season, and punched a record number of dance cards with eight, but none of its members advanced to Indy. Meanwhile, the maligned Southeastern Conference put two teams in the Final Four—and neither was named Kentucky.

And in the end, a big-haired kid who began the season on zero All-America lists wound up as the star of the biggest stage—sharing it with an unlikely gang from George Mason.

victory. Then, in a national title game expected to be evenly fought, Florida whipped lordly UCLA even worse, winning 73-57.

The Gators, who had been tournament underachievers for the previous five years, were untouchable this time around. They won their six games by margins of 26, 22, four, 13, 15 and 16 points – the highest average margin of victory in the tournament in five years.

Noah showcased his versatility in the NCAAs, averaging 16.2 points, 9.5 rebounds, 4.8 blocks,

AP/Wide World Photos

DICK VITALE'S

Biggest Stories of the Year in **College Basketball**

10 **No #1 seeds at Final Four.** Connecticut, Duke, Memphis and Villanova all fell short of a trip to Indianapolis. The only other time the four top seeds failed to make the Final Four was 1980.

09 **The passing of a legend.** DePaul's Ray Meyer passed away at age 92. He coached the Blue Demons for 42 years and broadcast their games for over a decade more.

08 **UCLA shows its muscle.** Ben Howland's team won the Pac-10 regular-season title, conference tournament and made the Final Four. The backcourt of Jordan Farmar and Arron Afflalo was one of the best in America.

07 **Two SEC teams in the Final Four.** This was supposed to be a "down" year in that conference after so many players left for the NBA early. With Glen "Big Baby" Davis and Tyrus Thomas leading the way, LSU joined Florida in Indianapolis.

06 **Surprising North Carolina.** With the top seven scorers from the 2004-05 championship team gone, Roy Williams did a magnificent job getting the Tar Heels back into the NCAA tournament. That earned Williams my Coach of the Year honors.

05 **Big East's Elite Eight.** An NCAA tournament record eight teams (Connecticut, Georgetown, Marquette, Pittsburgh, Seton Hall, Syracuse, Villanova and West Virginia) from the recently reshuffled conference made the big dance.

04 **J.J. Redick breaks ACC scoring record.** He shattered the conference record held for 51 years by Wake Forest's Dickie Hemric and finished his career with 2,769 points and a record 457 3-pointers.

 **Dick Vitale** coached the Pistons and the University of Detroit before broadcasting ESPN's first college basketball game in 1979.

03 **Adam Morrison and Redick battle for Player of the Year honors.** The Gonzaga and Duke stars put on some magical performances all season long and finished 1-2 in the NCAA Division 1 scoring list.

02 **George Mason makes the Final Four as an #11 seed.** Cinderella came all the way from Fairfax, Virginia to the big time by beating Michigan State, North Carolina, Wichita State and Connecticut. A salute to Patriots head coach Jim Larranaga!

01 **Florida wins national champi- onship.** Billy Donovan's team goes from being unranked in the preseason and a #3 seed in NCAA tournament to cutting down the nets in Indianapolis.

Gonzaga's **Adam Morrison** led the nation in scoring and despite all the perceived East Coast bias, or maybe because of it, shared two Player of the Year awards with Duke's J.J. Redick.

>> As an 11-seed George Mason shocked the nation and reached the Final Four, knocking off some of the best known college pro- grams in the country along the way. **>> Did you know that Mason was not the first 11-seed to reach a Final Four? >>** LSU was

DID YOU KNOW?

an 11-seed in 1986 when **Dale Brown's Tigers** made it to the national semifinals before bowing out to Denny Crum's Louisville Cardinals and the Tournament's Most Outstanding Player Pervis Ellison. **>> George Mason and LSU share the record** for the lowest seed to reach the Final Four.

2005-2006
Season in Review

SPORTS ALMANAC

Final Regular Season AP Men's Top 25 Poll
Taken **before** start of NCAA tournament.

The sportswriters & broadcasters poll; first place votes in parentheses; records through Monday, March 14, 2006; total points (based on 25 for 1st, 24 for 2nd, etc.); record in NCAA tourney and team lost to; head coach (career years and record including 2006 postseason), and preseason ranking. Teams in **bold** type went on to reach NCAA Final Four. George Mason, which did not make the AP Top 25, was the fourth Final Four team.

		Mar. 13 Record	Points	NCAA Recap	Head Coach	Preseason Rank
1	Duke (59)	30-3	1783	2-1 (LSU)	Mike Krzyzewski (31 yrs: 753-250)	1
2	Connecticut (11)	27-3	1709	3-1 (George Mason)	Jim Calhoun (34 yrs: 733-314)	3
3	Villanova (1)	25-4	1626	3-1 (Florida)	Jay Wright (12 yrs: 226-144)	5
4	Memphis	30-3	1610	3-1 (UCLA)	John Calipari (14 yrs: 337-129)	12
5	Gonzaga (1)	27-3	1509	2-1 (UCLA)	Mark Few (7 yrs: 188-41)	8
6	Ohio St.	25-5	1347	1-1 (Florida)	Thad Matta (6 yrs: 148-49)	NR
7	Boston College	26-7	1243	2-1 (Villanova)	Al Skinner (18 yrs: 313-254)	11
	UCLA	27-6	1243	5-1 (Florida)	Ben Howland (11 yrs: 229-134)	19
9	Texas	27-6	1215	3-1 (LSU)	Rick Barnes (19 yrs: 393-210)	NR
10	North Carolina	27-6	1060	1-1 (George Mason)	Roy Williams (18 yrs: 498-121)	NR
11	**Florida**	27-6	1006	6-0	Billy Donovan (12 yrs: 260-119)	NR
12	Kansas	25-7	1001	0-1 (Bradley)	Bill Self (12 yrs: 279-129)	NR
13	Illinois	25-6	907	1-1 (Washington)	Bruce Weber (8 yrs: 192-70)	17
14	George Washington	26-2	890	1-1 (Duke)	Karl Hobbs (5 yrs: 91-56)	21
15	Iowa	25-8	825	0-1 (Northwestern St.)	Steve Alford (15 yrs: 291-169)	20
16	Pittsburgh	24-7	816	1-1 (Bradley)	Jamie Dixon (3 yrs: 76-22)	NR
17	Washington	24-6	623	2-1 (Connecticut)	Lorenzo Romar (10 yrs: 177-130)	NR
18	Tennessee	21-7	572	1-1 (Wichita St.)	Bruce Pearl (14 yrs: 339-92)	NR
19	**LSU**	23-8	533	4-1 (UCLA)	John Brady (14 yrs: 256-188)	NR
20	Nevada	27-5	413	0-1 (Montana)	Mark Fox (2 yrs: 52-13)	22
21	Syracuse	23-11	377	0-1 (Texas A&M)	Jim Boeheim (30 yrs: 726-253)	16
22	West Virginia	20-10	312	2-1 (Texas)	John Beilein (24 yrs: 449-266)	14
23	Georgetown	21-9	177	2-1 (Florida)	John Thompson III (6 yrs: 110-65)	NR
24	Oklahoma	20-8	131	0-1 (WI-Milwaukee)	Kelvin Sampson (23 yrs: 456-256)	6
25	UAB	24-6	130	0-1 (Kentucky)	Mike Anderson (4 yrs: 89-41)	NR

Others receiving votes: 26. **Bucknell** 91 points; 27. **Michigan St.** 57; 28. **Arkansas** 46; 29. **N.C. State** 28; 30. **Southern Illinois** 28; 31. **San Diego St.** and **Texas A&M** 17; 33. **Marquette** 14; 34. **NC-Wilmington** 13; 35. **Wichita St.** 9; 36. **Kentucky** 5; 37. **Arizona** 4; 38. **California** 3; 39. **Cincinnati, Kent St., Missouri St.** 2; 42. **Montana, Pacific, Utah St., Winthrop** 1.

NCAA Men's Division I Tournament Seeds

ATLANTA	OAKLAND	WASHINGTON D.C.	MINNEAPOLIS
1 Duke (30-3)	1 Memphis (30-3)	1 Connecticut (27-3)	1 Villanova (25-4)
2 Texas (27-6)	2 UCLA (27-6)	2 Tennessee (21-7)	2 Ohio St. (25-5)
3 Iowa (23-7)	3 Gonzaga (27-3)	3 North Carolina (22-7)	3 Florida (27-6)
4 LSU (23-8)	4 Kansas (25-7)	4 Illinois (25-6)	4 Boston College (26-7)
5 Syracuse (23-11)	5 Pittsburgh (24-7)	5 Washington (24-6)	5 Nevada (27-5)
6 West Virginia (20-10)	6 Indiana (18-11)	6 Michigan St. (22-11)	6 Oklahoma (20-8)
7 California (20-10)	7 Marquette (20-10)	7 Wichita State (24-8)	7 Georgetown (21-9)
8 George Washington (26-2)	8 Arkansas (22-9)	8 Kentucky (21-12)	8 Arizona (19-12)
9 NC-Wilmington (25-7)	9 Bucknell (26-4)	9 UAB (24-6)	9 Wisconsin (19-11
10 N.C. State (21-9)	10 Alabama (17-12)	10 Seton Hall (18-11)	10 Northern Iowa (23-9)
11 So. Illinois (22-10)	11 San Diego St. (24-8)	11 George Mason (23-7)	11 Wisc-Milwaukee (21-8)
12 Texas A&M (21-8)	12 Kent State (25-8)	12 Utah St. (23-8)	12 Montana (23-6)
13 Iona (23-7)	13 Bradley (20-10)	13 Air Force (24-6)	13 Pacific (24-7)
14 Northwestern St. (25-7)	14 Xavier (21-10)	14 Murray St. (24-6)	14 South Alabama (24-6)
15 Pennsylvania (20-8)	15 Belmont (20-10)	15 Winthrop (23-7)	15 Davidson (20-10)
16 Southern (19-12)	16 Oral Roberts (21-11)	16 Albany (21-10)	16 Monmouth* (19-14)

*Monmouth defeated Hampton, 71-49, in the NCAA Tournament "opening-round" play-in game at Dayton, Ohio for a berth in the field of 64.

2006 NCAA Tournament Men's Division

Washington, D.C. Region

1st ROUND March 17-18	2nd ROUND March 19-20	SWEET 16 March 23-24	ELITE EIGHT March 25-26
(1) UConn 72	UConn 87	UConn 98	UConn 84
(16) Albany 59			
(8) Kentucky 69	Kentucky 83		
(9) UAB 64			
(5) Washington 75	Washington 67	Washington 92	George Mason 86
(12) Utah St. 61			
(4) Illinois 78	Illinois 64		
(13) Air Force 69			
(6) Michigan St. 65	George Mason 65	George Mason 63	
(11) Geo. Mason 75			
(3) N. Carolina 69	North Carolina 60		
(14) Murray St. 65			
(7) Wichita St. 86	Wichita St. 80	Wichita St. 55	
(10) Seton Hall 66			
(2) Tennessee 63	Tennessee 73		
(15) Winthrop 61			

Minneapolis Region

Play-in Game to Minneapolis (16) seed: Monmouth 71, Hampton 49

1st ROUND March 17-18	2nd ROUND March 19-20	SWEET 16 March 23-24	ELITE EIGHT March 25-26
(1) Villanova 58	Villanova 82	Villanova 60	Villanova 62
(16) Monmouth 45			
(8) Arizona 94	Arizona 78		
(9) Wisconsin 75			
(5) Nevada 79	Montana 56	Boston College 59	
(12) Montana 87			
(4) Boston Coll. 88	Boston College 69		
(13) Pacific 76			
(6) Oklahoma 74	Wi-Milwaukee 60	Florida 57	Florida 75
(11) Wi-Milw. 82			
(3) Florida 76	Florida 82		
(14) S. Alabama 50			
(7) Georgetown 54	Georgetown 70	Georgetown 53	
(10) N. Iowa 49			
(2) Ohio St. 70	Ohio St. 52		
(15) Davidson 62			

FINAL FOUR April 1 (right)

George Mason 58, Florida 73

NATIONAL CHAMPIONSHIP

Florida 73
UCLA 57

RCA Dome
Indianapolis, Ind.
Monday, April 3, 2006

FINAL FOUR April 1 (left)

LSU 45, UCLA 59

Atlanta Region

1st ROUND March 16-17	2nd ROUND March 18-19	SWEET 16 March 23-24	ELITE EIGHT March 25-26
(1) Duke 70	Duke 74	Duke 54	LSU 70
(16) Southern 54			
(8) Geo. Wash. 88	Geo. Wash. 61		
(9) NC-Wilm. 85			
(5) Syracuse 58	Texas A&M 57	LSU 62	
(12) Texas A&M 66			
(4) LSU 80	LSU 58		
(13) Iona 64			
(6) West Va. 64	West Virginia 67	West Virginia 71	Texas 60
(11) So. Illinois 46			
(3) Iowa 63	N'western St. 54		
(14) N'western St. 64			
(10) California 52	N.C. State 54	Texas 74	
(10) N.C. State 58			
(2) Texas 60	Texas 75		
(15) Penn 52			

Oakland Region

1st ROUND March 16-17	2nd ROUND March 18-19	SWEET 16 March 23-24	ELITE EIGHT March 25-26
(1) Memphis 94	Memphis 72	Memphis 80	Memphis 45
(16) O. Roberts 78			
(8) Arkansas 55	Bucknell 56		
(9) Bucknell 59			
(5) Pittsburgh 79	Pittsburgh 66	Bradley 64	
(12) Kent St. 64			
(4) Kansas 73	Bradley 72		
(13) Bradley 77			
(6) Indiana 87	Indiana 80	Gonzaga 71	UCLA 50
(11) SDSU 83			
(3) Gonzaga 79	Gonzaga 90		
(14) Xavier 75			
(7) Marquette 85	Alabama 59	UCLA 73	
(10) Alabama 90			
(2) UCLA 78	UCLA 62		
(15) Belmont 44			

2006 FINAL FOUR INDIANAPOLIS

NCAA Men's Championship Game

68th NCAA Division I Championship Game. **Date:** Monday, April 3, at the RCA Dome in Indianapolis. **Coaches:** Billy Donovan of Florida and Ben Howland of UCLA. **Favorite:** Florida by 1.
Attendance: 43,168; **Officials:** Jim Burr, John Cahill, Tony Greene. **TV Rating:** 11.2/18 share (CBS).

Florida 73

	Min	FG M-A	FT M-A	Pts	Reb O-T	A	PF
Corey Brewer	.37	4-12	1-3	11	3-7	4	3
Joakim Noah	.33	7-9	2-2	16	2-9	3	2
Al Horford	.24	5-8	4-5	14	2-7	3	2
Taurean Green	.36	1-9	0-1	2	0-4	8	1
Lee Humphrey	.36	4-8	3-3	15	0-1	2	1
Adrian Moss	.10	3-6	3-4	9	2-6	0	0
Walter Hodge	.12	0-3	0-0	0	0-1	1	1
Chris Richard	.12	2-3	2-2	6	0-0	0	3
TOTALS	.200	26-58	15-20	73	9-35	21	13

Three-point FG: 6-19 (Humphrey 4-8, Green 0-7, Brewer 2-3, Hodge 0-1); **Blocked Shots:** 10 (Noah 6, Horford 2, Richard, Brewer); **Turnovers:** 6 (Noah 2, Brewer 2, Horford, Green); **Steals:** 7 (Brewer 3, Hodge 2, Green, Noah); **Percentages:** 2-Pt FG (.513), 3-Pt FG (.316), Total FG (.448), Free Throws (.750).

UCLA 57

	Min	FG M-A	FT M-A	Pts	Reb O-T	A	PF
Cedric Bozeman	.25	2-3	5-6	9	0-3	3	2
L. Mbah a Moute	.32	3-9	0-0	6	3-10	1	4
Ryan Hollins	.26	4-10	2-2	10	5-10	0	2
Jordan Farmar	.34	8-21	1-2	18	0-2	4	2
Arron Afflalo	.32	3-10	2-2	10	0-2	1	2
Darren Collison	.21	0-3	0-0	0	1-3	1	3
Alfred Aboya	.14	1-1	0-2	2	2-3	1	2
Lorenzo Mata	.9	1-4	0-0	2	2-5	0	3
Michael Roll	.7	0-0	0-0	0	0-0	0	2
TOTALS	.200	22-61	10-14	57	13-38	11	22

Three-point FGs: 3-17 (Afflalo 2-7, Farmar 1-8, Mbah a Moute 0-2); **Blocked Shots:** 1 (Hollins); **Turnovers:** 12 (Afflalo 3, Collison 3, Bozeman 2, Farmar 2, Hollins, Mata); **Steals:** 3 (Farmar 2, Afflalo 1). **Percentages:** 2-Pt FG (.432), 3-Pt FG (.176), Total FG (.361), Free Throws (.714).

Florida (SEC)	.36	37 —	**73**
UCLA (Pac-10)	.25	32 —	**57**

Final ESPN/USA Today Coaches' Poll

Taken **after** NCAA Tournament.
Voted on by a panel of 31 Division I head coaches following the NCAA tournament; first place votes in parentheses with total points (based on 25 for 1st, 24 for 2nd, etc.). Schools on major probation are ineligible to be ranked.

		W-L	Pts	Before NCAAs W-L	Rank
1	Florida (31)	.33-6	775	27-6	10
2	UCLA	.32-7	739	27-6	8
3	LSU	.27-9	666	23-8	18
4	Connecticut	.30-4	658	27-3	2
5	Villanova	.28-5	620	25-4	4
6	Memphis	.33-4	607	30-3	3
7	Duke	.32-4	585	30-3	1
8	George Mason	.27-8	564	23-7	NR
9	Texas	.30-7	542	27-6	9
10	Gonzaga	.29-4	503	27-3	5
11	Boston College	.28-8	463	26-7	7
12	Washington	.26-7	403	24-6	17
13	Ohio St.	.26-6	354	25-5	6
14	North Carolina	.23-8	312	22-7	12
15	West Virginia	.22-11	300	20-10	23
16	Georgetown	.23-10	296	21-9	24
17	Illinois	.26-7	261	25-6	14
18	Pittsburgh	.25-8	247	24-7	16
19	George Washington	.27-3	221	26-2	11
20	Tennessee	.22-8	198	21-7	19
21	Wichita State	.26-9	169	24-8	NR
22	Kansas	.25-8	155	25-7	13
23	Iowa	.25-9	109	25-8	15
24	Bradley	.22-11	106	20-10	NR
25	Bucknell	.27-5	51	26-4	NR

Others receiving votes: 26. **N.C. State** (23 pts); 27. **Nevada** (18); 28. **Syracuse** (16); 29. **UAB** (16); 30. **Indiana** (14); 31. **Alabama** and **Oklahoma** (13); 33. **Arizona** (12); 34. **Kentucky** and **Nevada** (10); 36. **California** (6); 37. **Texas A&M** (5); 38. **South Carolina** (4); 39. **Pacifia** (3); 40. **San Diego St., Wisc-Milwaukee, Northwestern St.** and **NC-Wilmington** (2).

THE FINAL FOUR

at the RCA Dome in Indianapolis.
(April 1-3, 2006).

Semifinal — Game One

Minneapolis Regional champ Florida vs. Washington, D.C. Regional champ George Mason; Saturday, Apr. 1 (6:07 p.m. tipoff). **Coaches:** Billy Donovan, Florida and Jim Larranaga, George Mason. **Favorite:** Florida by 6.

George Mason (Colonial)	.26	32— **58**
Florida (SEC)	.31	42— **73**

High scorers— Jai Lewis & Tony Skinn, George Mason (13) and Lee Humphrey & Corey Brewer, Florida (19); **Att—** 43,168.

Semifinal — Game Two

Oakland Regional champion UCLA vs. Atlanta Regional champ LSU; Saturday, Apr. 1 (9:21 p.m. tipoff). **Coaches:** Ben Howland, UCLA and John Brady, LSU. **Favorite:** LSU by 2.

LSU (SEC)	.24	21— **45**
UCLA (Pac-10)	.39	20— **59**

High scorers— Glenn Davis (14) and L. Mbah a Moute, UCLA (17); **Att—** 43,168.

Most Outstanding Player

Joakim Noah, Florida sophomore forward/center. SEMIFINAL—26 minutes, 12 points, 8 rebounds, 2 assists, 4 blocks; FINAL—33 minutes, 16 points, 9 rebounds, 3 assists, 6 blocks.

All-Final Four Team

Joakim Noah, forward Corey Brewer and guards Taurean Green and Lee Humphrey of Florida and guard Jordan Farmar of UCLA.

NCAA Finalists' Tournament and Season Statistics

At least 10 games played during the overall season.

Florida (33-6)

| | NCAA Tournament | | | | | | Overall Season | | | | |
| | | | —Per Game— | | | | | | —Per Game— | | |
	Gm	FG %	TPts	Pts	Reb	Ast	Gm	FG %	TPts	Pts	Reb	Ast
Joakim Noah	6	.550	97	16.2	9.5	3.2	39	.627	552	14.2	7.1	2.1
Corey Brewer	6	.469	83	13.8	4.8	2.3	39	.468	494	12.7	4.8	3.3
Lee Humphrey	6	.455	77	12.8	2.0	1.5	38	.475	415	10.9	1.9	1.8
Al Horford	6	.569	71	11.8	10.0	2.5	39	.608	442	11.3	7.6	2.0
Taurean Green	6	.275	63	10.5	3.0	3.8	39	.366	519	13.3	2.9	4.7
Chris Richard	6	.600	23	3.8	2.0	0.5	39	.698	232	5.9	3.6	0.5
Adrian Moss	6	.462	15	2.5	3.3	0.0	39	.465	122	3.1	2.4	0.5
Walter Hodge	6	.154	5	0.8	1.5	0.7	39	.387	150	3.8	1.1	1.2
David Huertas	4	.333	2	0.5	0.8	0.3	35	.378	87	2.5	1.5	0.7
Garrett Tyler	2	—	0	0.0	0.0	0.0	16	.417	17	1.1	0.6	0.0
Jack Berry	2	—	0	0.0	0.0	0.0	15	.375	8	0.5	0.4	0.0
Brett Swanson	2	—	0	0.0	0.0	0.0	16	.364	14	0.9	0.3	0.1
FLORIDA	6	.458	436	72.7	39.8	14.7	39	.500	3052	78.3	35.9	16.7
OPPONENTS	6	.347	340	56.7	33.8	9.7	39	.399	2478	63.5	32.3	11.1

Three-pointers: NCAA TOURNAMENT—Humphrey (22-48), Brewer (13-25), Green (9-35), Hodge (1-7), Huertas (1-5), Noah (0-1), Moss (0-2), Team (45-119 for .378 pct.); OVERALL— Humphrey (133-246), Green (88-229), Brewer (42-120), Hodge (28-76), Huertas (12-36), Swanson (2-9), Moss (2-11), Tyler (1-4), Berry (1-4), Horford (0-2), Noah (0-1), Team 289-738 for .392 pct.).

UCLA (32-7)

| | NCAA Tournament | | | | | | Overall Season | | | | |
| | | | —Per Game— | | | | | | —Per Game— | | |
	Gm	FG %	TPts	Pts	Reb	Ast	Gm	FG %	TPts	Pts	Reb	Ast
Arron Afflalo	6	.339	69	11.5	3.7	0.7	39	.462	618	15.8	4.2	1.8
Jordan Farmar	6	.370	75	12.5	1.8	4.2	37	.410	498	13.5	2.6	5.1
Luc Mbah a Moute	6	.533	65	10.8	8.3	2.2	39	.538	354	9.1	8.2	1.3
Cedric Bozeman	6	.407	34	5.7	4.5	2.8	31	.500	235	7.6	3.3	2.3
Ryan Hollins	6	.719	64	10.7	6.3	0.3	33	.619	231	7.0	4.8	0.3
Darren Collison	6	.370	28	4.7	2.0	1.5	39	.402	215	5.5	1.8	2.3
Lorenzo Mata	6	.455	13	2.2	3.7	0.0	21	.500	76	3.6	3.9	0.0
Alfred Aboya	6	.556	11	1.8	1.7	0.3	33	.640	119	3.6	2.4	0.4
Michael Roll	6	.176	11	1.5	0.3	0.5	38	.369	131	3.4	0.9	0.9
Ryan Wright	2	.500	6	3.0	3.5	0.0	31	.566	73	2.4	1.5	0.0
Michael Fey	2	1.000	2	1.0	0.0	0.5	18	.481	31	1.7	1.3	0.1
Janou Rubin	2	.500	3	1.5	1.0	0.5	18	.545	16	0.9	0.7	0.3
UCLA	6	.429	379	63.2	36.0	12.8	39	.473	2642	67.7	33.4	13.9
OPPONENTS	6	.383	337	56.2	34.2	8.8	39	.415	2288	58.7	28.9	10.9

Three-pointers: NCAA TOURNAMENT— Farmar (12-39), Afflalo (11-34), Roll (3-13), Bozeman (1-7), Collison (1-5), Mbah a Moute (0-3), Rubin (1-1), Team (29-102 for .284 pct.); OVERALL— Afflalo (83-227), Farmar (63-189), Roll (36-94), Bozeman (22-56), Collison (19-58), Shipp (6-13), Mbah a Moute (5-38), Rubin (2-4), Aboya (0-2), Mata (0-1), Team (236-682 for .346 pct.).

Florida's Schedule

Reg. Season
(23-6)

W	St. Peter's		.80-51
W	Albany		.83-64
W	Wake Forest		.77-72
W	Syracuse		.75-70
W	Florida St.		.74-66
W	Alabama St.		.87-60
W	UCF		.80-47
W	at Providence		.87-77
W	Bethune-Cookman		88-58
W	Jacksonville		.101-58
W	at Miami-FL		.77-67
W	Florida A&M		.84-47
W	Morgan St.		.92-49
W	at Georgia		.90-72
W	Mississippi St.		.75-60
W	Auburn		.85-57
W	Savannah St.		.113-62
L	at Tennessee		.76-80
L	at South Carolina		62-68
W	Vanderbilt		.73-68
W	at Mississippi		.69-58

W	Kentucky		.95-80
L	South Carolina		.67-71
W	LSU		.71-62
W	at Vanderbilt		.73-68
L	at Arkansas		.81-85 OT
L	Tennessee		.72-76
L	at Alabama		.77-82
W	Georgia		.77-66
W	at Kentucky		.74-71

SEC Tourney
(3-0)

W	Arkansas		.74-71
W	LSU		.81-65
W	South Carolina		.49-47

NCAA Tourney
(6-0)

W	South Alabama		.76-50
W	Wisc-Milwaukee		.82-60
W	Georgetown		.57-53
W	Villanova		.75-62
W	George Mason		.73-58
W	UCLA		.73-57

UCLA's Schedule

Reg. Season
(26-6)

W	NMSU		.83-70
W	Temple		.54-47
W	DSUM		.56-37
L	Memphis		.80-88
W	Drexel		.57-56
W	Albany		.73-65
W	CSU		.69-57
W	Nevada		.67-56
W	at Michigan		.68-61
W	Wagner		.74-72
W	Sacramento St.		.86-56
W	Stanford		.71-54
L	California		.61-68
W	at Arizona		.85-79
W	at Arizona St.		.61-60
W	Washington St.		.63-61
L	Washington		.65-69
W	USC		.66-45
L	West Virginia		.56-60
W	at Oregon		.56-49
W	at Oregon St.		.63-54

W	Arizona St.		.69-60
W	Arizona		.84-73
W	at Washington St.		50-30
L	at Washington		.67-70
L	at USC		.68-71
W	OSU		.78-60
W	Oregon		.70-53
W	at California		.67-58
W	at Stanford		.75-54

Pac-10 Tourney
(3-0)

W	Oregon St.		.79-47
W	Arizona		.71-59
W	California		.71-52

NCAA Tourney
(5-1)

W	Belmont		.78-44
W	Alabama		.62-59
W	Gonzaga		.73-71
W	Memphis		.50-45
W	LSU		.59-45
L	Florida		.57-73

Final NCAA Men's Division I Standings

Conference records include regular season games only. Overall records include all postseason tournament games.

America East Conference

Team	Conference W	L	Pct	Overall W	L	Pct
*Albany	13	3	.812	21	11	.656
Binghamton	12	4	.750	16	13	.552
Boston University	9	7	.562	12	16	.429
Hartford	9	7	.562	13	15	.464
New Hampshire	8	8	.500	12	17	.414
Vermont	7	9	.438	13	17	.433
Maine	7	9	.438	12	16	.429
UMBC	5	11	.312	10	19	.345
Stony Brook	2	14	.125	4	24	.143

Conf. Tourney Final: Albany 80, Vermont 67.
*NCAA Tourney (0-1): Albany (0-1).

Atlantic Coast Conference

Team	Conference W	L	Pct	Overall W	L	Pct
*Duke	14	2	.875	32	4	.889
*North Carolina	12	4	.750	23	8	.742
*Boston College	11	5	.688	28	8	.778
*N.C. State	10	6	.625	22	10	.688
†Florida St	9	7	.562	20	10	.667
†Maryland	8	8	.500	19	13	.594
†Virginia	7	9	.438	15	15	.500
†Miami-FL	7	9	.438	18	16	.529
†Clemson	7	9	.438	19	13	.594
Virginia Tech	4	12	.250	14	16	.467
Georgia Tech	4	12	.250	11	17	.393
†Wake Forest	3	13	.188	17	17	.500

Conf. Tourney Final: Duke 78, Boston College 76.
*NCAA Tourney (6-4): Boston College (2-1), Duke (2-1), North Carolina (1-1), N.C. State (1-1).
†NIT (4-6): Miami-FL (2-1), Clemson (1-1), Florida St. (1-1), Virginia (0-1), Maryland (0-1), Wake Forest (0-1), .

Atlantic Sun Conference

Team	Conference W	L	Pct	Overall W	L	Pct
†Lipscomb	15	5	.750	21	11	.656
*Belmont	15	5	.750	20	11	.645
Florida Atlantic	14	6	.700	15	13	.536
Gardner-Webb	13	7	.650	17	12	.586
East Tennesse St.	12	8	.600	15	13	.536
Stetson	11	9	.550	14	18	.438
Campbell	9	11	.450	10	18	.357
Mercer	7	13	.350	9	19	.321
Jacksonville	1	19	.050	1	26	.037

Conf. Tourney Final: Belmont 74, Lipscomb 69 OT.
*NCAA Tourney (0-1): Belmont (0-1).
†NIT (0-1): Lipscomb (0-1).

Atlantic 10 Conference

Team	Conference W	L	Pct	Overall W	L	Pct
*George Washington	16	0	1.000	27	3	.900
†Charlotte	11	5	.688	19	13	.594
La Salle	10	6	.625	18	10	.643
Saint Louis	10	6	.625	16	13	.552
†St. Joseph's	9	7	.563	19	14	.576
Fordham	9	7	.563	16	16	.500
Massachusetts	8	8	.500	13	15	.464
Rhode Island	8	8	.500	14	14	.500
†Temple	8	8	.500	17	15	.531
*Xavier	8	8	.500	21	11	.656
Richmond	6	10	.375	13	17	.433
Dayton	6	10	.375	14	17	.452
St. Bonaventure	2	14	.125	8	19	.296
Duquesne	1	15	.063	3	24	.111

Conf. Tourney Final: Xavier 62, St. Joseph's 61.
*NCAA Tourney (1-2): G. Washington (1-1), Xavier (0-1).
†NIT (2-3): Charlotte (1-1), St. Joseph's (1-1), Temple (0-1).

Big East Conference

East	Conference W	L	Pct	Overall W	L	Pct
*Connecticut	14	2	.875	30	4	.882
*Villanova	14	2	.875	28	5	.848
*West Virginia	11	5	.688	22	11	.667
*Marquette	10	6	.625	20	11	.645
*Georgetown	10	6	.625	23	10	.697
*Pittsburgh	10	6	.625	25	8	.758
*Seton Hall	9	7	.562	18	12	.600
*Cincinnati	8	8	.500	21	13	.618
*Syracuse	7	9	.438	23	12	.657
*Rutgers	7	9	.438	19	14	.576
†Louisville	6	10	.375	21	13	.618
†Notre Dame	6	10	.375	16	14	.533
St. John's	5	11	.312	12	15	.444
Providence	5	11	.312	12	15	.444
DePaul	5	11	.312	12	15	.444
USF	1	15	.063	7	22	.241

Conf. Tourney Final: Syracuse 65, Pittsburgh 61.
*NCAA Tourney (11-8): Connecticut (3-1), Villanova (2-1), West Virginia (2-1), Georgetown (2-1), Pittsburgh (1-1), Marquette (0-1), Seton Hall (0-1), Syracuse (0-1).
†NIT (7-4): Louisville (3-1), Cincinnati (2-1), Rutgers (1-1), Notre Dame (1-1).

Big Sky Conference

Team	Conference W	L	Pct	Overall W	L	Pct
†Northern Arizona	12	3	.800	21	11	.656
*Montana	10	4	.714	24	7	.774
Eastern Washington	9	5	.643	15	15	.500
Montana St	7	7	.500	15	15	.500
Sacramento St.	5	9	.357	15	15	.500
Portland St.	5	9	.357	12	16	.429
Idaho St	4	10	.286	13	14	.481
Weber St	4	10	.286	10	17	.370

Conf. Tourney Final: Montana 73, No. Arizona 60.
*NCAA Tourney (1-1): Montana (1-1).
†NIT (0-1): Northern Arizona (0-1).

Big South Conference

Team	Conference W	L	Pct	Overall W	L	Pct
*Winthrop	13	3	.812	23	8	.742
Coastal Carolina	12	4	.750	20	10	.667
Birmingham-Southern	12	4	.750	19	9	.679
Radford	9	7	.562	16	13	.552
High Point	8	8	.500	16	13	.552
Charleston Southern	7	9	.438	13	16	.448
NC-Asheville	6	10	.375	9	19	.321
Liberty	3	13	.188	7	23	.233
VMI	2	14	.125	7	20	.259

Conf. Tourney Final: Winthrop 51, Coastal Carolina 50.
*NCAA Tourney (0-1): Winthrop (0-1).

Division I Independents

Team	Overall W	L	Pct
Texas A&M-Corpus Christi	20	8	.714
North Dakota St.	16	12	.571
Utah Valley St.	16	13	.552
IPFW	10	18	.357
Longwood	10	20	.333
South Dakota St.	9	20	.310
UC-Davis	8	20	.286
Texas-Pan American	7	24	.226
Northern Colorado	5	24	.172
Savannah St.	2	28	.067

Final NCAA Men's Division I Standings (Cont.)

Big Ten Conference

Team	Conference			Overall		
	W	L	Pct	W	L	Pct
*Ohio St	12	4	.750	26	6	.812
*Illinois	11	5	.688	26	7	.788
*Iowa	11	5	.688	25	9	.735
*Wisconsin	9	7	.562	19	12	.613
*Indiana	9	7	.562	19	12	.613
†Michigan	8	8	.500	22	11	.667
*Michigan St	8	8	.500	22	12	.647
†Penn St	6	10	.375	15	15	.500
Northwestern	6	10	.375	14	15	.483
†Minnesota	5	11	.312	16	15	.516
Purdue	3	13	.188	9	19	.321

Conf. Tourney Final: Iowa 67, Ohio St. 60.
***NCAA Tourney (3-6):** Ohio St. (1-1), Illinois (1-1), Indiana (1-1), Michigan St. (0-1), Wisconsin (0-1), Iowa (0-1).
†NIT (4-3): Michigan (4-1), Minnesota (1-1), Penn St. (0-1).

Big 12 Conference

Team	Conference			Overall		
	W	L	Pct	W	L	Pct
*Texas	13	3	.813	30	7	.811
*Kansas	13	3	.813	25	8	.758
*Oklahoma	11	5	.688	20	9	.690
*Texas A&M	10	6	.625	22	9	.710
†Colorado	9	7	.563	20	10	.667
†Nebraska	7	9	.438	19	14	.576
†Oklahoma St.	6	10	.375	17	16	.515
Texas Tech	6	10	.375	15	17	.469
Kansas St	6	10	.375	15	13	.536
Iowa St.	6	10	.375	16	14	.533
Missouri	5	11	.313	12	16	.429
Baylor	4	12	.250	4	13	.235

Conf. Tourney Final: Kansas 80, Texas 68.
***NCAA Tourney (4-4):** Texas (3-1), Texas A&M (1-1), Kansas (0-1), Oklahoma (0-1).
†NIT (0-3): Colorado (0-1), Nebraska (0-1), Oklahoma St. (0-1).

Big West Conference

Team	Conference			Overall		
	W	L	Pct	W	L	Pct
*Pacific	12	2	.857	24	8	.750
UC-Irvine	10	4	.714	16	13	.552
Long Beach St	9	5	.643	18	12	.600
Cal Poly	7	7	.500	10	19	.345
UC-Santa Barbara	6	8	.429	15	14	.517
Cal St.-Fullerton	5	9	.357	16	13	.552
Cal St.-Northridge	4	10	.286	11	17	.393
UC-Riverside	3	11	.214	5	23	.179

Conf. Tourney Final: Pacific 78, Long Beach St. 70.
***NCAA Tourney (0-1):** Pacific (0-1).

Conference USA

Team	Conference			Overall		
	W	L	Pct	W	L	Pct
*Memphis	13	1	.929	33	4	.892
*Ala-Birmingham	12	2	.857	24	7	.774
†UTEP	11	3	.786	21	10	.677
†Houston	9	5	.643	21	10	.677
UCF	7	7	.500	14	15	.429
Tulsa	6	8	.429	11	17	.393
Rice	6	8	.429	12	16	.429
Tulane	6	8	.429	12	17	.414
Marshall	5	9	.357	12	16	.429
SMU	4	10	.286	13	16	.448
So. Mississippi	3	11	.214	10	21	.323
East Carolina	2	12	.143	8	20	.286

Conf. Tourney Final: Memphis 57, UAB 46.
***NCAA Tourney (3-2):** Memphis (3-1), UAB (0-1).
†NIT (2-2): Houston (1-1), UTEP (1-1).

Colonial Athletic Association

Team	Conference			Overall		
	W	L	Pct	W	L	Pct
*George Mason	15	3	.833	27	8	.771
*NC-Wilmington	15	3	.833	25	8	.758
†Hofstra	14	4	.778	26	7	.788
†Old Dominion	13	5	.722	24	10	.706
Northeastern	12	6	.667	19	11	.633
Va. Commonwealth	11	7	.611	19	10	.655
Drexel	8	10	.444	15	16	.484
Towson	8	10	.444	12	16	.429
Delaware	4	14	.222	9	21	.300
William & Mary	3	15	.167	8	20	.286
Georgia St.	3	15	.167	7	22	.241
James Madison	2	16	.111	5	23	.179

Conf. Tourney Final: NC-Wilmington 78, Hofstra 67.
***NCAA Tourney (4-2):** George Mason (4-1), NC-Wilmington (0-1).
†NIT (5-2): Hofstra (2-1), Old Dominion (3-1).

Horizon League

Team	Conference			Overall		
	W	L	Pct	W	L	Pct
*WI-Milwaukee	12	4	.750	22	9	.710
*Butler	11	5	.688	20	13	.606
WI-Green Bay	8	8	.500	16	14	.484
Loyola-IL	8	8	.500	19	11	.633
Illinois-Chicago	8	8	.500	16	15	.516
Detroit	8	8	.500	16	16	.500
Wright St	8	8	.500	13	15	.464
Cleveland St.	5	11	.313	10	18	.357
Youngstown St.	4	12	.250	7	21	.250

Conf. Tourney Final: WI-Milwaukee 87, Butler 71.
***NCAA Tourney (1-1):** WI-Milwaukee (1-1).
†NIT (1-1): Butler (1-1).

Ivy League

Team	Conference			Overall		
	W	L	Pct	W	L	Pct
*Pennsylvania	12	2	.857	20	9	.690
Princeton	10	4	.714	12	15	.444
Cornell	8	6	.571	13	15	.464
Yale	7	7	.500	15	14	.517
Brown	6	8	.429	10	17	.370
Harvard	5	9	.357	13	14	.481
Columbia	4	10	.286	11	16	.407
Dartmouth	4	10	.286	6	21	.222

Conf. Tourney Final: Ivy League has no tournament.
***NCAA Tourney (0-1):** Penn (0-1).

Metro Atlantic Athletic Conference

Team	Conference			Overall		
	W	L	Pct	W	L	Pct
†Manhattan	14	4	.778	20	11	.645
*Iona	13	5	.722	23	7	.767
Marist	12	6	.667	19	10	.655
Siena	10	8	.556	15	13	.536
Saint Peter's	9	9	.500	17	15	.531
Loyola	8	10	.444	15	13	.536
Niagara	7	11	.389	11	18	.379
Fairfield	7	11	.389	9	19	.321
Canisius	6	12	.333	9	20	.310
Rider	4	14	.222	8	20	.286

Conf. Tourney Final: Iona 64, Saint Peter's 61.
***NCAA Tourney (0-1):** Iona (0-1).
†NIT (2-1): Manhattan (2-1).

Mid-American Conference

East	Conference			Overall		
	W	L	Pct	W	L	Pct
*Kent St.	15	3	.833	25	9	.735
†Akron	14	4	.778	23	10	.697
†Miami-OH	14	4	.778	18	11	.621
Ohio	10	8	.556	19	11	.633
Buffalo	8	10	.444	19	13	.594
Bowling Green	5	13	.278	9	21	.300
West	W	L	Pct	W	L	Pct
N. Illinois	12	6	.667	17	11	.607
Toledo	10	8	.556	20	11	.645
Western Mich	10	8	.556	14	18	.438
Ball St.	6	12	.333	10	18	.556
Eastern Mich	3	15	.167	7	21	.250
Central Mich	1	17	.055	4	24	.143

Conf. Tourney Final: Kent St. 71, Toledo 66.
*NCAA Tourney (0-1): Kent St. (0-1).
†NIT (0-2): Akron (0-1), Miami-OH (0-1).

Mid-Continent Conference

Team	Conference			Overall		
	W	L	Pct	W	L	Pct
*Oral Roberts	13	3	.813	21	12	.636
IUPUI	13	3	.813	19	10	.655
Missouri-KC	11	5	.688	14	14	.500
Valparaiso	8	8	.500	17	12	.586
Southern Utah	8	8	.500	10	20	.333
Chicago St.	8	8	.500	11	19	.367
Oakland	6	10	.375	11	18	.379
Western Illinois	3	13	.188	7	21	.250
Centenary	2	14	.125	4	23	.148

Conf. Tourney Final: Oral Roberts 85, Chicago St. 72.
*NCAA Tourney (1-1): Oral Roberts (1-1).

Mid-Eastern Athletic Conference

Team	Conference			Overall		
	W	L	Pct	W	L	Pct
†Delaware St.	16	2	.889	21	14	.600
Coppin St.	12	6	.667	12	18	.400
Bethune-Cookman	11	7	.611	15	15	.500
S.C. State	11	7	.611	14	16	.467
*Hampton	10	8	.556	16	16	.500
Florida A&M	10	8	.556	14	17	.452
Norfolk St.	10	8	.556	13	18	.419
N. Carolina A&T	6	12	.333	13	18	.419
Howard	5	13	.278	7	22	.241
MD-Eastern Shore	4	14	.222	7	22	.241
Morgan St.	4	17	.222	4	26	.133

Conf. Tourney Final: Hampton 60, Delaware St. 56.
*NCAA Tourney (0-1): Hampton (0-1).
†NIT (1-1): Delaware St. (1-1).

Missouri Valley Conference

Team	Conference			Overall		
	W	L	Pct	W	L	Pct
*Wichita St.	14	4	.778	26	9	.743
†Missouri St.	12	6	.667	22	9	.710
*Southern Illinois	12	6	.667	22	11	.667
†Creighton	12	6	.667	20	10	.667
*Northern Iowa	11	7	.611	23	10	.697
*Bradley	11	7	.611	22	11	.667
Drake	5	13	.278	12	19	.387
Evansville	5	13	.278	10	19	.345
Indiana St.	4	14	.222	13	16	.448
Illinois St.	4	14	.222	9	19	.321

Conf. Tourney Final: So. Illinois 59, Bradley 46.
*NCAA Tourney (4-4): Wichita St. (2-1), Bradley (2-1), So. Illinois (0-1), Northern Iowa (0-1).
†NIT (3-2): Creighton (1-1), Missouri. St. (2-1).

Mountain West Conference

Team	Conference			Overall		
	W	L	Pct	W	L	Pct
*San Diego St.	13	3	.813	24	9	.727
*Air Force	12	4	.750	24	7	.774
*BYU	12	4	.750	20	9	.690
UNLV	10	6	.625	17	13	.567
New Mexico	8	8	.500	17	13	.567
Utah	6	10	.375	14	15	.483
Wyoming	5	11	.312	14	18	.438
Colorado St.	4	12	.250	16	15	.516
TCU	2	14	.125	6	25	.194

Conf. Tourney Final: San Diego St. 69, Wyoming 64 OT.
*NCAA Tourney (0-2): San Diego St. (0-1), Air Force (0-1).
†NIT (0-1): BYU (0-1).

Northeast Conference

Team	Conference			Overall		
	W	L	Pct	W	L	Pct
†Fairleigh Dickinson	14	4	.778	20	12	.625
Central Connecticut St.	13	5	.722	18	11	.621
*Monmouth	12	6	.667	19	15	.559
Mt. St. Mary's	11	7	.611	13	17	.433
Robert Morris	10	8	.556	15	14	.517
LIU Brooklyn	9	9	.500	12	16	.429
Sacred Heart	8	10	.444	11	17	.393
Quinnipiac	7	11	.389	12	16	.429
St. Francis-NY	7	11	.389	10	17	.370
Wagner	6	12	.333	13	14	.481
St. Francis-PA	6	12	.333	4	24	.143

Conf. Tourney Final: Monmouth 49, Fairleigh Dickinson 48.
*NCAA Tourney (1-1): Monmouth (1-1).
†NIT (0-1): Fairleigh Dickinson (0-1).

Ohio Valley Conference

Team	Conference			Overall		
	W	L	Pct	W	L	Pct
*Murray St	17	3	.850	24	7	.774
Samford	14	6	.700	20	11	.645
Tennessee Tech	13	7	.650	19	12	.613
Jacksonville St.	12	8	.600	16	13	.552
Austin Peay	11	9	.550	17	14	.548
Eastern Kentucky	11	9	.550	14	16	.467
Tennessee St	11	9	.550	13	15	.464
Tennessee-Martin	9	11	.450	13	15	.464
Eastern Illinois	5	15	.250	6	21	.222
SE Missouri St	4	16	.200	7	20	.259
Morehead St	3	17	.150	4	23	.148

Conf. Tourney Final: Murray St. 74, Samford 57.
*NCAA Tourney (0-1): Murray St. (0-1).

Pacific-10 Conference

Team	Conference			Overall		
	W	L	Pct	W	L	Pct
*UCLA	14	4	.778	32	7	.821
*Washington	13	5	.722	26	7	.788
*California	12	6	.667	20	11	.645
*Arizona	11	7	.611	20	13	.606
†Stanford	11	7	.611	16	14	.533
USC	8	10	.444	17	13	.567
Oregon	7	11	.389	15	18	.455
Oregon St	5	13	.278	13	18	.419
Arizona St	5	13	.278	11	17	.393
Washington St	4	12	.222	11	17	.393

Conf. Tourney Final: UCLA 71, California 52.
*NCAA Tourney (8-4): UCLA (5-1), Washington (2-1), Arizona (1-1), California (0-1).
†NIT (1-1): Stanford (1-1).

Final NCAA Men's Division I Standings (Cont.)

Patriot League

Team	Conference W	L	Pct	Overall W	L	Pct
*Bucknell	14	0	1.000	27	5	.844
Holy Cross	11	3	.786	20	12	.625
Lehigh	11	3	.786	19	12	.613
American	7	7	.500	12	17	.414
Lafayette	5	9	.357	11	17	.393
Colgate	4	10	.286	10	19	.345
Navy	3	11	.214	10	18	.357
Army	1	13	.071	5	22	.185

Conf. Tourney Final: Bucknell 74, Holy Cross 59.
*****NCAA Tourney (1-1):** Bucknell (1-1).

Southeastern Conference

Eastern Div.	Conference W	L	Pct	Overall W	L	Pct
*Tennessee	12	4	.750	22	8	.733
*Florida	10	6	.625	33	6	.846
*Kentucky	9	7	.563	22	13	.629
†Vanderbilt	7	9	.438	17	13	.567
†South Carolina	6	10	.375	23	15	.605
Georgia	5	11	.313	15	15	.500

Western Div.	Conference W	L	Pct	Overall W	L	Pct
*LSU	14	2	.875	27	9	.750
*Alabama	10	6	.625	18	13	.581
*Arkansas	10	6	.625	22	10	.688
Mississippi St	5	11	.313	15	15	.500
Auburn	4	12	.250	12	16	.429
Mississippi	4	12	.250	14	16	.467

Conf. Tourney Final: Florida 49, South Carolina 47.
*****NCAA Tourney (13-5):** Florida (6-0), LSU (4-1), Kentucky (1-1), Alabama (1-1), Tennessee (1-1), Arkansas (0-1).
†NIT (5-1): South Carolina (5-0), Vanderbilt (0-1).

Southern Conference

North Div.	Conference W	L	Pct	Overall W	L	Pct
Elon	10	4	.714	15	14	.517
Chattanooga	8	6	.571	19	13	.594
W. Carolina	7	7	.500	13	17	.433
Appalachian St.	6	8	.429	14	16	.467
NC-Greensboro	4	10	.286	12	19	.387

South Div.	Conference W	L	Pct	Overall W	L	Pct
†Georgia Southern	11	4	.733	20	10	.667
*Davidson	10	5	.667	20	11	.645
College of Charleston	9	6	.600	17	11	.607
Furman	8	7	.533	15	13	.536
Wofford	6	9	.400	11	18	.379
The Citadel	1	14	.067	10	21	.323

Conf. Tourney Final: Davidson 80, Chattanooga 55.
*****NCAA Tourney (0-1):** Davidson (0-1).
†NIT (0-1): Georgia Southern (0-1).

Best in Show

Conferences with the most wins in the 2006 NCAA tournament. Number of tourney teams in parenthesis.

Conference	W-L	Pct.
SEC (6)	13-5	.722
Big East (8)	11-8	.579
Pac-10 (4)	8-4	.667
ACC (4)	6-4	.600
Colonial (2)	4-2	.667
Big 12 (4)	4-4	.500
Missouri Valley (4)	4-4	.500

Southland Conference

Team	Conference W	L	Pct	Overall W	L	Pct
*Northwestern St.	15	1	.938	26	8	.765
Sam Houston St.	11	5	.688	22	9	.710
SE Louisiana	10	6	.625	16	12	.571
Stephen F. Austin	9	7	.563	17	12	.586
Lamar	9	7	.563	17	14	.548
McNeese St.	9	7	.563	14	14	.500
Texas-Arlington	7	9	.438	14	16	.467
Texas-San Antonio	6	10	.375	11	17	.393
Louisiana-Monroe	6	10	.375	10	18	.357
Nicholls St.	5	11	.313	9	18	.333
Texas St.	1	15	.063	3	24	.111

Conf. Tourney Final: Northwestern St. 95, Sam Houston St. 87
*****NCAA Tourney (1-1):** Northwestern St. (1-1).

Southwestern Athletic Conference

Team	Conference W	L	Pct	Overall W	L	Pct
*Southern	15	3	.833	19	13	.594
Grambling St.	11	7	.611	14	13	.519
Alabama A&M	11	7	.611	13	13	.500
Jackson St.	10	8	.556	15	17	.469
Alabama St	10	8	.556	12	18	.400
Miss. Valley St.	9	9	.500	9	19	.321
Ark-Pine Bluff	8	10	.444	13	16	.448
Alcorn St.	8	10	.444	8	20	.286
Texas Southern	6	12	.333	8	22	.267
Prairie View A&M	2	16	.111	5	24	.172

Conf. Tourney Final: Southern 57, Ark-Pine Bluff 44.
*****NCAA Tourney (0-1):** Southern (0-1).

Sun Belt Conference

East Div.	Conference W	L	Pct	Overall W	L	Pct
†Western Kentucky	12	2	.857	23	8	.742
Middle Tennessee	8	6	.571	16	12	.571
Arkansas St	7	7	.500	12	18	.400
Arkansas-Little Rock	5	9	.357	14	15	.483
Florida International	4	10	.286	8	20	.286

West Div.	Conference W	L	Pct	Overall W	L	Pct
*South Alabama	12	3	.800	24	7	.774
Louisiana-Lafayette	7	8	.467	13	16	.448
Denver	7	8	.467	16	15	.516
New Orleans	6	9	.400	10	19	.345
North Texas	6	9	.400	14	14	.500
Troy	6	9	.400	14	15	.483

Conf. Tourney Final: South Alabama 95, Western Kentucky 70.
*****NCAA Tourney (0-1):** South Alabama (0-1).
†NIT (0-1): Western Kentucky (0-1).

West Coast Conference

Team	Conference W	L	Pct	Overall W	L	Pct
*Gonzaga	14	0	1.000	29	4	.879
St. Mary's-CA	8	6	.571	17	12	.586
Loyola Marymount	8	6	.571	12	18	.400
San Francisco	7	7	.500	11	17	.393
San Diego	6	8	.429	18	12	.600
Santa Clara	5	9	.357	13	16	.448
Portland	5	9	.357	11	18	.379
Pepperdine	3	11	.214	7	20	.259

Conf. Tourney Final: Gonzaga 68, Loyola Marymount 67.
*****NCAA Tourney (2-1):** Gonzaga (2-1).

Western Athletic Conference

Team	Conference			Overall		
	W	L	Pct	W	L	Pct
*Nevada	13	3	.813	27	6	.818
*Utah St.	11	5	.688	23	9	.719
†Louisiana Tech	11	5	.688	20	13	.606
Hawaii	10	6	.625	17	11	.607
New Mexico St.	10	6	.625	16	14	.533
Fresno St.	8	8	.500	15	13	.536
Boise St.	6	10	.375	14	15	.483
San Jose St	2	14	.125	6	25	.194
Idaho	1	15	.063	4	25	.138

Conf. Tourney Final: Nevada 70, Utah St. 63 OT.
*NCAA Tourney (0-2): Nevada (0-1), Utah St. (0-1).
†NIT (0-1): Louisiana Tech (0-1).

NCAA Tourney Expansion Not Imminent

The National Association of Basketball Coaches floated a plan to vastly expand the NCAA's Field of 65. A plan to nearly double the number of teams, creating a **128-team post-season tournament** surfaced in June 2006 but was not adopted by the NCAA. Even a smaller plan which proposed adding three to seven teams to the two that meet in the NCAA "Opening Round" play-in game each year in Dayton, Ohio the Tuesday night before the tourney. The ideas may have been spurred by **George Mason's Final Four run** in the 2006 tournament. GMU was an at-large team from the mid-major **Colonial Athletic Association** and was one of the last teams picked for the tournament. It's going to get harder to get into the consolation bracket as well. The NCAA, which now owns and operates the **NIT** announced it's contracting the NIT field to 32 teams from the 40 that have particiapted since 2002.

Annual Awards

Players of the Year

J.J. Redick, Duke, G . . . . . . AP, Wooden, Naismith, Rupp, co-USBWA, co-NABC
Adam Morrison, Gonzaga, F . . . . . .co-USBWA, co-NABC

Wooden Award Voting

Presented since 1977 by the Los Angeles Athletic Club and named after the former Purdue All-America and UCLA coach John Wooden. Voting done by 1,047-member panel of national media; candidates must have a cumulative college grade point average of 2.0 (out of 4.0) and be making progress toward graduation.

		Cl	Pos	Pts
1	J.J. Redick, Duke	Sr.	G	4646
2	Adam Morrison, Gonzaga	Jr.	F	4574
3	Shelden Williams, Duke	Sr.	F	2142
4	Randy Foye, Villanova	Sr.	G	2050
5	Brandon Roy, Washington	Sr.	G	1885
6	Allan Ray, Villanova	Sr.	G	1469
7	Dee Brown, Illinois	Sr.	G	1404
8	Kevin Pittsnoggle, West Va.	Sr.	F/C	1251
9	Glen Davis, LSU	So.	F	1232
10	Craig Smith, Boston College	Sr.	F	1173

Defensive Player of the Year

Formerly the Henry Iba Award, for defensive skills, sportsmanship and dedication; first presented by the Rotary Club of River Oaks in Houston in 1987 and named after the late Oklahoma State and U.S. Olympic team coach. Voting done by the National Association of Basketball Coaches.

Shelden Williams, Duke, F

Div. II and III Awards

Awarded by the National Association of Basketball Coaches.

Players of the Year
Div. II . . . . .Darius Hargrove, Va. Union
& Turner Trofholz, S. Dakota
Div. III . . . . .Brandon Adair, Virginia Wesleyan

Coaches of the Year

Roy Williams, North Carolina . . . . .AP, USBWA
Jay Wright, Villanova . . . . .NABC, Naismith

Consensus All-America Teams

The NCAA Division I players cited most frequently by the following All-America selectors: Associated Press, U.S. Basketball Writers, National Association of Basketball Coaches and Wooden Award Committee. (*) indicates unanimous first team selection. Holdover from the 2004-05 first team are in **bold** type.

First Team

	Class	Hgt	Pos
J.J. Redick*, Duke	Sr.	6-4	G
Randy Foye*, Villanova	Sr.	6-4	G
Adam Morrison*, Gonzaga	Jr.	6-8	F
Shelden Williams*, Duke	Sr.	6-9	F
Brandon Roy, Washington	Sr.	6-6	G

Second Team

	Class	Hgt	Pos
Dee Brown, Illinois	Sr.	6-0	G
Allan Ray, Villanova	Sr.	6-2	G
Rodney Carney, Memphis	Sr.	6-7	F
Rudy Gay, Connecticut	Sr.	6-7	F
Craig Smith, Boston College	Sr.	6-7	F

Third Team

	Class	Hgt	Pos
Glen Davis, LSU	So.	6-9	F
Leon Powe, California	So.	6-8	F
P.J. Tucker, Texas	Jr.	6-5	F
Kevin Pittsnoggle, West Virginia	Sr.	6-11	C
Nick Fazekas, Nevada	Jr.	6-11	F

Also mentioned: Tyler Hansbrough (North Carolina).

Despite, or perhaps because of, the much-publicized conference turnover in 2005, the expanded 16-team Big East "mega conference" landed a record 8 teams in the 2006 NCAA tournament. **Did you know***, the previous record of seven teams in a single tournament was held by the Big Ten, which accomplished the feat four times (1990, 1994, 1999, 2001), and the Big East (1991)?*

DID YOU KNOW?

NCAA Men's Division I Leaders

Includes games through NCAA and NIT tourneys.

INDIVIDUAL

Scoring

	Cl	Gm	FG%	3FG/Att	FT%	Reb	Ast	Stl	Blk	Pts	Avg	Hi
Adam Morrison, Gonzaga	Jr.	33	.496	74/173	.772	182	58	35	11	926	28.1	44
J.J. Redick, Duke	Sr.	36	.470	139/330	.863	71	95	52	2	964	26.8	41
Keydren Clark, St. Peter's	Sr.	32	.393	105/322	.892	132	140	80	8	840	26.3	43
Andre Collins, Loyola-MD	Sr.	28	.414	118/322	.414	100	131	67	4	730	26.1	39
Brion Rush, Grambling	Sr.	21	.409	54/173	.832	146	71	48	1	541	25.8	53
Quincy Douby, Rutgers	Jr.	33	.462	116/289	.847	141	103	58	27	839	25.4	41
Steve Burtt, Iona	Sr.	31	.446	96/236	.824	103	79	22	2	780	25.2	37
Rodney Stuckey, Eastern Wash.	Fr.	30	.490	55/148	.760	144	123	66	8	726	24.2	45
Alan Daniels, Lamar	Sr.	31	.436	75/247	.665	207	92	72	21	730	23.5	41
Trey Johnson, Jackson St.	Jr.	32	.455	67/152	.750	155	73	46	2	751	23.5	40
Whit Holcomb-Faye, Radford . .	Sr.	29	.395	83/248	.809	83	116	33	2	669	23.1	37
Larry Blair, Liberty	Jr.	30	.405	64/180	.803	140	80	61	11	679	22.6	38
Tim Smith, East Tenn. St.	Sr.	28	.448	41/125	.730	127	126	95	1	617	22.0	37
Roy Booker, SE Mo. St.	Sr.	27	.353	73/233	.825	129	47	17	1	594	22.0	30
Morris Almond, Rice	Sr.	28	.500	48/108	.795	163	32	39	19	612	21.9	40
Nick Fazekas, Nevada	Jr.	33	.529	31/107	.846	342	68	36	49	721	21.8	37
Elton Nesbitt, Ga. Southern . . .	Sr.	30	.424	103/264	.803	105	89	60	3	651	21.7	36
Jose Juan Barea, Northeastern .	Sr.	29	.400	66/227	.764	129	244	37	0	610	21.0	32
Caleb Green, Oral Roberts	Jr.	33	.527	3/10	.763	290	53	34	11	686	20.8	33
Kenny Adeleke, Hartford	Sr.	28	.592	0/0	.594	366	17	29	48	579	20.7	31

Rebounding

	Cl	Gm	No	Avg
Paul Millsap, Louisiana Tech	Jr.	33	438	13.3
Kenny Adeleke, Hartford	Sr.	28	366	13.1
Rashad Jose-Jennings, Ark-Little Rock	Jr.	29	329	11.3
Curtis Withers, Charlotte	Sr.	32	362	11.3
Ivan Almonte, Florida Int'l	Sr.	25	281	11.2
Marcus Slaughter, San Diego St. . . .	Jr.	30	329	11.0
Justin Williams, Wyoming	Sr.	30	329	11.0
Yemi Nicholson, Denver	Sr.	31	339	10.9
Harding Nana, Delaware	Sr.	30	326	10.9
Ricky Woods, SE Louisiana	Sr.	28	304	10.9
John Bowler, Eastern Michigan	Sr.	28	301	10.8
Corey Rouse, East Carolina	Sr.	28	301	10.8
Shelden Williams, Duke	Sr.	36	384	10.7
Aaron Gray, Pittsburgh	Jr.	33	345	10.5
Nick Fazekas, Nevada	Jr.	33	342	10.4
Obie Nwadike, C. Conn. St.	Sr.	29	299	10.3
Tim Parham, MD-Eastern Shore	Sr.	29	299	10.3
Todd Sowell, St. Peter's	So.	32	326	10.2
Leon Powe, California	So.	27	273	10.1
Matthew Knight, Loy. Marymount . . .	Jr.	30	299	10.0

Assists

	Cl	Gm	No	Avg
Jared Jordan, Marist	Jr.	29	247	8.5
Jose Juan Barea, Northeastern	Sr.	29	244	8.4
Terrell Everett, Oklahoma	Sr.	29	199	6.9
Walker Russell, Jacksonville St.	Sr.	29	197	6.8
Kenny Grant, Davidson	Sr.	31	208	6.7
Bobby Dixon, Troy	Sr.	29	192	6.6
Aaron Fitzgerald, UC-Irvine	Sr.	29	190	6.6
Chris Quinn, Notre Dame	Sr.	29	187	6.4
Cardell Johnson, UAB	Sr.	31	194	6.8
Will Blalock, Iowa St.	Jr.	30	184	6.1
Josh Wilson, Northern Arizona	Fr.	32	195	6.1
T.J. McCullough, Gardner-Webb . . .	Sr.	28	170	6.1
Lorenzo Williams, Rice	Jr.	28	170	6.1
Aubrey Conerly, Jacksonville	Sr.	27	161	6.0
Gerry McNamara, Syracuse	Sr.	35	207	5.9
Kevin Bell, Fresno St.	So.	28	165	5.9
Zack Wright, Ark-Little Rock	Jr.	28	164	5.9
Dee Brown, Illinois	Sr.	33	191	5.8
Jamie McNeilly, New Orleans	Jr.	29	164	5.7
Jejuan Plair, Sam Houston St.	Jr.	31	175	5.6

Field Goal Percentage

Minimum 5 Field Goals made per game.

	Cl	Gm	FG	FGA	Pct
Randall Hanke, Providence . . .	So.	27	149	220	67.7
Cedric Smith, Texas A&M-CC . .	Jr.	27	139	210	66.2
Joakim Noah, Florida	So.	39	202	322	62.7
James Augustine, Illinois	Sr.	33	174	279	62.4
Michael Harrison, Colorado St. .	Jr.	31	160	257	62.3
Kyle Hines, NC-Greensboro . .	So.	30	239	384	62.2
Nate Harris, Utah St.	Sr.	32	215	346	62.1
Eric Williams, Wake Forest . . .	Sr.	34	223	360	61.9
Kibwe Trim, Sacred Heart	Sr.	28	194	314	61.8
Michael Southall, LA-Lafayette .	Sr.	28	164	266	61.7
Andrew Strait, Montana	Sr.	31	223	363	61.4
Yemi Nicholson, Denver	Sr.	31	238	395	60.3
Chris Daniels, Tex A&M-CC . . .	Jr.	27	160	266	60.2
Tim Pollitz, Miami-OH	So.	26	144	241	59.8
Ra'Sean Dickey, Georgia Tech .	So.	28	148	248	59.7

Free Throw Percentage

Minimum 2.5 Free Throws made per game.

	Cl	Gm	FT	FTA	Pct
Blake Ahearn, SW Mo. St.	Jr.	31	117	125	93.6
Jermaine Anderson, UNH	Jr.	26	68	74	91.9
Shawan Robinson, Clemson . . .	Sr.	32	84	92	91.3
Derek Raivio, Gonzaga	Jr.	31	83	91	91.2
Adam Vogelsberg, Mid. Tenn. .	Jr.	28	108	119	90.8
Gerry McNamara, Syracuse . .	Sr.	35	111	123	90.2
Andre Collins, Loyola-MD	Sr.	28	101	112	90.2
Chris Hernandez, Stanford . . .	Sr.	30	109	121	90.1
Daniel Horton, Michigan	Sr.	33	136	151	90.1
Walker Russell, Jacksonville St. .	Sr.	29	112	125	89.6
Chris Stephens, Oregon St. . . .	Sr.	31	83	93	89.2
Ronald Steele, Alabama	So.	31	124	139	89.2
Keydren Clark, St. Peter's	Sr.	32	189	212	89.2
Jim Goffredo, Harvard	Jr.	26	73	82	89.0
Allan Ray, Villanova	Sr.	32	112	126	88.9

Gonzaga
Adam Morrison
Scoring

Louisiana Tech
Paul Millsap
Rebounds

Northeastern
Shawn James
Blocks

Marist
Jared Jordan
Assists

3-Pt Field Goal Percentage
Minimum 2.5 Three-Point FGs made per game.

	Cl	Gm	FG	FGA	Pct
Stephen Sir, Northern Arizona	Sr.	32	93	190	48.9
Josh Alexander, S.F. Austin	Fr.	29	73	153	47.7
J. Robert Merritt, Samford	Sr.	31	120	252	47.6
Ross Schraeder, UC Irvine	Sr.	29	74	156	47.4
Chris Hernandez, Stanford	Sr.	30	75	159	47.2
Steve Novak, Marquette	Sr.	31	121	259	46.7
James Collins, Birmingham-So.	Sr.	27	70	151	46.4
Lee Humphrey, Florida	Jr.	38	113	246	45.9
B.J. Spencer, Jacksonville St.	Sr.	27	82	179	45.8
Martin Samarco, Bowling Green	Sr.	29	100	219	45.7
Josh Goodwin, Belmont	Jr.	31	82	180	45.6
Jaycee Carroll, Utah St.	So.	32	93	206	45.1

3-Pt Field Goals Per Game

	Cl	Gm	No	Avg
Andre Collins, Loyola-MD	Sr.	28	118	4.2
Jack Leasure, Coastal Caro.	So.	30	125	4.2
Steve Novak, Marquette	Sr.	31	121	3.9
J. Robert Merritt, Samford	Sr.	31	120	3.9
J.J. Redick, Duke	Sr.	36	139	3.9
Eric Smith, Campbell	Jr.	28	107	3.8
Chris Lofton, Tennessee	So.	30	114	3.8
Will Whitington, Marist	Jr.	29	103	3.6
Quincy Douby, Rutgers	Jr.	33	116	3.5
Martin Samarco, Bowling Green	Sr.	29	100	3.4
Elton Nesbitt, Georgia Southern	Sr.	30	103	3.4

Blocked Shots

	Cl	Gm	No	Avg
Shawn James, Northeastern	So.	30	196	6.5
Justin Williams, Wyoming	Sr.	30	163	5.4
Stephane Lasme, UMass	Jr.	28	108	3.9
Shelden Williams, Duke	Sr.	36	137	3.8
Slim Millien, Idaho St.	Sr.	27	93	3.4
Eric Hicks, Cincinnati	Sr.	34	113	3.3
Michael Southall, LA-Lafayette	Sr.	28	93	3.3
Hilton Armstrong, UConn	Sr.	34	107	3.1
Tyrus Thomas, LSU	Fr.	32	99	3.1
Solomon Jones, South Florida	Sr.	29	89	3.1
Andrea Crosariol, Fairleigh Dickinson	Jr.	32	96	3.0
Mickell Gladness, Alabama A&M	So.	26	77	3.0
Patrick O'Bryant, Bradley	So.	25	72	2.9

Steals

	Cl	Gm	No	Avg
Tim Smith, East Tenn. St.	Sr.	28	95	3.4
Oliver Lafayette, Houston	Jr.	31	105	3.4
Obie Trotter, Alabama A&M	Sr.	26	87	3.3
Ibrahim Jaaber, Penn	Jr.	29	96	3.3
Kevin Hamilton, Holy Cross	Sr.	31	102	3.3
Bobby Dixon, Troy	Sr.	29	88	3.0
Bryan Mullins, Southern Illinois	Fr.	33	94	2.8
Quinton Day, UMKC	Jr.	27	76	2.8
Mardy Collins, Temple	Sr.	32	89	2.8
Ricky Hickman, NC-Greensboro	Jr.	28	77	2.8
DaShawn Freeman, Sacramento St.	Sr.	30	82	2.7

Single Game Highs

Points

No		Opponent	Date
53	Brion Rush, Grambling	Southern U.	Feb. 4
45	Rodney Stuckey, E. Wash.	N. Arizona	Jan. 5
44	Adam Morrison, Gonzaga	LMU	Feb. 18
43	Keydren Clark, St. Peter's	Canisius	Feb. 24
43	Adam Morrison, Gonzaga	Washington	Dec. 4
43	Adam Morrison, Gonzaga	Michigan St.	Nov. 22

Rebounds

No		Opponent	Date
30	Rashad Jones-Jennings, Ark-L.R.	Ark-P.B.	Dec. 13
28	Paul Millsap, La. Tech	San Jose St.	Feb. 15
23	Paul Millsap, La. Tech	Hawaii	Mar. 4
23	Greg Brunner, Iowa	Minnesota	Jan. 18

Assists

No		Opponent	Date
16	Bobby Dixon, Troy	Western Ky.	Jan. 19
16	Jared Jordan, Marist	Rider	Jan. 15

Blocks

No		Opponent	Date
12	Justin Williams, Wyoming	Utah	Mar. 10
11	Justin Williams, Wyoming	BYU	Feb. 18
11	Shawn James, Northeastern	JMU	Feb. 15
11	Michael Southall, LA-Lafayette	N. Tex.	Jan. 5

Steals

No		Opponent	Date
12	Carldell Johnson, UAB	So. Carolina St.	Nov. 27
10	Ricky Woods, SE Louisiana	Lamar	Mar. 3
10	Obie Trotter, Ala. A&M	Jarvis Christian	Nov. 26
10	Ricky Soliver, Iona	Portland St.	Nov. 25

3-point FGs

No		Opponent	Date
11	Josh Goodwin, Belmont	E. Tenn. St.	Dec. 1
10	Chris Riouse, Oral Roberts	Oakland	Feb. 9
10	Jaycee Carroll, Utah St.	New Mex. St.	Feb. 2

NCAA Men's Division I Leaders (Cont.)
TEAM

Scoring Offense

	Gm	W-L	Pts	Avg
Long Beach St.	.30	18-12	2498	83.3
Campbell	.28	10-18	2319	82.8
Texas A&M-Corpus Christi	.28	20-8	2307	82.4
Washington	.33	26-7	2706	82.0
Connecticut	.34	30-4	2781	81.8
East Tenn. St.	.28	15-13	2284	81.6
Duke	.36	32-4	2921	81.1
Belmont	.31	20-11	2499	80.6
Tennessee	.30	22-8	2413	80.4
Lamar	.31	17-14	2487	80.2

Scoring Defense

	Gm	W-L	Pts	Avg
Air Force	.31	24-7	1695	54.7
Princeton	.27	12-15	1500	55.6
Bucknell	.32	27-5	1785	55.8
Southern Ill.	.33	22-11	1864	56.5
Delaware St.	.35	21-14	2011	57.5
Washington St.	.28	11-17	1616	57.7
Northern Iowa	.33	23-10	1907	57.8
Richmond	.30	13-17	1735	57.8
Northwestern	.29	14-15	1697	58.5
UCLA	.39	32-7	2288	58.7

Scoring Margin

	Off	Def	Mar
Texas A&M-Corpus Christi	.82.4	67.4	15.0
Texas	.75.2	60.3	14.9
Florida	.78.3	63.5	14.7
Connecticut	.81.8	67.1	14.6
Memphis	.80.0	65.5	14.6
Kansas	.75.2	61.3	13.8
Duke	.81.1	68.1	13.0
Winthrop	.73.4	61.2	12.2
Washington	.82.0	69.9	12.1
Illinois	.70.0	58.7	11.3

Won-Lost Percentage

	W	L	Pct
George Washington	.27	3	90.0
Memphis	.33	4	89.2
Duke	.32	4	88.9
Connecticut	.30	4	88.2
Gonzaga	.29	4	87.9
Villanova	.28	5	84.8
Florida	.33	6	84.6
Bucknell	.27	5	84.4
UCLA	.32	7	82.1
Nevada	.27	6	81.8

Field Goal Percentage

	FG	FGA	Pct
Texas A&M-Corpus Christi	.837	1671	50.1
Florida	.1061	2120	50.0
Utah St.	.853	1714	49.8
Belmont	.897	1819	49.3
Montana	.876	1781	49.2
Colorado St.	.801	1630	49.1
Marist	.790	1613	49.0
Northern Arizona	.856	1754	48.8
Duke	.979	2011	48.7
Pacific	.858	1763	48.7

Field Goal Percentage Defense

	FG	FGA	Pct
Kansas	.702	1896	37.0
Memphis	.795	2094	38.0
Iowa	.732	1924	38.0
Connecticut	.842	2200	38.3
Texas	.805	2097	38.4
Lehigh	.643	1672	38.5
Bucknell	.596	1548	38.5
LA-Lafayette	.659	1707	38.6
Texas A&M-Corpus Christi	.617	1596	38.7
George Mason	.760	1958	38.8

Rebound Margin

	Off	Def	Mar
Texas	.40.5	29.9	10.6
Connecticut	.43.8	34.3	9.5
College of Charleston	.41.9	32.8	9.0
Oklahoma	.36.6	27.7	8.9
North Carolina	.39.9	31.8	8.1
LSU	.40.2	32.4	7.8
Pittsburgh	.38.8	31.2	7.6
St. John's	.38.1	31.2	6.9
Memphis	.41.3	34.6	6.7
Wake Forest	.39.4	33.0	6.4

Free Throw Percentage

	FT	FTA	Pct
St. joseph's	.525	657	79.9
New Hampshire	.357	455	78.5
Gonzaga	.667	853	78.2
Princeton	.266	344	77.3
Michigan St.	.524	681	76.9
Stanford	.500	655	76.3
Duke	.689	905	76.1
Gardner-Webb	.340	447	76.1
Davidson	.416	547	76.1
Siena	.476	627	75.9

3-point FG Percentage

	3PT	3PTA	Pct
Southern Utah	.226	527	42.9
UC-Irvine	.249	593	42.0
Portland St.	.201	498	40.4
Air Force	.276	684	40.4
Notre Dame	.288	715	40.3
Iona	.196	488	40.2
Utah St.	.232	579	40.1
Florida Atlantic	.216	541	39.9
Northern Arizona	.200	503	39.8
San Diego	.227	572	39.7

3-point FG Made Per Game

	Gm	No	Avg
Troy	.29	344	11.9
West Virginia	.33	337	10.2
Campbell	.28	276	9.9
Samford	.31	298	9.6
Notre Dame	.30	288	9.6
Fresno St.	.28	265	9.5
Houston	.31	286	9.2
Butler	.33	300	9.1
N.C. State	.32	288	9.0
Robert Morris	.29	260	9.0

Assists Per Game

	Gm	No	Avg
Texas A&M-Corpus Christi	28	550	19.6
Sam Houston St.	31	574	18.5
Davidson	31	567	18.3
Montana	31	565	18.2
Kansas	33	589	17.8
North Carolina	31	552	17.8
Boston College	36	639	17.8
Valparaiso	29	512	17.7
West Virginia	33	576	17.5
Northwestern St.	34	589	17.3

Blocks Per Game

	Gm	No	Avg
Connecticut	34	298	8.8
Northeastern	30	240	8.0
Massachusetts	28	202	7.2
Wyoming	32	221	6.9
Idaho St.	27	179	6.6
LSU	36	236	6.6
Colorado St.	31	202	6.5
Memphis	37	235	6.4
Fairleigh Dickinson	32	203	6.3
Syracuse	35	221	6.3

Steals Per Game

	Gm	No	Avg
Houston	31	385	12.4
Clemson	32	352	11.0
UAB	31	337	10.9
East Tenn. St.	28	288	10.3
Tennessee	30	301	10.0
Temple	32	318	9.9
McNeese St.	28	278	9.9
Sacramento St.	30	295	9.8
Kansas	33	323	9.8
Penn	29	283	9.8

2005-06 NCAA Div. 1
Attendance Leaders

Team	Gms	Attendance	Average
Kentucky	15	341,445	22,763
Syracuse	19	410,153	21,587
North Carolina	17	344,071	20,239
Louisville	22	402,963	18,316
Tennessee	15	269,310	17,954
Maryland	17	291,961	17,174
Wisconsin	16	274,272	17,142
Indiana	13	220,343	16,949
Illinois	16	265,888	16,618
Kansas	16	260,800	16,300
Ohio St.	17	261,622	15,389
Arkansas	16	239,336	14,958
Memphis	20	297,328	14,866
Michigan St.	14	206,626	14,759
Wake Forest	18	263,970	14,665
Arizona	14	204,213	14,586
North Carolina St.	18	260,509	14,472
Marquette	16	223,983	13,998
Connecticut	16	223,176	13,948
Creighton	17	236,313	13,900
New Mexico	17	227,575	13,386
Texas	17	221,415	13,024
Dayton	17	211,176	12,422
Vanderbilt	16	195,159	12,197
Iowa	17	204,102	12,006

Underclassmen in NBA Draft

Thirty-seven collegiate players and 10 international players forfeited their college eligibility and declared for the 2006 NBA Draft which took place at Madison Square Garden in New York City on June 28.

Fifty-seven American and International players (including Nevada Junior forward Nick Fazekas), who initially declared themselves eligible for the 2006 NBA Draft withdrew their names before the June 18 deadline. Under the new collective bargaining agreement signed following the 2005 NBA draft players from the United States will now have to wait one year after the date their high school class graduates. International players must turn 19 years old by the end of the calendar year. First round selections in **bold** type.

	Cl	Drafted by	Overall Pick
LaMarcus Aldridge, Texas	So.	Chicago	2
Pape-Philippe Amagou, France	NA	not drafted	—
Renaldo Balkman, S. Caro.	Jr.	New York	20
Andrea Bargnani, Italy	NA	Toronto	1
Will Blalock, Iowa St.	Jr.	Detroit	60
Josh Boone, UConn	Jr.	New Jersey	23
Ronnie Brewer, Arkansas	Jr.	Utah	14
Shannon Brown, Michigan St.	Jr.	Cleveland	25
Derek Burditt, Bliin College (TX)	So.	not drafted	—
Travis DeGroat, Delta St.	Jr.	not drafted	—
Guillermo Diaz, Miami-FL	Jr.	LA Clipperrs	52
Quincy Douby, Rutgers	Jr.	Sacramento	19
Mike Efevberha, CS-Northridge	Jr.	not drafted	—
Lior Eliyahu, Israel	NA	Orlando	44
Jordan Farmar, UCLA	So.	LA Lakers	26
Joel Freeland, Spain	NA	not drafted	—
Thomas Gardner, Missouri	Jr.	not drafted	—
Rudy Gay, UConn	So.	Houston	8
Daniel Gibson, Texas	Jr.	Cleveland	42
LeShawn Hammett, St. Francis	Jr.	not drafted	—
Tedric Hill, Gulf Coast CC (FL)	So.	not drafted	—
Donald Jeffes, Roxbury CC (MA)	So.	not drafted	—
Alexander Johnson, Fla. St.	Jr.	Indiana	45
David Johnson, Clinton JC (SC)	So.	not drafted	—
Mark Konecny, Lambuth U. (TN)	Jr.	not drafted	—
Kyle Lowry, Villanova	So.	Memphis	24
Damir Markota, Croatia	NA	San Antonio	59
Paul Millsap, La. Tech	Jr.	Utah	47
Matt Mitchell, Southern	Jr.	not drafted	—
Adam Morrison, Gonzaga	Jr.	Charlotte	3
Patrick O'Bryant, Bradley	So.	Golden St.	9
Oleksiy Pecherov, Ukraine	NA	Washington	18
Kosta Perovic, Serbia & Monte.	NA	Golden St.	38
Danilo Pinnock, Geo. Wash.	Jr.	Dallas	58
Leon Powe, California	Jr.	Denver	49
Sergio Rodriguez, Spain	NA	not drafted	—
Rajon Rondo, Kentucky	So.	Phoenix	21
Saer Sene, Belgium	NA	not drafted	—
Cedric Simmons, N.C. State	So.	N.O./Okla	15
Marcus Slaughter, San Diego St.	Jr.	not drafted	—
Curtis Stinson, Iowa St.	Jr.	not drafted	—
Tyrus Thomas, LSU	Fr.	Portland	4
P.J. Tucker, Texas	Jr.	Toronto	35
Ejike Ugboaja, Nigeria	NA	Cleveland	55
Darius Washington Jr., Memphis	So.	not drafted	—
Marcus Williams, UConn	Jr.	New Jersey	22
Shawne Williams, Memphis	Fr.	Indiana	17

Other 2006 Men's Tournaments

NIT Tournament

The 69th annual National Invitation Tournament had a 40-team field. First four rounds played on home courts of higher seeded teams. Semifinal and Championship games played Mar 28-30 at Madison Square Garden in New York City.

Opening Round

Manhattan 80 . . . . .Fairleigh Dickinson 77
Butler 53 .Miami-OH 52
Akron 80 . . . . .OT . . . . .Temple 73
Charlotte 77 . . . . .Georgia Southern 61
Rutgers 76 . . . . .Penn St. 71
Delaware St. 58 . . . . .Northern Arizona 53
UTEP 85 . . . . .Lipscomb 66
Stanford 65 . . . . .Virginia 49

1st Round

South Carolina 74 . . . . .Western Kentucky 55
Notre Dame 79 . . . . .Vanderbilt 69
Clemson 69 . . . . .Louisiana Tech 53
Minnesota 73 .Wake Forest 58
Houston 77 . . . . .BYU 67
Miami-FL 62 . . . . .Oklahoma 58
Old Dominion 79 . . . . .Colorado 61
Hofstra 73 . . . . .Nebraska 62
Saint Joseph's 71 . . . . .Rutgers 62
Michigan 82 . . . . .UTEP 67
Creighton 71 . . . . .Akron 60
Florida St. 67 . . . . .Butler 63
Louisville 71 . . . . .Delaware St. 54
Missouri St. 76 .Stanford 67
Cincinnati 86 . . . . .Charlotte 80
Manhattan 87 . . . . .Maryland 84

2nd Round

Hostra 77 . . . . .OT . . . . . . .Saint Joseph's 75
Michigan 87 . . . . .2OT . . . . .Notre Dame 84
Louisville 74 . . . . .Clemson 68
Miami-FL 53 . . . . .Creighton 52
Missouri St. 60 .Houston 59
Old Dominion 70 . . . . .Manhattan 66
South Carolina 69 . . . . . .OT . . . . . . .Florida St. 68
Cincinnati 76 . . . . .Minnesota 62

Quarterfinals

Old Dominion 61 . . . . .Hofstra 51
Michigan 71 .Miami-FL 65
Louisville 74 .Missouri St. 56
South Carolina 65 . . . . .Cincinnati 62

Semifinals

Michigan 66 . . . . .Old Dominion 43
South Carolina 78 . . . . .Louisville 63

Championship

South Carolina 76 . . . . .Michigan 64

Tournament MVPs

NIT

Renaldo Balkman, South Carolina forward

NCAA Division II

John Smith, Winona St. forward

NCAA Division III

Ton Ton Balenga, Va. Wesleyan guard

NAIA Division I

Evan Patterson, Texas Wesleyan forward

NAIA Division II

Michael Bonaparte, Coll. of the Ozarks forward

NCAA Division II

The eight regional winners of the 64-team field: NORTHEAST—Stonehill (26-6); EAST—Barton (28-3); SOUTH ATLANTIC—Virginia Union (27-6); SOUTH—Montevallo (29-4); SOUTH CENTRAL—Tarleton St. (27-6); GREAT LAKES—SIU Edwardsville (25-6); NORTH CENTRAL—Winona St. (29-4); WEST—Seattle Pacific (25-5).

The Elite Eight was played March 22-25, at Springfield, Massachusetts. There was no Third Place game.

Quarterfinals

Seattle Pacific 79 . . . . .Montevallo 65
Virginia Union 60 . . . .-. . . .SIU Edwardsville 58
Winona St. 86 . . . . .OT . . . . .Barton 78
Stonehill 69 . . . . .Tarleton St. 59

Semifinals

Virginia Union 68 . . . . .Seattle Pacific 63
Winona St. 83 . . . . .Stonehill 73

Championship

Winona St. 73 . . . . .Virginia Union 61

NCAA Division III

The four regional winners of the 48-team field: Illinois Wesleyan (24-6), Virginia Wesleyan (28-3), Amherst (28-2), Wittenberg (29-3).

The Final Four was played March 17-18, at Salem Civic Center in Salem, Va.

Semifinals

Virginia Wesleyan 81 . . . . .Illinois Wesleyan 79
Wittenberg 64 . . . . .Amherst 60

Third Place

Illinois Wesleyan 71 . . . . .Amherst 68

Championship

Virginia Wesleyan 59 . . . . .Wittenberg 56

NAIA Division I

The quarterfinalists, in alphabetical order, after two rounds of the 32-team NAIA tournament: Azusa Pacific, Calif. (30-6); Carroll, Mont. (30-4); Lindsey Wilson (24-10); Oklahoma Baptist (30-6); Oklahoma City (28-7); Olivet Nazarene (23-11); Robert Morris (31-3); Texas Wesleyan (23-9).

All tournament games played, March 18-21, at the Municipal Auditorium, Kansas City, Mo. There was no Third Place game.

Quarterfinals: Oklahoma Baptist def. Olivet Nazarene 91-75; Oklahoma City def. Lindsey Wilson, 77-67; Robert Morris def. Azusa Pacific, 94-91 OT; Texas Wesleyan def. Carroll, 73-70.

Semifinals: Oklahoma City def. Robert Morris, 94-92; Texas Wesleyan def. Oklahoma Baptist, 83-72.

Championship: Texas Wesleyan def. Oklahoma City, 67-65.

NAIA Division II

The quarterfinalists, in alphabetical order, after two rounds of the 32-team NAIA tournament: Huntington, Indiana (31-5), Lindenwood, Missouri (26-9); Mayville St., N.D. (27-6); MidAmerica Nazarene, Kansas (25-10); Mount Vernon Nazarene, Ohio (27-9); Morningside, Iowa (28-7); Ozarks, Missouri (27-6); Wash, Ohio (27-7).

All tournament games played, March 11-14, at Keeter Gymnasium in Point Lookout, Missouri. There was no Third Place game.

Quarterfinals: Huntington def. Morningside, 82-70; Lindenwood def. Mount Vernon Nazarene, 95-86; Ozarks def. Mayville St., 80-61; MidAmerica Nazarene def. Walsh, 74-68.

Semifinals: Ozarks def. Lindenwood, 88-69; Huntington def. MidAmerica Nazarene, 78-68.

Championship: Ozarks def. Huntington, 74-56.

Final Regular Season AP Women's Top 25 Poll

Taken **before** start of NCAA tournament.

The sportswriters & broadcasters poll: first place votes in parentheses; records through Sunday, March 12, 2006; total points (based on 25 for 1st, 24 for 2nd, etc.); record in NCAA tourney and team lost to; head coach (career years and career record including 2006 postseason), and preseason ranking. Teams in **bold** type went on to reach the NCAA Final Four.

		Mar. 12 Record	Points	NCAA Recap	Head Coach	Preseason Rank
1	**North Carolina** (46)	29-1	1,150	4-1 (Maryland)	Sylvia Hatchell (31 yrs: 717-268)	7
2	Ohio St.	28-2	1,056	1-1 (Boston College)	Jim Foster (28 yrs: 605-253)	4
3	**Maryland**	28-4	1,008	6-0	Brenda Frese (7 yrs: 141-75)	14
4	**Duke**	26-3	1,001	5-1 (Maryland)	Gail Goestenkors (14 yrs: 364-97)	1
5	LSU	27-3	967	4-1 (Duke)	Pokey Chatman (2 yrs: 64-7)	3
6	Tennessee	28-4	943	3-1 (North Carolina)	Pat Summitt (32 yrs: 913-177)	2
7	Oklahoma	26-4	901	2-1 (Stanford)	Sherri Coale (6 yrs: 151-50)	NR
8	Connecticut	27-4	853	3-1 (Duke)	Geno Auriemma (21 yrs: 587-116)	9
9	Rutgers	25-3	804	2-1 (Tennessee)	C. Vivian Stringer (35 yrs: 750-251)	5
10	Baylor	22-5	718	2-1 (Maryland)	Kim Mulkey-Robertson (6 yrs: 155-44)	6
11	Purdue	24-5	622	2-1 (North Carolina)	Kristy Curry (7 yrs: 179-50)	19
12	Georgia	21-8	598	2-1 (Connecticut)	Andy Landers (27 yrs: 657-208)	8
13	Stanford	23-6	564	3-1 (LSU)	Tara VanDerveer (27 yrs: 660-179)	11
	DePaul	25-5	564	2-1 (LSU)	Doug Bruno (20 yrs: 375-216)	18
15	Arizona St.	24-6	489	1-1 (Utah)	Charli Turner Thorne (13 yrs: 212-169)	20
16	Michigan St.	22-9	449	2-1 (Duke)	Joanne P. McCallie (14 yrs: 291-138)	10
17	Louisiana Tech	23-4	374	0-1 (Florida St.)	Chris Long (1 yr: 26-5)	NR
18	Utah	21-6	346	2-1 (Maryland)	Elaine Elliott (23 yrs: 487-193)	22
19	Temple	23-7	317	0-1 (Hartford)	Dawn Staley (6 yrs: 125-59)	21
20	Texas A&M	22-7	197	0-1 (TCU)	Gary Blair (21 yrs: 456-206)	NR
21	UCLA	19-10	188	1-1 (Purdue)	Kathy Olivier (13 yrs: 201-175)	NR
22	Brigham Young	23-4	187	1-1 (Oklahoma)	Jeff Judkins (5 yrs: 103-52)	NR
23	Bowling Green	28-2	168	0-1 (UCLA)	Curt Miller (5 yrs: 93-56)	NR
24	New Mexico	21-8	87	1-1 (Baylor)	Don Flanagan (11 yrs: 239-104)	NR
25	Minnesota	19-9	83	0-1 (Washington)	Pam Borton (8 yrs: 164-79)	16

Others receiving votes: 26. **Vanderbilt** (20-10, 53 points); 27. **Florida** (21-8, 51); 28. **Kentucky** (21-8, 44); 29. **Tulsa** (25-5, 33); 30. **Chattanooga** (27-3, 26); 31 **St. John's** (21-7, 20); 32. **N.C. State** (19-11, 17); 33. **George Washington** (22-8, 15); 34. **Virginia Tech** (20-9, 14); 35. **Boston College** (19-11, 11), 36. **Florida St.** (19-9, 7), 37. **Indiana St.** (26-5, 6) and **Old Dominion** (22-8, 6); 39. **Hartford** (26-3, 4); 40. **Virginia** (18-11, 3) and **Wyoming** (20-8, 3); 42. **Liberty** (24-5, 2); 43. **Army** (19-10, 1).

NCAA Women's Division I Tournament Seeds

	CLEVELAND		ALBUQUERQUE		BRIDGEPORT		SAN ANTONIO
1	North Carolina (29-1)	1	Ohio St. (28-2)	1	Duke (26-3)	1	LSU (27-3)
2	Tennessee (28-4)	2	Maryland (28-4)	2	Connecticut (22-8)	2	Oklahoma (29-4)
3	Rutgers (25-4)	3	Baylor (24-6)	3	Georgia (21-8)	3	Stanford (23-7)
4	Purdue (24-6)	4	Arizona St. (24-6)	4	Michigan St. (22-9)	4	DePaul (25-6)
5	UCLA (20-10)	5	Utah (24-6)	5	Kentucky (21-8)	5	N.C. State (19-11)
6	Texas A&M (23-8)	6	Florida (21-8)	6	Temple (24-7)	6	Florida St. (19-9)
7	G. Washington (22-8)	7	St. John's (21-7)	7	Virginia Tech (20-9)	7	BYU (25-5)
8	Vanderbilt (20-10)	8	Boston College (19-11)	8	USC (18-11)	8	Minnesota (19-9)
9	Louisville (19-9)	9	Notre Dame (18-11)	9	South Florida (18-11)	9	Washington (18-10)
10	Old Dominion (22-8)	10	California (18-11)	10	Missouri (21-9)	10	Iowa (17-11)
11	TCU (18-11)	11	New Mexico (21-9)	11	Hartford (26-3)	11	Louisiana Tech (26-4)
12	Bowling Green (28-2)	12	Mid. Tenn. St. (20-10)	12	Chattanooga (27-3)	12	Tulsa (25-5)
13	Missouri St. (17-14)	13.	Stephen. F. Austin (23-7)	13	Wisc-Milwaukee (21-8)	13	Liberty (24-5)
14	Dartmouth (23-6)	14	N. Arizona (21-10)	14	Marist (23-6)	14	SE Missouri St. (20-8)
15	Army (19-10)	15	Sacred Heart (26-4)	15	Coppin St. (22-8)	15	Pepperdine (14-16)
16	UC-Riverside (16-14)	16	Oakland (15-15)	16	Southern (20-10)	16	Florida Atlantic (20-10)

Maryland erased a 13-point deficit with 15 minutes remaining in the second half to beat Duke in overtime at the 2006 NCAA women's national championship game in Boston. It was the second largest comeback in women's national championship game history. **Did you know**, Louisiana Tech holds the record with its 14-point comeback to beat Auburn 56-54 at the 1988 Final Four?

2006 NCAA Tournament Women's Division

Cleveland Region

1st ROUND March 18-19

- (1) N. Carolina 75
- (16) UC-Riverside 51
- (8) Vanderbilt 76
- (9) Louisville 64
- (5) UCLA 74
- (12) Bowl. Green 61
- (4) Purdue 73
- (13) Missouri St. 52
- (6) Texas A&M 65
- (11) TCU 69
- (3) Rutgers 63
- (14) Dartmouth 58
- (7) Geo. Wash. 87
- (10) ODU 72
- (2) Tennessee 102
- (15) Army 54

2nd ROUND March 20-21

- North Carolina 89
- Vanderbilt 70
- UCLA 54
- Purdue 61
- TCU 48
- Rutgers 68
- Geo. Wash. 53
- Tennessee 66

Sweet 16 March 25-26

- North Carolina 70
- Purdue 68
- Rutgers 69
- Tennessee 76

Elite Eight March 27-28

- North Carolina 75
- Tennessee 63

Cleveland → North Carolina 70

Albuquerque Region

1st ROUND March 18-19

- (1) Ohio St. 68
- (16) Oakland 45
- (8) Boston Coll. 78
- (9) Notre Dame 61
- (5) Utah 76
- (12) Mid. Tenn. 71
- (4) Arizona St. 80
- (13) SFA 61
- (6) Florida 59
- (11) N. Mexico 83
- (3) Baylor 74
- (14) N. Arizona 56
- (7) St. John's 78
- (10) Cal 68
- (2) Maryland 95
- (15) Sacred Heart 54

2nd ROUND March 20-21

- Ohio St. 69
- Boston College 79
- Utah 86
- Arizona St. 65
- New Mexico 67
- Baylor 87
- St. John's 74
- Maryland 81

Sweet 16 March 25-26

- Boston College 54
- Utah 57
- Baylor 63
- Maryland 82

Elite Eight March 27-28

- Utah 65
- Maryland 75

Albuquerque → Maryland 81

Bridgeport Region

1st ROUND March 18-19

- (1) Duke 96
- (16) Southern 27
- (8) USC 67
- (9) S. Florida 65
- (5) Kentucky 69
- (12) Chattanooga 59
- (4) Michigan St. 65
- (13) Wisc-Milw. 46
- (6) Temple 58
- (11) Hartford 64
- (3) Georgia 75
- (14) Marist 60
- (7) Va. Tech 82
- (10) Missouri 51
- (2) Connecticut 77
- (15) Coppin St. 54

2nd ROUND March 20-21

- Duke 85
- USC 51
- Kentucky 63
- Michigan St. 67
- Hartford 54
- Georgia 73
- Virginia Tech 56
- Connecticut 79

Sweet 16 March 25-26

- Duke 86
- Michigan St. 61
- Georgia 75
- Connecticut 77

Elite Eight March 27-28

- Duke 63
- Connecticut 61

Bridgeport → Duke 64

San Antonio Region

1st ROUND March 18-19

- (1) LSU 72
- (16) Fla. Atlantic 48
- (8) Minnesota 69
- (9) Washington 73
- (5) N.C. State 61
- (12) Tulsa 68
- (4) DePaul 43
- (13) Liberty 80
- (6) Florida St. 71
- (11) La. Tech 72
- (9) Stanford 88
- (14) SE Missouri 45
- (7) BYU 67
- (10) Iowa 62
- (2) Oklahoma 78
- (15) Pepperdine 66

2nd ROUND March 20-21

- LSU 72
- Washington 49
- Tulsa 67
- DePaul 71
- Florida St. 70
- Stanford 88
- BYU 70
- Oklahoma 86

Sweet 16 March 25-26

- LSU 66
- DePaul 56
- Stanford 88
- Oklahoma 74

Elite Eight March 27-28

- LSU 62
- Stanford 59

San Antonio → LSU 45

FINAL FOUR April 2

- North Carolina 70
- Maryland 81

- Duke 64
- LSU 45

NATIONAL CHAMPIONSHIP

- Maryland 78
- Duke 75

TD Banknorth Garden
Boston, Massachusetts
Tuesday, April 4, 2006

NCAA Championship Game

Apr. 4, 2006 at TD Banknorth Garden in Boston, Mass.

Maryland 78

	Min	FG M-A	FT M-A	Pts	Reb O-T	A	PF
Laura Harper	37	6-14	4-6	16	4-7	0	4
Marissa Coleman	36	4-12	2-2	10	1-14	2	2
Crystal Langhorne	38	4-6	4-6	12	2-7	4	4
Kristi Toliver	43	6-18	2-2	16	1-3	4	2
Shay Doron	36	4-9	6-6	16	0-3	1	4
Ashleigh Newman	17	1-3	1-2	4	0-0	0	3
Charmaine Carr	3	0-0	0-0	0	1-1	0	0
Jade Perry	15	2-3	0-0	4	0-2	0	1
TOTALS	225	27-65	19-24	78	10-42	0	20

Three-point FG: 5-14 (Doron 2-6, Toliver 2-6, Newman 1-2, Coleman 0-2); **Blocked Shots:** 0; **Turnovers:** 16 (Doron 4, Coleman 3, Toliver 3, Harper 2, Newman 2, Perry 2); **Steals:** 10 (Doron 4, Lanhorne 2, Toliver 2, Coleman, Newman); **Percentages:** 3-Pt FG (.357); Total FG (.415); Free Throws (.792).

Duke 75

	Min	FG M-A	FT M-A	Pts	Reb O-T	A	PF
Mistie Williams	36	1-8	1-3	3	0-3	3	3
Wanisha Smith	8	0-2	0-0	0	1-4	0	1
Alison Bales	41	7-11	5-6	19	3-12	1	4
Lindsey Harding	38	6-14	4-5	16	0-3	1	5
Monique Currie	37	7-16	8-9	22	3-6	4	4
Abby Waner	37	1-6	2-3	5	3-4	4	1
Chante Black	13	0-2	0-0	0	0-3	1	3
Jessica Foley	15	3-6	2-2	10	1-1	0	0
TOTALS	225	25-65	22-28	75	12-41	14	21

Three-point FG: 3-11 (Foley 2-5, Waner 1-3, Harding 0-1, Currie 0-1); **Blocked Shots:** 5 (Bales 3, Williams 2); **Turnovers:** 16 (Harding 4, Currie 4, Waner 2, Williams 2, Smith 2 Foley); **Steals:** 11 (Harding 4, Currie 2, Waner 2, Williams, Smith, Bales); **Percentages:** 3-Pt FG (.273); Total FG (.385); Free Throws (.786).

	1	2	OT	F
Maryland (ACC)	28	42	8	— 78
Duke (ACC)	38	32	5	— 75

Technical Fouls: None. **Attendance:** 18,642. **Officials:** Lisa Mattingly, Bob Trammell, Tina Napier.

Final ESPN/USA Today Coaches' Poll

Taken **after** NCAA tournament.

Voted on by panel of 31 women's coaches and media following the NCAA tournament: first place votes in parentheses.

		Pts			Pts
1	Maryland (31)	.775	14	Baylor	.436
2	Duke	.744	15	DePaul	.356
3	North Carolina	.689	16	Michigan St.	.289
4	LSU	.679	17	Arizona St.	.228
5	Tennessee	.641	18	UCLA	.173
6	Connecticut	.619	19	Boston College	.162
7	Stanford	.536	20	BYU	.161
8	Oklahoma	.499	21	New Mexico	.108
9	Rutgers	.494	22	Vanderbilt	.103
10	Ohio St.	.463	23	Temple	.81
11	Purdue	.460	24	Louisiana Tech	.79
12	Utah	.447	25	George Washington	64
13	Georgia	.437			

WOMEN'S FINAL FOUR

at Boston, Mass. (April 2-4).

Semifinals

Maryland 81 . . . . .North Carolina 70
Duke 64 . . . . .LSU 45

Championship

Maryland 78 . . . . .OT . . . . .Duke 75

Final Records: Maryland (35-4), North Carolina (33-2), Duke (31-5), LSU (31-4).

Most Outstanding Player: Laura Harper, Maryland forward. SEMIFINAL—31 minutes, 24 points, 9 rebounds, 0 assists; FINAL—37 minutes, 16 points, 7 rebounds, 0 assists.

All-Tournament Team: Harper and Kristi Toliver of Maryland, Alison Bales and Monique Currie of Duke, Erlana Larkins, North Carolina.

Annual Awards

Player of the Year

Seimone Augustus, LSU . . . . .AP, Wade, Wooden, Broderick, Naismith,

Ivory Latta, North Carolina . . . . .USBWA

Coaches of the Year

Sylvia Hatchell, North Carolina . . . .AP, Naismith, USBWA WBCA

Consensus All-America Team

The NCAA Division I players cited most frequently by the Associated Press, US Basketball Writers Association and the Women's Basketball Coaches Association. Holdovers from 2004-05 All-America first team are in **bold** type; (*) indicates unanimous first team selection.

First Team

	Class	Hgt	Pos
Seimone Augustus*, LSU	Sr.	6-1	G
Monique Currie, Duke	Sr.	6-0	G
Courtney Paris, Oklahoma	Fr.	6-4	C
Sophia Young, Baylor	Sr.	6-1	F
Ivory Latta, North Carolina	Jr.	5-6	G

Second Team

	Class	Hgt	Pos
Jessica Davenport, Ohio St.	Jr.	6-5	C
Candice Wiggins, Stanford	So.	5-11	G
Candace Parker, Tennessee	Fr.	6-3	F
Cappie Pondexter, Rutgers	Sr.	5-9	G
Crystal Langhorne, Maryland	So.	6-2	F

Players also named: Tasha Humphrey, Georgia; Khara Smith, DePaul; Sylvia Fowles, LSU; Kim Smith, Utah; Candice Dupree, Temple.

Other Women's Tournaments

WNIT (Mar. 31 at Manhattan, Kansas): Final— Kansas St. def. Marquette, 77-65.
NCAA Division II (Mar. 25 at Hot Springs, Arkansas): Grand Valley St. def. AIC, 58-52.
NCAA Division III (Mar. 18 at Springfield, Mass.): Hope College def. Southern Maine, 69-56.
NAIA Division I (Mar. 21 at Jackson, Tenn.): Final— Union (Tenn.) def. Lubbock Christian, 79-62.
NAIA Division II (Mar. 14 at Sioux City, Iowa): Final— Hastings (Neb.) def. Ozarks (Mo.), 58-39.

NCAA Women's Division I Leaders
Includes games through NCAA and WNIT tourneys.

INDIVIDUAL

Scoring

	Cl	Gm	Pts	Avg
Seimone Augustus, LSU	Sr.	35	795	22.7
Sophia Young, Baylor	Sr.	33	736	22.3
Jessica Dickson, S. Florida	Jr.	31	682	22.0
Courtney Paris, Oklahoma	Fr.	36	788	21.9
Candice Wiggins, Stanford	So.	34	740	21.8
Cappie Pondexter, Rutgers	Sr.	32	690	21.6
Nefertiti Walker, Stetson	Sr.	27	581	21.5
Chrissy Givens, Mid. Tenn St.	Jr.	31	667	21.5
Tamara James, Miami-FL	Sr.	30	645	21.5
Tara Boothe, Xavier	Sr.	30	644	21.5
Emily Christian, Tennessee Tech	Sr.	32	686	21.4
Lindsay Shearer, Kent St.	Jr.	30	623	20.8
Crystal Kelly, Western Ky.	So.	34	687	20.2
Kari Koch, Missouri St.	Sr.	32	646	20.2
Tasha Humphrey, Georgia	So.	31	624	20.1
Alysha Clark, Belmont	Fr.	30	599	20.0
Tatiana Conceicao, SE Missouri St.	Sr.	31	601	19.4
Kim Smith, Utah	Sr.	34	655	19.3
B.J. Banjo, E. Tenn. St.	Sr.	27	516	19.1
Terra Wallace, TX-Arlington	Jr.	29	553	19.1

Assists

	Cl	Gm	No	Avg
Lyndsey Medders, Iowa St.	Jr.	28	215	7.7
Shona Thorburn, Utah	Sr.	34	242	7.1
Sally Skeldon, Mercer	Jr.	26	179	6.9
Dee Davis, Vanderbilt	Jr.	31	212	6.8
Ashley Langford, Tulane	Fr.	26	171	6.6
Melanie Boeglin, Indiana St.	Sr.	33	217	6.6
Claire Sullivan, Lehigh	So.	28	180	6.4
Erin Grant, Texas Tech	Sr.	29	183	6.3
Sharnee Zoll, Virginia	So.	32	201	6.3
Iva Milevoj, Winthrop	Sr.	29	179	6.2
Carolyn Kieger, Marquette	Sr.	32	196	6.1
Nikki Blue, UCLA	Sr.	32	189	5.9
Shuteamia Brayboy, Fla. Atlantic	So.	31	181	5.8
Angela Tisdale, Baylor	So.	30	175	5.8
Alisa Kresge, Marist	Jr.	30	174	5.8

Rebounding

	Cl	Gm	No	Avg
Courtney Paris, Oklahoma	Fr.	36	539	15.0
Ashley Haynes, Austin Peay	Sr.	28	374	13.4
Jillian Robbins, Tulsa	Jr.	32	409	12.8
Kyra Kaylor, William & Mary	So.	28	334	11.9
Sylvia Fowles, LSU	So.	35	407	11.6
LaKrisha Brown, Morehead St.	Sr.	29	336	11.6
Khara Smith, DePaul	Sr.	34	385	11.3
Quanitra Hollingsworth, VCU	Fr.	28	311	11.1
Meredith Alexis, James Madison	Jr.	31	339	10.9
Jenny Callan, Lehigh	Sr.	28	306	10.9
Alysha Clark, Belmont	Fr.	30	327	10.9
Dana Ferraro, Stony Brook	So.	30	327	10.9
Yolando Jones, LA-Lafayette	Jr.	28	305	10.9
Antoinette Wells, Wichita St.	Sr.	28	305	10.9
Gabriella Guegbelet, C. Conn. St.	Jr.	29	315	10.9

Blocked Shots

	Cl	Gm	No	Avg
Brooke McAfee, IUPUI	Sr.	28	137	4.9
Cassie Hager, UNI	Sr.	30	128	4.3
Zane Teilane, Western Ill.	Sr.	30	125	4.2
Marita Payne, Auburn	Sr.	29	107	3.7
Sarah Beato, Columbia	Sr.	27	96	3.6
Alison Bales, Duke	Jr.	35	120	3.4

Steals

	Cl	Gm	No	Avg
Sherill Baker, Georgia	Sr.	32	149	4.7
Leilani Mitchell, Idaho	Jr.	29	115	4.0
Kristen Boone, NC-Greensboro	So.	26	101	3.9
Tanya Rhodes, Rhode Island	Sr.	26	99	3.8
Megan Ballard, Colgate	Sr.	29	106	3.7
Lisa Willis, UCLA	Sr.	32	115	3.6

High-Point Games

Pts	Opponent	Date
46 Melanie Boeglin, Indiana St.	Drake	Jan. 26
46 Crystal Smith, Iowa	La. Tech	Nov. 22

TEAM

Scoring Offense

	Gm	W-L	Pts	Avg
Duke	35	31-4	3009	86.0
Maryland	38	34-4	3166	83.3
North Carolina	35	33-2	2877	82.2
Georgia	32	23-9	2554	79.8
Stanford	34	26-8	2671	78.6
Tennessee	36	31-5	2819	78.3
UCLA	32	21-11	2475	77.3
Idaho St.	30	17-13	2313	77.1
Oklahoma	36	31-5	2748	76.3
Indiana St.	33	27-6	2512	76.1
Miami-FL	30	17-13	2274	75.8
DePaul	34	27-7	2558	75.2

Scoring Defense

	Gm	W-L	Pts	Avg
Texas-Arlington	29	20-9	1495	51.6
Rutgers	32	27-5	1661	51.9
Western Ill.	30	23-7	1560	52.0
Ohio St.	32	29-3	1694	52.9
LSU	35	31-4	1866	53.3
Delaware St.	30	21-9	1602	53.4
Coppin St.	31	22-9	1658	53.5
Delaware	30	22-8	1638	54.6
Hartford	31	27-4	1698	54.8
Marist	30	23-7	1656	55.2
George Washington	32	23-9	1767	55.2
Temple	32	24-8	1767	55.2

Scoring Margin

	Off	Def	Mar
Duke	86.0	58.2	27.7
North Carolina	82.2	59.9	22.3
LSU	74.1	53.3	20.8
Ohio St.	71.5	52.9	18.6
Maryland	83.3	65.0	18.3
Tennessee	78.3	61.0	17.3
Connecticut	72.8	55.6	17.1
Georgia	79.8	64.1	15.7
Stanford	78.6	62.9	15.7

2005-06 NCAA Div. 1 Attendance Leaders

Team	Gms	Attendance	Average
Tennessee	14	214,980	15,356
Texas Tech	14	167,081	11,935
Connecticut	22	253,465	11,521
New Mexico	18	186,376	10,354
Minnesota	14	116,601	8,329

1901-2006
Through the Years

National Champions and NCAA Final Four

The Helms Foundation of Los Angeles, under the direction of founder Bill Schroeder, selected national college basketball champions from 1942-82 and researched retroactive picks from 1901-41. The first NIT tournament and then the NCAA tournament have settled the national championship since 1938, but there are four years (1939, '40, '44 and '54) where the Helms selections differ. In 1939, Helms picked undefeated LIU-Brooklyn (24-0), winners of the NIT. In 1940, Helms picked USC (20-3) although they were beaten by Kansas in the West Regionals of the NCAA tourney. In 1944, Helms picked unbeaten Army (15-0). Army did not lift its policy barring postseason play until the 1961 NIT. In 1954, Helms chose unbeaten Kentucky (25-0), even though Kentucky refused its NCAA bid after seniors Cliff Hagan, Frank Ramsey and Lou Tsioropoulos were declared ineligible.

Multiple champions (1901-37): Chicago, Columbia and Wisconsin (3); Kansas, Minnesota, Notre Dame, Penn, Pittsburgh, Syracuse and Yale (2).

Multiple champions (since 1938): UCLA (11); Kentucky (7); Indiana (5); North Carolina (4); Duke (3); Cincinnati, Connecticut, Kansas, Louisville, Michigan St., N.C. State, Oklahoma A&M (now Oklahoma St.) and San Francisco (2).

Year		Record	Head Coach	Outstanding Player
1901	Yale	10-4	No coach	G.M. Clark, F
1902	Minnesota	11-0	Louis Cooke	W.C. Deering, F
1903	Yale	15-1	W.H. Murphy	R.B. Hyatt, F
1904	Columbia	17-1	No coach	Harry Fisher, F
1905	Columbia	19-1	No coach	Harry Fisher, F
1906	Dartmouth	16-2	No coach	George Grebenstein, F
1907	Chicago	22-2	Joseph Raycroft	John Schommer, C
1908	Chicago	21-2	Joseph Raycroft	John Schommer, C
1909	Chicago	12-0	Joseph Raycroft	John Schommer, C
1910	Columbia	11-1	Harry Fisher	Ted Kiendl, F
1911	St. John's-NY	14-0	Claude Allen	John Keenan, F/C
1912	Wisconsin	15-0	Doc Meanwell	Otto Stangel, F
1913	Navy	9-0	Louis Wenzell	Laurence Wild, F
1914	Wisconsin	15-0	Doc Meanwell	Gene Van Gent, C
1915	Illinois	16-0	Ralph Jones	Ray Woods, G
1916	Wisconsin	20-1	Doc Meanwell	George Levis, F
1917	Washington St	25-1	Doc Bohler	Roy Bohler, G
1918	Syracuse	16-1	Edmund Dollard	Joe Schwarzer, G
1919	Minnesota	13-0	Louis Cooke	Arnold Oss, F
1920	Penn	22-1	Lon Jourdet	George Sweeney, F
1921	Penn	21-2	Edward McNichol	Danny McNichol, G
1922	Kansas	16-2	Phog Allen	Paul Endacott, G
1923	Kansas	17-1	Phog Allen	Paul Endacott, G
1924	North Carolina	25-0	Bo Shepard	Jack Cobb, F
1925	Princeton	21-2	Al Wittmer	Art Loeb, G
1926	Syracuse	19-1	Lew Andreas	Vic Hanson, F
1927	Notre Dame	19-1	George Keogan	John Nyikos, C
1928	Pittsburgh	21-0	Doc Carlson	Chuck Hyatt, F
1929	Montana St.	36-2	Schubert Dyche	John (Cat) Thompson, F
1930	Pittsburgh	23-2	Doc Carlson	Chuck Hyatt, F
1931	Northwestern	16-1	Dutch Lonborg	Joe Reiff, C
1932	Purdue	17-1	Piggy Lambert	John Wooden, G
1933	Kentucky	20-3	Adolph Rupp	Forest Sale, F
1934	Wyoming	26-3	Willard Witte	Les Witte, G
1935	NYU	19-1	Howard Cann	Sid Gross, F
1936	Notre Dame	22-2-1	George Keogan	John Moir, F
1937	Stanford	25-2	John Bunn	Hank Luisetti, F

Year		Record	Winner	Head Coach	Outstanding Player
1938	Temple	23-2	NIT	James Usilton	Meyer Bloom, G

Year	Champion	Runner-up	Score	Final Two		Third Place
1939	Oregon	Ohio St.	46-33	@ Evanston, IL	Oklahoma	Villanova
1940	Indiana	Kansas	60-42	@ Kansas City	Duquesne	USC
1941	Wisconsin	Washington St.	39-34	@ Kansas City	Arkansas	Pittsburgh
1942	Stanford	Dartmouth	53-38	@ Kansas City	Colorado	Kentucky
1943	Wyoming	Georgetown	46-34	@ New York	DePaul	Texas
1944	Utah	Dartmouth	42-40 (OT)	@ New York	Iowa St.	Ohio St.
1945	Oklahoma A&M	NYU	49-45	@ New York	Arkansas	Ohio St.

NCAA Final Four (Cont.)

Year	Champion	Runner-up	Score	Final Two	Third Place	Fourth Place
1946	Oklahoma A&M	North Carolina	43-40	@ New York	Ohio St.	California
1947	Holy Cross	Oklahoma	58-47	@ New York	Texas	CCNY
1948	Kentucky	Baylor	58-42	@ New York	Holy Cross	Kansas St.
1949	Kentucky	Oklahoma A&M	46-36	@ Seattle	Illinois	Oregon St.
1950	CCNY	Bradley	71-68	@ New York	N.C. State	Baylor
1951	Kentucky	Kansas St.	68-58	@ Minneapolis	Illinois	Oklahoma A&M

Year	Champion	Runner-up	Score	Third Place	Fourth Place	Final Four
1952	Kansas	St. John's	80-63	Illinois	Santa Clara	@ Seattle
1953	Indiana	Kansas	69-68	Washington	LSU	@ Kansas City
1954	La Salle	Bradley	92-76	Penn St.	USC	@ Kansas City
1955	San Francisco	La Salle	77-63	Colorado	Iowa	@ Kansas City
1956	San Francisco	Iowa	83-71	Temple	SMU	@ Evanston, IL
1957	North Carolina	Kansas	54-53 (3OT)	San Francisco	Michigan St.	@ Kansas City
1958	Kentucky	Seattle	84-72	Temple	Kansas St.	@ Louisville
1959	California	West Virginia	71-70	Cincinnati	Louisville	@ Louisville
1960	Ohio St.	California	75-55	Cincinnati	NYU	@ San Francisco
1961	Cincinnati	Ohio St.	70-65 (OT)	St. Joseph's-PA	Utah	@ Kansas City
1962	Cincinnati	Ohio St.	71-59	Wake Forest	UCLA	@ Louisville
1963	Loyola-IL	Cincinnati	60-58 (OT)	Duke	Oregon St.	@ Louisville
1964	UCLA	Duke	98-83	Michigan	Kansas St.	@ Kansas City
1965	UCLA	Michigan	91-80	Princeton	Wichita St.	@ Portland, OR
1966	Texas Western	Kentucky	72-65	Duke	Utah	@ College Park, MD
1967	UCLA	Dayton	79-64	Houston	North Carolina	@ Louisville
1968	UCLA	North Carolina	78-55	Ohio St.	Houston	@ Los Angeles
1969	UCLA	Purdue	92-72	Drake	North Carolina	@ Louisville
1970	UCLA	Jacksonville	80-69	New Mexico St.	St. Bonaventure	@ College Park, MD
1971	UCLA	Villanova	68-62	Western Ky.	Kansas	@ Houston
1972	UCLA	Florida St.	81-76	North Carolina	Louisville	@ Los Angeles
1973	UCLA	Memphis St.	87-66	Indiana	Providence	@ St. Louis
1974	N.C. State	Marquette	76-64	UCLA	Kansas	@ Greensboro, NC
1975	UCLA	Kentucky	92-85	Louisville	Syracuse	@ San Diego
1976	Indiana	Michigan	86-68	UCLA	Rutgers	@ Philadelphia
1977	Marquette	North Carolina	67-59	UNLV	NC-Charlotte	@ Atlanta
1978	Kentucky	Duke	94-88	Arkansas	Notre Dame	@ St. Louis
1979	Michigan St.	Indiana St.	75-64	DePaul	Penn	@ Salt Lake City
1980	Louisville	UCLA	59-54	Purdue	Iowa	@ Indianapolis
1981	Indiana	North Carolina	63-50	Virginia	LSU	@ Philadelphia

Year	Champion	Runner-up	Score	Third Place		Final Four
1982	North Carolina	Georgetown	63-62	Houston	Louisville	@ New Orleans
1983	N.C. State	Houston	54-52	Georgia	Louisville	@ Albuquerque
1984	Georgetown	Houston	84-75	Kentucky	Virginia	@ Seattle
1985	Villanova	Georgetown	66-64	Memphis St.	St. John's	@ Lexington
1986	Louisville	Duke	72-69	Kansas	LSU	@ Dallas
1987	Indiana	Syracuse	74-73	Providence	UNLV	@ New Orleans
1988	Kansas	Oklahoma	83-79	Arizona	Duke	@ Kansas City
1989	Michigan	Seton Hall	80-79 (OT)	Duke	Illinois	@ Seattle
1990	UNLV	Duke	103-73	Arkansas	Georgia Tech	@ Denver
1991	Duke	Kansas	72-65	North Carolina	UNLV	@ Indianapolis
1992	Duke	Michigan	71-51	Cincinnati	Indiana	@ Minneapolis
1993	North Carolina	Michigan	77-71	Kansas	Kentucky	@ New Orleans
1994	Arkansas	Duke	76-72	Arizona	Florida	@ Charlotte
1995	UCLA	Arkansas	89-78	North Carolina	Oklahoma St.	@ Seattle
1996	Kentucky	Syracuse	76-67	UMass	Mississippi St.	@ E. Rutherford, NJ
1997	Arizona	Kentucky	84-79 (OT)	Minnesota	North Carolina	@ Indianapolis
1998	Kentucky	Utah	78-69	Stanford	North Carolina	@ San Antonio
1999	Connecticut	Duke	77-74	Michigan St.	Ohio St.	@ St. Petersburg, FL
2000	Michigan St.	Florida	89-76	Wisconsin	North Carolina	@ Indianapolis
2001	Duke	Arizona	82-72	Michigan St.	Maryland	@ Minneapolis
2002	Maryland	Indiana	64-52	Oklahoma	Kansas	@ Atlanta
2003	Syracuse	Kansas	81-78	Marquette	Texas	@ New Orleans
2004	Connecticut	Georgia Tech	82-73	Duke	Oklahoma St.	@ San Antonio
2005	North Carolina	Illinois	75-70	Michigan St.	Louisville	@ St. Louis
2006	Florida	UCLA	73-57	George Mason	LSU	@ Indianapolis

Note: Six teams have had their standing in the Final Four vacated for using ineligible players: 1961–St. Joseph's-PA (3rd place); 1971–Villanova (Runner-up) and Western Kentucky (3rd); 1980–UCLA (Runner-up); 1985–Memphis St. (3rd); 1996–UMass (3rd).

Most Outstanding Player

A Most Outstanding Player has been selected every year of the NCAA tournament. Winners who did not play for the tournament champion are listed in **bold** type. The 1939 and 1951 winners are unofficial and not recognized by the NCAA. Statistics listed are for Final Four games only.

Multiple winners: Lew Alcindor (3); Alex Groza, Bob Kurland, Jerry Lucas and Bill Walton (2).

Year		Gm	FGM	Pct	3PTM	3PTA	FTM	Pct	Reb	Ast	Blk	Stl	PPG
1939	**Jimmy Hull**, Ohio St.	2	15	—	—	—	10	.833	—	—	—	—	20.0
1940	Marv Huffman, Indiana	2	7	—	—	—	4	—	—	—	—	—	9.0
1941	John Kotz, Wisconsin	2	8	—	—	—	6	—	—	—	—	—	11.0
1942	Howie Dallmar, Stanford	2	8	—	—	—	4	.667	—	—	—	—	10.0
1943	Kenny Sailors, Wyoming	2	10	—	—	—	8	.727	—	—	—	—	14.0
1944	Arnie Ferrin, Utah	2	11	—	—	—	6	—	—	—	—	—	14.0
1945	Bob Kurland, Okla. A&M	2	16	—	—	—	5	—	—	—	—	—	18.5
1946	Bob Kurland, Okla. A&M	2	21	—	—	—	10	.667	—	—	—	—	26.0
1947	George Kaftan, Holy Cross	2	18	—	—	—	12	.706	—	—	—	—	24.0
1948	Alex Groza, Kentucky	2	16	—	—	—	5	—	—	—	—	—	18.5
1949	Alex Groza, Kentucky	2	19	—	—	—	14	—	—	—	—	—	26.0
1950	Irwin Dambrot, CCNY	2	12	.429	—	—	4	.500	—	—	—	—	14.0
1951	**Bill Spivey**, Kentucky	2	20	.400	—	—	10	.625	37	—	—	—	25.0
1952	Clyde Lovellette, Kansas	2	24	—	—	—	18	—	—	—	—	—	33.0
1953	**B.H. Born**, Kansas	2	17	—	—	—	17	—	—	—	—	—	25.5
1954	Tom Gola, La Salle	2	12	—	—	—	14	—	—	—	—	—	19.0
1955	Bill Russell, San Francisco	2	19	—	—	—	9	—	—	—	—	—	23.5
1956	**Hal Lear**, Temple	2	32	—	—	—	16	—	—	—	—	—	40.0
1957	**Wilt Chamberlain**, Kansas	2	18	.514	—	—	19	.704	25	—	—	—	32.5
1958	**Elgin Baylor**, Seattle	2	18	.340	—	—	12	.750	41	—	—	—	24.0
1959	**Jerry West**, West Virginia	2	22	.667	—	—	22	.688	25	—	—	—	33.0
1960	Jerry Lucas, Ohio St.	2	16	.667	—	—	3	1.000	23	—	—	—	17.5
1961	**Jerry Lucas**, Ohio St.	2	20	.714	—	—	16	.941	25	—	—	—	28.0
1962	Paul Hogue, Cincinnati	2	23	.639	—	—	12	.632	38	—	—	—	29.0
1963	**Art Heyman**, Duke	2	18	.409	—	—	15	.682	19	—	—	—	25.5
1964	Walt Hazzard, UCLA	2	11	.550	—	—	8	.667	10	—	—	—	15.0
1965	**Bill Bradley**, Princeton	2	34	.630	—	—	19	.950	24	—	—	—	43.5
1966	**Jerry Chambers**, Utah	2	25	.532	—	—	20	.833	35	—	—	—	35.0
1967	Lew Alcindor, UCLA	2	14	.609	—	—	11	.458	38	—	—	—	19.5
1968	Lew Alcindor, UCLA	2	22	.629	—	—	9	.900	34	—	—	—	26.5
1969	Lew Alcindor, UCLA	2	23	.676	—	—	16	.640	41	—	—	—	31.0
1970	Sidney Wicks, UCLA	2	15	.714	—	—	9	.600	34	—	—	—	19.5
1971	**Howard Porter**, Villanova	2	20	.488	—	—	7	.778	24	—	—	—	23.5
1972	Bill Walton, UCLA	2	20	.690	—	—	17	.739	41	—	—	—	28.5
1973	Bill Walton, UCLA	2	28	.824	—	—	2	.400	30	—	—	—	29.0
1974	David Thompson, N.C. State	2	19	.514	—	—	11	.786	17	—	—	—	24.5
1975	Richard Washington, UCLA	2	23	.548	—	—	8	.727	20	—	—	—	27.0
1976	Kent Benson, Indiana	2	17	.500	—	—	7	.636	18	—	—	—	20.5
1977	Butch Lee, Marquette	2	11	.344	—	—	8	1.000	6	2	1	1	15.0
1978	Jack Givens, Kentucky	2	28	.651	—	—	8	.667	17	4	1	3	32.0
1979	Magic Johnson, Michigan St.	2	17	.680	—	—	19	.864	17	3	0	2	26.5
1980	Darrell Griffith, Louisville	2	23	.622	—	—	11	.688	7	15	0	2	28.5
1981	Isiah Thomas, Indiana	2	14	.560	—	—	9	.818	4	9	3	4	18.5
1982	James Worthy, N. Carolina	2	20	.741	—	—	2	.286	8	9	0	4	21.0
1983	**Akeem Olajuwon**, Houston	2	16	.552	—	—	9	.643	40	3	2	5	20.5
1984	Patrick Ewing, Georgetown	2	8	.571	—	—	2	1.000	18	1	15	1	9.0
1985	Ed Pinckney, Villanova	2	8	.571	—	—	12	.750	15	6	3	0	14.0
1986	Pervis Ellison, Louisville	2	15	.600	—	—	6	.750	24	2	3	1	18.0
1987	Keith Smart, Indiana	2	14	.636	0	1	7	.778	7	7	0	2	17.5
1988	Danny Manning, Kansas	2	25	.556	0	1	6	.667	17	4	8	9	28.0
1989	Glen Rice, Michigan	2	24	.490	7	16	4	1.000	16	1	0	3	29.5
1990	Anderson Hunt, UNLV	2	19	.613	9	16	2	.500	4	9	1	1	24.5
1991	Christian Laettner, Duke	2	12	.545	1	1	21	.913	17	2	1	2	23.0
1992	Bobby Hurley, Duke	2	10	.417	7	12	8	.800	3	11	0	3	17.5
1993	Donald Williams, N. Carolina	2	15	.652	10	14	10	1.000	4	1	0	2	25.0
1994	Corliss Williamson, Arkansas	2	21	.500	0	0	10	.714	21	8	3	4	26.0
1995	Ed O'Bannon, UCLA	2	16	.457	3	8	10	.769	25	3	1	7	22.5
1996	Tony Delk, Kentucky	2	15	.417	8	16	6	.546	9	2	3	2	22.0
1997	Miles Simon, Arizona	2	17	.459	3	10	17	.773	8	6	0	1	27.0
1998	Jeff Sheppard, Kentucky	2	16	.552	4	10	7	.778	10	7	0	4	21.5
1999	Richard Hamilton, Connecticut	2	20	.513	3	7	8	.727	12	4	1	2	25.5

Most Outstanding Player (Cont.)

Year		Gm	FGM	Pct	3PTM	3PTA	FTM	Pct	Reb	Ast	Blk	Stl	PPG
2000	Mateen Cleaves, Michigan St. . . .2	8	.444	3	4	10	.833	6	5	0	2	14.5
2001	Shane Battier, Duke 2	13	.464	5	12	12	.706	19	8	6	2	21.5
2002	Juan Dixon, Maryland 2	16	.593	7	15	12	.800	8	5	0	7	25.5
2003	Carmelo Anthony, Syracuse 2	19	.543	6	9	9	.818	24	8	0	4	26.5
2004	Emeka Okafor, Connecticut 2	17	.654	0	0	8	.533	22	2	4	1	21.0
2005	Sean May, North Carolina 2	19	.655	0	0	10	.714	17	5	2	1	24.0
2006	Joakim Noah, Florida 2	12	.600	0	1	4	1.000	17	5	10	2	14.0

Seeds at the Final Four

NCAA champions in **bold** type.

Year	Seeds (Total)	Teams
1979	1,2,2,9 (14)	Indiana St., **Michigan St.**, DePaul, Pennsylvania
1980	2,5,6,8 (21)	**Louisville**, Iowa, Purdue, UCLA
1981	1,1,2,3 (7)	Virginia, LSU, North Carolina, **Indiana**
1982	1,1,3,6 (11)	**North Carolina**, Georgetown, Louisville, Houston
1983	1,1,4,6 (12)	Houston, Louisville, Georgia, **N.C. State**
1984	1,1,2,7 (11)	Kentucky, **Georgetown**, Houston, Virginia
1985	1,1,2,8 (12)	St. John's, Georgetown, Memphis, **Villanova**
1986	1,1,2,11 (15)	Duke, Kansas, **Louisville**, LSU
1987	1,1,2,6 (10)	UNLV, **Indiana**, Syracuse, Providence
1988	1,1,2,6 (10)	Arizona, Oklahoma, Duke, **Kansas**
1989	1,2,3,3 (9)	Illinois, Duke, Seton Hall, **Michigan**
1990	1,3,4,4 (12)	**UNLV**, Duke, Georgia Tech, Arkansas
1991	1,1,2,3 (7)	UNLV, North Carolina, **Duke**, Kansas
1992	1,2,4,6 (13)	**Duke**, Indiana, Cincinnati, Michigan
1993	1,1,1,2 (5)	**North Carolina**, Kentucky, Michigan, Kansas
1994	1,2,2,3 (8)	**Arkansas**, Arizona, Duke, Florida
1995	1,2,2,4 (9)	**UCLA**, Arkansas, North Carolina, Oklahoma St.
1996	1,1,4,5 (11)	**Kentucky**, Massachusetts, Syracuse, Mississippi St.
1997	1,1,1,4 (7)	Kentucky, North Carolina, Minnesota, **Arizona**
1998	1,2,3,3 (9)	North Carolina, **Kentucky**, Stanford, Utah
1999	1,1,1,4 (7)	**Connecticut**, Duke, Michigan St., Ohio St.
2000	1,5,8,8 (22)	**Michigan St.**, Florida, Wisconsin, North Carolina
2001	1,1,2,3 (7)	**Duke**, Michigan St., Arizona, Maryland
2002	1,1,2,5 (9)	**Maryland**, Kansas, Oklahoma, Indiana
2003	1,2,3,3 (9)	Texas, Kansas, **Syracuse**, Marquette
2004	1,2,2,3 (8)	Duke, **Connecticut,** Oklahoma St., Georgia Tech
2005	1,1,4,5 (11)	**North Carolina**, Illinois, Louisville, Michigan St.
2006	2,3,4,11 (20)	UCLA, **Florida**, LSU, George Mason

Note: teams were not seeded before 1979.

All-Time Seeds Records

All-time records of NCAA tournament seeds since tourney began seeding teams in 1979. Records are through the 2006 NCAA Tournament. Note that 1st refers to championships. 2nd refers to runners-up and FF refers to Final Four appearances not including 1st and 2nd place finishes.

Seed	W	L	Pct.	1st	2nd	FF
1	341	99	.775	14	10	21
2	249	106	.701	6	7	11
3	181	108	.626	4	5	5
4	156	111	.584	1	1	8
5	131	113	.537	0	2	3
6	149	110	.575	2	1	3
7	95	112	.459	0	0	1
8	85	111	.434	1	1	2
9	64	113	.367	0	0	1
10	76	112	.404	0	0	0
11	49	108	.312	0	0	2
12	47	108	.303	0	0	0
13	22	88	.200	0	0	0
14	17	88	.162	0	0	0
15	4	88	.043	0	0	0
16	0	88	.000	0	0	0

Teams in Both NCAA and NIT

Fourteen teams played in both the NCAA and NIT tournaments from 1940-52. Colorado (1940), Utah (1944), Kentucky (1949) and BYU (1951) won one of the titles, while CCNY won two in 1950, beating Bradley in both championship games.

Year		NIT	NCAA
1940	Colorado	**Won Final**	Lost 1st Rd
	Duquesne	Lost Final	Lost 2nd Rd
1944	Utah	Lost 1st Rd	**Won Final**
1949	Kentucky	Lost 2nd Rd	**Won Final**
1950	CCNY	**Won Final**	**Won Final**
	Bradley	Lost Final	Lost Final
1951	BYU	**Won Final**	Lost 2nd Rd
	St. John's	Lost 3rd Rd	Lost 2nd Rd
	N.C. State	Lost 2nd Rd	Lost 2nd Rd
	Arizona	Lost 2nd Rd	Lost 1st Rd
1952	St. John's	Lost 2nd Rd	Lost Final
	Dayton	Lost Final	Lost 1st Rd
	Duquesne	Lost 3rd Rd	Lost 2nd Rd

With losses by Memphis, Villanova and Connecticut in the Elite Eight (Duke lost to LSU in the Sweet 16), the last No. 1 seeds were eliminated at the 2006 NCAA tournament, and the top seed from each region did not make the Final Four. **Did you know,** that it was only the second time since teams were first seeded in 1979? The only other time all the number one seeds bowed out before the Final Four was in 1980. See the table (**Seeds at the Final Four**) above for more details.

NCAA Tournament Appearances

App		W-L	F4	Championships	App		W-L	F4	Championships
48	Kentucky	.99-43	13	7 (1948-49, 51, 58, 78, 96, 98)	24	Oklahoma	.31-24	4	None
40	UCLA	.90-33	16	11 (1964-65,67-73,75,95)	24	Texas	.28-27	3	None
38	N. Carolina	.89-36	16	4 (1957,82,93, 2005)	23	Princeton	.13-27	1	None
34	Kansas	.68-34	11	2 (1952,88)	23	Georgetown	.40-22	4	1 (1984)
33	Indiana	.59-28	8	5 (1940,53,76,81,87)	23	Ohio St.	.38-22	9	1 (1960)
32	Louisville	.53-34	8	2 (1980,86)	22	Kansas St.	.27-26	4	None
31	Syracuse	.48-31	4	1 (2003)	22	DePaul	.21-25	2	None
30	Duke	.85-27	14	3 (1991-92, 2001)	22	Oklahoma St.	.37-21	6	2 (1945-46)
27	St. John's	.27-29	2	None	22	Iowa	.27-24	3	None
27	Notre Dame	.29-31	1	None	22	Pennsylvania	.13-24	1	None
27	Arkansas	.39-27	6	1 (1994)	22	N.C. State	.32-21	3	2 (1974,83)
27	Connecticut	.42-26	2	2 (1999, 2004)	21	Missouri	.18-21	0	None
27	Villanova	.42-27	3	1 (1985)	21	BYU	.11-24	0	None
26	Utah	.35-29	4	1 (1944)	21	Maryland	.35-20	2	1 (2002)
26	Illinois	.38-26	5	None	20	Michigan	.41-19	6	1 (1989)
25	Temple	.31-25	2	None	20	Purdue	.27-20	2	None
25	Arizona	.41-24	3	1 (1997)	20	Wake Forest	.27-20	1	None
24	Cincinnati	.40-23	6	2 (1961-62)	20	West Virginia	.18-20	1	None
24	Marquette	.32-25	3	1 (1977)	20	Michigan St.	.40-19	7	1 (1989)

Note: Although all NCAA tournament appearances are included above, the NCAA has officially voided the records of Villanova (4-1) and Western Ky. (4-1) in 1971; UCLA (5-1) in 1980 and again (0-1) in 1999; Oregon St. (2-3) from 1980-82; DePaul (6-4) from 1986-89; N.C. State (0-2) from 1987-88; Kentucky (2-1) and Maryland (1-1) in 1988; Missouri (3-1) in 1994; Connecticut (2-1) and Purdue (1-1) in 1996; Arizona (0-1) in 1999.

All-Time NCAA Division I Tournament Leaders

Through 2006; minimum of six games; **Last** column indicates final year played.

CAREER

Scoring

	Points	Yrs	Last	Gm	Pts
1	Christian Laettner, Duke	.4	1992	23	407
2	Elvin Hayes, Houston	.3	1968	13	358
3	Danny Manning, Kansas	.4	1988	16	328
4	Oscar Robertson, Cincinnati	.3	1960	10	324
5	Glen Rice, Michigan	.4	1989	13	308
6	Lew Alcindor, UCLA	.3	1969	12	304
7	Bill Bradley, Princeton	.3	1965	9	303
	Corliss Williamson, Arkansas	.3	1995	15	303
9	Juan Dixon, Maryland	.4	2002	16	294
10	Austin Carr, Notre Dame	.3	1971	7	289

	Average	Yrs	Last	Pts	Avg
1	Austin Carr, Notre Dame	.3	1971	289	41.3
2	Bill Bradley, Princeton	.3	1965	303	33.7
3	Oscar Robertson, Cincinnati	.3	1960	324	32.4
4	Jerry West, West Virginia	.3	1960	275	30.6
5	Bob Pettit, LSU	.2	1954	183	30.5
6	Dan Issel, Kentucky	.3	1970	176	29.3
	Jim McDaniels, Western Ky	.2	1971	176	29.3
8	Dwight Lamar, SW Louisiana	.2	1973	175	29.2
9	Bo Kimble, Loyola-CA	.3	1990	204	29.1
10	David Robinson, Navy	.3	1987	200	28.6

Rebounds

	Total	Yrs	Last	Gm	No
1	Elvin Hayes, Houston	.3	1968	13	222
2	Lew Alcindor, UCLA	.3	1969	12	201
3	Jerry Lucas, Ohio St.	.3	1962	12	197
4	Nick Collison, Kansas	.4	2003	16	181
5	Bill Walton, UCLA	.3	1974	12	176
6	Christian Laettner, Duke	.4	1992	23	169
7	Tim Duncan, Wake Forest	.4	1997	11	165
8	Paul Hogue, Cincinnati	.3	1962	12	160
9	Sam Lacey, New Mexico St.	.3	1970	11	157
10	Derrick Coleman, Syracuse	.4	1990	14	155

	Average	Yrs	Last	Reb	Avg
1	Johnny Green, Michigan St.	.2	1959	118	19.7
2	Artis Gilmore, Jacksonville	.2	1971	115	19.2
3	Paul Silas, Creighton	.3	1964	111	18.5
4	Len Chappell, Wake Forest	.2	1962	137	17.1
5	Elvin Hayes, Houston	.3	1968	222	17.1
6	Lew Alcindor, UCLA	.3	1969	201	16.8
7	Jerry Lucas, Ohio St.	.3	1962	197	16.4
8	Tim Duncan, Wake Forest	.4	1997	165	15.0
9	Bill Walton, UCLA	.3	1974	176	14.7
10	Sam Lacey, New Mexico St.	.3	1970	157	14.3

3-Pt Field Goals

	Total	Yrs	Last	Gm	No
1	Bobby Hurley, Duke	.4	1993	20	42
2	Tony Delk, Kentucky	.4	1996	17	40
3	Jeff Fryer, Loyola-CA	.3	1990	7	38
	Donald Williams, North Carolina	.4	1995	15	38
	Juan Dixon, Maryland	.4	2002	16	38

Assists

	Total	Yrs	Last	Gm	No
1	Bobby Hurley, Duke	.4	1993	20	145
2	Ed Cota, N. Carolina	.4	2000	16	118
3	Sherman Douglas, Syracuse	.4	1989	14	106
4	Greg Anthony, UNLV	.3	1991	15	100
	Aaron Miles, Kansas	.3	2004	15	100

SINGLE TOURNAMENT

Scoring

	Points	Year	Gm	Pts
1	Glen Rice, Michigan	1989	6	184
2	Bill Bradley, Princeton	1965	5	177
3	Elvin Hayes, Houston	1968	5	167
4	Danny Manning, Kansas	1988	6	163
5	Hal Lear, Temple	1956	5	160
	Jerry West, West Virginia	1959	5	160

	Average	Year	Gm	Pts	Avg
1	Austin Carr, Notre Dame	1970	3	158	52.7
2	Austin Carr, Notre Dame	1971	3	125	41.7
3	Jerry Chambers, Utah	1966	4	143	35.8
	Bo Kimble, Loyola-CA	1990	4	143	35.8
5	Bill Bradley, Princeton	1965	5	177	35.4
6	Clyde Lovellette, Kansas	1952	4	141	35.3

Rebounds

Total	Year	Gm	No	Avg
1 Elvin Hayes, Houston	1968	5	97	19.4
2 Artis Gilmore, Jacksonville	1970	5	93	18.6
3 Elgin Baylor, Seattle	1958	5	91	18.2
4 Sam Lacey, New Mexico St.	1970	5	90	18.0
5 Clarence Glover, Western Ky	1971	5	89	17.8
6 Len Chappell, Wake Forest	1962	5	86	17.2

Assists

Total	Year	Gm	No	Avg
1 Mark Wade, UNLV	1987	5	61	12.2
2 Rumeal Robinson, Michigan	1989	6	56	9.3
3 T.J. Ford, Texas	2003	5	51	10.2
4 Sherman Douglas, Syracuse	1987	6	49	8.2
5 Bobby Hurley, Duke	1992	6	47	7.8
6 Lazarus Sims, Syracuse	1996	6	46	7.7

SINGLE GAME

Scoring

Points	Year	Pts
1 Austin Carr, Notre Dame vs Ohio Univ	1970	61
2 Bill Bradley, Princeton vs Wichita St.	1965	58
3 Oscar Robertson, Cincinnati vs Arkansas	1958	56
4 Austin Carr, Notre Dame vs Kentucky	1970	52
Austin Carr, Notre Dame vs TCU	1971	52
6 David Robinson, Navy vs Michigan	1987	50
7 Elvin Hayes, Houston vs Loyola-IL	1968	49
8 Hal Lear, Temple vs SMU	1956	48
9 Austin Carr, Notre Dame vs Houston	1971	47
10 Dave Corzine, DePaul vs Louisville	1978	46
11 Bob Houbregs, Washington vs Seattle	1953	45
Austin Carr, Notre Dame vs Iowa	1970	45
Bo Kimble, Loyola-CA vs New Mexico St.	1990	45
14 Seven players tied with 44 each.		

Rebounds

Total	Year	No
1 Fred Cohen, Temple vs UConn	1956	34
2 Nate Thurmond, Bowl. Green vs Miss. St.	1963	31
3 Jerry Lucas, Ohio St. vs Kentucky	1961	30
4 Toby Kimball, UConn vs St. Joseph's-PA	1965	29
5 Elvin Hayes, Houston vs Pacific	1966	28
6 Four players tied with 27 each.		

Assists

Total	Year	No
1 Mark Wade, UNLV vs Indiana	1987	18
2 Sam Crawford, N. Mexico St. vs Nebraska	1993	16
3 Kenny Patterson, DePaul vs Syracuse	1985	15
Keith Smart, Indiana vs Auburn	1987	15
Pepe Sanchez, Temple vs. Lafayette	2000	15

SINGLE FINAL FOUR GAME

Letters in the **Year** column indicate the following: C for Consolation Game, F for Final and S for Semifinal.

Scoring

Points	Year	Pts
1 Bill Bradley, Princeton vs Wichita St	1965-C	58
2 Hal Lear, Temple vs SMU	1956-C	48
3 Bill Walton, UCLA vs Memphis St	1973-F	44
4 Bob Houbregs, Washington vs LSU	1953-C	42
Jack Egan, St. Joseph's-PA vs Utah	1961-C	42*
Gail Goodrich, UCLA vs Michigan	1965-C	42
7 Jack Givens, Kentucky vs Duke	1978-F	41
8 Oscar Robertson, Cincinnati vs L'ville	1959-C	39
Al Wood, N. Carolina vs Virginia	1981-S	39
10 Jerry West, West Va. vs Louisville	1959-S	38
Jerry Chambers, Utah vs Texas Western	1966-S	38
Freddie Banks, UNLV vs Indiana	1987-S	38
*Four overtimes.		

3-Pt Field Goals

Total	Year	No
1 Freddie Banks, UNLV vs. Indiana	1987-S	10
2 Four players tied with 7 each.		

Rebounds

Total	Year	No
1 Bill Russell, San Francisco vs Iowa	1956-F	27
2 Elvin Hayes, Houston vs UCLA	1967-S	24
3 Bill Russell, San Francisco vs SMU	1956-S	23
4 Elgin Baylor, Seattle vs Kansas St.	1958-S	22
Tom Sanders, NYU vs Ohio St.	1960-S	22
Larry Kenon, Memphis vs Providence	1973-S	22
Akeem Olajuwon, Houston vs Louisville	1983-S	22
8 Bill Spivey, Kentucky vs Kansas St.	1951-S	21
Lew Alcindor, UCLA vs Drake	1969-C	21
Artis Gilmore, Jacksonville vs St. Bonav.	1970-S	21
Bill Walton, UCLA vs Louisville	1972-S	21
Nick Collison, Kansas vs Syracuse	2003-C	21

Assists

Total	Year	No
1 Mark Wade, UNLV vs Indiana	1987-S	18
2 T.J. Ford, Texas vs. Syracuse	2003-C	13
3 Rumeal Robinson, Michigan vs Illinois	1989-S	12
Edgar Padilla, UMass vs. Ky.	1996-S	12
5 Michael Jackson, G'town vs St. John's	1985-S	11
Milt Wagner, Louisville vs LSU	1986-S	11
Rumeal Robinson, Mich. vs Seton Hall	1989-F	11*
Steve Blake, Maryland vs. Kansas	2002-S	11
*Overtime.		

Blocked Shots

Total	Year	No
1 Danny Manning, Kansas vs Duke	1988-S	6
Marcus Camby, UMass vs Kentucky	1996-S	6
Joakim Noah, Florida vs UCLA	2006-C	6

Steals

Total	Year	No
1 Tommy Amaker, Duke vs. Louisville	1986-C	7
Mookie Blaylock, Oklahoma vs. Kansas	1988-C	7
3 Gilbert Arenas, Arizona vs Michigan St.	2001-S	6

Triple Doubles

Total	Year	No
1 Oscar Robertson, Cincinnati vs. Louisville	1959-C	1
Magic Johnson, Mich. St. vs. Penn	1979-S	1

Note: Robertson had 39 pts, 17 rebs and 10 asts; Johnson had 29 pts, 10 rebs, 10 asts

---

Most Popular Final Four Sites

The NCAA has staged its Men's Division I championship—the Final Two (1939-51) and Final Four (since 1952)—at 33 different arenas and indoor stadiums in 27 different cities. The following facilities have all hosted the event more than twice.

No	Arena	Years
9	Municipal Auditorium (KC)	1940-42, 53-55, 57, 61, 64
7	Madison Sq. Garden (NYC)	1943-48, 50
6	Freedom Hall (Louisville)	1958-59, 62-63, 67, 69
4	Superdome (New Orleans)	1982, 87, 93, 2003
	RCA Dome (Indianapolis)	1991, 97, 2000, 2006
3	Kingdome (Seattle)	1984, 89, 95

NIT Championship

The National Invitation Tournament began under the sponsorship of the Metropolitan New York Basketball Writers Association in 1938. The NIT is now administered by the Metropolitan Intercollegiate Basketball Association. All championship games have been played at Madison Square Garden. **Multiple winners:** St. John's (6); Bradley (4); Michigan (3); BYU, Dayton, Kentucky, LIU-Brooklyn, Minnesota, Providence, South Carolina, Temple, Tulsa, Virginia and Virginia Tech (2).

Year	Winner	Score	Loser	Year	Winner	Score	Loser
1938	Temple	60-36	Colorado	1973	Virginia Tech	92-91 (OT)	Notre Dame
1939	LIU-Brooklyn	44-32	Loyola-IL	1974	Purdue	97-81	Utah
1940	Colorado	51-40	Duquesne	1975	Princeton	80-69	Providence
1941	LIU-Brooklyn	56-42	Ohio Univ.	1976	Kentucky	71-67	NC-Charlotte
1942	West Virginia	47-45	Western Ky.	1977	St. Bonaventure	94-91	Houston
1943	St. John's	48-27	Toledo	1978	Texas	101-93	N.C. State
1944	St. John's	47-39	DePaul	1979	Indiana	53-52	Purdue
1945	DePaul	71-54	Bowling Green	1980	Virginia	58-55	Minnesota
1946	Kentucky	46-45	Rhode Island	1981	Tulsa	86-84 (OT)	Syracuse
1947	Utah	49-45	Kentucky	1982	Bradley	67-58	Purdue
1948	Saint Louis	65-52	NYU	1983	Fresno St.	69-60	DePaul
1949	San Francisco	48-47	Loyola-IL	1984	Michigan	83-63	Notre Dame
1950	CCNY	69-61	Bradley	1985	UCLA	65-62	Indiana
1951	BYU	62-43	Dayton	1986	Ohio St.	73-63	Wyoming
1952	La Salle	75-64	Dayton	1987	Southern Miss.	84-80	La Salle
1953	Seton Hall	58-46	St. John's	1988	Connecticut	72-67	Ohio St.
1954	Holy Cross	71-62	Duquesne	1989	St. John's	73-65	Saint Louis
1955	Duquesne	70-58	Dayton	1990	Vanderbilt	74-72	Saint Louis
1956	Louisville	93-80	Dayton	1991	Stanford	78-72	Oklahoma
1957	Bradley	84-83	Memphis St.	1992	Virginia	81-76 (OT)	Notre Dame
1958	Xavier-OH	78-74 (OT)	Dayton	1993	Minnesota	62-61	Georgetown
1959	St. John's	76-71 (OT)	Bradley	1994	Villanova	80-73	Vanderbilt
1960	Bradley	88-72	Providence	1995	Virginia Tech	65-64 (OT)	Marquette
1961	Providence	62-59	Saint Louis	1996	Nebraska	60-56	St. Joseph's
1962	Dayton	73-67	St. John's	1997	Michigan	82-72	Florida St.
1963	Providence	81-66	Canisius	1998	Minnesota	79-72	Penn St.
1964	Bradley	86-54	New Mexico	1999	California	61-60	Clemson
1965	St. John's	55-51	Villanova	2000	Wake Forest	71-61	Notre Dame
1966	BYU	97-84	NYU	2001	Tulsa	79-60	Alabama
1967	Southern Illinois	71-56	Marquette	2002	Memphis	72-62	South Carolina
1968	Dayton	61-48	Kansas	2003	St. John's	70-67	Georgetown
1969	Temple	89-76	Boston Coll.	2004	Michigan	62-55	Rutgers
1970	Marquette	65-53	St. John's	2005	South Carolina	60-57	St. Joseph's
1971	North Carolina	84-66	Georgia Tech	2006	South Carolina	76-64	Michigan
1972	Maryland	100-69	Niagara				

Most Valuable Player

A Most Valuable Player has been selected every year of the NIT tournament. Winners who did not play for the tournament champion are listed in **bold** type. Note the all-time team listed below was selected by a media panel on Mar. 15, 1997.

Multiple winners: None. However, Tom Gola of La Salle is the only player to be named MVP in the NIT (1952) and Most Outstanding Player of the NCAA tournament (1954).

Year
1938 Don Shields, Temple
1939 **Bill Lloyd**, St. John's
1940 Bob Doll, Colorado
1941 **Frank Baumholtz**, Ohio U.
1942 Rudy Baric, West Virginia
1943 Harry Boykoff, St. John's
1944 Bill Kotsores, St. John's
1945 George Mikan, DePaul
1946 **Ernie Calverley**, Rhode Island
1947 Vern Gardner, Utah
1948 Ed Macauley, Saint Louis
1949 Don Lofgran, San Francisco
1950 Ed Warner, CCNY
1951 Roland Minson, BYU
1952 Tom Gola, La Salle
    & Norm Grekin, La Salle
1953 Walter Dukes, Seton Hall
1954 Togo Palazzi, Holy Cross
1955 **Maurice Stokes**, St. Francis-PA
1956 Charlie Tyra, Louisville
1957 **Win Wilfong**, Memphis St.
1958 Hank Stein, Xavier-OH
1959 Tony Jackson, St. John's
1960 **Lenny Wilkens**, Providence
1961 Vinny Ernst, Providence
1962 Bill Chmielewski, Dayton
1963 Ray Flynn, Providence

Year
1964 Lavern Tart, Bradley
1965 Ken McIntyre, St. John's
1966 **Bill Melchionni**, Villanova
1967 Walt Frazier, So. Illinois
1968 Don May, Dayton
1969 **Terry Driscoll**, Boston College
1970 Dean Meminger, Marquette
1971 Bill Chamberlain, N. Carolina
1972 Tom McMillen, Maryland
1973 **John Shumate**, Notre Dame
1974 **Mike Sojourner**, Utah
1975 **Ron Lee**, Oregon
1976 **Cedric Maxwell**, NC-Charlotte
1977 Greg Sanders, St. Bonaventure
1978 Ron Baxter, Texas
    & Jim Krivacs, Texas
1979 Clarence Carter, Indiana
    & Ray Tolbert, Indiana
1980 Ralph Sampson, Virginia
1981 Greg Stewart, Tulsa
1982 Mitchell Anderson, Bradley
1983 Ron Anderson, Fresno St.
1984 Tim McCormick, Michigan
1985 Reggie Miller, UCLA
1986 Brad Sellers, Ohio St.
1987 Randolph Keys, So. Miss.
1988 Phil Gamble, Connecticut

Year
1989 Jayson Williams, St. John's
1990 Scott Draud, Vanderbilt
1991 Adam Keefe, Stanford
1992 Bryant Stith, Virginia
1993 Voshon Lenard, Minnesota
1994 **Doremus Bennerman**, Siena
1995 Shawn Smith, Va. Tech
1996 Erick Strickland, Nebraska
1997 Robert Traylor, Michigan
1998 Kevin Clark, Minnesota
1999 Sean Lampley, California
2000 Robert O'Kelley, Wake Forest
2001 Marcus Hill, Tulsa
2002 Dajuan Wagner, Memphis
2003 Marcus Hatten, St. John's
2004 Daniel Horton, Michigan
2005 Carlos Powell, South Carolina
2006 Renaldo Balkman, South Carolina

All-Time NIT Team

Walt Frazier, S. Illinois
George Mikan, DePaul
Tom Gola, La Salle
Maurice Stokes, St. Francis-PA
Ralph Beard, Kentucky

All-Time Winningest Division I Teams
Top 25 Winning Percentage

Division I schools with best winning percentages through 2005-06 season (including tournament games). Years in Division I only; minimum 20 years. NCAA tournament columns indicate years in tournament, record and number of championships.

		First Year	Yrs	Games	Won	Lost	Tied	Pct	NCAA Tourney Yrs	W-L	Titles
1	Kentucky	1903	103	2523	1926	596	1	.764	48	99-43	7
2	North Carolina	1911	96	2572	1883	689	0	.732	38	89-36	4
3	UNLV	1959	48	1383	980	403	0	.709	14	30-13	1
4	Kansas	1899	108	2650	1873	777	0	.707	34	68-34	2
5	Duke	1906	101	2587	1796	791	0	.694	30	85-27	3
6	UCLA	1920	87	2288	1580	708	0	.691	40	90-33	11
7	Syracuse	1901	105	2451	1680	771	0	.685	31	48-31	1
8	St. John's	1908	99	2506	1689	817	0	.676	27	27-29	0
9	Western Kentucky	1915	87	2277	1525	752	0	.670	19	15-20	0
10	Utah	1909	98	2398	1584	814	0	.661	26	35-29	1
11	Illinois	1906	101	2358	1546	812	0	.656	26	38-26	0
12	Louisville	1912	92	2311	1505	816	0	.651	32	53-34	2
13	Arizona	1905	101	2326	1508	818	0	.648	25	41-24	1
14	Indiana	1901	106	2454	1589	865	0	.648	33	59-28	5
15	Arkansas	1924	83	2209	1429	780	0	.647	27	39-27	1
16	Chattanooga	1978	29	868	559	309	0	.644	9	3-9	0
17	Temple	1895	110	2573	1656	917	0	.644	25	31-25	0
18	Notre Dame	1898	101	2459	1581	887	1	.643	27	29-31	0
19	Pennsylvania	1897	106	2518	1612	904	2	.641	22	13-24	0
20	Connecticut	1901	103	2238	1427	811	0	.638	27	42-26	2
21	Murray St.	1926	81	2110	1343	768	0	.636	13	1-13	0
22	Cincinnati	1902	105	2374	1511	863	0	.636	24	40-23	2
23	Villanova	1921	86	2249	1431	813	0	.636	27	42-27	1
24	DePaul	1924	83	2064	1312	752	0	.636	22	21-25	0
25	Weber St.	1963	44	1255	785	443	0	.633	13	6-14	0

Top 35 All-Time Victories

Division I schools with most victories through 2005-06 (including postseason tournaments). Minimum 20 years in Division I.

		Wins			Wins			Wins			Wins
1	Kentucky	1926	10	Utah	1584	19	Arizona	1508	28	Villanova	1431
2	North Carolina	1883	11	Notre Dame	1581	20	Texas	1507	29	Oklahoma	1430
3	Kansas	1873	12	UCLA	1580	21	Louisville	1505	30	Arkansas	1429
4	Duke	1796	13	Oregon St.	1559	22	BYU	1501	31	Alabama	1427
5	St. John's	1689	14	Illinois	1546	23	Purdue	1491		Connecticut	1427
6	Syracuse	1680	15	Washington	1529	24	N.C. State	1483	33	St. Joseph's	1421
7	Temple	1656	16	Western Ky.	1525	25	West Virginia	1474	34	Iowa	1420
8	Penn	1612	17	Princeton	1522	26	Bradley	1473	35	Oklahoma St.	1413
9	Indiana	1589	18	Cincinnati	1511	27	Ohio St	1435			

Top 25 Single-Season Victories

Division I schools with most victories in a season through 2005-06 (including postseason tournaments). NCAA champions in **bold** type.

		Year	W-L			Year	W-L
1	UNLV	1987	37-2	16	UNLV	1991	34-1
	Duke	1999	37-2		**Connecticut**	1999	34-2
	Illinois	2005	37-2		Duke	1992	34-2
	Duke	1986	37-3		**Kentucky**	1996	34-2
5	**Kentucky**	1948	36-3		Kansas	1997	34-2
6	Massachusetts	1996	35-2		Kentucky	1947	34-3
	Georgetown	1985	35-3		**Georgetown**	1984	34-3
	Arizona	1988	35-3		Arkansas	1991	34-4
	Duke	2001	35-4		**N. Carolina**	1993	34-4
	Kansas	1986	35-4		N. Carolina	1998	34-4
	Kansas	1998	35-4				
	Kentucky	1998	35-4				
	Oklahoma	1988	35-4				
	UNLV	1990	35-5				
	Kentucky	1997	35-5				

*NCAA later stripped UMass of its four 1996 tournament victories after learning that center Marcus Camby accepted gifts from an agent.

Division I Winning Streaks
Full Season
(including tournaments)

No		Seasons	Broken by	Score
88	UCLA	1971-74	Notre Dame	71-70
60	San Francisco	1955-57	Illinois	62-33
47	UCLA	1966-68	Houston	71-69
45	UNLV	1990-91	Duke	79-77
44	Texas	1913-17	Rice	24-18
43	Seton Hall	1939-41	LIU-Bklyn	49-26
43	LIU-Brooklyn	1935-37	Stanford	45-31
41	UCLA	1968-69	USC	46-44
39	Marquette	1970-71	Ohio St.	60-59
37	Cincinnati	1962-63	Wichita St.	65-64
37	North Carolina	1957-58	West Virginia	75-64

Home Court

No		Seasons	Broken By	Score
129	Kentucky	1943-55	Georgia Tech	59-58
99	St. Bonaventure	1948-61	Detroit	77-70
98	UCLA	1970-76	Oregon	65-45
86	Cincinnati	1957-64	Kansas	51-47
81	Arizona	1945-51	Kansas St.	76-57
81	Marquette	1967-73	Notre Dame	71-69
80	Lamar	1978-84	Louisiana Tech	68-65

Associated Press Final Polls

Taken before NCAA, NIT and Collegiate Commissioner's Association (1974-75) tournaments.

The Associated Press introduced its weekly college basketball poll of sportswriters (later, sportswriters and broadcasters) during the 1948-49 season.

Since the NCAA Division I tournament has determined the national champion since 1939, the final AP poll ranks the nation's best teams through the regular season and conference tournaments.

Except for four seasons (see AP Post-Tournament Final Polls), the final AP poll has been released prior to the NCAA and NIT tournaments and has gone from a Top 10 (1949 and 1963-67) to a Top 20 (1950-62 and 1968-89) to a Top 25 (since 1990). Tournament champions are in **bold** type.

1949

		Before Tourns	Head Coach	Final Record
1	**Kentucky**	.29-1	Adolph Rupp	32-2
2	Oklahoma A&M	.21-4	Hank Iba	23-5
3	Saint Louis	.22-3	Eddie Hickey	22-4
4	Illinois	.19-3	Harry Combes	21-4
5	Western Ky.	.25-3	Ed Diddle	25-4
6	Minnesota	.18-3	Ozzie Cowles	same
7	Bradley	.25-6	Forddy Anderson	27-8
8	**San Francisco**	.21-5	Pete Newell	25-5
9	Tulane	.24-4	Cliff Wells	same
10	Bowling Green	.21-6	Harold Anderson	24-7

NCAA Final Four (at Edmundson Pavilion, Seattle): **Third Place**—Illinois 57, Oregon St. 53. **Championship**—Kentucky 46, Oklahoma A&M 36.

NIT Final Four (at Madison Square Garden): **Semifinals**—San Francisco 49, Bowling Green 39; Loyola-IL 55, Bradley 50. **Third Place**—Bowling Green 82, Bradley 77. **Championship**—San Francisco 48, Loyola-IL 47.

1950

		Before Tourns	Head Coach	Final Record
1	Bradley	.28-3	Forddy Anderson	32-5
2	Ohio St.	.21-3	Tippy Dye	22-4
3	Kentucky	.25-4	Adolph Rupp	25-5
4	Holy Cross	.27-2	Buster Sheary	27-4
5	N.C. State	.25-5	Everett Case	27-6
6	Duquesne	.22-5	Dudey Moore	23-6
7	UCLA	.24-5	John Wooden	24-7
8	Western Ky.	.24-5	Ed Diddle	25-6
9	St. John's	.23-4	Frank McGuire	24-5
10	La Salle	.20-3	Ken Loeffler	21-4
11	Villanova	.25-4	Al Severance	same
12	San Francisco	.19-6	Pete Newell	19-7
13	LIU-Brooklyn	.20-4	Clair Bee	20-5
14	Kansas St.	.17-7	Jack Gardner	same
15	Arizona	.26-4	Fred Enke	26-5
16	Wisconsin	.17-5	Bud Foster	same
17	San Jose St.	.21-7	Walter McPherson	same
18	Washington St.	.19-13	Jack Friel	same
19	Kansas	.14-11	Phog Allen	same
20	Indiana	.17-5	Branch McCracken	same

Note: Unranked **CCNY**, coached by Nat Holman, won both the NCAAs and NIT. The Beavers entered the postseason at 17-5 and had a final record of 24-5.

NCAA Final Four (at Madison Square Garden): **Third Place**—N. Carolina St. 53, Baylor 41. **Championship**—CCNY 71, Bradley 68.

NIT Final Four (at Madison Square Garden): **Semifinals**—Bradley 83, St. John's 72; CCNY 62, Duquesne 52. **Third Place**—St. John's 69, Duquesne 67 (OT). **Championship**—CCNY 69, Bradley 61.

1951

		Before Tourns	Head Coach	Final Record
1	**Kentucky**	.28-2	Adolph Rupp	32-2
2	Oklahoma A&M	.27-4	Hank Iba	29-6
3	Columbia	.22-0	Lou Rossini	22-1
4	Kansas St.	.22-3	Jack Gardner	25-4
5	Illinois	.19-4	Harry Combes	22-5
6	Bradley	.32-6	Forddy Anderson	same
7	Indiana	.19-3	Branch McCracken	same
8	N.C. State	.29-4	Everett Case	30-7
9	St. John's	.22-3	Frank McGuire	26-5
10	Saint Louis	.21-7	Eddie Hickey	22-8
11	**BYU**	.22-8	Stan Watts	26-10
12	Arizona	.24-4	Fred Enke	24-6
13	Dayton	.24-4	Tom Blackburn	27-5
14	Toledo	.23-8	Jerry Bush	same
15	Washington	.22-5	Tippy Dye	24-6
16	Murray St.	.21-6	Harlan Hodges	same
17	Cincinnati	.18-3	John Wiethe	18-4
18	Siena	.19-8	Dan Cunha	same
19	USC	.21-6	Forrest Twogood	same
20	Villanova	.25-6	Al Severance	25-7

NCAA Final Four (at Williams Arena, Minneapolis): **Third Place**—Illinois 61, Oklahoma St. 46. **Championship**—Kentucky 68, Kansas St. 58.

NIT Final Four (at Madison Sq. Garden): **Semifinals**—Dayton 69, St. John's 62 (OT); BYU 69, Seton Hall 59. **Third Place**—St. John's 70, Seton Hall 68 (2 OT). **Championship**—BYU 62, Dayton 43.

1952

		Before Tourns	Head Coach	Final Record
1	Kentucky	.28-2	Adolph Rupp	29-3
2	Illinois	.19-3	Harry Combes	22-4
3	Kansas St.	.19-5	Jack Gardner	same
4	Duquesne	.21-1	Dudey Moore	23-4
5	Saint Louis	.22-6	Eddie Hickey	23-8
6	Washington	.25-6	Tippy Dye	same
7	Iowa	.19-3	Bucky O'Connor	same
8	**Kansas**	.24-3	Phog Allen	28-3
9	West Virginia	.23-4	Red Brown	same
10	St. John's	.22-3	Frank McGuire	25-5
11	Dayton	.24-3	Tom Blackburn	28-5
12	Duke	.24-6	Harold Bradley	same
13	Holy Cross	.23-3	Buster Sheary	24-4
14	Seton Hall	.24-3	Honey Russell	25-3
15	St. Bonaventure	.19-5	Ed Melvin	21-6
16	Wyoming	.27-6	Everett Shelton	28-7
17	Louisville	.20-5	Peck Hickman	20-6
18	Seattle	.29-7	Al Brightman	29-8
19	UCLA	.19-10	John Wooden	19-12
20	SW Texas St.	.30-1	Milton Jowers	same

Note: Unranked La Salle, coached by Ken Loeffler, won the NIT. The Explorers entered the postseason at 21-7 and had a final record of 25-7.

NCAA Final Four (at Edmundson Pavillion, Seattle): **Semifinals**—St. John's 61, Illinois 59; Kansas 74, Santa Clara 59. **Third Place**—Illinois 67, Santa Clara 64. **Championship**—Kansas 80, St. John's 63.

NIT Final Four (at Madison Sq. Garden): **Semifinals**—La Salle 59, Duquesne 46; Dayton 69, St. Bonaventure 62. **Third Place**—St. Bonaventure 48, Duquesne 34. **Championship**—La Salle 75, Dayton 64.

Associated Press Final Polls (Cont.)

1953

		Before Tourns	Head Coach	Final Record
1	**Indiana** 18-3		Branch McCracken	23-3
2	La Salle 25-2		Ken Loeffler	25-3
3	Seton Hall 28-2		Honey Russell	31-2
4	Washington . . .27-2		Tippy Dye	30-3
5	LSU 22-1		Harry Rabenhorst	24-3
6	Kansas 16-5		Phog Allen	19-6
7	Oklahoma A&M .22-6		Hank Iba	23-7
	Kansas St. 17-4		Jack Gardner	same
9	Western Ky. 25-5		Ed Diddle	25-6
10	Illinois 18-4		Harry Combes	same
11	Oklahoma City . .18-4		Doyle Parrick	18-6
12	N.C. State 26-6		Everett Case	same
13	Notre Dame . . .17-4		John Jordan	19-5
14	Louisville 21-5		Peck Hickman	22-6
	Seattle 27-3		Al Brightman	29-4
16	Miami-OH 17-5		Bill Rohr	17-6
16	Eastern Ky. 16-8		Paul McBrayer	16-9
18	Duquesne 18-7		Dudey Moore	21-8
	Navy 16-4		Ben Carnevale	16-5
20	Holy Cross 18-5		Buster Sheary	20-6

NCAA Final Four (at Municipal Auditorium, Kansas City): **Semifinals**–Indiana 80, LSU 67; Kansas 79, Washington 53. **Third Place**–Washington 88, LSU 69. **Championship**–Indiana 69, Kansas 68.

NIT Final Four (at Madison Sq. Garden): **Semifinals**–Seton Hall 74, Manhattan 56; St. John's 64, Duquesne 55. **Third Place**–Duquesne 81, Manhattan 67. **Championship**–Seton Hall 58, St. John's 46.

1955

		Before Tourns	Head Coach	Final Record
1	**San Francisco** .23-1		Phil Woolpert	28-1
2	Kentucky 22-2		Adolph Rupp	23-3
3	La Salle 22-4		Ken Loeffler	26-5
4	N.C. State 28-4		Everett Case	same
5	Iowa 17-5		Bucky O'Connor	19-7
6	**Duquesne** 19-4		Dudey Moore	22-4
7	Utah 23-3		Jack Gardner	24-4
8	Marquette 22-2		Jack Nagle	24-3
9	Dayton 23-3		Tom Blackburn	25-4
10	Oregon St. 21-7		Slats Gill	22-8
11	Minnesota 15-7		Ozzie Cowles	same
12	Alabama 19-5		Johnny Dee	same
13	UCLA 21-5		John Wooden	same
14	G. Washington . .24-6		Bill Reinhart	same
15	Colorado 16-5		Bebe Lee	19-6
16	Tulsa 20-6		Clarence Iba	21-7
17	Vanderbilt 16-6		Bob Polk	same
18	Illinois 17-5		Harry Combes	same
19	West Virginia . .19-10		Fred Schaus	19-11
20	Saint Louis 19-7		Eddie Hickey	20-8

NCAA Final Four (at Municipal Auditorium, Kansas City): **Semifinals**–La Salle 76, Iowa 73; San Francisco 62, Colorado 50. **Third Place**–Colorado 75, Iowa 74. **Championship**–San Francisco 77, La Salle 63.

NIT Final Four (at Madison Square Garden): **Semifinals**–Dayton 79, St. Francis-PA 73 (OT); Duquesne 65, Cincinnati 51. **Third Place**–Cincinnati 96, St. Francis-PA 91 (OT). **Championship**–Duquesne 70, Dayton 58.

1954

		Before Tourns	Head Coach	Final Record
1	Kentucky 25-0		Adolph Rupp	same*
2	Indiana 19-3		Branch McCracken	20-4
3	Duquesne 24-2		Dudey Moore	26-3
4	Western Ky. 28-1		Ed Diddle	29-3
5	Oklahoma A&M .23-4		Hank Iba	24-5
6	Notre Dame . . .20-2		John Jordan	22-3
7	Kansas 16-5		Phog Allen	same
8	**Holy Cross** . . .23-2		Buster Sheary	26-2
9	LSU 21-3		Harry Rabenhorst	21-5
10	**La Salle** 21-4		Ken Loeffler	26-4
11	Iowa 17-5		Bucky O'Connor	same
12	Duke 22-5		Harold Bradley	same
13	Colorado A&M . .22-5		Bill Strannigan	22-7
14	Illinois 17-5		Harry Combes	same
15	Wichita 27-3		Ralph Miller	27-4
16	Seattle 26-1		Al Brightman	26-2
17	N.C. State 26-6		Everett Case	28-7
18	Dayton 24-6		Tom Blackburn	25-7
	Minnesota 17-5		Ozzie Cowles	same
20	Oregon St. 19-10		Slats Gill	same
	UCLA 18-7		John Wooden	same
	USC 17-12		Forrest Twogood	19-14

*Kentucky turned down invitation to NCAA tournament after NCAA declared seniors Cliff Hagan, Frank Ramsey and Lou Tsioropoulos ineligible for postseason play.

NCAA Final Four (at Municipal Auditorium, Kansas City): **Semifinals**–La Salle 69, Penn St. 54; Bradley 74, USC 72. **Third Place**–Penn St. 70, USC 61. **Championship**–La Salle 92, Bradley 76.

NIT Final Four (at Madison Square Garden): **Semifinals**–Duquesne 66, Niagara 51; Holy Cross 75, Western Ky. 69. **Third Place**–Niagara 71, Western Ky. 65. **Championship**–Holy Cross 71, Duquesne 62.

1956

		Before Tourns	Head Coach	Final Record
1	**San Francisco** .25-0		Phil Woolpert	29-0
2	N.C. State 24-3		Everett Case	24-4
3	Dayton 23-3		Tom Blackburn	25-4
4	Iowa 17-5		Bucky O'Connor	20-6
5	Alabama 21-3		Johnny Dee	same
6	**Louisville** 23-3		Peck Hickman	26-3
7	SMU 22-2		Doc Hayes	25-4
8	UCLA 21-5		John Wooden	22-6
9	Kentucky 19-5		Adolph Rupp	20-6
10	Illinois 18-4		Harry Combes	same
11	Oklahoma City . .18-6		Abe Lemons	20-7
12	Vanderbilt 19-4		Bob Polk	same
13	North Carolina . .18-5		Frank McGuire	same
14	Holy Cross 22-4		Roy Leenig	22-5
15	Temple 23-3		Harry Litwack	27-4
16	Wake Forest 19-9		Murray Greason	same
17	Duke 19-7		Harold Bradley	same
18	Utah 21-5		Jack Gardner	22-6
19	Oklahoma A&M .18-8		Hank Iba	18-9
20	West Virginia . .21-8		Fred Schaus	21-9

NCAA Final Four (at McGaw Hall, Evanston, IL): **Semifinals**–Iowa 83, Temple 76; San Francisco 86, SMU 68. **Third Place**–Temple 90, SMU 81. **Championship**–San Francisco 83, Iowa 71.

NIT Final Four (at Madison Square Garden): **Semifinals**–Dayton 89, St. Francis-NY 58; Louisville 89, St. Joseph's-PA 79. **Third Place**–St. Joseph's-PA 93, St. Francis-NY 82. **Championship**–Louisville 93, Dayton 80.

1957

		Before Tourns	Head Coach	Final Record
1	**N. Carolina**	.27-0	Frank McGuire	32-0
2	Kansas	.21-2	Dick Harp	24-3
3	Kentucky	.22-4	Adolph Rupp	23-5
4	SMU	.21-3	Doc Hayes	22-4
5	Seattle	.24-2	John Castellani	24-3
6	Louisville	.21-5	Peck Hickman	same
7	West Va.	.25-4	Fred Schaus	25-5
8	Vanderbilt	.17-5	Bob Polk	same
9	Oklahoma City	.17-8	Abe Lemons	19-9
10	Saint Louis	.19-7	Eddie Hickey	19-9
11	Michigan St.	.14-8	Forddy Anderson	16-10
12	Memphis St.	.21-5	Bob Vanatta	24-6
13	California	.20-4	Pete Newell	21-5
14	UCLA	.22-3	John Wooden	same
15	Mississippi St.	.17-8	Babe McCarthy	same
16	Idaho St.	.24-2	John Grayson	25-4
17	Notre Dame	.18-7	John Jordan	20-8
18	Wake Forest	.19-9	Murray Greason	same
19	Canisius	.20-5	Joe Curran	22-6
20	Oklahoma A&M	.17-9	Hank Iba	same

Note: Unranked **Bradley**, coached by Chuck Orsborn, won the NIT. The Braves entered the tourney at 19-7 and had a final record of 22-7.

NCAA Final Four (at Municipal Auditorium, Kansas City): **Semifinals**–North Carolina 74, Michigan St. 70 (3 OT); Kansas 80, San Francisco 56. **Third Place**–San Francisco 67, Michigan St. 60. **Championship**–North Carolina 54, Kansas 53 (3 OT).

NIT Final Four (at Madison Square Garden): **Semifinals**–Memphis St. 80, St. Bonaventure 78; Bradley 78, Temple 66. **Third Place**–Temple 67, St. Bonaventure 50. **Championship**–Bradley 84, Memphis St. 83.

1958

		Before Tourns	Head Coach	Final Record
1	West Virginia	.26-1	Fred Schaus	26-2
2	Cincinnati	.24-2	George Smith	25-3
3	Kansas St.	.20-3	Tex Winter	22-5
4	San Francisco	.24-1	Phil Woolpert	25-2
5	Temple	.24-2	Harry Litwack	27-3
6	Maryland	.20-6	Bud Millikan	22-7
7	Kansas	.18-5	Dick Harp	same
8	Notre Dame	.22-4	John Jordan	24-5
9	**Kentucky**	.19-6	Adolph Rupp	23-6
10	Duke	.18-7	Harold Bradley	same
11	Dayton	.23-3	Tom Blackburn	25-4
12	Indiana	.12-10	Branch McCracken	13-11
13	North Carolina	.19-7	Frank McGuire	same
14	Bradley	.20-6	Chuck Orsborn	20-7
15	Mississippi St.	.20-5	Babe McCarthy	same
16	Auburn	.16-6	Joel Eaves	same
17	Michigan St.	.16-6	Forddy Anderson	same
18	Seattle	.20-6	John Castellani	24-7
19	Oklahoma St.	.19-7	Hank Iba	21-8
20	N.C. State	.18-6	Everett Case	same

Note: Unranked **Xavier-OH**, coached by Jim McCafferty, won the NIT. The Musketeers entered the tourney at 15-11 and had a final record of 19-11.

NCAA Final Four (at Freedom Hall, Louisville): **Semifinals**–Kentucky 61, Temple 60; Seattle 73, Kansas St. 51. **Third Place**–Temple 67, Kansas St. 57. **Championship**–Kentucky 84, Seattle 72.

NIT Final Four (at Madison Square Garden): **Semifinals**–Dayton 80, St. John's 56; Xavier-OH 72, St. Bonaventure 53. **Third Place**–St. Bonaventure 84, St. John's 69. **Championship**–Xavier-OH 78, Dayton 74 (OT).

1959

		Before Tourns	Head Coach	Final Record
1	Kansas St.	.24-1	Tex Winter	25-2
2	Kentucky	.23-2	Adolph Rupp	24-3
3	Mississippi St.	.24-1	Babe McCarthy	same*
4	Bradley	.23-3	Chuck Orsborn	25-4
5	Cincinnati	.23-3	George Smith	26-4
6	N.C. State	.22-4	Everett Case	same
7	Michigan St.	.18-3	Forddy Anderson	19-4
8	Auburn	.20-2	Joel Eaves	same
9	North Carolina	.20-4	Frank McGuire	20-5
10	West Virginia	.25-4	Fred Schaus	29-5
11	**California**	.21-4	Pete Newell	25-4
12	Saint Louis	.20-5	John Benington	20-6
13	Seattle	.23-6	Vince Cazzetta	same
14	St. Joseph's-PA	.22-3	Jack Ramsay	22-5
15	St. Mary's-CA	.18-5	Jim Weaver	19-6
16	TCU	.19-5	Buster Brannon	20-6
17	Oklahoma City	.20-6	Abe Lemons	20-7
18	Utah	.21-5	Jack Gardner	21-7
19	St. Bonaventure	.20-2	Eddie Donovan	20-3
20	Marquette	.23-7	Eddie Hickey	23-6

*Mississippi St. turned down invitation to NCAA tournament because it was an integrated event.

Note: Unranked **St. John's**, coached by Joe Lapchick, won the NIT. The Redmen entered the tourney at 16-6 and had a final record of 20-6.

NCAA Final Four (at Freedom Hall, Louisville): **Semifinals**–West Virginia 94, Louisville 79; California 64, Cincinnati 58. **Third Place**–Cincinnati 98, Louisville 85. **Championship**–California 71, West Virginia 70.

NIT Final Four (at Madison Square Garden): **Semifinals**–Bradley 59, NYU 57; St. John's 76, Providence 55. **Third Place**–NYU 71, Providence 57. **Championship**–St. John's 76, Bradley 71 (OT).

1960

		Before Tourns	Head Coach	Final Record
1	Cincinnati	.25-1	George Smith	28-2
2	California	.24-1	Pete Newell	28-2
3	**Ohio St.**	.21-3	Fred Taylor	25-3
4	**Bradley**	.24-2	Chuck Orsborn	27-2
5	West Virginia	.24-4	Fred Schaus	26-5
6	Utah	.24-2	Jack Gardner	26-3
7	Indiana	.20-4	Branch McCracken	same
8	Utah St.	.22-4	Cecil Baker	24-5
9	St. Bonaventure	.19-3	Eddie Donovan	21-5
10	Miami-FL	.23-3	Bruce Hale	23-4
11	Auburn	.19-3	Joel Eaves	same
12	NYU	.19-4	Lou Rossini	22-5
13	Georgia Tech	.21-5	Whack Hyder	22-6
14	Providence	.21-4	Joe Mullaney	24-5
15	Saint Louis	.19-7	John Benington	19-8
16	Holy Cross	.20-5	Roy Leenig	20-6
17	Villanova	.19-5	Al Severance	20-6
18	Duke	.15-10	Vic Bubas	17-11
19	Wake Forest	.21-7	Bones McKinney	same
20	St. John's	.17-7	Joe Lapchick	17-8

NCAA Final Four (at the Cow Palace, San Fran.): **Semifinals**–Ohio St. 76, NYU 54; California 77, Cincinnati 69. **Third Place**–Cincinnati 95, NYU 71. **Championship**–Ohio St. 75, California 55.

NIT Final Four (at Madison Square Garden): **Semifinals**–Bradley 82, St. Bonaventure 71; Providence 68, Utah St. 62. **Third Place**–Utah St. 99, St. Bonaventure 93. **Championship**–Bradley 88, Providence 72.

Associated Press Final Polls (Cont.)

1961

		Before Tourns	Head Coach	Final Record
1	Ohio St.	24-0	Fred Taylor	27-1
2	**Cincinnati**	23-3	Ed Jucker	27-3
3	St. Bonaventure	22-3	Eddie Donovan	24-4
4	Kansas St.	22-3	Tex Winter	23-4
5	North Carolina	19-4	Frank McGuire	same
6	Bradley	21-5	Chuck Orsborn	same
7	USC	20-6	Forrest Twogood	21-8
8	Iowa	18-6	S. Scheuerman	same
9	West Virginia	23-4	George King	same
10	Duke	22-6	Vic Bubas	same
11	Utah	21-6	Jack Gardner	23-8
12	Texas Tech	14-9	Polk Robison	15-10
13	Niagara	16-4	Taps Gallagher	16-5
14	Memphis St.	20-2	Bob Vanatta	20-3
15	Wake Forest	17-10	Bones McKinney	19-11
16	St. John's	20-4	Joe Lapchick	20-5
17	St. Joseph's-PA	22-4	Jack Ramsay	25-5
18	Drake	19-7	Maury John	same
19	Holy Cross	19-4	Roy Leenig	22-5
20	Kentucky	18-8	Adolph Rupp	19-9

Note: Unranked **Providence**, coached by Joe Mullaney, won the NIT. The Friars entered the tourney at 20-5 and had a final record of 24-5.
NCAA Final Four (at Municipal Auditorium, Kansas City): **Semifinals**–Ohio St. 95, St. Joseph's-PA 69; Cincinnati 82, Utah 67. **Third Place**–St. Joseph's-PA 127, Utah 120 (4 OT). **Championship**–Cincinnati 70, Ohio St. 65 (OT).
NIT Final Four (at Madison Square Garden) **Semifinals**–St. Louis 67, Dayton 60; Providence 90, Holy Cross 83 (OT). **Third Place**–Holy Cross 85, Dayton 67. **Championship**–Providence 62, St. Louis 59.

1962

		Before Tourns	Head Coach	Final Record
1	Ohio St.	23-1	Fred Taylor	26-2
2	**Cincinnati**	25-2	Ed Jucker	29-2
3	Kentucky	22-2	Adolph Rupp	23-3
4	Mississippi St.	19-6	Babe McCarthy	same
5	Bradley	21-6	Chuck Orsborn	21-7
6	Kansas St.	22-3	Tex Winter	same
7	Utah	23-3	Jack Gardner	same
8	Bowling Green	21-3	Harold Anderson	same
9	Colorado	18-6	Sox Walseth	19-7
10	Duke	20-5	Vic Bubas	same
11	Loyola-IL	21-3	George Ireland	23-4
12	St. John's	19-4	Joe Lapchick	21-5
13	Wake Forest	18-8	Bones McKinney	22-9
14	Oregon St.	22-4	Slats Gill	24-5
15	West Virginia	24-5	George King	24-6
16	Arizona St.	23-3	Ned Wulk	23-4
17	Duquesne	20-5	Red Manning	22-7
18	Utah St.	21-5	Ladell Andersen	22-7
19	UCLA	16-9	John Wooden	18-11
20	Villanova	19-6	Jack Kraft	21-7

Note: Unranked **Dayton**, coached by Tom Blackburn, won the NIT. The Flyers entered the tourney at 20-6 and had a final record of 24-6.
NCAA Final Four (at Freedom Hall, Louisville): **Semifinals**–Ohio St. 84, Wake Forest 68; Cincinnati 72, UCLA 70. **Third Place**–Wake Forest 82, UCLA 80. **Championship**–Cincinnati 71, Ohio St. 59.
NIT Final Four (at Madison Square Garden): **Semifinals**–Dayton 98, Loyola-IL 82; St. John's 76, Duquesne 65. **Third Place**–Loyola-IL 95, Duquesne 84. **Championship**–Dayton 73, St. John's 67.

1963

AP ranked only 10 teams from the 1962-63 season through 1967-68.

		Before Tourns	Head Coach	Final Record
1	Cincinnati	23-1	Ed Jucker	26-2
2	Duke	24-2	Vic Bubas	27-3
3	**Loyola-IL**	24-2	George Ireland	29-2
4	Arizona St.	24-2	Ned Wulk	26-3
5	Wichita	19-7	Ralph Miller	19-8
6	Mississippi St.	21-5	Babe McCarthy	22-6
7	Ohio St.	20-4	Fred Taylor	same
8	Illinois	19-5	Harry Combes	20-6
9	NYU	17-3	Lou Rossini	18-5
10	Colorado	18-6	Sox Walseth	19-7

Note: Unranked **Providence**, coached by Joe Mullaney, won the NIT. The Friars entered the tourney at 21-4 and had a final record of 24-4.
NCAA Final Four (at Freedom Hall, Louisville): **Semifinals**–Loyola-IL 94, Duke 75; Cincinnati 80, Oregon St. 46. **Third Place**–Duke 85, Oregon St. 63. **Championship**–Loyola-IL 60, Cincinnati 58 (OT).
NIT Final Four (at Madison Square Garden): **Semifinals**–Providence 81, Marquette 64; Canisius 61, Villanova 46. **Third Place**–Marquette 66, Villanova 58. **Championship**–Providence 81, Canisius 66.

1964

AP ranked only 10 teams from the 1962-63 season through 1967-68.

		Before Tourns	Head Coach	Final Record
1	**UCLA**	26-0	John Wooden	30-0
2	Michigan	20-4	Dave Strack	23-5
3	Duke	23-4	Vic Bubas	26-5
4	Kentucky	21-4	Adolph Rupp	21-6
5	Wichita	22-5	Ralph Miller	23-6
6	Oregon St.	25-3	Slats Gill	25-4
7	Villanova	22-3	Jack Kraft	24-4
8	Loyola-IL	20-5	George Ireland	22-6
9	DePaul	21-3	Ray Meyer	21-4
10	Davidson	22-4	Lefty Driesell	same

Note: Unranked **Bradley**, coached by Chuck Orsborn, won the NIT. The Braves entered the tourney at 20-6 and finished with a record of 23-6.
NCAA Final Four (at Municipal Auditorium, Kansas City): **Semifinals**–Duke 91, Michigan 80; UCLA 90, Kansas St. 84. **Third Place**–Michigan 100, Kansas St. 90. **Championship**–UCLA 98, Duke 83.
NIT Final Four (at Madison Square Garden): **Semifinals**–New Mexico 72, NYU 65; Bradley 67, Army 52. **Third Place**–Army 60, NYU 59. **Championship**–Bradley 86, New Mexico 54.

Undefeated National Champions	
Seven NCAA seasons have ended with an undefeated national champion. UCLA has accomplished the feat four times.	
Year	**W-L**
1956 San Francisco	29-0
1957 North Carolina	32-0
1964 UCLA	30-0
1967 UCLA	30-0
1972 UCLA	30-0
1973 UCLA	30-0
1976 Indiana	32-0

1965

AP ranked only 10 teams from the 1962-63 season through 1967-68.

		Before Tourns	Head Coach	Final Record
1	Michigan	21-3	Dave Strack	24-4
2	**UCLA**	24-2	John Wooden	28-2
3	St. Joseph's-PA	25-1	Jack Ramsay	26-3
4	Providence	22-1	Joe Mullaney	24-2
5	Vanderbilt	23-3	Roy Skinner	24-4
6	Davidson	24-2	Lefty Driesell	same
7	Minnesota	19-5	John Kundla	same
8	Villanova	21-4	Jack Kraft	23-5
9	BYU	21-5	Stan Watts	21-7
10	Duke	20-5	Vic Bubas	same

Note: Unranked **St. John's**, coached by Joe Lapchick, won the NIT. The Redmen entered the tourney at 17-8 and finished with a record of 21-8.

NCAA Final Four (at Memorial Coliseum, Portland, OR): **Semifinals**–Michigan 93, Princeton 76; UCLA 108, Wichita St. 89. **Third Place**–Princeton 118, Wichita St. 82. **Championship**–UCLA 91, Michigan 80.

NIT Final Four (at Madison Square Garden): **Semifinals**–Villanova 91, NYU 69; St. John's 67, Army 60. **Third Place**–Army 75, NYU 74. **Championship**– St. John's 55, Villanova 51.

1966

AP ranked only 10 teams from the 1962-63 season through 1967-68.

		Before Tourns	Head Coach	Final Record
1	Kentucky	24-1	Adolph Rupp	27-2
2	Duke	23-3	Vic Bubas	26-4
3	**Texas Western**	23-1	Don Haskins	28-1
4	Kansas	22-3	Ted Owens	23-4
5	St. Joseph's-PA	22-4	Jack Ramsay	24-5
6	Loyola-IL	22-2	George Ireland	22-3
7	Cincinnati	21-5	Tay Baker	21-7
8	Vanderbilt	22-4	Roy Skinner	same
9	Michigan	17-7	Dave Strack	18-8
10	Western Ky.	23-2	Johnny Oldham	25-3

Note: Unranked **BYU**, coached by Stan Watts, won the NIT. The Cougars entered the tourney at 17-5 and had a final record of 20-5.

NCAA Final Four (at Cole Fieldhouse, College Park, MD): **Semifinals**–Kentucky 83, Duke 79; Texas Western 85, Utah 78. **Third Place**–Duke 79, Utah 77. **Championship**–Texas Western 72, Kentucky 65.

NIT Final Four (at Madison Square Garden): **Semifinals**–BYU 66, Army 60; NYU 69, Villanova 63. **Third Place**–Villanova 76, Army 65. **Championship**–BYU 97, NYU 84.

1967

AP ranked only 10 teams from the 1962-63 season through 1967-68.

		Before Tourns	Head Coach	Final Record
1	**UCLA**	26-0	John Wooden	30-0
2	Louisville	23-3	Peck Hickman	23-5
3	Kansas	22-3	Ted Owens	23-4
4	North Carolina	24-4	Dean Smith	26-6
5	Princeton	23-2	B. van Breda Kolff	25-3
6	Western Ky.	23-2	Johnny Oldham	23-3
7	Houston	23-3	Guy Lewis	27-4
8	Tennessee	21-5	Ray Mears	21-7
9	Boston College	19-2	Bob Cousy	21-3
10	Texas Western	20-5	Don Haskins	22-6

Note: Unranked **Southern Illinois**, coached by Jack Hartman, won the NIT. The Salukis entered the tourney at 20-2 and had a final record of 24-2.

NCAA Final Four (at Freedom Hall, Louisville): **Semifinals**–Dayton 76, N. Carolina 62; UCLA 73, Houston 58. **Third Place**–Houston 84, N. Carolina 62. **Championship**–UCLA 79, Dayton 64.

NIT Final Four (at Madison Square Garden): **Semifinals**–Marquette 83, Marshall 78; Southern Ill. 79, Rutgers 70. **Third Place**–Rutgers 93, Marshall 76. **Championship**–Southern Ill. 71, Marquette 56.

1968

AP ranked only 10 teams from the 1962-63 season through 1967-68.

		Before Tourns	Head Coach	Final Record
1	Houston	28-0	Guy Lewis	31-2
2	**UCLA**	25-1	John Wooden	29-1
3	St. Bonaventure	22-0	Larry Weise	23-2
4	North Carolina	25-3	Dean Smith	28-4
5	Kentucky	21-4	Adolph Rupp	22-5
6	New Mexico	23-3	Bob King	23-5
7	Columbia	21-4	Jack Rohan	23-5
8	Davidson	22-4	Lefty Driesell	24-5
9	Louisville	20-6	John Dromo	21-7
10	Duke	21-5	Vic Bubas	22-6

Note: Unranked **Dayton**, coached by Don Donoher, won the NIT. The Flyers entered the tourney at 17-9 and had a final record of 21-9.

NCAA Final Four (at the Sports Arena, Los Angeles): **Semifinals**–North Carolina 80, Ohio St. 66; UCLA 101, Houston 69. **Third Place**–Ohio St. 89, Houston 85. **Championship**–UCLA 78, North Carolina 55.

NIT Final Four (at Madison Square Garden): **Semifinals**–Dayton 76, Notre Dame 74 (OT); Kansas 58, St. Peter's 46. **Third Place**–Notre Dame 81, St.Peter's 78. **Championship**–Dayton 61, Kansas 48.

All-Time AP Top 20

The composite AP Top 20 from the 1948-49 season through 2005-06, based on the final regular season rankings of each year. The final AP poll has been taken before the NCAA and NIT tournaments each season since 1949 except in 1953 and '54 and again in 1974 and '75 when the final poll came out after the postseason. Team point totals are based on 20 points for all 1st place finishes, 19 for each 2nd, etc. Also listed are the number of times ranked No.1 by AP going into the tournaments, and times ranked in the pre-tournament Top 10 and Top 20.

		Pts	No.1	Top 10	Top 20			Pts	No.1	Top 10	Top 20
1	Kentucky	672	8	38	45	11	Michigan	200	2	10	15
2	North Carolina	542	5	30	39	12	Ohio St	191	2	11	14
3	Duke	482	7	27	36	13	Notre Dame	190	0	12	18
4	UCLA	463	7	23	36	14	Marquette	187	0	12	17
5	Kansas	378	1	19	30	15	N.C. State	182	1	9	17
6	Indiana	293	4	16	24	16	Syracuse	179	0	9	20
7	Cincinnati	259	2	13	19	17	UNLV	173	2	8	13
8	Louisville	257	0	12	24	18	Arkansas	166	0	9	15
9	Arizona	245	1	12	20	19	Maryland	160	0	8	17
10	Illinois	235	1	10	24	20	Oklahoma	157	1	7	13

Associated Press Final Polls (Cont.)

1969

		Before Tourns	Head Coach	Final Record
1	UCLA	.25-1	John Wooden	29-1
2	La Salle	.23-1	Tom Gola	same*
3	Santa Clara	.26-1	Dick Garibaldi	27-2
4	North Carolina	.25-3	Dean Smith	27-5
5	Davidson	.24-2	Lefty Driesell	26-3
6	Purdue	.20-4	George King	23-5
7	Kentucky	.22-4	Adolph Rupp	23-5
8	St. John's	.22-4	Lou Carnesecca	23-6
9	Duquesne	.19-4	Red Manning	21-5
10	Villanova	.21-4	Jack Kraft	21-5
11	Drake	.23-4	Maury John	26-5
12	New Mexico St.	.23-3	Lou Henson	24-5
13	South Carolina	.20-6	Frank McGuire	21-7
14	Marquette	.22-4	Al McGuire	24-5
15	Louisville	.20-5	John Dromo	21-6
16	Boston College	.21-3	Bob Cousy	24-4
17	Notre Dame	.20-6	Johnny Dee	20-7
18	Colorado	.20-6	Sox Walseth	21-7
19	Kansas	.20-6	Ted Owens	20-7
20	Illinois	.19-5	Harvey Schmidt	same

*On probation

Note: Unranked **Temple,** coached by Harry Litwack, won the NIT. The Owls entered the tourney at 18-8 and finished with a record of 22-8.

NCAA Final Four (at Freedom Hall, Louisville): **Semifinals**—Purdue 92, N. Carolina 65; UCLA 85, Drake 82. **Third Place**—Drake 104, N. Carolina 84. **Championship**—UCLA 92, Purdue 72.

NIT Final Four (at Madison Square Garden): **Semifinals**—Temple 63, Tennessee 58; Boston College 73, Army 61. **Third Place**—Tennessee 64, Army 52. **Championship**—Temple 89, Boston College 76.

1971

		Before Tourns	Head Coach	Final Record
1	UCLA	.25-1	John Wooden	29-1
2	Marquette	.26-0	Al McGuire	28-1
3	Penn	.26-0	Dick Harter	28-1
4	Kansas	.25-1	Ted Owens	27-3
5	USC	.24-2	Bob Boyd	24-2
6	South Carolina	.23-4	Frank McGuire	23-6
7	Western Ky.	.20-5	John Oldham	24-6
8	Kentucky	.22-4	Adolph Rupp	22-6
9	Fordham	.25-1	Digger Phelps	26-3
10	Ohio St.	.19-5	Fred Taylor	20-6
11	Jacksonville	.22-3	Tom Wasdin	22-4
12	Notre Dame	.19-7	Johnny Dee	20-9
13	N. Carolina	.22-6	Dean Smith	26-6
14	Houston	.20-6	Guy Lewis	22-7
15	Duquesne	.21-3	Red Manning	21-4
16	Long Beach St.	.21-4	Jerry Tarkanian	23-5
17	Tennessee	.20-6	Ray Mears	21-7
18	Villanova	.19-5	Jack Kraft	23-6
19	Drake	.20-7	Maury John	21-8
20	BYU	.18-9	Stan Watts	18-11

NCAA Final Four (at the Astrodome, Houston): **Semifinals**—Villanova 92, Western Ky. 89 (2 OT); UCLA 68, Kansas 60. **Third Place**—Western Ky. 77, Kansas 75. **Championship**—UCLA 68, Villanova 62.

NIT Final Four (at Madison Square Garden): **Semifinals**—N. Carolina 73, Duke 69; Ga.Tech 76, St. Bonaventure 71 (2 OT). **Third Place**—St. Bonaventure 92, Duke 88 (OT). **Championship**—N. Carolina 84, Ga. Tech 66.

1970

		Before Tourns	Head Coach	Final Record
1	Kentucky	.25-1	Adolph Rupp	26-2
2	UCLA	.24-2	John Wooden	28-2
3	St. Bonaventure	.22-1	Larry Weise	25-3
4	Jacksonville	.23-1	Joe Williams	27-2
5	New Mexico St.	.23-2	Lou Henson	27-3
6	South Carolina	.25-3	Frank McGuire	25-3
7	Iowa	.19-4	Ralph Miller	20-5
8	Marquette	.22-3	Al McGuire	26-3
9	Notre Dame	.20-6	Johnny Dee	21-8
10	N.C. State	.22-6	Norm Sloan	23-7
11	Florida St.	.23-3	Hugh Durham	23-3
12	Houston	.24-3	Guy Lewis	25-5
13	Penn	.25-1	Dick Harter	25-2
14	Drake	.21-6	Maury John	22-7
15	Davidson	.22-4	Terry Holland	22-5
16	Utah St.	.20-6	Ladell Andersen	22-7
17	Niagara	.21-5	Frank Layden	22-7
18	Western Ky.	.22-2	John Oldham	22-3
19	Long Beach St.	.23-3	Jerry Tarkanian	24-5
20	USC	.18-8	Bob Boyd	18-8

NCAA Final Four (at Cole Fieldhouse, College Park, MD): **Semifinals**—Jacksonville 91, St. Bonaventure 83; UCLA 93, New Mexico St. 77. **Third Place**—N. Mexico St. 79, St. Bonaventure 73. **Championship**—UCLA 80, Jacksonville 69.

NIT Final Four (at Madison Square Garden): **Semifinals**—St. John's 60, Army 59; Marquette 101, LSU 79. **Third Place**—Army 75, LSU 68. **Championship**—Marquette 65, St. John's 53.

1972

		Before Tourns	Head Coach	Final Record
1	UCLA	.26-0	John Wooden	30-0
2	North Carolina	.23-4	Dean Smith	26-5
3	Penn	.23-2	Chuck Daly	25-3
4	Louisville	.23-4	Denny Crum	26-5
5	Long Beach St.	.23-3	Jerry Tarkanian	25-4
6	South Carolina	.22-4	Frank McGuire	24-5
7	Marquette	.24-2	Al McGuire	25-4
8	SW Louisiana	.23-3	Beryl Shipley	25-4
9	BYU	.21-4	Stan Watts	21-5
10	Florida St.	.23-5	Hugh Durham	27-6
11	Minnesota	.17-6	Bill Musselman	18-7
12	Marshall	.23-3	Carl Tacy	23-4
13	Memphis St.	.21-6	Gene Bartow	21-7
14	Maryland	.23-5	Lefty Driesell	27-5
15	Villanova	.19-6	Jack Kraft	20-8
16	Oral Roberts	.25-1	Ken Trickey	26-2
17	Indiana	.17-7	Bob Knight	17-8
18	Kentucky	.20-6	Adolph Rupp	21-7
19	Ohio St.	.18-6	Fred Taylor	same
20	Virginia	.21-6	Bill Gibson	21-7

NCAA Final Four (at the Sports Arena, Los Angeles): **Semifinals**—Florida St. 79, N. Carolina 75; UCLA 96, Louisville 77. **Third Place**—N. Carolina 105, Louisville 91. **Championship**—UCLA 81, Florida St. 76.

NIT Final Four (at Madison Square Garden): **Semifinals**—Maryland 91, Jacksonville 77; Niagara 69, St. John's 67. **Third Place**—Jacksonville 83, St. John's 80. **Championship**—Maryland 100, Niagara 69.

1973

	Before Tourns	Head Coach	Final Record
1	UCLA 26-0	John Wooden	30-0
2	N.C. State 27-0	Norm Sloan	same*
3	Long Beach St. . .24-2	Jerry Tarkanian	26-3
4	Providence 24-2	Dave Gavitt	27-4
5	Marquette 23-3	Al McGuire	25-4
6	Indiana 19-5	Bob Knight	22-6
7	SW Louisiana . . .23-2	Beryl Shipley	24-5
8	Maryland 22-6	Lefty Driesell	23-7
9	Kansas St. 22-4	Jack Hartman	23-5
10	Minnesota 20-4	Bill Musselman	21-5
11	North Carolina . .22-7	Dean Smith	25-8
12	Memphis St. . . .21-5	Gene Bartow	24-6
13	Houston 23-3	Guy Lewis	23-4
14	Syracuse 22-4	Roy Danforth	24-5
15	Missouri 21-5	Norm Stewart	21-6
16	Arizona St. 18-7	Ned Wulk	19-9
17	Kentucky 19-7	Joe B. Hall	20-8
18	Penn 20-5	Chuck Daly	21-7
19	Austin Peay 21-5	Lake Kelly	22-7
20	San Francisco . . .22-4	Bob Gaillard	23-5

*N.C. State was ineligible for NCAA tournament for using improper methods to recruit David Thompson.
Note: Unranked **Virginia Tech**, coached by Don DeVoe, won the NIT. The Hokies entered the tourney at 18-5 and finished with a record of 22-5.
NCAA Final Four (at The Arena, St. Louis): **Semifinals**-Memphis St. 98, Providence 85; UCLA 70, Indiana 59. **Third Place**-Indiana 97, Providence 79. **Championship**-UCLA 87, Memphis St. 66.
NIT Final Four (at Madison Square Garden): **Semifinals**-Va. Tech 74, Alabama 73; Notre Dame 78, N. Carolina 71. **Third Place**-N. Carolina 88, Alabama 69. **Championship**-Va. Tech 92, Notre Dame 91 (OT).

1974

	Before Tourns	Head Coach	Final Record
1	N.C. State 26-1	Norm Sloan	30-1
2	UCLA 23-3	John Wooden	26-4
3	Notre Dame 24-2	Digger Phelps	26-3
4	Maryland 23-5	Lefty Driesell	same
5	Providence 26-3	Dave Gavitt	28-4
6	Vanderbilt 23-3	Roy Skinner	23-5
7	Marquette 22-4	Al McGuire	26-5
8	North Carolina . .22-5	Dean Smith	22-6
9	Long Beach St. . .24-2	Lute Olson	same
10	Indiana 20-5	Bob Knight	23-5
11	Alabama 22-4	C.M. Newton	same
12	Michigan 21-4	Johnny Orr	22-5
13	Pittsburgh 23-3	Buzz Ridl	25-4
14	Kansas 21-5	Ted Owens	23-7
15	USC 22-4	Bob Boyd	24-5
16	Louisville 21-6	Denny Crum	21-7
17	New Mexico . . .21-6	Norm Ellenberger	22-7
18	South Carolina . .22-4	Frank McGuire	22-5
19	Creighton 22-6	Eddie Sutton	23-7
20	Dayton 19-7	Don Donoher	20-9

NCAA Final Four (at Greensboro, NC, Coliseum): **Semifinals**-N.C. State 80, UCLA 77 (2 OT); Marquette 64, Kansas 51. **Third Place**-UCLA 78, Kansas 61. **Championship**-N.C. State 76, Marquette 64.
NIT Final Four (at Madison Square Garden): **Semifinals**-Purdue 78, Jacksonville 63; Utah 117, Boston Col. 93. **Third Place**-Boston Col. 87, Jacksonville 77. **Championship**-Purdue 87, Utah 81.
CCA Final Four (at The Arena, St. Louis): **Semifinals**-Indiana 73, Toledo 72; USC 74, Bradley 73. **Championship**-Indiana 85, USC 60.

1975

	Before Tourns	Head Coach	Final Record
1	Indiana 29-0	Bob Knight	31-1
2	UCLA 23-3	John Wooden	28-3
3	Louisville 24-2	Denny Crum	28-3
4	Maryland 22-4	Lefty Driesell	24-5
5	Kentucky 22-4	Joe B. Hall	26-5
6	North Carolina . .21-7	Dean Smith	23-8
7	Arizona St. 23-3	Ned Wulk	25-4
8	N.C.State 22-6	Norm Sloan	22-6
9	Notre Dame . . .18-8	Digger Phelps	19-10
10	Marquette 23-3	Al McGuire	23-4
11	Alabama 22-4	C.M. Newton	22-5
12	Cincinnati 21-5	Gale Catlett	23-6
13	Oregon St. 18-10	Ralph Miller	19-12
14	Drake 16-10	Bob Ortegel	19-10
15	Penn 23-4	Chuck Daly	23-5
16	UNLV 22-4	Jerry Tarkanian	24-5
17	Kansas St. 18-8	Jack Hartman	20-9
18	USC 18-7	Bob Boyd	18-8
19	Centenary 25-4	Larry Little	same
20	Syracuse 20-7	Roy Danforth	23-9

NCAA Final Four (at San Diego Sports Arena): **Semifinals**-Kentucky 95, Syracuse 79; UCLA 75, Louisville 74 (OT). **Third Place**-Louisville 96, Syracuse 88 (OT). **Championship**-UCLA 92, Kentucky 85.
NIT Championship (at Madison Sq. Garden): Princeton 80, Providence 69. No Top 20 teams played in NIT.
CCA Championship (at Freedom Hall, Louisville): Drake 83, Arizona 76. No.14 Drake and No.18 USC were only Top 20 teams in CCA.

1976

	Before Tourns	Head Coach	Final Record
1	Indiana 27-0	Bob Knight	32-0
2	Marquette 25-1	Al McGuire	27-2
3	UNLV 28-1	Jerry Tarkanian	29-2
4	Rutgers 28-0	Tom Young	31-2
5	UCLA 24-3	Gene Bartow	28-4
6	Alabama 22-4	C.M. Newton	23-5
7	Notre Dame 22-5	Digger Phelps	23-6
8	North Carolina . .25-3	Dean Smith	25-4
9	Michigan 21-6	Johnny Orr	25-7
10	Western Mich. . .24-2	Eldon Miller	25-3
11	Maryland 22-6	Lefty Driesell	same
12	Cincinnati 25-5	Gale Catlett	25-6
13	Tennessee 21-5	Ray Mears	21-6
14	Missouri 24-4	Norm Stewart	26-5
15	Arizona 22-8	Fred Snowden	24-9
16	Texas Tech 24-5	Gerald Myers	25-6
17	DePaul 19-8	Ray Meyer	20-9
18	Virginia 18-11	Terry Holland	18-12
19	Centenary 22-5	Larry Little	same
20	Pepperdine 21-5	Gary Colson	22-6

NCAA Final Four (at the Spectrum, Phila.); **Semifinals**-Michigan 86, Rutgers 70; Indiana 65, UCLA 51. **Third Place**-UCLA 106, Rutgers 92. **Championship**-Indiana 86, Michigan 68.
NIT Championship (at Madison Square Garden): Kentucky 71, NC-Charlotte 67. No Top 20 teams played in NIT.

Associated Press Final Polls (Cont.)

1977

		Before Tourns	Head Coach	Final Record
1	Michigan	.24-3	Johnny Orr	26-4
2	UCLA	.24-3	Gene Bartow	25-4
3	Kentucky	.24-3	Joe B. Hall	26-4
4	UNLV	.25-2	Jerry Tarkanian	29-3
5	North Carolina	.24-4	Dean Smith	28-5
6	Syracuse	.25-3	Jim Boeheim	26-4
7	**Marquette**	.20-7	Al McGuire	25-7
8	San Francisco	.29-1	Bob Gaillard	29-2
9	Wake Forest	.20-7	Carl Tacy	22-8
.10	Notre Dame	.21-6	Digger Phelps	22-7
11	Alabama	.23-4	C.M. Newton	25-6
12	Detroit	.24-3	Dick Vitale	25-4
13	Minnesota	.24-3	Jim Dutcher	same*
14	Utah	.22-6	Jerry Pimm	23-7
15	Tennessee	.22-5	Ray Mears	22-6
16	Kansas St.	.23-6	Jack Hartman	24-7
17	NC-Charlotte	.25-3	Lee Rose	28-5
18	Arkansas	.26-1	Eddie Sutton	26-2
19	Louisville	.21-6	Denny Crum	21-7
20	VMI	.25-3	Charlie Schmaus	26-4

*On probation

NCAA Final Four (at the Omni, Atlanta): **Semifinals**—Marquette 51, NC-Charlotte, 49; N. Carolina 84, UNLV 83. **Third Place**—UNLV 106, NC-Charlotte 94. **Championship**—Marquette 67, N. Carolina 59.
NIT Championship (at Madison Square Garden): St. Bonaventure 94, Houston 91. No.11 Alabama was only Top 20 team in NIT.

1978

		Before Tourns	Head Coach	Final Record
1	**Kentucky**	.25-2	Joe B. Hall	30-2
2	UCLA	.24-2	Gary Cunningham	25-3
3	DePaul	.25-2	Ray Meyer	27-3
4	Michigan St.	.23-4	Jud Heathcote	25-5
5	Arkansas	.28-3	Eddie Sutton	32-3
6	Notre Dame	.20-6	Digger Phelps	23-8
7	Duke	.23-6	Bill Foster	27-7
8	Marquette	.24-3	Hank Raymonds	24-4
9	Louisville	.22-6	Denny Crum	23-7
10	Kansas	.24-4	Ted Owens	24-5
11	San Francisco	.22-5	Bob Gaillard	23-6
12	New Mexico	.24-3	Norm Ellenberger	24-4
13	Indiana	.20-7	Bob Knight	21-8
14	Utah	.22-5	Jerry Pimm	23-6
15	Florida St.	.23-5	Hugh Durham	23-6
16	North Carolina	.23-7	Dean Smith	23-8
17	**Texas**	.22-5	Abe Lemons	26-5
18	Detroit	.24-3	Dave Gaines	25-4
19	Miami-OH	.18-8	Darrell Hedric	19-9
20	Penn	.19-7	Bob Weinhauer	20-8

NCAA Final Four (at the Checkerdome, St. Louis): **Semifinals**—Kentucky 64, Arkansas 59; Duke 90, Notre Dame 86. **Third Place**—Arkansas 71, Notre Dame 69. **Championship**—Kentucky 94, Duke 88.
NIT Championship (at Madison Square Garden): Texas 101, N.C. State 93. No. 17 Texas and No. 18 Detroit were only Top 20 teams in NIT.

1979

		Before Tourns	Head Coach	Final Record
1	Indiana St.	.29-0	Bill Hodges	33-1
2	UCLA	.23-4	Gary Cunningham	25-5
3	**Michigan St.**	.21-6	Jud Heathcote	26-6
4	Notre Dame	.22-5	Digger Phelps	24-6
5	Arkansas	.23-4	Eddie Sutton	25-5
6	DePaul	.22-5	Ray Meyer	26-6
7	LSU	.22-5	Dale Brown	23-6
8	Syracuse	.25-3	Jim Boeheim	26-4
9	North Carolina	.23-5	Dean Smith	23-6
10	Marquette	.21-6	Hank Raymonds	22-7
11	Duke	.22-7	Bill Foster	22-8
12	San Francisco	.21-6	Dan Belluomini	22-7
13	Louisville	.23-7	Denny Crum	24-8
14	Penn	.21-5	Bob Weinhauer	25-7
15	Purdue	.23-7	Lee Rose	27-8
16	Oklahoma	.20-9	Dave Bliss	21-10
17	St. John's	.18-10	Lou Carnesecca	21-11
18	Rutgers	.21-8	Tom Young	22-9
19	Toledo	.21-6	Bob Nichols	22-7
20	Iowa	.20-7	Lute Olson	20-8

NCAA Final Four (at Special Events Center, Salt Lake City): **Semifinals**—Michigan St. 101, Penn 67; Indiana St. 76, DePaul 74; **Championship**—Michigan St. 75, Indiana St. 64.
NIT Championship (at Madison Square Garden): Indiana 53, Purdue 52. No. 15 Purdue was the only Top 20 team in NIT.

1980

		Before Tourns	Head Coach	Final Record
1	DePaul	.26-1	Ray Meyer	26-2
2	**Louisville**	.28-3	Denny Crum	33-3
3	LSU	.24-5	Dale Brown	26-6
4	Kentucky	.28-5	Joe B. Hall	29-6
5	Oregon St.	.26-3	Ralph Miller	26-4
6	Syracuse	.25-3	Jim Boeheim	26-4
7	Indiana	.20-7	Bob Knight	21-8
8	Maryland	.23-6	Lefty Driesell	24-7
9	Notre Dame	.20-7	Digger Phelps	20-8
10	Ohio St.	.24-5	Eldon Miller	21-8
11	Georgetown	.24-5	John Thompson	26-6
12	BYU	.24-4	Frank Arnold	24-5
13	St. John's	.24-4	Lou Carnesecca	24-5
14	Duke	.22-8	Bill Foster	24-9
15	North Carolina	.21-7	Dean Smith	21-8
16	Missouri	.23-5	Norm Stewart	25-6
17	Weber St.	.26-2	Neil McCarthy	26-3
18	Arizona St.	.21-6	Ned Wulk	22-7
19	Iona	.28-4	Jim Valvano	29-5
20	Purdue	.19-9	Lee Rose	23-10

NCAA Final Four (at Market Square Arena, Indianapolis): **Semifinals**—Louisville 80, Iowa 72; UCLA 67, Purdue 62; **Championship**—Louisville 59, UCLA 54.
NIT Championship (at Madison Square Garden): Virginia 58, Minnesota 55. No Top 20 teams played in NIT.

1981

		Before Tourns	Head Coach	Final Record
1	DePaul	27-1	Ray Meyer	27-2
2	Oregon St.	26-1	Ralph Miller	26-2
3	Arizona St.	24-3	Ned Wulk	24-4
4	LSU	28-3	Dale Brown	31-5
5	Virginia	25-3	Terry Holland	29-4
6	North Carolina	25-7	Dean Smith	29-8
7	Notre Dame	22-5	Digger Phelps	23-6
8	Kentucky	22-5	Joe B. Hall	22-6
9	**Indiana**	21-9	Bob Knight	26-9
10	UCLA	20-6	Larry Brown	20-7
11	Wake Forest	22-6	Carl Tacy	22-7
12	Louisville	21-8	Denny Crum	21-9
13	Iowa	21-6	Lute Olson	21-7
14	Utah	24-4	Jerry Pimm	25-5
15	Tennessee	20-7	Don DeVoe	21-8
16	BYU	22-6	Frank Arnold	25-7
17	Wyoming	23-5	Jim Brandenburg	24-6
18	Maryland	20-9	Lefty Driesell	21-10
19	Illinois	20-7	Lou Henson	21-8
20	Arkansas	22-7	Eddie Sutton	24-8

NCAA Final Four (at the Spectrum, Phila.): **Semifinals**–N. Carolina 78, Virginia 65; Indiana 67, LSU 49. **Third Place**–Virginia 78, LSU 74. **Championship**–Indiana 63, N. Carolina 50.

NIT Championship (at Madison Square Garden): Tulsa 86, Syracuse 84. No Top 20 teams played in NIT.

1982

		Before Tourns	Head Coach	Final Record
1	**N. Carolina**	27-2	Dean Smith	32-2
2	DePaul	26-1	Ray Meyer	26-2
3	Virginia	29-3	Terry Holland	30-4
4	Oregon St.	23-4	Ralph Miller	25-5
5	Missouri	26-3	Norm Stewart	27-4
6	Georgetown	26-6	John Thompson	30-7
7	Minnesota	22-5	Jim Dutcher	23-6
8	Idaho	26-2	Don Monson	27-3
9	Memphis St.	23-4	Dana Kirk	24-5
10	Tulsa	24-5	Nolan Richardson	24-6
11	Fresno St.	26-2	Boyd Grant	27-3
12	Arkansas	23-5	Eddie Sutton	23-6
13	Alabama	23-6	Wimp Sanderson	24-7
14	West Virginia	26-3	Gale Catlett	27-4
15	Kentucky	22-7	Joe B. Hall	22-8
16	Iowa	20-7	Lute Olson	21-8
17	Ala-Birmingham	23-5	Gene Bartow	25-6
18	Wake Forest	20-8	Carl Tacy	21-9
19	UCLA	21-6	Larry Farmer	21-6
20	Louisville	20-9	Denny Crum	23-10

NCAA Final Four (at the Superdome, New Orleans): **Semifinals**–N. Carolina 68, Houston 63; Georgetown 50, Louisville 46. **Championship**–N. Carolina 63, Georgetown 62.

NIT Championship (at Madison Square Garden): Bradley 67, Purdue 58. No Top 20 teams played in NIT.

1983

		Before Tourns	Head Coach	Final Record
1	Houston	27-2	Guy Lewis	31-3
2	Louisville	29-3	Denny Crum	32-4
3	St. John's	27-4	Lou Carnesecca	28-5
4	Virginia	27-4	Terry Holland	29-5
5	Indiana	23-5	Bob Knight	24-6
6	UNLV	28-2	Jerry Tarkanian	28-3
7	UCLA	23-5	Larry Farmer	23-6
8	North Carolina	26-7	Dean Smith	28-8
9	Arkansas	25-3	Eddie Sutton	26-4
10	Missouri	26-7	Norm Stewart	26-8
11	Boston College	24-6	Gary Williams	25-7
12	Kentucky	22-7	Joe B. Hall	23-8
13	Villanova	22-7	Rollie Massimino	24-8
14	Wichita St.	25-3	Gene Smithson	same*
15	Tenn-Chatt.	26-3	Murray Arnold	26-4
16	**N.C. State**	20-10	Jim Valvano	26-10
17	Memphis St.	22-7	Dana Kirk	23-8
18	Georgia	21-9	Hugh Durham	24-10
19	Oklahoma St.	24-6	Paul Hansen	24-7
20	Georgetown	21-9	John Thompson	22-10

*On probation

NCAA Final Four (at The Pit, Albuquerque, NM): **Semifinals**–N.C. State 67, Georgia 60; Houston 94, Louisville 81. **Championship**–N.C. State 54, Houston 52.

NIT Championship (at Madison Square Garden): Fresno St. 69, DePaul 60. No Top 20 teams played in NIT.

1984

		Before Tourns	Head Coach	Final Record
1	North Carolina	27-2	Dean Smith	28-3
2	**Georgetown**	29-3	John Thompson	34-3
3	Kentucky	26-4	Joe B. Hall	29-5
4	DePaul	26-2	Ray Meyer	27-3
5	Houston	28-4	Guy Lewis	32-5
6	Illinois	24-4	Lou Henson	26-5
7	Oklahoma	29-4	Billy Tubbs	29-5
8	Arkansas	25-6	Eddie Sutton	25-7
9	UTEP	27-3	Don Haskins	27-4
10	Purdue	22-6	Gene Keady	22-7
11	Maryland	23-7	Lefty Driesell	24-8
12	Tulsa	27-3	Nolan Richardson	27-4
13	UNLV	27-5	Jerry Tarkanian	29-6
14	Duke	24-9	Mike Krzyzewski	24-10
15	Washington	24-6	Marv Harshman	24-7
16	Memphis St.	24-6	Dana Kirk	26-7
17	Oregon St.	22-6	Ralph Miller	22-7
18	Syracuse	22-8	Jim Boeheim	23-9
19	Wake Forest	21-8	Carl Tacy	23-9
20	Temple	25-4	John Chaney	26-5

NCAA Final Four (at the Kingdome, Seattle): **Semifinals**–Houston 49, Virginia 47 (OT); Georgetown 53, Kentucky 40. **Championship**–Georgetown 84, Houston 75.

NIT Championship (at Madison Square Garden): Michigan 83, Notre Dame 63. No Top 20 teams played in NIT.

Highest-Rated College Games on TV

The dozen highest-rated college basketball games seen on U.S. television have been NCAA tournament championship games, led by the 1979 Michigan State-Indiana State final that featured Magic Johnson and Larry Bird.

Listed below are the finalists (winning team first), date of game, TV network, and TV rating and audience share (according to Nielson Media Research).

		Date	Net	Rtg/Sh
1	Michigan St.-Indiana St.	3/26/79	NBC	24.1/38
2	Villanova-Georgetown	4/1/85	CBS	23.3/33
3	Duke-Michigan	4/6/92	CBS	22.7/35
4	N.C. State-Houston	4/4/83	CBS	22.3/32
5	N. Carolina-Michigan	4/5/93	CBS	22.2/34
6	Arkansas-Duke	4/4/94	CBS	21.6/33
7	N. Carolina-Georgetown	3/29/82	CBS	21.6/31
8	UCLA-Kentucky	3/31/75	NBC	21.3/33
9	Michigan-Seton Hall	4/3/89	CBS	21.3/33
10	Louisville-Duke	3/31/86	CBS	20.7/31
11	Indiana-N. Carolina	3/30/81	NBC	20.7/29
12	UCLA-Memphis St.	3/26/73	NBC	20.5/32

Associated Press Final Polls (Cont.)

1985

		Before Tourns	Head Coach	Final Record
1	Georgetown	30-2	John Thompson	35-3
2	Michigan	25-3	Bill Frieder	26-4
3	St. John's	27-3	Lou Carnesecca	31-4
4	Oklahoma	28-5	Billy Tubbs	31-6
5	Memphis St.	27-3	Dana Kirk	31-4
6	Georgia Tech	24-7	Bobby Cremins	27-8
7	North Carolina	24-8	Dean Smith	27-9
8	Louisiana Tech	27-2	Andy Russo	29-3
9	UNLV	27-3	Jerry Tarkanian	28-4
10	Duke	22-7	Mike Krzyzewski	23-8
11	VCU	25-5	J.D. Barnett	26-6
12	Illinois	24-8	Lou Henson	26-9
13	Kansas	25-7	Larry Brown	26-8
14	Loyola-IL	25-5	Gene Sullivan	27-6
15	Syracuse	21-8	Jim Boeheim	22-9
16	N.C. State	20-9	Jim Valvano	23-10
17	Texas Tech	23-7	Gerald Myers	23-8
18	Tulsa	23-7	Nolan Richardson	23-8
19	Georgia	21-8	Hugh Durham	22-9
20	LSU	19-9	Dale Brown	19-10

Note: Unranked **Villanova**, coached by Rollie Massimino, won the NCAAs. The Wildcats entered the tourney at 19-10 and had a final record of 25-10.
NCAA Final Four (at Rupp Arena, Lexington, KY): **Semifinals**– Georgetown 77, St. John's 59; Villanova 52, Memphis St. 45. **Championship**–Villanova 66, Georgetown 64.
NIT Championship (at Madison Square Garden): UCLA 65, Indiana 62. No Top 20 teams played in NIT.

1987

		Before Tourns	Head Coach	Final Record
1	UNLV	33-1	Jerry Tarkanian	37-2
2	North Carolina	29-3	Dean Smith	32-4
3	**Indiana**	24-4	Bob Knight	30-4
4	Georgetown	26-4	John Thompson	29-5
5	DePaul	26-2	Joey Meyer	28-3
6	Iowa	27-4	Tom Davis	30-5
7	Purdue	24-4	Gene Keady	25-5
8	Temple	31-3	John Chaney	32-4
9	Alabama	26-4	Wimp Sanderson	28-5
10	Syracuse	26-6	Jim Boeheim	31-7
11	Illinois	23-7	Lou Henson	23-8
12	Pittsburgh	24-7	Paul Evans	25-8
13	Clemson	25-5	Cliff Ellis	25-6
14	Missouri	24-9	Norm Stewart	24-10
15	UCLA	24-6	Walt Hazzard	25-7
16	New Orleans	25-3	Benny Dees	26-4
17	Duke	22-8	Mike Krzyzewski	24-9
18	Notre Dame	22-7	Digger Phelps	24-8
19	TCU	23-6	Jim Killingsworth	24-7
20	Kansas	23-10	Larry Brown	25-11

NCAA Final Four (at the Superdome, New Orleans): **Semifinals**–Syracuse 77, Providence 63; Indiana 97, UNLV 93. **Championship**–Indiana 74, Syracuse 73.
NIT Championship (at Madison Square Garden): Southern Miss. 84, La Salle 80. No Top 20 teams played in NIT.

1986

		Before Tourns	Head Coach	Final Record
1	Duke	32-2	Mike Krzyzewski	37-3
2	Kansas	31-3	Larry Brown	35-4
3	Kentucky	29-3	Eddie Sutton	32-4
4	St. John's	30-4	Lou Carnesecca	31-5
5	Michigan	27-4	Bill Frieder	28-5
6	Georgia Tech	25-6	Bobby Cremins	27-7
7	**Louisville**	26-7	Denny Crum	32-7
8	North Carolina	26-5	Dean Smith	28-6
9	Syracuse	25-5	Jim Boeheim	26-6
10	Notre Dame	23-5	Digger Phelps	23-6
11	UNLV	31-4	Jerry Tarkanian	33-5
12	Memphis St.	27-5	Dana Kirk	28-6
13	Georgetown	23-7	John Thompson	24-8
14	Bradley	31-2	Dick Versace	32-3
15	Oklahoma	25-8	Billy Tubbs	26-9
16	Indiana	21-7	Bob Knight	21-8
17	Navy	27-4	Paul Evans	30-5
18	Michigan St.	21-7	Jud Heathcote	23-8
19	Illinois	21-9	Lou Henson	22-10
20	UTEP	27-5	Don Haskins	27-6

NCAA Final Four (at Reunion Arena, Dallas): **Semifinals**–Duke 71, Kansas 67; Louisville 88, LSU 77. **Championship**–Louisville 72, Duke 69.
NIT Championship (at Madison Square Garden): Ohio St. 73, Wyoming 63. No Top 20 teams played in NIT.

1988

		Before Tourns	Head Coach	Final Record
1	Temple	29-1	John Chaney	32-2
2	Arizona	31-2	Lute Olson	35-3
3	Purdue	27-3	Gene Keady	29-4
4	Oklahoma	30-3	Billy Tubbs	35-4
5	Duke	24-6	Mike Krzyzewski	28-7
6	Kentucky	25-5	Eddie Sutton	27-6
7	North Carolina	24-6	Dean Smith	27-7
8	Pittsburgh	23-6	Paul Evans	24-7
9	Syracuse	25-8	Jim Boeheim	26-9
10	Michigan	24-7	Bill Frieder	26-8
11	Bradley	26-4	Stan Albeck	26-5
12	UNLV	27-5	Jerry Tarkanian	28-6
13	Wyoming	26-5	Benny Dees	26-6
14	N.C. State	24-7	Jim Valvano	24-8
15	Loyola-CA	27-3	Paul Westhead	28-4
16	Illinois	22-9	Lou Henson	23-10
17	Iowa	22-9	Tom Davis	24-10
18	Xavier-OH	26-3	Pete Gillen	26-4
19	BYU	25-5	Ladell Andersen	26-6
20	Kansas St.	22-8	Lon Kruger	25-9

Note: Unranked **Kansas**, coached by Larry Brown, won the NCAAs. The Jayhawks entered the tourney at 21-11 and had a final record of 27-11.
NCAA Final Four (at Kemper Arena, Kansas City): **Semifinals**–Kansas 66, Duke 59; Oklahoma 86, Arizona 78. **Championship**–Kansas 83, Oklahoma 79.
NIT Championship (at Madison Square Garden): Connecticut 72, Ohio St. 67. No Top 20 teams played in NIT.

1989

		Before Tourns	Head Coach	Final Record
1	Arizona	27-3	Lute Olson	29-4
2	Georgetown	26-4	John Thompson	29-5
3	Illinois	27-4	Lou Henson	31-5
4	Oklahoma	28-5	Billy Tubbs	30-6
5	North Carolina	27-7	Dean Smith	29-8
6	Missouri	27-7	Norm Stewart & Rich Daly*	29-8
7	Syracuse	27-7	Jim Boeheim	30-8
8	Indiana	25-7	Bob Knight	27-8
9	Duke	24-7	Mike Krzyzewski	28-8
10	**Michigan**	24-7	Bill Frieder (24-7) & Steve Fisher (6-0)	30-7
11	Seton Hall	26-6	P.J. Carlesimo	31-7
12	Louisville	22-8	Denny Crum	24-9
13	Stanford	26-6	Mike Montgomery	26-7
14	Iowa	22-9	Tom Davis	23-10
15	UNLV	26-7	Jerry Tarkanian	29-8
16	Florida St.	22-7	Pat Kennedy	22-8
17	West Virginia	25-4	Gale Catlett	26-5
18	Ball State	28-2	Rick Majerus	29-3
19	N.C. State	20-8	Jim Valvano	22-9
20	Alabama	23-7	Wimp Sanderson	23-8

NCAA Final Four (at The Kingdome, Seattle): **Semifinals**—Seton Hall 95, Duke 78; Michigan 83, Illinois 81. **Championship**—Michigan 80, Seton Hall 79 (OT).
NIT Championship (at Madison Square Garden): St. John's 73, St. Louis 65. No Top 20 teams played in NIT.
*Norm Stewart's assistant Rich Daly personally took over for his ailing boss (Daly coached the final 14 games of the season) but returned to his role as an assistant when Stewart recovered before the start of the following season.

1990

		Before Tourns	Head Coach	Final Record
1	Oklahoma	26-4	Billy Tubbs	27-5
2	**UNLV**	29-5	Jerry Tarkanian	35-5
3	Connecticut	28-5	Jim Calhoun	31-6
4	Michigan St.	26-5	Jud Heathcote	28-6
5	Kansas	29-4	Roy Williams	30-5
6	Syracuse	24-6	Jim Boeheim	26-7
7	Arkansas	26-4	Nolan Richardson	30-5
8	Georgetown	23-6	John Thompson	24-7
9	Georgia Tech	24-6	Bobby Cremins	28-7
10	Purdue	21-7	Gene Keady	22-8
11	Missouri	26-5	Norm Stewart	26-6
12	La Salle	29-1	Speedy Morris	30-2
13	Michigan	22-7	Steve Fisher	23-8
14	Arizona	24-6	Lute Olson	25-7
15	Duke	24-8	Mike Krzyzewski	29-9
16	Louisville	26-7	Denny Crum	27-8
17	Clemson	24-8	Cliff Ellis	26-9
18	Illinois	21-7	Lou Henson	21-8
19	LSU	22-8	Dale Brown	23-9
20	Minnesota	20-8	Clem Haskins	23-9
21	Loyola-CA	23-5	Paul Westhead	26-6
22	Oregon St.	22-6	Jim Anderson	22-7
23	Alabama	24-8	Wimp Sanderson	26-9
24	New Mexico St.	26-4	Neil McCarthy	26-5
25	Xavier-OH	26-4	Pete Gillen	28-5

NCAA Final Four (at McNichols Sports Arena, Denver): **Semifinals**—Duke 97, Arkansas 83; UNLV 90, Georgia Tech 81. **Championship**—UNLV 103, Duke 73.
NIT Championship (at Madison Square Garden): Vanderbilt 74, St.Louis 72. No Top 25 teams played in NIT.

1991

		Before Tourns	Head Coach	Final Record
1	UNLV	30-0	Jerry Tarkanian	34-1
2	Arkansas	31-3	Nolan Richardson	34-4
3	Indiana	27-4	Bob Knight	29-5
4	North Carolina	25-5	Dean Smith	29-6
5	Ohio St.	25-3	Randy Ayers	27-4
6	**Duke**	26-7	Mike Krzyzewski	32-7
7	Syracuse	26-5	Jim Boeheim	26-6
8	Arizona	26-6	Lute Olson	28-7
9	Kentucky	22-6	Rick Pitino	same*
10	Utah	28-3	Rick Majerus	30-4
11	Nebraska	26-7	Danny Nee	26-8
12	Kansas	22-7	Roy Williams	27-8
13	Seton Hall	22-8	P.J. Carlesimo	25-9
14	Oklahoma St.	22-7	Eddie Sutton	24-8
15	New Mexico St.	23-5	Neil McCarthy	23-6
16	UCLA	25-3	Jim Harrick	23-9
17	E.Tennessee St.	28-4	Alan LaForce	28-5
18	Princeton	24-2	Pete Carril	24-3
19	Alabama	21-9	Wimp Sanderson	23-10
20	St. John's	20-8	Lou Carnesecca	23-9
21	Mississippi St.	20-8	Richard Williams	20-9
22	LSU	20-9	Dale Brown	20-10
23	Texas	22-8	Tom Penders	23-9
24	DePaul	20-8	Joey Meyer	20-9
25	Southern Miss.	21-7	M.K. Turk	21-8

*On probation

NCAA Final Four (at the Hoosier Dome, Indianapolis): **Semifinals**—Kansas 79, North Carolina 73; Duke 79, UNLV 77. **Championship**—Duke 72, Kansas 65.
NIT Championship (at Madison Square Garden): Stanford 78, Oklahoma 72. No Top 25 teams played in NIT.

1992

		Before Tourns	Head Coach	Final Record
1	**Duke**	28-2	Mike Krzyzewski	34-2
2	Kansas	26-4	Roy Williams	27-5
3	Ohio St.	23-5	Randy Ayers	26-6
4	UCLA	25-4	Jim Harrick	28-5
5	Indiana	23-6	Bob Knight	27-7
6	Kentucky	26-6	Rick Pitino	29-7
7	UNLV	26-2	Jerry Tarkanian	same*
8	USC	23-5	George Raveling	24-6
9	Arkansas	25-7	Nolan Richardson	26-8
10	Arizona	24-6	Lute Olson	24-7
11	Oklahoma St.	26-7	Eddie Sutton	28-8
12	Cincinnati	25-4	Bob Huggins	29-5
13	Alabama	25-8	Wimp Sanderson	26-9
14	Michigan St.	21-7	Jud Heathcote	22-8
15	Michigan	20-8	Steve Fisher	25-9
16	Missouri	20-8	Norm Stewart	21-9
17	Massachusetts	28-4	John Calipari	30-5
18	North Carolina	21-9	Dean Smith	23-10
19	Seton Hall	21-8	P.J. Carlesimo	23-9
20	Florida St.	20-9	Pat Kennedy	22-10
21	Syracuse	21-9	Jim Boeheim	22-10
22	Georgetown	21-9	John Thompson	22-10
23	Oklahoma	21-8	Billy Tubbs	21-9
24	DePaul	20-8	Joey Meyer	20-9
25	LSU	20-9	Dale Brown	21-10

*On probation

NCAA Final Four (at the Metrodome, Minneapolis): **Semifinals**—Michigan 76, Cincinnati 72; Duke 81, Indiana 78. **Championship**—Duke 71, Michigan 51.
NIT Championship (at Madison Square Garden): Virginia 81, Notre Dame 76 (OT). No Top 25 teams played in NIT.

Associated Press Final Polls (Cont.)

1993

		Before Tourns	Head Coach	Final Record
1	Indiana	28-3	Bob Knight	31-4
2	Kentucky	26-3	Rick Pitino	30-4
3	Michigan	26-4	Steve Fisher	31-5
4	**N. Carolina**	28-4	Dean Smith	34-4
5	Arizona	24-3	Lute Olson	24-4
6	Seton Hall	27-6	P.J. Carlesimo	28-7
7	Cincinnati	24-4	Bob Huggins	27-5
8	Vanderbilt	26-5	Eddie Fogler	28-6
9	Kansas	25-6	Roy Williams	29-7
10	Duke	23-7	Mike Krzyzewski	24-8
11	Florida St.	22-9	Pat Kennedy	25-10
12	Arkansas	20-8	Nolan Richardson	22-9
13	Iowa	22-8	Tom Davis	23-9
14	Massachusetts	23-6	John Calipari	24-7
15	Louisville	20-8	Denny Crum	22-9
16	Wake Forest	19-8	Dave Odom	21-9
17	New Orleans	26-3	Tim Floyd	26-4
18	Georgia Tech	19-10	Bobby Cremins	19-11
19	Utah	23-6	Rick Majerus	24-7
20	Western Ky.	24-5	Ralph Willard	26-6
21	New Mexico	24-6	Dave Bliss	24-7
22	Purdue	18-9	Gene Keady	18-10
23	Oklahoma St.	19-8	Eddie Sutton	20-9
24	New Mexico St.	25-7	Neil McCarthy	26-8
25	UNLV	21-7	Rollie Massimino	21-8

NCAA Final Four (at the Superdome, New Orleans): **Semifinals**–North Carolina 78, Kansas 68; Michigan 81, Kentucky 78 (OT). **Championship**–North Carolina 77, Michigan 71.

NIT Championship (at Madison Square Garden): Minnesota 62, Georgetown 61. No. 25 UNLV was the only Top 25 team that played in the NIT.

1995

		Before Tourns	Head Coach	Final Record
1	UCLA	25-2	Jim Harrick	31-2
2	Kentucky	25-4	Rick Pitino	28-5
3	Wake Forest	24-5	Dave Odom	26-6
4	North Carolina	24-5	Dean Smith	28-6
5	Kansas	23-5	Roy Williams	25-6
6	Arkansas	27-6	Nolan Richardson	32-7
7	Massachusetts	26-4	John Calipari	26-5
8	Connecticut	25-4	Jim Calhoun	28-5
9	Villanova	25-7	Steve Lappas	25-8
10	Maryland	24-7	Gary Williams	26-8
11	Michigan St.	22-5	Jud Heathcote	22-6
12	Purdue	24-6	Gene Keady	25-7
13	Virginia	22-8	Jeff Jones	25-9
14	Oklahoma St.	23-9	Eddie Sutton	27-10
15	Arizona	23-7	Lute Olson	23-8
16	Arizona St.	22-8	Bill Frieder	24-9
17	Oklahoma	23-8	Kelvin Sampson	23-9
18	Mississippi St.	20-7	Richard Williams	22-8
19	Utah	27-5	Rick Majerus	28-6
20	Alabama	22-9	David Hobbs	23-10
21	Western Ky.	26-3	Matt Kilcullen	27-4
22	Georgetown	19-9	John Thompson	21-10
23	Missouri	19-8	Norm Stewart	20-9
24	Iowa St.	22-10	Tim Floyd	23-11
25	Syracuse	19-9	Jim Boeheim	20-10

NCAA Final Four (at the Kingdome, Seattle): **Semifinals**– UCLA 74, Oklahoma St. 61; Arkansas 75, North Carolina 68. **Championship**– UCLA 89, Arkansas 78.

NIT Championship (at Madison Square Garden):Virginia Tech 65, Marquette 64 (OT). No top 25 teams played in NIT.

1994

		Before Tourns	Head Coach	Final Record
1	North Carolina	27-6	Dean Smith	28-7
2	**Arkansas**	25-3	Nolan Richardson	31-3
3	Purdue	26-4	Gene Keady	29-5
4	Connecticut	27-4	Jim Calhoun	29-5
5	Missouri	25-3	Norm Stewart	28-4
6	Duke	23-5	Mike Krzyzewski	28-6
7	Kentucky	26-6	Rick Pitino	27-7
8	Massachusetts	27-6	John Calipari	28-7
9	Arizona	25-5	Lute Olson	29-6
10	Louisville	26-5	Denny Crum	28-6
11	Michigan	21-7	Steve Fisher	24-8
12	Temple	22-7	John Chaney	23-8
13	Kansas	25-7	Roy Williams	27-8
14	Florida	25-7	Lon Kruger	29-8
15	Syracuse	21-6	Jim Boeheim	23-7
16	California	22-7	Todd Bozeman	22-8
17	UCLA	21-6	Jim Harrick	21-7
18	Indiana	19-8	Bob Knight	21-9
19	Oklahoma St.	23-9	Eddie Sutton	24-10
20	Texas	25-7	Tom Penders	26-8
21	Marquette	22-8	Kevin O'Neill	24-9
22	Nebraska	20-9	Danny Nee	20-10
23	Minnesota	20-11	Clem Haskins	21-12
24	Saint Louis	23-5	Charlie Spoonhour	23-6
25	Cincinnati	22-9	Bob Huggins	22-10

NCAA Final Four (at the Charlotte Coliseum): **Semifinals**– Arkansas 91, Arizona 82; Duke 70, Florida 65. **Championship**– Arkansas 76, Duke 72.

NIT Championship (at Madison Square Garden): Villanova 80, Vanderbilt 73. No top 25 teams played in NIT.

1996

		Before Tourns	Head Coach	Final Record
1	Massachusetts	31-1	John Calipari	35-2
2	**Kentucky**	28-2	Rick Pitino	34-2
3	Connecticut	30-2	Jim Calhoun	32-3
4	Georgetown	26-7	John Thompson	29-8
5	Kansas	26-4	Roy Williams	29-5
6	Purdue	25-5	Gene Keady	26-6
7	Cincinnati	25-4	Bob Huggins	28-5
8	Texas Tech	28-1	James Dickey	30-2
9	Wake Forest	23-5	Dave Odom	26-6
10	Villanova	25-6	Steve Lappas	26-7
11	Arizona	24-6	Lute Olson	26-7
12	Utah	25-6	Rick Majerus	27-7
13	Georgia Tech	22-11	Bobby Cremins	24-12
14	UCLA	23-7	Jim Harrick	23-8
15	Syracuse	24-8	Jim Boeheim	29-9
16	Memphis	22-7	Larry Finch	22-8
17	Iowa St.	23-8	Tim Floyd	24-9
18	Penn St.	21-6	Jerry Dunn	21-7
19	Mississippi St.	22-7	Richard Williams	26-8
20	Marquette	22-7	Mike Deane	23-8
21	Iowa	22-8	Tom Davis	23-9
22	Virginia Tech	22-5	Bill Foster	23-6
23	New Mexico	27-4	Dave Bliss	28-5
24	Louisville	20-11	Denny Crum	22-12
25	North Carolina	20-10	Dean Smith	21-11

NCAA Final Four (at the Meadowlands, E. Rutherford, N.J.): **Semifinals**– Kentucky 81, Massachusetts 74; Syracuse 77, Mississippi St. 69. **Championship**– Kentucky 76, Syracuse 67.

NIT Championship (at Madison Square Garden): Nebraska 60, St. Joseph's 56. No top 25 teams played in NIT.

1997

	Before Tourns	Head Coach	Final Record
1	Kansas 32-1	Roy Williams	34-2
2	Utah 26-3	Rick Majerus	29-4
3	Minnesota 27-3	Clem Haskins	31-4
4	North Carolina . .24-6	Dean Smith	28-7
5	Kentucky 30-4	Rick Pitino	35-5
6	South Carolina . .24-7	Eddie Fogler	24-8
7	UCLA 21-7	Steve Lavin	24-8
8	Duke 23-8	Mike Krzyzewski	24-9
9	Wake Forest 23-6	Dave Odom	24-7
10	Cincinnati 25-7	Bob Huggins	26-8
11	New Mexico 24-7	Dave Bliss	25-8
12	St. Joseph's 24-6	Phil Martelli	26-7
13	Xavier 22-5	Skip Prosser	23-6
14	Clemson 21-9	Rick Barnes	23-10
15	**Arizona** 19-9	Lute Olson	25-9
16	Charleston 28-2	John Kresse	29-3
17	Georgia 24-8	Tubby Smith	24-9
18	Iowa St. 20-8	Tim Floyd	22-9
19	Illinois 21-9	Lon Kruger	22-10
20	Villanova 23-9	Steve Lappas	24-10
21	Stanford 20-7	Mike Montgomery	22-8
22	Maryland 21-10	Gary Williams	21-11
23	Boston College . .21-8	Jim O'Brien	22-9
24	Colorado 21-9	Ricardo Patton	22-10
25	Louisville 23-8	Denny Crum	26-9

NCAA Final Four (at the RCA Dome, Indianapolis):
Semifinals– Kentucky 78, Minnesota 69; Arizona 66, North Carolina 58. **Championship**– Arizona 84, Kentucky 79 (OT).

NIT Championship (at Madison Square Garden): Michigan 82, Florida St. 72. No top 25 teams played in NIT.

1998

	Before Tourns	Head Coach	Final Record
1	North Carolina . .30-3	Bill Guthridge	34-4
2	Kansas 34-3	Roy Williams	35-4
3	Duke 29-3	Mike Krzyzewski	32-4
4	Arizona 27-4	Lute Olson	30-5
5	**Kentucky** 29-4	Tubby Smith	35-4
6	Connecticut 29-4	Jim Calhoun	32-5
7	Utah 25-3	Rick Majerus	30-4
8	Princeton 26-1	Bill Carmody	27-2
9	Cincinnati 26-5	Bob Huggins	27-6
10	Stanford 26-4	Mike Montgomery	30-5
11	Purdue 26-7	Gene Keady	28-8
12	Michigan 24-8	Brian Ellerbe	25-9
13	Mississippi 22-6	Rob Evans	22-7
14	South Carolina . .23-7	Eddie Fogler	23-8
15	TCU 27-5	Billy Tubbs	27-6
16	Michigan St. 20-7	Tom Izzo	22-8
17	Arkansas 23-8	Nolan Richardson	24-9
18	New Mexico 23-7	Dave Bliss	24-8
19	UCLA 22-8	Steve Lavin	24-9
20	Maryland 19-10	Gary Williams	21-11
21	Syracuse 24-8	Jim Boeheim	26-9
22	Illinois 22-9	Lon Kruger	23-10
23	Xavier 22-7	Skip Prosser	22-8
24	Temple 21-8	John Chaney	21-9
25	Murray St. 29-3	Mark Gottfried	24-6

NCAA Final Four (at the Alamodome, San Antonio):
Semifinals– Kentucky 86, Stanford 85 (OT); Utah 65, North Carolina 59. **Championship**– Kentucky 78, Utah 69.

NIT Championship (at Madison Square Garden): Minnesota 79, Penn St. 72. No top 25 teams played in NIT.

AP Post-Tournament Final Polls

The final AP Top 20 poll has been released after the NCAA tournament and NIT four times– in 1953 and '54 and again in 1974 and '75. Those four polls are listed below; teams that were not included in the last regular season polls are in *CAPITAL* italic letters.

1953

		Final Record
1	Indiana	23-3
2	Seton Hall	31-2
3	Kansas	19-6
4	Washington	30-3
5	LSU	24-3
6	La Salle	25-3
7	*ST. JOHN'S*	17-6
8	Okla. A&M	23-7
9	Duquesne	21-8
10	Notre Dame	19-5
11	Illinois	18-4
12	Kansas St.	17-4
13	Holy Cross	20-6
14	Seattle	29-4
15	*WAKE FOREST*	22-7
16	*SANTA CLARA*	20-7
17	Western Ky.	25-6
18	N.C. State	26-6
19	*DEPAUL*	19-9
20	*SW MISSOURI*	24-4

1954

		Final Record
1	Kentucky	25-0
2	La Salle	26-4
3	Holy Cross	26-2
4	Indiana	20-4
5	Duquesne	26-3
6	Notre Dame	22-3
7	*BRADLEY*	19-13
8	Western Ky.	29-3
9	*PENN ST.*	18-6
10	Okla. A&M	24-5
11	USC	19-14
12	*GEO. WASH.*	23-3
13	Iowa	17-5
14	LSU	21-5
15	Duke	22-6
16	*NIAGARA*	24-6
17	Seattle	26-2
18	Kansas	16-5
19	Illinois	17-5
20	*MARYLAND*	23-7

1974

		Final Record
1	N.C. State	30-1
2	UCLA	26-4
3	Marquette	26-5
4	Maryland	23-5
5	Notre Dame	26-3
6	Michigan	22-5
7	Kansas	23-7
8	Providence	28-4
9	Indiana	23-5
10	Long Beach St.	24-2
11	*PURDUE*	22-8
12	North Carolina	22-6
13	Vanderbilt	23-5
14	Alabama	22-4
15	*UTAH*	22-8
16	Pittsburgh	25-4
17	USC	24-5
18	*ORAL ROBERTS*	23-6
19	South Carolina	22-5
20	Dayton	20-9

1975

		Final Record
1	UCLA	28-3
2	Kentucky	26-5
3	Indiana	31-1
4	Louisville	28-3
5	Maryland	24-5
6	Syracuse	23-9
7	N.C. State	22-6
8	Arizona St.	25-4
9	North Carolina	23-8
10	Alabama	22-5
11	Marquette	23-4
12	*PRINCETON*	22-8
13	Cincinnati	23-6
14	Notre Dame	19-10
15	Kansas St.	20-9
16	Drake	19-10
17	UNLV	24-5
18	Oregon St.	19-12
19	*MICHIGAN*	19-8
20	Penn	23-5

Pre-Tournament Records

1953– St. John's (Al DeStefano, 14-5); Wake Forest (Murray Greason, 21-6); Santa Clara (Bob Feerick, 18-6); DePaul (Ray Meyer, 18-7); SW Missouri St. (Bob Vanatta, 19-4 before NAIA tourney). **1954**– Bradley (Forddy Anderson, 15-12); Penn St. (Elmer Gross, 14-5); George Washington (Bill Reinhart, 23-2); Niagara (Taps Gallagher, 22-5); Maryland (Bud Millikan, 23-7). **1974**– Purdue (Fred Schaus, 18-8); Utah (Bill Foster, 19-7); Oral Roberts (Ken Trickey, 21-5). **1975**– Princeton (Pete Carril, 18-8); Michigan (Johnny Orr, 19-7).

Associated Press Final Polls (Cont.)

1999

		Before Tourns	Head Coach	Final Record
1	Duke	32-1	Mike Krzyzewski	37-2
2	Michigan St.	29-4	Tom Izzo	33-5
3	**Connecticut**	28-2	Jim Calhoun	34-2
4	Auburn	27-3	Cliff Ellis	29-4
5	Maryland	26-5	Gary Williams	28-6
6	Utah	27-4	Rick Majerus	28-5
7	Stanford	25-6	Mike Montgomery	26-7
8	Kentucky	25-8	Tubby Smith	28-9
9	St. John's	25-8	Mike Jarvis	28-9
10	Miami-FL	22-6	Leonard Hamilton	23-7
11	Cincinnati	26-5	Bob Huggins	27-6
12	Arizona	22-6	Lute Olson	22-7
13	North Carolina	24-9	Bill Guthridge	24-10
14	Ohio St.	23-8	Jim O'Brien	27-9
15	UCLA	22-8	Steve Lavin	22-9
16	College of Charleston	28-2	John Kresse	28-3
17	Arkansas	22-10	Nolan Richardson	23-11
18	Wisconsin	22-9	Dick Bennett	22-10
19	Indiana	22-10	Bobby Knight	23-11
20	Tennessee	20-8	Jerry Green	21-9
21	Iowa	18-9	Tom Davis	20-10
22	Kansas	22-9	Roy Williams	23-10
23	Florida	20-8	Billy Donovan	22-9
24	NC-Charlotte	22-10	Bob Lutz	23-11
25	New Mexico	24-8	Dave Bliss	25-9

NCAA Final Four (at the Tropicana Field, St. Petersburg): **Semifinals**— Duke 68, Michigan St. 62; Connecticut 64, Ohio St. 58. **Championship**— Connecticut 77, Duke 74.
NIT Championship (at Madison Square Garden): California 61, Clemson 60. No top 25 teams played in NIT.

2000

		Before Tourns	Head Coach	Final Record
1	Duke	27-4	Mike Krzyzewski	29-5
2	**Michigan St.**	26-7	Tom Izzo	32-7
3	Stanford	26-3	Mike Montgomery	27-4
4	Arizona	26-6	Lute Olson	27-7
5	Temple	26-5	John Chaney	27-6
6	Iowa St.	29-4	Larry Eustachy	32-5
7	Cincinnati	28-3	Bob Huggins	29-4
8	Ohio St.	22-6	Jim O'Brien	23-7
9	St. John's	24-7	Mike Jarvis	25-8
10	LSU	26-5	John Brady	28-6
11	Tennessee	24-6	Jerry Green	26-7
12	Oklahoma	26-6	Kelvin Sampson	27-7
13	Florida	24-7	Billy Donovan	29-8
14	Oklahoma St.	24-6	Eddie Sutton	27-7
15	Texas	23-8	Rick Barnes	24-9
16	Syracuse	26-6	Jim Boeheim	26-6
17	Maryland	24-9	Gary Williams	25-10
18	Tulsa	29-4	Bill Self	32-5
19	Kentucky	22-9	Tubby Smith	23-10
20	Connecticut	24-9	Jim Calhoun	25-10
21	Illinois	21-9	Lon Kruger	22-10
22	Indiana	20-8	Bobby Knight	20-9
23	Miami-FL	21-10	Leonard Hamilton	23-11
24	Auburn	23-9	Cliff Ellis	24-10
25	Purdue	21-9	Gene Keady	24-10

NCAA Final Four (at the RCA Dome, Indianapolis): **Semifinals**— Michigan St. 53, Wisconsin 41; Florida 71, North Carolina 59. **Championship**— Michigan St. 89, Florida 76.
NIT Championship (at Madison Square Garden): Wake Forest 71, Notre Dame 61. No top 25 teams played in NIT.

2001

		Before Tourns	Head Coach	Final Record
1	**Duke**	29-4	Mike Krzyzewski	35-4
2	Stanford	28-2	Mike Montgomery	31-3
3	Michigan St.	24-4	Tom Izzo	28-5
4	Illinois	24-7	Bill Self	27-8
5	Arizona	23-7	Lute Olson	28-8
6	North Carolina	25-6	Matt Doherty	26-7
7	Boston College	26-4	Al Skinner	27-5
8	Florida	23-6	Billy Donovan	24-7
9	Kentucky	22-9	Tubby Smith	24-10
10	Iowa St.	25-5	Larry Eustachy	25-6
11	Maryland	21-10	Gary Williams	25-11
12	Kansas	24-6	Roy Williams	26-7
13	Oklahoma	26-6	Kelvin Sampson	26-7
14	Mississippi	25-7	Rod Barnes	27-8
15	UCLA	21-8	Steve Lavin	23-9
16	Virginia	20-8	Pete Gillen	20-9
17	Syracuse	24-8	Jim Boeheim	25-9
18	Texas	25-8	Rick Barnes	25-9
19	Notre Dame	19-9	Mike Brey	20-10
20	Indiana	21-12	Mike Davis	21-13
21	Georgetown	23-7	Craig Esherick	25-8
22	St. Joseph's	25-6	Phil Martelli	26-7
23	Wake Forest	19-10	Dave Odom	19-11
24	Iowa	22-11	Steve Alford	23-12
25	Wisconsin	18-10	Dick Bennett (2-1) & Brad Soderberg (16-10)	18-11

NCAA Final Four (at the HHH Metrodome, Minneapolis): **Semifinals**–Duke 95, Maryland 84; Arizona 80, Michigan St. 61. **Championship**–Duke 82, Arizona 72.
NIT Championship (at Madison Square Garden): Tulsa 79, Alabama 60. No top 25 teams played in NIT.

2002

		Before Tourns	Head Coach	Final Record
1	Duke	29-3	Mike Krzyzewski	32-4
2	Kansas	29-3	Roy Williams	33-4
3	Oklahoma	27-4	Kelvin Sampson	31-5
4	**Maryland**	26-4	Gary Williams	32-4
5	Cincinnati	30-3	Bob Huggins	31-4
6	Gonzaga	29-3	Mark Few	29-4
7	Arizona	22-9	Lute Olson	24-10
8	Alabama	26-7	Mark Gottfried	27-8
9	Pittsburgh	27-5	Ben Howland	29-6
10	Connecticut	24-6	Jim Calhoun	27-7
11	Oregon	23-8	Ernie Kent	26-9
12	Marquette	26-6	Tom Crean	26-7
13	Illinois	24-8	Bill Self	26-9
14	Ohio St.	23-7	Jim O'Brien	24-8
15	Florida	22-8	Billy Donovan	22-9
16	Kentucky	20-9	Tubby Smith	22-10
17	Mississippi St.	26-7	Rick Stansbury	27-8
18	USC	22-9	Henry Bibby	22-10
19	Western Ky.	28-3	Dennis Felton	28-4
20	Oklahoma St.	23-8	Eddie Sutton	23-9
21	Miami-FL	24-7	Perry Clark	24-8
22	Xavier	25-5	Thad Matta	26-6
23	Georgia	21-9	Jim Harrick	22-10
24	Stanford	19-9	Mike Montgomery	20-10
25	Hawaii	27-5	Riley Wallace	27-6

NCAA Final Four (at the Georgia Dome, Atlanta): **Semifinals**–Maryland 97, Kansas 88; Indiana 73, Oklahoma 64. **Championship**–Maryland 64, Indiana 52.
NIT Championship (at Madison Square Garden): Memphis 72, South Carolina 62. No top 25 teams played in NIT.

2003

		Before Tourns	Head Coach	Final Record
1	Kentucky	29-3	Tubby Smith	32-4
2	Arizona	25-3	Lute Olson	28-4
3	Oklahoma	24-6	Kelvin Sampson	27-7
4	Pittsburgh	26-4	Ben Howland	28-5
5	Texas	22-6	Rick Barnes	26-7
6	Kansas	25-7	Roy Williams	30-8
7	Duke	24-6	Mike Krzyzewski	26-7
8	Wake Forest	24-5	Skip Prosser	25-6
9	Marquette	23-5	Tom Crean	27-6
10	Florida	24-7	Billy Donovan	25-8
11	Illinois	24-6	Bill Self	25-7
12	Xavier	25-5	Thad Matta	26-6
13	**Syracuse**	24-5	Jim Boeheim	30-5
14	Louisville	24-6	Rick Pitino	25-7
15	Creighton	29-4	Dana Altman	29-5
16	Dayton	25-5	Oliver Purnell	25-6
17	Maryland	19-9	Gary Williams	21-10
18	Stanford	23-8	Mike Montgomery	23-9
19	Memphis	23-6	John Calipari	23-7
20	Mississippi St.	21-9	Rick Stansbury	21-10
21	Wisconsin	22-7	Bo Ryan	24-8
22	Notre Dame	22-9	Mike Brey	24-10
23	Connecticut	21-9	Jim Calhoun	23-10
24	Missouri	21-10	Quin Snyder	22-11
25	Georgia	19-8	Jim Harrick	same*

*Georgia chose not to participate in any postseason tournaments due to an investigation into academic fraud.
NCAA Final Four (at the Superdome, New Orleans):
Semifinals–Syracuse 95, Texas 84; Kansas 94, Marquette 61. **Championship**–Syracuse 81, Kansas 78.
NIT Championship (at Madison Square Garden): St. John's 70, Georgetown 67. No top 25 teams played in NIT.

2004

		Before Tourns	Head Coach	Final Record
1	Stanford	29-1	Mike Montgomery	30-2
2	Kentucky	26-4	Tubby Smith	27-5
3	Gonzaga	27-2	Mark Few	28-3
4	Oklahoma St.	27-3	Eddie Sutton	31-4
5	St. Joseph's	27-1	Phil Martelli	30-2
6	Duke	27-5	Mike Krzyzewski	31-6
7	Connecticut	27-6	Jim Calhoun	33-6
8	Mississippi St.	25-3	Rick Stansbury	26-4
9	Pittsburgh	29-4	Jamie Dixon	31-5
10	Wisconsin	24-6	Bo Ryan	25-7
11	Cincinnati	24-6	Bob Huggins	25-7
12	Texas	23-7	Rick Barnes	25-8
13	illinois	24-6	Bruce Weber	26-7
14	Georgia Tech	23-9	Paul Hewitt	28-10
15	N.C. State	20-9	Herb Sendek	21-10
16	Kansas	21-8	Bill Self	24-9
17	Wake Forest	19-9	Skip Prosser	21-10
18	North Carolina	18-10	Roy Williams	19-11
19	Maryland	19-11	Gary Williams	20-12
20	Syracuse	21-7	Jim Boeheim	23-8
21	Providence	20-8	Tim Welsh	20-9
22	Arizona	20-9	Lute Olson	20-10
23	So. Illinois	25-4	Matt Painter	25-5
24	Memphis	21-7	John Calipari	22-8
25	Boston College	23-9	Al Skinner	24-10
	Utah St.	25-3	Stew Morrill	25-4

NCAA Final Four (at the Alamodome, San Antonio):
Semifinals–Georgia Tech 67, Oklahoma St. 65; Connecticut 79, Duke 78. **Championship**–Connecticut 82, Georgia Tech 73.
NIT Championship (at Madison Square Garden): Michigan 62, Rutgers 55. No. 25 Utah St. was the only Top 25 team that played in the NIT.

2005

		Before Tourns	Head Coach	Final Record
1	Illinois	32-1	Bruce Weber	37-2
2	North Carolina	27-4	Roy Williams	33-4
3	Duke	25-5	Mike Krzyzewski	27-6
4	Louisville	29-4	Rick Pitino	33-5
5	Wake Forest	26-5	Skip Prosser	27-6
6	Oklahoma St.	24-6	Eddie Sutton	26-7
7	Kentucky	25-5	Tubby Smith	28-6
8	Washington	27-5	Lorenzo Romar	29-6
9	Arizona	27-6	Lute Olson	30-7
10	Gonzaga	25-4	Mark Few	26-5
11	Syracuse	27-6	Jim Boeheim	27-7
12	Kansas	23-6	Bill Self	23-7
13	Connecticut	22-7	Jim Calhoun	23-8
14	Boston College	24-4	Al Skinner	25-5
15	Michigan St.	22-6	Tom Izzo	26-7
16	Florida	23-7	Billy Donovan	24-8
17	Oklahoma	24-7	Kelvin Sampson	25-8
18	Utah	27-5	Ray Giacoletti	29-6
19	Villanova	22-7	Jay Wright	24-8
20	Wisconsin	22-8	Bo Ryan	25-9
21	Alabama	24-7	Mark Gottfried	24-8
22	Pacific	26-3	Bob Thomason	27-4
23	Cincinnati	24-7	Bob Huggins	25-8
24	Texas Tech	20-10	Bob Knight	22-11
25	Georgia Tech	19-11	Paul Hewitt	20-12

NCAA Final Four (at the Edward Jones Dome, St. Louis):
Semifinals–Illinois 72, Louisville 57; North Carolina 87, Michigan St. 71. **Championship**–North Carolina 75, Illinois 70.
NIT Championship (at Madison Square Garden): South Carolina 60, St. Joseph's 57. No top 25 teams played in NIT.

2006

		Before Tourns	Head Coach	Final Record
1	Duke	30-3	Mike Krzyzewski	32-4
2	Connecticut	27-3	Jim Calhoun	30-4
3	Villanova	25-4	Jay Wright	28-5
4	Memphis	30-3	John Calipari	33-4
5	Gonzaga	27-3	Mark Few	29-4
6	Ohio St.	25-5	Thad Matta	26-6
7	Boston College	26-7	Al Skinner	28-8
	UCLA	27-6	Ben Howland	32-7
9	Texas	27-6	Rick Barnes	30-7
10	North Carolina	27-4	Roy Williams	33-4
11	Florida	23-7	Billy Donovan	24-8
12	Kansas	25-7	Bill Self	25-8
13	Illinois	25-6	Bruce Weber	26-7
14	Geo. Washington	26-2	Karl Hobbs	27-3
15	Iowa	25-8	Steve Alford	25-9
16	Pittsburgh	24-7	Jamie Dixon	25-8
17	Washington	24-6	Lorenzo Romar	26-7
18	Tennessee	21-7	Bruce Pearl	22-8
19	LSU	23-8	John Brady	27-9
20	Nevada	27-5	Mark Fox	27-6
21	Syracuse	23-11	Jim Boeheim	23-12
22	West Virginia	20-10	John Beilein	22-11
23	Georgetown	21-9	John Thompson III	23-10
24	Oklahoma	20-8	Kelvin Sampson	20-9
25	UAB	24-6	Mike Anderson	24-7

NCAA Final Four (at the RCA Dome, Indianapolis):
Semifinals–Florida 73, George Mason 58; UCLA 59, LSU 45. **Championship**–Florida 73, UCLA 57.
NIT Championship (at Madison Square Garden): South Carolina 76, Michigan 64. No top 25 teams played in NIT

Annual NCAA Division I Leaders
Scoring

The NCAA did not begin keeping individual scoring records until the 1947-48 season. All averages include postseason games where applicable.

Multiple winners: Pete Maravich and Oscar Robertson (3); Keydren Clark, Darrell Floyd, Charles Jones, Harry Kelly, Frank Selvy and Freeman Williams (2).

Year		Gm	Pts	Avg	Year		Gm	Pts	Avg
1948	Murray Wier, Iowa	19	399	21.0	1978	Freeman Williams, Portland St.	27	969	35.9
1949	Tony Lavelli, Yale	30	671	22.4	1979	Lawrence Butler, Idaho St	27	812	30.1
1950	Paul Arizin, Villanova	29	735	25.3	1980	Tony Murphy, Southern-BR	29	932	32.1
1951	Bill Mlkvy, Temple	25	731	29.2	1981	Zam Fredrick, S. Carolina	27	781	28.9
1952	Clyde Lovellette, Kansas	28	795	28.4	1982	Harry Kelly, Texas Southern	29	862	29.7
1953	Frank Selvy, Furman	25	738	29.5	1983	Harry Kelly, Texas Southern	29	835	28.8
1954	Frank Selvy, Furman	29	1209	41.7	1984	Joe Jakubick, Akron	27	814	30.1
1955	Darrell Floyd, Furman	25	897	35.9	1985	Xavier McDaniel, Wichita St	31	844	27.2
1956	Darrell Floyd, Furman	28	946	33.8	1986	Terrance Bailey, Wagner	29	854	29.4
1957	Grady Wallace, S. Carolina	29	906	31.2	1987	Kevin Houston, Army	29	953	32.9
1958	Oscar Robertson, Cincinnati	28	984	35.1	1988	Hersey Hawkins, Bradley	31	1125	36.3
1959	Oscar Robertson, Cincinnati	30	978	32.6	1989	Hank Gathers, Loyola-CA	31	1015	32.7
1960	Oscar Robertson, Cincinnati	30	1011	33.7	1990	Bo Kimble, Loyola-CA	32	1131	35.3
1961	Frank Burgess, Gonzaga	26	842	32.4	1991	Kevin Bradshaw, US Int'l	28	1054	37.6
1962	Billy McGill, Utah	26	1009	38.8	1992	Brett Roberts, Morehead St	29	815	28.1
1963	Nick Werkman, Seton Hall	22	650	29.5	1993	Greg Guy, Texas-Pan Am	19	556	29.3
1964	Howie Komives, Bowling Green	23	844	36.7	1994	Glenn Robinson, Purdue	34	1030	30.3
1965	Rick Barry, Miami-FL	26	973	37.4	1995	Kurt Thomas, TCU	27	781	28.9
1966	Dave Schellhase, Purdue	24	781	32.5	1996	Kevin Granger, Texas Southern	24	648	27.0
1967	Jimmy Walker, Providence	28	851	30.4	1997	Charles Jones, LIU-Brooklyn	30	903	30.1
1968	Pete Maravich, LSU	26	1138	43.8	1998	Charles Jones, LIU-Brooklyn	30	869	29.0
1969	Pete Maravich, LSU	26	1148	44.2	1999	Alvin Young, Niagara	29	728	25.1
1970	Pete Maravich, LSU	31	1381	44.5	2000	Courtney Alexander, Fresno St.	27	669	24.8
1971	Johnny Neumann, Ole Miss	23	923	40.1	2001	Ronnie McCollum, Centenary	27	787	29.1
1972	Dwight Lamar, SW La	29	1054	36.3	2002	Jason Conley, VMI	28	820	29.3
1973	Bird Averitt, Pepperdine	25	848	33.9	2003	Ruben Douglas, New Mexico	28	783	28.0
1974	Larry Fogle, Canisius	25	835	33.4	2004	Keydren Clark, St. Peter's	29	775	26.7
1975	Bob McCurdy, Richmond	26	855	32.9	2005	Keydren Clark, St. Peter's	28	721	25.8
1976	Marshall Rodgers, Texas-Pan Am	25	919	36.8	2006	Adam Morrison, Gonzaga	33	926	28.1
1977	Freeman Williams, Portland St.	26	1010	38.8					

Rebounds

The NCAA did not begin keeping individual rebounding records until the 1950-51 season. From 1956-62, the championship was decided on highest percentage of recoveries out of all rebounds made by both teams in all games. All averages include postseason games where applicable.

Multiple winners: Paul Millsap (3); Artis Gilmore, Jerry Lucas, Xavier McDaniel, Kermit Washington and Leroy Wright (2).

Year		Gm	No	Avg	Year		Gm	No	Avg
1951	Ernie Beck, Penn	27	556	20.6	1979	Monti Davis, Tennessee St.	26	421	16.2
1952	Bill Hannon, Army	17	355	20.9	1980	Larry Smith, Alcorn State	26	392	15.1
1953	Ed Conlin, Fordham	26	612	23.5	1981	Darryl Watson, Miss. Valley St.	27	379	14.0
1954	Art Quimby, Connecticut	26	588	22.6	1982	LaSalle Thompson, Texas	27	365	13.5
1955	Charlie Slack, Marshall	21	538	25.6	1983	Xavier McDaniel, Wichita St.	28	403	14.4
1956	Joe Holup, G. Washington	26	604	25.6	1984	Akeem Olajuwon, Houston	37	500	13.5
1957	Elgin Baylor, Seattle	25	508	23.5	1985	Xavier McDaniel, Wichita St.	31	460	14.8
1958	Alex Ellis, Niagara	25	536	26.2	1986	David Robinson, Navy	35	455	13.0
1959	Leroy Wright, Pacific	26	652	23.8	1987	Jerome Lane, Pittsburgh	33	444	13.5
1960	Leroy Wright, Pacific	17	380	23.4	1988	Kenny Miller, Loyola-IL	29	395	13.6
1961	Jerry Lucas, Ohio St.	27	470	19.8	1989	Hank Gathers, Loyola-CA	31	426	13.7
1962	Jerry Lucas, Ohio St.	28	499	21.1	1990	Anthony Bonner, St. Louis	33	456	13.8
1963	Paul Silas, Creighton	27	557	20.6	1991	Shaquille O'Neal, LSU	28	411	14.7
1964	Bob Pelkington, Xavier-OH	26	567	21.8	1992	Popeye Jones, Murray St.	30	431	14.4
1965	Toby Kimball, Connecticut	23	483	21.0	1993	Warren Kidd, Mid. Tenn. St.	26	386	14.8
1966	Jim Ware, Oklahoma City	29	607	20.9	1994	Jerome Lambert, Baylor	24	355	14.8
1967	Dick Cunningham, Murray St.	22	479	21.8	1995	Kurt Thomas, TCU	27	393	14.6
1968	Neal Walk, Florida	25	494	19.8	1996	Marcus Mann, Miss. Valley St.	29	394	13.6
1969	Spencer Haywood, Detroit	22	472	21.5	1997	Tim Duncan, Wake Forest	31	457	14.7
1970	Artis Gilmore, Jacksonville	28	621	22.2	1998	Ryan Perryman, Dayton	33	412	12.5
1971	Artis Gilmore, Jacksonville	26	603	23.2	1999	Ian McGinnis, Dartmouth	26	317	12.2
1972	Kermit Washington, American	23	455	19.8	2000	Darren Phillip, Fairfield	29	405	14.0
1973	Kermit Washington, American	22	439	20.0	2001	Chris Marcus, Western Ky.	31	374	12.1
1974	Marvin Barnes, Providence	32	597	18.7	2002	Jeremy Bishop, Quinnipiac	29	347	12.0
1975	John Irving, Hofstra	21	323	15.4	2003	Brandon Hunter, Ohio	30	378	12.6
1976	Sam Pellom, Buffalo	26	420	16.2	2004	Paul Millsap, Louisiana Tech	30	374	12.5
1977	Glenn Mosley, Seton Hall	29	473	16.3	2005	Paul Millsap, Louisiana Tech	29	360	12.4
1978	Ken Williams, N. Texas	28	411	14.7	2006	Paul Millsap, Louisiana Tech	33	438	13.3

Assists

The NCAA did not begin keeping individual assist records until the 1983-84 season. All averages include postseason games where applicable.

Multiple winner: Avery Johnson (2).

Year		Gm	No	Avg
1984	Craig Lathen, IL-Chicago	29	274	9.45
1985	Rob Weingard, Hofstra	24	228	9.50
1986	Mark Jackson, St. John's	36	328	9.11
1987	Avery Johnson, Southern-BR	31	333	10.74
1988	Avery Johnson, Southern-BR	30	399	13.30
1989	Glenn Williams, Holy Cross	28	278	9.93
1990	Todd Lehmann, Drexel	28	260	9.29
1991	Chris Corchiani, N.C. State	31	299	9.65
1992	Van Usher, Tennessee Tech	29	254	8.76
1993	Sam Crawford, N. Mexico St.	34	310	9.12
1994	Jason Kidd, California	30	272	9.06
1995	Nelson Haggerty, Baylor	28	284	10.14
1996	Raimonds Miglinieks, UC-Irvine	27	230	8.52
1997	Kenny Mitchell, Dartmouth	26	203	7.81
1998	Ahlon Lewis, Arizona St.	32	294	9.19
1999	Doug Gottlieb, Oklahoma St.	34	299	8.79
2000	Mark Dickel, UNLV	31	280	9.03
2001	Markus Carr, CS-Northridge	32	286	8.94
2002	T.J. Ford, Texas	33	273	8.27
2003	Martell Bailey, Illinois-Chicago	30	244	8.13
2004	Greg Day, Troy St.	31	256	8.26
2005	Damitrius Coleman, Mercer	28	224	8.00
	& Will Funn, Portland St.	28	224	8.00
2006	Jared Jordan, Marist	29	247	8.52

Blocked Shots

The NCAA did not begin keeping individual blocked shots records until the 1985-86 season. All averages include postseason games where applicable.

Multiple winners: Keith Closs, David Robinson and Tarvis Williams (2).

Year		Gm	No	Avg
1986	David Robinson, Navy	35	207	5.91
1987	David Robinson, Navy	32	144	4.50
1988	Rodney Blake, St. Joe's-PA	29	116	4.00
1989	Alonzo Mourning, G'town	34	169	4.97
1990	Kenny Green, Rhode Island	26	124	4.77
1991	Shawn Bradley, BYU	34	177	5.21
1992	Shaquille O'Neal, LSU	30	157	5.23
1993	Theo Ratliff, Wyoming	28	124	4.43
1994	Grady Livingston, Howard	26	115	4.42
1995	Keith Closs, Cen. Conn. St.	26	139	5.35
1996	Keith Closs, Cen. Conn. St.	28	178	6.36
1997	Adonal Foyle, Colgate	28	180	6.43
1998	Jerome James, Florida A&M	27	125	4.63
1999	Tarvis Williams, Hampton	27	135	5.00
2000	Ken Johnson, Ohio St.	30	161	5.37
2001	Tarvis Williams, Hampton	32	147	4.59
2002	Wojciech Myrda, La-Monroe	32	172	5.38
2003	Emeka Okafor, Connecticut	33	156	4.73
2004	Anwar Ferguson, Houston	27	111	4.11
2005	Deng Gai, Fairfield	30	165	5.50
2006	Shawn James, Northeastern	30	196	6.53

All-Time NCAA Division I Individual Leaders

Through 2005-06; includes regular season and tournament games; **Last** column indicates final year played.

CAREER

Scoring

	Points	Yrs	Last	Gm	Pts
1	Pete Maravich, LSU	3	1970	83	3667
2	Freeman Williams, Port. St.	4	1978	106	3249
3	Lionel Simmons, La Salle	4	1990	131	3217
4	Alphonso Ford, Miss. Val. St.	4	1993	109	3165
5	Harry Kelly, Texas Southern	4	1983	110	3066
6	Hersey Hawkins, Bradley	4	1988	125	3008
7	Oscar Robertson, Cincinnati	3	1960	88	2973
8	Danny Manning, Kansas	4	1988	147	2951
9	Alfredrick Hughes, Loyola-IL	4	1985	120	2914
10	Elvin Hayes, Houston	3	1968	93	2884
11	Larry Bird, Indiana St.	3	1979	94	2850
12	Otis Birdsong, Houston	4	1977	116	2832
13	Kevin Bradshaw, Beth-Cook/US Int'l	4	1991	111	2804
14	Allan Houston, Tennessee	4	1993	128	2801
15	J.J. Redick, Duke	4	2006	139	2769
16	Hank Gathers, USC/Loyola-CA	4	1990	117	2723
17	Reggie Lewis, Northeastern	4	1987	122	2708
18	Daren Queenan, Lehigh	4	1988	118	2703
19	Byron Larkin, Xavier-OH	4	1988	121	2696
20	David Robinson, Navy	4	1987	127	2669

	Average	Yrs	Last	Pts	Avg
1	Pete Maravich, LSU	3	1970	3667	44.2
2	Austin Carr, Notre Dame	3	1971	2560	34.6
3	Oscar Robertson, Cinn	3	1960	2973	33.8
4	Calvin Murphy, Niagara	3	1970	2548	33.1
5	Dwight Lamar, SW La	2	1973	1862	32.7
6	Frank Selvy, Furman	3	1954	2538	32.5
7	Rick Mount, Purdue	3	1970	2323	32.3
8	Darrell Floyd, Furman	3	1956	2281	32.1
9	Nick Werkman, Seton Hall	3	1964	2273	32.0
10	Willie Humes, Idaho St.	2	1971	1510	31.5
11	William Averitt, Pepperdine	2	1973	1541	31.4
12	Elgin Baylor, Idaho/Seattle	3	1958	2500	31.3
13	Elvin Hayes, Houston	3	1968	2884	31.0
14	Freeman Williams, Port. St.	4	1978	3249	30.7
15	Larry Bird, Indiana St.	3	1979	2850	30.3
16	Bill Bradley, Princeton	3	1965	2503	30.2
17	Rich Fuqua, Oral Roberts	2	1973	1617	29.9
18	Wilt Chamberlain, Kansas	2	1958	1433	29.9
19	Rick Barry, Miami-FL	3	1965	2298	29.8
20	Doug Collins, Illinois St.	3	1973	2240	29.1

	Field Goal Pct.	Yrs	Last	FG	FGA	Pct
1	Steve Johnson, Ore. St.	4	1981	828	1222	.678
2	Michael Bradley, Kentucky/ Villanova	3	2001	441	651	.677
3	Murray Brown, Fla. St.	4	1980	566	847	.668
4	Lee Campbell, M.Tenn St./ SW Mo.St.	3	1990	411	618	.665
5	Warren Kidd, M.Tenn.St.	3	1993	496	747	.664
6	Todd MacCulloch, Wash.	4	1999	702	1058	.664
7	Joe Senser, West Chester	4	1979	476	719	.662
8	Kevin Magee, UC-Irvine	2	1982	552	841	.656
9	Orlando Phillips, Pepperdine	2	1983	404	618	.654
10	Bill Walton, UCLA	3	1974	747	1147	.651

Note: minimum 400 FGs made and an average of four per game.

	Free Throw Pct.	Yrs	Last	FT	FTA	Pct
1	Gary Buchanan, Villanova	4	2003	324	355	.913
2	J.J. Redick, Duke	4	2006	662	726	.912
3	Greg Starrick, Ky/So.Ill	4	1972	341	375	.909
4	Jack Moore, Nebraska	4	1982	446	495	.901
5	Steve Henson, Kansas St.	4	1990	361	401	.900
6	Steve Alford, Indiana	4	1987	535	596	.898
7	Bob Lloyd, Rutgers	3	1967	543	605	.898
8	Jim Barton, Dartmouth	4	1989	394	440	.895
9	Tommy Boyer, Arkansas	3	1963	315	353	.892
10	Kyle Korver, Creighton	4	2003	312	350	.891

Note: minimum 300 FTs made and an average of 2.5 per game.

All-Time NCAA Division I Individual Leaders (Cont.)
Rebounds

Total (before 1973)	Yrs	Last	Gm	No
1 Tom Gola, La Salle	4	1955	118	2201
2 Joe Holup, G. Washington	4	1956	104	2030
3 Charlie Slack, Marshall	4	1956	88	1916
4 Ed Conlin, Fordham	4	1955	102	1884
5 Dickie Hemric, Wake Forest	4	1955	104	1802
6 Paul Silas, Creighton	3	1964	81	1751
7 Art Quimby, Connecticut	4	1955	80	1716
8 Jerry Harper, Alabama	4	1956	93	1688
9 Jeff Cohen, Wm. & Mary	4	1961	103	1679
10 Steve Hamilton, Morehead St.	4	1958	102	1675

Total (since 1973)	Yrs	Last	Gm	No
1 Tim Duncan, Wake Forest	4	1997	128	1570
2 Derrick Coleman, Syracuse	4	1990	143	1537
3 Malik Rose, Drexel	4	1996	120	1514
4 Ralph Sampson, Virginia	4	1983	132	1511
5 Pete Padgett, Nevada-Reno	4	1976	104	1464
6 Lionel Simmons, La Salle	4	1990	131	1429
7 Anthony Bonner, St. Louis	4	1990	133	1424
8 Tyrone Hill, Xavier-OH	4	1990	126	1380
9 Popeye Jones, Murray St.	4	1992	123	1374
10 Michael Brooks, La Salle	4	1980	114	1372

Average (before 1973)	Yrs	Last	Gm	Avg
1 Artis Gilmore, Jacksonville	2	1971	1224	22.7
2 Charlie Slack, Marshall	4	1956	1916	21.8
3 Paul Silas, Creighton	3	1964	1751	21.6
4 Leroy Wright, Pacific	3	1960	1442	21.5
5 Art Quimby, Connecticut	4	1955	1716	21.5

Note: minimum 800 rebounds.

Average (since 1973)	Yrs	Last	Gm	Avg
1 Glenn Mosley, Seton Hall	4	1977	1263	15.2
2 Bill Campion, Manhattan	3	1975	1070	14.2
3 Pete Padgett, Nevada-Reno	4	1976	1464	14.1
4 Bob Warner, Maine	4	1976	1304	13.6
5 Shaquille O'Neal, LSU	3	1992	1217	13.5

Note: minimum 650 rebounds.

Assists

Total	Yrs	Last	Gm	No
1 Bobby Hurley, Duke	4	1993	140	1076
2 Chris Corchiani, N.C. State	4	1991	124	1038
3 Ed Cota, N. Carolina	4	2000	138	1030
4 Keith Jennings, E. Tenn. St.	4	1991	127	983
5 Steve Blake, Maryland	4	2003	138	972
6 Sherman Douglas, Syracuse	4	1989	138	960
7 Tony Miller, Marquette	4	1995	123	956
8 Aaron Miles, Kansas	4	2005	138	954
9 Greg Anthony, Portland/UNLV	4	1991	138	950
10 Doug Gottlieb, ND/Okla St.	4	2000	124	947

Average	Yrs	Last	No	Avg
1 Avery Johnson, Southern	2	1988	732	12.00
2 Sam Crawford, N. Mexico St.	2	1993	592	8.84
3 Mark Wade, Okla/UNLV	3	1987	693	8.77
4 Chris Corchiani, N.C. State	4	1991	1038	8.37
5 Taurence Chisholm, Delaware	4	1988	877	7.97
6 Van Usher, Tennessee Tech	3	1992	676	7.95
7 Anthony Manuel, Bradley	3	1989	855	7.92
8 Chico Fletcher, Ark. St.	4	2000	893	7.83
9 Gary Payton, Oregon St.	4	1990	938	7.82
10 Orlando Smart, San Francisco	4	1994	902	7.78

Note: minimum 550 assists.

Blocked Shots

Average	Yrs	Last	No	Avg
1 Keith Closs, Cen. Conn. St.	2	1996	317	5.87
2 Adonal Foyle, Colgate	3	1997	492	5.66
3 David Robinson, Navy	2	1987	351	5.24
4 Wojciech Mydra, LA-Monroe	4	2002	535	4.65
5 Shaquille O'Neal, LSU	3	1992	412	4.58

Note: minimum 225 blocked shots.

Steals

Average	Yrs	Last	No	Avg
1 Desmond Cambridge, Ala. A&M	3	2002	330	3.93
2 Mookie Blaylock, Oklahoma	2	1989	281	3.80
3 Ronn McMahon, Eastern Wash.	3	1990	225	3.52
4 Eric Murdock, Providence	4	1991	376	3.21
5 Van Usher, Tennessee Tech	3	1992	270	3.18

Note: minimum 225 steals.

3-PT Field Goals

3-Pt Field Goals Made	Yrs	Last	Gm	3FG
1 J.J. Redick, Duke	4	2006	139	457
2 Curtis Staples, Virginia	4	1998	122	413
3 Keith Veney, Lamar/Marshall	4	1997	111	409
4 Doug Day, Radford	4	1993	117	401
5 Michael Watson, Missouri-KC	4	2004	117	391

3-Pt Field Goals/Game	Yrs	Last	3FG	Avg
1 Timothy Pollard, Miss. Vall	2	1989	256	4.57
2 Sydney Grider, LA-Lafayette	2	1990	253	4.36
3 Brian Merriweather, TX-Pan Am	3	2001	332	3.95
4 Josh Heard, Tenn. Tech	2	2000	210	3.82
5 Kareem Townes, La Salle	3	1995	300	3.70

3-Pt Field Goal Pct.	Yrs	Last	3FG	Att	Pct
1 Tony Bennett, Wisc-GB	4	1992	290	584	.497
2 David Olson, Eastern Ill.	4	1992	262	562	.466
3 Ross Land, N. Arizona	4	2000	308	664	.464
4 Dan Dickau, Washington/ Gonzaga	4	2002	215	465	.462
5 Sean Jackson, Ohio/ Princeton	4	1992	243	528	.460

Note: minimum 200 3FGs made and an average of two per game.

SINGLE SEASON
Scoring

Points	Year	Gm	Pts
1 Pete Maravich, LSU	1970	31	1381
2 Elvin Hayes, Houston	1968	33	1214
3 Frank Selvy, Furman	1954	29	1209
4 Pete Maravich, LSU	1969	26	1148
5 Pete Maravich, LSU	1968	26	1138
6 Bo Kimble, Loyola-CA	1990	32	1131
7 Hersey Hawkins, Bradley	1988	31	1125
8 Austin Carr, Notre Dame	1970	29	1106
9 Austin Carr, Notre Dame	1971	29	1101
10 Otis Birdsong, Houston	1977	36	1090

Average	Year	Gm	Pts	Avg
1 Pete Maravich, LSU	1970	31	1381	44.5
2 Pete Maravich, LSU	1969	26	1148	44.2
3 Pete Maravich, LSU	1968	26	1138	43.8
4 Frank Selvy, Furman	1954	29	1209	41.7
5 Johnny Neumann, Ole Miss	1971	23	923	40.1
6 Freeman Williams, Port. St.	1977	26	1010	38.8
7 Billy McGill, Utah	1962	26	1009	38.8
8 Calvin Murphy, Niagara	1968	24	916	38.2
9 Austin Carr, Notre Dame	1970	29	1106	38.1
10 Austin Carr, Notre Dame	1971	29	1101	38.0

Field Goal Pct.

		Year	FG	FGA	Pct
1	Steve Johnson, Oregon St.	1981	235	315	.746
2	Dwayne Davis, Florida	1989	179	248	.722
3	Keith Walker, Utica	1985	154	216	.713
4	Steve Johnson, Oregon St.	1980	211	297	.710
5	Adam Mark, Belmont	2002	150	212	.708

Free Throw Pct.

		Year	FT	FTA	Pct
1	Blake Ahearn, SW Mo. St.	2004	117	120	.975
2	Craig Collins, Penn St.	1985	94	98	.959
3	J.J. Redick, Duke	2004	143	150	.953
4	Rod Foster, UCLA	1982	95	100	.950
5	Clay McKnight, Pacific	2000	74	78	.949

3-Pt Field Goal Pct.

		Year	3FG	Att	Pct
1	Glenn Tropf, Holy Cross	1988	52	82	.634
2	Sean Wightman, W. Mich.	1992	48	76	.632
3	Keith Jennings, E. Tenn. St.	1991	84	142	.592
4	Dave Calloway, Monmouth	1989	48	82	.585
5	Steve Kerr, Arizona	1988	114	199	.573

Assists

	Average	Year	Gm	No	Avg
1	Avery Johnson, Southern-BR	1988	30	399	13.3
2	Anthony Manuel, Bradley	1988	31	373	12.0
3	Avery Johnson, Southern-BR	1987	31	333	10.7
4	Mark Wade, UNLV	1987	38	406	10.7
5	Nelson Haggerty, Baylor	1995	28	284	10.1
6	Glenn Williams, Holy Cross	1989	28	278	9.9
7	Chris Corchiani, N.C. State	1991	31	299	9.7
8	Tony Fairley, Charleston-So.	1987	28	270	9.6
9	Tyrone Bogues, Wake Forest	1987	29	276	9.5
10	Ron Weingard, Hofstra	1985	24	228	9.5

Rebounds

	Average (before 1973)	Year	Gm	No	Avg
1	Charlie Slack, Marshall	1955	21	538	25.6
2	Leroy Wright, Pacific	1959	26	652	25.1
3	Art Quimby, Connecticut	1955	25	611	24.4
4	Charlie Slack, Marshall	1956	22	520	23.6
5	Ed Conlin, Fordham	1953	26	612	23.5

	Average (since 1973)	Year	Gm	No	Avg
1	Kermit Washington, American	1973	25	511	20.4
2	Marvin Barnes, Providence	1973	30	571	19.0
3	Marvin Barnes, Providence	1974	32	597	18.7
4	Pete Padgett, Nevada	1973	26	462	17.8
5	Jim Bradley, Northern Ill	1973	24	426	17.8

Blocked Shots

	Average	Year	Gm	No	Avg
1	Shawn James, Northeastern	2006	30	196	6.53
2	Adonal Foyle, Colgate	1997	28	180	6.42
3	Keith Closs, Cen. Conn. St.	1996	28	178	6.36
4	David Robinson, Navy	1986	35	207	5.91
5	Deng Gai, Fairfield	2005	30	165	5.50
6	Shawn James, Northeastern	2005	25	136	5.44

Steals

	Average	Year	Gm	No	Avg
1	Desmond Cambridge, Ala. A&M	2002	29	160	5.52
2	Darron Brittman, Chicago St.	1986	28	139	4.96
3	Aldwin Ware, Florida A&M	1988	29	142	4.90
4	John Linehan, Providence	2002	31	139	4.48
5	Ronn McMahon, East Wash	1990	29	130	4.48

SINGLE GAME

Scoring

	Points vs Div. I Team	Year	Pts
1	Kevin Bradshaw, US Int'l vs Loyola-CA	1991	72
2	Pete Maravich, LSU vs Alabama	1970	69
3	Calvin Murphy, Niagara vs Syracuse	1969	68
4	Jay Handlan, Wash. & Lee vs Furman	1951	66
	Pete Maravich, LSU vs Tulane	1969	66
	Anthony Roberts, Oral Rbts vs N.C. A&T	1977	66
7	Anthony Roberts, Oral Rbts vs Ore	1977	65
	Scott Haffner, Evansville vs Dayton	1989	65
9	Pete Maravich, LSU vs Kentucky	1970	64
10	Johnny Neumann, Ole Miss vs LSU	1971	63
	Hersey Hawkins, Bradley vs Detroit	1988	63

	Points vs Non-Div. I Team	Year	Pts
1	Frank Selvy, Furman vs Newberry	1954	100
2	Paul Arizin, Villanova vs Phi. NAMC	1949	85
3	Freeman Williams, Port. St. vs Rocky Mt	1978	81
4	Bill Mlkvy, Temple vs Wilkes	1951	73
5	Freeman Williams, Port. St. vs So. Ore	1977	71
6	Darrell Floyd, Furman vs Morehead St.	1955	67

Note: Bevo Francis of Division II Rio Grande (Ohio) scored an overall collegiate record 113 points against Hillsdale in 1954. He also scored 84 against Alliance and 82 against Bluffton that same season.

3-Pt Field Goals

		Year	No
1	Keith Veney, Marshall vs Morehead St.	1996	15
2	Dave Jamerson, Ohio U. vs Charleston	1989	14
	Askia Jones, Kansas St. vs Fresno St.	1994	14
	Ronald Blackshear, Marshall vs. Akron	2002	14
5	Gary Bossert, Niagara vs Siena	1987	12
	Darrin Fitzgerald, Butler vs Detroit	1987	12
	Al Dillard, Arkansas vs Delaware St.	1993	12
	Mitch Taylor, South-BR vs La. Christian	1995	12
	David McMahan, Winthrop vs C. Carolina	1996	12
	Clarence Gilbert, Missouri vs Colorado	2002	12
	Terrence Woods, Fla. A&M vs Coppin St.	2003	12

Assists

		Year	No
1	Tony Fairley, Baptist vs Armstrong St.	1987	22
	Avery Johnson, Southern-BR vs TX-South	1988	22
	Sherman Douglas, Syracuse vs Providence	1989	22
4	Mark Wade, UNLV vs Navy	1986	21
	Kelvin Scarborough, N. Mexico vs Hawaii	1987	21
	Anthony Manuel, Bradley vs UC-Irvine	1987	21
	Avery Johnson, Southern-BR vs Ala. St.	1988	21

Rebounds

	Total (before 1973)	Year	No
1	Bill Chambers, Wm. & Mary vs Virginia	1953	51
2	Charlie Slack, Marshall vs M. Harvey	1954	43
3	Tom Heinsohn, Holy Cross vs BC	1955	42
4	Art Quimby, UConn vs BU	1955	40
5	Three players tied with 39 each.		

	Total (since 1973)	Year	No
1	Larry Abney, Fresno St. vs SMU	2000	35
2	David Vaughn, Oral Roberts vs Brandeis	1973	34
3	Robert Parish, Centenary vs So. Miss	1973	33
4	Durand Macklin, LSU vs Tulane	1976	32
	Jervaughn Scales, South-BR vs Grambling	1994	32

Blocked Shots

		Year	No
1	David Robinson, Navy vs NC-Wilmington	1986	14
	Shawn Bradley, BYU vs Eastern Ky	1990	14
	Roy Rogers, Alabama vs Georgia	1996	14
	Loren Woods, Arizona vs Oregon	2000	14
5	Seven players tied with 13 each.		

Steals

		Year	No
1	Mookie Blaylock, Oklahoma vs Centenary	1987	13
	Mookie Blaylock, Oklahoma vs Loyola-CA	1988	13
3	Kenny Robertson, Cleve. St. vs Wagner	1988	12
	Terry Evans, Oklahoma vs Florida A&M	1993	12
	Richard Duncan, Mid. Tenn St. vs E. Ky.	1999	12
	Greedy Daniels, TCU vs Ark-Pine Bluff	2001	12
	Jehiel Lewis, Navy vs Bucknell	2002	12

Players of the Year and Top Draft Picks

Consensus College Players of the Year and first overall selections in NBA draft since the abolition of the NBA's territorial draft in 1966. Top draft picks who became Rookie of the Year are in **bold** type; (*) indicates top draft pick chosen as junior, (**) indicates top draft pick chosen as sophomore, (†) indicates top draft pick chosen as a high school senior. Only five players have been the unanimous college player of the year, the first overall pick in the NBA draft and then the NBA Rookie of the year.

Year	Player of the Year	Top Draft Pick
1966	Cazzie Russell, Mich.	Cazzie Russell, NY
1967	Lew Alcindor, UCLA	Jimmy Walker, Det.
1968	Elvin Hayes, Houston	Elvin Hayes, SD
1969	Lew Alcindor, UCLA	**Lew Alcindor**, Mil.
1970	Pete Maravich, LSU	Bob Lanier, Det.
1971	Sidney Wicks, UCLA	Austin Carr, Cle.
1972	Bill Walton, UCLA	LaRue Martin, Por.
1973	Bill Walton, UCLA	Doug Collins, Phi.
1974	Bill Walton, UCLA	Bill Walton, Por.
1975	David Thompson, N.C. St.	David Thompson, Atl.
1976	Scott May, Indiana	John Lucas, Hou.
1977	Marques Johnson, UCLA	Kent Benson, Ind.
1978	Butch Lee, Marquette	
	& Phil Ford, N. Caro.	Mychal Thompson, Por.
1979	Larry Bird, Indiana St.	Magic Johnson, LAL**
1980	Mark Aguirre, DePaul	Joe Barry Carroll, G. St.
1981	Ralph Sampson, Va.	
	& Danny Ainge, BYU	Mark Aguirre, Dal.
1982	Ralph Sampson, Va.	James Worthy, LAL*
1983	Ralph Sampson, Va.	**Ralph Sampson**, Hou.
1984	Michael Jordan, N. Caro.	Akeem Olajuwon, Hou.
1985	Patrick Ewing, Georgetown	
	& Chris Mullin, St. John's	**Patrick Ewing**, NY
1986	Walter Berry, St. John's	Brad Daugherty, Cle.
1987	David Robinson, Navy	**David Robinson**, SA
1988	Hersey Hawkins, Bradley	
	& Danny Manning, Kan.	Danny Manning, LAC

Year	Player of the Year	Top Draft Pick
1989	Sean Elliott, Arizona	
	& Danny Ferry, Duke	Pervis Ellison, Sac.
1990	Lionel Simmons, La Salle	**Derrick Coleman**, NJ
1991	Larry Johnson, UNLV	
	& Shaquille O'Neal, LSU	**Larry Johnson**, Cha.
1992	Christian Laettner, Duke	**Shaquille O'Neal**, Orl.*
1993	Calbert Cheaney, Ind.	**Chris Webber**, Orl.**
1994	Glenn Robinson, Purdue	Glenn Robinson, Mil.*
1995	Ed O'Bannon, UCLA	
	& Joe Smith, Maryland	Joe Smith, G. St.**
1996	Marcus Camby, UMass	**Allen Iverson**, Phi.**
1997	Tim Duncan, Wake Forest	**Tim Duncan**, SA
1998	Antawn Jamison, N. Caro.	M. Olowokandi, LAC
1999	Elton Brand, Duke	**Elton Brand**, Chi.**
2000	Kenyon Martin, Cincinnati	Kenyon Martin, NJ
2001	Shane Battier, Duke	
	& Jason Williams, Duke	Kwame Brown, Wash.†
2002	Jason Williams, Duke	
	& Drew Gooden, Kansas	Yao Ming, Hou.
2003	T.J. Ford, Texas	
	& David West, Xavier	**LeBron James**, Cle.†
2004	Jameer Nelson, St. Joseph's	
	& Emeka Okafor, UConn	Dwight Howard, Orl.†
2005	Andrew Bogut, Utah	Andrew Bogut, Mil.**
2006	J.J. Redick, Duke	
	& Adam Morrison, Gonz.	Andrea Bargnani, Tor.

Annual Awards

UPI picked the first national Division I Player of the Year in 1955. Since then, the U.S. Basketball Writers Assn. (1959), the Associated Press Player of the Year (1961), the Atlanta Tip-Off Club (1969), the National Assn. of Basketball Coaches (1975), and the LA Athletic Club's John Wooden Award (1977) have joined in. UPI discontinued its award in 1997. Since 1977, the first year all the following awards were given out, the same player has won all of them in the same season 14 times: Marques Johnson in 1977, Larry Bird in 1979, Ralph Sampson in both 1982 and '83, Michael Jordan in 1984, David Robinson in 1987, Lionel Simmons in 1990, Calbert Cheaney in 1993, Glenn Robinson in 1994, Tim Duncan in 1997, Antawn Jamison in 1998, Elton Brand in 1999, Kenyon Martin in 2000 and Andrew Bogut in 2005.

Wooden Award

Voted on by a panel of coaches, sportswriters and broadcasters and first presented in 1977 by the Los Angeles Athletic Club in the name of former Purdue All-American and UCLA coach John Wooden. Unlike the other five player of the year awards, candidates for the Wooden must have a minimum grade point average of 2.00 (out of 4.00).

Multiple winners: Ralph Sampson (2).

Year		Year		Year	
1977	Marques Johnson, UCLA	1987	David Robinson, Navy	1997	Tim Duncan, Wake Forest
1978	Phil Ford, North Carolina	1988	Danny Manning, Kansas	1998	Antawn Jamison, N. Carolina
1979	Larry Bird, Indiana St.	1989	Sean Elliott, Arizona	1999	Elton Brand, Duke
1980	Darrell Griffith, Louisville	1990	Lionel Simmons, La Salle	2000	Kenyon Martin, Cincinnati
1981	Danny Ainge, BYU	1991	Larry Johnson, UNLV	2001	Shane Battier, Duke
1982	Ralph Sampson, Virginia	1992	Christian Laettner, Duke	2002	Jason Williams, Duke
1983	Ralph Sampson, Virginia	1993	Calbert Cheaney, Indiana	2003	T.J. Ford, Texas
1984	Michael Jordan, N. Carolina	1994	Glenn Robinson, Purdue	2004	Jameer Nelson, St. Joseph's
1985	Chris Mullin, St. John's	1995	Ed O'Bannon, UCLA	2005	Andrew Bogut, Utah
1986	Walter Berry St. John's	1996	Marcus Camby, UMass	2006	J.J. Redick, Duke

United Press International

Voted on by a panel of UPI college basketball writers and first presented in 1955.
Multiple winners: Oscar Robertson, Ralph Sampson and Bill Walton (3); Lew Alcindor and Jerry Lucas (2).

Year		Year		Year	
1955	Tom Gola, La Salle	1963	Art Heyman, Duke	1971	Austin Carr, Notre Dame
1956	Bill Russell, San Francisco	1964	Gary Bradds, Ohio St.	1972	Bill Walton, UCLA
1957	Chet Forte, Columbia	1965	Bill Bradley, Princeton	1973	Bill Walton, UCLA
1958	Oscar Robertson, Cincinnati	1966	Cazzie Russell, Michigan	1974	Bill Walton, UCLA
1959	Oscar Robertson, Cincinnati	1967	Lew Alcindor, UCLA	1975	David Thompson, N.C. State
1960	Oscar Robertson, Cincinnati	1968	Elvin Hayes, Houston	1976	Scott May, Indiana
1961	Jerry Lucas, Ohio St.	1969	Lew Alcindor, UCLA	1977	Marques Johnson, UCLA
1962	Jerry Lucas, Ohio St.	1970	Pete Maravich, LSU	1978	Butch Lee, Marquette

Year		Year		Year	
1979	Larry Bird, Indiana St.	1986	Walter Berry, St. John's	1993	Calbert Cheaney, Indiana
1980	Mark Aguirre, DePaul	1987	David Robinson, Navy	1994	Glenn Robinson, Purdue
1981	Ralph Sampson, Virginia	1988	Hersey Hawkins, Bradley	1995	Joe Smith, Maryland
1982	Ralph Sampson, Virginia	1989	Danny Ferry, Duke	1996	Ray Allen, UConn
1983	Ralph Sampson, Virginia	1990	Lionel Simmons, La Salle	1997	award discontinued
1984	Michael Jordan, N. Carolina	1991	Shaquille O'Neal, LSU		
1985	Chris Mullin, St. John's	1992	Jim Jackson, Ohio St.		

U.S. Basketball Writers Association

Voted on by the USBWA and first presented in 1959.

Multiple winners: Ralph Sampson and Bill Walton (3); Lew Alcindor, Jerry Lucas and Oscar Robertson (2).

Year		Year		Year	
1959	Oscar Robertson, Cincinnati	1976	Adrian Dantley, Notre Dame	1993	Calbert Cheaney, Indiana
1960	Oscar Robertson, Cincinnati	1977	Marques Johnson, UCLA	1994	Glenn Robinson, Purdue
1961	Jerry Lucas, Ohio St.	1978	Phil Ford, North Carolina	1995	Ed O'Bannon, UCLA
1962	Jerry Lucas, Ohio St.	1979	Larry Bird, Indiana St.	1996	Marcus Camby, UMass
1963	Art Heyman, Duke	1980	Mark Aguirre, DePaul	1997	Tim Duncan, Wake Forest
1964	Walt Hazzard, UCLA	1981	Ralph Sampson, Virginia	1998	Antawn Jamison, N. Carolina
1965	Bill Bradley, Princeton	1982	Ralph Sampson, Virginia	1999	Elton Brand, Duke
1966	Cazzie Russell, Michigan	1983	Ralph Sampson, Virginia	2000	Kenyon Martin, Cincinnati
1967	Lew Alcindor, UCLA	1984	Michael Jordan, N. Carolina	2001	Shane Battier, Duke
1968	Elvin Hayes, Houston	1985	Chris Mullin, St. John's	2002	Jason Williams, Duke
1969	Lew Alcindor, UCLA	1986	Walter Berry, St. John's	2003	David West, Xavier
1970	Pete Maravich, LSU	1987	David Robinson, Navy	2004	Jameer Nelson, St. Joseph's
1971	Sidney Wicks, UCLA	1988	Hersey Hawkins, Bradley	2005	Andrew Bogut, Utah
1972	Bill Walton, UCLA	1989	Danny Ferry, Duke	2006	Adam Morrison, Gonzaga
1973	Bill Walton, UCLA	1990	Lionel Simmons, La Salle		& J.J. Redick, Duke
1974	Bill Walton, UCLA	1991	Larry Johnson, UNLV		
1975	David Thompson, N.C. State	1992	Christian Laettner, Duke		

Associated Press Player of the Year

Voted on by AP sportswriters and broadcasters.

Multiple winners: Ralph Sampson (3); Lew Alcindor, Jerry Lucas, David Thompson and Bill Walton (2).

Year		Year		Year	
1961	Jerry Lucas, Ohio St.	1977	Marques Johnson, UCLA	1993	Calbert Cheaney, Indiana
1962	Jerry Lucas, Ohio St.	1978	Butch Lee, Marquette	1994	Glenn Robinson, Purdue
1963	Art Heyman, Duke	1979	Larry Bird, Indiana St.	1995	Joe Smith, Maryland
1964	Gary Bradds, Ohio St.	1980	Mark Aguirre, DePaul	1996	Marcus Camby, UMass
1965	Bill Bradley, Princeton	1981	Ralph Sampson, Virginia	1997	Tim Duncan, Wake Forest
1966	Cazzie Russell, Michigan	1982	Ralph Sampson, Virginia	1998	Antawn Jamison, N. Carolina
1967	Lew Alcindor, UCLA	1983	Ralph Sampson, Virginia	1999	Elton Brand, Duke
1968	Elvin Hayes, Houston	1984	Michael Jordan, N. Carolina	2000	Kenyon Martin, Cincinnati
1969	Lew Alcindor, UCLA	1985	Patrick Ewing, Georgetown	2001	Shane Battier, Duke
1970	Pete Maravich, LSU	1986	Walter Berry, St. John's	2002	Jason Williams, Duke
1971	Austin Carr, Notre Dame	1987	David Robinson, Navy	2003	David West, Xavier
1972	Bill Walton, UCLA	1988	Hersey Hawkins, Bradley	2004	Jameer Nelson, St. Joseph's
1973	Bill Walton, UCLA	1989	Sean Elliott, Arizona	2005	Andrew Bogut, Utah
1974	David Thompson, N.C. State	1990	Lionel Simmons, La Salle	2006	J.J. Redick, Duke
1975	David Thompson, N.C. State	1991	Shaquille O'Neal, LSU		
1976	Scott May, Indiana	1992	Christian Laettner, Duke		

Naismith Award

Voted on by a panel of coaches, sportswriters and broadcasters and first presented in 1969 by the Atlanta Tip-Off Club in 1969 in the name of the inventor of basketball, Dr. James Naismith.

Multiple winners: Ralph Sampson and Bill Walton (3).

Year		Year		Year	
1969	Lew Alcindor, UCLA	1982	Ralph Sampson, Virginia	1995	Joe Smith, Maryland
1970	Pete Maravich, LSU	1983	Ralph Sampson, Virginia	1996	Marcus Camby, UMass
1971	Austin Carr, Notre Dame	1984	Michael Jordan, N. Carolina	1997	Tim Duncan, Wake Forest
1972	Bill Walton, UCLA	1985	Patrick Ewing, Georgetown	1998	Antawn Jamison, N. Carolina
1973	Bill Walton, UCLA	1986	Johnny Dawkins, Duke	1999	Elton Brand, Duke
1974	Bill Walton, UCLA	1987	David Robinson, Navy	2000	Kenyon Martin, Cincinnati
1975	David Thompson, N.C. State	1988	Danny Manning, Kansas	2001	Shane Battier, Duke
1976	Scott May, Indiana	1989	Danny Ferry, Duke	2002	Jason Williams, Duke
1977	Marques Johnson, UCLA	1990	Lionel Simmons, La Salle	2003	T.J. Ford, Texas
1978	Butch Lee, Marquette	1991	Larry Johnson, UNLV	2004	Jameer Nelson, St. Joseph's
1979	Larry Bird, Indiana St.	1992	Christian Laettner, Duke	2005	Andrew Bogut, Utah
1980	Mark Aguirre, DePaul	1993	Calbert Cheaney, Indiana	2006	J.J. Redick, Duke
1981	Ralph Sampson, Virginia	1994	Glenn Robinson, Purdue		

National Association of Basketball Coaches

Voted on by the National Assn. of Basketball Coaches and presented by the Eastman Kodak Co. from 1975-94.
Multiple winners: Ralph Sampson and Jason Williams (2).

Year		Year		Year	
1975	David Thompson, N.C. State	1987	David Robinson, Navy	1999	Elton Brand, Duke
1976	Scott May, Indiana	1988	Danny Manning, Kansas	2000	Kenyon Martin, Cincinnati
1977	Marques Johnson, UCLA	1989	Sean Elliott, Arizona	2001	Jason Williams, Duke
1978	Phil Ford, North Carolina	1990	Lionel Simmons, La Salle	2002	Jason Williams, Duke
1979	Larry Bird, Indiana St.	1991	Larry Johnson, UNLV		& Drew Gooden, Kansas
1980	Michael Brooks, La Salle	1992	Christian Laettner, Duke	2003	Nick Collison, Kansas
1981	Danny Ainge, BYU	1993	Calbert Cheaney, Indiana	2004	Jameer Nelson, St. Joseph's
1982	Ralph Sampson, Virginia	1994	Glenn Robinson, Purdue		& Emeka Okafor, Connecticut
1983	Ralph Sampson, Virginia	1995	Shawn Respert, Mich. St.	2005	Andrew Bogut, Utah
1984	Michael Jordan, N. Carolina	1996	Marcus Camby, UMass	2006	J.J. Redick, Duke
1985	Patrick Ewing, Georgetown	1997	Tim Duncan, Wake Forest		& Adam Morrison, Gonzaga
1986	Walter Berry, St. John's	1998	Antawn Jamison, N. Carolina		

All-Time Winningest Division I Coaches

Minimum of 10 seasons as Division I head coach; regular season and tournament games included; coaches active during 2005-06 in **bold** type.

Top 30 Winning Percentage

		Yrs	W	L	Pct
1	Clair Bee	21	412	87	.826
2	Adolph Rupp	41	876	190	.822
3	John Wooden	29	664	162	.804
4	**Roy Williams**	18	493	124	.799
5	John Kresse	23	560	143	.797
6	Jerry Tarkanian	31	778	202	.794
7	Dean Smith	36	879	254	.776
8	Harry Fisher	13	147	44	.770
9	Frank Keaney	27	387	117	.768
10	George Keogan	24	385	117	.767
11	Jack Ramsay	11	231	71	.765
12	Vic Bubas	10	213	67	.761
13	**Mike Krzyzewski**	31	753	250	.751
14	Chick Davies	21	314	106	.748
15	Ray Mears	21	399	135	.747
16	**Jim Boeheim**	30	726	253	.742
17	Rick Majerus	20	431	151	.741
18	Bob Huggins	24	567	199	.740
19	Al McGuire	20	405	143	.739
20	Everett Case	18	376	133	.739
21	Phog Allen	48	746	264	.739
22	**John Calipari**	14	337	129	.739
23	**Lute Olson**	33	760	270	.738
24	Walter Meanwell	22	280	101	.735
25	**Tubby Smith**	15	365	133	.733
26	**Rick Pitino**	20	470	172	.732
27	Lew Andreas	25	355	134	.726
28	Lou Carnesecca	24	526	200	.725
29	Fred Schaus	12	251	96	.723
30	Cam Henderson	35	630	243	.722

Top 30 Victories

		Yrs	W	L	Pct
1	Dean Smith	36	879	254	.776
2	Adolph Rupp	41	876	190	.822
3	**Bob Knight**	40	869	350	.713
4	Jim Phelan	49	830	524	.613
5	**Eddie Sutton**	36	798	315	.717
6	Lefty Driesell	41	786	394	.666
7	Lou Henson	41	779	408	.656
8	Jerry Tarkanian	31	778	202	.794
9	Hank Iba	41	767	338	.694
10	**Lute Olson**	33	760	270	.738
11	Ed Diddle	42	759	302	.715
12	**Mike Krzyzewski**	31	753	250	.751
13	Phog Allen	48	746	264	.739
14	**John Chaney**	34	741	312	.704
15	**Jim Calhoun**	34	733	314	.700
16	Norm Stewart	38	731	375	.661
17	**Jim Boeheim**	30	726	253	.742
18	Ray Meyer	42	724	354	.672
19	Don Haskins	38	719	353	.671
20	Denny Crum	30	675	295	.696
21	John Wooden	29	664	162	.804
22	Ralph Miller	38	657	382	.632
23	Marv Harshman	40	654	449	.593
24	Gene Bartow	34	647	353	.647
25	**Billy Tubbs**	31	641	340	.653
26	Hugh Durham	37	633	429	.596
27	Cam Henderson	35	630	243	.722
28	Norm Sloan	37	624	393	.614
29	Slats Gill	36	599	392	.604
30	Abe Lemons	34	597	344	.634

Note: Clarence (Bighouse) Gaines of Division II Winston-Salem St. (1947-93) retired after the 1992-93 season to finish his 47-year career ranked No. 3 on the all-time NCAA list of all coaches regardless of division. His record is 828-446 with a .650 winning percentage.

Where They Coached

Allen–Baker (1906-08), Kansas (1908-09), Haskell (1909), Central Mo. St. (1913-19), Kansas (1920-56); **Andreas**–Syracuse (1925-43; 45-50); **Bartow**–Central Mo. St. (1962-64), Valparaiso (1965-70), Memphis St. (1971-74), Illinois (1975), UCLA (1976-77), UAB (1979-96); **Bee**–Rider (1929-31), LIU-Brooklyn (1932-45, 46-51); **Boeheim**–Syracuse (1977–); **Bubas**–Duke (1960-69); **Calhoun**–Northeastern (1973-86), Connecticut (1987–); **Calipari**–Massachusetts (1988-96), Memphis (2000—); **Carnesecca**–St. John's (1966-70, 74-92); **Case**–N.C. State (1947-64); **Chaney**–Cheyney St. (1973-82), Temple (1983-2006); **Crum**–Louisville (1972-01); **Davies**–Duquesne (1925-43, 47-48); **Diddle**–Western Ky. (1923-64); **Driesell**–Davidson (1961-69), Maryland (1970-86), J. Madison (1989-97), Georgia St. (1997-2003); **Durham**–Florida St. (1967-78), Georgia (1979-95), Jacksonville (1999-05); **Fisher**–Columbia (1907-16), Army (1922-23, 25), **Gill**–Oregon St. (1929-64); **Harshman**–Pacific Lutheran (1946-58), Wash. St. (1959-71), Washington (1972-85); **Haskins**–UTEP (1962-99); **Henderson**–Muskingum (1920-22), Davis & Elkins (1923-35), Marshall (1936-55); **Henson**–Hardin-Simmons (1963-66), N. Mexico St. (1967-75), Illinois (1976-96), N. Mexico St. (1997-05); **Huggins**–Walsh (1981-83), Akron (1985-89), Cincinnati (1990-05), Kansas St. (2006—); **Iba**–NW Missouri St. (1930-33), Colorado (1934), Oklahoma St. (1935-70); **Keaney**–Rhode Island (1921-48); **Keogan**–St. Louis (1916), Allegheny (1919), Valparaiso (1920-21), Notre Dame (1924-43); **Knight**–Army (1966-71), Indiana (1972-00), Texas Tech (2001–); **Kresse**–Charleston (1979-2002); **Krzyzewski**–Army (1976-80), Duke (1981–).

Lemons–Okla. City (1956-73), Pan American (1974-76), Texas (1977-82), Okla. City (1984-90); **Majerus**–Marquette (1984-86), Ball St. (1988-89), Utah (1991-2003); **Meanwell**–Wisconsin (1912-17, 21-34), Missouri (1918-20); **Mears**–Wittenberg (1957-62), Tennessee (1963-77); **Meyer**–DePaul (1943-84); **Miller**–Wichita St. (1952-64), Iowa (1965-70), Oregon St. (1971-89); **Olson**–Long Beach St. (1974), Iowa (1975-83), Arizona (1984–); **Phelan**– Mount St. Mary's (1955-2003); **Pitino**–Boston Univ. (1979-83), Providence (1986-87), Kentucky (1989-97), Louisville (2001–).
Ramsay–St. Joseph's-PA (1956-66); **Rupp**–Kentucky (1931-72); **Schaus**–West Va. (1955-60), Purdue (1973-78); **Sloan**–Presbyterian (1952-55), Citadel (1957-60), Florida (1961-66), N.C. State (1967-80), Florida (1981-89); **D. Smith**–North Carolina (1962-97); **T. Smith**–Tulsa (1992-95), Georgia (1996-97), Kentucky (1998–); **Stewart**–No. Iowa (1962-67), Missouri (1968-99); **Sutton**–Creighton (1970-74), Arkansas (1975-85), Kentucky (1986-89), Oklahoma St. (1991-2006); **Tarkanian**–Long Beach St. (1969-73), UNLV (1974-92), Fresno St. (1995-2002); **Tubbs**–Southwestern (1971-73), Lamar (1976-80, 2003-06), Oklahoma (1981-94), TCU (1995-2002); **Williams**–Kansas (1989-2003), North Carolina (2003–); **Wooden**–Indiana St. (1947-48), UCLA (1949-75).

Most NCAA Tournaments

Through 2006; listed are number of appearances, overall tournament record, times reaching Final Four, and number of NCAA championships. (*) denotes that actual records are different from official NCAA records.

App		W-L	F4	Championships
27	Dean Smith	65-27	11	2 (1982, 93)
27	**Lute Olson***	46-27	5	1 (1997)
26	**Bob Knight**	44-22	5	3 (1976, 81, 87)
26	**Eddie Sutton***	39-26	2	None
25	**Jim Boeheim**	40-24	3	1 (2003)
23	Denny Crum	42-23	6	2 (1980, 86)
22	**Mike Krzyzewski**	68-19	9	3 (1991-92, 2001)
20	Adolph Rupp	30-18	6	4 (1948-49, 51, 58)
20	John Thompson	34-19	3	1 (1984)
19	Lou Henson	19-20	2	None
19	**Jim Calhoun***	41-17	2	2 (1999, 2004)
18	Lou Carnesecca	17-20	1	None
18	Jerry Tarkanian	38-18	4	1 (1990)
18	Gene Keady*	19-18	0	None
17	**John Chaney**	23-17	0	None
17	**Roy Williams**	42-16	5	1 (2005)
16	John Wooden	47-10	12	10 (1964-65, 67-73, 75)
16	Norm Stewart*	12-16	0	None
16	Nolan Richardson	26-15	3	1 (1994)
16	Jim Harrick	18-15	1	1 (1995)
15	Digger Phelps	17-17	1	None
15	**Bob Huggins**	20-14	1	None
14	Don Haskins	14-13	1	1 (1966)
14	Guy Lewis	26-18	5	None
14	**Gary Williams**	26-13	2	1 (2002)
14	**Rick Barnes**	14-14	1	None

Active Coaches' Victories

Minimum five seasons in Division I.

		Yrs	W	L	Pct
1	Bob Knight, Texas Tech	40	**869**	350	.713
2	Lute Olson, Arizona	33	**760**	270	.738
3	Mike Krzyzewski, Duke	31	**753**	250	.751
4	Jim Calhoun, UConn	34	**733**	314	.700
5	Jim Boeheim, Syracuse	30	**726**	253	.742
6	Tom Davis, Drake	31	**580**	341	.630
7	Bob Huggins, Kansas St.	24	**567**	199	.740
8	Tom Penders, Houston	32	**566**	385	.595
9	Gary Williams, Maryland	28	**560**	319	.637
10	Homer Drew, Valparaiso	29	**555**	347	.615
11	Ben Braun, California	29	**523**	364	.590
12	Pat Douglass, UC-Irvine	25	**514**	238	.684
13	Bo Ryan, Wisconsin	22	**495**	152	.765
14	Rick Byrd, Belmont	25	**493**	284	.634
	Roy Williams, North Carolina	18	**493**	124	.799
16	Rick Pitino, Louisville	20	**470**	172	.732
17	Kelvin Sampson, Indiana	23	**456**	256	.640
18	Bobby Cremins, C. of Charleston	25	**454**	307	.597
19	John Beilein, West Virginia	24	**449**	266	.628
20	Pat Kennedy, Towson	26	**433**	351	.552
21	Dave Bike, Sacred Heart	28	**427**	387	.525
22	Don Maestri, Troy	24	**408**	280	.593
	Stew Morrill, Utah St.	20	**408**	201	.670
24	L. Vann Pettaway, Ala. A&M	20	**397**	194	.672
25	Rick Barnes, Texas	19	**393**	210	.652
26	Mike Deane, Wagner	22	**381**	267	.588
27	Tom Green, Fairleigh Dickinson	23	**378**	292	.564
28	Dave Odom, South Carolina	20	**377**	245	.606
29	Tubby Smith, Kentucky	15	**365**	133	.733
30	Jim Larranaga, George Mason	22	**364**	274	.571

Annual Awards

UPI picked the first national Division I Coach of the Year in 1955. Since then, the U.S. Basketball Writers Assn. (1959), AP (1967), the National Assn. of Basketball Coaches (1969), and the Atlanta Tip-Off Club (1987) have joined in. Since 1987, the first year all five awards were given out, no coach has won all of them in the same season.

United Press International

Voted on by a panel of UPI college basketball writers and first presented in 1955.
Multiple winners: John Wooden (6); Bob Knight, Ray Meyer, Adolph Rupp, Norm Stewart, Fred Taylor and Phil Woolpert (2).

Year	Year	Year
1955 Phil Woolpert, San Francisco	1970 John Wooden, UCLA	1985 Lou Carnesecca, St. John's
1956 Phil Woolpert, San Francisco	1971 Al McGuire, Marquette	1986 Mike Krzyzewski, Duke
1957 Frank McGuire, North Carolina	1972 John Wooden, UCLA	1987 John Thompson, Georgetown
1958 Tex Winter, Kansas St.	1973 John Wooden, UCLA	1988 John Chaney, Temple
1959 Adolph Rupp, Kentucky	1974 Digger Phelps, Notre Dame	1989 Bob Knight, Indiana
1960 Pete Newell, California	1975 Bob Knight, Indiana	1990 Jim Calhoun, Connecticut
1961 Fred Taylor, Ohio St.	1976 Tom Young, Rutgers	1991 Rick Majerus, Utah
1962 Fred Taylor, Ohio St.	1977 Bob Gaillard, San Francisco	1992 Perry Clark, Tulane
1963 Ed Jucker, Cincinnati	1978 Eddie Sutton, Arkansas	1993 Eddie Fogler, Vanderbilt
1964 John Wooden, UCLA	1979 Bill Hodges, Indiana St.	1994 Norm Stewart, Missouri
1965 Dave Strack, Michigan	1980 Ray Meyer, DePaul	1995 Leonard Hamilton, Miami-FL
1966 Adolph Rupp, Kentucky	1981 Ralph Miller, Oregon St.	1996 Gene Keady, Purdue
1967 John Wooden, UCLA	1982 Norm Stewart, Missouri	1997 award discontinued
1968 Guy Lewis, Houston	1983 Jerry Tarkanian, UNLV	
1969 John Wooden, UCLA	1984 Ray Meyer, DePaul	

Annual Awards (Cont.)
U.S. Basketball Writers Association
Voted on by the USBWA and first presented in 1959.

Multiple winners: John Wooden (5); Bob Knight (3); Lou Carnesecca, John Chaney, Ray Meyer, Fred Taylor and Roy Williams (2).

Year	Year	Year
1959 Eddie Hickey, Marquette	1975 Bob Knight, Indiana	1991 Randy Ayers, Ohio St.
1960 Pete Newell, California	1976 Bob Knight, Indiana	1992 Perry Clark, Tulane
1961 Fred Taylor, Ohio St.	1977 Eddie Sutton, Arkansas	1993 Eddie Fogler, Vanderbilt
1962 Fred Taylor, Ohio St.	1978 Ray Meyer, DePaul	1994 Charlie Spoonhour, St. Louis
1963 Ed Jucker, Cincinnati	1979 Dean Smith, North Carolina	1995 Kelvin Sampson, Oklahoma
1964 John Wooden, UCLA	1980 Ray Meyer, DePaul	1996 Gene Keady, Purdue
1965 Butch van Breda Kolff, Princeton	1981 Ralph Miller, Oregon St.	1997 Clem Haskins, Minnesota
1966 Adolph Rupp, Kentucky	1982 John Thompson, Georgetown	1998 Tom Izzo, Michigan St.
1967 John Wooden, UCLA	1983 Lou Carnesecca, St. John's	1999 Cliff Ellis, Auburn
1968 Guy Lewis, Houston	1984 Gene Keady, Purdue	2000 Larry Eustachy, Iowa St.
1969 Maury John, Drake	1985 Lou Carnesecca, St. John's	2001 Al Skinner, Boston College
1970 John Wooden, UCLA	1986 Dick Versace, Bradley	2002 Ben Howland, Pittsburgh
1971 Al McGuire, Marquette	1987 John Chaney, Temple	2003 Tubby Smith, Kentucky
1972 John Wooden, UCLA	1988 John Chaney, Temple	2004 Phil Martelli, St. Joseph's
1973 John Wooden, UCLA	1989 Bob Knight, Indiana	2005 Bruce Weber, Illinois
1974 Norm Sloan, N.C. State	1990 Roy Williams, Kansas	2006 Roy Williams, North Carolina

Associated Press
Voted on by AP sportswriters and broadcasters and first presented in 1967.

Multiple winners: John Wooden (5); Bob Knight (3); Guy Lewis, Ray Meyer, Ralph Miller, Eddie Sutton and Roy Williams (2).

Year	Year	Year
1967 John Wooden, UCLA	1981 Ralph Miller, Oregon St.	1995 Kelvin Sampson, Oklahoma
1968 Guy Lewis, Houston	1982 Ralph Miller, Oregon St.	1996 Gene Keady, Purdue
1969 John Wooden, UCLA	1983 Guy Lewis, Houston	1997 Clem Haskins, Minnesota
1970 John Wooden, UCLA	1984 Ray Meyer, DePaul	1998 Tom Izzo, Michigan St.
1971 Al McGuire, Marquette	1985 Bill Frieder, Michigan	1999 Cliff Ellis, Auburn
1972 John Wooden, UCLA	1986 Eddie Sutton, Kentucky	2000 Larry Eustachy, Iowa St.
1973 John Wooden, UCLA	1987 Tom Davis, Iowa	2001 Matt Doherty, North Carolina
1974 Norm Sloan, N.C. State	1988 John Chaney, Temple	2002 Ben Howland, Pittsburgh
1975 Bob Knight, Indiana	1989 Bob Knight, Indiana	2003 Tubby Smith, Kentucky
1976 Bob Knight, Indiana	1990 Jim Calhoun, Connecticut	2004 Phil Martelli, St. Joseph's
1977 Bob Gaillard, San Francisco	1991 Randy Ayers, Ohio St.	2005 Bruce Weber, Illinois
1978 Eddie Sutton, Arkansas	1992 Roy Williams, Kansas	2006 Roy Williams, North Carolina
1979 Bill Hodges, Indiana St.	1993 Eddie Fogler, Vanderbilt	
1980 Ray Meyer, DePaul	1994 Norm Stewart, Missouri	

National Association of Basketball Coaches
Voted on by NABC membership and first presented in 1969.

Multiple winners: John Wooden (3); Gene Keady and Mike Krzyzewski (2).

Year	Year	Year
1969 John Wooden, UCLA	1982 Don Monson, Idaho	1996 John Calipari, UMass
1970 John Wooden, UCLA	1983 Lou Carnesecca, St. John's	1997 Clem Haskins, Minnesota
1971 Jack Kraft, Villanova	1984 Marv Harshman, Washington	1998 Bill Guthridge, N. Carolina
1972 John Wooden, UCLA	1985 John Thompson, Georgetown	1999 Mike Krzyzewski, Duke
1973 Gene Bartow, Memphis St.	1986 Eddie Sutton, Kentucky	& Jim O'Brien, Ohio St.
1974 Al McGuire, Marquette	1987 Rick Pitino, Providence	2000 Gene Keady, Purdue
1975 Bob Knight, Indiana	1988 John Chaney, Temple	2001 Tom Izzo, Michigan St.
1976 Johnny Orr, Michigan	1989 P.J. Carlesimo, Seton Hall	2002 Kelvin Sampson, Oklahoma
1977 Dean Smith, North Carolina	1990 Jud Heathcote, Michigan St.	2003 Tubby Smith, Kentucky
1978 Bill Foster, Duke	1991 Mike Krzyzewski, Duke	2004 Phil Martelli, St. Joseph's
& Abe Lemons, Texas	1992 George Raveling, USC	& Mike Montgomery, Stanford
1979 Ray Meyer, DePaul	1993 Eddie Fogler, Vanderbilt	2005 Bruce Weber, Illinois
1980 Lute Olson, Iowa	1994 Nolan Richardson, Arkansas	2006 Jay Wright, Villanova
1981 Ralph Miller, Oregon St.	& Gene Keady, Purdue	
& Jack Hartman, Kansas St.	1995 Jim Harrick, UCLA	

Naismith Award
Voted on by a panel of coaches, sportswriters and broadcasters and first presented by the Atlanta Tip-Off Club in 1987 in the name of the inventor of basketball, Dr. James Naismith.

Multiple winner: Mike Krzyzewski (3).

Year	Year	Year
1987 Bob Knight, Indiana	1994 Nolan Richardson, Arkansas	2001 Rod Barnes, Mississippi
1988 Larry Brown, Kansas	1995 Jim Harrick, UCLA	2002 Ben Howland, Pittsburgh
1989 Mike Krzyzewski, Duke	1996 John Calipari, UMass	2003 Tubby Smith, Kentucky
1990 Bobby Cremins, Georgia Tech	1997 Roy Williams, Kansas	2004 Phil Martelli, St. Joseph's
1991 Randy Ayers, Ohio St.	1998 Bill Guthridge, N. Carolina	2005 Bruce Weber, Illinois
1992 Mike Krzyzewski, Duke	1999 Mike Krzyzewski, Duke	2006 Jay Wright, Villanova
1993 Dean Smith, North Carolina	2000 Mike Montgomery, Stanford	

Player of the Year and NBA MVP

College Players of the Year who have gone on to win the NBA's Most Valuable Player award:

Bill Russell COLLEGE–San Francisco (1956); PROS–Boston Celtics (1958, 1961, 1962, 1963 and 1965).

Oscar Robertson COLLEGE–Cincinnati (1958, 1959 and 1960); PROS–Cincinnati Royals (1964).

Kareem Abdul-Jabbar COLLEGE–UCLA (1967 and 1969); PROS–Milwaukee Bucks (1971, 1972 and 1974) and LA Lakers (1976, 1977 and 1980).

Bill Walton COLLEGE–UCLA (1972, 1973 and 1974); PROS–Portland Trail Blazers (1978).

Larry Bird COLLEGE–Indiana St. (1979); PROS–Boston Celtics (1984, 1985, and 1986).

Michael Jordan COLLEGE–North Carolina (1984); PROS–Chicago Bulls (1988, 1991, 1992, 1996 and 1998).

David Robinson COLLEGE–Navy (1987); PROS–San Antonio Spurs (1995).

Shaquille O'Neal COLLEGE–LSU (1991); PROS–LA Lakers (2000).

Tim Duncan COLLEGE–Wake Forest (1997); PROS–San Antonio Spurs (2002, 2003).

Other Men's Champions

The NCAA has sanctioned national championship tournaments for Division II since 1957 and Division III since 1975. The NAIA sanctioned a single tournament from 1937-91, then split into two divisions in 1992.

NCAA Div. II Finals

Multiple winners: Kentucky Wesleyan (8); Evansville (5); CS-Bakersfield and Virginia Union (3); Metropolitan State, North Alabama (2).

Year	Winner	Score	Loser	Year	Winner	Score	Loser
1957	Wheaton, IL	89-65	Ky. Wesleyan	1982	Dist. of Columbia	73-63	Florida Southern
1958	South Dakota	75-53	St. Michael's, VT	1983	Wright St., OH	92-73	Dist. of Columbia
1959	Evansville, IN	83-67	SW Missouri St.	1984	Central Mo. St.	81-77	St. Augustine's, NC
1960	Evansville	90-69	Chapman, CA	1985	Jacksonville St.	74-73	South Dakota St.
1961	Wittenberg, OH	42-38	SE Missouri St.	1986	Sacred Heart, CT	93-87	SE Missouri St.
1962	Mt. St. Mary's, MD	58-57*	CS-Sacramento	1987	Ky. Wesleyan	92-74	Gannon, PA
1963	South Dakota St.	42-40	Wittenberg, OH	1988	Lowell, MA	75-72	AK-Anchorage
1964	Evansville	72-59	Akron, OH	1989	N.C. Central	73-46	SE Missouri St.
1965	Evansville	85-82*	Southern Illinois	1990	Ky. Wesleyan	93-79	CS-Bakersfield
1966	Ky. Wesleyan	54-51	Southern Illinois	1991	North Alabama	79-72	Bridgeport, CT
1967	Winston-Salem, NC	77-74	SW Missouri St.	1992	Virginia Union	100-75	Bridgeport
1968	Ky. Wesleyan	63-52	Indiana St.	1993	CS-Bakersfield	85-72	Troy St., AL
1969	Ky. Wesleyan	75-71	SW Missouri St.	1994	CS-Bakersfield	92-86	Southern Ind.
1970	Phila. Textile	76-65	Tennessee St.	1995	Southern Indiana	71-63	UC-Riverside
1971	Evansville	97-82	Old Dominion, VA	1996	Fort Hays St.	70-63	N. Kentucky
1972	Roanoke, VA	84-72	Akron, OH	1997	CS-Bakersfield	57-56	N. Kentucky
1973	Ky. Wesleyan	78-76*	Tennessee St.	1998	UC-Davis	83-77	Ky. Wesleyan
1974	Morgan St., MD	67-52	SW Missouri St.	1999	Ky. Wesleyan	75-60	Metropolitan St.
1975	Old Dominion	76-74	New Orleans	2000	Metropolitan St.	97-79	Ky. Wesleyan
1976	Puget Sound, WA	83-74	Tennessee-Chatt.	2001	Ky. Wesleyan	72-63	Washburn, KS
1977	Tennessee-Chatt.	71-62	Randolph-Macon	2002	Metropolitan St.	80-72	Ky. Wesleyan
1978	Cheyney, PA	47-40	WI-Green Bay	2003	Northeastern St., OK	75-64	Ky. Wesleyan
1979	North Alabama	64-50	WI-Green Bay	2004	Kennesaw St., GA	84-59	Southern Indiana
1980	Virginia Union	80-74	New York Tech	2005	Virginia Union	63-58	Bryant
1981	Florida Southern	73-68	Mt. St. Mary's, MD	2006	Winona St., MN	73-61	Virginia Union
				*Overtime			

NCAA Div. III Finals

Multiple winners: North Park (5); WI-Platteville (4); Calvin, Potsdam St., Scranton, WI-Stevens Point and WI-Whitewater (2).

Year	Winner	Score	Loser	Year	Winner	Score	Loser
1975	LeMoyne-Owen, TN	57-54	Glassboro St., NJ	1991	WI-Platteville	81-74	Franklin Marshall
1976	Scranton, PA	60-57	Wittenberg, OH	1992	Calvin, MI	62-49	Rochester, NY
1977	Wittenberg, OH	79-66	Oneonta St., NY	1993	Ohio Northern	71-68	Augustana, IL
1978	North Park, IL	69-57	Widener, PA	1994	Lebanon Valley, PA	66-59*	NYU
1979	North Park, IL	66-62	Potsdam St., NY	1995	WI-Platteville	69-55	Manchester, IN
1980	North Park, IL	83-76	Upsala, NJ	1996	Rowan, NJ	100-93	Hope, MI
1981	Potsdam St., NY	67-65*	Augustana, IL	1997	Illinois Wesleyan	89-86	Neb-Wesleyan
1982	Wabash, IN	83-62	Potsdam St., NY	1998	WI-Platteville	69-56	Hope, MI
1983	Scranton, PA	64-63	Wittenberg, OH	1999	WI-Platteville	76-75**	Hampden-Sydney
1984	WI-Whitewater	103-86	Clark, MA	2000	Calvin, MI	79-74	WI-Eau Claire
1985	North Park, IL	72-71	Potsdam St., NY	2001	Catholic, DC	76-62	Wm. Paterson
1986	Potsdam St., NY	76-73	LeMoyne-Owen, TN	2002	Otterbein	102-83	Elizabethtown
1987	North Park, IL	106-100	Clark, MA	2003	Williams, MA	67-65	Gustavus Adolphus
1988	Ohio Wesleyan	92-70	Scranton, PA	2004	WI-Stevens Point	84-82	Williams
1989	WI-Whitewater	94-86	Trenton St., NJ	2005	WI-Stevens Point	73-49	Rochester
1990	Rochester, NY	43-42	DePauw, IN	2006	Virginia Wesleyan	59-56	Wittenberg
				*Overtime			
				**Double overtime			

NAIA Finals, 1937-91

Multiple winners: Grand Canyon, Hamline, Kentucky St. and Tennessee St. (3); Central Missouri, Central St., Fort Hays St. and SW Missouri St. (2).

Year	Winner	Score	Loser
1937	Central Missouri	35-24	Morningside, IA
1938	Central Missouri	45-30	Roanoke, VA
1939	Southwestern, KS	32-31	San Diego St.
1940	Tarkio, MO	52-31	San Diego St.
1941	San Diego St.	36-32	Murray St., KY
1942	Hamline, MN	33-31	SE Oklahoma
1943	SE Missouri St.	34-32	NW Missouri St.
1944	Not held		
1945	Loyola-LA	49-36	Pepperdine, CA
1946	Southern Illinois	49-40	Indiana St.
1947	Marshall, WV	73-59	Mankato St., MN
1948	Louisville, KY	82-70	Indiana St.
1949	Hamline, MN	57-46	Regis, CO
1950	Indiana St.	61-47	East Central, OK
1951	Hamline, MN	69-61	Millikin, IL
1952	SW Missouri St.	73-64	Murray St., KY
1953	SW Missouri St.	79-71	Hamline, MN
1954	St.Benedict's, KS	62-56	Western Illinois
1955	East Texas St.	71-54	SE Oklahoma
1956	McNeese St., LA	60-55	Texas Southern
1957	Tennessee St.	92-73	SE Oklahoma
1958	Tennessee St.	85-73	Western Illinois
1959	Tennessee St.	97-87	Pacific-Luth., WA
1960	SW Texas St.	66-44	Westminster, PA
1961	Grambling, LA	95-75	Georgetown, KY
1962	Prairie View, TX	62-53	Westminster, PA
1963	Pan American, TX	73-62	Western Carolina
1964	Rockhurst, MO	66-56	Pan American, TX
1965	Central St., OH	85-51	Oklahoma Baptist
1966	Oklahoma Baptist	88-59	Georgia Southern
1967	St.Benedict's, KS	71-65	Oklahoma Baptist
1968	Central St., OH	51-48	Fairmont St., WV
1969	Eastern N. Mex	99-76	MD-Eastern Shore
1970	Kentucky St.	79-71	Central Wash.
1971	Kentucky St.	102-82	Eastern Michigan
1972	Kentucky St.	71-62	WI-Eau Claire
1973	Guilford, NC	99-96	MD-Eastern Shore
1974	West Georgia	97-79	Alcorn St., MS

Year	Winner	Score	Loser
1975	Grand Canyon, AZ	65-54	M'western St., TX
1976	Coppin St., MD	96-91	Henderson St., AR
1977	Texas Southern	71-44	Campbell, NC
1978	Grand Canyon	79-75	Kearney St., NE
1979	Drury, MO	60-54	Henderson St., AR
1980	Cameron, OK	84-77	Alabama St.
1981	Beth. Nazarene, OK	86-85*	AL-Huntsville
1982	SC-Spartanburg	51-38	Biola, CA
1983	Charleston, SC	57-53	WV-Wesleyan
1984	Fort Hays St., KS	48-46*	WI-Stevens Pt.
1985	Fort Hays St.	82-80*	Wayland Bapt., TX
1986	David Lipscomb, TN	67-54	AR-Monticello
1987	Washburn, KS	79-77	West Virginia St.
1988	Grand Canyon	88-86*	Auburn-Montg, AL
1989	St.Mary's, TX	61-58	East Central, OK
1990	Birm-Southern, AL	88-80	WI-Eau Claire
1991	Oklahoma City	77-74	Central Arkansas

NAIA Div. I Finals

NAIA split tournament into two divisions in 1992.

Multiple winners: Life, GA and Oklahoma City (3).

Year	Winner	Score	Loser
1992	Oklahoma City	82-73*	Central Arkansas
1993	Hawaii Pacific	88-83	Okla. Baptist
1994	Oklahoma City	99-81	Life, GA
1995	Birm-Southern	92-76	Pfeiffer, NC
1996	Oklahoma City	86-80	Georgetown, KY
1997	Life, GA	73-64	Okla. Baptist
1998	Georgetown, KY	83-69	So. Nazarene
1999	Life, GA	63-60	Mobile, AL
2000	Life, GA	61-59	Georgetown, KY
2001	Faulkner, AL	63-59	Science & Arts, OK
2002	Science & Arts, OK	96-79	Okla. Baptist
2003	Concordia, CA	88-84*	Mountain St., WV
2004	Mountain St., WV	74-70	Concordia, CA
2005	John Brown	65-55	Azusa Pacific
2006	Texas Wesleyan	67-65	Oklahoma City

*Overtime

NAIA Div. II Finals

NAIA split tournament into two divisions in 1992.

Multiple winners: Bethel, IN (3), Northwestern, IA (2).

Year	Winner	Score	Loser
1992	Grace, IN	85-79*	Northwestern, IA
1993	Williamette, OR	63-56	Northern St., SD
1994	Eureka, IL	98-95*	Northern St.
1995	Bethel, IN	103-95*	NW Nazarene, ID
1996	Albertson, ID	81-72*	Whitworth, WA
1997	Bethel, IN	95-94	Siena Heights, MI
1998	Bethel, IN	89-87	Oregon Tech
1999	Cornerstone, MI	113-109	Bethel

Year	Winner	Score	Loser
2000	Embry-Riddle, FL	75-63	Ozarks, MO
2001	Northwestern, IA	82-78	Mid. Am. Nazarene, KS
2002	Evangel, MO	84-61	Robert Morris, IL
2003	Northwestern, IA	77-57	Bethany, KS
2004	Oregon Tech	81-72	Bellevue, NE
2005	Walsh, OH	81-70	Concordia, NE
2006	Ozarks, MO	74-56	Huntington, IN

WOMEN

NCAA Final Four

Replaced the Association of Intercollegiate Athletics for Women (AIAW) tournament in 1982 as the official playoff for the national championship.

Multiple winners: Tennessee (6); Connecticut (5); Louisiana Tech, Stanford and USC (2)

Year	Champion	Head Coach	Score	Runner-up	Third Place	
1982	Louisiana Tech	Sonya Hogg	76-62	Cheyney	Maryland	Tennessee
1983	USC	Linda Sharp	69-67	Louisiana Tech	Georgia	Old Dominion
1984	USC	Linda Sharp	72-61	Tennessee	Cheyney	Louisiana Tech
1985	Old Dominion	Marianne Stanley	70-65	Georgia	NE Louisiana	Western Ky.
1986	Texas	Jody Conradt	97-81	USC	Tennessee	Western Ky.
1987	Tennessee	Pat Summitt	67-44	Louisiana Tech	Long Beach St.	Texas
1988	Louisiana Tech	Leon Barmore	56-54	Auburn	Long Beach St.	Tennessee
1989	Tennessee	Pat Summitt	76-60	Auburn	Louisiana Tech	Maryland
1990	Stanford	Tara VanDerveer	88-81	Auburn	Louisiana Tech	Virginia
1991	Tennessee	Pat Summitt	70-67 (OT)	Virginia	Connecticut	Stanford

Year	Champion	Head Coach	Score	Runner-up	—Third Place—	
1992	Stanford	Tara VanDerveer	78-62	Western Kentucky	SW Missouri St.	Virginia
1993	Texas Tech	Marsha Sharp	84-82	Ohio St.	Iowa	Vanderbilt
1994	N. Carolina	Sylvia Hatchell	60-59	Louisiana Tech	Alabama	Purdue
1995	Connecticut	Geno Auriemma	70-64	Tennessee	Georgia	Stanford
1996	Tennessee	Pat Summitt	83-65	Georgia	Connecticut	Stanford
1997	Tennessee	Pat Summitt	68-59	Old Dominion	Stanford	Notre Dame
1998	Tennessee	Pat Summitt	93-75	Louisiana Tech	Arkansas	N.C. State
1999	Purdue	Carolyn Peck	62-45	Duke	Louisiana Tech	Georgia
2000	Connecticut	Geno Auriemma	71-52	Tennessee	Penn St.	Rutgers
2001	Notre Dame	Muffet McGraw	68-66	Purdue	Connecticut	SW Missouri St.
2002	Connecticut	Geno Auriemma	82-70	Oklahoma	Tennessee	Duke
2003	Connecticut	Geno Auriemma	73-68	Tennessee	Texas	Duke
2004	Contecticut	Geno Auriemma	70-61	Tennessee	LSU	Minnesota
2005	Baylor	Kim Mulkey-Robertson	84-62	Michigan St.	LSU	Tennessee
2006	Maryland	Brenda Frese	78-75 (OT)	Duke	North Carolina	LSU

Final Four sites: 1982 (Norfolk, Va.), **1983** (Norfolk, Va.), **1984** (Los Angeles), **1985** (Austin), **1986** (Lexington), **1987** (Austin), **1988** (Tacoma), **1989** (Tacoma), **1990** (Knoxville), **1991** (New Orleans), **1992** (Los Angeles), **1993** (Atlanta), **1994** (Richmond), **1995** (Minneapolis), **1996** (Charlotte), **1997** (Cincinnati), **1998** (Kansas City), **1999** (San Jose), **2000** (Philadelphia), **2001** (St. Louis), **2002** (San Antonio), **2003** (Atlanta), **2004** (New Orleans), **2005** (Indianapolis), **2006** (Boston), **2007** (Cleveland), **2008** (Tampa), **2009** (St. Louis), **2010** (San Antonio).

Most Outstanding Player

A Most Outstanding Player has been selected every year of the NCAA tournament. Winner who did not play for the tournament champion is listed in **bold,** type.

Multiple winners: Chamique Holdsclaw, Cheryl Miller and Diana Taurasi (2).

Year
1982 Janice Lawrence, La. Tech
1983 Cheryl Miller, USC
1984 Cheryl Miller, USC
1985 Tracy Claxton, Old Dominion
1986 Clarissa Davis, Texas
1987 Tonya Edwards, Tennessee
1988 Erica Westbrooks, La. Tech
1989 Bridgette Gordon, Tennessee
1990 Jennifer Azzi, Stanford

Year
1991 **Dawn Staley**, Virginia
1992 Molly Goodenbour, Stanford
1993 Sheryl Swoopes, Texas Tech
1994 Charlotte Smith, N. Carolina
1995 Rebecca Lobo, Connecticut
1996 Michelle Marciniak, Tennessee
1997 Chamique Holdsclaw, Tenn.
1998 Chamique Holdsclaw, Tenn.
1999 Ukari Figgs, Purdue

Year
2000 Shea Ralph, Connecticut
2001 Ruth Riley, Notre Dame
2002 Swin Cash, Connecticut
2003 Diana Taurasi, Connecticut
2004 Diana Taurasi, Connecticut
2005 Sophia Young, Baylor
2006 Laura Harper, Maryland

All-Time NCAA Division I Tournament Leaders

Through 2005-06; minimum of six games; **Last** column indicates final year played.

CAREER

Scoring

	Total Points	Yrs	Last	Pts	Avg
1	Chamique Holdsclaw, Tennessee	4	1999	**479**	21.8
2	Diana Taurasi, Connecticut	4	2004	**430**	18.7
3	Bridgette Gordon, Tenn	4	1989	**388**	21.6
4	Alana Beard, Duke	4	2004	**352**	18.5
5	Cheryl Miller, USC	4	1986	**333**	20.8
6	Katie Douglas, Purdue	4	2001	**318**	14.4
7	Janice Lawrence, La. Tech	3	1984	**312**	22.3
8	Penny Toler, S. Diego St/L. Beach St	4	1989	**291**	22.4
9	Ruth Riley, Notre Dame	4	2001	**276**	19.7
10	Dawn Staley, Virginia	4	1992	**274**	18.3

Rebounds

	Total Rebounds	Yrs	Last	No	Avg
1	Chamique Holdsclaw, Tennessee	4	1999	**196**	8.9
2	Cheryl Miller, USC	4	1986	**170**	10.6
3	Sheila Frost, Tennessee	4	1989	**162**	9.0
4	Val Whiting, Stanford	4	1993	**161**	10.1
5	Venus Lacy, La. Tech	3	1990	**148**	10.6
6	Bridgette Gordon, Tennessee	4	1989	**142**	7.9
	Tamika Catchings, Tennessee	3	2000	**142**	7.9
8	Kirsten Cummings, Long Beach St.	4	1985	**136**	10.5
9	Gwen Jackson, Tennessee	4	2003	**133**	6.7
10	Swin Cash, Connecticut	4	2002	**130**	6.5
	Nora Lewis, Louisiana Tech	3	1989	**130**	9.3

Assists

	Total Assists	Yrs	Last	No	Avg
1	Temeka Johnson, LSU	4	2005	**136**	8.5
2	Teresa Witherspoon, La. Tech	4	1988	**127**	7.9
3	Diana Taurasi, Connecticut	4	2004	**106**	4.3

Steals

	Total Steals	Yrs	Last	No	Avg
1	Ticha Penicheiro, Old Dominion	4	1998	**61**	4.7
2	Kelly Miller, Georgia	4	2001	**56**	4.7

SINGLE GAME

Scoring

		Year	Pts
1	Lorri Bauman, Drake vs Maryland	1982	50
2	Sheryl Swoopes, Texas Tech vs Ohio St	1993	47
3	Barbara Kennedy, Clemson vs Penn St	1982	43
4	Jackie Stiles, SW Mo. St. vs. Duke	2001	41
5	LaTaunya Pollard, L. Beach St. vs Howard	1982	40
	Cindy Brown, L. Beach St. vs Ohio St	1987	40
	Tamika Whitmore, Memphis vs. YSU	1998	40
	Tara Mitchem, SW Mo. St. vs. Toledo	2001	40

Rebounds

		Year	No
1	Cheryl Taylor, Tenn. Tech vs Georgia	1985	23
	Charlotte Smith, N. Car. vs La. Tech	1994	23
3	Daedra Charles, Tenn. vs SW Missouri	1991	22

Assists

		Year	No
1	Anne Troyan, Penn St. vs. N.C. State	1983	19
2	Tasha Pointer, Rutgers vs. S.F. Austin	2001	18
3	Three tied at 17 each.		

Associated Press Final Top 10 Polls

The Associated Press weekly women's college basketball poll was begun by Mel Greenberg of *The Philadelphia Inquirer* during the 1976-77 season. Although the poll was started as a Top 20 in 1977 and was expanded to a Top 25 in 1990, only the Top 10 from each poll are listed below due to space constraints. The Association of Intercollegiate Athletics for Women (AIAW) Tournament determined the Division I national champion from 1972-81. The NCAA began its women's Division I tournament in 1982. The final AP Polls were taken before the NCAA tournament. Eventual national champions are in **bold** type.

1977
1 **Delta St.**
2 Immaculata
3 St. Joseph's-PA
4 CS-Fullerton
5 Tennessee
6 Tennessee Tech
7 Wayland Baptist
8 Montclair St.
9 S.F. Austin St.
10 N.C. State

1982
1 **Louisiana Tech**
2 Cheyney
3 Maryland
4 Tennessee
5 Texas
6 USC
7 Old Dominion
8 Rutgers
9 Long Beach St.
10 Penn St.

1987
1 Texas
2 Auburn
3 Louisiana Tech
4 Long Beach St.
5 Rutgers
6 Georgia
7 **Tennessee**
8 Mississippi
9 Iowa
10 Ohio St.

1992
1 Virginia
2 Tennessee
3 **Stanford**
4 S.F. Austin St.
5 Mississippi
6 Miami-FL
7 Iowa
8 Maryland
9 Penn St.
10 SW Missouri St.

1997
1 Connecticut
2 Old Dominion
3 Stanford
4 North Carolina
5 Louisiana Tech
6 Georgia
7 Florida
8 Alabama
9 LSU
10 **Tennessee**

2002
1 **Connecticut**
2 Oklahoma
3 Duke
4 Vanderbilt
5 Stanford
6 Tennessee
7 Baylor
8 Louisiana Tech
9 Purdue
10 Iowa St.

1978
1 Tennessee
2 Wayland Baptist
3 N.C. State
4 Montclair St.
5 **UCLA**
6 Maryland
7 Queens-NY
8 Valdosta St.
9 Delta St.
10 LSU

1983
1 **USC**
2 Louisiana Tech
3 Texas
4 Old Dominion
5 Cheyney
6 Long Beach St.
7 Maryland
8 Penn St.
9 Georgia
10 Tennessee

1988
1 Tennessee
2 Iowa
3 Auburn
4 Texas
5 **Louisiana Tech**
6 Ohio St.
7 Long Beach St.
8 Rutgers
9 Maryland
10 Virginia

1993
1 Vanderbilt
2 Tennessee
3 Ohio St.
4 Iowa
5 **Texas Tech**
6 Stanford
7 Auburn
8 Penn St.
9 Virginia
10 Colorado

1998
1 **Tennessee**
2 Old Dominion
3 Connecticut
4 Louisiana Tech
5 Stanford
6 Texas Tech
7 North Carolina
8 Duke
9 Arizona
10 N.C. State

2003
1 **Connecticut**
2 Duke
3 LSU
4 Tennessee
5 Texas
6 Louisiana Tech
7 Texas Tech
8 Kansas St.
9 Stanford
10 Purdue

1979
1 **Old Dominion**
2 Louisiana Tech
3 Tennessee
4 Texas
5 S.F. Austin St.
6 UCLA
7 Rutgers
8 Maryland
9 Cheyney
10 Wayland Baptist

1984
1 Texas
2 Louisiana Tech
3 Georgia
4 Old Dominion
5 **USC**
6 Long Beach St.
7 Kansas St.
8 LSU
9 Cheyney
10 Mississippi

1989
1 **Tennessee**
2 Auburn
3 Louisiana Tech
4 Stanford
5 Maryland
6 Texas
7 Long Beach St.
8 Iowa
9 Colorado
10 Georgia

1994
1 Tennessee
2 Penn St.
3 Connecticut
4 **North Carolina**
5 Colorado
6 Louisiana Tech
7 USC
8 Purdue
9 Texas Tech
10 Virginia

1999
1 **Purdue**
2 Tennessee
3 Louisiana Tech
4 Colorado St.
5 Old Dominion
6 Connecticut
7 Rutgers
8 Notre Dame
9 Texas Tech
10 Duke

2004
1 Duke
2 Tennessee
3 Purdue
4 Texas
5 Penn St.
6 **Connecticut**
7 Louisiana Tech
8 Kansas St.
9 Houston
10 Stanford

1980
1 **Old Dominion**
2 Tennessee
3 Louisiana Tech
4 South Carolina
5 S.F. Austin St.
6 Maryland
7 Texas
8 Rutgers
9 Long Beach St.
10 N.C. State

1985
1 Texas
2 NE Louisiana
3 Long Beach St.
4 Louisiana Tech
5 **Old Dominion**
6 Mississippi
7 Ohio St.
8 Georgia
9 Penn St.
10 Auburn

1990
1 Louisiana Tech
2 **Stanford**
3 Washington
4 Tennessee
5 UNLV
6 S.F. Austin St.
7 Georgia
8 Texas
9 Auburn
10 Iowa

1995
1 **Connecticut**
2 Colorado
3 Tennessee
4 Stanford
5 Texas Tech
6 Vanderbilt
7 Penn St.
8 Louisiana Tech
9 Western Ky.
10 Virginia

2000
1 **Connecticut**
2 Tennessee
3 Louisiana Tech
4 Georgia
5 Notre Dame
6 Penn St.
7 Iowa St.
8 Rutgers
9 UC-Santa Barbara
10 Duke

2005
1 Stanford
2 LSU
3 Tennessee
4 North Carolina
5 **Baylor**
6 Michigan St.
7 Duke
8 Ohio St.
9 Rutgers
10 Connecticut

1981
1 **Louisiana Tech**
2 Tennessee
3 Old Dominion
4 USC
5 Cheyney
6 Long Beach St.
7 UCLA
8 Maryland
9 Rutgers
10 Kansas

1986
1 **Texas**
2 Georgia
3 USC
4 Louisiana Tech
5 Western Ky.
6 Virginia
7 Auburn
8 Long Beach St.
9 LSU
10 Rutgers

1991
1 Penn St.
2 Virginia
3 Georgia
4 **Tennessee**
5 Purdue
6 Auburn
7 N.C. State
8 LSU
9 Arkansas
10 Western Ky.

1996
1 Louisiana Tech
2 Connecticut
3 Stanford
4 **Tennessee**
5 Georgia
6 Old Dominion
7 Iowa
8 Penn St.
9 Texas Tech
10 Alabama

2001
1 Connecticut
2 **Notre Dame**
3 Tennessee
4 Georgia
5 Duke
6 Louisiana Tech
7 Oklahoma
8 Iowa St.
9 Purdue
10 Vanderbilt

2006
1 North Carolina
2 Ohio St.
3 **Maryland**
4 Duke
5 LSU
6 Tennessee
7 Oklahoma
8 Connecticut
9 Rutgers
10 Baylor

All-Time AP Top 10

The composite AP Top 10 from the 1976-77 season through 2005-06, based on the final regular season rankings of each year. Team points are based on 10 points for all 1st place finishes, 9 for each 2nd, etc. Also listed are the number of times ranked No. 1 by AP going into the tournaments, and times ranked in the pre-tournament Top 10.

		Pts	No.1	Top 10			Pts	No.1	Top 10
1	Tennessee	211	5	28	6	Stanford	77	1	12
2	Louisiana Tech	173	4	24	7	Georgia	72	0	13
3	Connecticut	99	6	13	8	Penn St.	52	1	11
4	Texas	93	4	18	9	Duke	49	1	9
5	Old Dominion	81	2	11	10	Long Beach St.	45	0	10

All-Time Winningest Division I Teams

Division I schools with best winning percentages (with a minimum of 350 victories) and most victories through 2005-06 (including postseason tournaments). Although official NCAA women's basketball records didn't begin until the 1981-82 season, results from previous seasons are included below.

Top 15 Winning Percentage

		Yrs	W	L	Pct
1	Louisiana Tech	32	899	154	.854
2	Tennessee	61	1006	234	.811
3	Texas	32	803	258	.757
4	Old Dominion	37	817	273	.750
5	Montana	32	676	236	.741
6	Stephen F. Austin St.	34	773	284	.731
7	Utah	32	675	256	.725
8	Stanford	32	687	263	.723
9	Connecticut	32	681	278	.710
10	Penn St.	42	724	297	.709
11	Rutgers	32	675	281	.706
12	Georgia	33	694	293	.703
13	Texas Tech	31	704	299	.702
14	Tennessee Tech	36	771	329	.701
15	Auburn	35	689	300	.697

Top 15 Victories

		Yrs	W	L	Pct
1	Tennessee	61	1006	234	.811
2	Louisiana Tech	32	899	154	.854
3	Old Dominion	37	817	273	.750
4	Texas	32	803	258	.757
5	James Madison	84	781	447	.636
6	Stephen F. Austin St.	34	773	284	.731
7	Tennessee Tech	36	771	329	.701
8	Long Beach St.	44	758	349	.685
9	Ohio St.	41	725	328	.689
10	Penn St.	42	724	297	.709
	Richmond	86	724	489	.594
12	Western Kentucky	44	720	349	.674
13	Texas Tech	31	704	299	.702
14	Kansas St.	38	697	416	.626
15	Georgia	33	694	293	.703

Annual NCAA Division I Leaders

All averages include postseason games

Scoring

Multiple winners: Cindy Blodgett, Andrea Congreaves and Jackie Stiles (2).

Year		Gm	Pts	Avg
1982	Barbara Kennedy, Clemson	31	908	29.3
1983	LaTaunya Pollard, L. Beach St	31	907	29.3
1984	Deborah Temple, Delta St	28	873	31.2
1985	Anucha Browne, Northwestern	28	855	30.5
1986	Wanda Ford, Drake	30	919	30.6
1987	Tresa Spaulding, BYU	28	810	28.9
1988	LeChandra LeDay, Grambling	28	850	30.4
1989	Patricia Hoskins, Miss. Valley	27	908	33.6
1990	Kim Perrot, SW Louisiana	28	839	30.0
1991	Jan Jensen, Drake	30	888	29.6
1992	Andrea Congreaves, Mercer	28	925	33.0
1993	Andrea Congreaves, Mercer	26	805	31.0
1994	Kristy Ryan, CS-Sacramento	26	727	28.0
1995	Koko Lahanas, CS-Fullerton	29	778	26.8
1996	Cindy Blodgett, Maine	32	889	27.8
1997	Cindy Blodgett, Maine	30	810	27.0
1998	Allison Feaster, Harvard	28	797	28.5
1999	Tamika Whitmore, Memphis	32	843	26.3
2000	Jackie Stiles, SW Missouri St.	32	890	27.8
2001	Jackie Stiles, SW Missouri St.	35	1062	30.3
2002	Kelly Mazzante, Penn St.	35	872	24.9
2003	Chandi Jones, Houston	28	770	27.5
2004	Emily Faurholt, Idaho	29	737	25.4
2005	Tan White, Mississippi St.	29	681	23.5
2006	Seimone Augustus, LSU	35	795	22.7

Rebounds

Multiple winner: Patricia Hoskins (2).

Year		Gm	No	Avg
1982	Anne Donovan, Old Dominion	28	412	14.7
1983	Deborah Mitchell, Miss. Col	28	447	16.0
1984	Joy Kellog, Oklahoma City	23	373	16.2
1985	Rosina Pearson, Beth-Cookman	26	480	18.5
1986	Wanda Ford, Drake	30	506	16.9
1987	Patricia Hoskins, Miss. Valley St.	28	476	17.0
1988	Katie Beck, East Tenn. St.	25	441	17.6
1989	Patricia Hoskins, Miss. Valley St.	27	440	16.3
1990	Pam Hudson, Northwestern St	29	438	15.1
1991	Tarcha Hollis, Grambling	29	443	15.3
1992	Christy Greis, Evansville	28	383	13.7
1993	Ann Barry, Nevada	25	355	14.2
1994	DeShawne Blocker, E. Tenn. St.	26	450	17.3
1995	Tera Sheriff, Jackson St.	29	401	13.8
1996	Dana Wynne, Seton Hall	29	372	12.8
1997	Etolia Mitchell, Georgia St.	25	330	13.2
1998	Alisha Hill, Howard	30	397	13.2
1999	Monica Logan, UMBC	27	364	13.5
2000	Malveata Johnson, N.C. A&T	27	363	13.4
2001	Andrea Gardner, Howard	31	439	14.2
2002	Mandi Carver, Idaho St.	27	336	12.4
2003	Jennifer Butler, Massachusetts	28	412	14.7
2004	Ashlee Kelly, Quinnipiac	29	392	13.5
2005	Sancho Lyttle, Houston	30	362	12.1
2006	Courtney Paris, Oklahoma	36	539	15.0

Note: Wanda Ford (1986) and Patricia Hoskins (1989) each led the country in scoring and rebounds in the same year.

All-Time NCAA Division I Individual Leaders

Through 2005-06; includes regular season and tournament games; Official NCAA women's basketball records began with 1981-82 season. Players who competed earlier than that are not included below; **Last** column indicates final year played.

CAREER

Scoring

	Average	Yrs	Last	Pts	Avg
1	Patricia Hoskins, Miss. Valley St.	4	1989	3122	28.4
2	Sandra Hodge, New Orleans	4	1984	2860	26.7
3	Jackie Stiles, SW Mo. St.	4	2001	3206	26.1
4	Lorri Bauman, Drake	4	1984	3115	26.0
5	Andrea Congreaves, Mercer	4	1993	2796	25.9
6	Cindy Blodgett, Maine	4	1998	3005	25.5
7	Valorie Whiteside, Aplach St.	4	1988	2944	25.4
8	Joyce Walker, LSU	4	1984	2906	24.8
9	Tarcha Hollis, Grambling	4	1991	2058	24.2
10	Korie Hlede, Duquesne	4	1998	2631	24.1

Rebounds

	Average	Yrs	Last	Reb	Avg
1	Wanda Ford, Drake	4	1986	1887	16.1
2	Patricia Hoskins, Miss. Valley St.	4	1989	1662	15.1
3	Tarcha Hollis, Grambling	4	1991	1185	13.9
4	Katie Beck, East Tenn. St.	4	1988	1404	13.4
5	Marilyn Stephens, Temple	4	1984	1519	13.0
6	Natalie Williams, UCLA	4	1994	1137	12.8
7	Cheryl Taylor, Tenn. Tech	4	1987	1532	12.8
8	DeShawne Blocker, E. Tenn. St.	4	1995	1361	12.7
9	Olivia Bradley, West Virginia	4	1985	1484	12.7
10	Judy Mosley, Hawaii	4	1990	1441	12.6

SINGLE SEASON

Scoring

	Average	Year	Gm	Pts	Avg
1	Patricia Hoskins, Miss. Valley St.	1989	27	908	33.6
2	Andrea Congreaves, Mercer	1992	28	925	33.0
3	Deborah Temple, Delta St.	1984	28	873	31.2
4	Andrea Congreaves, Mercer	1993	26	805	31.0
5	Wanda Ford, Drake	1986	30	919	30.6
6	Anucha Browne, Northwestern	1985	28	855	30.5
7	LeChandra LeDay, Grambling	1988	28	850	30.4
8	Jackie Stiles, SW Mo. St.	2001	35	1062	30.3
9	Kim Perrot, SW Louisiana	1990	28	841	30.0
10	Tina Hutchinson, San Diego St.	1984	30	898	29.9

SINGLE GAME

Scoring

		Year	Pts
1	Cindy Brown, Long Beach St. vs San Jose St.	1987	60
2	Lorri Bauman, Drake vs SW Missouri St.	1984	58
	Kim Perrot, SW La. vs SE La	1990	58
4	Jackie Stiles, SW Mo. St. vs Evansville	2000	56
5	Patricia Hoskins, Miss. Valley St. vs South-BR	1989	55
	Patricia Hoskins, Miss. Valley St. vs Ala. St.	1989	55
7	Wanda Ford, Drake vs SW Missouri St.	1986	54
	Anjinea Hopson, Grambling vs Jackson St.	1994	54
	Mary Lowry, Baylor vs Texas	1994	54
10	Chris Starr, Nevada vs CS-Sacramento	1983	53
	Felisha Edwards, NE La. vs Southern Miss	1991	53
	Sheryl Swoopes, Texas Tech vs Texas	1993	53

All-Time Winningest Division I Coaches

Minimum of 10 seasons as Division I head coach; regular season and tournament games included.

Top 10 Winning Percentage

		Yrs	W	L	Pct
1	Leon Barmore, La. Tech	20	576	87	.869
2	**Pat Summitt**, Tennessee	32	913	177	.838
3	**Geno Auriemma**, Connecticut	21	589	116	.835
4	**Gail Goestenkors**, Duke	14	364	97	.790
5	**Tara VanDerveer**, Stanford	27	660	179	.787
6	Bill Sheahan, Mt. St. Mary's	17	372	104	.782
7	**Robin Selvig**, Montana	28	645	188	.774
8	Marsha Sharp, Texas Tech	23	556	175	.761
9	**Andy Landers**, Georgia	27	657	208	.760
10	**Jody Conradt**, Texas	37	882	293	.751

Top 10 Victories

		Yrs	W	L	Pct
1	**Pat Summitt**, Tennessee	32	913	177	.838
2	**Jody Conradt**, Texas	37	882	293	.751
3	**C. Vivian Stringer**, Rutgers	34	750	251	.749
4	**Sylvia Hatchell**, N. Carolina	31	717	268	.728
5	Sue Gunter, LSU	34	708	308	.697
6	**Kay Yow**, N.C. State	35	693	320	.685
7	Rene Portland, Penn St.	30	681	249	.732
8	**Tara VanDerveer**, Stanford	27	660	179	.787
9	**Andy Landers**, Georgia	27	657	208	.760
10	**Theresa Grentz**, Illinois	32	652	299	.686

Note: active coaches in **bold** type and listed with current teams. Retired coached listed with last team coached.

Annual Awards

The Broderick Award was first given out to the Women's Division I or Large School Player of the Year in 1977. Since then, the National Assn. for Girls and Women in Sports (1978), the Women's Basketball Coaches Assn. (1983), the Atlanta Tip-Off Club (1983) and the Associated Press (1995) have joined in.

Since 1983, the first year as many as four awards were given out, the same player has won all of them in the same season twice: Cheryl Miller of USC in 1985 and Rebecca Lobo of Connecticut in 1995.

Associated Press

Voted on by AP sportswriters and broadcasters and first presented in 1995.
Multiple winner: Seimone Augustus and Chamique Holdsclaw (2).

Year	Year	Year
1995 Rebecca Lobo, Connecticut	1999 Chamique Holdsclaw, Tennessee	2003 Diana Taurasi, Connecticut
1996 Jennifer Rizzotti, Connecticut	2000 Tamika Catchings, Tennessee	2004 Alana Beard, Duke
1997 Kara Wolters, Connecticut	2001 Ruth Riley, Notre Dame	2005 Seimone Augustus, LSU
1998 Chamique Holdsclaw, Tennessee	2002 Sue Bird, Connecticut	2006 Seimone Augustus, LSU

Broderick Award

Voted on by a national panel of women's collegiate athletic directors and first presented by the late Thomas Broderick, an athletic outfitter, in 1977. Honda has presented the award since 1987. Basketball Player of the Year is one of 10 nominated for Collegiate Woman Athlete of the Year; (*) indicates player also won Athlete of the Year.
Multiple winners: Seimone Augustus, Chamique Holdsclaw, Nancy Lieberman, Cheryl Miller, Dawn Staley and Diana Taurasi (2).

Year	Year	Year
1977 Lucy Harris, Delta St.*	1979 Nancy Lieberman, Old Dominion*	1981 Lynette Woodard, Kansas
1978 Ann Meyers, UCLA*	1980 Nancy Lieberman, Old Dominion*	1982 Pam Kelly, La. Tech

Year	Year	Year
1983 Anne Donovan, Old Dominion	1991 Dawn Staley, Virginia	1999 Stephanie White-McCarty, Purdue
1984 Cheryl Miller, USC*	1992 Dawn Staley, Virginia	2000 Shea Ralph, Connecticut
1985 Cheryl Miller, USC	1993 Sheryl Swoopes, Texas Tech	2001 Jackie Stiles, SW Missouri St.*
1986 Kamie Ethridge, Texas*	1994 Lisa Leslie, USC	2002 Sue Bird, Connecticut
1987 Katrina McClain, Georgia	1995 Rebecca Lobo, Connecticut	2003 Diana Taurasi, Connecticut
1988 Teresa Weatherspoon, La. Tech*	1996 Jennifer Rizzotti, Connecticut	2004 Diana Taurasi, Connecticut
1989 Bridgette Gordon, Tennessee	1997 Chamique Holdsclaw, Tennessee	2005 Seimone Augustus, LSU
1990 Jennifer Azzi, Stanford	1998 Chamique Holdsclaw, Tennessee*	2006 Seimone Augustus, LSU

Wade Trophy

Originally voted on by the National Assn. for Girls and Women in Sports (NAGWS) and awarded for academics and community service as well as player performance. First presented in 1978 in the name of former Delta St. coach Lily Margaret Wade. Since 2002, the trophy has been awarded to the Women's Basketball Coaches Association player of the year.

Multiple winner: Seimone Augustus and Nancy Lieberman (2).

Year	Year	Year
1978 Carol Blazejowski, Montclair St.	1988 Teresa Weatherspoon, La. Tech	1998 Ticha Penicheiro, Old Dominion
1979 Nancy Lieberman, Old Dominion	1989 Clarissa Davis, Texas	1999 Stephanie White-McCarty, Purdue
1980 Nancy Lieberman, Old Dominion	1990 Jennifer Azzi, Stanford	2000 Edwina Brown, Texas
1981 Lynette Woodard, Kansas	1991 Daedra Charles, Tennessee	2001 Jackie Stiles, SW Missouri St.
1982 Pam Kelly, La. Tech	1992 Susan Robinson, Penn St.	2002 Sue Bird, Connecticut
1983 LaTaunya Pollard, L. Beach St.	1993 Karen Jennings, Nebraska	2003 Diana Taurasi, Connecticut
1984 Janice Lawrence, La. Tech	1994 Carol Ann Shudlick, Minnesota	2004 Alana Beard, Duke
1985 Cheryl Miller, USC	1995 Rebecca Lobo, Connecticut	2005 Seimone Augustus, LSU
1986 Kamie Ethridge, Texas	1996 Jennifer Rizzotti, Connecticut	2006 Seimone Augustus, LSU
1987 Shelly Pennefather, Villanova	1997 DeLisha Milton, Florida	

Naismith Trophy

Voted on by a panel of coaches, sportswriters and broadcasters and first presented in 1983 by the Atlanta Tip-Off Club in the name of the inventor of basketball, Dr. James Naismith.

Multiple winners: Cheryl Miller (3); Seimone Augustus, Clarissa Davis, Chamique Holdsclaw, Dawn Staley and Diana Taurasi (2).

Year	Year	Year
1983 Anne Donovan, Old Dominion	1991 Dawn Staley, Virgina	1999 Chamique Holdsclaw, Tennessee
1984 Cheryl Miller, USC	1992 Dawn Staley, Virginia	2000 Tamika Catchings, Tennessee
1985 Cheryl Miller, USC	1993 Sheryl Swoopes, Texas Tech	2001 Ruth Riley, Notre Dame
1986 Cheryl Miller, USC	1994 Lisa Leslie, USC	2002 Sue Bird, Connecticut
1987 Clarissa Davis, Texas	1995 Rebecca Lobo, Connecticut	2003 Diana Taurasi, Connecticut
1988 Sue Wicks, Rutgers	1996 Saudia Roundtree, Georgia	2004 Diana Taurasi, Connecticut
1989 Clarissa Davis, Texas	1997 Kate Starbird, Stanford	2005 Seimone Augustus, LSU
1990 Jennifer Azzi, Stanford	1998 Chamique Holdsclaw, Tennessee	2006 Seimone Augustus, LSU

Women's Basketball Coaches Association

Voted on by the WBCA and first presented by Champion athletic outfitters in 1983.

Multiple winners: Chamique Holdsclaw, Cheryl Miller and Dawn Staley (2).

Year	Year	Year
1983 Anne Donovan, Old Dominion	1990 Venus Lacy, La. Tech	1997 Kate Starbird, Stanford
1984 Janice Lawrence, La. Tech	1991 Dawn Staley, Virgina	1998 Chamique Holdsclaw, Tennessee
1985 Cheryl Miller, USC	1992 Dawn Staley, Virginia	1999 Chamique Holdsclaw, Tennessee
1986 Cheryl Miller, USC	1993 Sheryl Swoopes, Texas Tech	2000 Tamika Catchings, Tennessee
1987 Katrina McClain, Georgia	1994 Lisa Leslie, USC	2001 Ruth Riley, Notre Dame
1988 Michelle Edwards, Iowa	1995 Rebecca Lobo, Connecticut	2002 merged with Wade Trophy
1989 Clarissa Davis, Texas	1996 Saudia Roundtree, Georgia	

Wooden Award

Voted on by a panel of coaches, sportswriters and broadcasters and first presented in 2004 by the Los Angeles Athletic Club in the name of former Purdue All-American and UCLA coach John Wooden. Unlike the other player of the year awards, candidates for the Wooden must have a minimum grade point average of 2.00 (out of 4.00).

Multiple winner: Seimone Augustus (2).

Year	Year	Year
2004 Alana Beard, Duke	2005 Seimone Augustus, LSU	2006 Seimone Augustus, LSU

Coach of the Year Award

Voted on by the Women's Basketball Coaches Assn. and first presented by Converse athletic outfitters in 1983.

Multiple winners: Geno Auriemma and Pat Summitt (3), Jody Conradt, Rene Portland and Vivian Stringer (2).

Year	Year	Year
1983 Pat Summitt, Tennessee	1991 Rene Portland, Penn St.	1999 Carolyn Peck, Purdue
1984 Jody Conradt, Texas	1992 Ferne Labati, Miami-FL	2000 Geno Auriemma, Connecticut
1985 Jim Foster, St. Joseph's-PA	1993 Vivian Stringer, Iowa	2001 Muffet McGraw, Notre Dame
1986 Jody Conradt, Texas	1994 Marsha Sharp, Texas Tech	2002 Geno Auriemma, Connecticut
1987 Theresa Grentz, Rutgers	1995 Pat Summitt, Tennessee	2003 Gail Goestenkors, Duke
1988 Vivian Stringer, Iowa	1996 Leon Barmore, La. Tech	2004 Rene Portland, Penn St.
1989 Tara VanDerveer, Stanford	1997 Geno Auriemma, Connecticut	2005 Pokey Chatman, LSU
1990 Kay Yow, N.C. State	1998 Pat Summitt, Tennessee	2006 Sylvia Hatchell, N. Carolina

Other Women's Champions

The NCAA has sanctioned national championship tournaments for Division II and Division III since 1982. The NAIA sanctioned a single tournament from 1981-91, then split in to two divisions in 1992. (*) denotes overtime.

NCAA Div. II Finals

Multiple winners: North Dakota St. and Cal Poly Pomona (5); Delta St. and North Dakota (3).

Year	Winner	Score	Loser
1982	Cal Poly Pomona	93-74	Tuskegee, AL
1983	Virginia Union	73-60	Cal Poly Pomona
1984	Central Mo.St.	80-73	Virginia Union
1985	Cal Poly Pomona	80-69	Central Mo.St.
1986	Cal Poly Pomona	70-63	North Dakota St.
1987	New Haven, CT	77-75	Cal Poly Pomona
1988	Hampton, VA	65-48	West Texas St.
1989	Delta St., MS	88-58	Cal Poly Pomona
1990	Delta St., MS	77-43	Bentley, MA
1991	North Dakota St.	81-74	SE Missouri St.
1992	Delta St., MS	65-63	North Dakota St.
1993	North Dakota St.	95-63	Delta St.
1994	North Dakota St.	89-56	CS-San Bernadino
1995	North Dakota St.	98-85	Portland St.
1996	North Dakota St.	104-78	Shippensburg, PA
1997	North Dakota	94-78	S. Indiana
1998	North Dakota	92-76	Emporia St.
1999	North Dakota	80-63	Arkansas Tech
2000	Northern Kentucky	71-62	North Dakota St.
2001	Cal Poly Pomona	87-80*	North Dakota
2002	Cal Poly Pomona	74-62	SE Oklahoma St.
2003	South Dakota St.	65-60	Northern Kentucky
2004	California, PA	75-72	Drury
2005	Washburn	70-53	Seattle Pacific
2006	Grand Valley St.	58-52	AIC

NCAA Div. III Finals

Multiple winners: Washington (4); Capital, Elizabethtown, Hope and WI-Stevens Point (2).

Year	Winner	Score	Loser
1982	Elizabethtown, PA	67-66*	NC-Greensboro
1983	North Central, IL	83-71	Elizabethtown, PA
1984	Rust College, MS	51-49	Elizabethtown, PA
1985	Scranton, PA	68-59	New Rochelle, NY
1986	Salem St., MA	89-85	Bishop, TX
1987	WI-Stevens Pt.	81-74	Concordia, MN
1988	Concordia, MN	65-57	St. John Fisher, NY
1989	Elizabethtown, PA	66-65	CS-Stanislaus
1990	Hope, MI	65-63	St. John Fisher
1991	St. Thomas, MN	73-55	Muskingum, OH
1992	Alma, MI	79-75	Moravian, PA
1993	Central Iowa	71-63	Capital, OH
1994	Capital, OH	82-63	Washington, MO
1995	Capital, OH	59-55	WI-Oshkosh
1996	WI-Oshkosh	66-50	Mt. Union, OH
1997	NYU	72-70	WI-Eau Claire
1998	Washington, MO	77-69	So. Maine
1999	Washington, MO	74-65	Col.of St. Benedict, MN
2000	Washington, MO	79-33	So. Maine
2001	Washington, MO	67-45	Messiah, PA
2002	WI-Stevens Pt.	67-65	St. Lawrence, NY
2003	Trinity, TX	60-58	E. Connecticut St.
2004	Wilmington	59-53	Bowdoin
2005	Millikin	70-50	Randolph-Macon
2006	Hope, MI	69-56	Southern Maine

NAIA Finals

Multiple winners: One tournament–SW Oklahoma (4); Div. I tourney–Southern Nazarene (6), Oklahoma City (4); Union (3); Arkansas Tech (2); Div. II tourney–Hastings (3); Morningside, Northern St. and Western Oregon (2).

Year	Winner	Score	Loser
1981	Kentucky St.	73-67	Texas Southern
1982	SW Oklahoma	80-45	Mo. Southern
1983	SW Oklahoma	80-68	AL-Huntsville
1984	NC-Asheville	72-70*	Portland, OR
1985	SW Oklahoma	55-54	Saginaw Val., MI
1986	Francis Marion, SC	75-65	Wayland Baptist, TX
1987	SW Oklahoma	60-58	North Georgia
1988	Oklahoma City	113-95	Claflin, SC
1989	So. Nazarene, OK	98-96	Claflin, SC
1990	Oklahoma City	82-75	AR-Monticello
1991	Ft. Hays St., KS	57-53	SW Oklahoma
1992	I– Arkansas Tech	84-68	Wayland Baptist, TX
	II– Northern St., SD	73-56	Tarleton St., TX
1993	I– Arkansas Tech	76-75	Union, TN
	II– No. Montana	71-68	Northern St., SD
1994	I– So. Nazarene	97-74	David Lipscomb, TN
	II– Northern St., SD	48-45	Western Oregon
1995	I– So. Nazarene	78-77	SE Oklahoma
	II– Western Oregon	75-67	NW Nazarene, ID
1996	I– So. Nazarene	80-79	SE Oklahoma
	II– Western Oregon	80-77	Huron, SD

Year	Winner	Score	Loser
1997	I– So. Nazarene	78-73	Union, TN
	II– NW Nazarene	64-46	Black Hills St., SD
1998	I– Union, TN	73-70	So. Nazarene
	II– Walsh, OH	73-66	Mary Hardin-Baylor
1999	I– Oklahoma City	72-55	Simon Fraser, B.C.
	II– Shawnee St., OH	80-65	St. Francis, IN
2000	I– Oklahoma City	64-55	Simon Fraser, B.C.
	II– Mary, N.D.	59-49	Northwestern, IA
2001	I– Oklahoma City	69-52	Auburn Montgomery, AL
	II– Northwestern, IA	77-50	Albertson, ID
2002	I– Oklahoma City	82-73	So. Nazarene
	II– Hastings, NE	73-69	Cornerstone, MI
2003	I– So. Nazarene	71-70	Oklahoma City
	II– Hastings, NE	59-53	Dakota Wesleyan
2004	I– So. Nazarene	77-61	Oklahoma City
	II– Morningside	70-62	Mary, N.D.
2005	I– Union, TN	67-63	Oklahoma City
	II– Morningside	75-65	Cedarville, OH
2006	I– Union, TN	79-62	Lubbock Christian
	II– Hastings, NE	58-39	Ozarks, MO

AIAW Finals

The Association of Intercollegiate Athletics for Women Large College tournament determined the women's national champion for 10 years until supplanted by the NCAA.

In 1982, most Division I teams entered the first NCAA tournament rather than the last one staged by the AIAW.

Year	Winner	Score	Loser
1972	Immaculata, PA	52-48	West Chester, PA
1973	Immaculata, PA	59-52	Queens College, NY
1974	Immaculata, PA	68-53	Mississippi College
1975	Delta St., MS	90-81	Immaculata, PA
1976	Delta St., MS	69-64	Immaculata, PA
1977	Delta St., MS	68-55	LSU

Year	Winner	Score	Loser
1978	UCLA	90-74	Maryland
1979	Old Dominion	75-65	Louisiana Tech
1980	Old Dominion	68-53	Tennessee
1981	Louisiana Tech	79-59	Tennessee
1982	Rutgers	83-77	Texas

PRO
BASKETBALL

2005 / 2006 YEAR IN REVIEW

Phoenix point guard **Steve Nash** wrapped his arms around another MVP trophy in 2006.

HEAT RISES

Dwyane Wade, Shaq, Pat Riley and a gang of cast-offs came from behind to beat Dallas and bring a title to South Florida.

THEY CALLED HIM CRAZY, nuts, out of his mind. Pundits, players, prognosticators and fans alike thought Pat Riley had lost hold of his senses.

When the president of the Miami Heat revamped a roster that had fallen just a few nagging injuries short of the NBA Finals with a group of hyped-up, past-their-prime, so-called prima donnas, the common sentiment was that Riley, in search of his fifth title and first in 18 years, had become both desperate and delusional.

Yet, in the end, with champagne flowing down his Armani suit and joy smoothing his wrinkled brow, Riley knew best.

The 2005-2006 NBA season will be remembered for many things: Kobe Bryant's 81-point masterpiece, the Dallas Mavericks' first trip to the Finals, LeBron James' playoff appearance, Steve Nash's successful defense of his MVP award.

But more than anything, it will be remembered as the year the Heat beat the odds and defied the skeptics in winning the franchise's first championship.

"This team believed all along, even though we had a lot of doubters," Heat star Dwyane Wade said.

"My license plates on my car say 'Doubt It' because everybody doubted us. But not anymore."

Wade was perhaps the only Heat player who was not doubted. Even so, few thought he could reach the high level he did in leading Miami to a 4-games-to-2 victory over Dallas in the Finals. With an aging Shaquille O'Neal rendered largely ineffective by the Mavericks' swarming double- and triple-teams, Wade averaged 34.7 points and 7.8 rebounds to pick up the slack and the Finals MVP trophy. Down two games to none in the series, Miami's stunning rebound, in which they won four

Chris Broussard is a senior writer at *ESPN The Magazine.*

Miami's **Dwyane Wade** lifted his game and the Heat to another level, carrying the franchise to its first NBA championship.

straight games, was arguably the greatest comeback in Finals history.

The road to the ring was anything but smooth, though. It began with an offseason of turmoil in which Riley dropped hints that he missed coaching. He then pulled off the largest trade in NBA history, a five-team, 13-player deal that brought Antoine Walker, Jason Williams and James Posey to Miami. When he followed that by signing 37-year-old point guard Gary Payton as a free agent, speculation that Riley would soon replace coach Stan Van Gundy grew rampant.

The thinking was that Riley had—perhaps purposely—added too many egos for the successful but ring-less Van Gundy to control. Could Van Gundy get former all-star Walker to be happy as a third option behind O'Neal and Wade? Could he get the notoriously stubborn Payton to accept backing up Williams, who'd been known as a problem child himself for much of his career? Did O'Neal, who'd complained about Van Gundy's use of him in last year's playoffs, and inspirational leader Alonzo Mourning want Riley on the bench?

With rumors swirling, O'Neal out with injury, and many in Miami clamoring for Riley to take over, Van Gundy resigned in December

LA Laker **Kobe Bryant** led the NBA in scoring, thanks in part to the monster night he had against the Toronto Raptors in January 2006, scoring 81 points, the second highest total in league history.

Riley's mishmash crew was just about left for dead.

Then the transformation took place.

Inspired by Riley's battle cry of "15 Strong," a reference to the unity of the Heat's entire roster, Miami swept the next four games from New Jersey and then upset the defending Eastern Conference champion Detroit Pistons fairly easily in six games.

Still, doubt was about when the Heat met Dallas in the Finals. The young, athletic, deep and big Mavericks had upset defending champion San Antonio, and on paper, there was little reason to believe Miami could prevail. When the Mavericks won the first two games by a combined 24 points and built a 13-point fourth-quarter lead in Game 3, a four-game sweep seemed to be a strong possibility.

But Wade scored 15 in the fourth, Payton hit his only jumper of the game to break a tie with 9 seconds left, and the Heat rallied to win. Then, they took Game 4 in a blowout, Game 5 in overtime and in Game 6, they overcame a double-digit deficit on the Mavericks' home floor.

"The road to success is paved with adversity," said Mourning, whose admirable quest for a championship finally ended in success.

"We drove down that road as a team."

after the Heat trudged to an 11-10 record.

But while the returns of Riley and O'Neal brought improvement, Miami was far from a favorite when it ended the regular season at 52-30. When lightly regarded Chicago gave the Heat a scare in the first round before going down in six games and high-powered New Jersey blew Miami out in the Heat's second-round home opener,

AP/Wide World Photos

CHRIS BROUSSARD'S

10

Greatest Stories of the Year in **Pro Basketball**

10 Go West Young Team. With New Orleans devastated by Hurricane Katrina, the Hornets temporarily relocated to Oklahoma City. The move, along with the emergence of sensational rookie Chris Paul, renewed excitement in the franchise. After finishing last in attendance the previous season, the Hornets sold out 18 of their 36 games in Oklahoma City. There was just as much improvement on the court, as Paul led Coach Byron Scott's youthful club to a 20-game upgrade and near playoff berth.

09 Lighting It Up. For the first time in 24 years, three players averaged 30 or more points per game. Kobe Bryant paced everyone with a 35.4 point average, followed by Allen Iverson (33.0) and LeBron James (31.4). The last trio to do that was George Gervin, Moses Malone and Adrian Dantley in the 1981-82 season. A little perspective: in the entire decade of the '90s, Michael Jordan was the only player to average 30 or more for a season.

08 Clippin' the Script. After acquiring Sam Cassell and Cuttino Mobley in the offseason, the Los Angeles Clippers reached the playoffs for the first time since 1997. Behind their new crew and their old star, MVP candidate Elton Brand, the Clippers advanced to the second round before losing to Phoenix in seven games. It was the first time in 30 years the franchise got out of the first round.

07 Dream Job? Hailed—unofficially, of course—as the league's best coach after leading Detroit to consecutive Finals appearances, Larry Brown left for his "dream job" and roughly $11 million a year in his hometown of New York. Brown was expected to lead the talented yet chemistry-challenged Knicks to at least 40 wins, but instead the team imploded. Appearing overmatched, Brown used an inexplicable 42 different starting lineups and clashed publicly with star point guard Stephon Marbury. After the season the coach was fired.

06 Back to Back. Proving that his 2005 MVP season was no fluke, Steve Nash went out and won the award again by leading Phoenix to 54 wins despite losing superstar forward Amare Stoudemire for all but three games and star guard Joe Johnson in an offseason trade to Atlanta. Nash, only the fourth point guard ever to win the award, joined Magic Johnson as the only ones to win it more than once.

05 Goodbye and Good Riddance. The league's most controversial man, Ron Artest, repaid Indiana for supporting him through "The Malice at the Palace" by asking to be traded after hearing his name mentioned in trade rumors with Peja Stojakovic in December. After almost two months of league-wide talks and speculation, Indiana finally sent Artest to Sacramento for—guess who?—Peja Stojakovic. With his tough, defensive mentality, Artest transformed the Kings almost overnight, leading them on an improbable run to the playoffs.

04 The Little General. In his first full season as a head coach, Avery Johnson erased Dallas' longstanding and well-deserved reputation as a perennial pretender whose Achilles' Heel is softness. Heightening the focus on defense and getting superstar Dirk Nowitzki to become a more versatile offensive player, Johnson led the Mavericks to 60 wins and their first ever appearance in the NBA Finals. The Mavs' newfound toughness, both mentally and physically, was most apparent in their seven-game upset of defending champion San Antonio in the second round.

03 Blown Gasket. After running to the league's best record under first-year coach Flip Saunders and his offensive-minded approach, the Pistons stalled big time in the playoffs. No longer the defensive stalwarts they were under Larry Brown, the Pistons barely survived LeBron James and the Cleveland Cavaliers before falling to Miami in the conference finals. Finger pointing and bickering accompanied the collapse, and disgruntled team leader Ben Wallace ended up leaving after the season to play in Chicago.

02 81. In arguably the most impressive offensive performance in regular season history, Kobe Bryant scored an astounding 81 points in a 122-104 victory over Toronto on January 22. Second only to the 100 points Wilt Chamberlain scored in 1962, Bryant posted 55 after halftime to erase an 18-point third quarter deficit for the Lakers. Hitting 28 of 46 shots, including seven 3-pointers, plus 18 of 20 free throws, Bryant joined Chamberlain, David Thompson, Elgin Baylor and David Robinson as the only players to score 70 points in a game.

01 The Heat Is On. Miami's improbable championship run was a defining moment for several. Shaquille O'Neal's fourth ring was his first without Kobe Bryant and gave him one more than Tim Duncan, the only contemporary in his class. Dwyane Wade became the first of the heralded draft class of 2003 to win a title. Alonzo Mourning's career-long quest for a championship, one made tougher by a kidney transplant in 2003, ended triumphantly. And in perhaps the finest coaching job of his career, Pat Riley finally won it all without Kareem Abdul-Jabbar and Magic Johnson.

2005-2006
Season in Review

Final NBA Standings

Division champions (*) and playoff qualifiers (†) are noted. Number of seasons listed after each head coach refers to current tenure with club.

Western Conference

Northwest Div.	W	L	Pct	GB	Per Game For	Opp
*Denver	44	38	.537	—	100.3	100.1
Utah	41	41	.500	3	92.4	95.0
Seattle	35	47	.427	9	102.6	105.6
Minnesota	33	49	.402	11	91.7	93.6
Portland	21	61	.256	23	88.8	98.3

Head Coaches: Den— George Karl (2nd season); **Utah**—Jerry Sloan (18th); **Sea**—Bob Weiss (1st, 13-17) was fired and replaced by asst. Bob Hill (23-30) on Jan. 3, 2006; **Min**—Dwane Casey (1st); **Port**—Nate McMillan (1st).

Pacific Div.	W	L	Pct	GB	Per Game For	Opp
*Phoenix	54	28	.659	—	108.4	102.8
†LA Clippers	47	35	.573	7	97.2	95.6
†LA Lakers	45	37	.549	9	99.4	96.9
†Sacramento	44	38	.537	10	98.9	97.3
Golden St.	34	48	.415	20	98.5	99.8

Head Coaches: Pho—Mike D'Antoni (3rd season); **LAC**—Mike Dunleavy (3rd); **LAL**—Phil Jackson (1st); **Sac**—Rick Adelman (8th); **G.St.**—Mike Montgomery (2nd).

Southwest Div.	W	L	Pct	GB	Per Game For	Opp
*San Antonio	63	19	.768	—	95.6	88.8
†Dallas	60	22	.732	3	99.1	93.1
†Memphis	49	33	.598	14	92.2	88.5
New Orleans/ Oklahoma City	38	44	.463	25	92.8	95.6
Houston	34	48	.415	29	90.1	91.7

Head Coaches: SA—Gregg Popovich (10th season); **Dal**—Avery Johnson (2nd); **Hou**—Jeff Van Gundy (3rd); **Mem**—Mike Fratello (2nd); **NO/Okla**—Byron Scott (2nd).

Eastern Conference

Atlantic Div.	W	L	Pct	GB	Per Game For	Opp
*New Jersey	49	33	.598	—	93.8	92.4
Philadelphia	38	44	.463	11	99.4	101.3
Boston	33	49	.402	16	98.0	99.5
Toronto	27	55	.329	22	101.1	104.0
New York	23	59	.280	26	95.6	102.0

Head Coaches: NJ—Lawrence Frank (3rd season); **Phi**—Jim O'Brien (2nd); **Bos**—Doc Rivers (2nd); **Tor**—Sam Mitchell (2nd); **NY**—Larry Brown (1st).

Central Div.	W	L	Pct	GB	Per Game For	Opp
*Detroit	64	18	.780	—	96.8	90.2
†Cleveland	50	32	.610	14	97.6	95.4
†Indiana	41	41	.500	23	93.9	92.0
†Chicago	41	41	.500	23	97.8	97.2
†Milwaukee	40	42	.488	24	97.8	98.8

Head Coaches: Det—Flip Saunders (1st season); **Cle**—Mike Brown (1st); **Ind**—Rick Carlisle (3rd); **Chi**—Scott Skiles (3rd); **Mil**—Terry Stotts (1st).

Southeast Div.	W	L	Pct	GB	Per Game For	Opp
*Miami	52	30	.634	—	99.9	96.0
†Washington	42	40	.512	10	101.7	99.8
Orlando	36	46	.439	16	94.9	96.0
Charlotte	26	56	.317	26	96.9	100.9
Atlanta	26	56	.317	26	97.2	102.0

Head Coaches: Mia—Stan Van Gundy (11-10, 3rd season) resigned on Dec. 12, 2005 and was replaced by team president Pat Riley (41-20); **Wash**—Eddie Jordan (3rd); **Orl**—Brian Hill (1st). **Cha**—Bernie Bickerstaff (2nd); **Atl**—Mike Woodson (2nd).

Overall Conference Standings

Sixteen teams—eight from each conference—qualify for the NBA Playoffs; (*) indicates division champions.

Western Conference

		W	L	Home	Away	Conf	Div
1	San Antonio*	63	19	34-7	29-12	42-10	13-3
2	Phoenix*	54	28	31-10	23-18	32-20	10-6
3	Denver	44	38	26-15	18-23	25-27	10-6
4	Dallas	60	22	34-7	26-15	37-15	13-3
5	Memphis	49	33	30-11	19-22	31-21	6-10
6	LA Clippers	47	35	27-14	20-21	27-25	7-9
7	LA Lakers	45	37	27-14	18-23	27-25	9-7
8	Sacramento	44	38	27-14	17-24	30-22	10-6
	Utah	41	41	22-19	19-22	26-26	11-5
	N.O./OK City	38	44	24-17	14-27	25-27	7-9
	Seattle	35	47	22-19	13-28	20-32	10-6
	Houston	34	48	15-26	19-22	19-33	1-15
	Golden St.	34	48	21-20	13-28	19-33	4-12
	Minnesota	33	49	24-17	9-32	20-32	6-10
	Portland	21	61	15-26	6-35	10-42	3-13

Eastern Conference

		W	L	Home	Away	Conf	Div
1	Detroit*	64	18	37-4	27-14	39-13	13-3
2	Miami*	52	30	31-10	21-20	35-17	13-3
3	New Jersey*	49	33	29-12	20-21	33-19	10-6
4	Cleveland	50	32	31-10	19-22	34-18	11-5
5	Washington	42	40	27-14	15-26	29-23	8-8
6	Indiana	41	41	27-14	14-27	24-28	6-10
7	Chicago	41	41	21-20	20-21	30-22	4-12
8	Milwaukee	40	42	25-16	15-26	29-23	6-10
	Philadelphia	38	44	23-18	15-26	22-30	10-6
	Orlando	36	46	26-15	10-31	24-28	9-7
	Boston	33	49	21-20	12-29	19-33	10-6
	Toronto	27	55	15-26	12-29	20-32	6-10
	Charlotte	26	56	17-24	9-32	18-34	5-11
	Atlanta	26	56	18-23	8-33	19-33	5-11
	New York	23	59	15-26	8-33	15-37	4-12

2006 NBA All-Star Game

East, 122-120

55th NBA All-Star Game. **Date:** Feb. 19, at the Toyota Center in Houston; **Coaches:** Flip Saunders, Detroit (East) and Avery Johnson, Dallas (West); **MVP:** LeBron James, East (15 points, 9 assists, 5 steals); Starters chosen by fan vote, (Houston's Yao Ming was the leading vote-getter for the second straight season receiving 2,342,738 votes); bench chosen by conference coaches' vote.

Western Conference

Pos	Starters	Min	FG M-A	Pts	Reb	A
G	Kobe Bryant, LAL	26	4-11	8	7	8
G	Steve Nash, Pho	28	1-2	2	5	6
F	Tracy McGrady, Hou	27	15-26	36	0	2
F	Tim Duncan, SA	21	6-7	15	10	1
C	Yao Ming, Hou	19	2-5	5	2	1
	Bench					
F	Kevin Garnett, Min	16	1-9	2	9	4
F	Shawn Marion, Pho	17	5-9	14	8	0
G	Tony Parker, SA	20	3-8	8	0	4
C	Pau Gasol, Mem	14	0-3	0	12	1
F	Dirk Nowitzki, Dal	16	4-8	10	6	0
F	Elton Brand, LAC	17	6-11	12	7	0
G	Ray Allen, Sea	16	4-13	8	2	1
	TOTALS	240	51-112	120	68	28

Three-Point FG: 4-26 (McGrady 4-10, Bryant 0-5, Allen 1-7, Nowitzki 0-3, Parker 0-1); **Free Throws:** 14-24 (Marion 4-7, Duncan 3-3, McGrady 2-7, Nowitzki 2-3, Parker 2-2, Ming 1-2); **Percentages:** FG (.455), Three-Pt. FG (.154), Free Throws (.583); **Turnovers:** 23 (Duncan 5, Parker 5, Bryant 3, Brand 3, Nash 2, Garnett 2, McGrady, Gasol, Allen); **Steals:** 10 (Bryant 3, McGrady, Duncan, Ming, Nash, Garnett, Marion, Brand); **Blocked Shots:** 2 (Duncan, Marion); **Fouls:** 22 (Bryant 5, Duncan 2, Ming 2, Nash 2, Nowitzki 2, Brand 2, Allen 2, McGrady, Garnett, Marion, Parker, Gasol).

Eastern Conference

Pos	Starters	Min	FG M-A	Pts	Reb	A
G	Allen Iverson, Phi	26	5-14	12	2	2
G	Dwyane Wade, Mia	31	9-11	20	4	3
F	LeBron James, Cle	31	12-21	29	6	2
F	Vince Carter, NJ	18	2-5	5	4	2
C	Shaquille O'Neal, Mia	23	7-9	17	9	4
	Bench					
C	Ben Wallace, Det	24	0-1	0	8	2
F	Rasheed Wallace, Det	17	1-6	2	2	0
F	Chris Bosh, Tor	17	3-7	8	8	2
G	Richard Hamilton, Det	13	3-7	6	0	1
G	Gilbert Arenas, Wash.	10	0-4	1	0	1
G	Paul Pierce, Bos	15	3-6	7	2	1
G	Chauncey Billups, Det	16	6-10	15	4	7
	TOTALS	240	51-101	122	49	27

Three-Point FG: 6-21 (James 4-10, Billups 2-5, R. Wallace 0-4, Arenas 0-2); **Free Throws:** 14-28 (O'Neal 3-5, Wade 2-2, Iverson 2-4, Bosh 2-3, Carter 1-2, James 1-5, Billups 1-1, Pierce 1-2, Arenas 1-2, Wallace 0-2); **Percentages:** FG (.505), Three-Pt. FG (.286), Free Throws (.500); **Turnovers:** 16 (Wade 3, Iverson 3, Carter 2, O'Neal 2, Billups 2, Bosh, Hamilton, James, Arenas); **Steals:** 12 (B. Wallace 3, James 2, Wade 2, Carter, O'Neal, R. Wallace, Pierce, Arenas); **Blocked Shots:** 3 (B. Wallace 2, Wade); **Fouls:** 19 (O'Neal 5, Carter 3, B. Wallace 3, James 2, Wade, Bosh, Hamilton, Billups, R. Wallace, Arenas).

	1	2	3	4	F
East	28	25	41	28	122
West	28	42	27	23	120

Halftime— West, 70-53; **Third Quarter—** West, 97-94; **Technical Fouls—** none; **Officials—** #27 Dick Bavetta, #14 Joe DeRosa, #57 Greg Willard; **Attendance—** 18,652; **TV Rating—** 5.2 (TNT).

NBA 3-point Shootout

Six players are invited to compete in the annual three-point shooting contest held during All-Star Weekend, since 1986. Each shooter has 60 seconds to shoot the 25 balls in five racks outside the three-point line. Each ball is worth one point, except the last ball in each rack, which is worth two points. Highest scores advance. First prize: $35,000.

First Round	Pts
Ray Allen, Seattle	19
Gilbert Arenas, Washington	14
Dirk Nowitzki, Dallas	14
Failed to advance	**Pts**
Jason Terry, Dallas	13
Quentin Richardson, New York	12
Chauncey Billups, Detroit	12

Finals	Pts
Dirk Nowitzki	18
Gilbert Arenas	16
Ray Allen	15

Slam Dunk Contest

The Dunk contest was held annually from 1984-97 before being replaced by the 2Ball competition. It made its return in 2000. The competitors are selected based on "the creativity and artistry they have displayed in dunking" over the course of the season. The dunks are judged by five judges on a scale from six to ten. The top two scorers from the first round advance to the final round and attempt two dunks. The combined score of the two dunks determines the winner. First prize: $35,000.

First Round	Pts
Andre Iguodala, Philadelphia	95
Nate Robinson, New York	93
Failed to advance	**Pts**
Hakim Warrick, Memphis	86
Josh Smith, Atlanta	81

Finals	Score
Nate Robinson tied Andre Iguodala	94-94

Robinson won the first ever dunk-off, 47-46.

In 2007, the **NBA All-Star Weekend** is headed to **Las Vegas, Nevada** for the first time ever. As part of the deal casinos have agreed not to take any bets on the game. It will be the first time the event will be held in a non-NBA city. Looking even further ahead, the All-Star Game will return to a city that still has an NBA team (at least part-time) despite a natural catastrophe. The NBA announced that the 57th All-Star Game will be played at **New Orleans Arena** on Feb. 17, 2008. It's the first time a major sporting event has been scheduled in New Orleans in the aftermath of **Hurricane Katrina**.

LA Lakers
Kobe Bryant
Scoring

Minnesota
Kevin Garnett
Rebounding

Charlotte
Gerald Wallace
Steals

Phoenix
Steve Nash
Assists

NBA Regular Season Individual Leaders

Scoring
(*indicates rookie)

	Gm	Min	FG	FG%	3pt/Att	FT	FT%	Reb	Ast	Stl	Blk	Pts	Avg	Hi
Kobe Bryant, LAL	.80	3277	978	45.0	180/518	696	85.0	425	360	147	30	2832	35.4	81
Allen Iverson, Phi	.72	3103	815	44.7	72/223	675	81.4	232	532	140	10	2377	33.0	53
LeBron James, Cle	.79	3361	875	48.0	127/379	601	73.8	556	521	123	66	2478	31.4	52
Gilbert Arenas, Wash	.80	3384	746	44.7	199/540	655	82.0	280	484	161	25	2346	29.3	47
Dwyane Wade, Mia	.75	2892	699	49.5	13/76	629	78.3	430	503	146	58	2040	27.2	44
Paul Pierce, Bos	.79	3084	689	47.1	111/314	627	77.2	530	375	107	34	2116	26.8	50
Dirk Nowitzki, Dal	.81	3089	751	48.0	110/271	539	90.1	226	226	58	83	2151	26.6	51
Carmelo Anthony, Den	.80	2941	756	48.1	37/152	573	80.8	394	216	88	42	2122	26.5	45
Michael Redd, Milw	.80	3130	682	45.0	163/413	501	87.7	342	229	95	5	2028	25.4	43
Ray Allen, Sea	.78	3022	681	45.4	269/653	324	90.3	332	286	105	16	1955	25.1	42
Elton Brand, LAC	.79	3099	756	52.7	1/3	440	77.5	790	208	81	201	1953	24.7	44
Vince Carter, NJ	.79	2906	653	43.0	125/367	480	79.9	462	338	94	53	1911	25.2	51
Jason Richardson, G.St.	.75	2877	641	44.6	183/477	276	67.3	438	232	97	37	1741	23.2	44
Chris Bosh, Tor	.70	2751	549	50.5	0/13	474	81.6	647	181	50	79	1572	22.5	37
Shawn Marion, Pho	.81	3263	716	52.5	96/290	241	80.9	959	143	160	137	1769	21.8	44
Kevin Garnett, Min	.76	2957	626	52.6	8/30	396	81.0	966	308	104	107	1656	21.8	37
Mike Bibby, Sac	.82	3167	597	43.2	192/497	342	84.9	444	82	10	10	1728	21.1	44
Antawn Jamison, Wash	.82	3288	660	44.2	147/373	217	73.1	765	158	90	12	1684	20.5	37
Pau Gasol, Mem	.80	3135	600	50.3	3/12	425	68.9	713	371	46	153	1628	20.4	44
Mike James, Tor	.79	2925	576	46.9	169/382	283	83.7	262	460	72	3	1604	20.3	39
Chris Webber, Phi	.75	2893	617	43.4	617/1422	263	75.6	741	256	103	62	1518	20.2	34
Joe Johnson, Atl	.82	3340	632	45.3	128/360	261	79.1	335	536	103	31	1653	20.2	42
Richard Hamilton, Det	.80	2825	649	49.1	55/120	256	84.5	256	275	52	16	1609	20.1	40
Rashard Lewis, Sea	.78	2876	538	46.7	142/370	350	81.8	390	182	102	50	1568	20.1	45
Richard Jefferson, NJ	.78	3059	495	49.3	60/188	471	81.2	534	297	59	17	1521	19.5	40
Ricky Davis, Bos-Min	.78	3207	584	44.8	73/242	275	79.7	351	394	91	17	1516	19.4	35
Wally Szczerbiak, Min-Bos	72	2729	493	48.7	102/255	278	89.7	313	213	40	19	1366	19.0	34
Tony Parker, SA	.80	2715	623	54.8	11/36	253	70.7	261	460	83	4	1510	18.9	38
Steve Nash, Pho	.79	2796	541	51.2	150/342	257	92.1	333	826	61	12	1489	18.8	31
Al Harrington, Atl	.76	2782	551	45.2	66/191	243	69.4	523	238	85	14	1411	18.6	35

Rebounds

	Gm	Off	Def	Tot	Avg
Kevin Garnett, Min	.76	214	752	966	12.7
Dwight Howard, Orl	.82	288	734	1022	12.5
Shawn Marion, Pho	.81	249	710	959	11.8
Ben Wallace, Det	.82	301	622	923	11.3
Tim Duncan, SA	.80	231	650	881	11.0
Troy Murphy, G.St.	.74	195	548	743	10.0
Elton Brand, LAC	.79	236	554	790	10.0
Chris Webber, Phi	.75	184	557	741	9.9
Chris Kaman, LAC	.78	187	563	750	9.6
Jamaal Magloire, Mil	.82	220	558	778	9.5
Antawn Jamison, Wash	.82	167	598	765	9.3
Chris Bosh, Tor	.70	204	443	647	9.2
Lamar Odom, LAL	.80	181	556	737	9.2
Mehmet Okur, Utah	.82	211	535	746	9.1
Tyson Chandler, Chi	.79	265	449	714	9.0

Assists

	Gm	Ast	Avg
Steve Nash, Pho	.79	826	10.5
Baron Davis, G.St.	.54	480	8.9
Brevin Knight, Cha	.69	610	8.8
Chauncey Billups, Det	.81	699	8.6
Jason Kidd, NJ	.80	672	8.4
Andre Miller, Den	.82	674	8.2
Chris Paul*, NO/OKC	.78	611	7.8
Allen Iverson, Phi	.72	532	7.4
Luke Ridnour, Sea	.79	550	7.0
Rafer Alston, Hou	.63	425	6.7
Dwyane Wade, Mia	.75	503	6.7
LeBron James, Cle	.79	522	6.6
T.J. Ford, Milw	.72	473	6.6
Joe Johnson, Atl	.82	536	6.5
Kirk Hinrich, Chi	.81	514	6.3

Field Goal Pct.

	Gm	FG	Att	Pct
Shaquille O'Neal, Mia	.59	480	800	.600
Eddy Curry, NY	.72	336	597	.563
Tony Parker, SA	.80	623	1136	.548
Gerald Wallace, Cha	.55	317	589	.538
Andrew Bogut*, Milw	.82	323	606	.533
Dwight Howard, Orl	.82	468	881	.531
Elton Brand, LAC	.79	756	1435	.527
Boris Diaw, Pho	.81	449	853	.526
Kevin Garnett, Minn	.76	626	1191	.526
Shareef Abdur-Rahim, Sac	.72	332	632	.525

Free Throw Pct.

	Gm	FT	Att	Pct
Steve Nash, Pho	.79	257	279	.921
Peja Stojakovic, Ind-Sac	.71	238	260	.915
Ray Allen, Sea	.78	324	359	.903
Dirk Nowitzki, Dal	.81	539	598	.901
Wally Szczerbiak, Bos-Minn	.72	278	310	.897
Chauncey Billups, Det	.81	465	520	.894
Jerry Stackhouse, Dal	.55	195	221	.882
Michael Redd, Milw	.80	501	571	.877
Luke Ridnour, Sea	.79	199	227	.877
Earl Boykins, Den	.60	152	174	.874

3-Point Field Goal Pct.

	Gm	3FG	Att	Pct
Richard Hamilton, Det	.80	55	120	.458
Tyronn Lue, Atl	.51	58	127	.457
Leandro Barbosa, Pho	.57	87	196	.444
Mike James, Tor	.79	169	382	.442
Raja Bell, Pho	.79	150	342	.439
Ben Gordon, Chi	.80	166	382	.435
Chauncey Billups, Det	.81	184	425	.433
Bruce Bowen, SA	.82	104	245	.424
Jameer Nelson, Orl	.62	70	165	.424
Charile Bell, Milw	.59	71	168	.423
Matt Bonner, Tor	.78	102	243	.420

High-Point Games

	Opp	Date	FG-FT—Pts
Kobe Bryant, LAL	vs. Tor	1/22/06	28-18—81
Kobe Bryant, LAL	vs. Dal	12/20/05	18-22—62
Allen Iverson, Phi	vs. Atl	12/23/05	17-19—53
LeBron James, Cle	vs. Milw	12/10/05	19-9—52
LeBron James, Cle	vs. Utah	1/21/06	19-9—51
Dirk Nowitzki, Dal	vs. G.St	3/23/06	16-16—51
Kobe Bryant, LAL	vs. Sac	1/19/06	17-13—51
Kobe Bryant, LAL	vs. Pho	4/7/06	19-8—51
Vince Carter, NJ	vs. Mia	12/23/05	13-23—51

Blocked Shots

	Gm	Blk	Avg
Marcus Camby, Den	.56	184	3.29
Andrei Kirilenko, Utah	.69	220	3.19
Alonzo Mourning, Mia	.65	173	2.66
Josh Smith, Atl	.80	208	2.60
Elton Brand, LAC	.79	201	2.54
Samuel Dalembert, Phi	.66	160	2.42
Joel Przybilla, Port	.56	130	2.32
Jermaine O'Neal, Ind	.51	117	2.29
Ben Wallace, Det	.82	181	2.21
Eddie Griffin, Minn	.70	148	2.11

Steals

	Gm	Stl	Avg
Gerald Wallace, Cha	.55	138	2.51
Brevin Knight, Cha	.69	157	2.28
Chris Paul*, NO/OkC	.78	175	2.24
Gilbert Arenas, Wash	.80	161	2.01
Shawn Marion, Pho	.81	160	1.98
Dwyane Wade, Mia	.75	146	1.95
Allen Iverson, Phi	.72	140	1.94
Jason Kidd, NJ	.80	150	1.88
Kobe Bryant, LAL	.80	147	1.84
Ben Wallace, Det	.82	146	1.78

Rookie Leaders

Scoring

	Gm	FG	FT	Pts	Avg
Chris Paul, NO/OkC	.78	407	394	1258	16.1
Charlie Villanueva, Tor	.81	435	113	1053	13.0
Raymond Felton, Cha	.80	345	161	948	11.8
Deron Williams, Utah	.80	339	95	864	10.8
Andrew Bogut, Milw	.82	323	122	768	9.4

Field Goal Pct.

	Gm	FG	Att	Pct
Andrew Bogut, Milw	.82	323	606	.533
Channing Frye, NY	.65	305	640	.477
Charlie Villanueva, Tor	.81	435	940	.463
Chris Paul, NO/OkC	.78	407	947	.430
Deron Williams, Utah	.80	339	805	.421

Rebounds

	Gm	Off	Def	Tot	Avg
Andrew Bogut, Milw	.82	189	384	573	7.0
Charlie Villanueva, Tor	.81	181	340	521	6.4
Chris Paul, NO/OkC	.78	61	339	400	5.1
Danny Granger, Ind	.78	131	253	384	4.9
Marvin Williams, Atl	.79	122	261	383	4.8

Assists

	Gm	No	Avg
Chris Paul, NO/OkC	.78	611	7.8
Raymond Felton, Cha	.80	446	5.6
Deron Williams, Utah	.80	359	4.5
Sarunas Jasikevicius, Ind	.75	227	3.0
Jarrett Jack, Port	.79	219	2.8

Personal Fouls

Al Harrington, Atl	.301
Tyson Chandler, Chi	.298
Nenad Krstic, NJ	.297
Zaza Pachulia, Atl	.286
Gilbert Arenas, Wash	.286
Mehmet Okur, Utah	.285
Zydrunas Ilgauskas, Cle	.280
Dwight Howard, Orl	.277

Disqualifications

Tyson Chandler, Chi	.14
Samuel Dalembert, Phi	.9
Nenad Krstic, NJ	.9
Bobby Simmons, Milw	.8
Jarron Collins, Utah	.7
Jason Collins, NJ	.7
Four players tied	.6

Turnovers

Gilbert Arenas, Wash	.297
Steve Nash, Pho	.276
Paul Pierce, Bos	.273
Dwyane Wade, Mia	.268
Joe Johnson, Atl	.267
LeBron James, Cle	.260
Andre Miller, Den	.256
Kobe Bryant, LAL	.250

Triple Doubles

Jason Kidd, NJ	.8
LeBron James, Cle	.5
Boris Diaw, Pho	.4
Lamar Odom, Pho	.2
Andrei Kirilenko, Utah	.2
Chris Paul*, NO/OkC	.2
Dwyane Wade, Mia	.2
Twelve players tied	.1

Double Doubles

Kevin Garnett, Minn	.62
Shawn Marion, Pho	.60
Dwight Howard, Orl	.60
Tim Duncan, SA	.52
Elton Brand, LAC	.45
Steve Nash, Pho	.43
Chris Webber, Phi	.38
Three players tied	.35

Technical Fouls

Rasheed Wallace, Det	.19
Kobe Bryant, LAL	.15
Allen Iverson, Phi	.13
Stephen Jackson, Ind	.12
Carmelo Anthony, Den	.10
Andre Miller, Den	.10
Ruben Patterson, Den	.10
Eleven players tied	.9

Team by Team Statistics

Players who competed for more than one team during the regular season are listed with their final club; (*) indicates rookies.

Atlanta Hawks

	Gm	FG%	Tpts	PPG	RPG	APG
Joe Johnson	.82	.453	1653	20.2	4.1	6.5
Al Harrington	.76	.452	1411	18.6	6.9	3.1
Zaza Pachulia	.74	.451	911	11.7	7.9	1.7
Josh Smith	.80	.425	902	11.3	6.6	2.4
Tyronn Lue	.51	.459	560	11.0	1.6	3.1
Josh Childress	.74	.552	742	10.0	5.2	1.8
Salim Stoudamire*	.61	.415	589	9.7	1.9	1.2
Marvin Williams*	.79	.443	672	8.5	4.8	0.8
Anthony Grundy	.12	.500	52	4.3	1.4	0.8
Royal Ivey	.73	.439	260	3.6	1.3	1.0
John Edwards	.40	.484	70	1.8	1.2	0.1
Esteban Batista	.57	.425	101	1.8	2.5	0.1
Donta Smith	.23	.556	38	1.7	0.6	0.4

Triple Doubles: Johnson (1). **3-pt FG leader:** Johnson (128). **Steals leader:** Johnson (103). **Blocks leader:** Smith (208).

Signed: G Grundy (Mar. 27).

Boston Celtics

	Gm	FG%	Tpts	PPG	RPG	APG
Paul Pierce	.79	.471	2116	26.8	6.7	4.7
Wally Szczerbiak	.72	.487	1366	19.0	4.3	3.0
Delonte West	.71	.487	836	11.8	4.1	4.6
Al Jefferson	.59	.499	464	7.9	5.1	0.5
Raef LaFrentz	.82	.431	639	7.8	5.0	1.4
Ryan Gomes*	.61	.487	461	7.6	4.9	1.0
Tony Allen	.51	.471	369	7.2	2.2	1.3
Gerald Green*	.32	.478	167	5.2	1.3	0.6
Kendrick Perkins	.68	.515	354	5.2	5.9	1.0
Michael Olowokandi	.48	.446	238	5.0	4.6	0.5
Dan Dickau	.19	.370	62	3.3	0.8	2.1
Orien Greene*	.80	.395	254	3.2	1.8	1.6
Brian Scalabrine	.71	.383	205	2.9	1.6	0.7
Dwayne Jones	.14	.400	14	1.0	2.2	0.1

Triple Doubles: Pierce (1). **3-pt FG leader:** LaFrentz (112). **Steals leaders:** Pierce (107). **Blocks leader:** Perkins (105).

Acquired: F Szczerbiak, C Olowokandi, C Jones and a future first round draft pick from Minnesota for G Marcus Banks, C Mark Blount, G Ricky Davis, F Justin Reed and two conditional second round draft picks (Jan. 26).

Charlotte Bobcats

	Gm	FG%	Tpts	PPG	RPG	APG
Gerald Wallace	.55	.538	836	15.2	7.5	1.7
Emeka Okafor	.26	.415	344	13.2	10.0	1.2
Brevin Knight	.69	.399	871	12.6	3.2	8.8
Primoz Brezec	.79	.517	982	12.4	5.6	0.6
Raymond Felton*	.80	.391	948	11.9	3.3	5.6
Jumaine Jones	.76	.405	799	10.5	4.9	0.8
Kareem Rush	.47	.386	474	10.1	2.2	1.1
Melvin Ely	.57	.508	560	9.8	4.9	1.3
Sean May*	.23	.409	189	8.2	4.7	1.0
Matt Carroll	.78	.403	594	7.6	2.0	0.4
Bernard Robinson*	.66	.430	422	6.4	3.3	1.2
Alan Anderson	.36	.414	207	5.8	1.9	0.9
Jake Voskuhl	.41	.433	270	5.3	3.6	0.8
Lonny Baxter	.41	.433	118	2.9	2.9	0.1
Kevin Burleson	.39	.250	70	1.8	0.7	1.2

Triple Doubles: none. **3-pt FG leader:** Jones (115). **Steals leaders:** Knight (157). **Blocks leader:** Wallace (115).

Acquired: F Baxter from Houston for G Keith Bogans (Feb. 9).

Chicago Bulls

	Gm	FG%	Tpts	PPG	RPG	APG
Ben Gordon	.80	.422	1349	16.9	2.7	3.0
Kirk Hinrich	.81	.418	1284	15.9	3.6	6.3
Luol Deng	.78	.463	1112	14.3	6.6	1.9
Andres Nocioni	.82	.461	1063	13.0	6.1	1.4
Darius Songaila	.62	.481	568	9.2	4.0	1.4
Chris Duhon	.74	.400	647	8.7	3.0	5.0
Michael Sweetney	.66	.450	533	8.1	5.3	0.9
Tyson Chandler	.79	.565	417	5.3	9.0	1.0
Malik Allen	.54	.490	266	4.9	2.6	0.4
Jannero Pargo	.57	.373	274	4.8	1.1	1.6
Othella Harrington	.72	.495	347	4.8	2.1	0.5
Eddie Basden	.19	.405	39	2.1	1.5	0.4
Eric Piatkowski	.29	.393	59	2.0	0.8	0.4
Luke Schenscher	.20	.615	36	1.8	1.5	0.4
James Thomas	.22	.526	28	1.3	1.8	0.0
Randy Holcomb	.4	1.000	2	0.5	0.3	0.0
Randy Livingston	.5	.000	0	0.0	0.8	0.2

Triple Doubles: Duhon (1). **3-pt FG leader:** Gordon (166). **Steals leader:** Hinrich (94). **Blocks leader:** Chandler (104).

Signed: F Holcomb (Jan. 5.), F Thomas (Jan. 27), C Schenscher (Mar. 5).

Cleveland Cavaliers

	Gm	FG%	Tpts	PPG	RPG	APG
LeBron James	.79	.480	2478	31.4	7.0	6.6
Zydrunas Ilgauskas	.78	.506	1217	15.6	7.6	1.2
Larry Hughes	.36	.409	558	15.5	4.5	3.6
Ronald Murray	.76	.418	851	11.2	2.0	2.6
Drew Gooden	.79	.512	845	10.7	8.4	0.7
Donyell Marshall	.81	.395	750	9.3	6.1	0.7
Damon Jones	.82	.387	552	6.7	1.6	2.1
Eric Snow	.82	.409	391	4.8	2.4	4.2
Anderson Varejao	.48	.527	219	4.6	4.9	0.4
Aleksandar Pavlovic	.53	.410	241	4.5	1.5	0.5
Stephen Graham	.22	.389	58	2.6	1.2	0.3
Luke Jackson	.36	.341	96	2.7	1.1	0.7
Alan Henderson	.51	.516	127	2.5	2.7	0.2
Ira Newble	.36	.298	48	1.3	1.6	0.3
M. Andriuskevicius	.6	.000	0	0.0	0.7	0.0

Triple Doubles: James (5). **3-pt FG leader:** Jones (140). **Steals leader:** James (123). **Blocks leader:** Ilgauskas (136).

Signed: F Graham (Feb. 6).

Dallas Mavericks

	Gm	FG%	Tpts	PPG	RPG	APG
Dirk Nowitzki	.81	.480	2151	26.6	9.0	2.8
Jason Terry	.80	.474	1371	17.1	2.0	3.8
Josh Howard	.59	.471	923	15.6	6.3	1.9
Jerry Stackhouse	.55	.401	715	13.0	2.8	2.9
Marquis Daniels	.62	.480	634	10.2	3.6	2.8
Devin Harris	.56	.469	554	9.9	2.2	3.2
Keith Van Horn	.53	.424	472	8.9	3.6	0.7
Erick Dampier	.82	.493	469	5.7	7.8	0.6
Adrian Griffin	.52	.480	237	4.6	4.4	1.7
Doug Christie	.7	.346	26	3.7	1.9	2.0
Rawle Marshall	.23	.400	71	3.1	1.3	0.4
Josh Powell	.37	.457	110	3.0	2.2	0.2
Pavel Podkolzin	.1	.000	3	3.0	7.0	0.0
DeSagana Diop	.81	.487	190	2.3	4.6	0.3
Darrell Armstrong	.62	.336	130	2.1	1.3	1.4
Didier Illunga-Mbenga	43	.533	74	1.7	1.3	0.0

Triple Doubles: none. **3-pt FG leader:** Terry (171). **Steals leader:** Terry (100). **Blocks leader:** Diop (146).

Denver Nuggets

	Gm	FG%	Tpts	PPG	RPG	APG
Carmelo Anthony	..80	.481	2122	26.5	4.9	2.7
Andre Miller	..82	.463	1126	13.7	4.3	8.2
Kenyon Martin	56	.495	720	12.9	6.3	1.4
Marcus Camby	56	.465	716	12.8	11.9	2.1
Earl Boykins	60	.410	756	12.6	1.4	3.8
Ruben Patterson	...71	.515	858	12.1	3.4	1.8
Greg Buckner	73	.434	491	6.7	2.9	1.7
DerMarr Johnson	..58	.431	354	6.1	1.7	0.9
Reggie Evans	67	.489	135	5.6	7.5	0.6
Eduardo Najera	...64	.422	347	5.4	5.1	0.8
Francisco Elson	72	.532	352	4.9	4.7	0.7
Charles Smith	22	.417	80	3.6	0.7	0.4
Howard Eisley	...32	.330	101	3.2	1.0	2.2
Linas Kleiza	.61	.445	213	3.2	1.9	0.2
Julius Hodge*	14	.385	13	0.9	0.5	0.4
Nene	1	.000	0	0.0	0.0	0.0

Triple Doubles: none. **3-pt FG leader:** Buckner (86).
Steals leader: Miller (106). **Blocks leader:** Camby (184).
Acquired: F Patterson and F Smith from Portland for G Voshon Lenard (Feb. 23); F Evans from Seattle for G Earl Watson, F Byron Russell and a second round draft pick.
Signed: G Eisley (Mar. 3).

Detroit Pistons

	Gm	FG%	Tpts	PPG	RPG	APG
Richard Hamilton	..80	.491	1609	20.1	3.2	3.4
Chauncey Billups	...81	.418	1495	18.5	3.1	8.6
Rasheed Wallace	..80	.430	1209	15.1	6.8	2.3
Tayshaun Prince	..82	.455	1156	14.1	4.2	2.3
Antonio McDyess	..82	.509	638	7.8	5.3	1.1
Tony Delk	24	.441	182	7.6	2.2	1.4
Ben Wallace	82	.510	597	7.3	11.3	1.9
Amir Johnson*	3	.700	20	6.7	1.3	1.0
Maurice Evans	80	.452	403	5.0	2.0	0.8
Carlos Delfino	..68	.403	247	3.6	1.7	0.6
Kelvin Cato	27	.429	98	3.6	2.6	0.1
Lindsey Hunter	...30	.370	87	2.9	1.3	2.1
Jason Maxiell*	..26	.426	60	2.3	1.1	0.1
Alex Acker*	5	.250	9	1.8	1.0	0.8
Dale Davis	28	.375	26	0.9	1.9	0.2

Triple Doubles: none. **3-pt FG leader:** Billups (165).
Steals leader: Wallace (106). **Blocks leader:** Wallace (176).
Acquired: C Cato and a 2006 first round draft pick from Orlando for F Darko Milicic and G Carlos Arroyo.
Signed: G Delk (Mar. 1).

Golden St. Warriors

	Gm	FG%	Tpts	PPG	RPG	APG
Jason Richardson	...75	.673	1741	23.2	5.8	3.1
Baron Davis	54	.389	967	17.9	4.4	8.9
Troy Murphy	74	.433	1035	14.0	10.0	1.4
Derek Fisher	82	.410	1089	13.3	2.6	4.3
Mike Dunleavy	81	.406	932	11.5	4.9	2.9
Mickael Pietrus	82	.404	481	9.3	3.1	0.8
Ike Diogu	69	.524	486	7.0	3.3	0.4
Monta Ellis*	49	.415	334	6.8	2.1	1.6
Adonal Foyle	77	.507	345	4.5	5.5	0.4
Andris Biedrins	...68	.638	258	3.8	4.2	0.4
Will Bynum	15	.404	54	3.6	0.8	1.3
Zarko Cabarkapa	...61	.385	199	3.3	1.8	0.3
Chris Taft*	17	.605	47	2.8	2.1	0.1
Calbert Cheaney	...42	.389	92	2.2	1.5	0.5
Aaron Miles	19	.333	16	0.8	0.7	1.3

Triple Doubles: Davis (1). **3-pt FG leader:** Richardson (125). **Steals leader:** Richardson (105). **Blocks leader:** Foyle (159).
Signed: G Bynum (Mar. 27).

Houston Rockets

	Gm	FG%	Tpts	PPG	RPG	APG
Tracy McGrady	47	.406	1147	24.4	6.5	4.8
Yao Ming	57	.519	1271	22.3	10.2	1.5
Rafer Alston	63	.379	761	12.1	4.0	6.7
Juwan Howard	80	.459	942	11.8	6.7	1.4
David Wesley	71	.403	702	9.9	2.5	2.9
Stromile Swift	66	.491	586	8.9	4.4	0.4
Luther Head*	80	.403	707	8.8	3.3	2.7
Keith Bogans	72	.395	622	8.6	3.5	1.8
Jon Barry	20	.385	86	4.3	1.6	1.3
Richie Frahm	33	.390	108	3.3	1.0	0.6
Chuck Hayes	40	.562	147	3.7	4.5	0.4
Dikembe Mutombo	..64	.526	169	2.6	4.8	0.1
John Lucas III	13	.389	30	2.3	0.4	0.9
Rick Brunson	27	.389	54	2.0	0.8	1.3
Ryan Bowen	68	.298	88	1.3	1.3	0.4
Maciej Lampe	6	.182	4	0.7	1.5	0.3

Triple Doubles: none. **3-pt FG leader:** Head (113).
Steals leader: Alston (101). **Blocks leader:** Ming (94).
Acquired: G Bogans from Charlotte for F Lonny Baxter (Feb. 9); C Lampe from New Orleans/Oklahoma City for G Moochie Norris (Feb. 13).
Signed: F Davis (Dec. 29), F Lucas (Jan. 8), F Hayes (Jan. 28).

Indiana Pacers

	Gm	FG%	Tpts	PPG	RPG	APG
Jermaine O'Neal	...51	.472	1024	20.1	9.3	2.6
Peja Stojakovic	...71	.437	1290	18.2	5.8	1.9
Stephen Jackson	...81	.411	1329	16.4	3.9	2.8
Fred Jones	68	.417	651	9.6	2.5	2.3
Jamaal Tinsley	42	.409	390	9.3	3.2	5.0
Anthony Johnson	..75	.443	691	9.2	2.2	4.3
Austin Croshere	...50	.463	408	8.2	5.3	1.2
Danny Granger*	...78	.462	587	7.5	4.9	1.2
Sarunas Jasikevicius*	75	.396	547	7.3	2.0	3.0
Jeff Foster	63	.552	372	5.9	9.1	0.8
David Harrison	...67	.503	385	5.7	3.8	0.2
Jonathan Bender	...2	.800	10	5.0	2.0	1.0
Scot Pollard	45	.455	169	3.8	4.8	0.5
Eddie Gill	41	.222	45	1.1	0.4	0.3
Samaki Walker	7	.000	2	0.3	0.4	0.0

Triple Doubles: none. **3-pt FG leader:** Stojakovic (162).
Steals leader: Jackson (104). **Blocks leader:** O'Neal (117).
Acquired: F Peja Stojakovic from Sacramento for F Ron Artest (Jan. 25).

Los Angeles Clippers

	Gm	FG%	Tpts	PPG	RPG	APG
Elton Brand	79	.527	1953	24.7	10.0	2.6
Corey Maggette	..32	.445	570	17.8	5.3	2.1
Sam Cassell	78	.443	1345	17.2	3.7	6.3
Cuttino Mobley	...79	.426	1170	14.8	4.3	3.0
Chris Kaman	78	.523	932	11.9	9.6	1.0
Vladimir Radmanovic	77	.407	755	9.8	4.6	1.8
Shaun Livingston	...61	.427	352	5.8	3.0	4.5
Quinton Ross	67	.422	317	4.7	2.5	1.2
Zeljko Rebraca	...29	.542	135	4.7	2.2	0.3
Daniel Ewing*	...66	.380	252	3.8	1.3	1.3
Vin Baker	8	.467	27	3.4	2.4	0.5
James Singleton	...59	.510	203	3.4	3.3	0.5
Walter McCarty	...36	.333	88	2.4	1.9	0.6
Boniface Ndong	...23	.415	50	2.2	1.6	0.3
Yaroslav Korolev	...24	.300	27	1.1	0.5	0.4
Anthony Goldwire	...3	.143	2	0.7	0.3	0.7

Triple Doubles: none. **3-pt FG leader:** Radmanovic (138). **Steals leader:** Mobley (93). **Blocks leader:** Brand (201).

Los Angeles Lakers

	Gm	FG%	Tpts	PPG	RPG	APG
Kobe Bryant	80	.450	2832	35.4	5.3	4.5
Lamar Odom	80	.481	1186	14.8	9.2	5.5
Smush Parker	82	.447	941	11.5	3.3	3.7
Chris Mihm	59	.501	604	10.2	6.3	1.0
Brian Cook	81	.511	642	7.9	3.4	0.9
Kwame Brown	72	.526	536	7.4	6.6	1.0
Devean George	71	.400	448	6.3	3.9	1.0
Luke Walton	69	.412	345	5.0	3.6	2.3
Laron Profit	25	.476	104	4.2	1.7	0.6
Sasha Vujacic	82	.346	321	3.9	1.9	1.7
Jim Jackson	40	.294	121	3.0	1.9	0.9
Ronny Turiaf*	23	.500	45	2.0	1.6	0.3
Andrew Bynum*	46	.402	74	1.6	1.7	0.2
Von Wafer*	16	.158	20	1.3	0.5	0.3
Slava Medvedenko	2	.500	2	1.0	0.0	0.5
Devin Green	27	.214	25	0.9	0.9	0.3
Aaron McKie	14	.250	7	0.5	1.4	0.8

Triple Doubles: Odom (2). **3-pt FG leader:** Bryant (180). **Steals leader:** Bryant (147). **Blocks leader:** Mihm (73).
Signed: G Jackson (Mar. 6).

Memphis Grizzlies

	Gm	FG%	Tpts	PPG	RPG	APG
Pau Gasol	80	.503	1628	20.4	8.9	4.6
Mike Miller	74	.466	1014	13.7	5.4	2.7
Eddie Jones	75	.404	885	11.8	3.7	2.4
Damon Stoudamire	27	.397	317	11.7	3.5	4.7
Bobby Jackson	71	.382	808	11.4	3.1	2.7
Shane Battier	81	.488	818	10.1	5.3	1.7
Chucky Atkins	71	.394	678	9.5	1.7	2.8
Lorenzen Wright	78	.478	454	5.8	5.1	0.6
Jake Tsakalidis	51	.606	257	5.0	4.2	0.3
Hakim Warrick*	68	.443	278	4.1	2.1	0.4
Dahntay Jones	71	.414	281	4.0	1.5	0.5
Brian Cardinal	36	.414	124	3.4	1.5	0.9
Anthony Roberson	16	.452	35	2.2	0.4	0.3
Antonio Burks	57	.354	113	2.0	0.6	1.3
Lawrence Roberts	33	.455	51	1.5	1.5	0.2

Triple Doubles: Gasol and Miller (1). **3-pt FG leader:** Miller (138). **Steals leader:** Jones (131). **Blocks leader:** Gasol (153).
Signed: G Atkins (Jan. 23).

Miami Heat

	Gm	FG%	Tpts	PPG	RPG	APG
Dwyane Wade	75	.495	2040	27.2	5.7	6.7
Shaquille O'Neal	59	.600	1181	20.0	9.2	1.9
Jason Williams	59	.442	728	12.3	2.4	4.9
Antoine Walker	82	.435	1000	12.2	5.1	2.0
Udonis Haslem	81	.508	757	9.3	7.8	1.2
Alonzo Mourning	65	.597	509	7.8	5.5	0.2
Gary Payton	81	.420	626	7.7	2.9	3.2
James Posey	67	.403	483	7.2	4.8	1.3
Derek Anderson	43	.356	349	8.1	3.3	2.3
Jason Kapono	51	.446	207	4.1	1.4	0.7
Wayne Simien*	43	.483	146	3.4	2.0	0.2
Michael Doleac	31	.420	98	3.2	2.7	0.3
Dorell Wright	20	.465	58	2.9	1.6	0.4
Shandon Anderson	48	.429	126	2.6	1.7	0.6
Earl Barron	8	.313	13	1.6	1.3	0.0
Matt Walsh	2	1.000	2	1.0	0.0	0.0

Triple Doubles: Wade (2), O'Neal (1). **3-pt FG leader:** Walker (137). **Steals leader:** Wade (146). **Blocks leader:** Mourning (173).

Milwaukee Bucks

	Gm	FG%	Tpts	PPG	RPG	APG
Michael Redd	80	.450	2028	25.4	4.3	2.9
Bobby Simmons	75	.453	1002	13.4	4.4	2.3
T.J. Ford	72	.416	878	12.2	4.3	6.6
Maurice Williams	58	.424	703	12.1	2.5	4.0
Andrew Bogut*	82	.533	768	9.4	7.0	2.3
Jamaal Magloire	82	.467	752	9.2	9.5	0.7
Joe Smith	44	.475	379	8.6	5.2	0.7
Charlie Bell	59	.439	494	8.4	2.0	2.2
Dan Gadzuric	74	.553	383	5.2	3.1	0.3
Toni Kukoc	65	.389	317	4.9	2.3	2.1
Jiri Welsch	58	.387	251	4.3	1.9	1.1
Jermaine Jackson	30	.423	35	1.2	0.9	0.8
Reece Gaines	12	.500	13	1.1	0.0	0.3
Ervin Johnson	18	.412	15	0.8	1.3	0.1

Triple Doubles: Bell (1). **3-pt FG leader:** Redd (163).
Steals leader: Ford (104). **Blocks leader:** Magliore (80).
Signed: G Jackson (Dec. 15).

Minnesota Timberwolves

	Gm	FG%	Tpts	PPG	RPG	APG
Kevin Garnett	76	.526	1656	21.8	12.7	4.1
Ricky Davis	78	.448	1516	19.4	4.5	5.1
Mark Blount	81	.508	914	11.3	4.5	1.2
Marcus Banks	58	.468	578	10.0	2.3	3.8
Troy Hudson	36	.381	342	9.5	1.2	2.9
Trenton Hassell	77	.464	710	9.2	2.8	2.6
Bracey Wright	7	.412	62	8.9	2.6	0.7
Rashad McCants*	79	.450	627	7.9	1.8	0.8
Marko Jaric	75	.399	587	7.8	3.1	3.9
Eddie Griffin	70	.351	320	4.6	5.6	0.6
Justin Reed	72	.403	325	4.5	1.7	0.6
Anthony Carter	45	.387	150	3.3	1.4	2.2
Ronald Dupree	36	.524	80	2.2	1.4	0.4
Mark Madsen	62	.409	74	1.2	1.5	2.3

Triple Doubles: Garnett (1). **3-pt FG leader:** Davis (73). **Steals leader:** Jaric (108). **Blocks leader:** Griffin (148).

New Jersey Nets

	Gm	FG%	Tpts	PPG	RPG	APG
Vince Carter	79	.430	1911	24.2	5.8	4.3
Richard Jefferson	78	.493	1521	19.5	6.8	3.8
Nenad Krstic	80	.507	1080	13.5	6.4	1.1
Jason Kidd	80	.404	1065	13.3	7.3	8.4
Clifford Robinson	80	.427	550	6.9	3.3	1.1
Jeff McInnis	28	.441	149	5.3	1.8	1.9
Bostjan Nachbar	36	.346	157	4.4	1.7	0.8
Jason Collins	71	.397	255	3.6	4.8	1.0
Lamond Murray	57	.398	196	3.4	2.3	0.2
Scott Padgett	62	.353	211	3.4	2.3	0.2
Jacque Vaughn	80	.437	274	3.4	1.1	1.5
Zoran Planinic	56	.361	191	3.4	1.3	0.9
Derrick Zimmerman	2	.667	4	2.0	2.0	3.5
Antoine Wright*	39	.358	70	1.8	0.8	0.3
John Thomas	16	.400	15	0.9	1.3	0.1

Triple Doubles: Kidd (8), Carter (1). **3-pt FG leader:** Kidd (139).
Steals leader: Kidd (150). **Blocks leaders:** Krstic (63).
Acquired: F Nachbar from New Orleans/Oklahoma City for F Marc Jackson and F Linton Johnson III (Feb. 23).

NBA Points+Rebounds+Assists Leaders

	PPG	RPG	APG	Avg
Kobe Bryant, LAL	35.4	5.3	4.5	45.2
LeBron James, Cle	31.4	7.0	6.6	45.0
Allen Iverson, Phi	33.0	3.2	7.4	43.6
Dwyane Wade, Mia	27.2	5.7	6.7	39.6
Gilbert Arenas, Wash	29.3	3.5	6.1	38.9
Kevin Garnett, Min	21.8	12.7	4.1	38.6

New Orleans/Oklahoma City Hornets

	Gm	FG%	Tpts	PPG	RPG	APG
David West	.74	.512	1262	17.1	7.4	1.2
Chris Paul*	.78	.430	1258	16.1	5.1	7.8
Speedy Claxton	.71	.413	871	12.3	2.7	4.8
Desmond Mason	.70	.399	757	10.8	4.3	0.9
P.J. Brown	.75	.461	677	9.0	7.3	1.2
Rasual Butler	.79	.406	685	8.7	2.9	0.5
Kirk Snyder	.68	.453	542	8.0	2.4	1.5
J.R. Smith	.55	.393	423	7.7	2.0	1.1
Marcus Fizer	.3	.529	20	6.7	2.3	0.3
Marc Jackson	.64	.472	415	6.5	3.4	0.7
Chris Andersen	.32	.571	161	5.0	4.8	0.2
Aaron Williams	.48	.517	222	4.6	3.8	0.4
Linton Johnson III	.36	.409	153	4.3	3.4	0.4
Moochie Norris	.45	.411	125	2.8	1.2	1.1
Brandon Bass*	.29	.400	68	2.3	2.3	0.1
Arvydas Macijauskas	19	.341	44	2.3	0.5	0.3
Jackson Vroman	.41	.394	73	1.8	2.1	0.3

Triple Doubles: Paul (2). **3-pt FG leader:** Butler (92).
Steals leader: Paul (175). **Blocks leader:** West (64).
Acquired: C Williams from Toronto for a 2006 and 2009 second round draft pick (Feb. 3); G Norris from Houston for C Maciej Lampe (Feb. 13); F Jackson and F Johnson from New Jersey for F Bostjan Nachbar (Feb. 23).
Signed: F Fizer (Apr. 1).

New York Knicks

	Gm	FG%	Tpts	PPG	RPG	APG
Stephon Marbury	.60	.451	977	16.3	2.9	6.4
Steve Francis	.70	.435	1005	14.4	4.1	4.9
Jamal Crawford	.79	.416	1128	14.3	3.1	3.8
Eddy Curry	.72	.563	979	13.6	6.0	0.3
Jalen Rose	.72	.423	887	12.3	2.9	2.5
Channing Frye*	.65	.477	802	12.3	5.8	0.8
Nate Robinson*	.72	.407	670	9.3	2.3	2.0
Quentin Richardson	.55	.355	451	8.2	4.2	1.6
Qyntel Woods	.49	.508	329	6.7	3.9	1.0
Maurice Taylor	.67	.468	422	6.3	3.4	0.8
Jackie Butler	.55	.544	292	5.3	3.3	0.5
David Lee	.67	.596	345	5.1	4.5	0.6
Malik Rose	.72	.474	318	4.4	3.6	0.9
Jerome James	.44	.463	137	3.1	2.1	0.8
Ime Udoka	.8	.375	22	2.8	2.1	0.8

Triple Doubles: none. **3-pt FG leader:** Crawford (101).
Steals leader: Marbury (63). **Blocks leader:** Curry (56).
Acquired: G Francis from Orlando for F Trevor Ariza and G Anfernee Hardaway.
Signed: F/G Woods (Dec. 6); G/F Udoka (Apr. 6).

Orlando Magic

	Gm	FG%	Tpts	PPG	RPG	APG
Dwight Howard	.82	.531	1292	15.8	12.5	1.5
Grant Hill	.21	.490	318	15.1	3.8	2.3
Hedo Turkoglu	.78	.454	1165	14.9	4.3	2.8
Jameer Nelson	.62	.483	905	14.6	2.9	4.9
DeShawn Stevenson	.82	.460	900	11.0	2.9	2.0
Keyon Dooling	.50	.440	470	9.4	1.6	2.2
Tony Battie	.82	.507	649	7.9	5.6	0.6
Carlos Arroyo	.77	.444	449	5.8	1.7	3.0
Pat Garrity	.57	.417	282	4.9	1.9	0.7
Darko Milicic	.55	.509	266	4.8	2.7	0.7
Trevor Ariza	.57	.412	264	4.6	3.8	1.1
Travis Diener*	.23	.420	88	3.8	0.9	0.7
Mario Kasun	.28	.449	80	2.9	2.1	0.1
Bo Outlaw	.32	.603	75	2.3	2.4	0.4
Stacey Augmon	.36	.342	71	2.0	1.5	0.6
Terence Morris	.22	.327	35	1.6	1.7	0.2

Triple Doubles: Steve Francis (1). **3-pt FG leader:** Turkoglu (114). **Steals leader:** Turkoglu and Nelson (70).
Blocks leader: Howard (115).
Acquired: F Ariza and G Anfernee Hardaway from New York for G Steve Francis.

Philadelphia 76ers

	Gm	FG%	Tpts	PPG	RPG	APG
Allen Iverson	.72	.447	2377	33.0	3.2	7.4
Chris Webber	.75	.434	1518	20.2	9.9	3.4
Andre Iguodala	.82	.500	1007	12.3	5.9	3.1
Kyle Korver	.82	.430	939	11.5	3.3	2.0
John Salmons	.82	.420	619	7.5	2.7	2.7
Samuel Dalembert	.66	.531	485	7.3	8.2	0.4
Willie Green	.10	.424	70	7.0	1.5	0.5
Steven Hunter	.69	.601	421	6.1	3.9	0.2
Lee Nailon	.22	.500	93	4.2	1.9	0.3
Matt Barnes	.56	.500	175	3.1	2.2	0.5
Kevin Ollie	.70	.431	192	2.7	1.4	1.4
Shavlik Randolph*	.57	.454	131	2.3	2.3	0.3
Zendon Hamilton	.12	.500	26	2.2	0.9	0.0
Louis Williams*	.30	.442	56	1.9	0.6	0.3
Michael Bradley	.46	.405	67	1.5	2.3	0.4
Deng Gai	.2	.000	0	0.0	0.0	0.0

Triple Doubles: none. **3-pt FG leader:** Korver (184).
Steals leader: Iverson (140). **Blocks leader:** Dalembert (160). **Signed:** C Hamilton (Feb. 2).

Phoenix Suns

	Gm	FG%	Tpts	PPG	RPG	APG
Shawn Marion	.81	.525	1769	21.8	11.8	1.8
Steve Nash	.79	.512	1489	18.8	4.2	10.5
Raja Bell	.79	.457	1162	14.7	3.2	2.6
Boris Diaw	.81	.526	1080	13.3	6.9	6.2
Leandro Barbosa	.57	.481	744	13.1	2.6	2.8
Tim Thomas	.29	.431	300	10.3	4.5	0.7
Eddie House	.81	.422	796	9.8	1.6	1.8
James Jones	.75	.418	699	9.3	3.4	0.8
Amare Stoudemire	.3	.333	26	8.7	5.3	0.7
Kurt Thomas	.53	.486	455	8.6	7.8	1.1
Pat Burke	.42	.496	141	3.4	1.7	0.4
Brian Grant	.21	.415	61	2.9	2.7	0.3
Dijon Thompson*	.10	.440	28	2.8	1.1	0.1
Nikoloz Tskitishvili	.17	.351	36	2.1	1.3	0.2
Sharrod Ford	.3	.667	4	1.3	1.0	0.0
Josh Davis	.6	.286	6	1.0	0.7	0.2

Triple Doubles: Diaw (4), Nash (1). **3-pt FG leader:** Bell (197). **Steals leader:** Marion (160). **Blocks leader:** Marion (137).
Signed: F Davis (Jan. 9). **Acquired:** F Tskitishvili from Minnesota for a 2006 second round draft pick (Jan. 26).

Portland Trail Blazers

	Gm	FG%	Tpts	PPG	RPG	APG
Zach Randolph	.74	.436	1333	18.0	8.0	1.9
Darius Miles	.40	.461	559	14.0	4.6	1.8
Juan Dixon	.76	.435	935	12.3	2.3	2.0
Sebastian Telfair	.68	.394	643	9.5	1.8	3.6
Steve Blake	.68	.438	560	8.2	2.1	4.5
Voshon Lenard	.26	.393	191	7.3	1.8	1.6
Jarrett Jack*	.79	.442	526	6.7	2.0	2.8
Martell Webster*	.61	.399	404	6.6	2.1	0.6
Joel Przybilla	.56	.548	344	6.1	7.0	0.8
Travis Outlaw	.69	.440	400	5.8	2.7	0.5
Viktor Khryapa	.69	.462	403	5.8	4.4	1.3
Theo Ratliff	.55	.571	270	4.9	5.1	0.5
Brian Skinner	.65	.513	191	2.9	3.5	0.5
Ha Seung-Jin	.27	.581	44	1.6	1.8	0.0

Triple Doubles: none. **3-pt FG leader:** Blake (76).
Steals leader: Telfair (66). **Blocks leader:** Przybilla (130).
Acquired: G Lenard from Denver for F Ruben Patterson and F Charles Smith (Feb. 23); F Skinner from Sacramento for C Vitaly Potapenko and F Segei Monia (Feb. 23).

Sacramento Kings

	Gm	FG%	Tpts	PPG	RPG	APG
Mike Bibby	82	.432	1728	21.1	2.9	5.4
Ron Artest	56	.404	984	17.6	5.1	3.6
Brad Miller	79	.495	1182	15.0	7.8	4.7
Bonzi Wells	52	.463	707	13.6	7.7	2.8
Shareef Abdur-Rahim	72	.525	887	12.3	5.0	2.1
Kevin Martin	72	.480	778	10.8	3.6	1.3
Kenny Thomas	82	.505	748	9.1	7.5	2.0
Francisco Garcia*	67	.400	377	5.6	2.8	1.4
Corliss Williamson	37	.417	126	3.4	1.8	0.4
Jason Hart	66	.389	218	3.3	1.1	1.1
Sergei Monia	26	.333	77	3.0	2.0	0.7
Vitaly Potapenko	33	.521	84	2.5	1.9	0.3
Ronnie Price	29	.362	60	2.1	0.5	0.4
Jamal Sampson	12	.714	10	0.8	1.5	0.4

Triple Doubles: Thomas (1). **3-pt FG leader:** Bibby (192). **Steals leader:** Artests (122). **Blocks leader:** Miller (62).
Acquired: C Potapenko and F Monia from Portland for F Brian Skinner (Feb. 23).

San Antonio Spurs

	Gm	FG%	Tpts	PPG	RPG	APG
Tony Parker	80	.548	1510	18.9	3.3	5.8
Tim Duncan	80	.484	1485	18.6	11.0	3.2
Manu Ginobili	65	.462	981	15.1	3.5	3.6
Michael Finley	77	.412	780	10.1	3.2	1.5
Bruce Bowen	82	.433	619	7.5	3.9	1.5
Nazr Mohammed	80	.504	493	6.2	5.2	0.5
Brent Barry	74	.452	435	5.8	2.1	1.7
Nick Van Exel	65	.397	355	5.5	1.4	1.9
Beno Udrih	54	.455	275	5.1	1.0	1.7
Robery Horry	63	.384	321	5.1	3.8	1.3
Rasho Nesterovic	80	.515	362	4.5	3.9	0.4
Sean Marks	25	.521	81	3.2	1.7	0.3
Melvin Sanders	16	.485	41	2.6	1.4	0.2
Alex Scales	1	.000	0	0.0	0.0	0.0

Triple Doubles: none. **3-pt FG leader:** Finley (110).
Steals leader: Ginobili (101). **Blocks leader:** Duncan (162).
Signed: G Sanders (Nov. 10).

Seattle Supersonics

	Gm	FG%	Tpts	PPG	RPG	APG
Ray Allen	78	.454	1955	25.1	4.3	3.7
Rashard Lewis	78	.467	1568	20.1	5.0	2.3
Luke Ridnour	79	.418	910	11.5	3.0	7.0
Earl Watson	70	.430	623	8.9	2.3	4.1
Chris Wilcox	77	.571	626	8.1	5.3	0.7
Nick Collison	66	.525	493	7.5	5.6	1.1
Damien Wilkins	82	.444	536	6.5	2.3	1.3
Robert Swift	47	.515	301	6.4	5.6	0.2
Johan Petro	68	.510	353	5.2	4.4	0.2
Danny Fortson	23	.529	87	3.8	3.4	0.1
Mikki Moore	47	.435	154	3.3	2.8	0.6
Mateen Cleaves	27	.352	73	2.7	0.5	1.6
Mike Wilks	47	.322	86	1.8	0.8	0.7
Noel Felix	12	.240	18	1.5	1.1	0.2

Triple Doubles: none. **3-pt FG leader:** Allen (269).
Steals leader: Ridnour (123). **Blocks leader:** Swift (56).
Acquired: G Watson, F Byron Russell and a second round draft pick from Denver for F Reggie Evans.
Signed: F Felix (Mar. 13).

Toronto Raptors

	Gm	FG%	Tpts	PPG	RPG	APG
Chris Bosh	70	.505	1572	22.5	9.2	2.6
Mike James	79	.469	1604	20.3	3.3	5.8
Morris Peterson	82	.436	1374	16.8	4.6	2.3
Charlie Villanueva*	81	.463	1053	13.0	6.4	1.1
Matt Bonner	78	.448	583	7.5	3.6	0.7
Joey Graham*	80	.478	533	6.7	3.1	0.8
Jose Calderon	64	.423	349	5.5	2.2	4.5
Antonio Davis	44	.432	35	4.9	4.7	0.5
Andre Barrett	19	.365	87	4.6	1.3	2.7
Pape Sow	42	.431	147	3.5	3.5	0.2
Eric Williams	28	.387	91	3.3	1.8	0.5
Darrick Martin	40	.351	102	2.6	0.5	1.4
Loren Woods	27	.475	62	2.3	4.1	0.1
Rafael Araujo	52	.366	121	2.3	2.8	0.3
Alvin Williams	1	.000	1	1.0	3.0	1.0

Triple Doubles: none. **3-pt FG leader:** Peterson (177).
Steals leader: Peterson (104). **Blocks leader:** Bosh (79).
Acquired: F. Davis from New York for G Jalen Rose, a 2006 first round draft pick and chas. (Feb. 3).
Signed: G Martin (Nov. 16), G Barrett (Mar. 25).

Utah Jazz

	Gm	FG%	Tpts	PPG	RPG	APG
Mehmet Okur	82	.460	1472	18.0	9.1	2.4
Carlos Boozer	33	.549	537	16.3	8.6	2.7
Andrei Kirilenko	69	.460	1054	15.3	8.0	4.3
Matt Harpring	71	.475	885	12.5	5.2	1.4
Deron Williams	80	.421	864	10.8	2.4	4.5
Gordan Giricek	37	.433	393	10.6	1.9	1.7
Devin Brown	81	.393	611	7.5	2.6	1.3
Milt Palacio	71	.424	441	6.2	1.9	2.7
Keith McLeod	66	.353	370	5.6	1.2	2.3
Jarron Collins	79	.461	415	5.3	4.2	1.2
C.J. Miles*	23	.368	79	3.4	1.7	0.7
Andre Owens	23	.365	69	3.0	0.9	0.3
Kris Humphries	62	.379	188	3.0	2.5	0.5
Greg Ostertag	60	.492	146	2.4	3.8	1.0
Robert Whaley*	23	.404	49	2.1	1.9	0.7

Triple Doubles: Kirilenko (2). **3-pt FG leader:** Williams (91). **Steals leader:** Kirilenko (102). **Blocks leader:** Kirilenko (220).

Washington Wizards

	Gm	FG%	Tpts	PPG	RPG	APG
Gilbert Arenas	80	.447	2346	29.3	3.5	6.1
Antawn Jamison	82	.442	1684	20.5	9.3	1.9
Caron Butler	75	.455	1318	17.6	6.2	2.5
Antonio Davis	80	.418	767	9.6	2.2	3.6
Jarvis Hayes	21	.421	196	9.3	3.6	1.3
Brendan Haywood	79	.514	575	7.3	5.9	0.6
Jared Jeffries	77	.451	489	6.4	4.9	1.9
Etan Thomas	71	.533	337	4.7	3.9	0.2
Donell Taylor	51	.390	140	2.7	1.0	0.9
Billy Thomas	17	.325	38	2.2	0.8	0.5
Andray Blatche*	29	.388	65	2.2	1.3	0.3
Awvee Storey	25	.390	43	1.7	0.9	0.2
Calvin Booth	33	.426	46	1.4	1.6	0.4
Michael Ruffin	76	.442	105	1.4	3.6	0.4

Triple Doubles: none. **3-pt FG leader:** Arenas (199).
Steals leader: Arenas (161). **Blocks leader:** Haywood (104).
Signed: G Thomas (Feb. 24).

NBA Regular Season Team Leaders

OFFENSE

WEST	—Per Game— Pts	Reb	Ast	FG%	3Pt%	FT%
Phoenix	108.4	41.8	26.6	.479	.399	.806
Seattle	102.6	39.6	20.7	.459	.371	.785
Denver	100.3	41.3	23.4	.461	.325	.744
LA Lakers	99.4	42.2	21.1	.453	.349	.745
Dallas	99.1	42.2	18.0	.462	.374	.783
Sacramento	98.9	40.5	22.3	.454	.351	.784
Golden St.	98.5	42.3	20.7	.433	.341	.718
LA Clippers	97.2	43.1	20.8	.464	.344	.791
San Antonio	95.6	41.5	20.9	.472	.385	.702
N.O./Okla. City	92.8	40.2	18.5	.440	.339	.758
Utah	92.4	42.1	21.6	.442	.336	.719
Memphis	92.2	39.2	19.3	.448	.374	.711
Minnesota	91.7	39.4	20.9	.456	.329	.758
Houston	90.1	41.6	19.3	.433	.332	759
Portland	88.8	37.7	18.2	.445	.349	.689

EAST	—Per Game— Pts	Reb	Ast	FG%	3Pt%	FT%
Washington	101.7	41.2	18.6	.447	.357	.785
Toronto	101.1	38.5	19.4	.454	.375	.791
Miami	99.9	43.1	20.6	.478	.345	.700
Philadelphia	99.4	40.2	20.2	.458	.364	.760
Boston	98.0	39.6	20.9	.467	.362	.755
Chicago	97.8	42.8	22.0	.446	.379	.738
Milwaukee	97.8	41.2	21.6	.453	.380	.738
Cleveland	97.6	42.3	19.0	.454	.339	.729
Atlanta	97.2	40.3	19.8	.454	.367	.750
Charlotte	96.9	39.8	20.9	.433	.339	.729
Detroit	96.8	40.5	24.0	.455	.384	.727
New York	95.6	41.4	17.9	.455	.362	.726
Orlando	94.9	40.2	18.2	.472	.376	.730
Indiana	93.9	42.2	19.9	.444	.349	.737
New Jersey	93.8	41.0	23.0	.440	.330	.758

DEFENSE

WEST	—Per Game— Pts	Reb	Ast	FG%	3Pt%	FT%
Memphis	88.5	39.2	19.6	.436	.334	.754
San Antonio	88.8	41.5	16.3	.436	.334	.754
Houston	91.7	41.6	20.1	.429	.369	.731
Dallas	93.1	42.2	17.5	.443	.361	.752
Minnesota	93.6	39.4	19.0	.441	.364	.736
Utah	95.0	42.1	18.4	.449	.378	.746
N.O./Okla. City	95.6	40.2	19.3	.459	.367	.760
LA Clippers	95.6	43.1	21.5	.435	.347	.732
LA Lakers	96.9	42.2	21.1	.450	.353	.747
Sacramento	97.3	40.5	21.1	.454	.351	.747
Portland	98.3	37.7	21.2	.469	.381	.760
Golden State	99.8	42.3	22.3	.457	.351	.743
Denver	100.1	41.3	23.9	.454	.358	.736
Phoenix	102.8	41.8	18.9	.454	.363	.731
Seattle	105.6	39.6	24.1	.485	.375	.760

EAST	—Per Game— Pts	Reb	Ast	FG%	3Pt%	FT%
Detroit	90.2	40.5	18.8	.452	.325	.736
Indiana	92.0	42.2	18.5	.435	.343	.734
New Jersey	92.4	41.0	20.0	.439	.348	.741
Cleveland	95.4	42.3	20.3	.455	.356	.742
Orlando	96.0	40.2	20.0	.454	.357	.732
Miami	96.0	43.1	19.5	.440	.361	.739
Chicago	97.2	42.8	20.1	.426	.351	.777
Milwaukee	98.8	41.2	22.5	.466	.354	.747
Boston	99.5	39.6	21.5	.456	.353	.743
Washington	99.8	41.2	21.5	.465	.363	.745
Charlotte	100.9	39.8	22.9	.478	.356	.737
Philadelphia	101.3	40.2	23.0	.463	.351	.762
Atlanta	102.0	40.3	20.6	.478	.368	.745
New York	102.0	41.4	21.3	.467	.378	.753
Toronto	104.0	38.5	23.6	.491	.373	.748

Playoff Series Summaries

WESTERN CONFERENCE

FIRST ROUND (Best of 7)

(1) San Antonio Spurs 4, (8) Sacramento Kings 2

Date	Winner	Home Court
Apr. 22	Spurs, 122-88	at San Antonio
Apr. 25	Spurs, 128-119 OT	at San Antonio
Apr. 28	Kings, 94-93	at Sacramento
Apr. 30	Kings, 102-84	at Sacramento
May 2	Spurs, 109-98	at San Antonio
May 5	Spurs, 105-83	at Sacramento

(2) Phoenix Suns 4, (7) LA Lakers 3

Date	Winner	Home Court
Apr. 23	Suns, 107-102	at Phoenix
Apr. 26	Lakers, 99-93	at Phoenix
Apr. 28	Lakers, 99-92	at Los Angeles
Apr. 30	Lakers, 99-98 OT	at Los Angeles
May 2	Suns, 114-97	at Phoenix
May 4	Suns 126-118 OT	at Los Angeles
May 6	Suns, 121-90	at Phoenix

(6) LA Clippers 4, (3) Denver Nuggets 1

Date	Winner	Home Court
Apr. 22	Clippers, 89-87	at Los Angeles
Apr. 24	Clippers, 98-87	at Los Angeles
Apr. 27	Nuggets, 94-87	at Denver
Apr. 29	Clippers, 100-86	at Los Angeles
May 1	Clippers, 101-83	at Los Angeles

(4) Dallas Mavericks 4, (5) Memphis Grizzlies 0

Date	Winner	Home Court
Apr. 23	Mavericks, 103-93	at Dallas
Apr. 26	Mavericks, 94-79	at Dallas
Apr. 29	Mavericks, 94-89	at Memphis
May 1	Mavericks, 102-76	at Memphis

SEMIFINALS (Best of 7)

(4) Dallas Mavericks 4, (1) San Antonio Spurs 3

Date	Winner	Home Court
May 7	Spurs, 87-85	at San Antonio
May 9	Mavericks, 113-91	at San Antonio
May 13	Mavericks, 104-103	at Dallas
May 15	Mavericks, 123-118 OT	at Dallas
May 17	Spurs, 98-97	at San Antonio
May 19	Spurs, 91-86	at Dallas
May 22	Mavericks, 119-111 OT	at San Antonio

(2) Phoenix Suns 4, (6) LA Clippers 3

Date	Winner	Home Court
May 8	Suns, 130-123	at Phoenix
May 10	Clippers, 122-97	at Phoenix
May 12	Suns, 94-91	at Los Angeles
May 14	Clippers, 114-107	at Los Angeles
May 16	Suns, 125-118 2 OT	at Phoenix
May 18	Clippers, 118-106	at Los Angeles
May 22	Suns, 127-107	at Phoenix

CHAMPIONSHIP (Best of 7)

(4) Dallas Mavericks 4, (2) Phoenix Suns 2

Date	Winner	Home Court
May 24	Suns, 121-118	at Dallas
May 26	Mavericks, 105-98	at Dallas
May 28	Mavericks, 95-88	at Phoenix
May 30	Suns, 106-86	at Phoenix
June 1	Mavericks, 117-101	at Dallas
June 3	Mavericks, 102-93	at Phoenix

2006 NBA PLAYOFFS

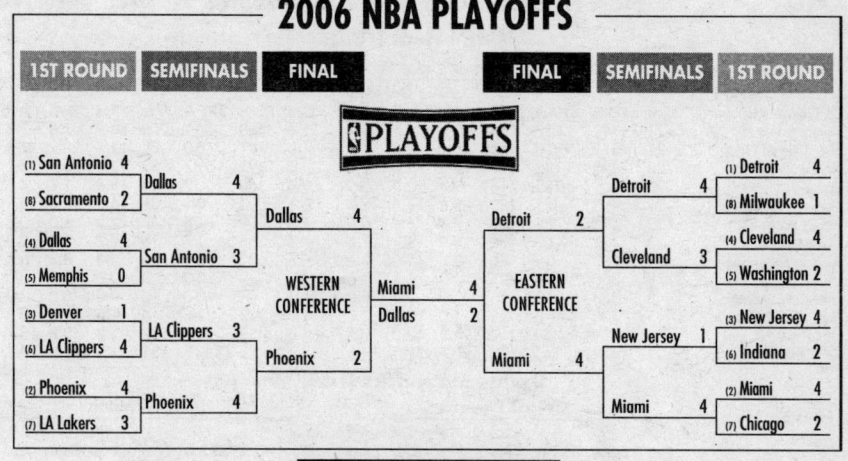

| 1ST ROUND | SEMIFINALS | FINAL | | FINAL | SEMIFINALS | 1ST ROUND |

PLAYOFFS

(1) San Antonio 4
(8) Sacramento 2
Dallas 4

(4) Dallas 4
(5) Memphis 0
San Antonio 3

Dallas 4

(3) Denver 1
(6) LA Clippers 4
LA Clippers 3

(2) Phoenix 4
(7) LA Lakers 3
Phoenix 4

Phoenix 2

WESTERN CONFERENCE

Miami 4
Dallas 2

Detroit 2

Detroit 4
Cleveland 3

New Jersey 1

Miami 4

EASTERN CONFERENCE

(1) Detroit 4
(8) Milwaukee 1

(4) Cleveland 4
(5) Washington 2

(3) New Jersey 4
(6) Indiana 2

(2) Miami 4
(7) Chicago 2

Detroit 4

Cleveland 3

New Jersey 1

Miami 4

EASTERN CONFERENCE

FIRST ROUND (Best of 7)

(1) Detroit Pistons 4, (8) Milwaukee Bucks 1

Date	Winner	Home Court
Apr. 23	Pistons, 92-74	at Detroit
Apr. 26	Pistons, 109-98	at Detroit
Apr. 29	Bucks, 124-104	at Milwaukee
May 1	Pistons, 109-99	at Milwaukee
May 3	Pistons, 122-93	at Detroit

(3) New Jersey Nets 4, (6) Indiana Pacers 2

Date	Winner	Home Court
Apr. 23	Pacers, 90-88	at New Jersey
Apr. 25	Nets, 90-75	at New Jersey
Apr. 27	Pacers, 107-95	at Indiana
Apr. 29	Nets, 97-88	at Indiana
May 2	Nets, 92-86	at New Jersey
May 4	Nets, 96-90	at Indiana

(2) Miami Heat 4, (7) Chicago Bulls 2

Date	Winner	Home Court
Apr. 22	Heat, 111-106	at Miami
Apr. 24	Heat, 115-108	at Miami
Apr. 27	Bulls, 109-90	at Chicago
Apr. 30	Bulls, 93-87	at Chicago
May 2	Heat, 92-78	at Miami
May 4	Heat, 113-96	at Chicago

(4) Cleveland Cavaliers 4, (5) Wash. Wizards 2

Date	Winner	Home Court
Apr. 22	Cavaliers, 97-86	at Cleveland
Apr. 25	Wizards, 89-84	at Cleveland
Apr. 28	Cavaliers, 97-96	at Washington
Apr. 30	Wizards, 106-96	at Washington
May 3	Cavaliers, 121-120 OT	at Cleveland
May 5	Cavaliers, 114-113 OT	at Washington

SEMIFINALS (Best of 7)

(1) Detroit Pistons 4, (4) Cleveland Cavaliers 3

Date	Winner	Home Court
May 7	Pistons, 113-86	at Detroit
May 9	Pistons, 97-91	at Detroit
May 13	Cavaliers, 86-77	at Cleveland
May 15	Cavaliers, 74-72	at Cleveland
May 17	Cavaliers, 86-84	at Detroit
May 19	Pistons, 84-82	at Cleveland
May 21	Pistons, 79-61	at Detroit

(2) Miami Heat 4, (3) New Jersey Nets 1

Date	Winner	Home Court
May 8	Nets, 100-88	at Miami
May 10	Heat, 111-89	at Miami
May 12	Heat, 103-92	at New Jersey
May 14	Heat, 102-92	at New Jersey
May 16	Heat, 106-105	at Miami

CHAMPIONSHIP (Best of 7)

(2) Miami Heat 4, (1) Detroit Pistons 2

Date	Winner	Home Court
May 23	Heat, 91-86	at Detroit
May 25	Pistons, 92-88	at Detroit
May 27	Heat, 98-83	at Miami
May 29	Heat, 89-78	at Miami
May 31	Pistons, 91-78	at Detroit
June 2	Heat, 95-78	at Miami

The Finals

NBA FINALS (Best of 7)

	W-L	Avg.	Leading Scorer
Dallas	2-4	91.8	D. Nowitzki (22.8)
Miami	4-2	92.8	D. Wade (34.7)

Date	Winner	Home Court
June 8	Mavericks, 90-80	at Dallas
June 11	Mavericks, 99-85	at Dallas
June 13	Heat, 98-96	at Miami
June 15	Heat, 98-74	at Miami
June 18	Heat, 101-100 OT	at Miami
June 20	Heat, 95-92	at Dallas

Finals MVP

Dwyane Wade, Miami, G
34.7 ppg, 7.8 rpg, 3.8 apg, 2.7 spg

NBA Finalists' Composite Box Scores
Miami Heat (16-7)

		Overall Playoffs			—Per Game—					Finals vs. Dallas			—Per Game—		
(3 Game Min.)	Gm	FG%	3PT-A	TPts	Pts	Reb	Ast	Gm	FG%	3PT-A	TPts	Pts	Reb	Ast
Dwyane Wade	23	.497	14-37	654	28.4	5.9	5.7	6	.468	3-11	208	34.7	7.8	3.8
Shaquille O'Neal	23	.612	0-0	424	18.4	9.8	1.7	6	.607	0-0	82	13.7	10.2	2.8
Antoine Walker	23	.403	48-148	307	13.3	5.6	2.4	6	.391	10-37	83	13.8	5.5	2.2
Jason Williams	23	.405	26-95	214	9.3	2.0	3.9	6	.360	10-29	53	8.8	1.8	4.7
Udonis Haslem	22	.493	0-1	189	8.6	7.4	0.8	6	.500	0-0	39	6.5	6.2	0.3
James Posey	22	.430	35-83	160	7.3	5.7	0.9	6	.419	8-20	44	7.3	6.0	0.3
Gary Payton	23	.422	17-58	133	5.8	1.7	1.6	6	.368	1-7	16	2.7	2.0	2.0
Alonzo Mourning	21	.703	0-0	80	3.8	2.9	0.1	6	.692	0-0	26	4.3	3.2	0.0
Derek Anderson	8	.300	5-14	24	3.0	1.1	0.6	0	—	0-0	0	0.0	0.0	0.0
Michael Doleac	8	.538	0-0	16	2.0	2.8	0.0	1	—	0-0	0	0.0	0.0	0.0
Shandon Anderson	13	.308	1-3	13	1.0	0.9	0.3	4	.333	2-6	6	1.5	1.8	0.8
HEAT	23	.481	146-439	2214	96.3	42.0	17.5	6	.458	32-105	557	92.8	43.8	16.7
OPPONENTS	23	.429	143-441	2127	92.5	39.1	17.5	6	.422	33-116	551	91.8	41.8	15.8

Dallas Mavericks (14-9)

		Overall Playoffs			—Per Game—					Finals vs. Miami			—Per Game—		
	Gm	FG%	3PT-A	TPts	Pts	Reb	Ast	Gm	FG%	3PT-A	TPts	Pts	Reb	Ast
Dirk Nowitzki	23	.468	23-67	620	27.0	11.7	2.9	6	.390	6-24	137	22.8	10.8	2.5
Jason Terry	22	.442	31-101	416	18.9	2.9	3.8	6	.478	13-41	132	22.0	2.2	3.5
Josh Howard	23	.453	24-65	384	16.7	7.4	1.4	6	.388	5-19	88	14.7	8.2	1.8
Jerry Stackhouse	22	.402	22-65	302	13.7	2.8	2.5	6	.355	7-19	64	12.8	3.4	3.0
Devin Harris	23	.480	0-8	216	9.4	1.7	2.2	6	.364	0-3	44	7.3	0.8	2.8
Erick Dampier	19	.540	0-1	95	5.0	6.7	0.3	6	.722	0-0	34	5.7	8.2	0.3
Adrian Griffin	20	.542	0-0	71	3.6	3.6	1.2	6	.563	0-0	18	3.0	3.2	0.8
Keith Van Horn	14	.339	8-28	51	3.6	2.3	0.1	5	.273	1-6	7	1.4	1.2	0.0
Marquis Daniels	20	.446	2-5	68	3.4	1.1	1.3	6	.545	1-3	17	2.8	0.5	1.3
DeSagana Diop	22	.615	0-0	59	2.7	5.0	0.1	6	.500	0-0	10	1.7	3.3	0.2
Darrell Armstrong	11	.200	0-7	8	0.7	0.6	0.2	1	.000	0-1	0	0.0	1.0	0.0
Didier Ilunga-Mbenga	7	.333	0-0	4	0.6	1.1	0.0	2	—	0-0	0	0.0	1.0	0.0
Josh Powell	6	.000	0-0	0	0.0	0.3	0.2	1	.000	0-0	0	0.0	1.0	0.0
MAVERICKS	23	.451	110-347	2294	99.7	42.7	15.3	6	.422	33-116	551	91.8	41.8	15.8
OPPONENTS	23	.470	122-354	2200	95.7	38.3	16.1	6	.458	32-105	557	92.8	43.8	16.7

NBA Playoff Leaders

Scoring Average

	Gm	FG	FT	Pts	Avg
Gilbert Arenas, Wash	6	65	54	204	34.0
LeBron James, Cle	13	146	87	400	30.8
Vince Carter, NJ	11	113	86	326	29.6
Dwyane Wade, Mia	23	219	202	654	28.4
Kobe Bryant, LAL	7	72	37	195	27.9
Michael Redd, Mllw	5	44	41	136	27.2
Dirk Nowitzki, Dal	23	196	205	620	27.0
Tin Duncan, SA	13	121	94	336	25.8
Elton Brand, LAC	12	124	57	305	25.4
Bonzi Wells, Sac	6	53	28	139	23.2

Total Points

	Gm	FG	FT	Pts	Avg
Dwyane Wade, Mia	23	219	202	654	28.4
Dirk Nowitzki, Dal	23	196	205	620	27.0
Shaquille O'Neal, Mia.	23	178	68	424	18.4
Jason Terry, Dal	22	163	59	416	18.9
Shawn Marion, Pho	20	163	59	407	20.4
Steve Nash, Pho	20	146	83	407	20.4

Rebounds

	Gm	Off	Def	Tot	Avg
Bonzi Wells, Sac	6	25	47	72	12.0
Dirk Nowitzki, Dal	23	47	221	268	11.7
Shawn Marion, Pho	20	57	176	233	11.6
Marcus Camby, Den	5	13	42	55	11.0
Lamar Odom, LAL	7	15	62	77	11.0

Assists

	Gm	No	Avg
Steve Nash, Pho	20	204	10.2
Jason Kidd, NJ	11	106	9.6
Kirk Hinrich, Chi	6	46	7.7
Andre Miller, Den	5	36	7.2
Chauncey Billups, Det	18	117	6.5

Final Playoff Standings

ranked by victories

	Gm	W	L	Pct	Per Game For	Opp
Miami Heat	23	16	7	.697	96.3	92.5
Dallas Mavericks	23	14	9	.609	99.7	95.7
Detroit Pistons	18	10	8	.556	91.7	88.5
Phoenix Suns	20	10	10	.500	107.2	106.0
Cleveland	13	7	6	.538	90.4	92.5
San Antonio	13	7	6	.538	103.1	100.8
LA Clippers	12	7	5	.583	105.7	101.9
New Jersey	11	5	6	.455	94.2	95.1
LA Lakers	7	3	4	.429	100.6	107.3
Washington	6	2	4	.333	101.7	101.5
Chicago	6	2	4	.333	98.3	101.3
Sacramento	6	2	4	.333	97.3	106.8
Indiana	6	2	4	.333	89.3	93.0
Denver	5	2	4	.333	87.4	95.0
Memphis	4	0	4	.000	84.3	98.3

Annual Awards

Most Valuable Player

The Maurice Podoloff Trophy; voting by 125-member panel of local and national pro basketball writers and broadcasters. Each ballot has five entries; points awarded on 10-7-5-3-1 basis.

	1st	2nd	3rd	4th	5th	Pts
Steve Nash, Phoenix	.57	32	20	8	6	924
LeBron James, Cleveland	.16	41	33	23	7	688
Dirk Nowitzki, Dallas	.14	22	25	36	17	544
Kobe Bryant, LA Lakers	.22	11	18	22	30	483
Chauncey Billups, Detroit	.15	13	22	18	25	430
Dwyane Wade, Miami	.0	3	4	9	19	87
Elton Brand, LA Clippers	.1	1	2	3	14	50
Tim Duncan, San Antonio	.0	2	0	6	1	33
Tony Parker, San Antonio	.0	0	1	0	4	9
Allen Iverson, Philadelphia	.0	0	0	0	1	1
Shawn Marion, Phoenix	.0	0	0	0	1	1

All-NBA Teams

Voting by a 126-member panel of local and national pro basketball writers and broadcasters. Each ballot has entries for three teams; points awarded on 5-3-1 basis. First Team repeaters from 2004-05 are in **bold** type.

Pos	First Team	1st	Pts
F	LeBron James, Cleveland	.116	610
F	Dirk Nowitzki, Dallas	.107	584
C	**Shaquille O'Neal**, Miami	.45	402
G	Kobe Bryant, LA Lakers	.110	597
G	Steve Nash, Phoenix	.106	583

Pos	Second Team	1st	Pts
F	Tim Duncan, San Antonio	.17	277
F	Elton Brand, LA Clippers	.15	309
C	Ben Wallace, Detroit	.44	263
G	Dwyane Wade, Miami	.13	373
G	Chauncey Billups, Detroit	.21	378

Pos	Third Team	1st	Pts
F	Carmelo Anthony, Denver	.0	97
F	Shawn Marion, Phoenix	.4	270
C	Yao Ming, Houston	.30	261
G	Allen Iverson, Philadelphia	.1	104
G	Gilbert Arenas, Washington	.0	79

Other players receiving votes: Kevin Garnett, Minn., 94; Tony Parker, SA, 66; Pau Gasol, Mem., 49; Vince Carter, NJ, 47; Paul Pierce, Bos., 29; Jason Kidd, NJ, 20; Dwight Howard, Orl., 11; Marcus Camby, Den., 9; Richard Hamilton, Det., 9; Rasheed Wallace, Det., 8; Zydrunas Ilgauskas, Cleveland, 5; Nenad Krsitc, NJ, 5; Ray Allen, Sea., 4; Mehmet Okur, Utah, 4; Michael Redd, Milw., 4; Brad Miller, Sac., 3; Joe Johnson, Atl., 2; Sam Cassell, LAC, 2; Mike Bibby, Sac., 1; Chris Bosh, Tor., 1; Boris Diaw, Phoenix, 1; Antawn Jamison, Wash., 1; Andrei Kirilenko, Utah, 1; Chris Kaman, LAC, 1; Chris Paul, NO/Okla. City, 1.

Rookie of the Year

The Eddie Gottlieb Trophy; voting by 125-member panel of local and national pro basketball writers and broadcasters. Each ballot has entries for three players; points awarded on 5-3-1 basis.

	1st	2nd	3rd	Pts
Chris Paul, NO/Okla. City	.124	1	0	623
Charlie Villanueva, Toronto	.0	73	29	248
Andrew Bogut, Milwaukee	.0	23	29	98
Raymond Felton, Charlotte	.0	19	22	79
Channing Frye, New York	.0	4	29	41
Deron Williams, Utah	.1	5	11	31
Luther Head, Houston	.0	0	2	2
Danny Granger, Indiana	.0	0	2	2
Ryan Gomes, Boston	.0	0	1	1

All-Defensive Teams

Voting by NBA head coaches. Each ballot has entries for two teams; two points given for 1st team, one for 2nd. Coaches cannot vote for own players. First Team repeaters from 2004-05 are in **bold** type.

Pos	First Team	1st	Pts
F	Andrei Kirilenko, Utah	.19	44
F	Ron Artest, Sacramento	.11	30
C	**Ben Wallace**, Detroit	.26	54
G	**Bruce Bowen**, San Antonio	.26	55
G	Jason Kidd, New Jersey	.9	28
G	Kobe Bryant, LA Lakers	.12	28

Pos	Second Team	1st	Pts
F	Tim Duncan, San Antonio	.7	23
F	Kevin Garnett, Minnesota	.4	10
F	Tayshaun Prince, Detroit	.3	13
C	Marcus Camby, Denver	.2	15
G	Chauncey Billups, Detroit	.7	23

Coach of the Year

The Red Auerbach Trophy; voting by a 124-member panel of local and national pro basketball writers and broadcasters.

Top Vote-getters	1st	2nd	3rd	Pts
Avery Johnson, Dallas	.63	29	17	419
Mike D'Antoni, Phoenix	.27	31	19	247
Flip Saunders, Detroit	.18	36	25	223
Mike Dunleavy, LA Clippers	.5	15	18	88
Byron Scott, NO/Okla. City	.7	3	13	57
Gregg Popovich, San Antonio	.2	3	6	25
Phil Jackson, LA Clippers	.1	1	5	13
Mike Brown, Cleveland	.1	0	4	9
Lawrence Frank, New Jersey	.0	2	2	8
Scott Skiles, Chicago	.0	2	2	8

All-Rookie Team

Voting by NBA's 30 head coaches, who cannot vote for players on their team. Each ballot has entries for two five-man teams, regardless of position; Coaches are not permitted to vote for players on their own team. two points given for 1st team, one for 2nd. First team votes in parentheses.

First Team	College	Pts
Chris Paul, NO/Okla. City (29)	Wake Forest	58
Charlie Villanueva, Toronto (27)	Connecticut	56
Andrew Bogut, Milwaukee (26)	Utah	55
Deron Williams, Utah (18)	Illinois	46
Channing Frye, New York (17)	Arizona	45

Second Team	College	Pts
Danny Granger, Indiana (14)	New Mexico	43
Raymond Felton, Charlotte (14)	North Carolina	40
Luther Head, Houston (4)	Illinois	28
Marvin Williams, Atlanta	North Carolina	15
Ryan Gomes, Boston	Providence	14

Other players receiving votes: Sarunas Jasikevicius, Ind., 12; Ike Diogu, G. St., 8; Nate Robinson, NY, 7; Rashad McCants, Minn., 6; Johan Petro, Sea., 6; Jose Calderon, Tor. 3; Jarrett Jack, Port., 3; Joey Graham, Tor., 2; Martell Webster, Port., 2; Salim Stoudamire, Atl., 1

J. Walter Kennedy Citizenship Award

The award, named for the NBA's second commissioner, is presented annually by the Professional Basketball Writers Association to honor an NBA player or coach "for outstanding community service and commitment to serve and give of his time outside the arena." The five finalists this season were Garnett, Ron Artest of the Sacramento Kings, Chauncey Billups of the Detroit Pistons, Steve Nash of the Phoenix Suns and Michael Redd of the Milwaukee Bucks.

Kevin Garnett, Minnesota

Sixth-Man Award

Voted on by a 123-member panel of local and national pro basketball writers and broadcasters. Each ballot has entries for three players; points awarded on 5-3-1 basis.

	1st	2nd	3rd	Pts
Mike Miller, Memphis	88	18	7	501
Speedy Claxton, NO/Okla. City	14	38	21	205
Jerry Stackhouse, Dallas	12	25	27	162
Antonio McDyess, Detroit	5	12	16	77
Earl Boykins, Denver	0	7	13	34
Alonzo Mourning, Miami	1	6	4	27
Leandro Barbosa, Phoenix	1	3	10	24
Mo Williams, Milwaukee	1	3	5	19
Michael Finley, San Antonio	0	2	4	10

Most Improved Player Award

Voted on by a 124-member panel of local and national pro basketball writers and broadcasters. Each ballot has entries for three players; points awarded on 5-3-1 basis.

	1st	2nd	3rd	Pts
Boris Diaw, Phoenix	80	28	5	489
David West, NO/Okla. City	22	52	17	283
Nenad Krstic, New Jersey	4	12	9	65
Gerald Wallace, Charlotte	3	6	13	46
Chris Bosh, Toronto	3	6	10	43
Andres Nocioni, Chicago	4	1	6	29
Tony Parker, San Antonio	3	2	8	29
Mike James, Toronto	1	4	4	21
Carmelo Anthony, Denver	2	1	6	19
Jameer Nelson, Orlando	1	1	10	18

Defensive Player of the Year Award

Voted on by a 124-member panel of local and national pro basketball writers and broadcasters.

Top Vote-getters	1st	2nd	3rd	Pts
Ben Wallace, Detroit	58	39	13	420
Bruce Bowen, San Antonio	38	33	19	308
Andrei Kirilenko, Utah	12	11	28	121
Ron Artest, Sacramento	6	7	14	65
Marcus Camby, Denver	3	9	13	55
Tim Duncan, San Antonio	3	7	6	42
Shawn Marion, Phoenix	0	7	12	33
Alonzo Mourning, Miami	4	2	3	29
Gerald Wallace, Charlotte	0	7	6	27

Sportsmanship Award

Each of the 30 NBA teams nominated one player from their roster "who best represents the ideals of sportsmanship on the court," then a panel of former NBA players (John Crotty, John Celestand, Eddie Johnson, Steve Mix and Kenny Smith) selected the six divisional winners from the pool of nominees. The award winner is chosen from the divisional winners in vote by a panel of local and national pro basketball writers and broadcasters. The winner receives the Joe Dumars Trophy, named for the Detroit Pistons guard who won the inaugural sportsmanship award in 1996.

	1st	2nd	3rd	4th	5th	6th	Pts
Elton Brand, LAC	83	84	52	38	28	19	2326
Shaquille O'Neal, Mia	73	62	58	34	33	44	2080
Yao Ming, Hou	34	41	60	56	61	52	1678
Jacque Vaughn, NJ	48	41	46	44	56	69	1676
Luol Deng, Chi	34	42	42	60	60	66	1592
Andrei Kirilenko, Utah	32	34	46	72	66	54	1592

2006 College Draft

First and second round picks at the 60th annual NBA Draft held June 28, 2006 held in New York City at the Theatre at Madison Square Garden. The order of the first 14 positions were determined by a Draft Lottery held May 23, in Secaucus, N.J. Positions 15 through 30 reflect regular season records in reverse order. Underclassmen are listed in CAPITAL letters.

First Round

	Team		Pos
1	Toronto	Andrea Bargnani, Italy	F
2	Chicago	LaMARCUS ALDRIDGE, Texas	F
3	Charlotte	ADAM MORRISON, Gonzaga	F
4	Portland	TYRUS THOMAS, LSU	F
5	Atlanta	Shelden Williams, Duke	F
6	Minnesota	Brandon Roy, Washington	G
7	Boston	Randy Foye, Villanova	G
8	Houston	RUDY GAY, Connecticut	F
9	Golden State	PATRICK O'BRYANT, Bradley	C
10	Seattle	Saer Sene, Senegal	F
11	Orlando	J.J. Redick, Duke	G
12	NO/Okla. City	Hilton Armstrong, UConn	C
13	Philadelphia	Thabo Sefolosha, Switzerland	G
14	Utah	RONNIE BREWER, Arkansas	G
15	NO/Okla. City	Cedric Simmons, N.C. State	F
16	Chicago	Rodney Carney, Memphis	F
17	Indiana	SHAWNE WILLIAMS, Memphis	F
18	Washington	Oleksiy Pecherov, Ukraine	C
19	Sacramento	QUINCY DOUBY, Rutgers	G
20	New York	RENALDO BALKMAN, So. Carolina	F
21	Phoenix	Rajon Rondo, Kentucky	G
22	New Jersey	MARCUS WILLIAMS, Connecticut	G
23	New Jersey	Josh Boone, Connecticut	F
24	Memphis	KYLE LOWRY, Villanova	G
25	Cleveland	Shannon Brown, Mich. St.	G
26	LA Lakers	JORDAN FARMAR, UCLA	G
27	Phoenix	Sergio Rodriguez, Spain	G
28	Dallas	Maurice Ager, Michigan St.	G
29	New York	Mardy Collins, Temple	G
30	Portland	Joel Freeland, United Kingdom	F

Second Round

	Team		Pos
31	Portland	James White, Cincinnati	G
32	Houston	Steve Novak, Marquette	F
33	Atlanta	Solomon Jones, South Florida	F
34	LA Clippers	Paul Davis, Michigan St.	C
35	Toronto	P.J. TUCKER, Texas	F
36	Minnesota	Craig Smith, Boston College	F
37	Minnesota	Bobby Jones, Washington	F
38	Golden St.	Kosta Perovic, Serbia	F
39	Milwaukee	David Noel, North Carolina	F
40	Seattle	Denham Brown, Connecticut	G
41	Orlando	James Augustine, Illinois	F
42	Cleveland	DANIEL GIBSON, Texas	G
43	NO/Okla. City	Marcus Vinicius, Brazil	F
44	Orlando	Lior Eliyahu, Israel	F
45	Indiana	Alexander Johnson, Florida St.	F
46	Utah	Dee Brown, Illinois	G
47	Utah	PAUL MILLSAP, La. Tech	F
48	Washington	Vladimir Veremeenko, Belarus	F
49	Denver	Leon Powe, California	F
50	Charlotte	Ryan Hollins, UCLA	C
51	LA Lakers	Cheick Samb, Senegal	C
52	LA Clippers	GUILLERMO DIAZ, Miami	G
53	Seattle	Yotam Halperin, Israel	G
54	New Jersey	Hassan Adams, Arizona	G
55	Cleveland	Ejike Ugboaja, Nigeria	F
56	Toronto	Edin Bavcic, Bosnia	F
57	Minnesota	Loukas Mavrokefalidis, Greece	C
58	Dallas	J.R. PINNOCK, George Washington	G
59	San Antonio	Damir Markota, Croatia	F
60	Detroit	WILL BLALOCK, Iowa St.	G

Continental Basketball Association
Final Standings

QW refers to quarters won. Teams get 3 points for a win, 1 point for each quarter won and ½ point for any quarters tied. The three highest quarter-point averages in each conference qualify for the playoffs. (*) denotes playoff qualifiers.

Eastern	W	L	Home	Away	QW	Pts	Avg
*Gary Steelheads	29	19	19-5	10-14	110.0	197.0	4.1
*Rockford Lightning	30	18	18-6	12-12	102.0	192.0	4.0
*Albany Patroons	20	28	13-11	7-17	89.0	149.0	3.1
Michgan Mayhem	8	40	7-17	1-23	71.0	95.0	2.0

Western	W	L	Home	Away	QW	Pts	Avg
*Yakama Sun Kings	31	17	16-8	15-9	102.5	195.5	4.1
*Sioux Falls Skyforce	30	18	21-3	9-15	104.0	194.0	4.0
*Idaho Stampede	25	23	17-7	8-16	101.5	176.5	3.7
Dakota Wizards	19	29	16-8	3-21	88.0	145.0	3.0

Playoffs

The constantly evolving CBA used a **new playoff format** for the 2005-06 season. The three highest quarter-point averages in each conference qualify for the playoffs. The six teams are seeded and each play three games in the first round in a round-robin format versus the three playoff qualifiers from the opposite conference. The seeds were as follows: **Gary** (1A), **Yakama** (1B), **Sioux Falls** (2A), **Rockford** (2B), **Idaho** (3A), **Albany** (3B). The two teams that accumulated the most total quarter points in their respective three first-round games (Yakama and Gary) advanced to play in the CBA Finals where the Sun Kings defeated the Steelheads two games to one, with the road team winning all three contests.

CBA Finals
(best of three)

Yakama vs. Gary

Mar. 23 Gary 119 . . . . .at Yakama 103
Mar. 26 Yakama 91 . . . . .at Gary 87
Mar. 27 Yakama 111 . . . . .at Gary 101

Yakama wins series, 2 games to 1

CBA Annual Awards

Most Valuable Player
Anthony Goldwire, Yakama

Newcomer of the Year
James Thomas, Albany

Rookie of the Year
Roger Powell, Rockford

Def. Player of the Year
Noel Felix, Sioux Falls

Coach of the Year
Jaren Jackson, Gary

CBA Regular Season Individual Leaders

Scoring

	Gm	Pts	Avg
T.J. Thompson, Albany	47	1194	25.4
Ronnie Fields, Rockford	47	1044	22.2
Roger Powell, Rockford	48	1013	21.1
Marlon Parmer, Rockford	44	918	20.9
Antwain Barbour, Yakama	46	938	20.4
Matt Freije, Idaho	28	546	19.5
Randy Holcomb, Albany	34	652	19.2
Jamario Moon, Albany	30	552	18.4

Assists

	Gm	Ast	Avg
Corey Williams, Sioux Falls	27	264	9.8
Anthony Goldwire, Yakama	40	341	8.5
Marlon Parmer, Rockford	44	322	7.3
Cheyne Gadson, Yakama	25	166	6.6
Eric Chatfield, Gary	45	244	5.4
T.J. Thompson, Albany	47	244	5.2
Jason Boucher, Michigan	42	214	5.1
Eddy Barlow, Idaho	47	199	4.2

Rebounding

	Gm	Reb	Avg
Eric Chenowith, Idaho	47	595	12.7
Chris Alexander, Gary	44	403	9.2
Rosell Ellis, Yakama	28	251	9.0
Carl Mitchell, Gary	47	413	8.8
Sidney Holmes, Rockford	47	405	8.6
Damion Dantzler, Dakota	40	320	8.0
Jamar Brown, Michigan	43	327	7.6
Leonard White, Yakama	43	325	7.6

Steals

	Gm	Stl	Avg
Ronnie Fields, Rockford	47	109	2.3
Jason Boucher, Michigan	42	97	2.3
Rosell Ellis, Yakama	28	60	2.1
Jamario Moon, Albany	30	63	2.1
Corey Williams, Sioux Falls	27	54	2.0
T.J. Thompson, Albany	47	86	1.8
Karlton Mims, Gary	43	73	1.7
Antwain Barbour, Yakama	46	76	1.7

Field Goal Pct.

	FGM	FGA	Pct
Chris Sockwell, Albany	182	284	0.64
Kenyon Gamble, Rockford	72	114	0.63
John Jackson, Rockford	180	284	0.61
Sidney Holmes, Rockford	145	249	0.58
Roger Powell, Rockford	361	633	0.57
Lawrence Nelson, Rockford	93	164	0.56
Chris Alexander, Gary	141	256	0.55
Damond Williams, Dakota	118	215	.054

Free Throw Pct.

	FTM	FTA	Pct
Brian Chase, Gary	105	115	0.91
Cordell Henry, Rockford	139	157	0.88
Jason Boucher, Michigan	111	126	0.88
Anthony Goldwire, Yakama	164	189	0.86
James Maye, Dakota	76	88	0.86
T.J. Thompson, Albany	237	276	0.85
Jermaine Blackburn, Idaho	68	82	0.82
Noel Felix, Sioux Falls	126	154	0.81

National Basketball Association Development League

The newly redubbed D-League is a feeder league founded by the NBA in 2001. (*) denotes playoff qualifiers.

2006 Final Standings

	W	L	Pct	GB
*Fort Worth Flyers	28	20	.583	—
*Albuquerque Thunderbirds	26	22	.542	2
*Florida Flame	25	23	.521	3
*Roanoke Dazzle	25	23	.521	3
Arkansas RimRockers	24	24	.500	4
Austin Toros	24	24	.500	4
Tulsa 66ers	24	24	.500	4
Fayetteville Patriots	16	32	.333	12

Regular Season Individual Leaders

Scoring

	Gm	Pts	Avg
Bracey Wright, Florida	30	659	22.0
Isiah Victor, Roanoke	45	844	18.8
Erik Daniels, Fayetteville	46	811	17.6
Tierre Brown, Albuquerque	32	551	17.2
John Lucas, Tulsa	35	590	16.9
Ramel Curry, Austin	44	740	16.8
Desmon Farmer, Tulsa	48	789	16.4
Peter Ramos, Roanoke	43	641	14.9
Clay Tucker, Arkansas	47	662	14.1
Bernard King, Tulsa	34	452	13.3

Rebounds

	Gm	Reb	Avg
Erik Daniels, Fayetteville	46	372	8.1
Isiah Victor, Roanoke	45	360	8.0
Peter Ramos, Roanoke	43	333	7.7
Duane Erwin, Florida	30	229	7.6
Marcus Douthit, Alburquerque	42	303	7.2
Jamar Smith, Austin	48	344	7.2

Assists

	Gm	Ast	Avg
Kareem Reid, Arkansas	48	391	8.1
Will Conroy, Tulsa	47	314	6.7
Aaron Miles, Fort Worth	27	178	6.6
Tierre Brown, Albuquerque	32	208	6.5
Derrick Zimmerman, Austin	45	290	6.4
Bernard King, Tulsa	34	154	4.5

Steals

	Gm	Stl	Avg
Derrick Zimmerman, Austin	45	87	1.9
Bryant Matthews, Roanoke	45	75	1.7
Kareem Reid, Arkansas	48	76	1.6
John Lucas, Tulsa	35	55	1.6
Will Conroy, Tulsa	47	71	1.5
Tierre Brown, Albuquerque	32	48	1.5

Field Goal Pct.

	FG	FGA	Pct
Shawnson Johnson, Tulsa	135	217	.622
Peter Ramos, Roanoke	266	452	.588
D'or Fischer, Roanoke	65	112	.580
Jason Clark, Roanoke	44	77	.571
Ayodeji Akindele, Fort Worth	122	222	.550
George Leach, Florida	164	300	.547

Blocks

	Gm	Blk	Avg
Cezary Trybanski, Tulsa	45	88	2.0
Peter Ramos, Roanoke	43	78	1.8
George Leach, Florida	47	65	1.4
D'or Fischer, Roanoke	26	34	1.3
Andreas Glyniadakis, Albuquerque	38	48	1.3
Marcus Douthit, Albuquerque	42	45	1.1

Playoffs

Semifinals

Apr. 15 at Albuquerque, N.M.

	1	2	3	4	F
Florida Flame	19	19	15	18	– 71
Albuquerque Thunderbirds	16	16	30	18	– 80

Apr. 15 at Fort Worth, Tex.

	1	2	3	4	F
Roanoke Dazzle	12	21	17	28	– 78
Fort Worth Flyers	25	14	22	26	– 87

Final

Apr. 22 at Fort Worth, Tex.   **Attendance:** 3,518

	1	2	3	4	F
Albuquerque Thunderbirds	28	30	29	32	– 119
Fort Worth Flyers	21	25	28	34	– 108

Annual Awards

Most Valuable Player . . . . .Marcus Fizer, Austin
Rookie of the Year . . . . .Will Bynum, Roanoke
Defensive P.O.Y. . . . . .Derrick Zimmerman, Austin

All-NBDL First Team

There were no holdovers from 2004-05 first team.

Pos		Team
F	Marcus Fizer	Austin
F	Ime Udoka	Fort Worth
G	Andre Barrett	Florida
G	Will Bynum	Roanoke
G	Anthony Grundy	Roanoke

All-NBDL Second Team

Pos		Team
F	Erik Daniels	Fayetteville
F	Jabar Smith	Austin
F	Isiah Victor	Roanoke
C	Scott Merritt	Austin
C	Luke Schenscher	Fort Worth
G	John Lucas III	Tulsa

More Changes Come to D-League

Seven new markets, including four franchises (Bismarck, N.D., Boise, Idaho, Broomfield, Colo., and Sioux Falls, S.D.) from the Continental Basketball Association (CBA), are included in the roster of 12 teams that will comprise the 2006-07 NBA Development League. The **Arkansas RimRockers** (Little Rock), **Austin Toros** (Texas), **Dakota Wizards** (Bismarck, N.D.), **Fort Worth Flyers** (Texas), **Sioux Falls Skyforce** (S.D.) and **Tulsa 66ers** (Okla.) will comprise the Eastern Division. The **Albuquerque Thunderbirds** (N.M.), **Anaheim Arsenal** (Calif.), **Bakersfield Jam** (Calif.), **Colorado 14ers** (Broomfield), **Idaho Stampede** (Boise), **Los Angeles D-Fenders** make up the Western Division.

The **Florida Flame** will not field a team in 2006-07 due to difficulties in arena scheduling. Members of the Flame ownership group are examining alternate venues with plans to return for the 2007-08 season.

With the addition to the 'D-League' of the expansion L.A. D-Fenders, the Los Angeles Lakers have become the first NBA team to own an NBA Development League team. The D-Fenders, whose name was chosen through a internet fan poll, will play their home games at the **Staples Center**, home to the Lakers and the NBA's L.A. Clippers. The D-Fenders games will take place either before or after Lakers home games.

2006 FIBA World Championships

Fifteenth World Basketball Championship held Aug. 19–Sept. 3, 2006 at Tokyo, Japan.

First Round

Two points for a win and one for a loss; (*) indicated team advanced to quarterfinals.

Group A	W	L	For	Opp	Pts
*Argentina	5	0	464	339	10
*France	3	2	353	329	8
*Nigeria	2	3	371	393	7
*Serbia & Montenegro	2	3	409	352	7
Lebanon	2	3	357	451	7
Venezuela	1	4	336	426	6

Group B	W	L	For	Opp	Pts
*Spain	5	0	476	336	10
*Germany	4	1	421	384	9
*Angola	3	2	451	406	8
*New Zealand	2	3	345	393	7
Japan	1	4	322	393	6
Panama	0	5	326	429	5

Group C	W	L	For	Opp	Pts
*Greece	5	0	404	358	10
*Turkey	4	1	370	358	9
*Lithuania	3	2	413	353	8
*Australia	2	3	370	349	7
Brazil	1	4	399	392	6
Qatar	0	5	310	456	5

Group D	W	L	For	Opp	Pts
*United States	5	0	543	428	10
*Italy	4	1	386	367	9
*Slovenia	2	3	434	433	7
*China	2	3	424	455	7
Puerto Rico	2	3	432	440	7
Senegal	0	5	355	451	5

Round of 16

Argentina 79 ....New Zealand 62
Turkey 90 ....Slovenia 84
Spain 87 ....Serbia & Montenegro 75
Lithuania 71 ....Italy 68
Greece 95 ....China 64
France 68 ....Angola 62
United States 113 ....Australia 73
Germany 78 ....Nigeria 77

Quarterfinals

Argentina 83 .... Turkey 58
Spain 89 ....Lithuania 67
Greece 73 ....France 56
United States 85 ....Germany 65

Semifinals

Spain 75 ....Argentina 74
Greece 101 ....United States 95

Bronze Medal

United States 96 ....Argentina 81

Gold Medal

Spain 70 ....Greece 47

Tournament MVP

Pau Gasol, Spain, F
21.3 ppg, 9.4 rpg and 2.4 bpg.

Tournament Individual Leaders

Scoring

	Gm	Pts	Avg
Yao Ming, China	6	152	25.3
Dirk Nowitzki, Germany	9	209	23.2
Pau Gasol, Spain	8	170	21.3
Carlos Arroyo, Puerto Rico	5	106	21.2
Elias Ayuso, Puerto Rico	5	106	21.2
Carmelo Anthony, USA	9	179	19.9
Dwyane Wade, USA	8	154	19.3
Fadi El Khatib, Lebanon	5	94	18.8

Rebounding

	Gm	Reb	Avg
Richard Lugo, Venezuela	5	57	11.4
Pau Gasol, Spain	8	75	9.4
Dirk Nowitzki, Germany	9	83	9.2
Darko Milicic, Serbia & Montenegro	6	56	9.3
Yao Ming, China	6	54	9.0

Assists

	Gm	Ast	Avg
Juan Ignacio Sanchez, Argentina	9	52	5.8
Carlos Arroyo, Puerto Rico	5	26	5.2
Chris Paul, USA	9	44	4.9
Liu Wei, China	6	27	4.5
LeBron James, USA	9	37	4.1

Women's National Basketball Association

2006 WNBA Final Standings

Conference champions (*) and playoff qualifiers (†) are noted. GB refers to Games Behind leader. Number of seasons listed after each head coach refers to current tenure with club.

Eastern Conference

	W	L	Pct	GB	Home	Road
*Connecticut	26	8	.765	–	14-3	12-5
†Detroit	23	11	.676	3	14-3	9-8
†Indiana	21	13	.618	5	12-5	9-8
†Washington	18	16	.529	8	13-4	5-12
New York	11	23	.324	15	7-10	4-13
Charlotte	11	23	.324	15	6-14	7-10
Chicago	5	29	.147	21	3-14	2-15

2005 Standings: 1. Connecticut (26-8); 2. Indiana (21-13); 3. New York (18-16); 4. Detroit (16-18); 5. Washington (16-18); 6. Charlotte (6-28).

Western Conference

	W	L	Pct	GB	Home	Road
*Los Angeles	25	9	.735	–	15-2	10-7
†Sacramento	21	13	.618	4	14-3	7-10
†Houston	18	16	.529	7	12-5	6-11
†Seattle	18	16	.529	7	9-8	9-8
Phoenix	18	16	.529	7	10-7	8-9
San Antonio	13	21	.382	12	6-11	7-10
Minnesota	10	24	.294	15	8-9	2-15

2005 Standings: 1. Sacramento (25-9); 2. Seattle (20-14); 3. Houston (19-15); 4. Los Angeles (17-17); 5. Phoenix (16-18); 6. Minnesota (14-20); 7. San Antonio (7-27).

WNBA Regular Season Individual Leaders

Scoring

	Gm	Pts	Avg
Diana Taurasi, Phoenix	34	260	25.3
Seimone Augustus, Minnesota	34	744	21.9
Lisa Leslie, Los Angeles	34	680	20.0
Lauren Jackson, Seattle	30	585	19.5
Cappie Pondexter, Phoenix	32	624	19.5
Alana Beard, Washington	32	614	19.2

Rebounds

	Gm	Reb	Avg
Cheryl Ford, Detroit	32	363	11.3
Taj McWilliams-Franklin, Connecticut	32	306	9.6
Lisa Leslie, Los Angeles	34	323	9.5
Michelle Snow, Houston	34	269	7.9
Lauren Jackson, Seattle	30	230	7.7
Sophia Young, San Antonio	34	257	7.6

Field Goal Pct.

	FGM	FGA	Pct
Erin Buescher, Sacramento	117	218	.537
Lauren Jackson, Seattle	193	361	.535
Bernadette Ngoyisa, Chicago	122	231	.528

Assists

	Gm	Ast	Avg
Nikki Teasley, Washington	34	183	5.4
Temeka Johnson, Los Angeles	32	161	5.0
Sue Bird, Seattle	34	162	4.8

Steals

	Gm	Stl	Avg
Tamika Catchings, Indiana	32	94	2.9
Tully Bevilaqua, Indiana	34	71	2.1
Sheryl Swoopes, Houston	31	64	2.1

Blocks

	Gm	Blk	Avg
Margo Dydek, Connecticut	34	85	2.5
Tammy Sutton-Brown, Charlotte	30	55	1.8
Lauren Jackson, Seattle	30	51	1.7

WNBA Playoffs

First Round (Best of 3)

Western Conference

Sacramento vs. Houston

Aug. 17 Sacramento 93 . . . . .at Houston 78
Aug. 19 at Sacramento 92 . . . . .Houston 64
Sacramento Monarchs win series, 2-0

Seattle vs. Los Angeles

Aug. 18 at Seattle 84 . . . . .Los Angeles 72
Aug. 20 at Los Angeles 78 . . . . .Seattle 70
Aug. 22 at Los Angeles 68 . . . . .Seattle 63
Los Angeles Sparks win series, 2-1

Eastern Conference

Detroit vs. Indiana

Aug. 17 Detroit 68 . . . . .at Indiana 56
Aug. 19 at Detroit 98 . . . . .Indiana 83
Detroit Shock win series, 2-0

Connecticut vs. Washington

Aug. 18 Connecticut 76 . . . . .at Washington 61
Aug. 20 at Connecticut 68 . . . . .Washington 65
Connecticut Sun win series, 2-0

Conference Finals (Best of 3)

Eastern

Connecticut vs. Detroit

Aug. 24 at Detroit 70 . . . . .Connecticut 59
Aug. 26 at Connecticut 77 . . . . .Detroit 68
Aug. 27 Detroit 79 . . . . .at Connecticut 55
Detroit Shock win series, 2-1

Western

Sacramento vs. Houston

Aug. 24 Sacramento 64 . . . . .at Los Angeles 61
Aug. 26 at Sacramento 72 . . . . .Los Angeles 58
Sacramento Monarchs win series, 2-0

Annual Awards

Most Valuable Player . . . . .Lisa Leslie, LA
Rookie of the Year . . . . .Seimone Augustus, Minn.
Most Improved . . . . .Erin Buescher, Sac.
Def. Player of the Year . . .Tamika Catchings, Ind.
Coach of the Year . . . . .Mike Thibault, Conn.
Kim Perrot Sportsmanship
Award . . . . .Dawn Staley, Hou.

All-WNBA First Team

Holdover from 2004-05 team is in **bold** type.

Pos	
F	Tamika Catchings, Indiana
F	**Lauren Jackson**, Seattle
C	Lisa Leslie, Los Angeles
G	Diana Taurasi, Phoenix
G	Katie Douglas, Connecticut

Championship Series (Best of 5)

Detroit vs. Sacramento

Detroit wins series, 3 games to 2

	W-L	Avg	Leading Scorer
Sacramento Monarchs	.2-3	74.8	Griffin (13.4 ppg)
Detroit Shock	.3-2	73.0	Nolan (17.8 ppg)

Date	Winner	Home Court
Aug. 30 . . . . .Monarchs, 95-71		at Detroit
Sept. 1 . . . . .Shock, 73-63		at Detroit
Sept. 3 . . . . .Monarchs, 89-69		at Sacramento
Sept. 6 . . . . .Shock, 72-52		at Sacramento
Sept. 9 . . . . .Shock, 80-75		at Detroit

Finals MVP: Deanna Nolan, Detroit, G/F (17.8 ppg, 4.2 rpg, 2.8 apg).

2006 WNBA Draft

First Round

Pick	Team	Player, College, Pos
1	Minnesota	Seimone Augustus, LSU, G
2	Phoenix	Cappie Pondexter, Rutgers, G
3	Charlotte	Monique Currie, Duke, G
4	San Antonio	Sophia Young, Baylor, F
5	Los Angeles	Lisa Willis, UCLA, G
6	Chicago	Candice Dupree, Temple, F
7	Minnesota	Shona Thorburn, Utah, G
8	Washington	Tamara James, Miami-FL, G
9	Indiana	La'Tangela Atkinson, N. Caro., F
10	Charlotte	Tye'sha Fluker, Tennessee, C
11	Seattle	Barbara Turner, Connecticut, G
12	New York	Sherill Baker, Georgia, G
13	Sacramento	Kim Smith, Utah, F
14	Sacramento	Scholanda Houston, LSU, G

1938-2006
Through the Years

SPORTS ALMANAC

The NBA Finals

Although the National Basketball Association traces its first championship back to the 1946-47 season, the league was then called the Basketball Association of America (BAA). It did not become the NBA until after the 1948-49 season when the BAA and the National Basketball League (NBL) agreed to merge.

In the chart below, the Eastern finalists (representing the NBA Eastern Division from 1947-70, and the NBA Eastern Conference since 1971) are listed in CAPITAL letters. Also, each NBA champion's wins and losses are noted in parentheses after the series score.

Multiple winners: Boston (16); Minneapolis-LA Lakers (14); Chicago Bulls (6); Detroit, Phi-SF-Golden St. Warriors, San Antonio and Syracuse Nationals-Phi. 76ers (3); Houston, New York (2).

Year	Winner	Head Coach	Series	Loser	Head Coach
1947	PHILADELPHIA WARRIORS	Eddie Gottlieb	4-1 (WWWLW)	Chicago Stags	Harold Olsen
1948	Baltimore Bullets	Buddy Jeannette	4-2 (LWWWLW)	PHILA. WARRIORS	Eddie Gottlieb
1949	Minneapolis Lakers	John Kundla	4-2 (WWWLLW)	WASH. CAPITOLS	Red Auerbach
1950	Minneapolis Lakers	John Kundla	4-2 (WLWWLW)	SYRACUSE	Al Cervi
1951	Rochester	Les Harrison	4-3 (WWWLLLW)	NEW YORK	Joe Lapchick
1952	Minneapolis Lakers	John Kundla	4-3 (WLWLWLW)	NEW YORK	Joe Lapchick
1953	Minneapolis Lakers	John Kundla	4-1 (LWWWW)	NEW YORK	Joe Lapchick
1954	Minneapolis Lakers	John Kundla	4-3 (WLWLWLW)	SYRACUSE	Al Cervi
1955	SYRACUSE	Al Cervi	4-3 (WWLLLWW)	Ft. Wayne Pistons	Charley Eckman
1956	PHILADELPHIA WARRIORS	George Senesky	4-1 (WLWWW)	Ft. Wayne Pistons	Charley Eckman
1957	BOSTON	Red Auerbach	4-3 (LWLWLWW)	St. Louis Hawks	Alex Hannum
1958	St. Louis Hawks	Alex Hannum	4-2 (WLWLWW)	BOSTON	Red Auerbach
1959	BOSTON	Red Auerbach	4-0	Mpls. Lakers	John Kundla
1960	BOSTON	Red Auerbach	4-3 (WLWLWLW)	St. Louis Hawks	Ed Macauley
1961	BOSTON	Red Auerbach	4-1 (WWLWW)	St. Louis Hawks	Paul Seymour
1962	BOSTON	Red Auerbach	4-3 (WLLWLWW)	LA Lakers	Fred Schaus
1963	BOSTON	Red Auerbach	4-2 (WWLWLW)	LA Lakers	Fred Schaus
1964	BOSTON	Red Auerbach	4-1 (WWLWW)	SF Warriors	Alex Hannum
1965	BOSTON	Red Auerbach	4-1 (WWLWW)	LA Lakers	Fred Schaus
1966	BOSTON	Red Auerbach	4-3 (LWWWLLW)	LA Lakers	Fred Schaus
1967	PHILADELPHIA 76ERS	Alex Hannum	4-2 (WLWWLW)	SF Warriors	Bill Sharman
1968	BOSTON	Bill Russell	4-2 (WLWLWW)	LA Lakers	B.van Breda Kolff
1969	BOSTON	Bill Russell	4-3 (LLWWLWW)	LA Lakers	B.van Breda Kolff
1970	NEW YORK	Red Holzman	4-3 (WLWLWLW)	LA Lakers	Joe Mullaney
1971	Milwaukee	Larry Costello	4-0	BALT. BULLETS	Gene Shue
1972	LA Lakers	Bill Sharman	4-1 (LWWWW)	NEW YORK	Red Holzman
1973	NEW YORK	Red Holzman	4-1 (LWWWW)	LA Lakers	Bill Sharman
1974	BOSTON	Tommy Heinsohn	4-3 (WLWLWLW)	Milwaukee	Larry Costello
1975	Golden St. Warriors	Al Attles	4-0	WASH. BULLETS	K.C. Jones
1976	BOSTON	Tommy Heinsohn	4-2 (WWLLWW)	Phoenix	John MacLeod
1977	Portland	Jack Ramsay	4-2 (LLWWWW)	PHILA. 76ERS	Gene Shue
1978	WASHINGTON BULLETS	Dick Motta	4-3 (LWLWLWW)	Seattle	Lenny Wilkens
1979	Seattle	Lenny Wilkens	4-1 (LWWWW)	WASH. BULLETS	Dick Motta
1980	LA Lakers	Paul Westhead	4-2 (WLWLWW)	PHILA. 76ERS	Billy Cunningham
1981	BOSTON	Bill Fitch	4-2 (WLWLWW)	Houston	Del Harris
1982	LA Lakers	Pat Riley	4-2 (WLWWLW)	PHILA. 76ERS	Billy Cunningham
1983	PHILADELPHIA 76ERS	Billy Cunningham	4-0	LA Lakers	Pat Riley
1984	BOSTON	K.C. Jones	4-3 (LWLWLWW)	LA Lakers	Pat Riley
1985	LA Lakers	Pat Riley	4-2 (LWWWLW)	BOSTON	K.C. Jones
1986	BOSTON	K.C. Jones	4-2 (WWLLWW)	Houston	Bill Fitch
1987	LA Lakers	Pat Riley	4-2 (WWLWLW)	BOSTON	K.C. Jones
1988	LA Lakers	Pat Riley	4-3 (LWWLLWW)	DETROIT PISTONS	Chuck Daly
1989	DETROIT	Chuck Daly	4-0	LA Lakers	Pat Riley
1990	DETROIT	Chuck Daly	4-1 (WLWWW)	Portland	Rick Adelman
1991	CHICAGO	Phil Jackson	4-1 (LWWWW)	LA Lakers	Mike Dunleavy
1992	CHICAGO	Phil Jackson	4-2 (WLWWLW)	Portland	Rick Adelman
1993	CHICAGO	Phil Jackson	4-2 (WWLWLW)	Phoenix	Paul Westphal
1994	Houston	Rudy Tomjanovich	4-3 (WLWLLWW)	NEW YORK	Pat Riley
1995	Houston	Rudy Tomjanovich	4-0	ORLANDO	Brian Hill
1996	CHICAGO	Phil Jackson	4-2 (WWWLLW)	Seattle	George Karl
1997	CHICAGO	Phil Jackson	4-2 (WWLLWW)	Utah	Jerry Sloan
1998	CHICAGO	Phil Jackson	4-2 (LWWWLW)	Utah	Jerry Sloan

The NBA Finals (Cont.)

Year	Winner	Head Coach	Series	Loser	Head Coach
1999	San Antonio	Gregg Popovich	4-1 (WWLWW)	NEW YORK	Jeff Van Gundy
2000	LA Lakers	Phil Jackson	4-2 (WWLWLW)	INDIANA	Larry Bird
2001	LA Lakers	Phil Jackson	4-1 (LWWWW)	PHILA. 76ERS	Larry Brown
2002	LA Lakers	Phil Jackson	4-0	NEW JERSEY	Byron Scott
2003	San Antonio	Gregg Popovich	4-2 (WLWLWW)	NEW JERSEY	Byron Scott
2004	DETROIT	Larry Brown	4-1 (WLWWW)	LA Lakers	Phil Jackson
2005	San Antonio	Gregg Popovich	4-3 (WWLLWLW)	DETROIT	Larry Brown
2006	MIAMI	Pat Riley	4-2 (LLWWWW)	Dallas	Avery Johnson

Note: Four finalists were led by player-coaches: **1948**—Buddy Jeannette (guard) of Baltimore; **1950**—Al Cervi (guard) of Syracuse; **1968**—Bill Russell (center) of Boston; **1969**—Bill Russell (center) of Boston.

Most Valuable Player

Winner who did not play for the NBA champion is in **bold** type.

Multiple winners: Michael Jordan (6); Tim Duncan, Magic Johnson and Shaquille O'Neal (3); Kareem Abdul-Jabbar, Larry Bird, Hakeem Olajuwon and Willis Reed (2).

Year		Year		Year	
1969	**Jerry West**, LA Lakers, G	1982	Magic Johnson, LA Lakers, G	1995	Hakeem Olajuwon, Houston, C
1970	Willis Reed, New York, C	1983	Moses Malone, Philadelphia, C	1996	Michael Jordan, Chicago, G
1971	Lew Alcindor, Milwaukee, C	1984	Larry Bird, Boston, F	1997	Michael Jordan, Chicago, G
1972	Wilt Chamberlain, LA Lakers, C	1985	K. Abdul-Jabbar, LA Lakers, C	1998	Michael Jordan, Chicago, G
1973	Willis Reed, New York, C	1986	Larry Bird, Boston, F	1999	Tim Duncan, San Antonio, F/C
1974	John Havlicek, Boston, F	1987	Magic Johnson, LA Lakers, G	2000	Shaquille O'Neal, LA Lakers, C
1975	Rick Barry, Golden State, F	1988	James Worthy, LA Lakers, F	2001	Shaquille O'Neal, LA Lakers, C
1976	Jo Jo White, Boston, G	1989	Joe Dumars, Detroit, G	2002	Shaquille O'Neal, LA Lakers, C
1977	Bill Walton, Portland, C	1990	Isiah Thomas, Detroit, G	2003	Tim Duncan, San Antonio, F/C
1978	Wes Unseld, Washington, C	1991	Michael Jordan, Chicago, G	2004	Chauncey Billups, Detroit, G
1979	Dennis Johnson, Seattle, G	1992	Michael Jordan, Chicago, G	2005	Tim Duncan, San Antonio, F/C
1980	Magic Johnson, LA Lakers, G/C	1993	Michael Jordan, Chicago, G	2006	Dwyane Wade, Miami, G
1981	Cedric Maxwell, Boston, F	1994	Hakeem Olajuwon, Houston, C		

Note: Lew Alcindor changed his name to Kareem Abdul-Jabbar after the 1970-71 season.

All-Time NBA Playoff Leaders

Through the 2006 playoffs.

CAREER

Years listed indicate number of playoff appearances. Players active in 2006 in **bold** type. DNP indicates player that was active in 2006 but did not participate in playoffs.

Points

		Yrs	Gm	Pts	Avg
1	Michael Jordan	13	179	**5987**	33.4
2	Kareem Abdul-Jabbar	18	237	**5762**	24.3
3	**Shaquille O'Neal**	13	194	**4970**	25.6
4	Karl Malone	19	193	**4761**	24.7
5	Jerry West	13	153	**4457**	29.1
6	Larry Bird	12	164	**3897**	23.8
7	John Havlicek	13	172	**3776**	22.0
8	Hakeem Olajuwon	15	145	**3755**	25.9
9	Magic Johnson	13	190	**3701**	19.5
10	Scottie Pippen	16	208	**3642**	17.5
11	Elgin Baylor	12	134	**3623**	27.0
12	Wilt Chamberlain	13	160	**3607**	22.5
13	Kevin McHale	13	169	**3182**	18.8
14	Dennis Johnson	13	180	**3116**	17.3
15	Julius Erving	11	141	**3088**	21.9
16	James Worthy	9	143	**3022**	21.1
17	Clyde Drexler	15	145	**2963**	20.4
18	Sam Jones	12	154	**2909**	18.9
19	**Tim Duncan**	8	118	**2838**	24.1
20	Charles Barkley	13	123	**2833**	23.0

Scoring Average

Minimum of 25 games or 700 points.

		Yrs	Gm	Pts	Avg
1	Michael Jordan	13	179	5987	33.4
2	**Allen Iverson** (DNP)	6	62	1899	30.6
3	Jerry West	13	153	4457	29.1
4	Elgin Baylor	12	134	3623	27.0
5	George Gervin	9	59	1592	27.0
6	Hakeem Olajuwon	15	145	3755	25.9
7	Dominique Wilkins	9	55	1421	25.8
8	**Dirk Nowitzki**	8	76	1952	25.7
9	**Shaquille O'Neal**	13	194	4970	25.6
10	Bob Pettit	9	88	2240	25.5
11	**Dwyane Wade**	3	50	1272	25.4
12	Rick Barry	7	74	1833	24.8
13	Karl Malone	19	193	4761	24.7
14	**Paul Pierce** (DNP)	4	37	908	24.5
15	Bernard King	5	28	687	24.5
16	Alex English	10	68	1661	24.4
17	Kareem Abdul-Jabbar	18	237	5762	24.3
18	Paul Arizin	8	49	1186	24.2
19	**Tim Duncan**	8	118	2838	24.1
20	Larry Bird	12	164	3897	23.8

Field Goals

		Yrs	FG	Att	Pct
1	Kareem Abdul-Jabbar	18	**2356**	4422	.533
2	Michael Jordan	13	**2188**	4497	.487
3	**Shaquille O'Neal**	12	**1759**	3132	.562
4	Karl Malone	19	**1743**	3768	.463
5	Jerry West	13	**1622**	3460	.469
6	Hakeem Olajuwon	15	**1504**	2847	.528
7	Larry Bird	12	**1458**	3090	.472
8	John Havlicek	13	**1451**	3329	.436
9	Wilt Chamberlain	13	**1425**	2728	.522
10	Elgin Baylor	12	**1388**	3161	.439

Free Throws

		Yrs	FT	Att	Pct
1	Michael Jordan	13	**1463**	1766	.828
2	Karl Malone	19	**1269**	1725	.736
3	Jerry West	13	**1213**	1507	.805
4	Kareem Abdul-Jabbar	18	**1050**	1419	.740
5	Magic Johnson	12	**1040**	1241	.838
6	**Shaquille O'Neal**	12	**1028**	1995	.515
7	Larry Bird	12	**901**	1012	.891
8	John Havlicek	13	**874**	1046	.836
9	Elgin Baylor	12	**847**	1101	.769
10	Scottie Pippen	16	**772**	1067	.724

Assists

		Yrs	Gm	No	Avg
1	Magic Johnson	13	190	**2346**	12.3
2	John Stockton	19	182	**1839**	10.1
3	Larry Bird	12	164	**1062**	6.5
4	Scottie Pippen	16	208	**1048**	5.0
5	Michael Jordan	13	179	**1022**	5.7

Rebounds

		Yrs	Gm	No	Avg
1	Bill Russell	13	165	**4104**	24.9
2	Wilt Chamberlain	13	160	**3913**	24.5
3	Kareem Abdul-Jabbar	18	237	**2481**	10.5
4	**Shaquille O'Neal**	13	194	**2367**	12.2
5	Karl Malone	19	193	**2062**	10.7

Appearances

	No		No
Karl Malone	19	Sam Perkins	15
John Stockton	19	Jerome Kersey	15
Kareem Abdul-Jabbar	18	Tree Rollins	15
Robert Parish	16	Charles Oakley	15
Scottie Pippen	16	Dolph Schayes	15
Terry Porter	16	Clyde Drexler	15

Games Played

	No		No
K. Abdul-Jabbar	237	Byron Scott	183
Robert Horry	211	John Stockton	182
Scottie Pippen	208	Dennis Johnson	180
Shaquille O'Neal	194	Michael Jordan	179
Danny Ainge	193	John Havlicek	172
Karl Malone	193	Kevin McHale	169
Magic Johnson	190	Michael Cooper	168
Robert Parish	184	Bill Russell	165

SINGLE GAME

Points

	Date	FG-FT–Pts
Michael Jordan, Chi at Bos*	4/20/86	22-19–63
Elgin Baylor, LA at Bos	4/14/62	22-17–61
Wilt Chamberlain, Phi vs Syr	3/22/62	22-12–56
Michael Jordan, Chi at Mia	4/29/92	20-16–56
Charles Barkley, Pho vs G.St.	5/4/94	23- 7–56
Rick Barry, SF vs Phi	4/18/67	22-11–55
Michael Jordan, Chi vs Cle	5/1/88	24- 7–55
Michael Jordan, Chi vs Pho	4/16/93	21-13–55
Michael Jordan, Chi vs. Wash	4/27/97	22-10–55

*Double overtime.

Field Goals

	Date	FG	Att
Wilt Chamberlain, Phi vs Syr	3/14/60	24	42
John Havlicek, Bos vs Atl	4/1/73	24	36
Michael Jordan, Chi vs Cle	5/1/88	24	45

Eight tied with 22 each.

Miscellaneous

3-Pt Field Goals

	Date	No
Rex Chapman, Pho at Sea	4/25/97	9
Dan Majerle, Pho vs Sea	6/1/93	8
Allen Iverson, Phi vs Tor	5/16/01	8

Nine tied with 7 each.

Assists

	Date	No
Magic Johnson, LA vs Pho	5/15/84	24
John Stockton, Utah at LA Lakers	5/17/88	24
Magic Johnson, LA Lakers at Port	5/3/85	23
John Stockton, Utah vs Port	4/25/96	23
Doc Rivers, Atl vs Bos	5/16/88	22

Four tied with 21 each.

Rebounds

	Date	No
Wilt Chamberlain, Phi vs Bos	4/5/67	41
Bill Russell, Bos vs Phi	3/23/58	40
Bill Russell, Bos vs St.L	3/29/60	40
Bill Russell, Bos vs LA*	4/18/62	40

Three tied with 39 each.
*Overtime.

Appearances in NBA Finals

Standings of all NBA teams that have reached the NBA Finals since 1947.

App		Titles	Last Won
28	Minneapolis-LA Lakers	14	2002
19	Boston Celtics	16	1986
9	Syracuse Nats-Phila. 76ers	3	1983
8	New York Knicks	2	1973
7	Ft. Wayne-Detroit Pistons	3	2004
6	Chicago Bulls	6	1998
6	Phila-SF-Golden St. Warriors	3	1975
4	Houston Rockets	2	1995
4	St. Louis Hawks	1	1958
4	Baltimore-Washington Bullets	1	1978
3	San Antonio Spurs	3	2005
3	Portland Trail Blazers	1	1977
3	Seattle SuperSonics	1	1979
2	Milwaukee Bucks	1	1971
2	New Jersey Nets	0	—
2	Phoenix Suns	0	—
2	Utah Jazz	0	—
1	Baltimore Bullets	1	1948
1	Rochester Royals	1	1951
1	Miami Heat	1	2006
1	Chicago Stags	0	—
1	Orlando Magic	0	—
1	Washington Capitols	0	—
1	Indiana Pacers	0	—

Change of address: The St. Louis Hawks now play in Atlanta and the Rochester Royals are now the Sacramento Kings.
Teams now defunct: Baltimore Bullets (1947-55), Chicago Stags (1946-50) and Washington Capitols (1946-51).

NBA FINALS

Points

Series		Year	Pts
4-Gm	Shaquille O'Neal, LAL vs NJ	2002	145
5-Gm	Allen Iverson, Phi vs LAL	2001	178
6-Gm	Michael Jordan, Chi vs Pho	1993	246
7-Gm	Elgin Baylor, LA vs Bos	1962	284

Field Goals

Series		Year	No
4-Gm	Hakeem Olajuwon, Hou vs Orl	1995	56
5-Gm	Allen Iverson, Phi vs LAL	2001	66
6-Gm	Michael Jordan, Chi vs Pho	1993	101
7-Gm	Elgin Baylor, LA vs Bos	1962	101

Assists

Series		Year	No
4-Gm	Bob Cousy, Bos vs Mpls	1959	51
5-Gm	Magic Johnson, LAL vs Chi	1991	62
6-Gm	Magic Johnson, LAL vs Bos	1985	84
7-Gm	Magic Johnson, LA vs Bos	1984	95

Rebounds

Series		Year	No
4-Gm	Bill Russell, Bos vs Mpls	1959	118
5-Gm	Bill Russell, Bos vs St.L	1961	144
6-Gm	Wilt Chamberlain, Phi vs SF	1967	171
7-Gm	Bill Russell, Bos vs LA	1962	189

NBA All-Star Game

The NBA staged its first All-Star Game before 10,094 at Boston Garden on March 2, 1951. From that year on, the game has matched the best players in the East against the best in the West. Winning coaches are listed first. East leads series, 34-19.

Multiple MVP winners: Bob Pettit (4); Michael Jordan and Oscar Robertson (3); Bob Cousy, Julius Erving, Allen Iverson, Magic Johnson, Karl Malone, Shaquille O'Neal and Isiah Thomas (2).

Year		Host	Coaches	Most Valuable Player
1951	East 111, West 94	Boston	Joe Lapchick, John Kundla	Ed Macauley, Boston
1952	East 108, West 91	Boston	Al Cervi, John Kundla	Paul Arizin, Philadelphia
1953	West 79, East 75	Ft. Wayne	John Kundla, Joe Lapchick	George Mikan, Minneapolis
1954	East 98, West 93 (OT)	New York	Joe Lapchick, John Kundla	Bob Cousy, Boston
1955	East 100, West 91	New York	Al Cervi, Charley Eckman	Bill Sharman, Boston
1956	West 108, East 94	Rochester	Charley Eckman, George Senesky	Bob Pettit, St. Louis
1957	East 109, West 97	Boston	Red Auerbach, Bobby Wanzer	Bob Cousy, Boston
1958	East 130, West 118	St. Louis	Red Auerbach, Alex Hannum	Bob Pettit, St. Louis
1959	West 124, East 108	Detroit	Ed Macauley, Red Auerbach	Bob Pettit, St. Louis
				& Elgin Baylor, Minneapolis
1960	East 125, West 115	Philadelphia	Red Auerbach, Ed Macauley	Wilt Chamberlain, Philadelphia
1961	West 153, East 131	Syracuse	Paul Seymour, Red Auerbach	Oscar Robertson, Cincinnati
1962	West 150, East 130	St. Louis	Fred Schaus, Red Auerbach	Bob Pettit, St. Louis
1963	East 115, West 108	Los Angeles	Red Auerbach, Fred Schaus	Bill Russell, Boston
1964	East 111, West 107	Boston	Red Auerbach, Fred Schaus	Oscar Robertson, Cincinnati
1965	East 124, West 123	St. Louis	Red Auerbach, Alex Hannum	Jerry Lucas, Cincinnati
1966	East 137, West 94	Cincinnati	Red Auerbach, Fred Schaus	Adrian Smith, Cincinnati
1967	West 135, East 120	San Francisco	Fred Schaus, Red Auerbach	Rick Barry, San Francisco
1968	East 144, West 124	New York	Alex Hannum, Bill Sharman	Hal Greer, Philadelphia
1969	East 123, West 112	Baltimore	Gene Shue, Richie Guerin	Oscar Robertson, Cincinnati
1970	East 142, West 135	Philadelphia	Red Holzman, Richie Guerin	Willis Reed, New York
1971	West 108, East 107	San Diego	Larry Costello, Red Holzman	Lenny Wilkens, Seattle
1972	West 112, East 110	Los Angeles	Bill Sharman, Tom Heinsohn	Jerry West, Los Angeles
1973	East 104, West 84	Chicago	Tom Heinsohn, Bill Sharman	Dave Cowens, Boston
1974	West 134, East 123	Seattle	Larry Costello, Tom Heinsohn	Bob Lanier, Detroit
1975	East 108, West 102	Phoenix	K.C. Jones, Al Attles	Walt Frazier, New York
1976	East 123, West 109	Philadelphia	Tom Heinsohn, Al Attles	Dave Bing, Washington
1977	West 125, East 124	Milwaukee	Larry Brown, Gene Shue	Julius Erving, Philadelphia
1978	East 133, West 125	Atlanta	Billy Cunningham, Jack Ramsay	Randy Smith, Buffalo
1979	West 134, East 129	Detroit	Lenny Wilkens, Dick Motta	David Thompson, Denver
1980	East 144, West 136 (OT)	Washington	Billy Cunningham, Lenny Wilkens	George Gervin, San Antonio
1981	East 123, West 120	Cleveland	Billy Cunningham, John MacLeod	Nate Archibald, Boston
1982	East 120, West 118	New Jersey	Bill Fitch, Pat Riley	Larry Bird, Boston
1983	East 132, West 123	Los Angeles	Billy Cunningham, Pat Riley	Julius Erving, Philadelphia
1984	East 154, West 145 (OT)	Denver	K.C. Jones, Frank Layden	Isiah Thomas, Detroit
1985	West 140, East 129	Indiana	Pat Riley, K.C. Jones	Ralph Sampson, Houston
1986	East 139, West 132	Dallas	K.C. Jones, Pat Riley	Isiah Thomas, Detroit
1987	West 154, East 149 (OT)	Seattle	Pat Riley, K.C. Jones	Tom Chambers, Seattle
1988	East 138, West 133	Chicago	Mike Fratello, Pat Riley	Michael Jordan, Chicago
1989	West 143, East 134	Houston	Pat Riley, Lenny Wilkens	Karl Malone, Utah
1990	East 130, West 113	Miami	Chuck Daly, Pat Riley	Magic Johnson, LA Lakers
1991	East 116, West 114	Charlotte	Chris Ford, Rick Adelman	Charles Barkley, Philadelphia
1992	West 153, East 113	Orlando	Don Nelson, Phil Jackson	Magic Johnson, LA Lakers
1993	West 135, East 132 (OT)	Salt Lake City	Paul Westphal, Pat Riley	Karl Malone, Utah
				& John Stockton, Utah
1994	East 127, West 118	Minneapolis	Lenny Wilkens, George Karl	Scottie Pippen, Chicago
1995	West 139, East 112	Phoenix	Paul Westphal, Brian Hill	Mitch Richmond, Sacramento
1996	East 129, West 118	San Antonio	Phil Jackson, George Karl	Michael Jordan, Chicago
1997	East 132, West 120	Cleveland	Doug Collins, Rudy Tomjanovich	Glen Rice, Charlotte
1998	East 135, West 114	New York	Larry Bird, George Karl	Michael Jordan, Chicago
1999	Not held—due to lockout			
2000	West 137, East 126	Oakland	Phil Jackson, Jeff Van Gundy	Tim Duncan, San Antonio
				& Shaquille O'Neal, LA Lakers
2001	East 111, West 110	Washington	Larry Brown, Rick Adelman	Allen Iverson, Philadelphia
2002	West 135, East 120	Philadelphia	Don Nelson, Byron Scott	Kobe Bryant, LA Lakers
2003	West 155, East 145 (2 OT)	Atlanta	Rick Adelman, Isiah Thomas	Kevin Garnett, Minnesota
2004	West 136, East 132	Los Angeles	Flip Saunders, Rick Carlisle	Shaquille O'Neal, LA Lakers
2005	East 125, West 115	Denver	Stan Van Gundy, Gregg Popovich	Allen Iverson, Philadelphia
2006	East 122, West 120	Houston	Flip Saunders, Avery Johnson	LeBron James, Cleveland

NBA Franchise Origins

Here is what the current 30 teams in the National Basketball Association have to show for the years they have put in as members of the National Basketball League (NBL), Basketball Association of America (BAA), the NBA, and the American Basketball Association (ABA). League titles are noted by year won.

Western Conference

	First Season	League Titles	Franchise Stops
Dallas Mavericks	1980-81 (NBA)	None	•Dallas (1980–)
Denver Nuggets	1967-68 (ABA)	None	•Denver (1967–)
Golden St. Warriors	1946-47 (BAA)	1 BAA (1947)	•Philadelphia (1946-62)
		2 NBA (1956, 75)	San Francisco (1962-71)
			Oakland (1971–)
Houston Rockets	1967-68 (NBA)	2 NBA (1994-95)	•San Diego (1967-71)
			Houston (1971–)
Los Angeles Clippers	1970-71 (NBA)	None	•Buffalo (1970-78)
			San Diego (1978-84)
			Los Angeles (1984–)
Los Angeles Lakers	1947-48 (NBL)	1 NBL (1948)	•Minneapolis (1947-60)
		1 BAA (1949)	Los Angeles (1960-67)
		14 NBA (1950,52-54,72,	Inglewood, CA (1967-99)
		80,82,85,87-88,00-02)	Los Angeles (1999–)
Memphis Grizzlies	1995-96 (NBA)	None	•Vancouver (1995-01)
			Memphis, TN (2001–)
Minnesota Timberwolves	1989-90 (NBA)	None	•Minneapolis (1989–)
New Orleans/			
Oklahoma City Hornets	1988-89 (NBA)	None	•Charlotte (1988-2002)
			New Orleans (2002–)
			Oklahoma City (2005–)
Phoenix Suns	1968-69 (NBA)	None	•Phoenix (1968–)
Portland Trail Blazers	1970-71 (NBA)	1 NBA (1977)	•Portland (1970–)
Sacramento Kings	1945-46 (NBL)	1 NBL (1946)	•Rochester, NY (1945-58)
		1 NBA (1951)	Cincinnati (1958-72)
			KC-Omaha (1972-75)
			Kansas City (1975-85)
			Sacramento (1985–)
San Antonio Spurs	1967-68 (ABA)	3 NBA (1999, 2003, 05)	•Dallas (1967-73)
			San Antonio (1973–)
Seattle SuperSonics	1967-68 (NBA)	1 NBA (1979)	•Seattle (1967–)
Utah Jazz	1974-75 (NBA)	None	•New Orleans (1974-79)
			Salt Lake City (1979–)

Eastern Conference

	First Season	League Titles	Franchise Stops
Atlanta Hawks	1946-47 (NBL)	1 NBA (1958)	•Tri-Cities (1946-51)
			Milwaukee (1951-55)
			St. Louis (1955-68)
			Atlanta (1968–)
Boston Celtics	1946-47 (BAA)	16 NBA (1957,59-66,68-69	•Boston (1946–)
		74,76,81,84,86)	
Charlotte Bobcats	2004-05 (NBA)	None	•Charlotte (2004–)
Chicago Bulls	1966-67 (NBA)	6 NBA (1991-93,96-98)	•Chicago (1966–)
Cleveland Cavaliers	1970-71 (NBA)	None	•Cleveland (1970-74)
			Richfield, OH (1974-94)
			Cleveland (1994–)
Detroit Pistons	1941-42 (NBL)	2 NBL (1944-45)	•Ft. Wayne, IN (1941-57)
		3 NBA (1989-90, 2004)	Detroit (1957-78)
			Pontiac, MI (1978-88)
			Auburn Hills, MI (1988–)
Indiana Pacers	1967-68 (ABA)	3 ABA (1970,72-73)	•Indianapolis (1967–)
Miami Heat	1988-89 (NBA)	1 NBA (2006)	•Miami (1988–)
Milwaukee Bucks	1968-69 (NBA)	1 NBA (1971)	•Milwaukee (1968–)
New Jersey Nets	1967-68 (ABA)	2 ABA (1974,76)	•Teaneck, NJ (1967-68)
			Commack, NY (1968-69)
			W. Hempstead, NY (1969-71)
			Uniondale, NY (1971-77)
			Piscataway, NJ (1977-81)
			E. Rutherford, NJ (1981–)
New York Knicks	1946-47 (BAA)	2 NBA (1970,73)	•New York (1946–)
Orlando Magic	1989-90 (NBA)	None	•Orlando, FL (1989–)
Philadelphia 76ers	1949-50 (NBA)	3 NBA (1955,67,83)	•Syracuse, NY (1949-63)
			Philadelphia (1963–)
Toronto Raptors	1995-96 (NBA)	None	•Toronto (1995–)
Washington Wizards	1961-62 (NBA)	1 NBA (1978)	•Chicago (1961-63)
			Baltimore (1963-73)
			Landover, MD (1973–)

Note: The Tri-Cities Blackhawks represented Moline and Rock Island, Ill., and Davenport, Iowa.

The Growth of the NBA

Of the 11 franchises that comprised the Basketball Association of America (BAA) at the start of the 1946-47 season, only three remain—the Boston Celtics, New York Knickerbockers and Golden State Warriors (originally Philadelphia Warriors).

Just before the start of the 1948-49 season, four teams from the more established **National Basketball League** (NBL)—the Ft. Wayne Pistons (now Detroit), Indianapolis Jets, Minneapolis Lakers (now Los Angeles) and Rochester Royals (now Sacramento Kings)—joined the BAA.

A year later, the six remaining NBL franchises—Anderson (Ind.), Denver, Sheboygan (Wisc.), the Syracuse Nationals (now Philadelphia 76ers), Tri-Cities Blackhawks (now Atlanta Hawks) and Waterloo (Iowa)—joined along with the new Indianapolis Olympians and the BAA became the 17-team **National Basketball Association**.

The NBA was down to 10 teams by the 1950-51 season and slipped to eight by 1954-55 with Boston, New York, Philadelphia and Syracuse in the Eastern Division, and Ft. Wayne, Milwaukee (formerly Tri-Cities), Minneapolis and Rochester in the West.

By 1960, five of those surviving eight teams had moved to other cities but by the end of the decade the NBA was a 14-team league. It also had a rival, the **American Basketball Association**, which began play in 1967 with a red, white and blue ball, a three-point line and 11 teams. After a nine-year run, the ABA merged four clubs—the Denver Nuggets, Indiana Pacers, New York Nets and San Antonio Spurs—with the NBA following the 1975-76 season. The NBA adopted the three-point shot in 1979-80.

Expansion/Merger Timetable
For teams currently in NBA.

1948—Added NBL's Ft. Wayne Pistons (now Detroit), Minneapolis Lakers (now Los Angeles) and Rochester Royals (now Sacramento Kings); **1949**—Syracuse Nationals (now Philadelphia 76ers) and Tri-Cities Blackhawks (now Atlanta Hawks).

1961—Chicago Packers (now Washington Wizards); **1966**—Chicago Bulls; **1967**—San Diego Rockets (now Houston) and Seattle SuperSonics; **1968**—Milwaukee Bucks and Phoenix Suns.

1970—Buffalo Braves (now Los Angeles Clippers), Cleveland Cavaliers and Portland Trail Blazers; **1974**—New Orleans Jazz (now Utah); **1976**—added ABA's Denver Nuggets, Indiana Pacers, New York Nets (now New Jersey) and San Antonio Spurs.

1980—Dallas Mavericks; **1988**—Charlotte Hornets and Miami Heat; **1989**—Minnesota Timberwolves and Orlando Magic.

1995—Toronto Raptors and Vancouver Grizzlies (Now Memphis).

2004—Charlotte Bobcats.

City and Nickname Changes

1951—Tri-Cities Blackhawks, who divided home games between Moline and Rock Island, Ill., and Davenport, Iowa, move to Milwaukee and become the Hawks; **1955**—Milwaukee Hawks move to St. Louis; **1957**—Ft. Wayne Pistons move to Detroit, while Rochester Royals move to Cincinnati.

1960—Minneapolis Lakers move to Los Angeles; **1962**—Chicago Packers renamed Zephyrs, while Philadelphia Warriors move to San Francisco; **1963**—Chicago Zephyrs move to Baltimore and become Bullets, while Syracuse Nationals move to Philadelphia and become the 76ers; **1968**—St. Louis Hawks move to Atlanta.

1971—San Diego Rockets move to Houston, while San Francisco Warriors move to Oakland and become Golden State Warriors; **1972**—Cincinnati Royals move to Midwest, divide home games between Kansas City, Mo., and Omaha, Neb., and become Kings; **1973**—Baltimore Bullets move to Landover, Md., outside Washington and become Capital Bullets; **1974**—Capital Bullets renamed Washington Bullets; **1975**—KC-Omaha Kings settle in Kansas City; **1977**—New York Nets move from Uniondale, N.Y., to Piscataway, N.J. (later East Rutherford) and become New Jersey Nets; **1978**—Buffalo Braves move to San Diego and become the Clippers; **1979**—New Orleans Jazz move to Salt Lake City and become Utah Jazz.

1984—San Diego Clippers move to Los Angeles; **1985**—Kansas City Kings move to Sacramento.

1997—Washington Bullets become Washington Wizards.

2001—Vancouver Grizzlies move to Memphis, Tenn.; **2002**—Charlotte Hornets move to New Orleans; **2005**—New Orleans Hornets become New Orleans/Oklahoma City Hornets and divide home games between New Orleans and Oklahoma City in aftermath of Hurricane Katrina.

Defunct NBA Teams
Teams that once played in the BAA and NBA, but no longer exist.

Anderson (Ind.)—Packers (1949-50); **Baltimore**—Bullets (1947-55); **Chicago**—Stags (1946-50); **Cleveland**—Rebels (1946-47); **Denver**—Nuggets (1949-50); **Detroit**—Falcons (1946-47); **Indianapolis**—Jets (1948-49) and Olympians (1949-53); **Pittsburgh**—Ironmen (1946-47); **Providence**—Steamrollers (1946-49); **St. Louis**—Bombers (1946-50); **Sheboygan (Wisc.)**—Redskins (1949-50); **Toronto**—Huskies (1946-47); **Washington**—Capitols (1946-51); **Waterloo (Iowa)**—Hawks (1949-50).

ABA Teams (1967-76)

Anaheim—Amigos (1967-68, moved to LA); **Baltimore**—Claws (1975, never played); **Carolina**—Cougars (1969-74, moved to St. Louis); **Dallas**—Chaparrals (1967-73, called Texas Chaparrals in 1970-71, moved to San Antonio); **Denver**—Rockets (1967-76, renamed Nuggets in 1974-76); **Miami**—Floridians (1968-72, called simply Floridians from 1970-72).

Houston—Mavericks (1967-69, moved to North Carolina); **Indiana**—Pacers (1967-76); **Kentucky**—Colonels (1967-76); **Los Angeles**—Stars (1968-70, moved to Utah); **Memphis**—Pros (1970-75, renamed Tams in 1972 and Sounds in 1974, moved to Baltimore); **Minnesota**—Muskies (1967-68, moved to Miami) and Pipers (1968-69, moved back to Pittsburgh); **New Jersey**—Americans (1967-68, moved to New York).

New Orleans—Buccaneers (1967-70, moved to Memphis); **New York**—Nets (1968-76); **Oakland**—Oaks (1967-69, moved to Washington); **Pittsburgh**—Pipers (1967-68, moved to Minnesota), Pipers (1969-72, renamed Condors in 1970); **St. Louis**—Spirits of St. Louis (1974-76); **San Antonio**—Spurs (1973-76); **San Diego**—Conquistadors (1972-75, renamed Sails in 1975); **Utah**—Stars (1970-75); **Virginia**—Squires (1970-76); **Washington**—Caps (1969-70, moved to Virginia).

Annual NBA Leaders
Scoring

Decided by total points from 1947-69, and per game average since 1970. A lockout in 1999 shortened the regular season to 50 games.

Multiple winners: Michael Jordan (10); Wilt Chamberlain (7); George Gervin and Allen Iverson (4); Neil Johnston, Bob McAdoo and George Mikan (3); Kareem Abdul-Jabbar, Paul Arizin, Adrian Dantley, Tracy McGrady, Shaquille O'Neal and Bob Pettit (2).

Year		Gm	Pts	Avg	Year		Gm	Pts	Avg
1947	Joe Fulks, Phi	.60	1389	23.2	1979	George Gervin, SA	.80	2365	29.6
1948	Max Zaslofsky, Chi	.48	1007	21.0	1980	George Gervin, SA	.78	2585	33.1
1949	George Mikan, Mpls	.60	1698	28.3	1981	Adrian Dantley, Utah	.80	2452	30.7
1950	George Mikan, Mpls	.68	1865	27.4	1982	George Gervin, SA	.79	2551	32.3
1951	George Mikan, Mpls	.68	1932	28.4	1983	Alex English, Den	.82	2326	28.4
1952	Paul Arizin, Phi	.66	1674	25.4	1984	Adrian Dantley, Utah	.79	2418	30.6
1953	Neil Johnston, Phi	.70	1564	22.3	1985	Bernard King, NY	.55	1809	32.9
1954	Neil Johnston, Phi	.72	1759	24.4	1986	Dominique Wilkins, Atl	.78	2366	30.3
1955	Neil Johnston, Phi	.72	1631	22.7	1987	Michael Jordan, Chi	.82	3041	37.1
1956	Bob Pettit, St.L	.72	1849	25.7	1988	Michael Jordan, Chi	.82	2868	35.0
1957	Paul Arizin, Phi	.71	1817	25.6	1989	Michael Jordan, Chi	.81	2633	32.5
1958	George Yardley, Det	.72	2001	27.8	1990	Michael Jordan, Chi	.82	2753	33.6
1959	Bob Pettit, St.L	.72	2105	29.2	1991	Michael Jordan, Chi	.82	2580	31.5
1960	Wilt Chamberlain, Phi	.72	2707	37.6	1992	Michael Jordan, Chi	.80	2404	30.1
1961	Wilt Chamberlain, Phi	.79	3033	38.4	1993	Michael Jordan, Chi	.78	2541	32.6
1962	Wilt Chamberlain, Phi	.80	4029	50.4	1994	David Robinson, SA	.80	2383	29.8
1963	Wilt Chamberlain, SF	.80	3586	44.8	1995	Shaquille O'Neal, Orl	.79	2315	29.3
1964	Wilt Chamberlain, SF	.80	2948	36.9	1996	Michael Jordan, Chi	.82	2491	30.4
1965	Wilt Chamberlain, SF-Phi	.73	2534	34.7	1997	Michael Jordan, Chi	.82	2431	29.7
1966	Wilt Chamberlain, Phi	.79	2649	33.5	1998	Michael Jordan, Chi	.82	2357	28.7
1967	Rick Barry, SF	.78	2775	35.6	1999	Allen Iverson, Phi	.48	1284	26.8
1968	Dave Bing, Det	.79	2142	27.1	2000	Shaquille O'Neal, LAL	.79	2344	29.7
1969	Elvin Hayes, SD	.82	2327	28.4	2001	Allen Iverson, Phi	.71	2207	31.1
1970	Jerry West, LA	.74	2309	31.2	2002	Allen Iverson, Phi	.60	1883	31.4
1971	Lew Alcindor, Mil	.82	2596	31.7	2003	Tracy McGrady, Orl	.75	2407	32.1
1972	Kareem Abdul-Jabbar, Mil	.81	2822	34.8	2004	Tracy McGrady, Orl	.67	1878	28.0
1973	Nate Archibald, KC-Omaha	.80	2719	34.0	2005	Allen Iverson, Phi	.75	2302	30.7
1974	Bob McAdoo, Buf	.74	2261	30.6	2006	Kobe Bryant, LAL	.80	2832	35.4
1975	Bob McAdoo, Buf	.82	2831	34.5					
1976	Bob McAdoo, Buf	.78	2427	31.1					
1977	Pete Maravich, NO	.73	2273	31.1					
1978	George Gervin, SA	.82	2232	27.2					

Note: Lew Alcindor changed his name to Kareem Abdul-Jabbar after the 1970-71 season.

Rebounds

Decided by total rebounds from 1951-69 and per game average since 1970.
Multiple winners: Wilt Chamberlain (11); Dennis Rodman (7); Moses Malone (6); Bill Russell (4); Kevin Garnett (3); Elvin Hayes, Dikembe Mutombo, Hakeem Olajuwon and Ben Wallace (2).

Year		Gm	No	Avg	Year		Gm	No	Avg
1951	Dolph Schayes, Syr	.66	1080	16.4	1970	Elvin Hayes, SD	.82	1386	16.9
1952	Larry Foust, Ft. Wayne	.66	880	13.3	1971	Wilt Chamberlain, LA	.82	1493	18.2
	& Mel Hutchins, Mil	.66	880	13.3	1972	Wilt Chamberlain, LA	.82	1572	19.2
1953	George Mikan, Mpls	.70	1007	14.4	1973	Wilt Chamberlain, LA	.82	1526	18.6
1954	Harry Gallatin, NY	.72	1098	15.3	1974	Elvin Hayes, Cap*	.81	1463	18.1
1955	Neil Johnston, Phi	.72	1085	15.1	1975	Wes Unseld, Wash	.73	1077	14.8
1956	Bob Pettit, St.L	.72	1164	16.2	1976	Kareem Abdul-Jabbar, LA	.82	1383	16.9
1957	Maurice Stokes, Roch	.72	1256	17.4	1977	Bill Walton, Port	.65	934	14.4
1958	Bill Russell, Bos	.69	1564	22.7	1978	Len Robinson, NO	.82	1288	15.7
1959	Bill Russell, Bos	.70	1612	23.0	1979	Moses Malone, Hou	.82	1444	17.6
1960	Wilt Chamberlain, Phi	.72	1941	27.0	1980	Swen Nater, SD	.81	1216	15.0
1961	Wilt Chamberlain, Phi	.79	2149	27.2	1981	Moses Malone, Hou	.80	1180	14.8
1962	Wilt Chamberlain, Phi	.80	2052	25.7	1982	Moses Malone, Hou	.81	1188	14.7
1963	Wilt Chamberlain, SF	.80	1946	24.3	1983	Moses Malone, Phi	.78	1194	15.3
1964	Bill Russell, Bos	.78	1930	24.7	1984	Moses Malone, Phi	.71	950	13.4
1965	Bill Russell, Bos	.78	1878	24.1	1985	Moses Malone, Phi	.79	1031	13.1
1966	Wilt Chamberlain, Phi	.79	1943	24.6	1986	Bill Laimbeer, Det	.82	1075	13.1
1967	Wilt Chamberlain, Phi	.81	1957	24.2	1987	Charles Barkley, Phi	.68	994	14.6
1968	Wilt Chamberlain, Phi	.82	1952	23.8	1988	Michael Cage, LAC	.72	938	13.0
1969	Wilt Chamberlain, LA	.81	1712	21.1	1989	Hakeem Olajuwon, Hou	.82	1105	13.5

*The Baltimore Bullets moved to Landover, Md. in 1973-74 and became first the Capital Bullets, then the Washington Bullets in 1974-75.

Rebounds (Cont.)

Year		Gm	No	Avg	Year		Gm	No	Avg
1990	Hakeem Olajuwon, Hou	82	1149	14.0	1999	Chris Webber, Sac	42	545	13.0
1991	David Robinson, SA	82	1063	13.0	2000	Dikembe Mutombo, Atl	82	1157	14.1
1992	Dennis Rodman, Det	82	1530	18.7	2001	Dikembe Mutombo, Atl-Phi	75	1015	13.5
1993	Dennis Rodman, Det	62	1232	18.3	2002	Ben Wallace, Det	80	1039	13.0
1994	Dennis Rodman, SA	79	1132	17.3	2003	Ben Wallace, Det	73	1126	15.4
1995	Dennis Rodman, SA	49	823	16.8	2004	Kevin Garnett, Min	82	1139	13.9
1996	Dennis Rodman, Chi	64	952	14.9	2005	Kevin Garnett, Min	82	1108	13.5
1997	Dennis Rodman, Chi	55	883	16.1	2006	Kevin Garnett, Min	76	966	12.7
1998	Dennis Rodman, Chi	80	1201	15.0					

Assists

Decided by total assists from 1952-69 and per game average since 1970.

Multiple winners: John Stockton (9); Bob Cousy (8); Oscar Robertson (6); Jason Kidd (5); Magic Johnson and Kevin Porter (4); Steve Nash, Andy Phillip and Guy Rodgers (2).

Year		No	Year		No	Year		APG
1947	Ernie Calverley, Prov	202	1967	Guy Rodgers, Chi	908	1987	Magic Johnson, LAL	12.2
1948	Howie Dallmar, Phi	120	1968	Wilt Chamberlain, Phi	702	1988	John Stockton, Utah	13.8
1949	Bob Davies, Roch	321	1969	Oscar Robertson, Cin	772	1989	John Stockton, Utah	13.6
1950	Dick McGuire, NY	386	1970	Lenny Wilkens, Sea	9.1	1990	John Stockton, Utah	14.5
1951	Andy Phillip, Phi	414	1971	Norm Van Lier, Chi	10.1	1991	John Stockton, Utah	14.2
1952	Andy Phillip, Phi	539	1972	Jerry West, LA	9.7	1992	John Stockton, Utah	13.7
1953	Bob Cousy, Bos	547	1973	Nate Archibald, KC-O	11.4	1993	John Stockton, Utah	12.0
1954	Bob Cousy, Bos	518	1974	Ernie DiGregorio, Buf	8.2	1994	John Stockton, Utah	12.6
1955	Bob Cousy, Bos	557	1975	Kevin Porter, Wash	8.0	1995	John Stockton, Utah	12.3
1956	Bob Cousy, Bos	642	1976	Slick Watts, Sea	8.1	1996	John Stockton, Utah	11.2
1957	Bob Cousy, Bos	478	1977	Don Buse, Ind	8.5	1997	Mark Jackson, Den-Ind	11.4
1958	Bob Cousy, Bos	463	1978	Kevin Porter, Det-NJ	10.2	1998	Rod Strickland, Wash	10.5
1959	Bob Cousy, Bos	557	1979	Kevin Porter, Det	13.4	1999	Jason Kidd, Pho	10.8
1960	Bob Cousy, Bos	715	1980	M.R. Richardson, NY	10.1	2000	Jason Kidd, Pho	10.1
1961	Oscar Robertson, Cin	690	1981	Kevin Porter, Wash	9.1	2001	Jason Kidd, Pho	9.8
1962	Oscar Robertson, Cin	899	1982	Johnny Moore, SA	9.6	2002	Andre Miller, Cle	10.9
1963	Guy Rodgers, SF	825	1983	Magic Johnson, LA	10.5	2003	Jason Kidd, NJ	8.9
1964	Oscar Robertson, Cin	868	1984	Magic Johnson, LA	13.1	2004	Jason Kidd, NJ	9.2
1965	Oscar Robertson, Cin	861	1985	Isiah Thomas, Det	13.9	2005	Steve Nash, Dal	11.5
1966	Oscar Robertson, Cin	847	1986	Magic Johnson, LAL	12.6	2006	Steve Nash, Pho	10.5

Field Goal Percentage

Multiple winners: Wilt Chamberlain and Shaquille O'Neal (9); Artis Gilmore (4); Neil Johnston (3); Bob Feerick, Johnny Green, Alex Groza, Cedric Maxwell, Kevin McHale, Gheorghe Muresan, Kenny Sears and Buck Williams (2).

Year		Pct	Year		Pct	Year		Pct
1947	Bob Feerick, Wash	.401	1967	Wilt Chamberlain, Phi	.683	1987	Kevin McHale, Bos	.604
1948	Bob Feerick, Wash	.340	1968	Wilt Chamberlain, Phi	.595	1988	Kevin McHale, Bos	.604
1949	Arnie Risen, Roch	.423	1969	Wilt Chamberlain, LA	.583	1989	Dennis Rodman, Det	.595
1950	Alex Groza, Indpls	.478	1970	Johnny Green, Cin	.559	1990	Mark West, Pho	.625
1951	Alex Groza, Indpls	.470	1971	Johnny Green, Cin	.587	1991	Buck Williams, Port	.602
1952	Paul Arizin, Phi	.448	1972	Wilt Chamberlain, LA	.649	1992	Buck Williams, Port	.604
1953	Neil Johnston, Phi	.452	1973	Wilt Chamberlain, LA	.727	1993	Cedric Ceballos, Pho	.576
1954	Ed Macauley, Bos	.486	1974	Bob McAdoo, Buf	.547	1994	Shaquille O'Neal, Orl	.599
1955	Larry Foust, Ft.W.	.487	1975	Don Nelson, Bos	.539	1995	Chris Gatling, G.St	.633
1956	Neil Johnston, Phi	.457	1976	Wes Unseld, Wash	.561	1996	Gheorghe Muresan, Wash	.584
1957	Neil Johnston, Phi	.447	1977	K. Abdul-Jabbar, LA	.579	1997	Gheorghe Muresan, Wash	.604
1958	Jack Twyman, Cin	.452	1978	Bobby Jones, Den	.578	1998	Shaquille O'Neal, LAL	.584
1959	Kenny Sears, NY	.490	1979	Cedric Maxwell, Bos	.584	1999	Shaquille O'Neal, LAL	.576
1960	Kenny Sears, NY	.477	1980	Cedric Maxwell, Bos	.609	2000	Shaquille O'Neal, LAL	.574
1961	Wilt Chamberlain, Phi	.509	1981	Artis Gilmore, Chi	.670	2001	Shaquille O'Neal, LAL	.572
1962	Walt Bellamy, Chi	.519	1982	Artis Gilmore, Chi	.652	2002	Shaquille O'Neal, LAL	.579
1963	Wilt Chamberlain, SF	.528	1983	Artis Gilmore, SA	.626	2003	Eddy Curry, Chi	.585
1964	Jerry Lucas, Cin	.527	1984	Artis Gilmore, SA	.631	2004	Shaquille O'Neal, LAL	.584
1965	W. Chamberlain, SF-Phi	.510	1985	James Donaldson, LAC	.637	2005	Shaquille O'Neal, Mia	.601
1966	Wilt Chamberlain, Phi	.540	1986	Steve Johnson, SA	.632	2006	Shaquille O'Neal, Mia	.600

Free Throw Percentage

Multiple winners: Bill Sharman (7); Rick Barry (6); Reggie Miller (5); Larry Bird (4); Mark Price and Dolph Schayes (3); Mahmoud Abdul-Rauf, Larry Costello, Ernie DiGregorio, Bob Feerick, Kyle Macy, Calvin Murphy, Oscar Robertson and Larry Siegfried (2).

Year		Pct	Year		Pct	Year		Pct
1947	Fred Scolari, Wash	.811	1952	Bob Wanzer, Roch	.904	1957	Bill Sharman, Bos	.905
1948	Bob Feerick, Wash	.788	1953	Bill Sharman, Bos	.850	1958	Dolph Schayes, Syr	.904
1949	Bob Feerick, Wash	.859	1954	Bill Sharman, Bos	.844	1959	Bill Sharman, Bos	.932
1950	Max Zaslofsky, Chi	.843	1955	Bill Sharman, Bos	.897	1960	Dolph Schayes, Syr	.892
1951	Joe Fulks, Phi	.855	1956	Bill Sharman, Bos	.867	1961	Bill Sharman, Bos	.921

Free Throw Percentage (Cont.)

Year	Pct	Year	Pct	Year	Pct
1962 Dolph Schayes, Syr	.896	1977 Ernie DiGregorio, Buf	.945	1992 Mark Price, Cle	.947
1963 Larry Costello, Syr	.881	1978 Rick Barry, G.St.	.924	1993 Mark Price, Cle	.948
1964 Oscar Robertson, Cin	.853	1979 Rick Barry, Hou	.947	1994 M. Abdul-Rauf, Den	.956
1965 Larry Costello, Phi	.877	1980 Rick Barry, Hou	.935	1995 Spud Webb, Sac	.934
1966 Larry Siegfried, Bos	.881	1981 Calvin Murphy, Hou	.958	1996 M. Abdul-Rauf, Den	.930
1967 Adrian Smith, Cin	.903	1982 Kyle Macy, Pho	.899	1997 Mark Price, G.St.	.906
1968 Oscar Robertson, Cin	.873	1983 Calvin Murphy, Hou	.920	1998 Chris Mullin, Ind	.939
1969 Larry Siegfried, NY	.864	1984 Larry Bird, Bos	.888	1999 Reggie Miller, Ind	.915
1970 Flynn Robinson, Mil	.898	1985 Kyle Macy, Pho	.907	2000 Jeff Hornacek, Utah	.950
1971 Chet Walker, Chi	.859	1986 Larry Bird, Bos	.896	2001 Reggie Miller, Ind	.928
1972 Jack Marin, Bal	.894	1987 Larry Bird, Bos	.910	2002 Reggie Miller, Ind	.911
1973 Rick Barry, G.St.	.902	1988 Jack Sikma, Mil	.922	2003 Allan Houston, NY	.919
1974 Ernie DiGregorio, Buf	.902	1989 Magic Johnson, LAL	.911	2004 Predrag Stojakovic, Sac	.927
1975 Rick Barry, G.St.	.904	1990 Larry Bird, Bos	.930	2005 Reggie Miller, Ind	.933
1976 Rick Barry, G.St.	.923	1991 Reggie Miller, Ind	.918	2006 Steve Nash, Pho	.921

Three-Point Field Goal Percentage

Multiple winners: Craig Hodges, Steve Kerr (2)

Year	Pct	Year	Pct	Year	Pct
1980 Fred Brown, Sea	.443	1989 Jon Sundvold, Mia	.522	1998 Dale Ellis, Sea	.464
1981 Brian Taylor, SD	.383	1990 Steve Kerr, Cle	.507	1999 Dell Curry, Milw	.476
1982 Campy Russell, NY	.439	1991 Jim Les, Sac	.461	2000 Hubert Davis, Dal	.491
1983 Mike Dunleavy, SA	.345	1992 Dana Barros, Sea	.446	2001 Brent Barry, Sea	.476
1984 Darrell Griffith, Utah	.361	1993 B.J. Armstrong, Chi	.453	2002 Steve Smith, SA	.472
1985 Byron Scott, LAL	.433	1994 Tracy Murray, Por	.459	2003 Bruce Bowen, SA	.441
1986 Craig Hodges, Milw	.451	1995 Steve Kerr, Chi	.524	2004 Anthony Peeler, Sac	.482
1987 Kiki Vandeweghe, Por	.481	1996 Tim Legler, Wash	.522	2005 Fred Hoiberg, Min	.483
1988 Craig Hodges, Milw-Pho	.491	1997 Glen Rice, Cha	.470	2006 Richard Hamilton, Det	.458

Blocked Shots

Multiple winners: Kareem Abdul-Jabbar and Mark Eaton (4); George Johnson, Dikembe Mutombo, Hakeem Olajuwon and Theo Ratliff (3); Manute Bol, Marcus Camby and Alonzo Mourning (2).

Year	Gm	No	Avg
1974 Elmore Smith, LA	.81	393	4.85
1975 Kareem Abdul-Jabbar, Mil	.65	212	3.26
1976 Kareem Abdul-Jabbar, LA	.82	338	4.12
1977 Bill Walton, Port	.65	211	3.25
1978 George Johnson, NJ	.81	274	3.38
1979 Kareem Abdul-Jabbar, LA	.80	316	3.95
1980 Kareem Abdul-Jabbar, LA	.82	280	3.41
1981 George Johnson, SA	.82	278	3.39
1982 George Johnson, SA	.75	234	3.12
1983 Tree Rollins, Atl	.80	343	4.29
1984 Mark Eaton, Utah	.82	351	4.28
1985 Mark Eaton, Utah	.82	456	5.56
1986 Manute Bol, Wash	.80	397	4.96
1987 Mark Eaton, Utah	.79	321	4.06
1988 Mark Eaton, Utah	.82	304	3.71
1989 Manute Bol, G.St.	.80	345	4.31
1990 Akeem Olajuwon, Hou	.82	376	4.59
1991 Hakeem Olajuwon, Hou	.56	221	3.95
1992 David Robinson, SA	.68	305	4.49
1993 Hakeem Olajuwon, Hou	.82	342	4.17
1994 Dikembe Mutombo, Den	.82	336	4.10
1995 Dikembe Mutombo, Den	.82	321	3.91
1996 Dikembe Mutombo, Den	.74	332	4.49
1997 Shawn Bradley, Dal-NJ	.73	248	3.40
1998 Marcus Camby, Tor	.63	230	3.65
1999 Alonzo Mourning, Mia	.46	180	3.91
2000 Alonzo Mourning, Mia	.79	294	3.72
2001 Theo Ratliff, Phi-Atl	.50	187	3.74
2002 Ben Wallace, Det	.80	278	3.48
2003 Theo Ratliff, Atl	.81	262	3.23
2004 Theo Ratliff, Atl-Port	.85	307	3.61
2005 Andrei Kirilenko, Utah	.41	136	3.32
2006 Marcus Camby, Den	.56	184	3.29

Steals

Multiple winners: Allen Iverson, Michael Jordan, Micheal Ray Richardson and Alvin Robertson (3); Mookie Blaylock, Magic Johnson and John Stockton (2).

Year	Gm	No	Avg
1974 Larry Steele, Port	.81	217	2.68
1975 Rick Barry, G.St.	.80	228	2.85
1976 Slick Watts, Sea	.82	261	3.18
1977 Don Buse, Ind	.81	281	3.47
1978 Ron Lee, Pho	.82	225	2.74
1979 M.L. Carr, Det	.80	197	2.46
1980 Micheal Ray Richardson, NY	.82	265	3.23
1981 Magic Johnson, LA	.37	127	3.43
1982 Magic Johnson, LA	.78	208	2.67
1983 Micheal Ray Richardson, G. ST-NJ	.64	182	2.84
1984 Rickey Green, Utah	.81	215	2.65
1985 Micheal Ray Richardson, NJ	.82	243	2.96
1986 Alvin Robertson, SA	.82	301	3.67
1987 Alvin Robertson, SA	.81	260	3.21
1988 Michael Jordan, Chi	.82	259	3.16
1989 John Stockton, Utah	.82	263	3.21
1990 Michael Jordan, Chi	.82	227	2.77
1991 Alvin Robertson, SA	.81	246	3.04
1992 John Stockton, Utah	.82	244	2.98
1993 Michael Jordan, Chi	.78	221	2.83
1994 Nate McMillan, Sea	.73	216	2.96
1995 Scottie Pippen, Chi	.79	232	2.94
1996 Gary Payton, Sea	.81	231	2.85
1997 Mookie Blaylock, Atl	.78	212	2.72
1998 Mookie Blaylock, Atl	.70	183	2.61
1999 Kendall Gill, NJ	.50	134	2.68
2000 Eddie Jones, Cha	.72	192	2.67
2001 Allen Iverson, Phi	.71	178	2.51
2002 Allen Iverson, Phi	.60	168	2.80
2003 Allen Iverson, Phi	.82	225	2.74
2004 Baron Davis, NO	.67	158	2.36
2005 Larry Hughes, Wash	.61	176	2.89
2006 Gerald Wallace, Cha	.55	138	2.51

Note: Akeem Olajuwon changed the spelling of his first name to Hakeem during the 1990-91 season.

All-Time NBA Regular Season Leaders
Through the 2005-06 regular season.
CAREER
Players active in 2005-06 in **bold** type.

Points

		Yrs	Gm	Pts	Avg
1	Kareem Abdul-Jabbar	.20	1560	**38,387**	24.6
2	Karl Malone	.19	1476	**36,928**	25.0
3	Michael Jordan	.15	1072	**32,292**	30.1
4	Wilt Chamberlain	.14	1045	**31,419**	30.1
5	Moses Malone	.19	1329	**27,409**	20.6
6	Elvin Hayes	.16	1303	**27,313**	21.0
7	Hakeem Olajuwon	.18	1238	**26,946**	21.8
8	Oscar Robertson	.14	1040	**26,710**	25.7
9	Dominique Wilkins	.15	1074	**26,668**	24.8
10	John Havlicek	.16	1270	**26,395**	20.8
11	Alex English	.15	1193	**25,613**	21.5
12	Reggie Miller	.18	1389	**25,279**	18.2
13	Jerry West	.14	932	**25,192**	27.0
14	Patrick Ewing	.17	1183	**24,815**	21.0
15	**Shaquille O'Neal**	.14	941	**24,764**	26.3
16	Charles Barkley	.16	1073	**23,757**	22.1
17	Robert Parish	.21	1611	**23,334**	14.5
18	Adrian Dantley	.15	955	**23,177**	24.3
19	Elgin Baylor	.14	846	**23,149**	27.4
20	Clyde Drexler	.15	1086	**22,195**	20.4
21	Larry Bird	.13	897	**21,791**	24.3
22	Hal Greer	.15	1122	**21,586**	19.2
23	**Gary Payton**	.16	1267	**21,455**	16.9
24	Walt Bellamy	.14	1043	**20,941**	20.1
25	Bob Pettit	.11	792	**20,880**	26.4
26	David Robinson	.14	987	**20,790**	21.1
27	George Gervin	.10	791	**20,708**	26.2
28	Mitch Richmond	.14	976	**20,497**	21.0
29	Tom Chambers	.16	1107	**20,049**	18.1
30	John Stockton	.19	1504	**19,711**	13.1

Scoring Average
Minimum of 400 games or 10,000 points.

		Yrs	Gm	Pts	Avg
1	Michael Jordan	.15	1072	32,292	30.1
2	Wilt Chamberlain	.14	1045	31,419	30.1
3	**Allen Iverson**	.10	682	19,115	28.0
4	Elgin Baylor	.14	846	23,149	27.4
5	Jerry West	.14	932	25,192	27.0
6	Bob Pettit	.11	792	20,880	26.4
7	**Shaquille O'Neal**	.14	941	24,764	26.3
8	George Gervin	.10	791	20,708	26.2
9	Oscar Robertson	.14	1040	26,710	25.7
10	Karl Malone	.19	1476	36,928	25.0
11	Dominique Wilkins	.15	1074	26,668	24.8
12	Kareem Abdul-Jabbar	.20	1560	38,387	24.6
13	Larry Bird	.13	897	21,791	24.3
14	Adrian Dantley	.15	955	23,177	24.3
15	Pete Maravich	.10	658	15,948	24.2
16	**Vince Carter**	.8	539	12,900	23.9
17	**Kobe Bryant**	.10	707	16,866	23.9
18	**Paul Pierce**	.8	605	14,202	23.5
19	Rick Barry	.10	794	18,395	23.2
20	Paul Arizin	.10	713	16,266	22.8
21	George Mikan	.9	520	11,764	22.6
22	Bernard King	.14	874	19,655	22.5
23	**Tracy McGrady**	.9	612	13,570	22.2
24	Charles Barkley	.16	1073	23,757	22.1
25	David Thompson	.8	509	11,264	22.1
26	**Tim Duncan**	.9	666	14,689	22.1
27	Bob McAdoo	.14	852	18,787	22.1
28	**Dirk Nowitzki**	.8	603	13,257	22.0
29	Julius Erving	.11	836	18,364	22.0
30	Geoff Petrie	.6	446	9,732	21.8

Assists

		Yrs	Gm	No	Avg
1	John Stockton	.19	1504	**15,806**	10.5
2	Mark Jackson	.17	1296	**10,334**	8.0
3	Magic Johnson	.13	906	**10,141**	11.2
4	Oscar Robertson	.14	1040	**9,887**	9.5
5	Isiah Thomas	.13	979	**9,061**	9.3
6	**Gary Payton**	.16	1267	**8,765**	6.9
7	Rod Strickland	.17	1094	**7,987**	7.3
8	**Jason Kidd**	.12	866	**7,955**	9.2
9	Maurice Cheeks	.15	1101	**7,392**	6.7
10	Lenny Wilkens	.15	1077	**7,211**	6.7
11	Terry Porter	.17	1274	**7,160**	5.6
12	Tim Hardaway	.13	867	**7,095**	8.2

Steals

		Yrs	Gm	No
1	John Stockton	.19	1504	3265
2	Michael Jordan	.15	1072	2514
3	**Gary Payton**	.16	1267	2402
4	Maurice Cheeks	.15	1101	2310
5	Scottie Pippen	.17	1178	2307

Note: Steals have only been an official stat since the 1973-74 season.

Blocked Shots

		Yrs	Gm	No
1	Hakeem Olajuwon	.18	1238	3830
2	Kareem Abdul-Jabbar	.20	1560	3189
3	**Dikembe Mutombo**	.15	1073	3154
4	Mark Eaton	.11	875	3064
5	David Robinson	.14	987	2954

Note: Blocked shots have only been an official stat since the 1973-74 season. Also, note that if ABA records are included, consider the following block totals: Artis Gilmore (3,178).

Rebounds

		Yrs	Gm	No	Avg
1	Wilt Chamberlain	.14	1045	**23,924**	22.9
2	Bill Russell	.13	963	**21,620**	22.5
3	Kareem Abdul-Jabbar	.20	1560	**17,440**	11.2
4	Elvin Hayes	.16	1303	**16,279**	12.5
5	Moses Malone	.19	1329	**16,212**	12.2
6	Karl Malone	.19	1476	**14,968**	10.1
7	Robert Parish	.21	1611	**14,715**	9.1
8	Nate Thurmond	.14	964	**14,464**	15.0
9	Walt Bellamy	.14	1043	**14,241**	13.7
10	Wes Unseld	.13	984	**13,769**	14.0
11	Hakeem Olajuwon	.18	1238	**13,748**	11.1
12	Buck Williams	.17	1307	**13,017**	10.0

Note: If rebounds accumulated in the ABA are included, consider the following totals: Moses Malone (17,834) and Artis Gilmore (16,330).

Games Played

		Yrs	Career	Gm
1	Robert Parish	.21	1976-97	1611
2	Kareem Abdul-Jabbar	.20	1970-89	1560
3	John Stockton	.19	1984-03	1504
4	Karl Malone	.19	1985-04	1476
5	Kevin Willis	.19	1985-05	1419

Note: If ABA records are included, consider the following game totals: Moses Malone (1,455).

Field Goals

		Yrs	FG	Att	Pct
1	Kareem Abdul-Jabbar	.20	15,837	28,307	.559
2	Karl Malone	.19	13,528	26,210	.516
3	Wilt Chamberlain	.14	12,681	23,497	.540
4	Michael Jordan	.15	12,192	24,537	.497
5	Elvin Hayes	.16	10,976	24,272	.452
6	Hakeem Olajuwon	.18	10,749	20,991	.512
7	Alex English	.15	10,659	21,036	.507
8	John Havlicek	.16	10,513	23,930	.439
9	Dominique Wilkins	.15	9,963	21,589	.461
10	**Shaquille O'Neal**	.13	9,808	16,915	.580
11	Patrick Ewing	.17	9,702	19,241	.504
12	Robert Parish	.21	9,614	17,914	.537

Note: If field goals made in the ABA are included, consider these NBA-ABA totals: Julius Erving (11,818), Dan Issel (10,431), George Gervin (10,368), Moses Malone (10,277) and Rick Barry (9,695).

Free Throws

		Yrs	FT	Att	Pct
1	Karl Malone	.19	9787	13,188	.742
2	Moses Malone	.19	8531	11,090	.769
3	Oscar Robertson	.14	7694	9,185	.838
4	Michael Jordan	.15	7327	8,772	.835
5	Jerry West	.14	7160	8,801	.814
6	Dolph Schayes	.16	6979	8,273	.844
7	Adrian Dantley	.15	6832	8,351	.818
8	Kareem Abdul-Jabbar	.20	6712	9,304	.721
9	Charles Barkley	.16	6349	8,643	.734
10	Reggie Miller	.18	6237	7,026	.888
11	Bob Pettit	.11	6182	8,119	.761
12	Wilt Chamberlain	.14	6057	11,862	.511

Note: If free throws made in the ABA are included, consider these totals: Moses Malone (9,018), Dan Issel (6,591), and Julius Erving (6,256).

Free Throw Percentage

		Yrs	FT	Att	Pct
1	Mark Price	.12	2135	2362	.904
2	Rick Barry	.10	3818	4243	.900
3	**Steve Nash**	.10	1726	1926	.896
4	**Peja Stojakovic**	.8	1864	2086	.894
5	Calvin Murphy	.13	3445	3864	.892

Note: If ABA records are included, consider the following free throw percentage: Rick Barry (5713-6397 for .893)

3-Pt Field Goal Pct.

(minimum 250 3-pt FGs made)

		Yrs	Gm	Pct	3FGM
1	Steve Kerr	.15	910	.454	726
2	Hubert Davis	.12	685	.441	728
3	Drazen Petrovic	.4	290	.437	255
4	Tim Legler	.10	310	.431	260
5	B.J. Armstrong	.11	747	.425	436

3-Pt Field Goals Made

		Yrs	Gm	Pct	3FGM
1	Reggie Miller	.18	1389	.395	2560
2	**Ray Allen**	.10	735	.399	1755
3	Dale Ellis	.17	1209	.403	1719
4	Glen Rice	.15	1000	.400	1559
5	Tim Hardaway	.14	867	.355	1542

Minutes Played

		Gm	MPG	Min
1	Kareem Abdul-Jabbar	.1560	36.8	57,446
2	Karl Malone	.1476	37.2	54,852
3	Elvin Hayes	.1303	38.4	50,000
4	Wilt Chamberlain	.1045	45.8	47,859
5	John Stockton	.1504	31.8	47,764

Triple-Doubles

		Yrs	Gm	No
1	Oscar Robertson	.14	1040	181
2	Magic Johnson	.13	906	138
3	Wilt Chamberlain	.14	1045	78
4	**Jason Kidd**	.12	866	75
5	Larry Bird	.13	897	59

Note: The triple-double totals of Oscar Robertson and Wilt Chamberlain do not include games in which they may have recorded a triple-double with double-digit blocks and/or steals, since those stats have only been official since the 1973-74 season.

Personal Fouls

		Yrs	Gm	Fouls	DQ
1	Kareem Abdul-Jabbar	.20	1560	4657	48
2	Karl Malone	.19	1476	4578	28
3	Robert Parish	.21	1611	4443	86
4	Charles Oakley	.19	1282	4421	63
5	Hakeem Olajuwon	.18	1238	4383	80

Note: If ABA records are included, consider the following personal foul totals: Artis Gilmore (4,529) and Caldwell Jones (4,436).

Disqualifications

		Yrs	Gm	No
1	Vern Mikkelsen	.10	699	127
2	Walter Dukes	.8	553	121
3	Shawn Kemp	.14	1051	115
4	Charlie Share	.8	555	105
5	Paul Arizin	.10	713	101

NBA-ABA Top 20

Points

All-Time combined regular season scoring leaders, including ABA service (1968-76). NBA players with ABA experience are listed in CAPITAL letters. Players active during 2005-06 are in **bold** type.

		Yrs	Pts	Avg
1	Kareem Abdul-Jabbar	.20	38,387	24.6
2	Karl Malone	.19	36,928	25.0
3	Wilt Chamberlain	.14	31,419	30.1
4	Michael Jordan	.15	32,292	30.1
5	JULIUS ERVING	.16	30,026	24.2
6	MOSES MALONE	.21	29,580	20.3
7	DAN ISSEL	.15	27,482	22.6
8	Elvin Hayes	.16	27,313	21.0
9	Hakeem Olajuwon	.18	26,946	21.8
10	Oscar Robertson	.14	26,710	25.7
11	Dominique Wilkins	.15	26,668	24.8
12	GEORGE GERVIN	.14	26,595	25.1
13	John Havlicek	.16	26,395	20.8
14	Alex English	.15	25,613	21.5
15	RICK BARRY	.14	25,279	24.8
	Reggie Miller	.18	25,279	18.2
17	Jerry West	.14	25,192	27.0
18	ARTIS GILMORE	.17	24,941	18.8
19	Patrick Ewing	.17	24,815	21.0
20	**Shaquille O'Neal**	.14	24,764	26.3

ABA Totals: BARRY (4 yrs, 226 gm, 6884 pts, 30.5 avg); ERVING (5 yrs, 407 gm, 11,662 pts, 28.7 avg); GERVIN (4 yrs, 269 gm, 5887 pts, 21.9 avg); GILMORE (5 yrs, 420 gm, 9362 pts, 22.3 avg); ISSEL (6 yrs, 500 gm, 12,823 pts, 25.6 avg); MALONE (2 yrs, 126 gm, 2171 pts, 17.2 avg).

All-Time NBA Regular Season Leaders (Cont.)

SINGLE SEASON

Scoring Average

		Season	Avg
1	Wilt Chamberlain, Phi	1961-62	50.4
2	Wilt Chamberlain, SF	1962-63	44.8
3	Wilt Chamberlain, Phi	1960-61	38.4
4	Elgin Baylor, LA	1961-62	38.3
5	Wilt Chamberlain, Phi	1959-60	37.6
6	Michael Jordan, Chi	1986-87	37.1
7	Wilt Chamberlain, SF	1963-64	36.9
8	Rick Barry, SF	1966-67	35.6
9	Kobe Bryant, LAL	2005-06	35.4
10	Michael Jordan, Chi	1987-88	35.0

Field Goal Pct.

		Season	Pct
1	Wilt Chamberlain, LA	1972-73	.727
2	Wilt Chamberlain, SF	1966-67	.683
3	Artis Gilmore, Chi	1980-81	.670
4	Artis Gilmore, Chi	1981-82	.652
5	Wilt Chamberlain, LA	1971-72	.649

Free Throw Pct.

		Season	Pct
1	Calvin Murphy, Hou	1980-81	.958
2	Mahmoud Abdul-Rauf, Den.	1993-94	.956
3	Mark Price, Cle	1992-93	.948
4	Mark Price, Cle	1991-92	.947
	Rick Barry, Hou	1978-79	.947

3-Pt Field Goal Pct.

		Season	Pct
1	Steve Kerr, Chi	1994-95	.524
2	Jon Sundvold, Mia	1988-89	.522
3	Tim Legler, Wash	1995-96	.522
4	Steve Kerr, Chi	1995-96	.515
5	Detlef Schrempf, Sea	1994-95	.514

Personal Fouls

		Season	No
1	Darryl Dawkins, NJ	1983-84	386
2	Darryl Dawkins, NJ	1982-83	379

Assists

		Season	Avg
1	John Stockton, Utah	1989-90	14.5
2	John Stockton, Utah	1990-91	14.2
3	Isiah Thomas, Det	1984-85	13.9
4	John Stockton, Utah	1987-88	13.8
5	John Stockton, Utah	1991-92	13.7
6	John Stockton, Utah	1988-89	13.6
7	Kevin Porter, Det	1978-79	13.4
8	Magic Johnson, LAL	1983-84	13.1
9	Magic Johnson, LAL	1988-89	12.8
10	John Stockton, Utah	1993-94	12.6

Rebounds

		Season	Avg
1	Wilt Chamberlain, Phi	1960-61	27.2
2	Wilt Chamberlain, Phi	1959-60	27.0
3	Wilt Chamberlain, Phi	1961-62	25.7
4	Bill Russell, Bos	1963-64	24.7
5	Wilt Chamberlain, Phi	1965-66	24.6

Blocked Shots

		Season	Avg
1	Mark Eaton, Utah	1984-85	5.56
2	Manute Bol, Wash	1985-86	4.96
3	Elmore Smith, LA	1973-74	4.85
4	Mark Eaton, Utah	1985-86	4.61
5	Hakeem Olajuwon, Hou	1989-90	4.59

Steals

		Season	Avg
1	Alvin Robertson, SA	1985-86	3.67
2	Don Buse, Ind	1976-77	3.47
3	Magic Johnson, LAL	1980-81	3.43
4	Micheal Ray Richardson, NY	1979-80	3.23
5	Alvin Robertson, SA	1986-87	3.21

Turnovers

		Season	No
1	Artis Gilmore, Chi	1977-78	366
2	Kevin Porter, Det/NJ	1977-78	360

SINGLE GAME

Points

	Date	FG-FT	Pts
Wilt Chamberlain, Phi vs NY†	3/2/62	36-28–	100
Kobe Bryant, LAL vs. Tor	1/22/06	28-18–	81
Wilt Chamberlain, Phi vs LA***	12/8/61	31-16–	78
Wilt Chamberlain, Phi vs Chi	1/13/62	29-15–	73
Wilt Chamberlain, SF at NY	11/16/62	29-15–	73
David Thompson, Den at Det	4/9/78	28-17–	73
Wilt Chamberlain, SF at LA	11/3/62	29-14–	72
Elgin Baylor, LA at NY	11/15/60	28-15–	71
David Robinson, SA at LAC	4/24/94	26-18–	71
Wilt Chamberlain, SF at Syr	3/10/63	27-16–	70
Michael Jordan, Chi at Cle*	3/28/90	23-21–	69
Wilt Chamberlain, Phi at Chi	12/16/67	30- 8–	68
Pete Maravich, NO vs NYK	2/25/77	26-16–	68
Wilt Chamberlain, Phi vs NY	3/9/61	27-13–	67
Wilt Chamberlain, Phi at St. L	2/17/62	26-15–	67
Wilt Chamberlain, Phi vs NY	2/25/62	25-17–	67
Wilt Chamberlain, SF vs LA	1/11/63	28-11–	67
Wilt Chamberlain, LA vs Pho	2/9/69	29- 8–	66
Wilt Chamberlain, Phi at Cin	2/13/62	24-17–	65
Wilt Chamberlain, Phi at St. L	2/27/62	25-15–	65
Wilt Chamberlain, Phi vs LA	2/7/66	28- 9–	65
Elgin Baylor, Mpls vs Bos	11/8/59	25-14–	64
Rick Barry, G.St. vs Port	3/26/74	30- 4–	64
Michael Jordan, Chi vs Orl	1/16/93	27- 9–	64

*Overtime   ***Triple overtime.
†Game was played at Hershey, Penn.

Field Goals

	Date	FG	Att
Wilt Chamberlain, Phi vs NY	3/2/62	36	63
Wilt Chamberlain, Phi vs LA***	12/8/61	31	62
Wilt Chamberlain, Phi at Chi	12/16/67	30	40
Rick Barry, G.St. vs Port	2/26/74	30	45

Wilt Chamberlain made 29 four times.
***Triple overtime.

Free Throws

	Date	FT	Att
Wilt Chamberlain, Phi vs NY	3/2/62	28	32
Adrian Dantley, Utah vs Hou	1/4/84	28	29
Adrian Dantley, Utah vs Den	11/25/83	27	31
Adrian Dantley, Utah vs Dal	10/31/80	26	29
Michael Jordan, Chi vs NJ	2/26/87	26	27

3-Pt Field Goals

	Date	No
Kobe Bryant, LAL vs Sea	1/7/03	12
Dennis Scott, Orl vs Atl	4/18/96	11
Ray Allen, Milw vs Char	4/14/02	10
Brian Shaw, Mia at Mil	4/8/93	10
Joe Dumars, Det vs Min	11/8/94	10
George McCloud, Dal vs Pho	12/16/95	10*

Many tied with 9 each
* Overtime

Assists

	Date	No
Scott Skiles, Orl vs Den	12/30/90	30
Kevin Porter, NJ vs Hou	2/24/78	29
Bob Cousy, Bos vs Mpls	2/27/59	28
Guy Rodgers, SF vs St.L	3/14/63	28
John Stockton, Utah vs SA	1/15/91	28

Rebounds

	Date	No
Wilt Chamberlain, Phi vs Bos	11/24/60	55
Bill Russell, Bos vs Syr	2/5/60	51
Bill Russell, Bos vs Phi	11/16/57	49
Bill Russell, Bos vs Det	3/11/65	49
Wilt Chamberlain, Phi vs Syr	2/6/60	45
Wilt Chamberlain, Phi vs LA	1/21/61	45

Blocked Shots

	Date	No
Elmore Smith, LA vs Port	10/28/73	17
Manute Bol, Wash vs Atl	1/25/86	15
Manute Bol, Wash vs Ind	2/26/87	15
Shaquille O'Neal, Orl at NJ	11/20/93	15

Steals

	Date	No
Larry Kenon, San Antonio at KC	12/26/76	11
Kendall Gill, NJ vs Mia.	4/3/99	11

14 different players tied with 10 each, including Alvin Robertson, who had 10 steals in a game four times.

All-Time Winningest NBA Coaches

Top 25 NBA career victories through the 2005-06 season. Career, regular season and playoff records are noted along with NBA titles won. Coaches active during 2005-06 season in **bold** type.

			Career			Regular Season			Playoffs			
		Yrs	W	L	Pct	W	L	Pct	W	L	Pct	NBA Titles
1	Lenny Wilkens	32	1412	1253	.530	1332	1155	.536	80	98	.449	1 (1979)
2	**Pat Riley**	22	1322	696	.655	1151	589	.661	171	107	.615	5 (1982,85,87-88, 2006)
3	Don Nelson	27	1260	965	.566	1190	880	.575	70	85	.452	None
4	**Larry Brown**	23	1110	889	.555	1010	800	.558	100	89	.529	1 (2004)
5	**Jerry Sloan**	21	1062	738	.590	984	658	.599	78	80	.494	None
6	**Phil Jackson**	15	1055	426	.712	877	353	.713	178	73	.709	9 (1991-93,96-98,00-02)
7	Red Auerbach	20	1037	548	.654	938	479	.662	99	69	.589	9 (1957, 59-66)
8	Bill Fitch	25	999	1160	.463	944	1106	.460	55	54	.505	1 (1981)
9	Dick Motta	25	991	1087	.477	935	1017	.479	56	70	.444	1 (1978)
10	Jack Ramsay	21	908	841	.519	864	783	.525	44	58	.431	1 (1977)
11	Cotton Fitzsimmons	21	867	824	.513	832	775	.518	35	49	.417	None
12	**George Karl**	18	845	620	.577	784	545	.590	61	75	.449	None
13	**Rick Adelman**	16	822	581	.586	752	481	.610	70	68	.507	None
14	Gene Shue	22	814	908	.473	784	861	.477	30	47	.390	None
15	Red Holzman	18	754	652	.536	696	604	.535	58	48	.547	2 (1970, 73)
	John MacLeod	18	754	711	.515	707	657	.518	47	54	.465	None
17	Chuck Daly	14	713	488	.594	638	437	.593	75	51	.595	2 (1989-90)
18	**Mike Fratello**	16	681	529	.566	661	524	.558	20	5	.323	None
19	Doug Moe	15	661	579	.533	628	529	.543	33	50	.398	None
20	K.C. Jones	10	603	309	.661	522	252	.674	81	57	.587	2 (1984,86)
21	**Gregg Popovich**	10	594	299	.665	518	252	.673	76	47	.618	3 (1999, 2003, 05)
	Del Harris	14	594	507	.540	556	457	.549	38	50	.432	None
23	Al Attles	14	588	548	.518	557	518	.518	31	30	.508	1 (1975)
24	Rudy Tomjanovich	13	578	455	.560	527	416	.559	51	39	.567	2 (1994-95)
25	**Mike Dunleavy**	13	548	524	.511	510	524	.493	38	33	.535	None

Note: The NBA does not recognize records from the National Basketball League (1937-49), the American Basketball League (1961-62) or the American Basketball Assn. (1968-76), so the following NBL, ABL and ABA overall coaching records are not included above: NBL—**John Kundla** (51-19 and a title in 1 year). ABA—**Larry Brown** (249-129 in 4 yrs), **Alex Hannum** (194-164 and one title in 4 yrs), **K.C. Jones** (30-58 in 1 yr), **Kevin Loughery** (189-95 and one title in 3 yrs).

Where They Coached

Adelman—Portland (1988-94), Golden State (1995-97), Sacramento (1998-06); **Attles**—Golden St. (1970-80,80-83); **Auerbach**—Washington (1946-49), Tri-Cities (1949-50), Boston (1950-66); **Brown**—Denver (1976-79), New Jersey (1981-83), San Antonio (1988-92), LA Clippers (1992-93), Indiana (1993-97), Philadelphia (1997-2003), Detroit (2003-05), New York (2005-06); **Daly**—Cleveland (1981-82), Detroit (1983-92), New Jersey (1992-94), Orlando (1997-99); **Dunleavy**—L.A. Lakers (1990-91), Milwaukee (1992-1995), Portland (1997-2000), L.A. Clippers (2003–); **Fitch**—Cleveland (1970-79), Boston (1979-83), Houston (1983-88), New Jersey (1989-92), LA Clippers (1994-98); **Fitzsimmons**—Phoenix (1970-72), Atlanta (1972-76), Buffalo (1977-78), Kansas City (1978-84), San Antonio (1984-86), Phoenix (1988-92, 95-96); **Fratello**—Atlanta (1980-90), Cleveland (1993-99), Memphis (2004—).

Harris—Houston (1979-83), Milwaukee (1987-92), LA Lakers (1994-99); **Holzman**—Milwaukee-St. Louis Hawks (1954-57), NY Knicks (1968-77,78-82); **Jackson**—Chicago (1989-98), LA Lakers (1999-2004, 05–); **Jones**—Washington (1973-76), Boston (1983-88), Seattle (1990-92); **Karl**—Cleveland (1984-86); Golden St. (1986-88), Seattle (1991-98), Milwaukee (1999-2003), Denver (2004—); **MacLeod**—Phoenix (1973-87), Dallas (1987-89), NY Knicks (1990-91); **Moe**—San Antonio (1976-80), Denver (1981-90), Philadelphia (1992-93).

Motta—Chicago (1968-76), Washington (1976-80), Dallas (1980-87), Sacramento (1990-91), Dallas (1994-96), Denver (1997); **Nelson**—Milwaukee (1976-87), Golden St. (1988-95, 2006—), New York (1995-96), Dallas (1997-2005); **Popovich**— San Antonio (1996—); **Ramsay**—Philadelphia (1968-72), Buffalo (1972-76), Portland (1976-86), Indiana (1986-89); **Riley**—LA Lakers (1981-90), New York (1991-95), Miami (1995-2003, 05–); **Shue**—Baltimore (1967-73), Philadelphia (1973-77), San Diego Clippers (1978-80), Washington (1980-86), LA Clippers (1987-89); **Sloan**—Chicago (1979-82), Utah (1988–); **Tomjanovich**—Houston (1991-2003), LA Lakers (2004-05); **Wilkens**—Seattle (1969-72), Portland (1974-76), Seattle (1977-85), Cleveland (1986-93), Atlanta (1993-2000), Toronto (2000-03), New York (2004-05).

All-Time Winningest NBA Coaches (Cont.)

Top Winning Percentages

Minimum of 350 victories, including playoffs; coaches active during 2005-06 season in **bold** type.

		Yrs	W	L	Pct
1	**Phil Jackson**	.15	1055	426	**.712**
2	Billy Cunningham	.8	520	235	**.689**
3	**Gregg Popovich**	.10	594	299	**.665**
4	K.C. Jones	.10	603	309	**.661**
5	**Pat Riley**	.22	1322	696	**.655**
6	Red Auerbach	.20	1037	548	**.654**
7	Tommy Heinsohn	.9	474	296	**.616**
8	Chuck Daly	.14	713	488	**.594**
9	Larry Costello	.10	467	323	**.591**
10	**Jerry Sloan**	.21	1062	738	**.590**
11	John Kundla	.11	485	338	**.589**
12	**Rick Adelman**	.16	822	581	**.586**
13	Bill Sharman	.7	368	267	**.580**
14	**George Karl**	.18	845	620	**.577**
15	Al Cervi	.9	359	267	**.573**
16	**Phil "Flip" Saunders**	.11	502	383	**.567**
17	Don Nelson	.27	1260	965	**.566**
18	Joe Lapchick	.9	356	277	**.562**
19	**Jeff Van Gundy**	.10	419	328	**.561**
20	Rudy Tomjanovich	.13	578	455	**.560**
21	**Larry Brown**	.23	1110	889	**.555**
22	Bill Russell	.8	375	317	**.542**
23	Del Harris	.14	594	507	**.540**
24	Alex Hannum	.12	518	446	**.537**
25	Red Holzman	.18	754	652	**.536**
26	Doug Moe	.15	661	579	**.533**
27	Lenny Wilkens	.32	1412	1253	**.530**
28	**Mike Fratello**	.16	681	546	**.525**
29	Richie Guerin	.8	353	325	**.521**
30	Jack Ramsay	.21	908	841	**.519**

Active Coaches' Victories

Through 2005-06 season, including playoffs.

		Yrs	W	L	Pct
1	Pat Riley, Miami	.22	**1322**	696	.655
2	Don Nelson, Golden St.	.27	**1260**	965	.566
3	Jerry Sloan, Utah	.21	**1062**	738	.590
4	Phil Jackson, LA Lakers	.15	**1055**	426	.712
5	George Karl, Denver	.18	**845**	620	.577
6	Mike Fratello, Memphis	.16	**681**	546	.525
7	Gregg Popovich, San Antonio	.10	**594**	299	.665
8	Mike Dunleavy, LA Clippers	.14	**548**	557	.496
9	Flip Saunders, Detroit	.11	**502**	383	.567
10	Jeff Van Gundy, Houston	.10	**419**	328	.561
11	Bernie Bickerstaff, Charlotte	.12	**394**	489	.446
12	Bob Hill, Seattle	.8	**296**	262	.530
13	Brian Hill, Orlando	.8	**276**	291	.487
	Rick Carlisle, Indiana	.5	**276**	196	.585
15	Doc Rivers, Boston	.7	**257**	268	.490
16	Nate McMillan, Portland	.6	**241**	252	.489
17	Scott Skiles, Chicago	.6	**232**	218	.516
18	Byron Scott, N.O./Okla. City	.7	**230**	262	.467
19	Maurice Cheeks, Philadelphia	.5	**203**	190	.517
20	Mike D'Antoni, Phoenix	.4	**170**	140	.548
21	Eddie Jordan, Washington	.5	**151**	208	.421
22	Isiah Thomas, New York	.3	**136**	125	.521
23	Lawrence Frank, New Jersey	.3	**128**	102	.557
24	Avery Johnson, Dallas	.2	**96**	40	.706
25	Terry Stotts, Milwaukee	.3	**93**	131	.415
26	Eric Musselman, Sacramento	.2	**75**	89	.457
27	Sam Mitchell, Toronto	.2	**60**	104	.366
28	Mike Brown, Cleveland	.1	**57**	38	.600
29	Mike Woodson, Atlanta	.2	**39**	125	.238
30	Dwane Casey, Minnesota	.1	**33**	49	.402

Annual Awards
Most Valuable Player

The Maurice Podoloff Trophy for regular season MVP. Named after the first commissioner (then president) of the NBA. Winners first selected by the NBA players (1956-80) then a national panel of pro basketball writers and broadcasters (since 1981). Winners' scoring averages are provided; (*) indicates led league.

Multiple winners: Kareem Abdul-Jabbar (6); Michael Jordan and Bill Russell (5); Wilt Chamberlain (4); Larry Bird, Magic Johnson and Moses Malone (3); Tim Duncan, Karl Malone, Steve Nash and Bob Pettit (2).

Year		Avg	Year		Avg
1956	Bob Pettit, St. Louis, F	25.7*	1982	Moses Malone, Houston, C	31.1
1957	Bob Cousy, Boston, G	20.6	1983	Moses Malone, Philadelphia, C	24.5
1958	Bill Russell, Boston, C	16.6	1984	Larry Bird, Boston, F	24.2
1959	Bob Pettit, St. Louis, F	29.2*	1985	Larry Bird, Boston, F	28.7
1960	Wilt Chamberlain, Philadelphia, C	37.6*	1986	Larry Bird, Boston, F	25.8
1961	Bill Russell, Boston, C	16.9	1987	Magic Johnson, LAL, G	23.9
1962	Bill Russell, Boston, C	18.9	1988	Michael Jordan, Chicago, G	35.0*
1963	Bill Russell, Boston, C	16.8	1989	Magic Johnson, LAL, G	22.5
1964	Oscar Robertson, Cincinnati, G	31.4	1990	Magic Johnson, LAL, G	22.3
1965	Bill Russell, Boston, C	14.1	1991	Michael Jordan, Chicago, G	31.5*
1966	Wilt Chamberlain, Philadelphia, C	33.5*	1992	Michael Jordan, Chicago, G	30.1*
1967	Wilt Chamberlain, Philadelphia, C	24.1	1993	Charles Barkley, Phoenix, F	25.6
1968	Wilt Chamberlain, Philadelphia, C	24.3	1994	Hakeem Olajuwon, Houston, C	27.3
1969	Wes Unseld, Baltimore, C	13.8	1995	David Robinson, San Antonio, C	27.6
1970	Willis Reed, New York, C	21.7	1996	Michael Jordan, Chicago, G	30.4*
1971	Lew Alcindor, Milwaukee, C	31.7*	1997	Karl Malone, Utah, F	27.4
1972	Kareem Abdul-Jabbar, Milwaukee, C	34.8*	1998	Michael Jordan, Chicago, G	28.7*
1973	Dave Cowens, Boston, C	20.5	1999	Karl Malone, Utah, F	23.8
1974	Kareem Abdul-Jabbar, Milwaukee, C	27.0	2000	Shaquille O'Neal, LAL, C	29.7*
1975	Bob McAdoo, Buffalo, F	34.5*	2001	Allen Iverson, Philadelphia, G	31.1*
1976	Kareem Abdul-Jabbar, LA, C	27.7	2002	Tim Duncan, San Antonio, F/C	25.5
1977	Kareem Abdul-Jabbar, LA, C	26.2	2003	Tim Duncan, San Antonio, F/C	23.3
1978	Bill Walton, Portland, C	18.9	2004	Kevin Garnett, Minnesota, F	24.2
1979	Moses Malone, Houston, C	24.8	2005	Steve Nash, Phoenix, G	15.5
1980	Kareem Abdul-Jabbar, LA, C	24.8	2006	Steve Nash, Phoenix, G	18.8
1981	Julius Erving, Philadelphia, F	24.6			

Note: Lew Alcindor changed his name to Kareem Abdul-Jabbar after the 1970-71 season.

Rookie of the Year

The Eddie Gottlieb Trophy for outstanding rookie of the regular season. Named after the pro basketball pioneer and owner-coach of the first NBA champion Philadelphia Warriors. Winners selected by a national panel of pro basketball writers and broadcasters. Winners' scoring averages provided; (*) indicates led league; winners who were also named MVP are in **bold** type.

Year		Avg	Year		Avg
1953	Don Meineke, Ft. Wayne, F	10.8	1980	Larry Bird, Boston, F	21.3
1954	Ray Felix, Baltimore, C	17.6	1981	Darrell Griffith, Utah, G	20.6
1955	Bob Pettit, Milwaukee Hawks, F	20.4	1982	Buck Williams, New Jersey, F	15.5
1956	Maurice Stokes, Rochester, F/C	16.8	1983	Terry Cummings, San Diego, F	23.7
1957	Tommy Heinsohn, Boston, F	16.2	1984	Ralph Sampson, Houston, C	21.0
1958	Woody Sauldsberry, Philadelphia, F/C	12.8	1985	Michael Jordan, Chicago, G	28.2
1959	Elgin Baylor, Minneapolis, F	24.9	1986	Patrick Ewing, New York, C	20.0
1960	**Wilt Chamberlain**, Philadelphia, C	37.6*	1987	Chuck Person, Indiana, F	18.8
1961	Oscar Robertson, Cincinnati, G	30.5	1988	Mark Jackson, New York, G	13.6
1962	Walt Bellamy, Chicago Packers, C	31.6	1989	Mitch Richmond, Golden St., G	22.0
1963	Terry Dischinger, Chicago Zephyrs, F	25.5	1990	David Robinson, San Antonio, C	24.3
1964	Jerry Lucas, Cincinnati, F/C	17.7	1991	Derrick Coleman, New Jersey, F	18.4
1965	Willis Reed, New York, C	19.5	1992	Larry Johnson, Charlotte, F	19.2
1966	Rick Barry, San Francisco, F	25.7	1993	Shaquille O'Neal, Orlando, C	23.4
1967	Dave Bing, Detroit, G	20.0	1994	Chris Webber, Golden St., F	17.5
1968	Earl Monroe, Baltimore, G	24.3	1995	Grant Hill, Detroit, F	19.9
1969	**Wes Unseld**, Baltimore, C	13.8		& Jason Kidd, Dallas, G	11.7
1970	Lew Alcindor, Milwaukee Bucks, C	28.8	1996	Damon Stoudamire, Toronto, G	19.0
1971	Dave Cowens, Boston, C	17.0	1997	Allen Iverson, Philadelphia, G	23.5
	& Geoff Petrie, Portland, G	24.8	1998	Tim Duncan, San Antonio, F/C	21.6
1972	Sidney Wicks, Portland, F	24.5	1999	Vince Carter, Toronto, F	18.3
1973	Bob McAdoo, Buffalo, C/F	18.0	2000	Elton Brand, Chicago, F	20.1
1974	Ernie DiGregorio, Buffalo, G	15.2		& Steve Francis, Houston, G	18.0
1975	Keith Wilkes, Golden St., F	14.2	2001	Mike Miller, Orlando, G/F	11.9
1976	Alvan Adams, Phoenix, C	19.0	2002	Pau Gasol, Memphis, F	17.6
1977	Adrian Dantley, Buffalo, F	20.3	2003	Amare Stoudemire, Phoenix, F	13.5
1978	Walter Davis, Phoenix, G	24.2	2004	LeBron James, Cleveland, F	20.9
1979	Phil Ford, Kansas City, G	15.9	2005	Emeka Okafor, Charlotte, C	15.1
			2006	Chris Paul, NO/Okla. City, G	16.1

Note: The Chicago Packers changed their name to the Zephyrs after 1961-62 season. Also, Lew Alcindor changed his name to Kareem Abdul-Jabbar after the 1970-71 season.

Number One Draft Choices

Overall first choices in the NBA draft since the abolition of the territorial draft in 1966. Players who became Rookie of the Year are in **bold** type. The draft lottery began in 1985.

Year		Overall 1st Pick	Year		Overall 1st Pick
1966	New York	Cazzie Russell, Michigan	1987	San Antonio	**David Robinson**, Navy
1967	Detroit	Jimmy Walker, Providence	1988	LA Clippers	Danny Manning, Kansas
1968	San Diego	Elvin Hayes, Houston	1989	Sacramento	Pervis Ellison, Louisville
1969	Milwaukee	**Lew Alcindor**, UCLA	1990	New Jersey	**Derrick Coleman**, Syracuse
1970	Detroit	Bob Lanier, St. Bonaventure	1991	Charlotte	**Larry Johnson**, UNLV
1971	Cleveland	Austin Carr, Notre Dame	1992	Orlando	**Shaquille O'Neal**, LSU
1972	Portland	LaRue Martin, Loyola-Chicago	1993	Orlando	**Chris Webber**, Michigan
1973	Philadelphia	Doug Collins, Illinois St.	1994	Milwaukee	Glenn Robinson, Purdue
1974	Portland	Bill Walton, UCLA	1995	Golden St.	Joe Smith, Maryland
1975	Atlanta	David Thompson, N.C. State	1996	Philadelphia	**Allen Iverson**, Georgetown
1976	Houston	John Lucas, Maryland	1997	San Antonio	**Tim Duncan**, Wake Forest
1977	Milwaukee	Kent Benson, Indiana	1998	LA Clippers	Michael Olowokandi, Pacific
1978	Portland	Mychal Thompson, Minnesota	1999	Chicago	**Elton Brand**, Duke
1979	LA Lakers	Magic Johnson, Michigan St.	2000	New Jersey	Kenyon Martin, Cincinnati
1980	Golden St	Joe Barry Carroll, Purdue	2001	Washington	Kwame Brown, Glynn Acad.
1981	Dallas	Mark Aguirre, DePaul	2002	Houston	Yao Ming, China
1982	LA Lakers	James Worthy, N. Carolina	2003	Cleveland	**LeBron James**, St. Vincent/St. Mary
1983	Houston	**Ralph Sampson**, Virginia	2004	Orlando	Dwight Howard, SW Atlanta Christ.
1984	Houston	Akeem Olajuwon, Houston	2005	Milwaukee	Andrew Bogut, Utah
1985	New York	**Patrick Ewing**, Georgetown	2006	Toronto	Andrea Bargnani, Italy
1986	Cleveland	Brad Daugherty, N. Carolina			

Note: Lew Alcindor changed his name to Kareem Abdul-Jabbar after the 1970-71 season; Akeem Olajuwon changed his first name to Hakeem in 1991; in 1975 David Thompson signed with Denver of the ABA and did not play for Atlanta; David Robinson joined NBA for 1989-90 season after fulfilling military obligation.

Sixth Man Award

Awarded to the Best Player Off the Bench for the regular season. Winners selected by a national panel of pro basketball writers and broadcasters.

Multiple winners: Kevin McHale, Ricky Pierce and Detlef Schrempf (2).

Year		Year		Year	
1983	Bobby Jones, Phi., F	1991	Detlef Schrempf, Ind., F	1999	Darrell Armstrong, Orl., G
1984	Kevin McHale, Bos., F	1992	Detlef Schrempf, Ind., F	2000	Rodney Rogers, Pho., F
1985	Kevin McHale, Bos., F	1993	Cliff Robinson, Port., F	2001	Aaron McKie, Phi., G
1986	Bill Walton, Bos., F/C	1994	Dell Curry, Char., G	2002	Corliss Williamson, Det., F
1987	Ricky Pierce, Mil., G/F	1995	Anthony Mason, NY, F	2003	Bobby Jackson, Sac., G
1988	Roy Tarpley, Dal., F	1996	Toni Kukoc, Chi., F	2004	Antawn Jamison, Dal., F
1989	Eddie Johnson, Pho., F	1997	John Starks, NY, G	2005	Ben Gordon, Chicago, G
1990	Ricky Pierce, Mil., G/F	1998	Danny Manning, Pho., F	2006	Mike Miller, Memphis, G

Defensive Player of the Year

Awarded to the Best Defensive Player for the regular season. Winners selected by a national panel of pro basketball writers and broadcasters.

Multiple winners: Dikembe Mutombo and Ben Wallace (4); Mark Eaton, Sidney Moncrief, Alonzo Mourning, Hakeem Olajuwon and Dennis Rodman (2).

Year		Year		Year	
1983	Sidney Moncrief, Mil., G	1991	Dennis Rodman, Det., F	1999	Alonzo Mourning, Mia., C
1984	Sidney Moncrief, Mil., G	1992	David Robinson, SA, C	2000	Alonzo Mourning, Mia., C
1985	Mark Eaton, Utah, C	1993	Hakeem Olajuwon, Hou., C	2001	Dikembe Mutombo, Atl.-Phi., C
1986	Alvin Robertson, SA, G	1994	Hakeem Olajuwon, Hou., C	2002	Ben Wallace, Det., C/F
1987	Michael Cooper, LAL, F	1995	Dikembe Mutombo, Den., C	2003	Ben Wallace, Det., C/F
1988	Michael Jordan, Chi., G	1996	Gary Payton, Sea., G	2004	Ron Artest, Ind., F
1989	Mark Eaton, Utah, C	1997	Dikembe Mutombo, Atl., C	2005	Ben Wallace, Det., C/F
1990	Dennis Rodman, Det., F	1998	Dikembe Mutombo, Atl., C	2006	Ben Wallace, Det., C/F

Most Improved Player

Awarded to the Most Improved Player for the regular season. Winners selected by a national panel of pro basketball writers and broadcasters.

Year		Year		Year	
1986	Alvin Robertson, SA, G	1993	Mahmoud Abdul-Rauf, Den., G	2000	Jalen Rose, Ind., G
1987	Dale Ellis, Sea., G	1994	Don MacLean, Wash., F	2001	Tracy McGrady, Orl., F
1988	Kevin Duckworth, Port., C	1995	Dana Barros, Phi., G	2002	Jermaine O'Neal, Ind., F
1989	Kevin Johnson, Pho., G	1996	Gheorghe Muresan, Wash., C	2003	Gilbert Arenas, G.St., G
1990	Rony Seikaly, Mia., C	1997	Isaac Austin, Miami, C	2004	Zach Randolph, Port., F
1991	Scott Skiles, Orl., G	1998	Alan Henderson, Atl., F	2005	Bobby Simmons, LAC, F
1992	Pervis Ellison, Wash., C	1999	Darrell Armstrong, Orl., G	2006	Boris Diaw, Phoenix, G

Coach of the Year

The Red Auerbach Trophy for outstanding coach of the year. Renamed in 1967 for the former Boston coach who led the Celtics to nine NBA titles. Winners selected by a national panel of pro basketball writers and broadcasters. Previous season and winning season records are provided; (*) indicates division title.

Multiple winners: Don Nelson and Pat Riley (3); Hubie Brown, Bill Fitch, Cotton Fitzsimmons and Gene Shue (2).

Year			Improvement	Year			Improvement
1963	Harry Gallatin, St. L	.29-51	to 48-32	1985	Don Nelson, Mil	.50-32*	to 59-23*
1964	Alex Hannum, SF	.31-49	to 48-32*	1986	Mike Fratello, Atl	.34-48	to 50-32
1965	Red Auerbach, Bos	.59-21*	to 61-18*	1987	Mike Schuler, Port	.40-42	to 49-33
1966	Dolph Schayes, Phi	.40-40	to 55-25*	1988	Doug Moe, Den	.37-45	to 54-28*
1967	Johnny Kerr, Chi	.Expan.	to 33-48	1989	Cotton Fitzsimmons, Pho	.28-54	to 55-27
1968	Richie Guerin, St. L	.39-42	to 56-26*	1990	Pat Riley, LA Lakers	.57-25*	to 63-19*
1969	Gene Shue, Balt	.36-46	to 57-25*	1991	Don Chaney, Hou	.41-41	to 52-30
1970	Red Holzman, NY	.54-28	to 60-22*	1992	Don Nelson, GS	.44-38	to 55-27
1971	Dick Motta, Chi	.39-43	to 51-31	1993	Pat Riley, NY	.51-31	to 60-22
1972	Bill Sharman, LA	.48-34*	to 69-13*	1994	Lenny Wilkens, Atl	.43-39	to 57-25*
1973	Tommy Heinsohn, Bos	.56-26*	to 68-14*	1995	Del Harris, LA Lakers	.33-49	to 48-34
1974	Ray Scott, Det	.40-42	to 52-30	1996	Phil Jackson, Chi	.47-35	to 72-10*
1975	Phil Johnson, KC-Omaha	.33-49	to 44-38	1997	Pat Riley, Mia	.42-40	to 61-21
1976	Bill Fitch, Cle	.40-42	to 49-33*	1998	Larry Bird, Ind	.39-43	to 58-24
1977	Tom Nissalke, Hou	.40-42	to 49-33*	1999	Mike Dunleavy, Port.	.46-36	to 35-15*
1978	Hubie Brown, Atl	.31-51	to 41-41	2000	Doc Rivers, Orlando	.33-17	to 41-41
1979	Cotton Fitzsimmons, KC	.31-51	to 48-34*	2001	Larry Brown, Phila.	.49-33	to 56-26*
1980	Bill Fitch, Bos	.29-53	to 61-21*	2002	Rick Carlisle, Det	.32-50	to 50-32*
1981	Jack McKinney, Ind	.37-45	to 44-38	2003	Gregg Popovich, SA	.58-24*	to 60-22*
1982	Gene Shue, Wash	.39-43	to 43-39	2004	Hubie Brown, Mem.	.28-54	to 50-32
1983	Don Nelson, Mil	.55-27*	to 51-31*	2005	Mike D'Antoni, Pho	.29-53	to 62-30*
1984	Frank Layden, Utah	.30-52	to 45-37*	2006	Avery Johnson, Dal	.58-24	to 60-22*

NBA's 50 Greatest Players

In October 1996, as part of its 50th anniversary celebration, the NBA named the 50 greatest players in league history. The voting was done by a league-approved panel of media, former players and coaches, current and former general managers and team executives. The players are listed alphabetically along with the dates of their professional careers and positions. Shaquille O'Neal, the only player active in 2005-06, is in **bold** type.

Player	Pos	Player	Pos	Player	Pos
Kareem Abdul-Jabbar, 1969-89	C	George Gervin, 1972-86	G	Robert Parish, 1976-97	C
Nate Archibald, 1970-84	G	Hal Greer, 1958-73	G	Bob Pettit, 1954-65	F/C
Paul Arizin, 1950-61	F/G	John Havlicek, 1962-78	F/G	Scottie Pippen, 1987-2005	F
Charles Barkley, 1984-00	F	Elvin Hayes, 1968-84	F/C	Willis Reed, 1964-74	C
Rick Barry, 1965-80	F	Magic Johnson, 1979-91, 96	G	Oscar Robertson, 1960-74	G
Elgin Baylor, 1958-72	F	Sam Jones, 1957-69	G	David Robinson, 1989-2003	C
Dave Bing, 1966-78	G	Michael Jordan, 1984-93,	G	Bill Russell, 1956-69	C
Larry Bird, 1979-92	F	95-98, 01-03		Dolph Schayes, 1948-64	F/C
Wilt Chamberlain, 1959-73	C	Jerry Lucas, 1963-74	F/C	Bill Sharman, 1950-61	G
Bob Cousy, 1950-63, 69-70	G	Karl Malone, 1985-2005	F	John Stockton, 1984-2003	G
Dave Cowens, 1970-80, 1982-83	C	Moses Malone, 1974-95	C	Isiah Thomas, 1981-94	G
Billy Cunningham, 1965-76	G	Pete Maravich, 1970-80	G	Nate Thurmond, 1963-77	C/F
Dave DeBusschere, 1962-74	F	Kevin McHale, 1980-93	F	Wes Unseld, 1968-81	C/F
Clyde Drexler, 1983-98	G	George Mikan, 1946-54, 55-56	C	Bill Walton, 1974-88	C
Julius Erving, 1971-87	F	Earl Monroe, 1967-80	G	Jerry West, 1960-74	G
Patrick Ewing, 1985-2002	C	Hakeem Olajuwon, 1984-2002	C	Lenny Wilkens, 1960-75	G
Walt Frazier, 1967-80	G	**Shaquille O'Neal**, 1992—	C	James Worthy, 1982-94	F

Note: Rick Barry, Billy Cunningham, Julius Erving, George Gervin and Moses Malone all played part of their pro careers in the ABA.

NBA's 10 Greatest Coaches

In December 1996, as part of its 50th anniversary celebration, the NBA named the 10 greatest coaches in league history. The voting was done by a league-approved panel of media. The coaches are listed alphabetically along with the dates of their professional coaching careers and overall records, including playoff games, and number of NBA titles won. Active coaches are in **bold** type.

Coach	W	L	Pct.	Titles	Coach	W	L	Pct.	Titles
Red Auerbach, 1946-66	1037	548	.654	9	John Kundla, 1947-59	485	338	.589	5
Chuck Daly, 1981-94, 97-99	713	488	.594	2	**Don Nelson**, 1976-96,				
Bill Fitch, 1970-98	999	1160	.463	1	97-05, 06–	1260	965	.566	0
Red Holzman, 1953-82	754	652	.536	2	Jack Ramsay, 1968-89	908	841	.519	1
Phil Jackson, 1989-98,					**Pat Riley**, 1981-2003, 05–	1322	696	.655	5
99-04, 05–	1055	426	.712	9	Lenny Wilkens, 1969-2005	1412	1253	.530	1
					TOTALS	9945	7367	.574	35

World Championships

The World Basketball Championships for men and women have been played regularly at four-year intervals (give or take a year) since 1970. The men's tournament began in 1950 and the women's in 1953. The Federation Internationale de Basketball Amateur (FIBA), which governs the World and Olympic tournaments, was founded in 1932. FIBA first allowed professional players from the NBA to participate in 1994. A team of collegians represented the USA in 1998.

Men

Multiple wins: Yugoslavia (5); Soviet Union and USA (3); Brazil (2).

Year	
1950	**Argentina**, United States, Chile
1954	**United States**, Brazil, Philippines
1959	**Brazil**, United States, Chile
1963	**Brazil**, Yugoslavia, Soviet Union
1967	**Soviet Union**, Yugoslavia, Brazil
1970	**Yugoslavia**, Brazil, Soviet Union
1974	**Soviet Union**, Yugoslavia, United States
1978	**Yugoslavia**, Soviet Union, Brazil
1982	**Soviet Union**, United States, Yugoslavia
1986	**United States**, Soviet Union, Yugoslavia
1990	**Yugoslavia**, Soviet Union, United States
1994	**United States**, Russia, Croatia
1998	**Yugoslavia**, Russia, United States
2002	**Yugoslavia**, Argentina, Germany
2006	**Spain**, Greece, United States
2010	at Turkey

Women

Multiple wins: USA (7); Soviet Union (6).

Year	
1953	**United States**, Chile, France
1957	**United States**, Soviet Union, Czechoslovakia
1959	**Soviet Union**, Bulgaria, Czechoslovakia
1964	**Soviet Union**, Czechoslovakia, Bulgaria
1967	**Soviet Union**, South Korea, Czechoslovakia
1971	**Soviet Union**, Czechoslovakia, Brazil
1975	**Soviet Union**, Japan, Czechoslovakia
1979	**United States**, South Korea, Canada
1983	**Soviet Union**, United States, China
1986	**United States**, Soviet Union, Canada
1990	**United States**, Yugoslavia, Cuba
1994	**Brazil**, China, United States
1998	**United States**, Russia, Australia
2002	**United States**, Russia, Australia
2006	**Australia**, Russia, United States
2010	TBD

American Basketball Association
ABA Finals

The original American Basketball Assn. began play in 1967-68 as a 10-team rival of the 21-year-old NBA. The ABA, which introduced the three-point basket, a multi-colored ball and the All-Star Game Slam Dunk Contest, lasted nine seasons before folding following the 1975-76 season. Four ABA teams–Denver, Indiana, New York and San Antonio–survived to enter the NBA in 1976-77. The NBA also adopted the three-point basket (in 1979-80) and the All-Star Game Slam Dunk Contest. The older league, however, refused to take in the ABA ball.

Multiple winners: Indiana (3); New York (2).

Year	Winner	Head Coach	Series	Loser	Head Coach
1968	Pittsburgh Pipers	Vince Cazzetta	4-3 (WLLWLWW)	New Orleans Bucs	Babe McCarthy
1969	Oakland Oaks	Alex Hannum	4-1 (WLWWW)	Indiana Pacers	Bob Leonard
1970	Indiana Pacers	Bob Leonard	4-2 (WWLWLW)	Los Angeles Stars	Bill Sharman
1971	Utah Stars	Bill Sharman	4-3 (WWLLWLW)	Kentucky Colonels	Frank Ramsey
1972	Indiana Pacers	Bob Leonard	4-2 (WLWLWW)	New York Nets	Lou Carnesecca
1973	Indiana Pacers	Bob Leonard	4-3 (WLLWLWW)	Kentucky Colonels	Joe Mullaney
1974	New York Nets	Kevin Loughery	4-1 (WWWLW)	Utah Stars	Joe Mullaney
1975	Kentucky Colonels	Hubie Brown	4-1 (WWWLW)	Indiana Pacers	Bob Leonard
1976	New York Nets	Kevin Loughery	4-2 (WLWLWLW)	Denver Nuggets	Larry Brown

Most Valuable Player

Winners' scoring averages provided; (*) indicates led league.

Multiple winners: Julius Erving (3); Mel Daniels (2).

Year		Avg
1968	Connie Hawkins, Pittsburgh, C	26.8*
1969	Mel Daniels, Indiana, C	24.0
1970	Spencer Haywood, Denver, C	30.0*
1971	Mel Daniels, Indiana, C	21.0
1972	Artis Gilmore, Kentucky, C	23.8
1973	Billy Cunningham, Carolina, F	24.1
1974	Julius Erving, New York, F	27.4*
1975	George McGinnis, Indiana, F	29.8*
	& Julius Erving, New York, F	27.9
1976	Julius Erving, New York, F	29.3*

Rookie of the Year

Winners' scoring averages provided; (*) indicates led league. Rookies who were also named Most Valuable Player are in **bold** type.

Year		Avg
1968	Mel Daniels, Minnesota, C	22.2
1969	Warren Armstrong, Oakland, G	21.5
1970	**Spencer Haywood**, Denver, C	30.0*
1971	Dan Issel, Kentucky, C	29.8*
	& Charlie Scott, Virginia, G	27.1
1972	**Artis Gilmore**, Kentucky, C	23.8
1973	Brian Taylor, New York, G	15.3
1974	Swen Nater, Virginia-SA, C	14.1
1975	Marvin Barnes, St. Louis, C	24.0
1976	David Thompson, Denver, F	26.0

Note: Warren Armstrong changed his name to Warren Jabali after the 1970-71 season.

Coach of the Year

Previous season and winning season records are provided; (*) indicates division title.

Multiple winner: Larry Brown (3).

Year			Improvement
1968	Vince Cazzetta, Pittsburgh		54-24*
1969	Alex Hannum, Oakland 22-56	to	60-18*
1970	Joe Belmont, Denver 44-34	to	51-33*
	& Bill Sharman, LA Stars 33-45	to	43-41
1971	Al Bianchi, Virginia 44-40	to	55-29*
1972	Tom Nissalke, Dallas 30-54	to	42-42
1973	Larry Brown, Carolina 35-49	to	57-27*
1974	Babe McCarthy, Kentucky . .56-28	to	53-31
	& Joe Mullaney, Utah 55-29*	to	51-33*
1975	Larry Brown, Denver 37-47	to	65-19*
1976	Larry Brown, Denver 65-19*	to	60-24*

Scoring Leaders

Scoring championship decided by per game point average every season.

Multiple winner: Julius Erving (3).

Year		Gm	Avg	Pts
1968	Connie Hawkins, Pittsburgh 70	1875	26.8	
1969	Rick Barry, Oakland 35	1190	34.0	
1970	Spencer Haywood, Denver 84	2519	30.0	
1971	Dan Issel, Kentucky 83	2480	29.8	
1972	Charlie Scott, Virginia 73	2524	34.6	
1973	Julius Erving, Virginia 71	2268	31.9	
1974	Julius Erving, New York 84	2299	27.4	
1975	George McGinnis, Indiana 79	2353	29.8	
1976	Julius Erving, New York 84	2462	29.3	

ABA All-Star Game

The ABA All-Star Game was an Eastern Division vs. Western Division contest from 1968-75. League membership had dropped to seven teams by 1976, the ABA's last season, so the team in first place at the break (Denver) played an All-Star team made up from the other six clubs.

Series: East won 5, West 3 and Denver 1.

Year	Result	Host	Coaches	Most Valuable Player
1968	East 126, West 120	Indiana	Jim Pollard, Babe McCarthy	Larry Brown, New Orleans
1969	West 133, East 127	Louisville	Alex Hannum, Gene Rhodes	John Beasley, Dallas
1970	West 128, East 98	Indiana	Babe McCarthy, Bob Leonard	Spencer Haywood, Denver
1971	East 126, West 122	Carolina	Al Bianchi, Bill Sharman	Mel Daniels, Indiana
1972	East 142, West 115	Louisville	Joe Mullaney, Ladell Andersen	Dan Issel, Kentucky
1973	West 123, East 111	Utah	Ladell Andersen, Larry Brown	Warren Jabali, Denver
1974	East 128, West 112	Virginia	Babe McCarthy, Joe Mullaney	Artis Gilmore, Kentucky
1975	East 151, West 124	San Antonio	Kevin Loughery, Larry Brown	Freddie Lewis, St. Louis
1976	Denver 144, ABA 138	Denver	Larry Brown, Kevin Loughery	David Thompson, Denver

Continental Basketball Association

Originally named the Eastern Pennsylvania Basketball League when it formed on April 23, 1946, the league changed names several times before becoming known as the Eastern Basketball Association. In 1978, the EBA was redubbed the CBA. The CBA suspended operations following the 2000 season but reorganized for the 2001-02 season.

Multiple champions: Allentown and Wilkes-Barre (8); Yakima/Yakama (4); Scranton, Tampa Bay, and Williamsport (3); Albany, Dakota, La Crosse, Pottsville, Rochester, Sioux Falls and Wilmington (2).

League Champions

Year		Year		Year		Year	
1947	Wilkes-Barre Barons	1963	Allentown Jets	1977	Scranton Apollos	1992	La Crosse Catbirds
1948	Reading Keys	1964	Camden Bullets	1978	Wilkes-Barre Barons	1993	Omaha Racers
1949	Pottsville Packers	1965	Allentown Jets	1979	Rochester Zeniths	1994	Quad City Thunder
1950	Williamsport Billies	1966	Wilmington Blue	1980	Anchorage Northern	1995	Yakima Sun Kings
1951	Sunbury Mercuries		Bombers		Knights	1996	Sioux Falls Skyforce
1952	Pottsville Packers	1967	Wilmington Blue	1981	Rochester Zeniths	1997	Oklahoma City
1953	Williamsport Billies		Bombers	1982	Lancaster Lightning		Calvary
1954	Williamsport Billies	1968	Allentown Jets	1983	Detroit Spirits	1998	Quad City Thunder
1955	Wilkes-Barre Barons	1969	Wilkes-Barre Barons	1984	Albany Patroons	1999	Connecticut Pride
1956	Wilkes-Barre Barons	1970	Allentown Jets	1985	Tampa Bay Thrillers	2000	Yakima Sun Kings
1957	Scranton Miners	1971	Scranton Apollos	1986	Tampa Bay Thrillers	2001	suspended play
1958	Wilkes-Barre Barons	1972	Allentown Jets	1987	Rapid City Thrillers*	2002	Dakota Wizards
1959	Wilkes-Barre Barons	1973	Wilkes-Barre Barons	1988	Albany Patroons	2003	Yakima Sun Kings
1960	Easton Madisons	1974	Hartford Capitols	1989	Tulsa Fast Breakers	2004	Dakota Wizards
1961	Baltimore Bullets	1975	Allentown Jets	1990	La Crosse Catbirds	2005	Sioux Falls Skyforce
1962	Allentown Jets	1976	Allentown Jets	1991	Wichita Falls Texans	2006	Yakama Sun Kings

*The Tampa Bay Thrillers moved to Rapid City, S.D. at the end of the 1987 regular season. The Yakima Sun Kings changed the spelling of their name to Yakama after they were purchased by the Yakama Indiana Nation in 2005.

National Basketball Association Development League

The D League was founded in 2001 as an eight-team player and coach development league owned and operated by the NBA. Until recently, the individual teams did not have a direct relationship with NBA clubs but occasionally players and coaches were called up to the NBA. The NBDL champion was determined in a best-of-three championship series for the first two seasons of the league before changing the format to a single-game playoff in 2004.

The league has expanded and contracted in the years since its founding and some franchises have relocated. In 2005, the league dropped the NBDL acronym and officially adopted the name D-League. Also, the NBA announced that each D-League team would now be officially affiliated with one or more NBA teams, making it more of a true minor league system, where players can be sent down to gain experience and called-up when the big league team has a need. Here are the NBA assignments for the 12 D-League teams, entering the 2006-07 season: ALBUQUERQUE—Cleveland Cavaliers, Indiana Pacers, Phoenix Suns; ANAHEIM—LA Clippers, Portland Trail Blazers, Orlando Magic; ARKANSAS—Atlanta Hawks, Memphis Grizzlies, Miami Heat; AUSTIN—Boston Celtics, Houston Rockets, San Antonio Spurs; BAKERSFIELD—Golden St. Warriors, Sacramento Kings; COLORADO—Denver Nuggets, New Jersey Nets, Toronto Raptors; DAKOTA—Chicago Bulls, Washington Wizards; Idaho—Seattle SuperSonics, Utah Jazz; FORT WORTH—Charlotte Bobcats, Dallas Mavericks, Philadelphia 76ers; LOS ANGELES—LA Lakers; SIOUX FALLS—Detroit Pistons, Minnesota Timberwolves; TULSA—Milwaukee Bucks, New Orleans/Oklahoma City Hornets, New York Knicks.

League Champions

Multiple champions: Asheville (2).

Year	Champions	Head Coach	Score	Runners-up	Head Coach
2002	Greenville Groove	Milton Barnes	2-0	No. Charleston Lowgators	Alex English
2003	Mobile Revelers	Sam Vincent	2-1 (WLW)	Fayetteville Patriots	Jeff Capel
2004	Asheville Altitude	Joey Meyer	108-106 OT	Huntsville Flight	Ralph Lewis
2005	Asheville Altitude	Joey Meyer	90-67	Columbus Riverdragons	Jeff Malone
2006	Albuquerque Thunderbirds	Michael Cooper	119-108	Fort Worth Flyers	Sam Vincent

Annual Awards

Most Valuable Player

Winner's scoring averages provided; (*) indicates led league.

Year		PPG
2002	Ansu Sesay, Greenville, F	16.5
2003	Devin Brown, Fayetteville, G	16.9
2004	Tierre Brown, Charleston, G	18.6
2005	Matt Carroll, Roanoke, G	20.1*
2006	Marcus Fizer, Austin, F	22.7

Rookie of the Year

Year	
2002	Fred House, N. Charleston
2003	Devin Brown, Fayetteville
2004	Desmond Penigar, Asheville
2005	James Thomas, Roanoke
2006	Will Bynum, Roanoke

Defensive Player of the Year

Year	
2002	Jeff Myers, Greenville
2003	Mikki Moore, Roanoke
2004	Karim Shabazz, Charleston
2005	Derrick Zimmerman, Columbus
2006	Derrick Zimmerman, Austin

Scoring Champion

Scoring championship decided by per game point average every season.

Year		PPG
2002	Isaac Fontaine, Mobile	17.4
2003	Nate Johnson, Columbus	19.5
2004	Desmond Penigar, Asheville	19.6
2005	Isiah Victor, Roanoke	19.5
2006	Bracey Wright, Florida	22.0

WOMEN
Women's National Basketball Association

The WNBA, owned and operated by the NBA, began play in 1997 as an eight-team summer league. The league added two teams prior to its second season (1998), then added two more teams before its third season in 1999. Four additional teams were added before the 2000 season, bringing the total number of teams to 16. Prior to the 2003 season two franchises were relocated and two were contracted and one franchise folded before the 2004 season. One team (Chicago Sky) was added for the 2006 season bringing the total back to 14. The WNBA champion was determined by a single-game playoff in the league's 1997 inaugural season, before going to a best-of-three championship series in 1998 and a best-of-five championship series starting in 2005.

Multiple winners: Houston (4); Detroit and Los Angeles (2).

Year	Champions	Head Coach	Series	Runners-up	Head Coach
1997	Houston Comets	Van Chancellor	65-51	New York Liberty	Nancy Darsch
1998	Houston Comets	Van Chancellor	2-1 (LWW)	Phoenix Mercury	Cheryl Miller
1999	Houston Comets	Van Chancellor	2-1 (WLW)	New York Liberty	Richie Adubato
2000	Houston Comets	Van Chancellor	2-0	New York Liberty	Richie Adubato
2001	Los Angeles Sparks	Michael Cooper	2-0	Charlotte Sting	Anne Donovan
2002	Los Angeles Sparks	Michael Cooper	2-0	New York Liberty	Richie Adubato
2003	Detroit Shock	Bill Laimbeer	2-1 (LWW)	Los Angeles Sparks	Michael Cooper
2004	Seattle Storm	Anne Donovan	2-1 (LWW)	Connecticut Sun	Mike Thibault
2005	Sacramento Monarchs	John Whisenant	3-1 (WLWW)	Connecticut Sun	Mike Thibault
2006	Detroit Shock	Bill Laimbeer	3-2 (LWLWW)	Sacramento Monarchs	John Whisenant

Championship MVPs: 1997-Cynthia Cooper, Houston; 1998-Cynthia Cooper, Houston; 1999-Cynthia Cooper, Houston; 2000-Cynthia Cooper, Houston; 2001-Lisa Leslie, Los Angeles; 2002-Lisa Leslie, Los Angeles; 2003-Ruth Riley, Detroit; 2004-Betty Lennox, Seattle; 2005-Yolanda Griffith, Sacramento; 2006-Deanna Nolan, Detroit.

Annual Awards

Most Valuable Player

Winner's scoring averages provided; (*) indicates led league.

Multiple winners: Sheryl Swoopes and Lisa Leslie (3); Cynthia Cooper (2).

Year		Avg
1997	Cynthia Cooper, Houston	22.2*
1998	Cynthia Cooper, Houston	22.7*
1999	Yolanda Griffith, Sacramento	18.8
2000	Sheryl Swoopes, Houston	20.7*
2001	Lisa Leslie, Los Angeles	19.5
2002	Sheryl Swoopes, Houston	18.5
2003	Lauren Jackson, Seattle	21.2*
2004	Lisa Leslie, Los Angeles	17.6
2005	Sheryl Swoopes, Houston	18.6*
2006	Lisa Leslie, Los Angeles	20.0

Coach of the Year

Previous season and winning season's record are provided; (*) indicates division title.

Multiple winner: Van Chancellor (3).

Year		Improvement
1997	Van Chancellor, Houston	18-10*
1998	Van Chancellor, Houston	18-10 to 27-3*
1999	Van Chancellor, Houston	27-3 to 26-6*
2000	Michael Cooper, Los Angeles	20-12 to 28-4*
2001	Dan Hughes, Cleveland	17-15 to 22-10*
2002	Marianne Stanley, Washington	10-22 to 17-15
2003	Bill Laimbeer, Detroit	9-23 to 25-9*
2004	Suzie McConnell Serio, Minn.	18-16 to 18-16
2005	John Whisenant, Sacramento	18-16 to 25-9*
2006	Mike Thibault, Connecticut	26-8 to 26-8*

Rookie of the Year

Year		Year	
1998	Tracy Reid, Cha	2002	Tamika Catchings, Ind
1999	Chamique Holdsclaw, Wash	2003	Cheryl Ford, Det
2000	Betty Lennox, Minn	2004	Diana Taurasi, Pho
2001	Jackie Stiles, Port	2005	Temeka Johnson, Was
		2006	Seimone Augustus, Minn

Defensive Player of the Year

Multiple winners: Sheryl Swoopes (3); Tamika Catchings and Teresa Weatherspoon (2).

Year		Year	
1997	Teresa Weatherspoon, NY	2001	Debbie Black, Mia
1998	Teresa Weatherspoon, NY	2002	Sheryl Swoopes, Hou
1999	Yolanda Griffith, Sac	2003	Sheryl Swoopes, Hou
2000	Sheryl Swoopes, Hou	2004	Lisa Leslie, LA
		2005	Tamika Catchings, Ind
		2006	Tamika Catchings, Ind

WNBA Number One Draft Picks

Year	Overall First Pick
1997	Utah Starzz	Dena Head
1998	Utah Starzz	Margo Dydek
1999	Washington Mystics	Chamique Holdsclaw
2000	Cleveland Rockers	Ann Wauters
2001	Seattle Storm	Lauren Jackson
2002	Seattle Storm	Sue Bird
2003	Cleveland Rockers	LaToya Thomas
2004	Phoenix Mercury	Diana Taurasi
2005	Charlotte Sting	Janel McCarville
2006	Minnesota Lynx	Seimone Augustus

American Basketball League (1997-98)
League Champions

Each ABL champion's wins and losses are noted in parentheses after the series score. Due largely to competition from the WNBA, the ABL folded before the 1999 season.

Year	Champions	Head Coach	Series	Runners-up	Head Coach
1997	Columbus Quest	Brian Agler	3-2 (WLLWW)	Richmond Rage	Lisa Boyer
1998	Columbus Quest	Brian Agler	3-2 (LLWWW)	Long Beach StingRays	Maura McHugh

Most Valuable Player
(*) indicates led league.

Year		PPG
1997	Nikki McCray, Columbus	19.9
1998	Natalie Williams, Portland	21.9*

Coach of the Year
(*) indicates division title.

Year		Improvement
1997	Brian Agler, Columbus	31-9*
1998	Lin Dunn, Portland	14-26 to 27-17

HOCKEY

This facial expression from **Rod Brind'Amour** helps explain what it's like to win a Stanley Cup after 17 years.

BACK IN
BUSINESS

After its one-year hiatus, the NHL returned to the ice in 2005-06 with a myriad of rule changes and a crop of talented rookies.

MANY TIMES DURING THE contentious 10-month lockout that killed the 2004-05 NHL season, commissioner Gary Bettman and his No. 2 man Bill Daly told the media that their research led them to believe that fans were willing to sacrifice a season if it meant getting the league on secure financial footing.

We media, always a cynical bunch, found it hard to believe that hockey fans would be so quick to forgive. There was a feeling — at least among those who cover the game — that the league would pay a significant price at the box office for its civil war.

As it turned out, the commissioner and his sidekick were right on the money. The fans did come back. And, oddly enough, they returned in record numbers.

"We had an extremely strong 2005-06 season," said a vindicated Bettman. "We set new marks for attendance and revenues. And, the game on the ice is as good, if not better, than it has ever been."

A big reason for the league's bounce-back success was its new look. Bettman and Co. gave the game a total makeover. On opening night, the league was re-launched with several new wrinkles and an improved standard of enforcement on some long-standing rules like hooking and holding.

Bettman's "new" NHL would emphasize speed and skill. Teams trying to play the clutch-and-grab game that dominated the league's landscape in the several seasons before the lockout would have to adjust or spend an awful lot of time killing penalties.

With the game's top offensive wizards free to work their magic, fans were treated to a more exciting brand of hockey. On the whole, goal scoring was up 18 percent over the 2003-04 season, the largest single season increase since 1929 when the league introduced forward passing in all three zones. Seven skaters surpassed the 100-point plateau, while five snipers netted 50 or more goals. As a point of comparison, in the past three seasons

 E.J. Hradek is a senior hockey writer for ESPN The Magazine.

AP/Wide World Photos

Hurricanes' goalie **Cam Ward** became the fourth rookie, and first since Ron Hextall in 1987, to be awarded the Conn Smythe Trophy as playoff MVP.

combined, there were just three 100-point scorers and only two 50-goal men. If Bettman was looking to pump up the offense (and he was), the commissioner succeeded in that mission.

Perhaps the most noticeable new wrinkle was the decision to adopt the shootout as a way to break regular season ties. While some hardcore traditionalists bristled at the idea of deciding a game with penalty shots, most fans seemed genuinely energized by the one-on-one showdowns between the goalie and shooter. Crowds around the league consistently rose to their feet to witness the game's final act.

On Nov. 26, an extended 15-round shootout between the Washington Capitals and New York Rangers pro-

duced one of the regular season's most memorable moments. Rangers journeyman defenseman Marek Malik, who wasn't previously known for anything involving offense, used a stick-between-the-legs trick shot to beat Caps goalie Olaf Kolzig. Malik's slick, slight-of-hand game-winner created some early-season buzz for the league, as it was replayed on highlight shows throughout North America.

It didn't, however, get more replay time than the amazing goal scored by Caps rookie sensation Alexander Ovechkin against the Phoenix Coyotes during a Jan. 16th contest at the Glendale Arena. After falling to the ice, Ovechkin managed to get his stick behind his head to swat the puck past

AP/Wide World Photos

NHL legend **Mario Lemieux**, right, retired in late January, but with the emergence of **Sidney Crosby** and fellow rookie Alexander Ovechkin, he leaves the game in good hands.

stunned goalie Brian Boucher. Without a doubt, Ovechkin's amazing tally was the goal of the season.

The Calder Trophy race between Ovechkin and fellow fab freshman Sidney Crosby (Pittsburgh Penguins) also created a lot of excitement for a league seeking new stars. Both talented youngsters were among the list of 100-point scorers. Ovechkin, who would later skate away with Rookie honors, also etched his name on the list of 50-goal scorers. Despite their tremendous individual talent, neither Ovechkin nor Crosby could lead their respective teams to the playoffs.

The postseason, which was pushed back by two weeks because of the league's participation in the 2006 Winter Olympics, provided more thrills for hungry hockey fans. In the Western Conference, the top four seeds — including the Presidents' Trophy winning Detroit Red Wings — were eliminated in the first round. It was the first time since the league adopted its current playoff format in 1993-94 that such a string of upsets had occurred.

In the end, the conference's lowest seeded team, the Edmonton Oilers, advanced to the Stanley Cup finals to meet the Eastern Conference champion Carolina Hurricanes. The Oilers and Hurricanes, both small market clubs that benefited from Bettman's new economic order, played a fiercely competitive series that came down to a seventh game. On home ice, in front of a wild sellout crowd at the RBC Center in Raleigh, the Canes captured their first Cup with a 3-1 victory.

Carolina's veteran captain Rod Brind'Amour was so excited to get his hands on the silver chalice, he raised it over his head and skated away without posing for the traditional photo with Bettman. Despite the unintended snub, Bettman had to smile. He and his league had gone through the darkness of a lost season.

And somehow, they both survived.

E.J. HRADEK'S

10

Biggest Stories of the Year in **Hockey**

10 Here Today, Gone Tomorrow.

Stud defenseman Chris Pronger led the Oilers on an unexpected run to the Stanley Cup finals. Edmonton's magical playoff run ended with a Game 7 loss in Carolina. Then, just days later, Pronger stunned the Oiler faithful by requesting a trade, citing "personal reasons." On July 3, Edmonton general manager Kevin Lowe grants Pronger's wish, dealing him to Anaheim.

09 Do You Know the Way to San Jose?

On Nov. 30, after a slow start to the new season, the Boston Bruins shocked the hockey world by trading franchise center Joe Thornton to the San Jose Sharks for Brad Stuart, Marco Sturm and Wayne Primeau. Thornton quickly settled into life in his new home on the left coast. By season's end, he'd piled up a league-best 125 points and helped the Sharks into the Western Conference semifinals. In June, he was awarded the Hart Trophy as the league's MVP.

08 New Kids on the Block.

Rookies Alexander Ovechkin and Sidney Crosby wowed fans with their season-long battle for the Calder Trophy. Both players hit the 100-point plateau, becoming just the sixth and seventh rookies to do so. In fact, at age 18, Crosby became the youngest player to ever crack the century mark. Still, Ovechkin skated away with the Calder.

07 Hull of a Career.

On Oct. 15, just five games into the season, legendary goal-scorer and colorful character Brett Hull announced his retirement. Hull made the final decision after consulting with Coyotes GM Michael Barnett and head coach Wayne Gretzky. The 41-year-old sniper finished his brilliant career with 741 goals, ranking him third on the all-time list.

06 No More Ties.

The introduction of the shootout created quite a stir around NHL rinks. Most fans embraced the idea of breaking regular season ties with a penalty-shot competition. Stars rookie Jussi Jokinen led the league with 10 shootout goals; while goaltenders Martin Brodeur (Devils), Rick DiPietro (Islanders) and Marty Turco (Stars) each recorded a league-high eight shootout wins.

05 Au Revoir, Monsieur Lemieux.

After being sidelined by an irregular heartbeat, 40-year-old Penguins owner/captain/legend

Mario Lemieux decides to retire on Jan. 25. It was the second - and seemingly final - retirement for Lemieux, who had returned to the ice in 2000, three years after his first retirement in 1997. Super Mario finished his career with 1,723 points in just 915 games.

04 Operation Slapshot.

The league's comeback season took a strange turn on Feb. 7 when New Jersey law enforcement officials announced that they were investigating a gambling ring that allegedly involved Coyotes assistant coach Rick Tocchet, who took a leave of absence from the club after being formally charged in the case. The story quickly grew into a tabloid sensation when Wayne Gretzky's wife, Janet, was alleged to have been among those who placed bets with Tocchet. She was not charged with any wrongdoing.

03 Swedish Gold.

The NHL closed its doors for a 15-day, mid-season break to allow its players to participate in the Winter Olympics in Torino, Italy. Team Sweden, which suffered a humiliating loss to lightly regarded Latvia at the '02

Games, redeemed itself by edging rival Finland, 3-2, in the Gold Medal game.

02 Hurricane Season.

On June 19, the Carolina Hurricanes clinched the franchise's first-ever Stanley Cup with a 3-1 victory over the Edmonton Oilers in Game 7 of the final series. The Hurricanes, who moved from Hartford in 1997, had opened a 3-1 series lead, but dropped the next two games to set up the decisive contest. Carolina rookie goalie Cam Ward was awarded the Conn Smythe Trophy as playoff MVP.

01 New Season, New League.

The NHL re-opened for business on Oct. 5 with 15 games featuring all 30 clubs. After losing a season to a prolonged labor battle, the league returned with several new rules and a commitment to maintain a higher standard of enforcement on obstruction fouls like hooking and holding. Commissioner Gary Bettman and his staff were determined to create a faster, more skilled on-ice product. And, for the most part, they succeeded.

In 2005-06, rookie senation Alexander Ovechkin scored 52 of the Capitals' 237 goals (21.9 percent). Only Teemu Selanne had a higher percentage of his team's goals as rookie, when he netted 76 of the Winnipeg Jets' 322 goals (23.6 percent) in 1992-93.

2005-2006
Season in Review

ESPN
SPORTS ALMANAC

Final NHL Standings

Division champions (*) and playoff qualifiers (†) are noted. Teams get two points for a win and one point for an overtime loss (OL) and a shootout loss (SL). Number of seasons listed after each head coach refers to current tenure with club through 2005-06 season.

Western Conference
Central Division

	W	L	OL	SL	Pts	GF	GA
*Detroit	58	16	5	3	124	305	209
†Nashville	49	25	5	3	106	259	227
Columbus	35	43	1	3	74	223	279
Chicago	26	43	7	6	65	211	285
St. Louis	21	46	7	8	57	197	292

Head Coaches: Det—Mike Babcock (1st season); **Nash**—Barry Trotz (7th); **Clb**—Gerard Gallant (2nd); **Chi**—Trent Yawney (1st); **St.L**—Mike Kitchen (2nd).

Northwest Division

	W	L	OL	SL	Pts	GF	GA
*Calgary	46	25	4	7	103	218	200
†Colorado	43	30	4	6	95	283	257
†Edmonton	41	28	4	9	95	256	251
Vancouver	42	32	4	4	92	256	255
Minnesota	38	36	5	3	84	231	215

Head Coaches: Calg—Darryl Sutter (3rd season); **Col**—Joel Quenneville (1st); **Edm**—Craig MacTavish (5th); **Van**—Marc Crawford (7th); **Min**—Jacques Lemaire (5th).
Note: Colorado finishes 2nd (and 7th in the conference) due to a higher win total than Edmonton.

Pacific Division

	W	L	OL	SL	Pts	GF	GA
*Dallas	53	23	5	1	112	265	218
†San Jose	44	27	4	7	99	266	242
†Anaheim	43	27	5	7	98	254	229
Los Angeles	42	35	4	1	89	249	270
Phoenix	38	39	2	3	81	246	271

Head Coaches: Dal—Dave Tippett (3rd season); **SJ**—Ron Wilson (3rd); **Ana**—Randy Carlyle (1st); **LA**—Andy Murray (6th, 37-28-5) was fired on March 21 and replaced by John Torchetti (5-7-0); **Pho**—Wayne Gretzky.

Eastern Conference
Northeast Division

	W	L	OL	SL	Pts	GF	GA
*Ottawa	52	21	3	6	113	314	211
†Buffalo	52	24	1	5	110	291	239
†Montreal	42	31	6	3	93	243	247
Toronto	41	33	1	7	90	257	270
Boston	29	37	8	8	74	230	266

Head Coaches: Ott—Bryan Murray (1st season); **Buf**—Lindy Ruff (8th); **Mon**—Claude Julien (3rd, 19-16-6) was fired on Jan. 14 and replaced by GM Bob Gainey (23-15-3); **Tor**—Pat Quinn (7th); **Bos**—Mike Sullivan (2nd).

Atlantic Division

	W	L	OL	SL	Pts	GF	GA
*New Jersey	46	27	5	4	101	242	229
†Philadelphia	45	26	5	6	101	267	259
†NY Rangers	44	26	8	4	100	257	215
NY Islanders	36	40	3	3	78	230	278
Pittsburgh	22	46	8	6	58	244	316

Head Coaches: NJ—Larry Robinson (1st season, 14-13-5) resigned on Dec. 19 and was replaced by GM Lou Lamoriello (32-14-4); **Phi**—Ken Hitchcock (3rd); **NYR**—Tom Renney (2nd); **NYI**—Steve Stirling (2nd, 18-22-2) was fired on Jan. 11 and replaced by asst. Brad Shaw (18-18-4); **Pit**—Ed Olczyk (2nd, 8-17-6) was fired on Dec. 15 and replaced by Michel Therrien (14-29-8).

Southeast Division

	W	L	OL	SL	Pts	GF	GA
*Carolina	52	22	6	2	112	294	260
†Tampa Bay	43	33	2	4	92	252	260
Atlanta	41	33	3	5	90	281	275
Florida	37	34	6	5	85	240	257
Washington	29	41	6	6	70	237	306

Head Coaches: Car—Peter Laviolette (2nd season); **TB**—John Tortorella (5th); **Atl**—Bob Hartley (3rd); **Fla**—Jacques Martin (1st); **Wash**—Glen Hanlon (2nd).

Home & Away, Division Records

Sixteen teams—eight from each conference—qualify for the Stanley Cup Playoffs; (*) indicates division champions.

Western Conference

		Pts	Home	Away	Div
1	Detroit*	124	27-9-3-2	31-7-2-1	25-3-2-2
2	Dallas*	112	28-11-2-0	25-12-3-1	17-11-3-1
3	Calgary*	103	30-7-1-3	16-18-3-4	20-8-3-1
4	Nashville	106	32-8-0-1	17-17-5-2	23-8-1-0
5	San Jose	99	25-9-1-6	19-18-3-1	16-10-3-3
6	Anaheim	98	26-10-2-3	17-17-3-4	18-9-2-3
7	Colorado	95	25-10-0-6	18-20-3-0	16-12-1-3
8	Edmonton	95	20-15-2-4	21-13-2-5	15-15-0-2
	Vancouver	92	25-10-3-3	17-22-1-1	15-12-2-3
	Los Angeles	89	26-14-1-0	16-21-3-1	14-14-3-1
	Minnesota	84	23-16-1-1	15-20-4-2	14-17-1-0
	Phoenix	81	19-18-1-3	19-21-1-0	15-15-1-1
	Columbus	74	23-18-0-0	12-25-1-3	15-15-1-1
	Chicago	65	16-19-4-2	10-24-3-4	11-17-2-2
	St. Louis	57	12-23-3-3	9-23-4-5	7-20-3-2

Eastern Conference

		Pts	Home	Away	Div
1	Ottawa*	113	29-9-1-2	23-12-2-4	20-8-1-3
2	Carolina*	112	31-8-2-0	21-14-4-2	18-11-3-0
3	New Jersey*	101	27-11-2-1	19-16-3-3	16-12-1-3
4	Buffalo	110	27-11-1-2	25-13-0-3	21-9-1-1
5	Philadelphia	101	22-13-4-2	23-13-1-4	19-9-2-2
6	NY Rangers	100	25-10-5-1	19-16-3-3	18-9-4-1
7	Montreal	93	24-13-3-1	18-18-3-2	18-9-5-0
8	Tampa Bay	92	25-14-1-1	18-19-1-3	16-11-2-3
	Toronto	90	26-12-1-2	15-21-0-5	11-16-1-4
	Atlanta	90	24-13-2-2	17-20-1-3	17-10-2-3
	Florida	85	25-11-1-4	12-23-5-1	18-11-0-3
	NY Islanders	78	20-18-2-1	16-22-1-2	15-15-1-1
	Boston	74	16-15-4-6	13-22-4-2	10-19-1-2
	Washington	70	16-18-2-5	13-23-4-1	11-14-3-4
	Pittsburgh	58	12-21-5-3	10-25-3-3	12-14-2-4

San Jose Sharks
Joe Thornton
Scoring, Assists

Detroit Red Wings
Nicklas Lidstrom
Defensemen Points

Washington Capitals
Alexander Ovechkin
Rookie Points, Shots

Calgary Flames
Miikka Kiprusoff
GAA, ShO, Min.

NHL Regular Season Individual Leaders

(*) indicates rookie eligible for Calder Trophy.

Scoring

	Pos	Gm	G	A	Pts	+/-	PM	PP	SH	GW	Shots	Pct
Joe Thornton, Bos.-SJ	C	81	29	96	**125**	31	61	11	0	6	195	14.9
Jaromir Jagr, NY Rangers	R	82	54	69	**123**	34	72	24	0	9	368	14.7
Alexander Ovechkin*, Washington	L	81	52	54	**106**	2	52	21	3	5	425	12.2
Dany Heatley, Ottawa	L	82	50	53	**103**	29	86	23	2	7	300	16.7
Daniel Alfredsson, Ottawa	R	77	43	60	**103**	29	50	16	5	8	249	17.3
Sidney Crosby*, Pittsburgh	C	81	39	63	**102**	-1	110	16	0	5	278	14.0
Eric Staal, Carolina	C	82	45	55	**100**	-8	81	19	4	4	279	16.1
Ilya Kovalchuk, Atlanta	L	78	52	46	**98**	-6	68	27	0	7	323	16.1
Marc Savard, Atlanta	C	82	28	69	**97**	7	100	14	1	4	212	13.2
Jonathan Cheechoo, San Jose	R	82	56	37	**93**	23	58	24	2	11	317	17.7
Marian Hossa, Atlanta	R	80	39	53	**92**	17	67	14	7	7	341	11.4
Brad Richards, Tampa Bay	C	82	23	68	**91**	0	32	7	4	0	282	8.2
Teemu Selanne, Anaheim	R	80	40	50	**90**	28	44	18	0	5	267	15.0
Jason Spezza, Ottawa	C	68	19	71	**90**	23	33	7	0	5	156	12.2
Brian Gionta, New Jersey	R	82	48	41	**89**	18	46	24	1	10	291	16.5
Olli Jokinen, Florida	C	82	38	51	**89**	14	88	14	1	9	351	10.8
Joe Sakic, Colorado	C	82	32	55	**87**	10	60	10	0	6	263	12.2
Pavel Datsyuk, Detroit	C	75	28	59	**87**	26	22	11	0	4	145	19.3
Patrick Marleau, San Jose	C	82	34	52	**86**	-12	26	20	1	4	260	13.1

Three tied with 85 points.

Goals

Cheechoo, SJ	.56
Jagr, NYR	.54
Kovalchuk, Atl	.52
Ovechkin*, Wash	.52
Heatley, Ott	.50
Gionta, NJ	.48
Gagne, Phi	.47
Staal, Car	.45
Alfredsson, Ott	.43
Selanne, Ana	.40
Shanahan, Det	.40

Three tied with 39.

Assists

Thornton, Bos-SJ	.96
Spezza, Ott	.71
Jagr, NYR	.69
Savard, Atl	.69
Richards, TB	.68
Lidstrom, Det	.64
Crosby*, Pit	.63
Alfredsson, Ott	.60
Datsyuk, Det	.59
Zubov, Dal	.58
Hemsky, Edm	.58
Kaberle, Tor	.58

Defensemen Points

Lidstrom, Det	.80
Zubov, Dal	.71
McCabe, Tor	.68
Visnovsky, LA	.67
Kaberle, Tor	.67
Niedermayer, Ana	.63
Schneider, Det	.59
Gonchar, Pit	.58
Pronger, Edm	.56
Boyle, TB	.53
Blake, Col	.51

Rookie Points

Ovechkin, Wash	.106
Crosby, Pit	.102
Boyes, Bos	.69
Jokinen, Dal	.55
Svatos, Col	.50
Phaneuf, Calg	.49
Vanek, Buf	.48
Prucha, NYR	.47
Steen, Tor	.45
Wellwood, Tor	.45
Carter, Phi	.42
Kunitz, Atl-Ana	.41

Plus/Minus

Redden, Ott	.+35
Rozsival, NYR	.+35
Jagr, NYR	.+34
Meszaros*, Ott	.+34
Schneider, Det	.+33
Thornton, Bos-SJ	.+31
Gagne, Phi	.+31
Nylander, NYR	.+31
Morrow, Dal	.+30

Game Winning Goals

Cheechoo, SJ	.11
Gionta, NJ	.10
Svatos*, Col	.9
Zetterberg, Det	.9
Jagr, NYR	.9
Jokinen, Fla	.9

Four tied with 8.

Power Play Goals

Kovalchuk, Atl	.27
Jagr, NYR	.24
Cheechoo, SJ	.24
Gionta, NJ	.24
Heatley, Ott	.23
Ovechkin*, Wash	.21
Marleau, SJ	.20

Three tied with 19.

Short-Handed Goals

Hossa, Atl	.7
Vermette, Ott	.6
Demitra, LA	.5
Pettinger, Wash	.5
Alfredsson, Ott	.5
Malone, Pit	.5
Rolston, Min	.5

Eleven tied with 4.

Shots

Ovechkin*, Wash . . .425
Jagr, NYR 368
Jokinen, Fla 351
Hossa, Atl 341
Gagne, Phi 334
Kovalchuk, Atl 323
Cheechoo, SJ 317
Bergeron, Bos 310
Lecavalier, TB 309
Blake, NYI 304
Heatley, Ott 300

Shooting Pct.
(Min. 82 shots)

Tanguay, Col 23.2
Prucha, NYR 23.1
Carter, Van 22.6
Parrish, NYI-LA 21.2
Holmstrom, Det 20.7
Eaves*, Ott 20.0
Svatos*, Col 19.4
Datsyuk, Det 19.2
Arnott, Dal 19.2
Brunette, Col 18.6

Penalty Minutes

Avery, LA 257
Witt, Wash-Nash 209
Neil, Ott 204
Morrow, Dal 183
Barnaby, Chi 178
Ott, Dal 178
Fedoruk, Ana 174
Brashear, Phi 166
Shelley, Clb 163
Hordichuk, Nash . . .163
Erskine, Dal-NYI 161

Minutes/Game
(Min. 50 Games)

McCabe, Tor 28:17
Kaberle, Tor 28:10
Lidstrom, Det 28:06
Pronger, Edm 27:59
Chara, Ott 27:11
Zubov, Dal 26:26
Ohlund, Van 25:40
Rafalski, NJ 25:31
Niedermayer, Ana . .25:30
Bouwmeester, Fla . . .25:29

Goaltending
(Minimum 24 games)

	Gm	Min	GAA	Record	GA	Shots	Sv%	EN	Sho	G	A	Pts	PM
Miikka Kiprusoff, Calgary 74		4380	2.07	42-20-11	151	1951	.923	5	10	0	2	2	10
Dominik Hasek, Ottawa 43		2584	2.09	28-10-4	90	1202	.925	1	5	0	0	0	16
Manny Legace, Detroit 51		2905	2.19	37-8-3	106	1244	.915	1	7	0	1	1	0
Cristobal Huet, Montreal 36		2103	2.20	18-11-4	77	1085	.929	1	7	0	0	0	0
Henrik Lundqvist*, NY Rangers . . .53		3112	2.24	30-12-9	116	1485	.922	2	2	0	2	2	0
Manny Fernandez, Minnesota . . .58		3411	2.29	30-18-7	130	1612	.919	3	1	0	3	3	6
Ilja Bryzgalov*, Anaheim 31		1575	2.51	13-12-1	66	733	.910	2	1	0	2	2	4
Marty Turco, Dallas 68		3910	2.55	41-19-5	166	1624	.898	2	3	0	2	2	28
Vesa Toskala, San Jose 37		2039	2.56	23-7-4	87	878	.901	1	2	0	1	1	4
Martin Brodeur, New Jersey 73		4365	2.57	43-23-7	187	2105	.911	2	5	0	3	3	4
Ryan Miller*, Buffalo 48		2862	2.60	30-14-3	124	1440	.914	3	1	0	2	2	0
Curtis Sanford*, St. Louis 34		1830	2.66	13-13-5	81	885	.908	4	3	0	0	0	0
Jean Sebastien Giguere, Anaheim .60		3381	2.66	30-15-11	150	1692	.911	4	2	0	0	0	20
Tomas Vokoun, Nashville 61		3601	2.67	36-18-7	160	1984	.919	1	4	0	2	2	26
Dwayne Roloson, Min-Edm 43		2524	2.73	14-24-5	115	1256	.908	4	2	0	1	1	8

Wins

Brodeur, NJ 43
Kiprusoff, Calg 42
Turco, Dal 41
Gerber, Car 38
Legace, Det 37
Vokoun, Nash 36
Luongo, Fla 35
Auld, Van 33
Joseph, Pho 32
Garon, LA 31
Five tied with 30.

Shutouts

Kiprusoff, Calg. 10
Huet, Mon 7
Legace, Det 7
Brodeur, NJ 5
Grahame, TB 5
Hasek, Ott 5
Garon, LA 4
Joseph, Pho 4
Luongo, Fla 4
Vokoun, Nash 4
Five tied with 3.

Save Pct.

Huet, Mon 929
Hasek, Ott 925
Kiprusoff, Calg 923
Lundqvist*, NYR 922
Fernandez, Min 919
Vokoun, Nash 919
Thomas, Bos 917
Legace, Det 915
Luongo, Fla 914
Miller*, Buf 914
Giguere, Ana 911

Minutes Played

Kiprusoff, Calg 4380
Brodeur, NJ 4365
Luongo, Fla 4305
Turco, Dal 3910
Auld, Van 3859
Vokoun, Nash 3601
DiPietro, NYI 3572
Kolzig, Wash 3506
Gerber, Car 3493
Garon, LA 3446
Joseph, Pho 3424

Team Goaltending

WESTERN	GAA	Mins	GA	Shots	Sv%	EN	SO	EASTERN	GAA	Mins	GA	Shots	Sv%	EN	SO
Calgary	2.32	4984	193	2261	.915	5	10	Ottawa	2.47	4975	205	2344	.913	1	8
Detroit	2.47	4972	205	2180	.906	4	9	NY Rangers .	2.53	4997	211	2358	.911	4	2
Minnesota .	2.56	4974	212	2460	.914	6	3	New Jersey .	2.70	5007	225	2403	.906	3	5
Dallas	2.60	5011	217	2099	.897	3	3	Buffalo	2.82	4986	234	2502	.906	5	2
Anaheim . . .	2.67	4987	222	2431	.909	6	3	Montreal . . .	2.94	4978	244	2507	.903	5	8
Nashville . . .	2.70	4980	224	2663	.916	1	6	Florida	3.02	5006	252	2853	.912	5	4
San Jose . .	2.82	4996	235	2180	.892	4	5	Philadelphia	3.04	4995	253	2372	.893	7	3
Edmonton . .	2.89	5027	242	2095	.884	5	2	Tampa Bay .	3.07	4997	256	2260	.887	10	7
Colorado . . .	3.02	4982	251	2415	.896	7	5	Boston	3.10	4997	258	2633	.902	6	2
Vancouver . .	3.03	4978	251	2466	.898	4	0	Carolina . . .	3.10	4997	258	2497	.897	5	4
Phoenix . . .	3.23	4976	268	2480	.892	8	4	Toronto . . .	3.16	4994	263	2509	.895	6	3
Los Angeles	3.24	4975	269	2459	.891	9	5	Atlanta . . .	3.25	4986	270	2483	.891	6	6
Columbus . . .	3.31	4996	276	2762	.900	8	1	NY Islanders	3.30	5001	275	2549	.892	12	5
Chicago	3.35	4997	279	2417	.885	6	2	Washington .	3.60	5006	300	2880	.896	9	1
St. Louis . . .	3.41	5001	284	2510	.887	11	3	Pittsburgh .	3.73	4985	310	2723	.886	7	2

2006 NHL All-Star Game Canceled

In the NHL's new collective bargaining agreement signed in 2005, it was decided that the All-Star Game will no longer be played during Olympic years. The 2007 game will be played in Dallas. See the Olympics chapter for 2006 Turin results.

Power Play/Penalty Killing

Power play and penalty killing conversions. Power play: No—number of opportunities; GF—goals for; Pct—percentage. Penalty killing: No—number of times shorthanded; GA—goals against; Pct—percentage of penalties killed; SH—shorthanded goals for.

WESTERN	—Power Play—			—Penalty Killing—				EASTERN	—Power Play—			—Penalty Killing—			
	No	GF	Pct	No	GA	Pct	SH		No	GF	Pct	No	GA	Pct	SH
Detroit	461	102	**22.1**	461	67	85.5	7	Toronto	501	107	**21.4**	496	99	80.0	14
Colorado	473	89	**18.8**	447	69	84.6	11	Buffalo	477	101	**21.2**	439	59	86.6	10
Nashville	512	94	**18.4**	533	82	84.6	12	Ottawa	490	102	**20.8**	476	73	84.7	25
Vancouver	526	96	**18.3**	512	93	81.8	6	Montreal	463	89	**19.2**	481	91	81.1	10
San Jose	500	91	**18.2**	399	77	80.7	10	Pittsburgh	495	94	**19.0**	533	113	78.8	13
Calgary	478	87	**18.2**	508	80	84.3	8	NY Rangers	440	83	**18.9**	486	79	83.7	4
Anaheim	480	87	**18.1**	510	84	83.5	9	Atlanta	528	100	**18.9**	491	102	79.2	13
Edmonton	485	88	**18.1**	478	76	84.1	15	Philadelphia	444	80	**18.0**	465	97	79.1	19
Dallas	498	88	**17.7**	504	82	83.7	10	Carolina	531	95	**17.9**	445	81	81.8	17
Phoenix	541	96	**17.7**	513	98	80.9	4	New Jersey	439	78	**17.8**	348	63	81.9	3
Minnesota	453	77	**17.0**	436	55	87.4	11	NY Islanders	450	76	**16.9**	476	99	79.2	5
St. Louis	512	75	**14.6**	461	82	82.2	6	Tampa Bay	485	81	**16.7**	390	72	81.5	11
Columbus	451	64	**14.2**	523	95	81.8	10	Florida	411	63	**15.3**	514	91	82.3	5
Los Angeles	541	77	**14.2**	489	104	78.7	15	Boston	418	62	**14.8**	479	78	83.7	9
Chicago	417	51	**12.2**	547	88	83.9	6	Washington	490	72	**14.7**	550	116	78.9	15

Shootout Records

Beginning with the 2005-06 NHL season, a shootout decides the game's winner if the score is still tied after a five-minute, four-on-four sudden death overtime. In the shootout, each team takes three shots. The team with the most goals after those six shots is the winner. If the score remains tied, the shootout goes to a sudden death format.

Of the 1230 NHL games played in 2005-06, 145 were decided via the shootout (11.79 percent). Players attempted 981 shots and scored 330 goals (33.64 percent). The tables below show each team's record in shootouts, along with their goals (G) and shots (Sh) for and against. Teams are ranked by wins.

Western Conference

			For		Against	
	GP	Record	G	Sh	G	Sh
1 Dallas	13	12-1	24	42	9	41
2 Columbus	11	8-3	15	43	9	44
3 Edmonton	16	7-9	19	53	23	54
4 Los Angeles	7	6-1	10	20	3	21
5 Nashville	9	6-3	12	25	8	25
6 Minnesota	8	5-3	9	31	7	30
7 Detroit	7	4-3	12	25	9	25
8 Phoenix	7	4-3	7	24	7	25
9 Vancouver	8	4-4	7	23	9	24
10 St. Louis	12	4-8	10	38	16	37
11 Colorado	9	3-6	6	30	11	31
12 Anaheim	10	3-7	8	31	12	31
13 Chicago	8	2-6	10	31	14	29
14 Calgary	9	2-7	6	29	12	26
15 San Jose	8	1-7	7	29	14	29

Eastern Conference

			For		Against	
	GP	Record	G	Sh	G	Sh
1 NY Islanders	12	9-3	19	41	12	44
2 New Jersey	13	9-4	18	45	12	45
3 Carolina	10	8-2	17	34	10	36
4 NY Rangers	11	7-4	18	49	15	50
5 Washington	13	7-6	18	54	17	57
6 Tampa Bay	10	6-4	12	27	9	27
7 Atlanta	10	5-5	11	36	11	34
8 Buffalo	10	5-5	12	32	11	30
9 Florida	9	4-5	8	31	9	31
10 Philadelphia	10	4-6	11	33	14	32
11 Toronto	10	3-7	4	24	10	24
12 Montreal	5	2-3	4	14	4	15
13 Ottawa	8	2-6	4	23	8	21
14 Boston	10	2-8	6	36	12	36
15 Pittsburgh	7	1-6	6	28	13	27

Individual Shootout Leaders

Leading shootout scorers (ranked by goals) and goaltenders (ranked by wins) during the 2005-06 season.

Shooters

	Goals	Shots	Pct	GDG
Jussi Jokinen, Dal	10	13	76.9	3
Viktor Kozlov, NJ	8	12	66.7	5
Miroslav Satan, NYI	7	10	70.0	5
Sergei Zubov, Dal	7	12	58.3	4
Brad Richards, TB	6	9	66.7	4
Jaroslav Balastik, Clb	6	9	66.7	3
Matt Cullen, Car	6	9	66.7	2
Alexander Ovechkin, Wash	6	13	46.2	3

Note: GDG denotes Game Deciding Goals

Goaltenders

	W-L	GA	Shots	SV%
Marty Turco, Dal	8-1	6	24	.750
Martin Brodeur, NJ	8-3	9	38	.763
Rick DiPietro, NYI	8-3	12	41	.707
Martin Gerber, Car	7-2	10	33	.697
Kari Lehtonen, Atl	5-0	3	20	.850
Michael Morrison, Edm-Ott	5-2	6	24	.750
Ten tied with 4 wins.				

Team by Team Statistics

High scorers and goaltenders with at least ten games played. Players who competed for more than one team during the regular season are listed with their final club; (*) indicates rookies eligible for Calder Trophy. Player positions are noted as follows: C—Center, L—Left wing, R—Right wing, D—Defenseman.

Mighty Ducks of Anaheim

Top Scorers	Gm	G	A	Pts	+/-	PM	PP
Teemu Selanne, R	.80	40	50	90	28	44	18
Andy McDonald, C	.82	34	51	85	24	32	13
Scott Niedermayer, D	.82	13	50	63	8	96	9
Joffrey Lupul, R	.81	28	25	53	-13	48	12
Chris Kunitz*, L	.69	19	22	41	16	71	5
ATL	.2	0	0	0	-3	2	0
ANA	.67	19	22	41	19	69	5
Rob Niedermayer, C	.76	15	24	39	-5	89	4
Ryan Getzlaf, C	.57	14	25	39	6	22	10
Francois Beauchemin*, D	72	8	28	36	2	52	4
CLB	.11	0	2	2	-6	11	0
ANA	.61	8	26	34	8	41	4
Todd Marchant, C	.79	9	25	34	2	66	0
CLB	.18	3	6	9	-1	20	0
ANA	.61	6	19	25	3	46	0
Jonathan Hedstrom, R	.79	13	14	27	2	48	2
Corey Perry*, R	.56	13	12	25	1	50	4
Todd Fedoruk, L	.76	4	19	23	6	174	0
Samuel Pahlsson, C	.82	11	10	21	-1	34	0
Ruslan Salei, D	.78	1	18	19	17	114	0

Acquired: D Beauchemin and R Tyler Wright from Clb. for C Sergei Fedorov and an '06 5th-round pick (Nov. 15). **Claimed:** L Kunitz off waivers from Nash. (Oct. 18); C Marchant off waivers from Clb. (Nov. 21).

Goalies (10 Gm)	Gm	Min	GAA	Record	SV%
Ilja Bryzgalov*	.31	1575	2.51	13-12-1	.909
Jean Sebastien Giguere	60	3381	2.66	30-15-11	.911
ANAHEIM	.82	4987	2.67	43-27-12	.909

Shutouts: Giguere (2), Bryzgalov (1). **Assists:** Bryzgalov (2). **PM:** Giguere (20), Bryzgalov (4).

Atlanta Thrashers

Top Scorers	Gm	G	A	Pts	+/-	PM	PP
Ilya Kovalchuk, L	.78	52	46	98	-6	68	27
Marc Savard, C	.82	28	69	97	7	100	14
Marian Hossa, R	.80	39	53	92	17	67	14
Vyacheslav Kozlov, L	.82	25	46	71	14	33	8
Peter Bondra, R	.60	21	18	39	-3	40	8
Jaroslav Modry, D	.79	7	31	38	-9	76	5
Greg de Vries, D	.82	7	28	35	1	76	3
Scott Mellanby, R	.71	12	22	34	5	55	3
Bobby Holik, C	.64	15	18	33	-6	79	5
Niclas Havelid, D	.82	4	28	32	9	48	2
Andy Sutton, D	.76	8	17	25	13	144	2
Patrik Stefan, C	.64	10	14	24	3	36	2
Serge Aubin, C	.74	7	17	24	-4	79	1
Jim Slater*, C	.71	10	10	20	1	46	1
Ronald Petrovicky, R	.60	8	12	20	-8	62	2
Steve McCarthy, D	.67	9	7	16	3	51	2
VAN	.51	2	4	6	3	43	0
ATL	.16	7	3	10	0	8	2
Brad Larsen, C	.62	7	8	15	-3	21	0
Jean-Pierre Vigier, R	.41	4	6	10	-4	40	1
Garnet Exelby, D	.75	1	9	10	11	75	0

Acquired: D McCarthy from Van. for an '07 4th-round pick (Mar. 9).

Goalies (10 Gm)	Gm	Min	GAA	Record	SV%
Mike Dunham	.17	779	2.77	8-5-2	.893
Kari Lehtonen*	.38	2166	2.94	20-15-0	.906
Michael Garnett*	.24	1271	3.45	10-7-4	.885
ATLANTA	.82	4986	3.25	41-33-8	.891

Shutouts: Lehtonen and Garnett (2), Dunham (1). **Assists:** Garnett (2), Lehtonen (1). **PM:** Lehtonen (4).

Boston Bruins

Top Scorers	Gm	G	A	Pts	+/-	PM	PP
Patrice Bergeron, C	.81	31	42	73	3	22	12
Brad Boyes*, C	.82	26	43	69	11	30	8
Marco Sturm, L	.74	29	30	59	6	48	8
SJ	.23	6	10	16	-8	16	3
BOS	.51	23	20	43	14	32	5
Glen Murray, R	.64	24	29	53	-8	52	6
Brad Stuart, D	.78	12	31	43	-8	52	7
SJ	.23	2	10	12	-2	14	1
BOS	.55	10	21	31	-6	38	6
Marty Reasoner, C	.77	11	23	34	-14	28	6
EDM	.58	9	17	26	-12	20	5
BOS	.19	2	6	8	-2	8	1
Brian Leetch, D	.61	5	27	32	-10	36	4
P.J. Axelsson, L	.59	10	18	28	-3	4	1
Brad Isbister, L	.58	6	17	23	-2	46	1
Wayne Primeau, C	.71	11	11	22	-16	57	1
SJ	.21	5	3	8	-6	17	1
BOS	.50	6	8	14	-10	40	0
Travis Green, C	.82	10	12	22	-2	79	0
David Tanabe, D	.75	4	16	20	-5	56	0
PHO	.21	0	4	4	-5	8	0
BOS	.54	4	12	16	0	48	0
Jiri Slegr, D	.32	5	11	16	-2	56	4

Acquired: D Tanabe from Pho. for C Dave Scatchard (Nov. 18); L Sturm, D Stuart and C Primeau from SJ for C Joe Thornton (Nov. 30); C Reasoner, C Yan Stastny and an '06 2nd-round pick from Edm. for L Sergei Samsonov (Mar. 9).

Goalies (10 Gm)	Gm	Min	GAA	Record	SV%
Hannu Toivonen*	.20	1163	2.63	9-5-4	.914
Tim Thomas	.38	2187	2.77	12-13-10	.917
Andrew Raycroft	.30	1619	3.71	8-19-2	.879
BOSTON	.82	4997	3.10	29-37-16	.902

Shutouts: Toivonen and Thomas (1). **Assists:** Thomas (1). **PM:** Toivonen (6), Thomas (4).

Buffalo Sabres

Top Scorers	Gm	G	A	Pts	+/-	PM	PP
Maxim Afinogenov, R	.77	22	51	73	6	84	11
Chris Drury, C	.81	30	37	67	-11	32	16
Ales Kotalik, R	.82	25	37	62	-3	62	10
Daniel Briere, C	.48	25	33	58	3	48	11
Tim Connolly, C	.63	16	39	55	5	28	7
Thomas Vanek*, L	.81	25	23	48	-11	72	11
Derek Roy, C	.70	18	28	46	1	57	5
Brian Campbell, D	.79	12	32	44	-14	16	5
Jochen Hecht, C	.64	18	24	42	10	34	4
Jean-Pierre Dumont, R	.54	20	20	40	-1	38	9
Teppo Numminen, D	.75	2	38	40	6	36	0
Jason Pominville*, R	.57	18	12	30	-4	22	10
Paul Gaustad*, C	.78	9	15	24	4	65	0
Mike Grier, R	.81	7	16	23	-7	28	0
Henrik Tallander, D	.82	6	15	21	10	74	0
Dmitri Kalinin, D	.55	2	16	18	14	54	0
Toni Lydman, D	.75	1	16	17	9	82	0
Jay McKee, D	.75	5	11	16	0	57	0
Taylor Pyatt, L	.41	6	6	12	-1	33	0
Rory Fitzpatrick, D	.56	4	5	9	-18	50	2
Adam Mair, C	.40	2	5	7	-2	47	0

Goalies (10 Gm)	Gm	Min	GAA	Record	Sv%
Ryan Miller*	.48	2862	2.60	30-14-3	.914
Martin Biron	.35	1934	2.89	21-8-3	.905
BUFFALO	.82	4986	2.82	52-24-6	.906

Shutouts: Miller and Biron (1). **Assists:** Miller (2), Biron (1). **PM:** Biron (10).

Calgary Flames

Top Scorers	Gm	G	A	Pts	+/-	PM	PP
Jarome Iginla, R	.82	35	32	67	5	86	17
Daymond Langkow, C	.82	25	34	59	2	46	11
Dion Phaneuf*, D	.82	20	29	49	5	93	16
Kristian Huselius, R	.78	20	27	47	-9	40	8
FLA	.24	5	3	8	-11	4	2
CALG	.54	15	24	39	2	36	6
Tony Amonte, R	.80	14	28	42	3	43	3
Chuck Kobasew, R	.77	20	11	31	-10	64	10
Andrew Ference, D	.82	4	27	31	-12	85	2
Jamie Lundmark, C	.53	10	19	29	-1	62	2
NYR	.3	1	0	1	-2	6	0
PHO	.38	5	13	18	-1	36	1
CALG	.12	4	6	10	2	20	1
Mike Leclerc, L	.50	10	16	26	0	37	4
PHO	.35	9	12	21	0	29	4
CALG	.15	1	4	5	0	8	0
Roman Hamrlik, D	.51	7	19	26	8	56	1
Matthew Lombardi, C	.55	6	20	26	-1	48	1
Robyn Regehr, D	.68	6	20	26	6	67	5
Chris Simon, L	.72	8	14	22	0	94	2
Shean Donovan, R	.80	9	11	20	9	82	0
Jordan Leopold, D	.74	2	18	20	6	68	2

Acquired: R Huselius from Fla. for D Steve Montador and C Dustin Johner (Dec. 2); L Leclerc and G Boucher from Pho. for C Steve Reinprecht and G Philippe Sauve (Feb. 1); C Lundmark from Pho. for an '06 4th-round pick (Mar. 9).

Goalies (10 Gm)	Gm	Min	GAA	Record	SV%
Miikka Kiprusoff	.74	4380	2.07	42-20-11	.923
Brian Boucher	.14	694	4.15	4-8-0	.871
PHO	.11	512	3.87	3-6-0	.877
CALG	.3	182	4.95	1-2-0	.854
CALGARY	.82	4984	2.32	46-25-11	.915

Shutouts: Kiprusoff (10). **Assists:** Kiprusoff (2). **PM:** Kiprusoff (10), Boucher (2).

Carolina Hurricanes

Top Scorers	Gm	G	A	Pts	+/-	PM	PP
Eric Staal, C	.82	45	55	100	-8	81	19
Justin Williams, R	.82	31	45	76	1	60	8
Cory Stillman, L	.72	21	55	76	-9	32	10
Rod Brind'Amour, C	.78	31	39	70	8	68	19
Mark Recchi, R	.83	28	36	64	-36	68	11
PIT	.63	24	33	57	-28	56	11
CAR	.20	4	3	7	-8	12	2
Erik Cole, L	.60	30	29	59	19	54	3
Doug Weight, C	.70	15	42	57	-17	75	9
ST.L	.47	11	33	44	-11	50	7
CAR	.23	4	9	13	-6	25	2
Ray Whitney, L	.63	17	38	55	0	42	12
Matt Cullen, C	.78	25	24	49	4	40	8
Frantisek Kaberle, D	.77	6	38	44	8	46	1
Bret Hedican, D	.74	5	22	27	11	58	2
Aaron Ward, D	.71	6	19	25	2	62	0
Kevyn Adams, C	.82	15	8	23	0	36	0
Oleg Tverdovsky, D	.72	3	20	23	-1	37	0
Craig Adams, R	.67	10	11	21	1	51	1
Mike Commodore, D	.72	3	10	13	12	138	0
Chad LaRose*, R	.49	1	12	13	7	35	0
Andrew Ladd*, L	.29	6	5	11	0	4	3
Andrew Hutchinson*, D	36	3	8	11	-2	18	2

Acquired: C Weight and L Erkki Rajamaki from St.L for R Jesse Boulerice, C Mike Zigomanis, a minor leaguer and 3 draft picks (Jan. 30); R Recchi from Pit. for L Niklas Nordgren, C Krys Kolanos and an '07 2nd-round pick (Mar. 9).

Goalies (10 Gm)	Gm	Min	GAA	Record	Sv%
Martin Gerber	.60	3493	2.78	38-14-6	.906
Cam Ward*	.28	1484	3.68	14-8-2	.882
CAROLINA	.82	4997	3.10	52-22-8	.897

Shutouts: Gerber (3), Combined — Gerber and Ward (1). **Assists:** Gerber and Ward (2). **PM:** Gerber (4).

Chicago Blackhawks

Top Scorers	Gm	G	A	Pts	+/-	PM	PP
Kyle Calder, L	.79	26	33	59	-4	52	6
Mark Bell, L	.82	25	23	48	-14	107	11
Radim Vrbata, R	.61	15	24	39	4	22	6
CAR	.16	2	3	5	0	6	1
CHI	.45	13	21	34	4	16	5
Rene Bourque*, L	.77	16	18	34	3	56	4
Brent Seabrook*, D	.69	5	27	32	5	60	1
Patrick Sharp, R	.72	14	17	31	5	46	1
PHI	.22	5	3	8	4	10	1
CHI	.50	9	14	23	1	36	0
Martin Lapointe, R	.82	14	17	31	-30	106	6
Matthew Barnaby, R	.82	8	20	28	-11	178	0
Jim Vandermeer, D	.76	6	18	24	-2	116	2
Pavel Vorobiev*, R	.39	9	12	21	-2	34	2
Duncan Keith*, D	.81	9	12	21	-11	79	1
Mikael Holmqvist, C	.72	10	10	20	-14	16	2
Brandon Bochenski*, R	.40	8	9	17	-2	22	2
OTT	.20	6	7	13	7	14	2
CHI	.20	2	2	4	-9	8	0
Mark Cullen, C	.29	7	9	16	7	2	0
Curtis Brown, C	.71	5	10	15	-9	38	0
James Wisniewski*, D	.19	2	5	7	0	36	0
Milan Bartovic*, R	.24	1	6	7	0	8	0
Jassen Cullimore, D	.54	1	6	7	-24	53	1

Acquired: C Sharp and R Eric Meloche from Phi. for R Matt Ellison and an '06 3rd-round pick (Dec. 6); R Vrbata from Car. for future condsid. (Dec. 30); R Bochenski and an '06 2nd-round pick from Ott. for C Tyler Arnason (Mar. 9).

Goalies (10 Gm)	Gm	Min	GAA	Record	SV%
Adam Munro*	.10	501	2.99	3-5-2	.893
Craig Anderson	.29	1553	3.32	6-12-4	.886
Nikolai Khabibulin	.50	2815	3.35	17-26-6	.886
CHICAGO	.82	4997	3.35	26-43-13	.885

Shutouts: Munro and Anderson (1). **Assists:** Munro, Anderson and Khabibulin (1). **PM:** Anderson (14), Khabibulin (10).

Colorado Avalanche

Top Scorers	Gm	G	A	Pts	+/-	PM	PP
Joe Sakic, C	.82	32	55	87	10	60	10
Alex Tanguay, L	.71	29	49	78	8	46	8
Andrew Brunette, L	.82	24	39	63	9	48	11
Milan Hejduk, R	.74	24	34	58	13	24	14
Rob Blake, D	.81	14	37	51	2	94	7
Marek Svatos*, R	.61	32	18	50	0	60	12
Josh-Michael Liles, D	.82	14	35	49	5	44	6
Pierre Turgeon, C	.62	16	30	46	1	32	7
Ian Laperriere, R	.82	21	24	45	3	116	1
Brett McLean, C	.82	9	31	40	-7	51	1
Patrice Brisebois, D	.80	10	28	38	1	55	4
Brett Clark, D	.80	9	27	36	3	56	4
Antti Laaksonen, L	.81	16	18	34	-2	40	0
Jim Dowd, C	.78	5	13	18	-11	40	0
CHI	.60	3	12	15	-5	38	0
COL	.18	2	1	3	-6	2	0
Steve Konowalchuk, L	.21	6	9	15	5	14	1
Karlis Skrastins, D	.82	3	11	14	-7	65	0
Dan Hinote, R	.73	5	8	13	-5	48	0
Brad Richardson*, C	.41	3	10	13	0	12	1
Cody McCormick, C	.45	4	4	8	1	29	0
Bob Boughner, D	.41	1	6	7	2	54	0

Acquired: G Theodore from Mon. for G David Aebischer (Mar. 8); C Dowd from Chi. for an '06 4th-round pick (Mar. 9).

Goalies (10 Gm)	Gm	Min	GAA	Record	SV%
Peter Budaj*	.34	1803	2.86	14-10-6	.900
Jose Theodore	.43	2410	3.41	18-18-6	.882
MON	.38	2114	3.46	17-15-5	.881
COL	.5	296	3.04	1-3-1	.885
COLORADO	.82	4982	3.02	43-30-9	.896

Shutouts: Budaj (2). **Assists:** Budaj, Theodore and Vitaliy Kolesnik (1). **PM:** Budaj (4), Theodore and Kolesnik (2).

Columbus Blue Jackets

Top Scorers	Gm	G	A	Pts	+/-	PM	PP
David Vyborny, R	.80	22	43	65	-9	50	5
Rick Nash, L	.54	31	23	54	5	51	11
Nikolai Zherdev, R	.73	27	27	54	-13	50	10
Sergei Fedorov, C	.67	12	32	44	-2	66	3
ANA	.5	0	1	1	-1	2	0
CLB	.62	12	31	43	-1	64	3
Jan Hrdina, C	.75	10	23	33	-8	78	4
Bryan Berard, D	.44	12	20	32	-29	32	11
Manny Malhotra, C	.58	10	21	31	1	41	1
Jason Chimera, L	.80	17	13	30	-10	95	1
Trevor Letowski, R	.81	10	18	28	-2	36	1
Duvie Westcott, D	.78	6	22	28	1	133	1
Jaroslav Balastik*, L	.66	12	10	22	-1	26	7
Adam Foote, D	.65	6	16	22	-16	89	2
Rostislav Klesla, D	.51	6	13	19	-4	75	2
Ron Hainsey, D	.55	2	15	17	13	43	1
Dan Fritsche*, C	.59	6	7	13	-14	22	0
Mark Hartigan, C	.33	9	3	12	-1	22	3
Jody Shelley, L	.80	3	7	10	-4	163	0
Aaron Johnson, D	.26	2	6	8	-1	23	1
Radoslav Suchy, D	.79	1	7	8	-8	30	0

Acquired: L Chimera, D Cale Hulse and R Michael Rupp from Pho. for L Geoff Sanderson and R Tim Jackman (Oct. 8); C Fedorov and an '06 5th-round pick from Ana. for D Francois Beauchemin and R Tyler Wright (Nov. 15).

Goalies (10 Gm)	Gm	Min	GAA	Record	SV%
Pascal Leclaire*	.33	1804	3.23	11-15-3	.911
Marc Denis	.49	2786	3.25	21-25-1	.900
COLUMBUS	.82	4996	3.31	35-43-4	.900

Shutouts: Denis (1). **Assists:** Leclaire and Denis (1). **PM:** Leclaire and Denis (2).

Dallas Stars

Top Scorers	Gm	G	A	Pts	+/-	PM	PP
Mike Modano, C	.78	27	50	77	23	58	12
Jason Arnott, C	.81	32	44	76	13	102	11
Sergei Zubov, D	.78	13	58	71	20	46	9
Brenden Morrow, L	.81	23	42	65	30	183	8
Jussi Jokinen*, L	.81	17	38	55	2	30	8
Jere Lehtinen, R	.80	33	19	52	9	30	14
Philippe Boucher, D	.66	16	27	43	28	77	8
Bill Guerin, R	.70	13	27	40	0	115	3
Stu Barnes, C	.78	15	21	36	9	44	0
Niko Kapanen, C	.81	14	21	35	-10	36	5
Antti Miettinen*, R	.79	11	20	31	0	46	4
Steve Ott, C	.82	5	17	22	1	178	0
Niklas Hagman, L	.84	8	13	21	-10	18	0
FLA	.30	2	4	6	-8	2	0
DAL	.54	6	9	15	-2	16	0
Stephane Robidas, D	.75	5	15	20	15	67	1
Janne Niinimaa, D	.63	3	13	16	-12	86	1
NYI	.41	1	9	10	-7	62	0
DAL	.22	2	4	6	-5	24	1
Trevor Daley, D	.81	3	11	14	-2	87	0
Jon Klemm, D	.76	4	7	11	-3	60	1
Willie Mitchell, D	.80	2	8	10	19	113	0
MIN	.64	2	6	8	15	87	0
DAL	.16	0	2	2	4	26	0

Acquired: L Hagman from Fla. for an '07 7th-round pick (Dec. 12); D Niinimaa and an '07 5th-round pick from NYI for D John Erskine and an '06 2nd-round pick (Jan. 10); D Mitchell and an '07 2nd-round pick from MIN. for D Martin Skoula and D Shawn Belle (Mar. 9).

Goalies (10 Gm)	Gm	Min	GAA	Record	SV%
Marty Turco	.68	3910	2.55	41-19-5	.898
Johan Hedberg	.19	1079	2.67	12-4-1	.898
DALLAS	.82	5011	2.60	53-23-6	.897

Shutouts: Turco (3). **Assists:** Turco and Hedberg (2). **PM:** Turco (28), Hedberg (6).

Detroit Red Wings

Top Scorers	Gm	G	A	Pts	+/-	PM	PP
Pavel Datsyuk, C	.75	28	59	87	26	22	11
Henrik Zetterberg, L	.77	39	46	85	29	30	17
Brendan Shanahan, L	.82	40	41	81	29	105	14
Nicklas Lidstrom, D	.80	16	64	80	21	50	9
Robert Lang, C	.72	20	42	62	17	72	8
Tomas Holmstrom, L	.81	29	30	59	14	66	11
Mathieu Schneider, D	.72	21	38	59	33	86	11
Jason Williams, C	.80	21	37	58	4	26	6
Mikael Samuelsson, R	.71	23	22	45	27	42	7
Steve Yzerman, C	.61	14	20	34	8	18	4
Kris Draper, C	.80	10	22	32	3	58	0
Jason Woolley, D	.53	1	18	19	3	28	0
Johan Franzen*, D	.80	12	4	16	4	36	0
Mark Mowers, R	.46	4	11	15	13	16	0
Daniel Cleary, R	.77	3	12	15	5	40	0
Andreas Lilja, D	.82	2	13	15	18	98	0
Brett Lebda*, D	.46	3	9	12	9	20	1
Kirk Maltby, L	.82	5	6	11	-9	80	0
Chris Chelios, D	.81	4	7	11	22	108	1
Niklas Kronwall*, D	.27	1	8	9	11	28	1

Goalies (10 Gm)	Gm	Min	GAA	Record	Sv%
Manny Legace	.51	2905	2.19	37-8-3	.915
Chris Osgood	.32	1846	2.76	20-6-5	.897
DETROIT	.82	4972	2.47	58-16-8	.906

Shutouts: Legace (7), Osgood (2). **Assists:** Legace (1). **PM:** Osgood (8).

Edmonton Oilers

Top Scorers	Gm	G	A	Pts	+/-	PM	PP
Ales Hemsky, R	.81	19	58	77	-5	64	7
Shawn Horcoff, C	.79	22	51	73	0	85	3
Jarret Stoll, C	.82	22	46	68	4	74	11
Ryan Smyth, L	.75	36	30	66	-5	58	19
Chris Pronger, D	.80	12	44	56	2	74	10
Sergei Samsonov, L	.74	23	30	53	-3	28	10
BOS	.55	18	19	37	-3	22	6
EDM	.19	5	11	16	0	6	4
Jaroslav Spacek, D	.76	12	31	43	11	96	4
CHI	.45	7	17	24	8	72	1
EDM	.31	5	14	19	3	24	3
Raffi Torres, L	.82	27	14	41	4	50	6
Fernando Pisani, R	.80	18	19	37	5	42	4
Marc-Andre Bergeron, D	75	15	20	35	3	38	8
Radek Dvorak, R	.64	8	20	28	-2	26	2
Steve Staios, D	.82	8	20	28	10	84	1
Ethan Moreau, L	.74	11	16	27	6	87	2
Michael Peca, C	.71	9	14	23	-4	56	2
Jason Smith, D	.76	4	13	17	1	84	0
Dick Tarnstrom, D	.55	6	8	14	-15	76	4
PIT	.33	5	5	10	-10	52	4
EDM	.22	1	3	4	-5	24	0
Georges Laraque, R	.72	2	10	12	-5	73	0
Igor Ulanov, D	.37	3	6	9	-11	29	1
Todd Harvey, L	.63	5	2	7	-7	32	0

Acquired: D Spacek from Chi. for L Tony Salmelainen (Jan. 26); D Tarnstrom from Pit. for R Jani Rita and D Cory Cross (Jan. 26); G Roloson from Min. for an '06 1st-round pick (Mar. 8); L Samsonov from Bos. for C Marty Reasoner, C Yan Stastny and an '06 2nd-round pick (Mar. 9).

Goalies (10 Gm)	Gm	Min	GAA	Record	Sv%
Dwayne Roloson	.43	2524	2.73	14-24-5	.908
MIN	.24	1361	3.00	6-17-1	.910
EDM	.19	1163	2.42	8-7-4	.905
Ty Conklin	.18	922	2.80	8-5-1	.880
Jussi Markkanen	.37	2016	3.13	15-12-6	.880
EDMONTON	.82	4994	2.89	41-28-13	.884

Shutouts: Roloson (2); Conklin (1). **Assists:** Roloson and Markkanen (1). **PM:** Roloson (8), Conklin (2).

Florida Panthers

Top Scorers	Gm	G	A	Pts	+/-	PM	PP
Olli Jokinen, C	.82	38	51	89	14	88	14
Joe Nieuwendyk, C	.65	26	30	56	-2	46	7
Jozef Stumpel, C	.74	15	37	52	11	26	3
Nathan Horton, R	.71	28	19	47	8	89	3
Jay Bouwmeester, D	.82	5	41	46	1	79	0
Martin Gelinas, L	.82	17	24	41	27	80	4
Gary Roberts, L	.58	14	26	40	4	51	4
Chris Gratton, C	.76	17	22	39	6	104	4
Mike Van Ryn, D	.80	8	29	37	15	90	3
Juraj Kolnik, R	.77	15	20	35	1	40	4
Jon Sim, R	.72	17	15	32	-7	54	8
PHI	.39	7	7	14	-6	28	4
FLA	.33	10	8	18	-1	26	4
Ric Jackman, D	.64	7	23	30	-20	52	3
PIT	.49	6	22	28	-20	46	3
FLA	.15	1	1	2	0	6	0
Stephen Weiss, C	.41	9	12	21	-2	22	5
Rostislav Olesz*, C	.59	8	13	21	-4	24	0
Sean Hill, D	.78	2	18	20	3	80	1
Lukas Krajicek*, D	.67	2	14	16	1	50	2
Joel Kwiatkowski, D	.73	4	8	12	3	86	1
Gregory Campbell*, C	.64	3	6	9	-11	40	0
Steve Montador, D	.58	2	5	7	4	79	0
CALG	.7	1	0	1	0	11	0
FLA	.51	1	5	6	4	68	0

Acquired: D Montador and C Dustin Johner from Calg. for R Kristian Huselius (Dec. 2); R Sim from Phi. for an '07 6th-round pick (Jan. 23); D Jackman from Pit. for C Petr Taticek (Mar. 9).

Goalies (10 Gm)	Gm	Min	GAA	Record	Sv%
Roberto Luongo	.75	4305	2.97	35-30-9	.914
Jamie McLennan	.17	678	3.01	2-4-2	.906
FLORIDA	.82	5006	3.02	37-34-11	.912

Shutouts: Luongo (4). **Assists:** Luongo (3). **PM:** Luongo (2).

Los Angeles Kings

Top Scorers	Gm	G	A	Pts	+/-	PM	PP
Lubomir Visnovsky, D	.80	17	50	67	7	50	10
Craig Conroy, C	.78	22	44	66	13	78	5
Pavol Demitra, C	.58	25	37	62	21	42	7
Michael Camalleri, C	.80	26	29	55	-14	50	15
Alexander Frolov, L	.69	21	33	54	17	40	4
Mark Parrish, R	.76	29	20	49	-23	20	16
NYI	.57	24	17	41	-14	16	13
LA	.19	5	3	8	-9	4	3
Derek Armstrong, C	.62	13	28	41	2	46	7
Joseph Corvo, D	.81	14	26	40	16	38	7
Sean Avery, C	.75	15	24	39	-5	257	1
Eric Belanger, C	.65	17	20	37	-5	62	5
Dustin Brown, R	.79	14	14	28	-10	80	6
Brent Sopel, D	.68	2	26	28	-13	70	2
NYI	.57	2	25	27	-9	64	2
LA	.11	0	1	1	-4	6	0
Mattias Norstrom, D	.77	4	23	27	-3	58	2
Luc Robitaille, L	.65	15	9	24	-6	52	3
Jeremy Roenick, C	.58	9	13	22	-5	36	2
Tom Kostopoulos, R	.76	8	14	22	-8	100	0
Tim Gleason, D	.78	2	19	21	0	77	0
Nathan Dempsey, D	.53	2	11	13	0	48	0
Jeff Cowan, L	.46	8	1	9	0	8	73	0
Mike Weaver, D	.53	0	9	9	-3	14	0

Acquired: R Parrish and D Sopel from NYI for D Denis Grebeshkov, L Jeff Tambellini and an '06 3rd-round pick (Mar. 8).

Goalies (10 Gm)	Gm	Min	GAA	Record	Sv%
Jason LaBarbera*	.29	1433	2.89	11-9-2	.900
Mathieu Garon	.63	3446	3.22	31-26-3	.894
LOS ANGELES	.82	4975	3.24	42-35-5	.891

Shutouts: Garon (4), LaBarbera (1). **Assists:** Garon (3), LaBarbera (1). **PM:** Garon (8).

Minnesota Wild

Top Scorers	Gm	G	A	Pts	+/-	PM	PP
Brian Rolston, C	.82	34	45	79	14	50	15
Marian Gaborik, R	.65	38	28	66	6	64	10
Pierre-Marc Bouchard, R	.80	17	42	59	3	28	7
Todd White, C	.61	19	21	40	-1	18	5
Randy Robitaille, C	.67	12	28	40	-5	54	7
Wes Walz, C	.82	19	18	37	7	61	1
Marc Chouinard, C	.74	14	16	30	1	34	6
Kurtis Foster*, D	.58	10	18	28	-3	60	6
Alexandre Daigle, C	.46	5	23	28	-6	12	2
Pascal Dupuis, L	.67	10	16	26	-10	40	4
Filip Kuba, D	.65	6	19	25	0	44	1
Mikko Koivu*, C	.64	6	15	21	-9	40	3
Martin Skoula, D	.78	5	16	21	6	46	3
DAL	.61	4	11	15	6	36	3
MIN	.17	1	5	6	0	10	0
Andrei Zyuzin, D	.57	7	11	18	-12	50	4
Daniel Tjarnqvist, D	.60	3	15	18	-11	32	3
Stephane Veilleux, L	.71	7	9	16	-13	63	0
Brent Burns, D	.72	4	12	16	-7	32	1
Nick Schultz, D	.79	2	12	14	2	43	0
Kyle Wanvig, R	.51	4	8	12	-8	64	1
Mattias Weinhandl, R	.68	4	7	11	-4	24	0
NYI	.53	2	4	6	-4	14	0
MIN	.15	2	3	5	0	10	0
Derek Boogaard*, L	.65	2	4	6	2	158	0

Acquired: D Skoula and D Shawn Belle from Dal. for D Willie Mitchell and an '07 2nd-round pick (Mar. 9). **Claimed:** R Weinhandl off waivers from NYI (Mar. 4).

Goalies (10 Gm)	Gm	Min	GAA	Record	Sv%
Manny Fernandez	.58	3411	2.29	30-18-7	.919
MINNESOTA	.82	4974	2.56	38-36-8	.914

Shutouts: Fernandez and Josh Harding* (1). **Assists:** Fernandez (3). **PM:** Fernandez (6).

Montreal Canadiens

Top Scorers	Gm	G	A	Pts	+/-	PM	PP
Alexei Kovalev, R	.69	23	42	65	-1	76	9
Saku Koivu, C	.72	17	45	62	1	70	5
Michael Ryder, R	.81	30	25	55	-5	40	18
Mike Ribeiro, C	.79	16	35	51	-6	36	8
Andrei Markov, D	.67	10	36	46	13	74	6
Jan Bulis, C	.73	20	20	40	2	50	6
Sheldon Souray, D	.75	12	27	39	-11	116	7
Chris Higgins*, C	.80	23	15	38	-1	26	7
Craig Rivet, D	.82	7	27	34	-5	109	5
Richard Zednik, R	.67	16	14	30	-2	48	6
Tomas Plekanec, C	.67	9	20	29	4	32	1
Steve Begin, C	.76	11	12	23	9	113	1
Francois Bouillon, D	.67	3	19	22	-6	34	3
Radek Bonk, C	.61	6	15	21	-3	52	0
Mathieu Dandenault, D	.82	5	15	20	8	83	0
Alexander Perezhogin*, R	.67	9	10	19	5	38	3
Niklas Sundstrom, R	.55	6	9	15	-6	30	0
Pierre Dagenais, R	.32	5	7	12	-5	16	2
Mark Streit, D	.48	2	9	11	-6	28	2
Aaron Downey, R	.42	3	4	7	2	95	0
ST.L	.17	2	0	2	0	45	0
MON	.25	1	4	5	2	50	0

Acquired: G Aebischer from Col. for G Jose Theodore (Mar. 8). **Claimed:** R Downey off waivers from St.L (Jan. 23).

Goalies (10 Gm)	Gm	Min	GAA	Record	Sv%
Cristobal Huet	.36	2103	2.20	18-11-4	.929
David Aebischer	.50	2895	3.09	29-17-2	.899
COL	.43	2477	2.98	25-14-2	.900
MON	.7	418	3.73	4-3-0	.892
MONTREAL	.82	4978	2.94	42-31-9	.892

Shutouts: Huet (7), Aebischer (3), Yann Danis (1). **Assists:** Aebischer (3). **PM:** Aebischer (16).

Nashville Predators

Top Scorers	Gm	G	A	Pts	+/-	PM	PP
Paul Kariya, L	82	31	54	85	-6	40	14
Steve Sullivan, R	69	31	37	68	2	50	13
Mike Sillinger, C	79	32	31	63	-17	63	14
ST.L	48	22	19	41	-17	49	11
NASH	31	10	12	22	0	14	3
Yanic Perreault, C	69	22	35	57	-3	30	10
Kimmo Timonen, D	79	11	39	50	-3	74	8
Martin Erat, L	80	20	29	49	0	76	5
Marek Zidlicky, D	67	12	37	49	8	82	10
Scott Hartnell, L	81	25	23	48	8	101	10
Dan Hamhuis, D	82	7	31	38	11	70	4
Adam Hall, R	75	14	15	29	0	40	10
David Legwand, C	44	7	19	26	3	34	0
Scottie Upshall, R	48	8	16	24	14	34	1
Greg Johnson, C	68	11	8	19	5	10	0
Scott Walker, R	33	5	11	16	2	36	1
Ryan Suter*, D	71	1	15	16	7	66	0
Jerred Smithson, C	66	5	9	14	9	54	0
Brendan Witt, D	75	1	13	14	0	209	0
WASH	58	1	10	11	-5	141	0
NASH	17	0	3	3	5	68	0
Darcy Hordichuk, L	74	7	6	13	9	163	0
Vernon Fiddler, C	40	8	4	12	-2	42	3
Danny Markov, D	58	0	11	11	9	62	0
Jordin Tootoo, R	34	4	6	10	9	55	0
Shea Weber, D	28	2	8	10	8	42	2

Acquired: C Sillinger from St.L for R Timofei Shishkanov (Jan. 29); D Witt from Wash. for C Kris Beech and an '06 1st-round pick (Mar. 9).

Goalies (10 Gm)	Gm	Min	GAA	Record	Sv%
Chris Mason	23	1227	2.54	12-5-1	.913
Tomas Vokoun	61	3601	2.67	36-18-7	.919
NASHVILLE	82	4980	2.70	49-25-8	.916

Shutouts: Vokoun (4), Mason (2). **Assists:** Vokoun (2). **PM:** Vokoun.

New Jersey Devils

Top Scorers	Gm	G	A	Pts	+/-	PM	PP
Brian Gionta, R	82	48	41	89	18	46	24
Scott Gomez, C	82	33	51	84	8	42	9
Jamie Langenbrunner, R	80	19	34	53	-1	74	8
Brian Rafalski, D	82	6	43	49	0	36	3
Patrik Elias, C	38	16	29	45	11	20	6
Sergei Brylin, L	82	15	22	37	-4	46	4
Paul Martin, D	80	5	32	37	1	32	3
John Madden, C	82	16	20	36	-7	36	0
Zach Parise*, C	81	14	18	32	-1	28	2
Alexander Mogilny, R	34	12	13	25	-7	6	7
Viktor Kozlov, R	69	12	13	25	0	16	2
Grant Marshall, R	76	8	17	25	-18	70	4
Brad Lukowich, D	75	2	19	21	0	40	0
NYI	57	1	12	13	-3	32	0
NJ	18	1	7	8	3	8	0
Jay Pandolfo, L	82	10	10	20	2	16	0
Colin White, D	73	3	14	17	-2	91	1
Ken Klee, D	74	3	12	15	-4	80	1
TOR	56	3	12	15	-1	66	1
NJ	18	0	0	0	-3	14	0
Richard Matvichuk, D	62	1	10	11	2	40	0
Erik Rasmussen, C	67	5	5	10	-4	32	1
Vladimir Malakhov, D	29	4	5	9	-9	26	3
Dan McGillis, D	27	0	6	6	-5	36	0
Tommy Albelin, D	36	0	6	6	4	2	0

Acquired: D Klee from Tor. for R Aleksander Suglobov (Mar. 8); D Lukowich from NYI for an '06 3rd-round pick (Mar. 9).

Goalies (10 Gm)	Gm	Min	GAA	Record	Sv%
Martin Brodeur	73	4365	2.57	43-23-7	.911
Scott Clemmensen	13	627	3.35	3-4-2	.881
NEW JERSEY	82	5007	2.70	46-27-9	.906

Shutouts: Brodeur (5). **Assists:** Brodeur (3). **PM:** Brodeur (4).

New York Islanders

Top Scorers	Gm	G	A	Pts	+/-	PM	PP
Miroslav Satan, R	82	35	31	66	-8	54	17
Alexei Yashin, C	82	28	38	66	-14	68	10
Jason Blake, L	76	28	29	57	0	60	12
Mike York, C	75	13	39	52	-9	30	4
Trent Hunter, R	82	16	19	35	-9	34	5
Shawn Bates, C	66	15	19	34	-11	60	1
Chris Campoli*, D	80	9	25	34	-16	46	2
Alexei Zhitnik, D	59	5	24	29	4	88	3
Arron Asham, R	63	9	15	24	-5	103	2
Robert Nilsson*, R	53	6	14	20	-6	26	1
Radek Martinek, D	74	1	16	17	-9	32	0
Sean Bergenheim*, L	28	4	5	9	-11	20	0
Joel Bouchard, D	25	1	9	10	5	23	0
Jeffrey Hamilton, C	13	2	6	8	0	8	1
Wyatt Smith, C	42	0	8	8	-7	26	0
Bruno Gervais*, D	27	3	4	7	-1	8	1
Denis Grebeshkov*, D	29	0	5	5	-12	20	0
LA	8	0	2	2	-4	12	0
NYI	21	0	3	3	-8	8	0
Eric Godard, R	57	2	4	6	-2	115	0
Jeff Tambellini*, L	25	1	3	4	1	10	0
LA	4	0	0	0	-1	2	0
NYI	21	1	3	4	2	8	0

Acquired: D Grebeshkov, L Tambellini and an '06 3rd-round pick from LA for R Mark Parrish and D Brent Sopel (Mar. 8).

Goalies (10 Gm)	Gm	Min	GAA	Record	Sv%
Rick DiPietro	63	3572	3.02	30-24-8	.900
Garth Snow	20	1096	3.72	4-13-1	.886
NY ISLANDERS	82	5001	3.30	36-40-6	.892

Shutouts: DiPietro (1). **Assists:** DiPietro (1). **PM:** DiPietro (28), Snow (2).

New York Rangers

Top Scorers	Gm	G	A	Pts	+/-	PM	PP
Jaromir Jagr, R	82	54	69	123	34	72	24
Michael Nylander, C	81	23	56	79	31	76	6
Martin Straka, L	82	22	54	76	17	42	4
Martin Rucinsky, L	52	16	39	55	10	56	4
Petr Sykora, R	74	23	28	51	6	50	8
ANA	34	7	13	20	1	28	1
NYR	40	16	15	31	5	22	7
Petr Prucha*, R	68	30	17	47	3	32	16
Steve Rucchin, C	72	13	23	36	6	10	4
Michal Rozsival, D	82	5	25	30	35	90	3
Jason Ward, R	81	10	18	28	-4	44	0
Fedor Tyutin*, D	77	6	19	25	1	58	4
Tom Poti, D	73	3	20	23	16	70	2
Sandis Ozolinsh, D	36	6	14	20	-2	28	2
ANA	17	3	3	6	-4	8	0
NYR	19	3	11	14	2	20	2
Dominic Moore*, C	82	9	9	18	4	28	2
Marek Malik, D	74	2	16	18	28	78	0
Marcel Hossa, L	64	10	6	16	-6	28	3
Blair Betts, C	66	8	2	10	-10	24	0
Jed Ortmeyer, R	78	5	2	7	2	38	0
Jason Strudwick, D	65	3	4	7	-10	66	0
Darius Kasparaitis, D	67	0	6	6	7	97	0
Ryan Hollweg*, L	52	2	3	5	-3	84	0

Acquired: R Sykora and an '07 4th-round pick from Ana. for D Maxim Kondratiev (Jan. 8); D Ozolinsh from Ana. for an '06 3rd-round pick (Mar. 9).

Goalies (10 Gm)	Gm	Min	GAA	Record	Sv%
Henrik Lundqvist*	53	3112	2.24	30-12-9	.922
Kevin Weekes	32	1850	2.95	14-14-3	.895
NY RANGERS	82	4997	2.53	44-26-12	.911

Shutouts: Lundqvist (2). **Assists:** Lundqvist (2), Weekes (1). **PM:** Weekes (4).

Ottawa Senators

Top Scorers	Gm	G	A	Pts	+/-	PM	PP
Dany Heatley, L	.82	50	53	103	29	86	23
Daniel Alfredsson, R	.77	43	60	103	29	50	16
Jason Spezza, C	.68	19	71	90	23	33	7
Peter Schaefer, L	.82	20	30	50	16	40	4
Wade Redden, D	.65	10	40	50	35	63	8
Bryan Smolinski, C	.81	17	31	48	8	46	4
Tyler Arnason, C	.79	13	32	45	1	44	5
CHI	.60	13	28	41	5	40	5
OTT	.19	0	4	4	-4	4	0
Mike Fisher, C	.68	22	22	44	23	64	2
Zdeno Chara, D	.71	16	27	43	17	135	10
Andrej Meszaros*, D	.82	10	29	39	34	61	5
Brian Pothier, D	.77	5	30	35	29	59	3
Antoine Vermette, C	.82	21	12	33	17	44	1
Chris Neil, R	.79	16	17	33	9	204	8
Chris Kelly*, C	.82	10	20	30	21	76	1
Patrick Eaves*, R	.58	20	9	29	7	22	5
Vaclav Varada, L	.76	5	16	21	2	50	1
Chris Phillips, D	.69	1	18	19	19	90	0
Anton Volchenkov, D	.75	4	13	17	21	53	0
Martin Havlat, C	.18	9	7	16	6	4	2
Christoph Schubert*, D	56	4	6	10	4	48	0
Brian McGrattan*, R	.60	2	3	5	0	141	0

Acquired: C Arnason from Chi. for R Brandon Bochenski and an '06 2nd-round pick (Mar. 9). **Claimed:** G Morrison off waivers from Edm. (Mar. 9).

Goalies (10 Gm)	Gm	Min	GAA	Record	Sv%
Dominik Hasek	.43	2584	2.09	28-10-4	.925
Ray Emery*	.39	2168	2.82	23-11-4	.902
Michael Morrison	.25	1099	2.95	11-4-3	.882
EDM	.21	892	2.83	10-4-2	.884
OTT	.4	207	3.48	1-0-1	.875
OTTAWA	.82	4975	2.47	52-21-9	.913

Shutouts: Hasek (5), Emery (3). **Assists:** Emery and Morrison (1). **PM:** Hasek (16), Emery and Morrison (2).

Philadelphia Flyers

Top Scorers	Gm	G	A	Pts	+/-	PM	PP
Simon Gagne, L	.72	47	32	79	31	38	12
Peter Forsberg, C	.60	19	56	75	21	46	8
Mike Knuble, R	.82	34	31	65	25	80	13
Joni Pitkanen, D	.58	13	33	46	22	78	5
Michal Handzus, C	.73	11	33	44	-2	38	2
Jeff Carter*, C	.81	23	19	42	10	40	6
R.J. Umberger*, C	.73	20	18	38	9	18	5
Sami Kapanen, R	.58	12	22	34	-9	12	3
Mike Richards*, C	.79	11	23	34	6	65	1
Frederick Meyer*, D	.57	6	21	27	10	33	2
Niko Dimitrakos, R	.64	9	16	25	4	32	1
SJ	.45	4	12	16	0	26	0
PHI	.19	5	4	9	4	6	1
Petr Nedved, C	.53	7	18	25	-14	70	3
PHO	.25	2	9	11	-6	34	1
PHI	.28	5	9	14	-8	36	2
Kim Johnsson, D	.47	6	19	25	5	34	3
Eric Desjardins, D	.45	4	20	24	3	56	3
Mike Rathje, D	.79	3	21	24	22	46	1
Derian Hatcher, D	.77	4	13	17	2	93	1
Brian Savage, L	.66	9	5	14	-18	28	4
Branko Radivojevic, R	.64	8	6	14	-6	44	1

Acquired: C Nedved from Pho. for D Dennis Seidenberg (Jan. 20); R Dimitrakos from SJ for an '06 3rd-round pick (Mar. 9).

Goalies (10 Gm)	Gm	Min	GAA	Record	Sv%
Robert Esche	.40	2286	2.97	22-11-5	.897
Antero Niittymaki*	.46	2690	2.97	23-15-6	.895
PHILADELPHIA	.82	4995	3.04	45-26-11	.893

Shutouts: Niittymaki (2), Esche (1). **Assists:** Esche (3), Niittymaki (1). **PM:** Esche (4).

Phoenix Coyotes

Top Scorers	Gm	G	A	Pts	+/-	PM	PP
Shane Doan, R	.82	30	36	66	-9	123	17
Mike Comrie, C	.80	30	30	60	2	55	10
Ladislav Nagy, L	.51	15	41	56	8	74	7
Mike Johnson, R	.80	16	38	54	7	50	6
Steve Reinprecht, C	.80	22	30	52	11	32	9
CALG	.52	10	19	29	10	24	5
PHO	.28	12	11	23	1	8	4
Paul Mara, D	.78	15	32	47	-12	70	8
Geoff Sanderson, L	.77	25	21	46	-15	58	11
CLB	.2	0	0	0	-1	0	0
PHO	.75	25	21	46	-14	58	11
Keith Ballard*, D	.82	8	31	39	-18	99	1
Dave Scatchard, C	.63	15	18	33	-13	112	5
BOS	.16	4	6	10	-2	28	1
PHO	.47	11	12	23	-11	84	4
Oleg Kvasha, L	.64	13	19	32	3	38	1
NYI	.49	9	12	21	-2	32	1
PHO	.15	4	7	11	5	6	0
Derek Morris, D	.53	6	21	27	-7	54	4
Oleg Saprykin, L	.67	11	14	25	-16	50	3
Zbynek Michalek*, D	.82	9	15	24	4	62	5
Fredrik Sjostrom, R	.75	6	17	23	1	42	1

Acquired: L Sanderson and R Tim Jackman from Clb. for L Jason Chimera, D Cale Hulse and R Michael Rupp (Oct. 8); C Scatchard from Bos. for D David Tanabe (Nov. 18); C Reinprecht and G Philippe Sauve from Calg. for L Mike Leclerc and G Brian Boucher (Feb. 1); L Kvasha and an '06 5th-round pick from NYI for an '06 3rd-round pick (Mar. 9).

Goalies (15 Gm)	Gm	Min	GAA	Record	Sv%
Curtis Joseph	.60	3424	2.91	32-21-3	.902
David Leneveu*	.15	814	3.24	3-8-2	.886
PHOENIX	.82	4976	3.23	38-39-5	.892

Shutouts: Joseph (4). **Assists:** Joseph (1). **PM:** Philippe Sauve (21), Joseph (18).

Pittsburgh Penguins

Top Scorers	Gm	G	A	Pts	+/-	PM	PP
Sidney Crosby*, C	.81	39	63	102	-1	110	16
Sergei Gonchar, D	.75	12	46	58	-13	100	8
John LeClair, L	.73	22	29	51	-24	61	8
Ryan Malone, L	.77	22	22	44	-22	63	10
Zigmund Palffy, R	.42	11	31	42	5	12	2
Colby Armstrong*, R	.47	16	24	40	15	58	7
Ryan Whitney*, D	.68	6	32	38	-7	85	2
Michel Ouellet*, R	.50	16	16	32	-13	16	11
Andy Hilbert, C	.47	12	15	27	4	38	3
CHI	.28	5	4	9	-4	22	0
PIT	.19	7	11	18	8	16	3
Tomas Surovy, L	.53	12	13	25	-13	45	3
Mario Lemieux, C	.26	7	15	22	-16	16	3
Eric Boguniecki, R	.47	6	10	16	-3	33	2
ST.L	.9	1	4	5	-1	4	1
PIT	.38	5	6	11	-2	29	1
Josef Melichar, D	.72	3	12	15	-2	66	0
Erik Christensen*, C	.33	6	7	13	-3	34	2
Jani Rita*, R	.51	4	10	14	-6	10	0
EDM	.21	3	0	3	0	6	0
PIT	.30	3	4	7	-6	4	0
Konstantin Koltsov, R	.60	3	6	9	-10	20	0
Brooks Orpik, D	.64	3	6	9	-3	124	0

Acquired: R Boguniecki from St.L for D Steve Poapst (Dec. 9); R Rita and D Cory Cross from Edm. for D Dick Tarnstrom (Jan. 26). **Claimed:** C Hilbert off waivers from Chi. (Mar. 9).

Goalies (10 Gm)	Gm	Min	GAA	Record	Sv%
Marc-Andre Fleury	.50	2809	3.25	13-27-6	.898
Sebastien Caron	.26	1312	3.98	8-9-5	.881
Jocelyn Thibault	.16	807	4.46	1-9-3	.876
PITTSBURGH	.82	4985	3.73	22-46-14	.886

Shutouts: Fleury and Caron (1). **Assists:** Fleury and Caron (1). **PM:** Thibault (2).

St. Louis Blues

Top Scorers	Gm	G	A	Pts	+/-	PM	PP
Scott Young, R	.79	18	31	49	-32	52	10
Petr Cajanek, C	.71	10	31	41	-22	54	3
Dean McAmmond, C	.78	15	22	37	-25	32	4
Keith Tkachuk, L	.41	15	21	36	-15	46	10
Lee Stempniak*, R	.57	14	13	27	-10	22	5
Jay McClement*, C	.67	6	21	27	-23	30	1
Jamal Mayers, R	.67	15	11	26	-22	129	0
Dallas Drake, R	.62	2	24	26	-13	59	1
Dennis Wideman*, D	.67	8	16	24	-31	83	5
Christian Backman, D	.52	6	12	18	-15	48	3
Kevin Dallman*, D	.67	4	10	14	-14	29	3
BOS	.21	0	1	1	1	8	0
ST.L	.46	4	9	13	-15	21	3
Mike Glumac*, R	.33	7	5	12	-8	33	5
Mark Rycroft, R	.80	6	4	10	-14	46	0
Barret Jackman, D	.63	4	6	10	-6	156	0
Eric Brewer, D	.32	6	3	9	-17	45	1
Vladimir Orszagh, R	.16	4	5	9	-2	14	1
Ryan Johnson, C	.65	3	6	9	-21	33	1
Jeff Hoggan, R	.52	2	6	8	-16	34	0
Simon Gamache*, L	.26	3	4	7	-5	10	0
NASH	.11	0	0	0	-6	0	0
ST.L	.15	3	4	7	1	10	0
Trent Whitfield, C	.30	2	5	7	-3	14	1

Claimed: L Gamache off waivers from Nash. (Nov. 29); D Dallman off waivers from Bos. (Dec. 3). **Waived:** L Gamache (Jan. 28).

Goalies (15 Gm)	Gm	Min	GAA	Record	SV%
Curtis Sanford*	.34	1830	2.66	13-13-5	.908
Jason Bacashihua*	.19	966	3.23	4-10-1	.899
Patrick Lalime	.31	1699	3.64	4-18-8	.881
ST. LOUIS	.82	5001	3.41	24-46-15	.887

Shutouts: Sanford (3). **Assists:** Bacashihua (1). **PM:** none.

San Jose Sharks

Top Scorers	Gm	G	A	Pts	+/-	PM	PP
Joe Thornton, C	.81	29	96	125	31	61	11
BOS	.23	9	24	33	0	6	3
SJ	.58	20	72	92	31	55	8
Jonathan Cheechoo, R	82	56	37	93	23	58	24
Patrick Marleau, C	.82	34	52	86	-12	26	20
Nils Ekman, L	.77	21	36	57	20	54	5
Tom Preissing, D	.74	11	32	43	17	26	2
Milan Michalek*, R	.81	17	18	35	1	45	4
Steve Bernier*, R	.39	14	13	27	4	35	2
Alyn McCauley, C	.76	12	14	26	-3	30	4
Mark Smith, C	.80	9	15	24	3	97	2
Ville Nieminen, L	.70	8	16	24	7	63	0
NYR	.48	5	12	17	10	53	0
SJ	.22	3	4	7	-3	10	0
Scott Hannan, D	.81	6	18	24	7	58	2
Christian Ehrhoff, D	.64	5	18	23	10	32	2
Kyle McLaren, D	.77	2	21	23	6	66	0
Grant Stevenson*, C	.47	10	12	22	-7	14	5
Marcel Goc*, C	.81	8	14	22	-7	22	2
Scott Thornton, L	.71	10	11	21	-8	84	1
Matthew Carle*, D	.12	3	3	6	-2	14	2
Patrick Rissmiller, C	.18	3	3	6	1	8	1
Rob Davison, D	.69	1	5	6	6	76	0
Josh Gorges, D	.49	0	6	6	5	31	0

Acquired: C Thornton from Bos. for L Marco Sturm, D Brad Stuart and C Wayne Primeau (Nov. 30); L Nieminen from NYR for an '06 3rd-round pick (Mar. 8).

Goalies (10 Gm)	Gm	Min	GAA	Record	Sv%
Vesa Toskala	.37	2039	2.56	23-7-4	.901
Evgeni Nabokov	.45	2575	3.10	16-19-7	.885
SAN JOSE	.82	4996	2.82	44-27-11	.892

Shutouts: Toskala (2), Nabokov and Nolan Schaefer (1). Nabokov and Schaefer also shared a shutout. **Assists:** Toskala and Nabokov (1). **PM:** Nabokov (18), Toskala (4), Schaefer (2).

Tampa Bay Lightning

Top Scorers	Gm	G	A	Pts	+/-	PM	PP
Brad Richards, C	.82	23	68	91	0	32	7
Vaclav Prospal, C	.81	25	55	80	-3	50	10
Vincent LeCavalier, C	.80	35	40	75	0	90	13
Martin St. Louis, R	.80	31	30	61	-3.	38	9
Fredrik Modin, L	.77	31	23	54	5	56	12
Dan Boyle, D	.79	15	38	53	-8	38	6
Ruslan Fedotenko, R	.80	26	15	41	-4	44	4
Pavel Kubina, D	.76	5	33	38	-12	96	4
Ryan Craig*, C	.48	15	13	28	-4	6	6
Darryl Sydor, D	.80	4	19	23	-18	30	1
Dave Andreychuk, L	.42	6	12	18	-13	16	4
Paul Ranger*, D	.76	1	17	18	5	58	0
Rob DiMaio, R	.61	4	13	17	-7	30	2
Evgeny Artyukhin*, R	.72	4	13	17	-4	90	1
Dimitry Afanasenkov, L	.68	9	6	15	-7	16	1
Cory Sarich, D	.82	1	14	15	-2	79	0
Tim Taylor, C	.82	7	6	13	-12	22	0
Nolan Pratt, D	.82	0	9	9	7	60	0
Martin Cibak, C	.65	2	6	8	-9	22	0
Norman Milley*, R	.14	2	1	3	-2	4	1

Five tied with 1 point each.

Goalies (10 Gm)	Gm	Min	GAA	Record	SV%
Sean Burke	.35	1713	2.80	14-10-4	.895
John Grahame	.57	3152	3.06	29-22-1	.889
TAMPA BAY	.82	4997	3.07	43-33-6	.887

Shutouts: Grahame (5), Burke (2). **Assists:** Burke and Grahame (1). **PM:** Grahame (14), Burke (10).

Toronto Maple Leafs

Top Scorers	Gm	G	A	Pts	+/-	PM	PP
Mats Sundin, C	.70	31	47	78	7	58	16
Bryan McCabe, D	.73	19	49	68	-1	116	19
Tomas Kaberle, D	.82	9	58	67	-1	46	6
Darcy Tucker, R	.74	28	33	61	-12	100	18
Jason Allison, C	.66	17	43	60	-18	76	9
Alex Steen*, C	.75	18	27	45	-9	42	9
Kyle Wellwood*, C	.81	11	34	45	0	14	3
Alexei Ponikarovsky, L	.81	21	17	38	15	68	2
Jeff O'Neill, C	.74	19	19	38	-19	64	14
Nik Antropov, C	.57	12	19	31	13	56	2
Chad Kilger, L	.79	17	11	28	-6	63	1
Matt Stajan, C	.80	15	12	27	5	50	3
Eric Lindros, C	.33	11	11	22	-3	43	4
Tie Domi, R	.77	5	11	16	-10	109	1
Alexander Khavanov, D	64	6	6	12	-11	60	2
Luke Richardson, D	.65	1	10	11	-19	71	0
CLB	.44	1	6	7	-18	30	0
TOR	.21	0	3	3	-1	41	0
Clarke Wilm, C	.60	1	7	8	-15	43	0
Aki Berg, D	.75	0	8	8	-5	56	0
Carlo Colaiacovo*, D	.21	2	5	7	0	17	1
Ian White*, D	.12	1	5	6	2	10	0
John Pohl, C	.7	3	1	4	2	4	1
Wade Belak, D	.55	0	3	3	-13	109	0

Six tied with 1 point each.

Acquired: D Richardson from Clb. for a conditional draft pick (Mar. 8).

Goalies (10 Gm)	Gm	Min	GAA	Record	Sv%
Jean-Sebastien Aubin	.11	677	2.22	9-0-2	.924
Mikael Tellqvist*	.25	1399	3.13	10-11-2	.895
Ed Belfour	.49	2897	3.29	22-22-4	.892
TORONTO	.82	4994	3.16	41-33-8	.895

Shutouts: Tellqvist (2), Aubin (1). **Assists:** Belfour (1). **PM:** Belfour (12).

Vancouver Canucks

Top Scorers

Top Scorers	Gm	G	A	Pts	+/-	PM	PP
Markus Naslund, L	.81	32	47	79	-19	66	13
Henrik Sedin, C	.82	18	57	75	11	56	5
Todd Bertuzzi, R	.82	25	46	71	-17	120	12
Daniel Sedin, L	.82	22	49	71	7	34	11
Brendan Morrison, C	.82	19	37	56	-1	84	8
Anson Carter, R	.81	33	22	55	-1	41	15
Nolan Baumgartner, D	.70	5	29	34	11	30	4
Mattias Ohlund, D	.78	13	20	33	-6	92	8
Sami Salo, D	.59	10	23	33	9	38	9
Ed Jovanovski, D	.44	8	25	33	-8	58	6
Ryan Kesler, C	.82	10	13	23	1	79	1
Keith Carney, D	.79	2	18	20	8	62	1
ANA	.61	2	16	18	13	48	1
VAN	.18	0	2	2	-5	14	0
Matt Cooke, C	.45	8	10	18	-8	71	0
Richard Park, R	.60	8	10	18	-2	29	0
Jarkko Ruutu, L	.82	10	7	17	1	142	2
Bryan Allen, D	.77	7	10	17	4	115	1
Eric Weinrich, D	.75	1	16	17	-23	52	1
ST.L	.59	1	16	17	-10	44	1
VAN	.16	0	0	0	-13	8	0

Acquired: D Carney and D Juha Alen from Ana. for D Brett Skinner and an '06 2nd-round pick (Mar. 9); D Weinrich from St.L for D Tomas Mojzis and an '06 3rd-round pick (Mar. 9).

Goalies (10 Gm)

Goalies (10 Gm)	Gm	Min	GAA	Record	SV%
Alexander Auld	.67	3859	2.94	33-26-6	.902
Dan Cloutier	.13	681	3.17	8-3-1	.892
VANCOUVER	.82	4978	3.03	42-32-8	.898

Shutouts: none. **Assists:** Auld (2). **PM:** Auld and Cloutier (4), Maxime Ouellet* and Mika Noronen (2).

Washington Capitals

Top Scorers

Top Scorers	Gm	G	A	Pts	+/-	PM	PP
Alexander Ovechkin*, L	.81	52	54	106	2	52	21
Dainius Zubrus, R	.71	23	34	57	3	84	13
Jeff Halpern, C	.70	11	33	44	-8	79	6
Brian Willsie, R	.82	19	22	41	-19	77	8
Chris Clark, R	.78	20	19	39	9	110	1
Matt Pettinger, L	.71	20	18	38	-2	39	4
Ben Clymer, L	.77	16	17	33	-7	72	3
Brian Sutherby, C	.76	14	16	30	-17	73	0
Jamie Heward, D	.71	7	21	28	-5	54	4
Bryan Muir, D	.72	8	18	26	-9	72	4
Brooks Laich*, C	.73	7	14	21	-9	26	1
Matt Bradley, R	.74	7	12	19	-8	72	0
Steve Eminger, D	.66	5	13	18	-12	81	1
Shaone Morrisonn, D	.80	1	13	14	7	91	0
Mathieu Biron, D	.52	4	9	13	-11	50	3
Andrew Cassels, C	.31	4	8	12	-3	14	2
Ivan Majesky, D	.57	1	8	9	-2	66	0
Rico Fata, C	.47	3	4	7	-4	22	1
Nolan Yonkman*, D	.38	0	7	7	1	86	0
Petr Sykora, C	.10	2	2	4	0	6	0
Jakup Klepis*, C	.25	1	3	4	-11	8	0

Goalies (10 Gm)

Goalies (10 Gm)	Gm	Min	GAA	Record	Sv%
Brent Johnson	.26	1413	3.44	9-12-1	.905
Olaf Kolzig	.59	3506	3.53	20-28-11	.896
WASHINGTON	.82	5006	3.60	29-41-12	.896

Shutouts: Johnson (1). **Assists:** Kolzig (3). **PM:** Johnson and Kolzig (14).

2006 NHL Entry Draft

Top 50 selections at the 44th annual NHL Entry Draft held June 24, 2006, at General Motors Place in Vancouver. First 30 picks are first-round selections, 31-50 are second round. The order of the first 14 positions were determined by a draft lottery of non-playoff teams held April 20 in New York City. Only the worst five teams from the 2005-06 regular season had the chance to win the first overall pick. No team could move up more than four spots in the draft order or drop more than one position. Positions 15 through 30 reflect regular season records in reverse order.

Top 50 Selections

	Team	Player, Last Team	Pos
1	St. Louis	Erik Johnson, US National U-18	D
2	Pittsburgh	Jordan Staal, Peterborough (OHL)	C
3	Chicago	Jonathan Toews, Nort Dakota (WCHA)	C
4	Washington	Nicklas Backstrom, Brynas (Swe)	C
5	Boston	Phil Kessel, Minnesota (WCHA)	C
6	Columbus	Derick Brassard, Drummondville (QMJHL)	C
7	NY Islanders	Kyle Okposo, Des Moines (USHL)	R
8	Phoenix	Peter Mueller, Everett (WHL)	C
9	Minnesota	James Sheppard, Cape Breton (QMJHL)	C
10	Florida	Michael Frolik, Kladno (Cze)	C
11	Los Angeles	Jonathan Bernier, Lewiston (QMJHL)	G
12	Atlanta	Bryan Little, Barrie (OHL)	C
13	Toronto	Jiri Tlusty, Kladno (CZE)	C
14	Vancouver	Michael Grabner, Spokane (WHL)	R
15	Tampa Bay	Riku Helenius, Ilves (Fin)	G
16	a-San Jose	Ty Wishart, Prince George (WHL)	D
17	b-Los Angeles	Trevor Lewis, Des Moines (USHL)	C
18	Colorado	Chris Stewart, Kingston (OHL)	R
19	Anaheim	Mark Mitera, Michigan (CCHA)	D
20	c-Montreal	David Fischer, Apple Valley, MN (HS)	D
21	NY Rangers	Bobby Sanguinetti, Owen Sound (OHL)	D
22	Philadelphia	Claude Giroux, Gatineau (QMJHL)	R
23	d-Washington	Semen Varlamov, Yaroslavl 2 (RUS)	G
24	Buffalo	Dennis Persson, Vasteras (Swe)	D
25	e-St. Louis	Patrik Berglund, Vasteras (Swe)	C
26	Calgary	Leland Irving, Everett (WHL)	G
27	Dallas	Ivan Vishnevskiy, Rouyn Noranda (QMJHL)	D
28	Ottawa	Nick Foligno, Sudbury (OHL)	L
29	f-Phoenix	Chris Summers, US National U-18	D
30	g-New Jersey	Matthew Corrente, Saginaw (OHL)	D
31	St. Louis	Tomas Kana, Vitkovice (Cze)	C
32	Pittsburgh	Carl Sneep, Brainerd, MN (HS)	D
33	Chicago	Igor Makarov, Krylja (Rus)	R
34	Washington	Michal Neuvirth, Sparta Jr. (Cze)	G
35	h-Washington	Francois Bouchard, Baie Comeau (QMJHL)	R
36	i-San Jose	Jamie McGinn, Ottawa (IHL)	L
37	Boston	Yuri Alexandrov, Cherepovec (Rus)	D
38	j-Anaheim	Bryce Swan, Halifax (QMJHL)	R
39	k-Philadelphia	Andreas Nodl, Sioux Falls (USHL)	R
40	Minnesota	Ondrej Fiala, Everett (WHL)	C
41	l-Detroit	Cory Emmerton, Kingston (OHL)	C
42	m-Philadelphia	Michael Ratchuk, US Nat'l U-18	D
43	Atlanta	Riley Holzapfel, Moose Jaw (WHL)	C
44	Toronto	Nikolai Kulemin, Magnitogorsk (Rus)	L
45	Edmonton	Jeff Petry, Des Moines (USHL)	D
46	n-Buffalo	Jhonas Enroth, Sodertalje (Swe)	G
47	o-Detroit	Shawn Matthias, Belleville (OHL)	C
48	Los Angeles	Joe Ryan, Quebec (QMJHL)	D
49	Montreal	Ben Maxwell, Kootenay (WHL)	C
50	p-Boston	Milan Lucic, Vancouver (WHL)	L

Acquired picks: a–from Mon; **b**–from Edm; **c**–from SJ; **d**–from Nash; **e**–from NJ; **f**–from Det; **g**–from Car; **h**–from Bos; **i**–from Clb; **j**–from NYI; **k**–from Pho; **l**–from Fla; **m**–from LA; **n**–from Van; **o**–from TB; **p**–from Edm.

Stanley Cup Playoffs

QUARTERFINALS	SEMIFINALS	FINALS		FINALS	SEMIFINALS	QUARTERFINALS

(1) Detroit 2
(8) Edmonton 4 — Edmonton 4
Edmonton 4
(4) Nashville 1
(5) San Jose 4 — San Jose 2
WESTERN CONFERENCE — Carolina 4 / Edmonton 3
(2) Dallas 1
(7) Colorado 4 — Colorado 0
Anaheim 1
(3) Calgary 3
(6) Anaheim 4 — Anaheim 4

EASTERN CONFERENCE

Ottawa 1 — Buffalo 3
(1) Ottawa 4
(8) Tampa Bay 1
Buffalo 4
(4) Buffalo 4
(5) Philadelphia 2
Carolina 4 — Carolina 4
(2) Carolina 4
(7) Montreal 1
New Jersey 1
(3) New Jersey 4
(6) NY Rangers 0

Stanley Cup Playoffs
Series Summaries
WESTERN CONFERENCE

FIRST ROUND (Best of 7)

	W-L	GF	Leading Scorers
Edmonton	4-2	19	Pronger (2-5–7)
			& Horcoff (1-6–7)
Detroit	2-4	17	Schneider (1-7–8)

Date	Winner	Home Ice
April 21	Red Wings, 3-2 (2OT)	at Detroit
April 23	Oilers, 4-2	at Detroit
April 25	Oilers, 4-3 (2OT)	at Edmonton
April 27	Red Wings, 4-2	at Edmonton
April 29	Oilers, 3-2	at Detroit
May 1	Oilers, 4-3	at Edmonton

	W-L	GF	Leading Scorers
Colorado	4-1	18	Three tied with 7 pts.
Dallas	1-4	15	Morrow (1-5–6)
			& Zubov (1-5–6)

Date	Winner	Home Ice
April 22	Avalanche, 5-2	at Dallas
April 24	Avalanche, 5-4 (OT)	at Dallas
April 26	Avalanche, 4-3 (OT)	at Colorado
April 28	Stars, 4-1	at Colorado
April 30	Avalanche, 3-2 (OT)	at Dallas

	W-L	GF	Leading Scorers
Anaheim	4-3	17	Selanne (3-3–6)
Calgary	3-4	16	Iginla (5-3–8)

Date	Winner	Home Ice
April 21	Flames, 2-1 (OT)	at Calgary
April 23	Mighty Ducks, 4-3	at Calgary
April 25	Flames, 5-2	at Anaheim
April 27	Mighty Ducks, 3-2 (OT)	at Anaheim
April 29	Flames, 3-2	at Calgary
May 1	Mighty Ducks, 2-1	at Anaheim
May 3	Mighty Ducks, 3-0	at Calgary

Shutout: Bryzgalov, Anaheim.

	W-L	GF	Leading Scorers
San Jose	4-1	17	Marleau (7-1–8)
Nashville	1-4	10	Kariya (2-5–7)

Date	Winner	Home Ice
April 21	Predators, 4-3	at Nashville
April 23	Sharks, 3-0	at Nashville
April 25	Sharks, 4-1	at San Jose
April 27	Sharks, 5-4	at San Jose
April 30	Sharks, 2-1	at Nashville

Shutout: Toskala, San Jose.

SEMIFINALS (Best of 7)

	W-L	GF	Leading Scorers
Edmonton	4-2	19	Horcoff (4-3–7)
			& Smyth (2-5–7)
San Jose	2-4	12	Marleau (2-4–6)

Date	Winner	Home Ice
May 7	Sharks, 2-1	at San Jose
May 8	Sharks, 2-1	at San Jose
May 10	Oilers, 3-2 (3OT)	at Edmonton
May 12	Oilers, 6-3	at Edmonton
May 14	Oilers, 6-3	at San Jose
May 17	Oilers, 2-0	at Edmonton

Shutouts: Roloson, Edmonton.

	W-L	GF	Leading Scorers
Anaheim	4-0	16	Lupul (6-1–7)
Colorado	0-4	4	Four tied with 2 pts.

Date	Winner	Home Ice
May 5	Mighty Ducks, 5-0	at Anaheim
May 7	Mighty Ducks, 3-0	at Anaheim
May 9	Mighty Ducks, 4-3 (OT)	at Colorado
May 11	Mighty Ducks, 4-1	at Colorado

Shutouts: Bryzgalov (2).

CHAMPIONSHIP (Best of 7)

	W-L	GF	Leading Scorers
Edmonton	4-1	16	Peca (3-2–5)
			& Pronger (2-3–5)
Anaheim	1-4	13	Marchant (1-4–5)

Date	Winner	Home Ice
May 19	Oilers, 3-1	at Anaheim
May 21	Oilers, 3-1	at Anaheim
May 23	Oilers, 5-4	at Edmonton
May 25	Mighty Ducks, 6-3	at Edmonton
May 27	Oilers, 2-1	at Anaheim

EASTERN CONFERENCE

FIRST ROUND (Best of 7)

	W-L	GF	Leading Scorers
Ottawa	4-1	23	Three tied with 10 pts.
Tampa Bay	1-4	13	Richards (3-5–8)

Date	Winner	Home Ice
April 21	Senators, 4-1	at Ottawa
April 23	Lightning, 4-3	at Ottawa
April 25	Senators, 8-4	at Tampa Bay
April 27	Senators, 5-2	at Tampa Bay
April 29	Senators, 3-2	at Ottawa

	W-L	GF	Leading Scorers
New Jersey	4-0	17	Elias (5-6–11)
NY Rangers	0-4	4	Betts (1-1–2)

Date	Winner	Home Ice
April 22	Devils, 6-1	at New Jersey
April 24	Devils, 4-1	at New Jersey
April 26	Devils, 3-0	at New York
April 29	Devils, 4-2	at New York

Shutout: Brodeur, New Jersey.

	W-L	GF	Leading Scorers
Carolina	4-2	15	Staal (2-6–8)
Montreal	2-4	17	Kovalev (4-3–7)

Date	Winner	Home Ice
April 22	Canadiens, 6-1	at Carolina
April 24	Canadiens, 6-5 (2OT)	at Carolina
April 26	Hurricanes, 2-1 (OT)	at Montreal
April 28	Hurricanes, 3-2	at Montreal
April 30	Hurricanes, 2-1	at Carolina
May 2	Hurricanes, 2-1 (OT)	at Montreal

	W-L	GF	Leading Scorers
Buffalo	4-2	27	Briere (3-6–9)
			Drury (3-6–9)
Philadelphia	2-4	14	Forsberg (4-4–8)

Date	Winner	Home Ice
April 22	Sabres, 3-2 (2OT)	at Buffalo
April 24	Sabres, 8-2	at Buffalo
April 26	Flyers, 4-2	at Philadelphia
April 28	Flyers, 5-4	at Philadelphia
April 30	Sabres, 3-0	at Buffalo
May 2	Sabres, 7-1	at Philadelphia

Shutouts: Miller, Buffalo.

SEMIFINALS (Best of 7)

	W-L	GF	Leading Scorers
Buffalo	4-1	16	Roy (2-5–7)
Ottawa	1-4	13	Alfredsson (1-5–6)

Date	Winner	Home Ice
May 5	Sabres, 7-6 (OT)	at Ottawa
May 8	Sabres, 2-1	at Ottawa
May 10	Sabres, 3-2 (OT)	at Buffalo
May 11	Senators, 2-1	at Buffalo
May 13	Sabres, 3-2 (OT)	at Ottawa

	W-L	GF	Leading Scorers
Carolina	4-1	17	Staal (3-4–7)
New Jersey	1-4	10	Three tied with 5 pts.

Date	Winner	Home Ice
May 6	Hurricanes, 6-0	at Carolina
May 8	Hurricanes, 3-2 (OT)	at Carolina
May 10	Hurricanes, 3-2	at New Jersey
May 13	Devils, 5-1	at New Jersey
May 14	Hurricanes, 4-1	at Carolina

Shutout: Ward, Carolina.

CHAMPIONSHIP (Best of 7)

	W-L	GF	Leading Scorers
Carolina	4-3	22	Stillman (3-7–10)
Buffalo	3-4	17	Briere (4-2–6)

Date	Winner	Home Ice
May 20	Sabres, 3-2	at Carolina
May 22	Hurricanes, 4-3	at Carolina
May 24	Sabres, 4-3	at Buffalo
May 26	Hurricanes, 4-0	at Buffalo
May 28	Hurricanes, 4-3 (OT)	at Buffalo
May 30	Sabres, 2-1 (OT)	at Buffalo
June 1	Hurricanes, 4-2	at Carolina

Shutouts: Gerber, Carolina.

Conn Smythe Trophy (Playoff MVP)
Cam Ward, Carolina, G
23 games, 15-8, 2.14 GAA, .920 Save Pct., 2 ShO

STANLEY CUP FINALS (Best of 7)

	W-L	GF	Leading Scorers
Carolina	4-3	19	Staal (2-6–8)
Edmonton	3-4	16	Pisani (5-1–6)
			& Hemsky (2-4–6)

Date	Winner	Home Ice
June 5	Hurricanes, 5-4	at Carolina
June 7	Hurricanes, 5-0	at Carolina
June 10	Oilers, 2-1	at Edmonton
June 12	Hurricanes, 2-1	at Edmonton
June 14	Oilers, 4-3 (OT)	at Carolina
June 17	Oilers, 4-0	at Edmonton
June 19	Hurricanes, 3-1	at Carolina

Shutouts: Ward, Carolina; Markkanen, Edmonton.

Stanley Cup Finals Box Scores

Game 1

Monday, June 5, at Carolina

Edmonton	1	2	1	—4
Carolina	0	1	4	—5

1st Period: EDM—Pisani 10 (Torres, Spacek), 8:18.
2nd Period: EDM—Pronger 5 (unassisted), 10:36 (penalty shot); EDM—Moreau 2 (Greene), 16:23; CAR—Brind'Amour 10 (Williams, Stillman), 17:17.
3rd Period: CAR—Whitney 7 (Weight, Ladd), 1:40; CAR—Whitney 8 (Recchi, Staal), 5:09 (pp); CAR—Williams 6 (LaRose, A. Ward), 10:02 (sh); EDM—Hemsky 5 (Stoll, Pronger), 13:31 (pp); CAR—Brind'Amour 11 (unassisted), 19:28.
Shots on Goal: Edmonton—8-12-18—38; Carolina—8-7-11—26. **Power plays:** Edmonton 1-7; Carolina 1-5.
Goalies: Edmonton, Roloson (23 shots, 19 saves), Conklin (3 shots, 2 saves); Carolina, C. Ward (38 shots, 34 saves). **Attendance:** 18,797 (18,730).

Game 2

Wednesday, June 7, at Carolina

Edmonton	0	0	0	—0
Carolina	1	2	2	—5

1st Period: CAR—Ladd 2 (Staal, Kaberle), 6:21.
2nd Period: CAR—Kaberle 3 (Whitney, Cullen), 10:28 (pp); CAR—Stillman 8 (Wallin, Williams), 19:57.
3rd Period: CAR—Weight 3 (Recchi, Cullen), 2:21 (pp); CAR—Recchi 6 (Kaberle, Cullen), 4:12 (pp).
Shots on Goal: Edmonton—6-10-9—25; Carolina—8-10-8—26. **Power plays:** Edmonton 0-6; Carolina 3-10.
Goalies: Edmonton, Markkanen (26 shots, 21 saves); Carolina, C. Ward (25 shots, 25 saves). **Attendance:** 18,928 (18,730).

Game 3

Saturday, June 10, at Edmonton

Carolina	0	0	1	—1
Edmonton	1	0	1	—2

1st Period: EDM—Horcoff 6 (Spacek, Hemsky), 2:31.
3rd Period: CAR—Brind'Amour 12 (Stillman), 9:09; EDM—Smyth 6 (Hemsky, Spacek), 17:45.
Shots on Goal: Carolina—6-8-11—25; Edmonton—9-11-10—30. **Power plays:** Carolina 0-5; Edmonton 0-7.
Goalies: Carolina, C. Ward (30 shots, 28 saves); Edmonton, Markkanen (25 shots, 24 saves). **Attendance:** 16,839 (16,839).

Game 4

Monday, June 12, at Edmonton

Carolina	1	1	0	—2
Edmonton	1	0	0	—2

1st Period: EDM—Samsonov 4 (Dvorak, Stoll), 8:40; CAR—Stillman 9 (Kaberle, Staal), 9:09 (pp).
2nd Period: CAR—Recchi 7 (Staal, Stillman), 15:56.
Shots on Goal: Carolina—4-11-5—20; Edmonton—8-8-5—21. **Power plays:** Carolina 1-6; Edmonton 0-5.
Goalies: Carolina, C. Ward (21 shots, 20 saves); Edmonton, Markkanen (20 shots, 18 saves). **Attendance:** 16,839 (16,839).

Stanley Cup Scoring Leaders

(incl. all playoff games)

	Gm	G	A	Pts	+/-	PM	PP
Eric Staal, Car	25	9	19	**28**	0	8	7
Cory Stillman, Car	25	9	17	**26**	12	14	4
Chris Pronger, Edm	24	5	16	**21**	10	26	3
Daniel Briere, Buf	18	8	11	**19**	0	12	3
Shawn Horcoff, Edm	24	7	12	**19**	4	12	1

Five tied with 18 pts. each.

Game 5

Wednesday, June 14, at Carolina

Edmonton	3	0	0	1	—4
Carolina	2	1	0	0	—3

1st Period: EDM—Pisani 11 (Pronger, Torres), 0:16; CAR—Staal 8 (Weight, Hedican), 5:54 (pp); CAR—Whitney 9 (Staal, Recchi), 10:16 (pp); EDM—Hemsky 6 (Tarnstrom, Staios), 13:25 (pp); EDM—Peca 6 (Hemsky, Pronger), 19:42.
2nd Period: CAR—Staal 9 (Whitney, Stillman), 9:56 (pp).
Overtime: EDM—Pisani 12 (unassisted), 3:31 (sh).
Shots on Goal: Edmonton—10-7-5-7—29; Carolina—14-8-2-0—24. **Power plays:** Edmonton 1-7; Carolina 3-7.
Goalies: Edmonton, Markkanen (24 shots, 21 saves); Carolina, C. Ward (29 shots, 25 saves). **Attendance:** 18,974 (18,730).

Game 6

Saturday, June 17, at Edmonton

Carolina	0	0	0	—0
Edmonton	0	2	2	—4

2nd Period: EDM—Pisani 13 (Hemsky, Spacek), 1:45 (pp); EDM—Torres 4 (Staios, Pisani), 9:54.
3rd Period: EDM—Peca 7 (Peca, Spacek), 3:04 (pp); EDM—Horcoff 7 (Dvorak, Tarnstrom), 13:05 (pp).
Shots on Goal: Carolina—3-4-9—16; Edmonton—10-11-13—34. **Power plays:** Carolina 0-6; Edmonton 3-9.
Goalies: Carolina, C. Ward (34 shots, 30 saves); Edmonton, Markkanen (16 shots, 16 saves). **Attendance:** 16,839 (16,839).

Game 7

Monday, June 19, at Carolina

Edmonton	0	0	1	—1
Carolina	1	1	1	—3

1st Period: CAR—A. Ward 2 (Recchi, Cullen), 1:26.
2nd Period: CAR—Kaberle 4 (Stillman, Cullen), 4:18 (pp).
3rd Period: EDM—Smyth 7 (Murray, Torres), 1:03; CAR—Williams 7 (Staal, Hedican), 18:59 (en).
Shots on Goal: Edmonton—5-8-10—23; Carolina—10-11-6—27. **Power plays:** Edmonton 0-4; Carolina 1-5.
Goalies: Edmonton, Markkanen (26 shots, 24 saves); Carolina, C. Ward (23 shots, 22 saves). **Attendance:** 18,928 (18,730).

Final Stanley Cup Standings

				—Goals—		
	Gm	W	L	For	Opp	Dif
Carolina	25	16	9	73	60	+13
Edmonton	24	15	9	70	61	+9
Buffalo	18	11	7	60	49	+11
Anaheim	16	9	7	46	36	+10
San Jose	11	6	5	29	29	0
New Jersey	9	5	4	27	21	+6
Ottawa	10	5	5	36	29	+7
Colorado	9	4	5	22	31	-9
Calgary	7	3	4	16	17	-1
Montreal	6	2	4	17	15	+2
Detroit	6	2	4	17	19	-2
Philadelphia	6	2	4	14	27	-13
Dallas	5	1	4	15	18	-3
Nashville	5	1	4	10	17	-7
Tampa Bay	5	1	4	13	23	-10
NY Rangers	4	0	4	4	17	-13

Finalists' Composite Box Scores

Carolina Hurricanes (16-9)

Top Scorers	Pos	Overall Playoffs								Finals vs Edmonton							
		Gm	G	A	Pts	+/-	PM	PP	S	Gm	G	A	Pts	+/-	PM	PP	S
Eric Staal	C	25	9	19	28	0	8	7	87	7	2	6	8	-2	4	2	16
Cory Stillman	L	25	9	17	26	12	14	4	75	7	2	5	7	3	4	1	22
Rod Brind'Amour	C	25	12	6	18	9	16	6	75	7	3	0	3	1	6	0	14
Justin Williams	R	25	7	11	18	12	34	0	71	7	2	2	4	3	4	0	15
Matt Cullen	C	25	4	14	18	2	12	2	56	7	0	5	5	1	6	0	12
Mark Recchi	R	25	7	9	16	-5	18	2	45	7	2	4	6	-1	2	1	12
Doug Weight	C	23	3	13	16	-3	20	2	35	5	1	2	3	0	2	1	7
Ray Whitney	L	24	9	6	15	-1	14	5	40	7	3	2	5	0	10	2	12
Frantisek Kaberle	D	25	4	9	13	-7	8	3	35	7	2	3	5	-3	2	2	14
Bret Hedican	D	25	2	9	11	6	42	0	23	7	0	2	2	2	18	0	2
Andrew Ladd	L	17	2	3	5	0	4	0	13	7	1	1	2	-1	2	0	6
Aaron Ward	D	25	2	3	5	0	18	0	18	7	1	1	2	1	6	0	3
Niclas Wallin	D	25	1	4	5	3	14	0	19	7	0	1	1	0	4	0	3
Mike Commodore	D	25	2	2	4	1	33	0	27	7	0	0	0	2	6	0	8
Glen Wesley	D	25	0	2	2	1	16	0	15	7	0	0	0	-1	6	0	4
Chad LaRose	R	21	0	1	1	-2	10	0	15	3	0	1	1	0	0	0	2
Cam Ward	G	23	0	1	1	0	0	0	0	7	0	0	0	0	0	0	0

Overtime goals—OVERALL (Stillman 2, Staal, Wallin); FINALS (none). **Shorthanded goals**—OVERALL—(Williams, Commodore); FINALS (Williams). **Power Play conversions**—OVERALL (31 for 129, 24.0%); FINALS (11 for 44, 25.0%).

Goaltending	Gm	Min	GAA	GA	SA	Sv%	W-L	Gm	Min	GAA	GA	SA	Sv%	W-L
Cam Ward	23	1320	2.14	47	584	.920	15-8	7	422	2.28	16	200	.920	4-3
Martin Gerber	6	221	3.53	13	90	.856	1-1	0	0	—	0	0	—	0-0
TOTAL	25	1547	2.33	60	674	.911	16-9	7	423	2.27	16	200	.920	4-3

Empty Net Goals—OVERALL (none), FINALS (none). **Shutouts**—OVERALL (Ward 2, Gerber), FINALS (Ward). **Assists**—OVERALL (Ward), FINALS (none). **Penalty Minutes**—OVERALL (Gerber 4), FINALS (none).

Edmonton Oilers (15-9)

Top Scorers	Pos	Overall Playoffs								Finals vs Carolina							
		Gm	G	A	Pts	+/-	PM	PP	S	Gm	G	A	Pts	+/-	PM	PP	S
Chris Pronger	D	24	5	16	21	10	26	3	61	7	1	3	4	1	8	0	23
Shawn Horcoff	C	24	7	12	19	4	12	1	41	7	2	0	2	-5	4	1	9
Fernando Pisani	R	24	14	4	18	4	10	3	49	7	5	1	6	1	2	1	17
Ales Hemsky	R	24	6	11	17	-3	14	4	47	7	2	4	6	-1	2	2	15
Ryan Smyth	L	24	7	9	16	-2	22	4	61	7	2	0	2	-3	6	1	17
Sergei Samsonov	L	24	4	11	15	2	14	1	40	7	1	0	1	1	2	0	11
Jaroslav Spacek	D	24	3	11	14	-3	24	2	43	7	0	5	5	2	8	0	12
Michael Peca	C	24	6	5	11	5	20	0	43	7	1	1	2	2	2	0	15
Raffi Torres	L	22	4	7	11	2	16	1	42	7	1	3	4	1	4	0	13
Jarret Stoll	C	24	4	6	10	-4	24	2	49	7	0	2	2	1	4	0	13
Steve Staios	D	24	1	5	6	0	28	1	28	7	0	0	0	2	8	0	9
Jason Smith	D	24	1	4	5	5	16	0	14	7	0	0	0	-1	6	0	4
Rem Murray	C	24	0	4	4	0	2	0	14	7	0	1	1	-1	0	0	6
Marc-Andre Bergeron	D	18	2	1	3	0	14	2	17	2	0	0	0	-2	2	0	2
Ethan Moreau	L	21	2	1	3	0	19	0	40	7	1	0	1	0	6	0	14
Brad Winchester	C	10	1	2	3	0	4	0	9	0	0	0	0	0	0	0	0
Todd Harvey	L	10	1	1	2	0	4	0	6	0	0	0	0	0	0	0	1
Georges Laraque	R	15	1	1	2	2	44	0	6	4	0	0	0	-1	17	0	1
Dick Tarnstrom	D	12	0	2	2	1	10	0	7	5	0	2	2	1	6	0	3
Radek Dvorak	R	16	0	2	2	-1	4	0	32	7	0	2	2	1	4	0	12
Dwayne Roloson	G	18	0	2	2	0	14	0	0	1	0	0	0	0	0	0	0
Toby Petersen	C	2	0	1	1	0	0	0	3	0	0	0	0	0	0	0	0
Matt Greene	D	18	0	1	1	1	34	0	4	7	0	1	1	1	14	0	3

Overtime goals—OVERALL (Horcoff, Pisani, Stoll); FINALS (Pisani). **Shorthanded goals**— OVERALL (Horcoff, Pisani, Peca); FINALS (Pisani). **Power Play conversions**—OVERALL (24 for 141, 17.0%); FINALS (5 for 45, 11.1%).

Goaltending	Gm	Min	GAA	GA	SA	Sv%	W-L	Gm	Min	GAA	GA	SA	Sv%	W-L
Jussi Markkanen	6	360	2.17	13	137	.905	3-3	6	360	2.16	13	137	.905	3-3
Dwayne Roloson	18	1160	2.33	45	618	.927	12-5	1	54	4.44	4	23	.826	0-0
Ty Conklin	1	6	10.00	1	3	.667	0-1	1	6	10.00	1	3	.667	0-1
TOTAL	24	1537	2.38	61	760	.920	15-9	7	423	2.70	19	163	.883	3-4

Empty Net Goals—OVERALL (2), FINALS (1). **Shutouts**—OVERALL (Markkanen, Roloson), FINALS (Markkanen). **Assists**—OVERALL (Roloson 2), FINALS (none). **Penalty Minutes**—OVERALL (Roloson 14), FINALS (none).

Annual Awards

Voting for the Hart, Calder, Norris, Lady Byng, Selke, and Masterton Trophies is conducted after the regular season by the Professional Hockey Writers' Association. The Vezina Trophy is selected by the NHL general managers, while the Jack Adams Award is selected by NHL broadcasters. Points are awarded on 10-7-5-3-1 basis except for the Vezina Trophy and the Adams Award which are awarded 5-3-1.

Hart Trophy
For Most Valuable Player

	Pos	1st	2nd	3rd	4th	5th	Pts
Joe Thornton, Bos-SJ	C	67	48	9	1	4—	1058
Jaromir Jagr, NYR	R	48	49	30	0	1—	974
Miikka Kiprusoff, Calg	G	10	24	45	20	8—	561
Eric Staal, Car	C	0	0	9	18	22—	121
Daniel Alfredsson, Ott	R	0	2	6	20	15—	119

Calder Trophy
For Rookie of the Year

	Pos	1st	2nd	3rd	4th	5th	Pts
Alexander Ovechkin, Wash	L	124	5	0	0	0—	1275
Sidney Crosby, Pit	C	4	95	19	10	1—	831
Dion Phaneuf, Calg	D	0	16	72	35	3—	580
Henrik Lundqvist, NYR	G	1	13	34	60	4—	455
Brad Boyes, Bos	C	0	0	1	7	22—	48

Norris Trophy
For Best Defenseman

	1st	2nd	3rd	4th	5th	Pts
Nicklas Lidstrom, Det	91	28	8	2	0—	1152
Scott Niedermayer, Ana	29	57	16	15	3—	817
Sergei Zubov, Dal	0	21	42	31	14—	464
Zdeno Chara, Ott	5	14	35	30	17—	430
Wade Redden, Ott	0	1	12	12	12—	115

Vezina Trophy
For Outstanding Goaltender

	1st	2nd	3rd	Pts
Miikka Kiprusoff, Calg	25	5	0—	140
Martin Brodeur, NJ	2	10	8—	48
Henrik Lundqvist, NYR	2	9	4—	41
Tomas Vokoun, Nash	1	1	7—	15
Manny Legace, Det	0	1	3—	6
Marty Turco, Dal	0	1	3—	6

Lady Byng Trophy
For Sportsmanship and Gentlemanly Play

	Pos	1st	2nd	3rd	4th	5th	Pts
Pavel Datsyuk, Det	C	41	21	14	12	6—	669
Brad Richards, TB	C	12	23	21	15	11—	442
Patrick Marleau, SJ	C	13	16	15	7	18—	356
Daniel Alfredsson, Ott	R	9	8	5	5	4—	190
Teemu Selanne, Ana	R	5	6	6	6	4—	144

Selke Trophy
For Best Defensive Forward

	Pos	1st	2nd	3rd	4th	5th	Pts
Rod Brind'Amour, Car	C	80	16	5	5	2—	954
Jere Lehtinen, Dal	R	9	41	27	15	10—	567
Mike Fisher, Ott	C	5	6	8	13	8—	179
Daniel Alfredsson, Ott	R	5	5	8	5	3—	143
John Madden, NJ	C	2	6	9	9	8—	142

Adams Award
For Coach of the Year

	1st	2nd	3rd	Pts
Lindy Ruff, Buf	20	15	10—	155
Peter Laviolette, Car	20	16	6—	154
Tom Renney, NYR	13	18	8—	127
Barry Trotz, Nash	2	5	12—	37
Mike Babcock, Det	4	2	2—	28

AP/Wide World Photos

San Jose's **Joe Thornton** took home the Art Ross and Hart Trophies at the NHL awards ceremony on June 22.

Other Awards

Lester B. Pearson Award (NHL Players Assn. MVP)—Jaromir Jagr, NYR

Jennings Trophy (goaltenders with a minimum of 25 games played for team with fewest goals against)—Miikka Kiprusoff, Calg.

Maurice "Rocket" Richard Trophy (regular season goal-scoring leader)—Jonathan Cheechoo, SJ

Art Ross Trophy (regular season points leader)—Joe Thornton, SJ

Masterton Trophy (perseverance, sportsmanship, and dedication to hockey)—Teemu Selanne, Ana.

King Clancy Trophy (leadership and humanitarian contributions to community)—Olaf Kolzig, Wash.

Lester Patrick Trophy (outstanding service to hockey in the U.S.)—TBA.

All-NHL Team

Voting by PHWA. Holdovers from 2003-04 first team in **bold**.

	First Team		Second Team
G	Miikka Kiprusoff, Calg	G	Martin Brodeur, NJ
D	**Scott Niedermayer**, Ana	D	Zdeno Chara, Ott
D	Nicklas Lidstrom, Det	D	Sergei Zubov, Dal
C	Joe Thornton, Bos-SJ	C	Eric Staal, Car
R	Jaromir Jagr, NYR	R	Daniel Alfredsson, Ott
L	Alexander Ovechkin, Wash	L	Dany Heatley, Ott

All-Rookie Team

Voting by PHWA.

Pos		Pos	
G	Henrik Lundqvist, NYR	F	Brad Boyes, Bos
D	Andrej Meszaros, Ott	F	Sidney Crosby, Pit
D	Dion Phaneuf, Calg	F	Alexander Ovechkin, Wash

COLLEGE HOCKEY

NCAA Men's Division I

Final regular season standings; overall records, including all postseason tournament games, in parentheses.

Atlantic Hockey

	W	L	T	Pts	GF	GA
*Holy Cross (27-10-2)	19	7	2	40	98	65
Mercyhurst (22-13-1)	19	8	1	39	119	87
Sacred Heart (21-12-2)	18	8	2	38	92	55
Bentley (15-17-5)	11	12	5	27	75	82
Army (12-18-6)	10	12	6	26	64	67
Connecticut (11-23-2)	9	18	1	19	79	106
Canisius (10-23-2)	8	18	2	18	68	87
American Int'l (6-21-5)	6	17	5	17	64	110

Conf. Tourney Final: Holy Cross 5, Bentley 2.
*NCAA Tourney (1-1): Holy Cross (1-1).

Central Collegiate Hockey Assn.

	W	L	T	Pts	GF	GA
*Miami-OH (26-9-4)	20	6	2	42	96	57
*Michigan St. (25-12-8)	14	7	7	35	82	66
*Michigan (21-15-5)	13	10	5	31	102	82
N. Michigan (22-16-2)	14	12	2	30	83	79
*Nebraska-Omaha (20-15-6)	12	10	6	30	99	90
Lake Superior (15-14-7)	11	12	5	27	75	70
Ferris St. (17-15-8)	10	11	7	27	77	81
Alaska-Fairbanks (18-16-5)	11	13	4	26	64	79
Notre Dame (13-19-4)	11	13	4	26	75	76
Ohio State (15-19-5)	11	14	3	25	72	71
W. Michigan (10-24-6)	7	16	5	19	69	115
Bowling Green (13-23-2)	8	18	2	18	83	111

Conf. Tourney Final: Michigan St. 2, Miami-OH 1.
*NCAA Tourney (1-4): Miami-OH (0-1), Michigan St. (1-1), Michigan (0-1), Nebraska-Omaha (0-1).

College Hockey America

	W	L	T	Pts	GF	GA
Niagara (20-15-1)	13	6	1	27	78	62
Alab.-Huntsville (19-13-2)	12	7	1	25	66	57
*Bemidji State (20-14-3)	12	7	1	25	72	46
Air Force (11-20-1)	8	12	0	16	60	74
Robert Morris (12-20-3)	7	11	2	16	51	66
Wayne State (6-23-6)	3	12	5	11	59	81

Conf. Tourney Final: Bemidji St. 4, Niagara 2.
*NCAA Tourney (0-1): Bemidji St. (0-1).

ECAC Hockey League

	W	L	T	Pts	GF	GA
Dartmouth (19-12-2)	14	6	2	30	84	56
Colgate (20-13-6)	14	6	2	30	66	46
*Cornell (22-9-4)	13	6	3	29	61	48
*Harvard (21-12-2)	13	8	1	27	63	59
St. Lawrence (21-17-2)	12	9	1	25	74	66
Union (16-16-6)	9	9	4	22	48	53
Rensselaer (14-17-6)	8	8	6	22	53	56
Clarkson (18-17-3)	9	11	2	20	61	70
Quinnipiac (20-18-1)	8	13	1	17	70	74
Princeton (10-18-3)	7	12	3	17	62	69
Yale (10-20-3)	6	14	2	14	65	83
Brown (5-20-7)	3	14	5	11	45	72

Conf. Tourney Final: Harvard 6, Cornell 2.
*NCAA Tourney (1-2): Cornell (1-1); Harvard (0-1).

Hockey East Association

	W	L	T	Pts	GF	GA
*Boston University (26-10-4)	17	7	3	37	89	67
*Boston College (26-13-3)	17	8	2	36	86	58
*Maine (28-12-2)	17	8	2	36	93	60
*New Hampshire (20-13-7)	14	7	6	34	85	63
Providence (17-16-3)	14	10	3	31	78	67
Vermont (18-14-6)	10	11	6	26	65	62
UMass-Lowell (14-20-2)	11	14	2	24	74	96
UMass-Amherst (13-21-2)	10	15	2	22	60	77
Northeastern (3-24-7)	3	17	7	13	57	88
Merrimack (6-23-5)	3	19	5	11	43	92

Conf. Tourney Final: B.U. 2, B.C. 1 (OT).
*NCAA Tourney (6-4): Boston University (1-1); Boston College (3-1), Maine (2-1), New Hampshire (0-1).

Western Collegiate Hockey Assn.

	W	L	T	Pts	GF	GA
*Minnesota (27-9-5)	20	5	3	43	107	64
Denver (21-15-3)	17	8	3	37	98	78
*Wisconsin (30-10-3)	17	8	3	37	98	60
*North Dakota (29-16-1)	16	12	0	32	104	76
*Colorado College (24-16-2)	15	11	2	32	94	75
St. Cloud St. (22-16-4)	13	13	2	28	79	62
Minnesota St. (17-18-4)	12	13	3	27	93	88
Michigan Tech (7-25-6)	6	16	6	18	54	113
Minnesota Duluth (11-25-4)	6	19	3	15	62	114
Alaska-Anchorage (6-27-3)	4	21	3	11	51	110

Conf. Tourney Final: Minnesota 5, North Dakota 4.
*NCAA Tourney (6-3): Minnesota (0-1), Wisconsin (4-0), North Dakota (2-1), Colorado College (0-1).

Independent

	W	L	T	Pts	GF	GA
Rochester Institute of Tech.	6	22	2	14	85	110

USCHO.com/CSTV
Division I Men's Poll

Compiled **before** the NCAA tournament. Voting panel consists of 28 Div. I coaches and 12 writers from across the country. First place votes are in parentheses. Teams in **bold** type went on to reach the NCAA Frozen Four.

		League	W	L	T	Pts
1	Boston University (20)	HEA	25	9	4	758
2	**Wisconsin** (15)	WCHA	26	10	3	751
3	Minnesota (5)	WCHA	27	8	5	719
4	Michigan St.	CCHA	24	11	8	694
5	Miami-OH	CCHA	26	8	4	638
6	**North Dakota**	WCHA	27	15	1	596
7	Harvard	ECAC	21	11	2	544
8	Cornell	ECAC	21	8	4	508
9	**Boston College**	HEA	23	12	3	486
10	**Maine**	HEA	26	11	2	454

Hobey Baker Award

For men's College Hockey Player of the Year. Voting is done by a 25-member panel of college hockey personnel, national al media, and pro scouts, plus a one percent fan vote.

	Cl	Pos
Winner: Matt Carle, Denver	Jr.	D

NCAA Division I Tournament

Regional seeds in parentheses

East Regional

Held in Albany, N.Y., March 25-26.

First Round

(1) Michigan St. 1 . . . .(4) New Hampshire 0
(3) Maine 6 . . . . .OT . . . .(2) Harvard 1

Second Round

Maine 5 .Michigan St. 4

Northeast Regional

Held in Worcester, Mass., March 24-25.

First Round

(1) Boston University 9 . . . .(4) Nebraska-Omaha 2
(3) Boston College 5 . . . .(2) Miami-OH 0

Second Round

Boston College 5 . . . . .Boston University 0

West Regional

Held in Grand Forks, N.D., March 24-25.

First Round

(4) Holy Cross 4 . . . . . . .OT . . . .(1) Minnesota 3
(2) North Dakota 5 . . . .(3) Michigan 1

Second Round

North Dakota 5 . . . . .Holy Cross 2

Midwest Regional

Held in Green Bay, Wis., March 25-26.

First Round

(1) Wisconsin 4 . . . . (4) Bemidji St. 0
(2) Cornell 3 . . . .(3) Colorado College 2

Second Round

Wisconsin 1 . . . . .3OT . . . . .Cornell 0

The Frozen Four

Held at the Bradley Center in Milwaukee, Wis., April 6 and April 8. Single elimination; no consolation game.

Semifinals

Boston College 6 . . . . .North Dakota 5
Wisconsin 5 . . . . .Maine 2

Championship Game

Wisconsin, 2-1

Boston College (HEA) 1   0   0   —1
Wisconsin (WCHA) 0   1   1   —2

1st Period: BC—Gannon 5 (Bertram), 9:01.
2nd Period: WIS—Earl 24 (Burish, Pavelski), 1:17.
3rd Period: WIS—Gilbert 12 (Pavelski, Burish), 9:32 (pp).

Shots on Goal: Boston College—9-10-4—23; Wisconsin—17-11-11—39.

Power plays: Boston College 0-4; Wisconsin 1-8.

Goalies: Boston College—Schneider (39 shots, 37 saves); Wisconsin—Elliott (23 shots, 22 saves).

Attendance: 17,758. **Time:** 2:30.

Most Outstanding Player: Robbie Earl, Wisconsin junior forward: SEMIFINAL—2 gaols, 1 assist; FINAL—1 goal.

All-Tournament Team: Earl, goaltender Brian Elliott, forward Adam Burish and defenseman Tom Gilbert of Wisconsin; forward Chris Collins and defenseman Brett Motherwell of Boston College.

Division I Leaders

Scoring

(Minimum 20 games)	Cl	Gm	G	A	Pts	Avg
Dave Borrelli, Mercyhurst	. . .Sr.	33	28	23	51	**1.55**
Ryan Potulny, Minnesota	. . .Jr.	41	38	25	63	**1.54**
Chris Collins, B.C.	. . . . . . .Sr.	42	34	29	63	**1.50**
Ben Cottreau, Mercyhurst	. .So.	35	17	34	51	**1.46**
Pierre-Luc O'Brien, S. Heart	. .Jr.	35	19	31	50	**1.43**

Goaltending

(Minimum 15 games)	Cl	Record	Sv%	GAA
Brian Elliott, Wisconsin	. . . Jr.	27-5-3	.938	**1.55**
Charlie Effinger, Miami-OH	.So.	12-4-3	.931	**1.83**
Jeff Lerg, Michigan St.	. . .Fr.	17-6-6	.928	**1.96**
Joe Fallon, Vermont	. . . . .So.	14-14-5	.907	**2.02**
Jeff Zatkoff, Miami-OH	. . . .Fr.	14-5-1	.928	**2.02**

Division III Championship

March 18-19 at First Arena in Elmira, N.Y.

Semifinals

St. Norbert (Wis.) 5 . . . . . .OT . . . . .Hobart (NY) 4
Middlebury (Vt.) 2 . . . . .Elmira (NY) 1

Championship

Middlebury 3 . . . .–. . . . . .St. Norbert 0

Final records: Middlebury (26-2-2); St. Norbert (25-5-2); Hobart (20-8-0); Elmira (18-9-2).

Women's College Hockey

NCAA Division I Frozen Four

March 24 and 26 at Mariucci Arena in Minneapolis, Minn.

Semifinals

Wisconsin 1 . . . . .St. Lawrence 0
Minnesota 5 .New Hampshire 4

Championship

Wisconsin 3 . . . . .Minnesota 0

Final records: Wisconsin (36-4-1); Minnesota (29-11-1); St. Lawrence (31-5-2); New Hampshire (33-3-1).

All-Tournament Team: Goaltender Jessie Vetter (Most Outstanding), forward Jinelle Zaugg and defenseman Bobbi-Jo Slusar of Wisconsin; forward Bobbi Ross and defenseman Ashley Albrecht of Minnesota; forward Jennifer Hitchcock of UNH.

NCAA Division III Championship

March 17-18 at Stafford Arena in Plattsburgh, N.Y.

Semifinals

Middlebury (Vt.) 2 . . . . .Gustavus Adolphus (Minn.) 1
Plattsburgh St. (NY) 4 . . . . .Wis.-Stevens Point 1

Third Place

Wis.-Stevens Point 2 . . . . .Gustavus Adolphus 0

Championship

Middlebury 3 .Plattsburgh St. 1

Final records: Middlebury (27-2-0); Plattsburgh St. (26-3-1); Wis.-Stevens Point (21-5-4); Gustavus Adolphus (22-5-2).

Patty Kazmaier Award

For women's College Hockey Player of the Year. Voting is done by a 13-member panel of national media, varsity coaches, and one USA Hockey member.

	Cl	Pos
Winner: Sara Bauer, Wisconsin	. . . . .Jr.	F

MINOR LEAGUE HOCKEY

American Hockey League

Division champions (*) and playoff qualifiers (†) are noted. **OTL** denotes any game that was tied at the end of regulation and lost during a five-minute overtime period. If the game is tied after the overtime period, a shootout ensues with each team getting five attempts to score on a breakaway from the red line. Shootout Losses are listed as **SOL**. Teams are awarded two points for a win (regulation, overtime or shootout), one point for an OTL or SOL, and zero points for a regulation loss.

Eastern Conference

Atlantic Division

Team (Affiliate)	W	L	OTL	SOL	Pts
*Portland (Ana)	.53	19	5	3	114
†Hartford (NYR)	.48	24	2	6	104
†Manchester (LA)	.43	30	3	4	93
†Providence (Bos)	.43	31	1	5	92
Lowell (Car/Col)	.29	37	6	8	72
Springfield (TB)	.28	43	3	6	65
Albany (NJ)	.25	48	4	3	57

East Division

Team (Affiliate)	W	L	OTL	SOL	Pts
*Wilkes-Barre/Scran. (Pit)	.51	18	5	6	113
†Hershey (Wash)	.44	21	5	10	103
†Norfolk (Chi)	.43	29	4	4	94
*Bridgeport Sound (NYI)	.38	33	6	3	85
Binghamton (Ott)	.35	37	4	4	78
Philadelphia (Phi)	.34	37	2	7	77

Western Conference

North Division

Team (Affiliate)	W	L	OTL	SOL	Pts
*Grand Rapids (Det)	.55	20	1	4	115
†Syracuse (Clb)	.47	25	5	3	102
†Manitoba (Van)	.44	24	7	5	100
†Toronto (Tor)	.41	29	6	4	92
Rochester (Buf)	.37	39	2	2	78
Hamilton (Mon/Dal) . . .	.35	41	0	4	74
Cleveland (SJ)	.27	48	2	3	59

West Division

Team (Affiliate)	W	L	OTL	SOL	Pts
*Milwaukee (Nash)	.49	21	6	4	108
†Houston (Min)	.50	24	3	3	106
†Peoria (St. Louis)	.46	26	3	5	100
†Iowa (Dal/Edm)	.41	31	1	7	90
Chicago (Atl)	.36	32	4	.8	84
Omaha Ak-Sar-Ben (Calg)	35	31	3	11	84
San Antonio (Pho)	.23	50	3	4	53

Scoring Leaders

	Gm	G	A	Pts	PM
Kirby Law, Hou.	80	43	67	110	95
Erik Westrum, Hou	71	34	64	98	138
Jiri Hudler, GR	76	36	60	96	56
Patrick O'Sullivan, Hou	78	47	46	93	64
Darren Haydar, Mil.	80	35	57	92	50

Goaltending Leaders

(At least 1560 minutes)	GP	GAA	Sv%	Record
Dany Sabourin, WBS	.49	2.26	.922	30-14-4
Wade Flaherty, Man	.49	2.40	.919	26-17-4
Brent Krahn, Oma	.57	2.50	.912	26-20-9

Calder Cup Finals

	W-L	GF	Leading Scorers
Hershey	.4-2	25	Beech (6-3–9)
			& Fleischmann (2-7–9)
Milwaukee	.2-4	14	Haydar (4-3–7)

Date	Winner	Home Ice
June 2	.Milwaukee, 2-1	at Milwaukee
June 3	.Hershey, 6-3	at Milwaukee
June 10	.Milwaukee, 2-0	at Hershey
June 11	.Hershey, 7-2	at Hershey
June 11	.Hershey, 6-4	at Hershey
June 11	.Hershey, 5-1	at Milwaukee

Playoff MVP: Frederic Cassivi, Hershey, G

IIHF World Hockey Championships

Qualifying Round standings and Playoff Round results from the 2006 IIHF Men's World Hockey Championships held May 5-21 in Riga, Latvia. Top four teams from each group (*) advanced to the single-elimination Playoff Round.

Qualifying Round

	W-L-T	Pts	GF	GA
*Canada	.4-1-0	8	28	10
*Finland	.3-1-1	7	17	7
*United States	.3-2-0	6	11	10
*Czech Republic	.2-1-2	6	14	12
Latvia	.1-2-1	3	7	23
Norway	.0-5-0	0	5	20

	W-L-T	Pts	GF	GA
*Russia	.4-0-1	9	22	11
*Sweden	.2-1-2	6	17	15
*Belarus	.3-2-0	6	16	10
*Slovakia	.2-2-1	5	19	10
Switzerland	.1-2-2	4	12	15
Ukraine	.0-5-0	0	4	29

Quarterfinals

Sweden 6	United States 0
Canada 4	Slovakia 1
Czech Republic 4 . . . . .OT	Russia 3
Finland 3	Belarus 1

Semifinals

Czech Republic 3	Finland 1
Sweden 5	Canada 4

Bronze Medal Game

Finland 5	Canada 0

Gold Medal Game

Sweden 4	Czech Republic 0

All-Star Team (selected by media): **G—** Andrei Mezin, Belarus; **D—** Petteri Nummelin, Finland and Niklas Kronwall, Sweden (MVP); **F—** Sidney Crosby, Canada; David Vyborny, Czech Republic and Alexander Ovechkin, Russia.

Note: There was no IIHF Women's World Championships played in 2006 due to the Turin Olympics. They will resume in 2007.

1893-2006
Through the Years

SPORTS ALMANAC

The Stanley Cup

The Stanley Cup was originally donated to the Canadian Amateur Hockey Association by Sir Frederick Arthur Stanley, Lord Stanley of Preston and 16th Earl of Derby, who had become interested in the sport while Governor General of Canada from 1888 to 1893. Stanley wanted the trophy to be a challenge cup, contested for each year by the best amateur hockey teams in Canada.

In 1893, the Cup was presented without a challenge to the AHA champion Montreal Amateur Athletic Association team. Every year since, however, there has been a playoff. In 1914, Cup trustees limited the field challenging for the trophy to the champion of the eastern professional National Hockey Association (NHA, organized in 1910) and the western professional Pacific Coast Hockey Association (PCHA, organized in 1912).

The NHA disbanded in 1917 and the National Hockey League (NHL) was formed. From 1918 to 1926, the NHL and PCHA champions played for the Cup with the Western Canada Hockey League (WCHL) champion joining in a three-way challenge in 1923 and '24. The PCHA disbanded in 1924, while the WCHL became the Western Hockey League (WHL) for the 1925-26 season and folded the following year. The NHL playoffs have decided the winner of the Stanley Cup ever since.

Champions, 1893-1917

Multiple winners: Montreal Victorias and Montreal Wanderers (4); Montreal Amateur Athletic Association and Ottawa Silver Seven (3); Montreal Shamrocks, Ottawa Senators, Quebec Bulldogs and Winnipeg Victorias (2).

Year		Year		Year	
1893	Montreal AAA	1901	Winnipeg Victorias	1909	Ottawa Senators
1894	Montreal AAA	1902	Montreal AAA	1910	Montreal Wanderers
1895	Montreal Victorias	1903	Ottawa Silver Seven	1911	Ottawa Senators
1896	(Feb.) Winnipeg Victorias	1904	Ottawa Silver Seven	1912	Quebec Bulldogs
	(Dec.) Montreal Victorias	1905	Ottawa Silver Seven	1913	Quebec Bulldogs
1897	Montreal Victorias	1906	Montreal Wanderers	1914	Toronto Blueshirts (NHA)
1898	Montreal Victorias	1907	(Jan.) Kenora Thistles	1915	Vancouver Millionaires (PCHA)
1899	Montreal Shamrocks		(Mar.) Montreal Wanderers	1916	Montreal Canadiens (NHA)
1900	Montreal Shamrocks	1908	Montreal Wanderers	1917	Seattle Metropolitans (PCHA)

Champions Since 1918

Multiple winners: Montreal Canadiens (23); Toronto Arenas-St. Pats-Maple Leafs (13); Detroit Red Wings (10); Boston Bruins and Edmonton Oilers (5); NY Islanders, NY Rangers and Ottawa Senators (4); Chicago Blackhawks and New Jersey Devils (3); Colorado Avalanche, Montreal Maroons, Philadelphia Flyers and Pittsburgh Penguins (2).

Year	Winner	Head Coach	Series	Loser	Head Coach
1918	Toronto Arenas	Dick Carroll	3-2 (WLWLW)	Vancouver (PCHA)	Frank Patrick
1919	No Decision*				
1920	Ottawa	Pete Green	3-2 (WWLLW)	Seattle (PCHA)	Pete Muldoon
1921	Ottawa	Pete Green	3-2 (LWWLW)	Vancouver (PCHA)	Frank Patrick
1922	Toronto St. Pats	Eddie Powers	3-2 (LWLWW)	Vancouver (PCHA)	Frank Patrick
1923	Ottawa	Pete Green	3-1 (WLWW)	Vancouver (PCHA)	Frank Patrick
			2-0	Edmonton (WCHL)	K.C. McKenzie
1924	Montreal	Leo Dandurand	2-0	Vancouver (PCHA)	Frank Patrick
			2-0	Calgary (WCHL)	Eddie Oatman
1925	Victoria (WCHL)	Lester Patrick	3-1 (WWLW)	Montreal	Leo Dandurand
1926	Montreal Maroons	Eddie Gerard	3-1 (WWLW)	Victoria (WHL)	Lester Patrick
1927	Ottawa	Dave Gill	2-0-2 (TWTW)	Boston	Art Ross
1928	NY Rangers	Lester Patrick	3-2 (LWLWW)	Montreal Maroons	Eddie Gerard
1929	Boston	Cy Denneny	2-0	NY Rangers	Lester Patrick
1930	Montreal	Cecil Hart	2-0	Boston	Art Ross
1931	Montreal	Cecil Hart	3-2 (WLLWW)	Chicago	Art Duncan
1932	Toronto	Dick Irvin	3-0	NY Rangers	Lester Patrick
1933	NY Rangers	Lester Patrick	3-1 (WWLW)	Toronto	Dick Irvin
1934	Chicago	Tommy Gorman	3-1 (WWLW)	Detroit	Jack Adams
1935	Montreal Maroons	Tommy Gorman	3-0	Toronto	Dick Irvin
1936	Detroit	Jack Adams	3-1 (WWLW)	Toronto	Dick Irvin
1937	Detroit	Jack Adams	3-2 (LWLWW)	NY Rangers	Lester Patrick
1938	Chicago	Bill Stewart	3-1 (WLWW)	Toronto	Dick Irvin
1939	Boston	Art Ross	4-1 (WLWWW)	Toronto	Dick Irvin

* The 1919 finals were cancelled after five games due to an influenza epidemic with Montreal and Seattle (PCHA) tied at 2-2-1.

The Stanley Cup (Cont.)

Year	Winner	Head Coach	Series	Loser	Head Coach
1940	NY Rangers	Frank Boucher	4-2 (WWLLWW)	Toronto	Dick Irvin
1941	Boston	Cooney Weiland	4-0	Detroit	Jack Adams
1942	Toronto	Hap Day	4-3 (LLLWWWW)	Detroit	Jack Adams
1943	Detroit	Ebbie Goodfellow	4-0	Boston	Art Ross
1944	Montreal	Dick Irvin	4-0	Chicago	Paul Thompson
1945	Toronto	Hap Day	4-3 (WWWWLLLW)	Detroit	Jack Adams
1946	Montreal	Dick Irvin	4-1 (WWWLW)	Boston	Dit Clapper
1947	Toronto	Hap Day	4-2 (LWWWLW)	Montreal	Dick Irvin
1948	Toronto	Hap Day	4-0	Detroit	Tommy Ivan
1949	Toronto	Hap Day	4-0	Detroit	Tommy Ivan
1950	Detroit	Tommy Ivan	4-3 (WLWLLWW)	NY Rangers	Lynn Patrick
1951	Toronto	Joe Primeau	4-1 (WLWWW)	Montreal	Dick Irvin
1952	Detroit	Tommy Ivan	4-0	Montreal	Dick Irvin
1953	Montreal	Dick Irvin	4-1 (WLWWW)	Boston	Lynn Patrick
1954	Detroit	Tommy Ivan	4-3 (WLWWLLW)	Montreal	Dick Irvin
1955	Detroit	Jimmy Skinner	4-3 (WWLWLW)	Montreal	Dick Irvin
1956	Montreal	Toe Blake	4-1 (WWWLW)	Detroit	Jimmy Skinner
1957	Montreal	Toe Blake	4-1 (WWWLW)	Boston	Milt Schmidt
1958	Montreal	Toe Blake	4-2 (WLWLWW)	Boston	Milt Schmidt
1959	Montreal	Toe Blake	4-1 (WWLWW)	Toronto	Punch Imlach
1960	Montreal	Toe Blake	4-0	Toronto	Punch Imlach
1961	Chicago	Rudy Pilous	4-2 (WLWLWW)	Detroit	Sid Abel
1962	Toronto	Punch Imlach	4-2 (WWWLLW)	Chicago	Rudy Pilous
1963	Toronto	Punch Imlach	4-1 (WWLWW)	Detroit	Sid Abel
1964	Toronto	Punch Imlach	4-3 (WLLWLWW)	Detroit	Sid Abel
1965	Montreal	Toe Blake	4-3 (WWWLLW)	Chicago	Billy Reay
1966	Montreal	Toe Blake	4-2 (LLWWWW)	Detroit	Sid Abel
1967	Toronto	Punch Imlach	4-2 (LWWLWW)	Montreal	Toe Blake
1968	Montreal	Toe Blake	4-0	St. Louis	Scotty Bowman
1969	Montreal	Claude Ruel	4-0	St. Louis	Scotty Bowman
1970	Boston	Harry Sinden	4-0	St. Louis	Scotty Bowman
1971	Montreal	Al MacNeil	4-3 (LLWWLWW)	Chicago	Billy Reay
1972	Boston	Tom Johnson	4-2 (WWLWLW)	NY Rangers	Emile Francis
1973	Montreal	Scotty Bowman	4-2 (WWLWLW)	Chicago	Billy Reay
1974	Philadelphia	Fred Shero	4-2 (LWWWLW)	Boston	Bep Guidolin
1975	Philadelphia	Fred Shero	4-2 (WWLLWW)	Buffalo	Floyd Smith
1976	Montreal	Scotty Bowman	4-0	Philadelphia	Fred Shero
1977	Montreal	Scotty Bowman	4-0	Boston	Don Cherry
1978	Montreal	Scotty Bowman	4-2 (WLWWLW)	Boston	Don Cherry
1979	Montreal	Scotty Bowman	4-1 (LWWWW)	NY Rangers	Fred Shero
1980	NY Islanders	Al Arbour	4-2 (WLWWLW)	Philadelphia	Pat Quinn
1981	NY Islanders	Al Arbour	4-1 (WWWLW)	Minnesota	Glen Sonmor
1982	NY Islanders	Al Arbour	4-0	Vancouver	Roger Neilson
1983	NY Islanders	Al Arbour	4-0	Edmonton	Glen Sather
1984	Edmonton	Glen Sather	4-1 (WLWWW)	NY Islanders	Al Arbour
1985	Edmonton	Glen Sather	4-1 (LWWWW)	Philadelphia	Mike Keenan
1986	Montreal	Jean Perron	4-1 (LWWWW)	Calgary	Bob Johnson
1987	Edmonton	Glen Sather	4-3 (WWLWLLW)	Philadelphia	Mike Keenan
1988	Edmonton	Glen Sather	4-0	Boston	Terry O'Reilly
1989	Calgary	Terry Crisp	4-2 (WLLWWW)	Montreal	Pat Burns
1990	Edmonton	John Muckler	4-1 (WWLWW)	Boston	Mike Milbury
1991	Pittsburgh	Bob Johnson	4-2 (LWLWWW)	Minnesota	Bob Gainey
1992	Pittsburgh	Scotty Bowman	4-0	Chicago	Mike Keenan
1993	Montreal	Jacques Demers	4-1 (LWWWW)	Los Angeles	Barry Melrose
1994	NY Rangers	Mike Keenan	4-3 (LWWWLLW)	Vancouver	Pat Quinn
1995	New Jersey	Jacques Lemaire	4-0	Detroit	Scotty Bowman
1996	Colorado	Marc Crawford	4-0	Florida	Doug MacLean
1997	Detroit	Scotty Bowman	4-0	Philadelphia	Terry Murray
1998	Detroit	Scotty Bowman	4-0	Washington	Ron Wilson
1999	Dallas	Ken Hitchcock	4-2 (LWLWWW)	Buffalo	Lindy Ruff
2000	New Jersey	Larry Robinson	4-2 (WLWWLW)	Dallas	Ken Hitchcock
2001	Colorado	Bob Hartley	4-3 (WLWLWLW)	New Jersey	Larry Robinson
2002	Detroit	Scotty Bowman	4-1 (LWWWW)	Carolina	Paul Maurice
2003	New Jersey	Pat Burns	4-3 (WWLLWLW)	Anaheim	Mike Babcock
2004	Tampa Bay	John Tortorella	4-3 (LWLWLWW)	Calgary	Darryl Sutter
2005	Not held*				
2006	Carolina	Peter Laviolette	4-3 (WWLWLLW)	Edmonton	Craig MacTavish

* The lack of a labor agreement between the owners and NHLPA and the ensuing owners' lockout, canceled the 2004-05 season.

M.J. O'Brien Trophy

Donated by Canadian mining magnate M.J. O'Brien, whose son Ambrose founded the National Hockey Association in 1910. Originally presented to the NHA champion until the league's demise in 1917, the trophy then passed to the NHL champion through 1927. It was awarded to the NHL's Canadian Division winner from 1927-38 and the Stanley Cup runner-up from 1939-50 before being retired in 1950.

NHA winners included the Montreal Wanderers (1910), original Ottawa Senators (1911 and '15), Quebec Bulldogs (1912 and '13), Toronto Blueshirts (1914) and Montreal Canadiens (1916 and '17).

Conn Smythe Trophy

The Most Valuable Player of the Stanley Cup Playoffs, as selected by the Pro Hockey Writers Association. Presented since 1965 by Maple Leaf Gardens Limited in the name of the former Toronto coach, GM and owner, Conn Smythe. Winners who did not play for the Cup champion are in **bold** type.

Multiple winners: Patrick Roy (3); Wayne Gretzky, Mario Lemieux, Bobby Orr and Bernie Parent (2).

Year		Year		Year	
1965	Jean Beliveau, Mon., C	1979	Bob Gainey, Mon., LW	1993	Patrick Roy, Mon., G
1966	**Roger Crozier**, Det., G	1980	Bryan Trottier, NYI, C	1994	Brian Leetch, NYR, D
1967	Dave Keon, Tor., C	1981	Butch Goring, NYI, C	1995	Claude Lemieux, NJ, RW
1968	**Glenn Hall**, St.L., G	1982	Mike Bossy, NYI, RW	1996	Joe Sakic, Col., C
1969	Serge Savard, Mon., D	1983	Billy Smith, NYI, G	1997	Mike Vernon, Det., G
1970	Bobby Orr, Bos., D	1984	Mark Messier, Edm., LW	1998	Steve Yzerman, Det., C
1971	Ken Dryden, Mon., G	1985	Wayne Gretzky, Edm., C	1999	Joe Nieuwendyk, Dal., C
1972	Bobby Orr, Bos., D	1986	Patrick Roy, Mon., G	2000	Scott Stevens, NJ, D
1973	Yvan Cournoyer, Mon., RW	1987	**Ron Hextall**, Phi., G	2001	Patrick Roy, Col., G
1974	Bernie Parent, Phi., G	1988	Wayne Gretzky, Edm., C	2002	Nicklas Lidstrom, Det., D
1975	Bernie Parent, Phi., G	1989	Al MacInnis, Calg., D	2003	**J-S Giguere**, Ana., G
1976	**Reggie Leach**, Phi., RW	1990	Bill Ranford, Edm., G	2004	Brad Richards, TB, C
1977	Guy Lafleur, Mon., RW	1991	Mario Lemieux, Pit., C	2005	Not awarded
1978	Larry Robinson, Mon., D	1992	Mario Lemieux, Pit., C	2006	Cam Ward, Car., G

Note: Ken Dryden (1971), Patrick Roy (1986), Ron Hextall (1987) and Cam Ward (2006) are the only players to win as rookies.

All-Time Stanley Cup Playoff Leaders
CAREER

Stanley Cup Playoff leaders through 2006. Years listed indicate number of playoff appearances. Players active in 2005-06 are in **bold** type; (DNP) indicates player that was active in 2005-06 but did not participate in playoffs.

Scoring

Points

		Yrs	Gm	G	A	Pts
1	Wayne Gretzky	16	208	122	260	382
2	Mark Messier	17	236	109	186	295
3	Jari Kurri	14	200	106	127	233
4	Glenn Anderson	15	225	93	121	214
5	Paul Coffey	16	194	59	137	196
6	**Brett Hull** (DNP)	19	202	103	87	190
7	Doug Gilmour	17	182	60	128	188
8	**Steve Yzerman**	20	196	70	115	185
9	Bryan Trottier	17	221	71	113	184
10	Ray Bourque	21	214	41	139	180
11	**Joe Sakic**	12	162	82	96	178
12	Jean Beliveau	17	162	79	97	176
13	Denis Savard	16	169	66	109	175
14	**Mario Lemieux** (DNP)	8	107	76	96	172
15	Denis Potvin	14	185	56	108	164
16	**Sergei Fedorov** (DNP)	13	162	50	113	163
17	**Peter Forsberg**	11	139	61	101	162
18	Mike Bossy	10	129	85	75	160
	Gordie Howe	20	157	68	92	160
	Bobby Smith	13	184	64	96	160
	Al MacInnis	19	177	39	121	160
22	Claude Lemieux	17	233	80	78	158
23	Adam Oates	15	163	42	114	156
24	**Jaromir Jagr**	13	149	67	88	155
25	Larry Murphy	20	215	37	115	152

Goals

		Yrs	Gm	G
1	Wayne Gretzky	16	208	122
2	Mark Messier	17	236	109
3	Jari Kurri	15	200	106
4	**Brett Hull** (DNP)	19	202	103
5	Glenn Anderson	15	225	93
6	Mike Bossy	10	129	85
7	Maurice Richard	15	133	82
	Joe Sakic	12	162	82
9	Claude Lemieux	17	233	80
10	Jean Beliveau	17	162	79

Assists

		Yrs	Gm	A
1	Wayne Gretzky	16	208	260
2	Mark Messier	17	236	186
3	Ray Bourque	21	214	139
4	Paul Coffey	16	194	137
5	Doug Gilmour	17	182	128
6	Jari Kurri	15	200	127
7	Glenn Anderson	15	225	121
	Al MacInnis	19	177	121
9	Larry Robinson	20	227	116
10	**Steve Yzerman**	20	196	115
	Larry Murphy	20	215	115

The Stanley Cup (Cont.)

Goaltending
Wins

		Gm	W-L	Pct	GAA
1	Patrick Roy	247	151-94	.616	2.30
2	Grant Fuhr	150	92-50	.648	2.92
3	**Martin Brodeur**	153	89-64	.582	1.89
4	Billy Smith	132	88-36	.710	2.73
	Ed Belfour (DNP)	161	88-68	.564	2.17
6	Ken Dryden	112	80-32	.714	2.40
7	Mike Vernon	138	77-56	.579	2.68
8	Jacques Plante	112	71-37	.657	2.17
9	Andy Moog	132	68-57	.544	3.04
10	**Curtis Joseph** (DNP)	131	62-66	.484	2.44

Shutouts

		Gm	GAA	No
1	Patrick Roy	247	2.30	23
2	**Martin Brodeur**	153	1.89	21
3	**Curtis Joseph** (DNP)	131	2.44	16
4	Clint Benedict	48	1.80	15
	Jacques Plante	112	2.17	15

Appearances in Cup Finals

Standings of all teams that have reached the Stanley Cup championship round, since 1918.

App		Cups	Last Won
32	Montreal Canadiens	23 *	1993
22	Detroit Red Wings	10	2002
21	Toronto Maple Leafs	13 †	1967
17	Boston Bruins	5	1972
10	New York Rangers	4	1994
10	Chicago Blackhawks	3	1961
7	Edmonton Oilers	5	1990
7	Philadelphia Flyers	2	1975
5	New York Islanders	4	1983
5	Vancouver Millionaires (PCHA)	0	—
4	(original) Ottawa Senators	4	1927
4	Minnesota/Dallas (North) Stars	1	1999
4	New Jersey Devils	3	2003
3	Montreal Maroons	2	1935
3	Calgary Flames	1	1989
3	St. Louis Blues	0	—
2	Colorado Avalanche	2	2001
2	Pittsburgh Penguins	2	1992
2	Carolina Hurricanes	1	2006
2	Victoria Cougars (WCHL-WHL)	1	1925
2	Buffalo Sabres	0	—
2	Seattle Metropolitans (PCHA)	0	—
2	Vancouver Canucks	0	—
1	Tampa Bay Lightning	1	2004
1	Mighty Ducks of Anaheim	0	—
1	Calgary Tigers (WCHL)	0	—
1	Edmonton Eskimos (WCHL)	0	—
1	Florida Panthers	0	—
1	Los Angeles Kings	0	—
1	Washington Capitals	0	—

*Les Canadiens also won the Cup in 1916 for a total of 24. Also, their final with Seattle in 1919 was cancelled due to an influenza epidemic that claimed the life of the Habs' Joe Hall.

†Toronto has won the Cup under three nicknames— Arenas (1918), St. Pats (1922) and Maple Leafs (1932,42,45,47-49,51,62-64,67).

Teams now defunct (7): Calgary Tigers, Edmonton Eskimos, Montreal Maroons, (original) Ottawa Senators, Seattle, Vancouver Millionaires and Victoria. Edmonton (1923) and Calgary (1924) represented the WCHL and later the WHL, while Vancouver (1918,1921-24) and Seattle (1919-20) played out of the PCHA.

Goals Against Average
Minimum of 50 games played

		Gm	Min	GA	GAA
1	**Martin Brodeur**	153	9533	300	1.89
2	George Hainsworth	52	3486	112	1.93
3	Turk Broda	101	6389	211	1.98
4	**Dominik Hasek** (DNP)	97	5972	202	2.03
5	Jacques Plante	112	6652	240	2.16
6	**Ed Belfour** (DNP)	161	9945	359	2.17
7	**Chris Osgood** (DNP)	87	5085	190	2.24
8	**N. Khabibulin** (DNP)	57	3464	131	2.27
9	Patrick Roy	247	15209	584	2.30
10	Ken Dryden	112	6846	274	2.40

Note: Clint Benedict had an average of 1.80 but played in only 48 games.

Games Played

		Yrs	Gm
1	Patrick Roy, Mon-Col	17	247
2	**Ed Belfour**, Chi-Dal-Tor (DNP)	13	161
3	**Martin Brodeur**, New Jersey	12	153
4	Grant Fuhr, Edm-Buf-St.L	14	150
5	Mike Vernon, Calg-Det-SJ-Fla	14	138

Miscellaneous
Championships

		Yrs	Cups
1	Henri Richard, Montreal	18	11
2	Yvan Cournoyer, Montreal	15	10
	Jean Beliveau, Montreal	17	10
4	Claude Provost, Montreal	14	9
5	Jacques Lemaire, Montreal	11	8
	Maurice Richard, Montreal	15	8
	Red Kelly, Detroit-Toronto	19	8

Years in Playoffs

		Yrs	Gm
1	**Chris Chelios**, Mon-Chi-Det	21	228
	Ray Bourque, Boston-Colorado	21	214
3	Gordie Howe, Detroit-Hartford	20	157
	Larry Robinson, Montreal-Los Angeles	20	227
	Larry Murphy, LA-Wash-Min-Pit-Tor-Det	20	215
	Scott Stevens, Wash-St.L-NJ	20	233
	Steve Yzerman, Detroit	20	196

Games Played

		Yrs	Gm
1	Patrick Roy, Montreal-Colorado	17	247
2	Mark Messier, Edm-NYR-Van	17	236
3	Claude Lemieux, Mon-NJ-Col-Pho-Dal	17	233
	Scott Stevens, Wash-St.L-NJ	20	233
5	Guy Carbonneau, Mon-St.L-Dal	17	231

Penalty Minutes

		Yrs	Gm	Min
1	Dale Hunter, Que-Wash-Col	18	186	729
2	Chris Nilan, Mon-NYR-Bos-Mon	12	111	541
3	Claude Lemieux, Mon-NJ-Col-Pho-Dal	17	233	529
4	Rick Tocchet, Phi-Pit-Bos-Pho	13	145	471
5	Willi Plett, Atl-Calg-Min-Bos	10	83	466

SINGLE SEASON

Points

		Year	Gm	G	A	Pts
1	Wayne Gretzky, Edm	1985	18	17	30	47
2	Mario Lemieux, Pit	1991	23	16	28	44
3	Wayne Gretzky, Edm	1988	19	12	31	43
4	Wayne Gretzky, LA	1993	24	15	25	40
5	Wayne Gretzky, Edm	1983	16	12	26	38
6	Paul Coffey, Edm	1985	18	12	25	37
7	Mike Bossy, NYI	1981	18	17	18	35
	Wayne Gretzky, Edm	1984	19	13	22	35
	Doug Gilmour, Tor	1993	21	10	25	35
10	Six tied with 34 each.					

Goals

		Year	Gm	No
1	Reggie Leach, Philadelphia	1976	16	19
	Jari Kurri, Edmonton	1985	18	19
3	Joe Sakic, Colorado	1996	22	18
4	Seven tied with 17 each, incl. 3 times by Mike Bossy.			

Assists

		Year	Gm	No
1	Wayne Gretzky, Edmonton	1988	19	31
2	Wayne Gretzky, Edmonton	1985	18	30
3	Wayne Gretzky, Edmonton	1987	21	29
4	Mario Lemieux, Pittsburgh	1991	23	28
5	Wayne Gretzky, Edmonton	1983	16	26

Goaltending

Wins

1 Sixteen tied with 16 each.

Shutouts

		Year	Gm	No
1	Martin Brodeur, New Jersey	2003	24	7
2	Dominik Hasek, Detroit	2002	23	6
3	J-S Giguere, Anaheim	2003	21	5
	Nikolai Khabibulin, Tampa Bay	2004	23	5
	Miikka Kiprusoff, Calgary	2004	26	5

Goals Against Average

	(Min. 8 games played)	Year	Gm	Min	GA	GAA
1	Terry Sawchuk, Det	1952	8	480	5	0.63
2	Clint Benedict, Mon-M	1928	9	555	8	0.89
3	Turk Broda, Tor	1951	9	509	9	1.06
4	Dave Kerr, NYR	1937	9	553	10	1.11
5	Jacques Plante, Mon	1960	8	489	11	1.35

Note: Average determined by games played through 1942-43 season and by minutes played since then.

SINGLE SERIES

Points

	Year	Rd	G-A—Pts
Rick Middleton, Bos vs Buf	1983	DF	5-14—19
Wayne Gretzky, Edm vs Chi	1985	CF	4-14—18
Mario Lemieux, Pit vs Wash	1992	DSF	7-10—17
Barry Pederson, Bos vs Buf	1983	DF	7-9—16
Doug Gilmour, Tor vs SJ	1994	CSF	3-13—16

Goals

	Year	Rd	No
Jari Kurri, Edm vs Chi	1985	CF	12
Newsy Lalonde, Mon vs Ott	1919	SF*	11
Tim Kerr, Phi vs Pit	1989	DF	10
Five tied with 9 each.			

*NHL final prior to Stanley Cup series with Seattle (PCHA).

Assists

	Year	Rd	No
Rick Middleton, Bos vs Buf	1983	DF	14
Wayne Gretzky, Edm vs Chi	1985	CF	14
Wayne Gretzky, Edm vs LA	1987	DSF	13
Doug Gilmour, Tor vs SJ	1994	CSF	13
Four tied with 11 each.			

SINGLE GAME

Points

	Date	G	A	Pts
Patrik Sundstrom, NJ vs Wash	4/22/88	3	5	8
Mario Lemieux, Pit vs Phi	4/25/89	5	3	8
Wayne Gretzky, Edm at Calg	4/17/83	4	3	7
Wayne Gretzky, Edm at Win	4/25/85	3	4	7
Wayne Gretzky, Edm vs LA	4/9/87	1	6	7

Goals

	Date	No
Newsy Lalonde, Mon vs Ott	3/1/19	5
Maurice Richard, Mon vs Tor	3/23/44	5
Darryl Sittler, Tor vs Phi	4/22/76	5
Reggie Leach, Phi vs Bos	5/6/76	5
Mario Lemieux, Pit vs Phi	4/25/89	5

Assists

	Date	No
Mikko Leinonen, NYR vs Phi	4/8/82	6
Wayne Gretzky, Edm vs LA	4/9/87	6
11 tied with 5 each.		

NHL All-Star Game

Three benefit NHL All-Star Games were staged in the 1930s for forward Ace Bailey and the families of Howie Morenz and Babe Siebert. Bailey, of Toronto, suffered a fractured skull on a career-ending check by Boston's Eddie Shore. Morenz, the Montreal Canadiens' legend, died of a heart attack at 35 after a severely broken leg ended his career. Siebert, who played with both Montreal teams, drowned at age 35.

The All-Star Game was revived at the start of the 1947-48 season as an annual exhibition match between the defending Stanley Cup champion and all-stars from the league's other five teams. The format has changed several times since then. The game was moved to midseason in 1966-67 and became an East vs. West contest in 1968-69. The Eastern (East, 1968-1974; Wales, 1975-93) Conference leads the series 19-8-1. From 1998-2002, the East-West format was abandoned for one pitting North America vs. the rest of the world (N. America leads that series 3-2). In 2003 the game returned to East vs. West. Beginning in 2006, the game will no longer be played during Olympic years.

Benefit Games

Date	Occasion		Host	Coaches
2/14/34	Ace Bailey Benefit	Toronto 7, All-Stars 3	Toronto	Dick Irvin, Lester Patrick
11/3/37	Howie Morenz Memorial	All-Stars 6, Montreals* 5	Montreal	Jack Adams, Cecil Hart
10/29/39	Babe Seibert Memorial	All-Stars 5, Canadiens 3	Montreal	Art Ross, Pit Lepine

*Combined squad of Montreal Canadiens and Montreal Maroons.

NHL All-Star Game (Cont.)

All-Star Games

Multiple MVP winners: Wayne Gretzky and Mario Lemieux (3); Bobby Hull and Frank Mahovlich (2).

Year		Host	Coaches	Most Valuable Player
1947	All-Stars 4, Toronto 3	Toronto	Dick Irvin, Hap Day	No award
1948	All-Stars 3, Toronto 1	Chicago	Tommy Ivan, Hap Day	No award
1949	All-Stars 3, Toronto 1	Toronto	Tommy Ivan, Hap Day	No award
1950	Detroit 7, All-Stars 1	Detroit	Tommy Ivan, Lynn Patrick	No award
1951	1st Team 2, 2nd Team 2	Toronto	Joe Primeau, Hap Day	No award
1952	1st Team 1, 2nd Team 1	Detroit	Tommy Ivan, Dick Irvin	No award
1953	All-Stars 3, Montreal 1	Montreal	Lynn Patrick, Dick Irvin	No award
1954	All-Stars 2, Detroit 2	Detroit	King Clancy, Jim Skinner	No award
1955	Detroit 3, All-Stars 1	Detroit	Jim Skinner, Dick Irvin	No award
1956	All-Stars 1, Montreal 1	Montreal	Jim Skinner, Toe Blake	No award
1957	All-Stars 5, Montreal 3	Montreal	Milt Schmidt, Toe Blake	No award
1958	Montreal 6, All-Stars 3	Montreal	Toe Blake, Milt Schmidt	No award
1959	Montreal 6, All-Stars 1	Montreal	Toe Blake, Punch Imlach	No award
1960	All-Stars 2, Montreal 1	Montreal	Punch Imlach, Toe Blake	No award
1961	All-Stars 3, Chicago 1	Chicago	Sid Abel, Rudy Pilous	No award
1962	Toronto 4, All-Stars 1	Toronto	Punch Imlach, Rudy Pilous	Eddie Shack, Tor., RW
1963	All-Stars 3, Toronto 3	Toronto	Sid Abel, Punch Imlach	Frank Mahovlich, Tor., LW
1964	All-Stars 3, Toronto 2	Toronto	Sid Abel, Punch Imlach	Jean Beliveau, Mon., C
1965	All-Stars 5, Montreal 2	Montreal	Billy Reay, Toe Blake	Gordie Howe, Det., RW
1966	No game (see below)			
1967	Montreal 3, All-Stars 0	Montreal	Toe Blake, Sid Abel	Henri Richard, Mon., C
1968	Toronto 4, All-Stars 3	Toronto	Punch Imlach, Toe Blake	Bruce Gamble, Tor., G
1969	West 3, East 3	Montreal	Scotty Bowman, Toe Blake	Frank Mahovlich, Det., LW
1970	East 4, West 1	St. Louis	Claude Ruel, Scotty Bowman	Bobby Hull, Chi., LW
1971	West 2, East 1	Boston	Scotty Bowman, Harry Sinden	Bobby Hull, Chi., LW
1972	East 3, West 2	Minnesota	Al MacNeil, Billy Reay	Bobby Orr, Bos., D
1973	East 5, West 4	NY Rangers	Tom Johnson, Billy Reay	Greg Polis, Pit., LW
1974	West 6, East 4	Chicago	Billy Reay, Scotty Bowman	Garry Unger, St.L., C
1975	Wales 7, Campbell 1	Montreal	Bep Guidolin, Fred Shero	Syl Apps Jr., Pit., C
1976	Wales 7, Campbell 5	Philadelphia	Floyd Smith, Fred Shero	Peter Mahovlich, Mon., C
1977	Wales 4, Campbell 3	Vancouver	Scotty Bowman, Fred Shero	Rick Martin, Buf., LW
1978	Wales 3, Campbell 2 (OT)	Buffalo	Scotty Bowman, Fred Shero	Billy Smith, NYI, G
1979	No game (see below)			
1980	Wales 6, Campbell 3	Detroit	Scotty Bowman, Al Arbour	Reggie Leach, Phi., RW
1981	Campbell 4, Wales 1	Los Angeles	Pat Quinn, Scotty Bowman	Mike Liut, St.L., G
1982	Wales 4, Campbell 2	Washington	Al Arbour, Glen Sonmor	Mike Bossy, NYI, RW
1983	Campbell 9, Wales 3	NY Islanders	Roger Neilson, Al Arbour	Wayne Gretzky, Edm., C
1984	Wales 7, Campbell 6	New Jersey	Al Arbour, Glen Sather	Don Maloney, NYR, LW
1985	Wales 6, Campbell 4	Calgary	Al Arbour, Glen Sather	Mario Lemieux, Pit., C
1986	Wales 4, Campbell 3 (OT)	Hartford	Mike Keenan, Glen Sather	Grant Fuhr, Edm., G
1987	No game (see below)			
1988	Wales 6, Campbell 5 (OT)	St. Louis	Mike Keenan, Glen Sather	Mario Lemieux, Pit., C
1989	Campbell 9, Wales 5	Edmonton	Glen Sather, Terry O'Reilly	Wayne Gretzky, LA, C
1990	Wales 12, Campbell 7	Pittsburgh	Pat Burns, Terry Crisp	Mario Lemieux, Pit., C
1991	Campbell 11, Wales 5	Chicago	John Muckler, Mike Milbury	Vincent Damphousse, Tor., LW
1992	Campbell 10, Wales 6	Philadelphia	Bob Gainey, Scotty Bowman	Brett Hull, St.L., RW
1993	Wales 16, Campbell 6	Montreal	Scotty Bowman, Mike Keenan	Mike Gartner, NYR, RW
1994	East 9, West 8	NY Rangers	Jacques Demers, Barry Melrose	Mike Richter, NYR, G
1995	No game (see below)			
1996	East 5, West 4	Boston	Doug MacLean, Scotty Bowman	Ray Bourque, Bos., D
1997	East 11, West 7	San Jose	Doug MacLean, Ken Hitchcock	Mark Recchi, Mon., RW
1998	North America 8, World 7	Vancouver	Jacques Lemaire, Ken Hitchcock	Teemu Selanne, Ana., RW
1999	North America 8, World 6	Tampa	Ken Hitchcock, Lindy Ruff	Wayne Gretzky, NYR, C
2000	World 9, North America 4	Toronto	Scotty Bowman, Pat Quinn	Pavel Bure, Fla., RW
2001	North America 14, World 12	Denver	Joel Quenneville, Jacques Martin	Bill Guerin, Bos., RW
2002	World 8, North America 5	Los Angeles	Scotty Bowman, Pat Quinn	Eric Daze, Chi., LW
2003	West 6, East 5 (OT)†	Florida	Marc Crawford, Jacques Martin	Dany Heatley, Atl., RW
2004	East 6, West 4	Minnesota	Pat Quinn, Dave Lewis	Joe Sakic, Col., C
2005	No game (see below)			
2006	No game (see below)			

†After a five-minute scoreless overtime, the game was settled by a shootout. The West outscored the East, 3-1.

No All-Star Game: in 1966 (moved from start of season to mid-season); in 1979 (replaced by Challenge Cup series with USSR); in 1987 (replaced by Rendez-Vous '87 series with USSR); in 1995 (canceled when NHL lockout shortened season to 48 games); in 2005 (NHL lockout canceled the entire season); in 2006 (game no longer played in Olympic years).

NHL Franchise Origins

Here is what the current 30 teams in the National Hockey League have to show for the years they have put in as members of the NHL, the early National Hockey Association (NHA) and the more recent World Hockey Association (WHA). League titles and Stanley Cup championships are noted by year won. The Stanley Cup has automatically gone to the NHL champion since the 1926-27 season. Following the 1992-93 season, the NHL renamed the Clarence Campbell Conference the Western Conference, while the Prince of Wales Conference became the Eastern Conference.

Western Conference

	First Season	League Titles	Franchise Stops
Anaheim Ducks	1993-94 (NHL)	None	•Anaheim, CA (1993—)
Calgary Flames	1972-73 (NHL)	1 Cup (1989)	•Atlanta (1972-80)
			Calgary (1980—)
Chicago Blackhawks	1926-27 (NHL)	3 Cups (1934,38,61)	•Chicago (1926—)
Colorado Avalanche	1972-73 (WHA)	1 WHA (1977)	•Quebec City (1972-95)
		2 Cups (1996, 2001)	Denver (1995—)
Columbus Blue Jackets	2000-01 (NHL)	None	•Columbus, OH (2000—)
Dallas Stars	1967-68 (NHL)	1 Cup (1999)	•Bloomington, MN (1967-93)
			Dallas (1993—)
Detroit Red Wings	1926-27 (NHL)	10 Cups (1936-37,43,50,52,54-	•Detroit (1926—)
		55,97,98, 2002)	
Edmonton Oilers	1972-73 (WHA)	5 Cups (1984-85,87-88,90)	•Edmonton (1972—)
Los Angeles Kings	1967-68 (NHL)	None	•Inglewood, CA (1967-99)
			Los Angeles (1999—)
Minnesota Wild	2000-01 (NHL)	None	•St. Paul, MN (2000—)
Nashville Predators	1998-99 (NHL)	None	•Nashville, TN (1998—)
Phoenix Coyotes	1972-73 (WHA)	3 WHA (1976, 78-79)	•Winnipeg (1972-96)
			Phoenix (1996—)
St. Louis Blues	1967-68 (NHL)	None	•St. Louis (1967—)
San Jose Sharks	1991-92 (NHL)	None	•San Francisco (1991-93)
			San Jose (1993—)
Vancouver Canucks	1970-71 (NHL)	None	•Vancouver (1970—)

Eastern Conference

	First Season	League Titles	Franchise Stops
Atlanta Thrashers	1999-00 (NHL)	None	•Atlanta (1999—)
Boston Bruins	1924-25 (NHL)	5 Cups (1929,39,41,70,72)	•Boston (1924—)
Buffalo Sabres	1970-71 (NHL)	None	•Buffalo (1970—)
Carolina Hurricanes	1972-73 (WHA)	1 WHA (1973)	•Boston (1972-74)
		1 Cup (2006)	W. Springfield, MA (1974-75)
			Hartford, CT (1975-78)
			Springfield, MA (1978-80)
			Hartford (1980-97)
			Greensboro, NC (1997-99)
			Raleigh, NC (1999—)
Florida Panthers	1993-94 (NHL)	None	•Miami (1993-98)
			Sunrise, FL (1998—)
Montreal Canadiens	1909-10 (NHA)	2 NHA (1916-17)	•Montreal (1909—)
		2 NHL (1924-25)	
		24 Cups (1916,24,30-	
		31,44,46,53,56-60,65-66,68-	
		69,71,73,76-79,86,93)	
New Jersey Devils	1974-75 (NHL)	3 Cups (1995, 2000,03)	•Kansas City (1974-76)
			Denver (1976-82)
			E. Rutherford, NJ (1982—)
New York Islanders	1972-73 (NHL)	4 Cups (1980-83)	•Uniondale, NY (1972—)
New York Rangers	1926-27 (NHL)	4 Cups (1928,33,40,94)	•New York (1926—)
Ottawa Senators	1992-93 (NHL)	None	•Ottawa (1992-1996)
			Kanata, Ont. (1996—)
Philadelphia Flyers	1967-68 (NHL)	2 Cups (1974-75)	•Philadelphia (1967—)
Pittsburgh Penguins	1967-68 (NHL)	2 Cups (1991-92)	•Pittsburgh (1967—)
Tampa Bay Lightning	1992-93 (NHL)	1 Cup (2004)	•Tampa, FL (1992-93)
			St. Petersburg, FL (1993-96)
			Tampa, FL (1996—)
Toronto Maple Leafs	1916-17 (NHA)	2 NHL (1918,22)	•Toronto (1916—)
		13 Cups (1918,22,32,42,45,	
		47-49,51,62-64,67)	
Washington Capitals	1974-75 (NHL)	None	•Landover, MD (1974-97)
			Washington, D.C. (1997—)

Note: The Hartford Civic Center roof collapsed after a snowstorm in January 1978, forcing the Whalers to move their home games to Springfield, Mass., for two years.

The Growth of the NHL

Of the four franchises that comprised the National Hockey League (NHL) at the start of the 1917-18 season, only two remain—the Montreal Canadiens and the Toronto Maple Leafs (originally the Toronto Arenas). From 1919-26, eight new teams joined the league, but only four—the Boston Bruins, Chicago Blackhawks (originally Black Hawks), Detroit Red Wings (originally Cougars) and New York Rangers—survived.

It was 41 years before the NHL expanded again, doubling in size for the 1967-68 season with new teams in Bloomington (Minn.), Los Angeles, Oakland, Philadelphia, Pittsburgh and St. Louis. The league had 16 clubs by the start of the 1972-73 season, but it also had a rival in the **World Hockey Association,** which debuted that year with 12 teams.

The NHL added two more teams in 1974 and merged the struggling Cleveland Barons (originally the Oakland Seals) and Minnesota North Stars in 1978, before absorbing four WHA clubs—the Edmonton Oilers, Hartford Whalers, Quebec Nordiques and Winnipeg Jets—in time for the 1979-80 season. Seven expansion teams joined the league in the 1990s, with two more being added in 2000 to make it an even 30.

Expansion/Merger Timetable

For teams currently in NHL.

1919—Quebec Bulldogs finally take the ice after sitting out NHL's first two seasons; **1924**—Boston Bruins and Montreal Maroons; **1925**—New York Americans and Pittsburgh Pirates; **1926**—Chicago Black Hawks (now Blackhawks), Detroit Cougars (now Red Wings) and New York Rangers; **1932**—Ottawa Senators return after sitting out 1931-32 season.

1967—California-Oakland Seals (later Cleveland Barons), Los Angeles Kings, Minnesota North Stars, Philadelphia Flyers, Pittsburgh Penguins and St. Louis Blues.

1970—Buffalo Sabres and Vancouver Canucks; **1972**—Atlanta Flames (now Calgary) and New York Islanders; **1974**—Kansas City Scouts (now New Jersey Devils) and Washington Capitals; **1978**—Cleveland Barons merge with Minnesota North Stars (now Dallas Stars) and team remains in Minnesota; **1979**—added WHA's Edmonton Oilers, Hartford Whalers (now Carolina Hurricanes), Quebec Nordiques (now Colorado Avalanche) and Winnipeg Jets (now Phoenix Coyotes).

1991—San Jose Sharks; **1992**—Ottawa Senators and Tampa Bay Lightning; **1993**—Mighty Ducks of Anaheim and Florida Panthers; **1998**—Nashville Predators; **1999**—Atlanta Thrashers.

2000—Columbus Blue Jackets and Minnesota Wild.

City and Nickname Changes

1919—Toronto Arenas renamed St. Pats; **1920**—Quebec Bulldogs move to Hamilton and become Tigers (will fold in 1925); **1926**—Toronto St. Pats renamed Maple Leafs; **1929**—Detroit Cougars renamed Falcons.

1930—Pittsburgh Pirates move to Philadelphia and become Quakers (will fold in 1931); **1932**—Detroit Falcons renamed Red Wings; **1934**—Ottawa Senators move to St. Louis and become Eagles (will fold in 1935); **1941**—New York Americans renamed Brooklyn Americans (will fold in 1942).

1967—California Seals renamed Oakland Seals three months into first season; **1970**—Oakland Seals renamed California Golden Seals; **1975**—California Golden Seals renamed Seals; **1976**—California Seals move to Cleveland and become Barons, while Kansas City Scouts move to Denver and become Colorado Rockies; **1978**—Cleveland Barons merge with Minnesota North Stars and become Minnesota North Stars.

1980—Atlanta Flames move to Calgary; **1982**—Colorado Rockies move to East Rutherford, N.J., and become New Jersey Devils; **1986**—Chicago Black Hawks renamed Blackhawks; **1993**—Minnesota North Stars move to Dallas and become Stars. **1995**—Quebec Nordiques move to Denver and become Colorado Avalanche; **1996**—Winnipeg Jets move to Phoenix and become Coyotes; **1997**—Hartford Whalers move to Greensboro, N.C. and become Carolina Hurricanes; **1999**—Carolina Hurricanes move to Raleigh, N.C.; **2006**—Mighty Ducks of Anaheim renamed Anaheim Ducks.

Defunct NHL Teams

Teams that once played in the NHL, but no longer exist.

Brooklyn—Americans (1941-42, formerly NY Americans from 1925-41); **Cleveland**—Barons (1976-78, originally California-Oakland Seals from 1967-76); **Hamilton (Ont.)**—Tigers (1920-25, originally Quebec Bulldogs from 1919-20); **Montreal**—Maroons (1924-38) and Wanderers (1917-18); **New York**—Americans (1925-41, later Brooklyn Americans for 1941-42); **Oakland**—Seals (1967-76, also known as California Seals and Golden Seals and later Cleveland Barons from 1976-78); **Ottawa**—Senators (1917-31 and 1932-34, later St. Louis Eagles for 1934-35); **Philadelphia**—Quakers (1930-31, originally Pittsburgh Pirates from 1925-30); **Pittsburgh**—Pirates (1925-30, later Philadelphia Quakers for 1930-31); **Quebec**—Bulldogs (1919-20, later Hamilton Tigers from 1920-25); **St. Louis**—Eagles (1934-35), originally Ottawa Senators (1917-31 and 1932-34).

WHA Teams (1972-79)

Baltimore—Blades (1975); **Birmingham**—Bulls (1976-78); **Calgary**—Cowboys (1975-77); **Chicago**—Cougars (1972-75); **Cincinnati**—Stingers (1975-79); **Cleveland**—Crusaders (1972-76, moved to Minnesota); **Denver**—Spurs (1975-76, moved to Ottawa); **Edmonton**—Oilers (1972-79, originally called Alberta Oilers in 1972-73); **Houston**—Aeros (1972-78); **Indianapolis**—Racers (1974-78).

Los Angeles—Sharks (1972-74, moved to Michigan); **Michigan**—Stags (1974-75, moved to Baltimore); **Minnesota**—Fighting Saints (1972-76) and New Fighting Saints (1976-77); **New England**—Whalers (1972-79, played in Boston from 1972-74, West Springfield, MA from 1974-75, Hartford from 1975-78 and Springfield, MA in 1979); **New Jersey**—Knights (1973-74, moved to San Diego); **New York**—Raiders (1972-73, renamed Golden Blades in 1973, moved to New Jersey).

Ottawa—Nationals (1972-73, moved to Toronto) and Civics (1976); **Philadelphia**—Blazers (1972-73, moved to Vancouver); **Phoenix**—Roadrunners (1974-77); **Quebec**—Nordiques (1972-79); **San Diego**—Mariners (1974-77); **Toronto**—Toros (1973-76, moved to Birmingham, AL); **Vancouver**—Blazers (1973-75, moved to Calgary); **Winnipeg**—Jets (1972-79).

Annual NHL Leaders
Art Ross Trophy (Scoring)

Given to the player who leads the league in points scored and named after the former Boston Bruins general manager-coach. First presented in 1948, names of prior leading scorers have been added retroactively. A tie for the scoring championship is broken three ways: 1. total goals; 2. fewest games played; 3. first goal scored.

Multiple winners: Wayne Gretzky (10); Gordie Howe and Mario Lemieux (6); Phil Esposito and Jaromir Jagr (5); Stan Mikita (4); Bobby Hull and Guy Lafleur (3); Max Bentley, Charlie Conacher, Bill Cook, Bernie Geoffrion, Elmer Lach, Newsy Lalonde, Joe Malone, Dickie Moore, Howie Morenz, Bobby Orr and Sweeney Schriner (2).

Year	Player	Gm	G	A	Pts
1918	Joe Malone, Mon	20	44	0	44
1919	Newsy Lalonde, Mon	17	23	9	32
1920	Joe Malone, Que	24	39	6	45
1921	Newsy Lalonde, Mon	24	33	8	41
1922	Punch Broadbent, Ott	24	32	14	46
1923	Babe Dye, Tor	22	26	11	37
1924	Cy Denneny, Ott	21	22	1	23
1925	Babe Dye, Tor	29	38	6	44
1926	Nels Stewart, Maroons	36	34	8	42
1927	Bill Cook, NYR	44	33	4	37
1928	Howie Morenz, Mon	43	33	18	51
1929	Ace Bailey, Tor	44	22	10	32
1930	Cooney Weiland, Bos	44	43	30	73
1931	Howie Morenz, Mon	39	28	23	51
1932	Busher Jackson, Tor	48	28	25	53
1933	Bill Cook, NYR	48	28	22	50
1934	Charlie Conacher, Tor	42	32	20	52
1935	Charlie Conacher, Tor	47	36	21	57
1936	Sweeney Schriner, NYA	48	19	26	45
1937	Sweeney Schriner, NYA	48	21	25	46
1938	Gordie Drillon, Tor	48	26	26	52
1939	Toe Blake, Mon	48	24	23	47
1940	Milt Schmidt, Bos	48	22	30	52
1941	Bill Cowley, Bos	46	17	45	62
1942	Bryan Hextall, NYR	48	24	32	56
1943	Doug Bentley, Chi	50	33	40	73
1944	Herbie Cain, Bos	48	36	46	82
1945	Elmer Lach, Mon	50	26	54	80
1946	Max Bentley, Chi	47	31	30	61
1947	Max Bentley, Chi	60	29	43	72
1948	Elmer Lach, Mon	60	30	31	61
1949	Roy Conacher, Chi	60	26	42	68
1950	Ted Lindsay, Det	69	23	55	78
1951	Gordie Howe, Det	70	43	43	86
1952	Gordie Howe, Det	70	47	39	86
1953	Gordie Howe, Det	70	49	46	95
1954	Gordie Howe, Det	70	33	48	81
1955	Bernie Geoffrion, Mon	70	38	37	75
1956	Jean Beliveau, Mon	70	47	41	88
1957	Gordie Howe, Det	70	44	45	89
1958	Dickie Moore, Mon	70	36	48	84
1959	Dickie Moore, Mon	70	41	55	96
1960	Bobby Hull, Chi	70	39	42	81
1961	Bernie Geoffrion, Mon	64	50	45	95
1962	Bobby Hull, Chi	70	50	34	84
1963	Gordie Howe, Det	70	38	48	86
1964	Stan Mikita, Chi	70	39	50	89
1965	Stan Mikita, Chi	70	28	59	87
1966	Bobby Hull, Chi	65	54	43	97
1967	Stan Mikita, Chi	70	35	62	97
1968	Stan Mikita, Chi	72	40	47	87
1969	Phil Esposito, Bos	74	49	77	126
1970	Bobby Orr, Bos	76	33	87	120
1971	Phil Esposito, Bos	78	76	76	152
1972	Phil Esposito, Bos	76	66	67	133
1973	Phil Esposito, Bos	78	55	75	130
1974	Phil Esposito, Bos	78	68	77	145
1975	Bobby Orr, Bos	80	46	89	135
1976	Guy Lafleur, Mon	80	56	69	125
1977	Guy Lafleur, Mon	80	56	80	136
1978	Guy Lafleur, Mon	79	60	72	132
1979	Bryan Trottier, NYI	76	47	87	134
1980	Marcel Dionne, LA	80	53	84	137
1981	Wayne Gretzky, Edm	80	55	109	164
1982	Wayne Gretzky, Edm	80	92	120	212
1983	Wayne Gretzky, Edm	80	71	125	196
1984	Wayne Gretzky, Edm	74	87	118	205
1985	Wayne Gretzky, Edm	80	73	135	208
1986	Wayne Gretzky, Edm	80	52	163	215
1987	Wayne Gretzky, Edm	79	62	121	183
1988	Mario Lemieux, Pit	77	70	98	168
1989	Mario Lemieux, Pit	76	85	114	199
1990	Wayne Gretzky, LA	73	40	102	142
1991	Wayne Gretzky, LA	78	41	122	163
1992	Mario Lemieux, Pit	64	44	87	131
1993	Mario Lemieux, Pit	60	69	91	160
1994	Wayne Gretzky, LA	81	38	92	130
1995	Jaromir Jagr, Pit	48	32	38	70
1996	Mario Lemieux, Pit	70	69	92	161
1997	Mario Lemieux, Pit	76	50	72	122
1998	Jaromir Jagr, Pit	77	35	67	102
1999	Jaromir Jagr, Pit	81	44	83	127
2000	Jaromir Jagr, Pit	63	42	54	96
2001	Jaromir Jagr, Pit	81	52	69	121
2002	Jarome Iginla, Calg	82	52	44	96
2003	Peter Forsberg, Col	75	29	77	106
2004	Martin St. Louis, TB	82	38	56	94
2006	Joe Thornton, Bos-SJ	81	29	96	125

Note: The three times players have tied for total points in one season the player with more goals has won the trophy. In 1961-62, Hull outscored Andy Bathgate of NY Rangers, 50 goals to 28. In 1979-80, Dionne outscored Wayne Gretzky of Edmonton, 53-51. In 1995, Jagr outscored Eric Lindros of Philadelphia, 32-29.

Goals

Multiple winners: Bobby Hull (7); Phil Esposito (6); Charlie Conacher, Wayne Gretzky, Gordie Howe and Maurice Richard (5); Bill Cooke, Babe Dye, Brett Hull, Mario Lemieux, Pavel Bure and Teemu Selanne (3); Jean Beliveau, Doug Bentley, Peter Bondra, Mike Bossy, Bernie Geoffrion, Bryan Hextall, Jarome Iginla, Joe Malone and Nels Stewart (2).

Year		No
1918	Joe Malone, Mon	44
1919	Odie Cleghorn, Mon	23
	& Newsy Lalonde, Mon	23
1920	Joe Malone, Que	39
1921	Babe Dye, Ham-Tor	35
1922	Punch Broadbent, Ott	32
1923	Babe Dye, Tor	26
1924	Cy Denneny, Ott	22
1925	Babe Dye, Tor	38
1926	Nels Stewart, Maroons	34
1927	Bill Cook, NYR	33
1928	Howie Morenz, Mon	33
1929	Ace Bailey, Tor	22
1930	Cooney Weiland, Bos	43
1931	Charlie Conacher, Tor	31
1932	Charlie Conacher, Tor	34
	& Bill Cook, NYR	34
1933	Bill Cook, NYR	28
1934	Charlie Conacher, Tor	32
1935	Charlie Conacher, Tor	36
1936	Charlie Conacher, Tor	23
	& Bill Thoms, Tor	23
1937	Larry Aurie, Det	23
	& Nels Stewart, Bos-NYA	23
1938	Gordie Drillon, Tor	26
1939	Roy Conacher, Bos	26
1940	Bryan Hextall, NYR	24
1941	Bryan Hextall, NYR	26
1942	Lynn Patrick, NYR	32
1943	Doug Bentley, Chi	33

Annual NHL Leaders (Cont.)

Year		No	Year		No	Year		No
1944	Doug Bentley, Chi.	38	1966	Bobby Hull, Chi	54	1987	Wayne Gretzky, Edm	62
1945	Maurice Richard, Mon	50	1967	Bobby Hull, Chi	52	1988	Mario Lemieux, Pit	70
1946	Gaye Stewart, Tor	37	1968	Bobby Hull, Chi	44	1989	Mario Lemieux, Pit	85
1947	Maurice Richard, Mon	45	1969	Bobby Hull, Chi	58	1990	Brett Hull, St.L	72
1948	Ted Lindsay, Det	33	1970	Phil Esposito, Bos	43	1991	Brett Hull, St.L	86
1949	Sid Abel, Det	28	1971	Phil Esposito, Bos	76	1992	Brett Hull, St.L	70
1950	Maurice Richard, Mon	43	1972	Phil Esposito, Bos	66	1993	Alexander Mogilny, Buf.	76
1951	Gordie Howe, Det	43	1973	Phil Esposito, Bos	55		& Teemu Selanne, Win	76
1952	Gordie Howe, Det	47	1974	Phil Esposito, Bos	68	1994	Pavel Bure, Van	60
1953	Gordie Howe, Det	49	1975	Phil Esposito, Bos	61	1995	Peter Bondra, Wash	34
1954	Maurice Richard, Mon	37	1976	Reggie Leach, Phi	61	1996	Mario Lemieux, Pit	69
1955	Bernie Geoffrion, Mon	38	1977	Steve Shutt, Mon	60	1997	Keith Tkachuk, Pho	52
	& Maurice Richard, Mon.	38	1978	Guy Lafleur, Mon	60	1998	Teemu Selanne, Ana	52
1956	Jean Beliveau, Mon	47	1979	Mike Bossy, NYI	69		& Peter Bondra, Wash	52
1957	Gordie Howe, Det	44	1980	Danny Gare, Buf	56	1999	Teemu Selanne, Ana	47
1958	Dickie Moore, Mon	36		Charlie Simmer, LA	56	2000	Pavel Bure, Fla	58
1959	Jean Beliveau, Mon	45		& Blaine Stoughton, Hart.	56	2001	Pavel Bure, Fla	59
1960	Bronco Horvath, Bos.	39	1981	Mike Bossy, NYI	68	2002	Jarome Iginla, Calg.	52
	& Bobby Hull, Chi	39	1982	Wayne Gretzky, Edm	92	2003	Milan Hejduk, Col.	50
1961	Bernie Geoffrion, Mon	50	1983	Wayne Gretzky, Edm	71	2004	Jarome Iginla, Calg.	41
1962	Bobby Hull, Chi	50	1984	Wayne Gretzky, Edm	87		Ilya Kovalchuk, Atl	41
1963	Gordie Howe, Det	38	1985	Wayne Gretzky, Edm	73		& Rick Nash, Clb	41
1964	Bobby Hull, Chi	43	1986	Jari Kurri, Edm	68	2006	Jonathan Cheechoo, SJ	56
1965	Norm Ullman, Tor	42						

Assists

Multiple winners: Wayne Gretzky (16); Bobby Orr (5); Adam Oates, Frank Boucher, Bill Cowley, Phil Esposito, Gordie Howe, Jaromir Jagr, Elmer Lach, Mario Lemieux, Stan Mikita and Joe Primeau (3); Syl Apps, Andy Bathgate, Jean Beliveau, Doug Bentley, Art Chapman, Bobby Clarke, Ron Francis, Ted Lindsay, Bert Olmstead, Henri Richard and Bryan Trottier (2).

Year		No	Year		No	Year		No
1918	No official records kept.		1949	Doug Bentley, Chi.	43	1979	Bryan Trottier, NYI	87
1919	Newsy Lalonde, Mon	9	1950	Ted Lindsay, Det	55	1980	Wayne Gretzky, Edm	86
1920	Corbett Denneny, Tor	12	1951	Gordie Howe, Det	43	1981	Wayne Gretzky, Edm	109
1921	Louis Berlinquette, Mon	9		& Teeder Kennedy, Tor	43	1982	Wayne Gretzky, Edm	120
	Harry Cameron, Tor	9	1952	Elmer Lach, Mon	50	1983	Wayne Gretzky, Edm	125
	& Joe Matte, Ham	9	1953	Gordie Howe, Det	46	1984	Wayne Gretzky, Edm	118
1922	Punch Broadbent, Ott	14	1954	Gordie Howe, Det	48	1985	Wayne Gretzky, Edm	135
	& Leo Reise, Ham	14	1955	Bert Olmstead, Mon	48	1986	Wayne Gretzky, Edm	163
1923	Ed Bouchard, Ham	12	1956	Bert Olmstead, Mon	56	1987	Wayne Gretzky, Edm	121
1924	King Clancy, Ott	8	1957	Ted Lindsay, Det	55	1988	Wayne Gretzky, Edm	109
1925	Cy Denneny, Ott	15	1958	Henri Richard, Mon	52	1989	Wayne Gretzky, LA	114
1926	Frank Nighbor, Ott	13	1959	Dickie Moore, Mon	55		& Mario Lemieux, Pit	114
1927	Dick Irvin, Chi	18	1960	Don McKenney, Bos	49	1990	Wayne Gretzky, LA	102
1928	Howie Morenz, Mon	18	1961	Jean Beliveau, Mon	58	1991	Wayne Gretzky, LA	122
1929	Frank Boucher, NYR	16	1962	Andy Bathgate, NYR	56	1992	Wayne Gretzky, LA	90
1930	Frank Boucher, NYR	36	1963	Henri Richard, Mon	50	1993	Adam Oates, Bos.	97
1931	Joe Primeau, Tor	32	1964	Andy Bathgate, NYR-Tor	58	1994	Wayne Gretzky, LA	92
1932	Joe Primeau, Tor	37	1965	Stan Mikita, Chi	59	1995	Ron Francis, Pit	48
1933	Frank Boucher, NYR	28	1966	Jean Beliveau, Mon	48	1996	Ron Francis, Pit	92
1934	Joe Primeau, Tor	32		Stan Mikita, Chi	48		& Mario Lemieux, Pit	92
1935	Art Chapman, NYA	34		& Bobby Rousseau, Mon.	48	1997	Mario Lemieux, Pit	72
1936	Art Chapman, NYA	28	1967	Stan Mikita, Chi.	62		& Wayne Gretzky, NYR	72
1937	Syl Apps, Tor	29	1968	Phil Esposito, Bos	49	1998	Jaromir Jagr, Pit	67
1938	Syl Apps, Tor	29	1969	Phil Esposito, Bos	77		& Wayne Gretzky, NYR	67
1939	Bill Cowley, Bos	34	1970	Bobby Orr, Bos	87	1999	Jaromir Jagr, Pit	83
1940	Milt Schmidt, Bos	30	1971	Bobby Orr, Bos	102	2000	Mark Recchi, Phi	63
1941	Bill Cowley, Bos	45	1972	Bobby Orr, Bos	80	2001	Jaromir Jagr, Pit	69
1942	Phil Watson, NYR	37	1973	Phil Esposito, Bos	75		& Adam Oates, Wash	69
1943	Bill Cowley, Bos	45	1974	Bobby Orr, Bos	90	2002	Adam Oates, Wash-Phi.	64
1944	Clint Smith, Chi	49	1975	Bobby Clarke, Phi	89	2003	Peter Forsberg, Col.	77
1945	Elmer Lach, Mon	54		& Bobby Orr, Bos.	89	2004	Scott Gomez, NJ	56
1946	Elmer Lach, Mon	34	1976	Bobby Clarke, Phi	89		& Martin St. Louis, TB	56
1947	Billy Taylor, Det	46	1977	Guy Lafleur, Mon	80	2006	Joe Thornton, Bos-SJ	96
1948	Doug Bentley, Chi.	37	1978	Bryan Trottier, NYI	77			

Goals Against Average

Average determined by games played through 1942-43 season and by minutes played since then. Minimum of 15 games from 1917-18 season through 1925-26; minimum of 25 games since 1926-27 season. Not to be confused with the Vezina Trophy. Goaltenders who posted the season's lowest goals against average, but did not win the Vezina are in **bold** type.

Multiple winners: Jacques Plante (9); Clint Benedict and Bill Durnan (6); Johnny Bower, Ken Dryden and Tiny Thompson (4); Patrick Roy and Georges Vezina (3); Ed Belfour, Frankie Brimsek, Turk Broda, George Hainsworth, Dominik Hasek, Miikka Kiprusoff, Harry Lumley, Bernie Parent, Pete Peeters, Terry Sawchuk and Marty Turco (2).

Year	GAA	Year	GAA	Year	GAA
1918 Georges Vezina, Mon	3.82	1948 Turk Broda, Tor	2.38	1978 Ken Dryden, Mon	2.05
1919 Clint Benedict, Ott	2.94	1949 Bill Durnan, Mon	2.10	1979 Ken Dryden, Mon	2.30
1920 Clint Benedict, Ott	2.67	1950 Bill Durnan, Mon	2.20	1980 Bob Sauve, Buf	2.36
1921 Clint Benedict, Ott	3.13	1951 Al Rollins, Tor	1.77	1981 Richard Sevigny, Mon	2.40
1922 Clint Benedict, Ott	3.50	1952 Terry Sawchuk, Det	1.90	1982 **Denis Herron,** Mon	2.64
1923 Clint Benedict, Ott	2.25	1953 Terry Sawchuk, Det	1.90	1983 Pete Peeters, Bos	2.36
1924 Georges Vezina, Mon	2.00	1954 Harry Lumley, Tor	1.86	1984 **Pat Riggin,** Wash	2.66
1925 Georges Vezina, Mon	1.87	1955 **Harry Lumley,** Tor	1.94	1985 **Tom Barrasso,** Buf	2.66
1926 Alex Connell, Ott	1.17	1956 Jacques Plante, Mon	1.86	1986 **Bob Froese,** Phi	2.55
1927 **Clint Benedict,** Mon-M	1.51	1957 Jacques Plante, Mon	2.02	1987 **Brian Hayward,** Mon	2.81
1928 Geo. Hainsworth, Mon	1.09	1958 Jacques Plante, Mon	2.11	1988 **Pete Peeters,** Wash	2.78
1929 Geo. Hainsworth, Mon	0.98	1959 Jacques Plante, Mon	2.16	1989 Patrick Roy, Mon	2.47
1930 Tiny Thompson, Bos	2.23	1960 Jacques Plante, Mon	2.54	1990 **Mike Liut,** Hart-Wash	2.53
1931 Roy Worters, NYA	1.68	1961 Johnny Bower, Tor	2.50	1991 Ed Belfour, Chi	2.47
1932 Chuck Gardiner, Chi	1.92	1962 Jacques Plante, Mon	2.37	1992 Patrick Roy, Mon	2.36
1933 Tiny Thompson, Bos	1.83	1963 **Jacques Plante,** Mon	2.49	1993 **Felix Potvin,** Tor	2.50
1934 **Wilf Cude,** Det-Mon	1.57	1964 **Johnny Bower,** Tor	2.11	1994 Dominik Hasek, Buf	1.95
1935 Lorne Chabot, Chi	1.83	1965 Johnny Bower, Tor	2.38	1995 Dominik Hasek, Buf	2.11
1936 Tiny Thompson, Bos	1.71	1966 **Johnny Bower,** Tor	2.25	1996 **Ron Hextall,** Phi	2.17
1937 Norm Smith, Det	2.13	1967 Glenn Hall, Chi	2.38	1997 **Martin Brodeur,** NJ	1.88
1938 Tiny Thompson, Bos	1.85	1968 Gump Worsley, Mon	1.98	1998 **Ed Belfour,** Dal	1.88
1939 Frankie Brimsek, Bos	1.58	1969 **Jacques Plante,** St.L	1.96	1999 **Ron Tugnutt,** Ott	1.79
1940 Dave Kerr, NYR	1.60	1970 **Ernie Wakely,** St.L	2.11	2000 **Brian Boucher,** Phi	1.91
1941 Turk Broda, Tor	2.06	1971 **Jacques Plante,** Tor	1.88	2001 **Marty Turco,** Dal	1.90
1942 Frankie Brimsek, Bos	2.45	1972 Tony Esposito, Chi	1.77	2002 **Patrick Roy,** Col	1.94
1943 John Mowers, Det	2.47	1973 Ken Dryden, Mon	2.26	2003 **Marty Turco,** Dal	1.72
1944 Bill Durnan, Mon	2.18	1974 Bernie Parent, Phi	1.89	2004 **Miikka Kiprusoff,** Calg	1.69
1945 Bill Durnan, Mon	2.42	1975 Bernie Parent, Phi	2.03	2006 Miikka Kiprusoff, Calg	2.07
1946 Bill Durnan, Mon	2.60	1976 Ken Dryden, Mon	2.03		
1947 Bill Durnan, Mon	2.30	1977 Bunny Larocque, Mon	2.09		

Penalty Minutes

Multiple winners: Red Horner (8); Gus Mortson and Dave Schultz (4); Bert Corbeau, Lou Fontinato and Tiger Williams (3); Sean Avery, Matthew Barnaby, Billy Boucher, Carl Brewer, Red Dutton, Pat Egan, Bill Ezinicki, Joe Hall, Tim Hunter, Keith Magnuson, Chris Nilan, Jimmy Orlando and Rob Ray (2).

Year	Min	Year	Min	Year	Min
1918 Joe Hall, Mon	60	1948 Bill Barilko, Tor	147	1978 Dave Schultz, LA-Pit	405
1919 Joe Hall, Mon	85	1949 Bill Ezinicki, Tor	145	1979 Tiger Williams, Tor	298
1920 Cully Wilson, Tor	79	1950 Bill Ezinicki, Tor	144	1980 Jimmy Mann, Win	287
1921 Bert Corbeau, Mon	86	1951 Gus Mortson, Tor	142	1981 Tiger Williams, Van	343
1922 Sprague Cleghorn, Mon	63	1952 Gus Kyle, Bos	127	1982 Paul Baxter, Pit	409
1923 Billy Boucher, Mon	52	1953 Maurice Richard, Mon	112	1983 Randy Holt, Wash	275
1924 Bert Corbeau, Tor	55	1954 Gus Mortson, Chi	132	1984 Chris Nilan, Mon	338
1925 Billy Boucher, Mon	92	1955 Fern Flaman, Bos	150	1985 Chris Nilan, Mon	358
1926 Bert Corbeau, Tor	121	1956 Lou Fontinato, NYR	202	1986 Joey Kocur, Det	377
1927 Nels Stewart, Mon-M	133	1957 Gus Mortson, Chi	147	1987 Tim Hunter, Calg	361
1928 Eddie Shore, Bos	165	1958 Lou Fontinato, NYR	152	1988 Bob Probert, Det	398
1929 Red Dutton, Mon-M	139	1959 Ted Lindsay, Chi	184	1989 Tim Hunter, Calg	375
1930 Joe Lamb, Ott	119	1960 Carl Brewer, Tor	150	1990 Basil McRae, Min	351
1931 Harvey Rockburn, Det	118	1961 Pierre Pilote, Chi	165	1991 Rob Ray, Buf	350
1932 Red Dutton, NYA	107	1962 Lou Fontinato, Mon	167	1992 Mike Peluso, Chi	408
1933 Red Horner, Tor	144	1963 Howie Young, Det	273	1993 Marty McSorley, LA	399
1934 Red Horner, Tor	146	1964 Vic Hadfield, NYR	151	1994 Tie Domi, Win	347
1935 Red Horner, Tor	125	1965 Carl Brewer, Tor	177	1995 Enrico Ciccone, TB	225
1936 Red Horner, Tor	167	1966 Reg Fleming, Bos-NYR	166	1996 Matthew Barnaby, Buf	335
1937 Red Horner, Tor	124	1967 John Ferguson, Mon	177	1997 Gino Odjick, Van	371
1938 Red Horner, Tor	82	1968 Barclay Plager, St.L	153	1998 Donald Brashear, Van	372
1939 Red Horner, Tor	85	1969 Forbes Kennedy, Phi-Tor	219	1999 Rob Ray, Buf	261
1940 Red Horner, Tor	87	1970 Keith Magnuson, Chi	213	2000 Denny Lambert, Atl	219
1941 Jimmy Orlando, Det	99	1971 Keith Magnuson, Chi	291	2001 Matthew Barnaby, Pit-TB	265
1942 Pat Egan, NYA	124	1972 Bryan Watson, Pit	212	2002 Peter Worrell, Fla	354
1943 Jimmy Orlando, Det	99	1973 Dave Schultz, Phi	259	2003 Jody Shelley, Clb	249
1944 Mike McMahon, Mon	98	1974 Dave Schultz, Phi	348	2004 Sean Avery, LA	261
1945 Pat Egan, Bos	86	1975 Dave Schultz, Phi	472	2006 Sean Avery, LA	257
1946 Jack Stewart, Det	73	1976 Steve Durbano, Pit-KC	370		
1947 Gus Mortson, Tor	133	1977 Tiger Williams, Tor	338		

All-Time NHL Regular Season Leaders
Through 2006 regular season.

CAREER
Players active during 2006 season in **bold** type.

Points

		Yrs	Gm	G	A	Pts
1	Wayne Gretzky	20	1487	894	1963	2857
2	Mark Messier	25	1756	694	1193	1887
3	Gordie Howe	26	1767	801	1049	1850
4	Ron Francis	23	1731	549	1249	1798
5	Marcel Dionne	18	1348	731	1040	1771
6	**Steve Yzerman**	22	1514	692	1063	1755
7	**Mario Lemieux**	17	915	690	1033	1723
8	Phil Esposito	18	1282	717	873	1590
9	Ray Bourque	22	1612	410	1169	1579
10	Paul Coffey	21	1409	396	1135	1531
11	**Joe Sakic**	17	1237	574	915	1489
12	Stan Mikita	22	1394	541	926	1467
13	**Jaromir Jagr**	15	1109	591	841	1432
14	Bryan Trottier	18	1279	524	901	1425
15	Adam Oates	19	1337	341	1079	1420
16	Doug Gilmour	20	1474	450	964	1414
17	Dale Hawerchuk	16	1188	518	891	1409
18	Jari Kurri	17	1251	601	797	1398
19	**Luc Robitaille**	19	1431	668	726	1394
20	**Brett Hull**	20	1269	741	650	1391
21	John Bucyk	23	1540	556	813	1369
22	Guy Lafleur	17	1126	560	793	1353
23	**Dave Andreychuk**	23	1639	640	698	1338
	Denis Savard	17	1196	473	865	1338
25	Mike Gartner	19	1432	708	627	1335
26	Gilbert Perreault	17	1191	512	814	1326
27	**Pierre Turgeon**	18	1277	511	809	1320
28	Alex Delvecchio	24	1549	456	825	1281
29	Al MacInnis	23	1416	340	934	1274
30	Jean Ratelle	21	1281	491	776	1267

Goals

		Yrs	Gm	No
1	Wayne Gretzky	20	1487	894
2	Gordie Howe	26	1767	801
3	**Brett Hull**	20	1269	741
4	Marcel Dionne	18	1348	731
5	Phil Esposito	18	1282	717
6	Mike Gartner	19	1432	708
7	Mark Messier	25	1756	694
8	**Steve Yzerman**	22	1514	692
9	**Mario Lemieux**	17	915	690
10	**Luc Robitaille**	19	1431	668
11	**Dave Andreychuk**	23	1639	640
12	Bobby Hull	16	1063	610
13	Dino Ciccarelli	19	1232	608
14	Jari Kurri	17	1251	601
15	**Brendan Shanahan**	18	1350	598
16	**Jaromir Jagr**	15	1109	591
17	**Joe Sakic**	17	1237	574
18	Mike Bossy	10	752	573
19	Guy Lafleur	17	1126	560
20	**Joe Nieuwendyk**	19	1242	559
21	John Bucyk	23	1540	556
22	Ron Francis	23	1731	549
23	Michel Goulet	15	1089	548
24	Maurice Richard	18	978	544
25	Stan Mikita	22	1394	541
26	Frank Mahovlich	18	1181	533
27	Bryan Trottier	18	1279	524
28	Pat Verbeek	20	1424	522
29	Dale Hawerchuk	16	1188	518
30	Gilbert Perreault	17	1191	512

Assists

		Yrs	Gm	No
1	Wayne Gretzky	20	1487	1963
2	Ron Francis	23	1731	1249
3	Mark Messier	25	1756	1193
4	Ray Bourque	22	1612	1169
5	Paul Coffey	21	1409	1135
6	Adam Oates	19	1337	1079
7	**Steve Yzerman**	22	1514	1063
8	Gordie Howe	26	1767	1049
9	Marcel Dionne	18	1348	1040
10	**Mario Lemieux**	17	915	1033
11	Doug Gilmour	20	1474	964
12	Al MacInnis	23	1416	934
13	Larry Murphy	21	1615	929
14	Stan Mikita	22	1394	926
15	**Joe Sakic**	17	1237	915
16	Bryan Trottier	18	1279	901
17	Phil Housley	21	1495	894
18	Dale Hawerchuk	16	1188	891
19	Phil Esposito	18	1282	873
20	Denis Savard	17	1196	865

Penalty Minutes

		Yrs	Gm	Min
1	Tiger Williams	14	962	3966
2	Dale Hunter	19	1407	3565
3	**Tie Domi**	16	1020	3515
4	Marty McSorley	17	961	3381
5	Bob Probert	16	935	3300
6	Rob Ray	15	900	3207
7	Craig Berube	17	1054	3149
8	Tim Hunter	16	815	3146
9	Chris Nilan	13	688	3043
10	Rick Tocchet	18	1144	2972
11	Pat Verbeek	20	1424	2905
12	**Chris Chelios**	22	1476	2803
13	Dave Manson	16	1103	2792
14	Scott Stevens	22	1635	2785
15	Willi Plett	12	834	2572

NHL-WHA Top 10

All-time regular season scoring leaders, including games played in World Hockey Association (1972-79). NHL players with WHA experience are listed in CAPITAL letters. Players active during 2006 are in **bold** type.

Points

		Yrs	G	A	Pts
1	WAYNE GRETZKY	21	940	2027	2967
2	GORDIE HOWE	32	975	1383	2358
3	MARK MESSIER	26	695	1203	1898
4	BOBBY HULL	23	913	895	1808
5	Ron Francis	23	549	1249	1798
6	Marcel Dionne	18	731	1040	1771
7	**Steve Yzerman**	22	692	1063	1755
8	**Mario Lemieux**	17	690	1033	1723
9	Phil Esposito	18	717	873	1590
10	Ray Bourque	22	410	1169	1579

WHA Totals: GRETZKY (1 yr, 80 gm, 46-64—110); HOWE (6 yrs, 419 gm, 174-334—508); MESSIER (1 yr, 52 gm, 1-10—11); HULL (7 yrs, 411 gm, 303-335—638).

Years Played

		Yrs	Career	Gm
1	Gordie Howe	26	1946-71, 79-80	1767
2	Mark Messier	25	1979-2004	1756
3	Alex Delvecchio	24	1950-74	1549
	Tim Horton	24	1949-50, 51-74	1446
5	Ron Francis	23	1981-2004	1731
	Dave Andreychuk	23	1982–	1639
	John Bucyk	23	1955-78	1540
	Al MacInnis	23	1982-2004	1416
9	Scott Stevens	22	1982-2004	1635
	Ray Bourque	22	1979-2001	1612
	Steve Yzerman	22	1983-2006	1514
	Chris Chelios	22	1984–	1476
	Stan Mikita	22	1958-80	1394
	Doug Mohns	22	1953-75	1390
	Dean Prentice	22	1952-74	1378

Note: Combined NHL-WHA years played: Howe (32); Messier (26); Howell (24); Bobby Hull (23); Norm Ullman, Eric Nesterenko, Frank Mahovlich and Dave Keon (22).

Games Played

		Yrs	Career	Gm
1	Gordie Howe	26	1946-71, 79-80	1767
2	Mark Messier	25	1979-2004	1756
3	Ron Francis	23	1981-2004	1731
4	**Dave Andreychuk**	23	1982–	1639
5	Scott Stevens	22	1982-2004	1635
6	Larry Murphy	21	1980–2001	1615
7	Ray Bourque	22	1979–2001	1612
8	Alex Delvecchio	24	1950–74	1549
9	John Bucyk	23	1955–78	1540
10	**Steve Yzerman**	22	1983-2006	1514
11	Phil Housley	21	1982–2003	1495
12	Wayne Gretzky	20	1979–99	1487
13	**Chris Chelios**	22	1984–	1476
14	Doug Gilmour	20	1983–2003	1474
15	Tim Horton	24	1949–50, 51–74	1446

Note: Combined NHL-WHA games played: Howe (2,186); Messier (1,808), Dave Keon (1,597), Harry Howell (1,581), Gretzky (1,567), Norm Ullman (1,554), Gartner (1,510) and Bobby Hull (1,474).

Goaltending

Wins

		Yrs	Gm	W	L	T	Pct
1	Patrick Roy	19	1029	**551**	315	131	.618
2	**Ed Belfour**	17	905	**457**	303	111	.588
3	Terry Sawchuk	21	971	**447**	330	172	.562
4	**Martin Brodeur**	13	813	**446**	240	105	.630
5	Jacques Plante	18	837	**434**	247	146	.614
6	**Curtis Joseph**	16	858	**428**	310	90	.571
7	Tony Esposito	16	886	**423**	306	152	.566
8	Glenn Hall	18	906	**407**	326	163	.545
9	Grant Fuhr	19	868	**403**	295	114	.567
10	Mike Vernon	19	781	**385**	273	92	.575
11	John Vanbiesbrouck	20	882	**374**	346	119	.517
12	Andy Moog	18	713	**372**	209	88	.622
13	Tom Barrasso	19	777	**369**	277	86	.563
14	Rogie Vachon	16	795	**355**	291	127	.541
15	Gump Worsley	21	861	**335**	352	150	.490
16	Harry Lumley	16	804	**330**	329	143	.501
17	**Chris Osgood**	12	600	**325**	183	66	.624
18	**Dominik Hasek**	14	638	**324**	202	82	.600
19	**Sean Burke**	17	797	**318**	331	101	.491
20	Billy Smith	18	680	**305**	233	105	.556

Losses

		Yrs	Gm	W	L	T	Pct
1	Gump Worsley	21	861	335	**352**	150	.490
2	Gilles Meloche	18	788	270	**351**	131	.446
3	John Vanbiesbrouck	20	882	374	**346**	119	.517
4	Terry Sawchuk	21	971	447	**330**	172	.562
5	**Sean Burke**	17	797	318	**331**	101	.491

Shutouts

		Yrs	Games	No
1	Terry Sawchuk	21	971	103
2	George Hainsworth	11	465	94
3	Glenn Hall	18	906	84
4	Jacques Plante	18	837	82
5	Alex Connell	12	417	81
	Tiny Thompson	12	553	81
7	**Martin Brodeur**	13	813	80
8	Tony Esposito	16	886	76
9	**Ed Belfour**	17	905	75
10	Lorne Chabot	11	411	73
11	Harry Lumley	16	804	71
12	**Dominik Hasek**	14	638	68
13	Roy Worters	12	484	66
	Patrick Roy	19	1029	66
15	Turk Broda	14	629	62

Goals Against Average

Minimum of 300 games played.

Before 1950

		Gm	Min	GA	GAA
1	George Hainsworth	465	29,415	937	1.91
2	Alex Connell	417	26,050	830	1.91
3	Chuck Gardiner	316	19,687	664	2.02
4	Lorne Chabot	411	25,307	860	2.04
5	Tiny Thompson	553	34,175	1183	2.08

Since 1950

		Gm	Min	GA	GAA
1	**Martin Brodeur**	813	47,876	1760	2.21
2	**Dominik Hasek**	638	37,146	1374	2.22
3	Ken Dryden	397	23,352	870	2.24
4	Roman Turek	328	19,095	734	2.31
5	Jacques Plante	837	49,533	1965	2.38
6	**Evgeni Nabokov**	303	17,273	705	2.45
7	**Chris Osgood**	600	34,450	1409	2.45
8	**Ed Belfour**	905	52,405	2165	2.48
9	**Patrick Lalime**	353	20,252	841	2.49
10	Glen Hall	906	53,484	2222	2.49

NHL-WHA Top 10

All-time regular season wins leaders, including games played in World Hockey Association (1972-79). NHL goaltenders with WHA experience are listed in CAPITAL letters. Players active during 2006 are in bold type.

Wins

		Yrs	W	L	T	Pct
1	Patrick Roy	19	**551**	315	131	.618
2	**Ed Belfour**	17	**457**	303	111	.588
3	JACQUES PLANTE	19	**449**	261	147	.610
4	Terry Sawchuk	21	**447**	330	172	.562
5	**Martin Brodeur**	13	**446**	240	105	.630
6	**Curtis Joseph**	16	**428**	310	90	.571
7	Tony Esposito	16	**423**	306	152	.566
8	Glenn Hall	18	**407**	326	163	.545
9	Grant Fuhr	19	**403**	295	114	.567
10	Mike Vernon	19	**385**	273	92	.575

WHA Totals: PLANTE (1 yr, 31 gm, 15-14-1).

All-Time NHL Regular Season Leaders (Cont.)
SINGLE SEASON

Scoring
Points

		Season	G	A	Pts
1	Wayne Gretzky, Edm	1985-86	52	163	215
2	Wayne Gretzky, Edm	1981-82	92	120	212
3	Wayne Gretzky, Edm	1984-85	73	135	208
4	Wayne Gretzky, Edm	1983-84	87	118	205
5	Mario Lemieux, Pit	1988-89	85	114	199
6	Wayne Gretzky, Edm	1982-83	71	125	196
7	Wayne Gretzky, Edm	1986-87	62	121	183
8	Mario Lemieux, Pit	1987-88	70	98	168
	Wayne Gretzky, LA	1988-89	54	114	168
10	Wayne Gretzky, Edm	1980-81	55	109	164
11	Wayne Gretzky, LA	1990-91	41	122	163
12	Mario Lemieux, Pit	1995-96	69	92	161
13	Mario Lemieux, Pit	1992-93	69	91	160
14	Steve Yzerman, Det	1988-89	65	90	155
15	Phil Esposito, Bos	1970-71	76	76	152
16	Bernie Nicholls, LA	1988-89	70	80	150
17	Jaromir Jagr, Pit	1995-96	62	87	149
	Wayne Gretzky, Edm	1987-88	40	109	149
19	Pat LaFontaine, Buf	1992-93	53	95	148
20	Mike Bossy, NYI	1981-82	64	83	147

WHA 150 points or more: 154—Marc Tardif, Que. (1977-78).

Goals

		Season	Gm	No
1	Wayne Gretzky, Edm	1981-82	80	92
2	Wayne Gretzky, Edm	1983-84	74	87
3	Brett Hull, St.L	1990-91	78	86
4	Mario Lemieux, Pit	1988-89	76	85
5	Alexander Mogilny, Buf.	1992-93	77	76
	Phil Esposito, Bos	1970-71	78	76
	Teemu Selanne, Win	1992-93	84	76
8	Wayne Gretzky, Edm	1984-85	80	73
9	Brett Hull, St.L	1989-90	80	72
10	Jari Kurri, Edm	1984-85	73	71
	Wayne Gretzky, Edm	1982-83	80	71
12	Brett Hull, St.L	1991-92	73	70
	Mario Lemieux, Pit	1987-88	77	70
	Bernie Nicholls, LA	1988-89	79	70
15	Mario Lemieux, Pit	1992-93	60	69
	Mario Lemieux, Pit	1995-96	70	69
	Mike Bossy, NYI	1978-79	80	69
18	Phil Esposito, Bos	1973-74	78	68
	Jari Kurri, Edm	1985-86	78	68
	Mike Bossy, NYI	1980-81	79	68

WHA 70 goals or more: 77—Bobby Hull, Win. (1974-75); 75—Real Cloutier, Que. (1978-79); 71—Marc Tardif, Que. (1975-76); 70—Anders Hedberg, Win. (1976-77).

Assists

		Season	Gm	No
1	Wayne Gretzky, Edm	1985-86	80	163
2	Wayne Gretzky, Edm	1984-85	80	135
3	Wayne Gretzky, Edm	1982-83	80	125
4	Wayne Gretzky, LA	1990-91	78	122
5	Wayne Gretzky, Edm	1986-87	79	121
6	Wayne Gretzky, Edm	1981-82	80	120
7	Wayne Gretzky, Edm	1983-84	74	118
8	Mario Lemieux, Pit	1988-89	76	114
	Wayne Gretzky, LA	1988-89	78	114
10	Wayne Gretzky, Edm	1987-88	64	109
	Wayne Gretzky, Edm	1980-81	80	109
12	Wayne Gretzky, LA	1989-90	73	102
	Bobby Orr, Bos	1970-71	78	102
14	Mario Lemieux, Pit	1987-88	77	98
15	Adam Oates, Bos	1992-93	84	97

WHA 95 assists or more: 106—Andre Lacroix, San Diego (1974-75).

Goaltending
Wins

		Season	Record
1	Bernie Parent, Phi	1973-74	47-13-12
2	Bernie Parent, Phi	1974-75	44-14-9
	Terry Sawchuk, Det	1950-51	44-13-13
	Terry Sawchuk, Det	1951-52	44-14-12
5	Martin Brodeur, NJ	1999-00	43-20-8
	Martin Brodeur, NJ	1997-98	43-17-8
	Martin Brodeur, NJ	2005-06	43-23-0
	Tom Barrasso, Pit	1992-93	43-14-5
	Ed Belfour, Chi	1990-91	43-19-7
10	Seven tied with 42 wins each.		

Most WHA wins in one season: 44—Richard Brodeur, Que. (1975-76).

Losses

		Season	Record
1	Gary Smith, Cal	1970-71	19-48-4
2	Al Rollins, Chi	1953-54	12-47-7
3	Peter Sidorkiewicz, Ott	1992-93	8-46-3
4	Harry Lumley, Chi	1951-52	17-44-9
5	Three tied with 41 losses each.		

Most WHA losses in one season: 36—Don McLeod, Van. (1974-75) and Andy Brown, Ind. (1974-75).

Shutouts

		Season	Gm	No
1	George Hainsworth, Mon	1928-29	44	22
2	Alex Connell, Ott	1925-26	36	15
	Alex Connell, Ott	1927-28	44	15
	Hal Winkler, Bos	1927-28	44	15
	Tony Esposito, Chi	1969-70	63	15

Most WHA shutouts in one season: 5—Gerry Cheevers, Cle. (1972-73) and Joe Daly, Win. (1975-76).

Goals Against Average
Before 1950

		Season	Gm	GAA
1	George Hainsworth, Mon	1928-29	44	0.98
2	George Hainsworth, Mon	1927-28	44	1.09
3	Alex Connell, Ott	1925-26	36	1.17
4	Tiny Thompson, Bos	1928-29	44	1.18
5	Roy Worters, NY Americans	1928-29	38	1.21

Since 1950

		Season	Gm	GAA
1	Miikka Kiprusoff, Calg	2003-04	38	1.69
2	Marty Turco, Dal	2002-03	55	1.72
3	Tony Esposito, Chi	1971-72	48	1.77
4	Al Rollins, Tor	1950-51	40	1.77
5	Ron Tugnutt, Ott	1998-99	43	1.79

Penalty Minutes

		Season	PM
1	Dave Schultz, Phi	1974-75	472
2	Paul Baxter, Pit	1981-82	409
3	Mike Peluso, Chi	1991-92	408
4	Dave Schultz, LA-Pit	1977-78	405
5	Marty McSorley, LA	1992-93	399
6	Bob Probert, Det	1987-88	398
7	Basil McRae, Min	1987-88	382
8	Joey Kocur, Det	1985-86	377
9	Tim Hunter, Calg	1988-89	375
10	Donald Brashear, Van	1997-98	372

WHA 355 minutes or more: 365—Curt Brackenbury, Min-Que. (1975-76).

SINGLE GAME

Points

	Date	G-A—Pts
Darryl Sittler, Tor vs Bos	2/7/76	6-4—10
Maurice Richard, Mon vs Det	12/28/44	5-3— 8
Bert Olmstead, Mon vs Chi	1/9/54	4-4— 8
Tom Bladon, Phi vs Cle	12/11/77	4-4— 8
Bryan Trottier, NYI vs NYR	12/23/78	5-3— 8
Peter Stastny, Que at Wash	2/22/81	4-4— 8
Anton Stastny, Que at Wash	2/22/81	3-5— 8
Wayne Gretzky, Edm vs NJ	11/19/83	3-5— 8
Wayne Gretzky, Edm vs Min	1/4/84	4-4— 8
Paul Coffey, Edm vs Det	3/14/86	2-6— 8
Mario Lemieux, Pit vs St.L	10/15/88	2-6— 8
Bernie Nicholls, LA vs Tor	12/1/88	2-6— 8
Mario Lemieux, Pit vs NJ	12/31/88	5-3— 8

Goals

	Date	No
Joe Malone, Que vs Tor	1/31/20	7
Newsy Lalonde, Mon vs Tor	1/10/20	6
Joe Malone, Que vs Ott	3/10/20	6
Corb Denneny, Tor vs Ham	1/26/21	6
Cy Denneny, Ott vs Ham	3/7/21	6
Syd Howe, Det vs NYR	2/3/44	6
Red Berenson, St.L at Phi	11/7/68	6
Darryl Sittler, Tor vs Bos	2/7/76	6

Assists

	Date	No
Billy Taylor, Det at Chi	3/16/47	7
Wayne Gretzky, Edm vs Wash	2/15/80	7
Wayne Gretzky, Edm at Chi	12/11/85	7
Wayne Gretzky, Edm vs Que	2/14/86	7
24 players tied with 6 each.		

Penalty Minutes

	Date	Min
Randy Holt, LA at Phi	3/11/79	67
Brad Smith, Tor vs Det	11/15/86	57
Reed Low, St.L at Calg	2/28/02	57
Frank Bathe, Phi vs LA	3/11/79	55
Reed Low, St.L at Det	12/31/02	53
Russ Anderson, Pit vs Edm	1/19/80	51

Penalties

	Date	No
Chris Nilan, Bos vs Har	3/31/91	10*
Nine tied with 9 each.		

* Nilan accumulated six minors, two majors, one 10-minute misconduct and one game misconduct.

All-Time Winningest NHL Coaches

Top 20 NHL career victories through the 2005-06 season. Career, regular season and playoff records are noted along with NHL titles won. Coaches active during 2005-06 season in **bold** type. In the following tables, overtime and shootout losses are considered losses.

		Career				Regular Season				Playoffs			
		Yrs	W	L	T	Pct	W	L	T	Pct	W	L	T	Pct	Stanley Cups
1	Scotty Bowman	30	**1467**	714	313	.651	1244	584	313	.654	223	130	0	.632	9 (1973, 76-79, 92, 97-98, 2002)
2	Al Arbour	22	**904**	663	248	.566	781	577	248	.564	123	86	0	.589	4 (1980-83)
3	Dick Irvin	26	**790**	609	228	.556	690	521	226	.559	100	88	2	.532	4 (1932,44,46,53)
4	**Pat Quinn**	19	**751**	596	154	.552	657	507	154	.557	94	89	0	.514	None
5	Mike Keenan	18	**675**	560	147	.542	584	491	147	.538	91	69	0	.569	1 (1994)
6	**Bryan Murray**	15	**604**	492	131	.546	565	443	131	.554	39	49	0	.443	None
7	Billy Reay	16	**599**	445	175	.563	542	385	175	.571	57	60	0	.487	None
8	Glen Sather	13	**586**	351	122	.611	497	314	121	.598	89	37	1	.705	4 (1984-85,87-88)
9	Toe Blake	13	**582**	292	159	.640	500	255	159	.634	82	37	0	.689	8 (1956-60,65-66,68)
10	Pat Burns	14	**579**	438	151	.560	501	367	151	.566	78	71	0	.523	1 (2003)
11	Roger Neilson	16	**511**	436	159	.534	460	381	159	.540	51	55	0	.481	None
12	**Jacques Martin**	12	**482**	418	119	.531	444	371	119	.539	38	47	0	.447	None
13	Brian Sutter	13	**479**	477	140	.501	451	437	140	.507	28	40	0	.412	None
14	Ken Hitchcock	10	**473**	305	88	.597	407	254	88	.602	66	51	0	.564	1 (1999)
15	**Jacques Lemaire**	12	**465**	397	124	.534	408	353	124	.531	57	44	0	.564	1 (1995)
	Jack Adams	21	**465**	442	162	.511	413	390	161	.512	52	52	1	.500	3 (1936-37, 43)
17	Jacques Demers	14	**464**	510	130	.479	409	467	130	.471	55	43	0	.561	1 (1993)
18	**Darryl Sutter**	11	**456**	404	101	.527	409	350	101	.534	47	54	0	.465	None
19	**Marc Crawford**	11	**454**	349	103	.558	411	309	103	.562	43	40	0	.518	1 (1996)
20	**Ron Wilson**	12	**453**	444	101	.505	418	408	101	.505	35	36	0	.493	None

Where They Coached

Adams—Toronto (1922-23), Detroit (1927-47); **Arbour**—St. Louis (1970-73), NY Islanders (1973-86,88-94); **Blake**—Montreal (1955-68); **Bowman**—St. Louis (1967-71), Montreal (1971-79), Buffalo (1979-87), Pittsburgh (1991-93), Detroit (1993-2002); **Burns**—Montreal (1988-92), Toronto (1992-96), Boston (1997-2000), New Jersey (2002-03); **Crawford**—Quebec/Colorado (1994-98), Vancouver (98-2006), Los Angeles (2006–); **Demers**—Quebec (1979-80), St. Louis (1983-86), Detroit (1986-90), Montreal (1992-95), Tampa Bay (1997-99).

Hitchcock—Dallas (1996-2002), Philadelphia (2002–); **Irvin**—Chicago (1930-31,55-56), Toronto (1931-40), Montreal (1940-55); **Keenan**—Philadelphia (1984-88), Chicago (1988-92), NY Rangers (1993-94), St. Louis (1994-96), Vancouver (1997-99), Boston (2000-01), Florida (2001-03); **Lemaire**—Montreal (1984-85), New Jersey (1993-98), Minnesota (2000–); **Martin**—St. Louis (1986-88), Ottawa (1995-2004), Florida (2004–); **Murray**—Washington (1982-90), Detroit (1990-93), Florida (1997-98), Anaheim (2001-02), Ottawa (2004–).

Neilson—Toronto (1977-79), Buffalo (1979-81), Vancouver (1982-83), Los Angeles (1984), NY Rangers (1989-93), Florida (1993-95), Philadelphia (1998-00), Ottawa (2002); **Quinn**—Philadelphia (1978-82), Los Angeles (1984-87), Vancouver (1990-94, 96), Toronto (1998-2006); **Reay**—Toronto (1957-59), Chicago (1963-77); **Sather**—Edmonton (1979-89, 93-94), NY Rangers (2003-04); **B. Sutter**—St. Louis (1988-92), Boston (1992-95), Calgary (1997-2000), Chicago (2001-05); **D. Sutter**—Chicago (1992-95), San Jose (1997-02), Calgary (2002-06); **Wilson**—Anaheim (1993-97), Washington (1997-2002), San Jose (2002–).

Top Winning Percentages

Minimum of 275 victories, including playoffs.

		Yrs	W	L	T	Pct.
1	Scotty Bowman	30	1467	714	313	**.651**
2	Toe Blake	13	582	292	159	**.640**
3	Glen Sather	13	586	351	122	**.611**
4	Fred Shero	10	451	272	119	**.606**
5	Don Cherry	6	281	177	77	**.597**
6	**Ken Hitchcock**	10	473	305	88	**.597**
7	Tommy Ivan	9	324	205	111	**.593**
8	**Bob Hartley**	7	335	246	61	**.569**
9	**Joel Quenneville**	9	388	287	77	**.567**
10	Al Arbour	22	904	663	248	**.566**
11	Billy Reay	16	599	445	175	**.563**
12	Emile Francis	13	433	326	112	**.561**
13	Pat Burns	14	579	438	151	**.560**
14	**Marc Crawford**	11	454	349	103	**.558**
15	Hap Day	10	308	237	81	**.557**
16	Dick Irvin	26	790	609	228	**.556**
17	Lester Patrick	13	312	242	115	**.552**
18	Art Ross	18	393	310	95	**.552**
19	**Pat Quinn**	19	751	596	154	**.552**
20	Bob Johnson	6	275	223	58	**.547**
21	**Bryan Murray**	15	604	492	131	**.546**
22	Terry Murray	11	406	331	89	**.545**
23	Mike Keenan	18	675	560	147	**.542**
24	**Jacques Lemaire**	12	465	397	124	**.534**
25	Roger Neilson	16	511	436	159	**.534**
26	**Lindy Ruff**	8	348	302	78	**.532**
27	**Jacques Martin**	12	482	418	119	**.531**
28	Punch Imlach	15	439	384	148	**.528**
29	**Darryl Sutter**	11	456	404	101	**.527**
30	Terry Crisp	9	310	286	78	**.518**

Active Coaches' Victories

Records through 2005-06 season, including playoffs.

		Yrs	W	L	T	Pct.
1	Bryan Murray, Ott.	15	604	492	131	.546
2	Jacques Martin, Fla.	12	482	418	119	.531
3	Ken Hitchcock, Phi.	10	473	305	88	.597
4	Jacques Lemaire, Min.	12	465	397	124	.534
5	Marc Crawford, LA	11	454	349	103	.558
6	Ron Wilson, SJ	12	453	444	101	.505
7	Joel Quenneville, Col	9	388	287	77	.567
8	Lindy Ruff, Buf.	8	348	302	78	.532
9	Bob Hartley, Atl.	7	335	246	61	.569
10	Paul Maurice, Tor.	9	285	325	99	.472
11	Barry Trotz, Nash.	7	235	290	60	.453
12	Craig MacTavish, Edm.	5	209	190	47	.521
13	John Tortorella, TB	6	186	191	37	.494
14	Peter Laviolette, Car.	4	169	141	25	.542
15	Dave Tippett, Dal.	3	148	92	28	.604
16	Mike Babcock, Det.	3	144	110	19	.562
17	Alain Vigneault, Van.	4	113	128	35	.473
18	Dave Lewis, Bos.	2	106	58	21	.630
19	Michel Therrien, Pit.	4	97	133	23	.429
20	Tom Renney, NYR	4	88	110	9	.447
21	Ted Nolan, NYI	2	78	79	19	.497
22	Claude Julien, NJ	3	76	84	11	.477
23	Randy Carlyle, Ana.	1	52	46	0	.531
24	Gerard Gallant, Clb.	2	51	72	4	.417
25	Glen Hanlon, Wash.	2	44	83	9	.357
26	Wayne Gretzky, Pho.	1	38	44	0	.463
27	Mike Kitchen, St.L	2	31	68	4	.320
28	Trent Yawney, Chi.	1	26	56	0	.317
29	Jim Playfair, Calg.	0	0	0	0	.000
	Guy Carbonneau, Mon.	0	0	0	0	.000

Annual Awards

Note that due to the owners' lockout and cancellation of the 2004-05 season, no awards were given out in 2005.

Hart Memorial Trophy

Awarded to the player "adjudged to be the most valuable to his team" and named after Cecil Hart, the former manager-coach of the Montreal Canadiens. Winners selected by Pro Hockey Writers Assn. (PHWA). Winners' scoring statistics or goaltender W-L records and goals against average are provided; (*) indicates led or tied for league lead.

Multiple winners: Wayne Gretzky (9); Gordie Howe (6); Eddie Shore (4); Bobby Clarke, Mario Lemieux, Howie Morenz and Bobby Orr (3); Jean Beliveau, Bill Cowley, Phil Esposito, Dominik Hasek, Bobby Hull, Guy Lafleur, Mark Messier, Stan Mikita and Nels Stewart (2).

Year		G	A	Pts	Year		G	A	Pts
1924	Frank Nighbor, Ottawa, C	10	3	13	1951	Milt Schmidt, Bos., C	22	39	61
1925	Billy Burch, Hamilton, C	20	4	24	1952	Gordie Howe, Det., RW	47	39	86*
1926	Nels Stewart, Maroons, C	34	8	42*	1953	Gordie Howe, Det., RW	49	46	95*
1927	Herb Gardiner, Mon., D	6	6	12	1954	Al Rollins, Chi., G	12-47-7;		3.23
1928	Howie Morenz, Mon., C	33	18	51	1955	Ted Kennedy, Tor., C	10	42	52
1929	Roy Worters, NYA, G	16-13-9;		1.21	1956	Jean Beliveau, Mon., C	47	41	88
1930	Nels Stewart, Maroons, C	39	16	55	1957	Gordie Howe, Det.,RW	44	45	89*
1931	Howie Morenz, Mon., C	28	23	51*	1958	Gordie Howe, Det., RW	33	44	77
1932	Howie Morenz, Mon., C	24	25	49	1959	Andy Bathgate, NYR, RW	40	48	88
1933	Eddie Shore, Bos., D	8	27	35	1960	Gordie Howe, Det., RW	28	45	73
1934	Aurel Joliat, Mon., LW	22	15	37	1961	Bernie Geoffrion, Mon., RW	50	45	95*
1935	Eddie Shore, Bos., D	7	26	33	1962	Jacques Plante, Mon., G	42-14-14;		2.37*
1936	Eddie Shore, Bos., D	3	16	19	1963	Gordie Howe, Det., RW	38	48	86*
1937	Babe Siebert, Mon., D	8	20	28	1964	Jean Beliveau, Mon., C	28	50	78
1938	Eddie Shore, Bos., D	3	14	17	1965	Bobby Hull, Chi., LW	39	32	71
1939	Toe Blake, Mon., LW	24	23	47*	1966	Bobby Hull, Chi., LW	54	43	97*
1940	Ebbie Goodfellow, Det., D	11	17	28	1967	Stan Mikita, Chi., C	35	62	97*
1941	Bill Cowley, Bos., C	17	45	62*	1968	Stan Mikita, Chi., C	40	47	87*
1942	Tommy Anderson, NYA, D	12	29	41	1969	Phil Esposito, Bos., C	49	77	126*
1943	Bill Cowley, Bos., C	27	45	72	1970	Bobby Orr, Bos., D	33	87	120*
1944	Babe Pratt, Tor., D	17	40	57	1971	Bobby Orr, Bos., D	37	102	139
1945	Elmer Lach, Mon., C	26	54	80*	1972	Bobby Orr, Bos., D	37	80	117
1946	Max Bentley, Chi., C	31	30	61*	1973	Bobby Clarke, Phi., C	37	67	104
1947	Maurice Richard, Mon., RW	45	26	71	1974	Phil Esposito, Bos., C	68	77	145*
1948	Buddy O'Connor, NYR, C	24	36	60	1975	Bobby Clarke, Phi., C	27	89	116
1949	Sid Abel, Det., C	28	26	54	1976	Bobby Clarke, Phi., C	30	89	119
1950	Chuck Rayner, NYR, G	28-30-11;		2.62	1977	Guy Lafleur, Mon., RW	56	80	136*

Year		G	A	Pts	Year		G	A	Pts
1978	Guy Lafleur, Mon., RW	60	72	132*	1992	Mark Messier, NYR, C	35	72	107
1979	Bryan Trottier, NYI., C	47	87	134*	1993	Mario Lemieux, Pit., C	69	91	160*
1980	Wayne Gretzky, Edm., C	51	86	137*	1994	Sergei Fedorov, Det., C	56	64	120
1981	Wayne Gretzky, Edm., C	55	109	164*	1995	Eric Lindros, Phi., C	29	41	70*
1982	Wayne Gretzky, Edm., C	92	120	212*	1996	Mario Lemieux, Pit., C	69	92	161*
1983	Wayne Gretzky, Edm., C	71	125	196*	1997	Dominik Hasek, Buf., G	37-20-10;		2.27
1984	Wayne Gretzky, Edm., C	87	118	205*	1998	Dominik Hasek, Buf., G	33-23-13;		2.09
1985	Wayne Gretzky, Edm., C	73	135	208*	1999	Jaromir Jagr, Pit., RW	44	83	127*
1986	Wayne Gretzky, Edm., C	52	163	215*	2000	Chris Pronger, St.L, D	14	48	62
1987	Wayne Gretzky, Edm., C	62	121	183*	2001	Joe Sakic, Col., C	54	64	118
1988	Mario Lemieux, Pit., C	70	98	168*	2002	Jose Theodore, Mon., G	30-24-10;		2.11
1989	Wayne Gretzky, LA, C	54	114	168	2003	Peter Forsberg, Col., C	29	77	106*
1990	Mark Messier, Edm., C	45	84	129	2004	Martin St. Louis, TB, RW	38	56	94*
1991	Brett Hull, St. L., RW	86	45	131	2006	Joe Thornton, Bos-SJ	29	96	125*

Calder Memorial Trophy

Awarded to the most outstanding rookie of the year and named after Frank Calder, the late NHL president (1917-43). Since the 1990-91 season, all eligible candidates must not have attained their 26th birthday by Sept. 15 of their rookie year. Winners selected by PHWA. Winners' scoring statistics or goaltender W-L record & goals against average are provided.

Year		G	A	Pts	Year		G	A	Pts
1933	Carl Voss, NYR-Det., C	8	15	23	1970	Tony Esposito, Chi., G	38-17-8;		2.17
1934	Russ Blinco, Maroons, C	14	9	23	1971	Gilbert Perreault, Buf., C	38	34	72
1935	Sweeney Schriner, NYA, LW	18	22	40	1972	Ken Dryden, Mon., G	39-8-15;		2.24
1936	Mike Karakas, Chi., G	21-19-8;		1.92	1973	Steve Vickers, NYR, LW	30	23	53
1937	Syl Apps, Tor., C	16	29	45	1974	Denis Potvin, NYI, D	17	37	54
1938	Cully Dahlstrom, Chi., C	10	9	19	1975	Eric Vail, Atl., LW	39	21	60
1939	Frankie Brimsek, Bos., G	33-9-1;		1.58	1976	Bryan Trottier, NYI, C	32	63	95
1940	Kilby MacDonald, NYR, LW	15	13	28	1977	Willi Plett, Atl., RW	33	23	56
1941	John Quilty, Mon., C	18	16	34	1978	Mike Bossy, NYI, RW	53	38	91
1942	Knobby Warwick, NYR, RW	16	17	33	1979	Bobby Smith, Min., C	30	44	74
1943	Gaye Stewart, Tor., LW	24	23	47	1980	Ray Bourque, Bos., D	17	48	65
1944	Gus Bodnar, Tor., C	22	40	62	1981	Peter Stastny, Que., C	39	70	109
1945	Frank McCool, Tor., G	24-22-4;		3.22	1982	Dale Hawerchuk, Win., C	45	58	103
1946	Edgar Laprade, NYR, C	15	19	34	1983	Steve Larmer, Chi., RW	43	47	90
1947	Howie Meeker, Tor., RW	27	18	45	1984	Tom Barrasso, Buf., G	26-12-3;		2.84
1948	Jim McFadden, Det., C	24	24	48	1985	Mario Lemieux, Pit., C	43	57	100
1949	Penny Lund, NYR, RW	14	16	30	1986	Gary Suter, Calg., D	18	50	68
1950	Jack Gelineau, Bos., G	22-30-15;		3.28	1987	Luc Robitaille, LA, LW	45	39	84
1951	Terry Sawchuk, Det., G	44-13-13;		1.99	1988	Joe Nieuwendyk, Calg., C	51	41	92
1952	Bernie Geoffrion, Mon., RW	30	24	54	1989	Brian Leetch, NYR, D	23	48	71
1953	Gump Worsley, NYR, G	13-29-8;		3.06	1990	Sergei Makarov, Calg., RW	24	62	86
1954	Camille Henry, NYR, LW	24	15	39	1991	Ed Belfour, Chi., G	43-19-7;		2.47
1955	Ed Litzenberger, Mon-Chi., RW	23	28	51	1992	Pavel Bure, Van., RW	34	26	60
1956	Glenn Hall, Det., G	30-24-16;		2.11	1993	Teemu Selanne, Win., RW	76	56	132
1957	Larry Regan, Bos., RW	14	19	33	1994	Martin Brodeur, NJ, G	27-11-8;		2.40
1958	Frank Mahovlich, Tor., LW	20	16	36	1995	Peter Forsberg, Que., C	15	35	50
1959	Ralph Backstrom, Mon., C	18	22	40	1996	Daniel Alfredsson, Ott., RW	26	35	61
1960	Billy Hay, Chi., C	18	37	55	1997	Bryan Berard, NYI, D	8	40	48
1961	Dave Keon, Tor., C	20	25	45	1998	Sergei Samsonov, Bos., LW	22	25	47
1962	Bobby Rousseau, Mon., RW	21	24	45	1999	Chris Drury, Col., C	20	24	44
1963	Kent Douglas, Tor., D	7	15	22	2000	Scott Gomez, NJ, C	19	51	70
1964	Jacques Laperriere, Mon., D	2	28	30	2001	Evgeni Nabokov, SJ, G	32-21-7;		2.19
1965	Roger Crozier, Det., G	40-23-7;		2.42	2002	Dany Heatley, Atl., RW	26	41	67
1966	Brit Selby, Tor., LW	14	13	27	2003	Barret Jackman, St.L, D	3	16	19
1967	Bobby Orr, Bos., D	13	28	41	2004	Andrew Raycroft, Bos., G	29-18-9;		2.05
1968	Derek Sanderson, Bos., C	24	25	49	2006	Alexander Ovechkin, Wash, L	52	54	106
1969	Danny Grant, Min., LW	34	31	65					

Vezina Trophy

From 1927-80, given to the principal goaltender(s) on the team allowing the fewest goals during the regular season. Trophy named after 1920's goalie Georges Vezina of the Montreal Canadiens, who died of tuberculosis in 1926. Since the 1980-81 season, the trophy has been awarded to the most outstanding goaltender of the year as selected by the league's general managers.

Multiple Winners: Jacques Plante (7, one of them shared); Bill Durnan and Dominik Hasek (6); Ken Dryden (5, three shared); Bunny Larocque (4, all shared); Terry Sawchuk (4, one shared); Tiny Thompson (4); Tony Esposito (3, one shared); George Hainsworth (3); Glenn Hall (3, two shared); Patrick Roy (3); Ed Belfour (2); Johnny Bower (2, one shared); Frankie Brimsek (2); Turk Broda (2); Martin Brodeur (2); Chuck Gardiner (2); Charlie Hodge (2, one shared); Bernie Parent (2, one shared); Gump Worsley (2, both shared).

Year		Record	GAA	Year		Record	GAA
1927	George Hainsworth, Mon	28-14-2	1.52	1930	Tiny Thompson, Bos	38-5-1	2.23
1928	George Hainsworth, Mon	26-11-7	1.09	1931	Roy Worters, NYA	18-16-10	1.68
1929	George Hainsworth, Mon	22-7-15	0.98	1932	Chuck Gardiner, Chi	18-19-11	1.92

Annual Awards (Cont.)

Year		Record	GAA	Year		Record	GAA
1933	Tiny Thompson, Bos	25-15-8	1.83	1971	Ed Giacomin, NYR	27-10-7	2.16
1934	Chuck Gardiner, Chi	20-17-11	1.73		& Gilles Villemure, NYR	22-8-4	2.30
1935	Lorne Chabot, Chi	26-17-5	1.83	1972	Tony Esposito, Chi	31-10-6	1.77
1936	Tiny Thompson, Bos	22-20-6	1.71		& Gary Smith, Chi	14-5-6	2.42
1937	Norm Smith, Det	25-14-9	2.13	1973	Ken Dryden, Mon	33-7-13	2.26
1938	Tiny Thompson, Bos	30-11-7	1.85	1974	(Tie) Bernie Parent, Phi	47-13-12	1.89
1939	Frankie Brimsek, Bos.	33-9-1	1.58		Tony Esposito, Chi	34-14-21	2.04
1940	Dave Kerr, NYR	27-11-10	1.60	1975	Bernie Parent, Phi.	44-14-10	2.03
1941	Turk Broda, Tor	28-14-6	2.06	1976	Ken Dryden, Mon	42-10-8	2.03
1942	Frankie Brimsek, Bos.	24-17-6	2.45	1977	Ken Dryden, Mon	41-6-8	2.14
1943	John Mowers, Det	25-14-11	2.47		& Bunny Larocque, Mon	19-2-4	2.09
1944	Bill Durnan, Mon	38-5-7	2.18	1978	Ken Dryden, Mon	37-7-7	2.05
1945	Bill Durnan, Mon	38-8-4	2.42		& Bunny Larocque, Mon.	22-3-4	2.67
1946	Bill Durnan, Mon	24-11-5	2.60	1979	Ken Dryden, Mon	30-10-7	2.30
1947	Bill Durnan, Mon	34-16-10	2.30		& Bunny Larocque, Mon.	22-7-4	2.84
1948	Turk Broda, Tor	32-15-13	2.38	1980	Bob Sauve, Buf	20-8-4	2.36
1949	Bill Durnan, Mon	28-23-9	2.10		& Don Edwards, Buf.	27-9-12	2.57
1950	Bill Durnan, Mon	26-21-17	2.20	1981	Richard Sevigny, Mon.	20-4-3	2.40
1951	Al Rollins, Tor.	27-5-8	1.77		Denis Herron, Mon.	6-9-6	3.50
1952	Terry Sawchuk, Det.	44-14-12	1.90		& Bunny Larocque, Mon.	16-9-3	3.03
1953	Terry Sawchuk, Det.	32-15-16	1.90	1982	Billy Smith, NYI	32-9-4	2.97
1954	Harry Lumley, Tor	32-24-13	1.86	1983	Pete Peeters, Bos	40-11-9	2.36
1955	Terry Sawchuk, Det.	40-17-11	1.96	1984	Tom Barrasso, Buf.	26-12-3	2.84
1956	Jacques Plante, Mon.	42-12-10	1.86	1985	Pelle Lindbergh, Phi	40-17-7	3.02
1957	Jacques Plante, Mon.	31-18-12	2.02	1986	John Vanbiesbrouck, NYR	31-21-5	3.32
1958	Jacques Plante, Mon.	34-14-8	2.11	1987	Ron Hextall, Phi	37-21-6	3.00
1959	Jacques Plante, Mon.	38-16-13	2.16	1988	Grant Fuhr, Edm.	40-24-9	3.43
1960	Jacques Plante, Mon.	40-17-12	2.54	1989	Patrick Roy, Mon	33-5-6	2.47
1961	Johnny Bower, Tor	33-15-10	2.50	1990	Patrick Roy, Mon	31-16-5	2.53
1962	Jacques Plante, Mon.	42-14-14	2.37	1991	Ed Belfour, Chi.	43-19-7	2.47
1963	Glenn Hall, Chi	30-20-16	2.55	1992	Patrick Roy, Mon.	36-22-8	2.36
1964	Charlie Hodge, Mon	33-18-11	2.26	1993	Ed Belfour, Chi.	41-18-11	2.59
1965	Johnny Bower, Tor	13-13-8	2.38	1994	Dominik Hasek, Buf	30-20-6	1.95
	& Terry Sawchuk, Tor	17-13-6	2.56	1995	Dominik Hasek, Buf	19-14-7	2.11
1966	Gump Worsley, Mon	29-14-6	2.36	1996	Jim Carey, Wash	35-24-9	2.26
	& Charlie Hodge, Mon	12-7-2	2.58	1997	Dominik Hasek, Buf	37-20-10	2.27
1967	Glenn Hall, Chi	19-5-5	2.38	1998	Dominik Hasek, Buf	33-23-13	2.09
	& Denis Dejordy, Chi	22-12-7	2.46	1999	Dominik Hasek, Buf	30-18-14	1.87
1968	Gump Worsley, Mon	19-9-8	1.98	2000	Olaf Kolzig, Wash	41-20-11	2.24
	& Rogie Vachon, Mon	23-13-2	2.48	2001	Dominik Hasek, Buf	37-24-4	2.11
1969	Jacques Plante, St.L	18-12-6	1.96	2002	Jose Theodore, Mon.	30-24-10	2.11
	& Glenn Hall, St.L	19-12-8	2.17	2003	Martin Brodeur, NJ.	41-23-9	2.02
1970	Tony Esposito, Chi	38-17-8	2.17	2004	Martin Brodeur, NJ.	38-26-11	2.03
				2006	Miikka Kiprusoff, Calg	42-20-11	2.07

Lady Byng Memorial Trophy

Awarded to the player "adjudged to have exhibited the best type of sportsmanship and gentlemanly conduct combined with a high standard of playing ability" and named after Lady Evelyn Byng, the wife of former Canadian Governor General (1921-26) Baron Byng of Vimy. Winners selected by PHWA.

Multiple winners: Frank Boucher (7); Wayne Gretzky (5); Red Kelly (4); Bobby Bauer, Mike Bossy, Alex Delvecchio and Ron Francis (3); Johnny Bucyk, Marcel Dionne, Paul Kariya, Dave Keon, Stan Mikita, Joey Mullen, Frank Nighbor, Jean Ratelle, Clint Smith and Sid Smith (2).

Year		Year		Year	
1925	Frank Nighbor, Ott., C	1943	Max Bentley, Chi., C	1961	Red Kelly, Tor., D
1926	Frank Nighbor, Ott., C	1944	Clint Smith, Chi., C	1962	Dave Keon, Tor., C
1927	Billy Burch, NYA, C	1945	Bill Mosienko, Chi., RW	1963	Dave Keon, Tor., C
1928	Frank Boucher, NYR, C	1946	Toe Blake, Mon., LW	1964	Ken Wharram, Chi., RW
1929	Frank Boucher, NYR, C	1947	Bobby Bauer, Bos., RW	1965	Bobby Hull, Chi., LW
1930	Frank Boucher, NYR, C	1948	Buddy O'Connor, NYR, C	1966	Alex Delvecchio, Det., LW
1931	Frank Boucher, NYR, C	1949	Bill Quackenbush, Det., D	1967	Stan Mikita, Chi., C
1932	Joe Primeau, Tor., C	1950	Edgar Laprade, NYR, C	1968	Stan Mikita, Chi., C
1933	Frank Boucher, NYR, C	1951	Red Kelly, Det., D	1969	Alex Delvecchio, Det., LW
1934	Frank Boucher, NYR, C	1952	Sid Smith, Tor., LW	1970	Phil Goyette, St.L., C
1935	Frank Boucher, NYR, C	1953	Red Kelly, Det., D	1971	Johnny Bucyk, Bos., LW
1936	Doc Romnes, Chi., F	1954	Red Kelly, Det., D	1972	Jean Ratelle, NYR, C
1937	Marty Barry, Det., C	1955	Sid Smith, Tor., LW	1973	Gilbert Perreault, Buf., C
1938	Gordie Drillon, Tor., RW	1956	Earl Reibel, Det., C	1974	Johnny Bucyk, Bos., LW
1939	Clint Smith, NYR, C	1957	Andy Hebenton, NYR, RW	1975	Marcel Dionne, Det., C
1940	Bobby Bauer, Bos., RW	1958	Camille Henry, NYR, LW	1976	Jean Ratelle, NY-Bos., C
1941	Bobby Bauer, Bos., RW	1959	Alex Delvecchio, Det., LW	1977	Marcel Dionne, LA, C
1942	Syl Apps, Tor., C	1960	Don McKenney, Bos., C	1978	Butch Goring, LA, C

Year		Year		Year	
1979	Bob MacMillan, Atl., RW	1988	Mats Naslund, Mon., LW	1997	Paul Kariya, Ana., LW
1980	Wayne Gretzky, Edm., C	1989	Joey Mullen, Calg., RW	1998	Ron Francis, Pit., C
1981	Rick Kehoe, Pit., RW	1990	Brett Hull, St.L., RW	1999	Wayne Gretzky, NYR, C
1982	Rick Middleton, Bos., RW	1991	Wayne Gretzky, LA, C	2000	Pavol Demitra, St.L, RW
1983	Mike Bossy, NYI, RW	1992	Wayne Gretzky, LA, C	2001	Joe Sakic, Col., C
1984	Mike Bossy, NYI, RW	1993	Pierre Turgeon, NYI, C	2002	Ron Francis, Car., C
1985	Jari Kurri, Edm., RW	1994	Wayne Gretzky, LA, C	2003	Alexander Mogilny, Tor., RW
1986	Mike Bossy, NYI, RW	1995	Ron Francis, Pit., C	2004	Brad Richards, TB, C
1987	Joey Mullen, Calg., RW	1996	Paul Kariya, Ana., LW	2006	Pavel Datsyuk, Det., C

Note: Bill Quackenbush and Red Kelly are the only defensemen to win the Lady Byng.

James Norris Memorial Trophy

Awarded to the most outstanding defenseman of the year and named after James Norris, the late Detroit Red Wings owner-president. Winners selected by PHWA.

Multiple winners: Bobby Orr (8); Doug Harvey (7); Ray Bourque (5); Nicklas Lidstrom (4); Chris Chelios, Paul Coffey, Pierre Pilote and Denis Potvin (3); Rod Langway, Brian Leetch and Larry Robinson (2).

Year		Year		Year	
1954	Red Kelly, Detroit	1972	Bobby Orr, Boston	1990	Ray Bourque, Boston
1955	Doug Harvey, Montreal	1973	Bobby Orr, Boston	1991	Ray Bourque, Boston
1956	Doug Harvey, Montreal	1974	Bobby Orr, Boston	1992	Brian Leetch, NY Rangers
1957	Doug Harvey, Montreal	1975	Bobby Orr, Boston	1993	Chris Chelios, Chicago
1958	Doug Harvey, Montreal	1976	Denis Potvin, NY Islanders	1994	Ray Bourque, Boston
1959	Tom Johnson, Montreal	1977	Larry Robinson, Montreal	1995	Paul Coffey, Detroit
1960	Doug Harvey, Montreal	1978	Denis Potvin, NY Islanders	1996	Chris Chelios, Chicago
1961	Doug Harvey, Montreal	1979	Denis Potvin, NY Islanders	1997	Brian Leetch, NY Rangers
1962	Doug Harvey, NY Rangers	1980	Larry Robinson, Montreal	1998	Rob Blake, Los Angeles
1963	Pierre Pilote, Chicago	1981	Randy Carlyle, Pittsburgh	1999	Al MacInnis, St. Louis
1964	Pierre Pilote, Chicago	1982	Doug Wilson, Chicago	2000	Chris Pronger, St. Louis
1965	Pierre Pilote, Chicago	1983	Rod Langway, Washington	2001	Nicklas Lidstrom, Detroit
1966	Jacques Laperriere, Montreal	1984	Rod Langway, Washington	2002	Nicklas Lidstrom, Detroit
1967	Harry Howell, NY Rangers	1985	Paul Coffey, Edmonton	2003	Nicklas Lidstrom, Detroit
1968	Bobby Orr, Boston	1986	Paul Coffey, Edmonton	2004	Scott Niedermayer, NJ
1969	Bobby Orr, Boston	1987	Ray Bourque, Boston	2006	Nicklas Lidstrom, Detroit
1970	Bobby Orr, Boston	1988	Ray Bourque, Boston		
1971	Bobby Orr, Boston	1989	Chris Chelios, Montreal		

Frank Selke Trophy

Awarded to the outstanding defensive forward of the year and named after the late Montreal Canadiens general manager. Winners selected by the PHWA.

Multiple winners: Bob Gainey (4); Guy Carbonneau and Jere Lehtinen (3); Sergei Fedorov and Michael Peca (2).

Year		Year		Year	
1978	Bob Gainey, Mon., LW	1988	Guy Carbonneau, Mon., C	1998	Jere Lehtinen, Dal., RW
1979	Bob Gainey, Mon., LW	1989	Guy Carbonneau, Mon., C	1999	Jere Lehtinen, Dal., RW
1980	Bob Gainey, Mon., LW	1990	Rick Meagher, St.L., C	2000	Steve Yzerman, Det., C
1981	Bob Gainey, Mon., LW	1991	Dirk Graham, Chi., RW	2001	John Madden, NJ, LW
1982	Steve Kasper, Bos., C	1992	Guy Carbonneau, Mon., C	2002	Michael Peca, NYI, C
1983	Bobby Clarke, Phi., C	1993	Doug Gilmour, Tor., C	2003	Jere Lehtinen, Dal., RW
1984	Doug Jarvis, Wash., C	1994	Sergei Fedorov, Det., C	2004	Kris Draper, Det., C
1985	Craig Ramsay, Buf., LW	1995	Ron Francis, Pit., C	2006	Rod Brind'Amour, Car., C
1986	Troy Murray, Chi., C	1996	Sergei Fedorov, Det., C		
1987	Dave Poulin, Phi., C	1997	Michael Peca, Buf., C		

Jack Adams Award

Awarded to the coach "adjudged to have contributed the most to his team's success" and named after the late Detroit Red Wings coach and general manager. Winners selected by NHL Broadcasters' Assn.; (*) indicates division champion.

Multiple winners: Pat Burns (3); Scotty Bowman, Jacques Demers and Pat Quinn (2).

Year		Improvement		Year		Improvement	
1974	Fred Shero, Phi.	37-30-11	to 50-16-12*	1990	Bob Murdoch, Win	26-42-12	to 37-32-11
1975	Bob Pulford, LA	41-14-23	to 37-35-8	1991	Brian Sutter, St.L	37-34-9	to 47-22-11
1976	Don Cherry, Bos	40-26-14	to 48-15-17*	1992	Pat Quinn, Van	28-43-9	to 42-26-12*
1977	Scotty Bowman, Mon	58-11-11*	to 60-8-12*	1993	Pat Burns, Tor	30-43-7	to 44-29-11
1978	Bobby Kromm, Det	6-55-9	to 32-34-14	1994	Jacques Lemaire, NJ	40-37-7	to 47-25-12
1979	Al Arbour, NYI	48-17-15*	to 51-15-14*	1995	Marc Crawford, Que	34-42-8	to 30-13-5*
1980	Pat Quinn, Phi	40-25-15	to 48-12-20*	1996	Scotty Bowman, Det	33-11-4*	to 62-13-7*
1981	Red Berenson, St.L	34-34-12	to 45-18-17*	1997	Ted Nolan, Buf	33-42-7	to 40-30-12*
1982	Tom Watt, Win	9-57-14	to 33-33-14	1998	Pat Burns, Bos	26-47-9	to 39-30-13
1983	Orval Tessier, Chi	30-38-12	to 47-23-10	1999	Jacques Martin, Ott	34-33-15	to 44-23-15*
1984	Bryan Murray, Wash	39-25-16	to 48-27-5	2000	Joel Quenneville, St.L.	37-32-13	to 51-20-11*
1985	Mike Keenan, Phi	44-26-10	to 53-20-7*	2001	Bill Barber, Phi	45-25-12	to 43-25-11-3
1986	Glen Sather, Edm	49-20-11*	to 56-17-7*	2002	Bob Francis, Pho	35-27-17-3	to 40-27-9-6
1987	Jacques Demers, Det	17-57-6	to 34-36-10	2003	Jacques Lemaire, Minn.	26-35-12-9	to 42-29-10-1
1988	Jacques Demers, Det	34-36-10	to 41-28-11*	2004	John Tortorella, TB	36-25-16-5	to 46-22-8-6*
1989	Pat Burns, Mon	45-22-13	to 53-18-9*	2006	Lindy Ruff, Buf	37-34-7-4	to 52-24-1-5

Annual Awards (Cont.)
Lester B. Pearson Award

Awarded to the season's most outstanding player and named after the former diplomat, Nobel Peace Prize winner and Canadian prime minister. Winners selected by the NHL Players Association.

Multiple winners: Wayne Gretzky (5); Mario Lemieux (4); Jaromir Jagr and Guy Lafleur (3); Marcel Dionne, Phil Esposito, Dominik Hasek and Mark Messier (2).

Year		Year		Year	
1971	Phil Esposito, Bos., C	1983	Wayne Gretzky, Edm., C	1995	Eric Lindros, Phi., C
1972	Jean Ratelle, NYR, C	1984	Wayne Gretzky, Edm., C	1996	Mario Lemieux, Pit., C
1973	Bobby Clarke, Phi., C	1985	Wayne Gretzky, Edm., C	1997	Dominik Hasek, Buf., G
1974	Phil Esposito, Bos., C	1986	Mario Lemieux, Pit., C	1998	Dominik Hasek, Buf., G
1975	Bobby Orr, Bos., D	1987	Wayne Gretzky, Edm., C	1999	Jaromir Jagr, Pit., RW
1976	Guy Lafleur, Mon., RW	1988	Mario Lemieux, Pit., C	2000	Jaromir Jagr, Pit., RW
1977	Guy Lafleur, Mon., RW	1989	Steve Yzerman, Det., C	2001	Joe Sakic, Col., C
1978	Guy Lafleur, Mon., RW	1990	Mark Messier, Edm., C	2002	Jarome Iginla, Calg., RW
1979	Marcel Dionne, LA, C	1991	Brett Hull, St.L., RW	2003	Markus Naslund, Van., LW
1980	Marcel Dionne, LA, C	1992	Mark Messier, NYR, C	2004	Martin St. Louis, TB, RW
1981	Mike Liut, St.L., G	1993	Mario Lemieux, Pit., C	2006	Jaromir Jagr, NYR
1982	Wayne Gretzky, Edm., C	1994	Sergei Fedorov, Det., C		

King Clancy Memorial Trophy

Awarded to the player who "best exemplifies leadership on and off the ice and who has made a noteworthy humanitarian contribution to his community" and named after former player, coach, official and executive Frank "King" Clancy. Presented by the NHL's Board of Governors.

Year		Year		Year	
1988	Lanny McDonald, Calg., RW	1994	Adam Graves, NYR, LW	2000	Curtis Joseph, Tor., G
1989	Bryan Trottier, NYI, C	1995	Joe Nieuwendyk, Calg., C	2001	Shjon Podein, Col., LW
1990	Kevin Lowe, Edm., D	1996	Kris King, Win., LW	2002	Ron Francis, Car., C
1991	Dave Taylor, LA, RW	1997	Trevor Linden, Van., C	2003	Brendan Shanahan, Det., LW
1992	Ray Bourque, Bos., D	1998	Kelly Chase, St.L, RW	2004	Jarome Iginla, Calg., RW
1993	Dave Poulin, Bos., C	1999	Rob Ray, Buf., RW	2006	Olaf Kolzig, Wash., G

Bill Masterton Trophy

Awarded to the player who "best exemplifies the qualities of perseverance, sportsmanship and dedication to hockey" and named after the 29-year-old rookie center of the Minnesota North Stars who died of a head injury sustained in a 1968 NHL game. Presented by the PHWA.

Year		Year		Year	
1968	Claude Provost, Mon., RW	1981	Blake Dunlop, St.L., C	1994	Cam Neely, Bos., RW
1969	Ted Hampson, Oak., C	1982	Chico Resch, Colo., G	1995	Pat LaFontaine, Buf., C
1970	Pit Martin, Chi., C	1983	Lanny McDonald, Calg., RW	1996	Gary Roberts, Calg., LW
1971	Jean Ratelle, NYR, C	1984	Brad Park, Det., D	1997	Tony Granato, SJ, LW
1972	Bobby Clarke, Phi., C	1985	Anders Hedberg, NYR, RW	1998	Jamie McLennan, St.L, G
1973	Lowell MacDonald, Pit., RW	1986	Charlie Simmer, Bos., LW	1999	John Cullen, TB, C
1974	Henri Richard, Mon., C	1987	Doug Jarvis, Hart., C	2000	Ken Daneyko, NJ, D
1975	Don Luce, Buf., C	1988	Bob Bourne, LA, C	2001	Adam Graves, NYR, LW
1976	Rod Gilbert, NYR, RW	1989	Tim Kerr, Phi., C	2002	Saku Koivu, Mon., C
1977	Ed Westfall, NYI, RW	1990	Gord Kluzak, Bos., D	2003	Steve Yzerman, Det., C
1978	Butch Goring, LA, C	1991	Dave Taylor, LA, RW	2004	Bryan Berard, Chi., D
1979	Serge Savard, Mon., D	1992	Mark Fitzpatrick, NYI, G	2006	Teemu Selanne, Ana., R
1980	Al MacAdam, Min., RW	1993	Mario Lemieux, Pit., C		

Number One Draft Choices

Overall first choices in the NHL draft since the league staged its first universal amateur draft in 1969. Players are listed with team that selected them; those who became Rookie of the Year are in **bold** type.

Year		Year		Year	
1969	Rejean Houle, Mon., LW	1982	Gord Kluzak, Bos., D	1995	**Bryan Berard,** Ott., D
1970	**Gilbert Perreault,** Buf., C	1983	Brian Lawton, Min., C	1996	Chris Phillips, Ott., D
1971	Guy Lafleur, Mon., RW	1984	**Mario Lemieux,** Pit., C	1997	Joe Thornton, Bos., C
1972	Billy Harris, NYI, RW	1985	Wendel Clark, Tor., LW/D	1998	Vincent Lecavalier, TB, C
1973	**Denis Potvin,** NYI, D	1986	Joe Murphy, Det., C	1999	Patrik Stefan, Atl., C
1974	Greg Joly, Wash., D	1987	Pierre Turgeon, Buf., C	2000	Rick DiPietro, NYI, G
1975	Mel Bridgman, Phi., C	1988	Mike Modano, Min., C	2001	Ilya Kovalchuk, Atl., RW
1976	Rick Green, Wash., D	1989	Mats Sundin, Que., RW	2002	Rick Nash, Clb., LW
1977	Dale McCourt, Det., C	1990	Owen Nolan, Que., RW	2003	Marc-Andre Fleury, Pit., G
1978	**Bobby Smith,** Min., C	1991	Eric Lindros, Que., C	2004	**Alexander Ovechkin,** Wash., LW
1979	Rob Ramage, Colo., D	1992	Roman Hamrlik, TB, D		
1980	Doug Wickenheiser, Mon., C	1993	Alexandre Daigle, Ott., C	2005	Sidney Crosby, Pit., C
1981	**Dale Hawerchuk,** Win., C	1994	Ed Jovanovski, Fla., D	2006	Erik Johnson, St.L, D

World Hockey Association
WHA Finals

The World Hockey Association began play in 1972-73 as a 12-team rival of the 56-year-old NHL. The WHA played for the AVCO World Trophy in its seven playoff finals (Avco Financial Services underwrote the playoffs).

Multiple winners: Winnipeg (3); Houston (2).

Year	Winner	Head Coach	Series	Loser	Head Coach
1973	New England Whalers	Jack Kelley	4-1 (WWLWW)	Winnipeg Jets	Bobby Hull
1974	Houston Aeros	Bill Dineen	4-0	Chicago Cougars	Pat Stapleton
1975	Houston Aeros	Bill Dineen	4-0	Quebec Nordiques	Jean-Guy Gendron
1976	Winnipeg Jets	Bobby Kromm	4-0	Houston Aeros	Bill Dineen
1977	Quebec Nordiques	Marc Boileau	4-3 (LWLWWLW)	Winnipeg Jets	Bobby Kromm
1978	Winnipeg Jets	Larry Hillman	4-0	NE Whalers	Harry Neale
1979	Winnipeg Jets	Larry Hillman	4-2 (WWLWLW)	Edmonton Oilers	Glen Sather

Playoff MVPs—1973—No award; **1974**—No award; **1975**—Ron Grahame, Houston, G; **1976**—Ulf Nilsson, Winnipeg, C; **1977**—Serg Bernier, Quebec, C; **1978**—Bobby Guindon, Winnipeg, C; **1979**—Rich Preston, Winnipeg, RW.

Most Valuable Player
(Gordie Howe Trophy, 1976-79)

Year		G	A	Pts
1973	Bobby Hull, Win., LW	.51	52	103
1974	Gordie Howe, Hou., RW	.31	69	100
1975	Bobby Hull, Win., LW	.77	65	142
1976	Marc Tardif, Que., LW	.71	77	148
1977	Robbie Ftorek, Pho., C	.46	71	117
1978	Marc Tardif, Que., LW	.65	89	154
1979	Dave Dryden, Edm., G	.41-17-2;2.89		

Scoring Leaders

Year		Gm	G	A	Pts
1973	Andre Lacroix, Phi	.78	50	74	124
1974	Mike Walton, Min	.78	57	60	117
1975	Andre Lacroix, S. Diego	.78	41	106	147
1976	Marc Tardif, Que	.81	71	77	148
1977	Real Cloutier, Que	.76	66	75	141
1978	Marc Tardif, Que	.78	65	89	154
1979	Real Cloutier, Que	.77	75	54	129

Note: In 1979, 18 year-old Rookie of the Year Wayne Gretzky finished third in scoring (46-64—110).

Rookie of the Year

Year		G	A	Pts
1973	Terry Caffery, N. Eng., C	.39	61	100
1974	Mark Howe, Hou., LW	.38	41	79
1975	Anders Hedberg, Win., RW	.53	47	100
1976	Mark Napier, Tor., RW	.43	50	93
1977	George Lyle, N. Eng., LW	.39	33	72
1978	Kent Nilsson, Win., C	.42	65	107
1979	Wayne Gretzky, Ind.-Edm., C	.46	64	110

Best Goaltender

Year		Record	GAA
1973	Gerry Cheevers, Cleveland	.32-20-0	2.84
1974	Don McLeod, Houston	.33-13-3	2.56
1975	Ron Grahame, Houston	.33-10-0	3.03
1976	Michel Dion, Indianapolis	.14-15-1	2.74
1977	Ron Grahame, Houston	.27-10-2	2.74
1978	Al Smith, New England	.30-20-3	3.22
1979	Dave Dryden, Edmonton	.41-17-2	2.89

Best Defenseman

Year	
1973	J.C. Tremblay, Quebec
1974	Pat Stapleton, Chicago
1975	J.C. Tremblay, Quebec
1976	Paul Shmyr, Cleveland
1977	Ron Plumb, Cincinnati
1978	Lars-Erik Sjoberg, Winnipeg
1979	Rick Ley, New England

Coach of the Year

Year			Improvement
1973	Jack Kelley, N..Eng		46-30-2*
1974	Billy Harris, Tor	.35-39-4 to	41-33-4
1975	Sandy Hucul, Pho	.Expan. to	39-31-8
1976	Bobby Kromm, Win	.38-35-5	52-27-2*
1977	Bill Dineen, Hou	.53-27-0 * to	50-24-6*
1978	Bill Dineen, Hou	.50-24-6 * to	42-34-4
1979	John Brophy, Birm	.36-41-3 to	32-42-6

*Won Division.

WHA All-Star Game

The WHA All-Star Game was an Eastern Division vs Western Division contest from 1973-75. In 1976, the league's five Canadian-based teams played the nine teams in the US. Over the final three seasons–East played West in 1977; AVCO Cup champion Quebec played a WHA All-Star team in 1978; and in 1979, a full WHA All-Star team played a three-game series with Moscow Dynamo of the Soviet Union.

Year	Result	Host	Coaches	Most Valuable Player
1973	East 6, West 2	Quebec	Jack Kelley, Bobby Hull	Wayne Carleton, Ottawa
1974	East 8, West 4	St. Paul, MN	Jack Kelley, Bobby Hull	Mike Walton, Minnesota
1975	West 6, East 4	Edmonton	Bill Dineen, Ron Ryan	Rejean Houle, Quebec
1976	Canada 6, USA 1	Cleveland	Jean-Guy Gendron, Bill Dineen	Can—Real Cloutier, Que. USA—Paul Shmyr, Cleve.
1977	East 4, West 2	Hartford	Jacques Demers, Bobby Kromm	East—L. Levasseur, Min. West—W. Lindstrom, Win.
1978	Quebec 5, WHA 4	Quebec	Marc Boileau, Bill Dineen	Quebec—Marc Tardif WHA—Mark Howe, NE
1979	WHA def. Moscow Dynamo 3 games to none (4-2, 4-2, 4-3)	Edmonton	Larry Hillman, P. Iburtovich	No awards

World Championship
Men

The World Hockey Championship tournament has been played regularly since 1930. The International Ice Hockey Federation (IIHF), which governs both the World and Winter Olympic tournaments, considers the Olympic champions from 1920-68 to also be the World champions. However the IIHF has not recognized an Olympic champion as World champion since 1968. The IIHF has sanctioned separate World Championships in Olympic years four times–in 1972, 1976, 1992 and 2002. The world championship is officially vacant for the three Olympic years from 1980-88.

Multiple winners: Soviet Union/Russia and Canada (23); Sweden (8); Czechoslovakia (6) Czech Republic (5), USA (2).

Year		Year		Year		Year	
1920	Canada	1952	Canada	1971	Soviet Union	1990	Soviet Union
1924	Canada	1953	Sweden	1972	Czechoslovakia	1991	Sweden
1928	Canada	1954	Soviet Union	1973	Soviet Union	1992	Sweden
1930	Canada	1955	Canada	1974	Soviet Union	1993	Russia
1931	Canada	1956	Soviet Union	1975	Soviet Union	1994	Canada
1932	Canada	1957	Sweden	1976	Czechoslovakia	1995	Finland
1933	United States	1958	Canada	1977	Czechoslovakia	1996	Czech Republic
1934	Canada	1959	Canada	1978	Soviet Union	1997	Canada
1935	Canada	1960	United States	1979	Soviet Union	1998	Sweden
1936	Great Britain	1961	Canada	1980	Not held	1999	Czech Republic
1937	Canada	1962	Sweden	1981	Soviet Union	2000	Czech Republic
1938	Canada	1963	Soviet Union	1982	Soviet Union	2001	Czech Republic
1939	Canada	1964	Soviet Union	1983	Soviet Union	2002	Slovakia
1940-46	Not held	1965	Soviet Union	1984	Not held	2003	Canada
1947	Czechoslovakia	1966	Soviet Union	1985	Czechoslovakia	2004	Canada
1948	Canada	1967	Soviet Union	1986	Soviet Union	2005	Czech Republic
1949	Czechoslovakia	1968	Soviet Union	1987	Sweden	2006	Sweden
1950	Canada	1969	Soviet Union	1988	Not held		
1951	Canada	1970	Soviet Union	1989	Soviet Union		

Women

The women's World Hockey Championship tournament is governed by the International Ice Hockey Federation (IIHF).

Multiple winners: Canada (8).

Year		Year		Year		Year		Year	
1990	Canada	1994	Canada	1999	Canada	2001	Canada	2005	United States
1992	Canada	1997	Canada	2000	Canada	2004	Canada		

Canada vs. USSR Summits

The first competition between the Soviet National Team and the NHL took place Sept. 2-28, 1972. A team of NHL All-Stars emerged as the winner of the heralded 8-game series, but just barely–winning with a record of 4-3-1 after trailing 1-3-1.

Two years later a WHA All-Star team played the Soviet Nationals and could win only one game and tie three others in eight contests. Two other Canada vs USSR series took place during NHL All-Star breaks: the three-game Challenge Cup at New York in 1979, and the two-game Rendez-Vous '87 in Quebec City in 1987.

The NHL All-Stars played the USSR in a three-game Challenge Cup series in 1979.

1972 Team Canada vs. USSR

NHL All-Stars vs Soviet National Team.

Date	City	Result	Goaltenders
9/2	Montreal	USSR, 7-3	Tretiak/Dryden
9/4	Toronto	Canada, 4-1	Esposito/Tretiak
9/6	Winnipeg	Tie, 4-4	Tretiak/Esposito
9/8	Vancouver	USSR, 5-3	Tretiak/Dryden
9/22	Moscow	USSR, 5-4	Tretiak/Esposito
9/24	Moscow	Canada, 3-2	Dryden/Tretiak
9/26	Moscow	Canada, 4-3	Esposito/Tretiak
9/28	Moscow	Canada, 6-5	Dryden/Tretiak

Standings

	W	L	T	Pts	GF	GA
Team Canada (NHL)	4	3	1	9	32	32
Soviet Union	3	4	1	7	32	32

Leading Scorers

1. Phil Esposito, Canada, (7-6–13); **2.** Aleksandr Yakushev, USSR (7-4–11); **3.** Paul Henderson, Canada (7-2–9); **4.** Boris Shadrin, USSR (3-5–8); **5.** Valeri Kharlamov, USSR (3-4–7) and Vladimir Petrov, USSR (3-4–7).

1974 Team Canada vs. USSR

WHA All-Stars vs Soviet National Team.

Date	City	Result	Goaltenders
9/17	Quebec City	Tie, 3-3	Tretiak/Cheevers
9/19	Toronto	Canada, 4-1	Cheevers/Tretiak
9/21	Winnipeg	USSR, 8-5	Tretiak/McLeod
9/23	Vancouver	Tie, 5-5	Tretiak/Cheevers
10/1	Moscow	USSR, 3-2	Tretiak/Cheevers
10/3	Moscow	USSR, 5-2	Tretiak/Cheevers
10/5	Moscow	Tie, 4-4	Cheevers/Tretiak
10/6	Moscow	USSR, 3-2	Sidelnikov/Cheevers

Standings

	W	L	T	Pts	GF	GA
Soviet Union	4	1	3	11	32	27
Team Canada (WHA)	1	4	3	5	27	32

Leading Scorers

1. Bobby Hull, Canada (7-2–9); **2.** Aleksandr Yakushev, USSR (6-2–8), Ralph Backstrom, Canada (4-4–8) and Valeri Kharlamov, USSR (2-6–8); **5.** Gordie Howe, Canada (3-4–7), Andre Lacroix, Canada (1-6–7) and Vladimi Petrov, USSR (1-6–7).

1979 Challenge Cup Series

NHL All-Stars vs Soviet National Team

Date	City	Result	Goaltenders
2/8	New York	NHL, 4-2	K. Dryden/Tretiak
2/10	New York	USSR, 5-4	Tretiak/K. Dryden
2/11	New York	USSR, 6-0	Myshkin/Cheevers

Rendez-Vous '87

NHL All-Stars vs Soviet National Team

Date	City	Result	Goaltenders
2/11	Quebec	NHL, 4-3	Fuhr/Belosheykhin
2/13	Quebec	USSR, 5-3	Belosheykhin/Fuhr

The Canada Cup

After organizing the historic 8-game Team Canada-Soviet Union series of 1972, NHL Players Association executive director Alan Eagleson and the NHL created the Canada Cup in 1976. For the first time, the best players from the world's six major hockey powers—Canada, Czechoslovakia, Finland, Russia, Sweden and the USA—competed together in one tournament.

1976
Round Robin Standings

	W	L	T	Pts	GF	GA
Canada	4	1	0	8	22	6
Czechoslovakia	3	1	1	7	19	9
Soviet Union	2	2	1	5	23	14
Sweden	2	2	1	5	16	18
United States	1	3	1	3	14	21
Finland	1	4	0	2	16	42

Finals (Best of 3)

Date	City	Score
9/13	Toronto	Canada 6, Czechoslovakia 0
9/15	Montreal	Canada 5, Czechoslovakia 4 (OT)

Note: Darryl Sittler scored the winning goal for Canada at 11:33 in overtime to clinch the Cup, 2 games to none.

Leading Scorers

1. Victor Hluktov, USSR (5-4—9), Bobby Orr, Canada (2-7—9) and Denis Potvin, Canada (1-8—9); **4.** Bobby Hull, Canada (5-3—8) and Milan Novy, Czechoslovakia (5-3—8).

Team MVPs

Canada—Rogie Vachon   Sweden—Borje Salming
Czech.—Milan Novy   USA—Robbie Ftorek
USSR—Alexandr Maltsev   Finland—Matti Hagman
Tournament MVP—Bobby Orr, Canada

1981
Round Robin Standings

	W	L	T	Pts	GF	GA
Canada	4	0	1	9	32	13
Soviet Union	3	1	1	7	20	13
Czechoslovakia	2	1	2	6	21	13
United States	2	2	1	5	17	19
Sweden	1	4	0	2	13	20
Finland	0	4	1	1	6	31

Semifinals

Date	City	Score
9/11	Ottawa	USSR 4, Czechoslovakia 1
9/11	Montreal	Canada 4, United States 1

Finals

Date	City	Score
9/13	Montreal	USSR 8, Canada 1

Leading Scorers

1. Wayne Gretzky, Canada (5-7—12); **2.** Mike Bossy, Canada (8-3—11), Bryan Trottier, Canada (3-8—11), Guy Lafleur, Canada (2-9—11), Alexei Kasatonov, USSR (1-10—11).

All-Star Team

Goal—Vladislav Tretiak, USSR; **Defense**—Arnold Kadlec, Czech. and Alexei Kasatonov, USSR; **Forwards**—Mike Bossy, Canada, Gil Perreault, Canada, and Sergei Shepelev, USSR. **Tournament MVP**—Tretiak.

1984
Round Robin Standings

	W	L	T	Pts	GF	GA
Soviet Union	5	0	0	10	22	7
United States	3	1	1	7	21	13
Sweden	3	2	0	6	15	16
Canada	2	2	1	5	23	18
West Germany	0	4	1	1	13	29
Czechoslovakia	0	4	1	1	10	21

Semifinals

Date	City	Score
9/12	Edmonton	Sweden 9, United States 2
9/15	Montreal	Canada 3, USSR 2 (OT)

Note: Mike Bossy scored the winning goal for Canada at 12:29 in overtime.

Finals (Best of 3)

Date	City	Score
9/16	Calgary	Canada 5, Sweden 2
9/18	Edmonton	Canada 6, Sweden 5

Leading Scorers

1. Wayne Gretzky, Canada (5-7—12); **2.** Michel Goulet, Canada (5-6—11), Kent Nilsson, Sweden (3-8—11), Paul Coffey, Canada (3-8—11); **5.** Hakan Loob, Sweden (6-4—10).

All-Star Team

Goal—Vladimir Myshkin, USSR; **Defense**—Paul Coffey, Canada and Rod Langway, USA; **Forwards**—Wayne Gretzky, Canada, John Tonelli, Canada, and Sergei Makarov, USSR. **Tournament MVP**—Tonelli.

1987
Round Robin Standings

	W	L	T	Pts	GF	GA
Canada	3	0	2	8	19	13
Soviet Union	3	1	1	7	22	13
Sweden	3	2	0	6	17	14
Czechoslovakia	2	2	1	5	12	15
United States	2	3	0	4	13	14
Finland	0	5	0	0	9	23

Semifinals

Date	City	Score
9/8	Hamilton	USSR 4, Sweden 2
9/9	Montreal	Canada 5, Czechoslovakia 3

Finals (Best of 3)

Date	City	Score
9/11	Montreal	USSR 6, Canada 5 (OT)
9/13	Hamilton	Canada 6, USSR 5 (2 OT)
9/15	Hamilton	Canada 6, USSR 5

Note: In Game 1, Alexander Semak of USSR scored at 5:33 in overtime. In Game 2, Mario Lemieux of Canada scored at 10:01 in the second overtime period. Lemieux also won Game 3 on a goal with 1:26 left in regulation time.

Leading Scorers

1. Wayne Gretzky, Canada (3-18—21); **2.** Mario Lemieux, Canada (11-7—18); **3.** Sergei Makarov, USSR (7-8—15); **4.** Vladimir Krutov, USSR (7-7—14); **5.** Viacheslav Bykov, USSR (2-7—9); **6.** Ray Bourque, Canada (2-6—8).

All-Star Team

Goal—Grant Fuhr, Canada; **Defense**—Ray Bourque, Canada and Viacheslav Fetisov, USSR; **Forwards**—Wayne Gretzky, Canada, Mario Lemieux, Canada, and Vladimir Krutov, USSR. **Tournament MVP**—Gretzky.

1991

Round Robin Standings

	W	L	T	Pts	GF	GA
Canada	3	0	2	8	21	11
United States	4	1	0	8	19	15
Finland	2	2	1	5	10	13
Sweden	2	3	0	4	13	17
Soviet Union	1	3	1	3	14	14
Czechoslovakia	1	4	0	2	11	18

Semifinals

Date	City	Score
9/11	Hamilton	United States 7, Finland 3
9/12	Toronto	Canada 4, Sweden 0

Finals (Best of 3)

Date	City	Score
9/14	Montreal	Canada 4, United States 1
9/16	Hamilton	Canada 4, United States 2

Leading Scorers

1. Wayne Gretzky, Canada (4-8—12); **2.** Steve Larmer, Canada (6-5—11); **3.** Brett Hull, USA (2-7—9); **4.** Mike Modano, USA (2-7—9); **5.** Mark Messier, Canada (2-6—8).

All-Star Team

Goal—Bill Ranford, Canada; **Defense**—Al MacInnis, Canada and Chris Chelios, USA; **Forwards**—Wayne Gretzky, Canada, Jeremy Roenick, USA and Mats Sundin, Sweden. **Tournament MVP**—Bill Ranford.

The World Cup

Formed jointly by the NHL and the NHL Players Association in cooperation with the International Ice Hockey Federation. The inaugural World Cup held games in nine different cities throughout North America and Europe, the most ever by a single international hockey tournament.

1996

Round Robin Standings

European Pool	W	L	T	Pts	GF	GA
Sweden	3	0	0	6	14	3
Finland	2	1	0	4	17	11
Germany	1	2	0	2	11	15
Czech Republic	0	3	0	0	4	17

North American Pool	W	L	T	Pts	GF	GA
United States	3	0	0	6	19	8
Canada	2	1	0	4	11	10
Russia	1	2	0	2	12	14
Slovakia	0	3	0	0	10	18

Semifinals

Date	City	Score
9/7	Philadelphia	Canada 3, Sweden 2 (OT)
9/8	Ottawa	United States 5, Russia 2

Finals (Best of 3)

Date	City	Score
9/10	Philadelphia	Canada 4, United States 3 (OT)
9/12	Montreal	United States 5, Canada 2
9/14	Montreal	United States 5, Canada 2

Leading Scorers

1. Brett Hull, USA (7-4—11); **2.** John LeClair, USA (6-4—10); **3.** Mats Sundin, Sweden (4-3—7); Wayne Gretzky, Canada (3-4—7); Doug Weight, USA (3-4—7); Paul Coffey, Canada (0-7—7); Brian Leetch, USA (0-7—7).

All-Tournament Team

Goal—Mike Richter, USA; **Defense**—Calle Johansson, Sweden and Chris Chelios, USA; **Forwards**—Brett Hull, USA; John LeClair, USA and Mats Sundin, Sweden. **Tournament MVP**—Mike Richter, USA.

2004

Round Robin Standings

European Pool	W	L	T	Pts	GF	GA
Finland	2	0	1	5	11	4
Sweden	2	0	1	5	13	9
Czech Republic	1	2	0	2	10	10
Germany	0	3	0	0	4	15

North American Pool	W	L	T	Pts	GF	GA
Canada	3	0	0	6	10	3
Russia	2	1	0	4	9	6
United States	1	2	0	2	5	6
Slovakia	0	3	0	0	4	13

Semifinals

Date	City	Score
9/10	St. Paul, Minn.	Finland 2, United States 1
9/11	Toronto	Canada 4, Czech Rep. 3 (OT)

Championship Game

Date	City	Score
9/14	Toronto	Canada 3, Finland 2

Leading Scorers

1. Fredrik Modin, Sweden (4-4—8); **2.** Vincent Lecavalier, Canada (2-5—7); **3.** Keith Tkachuk, USA (5-1—6); Joe Sakic, Canada (4-2—6); Martin Havlat, Czech Republic (3-3—6); Kimmo Timonen, Finland (1-5—6); Joe Thornton, Canada (1-5—6); Mike Modano, USA (0-6—6); Daniel Alfredsson, Sweden (0-6—6).

All-Tournament Team

Goal—Martin Brodeur, Canada; **Defense**—Kimmo Timonen, Finland and Adam Foote, Canada; **Forwards**—Vincent Lecavalier, Canada; Saku Koivu, Finland and Fredrik Modin, Sweden. **Tournament MVP**—Vincent Lecavalier, Canada.

Note: See Olympics chapter for all men's and women's Olympic hockey results.

U.S. DIVISION I COLLEGE HOCKEY

NCAA Men's Frozen Four

The NCAA Division I hockey tournament began in 1948 and was played at the Broadmoor Ice Palace in Colorado Springs from 1948-57. Since 1958, the tournament has moved around the country, stopping for consecutive years only at Boston Garden from 1972-74. Consolation games to determine third place were played from 1949-89 and discontinued in 1990.

Multiple winners: Michigan (9); North Dakota and Denver (7); Wisconsin (6); Minnesota (5); Boston University (4); Lake Superior St. and Michigan Tech (3); Boston College, Colorado College, Cornell, Maine, Michigan St. and RPI (2).

Year	Champion	Head Coach	Score	Runner-up	Third Place
1948	Michigan	Vic Heyliger	8-4	Dartmouth	Colorado College and Boston College

Year	Champion	Head Coach	Score	Runner-up	Third Place	Score	Fourth Place
1949	Boston College	Snooks Kelley	4-3	Dartmouth	Michigan	10-4	Colorado Col.
1950	Colorado College	Cheddy Thompson	13-4	Boston Univ.	Michigan	10-6	Boston College
1951	Michigan	Vic Heyliger	7-1	Brown	Boston Univ.	7-4	Colorado College
1952	Michigan	Vic Heyliger	4-1	Colorado Col.	Yale	4-1	St. Lawrence
1953	Michigan	Vic Heyliger	7-3	Minnesota	RPI	6-3	Boston Univ.
1954	RPI	Ned Harkness	5-4 *	Minnesota	Michigan	7-2	Boston College
1955	Michigan	Vic Heyliger	5-3	Colorado Col.	Harvard	6-3	St. Lawrence
1956	Michigan	Vic Heyliger	7-5	Michigan Tech	St. Lawrence	6-2	Boston College
1957	Colorado College	Tom Bedecki	13-6	Michigan	Clarkson	2-1†	Harvard
1958	Denver	Murray Armstrong	6-2	North Dakota	Clarkson	5-1	Harvard
1959	North Dakota	Bob May	4-3 *	Michigan St.	Boston College	7-6†	St. Lawrence
1960	Denver	Murray Armstrong	5-3	Michigan Tech	Boston Univ.	7-6	St. Lawrence
1961	Denver	Murray Armstrong	12-2	St. Lawrence	Minnesota	4-3	RPI
1962	Michigan Tech	John MacInnes	7-1	Clarkson	Michigan	5-1	St. Lawrence
1963	North Dakota	Barry Thorndycraft	6-5	Denver	Clarkson	5-3	Boston College
1964	Michigan	Allen Renfrew	6-3	Denver	RPI	2-1	Providence
1965	Michigan Tech	John MacInnes	8-2	Boston College	North Dakota	9-5	Brown
1966	Michigan St.	Amo Bessone	6-1	Clarkson	Denver	4-3	Boston Univ.
1967	Cornell	Ned Harkness	4-1	Boston Univ.	Michigan St.	6-1	North Dakota
1968	Denver	Murray Armstrong	4-0	North Dakota	Cornell	6-1	Boston College
1969	Denver	Murray Armstrong	4-3	Cornell	Harvard	6-5†	Michigan Tech
1970	Cornell	Ned Harkness	6-4	Clarkson	Wisconsin	6-5	Michigan Tech
1971	Boston Univ.	Jack Kelley	4-2	Minnesota	Denver	1-0	Harvard
1972	Boston Univ.	Jack Kelley	4-0	Cornell	Wisconsin	5-2	Denver
1973	Wisconsin	Bob Johnson	4-2	Denver	Boston College	3-1	Cornell
1974	Minnesota	Herb Brooks	4-2	Michigan Tech	Boston Univ.	7-5	Harvard
1975	Michigan Tech	John MacInnes	6-1	Minnesota	Boston Univ.	10-5	Harvard
1976	Minnesota	Herb Brooks	6-4	Michigan Tech	Brown	8-7	Boston Univ.
1977	Wisconsin	Bob Johnson	6-5 *	Michigan	Boston Univ.	6-5	N. Hampshire
1978	Boston Univ.	Jack Parker	5-3	Boston College	Bowl. Green	4-3	Wisconsin
1979	Minnesota	Herb Brooks	4-3	North Dakota	Dartmouth	7-3	N. Hampshire
1980	North Dakota	Gino Gasparini	5-2	N. Michigan	Dartmouth	8-4	Cornell
1981	Wisconsin	Bob Johnson	6-3	Minnesota	Mich. Tech	5-2	N. Michigan
1982	North Dakota	Gino Gasparini	5-2	Wisconsin	Northeastern	10-4	N. Hampshire
1983	Wisconsin	Jeff Sauer	6-2	Harvard	Providence	4-3	Minnesota
1984	Bowling Green	Jerry York	5-4 *	Minn-Duluth	North Dakota	6-5†	Michigan St.
1985	RPI	Mike Addesa	2-1	Providence	Minn. Duluth	7-6†	Boston College
1986	Michigan St.	Ron Mason	6-5	Harvard	Minnesota	6-4	Denver
1987	North Dakota	Gino Gasparini	5-3	Michigan St.	Minnesota	6-3	Harvard
1988	Lake Superior St.	Frank Anzalone	4-3 *	St. Lawrence	Maine	5-2	Minnesota
1989	Harvard	Billy Cleary	4-3 *	Minnesota	Michigan St.	7-4	Maine

Year	Champion	Head Coach	Score	Runner-up	Third Place
1990	Wisconsin	Jeff Sauer	7-3	Colgate	Boston College and Boston Univ.
1991	Northern Michigan	Rick Comley	8-7 *	Boston Univ.	Maine and Clarkson
1992	Lake Superior St.	Jeff Jackson	5-3	Wisconsin	Michigan and Michigan St.
1993	Maine	Shawn Walsh	5-4	Lake Superior St.	Boston Univ. and Michigan
1994	Lake Superior St.	Jeff Jackson	9-1	Boston Univ.	Harvard and Minnesota
1995	Boston Univ.	Jack Parker	6-2	Maine	Michigan and Minnesota
1996	Michigan	Red Berenson	3-2 *	Colorado Col.	Vermont and Boston Univ.
1997	North Dakota	Dean Blais	6-4	Boston Univ.	Colorado College and Michigan
1998	Michigan	Red Berenson	3-2 *	Boston College	New Hampshire and Ohio St.
1999	Maine	Shawn Walsh	3-2 *	New Hampshire	Boston College and Michigan St.
2000	North Dakota	Dean Blais	4-2	Boston College	St. Lawrence and Maine
2001	Boston College	Jerry York	3-2 *	North Dakota	Michigan and Michigan St.
2002	Minnesota	Don Lucia	4-3 *	Maine	Michigan and New Hampshire
2003	Minnesota	Don Lucia	5-1	New Hampshire	Michigan and Cornell
2004	Denver	George Gwozdecky	1-0	Maine	Minnesota Duluth and Boston College
2005	Denver	George Gwozdecky	4-1	North Dakota	Colorado College and Minnesota
2006	Wisconsin	Mike Eaves	2-1	Boston College	North Dakota and Maine

*Championship game overtime goals: 1954—1:54; 1959—4:22; 1977—0: 23; 1984—7:11 in 4th OT; 1988—4:46; 1989—4:16; 1991—1:57 in 3rd OT; 1996—3:35; 1998—17:51; 1999—10:50; 2001—4:43; 2002—16:58.

†Consolation game overtimes ended in 1st OT except in 1957, '59, and '69, which all ended in 2nd OT.

Note: Runners-up Denver (1973) and Wisconsin (1992) had participation voided by the NCAA for using ineligible players.

U.S. Division I College Hockey (Cont.)
Tournament Most Outstanding Player

The Most Outstanding Players of each NCAA Div. I tournament since 1948. Winners of the award who did not play for the tournament champion are in **bold** type. In 1960, three players, none on the winning team, shared the award.

Multiple winners: Lou Angotti and Marc Behrend (2).

Year	Year	Year
1948 **Joe Riley,** Dartmouth, F	1967 Walt Stanowski, Cornell, D	1988 Bruce Hoffort, Lk. Superior, G
1949 **Dick Desmond,** Dart., G	1968 Gerry Powers, Denver, G	1989 Ted Donato, Harvard, F
1950 **Ralph Bevins,** Boston U., G	1969 Keith Magnuson, Denver, D	1990 Chris Tancill, Wisconsin, F
1951 **Ed Whiston,** Brown, G	1970 Dan Lodboa, Cornell, D	1991 Scott Beattie, No. Mich., F
1952 **Ken Kinsley,** Colo. Col., G	1971 Dan Brady, Boston U., G	1992 Paul Constantin, Lk. Superior, F
1953 John Matchefts, Mich., F	1972 Tim Regan, Boston, U., G	1993 Jim Montgomery, Maine, F
1954 Abbie Moore, RPI, F	1973 Dean Talafous, Wisc., F	1994 Sean Tallaire, Lk. Superior, F
1955 **Phil Hilton,** Colo. Col., D	1974 Brad Shelstad, Minn., G	1995 Chris O'Sullivan, Boston U., F
1956 Lorne Howes, Mich., G	1975 Jim Warden, Mich. Tech, G	1996 Brendan Morrison, Michigan, F
1957 Bob McCusker, Colo. Col., F	1976 Tom Vannelli, Minn., F	1997 Matt Henderson, N. Dakota, F
1958 Murray Massier, Denver, F	1977 Julian Baretta, Wisc., G	1998 Marty Turco, Michigan, G
1959 Reg Morelli, N. Dakota, F	1978 Jack O'Callahan, Boston U., D	1999 Alfie Michaud, Maine, G
1960 **Lou Angotti,** Mich. Tech, F;	1979 Steve Janaszak, Minn., G	2000 Lee Goren, N. Dakota, F
Bob Marquis, Boston U., F;	1980 Doug Smail, N. Dakota, F	2001 Chuck Kobasew, Boston College, F
& **Barry Urbanski,** BU, G	1981 Marc Behrend, Wisc., G	2002 Grant Potulny, Minnesota, F
1961 Bill Masterton, Denver, F	1982 Phil Sykes, N. Dakota, F	2003 Thomas Vanek, Minnesota, F
1962 Lou Angotti, Mich. Tech, F	1983 Marc Behrend, Wisc., G	2004 Adam Berkhoel, Denver, G
1963 Al McLean, N. Dakota, F	1984 Gary Kruzich, Bowl. Green, G	2005 Peter Mannino, Denver, G
1964 Bob Gray, Michigan, G	1985 **Chris Terreri,** Prov., G	2006 Robbie Earl, Wisconsin, F
1965 Gary Milroy, Mich. Tech, F	1986 Mike Donnelly, Mich. St., F	
1966 Gaye Cooley, Mich. St., G	1987 Tony Hrkac, N. Dakota, F	

Hobey Baker Award

College hockey's Player of the Year award; voted on by a national panel of sportswriters, broadcasters, college coaches and pro scouts (plus a fan vote beginning in 2003). First presented in 1981 by the Decathlon Athletic Club of Bloomington, Minn., in the name of the Princeton collegiate hockey and football star who was killed in a plane crash.

Year	Year	Year
1981 Neal Broten, Minnesota, F	1990 Kip Miller, Michigan St., F	1999 Jason Krog, UNH, F
1982 George McPhee, Bowl. Green, F	1991 Dave Emma, Boston College, F	2000 Mike Mottau, Boston College, D
1983 Mark Fusco, Harvard, D	1992 Scott Pellerin, Maine, F	2001 Ryan Miller, Michigan St., G
1984 Tom Kurvers, Minn. Duluth, D	1993 Paul Kariya, Maine, F	2002 Jordan Leopold, Minnesota, D
1985 Bill Watson, Minn. Duluth, F	1994 Chris Marinucci, Minn. Duluth, F	2003 Peter Sejna, Colorado Coll., F
1986 Scott Fusco, Harvard, F	1995 Brian Holzinger, Bowl. Green, F	2004 Junior Lessard, Minn. Duluth, F
1987 Tony Hrkac, North Dakota, F	1996 Brian Bonin, Minnesota, F	2005 Marty Sertich, Colorado Coll., F
1988 Robb Stauber, Minnesota, G	1997 Brendan Morrison, Michigan, F	2006 Matt Carle, Denver, D
1989 Lane MacDonald, Harvard, F	1998 Chris Drury, Boston U., F	

NCAA Women's Frozen Four

Women's college hockey was officially introduced as an NCAA Division I sport in 2000-01.

Multiple winner: Minnesota-Duluth (3); Minnesota (2).

Year	Champion	Head Coach	Score	Runner-up	Third Place	Score	Fourth Place
2001	Minnesota Duluth	Shannon Miller	4-2	St. Lawrence	Harvard	3-2	Dartmouth
2002	Minnesota Duluth	Shannon Miller	3-2	Brown	(tie) Niagara and Minnesota, 2-2		
2003	Minnesota Duluth	Shannon Miller	4-3*	Harvard	Dartmouth	4-2	Minnesota
2004	Minnesota	Laura Halldorson	6-2	Harvard	St. Lawrence	2-1	Dartmouth
2005	Minnesota	Laura Halldorson	4-3	Harvard	St. Lawrence	5-1	Dartmouth
2006	Wisconsin	Mark Johnson	3-0	Minnesota	New Hampshire and St. Lawrence (no game)		

*Championship game overtime goal: 2003—4:19 in 2nd OT.

Tournament Most Outstanding Player

The Most Outstanding Players of each NCAA Women's Division I tournament since 2001. Winner of the award who did not play for the tournament champion in **bold** type.

Year	Year	Year
2001 Maria Rooth, Minn. Duluth, F	2003 Caroline Ouellette, Minn. Duluth, F	2005 Natalie Darwitz, Minnesota, F
2002 **Kristy Zamora,** Brown, F	2004 Krissy Wendell, Minnesota, F	2006 Jessie Vetter, Wisconsin, G

Patty Kazmaier Award

Awarded annually to the women's Division I player who displays the highest standards of personal and team excellence during the season; voted on by a 13-member panel of national media, college coaches and one USA Hockey member. First presented in 1998, in the name of the Princeton collegiate hockey and lacrosse star who died in 1990 of a rare blood disease.

Multiple winner: Jennifer Botterill (2).

Year	Year	Year
1998 Brandy Fisher, New Hampshire, F	2001 Jennifer Botterill, Harvard, F	2004 Angela Ruggiero, Harvard, D
1999 A.J. Mleczko, Harvard, F	2002 Brooke Whitney, Northeastern, F	2005 Krissy Wendell, Minnesota, F
2000 Ali Brewer, Brown, G	2003 Jennifer Botterill, Harvard, F	2006 Sara Bauer, Wisconsin, F

FANTASY SPORTS

Chargers RB **LaDainian Tomlinson** has been a high first-rounder in most fantasy football drafts since 2002.

LIFE IS JUST
A FANTASY

ESPN's Eric Karabell discusses some of the strengths, weaknesses, similarities and differences between fantasy baseball and football.

THERE'S JUST NO STOPPING FANTASY SPORTS. With more than 15 million adult Americans engaging in some kind of fantasy game, it's pretty clear that fantasy has become part of the sports culture.

So which fantasy sport is your favorite? Studies show that fantasy football is by far the most popular, helped by the fact the athletes perform only once a week and the season is easier to manage. Fantasy baseball comes in second place, and has been played passionately for more than 25 years. But there's also fantasy basketball, hockey, fishing, golf, racing — you name the sport, there's a fantasy game for it.

Personally, I've played fantasy baseball and football leagues for more than 15 years, and I wouldn't give up either one. I've seen fantastic finishes, both wins and losses, in each sport. Which one do I prefer? C'mon, it's like choosing which of your children you like best.

As ESPN.com's Deputy Fantasy Editor, I'm often asked about strategies, both general and intricate, so let's make like George Carlin and take a look at the differences between football and baseball.

Rosters: In football, it's generally 16 players to a team, with half of them active. It's pretty simple to understand, and owners enjoy the freedom of using bench spots for whatever they want, with few restrictions. In baseball, most rosters go 22-24 deep, and there are far more positions to think about, with two-thirds of those players trying to score runs, and the rest attempting to prevent them. Unlike football, you don't just get one statistic (points). You have 10 or more categories to think about.

Season: In football, there are 17 weeks (thanks to the ever-annoying bye week). Normally this bye week seems to come at a time when the owner is least prepared for it. The other problem with 17 weeks is that your best players aren't always

---

Eric Karabell is the Deputy Fantasy Editor for ESPN.com, where he has worked for more than nine years. He's been an avid fantasy player for much longer.

AP/Wide World Photos

As he does for the Minnesota Twins, starter **Johan Santana** will solidify your fantasy baseball team's pitching and keep you in line for a title.

around when you need them the most. Peyton Manning is one of fantasy's top quarterbacks, but if the Colts have the division sewn up in Week 15, it's unlikely he'll be helping you the final week. Baseball is a marathon, 162 games over six months, so there are no days off, let alone a week. I like the longer season, which separates the people who pay attention from those who do not. If you win a baseball league, you know you deserved it.

Prime Position: In football it's all about the running backs, who score most of the points and carry your team. In baseball, everyone loves the home run, and first basemen and outfielders generally provide them.

Overrated Position: In every football draft, someone takes a kicker or defense four rounds too soon. These positions are unpredictable, and little separates the top kickers from the middle of the pack. In baseball, saves are often thought of too highly. Mariano Rivera might be baseball's best closer, but saves are saves, and guys like Bob Wickman provide them at a fraction of the cost.

Draft: This is the biggest day of the fantasy football season, and if you mess it up, you're toast. Lot of pressure here, though many early picks are easy to predict, and late ones are often meaningless. Baseball can take all day, and you have to do a lot more homework to fill more positions.

AP/Wide World Photos

If you took a flyer on Rams backup and former Arena League QB **Kurt Warner** back in your 1999 draft, you were likely rewarded with a fantasy football championship.

In baseball, closers on bad teams get overlooked until the end, as well as the numerous 20-home run corner outfielders who do little else.

Rookies: Take a chance on the running backs as long as playing time looks good, but avoid quarterbacks at all costs. Even the great Peyton Manning was an interception machine his first season. In baseball, look for base stealers and strikeout arms, then deal your rookies in July before they hit a wall.

Specialists: In football the goal line running backs like Brandon Jacobs find their way onto teams, even if all they provide are the occasional touchdown. It's still worth it. In baseball, with so many more categories, you can afford to draft a few save guys who don't help anywhere else, or a stolen base guy with no power. The five-category baseball player is rare.

Overreacting: In football, with one game a week, a big performance tends to become worth much more than it should be, which leads to instant trade discussions. In baseball, fantasy owners get a much better sample size. Trends can be examined, so knee-jerk trades are less frequent.

Trash Talk: Fantasy baseball (rotisserie-style) is more individual, so trash talk is less a part of the game. In football, however, weekly head-to-head matchups between friends have made trash talk a staple — even a necessity — for any good league.

First round: In football there are running backs, running backs, and more running backs, with the occasional Manning or Moss mixed in. In baseball, it's usually Pujols, A-Rod and anything goes.

Late Rounds: In football, kickers and defenses are normally interchangeable, and therefore it's smart to wait until the final rounds so you can build up as much running back and wide receiver depth as possible.

Fantasy Football Top Performers

Time to relive all of your draft-day steals for the past 10 years. Listed are the top 20 fantasy football performers from 1996-2005. The scoring system used to devise the rankings is based on a combination of yardage accumulated and touchdowns scored/thrown. Note that TD shown below refer to passing touchdowns for quarterbacks, and total touchdowns for all others. (*) denotes rookie.

1996

Favre dominates in his only Super Bowl-winning season.

	Player	Pos	Key Statistics
1	Brett Favre, GB	QB	3899 passing yards, 39 TD
2	Vinny Testaverde, Bal.	QB	4177 passing yards, 33 TD
3	Terry Allen, Wash.	RB	1353 rushing yards, 21 TD
4	Terrell Davis, Den.	RB	1538 rushing yards, 15 TD
5	Mark Brunell, Jax	QB	4367 passing yards, 19 TD
6	Ricky Watters, Phi.	RB	1411 rushing yards, 13 TD
7	John Elway, Den.	QB	3328 passing yards, 26 TD
8	Jeff Blake, Cin.	QB	3624 passing yards, 24 TD
9	Curtis Martin, NE	RB	1152 rushing yards, 17 TD
10	Drew Bledsoe, NE	QB	4086 passing yards, 27 TD
11	Emmitt Smith, Dal.	RB	1204 rushing yards, 15 TD
12	Barry Sanders, Det.	RB	1553 rushing yards, 10 TD
13	Jerome Bettis, Pit.	RB	1431 rushing yards, 11 TD
14	Michael Jackson, Bal.	WR	1201 receiving yards, 14 TD
15	Tony Martin, SD	WR	1171 receiving yards, 14 TD
16	Eddie George*, Hou.	RB	1368 rushing yards, 8 TD
17	Steve Young, SF	QB	2410 passing yards, 14 TD
18	Carl Pickens, Cin.	WR	1180 receiving yards, 12 TD
19	Jeff Hostetler, Oak.	QB	2548 passing yards, 23 TD
20	Jerry Rice, SF	WR	1254 receiving yards, 9 TD

1997

Electrifying Lion Barry Sanders joins the 2000-yard club.

	Player	Pos	Key Statistics
1	Barry Sanders, Det.	RB	2053 rushing yards, 14 TD
2	Terrell Davis, Den.	RB	1750 rushing yards, 15 TD
3	Brett Favre, GB	QB	3867 passing yards, 35 TD
4	Kordell Stewart, Pit.	QB	21 passing TD, 11 rushing TD
5	Jeff George, Oak.	QB	3917 passing yards, 29 TD
6	Dorsey Levens, GB	RB	1435 rushing yards, 12 TD
7	John Elway, Den.	QB	3635 passing yards, 27 TD
8	Steve McNair, Ten.	QB	14 passing TD, 8 rushing TD
9	Drew Bledsoe, NE	QB	3706 passing yards, 28 TD
10	Steve Young, SF	QB	3029 passing yards, 19 TD
11	Mark Brunell, Jax	QB	3281 passing yards, 18 TD
12	Jerome Bettis, Pit.	RB	1665 rushing yards, 9 TD
13	Warren Moon, Sea.	QB	3678 passing yards, 25 TD
14	K. Abdul-Jabbar, Mia.	RB	892 rushing yards, 16 TD
15	N. Kaufman, Oak.	RB	1294 rushing yards, 8 TD
16	Rob Moore, Ari.	WR	1584 receiving yards, 8 TD
17	Corey Dillon*, Cin.	RB	1129 rushing yards, 10 TD
18	Antonio Freeman, GB	WR	1243 receiving yards, 12 TD
19	Marshall Faulk, Ind.	RB	1054 rushing yards, 8 TD
20	Brad Johnson, Min.	QB	3036 passing yards, 20 TD

1998

TD cracks 2000; welcome to the top-20 Moss and Owens.

	Player	Pos	Key Statistics
1	Terrell Davis, Den.	RB	2008 rushing yards, 21 TD
2	Steve Young, SF	QB	36 passing TD, 6 rushing TD
3	Jamal Anderson, Atl	RB	1846 rushing yards, 14 TD
4	R. Cunningham, Min	QB	3704 passing yards, 34 TD
5	Marshall Faulk, Ind.	RB	2227 all-purpose yards, 10 TD
6	Fred Taylor*, Jax	RB	1223 rushing yards, 17 TD
7	Brett Favre, GB	QB	4212 passing yards, 31 TD
8	Garrison Hearst, SF	RB	1570 rushing yards, 9 TD
9	Steve McNair, Ten	QB	3228 passing yards, 15 TD
10	Vinny Testaverde, NYJ	QB	3256 passing yards, 29 TD
11	Emmitt Smith, Dal.	RB	1332 rushing yards, 15 TD
12	Randy Moss*, Min.	WR	1313 receiving yards, 17 TD
13	Antonio Freeman, GB	WR	1424 receiving yards, 14 TD
14	Chris Chandler, Atl.	QB	3154 passing yards, 25 TD
15	Curtis Martin, NYJ	RB	1287 rushing yards, 9 TD
16	Trent Green, Wash.	QB	3441 passing yards, 23 TD
17	Ricky Watters, Sea.	RB	1239 rushing yards, 9 TD
18	Robert Edwards*, NE	RB	1115 rushing yards, 12 TD
19	Jake Plummer, Ari.	QB	3737 passing yards, 17 TD
20	Terrell Owens, SF	WR	1097 receiving yards, 15 TD

1999

Warner breaks out with the most surprising year in fantasy football history. Manning and Harrison join the party.

	Player	Pos	Key Statistics
1	Kurt Warner, St.L	QB	4353 passing yards, 41 TD
2	Marhsall Faulk, St.L	RB	2429 all-purpose yards, 12 TD
3	Edgerrin James*, Ind.	RB	1553 rushing yards, 17 TD
4	Steve Beuerlein, Car.	QB	4436 passing yards, 36 TD
5	Rich Gannon, Oak.	QB	3840 passing yards, 24 TD
6	Peyton Manning, Ind.	QB	4135 passing yards, 26 TD
7	Stephen Davis, Wash.	RB	1405 rushing yards, 17 TD
8	Eddie George, Ten.	RB	1304 rushing yards, 13 TD
9	Marvin Harrison, Ind.	WR	1663 receiving yards, 12 TD
10	Brad Johnson, Wash.	QB	4005 passing yards, 24 TD
11	Emmitt Smith, Dal.	RB	1397 rushing yards, 13 TD
12	Randy Moss, Min.	WR	1413 receiving yards, 12 TD
13	Doug Flutie, Buf.	QB	3171 passing yards, 19 TD
14	Brett Favre, GB	QB	4091 passing yards, 22 TD
15	Dorsey Levens, GB	RB	1034 rushing yards, 10 TD
16	Charlie Garner, SF	RB	1229 rushing yards, 6 TD
17	Cris Carter, Min.	WR	1241 receiving yards, 13 TD
18	Curtis Martin, NYJ	RB	1464 rushing yards, 5 TD
19	Steve McNair, Ten.	QB	12 passing TD, 8 rushing TD
20	Jimmy Smith, Jax	WR	1636 receiving yards, 6 TD

2000

Faulk scores 26 total touchdowns (18 rushing, 8 receiving) to break Emmitt Smith's former single-season record of 25.

	Player	Pos	Key Statistics
1	Marshall Faulk, St.L	RB	2207 all-purpose yards, 26 TD
2	D. Culpepper, Min.	QB	33 passing TD, 7 rushing TD
3	Jeff Garcia, SF	QB	4278 passing yards, 31 TD
4	Edgerrin James, Ind.	RB	1709 rushing yards, 18 TD
5	Peyton Manning, Ind.	QB	4413 passing yards, 33 TD
6	Rich Gannon, Oak.	QB	3430 passing yards, 28 TD
7	Eddie George, Ten.	RB	1509 rushing yards, 16 TD
8	D. McNabb, Phi.	QB	21 passing TD, 6 rushing TD
9	Elvis Grbac, KC	QB	4169 passing yards, 28 TD
10	Mike Anderson*, Den.	RB	1500 rushing yards, 15 TD
11	Robert Smith, Min.	RB	1521 rushing yards, 10 TD
12	Fred Taylor, Jax	RB	1399 rushing yards, 14 TD
13	Ahman Green, GB	RB	1175 rushing yards, 13 TD
14	Curtis Martin, NYJ	RB	1204 rushing yards, 11 TD
15	Ricky Watters, Sea.	RB	1242 rushing yards, 9 TD
16	Randy Moss, Min.	WR	1437 receiving yards, 15 TD
17	Charlie Garner, SF	RB	1142 rushing yards, 10 TD
18	Mark Brunell, Jax	QB	3640 passing yards, 20 TD
19	Lamar Smith, Mia.	RB	1139 rushing yards, 16 TD
20	Marvin Harrison, Ind.	WR	1413 receiving yards, 14 TD

Fantasy Football Top Performers (Cont.)

2001

The Rams are at it again, at least until their meeting with the Pats in the Super Bowl; Priest Holmes has his bust-out season; how did Jay Fiedler get in there?

	Player	Pos	Key Statistics
1	Marshall Faulk, St.L	RB	2147 all-purpose yards, 21 TD
2	Kurt Warner, St.L	QB	4830 passing yards, 36 TD
3	Jeff Garcia, SF	QB	3538 passing yards, 32 TD
4	Priest Holmes, KC	RB	2169 all-purpose yards, 10 TD
5	Rich Gannon, Oak.	QB	3828 passing yards, 27 TD
6	Steve McNair, Ten.	QB	21 passing TD, 5 rushing TD
7	D. McNabb, Phi.	QB	3233 passing yards, 25 TD
8	Peyton Manning, Ind.	QB	4131 passing yards, 26 TD
9	Ahman Green, Gb	RB	1387 rushing yards, 11 TD
10	Brett Favre, GB	QB	3921 passing yards, 32 TD
11	Aaron Brooks, NO	QB	3832 passing yards, 26 TD
12	Shaun Alexander, Sea.	RB	1318 rushing yards, 16 TD
13	Curtis Martin, NYJ	RB	1513 rushing yards, 10 TD
14	Marvin Harrison, Ind.	WR	1524 receiving yards, 15 TD
15	Terrell Owens, SF	WR	1412 receiving yards, 16 TD
16	Kordell Stewart, Pit.	QB	14 passing TD, 5 rushing TD
17	Jay Fiedler, Mia.	QB	20 passing TD, 4 rushing TD
18	Corey Dillon, Cin.	RB	1315 rushing yards, 13 TD
19	L. Tomlinson*, SD	RB	1236 rushing yards, 10 TD
20	David Boston, Ari.	WR	1598 receiving yards, 8 TD

2002

Priest Holmes solidifies himself as a top pick; Ricky Williams enjoys South Beach; Clinton Portis has a fine rookie season.

	Player	Pos	Key Statistics
1	Priest Holmes, KC	RB	2287 all-purpose yards, 24 TD
2	Ricky Williams, Mia.	RB	1853 rushing yards, 17 TD
3	L. Tomlinson, SD	RB	1683 rushing yards, 15 TD
4	Rich Gannon, Oak.	QB	4689 passing yards, 26 TD
5	Michael Vick, Atl.	QB	16 passing TD, 8 rushing TD
6	D. Culpepper, Min.	QB	18 passing TD, 10 rushing TD
7	Clinton Portis*, Den.	RB	1508 rushing yards, 17 TD
8	Shaun Alexander, Sea.	RB	1175 rushing yards, 18 TD
9	Deuce McAllister, NO	RB	1388 rushing yards, 16 TD
10	Peyton Manning, Ind.	QB	4200 passing yards, 27 TD
11	Charlie Garner, Oak.	RB	1903 all-purpose yards, 11 TD
12	Steve McNair, Ten.	QB	3387 passing yards, 22 TD
13	Trent Green, KC	QB	3690 passing yards, 26 TD
14	Drew Bledsoe, Buf.	QB	4359 passing yards, 24 TD
15	Tiki Barber, NYG	RB	1989 all-purpose yards, 11 TD
16	Aaron Brooks, NO	QB	3572 passing yards, 27 TD
17	Jeff Garcia, SF	QB	3344 passing yards, 21 TD
18	Tom Brady, NE	QB	3764 passing yards, 28 TD
19	Travis Henry, Buf.	RB	1438 rushing yards, 14 TD
20	Marvin Harrison, Ind,	WR	1722 receiving yards, 11 TD

2003

Holmes sets a new single-season touchdown record; Jamal Lewis misses the single-season rushing mark by 39 yards.

	Player	Pos	Key Statistics
1	Priest Holmes, KC	RB	2110 all-purpose yards, 27 TD
2	L. Tomlinson, SD	RB	2370 all-purpose yards, 17 TD
3	Ahman Green, GB	RB	1883 rushing yards, 20 TD
4	Jamal Lewis, Bal.	RB	2066 rushing yards, 14 TD
5	D. Culpepper, Min.	QB	3479 passing yards, 25 TD
6	Clinton Portis, Den.	RB	1591 rushing yards, 14 TD
7	Peyton Manning, Ind.	QB	4267 passing yards, 29 TD
8	Randy Moss, Min.	WR	1632 receiving yards, 17 TD
9	Shaun Alexander, Sea.	RB	1435 rushing yards, 16 TD
10	Deuce McAllister, NO	RB	1641 rushing yards, 8 TD

	Player	Pos	Key Statistics
11	Trent Green, KC	QB	4039 passing yards, 24 TD
12	Matt Hasselbeck, Sea.	QB	3841 passing yards, 26 TD
13	Torry Holt, St.L	WR	1696 receiving yards, 12 TD
14	Steve McNair, Ten.	QB	24 passing TD, 4 rushing TD
15	Aaron Brooks, NO	QB	3546 passing yards, 24 TD
16	Fred Taylor, Jax	RB	1572 rushing yards, 7 TD
17	Jon Kitna, Cin.	QB	3591 passing yards, 26 TD
18	Jeff Garcia, SF	QB	18 passing TD, 7 rushing TD
19	Ricky Williams, Mia.	RB	1372 rushing yards, 10 TD
20	Brett Favre, GB	QB	3361 passing yards, 32 TD

2004

Manning breaks Marino's record for TD passes, still beaten out by Culpepper as the top fantasy scorer; Ricky Williams sticks it to keeper-league owners everywhere by retiring just before training camp.

	Player	Pos	Key Statistics
1	D. Culpepper, Min.	QB	4717 passing yards, 39 TD
2	Peyton Manning, Ind.	QB	4557 passing yards, 49 TD
3	Shaun Alexander, Sea.	RB	1696 rushing yards, 20 TD
4	Tiki Barber, NYG	RB	2096 all-purpose yards, 15 TD
5	D. McNabb, Phi.	QB	3875 passing yards, 31 TD
6	L. Tomlinson, SD	RB	1335 rushing yards, 18 TD
7	Curtis Martin, NYJ	RB	1697 rushing yards, 14 TD
8	Trent Green, KC	QB	4591 passing yards, 27 TD
9	Jake Plummer, Den	QB	4089 passing yards, 27 TD
10	Domanick Davis, Hou.	RB	1188 rushing yards, 14 TD
11	Edgerrin James, Ind.	RB	1548 rushing yards, 9 TD
12	Brett Favre, GB	QB	4088 passing yards, 30 TD
13	Jake Delhomme, Car.	QB	3886 passing yards, 29 TD
14	Corey Dillon, NE	RB	1635 rushing yards, 13 TD
15	Aaron Brooks, NO	QB	21 passing TD, 4 rushing TD
16	Drew Brees, SD	QB	3159 passing yards, 27 TD
17	M. Muhammad, Car.	WR	1405 receiving yards, 16 TD
18	Marc Bulger, St.L	QB	3964 passing yards, 21 TD
19	Tom Brady, NE	QB	3692 passing yards, 28 TD
20	Michael Vick, Atl.	QB	2313 passing yards, 14 TD

2005

It's Shaun Alexander's turn to set a new single-season touchdown record (28); Larry Johnson takes advantage of the KC offensive line; Carson Palmer is the top-scoring fantasy quarterback of the year.

	Player	Pos	Key Statistics
1	Shaun Alexander, Sea.	RB	1880 rushing yards, 28 TD
2	Larry Johnson, KC	RB	1750 rushing yards, 21 TD
3	L. Tomlinson, SD	RB	1462 rushing yards, 20 TD
4	Tiki Barber, NYG	RB	2390 all-purpose yards, 11 TD
5	Edgerrin James, Ind.	RB	1506 rushing yards, 14 TD
6	Carson Palmer, Cin.	QB	3836 passing yards, 32 TD
7	Tom Brady, NE	QB	4110 passing yards, 26 TD
8	Peyton Manning, Ind.	QB	3747 passing yards, 28 TD
9	Clinton Portis, Wash.	RB	1516 rushing yards, 11 TD
10	Steve Smith, Car.	WR	1563 receiving yards, 13 TD
11	Matt Hasselbeck, Sea.	QB	3459 passing yards, 24 TD
12	Rudi Johnson, Cin.	RB	1458 rushing yards, 12 TD
13	Eli Manning, NYG	QB	3762 passing yards, 24 TD
14	LaMont Jordan, Oak.	RB	1025 rushing yards, 11 TD
15	Jake Plummer, Den.	QB	3366 passing yards, 18 TD
16	Michael Vick, Atl.	QB	15 passing TD, 6 rushing TD
17	Drew Brees, SD	QB	3576 passing yards, 24 TD
18	Trent Green, KC	QB	4014 passing yards, 17 TD
19	Kerry Collins, Oak.	QB	3759 passing yards, 20 TD
20	Drew Bledsoe, Dal.	QB	3639 passing yards, 23 TD

Fantasy Baseball Top Performers

Listed are the top 10 fantasy baseball positional players and top five fantasy pitchers from 1996-2005. The rankings are based on a typical 5 x 5 scoring system, where the following stats are used: batting average, home runs, runs batted in, runs, stolen bases for hitters; and wins, saves, strikeouts, earned run average and WHIP (walks + hits per inning pitched) for pitchers. (*) denotes rookie.

1996

Coors Field provides three memorable performances, and who can forget the Brady Anderson 50-homer year?

Hitter	Pos	Avg	HR	RBI	SB	R
1 Ellis Burks, Col.	OF	.344	40	128	32	142
2 Barry Bonds, SF	OF	.308	42	129	40	122
3 Alex Rodriguez, Sea.	SS	.358	36	123	15	141
4 A. Galarraga, Col.	1B	.304	47	150	18	119
5 Ken Griffey Jr., Sea.	OF	.303	49	140	16	125
6 Albert Belle, Cle.	OF	.311	48	148	11	124
7 Brady Anderson, Bal.	OF	.297	50	110	21	117
8 Kenny Lofton, Cle.	OF	.317	14	67	75	132
9 Dante Bichette, Col.	OF	.313	31	141	31	114
10 Mo Vaughn, Bos.	1B	.326	44	143	2	118

Pitcher	Pos	W	Sv	ERA	WHIP	K
1 John Smoltz, Atl.	SP	24	0	2.94	1.00	276
2 Kevin Brown, Fla.	SP	17	0	1.89	0.94	159
3 Greg Maddux, Atl.	SP	15	0	2.72	1.03	172
4 Hideo Nomo, LA	SP	16	0	3.19	1.16	234
5 Trevor Hoffman, SD	RP	9	42	2.25	0.92	111

1997

Griffey's best season still not enough to win, while Rocket's first year in Canada takes pitching honors.

Hitter	Pos	Avg	HR	RBI	SB	R
1 Larry Walker, Col.	OF	.366	49	130	33	143
2 Ken Griffey Jr., Sea.	OF	.304	56	147	15	125
3 Jeff Bagwell, Hou.	1B	.286	43	135	31	109
4 A. Galarraga, Col.	1B	.318	41	140	15	120
5 Barry Bonds, SF	OF	.291	40	101	37	123
6 Mike Piazza, LA	C	.362	40	124	5	104
7 Craig Biggio, Hou.	2B	.309	22	81	47	146
8 M. McGwire, Oak-St.L	1B	.274	58	123	3	86
9 Frank Thomas, ChW	DH	.347	35	125	1	110
10 Raul Mondesi, LA	OF	.310	30	87	32	95

Pitcher	Pos	W	Sv	ERA	WHIP	K
1 Roger Clemens, Tor.	SP	21	0	2.05	1.03	292
2 Pedro Martinez, Mon.	SP	17	0	1.90	0.93	305
3 Randy Johnson, Sea.	SP	20	0	2.28	1.05	291
4 Curt Schilling, Phi.	SP	17	0	2.97	1.05	319
5 Greg Maddux, Atl.	SP	19	0	2.20	0.95	177

1998

The single-season homer mark gets broken by two hitters, but Sosa gets the nod with his stolen bases.

Hitter	Pos	Avg	HR	RBI	SB	R
1 Sammy Sosa, ChC	OF	.308	66	158	18	134
2 Alex Rodriguez, Sea.	SS	.310	42	124	46	123
3 Mark McGwire, St.L	1B	.299	70	147	1	130
4 Ken Griffey Jr., Sea.	OF	.284	56	146	20	120
5 Albert Belle, ChW	OF	.328	49	152	6	113
6 Vinny Castilla, Col.	3B	.319	46	144	5	108
7 Juan Gonzalez, Tex.	OF	.318	45	157	2	110
8 Barry Bonds, SF	OF	.303	37	122	28	120
9 Craig Biggio, Hou.	2B	.325	20	88	50	123
10 V. Guerrero, Mon.	OF	.324	38	109	11	108

Pitcher	Pos	W	Sv	ERA	WHIP	K
1 Greg Maddux, Atl.	SP	18	0	2.22	0.98	204
2 Roger Clemens, Tor.	SP	20	0	2.65	1.10	271
3 Kevin Brown, SD	SP	18	0	2.38	1.07	257
4 Pedro Martinez, Bos.	SP	19	0	2.89	1.09	251
5 Curt Schilling, Phi.	SP	15	0	3.25	1.11	300

1999

The power of power is evident as Bagwell's second 30-30 season gets trumped by Slammin' Sammy.

Hitter	Pos	Avg	HR	RBI	SB	R
1 Sammy Sosa, ChC	OF	.288	63	141	7	114
2 Jeff Bagwell, Hou.	1B	.304	42	126	30	143
3 Chipper Jones, Atl.	3B	.319	45	110	25	116
4 Mark McGwire, St.L	1B	.278	65	147	0	118
5 Ken Griffey Jr., Sea.	OF	.285	48	134	24	123
6 Manny Ramirez, Cle.	OF	.333	44	165	2	131
7 Shawn Green, Tor.	OF	.309	42	123	20	134
8 Ivan Rodriguez, Tex.	C	.332	35	113	25	116
9 Larry Walker, Col.	OF	.379	37	115	11	108
10 Roberto Alomar, Cle.	2B	.323	24	120	37	138

Pitcher	Pos	W	Sv	ERA	WHIP	K
1 Pedro Martinez, Bos.	SP	23	0	2.07	0.92	313
2 Randy Johnson, Ari.	SP	17	0	2.48	1.02	364
3 Kevin Millwood, Atl.	SP	18	0	2.68	1.00	205
4 Kevin Brown, LA	SP	18	0	3.00	1.07	221
5 Billy Wagner, Hou.	RP	4	39	1.57	0.78	124

2000

Todd Helton enjoys his best season to keep Jeff Bagwell at No. 2, while Pedro edges the Big Unit for the second straight season.

Hitter	Pos	Avg	HR	RBI	SB	R
1 Todd Helton, Col.	1B	.372	42	147	5	138
2 Jeff Bagwell, Hou.	1B	.310	47	132	9	152
3 Sammy Sosa, Chc	OF	.320	50	138	7	106
4 V. Guerrero, Mon.	OF	.345	44	123	9	101
5 Alex Rodriguez, Sea.	SS	.316	41	132	15	134
6 Darin Erstad, Ana.	OF	.355	25	100	28	121
7 Richard Hidalgo, Hou.	OF	.314	44	122	13	118
8 Barry Bonds, SF	OF	.306	49	106	11	129
9 Carlos Delgado, Tor.	1B	.344	41	137	0	115
10 Frank Thomas, ChW	DH	.328	43	143	1	115

Pitcher	Pos	W	Sv	ERA	WHIP	K
1 Pedro Martinez, Bos.	SP	18	0	1.74	0.74	284
2 Randy Johnson, Ari.	SP	19	0	2.64	1.12	347
3 Kevin Brown, LA	SP	13	0	2.58	0.99	216
4 Greg Maddux, Atl.	SP	19	0	3.00	1.07	190
5 Robb Nen, SF	RP	4	41	1.50	0.85	92

2001

Bonds breaks HR record for his only time as fantasy's top hitter.

Hitter	Pos	Avg	HR	RBI	SB	R
1 Barry Bonds, SF	OF	.328	73	137	13	129
2 Sammy Sosa, ChC	OF	.328	64	160	0	146
3 Alex Rodriguez, Tex.	SS	.318	52	135	18	133
4 Luis Gonzalez, Ari.	OF	.325	57	142	1	128
5 Todd Helton, Col.	1B	.336	49	146	7	132
6 Shawn Green, LA	OF	.297	49	125	20	121
7 V. Guerrero, Mon.	OF	.307	34	108	37	107
8 Larry Walker, Col.	OF	.350	38	123	14	107
9 Ichiro Suzuki, Sea.	OF	.350	8	69	56	127
10 Bret Boone, Sea.	2B	.331	37	141	5	118

Pitcher	Pos	W	Sv	ERA	WHIP	K
1 Randy Johnson, Ari.	SP	21	0	2.49	1.01	372
2 Curt Schilling, Ari.	SP	22	0	2.98	1.08	293
3 Mike Mussina, NYY	SP	17	0	3.15	1.07	214
4 Greg Maddux, Atl.	SP	17	0	3.05	1.06	173
5 Javier Vazquez, Mon.	SP	16	0	3.42	1.08	208

Fantasy Baseball Top Performers (Cont.)

2002

One homer from 40-40, Vlad keeps A-Rod a runner up, while a pair of Arizona hurlers dominate the mound again.

Hitter	Pos	Avg	HR	RBI	SB	R
1 V. Guerrero, Mon.	OF	.336	39	111	40	106
2 Alex Rodriguez, Tex.	SS	.300	57	142	9	125
3 Alfonso Soriano, NYY	2B	.300	39	102	41	128
4 Barry Bonds, SF	OF	.370	46	110	9	117
5 Jim Thome, Cle.	1B	.304	52	118	1	101
6 M. Ordonez, ChW	OF	.320	38	135	7	116
7 Jason Giambi, NYY	1B	.314	41	122	2	120
8 Sammy Sosa, ChC	OF	.288	49	108	2	122
9 Lance Berkman, Hou.	OF	.292	42	128	8	106
10 Miguel Tejada, Oak.	SS	.308	34	131	7	108

Pitcher	Pos	W	Sv	ERA	WHIP	K
1 Randy Johnson, Ari.	SP	24	0	2.32	1.03	334
2 Curt Schilling, Ari.	SP	23	0	3.23	0.97	316
3 Pedro Martinez, Bos.	SP	20	0	2.26	0.92	239
4 Eric Gagne, LA	RP	4	52	1.97	0.86	114
5 Barry Zito, Oak.	SP	23	0	2.75	1.13	182

2003

Welcome to the list, Albert. Two top-10 newcomers (Pujols and Schmidt) are tops for the year.

Hitter	Pos	Avg	HR	RBI	SB	R
1 Albert Pujols. St.L	1B	.359	43	124	5	137
2 Gary Sheffield, Atl.	OF	.330	39	132	18	126
3 Alez Rodriguez, Tex.	SS	.298	47	118	17	124
4 Alfonso Soriano, NYY	2B	.290	38	91	35	114
5 Todd Helton, Col.	1B	.358	33	117	0	135
6 Barry Bonds, SF	OF	.341	45	90	7	111
7 Carlos Beltran, KC	OF	.307	26	100	41	102
8 Carlos Delgado, Tor.	1B	.302	42	145	0	117
9 Manny Ramirez, Bos.	OF	.325	37	104	3	117
10 Bret Boone, Sea.	2B	.294	35	117	16	111

Pitcher	Pos	W	Sv	ERA	WHIP	K
1 Jason Schmidt, SF	SP	17	0	2.34	0.95	208
2 Eric Gagne, LA	RP	2	55	1.20	0.69	137
3 Mark Prior, ChC	SP	18	0	2.43	1.10	245
4 Roy Halladay, Tor.	SP	22	0	3.25	1.07	204
5 Esteban Loaiza, ChW	SP	21	0	2.90	1.11	207

2004

The Twins' Johan Santana finishes No. 1 among all players, a feat that will be duplicated the following two seasons.

Hitter	Pos	Avg	HR	RBI	SB	R
1 V. Guerrero, LAA	OF	.337	39	126	15	124
2 Albert Pujols, St.L	1B	.331	46	123	5	133
3 Adrian Beltre, LA	3B	.334	48	121	7	104
4 Barry Bonds, SF	OF	.362	45	101	6	129
5 C. Beltran, KC-Hou.	OF	.267	38	104	42	121
6 Bobby Abreu, Phi.	OF	.301	30	105	40	118
7 Alex Rodriguez, NYY	3B	.286	36	106	28	112
8 Manny Ramirez, Bos.	OF	.308	43	130	2	108
9 Miguel Tejada, Bal.	SS	.311	34	150	4	107
10 Ichiro Suzuki, Sea.	OF	.372	8	60	36	101

Pitcher	Pos	W	Sv	ERA	WHIP	K
1 Johan Santana, Min.	SP	20	0	2.61	0.92	265
2 Randy Johnson, Ari.	SP	16	0	2.60	0.90	290
3 Curt Schilling, Bos.	SP	21	0	3.26	1.06	203
4 Jason Schmidt, SF	SP	18	0	3.20	1.08	251
5 Roger Clemens, Hou.	SP	18	0	2.98	1.16	218

2005

A-Rod's third best season finally results in top fantasy hitter honors. Santana plays sweet music again.

Hitter	Pos	Avg	HR	RBI	SB	R
1 A. Rodriguez, NYY	3B	.321	48	130	21	124
2 Derrek Lee, ChC	1B	.335	46	107	15	120
3 Albert Pujols, St.L	1B	.330	41	117	16	129
4 David Ortiz, Bos.	DH	.300	47	148	1	119
5 Mark Texeira, Tex.	1B	.301	43	144	4	112
6 Manny Ramirez, Bos.	OF	.292	45	144	1	112
7 Jason Bay, Pit.	OF	.306	32	101	21	110
8 Andruw Jones, Atl.	OF	.263	51	128	5	95
9 Alfonso Soriano, Tex.	2B	.268	36	104	30	102
10 V. Guerrero, LAA	OF	.317	32	108	13	95

Pitcher	Pos	W	Sv	ERA	WHIP	K
1 Johan Santana, Min.	SP	16	0	2.87	0.97	238
2 Chris Carpenter, St.L	SP	21	0	2.83	1.06	213
3 Roger Clemens, Hou.	SP	13	0	1.87	1.01	185
4 Pedro Martinez, NYM	SP	15	0	2.82	0.95	208
5 Dontrelle Willis, Fla.	SP	22	0	2.63	1.13	170

2006

Pujols holds off the HR champ, SB leader and 40-40 entrant for his second fantasy hitting title.

Hitter	Pos	Avg	HR	RBI	SB	R
1 Albert Pujols, St.L	1B	.331	49	137	7	119
2 Ryan Howard, Phi.	1B	.313	58	149	0	104
3 Jose Reyes, NYM	SS	.300	19	81	64	122
4 A. Soriano, Wash.	OF	.277	46	95	41	119
5 David Ortiz, Bos.	DH	.287	54	137	1	115
6 Derek Jeter, NYY	SS	.343	14	97	34	118
7 Matt Holliday, Col.	OF	.326	34	114	10	119
8 Carlos Beltran, NYM	OF	.275	41	116	18	127
9 Chase Utley, Phi.	2B	.309	32	102	15	131
10 Lance Berkman, Hou.	OF	.315	45	136	3	95

Pitcher	Pos	W	Sv	ERA	WHIP	K
1 Johan Santana, Min.	SP	19	0	2.77	0.98	245
2 Chris Carpenter, St.L	SP	15	0	3.09	1.07	184
3 Brandon Webb, Ari.	SP	16	0	3.10	1.13	178
4 John Smoltz, Atl.	SP	16	0	3.49	1.19	211
5 Roy Oswalt, Hou.	SP	15	0	2.98	1.17	166

Alicia Hollowell whiffed a record 13 batters in the final game to lead Arizona to the Div. I softball title.

UNWANTED
ATTENTION

The alleged rape and beating of a woman by three members of the Duke lacrosse team sent shockwaves throughout the NCAA.

SMALL SPORTS ALWAYS WANT to get coverage on ESPN. Never do they want to simultaneously be on CNN. Such was the case in the spring of 2006 with the Duke lacrosse team.

Duke athletics in late March should have been making national headlines for other reasons. JJ Redick's magical career was coming to a close in men's basketball. The women's hoops team played its way into the national championship game. Even this men's lacrosse team was trying to get back to their sport's national title game, where they were the year before. Instead, all other sports were hidden in the shadows.

A rape allegation led to chaos on campus, and caught the eye of every major news outlet in the country. This wasn't a story about the lesser-known, still-growing sport, it was a story about race, class, underage drinking, and violence in athletes.

Three players on Duke's lacrosse team were accused of sexually assaulting an exotic dancer at an off-campus party in the middle of March.

Allegedly, they took her into a bathroom, then physically beat her, and raped her.

A couple of hours after the alleged incident took place, a 19-year-old sophomore lacrosse player wrote an e-mail to his teammates saying that he planned an encore event. The e-mail said he would "have some strippers over" and not only kill them, but commit other acts that are too graphic for these pages. The players suggest the e-mail was meant to be funny, and in reference to a movie. The e-mail's author was temporarily suspended from the university.

Thus began the fallout. Duke launched a series of internal investigations into everything from the school's response, to the truth of the alleged incident, to the behavior of the lacrosse players in general.

Dozens of television satellite trucks were parked along the streets as the media from all around the country

Mike Hall is the lead anchor for ESPNU.

AP/Wide World Photos

Frequent protests occured outside the Durham, N.C. house where a woman alleged she was raped by three men at a party thrown by the Duke lacrosse team.

came to Durham in hordes. They were in search of the latest bit of information, in what was becoming one of the biggest sports-related stories of the year.

After a few weeks, three members of the lacrosse team — David Evans, Reade Seligmann, and Collin Finnerty — were charged with first degree forcible rape, first degree sexual offense, and kidnapping.

But the details of the event go much deeper than that. The alleged victim was black, all three men were white. In fact, Duke's lacrosse team had 46 white players, and one black one. And the incident transpired in an area of North Carolina where racial tensions were already high.

For days, and weeks, students and Durham residents marched in protest. Candlelight vigils were held. Pots and pans were even banged outside of the house where the party occurred.

One section of the townspeople thought actions were not taken fast enough, nor severe enough. Another section thought the reaction was too harsh, and not enough proof existed to warrant the response.

With each new day, new information surfaced. And seemingly each day, old information was proven incorrect. Evidence began to mount. Negative back stories developed on both sides

AP/Wide World Photos

Duke lacrosse player **Reade Seligmann**, 20, confers with his attorney, Kirk Osborn, during court proceedings on May 18, 2006.

In the meantime, the lacrosse program received a generous heaping of backlash. Head coach Mike Pressler resigned, ending a 16-year tenure marked by three ACC championships. Recruits who had originally agreed to play at Duke, ultimately changed their minds. The future of the program remained uncertain as spring turned into summer.

When fall finally arrived, and with it a new school year, things in Durham had not been resolved. The rape case was still pending on the three young men, and wasn't set to go to court until spring of 2007. While the court date lingered, those involved moved on.

The lacrosse program was reinstated over the summer. John Danowski was hired as the team's new head coach. Formerly the coach at Hofstra, he also had existing ties to the team, as he is the father of Duke All-American attackman Matt Danowski. And four months after his resignation from Duke, coach Pressler found a job as head coach at Division II Bryant University in Rhode Island.

Whether the end result for the three men is innocent or guilty, the damage had been done. Who knows how long it will take for the incident to no longer be synonymous with Duke lacrosse. In a mostly white city, it's a black eye that may never fade.

of the case. DNA was tested, and no matches were found. All the while, sports were not happening.

Initially games that Duke was to play were forfeited. Later, the season was suspended. Finally, two weeks after the alleged incident took place, Duke's president Richard Brodhead made an announcement. His school's nationally ranked lacrosse team's season was canceled for the rest of the year.

MIKE HALL'S

Biggest Stories of the Year in **College Sports**

10 Cowboys Up. In Oklahoma City, not far from their home in Stillwater, the Cowboys of Oklahoma State win their fourth consecutive NCAA wrestling championship, over runner-up Minnesota in March. It is the 34th title for the dominant program and the third time it has won four or more titles in a row.

09 Wildcats over Wildcats. Arizona's Alicia Hollowell throws her third straight shutout and sets the Women's College World Series record for strikeouts (with 13) in a 5-0 win over Northwestern. The Wildcats win their seventh softball championship with a two-game sweep.

08 Kenyon Dominance. Gotta be honest...I've never actually seen a minute of the Kenyon Men's Swimming and Diving team. And I don't focus too much of my time on Division III sports. But they've now won 27 straight national titles—clearly that deserves recognition.

07 Beavers Prevail. Oregon State beats North Carolina in the best-of-three championship for its first College World Series title. The Beavers' opening-game 11-1 loss to Miami-FL and 4-3 loss to North Carolina make them the only team in CWS history to lose twice in Omaha and still win the national championship.

06 Upset Special. Holy Cross was a #4 seed (the lowest in hockey's NCAA tournament), and had never won a postseason game. But 53 seconds into overtime against top-seeded powerhouse Minnesota, Tyler McGregor uncorks a wrist shot that finds the back of the net and gives the Crusaders a 4-3 win, creating the greatest upset in college hockey history.

05 Best of the Best. J.J. Redick becomes the ACC's all time leading scorer. Think of the list of incredible basketball players to come through this conference: Michael Jordan, Christian Laettner, Tim Duncan...the list goes on. None of them scored more points than Redick's 2,769.

04 Cheese On Ice? Even more than cheese, they know hockey in Wisconsin. The Badgers men's team wins its sixth Division I national title... just days after the Badgers women won their first. It's the first time that's ever happened in Division I college hockey.

03 **George Who?** George Mason destroys brackets all over the country by making it to the NCAA men's basketball Final Four. People barely knew the man, let alone the school, let alone its men's basketball team. It's the deepest mid-major run ever in a six-round NCAA tournament.

02 **Duke Lacrosse Scandal.** It stayed in the headlines for weeks and weeks, touching off a nationwide debate about sports, race and class. And it left a scar that may never leave the program.

01 **Coming Up Roses.** It was #1 vs #2. Both teams were undefeated...and they were the *only* teams undefeated. It was the game that we all wanted from the first month of college football. And it lived up to the impossibly high hype, as Vince Young and the Texas Longhorns won a dramatic Rose Bowl, 41-38, in the final seconds over Reggie Bush and USC... and with it, the national championship.

The University of Oregon football team announced that it has **384 possible uniform combinations** for the 2006-07 season. According to a *USA Today* report, the Ducks will have to choose from the following before each game:

4 colors of jerseys: green, yellow, white and black
4 colors of pants: green, yellow, white and black
3 helmet options: green and white (with a yellow one in the works)
4 colors of socks
2 colors of shoes

(For those wondering: 4 x 4 x 3 x 4 x 2 = 384)

Uniform decisions are made by head coach Mike Bellotti and equipment manager Pat Conrad, and are kept a secret until game day. Paul Lukas, founder of Uni Watch, notes, "they're not very uniform." ESPNU anchor Mike Hall adds, "A nation is relieved, as only two forms of ugly wasn't nearly enough." Ouch.

NCAA Schools & Champions

SPORTS ALMANAC

NCAA Division I-A Football Schools
2006 Season
Conferences and coaches as of Sept. 30, 2006.

Joining Mid-American in 2007: TEMPLE from I-A Independent (affiliate member in 2005 & 2006).

	Nickname	Conference	Head Coach	Location	Colors
Air Force	Falcons	Mountain West	Fisher DeBerry	Colo. Springs, CO	Blue/Silver
Akron	Zips	Mid-American	J.D. Brookhart	Akron, OH	Blue/Gold
Alabama	Crimson Tide	SEC-West	Mike Shula	Tuscaloosa, AL	Crimson/White
Arizona	Wildcats	Pac-10	Mike Stoops	Tucson, AZ	Cardinal/Navy
Arizona St.	Sun Devils	Pac-10	Dirk Koetter	Tempe, AZ	Maroon/Gold
Arkansas	Razorbacks	SEC-West	Houston Nutt	Fayetteville, AR	Cardinal/White
Arkansas St.	Indians	Sun Belt	Steve Roberts	State Univ., AR	Scarlet/Black
Army	Cadets, Black Knights	Independent	Bobby Ross	West Point, NY	Black/Gold/Gray
Auburn	Tigers	SEC-West	Tommy Tuberville	Auburn, AL	Orange/Blue
Ball St.	Cardinals	Mid-American	Brady Hoke	Muncie, IN	Cardinal/White
Baylor	Bears	Big 12	Guy Morriss	Waco, TX	Green/Gold
Boise St.	Broncos	WAC	Chris Petersen	Boise, ID	Orange/Blue
Boston College	Eagles	ACC	Tom O'Brien	Chestnut Hill, MA	Maroon/Gold
Bowling Green	Falcons	Mid-American	Gregg Brandon	Bowling Green, OH	Orange/Brown
Brigham Young	Cougars	Mountain West	Bronco Mendenhall	Provo, UT	Blue/White/Tan
Buffalo	Bulls	Mid-American	Turner Gill	Buffalo, NY	Royal Blue/White
California	Golden Bears	Pac-10	Jeff Tedford	Berkeley, CA	Blue/Gold
Central Florida	Golden Knights	USA	George O'Leary	Orlando, FL	Black/Gold
Central Michigan	Chippewas	Mid-American	Brian Kelly	Mt. Pleasant, MI	Maroon/Gold
Cincinnati	Bearcats	Big East	Mark Dantonio	Cincinnati, OH	Red/Black
Clemson	Tigers	ACC	Tommy Bowden	Clemson, SC	Purple/Orange
Colorado	Buffaloes	Big 12	Dan Hawkins	Boulder, CO	Silver/Gold/Black
Colorado St.	Rams	Mountain West	Sonny Lubick	Ft. Collins, CO	Green/Gold
Connecticut	Huskies	Big East	Randy Edsall	Storrs, CT	Blue/White
Duke	Blue Devils	ACC	Ted Roof	Durham, NC	Royal Blue/White
East Carolina	Pirates	USA	Skip Holtz	Greenville, NC	Purple/Gold
Eastern Michigan	Eagles	Mid-American	Jeff Genyk	Ypsilanti, MI	Green/White
Florida	Gators	SEC-East	Urban Meyer	Gainesville, FL	Orange/Blue
Florida Atlantic	Owls	Sun Belt	H. Schnellenberger	Boca Raton, FL	Blue/Red
Florida Int'l	Golden Panthers	Sun Belt	Don Strock	Miami, FL	Blue/Gold
Florida St.	Seminoles	ACC	Bobby Bowden	Tallahassee, FL	Garnet/Gold
Fresno St.	Bulldogs	WAC	Pat Hill	Fresno, CA	Red/Blue
Georgia	Bulldogs	SEC-East	Mark Richt	Athens, GA	Red/Black
Georgia Tech	Yellow Jackets	ACC	Chan Gailey	Atlanta, GA	Old Gold/White
Hawaii	Warriors	WAC	June Jones	Honolulu, HI	Green/White
Houston	Cougars	USA	Art Briles	Houston, TX	Scarlet/White
Idaho	Vandals	WAC	Dennis Erickson	Moscow, ID	Silver/Gold
Illinois	Fighting Illini	Big Ten	Ron Zook	Champaign, IL	Orange/Blue
Indiana	Hoosiers	Big Ten	Terry Hoeppner	Bloomington, IN	Cream/Crimson
Iowa	Hawkeyes	Big Ten	Kirk Ferentz	Iowa City, IA	Old Gold/Black
Iowa St.	Cyclones	Big 12	Dan McCarney	Ames, IA	Cardinal/Gold
Kansas	Jayhawks	Big 12	Mark Mangino	Lawrence, KS	Crimson/Blue
Kansas St.	Wildcats	Big 12	Ron Prince	Manhattan, KS	Purple/White
Kent St.	Golden Flashes	Mid-American	Doug Martin	Kent, OH	Navy Blue/Gold
Kentucky	Wildcats	SEC-East	Rich Brooks	Lexington, KY	Blue/White
LSU	Fighting Tigers	SEC-West	Les Miles	Baton Rouge, LA	Purple/Gold
LA-Lafayette	Ragin' Cajuns	Sun Belt	Rickey Bustle	Lafayette, LA	Vermilion/White
LA-Monroe	Warhawks	Sun Belt	Charlie Weatherbie	Monroe, LA	Maroon/Gold
Louisiana Tech	Bulldogs	WAC	Jack Bicknell III	Ruston, LA	Red/Blue
Louisville	Cardinals	Big East	Bob Petrino	Louisville, KY	Red/Black/White
Marshall	Thundering Herd	USA	Mark Snyder	Huntington, WV	Green/White

NCAA Division I-A Football Schools (Cont.)

	Nickname	Conference	Head Coach	Location	Colors
Maryland	Terrapins, Terps	ACC	Ralph Friedgen	College Park, MD	Red/White/Black/Gold
Memphis	Tigers	USA	Tommy West	Memphis, TN	Blue/Gray
Miami-FL	Hurricanes	ACC	Larry Coker	Coral Gables, FL	Orange/Grn./Wt.
Miami-OH	RedHawks	Mid-American	Shane Montgomery	Oxford, OH	Red/White
Michigan	Wolverines	Big Ten	Lloyd Carr	Ann Arbor, MI	Maize/Blue
Michigan St.	Spartans	Big Ten	John L. Smith	E. Lansing, MI	Green/White
Middle Tennessee	Blue Raiders	Sun Belt	Rick Stockstill	Murfreesboro, TN	Royal Blue/White
Minnesota	Golden Gophers	Big Ten	Glen Mason	Minneapolis, MN	Maroon/Gold
Mississippi	Ole Miss, Rebels	SEC-West	Ed Orgeron	Oxford, MS	Cardinal/Navy Bl.
Mississippi St.	Bulldogs	SEC-West	Sylvester Croom	Starkville, MS	Maroon/White
Missouri	Tigers	Big 12	Gary Pinkel	Columbia, MO	Old Gold/Black
Navy	Midshipmen	Independent	Paul Johnson	Annapolis, MD	Navy Blue/Gold
Nebraska	Cornhuskers	Big 12	Bill Callahan	Lincoln, NE	Scarlet/Cream
Nevada	Wolf Pack	WAC	Chris Ault	Reno, NV	Silver/Blue
New Mexico	Lobos	Mountain West	Rocky Long	Albuquerque, NM	Cherry/Silver
New Mexico St.	Aggies	WAC	Hal Mumme	Las Cruces, NM	Crimson/White
North Carolina	Tar Heels	ACC	John Bunting	Chapel Hill, NC	Carolina Blue/Wt.
North Carolina St.	Wolfpack	ACC	Chuck Amato	Raleigh, NC	Red/White
North Texas	Mean Green	Sun Belt	Darrell Dickey	Denton, TX	Green/White
Northern Illinois	Huskies	Mid-American	Joe Novak	DeKalb, IL	Cardinal/Black
Northwestern	Wildcats	Big Ten	Pat Fitzgerald	Evanston, IL	Purple/White
Notre Dame	Fighting Irish	Independent	Charlie Weis	Notre Dame, IN	Gold/Blue
Ohio University	Bobcats	Mid-American	Frank Solich	Athens, OH	Hunter Green/Wt.
Ohio St.	Buckeyes	Big Ten	Jim Tressel	Columbus, OH	Scarlet/Gray
Oklahoma	Sooners	Big 12	Bob Stoops	Norman, OK	Crimson/Cream
Oklahoma St.	Cowboys	Big 12	Mike Gundy	Stillwater, OK	Orange/Black
Oregon	Ducks	Pac-10	Mike Bellotti	Eugene, OR	Green/Yellow
Oregon St.	Beavers	Pac-10	Mike Riley	Corvallis, OR	Orange/Black
Penn St.	Nittany Lions	Big Ten	Joe Paterno	University Park, PA	Blue/White
Pittsburgh	Panthers	Big East	Dave Wannstedt	Pittsburgh, PA	Blue/Gold
Purdue	Boilermakers	Big Ten	Joe Tiller	W. Lafayette, IN	Old Gold/Black
Rice	Owls	USA	Todd Graham	Houston, TX	Blue/Gray
Rutgers	Scarlet Knights	Big East	Greg Schiano	New Brunswick, NJ	Scarlet
San Diego St.	Aztecs	Mountain West	Chuck Long	San Diego, CA	Scarlet/Black
San Jose St.	Spartans	WAC	Dick Tomey	San Jose, CA	Gold/White/Blue
South Carolina	Gamecocks	SEC-East	Steve Spurrier	Columbia, SC	Garnet/Black
South Florida	Bulls	Big East	Jim Leavitt	Tampa, FL	Green/Gold
SMU	Mustangs	USA	Phil Bennett	Dallas, TX	Red/Blue
Southern Miss.	Golden Eagles	USA	Jeff Bower	Hattiesburg, MS	Black/Gold
Stanford	Cardinal	Pac-10	Walt Harris	Stanford, CA	Cardinal/White
Syracuse	Orange	Big East	Greg Robinson	Syracuse, NY	Orange
Temple	Owls	Independent	Al Golden	Philadelphia, PA	Cherry/White
Tennessee	Volunteers	SEC-East	Phillip Fulmer	Knoxville, TN	Orange/White
Texas	Longhorns	Big 12	Mack Brown	Austin, TX	Burnt Orange/Wt.
Texas A&M	Aggies	Big 12	Dennis Franchione	College Station, TX	Maroon/White
TCU	Horned Frogs	Mountain West	Gary Patterson	Ft. Worth, TX	Purple/White
Texas Tech	Red Raiders	Big 12	Mike Leach	Lubbock, TX	Scarlet/Black
Toledo	Rockets	Mid-American	Tom Amstutz	Toledo, OH	Blue/Gold
Troy	Trojans	Sun Belt	Larry Blakeney	Troy, AL	Cardinal/Slvr./Blk.
Tulane	Green Wave	USA	Chris Scelfo	New Orleans, LA	Olive Grn./Sky Bl.
Tulsa	Golden Hurricane	USA	Steve Kragthorpe	Tulsa, OK	Blue/Gold/Crimson
UAB	Blazers	USA	Watson Brown	Birmingham, AL	Green/Gold
UCLA	Bruins	Pac-10	Karl Dorrell	Los Angeles, CA	Blue/Gold
UNLV	Rebels	Mountain West	Mike Sanford	Las Vegas, NV	Scarlet/Gray
USC	Trojans	Pac-10	Pete Carroll	Los Angeles, CA	Cardinal/Gold
Utah	Utes	Mountain West	Kyle Whittingham	Salt Lake City, UT	Crimson/White
Utah St.	Aggies	WAC	Brent Guy	Logan, UT	Navy Blue/White
UTEP	Miners	USA	Mike Price	El Paso, TX	Orange/Blue/Silver
Vanderbilt	Commodores	SEC-East	Bobby Johnson	Nashville, TN	Black/Gold
Virginia	Cavaliers	ACC	Al Groh	Charlottesville, VA	Orange/Blue
Virginia Tech	Hokies, Gobblers	ACC	Frank Beamer	Blacksburg, VA	Orange/Maroon
Wake Forest	Demon Deacons	ACC	Jim Grobe	Winston-Salem, NC	Old Gold/Black
Washington	Huskies	Pac-10	Tyrone Willingham	Seattle, WA	Purple/Gold
Washington St.	Cougars	Pac-10	Bill Doba	Pullman, WA	Crimson/Gray
West Virginia	Mountaineers	Big East	Rich Rodriguez	Morgantown, WV	Old Gold/Blue
Western Michigan	Broncos	Mid-American	Bill Cubit	Kalamazoo, MI	Brown/Gold
Wisconsin	Badgers	Big Ten	Bret Bielema	Madison, WI	Cardinal/White
Wyoming	Cowboys	Mountain West	Joe Glenn	Laramie, WY	Brown/Gold

NCAA Division I-AA Football Schools
2006 Season
Conferences and coaches as of Sept. 30, 2006.

Joining Big Sky in 2006: NORTHERN COLORADO from Great West.
Joining Big South in 2007: PRESBYTERIAN COLLEGE from Division II.
Joining Mid Eastern in 2007: WINSTON-SALEM ST. from Division II (2006 as a I-AA Independent).
Joining Ohio Valley in 2007: AUSTIN PEAY ST. from Pioneer (program left Pioneer League after the 2005 season; spent 2006 as a I-AA Independent).
Joining Southland in 2007: CENTRAL ARKANSAS from Division II (2006 as a I-AA Independent).
Leaving Northeast in 2007: STONY BROOK to I-AA Independent.
New Conference in 2007: Colonial Athletic Association (12 teams) — DELAWARE, HOFSTRA, JAMES MADISON, MAINE, MASSACHUSETTS, NEW HAMPSHIRE, NORTHEASTERN, RHODE ISLAND, RICHMOND, TOWSON, VILLANOVA and WILLIAM & MARY from Atlantic 10 (conference will no longer sponsor football).
Joining Division I-AA in 2008: NORTH DAKOTA from Division II.
Joining Colonial Athletic Association in 2009: OLD DOMINION (resurrecting its football program).

	Nickname	Conference	Head Coach	Location	Colors
Alabama A&M	Bulldogs	SWAC	Anthony Jones	Huntsville, AL	Maroon/White
Alabama St.	Hornets	SWAC	Charles Coe	Montgomery, AL	Black/Gold
Albany	Great Danes	Northeast	Bob Ford	Albany, NY	Purple/Gold
Alcorn St.	Braves	SWAC	Johnny Thomas	Lorman, MS	Purple/Gold
Appalachian St.	Mountaineers	Southern	Jerry Moore	Boone, NC	Black/Gold
Ark.-Pine Bluff	Golden Lions	SWAC	Mo Forte	Pine Bluff, AR	Black/Gold
Austin Peay St.	Governors	Independent	Carroll McCray	Clarksville, TN	Red/White
Bethune-Cookman	Wildcats	Mid-Eastern	Alvin Wyatt	Daytona Beach, FL	Maroon/Gold
Brown	Bears	Ivy	Phil Estes	Providence, RI	Brown/Red/White
Bucknell	Bison	Patriot	Tim Landis	Lewisburg, PA	Orange/Blue
Butler	Bulldogs	Pioneer	Jeff Voris	Indianapolis, IN	Blue/White
Cal Poly	Mustangs	Great West	Rich Ellerson	San Luis Obispo, CA	Green/Gold
Central Arkansas	Bears	Independent	Clint Conque	Conway, AR	Purple/Gray
Central Conn. St.	Blue Devils	Northeast	Jeff McInerney	New Britain, CT	Blue/White
Charleston So.	Buccaneers	Big South	Jay Mills	Charleston, SC	Blue/Gold
Chattanooga	Mocs	Southern	Rodney Allison	Chattanooga, TN	Navy Blue/Old Gold
The Citadel	Bulldogs	Southern	Kevin Higgins	Charleston, SC	Blue/White
Coastal Carolina	Chanticleers	Big South	David Bennett	Conway, SC	Green/Bronze/Black
Colgate	Raiders	Patriot	Dick Biddle	Hamilton, NY	Maroon/White/Gray
Columbia	Lions	Ivy	Norries Wilson	New York, NY	Lt. Blue/White
Cornell	Big Red	Ivy	Jim Knowles	Ithaca, NY.	Carnelian/White
Dartmouth	Big Green	Ivy	Buddy Teevens	Hanover, NH	Green/White
Davidson	Wildcats	Pioneer	Tripp Merritt	Davidson, NC	Red/Black
Dayton	Flyers	Pioneer	Mike Kelly	Dayton, OH	Red/Blue
Delaware	Blue Hens	Atlantic 10	K.C. Keeler	Newark, DE	Blue/Gold
Delaware St.	Hornets	Mid-Eastern	Al Lavan	Dover, DE	Red/Blue
Drake	Bulldogs	Pioneer	Rob Ash	Des Moines, IA	Blue/White
Duquesne	Dukes	Metro Atlantic	Jerry Schmitt	Pittsburgh, PA	Red/Blue
Eastern Illinois	Panthers	Ohio Valley	Bob Spoo	Charleston, IL	Blue/Gray
Eastern Kentucky	Colonels	Ohio Valley	Danny Hope	Richmond, KY	Maroon/White
Eastern Washington	Eagles	Big Sky	Paul Wulff	Cheney, WA	Red/White
Elon	Phoenix	Southern	Pete Lembo	Elon, NC	Maroon/Gold
Florida A&M	Rattlers	Mid-Eastern	Rubin Carter	Tallahassee, FL	Orange/Green
Fordham	Rams	Patriot	Tom Masella	Bronx, NY	Maroon/White
Furman	Paladins	Southern	Bobby Lamb	Greenville, SC	Purple/White
Gardner-Webb	Bulldogs	Big South	Steve Patton	Boiling Springs, NC	Scarlet/Black
Georgetown	Hoyas	Patriot	Kevin Kelly	Washington, DC	Blue/Gray
Georgia Southern	Eagles	Southern	Brian VanGorder	Statesboro, GA	Blue/White
Grambling St.	Tigers	SWAC	Melvin Spears	Grambling, LA	Black/Gold
Hampton	Pirates	Mid-Eastern	Joe Taylor	Hampton, VA	Royal Blue/White
Harvard	Crimson	Ivy	Tim Murphy	Cambridge, MA	Crimson/Black/White
Hofstra	Pride	Atlantic 10	Dave Cohen	Hempstead, NY	Gold/White/Blue
Holy Cross	Crusaders	Patriot	Tom Gilmore	Worcester, MA	Royal Purple
Howard	Bison	Mid-Eastern	Rayford T. Petty	Washington, DC	Blue/Wt./Red
Idaho St.	Bengals	Big Sky	Larry Lewis	Pocatello, ID	Orange/Black
Illinois St.	Redbirds	Gateway	Denver Johnson	Normal, IL	Red/White
Indiana St.	Sycamores	Gateway	Lou West	Terre Haute, IN	Royal Blue/White
Iona	Gaels	Metro Atlantic	Fred Mariani	New Rochelle, NY	Maroon/Gold
Jackson St.	Tigers	SWAC	Rick Comegy	Jackson, MS	Blue/White
Jacksonville	Dolphins	Pioneer	Steve Gilbert	Jacksonville, FL	Green/White
Jacksonville St.	Gamecocks	Ohio Valley	Jack Crowe	Jacksonville, AL	Red/White
James Madison	Dukes	Atlantic 10	Mickey Matthews	Harrisonburg, VA	Purple/Gold
Lafayette	Leopards	Patriot	Frank Tavani	Easton, PA	Maroon/White

	Nickname	Conference	Head Coach	Location	Colors
La Salle	Explorers	Metro Atlantic	Tim Miller	Philadelphia, PA	Blue/Gold
Lehigh	Mountain Hawks	Patriot	Andy Coen	Bethlehem, PA	Brown/White
Liberty	Flames	Big South	Danny Rocco	Lynchburg, VA	Red/White/Blue
Maine	Black Bears	Atlantic 10	Jack Cosgrove	Orono, ME	Blue/White
Marist	Red Foxes	Metro Atlantic	Jim Parady	Poughkeepsie, NY	Red/White
Massachusetts	Minutemen	Atlantic 10	Don Brown	Amherst, MA	Maroon/White
McNeese St.	Cowboys	Southland	Tommy Tate	Lake Charles, LA	Blue/Gold
Miss. Valley St.	Delta Devils	SWAC	Willie Totten	Itta Bena, MS	Green/White
Missouri St.	Bears	Gateway	Terry Allen	Springfield, MO	Maroon/White
Monmouth	Hawks	Northeast	Kevin Callahan	W. Long Branch, NJ	Royal Blue/White
Montana	Grizzlies	Big Sky	Bobby Hauck	Missoula, MT	Maroon/Silver
Montana St.	Bobcats	Big Sky	Mike Kramer	Bozeman, MT	Blue/Gold
Morehead St.	Eagles	Pioneer	Matt Ballard	Morehead, KY	Blue/Gold
Morgan St.	Bears	Mid-Eastern	Donald Hill-Eley	Baltimore, MD	Blue/Orange
Murray St.	Racers	Ohio Valley	Matt Griffin	Murray, KY	Blue/Gold
New Hampshire	Wildcats	Atlantic 10	Sean McDonnell	Durham, NH	Blue/White
Nicholls St.	Colonels	Southland	Jay Thomas	Thibodaux, LA	Red/Gray
Norfolk State	Spartans	Mid-Eastern	Pete Adrian	Norfolk, VA	Green/Gold
North Carolina A&T	Aggies	Mid-Eastern	Lee Fobbs	Greensboro, NC	Blue/Gold
North Dakota St.	Bison	Great West	Craig Bohl	Fargo, ND	Green/Yellow
Northeastern	Huskies	Atlantic 10	Rocky Hager	Boston, MA	Red/Black
Northern Arizona	Lumberjacks	Big Sky	Jerome Souers	Flagstaff, AZ	Blue/Gold
Northern Colorado	Bears	Big Sky	Scott Downing	Greeley, CO	Blue/Gold
Northern Iowa	Panthers	Gateway	Mark Farley	Cedar Falls, IA	Purple/Old Gold
Northwestern St.	Demons	Southland	Scott Stoker	Natchitoches, LA	Purple/White
Pennsylvania	Quakers	Ivy	Al Bagnoli	Philadelphia, PA	Red/Blue
Portland St.	Vikings	Big Sky	Tim Walsh	Portland, OR	Green/White
Prairie View A&M	Panthers	SWAC	Henry Frazier	Prairie View, TX	Purple/Gold
Princeton	Tigers	Ivy	Roger Hughes	Princeton, NJ	Orange/Black
Rhode Island	Rams	Atlantic 10	Tim Stowers	Kingston, RI	Light Blue/Navy/Wt.
Richmond	Spiders	Atlantic 10	Dave Clawson	Richmond, VA	Red/Blue
Robert Morris	Colonials	Northeast	Joe Walton	Moon Township, PA	Blue/White
Sacramento St.	Hornets	Big Sky	Steve Mooshagian	Sacramento, CA	Green/Gold
Sacred Heart	Pioneers	Northeast	Paul Gorham	Fairfield, CT	Scarlet/White
St. Francis-PA	Red Flash	Northeast	Dave Opfar	Loretto, PA	Red/White
Saint Peter's	Peacocks	Metro Atlantic	Chris Taylor	Jersey City, NJ	Blue/White
Sam Houston St.	Bearkats	Southland	Todd Whitten	Huntsville, TX	Orange/White
Samford	Bulldogs	Ohio Valley	Bill Gray	Birmingham, AL	Crimson/Blue
San Diego	Toreros	Pioneer	Jim Harbaugh	San Diego, CA	Lt. Blue/Navy
Savannah St.	Tigers	Independent	Theo Lemon	Savannah, GA	Orange/Blue
South Carolina St.	Bulldogs	Mid-Eastern	Oliver Pough	Orangeburg, SC	Garnet/Blue
South Dakota St.	Jackrabbits	Great West	John Stiegelmeier	Brookings, SD	Yellow/Blue
SE Missouri St.	Redhawks	Ohio Valley	Tony Samuel	Cape Girardeau, MO	Red/Black
Southeastern Louisiana	Lions	Southland	Dennis Roland	Hammond, LA	Green/Gold
Southern-BR	Jaguars	SWAC	Pete Richardson	Baton Rouge, LA	Blue/Gold
Southern Illinois	Salukis	Gateway	Jerry Kill	Cardondale, IL	Maroon/White
Southern Utah	Thunderbirds	Great West	Wes Meier	Cedar City, UT	Scarlet/White
S.F. Austin St.	Lumberjacks	Southland	Robert McFarland	Nacogdoches, TX	Purple/White
Stony Brook	Seawolves	Northeast	Chuck Priore	Stony Brook, NY	Scarlet/Gray
Tennessee-Martin	Skyhawks	Ohio Valley	Jason Simpson	Martin, TN	Orange/White/Blue
Tennessee St.	Tigers	Ohio Valley	James Webster	Nashville, TN	Blue/White
Tennessee Tech	Golden Eagles	Ohio Valley	Mike Hennigan	Cookeville, TN	Purple/Gold
Texas Southern	Tigers	SWAC	Steve Wilson	Houston, TX	Maroon/Gray
Texas St.	Bobcats	Southland	David Bailiff	San Marcos, TX	Maroon/Gold
Towson	Tigers	Atlantic 10	Gordy Combs	Towson, MD	Gold/White
UC-Davis	Aggies	Great West	Bob Biggs	Davis, CA	Yale Blue/Gold
Valparaiso	Crusaders	Pioneer	Stacy Adams	Valparaiso, IN	Brown/Gold
Villanova	Wildcats	Atlantic 10	Andy Talley	Villanova, PA	Blue/White
VMI	Keydets	Big South	Jim Reid	Lexington, VA	Red/White/Yellow
Wagner	Seahawks	Northeast	Walt Hameline	Staten Island, NY	Green/White
Weber St.	Wildcats	Big Sky	Ron McBride	Ogden, UT	Royal Purple/White
Western Carolina	Catamounts	Southern	Kent Briggs	Cullowhee, NC	Purple/Gold
Western Illinois	Leathernecks	Gateway	Don Patterson	Macomb, IL	Purple/Gold
Western Kentucky	Hilltoppers	Gateway	David Elson	Bowling Green, KY	Red/White
William & Mary	Tribe	Atlantic 10	Jimmye Laycock	Williamsburg, VA	Green/Gold/Silver
Winston-Salem St.	Rams	Independent	Kermit Blount	Winston-Salem, NC	Red/White
Wofford	Terriers	Southern	Mike Ayers	Spartanburg, SC	Old Gold/Black
Yale	Bulldogs, Elis	Ivy	Jack Siedlecki	New Haven, CT	Yale Blue/White
Youngstown St.	Penguins	Gateway	Jon Heacock	Youngstown, OH	Red/White

NCAA Division I Basketball Schools
2006-2007 Season

Conferences and coaches as of Sept. 30, 2006.

Joining Big Sky in 2006-07: NORTHERN COLORADO from Independent.
Joining Southland in 2006-07: TEXAS A&M-CORPUS CHRISTI from Independent.
Joining Sun Belt in 2006-07: FLORIDA ATLANTIC from Atlantic Sun; LA-MONROE from Southland.
Joining Big South in 2007-08: PRESBYTERIAN COLLEGE from Division II.
Joining Big West in 2007-08: UC-DAVIS from Independent.
Joining Mid Eastern in 2007-08: WINSTON-SALEM ST. from Division II (2006-07 as an Independent).
Joining Southland in 2007-08: CENTRAL ARKANSAS from Division II (2006-07 as an Independent).
Leaving Big South in 2007-08: BIRMINGHAM SOUTHERN to Division III.
Joining Division I in 2008-09: NORTH DAKOTA from Division II.

	Nickname	Conference	Head Coach	Location	Colors
Air Force	Falcons	Mountain West	Jeff Bzdelik	Colo. Springs, CO	Blue/Silver
Akron	Zips	Mid-American	Keith Dambrot	Akron, OH	Blue/Gold
Alabama	Crimson Tide	SEC-West	Mark Gottfried	Tuscaloosa, AL	Crimson/White
Alabama A&M	Bulldogs	SWAC	Vann Pettaway	Huntsville, AL	Maroon/White
Alabama St.	Hornets	SWAC	Lewis Jackson	Montgomery, AL	Black/Gold
Albany	Great Danes	America East	Will Brown	Albany, NY	Purple/Gold
Alcorn St.	Braves	SWAC	Samuel West	Lorman, MS	Purple/Gold
American	Eagles	Patriot	Jeff Jones	Washington, DC	Red/Blue
Appalachian St.	Mountaineers	Southern	Houston Fancher	Boone, NC	Black/Gold
Arizona	Wildcats	Pac-10	Lute Olson	Tucson, AZ	Cardinal/Navy
Arizona St.	Sun Devils	Pac-10	Herb Sendek	Tempe, AZ	Maroon/Gold
Arkansas	Razorbacks	SEC-West	Stan Heath	Fayetteville, AR	Cardinal/White
Ark.-Little Rock	Trojans	Sun Belt	Steve Shields	Little Rock, AR	Silver/Black/Maroon
Ark.-Pine Bluff	Golden Lions	SWAC	Van Holt	Pine Bluff, AR	Black/Gold
Arkansas St.	Indians	Sun Belt	Dickey Nutt	State Univ., AR	Scarlet/Black
Army	Black Knights	Patriot	Jim Crews	West Point, NY	Black/Gold/Gray
Auburn	Tigers	SEC-West	Jeff Lebo	Auburn, AL	Orange/Blue
Austin Peay St.	Governors	Ohio Valley	Dave Loos	Clarksville, TN	Red/White
Ball St.	Cardinals	Mid-American	Ronny Thompson	Muncie, IN	Cardinal/White
Baylor	Bears	Big 12	Scott Drew	Waco, TX	Green/Gold
Belmont	Bruins	Atlantic Sun	Rick Byrd	Nashville, TN	Navy Blue/Red
Bethune-Cookman	Wildcats	Mid-Eastern	Clifford Reed	Daytona Beach, FL	Maroon/Gold
Binghamton	Bearcats	America East	Al Walker	Binghamton, NY	Green/Black/White
Birmingham Southern	Panthers	Big South	Mitch Cole	Birmingham, AL	Black/Gold
Boise St.	Broncos	WAC	Greg Graham	Boise, ID	Orange/Blue
Boston College	Eagles	ACC	Al Skinner	Chestnut Hill, MA	Maroon/Gold
Boston University	Terriers	America East	Dennis Wolff	Boston, MA	Scarlet/White
Bowling Green	Falcons	Mid-American	Dan Dakich	Bowling Green, OH	Orange/Brown
Bradley	Braves	Mo. Valley	Jim Les	Peoria, IL	Red/White
Brigham Young	Cougars	Mountain West	Dave Rose	Provo, UT	Blue/White/Tan
Brown	Bears	Ivy	Craig Robinson	Providence, RI	Brown/Cardinal/White
Bucknell	Bison	Patriot	Pat Flannery	Lewisburg, PA	Orange/Blue
Buffalo	Bulls	Mid-American	R. Witherspoon	Buffalo, NY	Royal Blue/White
Butler	Bulldogs	Horizon	Todd Lickliter	Indianapolis, IN	Blue/White
California	Golden Bears	Pac-10	Ben Braun	Berkeley, CA	Blue/Gold
Cal Poly	Mustangs	Big West	Kevin Bromley	San Luis Obispo, CA	Green/Gold
CS-Fullerton	Titans	Big West	Bob Burton	Fullerton, CA	Blue/Orange/White
CS-Northridge	Matadors	Big West	Bobby Braswell	Northridge, CA	Red/White/Black
Campbell	Camels	Atlantic Sun	Robbie Laing	Buies Creek, NC	Orange/Black
Canisius	Golden Griffins	Metro Atlantic	Tom Parrotta	Buffalo, NY	Blue/Gold
Centenary	Gents, Gentlemen	Mid-Continent	Rob Flaska	Shreveport, LA	Maroon/White
Central Arkansas	Bears	Independent	Rand Chappell	Conway, AR	Purple/Gray
Central Conn. St.	Blue Devils	Northeast	Howie Dickenman	New Britain, CT	Blue/White
Central Florida	Golden Knights	USA	Kirk Speraw	Orlando, FL	Black/Gold
Central Michigan	Chippewas	Mid-American	Ernie Zeigler	Mt. Pleasant, MI	Maroon/Gold
Charleston So.	Buccaneers	Big South	Barclay Radebaugh	Charleston, SC	Blue/Gold
Charlotte	49ers	Atlantic 10	Bobby Lutz	Charlotte, NC	Green/White
Chattanooga	Mocs	Southern	John Shulman	Chattanooga, TN	Navy Blue/Old Gold
Chicago St.	Cougars	Mid-Continent	Kevin Jones	Chicago, IL	Green/White
Cincinnati	Bearcats	Big East	Mick Cronin	Cincinnati, OH	Red/Black
The Citadel	Bulldogs	Southern	Ed Conroy	Charleston, SC	Blue/White
Clemson	Tigers	ACC	Oliver Purnell	Clemson, SC	Purple/Orange
Cleveland St.	Vikings	Horizon	Gary Waters	Cleveland, OH	Forest Green/White
Coastal Carolina	Chanticleers	Big South	Buzz Peterson	Conway, SC	Green/Bronze/Black
Colgate	Raiders	Patriot	Emmett Davis	Hamilton, NY	Maroon/Gray/White
College of Charleston	Cougars	Southern	Bobby Cremins	Charleston, SC	Maroon/White
Colorado	Buffaloes	Big 12	Ricardo Patton	Boulder, CO	Silver/Gold/Black

NCAA Division I Basketball Schools (Cont.)

	Nickname	Conference	Head Coach	Location	Colors
Colorado St.	Rams	Mountain West	Dale Layer	Ft. Collins, CO	Green/Gold
Columbia	Lions	Ivy	Joseph Jones	New York, NY	Lt. Blue/White
Connecticut	Huskies	Big East	Jim Calhoun	Storrs, CT	Blue/White
Coppin St.	Eagles	Mid-Eastern	Ron Mitchell	Baltimore, MD	Royal Blue/Gold
Cornell	Big Red	Ivy	Steve Donahue	Ithaca, NY	Carnelian/White
Creighton	Bluejays	Mo. Valley	Dana Altman	Omaha, NE	Blue/White
Dartmouth	Big Green	Ivy	Terry Dunn	Hanover, NH	Green/White
Davidson	Wildcats	Southern	Bob McKillop	Davidson, NC	Red/Black
Dayton	Flyers	Atlantic 10	Brian Gregory	Dayton, OH	Red/Blue
Delaware	Fightin' Blue Hens	Colonial	Monte Ross	Newark, DE	Blue/Gold
Delaware St.	Hornets	Mid-Eastern	Greg Jackson	Dover, DE	Red/Columbia Blue
Denver	Pioneers	Sun Belt	Terry Carroll	Denver, CO	Crimson/Gold
DePaul	Blue Demons	Big East	Jerry Wainwright	Chicago, IL	Scarlet/Blue
Detroit Mercy	Titans	Horizon	Perry Watson	Detroit, MI	Red/White/Blue
Drake	Bulldogs	Mo. Valley	Tom Davis	Des Moines, IA	Blue/White
Drexel	Dragons	Colonial	Bruiser Flint	Philadelphia, PA	Navy Blue/Gold
Duke	Blue Devils	ACC	Mike Krzyzewski	Durham, NC	Royal Blue/White
Duquesne	Dukes	Atlantic 10	Ron Everhart	Pittsburgh, PA	Red/Blue
East Carolina	Pirates	USA	Ricky Stokes	Greenville, NC	Purple/Gold
East Tenn. St.	Buccaneers	Atlantic Sun	Murry Bartow	Johnson City, TN	Blue/Gold
Eastern Illinois	Panthers	Ohio Valley	Mike Miller	Charleston, IL	Blue/Gray
Eastern Kentucky	Colonels	Ohio Valley	Jeff Neubauer	Richmond, KY	Maroon/White
Eastern Michigan	Eagles	Mid-American	Charles Ramsey	Ypsilanti, MI	Green/White
Eastern Washington	Eagles	Big Sky	Mike Burns	Cheney, WA	Red/White
Elon	Phoenix	Southern	Ernie Nestor	Elon, NC	Maroon/Gold
Evansville	Aces	Mo. Valley	Steve Merfeld	Evansville, IN	Purple/White
Fairfield	Stags	Metro Atlantic	Ed Cooley	Fairfield, CT	Cardinal Red
Fairleigh Dickinson	Knights	Northeast	Tom Green	Teaneck, NJ	Maroon/Blue
Florida	Gators	SEC-East	Billy Donovan	Gainesville, FL	Orange/Blue
Florida A&M	Rattlers	Mid-Eastern	Mike Gillespie	Tallahassee, FL	Orange/Green
Florida Atlantic	Owls	Sun Belt	Rex Walters	Boca Raton, FL	Blue/Red
Florida Int'l	Golden Panthers	Sun Belt	Sergio Rouco	Miami, FL	Blue/Gold
Florida St.	Seminoles	ACC	Leonard Hamilton	Tallahassee, FL	Garnet/Gold
Fordham	Rams	Atlantic 10	Dereck Whittenburg	Bronx, NY	Maroon/White
Fresno St.	Bulldogs	WAC	Steve Cleveland	Fresno, CA	Red/Blue
Furman	Paladins	Southern	Jeff Jackson	Greenville, SC	Purple/White
Gardner-Webb	Bulldogs	Atlantic Sun	Rick Scruggs	Boiling Springs, NC	Scarlet/Black
George Mason	Patriots	Colonial	Jim Larranaga	Fairfax, VA	Green/Gold
George Washington	Colonials	Atlantic 10	Karl Hobbs	Washington, DC	Buff/Blue
Georgetown	Hoyas	Big East	John Thompson III	Washington, DC	Blue/Gray
Georgia	Bulldogs, 'Dawgs	SEC-East	Dennis Felton	Athens, GA	Red/Black
Georgia Southern	Eagles	Southern	Jeff Price	Statesboro, GA	Blue/White
Georgia St.	Panthers	Colonial	Michael Perry	Atlanta, GA	Roy. Blue/White
Georgia Tech	Yellow Jackets	ACC	Paul Hewitt	Atlanta, GA	Old Gold/White
Gonzaga	Bulldogs, Zags	West Coast	Mark Few	Spokane, WA	Blue/White/Red
Grambling St.	Tigers	SWAC	Larry Wright	Grambling, LA	Black/Gold
Hampton	Pirates	Mid-Eastern	Kevin Nickelberry	Hampton, VA	Royal Blue/White
Hartford	Hawks	America East	Dan Leibovitz	W. Hartford, CT	Scarlet/White
Harvard	Crimson	Ivy	Frank Sullivan	Cambridge, MA	Crimson/Black/White
Hawaii	Rainbow Warriors	WAC	Riley Wallace	Honolulu, HI	Green/White
High Point	Panthers	Big South	Bart Lundy	High Point, NC	Purple/White
Hofstra	Pride	Colonial	Tom Pecora	Hempstead, NY	Blue/Gold/White
Holy Cross	Crusaders	Patriot	Ralph Willard	Worcester, MA	Royal Purple
Houston	Cougars	USA	Tom Penders	Houston, TX	Scarlet/White
Howard	Bison	Mid-Eastern	Gil Jackson	Washington, DC	Blue/White/Red
Idaho	Vandals	WAC	George Pfeifer	Moscow, ID	Silver/Gold
Idaho St.	Bengals	Big Sky	Joe O'Brien	Pocatello, ID	Orange/Black
Illinois	Fighting Illini	Big Ten	Bruce Weber	Champaign, IL	Orange/Blue
Illinois-Chicago	Flames	Horizon	Jim Collins	Chicago, IL	Navy Blue/Red
Illinois St.	Redbirds	Mo. Valley	Porter Moser	Normal, IL	Red/White
Indiana	Hoosiers	Big Ten	Kelvin Sampson	Bloomington, IN	Cream/Crimson
IPFW	Mastodons	Independent	Dane Fife	Fort Wayne, IN	Royal Blue/White
IUPUI	Jaguars	Mid-Continent	Ron Hunter	Indianapolis, IN	Red/Gold
Indiana St.	Sycamores	Mo. Valley	Royce Waltman	Terre Haute, IN	Blue/White
Iona	Gaels	Metro Atlantic	Jeff Ruland	New Rochelle, NY	Maroon/Gold
Iowa	Hawkeyes	Big Ten	Steve Alford	Iowa City, IA	Old Gold/Black
Iowa St.	Cyclones	Big 12	Greg McDermott	Ames, IA	Cardinal/Gold
Jackson St.	Tigers	SWAC	Tevester Anderson	Jackson, MS	Blue/White

	Nickname	Conference	Head Coach	Location	Colors
Jacksonville	Dolphins	Atlantic Sun	Cliff Warren	Jacksonville, FL	Green/White
Jacksonville St.	Gamecocks	Ohio Valley	Mike LaPlante	Jacksonville, AL	Red/White
James Madison	Dukes	Colonial	Dean Keener	Harrisonburg, VA	Purple/Gold
Kansas	Jayhawks	Big 12	Bill Self	Lawrence, KS	Crimson/Blue
Kansas St.	Wildcats	Big 12	Bob Huggins	Manhattan, KS	Purple/White
Kennesaw St.	Owls	Atlantic Sun	Tony Ingle	Kennesaw, GA	Black/Gold
Kent St.	Golden Flashes	Mid-American	Jim Christian	Kent, OH	Navy Blue/Gold
Kentucky	Wildcats	SEC-East	Tubby Smith	Lexington, KY	Blue/White
La Salle	Explorers	Atlantic 10	John Giannini	Philadelphia, PA	Blue/Gold
Lafayette	Leopards	Patriot	Fran O'Hanlon	Easton, PA	Maroon/White
Lamar	Cardinals	Southland	Steve Roccaforte	Beaumont, TX	Red/White
Lehigh	Mountain Hawks	Patriot	Bill Taylor	Bethlehem, PA	Brown/White
Liberty	Flames	Big South	Randy Dunton	Lynchburg, VA	Red/White/Blue
Lipscomb	Bisons	Atlantic Sun	Scott Sanderson	Nashville, TN	Purple/Gold
Long Beach St.	49ers	Big West	Larry Reynolds	Long Beach, CA	Black/Gold
Long Island	Blackbirds	Northeast	Jim Ferry	Brooklyn, NY	Black/Silver/Blue
Longwood	Lancers	Independent	Mike Gillian	Farmville, VA	Blue/White
LSU	Fighting Tigers	SEC-West	John Brady	Baton Rouge, LA	Purple/Gold
LA-Lafayette	Ragin' Cajuns	Sun Belt	Robert Lee	Lafayette, LA	Vermilion/White
LA-Monroe	Warhawks	Sun Belt	Orlando Early	Monroe, LA	Maroon/Gold
Louisiana Tech	Bulldogs	WAC	Keith Richard	Ruston, LA	Red/Blue
Louisville	Cardinals	Big East	Rick Pitino	Louisville, KY	Red/Black/White
Loyola Chicago	Ramblers	Horizon	Jim Whitesell	Chicago, IL	Maroon/Gold
Loyola Maryland	Greyhounds	Metro Atlantic	Jimmy Patsos	Baltimore, MD	Green/Gray
Loyola Marymount	Lions	West Coast	Rodney Tention	Los Angeles, CA	Crimson/Blue
Maine	Black Bears	America East	Ted Woodward	Orono, ME	Blue/White
Manhattan	Jaspers	Metro Atlantic	Barry Rohrssen	Riverdale, NY	Kelly Green/White
Marist	Red Foxes	Metro Atlantic	Matt Brady	Poughkeepsie, NY	Red/White
Marquette	Golden Eagles	Big East	Tom Crean	Milwaukee, WI	Blue/Gold
Marshall	Thundering Herd	USA	Ron Jirsa	Huntington, WV	Green/White
Maryland	Terrapins, Terps	ACC	Gary Williams	College Park, MD	Red/Wt./Black/Gold
MD-Balt. County	Retrievers	America East	Randy Monroe	Baltimore, MD	Black/Gold/Red
MD-Eastern Shore	Hawks	Mid-Eastern	Larry Lessett	Princess Anne, MD	Maroon/Gray
Massachusetts	Minutemen	Atlantic 10	Travis Ford	Amherst, MA	Maroon/White
McNeese St.	Cowboys	Southland	Dave Simmons	Lake Charles, LA	Blue/Gold
Memphis	Tigers	USA	John Calipari	Memphis, TN	Blue/Gray
Mercer	Bears	Atlantic Sun	Mark Slonaker	Macon, GA	Orange/Black
Miami-FL	Hurricanes	ACC	Frank Haith	Coral Gables, FL	Orange/Grn./White
Miami-OH	RedHawks	Mid-American	Charlie Coles	Oxford, OH	Red/White
Michigan	Wolverines	Big Ten	Tommy Amaker	Ann Arbor, MI	Maize/Blue
Michigan St.	Spartans	Big Ten	Tom Izzo	East Lansing, MI	Green/White
Middle Tennessee	Blue Raiders	Sun Belt	Kermit Davis Jr.	Murfreesboro, TN	Royal Blue/White
Minnesota	Golden Gophers	Big Ten	Dan Monson	Minneapolis, MN	Maroon/Gold
Mississippi	Ole Miss, Rebels	SEC-West	Andy Kennedy	Oxford, MS	Cardinal/Navy Blue
Mississippi St.	Bulldogs	SEC-West	Rick Stansbury	Starkville, MS	Maroon/White
Miss. Valley St.	Delta Devils	SWAC	James Green	Itta Bena, MS	Green/White
Missouri	Tigers	Big 12	Mike Anderson	Columbia, MO	Old Gold/Black
Missouri St.	Bears	Mo. Valley	Barry Hinson	Springfield, MO	Maroon/White
Missouri-KC	Kangaroos	Mid-Continent	Rich Zvosec	Kansas City, MO	Blue/Gold
Monmouth	Hawks	Northeast	Dave Calloway	W. Long Branch, NJ	Midnight Blue/White
Montana	Grizzlies	Big Sky	Wayne Tinkle	Missoula, MT	Copper/Silver/Gold
Montana St.	Bobcats	Big Sky	Brad Huse	Bozeman, MT	Blue/Gold
Morehead St.	Eagles	Ohio Valley	Donnie Tyndall	Morehead, KY	Blue/Gold
Morgan St.	Bears	Mid-Eastern	Todd Bozeman	Baltimore, MD	Blue/Orange
Mt. St. Mary's	Mountaineers	Northeast	Milan Brown	Emmitsburg, MD	Blue/White
Murray St.	Racers	Ohio Valley	Billy Kennedy	Murray, KY	Blue/Gold
Navy	Midshipmen	Patriot	Billy Lange	Annapolis, MD	Navy Blue/Gold
Nebraska	Cornhuskers	Big 12	Doc Sadler	Lincoln, NE	Scarlet/Cream
Nevada	Wolf Pack	WAC	Mark Fox	Reno, NV	Silver/Blue
New Hampshire	Wildcats	America East	Bill Herrion	Durham, NH	Blue/White
New Mexico	Lobos	Mountain West	Ritchie McKay	Albuquerque, NM	Cherry/Silver
New Mexico St.	Aggies	WAC	Reggie Theus	Las Cruces, NM	Crimson/White
New Orleans	Privateers	Sun Belt	Buzz Williams	New Orleans, LA	Royal Blue/Silver
Niagara	Purple Eagles	Metro Atlantic	Joe Mihalich	Lewiston, NY	Purple/White/Gold
Nicholls St.	Colonels	Southland	J.P. Piper	Thibodaux, LA	Red/Gray
Norfolk State	Spartans	Mid-Eastern	Dwight Freeman	Norfolk, VA	Green/Gold
North Carolina	Tar Heels	ACC	Roy Williams	Chapel Hill, NC	Carolina Blue/Wht.
North Carolina A&T	Aggies	Mid-Eastern	Jerry Eaves	Greensboro, NC	Blue/Gold
North Carolina St.	Wolfpack	ACC	Sidney Lowe	Raleigh, NC	Red/White
NC-Asheville	Bulldogs	Big South	Eddie Biedenbach	Asheville, NC	Royal Blue/White
NC-Greensboro	Spartans	Southern	Mike Dement	Greensboro, NC	Gold/White/Navy

NCAA Division I Basketball Schools (Cont.)

	Nickname	Conference	Head Coach	Location	Colors
NC-Wilmington	Seahawks	Colonial	Benny Moss	Wilmington, NC	Green/Gold/Navy
North Dakota St.	Bison	Independent	Tim Miles	Fargo, ND	Yellow/Green
North Florida	Ospreys	Atlantic Sun	Matt Kilcullen	Jacksonville, FL	Navy Blue/Gray
North Texas	Mean Green	Sun Belt	Johnny Jones	Denton, TX	Green/White
Northeastern	Huskies	Colonial	Bill Coen	Boston, MA	Red/Black
Northern Arizona	Lumberjacks	Big Sky	Mike Adras	Flagstaff, AZ	Blue/Gold
Northern Colorado	Bears	Big Sky	Tad Boyle	Greeley, CO	Blue/Gold
Northern Illinois	Huskies	Mid-American	Rob Judson	DeKalb, IL	Cardinal/Black
Northern Iowa	Panthers	Mo. Valley	Ben Jacobson	Cedar Falls, IA	Purple/Old Gold
Northwestern	Wildcats	Big Ten	Bill Carmody	Evanston, IL	Purple/White
Northwestern St.	Demons	Southland	Mike McConathy	Natchitoches, LA	Purple/Orange/Wt.
Notre Dame	Fighting Irish	Big Ten	Mike Brey	Notre Dame, IN	Gold/Blue
Oakland-MI	Golden Grizzlies	Mid-Continent	Greg Kampe	Rochester, MI	Black/Gold
Ohio University	Bobcats	Mid-American	Tim O'Shea	Athens, OH	Hunter Green/White
Ohio St.	Buckeyes	Big Ten	Thad Matta	Columbus, OH	Scarlet/Gray
Oklahoma	Sooners	Big 12	Jeff Capel	Norman, OK	Crimson/Cream
Oklahoma St.	Cowboys	Big 12	Sean Sutton	Stillwater, OK	Orange/Black
Old Dominion	Monarchs	Colonial	Blaine Taylor	Norfolk, VA	Slate Blue/Silver
Oral Roberts	Golden Eagles	Mid-Continent	Scott Sutton	Tulsa, OK	Navy Blue/White
Oregon	Ducks	Pac-10	Ernie Kent	Eugene, OR	Green/Yellow
Oregon St.	Beavers	Pac-10	Jay John	Corvallis, OR	Orange/Black
Pacific	Tigers	Big West	Bob Thomason	Stockton, CA	Orange/Black
Pennsylvania	Quakers	Ivy	Glen Miller	Philadelphia, PA	Red/Blue
Penn St.	Nittany Lions	Big Ten	Ed DeChellis	University Park, PA	Blue/White
Pepperdine	Waves	West Coast	Vance Walberg	Malibu, CA	Blue/Orange
Pittsburgh	Panthers	Big East	Jamie Dixon	Pittsburgh, PA	Gold/Blue
Portland	Pilots	West Coast	Eric Reveno	Portland, OR	Purple/White
Portland St.	Vikings	Big Sky	Ken Bone	Portland, OR	Green/White
Prairie View A&M	Panthers	SWAC	Byron Rimm II	Prairie View, TX	Purple/Gold
Princeton	Tigers	Ivy	Joe Scott	Princeton, NJ	Orange/Black
Providence	Friars	Big East	Tim Welsh	Providence, RI	Black/White
Purdue	Boilermakers	Big Ten	Matt Painter	W. Lafayette, IN	Old Gold/Black
Quinnipiac	Bobcats	Northeast	Joe DeSantis	Hamden, CT	Navy/Gold
Radford	Highlanders	Big South	Byron Samuels	Radford, VA	Blue/Red/Green/Wt.
Rhode Island	Rams	Atlantic 10	Jim Baron	Kingston, RI	Lt. Blue/White/Navy
Rice	Owls	USA	Willis Wilson	Houston, TX	Blue/Gray
Richmond	Spiders	Atlantic 10	Chris Mooney	Richmond, VA	Red/Blue
Rider	Broncs	Metro Atlantic	Tommy Dempsey	Lawrenceville, NJ	Cranberry/White
Robert Morris	Colonials	Northeast	Mark Schmidt	Moon Township, PA	Blue/Red/White
Rutgers	Scarlet Knights	Big East	Fred Hill Jr.	New Brunswick, NJ	Scarlet
Sacramento St.	Hornets	Big Sky	Jerome Jenkins	Sacramento, CA	Green/Gold
Sacred Heart	Pioneers	Northeast	Dave Bike	Fairfield, CT	Scarlet/White
St. Bonaventure	Bonnies	Atlantic 10	Anthony Solomon	St. Bonaventure, NY	Brown/White
St. Francis-NY	Terriers	Northeast	Brian Nash	Brooklyn, NY	Red/Blue
St. Francis-PA	Red Flash	Northeast	Bobby Jones	Loretto, PA	Red/White
St. John's	Red Storm	Big East	Norm Roberts	Jamaica, NY	Red/White
Saint Joseph's	Hawks	Atlantic 10	Phil Martelli	Philadelphia, PA	Crimson/Gray
Saint Louis	Billikens	Atlantic 10	Brad Soderberg	St. Louis, MO	Blue/White
Saint Mary's-CA	Gaels	West Coast	Randy Bennett	Moraga, CA	Red/Blue
Saint Peter's	Peacocks	Metro Atlantic	John Dunne	Jersey City, NJ	Blue/White
Sam Houston St.	Bearkats	Southland	Bob Marlin	Huntsville, TX	Orange/White
Samford	Bulldogs	Ohio Valley	Jimmy Tillette	Birmingham, AL	Red/Blue
San Diego	Toreros	West Coast	Brad Holland	San Diego, CA	Lt. Blue/Navy
San Diego St.	Aztecs	Mountain West	Steve Fisher	San Diego, CA	Scarlet/Black
San Francisco	Dons	West Coast	Jessie Evans	San Francisco, CA	Green/Gold
San Jose St.	Spartans	WAC	George Nessman	San Jose, CA	Gold/White/Blue
Santa Clara	Broncos	West Coast	Dick Davey	Santa Clara, CA	Bronco Red/White
Savannah St.	Tigers	Independent	Horace Broadnax	Savannah, GA	Orange/Blue
Seton Hall	Pirates	Big East	Bobby Gonzalez	South Orange, NJ	Blue/White
Siena	Saints	Metro Atlantic	Fran McCaffery	Loudonville, NY	Green/Gold
South Alabama	Jaguars	Sun Belt	John Pelphrey	Mobile, AL	Red/White/Blue
South Carolina	Gamecocks	SEC-East	Dave Odom	Columbia, SC	Garnet/Black
South Carolina St.	Bulldogs	Mid-Eastern	Jamal Brown	Orangeburg, SC	Garnet/Blue
South Dakota St.	Jackrabbits	Independent	Scott Nagy	Brookings, SD	Yellow/Blue
South Florida	Bulls	Big East	Robert McCullum	Tampa, FL	Green/Gold
SE Missouri St.	Redhawks	Ohio Valley	Scott Edgar	Cape Girardeau, MO	Red/Black
Southeastern Louisiana	Lions	Southland	Jim Yarbrough Jr.	Hammond, LA	Green/Gold
Southern-BR	Jaguars	SWAC	Rob Spivery	Baton Rouge, LA	Blue/Gold
Southern Illinois	Salukis	Mo. Valley	Chris Lowery	Carbondale, IL	Maroon/White

	Nickname	Conference	Head Coach	Location	Colors
SMU	Mustangs	USA	Matt Doherty	Dallas, TX	Red/Blue
Southern Miss	Golden Eagles	USA	Larry Eustachy	Hattiesburg, MS	Black/Gold
Southern Utah	Thunderbirds	Mid-Continent	Bill Evans	Cedar City, UT	Scarlet/White
Stanford	Cardinal	Pac-10	Trent Johnson	Stanford, CA	Cardinal/White
S.F. Austin St.	Lumberjacks	Southland	Danny Kaspar	Nacogdoches, TX	Purple/White
Stetson	Hatters	Atlantic Sun	Derek Waugh	DeLand, FL	Green/White
Stony Brook	Seawolves	America East	Steve Pikiell	Stony Brook, NY	Scarlet/Gray
Syracuse	Orange	Big East	Jim Boeheim	Syracuse, NY	Orange
Temple	Owls	Atlantic 10	Fran Dunphy	Philadelphia, PA	Cherry/White
Tennessee	Volunteers	SEC-East	Bruce Pearl	Knoxville, TN	Orange/White
Tenn-Martin	Skyhawks	Ohio Valley	Bret Campbell	Martin, TN	Orange/Wt./Blue
Tennessee St.	Tigers	Ohio Valley	Cy Alexander	Nashville, TN	Blue/White
Tennessee Tech	Golden Eagles	Ohio Valley	Mike Sutton	Cookeville, TN	Purple/Gold
Texas	Longhorns	Big 12	Rick Barnes	Austin, TX	Burnt Orange/White
Texas A&M	Aggies	Big 12	Billy Gillispie	College Station, TX	Maroon/White
TX A&M Corpus-Christi	Islanders	Southland	Ronnie Arrow	Corpus Christi, TX	Blue/Green/Silver
TCU	Horned Frogs	Mountain West	Neil Dougherty	Ft. Worth, TX	Purple/White
Texas Southern	Tigers	SWAC	Ronnie Courtney	Houston, TX	Maroon/Gray
Texas St.	Bobcats	Southland	Doug Davalos	San Marcos, TX	Maroon/Gold
Texas Tech	Red Raiders	Big 12	Bob Knight	Lubbock, TX	Scarlet/Black
TX-Arlington	Mavericks	Southland	Scott Cross	Arlington, TX	Royal Blue/White
TX-Pan American	Broncs	Independent	Tom Schuberth	Edinburg, TX	Green/White
TX-San Antonio	Roadrunners	Southland	Brooks Thompson	San Antonio, TX	Orange/Navy/White
Toledo	Rockets	Mid-American	Stan Joplin	Toledo, OH	Blue/Gold
Towson	Tigers	Colonial	Pat Kennedy	Towson, MD	Gold/White/Black
Troy	Trojans	Sun Belt	Don Maestri	Troy, AL	Cardinal/Silver/Black
Tulane	Green Wave	USA	Dave Dickerson	New Orleans, LA	Olive Grn./Sky Blue
Tulsa	Golden Hurricane	USA	Doug Wojcik	Tulsa, OK	Blue/Gold/Crimson
UAB	Blazers	USA	Mike Davis	Birmingham, AL	Green/Gold
UC-Irvine	Anteaters	Big West	Pat Douglass	Irvine, CA	Blue/Gold
UCLA	Bruins	Pac-10	Ben Howland	Los Angeles, CA	Blue/Gold
UC-Davis	Aggies	Independent	Gary Stewart	Davis, CA	Yale Blue/Gold
UC-Riverside	Highlanders	Big West	David Spencer	Riverside, CA	Blue/Gold
UC-Santa Barbara	Gauchos	Big West	Bob Williams	Santa Barbara, CA	Blue/Gold
UNLV	Runnin' Rebels	Mountain West	Lon Kruger	Las Vegas, NV	Scarlet/Gray
USC	Trojans	Pac-10	Tim Floyd	Los Angeles, CA	Cardinal/Gold
Utah	Utes, Runnin' Utes	Mountain West	Ray Giacoletti	Salt Lake City, UT	Crimson/White
Utah St.	Aggies	WAC	Stew Morrill	Logan, UT	Navy Blue/White
Utah Valley St.	Wolverines	Independent	Dick Hunsaker	Orem, UT	Green/Gold/White
UTEP	Miners	USA	Tony Barbee	El Paso, TX	Orange/Blue/Silver
Valparaiso	Crusaders	Mid-Continent	Homer Drew	Valparaiso, IN	Brown/Gold
Vanderbilt	Commodores	SEC-East	Kevin Stallings	Nashville, TN	Black/Gold
Vermont	Catamounts	America East	Mike Lonergan	Burlington, VT	Green/Gold
Villanova	Wildcats	Big East	Jay Wright	Villanova, PA	Blue/White
Virginia	Cavaliers	ACC	Dave Leitao	Charlottesville, VA	Orange/Blue
VCU	Rams	Colonial	Anthony Grant	Richmond, VA	Black/Gold
VMI	Keydets	Big South	Duggar Baucom	Lexington, VA	Red/White/Yellow
Virginia Tech	Hokies, Gobblers	ACC	Seth Greenberg	Blacksburg, VA	Orange/Maroon
Wagner	Seahawks	Northeast	Mike Deane	Staten Island, NY	Green/White
Wake Forest	Demon Deacons	ACC	Skip Prosser	Winston-Salem, NC	Old Gold/Black
Washington	Huskies	Pac-10	Lorenzo Romar	Seattle, WA	Purple/Gold
Washington St.	Cougars	Pac-10	Tony Bennett	Pullman, WA	Crimson/Gray
Weber St.	Wildcats	Big Sky	Randy Rahe	Ogden, UT	Purple/White
West Virginia	Mountaineers	Big East	John Beilein	Morgantown, WV	Old Gold/Blue
Western Carolina	Catamounts	Southern	Larry Hunter	Cullowhee, NC	Purple/Gold
Western Illinois	Leathernecks	Mid-Continent	Derek Thomas	Macomb, IL	Purple/Gold
Western Kentucky	Hilltoppers	Sun Belt	Darrin Horn	Bowling Green, KY	Red/White
Western Michigan	Broncos	Mid-American	Steve Hawkins	Kalamazoo, MI	Brown/Gold
Wichita St.	Shockers	Mo. Valley	Mark Turgeon	Wichita, KS	Yellow/Black
William & Mary	Tribe	Colonial	Tony Shaver	Williamsburg, VA	Green/Gold/Silver
Winston-Salem St.	Rams	Independent	Philip Stitt	Winston-Salem, NC	Red/White
Winthrop	Eagles	Big South	Gregg Marshall	Rock Hill, SC	Garnet/Gold
Wisconsin	Badgers	Big Ten	Bo Ryan	Madison, WI	Cardinal/White
WI-Green Bay	Phoenix	Horizon	Tod Kowalczyk	Green Bay, WI	Green/White/Red
WI-Milwaukee	Panthers	Horizon	Rob Jeter	Milwaukee, WI	Black/Gold
Wofford	Terriers	Southern	Mike Young	Spartanburg, SC	Old Gold/Black
Wright St.	Raiders	Horizon	Brad Brownell	Dayton, OH	Green/Gold
Wyoming	Cowboys	Mountain West	Steve McClain	Laramie, WY	Brown/Gold
Xavier	Musketeers	Atlantic 10	Sean Miller	Cincinnati, OH	Blue/Gray/White
Yale	Bulldogs, Elis	Ivy	James Jones	New Haven, CT	Yale Blue/White
Youngstown St.	Penguins	Horizon	Jerry Slocum	Youngstown, OH	Red/White

Scouts Inc. Evaluations

Listed are the top recruiting prospects for the 2007 high school graduating class for boys basketball, and the 2006 and 2007 graduating classes for football, as graded by the members of ESPN's Scouts Inc.

The analysts and talent evaluators at Scouts Inc. watch games, break down film and use their extensive experience and contacts in their respective sports to provide the deepest and most detailed scouting reports available.

For expanded lists and in-depth information on each recruit, as well as expert analysis on professional basketball, football, baseball and more, go to the "Scouts" tab on ESPN.com.

Basketball Top 25 — High School Class of 2007

List is as of Sept. 30, 2006 and subject to change.

	Name	Hometown	Position 1	Position 2	HT	WT	Grade
1	Kevin Love	Lake Oswego, OR	Center	Power Forward	6-9	255	98
2	Eric Gordon	Indianapolis, IN	Shooting Guard	—	6-5	205	98
3	Derrick Rose	Chicago, IL	Point Guard	—	6-3	195	97
4	O.J. Mayo	Cincinnati, OH	Shooting Guard	—	6-4	195	97
5	Kyle Singler	Medford, OR	Small Forward	—	6-8	215	97
6	William Walker	Cincinnati, OH	Small Forward	—	6-6	225	97
7	Johnny Flynn	Niagara Falls, NY	Point Guard	—	5-11	170	96
8	Nick Calathes	Winter Park, FL	Shooting Guard	Point Guard	6-5	180	96
9	Nolan Smith	Mouth of Wilson, VA	Shooting Guard	Point Guard	6-2	185	96
10	Jerry Bayless	Phoenix, AZ	Point Guard	Shooting Guard	6-3	185	96
11	Daniel Hackett	Bellflower, CA	Shooting Guard	Small Forward	6-5	205	96
12	Austin Freeman	Hyattsville, MD	Shooting Guard	—	6-5	215	96
13	Corey Stokes	Newark, NJ	Shooting Guard	Small Forward	6-6	215	96
14	Donte Greene	Towson, MD	Power Forward	—	6-8	215	96
15	Herb Pope	Aliquippa, PA	Power Forward	—	6-9	215	96
16	Michael Beasley	Mouth of Wilson, VA	Power Forward	—	6-9	230	96
17	Blake Griffin	Oklahoma City, OK	Power Forward	—	6-8	245	96
18	Patrick Patterson	Huntington, WV	Power Forward	—	6-8	245	96
19	E'Twaun Moore	East Chicago, IL	Point Guard	Shooting Guard	6-3	185	95
20	James Harden	Lakewood, CA	Shooting Guard	Small Forward	6-5	200	95
21	James Hickson	Marietta, GA	Center	Power Forward	6-9	235	95
22	Deandre Jordan	Houston, TX	Center	Power Forward	6-11	235	95
23	Jeff Allen	Chatham, VA	Power Forward	—	6-7	250	95
24	Kosta Koufos	Canton, OH	Center	—	7-1	250	95
25	Lacedarius Dunn	Monroe, LA	Shooting Guard	—	6-4	185	95

Top 25 NCAA Football Recruiting Classes of 2006

Listed are the NCAA programs with the best recruiting classes from the pool of 2006 high school seniors, along with respective letter grades. These grades and rankings are purely subjective and were assigned by Tom Luginbill, the national director of recruiting for Scouts Inc.

	School	Grade		School	Grade		School	Grade
1	Florida	A	10	Ohio State	A-	19	UCLA	B-
2	USC	A	11	Michigan	B+	20	Tennessee	B-
3	Texas	A	12	Auburn	B+	21	Louisville	B-
4	Georgia	A	13	Clemson	B	22	Texas A&M	B-
5	Notre Dame	A	14	Mississippi	B	23	Maryland	B-
6	Florida State	A-	15	Oklahoma State	B	24	Virginia Tech	B-
7	Oklahoma	A-	16	Pittsburgh	B	25	North Carolina	B-
8	LSU	A-	17	Miami-FL	B-			
9	Penn State	A-	18	Alabama	B-			

Football Top 30 — High School Class of 2006

	Name	Hometown	Position	HT	WT	Rank	Grade	NCAA School
1	Myron Rolle	Galloway, NJ	S	6-3	210	S#1	94	Florida State
2	Percy Harvin	Virginia Beach, VA	WR	6-1	188	WR#1	93	Florida
3	Vidal Hazelton	Chatham, VA	WR	6-2	195	WR#2	93	USC
4	Andre Smith	Birmingham, AL	OT	6-5	302	OT#1	93	Alabama
5	Mitch Mustain	Springdale, AR	QB	6-3	205	QB#1	93	Arkansas
6	DeMarco Murray	Las Vegas, NV	RB	6-1	190	RB#1	92	Oklahoma
7	Sergio Kindle	Dallas, TX	OLB	6-3	220	OLB#1	92	Texas
8	Taylor Mays	Seattle, WA	S	6-4	225	S#2	92	USC
9	Matthew Stafford	Highland Park, TX	QB	6-3	210	QB#2	91	Georgia
10	Micah Johnson	Ft. Campbell, KY	ILB	6-2	249	ILB#1	91	Kentucky
11	Antwine Perez	Camden, NJ	S	6-2	200	S#3	91	USC
12	Maurice Evans	Middle Village, NY	DE	6-3	250	DE#1	91	Penn State
13	Jevan Snead	Stephensville, TX	QB	6-4	210	QB#3	91	Texas
14	Stafon Johnson	Bellflower, CA	RB	6-1	210	RB#2	90	USC
15	Tim Tebow	St. Augustine, FL	QB	6-3	225	QB#4	90	Florida
16	Jai Eugene	Destrehan, LA	CB	5-11	175	CB#1	89	LSU
17	Al Woods	Elton, LA	DT	6-4	315	DT#1	89	LSU
18	Marcus Ball	Stone Mountain, GA	OLB	6-1	210	OLB#2	89	Florida State
19	Sam Young	Coral Springs, FL	OT	6-8	295	OT#2	89	Notre Dame
20	Brandon Warren	Alcoa, TN	TE	6-3	230	TE#1	89	Florida State
21	Gerald McCoy	Oklahoma City, OK	DT	6-5	290	DT#2	89	Oklahoma
22	Eddie Jones	Kilgore, TX	DE	6-2	230	DE#2	88	Texas
23	Allen Walker	Olive Branch, MS	S	6-2	200	S#4	88	Mississippi
24	Carl Johnson	Durham, NC	OT	6-6	325	OT#3	88	Florida
25	Reshad Jones	Atlanta, GA	S	6-2	177	S#5	88	Georgia
26	Allen Bradford	San Bernardino, CA	OLB	6-0	230	OLB#3	87	USC
27	Markeith Summers	Olive Branch, MS	WR	6-3	185	WR#3	87	Mississippi
28	Jim Barrie	Tampa, FL	OT	6-6	295	OT#4	87	Florida
29	Jermaine Cunningham	Stone Mountain, GA	DE	6-3	220	DE#3	87	Florida
30	Chris Wells	Akron, OH	RB	6-2	230	RB#3	86	Ohio State

Football Top 30 — High School Class of 2007

List is as of Sept. 30, 2006 and subject to change. Note that 2007 National Signing Day is in February, so the NCAA school's listed have been given only a verbal commitment at press time.

	Name	Hometown	Position	HT	WT	Rank	Grade	NCAA School
1	Jimmy Clausen	Westlake Village, CA	QB	6-3	200	QB#1	91	Notre Dame
2	Chris Galippo	Anaheim, CA	ILB	6-2	240	ILB#1	90	USC
3	Marc Tyler	Westlake Village, CA	RB	6-1	210	RB#1	89	USC
4	Noel Devine	North Fort Myers, FL	RB	5-8	180	RB#2	87	undecided
5	Michael McNeil	Mobile, AL	S	6-2	200	S#1	86	undecided
6	Martez Wilson	Chicago, IL	DE	6-4	230	DE#1	86	undecided
7	Eric Berry	Fairburn, GA	CB	6-0	180	CB#1	86	undecided
8	Marshall Jones	Westlake Village, CA	S	6-1	190	S#2	85	USC
9	Tyrod Taylor	Hampton, VA	QB	6-1	185	QB#2	85	Virginia Tech
10	Terrance Toliver	Hempstead, TX	WR	6-4	190	WR#1	85	undecided
11	Marvin Austin	Washington, DC	DT	6-2	290	DT#1	85	undecided
12	Brian Maddox	Anderson, SC	RB	6-2	215	RB#3	85	South Carolina
13	Willy Korn	Duncan, SC	QB	6-1	200	QB#3	85	Clemson
14	Gary Gray	Columbia, SC	CB	5-11	170	CB#2	84	Notre Dame
15	Arrelious Benn	Washington, DC	WR	6-1	205	WR#2	84	undecided
16	Golden Tate	Hendersonville, TN	CB	5-11	180	CB#3	84	undecided
17	J.R. Hemingway	Conway, SC	WR	6-2	205	WR#3	84	Michigan
18	Tray Allen	Grand Prairie, TX	OT	6-4	300	OT#1	84	Texas
19	John Chiles	Arlington, TX	WR	6-1	180	WR#4	84	Texas
20	Joe McKnight	River Ridge, LA	RB	6-0	190	RB#4	84	undecided
21	Christian Scott	Dallas, TX	S	6-0	179	S#3	84	undecided
22	Kerry Neal	Bunn, NC	DE	6-3	232	DE#2	84	Notre Dame
23	Israel Troupe	Tifton, GA	WR	6-1	205	WR#5	83	Georgia
24	Josh Oglesby	Milwaukee, WI	OT	6-7	320	OT#2	83	Wisconsin
25	Deonte Thompson	Belle Glade, FL	WR	6-0	186	WR#6	83	undecided
26	Chris Rainey	Lakeland, FL	RB	5-8	165	RB#5	83	Florida
27	D.J. Stafford	LaGrange, GA	DT	6-3	273	DT#2	83	undecided
28	Greg Little	Durham, NC	WR	6-3	210	WR#7	82	undecided
29	Allen Bailey	Darien, GA	DE	6-3	252	DE#3	82	undecided
30	Phelon Jones	Mobile, AL	CB	6-0	195	CB#4	82	Miami-FL

Idaho
Dennis Erickson
Idaho

San Diego St.
Chuck Long
Oklahoma to San Diego St.

College of Charleston
Bobby Cremins
College of Charleston

N.C. State
Sidney Lowe
Pistons to N.C. State

Coaching Changes

New head coaches were named at 11 Division 1-A and 21 Division 1-AA football schools while 62 Division 1 basketball schools changed head coaches during or after the 2005-06 season. Coaching changes listed below are as of September 30, 2006.

Division I-A Football

	Old Coach	Record	Why Left?	New Coach	Old Job
Boise St.	Dan Hawkins	9-4	to Colorado*	Chris Petersen	Off. coord., Boise St.
Buffalo	Jim Hofher	1-10	Fired	Turner Gill	Asst., NFL Green Bay
Colorado	Gary Barnett	7-5	Resigned†	Dan Hawkins	Coach, Boise St.
Idaho	Nick Holt	2-9	to USC**	Dennis Erickson	Coach, NFL San Fran.
Kansas St.	Bill Snyder	5-6	Retired	Ron Prince	Off. coord., Virginia
Middle Tennessee	Andy McCollum	4-7	Fired	Rick Stockstill	Asst., South Carolina
Northwestern	Randy Walker	7-5	deceased@	Pat Fitzgerald	Asst., Northwestern
Rice	Ken Hatfield	1-10	Resigned	Todd Graham	Asst., Tulsa
San Diego St.	Tom Craft	5-7	Fired	Chuck Long	Off. coord., Oklahoma
Temple	Bobby Wallace	0-11	Resigned	Al Golden	Def. coord., Virginia
Wisconsin	Barry Alvarez	10-3	Resigned	Bret Bielema	Def. coord., Wisconsin

* as head coach   ** as assistant coach
@ Walker died on June 29, 2006 of an apparent heart attack at the age of 52.
† Barnett (7-5) resigned on Dec. 8, 2005 and was replaced for the Champs Sports Bowl by defensive coordinator Mike Hankowitz (0-1).

Division I-AA Football

	Old Coach	Record	Why Left?	New Coach	Old Job
Butler	Kit Cartwright	0-11	fired	Jeff Voris	Coach, NAIA Carroll Coll.
Central Conn. St.	Tom Masella	7-4	to Fordham*	Jeff McInerney	Def. coord., Rhode Island
Columbia	Bob Shoop	2-8	fired	Norries Wilson	Off. coord., Connecticut
Elon	Paul Hamilton	3-8	resigned	Pete Lembo	Coach, Lehigh
Fordham	Ed Foley	2-9	resigned	Tom Masella	Coach, Central Conn. St.
Georgetown	Bob Benson	4-7	resigned	Kevin Kelly	Asst., Navy
Georgia Southern	Mike Sewak	8-4	fired	Brian VanGorder	Asst., NFL Jacksonville
Hofstra	Joe Gardi	7-4	retired	Dave Cohen	Def. coord., Delaware
Jackson St.	James Bell	2-9	fired†	Rick Comegy	Coach, D-II Tuskegee
La Salle	Phil Longo	4-7	to Minn. Duluth**	Tim Miller	Asst., La Salle
Lehigh	Pete Lembo	8-3	to Elon*	Andy Coen	Off. coord., Pennsylvania
Liberty	Ken Karcher	1-10	fired	Danny Rocco	Asst., Virginia
Missouri St.	Randy Ball	4-6	fired	Terry Allen	Asst., Iowa St.
Murray St.	Joe Pannunzio	2-9	fired	Matt Griffin	Coach, Tennessee-Martin
North Carolina A&T	George Small	3-8	fired	Lee Fobbs	Asst., Texas A&M
Northern Colorado	O. Kay Dalton	4-7	fired	Scott Downing	Asst., Nebraska
Savannah St.	Richard Basil	0-11	resigned	Theo Lemon	Coach, D-II Central St.
SE Missouri St.	Tim Billings	2-9	resigned	Tony Samuel	Asst., Purdue
Stony Brook	Sam Kornhauser	6-5	retired	Chuck Priore	Coach, D-III Trinity (Conn.)
Tennessee-Martin	Matt Griffin	6-5	to Murray St.*	Jason Simpson	Off. coord., Chattanooga
VMI	Cal McCombs	3-8	fired	Jim Reid	Asst., Syracuse

* as head coach   ** as assistant coach
† Bell (2-6) was fired on Oct. 31, 2005 and replaced for the final three games by assistant coach Daryl Jones (0-3).

Division I Basketball

	Old Coach	Record	Why Left?	New Coach	Old Job
Arizona St.	Rob Evans	11-17	fired	Herb Sendek	Coach, NC State
Ball St.	Tim Buckley	10-18	fired	Ronny Thompson	Asst., Arkansas
Birmingham South.	Duane Reboul	19-9	retired	Mitch Cole	Asst., Birmingham Southern
Brown	Glen Miller	10-17	to Penn*	Craig Robinson	Asst., Northwestern
Canisius	Mike MacDonald	9-20	fired	Tom Parrotta	Asst., Hofstra
Central Michigan	Jay Smith	4-24	resigned	Ernie Zeigler	Asst., UCLA
Cincinnati	Andy Kennedy	21-13	interim	Mick Cronin	Coach, Murray St.
The Citadel	Pat Dennis	10-21	resigned	Ed Conroy	Asst., Coastal Carolina
Cleveland St.	Mike Garland	10-18	resigned	Gary Waters	Coach, Rutgers
Coll. of Charleston	Tom Herrion	17-11	fired	Bobby Cremins	Former coach, Ga. Tech
Delaware	David Henderson	9-21	fired	Monte Ross	Asst., Saint Joseph's
Duquesne	Danny Nee	3-24	resigned	Ron Everhart	Coach, Northeastern
Fairfield	Tim O'Toole	9-19	resigned	Ed Cooley	Asst., Boston College
Florida Atlantic	Matt Doherty	15-13	to SMU*	Rex Walters	Asst., Florida Atlantic
Furman	Larry Davis	15-13	to Cincinnati**	Jeff Jackson	Asst., Vanderbilt
Hampton	Bobby Collins	16-16	resigned	Kevin Nickelberry	Asst., Clemson
Hartford	Larry Harrison	13-15	resigned	Dan Leibovitz	Asst, Temple
Idaho	Leonard Perry	4-25	fired	George Pfeifer	Asst., Idaho
Idaho St.	Doug Oliver	13-14	resigned	Joe O'Brien	Former Asst., Fla. Int'l
Indiana	Mike Davis	19-12	resigned	Kelvin Sampson	Coach, Oklahoma
Iowa St.	Wayne Morgan	16-14	fired	Greg McDermott	Coach, Northern Iowa
Kansas St.	Jim Wooldridge	15-13	fired	Bob Huggins	Former coach, Cincinnati
Lamar	Billy Tubbs	17-14	resigned	Steve Roccaforte	Asst., Lamar
Manhattan	Bobby Gonzalez	20-11	to Seton Hall*	Barry Rohrssen	Asst., Pittsburgh
McNeese St.	Tic Price	14-14	fired	Dave Simmons	Asst., Northwestern St.
Mississippi	Rod Barnes	14-16	fired	Andy Kennedy	Interim coach, Cincinnati
Missouri	Quin Snyder	12-16@	resigned	Mike Anderson	Coach, UAB
Montana	Larry Krystkowiak	24-7	to NBA Milwaukee**	Wayne Tinkle	Asst., Montana
Montana St.	Mick Durham	15-15	retired	Brad Huse	Asst., Montana
Morehead St.	Kyle Macy	4-23	resigned	Donnie Tyndall	Asst., Middle Tennessee
Morgan St.	Butch Beard	4-26	resigned	Todd Bozeman	Former coach, California
Murray St.	Mick Cronin	24-7	to Cincinnati*	Billy Kennedy	Asst., Miami-FL
Nebraska	Barry Collier	19-14	to Butler†	Doc Sadler	Coach, UTEP
New Orleans	Monte Towe	10-19	to NC State**	Buzz Williams	Asst., Texas A&M
North Carolina St.	Herb Sendek	22-10	to Arizona St.*	Sidney Lowe	Asst., NBA Detroit
NC-Wilmington	Brad Brownell	25-8	to Wright St.*	Benny Moss	Asst., Charlotte
Northeastern	Ron Everhart	19-11	to Duquesne*	Bill Coen	Asst., Boston College
Northern Colorado	Craig Rasmuson	5-24	resigned	Tad Boyle	Asst., Wichita St.
Northern Iowa	Greg McDermott	23-10	to Iowa St.	Ben Jacobson	Asst., Northern Iowa
Oklahoma	Kelvin Sampson	20-9	to Indiana*	Jeff Capel	Coach, VCU
Oklahoma St.	Eddie Sutton	17-16	retired	Sean Sutton	Asst., Oklahoma St.
Pennsylvania	Fran Dunphy	20-9	to Temple*	Glen Miller	Coach, Brown
Pepperdine	Paul Westphal	7-20	fired	Vance Walberg	Coach, Fresno City (juco)
Portland	Michael Holton	11-18	fired	Eric Reveno	Asst., Stanford
Prairie View A&M	Darrell Hawkins	5-24	interim	Byron Rimm II	Asst., Prairie View A&M
Rutgers	Gary Waters	19-14	to Cleveland St.*	Fred Hill Jr.	Asst., Rutgers
Saint Peter's	Bob Leckie	17-15	retires	John Dunne	Asst., Seton Hall
Seton Hall	Louis Orr	18-12	fired	Bobby Gonzalez	Coach, Manhattan
SMU	Jimmy Tubbs	13-16	fired	Matt Doherty	Coach, Florida Atlantic
South Carolina St.	Ben Betts Jr.	14-16	to Oklahoma**	Jamal Brown	Asst., Tennessee St.
SE Missouri St.	Gary Garner	7-20	fired	Scott Edgar	Asst., Tennessee
Temple	John Chaney	17-15	retired	Fran Dunphy	Coach, Penn
TX-Arlington	Eddie McCarter	14-16	resigned	Scott Cross	Asst., TX-Arlington
TX-Pan American	Robert Davenport	7-24	fired	Tom Schuberth	Asst., Central Florida
TX-San Antonio	Tim Carter	11-17	fired	Brooks Thompson	Asst., Arizona St.
Texas St.	Dennis Nutt	3-24	resigned	Doug Davalos	Coach, D-III Sul Ross St.
UAB	Mike Anderson	24-7	to Missouri*	Mike Davis	Coach, Indiana
UTEP	Doc Sadler	21-10	to Nebraska**	Tony Barbee	Asst., Memphis
VCU	Jeff Capel	19-10	to Oklahoma*	Anthony Grant	Asst., Florida
Washington St.	Dick Bennett	11-17	retired	Tony Bennett	Asst., Washington St.
Weber St.	Joe Cravens	10-17	fired	Randy Rahe	Asst., Utah
Wright St.	Paul Biancardi	13-15	resigned	Brad Brownell	Coach, NC-Wilmington

* as head coach   ** as assistant coach   † as athletic director

@ Snyder (10-11) resigned on Feb. 10, 2006 and was replaced for the remainder of the season by assistant Melvin Watkins (2-5).

2005-06 Directors' Cup

Sponsored by the United States Sports Academy (USSA). Developed as a joint effort between the National Association of Collegiate Directors of Athletics (NACDA) and USA Today. Introduced in 1993-94 to honor the nation's best overall NCAA Division I athletic department (combining men's and women's sports). Winners in NCAA Division II and III and NAIA were named for the first time following the 1995-96 season.

Standings are computed by NACDA with points awarded for each Div. I school's finish in 20 sports (top 10 scoring sports for both men and women). Div. II schools are awarded points in 14 sports (top 7 scoring sports for both men and women). Div III schools are awarded points in 18 sports (top 9 scoring sports for both men and women). NAIA schools are awarded points in 12 sports (top 6 scoring sports for both men and women). National champions in each sport earn 100 points, while 2nd through 64th-place finishers earn decreasing points depending on the size of the tournament field. Division I-A football points are based on the final ESPN/*USA Today* Coaches' Top 25 poll. Listed below are team conferences (for Div. I only), combined Final Four finishes (1st through 4th place) for men's and women's programs, overall points in **bold** type, and the previous year's ranking (for Div. I only).

Multiple winners: Stanford (12); Williams, MA (10); Simon Fraser, BC and UC-Davis (6); Grand Valley St., MI (3); Azusa Pacific, CA and Lindenwood, MO (2).

Division I

		Conf	1-2-3-4	Pts	04-05 Rank			Conf	1-2-3-4	Pts	04-05 Rank
1	Stanford	Pac-10	2-2-3-0	**1197.38**	1	14	Tennessee	SEC	0-0-2-0	**748.25**	8
2	UCLA	Pac-10	2-2-1-0	**1071.38**	3	15	Penn St.	Big Ten	0-2-2-1	**727.88**	20
3	Texas	Big 12	2-0-2-2	**966.00**	2	16	Minnesota	Big Ten	0-2-1-0	**725.25**	22
4	North Carolina	ACC	0-1-1-1	**952.75**	9	17	Florida St.	ACC	1-0-2-0	**713.00**	
5	Florida	SEC	1-1-1-1	**913.00**	6	18	Washington	Pac-10	1-0-0-0	**692.25**	14
6	Notre Dame	Big East	0-0-2-1	**905.50**	16	19	Nebraska	Big 12	0-2-1-1	**685.50**	21
7	California	Pac-10	1-0-0-1	**865.50**	15	20	LSU	SEC	0-2-2-0	**675.13**	23
8	Duke	ACC	1-2-2-0	**851.25**	5	21	Alabama	SEC	0-0-1-0	**674.50**	
9	Georgia	SEC	1-2-0-0	**850.75**	7	22	Wisconsin	Big Ten	3-0-0-0	**662.00**	19
10	USC	Pac-10	1-4-1-0	**840.00**	10	23	Texas A&M	Big 12	0-0-0-0	**649.50**	
11	Arizona	Pac-10	1-1-1-1	**831.63**	18	24	Michigan	Big Ten	0-0-0-0	**643.38**	4
12	Ohio St.	Big Ten	0-0-1-1	**799.25**	12	25	Auburn	SEC	3-0-0-0	**621.63**	17
13	Arizona St.	Pac-10	0-0-1-3	**784.63**	11						

Division II

		1-2-3-4	Pts			1-2-3-4	Pts
1	Grand Valley St., MI	3-1-0-3	**974.75**	14	Seattle Pacific	0-1-1-0	**405.00**
2	Abilene Christian, TX	1-3-0-0	**592.50**	15	Florida Southern	0-0-1-0	**404.00**
3	Nebraska-Omaha	2-0-0-0	**591.00**	16	Adams St., CO	1-1-2-1	**393.00**
4	Southern Ill. Edwardsville	0-0-1-0	**569.25**	17	Drury, MO	1-1-0-0	**388.50**
5	Cal State-Bakersfield	0-1-1-1	**518.00**	18	Barry, FL	0-1-1-0	**370.50**
6	UC San Diego	0-0-1-1	**497.50**	19	Northwest Missouri St.	0-1-0-0	**359.00**
7	Central Missouri St.	0-0-0-0	**483.75**	20	Tampa, FL	1-0-1-0	**358.00**
8	Cal State-Chico	0-1-2-1	**481.00**		West Florida	0-0-2-0	**358.00**
9	Minnesota St.-Mankato	0-0-0-0	**481.00**	22	Colorado School of Mines	0-0-0-0	**353.25**
10	Lynn, FL	0-1-3-1	**471.00**	23	North Dakota	0-0-2-1	**349.50**
11	UMass-Lowell	1-0-0-0	**445.25**	24	St. Cloud St, MN	0-0-1-0	**346.50**
12	Emporia St., KS	0-1-0-0	**413.50**	25	Western St., CO	1-0-1-0	**346.25**
13	Nebraska-Kearney	0-2-0-0	**407.50**				

Division III

		1-2-3-4	Pts			1-2-3-4	Pts
1	Williams, MA	1-3-1-2	**920.50**	14	Wisconsin-La Crosse	3-1-0-1	**479.00**
2	New Jersey	1-1-0-0	**790.25**	15	Messiah, PA	2-1-0-0	**474.25**
3	Middlebury, VT	2-1-1-0	**758.00**	16	Denison, OH	0-1-0-0	**467.75**
4	Emory, GA	3-0-1-0	**751.50**	17	Claremont-Mudd-Scripps, CA	0-0-1-0	**467.00**
5	Cortland, NY	1-0-1-0	**654.00**		Wartburg, IA	1-0-0-1	**467.00**
6	Tufts, MA	0-0-1-0	**602.00**	19	Rowan, NJ	0-0-1-0	**455.50**
7	Washington, MO	0-0-1-0	**579.50**	20	Redlands, CA	0-1-0-0	**439.50**
8	Trinity, TX	0-0-0-1	**574.00**	21	Bowdoin, ME	0-0-1-0	**433.00**
9	Calvin MI	0-1-0-0	**561.25**	22	Wisconsin Stevens Point	0-0-1-0	**431.00**
10	Gustavus Adolphus, MN	0-2-1-1	**544.00**	23	Wheaton, IL	0-0-1-0	**429.50**
11	Amherst, MA	0-0-1-1	**511.00**	24	Salisbury, MD	1-1-0-0	**410.00**
12	Hope, MI	1-0-0-0	**487.50**	25	Nebraska-Wesleyan	1-0-0-2	**409.00**
13	De Pauw, IN	0-0-1-0	**487.00**				

NAIA

		1-2-3-4	Pts			1-2-3-4	Pts
1	Azusa Pacific, CA	.0-3-2-1	**836.00**	14	Missouri Baptist	.2-0-1-0	**467.25**
2	Lindenwood, MO	.1-3-1-2	**754.00**	15	Cedarville, OH	.0-0-0-1	**453.25**
3	Lindsey Wilson, KY	.1-0-1-0	**614.00**	16	Lee, TN	.0-1-0-0	**453.00**
4	Oklahoma Baptist	.0-0-2-3	**612.50**	17	Indiana Wesleyan	.0-0-0-0	**446.00**
5	Simon Fraser, BC	.1-1-2-1	**611.00**	18	Cumberland, KY	.0-0-2-0	**441.00**
6	Concordia, CA	.0-1-0-0	**596.00**	19	Mobile, AL	.1-0-0-0	**429.00**
7	Embry Riddle, FL	.0-0-1-0	**555.50**	20	Malone, OH	.0-0-0-0	**427.75**
8	Point Loma Nazarene, CA	.0-0-1-0	**555.00**	21	Morningside, IA	.0-0-1-0	**424.00**
9	Berry, GA	.0-0-0-0	**529.00**		Vanguard, CA	.0-0-1-0	**424.00**
10	Oklahoma City	.2-1-0-0	**522.00**	23	California Baptist	.3-1-0-0	**404.50**
11	Savannah Art & Design, GA	.0-1-1-0	**503.00**	24	Aquinas, MI	.0-0-0-0	**402.50**
12	McKendree, IL	.0-0-0-0	**480.50**	25	Hastings, NE	.1-0-1-0	**400.00**
13	British Columbia	.0-1-1-1	**475.50**				

NCAA Division I Schools on Probation

As of Sept. 30, 2006, there were 30 Division I member institutions serving NCAA probations.

School	Sport	Yrs	Penalty To End	School	Sport	Yrs	Penalty To End
Fresno St.	M & W Basketball	4	12/3/06	Northern Illinois	W Basketball	1	8/2/07
	& M & W Soccer	4	12/3/06	Weber St.	Football	2	1/18/08
Alabama	Football	5	1/31/07	Texas St.-San Marcos	Numerous	3	3/9/08
Washington	Football	2	2/9/07	Stony Brook	Numerous	3	4/20/08
Gardner-Webb	Baseball	3	3/3/07	St. John's	M Basketball	2	5/9/08
	M & W Basketball	3	3/3/07	Oklahoma	M Basketball	2	5/23/08
	M Soccer	3	3/3/07		M & W Gymnastics	2	5/23/08
	& W Track	3	3/3/07	Georgia	M Basketball	4	8/3/08
Michigan	M Basketball	4	5/6/07	Florida International	Football	3	8/23/08
Bradley	M Basketball	1	5/18/07	Mississippi St.	Football	4	10/25/08
CS-Northridge	M Basketball	3	6/1/07	Ohio St.	M & W Basketball	3	3/8/09
St. Bonaventure	M Basketball	3	7/17/07		Football	3	3/8/09
TCU	M & W Indoor	2	9/21/07	Nicholls St.	M Basketball	4	5/8/09
	M & W Outdoor	2	9/21/07		Football	4	5/8/09
Memphis	M Cross Country	2	10/20/07	Savannah St.	Football	3	6/19/09
	W Volleyball	2	10/20/07	Alcorn St.	W Basketball	3	6/28/09
Arizona St.	Football	2	11/9/07	Florida A&M	Numerous	4	1/30/10
Missouri	M Basketball	3	11/10/07	Fresno St.	M Basketball	4	4/25/10
South Carolina	Football	2	11/15/07	Baylor	M Basketball	5	6/22/10
Georgia Tech	Numerous	2	11/16/07		Football	5	6/22/10

Remaining postseason and TV sanctions

2006-2007 postseason bans: Alcorn St. women's basketball; St. John's men's basketball, TCU men's and women's indoor and outdoor track (team participation).
2006-2007 television bans: None.

NCAA Graduation Rates Match All-Time High

The following table compares graduation rates of NCAA Division I student athletes with the entire student body in those schools. Years given denote the year in which students entered college. Rates are based on students who enrolled as freshmen, received an athletics scholarship and graduated in six years or less. All figures are percentages.

Source: NCAA Graduation Rates Report, 2005.

	1993	**1994**	**1995**	**1996**	**1997**	**1998**
All Student Athletes	58	58	60	62	62	62
Entire Student Body	56	56	58	59	60	60
Male Student Athletes	51	51	54	55	55	55
Male Student Body	54	54	56	56	57	57
Female Student Athletes	68	69	69	70	70	71
Female Student Body	59	59	61	62	63	63
Div. I-A Football Players	48	51	53	54	57	54
Male Basketball Players	42	40	43	44	44	43
Female Basketball Players	63	65	65	66	64	63

2005-06 NCAA Team Champions

The NCAA administers 88 championships in 23 sports (not including Division I-A football). In 2005-06, 68 different schools won titles (including I-A football champ Texas) and 15 won multiple titles.

Multiple winners: Three—AUBURN (Div. I women's swimming & diving, women's outdoor track); EMORY (Div. III women's swimming & diving, men's and women's tennis); GRAND VALLEY ST. (Div. II football, women's volleyball, women's basketball); MARYLAND (Div. I field hockey, men's soccer, women's basketball); WISCONSIN (Div. I men's cross country, men's and women's ice hockey); WISCONSIN-LA CROSSE (Div. III men's cross country, indoor and outdoor track).

Two—LINCOLN, MO (Div. II women's indoor and outdoor track); MESSIAH, PA (Div. III men's and women's soccer); MIDDLEBURY, VT (Div. III men's and women's ice hockey); NEB.-OMAHA (Div. II wrestling and women's soccer); OKLAHOMA ST. (Div. I wrestling and men's golf); STANFORD (Div. I women's cross country and tennis); TEXAS (Div. I-A football, Div. I women's indoor track); UCLA (National men's volleyball and women's water polo); WISCONSIN-OSHKOSH (Div. III women's indoor and outdoor track). Overall-titles in parentheses; (*) indicates defending champions.

FALL

Cross Country
Men

Div.	Winner	Runner-Up	Score
I	Wisconsin (4)	Arkansas	37-105
II	Western St., CO* (7)	Adams St., CO	51-108
III	Wis.-La Crosse (3)	Calvin, MI*	94-117

Women

Div.	Winner	Runner-Up	Score
I	Stanford (3)	Colorado*	146-181
II	Adams St., CO* (11)	Grand Valley St.	54-69
III	Geneseo St., NY (1)	Williams, MA*	88-107

Field Hockey

Div.	Winner	Runner-Up	Score
I	Maryland (4)	Duke	1-0
II	UMass-Lowell (1)	Bloomsburg, PA*	2-1 (2OT)
III	Salisbury, MD* (4)	Messiah, PA	1-0

Football

Div.	Winner	Runner-Up	Score
I-A	Texas (4)	USC*	41-38
I-AA	Appalachian St. (1)	Northern Iowa	21-16
II	Grand Valley St. (3)	Northwest Mo. St.	21-17
III	Mount Union, OH (8)	Wis.-Whitewater	35-28

Note: There is no official Div. I-A playoff. Texas defeated USC in the BCS Championship Game (Rose Bowl).

Soccer
Men

Div.	Winner	Runner-Up	Score
I	Maryland (2)	New Mexico	1-0
II	Fort Lewis, CO (1)	Franklin Pierce, NH	3-1
III	Messiah, PA* (4)	Gustavus Adolphus, MN	1-0

Women

Div.	Winner	Runner-Up	Score
I	Portland (2)	UCLA	4-0
II	Nebraska-Omaha (1)	Seattle Pacific	2-1 (OT)
III	Messiah, PA (1)	New Jersey	1-0

Volleyball
Women

Div.	Winner	Runner-Up	Score
I	Washington (1)	Nebraska	3-0
II	Grand Valley St. (1)	Nebraska-Kearney	3-0
III	Wis.-Whitewater (2)	Juniata, PA*	3-2

Water Polo
Men

Div.	Winner	Runner-Up	Score
National	USC (3)	Stanford	3-2

WINTER

Basketball
Men

Div.	Winner	Runner-Up	Score
I	Florida (1)	UCLA	73-57
II	Winona St., MN (1)	Virginia Union*	73-61
III	Virginia Wesleyan (1)	Wittenberg, OH	59-56

Women

Div.	Winner	Runner-Up	Score
I	Maryland (1)	Duke	78-75 (OT)
II	Grand Valley St. (1)	American Int'l	58-52
III	Hope, MI (2)	Southern Maine	69-56

Bowling
Women

Div.	Winner	Runner-Up	Score
Nat'l	Fairleigh Dickinson (1)	Alabama A&M	4-1

Fencing

Div.	Winner	Runner-Up	Score
Combined	Harvard (1)	Penn St.	165-159

Gymnastics

Div.	Winner	Runner-Up	Margin
Men	Oklahoma* (7)	Illinois	by .425
Women	Georgia* (7)	Utah	by .950

Ice Hockey
Men

Div.	Winner	Runner-Up	Score
I	Wisconsin (6)	Boston College	2-1
III	Middlebury, VT* (8)	St. Norbert, WI	3-0

Women

Div.	Winner	Runner-Up	Score
I	Wisconsin (1)	Minnesota*	3-0
III	Middlebury, VT* (3)	Plattsburgh, NY	3-1

Rifle

Div.	Winner	Runner-Up	Score
Combined	AK-Fairbanks (8)	Nebraska	4682-4666

Skiing

Div.	Winner	Runner-Up	Score
Combined	Colorado (16)	New Mexico	654-556

Swimming & Diving
Men

Div.	Winner	Runner-Up	Score
I	Auburn* (6)	Arizona	480.5-440.5
II	Drury, MO* (4)	CS-Bakersfield	669-543.5
III	Kenyon, OH* (27)	Denison, OH	498-345

Women

Div.	Winner		Runner-Up	Score
I	..........Auburn	(4)	Georgia*	518.5-515.5
II	.....Truman St., MO*	(6)	Drury, MO	664-505
III	.......Emory, GA*	(2)	Kenyon, OH	428-418

Indoor Track
Men

Div.	Winner		Runner-Up	Score
I	..........Arkansas*	(19)	LSU	53-45
II	..St. Augustine's, NC	(9)	Abilene Christian	66.5-55
III	.....Wis.-La Crosse*	(13)	Lincoln, PA	78-31

Women

Div.	Winner		Runner-Up	Score
I	............Texas	(6)	Stanford	51-36
II	.........Lincoln, MO	(2)	Abilene Christian	87-50.33
III	......Wis.-Oshkosh*	(6)	Williams, MA	44-38

Wrestling
Men

Div.	Winner		Runner-Up	Score
I	......Oklahoma St.*	(34)	Minnesota	122.5-84
II	......Neb.-Omaha*	(8)	Neb.-Kearney	117-98.5
III	.....Wartburg, IA	(5)	Wis.-La Crosse	145.5-106

SPRING
Baseball

Div.	Winner		Runner-Up	Score
I	.......Oregon St.	(1)	N. Carolina	3-4, 11-7, 3-2
II	.........Tampa	(4)	Cal State-Chico	3-2 (10 inn.)
III	......Marietta, OH	(4)	Wheaton, MA	7-2

Note: The Division I Championship Series is best-of-three.

Golf
Men

Div.	Winner		Runner-Up	Score
I	.......Oklahoma St.	(10)	Florida	1143-1146
II	...S. Carolina-Aiken*	(3)	Columbus St., GA	1148-1160
III	.....Neb.-Wesleyan	(1)	Redlands, CA	1193-1203

Women

Div.	Winner		Runner-Up	Score
I	..........Duke*	(4)	USC	1167-1177
II	.........Rollins, FL*	(4)	Ferris St., MI	919-925
III	.....Methodist, NC*	(10)	G. Adolphus, MN	1240-1316

Note: The Division II championship was weather-shortened.

Lacrosse
Men

Div.	Winner		Runner-Up	Score
I	..........Virginia	(4)	Massachusetts	15-7
II	......Le Moyne, NY	(2)	Dowling, NY	12-5
III	......Cortland, NY	(1)	Salisbury, MD*	13-12 (OT)

Women

Div.	Winner		Runner-Up	Score
I	..........Northwestern*	(2)	Dartmouth	7-4
II	.......Adelphi, NY	(2)	West Chester, PA	16-8
III	......New Jersey	(12)	Gettysburg, PA	10-4

Rowing
Women

Div.	Winner		Runner-Up	Score
I	........California*	(2)	Brown	66-66†
II	..Western Washington*	(2)	Barry, FL	20-15
III	.....Williams, MA	(2)	Ithaca, NY*	21-15

†Cal and Brown tied with 66 pts., but Cal was awarded the championship based on a higher finish in the Varsity Eights final.

Softball

Div.	Winner		Runner-Up	Score
I	..........Arizona	(7)	Northwestern	8-0, 5-0
II	.....Lock Haven, PA	(1)	Emporia St., KS	3-0
III	.....Rutgers-Camden	(1)	St. Thomas, MN*	3-2

Note: The Division I Championship Series is best-of-three.

Tennis
Men

Div.	Winner		Runner-Up	Score
I	........Pepperdine	(1)	Georgia	4-2
II	.....Valdosta St., GA	(1)	Lynn, FL	5-2
III	.......Emory, GA	(2)	Middlebury, VT	4-1

Women

Div.	Winner		Runner-Up	Score
I	........Stanford*	(15)	Miami-FL	4-1
II	.......BYU-Hawaii	(6)	Armstrong Atlantic*	5-3
III	.......Emory, GA*	(5)	Washington & Lee, VA	5-1

Outdoor Track
Men

Div.	Winner		Runner-Up	Score
I	..........Florida St.	(1)	LSU	67-51
II	....Abilene Christian*	(16)	St Augustine's, NC	80-77.5
III	.....Wis.-La Crosse	(1)	Lincoln, PA*	74.5-54

Women

Div.	Winner		Runner-Up	Score
I	............Auburn	(1)	USC	57-38
II	.......Lincoln, MO*	(4)	Abilene Christian	93-86
III	.......Wis-Oshkosh	(7)	Williams, MA	52-42

Volleyball
Men

Div.	Winner		Runner-Up	Score
National	.......UCLA	(19)	Penn St.	3-0

Water Polo
Women

Div.	Winner		Runner-Up	Score
National	.......UCLA*	(4)	USC	9-8

All-Time Team Champions
Division I - Top Ten

Combined NCAA Division I men's, women's and coed team champions through spring 2006.

	School	Men's	Women's	Coed	Total
1	UCLA	.70	29	0	99
2	Stanford	.57	35	0	92
3	USC	.73	11	0	83
4	Oklahoma St. .	.48	0	0	48
5	Arkansas	.43	0	0	43
6	LSU	.16	24	0	40
7	Texas	.17	22	0	39
8	Michigan	.30	2	0	32
9	North Carolina ..	.9	22	0	31
10	Penn State	.17	4	9	30

Note: Totals above do not reflect Division I-A football championships, which are not conducted by the NCAA. Coed championships include rifle, skiing and fencing (since 1990).

Source: NCAA

Ohio St.
Boaz Ellis
Fencing

Oklahoma
Jonathan Horton
Gymnastics

Georgia
Courtney Kupets
Gymnastics

Oklahoma St.
Johny Hendricks
Wrestling

2005-06 Division I Individual Champions
Repeat champions in **bold** type.

FALL
Cross Country

Men (10,000 meters)	**Time**
1 **Simon Bairu**, Wisconsin	29:15.9
2 Richard Kiplagat, Iona	29:21.9
3 Chris Solinsky, Wisconsin	29:27.8

Women (6,000 meters)	**Time**
1 Johanna Nilsson, Northern Arizona	19:33.9
2 Caroline Bierbaum, Columbia-Barnard	19:46.0
3 Stephanie Madia, Notre Dame	19:48.4

WINTER
Fencing
Men

Event		Score
Foil	**Boaz Ellis**, Ohio St.	15-9
Epee	Benji Ungar, Harvard	15-14
Sabre	Adam Crompton, Ohio St.	15-9

Women

Event		Score
Foil	Erzsebet Garay, St. John's	14-12
Epee	Katarzyna Trzopek, Penn St.	12-11
Sabre	Mariel Zagunis, Notre Dame	15-8

Gymnastics
Men

Event		Points
All-Around	Jonathan Horton, Oklahoma	56.000
Floor Exercise	Jonathan Horton, Oklahoma	9.575
Pommel Horse	Timothy McNeill, California	9.350
Rings	Jonathan Horton, Oklahoma	9.637
Vault	David Sender, Stanford	9.562
Parallel Bars	**Justin Spring**, Illinois	9.825
High Bar	Justin Spring, Illinois	9.700
	& Dylan Carney, Stanford (tie)	9.700

Women

Event		Points
All-Around	Courtney Kupets, Georgia	39.750
Vault	Ashley Miles, Alabama	9.9375
Uneven Bars	Courtney Kupets, Georgia	9.8500
	& Kristina Baskett, Utah (tie)	9.8500
Balance Beam	Courtney Kupets, Georgia	9.9125
	& April Burkholder, LSU (tie)	9.9125
Floor Exercise	Kate Richardson, UCLA	9.9500

Rifle
Combined
Number in parentheses denotes inner tens.
Smallbore

		Points
1	Jamie Beyerle, AK-Fairbanks	690.5
2	Shannon Wilson, Mississippi	688.5
3	James Hall, Jacksonville St.	685.3

Air Rifle

		Points
1	Kristina Fehlings, Nebraska	692.0
2	Jamie Beyerle, AK-Fairbanks	690.4
3	Matthew Rawlings, AK-Fairbanks	690.2

Skiing
Men

Event		Time
Slalom	Karl Johnson, Dartmouth	1:13.85
Giant Slalom	Scott Veenis, Utah	2:12.19
10-k Classic	John Stene, Dartmouth	27:57.7
20-k Freestyle	Kit Richmond, Colorado	55:14.7

Women

Event		Time
Slalom	Lucie Zikova, Colorado	1:22.77
Giant Slalom	Abbi Lathrop, Colby	2:16.85
5-k Classic	Jana Rehemaa, Colorado	16:29.6
15-k Freestyle	Jana Rehemaa, Colorado	46:27.4

Wrestling

Wgt	Champion	Runner-Up
125	**Joe Dubuque**, Indiana	T. Nickerson, Cornell
133	Matt Valenti, Penn	C. Fleeger, Purdue
141	Nate Gallick, Iowa St.	T. Ware, Oklahoma
149	Dustin Schlatter, Minnesota	T. Eustice, Iowa
157	Ben Cherrington, Boise St.	B. Stith, Ariz. St.
165	**Johny Hendricks**, Okla. St.	R. Churella, Mich.
174	Ben Askren, Missouri	J. Herbert, Northwestern
184	Shane Webster, Oregon	R. Kish, Minnesota
197	**Jake Rosholt**, Okla. St.	P. Davis, Penn St.
Hvy	Cole Konrad, Minnesota	S. Mocco, Okla. St.

Georgia

Kara Lynn Joyce
Swimming

LSU

Xavier Carter
Track & Field

USC

Virginia Powell
Track & Field

California

Suzi Babos
Tennis

Swimming & Diving

(*) indicates meet record.

Men

Event (yards)	Time
50 free . . . . .Cullen Jones, NC State	19.18
100 free . . . . .Garrett Weber-Gale, Texas	42.11
200 free . . . .**Simon Burnett**, Arizona	1:31.20*
500 free . . . .**Peter Vanderkaay**, Michigan	4:08.60*
1650 free . . . . . .Sebastien Rouault, Georgia	14:29.43
100 back . . . . .**Matt Grevers**, Northwestern	45.93
200 back . . . .**Ryan Lochte**, Florida	1:37.68*
100 breast . . . . .Henrique Barbosa, California	52.52
200 breast . . . . .Henrique Barbosa, California	1:53.97
100 butterfly . . . . .Lyndon Ferns, Arizona	45.89
200 butterfly . . . . .**Davis Tarwater**, Michigan	1:41.84
200 IM . . . .**Ryan Lochte**, Florida	1:40.55*
400 IM . . . . .Ryan Lochte, Florida	3:38.15*
200 free relay . . . . .Auburn	1:17.52
400 free relay . . . . .Arizona	2:48.39
800 free relay . . . . .Arizona	6:16.67
200 medley relay . . . . .Arizona	1:23.88*
400 medley relay . . . . .Arizona	3:06.08

Diving	Points
1-meter . . . . .Chris Colwill, Georgia	407.10
3-meter . . . . .Chris Colwill, Georgia	460.95
Platform . . . . .Steven Segerlin, Auburn	469.30

Women

Event (yards)	Time
50 free . . . . . .**Kara Lynn Joyce**, Georgia	21.63*
100 free . . . . . .**Kara Lynn Joyce**, Georgia	47.41
200 free . . . . .Kara Lynn Joyce, Georgia	1:43.96
500 free . . . . .Laura Conway, Georgia	4:40.01
1650 free . . . . .Hayley Peirsol, Auburn	15:49.48
100 back . . . . .Rachel Goh, Auburn	52.35
200 back . . . . .Helen Silver, California	1:53.01
100 breast . . . . . . .Jessica Hardy, California	1:00.02
200 breast . . . . .Rebecca Soni, USC	2:09.37
100 butterfly . . . . .**Mary DeScenza**, Georgia	51.56
200 butterfly . . . . .**Mary DeScenza**, Georgia	1:53.78
200 IM . . . . .Whitney Myers, Arizona	1:54.88
400 IM . . . . .Whitney Myers, Arizona	4:06.32
200 free relay . . . . .Arizona	1:27.98*
400 free relay . . . . .Arizona	3:12.77*
800 free relay . . . .**Georgia**	7:03.75
200 medley relay . . . .**Georgia**	1:37.24
400 medley relay . . . . .Arizona	3:31.70

Diving	Points
1-meter . . . . .Blythe Hartley, USC	353.50
3-meter . . . .**Blythe Hartley**, USC	373.15
Platform . . . . .Taryn Ignacio, Kentucky	335.30

Indoor Track

(*) indicates meet record.

Men

Event	Time
60 meters . . . . .Jacob Norman, Baylor	6.56
200 meters . . . . .Walter Dix, Florida St.	20.27
400 meters . . . . .Xavier Carter, LSU	45.28
800 meters . . . . .Jackson Langat, TCU	1:47.02
Mile . . . . .Christian Smith, Kansas St.	4:12.75
3000 meters . . **Chris Solinsky**, Wisconsin	7:59.68
5000 meters . . . . . .Josphat Boit, Arkansas	13:49.93
60-m hurdles . . . . . .Aries Merritt, Tennessee	7.51*
4x400-m relay . . . . .LSU	3:04.01
Distance medley relay . . . . .Arkansas	9:37.02

Event	Hgt/Dist
High Jump . . . .**Jesse Williams**, USC	7-6
Pole Vault . . . . .**Thomas Skipper**, Oregon	18-6½
Long Jump . . . . . .Arturs Abolins, Nebraska	26-7¼
Triple Jump . . . . . .Jaanus Uudmae, Arkansas	54-4½
Shot Put . . . . . . .Garrett Johnson, Florida St.	67-2¼
35-lb Throw . . . .**Spyridon Jullien**, Va. Tech	77-10¼
Heptathlon . . . . . . .Donovan Kilmartin, Texas	6048 pts.

Women

Event	Time
60 meters . . . . .Marshevet Hooker, Texas	7.20
200 meters . . .Shalonda Solomon, S. Carolina	22.57
400 meters . . . . . . .Kineke Alexander, Iowa	52.16
800 meters . . . .Heather Dorniden, Minnesota	2:05.64
Mile . . . . .Johanna Nilsson, N. Arizona	4:37.78
3000 meters . . . . .Johanna Nilsson, N. Arizona	9:06.61
5000 meters . . . . .Amy Hastings, Arizona St.	15:51.63
60-m hurdles . . . . . .**Virginia Powell**, USC	7.84*
4x400-m relay . . . . .LSU	3:29.33
Distance medley relay . . . . . .North Carolina	11:01.97

Event	Hgt/Dist
High Jump . .Sheena Gordon, North Carolina	6-1¼
Pole Vault . . . . .Chelsea Johnson, UCLA	14-9
Long Jump . . . . . .Marshevet Hooker, Texas	22-0¼
Triple Jump . . . . .Yvette Lewis, Hampton	45-1½
Shot Put . . . . .Michelle Carter, Texas	60-10¾
20-lb Throw . . . . .Jenny Dahlgren, Georgia	78-10½
Pentathlon . . . . .Jacquelyn Johnson, Ariz. St.	4287 pts.

SPRING

Golf

Men

		Total
1	Jonathan Moore, Oklahoma St. . .68-70-69-69—276	
2	Chris Kirk, Georgia . . . . .71-71-70-68—280	
	Kyle Reifers, Wake Forest. . . . . .65-70-73-72—280	

Golf (cont.)
Women

		Total
1	Dewi Schreefel, USC	.73-74-70-69—286
2	Jennie Lee, Duke	.73-72-72-71—288
3	Da Sol Chung, UNLV	.76-72-70-72—290

Tennis
Men

Singles— Benjamin Kohlleoffel (UCLA) def. Somdev Devvarman (Virginia), 6-1, 6-4.

Doubles— Kevin Anderson & Ryan Rowe (Illinois) def. Andre Begemann & Scott Doerner (Pepperdine), 6-2, 6-4.

Women

Singles— Suzi Babos (California) def. Lindsey Nelson (USC), 6-4, 6-1.

Doubles— Cristelle Grier & Alexis Prousis (Northwestern) def. Lucia Sainz & Katharina Winterhalter (Fresno St.), 6-4, 6-1.

Outdoor Track
(*) indicates meet record
Men

Event		Time
100 meters	Xavier Carter, LSU	10.09
200 meters	Walter Dix, Florida St.	20.30
400 meters	Xavier Carter, LSU	44.53
800 meters	Ryan Brown, Washington	1:46.29
1500 meters	Vincent Rono, South Alabama	3:44.07
5000 meters	Chris Solinsky, Wisconsin	14:11.71
10,000 meters	Josphat Boit, Arkansas	28:37.64
110-m hurdles	Aries Merritt, Tennessee	13.21*
400-m hurdles	Micheal Tinsley, Jackson St.	48.25
3000-m steeple	Josh McAdams, BYU	8:34.10
4x100-m relay	LSU	38.44
4x400-m relay	**LSU**	3:01.58

Event		Hgt/Dist
High Jump	**Jesse Williams**, USC	7-7¼
Pole Vault	Thomas Skipper, Oregon	18-8¼
Long Jump	Arturs Abolins, Nebraska	26-3
Triple Jump	Rafeeq Curry, Florida St.	54-9½
Shot Put	Garrett Johnson, Florida St.	66-7
Discus	Vikas Gowda, North Carolina	198-8
Javelin	Justin Ryncavage, North Carolina	243-4
Hammer	**Spyridon Jullien**, Virginia Tech	237-2
Decathlon	Jake Arnold, Arizona	7870 pts.

Women

Event		Time
100 meters	Amberly Nesbitt, S. Carolina	11.34
200 meters	Shalonda Solomon, S. Carolina	22.62
400 meters	Clora Williams, Texas A&M	51.11
800 meters	Rebekah Noble, Oregon	2:02.07
1500 meters	Amy Lia, Washington	4:14.63
5000 meters	Mary Cullen, Providence	16:01.39
10,000 meters	Victoria Jackson, Arizona St.	32:54.72
100-m hurdles	**Virginia Powell**, USC	12.48
400-m hurdles	Markita James, Auburn	54.47
3000-m steeple	Jennifer Barringer, Colorado	9:53.04
4x100-m relay	**Texas**	42.84
4x400-m relay	LSU	3:25.78*

Event		Hgt/Dist
High Jump	Destinee Hooker, Texas	6-2¼
Pole Vault	Lacy Janson, Floida St.	13-11¼
Long Jump	Jovanee Jarrett, Auburn	21-2½
Triple Jump	Tabia Charles, Miami-FL	44-11½
Shot Put	Laura Gerraughty, North Carolina	60-1¼
Discus	Dace Ruskule, Nebraska	180-10
Javelin	**Dana Pounds**, Air Force	190-3
Hammer	Jenny Dahlgren, Georgia	226-4
Heptathlon	Jacquelyn Johnson, Arizona St.	5939 pts.

Championships
Most Outstanding Players
Men

Baseball	Jonah Nickerson, Oregon St.
Basketball	Joakim Noah, Florida
Cross Country	Simon Bairu, Wisconsin*
Golf	Jonathan Moore, Oklahoma St.*
Gymnastics	Jonathan Horton, Oklahoma*
Ice Hockey	Robbie Earl, Wisconsin
Lacrosse	Matt Ward, Virginia
Soccer: Offense	Jason Garey, Maryland
Soccer: Defense	Chris Seitz, Maryland
Swimming	Ryan Lochte, Florida†
& Diving	Chris Colwill, Georgia†
Tennis	Benjamin Kohlleoffel, UCLA*
Track: Indoor	Xavier Carter, LSU†
Track: Outdoor	Xavier Carter, LSU†
Volleyball	Steve Klosterman, UCLA
Water Polo	Adam Shilling & Juraj Zatovic, USC
Wrestling	Ben Askren, Missouri

Women

Basketball	Laura Harper, Maryland
Bowling	Lisa Friscioni, Fairleigh Dickinson
Cross Country	Johanna Nilsson, Northern Arizona*
Golf	Dewi Schreefel, USC*
Gymnastics	Courtney Kupets, Georgia*
Ice Hockey	Jessie Vetter, Wisconsin
Lacrosse	Sarah Albrecht, Northwestern
Soccer: Offense	Christine Sinclair, Portland
Soccer: Defense	Cori Alexander, Portland
Softball	Alicia Hollowell, Arizona
Swimming	Kara Lynn Joyce, Georgia†
& Diving	Blythe Hartley, USC†
Tennis	Suzi Babos, California*
Track: Indoor	Marshevet Hooker, Texas†
Track: Outdoor	Virginia Powell, USC†
Volleyball	Christal Morrison, Washington
Water Polo	Kelly Rulon, UCLA

(*) indicates won individual or all-around NCAA championship; There were no official Outstanding Players in fencing, field hockey, I-AA football, rifle, rowing and skiing. (†) Outstanding players in Swimming & Diving and Indoor and Outdoor Track are the individuals earning the most points in the Championships.

2005-06 NAIA Team Champions
Total NAIA titles in that sport in parentheses.

FALL

Cross Country: MEN'S–Virginia Intermont (2); WOMEN'S–Simon Fraser, BC (8). **Football:** MEN'S– Carroll, MT (4). **Soccer:** MEN'S–Lindsey Wilson, KY (7); WOMEN'S–Martin Methodist, TN (1). **Volleyball:** WOMENS–California Baptist (2).

WINTER

Basketball: MEN'S–Division I: Texas Wesleyan (1) and Division II: Ozarks, MO (1); WOMEN'S–Division I: Union, TN (3) and Division II: Hastings, NE (3). **Swimming & Diving:** MEN'S–California Baptist (1); WOMEN'S– California Baptist (2). **Indoor Track:** MEN'S–Lindenwood, MO (3); WOMEN'S–Missouri Baptist (1). **Wrestling:** MEN'S–Dana, NE (2).

SPRING

Baseball: MEN'S–Lewis-Clark St., ID (14). **Golf:** MEN'S–Oklahoma City (5); WOMEN'S–Oklahoma City (2). **Softball:** WOMEN'S–Mobile, AL (1). **Tennis:** MEN'S–Auburn-Montgomery (6); WOMEN'S–Auburn-Montgomery (7). **Outdoor Track:** MEN'S–Dickinson St., ND (3); WOMEN'S–Missouri Baptist (1).

Annual NCAA Division I Team Champions

Men's and women's NCAA Division I team champions from cross country to wrestling. Also see team champions for baseball, basketball, bowling, football, golf, ice hockey, soccer and tennis in the appropriate chapters throughout the almanac. See pages 476-478 for the list of 2005-06 individual champions.

CROSS COUNTRY

Men

With two of the meet's top three finishers and five in the top 14, top-ranked Wisconsin coasted to its first men's cross country title since 1988 and fourth overall. Badger senior Simon Bairu took first for the second consecutive year, completing the 10,000-meter course in 29:15.9. Junior Chris Solinsky came in third, just six seconds behind race runner-up Richard Kiplagat. Wisconsin finished with just 37 points, well ahead of runner-up Arkansas with 105. (Terre Haute, IN; Nov. 21, 2005.)

Multiple winners: Arkansas (11); Michigan St. (8); UTEP (7); Oregon, Stanford, Villanova and Wisconsin (4); Drake, Indiana and Penn St. (3); Colorado, Iowa St., San Jose St. and Western Michigan (2).

Year		Year		Year		Year		Year	
1938	Indiana	1951	Syracuse	1965	Western Mich.	1979	UTEP	1993	Arkansas
1939	Michigan St.	1952	Michigan St.	1966	Villanova	1980	UTEP	1994	Iowa St.
1940	Indiana	1953	Kansas	1967	Villanova	1981	UTEP	1995	Arkansas
1941	Rhode Island	1954	Oklahoma St.	1968	Villanova	1982	Wisconsin	1996	Stanford
1942	Indiana	1955	Michigan St.	1969	UTEP	1983	Vacated	1997	Stanford
	& Penn St.	1956	Michigan St.	1970	Villanova	1984	Arkansas	1998	Arkansas
1943	Not held	1957	Notre Dame	1971	Oregon	1985	Wisconsin	1999	Arkansas
1944	Drake	1958	Michigan St.	1972	Tennessee	1986	Arkansas	2000	Arkansas
1945	Drake	1959	Michigan St.	1973	Oregon	1987	Arkansas	2001	Colorado
1946	Drake	1960	Houston	1974	Oregon	1988	Wisconsin	2002	Stanford
1947	Penn St.	1961	Oregon St.	1975	UTEP	1989	Iowa St.	2003	Stanford
1948	Michigan St.	1962	San Jose St.	1976	UTEP	1990	Arkansas	2004	Colorado
1949	Michigan St.	1963	San Jose St.	1977	Oregon	1991	Arkansas	2005	Wisconsin
1950	Penn St.	1964	Western Mich.	1978	UTEP	1992	Arkansas		

Women

Paced by three top-25 finishers, Stanford won its second NCAA women's cross country title in the last three years and third overall. The well-balanced Cardinal were led by sophomore Arianna Lambie in seventh and junior Kathleen Trotter in 15th. Stanford totaled 146 points to best defending champ Colorado (181) and Duke (185). (Terre Haute, IN; Nov. 21, 2005.)

Multiple winners: Villanova (7); BYU (4); Stanford (3); Colorado, Oregon, Virginia and Wisconsin (2).

Year		Year		Year		Year		Year	
1981	Virginia	1986	Texas	1991	Villanova	1996	Stanford	2001	BYU
1982	Virginia	1987	Oregon	1992	Villanova	1997	BYU	2002	BYU
1983	Oregon	1988	Kentucky	1993	Villanova	1998	Villanova	2003	Stanford
1984	Wisconsin	1989	Villanova	1994	Villanova	1999	BYU	2004	Colorado
1985	Wisconsin	1990	Villanova	1995	Providence	2000	Colorado	2005	Stanford

FENCING

Men & Women

Harvard edged Penn State, 165-159, to win its first NCAA fencing championship and fourth overall NCAA title for the Ivy League school. Sophomore Benji Ungar grabbed the only individual title for the Crimson with a 15-14 nailbiter over Ohio State's Denis Tolkachev in the finals of the men's epee. Buckeye Boaz Ellis was the tournament's only repeat winner, winning the men's foil for the third straight year. (Houston, TX; Mar. 16-29, 2006.)

Multiple winners: Penn St. (9); Notre Dame (3); Columbia/Barnard (2). **Note:** Prior to 1990, men and women held separate championships. Men's multiple winners included: NYU (12); Columbia (11); Wayne St. (7); Navy, Notre Dame and Penn (3); Illinois (2). Women's multiple winners included: Wayne St. (3); Yale (2).

Year		Year		Year		Year	
1990	Penn St.	1995	Penn St.	2000	Penn St.	2005	Notre Dame
1991	Penn St.	1996	Penn St.	2001	St. John's	2006	Harvard
1992	Columbia/Barnard	1997	Penn St.	2002	Penn St.		
1993	Columbia/Barnard	1998	Penn St.	2003	Notre Dame		
1994	Notre Dame	1999	Penn St.	2004	Ohio St.		

FIELD HOCKEY

Women

Maryland senior Jackie Ciconte scored the game's only goal early in the first half as top-ranked Maryland defeated Duke, 1-0, in the finals of the Division I Women's Field Hockey Championship. It was the Terrapins' first title since 1999 and fourth overall. It was the third straight championship match loss for the Blue Devils. Sophomore goalie Kathryn Mason recorded the shutout for Maryland, turning away all five of Duke's shots.(Louisville, KY; Nov. 20, 2005.)

Multiple winners: Old Dominion (9); Maryland and North Carolina (4); Wake Forest (3); Connecticut (2).

Year		Year		Year		Year		Year	
1981	Connecticut	1986	Iowa	1991	Old Dominion	1996	North Carolina	2001	Michigan
1982	Old Dominion	1987	Maryland	1992	Old Dominion	1997	North Carolina	2002	Wake Forest
1983	Old Dominion	1988	Old Dominion	1993	Maryland	1998	Old Dominion	2003	Wake Forest
1984	Old Dominion	1989	North Carolina	1994	J. Madison	1999	Maryland	2004	Wake Forest
1985	Connecticut	1990	Old Dominion	1995	North Carolina	2000	Old Dominion	2005	Maryland

Annual NCAA Division I Team Champions (Cont.)

GYMNASTICS

Men

Oklahoma's Jonathan Horton won the all-around title and lifted the Sooners to their second straight Division I gymnastics title and fourth in the last five years. The win capped a perfect season for Oklahoma, who amassed 221.4 points to edge runner-up Illinois (220.975) and third-place Stanford (218.375). Horton also took home individual titles in the rings and floor exercise. Justin Spring led the Illini with wins in the parallel bars and high bar. *(Norman, OK; Apr. 6-8, 2006.)*

Multiple winners: Penn St. (11); Illinois (9); Nebraska (8); Oklahoma (7); California and So. Illinois (4); Iowa St., Michigan, Ohio St. and Stanford (3); Florida St and UCLA (2).

Year	Year	Year	Year	Year
1938 Chicago	1957 Penn St.	1970 Michigan	1983 Nebraska	1998 California
1939 Illinois	1958 Michigan St.	& Michigan (T)	1984 UCLA	1999 Michigan
1940 Illinois	& Illinois	1971 Iowa St.	1985 Ohio St.	2000 Penn St.
1941 Illinois	1959 Penn St.	1972 So. Illinois	1986 Arizona St.	2001 Ohio St.
1942 Illinois	1960 Penn St.	1973 Iowa St.	1987 UCLA	2002 Oklahoma
1943-47 Not held	1961 Penn St.	1974 Iowa St.	1988 Nebraska	2003 Oklahoma
1948 Penn St.	1962 USC	1975 California	1989 Illinois	2004 Penn St.
1949 Temple	1963 Michigan	1976 Penn St.	1990 Nebraska	2005 Oklahoma
1950 Illinois	1964 So. Illinois	1977 Indiana St.	1991 Oklahoma	2006 Oklahoma
1951 Florida St.	1965 Penn St.	& Oklahoma	1992 Stanford	
1952 Florida St.	1966 So. Illinois	1978 Oklahoma	1993 Stanford	(T) indicates won tram-
1953 Penn St.	1967 So. Illinois	1979 Nebraska	1994 Nebraska	poline competition
1954 Penn St.	1968 California	1980 Nebraska	1995 Stanford	(1969-70).
1955 Illinois	1969 Iowa	1981 Nebraska	1996 Ohio St.	
1956 Illinois	& Michigan (T)	1982 Nebraska	1997 California	

Women

Suzanne Yoculan's powerhouse Georgia squad overcame an aggressive challenge by Utah and Alabama to win its second straight NCAA women's gymnastics title and seventh overall. The Bulldogs were led by freshman Olympian Courtney Kupets, who won the all-around title, as well as individual titles in the uneven bars (tied with Utah's Kristina Baskett) and balance beam (tied with LSU's April Burkholder). Since 1982, only four schools have won the title. *(Corvallis, OR; Apr. 20-22, 2006.)*

Multiple winners: Utah (9); Georgia (7); UCLA (5); Alabama (4).

Year	Year	Year	Year	Year
1982 Utah	1987 Georgia	1992 Utah	1997 UCLA	2002 Alabama
1983 Utah	1988 Alabama	1993 Georgia	1998 UCLA	2003 UCLA
1984 Utah	1989 Georgia	1994 Utah	1999 Georgia	2004 UCLA
1985 Utah	1990 Utah	1995 Utah	2000 UCLA	2005 Georgia
1986 Utah	1991 Alabama	1996 Alabama	2001 UCLA	2006 Georgia

LACROSSE

Men

Leading by just a goal at halftime, Virginia put on a ferocious second-half surge to beat Massachusetts, 15-7, in the Division I lacrosse title game for its fourth national championship. The win capped a perfect 17-0 season for the Cavaliers, while UMass fell to 13-5. Matt Poskay and tournament most outstanding player Matt Ward each netted five goals to lead Virginia. Ward's 16 tournament goals broke the record of 15 set by Syracuse's Gary Gait in 1990. *(Philadelphia, PA; May 29, 2006.)*

Multiple winners: Syracuse and Johns Hopkins (8); Princeton (6); North Carolina and Virginia (4); Cornell (3); Maryland (2).

Year	Year	Year	Year	Year
1971 Cornell	1979 Johns Hopkins	1987 Johns Hopkins	1995 Syracuse	2003 Virginia
1972 Virginia	1980 Johns Hopkins	1988 Syracuse	1996 Princeton	2004 Syracuse
1973 Maryland	1981 North Carolina	1989 Syracuse	1997 Princeton	2005 Johns Hopkins
1974 Johns Hopkins	1982 North Carolina	1990 Syracuse*	1998 Princeton	2006 Virginia
1975 Maryland	1983 Syracuse	1991 North Carolina	1999 Virginia	
1976 Cornell	1984 Johns Hopkins	1992 Princeton	2000 Syracuse	
1977 Cornell	1985 Johns Hopkins	1993 Syracuse	2001 Princeton	
1978 Johns Hopkins	1986 North Carolina	1994 Princeton	2002 Syracuse	

*Title was later vacated due to action by the NCAA Committee on Infractions.

Women

Northwestern defeated Dartmouth, 7-4, in the final match to win its second consecutive Division I women's lacrosse title. The Wildcats trailed, 4-3, in the second half but scored the final four goals of the game to take home the title. Aly Josephs scored four goals to lead the Wildcats, while tournament MVP Sarah Albrecht added two goals and assist. Northwestern improved its record to 20-1 and Dartmouth closed its season at 14-6. *(Boston, MA; May 28, 2006.)*

Multiple winners: Maryland (9); Princeton and Virginia (3); Northwestern, Penn St. and Temple (2).

Year	Year	Year	Year	Year
1982 Massachusetts	1987 Penn St.	1992 Maryland	1997 Maryland	2002 Princeton
1983 Delaware	1988 Temple	1993 Virginia	1998 Maryland	2003 Princeton
1984 Temple	1989 Penn St.	1994 Princeton	1999 Maryland	2004 Virginia
1985 New Hampshire	1990 Harvard	1995 Maryland	2000 Maryland	2005 Northwestern
1986 Maryland	1991 Virginia	1996 Maryland	2001 Maryland	2006 Northwestern

RIFLE
Men & Women

After a one-year hiatus, Alaska-Fairbanks reclaimed its spot atop the NCAA riflery world with its eighth national title and seventh in the last eight years. Jamie Beyerle paced the Nanooks with a win in the Smallbore competition and a runner-up finish in Air Rifle, won by Nebraska's Kristina Fehlings. Matt Rawlings was strong as usual for the Nanooks with a third-place finish in Air Rifle. Alaska-Fairbanks accumulated 4682 points to beat Nebraska (4666). (*Colorado Springs, CO; Mar. 10-11, 2006.*)

Multiple winners: West Virginia (13); Alaska-Fairbanks (8); Tennessee Tech (3); Murray St. (2).

Year	Year	Year	Year	Year
1980 Tenn. Tech	1986 West Virginia	1992 West Virginia	1998 West Virginia	2004 AK-Fairbanks
1981 Tenn. Tech	1987 Murray St.	1993 West Virginia	1999 AK-Fairbanks	2005 Army
1982 Tenn. Tech	1988 West Virginia	1994 AK-Fairbanks	2000 AK-Fairbanks	2006 AK-Fairbanks
1983 West Virginia	1989 West Virginia	1995 West Virginia	2001 AK-Fairbanks	
1984 West Virginia	1990 West Virginia	1996 West Virginia	2002 AK-Fairbanks	
1985 Murray St.	1991 West Virginia	1997 West Virginia	2003 AK-Fairbanks	

ROWING
NCAA Championships
Women

Top-ranked Princeton cruised to a six-plus second victory in the Varsity Eights, but the real battle was for second place as California nipped Brown by just .261 seconds to win its second consecutive NCAA rowing championship. California and Brown tied with 66 points each, but the Cal was awarded the title based on a higher finish in the Eights. Princeton finished the tournament in third place with 56 points, followed by Washington State (52). (*West Windsor, NJ; May 26-28, 2006.*)

Multiple winners: Brown (4); Washington (3); California (2).

Year	Overall winner	Varsity Eights	Year	Overall winner	Varsity Eights
1997	Washington	Washington	2002	Brown	Washington
1998	Washington	Washington	2003	Harvard	Harvard
1999	Brown	Brown	2004	Brown	Brown
2000	Brown	Brown	2005	California	California
2001	Washington	Washington	2006	California	Princeton

Intercollegiate Rowing Association Regatta
VARSITY EIGHTS
Men

The California crew rallied from behind to beat Princeton by almost two seconds for its 15th IRA Varsity Eights title. Brown placed third, while Harvard, Washington and Yale rounded out the field. (*Cooper River, Camden, NJ; June 1-3, 2006.*)

The IRA was formed in 1895 by several Northeastern colleges after Harvard and Yale quit the Rowing Association (established in 1871) to stage an annual race of their own. Since then the IRA Regatta has been contested over courses of varying lengths in Poughkeepsie, N.Y., Marietta, Ohio, Syracuse, N.Y. and Camden, N.J.

Distances: 4 miles (1895-97,1899-1916,1925-41); 3 miles (1898,1921-24,1947-49,1952-63,1965-67); 2 miles (1920,1950-51); 2000 meters (1964, since 1968).

Multiple winners: Cornell (24); California (15); Navy (13); Washington (11); Penn (9); Brown and Wisconsin (7); Syracuse (6); Columbia (4); Harvard and Princeton (3); Northeastern (2).

Year	Year	Year	Year	Year
1895 Columbia	1917-19 Not held	1941 Washington	1967 Penn	1989 Penn
1896 Cornell	1920 Syracuse	1942-46 Not held	1968 Penn	1990 Wisconsin
1897 Cornell	1921 Navy	1947 Navy	1969 Penn	1991 Northeastern
1898 Penn	1922 Navy	1948 Washington	1970 Washington	1992 Dartmouth,
1899 Penn	1923 Washington	1949 California	1971 Cornell	Navy & Penn†
1900 Penn	1924 Washington	1950 Washington	1972 Penn	1993 Brown
1901 Cornell	1925 Navy	1951 Wisconsin	1973 Wisconsin	1994 Brown
1902 Cornell	1926 Washington	1952 Navy	1974 Wisconsin	1995 Brown
1903 Cornell	1927 Columbia	1953 Navy	1975 Wisconsin	1996 Princeton
1904 Syracuse	1928 California	1954 Navy*	1976 California	1997 Washington
1905 Cornell	1929 Columbia	1955 Cornell	1977 Cornell	1998 Princeton
1906 Cornell	1930 Cornell	1956 Cornell	1978 Syracuse	1999 California
1907 Cornell	1931 Navy	1957 Cornell	1979 Brown	2000 California
1908 Syracuse	1932 California	1958 Cornell	1980 Navy	2001 California
1909 Cornell	1933 Not held	1959 Wisconsin	1981 Cornell	2002 California
1910 Cornell	1934 California	1960 California	1982 Cornell	2003 Harvard
1911 Cornell	1935 California	1961 California	1983 Brown	2004 Harvard
1912 Cornell	1936 Washington	1962 Cornell	1984 Navy	2005 Harvard
1913 Syracuse	1937 Washington	1963 Cornell	1985 Princeton	2006 California
1914 Columbia	1938 Navy	1964 California	1986 Brown	
1915 Cornell	1939 California	1965 Navy	1987 Brown	
1916 Syracuse	1940 Washington	1966 Wisconsin	1988 Northeastern	

*In 1954, Navy was disqualified because of an ineligible coxswain; no trophies were given.
†First dead heat in history of IRA Regatta.

Annual NCAA Division I Team Champions (Cont.)

National Rowing Championship
VARSITY EIGHTS
Men

National championship raced annually from 1982-96 in Bantam, Ohio over a 2,000-meter course on Lake Harsha. Winner received the Herschede Cup. Regatta discontinued in 1997.

Multiple winners: Harvard (6); Brown (3); Wisconsin (2).

Year	Champion	Time	Runner-up	Time	Year	Champion	Time	Runner-up	Time
1982	Yale	5:50.8	Cornell	5:54.15	1990	Wisconsin	5:52.5	Harvard	5:56.84
1983	Harvard	5:59.6	Washington	6:00.0	1991	Penn	5:58.21	Northeastern	5:58.48
1984	Washington	5:51.1	Yale	5:55.6	1992	Harvard	5:33.97	Dartmouth	5:34.28
1985	Harvard	5:44.4	Princeton	5:44.87	1993	Brown	5:54.15	Penn	5:56.98
1986	Wisconsin	5:57.8	Brown	5:59.9	1994	Brown	5:24.52	Harvard	5:25.83
1987	Harvard	5:35.17	Brown	5:35.63	1995	Brown	5:23.40	Princeton	5:25.83
1988	Harvard	5:35.98	Northeastern	5:37.07	1996	Princeton	5:57.47	Penn	6:03.28
1989	Harvard	5:36.6	Washington	5:38.93	1997	discontinued			

Women

National championship held over various distances at 10 different venues from 1979-96. Distances– 1000 meters (1979-81); 1500 meters (1982-83); 1000 meters (1984); 1750 meters (1985); 2000 meters (1986-88, 1991-96); 1852 meters (1989-90). Winner received the Ferguson Bowl. Regatta discontinued in 1997.

Multiple winners: Washington (7); Princeton (4); Boston University (2).

Year	Champion	Time	Runner-up	Time	Year	Champion	Time	Runner-up	Time
1979	Yale	3:06	California	3:08.6	1988	Washington	6:41.0	Yale	6:42.37
1980	California	3:05.4	Oregon St.	3:05.8	1989	Cornell	5:34.9	Wisconsin	5:37.5
1981	Washington	3:20.6	Yale	3:22.9	1991	Boston Univ.	7:03.2	Cornell	7:06.21
1982	Washington	4:56.4	Wisconsin	4:59.83	1992	Boston Univ.	6:28.79	Cornell	6:32.79
1983	Washington	4:57.5	Dartmouth	5:03.02	1993	Princeton	6:40.75	Washington	6:43.86
1984	Washington	3:29.48	Radcliffe	3:31.08	1994	Princeton	6:11.38	Yale	6:14.46
1985	Washington	5:28.4	Wisconsin	5:32.0	1995	Princeton	6:11.98	Washington	6:12.69
1986	Wisconsin	6:53.28	Radcliffe	6:53.34	1996	Brown	6:45.7	Princeton	6:49.3
1987	Washington	6:33.8	Yale	6:37.4	1997	discontinued			

The Harvard-Yale Regatta

Harvard made it seven in a row and 20 of the last 22 by defeating Yale at the 141st running of the Harvard/Yale Regatta held June 10-11, 2006. High winds created rough conditions throughout the four-mile Varsity Eights course on the Thames River in New London, Conn. Harvard's crew battled back from an early seven-seat deficit to finish in 23:22.6, almost eight seconds ahead of the Elis (23:30.4). Harvard was also victorious in the Second Varsity race, while Yale's freshman squad edged Harvard by under a second to prevent the sweep. The Harvard/Yale Regatta is the nation's oldest intercollegiate sporting event. Harvard holds an 88-53 series edge.

SKIING
Men & Women

Colorado dominated the Nordic races at the 2006 NCAA Skiing National Championships en route to its 16th overall title. Despite competing without a full 12-skier team, the Buffaloes amassed a total of 654 points to crush the rest of the field and record the fourth-largest margin of victory in Championships history. New Mexico finished second with 556 points, followed by Dartmouth with 537½. Colorado senior and Estonia native Jana Rehemaa won the women's 5-k classic and 15-k freestyle, while Kit Richmond won the men's 20-k freestyle event, leading an impressive 1-2-4 finish for the Buffaloes. Lucie Zikova added yet another individual title for Colorado, winning the women's slalom in 1:22.77. (*Steamboat Springs, CO; March 8-11, 2006.*)

Multiple winners: Denver (18); Colorado (16); Utah (10); Vermont (5); Dartmouth and Wyoming (2).

Year		Year		Year		Year		Year	
1954	Denver	1965	Denver	1976	Colorado	1986	Utah	1997	Utah
1955	Denver	1966	Denver		& Dartmouth	1987	Utah	1998	Colorado
1956	Denver	1967	Denver	1977	Colorado	1988	Utah	1999	Colorado
1957	Denver	1968	Wyoming	1978	Colorado	1989	Vermont	2000	Denver
1958	Dartmouth	1969	Denver	1979	Colorado	1990	Vermont	2001	Denver
1959	Colorado	1970	Denver	1980	Vermont	1991	Colorado	2002	Denver
1960	Colorado	1971	Denver	1981	Utah	1992	Vermont	2003	Utah
1961	Denver	1972	Colorado	1982	Colorado	1993	Utah	2004	New Mexico
1962	Denver	1973	Colorado	1983	Utah	1994	Vermont	2005	Denver
1963	Denver	1974	Colorado	1984	Utah	1995	Colorado	2006	Colorado
1964	Denver	1975	Colorado	1985	Wyoming	1996	Utah		

SOFTBALL
Women

All-American Alicia Hollowell threw two shutouts to lead the Arizona Wildcats to a two-game sweep of Northwestern for their seventh Division I softball title under head coach Mike Candrea. Arizona blanked Northwestern, 8-0 and 5-0, in the best-of-three series. They won 20 of their last 22 games and finished out the year at 54-11, while runner-up Northwestern fell to 50-15. Over the two-game series, Hollowell threw 14 innings, scattered ten hits and struck out 25 batters. She improved her overall record to 32-5 and was selected the tournament's most outstanding player.

Arizona's high-powered offense was paced by Taryne Mowatt, who went 5-for-7 in the series, leftfielder Autumn Champion (4-for-8 with 3 RBI) and catcher Callista Balcko (3-for-7 with 3 RBI). Hurler Eileen Canney took both losses for Northwestern, falling to 26-9 for the season. Leftfielder Katie Logan banged out three hits to lead Northwestern, while shortstop Tammy Williams added two hits. (*Oklahoma City, OK; June 1-6, 2006.*)

Multiple winners: UCLA (10); Arizona (7); Texas A&M (2).

Year	Year	Year	Year	Year
1982 UCLA	1987 Texas A&M	1992 UCLA	1997 Arizona	2002 California
1983 Texas A&M	1988 UCLA	1993 Arizona	1998 Fresno St.	2003 UCLA
1984 UCLA	1989 UCLA	1994 Arizona	1999 UCLA	2004 UCLA
1985 UCLA	1990 UCLA	1995 UCLA*	2000 Oklahoma	2005 Michigan
1986 CS-Fullerton	1991 Arizona	1996 Arizona	2001 Arizona	2006 Arizona

*Title was later vacated due to action by the NCAA Committee on Infractions.

SWIMMING & DIVING
Men

The Auburn Tigers took care of business once again, scoring 480½ points at the NCAA Division I Men's Swimming and Diving Championships to win their fourth consecutive title and sixth overall. Arizona finished runner-up with 440½ points while Stanford placed third with 362½. The well-balanced Auburn squad reached its meet-winning total with just two event victories — from the 200-yard freestyle relay squad and Steven Segerin in the platform dive. Florida ace Ryan Lochte won three individual events — the 200-yard freestyle and the 200-yard and 400-yard individual medleys — and in the process set three American records. California's Henrique Barbosa (100-yard and 200-yard breaststroke) and Georgia's Chris Colwill (1-meter and 3-meter dives) each recorded double wins, while Arizona's Simon Burnett grabbed the 200-yard freestyle title and led Arizona to four relay wins. (*Atlanta, GA; Mar. 23-25, 2006.*)

Multiple winners: Michigan and Ohio St. (11); Texas and USC (9); Stanford (8); Auburn and Indiana (6); Yale (4); California and Florida (2).

Year	Year	Year	Year	Year
1937 Michigan	1951 Yale	1965 USC	1979 California	1993 Stanford
1938 Michigan	1952 Ohio St.	1966 USC	1980 California	1994 Stanford
1939 Michigan	1953 Yale	1967 Stanford	1981 Texas	1995 Michigan
1940 Michigan	1954 Ohio St.	1968 UCLA	1982 UCLA	1996 Texas
1941 Michigan	1955 Ohio St.	1969 Indiana	1983 Florida	1997 Auburn
1942 Yale	1956 Ohio St.	1970 Indiana	1984 Florida	1998 Stanford
1943 Ohio St.	1957 Michigan	1971 Indiana	1985 Stanford	1999 Auburn
1944 Yale	1958 Michigan	1972 Indiana	1986 Stanford	2000 Texas
1945 Ohio St.	1959 Michigan	1973 Indiana	1987 Stanford	2001 Texas
1946 Ohio St.	1960 USC	1974 USC	1988 Texas	2002 Texas
1947 Ohio St.	1961 Michigan	1975 USC	1989 Texas	2003 Auburn
1948 Michigan	1962 Ohio St.	1976 USC	1990 Texas	2004 Auburn
1949 Ohio St.	1963 USC	1977 USC	1991 Texas	2005 Auburn
1950 Ohio St.	1964 USC	1978 Tennessee	1992 Stanford	2006 Auburn

Women

After a one-year hiatus, Auburn reclaimed the title at the Division I Women's Swimming and Diving Championships with a three-point victory over defending champion Georgia. The margin of victory was the second closest in NCAA history, behind only Georgia's 1½-point win over Stanford in 2001. The Lady Tigers accumulated 518½ points, while Georgia finished with 515½. Arizona placed third with 415 and played a vital role in Auburn's title as it edged Georgia in the 400-yard freestyle relay, the meet's final event, to secure the overall victory for Auburn. Hayley Peirsol (1650-yard freestyle) and Rachel Goh (100-yard backstroke) recorded individual wins for the Lady Tigers. Georgia's Kara Lynn Joyce won the 50-, 100- and 200-yard freestyle swims, while teammate Mary DeScenza won the 100- and 200-yard butterflies, becoming the first swimmer in NCAA history to win four consecutive 200-yard butterfly titles. (*Athens, GA; Mar. 16-18, 2006.*)

Multiple winners: Stanford (8); Texas (7); Auburn and Georgia (4).

Year	Year	Year	Year	Year
1982 Florida	1987 Texas	1992 Stanford	1997 USC	2002 Auburn
1983 Stanford	1988 Texas	1993 Stanford	1998 Stanford	2003 Auburn
1984 Texas	1989 Stanford	1994 Stanford	1999 Georgia	2004 Auburn
1985 Texas	1990 Texas	1995 Stanford	2000 Georgia	2005 Georgia
1986 Texas	1991 Texas	1996 Stanford	2001 Georgia	2006 Auburn

Annual NCAA Division I Team Champions (Cont.)

INDOOR TRACK

Men

Host Arkansas overcame the graduation of many of its 2005 stars to win its record 19th NCAA men's Division I indoor track and field title. The Razorbacks received individual titles from its distance-medley relay team, Josphat Boit in the 5,000-meters and Jaanus Uudmae in the triple jump, the latter clinching the championship for Arkansas with the final event remaining. The Razorbacks finished with 53 points, followed by LSU (45) and Florida State (41). LSU wide receiver Xavier Carter won the 400-meters, placed second to Florida State's Walter Dix in the 200 and anchored the Tigers to a win in the 4x400-meter relay. Wisconsin's Chris Solinsky (3000 meters), USC's Jesse Williams (high jump), Oregon's Thomas Skipper (pole vault) and Virginia Tech's Spyridon Jullien (weight throw) were all repeat champions. (*Fayetteville, AR; Mar. 10-11, 2006.*)

Multiple winners: Arkansas (19); UTEP (7); Kansas and Villanova (3); LSU and USC (2).

Year	Year	Year	Year	Year
1965 Missouri	1974 UTEP	1983 SMU	1992 Arkansas	2001 LSU
1966 Kansas	1975 UTEP	1984 Arkansas	1993 Arkansas	2002 Tennessee
1967 USC	1976 UTEP	1985 Arkansas	1994 Arkansas	2003 Arkansas
1968 Villanova	1977 Washington St.	1986 Arkansas	1995 Arkansas	2004 LSU
1969 Kansas	1978 UTEP	1987 Arkansas	1996 George Mason	2005 Arkansas
1970 Kansas	1979 Villanova	1988 Arkansas	1997 Arkansas	2006 Arkansas
1971 Villanova	1980 UTEP	1989 Arkansas	1998 Arkansas	
1972 USC	1981 UTEP	1990 Arkansas	1999 Arkansas	
1973 Manhattan	1982 UTEP	1991 Arkansas	2000 Arkansas	

Women

Sprinter Marshevet Hooker won the 60-meter dash and the long jump to lift Texas to its sixth NCAA women's indoor track title and first since 1999. The Longhorns finished with 51 points to beat runner-up Stanford (36) and Arizona State (30). Michelle Carter was the only other individual winner for Texas with her throw of 60-10¾ in the shot put. Northern Arizona's distance specialist Johanna Nilsson joined Hooker as the meet's only double champions, winning the mile and the 3,000-meters. USC's Virginia Powell was the meet's only repeat winner, capturing the 60-m hurdles for the second straight year, with a meet record 7.84 seconds. (*Fayetteville, AR; Mar. 10-11, 2006.*)

Multiple winners: LSU (11); Texas (6); Nebraska and UCLA (2).

Year	Year	Year	Year	Year
1983 Nebraska	1988 Texas	1993 LSU	1998 Texas	2003 LSU
1984 Nebraska	1989 LSU	1994 LSU	1999 Texas	2004 LSU
1985 Florida St.	1990 Texas	1995 LSU	2000 UCLA	2005 Tennessee
1986 Texas	1991 LSU	1996 LSU	2001 UCLA	2006 Texas
1987 LSU	1992 Florida	1997 LSU	2002 LSU	

OUTDOOR TRACK

Men

On the strength of three individual titles and three runner-up finishes, Florida State won its first title at the NCAA Division I Outdoor Track and Field Championships. Sprinter Walter Dix won the 200-meters in 20.30 seconds, Rafeeq Curry took the title in the triple jump and Garrett Johnson took honors in the shot put. The Seminoles tallied 67 points to finish in front of runner-up LSU (51) and Texas (36). LSU sophomore Xavier Carter became the first man since Jesse Owens to win four events in a single meet, winning the 100- and 400-meters and leading the 4x100 and 4x400 relay teams to victory. (*Sacramento, CA; June 6-10, 2006.*)

Multiple winners: USC (26); Arkansas (12); UCLA (8); UTEP (6); Illinois and Oregon (5); LSU and Stanford (4); Kansas and Tennessee (3); SMU (2).

Year	Year	Year	Year	Year
1921 Illinois	1939 USC	1957 Villanova	1974 Tennessee	1992 Arkansas
1922 California	1940 USC	1958 USC	1975 UTEP	1993 Arkansas
1923 Michigan	1941 USC	1959 Kansas	1976 USC	1994 Arkansas
1924 Not held	1942 USC		1977 Arizona St.	1995 Arkansas
1925 Stanford*	1943 USC	1960 Kansas	1978 UCLA & UTEP	1996 Arkansas
1926 USC*	1944 Illinois	1961 USC	1979 UTEP	1997 Arkansas
1927 Illinois*	1945 Navy	1962 Oregon		1998 Arkansas
1928 Stanford	1946 Illinois	1963 USC	1980 UTEP	1999 Arkansas
1929 Ohio St.	1947 Illinois	1964 Oregon	1981 UTEP	
	1948 Minnesota	1965 Oregon & USC	1982 UTEP	2000 Stanford
1930 USC	1949 USC	1966 UCLA	1983 SMU	2001 Tennessee
1931 USC		1967 USC	1984 Oregon	2002 LSU
1932 Indiana	1950 USC	1968 USC	1985 Arkansas	2003 Arkansas
1933 LSU	1951 USC	1969 San Jose St.	1986 SMU	2004 Arkansas
1934 Stanford	1952 USC	1970 BYU, Kansas	1987 UCLA	2005 Arkansas
1935 USC	1953 USC	& Oregon	1988 UCLA	2006 Florida St.
1936 USC	1954 USC	1971 UCLA	1989 LSU	
1937 USC	1955 USC	1972 UCLA		
1938 USC	1956 UCLA	1973 UCLA	1990 LSU	
			1991 Tennessee	

(*) indicates unofficial championship.

AP/Wide World Photos

Auburn's **Markita James**, center, won the women's 400m hurdles at the NCAA Track and Field Championships on June 10, after Texas' Melanie Walker was disqualified.

Women

Auburn's Markita James and Josanne Lucas went 1-2 in the 400-meter hurdles to lift the Tigers to their first title at the NCAA Division I Women's Outdoor Track and Field Championships. Auburn accumulated 57 points to finish well in front of runner-up USC (38) and South Carolina (37). Jovanee Jarrett gave the Tigers their other win with her leap of 21-2½ in the long jump. USC's Virginia Powell (100-meter hurdles), Air Force's Dana Pounds (javelin) and Texas' 4x100-meter relay squad were all repeat winners. LSU set a meet record (3:25.78) in the 4x400-meter relay. (*Sacramento, CA; June 6-10, 2006.*)

Multiple winners: LSU (13); Texas (4); UCLA (3).

Year	Year	Year	Year	Year
1982 UCLA	1987 LSU	1992 LSU	1997 LSU	2002 South Carolina
1983 UCLA	1988 LSU	1993 LSU	1998 Texas	2003 LSU
1984 Florida St.	1989 LSU	1994 LSU	1999 Texas	2004 UCLA
1985 Oregon	1990 LSU	1995 LSU	2000 LSU	2005 Texas
1986 Texas	1991 LSU	1996 LSU	2001 USC	2006 Auburn

VOLLEYBALL

Men

UCLA returned to the pinnacle of the men's volleyball world, winning its 19th title under legendary coach Al Scates at the NCAA Men's Volleyball Championships. The Bruins swept Penn State in the final match, 30-27, 30-27, 30-27, for their 14th straight victory and first title since 2000. Tournament most outstanding player Steve Klosterman recorded 14 kills and seven digs, while Damien Scott pounded out 12 kills to pace the Bruins attack. Matt Proper blasted 13 kills and Dan O'Dell chipped in 39 assists for the Nittany Lions. (*State College, PA; May 6, 2006.*)

Multiple winners: UCLA (19); Pepperdine (5); USC (4); BYU (3).

Year	Year	Year	Year	Year
1970 UCLA	1978 Pepperdine	1986 Pepperdine	1994 Penn St.	2002 Hawaii†
1971 UCLA	1979 UCLA	1987 UCLA	1995 UCLA	2003 Lewis, IL*
1972 UCLA	1980 USC	1988 UCLA	1996 UCLA	2004 BYU
1973 San Diego St.	1981 USC	1989 UCLA	1997 Stanford	2005 Pepperdine
1974 UCLA	1982 UCLA	1990 USC	1998 UCLA	2006 UCLA
1975 UCLA	1983 UCLA	1991 Long Beach St.	1999 BYU	
1976 UCLA	1984 UCLA	1992 Pepperdine	2000 UCLA	
1977 USC	1985 Pepperdine	1993 UCLA	2001 BYU	

†Title was later vacated due to action by the NCAA Committee on Infractions.
*Division II

Annual NCAA Division I Team Champions (Cont.)
Women

Christal Morrison registered 15 kills and nine digs to lead Washington to a stunning 3 games to 0 upset of top-ranked Nebraska at the Division I Women's Volleyball Championships. The Huskies took down the Cornhuskers, 30-26, 30-25, 30-26 for their first title. Washington finished the season at 32-1 while Nebraska, who had swept its previous five tournament opponents before the title match, closed out its season at 33-2. (San Antonio, TX; Dec. 17, 2005.)

Multiple winners: Stanford (6); Hawaii, Long Beach St., UCLA and USC (3); Nebraska and Pacific (2).

Year	Year	Year	Year	Year
1981 USC	1986 Pacific	1991 UCLA	1996 Stanford	2001 Stanford
1982 Hawaii	1987 Hawaii	1992 Stanford	1997 Stanford	2002 USC
1983 Hawaii	1988 Texas	1993 Long Beach St.	1998 Long Beach St.	2003 USC
1984 UCLA	1989 Long Beach St.	1994 Stanford	1999 Penn St.	2004 Stanford
1985 Pacific	1990 UCLA	1995 Nebraska	2000 Nebraska	2005 Washington

WATER POLO
Men

USC edged Stanford in a defensive struggle, 3-2, to win its third NCAA water polo title and second in the last three years. Trojan Pavol Valovic netted the game winner with three minutes remaining to propel the Trojans to the title. Goaltender Adam Shilling turned away nine shots while his Cardinal counterpart Sandy Hohener saved 11. Shilling and senior teammate Juraj Zatovic were selected co-MVPs of the tournament. (Lewisburg, PA; Dec. 4, 2005.)

Multiple winners: California (11); Stanford (10); UCLA (8); UC-Irvine and USC (3).

Year	Year	Year	Year	Year
1969 UCLA	1977 California	1985 Stanford	1993 Stanford	2001 Stanford
1970 UC-Irvine	1978 Stanford	1986 Stanford	1994 Stanford	2002 Stanford
1971 UCLA	1979 UC-S. Barbara	1987 California	1995 UCLA	2003 USC
1972 UCLA	1980 Stanford	1988 California	1996 UCLA	2004 UCLA
1973 California	1981 Stanford	1989 UC-Irvine	1997 Pepperdine	2005 USC
1974 California	1982 UC-Irvine	1990 California	1998 USC	
1975 California	1983 California	1991 California	1999 UCLA	
1976 Stanford	1984 California	1992 California	2000 UCLA	

Women

Sophomore Courtney Mathewson scored with one second left on the clock to lift UCLA to a 9-8 win over rival USC and its fourth NCAA women's water polo title in the last six years. USC had tied the see-saw affair, 8-8, with under a minute remaining to set the stage for Mathewson's thrilling, last-second goal. Junior Kelly Rulon recorded four goals for the Bruins while Patty Cardenas led USC with three. UCLA improved to 29-4 and USC fell to 27-3. (Davis, CA; May 14, 2006.)

Multiple winner: UCLA (4).

Year	Year	Year	Year	Year
2001 UCLA	2003 UCLA	2004 USC	2005 UCLA	2006 UCLA
2002 Stanford				

WRESTLING
Men

Johny Hendricks and Jake Rosholt each successfully defended their titles to lift Oklahoma State to its fourth consecutive NCAA Division I wrestling title and 34th overall. The Cowboys amassed a total of 122½ points to cruise to the championship ahead of runner-up Minnesota (84) and Oklahoma (80½). Hendricks beat Michigan's Ryan Churella in the 165-pound weight class and Rosholt followed with a 10-3 win over Penn State's Phil Davis (197 pounds). (Oklahoma City, OK; Mar. 16-18, 2006.)

Multiple winners: Oklahoma St. (34); Iowa (20); Iowa St. (8); Oklahoma (7); Minnesota (2).

Year	Year	Year	Year	Year
1928 Okla. A&M*	1943-45 Not held	1961 Okla. St.	1977 Iowa St.	1993 Iowa
1929 Okla. A&M	1946 Okla. A&M	1962 Okla. St.	1978 Iowa	1994 Okla. St.
1930 Okla. A&M	1947 Cornell Col.	1963 Oklahoma	1979 Iowa	1995 Iowa
1931 Okla. A&M*	1948 Okla. A&M	1964 Okla. St.	1980 Iowa	1996 Iowa
1932 Indiana*	1949 Okla. A&M	1965 Iowa St.	1981 Iowa	1997 Iowa
1933 Okla. A&M*	1950 Northern Iowa	1966 Okla. St.	1982 Iowa	1998 Iowa
& Iowa St.*	1951 Oklahoma	1967 Michigan St.	1983 Iowa	1999 Iowa
1934 Okla. A&M	1952 Oklahoma	1968 Okla. St.	1984 Iowa	2000 Iowa
1935 Okla. A&M	1953 Penn St.	1969 Iowa St.	1985 Iowa	2001 Minnesota
1936 Oklahoma	1954 Okla. A&M	1970 Iowa St.	1986 Iowa	2002 Minnesota
1937 Okla. A&M	1955 Okla. A&M	1971 Okla. St.	1987 Iowa St.	2003 Okla. St.
1938 Okla. A&M	1956 Okla. A&M	1972 Iowa St.	1988 Arizona St.	2004 Okla. St.
1939 Okla. A&M	1957 Oklahoma	1973 Iowa St.	1989 Okla. St.	2005 Okla. St.
1940 Okla. A&M	1958 Okla. St.	1974 Oklahoma	1990 Okla. St.	2006 Okla. St.
1941 Okla. A&M	1959 Okla. St.	1975 Iowa	1991 Iowa	
1942 Okla. A&M	1960 Oklahoma	1976 Iowa	1992 Iowa	

(*) indicates unofficial champions. **Note:** Oklahoma A&M became Oklahoma St. in 1958.

HALLS of FAME & AWARDS

After a long wait **Bruce Sutter** was finally inducted into the Baseball Hall of Fame in 2006.

HOWARD BRUCE SUTTER
CHICAGO, N.L., 1976-1980
ST. LOUIS, N.L., 1981-1984
ATLANTA, N.L., 1985-1988

A DOMINANT CLOSER WHO REVOLUTIONIZED THE SPLIT-FINGERED
FASTBALL, WHICH CONFOUNDED BATTERS. EARNED 300 SAVES AND
POSTED A 2.83 ERA WHILE OFTEN PITCHING TWO OR MORE INNINGS. A
SIX-TIME ALL-STAR SELECTION. RANKED AMONG THE TOP TEN IN

BASEBALL

National Baseball Hall of Fame & Museum

Established in 1935 by Major League Baseball to celebrate the game's 100th anniversary. **Address:** 25 Main Street, Cooperstown, NY 13326. **Telephone:** (607) 547-7200. **Web:** www.baseballhalloffame.org

Eligibility: In August 2001, the Hall of Fame announced changes in the way players are elected via the Veterans Committee. The voting done by Baseball Writers' Association of America remains unchanged. Nominated players must have played at least parts of 10 seasons in the major leagues and be retired for at least five. Certain nominated players not elected by the writers can become eligible via the Veterans Committee. The new Veterans Committee will be comprised of all living Hall of Famers as well as all living winners of the Ford Frick and J.G. Taylor Spink. Awards and three members of the old 15-member Veterans Committee with unexpired terms. There was no Veterans Committee vote in 2002. Beginning in 2003 the new Veterans Committee votes every two years on former players and every four years on managers, umpires and executives. Previously, the committee voted annually.

Also, the eligibility of all players that had been dropped from the ballots for not receiving five percent of the vote was restored and those players can now be immediately considered by the new Veterans Committee. The players on baseball's ineligible list are still excluded from consideration. Pete Rose is the only living ex-player on that list.

Class of 2006 (18): BBWAA vote— **Bruce Sutter**, Chicago Cubs (1976-1980), St. Louis Cardinals (1981-1984), Atlanta Braves (1985-1986, 1988); Special Committe Vote (from Negro Leagues)—Ray Brown, Willard Brown, Andy Cooper, Frank Grant, Pete Hill, Biz Mackey, Effa Manley, Jose Mendez, Alex Pompez, Cumberland Posey, Louis Santop, Mule Suttles, Ben Taylor, Cristobal Torriente, Sol White, J.L. Wikinson, Jud Wilson.

2006 Top vote-getters (520 BBWAA ballots cast, 390 needed to elect, 26 to remain on ballot): 1. **Bruce Sutter** (400), 2. **Jim Rice** (337), 3. **Rich Gossage** (336), 4. **Andre Dawson** (317), 5. **Bert Blyleven** (277), 6. **Lee Smith** (234), 7. **Jack Morris** (214), 8. **Tommy John** (154), 9. **Steve Garvey** (135), 10. **Alan Trammell** (92), 11. **Dave Parker** (75), 12. **Dave Concepcion** (65), 13. **Don Mattingly** (64), 14. **Orel Hershiser** (58). 15. **Dale Murphy** (56).

Elected first year on ballot (40): Hank Aaron, Ernie Banks, Johnny Bench, Wade Boggs, George Brett, Lou Brock, Rod Carew, Steve Carlton, Ty Cobb, Dennis Eckersley, Bob Feller, Bob Gibson, Reggie Jackson, Walter Johnson, Al Kaline, Sandy Koufax, Mickey Mantle, Christy Mathewson, Willie Mays, Willie McCovey, Paul Molitor, Joe Morgan, Eddie Murray, Stan Musial, Jim Palmer, Kirby Puckett, Brooks Robinson, Frank Robinson, Jackie Robinson, Babe Ruth, Nolan Ryan, Mike Schmidt, Tom Seaver, Ozzie Smith, Warren Spahn, Willie Stargell, Honus Wagner, Ted Williams, Dave Winfield, Carl Yastrzemski and Robin Yount.

Members are listed with years of induction; (+) indicates deceased members.

Catchers

Bench, Johnny 1989	+ Cochrane, Mickey 1947	+ Hartnett, Gabby 1955
Berra, Yogi 1972	+ Dickey, Bill 1954	+ Lombardi, Ernie 1986
+ Bresnahan, Roger 1945	+ Ewing, Buck 1939	+ Schalk, Ray 1955
+ Campanella, Roy 1969	+ Ferrell, Rick 1984	
Carter, Gary 2003	Fisk, Carlton 2000	

1st Basemen

+ Anson, Cap 1939	+ Connor, Roger 1976	McCovey, Willie 1986
+ Beckley, Jake 1971	+ Foxx, Jimmie 1951	+ Mize, Johnny 1981
+ Bottomley, Jim 1974	+ Gehrig, Lou 1939	Murray, Eddie 2003
+ Brouthers, Dan 1945	+ Greenberg, Hank 1956	Perez, Tony 2000
Cepeda, Orlando 1999	+ Kelly, George 1973	+ Sisler, George 1939
+ Chance, Frank 1946	Killebrew, Harmon 1984	+ Terry, Bill 1954

2nd Basemen

Carew, Rod 1991	+ Herman, Billy 1975	+ Robinson, Jackie 1962
+ Collins, Eddie 1939	+ Hornsby, Rogers 1942	Sandberg, Ryne 2005
Doerr, Bobby 1986	+ Lajoie, Nap 1937	Schoendienst, Red 1989
+ Evers, Johnny 1946	+ Lazzeri, Tony 1991	
+ Fox, Nellie 1997	Mazeroski, Bill 2001	**Designated Hitters**
+ Frisch, Frankie 1947	+ McPhee, Bid 2000	
+ Gehringer, Charlie 1949	Morgan, Joe 1990	Molitor, Paul 2004

Shortstops

Aparicio, Luis 1984	+ Jackson, Travis 1982	+ Tinker, Joe 1946
+ Appling, Luke 1964	+ Jennings, Hugh 1945	+ Vaughan, Arky 1985
+ Bancroft, Dave 1971	+ Maranville, Rabbit 1954	+ Wagner, Honus 1936
Banks, Ernie 1977	+ Reese, Pee Wee 1984	+ Wallace, Bobby 1953
+ Boudreau, Lou 1970	Rizzuto, Phil 1994	+ Ward, Monte 1964
+ Cronin, Joe 1956	+ Sewell, Joe 1977	Yount, Robin 1999
+ Davis, George 1998	Smith, Ozzie 2002	

3rd Basemen

+ Baker, Frank 1955	Kell, George 1983	Schmidt, Mike 1995
Boggs, Wade 2005	+ Lindstrom, Fred 1976	+ Traynor, Pie 1948
Brett, George 1999	+ Mathews, Eddie 1978	
+ Collins, Jimmy 1945	Robinson, Brooks 1983	

Center Fielders

+ Ashburn, Richie 1995	+ Doby, Larry 1998	+ Roush, Edd 1962
+ Averill, Earl 1975	+ Duffy, Hugh 1945	Snider, Duke 1980
+ Carey, Max 1961	+ Hamilton, Billy 1961	+ Speaker, Tris 1937
+ Cobb, Ty 1936	+ Mantle, Mickey 1974	+ Waner, Lloyd 1967
+ Combs, Earle 1970	Mays, Willie 1979	+ Wilson, Hack 1979
+ DiMaggio, Joe 1955	+ Puckett, Kirby 2001	

Left Fielders

Brock, Lou 1985	+ Kelley, Joe 1971	+ Simmons, Al 1953
+ Burkett, Jesse 1946	Kiner, Ralph 1975	+ Stargell, Willie 1988
+ Clarke, Fred 1945	+ Manush, Heinie 1964	+ Wheat, Zack 1959
+ Delahanty, Ed 1945	+ Medwick, Joe 1968	Williams, Billy 1987
+ Goslin, Goose 1968	Musial, Stan 1969	+ Williams, Ted 1966
+ Hafey, Chick 1971	+ O'Rourke, Jim 1945	Yastrzemski, Carl 1989

Right Fielders

Aaron, Hank 1982	Kaline, Al 1980	+ Ruth, Babe 1936
+ Clemente, Roberto 1973	+ Keeler, Willie 1939	+ Slaughter, Enos 1985
+ Crawford, Sam 1957	+ Kelly, King 1945	+ Thompson, Sam 1974
+ Cuyler, Kiki 1968	+ Klein, Chuck 1980	+ Waner, Paul 1952
+ Flick, Elmer 1963	+ McCarthy, Tommy 1946	Winfield, Dave 2001
+ Heilmann, Harry 1952	+ Ott, Mel 1951	+ Youngs, Ross 1972
+ Hooper, Harry 1971	+ Rice, Sam 1963	
Jackson, Reggie 1993	Robinson, Frank 1982	

Major League Baseball's All-Time Team — 1969 and 1997

The Baseball Writers' Association of America originally selected an all-time team as part of major league baseball's 100th anniversary, announcing the outcome of its vote on July 21, 1969. Vote totals were not released. Another vote was released when a panel of 36 BWAA members picked an all-time team for the *Classic Sports Network* just before the 1997 All-Star Game. This time vote totals were given, the single outfield category was divided into three (left, center and right) and two recently popularized positions—the designated hitter and relief pitcher—were added. In the most recent vote two points were awarded for first-place votes and one point for second place. Point totals follow the names with the number of first-place votes in parentheses. All-time team members are listed in **bold** type

1969 Vote

C **Mickey Cochrane**, Bill Dickey, Roy Campanella
1B **Lou Gehrig**, George Sisler, Stan Musial
2B **Rogers Hornsby**, Charlie Gehringer, Eddie Collins
SS **Honus Wagner**, Joe Cronin, Ernie Banks
3B **Pie Traynor**, Brooks Robinson, Jackie Robinson
OF **Babe Ruth, Ty Cobb, Joe DiMaggio**, Ted Williams, Tris Speaker, Willie Mays

RHP **Walter Johnson**, Christy Mathewson, Cy Young
LHP **Lefty Grove**, Sandy Koufax, Carl Hubbell
Mgr. **John McGraw**, Casey Stengel, Joe McCarthy

1969 Vote All-Time Outstanding Player: **Ruth**, Cobb, Wagner, DiMaggio

1997 Vote

C **Johnny Bench** (24) 52; Yogi Berra (4) 22; Roy Campanella (4) 17; Mickey Cochrane (1) 5; Bill Dickey (1) 4; Gabby Hartnett (1) 3; Carlton Fisk 2.

1B **Lou Gehrig** (31) 661/2; Jimmie Foxx (3) 19; George Sisler (2) 8; Willie McCovey 6; Hank Greenberg 21/2; Stan Musial, Eddie Murray, Mark McGwire and Frank Thomas 1.

2B **Rogers Hornsby** (17) 44; Joe Morgan (6) 23; Jackie Robinson (6) 15; Charley Gehringer (4) and Napoleon Lajoie (3) 11; Eddie Collins (1) 3; Rod Carew 2; Ryne Sandberg 1.

SS **Honus Wagner** (23) 55; Cal Ripken Jr. (6) 24; Ozzie Smith (5) 16; Ernie Banks (1) 8; Lou Boudreau and Luke Appling 1.

3B **Mike Schmidt** (21) 50; Brooks Robinson (13) 37; Eddie Mathews 5; George Brett (1) 8; Pie Traynor 3; Pete Rose (1) 2; Frank Baker, Al Rosen and Wade Boggs 1.

LF **Ted Williams** (32) 68; Stan Musial (4) 36; Pete Rose, Ralph Kiner, Rickey Henderson and Barry Bonds 1.

CF **Willie Mays** (25) 57; Ty Cobb (7) 22; Joe DiMaggio (3) 17; Mickey Mantle (1) 10; Tris Speaker 2.

RF **Babe Ruth** (31) 67; Hank Aaron (5) 36; Frank Robinson 2; Al Kaline, Roberto Clemente and Tony Gwynn 1.

DH **Paul Molitor** (22) 48; Harold Baines (3) 12; Don Baylor (1) 10; Edgar Martinez (2) 9; Ty Cobb (2) 6; Hal McRae (1) 5; Mickey Mantle (1) and Dave Parker (1) 3; Joe DiMaggio (1) 2; Lee May, Frank Robinson and Tony Oliva 1.

RHP **Walter Johnson** (9) 30, Cy Young (12) 25; Christy Mathewson (5) 18; Bob Feller (4) 10; Bob Gibson (2) 9; Nolan Ryan (2) 7; Tom Seaver (1) 3; Greg Maddux (1), Grover Cleveland Alexander and Juan Marichal 2.

LHP **Sandy Koufax** (11) 32; Warren Spahn (11) 28; Lefty Grove (8) 25; Steve Carlton (4) 12; Carl Hubbell (1); Whitey Ford (1); Eddie Plank (1) 2.

RP **Dennis Eckersley** (16) 40; Rollie Fingers (9) 29; Lee Smith (4) 13; Hoyt Wilhelm (3) 10; Rich Gossage (3) 9; Bruce Sutter (1) 6, Dan Quisenberry 1.

Mgr. **Casey Stengel** (6) 22, Joe McCarthy (6) 18; Connie Mack (7) 17; John McGraw (6) 14; Sparky Anderson (3) 11; Leo Durocher (2) 6; Dick Williams (1) 4; Billy Martin (1) 3; Al Lopez (1), Ned Hanlon (1), Whitey Herzog (1), Earl Weaver and Bobby Cox 2; Tony La Russa 1.

Baseball (Cont.)

Pitchers

+ Alexander, Grover 1938
+ Bender, Chief 1953
+ Brown, Mordecai 1949
  Bunning, Jim 1996
  Carlton, Steve 1994
+ Chesbro, Jack 1946
+ Clarkson, John 1963
+ Coveleski, Stan 1969
+ Dean, Dizzy 1953
+ Drysdale, Don 1984
  Eckersley, Dennis 2004
+ Faber, Red 1964
  Feller, Bob 1962
  Fingers, Rollie 1992
  Ford, Whitey 1974
+ Galvin, Pud 1965
  Gibson, Bob 1981
+ Gomez, Lefty 1972
+ Grimes, Burleigh 1964
+ Grove, Lefty 1947
+ Haines, Jess 1970

+ Hoyt, Waite 1969
+ Hubbell, Carl 1947
+ Hunter, Catfish 1987
  Jenkins, Ferguson 1991
+ Johnson, Walter 1936
+ Joss, Addie 1978
+ Keefe, Tim 1964
  Koufax, Sandy 1972
+ Lemon, Bob 1976
+ Lyons, Ted 1955
  Marichal, Juan 1983
+ Marquard, Rube 1971
+ Mathewson, Christy 1936
+ McGinnity, Joe 1946
  Niekro, Phil 1997
+ Newhouser, Hal 1992
+ Nichols, Kid 1949
  Palmer, Jim 1990
+ Pennock, Herb 1948
  Perry, Gaylord 1991
+ Plank, Eddie 1946

+ Radbourne, Old Hoss 1939
+ Rixey, Eppa 1963
  Roberts, Robin 1976
+ Ruffing, Red 1967
+ Rusie, Amos 1977
  Ryan, Nolan 1999
  Seaver, Tom 1992
+ Spahn, Warren 1973
  Sutter, Bruce 2006
  Sutton, Don 1998
+ Vance, Dazzy 1955
+ Waddell, Rube 1946
+ Walsh, Ed 1946
+ Welch, Mickey 1973
+ Wilhelm, Hoyt 1985
+ Willis, Vic 1995
+ Wynn, Early 1972
+ Young, Cy 1937

Managers

+ Alston, Walter 1983
  Anderson, Sparky 2000
+ Durocher, Leo 1994
+ Hanlon, Ned 1996
+ Harris, Bucky 1975
+ Huggins, Miller 1964

  Lasorda, Tommy 1997
  Lopez, Al 1977
+ Mack, Connie 1937
+ McCarthy, Joe 1957
+ McGraw, John 1937
+ McKechnie, Bill 1962

+ Robinson, Wilbert 1945
+ Selee, Frank 1999
+ Stengel, Casey 1966
  Weaver, Earl 1996

Umpires

+ Barlick, Al 1989
+ Chylak, Nestor 1999
+ Conlan, Jocko 1974

+ Connolly, Tom 1953
+ Evans, Billy 1973
+ Hubbard, Cal 1976

+ Klem, Bill 1953
+ McGowan, Bill 1992

From Negro Leagues

+ Bell, Cool Papa (OF) 1974
+ Brown, Ray (P) 2006
+ Brown, Willard (OF) 2006
+ Cooper, Andy (P) 2006
+ Charleston, Oscar (1B-OF) .1976
+ Dandridge, Ray (3B) 1987
+ Day, Leon (P-OF-2B) 1995
+ Dihigo, Martin (P-OF) 1977
+ Foster, Rube (P-Mgr) 1981
+ Foster, Willie (P) 1996

+ Gibson, Josh (C) 1972
+ Grant, Frank (2B) 2006
+ Hill, Pete (OF) 2006
+ Irvin, Monte (OF) 1973
+ Johnson, Judy (3B) 1975
+ Leonard, Buck (1B) 1972
+ Lloyd, Pop (SS) 1977
+ Mackey, Biz (C) 2006
+ Mendez, Jose (P) 2006
+ Paige, Satchel (P) 1971

+ Rogan, Wilber (P) 1998
+ Santop, Luis (C) 2006
+ Smith, Hilton 2001
+ Stearnes, Turkey (OF) 2000
+ Suttles, Mule (1B) 2006
+ Taylor, Ben (1B) 2006
+ Torriente, Cristobal (OF) . . .2006
+ Wells, Willie (SS) 1997
+ Williams, Joe (P) 1999
+ Wilson, Jud (3B) 2006

Pioneers and Executives

+ Barrow, Ed 1953
+ Bulkeley, Morgan 1937
+ Cartwright, Alexander 1938
+ Chadwick, Henry 1938
+ Chandler, Happy 1982
+ Comiskey, Charles 1939
+ Cummings, Candy 1939
+ Frick, Ford 1970
+ Giles, Warren 1979
+ Griffith, Clark 1946

+ Harridge, Will 1972
+ Hulbert, William 1995
+ Johnson, Ban 1937
+ Landis, Kenesaw 1944
+ MacPhail, Larry 1978
  MacPhail, Lee 1998
+ Manley, Effa 2006
+ Pompez, Alex 2006
+ Posey, Cumberland 2006
+ Rickey, Branch 1967

+ Spalding, Al 1939
+ White, Sol 2006
+ Veeck, Bill 1991
+ Weiss, George 1971
+ Wilkinson, J.L. 2006
+ Wright, George 1937
+ Wright, Harry 1953
+ Yawkey, Tom 1980

BASKETBALL

Naismith Memorial Basketball Hall of Fame

Established in 1949 by the National Association of Basketball Coaches in memory of the sport's inventor, Dr. James Naismith. Original Hall opened in 1968 and a renovated version of the Hall opened in 1985. A completely new building opened Sept. 28, 2002. **Address:** 1000 West Columbus Avenue, Springfield, MA 01105. **Telephone:** (413) 781-6500. **Web:** www.hoophall.com.

Eligibility: Nominated players and referees must be retired for five years, coaches must have coached 25 years or be retired for five, and contributors must have already completed their noteworthy service to the game. Voting done by 24-member honors committee made up of media representatives, Hall of Fame members and trustees. Any nominee not elected after five years becomes eligible for consideration by the Veterans' Committee after a five-year wait.

Class of 2006 (6): PLAYER—**Charles Barkley**, Philadelphia 76ers (1984-92), Phoenix Suns (1992-96), Houston Rockets (1996-2000); **Joe Dumars**, Detroit (1985-99), **Dominique Wilkins**, Atlanta Hawks (1982-94), LA Clippers (1994), Boston Celtics (1994-95), San Antonio Spurs (1996-97), Orlando MAgic (1998-99); COACH—**Geno Auriemma**; CONTRIBUTOR—**Dave Gavitt**; INTERNATIONAL—**Sandro Gamba**.

2006 finalists (nominated but not elected): PLAYERS—Bobby Jones, Gus Johnson, Bernard King and Chet Walker. COACHES—Jim Calhoun, Gene Keady and Harley Redin. CONTRIBUTOR—Dick Vitale. VETERAN—John Kerr. INTERNATIONAL—Hortencia Marcari.

Note: John Wooden, **Lenny Wilkens** and **Bill Sharman** are the only members to be inducted as both a player and a coach.

Members are listed with years of induction; (+) indicates deceased members.

Men

Abdul-Jabbar, Kareem ..1995	Goodrich, Gail 1996	Monroe, Earl 1990
Archibald, Nate 1991	Greer, Hal 1981	Murphy, Calvin 1993
Arizin, Paul 1977	+ Gruenig, Robert 1963	+ Murphy, Charles (Stretch) 1960
Barkley, Charles 2006	Hagan, Cliff 1977	+ Page, Harlan (Pat) 1962
+ Barlow, Thomas (Babe) ..1980	+ Hanson, Victor 1960	Parish, Robert 2003
Barry, Rick 1987	Havlicek, John 1983	+ Petrovic, Drazen 2002
Baylor, Elgin 1976	Hawkins, Connie 1992	Pettit, Bob 1970
+ Beckman, John 1972	Hayes, Elvin 1990	+ Phillip, Andy 1961
Bellamy, Walt 1993	Haynes, Marques 1998	+ Pollard, Jim 1977
Belov, Sergei 1992	Heinsohn, Tom 1986	Ramsey, Frank 1981
Bing, Dave 1990	+ Holman, Nat 1964	Reed, Willis 1981
Bird, Larry 1998	Houbregs, Bob 1987	Risen, Arnie 1998
+ Borgmann, Bennie 1961	Howell, Bailey 1997	Robertson, Oscar 1979
Bradley, Bill 1982	+ Hyatt, Chuck 1959	+ Roosma, John 1961
+ Brennan, Joe 1974	Issel, Dan 1993	Russell, Bill 1974
Cervi, Al 1984	+ Jeannette, Buddy 1994	+ Russell, John (Honey) ...1964
+ Chamberlain, Wilt 1978	+ Johnson, Bill (Skinny) ...1976	Schayes, Dolph 1972
+ Cooper, Charles (Tarzan) 1976	Johnson, Earvin (Magic) .2002	+ Schmidt, Ernest J 1973
+ Cosic, Kresimir 1996	+ Johnston, Neil 1990	Schommer, John 1959
Cousy, Bob 1970	Jones, K. C 1989	+ Sedran, Barney 1962
Cowens, Dave 1991	Jones, Sam 1983	Sharman, Bill 1975
Cunningham, Billy 1986	+ Krause, Edward (Moose) .1975	+ Steinmetz, Christian 1961
+ Davies, Bob 1969	Kurland, Bob 1961	Thomas, Isiah 2000
+ DeBernardi, Forrest ...1961	Lanier, Bob 1992	Thompson, David 1996
+ DeBusschere, Dave 1982	+ Lapchick, Joe 1966	+ Thompson, John (Cat) ...1962
+ Dehnert, Dutch 1968	Lovellette, Clyde 1988	Thurmond, Nate 1984
Drexler, Clyde 2004	Lucas, Jerry 1979	Twyman, Jack 1982
Dumars, Joe 2006	Luisetti, Hank 1959	Unseld, Wes 1988
+ Endacott, Paul 1971	Macauley, Ed 1960	+ Vandivier, Robert (Fuzzy) 1974
English, Alex 1997	Malone, Moses 2001	+ Wachter, Ed 1961
Erving, Julius (Dr. J) ...1993	+ Maravich, Pete 1987	Walton, Bill 1993
+ Foster, Bud 1964	Martin, Slater 1981	Wanzer, Bobby 1987
Frazier, Walt 1987	McAdoo, Bob 2000	West, Jerry 1979
+ Friedman, Marty 1971	+ McCracken, Branch 1960	Wilkens, Lenny 1989
+ Fulks, Joe 1977	+ McCracken, Jack 1962	Wilkins, Dominique 2006
+ Gale, Laddie 1976	+ McDermott, Bobby 1988	Wooden, John 1960
Gallatin, Harry 1991	McGuire, Dick 1993	Worthy, James 2003
+ Gates, William (Pop) ...1989	McHale, Kevin 1999	+ Yardley, George 1996
Gervin, George 1996	+ Mikan, George 1959	
Gola, Tom 1975	Mikkelsen, Vern 1995	

Women

Blazejowski, Carol 1994	Marcari, Hortencia 2005
Crawford, Joan 1997	Meyers, Ann 1993
Curry, Denise 1997	Miller, Cheryl 1995
Donovan, Anne 1995	Semenova, Uljana 1993
Harris-Stewart, Lucia ...1992	White, Nera 1992
Lieberman, Nancy 1996	Woodard, Lynette 2004

Teams

Buffalo Germans 1961
First Team 1959
Harlem Globetrotters 2002
New York Renaissance 1963
Original Celtics 1959

Referees

+ Enright, Jim 1978
+ Hepbron, George 1960
+ Hoyt, George 1961
+ Kennedy, Pat 1959

+ Leith, Lloyd 1982
+ Mihalik, Red 1986
+ Nucatola, John 1977
+ Quigley, Ernest (Quig) 1961

+ Shirley, J. Dallas 1979
+ Strom, Earl 1995
+ Tobey, Dave 1961
+ Walsh, David 1961

Coaches

+ Allen, Forrest (Phog) 1959
+ Anderson, Harold (Andy) . .1984
  Auerbach, Red 1968
  Barmore, Leon 2003
+ Barry, Sam 1978
+ Blood, Ernest (Prof) 1960
  Boeheim, Jim 2005
  Brown, Larry 2002
  Calhoun, Jim 2005
+ Cann, Howard 1967
+ Carlson, Henry (Doc) 1959
  Carnesecca, Lou 1992
  Carnevale, Ben 1969
  Carril, Pete 1997
+ Case, Everett 1981
  Chaney, John 2001
  Conradt, Jody 1998
  Crum, Denny 1994
  Daly, Chuck 1994
+ Dean, Everett 1966
+ Diaz-Miguel, Antonio 1997
+ Diddle, Ed 1971
+ Drake, Bruce 1972
  Gaines, Clarence (Bighouse) .1981

+ Gardner, Jack 1983
+ Gill, Amory (Slats) 1967
+ Gomelsky, Aleksandr 1995
+ Gunter, Sue 2005
+ Hannum, Alex 1998
  Harshman, Marv 1984
  Haskins, Don 1997
+ Hickey, Eddie 1978
+ Hobson, Howard (Hobby) . .1965
+ Holzman, Red 1986
+ Iba, Hank 1968
+ Julian, Alvin (Doggie) 1967
+ Keaney, Frank 1960
+ Keogan, George 1961
  Knight, Bob 1991
  Krzyzewski, Mike 2001
  Kundla, John 1995
+ Lambert, Ward (Piggy) 1960
+ Litwack, Harry 1975
+ Loeffler, Ken 1964
+ Lonborg, Dutch 1972
+ McCutchan, Arad 1980
+ McGuire, Al 1992
+ McGuire, Frank 1976
+ McLendon, John 1978

+ Meanwell, Walter (Doc) . . .1959
  Meyer, Ray 1978
+ Miller, Ralph 1988
  Moore, Billie 1999
  Newell, Pete 1978
+ Nikolic, Aleksandar 1998
  Olson, Lute 2002
  Ramsay, Jack 1992
  Rubini, Cesare 1994
+ Rupp, Adolph 1968
+ Sachs, Leonard 1961
  Sharman, Bill 2004
+ Shelton, Everett 1979
  Smith, Dean 1982
  Summitt, Pat 2000
+ Taylor, Fred 1986
  Thompson, John 1999
+ Wade, Margaret 1984
  Watts, Stan 1985
  Wilkens, Lenny 1998
  Wooden, John 1972
+ Woolpert, Phil 1992
  Wootten, Morgan 2000
  Yow, Kay 2002

Contributors

+ Abbott, Senda Berenson . . .1984
+ Bee, Clair 1967
+ Biasone, Danny 2000
  Brown, Hubie 2005
+ Brown, Walter A 1965
+ Bunn, John 1964
  Colangelo, Jerry 2004
+ Douglas, Bob 1971
+ Duer, Al 1981
  Embry, Wayne 1999
+ Fagan, Clifford B 1983
+ Fisher, Harry 1973
+ Fleisher, Larry 1991
  Gavitt, Dave 2006
+ Gottlieb, Eddie 1971
+ Gulick, Luther 1959
+ Harrison, Les 1979

+ Hearn, Francis (Chick) 2003
+ Hepp, Ferenc 1980
+ Hickox, Ed 1959
+ Hinkle, Tony 1965
+ Irish, Ned 1964
+ Jones, R. William 1964
+ Kennedy, Walter 1980
  Lemon, Meadowlark 2003
+ Liston, Emil (Liz) 1974
+ Mokray, Bill 1965
+ Morgan, Ralph 1959
+ Morgenweck, Frank (Pop) . .1962
+ Naismith, James 1959
  Newton, Charles M. 2000
+ O'Brien, John J. (Jack) 1961
+ O'Brien, Larry 1991
+ Olsen, Harold G 1959

+ Podoloff, Maurice 1973
+ Porter, Henry (H.V.) 1960
+ Reid, William A 1963
+ Ripley, Elmer 1972
+ St. John, Lynn W 1962
+ Saperstein, Abe 1970
+ Schabinger, Arthur 1961
+ Stagg, Amos Alonzo 1959
  Stankovic, Boris 1991
+ Steitz, Ed 1983
+ Taylor, Chuck 1968
+ Teague, Bertha 1984
+ Tower, Oswald 1959
+ Trester, Arthur (A.L.) 1961
+ Wells, Cliff 1971
+ Wilke, Lou 1982
+ Zollner, Fred 1999

National Collegiate Basketball Hall of Fame

Established in 2006 by the National Association of Basketball Coaches. The five inaugural honorees inducted into the new college basketball hall of fame in November 2006 represent each of the three categories that will be recognized every year—coach, player and contributor. They are part of a founding class of over 100 individuals who are already members of the Naismith Basketball Hall of Fame with roots in college basketball and will automatically be included in the National Collegiate Basketball Hall of Fame.

The remaining Founding Class members will be officially inducted over a period of years at the annual induction ceremony in Kansas City. The museum will be located at the Sprint Center which is currently under construction in Kansas City, Mo. and is scheduled to open in 2007.

Class of 2006 (5): PLAYERS—**Oscar Robertson**, Cincinnati (1957-60) and **Bill Russell**, San Francisco (1953-56); COACHES—**Dean Smith**, North Carolina (1962-97) and **John Wooden**, Indiana St. (1947-48), UCLA (1949-75); CONTRIBUTOR—**Dr. James Naismith**, inventor.

Players	Coaches	Contributors
Robertson, Oscar 2006	Smith, Dean 2006	Naismith, Dr. James 2006
Russell, Bill 2006	Wooden, John 2006	

BOWLING

International Bowling Hall of Fame & Museum

The National Bowling Hall is one museum with separate wings for honorees of the American Bowling Congress (ABC), Professional Bowlers' Association (PBA), Women's International Bowling Congress (WIBC) and Professional Women Bowlers Association (PWBA). In 2005 the ABC and WIBC merged, becoming the United States Bowling Congress. There are plans to merge the respective wings in the hall of fame and there will be no future inductions under the banner of the ABC or WIBC. **Address:** 111 Stadium Plaza, St. Louis, MO 63102. **Telephone:** (314) 231-6340. **Web:** www.bowlingmuseum.com

Professional Bowlers Association

Established in 1975. **Eligibility:** The criteria was revamped in 2002. Nominees must now be retired from full-time competition on the PBA Tour for a minimum of at least five years, or reached the age of 50, and must have won a minimum of 10 PBA Tour titles or two major titles.

Members are listed with years of induction; (+) indicates deceased members.

Performance

+ Allen, Bill 1983	+ Fazio, Buzz 1976	Roth, Mark 1987
+ Anthony, Earl 1986	Ferraro, Dave 1997	Salvino, Carmen 1975
Aulby, Mike 1996	+ Godman, Jim 1987	Semiz, Teata 1998
Berardi, Joe 1990	Hardwick, Billy 1977	Smith, Harry 1975
Bluth, Ray 1975	Holman, Marshall 1990	Soutar, Dave 1979
Bohn, Parker III 2000	Hudson, Tommy 1989	Stefanich, Jim 1980
Buckley, Roy 1992	Husted, Dave 1996	Voss, Brian 1994
Burton, Nelson Jr 1979	Johnson, Don 1977	Webb, Wayne 1993
Carter, Don 1975	Laub, Larry 1985	+ Weber, Dick 1975
Colwell, Paul 1991	Monacelli, Amleto 1997	Weber, Pete 1998
Cook, Steve 1993	Ozio, David 1995	+ Welu, Billy 1975
Davis, Dave 1978	Pappas, George 1986	Williams, Mark 1999
Dickinson, Gary 1988	Petraglia, John 1982	Williams, Walter Ray Jr. . . .1995
Durbin, Mike 1984	Ritger, Dick 1978	Zahn, Wayne 1981

Veterans

Allison, Glenn 1984	+ Joseph, Joe 1985	Schlegel, Ernie 1997
Asher, Barry 1988	Limongello, Mike 1994	+ St. John, Jim 1989
Baker, Tom 1999	Marzich, Andy 1990	Strampe, Bob 1987
Foremsky, Skee 1992	McCune, Don 1991	
Guenther, Johnny 1986	McGrath, Mike 1988	

Meritorious Service

+ Antenora, Joe 1993	+ Fitzgerald, Jim 2000	Nakano, Keijiro 1999
Archibald, John 1989	+ Frantz, Lou 1978	Pezzano, Chuck 1975
Clemens, Chuck 1994	Golden, Harry 1983	Reichert, Jack 1992
+ Elias, Eddie 1976	Hoffman, Ted Jr 1985	+ Richards, Joe 1976
Esposito, Frank 1975	Jowdy, John 1988	+ Schenkel, Chris 1976
Evans, Dick 1986	Kelley, Joe 1989	Stitzlein, Lorraine 1980
Fiorito, Matt 2004	Lichstein, Larry 1996	Thompson, Al 1991
Firestone, Raymond 1987	Luby, Mort Jr. 2004	Zeller, Roger 1995
Fisher, E.A. (Bud) 1984	+ Nagy, Steve 1977	

American Bowling Congress

Established in 1941 and open to professional and amateur bowlers. **Eligibility:** Nominated bowlers must have competed in at least 20 years of ABC tournaments. Voting done by 170-member panel made up of ABC officials, Hall of Fame members and media representatives..

Members are listed with years of induction; (+) indicates deceased members.

Performance

Allison, Glenn 1979	+ Brosius, Eddie 1976	+ Crimmins, Johnny 1962
+ Anthony, Earl 1986	+ Bujack, Fred 1967	Davis, Dave 1990
Asher, Barry 1998	Bunetta, Bill 1968	+ Daw, Charlie 1941
+ Asplund, Harold 1978	Burton, Nelson Jr 1981	+ Day, Ned 1952
Aulby, Mike 2001	+ Burton, Nelson Sr 1964	Dickinson, Gary 1992
Baer, Gordy 1987	+ Campi, Lou 1968	Duke, Norm 2002
Beach, Bill 1991	+ Carlson, Adolph 1941	+ Easter, Sarge 1963
+ Benkovic, Frank 1958	Carter, Don 1970	Ellis, Don 1981
Berlin, Mike 1994	+ Caruana, Frank 1977	+ Falcaro, Joe 1968
+ Billick, George 1982	+ Cassio, Marty 1972	+ Faragalli, Lindy 1968
+ Blouin, Jimmy 1953	+ Castellano, Graz 1976	+ Fazio, Buzz 1963
Bluth, Ray 1973	Chamberlain, Bob 2005	Fehr, Steve 1993
+ Bodis, Joe 1941	+ Clause, Frank 1980	+ Gersonde, Russ 1968
+ Bomar, Buddy 1966	Cohn, Alfred 1985	+ Gibson, Therm 1965
Bower, Gary 2001	Colwell, Paul 1999	+ Godman, Jim 1987
+ Brandt, Allie 1960	Couture, Pete 2004	Goike, Robert 1996

Bowling (Cont.)

+ Golembiewski, Billy 1979
　Griffo, Greg 1995
　Guenther, Johnny 1988
　Hanson, Bob 2004
　Hardwick, Billy 1985
　Hart, Bob 1994
+ Hennessey, Tom 1976
　Hoover, Dick 1974
　Horn, Bud 1992
　Howard, George 1986
　Jackson, Eddie 1988
+ Jackson, Lowell 2003
+ Johnson, Don 1982
　Johnson, Earl 1987
+ Joseph, Joe 1969
+ Jouglard, Lee 1979
+ Kartheiser, Frank 1967
+ Kawolics, Ed 1968
+ Kissoff, Joe 1976
+ Klares, John 1982
+ Knox, Billy 1954
+ Koster, John 1941
+ Krems, Eddie 1973
　Kristof, Joe 1968
+ Krumske, Paul 1968
+ Lange, Herb 1941
+ Lauman, Hank 1976
　Lewis, Mark 2004
　Lillard, Bill 1972
　Lindemann, Tony 1979
+ Lindsey, Mort 1941

+ Lippe, Harry 1989
　Lubanski, Ed 1971
+ Lucci, Vince Sr 1978
+ Marino, Hank 1941
+ Martino, John 1969
　Marzich, Andy 1993
　McGrath, Mike 1993
+ McMahon, Junie 1967
+ Meisel, Darold 1998
+ Mercurio, Skang 1967
+ Meyers, Norm 1984
+ Nagy, Steve 1963
+ Norris, Joe 1954
+ O'Donnell, Chuck 1968
　Pappas, George 1989
+ Patterson, Pat 1974
　Powell, John (Junior) 2000
　Ritger, Dick 1984
+ Rogoznica, Andy 1993
　Salvino, Carmen 1979
　Savoy, Todd 2005
　Schissler, Les 1991
　Schlegel, Ernie 1997
　Schroeder, Jim 1990
+ Schwoegler, Connie 1968
　Scudder, Don 1999
　Semiz, Teata 1991
+ Sielaff, Lou 1968
+ Sinke, Joe 1977
+ Sixty, Billy 1961
　Smith, Harry 1978

+ Smith, Jimmy 1941
　Soutar, Dave 1985
+ Sparando, Tony 1968
　Spigner, Bill 2001
+ Spinella, Barney 1968
+ Steers, Harry 1941
　Stefanich, Jim 1983
+ Stein, Otto Jr 1971
~ Stoudt, Bud 1991
　Strampe, Bob 1977
+ Thoma, Sykes 1971
　Toft, Rod 1991
+ Totsky, Mike 1996
　Tountas, Pete 1989
　Tucker, Bill 1988
　Tuttle, Tommy 1995
+ Varipapa, Andy 1957
+ Ward, Walter 1959
+ Weber, Dick 1970
　Weber, Pete 2002
+ Welu, Billy 1975
　Wilcox, John 1999
　Williams, Walter Ray Jr. ..2005
+ Wilman, Joe 1951
+ Wolf, Phil 1961
　Wonders, Rich 1990
+ Young, George 1959
　Zahn, Wayne 1980
　Zikes, Les 1983
+ Zunker, Gil 1941

Pioneers

+ Hall, William Sr. 1994
　Hirashima, Hiroto 1995
+ Karpf, Samuel 1993
+ Moore, Henry 1996
+ Pasdeloup, Frank 1993
+ Rhodman, Bill 1997

+ Satow, Masao 1994
+ Schutte, Louis 1993
　Shimada, Fuzzy 1997
+ Stein, Louis 1997
+ Thompson, William V. ...1993
+ Timm, Dr. Henry 1993

Meritorious Service

+ Allen, Lafayette Jr. 1994
+ Briell, Frank 1996
+ Carow, Rev. Charles 1995
+ Celestine, Sydney 1993
+ Curtis, Thomas 1993
+ de Freitas, Eric 1994

+ Allen, Harold 1966
　Archibald, John 1996
+ Baker, Frank 1975
+ Baumgarten, Elmer 1963
+ Bellisimo, Lou 1986
+ Bensinger, Bob 1969
　Borden, Fred 2002
+ Chase, LeRoy 1972
+ Coker, John 1980
+ Collier, Chuck 1963
+ Cruchon, Steve 1983
+ Ditzen, Walt 1973
+ Dobs, Darold 1999
+ Doehrman, Bill 1968
+ Elias, Eddie 1985
　Esposito, Frank 1997
　Evans, Dick 1992

+ Franklin, Bill 1992
+ Hagerty, Jack 1963
+ Hattstrom, H.A. (Doc) ...1980
+ Hermann, Cornelius 1968
+ Howley, Pete 1941
　James, Steve 2005
　Jensen, Mark 2002
　Jowdy, John 2001
+ Kennedy, Bob 1981
+ Langtry, Abe 1963
+ Levine, Sam 1971
+ Luby, David 1969
　Luby, Mort Jr. 1988
+ Luby, Mort Sr. 1974
　Matzelle, Al 1995
+ McCullough, Howard 1971
　Mormando, Nick 2003

+ Patterson, Morehead 1985
+ Petersen, Louie 1963
　Pezzano, Chuck 1982
　Picchietti, Remo 1993
　Pluckhahn, Bruce 1989
+ Raymer, Milt 1972
+ Reed, Elmer 1978
　Reichert, Jack 1998
　Rudo, Milt 1984
　Schenkel, Chris 1988
　Skelton, Max 2002
+ Sweeney, Dennis 1974
　Tessman, Roger 1994
+ Thum, Joe 1980
　Weinstein, Sam 1970
+ Whitney, Eli 1975
+ Wolf, Fred 1976

Women's International Bowling Congress

Established in 1953. **Eligibility:** Performance nominees must have won at least one WIBC Championship Tournament title, a WIBC Queens tournament title or an international competition title and have bowled in at least 15 national WIBC Championship Tournaments (unless injury or illness cut career short).

Members are listed with years of induction; (+) indicates deceased members.

Performance

　Abel, Joy 1984
　Adamek, Donna 1996
　Ann, Patty 1995
　Bolt, Mae 1978
　Bouvia, Gloria 1987
　Boxberger, Loa 1984

　Buckner, Pam 1990
+ Burling, Catherine 1958
+ Burns, Nina 1977
　Cantaline, Anita 1979
　Carter, LaVerne 1977
　Carter, Paula 1994

　Coburn, Doris 1976
　Coburn-Carroll, Cindy ...1998
　Costello, Pat 1986
　Costello, Patty 1989
　Daniels, Cheryl 2002
　Dryer, Pat 1978

Duggan, Anne Marie 2005	Johnson, Tish 2002	Rickard, Robbie 1994
Duval, Helen 1970	Kelly, Annese 1985	+ Robinson, Leona 1969
+ Fellmeth, Catherine 1970	Kelly, Linda 2003	Romeo, Robin 1995
Fiebig, Cora 2004	+ Knechtges, Doris 1983	+ Rump, Anita 1962
Fothergill, Dotty 1980	Kuczynski, Betty 1981	+ Ruschmeyer, Addie 1961
+ Fulton, Louise 2001	Ladewig, Marion 1964	+ Ryan, Esther 1963
+ Fritz, Deane 1966	+ Matthews, Merle 1974	+ Sablatnik, Ethel 1979
Garms, Shirley 1971	+ McCutcheon, Floretta 1956	Sandelin, Lucy 1999
Gianulias, Nikki 1997	Merrick, Marge 1980	+ Schulte, Myrtle 1965
+ Gloor, Olga 1976	+ Mikiel, Val 1979	+ Shablis, Helen 1977
Gonzalez, Ashie 1998	Miller-Mackey, Dana 2000	Sill, Aleta 1996
Graham, Linda 1992	Miller, Carol 1997	+ Simon, Violet (Billy) 1960
Graham, Mary Lou 1989	+ Miller, Dorothy 1954	+ Small, Tess 1971
+ Greenwald, Goldie 1953	Mivelaz, Betty 1991	+ Smith, Grace 1968
Grinfelds, Vesma 1991	Mohacsi, Mary 1994	Soutar, Judy 1976
+ Harman, Janet 1985	Morris, Betty 1983	+ Stockdale, Louise 1953
+ Hartrick, Stella 1972	Naccarato, Jeanne 1999	Toepfer, Elvira 1976
+ Hatch, Grayce 1953	Nichols, Lorrie Koch 1989	+ Twyford, Sally 1964
Havlish, Jean 1987	Norman, Carol 2001	Wagner, Lisa 2000
+ Hoffman, Martha 1979	Norman, Edie Jo 1993	+ Warmbier, Marie 1953
Holm, Joan 1974	Norton, Virginia 1988	Wene-Martin, Sylvia 1966
+ Humphreys, Birdie 1979	Notaro, Phyllis 1979	Wilkinson, Dorothy 1990
Ignizio, Millie Martorella . . .1975	Ortner, Bev 1972	+ Winandy, Cecelia 1975
Jacobson, D.D 1981	+ Powers, Connie 1973	Zimmerman, Donna 1982
+ Jaeger, Emma 1953	Reichley, Susie 2000	

Meritorious Service

+ Baetz, Helen 1977	+ Haas, Dorothy 1977	O'Connor, Billie 1992
+ Baker, Helen 1989	Hagin, Elaine 2000	+ Phaler, Emma 1965
+ Banker, Gladys 1994	+ Herold, Mitzi 1998	+ Porter, Cora 1986
+ Bayley, Clover 1992	+ Higley, Margaret 1969	+ Quin, Zoe 1979
Bennie, Bernice 2003	+ Hochstadter, Bee 1967	+ Rishling, Gertrude 1972
+ Berger, Winifred 1976	+ Kay, Nora 1964	Robinson, Jeanette 2000
+ Bohlen, Philena 1955	Keller, Pearl 1999	Rowe, Dorothy 2004
Borschuk, Lo 1988	+ Kelly, Ellen 1979	Simone, Anne 1991
+ Botkin, Freda 1986	Kelone, Theresa 1978	Sloan, Catherine 1985
Broyles, Sylvia 2005	+ Knepprath, Jeannette 1963	+ Speck, Berdie 1966
+ Chapman, Emily 1957	+ Lasher, Iolia 1967	Spitalnick, Mildred 1994
Chapman, Nancy 2002	+ Marrs, Mabel 1979	+ Spring, Alma 1979
+ Crowe, Alberta 1982	+ McBride, Bertha 1968	+ Switzer, Pearl 1973
Deitch, Joyce 2003	McLeary, Hazel 2000	+ Todd, Trudy 1993
+ Dornblaser, Gertrude 1979	+ Menne, Catherine 1979	+ Veatch, Georgia 1974
Duffy, Agnes 1987	Mitchell, Flora 1996	+ White, Mildred 1975
Finke, Gertrude 1990	Morton, Clara 2001	+ Wood, Ann 1970
+ Fisk, Rae 1983	+ Mraz, Jo 1959	

Professional Women Bowlers Hall of Fame

Established in 1995 by the Ladies Pro Bowlers Tour. The LPBT has since been renamed the Professional Women Bowlers Association and the PWBA Hall of Fame has since been folded into the International Bowling Hall of Fame. The PWBA has not inducted any new members since 2003.

Eligibility: Nominees in performance category must have at least five titles from organizations including All-Star, World Invitational, LPBT, WPBA, PWBA, TPA and LPBA.

Members are listed with year of induction; (+) indicates deceased member.

Performance

Adamek, Donna 1995	Grinfelds, Vesma 1997	Nichols, Lorrie . . . . :1996
Coburn-Carroll, Cindy 1997	Johnson, Tish 1998	Norton, Virginia 2003
Costello, Pat 1997	Ladewig, Marion 1995	Romeo, Robin 1996
Costello, Patty 1995	Martorella, Millie 1995	Sill, Aleta 1998
Duggan, Anne Marie 2003	Miller-Mackie, Dana 2002	Wagner, Lisa 1996
Fothergill, Dotty 1995	Morris, Betty 1995	
Gianulias, Nikki 1996	Naccarato, Jeanne 2002	

Pioneers

Able, Joy 1998	Coburn, Doris 1996	Ortner, Bev 1998
Boxberger, Loa 1997	Duval, Helen 1995	Soutar, Judy 1997
Carter, LaVerne 1995	Garms, Shirley 1995	Zimmerman, Donna 1996

Builders

+ Buehler, Janet 1996	Robinson, Jeanette 1996	+ Veatch, Georgia 1995
Keller, Pearl 1997	Sommer Jr., John 1997	

BOXING

International Boxing Hall of Fame

Established in 1984 and opened in 1989. **Address:** 1 Hall of Fame Drive, Canastota, NY 13032. **Telephone:** (315) 697-7095. **Web:** www.ibhof.com.

Eligibility: All nominees must be retired for five years. Voting done by 142-member panel made up of Boxing Writers' Association members and world-wide boxing historians.

Class of 2006 (12): MODERN ERA—**Michael Carbajal, Humberto Gonzalez, Edwin Rosario.** OLD TIMERS—**Lou Brouillard, Jimmy Slattery, Teddy Yarosz.** PIONEER—**Jem Carney;** NON-PARTICIPANTS—**Jarvis Astaire, Whitey Bimstein, Rodolfo Sabbatini.** OBSERVERS—**Hank Kaplan** and **Stanley Weston.**

Members are listed with year of induction; (+) indicates deceased member.

Modern Era

Ali, Muhammad 1990	Giardello, Joey 1993	+ Olson, Carl (Bobo) 2000
+ Angott, Sammy 1998	Gomez, Wilfredo 1995	Ortiz, Carlos 1991
+ Apostoli, Fred 2003	Gonzalez, Humberto 2006	+ Ortiz, Manuel 1996
Arguello, Alexis 1992	+ Graham, Billy 1992	Palomino, Carlos 2004
+ Armstrong, Henry 1990	+ Graziano, Rocky 1991	Papp, Laszlo 2001
Basilio, Carmen 1990	Griffith, Emile 1990	+ Pastrano, Willie 2001
Benitez, Wilfredo 1996	Hagler, Marvelous Marvin .1993	Patterson, Floyd 1991
Benvenuti, Nino 1992	Harada, Masahiko (Fighting) 1995	Pedroza, Eusebio 1999
+ Berg, Jackie (Kid) 1994	Jack, Beau 1991	Pep, Willie 1990
Bivins, Jimmy 1999	+ Jenkins, Lew 1999	+ Perez, Pascual . . . . :1995
+ Brown, Joe 1996	Jofre, Eder 1992	Pryor, Aaron 1996
Buchanan, Ken 2000	Johansson, Ingemar 2002	Qawi, Dwight Muhammad .2004
+ Burley, Charley 1992	Johnson, Harold 1993	Ramos, Ultiminio 2001
Canto, Miguel 1998	Laguna, Ismael 2001	+ Robinson, Sugar Ray 1990
Carbajal, Michael 2006	LaMotta, Jake 1990	+ Rodriguez, Luis 1997
+ Carter, Jimmy 2000	Leonard, Sugar Ray 1997	+ Rosario, Edwin 2006
+ Cerdan, Marcel 1991	+ Liston, Sonny 1991	+ Saddler, Sandy 1990
Cervantes, Antonio 1998	Locche, Nicolino 2003	+ Saldivar, Vicente 1999
Chacon, Bobby 2005	Loi, Duilio 2005	+ Sanchez, Salvador 1991
Chandler, Jeff 2000	+ Louis, Joe 1990	+ Schmeling, Max 1992
+ Charles, Ezzard 1990	Marciano, Rocky 1990	Spinks, Michael 1994
Cokes, Curtis 2003	+ Maxim, Joey 1994	+ Tiger, Dick 1991
+ Conn, Billy 1990	McCallum, Mike 2003	Torres, Jose 1997
Cuevas, Pipino 2002	McGuigan, Barry 2005	Turpin, Randy 2001
+ Elorde, Gabriel (Flash) 1993	+ Montgomery, Bob 1995	+ Walcott, Jersey Joe 1990
Fenech, Jeff 2002	+ Monzon, Carlos 1990	+ Williams, Ike 1990
Foreman, George 2003	+ Moore, Archie 1990	+ Wright, Chalky 1997
Foster, Bob 1990	Muhammad, Matthew Saad 1998	+ Zale, Tony 1991
Frazier, Joe 1990	Napoles, Jose 1990	Zaragoza, Daniel 2004
Fullmer, Gene 1991	Nelson, Azumah 2004	Zarate, Carlos 1994
Galaxy, Khaosai 1999	Norris, Terry 2005	+ Zivic, Fritzie 1993
+ Galindez, Victor 2002	Norton, Ken 1992	
Gavilan, Kid 1990	Olivares, Ruben 1991	

Old-Timers

+ Ambers, Lou 1992	+ Dillon, Jack 1995	+ Leonard, Benny 1990
+ Arizmendi, Baby 2004	+ Dixon, George 1990	+ Levinsky, Battling 2000
+ Attell, Abe 1990	+ Driscoll, Jim 1990	+ Lewis, John Henry . . . . . : . .1994
+ Baer, Max 1995	+ Dundee, Johnny 1991	+ Lewis, Ted (Kid) 1992
+ Barry, Jimmy 2000	+ Escobar, Sixto 2002	+ Loughran, Tommy 1991
+ Bass, Benny 2002	+ Fields, Jackie 2004	+ Lynch, Benny 1998
+ Battalino, Battling 2003	+ Fitzsimmons, Bob 1990	+ Lynch, Joe 2005
+ Berlenbach, Paul 2001	+ Flowers, Theodore (Tiger) . .1993	+ Mandell, Sammy 1998
+ Braddock, Jim 2001	+ Gans, Joe 1990	+ McAuliffe, Jack 1995
+ Britton, Jack 1990	+ Genaro, Frankie 1998	+ McCoy, Charles (Kid) 1991
+ Brouillard, Lou 2006	+ Gibbons, Mike 1992	+ McFarland, Packey 1992
+ Brown, Aaron (Dixie Kid) . .2002	+ Gibbons, Tommy 1993	+ McGovern, Terry 1990
+ Brown, Panama Al 1992	+ Greb, Harry 1990	+ McLarnin, Jimmy 1991
+ Burns, Tommy 1996	+ Griffo, Young 1991	+ McVey, Sam 1999
+ Canzoneri, Tony 1990	+ Harris, Harry 2002	+ Miller, Freddie 1997
+ Carpentier, Georges 1991	+ Herman, Pete 1997	+ Mitchell, Charley 2002
+ Chocolate, Kid 1991	+ Jackson, Peter 1990	+ Moran, Owen 2002
+ Choynski, Joe 1998	+ Jeanette, Joe 1997	+ Nelson, Battling 1992
+ Corbett, James J. 1990	+ Jeffries, James J 1990	+ O'Brien, Philadelphia Jack .1994
+ Corbett III, Young 2004	+ Johnson, Jack 1990	+ Papke, Billy 2001
+ Coulon, Johnny 1999	+ Kaplan, Louis (Kid) 2003	+ Petrolle, Billy 2000
+ Criqui, Eugene 2005	+ Ketchel, Stanley 1990	+ Ritchie, Willie 2004
+ Darcy, Les 1993	+ Kilbane, Johnny 1995	+ Rosenbloom, Maxie 1993
+ Delaney, Jack 1996	+ LaBarba, Fidel 1996	+ Ross, Barney 1990
+ Dempsey, Jack 1990	+ Langford, Sam 1990	+ Ryan, Tommy 1991
+ Dempsey, Jack (Nonpareil) .1992	+ Lavigne, George (Kid) 1998	+ Sharkey, Jack 1994

+ Sharkey, Tom 2003
+ Slattery, Jimmy 2006
+ Steele, Freddie 1999
+ Stribling, Young 1996
+ Taylor, Charles (Bud) 2005
+ Tendler, Lew 1999
+ Thil, Marcel 2005

+ Tunney, Gene 1990
+ Villa, Pancho 1994
+ Walcott, Joe (Barbados) . .1991
+ Walker, Mickey 1990
+ Welsh, Freddie 1997
+ Wilde, Jimmy 1990
+ Willard, Jess 2003

+ Williams, Kid 1996
+ Wills, Harry 1992
+ Wolgast, Ad 2000
+ Wolgast, Midget 2001
+ Yarosz, Teddy 2006

Pioneers

+ Aaron, Barney 2001
+ Baldwin, Caleb 2003
+ Belcher, Jem 1992
+ Brain, Ben 1994
+ Broughton, Jack 1990
+ Burke, James (Deaf) 1992
+ Carney, Jem 2006
+ Chambers, Arthur 2000
+ Cribb, Tom 1991
+ Donovan, Prof. Mike 1998
+ Duffy, Paddy 1994

+ Goss, Joe 2003
+ Edwards, Billy 2004
+ Figg, James 1992
+ Heenan, John C. 2002
+ Jackson, Gentleman John . .1992
+ Johnson, Tom 1995
+ King, Tom 1992
+ Langham, Nat 1992
+ Mace, Jem 1990
+ Mendoza, Daniel 1990
+ Molineaux, Tom 1997

+ Morrissey, John 1996
+ Pearce, Henry 1993
+ Randall, Jack 2005
+ Richmond, Bill 1999
+ Sam, Dutch 1997
+ Sam, Young Dutch 2002
+ Sayers, Tom 1990
+ Spring, Tom 1992
+ Sullivan, John L 1990
+ Thompson, William 1991
+ Ward, Jem 1995

Non-Participants

+ Andrews, Thomas S 1992
+ Arcel, Ray 1991
  Arum, Bob 1999
  Astaire, Jarvis 2006
+ Ballarati, Giuseppe 1999
  Benton, George 2001
+ Bimstein, Whitey 2006
+ Blackburn, Jack 1992
+ Brady, William A. 1998
+ Branchini, Umberto 2004
  Brenner, Teddy 1993
+ Cayton, Bill 2005
+ Chambers, John Graham . .1990
  Chargin, Don 2001
  Christodolou, Stanley 2004
  Clancy, Gil 1993
+ Coffroth, James W. 1991
+ Cohen, Irving 2002
+ D'Amato, Cus. 1995
  Dickson, Jeff 2000
+ Donovan, Arthur 1993
  Duff, Mickey 1999
  Dundee, Angelo 1992
+ Dundee, Chris 1994

+ Dunphy, Don 1993
+ Duva, Dan 2003
  Duva, Lou 1998
+ Eaton, Aileen 2002
+ Egan, Pierce 1991
+ Fleischer, Nat 1990
+ Fox, Richard K. 1997
+ Fragetta, Dewey 2003
  Fraser, Don 2005
+ Futch, Eddie 1994
+ Goldman, Charley 1992
+ Goldstein, Ruby 1994
  Goodman, Murray 1999
+ Humphreys, Joe 1997
+ Ichinose, Sam 2001
+ Jacobs, Jimmy 1993
+ Jacobs, Mike 1990
+ Johnston, Jimmy 1999
+ Kearns, Jack (Doc) 1990
  King, Don 1997
  Lectoure, Tito 2000
+ Liebling, A.J. 1992
+ Lonsdale, Lord 1990
+ Markson, Harry 1992

  Mercante, Arthur 1995
+ Morgan, Dan 2000
+ Muldoon, William 1996
  Odd, Gilbert 1995
+ O'Rourke, Tom 1999
+ Parker, Dan 1996
+ Parnassus, George 1991
  Peltz, J. Russell 2004
+ Queensberry, Marquis of . .1990
+ Rickard, Tex 1990
+ Rudd, Irving 1999
+ Sabbatini, Rodolfo 2006
+ Sarreal Lope 2005
+ Siler, George 1995
+ Silverman, Sam 2002
+ Solomons, Jack 1995
  Steward, Emanuel 1996
+ Taub, Sam 1994
+ Taylor, Herman 1998
  Viscusi, Lou 2004
+ Walker, James J. (Jimmy) . .1992
+ Weill, Al 2003

Observers

+ Bromberg, Lester 2001
+ Cannon, Jimmy 2002
+ Citro, Ralph 2001
  Fiske, Jack 2003
  Gallo, Bill 2001

  Gutteridge, Reg 2002
  Heinz, W.C. 2004
+ Jones, Jersey 2005
  Kaplan, Hank 2006
+ Mullan, Harry 2005

+ Nagler, Barney 2004
+ Runyon, Damon 2002
  Schulberg, Budd 2003
  Sugar, Bert 2005
+ Weston, Stanley 2006

Old *Ring* Hall Members Not in Int'l. Boxing Hall

Nat Fleischer, the late founder and editor-in-chief of *The Ring*, established his magazine's Boxing Hall of Fame in 1954, but it was abandoned after the 1987 inductions. One hundred and thirty members of the old *Ring* Hall have been elected to the International Hall since 1989. The 24 boxers and one sportswriter who have yet to be elected to the International Hall are listed below with their year of induction into the *Ring* Hall.

Modern Group

+ Garcia, Ceferino 1977

+ Lesnevich, Gus 1973

+ Shirai, Yoshio 1977

Old-Timers

+ Britt, Jimmy 1976
+ Chaney, George (K.O.) . . .1974
+ Corbett, Young II 1965

+ Houck, Leo 1969
+ Jeffra, Harry 1982
+ Klaus, Frank 1974

+ Maher, Peter 1978
+ Root, Jack 1961
+ Smith, Jeff 1969

Pioneers

+ Chandler, Tom 1972
+ Clark, Nobby 1971
+ Collyer, Sam 1964
+ Donnelly, Dan 1960
+ Gully, John 1959

+ Hyer, Jacob 1968
+ Hyer, Tom 1954
+ Jackling, Thomas 1985
+ Kilrain, Jack 1965
+ Price, Ned 1962

+ Ryan, Paddy 1973

Non-Participant

+ Daniel, Dan (sportswriter) . .1977

FOOTBALL

College Football Hall of Fame

Established in 1955 by the National Football Foundation. **Address:** 111 South St. Joseph St., South Bend, IN 46601. **Telephone:** (574) 235-9999. **Web:** www.collegefootball.org

Eligibility: Nominated players must be out of college 10 years and a first team All-America pick by a major selector during their careers; coaches must be retired three years or active and over 75 years old. Voting done by 12-member panel of athletic directors, conference and bowl officials and media representatives. The first year representatives from NCAA Div. I-AA, II, and III, and the NAIA were eligible for induction was 1996.

Class of 2006 (22): LARGE COLLEGE—RB **Bobby Anderson**, Colorado (1967-69); DB **Bennie Blades**, Miami-FL (1985-87); T **Carl Eller**, Minnesota (1961-63); DL **Steve Emtman**, Washington (1989-91); FS **Thomas Everett**, Baylor (1983-86); DT **Chad Hennings**, Air Force (1984-87); OG **Chip Kell**, Tennessee (1968-70); QB **Mike Phipps**, Purdue (1967-69); RB **Mike Rozier**, Nebraska (1981-83); LB **Jeff Siemon**, Stanford (1968-71); DT **Bruce Smith**, Virginia Tech (1981-84); RB **Emmitt Smith**, Florida (1987-89). QB **Charlie Ward**, Florida St. (1989,1991-93); COACHES—**Bobby Bowden**, Samford (1959-62), West Virginia (1970-75), Florida St. (1976—); **Joe Paterno**, Penn St. (1966—). SMALL COLLEGE—DB **Kevin Dent**, Jackson St. (1985-88); QB **John Friesz**, Idaho (1986-89); E **Ronnie Mallett**, Central Arkansas (1978-81); WR **Jerry Rice**, Miss. Valley St. (1981-84) SMALL COLLEGE COACHES—**Dick Farley**, Williams-MA (1987-2003); **John Gagliardi**, Carroll College (1949-52), Saint John's-MN (1952—); **Vernon "Skip" McCain**, Maryland St. (1948-63).

Note: Bobby Dodd and **Amos Alonzo Stagg** are the only members to be honored as both players and coaches.
Players are listed with *final year they played* in college and coaches are listed with year of induction; (+) indicates deceased members.

Players

+ Abell, Earl-Colgate 1915	+ Below, Marty-Wisconsin . . .1923	Campbell, Earl-Texas 1977
Agase, Alex-Purdue/Ill 1946	+ Benbrook, Al-Michigan 1910	+ Cannon, Jack-N.Dame 1929
+ Agganis, Harry-Boston U . . .1952	Bennett, Cornelius-Alabama 1986	Cappelletti, John-Penn St . . .1973
Albert, Frank-Stanford 1941	+ Berry, Charlie-Lafayette 1924	+ Carideo, Frank-N.Dame 1930
+ Aldrich, Ki-TCU 1938	+ Bertelli, Angelo-N.Dame 1943	+ Carney, Charles-Illinois 1921
+ Aldrich, Malcolm-Yale 1921	+ Berwanger, Jay-Chicago 1935	Caroline, J.C.-Illinois 1954
+ Alexander, Joe-Syracuse . . .1920	+ Bettencourt, L.-St.Mary's . . .1927	Carpenter, Bill-Army 1959
Allen, Marcus-USC 1981	Biletnikoff, Fred-Fla.St. 1964	+ Carpenter, Hunter-No. Carolina/
Alworth, Lance-Arkansas . . .1961	Blades, Benny-Miami,FL 1987	Virginia Tech 1905
+ Ameche, Alan-Wisconsin . . .1954	Blanchard, Doc-Army 1946	Carroll, Chas.-Washington . .1928
+ Ames, Knowlton-Princeton . . .1889	+ Blozis, Al-Georgetown 1941	Carter, Anthony-Michigan . .1982
+ Amling, Warren-Ohio St 1946	Bock, Ed-Iowa St 1938	Casanova, Tommy-LSU 1971
Anderson, Bob P.-Army 1959	Bomar, Lynn-Vanderbilt 1924	+ Casey, Edward-Harvard 1919
Anderson, Bobby-Colorado .1969	+ Bomeisler, Bo-Yale 1912	Casillas, Tony-Oklahoma . . .1985
Anderson, Dick-Colorado . . .1967	Booth, Albie-Yale 1931	Cassady, Howard-Ohio St . . .1955
Anderson, Donny-Tex.Tech . .1965	+ Borries, Fred-Navy 1934	+ Chamberlin, Guy-Neb.Wesleyan/
+ Anderson, Hunk-N.Dame . . .1921	+ Bosley, Bruce-West Va 1955	Nebraska 1915
Arnett, Jon-USC 1956	Bosseler, Don-Miami,FL 1956	Chapman, Sam-California . . .1937
Atkins, Doug-Tennessee 1952	Bottari, Vic-California 1938	Chappuis, Bob-Michigan . . .1947
Babich, Bob-Miami-OH 1968	Bowden, Murry-Dartmouth . .1970	+ Christman, Paul-Missouri . . .1940
+ Bacon, Everett-Wesleyan . . .1912	+ Boynton, Ben-Williams 1920	Clark, Dutch-Colo. Col. 1929
+ Bagnell, Reds-Penn 1950	+ Brewer, Charles-Harvard 1895	Cleary, Paul-USC 1947
+ Baker, Hobey-Princeton 1913	+ Bright, Johnny-Drake 1951	+ Clevenger, Zora-Indiana 1903
+ Baker, John-USC 1931	Brodie, John-Stanford 1956	Cloud, Jack-Wm. & Mary . . .1949
+ Baker, Moon-N'western 1926	+ Brooke, George-Penn 1895	+ Cochran, Gary-Princeton 1897
Baker, Terry-Oregon St 1962	Brosky, Al-Illinois 1952	+ Cody, Josh-Vanderbilt 1919
+ Ballin, Harold-Princeton 1914	Brown, Bob-Nebraska 1963	Coleman, Don-Mich.St 1951
+ Banker, Bill-Tulane 1929	Brown, Geo-Navy/S.Diego St .1947	+ Conerly, Charlie-Miss 1947
Banonis, Vince-Detroit 1941	+ Brown, Gordon-Yale 1900	Connor, George-HC/ND 1947
+ Barnes, Stan-California 1921	Brown, Jim-Syracuse 1956	+ Corbin, William-Yale 1888
+ Barrett, Charles-Cornell 1915	+ Brown, John, Jr.-Navy 1913	Corbus, William-Stanford . . .1933
+ Baston, Bert-Minnesota 1916	+ Brown, Johnny Mack-Ala . . .1925	Covert, Jimbo-Pittsburgh . . .1983
+ Battles, Cliff-WV Wesleyan . .1931	+ Brown, Tay-USC 1932	+ Cowan, Hector-Princeton 1889
Baugh, Sammy-TCU 1936	Brown, Tom-Minnesota 1960	+ Coy, Edward (Ted)-Yale 1909
Baughan, Maxie-Ga.Tech . . .1959	Browner, Ross-Notre Dame . .1977	+ Crawford, Fred-Duke 1933
+ Bausch, James-Wichita/	Budde, Brad-USC 1979	Crow, John David-Tex.A&M .1957
Kansas 1930	+ Bunker, Paul-Army 1902	+ Crowley, Jim-Notre Dame . . .1924
Beagle, Ron-Navy 1955	Burford, Chris-Stanford 1959	Csonka, Larry-Syracuse 1967
Beasley, Terry-Auburn 1971	+ Burris, Kurt-Oklahoma 1954	Curtis, Tom-Michigan 1969
Beban, Gary-UCLA 1967	Burton, Ron-N'western 1959	+ Cutter, Slade-Navy 1934
Bechtol, Hub-Tex.Tech/Texas 1946	Butkus, Dick-Illinois 1964	+ Czarobski, Ziggie-N.Dame .1947
Beck, Ray-Ga. Tech 1951	Butler, Kevin-Georgia 1984	Dale, Carroll-Va.Tech 1959
+ Beckett, John-Oregon 1916	+ Butler, Robert-Wisconsin 1913	+ Dalrymple, Gerald-Tulane . . .1931
Bednarik, Chuck-Penn 1948	+ Cafego, George-Tenn 1939	+ Dalton, John-Navy 1911
Behm, Forrest-Nebraska 1940	+ Cagle, Red-SWLa/Army 1929	+ Daly, Chas.-Harvard/Army . . .1902
Bell, Bobby-Minnesota 1962	+ Cain, John-Alabama 1932	Daniell, Averell-Pitt 1936
Bell, Ricky-USC 1976	Cameron, Ed-Wash.& Lee . . .1924	+ Daniell, James-Ohio St 1941
Bellino, Joe-Navy 1960	+ Campbell, David-Harvard . . .1901	+ Davies, Tom-Pittsburgh 1921

College Football Hall of Fame (Cont.)

+ Koch, Barton-Baylor 1930
+ Koppisch, Walt-Columbia . . . 1924
   Kramer, Ron-Michigan 1956
   Kroll, Alex-Yale/Rutgers 1961
   Krueger, Charlie-Tex. A&M . . . 1957
   Kutner, Malcolm-Texas 1941
   Kwalick, Ted-Penn St 1968
+ Lach, Steve-Duke 1941
   Lane, Myles-Dartmouth 1927
   Lattner, Johnny-N.Dame 1953
   Lauricella, Hank-Tenn 1951
+ Lautenschlaeger, Les-Tulane . 1925
+ Layden, Elmer-N.Dame 1924
+ Layne, Bobby-Texas 1947
+ Lea, Langdon-Princeton 1895
   Leaks, Roosevelt-Texas 1974
   LeBaron, Eddie-Pacific 1949
+ Leech, James-VMI 1920
+ Lester, Darrell-TCU 1935
   Levias, Jerry-SMU 1968
   Lewis, D.D.-Mississippi State . 1967
   Lilly, Bob-TCU 1960
   Little, Floyd-Syracuse 1966
+ Lio, Augie-Georgetown 1940
+ Locke, Gordon-Iowa 1922
   Long, Chuck-Iowa 1985
   Long, Mel-Toledo 1971
+ Loria, Frank-Virginia Tech . . . 1967
   Lott, Ronnie-USC 1980
+ Lourie, Don-Princeton 1921
   Lucas, Richie-Penn St 1959
+ Luckman, Sid-Columbia 1938
   Lujack, Johnny-N.Dame 1947
+ Lund, Pug-Minnesota 1934
   Lynch, Jim-Notre Dame 1966
   MacAfee, Ken Jr.-N. Dame . . . 1977
+ Macomber, Bart-Illinois 1916
   MacLeod, Robert-Dart. 1938
   Maegle, Dick-Rice 1954
+ Mahan, Eddie-Harvard 1915
   Majors, John-Tennessee 1956
+ Mallory, William-Yale 1923
   Mancha, Vaughn-Ala 1947
   Mandich, Joe-Michigan 1969
+ Mann, Gerald-SMU 1927
   Manning, Archie-Miss 1970
   Manske, Edgar-N'western . . . 1933
   Marinaro, Ed-Cornell 1971
   Marino, Dan-Pittsburgh 1982
+ Markov, Vic-Washington 1937
+ Marshall, Bobby-Minn 1906
   Martin, Jim-Notre Dame 1949
   Matson, Ollie-San-Fran 1951
   Matthews, Ray-TCU 1927
+ Maulbetsch, John-Adrian/
   Mich 1916
+ Mauthe, Pete-Penn St 1912
+ Maxwell,Robert-Chicago/
   Swarthmore 1905
   May, Mark-Pittsburgh 1980
   McAfee, George-Duke 1939
   McCallum, Napoleon-Navy . . 1985
   McCauley, Donald-N. Carolina 1970
+ McClung, Lee-Yale 1891
   McColl, Bill-Stanford 1951
+ McCormick, Jim-Princeton . . . 1907
   McDonald, Tommy-Okla 1956
+ McDowall, Jack-N.C.State . . . 1927
   McElhenny, Hugh-Wash 1951
+ McEver, Gene-Tennessee 1931
+ McEwan, John-Army 1916

+ McFadden, Banks-Clemson . 1939
   McFadin, Bud-Texas 1950
   McGee, Mike-Duke 1959
+ McGinley, Edward-Penn 1924
+ McGovern, John-Minn 1910
   McGraw, Thurman-Colo.St . 1949
+ McKeever, Mike-USC 1960
   McKenzie, Reggie-Michigan . 1971
+ McLaren, George-Pitt 1918
   McMahon, Jim-BYU 1981
+ McMillan, Dan-USC/Calif . . 1921
+ McMillin, Bo-Centre 1921
+ McWhorter, Bob-Georgia . . 1913
+ Mercer, LeRoy-Penn 1912
   Meredith, Don-SMU 1959
   Merritt, Frank-Army 1943
+ Metzger, Bert-N.Dame 1930
+ Meylan, Wayne-Nebraska . . 1967
   Michaels, Lou-Kentucky . . . 1957
   Michels, John-Tennessee . . . 1952
+ Mickal, Abe-LSU 1935
+ Miller, Creighton-N.Dame . . 1943
+ Miller, Don-Notre Dame . . . 1924
+ Miller, Eugene-Penn St 1913
+ Miller, Fred-Notre Dame . . . 1928
   Miller, Rip-Notre Dame 1924
+ Millner, Wayne-N.Dame . . . 1935
+ Milstead, C.A.-Wabash/Yale . 1923
+ Minds, John-Penn 1897
+ Minisi, Skip-Penn/Navy 1947
   Mitchell, Lydell-Penn St. . . . 1971
   Modzelewski, Dick-Md. 1952
+ Moffat, Alex-Princeton 1883
+ Molinski, Ed-Tenn 1940
+ Montgomery, Cliff-Columbia 1933
   Moomaw, Donn-UCLA 1952
+ Morley, William-Columbia . . 1901
   Morris, George-Ga.Tech . . . 1952
   Morris, Larry-Ga.Tech 1954
+ Morton, Bill-Dartmouth 1931
   Morton, Craig-California . . . 1964
+ Moscrip, Monk-Stanford . . . 1935
+ Muller, Brick-California 1922
   Musso, Johnny-Alabama . . . 1971
+ Nagurski, Bronko-Minn 1929
   Neighbors, Billy-Alabama . . 1961
+ Nevers, Ernie-Stanford 1925
+ Newell, Marshall-Harvard . . 1893
+ Newman, Harry-Michigan . . 1932
   Newsome, Ozzie-Alabama . . 1977
   Nielson, Gifford-BYU 1977
   Nobis, Tommy-Texas 1965
   Nomellini, Leo-Minnesota . . 1949
+ Oberlander, Andrew-Dart . . 1925
+ O'Brien, Davey-TCU 1938
+ O'Dea, Pat-Wisconsin 1899
   Odell, Bob-Penn 1943
+ O'Hearn, Jack-Cornell 1914
   Olds, Robin-Army 1942
+ Oliphant, Elmer-Army/Pur . . 1917
   Olsen, Merlin-Utah St 1961
   Onkotz, Dennis-Penn St. . . . 1969
+ Oosterbaan, Bennie-Mich . . 1927
   O'Rourke, Charles-BC 1940
+ Orsi, John-Colgate 1931
+ Osgood, Win-Cornell/Penn . 1894
   Osmanski, Bill-Holy Cross . . 1938
+ Outland, John-Penn. 1899
+ Owen, George-Harvard 1922
   Owens, Jim-Oklahoma 1949
   Owens, Steve-Oklahoma . . . 1969

   Page, Alan-Notre Dame . . . 1966
   Palumbo, Joe-Virginia 1951
+ Pardee, Jack-Texas A&M . . 1956
   Parilli, Babe-Kentucky 1951
   Parker, Ace-Duke 1936
   Parker, Jackie-Miss.St 1953
+ Parker, Jim-Ohio St 1956
+ Pazzetti, Vince-Wesleyan/
   Lehigh 1912
+ Peabody, Chub-Harvard . . . 1941
+ Peck, Robert-Pittsburgh . . . 1916
   Pellegrini, Bob-Maryland . . 1955
+ Pennock, Stan-Harvard 1914
   Pfann, George-Cornell 1923
+ Phillips, H.D.-Sewanee 1905
   Phillips, Loyd-Arkansas 1966
   Phipps, Mike-Purdue 1969
   Pihos, Pete-Indiana 1946
   Pingel, John-Michigan St . . 1938
+ Pinckert, Erny-USC 1931
   Plunkett, Jim-Stanford 1970
+ Poe, Arthur-Princeton 1899
+ Pollard, Fritz-Brown 1916
+ Poole, B.-Miss/NC/Army . . . 1948
   Powell, Marvin-USC 1976
   Pregulman, Merv-Michigan . 1943
+ Price, Eddie-Tulane 1949
   Pritchard, Ron-Arizona St. . . 1968
   Pruitt, Greg-Oklahoma 1972
+ Pund, Peter-Georgia Tech . . 1928
   Ramsey, G.-Wm&Mary 1942
   Rauch, John-Georgia 1948
   Redman, Rick-Wash 1964
+ Reeds, Claude-Oklahoma . . 1913
   Reid, Mike-Penn St 1969
   Reid, Steve-Northwestern . . 1936
+ Reid, William-Harvard 1899
   Reifsnyder, Bob-Navy 1958
   Renfro, Mel-Oregon 1963
+ Rentner, Pug-N'western 1932
   Ressler, Glenn-Penn St. 1964
+ Reynolds, Bob-Stanford . . . 1935
+ Reynolds, Bobby-Nebraska . 1952
   Rhino, Randy-Georgia Tech . 1974
   Rhome, Jerry-SMU/Tulsa . . . 1964
   Richter, Les-California 1951
   Richter, Pat-Wisconsin 1962
+ Riley, Jack-Northwestern . . . 1931
   Rimington, Dave-Nebraska . 1982
+ Rinehart, Chas.-Lafayette . . 1897
   Ritcher, Jim-NC St. 1979
   Roberts, J. D.-Oklahoma . . . 1953
+ Robeson, Paul-Rutgers 1918
   Robinson, Dave-Penn St. . . . 1962
   Robinson, Jerry-UCLA 1978
   Rocker, Tracy-Auburn 1988
+ Rodgers, Ira-West Va 1919
   Rodgers, Johnny-Nebraska . 1972
+ Rogers, Ed-Carlisle/Minn . . 1903
   Rogers, George-S. Carolina . 1980
   Roland, Johnny-Missouri . . . 1965
   Romig, Joe-Colorado 1961
+ Rosenberg, Aaron-USC 1933
+ Rote, Kyle-SMU 1950
+ Routt, Joe-Texas A&M 1937
   Rozier, Mike-Nebraska 1983
+ Salmon, Red-Notre Dame . . 1903
   Sanders, Barry-Okla. St. . . . 1988
   Sarkisian, Alex-Northwestern 1948
+ Sauer, George-Nebraska . . . 1933
   Savitsky, George-Penn 1947

College Football Hall of Fame (Cont.)

Coaches (Cont.)

Small College

Players

Coaches

Small College Coaches (Cont.)

eade, Bob 1998	Raymond, Tubby 2003	Sochor, James 1999
idd, Roy 2003	Reade, Bob 1998	+ Steinke, Gilbert 1996
lausing, Chuck 1998	Robinson, Eddie G. 1997	Strahm, Dick 2004
artinelli, Fred 1993	+ Richard, Charlie 2004	+ Tressel, Lee 1996
udra, Darrell 2000	Rutschman, Ad 1998	Waters, Frank 2000
umford, Ace 2001	+ Schipper, Ron 2000	Westering, Frosty 2005
licks, Billy 1999	Sherman, Edgar 1996	

Pro Football Hall of Fame

tablished in 1963 by National Football League to commemorate the sport's professional origins. **Address:** 2121 George
as Drive NW, Canton, OH 44708. **Telephone:** (330) 456-8207. **Web:** www.profootballhof.com

ligibility: Nominated players must be retired five years, coaches can still be active. Vot-
done by 39-member panel made up of media representatives from all 31 NFL cities (two from New York), one PFWA rep-
ntative and six selectors-at-large.

lass of 2006 (6): PLAYERS—QB **Troy Aikman**, Dallas Cowboys (1989-2000); LB **Harry Carson**, NY Giants (1976-
QB **Warren Moon**, Houston Oilers (1984-93), Minnesota Vikings (1994-96), Seattle Seahawks (1997-98), Kanasa City
efs (1999-2000); DE/DT **Reggie White**, Phiadelphia Eagles (1985-92), Green Bay Packers (1993-98), Carolina Pan-
s (2000); T **Rayfield Wright**, Dallas Cowboys (1967-79). COACHES—**John Madden**, Oakland Raiders (1969-78).

Quarterbacks

aikman, Troy 2006	+ Graham, Otto 1965	Parker, Clarence (Ace) 1972
augh, Sammy 1963	Griese, Bob 1990	Starr, Bart 1977
lanta, George (also PK) . .1981	+ Herber, Arnie 1966	Staubach, Roger 1985
radshaw, Terry 1989	Jurgensen, Sonny 1983	Tarkenton, Fran 1986
lark, Dutch 1963	Kelly, Jim 2002	Tittle, Y.A 1971
onzelman, Jimmy 1964	+ Layne, Bobby 1967	+ Unitas, Johnny 1979
awson, Len 1987	+ Luckman, Sid 1965	+ Van Brocklin, Norm 1971
riscoll, Paddy 1965	Marino, Dan 2005	+ Waterfield, Bob 1965
lway, John 2004	Montana, Joe 2000	Young, Steve 2005
outs, Dan 1993	Moon, Warren 2006	
riedman, Benny 2005	Namath, Joe 1985	

Running Backs

allen, Marcus 2003	+ Hinkle, Clarke 1964	+ Payton, Walter 1993
attles, Cliff 1968	Hornung, Paul 1986	Perry, Joe 1969
rown, Jim 1971	Johnson, John Henry 1987	+ Pollard, Fritz 2005
ampbell, Earl 1991	Kelly, Leroy 1994	Riggins, John 1992
anadeo, Tony 1974	+ Leemans, Tuffy 1978	Sanders, Barry 2004
sonka, Larry 1987	Matson, Ollie 1972	Sayers, Gale 1977
ickerson, Eric 1999	McAfee, George 1966	Simpson, O.J 1985
orsett, Tony 1994	McElhenny, Hugh 1970	+ Strong, Ken 1967
udley, Bill 1966	+ McNally, Johnny (Blood) . .1963	Taylor, Jim 1976
ifford, Frank 1977	Moore, Lenny 1975	+ Thorpe, Jim 1963
range, Red 1963	+ Motley, Marion 1968	Trippi, Charley 1968
uyon, Joe 1966	+ Nagurski, Bronko 1963	Van Buren, Steve 1965
arris, Franco 1990	+ Nevers, Ernie 1963	+ Walker, Doak 1986

Ends & Wide Receivers

lworth, Lance 1978	+ Hutson, Don 1963	Newsome, Ozzie 1999
adgro, Red 1981	Joiner, Charlie 1996	Pihos, Pete 1970
erry, Raymond 1973	Largent, Steve 1995	Smith, Jackie 1994
iletnikoff, Fred 1988	Lavelli, Dante 1975	Stallworth, John 2002
asper, Dave 2002	Lofton, James 2003	Swann, Lynn 2001
hamberlin, Guy 1965	Mackey, John 1992	Taylor, Charley 1984
itka, Mike 1988	Maynard, Don 1987	Warfield, Paul 1983
ears, Tom 1970	McDonald, Tommy 1998	Winslow, Kellen 1995
ewitt, Bill 1971	+ Millner, Wayne 1968	
irsch, Elroy (Crazylegs) . .1968	Mitchell, Bobby 1983	

Offensive Linemen

ednarik, Chuck (C-LB) 1967	Little, Larry (G) 1993	Shaw, Billy (G) 1999
rown, Bob (T) 2004	Mack, Tom (G) 1999	Shell, Art (T) 1989
rown, Roosevelt (T) 1975	McCormack, Mike (T) 1984	Slater, Jackie (T) 2001
eLamielleure, Joe (G) 2003	Mix, Ron (T-G) 1979	Stephenson, Dwight (C) 1998
ierdorf, Dan (T) 1996	Munchak, Mike (G) 2001	Upshaw, Gene (G) 1987
atski, Frank (C) 1985	Munoz, Anthony (T) 1998	Yary, Ron (T) 2001
regg, Forrest (T-G) 1977	+ Musso, George (T-G) 1982	+ Webster, Mike (C) 1997
roza, Lou (T-PK) 1974	Otto, Jim (C) 1980	Wright, Rayfield (T) 2006
annah, John (G) 1991	Parker, Jim (G) 1973	
ones, Stan (T-G-DT) 1991	Ringo, Jim (C) 1981	
anger, Jim (C) 1987	St. Clair, Bob (T) 1990	

Linemen (pre-World War II)

+ Edwards, Turk (T) 1969	+ Hubbard, Cal (T) 1963	+ Musso, George (T-G) 1
+ Fortmann, Dan (G) 1985	+ Kiesling, Walt (G) 1966	+ Stydahar, Joe (T) 1
+ Healey, Ed (T) 1964	+ Kinard, Bruiser (T) 1971	+ Trafton, George (C) 1
+ Hein, Mel (C) 1963	+ Lyman, Link (T) 1964	+ Turner, Bulldog (C) 1
+ Henry, Pete (T) 1963	+ Michalske, Mike (G) 1964	+ Wojciechowicz, Alex (C) . .1

Defensive Linemen

Atkins, Doug 1982	Hampton, Dan 2002	Robustelli, Andy 1
Bethea, Elvin 2003	Jones, Deacon 1980	Selmon, Lee Roy 1
+ Buchanan, Buck 1990	+ Jordan, Henry 1995	Stautner, Ernie 1
Creekmur, Lou 1996	Lilly, Bob 1980	+ Weinmeister, Arnie 1
Davis, Willie 1981	Long, Howie 2000	White, Randy 1
Donovan, Art 1968	Marchetti, Gino 1972	+ White, Reggie 2
Eller, Carl 2004	+ Nomellini, Leo 1969	Willis, Bill 1
+ Ford, Len 1976	Olsen, Merlin 1982	Youngblood, Jack 2
Greene, Joe 1987	Page, Alan 1988	

Linebackers

Bell, Bobby 1983	Ham, Jack 1988	Schmidt, Joe 1
Buoniconti, Nick 2001	Hendricks, Ted 1990	Singletary, Mike 1
Butkus, Dick 1979	Huff, Sam 1982	Taylor, Lawrence 1
Carson, Harry 2006	Lambert, Jack 1990	Wilcox, Dave 2
Connor, George (DT-OT) . . .1975	Lanier, Willie 1986	
+ George, Bill 1974	+ Nitschke, Ray 1978	

Defensive Backs

Adderley, Herb 1980	Houston, Ken 1986	Renfro, Mel 1
Barney, Lem 1992	Johnson, Jimmy 1994	+ Tunnell, Emlen 1
Blount, Mel 1989	Krause, Paul 1998	Wilson, Larry 1
Brown, Willie 1984	+ Lane, Dick (Night Train) . . .1974	Wood, Willie 1
+ Christiansen, Jack 1970	Lary, Yale 1979	
Haynes, Michael 1997	Lott, Ronnie 2000	

Placekicker

Stenerud, Jan 1

Coaches

+ Allen, George 2002	+ Halas, George 1963	Noll, Chuck 1
+ Brown, Paul 1967	+ Lambeau, Curly 1963	+ Owen, Steve 1
+ Ewbank, Weeb 1978	+ Landry, Tom 1990	Shula, Don 1
+ Flaherty, Ray 1976	Levy, Marv 2001	Stram, Hank 2
Gibbs, Joe 1996	+ Lombardi, Vince 1971	Walsh, Bill 1
Gillman, Sid 1983	Madden, John 2006	
Grant, Bud 1994	+ Neale, Earle (Greasy) 1969	

Contributors

+ Bell, Bert 1963	Hunt, Lamar 1972	+ Rooney, Art 1
+ Bidwill, Charles 1967	+ Mara, Tim 1963	Rooney, Dan 2
+ Carr, Joe 1963	Mara, Wellington 1997	+ Rozelle, Pete 1
Davis, Al 1992	+ Marshall, George 1963	Schramm, Tex 1
+ Finks, Jim 1995	+ Ray, Hugh (Shorty) 1966	
+ Halas, George 1963	+ Reeves, Dan 1967	

NFL's All-Time Team

Selected by the Pro Football Hall of Fame voters and released Aug. 1, 2000 as part of the NFL Century celebration

Offense	Defense
Wide Receivers: Don Hutson and Jerry Rice	**Ends:** Deacon Jones and Reggie White
Tight End: John Mackey	**Tackles:** Joe Greene and Bob Lilly
Tackles: Roosevelt Brown and Anthony Munoz	**Linebackers:** Dick Butkus, Jack Ham
Guards: John Hannah and Jim Parker	and Lawrence Taylor
Center: Mike Webster	**Cornerbacks:** Mel Blount
Quarterback: Johnny Unitas	and Dick (Night Train) Lane
Running Backs: Jim Brown and Walter Payton	**Safeties:** Ronnie Lott and Larry Wilson

Specialists

Placekicker: Jan Stenerud	**Punt Returner:** Deion Sanders
Punter: Ray Guy	**Special Teams:** Steve Tasker
Kick Returner: Gale Sayers	

GOLF

World Golf Hall of Fame

e World Golf Hall of Fame opened its doors in 1998 at the World Golf Village outside of Jacksonville, Fla. **Address:** One orld Golf Place, St. Augustine, FL 32092. **Telephone:** (904) 940-4000. **Web:** www.wghof.com/hof/hof.php **Eligibility:** ofessionals have three avenues into the WGHF. A PGA Tour player qualifies for the ballot if he has at least 10 victories in proved tournaments, or at least two victories among The Players Championship, Masters, U.S. Open, British Open and PGA ampionship, is at least 40 years old and has been a member of the Tour for 10 years. A senior PGA Tour player qualifies e has been a Senior Tour member for five years and has 20 wins between the PGA Tour and Senior Tour or five wins among e PGA majors, the Players Championship and the senior majors (U.S. Senior Open, Tradition, PGA Seniors' Championship d Senior Players Championship). Final selections for both Veteran's (for players who played bulk of their career before 974) and Lifetime Achievement Categories are made by the Executive Committee of the World Golf Hall of Fame, which cludes leaders from the major golf organizations.

Any player qualifying for the LPGA Hall automatically qualifies for the WGHF. Until 1999, nominees must have had played years on the LPGA tour and won 30 official events, including two major championships; 35 official events and one major; 40 official events and no majors. The eligibility requirements were loosened somewhat in 1999. The new guidelines are sed on a system which awards two points for winning a major and one point for winning other tournaments, the Vare troy (for lowest scoring average) and the player of the year award. Players must win at least one major, Vare trophy, or play- of the year award and accumulate a total of 27 points to be inducted. For players not eligible for either the PGA Tour or LPGA Hall of Fame, a body of over 300 international golf writers and historians will vote each year.

Members are listed with year of induction; (+) indicates deceased members.

Class of 2006 (5): MEN—**Larry Nelson**, **Henry Picard** and **Vijay Singh***. WOMEN—**Marilynn Smith**; CON-BUTORS—**Mark McCormack**.

*Vijay Singh was elected in 2005 but deferred his induction due to a scheduling conflict.

Men

Anderson, Willie 1975	Floyd, Ray 1989	Norman, Greg 2001
Aoki, Isao 2004	+ Guldahl, Ralph 1981	+ Ouimet, Francis 1974
Armour, Tommy 1976	+ Hagen, Walter 1974	Palmer, Arnold 1974
Ball, John, Jr 1977	+ Hilton, Harold 1978	+ Park, Willie Sr 2005
Ballesteros, Seve 1999	+ Hogan, Ben 1974	+ Picard, Henry 2006
Barnes, Jim 1989	Irwin, Hale 1992	Player, Gary 1974
Beman, Deane 2000	Jacklin, Tony 2002	Price, Nick 2003
Bolt, Tommy 2002	Jacobs, John 2000	+ Robertson, Allan 2001
Bonallack, Sir Michael 2000	+ Jones, Bobby 1974	+ Runyan, Paul 1990
Boros, Julius 1982	Kite, Tom 2004	+ Sarazen, Gene 1974
Braid, James 1976	Langer, Bernhard 2002	Sifford, Charlie 2004
Burke, Jack Jr. 2000	+ Little, Lawson 1980	Singh, Vijay 2006
Casper, Billy 1978	Littler, Gene 1990	+ Smith, Horton 1990
Coles, Neil 2000	+ Locke, Bobby 1977	+ Snead, Sam 1974
Cooper, Lighthorse Harry ..1992	+ Mangrum, Lloyd 1998	Stewart, Payne 2001
Cotton, Sir Henry 1980	+ Middlecoff, Cary 1986	+ Taylor, John H 1975
Crenshaw, Ben 2002	Miller, Johnny 1996	Thomson, Peter 1988
Demaret, Jimmy 1983	+ Morris, Tom Jr 1975	+ Travers, Jerry 1976
De Vicenzo, Roberto 1989	+ Morris, Tom Sr 1976	+ Travis, Walter 1979
Diegel, Leo 2003	+ Nelson, Byron 1974	Trevino, Lee 1981
Evans, Chick 1975	Nelson, Larry 2006	+ Vardon, Harry 1974
Faldo, Nick 1997	Nicklaus, Jack 1974	Watson, Tom 1988

Women

Alcott, Amy 1999	Inkster, Julie 2000	Sorenstam, Annika 2003
Berg, Patty 1974	Jameson, Betty 1951	Streit, Marlene Stewart 2004
Bradley, Pat 1986	King, Betsy 1995	Suggs, Louise 1979
Carner, JoAnne 1985	Lopez, Nancy 1989	+ Vare, Glenna Collett 1975
Caponi, Donna 2001	Mann, Carol 1977	Webb, Karrie 2005
Danjel, Beth 1999	Okamoto, Ayako 2005	+ Wethered, Joyce 1975
Hagge, Marlene 2002	Rankin, Judy 2000	Whitworth, Kathy 1982
Haynie, Sandra 1977	Rawls, Betsy 1987	Wright, Mickey 1976
Higuchi, Chako 2003	Sheehan, Patty 1993	+ Zaharias, Babe Didrikson ..1974
Howe, Dorothy C.H 1978	Smith, Marilynn 2006	

Contributors

Bell, Judy 2001	+ Harlow, Robert 1988	Rodriguez, Chi Chi 1992
Campbell, William 1990	+ Hope, Bob 1983	+ Ross, Donald 1977
Corcoran, Fred 1975	+ Jones, Robert Trent 1987	+ Solheim, Karsten 2001
Crosby, Bing 1978	+ MacKenzie, Alister 2005	+ Shore, Dinah 1994
Darwin, Bernard 2005	McCormack, Mark 2006	+ Tufts, Richard 1992
Dey, Joe 1975	+ Penick, Harvey 2002	
Graffis, Herb 1977	+ Roberts, Clifford 1978	

HOCKEY

Hockey Hall of Fame

Established in 1945 by the National Hockey League and opened in 1961. **Address:** BCE Place, 30 Yonge Street, Toront
Ontario, M5E 1X8. **Telephone:** (416) 360-7735. **Web:** www.hhof.com

Eligibility: Nominated players and referees must be retired three years. However that waiting period has now been waive
10 times. Players that have had the waiting period waived are indicated with an asterisk. Voting done by 18-member par
made up of pro and amateur hockey personalities and media representatives. A 15-member Veterans Committee that selecte
older players was eliminated in 2000.

Class of 2006 (4): PLAYERS—G **Patrick Roy**, Montreal Canadiens (1985-,96), Colorado Avalanche (1996-2003); **Te**
rance "Dick" Duff, Toronto Maple Leafs (1954-64), New York Rangers (1963-65), Montreal Canadiens (1965-1970), L
Angeles Kings (1969-71), Buffalo Sabres (1970-72). BUILDERS—**Herb Brooks**, coach; **Harley Hotchkiss**, owner.

Members are listed with year of induction; (+) indicates deceased members.

Forwards

+ Abel, Sid 1969	+ Gardner, Jimmy 1962	Neely, Cam ....200?
+ Adams, Jack 1959	Gartner, Mike 2001	+ Nighbor, Frank ....194?
+ Apps, Syl 1961	+ Geoffrion, Bernie 1972	+ Noble, Reg 1962
Armstrong, George 1975	+ Gerard, Eddie 1945	+ O'Connor, Buddy ......198?
+ Bailey, Ace 1975	Gilbert, Rod 1982	+ Oliver, Harry ....196?
+ Bain, Dan 1945	Gillies, Clark 2002	Olmstead, Bert ....198?
+ Baker, Hobey 1945	+ Gilmour, Billy 1962	+ Patrick, Lynn ....198?
Barber, Bill 1990	Goulet, Michel 1998	Perreault, Gilbert ....199?
+ Barry, Marty 1965	Gretzky, Wayne* 1999	+ Phillips, Tom ....194?
Bathgate, Andy 1978	+ Griffis, Si 1950	+ Primeau, Joe ....196?
+ Bauer, Bobby 1996	Hawerchuk, Dale 2001	Pulford, Bob ....199?
Beliveau, Jean* 1972	+ Hay, George 1958	+ Rankin, Frank ....196?
+ Bentley, Doug 1964	+ Hextall, Bryan 1969	Ratelle, Jean ....198?
+ Bentley, Max 1966	+ Hooper, Tom 1962	Richard, Henri ....197?
+ Blake, Toe 1966	+ Howe, Gordie* 1972	+ Richard, Maurice (Rocket)* .196?
Bossy, Mike 1991	+ Howe, Syd 1965	+ Richardson, George ...1950
+ Boucher, Frank 1958	Hull, Bobby 1983	+ Roberts, Gordie ......197?
+ Bowie, Dubbie 1945	+ Hyland, Harry 1962	+ Russel, Blair ....196?
+ Broadbent, Punch 1962	+ Irvin, Dick 1958	+ Russell, Ernie ....196?
Bucyk, John (Chief) ...1981	+ Jackson, Busher 1971	+ Ruttan, Jack 1962
+ Burch, Billy 1974	+ Joliat, Aurel 1947	Savard, Denis ....200?
Clarke, Bobby 1987	+ Keats, Duke 1958	+ Scanlan, Fred ....196?
+ Colville, Neil 1967	Kennedy, Ted (Teeder) ..1966	Schmidt, Milt ....196?
+ Conacher, Charlie ...1961	Keon, Dave 1986	+ Schriner, Sweeney 1962
Conacher, Roy 1998	+ Kharlamov, Valeri 2005	+ Seibert, Oliver ......196?
+ Cook, Bill 1952	Kurri, Jari 2001	Shutt, Steve ....199?
+ Cook, Bun 1995	Lach, Elmer 1966	+ Siebert, Babe ....196?
Cournoyer, Yvan 1982	Lafleur, Guy 1988	Sittler, Darryl ....198?
+ Cowley, Bill 1968	LaFontaine, Pat 2003	+ Smith, Alf 1962
+ Crawford, Rusty 1962	+ Lalonde, Newsy 1950	Smith, Clint ....199?
+ Darragh, Jack 1962	Laprade, Edgar 1993	+ Smith, Hooley ....197?
+ Davidson, Scotty 1950	Lemaire, Jacques 1984	+ Smith, Tommy ....197?
+ Day, Hap 1961	Lemieux, Mario* 1997	+ Stanley, Barney 1962
Delvecchio, Alex 1977	+ Lewis, Herbie 1989	Stastny, Peter ....199?
+ Denneny, Cy 1959	Lindsay, Ted* 1966	+ Stewart, Nels 1962
Dionne, Marcel 1992	+ MacKay, Mickey 1952	+ Stuart, Bruce ....196?
+ Drillon, Gordie 1975	Mahovlich, Frank 1981	+ Taylor, Fred (Cyclone) ...194?
+ Drinkwater, Graham ..1950	+ Malone, Joe 1950	+ Trihey, Harry ....195?
Duff, Dick 2006	+ Marshall, Jack 1965	Trottier, Bryan ....199?
Dumart, Woody 1992	+ Maxwell, Fred 1962	Ullman, Norm ....198?
+ Dunderdale, Tommy ...1974	McDonald, Lanny 1992	+ Walker, Jack ....196?
+ Dye, Babe 1970	+ McGee, Frank 1945	+ Walsh, Marty ....196?
Esposito, Phil 1984	+ McGimsie, Billy 1962	+ Watson, Harry (Whipper) .199?
+ Farrell, Arthur 1965	Mikita, Stan 1983	+ Watson, Harry (Moose) ...196?
Federko, Bernie 2002	Moore, Dickie 1974	+ Weiland, Cooney ......197?
+ Foyston, Frank 1958	+ Morenz, Howie 1945	+ Westwick, Harry (Rat) ...196?
+ Frederickson, Frank ..1958	+ Mosienko, Bill 1965	+ Whitcroft, Fred ......196?
Gainey, Bob 1992	Mullen, Joe 2000	

Referees & Linesmen

Armstrong, Neil 1991	+ Hayes, George 1988	+ Smeaton, J. Cooper ...196?
Ashley, John 1981	+ Hewitson, Bobby 1963	Storey, Red ....196?
Chadwick, Bill 1964	+ Ion, Mickey 1961	Udvari, Frank ....197?
D'Amico, John 1993	Pavelich, Matt 1987	van Hellemond, Andy ...199?
+ Elliott, Chaucer 1961	+ Rodden, Mike 1962	

Goaltenders

+ Benedict, Clint 1965	Giacomin, Eddie 1987	+ Plante, Jacques 1978
+ Bower, Johnny 1976	+ Hainsworth, George 1961	+ Rayner, Chuck 1973
+ Brimsek, Frankie 1966	Hall, Glenn 1975	Roy, Patrick 2006
+ Broda, Turk 1967	+ Hern, Riley 1962	+ Sawchuk, Terry* 1971
Cheevers, Gerry 1985	+ Holmes, Hap 1972	Smith, Billy 1993
Connell, Alex 1958	+ Hutton, J.B. (Bouse) 1962	+ Thompson, Tiny 1959
Dryden, Ken 1983	+ Lehman, Hughie 1958	Tretiak, Vladislav 1989
+ Durnan, Bill 1964	+ LeSueur, Percy 1961	+ Vezina, Georges 1945
Esposito, Tony 1988	· Lumley, Harry 1980	Worsley, Gump 1980
Fuhr, Grant 2003	+ Moran, Paddy 1958	+ Worters, Roy 1969
+ Gardiner, Chuck 1945	Parent, Bernie 1984	

Defensemen

Boivin, Leo 1986	+ Green, Wilf (Shorty) 1962	Pilote, Pierre 1975
+ Boon, Dickie 1952	+ Hall, Joe 1961	+ Pitre, Didier 1962
+ Bouchard, Butch 1966	+ Harvey, Doug 1973	Potvin, Denis 1991
+ Boucher, George 1960	Horner, Red 1965	+ Pratt, Babe 1966
Bourque, Ray 2004	+ Horton, Tim 1977	Pronovost, Marcel 1978
+ Cameron, Harry 1962	Howell, Harry 1979	+ Pulford, Harvey 1945
Clancy, King 1958	+ Johnson, Ching 1958	+ Quackenbush, Bill 1976
+ Clapper, Dit* 1947	+ Johnson, Ernie 1952	Reardon, Kenny 1966
Cleghorn, Sprague 1958	Johnson, Tom 1970	Robinson, Larry 1995
Coffey, Paul 2004	Kelly, Red* 1969	+ Ross, Art 1945
+ Conacher, Lionel 1994	Langway, Rod 2002	Salming, Borje 1996
+ Coulter, Art 1974	+ Laperriere, Jacques 1987	Savard, Serge 1986
+ Dutton, Red 1958	Lapointe, Guy 1993	+ Seibert, Earl 1963
Fetisov, Viacheslav 2001	+ Laviolette, Jack 1962	+ Shore, Eddie 1947
Flaman, Fernie 1990	+ Mantha, Sylvio 1960	+ Simpson, Joe 1962
Gadsby, Bill 1970	+ McNamara, George 1958	Stanley, Allan 1981
+ Gardiner, Herb 1958	Murphy, Larry 2004	+ Stewart, Jack 1964
+ Goheen, F.X. (Moose) 1952	Orr, Bobby* 1979	+ Stuart, Hod 1945
+ Goodfellow, Ebbie 1963	Park, Brad 1988	+ Wilson, Gordon (Phat) 1962
+ Grant, Mike 1950	+ Patrick, Lester 1947	

Builders

+ Adams, Charles 1960	+ Hewitt, Foster 1965	+ Patrick, Frank 1958
+ Adams, Weston W. Sr 1972	+ Hewitt, W.A 1945	+ Pickard, Allan 1958
+ Ahearn, Frank 1962	Hotchkiss, Harley 2006	+ Pilous, Rudy 1985
+ Ahearne, J.F. (Bunny) 1977	+ Hume, Fred 1962	Poile, Bud 1990
+ Allan, Sir Montagu 1945	Ilitch, Mike 2003	Pollock, Sam 1978
Allen, Keith 1992	+ Imlach, Punch 1984	+ Raymond, Donat 1958
Arbour, Al 1996	+ Ivan, Tommy 1964	+ Robertson, John Ross 1945
+ Ballard, Harold 1977	+ Jennings, Bill 1975	+ Robinson, Claude 1945
+ Bauer, Fr. David 1989	+ Johnson, Bob 1992	+ Ross, Philip 1976
+ Bickell, J.P. 1978	+ Juckes, Gordon 1979	+ Sabetzki, Gunther 1995
Bowman, Scotty 1991	+ Kilpatrick, John 1960	Sather, Glen 1997
+ Brooks, Herb 2006	Kilrea, Brian 2003	+ Selke, Frank 1960
+ Brown, George 1961	+ Knox, Seymour III 1993	Sinden, Harry 1983
+ Brown, Walter 1962	+ Leader, Al 1969	+ Smith, Frank 1962
+ Buckland, Frank 1975	+ LeBel, Bob 1970	+ Smythe, Conn 1958
Bush, Walter 2000	+ Lockhart, Tom 1965	Snider, Ed 1988
Butterfield, Jack 1980	+ Loicq, Paul 1961	+ Stanley, Lord of Preston . . .1945
+ Calder, Frank 1945	+ Mariucci, John 1985	+ Sutherland, James 1945
+ Campbell, Angus 1964	Mathers, Frank 1992	+ Tarasov, Anatoli 1974
+ Campbell, Clarence 1966	+ McLaughlin, Frederic 1963	Torrey, Bill 1995
+ Cattarinich, Joseph 1977	+ Milford, Jake 1984	+ Turner, Lloyd 1958
Costello, Murray 2005	+ Molson, Hartland 1973	+ Tutt, William Thayer 1978
+ Dandurand, Leo 1963	Morrison, Ian (Scotty) 1999	+ Voss, Carl 1974
+ Dilio, Frank 1964	+ Murray, Athol (Pere) 1998	+ Waghorne, Fred 1961
+ Dudley, George 1958	+ Nelson, Francis 1945	+ Wirtz, Arthur 1971
+ Dunn, James 1968	+ Neilson, Roger 2002	Wirtz, Bill 1976
Fletcher, Cliff 2004	+ Norris, Bruce 1969	Ziegler, John 1987
+ Francis, Emile 1982	+ Norris, James D 1962	
+ Gibson, Jack 1976	+ Norris, James Sr 1958	**Note:** Alan Eagleson was inducted
+ Gorman, Tommy 1963	+ Northey, William 1945	into the Hockey Hall of Fame in 1989
+ Griffiths, Frank A. 1993	+ O'Brien, J.A 1962	but resigned in 1998 after being found
+ Hanley, Bill 1986	O'Neill, Brian 1994	guilty of fraud.
+ Hay, Charles 1984	Page, Fred 1993	
+ Hendy, Jim 1968	Patrick, Craig 2001	

U.S. Hockey Hall of Fame

Established in 1968 by the Eveleth (Minn.) Civic Association Project H Committee and opened in 1973. **Address:** 801 Hat Trick Ave., P.O. Box 657, Eveleth, MN 55734. **Telephone:** (218) 744-5167. **Web:** www.ushockeyhall.com

Eligibility: Nominated players and referees must be American-born and retired five years; coaches must be American-born and must have coached predominantly American teams. Voting done by 12-member panel made up of Hall of Fame members and U.S. hockey officials.

Class of 2005 (4): PLAYERS—**Keith Christiansen, Lane MacDonald, Maurice "Moe" Roberts** and **Murray Williamson**.

Members are listed with year of induction; (+) indicates deceased members.

Players

+ Abel, Clarence (Taffy) 1973	Fusco, Mark 2002	Mayasich, John 1976
+ Baker, Hobey 1973	Fusco, Scott 2002	McCartan, Jack 1983
Bartholome, Earl 1977	+ Garrison, John 1974	Moe, Bill 1974
+ Bessone, Peter 1978	Garrity, Jack 1986	Morrow, Ken 1995
Blake, Bob 1985	+ Goheen, Frank (Moose) . . .1973	+ Moseley, Fred 1975
Boucha, Henry 1995	Grant, Wally 1994	Mullen, Joe 1998
+ Brimsek, Frankie 1973	+ Harding, Austie 1975	+ Murray, Hugh (Muzz) Sr . . .1987
Broten, Neal 2000	Housley, Phil 2004	+ Nelson, Hub 1978
Cavanagh, Joe 1994	Howe, Mark 2003	+ Nyrop, William D. 1997
+ Chaisson, Ray 1974	Iglehart, Stewart 1975	Olson, Eddie 1977
Chase, John 1973	Ikola, Willard 1990	+ Owen, George 1973
Christian, Bill 1984	Johnson, Mark 2004	+ Palmer, Winthrop 1973
Christian, Dave 2001	Johnson, Paul 2001	Paradise, Bob 1989
Christian, Roger 1989	Johnson, Virgil 1974	+ Purpur, Clifford (Fido) 1974
Christiansen, Keith 2005	+ Karakas, Mike 1973	Ramsey, Mike 2001
Cleary, Bill 1976	Kirrane, Jack 1987	Riley, Bill 1977
Cleary, Bob 1981	LaFontaine, Pat 2003	Riley, Joe 2002
+ Conroy, Tony 1975	+ Lane, Myles 1973	+ Roberts, Maurice 2005
Coppo, Paul 2004	Langevin, Dave 1993	+ Romnes, Elwin (Doc) 1973
Curran, Mike 1998	Langway, Rod 1999	+ Rondeau, Dick 1985
+ Dahlstrom, Carl (Cully) 1973	Larson, Reed 1996	Sheehy, Timothy 1997
+ Desjardins, Vic 1974	+ Linder, Joe 1975	Watson, Gordie 1999
+ Desmond, Richard 1988	+ LoPresti, Sam 1973	+ Williams, Tom 1981
Dill, Bob 1979	MacDonald, Lane 2005	Williamson, Murray 2005
Dougherty, Richard 2003	+ Mariucci, John 1973	+ Winters, Frank (Coddy) . . .1973
+ Everett, Doug 1974	Matchefts, John 1991	+ Yackel, Ken 1986
Ftorek, Robbie 1991	+ Mather, Bruce 1998	

Coaches

+ Almquist, Oscar 1983	Heyliger, Vic 1974	Pleban, Connie 1990
Bessone, Amo 1992	+ Holt Jr., Charles E. 1997	Ramsay, Mike 2001
+ Brooks, Herb 1990	Ikola, Willard 1990	Riley, Jack 1979
Ceglarski, Len 1992	+ Jeremiah, Eddie 1973	+ Ross, Larry 1988
+ Cunniff, John 2003	+ Johnson, Bob 1991	+ Thompson, Cliff 1973
+ Fullerton, James 1992	Johnson, Paul 2001	+ Stewart, Bill 1982
Gambucci, Sergio 1996	Kelley, Jack 1993	Watson, Sid 1999
+ Gordon, Malcolm 1973	+ Kelly, John (Snooks) 1974	+ Winsor, Ralph 1973
Harkness, Ned 1994	Nanne, Lou 1998	Woog, Doug 2002

Referee   ## Contributor

Chadwick, Bill 1974   + Schulz, Charles M. 1993

Administrators

+ Brown, George 1973	+ Jennings, Bill 1981	Ridder, Bob 1976
+ Brown, Walter 1973	+ Kahler, Nick 1980	Trumble, Hal 1970
Bush, Walter 1980	+ Lockhart, Tom 1973	+ Tutt, Thayer 1973
+ Clark, Don 1978	Marvin, Cal 1982	Wirtz, Bill 1967
Claypool, Jim 1995	Palazzari, Doug 2000	+ Wright, Lyle 1973
+ Gibson, J.L. (Doc) 1973	Patrick, Craig 1996	
Ilitch, Mike 2004	Pleau, Larry 2000	

Members of Both Hockey and U.S. Hockey Halls of Fame

Players	**Coaches**		**Builders**
Hobey Baker	Bob Johnson	George Brown	Bill Jennings
Frankie Brimsek	Herb Brooks	Walter Brown	Tom Lockhart
Frank (Moose) Goheen		Walter Bush	Craig Patrick
Rod Langway	**Referee**	Doc Gibson	Thayer Tutt
Pat LaFontaine	Bill Chadwick	Mike Ilitch	Bill Wirtz
John Mariucci			
Joe Mullen			

HORSE RACING

National Museum of Racing and Hall of Fame

Established in 1950 by the Saratoga Springs Racing Association and opened in 1955. **Address:** National Museum of Racing and Hall of Fame, 191 Union Ave., Saratoga Springs, NY 12866. **Telephone:** (518) 584-0400. **Web:** www.racingmuseum.org

Eligibility: Nominated horses must be retired five years; jockeys must be active at least 15 years; trainers must be active at least 25 years. Voting done by 125-member panel of horse racing media.

Class of 2006 (3): JOCKEY—**Bill Boland**. TRAINER—**Carl Hanford**. HORSES—**Cougar II**.

Members are listed with year of induction; (+) indicates deceased members.

Jockeys

+ Adams, Frank (Dooley)* . . . 1970	Fishback, Jerry* 1992	+ Patrick, Gil 1970
+ Adams, John 1965	+ Garner, Andrew (Mack) 1969	Pincay, Laffit Jr. 1975
+ Aitcheson, Joe Jr.* 1978	+ Garrison, Snapper 1955	+ Purdy, Sam 1970
+ Arcaro, Eddie 1958	+ Gomez, Avelino 1982	+ Reiff, John 1956
Atkinson, Ted 1957	+ Griffin, Henry 1956	+ Robertson, Alfred 1971
Baeza, Braulio 1976	+ Guerin, Eric 1972	Rotz, John L. 1983
Bailey, Jerry 1995	Hartack, Bill 1959	+ Sande, Earl 1955
+ Barbee, George 1996	Hawley, Sandy 1992	+ Shilling, Carroll 1970
+ Bassett, Carroll* 1972	+ Johnson, Albert 1971	+ Shoemaker, Bill 1958
Baze, Russell 1999	Krone, Julie 2000	+ Simms, Willie 1977
+ Blum, Walter 1987	+ Knapp, Willie 1969	+ Sloan, Todhunter 1955
Boland, Bill 2006	+ Kummer, Clarence 1972	Smith, Mike 2003
+ Bostwick, George H.* 1968	+ Kurtsinger, Charley 1967	+ Smithwick, A. Patrick* 1973
+ Boulmetis, Sam 1973	+ Loftus, Johnny 1959	Stevens, Gary 1997
+ Brooks, Steve 1963	Longden, Johnny 1958	+ Stout, James 1968
Brumfield, Don 1996	Maher, Danny 1955	+ Taral, Fred 1955
+ Burns, Tommy 1983	+ McAtee, Linus 1956	+ Tuckerman, Bayard Jr.* . . . 1973
+ Butwell, Jimmy 1984	McCarron, Chris 1989	Turcotte, Ron 1979
+ Byers, J.D. (Dolly) 1967	+ McCreary, Conn 1975	+ Turner, Nash 1955
Cauthen, Steve 1994	+ McKinney, Rigan 1968	Ussery, Robert 1980
+ Coltiletti, Frank 1970	+ McLaughlin, James 1955	Vasquez, Jacinto 1998
Cordero, Angel Jr. 1988	+ Miller, Walter 1955	Velasquez, Jorge 1990
+ Crawford, Robert (Specs)* . . 1973	+ Murphy, Isaac 1955	Walsh, Thomas* 2005
Day, Pat 1991	+ Neves, Ralph 1960	+ Westrope, Jack 2002
Delahoussaye, Eddie 1993	+ Notter, Joe 1963	+ Woolf, George 1955
Desormeaux, Kent 2004	+ O'Connor, Winnie 1956	+ Workman, Raymond 1956
+ Ensor, Lavelle (Buddy) 1962	+ Odom, George 1955	Ycaza, Manuel 1977
+ Fator, Laverne 1955	+ O'Neill, Frank 1956	
Fires, Earlie 2001	+ Parke, Ivan 1978	*Steeplechase jockey

Trainers

+ Barrera, Laz 1979	+ Hyland, John 1956	+ Parke, Burley 1986
+ Bedwell, H. Guy 1971	+ Jacobs, Hirsch 1958	+ Penna, Angel Sr. 1988
+ Brown, Edward D. 1984	Jerkens, H. Allen 1975	+ Pincus, Jacob 1988
Burch, Elliot 1980	Johnson, Philip 1997	+ Rogers, John 1955
+ Burch, Preston M. 1963	+ Johnson, William R. 1986	+ Rowe, James Sr. 1955
+ Burch, W.P. 1955	+ Jolley, LeRoy 1987	Schulhofer, Scotty 1992
+ Burlew, Fred 1973	+ Jones, Ben A. 1958	Sheppard, Jonathan 1990
+ Childs, Frank E. 1968	+ Jones, H.A. (Jimmy) 1959	+ Smith, Robert A. 1976
+ Clark, Henry 1982	+ Joyner, Andrew 1955	Smith, Tom 2001
+ Cocks, W. Burling 1985	Kelly, Tom 1993	+ Smithwick, Mike 1976
Conway, James P. 1996	+ Laurin, Lucien 1977	+ Stephens, Woody 1976
Croll, Jimmy 1994	+ Lewis, J. Howard 1969	Tenny, Mesh 1991
Delp, Bud 2002	Lukas, D. Wayne 1999	+ Thompson, H.J. 1969
Drysdale, Neil 2000	+ Luro, Horatio 1980	+ Trotsek, Harry 1984
+ Duke, William 1956	Mandella, Richard 2001	Van Berg, Jack 1985
+ Feustel, Louis 1964	+ Madden, John 1983	+ Van Berg, Marion 1970
+ Fitzsimmons, J. (Sunny Jim) . 1958	+ Maloney, Jim 1989	+ Veitch, Sylvester 1977
Frankel, Bobby 1995	Martin, Frank (Pancho) 1981	+ Walden, Robert 1970
+ Gaver, John M. 1966	McAnally, Ron 1990	Walsh, Michael 1997
Hanford, Carl 2006	+ McDaniel, Henry 1956	+ Ward, Sherrill 1978
+ Healey, Thomas 1955	McGaughey, Shug 2004	Watters, Sidney Jr. 2005
+ Hildreth, Samuel 1955	+ Miller, MacKenzie 1987	Whiteley, Frank Jr. 1978
+ Hine, Hubert (Sonny) 2003	+ Molter, William, Jr. 1960	+ Whittingham, Charlie 1974
+ Hirsch, Max 1959	Mott, Bill 1998	+ Williamson, Ansel 1998
Hirsch, W.J. (Buddy) 1982	+ Mulholland, Winbert 1967	Winfrey, W.C. (Bill) 1971
+ Hitchcock, Thomas Sr. 1973	+ Neloy, Eddie 1983	Zito, Nick 2005
+ Hughes, Hollie 1973	Nerud, John 1972	

Horse Racing (Cont.)

Horses

Year foaled in parentheses.

A.P. Indy (1989) 2000
+ Ack Ack (1966) 1986
Affectionately (1960) 1989
+ Affirmed (1975) 1980
All-Along (1979) 1990
+ Alsab (1939) 1976
+ Alydar (1975) 1989
Alysheba (1984) 1993
+ American Eclipse (1814) . . .1970
+ Armed (1941) 1963
+ Artful (1902) 1956
+ Arts and Letters (1966) 1994
+ Assault (1943) 1964
+ Battleship (1927) 1969
+ Bayakoa (1984) 1998
+ Bed O'Roses (1947) 1976
+ Beldame (1901) 1956
+ Ben Brush (1893) 1955
+ Bewitch (1945) 1977
+ Bimelech (1937) 1990
+ Black Gold (1919) 1989
+ Black Helen (1932) 1991
+ Blue Larkspur (1926) 1957
+ Bold 'n Determined (1977) .1997
+ Bold Ruler (1954) 1973
+ Bon Nouvel (1960) 1976
+ Boston (1833) 1955
+ Broomstick (1901) 1956
+ Buckpasser (1963) 1970
+ Busher (1942) 1964
+ Bushranger (1930) 1967
+ Cafe Prince (1970) 1985
+ Carry Back (1958) 1975
+ Cavalcade (1931) 1993
+ Challendon (1936) 1977
+ Chris Evert (1971) 1988
+ Cicada (1959) 1967
Cigar (1990) 2002
+ Citation (1945) 1959
+ Coaltown (1945) 1983
+ Colin (1905) 1956
+ Commando (1898) 1956
Cougar II (1969) 2006
+ Count Fleet (1940) 1961
+ Crusader (1923) 1995
+ Dahlia (1971) 1981
+ Damascus (1964) 1974
Dance Smartly (1989) 2003
+ Dark Mirage (1965) 1974
+ Davona Dale (1976) 1985
+ Desert Vixen (1970) 1979
+ Devil Diver (1939) 1980
+ Discovery (1931) 1969
+ Domino (1891) 1955
+ Dr. Fager (1964) 1971
Easy Goer (1986) 1997

+ Eight 30 (1936) 1994
+ Elkridge (1938) 1966
+ Emperor of Norfolk (1885) .1988
+ Equipoise (1928) 1957
+ Exceller (1973) 1999
+ Exterminator (1915) 1957
+ Fairmount (1921) 1985
+ Fair Play (1905) 1956
+ Firenze (1885) 1981
Flatterer (1979) 1994
Flawlessly (1989) 2004
+ Foolish Pleasure (1972) . . .1995
+ Forego (1971) 1979
+ Fort Marcy (1964) 1998
+ Gallant Bloom (1966) 1977
+ Gallant Fox (1927) 1957
+ Gallant Man (1954) 1987
+ Gallorette (1942) 1962
+ Gamely (1964) 1980
Genuine Risk (1977) 1986
+ Good and Plenty (1900) . . .1956
+ Go For Wand (1987) 1996
+ Granville (1933) 1997
+ Grey Lag (1918) 1957
+ Gun Bow (1960) 1999
+ Hamburg (1895) 1986
+ Hanover (1884) 1955
+ Henry of Navarre (1891) . . .1985
+ Hill Prince (1947) 1991
+ Hindoo (1878) 1955
Holy Bull (1991) 2001
+ Imp (1894) 1965
+ Jay Trump (1957) 1971
John Henry (1975) 1990
+ Johnstown (1936) 1992
+ Jolly Roger (1922) 1965
+ Kingston (1884) 1955
+ Kelso (1957) 1967
+ Kentucky (1861) 1983
Lady's Secret (1982) 1992
+ La Prevoyante (1970) 1995
+ L'Escargot (1963) 1977
+ Lexington (1850) 1955
Lonesome Glory (1989) . . .2005
+ Longfellow (1867) 1971
+ Luke Blackburn (1877) 1956
+ Majestic Prince (1966) 1988
+ Man o'War (1917) 1957
Maskette (1906) 2001
Miesque (1984) 1999
+ Miss Woodford (1880) 1967
+ Myrtlewood (1933) 1979
+ Nashua (1952) 1965
+ Native Dancer (1950) 1963
+ Native Diver (1959) 1978
+ Needles (1953) 2000

+ Neji (1950) 1966
+ Noor (1945) 2002
+ Northern Dancer (1961) . . .1976
+ Oedipus (1941) 1978
+ Old Rosebud (1911) 1968
+ Omaha (1932) 1965
+ Pan Zareta (1910) 1972
+ Parole (1873) 1984
Personal Ensign (1984) . . .1993
Paseana (1987) 2001
+ Peter Pan (1904) 1956
Precisionist (1983) 2003
Princess Rooney (1980) . . .1991
+ Real Delight (1949) 1987
+ Regret (1912) 1957
+ Reigh Count (1925) 1978
Riva Ridge (1969) 1998
+ Roamer (1911) 1981
+ Roseben (1901) 1956
+ Round Table (1954) 1972
+ Ruffian (1972) 1976
+ Ruthless (1864) 1975
+ Salvator (1886) 1955
+ Sarazen (1921) 1957
+ Seabiscuit (1933) 1958
+ Searching (1952) 1978
+ Seattle Slew (1974) 1981
+ Secretariat (1970) 1974
Serena's Song (1992) 2002
+ Shuvee (1966) 1975
+ Silver Spoon (1956) 1978
+ Sir Archy (1805) 1955
+ Sir Barton (1916) 1957
Skip Away (1993) 2004
Slew o' Gold (1980) 1992
+ Sun Beau (1925) 1996
+ Sunday Silence (1986) 1996
+ Stymie (1941) 1975
+ Susan's Girl (1969) 1976
+ Swaps (1952) 1966
+ Sword Dancer (1956) 1977
+ Sysonby (1902) 1956
+ Ta Wee (1966) 1994
+ Tim Tam (1955) 1985
+ Tom Fool (1949) 1960
+ Top Flight (1929) 1966
+ Tosmah (1961) 1984
+ Twenty Grand (1928) 1957
+ Twilight Tear (1941) 1963
+ War Admiral (1934) 1958
+ Whirlaway (1938) 1959
+ Whisk Broom II (1907) 1979
Winning Colors (1985) . . .2000
Zaccio (1976) 1990
+ Zev (1920) 1983

Exemplars of Racing

+ Hanes, John W 1982
+ Jeffords, Walter M 1973

+ Mellon, Paul 1989

Widener, George D 1971

MEDIA

National Sportscasters and Sportswriters Hall of Fame

Established in 1959 by the National Sportscasters and Sportswriters Association. **Address:** 322 East Innes St., Salisbury, NC 28144. **Telephone:** (704) 633-4275. **Web:** www.nssahalloffame.com. **Eligibility:** Nominees must be active for at least 25 years. Voting done by NSSA membership and other media representatives.

Class of 2006 (2): **W.O. McGeehan** and **Phil Rizzuto**.

Members are listed with year of induction; (+) indicates deceased members.

Sportscasters

+ Allen, Mel	1972	+ Gowdy, Curt	1981
+ Barber, Walter (Red)	1973	Harwell, Ernie	1989
Brennaman, Marty	2005	+ Hearn, Chick	1997
+ Brickhouse, Jack	1983	+ Hodges, Russ	1975
+ Buck, Jack	1990	+ Hoyt, Waite	1987
+ Caray, Harry	1989	+ Husing, Ted	1963
+ Cosell, Howard	1993	Jackson, Keith	1995
+ Dean, Dizzy	1976	+ McCarthy, Clem	1970
+ Dunphy, Don	1986	McKay, Jim	1987
+ Elson, Bob	1995	+ McNamee, Graham	1964
Enberg, Dick	1996	Michaels, Al	1998
Garagiola, Joe	2004	Miller, Jon	1999
+ Glickman, Marty	1992		

+ Murphy, Bob	2002
+ Nelson, Lindsey	1979
+ Prince, Bob	1986
Rizutto, Phil	2006
+ Schenkel, Chris	1981
+ Scott, Ray	1982
Scully, Vin	1991
Simpson, Jim	2000
+ Stern, Bill	1974
Summerall, Pat	1994
Whitaker, Jack	2001
Wolff, Bob	2003

Sportswriters

Anderson, Dave	1990	+ Grimsley, Will	1987
Bisher, Furman	1989	Heinz, W.C.	2001
Broeg, Bob	1997	Holtzman, Jerome	2004
+ Burick, Si	1985	Izenberg, Jerry	2000
+ Cannon, Jimmy	1986	Jenkins, Dan	1996
+ Carmichael, John P.	1994	Jenkins, Sally	2005
Collins, Bud	2002	+ Kieran, John	1971
+ Connor, Dick	1992	+ Lardner, Ring	1967
+ Considine, Bob	1980	+ McDonough, Will	2003
+ Daley, Arthur	1976	McGeehan, W.O.	2006
Deford, Frank	1998	+ Murphy, Jack	1988
Durslag, Mel	1995	+ Murray, Jim	1978
+ Gould, Alan	1990	Olderman, Murray	1993
+ Graham, Frank Sr.	1995		

+ Parker, Dan	1975
Pope, Edwin	1994
+ Povich, Shirley	1984
+ Rice, Grantland	1962
+ Runyon, Damon	1964
Russell, Fred	1988
Sherrod, Blackie	1991
+ Smith, Walter (Red)	1977
+ Spink, J.G. Taylor	1969
+ Steadman, John	1999
Vecsey, George	2001
+ Ward, Arch	1973
+ Woodward, Stanley	1974

MOTORSPORTS

Motorsports Hall of Fame of America

Established in 1989. **Mailing Address:** P.O. Box 194, Novi, MI 48376. **Telephone:** (248) 349-7223. **Web:** www.mshf.com. **Eligibility:** Nominees must be retired at least three years or engaged in their area of motorsports for at least 20 years. Areas include: open wheel, stock car, dragster, sports car, motorcycle, off road, power boat, air racing, land speed records, historic and at-large.

Class of 2006 (7): DRIVERS—**Nigel Mansell** (open wheel), **Hershel McGriff** (stock cars), **Chris Karamesines** (drag racing), **Elliott Forbes-Robinson** (sports cars), **Jeff Ward** (motocross), **Curtis Turner** (stock cars). CONTRIBUTORS—**Tom Carnegie**.

Members are listed with year of induction; (+) indicates deceased members.

Drivers

Allison, Bobby	1992	D'Eath, Tom	2000
Amato, Joe	2004	DeCoster, Roger	1994
Andretti, Mario	1990	+ DePalma, Ralph	1992
Arfons, Art	1991	+ DePaolo, Peter	1995
+ Baker, Buck	1998	+ Donahue, Mark	1990
+ Baker, Cannonball	1989	+ Earnhardt, Dale	2002
+ Bettenhausen, Tony	1997	Fittipaldi, Emerson	2001
Brabham, Geoff	2004	Flock, Tim	1999
Breedlove, Craig	1993	Follmer, George	1999
Bryan, Jimmy	1999	Forbes-Robinson, Elliott	2006
+ Campbell, Sir Malcolm	1994	Foster, Danny	2005
+ Cantrell, Bill	1992	Foyt, A.J.	1989
+ Chenoweth, Dean	1991	Garlits, Don	1989
+ Chevrolet, Gaston	2002	Glidden, Bob	1994
Chrisman, Art	1997	+ Gregg, Peter	2000
+ Clark, Jim	1990	Gurney, Dan	1991
+ Cook, Betty	1996	Hanauer, Chip	1995
+ Cooper, Earl	2001	Hannah, Bob	2000
Cunningham, Briggs	1997	+ Hanks, Sam	2000
+ Davis, Jim	1997	+ Harroun, Ray	2000

Hart, C.J.	1999
Haywood, Hurley	2005
Hill, Eddie	2002
Hill, Phil	1989
+ Hinnershitz, Tommy	2003
+ Holbert, Al	1993
+ Horn, Ted	1993
+ Hulme, Denis	1998
Ivo, Tommy	2005
Jarrett, Ned	1997
Jenkins, Bill (Grumpy)	1996
Johncock, Gordon	2002
Johnson, Junior	1991
Jones, Parnelli	1992
Kalitta, Connie	1992
Karamesines, Chris	2006
Kenyon, Mel	2003
+ Kurtis, Frank	1999
Lawson, Eddie	2002
Leonard, Joe	1991

Motorsports (Cont.)

+ Lockhart, Frank 1999
  Lorenzen, Fred 2001
+ McLaren, Bruce 1995
  Mann, Dick 1993
  Mansell, Nigel 2006
  Markle, Bart 1999
+ Mays, Rex 1995
  McEwen, Tom 2001
  McGriff, Hershel 2006
  Mears, Rick 1998
+ Meyer, Louis 1993
+ Miles, Ken 2001
+ Milton, Tommy 1998
  Muldowney, Shirley 1990
+ Muncy, Bill 1989
+ Murphy, Jimmy 1998
+ Musson, Ron 1993
  Nickelson, Don 1998
  Nixon, Gary 2003
+ Nordskog, Bob 1997

+ Oldfield, Barney 1989
  Ongais, Danny 2000
  Parks, Wally 1993
  Parsons, Benny 2005
+ Parsons, Johnnie 2004
  Pearson, David 1993
+ Petrali, Joe 1992
+ Petty, Lee 1996
  Petty, Richard 1989
  Prudhomme, Don 1991
  Rahal, Bobby 2004
  Resweber, Carroll 1998
  Redman, Brian 2002
+ Revson, Peter 1996
+ Roberts, Fireball 1995
  Roberts, Kenny 1990
  Rutherford, Johnny 1996
+ Ruttman, Troy 2005
  Seebold, Bill 1999
+ Shaw, Wilbur 1991

  Slovak, Mira 2001
  Smith, Malcolm 1996
  Sneva, Tom 2005
  Spencer, Freddie 2001
  Springsteen, Jay 2005
+ Thompson, Mickey 1990
+ Turner, Curtis 2006
  Unser, Al 1991
  Unser, Bobby 1994
  Vesco, Don 2004
+ Vukovich, Bill Sr 1992
  Waltrip, Darrell 2003
  Ward, Jeff 2006
  Ward, Rodger 1995
+ Wood, Gar 1990
  Yarborough, Cale 1994

Contributors

+ Agajanian, J.C 1992
  Bignotti, George 1993
+ Black, Keith 1995
  Bondurant, Bob 2003
+ Brawner, Clint 1998
  Carnegie, Tom 2006
  Chapman, Colin 1997
+ Chevrolet, Louis 1995
+ Donovan, Ed 2003
  Duesenberg, Fred 1997
  Economaki, Chris 1994
+ Ford, Henry 1996

+ France, Bill Jr. 2004
+ France, Bill Sr. 1990
+ Glick, Shav 2004
  Granatelli, Andy 2001
  Hall, Jim 1994
+ Holman, John 2005
+ Hulman, Tony 1991
+ Jones, Ted 2003
+ Kiekhaefer, Carl 1998
  Little, Bernie 1994
+ Miller, Harry 1999
+ Moody, Ralph 2005

+ Offenhauser, Fred 2002
  Penske, Roger 1995
+ Rickenbacker, Eddie 1994
+ Rose, Mauri 1996
  Shelby, Carroll 1992
  Simpson, Bill 2003
  Watson, A.J. 1996
  Wood, Glen 2000
  Wood, Leonard 2000
+ Yunick, Smokey 2000

International Motorsports Hall of Fame

Established in 1990 by the International Motorsports Hall of Fame Commission. **Mailing Address:** P.O. Box 1018, Talladega, AL 35161. **Telephone:** (256) 362-5002. **Web:** www.motorsportshalloffame.com.

  Eligibility: Nominees must be retired from their specialty in motorsports for five years. Voting done by 150-member panel made up of the world-wide auto racing media. Members are listed with year of induction; (+) indicates deceased members.

  Class of 2006 (5): DRIVERS—**Dale Earnhardt** (stock cars), **Harry Gant** (stock cars), **Janet Guthrie** (stock cars); CONTRIBUTORS—**H.A. "Humpy" Wheeler** and **Jack Roush**.

Drivers

  Allison, Bobby 1993
  Amato, Joe 2005
  Andretti, Mario 2000
+ Ascari, Alberto 1992
+ Baker, Buck 1990
  Bonnett, Neil 2001
+ Bettenhausen, Tony 1991
  Brabham, Jack 1990
  Bryan, Jimmy 2001
+ Campbell, Sir Malcolm 1990
+ Caracciola, Rudolph 1998
+ Clark, Jim 1990
+ DePalma, Ralph 1991
+ Donahue, Mark 1990
  Earnhardt, Dale 2006
+ Evans, Richie 1996
+ Fangio, Juan Manuel 1990
  Farmer, Charles 2004
  Fittipaldi, Emerson 2003
+ Flock, Tim 1991
  Foyt, A.J. 2000
  Gant, Harry 2006
  Glidden, Bob 2005
+ Gregg, Peter 1992
  Gurney, Dan 1990
  Guthrie, Janet 2006
  Hailwood, Mike 2001

+ Haley, Donald 1996
  Hanauer, Chip 2005
+ Hill, Graham 1990
  Hill, Phil 1991
+ Holbert, Al 1993
+ Hulme, Denis 2002
  Ickx, Jacky 2002
+ Isaac, Bobby 1996
  Jarrett, Ned 1991
  Johncock, Gordon 1999
  Johnson, Junior 1990
  Jones, Parnelli 1990
  Kenyon, Mel 2003
+ Kulwicki, Alan 2002
  Lauda, Niki 1993
  Lorenzen, Fred 1991
+ Lund, Tiny 1994
  Mansell, Chip 2005
+ Mays, Rex 1993
+ McLaren, Bruce 1991
+ Meyer, Louis 1992
  Moss, Stirling 1990
  Muldowney, Shirley 2004
+ Muncey, Bill 2004
+ Nuvolari, Tazio 1998
+ Oldfield, Barney 1990
  Parsons, Benny 1994

  Pearson, David 1993
+ Petty, Lee 1990
  Piquet, Nelson 2000
  Prodhomme, Don 2000
  Prost, Alain 1999
  Rahal, Bobby 2004
+ Richmond, Tim 2002
+ Roberts, Fireball 1990
  Roberts, Kenny 1992
  Rose, Mauri 1994
  Rutherford, Johnny 1996
  Scott, Wendell 1999
+ Senna, Ayrton 2000
+ Shaw, Wilbur 1991
  Smith, Louise 1999
  Stewart, Jackie 1990
  Surtees, John 1996
+ Thomas, Herb 1994
+ Turner, Curtis 1992
  Unser, Al Sr. 1998
  Unser, Bobby 1990
+ Vukovich, Bill 1991
  Waltrip, Darrell 2005
  Ward Rodger 1992
+ Weatherly, Joe 1994
  Wood, Glen 2002
  Yarborough, Cale 1993

Contributors

Bignotti, George 1993	+ France, Bill Sr 1990	+ Porsche, Ferdinand ......199(
Breedlove, Craig 2000	Granatelli, Andy 1992	+ Rickenbacker, Eddie 1992
+ Bugatti, Ettore 2002	+ Hulman, Tony 1990	Roush, Jack ....200(
+ Chapman, Colin 1994	Hyde, Harry 1999	Shelby, Carroll 199
+ Chevrolet, Louis 1992	Marcum, John 1994	+ Thompson, Mickey ....199(
+ Cunningham, Briggs 2003	+ Matthews, Banjo 1998	Watson, A.J. 2003
+ Ferrari, Enzo 1994	Moody, Ralph 1994	Wheeler, H.A. (Humpy) ...200(
+ Ford, Henry 1993	+ Offenhauser, Fred 2001	+ Yunick, Smokey ....199(
Fox, Ray 2003	Parks, Wally 1992	
France, Bill Jr. 2004	Penske, Roger 1998	

OLYMPICS

U.S. Olympic Hall of Fame

Established in 1983 by the United States Olympic Committee. **Mailing Address:** U.S. Olympic Committee, 1750 East Bou der Street, Colorado Springs, CO 80909. Plans for a permanent museum site have been suspended due to lack of funding **Telephone:** (719) 866-4529. **Web:** www.usoc.org

Eligibility: Nominated athletes must be four years removed from their last Olympic competition. Voting for membership i the Hall was suspended in 1993 but resumed in 2004. Voting from 1983-92 was done by National Sportscasters and Sport writers Association, Hall of Fame members and the USOC board members of directors. Beginning in 2004 the voting weigh was divided among U.S. Olympians, select U.S. Olympic family/media and fans.

Class of 2006: ATHLETES—**Evelyn Ashford** (track & field), **Rowdy Gaines** (swimming), **Bob Hayes** (track & field) **Shannon Miller** (gymnastics), **Kristi Yamaguchi** (figure skating), **Diana Golden-Brosnihan** (paralympian), COACH— **Herb Brooks**. VETERAN—**Jack Shea**. SPECIAL CONTRIBUTOR—**Dick Ebersol**.

Members are listed with year of induction; (+) indicates deceased members.

Teams

1956 Basketball Dick Boushka, Carl Cain, Chuck Darling, Bill Evans, Gib Ford, Burdy Haldorson, Bill Hougland, Bo Jeangerard, K.C. Jones, Bill Russell, Ron Tomsic, +Jim Walsh and coach +Gerald Tucker.

1960 Basketball Jay Arnette, Walt Bellamy, Bob Boozer, Terry Dischinger, Burdy Haldorson, Darrall Imhoff, Allen Kelley +Lester Lane, Jerry Lucas, Oscar Robertson, Adrian Smith, Jerry West and coach Pete Newell.

1964 Basketball Jim Barnes, Bill Bradley, Larry Brown, Joe Caldwell, Mel Counts, Richard Davies, Walt Hazzard, Luk Jackson, John McCaffrey, Jeff Mullins, Jerry Shipp, George Wilson and coach +Hank Iba.

1960 Ice Hockey Billy Christian, Roger Christian, Billy Cleary, Bob Cleary, Gene Grazia, Paul Johnson, Jack Kirrane, Joh Mayasich, Jack McCartan, Bob McKay, Dick Meredith, Weldon Olson, Ed Owen, Rod Paavola, Larry Palmer, Dick Roder heiser, +Tom Williams and coach Jack Riley.

1980 Ice Hockey Bill Baker, Neal Broten, Dave Christian, Steve Christoff, Jim Craig, Mike Eruzione, John Harrington, Stev Janaszak, Mark Johnson, Ken Morrow, Rob McClanahan, Jack O'Callahan, Mark Pavelich, Mike Ramsey, Buzz Schneide Dave Silk, Eric Strobel, Bob Suter, Phil Verchota, Mark Wells and coach +Herb Brooks.

1996 Women's Soccer Michelle Akers, Brandi Chastain, Amanda Cromwell, Joy Fawcett, Julie Foudy, Carin Gabarra, Mi Hamm, Mary Harvey, Kristine Lilly, Shannon MacMillan, Tiffeny Milbrett, Carla Overbeck, Cindy Parlow, Tiffany Roberts Briana Scurry, Thori Staples Bryan, Tisha Venturini, Saskia Webber, Staci Wilson and coach Tony DiCicco.

Alpine Skiing
Mahre, Phil 1992

Bobsled
+ Eagan, Eddie (see Boxing) .1983

Boxing
Clay, Cassius 1983
+ Eagan, Eddie (see Bobsled) .1983
Foreman, George 1990
Frazier, Joe 1989
Leonard, Sugar Ray 1985
Patterson, Floyd 1987

Coaches
+ Brooks, Herb 2006

Cycling
Carpenter-Phinney, Connie .1992

Diving
King, Miki 1992
Lee, Sammy 1990
Louganis, Greg 1985
McCormick, Pat 1985

Figure Skating
Albright, Tenley 1988
Button, Dick 1983
Fleming, Peggy 1983
Hamill, Dorothy 1991
Hamilton, Scott 1990
Yamaguchi, Kristi 2006

Gymnastics
Conner, Bart 1991
Retton, Mary Lou 1985
Miller, Shannon 2006
Vidmar, Peter 1991

Paralympian
Golden-Brosnihan, Diana ..2006

Rowing
+ Kelly, Jack Sr. 1990

Speed Skating
Blair, Bonnie 2004
Heiden, Eric 1983
Jansen, Dan 2004

Veterans
+ Shea, Jack 2006

Wrestling
Gable, Dan 1985

Contributors
+ Arledge, Roone 1989
+ Brundage, Avery 1983
+ Bushnell, Asa 1990
Ebersol, Dick 2006
Greenspan, Bud 2004
Hull, Col. Don 1992
+ Iba, Hank 1985

Swimming
Babashoff, Shirley 1987
Biondi, Matt 2004
Caulkins, Tracy ....199(
+ Daniels, Charles 1988
de Varona, Donna 1987
Evans, Janet 2004
Gaines, Rowdy ....200(
+ Kahanamoku, Duke 1984
+ Madison, Helene 1992
Meyer, Debbie ....198(
Naber, John 1984
Schollander, Don 1983
Spitz, Mark 1983
+ Weissmuller, Johnny 1983

Weight Lifting
+ Davis, John 1989
Kono, Tommy ....199(

+ Kane, Robert ....198(
+ Kelly, Jack Jr. 1992
McKay, Jim 1988
Miller, Don 1984
+ Simon, William 1991
Walker, LeRoy 1987

U.S. Olympic Hall of Fame (Cont.)
Track & Field

Ashford, Evelyn 2006	Hayes, Bob 2006	+ Owens, Jesse 1983
Beamon, Bob 1983	Jenner, Bruce 1986	+ Paddock, Charley 1991
Boston, Ralph 1985	Johnson, Rafer 1983	Richards, Bob 1983
Calhoun, Lee 1991	+ Joyner, Florence Griffith ...2004	+ Rudolph, Wilma 1983
Campbell, Milt 1992	Joyner-Kersee, Jackie 2004	+ Sheppard, Mel 1989
Coachman, Alice 2004	+ Kraenzlein, Alvin 1985	Shorter, Frank 1984
Davenport, Willie 1991	Lewis, Carl 1985	+ Thorpe, Jim 1983
Davis, Glenn 1986	Mathias, Bob 1983	Toomey, Bill 1984
Didrikson, Babe 1983	Mills, Billy 1984	Tyus, Wyomia 1985
Dillard, Harrison 1983	Morrow, Bobby 1989	Whitfield, Mal 1988
Evans, Lee 1989	Moses, Edwin 1985	+ Wykoff, Frank 1984
Ewry, Ray 1983	O'Brien, Parry 1984	
Fosbury, Dick 1992	Oerter, Al 1983	

SOCCER

National Soccer Hall of Fame

stablished in 1950 by the Philadelphia Oldtimers Association. First exhibit unveiled in Oneonta, NY in 1982. Moved into
ew Hall of Fame building in the summer of 1999. **Address:** 18 Stadium Circle, Oneonta, NY 13820. **Telephone:** (607)
32-3351. **Web:** www.soccerhall.org

   Eligibility: Players must have been retired as a player for at least three years, but for no more than 10 years He or she
ust have played at least 20 full international games for the United States. He or she must have played at least five sea-
ns in an American first-division professional league (NASL or MLS), and won the league championship, won the U.S.
pen Cup or been a league all-star at least once. Other categories include Veterans (included under Players) and Builders.
Voting done by a committee made up of Hall of Famers, U.S. Soccer officials and members of the national media.

Class of 2006 (4): Alexi Lalas, Carla Overbeck, Al Trost and **Philip Anschutz.**
Members are listed with home state and year of induction; (+) indicates deceased members.

Players

Akers, Michelle 2004	+ Fricker, Werner 1992	Nanoski, Jukey 1993
Alberto, Carlos 2003	+ Fryer, William J. 1951	Nelson, Johnny 2005
Annis, Robert 1976	Gabarra, Carin 2000	Nilsen, werner 2005
Auld, Andrew 1986	+ Gaetjens, Joe 1976	Ntsoelengoe, Ace (S.Afr.) ..2003
Bachmeier, Adolph 2002	+ Gallagher, James 1986	+ O'Brien, Shamus 1990
Bahr, Walter 1976	Gard, Gino 1976	Olaff, Gene 1971
Balboa, Marcelo 2005	+ Gentle, James 1986	+ Oliver, Arnie 1968
Barr, George 1983	Getzinger, Rudy 1991	Oliver, Len 1996
Beardsworth, Fred 1965	+ Glover, Teddy 1965	Overbeck, Carla 2006
Beckenbauer, Franz (Ger) .1998	Gonsalves, Billy 1950	Pariani, Gino 1976
Bernabei, Ray 1978	Gormley, Bob 1989	+ Patenaude, Bert 1971
Bogicevic, Vladislav (Yug) ..2002	+ Govier, Sheldon 1950	Pel|fe (Brazil) 1993
Bookie, Michael 1986	Granitza, Karl-Heinz (Ger) .2003	Ramos, Tab 2005
Borghi, Frank 1976	Gryzik, Joe 1973	+ Ratican, Harry 1950
Boulos, Frenchy 1980	Harker, Al 1979	+ Renzulli, Pete 1951
Brittan, Harold 1951	Harkes, John 2005	+ Roe, Jimmy 1997
Brown, David 1951	Heinrichs, April 1998	Roth, Werner 1989
Brown, George 1995	Higgins, Shannon 2002	Roy, Willy 1989
Brown, James 1986	Howard, Ted 2003	+ Ryan, Hun 1958
Caligiuri, Paul 2004	Hynes, John 1977	Salcedo Frabie 2005
Carenza, Joe 1982	+ Japp, John 1953	Schaller, Willy 1995
Caraffi, Ralph 1959	Keough, Harry 1976	Slone, Philip 1986
Chacurian, Chico 1992	Kropfelder, Nicholas 1996	+ Souza, Ed 1976
Chesney, Stan 1966	+ Kunter, Rudy 1963	Souza, Clarkie 1976
Child, Paul (Eng) 2003	Lalas, Alexi 2006	+ Spalding, Dick 1951
Chinaglia, Giorgio (Italy) ..2000	Lang, Millard 1950	+ Stark, Archie 1950
Clavijo, Fernando 2005	Lenarduzzi, Bob (Can) 2003	+ Swords, Thomas 1951
Colombo, Charlie 1976	+ Looby, Bill 2001	+ Tintle, Joseph 1952
Coombes, Geoff 1976	+ Maca, Joe 1976	+ Tracey, Ralph 1986
Craddock Jr., Robert 1976	Mausser, Arnie 2003	Trost, Al 2006
Danilo, Paul 1997	McBride, Pat 1994	+ Vaughn, Frank 1986
Davis, Rick 2001	+ McGhee, Bart 1986	+ Wallace, Frank 1976
Dick, Walter 1989	+ McGuire, John 1951	+ Weir, Alex 1975
Diorio, Nick 1974	+ McIlveney, Eddie 1976	Willey, Alan (Eng) 2003
Donelli, Buff 1954	McLaughlin, Bennie 1977	Wilson, Bruce (Can) 2003
Douglas, Jimmy 1953	+ Mieth, Werner 1974	+ Wilson, Peter 1950
Dunn, James 1974	+ Millar, Robert 1950	Wolanin, Adam 1976
Duggan, Thomas 1951	Monsen, Lloyd 1994	+ Wood, Alex 1986
Ely, Alexander 1997	Moore, Johnny 1997	Wynalda, Eric 2004
Ferguson, John 1950	+ Moorehouse, George 1986	Zerhusen, Al 1978
Fleming, Tom (Whitey) 2005	+ Morrison, Robert 1951	
Florie, Thomas 1986	Murphy, Edward 1998	

Builders

Abronzino, Umberto 1971	+ Fowler, Dan 1970	+ Morrissette, Bill 1967
Aimi, Milton 1991	+ Fowler, Peg 1979	+ Netto, Fred 1958
+ Alonso, Julie 1972	+ Garcia, Pete 1964	Newman, Ron 1992
+ Andersen, William 1956	+ Giesler, Walter 1962	+ Niotis, D.J. 1963
Anschutz, Philip 2006	+ Gould, David L. 1953	+ Palmer, William 1952
+ Ardizzone, John 1971	+ Greer, Don 1985	+ Pearson, Eddie 1990
+ Armstrong, James 1952	+ Guelker, Bob 1980	+ Peel, Peter 1951
+ Barriskill, Joe 1953	Guennel, Joe 1980	+ Peters, Wally 1967
Berling, Clay 1995	+ Healey, George 1951	Phillipson, Don 1987
+ Best, John O. 1982	+ Heilpern, Herb 1988	+ Piscopo, Giorgio 1978
+ Booth, Joseph 1952	+ Hemmings, William 1961	+ Pomeroy, Edgar 1955
+ Boxer, Matt 1961	Hermann, Robert 2001	+ Ramsden, Arnold 1957
Bradley, Gordon (Eng) 1996	+ Hudson, Maurice 1966	+ Reese, Doc 1957
+ Briggs, Lawrence E. 1978	Hunt, Lamar 1982	Ringsdorf, Gene 1979
+ Brock, John 1950	+ Iglehart, Alfredda 1951	Robbie, Elizabeth 2003
+ Brown, Andrew M. 1950	+ Jeffrey, William 1951	+ Robbie, Joe 2003
+ Cahill, Thomas W 1950	+ Johnston, Jack 1952	Ross, Steve 2003
+ Chyzowych, Walter 1997	+ Kabanica, Mike 1987	+ Rottenberg, Jack 1971
+ Coll, John 1986	Kehoe, Bob 1990	+ Sager, Tom 1968
+ Collins, George M. 1951	+ Kelly, Frank 1994	Saunders, Harry 1981
Collins, Peter 1998	+ Kempton, George 1950	Schellscheidt, Mannie 1990
+ Commander, Colin 1967	+ Klein, Paul 1953	+ Schillinger, Emil 1960
+ Cordery, Ted 1975	Kleinaitis, Al 1995	+ Schroeder, Elmer 1951
+ Craddock, Robert 1959	+ Kozma, Oscar 1964	+ Schwarz, Erno 1951
+ Craggs, Edmund 1969	+ Kracher, Frank 1983	+ Shields, Fred 1968
Craggs, George 1981	Kraft, Granny 1984	+ Single, Erwin 1981
+ Cummings, Wilfred R. 1953	+ Kraus, Harry 1963	+ Smith, Alfred 1951
+ Delach, Joseph 1973	+ Lamm, Kurt 1979	Smith, Patrick 1998
DeLuca, Enzo 1979	Larson, Bert 1988	Spath, Reinhold 1997
+ Donaghy, Edward J. 1951	+ Lewis, H. Edgar 1950	+ Steelink, Nicolaas 1971
+ Donnelly, George 1989	Lombardo, Joe 1984	Steinbrecher, Hank 2005
+ Dresmich, John W. 1968	Long, Denny 1993	Stern, Lee 2003
+ Duff, Duncan 1972	+ MacEwan, John J. 1953	+ Steur, August 1969
+ Edwards, Gene 1985	+ Magnozzi, Enzo 1977	+ Stewart, Douglas 1950
+ Epperlein, Rudy 1951	+ Maher, Jack 1970	+ Stone, Robert T 1971
Ertegun, Ahmet 2003	+ Manning, Dr. Randolf 1950	Toye, Clive 2003
Ertegun, Nesuhi 2003	+ Marre, John 1953	+ Triner, Joseph 1951
+ Fairfield, Harry 1951	+ McClay, Allan 1971	+ Walder, Jimmy 1971
Feibusch, Ernst 1984	+ McGrath, Frank 1978	+ Washauer, Adolph 1977
+ Fernley, John A. 1951	+ McGuire, Jimmy 1951	+ Webb, Tom 1987
+ Ferro, Charles 1958	+ McSkimming, Dent 1951	+ Weston, Victor 1956
+ Fishwick, George E. 1974	Merovich, Pete 1971	+ Woods, John W. 1952
+ Flamhaft, Jack 1964	Miller, Al 1995	Woosnam, Phil 1997
+ Fleming, Harry G. 1967	+ Miller, Milton 1971	+ Yeagley, Jerry 1989
+ Foulds, Pal 1953	+ Mills, Jimmy 1954	+ Young, John 1958
+ Foulds, Sam 1969	+ Moore, James F. 1971	+ Zampini, Dan 1963

SWIMMING

International Swimming Hall of Fame

Established in 1965 by the U.S. College Coaches' Swim Forum. **Address:** One Hall of Fame Drive, Ft. Lauderdale, FL 33316. **Telephone:** (954) 462-6536. **Web:** www.ishof.org.

Categories for induction are: swimming, diving, water polo, synchronized swimming, coaching, pioneers and contributors. Coaches and contributors are not included in the following list. Only U.S. men and women listed below.

Class of 2006 (2): U.S. MEN—**Joe Bottom** and **Tom Dolan.**

Members are listed with year of induction; (+) indicates deceased members.

U.S. Men

+ Anderson, Miller 1967	Clark, Earl 1972	Edgar, David 1996
Barrowman, Mike 1997	Clark, Steve 1966	+ Faricy, John 1990
Berkoff, David 2005	+ Cleveland, Dick 1991	+ Farrell, Jeff 1968
Biondi, Matt 1997	Clotworthy, Robert 1980	Fick, Peter 1978
+ Boggs, Phil 1985	+ Crabbe, Buster 1965	+ Flanagan, Ralph 1978
Bottom, Joe 2006	+ Daniels, Charlie 1965	Ford, Alan 1966
Breen, George 1975	Degener, Dick 1971	Furniss, Bruce 1987
+ Browning, Skippy 1975	DeMont, Rick 1990	Gaines, Rowdy 1995
Bruner, Mike 1988	Dempsey, Frank 1996	Garton, Tim 1997
Burton, Mike 1977	+ Desjardins, Pete 1966	+ Glancy, Harrison 1990
+ Cann, Tedford 1967	Dolan, Tom 2006	Goodell, Brian 1986
Carey, Rick 1993	Dysdale, Taylor 1994	+ Goodwin, Budd 1971

U.S. Women

TENNIS
International Tennis Hall of Fame

Originally the National Tennis Hall of Fame. Established in 1953 by James Van Alen and sanctioned by the U.S. Tennis Association in 1954. Renamed the International Tennis Hall of Fame in 1976. **Address:** 194 Bellevue Ave., Newport, RI 02840. **Telephone:** (401) 849-3990. **Web:** www.tennisfame.com

Eligibility: Nominated players must be five years removed from being a "significant factor" in competitive tennis. Voting done by members of the international tennis media. Due to space constraints only players are listed below.

Class of 2006 (3): **Patrick Rafter** and **Gabriela Sabatini**.

Members are listed with year of induction; (+) indicates deceased members.

Men

+ Adee, George 1964	+ Griffin, Clarence 1970	Pietrangeli, Nicola 1986
+ Alexander, Fred 1961	+ Hackett, Harold 1961	+ Quist, Adrian 1984
+ Allison, Wilmer 1963	Hewitt, Bob 1992	Rafter, Patrick 2006
+ Alonso, Manuel 1977	+ Hoad, Lew 1980	Ralston, Dennis 1987
Anderson, Malcolm 2000	+ Hovey, Fred 1974	+ Renshaw, Ernest 1983
+ Ashe, Arthur 1985	+ Hunt, Joe 1966	+ Renshaw, William 1983
+ Austin, Bunny 1997	+ Hunter, Frank 1961	+ Richards, Vincent 1961
Becker, Boris 2003	+ Johnston, Bill 1958	+ Riggs, Bobby 1967
+ Behr, Karl 1969	+ Jones, Perry 1970	Roche, Tony 1986
Borg, Bjorn 1987	Kelleher, Robert 2000	Rose, Mervyn 2001
+ Borotra, Jean 1976	Kodes, Jan 1990	Rosewall, Ken 1980
+ Bromwich, John 1984	Kramer, Jack 1968	Santana, Manuel 1984
+ Brookes, Norman 1977	+ Lacoste, Rene 1976	Savitt, Dick 1976
+ Brugnon, Jacques 1976	+ Larned, William 1956	Schroeder, Ted 1966
+ Budge, Don 1964	Larsen, Art 1969	+ Sears, Richard 1955
+ Campbell, Oliver 1955	Laver, Rod 1981	Sedgman, Frank 1979
+ Chace, Malcolm 1961	Lendl, Ivan 2001	Segura, Pancho 1984
+ Clark, Clarence 1983	+ Lott, George 1964	Seixas, Vic 1971
+ Clark, Joseph 1955	Mako, Gene 1973	+ Shields, Frank 1964
+ Clothier, William 1956	McEnroe, John 1999	+ Slocum, Henry 1955
+ Cochet, Henri 1976	McGregor, Ken 1999	Smith, Stan 1987
Connors, Jimmy 1998	+ McKinley, Chuck 1986	Stolle, Fred 1985
Cooper, Ashley 1991	+ McLoughlin, Maurice 1957	+ Talbert, Bill 1967
Courier, Jim 2005	McMillan, Frew 1992	+ Tilden, Bill 1959
+ Crawford, Jack 1979	+ McNeill, Don 1965	Trabert, Tony 1970
+ David, Herman 1998	Mulloy, Gardnar 1972	+ Van Ryn, John 1963
+ Doeg, John 1962	+ Murray, Lindley 1958	Vilas, Guillermo 1991
+ Doherty, Lawrence 1980	+ Myrick, Julian 1963	+ Vines, Ellsworth 1962
+ Doherty, Reginald 1980	Nastase, Ilie 1991	+ von Cramm, Gottfried 1977
+ Drobny, Jaroslav 1983	Newcombe, John 1986	+ Ward, Holcombe 1956
+ Dwight, James 1955	+ Nielsen, Arthur 1971	+ Washburn, Watson 1965
Edberg, Stefan 2004	Noah, Yannick 2005	+ Whitman, Malcolm 1955
Emerson, Roy 1982	Olmedo, Alex 1987	Wilander, Mats 2002
+ Etchebaster, Pierre 1978	+ Osuna, Rafael 1979	+ Wilding, Anthony 1978
Falkenburg, Bob 1974	+ Parker, Frank 1966	+ Williams, Richard 2nd 1957
Fraser, Neale 1984	+ Patterson, Gerald 1989	Wood, Sidney 1964
+ Garland, Chuck 1969	Patty, Budge 1977	+ Wrenn, Robert 1955
+ Gonzales, Pancho 1968	+ Perry, Fred 1975	+ Wright, Beals 1956
+ Grant, Bryan (Bitsy) 1972	+ Pettitt, Tom 1982	

Women

+ Atkinson, Juliette 1974	Goolagong Cawley, Evonne 1988	Osborne duPont, Margaret .1967
Austin, Tracy 1992	Graf, Steffi 2004	+ Palfrey Danzig, Sarah 1963
+ Barger-Wallach, Maud 1958	+ Hansell, Ellen 1965	Richey, Nancy 2003
Betz Addie, Pauline 1965	Hard, Darlene 1973	+ Roosevelt, Ellen 1975
+ Bjurstedt Mallory, Molla ...1958	Hart, Doris 1969	+ Round Little, Dorothy 1986
Bowrey, Lesley Turner 1997	Haydon Jones, Ann 1985	+ Ryan, Elizabeth 1972
Brough Clapp, Louise 1967	Heldman, Gladys 1979	Sabatini, Gabriela 2006
+ Browne, Mary 1957	+ Hotchkiss Wightman, Hazel 1957	+ Sears, Eleanora 1968
Bueno, Maria 1978	+ Jacobs, Helen Hull 1962	Shriver, Pam 2002
+ Cahill, Mabel 1976	King, Billie Jean 1987	Smith Court, Margaret 1979
Casals, Rosie 1996	+ Lenglen, Suzanne 1978	+ Sutton Bundy, May 1956
Cheney, Dorothy (Dodo) ...2004	Mandlikova, Hana 1994	+ Townsend Toulmin, Bertha ..1974
+ Connolly Brinker, Maureen ..1968	+ Marble, Alice 1964	Wade, Virginia 1989
+ Dod, Charlotte (Lottie) 1983	+ McKane Godfree, Kitty 1978	+ Wagner, Marie 1969
+ Douglass Chambers, Dorothy 1981	+ Moore, Elisabeth 1971	+ Wills Moody Roark, Helen ..1959
Dürr, Françoise 2003	Mortimer Barrett, Angela ..1993	
Evert, Chris 1995	Novotna, Jana 2005	
Fry Irvin, Shirley 1970	Navratilova, Martina 2000	
+ Gibson, Althea 1971	+ Nuthall Shoemaker, Betty ..1977	

TRACK & FIELD

National Track & Field Hall of Fame

Established in 1974 by the The Athletics Congress (now USA Track & Field). Originally located in Charleston, WV, the Hall moved to Indianapolis in 1983 and opened at the Hoosier Dome (now RCA Dome) in 1986. The Hall moved to Manhattan and reopened at the 168th Street Armory in early 2004. **Address:** 216 Fort Washington Ave., New York, NY 10032. **Telephone:** (212) 923-1803, ext. 10. **Web:** www.usatf.com/HallOfFame/TF/

Eligibility: Nominated athletes must be retired three years and coaches must have coached at least 20 years if retired or 35 years if still coaching. Voting done by 800-member panel made up of Hall of Fame and USA Track & Field officials, Hall of Fame members, current U.S. champions and members of the Track & Field Writers of America. Due to space contraints, the coaches and contributors are not listed below.

Class of 2005 (6): MEN—**Jim Fuchs** (thrower), **Roger Kingdom** (hurdles), **Mike Powell** (long jump), **Wes Santee** (middle distance), **Fred Wolcott** (hurdles). WOMEN—**Earlene Brown** (thrower). Members are listed with year of induction; (+) indicates deceased members.

Men

+ Albritton, Dave	1980	James, Larry	2003	+ Prefontaine, Steve	1976
Ashenfelter, Horace	1975	Jenkins, Charlie	1992	Prinstein, Meyer	2000
Banks, Willie	1999	Jenner, Bruce	1980	+ Ray, Joie	1976
+ Bausch, James	1979	+ Johnson, Cornelius	1994	+ Rice, Greg	1977
Beamon, Bob	1977	Johnson, Michael	2004	Richards, Rev. Bob	1975
Beatty, Jim	1990	Johnson, Rafer	1974	Robinson, Arnie	2000
Bell, Earl	2002	Jones, Hayes	1976	Rodgers, Bill	1999
Bell, Greg	1988	+ Kelley, John A.	1980	+ Rose, Ralph	1976
+ Boeckmann, Dee	1976	Kingdom, Roger	2005	Ryun, Jim	1980
Boston, Ralph	1974	Kiviat, Abel	1985	Salazar, Alberto	2001
+ Borican, Jonn	2000	+ Kraenzlein, Alvin	1974	Santee, Wes	2005
Bragg, Don	1996	Laird, Ron	1986	+ Scholz, Jackson	1977
+ Calhoun, Lee	1974	Larrabee, Mike	2003	Schul, Bob	1991
Campbell, Milt	1989	+ Lash, Don	1995	Scott, Steve	2002
Carlos, John	2003	+ Laskau, Henry	1997	Seagren, Bob	1986
Carr, Henry	1997	Lewis, Carl	2001	+ Sheppard, Mel	1976
+ Clark, Ellery	1991	Lindgren, Gerry	2004	+ Sheridan, Martin	1988
Conley, Mike	2004	Liquori, Marty	1995	Shorter, Frank	1989
Connolly, Harold	1984	Long, Dr. Dallas	1996	Silvester, Jay	1998
Courtney, Tom	1978	Marsh, Henry	2001	Sime, Dave	1981
+ Cunningham, Glenn	1974	+ Mathias, Bob	1974	+ Simpson, Robert	1974
+ Curtis, William	1979	Matson, Randy	1984	Smith, Tommie	1978
+ Davenport, Willie	1982	McCluskey, Joe	1996	+ Stanfield, Andy	1977
Davis, Glenn	1974	+ Meadows, Earle	1996	Steers, Les	1974
Davis, Harold	1974	+ Meredith, Ted	1982	Stones, Dwight	1998
Davis, Jack	2004	+ Metcalfe, Ralph	1975	+ Taylor, Frederick Morgan	2000
Davis, Otis	2004	+ Milburn, Rod	1993	+ Tewksbury, Dr. Walter	1996
Dillard, Harrison	1974	Mills, Billy	1976	Thomas, John	1985
Dumas, Charles	1990	Moore, Charles	1999	+ Thomson, Earl	1977
Evans, Lee	1983	Moore, Tom	1988	+ Thorpe, Jim	1975
+ Ewell, Barney	1986	Morrow, Bobby	1975	+ Tolan, Eddie	1982
+ Ewry, Ray	1974	+ Mortensen, Jess	1992	Toomey, Bill	1975
Flanagan, John	1975	Moses, Edwin	1994	+ Towns, Forrest (Spec)	1976
Fosbury, Dick	1981	+ Myers, Lawrence	1974	Warmerdam, Cornelius	1974
Foster, Greg	1998	Myricks, Larry	2001	Whitfield, Mal	1974
Fuchs, Jim	2005	Nehemiah, Renaldo	1997	Wilkins, Mac	1993
+ Gordien, Fortune	1979	O'Brien, Parry	1974	+ Williams, Archie	1992
Greene, Charles	1992	Oerter, Al	1974	Wohlhuter, Rick	1990
+ Hahn, Archie	1983	+ Osborn, Harold	1974	Wolcott, Fred	2005
+ Hardin, Glenn	1978	+ Owens, Jesse	1974	Woodruff, John	1978
+ Hayes, Bob	1976	+ Paddock, Charlie	1976	Wottle, Dave	1982
Held, Bud	1987	Patton, Mel	1985	+ Wykoff, Frank	1977
Hines, Jim	1979	+ Peacock, Eulace	1987	Young, George	1981
Houser, Bud	1979	Penel, John	2004	Young, Larry	2002
+ Hubbard, DeHart	1979	Powell, Mike	2005		

Women

Ashford, Evelyn	1997	Heritage, Doris Brown	1990	Schmidt, Kate	1994
Brisco, Valerie	1995	+ Jackson, Nell	1989	Seidler, Maren	2000
Brown, Earlene	2005	Joyner-Kersee, Jackie	2004	+ Shiley Newhouse, Jean	1993
Cheeseborough, Chandra	2000	Larrieu Smith, Francie	1998	Slaney, Mary	2003
Coachman, Alice	1975	Manning-Mims, Madeline	1984	+ Stephens, Helen	1975
+ Copeland, Lillian	1994	McDaniel, Mildred	1983	Torrence, Gwen	2002
+ Didrikson, Babe	1974	McGuire, Edith	1979	Tyus, Wyomia	1980
+ Faggs, Mae	1976	Ritter, Louise	1995	+ Walsh, Stella	1975
Ferrell, Barbara	1988	+ Robinson, Betty	1977	Watson, Martha	1987
+ Griffith Joyner, Florence	1995	+ Rudolph, Wilma	1974	White, Willye	1981
+ Hall Adams, Evelyne	1988	Samuelson, Joan	2004		

WOMEN

International Women's Sports Hall of Fame

Established in 1980 by the Women's Sports Foundation. **Address:** Women's Sports Foundation, Eisenhower Park, East Meadow, NY 11554. **Telephone:** (516) 542-4700.

Eligibility: Nominees' achievements and commitment to the development of women's sports must be internationally recognized. Athletes are elected in two categories—Pioneer (before 1960) and Contemporary (since 1960). Members are divided below by sport for the sake of easy reference; (*) indicates member inducted in Pioneer category. Coaching nominees must have coached at least 10 years. Members are listed with year of induction; (+) indicates deceased members.

Class of 2005 (3): PIONEER—**Katarina Witt** (figure skating); CONTEMPORARY—**Lusia Harris Stewart** (basketball); COACH—**Marjorie Wright** (softball).

Alpine Skiing
Cranz, Christl* 1991
+ Golden Brosnihan, Diana . .1997
Lawrence, Andrea Mead* . .1983
Moser-Proell, Annemarie . . .1982

Auto Racing
Guthrie, Janet 1980

Aviation
+ Coleman, Bessie* 1992
+ Earhart, Amelia* 1980
+ Marvingt, Marie* 1987

Badminton
Hashman, Judy Devlin* . . .1995

Baseball
Stone, Toni* 1993

Basketball
Meyers, Ann 1985
Miller, Cheryl 1991
Stewart, Lusia Harris 2005

Bowling
Ladewig, Marion* 1984

Cycling
Carpenter Phinney, Connie .1990

Diving
Gao, Min 2003
King, Micki 1983
McCormick, Pat* 1984
Riggin, Aileen* 1988

Equestrian
Hartel, Lis 1994

Fencing
Schacherer-Elek, Ilona* . . .1989

Figure Skating
Albright, Tenley* 1983
+ Blanchard, Theresa Weld* .1989
Fleming, Peggy 1981
Heiss Jenkins, Carol* 1992
+ Henie, Sonja* 1982
Protopopov, Ludmila 1992
Rodnina, Irena 1988
Scott-King, Barbara Ann* . .1997
Torvill, Jayne 2002
Witt, Katarina* 2005

Golf
Berg, Patty* 1980
Carner, JoAnne 1987
Haynie, Sandra 1999
Hicks, Betty* 1995
Jameson, Betty* 1999
Mann, Carol 1982
Rawls, Betsy* 1986
+ Sears, Eleanora 1984
Suggs, Louise* 1987
+ Vare, Glenna Collett* 1981
Whitworth, Kathy 1984
Wright, Mickey 1981
+ Zaharias, Babe Didrikson* .1980

Gymnastics
Caslavska, Vera 1991
Comaneci, Nadia 1990
Korbut, Olga 1982
Latynina, Larysa* 1985
Retton, Mary Lou 1993
Tourischeva, Lyudmila 1987

Orienteering
Kringstad, Annichen 1995

Shooting
Murdock, Margaret 1988

Softball
Joyce, Joan 1989

Speed Skating
+ Klein Outland, Kit* 1993
Young, Sheila 1981

Squash
McKay, Heather* 2003

Swimming
Caulkins, Tracy 1986
+ Chadwick, Florence* 1996
Curtis Cuneo, Ann* 1985
de Varona, Donna 1983
Ederle, Gertrude* 1980
Fraser, Dawn 1985
Hogshead-Makar, Nancy . .2004
Holm, Eleanor* 1980
Meagher, Mary T. 1993
Meyer-Reyes, Debbie 1987
Ruiz-Confronto, Tracie 2001

Tennis
Bueno, Maria Esther 2004
+ Connolly, Maureen* 1987
+ Dod, Charlotte (Lottie)* 1986
Evert, Chris 1981
+ Gibson, Althea* 1980
Goolagong Cawley, Evonne 1989
+ Hotchkiss Wightman, Hazel*1986
King, Billie Jean 1980
+ Lenglen, Suzanne* 1984
Navratilova, Martina 1984
Osbourne du Pont,Margaret*1998
+ Sears, Eleanora* 1984
Smith Court, Margaret 1986

Track & Field
Ashford, Evelyn 1997
Blankers-Koen, Fanny* 1982
Brisco, Valerie 2002
Cheng, Chi 1994
Coachman Davis, Alice* . .1991
Cuthbert, Betty* 2002
+ Faggs Star, Aeriwentha Mae* 1996
+ Griffith Joyner, Florence . .1998
Joyner-Kersee, Jackie 2003
Manning Mims, Madeline . .1987
Nelson, Marjorie Jackson* .2001
+ Rudolph, Wilma 1980
Samuelson, Joan Benoit . .1999
+ Stephens, Helen* 1983
Strickland de la Hunty, Shirley*1998
Szewinska, Irena 1992
Tyus, Wyomia 1981
Waitz, Grete 1995
White, Willye 1988
+ Zaharias, Babe Didrikson* .1980

Volleyball
+ Hyman, Flo 1986

Water Skiing
McGuire, Willa Worthington* 1990

Coaches
+ Applebee, Constance 1991
Backus, Sharron 1993
Carver, Chris 2001
Conradt, Judy 1995
Emery, Gail 1997
Franke, Nikki 2002
Green, Tina Sloan 1999
Grossfeld, Muriel 1991
Holum, Diana 1996
Jacket, Barbara 1995
+ Jackson, Nell 1990
Kanakogi, Rusty 1994
Kearney, Beverly 2004
Summitt, Pat Head 1990
VanDerveer, Tara 1998
Vollstedt, Linda 2003
+ Wade, Margaret 1992
Wright, Marjorie 2005

Women inducted in multiple categories

Babe Didrikson Zaharias is inducted for both golf and track and field; **Charlotte "Lottie" Dod** is inducted for tennis, as well as archery and golf; **Marie Marvingt** is inducted for aviation, as well as mountaineering; **Eleanora Sears** is inducted for golf, as well as polo and squash.

RETIRED NUMBERS

Major League Baseball

The New York Yankees have retired the most uniform numbers (14) in the major leagues; followed by the Brooklyn/Los Angeles Dodgers (10), the St. Louis Cardinals (9), the Chicago White Sox, the Pittsburgh Pirates and New York/San Francisco Giants (8). **Jackie Robinson** had his #42 retired by Major League Baseball in 1997. Players who were already wearing the number were allowed to continue to do so. Los Angeles had already retired Robinson's number so he's only listed with the Dodgers below. **Nolan Ryan** has had his number retired by three teams—#34 by Texas and Houston and #30 by California (now Los Angeles Angels of Anaheim). Six players and a manager have had their numbers retired by two teams: **Hank Aaron**—#44 by the Boston/Milwaukee/Atlanta Braves and the Milwaukee Brewers; **Rod Carew**—#29 by Minnesota and California (now Anaheim); **Rollie Fingers**—#34 by Milwaukee and Oakland; **Carlton Fisk**—#27 by Boston and #72 by the Chicago White Sox; **Reggie Jackson**— #9 by the Oakland Athletics and #44 by the New York Yankees; **Frank Robinson**—#20 by Cincinnati and Baltimore; **Casey Stengel**—#37 by the New York Yankees and New York Mets.

Number retired in 2006 (1): ST. LOUIS CARDINALS—#42 worn by **Bruce Sutter** (1981-84 with Cardinals).

American League

Two AL teams—the Seattle Mariners and the Toronto Blue Jays—have not retired any numbers. The Blue Jays have a "level of excellence" which includes Joe Carter (#29), Tony Fernandez (#1), Dave Stieb (#11), George Bell (#37), and Cito Gaston (#43). All numbers have been used in recent years, however.

Baltimore Orioles
4 Earl Weaver
5 Brooks Robinson
8 Cal Ripken Jr.
20 Frank Robinson
22 Jim Palmer
33 Eddie Murray

Boston Red Sox
1 Bobby Doerr
4 Joe Cronin
8 Carl Yastrzemski
9 Ted Williams
27 Carlton Fisk

Chicago White Sox
2 Nellie Fox
3 Harold Baines
4 Luke Appling
9 Minnie Minoso
11 Luis Aparicio
16 Ted Lyons
19 Billy Pierce
72 Carlton Fisk

Cleveland Indians
3 Earl Averill
5 Lou Boudreau
14 Larry Doby
18 Mel Harder
19 Bob Feller
21 Bob Lemon
455 Fans (# of consecutive sellouts)

Detroit Tigers
2 Charlie Gehringer
5 Hank Greenberg
6 Al Kaline
16 Hal Newhouser
23 Willie Horton

Kansas City Royals
5 George Brett
10 Dick Howser
20 Frank White

LA Angels of Anaheim
11 Jim Fregosi
26 Gene Autry
29 Rod Carew
30 Nolan Ryan
50 Jimmie Reese

Minnesota Twins
3 Harmon Killebrew
6 Tony Oliva
14 Kent Hrbek
29 Rod Carew
34 Kirby Puckett

Oakland Athletics
9 Reggie Jackson
27 Catfish Hunter
34 Rollie Fingers
43 Dennis Eckersley

New York Yankees
1 Billy Martin
3 Babe Ruth
4 Lou Gehrig
5 Joe DiMaggio
7 Mickey Mantle
8 Yogi Berra & Bill Dickey
9 Roger Maris
10 Phil Rizzuto
15 Thurman Munson
16 Whitey Ford
23 Don Mattingly
32 Elston Howard
37 Casey Stengel
44 Reggie Jackson
49 Ron Guidry

Tampa Bay Devil Rays
12 Wade Boggs

Texas Rangers
26 Johnny Oates
34 Nolan Ryan

National League

Three NL teams—the Arizona Diamondbacks, Colorado Rockies and Washington Nationals—have not retired any numbers. San Francisco has honored former NY Giants Christy Mathewson and John McGraw even though they played before numbers were worn. As did the Philadelphia Phillies for Grover Cleveland Alexander and Chuck Klein. The Montreal Expos had retired #8 for Gary Carter, #10 for Rusty Staub and Andre Dawson and #30 for Tim Raines but Washington has used those numbers.

Atlanta Braves
3 Dale Murphy
21 Warren Spahn
35 Phil Niekro
41 Eddie Mathews
44 Hank Aaron

Chicago Cubs
10 Ron Santo
14 Ernie Banks
23 Ryne Sandberg
26 Billy Williams

Cincinnati Reds
1 Fred Hutchinson
5 Johnny Bench
8 Joe Morgan
10 Sparky Anderson
18 Ted Kluszewski
20 Frank Robinson
24 Tony Perez

Florida Marlins
5 Carl Barger

Houston Astros
24 Jimmy Wynn
25 Jose Cruz
32 Jim Umbricht
33 Mike Scott
34 Nolan Ryan
40 Don Wilson
49 Larry Dierker

Los Angeles Dodgers
1 Pee Wee Reese
2 Tommy Lasorda
4 Duke Snider
19 Jim Gilliam
20 Don Sutton
24 Walter Alston
32 Sandy Koufax
39 Roy Campanella
42 Jackie Robinson
53 Don Drysdale

Milwaukee Brewers
4 Paul Molitor
19 Robin Yount
34 Rollie Fingers
44 Hank Aaron

New York Mets
14 Gil Hodges
37 Casey Stengel
41 Tom Seaver

Philadelphia Phillies
1 Richie Ashburn
14 Jim Bunning
20 Mike Schmidt
32 Steve Carlton
36 Robin Roberts

Pittsburgh Pirates
1 Billy Meyer
4 Ralph Kiner
8 Willie Stargell
9 Bill Mazeroski
20 Pie Traynor
21 Roberto Clemente
33 Honus Wagner
40 Danny Murtaugh

San Diego Padres
6 Steve Garvey
19 Tony Gwynn
31 Dave Winfield
35 Randy Jones

San Francisco Giants
3 Bill Terry
4 Mel Ott
11 Carl Hubbell
24 Willie Mays
27 Juan Marichal
30 Orlando Cepeda
36 Gaylord Perry
44 Willie McCovey

St. Louis Cardinals
1 Ozzie Smith
2 Red Schoendienst
6 Stan Musial
9 Enos Slaughter
14 Ken Boyer
17 Dizzy Dean
20 Lou Brock
42 Bruce Sutter
45 Bob Gibson
85 August (Gussie) Busch (age)

National Basketball Association

Boston has retired the most numbers (21) in the NBA, followed by Portland (9); the Rochester/Cincinnati Royals/K.C./Sacramento Kings, Syracuse Nats/Philadelphia 76ers and New York Knicks (8); Detroit, Los Angeles Lakers, Milwaukee and Phoenix Suns have (7); Cleveland and New Jersey have (6). **Wilt Chamberlain** is the only player to have his number retired by three teams: #13 by the LA Lakers, Golden State and Philadelphia; Nine players have had their numbers retired by two teams: **Kareem Abdul-Jabbar**—#33 by LA Lakers and Milwaukee; **Charles Barkley**—#34 by Philadelphia and Phoenix; **Clyde Drexler**—#22 by Houston and Portland; **Julius Erving**—#6 by Philadelphia and #32 by New Jersey; **Michael Jordan**—#23 by Chicago and Miami (in his honor); **Bob Lanier**—#16 by Detroit and Milwaukee; **Pete Maravich**—#7 by Utah and New Orleans; **Oscar Robertson**—#1 by Milwaukee and #14 by Sacramento; **Nate Thurmond**—#42 by Cleveland and Golden State. Miami retired #23 for **Michael Jordan** eventhough he never played for the team.

Numbers retired in 2005-06 (3): ATLANTA—#40 worn by **Jason Collier** (2003-05 with Hawks); INDIANA—#31 worn by **Reggie Miller** (1988-2005 with Pacers); UTAH—#32 worn by **Karl Malone** (1986-2003 with Jazz).

Eastern Conference

Two Eastern teams—the Charlotte Bobcats and Toronto Raptors—have not retired any numbers.

Atlanta Hawks
- 9 Bob Pettit
- 17 Ted Turner
- 21 Dominique Wilkins
- 23 Lou Hudson
- 40 Jason Collier

Chicago Bulls
- 4 Jerry Sloan
- 10 Bob Love
- 23 Michael Jordan
- 33 Scottie Pippen

Cleveland Cavaliers
- 7 Bingo Smith
- 22 Larry Nance
- 25 Mark Price
- 34 Austin Carr
- 42 Nate Thurmond
- 43 Brad Daugherty

Detroit Pistons
- 2 Chuck Daly
- 4 Joe Dumars
- 11 Isiah Thomas
- 15 Vinnie Johnson
- 16 Bob Lanier
- 21 Dave Bing
- 40 Bill Laimbeer

Boston Celtics
- 1 Walter A. Brown
- 2 Red Auerbach
- 3 Dennis Johnson
- 6 Bill Russell
- 10 Jo Jo White
- 14 Bob Cousy
- 15 Tom Heinsohn
- 16 Tom (Satch) Sanders
- 17 John Havlicek
- 18 Dave Cowens
- 19 Don Nelson
- 21 Bill Sharman
- 22 Ed Macauley
- 23 Frank Ramsey
- 24 Sam Jones
- 25 K.C. Jones
- 31 Cedric Maxwell
- 32 Kevin McHale
- 33 Larry Bird
- 35 Reggie Lewis
- 00 Robert Parish
- **Loscy** Jim Loscutoff (#18)
- **Radio mic** Johnny Most

Indiana Pacers
- 30 George McGinnis
- 31 Reggie Miller
- 34 Mel Daniels
- 35 Roger Brown
- 529 Bob "Slick" Leonard

Miami Heat
- 23 Michael Jordan

Milwaukee Bucks
- 1 Oscar Robertson
- 2 Junior Bridgeman
- 4 Sidney Moncrief
- 14 Jon McGlocklin
- 16 Bob Lanier
- 32 Brian Winters
- 33 Kareem Abdul-Jabbar

New York Knicks
- 10 Walt Frazier
- 12 Dick Barnett
- 15 Dick McGuire & Earl Monroe
- 19 Willis Reed
- 22 Dave DeBusschere
- 24 Bill Bradley
- 33 Patrick Ewing
- 613 Red Holzman

New Jersey Nets
- 3 Drazen Petrovic
- 4 Wendell Ladner
- 23 John Williamson
- 25 Bill Melchionni
- 32 Julius Erving
- 52 Buck Williams

Orlando Magic
- 6 Fans ("Sixth Man")

Philadelphia 76ers
- 2 Moses Malone
- 6 Julius Erving
- 10 Maurice Cheeks
- 13 Wilt Chamberlain
- 15 Hal Greer
- 24 Bobby Jones
- 32 Billy Cunningham
- 34 Charles Barkley
- **P.A. mic** Dave Zinkoff

Washington Wizards
- 11 Elvin Hayes
- 25 Gus Johnson
- 41 Wes Unseld

Western Conference

Two Western teams—the Los Angeles Clippers and Memphis Grizzlies—have not retired any numbers.

Dallas Mavericks
- 15 Brad Davis
- 22 Rolando Blackman

Denver Nuggets
- 2 Alex English
- 33 David Thompson
- 40 Byron Beck
- 44 Dan Issel
- 432 Doug Moe

Golden St. Warriors
- 13 Wilt Chamberlain
- 14 Tom Meschery
- 16 Al Attles
- 24 Rick Barry
- 42 Nate Thurmond

Houston Rockets
- 22 Clyde Drexler
- 23 Calvin Murphy
- 24 Moses Malone
- 34 Hakeem Olajuwon
- 45 Rudy Tomjanovich

Los Angeles Lakers
- 13 Wilt Chamberlain
- 22 Elgin Baylor
- 25 Gail Goodrich
- 32 Magic Johnson
- 33 Kareem Abdul-Jabbar
- 42 James Worthy
- 44 Jerry West
- **Radio mic** Chick Hearn

Minn. Timberwolves
- 2 Malik Sealy

New Orleans Hornets
- 7 Pete Maravich
- 13 Bobby Phills

Phoenix Suns
- 5 Dick Van Arsdale
- 6 Walter Davis
- 7 Kevin Johnson
- 9 Dan Majerle
- 24 Tom Chambers
- 33 Alvan Adams
- 34 Charles Barkley
- 42 Connie Hawkins
- 44 Paul Westphal
- 832 Cotton Fitzsimmons

Portland Trail Blazers
- 1 Larry Weinberg
- 13 Dave Twardzik
- 15 Larry Steele
- 20 Maurice Lucas
- 22 Clyde Drexler
- 32 Bill Walton
- 36 Lloyd Neal
- 45 Geoff Petrie
- 77 Jack Ramsay

Sacramento Kings
- 1 Nate Archibald
- 2 Mitch Richmond
- 6 Fans ("Sixth Man")
- 11 Bob Davies
- 12 Maurice Stokes
- 14 Oscar Robertson
- 27 Jack Twyman
- 44 Sam Lacey

San Antonio Spurs
- 13 James Silas
- 32 Sean Elliott
- 44 George Gervin
- 50 David Robinson
- 00 Johnny Moore

Seattle SuperSonics
- 1 Gus Williams
- 10 Nate McMillan
- 19 Lenny Wilkens
- 32 Fred Brown
- 43 Jack Sikma
- **Radio mic** Bob Blackburn

Utah Jazz
- 1 Frank Layden
- 7 Pete Maravich
- 12 John Stockton
- 14 Jeff Hornacek
- 32 Karl Malone
- 35 Darrell Griffith
- 53 Mark Eaton

Retired Numbers (Cont.)
National Football League

The Chicago Bears have retired the most uniform numbers (13) in the NFL; followed by the New York Giants (11); the Dallas Texans/Kansas City Chiefs, Boston-New England Patriots and San Francisco (8); the Baltimore-Indianapolis Colts (7); Detroit and Philadelphia (6); Cleveland (5). No player has ever had his number retired by more than one NFL team.
Number retired in 2005-06 (1): PHILADELPHIA—#92 worn by **Reggie White** (1985-92 with Eagles).

AFC

Four AFC teams—the Baltimore Ravens, Houston Texans, Jacksonville Jaguars and Oakland Raiders—have not retired any numbers.

Buffalo Bills
12 Jim Kelly

Cincinnati Bengals
54 Bob Johnson

Cleveland Browns
14 Otto Graham
32 Jim Brown
45 Ernie Davis
46 Don Fleming
76 Lou Groza

Denver Broncos
7   John Elway
18 Frank Tripucka
44 Floyd Little

Indianapolis Colts
19 Johnny Unitas
22 Buddy Young
24 Lenny Moore
70 Art Donovan
77 Jim Parker
82 Raymond Berry
89 Gino Marchetti

Kansas City Chiefs
3   Jan Stenerud
16 Len Dawson
28 Abner Haynes
33 Stone Johnson
36 Mack Lee Hill
63 Willie Lanier
78 Bobby Bell
86 Buck Buchanan

Miami Dolphins
12 Bob Griese
13 Dan Marino
39 Larry Csonka

New England Patriots
20 Gino Cappelletti
40 Mike Haynes
56 Andre Tippett
57 Steve Nelson
73 John Hannah
78 Bruce Armstrong
79 Jim Lee Hunt
89 Bob Dee

New York Jets
12 Joe Namath
13 Don Maynard
73 Joe Klecko

Pittsburgh Steelers
70 Ernie Stautner

San Diego Chargers
14 Dan Fouts
19 Lance Alworth

Tennessee Titans
34 Earl Campbell
43 Jim Norton
63 Mike Munchak
65 Elvin Bethea
74 Bruce Matthews

NFC

Dallas is the only NFC team that hasn't officially retired any numbers. The Falcons haven't issued uniform #10 (Steve Bartkowski) and #78 (Mike Kenn) since those players retired. The Cowboys have a "Ring of Honor" at Texas Stadium that includes 15 players, one coach and one president/GM—Troy Aikman, Tony Dorsett, Cliff Harris, Bob Hayes, Chuck Howley, Michael Irvin, Lee Roy Jordan, Tom Landry, Bob Lilly, Don Meredith, Don Perkins, Mel Renfro, Tex Schramm, Emmitt Smith, Roger Staubach, Randy White and Rayfield Wright.

Arizona Cardinals
8   Larry Wilson
40 Pat Tillman
77 Stan Mauldin
88 J.V. Cain
99 Marshall Goldberg

Atlanta Falcons
31 William Andrews
57 Jeff Van Note
60 Tommy Nobis

Carolina Panthers
51 Sam Mills

Chicago Bears
3   Bronko Nagurski
5   George McAfee
7   George Halas
28 Willie Galimore
34 Walter Payton
40 Gale Sayers
41 Brian Piccolo
42 Sid Luckman
51 Dick Butkus
56 Bill Hewitt
61 Bill George
66 Bulldog Turner
77 Red Grange

Detroit Lions
7   Dutch Clark
22 Bobby Layne
37 Doak Walker
56 Joe Schmidt
85 Chuck Hughes
88 Charlie Sanders

Green Bay Packers
3   Tony Canadeo
14 Don Hutson
15 Bart Starr
66 Ray Nitschke
92 Reggie White

Minnesota Vikings
10 Fran Tarkenton
53 Mick Tingelhoff
70 Jim Marshall
77 Korey Stringer
80 Cris Carter
88 Alan Page

New Orleans Saints
31 Jim Taylor
81 Doug Atkins

New York Giants
1   Ray Flaherty
4   Tuffy Leemans
7   Mel Hein
11 Phil Simms
14 Y.A. Tittle
16 Frank Gifford
32 Al Blozis
40 Joe Morrison
42 Charlie Conerly
50 Ken Strong
56 Lawrence Taylor

Philadelphia Eagles
15 Steve Van Buren
40 Tom Brookshier
44 Pete Retzlaff
60 Chuck Bednarik
70 Al Wistert
92 Reggie White
99 Jerome Brown

St. Louis Rams
7   Bob Waterfield
29 Eric Dickerson
74 Merlin Olsen
78 Jack Youngblood
85 Jack Youngblood

San Francisco 49ers
12 John Brodie
16 Joe Montana
34 Joe Perry
37 Jimmy Johnson
39 Hugh McElhenny
42 Ronnie Lott
70 Charlie Krueger
73 Leo Nomellini
79 Bob St. Clair
87 Dwight Clark

Seattle Seahawks
12 Fans ("12th Man")
80 Steve Largent

Tampa Bay Buccaneers
63 Lee Roy Selmon

Washington Redskins
33 Sammy Baugh

National Hockey League

The Boston Bruins have retired the most uniform numbers (10) in the NHL; followed by Montreal (7); N.Y. Islanders (6); Chicago and Detroit (5). Following his retirement in 1999, the NHL announced that the league would retire **Wayne Gretzky**'s #99. Three other players have had their numbers retired by two teams: **Gordie Howe**—#9 by Detroit and Hartford; **Bobby Hull**—#9 by Chicago and Winnipeg (now Phoenix); and **Ray Bourque**—#77 by Boston and Colorado.

Numbers retired in 2005-06 (5): MONTREAL—#5 worn by **Bernard Geoffrion** (1950-64 with Canadiens), #12 worn by **Dickie Moore** (1951-63 with Canadiens) and **Yvan Cournoyer** (1963-79 with Canadiens) #18 worn by **Serge Savard** (1967-81 with Canadiens) and #29 **Ken Dryden** (1971-79 with Canadiens). NY RANGERS—#11 for **Mark Messier** (1991-97, 2000-04 with Rangers). Detroit announced plans to retire **Steve Yzerman**'s #19 in 2007.

Eastern Conference

Five Eastern teams—the Atlanta Thrashers, Carolina Hurricanes, Florida Panthers, New Jersey Devils and Tampa Bay Lightning—have not retired any numbers. The Hartford Whalers had retired three numbers: #2 Rick Ley, #9 Gordie Howe and #19 John McKenzie. Mario Lemieux's retired #66 with Pittsburgh has been temporarily unretired during his recent comeback.

Boston Bruins
- 2 Eddie Shore
- 3 Lionel Hitchman
- 4 Bobby Orr
- 5 Dit Clapper
- 7 Phil Esposito
- 8 Cam Neely
- 9 John Bucyk
- 15 Milt Schmidt
- 24 Terry O'Reilly
- 77 Ray Bourque

Buffalo Sabres
- 2 Tim Horton
- 7 Rick Martin
- 11 Gilbert Perreault
- 14 Rene Robert

Montreal Canadiens
- 1 Jacques Plante
- 2 Doug Harvey
- 4 Jean Beliveau
- 5 Bernard Geoffrion
- 7 Howie Morenz
- 9 Maurice Richard
- 10 Guy Lafleur
- 12 Dickie Moore
- Yvan Cournoyer
- 16 Henri Richard
- 18 Serge Savard
- 29 Ken Dryden

New York Islanders
- 5 Denis Potvin
- 9 Clark Gillies
- 19 Bryan Trottier
- 22 Mike Bossy
- 23 Bob Nystrom
- 31 Billy Smith

New York Rangers
- 1 Eddie Giacomin
- 7 Rod Gilbert
- 11 Mark Messier
- 35 Mike Richter

Ottawa Senators
- 8 Frank Finnigan

Philadelphia Flyers
- 1 Bernie Parent
- 4 Barry Ashbee
- 7 Bill Barber
- 16 Bobby Clarke

Pittsburgh Penguins
- 21 Michel Briere
- 66 Mario Lemieux

Toronto Maple Leafs
- 5 Bill Barilko
- 6 Ace Bailey

Washington Capitals
- 5 Rod Langway
- 7 Yvon Labre
- 32 Dale Hunter

Western Conference

Four Western teams—the Columbus Blue Jackets, Mighty Ducks of Anaheim, Nashville Predators and San Jose Sharks—have not retired any numbers. Note, the Quebec Nordiques retired the numbers of J.C. Tremblay (3), Marc Tardif (8) and Michel Goulet (16) but these numbers have been worn since the team moved to Colorado. Detroit has not officially retired the numbers of Larry Aurie (6) and Vladimir Konstantinov (16) but has kept them "out of circulation." Similarly, St. Louis has not officially retired the number of Doug Wickenheiser (14) but has kept it out of circulation since his death in 1999.

Calgary Flames
- 9 Lanny McDonald

Chicago Blackhawks
- 1 Glenn Hall
- 9 Bobby Hull
- 18 Denis Savard
- 21 Stan Mikita
- 35 Tony Esposito

Colorado Avalanche
- 33 Patrick Roy
- 77 Ray Bourque

Dallas Stars
- 7 Neal Broten
- 8 Bill Goldsworthy
- 19 Bill Masterton

Detroit Red Wings
- 1 Terry Sawchuk
- 7 Ted Lindsay
- 9 Gordie Howe
- 10 Alex Delvecchio
- 12 Sid Abel
- 19 Steve Yzerman (2007)

Edmonton Oilers
- 3 Al Hamilton
- 7 Paul Coffey
- 17 Jari Kurri
- 31 Grant Fuhr
- 99 Wayne Gretzky

Los Angeles Kings
- 16 Marcel Dionne
- 18 Dave Taylor
- 30 Rogie Vachon
- 99 Wayne Gretzky

Minnesota Wild
- 1 Fans

Phoenix Coyotes
- 9 Bobby Hull
- 25 Thomas Steen

St. Louis Blues
- 3 Bob Gassoff
- 8 Barclay Plager
- 11 Brian Sutter
- 24 Bernie Federko

Vancouver Canucks
- 12 Stan Smyl

AWARDS

Associated Press Athletes of the Year

Selected annually by AP newspaper sports editors since 1931.

Male

The top 5 vote-getters: 1. **Lance Armstrong**, cycling, 30 votes; 2. **Reggie Bush**, football, 23; 3. **Peyton Manning**, football, 8; 4. **Roger Federer**, tennis and **Tiger Woods**, golf, 7.

Multiple winners: Lance Armstrong (4); Michael Jordan and Tiger Woods (3); Don Budge, Sandy Koufax, Carl Lewis, Joe Montana and Byron Nelson (2).

Year		Year		Year	
1931	**Pepper Martin**, baseball	1941	**Joe DiMaggio**, baseball	1951	**Dick Kazmaier**, col. football
1932	**Gene Sarazen**, golf	1942	**Frank Sinkwich**, col. football	1952	**Bob Mathias**, track
1933	**Carl Hubbell**, baseball	1943	**Gunder Haegg**, track	1953	**Ben Hogan**, golf
1934	**Dizzy Dean**, baseball	1944	**Byron Nelson**, golf	1954	**Willie Mays**, baseball
1935	**Joe Louis**, boxing	1945	**Byron Nelson**, golf	1955	**Hopalong Cassady**, col. football
1936	**Jesse Owens**, track	1946	**Glenn Davis**, college football		
1937	**Don Budge**, tennis	1947	**Johnny Lujack**, col. football	1956	**Mickey Mantle**, baseball
1938	**Don Budge**, tennis	1948	**Lou Boudreau**, baseball	1957	**Ted Williams**, baseball
1939	**Nile Kinnick**, college football	1949	**Leon Hart**, college football	1958	**Herb Elliott**, track
1940	**Tom Harmon**, college football	1950	**Jim Konstanty**, baseball	1959	**Ingemar Johansson**, boxing

Awards (Cont.)

Year		Year		Year	
1960	**Rafer Johnson**, track	1976	**Bruce Jenner**, track	1992	**Michael Jordan**, pro basketball
1961	**Roger Maris**, baseball	1977	**Steve Cauthen**, horse racing	1993	**Michael Jordan**, pro basketball
1962	**Maury Wills**, baseball	1978	**Ron Guidry**, baseball	1994	**George Foreman**, boxing
1963	**Sandy Koufax**, baseball	1979	**Willie Stargell**, baseball	1995	**Cal Ripken Jr.**, baseball
1964	**Don Schollander**, swimming	1980	**U.S. Olympic hockey team**	1996	**Michael Johnson**, track
1965	**Sandy Koufax**, baseball	1981	**John McEnroe**, tennis	1997	**Tiger Woods**, golf
1966	**Frank Robinson**, baseball	1982	**Wayne Gretzky**, hockey	1998	**Mark McGwire**, baseball
1967	**Carl Yastrzemski**, baseball	1983	**Carl Lewis**, track	1999	**Tiger Woods**, golf
1968	**Denny McLain**, baseball	1984	**Carl Lewis**, track	2000	**Tiger Woods**, golf
1969	**Tom Seaver**, baseball	1985	**Dwight Gooden**, baseball	2001	**Barry Bonds**, baseball
1970	**George Blanda**, pro football	1986	**Larry Bird**, pro basketball	2002	**Lance Armstrong**, cycling
1971	**Lee Trevino**, golf	1987	**Ben Johnson**, track	2003	**Lance Armstrong**, cycling
1972	**Mark Spitz**, swimming	1988	**Orel Hershiser**, baseball	2004	**Lance Armstrong**, cycling
1973	**O.J. Simpson**, pro football	1989	**Joe Montana**, pro football	2005	**Lance Armstrong**, cycling
1974	**Muhammad Ali**, boxing	1990	**Joe Montana**, pro football		
1975	**Fred Lynn**, baseball	1991	**Michael Jordan**, pro basketball		

Female

The top 5 vote-getters: 1. **Annika Sorenstam**, golf, 47 votes; 2. **Danica Patrick**, auto racing, 17; 3. **Maria Sharapova**, tennis, 5; 4. **Michelle Wie**, golf and **Venus Williams**, tennis, 4.

Multiple winners: Babe Didrikson Zaharias (6); Chris Evert (4); Patty Berg, Maureen Connolly and Annika Sorenstam (3); Tracy Austin, Althea Gibson, Billie Jean King, Nancy Lopez, Alice Marble, Martina Navratilova, Wilma Rudolph, Monica Seles, Kathy Whitworth and Mickey Wright (2).

Year		Year		Year	
1931	**Helene Madison**, swimming	1956	**Pat McCormick**, diving	1981	**Tracy Austin**, tennis
1932	**Babe Didrikson**, track	1957	**Althea Gibson**, tennis	1982	**Mary Decker Tabb**, track
1933	**Helen Jacobs**, tennis	1958	**Althea Gibson**, tennis	1983	**Martina Navratilova**, tennis
1934	**Virginia Van Wie**, golf	1959	**Maria Bueno**, tennis	1984	**Mary Lou Retton**, gymnastics
1935	**Helen Wills Moody**, tennis	1960	**Wilma Rudolph**, track	1985	**Nancy Lopez**, golf
1936	**Helen Stephens**, track	1961	**Wilma Rudolph**, track	1986	**Martina Navratilova**, tennis
1937	**Katherine Rawls**, swimming	1962	**Dawn Fraser**, swimming	1987	**Jackie Joyner-Kersee**, track
1938	**Patty Berg**, golf	1963	**Mickey Wright**, golf	1988	**Florence Griffith Joyner**, track
1939	**Alice Marble**, tennis	1964	**Mickey Wright**, golf	1989	**Steffi Graf**, tennis
1940	**Alice Marble**, tennis	1965	**Kathy Whitworth**, golf	1990	**Beth Daniel**, golf
1941	**Betty Hicks Newell**, golf	1966	**Kathy Whitworth**, golf	1991	**Monica Seles**, tennis
1942	**Gloria Callen**, swimming	1967	**Billie Jean King**, tennis	1992	**Monica Seles**, tennis
1943	**Patty Berg**, golf	1968	**Peggy Fleming**, skating	1993	**Sheryl Swoopes**, basketball
1944	**Ann Curtis**, swimming	1969	**Debbie Meyer**, swimming	1994	**Bonnie Blair**, speed skating
1945	**Babe Didrikson Zaharias**, golf	1970	**Chi Cheng**, track	1995	**Rebecca Lobo**, col. basketball
1946	**Babe Didrikson Zaharias**, golf	1971	**Evonne Goolagong**, tennis	1996	**Amy Van Dyken**, swimming
1947	**Babe Didrikson Zaharias**, golf	1972	**Olga Korbut**, gymnastics	1997	**Martina Hingis**, tennis
1948	**Fanny Blankers-Koen**, track	1973	**Billie Jean King**, tennis	1998	**Se Ri Pak**, golf
1949	**Marlene Bauer**, golf	1974	**Chris Evert**, tennis	1999	**U.S. Soccer Team**
1950	**Babe Didrikson Zaharias**, golf	1975	**Chris Evert**, tennis	2000	**Marion Jones**, track
1951	**Maureen Connolly**, tennis	1976	**Nadia Comaneci**, gymnastics	2001	**Jennifer Capriati**, tennis
1952	**Maureen Connolly**, tennis	1977	**Chris Evert**, tennis	2002	**Serena Williams**, tennis
1953	**Maureen Connolly**, tennis	1978	**Nancy Lopez**, golf	2003	**Annika Sorenstam**, golf
1954	**Babe Didrikson Zaharias**, golf	1979	**Tracy Austin**, tennis	2004	**Annika Sorenstam**, golf
1955	**Patty Berg**, golf	1980	**Chris Evert Lloyd**, tennis	2005	**Annika Sorenstam**, golf

USOC Sportsman & Sportswoman of the Year

To the outstanding overall male and female athletes from within the U.S. Olympic Committee member organizations. Winners are chosen from nominees of the national governing bodies for Olympic and Pan American Games and affiliated organizations. Voting is done by members of the national media, USOC board of directors and Athletes' Advisory Council.

Sportsman

Multiple winners: Lance Armstrong (4); Eric Heiden and Michael Johnson (3); Matt Biondi and Greg Louganis (2).

Year		Year		Year	
1974	**Jim Bolding**, track	1985	**Willie Banks**, track	1996	**Michael Johnson**, track
1975	**Clint Jackson**, boxing	1986	**Matt Biondi**, swimming	1997	**Pete Sampras**, tennis
1976	**John Naber**, swimming	1987	**Greg Louganis**, diving	1998	**Jonny Moseley**, skiing
1977	**Eric Heiden**, speed skating	1988	**Matt Biondi**, swimming	1999	**Lance Armstrong**, cycling
1978	**Bruce Davidson**, equestrian	1989	**Roger Kingdom**, track	2000	**Rulon Gardner**, wrestling
1979	**Eric Heiden**, speed skating	1990	**John Smith**, wrestling	2001	**Lance Armstrong**, cycling
1980	**Eric Heiden**, speed skating	1991	**Carl Lewis**, track	2002	**Lance Armstrong**, cycling
1981	**Scott Hamilton**, fig. skating	1992	**Pablo Morales**, swimming	2003	**Lance Armstrong**, cycling
1982	**Greg Louganis**, diving	1993	**Michael Johnson**, track	2004	**Michael Phelps**, swimming
1983	**Rick McKinney**, archery	1994	**Dan Jansen**, speed skating	2005	**Hunter Kemper**, triathlon
1984	**Edwin Moses**, track	1995	**Michael Johnson**, track		

Sportswoman

Multiple winners: Bonnie Blair, Tracy Caulkins, Jackie Joyner-Kersee, Picabo Street and Sheila Young Ochowicz (2).

Year		Year		Year	
'74	**Shirley Babashoff**, swimming	1984	**Tracy Caulkins**, swimming	1995	**Picabo Street**, skiing
'75	**Kathy Heddy**, swimming	1985	**Mary Decker Slaney**, track	1996	**Amy Van Dyken**, swimming
'76	**Sheila Young**, speedskating	1986	**Jackie Joyner-Kersee**, track	1997	**Tara Lipinski**, figure skating
'77	**Linda Fratianne**, fig. skating	1987	**Jackie Joyner-Kersee**, track	1998	**Picabo Street**, skiing
'78	**Tracy Caulkins**, swimming	1988	**Florence Griffith Joyner**, track	1999	**Jenny Thompson**, swimming
'79	**Sippy Woodhead**, swimming	1989	**Janet Evans**, swimming	2000	**Marion Jones**, track
'80	**Beth Heiden**, speed skating	1990	**Lynn Jennings**, track	2001	**Jennifer Capriati**, tennis
'81	**Sheila Ochowicz**, speed skating & cycling	1991	**Kim Zmeskal**, gymnastics	2002	**Sarah Hughes**, figure skating
'82	**Melanie Smith**, equestrian	1992	**Bonnie Blair**, speed skating	2003	**Michelle Kwan**, figure skating
'83	**Tamara McKinney**, skiing	1993	**Gail Devers**, track	2004	**Carly Patterson**, gymnastics
		1994	**Bonnie Blair**, speed skating	2005	**Katie Hoff**, swimming

UPI International Athletes of the Year

Selected annually by United Press International's European newspaper sports editors from 1974-95.

Male

Multiple winners: Sebastian Coe, Alberto Juantorena and Carl Lewis (2).

Year		Year		Year	
'74	**Muhammad Ali**, boxing	1982	**Daley Thompson**, track	1990	**Stefan Edberg**, tennis
'75	**Joao Oliveira**, track	1983	**Carl Lewis**, track	1991	**Sergei Bubka**, track
'76	**Alberto Juantorena**, track	1984	**Carl Lewis**, track	1992	**Kevin Young**, track
'77	**Alberto Juantorena**, track	1985	**Steve Cram**, track	1993	**Miguel Indurain**, cycling
'78	**Henry Rono**, track	1986	**Diego Maradona**, soccer	1994	**Johann Olav Koss**, speed skating
'79	**Sebastian Coe**, track	1987	**Ben Johnson**, track		
'80	**Eric Heiden**, speed skating	1988	**Matt Biondi**, swimming	1995	**Jonathan Edwards**, track
'81	**Sebastian Coe**, track	1989	**Boris Becker**, tennis	1996	discontinued

Female

Multiple winners: Nadia Comaneci, Steffi Graf, Marita Koch and Monica Seles (2).

Year		Year		Year	
'74	**Irena Szewinska**, track	1982	**Marita Koch**, track	1990	**Merlene Ottey**, track
'75	**Nadia Comaneci**, gymnastics	1983	**Jarmila Kratochvilova**, track	1991	**Monica Seles**, tennis
'76	**Nadia Comaneci**, gymnastics	1984	**Martina Navratilova**, tennis	1992	**Monica Seles**, tennis
'77	**Rosie Ackermann**, track	1985	**Mary Decker Slaney**, track	1993	**Wang Junxia**, track
'78	**Tracy Caulkins**, swimming	1986	**Heike Drechsler**, track	1994	**Le Jingyi**, swimming
'79	**Marita Koch**, track	1987	**Steffi Graf**, tennis	1995	**Gwen Torrence**, track
'80	**Hanni Wenzel**, alpine skiing	1988	**Florence Griffith Joyner**, track	1996	discontinued
'81	**Chris Evert Lloyd**, tennis	1989	**Steffi Graf**, tennis		

American-International Athlete Trophy

Formerly known as the Jesse Owens International Trophy, the trophy has been presented annually by the International Amateur Athletic Association since 1981 and selected by a worldwide panel of electors.

Multiple winners: Lance Armstrong, Michael Johnson and Marion Jones (2).

Year		Year		Year	
'81	**Eric Heiden**, speed skating	1990	**Roger Kingdom**, track	1997	**Michael Johnson**, track
'82	**Sebastian Coe**, track	1991	**Greg LeMond**, cycling	1998	**Haile Gebrselassie**, track
'83	**Mary Decker**, track	1992	**Mike Powell**, track	1999	**Marion Jones**, track
'84	**Edwin Moses**, track	1993	**Vitaly Scherbo**, gymnastics	2000	**Lance Armstrong**, cycling
'85	**Carl Lewis**, track	1994	**Wang Junxia**, track	2001	**Marion Jones**, track
'86	**Said Aouita**, track	1995	**Johann Olva Koss**, speed skating	2002	**Ian Thorpe**, swimming
'87	**Greg Louganis**, diving			2003	**Lance Armstrong**, cycling
'88	**Ben Johnson**, track	1996	**Michael Johnson**, track	2004	**Michael Phelps**, swimming

Honda-Broderick Cup

The outstanding collegiate woman athlete of the year in NCAA competition. Winner is chosen from nominees in each of the NCAA's 10 competitive sports. Final voting is done by member athletic directors. Award is named after founder and sportswear manufacturer Thomas Broderick.

Multiple winner: Tracy Caulkins (2).

Year			Year		
'77	**Lucy Harris**, Delta St	basketball	1987	**Mary T. Meagher**, California	swimming
'78	**Ann Meyers**, UCLA	basketball	1988	**Teresa Weatherspoon**, La. Tech	basketball
'79	**Nancy Lieberman**, Old Dominion	basketball	1989	**Vicki Huber**, Villanova	track
'80	**Julie Shea**, N.C. State	track & field	1990	**Suzy Favor**, Wisconsin	track
'81	**Jill Sterkel**, Texas	swimming	1991	**Dawn Staley**, Virginia	basketball
'82	**Tracy Caulkins**, Florida	swimming	1992	**Missy Marlowe**, Utah	gymnastics
'83	**Deitre Collins**, Hawaii	volleyball	1993	**Lisa Fernandez**, UCLA	softball
'84	**Tracy Caulkins**, Florida	swimming	1994	**Mia Hamm**, North Carolina	soccer
	& **Cheryl Miller**, USC	basketball	1995	**Rebecca Lobo**, UConn	basketball
'85	**Jackie Joyner**, UCLA	track & field	1996	**Jennifer Rizzotti**, UConn	basketball
'86	**Kamie Ethridge**, Texas	basketball	1997	**Cindy Daws**, Notre Dame	soccer

Awards (Cont.)

Year			Year		
1998	**Chamique Holdsclaw**, Tennessee	. . .basketball	2003	**Natasha Watley**, UCLA	. . . . .softbal
1999	**Misty May**, Long Beach St.	. . . . .volleyball	2004	**Tara Kirk**, Stanford	. . . . .swimming
2000	**Cristina Teuscher**, Columbia	. . . . . . .swimming	2005	**Ogonna Nnamani**, Stanford	. . . . . . .volleyba
2001	**Jackie Stiles**, SW Missouri St.	. . . . . .basketball	2006	**Christine Sinclair**, Portland	. . . . .socce
2002	**Angela Williams**, USC	. . . . .track			

Flo Hyman Award

Presented annually since 1987 by the Women's Sports Foundation for "exemplifying dignity, spirit and commitment to exce lence" and named in honor of the late captain of the 1984 U.S. Women's Volleyball team. Voting by WSF members.

Year		Year		Year	
1987	**Martina Navratilova**, tennis	1993	**Lynette Woodard**, basketball	1999	**Bonnie Blair**, speed skating
1988	**Jackie Joyner-Kersee**, track	1994	**Patty Sheehan**, golf	2000	**Monica Seles**, tennis
1989	**Evelyn Ashford**, track	1995	**Mary Lou Retton**; gymnastics	2001	**Lisa Leslie**, basketball
1990	**Chris Evert**, tennis	1996	**Donna de Varona**, swimming	2002	**Dot Richardson**, softball
1991	**Diana Golden**, skiing	1997	**Billie Jean King**, tennis	2003	**Nawal El Moutawakel**, trac
1992	**Nancy Lopez**, golf	1998	**Nadia Comaneci**, gymnastics	2004	**Kristi Yamaguchi**, fig. skating

James E. Sullivan Memorial Award

Presented annually by the Amateur Athletic Union since 1930. The Sullivan Award is named after the former AAU preside and given to the athlete who, "by his or her performance, example and influence as an amateur, has done the most durin the year to advance the cause of sportsmanship."

Duke senior **J.J. Redick** won the 76th Sullivan Award. The guard beat out several high-profile college football players inclu ing Reggie Bush and Vince Young, becoming the first men's basketball player to win the Sullivan Award since Bill Walton 1973. Redick also won the Associated Press and John Wooden Award as the national player of the year.

Year		Year		Year	
1930	**Bobby Jones**, golf	1956	**Pat McCormick**, diving	1982	**Mary Decker**, track
1931	**Barney Berlinger**, track	1957	**Bobby Morrow**, track	1983	**Edwin Moses**, track
1932	**Jim Bausch**, track	1958	**Glenn Davis**, track	1984	**Greg Louganis**, diving
1933	**Glenn Cunningham**, track	1959	**Parry O'Brien**, track	1985	**Joan B. Samuelson**, track
1934	**Bill Bonthron**, track	1960	**Rafer Johnson**, track	1986	**Jackie Joyner-Kersee**, track
1935	**Lawson Little**, golf	1961	**Wilma Rudolph**, track	1987	**Jim Abbott**, baseball
1936	**Glenn Morris**, track	1962	**Jim Beatty**, track	1988	**Florence Griffith Joyner**, trac
1937	**Don Budge**, tennis	1963	**John Pennel**, track	1989	**Janet Evans**, swimming
1938	**Don Lash**, track	1964	**Don Schollander**, swimming	1990	**John Smith**, wrestling
1939	**Joe Burk**, rowing	1965	**Bill Bradley**, basketball	1991	**Mike Powell**, track
1940	**Greg Rice**, track	1966	**Jim Ryun**, track	1992	**Bonnie Blair**, speed skating
1941	**Leslie MacMitchell**, track	1967	**Randy Matson**, track	1993	**Charlie Ward**, football
1942	**Cornelius Warmerdam**, track	1968	**Debbie Meyer**, swimming	1994	**Dan Jansen**, speed skating
1943	**Gilbert Dodds**, track	1969	**Bill Toomey**, track	1995	**Bruce Baumgartner**, wrestling
1944	**Ann Curtis**, swimming	1970	**John Kinsella**, swimming	1996	**Michael Johnson**, track
1945	**Doc Blanchard**, football	1971	**Mark Spitz**, swimming	1997	**Peyton Manning**, football
1946	**Arnold Tucker**, football	1972	**Frank Shorter**, track	1998	**Chamique Holdsclaw**,
1947	**John B. Kelly, Jr.**, rowing	1973	**Bill Walton**, basketball		basketball
1948	**Bob Mathias**, track	1974	**Rich Wohlhuter**, track	1999	**Coco and Kelly Miller**,
1949	**Dick Button**, skating	1975	**Tim Shaw**, swimming		basketball
1950	**Fred Wilt**, track	1976	**Bruce Jenner**, track	2000	**Rulon Gardner**, wrestling
1951	**Bob Richards**, track	1977	**John Naber**, swimming	2001	**Michelle Kwan**, figure skatin
1952	**Horace Ashenfelter**, track	1978	**Tracy Caulkins**, swimming	2002	**Sarah Hughes**, figure skating
1953	**Sammy Lee**, diving	1979	**Kurt Thomas**, gymnastics	2003	**Michael Phelps**, swimming
1954	**Mal Whitfield**, track	1980	**Eric Heiden**, speed skating	2004	**Paul Hamm**, gymnastics
1955	**Harrison Dillard**, track	1981	**Carl Lewis**, track	2005	**J.J. Redick**, basketball

ESPY Awards

The ESPY Awards, which represent the convergence of the sports and entertainment communities, were created by ESPN 1993 and are given for Excellence in Sports Performance in more than 30 categories. ESPYs are awarded by a panel of spo executives, journalists and retired athletes whose decisions are based on the performances of the nominees during the ye preceding the awards ceremony. Note that not all categories are listed below.

Breakthrough Athlete

Year		Year	
1993	Gary Sheffield, San Diego Padres	2000	Kurt Warner, St. Louis Rams
1994	Mike Piazza, Los Angeles Dodgers	2001	Daunte Culpepper, Minnesota Vikings
1995	Jeff Bagwell, Houston Astros	2002	Tom Brady, New England Patriots
1996	Hideo Nomo, Los Angeles Dodgers	2003	Alfonso Soriano, New York Yankees
1997	Tiger Woods, golf	2004	LeBron James, Cleveland Cavaliers
1998	Nomar Garciaparra, Boston Red Sox	2005	Dwyane Wade, Miami Heat
1999	Randy Moss, Minnesota Vikings	2006	Chris Paul, New Orleans Hornets

Best Coach/Manager

ar	
93	Jimmy Johnson, Dallas Cowboys
94	Jimmy Johnson, Dallas Cowboys
95	George Siefert, San Francisco 49ers
96	Gary Barnett, Northwestern
97	Joe Torre, New York Yankees
98	Jim Leyland, Florida Marlins
99	Joe Torre, New York Yankees
00	Joe Torre, New York Yankees
01	Joe Torre, New York Yankees
02	Phil Jackson, Los Angeles Lakers
03	Jon Gruden, Tampa Bay Buccaneers
04	Larry Brown, Detroit Pistons
05	Bill Belichick, New England Patriots
06	Bill Cowher, Pittsburgh Steelers

Best Comeback Athlete

ar	
93	Dave Winfield, Toronto Blue Jays
94	Mario Lemieux, Pittsburgh Penguins
95	Dan Marino, Miami Dolphins
96	Michael Jordan, Chicago Bulls
97	Evander Holyfield, boxer
98	Roger Clemens, Toronto Blue Jays
99	Eric Davis, Baltimore Orioles
00	Lance Armstrong, cycling
01	Andres Galarraga, baseball
02	Jennifer Capriati, tennis
03	Tommy Maddox, Pittsburgh Steelers
04	Bethany Hamilton, surfing
05	Mark Fields, Carolina Panthers
06	Tedy Bruschi, New England Patriots

Best Female Athlete

ar		Year	
93	Monica Seles, tennis	2000	Mia Hamm, soccer
94	Julie Krone, jockey	2001	Marion Jones, track
95	Bonnie Blair,	2002	V. Williams, tennis
	speed skater	2003	S. Williams, tennis
96	Rebecca Lobo,	2004	Diana Taurasi,
	basketball		basketball
97	Amy Van Dyken,	2005	Annika Sorenstam,
	swimming		golf
98	Mia Hamm, soccer	2006	Annika Sorenstam,
99	C. Holdsclaw,		golf
	college basketball		

Best Male Athlete

ar	
93	Michael Jordan, Chicago Bulls
94	Barry Bonds, San Francisco Giants
95	Steve Young, San Francisco 49ers
96	Cal Ripken, Baltimore Orioles
97	Michael Johnson, Olympic sprinter
98	Tiger Woods, golf
99	Mark McGwire, St. Louis Cardinals
00	Tiger Woods, golf
01	Tiger Woods, golf
02	Tiger Woods, golf
03	Lance Armstrong, cycling
04	Lance Armstrong, cycling
05	Lance Armstrong, cycling
06	Lance Armstrong, cycling

Outstanding Performance Under Pressure

ar	
93	Christian Laettner, Duke
94	Joe Carter, Toronto Blue Jays
95	Mark Messier, New York Rangers
96	Martin Brodeur, New Jersey Devils
97	Kerri Strug, Olympic gymnast
98	Terrell Davis, Denver Broncos
99	Mark O'Meara, golf

Best Team

Year		Year	
1993	Dallas Cowboys	2000	U.S. Women's
1994	Toronto Blue Jays		World Cup Team
1995	New York Rangers	2001	NY Yankees &
1996	UConn women's		Oklahoma football
	basketball	2002	Los Angeles Lakers
1997	New York Yankees	2003	Anaheim Angels
1998	Denver Broncos	2004	Detroit Pistons
1999	New York Yankees	2005	Boston Red Sox
		2006	Pittsburgh Steelers

Best Baseball Player

Year	
1993	Dennis Eckersley, Oakland A's
1994	Barry Bonds, San Francisco Giants
1995	Jeff Bagwell, Houston Astros
1996	Greg Maddux, Atlanta Braves
1997	Ken Caminiti, San Diego Padres
1998	Larry Walker, Colorado Rockies
1999	Mark McGwire, St. Louis Cardinals
2000	Pedro Martinez, Boston Red Sox
2001	Pedro Martinez, Boston Red Sox
2002	Barry Bonds, San Francisco Giants
2003	Barry Bonds, San Francisco Giants
2004	Barry Bonds, San Francisco Giants
2005	Albert Pujols, St. Louis Cardinals
2006	Albert Pujols, St. Louis Cardinals

Best NFL Player

Year	
1993	Emmitt Smith, Dallas Cowboys
1994	Emmitt Smith, Dallas Cowboys
1995	Barry Sanders, Detroit Lions
1996	Brett Favre, Green Bay Packers
1997	Brett Favre, Green Bay Packers
1998	Barry Sanders, Detroit Lions
1999	Terrell Davis, Denver Broncos
2000	Kurt Warner, St. Louis Rams
2001	Marshall Faulk, St. Louis Rams
2002	Marshall Faulk, St. Louis Rams
2003	Michael Vick, Atlanta Falcons
2004	Peyton Manning, Indianapolis Colts
2005	Peyton Manning, Indianapolis Colts
2006	Shaun Alexander, Seattle Seahawks

Best NBA Player

Year	
1993	Michael Jordan, Chicago Bulls
1994	Charles Barkley, Phoenix Suns
1995	Hakeem Olajuwon, Houston Rockets
1996	Hakeem Olajuwon, Houston Rockets
1997	Michael Jordan, Chicago Bulls
1998	Michael Jordan, Chicago Bulls
1999	Michael Jordan, Chicago Bulls
2000	Tim Duncan, San Antonio Spurs
2001	Shaquille O'Neal, Los Angeles Lakers
2002	Shaquille O'Neal, Los Angeles Lakers
2003	Tim Duncan, San Antonio Spurs
2004	Kevin Garnett, Minnesota Timberwolves
2005	Steve Nash, Phoenix Suns
2006	Dwyane Wade, Miami Heat

Best WNBA Player

Year	
1998	Cynthia Cooper, Houston Comets
1999	Cynthia Cooper, Houston Comets
2000	Cynthia Cooper, Houston Comets
2001	Sheryl Swoopes, Houston Comets
2002	Lisa Leslie, Los Angeles Sparks
2003	Lisa Leslie, Los Angeles Sparks
2004	Lauren Jackson, Seattle Storm
2005	Lauren Jackson, Seattle Storm
2006	Sheryl Swoopes, Houston Comets

Best NHL Player

Year	
1993	Mario Lemieux, Pittsburgh Penguins
1994	Mario Lemieux, Pittsburgh Penguins
1995	Mark Messier, New York Rangers
1996	Eric Lindros, Philadelphia Flyers
1997	Joe Sakic, Colorado Avalanche
1998	Mario Lemieux, Pittsburgh Penguins
1999	Dominik Hasek, Buffalo Sabres
2000	Dominik Hasek, Buffalo Sabres
2001	Chris Pronger, St. Louis Blues
2002	Jarome Iginla, Calgary Flames
2003	Jean-Sebastien Giguere, Anaheim Mighty Ducks
2004	Jarome Iginla, Calgary Flames
2005	not awarded
2006	Jaromir Jagr, NY Rangers

Outstanding College Football Performer of the Year

Year	
1993	Garrison Hearst, Georgia
1994	Charlie Ward, Florida State
1995	Rashaan Salaam, Colorado
1996	Eddie George, Ohio State
1997	Danny Wuerffel, Florida
1998	Peyton Manning, Tennessee
1999	Ricky Williams, Texas
2000	Michael Vick, Virginia Tech
2001	Chris Weinke, Florida State

Outstanding Men's College Basketball Performer of the Year

Year		Year	
1993	Christian Laettner, Duke	1998	Keith Van Horn, Utah
1994	Bobby Hurley, Duke	1999	Antawn Jamison, N. Carolina
1995	Grant Hill, Duke		
1996	Ed O'Bannon, UCLA	2000	Elton Brand, Duke
1997	Tim Duncan, Wake Forest	2001	Kenyon Martin, Cincinnati

Outstanding Women's College Basketball Performer of the Year

Year	
1993	Dawn Staley, Virginia
1994	Sheryl Swoopes, Texas Tech
1995	Charlotte Smith, North Carolina
1996	Rebecca Lobo, Connecticut
1997	Saudia Roundtree, Georgia
1998	Chamique Holdsclaw, Tennessee
1999	Chamique Holdsclaw, Tennessee
2000	Chamique Holdsclaw, Tennessee
2001	Tamika Catchings, Tennessee

Best Men's Tennis Player

Year		Year	
1993	Jim Courier	2000	Andre Agassi
1994	Pete Sampras	2001	Pete Sampras
1995	Pete Sampras	2002	Lleyton Hewitt
1996	Pete Sampras	2003	Andre Agassi
1997	Pete Sampras	2004	Andy Roddick
1998	Pete Sampras	2005	Roger Federer
1999	Pete Sampras	2006	Roger Federer

Best Women's Tennis Player

Year		Year	
1993	Monica Seles	2001	Venus Williams
1994	Steffi Graf	2002	Venus Williams
1995	A. Sanchez Vicario	2002	Venus Williams
1996	Steffi Graf	2003	Serena Williams
1997	Steffi Graf	2004	Serena Williams
1998	Martina Hingis	2005	Maria Sharapova
1999	Lindsay Davenport	2006	Venus Williams
2000	Lindsay Davenport		

Best Men's Golfer

Year		Year	
1993	Fred Couples	1999	Mark O'Meara
1994	Nick Price	2000	Tiger Woods
1995	Nick Price	2001	Tiger Woods
1996	Corey Pavin	2002	Tiger Woods
1997	Tom Lehman	2003	Tiger Woods
1998	Tiger Woods	2004	Phil Mickelson

Best Women's Golfer

Year		Year	
1993	Dottie Mochrie	1999	Annika Sorenstam
1994	Betsy King	2000	Julie Inkster
1995	Laura Davies	2001	Karrie Webb
1996	Annika Sorenstam	2002	Annika Sorenstam
1997	Karrie Webb	2003	Annika Sorenstam
1998	Annika Sorenstam	2004	Annika Sorenstam

Best Golfer

Year		Year	
2004	Tiger Woods	2005	Tiger Woods

Best Jockey

Year		Year	
1994	Mike Smith	2001	Kent Desormeaux
1995	Chris McCarron	2002	Victor Espinoza
1996	Jerry Bailey	2003	Jose Santos
1997	Jerry Bailey	2004	Stewart Elliot
1998	Gary Stevens	2005	Jeremy Rose
1999	Kent Desormeaux	2006	Edgar Prado
2000	Chris Antley		

Best Bowler

Year		Year	
1995	Norm Duke	2001	Walter Ray William
1996	Mike Aulby	2002	Pete Weber
1997	Bob Learn Jr.	2003	Walter Ray William
1998	Walter Ray Williams	2004	Pete Weber
1999	Walter Ray Williams	2005	Walter Ray William
2000	Parker Bohn III	2006	Walter Ray William

Best Driver

Year		Year	
1993	Nigel Mansell	2000	Dale Jarrett
1994	Nigel Mansell	2001	Bobby Labonte
1995	Al Unser Jr.	2002	Michael Schumach
1996	Jeff Gordon	2003	Tony Stewart
1997	Jimmy Vasser	2004	Dale Earnhardt Jr.
1998	Jeff Gordon	2005	Michael Schumach
1999	Jeff Gordon	2006	Tony Stewart

Best Men's Track Athlete

Year		Year	
1993	Kevin Young	2000	Michael Johnson
1994	Michael Johnson	2001	Maurice Greene
1995	Dennis Mitchell	2002	Maurice Greene
1996	Michael Johnson	2003	Tim Montgomery
1997	Michael Johnson	2004	Tom Pappas
1998	Wilson Kipketer	2005	not awarded
1999	Maurice Greene	2006	Justin Gatlin

Best Women's Track Athlete

Year		Year	
1993	Evelyn Ashford	2000	Marion Jones
1994	Gail Devers	2001	Marion Jones
1995	Gwen Torrence	2002	Marion Jones
1996	Kim Batten	2003	Gail Devers
1997	Marie-Jose Perec	2004	Gail Devers
1998	Marion Jones	2005	not awarded
1999	Marion Jones	2006	Allyson Felix

Game of the Year

Year	
1996	AFC championship between Colts and Steelers
1997	Rose Bowl, Ohio State edges Arizona St.
1998	Super Bowl XXXII, Broncos over Packers
1999-2001	not awarded
2002	World Series Game 7, Diamondbacks-Yankees
2003	Fiesta Bowl, Ohio State beat Miami-FL in OT
2004	Super Bowl XXXVIII, Patriots over Panthers
2005	ALCS Game 5, Red Sox beat Yankees
2006	Rose Bowl, Texas beat USC

Best Play

Year	
2002	Derek Jeter's throw in World Series Game 3.
2003	LSU's Hail Mary TD.
2004	New Orleans Saints' lateral
2005	Blake Hoffarber's last second 3-pointer from flat on his back.
2006	Tyrone Prothro's behind-the-back catch

Best Boxer

Year		Year	
1993	Riddick Bowe	2000	Roy Jones Jr.
1994	Evander Holyfield	2001	Felix Trinidad
1995	George Foreman	2002	Lennox Lewis
1996	Roy Jones Jr.	2003	Roy Jones Jr.
1997	Evander Holyfield	2004	Antonio Tarver
1998	Evander Holyfield	2005	Bernard Hopkins
1999	Oscar De La Hoya	2006	Oscar De La Hoya

Best Male College Athlete

Year	
2002	Cael Sanderson, Iowa St. wrestling
2003	Carmelo Anthony, Syracuse basketball
2004	Emeka Okafor, UConn basketball
2005	Matt Leinart, USC football
2006	Reggie Bush, USC football

Best Female College Athlete

Year	
2002	Sue Bird, UConn basketball
2003	Diana Taurasi, UConn basketball
2004	Diana Taurasi, UConn basketball
2005	Cat Osterman, Texas softball
2006	Cat Osterman, Texas softball

Best Male Soccer Player

Year		Year	
2002	Landon Donovan	2004	David Beckham
2003	Ronaldo		

Best Female Soccer Player

Year		Year	
2002	Tiffeny Milbrett	2004	Mia Hamm
2003	Katia		

Best Soccer Player

Year		Year	
2005	Mia Hamm, USA	2006	Ronaldinho, Brazil

Best U.S. Olympian

Year	
2006	Shaun White, snowboarding

Best Outdoors Athlete

Year	
2002	Kevin VanDam, fishing
2003	Jay Yelas, fishing
2004	Tina Bosworth, log rolling
2005	J.R. Salzman, lumberjack

Best Action Sports Athlete

Year	
2002	Kelly Clark, snowboarding
2003	Shaun White, snowboarding
2004	Award split into female and male categories

Best Male Action Sports Athlete

Year		Year	
2004	Ryan Nyquist, bike	2006	Shaun White, snowboarding
2005	Dave Mirra, bike		

Best Female Action Sports Athlete

Year	
2004	Dallas Friday, wakeboarding
2005	Sofia Mulanovich, surfing
2006	Hannah Teter, snowboarding

Best Male Athlete with a Disability

Year	
2005	Marlon Shirley, track & field
2006	Bobby Martin, football

Best Female Athlete with a Disability

Year	
2005	Erin Popovich, swimming
2006	Sarah Reinertsen, triathon

Best Sports Movie

Year		Year	
2002	The Rookie	2005	Friday Night Lights
2003	Bend it like Beckham	2006	Glory Road
2004	Miracle		

Best Record-Breaking Performance

Year	
2001	Pete Sampras, Grand Slam singles titles
2002	Tiger Woods, four straight Majors
2003	Emmitt Smith, NFL rushing record
2004	Eric Gagne, baseball consecutive saves
2005	Peyton Manning, NFL single-season TD passes
2006	Shaun Alexander, NFL single-season TDs scored

Best Upset

Year	
2004	Pistons over Lakers in NBA Finals
2005	#14 Bucknell over #3 Kansas in NCAA tournament

Best Moment

Year	
2006	Jason McElwaine, Greece-Athena HS basketball

Arthur Ashe Award for Courage

Presented since 1993 on the annual ESPN "ESPYs" telecast. Given to a member of the sports community who has exemplified the same courage, spirit and determination to help others despite personal hardship that characterized Arthur Ashe, the late tennis champion and humanitarian. Voting done by select 26-member committee of media and sports personalities.

Year		Year		Year	
1993	**Jim Valvano**, basketball	1999	**Billie Jean King**, tennis	2003	**Pat Tillman**, football & **Kevin Tillman**, baseball
1994	**Steve Palermo**, baseball	2000	**Dave Sanders**, Columbine H.S. coach		
1995	**Howard Cosell**, TV & radio			2004	**George Weah**, soccer
1996	**Loretta Clairborne**, special olympics	2001	**Cathy Freeman**, track	2005	**Emmanuel Ofosu Yeboah** & **Jim MacLaren**, disabled athletes
1997	**Muhammad Ali**, boxing	2002	**Todd Beamer, Mark Bingham, Tom Burnett** and **Jeremy Glick**, Flight 93		
1998	**Dean Smith**, college basketball			2006	**Afghanistan female soccer**

The Hickok Belt

Officially known as the S. Rae Hickok Professional Athlete of the Year Award and presented by the Kickik Manufacturing Co. of Arlington, Texas, from 1950-76. The trophy was a large belt of gold, diamonds and other jewels, reportedly worth $30,000 in 1976, the last year it was handed out. Voting was done by 270 newspaper sports editors from around the country.
Multiple winner: Sandy Koufax (2).

Year		Year		Year	
1950	**Phil Rizzuto**, baseball	1960	**Arnold Palmer**, golf	1970	**Brooks Robinson**, baseball
1951	**Allie Reynolds**, baseball	1961	**Roger Maris**, baseball	1971	**Lee Trevino**, golf
1952	**Rocky Marciano**, boxing	1962	**Maury Wills**, baseball	1972	**Steve Carlton**, baseball
1953	**Ben Hogan**, golf	1963	**Sandy Koufax**, baseball	1973	**O.J. Simpson**, football
1954	**Willie Mays**, baseball	1964	**Jim Brown**, football	1974	**Muhammad Ali**, boxing
1955	**Otto Graham**, football	1965	**Sandy Koufax**, baseball	1975	**Pete Rose**, baseball
1956	**Mickey Mantle**, baseball	1966	**Frank Robinson**, baseball	1976	**Ken Stabler**, football
1957	**Carmen Basilio**, boxing	1967	**Carl Yastrzemski**, baseball	1977	Discontinued
1958	**Bob Turley**, baseball	1968	**Joe Namath**, football		
1959	**Ingemar Johansson**, boxing	1969	**Tom Seaver**, baseball		

ABC's "Wide World of Sports" Athlete of the Year

Selected annually by the producers of ABC Sports since 1962.
Multiple winners: Greg LeMond and Tiger Woods (2).

Year		Year		Year	
1962	**Jim Beatty**, track	1975	**Jack Nicklaus**, golf	1989	**Greg LeMond**, cycling
1963	**Valery Brumel**, track	1976	**Nadia Comaneci**, gymnastics	1990	**Greg LeMond**, cycling
1964	**Don Schollander**, swimming	1977	**Steve Cauthen**, horse racing	1991	**Carl Lewis**, track
1965	**Jim Clark**, auto racing	1978	**Ron Guidry**, baseball		& **Kim Zmeskal**, gymnastics
1966	**Jim Ryun**, track	1979	**Willie Stargell**, baseball	1992	**Bonnie Blair**, speed skating
1967	**Peggy Fleming**, figure skating	1980	**U.S. Olympic hockey team**	1993	**Evander Holyfield**, boxing
1968	**Bill Toomey**, track	1981	**Sugar Ray Leonard**, boxing	1994	**Al Unser Jr.**, auto racing
1969	**Mario Andretti**, auto racing	1982	**Wayne Gretzky**, hockey	1995	**Miguel Indurlfain**, cycling
1970	**Willis Reed**, basketball	1983	**Australia II**, yachting	1996	**Michael Johnson**, track
1971	**Lee Trevino**, golf	1984	**Edwin Moses**, track	1997	**Tiger Woods**, golf
1972	**Olga Korbut**, gymnastics	1985	**Pete Rose**, baseball	1998	**Mark McGwire**, baseball
1973	**O.J. Simpson**, football	1986	**Debi Thomas**, figure skating	1999	**Lance Armstrong**, cycling
	& **Jackie Stewart**, auto racing	1987	**Dennis Conner**, yachting	2000	**Tiger Woods**, golf
1974	**Muhammad Ali**, boxing	1988	**Greg Louganis**, diving	2001	discontinued

Presidential Medal of Freedom

Since President John F. Kennedy established the Medal of Freedom as America's highest civilian honor in 1963, only 16 sports figures have won the award. Note that (*) indicates the presentation was made posthumously.

Year		President	Year		President
1963	**Bob Kiphuth**, swimming	Kennedy	1993	**Arthur Ashe***, tennis	Clinton
1976	**Jesse Owens**, track & field	Ford	2002	**Hank Aaron**, baseball	G.W. Bush
1977	**Joe DiMaggio**, baseball	Ford	2003	**John Wooden**, basketball	G.W. Bush
1983	**Paul (Bear) Bryant***, football	Reagan	2003	**Roberto Clemente***, baseball	G.W. Bush
1984	**Jackie Robinson***, baseball	Reagan	2004	**Arnold Palmer**, golf	G.W. Bush
1986	**Earl (Red) Blaik**, football	Reagan	2005	**Muhammad Ali**, boxing	G.W. Bush
1991	**Ted Williams**, baseball	G. Bush	2005	**Jack Nicklaus**, golf	G.W. Bush
1992	**Richard Petty**, auto racing	G. Bush	2005	**Frank Robinson**, baseball	G.W. Bush

Congressional Gold Medal

Since the American Revolution, the U.S. Congress has commissioned gold medals as its highest expression of national appreciation for distinguished achievements and contributions. The medals are produced by the U.S. Mint. Each medal honors a particular individual, institution or event. Only four sports figure have won the award but note that track legend **Wilma Rudolph** has been nominated for, but not yet awarded, the Congressional gold medal.

Year		Year	
1973	**Roberto Clemente**, baseball	1988	**Jesse Owens**, track & field
1982	**Joe Louis**, boxing	2005	**Jackie Robinson**, baseball

Time Person of the Year

Since Charles Lindbergh was named *Time* magazine's first Man of the Year for 1927, two individuals with significant sports credentials have won the honor.

Year	
1984	**Peter Ueberroth**, president of the Los Angeles Olympic Organizing Committee.
1991	**Ted Turner**, owner-president of Turner Broadcasting System, founder of CNN cable news network, owner of the Atlanta Braves (NL) and Atlanta Hawks (NBA), and former winning America's Cup skipper.

TROPHY CASE

From the first organized track meet at Olympia in 776 B.C., to the Turin Winter Olympics over 2,700 years later, championships have been officially recognized with prizes that are symbolically rich and eagerly pursued. Here are 15 of the most coveted trophies in America.

(Illustrations by Lynn Mercer Michaud)

America's Cup

First presented by England's Royal Yacht Squadron to the winner of an invitational race around the Isle of Wight on Aug. 22, 1851 . . . originally called the Hundred Guinea Cup . . . renamed after the U.S. boat America, winner of the first race . . . made of sterling silver and designed by London jewelers R. & G. Garrard . . . measures 2 feet, 3 inches high and weighs 16 lbs . . . originally cost 100 guineas ($500), now valued at $250,000 . . . bell-shaped base added in 1958 . . . challenged for every three to four years . . . trophy held by yacht club sponsoring winning boat . . . Cup was badly damaged when a Maori protester repeatedly smashed it with a sledgehammer on March 14, 1997. It was sent back to the original maker and fully restored.

Vince Lombardi Trophy

First presented at the AFL-NFL World Championship Game (now Super Bowl) on Jan. 15, 1967 . . . originally called the World Championship Game Trophy . . . renamed in 1971 in honor of former Green Bay Packers GM-coach and two-time Super Bowl winner Vince Lombardi, who died in 1970 as coach of Washington . . . made of sterling silver and designed by Tiffany & Co. of New York . . . measures 21 inches high and weighs 7 lbs (football depicted is regulation size) . . . valued at $12,500 . . . competed for annually . . . winning team keeps trophy.

Olympic Gold Medal

First presented by International Olympic Committee in 1908 (until then winners received silver medals) . . . second and third place finishers also got medals of silver and bronze for first time in 1908 . . . each medal must be at least 2.4 inches in diameter and 0.12 inches thick . . . tthe gold medal is actually made of silver, but must be gilded with at least 6 grams (0.21 ounces) of pure gold . . . the medals for the 1996 Atlanta Games were designed by Malcolm Grear Designers and produced by Reed & Barton of Taunton, Mass . . . 604 gold, 604 silver and 630 bronze medals were made . . . competed for every two years as Winter and Summer Games alternate . . . winners keep medals.

Awards (Cont.)

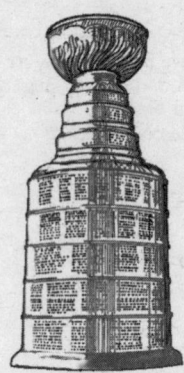

Stanley Cup

Donated by Lord Stanley of Preston, the Governor General of Canada and first presented in 1893 . . . original cup was made of sterling silver by an unknown London silversmith and measured 7 inches high with an 11½-inch diameter . . . in order to accommodate all the rosters of winning teams, the cup now measures 35½ inches high with a base 54 inches around and weighs 32 lbs . . . in order to add new names each year, bands on the trophy are often retired and displayed at the Hall of Fame . . . originally bought for 10 guineas ($48.67), it is now insured for $75,000 . . . actual cup retired to Hall of Fame and replaced in 1970 . . . presented to NHL playoff champion since 1918 . . . trophy loaned to winning team for one year.

World Cup

First presented by the Federation Internationale de Football Association (FIFA) . . . originally called the World Cup Trophy . . . renamed the Jules Rimet Cup (after the then FIFA president) in 1946, but retired by Brazil after that country's third title in 1970 . . . new World Cup trophy created in 1974 . . . designed by Italian sculptor Silvio Gazzaniga and made of solid 18 carat gold with two malachite rings inlaid at the base . . . measures 14.2 inches high and weighs 11 lbs . . . insured for $200,000 (U.S.) . . . competed for every four years . . . winning team gets gold-plated replica.

Commissioner's Trophy

First presented by the Commissioner of baseball to the winner of the 1967 World Series . . . also known as the World Championship Trophy . . . made of brass and gold plate with an ebony base and a baseball in the center made of pewter with a silver finish . . . designed by Balfour & Co. of Attleboro, Mass . . . 30 pennants represent 14 AL and 16 NL teams . . . measures 30 inches high and 36 inches around at the base and weighs 30 lbs . . . valued at $15,000 . . . competed for annually . . . winning team keeps trophy.

Larry O'Brien Trophy

First presented in 1978 to winner of NBA Finals . . . originally called the Walter A. Brown Trophy after the league pioneer and Boston Celtics owner (an earlier NBA championship bowl was also named after Brown) . . . renamed in 1984 in honor of outgoing commissioner O'Brien, who served from 1975-84 . . . made of sterling silver with 24 carat gold overlay and designed by Tiffany & Co. of New York . . . measures 2 feet high and weighs 14½ lbs (basketball depicted is regulation size) . . . valued at $13,500 . . . competed for annually . . . winning team keeps trophy.

Heisman Trophy

First presented in 1935 to the best college football player east of the Mississippi by the Downtown Athletic Club of New York . . . players across the entire country eligible since 1936 . . . originally called the DAC Trophy . . . renamed in 1936 following the death of DAC athletic director and former college coach John W. Heisman . . . made of bronze and designed by New York sculptor Frank Eliscu, it measures 13½ in. high, 6½ in. wide and 14 in. long at the base and weighs 25 lbs . . . valued at $2,000 . . . voting done by national media and former Heisman winners . . . trophy sponsor American Suzuki announced plans for limited fan voting starting in 1999 . . . awarded annually . . . winner keeps trophy.

James E. Sullivan Memorial Award

First presented by the Amateur Athletic Union (AAU) in 1930 as a gold medal and given to the nation's outstanding amateur athlete . . . trophy given since 1933 . . . named after the amateur sports movement pioneer, who was a founder and past president of AAU and the director of the 1904 Olympic Games in St. Louis . . . made of bronze with a marble base, it measures 17½ in. high and 11 in. wide at the base and weighs 13½ lbs . . . valued at $2,500 . . . voting done by AAU and USOC officials, former winners and selected media . . . awarded annually . . . winner keeps trophy.

Ryder Cup

Donated in 1927 by English seed merchant Samuel Ryder, who offered the gold cup for a biennial match between teams of golfing pros from Great Britain and the United States . . . the format changed in 1977 to include the best players on the European PGA Tour . . . made of 14 carat gold on a wood base and designed by Mappin and Webb of London . . . the golfer depicted on the top of the trophy is Ryder's friend and teaching pro Abe Mitchell . . . the cup measures 16 in. high and weighs 4 lbs . . . insured for $50,000 . . . competed for every two years at alternating European and U.S. sites . . . the cup is held by the PGA headquarters of the winning side.

Davis Cup

Donated by American college student and U.S. doubles champion Dwight F. Davis in 1900 and presented by the International Tennis Federation (ITF) to the winner of the annual 16-team men's competition . . . officially called the International Lawn Tennis Challenge Trophy . . . made of sterling silver and designed by Shreve, Crump and Low of Boston, the cup has a matching tray (added in 1921) and a very heavy two-tiered base containing rosters of past winning teams . . . it stands 34½ in. high and 108 in. around at the base and weighs 400 lbs . . . insured for $150,000 . . . competed for annually . . . trophy loaned to winning country for one year.

Borg-Warner Trophy

First presented by the Borg-Warner Automotive Co. of Chicago in 1936 to the winner of the Indianapolis 500 . . . replaced the Wheeler-Schebler Trophy which went to the 400-mile leader from 1911-32 . . . made of sterling silver with bas-relief sculptured heads of each winning driver and a gold bas-relief head of Tony Hulman, the owner of the Indy Speedway from 1945-77 . . . designed by Robert J. Hill and made by Gorham, Inc. of Rhode Island . . . measures 51½ in. high and weighs over 80 lbs . . . new base added in 1988 and the entire trophy restored in 1991 . . . competed for annually . . . insured for $1 million . . . trophy stays at Speedway Hall of Fame . . . winner gets a 14-in. high replica valued at $30,000.

NCAA Championship Trophy

First presented in 1952 by the NCAA to all 1st, 2nd and 3rd place teams in sports with sanctioned tournaments . . . 1st place teams receive gold-plated awards, 2nd place award is silver-plated and 3rd is bronze . . . replaced silver cup given to championship teams from 1939-51 . . . made of walnut, the trophy stands 24¾ in. high, 14⅛ in. wide and 4½ in. deep at the base and weighs 15 lbs . . . designed by Medallic Art Co. of Danbury, Conn. and made by House of Usher of Kansas City since 1990 . . . valued at $500 . . . competed for annually . . . winning teams keep trophies.

World Championship Belt

First presented in 1921 by the World Boxing Association, one of the three organizations (the World Boxing Council and International Boxing Federation are the others) generally accepted as sanctioning legitimate world championship fights . . . belt weighs 8 lbs. and is made of hand tanned leather . . . the outsized buckle measures 10½ in. high and 8 in. wide, is made of pewter with 24 carat gold plate and contains crystal and semi-precious stones . . . side panels of polished brass are for engraving title bout results . . . currently made by Champbelts by Ronn Scala in Pittsburgh . . . champions keep belts even if they lose their title.

World Championship Ring

Rings decorated with gems and engraving date back to ancient Egypt where the wealthy wore heavy gold and silver rings to indicate social status . . . championship rings in sports serve much the same purpose, indicating the wearer is a champion . . . As an example, the Dallas Cowboys' ring for winning Superbowl XXX on Jan. 28, 1996 was designed by Diamond Cutters International of Houston . . . each ring is made of 14 carat yellow gold, weighs 48-51 penny weights and features five trimmed marquis diamonds interlocking in the shape of the Cowboys' star logo as well as five more marquis diamonds (for the team's five Super Bowl wins) on a bed of 51 smaller diamonds . . . rings were appraised at over $30,000 each.

Jimmy Connors plants a smooch on his then fiancee, Chris Evert, on August 27, 1974. The duo combined for 263 all-time singles titles.

Sports Personalities

Nine hundred sixty-one entries dating back to the 19th century. Entries updated through Oct. 1, 2006.

Hank Aaron (b. Feb. 5, 1934): Baseball OF; led NL in HRs and RBI 4 times each and batting twice with Milwaukee and Atlanta Braves; MVP in 1957; played in 24 All-Star Games, all-time leader in HRs (755), RBI (2,297), total bases (6,856), 3rd in hits (3,771); won 3 Gold Gloves.

Kareem Abdul-Jabbar (b. Lew Alcindor, Apr. 16, 1947): Basketball C; led UCLA to 3 NCAA titles (1967-69); Final 4 MOP 3 times; Player of Year twice; led Milwaukee (1) and LA Lakers (5) to 6 NBA titles; playoff MVP twice (1971,85), regular season MVP 6 times (1971-72,74,76-77,80); retired in 1989 after 20 seasons as all-time leader in over 20 categories.

Andre Agassi (b. Apr. 29, 1970): Tennis; 60 career tournament wins including the career grand slam; Wimbledon (1992), U.S. Open (1994,99), Australian Open (1995,2000,01,03), French Open (1999); helped U.S. win 2 Davis Cup finals (1990,92); regained the world No. 1 ranking in 1999 for the first time since 1996; retired after the 2006 U.S. Open; married to former tennis star Steffi Graf.

Troy Aikman (b. Nov. 21, 1966): Football QB; consensus All-America at UCLA (1988); 1st overall pick in 1989 NFL Draft (by Dallas); led Cowboys to 3 Super Bowl titles (1992,93,95 seasons); MVP of Super Bowl XXVII; inducted into Pro Football HOF in 2006.

Marv Albert (b. June 12, 1941): Radio-TV; NBC announcer and broadcaster for the New York Knicks, Rangers and Giants who pleaded guilty to a misdemeanor assault charge amid embarrassing allegations of his sex life. Rehired to MSG and Turner networks in 1998 and NBC in '99.

Tenley Albright (b. July 18, 1935): Figure skater; 2-time world champion (1953,55); won Olympic silver (1952) and gold (1956) medals; became a surgeon.

Amy Alcott (b. Feb. 22, 1956): Golfer; 29 career wins, including five majors; inducted into World Golf Hall of Fame in 1999.

Grover Cleveland (Pete) Alexander (b. Feb. 26, 1887, d. Nov. 4, 1950): Baseball RHP; won 20 or more games 9 times; 373 career wins and 90 shutouts.

Muhammad Ali (b. Cassius Clay, Jan. 17, 1942): Boxer; 1960 Olympic light heavyweight champion; 3-time world heavyweight champ (1964-67, 1974-78,1978-79); defeated Sonny Liston (1964), George Foreman (1974) and Leon Spinks (1978) for title; fought Joe Frazier in 3 memorable bouts (1971-75), winning twice; adopted Black Muslim faith in 1964 and changed name; stripped of title in 1967 after conviction for refusing induction into U.S. Army; verdict reversed by Supreme Court in 1971; career record of 56-5 with 37 KOs and 19 successful title defenses; lit the flaming cauldron to signal the beginning of the 1996 Summer Olympics in Atlanta.

Forrest (Phog) Allen (b. Nov. 18, 1885, d. Sept. 16, 1974): Basketball; college coach 48 years; directed Kansas to NCAA title (1952); 746 wins.

Bobby Allison (b. Dec. 3, 1937): Auto racer; 3-time winner of Daytona 500 (1978,82,88); NASCAR national champ in 1983; father of Davey.

Davey Allison (b. Feb. 25, 1961, d. July 13, 1993): Auto racer; stock car Rookie of Year (1987); winner of 19 NASCAR races, including 1992 Daytona 500; killed at age 32 in helicopter accident at Talladega Superspeedway; son of Bobby.

Roberto Alomar (b. Feb. 5, 1968): Baseball; 10-time Gold Glove second baseman; MVP of 1992 ALCS; became known well beyond baseball for spitting in the face of umpire John Hirschbeck during final weekend of 1996 season; named MVP of 1998 All-Star Game.

Walter Alston (b. Dec. 1, 1911, d. Oct. 1, 1984): Baseball; managed Brooklyn-LA Dodgers 23 years, won 7 pennants and 4 World Series (1955,59,63,65); retired after 1976 season with 2,063 wins (2,040 regular season and 23 postseason).

Gary Anderson (b. July 16, 1959): Football K; all-time leading scorer in NFL history; had perfect regular season in 1998 (59/59 PAT, 35/35 FG); held NFL record for consecutive FG made (40, broken by M. Vanderjagt's 42); led AFC in scoring 3 times (1983-85 with Steelers) and NFC once (1998 with Vikings).

Sparky Anderson (b. Feb. 22, 1934): Baseball; only manager to win World Series in each league—Cincinnati in NL (1975-76) and Detroit in AL (1984); 5th-largest skipper on all-time career list with 2,228 wins (2,194 regular season and 34 postseason); inducted into the Baseball Hall of Fame in 2000.

Mario Andretti (b. Feb. 28, 1940): Auto racer; 4-time USAC-CART national champion (1965-66,69,84); only driver to win Daytona 500 (1967), Indy 500 (1969) and Formula One world title (1978); Indy 500 Rookie of Year (1965); retired after 1994 racing season ranked 1st in poles (67) and starts (407) and 2nd in wins (52) on all-time CART list; father of Michael and Jeff, uncle of John, grandfather of Marco.

Michael Andretti (b. Oct. 5, 1962): Auto racer; 1991 CART national champion with single-season record 8 wins; Indy 500 Rookie of Year (1984); left IndyCar circuit for ill-fated Formula One try in 1993; returned to IndyCar in 1994; son of Mario, father of Marco.

Earl Anthony (b. Apr. 27, 1938, d. Aug. 14, 2001): Bowler; 6-time PBA Bowler of Year; 41 career titles; first to earn $100,000 in 1 season (1975); first to earn $1 million in career; won 10 Majors (2 Tournament of Champions, 6 PBA National Championships and 2 ABC Masters).

Said Aouita (b. Nov. 2, 1959): Moroccan runner; won gold (5000m) and bronze (800m) in 1984 Olympics; won 5000m at 1987 World Championships; formerly held 2 world records recognized by IAAF—2000m and 5000m.

Luis Aparicio (b. Apr. 29, 1934): Baseball SS; retired as all-time leader in most games, assists and double plays by shortstop; led AL in stolen bases 9 times (1956-64); 506 career steals.

Al Arbour (b. Nov. 1, 1932): Hockey; coached NY Islanders to 4 straight Stanley Cup titles (1980-83); retired after 1993-94 season; 2nd on all-time career list with 904 wins (781 regular season and 123 postseason); elected to Hockey Hall of Fame in 1996.

Eddie Arcaro (b. Feb. 19, 1916, d. Nov. 14, 1997): Jockey; 2-time Triple Crown winner (Whirlaway in 1941, Citation in '48); he won Kentucky Derby 5 times, Preakness and Belmont 6 times each.

Roone Arledge (b. July 8, 1931, d. Dec. 5, 2002): Sports TV pioneer; innovator of live events, anthology shows, Olympic coverage, "Monday Night Football" and "Wide World of Sports"; ran ABC Sports from 1968-86; ran ABC News from 1977-98.

Henry Armstrong (b. Dec. 12, 1912, d. Oct. 22, 1988): Boxer; held feather-, light- and welterweight titles simultaneously in 1938; pro record 152-21-8 with 100 KOs.

Lance Armstrong (b. Sept. 18, 1971): Cyclist; Texan who made cycling history becoming the first 6-time, then 7-time winner of the Tour de France (1999-2005); returned from treatment for testicular cancer to become the world's top cyclist; 4-time AP Male Athlete of the Year.

Arthur Ashe (b. July 10, 1943, d. Feb. 6, 1993): Tennis; first black man to win U.S. Championship (1968) and Wimbledon (1975); 1st U.S. player to earn $100,000 in 1 year (1970); won Davis Cup as player (1968-70) and captain (1981-82); wrote black sports history, *Hard Road to Glory*; announced in 1992 that he was infected with AIDS virus from a blood transfusion during 1983 heart surgery; in 1997, the new home for the U.S. Open was named Arthur Ashe Stadium.

Evelyn Ashford (b. Apr. 15, 1957): Track & Field; winner of 4 Olympic gold medals—100m in 1984, and 4x100m in 1984, '88 and '92; also won silver medal in 100m in '88; member of 5 U.S. Olympic teams (1976-92); Inducted into Track and Field and Women's Sports Halls of Fame in 1997.

Red Auerbach (b. Sept. 20, 1917): Basketball; retired as winningest all-time coach (regular season and playoffs) in NBA history (now 7th); won 1,037 times in 20 years; as coach-GM, led Boston to a record 9 NBA titles, including 8 in a row (1959-66); also coached defunct Washington Capitols (1946-49); NBA Coach of the Year award named after him; retired as Celtics coach in 1966 and as GM in '84; club president from 1970 to 1997 and then again beginning in 2001.

Tracy Austin (b. Dec. 12, 1962): Tennis; youngest player to win U.S. Open (age 16 in 1979); won 2nd U.S. Open in '81; named AP Female Athlete of Year twice before she was 20; recurring neck and back injuries shortened career after 1983; youngest player ever inducted into Tennis Hall of Fame (age 29 in 1992).

Paul Azinger (b. Jan. 6, 1960): Golf; PGA Player of Year (1987); 12 career wins, including '93 PGA Championship; missed most of '94 season overcoming lymphoma (a form of cancer) in right shoulder blade; member of 4 U.S. Ryder Cup teams (1989,91,93,2002).

Bob Baffert (b. Jan. 13, 1953): Horse racing; 3-time Eclipse Award winner as outstanding trainer (1997-99); trained 3 Kentucky Derby winners (1997,98,02), 4 Preakness winners (1997,98,01,02) and 1 Belmont Stakes winner (2001); 4-time leading annual money leader for trainers (1998-01).

Donovan Bailey (b. Dec. 16, 1967): Track; Jamaican-born Canadian sprinter who set world record in the 100m (9.84) in gold medal-winning performance at 1996 Olympics which stood until '99; set indoor record in 50m (5.56) in 1996; member of Canadian 4x100 relay that won gold in 1996 Olympics.

Oksana Baiul (b. Feb. 26, 1977): Ukrainian figure skater; 1993 world champion at age 15; edged Nancy Kerrigan by a 5-4 judges' vote for 1994 Olympic gold medal.

Hobey Baker (b. Jan. 15, 1892, d. Dec. 21, 1918): Football and hockey star at Princeton (1911-14); member of college football and pro hockey Halls of Fame; college hockey Player of Year award named after him; killed in plane crash.

Seve Ballesteros (b. Apr. 9, 1957): Spanish golfer; has won British Open 3 times (1979,84,88) and Masters twice (1980,83); 3-time European Golfer of Year (1986,88,91); has led Europe to 5 Ryder Cup titles (1985,87,89,95,97).

Ernie Banks (b. Jan. 31, 1931): Baseball SS-1B; led NL in home runs and RBI twice each; 2-time MVP (1958-59) with Chicago Cubs; 512 career HRs.

Roger Bannister (b. Mar. 23, 1929): British runner; first to run mile in less than 4 minutes (3:59.4 on May 6, 1954).

Walter (Red) Barber (b. Feb. 17, 1908, d. Oct. 22, 1992): Radio-TV; renowned baseball play-by-play broadcaster for Cincinnati, Brooklyn and N.Y. Yankees from 1934-66; won Peabody Award for radio commentary in 1991.

Charles Barkley (b. Feb. 20, 1963): Basketball F; 5-time All-NBA 1st team with Philadelphia and Phoenix; U.S. Olympic Dream Team member in '92; NBA regular season MVP in 1993; currently a basketball announcer for TNT; inducted into Basketball Hall of Fame in 2006.

Leon Barmore (b. June 3, 1944): basketball coach; respected coach of Louisiana Tech Lady Techsters; career win pct. of .869 (576-87, 20 yrs) is best all-time; won national championship with Louisiana Tech in 1988.

Rick Barry (b. Mar. 28, 1944): Basketball F; only player to lead both NBA and ABA in scoring; 5-time All-NBA 1st team; Finals MVP with Golden St. in 1975. Perfected the underhand foul shot.

Sammy Baugh (b. Mar. 17, 1914): Football G, DB-P; led Washington to NFL titles in 1937 (his rookie year) and '42; led league in passing 6 times, punting 4 times and interceptions once.

Elgin Baylor (b. Sept. 16, 1934): Basketball; Most Outstanding Player of Final Four in 1958; led Minneapolis-LA Lakers to 8 NBA Finals; 10-time All-NBA 1st team (1959-65,67-69); LA Clippers' Vice President of Basketball Operations.

Bob Beamon (b. Aug. 29, 1946): Track & Field; won 1968 Olympic gold medal in long jump with world record (29-ft, 2½in.) that shattered old mark nearly 2 feet; record finally broken by 2 inches 1991 by Mike Powell.

Franz Beckenbauer (b. Sept. 11, 1945): Soccer; captain of West German World Cup champions 1974 then coached West Germany to World Cup title in 1990; invented sweeper position; played in U.S. for NY Cosmos (1977-80,83).

David Beckham (b. May 2, 1975): Soccer; English star perhaps known more for his good looks, 1999 marriage to former Spice Girl, Victoria Adams (Posh Spice), and his trademark free kick; captain the English national team from 2000-2006; scored goals in 3 different World Cups (1998,2002,2006); played for Manchester United (1993-95, 1995-2003) then Real Madrid (since 2003).

Boris Becker (b. Nov. 22, 1967): German tennis player; 3-time Wimbledon champion (1985-86,89); youngest male (17) to win Wimbledon; led country to 1st Davis Cup win in 1988; has also won U.S. (1989) and Australian (1991,96) Opens.

Chuck Bednarik (b. May 1, 1925): Football LB; 2-time All-America at Penn and 7-time All-Pro with NFL Eagles as both center (1950) and linebacker (1951-56); missed only 3 games in 14 seasons; led Eagles to 1960 NFL title as a 35-year-old two-way player.

Clair Bee (b. Mar. 2, 1896, d. May 20, 1983): Basketball coach who led LIU to 2 undefeated seasons (1936,39) and 2 NIT titles (1939,41); his teams won 95 percent of their games between 1931-51 including 43 in a row from 1935-37; coached NBA Baltimore Bullets from 1952-54, but was only 34-116; contributions to game include 1-3-1 zone defense, 3-second rule and NBA 24-second clock.

Bill Belichick (b. Apr. 16, 1952): Football; long-time assistant to Bill Parcells who became head coach of N.E. Patriots in 2000 and went on to win 3 Super Bowls; 2nd best playoff record in NFL history (11-2).

Jean Beliveau (b. Aug. 31, 1931): Hockey; led Montreal to 10 Stanley Cups in 17 playoffs; playoff MVP (1965); 2-time regular season MVP (1956,64).

Bert Bell (b. Feb. 25, 1895, d. Oct. 11, 1959): Football; team owner and 2nd NFL commissioner (1946-59); proposed college draft in 1935 and instituted blackout rule.

James (Cool Papa) Bell (b. May 17, 1903, Mar. 8, 1991): Baseball; member of the Negro Leagues; widely considered the fastest player ever to play baseball; also coached for the Kansas City Monarchs, teaching such players as Jackie Robinson; member of the National Baseball Hall of Fame.

Deane Beman (b. Apr. 22, 1938): Golf; 1st commissioner of PGA Tour (1974-94); introduced "stadium golf" and created The Players Championship; as player, won U.S. Amateur twice and British Amateur once; inducted into the World Golf Hall of Fame in 2000.

Johnny Bench (b. Dec. 7, 1947): Baseball C; led NL in HRs and RBI 3 times; 2-time regular season MVP (1970,72) with Cincinnati, World Series MVP in 1976; 389 career HRs.

Patty Berg (b. Feb. 13, 1918, d. Sept. 10, 2006): Golfer; 60 career pro wins, including 15 majors; 3-time AP Female Athlete of Year (1938,43,55).

Chris Berman (b. May 10, 1955): Radio-TV; 6-time national Sportscaster of Year famous for nicknames and jovial studio anchoring on ESPN; play-by-play man first year Brown University football team won the Ivy League (1976).

Yogi Berra (b. May 12, 1925): Baseball C; played ... 10 World Series winners with NY Yankees; holds ... S records for games played (75), at bats (259) and s (71); 3-time AL MVP (1951,54-55); managed both ...nkees (1964) and NY Mets (1973) to pennants.

Jay Berwanger (b. Mar. 19, 1914, d. June 26, ...002): Football HB; Univ. of Chicago star; won 1st ...eisman Trophy in 1935; top selection in the 1st-ever ...FL Draft (1936).

Gary Bettman (b. June 2, 1952): Hockey; former ...BA executive, who was named first commissioner of ...HL on Dec. 11, 1992; took office on Feb. 1, 1993; ...mmissioner during NHL lockout of 2004-05.

Abebe Bikila (b. Aug. 7, 1932, d. Oct. 25, ...973): Ethiopian runner; 1st to win consecutive Olympic ...arathons (1960,64).

Matt Biondi (b. Oct. 8, 1965): Swimmer; won 7 ...edals in 1988 Olympics, including 5 gold (3 indi-...dual, 3 relay); won a total of 11 medals (8 gold, ...silver and a bronze) in 3 Olympics (1984,88,92).

Larry Bird (b. Dec. 7, 1956): Basketball F; col-...ge Player of Year (1979) at Indiana St.; 1980 NBA ...ookie of Year; 9-time All-NBA 1st team; 3-time regu-... season MVP (1984-86); led Boston to 3 NBA titles ...981,84, 86); 2-time Finals MVP (1984,86); U.S. ...ympic Dream Team member in '92; inducted into ...all of Fame in 1998; in 1997, named coach of Indi-...a Pacers and won Coach of the Year honors in first ...ason; led the Pacers to the NBA Finals in 2000 but ...st in 6 games to the Lakers and retired; named pres-...ent of basketball operations of Pacers in 2003.

The Black Sox: Eight Chicago White Sox players ...ho were banned from baseball for life in 1921 for ...legedly throwing the 1919 World Series— RHP Eddie ...cotte (1884-1969), OF Happy Felsch (1891-1964), ... Chick Gandil (1887-1970), OF Shoeless Joe Jack-...n (1889-1951), INF Fred McMullin (1891-1952), SS ...vede Risberg (1894-1975), 3B-SS Buck Weaver ...890-1956), and LHP Lefty Williams (1893-1959).

Earl (Red) Blaik (b. Feb. 15, 1897, d. May 6, ...989): Football; coached Army to consecutive nation-...titles in 1944-45; 166 career wins and 3 Heisman ...nners (Blanchard, Davis, Dawkins).

Bonnie Blair (b. Mar. 18, 1964): Speed skater; ...ly American woman to win 5 Olympic gold medals ... Winter Games; won 500-meters in 1988, then 500 ...d 1,000m in both 1992 and '94; added 1,000m ...onze in 1988; Sullivan Award winner (1992); retired ... 31st birthday as reigning world sprint champ.

Hector (Toe) Blake (b. Aug. 21, 1912, d. May ...7, 1995): Hockey LW; led Montreal to 2 Stanley Cups ... a player and 8 more as coach; 1939 NHL MVP.

Felix (Doc) Blanchard (b. Dec. 11, 1924): Foot-...ll FB; 3-time All-America; led Army to national titles ... 1944-45; Glenn Davis' running mate; won Heis-...an Trophy and Sullivan Award in 1945.

George Blanda (b. Sept. 17, 1927): Football QB-...; was pro football's all-time leading scorer (2,002 ...ints) until 2000 when he was finally passed by kick-... Gary Anderson; led Houston to 2 AFL titles (1960-...); played 26 pro seasons; retired at age 48.

Fanny Blankers-Koen (b. Apr. 26, 1918, d. Jan. ...5, 2004): Dutch sprinter; 30-year-old mother of two, ...ho won 4 gold medals (100m, 200m, 800m hur-...es and 4x100m relay) at 1948 Olympics.

Drew Bledsoe (b. Feb. 14, 1972): Football QB; ...t overall pick in 1993 NFL draft (N.E. Patriots); one ... only 10 QBs in NFL history with 40,000 career ...ssing yards; traded to Buffalo before 2002 season; ...gned with Dallas in 2005.

Jim Boeheim (b. Nov. 17, 1944): Basketball; long-...e coach at Syracuse; finally won 1st NCAA title in ...003; entered 2006-07 with career record of 726-253.

Wade Boggs (b. June 15, 1958): Baseball 3B; 5 ... batting titles (1983,85-88) with Boston Red Sox; ...-time All-Star; two Gold Gloves; later played with ...Y Yankees and Tampa Bay; got 3000th career hit ...th a home run Aug. 7, 1999 against Cleveland; ...ducted into Hall of Fame in 2005.

Barry Bonds (b. July 24, 1964): Baseball OF; set MLB single-season HR record in 2001 with 73; 7-time NL MVP, 2 with Pittsburgh (1990,92) and 5 with San Francisco (1993,2001-04); one of only 4 men with 40 HRs and 40 SBs in same season (1996); became the 3rd player to reach 700 career HRs in 2004; holds major league record for single season (2004) and career walks; hit .370 in 2002 at age 38; passed Babe Ruth in 2006 for 2nd on the all-time HR list; finished sea-son with 734 (behind Aaron's 755), son of Bobby.

Bjorn Borg (b. June 6, 1956): Swedish tennis player; 2-time Player of Year (1979-80); won 6 French Opens and 5 straight Wimbledons (1976-80); led Swe-den to 1st Davis Cup win in 1975; retired in 1983 at age 26; attempted unsuccessful comeback in 1991.

Mike Bossy (b. Jan. 22, 1957): Hockey RW; led NY Isles to 4 Stanley Cups; playoff MVP in 1982; 50 goals or more 9 straight years; 573 career goals.

Ralph Boston (b. May 9, 1939): Track & Field; medaled in 3 consecutive Olympic long jumps— gold (1960), silver (1964), bronze (1968).

Ray Bourque (b. Dec. 28, 1960): Hockey D; 12-time All-NHL 1st team; won 5 Norris Trophies (1987-88,1990-91,94) with Boston; '96 All-Star Game MVP; all-time leader for points and assists by a defenseman; won 2001 Stanley Cup with Colorado then retired; elected to Hall of Fame in 2004.

Bobby Bowden (b. Nov. 8, 1929): Football; coached Florida St. to 2 national titles (1993,99); entered 2006 season as all-time wins leader in college football history with 359 victories including a 19-9-1 bowl record in 40 years as coach at Samford, West Va. and FSU; father of Clemson head coach Tommy and former Auburn coach Terry.

Riddick Bowe (b. Aug. 10, 1967): Boxer; former undisputed heavyweight champ who fought career-defin-ing trilogy with Evander Holyfield (1992-1995); won 1st meeting by decision, lost rematch in "Fan Man Fight," won last Holyfield fight by 8th-round KO.

Scotty Bowman (b. Sept. 18, 1933): Hockey coach; all-time winningest NHL coach in both regular season (1,244) and playoffs (223) over 30 seasons; coached a record nine Stanley Cup winners with Mon-treal (1973,76-79), Pittsburgh (1992) and Detroit (1997,98,2002); retired after 2001-02 season.

Jack Brabham (b. Apr. 2, 1926): Australian auto racer; 3-time Formula One champion (1959-60,66); 14 career wins; member of the Hall of Fame.

James J. Braddock (b. June 7, 1905, d. Nov. 29, 1974): Boxer; journeyman who won heavyweight belt in 10-1 upset of hard-hitting Max Baer in 1935.

Bill Bradley (b. July 28, 1943): Basketball F; 2-time All-America at Princeton; Player of the Year and Final 4 MOP in 1965; captain of gold medal-winning 1964 Olympic team; Sullivan Award winner (1965); led NY Knicks to 2 NBA titles (1970,73); U.S. Sena-tor (D, N.J.) 1979-95; ran for President in 2000.

Pat Bradley (b. Mar. 24, 1951): Golfer; 2-time LPGA Player of Year (1986,91); won career LPGA grand slam, including 3 du Maurier Classics; inducted into the LPGA Hall of Fame on Jan. 18, 1992; among all-time LPGA money leaders and tournament winners (31); cap-tained the 2000 U.S. Solheim Cup team.

Terry Bradshaw (b. Sept. 2, 1948): Football QB; led Pittsburgh to 4 Super Bowl titles (1975-76,79-80); 2-time Super Bowl MVP (1979-80) and regular sea-son MVP in 1978; Fox TV studio analyst.

Tom Brady (b. Aug. 3, 1977): Football QB; 6th-round draft pick (Michigan) who became 3-time Super Bowl winner with N.E. Patriots, 2-time Super Bowl MVP.

George Brett (b. May 15, 1953): Baseball 3B-1B; AL batting champion in 3 different decades (1976,80,90); MVP in 1980; led KC to World Series title in 1985; retired after 1993 season with 3,154 hits and .305 average; inducted into Hall of Fame in 1999.

Valerie Brisco-Hooks (b. July 6, 1960): Track & Field; won three gold medals at the 1984 Olympics (200 meters, 400 meters and 4x100 relay); first ath-lete to ever win the 200 and 400 in the same Olympics.

Lou Brock (b. June 18, 1939): Baseball OF; former all-time SB leader (938); led NL in SBs 8 times; led St. Louis to 2 WS titles (1964,67); 3,023 career hits.

Herb Brooks (b. Aug. 5, 1937, d. Aug. 11, 2003): Hockey; former U.S. Olympic player (1964,68) who coached 1980 "Miracle on Ice" team to gold medal and 2002 U.S. team to silver medal; coached Minnesota to 3 NCAA titles (1974,76,78); also coached 4 NHL teams.

Jim Brown (b. Feb. 17, 1936): Football FB; All-America at Syracuse (1956) and NFL Rookie of Year (1957); led NFL in rushing 8 times; 8-time All-Pro (1957-61,63-65); 3-time MVP (1958,63,65) with Cleveland; ran for 12,312 yards and scored 126 touchdowns in just 9 seasons; first player to reach the 100-touchdown milestone; member of pro and college football halls of fame.

Larry Brown (b. Sept. 14, 1940): Basketball; played in ACC, AAU, 1964 Olympics and ABA; 3-time assist leader (1968-70) and 3-time Coach of Year (1973,75-76) in ABA; coached ABA's Carolina and Denver and NBA's Denver, N.J., San Antonio, LA Clippers, Indiana, Philadelphia, Detroit and N.Y. Knicks, winning the 2004 NBA title with Pistons; also coached UCLA to NCAA Final (1980), Kansas to NCAA title (1988) and the USA men's basketball team to a disappointing bronze medal in Athens in 2004.

Mordecai (Three-Finger) Brown (b. Oct. 18, 1876, d. Feb. 14, 1948): Baseball; nickname derived from injury in a childhood accident that left him with three digits on right hand; injury gave him a particularly nasty curve ball; won the decisive game of the the 1907 World Series as a Chicago Cub; in 1908, first pitcher to record 4 consecutive shutouts and finished at 29-9; career record of 239-130 with lifetime ERA of 2.06; member of Hall of Fame.

Paul Brown (b. Sept. 7, 1908, d. Aug. 5, 1991): Football innovator; coached Ohio St. to national title in 1942; in pros, directed Cleveland Browns to 4 straight AAFC titles (1946-49) and 3 NFL titles (1950,54-55); formed Cincinnati Bengals as head coach and part owner in 1968 (reached playoffs in '70).

Valery Brumel (b. Apr. 14, 1942, d. Jan. 26, 2003): Soviet high jumper; dominated event from 1961-64; broke world record 5 times; won silver in 1960 Olympics and gold in 1964; highest jump was 7-5¾.

Avery Brundage (b. Sept. 28, 1887, d. May 5, 1975): Amateur sports czar for over 40 years as president of AAU (1928-35), U.S. Olympic Committee (1929-53) and Int'l Olympic Committee (1952-72).

Kobe Bryant (b. Aug. 23, 1978): Basketball; G/F for the LA Lakers; graduated from Lower Merion (Penn.) HS and made the jump directly to the NBA; youngest player (18 yrs., 2 mos., 11 days) ever to appear in an NBA game; became the youngest all-star in NBA history in 1998 and scored a team-high 18 points; won 3 consecutive titles with the Lakers (2000,01,02); accused of rape in 2003 but charges were dropped in 2004.

Paul (Bear) Bryant (b. Sept. 11, 1913, d. Jan. 26, 1983): Football; coached at 4 colleges over 38 years; directed Alabama to 6 national titles (1961,64-65,73,78-79); retired as the winningest coach of all-time (323-85-17 record) finally passed by Joe Paterno in 2001; 15 bowl wins, including 8 Sugar Bowls.

Sergey Bubka (b. Dec. 4, 1963): Ukrainian pole vaulter; 1st man to clear 20 feet both indoors and out (1991); holder of indoor (20-2) and outdoor (20-1¾) world records; 6-time world champion (1983, 87, 91, 93, 95, 97); won Olympic gold medal in 1988, but failed to clear any height in 1992 Games.

Buck Buchanan (b. Sept. 10, 1940, d. July 16, 1992): Football; played both ways in college at Grambling; first player chosen in the first AFL draft by the Dallas Texans who later became the KC Chiefs; missed one game in a 13-year pro career; played in six AFL All-Star games and two Pro Bowls at def. tackle; defensive star of the Chiefs team that won Super Bowl IV; later coached the New Orleans Saints and Cleveland Browns; member of Pro Football Hall of Fame.

Jack Buck (b. Aug. 21, 1924, d. June 18, 2002): Radio-TV; broadcast baseball games for St. Louis Cardinals from 1954-2001; CBS Radio voice for Monday Night Football (1978-96) and announcer for 1st televised AFL game in 1960; recipient of Baseball Hall of Fame's Ford Frick Award (1987) and Football Hall of Fame's Pete Rozelle Award (1996); received the Purple Heart in WWII; father of sportscaster Joe.

Don Budge (b. June 13, 1915, d. Jan. 26, 2000): Tennis; in 1938 became 1st player to win the Grand Slam— the French, Wimbledon, U.S. and Australian titles in 1 year; led U.S. to 2 Davis Cups (1937-38); turned pro in late '38.

Maria Bueno (b. Oct. 11, 1939): Brazilian tennis player; won 4 U.S. Championships (1959,63-64,66) and 3 Wimbledons (1959-60,64).

Leroy Burrell (b. Feb. 21, 1967): Track & Field; set former world record of 9.85 in 100 meters, July 6, 1994; previously held record (9.90) in 1991; member of 4 world record-breaking 4x100m relay teams.

Susan Butcher (b. Dec. 26, 1954, d. Aug. 5, 2006): Sled Dog racer; 4-time winner of Iditarod Trail race (1986-88,90).

Dick Butkus (b. Dec. 9, 1942): Football LB; 5-time All-America at Illinois (1963-64); All-Pro 7 of 9 NFL seasons with Chicago Bears; worked with XFL in 2001.

Dick Button (b. July 18, 1929): Figure skater; 5-time world champion (1948-52); 2-time Olympic champ (1948,52); Sullivan Award winner (1949); won Emmy Award as Best Analyst for 1980-81 TV season.

Walter Byers (b. Mar. 13, 1922): College athletics; 1st exec. director of NCAA, serving from 1951-88.

Frank Calder (b. Nov. 17, 1877, d. Feb. 4, 1943): Hockey; 1st NHL president (1917-43); guided league through its formative years; NHL's Rookie of the Year award named after him.

Jim Calhoun (b. May 10, 1942): Basketball; head coached UConn to 2 NCAA titles (1999, 2004); inducted into Basketball Hall of Fame in 2005.

Lee Calhoun (b. Feb. 23, 1933, d. June 22, 1989): Track & Field; won consecutive Olympic gold medals in the 110m hurdles (1956,60).

Walter Camp (b. Apr. 7, 1859, d. Mar. 14, 1925): Football coach and innovator; established scrimmage line, center snap, downs, 11 players per side; selected 1st All-America team (1889).

Roy Campanella (b. Nov. 19, 1921, d. June 26, 1993): Baseball C; 3-time NL MVP (1951,53,55); led Brooklyn to 5 pennants and 1st World Series title (1955); career cut short when paralyzed in 1958 car crash.

Clarence Campbell (b. July 9, 1905, d. June 24, 1984): Hockey; 3rd NHL president (1946-77), league tripled in size from 6 to 18 teams during his tenure.

Earl Campbell (b. Mar. 29, 1955): Football RB; won Heisman Trophy in 1977; led NFL in rushing 3 times; 3-time All-Pro; 2-time MVP (1978-79) at Houston.

John Campbell (b. Apr. 8, 1955): Harness racing; 5-time winner of Hambletonian (1987,88,90,95,98); 3-time Driver of Year; first driver to go over $100 million in career winnings.

Milt Campbell (b. Dec. 9, 1933): Track & Field; won silver medal in 1952 Olympic decathlon and gold medal in '56.

Jimmy Cannon (b. 1910, d. Dec. 5, 1973): Tough, opinionated New York sportswriter and essayist who viewed sports as an extension of show business; protégé of Damon Runyon; covered World War II for *Stars & Stripes.*

Jose Canseco (b. July 2, 1964): Baseball OF/DH; 1986 AL ROY and 1988 MVP with the Oakland A's; became the 1st player in MLB history with 40 HRs and 40 steals in a season (1988); retired in 2003 with 462 career HRs; admitted steroid use in 2005 book.

Tony Canzoneri (b. Nov. 6, 1908, d. Dec. 9, 1959): Boxer; 2-time world lightweight champion (1930-33,35-36); pro record 141-24-10 with 44 KOs.

Roberto Clemente explains the fine art of hitting to one of his adoring fans, nine-year-old Junior James, on September 25, 1961.

Jennifer Capriati (b. Mar. 29, 1976): Tennis; youngest Grand Slam semifinalist ever (age 14 in 1990 French Open); surprise gold medalist at 1992 Olympics; staged successful comeback, winning French Open (2001) and 2 Australian Opens (2001,02).

Harry Caray (b. Mar. 1, 1917, d. Feb. 18, 1998): Radio-TV; baseball play-by-play broadcaster for St. Louis Cardinals, Oakland, Chicago White Sox and Cubs 1945-98; father of sportscaster Skip and grandfather of sportscaster Chip.

Rod Carew (b. Oct. 1, 1945): Baseball 2B-1B; led AL in batting 7 times (1969,72-75,77-78) with Minnesota; MVP in 1977; had 3,053 career hits.

Steve Carlton (b. Dec. 22, 1944): Baseball LHP; won 20 or more games 6 times; 4-time Cy Young winner (1972,77,80,82) with Philadelphia; 329-244 career record; 4,136 career Ks.

JoAnne Carner (b. Apr. 4, 1939): Golfer; 5-time U.S. Amateur champion; 2-time U.S. Open champ; 3-time LPGA Player of Year (1974,81-82); 43 career wins.

Cris Carter (b. Nov. 25, 1965): Football; WR with Philadelphia (1987-89), Minnesota (1990-2001) and Miami (2002); twice caught 122 passes in a season (1994, '95), the first time establishing an NFL record for catches in a season that was beaten a year later; 2nd player to reach 1000 career catches.

Don Carter (b. July 29, 1926): Bowler; 6-time Bowler of Year (1953-54,57-58,60,62); voted Greatest of All-Time in 1970.

Joe Carter (b. Mar. 7, 1960): Baseball OF; 3-time All-America at Wichita St. (1979-81); won 1993 World Series for Toronto with 3-run HR in bottom of the 9th of Game 6.

Alexander Cartwright (b. Apr. 17, 1820, d. July 12, 1892): Baseball; engineer and draftsman who spread gospel of baseball from New York City to California gold fields; widely regarded as the father of modern game; his guidelines included setting 3 strikes for an out and 3 outs for each half inning.

Billy Casper (b. June 24, 1931): Golfer; 2-time PGA Player of Year (1966,70); has won U.S. Open (1959,66), Masters (1970), U.S. Senior Open (1983); compiled 51 PGA Tour wins and 9 on Senior Tour.

Tracy Caulkins (b. Jan. 11, 1963): Swimmer; won 3 gold medals (2 individual) at 1984 Olympics; set 5 world records and won 48 U.S. national titles from 1978-84; Sullivan Award winner (1978); 2-time Honda Broderick Cup winner (1982,84).

Steve Cauthen (b. May 1, 1960): Jockey; became youngest jockey (18) to win the Triple Crown with Affirmed in 1978; won a record $6.1 million in 1977, winning the Eclipse Award as the nation's top rider and the award for AP male athlete of the year.

Evonne Goolagong Cawley (b. July 31, 1951): Australian tennis player; won Australian Open 4 times, Wimbledon twice (1971,80), French once (1971).

Florence Chadwick (b. Nov. 9, 1917, d. Mar. 15, 1995): Dominant distance swimmer of 1950s; set English Channel records from France to England (1950) and England to France (1951 and '55).

Wilt Chamberlain (b. Aug. 21, 1936, d. Oct. 12, 1999): Basketball C; consensus All-America in 1957 and '58 at Kansas; Final Four MOP in 1957; led NBA in scoring 7 times and rebounding 11 times; 7-time All-NBA first team; 4-time MVP (1960,66-68) in Philadelphia; scored 100 points vs. NY Knicks in Hershey, Pa., Mar. 2, 1962; led 76ers (1967) and LA Lakers (1972) to NBA titles; Finals MVP in 1972.

A.B. (Happy) Chandler (b. July 14, 1898, d. June 15, 1991): Baseball; former Kentucky governor and U.S. Senator who succeeded Judge Landis as commissioner in 1945; backed Branch Rickey's move in 1947 to make Jackie Robinson 1st black player in major leagues; deemed too pro-player and ousted by owners in 1951.

Michael Chang (b. Feb. 22, 1972): Tennis; won the 1989 French Open, becoming the youngest men's champion of a grand slam event (17 years, 3 months.); went 11 consecutive years (1988-98) with at least one title; finished in top 10 in the ATP year-end rankings from 1992-97 (career high no. 2 in 1996).

Julio Cesar Chavez (b. July 12, 1962): Mexican boxer; world jr. welterweight champ (1989-94); also held titles as jr. lightweight (1984-87) and lightweight (1987-89); won over 100 bouts; 90-bout unbeaten streak ended 1/29/94 when Frankie Randall won title on split decision; Chavez won title back 4 months later.

Linford Christie (b. Apr. 2, 1960): British sprinter; won 100-meter gold medals at both 1992 Olympics (9.96) and '93 World Championships (9.87).

Jim Clark (b. Mar. 14, 1936, d. Apr. 7, 1968): Scottish auto racer; 2-time Formula One world champion (1963,65); won Indy 500 in 1965; killed in car crash.

Bobby Clarke (b. Aug. 13, 1949): Hockey C; led Philadelphia Flyers to consecutive Stanley Cups in 1974-75; 3-time regular season MVP (1973,75-76); currently Flyers GM.

Ron Clarke (b. Feb. 21, 1937): Australian runner; from 1963-70 set 17 world records in races from 2 miles to 20,000m; never won Olympic gold medal.

Roger Clemens (b. Aug. 4, 1962): Baseball RHP; twice fanned MLB record 20 batters in 9-inning game (April 29, 1986 & Sept. 18, 1996); won a record 7 Cy Young Awards with Boston (1986-87,91), Toronto (1997,98), N.Y. Yankees (2001) and Houston (2004); AL MVP in 1986; won 2 World Series with N.Y. (1999-2000); got 300th win in 2003; led majors in ERA in 2005 at age 43; 2nd to Nolan Ryan in career K's.

Roberto Clemente (b. Aug. 18, 1934, d. Dec. 31, 1972): Baseball OF; hit over .300 13 times with Pittsburgh; led NL in batting 4 times; World Series MVP in 1971; regular season MVP in 1966; had 3,000 career hits; killed in plane crash; MLB Man of the Year award is named for him.

Alice Coachman (b. Nov. 9, 1923): Track & Field; became the first black woman to win an Olympic gold medal with her win in the high jump in 1948 (London); broke the high school and college high jump records despite not wearing any shoes; member of the National Track & Field Hall of Fame.

Ty Cobb (b. Dec. 18, 1886, d. July 17, 1961): Baseball OF; all-time highest career batting average (.367); hit over .400 3 times; led AL in batting 12 times and stolen bases 6 times with Detroit; MVP in 1911; had 4,191 career hits, 2,245 career runs and 892 steals; played 24 years (22 with Detroit, 2 with Philadelphia); nicknamed "The Georgia Peach"; part of Baseball Hall of Fame's inaugural class.

Mickey Cochrane (b. Apr. 6, 1903, d. June 28, 1962): Baseball C; led Philadelphia A's (1929-30) and Detroit (1935) to 3 World Series titles; 2-time AL MVP (1928,34).

Sebastian Coe (b. Sept. 29, 1956): British runner; won gold medal in 1500m and silver medal in 800m at both 1980 and '84 Olympics; long-time world record holder in 800m and 1000m; elected to Parliament as Conservative in 1992.

Paul Coffey (b. June 1, 1961): Hockey D; 3-time Norris Trophy winner; member of 4 Stanley Cup champions at Edmonton (1984-85,87) and Pittsburgh (1991); ranks 10th on NHL all-time scoring list; elected to Hall of Fame in 2004.

Rocky Colavito (b. August 10, 1933): Baseball OF; six-time all-star who hit 374 HRs over his 14-year career; hugely popular in Cleveland where he played from 1955-59 and then 1965-67; led the league in HRs in 1959 with 42 and RBI in 1965 with 108; hit four consecutive HRs in one game.

Eddie Collins (b. May 2, 1887, d. Mar. 25, 1951): Baseball 2B; led Philadelphia A's (1910-11) and Chicago White Sox (1917) to 3 World Series titles; AL MVP in 1914; had 3,311 career hits and 743 stolen bases.

Nadia Comaneci (b. Nov. 12, 1961): Romanian gymnast; first to record perfect 10 in Olympics; won 3 individual golds at 1976 Olympics and 2 more in '80.

Lionel Conacher (b. May 24, 1901, d. May 26, 1954): Canada's greatest all-around athlete; NHL hockey (2 Stanley Cups), CFL football (1 Grey Cup), minor league baseball, soccer, lacrosse, track, amateur boxing champion; member of Parliament (1949-54).

Tony Conigliaro (b. Jan. 7, 1945, d. Feb. 24, 1990): Baseball OF; youngest (20 years old) to lead the AL in HRs (32 in 1965); hit in the face with a fastball in 1967; came back to hit 36 HRs in 1970 but was never the same.

Gene Conley (b. Nov. 10, 1930): Baseball and Basketball; played for World Series and NBA champions with Milwaukee Braves (1957) and Boston Celtics (1959-61); losing pitcher in 1954 All-Star Game and winning pitcher in 1955 Game; 91-96 record in 11 seasons.

Billy Conn (b. Oct. 8, 1917, d. May 29, 1993): Boxer; Pittsburgh native and world light heavyweight champion from 1939-41; nearly upset heavyweight champ Joe Louis in 1941 title bout, but was knocked out in 13th round; pro record 63-11-1 with 14 KOs.

Dennis Conner (b. Sept. 16, 1942): Sailing; 3-time America's Cup-winning skipper aboard *Freedom* (1980), *Stars & Stripes* (1987) and the *Stars & Stripes* catamaran (1988); only American skipper to lose Cup, first in 1983 when *Australia II* beat *Liberty* and again in '95 when New Zealand's *Black Magic* swept Conner and his *Stars & Stripes* crew aboard the borrowed *Young America.*

Maureen Connolly (b. Sept. 17, 1934, d. June 21, 1969): Tennis; 1st woman to win Grand Slam (in 1953 at age 18); horse riding accident ended her career in '54 at age 19; won 3 Wimbledons (1952-54), 3 U.S. Opens (1951-53), 2 French Opens (1953-54) and 1 Australian Open (1953); 3-time AP Female Athlete of Year (1951-53).

Jimmy Connors (b. Sept. 2, 1952): Tennis; No.1 player in world 5 times (1974-78); won 5 U.S. Opens, 2 Wimbledons and 1 Australian; rose from No. 936 at the close of 1990 to U.S. Open semifinals in 1991 at age 39; NCAA singles champ (1971); all-time leader in pro singles titles (109) and matches won at U.S. Open (98) and Wimbledon (84).

Jack Kent Cooke (b. Oct. 25, 1912, d. April 6, 1997): Football; sole owner of NFL Washington Redskins from 1985-97; teams won 2 Super Bowls (1988,92); also owned NBA Lakers and NHL Kings in LA; built LA Forum for $12 million in 1967.

Cynthia Cooper (b. April 14, 1963): Women's basketball G; won two NCAA basketball titles at USC (1983-84); won gold medal with U.S. team in 1988; 2-time WNBA MVP and 4-time league champion with Houston Comets; coach of WNBA's Phoenix Mercury 2001-02; coach of Prairie View A&M since 2005.

Angel Cordero Jr. (b. Nov. 8, 1942): Jockey; retired third on all-time list with 7,057 wins in 38,646 starts; won Kentucky Derby 3 times (1974,76,85), Preakness twice and Belmont once; 2-time Eclipse Award winner (1982-83).

Howard Cosell (b. Mar. 25, 1920, d. Apr. 23, 1995): Radio-TV; former ABC commentator on *Monday Night Football* and *Wide World of Sports,* who energized TV sports journalism with abrasive "tell it like it is" style.

Bob Costas (b. Mar. 22, 1952): Radio-TV; NBC broadcaster who has been anchor for NBA, NFL and Olympics as well as baseball play-by-play man; 15-time Emmy winner as studio host/play-by-play and 8-time National Sportscaster of Year.

James (Doc) Counsilman (b. Dec. 28, 1920, d. Jan. 4, 2004): Swimming; coached Indiana men's swim team to 6 NCAA championships (1968-73); coached the 1964 and '76 U.S. men's Olympic teams that won a combined 21 of 24 gold medals; in 1979 became oldest person (59) to swim English Channel; retired in 1990 with dual meet record of 287-36-1.

Fred Couples (b. Oct. 3, 1959): Golfer; 2-time PGA Tour Player of the Year (1991,92); 15 Tour victories, including 1992 Masters.

Jim Courier (b. Aug. 17, 1970): Tennis; No. 1 player in world in 1992, won 2 Australian Opens (1992-93) and 2 French Opens (1991-92); played on 1992 Davis Cup winner; Nick Bollettieri Academy classmate of Andre Agassi; entered Hall of Fame in 2005.

Margaret Smith Court (b. July 16, 1942): Australian tennis player; won Grand Slam in both singles (1970) and mixed doubles (1963 with Ken Fletcher); record 24 Grand Slam singles titles—11 Australian, 5 U.S., 5 French and 3 Wimbledon.

Bob Cousy (b. Aug. 9, 1928): Basketball G; led NBA in assists 8 times; 10-time All-NBA 1st team; 1957 MVP; led Boston to 6 NBA titles (1957,59-63); elected to Hall of Fame in 1970, one of NBA's 50 Greatest Players.

Buster Crabbe (b. Feb. 7, 1908, d. Apr. 23, 1983): Swimmer; 2-time Olympic freestyle medalist with bronze in 1928 (1500m) and gold in '32 (400m); became movie star and King of Serials as Flash Gordon and Buck Rogers.

Ben Crenshaw (b. Jan. 11, 1952): Golfer; co-NCAA champion with Tom Kite in 1972; battled Graves' disease in mid-1980s; 19 career Tour victories; won Masters for second time in 1995 and dedicated it to 90-year-old mentor Harvey Penick, who had died a week earlier; captain of 1999 Ryder Cup team.

Joe Cronin (b. Oct. 12, 1906, d. Sept. 7, 1984): Baseball SS; hit over .300 and drove in over 100 runs 8 times each; player-manager in Washington and Boston (1933-47); AL president (1959-73).

Larry Csonka (b. Dec. 25, 1946): Football RB; powerful runner and blocker who gained 8,081 yards in 11 seasons in the AFL and NFL; won two consecutive Super Bowls with the Miami Dolphins (1973-74) and was named MVP in the latter, rushing for 145 yards and two TDs; member of the College and Pro Football Halls of Fame; rescued from storm-tossed vessel by Coast Guard in Bering Sea in 2005.

Mark Cuban (b. July 31, 1958): Basketball; enthusiastic, outspoken owner of the Dallas Mavericks; co-creator of Broadcast.com, which he sold to Yahoo! in 1999 for roughly $5 billion in Yahoo! stock; purchased the Mavericks in 2000 for $280 million; has spent slightly less than that in fines to the NBA for, among other things, criticizing officials and getting involved in on-court fracases.

Ann Curtis (b. Mar. 6, 1926): Swimming; won two gold medals and one silver in 1948 Olympics; set four world and 18 U.S. records during career; first woman and swimmer to win Sullivan Award (1944).

Betty Cuthbert (b. Apr. 20, 1938): Australian runner; won gold medals in 100 and 200 meters and 4x100m relay at 1956 Olympics; also won 400m gold at 1964 Olympics.

Bjorn Dählie (b. June 19, 1967): Norwegian cross-country skier; winner of a record eight gold and 12 overall Winter Olympic medals from 1992-98.

Chuck Daly (b. July 20, 1930): Basketball; coached Detroit to two NBA titles (1989-90); also coached NBA "Dream Team" to gold medal in 1992 Olympics; retired in 1994 but returned in 1997 to coach Orlando Magic for two seasons.

John Daly (b. Apr. 28, 1966): Golfer; big hitter who was surprise winner of 1991 PGA Championship as unknown 25-year-old; battled through personal troubles in 1994 to return in '95 and win 2nd major at British Open, beating Italy's Costantino Rocca in 4-hole playoff; won first PGA Tour event in nine years at 2004 Buick Invitational; has admitted to accumulating somewhere in the range of $50-60 million in gambling losses.

Johnny Damon (b. Nov. 5, 1973): Baseball CF; long-haired lead-off man for the 2004 World Series champion Boston Red Sox; became a short-haired lead-off man when he was signed by NY Yankees in 2006.

Stanley Dancer (b. July 25, 1927, d. Sept. 8, 2005): Harness racing; winner of 4 Hambletonians; trainer-driver of Triple Crown winners in trotting (Nevele Pride in 1968 and Super Bowl in '72) and pacing (Most Happy Fella in 1970).

Beth Daniel (b. Oct. 14, 1956): Golfer; 33 career wins, including 1 major; inducted into World Golf Hall of Fame in 1999.

Alvin Dark (b. Jan. 7, 1922): Baseball IF and MGR; hit .322 to win the NL Rookie of the Year award in 1948 with the Boston Braves; won 994 games as a manager and led the Oakland A's to a World Series win in 1974.

Tamas Darnyi (b. June 3, 1967): Hungarian swimmer; 2-time double gold medal winner in 200m and 400m individual medley at 1988 and '92 Olympics; also won both events in 1986 and '91 world championships; set world records in both at '91 worlds; 1st swimmer to break 2 minutes in 200m IM (1:59:36).

Lindsay Davenport (b. June 8, 1976): Tennis player; became first American female ranked No. 1 in the world (1998) since Chris Evert in 1985; won U.S. Open (1998), Wimbledon (1999) and Australian Open (2000); won Olympic gold medal in 1996.

Al Davis (b. July 4, 1929): Football; GM-coach of Oakland 1963-66; helped force AFL-NFL merger as AFL commissioner in 1966; returned to Oakland as managing general partner and directed club to 3 Super Bowl wins (1977,81,84); defied fellow NFL owners and moved Raiders to LA in 1982; turned down owners' 1995 offer to build him a new stadium in LA and moved back to Oakland instead.

Dwight Davis (b. July 5, 1879, d. Nov. 28, 1945): Tennis; donor of Davis Cup; played for winning U.S. team in 1st two Cup finals (1900,02); won U.S. and Wimbledon doubles titles in 1901; Secretary of War (1925-29) under President Coolidge.

Ernie Davis (b. Dec. 14, 1939, d. May 18, 1963): Football; star running back at Syracuse University; first black player to win the Heisman Trophy in 1961; drafted by the Washington Redskins and traded to Cleveland but died the following year of leukemia before playing a pro game.

Glenn Davis (b. Dec. 26, 1924, d. Mar. 9, 2005): Football HB; 3-time All-America; led Army to national titles in 1944-45; Doc Blanchard's running mate; won Heisman Trophy in 1946.

John Davis (b. Jan. 12, 1921, d. July 13, 1984): Weightlifting; 6-time world champion; 2-time Olympic super-heavyweight champ (1948,52); undefeated from 1938-53.

Terrell Davis (b. Oct. 28, 1972): Football RB; 1998 NFL MVP, rushing for a league-leading 2,008 yards (4th all-time); played for two Super Bowl winners in Denver (XXXII and XXXIII), earning MVP honors in the former with Super Bowl-record 3 rushing touchdownss.

Pat Day (b. Oct. 13, 1953): Jockey; four-time Eclipse award winner (1984,86,87,91); became all-time leader in earnings in 2002; 4th all-time with 8,803 career victories; won Kentucky Derby (1992), five Preaknesses (1985,90,94-96) and three Belmonts (1989,94,2000); inducted into Hall of Fame in 1991; retired in 2005.

Ron Dayne (b. Mar. 14, 1978): Football RB; NCAA Div. I-A all-time leading rusher, gaining 6,397 yards at Wisconsin (1996-99); 1999 Heisman Trophy winner; selected in 1st round (11th overall) of 2000 NFL draft by NY Giants.

Dizzy Dean (b. Jan. 16 1911, d. July 17, 1974): Baseball RHP; led NL in strikeouts and complete games four times; last NL pitcher to win 30 games (30-7 in 1934); MVP in 1934 with St. Louis; 150-83 all-time record.

Dave DeBusschere (b. Oct. 16, 1940, d. May, 14, 2003): Basketball F; youngest coach in NBA history (24 in 1964); player-coach of Detroit Pistons (1964-67); played in 8 All-Star games; won 2 NBA titles as player with NY Knicks (1970, 73); ABA commissioner (1975-76); also pitched 2 seasons for Chicago White Sox (1962-63) with 3-4 record.

Pierre de Coubertin (b. Jan. 1, 1863, d. Sept. 2, 1937): French educator; father of the Modern Olympic Games; IOC president from 1896-1925.

Brian Deegan (b. May 9, 1975): Freestyle Motocross Rider; early pioneer of FMX, winner of 10 combined X Games medals, first rider to land a 360 in competition, WFA Series champ (1999), L.A. Coliseum Supercross winner (1999–125cc), experienced numerous life-threatening crashes, featured in over 20 motocross videos.

Anita DeFrantz (b. Oct. 4, 1952): Olympics; attorney who became the International Olympic Committee's first female vice president in 1997; first woman to represent U.S. on IOC (elected in 1986); member of USOC Executive Committee; member of bronze medal U.S. women's eight-oared shell at Montreal in 1976.

Oscar De La Hoya (b. Feb. 4, 1973): Boxer; 1992 Olympic gold medallist (lightweight); has held world titles in 4 weight classes (lightweight, super lightweight, welterweight and jr. middleweight); was unbeaten until losing WBC Welterweight belt to Felix Trinidad in a majority decision in 1999; later moved to jr. middleweight and won WBA and WBC belts; TKO'd in 9th round by champ Bernard Hopkins in their undisputed middleweight title fight in September 2004.

Cedric Dempsey (b. Apr. 14, 1932): College sports; succeeded Dick Schultz as NCAA executive director (title later changed to president) in 1993 and served until the end of 2002; former athletic director at Pacific (1967-79), San Diego St. (1979), Houston (1979-82) and Arizona (1983-93).

Jack Dempsey (b. June 24, 1895, d. May 31, 1983): Boxer; world heavyweight champion from 1919-26; lost title to Gene Tunney, then lost "Long Count" rematch in 1927 when he floored Tunney in 7th round but failed to retreat to neutral corner; pro record 64-6-9 with 49 KOs.

Bob Devaney (b. April 13, 1915, d. May 9, 1997): Football; head coach at Wyoming from 1957-1961; from 1962 to 1972 built Nebraska into a college football power; won two consecutive national championships in 1970-71; won eight Big Eight Conference titles; later served as Nebraska's athletic director.

Donna de Varona (b. Apr. 26, 1947): Swimming; won gold medals in 400 IM and 400 freestyle relay at 1964 Olympics; set 18 world records during career; co-founder of Women's Sports Foundation in 1974.

Gail Devers (b. Nov. 19, 1966): Track & Field; won Olympic gold medal in 100 meters in 1992 and '96; world champion in 100 meters (1993) and 100-meter hurdles (1993,95,99); overcame thyroid disorder (Graves' disease) that sidelined her in 1989-90 and nearly resulted in having both feet amputated.

Klaus Dibiasi (b. Oct. 6, 1947): Italian diver; won 3 consecutive Olympic gold medals in platform event (1968,72,76).

Eric Dickerson (b. Sept. 2, 1960): Football RB; led NFL in rushing 4 times (1983-84,86,88); ran for single-season record 2,105 yards in 1984; NFC Rookie of Year in 1983; All-Pro 5 times; traded from LA Rams to Indianapolis (Oct. 31, 1987) in 3-team, 10-player deal (including draft picks) that also involved Buffalo; 6th on all-time career rushing list with 13,259 yards in 11 seasons.

Harrison Dillard (b. July 8, 1923): Track & Field; only man to win Olympic gold medals in both sprints (100m in 1948) and hurdles (110m in 1952).

Joe DiMaggio (b. Nov. 25, 1914, d. Mar. 8, 1999): Baseball OF; hit safely in 56 straight games (1941); led AL in batting, HRs and RBI twice each; 3-time MVP (1939,41,47); hit .325 with 361 HRs over 13 seasons; led NY Yankees to 10 World Series titles.

Marcel Dionne (b. Aug. 3, 1951): Hockey C; fifth on NHL's all-time points list (1,771) and fourth on goals list (731) through 2006; tied Wayne Gretzky for the league lead in points (137) in 1980; scored 50 goals in a season 6 times; won the Lady Byng Trophy for gentlemanly play in 1975 and 1977; member of the Hockey Hall of Fame.

Mike Ditka (b. Oct. 18, 1939): Football; All-America at Pitt (1960); NFL Rookie of Year (1961); 5-time Pro Bowl tight end for Chicago Bears; returned to Chicago as head coach in 1982 and won Super Bowl XX in 1986; left Bears in 1992 and worked as a broadcaster at NBC for four years; coached the New Orleans Saints from 1997-99; compiled 127-101-0 record in 14 seasons; currently an analyst on ESPN.

Larry Doby (b. Dec. 13, 1924, d. June 18, 2003): Baseball OF; first black player in the AL; joined the Cleveland Indians in July 1947, three months after Jackie Robinson entered the Majors with the NL's Brooklyn Dodgers; an all-star centerfielder from 1949-55; managed the Chicago White Sox in 1978, becoming the second black major league manager; inducted into the Hall of Fame in 1998.

Charlotte (Lottie) Dod (b. Sept. 24, 1871, d. June 27, 1960): British athlete; was 5-time Wimbledon singles champion (1887-88,91-93); youngest player ever to win Wimbledon (15 in 1887); archery silver medalist at 1908 Olympics; member of national field hockey team in 1899; British Amateur golf champ in 1904.

Tony Dorsett (b. Apr. 7, 1954): Football RB; won Heisman Trophy leading Pitt to national title in 1976; 3rd all-time in NCAA Div. I-A rushing with 6,082 yards; led Dallas to Super Bowl title as NFC Rookie of Year (1977); NFC Player of Year (1981); rushed for 12,739 yards in 12 years.

James (Buster) Douglas (b. Apr. 7, 1960): Boxer; 42-1 shot who knocked out undefeated Mike Tyson in 10th round on Feb. 10, 1990 to win heavyweight title in Tokyo; 8½ months later, lost only title defense to Evander Holyfield by KO in 3rd round.

Vicki Manalo Draves (b. Dec. 31, 1924): Diver; First woman in olympic history to win gold medals in both platform diving and springboard diving; inducted into Int'l Swimming Hall of Fame in 1969.

The Dream Team Head coach Chuck Daly's "Best Ever" 12-man NBA All-Star squad that headlined the 1992 Summer Olympics in Barcelona and easily won the basketball gold medal; co-captained by Larry Bird and Magic Johnson, with veterans Charles Barkley, Clyde Drexler, Patrick Ewing, Michael Jordan, Karl Malone, Chris Mullin, Scottie Pippen, David Robinson, John Stockton and Duke's Christian Laettner.

Heike Drechsler (b. Dec. 16, 1964): German long jumper and sprinter; East German before reunification in 1991; set world long jump record (24-2¼) in 1988; won long jump gold medals at 1992 Olympics and 1983 and '93 World Championships; won silver medal in long jump and bronze medals in both 100- and 200-meter sprints at 1988 Olympics.

Ken Dryden (b. Aug. 8, 1947): Hockey G; led Montreal to 6 Stanley Cup titles; playoff MVP as rookie in 1971; won or shared 5 Vezina trophies; 2.24 career GAA.

Don Drysdale (b. July 23, 1936, d. July 3, 1993): Baseball RHP; led NL in strikeouts 3 times and games started 4 straight years; pitched record 6 shutouts in a row in 1968; won Cy Young (1962); had 209-166 record and hit 29 HRs in 14 years.

Charley Dumas (b. Feb. 12, 1937): U.S. high jumper; first man to clear 7 feet (7-0½) on June 29, 1956; won gold medal at 1956 Olympics.

Tim Duncan (b. Apr. 25, 1976): Basketball C/F; drafted first overall by San Antonio in 1997 NBA Draft; 7-footer who dominates on offense and defense; has won 3 NBA titles (1999, 2003, 2005) earning Finals MVP honors each time; 2-time NBA MVP (2002-03); 1997 College Player of the Year at Wake Forest; 1998 NBA Rookie of the Year.

Margaret Osborne du Pont (b. Mar. 4, 1918): Tennis; won 5 French, 7 Wimbledon and an unprecedented 25 U.S. national titles in singles, doubles and mixed doubles from 1941-62.

Roberto Duran (b. June 16, 1951): Panamanian boxer; one of only 6 fighters to hold 4 different world titles— lightweight (1972-79), welterweight (1980), junior middleweight (1983) and middleweight (1989-90); lost famous "No Mas" welterweight title bout when he quit in 8th round against Sugar Ray Leonard (1980); retired in 2002 at age 50 (104-16, 69 KOs).

Leo Durocher (b. July 27, 1905, d. Oct. 7, 1991): Baseball; managed in NL 24 years; won 2,015 games, including postseason; 3 pennants with Brooklyn (1941) and NY Giants (1951,54); won World Series in 1954.

Eddie Eagan (b. Apr. 26, 1898, d. June 14, 1967): Only athlete to win gold medals in both Summer and Winter Olympics (Boxing—1920, Bobsled—1932).

Alan Eagleson (b. Apr. 24, 1933): Hockey; Toronto lawyer, agent and 1st executive director of NHL Players Assn. (1967-90); midwived Team Canada vs. Soviet series (1972) and Canada Cup; charged with racketeering and defrauding NHLPA in indictment handed down by U.S. grand jury in 1994; was sentenced to 18 months in jail in Jan. 1998 after pleading guilty but only served 6 months; resigned from Hall of Fame in 1998.

Dale Earnhardt (b. Apr. 29, 1951, d. Feb. 18, 2001): Auto racer; 7-time NASCAR national champion (1980,86-87,90-91,93-94); Rookie of Year in 1979; was all-time NASCAR money leader with over $34 million won and 76 career wins when he died; finally won Daytona 500 in 1998 on 20th attempt; died in last lap crash at the 2001 Daytona 500.

James Easton (b. July 26, 1935): Olympics; archer and sporting goods manufacturer (Easton softball bats); one of 4 American delegates to the International Olympic Committee; president of International Archery Federation (FITA); member of LA Olympic Organizing Committee in 1984.

Dennis Eckersley (b. Oct. 3, 1954): Baseball P; began his career as a starter in 1975 with Cleveland; no-hit Angels in 1977; won 20 games in 1978 with Boston; moved to the bullpen after 12 seasons as a starter and became one of the best closers of all-time with Oakland; won 1992 AL Cy Young and MVP.

Stefan Edberg (b. Jan. 19, 1966): Swedish tennis player; 2-time No.1 player (1990-91); 2-time winner of Australian Open (1985,87), Wimbledon (1988,90) and U.S. Open (1991-92).

Gertrude Ederle (b. Oct. 23, 1906, d. Nov. 30, 2003): Swimmer; 1st woman to swim English Channel, breaking men's record by 2 hours in 1926; won 3 medals in 1924 Olympics.

Krisztina Egerszegi (b. Aug. 16, 1974): Hungarian swimmer; 3-time gold medal winner (100m and 200m backstroke and 400m IM) at 1992 Olympics; also won a gold (200m back) and silver (100m back) at 1988 Games; youngest (14) ever to win swimming gold. Won fifth gold medal (200m back) at '96 Games.

Lee Elder (b. July 14, 1934): Golf; in 1975, became the first black golfer to play in the Masters Tournament; also played in the 1977 Masters; member of the 1979 U.S. Ryder Cup team; played in South Africa's first integrated tournament in 1972.

Todd Eldredge (b. Aug. 28, 1971): Figure Skater; 6-time U.S. champion (1990,91,95,97,98,2002); 1996 World Champion; won U.S. titles at all three levels (novice, junior and senior); most decorated American figure skater without an Olympic medal.

Bill Elliott (b. Oct. 8, 1955): Auto racer; 2-time winner of Daytona 500 (1985,87); NASCAR national champ in 1988; 44 career NASCAR wins.

Herb Elliott (b. Feb. 25, 1938): Australian runner; undefeated from 1958-60; ran 17 sub-4:00 miles; 3 world records; won gold medal in 1500 meters at 1960 Olympics; retired at age 22.

Ernie Els (b. Oct. 17, 1969): Golfer; sweet swinging South African; 1994 PGA Tour Rookie of the Year and European Golfer of the Year; 2-time U.S. Open winner (1994,97); won 3rd major in 2002 British Open playoff; 15 PGA Tour wins.

John Elway (b. June 28, 1960): Football QB; All-American at Stanford; #1 overall pick in the 1983 draft; known for his last-minute, game-winning scoring drives; led Broncos to 3 Super Bowl losses before back-to-back wins in Super Bowl XXXII and XXXIII; 1987 NFL MVP; 4-time Pro Bowler; one of only three quarterbacks (Marino & Favre) to throw for over 50,000 yards.

Roy Emerson (b. Nov. 3, 1936): Australian tennis player; won 12 majors in singles— 6 Australian, 2 French, 2 Wimbledon and 2 U.S. from 1961-67.

Kornelia Ender (b. Oct. 25, 1958): East German swimmer; 1st woman to win 4 gold medals at one Olympics (1976), all in world-record time.

Julius Erving (b. Feb. 22, 1950): Basketball F; "Dr. J"; changed game in the ABA, then NBA with his "above-the-rim" style of play; in ABA (1971-76): 3-time MVP, 2-time playoff MVP, led NY Nets to 2 titles (1974,76); in NBA (1976-87): 5-time All-NBA 1st team, MVP in 1981, led Philadelphia 76ers to 1983 NBA title.

Phil Esposito (b. Feb. 20, 1942): Hockey C; 1st NHL player to score 100 points in a season (126 in 1969); 6-time All-NHL 1st team with Boston (1969-74); 2-time MVP (1969,74); 5-time scoring champ; star of 1972 Canada-Soviet series; former president-GM of Tampa Bay Lightning.

Janet Evans (b. Aug. 28, 1971): Swimmer; won 3 individual gold medals (400m & 800m freestyle, 400m IM) at 1988 Olympics; 1989 Sullivan Award winner; won 1 gold (800m) and 1 silver (400m) at 1992 Olympics.

Lee Evans (b. Feb. 25, 1947): Track & Field; dominant quarter-miler in world from 1966-72; world record in 400m set at 1968 Olympics stood 20 years.

Chris Evert (b. Dec. 21, 1954): Tennis; No. 1 player in world 5 times (1975-77,80-81); won at least 1 Grand Slam singles title every year from 1974-86; 18 majors in all— 7 French, 6 U.S., 3 Wimbledon and 2 Australian; retired after 1989 season with 154 singles titles and $8,896,195 in career earnings.

Weeb Ewbank (b. May 6, 1907, d. Nov. 18, 1998): Football; only coach to win NFL and AFL titles; led Baltimore to 2 NFL titles (1958-59) and NY Jets to Super Bowl III win.

Patrick Ewing (b. Aug. 5, 1962): Basketball C; 3-time All-America; led Georgetown to 3 NCAA Finals and 1984 title; Final 4 MOP in '84; 1986 NBA Rookie of Year with New York; All-NBA (1990); on U.S. Olympic gold medal-winning teams in 1984 and '92; named one of the NBA's 50 Greatest Players.

Ray Ewry (b. Oct. 14, 1873, d. Sept. 29, 1937): Track & Field; won 10 gold medals (although 2 are not recognized by IOC) over 4 consecutive Olympics (1900,04,06,08); all events he won (Standing HJ, LJ and TJ) were discontinued in 1912.

Nick Faldo (b. July 18, 1957): British golfer; 3-time winner of British Open (1987,90,92) and Masters (1989, 90, 96); 3-time European Golfer of Year (1989-90,92); PGA Player of the Year in 1990.

Juan Manuel Fangio (b. June 24, 1911, d. July 17, 1995): Argentine auto racer; 5-time F1 world champ (1951,54-57); 24 career wins, retired in 1958.

Marshall Faulk (b. Feb. 26, 1973): Football RB; 3-time consensus All-America at San Diego St.; 2-time NCAA Div. I-A rushing leader (1991-92); 2nd overall pick (Indianapolis) of the 1994 NFL draft; traded to St.L Rams in 1999; 3-time AP Offensive Player of the Year (1999-2001); NFL MVP in 2000 (AP/PFWA) and 2001 (Bell/PFWA); set NFL single season record with 26 TDs in 2000 (broken by P. Holmes's 27 in 2003).

Brett Favre (b. Oct. 10, 1969): Football; Strong-armed Southern Miss. QB drafted in 1991 in the 2nd round (33rd overall) by Atlanta; traded to Green Bay in 1992; 3-time league MVP (1995-97); 8-time Pro Bowl QB; led Packers to Super Bowl victory in 1997; holds NFL quarterback record for consecutive games started with over 200...and counting.

Sergei Fedorov (b. Dec. 13, 1969): Hockey C; first Russian to win NHL Hart Trophy as 1993-94 regular season MVP; 5-time All-Star and 3-time Stanley Cup winner (1997,98,2002) with Detroit.

Roger Federer (b. Aug. 8, 1984): Tennis; top-ranked men's tennis player since October, 2004, the third-longest streak as the ATP's #1 player (behind Lendl and Connors); winner of 9 Grand Slam events: Australian Open (2004,06), Wimbledon (2003-06); U.S. Open (2004-06); recorded a 55-match win streak in North America, broken by Andy Murray on Aug. 16, 2006; 2-time ATP Player of the Year (2004-05).

Donald Fehr (b. July 18, 1948): Baseball labor leader; protégé of Marvin Miller; executive director and general counsel of Major League Players Assn. since 1983; led players in 1994 "salary cap" strike that lasted eight months and resulted in first cancellation of World Series since 1904.

Bob Feller (b. Nov. 3, 1918): Baseball RHP; Hall of Fame fire-baller who led AL in strikeouts 7 times and wins 6 times with Cleveland Indians; threw 3 no-hitters and major league record 12 one-hitters; 266-162 record; amassed 2,581 Ks despite missing four seasons to military service during WWII.

Tom Ferguson (b. Dec. 20, 1950): Rodeo; 6-time All-Around champion (1974-79); 1st cowboy to win $100,000 in one season (1978); 1st to win $1 million in career (1986).

Herve Filion (b. Feb. 1, 1940): Harness racing; 10-time Driver of Year; only driver to win over 15,000 races.

Rollie Fingers (b. Aug. 25, 1946): Baseball RHP; mustachioed relief ace with 341 career saves; won AL MVP and Cy Young awards in 1981 with Milwaukee; World Series MVP in 1974 with Oakland; elected to Hall of Fame in 1992.

Charles O. Finley (b. Feb. 22, 1918, d. Feb. 19, 1997): Baseball owner; moved KC A's to Oakland in 1968; won 3 straight World Series from 1972-74; also owned teams in NHL and ABA.

Bobby Fischer (b. Mar. 9, 1943): Chess; at 15, became youngest international grandmaster in chess history; only American to hold world championship (1972-75); was stripped of title in 1975 after refusing to defend against Anatoly Karpov and became recluse; re-emerged to defeat old foe and former world champion Boris Spassky in 1992.

Carlton Fisk (b. Dec. 26, 1947): Baseball C; holds all-time major league record for games caught (2,229); also held HR record for catchers (351) until 2004 (Mike Piazza); AL Rookie of Year (1972) and 10-time All-Star; hit epic, 12th-inning Game 6 homer for Boston Red Sox in 1975 World Series; elected to the Hall of Fame in 2000.

Emerson Fittipaldi (b. Dec. 12, 1946): Brazilian auto racer; 2-time Formula One world champion (1972,74); 2-time winner of Indy 500 (1989,93); won overall IndyCar title in 1989.

Bob Fitzsimmons (b. May 26, 1863, d. Oct. 22, 1917): British boxer; held 3 world titles— middleweight (1881-97), heavyweight (1897-99) and light heavyweight (1903-05); pro record 40-11 with 32 KOs.

James (Sunny Jim) Fitzsimmons (b. July 23, 1874, d. Mar. 11, 1966): Horse racing; trained horses that won over 2,275 races, including 2 Triple Crown winners—Gallant Fox in 1930 and Omaha in '35.

Jim Fixx (b. Apr. 23, 1932, d. July 20, 1984): Running; author who popularized the sport of running; his 1977 bestseller *The Complete Book of Running*, is credited with helping start America's fitness revolution; ironically died of a heart attack while running.

Larry Fleisher (b. Sept. 26, 1930, d. May 4, 1989): Basketball; led NBA players union from 1961-89; increased average yearly salary from $9,400 in 1967 to $600,000 without a strike.

Peggy Fleming (b. July 27, 1948): Figure skating; 3-time world champion (1966-68); won Olympic gold medal in 1968.

Curt Flood (b. Jan. 18, 1938, d. Jan. 20, 1997): Baseball OF; played 15 years (1956-69,71) mainly with St. Louis; hit over .300 6 times with 7 Gold Gloves; refused trade to Phillies in 1969; lost challenge to baseball's reserve clause in Supreme Court in 1972 but his case helped bring free agency to MLB.

Ray Floyd (b. Sept. 14, 1942): Golfer; has 22 PGA victories in 4 decades; joined Senior PGA Tour in 1992 and has 14 Senior wins; has won Masters (1976), U.S. Open (1986), PGA twice (1969,82) and PGA Seniors Championship (1995); first player to win on PGA and Senior tours in same year (1992); member of 8 Ryder Cup teams and captain in 1989.

Doug Flutie (b. Oct. 23, 1962): Football QB; Boston College QB who threw famous 48-yard "Hail Mary" to defeat Miami on Nov. 23, 1984; 1984 Heisman Trophy winner; played in USFL, NFL and CFL; 6-time CFL MVP; led Calgary (1992) and Toronto (1996-97) to Grey Cup titles; on Jan. 1, he recorded the NFL's first drop kick since 1941; retired from football after the 2005 season (with New England).

Whitey Ford (b. Oct. 21, 1928): Baseball LHP; all-time leader in World Series wins (10); led AL in wins 3 times; won Cy Young and World Series MVP in 1961 with NY Yankees; 236-106 record.

George Foreman (b. Jan. 10, 1949): Boxer; Olympic heavyweight champ (1968); world heavyweight champ (1973-74, 94-95); lost title to Muhammad Ali (KO-8th) in '74; recaptured it on Nov. 5, 1994 at age 45 with a 10-round KO of WBA/IBF champ Michael Moorer, becoming the oldest man to win heavyweight crown; named AP Male Athlete of Year 20 years after losing title to Ali; stripped of WBA title in 1995 after declining to fight No. 1 contender; successfully defended title at age 46 against 26-year-old Axel Schulz in controversial maj. decision; gave up IBF title after refusing rematch with Schulz.

Dick Fosbury (b. Mar. 6, 1947): Track & Field; revolutionized high jump with back-first "Fosbury Flop"; won gold medal at 1968 Olympics.

Greg Foster (b. Aug. 4, 1958): Track & Field; 3-time winner of World Championship in 110-m hurdles (1983,87,91); won silver in 1984 Olympics; world indoor champion in 1991.

The Four Horsemen Senior backfield that led Notre Dame to national collegiate football championship in 1924; put together as sophomores by Irish coach Knute Rockne; immortalized by sportswriter Grantland Rice, whose report of the Oct. 19, 1924, Notre Dame-Army game began: "Outlined against a blue, gray October sky the Four Horsemen rode again..."; HB Jim Crowley (b. Sept. 10, 1902, d. Jan. 15, 1986), FB Elmer Layden (b. May 4, 1903, d. June 30, 1973), HB Don Miller (b. May 30, 1902, d. July 28, 1979) and QB Harry Stuhldreher (b. Oct. 14, 1901, d. Jan. 26, 1965).

The Four Musketeers French quartet that dominated men's tennis in 1920s and '30s, winning 8 straight French singles titles (1925-32), 6 Wimbledons in a row (1924-29) and 6 consecutive Davis Cups (1927-32)— Jean Borotra (b. Aug. 13, 1898, d. July 17, 1994), Jacques Brugnon (b. May 11, 1895, d. Mar. 20, 1978), Henri Cochet (b. Dec. 14, 1901, d. Apr. 1, 1987), Rene Lacoste (b. July 2, 1905, d. Oct. 13, 1996).

Nellie Fox (b. Dec. 25, 1927, d. Dec. 1, 1975): Baseball 2B; batted .306 in 1959 to win the AL MVP award with the pennant-winning Chicago White Sox; led the league in fielding percentage six times, hits four times and triples once; ended his 19-year career with 2,663 hits, 1,279 runs and .288 average.

Jimmie Foxx (b. Oct. 22, 1907, d. July 21, 1967): Baseball 1B; led AL in home runs 4 times and batting average twice; won Triple Crown in 1933; 3-time MVP (1932-33,38) with Philadelphia and Boston; hit 30 HRs or more 12 years in a row; 534 career HRs.

A.J. Foyt (b. Jan. 16, 1935): Auto racer; 7-time USAC-CART national champion (1960-61,63-64, 67,75,79); 4-time Indy 500 winner (1961,64, 67,77); only driver in history to win Indy 500, Daytona 500 (1972) and 24 Hours of LeMans (1967 with Dan Gurney); retired in 1993 as all-time CART wins leader with 67.

Bill France Sr. (b. Sept. 26, 1909, d. June 7, 1992): Stock car pioneer and promoter; founded NASCAR in 1948; guided race circuit through formative years; built both Daytona (Fla.) Int'l Speedway and Talladega (Ala.) Superspeedway.

Dawn Fraser (b. Sept. 4, 1937): Australian swimmer; won gold medals in 100m freestyle at 3 consecutive Olympics (1956,60,64).

Joe Frazier (b. Jan. 12, 1944): Boxer; 1964 Olympic heavyweight champion; world heavyweight champ (1970-73); decisioned former champ Muhammad Ali in March 1971 in one of the most anticipated prizefights in history, fought Ali twice more, losing both times including the "Thrilla in Manila" in 1975; pro record 32-4-1 with 27 KOs.

Walt Frazier (b. March 29, 1945): Basketball G; won the NBA championship twice (1970 and 73) with the New York Knicks; stole spotlight from teammate Willis Reed in Game 7 of 1970 Finals vs. the Lakers with 36 points, 19 assists and 5 steals; averaged 18.9 PPG and 6.1 APG over his career; four-time all-NBA and a member of the Hall of Fame; nicknamed "Clyde" after well-dressed gangster Clyde Barrow.

Cathy Freeman (b. Feb. 16, 1973): Track & Field; Australian Aborigine who lit the cauldron at the start of the 2000 Olympic Games in Sydney and later won gold in the 400-meters on her home soil; 2-time world champion in the 400-meters (1997,99).

Ford Frick (b. Dec. 19, 1894, d. Apr. 8, 1978): Baseball; sportswriter and radio announcer who served as NL president (1934-51) and commissioner (1951-65); convinced record-keepers to list Roger Maris' and Babe Ruth's season records separately; major leagues moved to West Coast and expanded from 16 to 20 teams during his tenure.

Frankie Frisch (b. Sept. 9, 1898, d. Mar. 12, 1973): Baseball 2B; played on 8 NL pennant winners in 19 years with NY and St. Louis; hit .300 or better 11 years in a row (1921-31); MVP in 1931; player-manager from 1933-37.

Dan Gable (b. Oct. 25, 1948): Wrestling; career wrestling record of 118-1 (Larry Owings beat him in his final collegiate match) at Iowa St., where he was a 2-time NCAA champ (1968,69) and tourney MVP in 1969 (137 lbs); won gold medal (149 lbs) at 1972 Olympics; coached Iowa to 9 straight NCAA titles (1978-86) and 15 overall in 21 years.

Eddie Gaedel (b. June 8, 1925, d. June 18, 1961): Baseball PH; St. Louis Browns' 3-foot-7 player whose career lasted one at bat (he walked) on Aug 19, 1951; hired as a publicity stunt by owner Bill Veeck.

Clarence (Big House) Gaines (b. May 21, 1924): Basketball; retired as coach of Div. II Winston-Salem in 1993 with 828-447 record in 47 years.

Alonzo (Jake) Gaither (b. Apr. 11, 1903, d. Feb. 18, 1994): Football; head coach at Florida A&M for 25 years; led Rattlers to 6 national black college titles; retired after 1969 season with record of 203-36-4 and a winning percentage of .844; coined phrase, "I like my boys agile, mobile and hostile."

Rulon Gardner (b. Aug. 16, 1971): Olympic wrestler; surprise winner of the super heavyweight Greco-Roman gold medal at the 2000 Sydney Games; beat unbeatable Russian legend Alexandre Kareline, 1-0; won 2000 Sullivan Award and USOC Sportsman of the Year Award; lost a toe to frostbite in 2002 but still took bronze medal in Athens (2004).

Cito Gaston (b. Mar. 17, 1944): Baseball; managed Toronto to consecutive World Series titles (1992-93); first black manager to win Series.

Justin Gatlin (b. Feb. 10, 1982): American sprinter; won 100m gold medal and 200m bronze at 2004 Summer Olympics in Athens; won 100m and 200m dashes at 2005 World Outdoor Championships; tied 100-m record (9.77) in May 2006; faces a possible 8-year ban and loss of his share of the record for a 2nd positive drug test later in the year (under appeal).

Lou Gehrig (b. June 19, 1903, d. June 2, 1941): Baseball 1B; played in 2,130 consecutive games from 1925-39 a major league record until Cal Ripken Jr. surpassed it in 1995; led AL in RBI 5 times and HRs 3 times; drove in 100 runs or more 13 years in a row; 2-time MVP (1927,36); hit .340 with 493 HRs over 17 seasons; led NY Yankees to 6 World Series titles; died at age 37 of Amyotrophic Lateral Sclerosis (ALS), a rare and incurable disease of the nervous system now better known as Lou Gehrig's disease.

Bernie Geoffrion (b. Feb. 14, 1931, d. Mar. 11, 2006): Hockey RW; credited with popularizing the slap shot, earning his nickname "Boom Boom"; scored 30 goals in 1952 to win the NHL's Calder Trophy (Rookie of the Year Award); won the MVP award (Hart) in 1955; became the second player in history to score 50 goals in one season; led the league in points in 1955 and 61; won 6 Stanley Cups with Montreal; member of the Hockey Hall of Fame.

George Gervin (b. April 27, 1952): Basketball G/F; joined the ABA in 1972 and came to the NBA with San Antonio in 1976; a five-time NBA all-star; led the league in scoring four times; scored 26,595 points with an average of 25.1 per game; known as the "Iceman" because of his cool style; elected to the Hall of Fame in 1996.

A. Bartlett Giamatti (b. Apr. 14, 1938, d. Sept. 1, 1989): Scholar and seventh commissioner of baseball; banned Pete Rose for life for betting on Major League games and associating with known gamblers; also served as the president of Yale (1978-86) and the National League (1986-89); father of character actor Paul.

Joe Gibbs (b. Nov. 25, 1940): Football; coached Washington to 3 Super Bowl titles in 12 seasons before retiring in 1993; owner of NASCAR racing team that won 1993 Daytona 500 and 2000 Winston Cup title; lured out of retirement to coach Redskins in 2004; began 2006 season with 157 wins, 12th on the all-time list.

Althea Gibson (b. Aug. 25, 1927, d. Sept. 28, 2003): Tennis; won both Wimbledon and U.S. championships in 1957 and '58; 1st African-American to play in either tourney and 1st to win each title.

Bob Gibson (b. Nov. 9, 1935): Baseball RHP; won 20 or more games 5 times; won 2 NL Cy Youngs (1968,70); MVP in 1968; led St. Louis to 2 World Series titles (1964,67); his ERA of 1.12 in 1968 is the lowest for a starter since 1914; 251-174 record.

Josh Gibson (b. Dec. 21, 1911, d. Jan. 20, 1947): Baseball C; the "Babe Ruth of the Negro Leagues"; Satchel Paige's battery mate with Pittsburgh Crawfords. The Negro Leagues did not keep accurate records but Gibson hit 84 home runs in one season and his Baseball Hall of Fame plaque says he hit "almost 800" home runs in his 17-year career.

Kirk Gibson (b. May 28, 1957): Baseball OF; All-America flanker at Mich. St. in 1978; chose baseball career and was AL playoff MVP with Detroit in 1984 and NL regular season MVP with Los Angeles in 1988; hit famous pinch-hit home run against Oakland's Dennis Eckersley in Game 1 of the 1988 World Series to vault the Dodgers to the title.

Frank Gifford (b. Aug. 16, 1930): Football HB; 4-time All-Pro (1955-57,59); NFL MVP in 1956; led NY Giants to 3 NFL title games; longtime TV sportscaster, beginning career in 1958 while still a player; scandal struck the married Gifford after he was videotaped in a compromising position with a former stewardess in 1997.

Sid Gillman (b. Oct. 26, 1911, d. Jan. 3, 2003): Football innovator; coach elected to both College and Pro Football Halls of Fame; led college teams at Miami-OH and Cincinnati to combined 81-19-2 record from 1944-54; coached LA Rams (1955-59) in NFL, then led LA-San Diego Chargers to 5 Western titles and 1 league championship in first six years of AFL.

George Gipp (b. Feb. 18, 1895, d. Dec. 14, 1920): Football HB; died of throat infection 2 weeks before he made All-America at Notre Dame; rushed for 2,341 yards, scored 156 points and averaged 38 yards a punt in 4 years (1917-20); inspiration for Knute Rockne's "Win one for the Gipper" speech.

Marc Girardelli (b. July 18, 1963): Luxembourg Alpine skier; Austrian native who refused to join Austrian Ski Federation because he wanted to be coached by his father; won unprecedented 5th overall World Cup title in 1993; winless at Olympics, although he won 2 silver medals in 1992.

Tom Glavine (b. Mar. 26, 1966): Baseball LHP; led the majors in wins from 1991-95 with 91; NL Cy Young winner in 1991 and '98; eight-time All-Star; World Series MVP with Atlanta in 1995; ended 2006 season with 290 career wins.

Tom Gola (b. Jan. 13, 1933): Basketball F; 4-time All-America and 1955 Player of Year at La Salle; MOP in 1952 NIT and '54 NCAA Final 4, leading Explorers to both titles; won NBA title as rookie with Philadelphia Warriors in 1956; 4-time NBA All-Star.

Marshall Goldberg (b. Oct. 24, 1917, d. Apr. 3, 2006): Football HB; 2-time consensus All-America at Pittsburgh (1937-38); led Pitt to national championship in 1937; played with NFL champion Chicago Cardinals 10 years later.

Lefty Gomez (b. Nov. 26, 1908, d. Feb. 17, 1989): Baseball LHP; 4-time 20-game winner with NY Yankees; holds World Series record for most wins (6) without a defeat; pitched on 5 world championship clubs in 1930s.

Pancho Gonzales (b. May 9, 1928, d. July 3, 1995): Tennis; won consecutive U.S. Championships in 1948-49 before turning pro at 21; dominated pro tour from 1950-61; in 1969 at age 41, played longest Wimbledon match ever (5:12), beating Charlie Pasarell 22-24,1-6,16-14,6-3,11-9.

Bob Goodenow (b. Oct. 29, 1952): Hockey; succeeded Alan Eagleson as executive director of NHL Players Association in 1990; led players out on 10-day strike (Apr. 1-10) in 1992, during 103-day owners' lockout in 1994-95 and lockout in 2004; resigned in 2005.

Roger Goodell (b. Feb. 19, 1959): Football; former NFL intern who rose quickly through the ranks and was elected to succeed Paul Tagliabue as the Commissioner of the league on Aug. 8, 2006; joined the NFL as an intern in 1981 after graduating from Washington & Jefferson College; also worked in P.R. for the N.Y. Jets, as assistant to AFC president Lamar Hunt, and in many positions for Tagliabue including Executive V.P. and COO from 2001-06.

Gail Goodrich (b. April 23, 1943): Basketball G; starred at UCLA and won two national championships in 1964 and 1965 under legendary coach John Wooden's tutelage; won the NBA championship with the L.A. Lakers in 1972 and led the team in scoring (25.9 ppg); averaged 18.6 ppg over his 14-year career.

Jeff Gordon (b. Aug. 4, 1971): Auto racer; 1993 NASCAR Rookie of Year; 4-time Winston Cup champion (1995,97,98,2001); won inaugural Brickyard 400 in 1994; became youngest winner (25) of the Daytona 500 in 1997, won Daytona 500 again in 1999 and 2005; in 1998 he tied Richard Petty for the modern-era record for wins in a single season with 13; NASCAR's all-time leading money winner; has 75 Winston/Nextel Cup career wins as of Sept. 2006.

Rich (Goose) Gossage (b. July 5, 1951): Baseball RHP; Nine-time All-Star (1975-78, 80-82, 84-85); intimidating relief pitcher; Fireman of the Year in 1975 with White Sox and 1978 with Yankees; led AL in saves with 26 (1975), 27 (1978); 1,002 career appearances; 310 saves.

Shane Gould (b. Nov. 23, 1956): Australian swimmer; set world records in 5 different women's freestyle events between July 1971 and Jan. 1972; won 3 gold medals, a silver and bronze in 1972 Olympics then retired at age 16.

Alf Goullet (b. Apr. 5, 1891, d. Mar. 11, 1995): Cycling; Australian who gained fame and fortune early in century as premier performer on U.S. 6-day bike race circuit; won 8 annual races at Madison Square Garden with 6 different partners from 1913-23.

Curt Gowdy (b. July 31, 1919, d. Feb. 20, 2006): Radio-TV; former radio voice of NY Yankees and then Boston Red Sox from 1949-66; TV play-by-play man for AFL, NFL and major league baseball; has broadcast World Series, All-Star Games, Rose Bowls, Super Bowls, Olympics and NCAA Final Fours for 3 networks; hosted "The American Sportsman."

Steffi Graf (b. June 14, 1969): German tennis player; won Grand Slam and Olympic gold medal in 1988 at age 19; won three of four majors in 1993, '95 and '96; won 22 Grand Slam singles titles— 7 at Wimbledon, 6 French, 5 U.S. and 4 Australian Opens, retired in 1999 as 3rd all-time with 107 career singles titles and as all-time tour leader in career earnings with over $21 million in prize money; married to fellow tennis great Andre Agassi.

Otto Graham (b. Dec. 6, 1921, d. Dec. 17, 2003): Football QB and basketball All-America at Northwestern; in pro ball, led Cleveland Browns to 7 league titles in 10 years, winning 4 AAFC championships (1946-49) and 3 NFL (1950,54-55); 5-time All-Pro; 2-time NFL MVP (1953,55).

Cammi Granato (b. Mar. 25, 1971): Hockey; American women's hockey pioneer; captain of U.S. team that won gold at the inaugural Olympic women's hockey competition in 1998 at Nagano; sister of NHL veteran Tony.

Red Grange (b. June 13, 1903, d. Jan. 28, 1991): Football HB; 3-time All-America at Illinois who brought 1st huge crowds to pro football when he signed with Chicago Bears in 1925; formed 1st AFL with manager-promoter C.C. Pyle in 1926, but league folded and he returned to Bears.

Bud Grant (b. May 20, 1927): Football and Basketball; only coach to win 100 games in both CFL and NFL and only member of both CFL and U.S. Pro Football Halls of Fame; led Winnipeg to 4 Grey Cup titles (1958-59,61-62) in 6 appearances, but his Minnesota Vikings lost all 4 Super Bowl attempts in 1970s; accumulated 122 CFL wins and 168 NFL wins; also All-Big Ten at Minnesota in both football and basketball in late 1940s; a 3-time CFL All-Star offensive end; also member of 1950 NBA champion Minneapolis Lakers.

Rocky Graziano (b. June 7, 1922, d. May 22, 1990): Boxer; world middleweight champion (1946-47); fought Tony Zale for title 3 times in 21 months, losing twice; pro record 67-10-6 with 52 KOs; movie "Somebody Up There Likes Me" based on his life.

Hank Greenberg (b. Jan. 1, 1911, d. Sept. 4, 1986): Baseball 1B/LF; slugging right-hander who led AL in HRs and RBI 4 times each; 2-time MVP (1935, 40) with Detroit; 331 career HRs, including 58 in 1938; elected to Hall of Fame in 1956.

Joe Greene (b. Sept. 24, 1946): Football DT; 5-time All-Pro (1972-74,77,79); led Pittsburgh to 4 Super Bowl titles in 1970s; nicknamed "Mean Joe."

Maurice Greene (b. July 23, 1974): Track & Field; world 100m champion in 1997, 99 and 2001 and 200m champion in 1999; former world record holder (9.79) in the 100m; won the gold medal in the 100m and 4x100m at the 2000 Sydney Olympics; took 100m bronze at 2004 Athens Olympics.

Bud Greenspan (b. Sept. 18, 1926): Filmmaker specializing in the Olympic Games; has won Emmy awards for 22-part "The Olympiad" (1976-77) and historical vignettes for ABC-TV's coverage of 1980 Winter Games; won 1994 Emmy award for edited special on Lillehammer Winter Olympics; won The Peabody Award in 1996 for his outstanding service in chronicling the Olympic Games.

Wayne Gretzky (b. Jan. 26, 1961): Hockey C; 10-time NHL scoring champion; 9-time regular season MVP (1979-87,89) and 9-time All-NHL first team; scored 200 points or more in a season 4 times; led Edmonton to 4 Stanley Cups (1984-85,87-88); 2-time playoff MVP (1985,88); traded to LA Kings (Aug. 9, 1988); broke Gordie Howe's all-time NHL goal scoring record of 801 on Mar. 23, 1994; all-time NHL leader in points (2857), goals (894) and assists (1963); also all-time Stanley Cup leader in points, goals and assists; spent the end of the 1996 season with the St. Louis Blues and then signed a free agent contract with the New York Rangers; retired in 1999 at age 38 with 61 NHL scoring records in 20 seasons; became part-owner of NHL's Coyotes in 2000 and stepped behind the bench as Coyotes head coach in 2005.

Bob Griese (b. Feb. 3, 1945): Football QB; 2-time All-Pro (1971,77); led Miami to undefeated season (17-0) in 1972 and consecutive Super Bowl titles (1973-74); father of Brian.

Ken Griffey Jr. (b. Nov. 21, 1969): Baseball OF; overall 1st pick of 1987 draft by Seattle; 10-time Gold Glove winner; 12-time All-Star; 1997 AL MVP; MVP of 1992 All-Star game at age 23; hit home runs in 8 consecutive games in 1993; son of Ken Sr. and in 1990 they became the first father-son combination to appear in the same major league lineup; traded to the Cincinnati Reds before the 2000 season but has been plagued with injuries; hit 27 homers in 2006 to reach 563 for his career.

Archie Griffin (b. Aug. 21, 1954): Football RB; only college player to win two Heisman Trophies (1974-75); rushed for 5,177 yards in career at Ohio St. and played in four straight Rose Bowls; drafted by Cincinnati Bengals and played 8 years in NFL.

Emile Griffith (b. Feb. 3, 1938): Boxer; world welterweight champion (1961,62-63,63-65); world middleweight champ (1966-67,67-68); pro record 85-24-2 with 23 KOs.

Dick Groat (b. Nov. 4, 1930): Basketball G and Baseball SS; 2-time basketball All-America at Duke and college Player of Year in 1951; won NL MVP award as shortstop with Pittsburgh in 1960; won World Series with Pirates (1960) and St. Louis (1964).

Lefty Grove (b. Mar. 6, 1900, d. May 23, 1975): Baseball LHP; won 20 or more games 8 times; led AL in ERA 9 times and strikeouts 7 times; 31-4 record and MVP in 1931 with Philadelphia; 300-141 record; real name: Robert Moses Grove.

Lou Groza (b. Jan. 25, 1924, d. Nov. 29, 2000): Football T-PK; 6-time All-Pro; played in 13 championship games for Cleveland from 1946-67; kicked winning field goal in 1950 NFL title game; 1,608 career points (1,349 in NFL).

Janet Guthrie (b. Mar. 7, 1938): Auto racer; in 1977, became 1st woman to race in Indianapolis 500; placed 9th at Indy in 1978.

Tony Gwynn (b. May 9, 1960): Baseball OF; 8-time NL batting champion (1984,87-89,94-97) with San Diego, 15-time All-Star; got 3,000th career hit Aug. 6, 1999 at Montreal; played basketball at San Diego St. leaving as school's all-time assist leader; drafted in 10th round of 1981 NBA draft by then San Diego Clippers; retired with 3,141 career hits.

Harvey Haddix (b. Sept. 18, 1925, d. Jan. 9, 1994): Baseball LHP; pitched 12 perfect innings for Pittsburgh, but lost to Milwaukee in the 13th, 1-0 (May 26, 1959); won Game 7 of 1960 World Series.

Walter Hagen (b. Dec. 21, 1892, d. Oct. 5, 1969): Pro golf pioneer; won 2 U.S. Opens (1914,19), 4 British Opens (1922,24,28-29), 5 PGA Championships (1921,24-27) and 5 Western Opens; 44 career PGA wins; 6-time U.S. Ryder Cup captain.

Marvin Hagler (b. May 23, 1954): Boxer; hardpunching world middleweight champion from 1980-87; enjoyed his nickname "Marvelous Marvin" so much he had his name legally changed; pro record of 62-3-2 with 52 KOs; retired after suffering 1987 upset loss to Sugar Ray Leonard.

Mika Hakkinen (b. Sept. 28, 1968): Finnish auto racer; won two consecutive Formula One world drivers championships in 1998 and '99; recorded eight wins in '98 and five in '99; 20 career F1 wins.

George Halas (b. Feb. 2, 1895, d. Oct. 31, 1983): Football pioneer; MVP in 1919 Rose Bowl; player-coach-owner of Chicago Bears from 1920-83; signed Red Grange in 1925; coached Bears for 40 seasons and won 8 NFL titles (1921,32-33,40-41,43,46,63); 2nd on all-time win list with 324 wins; elected to NFL Hall of Fame in 1963.

Dorothy Hamill (b. July 26, 1956): Figure skater; won Olympic gold medal and world championship in 1976; Ice Capades headliner from 1977-84; bought the financially-strapped Ice Capades in 1993 and sold it several years later.

Scott Hamilton (b. Aug. 28, 1958): Figure skater; 4-time world champion (1981-84); won gold medal at 1984 Olympics.

Mia Hamm (b. Mar. 17, 1972): Soccer F; all-time leading international scorer with 158 goals; member of three U.S. Olympic team (1996,2000,04), and four U.S. World Cup teams (1991,95,99,2003); made the U.S. National Team at 15; a three-time collegiate All-American; led UNC to four national titles (1989,90, 92,93); Two-time FIFA Women's World Player of the Year (2001-02); married to baseball's Nomar Garciaparra.

Tonya Harding (b. Nov. 12, 1970): Figure skater; 1991 and 1994 U.S. women's champion; involved in plot hatched by ex-husband Jeff Gillooly to injure rival Nancy Kerrigan and keep her off Olympic team; won '94 U.S. title in Kerrigan's absence; denied any role in assault and sued USOC to keep her spot in Olympics; finished 8th at Lillehammer (Kerrigan recovered and won silver medal); pleaded guilty on Mar. 16 to conspiracy to hinder investigation; stripped of 1994 title by U.S. Figure Skating Association.

Tom Harmon (b. Sept. 28, 1919, d. Mar. 17, 1990): Football HB; 2-time All-America at Michigan; won Heisman Trophy in 1940; played with AFL NY Americans in 1941 and NFL LA Rams (1946-47);World War II fighter pilot who won Silver Star and Purple Heart; became radio-TV commentator.

Franco Harris (b. Mar. 7, 1950): Football RB; ran for over 1,000 yards in a season 8 times; rushed for 12,120 yards in 13 years; led Pittsburgh to 4 Super Bowl titles.

Leon Hart (b. Nov. 2, 1928, d. Sept. 24, 2002): Football E; only player to win 3 national championships in college and 3 more in the NFL; won his titles at Notre Dame (1946-47,49) and with Detroit Lions (1952-53,57); 3-time All-America and last lineman to win Heisman Trophy (1949); All-Pro on both offense and defense in 1951.

Bill Hartack (b. Dec. 9, 1932): Jockey; won Kentucky Derby 5 times (1957,60,62,64,69), Preakness 3 times (1956,64,69), and the Belmont once (1960).

Doug Harvey (b. Dec. 19, 1924, d. Dec. 26, 1989): Hockey D; 10-time All-NHL 1st team; won Norris Trophy 7 times (1955-58,60-62); led Montreal to 6 Stanley Cups.

Dominik Hasek (b. Jan. 29, 1965): Czech hockey goaltender; 2-time NHL MVP (1997,98) with Buffalo; 6-time Vezina Trophy winner (1994,95,97,98,99, 2001); led Czech Republic to Olympic gold medal in 1998 at Nagano; won Stanley Cup with Detroit in 2002.

Billy Haughton (b. Nov. 2, 1923, d. July 15, 1986): Harness racing; 4-time winner of Hambletonian; trainer-driver of one Pacing Triple Crown winner (1968); 4,910 career wins.

João Havelange (b. May 8, 1916): Soccer; Brazilian-born president of Federation Internationale de Football Assoc. (FIFA) 1974-98; also member of International Olympic Committee.

John Havlicek (b. Apr. 8, 1940): Basketball F; played in three NCAA Finals at Ohio St. (1960-62); led Boston to eight NBA titles (1963-66,68-69,74,76); Finals MVP in 1974; four-time All-NBA 1st team; #17 retired by the Celtics.

Tony Hawk (b. May 12, 1968): Skateboarder; winner of 16 X Games medals; top-ranked vert skater for 12 consecutive years; in 1999, became the first person to land the 900; credited with inventing nearly 100 tricks; creator, Tony Hawk's Pro Skater bestselling video game franchise ($1billion+ in sales), autobiography appeared on The New York Times bestseller list (2000).

Bob Hayes (b. Dec. 20, 1942, d. Sept. 18, 2002): Track & Field and Football; won gold medal in 100m at 1964 Olympics; all-pro SE for Dallas in 1966; won Super Bowl with Cowboys in 1972; convicted of drug trafficking in 1979 and served 18 months of a 5-year sentence.

Elvin Hayes (b. Nov. 17, 1945): Basketball C; Known as "the Big E"; Overall number one pick of the 1968 NBA draft; three-time All-NBA first team (1975,77,79); 1978 Finals MVP; 12-time NBA all-star (1969-80); named to NBA's 50 Greatest Players; amassed 27,313 points and 16,279 rebounds; member of basketball Hall of Fame.

Woody Hayes (b. Feb. 14, 1913, d. Mar. 12, 1987): Football; coached Ohio St. to 6 national titles (1954,57,61,68,70) and 4 Rose Bowl victories; 238 career wins in 28 seasons at Denison, Miami-OH and OSU; his coaching career ended abruptly in 1978 after he attacked an opposing player on the sidelines after an interception.

Thomas Hearns (b. Oct. 18, 1958): Boxer; held world titles as welterweight, junior middleweight, middleweight and light heavyweight; four career losses came against Ray Leonard, Marvin Hagler and twice to Iran Barkley; pro record of 60-4-1, 46 KOs.

Eric Heiden (b. June 14, 1958): Speed skater; 3-time overall world champion (1977-79); won all 5 men's speed skating gold medals at 1980 Olympics, setting records in each; Sullivan Award winner (1980).

Mel Hein (b. Aug. 22, 1909, d. Jan. 31, 1992): Football; NFL All-Pro 8 straight years (1933-40); MVP in 1938 with Giants; didn't miss a game in 15 years.

John W. Heisman (b. Oct. 23, 1869, d. Oct. 3, 1936): Football; coached at 9 colleges from 1892-1927; won 185 games; Director of Athletics at Downtown Athletic Club in NYC (1928-36); DAC named Heisman Trophy after him.

Carol Heiss (b. Jan. 20, 1940): Figure skater; 5-time world champion (1956-60); won Olympic silver medal in 1956 and gold in '60; married 1956 men's gold medalist Hayes Jenkins.

Rickey Henderson (b. Dec. 25, 1958): Baseball OF; AL playoff MVP (1989) and AL regular season MVP (1990); set single-season base stealing record of 130 in 1982; led AL in steals a record 12 times; broke Lou Brock's all-time record of 938 on May 1, 1991; holds all-time MLB records in runs (2295), stolen bases (1406), and HRs as leadoff batter (81).

Sonja Henie (b. Apr. 8, 1912, d. Oct. 12, 1969): Norwegian figure skater; 10-time world champion (1927-36); won 3 consecutive Olympic gold medals (1928,32,36); became movie star.

Foster Hewitt (b. Nov. 21, 1902, d. Apr. 21, 1985): Radio-TV; Canada's premier hockey play-by-play broadcaster from 1923-81; coined phrase, "He shoots, he scores!"

Damon Hill (b. Sept. 17, 1960): British auto racer; 1996 Formula 1 champion; 22 F1 wins places him 10th all-time; retired following 1999 season; son of Graham.

Graham Hill (b. Feb. 15, 1929, d. Nov. 29, 1975): British auto racer; 2-time Formula One world champion (1962,68); won Indy 500 in 1966; killed in plane crash; father of Damon.

Phil Hill (b. Apr. 20, 1927): Auto racer; first U.S. driver to win Formula One championship (1961); 3 career wins (1958-64).

Sir Edmund Hillary (b. July 20, 1919): New Zealand mountaineer; On May 29, 1953, along with Sherpa Tenzing Norgay, Hillary became the first to reach summitt of Mt. Everest, the world's highest peak.

Martina Hingis (b. Sept. 30, 1980): Swiss tennis player; in March 1997 at 16 years, 6 months, she became the youngest No. 1 ranked player since the ranking system began in 1975; won Wimbledon (1997), U.S. Open (1997) and 3 Australian Opens (1997,98,99); first woman to surpass the $3 million mark in earnings for one season (1997).

Max Hirsch (b. July 30, 1880, d. Apr. 3, 1969): Horse racing; trained 1,933 winners from 1908-68; won Triple Crown with Assault in 1946.

Tommy Hitchcock (b. Feb. 11, 1900, d. Apr. 19, 1944): Polo; world class player at 20; achieved 10-goal rating 18 times from 1922-40.

Lew Hoad (b. Nov. 23, 1934, d. July 3, 1994): Australian tennis player; 2-time Wimbledon winner (1956-57); won Australian, French and Wimbledon titles in 1956, but missed capturing Grand Slam at Forest Hills when beaten by Ken Rosewall in 4-set final.

Gil Hodges (b. Apr. 4, 1924, d. Apr. 2, 1972): Baseball 1B-Manager; tied Major League record with four home runs in one game on Aug 31, 1950; won three Gold Gloves (1957-59); drove in 100 runs in seven consecutive seasons (1949-55); hit 370 home runs and 1,274 RBIs lifetime; won 660 games as a manager (Senators and Mets).

Mat Hoffman (b. Jan. 9, 1972): BMX; youngest pro in BMX history at age 16; world record holder for High Air on a BMX Bike (26.5 feet out of a 24-foot quarterpipe in 2001); invented over 100 staple BMX tricks; started the Bike Stunt Series (1992–televised by ESPN starting in 1995); founded the Hoffman Sports Association (1999 – governing body for major BMX events today).

Trevor Hoffman (b. Oct. 13, 1967): Baseball RHP; 2-time NL saves leader (1998, 2006); earned his 479th save on Sept, 24, 2006 to pass Lee Smith as the all-time major league leader (finished the season with 482); recorded seven 40-save seasons and one 50-save season (53 in 1998).

Ben Hogan (b. Aug. 13, 1912, d. July 25, 1997): Golfer; 4-time PGA Player of Year; one of only five players to win all four Grand Slam titles (others are Nicklaus, Player, Sarazen and Woods); won 4 U.S. Opens, 2 Masters, 2 PGAs and 1 British Open between 1946-53; nearly killed in Feb. 2, 1949 car accident, but came back to win 1950 U.S. Open just 16 months later; one of only two players (Woods) to win three of the four current majors in one year when he won Masters, U.S. Open and British Open in 1953 at age 41; third on all-time list with 64 career wins.

Chamique Holdsclaw (b. Aug. 9, 1977): Basketball F; 2-time national player of the year, leading Tennessee to 3 straight national championships (1996-98); 1998 Sullivan Award winner; top selection by the Washington Mystics in the 1999 WNBA draft; 1999 WNBA Rookie of the Year.

Eleanor Holm (b. Dec. 6, 1913, d. Jan. 31, 2004): Swimmer; won gold medal in 100m backstroke at 1932 Olympics; thrown off '36 U.S. team for drinking champagne in public and shooting craps on boat to Germany.

Nat Holman (b. Oct. 18, 1896, d. Feb. 12, 1995): Basketball pioneer; played with Original Celtics (1920-28); coached CCNY to both NCAA and NIT titles in 1950 (a year later, several of his players were caught up in a point-shaving scandal); 423 career wins.

Larry Holmes (b. Nov. 3, 1949): Boxer; heavyweight champion (WBC or IBF) from 1978-85; beat Gerry Cooney on a 13th-round TKO in their 1982 mega-fight; successfully defended title 20 times before losing to Michael Spinks; returned from first retirement in 1988 and was KO'd in 4th by champ Mike Tyson; launched second comeback in 1991; fought and lost title bids against Evander Holyfield in '92 and Oliver McCall in '95; pro record of 69-6 and 44 KOs.

Lou Holtz (b. Jan. 6, 1937): Football; coached Notre Dame to national title in 1988; 2-time Coach of Year (1977,88); also coached NFL's NY Jets for 13 games (3-10) in 1976.

Evander Holyfield (b. Oct. 19, 1962): Boxer; only man to win (and lose) world heavyweight title 4 times; Wore belt off and on from 1990-2001; defeated former champ Mike Tyson in 1996 to win WBA belt; in 1997 rematch, Tyson was DQ'd for twice biting his ear; former undisputed cruiserweight world (1987-88) champ before moving to heavyweight; returned to ring in Aug. 2006 with a 2nd-round TKO of Jeremy Bates.

Red Holzman (b. Aug. 10, 1920, d. Nov. 13, 1998): Basketball; played for NBL and NBA champions at Rochester (1946,51); coached NY Knicks to 2 NBA titles (1970,73); Coach of Year (1970); 754 career NBA wins.

Bernard Hopkins (b. Jan. 15, 1965): Boxer; became first undisputed world middleweight champion since Marvin Hagler when he upset undefeated Felix Trinidad with a 12th-round TKO in 2001 to unify belts; defended title for a division-record 20 times before finally losing belts on a split decision to Jermain Taylor in 2005; won decision over Antonio Tarver in June, 2006; retired with a record of 47-4-1 with 32 KOs.

Rogers Hornsby (b. Apr. 27, 1896, d. Jan. 5, 1963): Baseball 2B; hit .400 3 times, including .424 in 1924; led NL in batting 7 times; 2-time MVP (1925,29); career BA of .358 over 23 years is highest in NL.

Paul Hornung (b. Dec. 23, 1935): Football HB-PK; only Heisman Trophy winner to play for losing team (2-8 Notre Dame in 1956); 3-time NFL scoring leader (1959-61) at Green Bay; 176 points in 1960, an all-time record; MVP in 1961; suspended by NFL for 1963 season for betting on his own team.

Gordie Howe (b. Mar. 31, 1928): Hockey RW; played 32 seasons in NHL and WHA from 1946-80; led NHL in scoring 6 times; All-NHL 1st team 12 times; MVP 6 times in NHL (1952-53,57-58,60,63) with Detroit and once in WHA (1974) with Houston; ranks 2nd on all-time NHL list in goals (801) and 3rd in points (1,850); played with sons Mark and Marty at Houston (1973-77) and New England-Hartford (1977-80).

Cal Hubbard (b. Oct. 31, 1900, d. Oct. 17, 1977): Member of college football, pro football and baseball halls of fame; 9 years in NFL; 4-time All-Pro at end and tackle; AL umpire (1936-51).

William DeHart Hubbard (b. Nov. 25, 1903, d. June 23, 1976): Track & Field; won the long jump at the 1924 Olympics, becoming the first black athlete to win an Olympic gold medal in an individual event; set the long jump world record in 1925 (25-10¾) and tied the 100-yard dash record (9.6) in 1926.

Carl Hubbell (b. June 22, 1903, d. Nov. 21, 1988): Baseball LHP; led NL in wins and ERA 3 times each; 2-time MVP (1933,36) with NY Giants; fanned Ruth, Gehrig, Foxx, Simmons and Cronin in succession in 1934 All-Star Game; 253-154 career record.

Sam Huff (b. Oct. 4, 1934): Football LB; glamorized NFL's middle linebacker position with NY Giants from 1956-63; subject of "The Violent World of Sam Huff" TV special in 1961; helped club win 6 division titles and a world championship (1956).

Miller Huggins (b. Mar. 27, 1878, d. Sept. 25, 1929): Baseball; managed NY Yankees from 1918 until his death late in '29 season; led Yanks to 6 pennants and 3 World Series titles from 1921-28.

Bobby Hull (b. Jan. 3, 1939): Hockey LW; led NHL in scoring 3 times; 2-time MVP (1965-66) with Chicago; All-NHL first team 10 times; jumped to WHA in 1972, 2-time MVP there (1973,75) with Winnipeg; scored 913 goals in both leagues; father of Brett.

Brett Hull (b. Aug. 9, 1964): Hockey RW; NHL MVP in 1991 with St. Louis; holds single season RW scoring record with 86 goals; he and father Bobby have both won Hart (MVP), Lady Byng (sportsmanship) and All-Star Game MVP trophies; won 2 Stanley Cups.

Lamar Hunt (b. Aug. 2, 1932): Football/Soccer; Founder of the Kansas City Chiefs (formerly Dallas Texans); instrumental in forming the AFL in 1959 and merging the league with NFL in 1966; elected to the Pro Football HOF in 1972; AFC Championship trophy bear his name; investor/operator in MLS.

Jim (Catfish) Hunter (b. Apr. 8, 1946, d. Sept. 9, 1999): Baseball RHP; won 20 games or more 5 times (1971-75); played on 5 World Series winners with Oakland and NY Yankees; threw perfect game in 1968; won AL Cy Young Award in 1974; 224-166 career record.

Ibrahim Hussein (b. June 3, 1958): Kenyan distance runner; 3-time winner of Boston Marathon (1988,91-92) and 1st African runner to win in Boston; won New York Marathon in 1987.

Don Hutson (b. Jan. 31, 1913, d. June 24, 1997): Football E-PK; led NFL in receptions 8 times and interceptions once; 9-time All-Pro (1936,38-45) for Green Bay; 99 career TD catches.

Flo Hyman (b. July 31, 1954, d. Jan. 24, 1986): Volleyball; 3-time All-America spiker at Houston and captain of 1984 U.S. Women's Olympic team; died of heart attack caused by Marfan Syndrome during a match in Japan in 1986; namesake of award given out annually by the Women's Sports Foundation.

Hank Iba (b. Aug. 6, 1904, d. Jan. 15, 1993): Basketball; coached Oklahoma A&M to 2 straight NCAA titles (1945-46); 767 career wins in 41 years; coached U.S. Olympic team to 2 gold medals (1964,68), but lost to Soviets in controversial '72 final.

Punch Imlach (b. Mar. 15, 1918, d. Dec. 1, 1987): Hockey; directed Toronto to 4 Stanley Cups (1962-64,67) in 11 seasons as GM-coach.

Miguel Induráin (b. July 16, 1964): Spanish cyclist; won 5 straight Tour de Frances (1991-95), won gold in time trial at '96 Olympics; retired in 1997.

Juli Inkster (b. June 24, 1960): Golfer; 31 career LPGA victories; winner of 7 major LPGA tournaments and 3 consecutive U.S. Women's Amateur tournaments (1980-82); inducted into the World Golf Hall of Fame in 2000; LPGA Rookie of the Year in 1984.

Hale Irwin (b. June 3, 1945): Golfer; oldest player ever to win U.S. Open (45 in 1990); NCAA champion in 1967; 20 PGA victories, including 3 U.S. Opens (1974,79,90); 5-time Ryder Cup team member; joined Senior PGA Tour in 1995 and has already won 44 titles.

Allen Iverson (b. June 7, 1975): Basketball G; former Georgetown Hoya chosen first overall by the Philadelphia 76ers in the 1996 NBA Draft; NBA Rookie of the Year (1997); 3-time NBA scoring leader (2001-02,05) and steals leader (2001-02); voted regular season MVP in 2001 and led 76ers to NBA Finals.

Bo Jackson (b. Nov. 30, 1962): Baseball OF and Football RB; won Heisman Trophy in 1985 and MVP of baseball All-Star Game in 1989; starter for both baseball's KC Royals and NFL's LA Raiders in 1988 and '89; severely injured left hip Jan. 13, 1991, in NFL playoffs; waived by Royals but signed by Chicago White Sox in 1991; missed entire 1992 season recovering from hip surgery; played for White Sox in 1993 and California in '94 before retiring.

Joe Jackson (b. July 16, 1889, d. Dec. 5, 1951): Baseball OF; hit .300 or better 11 times; nicknamed "Shoeless Joe"; career average of .356, third highest all-time; was placed on MLB's ineligible list in 1921 following the Black Sox scandal in which he and 7 teammates were accused of fixing 1919 World Series.

Phil Jackson (b. Sept. 17, 1945): Basketball; NBA champion as reserve forward with New York in 1973 (injured when Knicks won in '70); coached Chicago to six NBA titles in eight years (1991-93, 96-98); coach of the year in 1996 and 97; returned to coach the LA Lakers in 1999 and won 3 more titles (2000,01,02); all-time leader in winning pct. for NBA coaches with 350 or more wins; left Lakers after 2004 Finals loss to Detroit but returned after one season; all-time NBA leader in playoff wins (178).

Reggie Jackson (b. May 18, 1946): Baseball OF; led AL in HRs 4 times; MVP in 1973; played on 5 World Series winners with Oakland and NY Yankees; 1977 Series MVP with 5 HRs; 563 career HRs; all-time strikeout leader (2,597); member of the Hall of Fame.

Dr. Robert Jackson (b. Aug. 6, 1932): Surgeon; revolutionized sports medicine by popularizing the use of arthroscopic surgery to treat injuries; learned technique from Japanese physician that allowed athletes to return quickly from potentially career-ending injuries.

Helen Jacobs (b. Aug. 6, 1908, d. June 2, 1997): Tennis; 4-time winner of U.S. Championship (1932-35); Wimbledon winner in 1936; lost 4 Wimbledon finals to arch-rival Helen Wills Moody.

Jaromir Jagr (b. Feb. 15, 1972): Czech Hockey RW; fifth overall pick by Pittsburgh (1990); NHL All-Rookie team (1991); NHL MVP (1999); Won Art Ross Trophy (1995,98,99,00,01); 7-time All-NHL First Team; NHL single season record for most points by a right wing (149); NHL single season record for most assists by a RW (87).

LeBron James (b. Dec. 30, 1984): Basketball; mega-hyped top overall pick in 2003 NBA Draft (Cleveland) straight out of high school; youngest-ever NBA Rookie of the Year (2004).

Dan Jansen (b. June 17, 1965): Speed skater; fell in 500m and 1,000m in 1988 Olympics just after sister Jane's death; placed 4th in 500m and didn't attempt 1,000m in 1992; fell in 500m at '94 Games, but finally won an Olympic medal with world record (1:12.43) effort in 1,000m, then took victory lap with baby daughter Jane in his arms; won 1994 Sullivan Award.

Dale Jarrett (b. Nov. 26, 1956): Auto racer; 1999 Winston Cup champion; 3-time Daytona 500 champion (1993,96,2000); son of driver Ned Jarrett.

James J. Jeffries (b. Apr. 15, 1875, d. Mar. 3, 1953): Boxer; world heavyweight champion (1899-1905); retired undefeated but came back to fight Jack Johnson in 1910 and lost (KO, 15th).

David Jenkins (b. June 29, 1936): Figure skater; brother of Hayes; 3-time world champion (1957-59); won gold medal at 1960 Olympics.

Hayes Jenkins (b. Mar. 23, 1933): Figure skater; 4-time world champion (1953-56); won gold medal at 1956 Olympics; married 1960 women's gold medalist Carol Heiss.

Bruce Jenner (b. Oct. 28, 1949): Track & Field; won gold medal in 1976 Olympic decathlon.

Jackie Jensen (b. Mar. 9, 1927, d. July 14, 1982): Football RB and Baseball OF; All-America at Cal in 1948; AL MVP with Boston Red Sox in 1958.

Derek Jeter (b. June 26, 1974): Baseball SS; 1st-round draft choice (6th overall) of the N.Y. Yankees in 1992; became Yankees' everyday starting shortstop in 1996 and the team hasn't missed the postseason since; won 4 World Series championships in his first 5 seasons (1996, 98-2000); MVP of the 2000 All-Star Game and World Series; named captain of the Yankees in 2003; all-time postseason hits leader.

Ben Johnson (b. Dec. 30, 1961): Canadian sprinter; set 100m world record (9.83) at 1987 World Championships; won 100m at 1988 Olympics, but flunked drug test and forfeited gold medal; 1987 world record revoked in '89 for admitted steroid use; returned drug-free in 1991, but performed poorly; banned for life by IAAF in 1993 for testing positive again.

Bob Johnson (b. Mar. 4, 1931, d. Nov. 26, 1991): Hockey; coached Pittsburgh Penguins to 1st Stanley Cup title in 1991; led Wisconsin to 3 NCAA titles (1973,77,81); also coached 1976 U.S. Olympic team and NHL Calgary Flames (1982-87).

Earvin (Magic) Johnson (b. Aug. 14, 1959): Basketball G; led Michigan St. to NCAA title in 1979 and was Final 4 MOP; All-NBA 1st team 9 times; 3-time MVP (1987,89-90); led LA Lakers to 5 NBA titles; 3-time Finals MVP (1980, 82, 87); 3rd all-time in NBA assists with 10,141; retired on Nov. 7, 1991 after announcing he was HIV-positive; returned to score 25 points in 1992 NBA All-Star Game; U.S. Olympic Dream Team co-captain; announced NBA comeback then retired again before start of 1992-93 season; named head coach of Lakers on Mar. 23, 1994, but finished season at 5-11 and quit; later became minority owner of team; came back a final time and played 32 games during 1995-96 season.

Jack Johnson (b. Mar. 31, 1878, d. June 10, 1946): Boxer; controversial heavyweight champion (1908-15) and 1st black to hold title; defeated Tommy Burns for crown at age 30; fled to Europe in 1913 after Mann Act conviction; lost title to Jess Willard in Havana, but claimed to have taken a dive; pro record 78-8-12 with 45 KOs.

Jimmy Johnson (b. July 16, 1943): Football; All-SWC defensive lineman on Arkansas' 1964 national championship team; coached U. of Miami-FL to national title in 1987; college record of 81-34-3 in 10 years; hired by old pal Jerry Jones to succeed Tom Landry in 1989; went 1-15 in '89, then led Cowboys to consecutive Super Bowl victories (1993-94); quit in 1994 after feuding with Jones; replaced Don Shula as Miami Dolphins head coach from 1996-99.

Judy Johnson (b. Oct. 26, 1899, d. June 13, 1989): Baseball IF; one of the great stars of the Negro Leagues; a terrific fielding third baseman who regularly batted over .300; when baseball integrated Johnson's playing days were over but he coached and scouted for the Philadelphia Athletics, Boston Braves and Philadelphia Phillies; member of Hall of Fame.

Junior Johnson (b. June 28, 1931): Auto Racing; won Daytona 500 in 1960; also won 13 NASCAR races in 1965, including the Rebel 300 at Darlington; retired from racing to become a highly successful car owner; his first driver was Bobby Allison.

Michael Johnson (b. Sep 13, 1967): Track & Field; Shattered world record in 200m (19.32) and set Olympic record in 400m (43.49) to become first man to win the gold in both races in the same Olympic Games at Atlanta in 1996; two-time world champion in 200 (1991,95) and four-time world champ in 400 (1993,95,97,99); set world record in 400m (43.18) at '99 world championships in Seville; won the 400 in Sydney in 2000 to become the only man to win the event in two consecutive Olympics; retired in 2001.

Rafer Johnson (b. Aug. 18, 1935): Track & Field; won silver medal in 1956 Olympic decathlon and gold medal in 1960.

Randy Johnson (b. Sept. 10, 1963): Baseball LHP; 6'10'' flamethrower; struck out over 300 batters 6 times (1993,98,99,00,01,02); led AL in Ks 4 times (1992-95) and NL 5 times (1999-2002,04); struck out 20 batters in a game (5/8/01); 5-time Cy Young Award winner with Seattle and Arizona (AL-1995, NL-1999-2002); won 3 games and co-MVP honors (Curt Schilling) in 2001 World Series; became oldest in baseball history to pitch a perfect game at age 40; signed free-agent deal with N.Y. Yankees in 2005.

Walter Johnson (b. Nov. 6, 1887, d. Dec. 10, 1946): Baseball RHP; nicknamed "Big Train;" Johnson had an overpowering fastball; won 20 games or more 10 straight years; led AL in ERA 5 times, wins 6 times and strikeouts 12 times; twice MVP (1913, 24) with Washington Senators; all-time leader in shutouts (110) and 2nd in wins (417); part of the Hall of Fame's inaugural class of 1936.

Ben A. Jones (b. Dec. 31, 1882, d. June 13, 1961): Horse racing; Calumet Farm trainer (1939-47); saddled 6 Kentucky Derby champions, including 2 Triple Crown winners—Whirlaway in 1941 and Citation in '48.

Bobby Jones (b. Mar. 17, 1902, d. Dec. 18, 1971): Won U.S. and British Opens plus U.S. and British Amateurs in 1930 to become golf's only Grand Slam winner ever; between 1922-30, he won 4 U.S. Opens, 5 U.S. Amateurs, 3 British Opens, and 1 British Amateur for 13 Major titles in all, a record that stood until Jack Nicklaus broke it; played in 6 Walker Cups; designed Augusta National (with Alister Mackenzie) and founded Masters tournament in 1934.

Deacon Jones (b. Dec. 9, 1938): Football DE; 5-time All-Pro (1965-69) with LA Rams; unofficially 3rd all-time in NFL sacks with 173½ in 14 years; inducted into Pro Football Hall of Fame in 1980.

Jerry Jones (b. Oct. 13, 1942): Football; owner-GM of Dallas Cowboys; maverick who bought declining team (3-13) and Texas Stadium for $140 million in 1989; hired pal Jimmy Johnson to replace legendary coach Tom Landry; their partnership led to 2 Super Bowl titles (1993-94); when feud developed, he fired Johnson and hired Barry Switzer and won Super Bowl in 1996; hired proven winner Bill Parcells as head coach in 2003 following three losing seasons.

Marion Jones (b. Oct. 12, 1975): Track & Field; American sprinter who won 3 golds (100m, 200m, 4x100m) at 2000 Sydney Olympics; 5-time world champion: 100m (1997,99), 200m (2001), 4x100m (1997, 2001); voted Women's Athlete of the Year by *Track & Field News* in 1997,98 and 2000; 1999 Jesse Owens Award winner; 2000 AP and USOC Female Athlete of the Year.

Roy Jones Jr. (b. Jan. 16, 1969): Boxing; robbed of gold medal at 1988 Olympics on a scoring error; still voted Outstanding Boxer of the Games; won IBF middleweight crown, beating Bernard Hopkins in 1993; moved up to super middleweight and won IBF title from James Toney in 1994; moved up to light heavyweight, winning WBC (1997), WBA (1998) and IBF titles (1999); made temporary move to heavyweight in 2003 and decisioned John Ruiz for WBA belt; lost WBC light heavyweight belt to Antonio Tarver in a 2nd round KO in 2004; knocked out in comeback fight with Glen Johnson in 2004; fought Tarver for a 3rd time in 2005.

Michael Jordan (b. Feb. 17, 1963): Basketball G; College Player of Year with North Carolina in 1984; NBA Rookie of the Year (1985); led NBA in scoring 7 years in a row (1987-93) and also 1996-98; 10-time All-NBA 1st team; 5-time regular season MVP (1988,91-92,96,98) and 6-time MVP of NBA Finals (1991-93,96-98); 3-time AP Male Athlete of Year; led U.S. Olympic team to gold in 1984 and '92; stunned sports world when he retired at age 30 on Oct. 6, 1993; signed as OF with Chi. White Sox and spent summer of '94 in AA with Birmingham; struggled with .204 average; made one of the most anticipated comebacks in sports history when he returned to the Bulls lineup on Mar. 19, 1995 but Bulls were eliminated by Orlando in 2nd round of playoffs later that season; led Bulls to NBA titles for the next 3 years for 6 titles in all (1991-93,96-98); retired in 1999; became pres. of Wash. Wizards before unretiring again in 2001 and returning to play with Wizards for 2 seasons; became part-owner of the Charlotte Bobcats in June, 2006.

Florence Griffith Joyner (b. Dec. 21, 1959, d. Sept. 21, 1998): Track & Field; set world records in 100 and 200m in 1988; won 3 gold medals at '88 Olympics (100m, 200m, 4x100m relay); Sullivan Award winner (1988); retired in 1989; named as co-chairperson of President's Council on Physical Fitness and Sports in 1993; sister-in-law of Jackie Joyner-Kersee; died of suffocation during an epileptic seizure in 1998.

Jackie Joyner-Kersee (b. Mar. 3, 1962): Track & Field; 2-time world champion in both long jump (1987,91) and heptathlon (1987,93); won heptathlon gold medals at 1988 and '92 Olympics and LJ gold at '88 Games; also won Olympic silver (1984) in heptathlon and bronze (1992,96) in LJ; Sullivan Award winner (1986); only woman to receive *The Sporting News* Man of Year award.

Alberto Juantorena (b. Nov. 21, 1950): Cuban runner; won 400m and 800m golds at 1976 Olympics.

Sonny Jurgensen (b. Aug. 23, 1934): Football QB; played 18 seasons with Philadelphia and Washington; led NFL in passing twice (1967,69); All-Pro in 1961; 255 career TD passes.

Duke Kahanamoku (b. Aug. 24, 1890, d. Jan. 22, 1968): Swimmer; won 3 gold medals and 2 silver over 3 Olympics (1912,20,24); also surfing pioneer.

Al Kaline (b. Dec. 19, 1934): Baseball; youngest player (at age 20) to win batting title (led AL with .340 in 1955); had 3,007 hits, 399 HRs in 22 years with Detroit.

Paul Kariya (b. Oct. 16, 1974): Hockey LW; first-ever selection of Anaheim (4th overall in 1993); led Maine to an NCAA Div. I national title in 1993; won Hobey Baker Award in 1993 as a freshman.

Anatoly Karpov (b. May 23, 1951): Chess; Soviet world champion from 1975-85; regained International Chess Federation (FIDE) championship in 1993 when countryman Garry Kasparov was stripped of title after forming new Professional Chess Association; held FIDE title until 1999.

Garry Kasparov (b. Apr. 13, 1963): Chess; Azerbaijani who became youngest player (22 years, 210 days) ever to win world championship as Soviet in 1985; defeated countryman Anatoly Karpov for title; split with International Chess Federation (FIDE) to form Professional Chess Association (PCA) in 1993; stripped of FIDE title in '93 but successfully defended PCA title against Briton Nigel Short; beat IBM supercomputer "Deep Blue" 4 games to 2 in 1996 much-publicized match in New York; lost rematch to computer in 1997; finally lost world title to Vladimir Kramnik in 2000.

Mike Keenan (b. Oct. 21, 1949): Hockey; coach who finally led NY Rangers to Stanley Cup title in 1994 after 53 unsuccessful years; ranked 5th all-time on NHL coaching wins list.

Kipchoge (Kip) Keino (b. Jan. 17, 1940): Kenyan runner; policeman who beat USA's Jim Ryun to win 1,500m gold medal at 1968 Olympics; won again in steeplechase at 1972 Summer Games; his success spawned long line of distance champions from Kenya.

Johnny A. Kelley (b. Sept. 6, 1907, d. Oct. 7, 2004): Distance runner; ran in his 61st and final Boston Marathon at age 84 in 1992, finishing in 5:58:36; won Boston twice (1935,45) and was 2nd seven times.

Jim Kelly (b. Feb. 14, 1960): Football QB; led Buffalo to four straight Super Bowls, and is only QB to lose four times; named to AFC Pro Bowl team 5 times; inducted into Pro Football Hall of Fame in 2002.

Leroy Kelly (b. May 20, 1942): Football; replaced Jim Brown in the Cleveland Browns backfield; in 1967, he led the NFL in rushing yards (1,205), rushing average (5.1 per carry) and rushing touchdowns (11).

Walter Kennedy (b. June 8, 1912, d. June 26, 1977): Basketball; 2nd NBA commissioner (1963-75), league doubled in size to 18 teams during his tenure.

Nancy Kerrigan (b. Oct. 13, 1969): Figure skating; 1993 U.S. women's champion and Olympic medalist in 1992 (bronze) and '94 (silver); victim of Jan. 6, 1994 assault at U.S. nationals in Detroit when Shane Stant clubbed her in right knee with metal baton after a practice session; conspiracy hatched by Jeff Gillooly, ex-husband of rival Tonya Harding; although unable to compete in nationals, she recovered and was granted berth on Olympic team; finished 2nd in Lillehammer to Oksana Baiul of Ukraine by a 5-4 judges' vote.

Billy Kidd (b. Apr. 13, 1943): Skiing; the first great Amercian male Alpine skier; first American male to win an Olympic medal with a silver in the slalom and a bronze in the Alpine combined in 1964; competed respectably with the great Jean-Claude Killy; won the world Alpine combined event in 1970, which was the first world championship for an American male.

Harmon Killebrew (b. June 29, 1936): Baseball 3B-1B; led AL in HRs 6 times and RBI 3 times; MVP in 1969 with Minnesota; 573 career HRs.

Jean-Claude Killy (b. Aug. 30, 1943): French alpine skier; 2-time World Cup champion (1967-68); won 3 gold medals at 1968 Olympics in Grenoble; co-president of 1992 Winter Games in Albertville; president of coordination commission for 2006 Turin Games.

Ralph Kiner (b. Oct. 27, 1922): Baseball OF; led NL in home runs 7 straight years (1946-52) with Pittsburgh; 369 career HRs and 1,015 RBI in 10 seasons; long-time NY Mets announcer.

Betsy King (b. Aug. -13, 1955): Golfer; 2-time LPGA Player of Year (1984,89); 3-time winner of Dinah Shore (1987,90,97) and 2-time winner of U.S. Open (1989,90); 34 overall Tour wins; 1st player in LPGA history to break $5 million mark in career earnings; member of LPGA Hall of Fame.

Billie Jean King (b. Nov. 22, 1943): Tennis; women's rights pioneer; Wimbledon singles champ 6 times; U.S. champ 4 times; first woman athlete to earn $100,000 in one year (1971); beat 55-year-old Bobby Riggs 6-4,6-3,6-3, in "Battle of the Sexes" to win $100,000 at Astrodome in 1973; founded the Women's Sports Foundation in 1974; captained the U.S. Olympic team in 1996 and 2000.

Don King (b. Aug. 20, 1931): Boxing promoter; first major black promoter who has controlled heavyweight title off and on since 1978; first big promotion was Muhammad Ali's fight against George Foreman in 1974; former numbers operator who served 4 years for manslaughter (1967-70); acquitted of tax evasion and fraud in 1985; also promoted Larry Holmes, Mike Tyson, Evander Holyfield, Roberto Duran and Julio Cesar Chavez among others; has been accused of bilking his fighters out of money; famous for his gravity-defying hairstyle and his catchphrase "Only in America!".

Karch Kiraly (b. Nov. 3, 1960): Volleyball; USA's preeminent volleyball player; led UCLA to three NCAA championships (1979,81,82); played on US national teams that won Olympic gold medals in 1984 and '88, world championships in '82 and '86; won the inaugural gold medal for Olympic beach volleyball with Kent Steffes in 1996.

Tom Kite (b. Dec. 9, 1949): Golfer; co-NCAA champion with Ben Crenshaw (1972); PGA Rookie of Year (1973); PGA Player of Year (1989); finally won 1st major with victory in 1992 U.S. Open at Pebble Beach; captain of 1997 US Ryder Cup team; 19 career PGA wins, played on the Champions tour since 2000 (currently has 9 wins).

Gene Klein (b. Jan. 29, 1921, d. Mar. 12, 1990): Horseman; won 3 Eclipse awards as top owner (1985-87); his filly Winning Colors won 1988 Kentucky Derby; also owned San Diego Chargers football team (1966-84).

Bob Knight (b. Oct. 25, 1940): Basketball; coached Indiana to 3 NCAA titles (1976,81,87); 3-time Coach of Year (1975-76,89); coached 1984 U.S. Olympic team to gold medal; his volatile temper finally cost him when he was fired from Indiana in Sept. 2000 after a string of unacceptable incidents that included choking one of his players; returned to coaching with Texas Tech in 2001; 3rd on all-time NCAA list with 869 wins in all.

Phil Knight (b. Feb. 24, 1938): Founder and chairman of Nike, Inc., the multi-billion dollar shoe and fitness company founded in 1972 and based in Beaverton, Ore.; named "The Most Powerful Man in Sports" by *The Sporting News* in 1992.

Bill Koch (b. June 7, 1955): Cross country skiing; first highly accomplished American male in his sport; first American male to win a cross country Olympic medal when he took home a silver in the 30-kilometer race in 1976; in 1982, he was the first American male to win the Nordic World Cup.

Tommy Kono (b. June 27, 1930): weight lifter; won 2 olympic gold medals for U.S. (1952,56) and 1 silver (1960); all 3 medals were in different weight classes; set world records in four different classes; inducted into U.S. Olympic Hall of Fame in 1990.

Olga Korbut (b. May 16, 1955): Soviet gymnast; became the media darling of the 1972 Olympics in Munich by winning 3 gold medals (balance beam, floor exercise and team all-around); came back in the 1976 Olympics in Montreal and was a part of the USSR's gold medal winning all-around team; first to perform back somersault on balance beam; was inducted into the International Women's Sports Hall of Fame in 1982, the first gymnast to be inducted.

Johann Olav Koss (b. Oct. 29, 1968): Norwegian speed skater; won three gold medals at 1994 Olympics in Lillehammer with world records in the 1,500m, 5,000m and 10,000m; also won 1,500m gold and 10,000m silver in 1992 Games; retired shortly after '94 Olympics.

Sandy Koufax (b. Dec. 30, 1935): Baseball LHP; led NL in strikeouts 4 times and ERA 5 straight years; won 3 Cy Young Awards (1963,65,66) with LA Dodgers; MVP in 1963; 2-time World Series MVP (1963, 65); threw perfect game against Chicago Cubs (1-0, Sept. 9, 1965) and had 3 other no-hitters, 40 shutouts and 137 complete games in a career that ended prematurely due to an arm injury.

Alvin Kraenzlein (b. Dec. 12, 1876, d. Jan. 6, 1928): Track & Field; won 4 individual gold medals in 1900 Olympics (60m, long jump and the 110m and 200m hurdles).

Jack Kramer (b. Aug. 1, 1921): Tennis; Wimbledon singles champ 1947; U.S. champ 1946-47; promoter and Open pioneer.

Lenny Krayzelburg (b. Sept. 28, 1975): Swimmer; born in Ukraine but became American citizen in 1995; won gold for U.S. in the 100m and 200m backstrokes at the 2000 Sydney Games; was also part of U.S. team that set a world record in the 4x100m medley relay in Sydney.

Ingrid Kristiansen (b. Mar. 21, 1956): Norwegian runner; 2-time Boston Marathon winner (1986,89); won New York City Marathon in 1989; former world record holder in the marathon.

Julie Krone (b. July 24, 1963): Jockey; only woman to ride winner in a Triple Crown race when she took 1993 Belmont Stakes aboard Colonial Affair; retired in 1999 as all-time winningest female jockey with over 3,000 wins; became the first female jockey named to hall of fame in 2000; came out of retirement in 2002, winning 2003 Breeders Cup race aboard Halfbridled.

Mike Krzyzewski (b. Feb. 13, 1947): Basketball; has coached Duke to 10 Final Four appearances and 3 NCAA titles (1991-92,2001); has coached at Army (1976-80) and Duke (1981–); inducted into Hall of Fame in 2001.

Bowie Kuhn (b. Oct. 28, 1926): Baseball Commissioner; Elected commissioner on Feb. 4, 1969 and served until Sept. 30, 1984; kept Willie Mays and Mickey Mantle out of baseball for their employment with casinos; handed down one-year suspensions of several players for drug involvement; nixed Charlie Finley's sale of three players for $3.5 million; baseball enjoyed unprecedented attendance and television contracts during his reign.

Alan Kulwicki (b. Dec. 14, 1954, d. Apr. 1, 1993): Auto racer; 1992 NASCAR national champion; 1st college grad and Northerner to win title; NASCAR Rookie of Year in 1986; famous for driving car backwards on victory lap; killed at age 38 in plane crash near Bristol, Tenn.

Michelle Kwan (b. July 7, 1980): Figure Skater; 1998 Olympic silver medalist at Nagano and 2002 bronze medalist at Salt Lake City; 9-time U.S. Champion (1996,98-05) and 5-time World Champ (1996,98,00,01,03); holds U.S. record with 8 career overall medals at the World Championships (5 gold, 3 silver); was U.S. alternate to the Olympics in 1994 as a 13-year-old.

Marion Ladewig (b. Oct. 30, 1914): Bowler; named Woman Bowler of the Year 9 times (1950-54,57-59,63).

Guy Lafleur (b. Sept. 20, 1951): Hockey RW; led NHL in scoring 3 times (1976-78); 2-time MVP (1977-78), played for 5 Stanley Cup winners in Montreal; playoff MVP in 1977; returned to NHL as player in 1988 after election to Hall of Fame; retired again in 1991 with 560 goals and 1,353 points.

Napoleon (Nap) Lajoie (b. Sept. 5, 1874, d. Feb. 7, 1959): Baseball 2B; led AL in batting 3 times (1901,03-04); batted .422 in 1901; hit .339 for career with 3,251 hits.

Jack Lambert (b. July 8, 1952): Football LB; 6-time All-Pro (1975-76,79-82); led Pittsburgh to 4 Super Bowl titles.

Floyd Landis (b. Oct. 14, 1975): Cycling; surprising winner of the 2006 Tour de France; 3rd American to win Tour; it was later revealed that 2 of his urine samples taken during the race tested positive for high testosterone levels; still held title as of Oct. 1, 2006, though disciplinary proceedings were ongoing.

Kenesaw Mountain Landis (b. Nov. 20, 1866, d. Nov. 25, 1944): U.S. District Court judge who became first baseball commissioner (1920-44); banned eight Chicago "Black Sox" from baseball for life for throwing 1919 World Series.

Tom Landry (b. Sept. 11, 1924, d. Feb. 12, 2000): Football; All-Pro DB for NY Giants (1954); coached Dallas for 29 years (1960-88); won 2 Super Bowls (1972,78); 3rd on NFL all-time list with 270 wins.

Steve Largent (b. Sept. 28, 1954): Football WR; retired in 1989 after 14 years in Seattle with then NFL records in passes caught (819) and TD passes caught (100); elected to U.S. House of Representatives (R, Okla.) in 1994 and Pro Football Hall of Fame in '95; ran for governor of Oklahoma in 2002 but suffered a narrow defeat.

Don Larsen (b. Aug. 7, 1929): Baseball RHP; NY Yankees hurler who pitched the only perfect game in World Series history— a 2-0 victory over Brooklyn in Game 5 of the 1956 Series (Oct. 8); Series MVP that year; had career record of 81-91 in 14 seasons with 6 clubs.

Tommy Lasorda (b. Sept. 22, 1927): Baseball; managed LA Dodgers to 2 World Series titles (1981,88) in 4 appearances; retired as manager during 1996 season with 1,599 regular-season wins in 21 years; named interim GM of Dodgers in 1998; member of Baseball Hall of Fame; managed gold-medal winning U.S. Olympic team in 2000 at Sydney.

Larissa Latynina (b. Dec. 27, 1934): Soviet gymnast; won total of 18 medals, (9 gold) in 3 Olympics (1956,60,64).

Nikki Lauda (b. Feb. 22, 1949): Austrian auto racer; 3-time world Formula One champion (1975, 77,84); 25 career wins from 1971-85.

Rod Laver (b. Aug. 9, 1938): Australian tennis player; undersized but big-hitting left-hander is only player to win Grand Slam twice (1962,69); Wimbledon champion 4 times (1st to earn $1 million in career prize money, won 11 Grand Slam and 47 professional singles titles.

Andrea Mead Lawrence (b. Apr. 19, 1932): Alpine skier; won 2 gold medals at 1952 Olympics.

Bobby Layne (b. Dec. 19, 1926, d. Dec. 1, 1986): Football QB; college star at Texas; master of 2-minute offense; led Detroit to 4 divisional titles and 3 NFL championships in 1950s.

Frank Leahy (b. Aug. 27, 1908, d. June 21, 1973): Football; coached Notre Dame to four national titles (1943,46-47,49); career record of 107-13-9 for a winning pct. of .864.

Sammy Lee (b. Aug. 1, 1920): Diving; won Olympic gold medals for U.S. in the platform diving event in 1948 and 1952, the first male diver in history to win 2 golds in that event; Sullivan Award winner (1953); former Dr. in U.S. Army; trained Greg Louganis.

Brian Leetch (b. Mar. 3, 1968): Hockey D; NHL Rookie of Year in 1989; won Norris Trophy as top defenseman in 1992; Conn Smythe Trophy winner as playoffs' MVP in 1994 when he helped lead NY Rangers to 1st Stanley Cup title in 54 years.

Jacques Lemaire (b. Sept. 7, 1945): Hockey C; member of 8 Stanley Cup champions in Montreal; scored 366 goals in 12 seasons; coached Canadiens (1983-85) and NJ Devils (1993-98), won 1995 Stanley Cup with New Jersey; returned to coaching with the expansion Minnesota Wild in 2000.

Mario Lemieux (b. Oct. 5, 1965): Hockey C; 6-time NHL scoring leader (1988-89,92-93,96-97); Rookie of Year (1985); 4-time All-NHL 1st team (1988-89,93,96); 3-time regular season MVP (1988,93,96); 3-time All-Star Game MVP; led Pittsburgh to consecutive Stanley Cup titles (1991 and '92) and was playoff MVP both years; won 1993 scoring title despite missing 24 games to undergo radiation treatments for Hodgkin's disease; missed 62 games during 1993-94 season and entire 1994-95 season due to back injuries and fatigue; returned in 1995-96 to lead NHL in scoring and win the MVP trophy; retired after 1996-97 season and inducted into the Hall of Fame; headed group of investors that bought bankrupt Penguins in 1999; made surprising return to the ice in 2001 as owner-player with Penguins; retired again in 2006.

Greg LeMond (b. June 26, 1961): American cyclist; 3-time Tour de France winner (1986,89-90); only non-European to win the event until Lance Armstrong in 1999; retired in Dec. 1994 after being diagnosed with a rare muscular disease known as mitochondrial myopathy.

Ivan Lendl (b. Mar. 7, 1960): Czech tennis player; No. 1 player in world 4 times (1985-87,89); won both French and U.S. Opens 3 times and Australian twice; owns 94 career tournament wins.

Suzanne Lenglen (b. May 24, 1899, d. July 4, 1938): French tennis player; dominated women's tennis from 1919-26; won both Wimbledon and French singles titles 6 times.

Sugar Ray Leonard (b. May 17, 1956): Boxer; light welterweight Olympic champ (1976); won world welterweight title in 1979 and 4 more titles; in 1987 he upset Marvin Hagler for the middleweight crown; retired and unretired several times, before ending his career for good in 1997 with record of 36-3-1 and 25 KOs following a TKO loss to Hector Camacho.

Walter (Buck) Leonard (b. Sept. 8, 1907, d. Nov. 27, 1997): Baseball 1B; won Negro League championship nine years in a row with the Homestead Grays; hit .391 in 1948 to lead the league; usually batted cleanup behind Josh Gibson; retired at the age of 48; member of the National Baseball Hall of Fame.

Lisa Leslie (b. July 7, 1972): Basketball C; 2-time WNBA Finals MVP (2001-02) with the champion Los Angeles Sparks; 3-time regular season MVP (2001,2004,2006); 3-time WNBA All-Star Game MVP (1999,2001-02); 3-time Olympic gold medalist (1996,2000,2004); consensus National Player of the Year at USC (1994).

Marv Levy (b. Aug. 3, 1928): Football; coached Buffalo to four consecutive Super Bowls, but is one of two coaches who are 0-4 (Bud Grant is the other); won 50 games and two CFL Grey Cups with Montreal (1974,77); returned to Bills as GM in 2006.

Bill Lewis (b. Nov. 30, 1868, d. Jan. 1, 1949): Football; college star at Amherst College and then Harvard; first black player to be selected as an All-American (1892-93); also the first black admitted to the American Bar Association (1911); was U.S. Assistant Attorney General.

Carl Lewis (b. July 1, 1961): Track & Field; won 9 Olympic gold medals; 4 in 1984 (100m, 200m, 4x100m, LJ), 2 in '88 (100m, LJ), 2 in '92 (4x100m, LJ) and 1 in '96 (LJ); has record 8 World Championship titles and 9 medals in all; Sullivan Award winner (1981); two-time AP Athlete of the Year (1983-84); in 1991, set world record in 100m with a 9.86 (since broken).

Lennox Lewis (b. Sept. 2, 1965): British boxer; won 1988 Olympic super heavyweight gold medal for Canada; was awarded WBC heavyweight belt when Riddick Bowe tossed it in a London trash can in 1993; lost title in a 2nd round TKO loss to Oliver McCall; won rematch 3 years later when McCall suffered emotional breakdown in the ring; unified titles in his rematch with Evander Holyfield in Nov. 1999; lost belts in upset loss to Hasim Rahman in April 2001 but took them back 7 months later; recorded 8th-round KO of Mike Tyson in June 2002.

Nancy Lieberman (b. July 1, 1958): Basketball; 3-time All-America and 2-time Player of Year (1979-80); led Old Dominion to consecutive AIAW titles in 1979 and '80; played in defunct WPBL and WABA and became 1st woman to play in men's pro league (USBL) in 1986; played in the inaugural season of the WNBA for the Phoenix Mercury and served as coach/GM of Detroit Shock (1998-2000).

Eric Lindros (b. Feb. 28, 1973): Hockey C; No. 1 pick in 1991 NHL draft by Quebec but sat out 1991-92 season rather than play for Nordiques; traded to Philadelphia in 1992 for 6 players, 2 No. 1 picks and $15 million; elected Flyers captain at age 22; won Hart Trophy as NHL MVP in 1995; 6-time NHL all-star; suffered series of concussions since 1999.

Tara Lipinski (b. June 10, 1982): Figure Skater; won the 1998 women's figure skating gold medal at the Olympics in Nagano, becoming the youngest in history (15 yrs., 7 mos.) to do so; she and Michelle Kwan gave the U.S. its first 1-2 finish in that event since 1956; 1997 U.S. and World champion; turned pro in April 1998.

Sonny Liston (b. May 8, 1932, d. Dec. 30, 1970): Boxer; heavyweight champion (1962-64), who knocked out Floyd Patterson twice in the first round, then lost title to Muhammad Ali (then Cassius Clay) in 1964; pro record of 50-4 with 39 KOs.

Vince Lombardi (b. June 11, 1913, d. Sept. 3, 1970): Football; coached Green Bay to five NFL titles; won first two Super Bowls (1967-68); died as NFL's alltime winningest coach with percentage of .740 (105-35-6); Super Bowl trophy named in his honor.

Johnny Longden (b. Feb. 14, 1907, d. Feb. 14, 2003): Jockey; first to win 6,000 races; rode Count Fleet to Triple Crown in 1943.

Jeannie Longo (b. Oct. 31, 1958): French cyclist; 12-time world cycling champion and 1996 olympic road race gold medallist.

Nancy Lopez (b. Jan. 6, 1957): Golfer; 4-time LPGA Player of the Year (1978-79,85,88); Rookie of Year (1977); 3-time winner of LPGA Championship; reached Hall of Fame by age 30 with 35 victories; 48 career wins.

Donna Lopiano (b. Sept. 11, 1946): Former basketball and softball star who was women's athletic director at Texas for 18 years before leaving to become executive director of Women's Sports Foundation in 1992.

Greg Louganis (b. Jan. 29, 1960): U.S. diver; widely considered the greatest diver in history; won platform and springboard gold medals at both 1984 and '88 Olympics; also won a silver medal at the 1976 Olympics at the age of 16; won five world championships and 47 U.S. National Diving titles; revealed on Feb. 22, 1995 that he has AIDS.

Joe Louis (b. May 13, 1914, d. Apr. 12, 1981): Boxer; world heavyweight champion from June 22, 1937 to Mar. 1, 1949; his reign of 11 years, 8 months longest in division history; successfully defended title 25 times; retired in 1949, but returned to lose title shot against successor Ezzard Charles in 1950 and then to Rocky Marciano in '51; pro record of 63-3 with 49 KOs.

Sid Luckman (b. Nov. 21, 1916, d. July 5, 1998): Football QB; 6-time All-Pro; led Chicago Bears to 4 NFL titles (1940-41,43,46); MVP in 1943.

Hank Luisetti (b. June 16, 1916, d. Dec. 17, 2002): Basketball F; 3-time All-America at Stanford (1936-38); revolutionized game with one-handed shot.

Johnny Lujack (b. Jan. 4, 1925): Football QB; led Notre Dame to three national titles (1943,46-47); won Heisman Trophy in 1947.

Darrell Wayne Lukas (b. Sept. 2, 1935): Horse racing; Eclipse-winning trainer who saddled Horses of Year Lady's Secret in 1988 and Criminal Type in 1990; first trainer to earn over $100 million in purses; led nation in earnings 14 times since 1983; Grindstone's Kentucky Derby win in 1996 gave him six Triple Crown wins in a row; has won Preakness 5 times, Kentucky Derby 4 times and Belmont 4 times; his most recent Triple Crown victory came in the 2000 Belmont with Commendable; leads all Breeders' Cup trainers with 16 victories.

Gen. Douglas MacArthur (b. Jan. 26, 1880, d. Apr. 5, 1964): Controversial U.S. general of World War II and Korea; president of U.S. Olympic Committee (1927-28); college football devotee; National Football Foundation MacArthur Bowl named after him.

Connie Mack (b. Dec. 22, 1862, d. Feb. 8, 1956): Baseball owner; managed Philadelphia A's until he was 87 (1901-50); all-time major league leader with 3,755, including World Series; won 9 AL pennants and 5 World Series (1910-11,13,29-30); also finished last 17 times.

Andy MacPhail (b. Apr. 5, 1953): Baseball; Former Chicago Cubs president/CEO who was GM of 2 World Series champions in Minnesota (1987,91); won first title at age 34; son of Lee, grandson of Larry.

Larry MacPhail (b. Feb. 3, 1890, d. Oct. 1, 1975): Baseball exec. and innovator; introduced major leagues to night games at Cincinnati (May 24, 1935); won pennant in Brooklyn (1941) and World Series with NY Yankees (1947); father of Lee, grandfather of Andy.

Lee MacPhail (b. Oct. 25, 1917): Baseball; AL president (1974-83); president of owners' Player Relations Committee (1984-85); also GM of Baltimore (1959-65) and NY Yankees (1967-74); son of Larry and father of Andy.

Wendy Macpherson (b. Jan. 28, 1968): Bowling; voted Bowler of the Decade for the 1990s; Major titles include the 1986 BPAA U.S. Open, 1988, 2000 and 2003 WIBC Queens and 1999 Sam's Town Invitational; annual PWBA money winner 4 times (1996, 97,99,2000).

John Madden (b. Apr. 10, 1936): Football and Radio-TV; won 112 games and a Super Bowl (1976 season) as coach of Oakland Raiders; has won 15 Emmy Awards since 1982 as NFL analyst; signed 4-year, $32 million deal with Fox in 1994— a richer contract than any NFL player at the time; joined Al Michaels in ABC's Monday Night Football booth in 2002 after 21 seasons alongside Pat Summerall; joined NBC for Sunday Night Football beginning in 2006.

Greg Maddux (b. Apr. 14, 1966): Baseball RHP; won unprecedented 4 straight NL Cy Young Awards with Cubs (1992) and Atlanta (1993-95); has led NL in ERA four times (1993-95,98); won 15th gold glove in 2005; only pitcher to win at least 15 games in 17 straight seasons (1988-2004); got his 300th win in 2004 (333 through 2006).

Larry Mahan (b. Nov. 21, 1943): Rodeo; 6-time All-Around world champion cowboy (1966-70,73).

Phil Mahre (b. May 10, 1957): Alpine skier; 3-time World Cup overall champ (1981-83); finished 1-2 with twin brother Steve in 1984 Olympic slalom.

Karl Malone (b. July 24, 1963): Basketball F; 11-time All-NBA 1st team (1989-99) with Utah; 2-time NBA MVP (1997,99); all-time NBA leader in free throws made (9,787), 2nd in career points (36,928) and field goals made (13,528); member of the 1992 and '96 Olympic gold medal teams; named one of the NBA's 50 greatest players.

Moses Malone (b. Mar. 23, 1955): Basketball C; signed with Utah of ABA out of high school at age 19; led NBA in rebounding 6 times; 4-time All-NBA 1st team; 3-time NBA MVP (1979,82-83); Finals MVP with Philadelphia in 1983; played 21 pro seasons.

Peyton Manning (b. Mar. 24, 1976): Football QB; graduated from Tennessee in 1998 and became the top overall pick by the Indianapolis Colts in the 1998 draft; 2-time Associated Press NFL MVP (2003-04); led AFC in passing efficiency 3 times (1998,2004-05); entered 2006 with 244 touchdown passes, tied for 12th on the all-time list; threw an NFL record 49 TD passes in 2004, breaking Dan Marino's record of 48; son of Archie, brother of Eli.

Nigel Mansell (b. Aug. 8, 1953): British auto racer; won 1992 Formula One driving championship with record 9 victories and 14 poles; quit Grand Prix circuit to race Indy cars in 1993; 1st rookie to win IndyCar title; 3rd driver to win IndyCar and F1 titles; returned to F1 after 1994 IndyCar season and won '94 Australian Grand Prix; left F1 again on May 23, 1995 with 31 wins and 32 poles in 15 years.

Mickey Mantle (b. Oct. 20, 1931, d. Aug. 13, 1995): Baseball CF; led AL in home runs 4 times; won Triple Crown in 1956; hit 52 HRs in 1956 and 54 in '61; 3-time MVP (1956-57,62); hit 536 career HRs; played in 12 World Series with NY Yankees and won 7 times; all-time World Series leader in HRs (18), RBI (40), runs (42) and strikeouts (54); inducted into Baseball Hall of Fame in 1974.

Diego Maradona (b. Oct. 30, 1960): Soccer F; captain and MVP of 1986 World Cup champion Argentina; also led national team to 1990 World Cup final; consensus Player of Decade in 1980s; led Napoli to 2 Italian League titles (1987,90) and UEFA Cup (1989); tested positive for cocaine and suspended 15 months by FIFA in 1991; returned to World Cup as Argentine captain in 1994, but was kicked out after two games when test found 5 banned substances in his urine.

Pete Maravich (b. June 27, 1947, d. Jan. 5, 1988): Basketball; NCAA scoring leader 3 times at LSU (1968-70); averaged NCAA-record 44.2 points a game over career; Player of Year in 1970; NBA scoring champ in '77 with New Orleans.

Alice Marble (b. Sept. 28, 1913, d. Dec. 13, 1990): Tennis; 4-time U.S. champion (1936,38-40); won Wimbledon in 1939; swept U.S. singles, doubles and mixed doubles from 1938-40.

Gino Marchetti (b. Jan. 2, 1927): Football DE; 8-time NFL All-Pro (1957-64) with Baltimore Colts.

Rocky Marciano (b. Sept. 1, 1923, d. Aug. 31, 1969): Boxer; heavyweight champion (1952-56); only heavyweight champ in history to retire undefeated; pro record of 49-0 with 43 KOs; killed in plane crash.

Juan Marichal (b. Oct. 20, 1938): Baseball RHP; won 21 or more games 6 times for S.F. Giants from 1963-69; ended 16-year career at 243-142.

Dan Marino (b. Sept. 15, 1961): Football QB; all-time NFL leader in career TD passes (420), passing yards (61,361), attempts (8,358) and completions (4,967); 4-time leading passer in AFC (1983-84,86,89); set NFL single-season records for TD passes (48) and passing yards (5,084) in 1984 (TD passes since broken by P. Manning with 49 in 2004).

Roger Maris (b. Sept. 10, 1934, d. Dec. 14, 1985): Baseball OF; broke Babe Ruth's season HR record with 61 in 1961 and held record until 1998 (Mark McGwire); 2-time AL MVP (1960-61) with NY Yankees; 275 HRs in 12 years.

Jim Marshall (b. Dec. 30, 1937): Football; long-time Vikings DE and NFL ironman; played in an NFL-record 282 consecutive games (1960-1979); also famous for picking up a fumble and running 66 yards the wrong way into the opponent's (49ers) endzone.

Billy Martin (b. May 16, 1928, d. Dec. 25, 1989): Baseball; 5-time manager of NY Yankees; won 2 pennants and 1 World Series (1977); also managed Minnesota, Detroit, Texas and Oakland; played on 5 Yankee world champions in 1950s.

Pedro Martinez (b. Oct. 25, 1971): Baseball RHP; one of baseball's premier pitchers; won 1997 NL Cy Young award with Montreal; traded to Boston Red Sox in Nov. 1997; 2-time AL Cy Young Award winner with Boston (1999,2000); signed with NY Mets in 2005.

Eddie Mathews (b. Oct. 13, 1931, d. Feb. 18, 2001): Baseball 3B; led NL in HRs twice (1953,59); hit 30 or more HRs 9 straight years; 512 career HRs.

Christy Mathewson (b. Aug. 12, 1880, d. Oct. 7, 1925): Baseball RHP; won 22 or more games 12 straight years (1903-14); 373 career wins; pitched 3 shutouts in 1905 World Series.

Bob Mathias (b. Nov. 17, 1930, d. Sept. 2, 2006): Track & Field; youngest winner of decathlon with gold medal in 1948 Olympics at age 17; first to repeat as decathlon champ in 1952; Sullivan Award winner (1948); 4-term member of U.S. Congress (R, Calif.) from 1967-74.

Ollie Matson (b. May 1, 1930): Football HB; All-America at San Francisco (1951); bronze medal winner in 400m at 1952 Olympics; 4-time All-Pro for NFL Chicago Cardinals (1954-57); traded to LA Rams for 9 players in 1959; accounted for 12,884 all-purpose yards and scored 73 TDs in 14 seasons.

Don Mattingly (b. Apr. 20, 1961): Baseball 1B; AL MVP (1985); won AL batting title in 1984 (.343); led majors with 145 RBI in 1985; led AL with 238 hits (Yankee record) and 53 doubles in 1986; won 9 Gold Glove Awards at 1B (1985-89, 91-94).

Willie Mays (b. May 6, 1931): Baseball OF; nicknamed the "Say Hey Kid"; led NL in HRs and stolen bases 4 times each; 2-time MVP (1954,65) with NY-SF Giants; Hall of Famer who played in 24 All-Star Games, earning MVP honors twice (1963,68); 12-time Gold Glove winner; 660 HRs, 1,903 RBI and 3,283 hits in career.

Bill Mazeroski (b. Sept. 5, 1936): Baseball 2B; career .260 hitter who won the 1960 World Series for Pittsburgh with a lead-off HR in the bottom of the 9th inning of Game 7; the pitcher was Ralph Terry of the NY Yankees, the count was 1-0 and the score was tied 9-9; also a sure-fielder, Maz won 8 Gold Gloves in 17 seasons.

Bob McAdoo (b. Sept. 25, 1951): Basketball F/C; 1972 Sporting News First Team All-American; NBA Rookie of the Year (1973); NBA MVP (1975); All-NBA First Team (1975); Led NBA in scoring three consecutive years (1974-76); 5-time All-Star (1974-78); two championships with LA Lakers (1982,85).

Joe McCarthy (b. Apr. 21, 1887, d. Jan. 13, 1978): Baseball; first manager to win pennants in both leagues (Chicago Cubs in 1929 and NY Yankees in 1932); greatest success came with Yankees when he won seven pennants and six World Series championships from 1936 to 1943; first manager to win four World Series in a row (1936-39); finished his career with the Boston Red Sox (1948-50); lifetime record of 2125-1333; member of Baseball Hall of Fame.

Pat McCormick (b. May 12, 1930): U.S. diver; won women's platform and springboard gold medals in both 1952 and '56 Olympics.

Willie McCovey (b. Jan. 10, 1938): Baseball 1B; led NL in HRs 3 times and RBI twice; MVP in 1969 with SF; 521 career HRs; indicted for tax evasion in July 1995, pled guilty; "McCovey Cove," the bay outside the rightfield fence at San Francisco's SBC Park is named for him.

John McEnroe (b. Feb. 16, 1959): Tennis; No.1 player in the world 4 times (1981-84); 4-time U.S. Open champ (1979-81,84); 3-time Wimbledon champ (1981,83-84); played on 5 Davis Cup winners (1978,79,81,82,92); won NCAA singles title (1978); finished career with 77 singles championships, 77 more in men's doubles (including 9 Grand Slam titles), and U.S. Davis Cup records for years played (13) and singles matches won (41).

John McGraw (b. Apr. 7, 1873, d. Feb. 25, 1934): Baseball; managed NY Giants to 9 NL pennants between 1905-24; won 3 World Series (1905,21-22); 2nd on all-time career list with 2,866 wins in 33 seasons (2,840 regular season and 26 World Series).

Frank McGuire (b. Nov. 8, 1916, d. Oct. 11, 1994): Basketball; winner of 731 games as high school, college and pro coach; won at least 100 games at 3 colleges— St. John's (103), North Carolina (164) and South Carolina (283); won 550 games in 30 college seasons; 1957 UNC team went 32-0 and beat Kansas 54-53 in triple OT to win NCAA title; coached NBA Philadelphia Warriors to 49-31 record in 1961-62 season, but refused to move with team to San Francisco.

Mark McGwire (b. Oct. 1, 1963): Baseball 1B; Sporting News college player of the year (1984); Member of 1984 U.S. Olympic baseball team; won AL Rookie of the Year and hit rookie-record 49 HRs in 1987; shattered Roger Maris' season home run record (61) in 1998 with St. Louis (70); followed that magical season with 65 HRs and 147 RBI in 1999.

Jim McKay (b. Sept. 24, 1921): Radio-TV; host and commentator of ABC's Olympic coverage and "Wide World of Sports" show since 1961; 12-time Emmy winner; also given Peabody Award in 1988 and Life Achievement Emmy in 1990; became part owner of Baltimore Orioles in 1993.

Tamara McKinney (b. Oct. 16, 1962): Skiing; first American woman to win overall Alpine World Cup championship (1983); won World Cup slalom (1984) and giant slalom titles twice (1981,83).

Denny McLain (b. Mar. 29, 1944): Baseball RHP; last pitcher to win 30 games (1968); 2-time Cy Young winner (1968-69) with Detroit; convicted of racketeering, extortion and drug possession in 1985, served 29 months of 25-year jail term, sentence overturned when court ruled he had not received a fair trial; he has faced subsequent legal troubles.

Rick Mears (b. Dec. 3, 1951): Auto racer; 3-time CART national champ (1979,81-82); 4-time winner of Indy 500 (1979,84,88,91) and only driver to win 6 Indy 500 poles; Indy 500 Rookie of Year (1978); retired in 1992 with 29 CART wins and 40 poles.

Mark Messier (b. Jan. 18, 1961): Hockey C; 2-time NHL MVP with Edmonton (1990) and NY Rangers (1992); captain of 1994 Rangers team that won 1st Stanley Cup since 1940; ranks 2nd in all-time playoff points, goals and assists; 2nd on all-time regular season points list (1,887); retired in 2005.

Mike Metzger (b. Nov. 19, 1975): Freestyle Motocross Rider; AMA National mini-bike champion (1990), credited as "The Godfather" of FMX for his early creative influences and trick inventions; first to land back-to-back backflips in competition (2002 X Games), winner of five X Games medals.

Debbie Meyer (b. Aug. 14, 1952): Swimmer; 1st swimmer to win 3 individual golds at 1 Olympics (1968).

Ann Meyers (b. Mar. 26, 1955): Basketball G; In 1974, became first high schooler to play for U.S. national team; 4-time All-American at UCLA (1976-79); member of 1976 U.S. Olympic team; Broderick Award and Cup winner (1978); Signed $50,000 no cut contract with NBA's Indiana Pacers (1980); married Dodger great Don Drysdale.

George Mikan (b. June 18, 1924, d. June 2, 2005): Basketball C; 3-time All-America (1944-46); led DePaul to NIT title (1945); led Minneapolis Lakers to 5 NBA titles in 6 years (1949-54); first commissioner of ABA (1967-69).

Stan Mikita (b. May 20, 1940): Hockey C; led NHL in scoring 4 times; won both MVP and Lady Byng awards in 1967 and '68 with Chicago.

Bode Miller (b. Oct. 12, 1977): Alpine Skier; won 2 silver medals at 2002 Winter Games; 2 golds, 1 silver at 2003 World Championships; 2nd overall in 2003 World Cup standings; 2004 Giant Slalom World Cup champion; 2005 Overall World Cup champ; came up empty at Turin Games in 2006.

Cheryl Miller (b. Jan. 3, 1964): Basketball; 3-time College Player of Year (1984-86); led USC to NCAA title and U.S. to Olympic gold medal in 1984; coached USC to 44-14 record in 2 years; coached WNBA's Phoenix Mercury for 4 years; sister of NBA's Reggie.

Del Miller (b. July 5, 1913, d. Aug. 19, 1996): Harness racing; driver, trainer, owner, breeder, seller and track owner; drove to 2,441 wins from 1929-90.

Marvin Miller (b. Apr. 14, 1917): Baseball labor leader; executive director of Players' Assn. from 1966-82; increased average salary from $19,000 to over $240,000; led 13-day strike in 1972 and 50-day walkout in '81.

Shannon Miller (b. Mar. 10, 1977): Gymnast; won 5 medals in 1992 Olympics and 2 golds in '96 Games; All-Around world champion in 1993 and '94.

Billy Mills (b. June 30, 1938): Track & Field; Native American who was upset winner of 10,000m gold medal at 1964 Olympics.

Bora Milutinovic (b. Sept. 7, 1944): Soccer; Serbian who coached U.S. national team from 1991-95; led Mexico (1986), Costa Rica ('90), USA ('94) and Nigeria ('98) into the 2nd round of the World Cup.

Dave Mirra (b. Apr. 4, 1974): BMX; medaled in every summer X Games since 1995; has 20 X Games medals (14 gold); first to do a double backflip on a BMX bike; nicknamed "Miracle Boy" after his brush with death when he was hit by a drunk driver (1994).

Tommy Moe (b. Feb. 17, 1970): Alpine skier; won Downhill gold and Super-G silver at 1994 Winter Olympics; 1st U.S. man to win 2 Olympic alpine medals in one year.

Paul Molitor (b. Aug. 22, 1956): Baseball DH-1B; All-America SS at Minnesota in 1976; spent 15 years with Milwaukee, then 3 each with Toronto and Minnesota; led Blue Jays to 2nd straight World Series title as MVP (1993); hit .418 in 2 Series appearances (1982,93); holds World Series game record with 5 hits.

Joe Montana (b. June 11, 1956): Football QB; led Notre Dame to national title in 1977; led San Francisco to 4 Super Bowl titles in 1980s; only 3-time Super Bowl MVP; 2-time NFL MVP (1989-90); led NFL in passing 5 times; traded to K.C. in 1993; ranks 5th all-time in passing efficiency (92.3), 273 career TD passes and 40,551 passing yards; inducted into Pro Football Hall of Fame in 2000.

Tim Montgomery (b. Jan. 25, 1975): American sprinter; broke world record in 100m with a 9.78 on Sept. 14, 2002; failed to qualify for 2004 Olympics.

Helen Wills Moody (b. Oct. 6, 1905, d. Jan. 1, 1998): Tennis; won 8 Wimbledon singles titles, 7 U.S. and 4 French from 1923-38.

Warren Moon (b. Nov. 18, 1956): Football QB; MVP of 1978 Rose Bowl with Washington; MVP of CFL with Edmonton in 1983; led Eskimos to 5 consecutive Grey Cup titles (1978-82) and was playoff MVP twice (1980,82); entered NFL in 1984 and played for 4 different teams; picked for 9 Pro Bowls; inducted into Pro Football Hall of Fame in 2006.

Archie Moore (b. Dec. 13, 1913, d. Dec. 9, 1998): Boxer; world light heavyweight champion (1952-60); pro record 199-26-8 with a record 145 KOs.

Noureddine Morceli (b. Feb. 28, 1970): Algerian runner; 3-time world champion at 1,500 meters (1991,93,95) and 1996 Olympic gold medal winner; former holder of world records in several middle distance events.

Howie Morenz (b. June 21, 1902, d. Mar. 8, 1937): Hockey C; 3-time NHL MVP (1928,31,32); led Montreal Canadiens to 3 Stanley Cups; voted Outstanding Player of the Half-Century in 1950.

Joe Morgan (b. Sept. 19, 1943): Baseball 2B; regular-season MVP both years he led Cincinnati to World Series titles (1975-76); 1,865 career walks; led NL in walks 4 times.

Bobby Morrow (b. Oct. 15, 1935): Track & Field; won 3 gold medals at 1956 Olympics (100m, 200m and 4x400m relay).

Willie Mosconi (b. June 27, 1913, d. Sept. 12, 1993): Pocket Billiards; 14-time world champion from 1941-57.

Annemarie Moser-Pröll (b. Mar. 27, 1953): Austrian alpine skier; won World Cup overall title 6 times (1971-75,79); all-time women's World Cup leader in career wins with 61; won Downhill in 1980 Olympics.

Edwin Moses (b. Aug. 31, 1955): Track & Field; won 400m hurdles at 1976 and '84 Olympics, bronze medal in '88; also winner of 122 consecutive races from 1977-87.

Stirling Moss (b. Sept. 17, 1929): Auto racer; won 194 of 466 career races and 16 Formula One events, but was never world champion.

Marion Motley (b. June 5, 1920, d. June 27, 1999): Football FB/LB; hard-charging runner who was all-time leading AAFC rusher; ran for over 4,700 yards and 31 TDs for Cleveland Browns (1946-53), leading the NFL in 1950; first black member of the Pro Football Hall of Fame.

Shirley Muldowney (b. June 19, 1940): Drag Racer; "Cha Cha"; women's racing pioneer; 3-time Winston drag racing Top Fuel champion (1977,80,82); recorded 18 career NHRA National Event Victories.

Anthony Munoz (b. Aug. 19, 1958): Football OT; drafted 3rd overall in 1980 out of USC; 11-time All-Pro with Cincinnati; member of NFL 75th Anniv. All-Time Team; elected to Hall of Fame in 1998.

Calvin Murphy (b. May 9, 1948): Basketball G; NBA All-Rookie team (1971); holds NBA single season free throw percentage (.958); third all-time career free throw pct. (.892); elected to Basketball Hall of Fame in 1992; only 5'9" and 165 pounds.

Dale Murphy (b. Mar. 12, 1956): Baseball OF; led NL in HRs and RBI twice; 2-time MVP (1982-83) with Atlanta; also played with Philadelphia and Colorado; retired in 1993 with 398 HRs.

Jack Murphy (b. Feb. 5, 1923, d. Sept. 24, 1980): Sports editor and columnist of *The San Diego Union* from 1951-80; instrumental in bringing AFL Chargers south from LA in 1961, landing Padres as NL expansion team in '69; and lobbying for San Diego stadium that would later bear his name.

Eddie Murray (b. Feb. 24, 1956): Baseball 1B-DH; AL Rookie of Year in 1977; became 20th player in history, but only 2nd switch hitter (after Pete Rose) to get 3,000 hits; one of only 4 men (Aaron, Mays and Palmiero) with 500 HRs and 3,000 hits.

Jim Murray (b. Dec. 29, 1919, d. Aug. 16, 1998): Sports columnist for *LA Times* 1961-98; 14-time Sportswriter of the Year; won Pulitzer Prize for commentary in 1990.

Ty Murray (b. Oct. 11, 1969): Rodeo cowboy; 7-time All-Around world champion (1989-94,98); Rookie of Year in 1988; youngest (age 20) to win All-Around title; set single season earnings mark with $297,896 in 1993; career hampered by injury.

Stan Musial (b. Nov. 21, 1920): Baseball OF-1B; led NL in batting 7 times and RBI 2 times; 3-time MVP (1943,46,48) with St. Louis; played in 24 All-Star Games; had 3,630 career hits (4th all-time) and .331 average.

John Naber (b. Jan. 20, 1956): Swimmer; won 4 gold medals and a silver in 1976 Olympics.

Bronko Nagurski (b. Nov. 3, 1908, d. Jan. 7, 1990): Football FB-T; All-America at Minnesota (1929); All-Pro with Chicago Bears (1932-34); charter member of college and pro Halls of Fame.

James Naismith (b. Nov. 6, 1861, d. Nov. 28, 1939): Canadian physical education instructor who invented basketball in 1891 at the YMCA Training School (now Springfield College) in Springfield, Mass.

Joe Namath (b. May 31, 1943): Football QB; signed for unheard-of $400,000 as rookie with AFL's NY Jets in 1965; 2-time All-AFL (1968-69) and All-NFL (1972); led Jets to Super Bowl upset as MVP in '69 after making brash prediction of victory.

Ilie Nastase (b. July 19, 1946): Romanian tennis player; No.1 in the world twice (1972-73); won U.S. (1972) and French (1973) Opens; has since entered Romanian politics.

Martina Navratilova (b. Oct. 18, 1956): Tennis player; No.1 player in the world 7 times (1978-79,82-86); won her record 9th Wimbledon singles title in 1990; also won 4 U.S. Opens, 3 Australian and 2 French; in all, won 18 Grand Slam singles titles, 41 Grand Slam doubles titles; all-time leader among men and women in singles titles (167); 3rd all-time on women's career money list with over $21 million; inducted into Int'l Tennis Hall of Fame in 2000; retired in 2006 after winning U.S. Open mixed doubles title.

Cosmas Ndeti (b. Nov. 24, 1971): Kenyan distance runner; winner of three consecutive Boston Marathons (1993-95); set what is still the course record of 2:07:15 in 1994.

Earle (Greasy) Neale (b. Nov. 5, 1891, d. Nov. 2, 1973): Baseball and Football; hit .357 for Cincinnati in 1919 World Series; also played with pre-NFL Canton Bulldogs; later coached Philadelphia Eagles to 2 NFL titles (1948-49).

Primo Nebiolo (b. July 14, 1923, d. Nov. 7, 1999): Italian president of International Amateur Athletic Federation (IAAF) since 1981; also an at-large member of International Olympic Committee; regarded as dictatorial, but credited with elevating track & field to world class financial status.

Byron Nelson (b. Feb. 4, 1912, d. Sept. 26, 2006): Golfer; 2-time winner of both Masters (1937,42) and PGA (1940,45); also U.S. Open champion in 1939; won 19 tournaments in 1945, including 11 in a row; also set all-time PGA stroke average with 68.33 strokes per round over 120 rounds in '45.

Lindsey Nelson (b. May 25, 1919, d. June 10, 1995): Radio-TV; all-purpose play-by-play broadcaster for CBS, NBC and others; 4-time Sportscaster of the Year (1959-62); voice of Cotton Bowl for 25 years and NY Mets from 1962-78; given Life Achievement Emmy Award in 1991.

Ernie Nevers (b. June 11, 1903, d. May 3, 1976): Football FB; earned 11 letters in four sports at Stanford; played pro football, baseball and basketball; scored 40 points for Chicago Cardinals in one NFL game (1929).

Paula Newby-Fraser (b. June 2, 1962): Zimbabwean triathlete; 8-time winner of Ironman Triathlon in Hawaii; established women's record of 8:55:28 in 1992.

John Newcombe (b. May 23, 1944): Australian tennis player; No.1 player in world 3 times (1967,70-71); won Wimbledon 3 times and U.S. and Australian championships twice each.

Pete Newell (b. Aug. 31, 1915): Basketball; coached at Univ. of San Francisco, Michigan St. and the Univ. of California; first coach to win NIT (San Francisco-1949), NCAA (California-1959) and Olympic gold medal (1960); later served as the general manager of the San Diego Rockets and LA Lakers in the NBA; member of Basketball Hall of Fame.

Jack Nicklaus (b. Jan. 21, 1940): Golfer; all-time leader in major tournament wins with 18— 6 Masters, 5 PGAs, 4 U.S. Opens and 3 British Opens; oldest player to win Masters (46 in 1986); PGA Player of Year 5 times (1967,72-73,75-76); named Golfer of the Century by PGA in 1988; 6-time Ryder Cup player and 2-time captain (1983,87); won NCAA title (1961) and 2 U.S. Amateurs (1959,61); 73 PGA Tour wins (2nd to Sam Snead's 82); fourth win in Tradition in 1996 gave him 8 majors on Senior PGA Tour; nicknamed "the Golden Bear."

Chuck Noll (b. Jan. 5, 1932): Football; coached Pittsburgh to 4 Super Bowl wins (1975-76,79-80); retired after 1991 season with 209 career wins (including playoffs) in 23 years.

Greg Norman (b. Feb. 10, 1955): Australian golfer; 73 tournament wins worldwide including 20 PGA Tour victories; 2-time British Open winner (1986,93); lost Masters by a stroke in both 1986 (to Jack Nicklaus) and '87 (to Larry Mize in sudden death); 1995 PGA Tour Player of the Year.

James D. Norris (b. Nov. 6, 1906, d. Feb. 25, 1966): Boxing promoter and NHL owner; president of International Boxing Club from 1949 until U.S. Supreme Court ordered its break-up (for anti-trust violations) in 1958; only NHL owner to win Stanley Cups in two cities: Detroit (1936-37,43) and Chicago (1961).

Paavo Nurmi (b. June 13, 1897, d. Oct. 2, 1973): Finnish runner; won 9 gold medals (6 individual) in 1920, '24 and '28 Olympics; from 1921-31 broke 23 world outdoor records in events ranging from 1,500 to 20,000 meters.

Dan O'Brien (b. July 18, 1966): Track & Field; Olympic decathlon gold medalist (1996); set former world record in decathlon (8,891 pts) in 1992, after shockingly failing to qualify for event at U.S. Olympic Trials; three-time gold medalist at World Championships (1991,93,95).

Larry O'Brien (b. July 7, 1917, d. Sept. 27, 1990): Basketball; former U.S. Postmaster General and 3rd NBA commissioner (1975-84), league absorbed 4 ABA teams and created salary cap during his term in office.

Parry O'Brien (b. Jan. 28, 1932): Track & Field; in 4 consecutive Olympics, won two gold medals, a silver and placed 4th in the shot put (1952-64).

Al Oerter (b. Sept. 19, 1936): Track & Field; his 4 discus gold medals in consecutive Olympics from 1956-68 is an unmatched Olympic record.

Sadaharu Oh (b. May 20, 1940): Baseball 1B; led Japan League in HRs 15 times; 9-time MVP for Tokyo Giants; all-time Japan League HR leader with 868 in 22 years.

WHO'S WHO

Hakeem Olajuwon (b. Jan. 21, 1963): Basketball C; Nigerian native who was All-America in 1984 and Final Four MOP in 1983 for Houston; overall 1st pick by Houston Rockets in 1984 NBA draft; led Rockets to back-to-back NBA titles (1994-95); regular season MVP (1994) and 2-time Finals MVP ('94-95); 6-time All-NBA 1st team (1987-89,93-95); all-time NBA blocks leader.

Jose Maria Olazabal (b. Feb. 5, 1966): Spanish golfer; has 28 worldwide victories including 2 Masters (1994,99); played on 6 European Ryder Cup teams.

Barney Oldfield (b. Jan. 29, 1878, d. Oct. 4, 1946): Auto racing pioneer; drove cars built by Henry Ford; first man to drive car a mile per minute (1903).

Walter O'Malley (b. Oct. 9, 1903, d. Aug. 9, 1979): Baseball owner; moved Brooklyn Dodgers to Los Angeles after 1957 season; won 4 World Series (1955,59,63,65).

Shaquille O'Neal (b. Mar. 6, 1972): Basketball C; 2-time All-America at LSU (1991-92); overall 1st pick (as a junior) by Orlando in 1992 NBA draft; Rookie of Year in 1993; 2-time NBA scoring leader (1995,2000); regular season MVP (2000) and 3-time NBA Finals MVP (2000,01,02); named one of the NBA's 50 Greatest Players; traded to Miami in 2004 and won a title with the Heat in 2006.

Bobby Orr (b. Mar. 20, 1948): Hockey D; league's only 8-time Norris Trophy winner as best defenseman (1968-75); credited with revolutionizing the position; 3-time Hart Trophy winner as NHL regular season MVP (1970-72); led NHL in scoring twice and assists 5 times; All-NHL 1st team 8 times; playoff MVP twice (1970,72) with Boston; career cut short due to a series of knee injuries.

Tom Osborne (b. Feb. 23, 1937): Football; Nebraska head coach from 1973-97; career record of 255-49-3; his win pct. of .836 is fifth all-time; won national championships in 1994 and '95 and shared national title with Michigan in '97; elected to U.S. Congress (R., Neb.) in 2000.

Mel Ott (b. Mar. 2, 1909, d. Nov. 21, 1958): Baseball OF; joined NY Giants at age 16; led NL in HRs 6 times; had 511 HRs and 1,860 RBI in 22 years.

Kristin Otto (b. Feb. 7, 1966): East German swimmer; 1st woman to win 6 gold medals (4 individual) at one Olympics (1988).

Francis Ouimet (b. May 8, 1893, d. Sept. 3, 1967): Golfer; won 1913 U.S. Open as 20-year-old amateur playing on Brookline, Mass. course where he used to caddie; won U.S. Amateur twice; 8-time Walker Cup player.

Jesse Owens (b. Sept. 12, 1913, d. Mar. 31, 1980): Track & Field; set 4 world records in one afternoon competing for Ohio State at the Big Ten Championships (May 25, 1935); a year later, he soundly debunked Adolf Hitler's "master race" claims, winning 4 gold medals (100m, 200m, 4x100m relay and long jump) at 1936 Summer Olympics in Berlin.

Alan Page (b. Aug. 7, 1945): Football DE; All-America at Notre Dame in 1966 and member of two national championship teams; 6-time NFL All-Pro and 1971 Player of Year with Minnesota Vikings; later a lawyer who was elected to Minnesota Supreme Court in 1992.

Satchel Paige (b. July 7, 1906, d. June 6, 1982): Baseball RHP; pitched 55 career no-hitters over 20 seasons in Negro Leagues, entered major leagues with Cleveland in 1948 at age 42; had 28-31 record in 5 years; returned to AL at age 59 to start 1 game for Kansas City in 1965 (went 3 innings, gave up a hit and got a strikeout; elected to Baseball Hall of Fame in 1971.

Se Ri Pak (b. Sept. 28, 1977): Golfer; won two Majors as an LPGA rookie in 1998 (LPGA Championship and U.S. Open); youngest player to win the U.S. Open (20); her win at the 2006 LPGA Championship gave her a total of 5 majors.

Arnold Palmer (b. Sept. 10, 1929): Golfer; winner of 4 Masters, 2 British Opens and a U.S. Open; 2-time PGA Player of Year (1960,62); 1st player to earn over $1 million in career (1968); annual PGA Tour money leader award named after him; 62 wins on PGA Tour and 10 more on Champions Tour; made 48 consecutive Masters starts.

Jim Palmer (b. Oct. 15, 1945): Baseball RHP; 3-time Cy Young Award winner (1973,75-76); won 20 or more games 8 times with Baltimore; elected to the Baseball Hall of Fame in 1990.

Bill Parcells (b. Aug. 22, 1941): Football; coached NY Giants to 2 Super Bowl titles (1987,91); retired after 1990 season then returned in 1993 as coach of New England; took hapless Pats from 2-14 in 1992 to Super Bowl (loss to Green Bay); coached the Jets for 3 seasons (1997-99), turning them from 1-15 doormat to AFC East champ in 2 years; retired again in 2000; returned in 2003 as head coach of the Cowboys.

Jack Pardee (b. Apr. 19, 1936): Football; All-America LB at Texas A&M; All-Pro with LA Rams (1963) and Washington (1971); 2-time NFL Coach of Year (1976,79); won 87 games in 11 seasons; only man hired as head coach in NFL, WFL, USFL and CFL.

Bernie Parent (b. Apr. 3, 1945): Hockey G; led Philadelphia Flyers to 2 Stanley Cups as playoff MVP (1974,75); 2-time Vezina Trophy winner; posted 55 career shutouts and 2.55 GAA in 13 seasons.

Joe Paterno (b. Dec. 21, 1926): Football; passed Bear Bryant in 2001 as all-time wins leader in college football (since passed himself by Bobby Bowden); coached Penn St. to 354-117-3 record, 21-10-1 bowl record and 2 national titles (1982,86) in 40 years; also had three unbeaten teams that didn't finish No. 1; 4-time Coach of Year (1968,78,82,86).

Craig Patrick (b. May 20, 1946): Hockey; 3rd generation Patrick to have name inscribed on Stanley Cup; GM of 2-time Cup champion Pittsburgh Penguins (1991-92); also captain of 1969 NCAA champion at Denver; assistant coach-GM of 1980 gold medal-winning U.S. Olympic team; grandson of Lester.

Lester Patrick (b. Dec. 30, 1883, d. June 1, 1960): Hockey; pro hockey pioneer as player, coach and general manager for 43 years; led NY Rangers to Stanley Cups as coach (1928,33) and GM (1940); grandfather of Craig.

Carly Patterson (b. Feb. 4, 1988): American gymnast; Olympic all-around champ at Athens in 2004.

Floyd Patterson (b. Jan. 4, 1935, d. May 11, 2006): Boxer; Olympic middleweight champ in 1952; world heavyweight champ (1956-59,60-62); 1st to regain heavyweight crown; fought Ingemar Johansson 3 times in 22 months from 1959-61, won last 2; pro record 55-8-1 (40 KOs).

Walter Payton (b. July 25, 1954, d. Nov. 1, 1999): Football RB; formerly NFL's all-time leading rusher with 16,726 yards (1984-2002, passed by Emmitt Smith); scored 125 career TDs; All-Pro 7 times with Chicago; led NFC in rushing 5 times (1976-80); league MVP in 1977 (AP & PFWA) and 1985 (Bell); won ring with Bears in Super Bowl XX; known as superb runner, receiver and blocker; nicknamed "Sweetness".

Calvin Peete (b. July 18, 1943): Golf; began playing golf at age 23; over $2 million in career earnings; selected to 2 U.S. Ryder Cup teams (1983,85).

Pelé (b. Oct. 23, 1940): Brazilian soccer F; given name— Edson Arantes do Nascimento; led Brazil to 3 World Cup titles (1958,62,70); came to U.S. in 1975 to play for NY Cosmos in NASL; scored 1,281 goals in 22 years including 12 goals in the World Cup; served as Brazil's minister of sport (1990-98); named IOC Athlete of the Century and FIFA's co-Player of the Century (along with Diego Maradona).

Roger Penske (b. Feb. 20, 1937): Auto racing; national sports car driving champion (1964); established racing team in 1961; co-founder of CART; Penske Racing has won 14 Indianapolis 500s and 11 CART points titles; announced move to IRL for 2002 season; won IRL points title with Sam Hornish Jr. in 2006.

Willie Pep (b. Sept. 19, 1922): Boxer; 2-time world featherweight champion (1942-48,49-50); pro record 230-11-1 with 65 KOs.

Marie-Jose Perec (b. 1968): Track & Field; French sprinter who became 2nd woman to win the 200m and 400m events in the same Olympics (1996); also won the 400 in 1992 Games.

Fred Perry (b. May 18, 1909, d. Feb. 2, 1995): British tennis player; 3-time Wimbledon champion (1934-36); first player to win all four Grand Slam singles titles, though not in same year; last native to win All-England men's title.

Gaylord Perry (b. Sept. 15, 1938): Baseball RHP; one of only four pitchers to win the Cy Young Award in both leagues; retired in 1983 with 314-265 record and 3,534 K over 22 years with 8 teams; brother Jim won 215 games for family total of 529.

Bob Pettit (b. Dec. 12, 1932): Basketball F; All-NBA 1st team 10 times (1955-64); 2-time MVP (1956,59) with St. Louis Hawks; first player to score 20,000 points.

Richard Petty (b. July 2, 1937): Auto racer; 7-time winner of Daytona 500; 7-time NASCAR national champ (1964,67,71-72,74-75,79); first stock car driver to win $1 million in career; all-time NASCAR leader in races won (200), poles (126) and wins in a single season (27 in 1967); son of Lee (55 career wins), father of Kyle (8 career wins), grandfather of Adam; nicknamed "The King".

Michael Phelps (b. June 30, 1985): American swimmer who attempted to break Mark Spitz's Olympic record of 7 gold medals in 2004 but "settled" for 6 golds and two bronzes in Athens.

Mike Piazza (b. Sept. 4, 1968): Baseball C; slugger who broke Carlton Fisk's MLB record for HRs by a catcher in 2004 with his 352nd; 11-time All-Star.

Laffit Pincay Jr. (b. Dec. 29, 1946): Jockey; 5-time Eclipse Award winner (1971,73-74,79,85); winner of 3 Belmonts and 1 Kentucky Derby (aboard Swale in 1984); retired as all-time winningest jockey with 9,531 career wins.

Scottie Pippen (b. Sept. 25, 1965): Basketball F; started on 6 NBA champions with Chicago (1991-93, 96-98); 3-time All-NBA first team (1994-96). Voted one of NBA's 50 Greatest Players.

Nelson Piquet (b. Aug. 17, 1952): Brazilian auto racer; 3-time Formula One world champion (1981,83, 87); left circuit in 1991 with 23 career wins.

Rick Pitino (b. Sept. 18, 1952): Basketball coach; won 1996 NCAA title at Kentucky; became coach and president of NBA's Celtics in 1997 but was unsuccessful, resigning in 2001; returned to college ranks with Louisville in 2005 became 1st to take 3 schools to the Final Four (Providence, Ky., Louisville).

Jacques Plante (b. Jan. 17, 1929, d. Feb. 27, 1986): Hockey G; led Montreal to 6 Stanley Cups (1953,56-60); won 7 Vezina Trophies; MVP in 1962; first goalie to regularly wear a mask; posted 82 shutouts with 2.38 GAA.

Gary Player (b. Nov. 1, 1936): South African golfer; 3-time winner of Masters (1961,74,78) and British Open (1959,68,74); one of only 5 players to win career Grand Slam (Hogan, Nicklaus, Sarazen and Woods); also won 2 PGAs, a U.S. Open and 2 U.S. Senior Opens.

Jim Plunkett (b. Dec. 5, 1947): Football QB; Heisman Trophy winner (Stanford) in 1970; AFL Rookie of the Year in 1971; led Oakland-LA Raiders to Super Bowl wins in 1981 and '84; MVP in '81.

Maurice Podoloff (b. Aug. 18, 1890, d. Nov. 24, 1985): Basketball; engineered merger of Basketball Assn. of America and National Basketball League into NBA in 1949; NBA commissioner (1949-63); league MVP trophy named after him.

Fritz Pollard (b. Jan. 27, 1894, d. May 11, 1986): Football; 1st black All-America RB (1916 at Brown); 1st black to play in Rose Bowl; 7-year NFL pro (1920-26); 1st black NFL coach, at Milwaukee and Hammond, Ind.

Sam Pollock (b. Dec. 15, 1925): Hockey GM; managed NHL Montreal Canadiens to 9 Stanley Cups in 14 years (1965-78).

Denis Potvin (b. Oct. 29, 1953): Hockey D; won Norris Trophy 3 times (1976,78-79); 5-time All-NHL 1st-team; led NY Islanders to 4 Stanley Cups.

Asafa Powell (b. Nov. 11, 1982): Track & Field; Jamaican sprinter who broke Tim Montgomery's 100m world record with a 9.77 on June 14, 2005.

Mike Powell (b. Nov. 10, 1963): Track & Field; broke Bob Beamon's 23-year-old long jump world record by 2 inches with leap of 29-ft., 4½ in. at the 1991 World Championships; Sullivan Award winner (1991); won long jump silver medals in 1988 and '92 Olympics; repeated as world champ in 1993.

Steve Prefontaine (b. Jan. 25, 1951, d. May 30, 1975): Track & Field; All-America distance runner at Oregon; first athlete to win same event at NCAA championships 4 straight years (5,000 meters from 1970-73); finished 4th in 5,000 at 1972 Munich Olympics; first athlete to endorse Nike running shoes; killed in a one-car accident.

Nick Price (b. Jan. 28, 1957): Zimbabwean golfer; PGA Tour Player of Year in 1993 and '94; became 1st since Nick Faldo in 1990 to win 2 Grand Slam titles in same year when he took British Open and PGA Championship in 1994; also won PGA in '92.

Alain Prost (b. Feb. 24, 1955): French auto racer; 4-time Formula One world champion (1985-86,89,93); retired after '93 season as all-time leader with 51 (passed by Michael Schumacher in 2001).

Kirby Puckett (b. Mar. 14, 1961, d. Mar. 6, 2006): Baseball OF; led Minnesota Twins to World Series titles in 1987 and '91; retired in 1996 due to an eye ailment with batting title (1989), 2,304 hits and a .318 career average in 12 seasons; elected to Hall of Fame in 2001.

C.C. Pyle (b. 1882, d. Feb. 3, 1939): Promoter; known as "Cash and Carry"; hyped Red Grange's pro football debut by arranging 1925 barnstorming tour with Chicago Bears; had Grange bolt NFL for new AFL in 1926 (AFL folded in '27); also staged two transcontinental footraces (1928-29), known as "Bunion Derbies."

Bobby Rahal (b. Jan. 10, 1953): Auto racer; 3-time PPG Cup champ (1986,87,92); 24 career Indy-Car wins, including 1986 Indy 500; current IRL team owner with TV's David Letterman; acted as interim president-CEO of CART in 2000.

Jack Ramsay (b. Feb. 21, 1925): Basketball; coach who won 239 college games with St. Joe's-PA in 11 seasons and 906 NBA games (including playoffs) with 4 teams over 21 years; led Portland to 1977 NBA title; placed 3rd in 1961 Final Four (later vacated).

Bill Rasmussen (b. Oct. 15, 1932): Radio-TV; unemployed radio broadcaster who founded ESPN, the nation's first 24-hour all-sports cable-TV network, in 1978; bought out by Getty Oil in 1981.

Willis Reed (b. June 25, 1942): Basketball C; led NY Knicks to NBA titles in 1970 and '73, Finals MVP both years; 1970 regular season MVP. Voted one of NBA's 50 Greatest Players; fought off serious injury and limped onto court just prior to Game 7 of the 1970 Finals, his dramatic entrance helped inspire his team to victory over Wilt Chamberlain's Lakers.

Pee Wee Reese (b. July 23, 1918, d. Aug. 14, 1999): Baseball SS; member of Brooklyn/Los Angeles Dodgers from 1940-58; led NL in runs scored (132) in 1949 and stolen bases (30) in 1952; hit over .300 in a season once (.309 in 1954); led the NL in putouts four times; real name was Harold H. Reese.

Mary Lou Retton (b. Jan. 24, 1968): Gymnast; won gold medal in women's All-Around at the 1984 Olympics; also won 2 silvers and 2 bronzes.

Grantland Rice (b. Nov. 1, 1880, d. July 13, 1954): First celebrated American sportswriter; chronicled the Golden Age of Sport in 1920s; immortalized Notre Dame's "Four Horsemen."

Jerry Rice (b. Oct. 13, 1962): Football WR; 2-time Div. I-AA All-America at Mississippi Valley St. (1983-84); won 3 Super Bowls with San Francisco (1989,90,95); 10-time All-Pro; regular season MVP in 1987 and Super Bowl MVP in 1989; all-time NFL leader in touchdowns (208), receptions (1549) and receiving yards (22,895); announced retirement in 2005 at age 42 after a 20-year NFL career.

Henri Richard (b. Feb. 29, 1936): Hockey C; leap year baby who played on more Stanley Cup championship teams (11) than anybody else; at 5-foot-7, known as the "Pocket Rocket"; brother of Maurice Richard.

Maurice Richard (b. Aug. 4, 1921, d. May 27, 2000): Hockey RW; the "Rocket"; 8-time NHL 1st team All-Star; MVP in 1947; 1st to score 50 goals in one season (1944-45); 544 career goals; played on 8 Stanley Cup winners in Montreal.

Bob Richards (b. Feb. 2, 1926): Track & Field; pole vaulter, ordained minister and original *Wheaties* pitchman, remains only 2-time Olympic pole vault champ (1952,56).

Tex Rickard (b. Jan. 2, 1870, d. Jan. 6, 1929): Promoter who handled boxing's first $1 million gate (Dempsey vs. Carpentier in 1921); built Madison Square Garden in 1925; founded NY Rangers as Garden tenant in 1926 and named NHL team after himself (Tex's Rangers); also built Boston Garden in 1928.

Eddie Rickenbacker (b. Oct. 8, 1890, d. July 23, 1973): Mechanic and auto racer; became America's top flying ace (22 kills) in World War I; owned Indianapolis Speedway (1927-45) and ran Eastern Air Lines (1938-59).

Branch Rickey (b. Dec. 20, 1881, d. Dec. 9, 1965): Baseball innovator; revolutionized game with creation of modern farm system while GM of St. Louis Cardinals (1917-42); integrated major leagues in 1947 as president-GM of Brooklyn Dodgers when he brought up Jackie Robinson (whom he had signed on Oct. 23, 1945); later GM of Pittsburgh Pirates.

Leni Riefenstahl (b. Aug. 22, 1902, d. Sept. 8, 2003): German filmmaker of 1930s; directed classic sports documentary "Olympia" on 1936 Berlin Summer Olympics; infamous, however, for also making 1934 Hitler propaganda film "Triumph of the Will."

Roy Riegels (b. Apr. 4, 1908, d. Mar. 26, 1993): Football; California center who picked up fumble in 2nd quarter of 1929 Rose Bowl and raced 70 yards in the wrong direction to set up a 2-point safety in 8-7 loss to Georgia Tech.

Bobby Riggs (b. Feb. 25, 1918, d. Oct. 25, 1995): Tennis; won Wimbledon (1939) and U.S. title twice (1939,41); legendary hustler who made his biggest score in 1973 as 55-year-old male chauvinist challenging the best women players; beat No. 1 Margaret Smith Court 6-2,6-1, but was thrashed by No. 2 Billie Jean King, 6-4,6-3,6-3 in nationally televised "Battle of the Sexes" on Sept. 20, before 30,492 at the Astrodome.

Pat Riley (b. Mar. 20, 1945): Basketball; coached LA Lakers to 4 of their 5 NBA titles in 1980s (1982,85,87-88); coached New York Knicks from 1991-95, then signed with Miami Heat as coach, team president and part-owner; coached Heat to NBA title in 2006; 3-time Coach of Year (1990,93,97); 2nd on list of all-time coaching victories behind Lenny Wilkens.

Cal Ripken Jr. (b. Aug. 24, 1960): Baseball SS; broke Lou Gehrig's major league Iron Man record of 2,130 consecutive games played on Sept. 6, 1995; record streak began on May 30, 1982 and ended Sept. 19, 1998 after 2,632 games; 2-time AL MVP (1983,91) for Baltimore; AL Rookie of Year (1982); AL starter in All-Star Game from 1984-2001; 2-time All-Star Game MVP (1991,2001); holds record for career home runs by a shortstop.

Phil Rizzuto (b. Sept. 25, 1918): Baseball SS; nicknamed "the Scooter"; AL MVP with the Yankees in 1950; 5-time All-Star; retired in 1956 and became Yankees radio and television announcer; elected to the Hall of Fame in 1994.

Oscar Robertson (b. Nov. 24, 1938): Basketball G; 3-time College Player of Year (1958-60) at Cincinnati; led 1960 U.S. Olympic team to gold medal; NBA Rookie of Year (1961); 9-time All-NBA 1st team; MVP in 1964 with Cincinnati Royals; NBA champion in 1971 with Milwaukee Bucks; 6-time annual NBA assist leader; 4th in career assists with 9,887; 8th in career points with 26,710.

Paul Robeson (b. Apr. 8, 1898, d. Jan. 23, 1976): Black 4-sport star and 2-time football All-America (1917-18) at Rutgers; 3-year NFL pro; also scholar, lawyer, singer, actor and political activist; long-tainted by Communist sympathies, he was finally inducted into College Football Hall of Fame in 1995.

Brooks Robinson (b. May 18, 1937): Baseball 3B; led AL in fielding 12 times from 1960-72 with Baltimore; AL MVP in 1964; World Series MVP in 1970; 16 Gold Gloves; entered Hall of Fame in 1983.

David Robinson (b. Aug. 6, 1965): Basketball C; 1987 College Player of Year at Navy; overall 1st pick by San Antonio in 1987 NBA draft; served in military (1987-89); NBA Rookie of Year (1990) and MVP (1995); 2-time All-NBA 1st team (1991,92); led NBA in scoring in 1994; member of 1988, '92 and '96 U.S. Olympic teams; won 2 NBA titles (1999, 2003).

Eddie Robinson (b. Feb. 13, 1919): Football; head coach at Div. I-AA Grambling from 1941-97; retired as winningest coach in college history (408-165-15), since passed by St. John's-Minn. (Div. III) coach John Gagliardi; led Tigers to 8 national black college titles.

Frank Robinson (b. Aug. 31, 1935): Baseball OF; won MVP in NL (1961) and AL (1966); Triple Crown winner and World Series MVP in 1966 with Baltimore; 6th on all-time home run list with 586; 1st black manager in major leagues with Cleveland in 1975; has also managed in San Francisco, Baltimore and Montreal/Washington; served as the league's VP of on-field operations (2000-01).

Jackie Robinson (b. Jan. 31, 1919, d. Oct. 24, 1972): Baseball 1B-2B-3B; 4-sport athlete at UCLA (baseball, basketball, football and track); hit .387 with Kansas City Monarchs of Negro Leagues in 1945; signed by Brooklyn Dodgers' Branch Rickey on Oct. 23, 1945. Played in minors (Montreal) in 1946 and broke Major League Baseball's color line in 1947; Rookie of Year in 1947 and NL's MVP in 1949; hit .311 over 10 seasons. His #42 was retired by Major League Baseball in 1997.

Sugar Ray Robinson (b. May 3, 1921, d. Apr. 12, 1989): Boxer; arguably the greatest pound-for-pound prizefighter of all-time; world welterweight champion (1946-51); 5-time middleweight champ; retired at age 45 with pro record of 174-19-6 (109 KOs).

Knute Rockne (b. Mar. 4, 1888, d. Mar. 31, 1931): Football; coached Notre Dame to 3 consensus national titles (1924,29,30), highest winning percentage in college history (.881) with record of 105-12-5 over 13 seasons; killed in plane crash.

Bill Rodgers (b. Dec. 23, 1947): Distance runner; won Boston and New York City marathons 4 times each from 1975-80.

Dennis Rodman (b. May 13, 1961): Basketball F; superb rebounder and defender; known for dyeing his hair and getting suspended; in 1997, he was suspended for 11 games for kicking a cameraman; led NBA in rebounding 7 straight years (1992-98); won 5 NBA titles with Detroit (1989,90) and Chicago (1996-98); 2-time defensive player of the year (1990-91).

Irina Rodnina (b. Sept. 12, 1949): Soviet figure skater; won 10 world championships and 3 Olympic gold medals in pairs competition from 1969-80.

Alex Rodriguez (b. July 27, 1975): Baseball 3B; led AL in hitting (.358) his first full season in the majors (1996); in 1998 became third player ever with 40 HRs and 40 steals in one season; signed a 10-year, $252m deal (the biggest in U.S. sports history) with Texas in 2000, won AL MVP in 2003; was traded to NY Yankees in 2004 and won AL MVP in 2005.

Juan (Chi Chi) Rodriguez (b. Oct. 23, 1935): Golfer; popular player with 8 PGA Tour victories and 22 Senior Tour wins; 1973 U.S. Ryder Cup Team.

Ronaldo (b. Sept. 22, 1976): Brazilian soccer F; named to the Brazilian National Team when he was 17; 3-time FIFA World Player of the Year (1996,97,2002); European Player of the Year in 1997 and 2002; named 1998 World Cup MVP; led Brazil to World Cup title in 2002, scoring 8 times including both of Brazil's goals in its win over Germany in the final; all-time leading scorer in World Cup history with 15 in 4 World Cups.

Art Rooney (b. Jan. 27, 1901, d. Aug. 25, 1988): Race track legend and pro football pioneer; bought Pittsburgh Steelers franchise in 1933 for $2,500; finally won NFL title with 1st of 4 Super Bowls in 1974 season.

Theodore Roosevelt (b. Oct. 27, 1858, d. Jan. 6, 1919): 26th President of the U.S.; physical fitness buff who boxed as undergraduate at Harvard; credited with presidential assist in forming of Intercollegiate Athletic Assn. (now NCAA) in 1905-06.

Mauri Rose (b. May 26, 1906, d. Jan. 1, 1981): Auto racer; 3-time winner of Indy 500 (1941,47-48).

Murray Rose (b. Jan. 6, 1939): Australian swimmer; won 3 gold medals at 1956 Olympics; added a gold, silver and bronze in 1960.

Pete Rose (b. Apr. 14, 1941): Baseball OF-IF; all-time hits leader with 4,256 and games leader with 3562; led NL in batting 3 times; regular-season MVP in 1973; World Series MVP in 1975; had 44-game hitting streak in '78; managed Cincinnati (1984-89); banned for life in 1989 for conduct detrimental to baseball (betting on baseball); convicted of tax evasion in 1990 and sentenced to 5 months in prison.

Ken Rosewall (b. Nov. 2, 1934): Tennis; won French and Australian singles titles at age 18; U.S. champ twice, but never won Wimbledon.

Mark Roth (b. Apr. 10, 1951): Bowler; 4-time PBA Player of Year (1977-79,84); has 34 tournament wins and over $1.6 million in career earnings.

Alan Rothenberg (b. Apr. 10, 1939): Soccer; president of U.S. Soccer 1990-98; surprised European skeptics by directing hugely successful 1994 World Cup tournament; successfully got oft-delayed outdoor Major League Soccer off ground in 1996.

Chad Rowan (Akebono) (b. May 8, 1969): Sumo Wrestling; 6-foot-9, 510-pound naturalized Japanese citizen born in Hawaii; first foreign grand champion in sumo wrestling's 2,000-year history.

Patrick Roy (b. Oct. 5, 1965): Hockey G; led Montreal to 2 Stanley Cup titles (1986,93) and won 3rd and 4th Cups with Colorado (1996,2001); 3-time playoff MVP (as rookie in 1986,93,2001); won Vezina Trophy 3 times (1989-90,92); led NHL in goals against average 3 times (1989,92,2002); all-time leader in career regular season wins (551) and playoff wins (151).

Pete Rozelle (b. Mar. 1, 1926, d. December 6, 1996): Football; NFL Commissioner from 1960-89; presided over growth of league from 12 to 28 teams, merger with AFL, creation of Super Bowl and advent of huge TV rights fees.

Wilma Rudolph (b. June 23, 1940, d. Nov. 12, 1994): Track & Field; won 3 gold medals (100m, 200m and 4x100m relay) at 1960 Olympics; also won relay silver in '56 Games at age 16; 2-time AP Athlete of Year (1960-61) and Sullivan Award winner in 1961; suffered from polio and wore leg braces until she was 9.

John Ruiz (b. Jan. 4, 1972): Boxer; defeated Evander Holyfield by decision in 2001 for the WBA heavyweight title; the first-ever Hispanic heavyweight champ; lost belt to Roy Jones Jr. on unanimous dec. in 2003.

Damon Runyon (b. Oct. 4, 1884, d. Dec. 10, 1946): Kansas native who gained fame as New York journalist, sports columnist and short-story writer; best known for 1932 story collection, "Guys and Dolls."

Adolph Rupp (b. Sept. 2, 1901, d. Dec. 10, 1977): Basketball; 2nd in all-time college coaching wins with 876; led Kentucky to 4 NCAA championships (1948-49,51,58) and 1 NIT title (1946).

Bill Russell (b. Feb. 12, 1934): Basketball C; won titles in college (with San Francisco in 1955,56), Olympics (1956) and pros; 5-time NBA MVP (1958,61,62,63,65); led Boston Celtics to an amazing 11 titles from 1957-69; 4-time NBA rebound leader (1958-59,64-65); 2nd on all-time rebound list with 21,620; became first black NBA (and major professional sports) head coach in 1966.

Babe Ruth (b. Feb. 6, 1895, d. Aug. 16, 1948): Baseball LHP-OF; two-time 20-game winner with Boston Red Sox (1916-17); had a 94-46 record with a 2.28 ERA; while he was 3-0 in the World Series with an ERA of 0.87; sold to New York Yankees for $100,000 in 1920; AL MVP in 1923; led AL in slugging average 13 times, HRs 12 times, RBI 6 times and batting once (.378 in 1924); hit 60 HRs in 1927 and at least 54 3 other times; ended career with Boston Braves in 1935 with 714 HRs, 2,211 RBI, 2,062 walks and a batting average of .342; remains all-time leader in slugging percentage (.690); member of the Hall of Fame's inaugural class of 1936.

Johnny Rutherford (b. Mar. 12, 1938): Auto racer; 3-time winner of Indy 500 (1974,76,80); CART national champion in 1980.

Nolan Ryan (b. Jan. 31, 1947): Baseball RHP; recorded 7 no-hitters against Kansas City and Detroit (1973), Minnesota (1974), Baltimore (1975), LA Dodgers (1981), Oakland A's (1990) and Toronto (1991 at age 44); 2-time 20-game winner (1973-74); 2-time NL leader in ERA (1981,87); led AL in strikeouts 9 times and NL twice in 27 years; retired after 1993 season with 324 wins, 292 losses and all-time records for strikeouts (5,714) and walks (2,795); number retired by three teams (California, Houston, Texas).

Samuel Ryder (b. Mar. 24, 1858, d. Jan. 2, 1936): Golf; English seed merchant who donated the Ryder Cup in 1927 for competition between pro golfers from Great Britain and the U.S.; made his fortune by coming up with idea of selling seeds in small packages.

Toni Sailer (b. Nov. 17, 1935): Austrian skier; 1st to win 3 alpine gold medals in Winter Olympics— taking downhill, slalom and giant slalom events in 1956.

Alberto Salazar (b. Aug. 7, 1958): Track and Field; broke 12-year-old record at New York Marathon in 1981 and broke Boston Marathon record in 1982; won three straight NY Marathons (1980-82).

Juan Antonio Samaranch (b. July 17, 1920): president of International Olympic Committee (1980-2001); the native of Barcelona was re-elected in 1996 after IOC's move in '95 to bump membership age limit to 80; replaced by Belgian Jacques Rogge.

Pete Sampras (b. Aug. 12, 1971): Tennis; No.1 in world (1993-98); youngest ever U.S. Open men's champ (19 years, 28 days) in 1990; his win at 2002 U.S. Open was record 14th grand slam singles title; won 2 Australian Opens (1994,97), 7 Wimbledons (1993-95, 1997-2000) and 5 U.S. Opens (1990,93, 95-96,2002); career money leader on ATP Tour.

Joan Benoit Samuelson (b. May 16, 1957): Distance runner; won Boston Marathon twice (1979,83); won first women's Olympic marathon in 1984 Games; Sullivan Award recipient in 1985.

Arantxa Sanchez-Vicario (b. Dec. 18, 1971): Spanish tennis player; won 29 singles titles including 3 French Opens (1989,94,98) and 1 U.S. Open (1994); 6 doubles and 4 mixed doubles grand slam titles.

Earl Sande (b. Nov. 13, 1898, d. Aug. 19, 1968): Jockey; rode Gallant Fox to Triple Crown in 1930; won 5 Belmonts and 3 Kentucky Derbies.

Barry Sanders (b. July 16, 1968): Football RB; won 1988 Heisman Trophy as junior at Oklahoma St.; all-time NCAA single season leader in rushing (2,628 yards), scoring (234 points) and TDs (39); 4-time NFL rushing leader with Detroit Lions (1990,94,96,97); NFC Rookie of Year (1988); 2-time NFL Player of Year (1991,97); NFC MVP (1994); rushed for 2,053 yards in 1997; No. 3 all-time rusher (15,269 yds); retired prior to 1999 season; inducted into Pro Football hall of Fame in 2004.

Deion Sanders (b. Aug. 9, 1967): Baseball OF and Football DB-KR-WR; 2-time All-America at Florida St. in football (1987-88); 7-time NFL All-Pro CB with Atlanta, San Fran. and Dallas (1991-94,96-98); led majors in triples (14) with Braves in 1992 and hit .533 in World Series that year; played on 2 Super Bowl winners (SF in XXIX, and Dallas in XXX); first 2-way starter in NFL since 1962 (Chuck Bednarik); only athlete to play in both World Series and Super Bowl.

Cael Sanderson (b. June 20, 1979): Wrestling; first 4-time undefeated NCAA college wrestling champion (1999-2002); went 159-0 during 4-year career at Iowa State; 4-time NCAA Most Outstanding Wrestler; won gold medal at Athens Games in 2004.

Abe Saperstein (b. July 4, 1901, d. Mar. 15, 1966): Basketball; founded all-black, Harlem Globetrotters barnstorming team in 1927; coached sharp-shooting comedians to 1940 world pro title in Chicago and established troupe as game's foremost goodwill ambassadors; also served as 1st commissioner of American Basketball League (1961-62).

Gene Sarazen (b. Feb. 27, 1902, d. May 13, 1999): Golfer; one of only five players to win all four Grand Slam titles (others are Hogan, Nicklaus, Player and Woods); won Masters, British Open, 2 U.S. Opens and 3 PGA titles between 1922-35; invented sand wedge in 1930.

Glen Sather (b. Sept. 2, 1943): Hockey; GM-coach of 4 Stanley Cup winners in Edmonton (1984-85,87-88) and GM-only for another in 1990; ranks 7th on all-time NHL coaching list with 586 wins (including playoffs); entered Hockey Hall of Fame in 1997; named Pres-GM of NY Rangers in 2000.

Terry Sawchuk (b. Dec. 28, 1929, d. May 31, 1970): Hockey G; recorded 103 shutouts in 21 NHL seasons; 4-time Vezina Trophy winner; played on 4 Stanley Cup winners at Detroit and Toronto; posted career 2.52 GAA.

Gale Sayers (b. May 30, 1943): Football HB; 2-time All-America at Kansas; NFL Rookie of Year (1965) and 5-time All-Pro with Chicago; scored then-record 22 TDs in rookie year; led league in rushing twice (1966,69).

Chris Schenkel (b. Aug. 21, 1923, d. Sept. 11, 2005): Radio-TV; 4-time Sportscaster of Year; easy-going baritone who covered basketball, bowling, football, golf and the Olympics for ABC and CBS; host of ABC's Pro Bowlers Tour for 33 years; received lifetime achievement Emmy Award in 1992.

Vitaly Scherbo (b. Jan. 13, 1972): Russian gymnast; winner of unprecedented 6 gold medals in gymnastics, including men's All-Around, for Unified Team in 1992 Olympics; also won 3 bronze in '96 Games.

Curt Schilling (b. Nov. 14, 1966): Baseball RHP; led majors in strikeouts twice (1997-98) with Philadelphia; 3-time 20-game winner with Arizona (2001-02,04); shared 2001 World Series MVP award with teammate Randy Johnson; traded to Boston and helped Red Sox end 86-year championship drought in 2004.

Mike Schmidt (b. Sept. 27, 1949): Baseball 3B; led NL in HRs 8 times; 3-time MVP (1980,81,86) with Philadelphia; 548 career HRs and 10 Gold Gloves; inducted into Hall of Fame in 1995.

Don Schollander (b. Apr. 30, 1946): Swimming; won 4 gold medals at 1964 Olympics, plus one gold and one silver in 1968; won Sullivan Award in 1964.

Dick Schultz (b. Sept. 5, 1929): Reform-minded executive director of NCAA from 1988-93; announced resignation on May 11, 1993 in wake of special investigator's report citing Univ. of Virginia with improper student-athlete loan program during Schultz's tenure as athletic director (1981-87); executive director of USOC 1995-2000.

Michael Schumacher (b. Jan. 3, 1969): German auto racer; Formula One's all-time win leader with 84 grand prix victories (and counting); 7-time world champion (1994-95,2000-04); broke his own F1 single-season record with 13 wins in 2004; announced retirement at the end of the 2006 F1 season.

Bob Seagren (b. Oct. 17, 1946): Track & Field; won gold medal in pole vault at 1968 Olympics; broke world outdoor record 5 times.

Tom Seaver (b. Nov. 17, 1944): Baseball RHP; won 3 Cy Young Awards (1969,73,75); led NL in K 5 times (1970,71,73,75,76); pitched no-hitter in 1978 for Cin.; had 311 wins, 3,640 strikeouts and 2.86 ERA over 20 years.

Peter Seitz (b. May 17, 1905, d. Oct. 17, 1983): Baseball arbitrator; ruled on Dec. 23, 1975 that players who perform for one season without a signed contract can become free agents; decision ushered in big money era for players.

Monica Seles (b. Dec. 2, 1973): Tennis; No. 1 in the world in 1991 and '92 after winning Australian, French and U.S. Opens both years; won 4 Australian, 3 French and 2 US Opens; winner of 30 singles titles in just 5 years before she was stabbed in the back by Steffi Graf fan Gunter Parche on Apr. 30, 1993 during match in Hamburg, Germany; spent remainder of 1993, all of '94 and most of '95 recovering; returned to tennis with win at the 1995 Canadian Open; won 1996 Australian Open; winner of 53 WTA tournaments.

Bud Selig (b. July 30, 1934): Baseball; Milwaukee car dealer who bought AL Seattle Pilots for $10.8 million in 1970 and moved team to Midwest; as de facto commissioner, he presided over 232-day players' strike that resulted in cancellation of World Series for first time since 1904; officially elected baseball's ninth commissioner on July 9, 1998; has overseen many changes in MLB including interleague play, wild card playoffs, and new steroid testing policy.

Frank Selke (b. May 7, 1893, d. July 3, 1985): Hockey; GM of 6 Stanley Cup champions in Montreal (1953,56-60); the annual NHL trophy for best defensive forward bears his name.

Ayrton Senna (b. Mar. 21, 1960, d. May 1, 1994): Brazilian auto racer; 3-time Formula One champion (1988,90-91); died as all-time F1 leader in poles (65) and 2nd in wins (41, currently in 3rd); killed in crash at Imola, Italy during '94 San Marino GP.

Wilbur Shaw (b. Oct. 13, 1902, d. Oct. 30, 1954): Auto racer; 3-time winner and 3-time runner-up of Indy 500 from 1933-1940.

Patty Sheehan (b. Oct. 27, 1956): Golfer; LPGA Player of Year in 1983; clinched entry into LPGA Hall of Fame with her 30th career win in 1993; her 6 major titles include 3 LPGA Champ. (1983-84,93), 2 U.S. Opens (1992,94) 1 Dinah Shore (1996).

Bill Shoemaker (b. Aug. 19, 1931, d. Oct. 12, 2003): Jockey; ranks 2nd all-time in career wins with 8,833 (passed by Laffit Pincay Jr. in Dec. 1999); 3-time Eclipse Award winner as jockey (1981) and special award recipient (1976,81); won 5 Belmonts, 4 Kentucky Derbys and 2 Preaknesses; oldest jockey to win Kentucky Derby (age 54, aboard Ferdinand in 1986); retired in 1990 to become trainer; paralyzed in 1991 auto accident but continued to train horses.

Eddie Shore (b. Nov. 25, 1902, d. Mar. 16, 1985): Hockey D; only NHL defenseman to win Hart Trophy as MVP 4 times (1933,35-36,38); led Boston Bruins to Stanley Cup titles in 1929 and '39; had 105 goals and 1,047 penalty minutes in 14 seasons.

Frank Shorter (b. Oct. 31, 1947): Track & Field; won gold medal in marathon at 1972 Olympics, 1st American to win in 64 years.

Don Shula (b. Jan. 4, 1930): Football; retired after 1995 season with an NFL-record 347 career wins (including playoffs) and a winning percentage of .665; took six teams to Super Bowl and won twice with Miami (VII, VIII); 4-time Coach of Year, twice with Baltimore (1964,68) and twice with Miami (1970-71); coached 1972 Dolphins to 17-0 record, the only undefeated team in NFL history.

Charlie Sifford (b. June 2, 1922): Golf; won the Hartford Open in 1967 with a final-round 64, becoming the first black player to win a PGA event; amassed over $1 million in career earnings; published his autobiography "Just Let Me Play" in 1992.

Al Simmons (b. May 22, 1902, d. May 26, 1956): Baseball OF; led AL in batting twice (1930-31) with Philadelphia A's and knocked in 100 runs or more 11 straight years (1924-34).

O.J. Simpson (b. July 9, 1947): Football RB; won Heisman Trophy in 1968 at USC; ran for 2,003 yards in NFL in 1973; All-Pro 5 times; MVP in 1973; rushed for 11,236 career yards; TV analyst and actor after career ended; arrested June 17, 1994 as suspect in double murder of ex-wife Nicole Brown Simpson and her friend Ronald Goldman; acquitted on Oct. 3, 1995 by a Los Angeles jury in criminal trial but forced to make financial reparations after losing wrongful death suit.

Vijay Singh (b. Feb. 22, 1963): Fijian golfer; temporarily dethroned Tiger Woods as world's top-ranked player in 2004; has 29 career PGA Tour wins including 1998 and 2004 PGA championships and 2000 Masters; 2003-04 PGA Tour money leader.

George Sisler (b. Mar. 24, 1893, d. Mar. 26, 1973): Baseball 1B; hit over .400 twice (1920,22) and batted over .300 in 13 of his 15 seasons; his MLB record of 257 hits (1920) was finally broken by Seattle's Ichiro Suzuki (262) in 2004; played most of his career with the St. Louis Browns; inducted into Baseball Hall of Fame in 1939.

Mary Decker Slaney (b. Aug. 4, 1958): U.S. middle distance runner; has held 7 separate American track & field records from the 800 to 10,000 meters; won both 1,500 and 3,000 meters at 1983 World Championships in Helsinki, but no Olympic medals.

Kelly Slater (b. Feb. 11, 1972): Surfer; 7-time world champion; member of the Surfers' Hall of Fame; started the new school movement of surfing; holds records for being the youngest (1992) and oldest (2005) world champion; earned the only perfect two-wave score at a WCT event, ties for most WCT event wins in a tour season, and in number of career WCT event wins, highest money-earner in the history of the ASP (Association of Surfing Professionals).

Raisa Smetanina (b. Feb. 29, 1952): Russian Nordic skier; all-time leading female Winter Olympics medalist with 10 cross country medals (4 gold, 5 silver and a bronze) in 5 appearances (1976,80,84, 88,92) for USSR and Unified Team.

Billy Smith (b. Dec. 12, 1950): Hockey G; led NY Islanders to 4 consecutive Stanley Cups (1980-83); won Vezina Trophy in 1982; Stanley Cup MVP in 1983.

Dean Smith (b. Feb. 28, 1931): Basketball; No. 1 on all-time NCAA coaches victory list (879 wins); led North Carolina to 25 NCAA tournaments in 34 years, reaching Final Four 10 times and winning championship twice (1982,93); coached U.S. Olympic team to gold medal in 1976.

Emmitt Smith (b. May 15, 1969): Football RB; NFL's all-time leading rusher (18,355 yards); also holds all-time record for rushing TDs (164); 4-time NFL rushing leader (1991-93,95); 11 straight 1,000-yard seasons (1991-2001) with Dallas Cowboys; regular season and Super Bowl MVP in 1993; played on three Super Bowl champions (1993,94,96).

John Smith (b. Aug. 9, 1965): Wrestler; 2-time NCAA champion for Oklahoma St. at 134 lbs (1987-88) and Most Outstanding Wrestler of '88 championships; 3-time world champion; gold medal winner at 1988 and '92 Olympics at 137 lbs; won Sullivan Award (1990); coached Oklahoma St. to 1994 NCAA title and brother Pat was Most Outstanding Wrestler.

Lee Smith (b. Dec. 4, 1957): Baseball RHP; 3-time NL saves leader (1983,91-92); retired as all-time saves leader with 478 (since passed by T. Hoffman); 10 seasons with 30+ saves, 3 times saved over 40.

Michelle Smith deBruin (b. Apr. 7, 1969): Irish swimmer; won three gold medals at the 1996 Olympics; accused of using performance-enhancing drugs but passed all tests until she was suspended for 4 years by FINA in 1998 for tampering with a urine sample.

Ozzie Smith (b. Dec. 26, 1954): Baseball SS; won 13 straight Gold Gloves (1980-92); played in 12 straight All-Star Games (1981-92); MVP of 1985 NL playoffs; all-time MLB assist leader (8,375); inducted into Baseball Hall of Fame in 2002.

Walter (Red) Smith (b. Sept. 25, 1905, d. Jan. 15, 1982): Sportswriter for newspapers in Philadelphia and New York from 1936-82; won Pulitzer Prize for commentary in 1976.

Conn Smythe (b. Feb. 1, 1895, d. Nov. 18, 1980): Hockey pioneer; built Maple Leaf Gardens in 1931; managed Toronto to 7 Stanley Cups.

Sam Snead (b. May 27, 1912, d. May 23, 2002): Golfer; won both Masters and PGA 3 times and British Open once; runner-up in U.S. Open 4 times; PGA Player of Year in 1949; oldest player (52 years, 10 months) to win PGA event with Greater Greensboro Open title in 1965; all-time PGA Tour career victory leader with 82.

Peter Snell (b. Dec. 17, 1938): Track & Field; New Zealander who won gold medal in 800m at 1960 Olympics, then won both the 800m and 1,500m at 1964 Games.

Duke Snider (b. Sept. 19, 1926): Baseball OF; hit 40 or more home runs five straight seasons (1953-57); led the league in runs scored 1953-55; played in six World Series with the Dodgers and batted .286 with 11 home runs; nicknamed "Duke of Flatbush"; in 18 seasons hit 407 home runs, scored 1,259 runs and had 1,333 RBI.

Annika Sorenstam (b. Oct. 9, 1970): Swedish golfer; has won 10 women's majors; 8-time Rolex Player of the Year (1995,97-98, 2001-05); shot an LPGA-record 59 in round 2 of the 2001 Standard Register Ping; LPGA all-time leading money winner; in 2003 she became first woman in 58 years to play on men's PGA Tour (via a sponsor's exemption); shot 71-74 but missed the cut at the Colonial by 4 strokes.

Sammy Sosa (b. Nov. 12, 1968): Baseball OF; slugging Chicago Cub who surpassed Roger Maris' season home run record (61), just after Mark McGwire did in 1998 and finished the year with 66; followed that up with seasons of 63, 50 and 64 HRs; 1998 NL MVP; 7-time All-Star; 588 career homers.

Javier Sotomayor (b. Oct. 13, 1967): Cuban high jumper; first man to clear 8 feet (8-0) on July 29, 1989; won gold medal at 1992 Olympics with jump of only 7-ft, 8-in.; broke world record with leap of 8-0½ in 1993; had a controversial drug suspension reduced, which allowed him to participate in 2000 Olympics; won the silver medal in Sydney with a leap of 7-7¼.

Warren Spahn (b. Apr. 23, 1921, d. Nov. 23, 2003): Baseball LHP; led NL in wins 8 times; won 20 or more games 13 times; Cy Young winner in 1957; most career wins (363) by a lefthander.

Tris Speaker (b. Apr. 4, 1888, d. Dec. 8, 1958): Baseball OF; all-time leader in outfield assists (449) and doubles (792); had .344 career BA and 3,515 hits.

J.G. Taylor Spink (b. Nov. 6, 1888, d. Dec. 7, 1962): Publisher of *The Sporting News* from 1914-62; BBWAA annual meritorious service award named after him.

Leon Spinks (b. July 11, 1953): Boxing; won heavyweight crown in split decision over Muhammad Ali in Feb. 1978; Ali regained title seven months later; won gold medal in light heavyweight division at 1976 Olympics; brother Michael won the heavyweight title in 1983; were the only brothers to hold world titles; known more for frequent traffic violations and lavish lifestyle than bouts late in career; filed for bankruptcy in 1986.

Mark Spitz (b. Feb. 10, 1950): American swimmer; set 23 world and 35 U.S. records; won all-time record 7 gold medals (4 individual, 3 relay) in 1972 Olympics; also won 4 medals (2 gold, a silver and a bronze) in 1968 Games for a total of 11; comeback attempt at age 41 foundered in 1991.

Latrell Sprewell (b. Sept. 8, 1970): Basketball G; former NBA All-Star who made headlines in 1997 for attacking Golden State Warriors head coach P.J. Carlesimo during a practice.

Lyn St. James (b. Mar. 13, 1947): Auto racer; one of just 4 women to qualify for the Indianapolis 500; best finish in the race came in 1992 when she came in 11th and won Indianapolis 500 Rookie of the Year.

Amos Alonzo Stagg (b. Aug. 16, 1862, d. Mar. 17, 1965): Football innovator; coached at U. of Chicago for 41 seasons and College of the Pacific for 14 more; 314-199-35 record; elected to both college football and basketball Halls of Fame.

Willie Stargell (b. Mar. 6, 1940, d. Apr. 9, 2001): Baseball OF-1B; "Pops"; led NL in home runs twice (1971,73); 475 career HRs; NL co-MVP and World Series MVP in 1979.

Bart Starr (b. Jan. 9, 1934): Football QB; led Green Bay to 5 NFL titles and 2 Super Bowl wins from 1961-67; regular season MVP in 1966; MVP of Super Bowls I and II.

Roger Staubach (b. Feb. 5, 1942): Football QB; Heisman Trophy winner as Navy junior in 1963; led Dallas to 2 Super Bowl titles (1972,78) and was Super Bowl MVP in 1972; 5-time leading passer in NFC (1971,73,77-79).

George Steinbrenner (b. July 4, 1930): Baseball; principal owner of NY Yankees since 1973; teams have won 10 pennants and 6 World Series (1977-78,96,98,99,00); has changed managers 21 times and GMs 11 times in 31 years; ordered by baseball commish Fay Vincent in 1990 to surrender control of club for dealings with small-time gambler; reinstated in 1993.

Casey Stengel (b. July 30, 1890, d. Sept. 29, 1975): Baseball; player for 14 years and manager for 25; outfielder and lifetime .284 hitter with 5 clubs (1912-25); guided NY Yankees to 10 AL pennants and 7 World Series titles from 1949-60; 1st NY Mets skipper from 1962-65.

Ingemar Stenmark (b. Mar. 18, 1956): Swedish alpine skier; 3-time World Cup overall champ (1976-78); posted 86 World Cup wins in 16 years; won 2 gold medals at 1980 Olympics.

Helen Stephens (b. Feb. 3, 1918, d. Jan. 17, 1994): Track & Field; set 3 world records in 100-yard dash and 4 more in 100 meters in 1935-36; won gold medals in 100 meters and 4x100-meter relay in 1936 Olympics; retired in 1937.

Woody Stephens (b. Sept. 1, 1913, d. Aug. 22, 1998): Horse racing; trainer who saddled an unprecedented 5 straight winners in Belmont Stakes (1982-86); also had two Kentucky Derby winners (1974,84) and one Preakness winner (1952); trained 1982 Horse of Year Conquistador Cielo; won Eclipse award as nation's top trainer in 1983.

David Stern (b. Sept. 22, 1942): Basketball; marketing expert and NBA commissioner since 1984; took office the year Michael Jordan turned pro; league has grown from 23 teams to 30 during his watch and opened offices worldwide; oversaw launch of WNBA in 1997.

Teófilo Stevenson (b. Mar. 29, 1952): Cuban boxer; won 3 consecutive gold medals as Olympic heavyweight (1972,76,80); was denied a chance to win a fourth when Cuba boycotted 1984 Los Angeles Games; did not turn pro.

Jackie Stewart (b. June 11, 1939): Auto racer; won 27 Formula One races and 3 world driving titles from 1965-73.

John Stockton (b. Mar. 26, 1962): Basketball G; all-time NBA leader in every major assist category, including most in a season (1,164) and most in a career (15,806); also the NBA's all-time leader in steals (3,265); All-NBA team in '94 and '95; member of 1992 and '96 US Olympic basketball teams; 10-time All-Star; played 19 seasons with Utah Jazz—18 of them with Karl Malone—perfecting the pick and roll.

Curtis Strange (b. Jan. 30, 1955): Golfer; won consecutive U.S. Open titles (1988-89); 3-time leading money winner on PGA Tour (1985,87-88); first PGA player to win $1 million in one year (1988); captain of the 2002 U.S. Ryder Cup team.

Picabo Street (b. Apr. 3, 1971): Skiing; 2-time Olympic medalist, gold (Super G in 1998) and silver (downhill in 1994); her 1995 World Cup downhill series title first-ever by U.S. woman, she repeated the feat in 1996.

Kerri Strug (b. Nov. 19, 1977): Gymnastics; delivered the most dramatic moment of the 1996 Summer Olympics when she completed a vault (9.712) after spraining her ankle; the second vault helped assure the first all-around gold medal for a US Women's gymnastics team.

Louise Suggs (b. Sept. 7, 1923): Golfer; won 11 majors and 58 LPGA events overall from 1949-62; founder and charter member of the LPGA; first woman elected to LPGA Hall of Fame (1951).

James E. Sullivan (b. Nov. 18, 1862, d. Sept. 16, 1914): Track & Field; pioneer who founded Amateur Athletic Union (AAU) in 1888; director of St. Louis Olympic Games in 1904; AAU's annual Sullivan Award for performance and sportsmanship named after him.

John L. Sullivan (b. Oct. 15, 1858, d. Feb. 2, 1918): Boxer; nicknamed "The Boston Strong Boy"; world heavyweight champion (1882-92); last of bare-knuckle champions, beating Jake Kilrain after 75 rounds in 1889; was knocked out by "Gentleman" Jim Corbett in the 21st round in 1892, never fought again.

Pat Summitt (b. June 14, 1952): Basketball; women's basketball coach at Tennessee (1974—); entered 2006-07 season as all-time leader in career victories with 913; coached 1984 US women's basketball team to its first Olympic gold medal; has coached Lady Vols to 6 national championships (1987, 89,91,96,97,98); her Lady Vols have made 9 of last 12 Final Fours.

Don Sutton (b. April 2, 1945): Baseball RHP; won 324 games and tossed 58 shutouts in his 23-year career; recorded NL record five career 1-hitters; played with Dodgers, Astros, Brewers, Athletics, Angels and was a 4-time All-Star; elected to Hall of Fame in 1998.

Ichiro Suzuki (b. Oct. 22, 1973): Baseball OF; became the 2nd player (Fred Lynn) to win AL Rookie of the Year and MVP in same year (2001); 1st Japanese-born position player to play in MLB; won 7 consecutive Japanese batting titles (1994-2000) and has won two more in AL with Seattle (2001,04); broke George Sisler's 84-year-old hits record with 262 in 2004.

Lynn Swann (b. Mar. 7, 1952): Football WR; played nine seasons with Pittsburgh (1974-82); appeared in four Super Bowls and had 16 catches for 364 yards and three TDs; named MVP of Super Bowl X for 4 catch, 161 yard, 1 TD performance.

Barry Switzer (b. Oct. 5, 1937): Football; coached Oklahoma to 3 national titles (1974-75,85); 4th on all-time winning pct list at .837 (157-29-4); resigned in 1989 after OU was slapped with 3-year NCAA probation; hired as Dallas Cowboys head coach in 1994 and led team to victory in Super Bowl XXX in 1996.

Sheryl Swoopes (b. Mar. 25, 1971): Basketball; forward for WNBA's Houston Comets; 4-time WNBA regular season MVP (2000,02,03,05); 3-time Olympic gold medalist (1996,2000,2004); led Texas Tech to Div. I NCAA championship in 1993; consensus National Player of the Year in 1993.

Paul Tagliabue (b. Nov. 24, 1940): Football; NFL attorney who was elected league's 4th commissioner in 1989 and served until his retirement in 2006; ushered in salary cap in 1994; the league expanded from 28 teams to 32 in his tenure.

Anatoli Tarasov (b. 1918, d. June 23, 1995): Hockey; coached Soviet Union to 9 straight world championships and 3 Olympic gold medals (1964, 68,72).

Jerry Tarkanian (b. Aug. 30, 1930): Basketball; amassed 778 wins in 31 years at Long Beach St., UNLV and Fresno St.; led UNLV to 4 Final Fours and 1 national title (1990); fought battle with NCAA over purity of UNLV program; quit as coach after going 26-2 in 1991-92; fired after 20 games (9-11) as coach of NBA San Antonio Spurs in 1992.

Fran Tarkenton (b. Feb. 3, 1940): Football QB; scrambling two-time NFL All-Pro (1973,75); 1975 Player of the Year; threw for 47,003 yards and 342 TDs (both former NFL records) in 18 seasons with Vikings and N.Y. Giants; selected to 9 Pro Bowls; inducted into Pro Football Hall of Fame in 1986.

Chuck Taylor (b. June 24, 1901, d. June 23, 1969): Converse traveling salesman whose name came to grace the classic, high-top canvas basketball sneakers known as "Chucks"; over 750 million pairs have been sold since 1917; he also ran clinics worldwide and edited Converse Basketball Yearbook (1922-68).

Lawrence Taylor (b. Feb. 4, 1959): Football LB; All-America at North Carolina (1980); only defensive player in NFL history to be consensus Player of Year (1986); led N.Y. Giants to Super Bowl titles in 1986 and '90 seasons; played in 10 Pro Bowls (1981-90); retired after 1993 season with 132½ sacks; had several drug-related arrests in retirement; inducted into Hall of Fame in 1999.

Marshall (Major) Taylor (b. Nov. 26, 1878, d. June 21, 1932): Cyclist; Considered one of the first African-American sports heroes; held 7 world cycling records at the turn of the century, racing mostly in Europe, Australia and New Zealand after being barred from many events in the U.S. due to racial prejudices; won the world one-mile championship in 1899.

Gustavo Thoeni (b. Feb. 28, 1951): Italian alpine skier; 4-time World Cup overall champion (1971-73,75); won giant slalom at 1972 Olympics.

Isiah Thomas (b. Apr. 30, 1961): Basketball; led Indiana to NCAA title as sophomore and Final 4 MOP in 1981; consensus All-America guard in '81; led Detroit to 2 NBA titles (1989,1990); NBA Finals MVP in 1990; 3-time All-NBA 1st team (1984-86); elected to Hall of Fame in 2000; currently president and head coach of the N.Y. Knicks.

Thurman Thomas (b. May 16, 1966): Football RB; 3-time AFC rushing leader (1990-91,93); 2-time All-Pro (1990-91); 1991 NFL Player of Year; led Buffalo to 4 straight Super Bowls (1991-94).

Daley Thompson (b. July 30, 1958): British Track & Field; won consecutive gold medals in decathlon at 1980 and '84 Olympics.

Jenny Thompson (b. Feb. 26, 1973): American swimmer; 8-time Olympic gold medalist (all in relays) and winner of 12 Olympic medals overall, more than any other American; competed in 5 Olympic Games (1988,92,96,2000,04).

John Thompson (b. Sept. 2, 1941): Basketball; coached centers Patrick Ewing, Alonzo Mourning and Dikembe Mutombo at Georgetown; reached NCAA tourney final 3 out of 4 years with Ewing, winning title in 1984; also led Hoyas to 6 Big East tourney titles; coached 1988 U.S. Olympic team to bronze medal; retired abruptly during 1999 season with 27-year mark of 596-239.

Bobby Thomson (b. Oct. 25, 1923): Baseball OF; career .270 hitter who won the 1951 NL pennant for the NY Giants with a 1-out, 3-run HR in the bottom of the 9th inning of Game 3 of a best-of-3 playoff with Brooklyn; the pitcher was Ralph Branca, the count was 0-1 and the Dodgers were ahead 4-2; the Giants had trailed Brooklyn by 13½ games on Aug. 11.

Ian Thorpe (b. Oct. 13, 1982): Australian swimmer; 5-time gold medalist; won 400m free at Sydney Olympics (breaking his own world record) and silver in 200m free; won gold and broke the world record in the 4x100m and 4x200 free relays; won 200m free and 400m free Olympic gold at Athens in 2004; 2002 Jesse Owens Award winner.

Jim Thorpe (b. May 28, 1887, d. Mar. 28, 1953): Native American multi-sport superstar; 2-time All-America halfback at Carlisle; won both pentathlon and decathlon gold medals at 1912 Olympics; stripped of medals a month later for playing semi-pro baseball prior to Games (medals restored in 1982); played major league baseball (1913-19) and pro football (1920-26,28); became first president of NFL (then known as the APFA) in 1920; chosen "Athlete of the Half Century" by AP in 1950.

Bill Tilden (b. Feb. 10, 1893, d. June 5, 1953): Tennis; won 7 U.S. and 3 Wimbledon titles in 1920s; led U.S. to 7 straight Davis Cup victories (1920-26).

Tinker to Evers to Chance Chicago Cubs double play combination from 1903-10; immortalized in poem by New York sportswriter Franklin P. Adams—SS Joe Tinker (1880-1948), 2B Johnny Evers (1883-1947) and 1B Frank Chance (1877-1924); all 3 managed the Cubs and made the Hall of Fame.

Y.A. Tittle (b. Oct. 24, 1926): Football QB; Yelberton Abraham Tittle played 17 years in AAFC and NFL; All-Pro 4 times; league MVP with San Francisco (1957) and NY Giants (1962, 63); passed for 28,339 career yards.

Alberto Tomba (b. Dec. 19, 1966): Italian alpine skier; winner of 5 Olympic medals (3 gold, 2 silver); became 1st alpine skier to win gold medals in 2 consecutive Winter Games when he won the slalom and giant slalom in 1988 then repeated in the GS in '92.

Dara Torres (b. April 15, 1967): Swimmer; her 9 career Olympic medals (4G, 1S, 4B) are the 2nd-most for an American woman.

Vladislav Tretiak (b. Apr. 25, 1952): Hockey G; led USSR to Olympic gold medals in 1972 and '76; starred for Soviets against Team Canada in 1972, and again in 2 Canada Cups (1976,81).

Lee Trevino (b. Dec. 1, 1939): Golfer; 2-time winner of 3 majors—U.S. Open (1968, 71), British Open (1971-72) and PGA (1974,84); PGA Tour Player of the Year (1971) and 3 times with Seniors (1990,92,94); 29 PGA Tour and 29 Champions Tour wins.

Felix Trinidad (b. Jan. 10, 1973): Puerto Rican boxer; former WBC/IBF welterweight champion; won WBC belt with a maj. dec. over Oscar De La Hoya in 1999; stepped up to jr. middleweight and won the WBA title from David Reid in 2000; moved to middleweight and suffered a 12th-round TKO to Bernard Hopkins in 2001 then retired; KO'd Ricardo Mayorga in 2004 comeback fight; lost to Winky Wright in 2005.

Bryan Trottier (b. July 17, 1956): Hockey C; led NY Islanders to 4 straight Stanley Cups (1980-83); Rookie of Year (1976); scoring champion (134 points) and regular season MVP in 1979; playoff MVP (1980); added 5th and 6th Cups with Pittsburgh in 1991 and '92; entered Hockey Hall of Fame in 1997.

Gene Tunney (b. May 25, 1897, d. Nov. 7, 1978): Boxer; world heavyweight champion from 1926-28; beat 31-year-old champ Jack Dempsey in unanimous 10 round decision in 1926; beat him again in famous "long count" rematch in '27; quit while still champion in 1928 with 65-1-1 record and 47 KOs.

Ted Turner (b. Nov. 19, 1938): Sportsman and TV mogul; skippered Courageous to America's Cup win in 1977; one-time owner of MLB Braves, NBA Hawks and NHL Thrashers; founder of CNN, TNT and TBS; founder of Goodwill Games; 1991 Time Man of Year.

Mike Tyson (b. June 30, 1966): Boxer; youngest (19) heavyweight champion ever (WBC in 1986); undisputed champ from 1987 until upset loss to 42-1 shot Buster Douglas on Feb. 10, 1990, in Tokyo; found guilty on Feb. 10, 1992, of raping 18-year-old Miss Black America contestant Desiree Washington in Indianapolis on July 19, 1991; sentenced to 6-year prison term; released May 9, 1995 after serving 3 years; reclaimed WBC and WBA belts with wins over Frank Bruno and Bruce Seldon in 1996; lost WBA title to Evander Holyfield in 1996; he bit Holyfield's ear twice during their 1997 WBA title rematch; was KO'd in 8th round by Lennox Lewis in 2002.

Wyomia Tyus (b. Aug. 29, 1945): Track & Field; 1st woman to win consecutive Olympic gold medals in 100m (1964-68).

Peter Ueberroth (b. Sept. 2, 1937): Organizer of 1984 Summer Olympics in LA; 1984 *Time* Man of Year; baseball commissioner from 1984-89; headed Rebuild Los Angeles for one year after 1992 riots; currently chairman of USOC.

Johnny Unitas (b. May 7, 1933, d. Sept. 11, 2002): Football QB; Big-game field general who led Baltimore Colts to 2 NFL titles (1958-59) and a Super Bowl win (1971); All-Pro 5 times; 3-time MVP (1959,64,67); selected to 10 Pro Bowls; passed for 40,239 career yards and 290 TDs.

Al Unser Jr. (b. Apr. 19, 1962): Auto racer; 2-time CART-IndyCar national champion (1990,94); 2-time Indy 500 winer (1992,94), giving Unser family 9 overall titles at the Brickyard; retired in 2004 with 31 CART wins in 19 years; left CART for Indy Racing League in 2000; son of Al and nephew of Bobby.

Al Unser Sr. (b. May 29, 1939): Auto racer; 3-time USAC-CART national champion (1970,83,85); 4-time winner of Indy 500 (1970-71,78,87); retired in 1994 with 39 wins; younger brother of Bobby and father of Al Jr.

Bobby Unser (b. Feb. 20, 1934): Auto racer; 2-time USAC-CART national champion (1968,74); 3-time winner of Indy 500 (1968,75,81); retired after 1981 season; fifth all-time with 35 career wins.

Gene Upshaw (b. Aug. 15, 1945): Football RB; 2-time All-AFL and 3-time All-NFL selection with Oakland; helped lead Raiders to 2 Super Bowl titles in 1976 and '80 seasons; executive director of NFL Players Assn. since 1987; agreed to application of salary cap in 1994.

Jim Valvano (b. Mar. 10, 1946, d. Apr. 28, 1993): Basketball; coach at N.C. State whose team upset Houston to win national title in 1983; in 19 seasons as a coach appeared in 8 NCAA tournaments; twice voted ACC Coach of the Year; career record 346-212; at N.C. State (1986-89) when a recruiting and admissions scandal forced him out of the job; worked as a broadcaster for ESPN and ABC; died after a year-long battle with cancer; The V Foundation for cancer research is named for him.

Norm Van Brocklin (b. Mar. 15, 1926, d. May 2, 1983): Football QB-P; led NFL in passing 3 times and punting twice; led LA Rams (1951) and Philadelphia (1960) to NFL titles; MVP in 1960.

Amy Van Dyken (b. Feb. 17, 1973): Swimming; first American woman to win four gold medals in one Olympics (1996); won the individual 50m freestyle, 100m butterfly, and was on the US team for the 4x100 freestyle and 4x50 medley; won gold at Sydney in 2000 as part of the US 4x100 freestyle relay.

Johnny Vander Meer (b. Nov. 2, 1914, d. Oct. 6, 1997): Baseball LHP; only major leaguer to pitch consecutive no-hitters (June 11 & 15, 1938).

Harold S. Vanderbilt (b. July 6, 1884, d. July 4, 1970): Sportsman; successfully defended America's Cup 3 times (1930, 34,37); also invented contract bridge in 1926.

Glenna Collett Vare (b. June 20, 1903, d. Feb. 10, 1989): Golfer; won record 6 U.S. Women's Amateur titles from 1922-35; "the female Bobby Jones."

Andy Varipapa (b. Mar. 31, 1891, d. Aug. 25, 1984): Bowler; trick-shot artist; won consecutive All-Star match game titles (1947-48) at age 55 and 56.

Bill Veeck (b. Feb. 9, 1914, d. Jan. 2, 1986): Maverick baseball executive; owned AL teams in Cleveland, St. Louis and Chicago from 1946-80; introduced ballpark giveaways, exploding scoreboards, Wrigley Field's ivy-covered walls and midget Eddie Gaedel; won World Series with Indians (1948) and pennant with White Sox (1959).

Jacques Villeneuve (b. Apr. 9, 1971): Canadian auto racer; won Indy 500 and IndyCar driving championship in 1995; jumped to Formula One racing in 1996 and won the F1 title in 1997.

Fay Vincent (b. May 29, 1938): Baseball; became 8th commissioner after death of A. Bartlett Giamatti in 1989; presided over World Series earthquake, owners' lockout and banishment of NY Yankees owner George Steinbrenner in his first year on the job; contentious relationship with owners resulted in his resignation on Sept. 7, 1992, four days after 18-9 "no confidence" vote.

Lasse Viren (b. July 22, 1949): Finnish runner; won gold medals at 5,000 and 10,000 meters in 1972 Munich Olympics; repeated 5,000/10,000 double in 1976 Games and added a fifth place finish in the marathon.

Dick Vitale (b. June 9, 1939): Broadcaster; Radio and television commentator for ESPN and ABC Sports known for his enthusiastic, almost spastic style; had successful college and pro basketball coaching career with the University of Detroit (1973-77) and the Detroit Pistons (1978-79).

Lanny Wadkins (b. Dec. 5, 1949): Golfer; member of 8 U.S. Ryder Cup teams and captain of 1995 team; won 1977 PGA Championship; 21 career PGA Tour wins.

Honus Wagner (b. Feb. 24, 1874, d. Dec. 6, 1955): Baseball SS; hit .300 for 17 consecutive seasons (1897-1913) with Louisville and Pittsburgh; led NL in batting 8 times; ended career with 3,430 career hits, a .329 average and 722 stolen bases.

Lisa Wagner (b. May 19, 1961): Bowler; 4-time LPBT Player of Year (1983,86,88,93); 1980's Bowler of Decade; first woman to earn $100,000 in a season; winner of 32 pro titles.

Grete Waitz (b. Oct. 1, 1953): Norwegian runner; 9-time winner of New York City Marathon from 1978-88; won silver medal at 1984 Olympics.

Jersey Joe Walcott (b. Jan. 31, 1914, d. Feb. 27, 1994): Boxer; oldest heavyweight (37) to win the championship (until George Foreman beat his record in 1994); lost four championship bouts before knocking out Ezzard Charles in the seventh round in 1951; lost the title the following year to Rocky Marciano; won 50 bouts, 30 by knockout, lost 17 and fought one draw as a professional; later became sheriff of Camden County, NJ.

Doak Walker (b. Jan. 1, 1927, d. Sept. 27, 1998): Football HB; won Heisman Trophy as SMU junior in 1948; led Detroit to 2 NFL titles (1952-53); All-Pro 4 times in 6 years.

Herschel Walker (b. Mar. 3, 1962): Football RB; led Georgia to national title as freshman in 1980; won Heisman in 1982 then jumped to upstart USFL in '83; signed by Dallas Cowboys after USFL folded; led NFL in rushing in 1988; traded to Minnesota in 1989 for 5 players and 6 draft picks.

Rusty Wallace (b. Aug. 14, 1956): Auto racing; NASCAR Winston Cup champion in 1989 and runner-up in 1980, 1988 and 1993; recorded 55 victories and won over $40 million in earnings in more than 25 years of racing; currently a racing analyst for ESPN.

Bill Walsh (b. Nov. 30, 1931): Football; Hall of Fame coach and GM of 3 Super Bowl winners with San Francisco (1982,85,89); retired after 1989 Super Bowl; returned to college coaching in 1992 for his second stint at Stanford; retired again after 1994 season; returned as 49er GM from 1999-2001.

Bill Walton (b. Nov. 5, 1952): Basketball C; 3-time College Player of Year (1972-74); led UCLA to 2 national titles (1972-73); led Portland to NBA title as MVP in 1977; regular season MVP in 1978; won 1986 NBA title with Boston.

Darrell Waltrip (b. Feb. 5, 1947): Auto racing; 3-time NASCAR Winston Cup champion (1981,82,85); 84 career Winston Cup wins and 59 poles.

Arch Ward (b. Dec. 27, 1896, d. July 9, 1955): Promoter and sports editor of *Chicago Tribune* from 1930-55; founder of baseball All-Star Game (1933), Chicago College All-Star Football Game (1934) and the All-America Football Conference (1946-49).

Charlie Ward (b. Oct. 12, 1970): Football QB and Basketball G; 1993 Heisman winner with national champion Florida St.; won Sullivan Award (1993); 3-year starter for FSU basketball team; 1st round pick of NY Knicks in 1994 NBA draft.

Glenn (Pop) Warner (b. Apr. 5, 1871, d. Sept. 7, 1954): Football innovator; coached at 7 colleges over 49 years; 319 career wins, 4th all-time; produced 47 All-Americas, including Jim Thorpe and Ernie Nevers.

Kurt Warner (b. June 22, 1971): Football QB; former Arena leaguer who led the St. Louis Rams to 2000 Super Bowl win; threw for a record 414 yards and was Super Bowl MVP; 2-time NFL MVP (1999,2001).

Tom Watson (b. Sept. 4, 1949): Golfer; 6-time PGA Player of the Year (1977-80,82,84); has won 5 British Opens, 2 Masters and a U.S. Open; 4-time Ryder Cup member and captain of 1993 team; 39 PGA tour wins; 8 Champions tour wins.

Danny Way (b. Apr. 15, 1974): Skateboarder; conceived the Megaramp (2002) and brought the Big Air event to the X Games (2004); set world records for longest distance jumped (79 feet–2004), height out of a ramp (23.5 feet– 2003), and highest bomb drop (28 feet–2006, from the guitar outside the Hard Rock Hotel in Las Vegas); first person to jump over the Great Wall of China without motorized aid (2005), two-time Thrasher Magazine Skater of the Year (1991, 2004).

Earl Weaver (b. Aug. 14, 1930): Baseball; managed the Baltimore Orioles to 6 Eastern Division titles, four AL pennants and a World Series victory in 1970; was ejected 91 times and suspended four times for outbursts against umpires; record of 1,480-1,060 from 1968-82 and 1985-86.

Alan Webb (b. Jan. 13, 1983): Track; on May 27, 2001 at the Prefontaine Classic, he ran a mile in 3:53.43 to break Jim Ryun's 36-year-old national high school record.

Karrie Webb (b. Dec. 21, 1974): Australian golfer; youngest woman (26) to win career Grand Slam; her win in the 2002 British Open made her the first player to win the "Super Grand Slam" (5 different majors) and gave her 6 major titles; won the 2006 Kraft Nabisco Championship to make it 7 majors; 2-time Rolex Player of the Year (1999-2000); entered Hall of Fame in 2005.

Dick Weber (b. Dec. 23, 1929, d. Feb. 13, 2005): Bowler; 3-time PBA Bowler of the Year (1961,63,65); won 30 PBA titles in 4 decades; father of Pete.

Pete Weber (b. Aug. 21, 1962): Bowler; 2nd on all-time PBA money list; 1990 PBA Rookie of the Year; inducted into PBA Hall of Fame (1998); has 31 PBA titles; son of Dick.

Johnny Weissmuller (b. June 2, 1904, d. Jan. 20 1984): American swimmer; won 3 gold medals (100m free, 400m free, 4x200m free) at 1924 Olympics and 2 more at 1928 Games (100m free and 4x200m free); set 51 world records; became Hollywood's most famous Tarzan.

Jerry West (b. May 28, 1938): Basketball G; 2-time All-America and NCAA Final 4 MOP (1959) at West Virginia; led 1960 U.S. Olympic team to gold medal; 10-time All-NBA 1st-team; NBA finals MVP (1969); led LA Lakers to NBA title once as player (1972) and then 6 more times (1980,82,85,87,88,00) as an executive in various positions with the club; hired as President of Basketball Ops. by Memphis Grizzlies in 2002; his silhouette serves as the NBA's logo.

Pernell Whitaker (b. Jan. 2, 1964): Boxer; won Olympic gold medal as lightweight in 1984; won 4 world championships as lightweight, jr. welterweight, welterweight and jr. middleweight; outfought but failed to beat Julio Cesar Chavez when 1993 welterweight title defense ended in controversial draw; pro record of 41-3-1 (17 KOs); nicknamed "Sweet Pea".

Bill White (b. Jan. 28, 1934): Baseball; former NL president and highest ranking black executive in sports from 1989-94; as 1st baseman, won 7 Gold Gloves and hit .286 with 202 HRs in 13 seasons.

Byron (Whizzer) White (b. June 8, 1917, d. Apr. 15, 2002): Football; All-America HB at Colorado (1937); signed with Pittsburgh in 1938 for the then largest contract in pro history ($15,800); took Rhodes Scholarship in 1939; returned to NFL in 1940 to lead league in rushing and retired in 1941; named to U.S. Supreme Court by President Kennedy in 1962 and stepped down in 1993.

Reggie White (b. Dec. 19, 1961, d. Dec. 26, 2004): Football DE; consensus All-America in 1983 at Tennessee; 7-time All-NFL (1986-92) with Philadelphia; won Super Bowl with Green Bay in 1997; 2nd all-time in NFL sacks (198).

Shaun White (b. Sept. 3, 1986): Snowboarder/Skateboarder; first athlete to compete in both Winter and Summer X Games; winner of 9 combined X Games medals; won an Olympic gold medal in 2006 for Halfpipe; won 2 Winter X Games gold medals in Slopestyle and SuperPipe (2003, 2006); nicknamed "The Flying Tomato."

Kathy Whitworth (b. Sept. 27, 1939): Golf; 7-time LPGA Player of the Year (1966-69,71-73); won 6 majors; 88 tour wins, most on LPGA or PGA tour.

Hoyt Wilhelm (b. July 26, 1923, d. Aug. 23, 2002): Baseball RHP; Knuckleballer who is 1st in games finished (651) and games won in relief (123); career ERA of 2.52 and 227 saves; 1st reliever inducted into Hall of Fame (1985); threw no-hitter vs. NY Yankees (1958); hit lone HR of career in first major league at bat (1952); won Purple Heart at Battle of the Bulge.

Lenny Wilkens (b. Oct. 28, 1937): Basketball; NBA's all-time winningest coach; MVP of 1960 NIT as Providence guard; played 15 years in NBA, including 4 as player-coach; 9-time All-Star and MVP of 1971 game; coached Seattle to 1979 NBA title; Coach of Year in 1994 with Atlanta; career record of 1412-1253 including playoffs with 7 NBA teams; coached USA basketball team to gold medal in 1996; member of the basketball hall of fame as player *and* coach.

Dominique Wilkins (b. Jan. 12, 1960): Basketball F; prolific scorer and ferocious dunker who led NBA in scoring (30.3 ppg) in 1986 with Atlanta; All-NBA 1st team in 1986; 2-time NBA slam dunk champion; nicknamed "The Human Highlight Film"; inducted into Basketball Hall of Fame in 2006.

Bud Wilkinson (b. Apr. 23, 1916, d. Feb. 9, 1994): Football; played on 1936 national championship team at Minnesota; coached Oklahoma to 3 national titles (1950, 55, 56); won 4 Orange and 2 Sugar Bowls; teams had winning streaks of 47 (1953-57) and 31 (1948-50); retired after 1963 season with 145-29-4 record in 17 years; also coached St. Louis of NFL to 9-20 record from 1978-79.

Ricky Williams (b. May 21, 1977): Football RB; became all-time NCAA Div. I-A leader in rushing yards (6,279) and TDs (75) at Texas but has been passed in both categories; 1998 Heisman Trophy winner; 5th overall in 1999 NFL draft by Saints; traded to Miami in 2002; stunned teammates when he retired suddenly just prior to 2004 season; returned in 2005; suspended from the NFL for 2006; instead played in CFL.

Serena Williams (b. Sept. 26, 1981): Tennis; first African-American woman to win a Grand Slam title since Althea Gibson in 1958 by winning the 1999 U.S. Open; has 7 career Grand Slam titles: 2 Wimbledons (2002-03), French Open (2002), 2 U.S. Opens (1999,02) and 2 Australian Opens (2003,05); has won career doubles Grand Slam with Venus.

Ted Williams (b. Aug. 30, 1918, d. July 5, 2002): Baseball OF; led AL in batting 6 times, and HRs and RBI 4 times each; won Triple Crown twice (1942,47); 2-time MVP (1946,49); last player to bat .400 when he hit .406 in 1941; Marine Corps combat pilot who missed 3 full seasons during WWII (1943-45) and most of two others (1952-53) during Korean War; hit .344 lifetime with 521 HRs in 19 years with Boston Red Sox; also known as avid fisherman; furor erupted following his death when plans to keep his body frozen at a cryogenic lab were made public.

Venus Williams (b. June 17, 1980): Tennis; won 3 Wimbledon (2000,01,05) and 2 U.S. Open (2000, 01) singles titles; 2000 Olympic singles and doubles (with sister Serena) gold medalist; recorded fastest serve in WTA history with 127 mph blast in 1998; won career doubles grand slam with Serena.

Walter Ray Williams Jr. (b. Oct. 6, 1959): Bowling and Horseshoes; 6-time PBA Bowler of Year (1986,93,96,97,98,2003); all-time leading money winner on the PBA Tour; has 42 all-time record PBA titles; also won 6 World Horseshoe Pitching titles.

Hack Wilson (b. Apr. 26, 1900, d. Nov. 23, 1948): Baseball; as a Chicago Cub, he produced one of baseball's most outstanding seasons in 1930 with 56 home runs, .356 batting average, 105 walks and, most amazingly, a major league record 191 RBIs that still stands; finished career with 244 HRs, 1,062 RBIs.

Dave Winfield (b. Oct. 3, 1951): Baseball OF-DH; selected in 4 major sports league drafts in 1973—NFL, NBA, ABA, and MLB; chose baseball and played in 12 All-Star Games over 22-year career; at age 41, helped lead Toronto to World Series title in 1992; 3,110 hits and 465 HRs.

Katarina Witt (b. Dec. 3, 1965): East German figure skater; 4-time world champion (1984-85,87-88); won consecutive Olympic gold medals (1984,88).

John Wooden (b. Oct. 14, 1910): Basketball; College Player of Year at Purdue in 1932; coached UCLA to 88 straight wins (1971-74), 10 national titles (1964-65,67-73,75); inducted into the Hall of Fame as both player and coach; career college coaching record of 664-162 over 29 years.

Tiger Woods (b. Dec. 30, 1975): Golfer; 3-time winner of U.S. Amateur (1994-96); won 6 events and broke the single season money record in his 1st full season on PGA Tour; won 1997 Masters by a record 18-under par and 13 strokes; won 2nd major at 1999 PGA Championship; in 2000 won the U.S. Open at Pebble Beach by a record 15 strokes, the British Open by 8 strokes and the PGA Championship in a playoff; held all 4 Major titles simultaneously with his win at 2001 Masters; has since won 6 more majors for a total of 12: 2 Masters (2002,05), 2002 U.S. Open, 2 British Opens (2005-06) and 2006 PGA Championship; all-time PGA Tour money leader; 1 of only 5 players to win all 4 Grand Slam titles (others are Hogan, Nicklaus, Player and Sarazen); 7-time PGA Tour player of the year.

Mickey Wright (b. Feb. 14, 1935): Golfer; won 3 of 4 majors (LPGA, U.S. Open, Titleholders) in 1961; 4-time winner of both U.S. Open and LPGA titles; 82 career wins including 13 majors.

Early Wynn (b. Jan. 6, 1920, d. Mar. 4, 1999): Baseball RHP; won 20 games 5 times; Cy Young winner in 1959; 300-244 record in 23 years.

Kristi Yamaguchi (b. July 12, 1971): Figure Skating; finished 2nd in the 1991 American nationals but won the world title that year; won the national, world and Olympic titles in 1992, then turned professional.

Cale Yarborough (b. Mar. 27, 1940): Auto racer; 3-time NASCAR national champion (1976-78); 4-time winner of Daytona 500 (1968,77,83-84); 83 career NASCAR wins.

Carl Yastrzemski (b. Aug. 22, 1939): Baseball OF; led AL in batting 3 times; won Triple Crown and MVP in 1967; had 3,419 hits and 452 HRs in 23 years with Boston Red Sox; member of Hall of Fame.

Cy Young (b. Mar. 29, 1867, d. Nov. 4, 1955): Baseball RHP; all-time leader in wins (511), losses (313), complete games (751) and innings pitched (7,356); had career 2.63 ERA in 22 years (1890-1911); 30-game winner 5 times and 20-game winner 11 other times; threw three no-hitters and a perfect game (1904); annual AL and NL pitching awards named after him.

Dick Young (b. Oct. 17, 1917, d. Aug. 31, 1987): Confrontational sportswriter for 44 years with NY tabloids; as baseball beat writer and columnist, he led change from flowery prose to hard-nosed reporting.

Sheila Young (b. Oct. 14, 1950): Speed skater and cyclist; 1st U.S. athlete to win 3 medals at Winter Olympics (1976); won speed skating overall and sprint cycling world titles in 1976.

Steve Young (b. Oct. 11, 1961): Football QB; All-America at BYU (1983); NFL Player of Year (1992) with SF 49ers; only QB to lead NFL in passer rating 4 straight years (1991-94); rating of 112.8 in 1994 is highest ever; threw record 6 TD passes in MVP performance in Super Bowl XXIX; retired with NFL records for highest passer rating (96.8) and completion pct. (64.4); 232 career TD passes and 33,124 yards.

Robin Yount (b. Sept. 16, 1955): Baseball SS-OF; AL MVP at 2 positions—as SS in 1982 and OF in '89; retired after 1993 season with 3,142 hits, 251 HRs and a major-league-record 123 sacrifice flies after 20 seasons with Brewers; inducted into Hall of Fame in 1999.

Steve Yzerman (b. May 9, 1965): Hockey C; Captained the Detroit Red Wings to 3 Stanley Cup wins (1997-98,2002); won the Conn Smythe Trophy as the playoff MVP in 1998; one of only 14 NHL players to score more than 600 goals; retired after 2005-06 with 692 goals and 1,755 career points.

Mario Zagalo (b. Aug. 9, 1931): Soccer; Brazilian forward who is one of only two men (Franz Beckenbauer is the other) to serve as both captain (1962) and coach (1970,94) of World Cup champion.

Babe Didrikson Zaharias (b. June 26, 1911, d. Sept. 27, 1956): All-around athlete who was chosen AP Female Athlete of Year 6 times from 1932-54; won 2 gold medals (javelin and 80-meter hurdles) and a silver (high jump) at 1932 Olympics; played baseball and acquired the nickname "Babe" for her tape measure home runs; real first name was Mildred; took up golf in 1935 and went on to win 55 pro and amateur events; won 10 majors, including 3 U.S. Opens (1948,50,54); helped found LPGA in 1949; chosen female "Athlete of the Half Century" by AP in 1950; when asked if there was anything she didn't play, she replied, "Yeah, dolls."

Tony Zale (b. May 29, 1913, d. March 20, 1997): Boxer; 2-time world middleweight champion (1941-47,48); fought Rocky Graziano for title 3 times in 21 months in 1947-48, winning twice; pro record 67-18-2 with 44 KOs.

Frank Zamboni (b. Jan. 16, 1901, d. July 27, 1988): Mechanic, ice salesman and skating rink owner in Paramount, Calif.; invented ice-resurfacing machine in 1949; now there are few skating rinks without one as thousands have been sold in over 35 countries.

Emil Zatopek (b. Sept. 19, 1922, d. Nov. 22, 2000): Czech distance runner; winner of 1948 Olympic gold medal at 10,000 meters; 4 years later, won unprecedented Olympic triple crown (5,000 meters, 10,000 meters and marathon) at 1952 Games in Helsinki.

Zinedine Zidane (b. June 23, 1972): French soccer player; 3-time FIFA World Player of the Year (1998, 2000, 2003); led host nation France to 1998 World Cup title, scoring twice in final against Brazil; a record $64m transfer fee sent the midfielder from Juventus to Real Madrid in 2001; led France to the World Cup final in 2006 (loss to Italy in penalty kicks); won Golden Ball as the tournament's most outstanding player, despite being given a red card in the 110th minute of the final for his notorious headbutt into the chest of Italy's Marco Materazzi.

John Ziegler (b. Feb. 9, 1934): Hockey; NHL president from 1977-92; negotiated settlement with rival WHA in 1979 that led to inviting four WHA teams (Edmonton, Hartford, Quebec and Winnipeg) to join NHL; stepped down June 12, 1992, 2 months after settling 10-day players' strike.

Pirmin Zurbriggen (b. Feb. 4, 1963): Swiss alpine skier; 4-time World Cup overall champ (1984,87-88,90) and 3-time runner-up; 40 World Cup wins in 10 years; won gold and bronze medals at 1988 Olympics.

Minority Firsts

Jackie Robinson's breaking of the baseball color barrier took on mythic status, but many other athletes of color entered their chosen sport or won major championships with decidedly less fanfare. This list attempts to chronicle their successes. Official sources were used where available; some entries are based on published reports at the time or anecdotal information.

African-American

Auto Racing

NASCAR driver: Charlie Scott, Daytona Beach, Fla., 1956
NASCAR winner: Wendell Scott, Jacksonville, Fla., 1963

Baseball

MLB player: Jackie Robinson, Brooklyn Dodgers, 1947
MLB coach: Buck O'Neil, Chicago Cubs, 1962
MLB manager: Frank Robinson, Cleveland Indians, 1975
Hall of Fame: Jackie Robinson, 1962

Boxing

Heavyweight champion: Jack Johnson, 1908

College Football

Player, major college: George Jewett, Michigan, 1890
Head coach, Div. I-A: Willie Jeffries, Wichita State, 1979
Heisman Trophy: Ernie Davis, Syracuse, 1961
Hall of Fame: Fritz Pollard, 1954

Golf

PGA Tour: Charlie Sifford, 1961
PGA winner: Peter Brown, Waco Open, 1964
Major winner: Tiger Woods, Masters, 1997
World Hall of Fame: Charlie Sifford, 2004
LPGA Tour: Althea Gibson, 1963

NBA

Player: Earl Lloyd, Washington Capitols, 1950
Coach: Bill Russell, Boston Celtics, 1968
Hall of Fame: Bill Russell, Boston Celtics, 1975

NFL

Player, pre-merger: Charles Follis, Shelby Athletic Club, 1902
QB: Willie Thrower, Chicago Bears, 1953
Head coach, pre-merger: Fritz Pollard, Akron Pros, 1921
Hall of Fame: Emlen Tunnell, New York Giants, 1967

NHL

Player: Willie O'Ree, Boston Bruins, 1958 (Canadian); Val James, Buffalo Sabres, 1982 (American)
Coach: Dirk Graham, Chicago Blackhawks, 1998 (Canadian)
Hall of Fame: Grant Fuhr (Canadian), Edmonton Oilers, 2003

Olympics

Summer Games
Gold medalist (men): DeHart Hubbard, long jump, 1924
Gold medalist (women): Alice Coachman, high jump, 1948
Winter Games
Gold medalist (men): Shani Davis, speedskating, 2006
Gold medalist (women): Vonetta Flowers, bobsled, 2002

Tennis

Grand Slam event: Althea Gibson, French Open, 1956; Arthur Ashe, U.S. Open, 1968
Hall of Fame: Althea Gibson, 1971; Arthur Ashe, 1985

Hispanic

Auto Racing

NASCAR driver: Frank Mundy, Strictly Stock Race #1 at Charlotte (N.C.) Speedway, 1949

Baseball

Player: Esteban Bellán, Troy, N.Y. Haymakers, 1871
Manager: Mike Gonzalez, St. Louis Cardinals, 1940
Hall of Fame: Roberto Clemente, 1973

Boxing

Heavyweight champion: John Ruiz, WBA, 2001

College Football

QB, starting, major college: Tom Flores, Pacific; Joe Kapp, California, 1956
Heisman Trophy: Jim Plunkett, Stanford, 1970
Head coach, major coll.: Marcelino Huerta, Wichita St., 1962

Golf

PGA Tour winner: Chi Chi Rodriguez, Denver Open, 1963
LPGA Tour winner: Fay Crocker, Serbin Open (Miami), 1955

NBA

Player: Butch Lee, Atlanta Hawks, 1979
Coach: Dick Versace, Indiana Pacers, 1989

NFL

Player: Lou Molinet, Frankford Yellowjackets, 1927
Quarterback: Tom Flores, Oakland Raiders (AFL), 1960
Head coach: Tom Fears, New Orleans Saints, 1967

NHL

Player: Bill Guerin, New Jersey Devils, 1991

Olympics

Summer Games
Medalist (men): Miguel Capriles, fencing, bronze, 1932
Winter Games
Gold medalist (men): Derek Parra, speedskating, 2006
Medalist (women): Jennifer Rodriguez, speedskating, bronze, 2002

Tennis

Grand Slam event: Pancho Gonzalez, U.S. Champ's, 1948

Asian

Auto Racing

NASCAR driver: George Tet, Grand National race #21, Charlotte (N.C.) Motor Speedway, 1960

Baseball

Player: Masanori Murakami, San Francisco Giants, 1964 (Japanese); Ryan Kurosaki, St. Louis Cardinals, 1975 (Japanese-American)

College Football

QB, starting: Roman Gabriel, NC State, 1959

Golf

PGA Tour winner: Isao Aoki, Hawaiian Open, 1983
LPGA Major winner: Chako Higuchi, LPGA Champ., 1977

NBA

Player: Wataru Misaka, New York Knicks, 1947

NFL

Player: Walter Achiu, Dayton Triangles, 1927
QB: Roman Gabriel, Los Angeles Rams, 1962

NHL

Player: Larry Kwong, New York Rangers, 1948 (Canadian)

Olympics

Summer Games
Gold medalist (men): Sammy Lee, diving, 1948
Gold medalist (women): Victoria Manalo Draves, diving, 1948
Winter Games
Gold medalist (men): Apolo Anton Ohno, short-track speed skating, 2002
Gold medalist (women): Kristi Yamaguchi, figure skating, 1992

Tennis

Grand Slam event: Michael Chang, French Open, 1988

BALLPARKS
& ARENAS

Our Home.
Our Team.
Be a Saint.

Just over a year after Hurricane Katrina shuttered the **Superdome**, the Saints returned to their New Orleans home.

Coming Attractions

SPORTS ALMANAC

2006

BASEBALL

St. Louis (NL): The Cardinals opened the new Busch Stadium (Anheuser-Busch Cos. Inc. is the title sponsor) on April 10, 2006 with a 6-4 win over Milwaukee behind starter Mark Mulder's 8+ innings pitched and two-run homer. The open-air, baseball-only park offers a spectacular view of the Gateway Arch and St. Louis skyline. The seating capacity is 46,861. The estimated cost of the project, including a new Cardinals Hall of Fame and Museum, is $387.5 million. The ballpark initially opened at a reduced seating capacity (about 40,000) but was fully functional by mid-season.

NFL FOOTBALL

Arizona (NFC): University of Phoenix Stadium opened with a 21-13 pre-season win against the defending Super Bowl champions Pittsburgh Steelers on Aug. 12, 2006. The 63,500-seat (expandable to 72,800 for major events) stadium is located in Glendale, Ariz. (15 miles west of Phoenix) on a site on the Loop 101 (Agua Fria Freeway) south of Glendale Avenue and adjacent to the new home of the NHL's Coyotes. The stadium has a partially retractable roof and features a natural grass field that can be rolled out into the parking lot to help it grow. The stadium will include 88 luxury suites (with space for 16 more) and 7,000 club seats; the cost of the complex is $455 million.

2007

NHL HOCKEY

New Jersey (East): Construction on a new 17,500-seat arena in Newark for the New Jersey Devils is well underway. Groundbreaking took place on Oct. 3, 2005. Funding from a new lease on Newark Airport will help pay for the project. The arena site is located in downtown Newark near Penn Station; estimated cost: $310 million of which the city will contribute $210 million. The arena will include 68 luxury suites and the opening is scheduled for August 2007, in time for the 2007-08 NHL season.

2008

BASEBALL

Washington (NL): The Nationals broke ground on a new ballpark on May 4, 2006. The stadium, to be built largely with public funds, will be owned by the D.C. Sports & Entertainment Commission. The site of the new ballpark is located along the Anacostia River at South Capitol and M Streets. The exterior design includes a lot of glass, similar to the new Washington Convention Center. Included in the ballpark's 41,000-seat capacity are approximately 22,000 seats in the lower bowl, 12,100 in the upper seating bowl, from where fans can see the U.S. Capitol building, 2,500 club seats and 1,112 suite seats. The project budget is currently set at $611 million. The home opener is scheduled for 2008.

NFL FOOTBALL

Indianapolis (AFC): Construction on Lucas Oil Stadium, the new home for the Colts, is well underway. Lucas Oil bought the stadium naming rights for 20 years for $120 million. The new glass and brick stadium will seat 63,000 (expandable to 70,000) and cost about $675 million. The new stadium will feature a retractable-roof and Fieldturf. It will be located in the parking lot across South Street from the RCA Dome, which will continue to serve as the Colts' home until the new stadium is completed. That is scheduled to be in time for the 2008 season. The project is expected to be funded largely from slot machine revenue.

2009

BASEBALL

New York (AL): The Yankees broke ground on the new Yankee Stadium on Aug. 16, 2006 to be located on the sites of Macombs Dam and Mullaly Parks. The plan also calls for a new waterfront park and esplanade along the Harlem River, major infrastructure improvements, and the construction of more than 5,000 new parking spaces. The Yankees agreed to privately finance the new $800 million facility with the city chipping in $135 million to replace parkland (and make the necessary infrastructure improvements) and the State on the hook for $70 million for the construction of new parking facilities. The new retro-styled park will have 51,000 seats, fewer than "The House that Ruth Built" but it will have a lot more luxury suites. The Yankees hired HOK Sport as their architect and the stadium is set to open in April 2009.

New York (NL): The New Mets Ballpark (title sponsor still pending) will seat approximately 45,000 and feature natural grass. Although the park will be located in Willets Point, Queens between Shea Stadium and 126th Street it will be designed to evoke memories of Brooklyn's long lost Ebbets Field. The asymmetrical outfield walls and generous dimensions (LF—335'; LC—379'; CF—408'; RC—391'; RF—330') should make for a traditional pitcher's park. The estimated cost of the ballpark and infrastructure improvements is $610 million. The Mets are expected to cover $420 million of the total. The deal includes a 40-year lease that will keep the Mets in New York until at least 2049. Construction is scheduled to be completed by April 2009.

NBA BASKETBALL

New Jersey (East): Nets owner Bruce Ratner has plans to move the team to Brooklyn and build a 19,000-seat, Frank Gehry-designed arena that will be a part of Atlantic Yards, a $4.2 billion office, residential and shopping complex. The plans still face small but vocal opposition from area residents and the arena is aiming to be open for business no sooner than 2009. The entire project is expected to take 10 years to complete. In 2006, local voters overwhelmingly elected politicians supporting the project over those in opposition. The Nets recently made arrangements to the stay at Continental Airlines Arena in the Meadowlands through at least the 2008-09 season, with a team option to extend their lease through the 2012-13 season.

AP/Wide World Photos

Arizona's brand new **University of Phoenix Stadium** opened in 2006. It boasts the nation's first retractable natural grass field which can be rolled outside the stadium on a 17-million pound tray when not in use to help the grass grow.

NFL FOOTBALL

Dallas (NFC): Construction on a new publicly funded stadium for the Cowboys in Arlington, Texas is underway. The 75,000-seat stadium will be located south of the Tom Landry Freeway, next door to the Texas Rangers' Ameriquest Field. As of September 2006, no detailed drawings of the new stadium have been released to the public. But the designs call for a retractable-roof stadium that would be expandable to hold up to 90,000 fans and cost an estimated $650 million. Adjacent to the new stadium will be a 1.2 million-square-foot shopping area called Glorypark. The home opener is set for the fall of 2009.

2010

BASEBALL

Minnesota (AL): The Hennepin County board of commissioners recently voted 4-3 to approve a Hennepin County sales tax that will pay for most of the $522 million open-air ballpark. The 0.15 percent sales tax (three cents on a $20 purchase) excludes clothing, food, medical supplies and automobiles. The Twins announced they would contribute $130 million toward the construction of the ballpark. The new ballpark will seat 42,000 including 72 suites and 4,000 club seats. It will be located at the Rapid Park site behind the Target Center, which is located at the convergence of I-394 and I-94, the Hiawatha Light Rail line and the proposed Northstar Commuter Rail line. The anticipated home opener is tenatively scheduled for 2010.

NFL FOOTBALL

New York (AFC/NFC): In the aftermath of the political defeat of their proposal to build a stadium on Manhattan's West Side, the New York Jets partnered with the New York Giants and announced plans for a joint venture to build a new 80,000-seat stadium in the Meadowlands. The stadium, which would be the second largest in the NFL, will include 10,000 club seats and 200 luxury suites. Plans could also include a retractable roof bringing the price tag for the privately financed stadium to $1 billion. The construction is currently scheduled for completion in 2010.

Other Ballpark & Stadia in the Works

After looking into the possibility of moving the team to San Jose, the Oakland A's are moving toward extending their lease at **McAfee Coliseum** through at least 2010 and potentially to 2014 with a series of one-year lease options.

The **Florida Marlins** continue on their long odyssey toward a new ballpark in south Florida. The *Miami Herald* reported in August 2006 that MLB has stepped into the process like never before and is pushing a downtown Miami site just south of the old Miami Arena. The new site is bordered by Northwest Fifth and Seventh streets and by Miami Avenue to the east and the Metrorail line to the west. The team is reportedly still $100 million short of the $430 million they need to build the ballpark. The current lease that the Marlins hold at Dolphin Stadium will expire in 2010.

The **Pittsburgh Penguins** are still working toward a replacement for the aging Mellon Arena. The new Pittsburgh mayor Luke Ravenstahl is currently at odds with the team on how to fund the project. The team and owner Mario Lemieux are still committed to working with the Ise of Capri Casinos Inc. plan to pledge $290 million toward construction of a new arena upon receiving a license to open a slot machine parlor. The mayor is proposing a "Plan B" which is bankrolled by other proposed casino ventures. The team is currently for sale and the current frontrunner is believed to be Canadian businessman Jim Balsillie who could have plans to relocate the team to Ontario. The team and local government has worked together on site acquisition, securing the parcel of land in the lower Hill and Uptown area on which to build a new arena.

Also, in 2006 the San Francisco 49ers announced their latest proposal to build a new 68,000-seat stadium at **Candlestick Point** to open for business in 2012. It would be built on landfill just southeast of the current Monster Park and would cost between $600 million and $800 million. If the deal, which still requires city approval, collapses a new stadium for the Niners could be constructed 45 miles south of the city in Santa Clara.

Home, Sweet Home

The home fields, home courts and home ice of the AL, NL, NBA, NFL, NHL, NCAA Division I-A college football and Division I basketball. Also included are MLS stadiums, Formula One, Champ Car, Indy Racing League and NASCAR auto racing tracks.

Attendance figures for the 2005 NFL regular season and the 2005-06 NBA and NHL regular seasons are provided. See Baseball chapter for 2006 AL and NL attendance figures.

MAJOR LEAGUE BASEBALL

American League

	Built	Capacity	LF	LCF	CF	RCF	RF	Field
Baltimore Orioles . . . . . **Oriole Park at Camden Yards**	1992	**48,190**	337	376	406	391	320	Grass
Boston Red Sox . . . . **Fenway Park**	1912	**38,805**	310	379	390*	380	302	Grass
Chicago White Sox . . . . **U.S. Cellular Field**	1991	**41,000**	330	377	400	372	335	Grass
Cleveland Indians . . . . **Jacobs Field**	1994	**43,068**	325	370	405	375	325	Grass
Detroit Tigers . . . . **Comerica Park**	2000	**40,120**	345	395	420	365	330	Grass
Kansas City Royals . . . . **Kauffman Stadium**	1973	**40,793**	330	375	400	375	330	Grass
Los Angeles Angels of Anaheim . . . . **Angel Stadium of Anaheim**	1966	**45,030**	365	387	400	370	365	Grass
Minnesota Twins . . . **Hubert H. Humphrey Metrodome**	1982	**48,678**	343	385	408	367	327	Turf
New York Yankees . . . . **Yankee Stadium**	1923	**57,478**	318	399	408	385	314	Grass
Oakland Athletics . . . . **McAfee Coliseum**	1966	**34,007†**	330	367	400	367	330	Grass
Seattle Mariners . . . . **SAFECO Field**	1999	**47,116**	331	390	405	387	327	Grass
Tampa Bay Devil Rays . . . . **Tropicana Field**	1990	**43,761**	315	370	404	370	322	Turf
Texas Rangers . . . . . . **Ameriquest Field in Arlington**	1994	**49,115**	332	390	400	381	325	Grass
Toronto Blue Jays . . . . **Rogers Centre**	1989	**50,516**	328	375	400	375	328	Turf

*The straightaway center-field fence at Fenway Park is 390 feet from home plate but the deepest part of center-field, a.k.a. "the Triangle," is 420 feet away. The left-field fence, known as "the Green Monster," is 37 feet tall. Two hundred and seventy seats were added to the top of the wall in 2003 replacing the 23-foot screen that previously topped the Monster.

†The Oakland A's have closed off the upper deck of McAfee Coliseum and covered the seats with a tarp. The stadium could accomodate 43,662 fans if the upper tier was reopened.

National League

	Built	Capacity	LF	LCF	CF	RCF	RF	Field
Arizona Diamondbacks . . . . **Chase Field**	1998	**49,033**	330	376	407	376	334	Grass
Atlanta Braves . . . . **Turner Field**	1996	**50,091**	335	380	401	390	330	Grass
Chicago Cubs . . . . **Wrigley Field**	1914	**39,111**	355	368	400	368	353	Grass
Cincinnati Reds . . . . **Great American Ball Park**	2003	**42,059**	328	379	404	370	325	Grass
Colorado Rockies . . . . **Coors Field**	1995	**50,449**	347	390	415	375	350	Grass
Florida Marlins . . . . **Dolphin Stadium**	1987	**36,331**	330	385	434	385	345	Grass
Houston Astros . . . . **Minute Maid Park**	2000	**40,950**	315	362	436	373	326	Grass
Los Angeles Dodgers . . . . **Dodger Stadium**	1962	**56,000**	330	385	395	385	330	Grass
Milwaukee Brewers . . . . **Miller Park**	2001	**42,400**	340	374	400	374	345	Grass
New York Mets . . . . **Shea Stadium**	1964	**56,749**	338	378	410	378	338	Grass
Philadelphia Phillies . . . . **Citizens Bank Park**	2004	**43,000**	329	369	401*	369	330	Grass
Pittsburgh Pirates . . . . **PNC Park**	2001	**37,898**	326	368	399*	375	324	Grass
St. Louis Cardinals . . . . **Busch Stadium**	2006	**46,000**	336	390	400	390	335	Grass
San Diego Padres . . . . **PETCO Park**	2004	**46,000**	334	367	396*	387	322	Grass
San Francisco Giants . . . . **AT&T Park**	2000	**41,467**	339	364	399	421	309	Grass
Washington Nationals . . . . **RFK Stadium**	1962	**45,250**	335	380	410	380	335	Grass

*The deepest part of PNC Park is 410 feet between straightaway center and left-center. The deepest part of Citizens Bank Park is 409 feet in part of left-center. The deepest part of PETCO Park is 411 feet in part of right-center.

Rank by Capacity

AL

New York	.57,478
Toronto	.50,516
Texas	.49,115
Minnesota	.48,678
Baltimore	.48,190
Seattle	.47,116
Los Angeles	.45,030
Tampa Bay	.43,761
Cleveland	.43,068
Chicago	.41,000
Kansas City	.40,793
Detroit	.40,120
Boston	.38,805
Oakland	.34,007

NL

New York	.56,749
Los Angeles	.56,000
Colorado	.50,449
Atlanta	.50,091
Arizona	.49,033
Montreal	.46,500
St. Louis	.46,000
San Diego	.46,000
Philadelphia	.43,000
Milwaukee	.42,400
Cincinnati	.42,059
San Francisco	.41,467
Houston	.40,950
Chicago	.39,111
Pittsburgh	.37,898
Florida	.36,331

Rank by Age

AL

Boston	.1912
New York	.1923
Los Angeles	.1966
Oakland	.1966
Kansas City	.1973
Minnesota	.1982
Toronto	.1989
Tampa Bay	.1990
Chicago	.1991
Baltimore	.1992
Cleveland	.1994
Texas	.1994
Seattle	.1999
Detroit	.2000

Note: New York's Yankee Stadium (AL) was rebuilt in 1976.

NL

Chicago	.1914
Los Angeles	.1962
New York	.1964
Montreal	.1976
Florida	.1987
Atlanta	.1993
Colorado	.1995
Arizona	.1998
Houston	.2000
San Francisco	.2000
Milwaukee	.2001
Pittsburgh	.2001
Cincinnati	.2003
Philadelphia	.2004
San Diego	.2004
St. Louis	.2006

Home Fields

Listed below are the principal home fields used through the years by current American and National League teams. The NL became a major league in 1876, the AL in 1901.

The capacity figures in the right-hand column indicate the largest seating capacity of the ballpark while the club played there. Capacity figures before 1915 (and the introduction of concrete grandstands) are sketchy at best and have been left blank.

American League

Baltimore Orioles

1901	Lloyd Street Grounds (Milwaukee) . . .	—
1902–53	Sportsman's Park II (St. Louis)	30,500
1954–91	Memorial Stadium (Baltimore)	53,371
1992–	Oriole Park at Camden Yards	48,190

Boston Red Sox

1901–11	Huntington Ave. Grounds	—
1912–	Fenway Park	38,815
	(1934 capacity—27,000)	

Chicago White Sox

1901–10	Southside Park	—
1910–90	Comiskey Park I	43,931
1991–	U.S. Cellular Field	41,000
	(2003 capacity—46,943)	

Cleveland Indians

1901–09	League Park I	—
1910–46	League Park II	21,414
1932–93	Cleveland Stadium	74,483
1994–	Jacobs Field	43,068

Detroit Tigers

1901–11	Bennett Park	—
1912–99	Tiger Stadium	46,945
2000–	Comerica Park	40,120
	(1912 capacity—23,000)	

Kansas City Royals

1969–72	Municipal Stadium	35,020
1973–	Kauffman Stadium	40,793
	(1973 capacity—40,762)	

Los Angeles Angels of Anaheim

1961	Wrigley Field (Los Angeles)	20,457
1962-65	Dodger Stadium	56,000
1966–	Angel Stadium of Anaheim	45,030
	(1966 capacity—43,250)	

Minnesota Twins

1901-02	American League Park (Washington, DC)	—
1903-60	Griffith Stadium	27,410
1960-81	Metropolitan Stadium	
	(Bloomington, MN)	45,919
1982–	HHH Metrodome (Minneapolis)	48,678
	(1982 capacity—54,000)	

New York Yankees

1901-02	Oriole Park (Baltimore)	—
1903-12	Hilltop Park (New York)	—
1913-22	Polo Grounds II	38,000
1923-73	Yankee Stadium I	67,224
1974-75	Shea Stadium	55,101
1976–	Yankee Stadium II	57,478
	(1976 capacity—57,145)	

Oakland Athletics

1901-08	Columbia Park (Philadelphia)	—
1909-54	Shibe Park	33,608
1955-67	Municipal Stadium (Kansas City) . . .	35,020
1968–	McAfee Coliseum	43,662
	(1968 capacity—48,621)	

Seattle Mariners

1977-99	The Kingdome	59,166
1999–	SAFECO Field	47,116

Tampa Bay Devil Rays

1990–	Tropicana Field	43,761

Texas Rangers

1961	Griffith Stadium (Washington, DC) . . .	27,410
1962-71	RFK Stadium	45,016
1972-93	Arlington Stadium (Texas)	43,521
1994–	Ameriquest Field in Arlington	49,115

Toronto Blue Jays

1977-89	Exhibition Stadium	43,737
1989–	Rogers Centre	50,516
	(1989 capacity—49,500)	

Ballpark Name Changes: ANAHEIM—**Angel Stadium of Anaheim,** originally Anaheim Stadium (1966-98), then Edison International Field of Anaheim (1998-2003); CHICAGO—**Comiskey Park I** originally White Sox Park (1910-12), then Comiskey Park in 1913, then White Sox Park again in 1962, then Comiskey Park again in 1976; **U.S. Cellular Field** originally Comiskey Park (1991-2002); CLEVELAND—**League Park** renamed Dunn Field in 1920, then League Park again in 1928; **Cleveland Stadium** originally Municipal Stadium (1932-74); DETROIT—**Tiger Stadium** originally Navin Field (1912-37), then Briggs Stadium (1938-60); KANSAS CITY—**Kauffman Stadium** originally Royals Stadium (1973-93); LOS ANGELES—**Dodger Stadium** referred to as Chavez Ravine by AL while Angels played there (1962-65); OAKLAND—**McAfee Coliseum** originally Oakland Alameda Coliseum (1968-98), then Network Associates Coliseum (1998-2004); PHILADELPHIA—**Shibe Park** renamed Connie Mack Stadium in 1953; ST. LOUIS—**Sportsman's Park** renamed Busch Stadium in 1953; WASHINGTON—**Griffith Stadium** originally National Park (1892-1920), **RFK Stadium** originally D.C. Stadium (1961-68); TEXAS—**Ameriquest Field in Arlington** originally The Ballpark in Arlington (1994-2004); TORONTO—**Rogers Centre** originally Skydome (1989-2005).

National League

Arizona Diamondbacks

1998–	Chase Field	49,033

Atlanta Braves

1876–94	South End Grounds I (Boston)	—
1894–1914	South End Grounds II	—
1915–52	Braves Field	40,000
1953–65	County Stadium (Milwaukee)	43,394
1966–96	Atlanta-Fulton County Stadium	52,769
	(1966 capacity—50,000)	
1997–	Turner Field	50,091

Chicago Cubs

1876–77	State Street Grounds	—
1878–84	Lakefront Park	—
1885–91	West Side Park	—
1891–93	Brotherhood Park	—
1893–1915	West Side Grounds	—
1916–	Wrigley Field	39,111
	(1916 capacity—16,000)	

Cincinnati Reds

1876–79	Avenue Grounds	—
1880	Bank Street Grounds	—
1890–1901	Redland Field I	—
1902–11	Palace of the Fans	—
1912–70	Crosley Field	29,603
1970–2002	Cinergy Field	40,007
	(1970 capacity—52,000)	
2003–	Great American Ball Park	42,059

THE WISE GUIDES BALLPARK GUIDE

The Major League ballpark has been so mythologized in American literature, compared to the great cathedrals and temples created by mankind. To that, we say: So what? Whether it's Wrigley or Fenway or the latest corporate-themed stadium, the ballpark is a shrine. It's where you catch a game and cheer on your team, but is also a place to be explored. No two are alike, so there is food and drink to sample and history to learn and interesting people to meet. That's the philosophy of Wise Guides Inc. and why we started writing our guide books; to celebrate these ballparks and stadiums, as well as the neighborhoods they sit in, and try to capture the entire experience of attending a game.

John and **Andy Buchanan**, Wise Guides Inc.

American League

Ameriquest Field in Arlington – The Rangers may not have much history to boast about but that doesn't mean you can't pick some up while here: the park features a museum, Legends of the Game Baseball, which includes many items on loan from Cooperstown and a 225-seat theater. There's also a Children's Learning Center for the kids.

Angel Stadium of Anaheim – This stadium opened 40 years ago and was also home to the NFL's Rams from 1980-94. It has since been converted to a baseball only facility and, in typical southern California style, is surrounded by thousands of parking spots.

Comerica Park – This park in downtown Detroit features a carousel, Ferris wheel and a fountain that spouts 'liquid fireworks.' Beyond the left field wall is a series of unique statues of six Tigers greats. And, for the first time in a while, a good team on the field.

Fenway Park – The Fenway Frank may get the pub but better yet are the grilled sausages with peppers and onions; the smell of these and other offerings on Yawkey Way is enough to turn a vegetarian. This oldest park in the majors is full of quirks, including the Green Monster and the bullpens in right field; late owner Thomas Yawkey put them there in 1940, reportedly to create a shorter home run arc for his new lefty slugger, Ted Williams.

Hubert H. Humphrey Metrodome – This place is pretty sterile but has hosted some exciting events in its 24 years: the Super Bowl ('92), two Final Fours ('92, '01), the All-Star Game ('85) and two World Series Game 7s ('87, '91), both won by the Twins. A new downtown, open-air facility is in the works.

Jacobs Field – The video screen at the Jake is the largest in the majors while the light towers rise some 200 feet and were designed to blend in with the city's smoke stacks and downtown high-rises. Sold out the season before Opening Day every year from 1995 to 2000.

Kauffman Stadium - Bo Jackson jacked the longest home run in stadium history on Sept. 14, 1986. Estimated at 475 feet, it was Jackson's first career home run. A major renovation is in the works for this 33-year-old park.

McAfee Coliseum – The A's share this building with the football Raiders, and tailgating is commonplace in the surrounding parking lots. One claim to fame (or not): first baseball stadium where 'The Wave' was performed.

Oriole Park at Camden Yards – Get some culture on your visit to Camden by visiting the nearby Babe Ruth Birthplace and Museum and the Sports Legends museum, housed in the historic Camden Station building. Boog's Barbeque, run by former Oriole star Boog Powell, is a delicious stop inside the park.

Rogers Centre – The former SkyDome opened in 1989 as the first of the luxury ballparks, with a retractable roof, skyboxes galore, restaurants and bars (the Hard Rock Café Toronto is here), and even a hotel overlooking the field.

Safeco Field – While Safeco has a retractable roof it does not enclose the park, so fans are spared the rain but not the chill. And if you're really looking for the outdoors experience, Safeco has 'parking spots' for more than 150 bicycles.

Tropicana Field – It may seem sacriligious, but the Devil Rays say this domed stadium incorporates a design from Ebbets Field in its soaring rotunda. The tilted roof and a cigar bar give it some character, but doubtful Ebbets ever hosted figure skating or motorcycle races.

U.S. Cellular Field – They lopped eight rows off the much-criticized upper deck a few years ago and put on a new roof, which was an improvement. Come prepared to eat because the concessions are varied and excellent; on the way in check out the home plate of old Comiskey Park in the parking lot across the street.

Yankee Stadium – The 'House That Ruth Built' opened on April 18, 1923, with (who else?) Ruth hitting a 3-run homer as the Yanks beat (who else?) the Red Sox. It has seen historic football games, legendary boxing matches, visits from popes and almost 40 World Series since. A new park next door is scheduled to open for the 2009 season.

National League

AT&T Park – No one upgraded like the Giants when they moved into this place in 2000 from cold and dingy Candlestick. Besides all the amenities of a modern ballpark and the incredible views of the bay, the team notes the park is situated in one of the sunniest and warmest spots of San Francisco. Take the ferry, which drops you off at a nearby terminal.

Busch Stadium – This brand new ballpark kept the same name as the old one and is also downtown in sight of the Arch. If you visit the Cardinals Hall of Fame you get two museums for the price of one - it shares space with the International Bowling Museum and Hall of Fame in a building adjacent to Busch.

Chase Field – The retractable roof can be opened or closed in just over four minutes -after closure the air conditioning kicks in and can lower the temperature by 30 degrees in three hours. Hit the Taste of the Majors concession stands for foods representing each National League city.

Citizens Bank Park – They made an effort in this new park to highlight local cuisine, including hoagies and cheesesteaks, and you're likely to see former Phillies slugger Greg Luzinski at Bull's' BBQ. It's located along Ashburn Alley, an outfield concourse of shops and concessions named for Phils legend Richie Ashburn.

Coors Field – Sit in the 20th row of the upper deck, which is painted purple amid a sea of green seats, and you'll be exactly one mile above sea level. Located in Denver's LoDo district, it's one of three National League ballparks named after a beer; there are none in the American League.

Dodger Stadium – Opened in 1962, this park is now one of the majors' oldest, but don't let that fool you; it's undergone various modernizations and the setting in Chavez Ravine remains maybe the best in baseball. Bring some headphones and tune in the incomparable Vin Scully calling the game on the radio.

Dolphin Stadium – This is really a football stadium, hence the name and address (Dan Marino Boulevard). It has plenty of parking (over 24,000 spots plus one helipad), the Fish Tank (a rentable hot tub near the Marlins bullpen) and the lovely Marlin Mermaids, the first cheerleaders in baseball.

Great American Ballpark – The Reds are the oldest baseball franchise and a visit to the team's Hall of Fame and Museum on the west side of the park is a great way to soak up some of that history. This new park has received mediocre architectural reviews but the same can't be said for the chilli-cheese dogs, which are must-have.

Miller Park – Brewers fans tailgate like no others in baseball, and the smell of grilled brats and sausages fills the parking lot before, and often after, games. To take in a game on the cheap, fill up at the tailgate and then get the $1, obstructed-view 'Uecker seats,' named for longtime Brewers broadcaster Bob Uecker.

Minute Maid Park – Trains are the theme here, from the refurbished Union Station that many fans enter through to the replica locomotive that runs inside; ironic, because almost all fans drive to the game. The huge glass wall in left field (hurricane-resistant glass) provides light and a view of downtown even when the retractable roof is closed.

Petco Park – Rather than knock down the 95-year-old Western Metal Supply Company Building the Padres incorporated it into their new ballpark. It stands in the left-field corner and now contains a restaurant, suites and bleachers on the roof. Petco is located downtown in the historic and lively Gaslamp Quarter.

PNC Park - Park downtown and walk across the Clemente Bridge to this intimate new field. Before entering, check out the statues of Pirates' greats Honus Wagner, Willie Stargell and Roberto Clemente. The right field wall at PNC rises to 21 feet in honor of Clemente (#21).

RFK Stadium – This place was built for the Redskins and Senators, and welcomed the Nationals in 2005 when they were moved from Montreal (remember the Expos?). Some of that Senators history remains in upper deck seats painted white to designate where long home runs from Frank Howard landed. The Nats hope to move into a new stadium in southeast Washington in a few years.

Shea Stadium – Joe Namath played here and so did the Beatles, and the Yankees called it home in 1974-75 when their park was being renovated. The Mets have been in Queens for more than 40 years and should be for decades to come – a new ballpark next door to Shea is expected to open by 2009.

Turner Field – The former Olympic Stadium hosted the opening and closing ceremonies in 1996 as well as all the track and field events, before being converted to a baseball-only facility. They've preserved a portion of the left-field wall over which Hank Aaron launched number 715, and it stands in the parking lot next door, the site of the old Fulton County Stadium.

Wrigley Field - The Bears played at Wrigley for 50 years and won four NFL championships there. Little-known fact: their 332 games are the most ever played by one team in a home stadium in NFL history. Head to the park early and hang out with the ballhawks on Waveland Avenue who shag batting practice homers.

WISE GUIDE™
FAN NAVIGATOR

Major League Baseball (Cont.)

Colorado Rockies
1993–94	Mile High Stadium (Denver)	76,100
1995–	Coors Field	50,449

Florida Marlins
1993–	Dolphin Stadium (Miami)	36,331
	(1993 capacity—47,662)	

Houston Astros
1962–64	Colt Stadium	32,601
1965–99	The Astrodome	54,370
	(1965 capacity—45,011)	
2000–	Minute Maid Park	40,950

Los Angeles Dodgers
1890	Washington Park I (Brooklyn)	—
1891–97	Eastern Park	—
1898–1912	Washington Park II	—
1913–55	Ebbets Field	31,497
1956–57	Ebbets Field	31,497
	& Roosevelt Stadium (Jersey City)	24,167
1958–61	Memorial Coliseum (Los Angeles)	93,600
1962–	Dodger Stadium	56,000

Milwaukee Brewers
1969	Sick's Stadium (Seattle)	59,166
1970–	County Stadium (Milwaukee)	53,192
2000	(1970 capacity—46,620)	
2001–	Miller Park	42,400

New York Mets
1962–63	Polo Grounds	55,987
1964–	Shea Stadium	56,749
	(1964 capacity—55,101)	

Philadelphia Phillies
1883–86	Recreation Park	—
1887–94	Huntington Ave. Grounds	—
1895–1938	Baker Bowl	18,800
1938–70	Shibe Park	33,608

Philadelphia Phillies (Cont.)
1971–2003	Veterans Stadium	62,418
2004–	Citizens Bank Park	43,000

Pittsburgh Pirates
1887–90	Recreation Park	—
1891–1909	Exposition Park	—
1909–70	Forbes Field	35,000
1970–2000	Three Rivers Stadium	47,687
	(1970 capacity—50,235)	
2001–	PNC Park	37,898

St. Louis Cardinals
1876–77	Sportsman's Park I	—
1885–86	Vandeventer Lot	—
1892–1920	Robison Field	18,000
1920–66	Sportsman's Park II	30,500
1966–2005	Busch Stadium	49,814
2006–	Busch Stadium II	46,000

San Diego Padres
1969–2003	Qualcomm Stadium	66,083
2004–	PETCO Park	46,000

San Francisco Giants
1876	Union Grounds (Brooklyn)	—
1883–88	Polo Grounds I (New York)	—
1889–90	Manhattan Field	—
1891–1957	Polo Grounds II	55,987
1958–59	Seals Stadium (San Francisco)	22,900
1960–99	3Com Park	63,000
	(1960 capacity—42,553)	
2000–	AT&T Park	41,467

Washington Nationals
1969–76	Jarry Park (Montreal)	28,000
1977–2002	Olympic Stadium	46,500
2003–04	Olympic Stadium	46,500
	& Hiram Bithon Stadium (San Juan)	18,000
2005–	RFK Stadium (Washington D.C.)	45,250

Ballpark Name Changes: ARIZONA—**Chase Field** originally named Bank One Ballpark (1998-2005); ATLANTA—**Atlanta-Fulton County Stadium** originally Atlanta Stadium (1966-74), **Turner Field** originally Centennial Olympic Stadium (1996); CHICAGO—**Wrigley Field** originally Weeghman Park (1914-17), then Cubs Park (1918-25); CINCINNATI—**Redland Field** originally League Park (1890-93), **Crosley Field** originally Redland Field II (1912-33) and **Cinergy Field** originally Riverfront Stadium (1970-96); FLORIDA—**Dolphin Stadium** originally Joe Robbie Stadium (1987-96), then Pro Player Stadium (1997-2004), then Dolphins Stadium (2004-06); HOUSTON—**Astrodome** originally Harris County Domed Stadium before it opened in 1965; **Enron Field** renamed Astros Field briefly and then Minute Maid Park in 2002; PHILADELPHIA—**Baker Field** originally Philadelphia Park (1895-1912), **Shibe Park** renamed Connie Mack Stadium in 1953; ST. LOUIS—**Robison Field** originally Vandeventer Lot, then League Park, then Cardinal Park all before becoming Robison Field in 1901, **Sportsman's Park** renamed Busch Stadium in 1953, and **Busch Stadium** originally Busch Memorial Stadium (1966-82); SAN DIEGO—**Qualcomm Stadium** originally San Diego Stadium (1967-81) and San Diego/Jack Murphy Stadium (1982-96); SAN FRANCISCO—**3Com Park** originally Candlestick Park (1960-95), **AT&T Park** originally Pacific Bell Park (2000-03), then SBC Park (2003-06).

NATIONAL BASKETBALL ASSOCIATION

Western Conference

		Location	Built	Capacity
Dallas Mavericks	American Airlines Center	Dallas, Texas	2001	**19,200**
Denver Nuggets	Pepsi Center	Denver, Colo.	1999	**19,099**
Golden State Warriors	Oakland Arena	Oakland, Calif.	1997	**19,596**
Houston Rockets	Toyota Center	Houston, Texas	2003	**18,300**
Los Angeles Clippers	Staples Center	Los Angeles, Calif.	1999	**18,694**
Los Angeles Lakers	Staples Center	Los Angeles, Calif.	1999	**18,997**
Memphis Grizzlies	FedEx Forum	Memphis, Tenn.	2004	**18,400**
Minnesota Timberwolves	Target Center	Minneapolis, Minn.	1990	**19,006**
New Orleans Hornets*	Ford Center & Maravich Assembly Center	Oklahoma City, Okla. Baton Rouge, La.	2002 1971	**19,675** **14,164**
Phoenix Suns	America West Arena	Phoenix, Ariz.	1992	**19,023**
Portland Trail Blazers	Rose Garden	Portland, Ore.	1995	**19,980**
Sacramento Kings	ARCO Arena	Sacramento, Calif.	1988	**17,317**
San Antonio Spurs	SBC Center	San Antonio, Texas	2002	**18,500**
Seattle SuperSonics	KeyArena at Seattle Center	Seattle, Wash.	1962	**17,072**
Utah Jazz	Delta Center	Salt Lake City, Utah	1991	**19,911**

*Due to the aftermath of Hurricane Katrina the New Orleans Hornets were forced out of New Orleans Arena and arranged to play 35 regular-season games at Oklahoma City's Ford Center and six games at LSU's Maravich Assembly Center.

Notes: Seattle's KeyArena was originally the Seattle Center Coliseum before being rebuilt in 1995; The Staples Center has different listed capacities for Clippers games and Lakers games because of different floor seating arrangements.

Eastern Conference

Team	Arena	Location	Built	Capacity
Atlanta Hawks	Philips Arena	Atlanta, Ga.	1999	19,445
Boston Celtics	TD Banknorth Garden	Boston, Mass.	1995	18,624
Charlotte Bobcats	Charlotte Bobcats Arena	Charlotte, N.C.	2005	18,500
Chicago Bulls	United Center	Chicago, Ill.	1994	21,711
Cleveland Cavaliers	The Quicken Loans Arena	Cleveland, Ohio	1994	20,562
Detroit Pistons	The Palace of Auburn Hills	Auburn Hills, Mich.	1988	22,076
Indiana Pacers	Conseco Fieldhouse	Indianapolis, Ind.	1999	18,345
Miami Heat	AmericanAirlines Arena	Miami, Fla.	1999	16,500
Milwaukee Bucks	Bradley Center	Milwaukee, Wisc.	1988	18,717
New Jersey Nets	Continental Airlines Arena	E. Rutherford, N.J.	1981	20,049
New York Knicks	Madison Square Garden	New York, N.Y.	1968	19,763
Orlando Magic	TD Waterhouse Centre	Orlando, Fla.	1989	17,248
Philadelphia 76ers	Wachovia Center	Philadelphia, Penn.	1996	20,444
Toronto Raptors	Air Canada Centre	Toronto, Ont.	1999	19,800
Washington Wizards	Verizon Center	Washington, D.C.	1997	20,674

Rank by Capacity

Western		Eastern	
Portland	19,980	Detroit	22,076
Utah	19,911	Chicago	21,711
New Orleans	19,675	Washington	20,674
Golden State	19,596	Cleveland	20,562
Dallas	19,200	Philadelphia	20,444
Denver	19,099	New Jersey	20,049
Phoenix	19,023	Toronto	19,800
Minnesota	19,006	New York	19,763
LA Lakers	18,997	Atlanta	19,445
LA Clippers	18,694	Milwaukee	18,717
San Antonio	18,500	Boston	18,624
Memphis	18,400	Charlotte	18,500
Houston	18,300	Indiana	18,345
Sacramento	17,317	Orlando	17,248
Seattle	17,072	Miami	16,500

Rank by Age

Western		Eastern	
Seattle	1962	New York	1968
Sacramento	1988	New Jersey	1981
Minnesota	1990	Detroit	1988
Utah	1991	Milwaukee	1988
Phoenix	1992	Orlando	1989
Portland	1995	Chicago	1994
Golden St.	1997	Cleveland	1994
Denver	1999	Boston	1995
LA Clippers	1999	Philadelphia	1996
LA Lakers	1999	Washington	1997
Dallas	2001	Toronto	1999
San Antonio	2002	Atlanta	1999
New Orleans	2002	Indiana	1999
Houston	2003	Miami	1999
Memphis	2004	Charlotte	2005

Note: The Seattle Center Coliseum was rebuilt and renamed KeyArena in 1995.

2005-06 NBA Attendance

Official overall attendance in the NBA for the 2005-06 season was 21,521,083 for an average per game crowd of 17,497 over 1,230 games. Teams in each conference are ranked by attendance over 41 home games based on total tickets distributed. Rank column refers to rank in entire league. Numbers in parentheses indicate conference rank in 2004-05. Note that in the aftermath of Hurricane Katrina, the Hornets split their home games between the Maravich Center in Baton Rouge and Ford Center in Oklahoma City.

Western Conference

	Team	Attendance	Rank	Average
1	Dallas (1)	824,993	3	20,121
2	LA Lakers (2)	774,189	7	18,882
3	San Antonio (4)	770,677	8	18,797
4	Utah (3)	751,621	9	18,332
5	Golden St. (13)	730,928	10	18,273
6	N.O./Okla. City (15)	744,920	11	18,168
7	Phoenix (5)	730,179	12	17,809
8	LA Clippers (9)	712,409	13	17,375
9	Sacramento (7)	709,997	14	17,317
10	Denver (6)	702,555	15	17,135
11	Seattle (12)	664,157	23	16,198
12	Minnesota (8)	648,167	25	15,808
13	Memphis (10)	647,533	26	15,793
14	Houston (14)	636,110	28	15,514
15	Portland (11)	617,199	30	15,053
	TOTAL	10,665,634	—	17,342

Eastern Conference

	Team	Attendance	Rank	Average
1	Detroit (1)	883,040	1	22,076
2	Chicago (2)	868,720	2	21,188
3	Miami (3)	818,149	4	19,954
4	Cleveland (5)	792,391	5	19,326
5	New York (4)	776,176	6	18,931
6	Washington (7)	684,889	16	17,122
7	Toronto (8)	699,242	17	17,054
8	Boston (10)	692,513	18	16,890
9	New Jersey (12)	691,543	19	16,866
10	Milwaukee (11)	681,337	20	16,617
11	Philadelphia (6)	677,248	21	16,518
12	Charlotte (15)	671,011	22	16,366
13	Indiana (9)	663,368	24	16,179
14	Orlando (13)	638,005	27	15,561
15	Atlanta (14)	617,817	29	15,068
	TOTAL	10,855,449	—	17,651

Home Courts

Listed below are the principal home courts used through the years by current NBA teams. The largest capacity of each arena is noted in the right-hand column. ABA arenas (1967-76) are included for Denver, Indiana, New Jersey and San Antonio.

Western Conference

Dallas Mavericks

1980–2000	Reunion Arena	18,187
2001–	American Airlines Center	19,200

Denver Nuggets

1967–75	Auditorium Arena	6,841
1975–99	McNichols Sports Arena	17,171
	(1975 capacity—16,700)	
1999–	Pepsi Center	19,099

Golden State Warriors

1946–52	Philadelphia Arena	7,777
1952–62	Convention Hall (Philadelphia)	9,200
	& Philadelphia Arena	7,777
1962–64	Cow Palace (San Francisco)	13,862
1964–66	Civic Auditorium	7,500
	& (USF Memorial Gym)	6,000
1966–67	Cow Palace, Civic Auditorium	
	& Oakland Coliseum Arena	15,000
1967–71	Cow Palace	14,500
1971–96	Oakland Coliseum Arena	15,025
	(1971 capacity—12,905)	
1996–97	San Jose Arena	18,500
1997–	The Arena in Oakland	19,596

Houston Rockets

1967–71	San Diego Sports Arena	14,000
1971–72	Hofheinz Pavilion (Houston)	10,218
1972–73	Hofheinz Pavilion	10,218
	& HemisFair Arena (San Antonio)	10,446
1973–75	Hofheinz Pavilion	10,218
1975–2002	Compaq Center	16,285
2003–	Toyota Center	18,300

Los Angeles Clippers

1970–78	Memorial Auditorium (Buffalo)	17,300
1978–84	San Diego Sports Arena	12,167
1985–94	Los Angeles Sports Arena	16,005
1994–99	Los Angeles Sports Arena	16,021
	& Arrowhead Pond	18,211
1999–	Staples Center	18,694

Los Angeles Lakers

1948–60	Minneapolis Auditorium	10,000
1960–67	Los Angeles Sports Arena	14,781
1967–99	Great Western Forum (Inglewood, CA)	17,505
	(1967 capacity—17,086)	
1999–	Staples Center	18,997

Memphis Grizzlies

1995–2001	General Motors Place (Vancouver)	19,193
2001–03	The Pyramid (Memphis, TN)	19,342
2004–	FedEx Forum	18,400

Minnesota Timberwolves

1989–90	Hubert H. Humphrey Metrodome	23,000
1990–	Target Center	19,006

New Orleans Hornets

1988–2002	Charlotte Coliseum	19,925
	(1988 capacity—23,500)	

New Orleans (Cont.)

2002–05	New Orleans Arena	18,500
2005-06	Ford Center (Oklahoma City)	19,675
	& Maravich Center (Baton Rouge)	14,164

Phoenix Suns

1968–92	Arizona Veterans' Memorial Coliseum	14,487
1992–	America West Arena	19,023

Portland Trail Blazers

1970–95	Memorial Coliseum	12,888
1995–	Rose Garden	19,980
	(1995 capacity—21,538)	

Sacramento Kings

1948–55	Edgarton Park Arena (Rochester, NY)	5,000
1955–58	Rochester War Memorial	10,000
1958–72	Cincinnati Gardens	11,438
1972–74	Municipal Auditorium (Kansas City)	9,929
	& Omaha (NE) Civic Auditorium	9,136
1974–78	Kemper Arena (Kansas City)	16,785
	& Omaha Civic Auditorium	9,136
1978–85	Kemper Arena	16,886
1985–88	ARCO Arena I	10,333
1988–	ARCO Arena II	17,317
	(1988 capacity—16,517)	

San Antonio Spurs

1967–70	Memorial Auditorium (Dallas)	8,088
	& Moody Coliseum (Dallas)	8,500
1970–71	Moody Coliseum	8,500
	Tarrant County	
	Convention Center (Ft. Worth)	13,500
	& Municipal Coliseum (Lubbock)	10,400
1971–73	Moody Coliseum	9,500
	& Memorial Auditorium	8,088
1973–93	HemisFair Arena (San Antonio)	16,057
1993–2002	The Alamodome	20,557
2002–	SBC Center	18,500

Seattle SuperSonics

1967–78	Seattle Center Coliseum	14,098
1978–85	Kingdome	40,192
1985–94	Seattle Center Coliseum	14,252
1994–95	Tacoma Dome	19,000
1995–	KeyArena at Seattle Center	17,072

Utah Jazz

1974–75	Municipal Auditorium (New Orleans)	7,853
	& Louisiana Superdome	47,284
1975–79	Superdome	47,284
1979–83	Salt Palace (Salt Lake City)	12,519
1983–84	Salt Palace	12,519
	& Thomas & Mack Center (Las Vegas)	18,500
1984–91	Salt Palace	12,616
1991–	Delta Center	19,911

Note: The Sacramento (then Kansas City) Kings played 30 home games at Kansas City Municipal Auditorium during the 1979-80 season after the Kemper Auditorium roof collapsed during a severe rain and wind storm on June 4, 1979.

Eastern Conference

Atlanta Hawks

1949–51	Wharton Field House (Moline, IL)	6,000
1951–55	Milwaukee Arena	11,000
1955–68	Kiel Auditorium (St. Louis)	10,000
1968–72	Alexander Mem. Coliseum (Atlanta)	7,166
1972–96	The Omni	16,378
1997–99	Georgia Dome	21,570
	& Alexander Mem. Coliseum	9,300
1999–	Philips Arena	19,445

Boston Celtics

1946–95	Boston Garden	14,890
1995–	TD Banknorth Garden	18,624

Note: From 1975-95 the Celtics played some regular season games at the Hartford Civic Center (15,418).

Charlotte Bobcats

2004-05	Charlotte Coliseum	19,925
2005–	Charlotte Arena	18,500

Chicago Bulls

1966–67	Chicago Amphitheater	11,002
1967–94	Chicago Stadium	18,676
1994–	United Center	21,711

Cleveland Cavaliers

1970–74	Cleveland Arena	11,000
1974–94	The Coliseum (Richfield, OH)	20,273
1994–	The Quicken Loans Arena	20,562

Detroit Pistons

1948–52	North Side H.S: Gym (Ft. Wayne, IN) . .	3,800
1952–57	Memorial Coliseum (Ft. Wayne)	9,306
1957–61	Olympia Stadium (Detroit)	14,000
1961–78	Cobo Arena	11,147
1978–88	Silverdome (Pontiac, MI)	22,366
1988–	The Palace of Auburn Hills	22,076

Indiana Pacers

1967–74	State Fairgrounds (Indianapolis) . .	9,479
1974–99	Market Square Arena	16,530
	(1974 capacity—17,287)	
1999–	Conseco Fieldhouse	18,345

Miami Heat

1988–99	Miami Arena	15,200
2000–	AmericanAirlines Arena	16,500

Milwaukee Bucks

1968–88	Milwaukee Arena (The Mecca)	11,052
1988–	Bradley Center	18,717

New Jersey Nets

1967–68	Teaneck (NJ) Armory	3,500
1968–69	Long Island Arena (Commack, NY)	6,500
1969–71	Island Garden (W. Hempstead, NY) . .	5,200
1971–77	Nassau Coliseum (Uniondale, NY)	15,500
1977–81	Rutgers Ath. Center (Piscataway, NJ) . .	9,050
1981–	Continental Airlines Arena (E. Ruth., NJ)	.20,049

New York Knicks

1946–68	Madison Sq. Garden III (50th St.) . .	18,496
1968–	Madison Sq. Garden IV (33rd St.) . . .	19,763
	(1968 capacity—19,694)	

Orlando Magic

1989–	TD Waterhouse Centre	17,248

Philadelphia 76ers

1949–51	State Fair Coliseum (Syracuse, NY) . .	.7,500
1951–63	Onondaga County (NY) War Memorial	.8,000
1963–67	Convention Hall (Philadelphia)	12,000
	& Philadelphia Arena	.7,777
1967–96	CoreStates Spectrum	18,136
1996–	Wachovia Center	.20,444

Toronto Raptors

1995–99	SkyDome	20,125
1999–	Air Canada Centre	19,800

Washington Wizards

1961–62	Chicago Amphitheater	11,000
1962–63	Chicago Coliseum	.7,100
1963–73	Baltimore Civic Center	12,289
1973–97	USAir Arena (Landover, MD)	18,756
1997–	Verizon Center	20,674

Note: From 1988-96 the Wizards (then Bullets) played four regular season games at Baltimore Arena (12,756).

Building Name Changes: BOSTON—**TD Banknorth Garden** originally FleetCenter (1995-2005); CLEVELAND—**The Quicken Loans Arena** originally Gund Arena (1994-2005); HOUSTON—**Compaq Center** originally The Summit (1975-97); NEW JERSEY—**Continental Airlines Arena** originally Byrne Meadowlands Arena (1981-96); ORLANDO—**TD Waterhouse Centre** originally Orlando Arena (1989-99); PHILADELPHIA—**Wachovia Center** originally the CoreStates Center (1996-98), then the First Union Center (1998-2003) and **CoreStates Spectrum** originally The Spectrum (1967-94); WASHINGTON—**USAir Arena** originally Capital Centre (1973-93); **Verizon Center** originally MCI Center (1997-2006).

NATIONAL FOOTBALL LEAGUE

American Football Conference

		Location	Built	Capacity	Field
Baltimore Ravens	**M&T Bank Stadium**	Baltimore, Md.	1998	**69,084**	Grass
Buffalo Bills	**Ralph Wilson Stadium**	Orchard Park, N.Y.	1973	**73,967**	Turf
Cincinnati Bengals	**Paul Brown Stadium**	Cincinnati, Ohio	2000	**65,352**	Grass
Cleveland Browns	**Cleveland Browns Stadium**	Cleveland, Ohio	1999	**73,200**	Grass
Denver Broncos	**INVESCO Field at Mile High**	Denver, Colo.	2001	**76,125**	Grass
Houston Texans	**Reliant Stadium**	Houston, Tex.	2002	**69,500**	Grass
Indianapolis Colts	**RCA Dome**	Indianapolis, Ind.	1984	**56,127**	Turf
Jacksonville Jaguars	**ALLTEL Stadium**	Jacksonville, Fla.	1995	**73,000**	Grass
Kansas City Chiefs	**Arrowhead Stadium**	Kansas City, Mo.	1972	**79,451**	Grass
Miami Dolphins	**Dolphin Stadium**	Miami, Fla.	1987	**75,540**	Grass
New England Patriots	**Gillette Stadium**	Foxboro, Mass.	2002	**68,000**	Grass
New York Jets	**Giants Stadium**	E. Rutherford, N.J.	1976	**80,062**	Turf
Oakland Raiders	**McAfee Coliseum**	Oakland, Calif.	1966	**63,132**	Grass
Pittsburgh Steelers	**Heinz Field**	Pittsburgh, Pa.	2001	**64,450**	Grass
San Diego Chargers	**Qualcomm Stadium**	San Diego, Calif.	1967	**71,294**	Grass
Tennessee Titans	**LP Field**	Nashville, Tenn.	1999	**68,798**	Grass

National Football Conference

		Location	Built	Capacity	Field
Arizona Cardinals	**University of Phoenix Stadium**	Glendale, Ariz.	2006	**63,500***	Grass
Atlanta Falcons	**Georgia Dome**	Atlanta, Ga.	1992	**71,228**	Turf
Carolina Panthers	**Bank of America Stadium**	Charlotte, N.C.	1996	**73,500**	Grass
Chicago Bears	**Soldier Field**	Chicago, Ill.	1924	**63,000**	Grass
Dallas Cowboys	**Texas Stadium**	Irving, Texas	1971	**65,639**	Turf
Detroit Lions	**Ford Field**	Detroit, Mich.	2002	**65,000**	Turf
Green Bay Packers	**Lambeau Field**	Green Bay, Wis.	1957	**72,515**	Grass
Minnesota Vikings	**Hubert H. Humphrey Metrodome**	Minneapolis, Minn.	1982	**64,121**	Turf
New Orleans Saints	**Louisiana Superdome**	New Orleans, La.	1975	**69,703**	Turf
New York Giants	**Giants Stadium**	E. Rutherford, N.J.	1976	**80,062**	Grass
Philadelphia Eagles	**Lincoln Financial Field**	Philadelphia, Pa.	2003	**68,532**	Grass
St. Louis Rams	**Edward Jones Dome**	St. Louis, Mo.	1995	**66,000**	Turf
San Francisco 49ers	**Monster Park**	San Francisco, Calif.	1960	**69,400**	Grass
Seattle Seahawks	**Qwest Field**	Seattle, Wash.	2002	**67,000**	Grass
Tampa Bay Buccaneers	**Raymond James Stadium**	Tampa, Fla.	1998	**65,657**	Grass
Washington Redskins	**FedEx Field**	Raljon, Md.	1997	**86,484**	Grass

*Cardinals Stadium is expandable to 73,000.

National Football League (Cont.)

Rank by Capacity

AFC		NFC	
NY Jets	80,062	Washington	86,484
Kansas City	79,451	NY Giants	80,062
Denver	76,125	Carolina	73,500
Miami	75,540	Green Bay	72,515
Buffalo	73,967	Atlanta	71,228
Cleveland	73,200	New Orleans	69,703
Jacksonville	73,000	San Francisco	69,400
San Diego	71,294	Philadelphia	68,532
Houston	69,500	Seattle	67,000
Baltimore	69,084	St. Louis	66,000
Tennessee	68,798	Tampa Bay	65,657
New England	68,000	Dallas	65,639
Cincinnati	65,352	Detroit	65,000
Pittsburgh	64,450	Minnesota	64,121
Oakland	63,132	Arizona	63,500
Indianapolis	56,127	Chicago	63,000

Rank by Age

AFC		NFC	
Oakland	1966	Chicago	1924
San Diego	1967	Green Bay	1957
Kansas City	1972	San Francisco	1960
Buffalo	1973	Dallas	1971
NY Jets	1976	New Orleans	1975
Indianapolis	1984	NY Giants	1976
Miami	1987	Minnesota	1982
Jacksonville	1995	Atlanta	1992
Baltimore	1998	St. Louis	1995
Cleveland	1999	Carolina	1996
Tennessee	1999	Washington	1997
Cincinnati	2000	Tampa Bay	1998
Denver	2001	Seattle	2002
Pittsburgh	2001	Detroit	2002
New England	2002	Philadelphia	2003
Houston	2002	Arizona	2006

Notes: Chicago's Soldier Field was rebuilt and Green Bay's Lambeau Field was renovated in 2003.

2005 NFL Attendance

Overall paid attendance in the NFL for the 2005 season was 17,200,324 for an average per game crowd of 67,189 over 256 games. Teams in each conference are ranked by attendance over eight home games. Rank column indicates rank in entire league. Numbers in parentheses indicate conference rank in 2004.

AFC

		Attendance	Rank	Average
1	Kansas City (2)	623,325	3	77,915
2	N.Y. Jets (1)	619,958	4	77,494
3	Denver (3)	608,790	5	76,098
4	Cleveland (4)	578,330	7	72,291
5	Miami (5)	575,256	8	71,907
6	Buffalo (6)	575,248	9	71,906
7	Baltimore (8)	563,076	11	70,384
8	Houston (7)	562,397	13	70,299
9	Tennessee (10)	553,192	14	69,149
10	New England (11)	550,048	15	68,756
11	San Diego (14)	529,916	18	66,239
12	Cincinnati (12)	526,469	19	65,808
13	Jacksonville (9)	525,519	20	65,689
14	Pittsburgh (13)	507,434	25	63,429
15	Indianapolis (15)	457,373	29	57,171
16	Oakland (16)	418,450	30	52,306
	TOTAL	8,774,781	—	68,553

NFC

		Attendance	Rank	Average
1	Washington (1)	716,999	1	89,624
2	NY Giants (2)	628,519	2	78,564
3	Carolina (3)	587,700	6	73,462
4	Atlanta (4)	565,106	10	70,638
5	Green Bay (5)	562,419	12	70,302
6	Philadelphia (6)	541,393	16	67,674
7	Seattle (7)	532,954	17	66,619
8	St. Louis (8)	523,685	21	65,460
9	San Francisco (10)	523,426	22	65,428
10	Tampa Bay (9)	521,741	23	65,217
11	Minnesota (12)	511,960	24	63,995
12	Dallas (13)	505,258	26	63,157
13	Chicago (15)	496,965	27	62,120
14	Detroit (14)	492,580	28	61,572
15	New Orleans (11)	417,270	31	52,158
16	Arizona (16)	297,568	32	42,509
	TOTAL	8,425,543	—	66,585

Home Fields

Listed below are the principal home fields used through the years by current NFL teams. The largest capacity of each stadium is noted in the right-hand column. All-America Football Conference stadiums (1946-49) are included for Cleveland and San Francisco.

AFC

Baltimore Ravens

1996–97	Memorial Stadium	65,000
1998–	M&T Bank Stadium	69,084

Buffalo Bills

1960–72	War Memorial Stadium	45,748
1973–	Ralph Wilson Stadium (Orchard Park, NY)	73,967
	(1973 capacity—80,020)	

Cincinnati Bengals

1968–69	Nippert Stadium (Univ. of Cincinnati)	26,500
1970–99	Cinergy Field	60,389
	(1970 capacity—56,200)	
2000–	Paul Brown Stadium	65,352

Cleveland Browns

1946–95	Cleveland Stadium	78,512
	(1946 capacity—85,703)	
1999–	Cleveland Browns Stadium	73,200

Denver Broncos

1960–2000	Mile High Stadium	76,123
	(1960 capacity—34,000)	
2001–	INVESCO Field at Mile High	76,125

Houston Texans

2002–	Reliant Stadium	69,500

Indianapolis Colts

1953–83	Memorial Stadium (Baltimore)	60,020
1984–	RCA Dome (Indianapolis)	56,127
	(1984 capacity—60,127)	

Jacksonville Jaguars

1995–	ALLTEL Stadium	73,000

Kansas City Chiefs

1960–62	Cotton Bowl (Dallas)	72,000
1963–71	Municipal Stadium (Kansas City)	47,000
1972–	Arrowhead Stadium	79,451
	(1972 capacity—78,097)	

Miami Dolphins

1966–86	Orange Bowl	.75,206
1987–	Dolphin Stadium	.75,540

New England Patriots

1960–62	Nickerson Field (Boston Univ.)	17,369
1963–68	Fenway Park	.33,379
1969	Alumni Stadium (Boston College)	.26,000
1970	Harvard Stadium	.37,300
1971-2001	Foxboro Stadium	.60,292
	(1971 capacity—61,114)	
2002–	Gillette Stadium (Foxboro, Mass.)	.68,000

New York Jets

1960–63	Polo Grounds	.55,987
1964–83	Shea Stadium	.60,372
1984–	Giants Stadium (E. Rutherford, NJ)	.80,062

Oakland Raiders

1960	Kesar Stadium (San Francisco)	.59,636
1961	Candlestick Park	.42,500
1962–65	Frank Youell Field (Oakland)	.20,000
1966–81	Oakland-Alameda County Coliseum	.54,587
1982–94	Memorial Coliseum (Los Angeles)	.67,800
1995–	McAfee Coliseum	.63,132

Pittsburgh Steelers

1933–57	Forbes Field	.35,000
1958–63	Forbes Field	.35,000
	& Pitt Stadium	.54,500
1964–69	Pitt Stadium	.54,500
1970–	Three Rivers Stadium	.59,600
2000	(1970 capacity—49,000)	
2001–	Heinz Field	.64,450

San Diego Chargers

1960	Memorial Coliseum (Los Angeles)	.92,604
1961–66	Balboa Stadium (San Diego)	.34,000
1967–	Qualcomm Stadium	.71,294
	(1967 capacity—54,000)	

Tennessee Titans

1960–64	Jeppesen Stadium (Houston)	.23,500
1965–67	Rice Stadium (Rice Univ.)	.70,000
1968-96	Astrodome	.59,969
1997	Liberty Bowl (Memphis)	.62,380
1998	Vanderbilt Stadium (Nashville)	.41,600
1999–	LP Field (Nashville)	.68,798

Stadium Name Changes: BALTIMORE—**M&T Bank Stadium** was originally named Ravens Stadium (1998-99) then was renamed PSInet Stadium (1999-2002) and renamed Ravens Stadium (2002-03); BUFFALO—**Ralph Wilson Stadium** originally Rich Stadium (1973-99); CINCINNATI—Cinergy Field originally Riverfront Stadium (1970-96); CLEVELAND—Cleveland Stadium originally Municipal Stadium (1932-74); DENVER—**Mile High Stadium** originally Bears Stadium (1948-66); INDIANAPOLIS—**RCA Dome** originally Hoosier Dome (1984-94); JACKSONVILLE—**ALLTEL Stadium** originally Jacksonville Municipal Stadium (1995-97); MIAMI—**Dolphins Stadium** originally Joe Robbie Stadium (1987-96), then Pro Player Stadium (1996-2005); NEW ENGLAND—Foxboro Stadium originally Schaefer Stadium (1971-82), then Sullivan Stadium (1983-89); **Gillette Stadium** originally CMGI Field; OAKLAND—**McAfee Coliseum** originally Oakland Alameda Coliseum (1995-99), Network Associates Coliseum (1999-2004); SAN DIEGO—**Qualcomm Stadium** originally San Diego Stadium (1967-81) then San Diego/Jack Murphy Stadium (1981-96); TENNESSEE—**LP Field** originally Adelphia Coliseum (1999-2001), then The Coliseum (2001-06).

- NFC

Arizona Cardinals

1920–21	Normal Field (Chicago)	.7,500
1922–25	Comiskey Park	.28,000
1926–28	Normal Field	.7,500
1929–59	Comiskey Park	.52,000
1960–65	Busch Stadium (St. Louis)	.34,000
1966–87	Busch Memorial Stadium	.54,392
1988-05	Sun Devil Stadium (Tempe, AZ)	.73,273
2006—	Univ. of Phoenix Stadium (Glendale)	.63,500

Atlanta Falcons

1966-91	Atlanta-Fulton County Stadium	.59,643
1992–	Georgia Dome	.71,228

Carolina Panthers

1995	Memorial Stadium (Clemson, SC)	.81,473
1996–	Bank of America Stadium	.73,500

Chicago Bears

1920	Staley Field (Decatur, IL)	—
1921–70	Wrigley Field (Chicago)	.37,741
1971–2001	Soldier Field	.66,944
	(1971 capacity—55,049)	
2002	Memorial Stadium (Champaign, IL)	.69,249
2003–	Soldier Field	.63,000

Dallas Cowboys

1960–70	Cotton Bowl	.72,132
1971–	Texas Stadium (Irving, TX)	.65,639
	(1971 capacity—65,101)	

Detroit Lions

1930–33	Spartan Stadium (Portsmouth, OH)	.8,200
1934–37	Univ. of Detroit Stadium	.25,000
1938–74	Tiger Stadium	.54,468
1975-2001	Pontiac Silverdome	.80,311
	(1975 capacity—80,638)	
2002–	Ford Field	.65,000

Green Bay Packers

1921–22	Hagemeister Brewery Park	—
1923–24	Bellevue Park	—
1925–56	City Stadium I	.24,800
1957–	Lambeau Field	.72,515
	(1957 capacity—32,150)	
	(2002 capacity—62,500)	

Note: The Packers played games in Milwaukee from 1933-94: at Borchert Field, State Fair Park and Marquette Stadium (1933-52), and County Stadium (1953-94).

Minnesota Vikings

1961–81	Metropolitan Stadium (Bloomington)	.48,446
1982–	HHH Metrodome (Minneapolis)	.64,121
	(1982 capacity—62,220)	

New Orleans Saints

1967–74	Tulane Stadium	.80,997
1975–2004	Louisiana Superdome	.69,703
	(1975 capacity—74,472)	
2005	Tiger Stadium (Baton Rouge)	.91,644
	& Alamodome (San Antonio)	.65,000
2006—	Louisiana Superdome	.69,703

Note: The Saints were unable to play at the Louisiana Superdome in the wake of Hurricane Katrina and played four home games at LSU's Tiger Stadium and three at the Alamodome in San Antonio in 2005.

New York Giants

1925–55	Polo Grounds II	.55,200
1956–73	Yankee Stadium I	.63,800
1973–74	Yale Bowl (New Haven, CT)	.70,896
1975	Shea Stadium	.60,372
1976–	Giants Stadium (E. Rutherford, NJ)	.80,062
	(1976 capacity—76,800)	

National Football League (Cont.)

Philadelphia Eagles

1933–35	Baker Bowl	18,800
1936–39	Municipal Stadium	73,702
1940	Shibe Park	33,608
1941	Municipal Stadium	73,702
1942	Shibe Park	33,608
1943	Forbes Field (Pittsburgh)	34,528
1944–57	Shibe Park	33,608
1958–70	Franklin Field (Univ. of Penn.)	60,546
1971–2002	Veterans Stadium	65,352
2003–	Lincoln Financial Field	68,532

St. Louis Rams

1937–42	Municipal Stadium (Cleveland)	85,703
1937	League Park (Cleveland)	—
1938	Shaw Stadium (Cleveland)	—
1937	League Park	—
1943	Suspended operations for one year.	
1944–45	Municipal Stadium	85,703
1946–79	Memorial Coliseum (Los Angeles)	92,604
1980–94	Anaheim Stadium	69,008
1995	Busch Stadium	60,000
1995–	Edward Jones Dome	66,000

San Francisco 49ers

1946–70	Kezar Stadium	59,636
1971–	Monster Park	69,400
(1971 capacity—61,246)		

Seattle Seahawks

1976–94	Kingdome	66,000
1994	Kingdome	66,400
	& Husky Stadium	72,500
1995–99	Kingdome	66,400
2000-01	Husky Stadium	72,500
2002–	Qwest Field	67,000

Tampa Bay Buccaneers

1976–97	Houlihan's Stadium	74,300
1998–	Raymond James Stadium	65,657

Washington Redskins

1932	Braves Field (Boston)	40,000
1933–36	Fenway Park	27,000
1937–60	Griffith Stadium (Washington, DC)	35,000
1961–97	RFK Stadium	56,454
1997–	FedEx Field (Raljon, MD)	86,484

Stadium Name Changes: ATLANTA—**Atlanta-Fulton County Stadium** originally Atlanta Stadium (1966-74); CAROLINA—**Bank of America Stadium** originally Ericsson Stadium (1996-2004); CHICAGO—**Wrigley Field** originally Cubs Park (1916-25); DETROIT—**Tiger Stadium** originally Navin Field (1912-37), then Briggs Stadium (1938-60), also, **Pontiac Silverdome** originally Pontiac Metropolitan Stadium (1975); GREEN BAY—**Lambeau Field** originally City Stadium II (1957-64); PHILADELPHIA—**Shibe Park** renamed Connie Mack Stadium in 1953; ST. LOUIS—**Busch Memorial Stadium** renamed Busch Stadium in 1983, **Edward Jones Dome** originally Trans World Dome (1995-99), then The Dome at America's Center (2000-01); SAN FRANCISCO—**Monster Park** originally Candlestick Park (1960-94), then 3Com Park (1995-2001) and again Candlestick Park (2001-04); SEATTLE—**Qwest Field** originally Seahawks Stadium (2002-04); TAMPA BAY—**Raymond James Stadium** originally Tampa Stadium (1976-96), then **Houlihan's Stadium** (1996-98); WASHINGTON—**RFK Stadium** originally D.C. Stadium (1961-68), also, **FedEx Field** originally Jack Kent Cooke Stadium (1997-99).

NATIONAL HOCKEY LEAGUE

Western Conference

	Arena	Location	Built	Capacity
Anaheim, Mighty Ducks of	**Honda Center**	Anaheim, Calif.	1993	**17,174**
Calgary Flames	**Pengrowth Saddledome**	Calgary, Alb.	1983	**17,135**
Chicago Blackhawks	**United Center**	Chicago, Ill.	1994	**20,500**
Colorado Avalanche	**Pepsi Center**	Denver, Colo.	1999	**18,007**
Columbus Blue Jackets	**Nationwide Arena**	Columbus, Ohio	2000	**18,136**
Dallas Stars	**American Airlines Center**	Dallas, Texas	2001	**18,532**
Detroit Red Wings	**Joe Louis Arena**	Detroit, Mich.	1979	**20,058**
Edmonton Oilers	**Rexall Place**	Edmonton, Alb.	1974	**16,839**
Los Angeles Kings	**Staples Center**	Los Angeles, Calif.	1999	**18,118**
Minnesota Wild	**Xcel Energy Center**	St. Paul, Minn.	2000	**18,064**
Nashville Predators	**Gaylord Entertainment Center**	Nashville, Tenn.	1994	**17,113**
Phoenix Coyotes	**Glendale Arena**	Glendale, Ariz.	2003	**17,500**
St. Louis Blues	**Scottrade Center**	St. Louis, Mo.	1994	**19,022**
San Jose Sharks	**HP Pavilion at San Jose**	San Jose, Calif.	1993	**17,496**
Vancouver Canucks	**General Motors Place**	Vancouver, B.C.	1995	**18,422**

Eastern Conference

	Arena	Location	Built	Capacity
Atlanta Thrashers	**Philips Arena**	Atlanta, Ga.	1999	**18,545**
Boston Bruins	**TD Banknorth Garden**	Boston, Mass.	1995	**17,565**
Buffalo Sabres	**HSBC Arena**	Buffalo, N.Y.	1996	**18,690**
Carolina Hurricanes	**RBC Center**	Raleigh, N.C.	1999	**18,730**
Florida Panthers	**BankAtlantic Center**	Sunrise, Fla.	1998	**19,250**
Montreal Canadiens	**Bell Centre**	Montreal, Que.	1996	**21,273**
New Jersey Devils	**Continental Airlines Arena**	E. Rutherford, N.J.	1981	**19,040**
New York Islanders	**Nassau Veterans' Mem. Coliseum**	Uniondale, N.Y.	1972	**16,234**
New York Rangers	**Madison Square Garden**	New York, N.Y.	1968	**18,200**
Ottawa Senators	**Scotiabank Place**	Kanata, Ont.	1996	**19,311**
Philadelphia Flyers	**Wachovia Center**	Philadelphia, Penn.	1996	**18,525**
Pittsburgh Penguins	**Mellon Arena**	Pittsburgh, Penn.	1961	**16,958**
Tampa Bay Lightning	**St. Pete Times Forum**	Tampa Bay, Fla.	1996	**19,758**
Toronto Maple Leafs	**Air Canada Centre**	Toronto, Ont.	1999	**18,819**
Washington Capitals	**Verizon Center**	Washington, D.C.	1997	**18,672**

Rank by Capacity

Western		Eastern	
Chicago	.20,500	Montreal	.21,273
Detroit	.20,058	Tampa Bay	.19,758
St. Louis	.19,022	Florida	.19,250
Dallas	.18,532	New Jersey	.19,040
Vancouver	.18,422	Toronto	.18,819
Columbus	.18,136	Carolina	.18,730
Los Angeles	.18,118	Buffalo	.18,690
Minnesota	.18,064	Washington	.18,672
Colorado	.18,007	Atlanta	.18,545
Phoenix	.17,500	Philadelphia	.18,523
San Jose	.17,496	Ottawa	.18,500
Anaheim	.17,174	NY Rangers	.18,200
Calgary	.17,135	Boston	.17,565
Nashville	.17,113	Pittsburgh	.16,958
Edmonton	.16,839	NY Islanders	.16,234

Rank by Age

Western		Eastern	
Edmonton	.1974	Pittsburgh	.1961
Detroit	.1979	NY Rangers	.1968
Calgary	.1983	NY Islanders	.1972
Anaheim	.1993	New Jersey	.1981
San Jose	.1993	Boston	.1995
Chicago	.1994	Montreal	.1996
St. Louis	.1994	Ottawa	.1996
Nashville	.1994	Buffalo	.1996
Vancouver	.1995	Philadelphia	.1996
Colorado	.1999	Tampa Bay	.1996
Los Angeles	.1999	Washington	.1997
Columbus	.2000	Florida	.1998
Minnesota	.2000	Toronto	.1999
Dallas	.2001	Carolina	.1999
Phoenix	.2003	Atlanta	.1999

2005-06 NHL Attendance

Official overall paid attendance for the 2005-06 season according to the NHL accounting office was 20,554,299 (paid tickets) for an average per game crowd of 16,711 over 1,230 games. Teams in each conference are ranked by attendance over 41 home games. Rank column refers to rank in entire league. Numbers in parentheses indicate conference rank in 2003-04.

Western Conference

		Attendance	Rank	Average
1	Detroit (1)	.822,706	3	20,066
2	Calgary (10)	.790,849	7	19,289
3	Vancouver (2)	.763,830	8	18,630
4	Minnesota (4)	.761,614	9	18,575
5	Colorado (6)	.738,287	11	18,007
6	Los Angeles (7)	.731,475	12	17,840
7	Dallas (5)	.730,979	13	17,828
8	Edmonton (8)	.690,143	15	16,832
9	San Jose (11)	.690,095	16	16,831
10	Columbus (9)	.688,655	17	16,796
11	Phoenix (12)	.638,871	22	15,582
12	Anaheim (13)	.619,380	24	15,106
13	Nashville (15)	.591,556	25	14,428
14	St. Louis (3)	.582,742	27	14,213
15	Chicago (14)	.546,075	29	13,318
	TOTAL	.10,387,257	—	16,890

Eastern Conference

		Attendance	Rank	Average
1	Montreal (1)	.872,194	1	21,273
2	Toronto (2)	.795,747	6	19,408
3	Philadelphia (3)	.805,783	4	19,653
4	NY Rangers (4)	.743,848	10	18,142
5	Tampa Bay (5)	.840,887	2	20,509
6	Ottawa (6)	.498,453	5	19,474
7	Florida (7)	.656,587	19	16,014
8	Buffalo (8)	.693,329	14	16,910
9	Boston (9)	.664,673	18	16,211
10	Atlanta (10)	.637,578	23	15,550
11	New Jersey (11)	.583,448	26	14,230
12	Washington (12)	.570,113	28	13,905
13	NY Islanders (13)	.516,973	30	12,609
14	Carolina (14)	.639,454	21	15,596
15	Pittsburgh (15)	.647,975	20	15,804
	TOTAL	.10,167,042	—	16,532

Note: Due to the lockout, there was no 2004-05 NHL season.

Home Ice

Listed below are the principal home buildings used through the years by current NHL teams. The largest capacity of each arena is noted in the right hand column. World Hockey Association arenas (1972-79) are included for Edmonton, Hartford (now Carolina), Quebec (now Colorado) and Winnipeg (now Phoenix).

Western Conference

Anaheim, Mighty Ducks of

1993–	Honda Center	.17,174

Calgary Flames

1972–80	The Omni (Atlanta)	.15,278
1980–83	Calgary Corral	.7,424
1983–	Pengrowth Saddledome	.17,135
	(1983 capacity—16,674)	

Chicago Blackhawks

1926–29	Chicago Coliseum	.5,000
1929–94	Chicago Stadium	.17,317
1994–	United Center	.20,500

Colorado Avalanche

1972–95	Le Colisee de Quebec	.15,399
1995–99	McNichols Arena (Denver)	.16,061
1999–	Pepsi Center	.18,007

Columbus Blue Jackets

2000–	Nationwide Arena	.18,136

Dallas Stars

1967–93	Met Center (Bloomington, MN)	.15,174
1993–2000	Reunion Arena (Dallas)	.17,001
2001–	American Airlines Center	.18,532

Detroit Red Wings

1926–27	Border Cities Arena (Windsor, Ont.)	.3,200
1927–79	Olympia Stadium (Detroit)	.16,700
1979–	Joe Louis Arena	.20,058

Edmonton Oilers

1972–74	Edmonton Gardens	.7,200
1974–	Rexall Place	.16,839
	(1974 capacity—15,513)	

Los Angeles Kings

1967–99	Great Western Forum (Inglewood)	.16,005
	(1967 capacity—15,651)	
1999–	Staples Center	.18,118

Note: The Kings played 17 games at Long Beach Sports Arena and LA Sports Arena at the start of the 1967-68 season.

Minnesota Wild

2000–	Xcel Energy Center (St. Paul)	.18,064

Nashville Predators

1998–	Gaylord Entertainment Center	.17,113

National Hockey League (Cont.)

Phoenix Coyotes

1972–96	Winnipeg Arena	15,393
	(1972 capacity—10,177)	
1996–2002	America West (Phoenix)	16,210
2003–	Glendale Arena (Glendale, Ariz.)	17,500

St. Louis Blues

1967–94	St. Louis Arena	17,188
1994–	Scottrade Center	19,022

San Jose Sharks

1991–93	Cow Palace (Daly City, CA)	11,100
1993–	HP Pavilion at San Jose	17,496

Vancouver Canucks

1970–95	Pacific Coliseum	16,150
1995–	General Motors Place	18,422

Building Name Changes: ANAHEIM—**Honda Center** originally Arrowhead Pond (1993-2006); CALGARY—**Pengrowth Saddledome** formerly named Canadian Airlines Saddledome (1996-2000) which was originally Olympic Saddledome (1983-95); DALLAS—**Met Center** in Minneapolis originally Metropolitan Sports Center (1967-82); EDMONTON—**Rexall Place** was formerly named Skyreach Centre (1999-2004) which was formerly named Edmonton Coliseum (1995-99) which was originally Northlands Coliseum (1974-94); LOS ANGELES—**Great Western Forum** originally The Forum (1967-88); NASHVILLE—**Gaylord Entertainment Center** originally Nashville Arena (1994-99); ST. LOUIS—**Scottrade Center** originally Kiel Center (1994-2000) then Savvis Center (2000-06), **St. Louis Arena** renamed The Checkerdome in 1977, then St. Louis Arena again in 1982; SAN JOSE—**HP Pavilion at San Jose** originally San Jose Arena (1993-2000), then Compaq Center at San Jose (2000-03).

Eastern Conference

Atlanta Thrashers

1999–	Philips Arena	18,545

Boston Bruins

1924–28	Boston Arena	6,200
1928–95	Boston Garden	14,448
1995–	TD Banknorth Garden	17,565

Buffalo Sabres

1970–96	Memorial Auditorium (The Aud)	16,284
	(1970 capacity—10,429)	
1996–	HSBC Arena	18,690

Carolina Hurricanes

1972–73	Boston Garden	14,442
1973–74	Boston Garden (regular season)	14,442
	West Springfield (MA) Big E (playoffs)	5,513
1974–75	West Springfield Big E	5,513
	& Hartford (CT) Civic Center	10,507
1975–77	Hartford Civic Center	10,507
1977–78	Hartford Civic Center	10,507
	& Springfield (MA) Civic Center	7,725
1978–79	Springfield Civic Center	7,725
1979–80	Springfield Civic Center	7,725
	& Hartford Civic Center II	14,250
1980–97	Hartford Civic Center II	15,635
1997–99	Greensboro Coliseum	21,500
1999–	RBC Center	18,730

Note: The Hartford Civic Center roof caved in January 1978, forcing the Whalers to move their home games to Springfield, MA for two years.

Florida Panthers

1993–98	Miami Arena	14,703
1998–	BankAtlantic Center	19,250

Montreal Canadiens

1910–21	Jubilee Arena	3,200
1913–18	Montreal Arena (Westmount)	6,000
1918–26	Mount Royal Arena	6,750
1926–68	Montreal Forum I	15,500
1968–96	Montreal Forum II	17,959
1996–	Bell Centre	21,273

New Jersey Devils

1974–76	Kemper Arena (Kansas City)	16,300
1976–82	McNichols Arena (Denver)	15,900
1982–	Continental Airlines Arena	19,040
	(1982 capacity—19,023)	

New York Islanders

1972–	Nassau Veterans' Mem. Coliseum	16,234
	(1972 capacity—14,500)	

New York Rangers

1925–68	Madison Square Garden III	15,925
1968–	Madison Square Garden IV	18,200
	(1968 capacity—17,250)	

Ottawa Senators

1992–96	Ottawa Civic Center	10,755
1996–	Scotiabank Place (Kanata)	19,311
	(1996 capacity—18,500)	

Philadelphia Flyers

1967–96	CoreStates Spectrum	17,380
	(1967 capacity—14,558)	
1996–	Wachovia Center	18,523

Pittsburgh Penguins

1967–	Mellon Arena	16,958
	(1967 capacity—12,508)	

Tampa Bay Lightning

1992–93	Expo Hall (Tampa)	10,500
1993–96	ThunderDome (St. Petersburg)	26,000
1996–	St. Pete Times Forum	19,758

Toronto Maple Leafs

1917–31	Mutual Street Arena	8,000
1931–99	Maple Leaf Gardens	15,746
	(1931 capacity—13,542)	
1999–	Air Canada Centre	18,819

Washington Capitals

1974–97	USAir Arena (Landover, MD)	18,130
1997–	Verizon Center	18,672

Building Name Changes: BOSTON—**TD Banknorth Garden** originally FleetCenter (1995-2005); BUFFALO—**HSBC Arena** originally Marine Midland Arena (1996-99); CALGARY—**Pengrowth Saddledome** originally Canadian Airlines Arena (1983-2000); CAROLINA—**RBC Center** originally Raleigh Entertainment and Sports Arena (1999-2002); DALLAS—**American Airlines Center** originally Reunion Arena (1993-2000); FLORIDA—**BankAtlantic Center** formerly named Office Depot Center (2002-05) and originally National Car Rental Center (1998-2002); MONTREAL—**Bell Centre** originally Molson Centre (1996-2002); NEW JERSEY—**Continental Airlines Arena** originally Meadowlands Arena (1982-96); OTTAWA—**Scotiabank Place** originally Corel Center; PHILADELPHIA—**Wachovia Center** originally the CoreStates Center (1996-98), then First Union Center (1998-2003) and **CoreStates Spectrum** originally The Spectrum (1967-94); PITTSBURGH—**Mellon Arena** originally Civic Arena (1967-2000); TAMPA BAY—**St. Pete Times Forum** originally Ice Palace (1996-2002); WASHINGTON—**USAir Arena** originally Capital Centre (1974-93); **Verizon Center** originally MCI Center (1997-2006).

AUTO RACING

Formula One, NASCAR Winston Cup, Champ Car and Indy Racing League (IRL) racing circuits. Qualifying records accurate as of Sept. 30, 2006. Capacity figures for NASCAR, Champ Car and IRL tracks are approximate and pertain to grandstand seating only. Standing room and hillside terrain seating featured at most road courses are not included.

Champ Car World Series

	Location	Miles	Qual.mph record	Set by	Seats
Burke Lakefront Airport	Cleveland, Ohio	2.106**	134.705	A.J. Allmendinger (2006)	36,000
Exhibition Place	Toronto, Ont.	1.755**	110.565	Gil de Ferran (1999)	60,000
Finning International Speedway	Edmonton, Alb.	1.973**	121.291	Sebastien Bourdais (2006)	70,000
Fundidora Park	Monterrey, Mexico	2.104*	103.401	Sebastien Bourdais (2006)	61,871
Circuit Gilles Villeneuve	Montreal, Que.	2.709*	122.726	Christiano da Matta (2002)	100,000
Grand Prix of Denver	Denver, Colo.	1.657**	100.941	Sebastien Bourdais (2006)	
Las Vegas Motor Speedway	Las Vegas, Nev.	1.500	206.186	Patrick Carpentier (2004)	126,000
Long Beach	Long Beach, Calif.	1.968**	105.924	Sebastien Bourdais (2006)	63,000
Autódromo Hermanos Rodriguez	Mexico City, Mexico	2.786*	116.733	Sebastien Bourdais (2004)	
The Milwaukee Mile	West Allis, Wisc.	1.032	185.500	Patrick Carpentier (1998)	45,000
Portland International Raceway	Portland, Ore.	1.964*	122.768	Helio Castroneves (2000)	50,000
Reliant Park	Houston, Tex.	1.69**	104.850	Mario Dominguez (2006)	
Road America	Elkhart Lake, Wisc.	4.048*	145.924	Dario Franchitti (2000)	10,000
San Jose Grand Prix	San Jose, Calif.	1.448**	106.040	Sebastien Bourdais (2006)	
Gold Coast-Surfers Paradise	Queensland, Australia	2.795**	111.547	Cristiano da Matta (2002)	55,000

*Road courses (not ovals). **Temporary street circuits.

IndyCar Series

Founded by Indianapolis Motor Speedway president Tony George, the IndyCar Series competes with Champ Car and fielded 14 races, anchored by the Indianapolis 500, in 2006.

	Location	Miles	Qual.mph Record	Set by	Seats
California Speedway	Fontana, Calif.	2.0	241.428†	Gil de Ferran (2000)*	92,109
Chicagoland Speedway	Joliet, Ill.	1.5	222.137	Robbie Buhl (2001)	75,000
Homestead-Miami Speedway	Homestead, Fla.	1.5	218.539	Sam Hornish Jr. (2006)	65,000
Indianapolis Motor Speedway	Indianapolis, Ind.	2.5	237.498	Arie Luyendyk (1996)*	250,000
Infineon Raceway	Sonoma, Calif.	2.26*	108.248	Ryan Briscoe (2005)	102,000
Kansas Speedway	Kansas City, Kan.	1.5	218.085	Scott Dixon (2003)	75,000
Kentucky Speedway	Sparta, Ky.	1.5	219.191	Scott Goodyear (2000)	70,000
Michigan Intl. Speedway	Brooklyn, Mich.	2.0	222.458	Tomas Scheckter (2003)	136,373
The Milwaukee Mile	West Allis, Wisc.	1.032	172.477	Helio Castroneves (2006)	45,000
Nashville Superspeedway	Nashville, Tenn.	1.33	206.211	Scott Dixon (2003)	50,000
Grand Prix of St. Petersburg	St. Petersburg, Fla.	1.8**	104.054	Dario Franchitti (2006)	
Texas Motor Speedway	Fort Worth, Texas	1.5	225.979	Billy Boat (1998)	154,861
Twin Ring Motegi	Motegi, Japan	1.549	206.996	Scott Dixon (2003)	50,000
Watkins Glen International	Watkins Glen, N.Y.	3.4	133.806	Helio Castroneves (2005)	35,000

*Road course. **Temporary street circuit. †Indicates world closed-course record for auto racing.

NEXTEL Cup

	Location	Miles	Qual.mph Record	Set by	Seats
Atlanta Motor Speedway	Hampton, Ga.	1.54	197.478	Geoff Bodine (1997)	124,000
Bristol Motor Speedway	Bristol, Tenn.	0.533	128.709	Ryan Newman (2003)	147,000
California Speedway	Fontana, Calif.	2.0	188.245	Kyle Busch (2005)	92,000
Chicagoland Speedway	Joliet, Ill.	1.5	188.147	Jimmie Johnson (2005)	75,000
Darlington International Raceway	Darlington, S.C.	1.366	173.797	Ward Burton (1996)	65,000
Daytona International Speedway	Daytona Beach, Fla.	2.5	210.364	Bill Elliott (1987)	168,000
Dover International Speedway	Dover, Del.	1.0	161.522	Jeremy Mayfield (2004)	140,000
Homestead-Miami Speedway	Homestead, Fla.	1.5	181.111	Jamie McMurray (2003)	72,000
Indianapolis Motor Speedway	Indianapolis, Ind.	2.5	186.293	Casey Mears (2004)	250,000+
Infineon Raceway	Sonoma, Calif.	1.99*	94.325	Jeff Gordon (2005)	42,500
Kansas Speedway	Kansas City, Kan.	1.5	180.856	Matt Kenseth (2005)	75,000
Las Vegas Motor Speedway	Las Vegas, Nev.	1.5	174.904	Kasey Kahne (2004)	126,000
Lowe's Motor Speedway	Concord, N.C.	1.5	193.216	Elliot Sadler (2005)	167,000
Martinsville Speedway	Martinsville, Va.	0.526	98.084	Tony Stewart (2005)	91,000
Michigan Speedway	Brooklyn, Mich.	2.0	194.232	Ryan Newman (2005)	136,384
New Hampshire Int'l Speedway	Loudon, N.H.	1.058	133.357	Ryan Newman (2003)	91,000
Phoenix International Raceway	Phoenix, Ariz.	1.0	135.854	Ryan Newman (2004)	76,812
Pocono Raceway	Long Pond, Penn.	2.5	172.533	Kasey Kahne (2004)	77,000
Richmond International Raceway	Richmond, Va.	0.75	129.983	Brian Vickers (2004)	107,097
Talladega Superspeedway	Talladega, Ala.	2.66	212.809	Bill Elliott (1987)	143,000
Texas Motor Speedway	Ft. Worth, Texas	1.5	194.224	Bill Elliott (2002)	154,861
Watkins Glen International	Watkins Glen, N.Y.	2.45*	181.068	Ricky Rudd (2000)	40,000

*Road courses (not ovals).

Formula One

Race track capacity figures unavailable.

Grand Prix		Miles	Qual.mph Record	Set by
Australian	**Albert Park** (Melbourne)	3.295	140.537	Michael Schumacher (2004)
Bahrain	**Bahrain International** (Sakhir)	3.366	134.432	Michael Schumacher (2004)
Belgian	**Spa-Francorchamps**	4.333	143.418	Mika Hakkinen (1998)
Brazilian	**Interlagos** (Sao Paulo)	2.684	193.747	Rubens Barrichello (2003)
British	**Silverstone** (Towcester)	3.194	148.043	Nigel Mansell (1992)
Canadian	**Circuit Gilles Villeneuve** (Montreal)	2.747	133.941	Juan Montoya (2002)
China	**Shanghai International**	3.387	129.867	Rubens Barrichello (2004)
European	**Nürburgring** (Nürburg, Germany)	2.822	135.959	Michael Schumacher (2001)
French	**Magny Cours** (Nevers)	2.641	159.757	Juan Montoya (2002)
German	**Hockenheim** (Germany)	2.796	204.450	Michael Schumacher (2002)
Hungarian	**Hungaroring** (Budapest)	2.468	122.410	Michael Schumacher (2005)
Italian	**Autodromo Nazionale di Monza** (Milan)	3.585	161.460	Juan Pablo Montoya (2002)
Japanese	**Suzuka** (Nagoya)	3.644	138.565	Michael Schumacher (2004)
Malaysian	**Sepang** (Kuala Lumpur)	3.444	133.220	Michael Schumacher (2004)
Monaco	**Monte Carlo** (Monaco)	2.082	141.595	Rubens Barrichello (2002)
San Marino	**Autodromo Enzo e Dino Ferrari** (Imola, Italy)	3.063	138.362	Jenson Button (2004)
Spanish	**Catalunya** (Barcelona)	2.937	140.935	Michael Schumacher (2004)
Turkish	**Otodrom** (Istanbul)	3.293	137.323	Kimi Raikkonen (2005)
United States	**Indianapolis Motor Speedway**	2.606	133.595	Rubens Barrichello (2004)

SOCCER

World's Premier Soccer Stadiums

(Listed alphabetically by city)

Stadium	Location	Seats	Stadium	Location	Seats
New Olympic	Athens, Greece	72,000	Old Trafford	Manchester, England	67,650
Eden Park	Auckland, New Zealand	50,000	Estadio Azteca	Mexico City, Mexico	106,000
Nou Camp	Barcelona, Spain	98,000	Meazza (San Siro)	Milan, Italy	85,700
Beijing National	Beijing, China	91,000	Centenario	Montevideo, Uruguay	76,609
Olympiastadion	Berlin, Germany	76,243	Luzhniki Stadion	Moscow, Russia	80,840
Népstadion	Budapest, Hungary	65,000	Olympiastadion	Munich, Germany	63,000
Antonio Liberti	Buenos Aires, Argentina	76,689	San Paolo	Naples, Italy	78,210
National	Cairo, Egypt	90,000	Stade de France	Paris, France	80,000
Salt Lake	Calcutta, India	120,000	Rungnado (May Day)	Pyongyang, N. Korea	150,000
Millennium	Cardiff, Wales	72,500	Maracana	Rio de Janeiro, Brazil	70,000
Westfalenstadion	Dortmund, Germany	68,600	King Fahd II	Riyadh, Saudi Arabia	79,000
Lansdowne Road	Dublin, Ireland	50,000	Olimpico	Rome, Italy	82,307
Celtic Park	Glasgow, Scotland	60,506	Nacional	Santiago, Chile	77,000
Hampden Park	Glasgow, Scotland	52,670	Morumbi	Sao Paulo, Brazil	80,000
Guangdong	Guanzhou, China	80,000	Chasmil	Seoul, S. Korea	100,000
FNB Stadium	Johannesburg, S. Africa	94,700	Stadium Australia	Sydney, Australia	80,000
Olympic Stadium	Kiev, Ukraine	83,160	Azadi	Tehran, Iran	100,000
new Estadio da Luz	Lisbon, Portugal	65,000	Delle Alpi	Turin, Italy	69,041
Wembley Stadium	Londo, England	90,000	Ernst Happel	Vienna, Austria	47,500
Santiago Bernabeu	Madrid, Spain	106,500	International	Yokohama, Japan	70,574

Major League Soccer

The 13-team MLS is the only U.S. Division I professional outdoor league sanctioned by FIFA and U.S. Soccer. Note that some capacity figures are approximate given the adjustments of football stadium seating to soccer.

Western Conference

	Stadium	Built	Seats	Field
CD Chivas USA	Home Depot Center	2003	27,000	Grass
Colorado Rapids	INVESCO Field	2001	17,500	Grass
FC Dallas	Pizza Hut Park	2005	21,193	Grass
Houston Dynamo	Robertson	1942	32,000	Grass
L.A. Galaxy	Home Depot Center	2003	27,000	Grass
Real Salt Lake	Rice-Eccles	1927	45,634	Grass

Eastern Conference

	Stadium	Built	Seats	Field
Chicago Fire	Toyota Park	2006	21,210	Grass
Columbus Crew	Columbus Crew	1999	22,555	Grass
D.C. United	RFK	1961	26,169	Grass
Kansas City Wizards	Arrowhead	1972	20,571	Grass
N.E. Revolution	Gillette	2002	21,000	Grass
Red Bull New York	Giants	1976	25,576	Grass
Toronto FC	BMO Field	2007	20,000	Turf

Note: Red Bull New York and Real Salt Lake both have plans to open new soccer specific stadiums in 2008. **Red Bull Park** is currently under construction in Harrison, N.J. The stadium will have a capacity of 25,000. **Sandy Stadium** is being built in Sandy, Utah, a suburb of Salt Lake City. The expected capacity of the stadium is 20,000.

Horse Racing
Triple Crown race tracks

Race	Racetrack	Seats	Infield
Kentucky Derby	Churchill Downs	48,500	65,000
Preakness Stakes	Pimlico Race Course	13,047	60,000
Belmont Stakes	Belmont Park	32,941	N/A

Record crowds: Kentucky Derby—163,628 (1974); Preakness—112,668 (2004); Belmont—120,139 (2004).
Note: Belmont Park does not open infield for Belmont Stakes.

Tennis
Grand Slam center courts

Event	Main Stadium	Seats
Australian Open	Melbourne Park	15,021
French Open	Stade Roland Garros	16,300
Wimbledon	Centre Court	13,813
U.S. Open	Arthur Ashe Stadium	22,547

COLLEGE BASKETBALL

The 50 Largest Arenas

The 50 largest arenas in Division I for the 2006-07 NCAA regular season. Note that (*) indicates part-time home court.

		Seats	Home Team			Seats	Home Team
1	Carrier Dome	33,000	Syracuse	26	Assembly Hall	16,450	Illinois
2	Thompson-Boling Arena	24,535	Tennessee	27	Allen Fieldhouse	16,300	Kansas
3	Rupp Arena	23,500	Kentucky	28	Hartford Civic Center	16,294	UConn*
4	Marriott Center	22,700	BYU	29	L.A. Sports Arena	16,161	USC
5	Dean Smith Center	21,800	N. Carolina	30	Save Mart Center	16,116	Fresno St.
6	Verizon Center	20,674	Georgetown*	31	Carver-Hawkeye Arena	15,500	Iowa
7	Continental Airlines Arena	20,049	Seton Hall		Pepsi Arena	15,500	Siena
8	Scottrade Center	20,000	Saint Louis	33	Bryce Jordan Center	15,261	Penn St.
9	RBC Center	19,722	N.C. State	34	John Paul Jones Arena	15,219	Virginia
10	Value City Arena	19,500	Ohio St.	35	United Spirit Arena	15,098	Texas Tech
11	Bud Walton Arena	19,200	Arkansas	36	Breslin Events Center	15,085	Michigan St.
12	Wachovia Center	19,010	Villanova*	37	Mizzou Arena	15,061	Missouri
13	Freedom Hall	18,865	Louisville	38	Coleman Coliseum	15,043	Alabama
14	Bradley Center	18,717	Marquette	39	Arena-Auditorium	15,028	Wyoming
15	Thomas & Mack Center	18,500	UNLV	40	Huntsman Center	15,000	Utah
16	Madison Square Garden	18,470	St. John's*	41	LJVM Coliseum	14,665	Wake Forest
17	FedEx Forum	18,400	Memphis	42	Williams Arena	14,625	Minnesota
18	University Arena (The Pit)	18,018	New Mexico	43	McKale Center	14,545	Arizona
19	Comcast Center	17,950	Maryland	44	Maravich Assembly Ctr	14,236	LSU
20	Colonial Center	17,600	South Carolina	45	Wells Fargo Arena	14,198	Arizona St.
21	Qwest Center Omaha	17,560	Creighton	46	Memorial Gym	14,168	Vanderbilt
22	Allstate Arena	17,500	DePaul	47	Mackey Arena	14,123	Purdue
23	Assembly Hall	17,456	Indiana	48	James H. Hilton Coliseum	14,092	Iowa St.
24	Herb Kohl Center	17,142	Wisconsin	49	WVU Coliseum	14,000	West Virginia
25	Frank Erwin Center	16,755	Texas	50	Crisler Arena	13,751	Michigan

Division I Conference Home Courts

NCAA Division I conferences for the 2006-07 season. Teams with home games in more than one arena are noted.

America East

	Home Floor	Seats
Albany	Rec & Convocation Ctr.	5,000
Binghamton	Events Center	5,142
Boston University	Case Gym	1,800
	& Agganis Arena	5,687
Hartford	Reich Family Pavilion	3,977
Maine	Alfond Arena	5,712
MD-Balt. County	RAC Arena	4,024
New Hampshire	Lundholm Gym	3,500
Stony Brook	SB Sports Complex	4,103
Vermont	Patrick Gym	3,266

Atlantic Sun

	Home Floor	Seats
Belmont	Curb Event Center	5,000
Campbell	Carter Gym	1,050
East Tennessee St.	Memorial Center	12,000
Gardner-Webb	Paul Porter Arena	5,000
Jacksonville	Swisher Gym	1,500
Kennesaw St.	KSU Convocation Center	4,500
Lipscomb	Allen Arena	5,028
Mercer	University Center	3,200
North Florida	UNF Arena	5,800
Stetson	Edmunds Center	5,000

Atlantic Coast

	Home Floor	Seats
Boston College	Silvio O. Conte Forum	8,606
Clemson	Littlejohn Coliseum	11,020
Duke	Cameron Indoor Stadium	9,314
Florida St.	Donald L. Tucker Center	12,200
Georgia Tech	Alexander Memorial Coliseum	9,191
Maryland	Comcast Center	17,950
Miami-FL	BankUnited Center	7,000
North Carolina	Dean Smith Center	21,800
N.C. State	RBC Center	19,722
Virginia	John Paul Jones Arena	15,219
Virginia Tech	Cassell Coliseum	10,052
Wake Forest	LJVM Coliseum	14,665

Atlantic 10

	Home Floor	Seats
Charlotte	Halton Arena	9,105
Dayton	U. of Dayton Arena	13,266
Duquesne	Palumbo Center	6,200
Fordham	Rose Hill Gym	3,470
George Washington	Smith Center	5,000
La Salle	Tom Gola Arena	4,000
Massachusetts	Mullins Center	9,493
Rhode Island	Ryan Center	7,657
Richmond	Robins Center	9,071
St. Bonaventure	Reilly Center	6,000
Saint Louis	Scottrade Center	20,000
St. Joseph's	Alumni Mem. Fieldhouse	3,200
Temple	Liacouras Center	10,206
Xavier-OH	Cintas Center	10,250

College Basketball (Cont.)

Big East

	Home Floor	Seats
Cincinnati	Fifth Third Arena	13,176
Connecticut	Gampel Pavilion	10,167
	& Hartford Civic Center	16,294
DePaul	Allstate Arena	17,500
Georgetown	Verizon Center	20,674
Louisville	Freedom Hall	18,865
Marquette	Bradley Center	18,717
Notre Dame	Joyce Center	11,418
Pittsburgh	Petersen Event Center	12,500
Providence	Dunkin Donuts Center	12,993
Rutgers	Louis Brown Athletic Center (The RAC)	9,000
St. John's	Carnesecca Arena	6,008
	& Madison Square Garden	18,470
Seton Hall	Continental Airlines Arena	20,049
South Florida	Sun Dome	10,411
Syracuse	Carrier Dome	33,000
Villanova	The Pavilion	6,500
	& Wachovia Center	19,010
West Virginia	WVU Coliseum	14,000

Big Sky

	Home Floor	Seats
Eastern Wash.	Reese Court	6,000
Idaho St.	Reed Gym	3,040
Montana	Dahlberg Arena	7,321
Montana St.	Worthington Arena	7,250
Northern Arizona	Walkup Skydome	7,000
Northern Colorado	Butler-Hancock Sports Pavilion	4,500
Portland St.	Stott Center	1,500
Sacramento St.	Hornets Nest	1,200
Weber St.	Dee Events Center	12,000

Big South

	Home Floor	Seats
Birmingham-Southern	Bill Battle Coliseum	2,000
Charleston Southern	CSU Fieldhouse	1,500
Coastal Carolina	Kimbel Gymnasium	1,037
High Point	Millis Center	2,565
Liberty	Vines Center	9,000
NC-Asheville	Justice Center	1,100
	& Asheville Civic Center	6,000
Radford	Dedmon Center	5,000
VMI	Cameron Hall	5,800
Winthrop	Winthrop Coliseum	6,100

Big Ten

	Home Floor	Seats
Illinois	Assembly Hall	16,450
Indiana	Assembly Hall	17,456
Iowa	Carver-Hawkeye Arena	15,500
Michigan	Crisler Arena	13,751
Michigan St.	Breslin Events Center	15,085
Minnesota	Williams Arena	14,625
Northwestern	Welsh-Ryan Arena	8,117
Ohio St.	Value City Arena	19,500
Penn St.	Bryce Jordan Center	15,261
Purdue	Mackey Arena	14,123
Wisconsin	Kohl Center	17,142

Men's Basketball Attendance Leaders

Schools ranked by average attendance for 2005-06 season.

	Gm	Attendance	Average
1 Kentucky	15	341,445	22,763
2 Syracuse	19	410,153	21,587
3 North Carolina	17	344,071	20,239
4 Louisville	22	402,963	18,316
5 Tennessee	15	269,310	17,954
6 Maryland	17	291,961	17,174

Big 12

	Home Floor	Seats
Baylor	Ferrell Center	10,284
Colorado	Coors Events Conference Ctr.	11,064
Iowa St.	Hilton Coliseum	14,092
Kansas	Allen Fieldhouse	16,300
Kansas St.	Bramlage Coliseum	13,595
Missouri	Mizzou Arena	15,061
Nebraska	Devaney Sports Center	13,500
Oklahoma	Lloyd Noble Center	12,000
Oklahoma St.	Gallagher-Iba Arena	13,611
Texas	Erwin Center	16,755
Texas A&M	Reed Arena	12,500
Texas Tech	United Spirit Arena	15,098

Big West

	Home Floor	Seats
Cal Poly	Mott Gym	3,032
CS-Fullerton	Titan Gym	4,000
CS-Northridge	The Matadome	1,600
Long Beach St.	The Walter Pyramid	5,000
Pacific	Alex G. Spanos Center	6,150
UC-Davis	The Pavilion	7,200
UC-Irvine	Bren Events Center	5,000
UC-Riverside	Student Rec. Center	3,168
UC-Santa Barbara	The Thunderdome	6,000

Colonial Athletic Association

	Home Floor	Seats
Delaware	Bob Carpenter Center	5,000
Drexel	Daskalakis Athletic Center	2,300
George Mason	Patriot Center	10,000
Georgia St.	GSU Sports Arena	4,500
Hofstra	Hofstra Arena	5,124
James Madison	JMU Convocation Center	7,156
Northeastern	Solomon Court	1,500
	& Matthews Arena	6,000
NC-Wilmington	Trask Coliseum	6,100
Old Dominion	Ted Constant Convocation Ctr.	8,650
Towson	Towson Center	5,000
VCU	Siegel Center	7,500
William & Mary	Kaplan Arena	8,600

Conference USA

	Home Floor	Seats
UAB	Bartow Arena	8,508
Central Fla.	UCF Arena	5,100
East Carolina	Williams Arena at Minges Coliseum	8,000
Houston	Hofheinz Pavilion	8,479
Marshall	Cam Henderson Center	9,043
Memphis	FedEx Forum	18,400
Rice	Autry Court	5,000
SMU	Moody Coliseum	8,998
Southern Miss	Reed Green Coliseum	8,095
Tulane	Fogelman Arena	3,600
Tulsa	Reynolds Center	8,355
UTEP	Haskins Center	12,000

Horizon League

	Home Floor	Seats
Butler	Hinkle Fieldhouse	11,043
Cleveland St.	Wolstein Center	13,610
Detroit Mercy	Calihan Hall	8,837
IL-Chicago	UIC Pavilion	8,000
Loyola-IL	Gentile Center	5,200
WI-Green Bay	Resch Center	10,400
WI-Milwaukee	U.S. Cellular Arena	10,783
Wright St.	Nutter Center	10,632
Youngstown St.	Beeghly Center	6,500

Ivy League

	Home Floor	Seats
Brown	Pizzitola Sports Center	2,800
Columbia	Levien Gymnasium	3,408
Cornell	Newman Arena	4,473
Dartmouth	Leede Arena	2,100
Harvard	Lavietes Pavilion	2,195
Penn	The Palestra	8,700
Princeton	Jadwin Gymnasium	6,854
Yale	Payne Whitney Gym	3,100

Metro Atlantic

	Home Floor	Seats
Canisius	Koessler Athletic Center	2,176
Fairfield	Arena at Harbor Yard	9,000
Iona	Hynes Athletic Center	2,611
Loyola-MD	Reitz Arena	3,000
Manhattan	Draddy Gymnasium	3,000
Marist	McCann Field House	3,944
Niagara	Gallagher Center	2,400
Rider	Alumni Gymnasium	1,650
St. Peter's	Yanitelli Center	3,200
Siena	Pepsi Arena	15,500

Mid-American

	Home Floor	Seats
Akron	JAR Arena	5,942
Ball St.	John E. Worthen Arena	11,500
Bowling Green	Anderson Arena	5,000
Buffalo	Alumni Arena	6,100
Central Mich.	Rose Arena	5,200
Eastern Mich.	Convocation Center	8,824
Kent St.	MAC Center	6,327
Miami-OH	Millett Hall	9,200
Northern Illinois	Convocation Center	9,100
Ohio Univ.	Convocation Center	13,000
Toledo	Savage Hall	9,000
Western Mich.	University Arena	5,421

Mid-Continent

	Home Floor	Seats
Centenary	Gold Dome	3,000
Chicago St.	Dickens Athletic Center	2,500
IUPUI	IUPUI Gym	2,000
Missouri-KC	Municipal Auditorium	9,827
	& Kemper Arena	18,646
Oakland	Athletics Center O'Rena	4,005
Oral Roberts	Mabee Center	10,575
Southern Utah	Centrum	5,300
Valparaiso	Athletics-Recreation Center	5,000
Western Ill.	Western Hall	5,139

Mid-Eastern Athletic

	Home Floor	Seats
Bethune-Cookman	Moore Gym	3,000
Coppin St.	Coppin Center	3,000
Delaware St.	Memorial Hall	3,000
Florida A&M	Gaither Gym	3,365
Hampton	Hampton Convocation Center	7,500
Howard	Burr Gym	2,200
MD-East.Shore	W.P. Hytche Center	5,500
Morgan St.	Hill Fieldhouse	4,500
Norfolk St.	Echols Hall	7,600
N. Carolina A&T	Corbett Sports Center	6,700
South Carolina St.	SHM Center	3,200
Winston-Salem St.	LJVM Coliseum Annex	4,000

Missouri Valley

	Home Floor	Seats
Bradley	Carver Arena	11,300
Creighton	Qwest Center Omaha	17,560
Drake	Knapp Center	7,002
Evansville	Roberts Stadium	11,600
Illinois St.	Redbird Arena	10,200
Indiana St.	Hulman Center	10,200
Missouri St.	Hammons Student Center	8,846
Northern Iowa	McLeod Center	6,000
	& UNI-Dome	10,000
Southern Ill.	SIU Arena	10,000
Wichita St.	Charles Koch Arena	10,400

Mountain West

	Home Floor	Seats
Air Force	Clune Arena	6,002
BYU	Marriott Center	22,700
Colorado St.	Moby Arena	8,745
UNLV	Thomas & Mack Center	18,500
New Mexico	The Pit	18,018
San Diego St.	Cox Arena at the Aztec Bowl	12,414
TCU	Daniel-Meyer Coliseum	7,201
Utah	Jon M. Huntsman Center	15,000
Wyoming	Arena-Auditorium	15,028

Northeast

	Home Floor	Seats
Central Conn. St.	Detrick Gym	3,200
Farleigh Dickinson	Rothman Center	5,000
LIU-Brooklyn	ARW Center	3,000
Monmouth	Boylan Gym	2,500
Mt. St. Mary's	Knott Arena	3,121
Quinnipiac	Burt Kahn Court	2,000
Robert Morris	Sewall Center	3,056
Sacred Heart	Pitt Center	2,100
St. Francis-NY	Pope Center	1,200
St. Francis-PA	DeGol Arena	3,500
Wagner	Spiro Sports Center	2,100

Ohio Valley

	Home Floor	Seats
Austin Peay	Dunn Center	9,000
Eastern Illinois	Lantz Arena	5,300
Eastern Ky.	McBrayer Arena	6,500
Jacksonville St.	Mathews Coliseum	5,500
Morehead St.	Johnson Arena	6,500
Murray St.	Regional Special Events Ctr.	8,602
Samford	Seibert Hall	4,000
SE Missouri St.	Show Me Center	7,000
Tennessee-Martin	Skyhawk Arena	6,700
Tennessee-Martin	Gentry Complex	10,500
Tennessee Tech	Eblen Center	10,152

Pacific-10

	Home Floor	Seats
Arizona	McKale Center	14,545
Arizona St.	Wells Fargo Arena	14,198
California	Haas Pavillion	11,877
Oregon	McArthur Court	9,087
Oregon St.	Gill Coliseum	10,400
Stanford	Maples Pavilion	7,391
UCLA	Pauley Pavilion	12,819
USC	LA Sports Arena	16,161
Washington	Bank of America Arena	10,000
Washington St.	Friel Court	11,566

NBA and College Buildings

Six division I teams play at least a portion of their home games in an NBA building and thanks to Hurricane Katrina one NBA team, the New Orleans Hornets, will be playing a portion of their home games on a college court in 2005-06.

Building	College	NBA Team	Building	College	NBA Team
Verizon Center	Georgetown	Wizards	Madison Square Garden	St. John's	Knicks
Continental Airlines Arena	Seton Hall	Nets	FedEx Forum	Memphis	Grizzlies
Wachovia Center	Villanova	76ers	Bradley Center	Marquette	Bucks

College Basketball (Cont.)

Patriot League

	Home Floor	Seats
American	Bender Arena	4,500
Army	Christl Arena	5,043
Bucknell	Gary A. Sojka Pavilion	4,000
Colgate	Cotterell Court	3,000
Holy Cross	Hart Recreation Center	3,600
Lafayette	Kirby Sports Center	3,500
Lehigh	Stabler Arena	5,600
Navy	Alumni Hall	5,710

Southeastern

Eastern	Home Floor	Seats
Florida	O'Connell Center	12,000
Georgia	Stegeman Coliseum	10,523
Kentucky	Rupp Arena	23,500
South Carolina	Colonial Center	17,600
Tennessee	Thompson-Boling Arena	24,535
Vanderbilt	Memorial Gymnasium	14,168
Western	**Home Floor**	**Seats**
Alabama	Coleman Coliseum	15,043
Arkansas	Bud Walton Arena	19,200
Auburn	Beard-Eaves-Memorial Coliseum	10,500
LSU	Maravich Assembly Center	14,164
Mississippi	Tad Smith Coliseum	8,700
Mississippi St.	Humphrey Coliseum	10,500

Southern

	Home Floor	Seats
Appalachian St.	Seby Jones Arena	8,325
The Citadel	McAlister Field House	6,200
Coll. of Charleston	John Kresse Arena	5,000
Davidson	Belk Arena	5,700
Elon	Koury Center	2,000
Furman	Timmons Arena	5,000
Ga. Southern	Hanner Fieldhouse	5,500
NC-Greensboro	Fleming Gymnasium	2,320
Chattanooga	McKenzie Arena	11,218
W. Carolina	Ramsey Center	7,286
Wofford	Johnson Arena	3,500

Southland

	Home Floor	Seats
Central Arkansas	Farris Center	5,500
Lamar	Montagne Center	10,080
McNeese St.	Burton Coliseum	8,000
Nicholls St.	Stopher Gym	3,800
Northwestern St.	Prather Coliseum	4,300
Sam Houston St.	Johnson Coliseum	6,172
SE Louisiana	University Center	7,500
S.F. Austin St.	W.R. Johnson Coliseum	7,200
Texas A&M-Corpus Christi	American Bank Center	8,156
TX-Arlington	Texas Hall	4,200
TX-San Antonio	Convocation Center	5,100
Texas St.	Strahan Coliseum	7,200

Southwestern Athletic

	Home Floor	Seats
Alabama A&M	Elmore Gymnasium	6,000
Alabama St.	Joe Reed Acadome	8,000
Alcorn St.	Whitney Complex	7,000
Arkansas-Pine Bluff	K.L. Johnson Complex	4,500
Grambling St.	Tiger Memorial Gym	4,500
Jackson St.	Williams Center	8,000
Miss.Valley St.	Harrison HPER Athletic Complex	6,000
Prairie View A&M	William Nicks Building	5,520
Southern-BR	Clark Activity Center	7,500
TX Southern	Health & P.E. Building	8,100

Sun Belt

	Home Floor	Seats
Arkansas-Little Rock	Stephens Center	5,600
Arkansas St	Convocation Center	10,563
Denver	Magness Arena	7,200
Fla. Atlantic	FAU Gym	5,000
Florida International	Pharmed Arena	5,000
LA-Lafayette	The Cajundome	11,550
LA-Monroe	Fant-Ewing Coliseum	7,085
Middle Tennessee	Murphy Cente	11,520
New Orleans	Lakefront Arena	8,933
North Texas	The Super Pit	10,032
South Alabama	Mitchell Center	10,000
Troy	Trojan Arena	4,000
Western Ky.	E.A. Diddle Arena	7,326

West Coast

	Home Floor	Seats
Gonzaga	McCarthey Athletic Center	6,000
Loyola Marymount	Gersten Pavilion	4,156
Pepperdine	Firestone Fieldhouse	3,104
Portland	Chiles Center	5,000
St. Mary's-CA	McKeon Pavilion	3,500
San Diego	Jenny Craig Pavilion	5,100
San Francisco	War Memorial Gym	5,300
Santa Clara	Leavey Center	5,000

Western Athletic

	Home Floor	Seats
Boise St.	Taco Bell Arena	12,380
Fresno St.	Save Mart Center	16,116
Hawaii	Stan Sheriff Center	10,300
Idaho	Cowan Spectrum	7,000
Louisiana Tech	Thomas Assembly Center	8,000
Nevada	Lawlor Events Center	11,200
New Mexico St.	Pan American Center	13,071
San Jose St.	The Event Center	5,000
Utah St.	Dee Glen Smith Spectrum	10,270

Independents

	Home Floor	Seats
IPFW	Memorial Coliseum	11,500
	& Hilliard Gates Sports Center	2,700
Longwood	Henry I. Willet Jr. Hall	2,522
North Dakota St.	Bison Sports Arena	6,000
Savannah St.	Wiley Gym	2,100
South Dakota St.	Frost Arena	8,500
Texas-Pan Am	Health/PE Fieldhouse	3,500
Utah Valley St.	McKay Center	8,000

Future NCAA Final Four Sites

Men

Year	Arena	Seats	Location
2007	Georgia Dome	40,000	Atlanta
2008	Alamodome	36,500	San Antonio
2009	Ford Field	65,000	Detroit
2010	Lucas Oil Stadium	63,000	Indianapolis
2011	Reliant Stadium	69,500	Houston

Women

Year	Arena	Seats	Location
2007	Quicken Loans Arena	20,562	Cleveland
2008	St. Pete Times Forum	19,758	Tampa
2009	Edward Jones Dome	66,000	St. Louis
2010	Alamodome	36,500	San Antonio
2011	Lucas Oil Stadium	63,000	Indianapolis

COLLEGE FOOTBALL

The 40 Largest I-A Stadiums

The 40 largest stadiums in NCAA Division I-A college football heading into the 2006 season. Note that (*) indicates stadium not on campus.

		Location	Seats	Home Team	Conference	Built	Field
1	Michigan Stadium	Ann Arbor, Mich.	107,501	Michigan	Big Ten	1927	Turf
2	Beaver Stadium	University Park, Penn.	107,282	Penn St.	Big Ten	1960	Grass
3	Neyland Stadium	Knoxville, Tenn.	104,079	Tennessee	SEC-East	1921	Grass
4	Ohio Stadium	Columbus, Ohio	101,568	Ohio St.	Big Ten	1922	Grass
5	Sanford Stadium	Athens, Ga.	92,746	Georgia	SEC-East	1929	Grass
6	LA Memorial Coliseum*	Los Angeles, Calif.	92,516	USC	Pac-10	1923	Grass
7	Tiger Stadium	Baton Rouge, La.	92,400	LSU	SEC-West	1924	Grass
8	Bryant-Denny Stadium	Tuscaloosa, Ala.	92,158	Alabama	SEC-West	1929	Grass
9	Rose Bowl*	Pasadena, Calif.	91,500	UCLA	Pac-10	1922	Grass
10	Ben Hill Griffin Stadium at Florida Field	Gainesville, Fla.	88,548	Florida	SEC-East	1929	Grass
11	Jordan-Hare Stadium	Auburn, Ala.	87,451	Auburn	SEC-West	1939	Grass
12	Darrell K. Royal-Texas Memorial Stadium	Austin, Texas	85,123	Texas	Big 12-South	1924	Grass
13	Kyle Field	College Station, Texas	82,600	Texas A&M	Big 12-South	1925	Grass
14	Doak Campbell Stadium	Tallahasse, Fla.	82,300	Florida St.	ACC	1950	Grass
15	Gaylord Family-Oklahoma Memorial Stadium	Norman, Okla.	82,112	Oklahoma	Big 12-South	1924	Grass
16	Memorial Stadium	Clemson, S.C.	81,474	Clemson	ACC	1942	Grass
17	Memorial Stadium	Lincoln, Neb.	81,067	Nebraska	Big 12-North	1923	Turf
18	Notre Dame Stadium	Notre Dame, Ind.	80,795	Notre Dame	Independent	1930	Grass
19	Camp Randall Stadium	Madison, Wis.	80,321	Wisconsin	Big Ten	1917	Turf
20	Williams-Brice Stadium	Columbia, S.C.	80,250	South Carolina	SEC-East	1934	Grass
21	Donald W. Reynolds Razorback Stadium	Fayetteville, Ark.	80,000	Arkansas	SEC-West	1938	Grass
22	Spartan Stadium	East Lansing, Mich.	75,005	Michigan St.	Big Ten	1957	Turf
23	Sun Devil Stadium	Tempe, Ariz.	73,379	Arizona St.	Pac-10	1959	Grass
24	Memorial Stadium	Berkeley, Calif.	73,347	California	Pac-10	1923	Turf
25	Husky Stadium	Seattle, Wash.	72,500	Washington	Pac-10	1920	Turf
26	Orange Bowl*	Miami, Fla.	72,319	Miami-FL	ACC	1935	Grass
27	Legion Field*	Birmingham, Ala.	71,594	UAB	USA	1927	Grass
28	Qualcomm Stadium	San Diego, Calif.	71,295	San Diego St.	Mountain West	1967	Grass
29	Kinnick Stadium	Iowa City, Iowa	70,585	Iowa	Big Ten	1929	Grass
30	Citrus Bowl*	Orlando, Fla.	70,188	Central Florida	USA	1936	Grass
31	Rice Stadium	Houston, Texas	70,000	Rice	USA	1950	Turf
32	Louisiana Superdome*	New Orleans, La.	69,767	Tulane	USA	1975	Turf
33	Memorial Stadium	Champaign, Ill.	69,249	Illinois	Big Ten	1923	Turf
34	Lincoln Financial Field*	Philadelphia, Penn.	68,532	Temple	Mid-American	2003	Grass
35	Memorial Stadium	Columbia, Mo.	68,349	Missouri	Big 12-North	1926	Turf
36	Commonwealth	Lexington, Ky.	67,606	Kentucky	SEC-East	1973	Grass
37	Lane Stadium	Blacksburg, Va.	66,233	Va. Tech	ACC	1965	Grass
38	Raymond James Stadium*	Tampa, Fla.	65,657	South Florida	Big East	1998	Grass
39	LaVell Edwards Stadium	Provo, Utah	65,524	BYU	Mountain West	1964	Grass
40	Heinz Field*	Pittsburgh, Penn.	64,450	Pittsburgh	Big East	2001	Grass

Note: The capacities for several stadiums including the Rose Bowl, Louisiana Superdome and Sun Devil Stadium are often listed differently for other events, such as bowl games, which they host.

2006 Conference Home Fields

NCAA Division I-A conference by conference listing includes member teams heading into the 2006 season. Note that (*) indicates stadium is not on campus. For the purposes of this list anything other than natural grass is called turf.

Atlantic Coast

Atlantic	Stadium	Built	Seats	Field
Boston College	Alumni	1957	44,500	Turf
Clemson	Memorial	1942	81,474	Grass
Florida St.	Doak Campbell	1950	82,300	Grass
Maryland	Byrd	1950	51,500	Grass
N.C. State	Carter-Finley	1966	53,800	Grass
Wake Forest	Groves	1968	31,500	Grass
Coastal	**Stadium**	**Built**	**Seats**	**Field**
Duke	Wallace Wade	1929	33,941	Grass
Georgia Tech	Bobby Dodd	1913	55,000	Grass
Miami-FL	Orange Bowl*	1935	72,319	Grass
No. Carolina	Kenan Memorial	1927	60,000	Grass
Virginia	Scott	1931	61,500	Grass
Virginia Tech	Lane	1965	66,233	Grass

Big East

	Stadium	Built	Seats	Field
Cincinnati	Nippert	1924	35,000	Turf
Connecticut	Rentschler Field*	2003	40,000	Grass
Louisville	Papa John's Cardinal	1998	42,000	Turf
Pittsburgh	Heinz Field*	2001	64,450	Grass
Rutgers	Rutgers	1994	41,500	Grass
South Florida	Raymond James*	1988	65,657	Grass
Syracuse	Carrier Dome	1980	51,000	Turf
West Virginia	Mountaineer Field	1980	60,000	Turf

College Football (Cont.)

Big Ten

	Stadium	Built	Seats	Field
Illinois	Memorial	1923	69,249	Turf
Indiana	Memorial	1960	52,354	Turf
Iowa	Kinnick	1929	70,585	Grass
Michigan	Michigan	1927	107,501	Turf
Michigan St.	Spartan	1957	75,005	Grass
Minnesota	HHH Metrodome*	1982	64,172	Turf
Northwestern	Ryan Field	1926	49,256	Grass
Ohio St.	Ohio	1922	101,568	Grass
Penn St.	Beaver	1960	107,282	Grass
Purdue	Ross-Ade	1924	62,500	Grass
Wisconsin	Camp Randall	1917	80,320	Turf

Big 12

North	Stadium	Built	Seats	Field
Colorado	Folsom Field	1924	53,750	Turf
Iowa St.	Jack Trice Field	1975	45,814	Grass
Kansas	Memorial	1921	50,250	Turf
Kansas St.	Snyder Family	1968	52,000	Turf
Missouri	Memorial	1926	68,349	Turf
Nebraska	Memorial	1923	81,067	Turf
South	**Stadium**	**Built**	**Seats**	**Field**
Baylor	Floyd Casey	1950	50,000	Grass
Oklahoma	Gaylord Family-Oklahoma Memorial	1924	82,112	Grass
Oklahoma St.	Boone Pickens	1920	50,614	Turf
Texas	Royal-Memorial	1924	85,123	Grass
Texas A&M	Kyle Field	1925	82,600	Grass
Texas Tech	Jones AT&T	1947	53,702	Turf

Note: The annual Oklahoma-Texas game has been played at the Cotton Bowl (capacity 68,252) in Dallas since 1937.

Conference USA

East	Stadium	Built	Seats	Field
UAB	Legion Field	1927	71,594	Grass
C. Florida	Citrus Bowl	1936	70,188	Grass
E. Carolina	Dowdy-Ficklen	1963	43,000	Grass
Marshall	Joan C. Edwards	1991	38,019	Turf
Memphis	Liberty Bowl*	1965	62,380	Grass
Southern Miss	M.M. Roberts	1976	33,000	Grass
West	**Stadium**	**Built**	**Seats**	**Field**
Houston	Robertson	1942	32,000	Grass
Rice	Rice	1950	70,000	Turf
SMU	Gerald J. Ford Stadium	2000	32,000	Grass
Tulane	Superdome*	1975	69,767	Turf
Tulsa	Skelly	1930	35,542	Turf
UTEP	Sun Bowl*	1963	51,500	Grass

Mid-American

	Stadium	Built	Seats	Field
Akron	Rubber Bowl*	1940	35,202	Turf
Ball St.	Scheumann	1967	25,400	Grass
Bowling Green	Doyt Perry	1966	28,599	Grass
Buffalo	UB	1993	29,013	Turf
Central Mich.	Kelly/Shorts	1972	30,199	Turf
Eastern Mich.	Rynearson	1969	30,200	Turf
Kent	Dix	1969	29,287	Turf
Miami-OH	Fred Yager	1983	24,286	Turf
Northern Ill.	Huskie	1965	31,000	Turf
Ohio Univ.	Peden	1929	24,000	Turf
Temple	Lincoln Financial Field*	2003	68,532	Grass
Toledo	Glass Bowl	1937	26,248	Turf
Western Mich.	Waldo	1939	30,200	Turf

I-A Independents

	Stadium	Built	Seats	Field
Army	Michie	1924	39,929	Turf
Navy	Navy-Marine Corps Memorial	1959	30,000	Turf
Notre Dame	Notre Dame	1930	80,795	Grass

Mountain West

	Stadium	Built	Seats	Field
Air Force	Falcon	1962	52,480	Turf
BYU	LaVell Edwards	1964	65,524	Grass
Colorado St.	Hughes	1968	34,000	Turf
New Mexico	University	1960	38,634	Grass
San Diego St.	Qualcomm*	1967	71,295	Grass
TCU	Amon G. Carter	1929	46,083	Grass
UNLV	Sam Boyd*	1971	36,800	Grass
Utah	Rice-Eccles	1927	45,017	Turf
Wyoming	War Memorial	1950	32,580	Turf

Pacific-10

	Stadium	Built	Seats	Field
Arizona	Arizona	1928	57,803	Grass
Arizona St.	Sun Devil	1958	73,379	Grass
California	Memorial	1923	73,347	Turf
Oregon	Autzen	1967	53,800	Turf
Oregon St.	Reser	1953	43,300	Turf
Stanford	Stanford	1921	50,000	Grass
UCLA	Rose Bowl*	1922	92,542	Grass
USC	LA Memorial Coliseum*	1923	92,516	Grass
Washington	Husky	1920	72,500	Turf
Washington St.	Martin	1972	37,600	Grass

Southeastern

East	Stadium	Built	Seats	Field
Florida	Florida Field	1929	90,000	Grass
Georgia	Sanford	1929	92,746	Grass
Kentucky	Commonwealth	1973	67,530	Grass
South Carolina	Williams-Brice	1934	80,250	Grass
Tennessee	Neyland	1921	104,079	Grass
Vanderbilt	Vanderbilt	1981	39,790	Grass
West	**Stadium**	**Built**	**Seats**	**Field**
Alabama	Bryant-Denny	1929	92,158	Grass
Arkansas	Donald W. Reynolds Razorback & War Memorial*	1938	80,000	Grass
Auburn	Jordan-Hare	1939	87,451	Grass
LSU	Tiger	1924	92,400	Grass
Mississippi	Vaught-Hemingway	1915	60,580	Grass
Miss. St.	Davis Wade	1915	55,082	Grass

Note: EAST–Vanderbilt Stadium was rebuilt in 1981.

Sun Belt

	Stadium	Built	Seats	Field
Arkansas St.	Indian	1974	33,410	Turf
Florida Atlantic	Lockhart	1959	20,450	Grass
Florida International	FIU	1995	17,103	Turf
LA-Lafayette	Cajun Field	1971	31,000	Grass
LA-Monroe	Malone	1978	30,427	Grass
Mid. Tenn. St.	Johnny 'Red' Floyd	1933	30,788	Turf
North Texas	Fouts Field	1952	30,500	Turf
Troy	Movie Gallery Veterans	1950	30,000	Turf

Western Athletic

	Stadium	Built	Seats	Field
Boise St.	Bronco	1970	30,000	Turf
Fresno St.	Bulldog	1980	41,031	Grass
Hawaii	Aloha*	1975	50,000	Turf
Idaho	Kibbie Dome	1975	16,000	Turf
Louisiana Tech	Joe Aillet	1968	30,600	Grass
Nevada	Mackay	1967	31,900	Grass
New Mexico St.	Aggie Memorial	1978	30,343	Grass
San Jose St.	Spartan	1933	30,456	Grass
Utah St.	Romney	1968	30,257	Grass

BUSINESS

You've got to hand it to him. In the end, **Drew Rosenhaus** got **Terrell Owens** the money he wanted. Next question.

DRUG BUSINESS

Allegations of performance-enhancing drug use led to sports' biggest off-field battles in 2006, often overshadowing the games.

TALK OF DRUG USE WAS RAMPANT IN 2006, AND ALMOST NO SPORT WAS SPARED.

Baseball entered the year ready to implement a new drug policy that increased penalties for failed tests and banned amphetamines as well as anabolic steroids. But it could not escape its recent, juice-soaked past.

In March, Mark Fainaru-Wada and Lance Williams, reporters for the *San Francisco Chronicle*, published *Game of Shadows*, a book detailing the connections between BALCO and numerous star athletes.

Game of Shadows pointed incriminating fingers at Barry Bonds, Jason Giambi and Gary Sheffield, reporting that BALCO founder Victor Conte put each of them on specific steroid regimens.

Bonds, who began 2006 just 47 home runs shy of Hank Aaron's all-time record, was dogged all year by the allegations. And Commissioner Bud Selig declined an official celebration when Bonds passed Babe Ruth to become the #2 home run hitter in major league history. For their part, Fainaru-Wada and Williams were sent to prison by a federal judge in September for failing to reveal the sources of confidential grand jury testimony they used in their reports.

In June, federal agents raided the home of Jason Grimsley, a journeyman relief pitcher for the Arizona Diamondbacks pitcher who reportedly told investigators that he used steroids, and named other players who were on the juice.

That began another round of speculation and stories about steroids. In early October, it was reported that pitchers Roger Clemens and Andy Pettitte, as well as Baltimore Orioles players Miguel Tejada, Brian Roberts and Jay Gibbons were implicated in Grimsley's statements. All players vehemently denied the accusations.

Through it all, home runs, which had dropped 8 percent in 2005,

 Peter Keating writes "The Biz" column for *ESPN The Magazine* and is the author of "Dingers! A Short History of the Long Ball."

AP/Wide World Photos

 *San Francisco Chronicle reporters* **Mark Fainaru-Wada**, left, and **Lance Williams**, authors of "Game of Shadows," were arrested for not revealing sources.

leading some analysts to predict a new, post-steroids era of small ball, actually bounced up 7.3 percent. And Major League Baseball set an all-time attendance record, as more than 75 million fans visited ballparks.

Go figure.

Of course, baseball wasn't the only sport to weather accusations about drug use. In July, details emerged that American cyclist Floyd Landis flunked a drug test during his victorious 2006 Tour de France. He of course denied any claims of doping, but a second sample confirmed an unnatural level and source of testosterone in his blood.

At various times, Landis and his representatives have blamed alcohol, a conspiracy, dehydration and thyroid medication for his failed drug test, turning him into a punchline for late-night comedians.

As we went to press, Landis was still in the appeal process. But the damage to his now disbanded team (Phonak) is already done. The damage to the sport of cycling, however, is ongoing.

For more information on Landis and various other drug-related stories of 2006, see the International Sports essay on page 618.

PETER KEATING'S

10 ⬇

Biggest Stories of the Year in Business

10 What will they think of next?

In July, Apple and Nike team to release the Nike + iPod Sports Kit, which features a small device that sits inside a Nike shoe, streams data to a Nano and keeps track of your time elapsed and calories burned while you run. The price is $29 plus the cost of the Nano and the shoes. In most cases, roughly $300.

09 Higher Education

The Arizona Cardinals ink one of the biggest naming rights deal in history on September 26 (see page 608 for more details). The for-profit University of Phoenix will pay the team $154.5 million over 20 years to affix its name to the Cardinals' new stadium in Glendale, Ariz.

08 National Debt

A group headed by real estate developer Theodore Lerner purchases the Washington Nationals for $450 million. Major League Baseball had taken control of the franchise in 2002 for $120 million and moved the club from Montreal to D.C. before the 2005 season.

07 T.O. gets his cash

Perhaps you've heard about this one. Four days after the Eagles release him on March 14, wide receiver Terrell Owens signs a tidy three-year contract with the Dallas Cowboys. Philadelphia had suspended Owens for the final nine games of the 2005 season after a series of infractions, and after he demanded a new deal just one season into a seven-year, $49 million contract. After a hamstring injury, Owens debuted for Dallas in a preseason game on August 31.

06 (Red) Bull Market

Red Bull, the energy drink maker, buys and renames Major League Soccer's MetroStars (now Red Bull New York) in March. The sale price of $100 million reportedly includes the team, plus part-ownership *of* and naming rights *to* a new soccer-only stadium Red Bull is building in Harrison, N.J.

05 World Baseball Classic

Major League Baseball, with cooperation from its players union, establishes the World Baseball Classic, in which teams from 16 countries compete and showcase baseball's international appeal. Despite much criticism over scheduling, the WBC comes off without a hitch from March 3 to 20, with Japan winning the four-round tournament.

Former league intern **Roger Goodell**, left, was selected to succeed Paul Tagliabue as NFL commissioner on August 8.

04 Online gambling takes a hit

The U.S. government effectively bans online gambling on October 13, when President Bush signs into law a bill making it illegal for banks and credit card companies to transfer payments to betting websites. An estimated 23 million Americans gambled $6 billion over the Internet last year.

03 Superdome is back in business

More than a year after Hurricane Katrina, the Superdome reopens for football on September 25, as the Saints defeat the Falcons, 23-3, on Monday Night Football. The stadium, which suffered 70 percent roof failure and extensive water damage, is still in the midst of a $185-million renovation. But it's ready for the NFL, and so are New Orleans fans, who bought more than 55,000 season tickets, a franchise record, for the 2006 season.

Among the Big Easy's other teams, the NBA Hornets are planning to return in 2007, and the AAA-baseball Zephyrs never left.

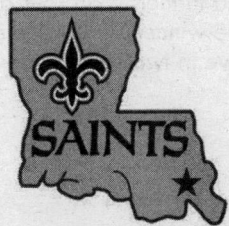

02 New NFL labor deal
The NFL and NFL Players Association conclude a new labor deal on March 8, extending their collective bargaining agreement through 2011. Owners had split over the issue of revenue sharing, but eventually reach an agreement whereby high-revenue clubs will put a reported $850 million into a pool to be split among low-revenue teams. Meanwhile, the league's salary cap will continue to rise, and players will get 59.5 percent of overall revenues.

Shortly after helping maintain labor peace, Paul Tagliabue, commissioner of the NFL for 16 years, announces he would retire. In August, he is succeeded by Roger Goodell, who started with the league as an intern in 1982 and rose to become its chief operating officer, and now commissioner.

01 Drug Scandals
Steroids and other performance-enhancing drugs grab headlines throughout the year. As it was in 2005, baseball is hit especially hard in the midst of Barry Bonds' pursuit of Hank Aaron's all-time home run mark, and Jason Grimsley's recent revelations.

Cycling, already reeling, is rocked further when Tour de France winner Floyd Landis tests positive in two samples.

Honorable Mention
(some not so honorable)

* Following the scandal involving the **Duke men's lacrosse** team and an alleged sexual assault, sales of merchandise bearing the team's name and logo jump.

* The St. Louis Cardinals open the new **Busch Stadium**. The team and other private developers are paying at least two-thirds of the ballpark's $646-million cost.

* Saints running back **Reggie Bush**, the #2 overall pick in the 2006 NFL draft, inks $5 million in endorsement deals with companies such as Adidas, General Motors and PepsiCo, the most ever for a rookie.

* The **Knicks spend** an NBA-record $123.6 million on player salaries in 2005-06, only to net 23 wins.

* Topps includes Royals minor leaguer **Alex Gordon** in its 2006 MLB card set by mistake, then pulls the release. Fans get their hands on some before the recall, however, sending the card's value to as much as $2,550 in trading among collectors.

2005-06 Top 50 TV Sports Events

Final 2005-06 network television ratings for the top nationally telecast sports events, according to Nielsen Media Research. Covers period from Sept. 1, 2005 through Aug. 31, 2006. Events are listed with ratings points and audience share; each ratings point represents 1,102,000 households and shares indicate percentage of TV sets in use.

Multiple entries: SPORTS—NFL Football (35); Winter Olympics (10); Major League Baseball (8); NCAA Football Bowl Games (3). NETWORKS—FOX (15); CBS (13); ABC and NBC (11) .

		Date	Net	Rtg/Sh
1	**Super Bowl XL** (Steelers vs Seahawks)	2/5/06	ABC	41.5/62
2	**AFC Championship Game** (Steelers at Broncos)	1/22/06	CBS	23.6/44
3	**Rose Bowl** (Texas vs USC)	1/4/06	ABC	21.7/35
4	**AFC Div. Playoff Game** (Steelers at Colts)	1/15/06	CBS	20.9/43
5	**NFC Championship Game** (Panthers at Seahawks)	1/22/06	FOX	20.7/31
6	**NFC Div. Playoff Game** (Panthers at Bears)	1/15/06	FOX	19.7/35
7	**AFC Wild Card Game** (Steelers at Bengals)	1/8/06	CBS	18.9/34
8	**AFC Div. Playoff Game** (Patriots at Broncos)	1/14/05	CBS	16.1/28
9	**NFC Div. Playoff Game** (Redskins at Seahawks)	1/14/05	FOX	15.8/31
10	**Winter Olympics** (Women's figure skating long program, men's aerials, snowboarding)	2/23/06	NBC	15.7/24
11	**Winter Olympics** (Women's figure skating short program, men's speedskating 1500m)	2/21/06	NBC	15.4/23
12	**NFL Regular Season Late Game** (Various teams)	11/27/05	FOX	15.3/27
13	**NFC Wild Card Game** (Panthers at Giants)	1/8/06	FOX	15.1/34
14	**NFL Monday Night Football** (Steelers at Colts)	11/28/05	ABC	14.8/23
15	**NFL Regular Season Late Game** (Various teams)	1/1/06	FOX	14.5/28
16	**NFL Monday Night Football** (Colts at Patriots)	11/7/05	ABC	14.3/23
17	**NFC Wild Card Game** (Redskins at Buccaneers)	1/7/06	ABC	14.2/29
18	**AFC Wild Card Game** (Jaguars at Patriots)	1/7/06	ABC	13.9/24
19	**NFL Regular Season Late Game** (Various teams)	9/11/05	FOX	13.7/27
	NFL Regular Season Late Game (Various teams)	12/4/05	CBS	13.7/25
	NFL Regular Season Early Game (Various teams)	12/18/05	CBS	13.7/31
22	**Winter Olympics** (Ice dancing final, men's GS final men's aerials)	2/20/06	NBC	13.5/21
23	**NFL Regular Season Late Game** (Various teams)	10/30/05	FOX	13.4/25
	NFL Regular Season Late Game (Various teams)	12/11/05	CBS	13.4/25
	Winter Olympics (Figure skating pairs short program, men's speedskating 5000m)	2/11/06	NBC	13.4/23
26	**NFL Regular Season Late Game** (Various teams)	11/20/05	CBS	13.3/24
	NFL Thanksgiving Day Late Game (Broncos at Cowboys)	11/24/05	CBS	13.3/34
	Winter Olympics (Men's downhill, short track men's 1500m, ski jumping)	2/12/06	NBC	13.3/20
29	**NFL Monday Night Football** (Eagles at Falcons)	9/12/05	ABC	13.0/22
	MLB World Series—Game 4 (White Sox at Astros)	10/26/05	FOX	13.0/21
31	**NFL Regular Season Late Game** (Various teams)	11/13/05	FOX	12.9/24
	Fiesta Bowl (Ohio St. vs Notre Dame)	1/2/06	ABC	12.9/21
33	**Winter Olympics** (Figure skating pairs free, women's halfpipe men's speedskating 500m)	2/13/06	NBC	12.8/19
34	**NFL Regular Season Early Game** (Various teams)	12/4/05	FOX	12.6/27
35	**NFL Monday Night Football** (Cowboys at Eagles)	11/14/05	ABC	12.4/20
36	**NFL Regular Season Late Game** (Various teams)	9/25/05	CBS	12.3/23
	NFL Regular Season Late Game (Various teams)	10/23/05	CBS	12.3/23
38	**Orange Bowl** (Penn St. vs Florida St.)	1/3/06	ABC	12.2/21
39	**NFL Regular Season Late Game** (Various teams)	10/2/05	FOX	12.0/23
40	**Winter Olympics** (Men's figure skating long program, men's snowboardcross)	2/16/06	NBC	11.9/19
41	**NFL Thursday Night—Season Opener** (Raiders at Patriots)	9/8/05	ABC	11.7/21
	NFL Regular Season Early Game (Various teams)	11/20/05	FOX	11.7/26
43	**NFL Regular Season Early Game** (Various teams)	12/11/05	FOX	11.6/25
	Winter Olympics (Ice dancing, women's Super G, women's speedskating 1000m)	2/19/06	NBC	11.6/18
45	**NFL Regular Season Late Game** (Various teams)	9/18/05	CBS	11.5/23
	NFL Regular Season Late Game (Various teams)	11/6/05	CBS	11.5/21
47	**NFL Regular Season Late Game** (Various teams)	12/18/05	FOX	11.4/22
48	**Winter Olympics** (Women's downhill, men's moguls, women's short track 500m)	2/15/06	NBC	11.3/18
	Winter Olympics (Men's Super G, men's speedskating 1000m, men's short track 1000m)	2/18/06	NBC	11.3/19
	NASCAR Daytona 500 (Jimmie Johnson wins)	2/19/06	NBC	11.3/23

Other top non-NFL TV sports events

		Date	Net	Rtg/Sh
51	**Winter Olympics** (Men's figure skating short program, women's speedskating 500m)	2/14/06	NBC	11.2/18
	Winter Olympics (Ice dancing, women's snowboardcross, men's skeleton)	2/17/06	NBC	11.2/19
	NCAA Men's Basketball Championship Game (Florida vs UCLA)	4/3/06	CBS	11.2/18
54	**MLB World Series—Game 2** (Astros at White Sox)	10/23/05	FOX	11.1/17
55	**MLB World Series—Game 3** (White Sox at Astros)	10/25/05	FOX	11.1/21
66	**Winter Olympics** (Women's slalom, women's aerials, women's speedskating 1500m)	2/22/06	NBC	10.0/15
	NBA Finals—Game 6 (Mavericks at Heat)	6/20/06	ABC	10.0/18

All-Time Top-Rated TV Programs

NFL Football dominates television's All-Time Top-Rated 50 Programs with 22 Super Bowls and the 1981 NFC Championship Game making the list. Rankings based on surveys taken from January 1961 through August 31, 2006; include only sponsored programs seen on individual networks; and programs under 30 minutes scheduled duration are excluded. Programs are listed with ratings points, audience share and number of households watching, according to Nielsen Media Research.

Multiple entries: The Super Bowl (22); "Roots" (7); "The Beverly Hillbillies" and "The Thorn Birds" (3); "The Bob Hope Christmas Show," "The Ed Sullivan Show," "Gone With The Wind" and 1994 Winter Olympics (2).

	Program	Episode/Game	Net	Date	Rating	Share	Households
1	M*A*S*H (series)	Final episode	CBS	2/28/83	60.2	77	50,150,000
2	Dallas (series)	"Who Shot J.R.?"	CBS	11/21/80	53.3	76	41,470,000
3	Roots (mini-series)	Part 8	ABC	1/30/77	51.1	71	36,380,000
4	Super Bowl XVI	49ers 26, Bengals 21	CBS	1/24/82	49.1	73	40,020,000
5	Super Bowl XVII	Redskins 27, Dolphins 17	NBC	1/30/83	48.6	69	40,480,000
6	XVII Winter Olympics	Women's Figure Skating	CBS	-2/23/94	48.5	64	45,690,000
7	Super Bowl XX	Bears 46, Patriots 10	NBC	1/26/86	48.3	70	41,490,000
8	Gone With the Wind (movie)	Part 1	NBC	11/7/76	47.7	65	33,960,000
9	Gone With the Wind (movie)	Part 2	NBC	11/8/76	47.4	64	33,750,000
10	Super Bowl XII	Cowboys 27, Broncos 10	CBS	1/15/78	47.2	67	34,410,000
11	Super Bowl XIII	Steelers 35, Cowboys 31	NBC	1/21/79	47.1	74	35,090,000
12	Bob Hope Special	Christmas Show	NBC	1/15/70	46.6	64	27,260,000
13	Super Bowl XVIII	Raiders 38, Redskins 9	CBS	1/22/84	46.4	71	38,800,000
	Super Bowl XIX	49ers 38, Dolphins 16	ABC	1/20/85	46.4	63	39,390,000
15	Super Bowl XIV	Steelers 31, Rams 19	CBS	1/20/80	46.3	67	35,330,000
16	Super Bowl XXX	Cowboys 27, Steelers 17	NBC	1/28/96	46.0	68	44,114,400
	ABC Theater (special)	"The Day After"	ABC	11/20/83	46.0	62	38,550,000
18	Roots (mini-series)	Part 6	ABC	1/28/77	45.9	66	32,680,000
	The Fugitive (series)	Final episode	ABC	8/29/67	45.9	72	25,700,000
20	Super Bowl XXI	Giants 39, Broncos 20	CBS	1/25/87	45.8	66	40,030,000
21	Roots (mini-series)	Part 5	ABC	1/27/77	45.7	71	32,540,000
22	Super Bowl XXVIII	Cowboys 30, Bills 13	NBC	1/30/94	45.5	66	42,860,000
	Cheers (series)	Final episode	NBC	5/20/93	45.5	64	42,360,500
24	The Ed Sullivan Show	Beatles' 1st appearance	CBS	2/9/64	45.3	60	23,240,000
25	Super Bowl XXVII	Cowboys 52, Bills 17	NBC	1/31/93	45.1	66	41,988,100
26	Bob Hope Special	Christmas Show	NBC	1/14/71	45.0	61	27,050,000
27	Roots (mini-series)	Part 3	ABC	1/25/77	44.8	68	31,900,000
28	Super Bowl XXXII	Broncos 31, Packers 24	NBC	1/25/98	44.5	67	43,630,000
29	Super Bowl XI	Raiders 32, Vikings 14	NBC	1/9/77	44.4	73	31,610,000
	Super Bowl XV	Raiders 27, Eagles 10	NBC	1/25/81	44.4	63	34,540,000
31	Super Bowl VI	Cowboys 24, Dolphins 3	CBS	1/16/72	44.2	74	27,450,000
32	XVII Winter Olympics	Women's Figure Skating	CBS	2/25/94	44.1	64	41,540,000
	Roots (mini-series)	Part 2	ABC	1/24/77	44.1	62	31,400,000
34	The Beverly Hillbillies (series)	Regular episode	CBS	1/8/64	44.0	65	22,570,000
35	Roots (mini-series)	Part 4	ABC	1/26/77	43.8	66	31,190,000
	The Ed Sullivan Show	Beatles' 2nd appearance	CBS	2/16/64	43.8	60	22,445,000
37	Super Bowl XXIII	49ers 20, Bengals 16	NBC	1/22/89	43.5	68	39,320,000
38	The Academy Awards	John Wayne wins Oscar	ABC	4/7/70	43.4	78	25,390,000
39	Super Bowl XXXI	Packers 35, Patriots 21	FOX	1/26/97	43.3	65	42,000,000
	Super Bowl XXXIV	Rams 23, Titans 16	ABC	1/30/00	43.3	63	43,618,000
41	The Thorn Birds (mini-series)	Part 3	ABC	3/29/83	43.2	62	35,990,000
42	The Thorn Birds (mini-series)	Part 4	ABC	3/30/83	43.1	62	35,900,000
43	NFC Championship Game	49ers 28, Cowboys 27	CBS	1/10/82	42.9	62	34,940,000
44	The Beverly Hillbillies (series)	Regular episode	CBS	1/15/64	42.8	62	21,960,000
45	Super Bowl VII	Dolphins 14, Redskins 7	NBC	1/14/73	42.7	72	27,670,000
46	The Thorn Birds (mini-series)	Part 2	ABC	3/28/83	42.5	59	35,400,000
47	Super Bowl IX	Steelers 16, Vikings 6	NBC	1/12/75	42.4	72	29,040,000
	The Beverly Hillbillies (series)	Regular episode	CBS	2/26/64	42.4	60	21,750,000
49	Super Bowl X	Steelers 21, Cowboys 17	CBS	1/18/76	42.3	78	29,440,000
	ABC Sunday Night Movie	"Airport"	ABC	11/11/73	42.3	63	28,000,000
	ABC Sunday Night Movie	"Love Story"	ABC	10/1/72	42.3	62	27,410,000
	Cinderella	Musical special	CBS	2/22/65	42.3	59	22,250,000
	Roots (mini-series)	Part 7	ABC	1/29/77	42.3	65	30,120,000

All-Time Top-Rated Cable TV Sports Events

All-time cable television for sports events, according to ESPN, Turner Sports research and The Sports Business Daily. Covers period from Sept. 1, 1980 through Aug. 31, 2006.

NFL Telecasts

		Date	Net	Rtg
1	Chicago at Minnesota	12/6/87	ESPN	17.6
2	Detroit at Miami	12/25/94	ESPN	15.1
3	Chicago at Minnesota	12/3/89	ESPN	14.7
4	Cleveland at San Fran	11/29/87	ESPN	14.2
5	Pittsburgh at Houston	12/30/90	ESPN	13.8

Non-NFL Telecasts

		Date	Net	Rtg
1	MLB: Chicago (NL)-St. Louis	9/7/98	ESPN	9.5
2	NBA: Detroit-Boston	6/1/88	TBS	8.8
3	NBA: Chicago-Detroit	5/31/89	TBS	8.2
4	NBA: Detroit-Boston	5/26/88	TBS	8.1
	MLB: Giants-Chicago (NL)	9/28/98	ESPN	8.0

ESPN The Magazine's Ultimate Standings
Fan Satisfaction Rankings

ESPN The Magazine, in conjunction with *SportsNation*, surveyed over 30,000 fans in order to rank the current 122 major men's professional sports franchises (MLB, NFL, NBA, NHL). The following eight criteria were used:

Bang for the Buck: Revenues directly from fans divided by wins in the past three years; **Fan Relations**: Ease of access to players, coaches and management; **Ownership**: Honesty; loyalty to players and city; **Affordability**: Price of tickets, parking and concessions; **Stadium Experience**: Friendliness of environment, quality of game-day promotions; **Players**: Effort on the field, likability off it; **Coach/Manager**: Strong on-field leadership; **Championships**: Titles already won or expected soon.

In 2005 and 2006, no NHL teams were ranked due to the 2004-05 lockout. NHL teams are placed at the end, ordered by their 2004 ranking. Also note that since the Charlotte Bobcats have not been in existence for three years, they could not be ranked in the "Bang for the Buck" category and therefore were not included in the overall ranking.

Team	League	2004	2005	2006
San Antonio Spurs	NBA	1	2	1
Detroit Pistons	NBA	4	1	2
Pittsburgh Steelers	NFL	16	9	3
Indianapolis Colts	NFL	40	3	4
LA Angels of Anaheim	MLB	6	5	5
Atlanta Falcons	NFL	70	7	6
St. Louis Cardinals	MLB	18	11	7
Carolina Panthers	NFL	42	12	8
Atlanta Braves	MLB	33	16	9
New England Patriots	NFL	13	4	10
Houston Astros	MLB	71	27	11
Indiana Pacers	NBA	17	10	12
Chicago White Sox	MLB	99	70	13
Denver Broncos	NFL	19	26	14
Dallas Mavericks	NBA	2	13	15
Jacksonville Jaguars	NFL	75	28	16
Milwaukee Brewers	MLB	112	45	17
Philadelphia Eagles	NFL	23	6	18
Cincinnati Bengals	NFL	74	43	19
Phoenix Suns	NBA	55	21	20
Houston Rockets	NBA	53	56	21
Tampa Bay Buccaneers	NFL	32	36	22
Miami Heat	NBA	79	18	23
Seattle Seahawks	NFL	54	59	24
Cleveland Indians	MLB	87	42	25
Kansas City Chiefs	NFL	5	24	26
Dallas Cowboys	NFL	36	39	27
New York Yankees	MLB	28	17	28
Denver Nuggets	NBA	68	48	29
Green Bay Packers	NFL	3	8	30
Buffalo Bills	NFL	96	15	31
Memphis Grizzlies	NBA	38	30	32
New York Giants	NFL	90	71	33
Tennessee Titans	NFL	7	19	34
Utah Jazz	NBA	26	20	35
Miami Dolphins	NFL	57	55	36
Washington Redskins	NFL	92	60	37
Minnesota Twins	MLB	51	29	38
Minnesota Timberwolves	NBA	29	14	39
Sacramento Kings	NBA	14	23	40
Texas Rangers	MLB	76	31	41
Oakland Athletics	MLB	66	38	42
Chicago Bears	NFL	103	69	43
Chicago Bulls	NBA	93	74	44
San Diego Chargers	NFL	118	37	45
Cleveland Cavaliers	NBA	82	34	46
Toronto Blue Jays	MLB	47	67	47
Philadelphia 76ers	NBA	35	40	48
San Diego Padres	MLB	62	47	49
St. Louis Rams	NFL	34	66	50
Arizona Diamondbacks	MLB	9	32	51
Milwaukee Bucks	NBA	46	51	52
Florida Marlins	MLB	24	25	53
Baltimore Ravens	NFL	22	22	54
New Orleans Hornets	NBA	30	83	55
San Francisco Giants	MLB	39	35	56
Seattle SuperSonics	NBA	60	33	57
Golden State Warriors	NBA	94	80	58
Washington Wizards	NBA	105	62	59
Cincinnati Reds	MLB	101	54	60
Los Angeles Lakers	NBA	31	49	61
Boston Red Sox	MLB	95	46	62
New York Jets	NFL	81	41	63
Washington Nationals	MLB	97	68	64
New Jersey Nets	NBA	80	76	65
Cleveland Browns	NFL	110	90	66
New York Mets	MLB	111	86	67
Pittsburgh Pirates	MLB	102	64	68
Detroit Lions	NFL	107	72	69
Boston Celtics	NBA	61	63	70
Oakland Raiders	NFL	104	84	71
Seattle Mariners	MLB	67	61	72
Chicago Cubs	MLB	45	57	73
Kansas City Royals	MLB	25	58	74
Colorado Rockies	MLB	100	85	75
Detroit Tigers	MLB	113	53	76
Orlando Magic	NBA	108	44	77
Los Angeles Clippers	NBA	86	65	78
Houston Texans	NFL	—	—	79
Baltimore Orioles	MLB	84	50	80
San Francisco 49ers	NFL	72	89	81
Los Angeles Dodgers	MLB	64	52	82
Philadelphia Phillies	MLB	58	78	83
Toronto Raptors	NBA	50	75	84
Tampa Bay Devil Rays	MLB	77	73	85
Arizona Cardinals	NFL	119	82	86
Atlanta Hawks	NBA	117	88	87
New York Knicks	NBA	116	77	88
Portland Trail Blazers	NBA	115	79	89
Minnesota Vikings	NFL	106	81	90
New Orleans Saints	NFL	78	87	91
Edmonton Oilers	NHL	8	—	—
Ottawa Senators	NHL	10	—	—
Minnesota Wild	NHL	11	—	—
Colorado Avalanche	NHL	12	—	—
Detroit Red Wings	NHL	15	—	—
Vancouver Canucks	NHL	20	—	—
St. Louis Blues	NHL	21	—	—
Tampa Bay Lightning	NHL	27	—	—
Anaheim Ducks	NHL	37	—	—
Philadelphia Flyers	NHL	41	—	—
Dallas Stars	NHL	43	—	—
New Jersey Devils	NHL	44	—	—
Los Angeles Kings	NHL	48	—	—
Columbus Blue Jackets	NHL	49	—	—
Calgary Flames	NHL	52	—	—
Nashville Predators	NHL	56	—	—
Atlanta Thrashers	NHL	59	—	—
Buffalo Sabres	NHL	63	—	—
Carolina Hurricanes	NHL	65	—	—
Phoenix Coyotes	NHL	69	—	—
Montreal Canadiens	NHL	73	—	—
San Jose Sharks	NHL	83	—	—
New York Islanders	NHL	85	—	—
Toronto Maple Leafs	NHL	88	—	—
Boston Bruins	NHL	89	—	—
Pittsburgh Penguins	NHL	91	—	—
Florida Panthers	NHL	98	—	—
Washington Capitals	NHL	109	—	—
New York Rangers	NHL	114	—	—
Chicago Blackhawks	NHL	120	—	—

Forbes Team Valuations

Current values of all 122 NBA, MLB, NHL and NFL teams, as calculated by *Forbes Magazine*. Values are based on figures from the 2005 season for the NFL and MLB, the 2004-05 season for the NBA and the 2003-04 season for the NHL (no NHL totals from 2004-05 due to lockout). Figures are in millions of dollars.

Avg. franchise values: NBA ($326 million), **MLB** ($376 million), **NHL** ($163 million) and **NFL** ($898 million).

	NBA		MLB		NHL		NFL
1	New York $543	1	NY Yankees $1026	1	NY Rangers $282	1	Washington $1423
2	LA Lakers 529	2	Boston 617	2	Toronto 280	2	New England . . .1176
3	Houston 422	3	NY Mets 604	3	Philadelphia 264	3	Dallas 1173
4	Chicago 409	4	LA Dodgers 482	4	Dallas 259	4	Houston 1043
5	Dallas 403	5	Chi. Cubs 448	5	Detroit 248	5	Philadelphia 1024
6	Detroit 402	6	Washington 440	6	Colorado 246	6	Denver 975
7	Phoenix 395	7	St. Louis 429	7	Boston 236	7	Cleveland 970
8	Miami 362	8	Seattle 428	8	Montreal 195	8	Tampa Bay 955
9	Cleveland 356	9	Philadelphia 424	9	Los Angeles 193	9	Baltimore 946
10	Boston 353	10	Houston 416	10	Chicago 178	10	Chicago 945
11	Philadelphia 351	11	San Francisco 410	11	Minnesota 163	11	Carolina 936
12	San Antonio 350	12	Atlanta 405	12	NY Islanders 160	12	Miami 912
13	Sacramento 345	13	LA Angels 368	13	Tampa Bay 150	13	Green Bay 911
14	Indiana 324	14	Baltimore 359	14	San Jose 149	14	Kansas City 894
15	Washington 318	15	San Diego 354	15	Vancouver 148	15	NY Giants 890
16	Minnesota 303	16	Texas 353	16	St. Louis 140	16	Seattle 888
17	Charlotte 300	17	Cleveland 352	17	Columbus 139	17	Tennessee 886
18	Memphis 294	18	Chi. White Sox . . .315	18	Phoenix 136	18	Pittsburgh 880
19	Denver 283	19	Arizona 305	19	Ottawa 125	19	NY Jets 876
20	Toronto 278	20	Colorado 298	20	New Jersey 124	20	St. Louis Rams 841
21	Utah 274	21	Detroit 292	21	Florida 121	21	Detroit 839
22	New Jersey 271	22	Toronto 286	22	Calgary 116	22	Indianapolis 837
23	Atlanta 262	23	Cincinnati 274	23	Washington 115	23	Cincinnati 825
24	LA Clippers 248	24	Pittsburgh 250	24	Nashville 111	24	Arizona 789
25	Orlando 247	25	Kansas City 239	25	Anaheim 108	25	Buffalo 756
26	Golden State 243	26	Milwaukee 235	26	Atlanta 106	26	Jacksonville 744
27	Seattle 234	27	Oakland 234	27	Edmonton 104	27	New Orleans 738
28	Milwaukee 231	28	Florida 226	28	Buffalo 103	28	Oakland 736
29	Portland 227	29	Minnesota 216	29	Pittsburgh 101	29	San Francisco 734
30	New Orleans 225	30	Tampa Bay 209	30	Carolina 100	30	San Diego 731
						31	Atlanta 730
						32	Minnesota 720

Reprinted by Permission of *Forbes Magazine*, copyright 2006 Forbes Inc.

Teams Bought in 2006

Five major league clubs acquired new majority owners from Oct. 7, 2005 through Sept. 30, 2006.

Major League Baseball

Cincinnati Reds: On Jan. 19, MLB owners unanimously approved the sale of the Reds from Carl Lindner to a group headed by Cincinnati produce mogul Robert Castellini. Terms of the deal were not disclosed, but the franchise is worth an estimated $270 million and the group reportedly purchased a 70 percent stake. Lindner had three similar offers but chose to sell to Castellini due to his ties to the city. The Castellini family founded a fruit and vegetable distributing company on the banks of the Ohio River in 1896. Castellini's group had to divest its interest in the St. Louis Cardinals before the deal could be approved.

Washington Nationals: On May 18, MLB owners unanimously approved the sale of the Nationals to a group headed by Theodore Lerner and former Atlanta Braves president Stan Kasten for $450 million. The franchise had previously been owned by the other 29 major league teams and operations were being run by the commissioner's office. Lerner, 80, is a real estate developer who grew up in Washington, D.C. The ownership group also includes his son, Mark, and two sons-in-law.

NBA Basketball

Seattle SuperSonics: On July 19, Starbucks chairman Howard Schultz and his group, the Basketball Club of Seattle, sold the SuperSonics and the WNBA's Seattle Storm for $350 million to the Professional Basketball Club LLC, headed by Oklahoma City businessman Clay Bennett. Rumors immediately began swirling that it was only a matter of time before the new ownership group moved the franchise to Oklahoma City, though Bennett denied such claims as long as a deal can be worked out with the city to replace or renovate the aging KeyArena.

NHL Hockey

Phoenix Coyotes: Co-owners Jerry Moyes and Steve Ellman announced their agreement on April 13 for Moyes to assume majority ownership control of the Coyotes, Glendale Arena and Arizona Sting (NLL). Ellman had been the team's chairman and governor. The deal was approved by the NHL board of governors on June 21. Terms of the deal were not disclosed. Wayne Gretzky, who is also the Coyote's head coach, will keep his minority ownership interest.

St. Louis Blues: On June 22, the NHL's board of governors approved the sale of the Blues and the Savvis Center from Bill and Nancy Laurie to Dave Checketts, Sports Capital Partners (SCP) and TowerBrook Capital Partners, L.P. for a reported $150 million. Checketts is also the owner of Real Salt Lake (MLS) and is the former president of Madison Square Garden, where he oversaw the operations of the New York Knicks, the New York Rangers and the New York Liberty (WNBA).

Team Payrolls

Team payrolls for active players during the 2005-06 season for the NBA and NHL, the 2005 season for the NFL and the 2006 season (as of opening day) for Major League Baseball. Figures are in millions of dollars. **Note:** The NFL, NHL and NBA use a salary cap to limit payrolls. The NFL's cap was $85.5 million in 2005, the NHL's cap was $39 million in 2005-06, and the NBA's cap was $49.5 million, though teams can circumvent the cap via bonuses and other exceptions. Note, however, that the totals listed below reflect actual player salaries, not salary cap numbers. **Sources**: USA Today, NHLPA, NFLPA and AP.

	NBA		MLB		NHL		NFL
1	New York $92.9	1	NY Yankees ...$198.7	1	New Jersey $44.9	1	Seattle $100.6
2	San Antonio 79.6	2	Boston 120.1	2	Vancouver 43.7	2	Atlanta 98.8
3	Dallas 68.3	3	LA Angels 103.6	3	Philadelphia 42.6	3	Oakland 98.2
4	Indiana 66.6	4	Chi. White Sox ..102.9	4	NY Rangers 41.5	4	New Orleans 96.0
5	Memphis 64.6	5	NY Mets 100.9	5	Colorado 41.0	5	Denver 95.4
6	New Jersey 61.6	6	LA Dodgers 99.2	6	Dallas 40.7	6	Baltimore 94.7
7	Sacramento 60.5	7	Chi Cubs 94.8	7	Detroit 39.6	7	New England 94.4
8	Philadelphia ...59.7	8	Atlanta 92.5	8	Tampa Bay 39.2	8	Carolina 90.2
9	Phoenix 59.7	9	Houston 92.1	9	Edmonton 38.5	9	Minnesota 85.4
10	Miami 59.7	10	San Francisco ...90.9	10	Los Angeles 37.9	10	Pittsburgh 84.2
11	Detroit 57.9	11	Seattle 87.9	11	Atlanta 37.2	11	Kansas City 83.4
12	Utah 57.8	12	Philadelphia 87.1	12	Ottawa 36.9	12	Jacksonville 83.3
13	Golden State ...57.5	13	St. Louis 86.9	13	Toronto 36.8	13	San Francisco ...82.8
14	Milwaukee 56.5	14	Detroit 82.3	14	Boston 36.7	14	NY Giants 82.4
15	Minnesota 54.3	15	Baltimore 72.6	15	Calgary 36.6	15	Dallas 82.2
16	LA Lakers 54.2	16	Toronto 71.9	16	Carolina 35.3	16	Houston 81.7
17	Denver 53.8	17	San Diego 68.9	17	Montreal 33.0	17	Buffalo 80.9
18	Orlando 52.9	18	Texas 65.1	18	Anaheim 32.1	18	Detroit 80.6
19	Boston 52.6	19	Minnesota 63.8	19	Nashville 31.6	19	NY Jets 79.3
20	Cleveland 51.8	20	Washington 63.3	20	NY Islanders 31.4	20	St. Louis 78.9
21	LA Clippers 51.3	21	Oakland 62.3	21	San Jose 31.0	21	San Diego 78.7
22	Portland 51.1	22	Cincinnati 59.2	22	Phoenix 30.4	22	Chicago 78.4
23	Washington 50.2	23	Arizona 58.9	23	Chicago 30.1	23	Indianapolis 77.4
24	Seattle 46.9	24	Cleveland 56.8	24	Columbus 30.1	24	Arizona 76.5
25	Houston 46.8	25	Milwaukee 50.5	25	Buffalo 28.5	25	Cincinnati 74.8
26	New Orleans ...43.6	26	Kansas City 47.3	26	St. Louis 28.5	26	Tampa Bay 73.8
27	Chicago 37.7	27	Pittsburgh 46.9	27	Florida 26.5	27	Cleveland 73.5
28	Atlanta 36.6	28	Colorado 40.8	28	Minnesota 25.2	28	Philadelphia 72.7
29	Toronto 34.6	29	Tampa Bay 35.4	29	Pittsburgh 23.1	29	Miami 70.9
30	Charlotte 30.3	30	Florida 14.3	30	Washington 18.9	30	Washington 66.1
						31	Green Bay 64.7
						32	Tennessee 61.3

Top 10 Salaries In Each Sport

The top 10 highest paid athletes in the NBA and NHL (2005-06 season), Major League Baseball (2006 - opening day) and the NFL (2005). Figures are in millions of dollars. Note that NFL figures include signing bonuses.
Sources: USA Today, Street & Smith's SportsBusiness Journal, NHLPA and AP.

NFL

		Position	Team	Salary
1	Michael Vick	Quarterback	Atlanta	$23.103
2	Matt Hasselbeck ..	Quarterback	Seattle	19.005
3	Orlando Pace	Off. Lineman	St. Louis	18.000
4	Walter Jones	Off. Lineman	Seattle	17.701
5	Tom Brady	Quarterback	New Eng.	15.654
6	Champ Bailey	Def. Back	Denver	13.508
7	Fred Smoot	Def. Back	Minnesota	12.300
8	Samari Rolle	Def. Back	Baltimore	12.001
9	Anthony Henry ...	Def. Back	Dallas	11.605
10	Jonathan Ogden ..	Off. Lineman	Baltimore	10.666
	League Avg			1.400

MLB

		Position	Team	Salary
1	Alex Rodriguez ...	Third Base	NY Yankees	$21.681
2	Derek Jeter	Shortstop	NY Yankees	20.600
3	Jason Giambi	First Base	NY Yankees	20.429
4	Jeff Bagwell	First Base	Houston	19.369
5	Barry Bonds	Left Field	San Fran.	19.331
6	Mike Mussina	Pitcher	NY Yankees	19.000
7	Manny Ramirez ...	Left Field	Boston	18.279
8	Todd Helton	First Base	Colorado	16.600
9	Andy Pettitte	Pitcher	Houston	16.428
10	Magglio Ordonez .	Right Field	Detroit	16.200
	League Avg			2.867

NBA

		Position	Team	Salary
1	Shaquille O'Neal ..	Center	Miami	$20.000
2	Chris Webber	Forward	Philadelphia	19.130
3	Michael Finley ...	Forward	San Antonio	18.612
4	Kevin Garnett	Forward	Minnesota	18.000
5	Allen Iverson	Guard	Philadelphia	16.450
	Stephon Marbury .	Guard	New York	16.450
7	Jason Kidd	Guard	New Jersey	16.440
8	Jermaine O'Neal ..	Forward	Indiana	16.430
9	Kobe Bryant	Guard	LA Lakers	15.950
10	Tim Duncan	Center	San Antonio	15.850
	League Avg			5.000

NHL

		Position	Team	Salary
1	Jaromir Jagr	Right Wing	NY Rangers	$8.360
2	Nicklas Lidstrom ..	Defense	Detroit	7.600
	Keith Tkachuk	Left Wing	St. Louis	7.600
	Alexei Yashin	Center	NY Islanders	7.600
5	Jarome Iginla	Right Wing	Calgary	7.000
6	Mats Sundin	Center	Toronto	6.840
7	Nikolai Khabibulin .	Goalie	Chicago	6.750
	Scott Niedermayer .	Defense	Anaheim	6.750
9	Bill Guerin	Right Wing	Dallas	6.738
10	Joe Sakic	Center	Colorado	6.665
	League Avg			1.460

Collective Bargaining Agreements

Listed are highlights from the collective bargaining agreements (CBAs) of the four major sports leagues. Note that the NFL has not released its newly signed agreement to the media or public, so the points highlighted below are widely reported, yet unconfirmed. **Sources:** League CBAs, league players' associations, *USA Today*

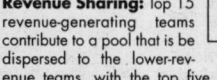

Expiration: Current agreement expires December 19, 2006.

Salary cap: None, though it does tax teams whose payrolls exceed agreed-upon limits, which vary from year to year.

Maximum player salary: None.

Minimum player salary: $327,000 (2006).

Free Agency: A player can become eligible for free agency after six years of MLB service.

Revenue Sharing: Each team contributes 34% of its Net Local Revenue into a pool, which is then divided equally among all teams.

Luxury Tax: Referred to by MLB as the "Competitive Balance Tax." In 2006 the tax threshold was $136.5 million. The amount of tax is charged on the difference between the threshold and the team's payroll and depends upon how many consecutive years the team has exceeded the tax threshold.

Steroid Policy (through 2008)**:** 50-game suspension for first offense, 100 games for second offense, lifetime ban for third offense. At least one regular season test.

Expiration: Current agreement is valid through the 2010-11 season, with a league option for an additional season.

Salary cap: In 2006-07, the cap is set at $53.135 million, while the minimum (75% of max.) is $39.85 million. The NBA operates under a soft salary cap and contains exceptions that allow teams to exceed the cap. For example, the Larry Bird exception allows a team to exceed the salary cap to re-sign its own free agents up to the players' maximum salary.

Maximum player salary: Depends on the number of years played, but rookie maximum in 2006-07 is $12.45 million and the maximun for a veteran with more than ten years played is $17.44 million (without bonuses).

Minimum player salary: Depends on the number of years played, but rookie minimum in 2006-07 is $412,718 and the minimum for a veteran with more than ten years played is $1.18 million.

Steroid Policy: 10-game suspension for first offense, 25 games for second, one year for third and a lifetime ban for a fourth. Up to four random tests per season.

Expiration: Agreement signed in March, 2006 is valid through 2011 season.

Salary cap: $102 million for 2006; $109 million for 2007. Future years to be determined by revenue.

Revenue Sharing: Top 15 revenue-generating teams contribute to a pool that is be dispersed to the lower-revenue teams, with the top five teams giving the most. Expected to add $850-900 million over the life of the contract.

Rookies: Players drafted in the first round of the draft can sign contracts longer than five years. Those drafted in rounds 2-7 can sign only four-year deals, preventing teams from locking up players who prove to be worth more than their initial contract allows.

Franchise Players: Teams can no longer protect a player with the "franchise" tag for more than two years. "Franchise" player becomes a "transition" player in the third year of his contract, so its easier for him to leave.

Steroid Policy: Four-game suspension for first offense, eight games for second offense, one-year ban for third offense. Players subject to at least one test per season.

Expiration: Agreement is valid until Sept. 15, 2011. However, the NHLPA has the option to terminate it on Sept. 15, 2009 or extend it to 2012.

Salary cap: In 2005-06, the cap was set at $39 million, while the minimum was set at $21.5 million. In 2006-07, those figures were upped to $44 million (maximum) and $28 million (minimum).

Maximum player salary: Players can earn no more than 20 percent of the salary cap (or $7.8 million in 2005-06).

Minimum player salary: $450,000 for 2005-06 and 2006-07, $475,000 in 2007-09 and $500,000 for 2009-11.

Revenue Sharing: All clubs are eligible for revenue sharing that are ranked in the bottom half (bottom 15) in league revenue and those that operate in cities with a demographic of 2.5 million or fewer TV households.

Steroid Policy: 20-game suspension for first offense, 60 games for second offense, lifetime ban for third offense. Players subject to up to two tests per season.

Highest and Lowest Ticket Prices

The most expensive and least expensive average ticket prices for NFL and MLB franchises for the 2006 season, and NBA and NHL franchises for the 2005-06 season. Note that average ticket prices for each league are as follows: **NFL** $58.95, **MLB** $22.21, **NBA** $45.92 and **NHL** $41.19. **Source:** *Team Marketing Report*

NFL

	Highest	Venue	Avg. Price
1	New England	Gillette Stadium	$90.89
2	NY Giants	Giants Stadium	71.59
3	NY Jets	Giants Stadium	71.32
4	Chicago	Soldier Field	68.89
5	Minnesota	HHH Metrodome	67.94

	Lowest	Venue	Avg. Price
1	Buffalo	Ralph Wilson Stadium	$39.37
2	Jacksonville	ALLTEL Stadium	40.16
3	Seattle	Qwest Field	44.78
4	Arizona	Sun Devil Stadium	44.98
5	Tennessee	The Coliseum	47.82

MLB

	Highest	Venue	Avg. Price
1	Boston	Fenway Park	$46.46
2	Chicago Cubs	Wrigley Field	34.30
3	St. Louis	Busch Stadium	29.78
4	NY Yankees	Yankee Stadium	28.27
5	Philadelphia	Citizens Bank Park	26.73

	Lowest	Venue	Avg. Price
1	Kansas City	Kauffman Stadium	$13.71
2	Colorado	Coors Field	14.72
3	Texas	Ameriquest Field	15.81
4	Florida	Dolphin Stadium	16.70
5	Atlanta	Turner Field	17.07

NBA

	Highest	Venue	Avg. Price
1	LA Lakers	Staples Center	$79.21
2	New York	Madison Sq. Garden	70.51
3	Sacramento	ARCO Arena	59.80
4	Boston	TD Banknorth Garden	55.93
5	Houston	Toyota Center	55.59

	Lowest	Venue	Avg. Price
1	Golden St.	The Arena in Oakland	$27.69
2	New Orleans	New Orleans Arena	31.00
3	Seattle	KeyArena	34.01
4	Denver	Pepsi Center	35.50
5	Charlotte	Charlotte Coliseum	36.61

NHL

	Highest	Venue	Avg. Price
1	Philadelphia	Wachovia Center	$54.81
2	New Jersey	Continental Airlines Arena	54.67
3	Vancouver	General Motors Place	54.08
4	Boston	TD Banknorth Garden	53.05
5	Minnesota	Xcel Energy Center	50.11

	Lowest	Venue	Avg. Price
1	Carolina	RBC Center	$26.15
2	Phoenix	Glendale Arena	27.37
3	Buffalo	HSBC Arena	29.73
4	Anaheim	Arrowhead Pond	30.32
5	San Jose	HP Pavilion	33.00

Commissioners and Presidents

Chief Executives of Established Major Sports Organizations since 1876. (*) indicates died in office.

Major League Baseball

Commissioner	Tenure
Kenesaw Mountain Landis*	1920–44
Albert (Happy) Chandler	1945–51
Ford Frick	1951–65
William Eckert	1965–68
Bowie Kuhn	1969–84
Peter Ueberroth	1984–89
A. Bartlett Giamatti*	1989
Fay Vincent	1989–92
Bud Selig†	1998–

†Served as interim commissioner from 1992-98.

National League

President	Tenure
Morgan G. Bulkeley	1876
William A. Hulbert*	1877–82
A.G. Mills	1883–84
Nicholas Young	1885–1902
Henry Pulliam*	1903–09
Thomas J. Lynch	1910–13
John K. Tener	1914–18
John A. Heydler	1918–34
Ford Frick	1935–51
Warren Giles	1951–69
Charles (Chub) Feeney	1970–86
A. Bartlett Giamatti	1987–89
Bill White	1989–94
Leonard Coleman	1994–99

Note: League president jobs were eliminated after the 1999 season.

American League

President	Tenure
Bancroft (Ban) Johnson	1901–27
Ernest Barnard*	1927–31
William Harridge	1931–59
Joe Cronin	1959–73
Lee McPhail	1974–83
Bobby Brown	1984–94
Gene Budig	1994–99

Note: League president jobs were eliminated after the 1999 season.

NBA

Commissioner	Tenure
Maurice Podoloff	1949–63
Walter Kennedy	1963–75
Larry O'Brien	1975–84
David Stern	1984–

NFL

President	Tenure
Jim Thorpe	1920
Joe Carr	1921–39
Carl Storck	1939–41

Commissioner	
Elmer Layden	1941–46
Bert Bell*	1946–59
Austin Gunsel	1959–60
Pete Rozelle	1960–89
Paul Tagliabue	1989–2006
Roger Goodell	2006–

NHL

President	Tenure
Frank Calder*	1917–43
Red Dutton	1943–46
Clarence Campbell	1946–77
John Ziegler	1977–92
Gil Stein	1992–93

Commissioner	
Gary Bettman	1993–

NCAA

President	Tenure
Walter Byers	1951–88
Dick Schultz	1988–93
Cedric Dempsey	1993–2002
Myles Brand	2003–

Note: Office was known as Executive Director until 1998.

IOC

President	Tenure
Demetrius Vikelas, Greece	1894–96
Baron Pierre de Coubertin, France	1896–1925
Count Henri de Baillet-Latour, Belgium	1925–42
Vacant	1942–46
J. Sigfried Edstrom, Sweden	1946–52
Avery Brundage, USA	1952–72
Lord Michael Killanin, Ireland	1972–80
Juan Antonio Samaranch, Spain	1980–2001
Jacques Rogge, Belgium	2001–

Pro Stadium Naming Rights

Names like Dodger Stadium, Fenway Park and Lambeau Field are a dying breed, as owners continue to sell their venues' naming rights to the highest bidder. Listed are the most lucrative sponsorship deals to date, ranked by the total amount over the life of the contract. Totals are as of Sept. 30, 2006.

	Facility	Sponsor	Home Teams	Price (Mill.)	Years	Avg/Yr (Mill.)	Expires
1	Reliant Stadium, Houston	Reliant Energy	Texans	$300.0	30	$10.00	2032
2	FedEx Field, Raljon, MD	Federal Express	Redskins	205.0	27	7.60	2025
3	American Airlines Center, Dallas	American Airlines	Mavericks, Stars	195.0	30	6.50	2030
4	Philips Arena, Atlanta	Royal Philips Electron.	Hawks, Thrashers	185.0	20	9.25	2019
5	Minute Maid Park, Houston	Minute Maid	Astros	170.0	28	6.07	2029
6	U. of Phoenix Stadium, Glendale	University of Phoenix	Cardinals	154.5	20	7.73	2025
7	Bank of America Stadium, Charlotte	Bank of America	Car. Panthers	140.0	20	7.00	2023
8	Lincoln Financial Field, Phila.	Lincoln Financial Group	Eagles	139.6	20	6.98	2022
9	Nationwide Arena, Columbus	Nationwide Insurance	Blue Jackets	135.0		indefinitely	
10	Lucas Oil Stadium*, Indianapolis	Lucas Oil Products	Colts	121.5	20	6.08	2028
11	Invesco Field at Mile High, Denver	Invesco Funds	Broncos	120.0	20	6.00	2021
	TD Banknorth Garden, Boston	TD Banknorth	Bruins, Celtics	120.0	20	6.00	2025
13	Staples Center, Los Angeles	Staples	Lakers, Clippers, LA Kings	116.0	20	5.80	2019
14	Citizens Bank Park, Philadelphia	Citizens Bank	Phillies	95.0	25	3.80	2029
	Toyota Center, Houston	Toyota	Rockets	95.0	20	4.75	2022
16	FedEx Forum, Memphis	Federal Express	Grizzlies	90.0	23	3.91	2026
	Gillette Stadium, Foxborough, MA	Gillette	Patriots	90.0	15	6.00	2016
18	Gaylord Ent. Center, Memphis	Gaylord Entertainment	Predators	80.0	20	4.00	2018
	RBC Center, Raleigh	RBC Centura Banks	Hurricanes	80.0	20	4.00	2022
20	Qwest Field, Seattle	Qwest Communications	Seahawks	75.0	15	5.00	2018
	Ameriquest Field, Arlington, TX	Ameriquest Capital	Texas Rangers	75.0	30	2.50	2033
	Great American Ballpark, Cincinnati	Great American Ins.	Reds	75.0	30	2.50	2032
	M&T Bank Stadium, Baltimore	M&T Bank	Ravens	75.0	15	5.00	2017
	Xcel Energy Center, St. Paul	Xcel Energy	Wild	75.0	25	3.00	2024

*scheduled to open in 2008.

Note: Nationwide privately financed 90 percent of the facility's construction costs. As part of the deal, the company secured naming rights to the venue indefinitely.

Source: *Street & Smith's SportsBusiness Journal* research

Television Rights

Major sports and their television deals as of Sept. 30, 2006.

League	Network	Yrs (Ends)	Amount
NFL	.ESPN (MNF)	8 (2013)	$8.8 billion
	NBC (Sun. nights)	6 (2011)	3.6 billion
	FOX (Sundays)	6 (2011)	4.4 billion
	CBS (Sundays)	6 (2011)	3.7 billion
	DirecTV (Sundays)	5 (2010)	3.5 billion
NBA	.ABC/ESPN	6 (2008)	$2.4 billion
	TNT	6 (2008)	2.2 billion
MLB	.ESPN	8 (2013)	2.368 billion
	FOX	7 (2013)	undisclosed
	TBS	7 (2013)	undisclosed

League	Network	Yrs (Ends)	Amount
NHL	.NBC	2 (2007)	— †
	Versus (formerly OLN)	2 (2007)	$135 million
NCAA Men's Hoops Tournament	.CBS	11 (2013)	$6 billion
NCAA Women's Hoops Tournament	.ESPN	11 (2013)	$200 million@
NCAA Football BCS	.ABC	8 (2014)	$300 million%
	FOX	6 (2010)	320 million%
NASCAR	.FOX, TNT ABC, ESPN, SPEED	8 (2014)	$4.48 billion
Olympics	.NBC	13 (2008)	$3.5 billion #
	NBC	9 (2012)	2.2 billion #
PGA Tour	.CBS, NBC,	6 (2012)	undisclosed
	The Golf Channel	15 (2021)	undisclosed
WNBA	.ABC/ESPN	6 (2008)	undisclosed

Super Bowl TV Rights

2006	ABC	2009	NBC	2012	NBC
2007	CBS	2010	CBS		
2008	FOX	2011	FOX		

† NBC and the NHL agreed to a two-year deal whereby the two entities share advertising revenues. NBC paid no rights fees and has an option to renew the deal for an additional two years.

@ Also included are all rights to the College World Series and various other NCAA championships.

% ABC and the Rose Bowl agreed to an eight-year deal (2007-2014) to include eight Rose Bowls and two other BCS title games. FOX and the BCS inked a deal worth an estimated $320 million which gives them rights to the Fiesta, Orange and Sugar bowls from 2007-10 and the BCS National Championship Game from 2007-09.

NBC paid approximately $3.5 billion for exclusive rights to the 1996 Summer Games (Atlanta), the 2000 Summer Games (Sydney), the 2002 Winter Games (Salt Lake City), the 2004 Summer Games (Athens), the 2006 Winter Games (Turin) and the 2008 Summer Games (Beijing). In July 2003, NBC announced a deal worth $2.2 billion which also gave them rights to the 2010 Winter Games (Vancouver) and the 2012 Summer Games (London).

Note: The NFL and NBA also have league-owned channels. The NFL Network shows preseason games, as well as an eight-game regular season package beginning in 2006. NBA TV offered 96 NBA regular season games during the 2005-06 season.

The Rich Get Richer

As if their gaudy multi-million dollar salaries, winnings and signing bonuses aren't enough, these athletes also fared pretty well on Madison Avenue. Listed are the most lucrative endorsement contracts of all time. Note that Michael Jordan signed a lifetime deal with Nike in 1989 for an undisclosed sum, but it is estimated that he still makes somewhere between $12-20 million per year. He is, however, omitted from the list below.

	Athlete	Sport	Company	Amount	Years	Per Year	Signed
1	Andre Agassi	Tennis	Nike	$120 million	10	$12.0 million	1995
2	Tiger Woods	Golf	Nike	100 million	5	20.0 million	2000
3	LeBron James	Basketball	Nike	90 million	7	12.9 million	2003
4	Grant Hill	Basketball	Fila	80 million	7	11.4 million	1997
5	Yao Ming	Basketball	Reebok	80 million	10	8.0 million	2003
6	David Beckham	Soccer	Gillette	61 million	5	12.2 million	2004
7	Serena Williams	Tennis	Nike	60 million	8	7.5 million	2003
8	Allen Iverson	Basketball	Reebok	50 million	10	5.0 million	1996
9	Kobe Bryant	Basketball	Nike	45 million	5	9.0 million	2003
10	Venus Williams	Tennis	Reebok	40 million	5	8.0 million	2000
	Shaquille O'Neal	Basketball	Reebok	40 million	5	8.0 million	1992

Top-Selling Sports Jerseys

LeBron or D-Wade? Reggie Bush or Vince Young? Mickey Mantle or Ted Williams? Which players's jersey is the most popular? Listed are currently the best-selling NBA, NFL and "throwback" jerseys. **NBA** figures are based on sales at the NBA Store in New York City and NBAstore.com, from the 2005-06 preseason until April 8, 2006. **NFL** figures are based on sales from April 1 to mid-July 2006. **Throwbacks** are based on sales from Sept. 1, 2005 to Sept. 1, 2006.

NBA

1 Dwyane Wade, Miami
2 LeBron James, Cleveland
3 Allen Iverson, Philadelphia
4 Kobe Bryant, LA Lakers
5 Stephon Marbury, New York
6 Shaquille O'Neal, Miami
7 Tracy McGrady, Houston
8 Carmelo Anthony, Denver
9 Vince Carter, New Jersey
10 Ben Wallace, Detroit (now Chi.)

Source: NBA.com

NFL

1 Reggie Bush, New Orleans
2 LaDainian Tomlinson, San Diego
3 Ben Roethlisberger, Pittsburgh
4 Troy Polamalu, Pittsburgh
5 Randy Moss, Oakland
6 Peyton Manning, Indianapolis
7 Chad Johnson, Cincinnati
8 Vince Young, Tennessee
9 Eli Manning, NY Giants
10 Hines Ward, Pittsburgh

Source: NFL

Throwbacks

1 Reggie White, Philadelphia, 1992
2 Mickey Mantle, NY Yankees, 1951
3 Ted Williams, Boston, 1939
4 Lawrence Taylor, NY Giants, 1990
5 Lou Gehrig, NY Yankees, 1939
6 Deion Sanders, San Fran., 1994
7 Jackie Robinson, Brooklyn, 1955
8 Steve Young, San Fran., 1994
9 Dick Butkus, Chicago, 1970
10 Randall Cunningham, Phila., 1992

Source: Mitchell & Ness Nostalgia Co.

Costliest Collectibles

Listed are the most expensive pieces of sports memorabilia ever sold, according to the following auction houses and other sources: Lelands, Guernsey's, Sotheby's, Christie's, Gotta Have It! Collectibles, Grey Flannel Auctions, Mastro Auctions and Hunt Auctions. Figures are as of Sept. 1, 2006. (*) indicates estimated amount paid.

	Item	Sold For
1	Mark McGwire 70th HR ball, 1998 HR chase (purchased by Todd McFarlane)	$3,005,000
2	Honus Wagner 1909 American Tobacco Co. "Gretzky" T206 PSA-8 baseball card	1,265,000
	Babe Ruth bat, first HR in Yankee Stadium	1,265,000
4	Babe Ruth sale contract (Red Sox to Yankees)	996,000
5	Babe Ruth 1933 inaugural All-Star Game HR ball	805,000
6	Barry Bonds 700th HR ball	804,129
7	SGC co. 1914 Cracker Jack complete baseball card set	800,000
8	Babe Ruth 1934 Tour of Japan Game Worn Uniform	787,859
9	Honus Wagner 1909 American Tobacco Co. "Gretzky" T206 PSA-8 baseball card	640,500
10	Barry Bonds 73rd HR (purchased by Todd McFarlane)	517,500
11	Honus Wagner 1909 American Tobacco Co. "Gretzky" T206 PSA-8 baseball card	500,000*
12	1921 Bath Ruth bat used in hitting record setting 59th HR	483,000
13	1869 Cincinnati Red Stockings Trophy Ball Collection (17)	473,383
14	Honus Wagner American Tobacco Co. "Frank Nagy" T206 GAI 3.5 baseball card	456,057
15	Honus Wagner 1909 American Tobacco Co. T206 "Gretzky" PSA-8 baseball card	451,000
	(purchased by Wayne Gretzky and then-owner of L.A. Kings Bruce McNall)	
16	1941 Bruce Smith (Minnesota RB) Heisman Trophy	395,240
17	Lou Gehrig's last game-used 1939 baseball glove	387,500
18	Joe DiMaggio's 1941 bat used during 56-game hitting streak	345,596
	(purchased by Hillerich & Bradsby, authenticity of streak-bat since called into question)	
19	Ty Cobb's 1928 signed Philadelphia A's jersey	332,550
20	Mickey Mantle's 1956 American League MVP Award	319,250
21	Mickey Mantle's 1956 Batting Champion of the Year Silver Bat Award	313,500
22	Lou Gehrig's signed 1927 Yankees road jersey	305,000
23	Roger Maris 1961 New York Yankees Home Pinstripe Jersey	302,106
24	Mickey Mantle's 1962 American League MVP Award	290,500
25	Jim Thorpe's 1916-1917 football jersey	284,350

The Peabody Award

Presented annually since 1940 for outstanding achievement in radio and television broadcasting. Named after Georgia banker and philanthropist George Foster Peabody, the awards are administered by the Henry W. Grady College of Journalism and Mass Communication at the University of Georgia.

Television

Year
1960 **CBS** for coverage of 1960 Winter and Summer Olympic Games
1966 ABC's **"Wide World of Sports"** (for Outstanding Achievement in Promotion of International Understanding).
1968 **ABC Sports** coverage of both the 1968 Winter and Summer Olympic Games.
1972 **ABC Sports** coverage of the 1972 Summer Olympics in Munich.
1973 **Joe Garagiola** of NBC Sports (for "The Baseball World of Joe Garagiola").
1976 **ABC Sports** coverage of both the 1976 Winter and Summer Olympic Games.
1984 **Roone Arledge**, president of ABC News & Sports (for significant contributions to news and sports programming).
1986 **WFAA-TV**, Dallas for its investigation of the Southern Methodist University football program.
1988 **Jim McKay** of ABC Sports (for pioneering efforts and career accomplishments in the world of TV sports).
1991 **CBS Sports** coverage of the 1991 Masters golf tournament
   & **HBO Sports** and **Black Canyon Productions** for the baseball special "When It Was A Game."
1995 **Kartemquin Educational Films** and **KTCA-TV** in St. Paul, MN, presented on PBS for "Hoop Dreams"
   & **Turner Original Productions** for the baseball special "Hank Aaron: Chasing the Dream."
1996 **HBO Sports** for its documentary "The Journey of the African-American Athlete"
   & **Bud Greenspan**, a personal award for excellence in chronicling the Olympic Games.
1997 **HBO Pictures** and **The Thomas Carter Company** for the original movie "Don King: Only in America."
1998 **KTVX-TV**, Salt Lake City for its investigation into the policies and practices of the IOC during the Olympic bribery scandal & **HBO Sports** for its ongoing series of sports documentaries.
1999 **WCPO-TV**, Cincinnati for its investigation of fraud and misrepresentation in the construction of new sports stadiums, **HBO Sports** for its documentary "Dare to Compete: The Struggle of Women in Sports," and its documentary "Fists of Freedom: The Story of the '68 Summer Games" & **ESPN** for its "SportsCentury" series.
2000 **HBO Sports** for its documentary "Ali-Frazier 1: One Nation...Divisible."
2001 **The Ciesla Foundation** and **Cinemax** for the documentary "The Life and Times of Hank Greenberg."
2002 **ESPN** for "The Complete Angler," its documentary celebrating nature, art and fly-fishing.
2005 **Showtime** and **Red Rock Entertainment** for the original movie "Edge of America," about an African-American teacher who agrees to coach the girls basketball team at an American Indian-reservation school in Utah.

Radio

Year
1974 **WSB** radio in Atlanta for "Henry Aaron: A Man with a Mission."
1991 **Red Barber** of National Public Radio (for his six decades as a broadcaster and his 10 years as a commentator on NPR's "Morning Edition").

National Emmy Awards
Sports Programming

Presented by the Academy of Television Arts and Sciences since 1948. Eligibility period covered the calendar year from 1948-57 and since 1988. Note that due to space constraints, not every award is listed below.

Multiple major award winners: ABC "Wide World of Sports" (20), NFL Films Football coverage (15); HBO "Real Sports with Bryant Gumbel" (13); ESPN "SportsCenter" and NBC Olympics coverage (11); CBS NFL Football coverage (10); ABC Olympics coverage and ABC "Monday Night Football" (9); ESPN "Outside the Lines" and FOX MLB coverage (8); CBS NCAA Basketball coverage, CBS "NFL Today" and ESPN "GameDay/Sunday NFL Countdown (5); ESPN "SportsCentury" series (4); ABC "The American Sportsman," ABC Indianapolis 500 coverage, CBS Golf coverage, CBS Tour de France coverage, FOX "NFL Sunday," HBO "Inside the NFL" and NBC Ironman Triathlon coverage (3); ABC Kentucky Derby coverage, ABC "Sportsbeat," Bud Greenspan Olympic specials, CBS Olympics coverage, ESPN "Speedworld," ESPN Sunday Night Football, ESPN Wimbledon coverage, MTV Sports series, The NBA on NBC and NBC World Series coverage (2).

1949
Coverage—"Wrestling" (KTLA, Los Angeles)

1950
Program—"Rams Football" (KNBH-TV, Los Angeles)

1954
Program—"Gillette Cavalcade of Sports" (NBC)

1965-66
Programs—"Wide World of Sports" (ABC), "Shell's Wonderful World of Golf" (NBC) and "CBS Golf Classic" (CBS)

1966-67
Program—"Wide World of Sports" (ABC)

1967-68
Program—"Wide World of Sports" (ABC)

1968-69
Program—"1968 Summer Olympics" (ABC)

1969-70
Programs—"NFL Football" (CBS) and "Wide World of Sports" (ABC)

1970-71

Program—"Wide World of Sports" (ABC)

1971-72

Program—"Wide World of Sports" (ABC)

1972-73

News Special—"Coverage of Munich Olympic Tragedy" (ABC)
Sports Programs—"1972 Summer Olympics" (ABC) and "Wide World of Sports" (ABC)

1973-74

Program—"Wide World of Sports" (ABC)

1974-75

Non-Edited Program— "Jimmy Connors vs. Rod Laver Tennis Challenge" (CBS)
Edited Program— "Wide World of Sports" (ABC)

1975-76

Live Special—"1975 World Series: Cincinnati vs. Boston" (NBC)
Live Series—"NFL Monday Night Football" (ABC)
Edited Specials—"1976 Winter Olympics" (ABC) and "Triumph and Tragedy: The Olympic Experience" (ABC)
Edited Series—"Wide World of Sports" (ABC)

1976-77

Live Special—"1976 Summer Olympics" (ABC)
Live Series—"The NFL Today/NFL Football" (CBS)
Edited Special—"1976 Summer Olympics Preview" (ABC)
Edited Series—"The Olympiad" (PBS)

1977-78

Live Special—"Muhammad Ali vs. Leon Spinks Heavyweight Championship Fight" (CBS)
Live Series—"The NFL Today/NFL Football" (CBS)
Edited Special—"The Impossible Dream: Ballooning Across the Atlantic" (CBS)
Edited Series—"The Way It Was" (PBS)

1978-79

Live Special—"Super Bowl XIII: Pittsburgh vs Dallas" (NBC)
Live Series—"NFL Monday Night Football" (ABC)
Edited Special—"Spirit of '78: The Flight of Double Eagle II" (ABC)
Edited Series—"The American Sportsman" (ABC)

1979-80

Live Special—"1980 Winter Olympics" (ABC)
Live Series—"NCAA College Football" (ABC)
Edited Special—"Gossamer Albatross: Flight of Imagination" (CBS)
Edited Series—"NFL Game of the Week" (NFL Films)

1980-81

Live Special—"1981 Kentucky Derby" (ABC)
Live Series—"PGA Golf Tour" (CBS)
Edited Special—"Wide World of Sports 20th Anniversary Show" (ABC)
Edited Series—"The American Sportsman" (ABC)

1981-82

Live Special—"1982 NCAA Basketball Final: North Carolina vs Georgetown" (CBS)
Live Series—"NFL Football" (CBS)
Edited Special—"1982 Indianapolis 500" (ABC)
Edited Series—"Wide World of Sports" (ABC)

1982-83

Live Special—"1982 World Series: St. Louis vs Milwaukee" (NBC)
Live Series—"NFL Football" (CBS)
Edited Special—"Wimbledon '83" (NBC)
Edited Series—"Wide World of Sports" (ABC)
Journalism—"ABC Sportsbeat" (ABC)

1983-84

No awards given

1984-85

Live Special—"1984 Summer Olympics" (ABC)
Live Series—No award given
Edited Special—"Road to the Super Bowl '85" (NFL Films)
Edited Series—"The American Sportsman" (ABC)
Journalism—"ABC Sportsbeat" (ABC), "CBS Sports Sunday" (CBS), Dick Schaap features (ABC) and 1984 Summer Olympic features (ABC)

1985-86

No awards given

1986-87

Live Special—"1987 Daytona 500" (CBS)
Live Series—"NFL Football" (CBS)
Edited Special—"Wide World of Sports 25th Anniversary Special" (ABC)
Edited Series—"Wide World of Sports" (ABC)

1987-88

Live Special—"1987 Kentucky Derby" (ABC)
Live Series—"NFL Monday Night Football" (ABC)
Edited Special—"Paris-Roubaix Bike Race" (CBS)
Edited Series—"Wide World of Sports" (ABC)

1988

Live Special—"1988 Summer Olympics" (NBC)
Live Series—"1988 NCAA Basketball" (CBS)
Edited Special—"Road to the Super Bowl '88" (NFL Films)
Edited Series—"Wide World of Sports" (ABC)
Studio Show—"NFL GameDay" (ESPN)
Journalism—1988 Summer Olympic reporting (NBC)

1989

Live Special—"1989 Indianapolis 500" (ABC)
Live Series—"NFL Monday Night Football" (ABC)
Edited Special—"Trans-Antarctica! The International Expedition" (ABC)
Edited Series—"This is the NFL" (NFL Films)
Studio Show—"NFL Today" (CBS)
Journalism—1989 World Series Game 3 earthquake coverage (ABC)

National Emmy Awards (Cont.)

1990

Live Special—"1990 Indianapolis 500" (ABC)
Live Series—"1990 NCAA Basketball Tournament" (CBS)
Edited Special—"Road to Super Bowl XXIV" (NFL Films)
Edited Series—"Wide World of Sports" (ABC)
Studio Show—"SportsCenter" (ESPN)
Journalism—"Outside the Lines: The Autograph Game" (ESPN)

1991

Live Special—"1991 NBA Finals: Chicago vs LA Lakers" (NBC)
Live Series—"1991 NCAA Basketball Tournament" (CBS)
Edited Special—"Wide World of Sports 30th Anniversary Special" (ABC)
Edited Series—"This is the NFL" (NFL Films)
Studio Show—"NFL GameDay" (ESPN) and "NFL Live" (NBC)
Journalism—"Outside the Lines: Steroids–Whatever It Takes" (ESPN)

1992

Live Special—"1992 Breeders' Cup" (NBC)
Live Series—"1992 NCAA Basketball Tournament" (CBS)
Edited Special—"1992 Summer Olympics" (NBC)
Edited Series—"MTV Sports" (MTV)
Studio Show—"The NFL Today" (CBS)
Journalism—"Outside the Lines: Portraits in Black and White" (ESPN)

1993

Live Special—"1993 World Series" (CBS)
Live Series—"Monday Night Football" (ABC)
Edited Special—"Road to the Super Bowl" (NFL Films)
Edited Series—"This is the NFL" (NFL Films)
Studio Show—"The NFL Today" (CBS)
Journalism (TIE)—"Outside the Lines: Mitch Ivey Feature" (ESPN) and "SportsCenter: University of Houston Football" (ESPN).
Feature—"Arthur Ashe: His Life, His Legacy" (NBC).

1994

Live Special—"NHL Stanley Cup Finals" (ESPN)
Live Series—"Monday Night Football" (ABC)
Edited Special—"Lillehammer '94: 16 Days of Glory" (Disney/Cappy Productions)
Edited Series—"MTV Sports" (MTV)
Studio Show—"NFL GameDay" (ESPN)
Journalism—"1994 Winter Olympic Games: Mossad feature" (CBS)
Feature (TIE)—"Heroes of Telemark" on Winter Olympic Games (CBS); and "SportsCenter: Vanderbilt running back Brad Gaines" (ESPN).

"Baseball" Wins Prime Time Emmy

Ken Burns's miniseries "Baseball" won the 1994 Emmy Award for Outstanding Informational Series. The nine-part documentary aired from Sept. 18-28, 1994 and ran more than 18 hours, drawing the largest audience in PBS history.

AP/Wide World Photos
NFL Films president **Steve Sabol** and founder, Ed Sabol, won the Lifetime Achievement Emmy Award in 2003.

1995

Live Special—"Cal Ripken 2131" (ESPN)
Live Series—"ESPN Speedworld" (ESPN)
Edited Special (quick turn-around)—"Outside the Lines: Play-ball–Opening Day in America" (ESPN)
Edited Special (long turn-around)—"Lillehammer, an Olympic Diary" (CBS)
Edited Series—"NFL Films Presents" (NFL Films)
Studio Show (TIE)—"NFL GameDay" (ESPN) and "FOX NFL Sunday"(FOX)
Journalism—"Real Sports with Bryant Gumbel: Broken Promises" (HBO)
Feature (TIE)—"SportsCenter: Jerry Quarry" (ESPN) and "Real Sports with Bryant Gumbel: Coach" (HBO).

1996

Live Special—"1996 World Series" (FOX)
Live Series—"ESPN Speedworld" (ESPN)
Edited Special—"Football America" (TNT/NFL Films)
Edited Series—"NFL Films Presents" (NFL Films)
Live Event Turnaround—"The Centennial Olympic Games" (NBC)
Studio Show—"SportsCenter" (ESPN)
Journalism—"Outside the Lines: AIDS in Sports" (ESPN)
Feature—"Real Sports with Bryant Gumbel: 1966 Texas Western NCAA Champs" (HBO).

1997

Live Special—"The NBA Finals" (NBC)
Live Series—"NFL Monday Night Football" (ABC)
Edited Special—"Ironman Triathlon World Championship" (NBC/World Triathlon Corporation)
Edited Series—"NFL Films Presents" (NFL Films)
Live Event Turnaround—"Outside The Lines: Inside The Kentucky Derby" (ESPN)
Studio Show—"FOX NFL Sunday" (FOX)
Journalism—"Real Sports with Bryant Gumbel: Pros and Cons" (HBO)
Feature—"NFL Films Presents: Eddie George" (NFL Films).

1998

Live Special—"McGwire's 62nd Home Run Game" (FOX)
Live Series—"NBC Golf Tour" (NBC)
Edited Special—"A Cinderella Season: The Lady Vols Fight Back" (HBO)
Edited Series—"Real Sports with Bryant Gumbel" (HBO)
Live Event Turnaround—"Wimbledon '98" (NBC)
Studio Show—"FOX NFL Sunday" (FOX)
Journalism (TIE)—"Real Sports with Bryant Gumbel: Winning At All Costs" (HBO) and "Real Sports with Bryant Gumbel: Diamond Bucks" (HBO)
Feature—"NFL Films Presents: Steve Mariucci" (ESPN2 and NFL Films).

1999

Live Special—"2000 MLB All-Star Game" (FOX)
Live Series—"MLB Regular Season" (FOX)
Edited Special—"Ironman Triathlon World Championship" (NBC)
Edited Series—"SportsCentury: 50 Greatest Athletes" (ESPN)
Live Event Turnaround—"The World Track & Field Championships" (NBC)
Studio Show—"MLB Pre-Game Show" (FOX)
Journalism—"Real Sports with Bryant Gumbel: Fake Golf Clubs" (HBO)
Feature—"NFL Films Presents: Lt. Kalsu" (ESPN2)

2000

Live Special—"2000 World Series" (FOX)
Live Series—"NFL Sunday Night Football" (ESPN)
Edited Special—"Hoops and Hoosiers: The Story of the Final Four 2000" (CBS)
Edited Series—"SportsCentury: The Top 50 & Beyond" (ESPN)
Live Event Turnaround—"The Games of the XXVII Olympiad" (NBC)
Studio Show—"FOX NFL Sunday" (FOX)
Journalism—"Real Sports with Bryant Gumbel: Dominican Free-For-All" (HBO)
Feature—"The Games of the XXVII Olympiad" (NBC)

2001

Live Special—"2001 World Series" (FOX)
Live Series—"NASCAR on FOX" (FOX)
Edited Special—"ABC's Wide World of Sports 40th Anniversary Special" (ABC)
Edited Series—"SportsCentury" (ESPN Classic)
Live Event Turnaround—"Tour de France" (CBS)
Studio Show—Weekly—"Sunday NFL Countdown" (ESPN)
Studio Show—Daily—"Inside the NBA" (TNT/TBS)
Journalism—"Real Sports with Bryant Gumbel: Amare Stoudemire" (HBO)
Feature—"NFL Films Presents: Gerry Faust—The Golden Dream" (ESPN2)
Documentary—"Do You Believe in Miracles? The Story of the 1980 U.S. Hockey Team" (HBO)

2002

Live Special—"XIX Olympic Winter Games" (NBC)
Live Series—"The NBA on NBC" (NBC)
Edited Special—"America's Heroes: The Bravest vs. The Finest" (NBC)
Edited Series—"Real Sports with Bryant Gumbel" (HBO)
Live Event Turnaround—"Tour de France" (CBS)
Studio Show—Weekly—"Inside the NFL" (HBO & NFL Films)
Studio Show—Daily—"Baseball Tonight" (ESPN)
Journalism—"Outside the Lines, Weekly: Eligibility for Sale" (ESPN) and "Outside the Lines, Weekly: Iraqi Atletes, Tales of Torture" (ESPN)
Long Feature—"SportsCenter: Flight 93" (ESPN)
Short Feature—"SportsCenter: Chris Paul" (ESPN), "XIX Olympic Winter Games: Bill Johnson" (NBC) and "XIX Olympic Winter Games: The Sheas" (NBC)
Documentary—"Our Greatest Hopes, Our Worst Fears: The Tragedy of the Munich Games" (ABC)

2003

Live Special— "MLB on FOX: Post Season" (FOX)
Live Series— "ESPN NFL Sunday Night Football" (ESPN)
Edited Special— "Ironman Triathlon World Championship" (NBC/World Triathlon Corporation)
Edited Series/Anthology—Legendary Nights" (HBO)
Live Event Turnaround—"Tour de France" (CBS)
Studio Show—Weekly—"Sunday NFL Countdown" (ESPN)
Studio Show—Daily—"SportsCenter" (ESPN)
Journalism—"Real Sports with Bryant Gumbel: Marcus Dixon" (HBO)
Editing—"Jim McKay — My World in My Words " (HBO)
The Dick Schaap Outstanding Writing Award— "Wimbledon — Where is Wimbledon" (ESPN)
Long Feature—"NFL Films Presents on The NFL Network: Big Charlie's" (NFL Network/NFL Films) and "Real Sports with Bryant Gumbel: Alex Zanardi" (HBO)
Short Feature—"SportsCenter: Picking Up Butch" (ESPN)
Documentary—"The Curse of the Bambino" (HBO/Black Canyon Productions/Clear Channel Entertainment Television)

2004

Live Special—"The Masters" (CBS)
Live Series—"ABC's NFL Monday Night Football" (ABC)
Edited Special—"Ironman Triathlon World Championship" (NBC/Ironman Productions)
Edited Series/Anthology—"Real Sports with Bryant Gumbel" (HBO)
Live Event Turnaround—"The Games of the XXVIII Olympiad" (NBC)
Studio Show—Weekly—"Inside the NFL" (HBO)
Studio Show—Daily—"SportsCenter" (ESPN)
Journalism—"Real Sports with Bryant Gumbel: Sport of Sheikhs" (HBO)
Editing (TIE)—"NFL Films Presents on NFL Network: Michael Zagaris" (NFL Network/NFL Films) and "Wimbledon on NBC: Patrick Stewart Tease and Closing Thoughts" (NBC)
The Dick Schaap Outstanding Writing Award— "Wimbledon on ESPN2—Wimbledon Reflections" (ESPN2)
Long Feature—"SportsCenter: Ben Comen" (ESPN)
Short Feature—"The Super Bowl Today: NFL Quarterbacks" (CBS)
Documentary—"The Games of the XXVIII Olympiad: Stylianos Kryiakides, The Journey of a Warrior" (NBC)

2005

Live Special—"134th British Open Championship" (TNT)
Live Series—"NASCAR on FOX" (FOX)
Edited Special—"CostasNOW: David Robinson—A Man In Full" (HBO)
Edited Series/Anthology—"SportsCentury" (ESPN Classic)
Live Event Turnaround—"Best of Winter X Games Nine" (ABC & ESPN Productions)
Studio Show—Weekly—"Inside the NFL" (HBO)
Studio Show—Daily—"Inside the NBA, Playoffs" (TNT)
Journalism—"Real Sports with Bryant Gumbel: Soccer Racism" (HBO)
Editing—"PGA Tour Sunday: Kevin Hall" (USA & PGA Tour Productions)
The Dick Schaap Outstanding Writing Award— "SportsCenter: Finding Bobby Fischer" (Jeremy Schaap, ESPN)
Long Feature—"Real Sports with Bryant Gumbel: The Hoyts" (HBO)
Short Feature—"Timeless: Lama Kunga" (ESPN2 & Red Line Films)
Documentary—"Rhythm in the Rope" (ESPN2)

Sportscasters of the Year
National Emmy Awards

An Emmy Award for Sportscasters was first introduced in 1968 and given for Outstanding Host/Commentator for the 1967-68 TV season. Two awards, one for Outstanding Host or Play-by-Play and the other for Outstanding Analyst, were first presented in 1981 for the 1980-81 season. Three awards, for Outstanding Studio Host, Play-by-Play and Studio Analyst, have been given since the 1993 season, and one more, Sports Event Analyst, was added in 1997.

Multiple winners: Bob Costas and John Madden (15); Jim McKay (9); Joe Buck and Cris Collinsworth (6); Dick Enberg and Al Michaels (4); Keith Jackson and Tim McCarver (3); Terry Bradshaw, James Brown and Joe Morgan (2). Note that Jim McKay has won a total of 12 Emmy awards: eight for Host/Commentator, one for Host/Play-by-Play, two for Sports Writing and one for News Commentary.

Season	Host/Commentator	Season	Host/Play-by-Play	Season	Analyst
1967-68	Jim McKay, ABC	1980-81	Dick Enberg, NBC	1980-81	Dick Button, ABC
1968-69	No award	1981-82	Jim McKay, ABC	1981-82	John Madden, CBS
1969-70	No award	1982-83	Dick Enberg, NBC	1982-83	John Madden, CBS
1970-71	Jim McKay, ABC	1983-84	No award	1983-84	No award
	& Don Meredith, ABC	1984-85	George Michael, NBC	1984-85	No award
1971-72	No award	1985-86	No award	1985-86	No award
1972-73	Jim McKay, ABC	1986-87	Al Michaels, ABC	1986-87	John Madden, CBS
1973-74	Jim McKay, ABC	1987-88	Bob Costas, NBC	1987-88	John Madden, CBS
1974-75	Jim McKay, ABC	1988	Bob Costas, NBC	1988	John Madden, CBS
1975-76	Jim McKay, ABC	1989	Al Michaels, ABC	1989	John Madden, CBS
1976-77	Frank Gifford, ABC	1990	Dick Enberg, NBC	1990	John Madden, CBS
1977-78	Jack Whitaker, CBS	1991	Bob Costas, NBC	1991	John Madden, CBS
1978-79	Jim McKay, ABC	1992	Bob Costas, NBC	1992	John Madden, CBS
1979-80	Jim McKay, ABC				

Studio Host

Year		Year		Year	
1993	Bob Costas, NBC	1998	James Brown, FOX	2002	Bob Costas, HBO/NBC
1994	Bob Costas, NBC	1999	James Brown, FOX	2003	Bob Costas, HBO/NBC
1995	Bob Costas, NBC	2000	Bob Costas, NBC	2004	Bob Costas, HBO/NBC
1996	Bob Costas, NBC	2001	Bob Costas, HBO &	2005	Bob Costas, HBO/NBC
1997	Dan Patrick, ESPN		Ernie Johnson, TNT/TBS		

Play-by-Play

Year		Year		Year	
1993	Dick Enberg, NBC	1998	Keith Jackson, ABC	2003	Joe Buck, FOX
1994	Keith Jackson, ABC	1999	Joe Buck, FOX	2004	Joe Buck, FOX
1995	Al Michaels, ABC	2000	Al Michaels, ABC	2005	Joe Buck, FOX
1996	Keith Jackson, ABC	2001	Joe Buck, FOX		
1997	Bob Costas, NBC	2002	Joe Buck, FOX		

Studio Analyst

Year		Year		Year	
1993	Billy Packer, CBS	1998	Cris Collinsworth, HBO/FOX	2003	Cris Collinsworth, HBO
1994	John Madden, FOX	1999	Terry Bradshaw, FOX	2004	Cris Collinsworth, HBO
1995	John Madden, FOX	2000	Steve Lyons, FOX	2005	Cris Collinsworth, HBO
1996	Howie Long, FOX	2001	Terry Bradshaw, FOX		
1997	Cris Collinsworth, HBO/NBC	2002	Cris Collinsworth, HBO		

Sports Events Analyst

Year		Year		Year	
1997	Joe Morgan, ESPN	2000	Tim McCarver, FOX	2003	John Madden, ABC
1998	John Madden, FOX	2001	Tim McCarver, FOX	2004	Joe Morgan, ESPN
1999	John Madden, FOX	2002	Tim McCarver, FOX	2005	John Madden, ABC

Lifetime Achievement Emmy Award

Year		Year		Year		Year	
1989	Jim McKay	1994	Howard Cosell	1999	Jack Buck	2004	Chet Simmons
1990	Lindsey Nelson	1995	Vin Scully	2000	Dick Enberg	2005	Bud Greenspan
1991	Curt Gowdy	1996	Frank Gifford	2001	Herb Granath		
1992	Chris Schenkel	1997	Jim Simpson	2002	Roone Arledge*		
1993	Pat Summerall	1998	Keith Jackson	2003	Ed and Steve Sabol		

*Arledge is the only recipient of two Lifetime Achievement Emmy Awards. In addition to sports, he won the lifetime award for "News and Documentary" in 2002.

National Sportscasters and Sportswriters Assn. Award

Sportscaster of the Year presented annually since 1959 by the National Sportscasters and Sportswriters Association, based in Salisbury, N.C. Voting is done by NSSA members and selected national media.

Multiple winners: Bob Costas (8); Chris Berman (6) Keith Jackson (5); Lindsey Nelson and Chris Schenkel (4); Joe Buck, Dick Enberg, Al Michaels and Vin Scully (3); Curt Gowdy, Jim Nantz and Ray Scott (2).

Year		Year		Year		Year	
1959	Lindsey Nelson	1971	Ray Scott	1982	Vin Scully	1994	Chris Berman
1960	Lindsey Nelson	1972	Keith Jackson	1983	Al Michaels	1995	Bob Costas
1961	Lindsey Nelson	1973	Keith Jackson	1984	John Madden	1996	Chris Berman
1962	Lindsey Nelson	1974	Keith Jackson	1985	Bob Costas	1997	Bob Costas
1963	Chris Schenkel	1975	Keith Jackson	1986	Al Michaels	1998	Jim Nantz
1964	Chris Schenkel	1976	Keith Jackson	1987	Bob Costas	1999	Dan Patrick
1965	Vin Scully	1977	Pat Summerall	1988	Bob Costas	2000	Bob Costas
1966	Curt Gowdy	1978	Vin Scully	1989	Chris Berman	2001	Chris Berman
1967	Chris Schenkel	1979	Dick Enberg	1990	Chris Berman	2002	Joe Buck
1968	Ray Scott	1980	Dick Enberg	1991	Bob Costas	2003	Joe Buck
1969	Curt Gowdy		& Al Michaels	1992	Bob Costas	2004	Joe Buck
1970	Chris Schenkel	1981	Dick Enberg	1993	Chris Berman	2005	Jim Nantz

The Pulitzer Prize

The Pulitzer Prizes for journalism, letters, drama and music have been presented annually since 1917 in the name of Joseph Pulitzer (1847-1911), the publisher of the *New York World*. Prizes are awarded by the president of Columbia University on the recommendation of a board of review. Sixteen Pulitzers have been awarded for newspaper sports reporting, sports commentary and sports photography.

News Coverage

1935 **Bill Taylor,** *NY Herald Tribune,* for his reporting on the 1934 America's Cup yacht races.

Special Citation

1952 **Max Kase**, *NY Journal-American,* for his reporting on the 1951 college basketball point-shaving scandal.

Meritorious Public Service

1954 *Newsday* (Garden City, N.Y.) for its expose of New York State's race track scandals and labor racketeering.

General Reporting

1956 **Arthur Daley**, *NY Times,* for his 1955 columns.

Investigative Reporting

1981 **Clark Hallas** & **Robert Lowe**, *(Tucson) Arizona Daily Star,* for their 1980 investigation of the University of Arizona athletic department.

1986 **Jeffrey Marx** & **Michael York,** Lexington (Ky.) *Herald-Leader,* for their 1985 investigation of the basketball program at the University of Kentucky and other major colleges.

Specialized Reporting

1985 **Randall Savage** & **Jackie Crosby,** Macon (Ga.) *Telegraph and News,* for their 1984 investigation of athletics and academics at the University of Georgia and Georgia Tech.

Beat Reporting

2000 **George Dohrmann**, St. Paul (Min.) *Pioneer Press,* for his investigation that revealed academic fraud in the men's basketball program at the University of Minnesota.

Feature Writing

1997 **Lisa Pollak**, *Baltimore Sun,* for her story about baseball umpire John Hirschbeck dealing with the death of one son and the illness of another from the same disease.

Commentary

1976 **Red Smith**, *NY Times,* for his 1975 columns.

1981 **Dave Anderson**, *NY Times,* for his 1980 columns.

1990 **Jim Murray**, *LA Times,* for his 1989 columns.

Photography

1949 **Nat Fein,** *NY Herald Tribune,* for his photo, "Babe Ruth Bows Out."

1952 **John Robinson** & **Don Ultang,** *Des Moines* (Iowa) *Register and Tribune,* for their sequence of six pictures of the 1951 Drake-Oklahoma A&M football game, in which Drake's Johnny Bright had his jaw broken.

1985 **The Photography Staff** of the *Orange County* (Calif.) *Register,* for their coverage of the 1984 Summer Olympics in Los Angeles.

1993 **William Snyder** & **Ken Geiger,** The *Dallas Morning News,* for their coverage of the 1992 Summer Olympics in Barcelona, Spain.

Red Smith Award

Presented annually by the Associated Press Sports Editors (APSE) to a person who has made "major contributions to sports journalism" and named in honor of the late newspaper columnist for the *New York Herald-Tribune* and *New York Times*.

Year		Year		Year	
1981	Red Smith, *NY Times*	1990	Dave Smith, *Dallas Morning News*	2000	Jerry Izenberg, *Newark Star Ledger*
1982	Jim Murray, *LA Times*	1991	Dave Kindred, *Nat'l Sports Daily*	2001	John Steadman, *Baltimore Sun*
1983	Shirley Povich, *Washington Post*	1992	Ed Storin, *Miami Herald*	2002	Dick Schaap, *ESPN*
1984	Fred Russell, *Nashville Banner*	1993	Tom McEwen, *Tampa Tribune*		"The Sports Reporters"
1985	Blackie Sherrod, *Dallas Morning News*	1994	Dave Anderson, *NY Times*	2003	George Solomon, *Washington Post*
		1995	Richard Sandler, *Newsday*	2004	Jimmy Cannon, NYC columnist
1986	Si Burick, *Dayton Daily News*	1996	Bill Dwyre, *LA Times*	2005	Mary Garber, *Winston-Salem Journal*
1987	Will Grimsley, AP	1997	Jerome Holtzman, *Chicago Tribune*		
1988	Furman Bisher, *Atlanta Journal*	1998	Sam Lacy, *Baltimore Afro-American*		
1989	Edwin Pope, *Miami Herald*	1999	Bud Collins, *Boston Globe*	2005	Joe McGuff, *Kansas City Star*

Sportswriter of the Year
NSSA Award

Presented annually since 1959 by the National Sportscasters and Sportswriters Association, based in Salisbury, N.C. Voting is done by NSSA members and selected national media.

Multiple winners: Jim Murray (14); Rick Reilly (10); Frank Deford (6); Red Smith (5); Will Grimsley (4); Peter Gammons (3).

Year		Year		Year	
1959	Red Smith, *NY Herald-Tribune*	1976	Jim Murray, *LA Times*	1993	Peter Gammons, *Boston Globe*
1960	Red Smith, *NY Herald-Tribune*	1977	Jim Murray, *LA Times*	1994	Rick Reilly, *Sports Ill.*
1961	Red Smith, *NY Herald-Tribune*	1978	Will Grimsley, AP	1995	Rick Reilly, *Sports Ill.*
1962	Red Smith, *NY Herald-Tribune*	1979	Jim Murray, *LA Times*	1996	Rick Reilly, *Sports Ill.*
1963	Arthur Daley, *NY Times*	1980	Will Grimsley, AP	1997	Dave Kindred, *The Sporting News*
1964	Jim Murray, *LA Times*	1981	Will Grimsley, AP		
1965	Red Smith, *NY Herald-Tribune*	1982	Frank Deford, *Sports Ill.*	1998	Mitch Albom, *Detroit Free Press*
1966	Jim Murray, *LA Times*	1983	Will Grimsley, AP	1999	Rick Reilly, *Sports Ill.*
1967	Jim Murray, *LA Times*	1984	Frank Deford, *Sports Ill.*	2000	Bob Ryan, *Boston Globe*
1968	Jim Murray, *LA Times*	1985	Frank Deford, *Sports Ill.*	2001	Rick Reilly, *Sports Ill.*
1969	Jim Murray, *LA Times*	1986	Frank Deford, *Sports Ill.*	2002	Rick Reilly, *Sports Ill.*
1970	Jim Murray, *LA Times*	1987	Frank Deford, *Sports Ill.*	2003	Rick Reilly, *Sports Ill.*
1971	Jim Murray, *LA Times*	1988	Frank Deford, *Sports Ill.*	2004	Rick Reilly, *Sports Ill.*
1972	Jim Murray, *LA Times*	1989	Peter Gammons, *Sports Ill.*	2005	Steve Rushin, *Sports Ill.*
1973	Jim Murray, *LA Times*	1990	Peter Gammons, *Boston Globe*		
1974	Jim Murray, *LA Times*	1991	Rick Reilly, *Sports Ill.*		
1975	Jim Murray, *LA Times*	1992	Rick Reilly, *Sports Ill.*		

Best Newspaper Sports Sections of 2005

Winners of the annual Associated Press Sports Editors contest for best daily and Sunday sports sections. Awards are divided into different categories, based on circulation figures. Selections are made by a committee of APSE members.

Circulation Over 250,000

Top 10 Daily		Top 10 Sunday	
Chicago Tribune	Los Angeles Times	Boston Globe	Indianapolis Star
Dallas Morning News	Miami Herald	Chicago Tribune	Kansas City Star
Detroit Free Press	Minneapolis Star Tribune	Dallas Morning News	Newark Star-Ledger
Fort Worth Star-Telegram	New York Times	Denver Post	Orlando Sentinel
Houston Chronicle	Philadelphia Inquirer	Fort Worth Star-Telegram	South Florida Sun-Sentinel

Circulation 100,000-250,000

Top 10 Daily		Top 10 Sunday	
Detroit News	Salt Lake Tribune	Charlotte Observer	Pittsburgh Post-Gazette
Hartford Courant	San Antonio Express-News	The State	St. Paul Pioneer Press
Memphis Commercial Appeal	Seattle Post-Intelligencer	(Columbia, SC)	Salt Lake Tribune
Palm Beach Post	Seattle Times	Lexington Herald-Leader	San Antonio Express-News
Riverside Press-Enterprise	Tampa Tribune	Louisville Courier-Journal	Wilmington (Del.) News Journal
		Palm Beach Post	

Best Sportswriting of 2005

Winners of the annual Associated Press Sports Editors Contest for best sportswriting in 2005. Eventual winners were chosen from five finalists in each writing division. Selections are made by a committee of APSE members. Note the investigative writing division included all circulation categories.

Circulation over 250,000

Column:	Joe Posnanski, *Kansas City Star*	**Game story:**	Dave Sheinin, *Washington Post*
Feature:	Amy Shipley, *Washington Post*	**Explanatory:**	Geoff Baker, *Toronto Star*
Breaking News:	Helene Elliott, *Los Angeles Times*	**Project:**	Shawn Windsor, *Detroit Free Press*

Circulation 100,000-250,000

Column:	Ian O'Connor, *White Plains Journal News*	**Game story:**	Adrian Wojnarowski, *Hackensack (N.J.) Record*
Feature:	Kent Babb, *The State (Columbia, S.C.)*		
Breaking News:	Gary Parrish, *Memphis Commercial Appeal*	**Explanatory:**	Larry Stone, *Seattle Times*
		Project:	Greg Bishop, *Seattle Times*

All Categories

Investigative: Bob Hohler, *Boston Globe*

INTERNATIONAL
SPORTS

2005 / 2006 YEAR IN REVIEW

American **Floyd Landis** won the Tour de France then was flagged as a cheater following a positive drug test.

IS ANYONE CLEAN?

Floyd Landis, Justin Gatlin and Marion Jones all faced charges of cheating in 2006 and despite good news for Jones, serious questions remain about the legitimacy of sports in the steroid age.

It was called a ride for the ages and it turns out it may have been too good to be true.

After capping perhaps the greatest comeback in Tour de France history and extending the USA's chokehold on the yellow jersey, American Floyd Landis tested positive for high levels of testosterone.

Testosterone is on the World Anti-Doping Agency's list of banned steroids but it is complicated to accurately test for because testosterone is a naturally occurring hormone in the human body.

Actually it was the ratio of testosterone to epitestosterone that landed Landis in trouble. The sample he provided to officials showed a ratio of 4:1, four times the average.

Landis steadfastly denied using any banned substance and claimed the testosterone must have been produced naturally.

If Landis had fallen back in the pack for good after suffering a collapse in the mountains then it might not be such a big story but the feat that made cycling fans wide-eyed and later raised eyebrows was his amazing resurrection in Stage 17, the final day in the Alps.

After losing his lead and falling behind by more than eight minutes to Spain's Oscar Pereiro, everyone was certain Landis was done.

Everyone but Landis.

His heroic performance sent a tasershock through the sport and vaulted him from 11th back to third just 30 seconds off the lead. He completed the comeback days later passing Pereiro for the win.

To many observers it wasn't a total shock that Landis should fail a drug test, considering that cycling has had a recent history thick with drug scandal. Tour organizers had high hopes in 2006 that it was a new era for the world's biggest bike race in two ways. They would be turning the page from scandal as well as the predictable dominance of retired seven-time winner Lance Armstrong.

It appeared that it could be the cleanest race in years. Especially after nine

Gerry Brown is Co-Editor of the ESPN Sports Almanac

AP/Wide World Photos

American **Justin Gatlin** broke the world record in the 100 meter dash, for about 48 hours. He currently shares the mark but could lose that too, pending arbitration on his failed drug test.

riders, including 1997 Tour de France winner Jan Ullrich and 2005 runner-up Ivan Basso, were bounced for suspicion of doping just before this year's race began.

With a constant cloud of suspicion raining allegations on the sport of professional cycling, it could ill afford another storm.

Then Hurricane Floyd blew in.

Drug testing is certainly not an exact science and the thing that makes the Landis case even more puzzling is the fact that he didn't fail previous tests from the 2006 Tour de France and taking steroids immediately preceding his miracle comeback would not have enhanced his performance that day.

In September, the Landis "B" sample confirmed the initial result and he was immediately fired by his team. His Tour title remains in limbo. The International Cycling Union has final say on whether he will officially lose the 2006 Tour de France victory.

Landis continues to deny the charges and is vigorously fighting the accusations.

Landis is actually the second former Armstrong teammate to get caught up in charges of doping.

Tyler Hamilton initially tested positive for blood doping after winning gold at the 2004 Athens Summer Olympics, but his "B" sample was mistakenly destroyed and he was able to keep his medal.

Hamilton would later fail a test at the 2004 Tour of Spain and was given a two-year ban.

Track star **Marion Jones** failed, then passed, a test for banned substances in 2006.

year ban from the sport but hopes to shorten the sentence in an arbitration hearing in order to be eligible to compete at the 2008 Beijing Summer Olympics.

Still, his career is in serious jeopardy and he claims he has no idea how the banned substances got into his system and denies that he knowingly cheated.

Perhaps the only bright news to come from the test tube this year was the happy ending to the swirling suspicions surrounding three-time gold medallist Marion Jones.

Jones has been accused in the past of using banned substances by both her ex-husband C.J. Hunter and BALCO founder Victor Conte.

It appeared that their accusations were on target after Jones initially tested positive for EPO after winning the 100 meters at the U.S. Track and Field Championships on June 23, but Jones' "B" sample came up clean and the sprinter was cleared.

Landis, Gatlin and Jones are far from the only athletes suspected of taking banned substances. It has become a major issue in baseball and other sports and, justly or not, until the day that truly reliable tests can be devised the haze of suspicion will always cover heroic performances like Floyd's stage for the ages with a shadow of doubt.

If cycling is the sickest sport at the global clinic then track and field is showing serious symptoms too. And forget bird flu, nearly every sport has been touched by the constant threat of a steroid pandemic.

American Justin Gatlin, the reigning Olympic champion in the 100 meter dash and co-holder of the world record, flunked a test for testosterone or other steroids at the Kansas Relays on April 22 but avoided a lifetime ban by agreeing to accept his positive test and aid in an ongoing anti-drug effort.

The 24-year-old Gatlin faces an 8-

For more information on baseball's battle with steroids see the Business essay on page 596.

AP/Wide World Photos

10

Biggest Stories of the Year in **International Sports**

10 Slew of swimming records fall. Twenty swimming world records were broken in 2006. Among the high water marks that were bested was Janet Evans' nearly 18-year-old mark in the women's 400 meter freestyle. Evans set what was the second oldest record on the books (see page 631) at the 1988 Seoul Summer Olympic Games. Laure Manaudou swam a 4:03.03 at the French Championships to eclipse Evans' long-standing record. Evans still holds the world records in the 800 meter free and 1500m free. Her mark in the 1500 meter free, which was set Mar. 26, 1988 in Orlando, Fla., is still the oldest swimming record currently standing.

09 Track Triple Crown. Ethiopia's Kenenisa Bekele becomes the first person to win world titles on three surfaces when he wins the men's 3000 meters at the 2006 World Indoor Track and Field Championships in Moscow. Bekele, 23, is also the reigning champion in the outdoor 10,000 meters as well as the World Cross-Country Championship.

08 Awesome Austrians. Austrian skiers, led by Benjamin Raich, cap a wunderbar year winning half of the World Cup titles, to go with their record 14 medals at the Turin Winter Olympics.

07 The Croation Sensation Janica Kostelic wins gold and silver at Turin then captures the overall and slalom titles on the World Cup circuit, winning events in all five disciplines along the way, becoming only the second woman ever to do so.

06 Blazing in Boston. Kicking off the new World Marathon Majors series, Kenya's Robert Kipkoech Cheruiyot "struggles" a bit down the home stretch but still sets a new course record at the 110th edition of the Boston Marathon, outpacing countryman Benjamin Maiyo by more than a minute in a time of 2:07:14. The Marathon Majors consist of the Boston, London, Berlin, Chicago and New York City Marathon.

05 Sweet 16. Delaware teenager Kimmie Meissner wins the women's World Figure Skating Championship in Calgary, Canada. Meissner, 16, took silver at the U.S Championship and finished sixth at the Turin Winter Games before skating a flawless long program at Worlds landing seven triple jumps including two triple-triple combinations. She became the first American to win a world figure skating title since Michelle Kwan in 2003.

04 World's Fastest Man? Not quite.

American sprinter Justin Gatlin apparently sets the world record in the men's 100 meters and earns the title of World's Fastest Man with a time of 9.76 seconds at an IAAF meet in Doha, Qatar on May 12, 2006. It is announced several days later, however, that his time was actually 9.766 and should have been rounded up to 9.77, giving him only a share of the world record (with Jamaica's Asafa Powell) instead of sole ownership. But before Powell and Gatlin can successfully arrange a highly anticipated showdown...

03 Gatlin tests positive.

The Olympic and world champion in the 100 meters reveals in July that he tested positive for "testosterone or its precursor" in April 2006 and again in a "B" sample several months later. He claims that he has no idea how he could have the substance in his system but later he accepts an eight-year ban from USA Track and Field, with plans to exhaust the appeals process hoping to regain eligibility before the 2008 Summer Olympics in Beijing. Gatlin will keep his share of the world record until his final appeal is ruled on.

02 Turning a Positive into a Negative.

After testing positive for the perfomance enhancer erythropoietin (EPO) on June 23, former Olympic champion Marion Jones declared her innocence. The highly decorated sprinter, winner of three gold medals (and two bronze) at the 2000 Sydney Summer Games, has been accused in the past by both her ex-husband C.J. Hunter and the infamous BALCO boss Victor Conte of using banned substances. And just when it looked like guilt by association and the positive test result would bring a disgraceful end to her comeback from childbirth she is exonerated when her "B" sample turns up clean in September.

01 Hurricane Floyd.

American Floyd Landis stages a stunning comeback after crumbling on the penultimate mountain stage at the first post-Armstrong Tour de France. Landis, nursing an arthritic hip, was left for dead by the leaders in the final climb of Stage 16, coughing up his lead and falling more than eight minutes behind Spain's Oscar Pereiro. But the next day Landis was amazingly reborn and reeled in all but 30 seconds of his deficit. Landis then won the race by dusting Pereiro in the final time trial. It was the eighth straight year that cycling's biggest race was won by an American, that is until it is announced that Landis tested positive for elevated levels of testosterone. Landis is appealing the verdict and will remain the official champion until a proper hearing. If stripped of the title, Landis would become the first winner in the race's 103-year history to lose the title for doping.

2005-2006
Season in Review

SPORTS ALMANAC

TRACK & FIELD

2006 IAAF World Athletics Final

The 4th annual IAAF World Athletics Final held in Stuttgart, Germany, Sept. 9-10, 2006. Total prize fund for the event is $3,020,000 with anyone setting a world record receiving an additional $100,000. Participants are decided according to the IAAF rankings in each event. Note that (CR) indicates championship meet record.

MEN

Event		Time	
100 meters	Asafa Powell, JAM	9.89	CR
200 meters	Tyson Gay, USA	19.68	CR
400 meters	Jeremy Wariner, USA	44.02	CR
800 meters	Mbulaeni Mulaudzi, RSA	1:46.99	
1500 meters	Alex Kipchirchir, KEN	3:32.76	CR
3000 meters	Tariku Bekele, ETH	7:38.98	
5000 meters	Kenenisa Bekele, ETH	13:48.62	
110m hurdles	Xiang Liu, CHN	12.93	CR
400m hurdles	Periklis Iakovakis, GRE	47.92	
3000m steeple	Paul Kipsiele Koech, KEN	8:01.37	

Event		Hgt/Dist
High Jump	Linus Thornblad, SWE	7-7¾
Pole Vault	Paul Burgess, AUS	19-1
Long Jump	Irving Saladino, PAN	27-7¼
Triple Jump	Yoandri Betanzos, CUB	57-8
Shot Put	Reese Hoffa, USA	69-0¾
Discus	Virgilijus Alekna, LIT	225-2 CR
Hammer	Koji Murofushi, JPN	267-1
Javelin	Andreas Thorkildsen, NOR	293-8

WOMEN

Event		Time	
100 meters	Sherone Simpson, JAM	10.89	
200 meters	Allyson Felix, USA	22.11	CR
400 meters	Sanya Richards, USA	49.25	CR
800 meters	Zulia Calatayud, CUB	1:59.02	CR
1500 meters	Maryam Yusuf Jamal, BRN	4:01.58	
3000 meters	Meseret Defar, ETH	8:34.22	CR
5000 meters	Tirunesh Dibaba, ETH	16:04.77	
100m hurdles	Michelle Perry, USA	12.52	
400m hurdles	Lashinda Demus, USA	53.42	
3000m steeple	Alesia Turava, BLR	9:27.08	

Event		Hgt/Dist	
High Jump	Kajsa Bergqvist, SWE	6-6	
Pole Vault	Yelena Isinbayeva, RUS	15-7	
Long Jump	Tatyana Lebedeva, RUS	22-8	
Triple Jump	Tatyana Lebedeva, RUS	48-7½	
Shot Put	Natallia Khoroneko, BLR	65-0	
Discus	Franka Dietzsch, GER	212-4	
Hammer	Betty Heidler, GER	247-6	CR
Javelin	Barbora Spotakova, CZR	217-2	

2006 IAAF World Cross Country Championships

The 34th IAAF World Cross Country Championships held in Fukuoka, Japan (April 1-2).

MEN

12 km	1. Kenenisa Bekele, Ethiopia	35:40
(7.45 mi)	2. Sileshi Sihine, Ethiopia	35:43
	3. Martin Irungu Mathathi, Kenya	35:44
	Best USA—Ryan Hall, 43rd	37:29

WOMEN

8 km	1. Tirunesh Dibaba, Ethiopia	25:21
(4.97 mi)	2. Lornah Kiplagat, Netherlands	25:26
	3. Meselech Melkamu, Ethiopia	25:38
	Best USA—Blake Russell, 11th	26:23

World Outdoor Records Set in 2006

World outdoor records set or equaled between Sept. 29, 2005 and Sept. 28, 2006; (p) indicates record is pending ratification by the IAAF.

MEN

Event	Name	Record	Old Mark	Former Holder
100 meters	**Justin Gatlin**, USA (tie)	9.77†	9.77	Asafa Powell (2005)
100 meters	**Asafa Powell**, JAM (tie)	9.77	9.77	Powell & Gatlin
100 meters	**Asafa Powell**, JAM (tie)	9.77p	9.77	Powell & Gatlin
4 x 800-m relay	**Kenya**	7:02.43p	7:03.89	Great Britain (1982)
110-m hurdles	**Xiang Liu**, CHN	12.88	12.91	Liu (2004) & Colin Jackson, GBR (1993)

WOMEN

Event	Name	Record	Old Mark	Former Holder
5000 meters	**Meseret Defar**, ETH	14:24.53	14:24.68	Elvan Abeylegesse, TUR (2004)
Hammer	**Tatyana Lysenko**, RUS	255-3p	254-0	Tatyana Lysenko, RUS (2006)

† Gatlin was originally thought to have broken the world record with a time of 9.76. Five days later, the IAAF announced that his actual time was 9.766 and should have been rounded up to 9.77, thus tying the record. In August, Gatlin was handed an eight-year ban and loss of his share of the record for a second positive drug test. His mark will stand, however, until the completion of his appeal process (which hadn't happened as of Sept. 28, 2006).

World, Olympic and American Records

As of Sept. 28, 2006

World outdoor records officially recognized by the International Amateur Athletics Federation (IAAF); (p) indicates record is pending ratification. (†) indicates record is pending appeal process. Note that marathon records are not officially recognized by the IAAF.

MEN

Running

Event		Time		Date Set	Location
100 meters:	World	9.77	**Asafa Powell**, Jamaica	June 14, 2005	Athens
		9.77†	**Justin Gatlin**, USA	May 12, 2006	Doha, QAT
		9.77	**Asafa Powell**, Jamaica	June 11, 2006	Gateshead, ENG
		9.77p	**Asafa Powell**, Jamaica	Aug. 18, 2006	Zurich
	Olympic	9.84	Donovan Bailey, Canada	July 27, 1996	Atlanta
	American	9.78	Tim Montgomery	Sept. 14, 2002	Paris
200 meters:	World	19.32	**Michael Johnson**, USA	Aug. 1, 1996	Atlanta
	Olympic	19.32	Johnson (same as World)	—	—
	American	19.32	Johnson (same as World)	—	—
400 meters:	World	43.18	**Michael Johnson**, USA	Aug. 26, 1999	Seville
	Olympic	43.49	Michael Johnson, USA	July 29, 1996	Atlanta
	American	43.18	Johnson (same as World)	—	—
800 meters:	World	1:41.11	**Wilson Kipketer**, Denmark	Aug. 24, 1997	Cologne
	Olympic	1:42.58	Vebjoern Rodal, Norway	July 31, 1996	Atlanta
	American	1:42.60	Johnny Gray	Aug. 28, 1985	Koblenz, W. Ger.
1000 meters:	World	2:11.96	**Noah Ngeny**, Kenya	Sept. 5, 1999	Rieti, ITA
	Olympic		Not an event	—	—
	American	2:13.9	Rick Wohlhuter	July 30, 1974	Oslo
1500 meters:	World	3:26.00	**Hicham El Guerrouj**, Morocco	July 14, 1998	Rome
	Olympic	3:32.07	Noah Ngeny, Kenya	Sept. 29, 2000	Sydney
	American	3:29.30	Bernard Lagat	Aug. 28, 2005	Rieti, ITA
Mile:	World	3:43.13	**Hicham El Guerrouj**, Morocco	July 7, 1999	Rome
	Olympic		Not an event	—	—
	American	3:47.69	Steve Scott	July 7, 1982	Oslo
2000 meters:	World	4:44.79	**Hicham El Guerrouj**, Morocco	Sept. 7, 1999	Berlin
	Olympic		Not an event	—	—
	American	4:52.44	Jim Spivey	Sept. 15, 1987	Lausanne, SWI
3000 meters:	World	7:20.67	**Daniel Komen**, Kenya	Sept. 1, 1996	Rieti, ITA
	Olympic		Not an event	—	—
	American	7:30.84	Bob Kennedy	Aug. 8, 1998	Monte Carlo
5000 meters:	World	12:37.35	**Kenenisa Bekele**, Ethiopia	May 31, 2004	Hengelo, NED
	Olympic	13:05.59	Said Aouita, Morocco	Aug. 11, 1984	Los Angeles
	American	12:58.21	Bob Kennedy	Aug. 14, 1996	Zurich
10,000 meters:	World	26:17.53	**Kenenisa Bekele**, Ethiopia	Aug. 26, 2005	Brussels
	Olympic	27:05.10	Kenenisa Bekele, Ethiopia	Aug. 20, 2004	Athens
	American	27:13.98	Meb Keflezighi	May 4, 2001	Stanford, Calif.
20,000 meters:	World	56:55.6	**Arturo Barrios**, Mexico	Mar. 30, 1991	La Fleche, FRA
	Olympic		Not an event	—	—
	American	58:15.0	Bill Rodgers	Aug. 9, 1977	Boston
Marathon:	World	2:04:55	**Paul Tergat**, KEN	Sept. 28, 2003	Berlin
	Olympic	2:09:21	Carlos Lopes, Portugal	Aug. 12, 1984	Los Angeles
	American	2:05:38	Khalid Khannouchi	Apr. 14, 2002	London

Relays

Event		Time		Date Set	Location
4 x 100m:	World	37.40	**USA** (Marsh, Burrell, Mitchell, C. Lewis)	Aug. 8, 1992	Barcelona
		37.40	**USA** (Drummond, Cason, Mitchell, Burrell)	Aug. 21, 1993	Stuttgart
	Olympic	37.40	USA (same as World - 1992)	—	—
	American	37.40	USA (same as World)	—	—
4 x 200m:	World	1:18.68	**USA** (Marsh, Burrell, Heard, C. Lewis)	Apr. 17, 1994	Walnut, Calif.
	Olympic		Not an event	—	—
	American	1:18.68	USA (same as World)	—	—
4 x 400m:	World	2:54.20	**USA** (Young, Pettigrew, Washington, Johnson)	July 22,1998	Uniondale, N.Y.
	Olympic	2:55.74	USA (Valmon, Watts, Johnson, S. Lewis)	Aug. 8, 1992	Barcelona
	American	2:54.20	USA (same as World)	—	—
4 x 800m:	World	7:02.43p	**Kenya** (Mutua, Yiampoy, Kombich, Bungei)	Aug. 25,2006	Brussels
	Olympic		Not an event	—	—
	American	7:02.82p	USA (Harris, Robinson, Burley, Krummenacker)	Aug. 25,2006	Brussels
4 x 1500m:	World	14:38.8	**West Germany** (Wessinghage, Hudak, Lederer, Fleschen)	Aug. 17, 1977	Cologne
	Olympic		Not an event	—	—
	American	14:46.3	USA (Aldredge, Clifford, Harbour, Duits)	June 24, 1979	Bourges, FRA

Steeplechase

Event	Time		Date Set	Location
3000 meters:	**World** 7:53.63	**Saif Saaeed Shaheen**, Qatar	Sept. 3, 2004	Brussels
	Olympic . . .8:05.51	Julius Kariuki, Kenya	Sept. 30, 1988	Seoul
	American . .8:08.82p	Daniel Lincoln	July 14, 2006	Rome

Note: A men's steeplechase course consists of 28 hurdles (3 feet high) and seven water jumps (12 feet long).

Hurdles

Event	Time		Date Set	Location
110 meters:	**World** 12.88	**Xiang Liu**, China	July 11, 2006	Lausanne
	Olympic 12.91	Xiang Liu, China	Aug. 27, 2004	Athens
	American 12.90	Dominique Arnold	July 11, 2006	Lausanne
400 meters:	**World** 46.78	**Kevin Young**, USA	Aug. 6, 1992	Barcelona
	Olympic 46.78	Young (same as World)	—	—
	American 46.78	Young (same as World)	—	—

Note: The 10 hurdles at 110 meters are 3 feet, 6 inches high and those at 400 meters are 3 feet.

Walking

Event	Time		Date Set	Location
20 km:	**World** . . .1:17:21	**Jefferson Perez**, Ecuador	Aug. 23, 2003	Paris
	Olympic . . .1:18:59	Robert Korzeniowski, Poland	Sept. 22, 2000	Sydney
	American . .1:22:02	Tim Seaman	May 22, 2004	Copenhagen, DEN
50 km:	**World** . . .3:35:29p	**Denis Nizhegorodov**, Russia	June 13, 2004	Cheboksary, RUS
	Olympic . . .3:38:29	Vyacheslav Ivanenko, USSR	Sept. 30, 1988	Seoul
	American . .3:48:04	Curt Clausen	May 2, 1999	Deauville, FRA

Field Events

Event	Mark		Date Set	Location
High Jump:	**World** 8-0½	**Javier Sotomayor**, Cuba	July 27, 1993	Salamanca, SPA
	Olympic 7-10	Charles Austin, USA	July 28, 1996	Atlanta
	American. . . . 7-10½	Charles Austin	Aug. 7, 1991	Zurich
Pole Vault:	**World** 20-1¾	**Sergey Bubka**, Ukraine	July 31, 1994	Sestriere, ITA
	Olympic 19-6¼	Tim Mack, USA	Aug. 27, 2004	Athens
	American. . . . 19-9¼	Jeff Hartwig	June 14, 2000	Jonesboro, Ark.
Long Jump:	**World** 29-4½	**Mike Powell**, USA	Aug. 30, 1991	Tokyo
	Olympic 29-2½	Bob Beamon, USA	Oct. 18, 1968	Mexico City
	American. . . . 29-4½	Powell (same as World)	—	—
Triple Jump:	**World**. 60- 0¼	**Jonathan Edwards**, GBR	Aug. 7, 1995	Göteborg, SWE
	Olympic 59-4¼	Kenny Harrison, USA	July 27, 1996	Atlanta
	American. . . . 59-4¼	Kenny Harrison (same as Olympic)	—	—
Shot Put:	**World** 75-10¼	**Randy Barnes**, USA	May 20, 1990	Los Angeles
	Olympic 73- 8¾	Ulf Timmermann, East Germany	Sept. 23, 1988	Seoul
	American. . . 75-10¼	Barnes (same as World)	—	—
Discus:	**World** 243-0	**Jurgen Schult**, East Germany	June 6, 1986	Neubrandenburg
	Olympic . . . 229-3½	Virgilijus Alekna, Lithuania	Aug. 23, 2004	Athens
	American. . . 237-4	Ben Plucknett	July 7, 1981	Stockholm
Javelin:	**World** 323-1	**Jan Zelezny**, Czech Republic	May 25, 1996	Jena, GER
	Olympic . . 295-10	Jan Zelezny, Czech Republic	Sept. 23, 2000	Sydney
	American. . . 287-8	Breaux Greer	Sept 19, 2004	Monaco
Hammer:	**World** 284-7	**Yuriy Sedykh**, USSR	Aug. 30, 1986	Stuttgart
	Olympic . . . 278-2	Sergey Litvinov, USSR	Sept. 26, 1988	Seoul
	American. . . 270-9	Lance Deal	Sept. 7, 1996	Milan

Note: The international weights for men—**Shot** (16 lbs); **Discus** (4 lbs/6.55 oz); **Javelin** (minimum 1 lb/12¼ oz.); **Hammer** (16 lbs).

Decathlon

	Points		Date Set	Location
Ten Events:	**World**. 9026	**Roman Sebrle**, Czech Republic	May 26-27, 2001	Gotzis, AUT
	Olympic. 8893	Roman Sebrle, Czech Republic	Aug. 23-24, 2004	Athens
	American 8891	Dan O'Brien	Sept. 4-5, 1992	Talence, FRA

Note: Sebrle's WR times and distances, in order over two days—**100m** (10.64); **LJ** (26-7¼); **Shot** (50-3½); **HJ** (6-11½); **400m** (47.79); **110m H** (13.92); **Discus** (157-3); **PV** (15-9); **Jav** (230-2); **1500m** (4:21.98).

World, Olympic and American Outdoor Records (Cont.)

WOMEN
Running

Event		Time		Date Set	Location
100 meters:	**World**	.......10.49	**Florence Griffith Joyner**, USA	July 16, 1988	Indianapolis
	Olympic	......10.62	Florence Griffith Joyner, USA	Sept. 24, 1988	Seoul
	American	......10.49	Griffith Joyner (same as World)	—	—
200 meters:	**World**	......21.34	**Florence Griffith Joyner**, USA	Sept. 29, 1988	Seoul
	Olympic	......21.34	Griffith Joyner (same as World)	—	—
	American	......21.34	Griffith Joyner (same as World)	—	—
400 meters:	**World**	......47.60	**Marita Koch**, East Germany	Oct. 6, 1985	Canberra, AUS
	Olympic	......48.25	Marie-Jose Perec, France	July 29, 1996	Atlanta
	American	......48.70p	Sanya Richards	Sept. 16, 2006	Athens
800 meters:	**World**	......1:53.28	**Jarmila Kratochvilova**, Czech.	July 26, 1983	Munich
	Olympic	......1:53.42	Nadezhda Olizarenko, USSR	July 27, 1980	Moscow
	American	......1:56.40	Jearl Miles-Clark	Aug. 11, 1999	Zurich
1000 meters:	**World**	......2:28.98	**Svetlana Masterkova**, Russia	Aug. 23, 1996	Brussels
	Olympic	....	Not an event		
	American	......2:31.80	Regina Jacobs	July 3, 1999	Brunswick, Me.
1500 meters:	**World**	......3:50.46	**Qu Yunxia**, China	Sept. 11, 1993	Beijing
	Olympic	......3:53.96	Paula Ivan, Romania	Oct. 1, 1988	Seoul
	American	......3:57.12	Mary Slaney	July 26, 1983	Stockholm
Mile:	**World**	......4:12.56	**Svetlana Masterkova**, Russia	Aug. 14, 1996	Zurich
	Olympic	....	Not an event	—	—
	American	......4:16.71	Mary Slaney	Aug. 21, 1985	Zurich
2000 meters:	**World**	......5:25.36	**Sonia O'Sullivan**, Ireland	July 8, 1994	Edinburgh
	Olympic	....	Not an event	—	—
	American	...... 5:32.7	Mary Slaney	Aug. 3, 1984	Eugene, Ore.
3000 meters:	**World**	......8:06.11	**Wang Junxia**, China	Sept. 13, 1993	Beijing
	Olympic	......8:26.53	Tatyana Samolenko, USSR	Sept. 25, 1988	Seoul
	American	......8:25.83	Mary Slaney	Sept. 7, 1985	Rome
5000 meters:	**World**	......14:24.53	**Meseret Defar**, Ethiopia	June 3, 2006	New York
	Olympic	......14:40.79	Gabriela Szabo, Romania	Sept. 25, 2000	Sydney
	American	......14:45.35	Regina Jacobs	July 27, 2000	Sacramento
10,000 meters:	**World**	......29:31.78	**Wang Junxia**, China	Sept. 8, 1993	Beijing
	Olympic	......30:17.49	Derartu Tulu, Ethiopia	Sept. 30, 2000	Sydney
	American	......30:50.32p	Deena Kastor	May 3, 2002	Stanford, Calif.
Marathon:	**World**	......2:15:25	**Paula Radcliffe**, Great Britain	Apr. 13, 2003	London
	Olympic	......2:23:14	Naoko Takahashi, Japan	Sept. 24, 2000	Sydney
	American	......2:19:36	Deena Kastor	Apr. 23, 2006	London

Relays

Event		Time		Date Set	Location
4 x 100m:	**World**	.....41.37	**East Germany** (Gladisch, Rieger, Auerswald, Gohr)	Oct. 6, 1985	Canberra, AUS
	Olympic	....41.60	East Germany (Muller, Wockel, Auerswald, Gohr)	Aug. 1, 1980	Moscow
	American	41.47	USA (Gaines, Jones, Miller, Devers)	Aug. 9, 1997	Athens
4 x 200m:	**World**	...1:27.46	**USA** (Jenkins, Colander-Richardson, Perry, Jones)	Apr. 29, 2000	Philadelphia
	Olympic	....	Not an event	—	—
	American	..1:27.46	USA (same as World)	—	—
4 x 400m:	**World**	...3:15.17	**USSR** (Ledovskaya, Nazarova, Pinigina, Bryzgina)	Oct. 1, 1988	Seoul
	Olympic	...3:15.17	USSR (same as World)	—	—
	American	..3:15.51	USA (Howard, Dixon, Brisco, Griffith Joyner)	Oct. 1, 1988	Seoul
4 x 800m:	**World**	...7:50.17	**USSR** (Olizarenko, Gurina, Borisova, Podyalovskaya)	Aug. 5, 1984	Moscow
	Olympic	....	Not an event	—	—
	American	..8:17.09	Athletics West (Addison, Arbogast, Decker Slaney, Mullen)	Apr. 24, 1983	Walnut, Calif.

Hurdles

Event		Time		Date Set	Location
100 meters:	**World**	......12.21	**Yordanka Donkova**, Bulgaria	Aug. 20, 1988	Stara Zagora, BUL
	Olympic	......12.37	Joanna Hayes, USA	Aug. 24, 2004	Athens
	American	......12.33	Gail Devers	July 23, 2000	Sacramento

400 meters:	World 52.34	Yuliya Pechonkina, Russia	Aug. 8, 2003	Tula, RUS
	Olympic 52.77	Fani Halkia, Greece	Aug. 22, 2004	Athens
	American 52.61	Kim Batten	Aug. 11, 1995	Göteborg, SWE

Note: The 10 hurdles at 110 meters are 3 feet, 6 inches high and those at 400 meters are 3 feet.

Walking

Event	Time		Date Set	Location
20 km:	World 1:25:41	Olimpiada Ivanova, Russia	Aug. 7, 2005	Helsinki
	Olympic 1:29:05	Wang Liping, China	Sept. 28, 2000	Sydney
	American 1:31:51	Michelle Rohl	May 13, 2000	Kenosha, Wis.

Steeplechase

Event	Time		Date Set	Location
3000 meters:	World 9:01.59	Gulnara Samitova, Russia	July 4, 2004	Heraklion, GRE
	Olympic	Not an event	—	—
	American 9:29.32	Briana Shook	July 31, 2004	Heusden-Zolder, BEL

Note: A women's steeplechase course consists of 28 hurdles (30 inches high) and seven water jumps (10 feet long).

Field Events

Event	Mark		Date Set	Location
High Jump:	World 6-10¼	Stefka Kostadinova, Bulgaria	Aug. 30, 1987	Rome
	Olympic 6-9	Yelena Slesarenko, Russia	Aug. 28, 2004	Athens
	American 6-8	Louise Ritter	July 8, 1988	Austin, Texas
	6-8	Louise Ritter	Sept. 30, 1988	Seoul
Pole Vault:	World 16-5¼	Yelena Isinbayeva, Russia	Aug. 12, 2005	Helsinki
	Olympic 16-1¼	Yelena Isinbayeva, Russia	Aug. 24, 2004	Athens
	American 15-10	Stacy Dragila	June 8, 2004	Ostrava, CZR
Long Jump:	World 24-8¼	Galina Chistyakova, USSR	June 11, 1988	Leningrad
	Olympic 24-3¼	Jackie Joyner-Kersee, USA	Sept. 29, 1988	Seoul
	American 24-7	Jackie Joyner-Kersee	May 22, 1994	New York
Triple Jump:	World 50-10¼	Inessa Kravets, Ukraine	Aug. 10, 1995	Göteborg, SWE
	Olympic 50-3½	Inessa Kravets, Ukraine	July 31, 1996	Atlanta
	American 47-5	Tiombe Hurd	July 11, 2004	Sacramento, Calif.
Shot Put:	World 74-3	Natalya Lisovskaya, USSR	June 7, 1987	Moscow
	Olympic 73-6¼	Ilona Slupianek, E. Germany	July 24, 1980	Moscow
	American 66-2½	Ramona Pagel	June 25, 1988	San Diego
Discus:	World 252-0	Gabriele Reinsch, E. Germany	July 9, 1988	Neubrandenburg
	Olympic 237-2½	Martina Hellmann, E. Germany	Sept. 29, 1988	Seoul
	American 227-10	Suzy Powell	Apr. 27, 2002	La Jolla, Calif.
Javelin:	World 235-3	Osleidys Menendez, Cuba	Aug. 14, 2005	Helsinki
	Olympic 234-8	Osleidys Menendez, Cuba	Aug. 27, 2004	Athens
	American . . 204-10	Kim Kreiner	May 28, 2006	San Mateo, Calif.
	204-10	Kim Kreiner	July 6, 2006	Arhus, DEN
Hammer:	World 255-3	Tatyana Lysenko, Russia	Aug. 15, 2006	Tallinn, EST
	Olympic . . . 246-1	Olga Kuzenkova, Russia	Aug. 25, 2004	Athens
	American . . 242-4	Erin Gilreath	June 25, 2005	Carson, Calif.

Note: The international weights for women—**Shot** (8 lbs/13 oz); **Discus** (2 lbs/3.27 oz); **Javelin** (minimum 1 lb/5.16 oz); **Hammer** (8 lbs/13 oz).

Heptathlon

Seven Events:	Points		Date Set	Location
	World 7291	Jackie Joyner-Kersee, USA	Sept. 23-24, 1988	Seoul
	Olympic 7291	Joyner-Kersee (same as World)	—	—
	American . . . 7291	Joyner-Kersee (same as World)	—	—

Note: Joyner-Kersee's WR times and distances, in order over two days—**100m H** (12.69); **HJ** (6 1¼); **Shot** (51-10); **200m** (22.56); **LJ** (23 10¼); **Jav** (149-10); **800m** (2:08.51).

World Indoor Records Set in 2006

World indoor records set or equaled between Sept. 30, 2005 and Sept. 28, 2006. (p) indicates pending ratification.

MEN

Event	Name	Record	Old Mark	Former Holder
4 x 400m relay . . . . .United States		3:01.96p	3:02.83	United States (1999)
(Clement, Spearmon, Williamson, Wariner)				

WOMEN

Event	Name	Record	Old Mark	Former Holder
1500 meters . . . . .Yelena Soboleva, RUS		3:58.28p	3:59.98	Regina Jacobs, USA (2003)
3000 meters . . . . . . .Liliya Shobukhova, RUS		8:27.86p	8:29.15	Berhane Adere, ETH (2002)
4 x 400m relay . . . . .Russia		3:23.37p	3:23.88	Russia (2004)
High Jump . . . . .Kajsa Bergqvist, SWE		6-9¾	6-9½	Heike Henkel, GER (1992)
Pole Vault . . . . .Yelena Isinbayeva, RUS		16-1¼	16-0¾	Yelena Isinbayeva, RUS (2005)

World and American Indoor Records

As of Sept. 28, 2006

World indoor records officially recognized by the International Amateur Athletics Federation (IAAF); (p) indicates record is pending ratification by the IAAF; (a) indicates record was set at an altitude over 1000 meters.

MEN
Running

Event		Time		Date Set	Location
50 meters:	World	5.56a	**Donovan Bailey**, Canada	Feb. 9, 1996	Reno, Nev.
		5.56	**Maurice Greene**, USA	Feb. 13, 1999	Los Angeles
	American	5.56	Greene (same as World)	Feb. 13, 1999	Los Angeles
60 meters:	World	6.39	**Maurice Greene**, USA	Feb. 3, 1998	Madrid
		6.39	**Maurice Greene**, USA	Mar. 3, 2001	Atlanta
	American	6.39	Greene (same as World)	—	—
200 meters:	World	19.92	**Frankie Fredericks**, Namibia	Feb. 18, 1996	Lievin, FRA
	American	20.10	Wallace Spearmon	Mar. 11, 2005	Fayetteville, Ark.
400 meters:	World	44.57	**Kerron Clement**, USA	Mar. 12, 2005	Fayetteville, Ark.
	American	44.57	Clement (same as World)	—	—
800 meters:	World	1:42.67	**Wilson Kipketer**, Denmark	Mar. 9, 1997	Paris
	American	1:45.00	Johnny Gray	Mar. 8, 1992	Sindelfingen, GER
1000 meters:	World	2:14.96	**Wilson Kipketer**, Denmark	Feb. 20, 2000	Birmingham, ENG
	American	2:17.86	David Krummenacker	Jan. 27, 2002	Boston
1500 meters:	World	3:31.18	**Hicham El Guerrouj**, Morocco	Feb. 2, 1997	Stuttgart
	American	3:33.34	Bernard Lagat	Feb. 11, 2005	Fayetteville, Ark.
Mile:	World	3:48.45	**Hicham El Guerrouj**, Morocco	Feb. 12, 1997	Ghent, BEL
	American	3:49.89	Bernard Lagat	Feb. 11, 2005	Fayetteville, Ark.
3000 meters:	World	7:24.90	**Daniel Komen**, Kenya	Feb. 6, 1998	Budapest
	American	7:39.23	Tim Broe	Jan. 27, 2002	Boston
5000 meters:	World	12:49.60	**Kenenisa Bekele**, Ethiopia	Feb. 20, 2004	Birmingham, ENG
	American	13:20.55	Doug Padilla	Feb. 12, 1982	New York

Note: The Mile run is 1,609.344 meters.

Hurdles

Event		Time		Date Set	Location
50 meters:	World	6.25	**Mark McKoy**, Canada	Mar. 5, 1986	Kobe, JPN
	American	6.35	Greg Foster	Jan. 27, 1985	Rosemont, Ill.
		6.35	Greg Foster	Jan. 31, 1987	Ottawa
60 meters:	World	7.30	**Colin Jackson**, Great Britain	Mar. 6, 1994	Sindelfingen, GER
	American	7.36	Greg Foster	Jan. 16, 1987	Los Angeles
		7.36	Allen Johnson	March 6, 2004	Budapest

Note: The hurdles for both distances are 3 feet, 6 inches high. There are four hurdles in the 50 meters and five in the 60.

Walking

Event		Time		Date Set	Location
5000 meters:	World	18:07.08	**Mikhail Shchennikov**, Russia	Feb. 14, 1995	Moscow
	American	19:15.88p	Tim Seaman	Feb. 25, 2006	Boston

Relays

Event		Time		Date Set	Location
4 x 200 meters:	World	1:22.11	**Great Britain**	Mar. 3, 1991	Glasgow
	American	1:22.71	National Team	Mar. 3, 1991	Glasgow
4 x 400 meters:	World	3:01.96p	**United States**	Feb. 11, 2006	Fayetteville, Ark.
	American	3:01.96p	National Team (same as World)	Feb. 11, 2006	Fayetteville, Ark.
4 x 800 meters:	World	7:13.94	**United States**	Feb. 6, 2000	Boston
	American	7:13.94	Global Athletics (same as World)	Feb. 6, 2000	Boston

Field Events

Event		Mark		Date Set	Location
High Jump:	World	7-11½	**Javier Sotomayor**, Cuba	Mar. 4, 1989	Budapest
	American	7-10½	Hollis Conway	Mar. 10, 1991	Seville
Pole Vault:	World	20-2	**Sergey Bubka**, Ukraine	Feb. 21, 1993	Donyetsk, UKR
	American	19-9	Jeff Hartwig	Mar. 10, 2002	Sindelfingen, GER
Long Jump:	World	28-10¼	**Carl Lewis**, USA	Jan. 27, 1984	New York
	American	28-10¼	Lewis (same as World)	—	—
Triple Jump:	World	58-6	**Aliecer Urrutia**, Cuba	Mar. 1, 1997	Sindelfingen, GER
		58-6	**Christian Olsson**, Sweden	Mar. 7, 2004	Budapest
	American	58-3¼	Mike Conley	Feb. 27, 1987	New York
Shot Put:	World	74-4¼	**Randy Barnes**, USA	Jan. 20, 1989	Los Angeles
	American	74-4¼	Barnes (same as World)	—	—

Note: The international shot put weight for men is 16 lbs.

Heptathlon

	Points		Date Set	Location
Seven Events:	**World** 6476	**Dan O'Brien**, USA	Mar. 13-14, 1993	Toronto
	American 6476	O'Brien (same as World)	–	–

Note: O'Brien's WR times and distances, in order over two days—**60m** (6.67); **LJ** (25-8¾); **SP** (52-6¾); **HJ** (6-11¾); **60m H** (7.85); **PV** (17-0¾); **1000m** (2:57.96).

WOMEN
Running

Event	Time		Date Set	Location
50 meters:	**World** 5.96	**Irina Privalova**, Russia	Feb. 9, 1995	Madrid
	American 6.02	Gail Devers	Feb. 21, 1999	Lievin, FRA
60 meters:	**World** 6.92	**Irina Privalova**, Russia	Feb. 11, 1993	Madrid
	6.92	**Irina Privalova**, Russia	Feb. 9, 1995	Madrid
	American 6.95	Gail Devers	Mar. 12, 1993	Toronto
	6.95	Marion Jones	Mar. 7, 1998	Maebashi, JPN
200 meters:	**World** 21.87	**Merlene Ottey**, Jamaica	Feb. 13, 1993	Lievin, FRA
	American 22.18	Michelle Collins	Mar. 15, 2003	Birmingham, ENG
400 meters:	**World** 49.59	**Jarmila Kratochvilova**, Czech.	Mar. 7, 1982	Milan
	American 50.64	Diane Dixon	Mar. 10, 1991	Seville
800 meters:	**World** 1:55.82	**Jolanda Ceplak**, Slovenia	Mar. 3, 2002	Vienna
	American . .1:58.71	Nicole Teter	Mar. 2, 2002	New York
1000 meters:	**World** 2:30.94	**Maria Mutola**, Mozambique	Feb. 25, 1999	Stockholm
	American . . .2:34.19	Jennifer Toomey	Feb. 20, 2004	Birmingham, ENG
1500 meters:	**World** . . .3:58.28p	**Yelena Soboleva**, Russia	Feb. 18, 2006	Moscow
	American . . .3:59.98	Regina Jacobs	Feb. 1, 2003	Boston
Mile:	**World** 4:17.14	**Doina Melinte**, Romania	Feb. 9, 1990	E. Rutherford, N.J.
	American . . .4:20.5	Mary Slaney	Feb. 19, 1982	San Diego
3000 meters:	**World** 8:27.86p	**Liliya Shobukhova**, Russia	Feb. 17, 2006	Moscow
	American . . .8:39.14	Regina Jacobs	Mar. 7, 1999	Maebashi, JPN
5000 meters:	**World** . . .14:32.93	**Tirunesh Dibaba**, Ethiopia	Jan. 29, 2005	Boston
	American . .15:07.33	Marla Runyan	Feb. 18, 2001	New York City

Note: The Mile run is 1,609.344 meters.

Hurdles

Event	Time		Date Set	Location
50 meters:	**World** 6.58	**Cornelia Oschkenat**, E. Ger.	Feb. 20, 1988	East Berlin
	American 6.67a	Jackie Joyner-Kersee	Feb. 10, 1995	Reno, Nev.
60 meters:	**World** 7.69	**Ludmila Engquist**, USSR	Feb. 4, 1990	Chelyabinsk, USSR
	American 7.74	Gail Devers	Mar. 1, 2003	Boston

Note: The hurdles for both distances are 2 feet, 9 inches high. There are four hurdles in the 50 meters and five in the 60.

Walking

Event	Time		Date Set	Location
3000 meters:	**World** . . .11:40.33	**Claudia Stef**, Romania	Jan. 30, 1999	Bucharest
	American . .12:20.79	Debbi Lawrence	Mar. 12, 1993	Toronto

Relays

Event	Time		Date Set	Location
4 x 200 meters:	**World** 1:32.41	**Russia**	Jan. 29, 2005	Glasgow
	American 1:33.24	National Team	Feb. 12, 1994	Glasgow
4 x 400 meters:	**World** . . . 3:23.37	**Russia**	Jan. 28, 2006	Glasgow
	American . 3:27.59	National Team	Mar. 7, 1999	Maebashi, JPN
4 x 800 meters:	**World** 8:18.71	**Russia**	Feb. 4, 1994	Moscow
	American . . . 8:25.5	Villanova	Feb. 7, 1987	Gainesville, Fla.

Field Events

Event	Mark		Date Set	Location
High Jump:	**World**. 6-9¾	**Kajsa Bergqvist**, Sweden	Feb. 4, 2006	Arnstadt, GER
	American 6-7	Tisha Waller	Feb. 28, 1998	Atlanta
Pole Vault:	**World**. 16-1¾	**Yelena Isinbayeva**, Russia	Feb. 12, 2006	Donetsk, UKR
	American 15-9¼	Stacy Dragila, USA	Mar. 6, 2004	Budapest
Long Jump:	**World**. 24-2¼	**Heike Drechsler**, E. Germany	Feb. 13, 1988	Vienna
	American 23-4¾	Jackie Joyner-Kersee	Mar. 5, 1994	Atlanta
Triple Jump:	**World**. 50-4¾	**Tatyana Lebedeva**, Russia	Mar. 6, 2004	Budapest
	American 46-8¼	Sheila Hudson	Mar. 4, 1995	Atlanta
Shot Put:	**World**. 73-10	**Helena Fibingerova**, Czech.	Feb. 19, 1977	Jablonec, CZE
	American 65-0¾	Ramona Pagel	Feb. 20, 1987	Inglewood, Calif.

Note: The international shotput weight for women is 8 lbs. and 13 oz.

Pentathlon

	Points		Date Set	Location
Five Events:	**World** 4991	**Irina Byelova**, Russia	Feb. 14-15, 1992	Berlin
	American 4753	DeDee Nathan	Mar. 4-5, 1999	Maebashi, JPN

Note: Byelova's WR times and distances, in order over two days—**60m H** (8.22); **HJ** (6-4); **SP** (43-5¾); **LJ** (21-1¾); **800m** (2:10.26).

2006 IAAF World Indoor Championships

The 11th IAAF World Indoor Championships in Athletics held in Moscow, Russia, March 10-12, 2006. Note that (CR) indicates championships meet record.

Final Medal Leaders

		G	S	B	Total			G	S	B	Total
1	Russia	8	5	5	18	8	Ethiopia	2	0	0	2
2	United States	7	4	2	13		Ukraine	2	0	0	2
3	Kenya	1	1	2	4		Cuba	0	1	1	2
4	Belarus	1	1	1	3		Spain	0	1	1	2
	Germany	1	1	1	3		Bahamas	0	0	2	2
	Poland	0	2	1	3	13	Twenty-one countries tied with 1 medal each.				
	Sweden	0	1	2	3						

MEN

Event		Time
60 meters	Leonard Scott, USA	6.50
400 meters	Alleyne Francique, GRN	45.54
800 meters	Wilfred Bungei, KEN	1:47.15
1500 meters	Ivan Heshko, UKR	3:42.08
3000 meters	Kenenisa Bekele, ETH	7:39.32
60m hurdles	Terrence Trammell, USA	7.43
4 x 400m relay	USA (Washington, Merritt, Campbell, Spearmon)	3:03.24

Event		Hgt/Dist
High Jump	Yaroslav Rybakov, RUS	7-9¼
Pole Vault	Brad Walker, USA	19-0½
Long Jump	Ignisious Gaisah, GHA	27-2¾
Triple Jump	Walter Davis, USA	58-2
Shot Put	Reese Hoffa, USA	72-6½
Heptathlon	Andre Niklaus, GER	6192 pts

WOMEN

Event		Time
60 meters	Me'Lisa Barber, USA	7.01
400 meters	Olesya Krasnomovets, RUS	50.04 CR
800 meters	M. de Lourdes Mutola, MOZ	1:58.90
1500 meters	Yuliya Chizhenko, RUS	4:04.70
3000 meters	Meseret Defar, ETH	8:38.80
60m hurdles	Derval O'Rourke, IRL	7.84
4 x 400m relay	Russia (Levina, Nazarova, Krasnomovets, Antyukh)	3:24.91

Event		Hgt/Dist
High Jump	Yelena Slesarenko, RUS	6-7½
Pole Vault	Yelena Isinbayeva, RUS	15-9
Long Jump	Tatyana Kotova, RUS	22-11¾
Triple Jump	Tatyana Lebedeva, RUS	49-0¾
Shot Put	Natallia Khoroneko, BLR	65-1
Pentathlon	Lyudmila Blonska, UKR	4685 pts

SWIMMING

World Swimming Records Set in 2006

World long course records set or equaled between Sept. 29, 2005 and Sept. 28, 2006; (*) indicates record is awaiting ratification. (r) indicates relay leadoff split.

MEN

Event	Name	Record	Old Mark	Former Holder
200m backstroke	**Aaron Peirsol,** USA	1:54.44	1:54.66	Aaron Peirsol, USA (2005)
100m breaststroke	**Brendan Hansen,** USA	59.13	59.30	Brendan Hansen, USA (2004)
200m breaststroke	**Brendan Hansen,** USA	2:08.74	2:09.04	Brendan Hansen, USA (2004)
	Brendan Hansen, USA	2:08.50	2:08.74	Brendan Hansen, USA (2006)
200m butterfly	**Michael Phelps,** USA	1:53.80	1:53.93	Michael Phelps, USA (2003)
200m IM	**Michael Phelps,** USA	1:55.84	1:55.94	Michael Phelps, USA (2003)
4x100m freestyle relay	**USA** (Phelps, Walker, Jones, Lezak)	3:12.46	3:13.77	South Africa (2004)

WOMEN

Event	Name	Record	Old Mark	Former Holder
100m freestyle	**Lisbeth Lenton,** AUS	53.42	53.52	Jodie Henry, AUS (2004)
	Britta Steffen, GER	53.30	53.42	Lisbeth Lenton, AUS (2006)
400m freestyle	**Laure Manaudou,** FRA	4:03.03	4:03.85	Janet Evans, USA (1988)
	Laure Manaudou, FRA	4:02.13	4:03.03	Laure Manaudou, FRA (2006)
50m backstroke	**Aleksandra Herasimenia,** BLR	28.19	28.19	(tie) Janine Pietsch, GER (2005)
50m breaststroke	**Jade Edmistone,** AUS	30.31	30.45	Jade Edmistone, AUS (2005)
100m breaststroke	**Leisel Jones,** AUS	1:05.71	1:06.20	Jessica Hardy, USA (2005)
	Leisel Jones, AUS	1:05.09	1:05.71	Leisel Jones, AUS (2006)
200m breaststroke	**Leisel Jones,** AUS	2:20.54	2:21.72	Leisel Jones, AUS (2005)
200m butterfly	**Jessicah Schipper,** AUS	2:05.40	2:05.61	Otylia Jedrejczak, POL (2005)
4x100m freestyle relay	**Germany** (Dallman, Goetz, Steffen, Liebs)	3:35.22	3:35.94	Australia (2004)
4x200m freestyle relay	**Germany** (Dallman, Samulski, Steffen, Liebs)	7:50.82	7:53.42	United States (2004)
4x100m medley relay	**Australia** (Edington, Jones, Schipper, Lenton)	3:56.30	3:57.32	Australia (2004)

World, Olympic and American Records
As of September 28, 2006

World long course records officially recognized by the Federation Internationale de Natation Amateur (FINA). Note that (p) indicates preliminary heat; (r) relay lead-off split; and (s) indicates split time. Note that (*) denotes that a record is awaiting ratification.

MEN
Freestyle

Distance		Time		Date Set	Location
50 meters:	**World**	21.64	**Aleksandr Popov**, Russia	June 16, 2000	Moscow
	Olympic	21.91	Aleksandr Popov, Unified Team	July 30, 1992	Barcelona
	American	21.76	Gary Hall Jr.	Aug. 15, 2000	Indianapolis
100 meters:	**World**	47.84p	**P. van den Hoogenband**, NED	Sept. 19, 2000	Sydney
	Olympic	47.84p	P. van den Hoogenband, NED (same as World)	—	
	American	48.17p	Jason Lezak	July 10, 2004	Long Beach, Calif.
200 meters:	**World**	1:44.06	**Ian Thorpe**, Australia	July 25, 2001	Fukuoka, JPN
	Olympic	1:44.71	Ian Thorpe, Australia	Aug. 16, 2004	Athens
	American	1:45.20	Michael Phelps	July 26, 2005	Montreal
400 meters:	**World**	3:40.08	**Ian Thorpe**, Australia	July 30, 2002	Manchester, GBR
	Olympic	3:40.59	Ian Thorpe, Australia	Sept. 16, 2000	Sydney
	American	3:44.11	Klete Keller	Aug. 14, 2004	Athens
800 meters:	**World**	7:38.65	**Grant Hackett**, Australia	July 27, 2005	Montreal
	Olympic		Not an event	—	
	American	7:45.63	Larsen Jensen	July 27, 2005	Montreal
1500 meters:	**World**	14:34.56	**Grant Hackett**, Australia	July 29, 2001	Fukuoka, JPN
	Olympic	14:43.40	Grant Hackett, Australia	Aug. 21, 2004	Athens
	American	14:45.29	Larsen Jensen	Aug. 21, 2004	Athens

Backstroke

Distance		Time		Date Set	Location
50 meters:	**World**	24.80	**Thomas Rupprath**, Germany	July 27, 2003	Barcelona
	Olympic		Not an event	—	
	American	24.99	Lenny Krayzelburg	Aug. 28, 1999	Sydney
100 meters:	**World**	53.17	**Aaron Peirsol**, USA	April 2, 2005	Indianapolis
	Olympic	53.45r	Aaron Peirsol, USA	Aug. 21, 2004	Athens
	American	53.17	Peirsol (same as World)	—	
200 meters:	**World**	1:54.44	**Aaron Peirsol**, USA	Aug. 19, 2006	Victoria, B.C.
	Olympic	1:54.95	Aaron Peirsol, USA	Aug. 19, 2004	Athens
	American	1:54.44	Peirsol (same as World)	—	

Breaststroke

Distance		Time		Date Set	Location
50 meters:	**World**	27.18	**Oleg Lisogor**, Ukraine	Aug. 1, 2002	Berlin
	Olympic		Not an event	—	
	American	27.39	Ed Moses	Mar. 31, 2001	Austin, Texas
100 meters:	**World**	59.13	**Brendan Hansen**, USA	Aug. 1, 2006	Irvine, Calif.
	Olympic	1:00.01p	Brendan Hansen, USA	Aug. 14, 2004	Athens
	American	59.13	Hansen (same as World)	—	
200 meters:	**World**	2:08.50	**Brendan Hansen**, USA	Aug. 20, 2006	Victoria, B.C.
	Olympic	2:09.44	Kosuke Kitajima, Japan	Aug. 18, 2004	Athens
	American	2:08.50	Hansen (same as World)	—	

Butterfly

Distance		Time		Date Set	Location
50 meters:	**World**	22.96	**Roland Schoeman**, South Africa	July 25, 2005	Montreal
	Olympic		Not an event	—	
	American	23.12	Ian Crocker	July 25, 2005	Montreal
100 meters:	**World**	50.40	**Ian Crocker**, USA	July 30, 2005	Montreal
	Olympic	51.25	Michael Phelps, USA	Aug. 20, 2004	Athens
	American	50.40	Crocker (same as World)	—	
200 meters:	**World**	1:53.80	**Michael Phelps**, USA	Aug. 17, 2006	Victoria, B.C.
	Olympic	1:54.04	Michael Phelps, USA	Aug. 17, 2004	Athens
	American	1:53.80	Phelps (same as World)	—	

Individual Medley

Distance		Time		Date Set	Location
200 meters:	**World**	1:55.84	**Michael Phelps**, USA	Aug. 20, 2006	Victoria, B.C.
	Olympic	1:57.14	Michael Phelps, USA	Aug. 19, 2004	Athens
	American	1:55.84	Phelps (same as World)	—	
400 meters:	**World**	4:08.26	**Michael Phelps**, USA	Aug. 14, 2004	Athens
	Olympic	4:08.26	Phelps (same as World)	—	
	American	4:08.26	Phelps (same as World)	—	

Swimming (Cont.)
Relays

Distance		Time		Date Set	Location
4x100m free:	**World**	. . . . 3:12.46	**USA** (Phelps, Walker, Jones, Lezak)	Aug. 19, 2006	Victoria, B.C.
	Olympic	. . . 3:13.17	South Africa (Schoeman, Ferns, Townsend, Neethling)	Aug. 15, 2004	Athens
	American	. . 3:12.46	USA (same as World)	—	—
4x200m free:	**World**	. . . . 7:04.66	**Australia** (Hackett, Klim, Kirby, Thorpe)	July 27, 2001	Fukuoka, JPN
	Olympic	. . . 7:07.05	Australia (Thorpe, Klim, Pearson, Kirby)	Sept. 19, 2000	Sydney
	American	. .7:05.28	USA (Phelps, Lochte, Vanderkaay, Keller)	Aug. 18, 2006	Victoria, B.C
4x100m medley:	**World**	3:30.68	**USA** (Peirsol, Hansen, Crocker, Lezak)	Aug. 21, 2004	Athens
	Olympic	. . . 3:30.68	USA (same as World)	—	—
	American	. . 3:30.68	USA (same as World)	—	—

WOMEN
Freestyle

Distance		Time		Date Set	Location
50 meters:	**World**	. . . . . 24.13p	**Inge de Bruijn**, Netherlands	Sept. 22, 2000	Sydney
	Olympic	. . . . 24.13p	de Bruijn (same as World)	—	—
	American	. . . 24.63	Dara Torres	Sept. 23, 2000	Sydney
100 meters:	**World**	. . . . . 53.30	**Britta Steffen**, Germany	Aug. 2, 2006	Budapest
	Olympic	. . . . . 53.52p	Jodie Henry, Australia	Aug. 18, 2004	Athens
	American	. . . 53.58	Amanda Weir	Aug. 5, 2006	Irvine, Calif.
200 meters:	**World**	. . . . 1:56.64	**Franziska van Almsick**, Ger.	Aug. 3, 2002	Berlin
	Olympic	. . . 1:57.65	Heike Friedrich, E. Germany	Sept. 21, 1988	Seoul
	American	. . 1:57.41r	Lindsay Benko	July 24, 2003	Barcelona
400 meters:	**World**	. . . . 4:02.13	**Laure Manaudou**, FRA	Aug. 6, 2006	Budapest
	Olympic	. . 4:03.85	Janet Evans, USA	Sept. 22, 1988	Seoul
	American	. . 4:03.85	Evans (same as Olympics)	—	—
800 meters:	**World**	. . 8:16.22	**Janet Evans**, USA	Aug. 20, 1989	Tokyo
	Olympic	. . 8:19.67	Brooke Bennett, USA	Sept. 22, 2000	Sydney
	American	. . 8:16.22	Evans (same as World)	—	—
1500 meters:	**World**	. . 15:52.10	**Janet Evans**, USA	Mar. 26, 1988	Orlando
	Olympic	. . . .	Not an event	—	—
	American	. 15:52.10	Evans (same as World)	—	—

Backstroke

Distance		Time		Date Set	Location
50 meters:	**World**	. . . . . 28.19	**Janine Pietsch**, Germany	May 25, 2005	Berlin
		28.19	**Aleksandra Herasimenia**, BLR	May 31, 2006	Minsk, BLR
	Olympic	. . . .	Not an event	—	—
	American	. . . 28.35	Natalie Coughlin	June 3, 2006	Zagreb, CRO
100 meters:	**World**	. . . . . 59.58	**Natalie Coughlin**, USA	Aug. 13, 2002	Ft. Lauderdale, Fla.
	Olympic	. . . 59.68r	Natalie Coughlin, USA	Aug. 21, 2004	Athens
	American	. . . . 59.58	Coughlin (same as World)	—	—
200 meters:	**World**	. . . . 2:06.62	**Krisztina Egerszegi**, Hungary	Aug. 25, 1991	Athens
	Olympic	. . 2:07.06	Krisztina Egerszegi, Hungary	July 31, 1992	Barcelona
	American	. . 2:08.53	Natalie Coughlin	Aug. 16, 2002	Ft. Lauderdale, Fla.

Breaststroke

Distance		Time		Date Set	Location
50 meters:	**World**	. . . . . 30.31	**Jade Edmistone**, Australia	Jan. 30, 2006	Melbourne, AUS
	Olympic	. . . .	Not an event	—	—
	American	. . . . 30.85	Jessica Hardy	July 31, 2005	Montreal
100 meters:	**World**	. . . . 1:05.09	**Leisel Jones**, AUS	Mar. 20, 2006	Melbourne, AUS
	Olympic	. . 1:06.64	Luo Xuejuan, China	Aug. 16, 2004	Athens
	American	. . 1:06.20p	Jessica Hardy	July 26, 2005	Montreal
200 meters:	**World**	. . . .2:20.54	**Leisel Jones**, AUS	Feb. 1, 2006	Melbourne, AUS
	Olympic	. . 2:23.37	Amanda Beard, USA	Aug. 19, 2004	Athens
	American	. . 2:22.44	Amanda Beard	July 12, 2004	Long Beach, Calif.

Butterfly

Distance		Time		Date Set	Location
50 meters:	World	25.57	**Anna-Karin Kammerling**, SWE	July 30, 2002	Berlin
	Olympic		Not an event	—	
	American	26.00	Jenny Thompson	July 26, 2003	Barcelona
100 meters:	World	56.61	**Inge de Bruijn**, Netherlands	Sept. 17, 2000	Sydney
	Olympic	56.61	de Bruijn (same as World)		
	American	57.58p	Dara Torres	Aug. 9, 2000	Indianapolis
200 meters:	World	2:05.40	**Jessicah Schipper**, Australia	Aug. 17, 2006	Victoria, B.C.
	Olympic	2:05.88	Misty Hyman, USA	Sept. 20, 2000	Sydney
	American	2:05.88	Hyman (same as Olympic)	—	

Individual Medley

Distance		Time		Date Set	Location
200 meters:	World	2:09.72	**Wu Yanyan**, China	Oct. 17, 1997	Shanghai
	Olympic	2:10.68	Yana Klochkova, Ukraine	Sept. 19, 2000	Sydney
	American	2:10.05	Katie Hoff	Aug. 1, 2006	Irvine, Calif.
400 meters:	World	4:33.59	**Yana Klochkova**, Ukraine	Sept. 16, 2000	Sydney
	Olympic	4:33.59	Klochkova, UKR (same as World)	—	—
	American	4:34.95	Kaitlin Sandeno	Aug. 14, 2004	Athens

Relays

Distance		Time		Date Set	Location
4x100m free:	World	3:35.22	**Germany** (Dallman, Goetz, Steffen, Liebs)	July 31, 2006	Budapest
	Olympic	3:35.94	**Australia** (Mills, Lenton, Thomas, Henry)	Aug. 14, 2004	Athens
	American	3:35.80	USA (Weir, Coughlin, Joyce, Nymeyer)	Aug. 19, 2006	Victoria, B.C.
4x200m free:	World	7:50.82	**Germany** (Dallman, Samulski, Steffen, Liebs)	Aug. 3, 2006	Budapest
	Olympic	7:53.42	USA (Coughlin, Piper, Vollmer, Sandeno)	Aug. 18, 2004	Athens
	American	7:53.42	USA (same as Olympic)	—	—
4x100m medley:	World	3:56.30	**Australia** (Edington, Jones, Schipper, Lenton)	Mar. 21, 2006	Melbourne, AUS
	Olympic	3:57.32	Australia (Rooney, Jones, Thomas, Henry)	Aug. 21, 2004	Athens
	American	3:58.30	USA (Bedford, Quann, Thompson, Torres)	Sept. 23, 2000	Sydney

2006 FINA Short Course World Championships

The 8th FINA Short Course (25m) World Championships held in Shanghai, China, April 5-9, 2006. Note that (WR) indicates world record and (CR) indicates championships meet record.

MEN

Event		Time	
50m free	Duje Draganja, CRO	21.38	
100m free	Ryk Neethling, RSA	47.24	
200m free	Ryk Neethling, RSA	1:43.51	
400m free	Yury Prilukov, RUS	3:38.08	
1500m free	Yury Prilukov, RUS	14:23.92	CR
50m back	Matthew Welsh, AUS	23.53	
100m back	Matthew Welsh, AUS	51.09	
200m back	Ryan Lochte, USA	1:49.05	WR
50m breast	Oleg Lisogor, UKR	26.39	CR
100m breast	Oleg Lisogor, UKR	58.14	CR
200m breast	Vladislav Polyakov, KAZ	2:06.95	
50m fly	Matthew Welsh, AUS	23.05	
100m fly	Kaio Almeida, BRA	51.07	
200m fly	Wu Peng, CHN	1:52.36	CR
100m I.M.	Ryk Neethling, RSA	52.42	CR
200m I.M.	Ryan Lochte, USA	1:53.31	WR
400m I.M	Ryan Lochte, USA	4:02.49	CR
4x100m free	Italy	3:10.74	
4x200m free	Italy	6:59.08	CR
4x100m medley	Australia	3:27.71	

WOMEN

Event		Time	
50m free	Lisbeth Lenton, AUS	23.97	
100m free	Lisbeth Lenton, AUS	52.33	
200m free	Yang Yu, CHN	1:54.94	
400m free	Kate Ziegler, USA	4:01.79	
800m free	Anastasia Ivanenko, RUS	8:11.99	CR
50m back	Janine Pietsch, GER	27.00	CR
100m back	Janine Pietsch, GER	58.02	CR
200m back	Margaret Hoelzer, USA	2:05.29	
50m breast	Jade Edmistone, AUS	30.22	
100m breast	Tara Kirk, USA	1:05.25	CR
200m breast	Qi Hui, CHN	2:20.72	
50m fly	Therese Alshammar, SWE	25.76	
100m fly	Lisbeth Lenton, AUS	56.61	
200m fly	Jessicah Schipper, AUS	2:05.11	CR
100m I.M.	Brooke Hanson, AUS	1:00.16	
200m I.M.	Qi Hui, CHN	2:09.33	
400m I.M	Qi Hui, CHN	4:34.28	
4x100m free	Netherlands	3:33.32	WR
4x200m free	Australia	7:46.96	
4x100m medley	Australia	3:51.84	WR

WINTER SPORTS

Alpine Skiing

World Cup Champions
Top Five Standings
MEN

Overall 1. Benjamin Raich, AUT (1410 pts); 2. Aksel Lund Svindal, NOR (1006); 3. Bode Miller, USA (928); 4. Daron Rahlves, USA (903); 5. Michael Walchhofer, AUT (855).

Downhill 1. Michael Walchhofer, AUT (522 pts); 2. Fritz Strobl, AUT (491); 3. Daron Rahlves, USA (444); 4. Marco Buechel, LIE (400); 5. Bode Miller, USA (340).

Slalom 1. Giorgio Rocca, ITA (547 pts); 2. Kalle Pallander, FIN (495); 3. Benjamin Raich, AUT (410); 4. Ted Ligety, USA (396); 5. Thomas Grandi, CAN (360).

Giant Slalom 1. Benjamin Raich, AUT (481 pts); 2. Massimiliano Blardone, ITA (442); 3. Fredrik Nyberg, SWE (414); 4. Davide Simoncelli, ITA (314); 5. Kalle Palander, FIN (306). *Best USA*—Bode Miller (9th, 108 pts).

Super G 1. Aksel Lund Svindal, NOR (284 pts); 2. Hermann Maier, AUT (282); 3. Daron Rahlves, USA (269); 4. Hannes Reichelt, AUT (250); 5. Kjetil Andre Aamodt, NOR (223).

Combined 1. Benjamin Raich, AUT (345 pts); 2. Bode Miller, USA & Michael Walchhofer, AUT (200); 4. Rainer Schoenfelder, AUT (182); 5. Kjetil Andre Aamodt, NOR (162).

Nation's Cup Champion: Austria

WOMEN

Overall 1. Janica Kostelic, CRO (1970 pts); 2. Anja Paerson, SWE (1662); 3. Michaela Dorfmeister, AUT (1364); 4. Nicole Hosp, AUT (1112); 5. Lindsey Kildow, USA (1067).

Downhill 1. Michaela Dorfmeister, AUT (498 pts); 2. Lindsey Kildow, USA (410); 3. Renate Goetschl, AUT (315); 4. Janica Kostelic, CRO (300); 5. Fraenzi Aufdenblatten, SUI (272).

Slalom 1. Janica Kostelic, CRO (740 pts); 2. Marlies Schild, AUT (550); 3. Anja Paerson, SWE (485); 4. Kathrin Zettel, AUT (399); 5. Tanja Poutiainen, FIN (320). *Best USA*—Lindsey Kildow (9th, 214 pts).

Giant Slalom 1. Anja Paerson, SWE (586 pts); 2. Maria Jose Rienda, ESP (537); 3. Janica Kostelic, CRO (464); 4. Nicole Hosp, AUT (461); 5. Genevieve Simard, CAN (343). *Best USA*—Julia Mancuso (11th, 212 pts).

Super G 1. Michaela Dorfmeister, AUT (626 pts); 2. Alexandra Meissnitzer, AUT (437); 3. Nadia Styger, SUI (360); 4. Lindsey Kildow, USA (326); 5. Janica Kostelic, CRO (266).

Combined 1. Janica Kostelic, CRO (200 pts); 2. Anja Paerson, SWE (160); 3. Lindsey Kildow, USA (110); 4. Marlies Schild, AUT (105); 5. Nicole Hosp, AUT (90).

Nation's Cup Champion: Austria

2006 U.S. Alpine Championships
at Sugarloaf, Maine (Mar. 24-29)
MEN

Downhill . . . . .Bode Miller, Bretton Woods, N.H.
Slalom . . . . .Ted Ligety, Park City, Utah
Giant Slalom . . . . .Bode Miller, Bretton Woods, N.H.
Super G . . . . .Daron Rahlves, Sugar Bowl, Calif.
Combined . . . . .Ted Ligety, Park City, Utah

WOMEN

Downhill . . . . .Kirsten Clark, Raymond, Maine
Slalom . . . . .Kaylin Richardson, Edina, Minn.
Giant Slalom . . . . .Caitlin Ciccone, Bethlehem, N.H.
Super G . . . . .Stacey Cook, Truckee, Calif.
Combined . . . . Julia Mancuso, Olympic Valley, Calif.

Freestyle Skiing

World Cup Champions
MEN

Overall . . . . .Tomas Kraus, Czech Republic
Aerials . . . . .Dmitri Dashinski, Belarus
Moguls . . . . .Dale Begg-Smith, Australia
Ski Cross . . . . .Tomas Kraus, Czech Republic
Halfpipe . . . . .Kalle Leinonen, Finland

WOMEN

Overall . . . . .Ophelie David, France
Aerials . . . . .Evelyne Leu, Switzerland
Moguls . . . . Jennifer Heil, Canada
Ski Cross . . . . .Ophelie David, France
Halfpipe . . . . .Anais Caradeux, France

2006 U.S. Freestyle Championships
at Killington, Vt. (March 23-26)
MEN

Aerials . . . . Jeret Peterson, Boise, Idaho
Moguls . . . . .David Babic, Washington, Vt.
Dual Moguls . . . . .Sho Kashima, Zephyr Cove, Nev.
Halfpipe . . . . .Scott Hibbert, Canada

WOMEN

Aerials . . . . .Kate Reed, Montrose, Colo.
Moguls . . . . .Hannah Kearney, Norwich, Vt.
Dual Moguls . . . . .Hannah Kearney, Norwich, Vt.
Halfpipe . . . . .Jennifer Hudak, Park City, Utah

Snowboarding

World Cup Champions
MEN

Halfpipe . . . . Jan Michaelis, Germany
Parallel Slalom . . . . .Simon Schoch, Switzerland
Snowboardcross . . . . .Jasey Jay Anderson, Canada
Big Air .Stefan Gimpl, Austria

WOMEN

Halfpipe . . . . .Manuela Laura Pesko, Switzerland
Parallel Slalom . . . . .Daniela Meuli, Switzerland
Snowboardcross . . . . .Dominique Maltais, Canada
Big Air . . . . .Manuela Laura Pesko, Switzerland

2006 U.S. Open Snowboarding Championships
at Stratton, Vt. (Mar. 14-19)
MEN

Halfpipe . . . . .Shaun White, Calrsbad, Calif.
Quarterpipe . . . . .Danny Davis, Highland, Mich.
Slopestyle . . . . .Shaun White, Carlsbad, Calif.

WOMEN

Halfpipe . . . . .Torah Bright, Australia
Quarterpipe . . . . . .Hana Beaman, Mammoth Lakes, Calif.
Slopestyle . . . . .Hana Beaman, Mammoth Lakes, Calif.

2005 Snowboardcross Championships
at Mt. Hood Meadows, Ore. (Dec. 16)
Men . . . . .Graham Watanabe, Sun Valley, Idaho
Women . . . . .Leslee Olson, Bend, Ore.

Nordic Skiing
World Cup Champions
MEN

Cross Country - Overall . . . . . . Tobias Angerer, Germany
Cross Country - Distance . . . . . . Tobias Angerer, Germany
Cross Country - Sprint . . . . Bjoern Lind, Sweden
Nordic Combined - Overall . . . . Hannu Manninen, Finland
Nordic Combined - Sprint . . . . . Hannu Manninen, Finland
Ski Jumping - Overall . . . . . Jakub Janda, Czech Republic
Ski Jumping - Four Hills . . . . Jakub Janda, Czech Republic
& Janne Ahonen, Finland (tie)
Ski Jumping - Nordic Tourn. . . . Thomas Morgenstern, Austria

WOMEN

Cross Country - Overall . . . . Marit Bjoergen, Norway
Cross Country - Distance . . . . . . Julija Tchepalova, Russia
Cross Country - Sprint . . . . Marit Bjoergen, Norway

2006 U.S. Cross Country Championships
at Soldier Hollow, Utah (Jan. 3-10)

MEN

Sprint . . . . Chris Cook, Rhinelander, Wis.
15-k Classic . . . . Kris Freeman, Andover, N.H.
30-k Pursuit . . . . Kris Freeman, Andover, N.H.
10-k Freestyle . . . . James Southam, Anchorage, Alaska
30-k Freestyle . . . . Andrew Johnson, Greensboro, Vt.

WOMEN

Sprint . . . . Kikkan Randall, Anchorage, Alaska
10-k Classic . . . . Kikkan Randall, Anchorage, Alaska
20-k Pursuit . . . . Wendy Wagner, Park City, Utah
5-k Freestyle . . . . Kikkan Randall, Anchorage, Alaska
& Liz Stephen, Montpelier, Vt. (tie)
15-k Freestyle . . . . Rebecca Dussault, Gunnison, Colo.

2006 U.S. Ski Jumping/ Nordic Combined Championships
at Steamboat Springs, Colo. (Jan. 20-21)

MEN

Nordic Combined . . Todd Lodwick, Steamboat Springs, Colo.
Normal Hill . . . . Clint Jones, Steamboat Springs, Colo.
Large Hill . . . . Todd Lodwick, Steamboat Springs, Colo.

WOMEN

Normal Hill . . . . Lindsey Van, Park City, Utah
Large Hill . . . . Lindsey Van, Park City, Utah

Speed Skating
World Cup Champions
MEN

100 meters . . . . Yuya Oikawa, Japan
500 meters . . . . Lee Kang-Seok, Korea
1000 meters . . . . Shani Davis, United States
1500 meters . . . . Chad Hedrick, United States
5000/10,000 meters . . . . . . Chad Hedrick, United States

WOMEN

100 meters . . . . Jenny Wolf, Germany
500 meters . . . . Jenny Wolf, Germany
1000 meters . . . . Anni Friesinger, Germany
1500 meters . . . . Anni Friesinger, Germany
3000/5000 meters . . . . Cindy Klassen, Canada

2006 World Allround Championships
at Calgary, Canada (Mar. 18-19)

MEN

500 meters . . . . Shani Davis, United States
1500 meters . . . . Shani Davis, United States
5000 meters . . . . Sven Kramer, Netherlands
10,000 meters . . . . Sven Kramer, Netherlands
All-Around . . . . Shani Davis, United States

WOMEN

500 meters . . . . Cindy Klassen, Canada
1500 meters . . . . Cindy Klassen, Canada
3000 meters . . . . Cindy Klassen, Canada
5000 meters . . . . Cindy Klassen, Canada
All-Around . . . . Cindy Klassen, Canada

2006 World Short Track Championships
at Minneapolis, Minn. (March 31-April 2)

MEN

500 meters . . . . Francois-Louis Tremblay, Canada
1000 meters . . . . Ahn Hyun-Soo, Korea
1500 meters . . . . Ahn Hyun-Soo, Korea
3000 meters . . . . Charles Hamelin, Canada
5000 meter relay . . . . Canada
All-Around . . . . Ahn Hyun-Soo, Korea

WOMEN

500 meters . . . . Wang Meng, China
1000 meters . . . . Jin Sun-Yu, Korea
1500 meters . . . . Jin Sun-Yu, Korea
3000 meters . . . . Jin Sun-Yu, Korea
3000 meter relay . . . . China
All-Around . . . . Jin Sun-Yu, Korea

Figure Skating

World Championships
at Calgary, Canada (March 20-26)

Men's —1. Stephane Lambiel, Switzerland; 2. Brian Joubert, France; 3. Evan Lysacek, USA; 4. Nobunari Oda, Japan; 5. Emanuel Sandhu, Canada.

Women's —1. Kimmie Meissner, USA; 2. Fumie Suguri, Japan; 3. Sasha Cohen, USA; 4. Elena Sokolova, Russia; 5. Yukari Nakano, Japan.

Pairs —1. Pang Qing & Tong Jian, China; 2. Zhang Dan & Zhang Hao, China; 3. Maria Petrova & Alexei Tikhonov, Russia; 4. Rena Inoue & John Baldwin, USA; 5. Valerie Marcoux & Craig Buntin, Canada.

Ice Dance —1. Albena Denkova & Maxim Staviski, Bulgaria; 2. Marie-France Dubreuil & Patrice Lauzon, Canada; 3. Tanith Belbin & Benjamin Agosto, USA; 4. Margarita Drobiazko & Povilas Vanagas, Lithuania; 5. Isabelle Delobel & Olivier Schoenfelder, France.

U.S. Championships
at St. Louis, Mo. (Jan. 7-15)

Men's . . . . Johnny Weir
Women's . . . . Sasha Cohen
Pairs . . . . Rena Inoue
& John Baldwin
Ice Dance . . . . Tanith Belbin
& Benjamin Agosto

European Championships
at Lyon, France (Jan. 16-22)

Men's . . . . Evgeni Plushenko, Russia
Women's . . . . Irina Slutskaya, Russia
Pairs . . . . Tatiana Totmianina
& Maxim Marinin, Russia
Ice Dance . . . . Tatiana Navka
& Roman Kostomarov, Russia

Cycling
2006 Tour de France

The 93rd Tour de France (July 1-23) ran 20 stages, covering 3,657 kilometers (2,272 miles) starting in Strasbourg, winding through the French countryside, passing through the Netherlands, Belgium, Luxembourg, Germany and Spain and finishing in Paris on the Avenue des Champs-Elysees. American Floyd Landis, riding for Team Phonak, made up nearly eight minutes during Stage 17 to regain his lead, and held on to win the Tour in 89 hours, 39 minutes and 30 seconds.

In the following weeks, it was revealed that two of Landis' urine samples taken after Stage 17 tested positive for high testosterone levels. Tour officials immediately denounced the win and declared runner-up Oscar Pereiro of Spain to be the race's winner. At press time, however, disciplinary proceedings were ongoing and Landis still officially held the title.

	Team	Behind		Team	Behind
1 Floyd Landis, USA	Phonak	—	6 Denis Menchov, RUS	Rabobank	7:06
2 Oscar Pereiro, ESP	CEP	0:57	7 Cyril Dessel, FRA	AG2R	8:41
3 Andreas Kloden, GER	T-Mobile	1:29	8 Christophe Moreau, France	AG2R	9:37
4 Carlos Sastre, ESP	CSC	3:13	9 Haimar Zubeldia, ESP	Euskaltel	12:05
5 Cadel Evans, AUS	Davitamon-Lotto	5:08	10 Michael Rogers, AUS	T-Mobile	15:07

Other Worldwide Champions

2006 Major UCI (Union Cycliste Internationale) Road results through Sept. 17. Note that in some instances, the date shown below is the final day of that particular race.

MEN

Race	Winner	Race	Winner
Jan. 22: Tour Down Under (AUS)	Robbie McEwen, AUS	Apr. 9: Paris-Roubaix (FRA)	Fabian Cancellara, SWI
Feb. 12: Tour de Langwaki (MAS)	David George, RSA	Apr. 16: Amstel Gold Race (NED)	Frank Schleck, LUX
Feb. 12: Mediterranean Tour (FRA)	Cyril Dessel, FRA	Apr. 20: Fleche Wallonne (BEL)	Alejandro Valverde, ESP
Feb. 16: Ruta del Sol (ESP)	Carlos Garcia Quesada, ESP	Apr. 23: Liege-Bastogne-Liege (BEL)	Alejandro Valverde, ESP
Feb. 16: Tour of Valencia (ESP)	Antonio Colom, ESP	Apr. 30: Tour de Romandie (SWI)	Cadel Evans, AUS
Feb. 25: Omloop Het Volk (BEL)	Philippe Gilbert, BEL	May 7: Four Days of Dunkirk (FRA)	Roberto Petito, ITA
Mar. 12: Paris-Nice (FRA)	Floyd Landis, USA	May 21: Tour of Catalunya (ESP)	David Canada, ESP
Mar. 14: Tirreno-Adriatico (ITA)	Thomas Dekker, NED	May 28: Giro d'Italia (ITA)	Ivan Basso, ITA
Mar. 18: Milan-San Remo (ITA)	Filippo Pozzato, ITA	June 11: Dauphine Libere (FRA)	Levi Leipheimer, USA
Mar. 26: Criterium Int'l (FRA)	Ivan Basso, ITA	June 18: Tour of Switzerland (SWI)	Jan Ullrich, GER
Apr. 2: Tour de Flanders (BEL)	Tom Boonen, BEL	June 30: Vattenfall Cyclassics (GER)	Oscar Freire Gomez, ESP
Apr. 5: Gent-Wevelgem (BEL)	Thor Hushovd, NOR	Aug. 9: Tour of Germany (GER)	Jens Voigt, GER
Apr. 8: Tour of the Basque Country (ESP)	Jose Angel Gomez Marchante, ESP	Aug. 12: San Sebastian Classic (ESP)	Xavier Florencio, ESP
		Sept. 17: Tour of Spain (ESP)	Alexandre Vinokourov, KAZ

WOMEN

Race	Winner	Race	Winner
Feb. 26: Geelong Women's Tour (AUS)	Ina Teutenberg, GER	June 11: Commerce Bank Liberty Classic (USA)	Regina Schleicher, GER
Mar. 5: Wellington WC (NZ)	Sarah Ulmer, NZ	July 9: Giro d'Italia Femminile (ITA)	Edita Pucinskaite, LTU
Apr. 2: Tour de Flanders (BEL)	M. Melchers-Van Poppel, NED	Aug. 26: GP of Plouay (FRA)	Nicole Brandli, SWI
Apr. 19: Fleche Wallonne (BEL)	Nicole Cooke, GBR	Sept. 3: Rotterdam Tour (NED)	Ina Teutenberg, GER
May 8: GP Feminas Castilla y Leon (ESP)	Nicole Cooke, GBR	Sept. 10: Tour of Nuremberg (GER)	Regina Schleicher, GER
May 21: Tour de L'Aude (FRA)	Amber Neben, USA		
May 27: Montreal World Cup (CAN)	Judith Arndt, GER		

Gymnastics
2005 World Championships

The 2005 Artistic Gymnastics World Championships held at Rod Laver Arena in Melbourne, Australia, November 22-27.

MEN		WOMEN	
All-Around	Hiroyuki Tomita, Japan	All-Around	Chellsie Memmel, United States
High Bar	Aljaz Pegan, Slovenia	Vault	Cheng Fei, China
Parallel Bars	Mitja Petkovsek, Slovenia	Uneven Bars	Anastasia Liukin, United States
Vault	Marian Dragulescu, Romania	Balance Beam	Anastasia Liukin, United States
Pommel Horse	Xiao Qin, China	Floor Exercise	Alicia Sacramone, United States
Rings	Yuri Van Gelder, Netherlands		
Floor Exercise	Diego Hypolito, Brazil		

Note: The 2006 World Championships were held October 14-22 in Aarhus, Denmark. For results, see the Updates chapter beginning on page 969.

Marathons
2006 Boston Marathon

The 110th edition of the Boston Marathon was held Monday, April 17, 2006 and run, as always, from Hopkinton through Ashland, Framingham, Natick, Wellesley, Newton and Brookline to Boston, Mass. Kenya's Robert Kipkoech Cheruiyot cruised through the Newton Hills, then broke away from the leading pack in mile 21. He labored in the final miles but still broke the tape in a course record 2:07:14, edging the previous record by one second. It was Cheruiyot's second Boston win. Country-man Benjamin Maiyo placed second, but perhaps most surprising was return to prominence by American men in Boston as they place third, fourth and fifth. No American has won Boston since Greg Meyer in 1983.

In the women's division, 25-year-old Kenyan Rita Jeptoo made her move in Brookline's Coolidge Corner with about three miles to go and held on to win in 2:23:38, beating runner-up Jelena Prokopcuka of Latvia by ten seconds. It was the first trip to the United States for Jeptoo and she made it a lucrative one, earning $100,000 for the win. Cheruiyot also took home $100,000 for his win, plus an additional $25,000 for setting a new course record. **Distance:** 26.2 miles.

MEN

		Time
1	Robert Kipkoech Cheruiyot, Kenya	2:07:14*
2	Benjamin Maiyo, Kenya	2:08:21
3	Meb Keflezighi, San Diego, CA	2:09:56
4	Brian Sell, Rochester, MI	2:10:55
5	Alan Culpepper, Lafayette, CO	2:11:02

* course record

WOMEN

		Time
1	Rita Jeptoo, Kenya	2:23:38
2	Jelena Prokopcuka, Latvia	2:23:48
3	Reiko Tosa, Japan	2:24:11
4	Bruna Genovese, Italy	2:25:28
5	Kiyoko Shimahara, Japan	2:26:52

Best USA: 13th—Emily Levan, Maine, 2:37:01

World Marathon Majors

On January 23, 2006, the Boston, London, Berlin, Chicago and New York City marathons collectively launched the World Marathon Majors – a new series offering a $1 million prize purse to be split equally between the top male and female marathoners in the world. The inaugural 2006-2007 series launched at the Boston Marathon on April 17, 2006 and will conclude at the New York City Marathon on November 4, 2007.

Other 2006 Winners

Osaka
Jan. 29 Women Catherine Ndereba, KEN ...2:25:05
(No men's division)

Tokyo
Feb. 12 Men Ambesse Tolossa, ETH 2:08:58
(No women's division)

Los Angeles
Mar. 19 Men Benson Cherono, KEN 2:08:40
Women Lidiya Grigoryeva, RUS 2:25:10

Rome
Mar. 26 Men David Kipkorir, KEN 2:08:38
Women Tetyana Hladyr, UKR ...2:25:44

Paris
Apr. 9 Men Gashaw Melese, ETH 2:08:03
Women Irina Timofeyeva, RUS 2:27:19

Rotterdam
Apr. 9 Men Sammy Korir, KEN 2:06:38
Women Mindaye Gishu, ETH 2:28:30

London
Apr. 23 Men Felix Limo, KEN 2:06:39
Women Deena Kastor, USA 2:19:36

Berlin
Sept. 24 Men Haile Gebrselassie, ETH ...2:05:56
Women Gete Wami, ETH 2:21:34

Late 2005

Chicago
Oct. 9 Men Felix Limo, KEN 2:07:02
Women Deena Kastor, USA 2:21:25

New York City
Nov. 6 Men Paul Tergat, KEN 2:09:30
Women Jelena Prokopcuka, LAT 2:24:41

Tokyo Women's
Nov. 20 Women Naoko Takahashi, JPN ...2:24:39

Fukuoka
Dec. 4 Men Dmytro Baranovskyy, UKR ...2:08:29
(No women's division)

Rowing
2006 World Championships
at Eton, Great Britain (August 20-27)

MEN

Eights	Germany, 5:21.85
Coxed Pairs	Serbia & Montenegro, 6:51.27
Coxed Fours	Germany, 6:05.77
Coxless Pairs	Australia, 6:18.00
Coxless Fours	Great Britain, 5:43.75
Single Sculls	Mahe Drysdale, New Zealand, 6:35.40
Double Sculls	France, 6:07.60
Quad Sculls	Poland, 5:38.99

WOMEN

Eights	United States, 5:55.50
Coxless Pairs	Canada, 6:54.68
Coxless Fours	Australia, 6:25.35
Single Sculls	Ekaterina Karsten-Khodotovich, Belarus, 7:11.02
Double Sculls	Australia, 6:47.67
Quad Sculls	Russia, 6:11.99

1882-2006
Through the Years

ESPN SPORTS ALMANAC

TRACK & FIELD

IAAF World Championships

While the Summer Olympics have served as the unofficial world outdoor championships for track and field throughout the centuries, a separate World Championship meet was started in 1983 by the International Amateur Athletic Federation (IAAF). The meet was held every four years from 1983-91, but began an every-other-year cycle in 1993. World Championship sites include Helsinki (1983, 2005), Rome (1987), Tokyo (1991), Stuttgart (1993), Göteborg, Sweden (1995), Athens (1997), Seville, Spain (1999), Edmonton (2001) and Paris (2003). Looking forward, the Championships will be held in Osaka, Japan (2007) and Berlin (2009). Note that (WR) indicates world record and (CR) indicates championship meet record.

MEN

Multiple gold medals (including relays): Michael Johnson (9); Carl Lewis (8); Sergey Bubka (6); Maurice Greene and Lars Riedel (5); Hicham El Guerrouj, Haile Gebrselassie, Allen Johnson, Ivan Pedroso, Antonio Pettigrew and Calvin Smith (4); Donovan Bailey, Tomas Dvorak, Greg Foster, John Godina, Werner Gunthor, Wilson Kipketer, Moses Kiptanui, Robert Korzeniowski, Dennis Mitchell, Noureddine Morceli, Dan O'Brien, Butch Reynolds and Jan Zelezny (3); Andrey Abduvaliyev, Virgilijus Alekena, Abel Anton, Kenenisa Bekele, Derrick Brew, Leroy Burrell, John Capel, Andre Cason, Stephane Diagana, Maurizio Damilano, Ladji Doucoure, Jon Drummond, Jonathan Edwards, Justin Gatlin, Jaouad Gharib, Colin Jackson, Ismael Kirui, Billy Konchellah, Sergey Litvinov, Tim Montgomery, Edwin Moses, Dwight Phillips, Mike Powell, Rashid Ramzi, Felix Sanchez, Saif Saaeed Shaheen, Javier Sotomayor, Angelo Taylor, Ivan Tikhon, Jeremy Wariner, Bernard Williams and Jerome Young (2).

100 Meters

Year		Time	
1983	Carl Lewis, USA	10.07	
1987	Carl Lewis, USA	9.93	
1991	Carl Lewis, USA	9.86	**WR**
1993	Linford Christie, GBR	9.87	
1995	Donovan Bailey, CAN	9.97	
1997	Maurice Greene, USA	9.86	
1999	Maurice Greene, USA	9.80	**CR**
2001	Maurice Greene, USA	9.82	
2003	Kim Collins, SKN	10.07	
2005	Justin Gatlin, USA	9.88	

Note: Ben Johnson was the original winner in 1987, but was stripped of his title and world record time (9.83) following his 1989 admission of drug taking.

200 Meters

Year		Time	
1983	Calvin Smith, USA	20.14	
1987	Calvin Smith, USA	20.16	
1991	Michael Johnson, USA	20.01	
1993	Frank Fredericks, NAM	19.85	
1995	Michael Johnson, USA	19.79	**CR**
1997	Ato Boldon, USA	20.04	
1999	Maurice Greene, USA	19.90	
2001	Konstantinos Kenteris, GRE	20.04	
2003	John Capel, USA	20.30	
2005	Justin Gatlin, USA	20.04	

400 Meters

Year		Time	
1983	Bert Cameron, JAM	45.05	
1987	Thomas Schonlebe, E. Ger	44.33	
1991	Antonio Pettigrew, USA	44.57	
1993	Michael Johnson, USA	43.65	
1995	Michael Johnson, USA	43.39	
1997	Michael Johnson, USA	44.12	
1999	Michael Johnson, USA	43.18	**WR**
2001	Avard Moncur, BAH	44.64	
2003	Jerome Young, USA	44.50	
2005	Jeremy Wariner, USA	43.93	

800 Meters

Year		Time	
1983	Willi Wülbeck, W. Ger	1:43.65	
1987	Billy Konchellah, KEN	1:43.06	**CR**
1991	Billy Konchellah, KEN	1:43.99	
1993	Paul Ruto, KEN	1:44.71	
1995	Wilson Kipketer, DEN	1:45.08	
1997	Wilson Kipketer, DEN	1:43.38	
1999	Wilson Kipketer, DEN	1:43.30	
2001	Andre Bucher, SWI	1:43.70	
2003	Djabir Said-Guerni, ALG	1:44.81	
2005	Rashid Ramzi, BRN	1:44.24	

1500 Meters

Year		Time	
1983	Steve Cram, GBR	3:41.59	
1987	Abdi Bile, SOM	3:36.80	
1991	Noureddine Morceli, ALG	3:32.84	
1993	Noureddine Morceli, ALG	3:34.24	
1995	Noureddine Morceli, ALG	3:33.73	
1997	Hicham El Guerrouj, MOR	3:35.83	
1999	Hicham El Guerrouj, MOR	3:27.65	**CR**
2001	Hicham El Guerrouj, MOR	3:30.68	
2003	Hicham El Guerrouj, MOR	3:31.77	
2005	Rashid Ramzi, BRN	3:37.88	

5000 Meters

Year		Time	
1983	Eammon Coghlan, IRL	13:28.53	
1987	Said Aouita, MOR	13:26.44	
1991	Yobes Ondieki, KEN	13:14.45	
1993	Ismael Kirui, KEN	13:02.75	
1995	Ismael Kirui, KEN	13:16.77	
1997	Daniel Komen, KEN	13:07.38	
1999	Salah Hissou, MOR	12:58.13	
2001	Richard Limo, KEN	13:00.77	
2003	Eliud Kipchoge, KEN	12:52.79	**CR**
2005	Benjamin Limo, KEN	13:32.55	

10,000 Meters

Year		Time	
1983	Alberto Cova, ITA	28:01.04	
1987	Paul Kipkoech, KEN	27:38.63	
1991	Moses Tanui, KEN	27:38.74	
1993	Haile Gebrselassie, ETH	27:46.02	
1995	Haile Gebrselassie, ETH	27:12.95	
1997	Haile Gebrselassie, ETH	27:24.58	
1999	Haile Gebrselassie, ETH	27:57.27	
2001	Charles Kamathi, KEN	27:53.25	
2003	Kenenisa Bekele, ETH	26:49.57	CR
2005	Kenenisa Bekele, ETH	27:08.33	

Marathon

Year		Time	
1983	Rob de Castella, AUS	2:10:03	
1987	Douglas Wakiihuri, KEN	2:11:48	
1991	Hiromi Taniguchi, JPN	2:14:57	
1993	Mark Plaatjes, USA	2:13:57	
1995	Martin-Fiz, SPA	2:11:41	
1997	Abel Anton, SPA	2:13:16	
1999	Abel Anton, SPA	2:13:36	
2001	Gezahegne Abera, ETH	2:12:42	
2003	Jaouad Gharib, MOR	2:08:31	CR
2005	Jaouad Gharib, MOR	2:10:10	

110-Meter Hurdles

Year		Time	
1983	Greg Foster, USA	.13.42	
1987	Greg Foster, USA	.13.21	
1991	Greg Foster, USA	.13.06	
1993	Colin Jackson, GBR	.12.91	WR
1995	Allen Johnson, USA	.13.00	
1997	Allen Johnson, USA	.12.93	
1999	Colin Jackson, GBR	.13.04	
2001	Allen Johnson, USA	.13.04	
2003	Allen Johnson, USA	.13.12	
2005	Ladji Doucoure, FRA	.13.07	

400-Meter Hurdles

Year		Time	
1983	Edwin Moses, USA	.47.50	
1987	Edwin Moses, USA	.47.46	
1991	Samuel Matete, ZAM	.47.64	
1993	Kevin Young, USA	.47.18	CR
1995	Derrick Adkins, USA	.47.98	
1997	Stephane Diagana, FRA	.47.70	
1999	Fabrizio Mori, ITA	.47.72	
2001	Felix Sanchez, DOM	.47.49	
2003	Felix Sanchez, DOM	.47.25	
2005	Bershawn Jackson, USA	.47.30	

3000-Meter Steeplechase

Year		Time	
1983	Patriz Ilg, W. Ger	.8:15.06	
1987	Francesco Panetta, ITA	.8:08.57	
1991	Moses Kiptanui, KEN	.8:12.59	
1993	Moses Kiptanui, KEN	.8:06.36	
1995	Moses Kiptanui, KEN	.8:04.16	CR
1997	Wilson B. Kipketer, KEN	.8:05.84	
1999	Christopher Koskei, KEN	.8:11.76	
2001	Reuben Kosgei, KEN	.8:15.16	
2003	Saif Saaeed Shaheen, QAT	.8:04.39	
2005	Saif Saaeed Shaheen, QAT	.8:13.31	

4 x 100-Meter Relay

Year		Time	
1983	United States	.37.86	WR
1987	United States	.37.90	
1991	United States	.37.50	WR
1993	United States	.37.48	CR
1995	Canada	.38.31	
1997	Canada	.37.86	
1999	United States	.37.59	
2001	United States	.37.96	
2003	United States	.38.06	
2005	France	.38.08	

4 x 400-Meter Relay

Year		Time	
1983	Soviet Union	3:00.79	
1987	United States	2:57.29	
1991	Great Britain	2:57.53	
1993	United States	2:54.29	WR
1995	United States	2:57.32	
1997	United States	2:56.47	
1999	United States	2:56.45	
2001	United States	2:57.54	
2003	France	2:58.88*	
2005	United States	2:56.91	

*The United States was stripped of its 2003 gold after lead runner Calvin Harrison's second doping violation. As a result, Tyree Washington, Derrick Brew and Jerome Young also lost their gold.

20-Kilometer Walk

Year		Time	
1983	Ernesto Canto, MEX	1:20.49	
1987	Maurizio Damilano, ITA	1:20.45	
1991	Maurizio Damilano, ITA	1:19.37	
1993	Valentin Massana, SPA	1:22.31	
1995	Michele Didoni, ITA	1:19.59	
1997	Daniel Garcia, MEX	1:21:43	
1999	Ilya Markov, RUS	1:23:34	
2001	Roman Rasskazov, RUS	1:20:31	
2003	Jefferson Perez, ECU	1:17:21	WR
2005	Jefferson Perez, ECU	1:18:35	

50-Kilometer Walk

Year		Time	
1983	Ronald Weigel, E. Ger	3:43:08	
1987	Hartwig Gauder, E. Ger	3:40:53	
1991	Aleksandr Potashov, USSR	3:53:09	
1993	Jesus Angel Garcia, SPA	3:41:41	
1995	Valentin Kononen, FIN	3:43.42	
1997	Robert Korzeniowski, POL	3:44:46	
1999	Ivano Brugnetti, ITA	3:47:54*	
2001	Robert Korzeniowski, POL	3:42:08	
2003	Robert Korzeniowski, POL	3:36:03	WR
2005	Sergey Kirdyapkin, RUS	3:38:08	

* Original winner German Skurygin, RUS, was stripped of his 1999 title after testing positive for a banned substance.

High Jump

Year		Height	
1983	Gennedy Avdeyenko, USSR	7- 7¼	
1987	Patrik Sjoberg, SWE	7- 9¾	
1991	Charles Austin, USA	7- 9¾	
1993	Javier Sotomayor, CUB	7-10½	CR
1995	Troy Kemp, BAH	7- 9¼	
1997	Javier Sotomayor, CUB	7- 9¼	
1999	Vyacheslav Voronin, RUS	7- 9¼	
2001	Martin Buss, GER	7- 8¾	
2003	Jacques Freitag, RSA	7- 8½	
2005	Yuriy Krymarenko, UKR	7- 7¼	

Track & Field (Cont.)

Pole Vault

Year		Height	
1983	Sergey Bubka, USSR	18- 8¼	
1987	Sergey Bubka, USSR	19- 2¼	
1991	Sergey Bubka, USSR	19- 6¼	
1993	Sergey Bubka, UKR	19- 8¼	
1995	Sergey Bubka, UKR	19- 5	
1997	Sergey Bubka, UKR	19- 8½	
1999	Maksim Tarasov, RUS	19- 9	
2001	Dmitri Markov, AUS	19-10¼	CR
2003	Giuseppe Gibilisco, ITA	19- 4¼	
2005	Rens Blom, NED	19- 0½	

Long Jump

Year		Distance	
1983	Carl Lewis, USA	28- 0¾	
1987	Carl Lewis, USA	28- 0¼	
1991	Mike Powell, USA	29- 4½	WR
1993	Mike Powell, USA	28- 2¼	
1995	Ivan Pedroso, CUB	28- 6½	
1997	Ivan Pedroso, CUB	27- 7½	
1999	Ivan Pedroso, CUB	28- 1	
2001	Ivan Pedroso, CUB	27- 6¾	
2003	Dwight Phillips, USA	27- 3¾	
2005	Dwight Phillips, USA	28- 2¾	

Triple Jump

Year		Distance	
1983	Zdzislaw Hoffmann, POL	57- 2	
1987	Khristo Markov, BUL	58- 9	
1991	Kenny Harrison, USA	58- 4	
1993	Mike Conley, USA	58- 7¼	
1995	Jonathan Edwards, GBR	60- 0¼	WR
1997	Yoelvis Quesada, CUB	58- 6¾	
1999	Charles Michael Friedek, GER	57- 8½	
2001	Jonathan Edwards, GBR	58- 9½	
2003	Christian Olsson, SWE	58- 1¾	
2005	Walter Davis, USA	57- 7¾	

Shot Put

Year		Distance	
1983	Edward Sarul, POL	70- 2¼	
1987	Werner Günthör SWI	72-11¼	CR
1991	Werner Günthör, SWI	71- 1¼	
1993	Werner Günthör, SWI	72- 1	
1995	John Godina, USA	70- 5¼	
1997	John Godina, USA	70- 4¼	
1999	C.J. Hunter, USA	71- 6	
2001	John Godina, USA	71- 9	
2003	Andrei Mikhnevich, BLR	71- 2	
2005	Adam Nelson, USA	71- 3½	

Discus

Year		Distance	
1983	Imrich Bugar, CZE	222- 2	
1987	Jurgen Schult, E. Ger	225- 6	
1991	Lars Riedel, GER	217- 2	
1993	Lars Riedel, GER	222- 2	
1995	Lars Riedel, GER	225- 7	
1997	Lars Riedel, GER	224-10	
1999	Anthony Washington, USA	226- 7	
2001	Lars Riedel, GER	228- 9	
2003	Virgilijus Alekna, LIT	228- 7	
2005	Virgilijus Alekna, LIT	230- 2	CR

Hammer Throw

Year		Distance	
1983	Sergey Litvinov, USSR	271- 3	
1987	Sergey Litvinov, USSR	272- 6	
1991	Yuri Sedykh, USSR	268- 0	
1993	Andrey Abduvaliyev, TAJ	267-10	
1995	Andrey Abduvaliyev, TAJ	267- 7	
1997	Heinz Weis, GER	268- 4	
1999	Karsten Kobs, GER	263- 3	
2001	Szymon Ziolkowski, POL	273- 7	
2003	Ivan Tikhon, BLR	272- 5	
2005	Ivan Tikhon, BLR	275- 2	CR

Javelin

Year		Distance	
1983	Detlef Michel, E. Ger	293-7	
1987	Seppo Raty, FIN	274-1	
1991	Kimmo Kinnunen, FIN	297-11	
1993	Jan Zelezny, CZR	282-1	
1995	Jan Zelezny, CZR	293-11	
1997	Marius Corbett, S. Afr.	290-0	
1999	Aki Parviainen, FIN	293-8	
2001	Jan Zelezny, CZR	304- 5	CR
2003	Sergey Makarov, RUS	280- 3	
2005	Andrus Varnik, EST	286- 0	

Decathlon

Year		Points	
1983	Daley Thompson, GBR	8714	
1987	Torsten Voss, E. Ger	8680	
1991	Dan O'Brien, USA	8812	
1993	Dan O'Brien, USA	8817	
1995	Dan O'Brien, USA	8695	
1997	Tomas Dvorak, CZR	8837	
1999	Tomas Dvorak, CZR	8744	
2001	Tomas Dvorak, CZR	8902	CR
2003	Tom Pappas, USA	8750	
2005	Bryan Clay, USA	8732	

WOMEN

Multiple gold medals (including relays): Gail Devers (5); Jearl Miles Clark, Jackie Joyner-Kersee and Marion Jones (4); Tirunesh Dibaba, Tatyana Samolenko Dorovskikh, Silke Gladisch, Marita Koch, Astrid Kumbernuss, Maria Mutola, Merlene Ottey, Gabriela Szabo and Gwen Torrence (3); Me'Lisa Barber, Hassiba Boulmerka, Sabine Braun, Olga Bryzgina, Hestrie Cloete, Mary Decker, Franka Dietzsch, Stacy Dragila, Heike Daute Drechsler, Lyudmila Narozhilenko Enquist, Cathy Freeman, Chryste Gaines, Trine Hattestad, Martina Optiz Hellmann, Olimpiada Ivanova, Stefka Kostadinova, Katrin Krabbe, Jarmila Kratochvilova, Tatyana Lebedeva, Mirela Manjani, Fiona May, Osleidys Menendez, Inger Miller, Yipsi Moreno, Marie-José Pérec, Yuliya Pechonkina, Zhanna Pintusevich-Block, Ana Quirot, Tatyana Tomashova and Huang Zhihong (2).

100 Meters

Year		Time	
1983	Marlies Gohr, E. Ger	10.97	
1987	Silke Gladisch, E. Ger	10.90	
1991	Katrin Krabbe, GER	10.99	
1993	Gail Devers, USA	10.81	
1995	Gwen Torrence, USA	10.85	
1997	Marion Jones, USA	10.83	
1999	Marion Jones, USA	10.70	CR
2001	Zhanna Pintusevich-Block, UKR	10.82	
2003	Torri Edwards, USA	10.93*	
2005	Lauryn Williams, USA	10.93	

*Original winner Kelli White, USA, was stripped of her medal.

200 Meters

Year		Time	
1983	Marita Koch, E. Ger	22.13	
1987	Silke Gladisch, E. Ger	21.74	CR
1991	Katrin Krabbe, GER	22.09	
1993	Merlene Ottey, JAM	21.98	
1995	Merlene Ottey, JAM	22.12	
1997	Zhanna Pintusevich, UKR	22.32	
1999	Inger Miller, USA	21.77	
2001	Marion Jones, USA	22.39	
2003	Anastasiya Kapachinskaya, RUS	22.38*	
2005	Allyson Felix, USA	22.16	

*Original winner Kelli White, USA, was stripped of her medal.

400 Meters

Year		Time	
1983	Jarmila Kratochvilova, CZE	.47.99	WR
1987	Olga Bryzgina, USSR	.49.38	
1991	Marie-José Pérec, FRA	.49.13	
1993	Jearl Miles, USA	.49.82	
1995	Marie-José Pérec, FRA	.49.28	
1997	Cathy Freeman, AUS	.49.77	
1999	Cathy Freeman, AUS	.49.67	
2001	Amy Mbacke Thiam, SEN	.49.86	
2003	Ana Guevara, MEX	.48.89	
2005	Tonique Williams-Darling, BAH	.49.55	

800 Meters

Year		Time	
1983	Jarmila Kratochvilova, CZE	.1:54.68	CR
1987	Sigrun Wodars, E. Ger	.1:55.26	
1991	Lilia Nurutdinova, USSR	.1:57.50	
1993	Maria Mutola, MOZ	.1:55.43	
1995	Ana Quirot, CUB	.1:56.11	
1997	Ana Quirot, CUB	.1:57.14	
1999	Ludmila Formanova, CZR	.1:56.68	
2001	Maria Mutola, MOZ	.1:57.17	
2003	Maria Mutola, MOZ	.1:59.89	
2005	Zulia Calatayud, CUB	.1:58.82	

1500 Meters

Year		Time	
1983	Mary Decker, USA	.4:00.90	
1987	Tatiana Samolenko, USSR	.3:58.56	
1991	Hassiba Boulmerka, ALG	.4:02.21	
1993	Liu Dong, CHN	.4:00.50	
1995	Hassiba Boulmerka, ALG	.4:02.42	
1997	Carla Sacramento, POR	.4:04.24	
1999	Svetlana Masterkova, RUS	.3:59.53	
2001	Gabriela Szabo, ROM	.4:00.57	
2003	Tatyana Tomashova, RUS	.3:58.52	CR
2005	Tatyana Tomashova, RUS	.4:00.35	

5000 Meters

Held as 3000-meter race from 1983-93

Year		Time	
1983	Mary Decker, USA	.8:34.62	
1987	Tatyana Samolenko, USSR	.8:38.73	
1991	T. Samolenko Dorovskikh, USSR	.8:35.82	
1993	Qu Yunxia, CHN	.8:28.71	
1995	Sonia O'Sullivan, IRL	.14:46.47	
1997	Gabriela Szabo, ROM	.14:57.68	
1999	Gabriela Szabo, ROM	.14:41.82	
2001	Olga Yegorova, RUS	.15:03.39	
2003	Tirunesh Dibaba, ETH	.14:51.72	
2005	Tirunesh Dibaba, ETH	.14:38.59	CR

10,000 Meters

Year		Time	
1983	Not held		
1987	Ingrid Kristiansen, NOR	.31:05.85	
1991	Liz McColgan, GBR	.31:14.31	
1993	Wang Junxia, CHN	.30:49.30	
1995	Fernanda Ribeiro, POR	.31:04.99	
1997	Sally Barsosio, KEN	.31:32.92	
1999	Gete Wami, ETH	.30:24.56	
2001	Derartu Tulu, ETH	.31:48.81	
2003	Berhane Adere, ETH	.30:04.18	CR
2005	Tirunesh Dibaba, ETH	.30:24.02	

3000-Meter Steeplechase

Year		Time
2005	Docus Inzikuru, UGA	.9:18.24

Marathon

Year		Time	
1983	Grete Waitz, NOR	.2:28:09	
1987	Rose Mota, POR	.2:25:17	
1991	Wanda Panfil, POL	.2:29:53	
1993	Junko Asari, JPN	.2:30:03	
1995	Manuela Machado, POR	.2:25:39	
1997	Hiromi Suzuki, JPN	.2:29:48	
1999	Jong Song-Ok, N. Kor	.2:26:59	
2001	Lidia Simon, ROM	.2:26:01	
2003	Catherine Ndereba, KEN	.2:23:55	
2005	Paula Radcliffe, GBR	.2:20:57	CR

100-Meter Hurdles

Year		Time	
1983	Bettine Jahn, E. Ger	.12.35^W	
1987	Ginka Zagorcheva, BUL	.12.34	CR
1991	Lyudmila Narozhilenko, USSR	.12.59	
1993	Gail Devers, USA	.12.46	
1995	Gail Devers, USA	.12.68	
1997	Ludmila Enquist, SWE	.12.50	
1999	Gail Devers, USA	.12.37	
2001	Anjanette Kirkland, USA	.12.42	
2003	Perdita Felicien, CAN	.12.53	
2005	Michelle Perry, USA	.12.66	

^{W} indicates wind-aided.

400-Meter Hurdles

Year		Time	
1983	Yekaterina Fesenko, USSR	.54.14	
1987	Sabine Busch, E. Ger	.53.62	
1991	Tatiana Ledovskaya, USSR	.53.11	
1993	Sally Gunnell, GBR	.52.74	WR
1995	Kim Batten, USA	.52.61	WR
1997	Nezha Bidouane, MOR	.52.97	
1999	Daima Pernia, CUB	.52.89	
2001	Nezha Bidouane, MOR	.53.34	
2003	Jana Pittman, AUS	.53.22	
2005	Yuliya Pechonkina, RUS	.52.90	

4 x 100-Meter Relay

Year		Time	
1983	East Germany	.41.76	
1987	United States	.41.58	
1991	Jamaica	.41.94	
1993	Russia	.41.49	
1995	United States	.42.12	
1997	United States	.41.47	CR
1999	Bahamas	.41.92	
2001	Germany	.42.32*	
2003	France	.41.78	
2005	United States	.41.78	

*The United States was stripped of its 2001 gold after lead runner Kelli White tested positive for a stimulant. As a result, Chryste Gaines, Inger Miller and Marion Jones also lost their gold.

4 x 400-Meter Relay

Year		Time	
1983	East Germany	.3:19.73	
1987	East Germany	.3:18.63	
1991	Soviet Union	.3:18.43	
1993	United States	.3:16.71	CR
1995	United States	.3:22.39	
1997	Germany	.3:20.92	
1999	Russia	.3:21.98	
2001	Jamaica	.3:20.65	
2003	United States	.3:22.63	
2005	Russia	.3:20.95	

Track & Field (Cont.)

20-Kilometer Walk
Held as 10-Kilometer race from 1987-97

Year		Time	
1983	Not held		
1987	Irina Strakhova, USSR	.44:12	
1991	Alina Ivanova, USSR	.42:57	
1993	Sari Essayah, FIN	.42:59	
1995	Irina Stankina, RUS	.42:13	
1997	Anna Sidoti, ITA	.42:55	
1999	Hongyu Liu, CHN	1:30:50	
2001	Olimpiada Ivanova, RUS	1:27:48	
2003	Yelena Nikolayeva, RUS	1:26:52	
2005	Olimpiada Ivanova, RUS	1:25:41	WR

High Jump

Year		Height	
1983	Tamara Bykova, USSR	.6- 7	
1987	Stefka Kostadinova, BUL	.6-10¼	WR
1991	Heike Henkel, GER	.6- 8¾	
1993	Ioamnet Quintero, CUB	.6- 6¼	
1995	Stefka Kostadinova, BUL	.6- 7	
1997	Hanne Haugland, NOR	.6- 6¼	
1999	Inga Babakova, UKR	.6- 6¼	
2001	Hestrie Cloete, RSA	.6- 6¾	
2003	Hestrie Cloete, RSA	.6- 9	
2005	Kajsa Bergqvist, SWE	.6- 7½	

Pole Vault

Year		Height	
1999	Stacy Dragila, USA	.15- 1	
2001	Stacy Dragila, USA	.15- 7	
2003	Svetlana Feofanova, RUS	.15- 7	
2005	Yelena Isinbayeva, RUS	16-5¼	WR

Long Jump

Year		Distance	
1983	Heike Daute, E. Ger	.23-10¼ᵂ	
1987	Jackie Joyner-Kersee, USA	.24- 1¾	CR
1991	Jackie Joyner-Kersee, USA	.24- 0¼	
1993	Heike Drechsler, GER	.23- 4	
1995	Fiona May, ITA	22-10¾ᵂ	
1997	Lyudmila Galkina, RUS	.23- 1¾	
1999	Niurka Montalvo, SPA	.23- 2	
2001	Fiona May, ITA	.23- 0½	
2003	Eunice Barber, FRA	22-11¼	
2005	Tianna Madison, USA	.22- 7¼	

ᵂ indicates wind-aided.

Triple Jump

Year		Distance	
1993	Ana Biryukova, RUS	46- 6¼	
1995	Inessa Kravets, UKR	50- 10¾	WR
1997	Sarka Kasparkova, CZE	49- 10½	
1999	Paraskevi Tsiamita, GRE	48- 10	
2001	Tatyana Lebedeva, RUS	50- 0½	
2003	Tatyana Lebedeva, RUS	49- 9¾	
2005	Trecia Smith, JAM	49- 7	

Shot Put

Year		Distance	
1983	Helena Fibingerova, CZE	.69- 0	
1987	Natalia Lisovskaya, USSR	.69- 8	CR
1991	Huang Zhihong, CHN	.68- 4	
1993	Huang Zhihong, CHN	.67- 6	
1995	Astrid Kumbernuss, GER	.69- 7½	
1997	Astrid Kumbernuss, GER	.67- 11½	
1999	Astrid Kumbernuss, GER	.65- 1½	
2001	Yanina Korolchik, BLR	.67- 7½	
2003	Svetlana Krivelyova, RUS	.67- 8¼	
2005	Nadezhda Ostapchuk, BLR	.67- 3½	

Discus

Year		Distance	
1983	Martina Opitz, E. Ger	.226- 2	
1987	Martina Opitz Hellmann, E. Ger	.235- 0	CR
1991	Tsvetanka Khristova, BUL	.233- 0	
1993	Olga Burova, RUS	.221- 1	
1995	Ellina Zvereva, BLR	.225- 2	
1997	Beatrice Faumuina, NZE	.219- 3	
1999	Franka Dietzsch, GER	.223- 6	
2001	Natalya Sadova, RUS	.224-11	
2003	Irina Yatchenko, BLR	.220-10	
2005	Franka Dietzsch, GER	.218- 4	

Hammer Throw

Year		Distance	
1999	Mihaela Melinte, ROM	.246-8¾	CR
2001	Yipsi Moreno, CUB	.231- 9	
2003	Yipsi Moreno, CUB	.240- 7	
2005	Olga Kuzenkova, RUS	.246- 5	

Javelin

Year		Distance	
1983	Tiina Lillak, FIN	.232- 4	
1987	Fatima Whitbread, GBR	.251- 5	CR
1991	Xu Demei, CHN	.225- 8	
1993	Trine Hattestad, NOR	.227- 0	
1995	Natalya Shikolenko, BLR	.221- 8	
1997	Trine Hattestad, NOR	.225- 8	
1999	Mirela Manjani-Tzelili, GRE	.220- 1	
2001	Osleidys Menendez, CUB	.228- 1	
2003	Mirela Manjani, GRE	.218- 3	
2005	Osleidys Menendez, CUB	.235- 3	WR

Heptathlon

Year		Points	
1983	Ramona Neubert, E. Ger	6770	
1987	Jackie Joyner-Kersee, USA	7128	CR
1991	Sabine Braun, GER	6672	
1993	Jackie Joyner-Kersee, USA	6837	
1995	Ghada Shouaa, SYR	6651	
1997	Sabine Braun, GER	6739	
1999	Eunice Barber, FRA	6861	
2001	Yelena Prokhorova, RUS	6694	
2003	Carolina Kluft, SWE	7001	
2005	Carolina Kluft, SWE	6887	

World Cross Country Championships
MEN

Multiple winners: Kenenisa Bekele, John Ngugi and Paul Tergat (5); Carlos Lopes (3); Mohammed Mourhit, Khalid Skah, William Sigei, John Treacy and Craig Virgin (2).

Year		Year		Year	
1973	Pekka Paivarinta, Finland	1980	Craig Virgin, USA	1987	John Ngugi, Kenya
1974	Eric DeBeck, Belgium	1981	Craig Virgin, USA	1988	John Ngugi, Kenya
1975	Ian Stewart, Scotland	1982	Mohammed Kedir, Ethiopia	1989	John Ngugi, Kenya
1976	Carlos Lopes, Portugal	1983	Bekele Debele, Ethiopia	1990	Khalid Skah, Morocco
1977	Leon Schots, Belgium	1984	Carlos Lopes, Portugal	1991	Khalid Skah, Morocco
1978	John Treacy, Ireland	1985	Carlos Lopes, Portugal	1992	John Ngugi, Kenya
1979	John Treacy, Ireland	1986	John Ngugi, Kenya	1993	William Sigei, Kenya

Year		Year		Year	
1994	William Sigei, Kenya	1999	Paul Tergat, Kenya	2004	Kenenisa Bekele, Ethiopia
1995	Paul Tergat, Kenya	2000	Mohammed Mourhit, Belgium	2005	Kenenisa Bekele, Ethiopia
1996	Paul Tergat, Kenya	2001	Mohammed Mourhit, Belgium	2006	Kenenisa Bekele, Ethiopia
1997	Paul Tergat, Kenya	2002	Kenenisa Bekele, Ethiopia		
1998	Paul Tergat, Kenya	2003	Kenenisa Bekele, Ethiopia		

WOMEN

Multiple winners: Grete Waitz (5); Lynn Jennings and Derartu Tulu (3); Zola Budd, Paola Cacchi, Tirunesh Dibaba, Maricica Puica, Paula Radcliffe, Annette Sergent, Carmen Valero and Gete Wami (2).

Year		Year		Year	
1973	Paola Cacchi, Italy	1985	Zola Budd, England	1997	Derartu Tulu, Ethiopia
1974	Paola Cacchi, Italy	1986	Zola Budd, England	1998	Sonia O'Sullivan, Ireland
1975	Julie Brown, USA	1987	Annette Sergent, France	1999	Gete Wami, Ethiopia
1976	Carmen Valero, Spain	1988	Ingrid Kristiansen, Norway	2000	Derartu Tulu, Ethiopia
1977	Carmen Valero, Spain	1989	Annette Sergent, France	2001	Paula Radcliffe, Gr. Britain
1978	Grete Waitz, Norway	1990	Lynn Jennings, USA	2002	Paula Radcliffe, Gr. Britain
1979	Grete Waitz, Norway	1991	Lynn Jennings, USA	2003	Werknesh Kidane, Ethiopia
1980	Grete Waitz, Norway	1992	Lynn Jennings, USA	2004	Benita Johnson, Australia
1981	Grete Waitz, Norway	1993	Albertina Dias, Portugal	2005	Tirunesh Dibaba, Ethiopia
1982	Maricica Puica, Romania	1994	Helen Chepngeno, Kenya	2006	Tirunesh Dibaba, Ethiopia
1983	Grete Waitz, Norway	1995	Derartu Tulu, Ethiopia		
1984	Maricica Puica, Romania	1996	Gete Wami, Ethiopia		

Marathons
Boston

America's oldest regularly contested foot race, the Boston Marathon is held on Patriots' Day every April. It has been run at four different distances: 24 miles, 1232 yards (1897-1923); 26 miles, 209 yards (1924-26); 26 miles, 385 yards (1927-52, since 1957); 25 miles, 958 yards (1953-56).

MEN

Multiple winners: Clarence DeMar (7); Gerard Cote and Bill Rodgers (4); Ibrahim Hussein, Cosmas Ndeti, Eino Oksanen and Leslie Pawson (3); Tarzan Brown, Jim Caffrey, Robert Kipkoech Cheruiyot, John A. Kelley, John Miles, Toshihiko Seko, Geoff Smith, Moses Tanui and Aurele Vandendriessche (2).

Year		Time	Year		Time
1897	John McDermott, New York	2:55:10	1933	Leslie Pawson, Rhode Island	2:31:01
1898	Ronald McDonald, Massachusetts	2:42:00	1934	Dave Komonen, Canada	2:32:53
1899	Lawrence Brignolia, Massachusetts	2:54:38	1935	John A. Kelley, Massachusetts	2:32:07
			1936	Ellison (Tarzan) Brown, Rhode Island	2:33:40
1900	Jim Caffrey, Canada	2:39:44	1937	Walter Young, Canada	2:33:20
1901	Jim Caffrey, Canada	2:29:23	1938	Leslie Pawson, Rhode Island	2:35:34
1902	Sam Mellor, New York	2:43:12	1939	Ellison (Tarzan) Brown, Rhode Island	2:28:51
1903	J.C. Lorden, Massachusetts	2:41:29			
1904	Mike Spring, New York	2:38:04	1940	Gerard Cote, Canada	2:28:28
1905	Fred Lorz, New York	2:38:25	1941	Leslie Pawson, Rhode Island	2:30:38
1906	Tim Ford, Massachusetts	2:45:45	1942	Joe Smith, Massachusetts	2:26:51
1907	Tom Longboat, Canada	2:24:24	1943	Gerard Cote, Canada	2:28:25
1908	Tom Morrissey, New York	2:25:43	1944	Gerard Cote, Canada	2:31:50
1909	Henri Renaud, New Hampshire	2:53:36	1945	John A. Kelley, Massachusetts	2:30:40
			1946	Stylianos Kyriakides, Greece	2:29:27
1910	Fred Cameron, Nova Scotia	2:28:52	1947	Yun Bok Suh, Korea	2:25:39
1911	Clarence DeMar, Massachusetts	2:21:39	1948	Gerard Cote, Canada	2:31:02
1912	Mike Ryan, Illinois	2:21:18	1949	Karle Leandersson, Sweden	2:31:50
1913	Fritz Carlson, Minnesota	2:25:14			
1914	James Duffy, Canada	2:25:01	1950	Kee Yonh Ham, Korea	2:32:39
1915	Edouard Fabre, Canada	2:31:41	1951	Shigeki Tanaka, Japan	2:27:45
1916	Arthur Roth, Massachusetts	2:27:16	1952	Doroteo Flores, Guatemala	2:31:53
1917	Bill Kennedy, New York	2:28:37	1953	Keizo Yamada, Japan	2:18:51
1918	World War relay race		1954	Veiko Karvonen, Finland	2:20:39
1919	Carl Linder, Massachusetts	2:29:13	1955	Hideo Hamamura, Japan	2:18:22
			1956	Antti Viskari, Finland	2:14:14
1920	Peter Trivoulidas, New York	2:29:31	1957	John J. Kelley, Connecticut	2:20:05
1921	Frank Zuna, New Jersey	2:18:57	1958	Franjo Mihalic, Yugoslavia	2:25:54
1922	Clarence DeMar, Massachusetts	2:18:10	1959	Eino Oksanen, Finland	2:22:42
1923	Clarence DeMar, Massachusetts	2:23:37			
1924	Clarence DeMar, Massachusetts	2:29:40	1960	Paavo Kotila, Finland	2:20:54
1925	Charles Mellor, Illinois	2:33:00	1961	Eino Oksanen, Finland	2:23:39
1926	John Miles, Nova Scotia	2:25:40	1962	Eino Oksanen, Finland	2:23:48
1927	Clarence DeMar, Massachusetts	2:40:22	1963	Aurele Vandendriessche, Belgium	2:18:58
1928	Clarence DeMar, Massachusetts	2:37:07	1964	Aurele Vandendriessche, Belgium	2:19:59
1929	John Miles, Nova Scotia	2:33:08	1965	Morio Shigematsu, Japan	2:16:33
			1966	Kenji Kimihara, Japan	2:17:11
1930	Clarence DeMar, Massachusetts	2:34:48	1967	David McKenzie, New Zealand	2:15:45
1931	James Henigan, Massachusetts	2:46:45	1968	Amby Burfoot, Connecticut	2:22:17
1932	Paul deBruyn, Germany	2:33:36			

Boston Marathon (Cont.)

Year		Time
1969	Yoshiaki Unetani, Japan	2:13:49
1970	Ron Hill, England	2:10:30
1971	Alvaro Mejia, Colombia	2:18:45
1972	Olavi Suomalainen, Finland	2:15:39
1973	Jon Anderson, Oregon	2:16:03
1974	Neil Cusack, Ireland	2:13:39
1975	Bill Rodgers, Massachusetts	2:09:55
1976	Jack Fultz, Pennsylvania	2:20:19
1977	Jerome Drayton, Canada	2:14:46
1978	Bill Rodgers, Massachusetts	2:10:13
1979	Bill Rodgers, Massachusetts	2:09:27
1980	Bill Rodgers, Massachusetts	2:12:11
1981	Toshihiko Seko, Japan	2:09:26
1982	Alberto Salazar, Oregon	2:08:52
1983	Greg Meyer, New Jersey	2:09:00
1984	Geoff Smith, England	2:10:34
1985	Geoff Smith, England	2:14:05
1986	Rob de Castella, Australia	2:07:51
1987	Toshihiko Seko, Japan	2:11:50
1988	Ibrahim Hussein, Kenya	2:08:43
1989	Abebe Mekonnen, Ethiopia	2:09:06

Year		Time
1990	Gelindo Bordin, Italy	2:08:19
1991	Ibrahim Hussein, Kenya	2:11:06
1992	Ibrahim Hussein, Kenya	2:08:14
1993	Cosmas Ndeti, Kenya	2:09:33
1994	Cosmas Ndeti, Kenya	2:07:15
1995	Cosmas Ndeti, Kenya	2:09:22
1996	Moses Tanui, Kenya	2:09:16
1997	Lameck Aguta, Kenya	2:10:34
1998	Moses Tanui, Kenya	2:07:34
1999	Joseph Chebet, Kenya	2:09:52
2000	Elijah Lagat, Kenya	2:09:47
2001	Lee Bong-Ju, South Korea	2:09:43
2002	Rodgers Rop, Kenya	2:09:02
2003	Robert Kipoech Cheruiyot, Kenya	2:10:11
2004	Timothy Cherigat, Kenya	2:10:37
2005	Hailu Negussie, Ethiopia	2:11:45
2006	Robert Kipoech Cheruiyot, Kenya	2:07:14*

*Course record.

WOMEN

Multiple winners: Catherine Ndereba (4); Rosa Mota, Uta Pippig and Fatuma Roba (3); Joan Benoit, Miki Gorman, Ingrid Kristiansen and Olga Markova (2).

Year		Time
1972	Nina Kuscsik, New York	3:08:58
1973	Jacqueline Hansen, California	3:05:59
1974	Miki Gorman, California	2:47:11
1975	Liane Winter, West Germany	2:42:24
1976	Kim Merritt, Wisconsin	2:47:10
1977	Miki Gorman, California	2:48:33
1978	Gayle Barron, Georgia	2:44:52
1979	Joan Benoit, Maine	2:35:15
1980	Jacqueline Gareau, Canada	2:34:28
1981	Allison Roe, New Zealand	2:26:46
1982	Charlotte Teske, West Germany	2:29:33
1983	Joan Benoit, Maine	2:22:43
1984	Lorraine Moller, New Zealand	2:29:28
1985	Lisa Larsen Weidenbach, Mass	2:34:06
1986	Ingrid Kristiansen, Norway	2:24:55
1987	Rosa Mota, Portugal	2:25:21
1988	Rosa Mota, Portugal	2:24:30
1989	Ingrid Kristiansen, Norway	2:24:33

Year		Time
1990	Rosa Mota, Portugal	2:25:23
1991	Wanda Panfil, Poland	2:24:18
1992	Olga Markova, CIS	2:23:43
1993	Olga Markova, Russia	2:25:27
1994	Uta Pippig, Germany	2:21:45
1995	Uta Pippig, Germany	2:25:11
1996	Uta Pippig, Germany	2:27:12
1997	Fatuma Roba, Ethiopia	2:26:23
1998	Fatuma Roba, Ethiopia	2:23:21
1999	Fatuma Roba, Ethiopia	2:23:25
2000	Catherine Ndereba, Kenya	2:26:11
2001	Catherine Ndereba, Kenya	2:23:53
2002	Margaret Okayo, Kenya	2:20:43*
2003	Svetlana Zakharova, Russia	2:25:20
2004	Catherine Ndereba, Kenya	2:24:27
2005	Catherine Ndereba, Kenya	2:25:13
2006	Rita Jeptoo, Kenya	2:23:38

*Course record.

New York City

Started in 1970, the New York City Marathon is run in the fall, usually on the first Sunday in November. The route winds through all of the city's five boroughs and finishes in Central Park.

MEN

Multiple winners: Bill Rodgers (4); Alberto Salazar (3); Tom Fleming, John Kagwe, Orlando Pizzolato and German Silva (2).

Year		Time	Year		Time	Year		Time
1970	Gary Muhrcke, USA	2:31:38	1983	Rod Dixon, NZE	2:08:59	1996	Giacomo Leone, ITA	2:09:54
1971	Norman Higgins, USA	2:22:54	1984	Orlando Pizzolato, ITA	2:14:53	1997	John Kagwe, KEN	2:08:12
1972	Sheldon Karlin, USA	2:27:52	1985	Orlando Pizzolato, ITA	2:11:34	1998	John Kagwe, KEN	2:08:45
1973	Tom Fleming, USA	2:21:54	1986	Gianni Poli, ITA	2:11:06	1999	Joseph Chebet, KEN	2:09:14
1974	Norbert Sander, USA	2:26:30	1987	Ibrahim Hussein, KEN	2:11:01			
1975	Tom Fleming, USA	2:19:27	1988	Steve Jones, WAL	2:08:20	2000	Abdelkhader El Mouaziz, MOR	2:10:08
1976	Bill Rodgers, USA	2:10:09	1989	Juma Ikangaa, TAN	2:08:01	2001	Tesfaye Jifar, ETH	2:07:43*
1977	Bill Rodgers, USA	2:11:28	1990	Douglas Wakiihuri, KEN	2:12:39	2002	Rodgers Rop, KEN	2:08:07
1978	Bill Rodgers, USA	2:12:12	1991	Salvador Garcia, MEX	2:09:28	2003	Martin Lel, KEN	2:10:30
1979	Bill Rodgers, USA	2:11:42	1992	Willie Mtolo, S. Afr.	2:09:29	2004	Hendrik Ramaala, RSA	2:09:28
1980	Alberto Salazar, USA	2:09:41	1993	Andres Espinosa, MEX	2:10:04	2005	Paul Tergat, KEN	2:09:30
1981	Alberto Salazar, USA	2:08:13	1994	German Silva, MEX	2:11:21			
1982	Alberto Salazar, USA	2:09:29	1995	German Silva, MEX	2:11:00	*Course record.		

WOMEN

Multiple winners: Grete Waitz (9); Miki Gorman, Nina Kuscsik, Margaret Okayo and Tegla Loroupe (2).

Year	Time	Year	Time	Year	Time
1970 No Finisher		1983 Grete Waitz, NOR	. . . .2:27:00	1996 Anuta Catuna, ROM	. .2:28:18
1971 Beth Bonner, USA	. . . .2:55:22	1984 Grete Waitz, NOR	. . . .2:29:30	1997 F. Rochat-Moser, SWI	.2:28:43
1972 Nina Kuscsik, USA	. .3:08:41	1985 Grete Waitz, NOR	. . . .2:28:34	1998 Franca Fiacconi, ITA	. .2:25:17
1973 Nina Kuscsik, USA	. .2:57:07	1986 Grete Waitz, NOR	. . . .2:28:06	1999 Adriana Fernandez, MEX	.2:25:06
1974 Katherine Switzer, USA	.3:07:29	1987 Priscilla Welch, GBR	. . .2:30:17	2000 Ludmila Petrova, RUS	. .2:25:45
1975 Kim Merritt, USA	. .2:46:14	1988 Grete Waitz, NOR	. . . .2:28:07	2001 Margaret Okayo, KEN	2:24:21
1976 Miki Gorman, USA	. .2:39:11	1989 Ingrid Kristiansen, NOR	.2:25:30	2002 Joyce Chepchumba, KEN	2:25:56
1977 Miki Gorman, USA	. .2:43:10	1990 Wanda Panfil, POL	. . .2:30:45	2003 Margaret Okayo, KEN	2:22:31*
1978 Grete Waitz, NOR	. .2:32:30	1991 Liz McColgan, GBR	. . .2:27:23	2004 Paula Radcliffe, GBR	. .2:23:10
1979 Grete Waitz, NOR	. .2:27:33	1992 Lisa Ondieki, AUS	. . .2:24:40	2005 Jelena Prokopcuka, LAT	2:24:41
1980 Grete Waitz, NOR	. .2:25:41	1993 Uta Pippig, GER	. . . .2:26:24	*Course record.	
1981 Allison Roe, NZE	. . . .2:25:29	1994 Tegla Loroupe, KEN	. .2:27:37		
1982 Grete Waitz, NOR	. .2:27:14	1995 Tegla Loroupe, KEN	. .2:28:06		

Annual Awards

Track & Field News Athletes of the Year

Voted on by an international panel of track and field experts and presented since 1959 for men and 1974 for women.

MEN

Multiple winners: Hicham El Guerrouj and Carl Lewis (3); Kenenisa Bekele, Sergey Bubka, Sebastian Coe, Haile Gebrselassie, Michael Johnson, Alberto Juantorena, Noureddine Morceli, Jim Ryun and Peter Snell (2).

Year	Event	Year	Event
1959 Martin Lauer, W. Germany	. . . . .110H/Decathlon	1983 Carl Lewis, USA	. . . . .100/200/Long Jump
1960 Rafer Johnson, USA	. . . . .Decathlon	1984 Carl Lewis, USA	. . . . .100/200/Long Jump
1961 Ralph Boston, USA	. . . .Long Jump/110 Hurdles	1985 Said Aouita, Morocco	. . . . .1500/5000
1962 Peter Snell, New Zealand	. . . . .800/1500	1986 Yuri Sedykh, USSR	. . . . .Hammer Throw
1963 C.K. Yang, Taiwan	. . . . . . .Decathlon/Pole Vault	1987 Ben Johnson, Canada	100
1964 Peter Snell, New Zealand	. . . . .800/1500	1988 Sergey Bubka, USSR	. . . . .Pole Vault
1965 Ron Clarke, Australia	. . . . .5000/10,000	1989 Roger Kingdom, USA	. . . .'. . .110 Hurdles
1966 Jim Ryun, USA	. . . . .800/1500	1990 Michael Johnson, USA	. . . . .200/400
1967 Jim Ryun, USA	1500	1991 Sergey Bubka, USSR	. . . . .Pole Vault
1968 Bob Beamon, USA	. . . . .Long Jump	1992 Kevin Young, USA	. . . . .400 Hurdles
1969 Bill Toomey, USA	. . . . .Decathlon	1993 Noureddine Morceli, Algeria	. .Mile/1500/3000
1970 Randy Matson, USA	. . . . .Shot Put	1994 Noureddine Morceli, Algeria	. .Mile/1500/3000
1971 Rod Milburn, USA	. . . . .110 Hurdles	1995 Haile Gebrselassie, Ethiopia	. . . . .5000/10,000
1972 Lasse Viren, Finland	. . . . .5000/10,000	1996 Michael Johnson, USA	. . . . .200/400
1973 Ben Jipcho, Kenya	. . . .1500/5000/Steeplechase	1997 Wilson Kipketer, Denmark	800
1974 Rick Wohlhuter, USA	. . . . .800/1500	1998 Haile Gebrselassie, Ethiopia	.3000/5000/10,000
1975 John Walker, New Zealand	. . . . .800/1500	1999 Hicham El Guerrouj, Morocco	. . . . . . .Mile/1500
1976 Alberto Juantorena, Cuba	. . . . .400/800	2000 Virgilijus Alekna, Lithuania	. . . . .Discus
1977 Alberto Juantorena, Cuba	. . . . .400/800	2001 Hicham El Guerrouj, Morocco	. . . . . . .Mile/1500
1978 Henry Rono, Kenya	. .5000/10,000/Steeplechase	2002 Hicham El Guerrouj, Morocco	. . . . . . .Mile/1500
1979 Sebastian Coe, Great Britain	. . . . . .800/1500	2003 Felix Sanchez, Dominican Republic	. .400 Hurdles
1980 Edwin Moses, USA	. . . . .400 Hurdles	2004 Kenenisa Bekele, Ethiopia	. . . . . . .5000/10,000
1981 Sebastian Coe, Great Britain	. . . . . .800/1500	2005 Kenenisa Bekele, Ethiopia	. . . . . . .5000/10,000
1982 Carl Lewis, USA	. . . . .100/200/Long Jump		

WOMEN

Multiple winners: Marita Koch (4); Marion Jones and Jackie Joyner-Kersee (3); Evelyn Ashford and Yelena Isinbayeva (2).

Year	Event	Year	Event
1974 Irena Szewinska, Poland	. . . . .100/200/400	1990 Merlene Ottey, Jamaica	. . . . .100/200
1975 Faina Melnik, USSR	. . . . .Shot Put/Discus	1991 Heike Henkel, Germany	. . . . .High Jump
1976 Tatiana Kazankina, USSR	. . . . .800/1500	1992 Heike Drechsler, Germany	. . . . .Long Jump
1977 Rosemarie Ackermann, E. Germany	. . .High Jump	1993 Wang Junxia, China	. . . .1500/3000/10,000
1978 Marita Koch, E. Germany	. . . . . . .100/200/400	1994 Jackie Joyner-Kersee, USA	. . .100H/Heptathlon/LJ
1979 Marita Koch, E. Germany	. . . . . . .100/200/400	1995 Sonia O'Sullivan, Ireland	. . .1500/3000/5000
1980 Ilona Briesenick, E. Germany	. . . . .Shot Put	1996 Svetlana Masterkova, Russia	. . . . .800/1500
1981 Evelyn Ashford, USA	. . . . .100/200	1997 Marion Jones, USA	. . . . .100/200
1982 Marita Koch, E. Germany	. . . . . . .100/200/400	1998 Marion Jones, USA	. . . . .100/200/LJ
1983 Jarmila Kratochvilova, Czech	. . . . .200/400/800	1999 Gabriela Szabo, Romania	. . . . .3000/5000
1984 Evelyn Ashford, USA	100	2000 Marion Jones, USA	. . . . .100/200/LJ
1985 Marita Koch, E. Germany	. . . . . . .100/200/400	2001 Stacy Dragila, USA	. . . . .Pole Vault
1986 Jackie Joyner-Kersee, USA . .Heptathlon/Long Jump		2002 Paula Radcliffe, Gr. Britain	.3000/5000/10k/Mar
1987 Jackie Joyner-Kersee, USA	. . .100H/Heptathlon/LJ	2003 Maria Mutola, Mozambique	800
1988 Florence Griffith Joyner, USA	. . . . .100/200	2004 Yelena Isinbayeva, Russia	. . . . .Pole Vault
1989 Ana Quirot, Cuba	. . . . .400/800	2005 Yelena Isinbayeva, Russia	. . . . .Pole Vault

SWIMMING & DIVING
FINA World Championships

While the Summer Olympics have served as the unofficial world championships for swimming and diving throughout the centuries, a separate World Championship meet was started in 1973 by the Federation Internationale de Natation Amateur (FINA). The meet has varied between being held every two years, every three years or every four years. Currently it is held every two years. Sites have been Belgrade (1973); Cali, COL (1975); West Berlin (1978); Guayaquil, ECU (1982); Madrid (1986); Perth (1991 & 98), Rome (1994), Fukuoka, JPN (2001), Barcelona (2003) and Montreal (2005). Looking forward, the Championships will be held in Melbourne (2007) and Rome (2009).

MEN

Most gold medals (including relays): Ian Thorpe (11); Grant Hackett (10); Michael Phelps (8); Jim Montgomery and Aaron Peirsol (7); Matt Biondi, Michael Klim and Aleksandr Popov (6); Rowdy Gaines and Brendan Hansen (5); Joe Bottom, Ian Crocker, Tamas Darnyi, Michael Gross, Tom Jager, David McCagg, Vladimir Salnikov, Tim Shaw and Matt Welsh (4); Billy Forrester, Andras Hargitay, Jason Lezak, Roland Matthes, John Murphy, Jeff Rouse, Norbert Rozsa and David Wilkie (3).

50-Meter Freestyle

Year		Time	
1973-82 Not held			
1986	Tom Jager, USA	.22.49	
1991	Tom Jager, USA	.22.16	
1994	Aleksandr Popov, RUS	.22.17	
1998	Bill Pilczuk, USA	.22.29	
2001	Anthony Ervin, USA	.22.09	
2003	Aleksandr Popov, RUS	.21.92	
2005	Roland Schoeman, RSA	.21.69	**CR**

100-Meter Freestyle

Year		Time	
1973	Jim Montgomery, USA	.51.70	
1975	Tim Shaw, USA	.51.25	
1978	David McCagg, USA	.50.24	
1982	Jorg Woithe, E. Ger	.50.18	
1986	Matt Biondi, USA	.48.94	
1991	Matt Biondi, USA	.49.18	
1994	Aleksandr Popov, RUS	.49.12	
1998	Aleksandr Popov, RUS	.48.93	
2001	Anthony Ervin, USA	.48.33	
2003	Aleksandr Popov, RUS	.48.42	
2005	Filippo Magnini, ITA	.48.12	**CR**

200-Meter Freestyle

Year		Time	
1973	Jim Montgomery, USA	1:53.02	
1975	Tim Shaw, USA	1:52.04	
1978	Billy Forrester, USA	1:51.02	
1982	Michael Gross, W. Ger	1:49.84	
1986	Michael Gross, W. Ger	1:47.92	
1991	Giorgio Lamberti, ITA	1:47.27	
1994	Antti Kasvio, FIN	1:47.32	
1998	Michael Klim, AUS	1:47.41	
2001	Ian Thorpe, AUS	1:44.06	**WR**
2003	Ian Thorpe, AUS	1:45.14	
2005	Michael Phelps, USA	1:45.20	

400-Meter Freestyle

Year		Time	
1973	Rick DeMont, USA	3:58.18	
1975	Tim Shaw, USA	3:54.88	
1978	Vladimir Salnikov, USSR	3:51.94	
1982	Vladimir Salnikov, USSR	3:51.30	
1986	Rainer Henkel, W. Ger	3:50.05	
1991	Jorg Hoffman, GER	3:48.04	
1994	Kieren Perkins, AUS	3:43.80	
1998	Ian Thorpe, AUS	3:46.29	
2001	Ian Thorpe, AUS	3:40.17	**WR**
2003	Ian Thorpe, AUS	3:42.58	
2005	Grant Hackett, AUS	3:42.91	

800-Meter Freestyle

Year		Time	
1973-98 Not held			
2001	Ian Thorpe, AUS	7:39.16	
2003	Grant Hackett, AUS	7:43.82	
2005	Grant Hackett, AUS	7:38.65	**WR**

1500-Meter Freestyle

Year		Time	
1973	Stephen Holland, AUS	15:31.85	
1975	Tim Shaw, USA	15:28.92	
1978	Vladimir Salnikov, USSR	15:03.99	
1982	Vladimir Salnikov, USSR	15:01.77	
1986	Rainer Henkel, W. Ger	15:05.31	
1991	Jorg Hoffman, GER	14:50.36	
1994	Kieren Perkins, AUS	14:50.52	
1998	Grant Hackett, AUS	14:51.70	
2001	Grant Hackett, AUS	14:34.56	**WR**
2003	Grant Hackett, AUS	14:43.14	
2005	Grant Hackett, AUS	14:42.58	

50-Meter Backstroke

Year		Time	
1973-98 Not held			
2001	Randall Bal, USA	.25.34	
2003	Thomas Rupprath, GER	.24.80	**WR**
2005	Aristeidis Grigoriadis, GRE	.24.95	

100-Meter Backstroke

Year		Time	
1973	Roland Matthes, E. Ger	.57.47	
1975	Roland Matthes, E. Ger	.58.15	
1978	Bob Jackson, USA	.56.36	
1982	Dirk Richter, E. Ger	.55.95	
1986	Igor Polianski, USSR	.55.58	
1991	Jeff Rouse, USA	.55.23	
1994	Martin Lopez-Zubero, SPA	.55.17	
1998	Lenny Krayzelburg, USA	.55.00	
2001	Matt Welsh, AUS	.54.31	
2003	Aaron Peirsol, USA	.53.61	**CR**
2005	Aaron Peirsol, USA	.53.62	

200-Meter Backstroke

Year		Time	
1973	Roland Matthes, E. Ger	2:01.87	
1975	Zoltan Varraszto, HUN	2:05.05	
1978	Jesse Vassallo, USA	2:02.16	
1982	Rick Carey, USA	2:00.82	
1986	Igor Polianski, USSR	1:58.78	
1991	Martin Zubero, SPA	1:59.52	
1994	Vladimir Selkov, RUS	1:57.42	
1998	Lenny Krayzelburg, USA	1:58.84	
2001	Aaron Peirsol, USA	1:57.13	
2003	Aaron Peirsol, USA	1:55.92	
2005	Aaron Peirsol, USA	1:54.66	**WR**

50-Meter Breaststroke

Year		Time
1973-98	Not held	
2001	Oleg Lisogor, UKR	.27.52
2003	James Gibson, GBR	.27.56
2005	Mark Warnecke, GER	.27.63

100-Meter Breaststroke

Year		Time
1973	John Hencken, USA	1:04.02
1975	David Wilkie, GBR	1:04.26
1978	Walter Kusch, W. Ger	1:03.56
1982	Steve Lundquist, USA	1:02.75
1986	Victor Davis, CAN	1:02.71
1991	Norbert Rozsa, HUN	1:01.45
1994	Norbert Rozsa, HUN	1:01.24
1998	Frederik deBurghgraeve, BEL	1:01.34
2001	Roman Sloudnov, RUS	1:00.16
2003	Kosuke Kitajima, JPN	.59.78
2005	Brendan Hansen, USA	.59.37 CR

200-Meter Breaststroke

Year		Time
1973	David Wilkie, GBR	2:19.28
1975	David Wilkie, GBR	2:18.23
1978	Nick Nevid, USA	2:18.37
1982	Victor Davis, CAN	2:14.77
1986	Jozsef Szabo, HUN	2:14.27
1991	Mike Barrowman, USA	2:11.23
1994	Norbert Rozsa, HUN	2:12.81
1998	Kurt Grote, USA	2:13.40
2001	Brendan Hansen, USA	2:10.69
2003	Kosuke Kitajima, JPN	2:09.42 WR
2005	Brendan Hansen, USA	2:09.85

50-Meter Butterfly

Year		Time
1973-98	Not held	
2001	Geoff Huegill, AUS	.23.50
2003	Matt Welsh, AUS	.23.43
2005	Roland Schoeman, RSA	.22.96 WR

100-Meter Butterfly

Year		Time
1973	Bruce Robertson, CAN	.55.69
1975	Greg Jagenburg, USA	.55.63
1978	Joe Bottom, USA	.54.30
1982	Matt Gribble, USA	.53.88
1986	Pablo Morales, USA	.53.54
1991	Anthony Nesty, SUR	.53.29
1994	Rafal Szukala, POL	.53.51
1998	Michael Klim, AUS	.52.25
2001	Lars Frolander, SWE	.52.10
2003	Ian Crocker, USA	.50.98
2005	Ian Crocker, USA	.50.40 WR

200-Meter Butterfly

Year		Time
1973	Robin Backhaus, USA	2:03.32
1975	Billy Forrester, USA	2:01.95
1978	Mike Bruner, USA	1:59.38
1982	Michael Gross, W. Ger	1:58.85
1986	Michael Gross, W. Ger	1:56.53
1991	Melvin Stewart, USA	1:55.69 WR
1994	Denis Pankratov, RUS	1:56.54
1998	Denys Sylantyev, UKR	1:56.61
2001	Michael Phelps, USA	1:54.58 WR
2003	Michael Phelps, USA	1:54.35 WR
2005	Pawel Korzeniowski, POL	1:55.02

200-Meter Individual Medley

Year		Time
1973	Gunnar Larsson, SWE	2:08.36
1975	Andras Hargitay, HUN	2:07.72
1978	Graham Smith, CAN	2:03.65
1982	Alexander Sidorenko, USSR	2:03.30
1986	Tamás Darnyi, HUN	2:01.57
1991	Tamás Darnyi, HUN	1:59.36
1994	Janis Sievinen, FIN	1:58.16
1998	Marcel Wouda, NET	2:01.18
2001	Massimiliano Rosolino, ITA	1:59.71
2003	Michael Phelps, USA	1:56.04 WR
2005	Michael Phelps, USA	1:56.68

400-Meter Individual Medley

Year		Time
1973	Andras Hargitay, HUN	4:31.11
1975	Andras Hargitay, HUN	4:32.57
1978	Jesse Vassallo, USA	4:20.05
1982	Ricardo Prado, BRA	4:19.78
1986	Tamás Darnyi, HUN	4:18.98
1991	Tamás Darnyi, HUN	4:12.36
1994	Tom Dolan, USA	4:12.30
1998	Tom Dolan, USA	4:14.95
2001	Alessio Boggiatto, ITA	4:13.15
2003	Michael Phelps, USA	4:09.09 WR
2005	Laszlo Cseh, HUN	4:09.63

4 x 100-Meter Freestyle Relay

Year		Time
1973	United States	3:27.18
1975	United States	3:24.85
1978	United States	3:19.74
1982	United States	3:19.26
1986	United States	3:19.98
1991	United States	3:17.15
1994	United States	3:16.90
1998	United States	3:16.69
2001	Australia	3:14.10
2003	Russia	3:14.06
2005	United States	3:13.77 CR

4 x 200-Meter Freestyle Relay

Year		Time
1973	United States	7:33.22
1975	West Germany	7:39.44
1978	United States	7:20.82
1982	United States	7:21.09
1986	East Germany	7:15.91
1991	Germany	7:13.50
1994	Sweden	7:17.34
1998	Australia	7:12.48
2001	Australia	7:04.66 WR
2003	Australia	7:08.58
2005	United States	7:06.58

4 x 100-Meter Medley Relay

Year		Time
1973	United States	3:49.49
1975	United States	3:49.00
1978	United States	3:44.63
1982	United States	3:40.84
1986	United States	3:41.25
1991	United States	3:39.66
1994	United States	3:37.74
1998	Australia	3:37.98
2001	Australia	3:35.35
2003	United States	3:31.54 WR
2005	United States	3:31.85

Swimming & Diving (Cont.)

WOMEN

Most gold medals (including relays): Kornelia Ender (8); Kristin Otto (7); Jenny Thompson (6); Inge De Bruijn, Hannah Stockbauer and Luo Xuejuan (5); Tracy Caulkins, Heike Friedrich, Le Jingyi, Leisel Jones, Jana Klochkova, Rosemarie Kother and Ulrike Richter (4); Hannalore Anke, Lu Bin, He Cihong, Natalie Coughlin, Janet Evans, Nicole Haislett, Katie Hoff, Lisbeth Lenton, Lui Limin, Birgit Meineke, Joan Pennington, Manuela Stellmach, Petria Thomas, Amy Van Dyken, Renate Vogel and Cynthia Woodhead (3).

50-Meter Freestyle

Year		Time
1973-82 Not held		
1986	Tamara Costache, ROM	.25.28
1991	Zhuang Yong, CHN	.25.47
1994	Le Jingyi, CHN	.24.51	WR
1998	Amy Van Dyken, USA	.25.15
2001	Inge de Bruijn, NED	.24.47
2003	Inge de Bruijn, NED	.24.47
2005	Lisbeth Lenton, AUS	.24.59

100-Meter Freestyle

Year		Time
1973	Kornelia Ender, E. Ger	.57.54
1975	Kornelia Ender, E. Ger	.56.50
1978	Barbara Krause, E. Ger	.55.68
1982	Birgit Meineke, E. Ger	.55.79
1986	Kristin Otto, E. Ger	.55.05
1991	Nicole Haislett, USA	.55.17
1994	Le Jingyi, CHN	.54.01	WR
1998	Jenny Thompson, USA	.54.95
2001	Inge de Bruijn, NED	.54.18
2003	Hanna-Maria Seppala, FIN	.54.37
2005	Jodie Henry, AUS	.54.18

200-Meter Freestyle

Year		Time
1973	Keena Rothhammer, USA	2:04.99
1975	Shirley Babashoff, USA	2:02.50
1978	Cynthia Woodhead, USA	1:58.53
1982	Annemarie Verstappen, NED	1:59.53
1986	Heike Friedrich, E. Ger	1:58.26
1991	Hayley Lewis, AUS	2:00.48
1994	Franziska Van Almsick, GER	1:56.78	WR
1998	Claudia Poll, CRC	1:58.90
2001	Giaan Rooney, AUS	1:58.57
2003	Alena Popchenko, BLR	1:58.32
2005	Solenne Figues, FRA	1:58.60

400-Meter Freestyle

Year		Time
1973	Heather Greenwood, USA	4:20.28
1975	Shirley Babashoff, USA	4:22.70
1978	Tracey Wickham, AUS	4:06.28	WR
1982	Carmela Schmidt. E. Ger	4:08.98
1986	Heike Friedrich, E. Ger	4:07.45
1991	Janet Evans, USA	4:08.63
1994	Yang Aihua, CHN	4:09.64
1998	Yan Chen, CHN	4:06.72
2001	Yana Klochkova, UKR	4:07.30
2003	Hannah Stockbauer, GER	4:06.75
2005	Laure Manaudou. FRA	4:06.44

800-Meter Freestyle

Year		Time
1973	Novella Calligaris, ITA	.8:52.97
1975	Jenny Turrall, AUS	.8:44.75
1978	Tracey Wickham, AUS	.8:25.94
1982	Kim Linehan, USA	.8:27.48
1986	Astrid Strauss, E. Ger	.8:28.24
1991	Janet Evans, USA	.8:24.05
1994	Janet Evans, USA	.8:29.85
1998	Brooke Bennett, USA	.8:28.71
2001	Hannah Stockbauer, GER	.8:24.66
2003	Hannah Stockbauer, GER	.8:23.66	CR
2005	Kate Ziegler, USA	.8:25.31

1500-Meter Freestyle

Year		Time
1973-98 Not held		
2001	Hannah Stockbauer, GER	16:01.02
2003	Hannah Stockbauer, GER	16:00.18	CR
2005	Kate Ziegler, USA	16:00.41

50-Meter Backstroke

Year		Time
1973-98 Not held		
2001	Haley Cope, USA	.28.51
2003	Nina Zhivanevskaya, ESP	.28.48	CR
2005	Giaan Rooney, AUS	.28.63

100-Meter Backstroke

Year		Time
1973	Ulrike Richter, E. Ger	1:05.42
1975	Ulrike Richter, E. Ger	1:03.30
1978	Linda Jezek, USA	1:02.55
1982	Kristin Otto, E. Ger	1:01.30
1986	Betsy Mitchell, USA	1:01.74
1991	Krisztina Egerszegi, HUN	1:01.78
1994	He Cihong, CHN	1:00.57
1998	Lea Maurer, USA	1:01.16
2001	Natalie Coughlin, USA	1:00.37
2003	Antje Buschschulte, GER	1:00.50
2005	Kirsty Coventry, ZIM	1:00.24

200-Meter Backstroke

Year		Time
1973	Melissa Belote, USA	2:20.52
1975	Birgit Treiber, E. Ger	2:15.46
1978	Linda Jezek, USA	2:11.93
1982	Cornelia Sirch, E. Ger	2:09.91
1986	Cornelia Sirch, E. Ger	2:11.37
1991	Krisztina Egerszegi, HUN	2:09.15
1994	He Cihong, CHN	2:07.40	CR
1998	Roxanna Maracineanu, FRA	2:11.26
2001	Diana Iuliana Mocanu, ROM	2:09.94
2003	Katy Sexton, GBR	2:08.74
2005	Kirsty Coventry, ZIM	2:08.52

50-Meter Breaststroke

Year		Time
1973-82 Not held		
2001	Luo Xuejuan, CHN	.30.84
2003	Luo Xuejuan, CHN	.30.67
2005	Jade Edmistone, AUS	.30.45	WR

100-Meter Breaststroke

Year		Time
1973	Renate Vogel, E. Ger	1:13.74
1975	Hannalore Anke, E. Ger	1:12.72
1978	Julia Bogdanova, USSR	1:10.31
1982	Ute Geweniger, E. Ger	1:09.14
1986	Sylvia Gerasch, E. Ger	1:08.11
1991	Linley Frame, AUS	1:08.81
1994	Samantha Riley, AUS	1:07.69
1998	Kristy Kowal, USA	1:08.42
2001	Luo Xuejuan, CHN	1:07.18
2003	Luo Xuejuan, CHN	1:06.80
2005	Leisel Jones, AUS	1:06.25

200-Meter Breaststroke

Year		Time	
1973	Renate Vogel, E. Ger	2:40.01	
1975	Hannalore Anke, E. Ger	2:37.25	
1978	Lina Kachushite, USSR	2:31.42	
1982	Svetlana Varganova, USSR	2:28.82	
1986	Silke Hoerner, E. Ger	2:27.40	
1991	Elena Volkova, USSR	2:29.53	
1994	Samantha Riley, AUS	2:26.87	
1998	Agnes Kovacs, HUN	2:25.45.	
2001	Agnes Kovacs, HUN	2:24.90	
2003	Amanda Beard, USA	2:22.99	
2005	Leisel Jones, AUS	2:21.72	WR

50-Meter Butterfly

Year		Time	
1973-98 Not held			
2001	Inge de Bruijn, NED	25.90	
2003	Inge de Bruijn, NED	25.84	CR
2005	Danni Miatke, AUS	26.11	

100-Meter Butterfly

Year		Time	
1973	Kornelia Ender, E. Ger	1:02.53	
1975	Kornelia Ender, E. Ger	1:01.24	
1978	Joan Pennington, USA	1:00.20	
1982	Mary T. Meagher, USA	59.41	
1986	Kornelia Gressler, E. Ger	59.51	
1991	Qian Hong, CHN	59.68	
1994	Liu Limin, CHN	58.98	
1998	Jenny Thompson, USA	58.46	
2001	Petria Thomas, AUS	58.27	
2003	Jenny Thompson, USA	57.96	
2005	Jessicah Schipper, AUS	57.23	CR

200-Meter Butterfly

Year		Time	
1973	Rosemarie Kother, E. Ger	2:13.76	
1975	Rosemarie Kother, E. Ger	2:15.92	
1978	Tracy Caulkins, USA	2:09.78	
1982	Ines Geissler, E. Ger	2:08.66	
1986	Mary T. Meagher, USA	2:08.41	
1991	Summer Sanders, USA	2:09.24	
1994	Liu Limin, CHN	2:07.25	
1998	Susie O'Neill, AUS	2:07.93	
2001	Petria Thomas, AUS	2:06.73	
2003	Otylia Jedrzejczak, POL	2:07.56	
2005	Otylia Jedrzejczak, POL	2:05.61	WR

200-Meter Individual Medley

Year		Time	
1973	Andre Huebner, E. Ger	2:20.51	
1975	Kathy Heddy, USA	2:19.80	
1978	Tracy Caulkins, USA	2:19.80	
1982	Petra Schneider, E. Ger	2:11.79	
1986	Kristin Otto, E. Ger	2:15.56	
1991	Lin Li, CHN	2:13.40	
1994	Lu Bin, CHN	2:12.34	
1998	Yanyan Wu, CHN	2:10.88	
2001	Maggie Bowen, USA	2:11.93	
2003	Yana Klochkova, UKR	2:10.75	
2005	Katie Hoff, USA	2:10.41	WR

400-Meter Individual Medley

Year		Time	
1973	Gudrun Wegner, E. Ger	4:57.71	
1975	Ulrike Tauber, E. Ger	4:52.76	
1978	Tracy Caulkins, USA	4:40.83	
1982	Petra Schneider, E. Ger	4:36.10	
1986	Kathleen Nord, E. Ger	4:43.75	
1991	Lin Li, CHN	4:41.45	
1994	Dai Guohong, CHN	4:39.14	
1998	Yan Chen, CHN	4:36.66	
2001	Yana Klochkova, UKR	4:36.98	
2003	Yana Klochkova, UKR	4:36.74	
2005	Katie Hoff, USA	4:36.07	CR

4 x 100-Meter Freestyle Relay

Year		Time	
1973	East Germany	3:52.45	
1975	East Germany	3:49.37	
1978	United States	3:43.43	
1982	East Germany	3:43.97	
1986	East Germany	3:40.57	
1991	United States	3:43.26	
1994	China	3:37.91	
1998	United States	3:42.11	
2001	Germany	3:39.58	
2003	United States	3:38.09	
2005	Australia	3:37.32	CR

4 x 200-Meter Freestyle Relay

Year		Time	
1973-82 Not held			
1986	East Germany	7:59.33	
1991	Germany	8:02.56	
1994	China	7:57.96	
1998	Germany	8:01.46	
2001	Great Britain	7:58.69	
2003	United States	7:55.70	
2005	United States	7:53.70	CR

4 x 100-Meter Medley Relay

Year		Time	
1973	East Germany	4:16.84	
1975	East Germany	4:14.74	
1978	United States	4:08.21	
1982	East Germany	4:05.80	
1986	East Germany	4:04.82	
1991	United States	4:06.51	
1994	China	4:01.67	
1998	United States	4:01.93	
2001	Australia	4:01.50	
2003	China	3:59.89	
2005	Australia	3:57.47	CR

Diving

Multiple Gold Medals: MEN—Greg Louganis and Dmitri Sautin (5); Phil Boggs and Alexandre Despatie (3); Klaus Dibiasi, Wang Feng, Hu Jia, Tian Liang and Yu Zhuocheng (2). WOMEN—Guo Jingjing (6); Irina Kalinina and Gao Min (3); Blythe Hartley, Irina Lashko, Fu Mingxia, Wu Mingxia and Li Ting (2).

MEN

1-Meter Springboard

Year		Pts
1973-86 Not Held		
1991	Edwin Jongejans, NED	588.51
1994	Evan Stewart, ZIM	382.14
1998	Yu Zhuocheng, CHN	417.54
2001	Wang Feng, CHN	444.03
2003	Xu Xiang, CHN	431.94
2005	Alexandre Despatie, CAN	489.69

3-Meter Springboard

Year		Pts
1973	Phil Boggs, USA	618.57
1975	Phil Boggs, USA	597.12
1978	Phil Boggs, USA	913.95
1982	Greg Louganis, USA	752.67
1986	Greg Louganis, USA	750.06
1991	Kent Ferguson, USA	650.25
1994	Yu Zhuocheng, CHN	655.44
1998	Dmitri Sautin, RUS	746.79
2001	Dmitri Sautin, RUS	725.82
2003	Alexander Dobroskok, RUS	788.37
2005	Alexandre Despatie, CAN	813.60

Swimming & Diving (Cont.)

Platform

Year		Pts
1973	Klaus Dibiasi, ITA	559.53
1975	Klaus Dibiasi, ITA	547.98
1978	Greg Louganis, USA	844.11
1982	Greg Louganis, USA	634.26
1986	Greg Louganis, USA	668.58
1991	Sun Shuwei, CHN	626.79
1994	Dmitri Sautin, RUS	634.71
1998	Dmitri Sautin, RUS	750.99
2001	Tian Liang, CHN	688.77
2003	Alexandre Despatie, CAN	716.91
2005	Hu Jia, CHN	698.01

3-Meter Synchronized

Year		Pts
1973-98	Not held	
2001	Peng Bo & Wang Kenan, CHN	342.63
2003	Alexander Dobroskok & Dmitri Sautin, RUS	369.18
2005	He Chong & Wang Feng, CHN	384.42

10-Meter Synchronized

Year		Pts
1973-98	Not held	
2001	Tian Liang & Hu Jia, CHN	361.41
2003	Mathew Helm & Robert Newbery, AUS	384.60
2005	Dmitry Dobrosok & Glen Galperin, RUS	392.88

WOMEN
1-Meter Springboard

Year		Pts
1973-86	Not held	
1991	Gao Min, CHN	478.26
1994	Chen Lixia, CHN	279.30
1998	Irina Lashko, RUS	296.07
2001	Blythe Hartley, CAN	300.81
2003	Irina Lashko, AUS	299.97
2005	Blythe Hartley, CAN	325.65

3-Meter Springboard

Year		Pts
1973	Christa Koehler, E. Ger	442.17
1975	Irina Kalinina, USSR	489.81
1978	Irina Kalinina, USSR	691.43
1982	Megan Neyer, USA	501.03
1986	Gao Min, CHN	582.90
1991	Gao Min, CHN	539.01
1994	Tan Shuping, CHN	548.49
1998	Yulia Pakhalina, RUS	544.52
2001	Guo Jingjing, CHN	596.67
2003	Guo Jingjing, CHN	617.94
2005	Guo Jingjing, CHN	645.54

Platform

Year		Pts
1973	Ulrike Knape, SWE	406.77
1975	Janet Ely, USA	403.89
1978	Irina Kalinina, USSR	412.71
1982	Wendy Wyland, USA	438.79
1986	Chen Lin, CHN	449.67
1991	Fu Mingxia, CHN	426.51
1994	Fu Mingxia, CHN	434.04
1998	Olena Zhupyna	550.41
2001	Xu Mian, CHN	532.65
2003	Emilie Heymans, CAN	597.45
2005	Laura Wilkinson, USA	564.87

3-Meter Synchronized

Year		Pts
1973-98	Not held	
2001	Wu Minxia & Guo Jingjing, CHN	347.31
2003	Wu Minxia & Guo Jingjing, CHN	357.30
2005	Li Ting & Guo Jingjing, CHN	351.60

10-Meter Synchronized

Year		Pts
1973-98	Not held	
2001	Duan Qing & Sang Xue, CHN	329.94
2003	Lao Lishi & Li Ting, CHN	344.58
2005	Jia Tong & Yuan Pei Lin, CHN	344.58

ALPINE SKIING

World Cup Overall Champions

World Cup Overall Champions (downhill and slalom events combined) since the tour was organized in 1967.

MEN

Multiple winners: Marc Girardelli (5); Hermann Maier, Gustavo Thoeni and Pirmin Zurbriggen (4); Phil Mahre and Ingemar Stenmark (3); Stephan Eberharter, Jean-Claude Killy, Lasse Kjus and Karl Schranz (2).

Year		Year		Year	
1967	Jean-Claude Killy, France	1981	Phil Mahre, USA	1995	Alberto Tomba, Italy
1968	Jean-Claude Killy, France	1982	Phil Mahre, USA	1996	Lasse Kjus, Norway
1969	Karl Schranz, Austria	1983	Phil Mahre, USA	1997	Luc Alphand, France
1970	Karl Schranz, Austria	1984	Pirmin Zurbriggen, Switzerland	1998	Hermann Maier, Austria
1971	Gustavo Thoeni, Italy	1985	Marc Girardelli, Luxembourg	1999	Lasse Kjus, Norway
1972	Gustavo Thoeni, Italy	1986	Marc Girardelli, Luxembourg	2000	Hermann Maier, Austria
1973	Gustavo Thoeni, Italy	1987	Pirmin Zurbriggen, Switzerland	2001	Hermann Maier, Austria
1974	Piero Gros, Italy	1988	Pirmin Zurbriggen, Switzerland	2002	Stephan Eberharter, Austria
1975	Gustavo Thoeni, Italy	1989	Marc Girardelli, Luxembourg	2003	Stephan Eberharter, Austria
1976	Ingemar Stenmark, Sweden	1990	Pirmin Zurbriggen, Switzerland	2004	Hermann Maier, Austria
1977	Ingemar Stenmark, Sweden	1991	Marc Girardelli, Luxembourg	2005	Bode Miller, USA
1978	Ingemar Stenmark, Sweden	1992	Paul Accola, Switzerland	2006	Benjamin Raich, Austria
1979	Peter Luescher, Switzerland	1993	Marc Girardelli, Luxembourg		
1980	Andreas Wenzel, Liechtenstein	1994	Kjetil Andre Aamodt, Norway		

WOMEN

Multiple winners: Annemarie Moser-Pröll (6); Janica Kostelic, Petra Kronberger and Vreni Schneider (3); Michela Figini, Nancy Greene, Erika Hess, Anja Paerson, Katja Seizinger, Maria Walliser and Hanni Wenzel (2).

Year		Year		Year	
1967	Nancy Greene, Canada	1981	Marie-Therese Nadig, SWI	1995	Vreni Schneider, Switzerland
1968	Nancy Greene, Canada	1982	Erika Hess, Switzerland	1996	Katja Seizinger, Germany
1969	Gertrud Gabi, Austria	1983	Tamara McKinney, USA	1997	Pernilla Wiberg, Sweden
1970	Michele Jacot, France	1984	Erika Hess, Switzerland	1998	Katja Seizinger, Germany
1971	Annemarie Pröll, Austria	1985	Michela Figini, Switzerland	1999	Alexandra Meissnitzer, Austria
1972	Annemarie Pröll, Austria	1986	Maria Walliser, Switzerland	2000	Renate Goetschl, Austria
1973	Annemarie Pröll, Austria	1987	Maria Walliser, Switzerland	2001	Janica Kostelic, Croatia
1974	Annemarie Pröll, Austria	1988	Michela Figini, Switzerland	2002	Michaela Dorfmeister, Austria
1975	Annemarie Moser-Pröll, Austria	1989	Vreni Schneider, Switzerland	2003	Janica Kostelic, Croatia
1976	Rosi Mittermaier, W. Germany	1990	Petra Kronberger, Austria	2004	Anja Paerson, Sweden
1977	Lise-Marie Morerod, Switzerland	1991	Petra Kronberger, Austria	2005	Anja Paerson, Sweden
1978	Hanni Wenzel, Liechtenstein	1992	Petra Kronberger, Austria	2006	Janica Kostelic, Croatia
1979	Annemarie Moser-Pröll, Austria	1993	Anita Wachter, Austria		
1980	Hanni Wenzel, Liechtenstein	1994	Vreni Schneider, Switzerland		

World Cup Event Champions

World Cup Champions in each individual event since the tour was organized in 1967.

MEN
Downhill

Multiple winners: Franz Klammer (5); Luc Alphand, Stephan Eberharter, Franz Heinzer and Peter Muller (3); Roland Collumbin, Marc Girardelli, Helmut Hoflehner, Hermann Maier, Bernard Russi, Karl Schranz, Michael Walchhofer and Pirmin Zurbriggen (2).

Year		Year		Year	
1967	Jean-Claude Killy, France	1980	Peter Muller, Switzerland	1993	Franz Heinzer, Switzerland
1968	Gerhard Nenning, Austria	1981	Harti Weirather, Austria	1994	Marc Girardelli, Luxembourg
1969	Karl Schranz, Austria	1982	Steve Podborski, Canada	1995	Luc Alphand, France
1970	Karl Schranz, Austria		Peter Muller, Switzerland	1996	Luc Alphand, France
	Karl Cordin, Austria	1983	Franz Klammer, Austria	1997	Luc Alphand, France
1971	Bernard Russi, Switzerland	1984	Urs Raber, Switzerland	1998	Andreas Schifferer, Austria
1972	Bernard Russi, Switzerland	1985	Helmut Hoflehner, Austria	1999	Lasse Kjus, Norway
1973	Roland Collumbin, Switzerland	1986	Peter Wirnsberger, Austria	2000	Hermann Maier, Austria
1974	Roland Collumbin, Switzerland	1987	Pirmin Zurbriggen, Switzerland	2001	Hermann Maier, Austria
1975	Franz Klammer, Austria	1988	Pirmin Zurbriggen, Switzerland	2002	Stephan Eberharter, Austria
1976	Franz Klammer, Austria	1989	Marc Girardelli, Luxembourg	2003	Stephan Eberharter, Austria
1977	Franz Klammer, Austria	1990	Helmut Hoflehner, Austria	2004	Stephan Eberharter, Austria
1978	Franz Klammer, Austria	1991	Franz Heinzer, Switzerland	2005	Michael Walchhofer, Austria
1979	Peter Muller, Switzerland	1992	Franz Heinzer, Switzerland	2006	Michael Walchhofer, Austria

Slalom

Multiple winners: Ingemar Stenmark (8); Alberto Tomba (4); Jean-Noel Augert and Marc Girardelli (3); Armin Bittner, Benjamin Raich, Thomas Sykora and Gustavo Thoeni (2).

Year		Year		Year	
1967	Jean-Claude Killy, France	1980	Ingemar Stenmark, Sweden	1994	Alberto Tomba, Italy
1968	Domeng Giovanoli, Switzerland	1981	Ingemar Stenmark, Sweden	1995	Alberto Tomba, Italy
1969	Jean-Noel Augert, France	1982	Phil Mahre, USA	1996	Sebastien Amiez, France
1970	Patrick Russel, France	1983	Ingemar Stenmark, Sweden	1997	Thomas Sykora, Austria
	Alain Penz, France	1984	Marc Girardelli, Luxembourg	1998	Thomas Sykora, Austria
1971	Jean-Noel Augert, France	1985	Marc Girardelli, Luxembourg	1999	Thomas Stangassinger, Austria
1972	Jean-Noel Augert, France	1986	Rok Petrovic, Yugoslavia	2000	Kjetil Andre Aamodt, Norway
1973	Gustavo Thoeni, Italy	1987	Bojan Krizaj, Yugoslavia	2001	Benjamin Raich, Austria
1974	Gustavo Thoeni, Italy	1988	Alberto Tomba, Italy	2002	Ivica Kostelic, Croatia
1975	Ingemar Stenmark, Sweden	1989	Armin Bittner, West Germany	2003	Kalle Palander, Finland
1976	Ingemar Stenmark, Sweden	1990	Armin Bittner, West Germany	2004	Rainer Schoenfelder, Austria
1977	Ingemar Stenmark, Sweden	1991	Marc Girardelli, Luxembourg	2005	Benjamin Raich, Austria
1978	Ingemar Stenmark, Sweden	1992	Alberto Tomba, Italy	2006	Giorgio Rocca, Italy
1979	Ingemar Stenmark, Sweden	1993	Tomas Fogdof, Sweden		

Giant Slalom

Multiple winners: Ingemar Stenmark (8); Michael von Gruenigen and Alberto Tomba (4); Hermann Maier and Pirmin Zurbriggen (3); Joel Gaspoz, Jean-Claude Killy, Phil Mahre, Benjamin Raich and Gustavo Thoeni (2).

Year		Year		Year	
1967	Jean-Claude Killy, France	1976	Ingemar Stenmark, Sweden	1984	Ingemar Stenmark, Sweden
1968	Jean-Claude Killy, France	1977	Heini Hemmi, Switzerland		Pirmin Zurbriggen, Switzerland
1969	Karl Schranz, Austria		Ingemar Stenmark, Sweden	1985	Marc Girardelli, Luxembourg
1970	Gustavo Thoeni, Italy	1978	Ingemar Stenmark, Sweden	1986	Joel Gaspoz, Switzerland
1971	Patrick Russel, France	1979	Ingemar Stenmark, Sweden	1987	Joel Gaspoz, Switzerland
1972	Gustavo Thoeni, Italy	1980	Ingemar Stenmark, Sweden		Pirmin Zurbriggen, Switzerland
1973	Hans Hinterseer, Austria	1981	Ingemar Stenmark, Sweden	1988	Alberto Tomba, Italy
1974	Piero Gros, Italy	1982	Phil Mahre, USA	1989	Pirmin Zurbriggen, Switzerland
1975	Ingemar Stenmark, Sweden	1983	Phil Mahre, USA		

Alpine Skiing (Cont.)

Year		Year		Year	
1990	Ole-Cristian Furuseth, Norway	1995	Alberto Tomba, Italy	2001	Hermann Maier, Austria
	Gunther Mader, Austria	1996	Michael von Gruenigen, SWI	2002	Frederic Covili, France
1991	Alberto Tomba, Italy	1997	Michael von Gruenigen, SWI	2003	Michael von Gruenigen, SWI
1992	Alberto Tomba, Italy	1998	Hermann Maier, Austria	2004	Bode Miller, USA
1993	Kjetil Andre Aamodt, Norway	1999	Michael von Gruenigen, SWI	2005	Benjamin Raich, Austria
1994	Christian Mayer, Austria	2000	Hermann Maier, Austria	2006	Benjamin Raich, Austria

Super G

Multiple winners: Hermann Maier (5); Pirmin Zurbriggen (4); Stephan Eberharter (2).

Year		Year		Year	
1986	Markus Wasmeier, W. Ger.	1993	Kjetil Andre Aamodt, Norway	2000	Hermann Maier, Austria
1987	Pirmin Zurbriggen, Switzerland	1994	Jan Einar Thorsen, Norway	2001	Hermann Maier, Austria
1988	Pirmin Zurbriggen, Switzerland	1995	Peter Runggaldier, Italy	2002	Stephan Eberharter, Austria
1989	Pirmin Zurbriggen, Switzerland	1996	Atle Skaardal, Norway	2003	Stephan Eberharter, Austria
1990	Pirmin Zurbriggen, Switzerland	1997	Luc Alphand, France	2004	Hermann Maier, Austria
1991	Franz Heinzer, Switzerland	1998	Hermann Maier, Austria	2005	Bode Miller, USA
1992	Paul Accola, Switzerland	1999	Hermann Maier, Austria	2006	Aksel Lund Svindal, Norway

Combined

Multiple winners: Marc Girardelli and Andreas Wenzel (4); Kjetil Andre Aamodt and Phil Mahre (3); Bode Miller, Benjamin Raich and Pirmin Zurbriggen (2).

Year		Year		Year	
1979	Andreas Wenzel, Liechtenstein	1988	Hubert Strolz, Austria	1997-99	Not awarded
1980	Andreas Wenzel, Liechtenstein	1989	Marc Girardelli, Luxembourg	2000	Kjetil Andre Aamodt, Norway
1981	Phil Mahre, USA	1990	Pirmin Zurbriggen, Switzerland	2001	Lasse Kjus, Norway
1982	Phil Mahre, USA	1991	Marc Girardelli, Luxembourg	2002	Kjetil Andre Aamodt, Norway
1983	Phil Mahre, USA	1992	Paul Accola, Switzerland	2003	Bode Miller, USA
1984	Andreas Wenzel, Liechtenstein	1993	Marc Girardelli, Luxembourg	2004	Bode Miller, USA
1985	Andreas Wenzel, Liechtenstein	1994	Kjetil Andre Aamodt, Norway	2005	Benjamin Raich, Austria
1986	Markus Wasmeier, W. Ger	1995	Marc Girardelli, Luxembourg	2006	Benjamin Raich, Austria
1987	Pirmin Zurbriggen, Switzerland	1996	Gunther Mader, Austria		

WOMEN
Downhill

Multiple winners: Annemarie Moser-Pröll (7), Michela Figini, Renate Goetschl and Katja Seizinger (4); Michaela Dorfmeister, Isolde Kostner, Isabelle Mir, Marie-Therese Nadig, Picabo Street, Bridgitte Totschnig-Habersatter and Maria Walliser (2).

Year		Year		Year	
1967	Marielle Goitschel, France	1980	Marie-Therese Nadig, SWI	1994	Katja Seizinger, Germany
1968	Isabelle Mir, France	1981	Marie-Therese Nadig, SWI	1995	Picabo Street, USA
	Olga Pall, Austria	1982	Marie-Cecile Gros-Gaudenier, FRA	1996	Picabo Street, USA
1969	Wiltrud Drexel, Austria	1983	Doris De Agostini, Switzerland	1997	Renate Goetschl, Austria
1970	Isabelle Mir, France	1984	Maria Walliser, Switzerland	1998	Katja Seizinger, Germany
1971	Annemarie Pröll, Austria	1985	Michela Figini, Switzerland	1999	Renate Goetschl, Austria
1972	Annemarie Pröll, Austria	1986	Maria Walliser, Switzerland	2000	Regina Haeusl, Germany
1973	Annemarie Pröll, Austria	1987	Michela Figini, Switzerland	2001	Isolde Kostner, Italy
1974	Annemarie Pröll, Austria	1988	Michela Figini, Switzerland	2002	Isolde Kostner, Italy
1975	Annemarie Moser-Pröll, Austria	1989	Michela Figini, Switzerland	2003	Michaela Dorfmeister, Austria
1976	Bridgitte Totschnig-Habersatter, AUT	1990	Katrin Gutensohn-Knopf, GER	2004	Renate Goetschl, Austria
1977	Bridgitte Totschnig-Habersatter, AUT	1991	Chantal Bournissen, SWI	2005	Renate Goetschl, Austria
1978	Annemarie Moser-Pröll, Austria	1992	Katja Seizinger, Germany	2006	Michaela Dorfmeister, Austria
1979	Annemarie Moser-Pröll, Austria	1993	Katja Seizinger, Germany		

Slalom

Multiple winners: Vreni Schneider (6); Erika Hess (5); Janica Kostelic (3); Marielle Goitschel, Britt Lafforgue, Lisa-Marie Morerod and Roswitha Steiner (2).

Year		Year		Year	
1967	Marielle Goitschel, France	1981	Erika Hess, Switzerland	1993	Vreni Schneider, Switzerland
1968	Marielle Goitschel, France	1982	Erika Hess, Switzerland	1994	Vreni Schneider, Switzerland
1969	Gertrud Gabl, Austria	1983	Erika Hess, Switzerland	1995	Vreni Schneider, Switzerland
1970	Ingrid Lafforgue, France	1984	Tamara McKinney, USA	1996	Elfi Eder, Austria
1971	Britt Lafforgue, France	1985	Erika Hess, Switzerland	1997	Pernilla Wiberg, Sweden
1972	Britt Lafforgue, France	1986	Roswitha Steiner, Austria	1998	Ylva Nowen, Sweden
1973	Patricia Emonet, France		Erika Hess, Switzerland	1999	Sabine Egger, Austria
1974	Christa Zechmeister, W. Germany	1987	Corrine Schmidhauser,	2000	Spela Pretnar, Slovenia
1975	Lisa-Marie Morerod, Switzerland		Switzerland	2001	Janica Kostelic, Croatia
1976	Rosi Mittermaier, W. Germany	1988	Roswitha Steiner, Austria	2002	Laure Pequegnot, France
1977	Lisa-Marie Morerod, Switzerland	1989	Vreni Schneider, Switzerland	2003	Janica Kostelic, Croatia
1978	Hanni Wenzel, Liechtenstein	1990	Vreni Schneider, Switzerland	2004	Anja Paerson, Sweden
1979	Regina Sackl, Austria	1991	Petra Kronberger, Austria	2005	Tanja Poutiainen, Finland
1980	Perrine Pelene, France	1992	Vreni Schneider, Switzerland	2006	Janica Kostelic, Croatia

Giant Slalom

Multiple winners: Vreni Schneider (5); Lisa-Marie Morerod, Annemarie Moser-Pröll and Anja Paerson (3); Martina Ertl, Nancy Greene, Carole Merle, Sonja Nef, Anita Wachter and Hanni Wenzel (2).

Year		Year		Year	
1967	Nancy Greene, Canada	1981	Marie-Therese Nadig, SWI	1994	Anita Wachter, Austria
1968	Nancy Greene, Canada	1982	Irene Epple, West Germany	1995	Vreni Schneider, Switzerland
1969	Marilyn Cochran, USA	1983	Tamara McKinney, USA	1996	Martina Ertl, Germany
1970	Michele Jacot, France	1984	Erika Hess, Switzerland	1997	Deborah Compagnoni, Italy
	Francoise Macchi, France	1985	Maria Keihl, West Germany	1998	Martina Ertl, Germany
1971	Annemarie Pröll, Austria		Michela Figini, Switzerland	1999	Alexandra Meissnitzer, Austria
1972	Annemarie Pröll, Austria	1986	Vreni Schneider, Switzerland	2000	Michaela Dorfmeister, Austria
1973	Monika Kaserer, Austria	1987	Vreni Schneider, Switzerland	2001	Sonja Nef, Switzerland
1974	Hanni Wenzel, Liechtenstein		Maria Walliser, Switzerland	2002	Sonja Nef, Switzerland
1975	Annemarie Moser-Pröll, Austria	1988	Mateja Svet, Yugoslavia	2003	Anja Paerson, Sweden
1976	Lisa-Marie Morerod, SWI	1989	Vreni Schneider, Switzerland	2004	Anja Paerson, Sweden
1977	Lisa-Marie Morerod, SWI	1990	Anita Wachter, Austria	2005	Tanja Poutiainen, Finland
1978	Lisa-Marie Morerod, SWI	1991	Vreni Schneider, Switzerland	2006	Anja Paerson, Sweden
1979	Christa Kinshofer, W. Ger.	1992	Carole Merle, France		
1980	Hanni Wenzel, Liechtenstein	1993	Carole Merle, France		

Super G

Multiple winners: Katja Seizinger (5); Carole Merle (4); Michaela Dorfmeister, Hilde Gerg and Renate Goetschl (2).

Year		Year		Year	
1986	Maria Kiehl, West Germany	1993	Katja Seizinger, Germany	2000	Renate Goetschl, Austria
1987	Maria Walliser, Switzerland	1994	Katja Seizinger, Germany	2001	Regine Cavagnoud, France
1988	Michela Figini, Switzerland	1995	Katja Seizinger, Germany	2002	Hilde Gerg, Germany
1989	Carole Merle, France	1996	Katja Seizinger, Germany	2003	Carole Montillet, France
1990	Carole Merle, France	1997	Hilde Gerg, Germany	2004	Renate Goetschl, Austria
1991	Carole Merle, France	1998	Katja Seizinger, Germany	2005	Michaela Dorfmeister, Austria
1992	Carole Merle, France	1999	Alexandra Meissnitzer, Austria	2006	Michaela Dorfmeister, Austria

Combined

Multiple winners: Brigitte Oertli (5); Janica Kostelic (4); Anita Wachter and Hanni Wenzel (3); Sabine Ginther, Renate Goetschl and Pernilla Wiberg (2).

Year		Year		Year	
1979	Annemarie Moser-Pröll, Austria	1987	Brigitte Oertli, Switzerland	1996	Anita Wachter, Austria
	Hanni Wenzel, Liechtenstein	1988	Brigitte Oertli, Switzerland	1997–99	Not Awarded
1980	Hanni Wenzel, Liechtenstein	1989	Brigitte Oertli, Switzerland	2000	Renate Goetschl, Austria
1981	Maria-Therese Nadig,	1989	Brigitte Oertli, Switzerland	2001	Janica Kostelic, Croatia
	Switzerland	1990	Anita Wachter, Austria	2002	Renate Goetschl, Austria
1982	Irene Epple, West Germany	1991	Sabine Ginther, Austria	2003	Janica Kostelic, Croatia
1983	Hanni Wenzel, Liechtenstein	1992	Sabine Ginther, Austria	2004	Not Awarded
1984	Erika Hess, Switzerland	1993	Anita Wachter, Austria	2005	Janica Kostelic, Croatia
1985	Brigitte Oertli, Switzerland	1994	Pernilla Wiberg, Sweden	2006	Janica Kostelic, Croatia
1986	Maria Walliser, Switzerland	1995	Pernilla Wiberg, Sweden		

FIGURE SKATING

World Champions

Skaters who won World and Olympic championships in the same year are listed in **bold** type.

MEN

Multiple winners: Ulrich Salchow (10); Karl Schafer (7); Dick Button (5); Willy Bockl, Kurt Browning, Scott Hamilton and Hayes Jenkins and Alexei Yagudin (4); Emmerich Danzer, Gillis Grafstrom, Gustav Hugel, David Jenkins, Fritz Kachler, Ondrej Nepela, Evgeni Plushenko and Elvis Stojko (3); Brian Boitano, Gilbert Fuchs, Jan Hoffmann, Felix Kaspar, Vladimir Kovalev, Stephane Lambiel and Tim Wood (2).

Year		Year		Year	
1896	Gilbert Fuchs, Germany	1908	**Ulrich Salchow**, Sweden	1926	Willy Bockl, Austria
1897	Gustav Hugel, Austria	1909	Ulrich Salchow, Sweden	1927	Willy Bockl, Austria
1898	Henning Grenander, Sweden	1910	Ulrich Salchow, Sweden	1928	Willy Bockl, Austria
1899	Gustav Hugel, Austria	1911	Ulrich Salchow, Sweden	1929	Gillis Grafstrom, Sweden
1900	Gustav Hugel, Austria	1912	Fritz Kachler, Austria	1930	Karl Schafer, Austria
1901	Ulrich Salchow, Sweden	1913	Fritz Kachler, Austria	1931	Karl Schafer, Austria
1902	Ulrich Salchow, Sweden	1914	Gosta Sandhal, Sweden	1932	**Karl Schafer**, Austria
1903	Ulrich Salchow, Sweden	1915-21	Not held	1933	Karl Schafer, Austria
1904	Ulrich Salchow, Sweden	1922	Gillis Grafstrom, Sweden	1934	Karl Schafer, Austria
1905	Ulrich Salchow, Sweden	1923	Fritz Kachler, Austria	1935	Karl Schafer, Austria
1906	Gilbert Fuchs, Germany	1924	**Gillis Grafstrom**, Sweden	1936	**Karl Schafer**, Austria
1907	Ulrich Salchow, Sweden	1925	Willy Bockl, Austria	1937	Felix Kaspar, Austria

Figure Skating (Cont.)

Year		Year		Year	
1938	Felix Kaspar, Austria	1968	Emmerich Danzer, Austria	1993	Kurt Browning, Canada
1939	Graham Sharp, Britain	1969	Tim Wood, USA	1994	Elvis Stojko, Canada
1940-46	Not held	1970	Tim Wood, USA	1995	Elvis Stojko, Canada
1947	Hans Gerschwiler, Switzerland	1971	Ondrej Nepela, Czechoslovakia	1996	Todd Eldredge, USA
1948	**Dick Button**, USA	1972	**Ondrej Nepela**, Czechoslovakia	1997	Elvis Stojko, Canada
1949	Dick Button, USA	1973	Ondrej Nepela, Czechoslovakia	1998	Alexei Yagudin, Russia
		1974	Jan Hoffmann, E. Germany	1999	Alexei Yagudin, Russia
1950	Dick Button, USA	1975	Sergie Volkov, USSR		
1951	Dick Button, USA	1976	**John Curry**, Britain	2000	Alexei Yagudin, Russia
1952	**Dick Button**, USA	1977	Vladimir Kovalev, USSR	2001	Evgeni Plushenko, Russia
1953	Hayes Jenkins, USA	1978	Charles Tickner, USA	2002	**Alexei Yagudin**, Russia
1954	Hayes Jenkins, USA	1979	Vladimir Kovalev, USSR	2003	Evgeni Plushenko, Russia
1955	Hayes Jenkins, USA			2004	Evgeni Plushenko, Russia
1956	**Hayes Jenkins**, USA	1980	Jan Hoffmann, E. Germany	2005	Stephane Lambiel, Switzerland
1957	David Jenkins, USA	1981	Scott Hamilton, USA	2006	Stephane Lambiel, Switzerland
1958	David Jenkins, USA	1982	Scott Hamilton, USA		
1959	David Jenkins, USA	1983	Scott Hamilton, USA		
1960	Alan Giletti, France	1984	**Scott Hamilton**, USA		
1961	Not held	1985	Alexander Fadeev, USSR		
1962	Donald Jackson, Canada	1986	Brian Boitano, USA		
1963	Donald McPherson, Canada	1987	Brian Orser, Canada		
1964	**Manfred Schnelldorfer**, W. Germany	1988	**Brian Boitano**, USA		
		1989	Kurt Browning, Canada		
1965	Alain Calmat, France	1990	Kurt Browning, Canada		
1966	Emmerich Danzer, Austria	1991	Kurt Browning, Canada		
1967	Emmerich Danzer, Austria	1992	**Viktor Petrenko**, CIS		

WOMEN

Multiple winners: Sonja Henie (10); Carol Heiss, Michelle Kwan and Herma Planck Szabo (5); Lily Kronberger and Katarina Witt (4); Sjoukje Dijkstra, Peggy Fleming and Meray Horvath (3); Tenley Albright, Linda Fratianne, Anett Poetzsch, Beatrix Schuba, Barbara Ann Scott, Gabriele Seyfert, Irina Slutskaya, Megan Taylor, Alena Vrzanova and Kristi Yamaguchi (2).

Year		Year		Year	
1906	Madge Syers, Britain	1949	Alena Vrzanova, Czechoslovakia	1980	**Anett Poetzsch**, E. Germany
1907	Madge Syers, Britain	1950	Alena Vrzanova, Czechoslovakia	1981	Denise Biellmann, Switzerland
1908	Lily Kronberger, Hungary	1951	Jeannette Altwegg, Britain	1982	Elaine Zayak, USA
1909	Lily Kronberger, Hungary	1952	Jacqueline Du Bief, France	1983	Rosalyn Sumners, USA
1910	Lily Kronberger, Hungary	1953	Tenley Albright, USA	1984	**Katarina Witt**, E. Germany
1911	Lily Kronberger, Hungary	1954	Gundi Busch, W. Germany	1985	Katarina Witt, E. Germany
1912	Meray Horvath, Hungary	1955	Tenley Albright, USA	1986	Debi Thomas, USA
1913	Meray Horvath, Hungary	1956	Carol Heiss, USA	1987	Katarina Witt, E. Germany
1914	Meray Horvath, Hungary	1957	Carol Heiss, USA	1988	**Katarina Witt**, E. Germany
1915-21	Not held	1958	Carol Heiss, USA	1989	Midori Ito, Japan
		1959	Carol Heiss, USA		
1922	Herma Planck-Szabo, Austria			1990	Jill Trenary, USA
1923	Herma Planck-Szabo, Austria	1960	**Carol Heiss**, USA	1991	Kristi Yamaguchi, USA
1924	**Herma Planck-Szabo**, AUT	1961	Not held	1992	**Kristi Yamaguchi**, USA
1925	Herma Planck-Szabo, Austria	1962	Sjoukje Dijkstra, Netherlands	1993	Oksana Baiul, Ukraine
1926	Herma Planck-Szabo, Austria	1963	Sjoukje Dijkstra, Netherlands	1994	Yuka Sato, Japan
1927	Sonja Henie, Norway	1964	**Sjoukje Dijkstra**, Netherlands	1995	Lu Chen, China
1928	**Sonja Henie**, Norway	1965	Petra Burka, Canada	1996	Michelle Kwan, USA
1929	Sonja Henie, Norway	1966	Peggy Fleming, USA	1997	Tara Lipinski, USA
1930	Sonja Henie, Norway	1967	Peggy Fleming, USA	1998	Michelle Kwan, USA
1931	Sonja Henie, Norway	1968	**Peggy Fleming**, USA	1999	Maria Butyrskaya, Russia
1932	**Sonja Henie**, Norway	1969	Gabriele Seyfert, E. Germany		
1933	Sonja Henie, Norway	1970	Gabriele Seyfert, E. Germany	2000	Michelle Kwan, USA
1934	Sonja Henie, Norway	1971	Beatrix Schuba, Austria	2001	Michelle Kwan, USA
1935	Sonja Henie, Norway	1972	**Beatrix Schuba**, Austria	2002	Irina Slutskaya, Russia
1936	**Sonja Henie**, Norway	1973	Karen Magnussen, Canada	2003	Michelle Kwan, USA
1937	Cecilia Colledge, Britain	1974	Christine Errath, E. Germany	2004	Shizuka Arakawa, Japan
1938	Megan Taylor, Britain	1975	Dianne DeLeeuw, Netherlands	2005	Irina Slutskaya, Russia
1939	Megan Taylor, Britain	1976	**Dorothy Hamill**, USA	2006	Kimmie Meissner, USA
1940-46	Not held	1977	Linda Fratianne, USA		
1947	Barbara Ann Scott, Canada	1978	Anett Poetzsch, E. Germany		
1948	**Barbara Ann Scott**, Canada	1979	Linda Fratianne, USA		

U.S. Champions

Skaters who won U.S., World and Olympic championships in same year are in **bold** type.

MEN

Multiple winners: Dick Button and Roger Turner (7); Todd Eldredge (6); Sherwin Badger and Robin Lee (5); Brian Boitano, Scott Hamilton, David Jenkins, Hayes Jenkins and Charles Tickner (4); Gordon McKellen, Nathaniel Niles, Johnny Weir, Michael Weiss and Tim Wood (3); Scott Allen, Christopher Bowman, Scott Davis, Eugene Turner and Gary Visconti (2).

Year		Year		Year		Year	
1914	Norman Scott	1940	Eugene Turner	1965	Gary Visconti	1989	Christopher Bowman
1915-17	Not held	1941	Eugene Turner	1966	Scott Allen	1990	Todd Eldredge
1918	Nathaniel Niles	1942	Robert Specht	1967	Gary Visconti	1991	Todd Eldredge
1919	Not held	1943	Arthur Vaughn	1968	Tim Wood	1992	Christopher Bowman
1920	Sherwin Badger	1944-45	Not held	1969	Tim Wood	1993	Scott Davis
1921	Sherwin Badger	1946	Dick Button			1994	Scott Davis
1922	Sherwin Badger	1947	Dick Button	1970	Tim Wood	1995	Todd Eldredge
1923	Sherwin Badger	1948	**Dick Button**	1971	John (Misha) Petkevich	1996	Rudy Galindo
1924	Sherwin Badger	1949	Dick Button	1972	Ken Shelley	1997	Todd Eldredge
1925	Nathaniel Niles	1950	Dick Button	1973	Gordon McKellen	1998	Todd Eldredge
1926	Chris Christenson	1951	Dick Button	1974	Gordon McKellen	1999	Michael Weiss
1927	Nathaniel Niles	1952	**Dick Button**	1975	Gordon McKellen	2000	Michael Weiss
1928	Roger Turner	1953	Hayes Jenkins	1976	Terry Kubicka	2001	Tim Goebel
1929	Roger Turner	1954	Hayes Jenkins	1977	Charles Tickner	2002	Todd Eldredge
1930	Roger Turner	1955	Hayes Jenkins	1978	Charles Tickner	2003	Michael Weiss
1931	Roger Turner	1956	**Hayes Jenkins**	1979	Charles Tickner	2004	Johnny Weir
1932	Roger Turner	1957	David Jenkins	1980	Charles Tickner	2005	Johnny Weir
1933	Roger Turner	1958	David Jenkins	1981	Scott Hamilton	2006	Johnny Weir
1934	Roger Turner	1959	David Jenkins	1982	Scott Hamilton		
1935	Robin Lee	1960	David Jenkins	1983	Scott Hamilton		
1936	Robin Lee	1961	Bradley Lord	1984	**Scott Hamilton**		
1937	Robin Lee	1962	Monty Hoyt	1985	Brian Boitano		
1938	Robin Lee	1963	Thomas Litz	1986	Brian Boitano		
1939	Robin Lee	1964	Scott Allen	1987	Brian Boitano		
				1988	**Brian Boitano**		

WOMEN

Multiple winners: Michelle Kwan and Maribel Vinson (9); Theresa Weld Blanchard and Gretchen Merrill (6); Tenley Albright, Peggy Fleming and Janet Lynn (5); Linda Fratianne and Carol Heiss (4); Dorothy Hamill, Beatrix Loughran, Rosalyn Summers, Joan Tozzer and Jill Trenary (3); Yvonne Sherman and Debi Thomas (2).

Year		Year		Year		Year	
1914	Theresa Weld	1940	Joan Tozzer	1964	Peggy Fleming	1988	Debi Thomas
1915-17	Not held	1941	Jane Vaughn	1965	Peggy Fleming	1989	Jill Trenary
1918	Rosemary Beresford	1942	Jane Sullivan	1966	Peggy Fleming	1990	Jill Trenary
1919	Not held	1943	Gretchen Merrill	1967	Peggy Fleming	1991	Tonya Harding
1920	Theresa Weld	1944	Gretchen Merrill	1968	**Peggy Fleming**	1992	**Kristi Yamaguchi**
1921	Theresa Blanchard	1945	Gretchen Merrill	1969	Janet Lynn	1993	Nancy Kerrigan
1922	Theresa Blanchard	1946	Gretchen Merrill	1970	Janet Lynn	1994	vacated*
1923	Theresa Blanchard	1947	Gretchen Merrill	1971	Janet Lynn	1995	Nicole Bobek
1924	Theresa Blanchard	1948	Gretchen Merrill	1972	Janet Lynn	1996	Michelle Kwan
1925	Beatrix Loughran	1949	Yvonne Sherman	1973	Janet Lynn	1997	Tara Lipinski
1926	Beatrix Loughran	1950	Yvonne Sherman	1974	Dorothy Hamill	1998	Michelle Kwan
1927	Beatrix Loughran	1951	Sonya Klopfer	1975	Dorothy Hamill	1999	Michelle Kwan
1928	Maribel Vinson	1952	Tenley Albright	1976	**Dorothy Hamill**	2000	Michelle Kwan
1929	Maribel Vinson	1953	Tenley Albright	1977	Linda Fratianne	2001	Michelle Kwan
1930	Maribel Vinson	1954	Tenley Albright	1978	Linda Fratianne	2002	Michelle Kwan
1931	Maribel Vinson	1955	Tenley Albright	1979	Linda Fratianne	2003	Michelle Kwan
1932	Maribel Vinson	1956	Tenley Albright	1980	Linda Fratianne	2004	Michelle Kwan
1933	Maribel Vinson	1957	Carol Heiss	1981	Elaine Zayak	2005	Michelle Kwan
1934	Suzanne Davis	1958	Carol Heiss	1982	Rosalyn Sumners	2006	Sasha Cohen
1935	Maribel Vinson	1959	Carol Heiss	1983	Rosalyn Sumners		
1936	Maribel Vinson	1960	**Carol Heiss**	1984	Rosalyn Sumners		
1937	Maribel Vinson	1961	Laurence Owen	1985	Tiffany Chin		
1938	Joan Tozzer	1962	Barbara Pursley	1986	Debi Thomas		
1939	Joan Tozzer	1963	Lorraine Hanlon	1987	Jill Trenary		

* Tonya Harding was stripped of the 1994 women's title and banned from membership in the U.S. Figure Skating Assn. for life on June 30, 1994 for violating the USFSA Code of Ethics after she pleaded guilty to a charge of conspiracy to hinder the prosecution related to the Jan. 6, 1994 attack on Nancy Kerrigan.

TOUR DE FRANCE

The world's premier cycling event, the Tour de France is staged throughout the country (sometimes passing through neighboring countries) over four weeks. The 1946 Tour, however, the first after World War II, was only a five-day race.

Multiple winners: Lance Armstrong (7); Jacques Anquetil, Bernard Hinault, Miguel Induráin and Eddy Merckx (5); Louison Bobet, Greg LeMond and Philippe Thys (3); Gino Bartali Ottavio Bottecchia, Fausto Coppi, Laurent Fignon, Nicholas Frantz, Firmin Lambot, André Leducq, Sylvere Maes,. Antonin Magne, Lucien Petit-Breton and Bernard Thevenet (2).

Year	Winner	Time (hrs:min:sec)
1903	Maurice Garin, France	94:33:14
1904	Henri Cornet, France	96:05:55
1905	Louis Trousselier, France	112:18:09
1906	René Pottier, France	185:47:26
1907	Lucien Petit-Breton, France	156:22:30
1908	Lucien Petit-Breton, France	156:09:31
1909	Francois Faber, Luxembourg	156:55:10
1910	Octave Lapize, France	163:52:38
1911	Gustave Garrigou, France	195:35:25
1912	Odile Defraye, Belgium	184:50:00
1913	Philippe Thys, Belgium	197:54:00
1914	Philippe Thys, Belgium	200:28:49
1915-18	Not held	
1919	Firmin Lambot, Belgium	231:07:15
1920	Philippe Thys, Belgium	228:36:13
1921	Léon Scieur, Belgium	221:50:00
1922	Firmin Lambot, Belgium	222:08:06
1923	Henri Pelissier, France	222:15:30
1924	Ottavio Bottecchia, Italy	226:18:21
1925	Ottavio Bottecchia, Italy	219:10:13
1926	Lucien Buysse, Belgium	238:44:25
1927	Nicholas Frantz, Luxembourg	198:16:42
1928	Nicholas Frantz, Luxembourg	192:48:58
1929	Maurice Dewaele, Belgium	186:39:16
1930	André Leducq, France	172:12:10
1931	Antonin Magne, France	177:10:03
1932	André Leducq, France	154:11:49
1933	Georges Speicher, France	147:51:37
1934	Antonin Magne, France	147:03:58
1935	Romain Maes, Belgium	141:32:00
1936	Sylvere Maes, Belgium	142:47:32
1937	Roger Lapebie, France	138:58:31
1938	Gino Bartali, Italy	148:29:12
1939	Sylvere Maes, Belgium	132:03:17
1940-45	Not held	
1946	Jean Lazarides, France	44:31:42
1947	Jean Robic, France	148:11:25
1948	Gino Bartali, Italy	147:10:36
1949	Fausto Coppi, Italy	149:40:49
1950	Ferdinand Kubler, Switzerland	145:36:56
1951	Hugo Koblet, Switzerland	142:20:14
1952	Fausto Coppi, Italy	151:57:20
1953	Louison Bobet, France	129:23:25
1954	Louison Bobet, France	140:06:50
1955	Louison Bobet, France	130:29:26
1956	Roger Walkowiak, France	124:01:16
1957	Jacques Anquetil, France	135:44:42
1958	Charly Gaul, Luxembourg	116:59:05
1959	Federico Bahamontes, Spain	113:50:54

Year	Winner	Time (hrs:min:sec)
1960	Gastone Nencini, Italy	112:08:42
1961	Jacques Anquetil, France	122:01:33
1962	Jacques Anquetil, France	114:31:54
1963	Jacques Anquetil, France	113:30:05
1964	Jacques Anquetil, France	127:09:44
1965	Felice Gimondi, Italy	116:42:06
1966	Lucien Aimar, France	117:34:21
1967	Roger Pingeon, France	136:53.50
1968	Jan Janssen, Netherlands	133:49:42
1969	Eddy Merckx, Belgium	116:16:02
1970	Eddy Merckx, Belgium	119:31:48
1971	Eddy Merckx, Belgium	96:45:14
1972	Eddy Merckx, Belgium	108:17:18
1973	Luis Ocana, Spain	122:25:34
1974	Eddy Merckx, Belgium	116:16:58
1975	Bernard Thevenet, France	114:35:31
1976	Lucien van Impe, Belgium	116:22:23
1977	Bernard Thevenet, France	115:38:30
1978	Bernard Hinault, France	108:18:00
1979	Bernard Hinault, France	103:06:50
1980	Joop Zoetemelk, Netherlands	109:19:14
1981	Bernard Hinault, France	96:19:38
1982	Bernard Hinault, France	92:08:46
1983	Laurent Fignon, France	105:07:52
1984	Laurent Fignon, France	112:03:40
1985	Bernard Hinault, France	113:24:23
1986	Greg LeMond, USA	110:35:19
1987	Stephen Roche, Ireland	115:27:42
1988	Pedro Delgado, Spain	84:27:53
1989	Greg LeMond, USA	87:38:35
1990	Greg LeMond, USA	90:43:20
1991	Miguel Induráin, Spain	101:01:20
1992	Miguel Induráin, Spain	100:49:30
1993	Miguel Induráin, Spain	95:57:09
1994	Miguel Induráin, Spain	103:38:38
1995	Miguel Induráin, Spain	92:44:59
1996	Bjarne Riis, Denmark	95:57:16
1997	Jan Ullrich, Germany	100:30:35
1998	Marco Pantani, Italy	92:49:46
1999	Lance Armstrong, USA	91:32:16
2000	Lance Armstrong, USA	92:33:08
2001	Lance Armstrong, USA	86:17:28
2002	Lance Armstrong, USA	82:05:12
2003	Lance Armstrong, USA	83:41:12
2004	Lance Armstrong, USA	83:36:02
2005	Lance Armstrong, USA	86:15:02
2006	Floyd Landis, USA	89:39:30

Note: Landis' 2006 win is currently under appeal (as of Sept. 28, 2006).

RUGBY

World Cup

The inaugural Rugby World Cup was held in 1987. Like soccer's World Cup, it is held every four years. Sixteen national teams were assembled for the first three tournaments but beginning in 1999, 20 teams played for the William Webb Ellis Cup, named for the game's inventor. The Rugby World Cup is now billed as the world's third largest athletic event, behind the Olympics and the soccer World Cup.

Year	Winner	Score	Runner up	Host Country
1987	New Zealand	29-9	France	Australia & New Zealand
1991	Australia	12-6	England	United Kingdom & France
1995	South Africa	15-12	New Zealand	South Africa
1999	Australia	35-12	France	Wales
2003	England	20-17	Australia	Australia

OLYMPIC GAMES

2005 / 2006 YEAR IN REVIEW

American snowboarder **Shaun White** flew to a halfpipe gold medal in spectacular fashion in 2006.

ITALIAN ICE

Some high profile Americans suffered meltdowns on the world stage while others stayed frosty and peaked in the Italian Alps.

THE TURIN OLYMPICS LIVED UP TO THE HYPE, if not so much the hyped. Much ink went to flamboyant favorites like skier Bode Miller and snowboarder Lindsey Jacobellis leading up to the Games, but it was the unknowns who became darlings when the torch went out.

Miller was arguably the best alpine skier the American team ever had, and his bold statements about skiing drunk only added to his renegade legend. But he partied more than he performed, and left Americans placing more pride in young slalom star Ted Ligety, who took the alpine combined gold.

Days later, on the women's side, Julia Mancuso took gold in the giant slalom and Lindsey Kildow bravely returned from a horrific crash in training to finish eighth in the downhill.

Snowboarder Lindsey Jacobellis' good looks, huge talent and expertise in the hot new sport of snowboard cross got her almost as much pre-Games love as Miller, but she turned a lead into a loss when she attempted a board trick in mid-air, lost her balance and tumbled to silver. That left the stage to X Games phenom Shaun White, who danced through the air to land gold in the halfpipe.

Another crossover legend, speed skater Chad Hedrick, did not fare as well as hoped. After only three years in the sport, the former inline skater did win three medals, including a gold in the 5000m, but he didn't match Eric Heiden's gold standard record five of 1980. Shani Davis became the first African American man to win a winter gold medal, winning his specialty, the 1000m, but his flat refusal to participate in a men's relay developed a rift between he and Hedrick, which at times overshadowed the accomplishments of the whole men's team. The spotlight

 **Eric Adelson** is a senior writer at ESPN The Magazine

AP/Wide World Photos

American **Lindsey Jacobellis** wiped out on a superfluous jump within sight of the finish line to blow the gold medal in the women's Olympic snowboardcross.

—and the Wheaties box—went instead to big-smiling North Carolina native Joey Cheek, who turned the final corner of the 500m to win gold. Cheek donated his USOC bonus to charity to help support children in poor nations. In short track, Apolo Anton Ohno matched his high expectations by winning gold in the 500 meters.

American figure skaters Johnny Weir and Sasha Cohen delighted stylistically, but also came up short in their bids for gold. The energetic Cohen silvered as the elegant Japanese skater, Shizuka Arakawa, won the individual event to bring home the only medal for Japan. As for the men, Russian Yevgney Plushenko completed his remarkable oeuvre with a gold, while Weir struggled to make it to the rink on time and failed to medal.

Pairs skating actually overshadowed the individual contests, as China's Zhang Dan got up from a terrible fall, restarted her program and, with partner Zhang Hao, won a silver medal. The usually smooth ice dancing competition was marred with falls, yet Russians Tatyana Navka and Roman Kostomarov won gold while Americans Tanith Belbin and Ben Agosto awed American fans on their way to silver.

In hockey, both heavily favored

Heavily hyped American **Bode Miller,** who was expected to threaten for four golds, straddled a slalom gate at the Turin Games and failed to win a medal in any event.

Canada and the aging Team USA crumbled and Finland dueled Scandinavian rival Sweden for the gold. The Three Crowns, behind the leadership of longtime national team members Mats Sundin, Peter Forsberg, and Nicklas Lidstrom—along with young goalie Henrik Lundqvist, won gold only 12 years after Forsberg's "stamp" goal announced Sweden's arrival as an international hockey power.

Sweden beat the U.S. on the women's side, but Canada took gold.

The Games' best story came from the overlooked sport of cross-country, as Norway's Frode Estil fell and lost 45 seconds at the start, then climbed furiously back into the lead group by the end of the race. He won silver, and some called the performance the greatest second place finish ever.

On the women's side, Canadian Sara Renner broke her ski pole yet medaled in pairs thanks to an assist from Norwegian coach Bjoernar Haakensmoen. The beautifully simple gesture became international news, and the coach received more than five tons of maple syrup in thanks from grateful Canadians.

"It was natural for me to do it, and I think anyone should have done it," Haakensmoen told the Associated Press.

"I didn't think about it. It was just a reflex...but the response has been unbelievable."

Despite the failure of its preordained stars, the American team finished second in the medal count, and held strong as an elite force in the Winter Games. However, as everyone from Miller to Cheek learned, potential rarely holds up like performance, and a good preamble never compares to a happy ending.

AP/Wide World Photos

ERIC ADELSON'S

Greatest Stories of the **Turin Winter Games**

10 **Greatest Hero:** The Wheaties box, and the best storyline, went to American speed-skater Joey Cheek, who won gold in the 500 meters and silver in the 1,000 then donated his USOC bonus money ($40,000) to Right to Play, the organization started by Norwegian speedskating legend Johann Olav Koss that uses sports to foster humanitarian aid in developing countries. Cheek's humility and spirit overshadowed not only the sparring between Hedrick and Davis, but every other storyline to emerge from Turin's stunning Oval Lingotto. He was elected by the U.S. team to serve as their flag-bearer at the Closing Ceremony.

09 **Greatest Unsung Nation:** The South Koreans continued to ascend in the sport of short-track speedskating, as the little nation that could, did, winning four out of the six individual golds up for grabs and both team golds. American Apolo Anton Ohno grew his soul patched legend with a win in the 500 meters.

08 **Greatest Stories:** Turin offered two events that became as inspirational as they were thrilling, and both occurred in cross-country skiing. Norwegian Frode Estil fell at the beginning of the pursuit and amazingly clawed all the way back to silver. And in the women's team sprint, Canadian Sara Renner broke her pole but finished second with team-mate Beckie Scott after a Norwegian coach offered up his pole. The gesture won the coach worldwide praise and many gallons of Canadian maple syrup.

07 **Greatest Soap Opera:** Drama usurped dominance in long-track speedskating, as the feud between Texan Chad Hedrick and Chicagoan Shani Davis stole the show. Hedrick fell short of his goal of winning five golds—winning only the 5,000 meters—but Davis became the first African-American male to win gold in the sport when he took the 1,000 meters. Meanwhile, the biggest hometown hero of the entire Games was dashing Italian Enrico Fabris, who won the 1,500 meters and then led his nation to gold in the team pursuit. Canadian Cindy Klassen broke a national record by winning her sixth career gold after entering the Games with only one.

06 **Greatest Mistake:** The frustration continued for the U.S. women's hockey team, as coach Ben Smith inexplicably left legend and leader Cammi Granato off the '06 team. That led to an historic upset at the hands of Sweden and a devastating bronze-medal finish.

05 Greatest Disappointment: A hugely disappointing stretch for North American hockey fans only got worse after a strike-wrecked NHL season when both Canada and the U.S. took early exits from gold-medal contention. Canada, stocked with NHL stars, somehow couldn't find a way to score, and the States, stocked with aging veterans, couldn't find a way to skate. Sweden did both, and the Three Crowns won gold to cement itself as an international powerhouse. The Canadian women outscored their first three opponents 36-1 on their way to gold.

04 Greatest Accomplishment: Americans' figure skating hopes rested on Michelle Kwan and Sasha Cohen, but Kwan pulled out before the Games because of injury and Cohen's falls cost her gold. That opened a curtain on the delightful and technically stunning Japanese skater Shizuka Arakawa, who became the first Asian-born woman to win Olympic figure skating gold. At 25, she also became the second oldest. Russian wonder Yevgeny Plushenko dominated the men's event to win his first Olympic gold, and American ice dancers Tanith Belbin and Benjamin Agosto captivated by winning silver.

03 Greatest Overestimation: American ski fans (and marketers) prepared for the coronation of the nation's "best-ever" downhill skier, but New Hampshire hero Bode Miller got crowned in Turin, going without a medal. His partying and pontificating won him iconoclastic reverence leading up to the Games, but it did not win him any patience after he missed the podium five times. Slalom expert Ted Ligety saved the Games for the U.S. Ski team by winning a surprise gold in Combined.

02 Greatest Revelation: Olympics fans found a sport of the future in the thrilling (and borderline dangerous) event of Snowboard Cross, where boarders race down a mountain in packs. American Seth Wescott became the first gold medalist in the new discipline, but blonde dervish Lindsey Jacobellis threw away a sure gold by blowing the landing on a backside method grab and falling during her final jump. She silvered.

01 Greatest Emergence: Red-headed X-Gamer Shaun White beamed during Opening Ceremonies and shined throughout the Games, leaping from wild popularity to icon status among the latest generation of American athletes. White posted an untouchable 46.8 in the half-pipe to win gold. On the women's side, Hannah Teter won gold with a 46.4.

2006
Games in Review

SPORTS ALMANAC

Final Medal Standings

Full results of the XXth Olympic Winter Games at Turin, Italy from Feb. 10-26, 2006. National medal stadings are not recognized by the IOC. The unofficial point totals are based on three points for every gold medal, two for each silver and one for each bronze. Eighty-four nations competed but only 26 medaled.

		G	S	B	Total	Points			G	S	B	Total	Points
1	Germany	11	12	6	29	63	14	Finland	0	6	3	9	15
2	**United States**	9	9	7	25	52	15	Estonia	3	0	0	3	9
3	Canada	7	10	7	24	48	16	Czech Republic	1	2	1	4	8
	Austria	9	7	7	23	48	17	Croatia	1	2	0	3	7
5	Russia	8	6	8	22	44	18	Australia	1	0	1	2	4
6	Norway	2	8	9	19	31	19	Poland	0	1	1	2	3
7	Sweden	7	2	5	14	30	20	Japan	1	0	0	1	3
8	Switzerland	5	4	5	14	28	21	Ukraine	0	0	2	2	2
9	South Korea	6	3	2	11	26		Belarus	0	1	0	1	2
10	Italy	5	0	6	11	21		Bulgaria	0	1	0	1	2
11	China	2	4	5	11	19		Great Britain	0	1	0	1	2
12	France	3	2	4	9	17		Slovakia	0	1	0	1	2
	Netherlands	3	2	4	9	17	26	Latvia	0	0	1	1	1

2002 Salt Lake City Top 10: 1. **Germany** (35 medals, 75 points); 2. **United States** (34 medals, 67 points); 3. **Norway** (24 medals, 53 points); 4. **Russia** (16 medals, 34 points); 5. **Canada** (17 medals, 32 points); 6. **Austria** (17 medals, 25 points); 7. **Italy** (12 medals, 24 points) & **France** (11 medals, 24 points); 9. **Switzerland** (11 medals, 19 points) & **Netherlands** (8 medals, 19 points).

Leading Medal Winners

(*) indicates at least one medal earned as preliminary member of eventual medal-winning relay team. USA medalists in bold type.

Men

No		Sport	G-S-B
4	Ahn Hyun-Soo, KOR	ST Speed Skating	3-0-1
3	Michael Greis, GER	Biathlon	3-0-0
3	Felix Gottwald, AUT	Nordic Combined	2-1-0
3	Sven Fischer, GER	Biathlon	2-0-1
3	Enrico Fabris, ITA	Speed Skating	2-0-1
3	Lee Ho-suk, KOR	ST Speed Skating	1-2-0
3	**Chad Hedrick**, USA	Speed Skating	1-1-1
3	Georg Hettich, GER	Nordic Combined	1-1-1
3	Lars Bystoel, NOR	Ski Jumping	1-0-2
3	**Apolo Anton Ohno**, USA	ST Speed Skating	1-0-2
2	Ole Einar Bjoerndalen, NOR	Biathlon	0-2-1
2	Benjamin Raich, AUT	Alpine Skiing	2-0-0
2	Andre Lange, GER	Bobsled	2-0-0
2	Kevin Kuske, GER	Bobsled	2-0-0
2	Bjoern Lind, SWE	Nordic Skiing	2-0-0
2	Thomas Morgenstern, AUT	Ski Jumping	2-0-0
2	**Shani Davis**, USA	Speed Skating	1-1-0
2	**Joey Cheek**, USA	Speed Skating	1-1-0
2	Andreas Kofler, AUT	Ski Jumping	1-1-0
2	Pietro Piller Cottrer, ITA	Nordic Skiing	1-0-1
2	Vincent Defrasne, FRA	Biathlon	1-0-1
2	Thobias Fredriksson, SWE	Nordic Skiing	1-0-1
2	Francois-Louis Tremblay, CAN	ST Speed Skating	0-2-0
2	Matti Hautamaeki, FIN	Ski Jumping	0-2-0
2	Hermann Maier, AUT	Alpine Skiing	0-1-1
2	Sven Kramer, NED	Speed Skating	0-1-1
2	Halvard Hanevold, NOR	Biathlon	0-1-1
2	Tobias Anderer, GER	Nordic Skiing	0-1-1
2	Magnus Moan, NOR	Nodric Combined	0-1-1
2	Carl Verheijen, NED	Speed Skating	0-0-2
2	Roar Ljoekelsoey, NOR	Ski Jumping	0-0-2
2	Martin Annen, SUI	Bobsled	0-0-2
2	Beat Hefti, SUI	Bobsled	0-0-2
2	Erben Wennemars, NED	Speedskating	0-0-2
2	Rainer Schoenfelder, AUT	Alpine Skiing	0-0-2

Women

No		Sport	G-S-B
5	Cindy Klassen, CAN	Speed Skating	1-2-2
3	Jin Sun-yu, KOR	ST Speed Skating	3-0-0
3	Kati Wilhelm, GER	Biathlon	1-2-0
3	Meng Wang, CHN	ST Speed Skating	1-1-1
3	Albina Akhatova, RUS	Biathlon	1-0-2
3	Anja Paerson, SWE	Alpine Skiing	1-0-2
3	Martina Glagow, GER	Biathlon	0-3-0
2	Svetlana Ishmouratova, RUS	Biathlon	2-0-0
2	Kristina Smigun, EST	Nordic Skiing	2-0-0
2	Michaela Dorfmeister, AUT	Alpine Skiing	2-0-0
2	Janica Kostelic, CRO	Alpine Skiing	1-1-0
2	Clara Hughes, CAN	Speed Skating	1-1-0
2	Choi Eun-kyung, KOR	ST Speed Skating	1-1-0
2	Katerina Neumannova, CZE	Nordic Skiing	1-1-0
2	Anna Carin Olofsson, SWE	Biathlon	1-1-0
2	Claudia Pechstein, GER	Speed Skating	1-1-0
2	Julija Tchepalova, RUS	Nordic Skiing	1-1-0
2	Ireen Wust, NED	Speed Skating	1-0-1
2	Anni Friesinger, GER	Speed Skating	1-0-1
2	Florence Baverel-Robert, FRA	Biathlon	1-0-1
2	E. Medvedeva-Abruzova, RUS	Nordic Skiing	1-0-1
2	Kristina Groves, CAN	Speed Skating	0-2-0
2	Claudia Kuenzel, GER	Speed Skating	0-2-0
2	Marlies Schild, AUT	Alpine Skiing	0-1-1
2	A. Leblanc-Boucher, CAN	ST Speed Skating	0-1-1

Medal Sports

Medal winners at the XXth Winter Olympic Games contested at Turin, Italy from Feb. 10-26, 2006.

ALPINE SKIING

Downhill and Super G, the two fastest events, consist of one run each. Slalom and giant slalom are two runs each. The combined event is one downhill run and two slalom runs. In all events, fastest combined time wins.
Medal Breakdown (10 events): **Fourteen medals**—Austria (4-5-5); **Four**—Sweden (1-0-3); **Three**—Croatia (1-2-0) and Switzerland (0-1-2); **Two**—France (1-1-0) and USA (2-0-0); **One**—Norway (1-0-0) and Finland (0-1-0)

MEN
Downhill

		Time
1	Antoine Deneriaz, FRA	1:48.80
2	Michael Walchofer, AUT	1:49.52
3	Bruno Kerne, SWI	1:49.82

Top 10 USA: 5th—Bode Miller (1:49.93). 10th—Daron Rahlves (1:50.33).

Slalom

		Time
1	Benjamin Raich, AUT	1:43.14
2	Reinfried Herbst, AUT	1:43.97
3	Rainer Schoenfelder, AUT	1:44.15

Best USA: 12th—James Cochran (1:45.68).

Giant Slalom

		Time
1	Benjamin Raich, AUT	2:35.00
2	Joel Chenal, FRA	2:35.07
3	Hermann Maier, AUT	2:35.16

Top 10 USA: 6th—Bode Miller (2:36.06).

Super G

		Time
1	Kjetil Andre Aamodt, NOR	1:30.65
2	Hermann Maier, AUT	1:30.78
3	Ambrosi Hoffman, SWI	1:30.98

Top 10 USA: 7th—Scott Macartney (1:31.23). 9th—Daron Rahlves (1:31.37).

Combined

		Time
1	Ted Ligety, USA	3:09.35
2	Ivica Kostelic, CRO	3:09.88
3	Rainer Schoenfelder, AUT	3:10.67

Next Best USA: 16th—Scott Macartney (3:13.05).

WOMEN
Downhill

		Time
1	Michaela Dorfmeister, AUT	1:56.49
2	Martina Schild, SWI	1:56.86
3	Anja Paerson, SWE	1:57.13

Top 10 USA: 7th—Julia Mancuso (1:57.71). 8th—Lindsey C. Kildow (1:57.78).

Slalom

		Time
1	Anja Paerson, SWE	1:29.04
2	Nicole Hosp, AUT	1:29.33
3	Marlies Schild, AUT	1:29.79

Top 10 USA: 10th—Sarah Schleper (1:31.38).

Giant Slalom

		Time
1	Julia Mancuso, USA	2:09.19
2	Tanja Poutianinen, FIN	2:09.86
3	Anna Ottosson, SWE	2:10.33

Next Best USA: 23rd—Stacey J. Cook (2:14.44).

Super G

		Time
1	Michaela Dorfmeister, AUT	1:32.47
2	Janica Kostelic, CRO	1:32.74
3	Alexandra Meissnitzer, AUT	1:33.06

Top 10 USA: 7th—Lindsey C. Kildow (1:33.42).

Combined

		Time
1	Janica Kostelic, CRO	2:51.08
2	Marlies Schild, AUT	2:51.58
3	Anja Paerson, SWE	2:51.63

Top 10 USA: 9th—Julia Mancuso (2:55.44).

BIATHLON

Cross country (any style) and rifle shooting (.22 caliber, small-bore, standing and prone). MT indicated missed targets.
Medal Breakdown (10 events): **Eleven medals**—Germany (5-4-2); **Six**—Norway (0-3-3); **Five**—Russia (2-1-2); **Four**—France (2-0-2); **Two**—Sweden (1-1-0); **One**—Poland (0-1-0), Ukraine (0-0-1).

MEN
10-km Sprint

		MT	Time
1	Sven Fischer, GER	0	26:11.6
2	Halvard Hanevold, NOR	0	26:19.8
3	Frode Andresen, NOR	1	26:31.3

Best USA: 37th—Tim Burke (28:27.8).

12.5-km Pursuit

		MT	Time
1	Vincent Defrasne, FRA	2	35:20.2
2	Ole Einar Bjoerndalen, NOR	3	35:22.9
3	Sven Fischer, GER	4	35:15.8

Best USA: 38th—Tim Burke (4 MT, 39:17.6).

15-km Mass Start

		MT	Time
1	Michael Greis, GER	1	47:20.0
2	Tomasz Sikora, POL	1	+6.3
3	Ole Einar Bjoerndalen, NOR	3	+12.3

Best USA: 13th—Jay Hakkinen (1 MT, +1:09.6).

20-km Individual

		MT	Time
1	Michael Greis, GER	1	54:23.0
2	Ole Einar Bjoerndalen, NOR	2	54:39.0
3	Halvard Hanevold, NOR	2	55:31.9

Top 10 USA: 10th—Jay Hakkinen (3 MT, 56:10.9).

4 x 7.5-km Relay

		MT	Time
1	Germany	1	1:21:51.5
2	Russia	0	1:22:12.4
3	France	0	1:22:35.1

GER—Rico Gross, Michael Roesch, Sven Fischer, Michael Greis; **RUS**—Ivan Tcherezov, Sergei Tchepikov, Pavel Rostovtsev, Nikolay Kruglov; **FRA**—Julien Robert, Vincent Defrasne, Ferreol Cannard, Raphael Poiree.

USA Entry: 9th—Jay Hakkinen, Tim Burke, Lowell Bailey, Jeremy Teela (1 MT, 1:24:23.4).

WOMEN

7.5-km Sprint

		MT	Time
1	Florence Baverel-Robert, FRA	0	22:31.4
2	Anna Carin Olofsson, SWE	1	22:33.8
3	Lilla Efremova, UKR	0	22:38.0

Best USA: 35th—Rachel Steer (1 MT, 24:29.6).

10-km Pursuit

		MT	Time
1	Kati Wilhelm, GER	2	36:43.6
2	Martina Glagow, GER	3	+1:13.6
3	Albina Akhatova, RUS	1	+1:21.4

Best USA: 39th—Rachel Steer (3 MT, +6:49.3).

12.5-km Mass Start

		MT	Time
1	Anna Carin Olofsson, SWE	1	40:36.5
2	Kati Wilhelm, GER	1	40:55.3
3	Uschi Disl, GER	3	41:18.4

Best USA: none.

15-km Individual

		MT	Time
1	Svetlana Ishmouratova, RUS	1	49:24.1
2	Martina Glagow, GER	2	50:34.9
3	Albina Akhatova, RUS	2	50:55.0

Best USA: 41th—Rachel Steer (3 MT, 55:48.3).

Note: Russia's Olga Pyleva initially won the silver medal but was stripped of her medal and expelled from the Games after testing positive for the stimulant carphedon.

4 x 7.5-km Relay

		MT	Time
1	Russia	0	1:16:12.5
2	Germany	1	1:17:03.2
3	France	0	1:18:38.7

RUS—Olga Zaitseva, Anna Bogaliy, Albina Akhatova, Svetlana Ishmouratova; **GER**—Andrea Henkel, Martina Glagow, Kati Wilhelm, Katrin Aprel **FRA**—Sandrine Bailly, Florence Baverel-Robert, Sylvie Becaert, Delphyne Peretto.

USA Entry: 15th—Tracy Barnes, Rachel Steer, Carolyn Treacy, Lanny Barnes (0 MT, 1:25:20.3).

BOBSLED

In all three Olympic bobsled events, teams make two runs on consecutive days for a total of four runs. The sled with the fastest total time (all runs count), figured to the hundredth of a second, is the winner.

Medal Breakdown (3 events): **Three medals**—Germany (3-0-0); **Two**—Switzerland (0-0-2); **One**—Canada (0-1-0); Russia (0-1-0); United States (0-1-0); Italy (0-0-1).

Two-Man

		Time
1	Germany I	3:43.38
2	Canada I	3:43.59
3	Switzerland I	3:43.73

GER I—Andre Lange & Kevin Kuske; **CAN I**—Pierre Lueders & Lascelles Brown; **SWI I**—Martin Annen & Beat Hefti.

Top 10 USA: 7th, **USA I**—Todd Hays & Pavle Jovanovic.

Two-Woman

		Time
1	Germany I	3:49.98
2	United States I	3:50.69
3	Italy I	3:51.01

GER I—Sandra Kiriasis & Anja Schneiderheinze; **USA I**—Shauna Rohbock & Valerie Fleming; **ITA I**—Gerda Wiessensteiner & Jennifer Isacco.

Other Top 10 USA: 6th, **USA II**—Jean Prahm & Vonetta Flowers.

Four-Man

		Time
1	Germany I	3:40.42
2	Russia I	3:40.55
3	Switzerland I	3:40.83

GER I—Andre Lange, Rene Hoppe, Kevin Kuske, Martin Putze; **RUS I**—Aleksandr Zoubkov, Filipp Egorov, Alexej Seliverstov, Alexey Voevoda; **SWI I**—Martin Annen, Thomas Lamparter, Beat Hefti, Cedric Grand.

Top 10 USA: 6th, **USA II**—Steve Holcomb, Curt Tomasevicz, Bill Schuffenhauer, Lorenzo Smith III; 7th, **USA I**—Todd Hays, Pavle Jovanovic, Steve Mesler, Brock Kreitzburg.

> ### STEROIDS STRIKE BOBSLEDDING!
> Brazil, the lone tropical nation to qualify for the bobsledding competition at Turin, was also the first team to have an athlete disqualified from the 2006 Winter Games for steroids. Sao Paulo's Armando dos Santos tested positive for nandrolone.

CROSS COUNTRY SKIING

There are two techniques in cross country: classical (parallel skis) and freestyle (skating style). The Sprint features a qualification round with the fastest 16 skiers moving on to elimination heats. Top two finishers in each heat advance until there is a four-skier final.

Medal breakdown (12 events): **Seven medals**—Russia (2-2-3); **Five**—Sweden (3-0-2); **Four**—Italy (2-0-2), Norway (0-3-1), Germany (0-3-1); **Three**—Estonia (3-0-0), Czech Republic (1-2-0); **Two**—Canada (1-1-0); **One**—France (0-1-0), Poland (0-0-1), Austria (0-0-1), Finland (0-0-1).

MEN

1.4-km Sprint

		Time
1	Bjoern Lind, SWE	2:26.5
2	Roddy Darragon, FRA	2:27.1
3	Thobias Fredriksson, SWE	2:27.8

15-km Classical

		Time
1	Andrus Veerpalu, EST	38:01.3
2	Lukas Bauer, CZE	38:15.8
3	Tobias Angerer, GER	38:20.5

Best USA: 22nd—Kris Freeman (39:57.4)

Team Sprint

		Time
1	Sweden	17:02.9
2	Norway	17:03.5
3	Russia	17:05.2

SWE—Thobias Fredrikssonn and Bjoern Lind; **NOR**—Jens Arne Svartedal and Tor Arne Hetland; **RUS**—Ivan Alypov and Vassili Rotschev.

30-km Combined Pursuit

		Time
1	Eugeni Dementiev, RUS	1:17:00.8
2	Frode Estil, NOR	1:17:01.4
3	Pietro Piller Cottrer, ITA	1:17:01.7

Cross Country Skiing (Cont.)
MEN

4 x 10–km Mixed Relay
		Time
1	Italy	1:43:45.7
2	Germany	1:44:01.4
3	Sweden	1:44:01.7

ITA—Fulvio Valbusa, Giorgio Di Centa, Pietro Piller Cottrer, Cristian Zorzi; **GER**—Andreas Schluetter, Jens Filbrich, Rene Sommerfeldt, Tobias Angerer; **SWE**—Mats Larsson, Johan Olsson, Anders Soedergren, Mathias Fredriksson.

USA Entry: 12th—Kris Freeman, Lars Floram, Andrew Johnson, Carl Swenson (1:48:44.2)

50–km Freestyle
		Time
1	Giorgio Di Centa, ITA	2:06:11.8
2	Eugeni Dementiev, RUS	2:06:12.6
3	Mikhail Botwinov, AUT	2:06:12.7

Best USA: 34th—Andrew Johnson (2:07:56.3)

WOMEN

1.2-km Sprint
		Time
1	Chandra Crawford, CAN	2:12.3
2	Claudia Kuenzel, GER	2:13.0
3	Alena Sidko, RUS	2:13.2

10-km Classical
		Time
1	Kristina Smigun, EST	27:51.4
2	Marit Bjorgen, NOR	28:12.7
3	Hilde G. Pedersen, NOR	28:14.0

Best USA: 50th—Wendy Wagner (31:41.0)

Team Sprint
		Time
1	Sweden	16:36.9
2	Canada	16:37.5
3	Finland	16:39.2

SWE—Anna Dahlberg and Lina Andersson; **CAN**—Sara Renner and Beckie Scott; **FIN**—Aino Kaisa Saarinen and Virpi Kuitunen.

USA Entry: 10th—Wendy Wagner and Kikkan Randall.

15-km Combined Pursuit
		Time
1	Kristina Smigun, EST	42:48.7
2	Katerina Neumannova, CZE	42:50.6
3	Evgenia Medvedeva-Abruzova, RUS	43:03.2

Best USA: 48th—Rebecca Dussault (47:53.7)

4 x 5-km Mixed Relay
		Time
1	Russia	54:47.7
2	Germany	54:57.7
3	Italy	54:58.7

RUS—Natalia Baranova-Masolkina, Larisa Kurkina, Yulia Tchepalova, Evgenia Medvedeva-Abruzova; **GER**—Stefanie Boehler, Viola Bauer, Evi Sachenbacher Stehle, Claudia Kuenzel; **ITA**—Arianna Follis, Gabriella Paruzzi, Antonella Confortola, Sabina Valbusa.

USA Entry: 14th—Wendy Wagner, Kikkan Randall, Sarah Konrad, Rebecca Dussault (57:58.4)

30–km Freestyle
		Time
1	Katerina Neumannova, CZE	1:22:25.4
2	Yulia Tchepalova, RUS	1:22:26.8
3	Justyna Kowalczyk, POL	1:22:27.5

Best USA: 32nd—Sarah Konrad (1:28:39.2)

CURLING

Teams attempt to slide a 20-kg (42 lbs) stone into a three-circle target six feet in diameter called the "house." The team with the stone closest to the center circle, the "tee," gets a point. All stones of the winning team which are closer to the center than is the nearest stone of the opponent are also given one point each. After 10 rounds or "ends" the team with the most points wins.

Medal Breakdown (2 events): Two medals—Canada (1-010); **One**—Sweden (1-0-0), Finland (0-1-0), Switzerland (0-1-0), United States (0-0-1).

MEN
Round Robin Standings

	W-L		W-L
*Finland	7-2	Norway	5-4
*Canada	6-3	Italy	4-5
*Great Britain	6-3	Germany	3-6
*United States	6-3	Sweden	3-6
Switzerland	5-4	New Zealand	0-9

*Advanced to the semifinal round.

Semifinals
Canada 11	United States 5
Finland 4	Great Britain 3

Bronze Medal
United States 8	Great Britain 6

Gold Medal
Canada 10	Finland 4

WOMEN
Round Robin Standings

	W-L		W-L
*Switzerland	7-2	Russia	5-4
*Sweden	7-2	Japan	4-5
*Canada	6-3	Denmark	2-7
*Norway	6-3	United States	2-7
Great Britain	5-4	Italy	1-8

*Advanced to the semifinal round.

Semifinals
Sweden 5	Norway 4
Switzerland 7	Canada 5

Bronze Medal
Canada 11	Norway 5

Gold Medal
Sweden 7	Switzerland 6

FIGURE SKATING

All four events consist of a short program (two minutes and 50 seconds) and a free skate, sometimes called the "long program" (max. 4:40 for men and 4:10 for women). The short program must contain eight required elements in any sequence. A new scoring system was put in place in the aftermath of the "skategate" controversy that struck the 2002 Salt Lake City Winter Games. Major changes include an expanded panel of 12 judges from which nine are chosen anonymously and at random and the high and low scores from each element are thrown out and the remaining seven scores are averaged.

Medal breakdown (4 events): **Four medals**—Russia (3-0-1); **Two**—United States (0-2-0), China (0-1-1); **One**—Japan (1-0-0), Switzerland (0-1-0), Canada (0-0-1), Ukraine (0-0-1).

MEN

		Pts
1	Yevgeny Plushenko, RUS	258.33
2	Stephane Lambiel, SWI	231.21
3	Jeffrey Buttle, CAN	227.59

Top 10 USA: 4th—Evan Lysacek (220.13); 5th—Johnny Weir (216.63); 7th—Matt Savoie (206.67).

Pairs

		Pts
1	Tatyana Totmiyanina & Maxim Marinin, RUS	204.48
2	Dan Zhang & Hao Zhang, CHN	189.73
3	Xue Shen & Hongbo Zhao, CHN	186.91

Top 10 USA: 7th—Rena Inoue & John Baldwin (175.01).

WOMEN

		Pts
1	Shizuka Arakawa, JPN	191.34
2	Sasha Cohen, USA	183.36
3	Irina Slutskaya, RUS	181.44

Other Top 10 USA: 6th—Kimmie Meissner (165.71); 7th—Emily Hughes (160.87).

Ice Dancing

		Pts
1	Tatyana Navka & Roman Kostomarov, RUS	200.64
2	Tanith Belbin & Ben Agosto, USA	196.06
3	Yelena Grushina & Ruslan Goncharov, UKR	195.85

Other USA Entries: 14th—Melissa Gregory & Denis Petukhov; 16th—Jamie Silverstein & Ryan O'Meara.

FREESTYLE SKIING

Aerials consist of two jumps wih points awarded for execution and precision (50%), height and distance (20%) and landing (30%). Moguls consist of turns executed on a bumpy course (50%), two aerials (25%) and elasped time (25%).

Medal breakdown (4 events): **Two medals**—China (1-1-0), Australia (1-0-1); **One**—Switzerland (1-0-0), Canada (1-0-0), Norway (0-1-0), Finland (0-1-0), Belarus (0-1-0), Russia (0-0-1), France (0-0-1), United States (0-0-1).

MEN
Aerials

		Pts
1	Xiaopeng Han, CHN	250.77
2	Dmitry Dashinski, BLR	248.68
3	Vladimir Lebedev, RUS	246.76

Top 10 USA: 7th—Jeret Peterson (237.48).

Moguls

		Pts
1	Dale Begg-Smith, AUS	26.77
2	Mikko Ronkainen, FIN	26.62
3	Toby Dawson, USA	26.30

Other Top 10 USA: 6th—Jeremy Bloom (25.17); 7th—Travis Mayer (24.91), 9th—Travis Cabral (24.38).

WOMEN
Aerials

		Pts
1	Evelyne Leu, SWI	202.55
2	Nina Li, CHN	197.39
3	Alisa Camplin, AUS	191.39

Top 10 USA: None.

Moguls

		Pts
1	Jennifer Heil, CAN	26.50
2	Kari Traa, NOR	25.65
3	Sandra Laoura, FRA	25.37

Best USA: 10th—Shannon Bahrke (22.82), 11th—Jillian Vogtli (22.72), 18th—Michelle Roark (20.04).

ICE HOCKEY

Medal breakdown (2 events): **Two medals**—Sweden (0-2-0); **One**—Canada (1-0-0), Finland (1-0-0), Czech Republic (0-0-1), United States (0-0-1).

MEN

Round Robin Standings

Group A	W-L-T	Pts	GF	GA
*Finland	5-0-0	10	19	2
*Switzerland	2-1-2	6	10	12
*Canada	3-0-2	6	15	9
*Czech Republic	2-3-0	4	14	12
Germany	0-3-2	2	7	16
Italy	0-3-2	2	9	23

Group B	W-L-T	Pts	GF	GA
*Slovakia	5-0-0	10	18	8
*Russia	4-1-0	8	23	11
*Sweden	3-2-0	6	15	12
*United States	1-3-1	3	13	13
Kazakhstan	1-4-0	2	9	16
Latvia	0-4-1	1	11	31

*Advanced to medal round.

Quarterfinals

Sweden 6 . . . . .Switzerland 2
Finland 4 . . . . .United States 3
Russia 2 . . . . .Canada 0
Czech Republic 3 . . . . .Slovakia 1

Semifinals

Sweden 7 . . . . .Czech Republic 3
Finland 4 . . . . .Russia 0

Bronze Medal

Czech Republic 3 . . . . .Russia 0

Gold Medal

Sweden 3 . . . . .Finland 2

Ice Hockey (Cont.)

MEN

Leading Scorers

	Gm	G	A	Pts	+/-
Teemu Selanne, FIN	8	6	5	11	7
Marian Hossa, SVK	6	5	5	10	9
Daniel Alfredsson, SWE	8	5	5	10	2
Saku Koivu, FIN	8	3	7	10	5
Ville Peltonen, FIN	8	4	5	9	4
Olli Jokinen, FIN	8	6	2	8	5
Jere Lehtinen, FIN	8	3	5	8	6
Mats Sundin, SWE	8	3	5	8	1
Martin Straka, CZE	8	2	6	8	4
Pavel Datsyuk, RUS	8	1	7	8	5

Leading Goaltenders

	Gm	Svs	GAA
Antero Niittymaki, FIN	6	156	1.34
Evgeni Nabokov, RUS	7	126	1.34
David Aebischer, SWI	4	110	2.10
Martin Brodeur, CAN	4	96	2.01
Peter Budaj, SVK	3	73	2.01
Vitaliy Yeremeyev, KAZ	6	137	2.33
Henrik Lundqvist, SWE	6	137	2.33
Rick DiPietro, USA	4	75	2.28

Gold Medal Game

Sunday, Feb. 26, 2006 at Palasport Olimpico

	1	2	3	F
Finland	1	1	0	2
Sweden	0	2	1	3

Scoring

1st PERIOD—Kimmo Timonen, FIN (Teemu Selanne) 14:14.

2nd PERIOD—Henrik Zetterberg, SWE (Mikael Samuelsson, Christian Backman) 4:42; Niklas Kronwall, SWE (Zetterberg) 13:24; Ville Peltonen, FIN (Jussi Jokinen, Olli Jokinen) 15:00.

3rd PERIOD—Nicklas Lidstrom (Mats Sundin, Peter Forsberg) 00:10.

Goaltenders

FINLAND—Antero Niittymaki (28 shots, 25 saves); SWEDEN—Henrik Lundqvist (27 shots, 25 saves).

Referee: Paul Devorski, Canada.

WOMEN

Round Robin Standings

Group A	W-L-T	Pts	GF	GA
*Canada	3-0-0	6	36	1
*Sweden	2-1-0	4	15	9
Russia	1-2-0	2	6	16
Italy	0-3-0	0	1	32
Group B	W-L-T	Pts	GF	GA
*United States	3-0-0	6	18	3
*Finland	2-1-0	4	10	7
Germany	1-2-0	2	2	9
Switzerland	0-3-0	0	1	12

*Advanced to medal round.

Placement Round: 7th place—Switzerland 11, Italy 0; 5th place—Germany 1, Russia 0.

Semifinals

Sweden 3	United States 2
Canada 6	Finland 0

Bronze Medal

United States 4 .... Finland 0

Gold Medal

Canada 4 .... Sweden 1

Scoring: 1st PERIOD—Gillian Apps, CAN (Hayley Wickenheiser), 3:15; Caroline Ouellette, CAN (Jayna Hefford, Jennifer Botterill), 12:13. 2nd PERIOD—Cherie Piper, CAN (Wickenheiser, Cheryl Pounder), 8:58; Hefford, CAN (Botterill, Sarah Vaillancourt). 3rd PERIOD—Gunilla Andersson, SWE (Erika Holst, Maria Rooth).

LUGE

Medal breakdown (3 events): **Four medals**—Germany (1-2-1); **Two**—Italy (1-0-1); **One**—Austria (1-0-0), Russia (0-1-0).

MEN
Singles

		Time
1	Armin Zoeggeler, ITA	3:26.088
2	Albert Demtschenko, RUS	3:26.198
3	Martins Rubenis, LAT	3:26.445

Top 10 USA: 4th—Tony Benshoof (3:26.598).

Doubles

		Time
1	Andreas Linger & Wolfgang Linger, AUT	1:34.497
2	Andre Florschuetz & Torsten Wustlich, GER	1:34.807
3	Oswald Haselrieder & Gerhard Plankensteiner, ITA	1:34.930

Top 10 USA: 8th—Preston Griffall & Dan Joye (1:35.410).

WOMEN
Singles

		Time
1	Sylke Otto, GER	3:07.979
2	Silke Kraushaar, GER	3:08.115
3	Tatjana Huefner, GER	3:08.460

Top 10 USA: 4th—Courtney Zablocki (3:08.852)

SKELETON

The event's named is derived from the prototype of today's sleds, which resembled human skeletons. The event was revived in 2002 after leaving the Olympic schedule following the 1948 Winter Games. Its similar to luge except athletes lie stomach-down and head-first. Two runs held on one day, and medals are awarded for lowest aggregate times.

Medal breakdown (2 events): **Three medals**—Canada (1-1-1); **Two**—Switzerland (1-0-1); **One**—Great Britain (0-1-0).

MEN
Singles

		Time
1	Duff Gibson, CAN	1:55.88
2	Jeff Pain, CAN	1:56.14
3	Gregor Staehli, SWI	1:56.80

Top 10 USA: 6th—Eric Bernotas (1:57.19).

WOMEN
Singles

		Time
1	Maya Pedersen, SWI	1:59.83
2	Shelley Rudman, GBR	2:01.06
3	Melissa Hollingsworth-Richards, CAN	2:01.41

Top 10 USA: 6th—Katie Uhlaender (2:02.30).

NORDIC COMBINED

Each event consists of a ski jump followed by a cross country race (freestyle). Using the Gundersen Method, the cross country starting order in all events is determined by finish in ski jump. This scoring system converts point differentials in the jumping portion of the event into exact time intervals that staggers the start of the cross country race. The **Jump** column shows the athlete's final jump score, in points, with place in parentheses. Cross country times shown are adjusted to include the competitors' staggered start time.

Sprint

One jump off large hill followed the next day by a 7.5-km cross country race.

		Jump	7.5-km
1	Felix Gottwald, AUT	112.1 (12)	18:29.0
2	Magnus Moan, NOR	111.8 (13)	18:34.4
3	Georg Hettich, GER	125.7 (1)	18:38.6

Top 10 USA: 9th—Todd Lodwick (107.3 (19), 19:11.4); 10th—Johnny Spillane (109.5 (14), 19:15.2).

Individual

Two jumps off normal hill followed the next day by a 15-km cross country race.

		Jump	15-km
1	Georg Hettich, GER	262.5 (1)	39:44.6
2	Felix Gottwald, AUT	234.5 (11)	39:54.4
3	Magnus Moan, NOR	237.5 (9)	40:00.8

Top 10 USA: 8th—Todd Lodwick (232.0 (13), 40:56.6).

Team

Two jumps off normal hill for each teams four skiers followed the next day by a 4x5-km cross country relay

		Jump	4x5-km
1	Austria	903.2 (2)	49:52.6
2	Germany	913.5 (1)	50:07.9
3	Finland	878.6 (4)	50:19.4

AUT—Michael Gruber, Christoph Bieler, Felix Gottwald, Mario Stecher; **GER**—Bjoern Kircheisen, Georg Hettich, Ronny Ackermann, Jens Gaiser; **FIN**—Antti Kuisma, Anssi Koivuranta, Jaakko Tallus, Hannu Manninen.

USA Entry: 7th—Johnny Spillane, Carl Van Loan, Bill Demong, Todd Lodwick (820.6 (8), 51:52.5).

SHORT TRACK SPEED SKATING

The short track oval is 111.12 meters (364 feet). Distance (laps): 500m (4½); 1000m (9); 1500m (13½); 3000m (27); 5000m (45).

Medal breakdown (8 events): Ten medals—South Korea (6-3-1); **Five**—China (1-1-3); **Four**—Canada (0-3-1); **Three**—USA (1-0-2); **One**—Bulgaria (0-1-0), Italy (0-0-1).

MEN

500 meters

		Time
1	Apolo Anton Ohno, USA	41.935
2	Francois-Louis Tremblay, CAN	42.002
3	Hyun-Soo Ahn, S. Kor	42.089

1000 meters

		Time
1	Hyun-Soo Ahn, S. Kor	1:26.739
2	Ho-Suk Lee, S. Kor	1:26.764
3	Apolo Anton Ohno, USA	1:26.927

Next Best USA: 4th—Rusty Smith (1:27.435).

1500 meters

		Time
1	Hyun-Soo Ahn, S. Kor	2:25.341
2	Ho-Suk Lee, S. Kor	2:25.600
3	Jiajun Li, CHN	1:26.927

Top 10 USA: 8th—Apolo Anton Ohno (2:24.789, Final B).

5000-m Relay

		Time
1	South Korea	6:43.376
2	Canada	6:43.707
3	United States	6:47.990

S.KOR—Hyun-Soo Ahn, Ho-Suk Lee, Oh Se-Jong, Seo Ho-Jin, Song Suk-Woo; **CAN**—Eric Bedard, Jonathan Guilmette, Charles Hamelin, Francois-Louis Tremblay, Mathieu Turcotte; **USA**—Alex Izykowski, J.P. Kepka, Anthony Lobello, Apolo Anton Ohno, Rusty Smith.

WOMEN

500 meters

		Time
1	Meng Wang, CHN	44.345
2	Evgenia Radanova, BUL	44.374
3	Anouk Leblanc-Boucher, CAN	44.759

Top 10 USA: 7th—Allison Baver (55.689, Final B).

1000 meters

		Time
1	Sun-Yu Jin, S. Kor	1:32.859
2	Meng Wang, CHN	1:33.079
3	Yang Yang (A), CHN	1:33.937

1500 meters

		Time
1	Sun-Yu Jin, S. Kor	2:23.494
2	Eun-Kyung Choi, S. Kor	2:24.069
3	Meng Wang, CHN	2:24.469

Top 10 USA: 8th—Hyo-Jung Kim, USA (2:29.978, Final B).

3000-m Relay

		Time
1	South Korea	4:17.040
2	Canada	4:17.336
3	Italy	4:20.030

S.KOR—Byun Chun-Sa, Eun-Kyung Choi, Jeon Da-Hye, Sun-Yu Jin, Yun-Mi Kang; **CAN**—Alanna Kraus, Anouk Leblanc-Boucher, Amanda Overland, Kalyna Roberge, Tania Vicent; **ITA**—Marta Capurso, Arianna Fontana, Cecilia Maffei, Katia Zini, Mara Zini.

USA Entry: 4th—Allison Beaver, Kimberly Derrick, Maria Garcia, Caroline Hallisey, Hyo-Jung Kim.

SKI JUMPING

Each competitor gets two jumps with points awarded for distance and style. The normal hill is 90 meters (295 feet) and the large hill is 120 meters (394 feet).
Medal breakdown (3 events): **Four medals**—Norway (1-0-3); **Three**—Austria (2-1-0); **Two**—Finland (0-2-0).

Normal Hill

		1st (m)	2nd (m)	Pts
1	Lars Bystoel, NOR 101.5		103.5	266.5
2	Matti Hautamaeaki, FIN . . .102.0		103.5	265.5
3	Roar Ljoekelsoey, NOR 102.5		102.5	264.5

Large Hill

		1st (m)	2nd (m)	Pts
1	Thomas Morgenstern, AUT .131.4		145.5	276.9
2	Andreas Kofler, AUT 135.7		141.1	276.8
3	Lars Bystoel, NOR 121.5		129.2	250.7

Team (Large Hill)

		Pts
1	Austria 984.0	
2	Finland 976.6	
3	Norway 950.1	

AUT—Andreas Widhoelzl, Andreas Kofler, Martin Koch, Thomas Morgenstern; **FIN**—Tami Kiuru, Janne Happonen, Janne Ahonen, Matti Hautamaeki; **NOR**—Lars Bystoel, Bjoern Einar Romoeren, Tommy Ingebrigtsen, Roar Ljoekelsoey.
USA Entry: 14th—Tommy Schwall, Anders Johnson, Clint Jones, Alan Alborn (286.8).

SNOWBOARDING

Olympic snowboarding is comprised of three events. In the **Halfpipe** athletes compete on a sloped U-shaped course performing a sequence of aerial tricks before a panel of judges. **Parallel Giant Slalom** consists of a qualifying round in which the top 16 finishers are ranked and placed in a seeded bracket to compete head-to-head in a single elimination tournament. **Snowboard cross**, which made its debut at Turin, is an untimed four-boarder downhill free-for-all.

Medal breakdown (3 events): **Seven medals**—United States (3-3-1); **Four**—Switzerland (3-1-0); **One**—Germany (0-1-0), Slovakia (0-1-0), Canada (0-0-1), Austria (0-0-1), Norway (0-0-1), Finland (0-0-1), France (0-0-1).

MEN

Halfpipe

Score referes to the boarders' highest after two runs.

		Score
1	Shaun White, USA 46.8	
2	Danny Kass, USA 44.0	
3	Markku Koski, FIN 41.5	

Other Top 10 USA: 4th—Mason Aguirre (40.3).

Parallel Giant Slalom

1. Philipp Schoch, SWI
2. Simon Schoch, SWI
3. Siegfried Grabner, AUT

Note: BIG FINAL (gold medal)— Philipp Schoch beats big brother Simon (+0.88, +0.73). SMALL FINAL (bronze medal)—Grabner def. Mathieu Bozzetto, FRA (DNF, +0.41).

Snowboard Cross

1. Seth Wescott, USA
2. Radoslav Zidek, SVK
3. Paul-Henri Delerue, FRA

Other Top 10 USA: 6th—Jason Smith.

WOMEN

Halfpipe

Score referes to the boarders' highest after two runs.

		Score
1	Hannah Teter, USA 46.4	
2	Gretchen Bleiler, USA 43.4	
3	Kjersti Buaas, NOR 42.0	

Other Top 10 USA: 4th—Kelly Clark (41.1), 6th—Elena Hight (37.8)

Parallel Giant Slalom

1. Daniela Meuli, SWI
2. Amelie Kober, GER
3. Rosey Fletcher, USA

Note: BIG FINAL (gold medal)— Daniela Meuli def. Amelie Kober (+0.21, +15.97). SMALL FINAL (bronze medal)—Rosey Fletcher def. Doris Guenther, AUT (+1.50, +0.69).

Snowboard Cross

1. Tanja Frieden, SWI
2. Lindsey Jacobellis, USA
3. Dominique Maltais, CAN

SPEED SKATING

The long track oval measures 400 meters (1,312 feet). Distance (laps): 500m (1¼ laps), 1000m (2½ laps), 1500m (3¾ laps), 3000m (7½ laps), 5000m (12½ laps), 10,000m (25 laps).
Medal breakdown (10 events): **Nine medals**—Netherlands (3-2-4); **Eight**—Canada (2-4-2); **Seven**—United States (3-3-1); **Three**—Germany (1-1-1), Italy (2-0-1), Russia (1-1-1); **Two**—China (0-1-1); **One**—South Korea (0-0-1).

MEN

500 meters

Times reflected are a combination of two heats with each skater racing once on the inside lane and once on the outside lane.

		Time
1	Joey Cheek, USA 69.76	
2	Dmitry Dorofeyev, RUS 70.41	
3	Lee Kang Seok, S. Kor. 70.43	

Next Best USA: 12th—Casey FitzRandolph (71.12).

1000 meters

		Time
1	Shani Davis, USA 1:08.89	
2	Joey Cheek, USA 1:09.16	
3	Erben Wennemars, NED .1:09.32	

Other Top 10 USA: 6th—Chad Hedrick (1:09.45); 9th—Casey FitzRandolph (1:09.74).

1500 meters

		Time
1	Enrico Fabris, ITA	1:45.97
2	Shani Davis, USA	1:46.13
3	Chad Hedrick, USA	1:46.22

Other Top 10 USA: 9th—Joey Cheek (1:47.52).

5000 meters

		Time
1	Chad Hedrick, USA	6:14.68
2	Sven Kramer, NED	6:16.40
3	Enrico Fabris, ITA	6:18.25

Other Top 10 USA: 7th—Shani Davis (6:23.08).

10,000 meters

		Time
1	Bob De Jong, NED	13:01.57
2	Chad Hedrick, USA	13:05.40
3	Carl Verheijen, NED	13:08.80

Next Best USA: 15th—Charles Ryan Leveille Cox (14:14.81).

Team Pursuit

1 Italy
2 Canada
3 Netherlands

ITA—Matteo Anesi, Enrico Fabris, Ippolito Sanfratello; **CAN**—Arne Dankers, Steven Elm, Justing Warsylewicz; **NED**—Sven Kramer, Mark Tuitert, Carl Verheijen.
USA Entry: 6th—KC Boutiette, Charles Ryan Leveille Cox, Clay Mull.

WOMEN

500 meters

Times reflected are a combination of two heats with each skater racing once on the inside lane and once on the outside lane.

		Time
1	Svetlana Zhurova, RUS	76.57
2	Manli Wang, CHN	76.78
3	Ren Hui, CHN	76.87

Best USA: 11th—Jennifer Rodriguez (77.70).

1000 meters

		Time
1	Marianne Timmer, NED	1:16.05
2	Cindy Klassen, CAN	1:16.09
3	Anni Friesinger, GER	1:16.11

Top 10 USA: 10th—Jennifer Rodriguez (1:17.47).

1500 meters

		Time
1	Cindy Klassen, CAN	1:55.27
2	Kristina Groves, CAN	1:56.74
3	Ireen Wust, NED	1:56.90

Top 10 USA: 8th—Jennifer Rodriguez, USA (1:59.30).

3000 meters

		Time
1	Ireen Wust, NED	4:02.43
2	Renate Groenewold, NED	4:03.48
3	Cindy Klassen, CAN	4:04.37

Best USA: 11th—Catherine Raney, USA (4:10.44).

5000 meters

		Time
1	Clara Hughes, CAN	6:59.07
2	Claudia Pechstein, GER	7:00.08
3	Cindy Klassen, CAN	7:00.57

Top 10 USA: 7th—Catherine Raney, USA (7:04.91).

Team Pursuit

1 Germany
2 Canada
3 Russia

GER—Daniela Anschuetz Thoms, Anni Friesinger, Claudia Pechstein; **CAN**—Kristina Groves, Clara Hughes, Christine Nesbitt; **RUS**—Yekaterina Abramova, Yekaterina Lobysheva, Svetlana Vysokova.

USA Entry: 5th—Margaret Crowley, Maria Lamb, Catherine

Turin Olympic Firsts

• Shizuka Arakawa won Japan's first ever ice skating gold medal.

• Freestyle skier Xiaopeng Han won the first ever gold medal on snow for China in the men's aerial competition.

• Swiss snowboarding siblings **Phillip** and **Simon Schoch** became the first brothers to win gold and silver in the same event (Parallel Giant Slalom) since the Mahre brothers (Phil and Steve) did it in the 1984 Men's Slalom (Alpine Skiing) at Sarajevo.

• For the first time, one country swept all three medals in the men's Alpine skiing slalom. Before the Austrian onslaught in 2006, three other nations had managed to win all three medals in an Alpine skiing event, but never in slalom.

• For the first time in Olympic history two Scandinavian teams, Finland and Sweden, played for the gold medal in men's ice hockey.

AP/Wide World Photos

1924-2006
Through the Years

SPORTS ALMANAC

The Winter Olympics

The move toward a winter version of the Olympics began in 1908 when figure skating made an appearance at the Summer Games in London. Ten-time world champion Ulrich Salchow of Sweden, who originated the backwards, one revolution jump that bears his name, and Madge Syers of Britain were the first singles champions. Germans Anna Hubler and Heinrich Berger won the pairs competition.

Organizers of the 1916 Summer Games in Berlin planned to introduce a "Skiing Olympia," featuring nordic events in the Black Forest, but the Games were cancelled after the outbreak of World War I in 1914.

The Games resumed in 1920 at Antwerp, Belgium, where figure skating returned and ice hockey was added as a medal event. Sweden's Gillis Grafstrom and Magda Julin took individual honors, while Ludovika and Walter Jakobsson were the top pair. In hockey, Canada won the gold medal with the United States second and Czechoslovakia third.

Despite the objections of Modern Olympics' founder Baron Pierre de Coubertin and the resistance of the Scandinavian countries, which had staged their own Nordic championships every four or five years from 1901-26 in Sweden, the International Olympic Committee sanctioned an "International Winter Sports Week" at Chamonix, France, in 1924. The 11-day event, which included nordic skiing, speed skating, figure skating, ice hockey and bobsledding, was a huge success and was retroactively called the first Olympic Winter Games.

Seventy years after those first cold weather Games, the 17th edition of the Winter Olympics took place in Lillehammer, Norway, in 1994. The event ended the four-year Olympic cycle of staging both Winter and Summer Games in the same year and began a new schedule that calls for the two Games to alternate every two years.

Year	No	Location	Dates	Nations	Most medals	USA medals
1924	I	Chamonix, FRA	Jan. 25-Feb. 4	16	Norway (4-7-6–17)	1-2-1–4 (3rd)
1928	II	St. Moritz, SWI	Feb. 11-19	25	Norway (6-4-5–15)	2-2-2– 6 (2nd)
1932	III	Lake Placid, USA	Feb. 4-15	17	USA (6-4-2–12)	6-4-2–12 (1st)
1936	IV	Garmisch-Partenkirchen, GER .	Feb. 6-16	28	Norway (7-5-3–15)	1-0-3– 4 (T-5th)
1940-**a**	–	Sapporo, JPN	Cancelled (WWII)			
1944	–	Cortina d'Ampezzo, ITA	Cancelled (WWII)			
1948	V	St. Moritz, SWI	Jan. 30-Feb. 8	28	Norway (4-3-3–10), Sweden (4-3-3–10) & Switzerland (3-4-3–10)	3-4-2– 9 (4th)
1952-**b**	VI	Oslo, NOR	Feb. 14-25	30	Norway (7-3-6–16)	4-6-1–11 (2nd)
1956-**c**	VII	Cortina d'Ampezzo, ITA	Jan. 26-Feb. 5	32	USSR (7-3-6–16)	2-3-2– 7 (T-4th)
1960	VIII	Squaw Valley, USA	Feb. 18-28	30	USSR (7-5-9–21)	3-4-3–10 (2nd)
1964	IX	Innsbruck, AUT	Jan. 29-Feb. 9	36	USSR (11-8-6–25)	1-2-3– 6 (7th)
1968-**d**	X	Grenoble, FRA	Feb. 6-18	37	Norway (6-6-2–14)	1-5-1– 7 (T-7th)
1972	XI	Sapporo, JPN	Feb. 3-13	35	USSR (8-5-3–16)	3-2-3– 8 (6th)
1976-**e**	XII	Innsbruck, AUT	Feb. 4-15	37	USSR (13-6-8–27)	3-3-4–10 (T-3rd)
1980	XIII	Lake Placid, USA	Feb. 14-23	37	E. Germany (9-7-7–23)	6-4-2–12 (3rd)
1984	XIV	Sarajevo, YUG	Feb. 7-19	49	USSR (6-10-9–25)	4-4-0– 8 (T-5th)
1988	XV	Calgary, CAN	Feb. 13-28	57	USSR (11-9-9–29)	2-1-3– 6 (T-8th)
1992-**f**	XVI	Albertville, FRA	Feb. 8-23	63	Germany (10-10-6–26)	5-4-2–11 (6th)
1994-**g**	XVII	Lillehammer, NOR	Feb. 12-27	67	Norway (10-11-5–26)	6-5-2–13 (T-5th)
1998	XVIII	Nagano, JPN	Feb. 7-22	72	Germany (12-9-8–29)	6-3-4–13 (5th)
2002	XIX	Salt Lake City, USA	Feb. 8-24	78	Germany (12-16-7–35)	10-13-11–34 (2nd)
2006	XX	Turin, ITA	Feb. 10-26	87	Germany (11-12-6–29)	9-9-7–25 (2nd)
2010	XXI	Vancouver, CAN	Feb. 12-28			

a–The 1940 Winter Games are originally scheduled for Sapporo, but Japan resigns as host in 1937 when the Sino-Japanese war breaks out. St. Moritz is the next choice, but the Swiss feel that ski instructors should not be considered professionals and the IOC withdraws its offer. Finally, Garmisch-Partenkirchen is asked to serve again as host, but the Germans invade Poland in 1939 and the Games are eventually cancelled.

b–Germany and Japan are allowed to rejoin the Olympic community for the first time since World War II. Though a divided country, the Germans send a joint East-West team through 1964.

c–The Soviet Union (USSR) participates in its first Winter Olympics and takes home the most medals, including the gold medal in ice hockey.

d–East Germany and West Germany officially send separate teams for the first time and will continue to do so through 1988.

e–The IOC grants the 1976 Winter Games to Denver in May 1970, but in 1972 Colorado voters reject a $5 million bond issue to finance the undertaking. Denver immediately withdraws as host and the IOC selects Innsbruck, the site of the 1964 Games, to take over.

f–Germany sends a single team after East and West German reunification in 1990 and the USSR competes as the Unified Team after the breakup of the Soviet Union in 1991.

g–The IOC moves the Winter Games' four-year cycle ahead two years in order to separate them from the Summer Games and alternate Olympics every two years.

Event-by-Event

Gold medal winners from 1924-2006 in the following events: Alpine Skiing, Biathlon, Bobsled, Cross Country Skiing, Curling, Figure Skating, Freestyle Skiing, Ice Hockey, Luge, Nordic Combined, Skeleton, Ski Jumping, Snowboarding and Speed Skating.

ALPINE SKIING

MEN

Multiple gold medals: Kjetil Andre Aamodt (4); Jean-Claude Killy, Toni Sailer and Alberto Tomba (3); Hermann Maier, Henri Oreiller, Benjamin Raich, Ingemar Stenmark and Markus Wasmeier (2).

Downhill

Year		Time	Year		Time
1948	Henri Oreiller, FRA	2:55.0	1980	Leonhard Stock, AUS	1:45.50
1952	Zeno Colò, ITA	2:30.8	1984	Bill Johnson, USA	1:45.59
1956	Toni Sailer, AUT	2:52.2	1988	Pirmin Zurbriggen, SWI	1:59.63
1960	Jean Vuarnet, FRA	2:06.0	1992	Patrick Ortlieb, AUT	1:50.37
1964	Egon Zimmermann, AUT	2:18.16	1994	Tommy Moe, USA	1:45.75
1968	Jean-Claude Killy, FRA	1:59.85	1998	Jean-Luc Cretier, FRA	1:50.11
1972	Bernhard Russi, SWI	1:51.43	2002	Fritz Strobl, AUT	1:39.13
1976	Franz Klammer AUT	1:45.73	2006	Antoine Deneriaz, FRA	1:48.80

Slalom

Year		Time	Year		Time
1948	Edi Reinalter, SWI	2:10.3	1980	Ingemar Stenmark, SWE	1:44.26
1952	Othmar Schneider, AUT	2:00.0	1984	Phil Mahre, USA	1:39.41
1956	Toni Sailer, AUT	3:14.7	1988	Alberto Tomba, ITA	1:39.47
1960	Ernst Hinterseer, AUT	2:08.9	1992	Finn Christian Jagge, NOR	1:44.39
1964	Pepi Stiegler, AUT	2:11.13	1994	Thomas Stangassinger, AUT	2:02.02
1968	Jean-Claude Killy, FRA	1:39.73	1998	Hans-Petter Buraas, NOR	1:49.31
1972	Francisco Ochoa, SPA	1:49.27	2002	Jean-Pierre Vidal, FRA	1:41.06
1976	Piero Gros, ITA	2:03.29	2006	Benjamin Raich, AUT	1:43.14

Giant Slalom

Year		Time	Year		Time
1952	Stein Eriksen, NOR	2:25.0	1984	Max Julen, SWI	2:41.18
1956	Toni Sailer, AUS	3:00.1	1988	Alberto Tomba, ITA	2:06.37
1960	Roger Staub, SWI	1:48.3	1992	Alberto Tomba, ITA	2:06.98
1964	Francois Bonlieu, FRA	1:46.71	1994	Markus Wasmeier, GER	2:52.46
1968	Jean-Claude Killy, FRA	3:29.28	1998	Hermann Maier, AUT	2:38.51
1972	Gustav Thöni, ITA	3:09.62	2002	Stephan Eberharter, AUT	2:23.28
1976	Heini Hemmi, SWI	3:26.97	2006	Benjamin Raich, AUT	2:35.00
1980	Ingemar Stenmark, SWE	2:40.74			

Super G

Year		Time	Year		Time
1988	Frank Piccard, FRA	1:39.66	1998	Hermann Maier, AUT	1:34.82
1992	Kjetil Andre Aamodt, NOR	1:13.04	2002	Kjetil Andre Aamodt, NOR	1:21.58
1994	Markus Wasmeier, GER	1:32.53	2006	Kjetil Andre Aamodt, NOR	1:30.65

Alpine Combined

Year		Points	Year		Time
1936	Franz Pfnür, GER	99.25	1994	Lasse Kjus, NOR	3:17.53
1948	Henri Oreiller, FRA	3.27	1998	Mario Reiter, AUT	3:08.06
1952-84	Not held		2002	Kjetil Andre Aamodt, NOR	3:17.56
1988	Hubert Strolz, AUT	36.55	2006	Ted Ligety, USA	3:09.35
1992	Josef Polig, ITA	14.58			

Athletes with Winter and Summer Medals

Only three athletes have won medals in both the Winter and Summer Olympics:

Eddie Eagan, USA–Light Heavyweight Boxing gold (1920) and Four-man Bobsled gold (1932).

Jacob Tullin Thams, Norway–Ski Jumping gold (1924) and 8-meter Yachting silver (1936).

Christa Luding-Rothenburger, East Germany–Speed Skating gold at 500 meters (1984) and 1,000m (1988), silver at 500m (1988) and bronze at 500m (1992) and Match Sprint Cycling silver (1988). Luding-Rothenburger is the only athlete to ever win medals in both Winter and Summer Games in the same year.

Gold Strike in the Mountains

With his age-defying gold medal performance at Sestriere, Italy in 2006, Norway's **Kjetil Andre Aamodt** became the first (and for 30 minutes only) skier in Olympic history to win four Alpine Skiing gold medals. The 34-year-old's gold at the 2006 Super G also made him the first Alpine skier to earn four medals in the same event (he won a bronze in 1994 to go with his three golds). Aamodt, is both the youngest *and* oldest alpine skier to win Olympic gold, first taking a gold medal in the Super G at 20 years old in 1992 at Albertville. Aamodt is also the only Alpine skier to win eight career Olympic medals.

Half an hour after Aamodt became the first Alpine skier to win four gold medals, **Janica Kostelic** of Croatia won the Alpine Combined to become the first woman to achieve the same feat. She also took the silver medal in the Super G and placed fourth in the slalom.

WOMEN

Multiple gold medals: Janica Kostelic (4), Deborah Compagnoni, Vreni Schneider and Katja Seizinger (3); Michaela Dorfmeister, Marielle Goitschel, Trude Jochum-Beiser, Petra Kronperger, Andrea Mead Lawrence, Rosi Mittermaier, Marie-Theres Nadig, Hanni Wenzel and Pernilla Wiberg (2).

Downhill

Year		Time	Year		Time
1948	Hedy Schlunegger, SWI	2:28.3	1980	Annemarie Moser-Pröll, AUT	1:37.52
1952	Trude Jochum-Beiser, AUT	1:47.1	1984	Michela Figini, SWI	1:13.36
1956	Madeleine Berthod, SWI	1:40.7	1988	Marina Kiehl, W. Ger	1:25.86
1960	Heidi Biebl, GER	1:37.6	1992	Kerrin Lee-Gartner, CAN	1:52.55
1964	Christl Haas, AUT	1:55.39	1994	Katja Seizinger, GER	1:35.93
1968	Olga Pall, AUT	1:40.87	1998	Katja Seizinger, GER	1:28.89
1972	Marie-Theres Nadig, SWI	1:36.68	2002	Carole Montillet, FRA	1:39.56
1976	Rosi Mittermaier, W. Ger	1:46.16	2006	Michaela Dorfmeister, AUT	1:56.49

Slalom

Year		Time	Year		Time
1948	Gretchen Fraser, USA	1:57.2	1980	Hanni Wenzel, LIE	1:25.09
1952	Andrea Mead Lawrence, USA	2:10.6	1984	Paoletta Magoni, ITA	1:36.47
1956	Renée Colliard, SWI	1:52.3	1988	Vreni Schneider, SWI	1:36.69
1960	Anne Heggtveit, CAN	1:49.6	1992	Petra Kronberger, AUT	1:32.68
1964	Christine Goitschel, FRA	1:29.86	1994	Vreni Schneider, SWI	1:56.01
1968	Marielle Goitschel, FRA	1:25.86	1998	Hilde Gerg, GER	1:32.40
1972	Barbara Cochran, USA	1:31.24	2002	Janica Kostelic, CRO	1:46.10
1976	Rosi Mittermaier, W. Ger	1:30.54	2006	Anja Paerson, SWE	1:29.04

Giant Slalom

Year		Time	Year		Time
1952	Andrea Mead Lawrence, USA	2:06.8	1984	Debbie Armstrong, USA	2:20.98
1956	Ossi Reichert, GER	1:56.5	1988	Vreni Schneider, SWI	2:06.49
1960	Yvonne Rügg, SWI	1:39.9	1992	Pernilla Wiberg, SWE	2:12.74
1964	Marielle Goitschel, FRA	1:52.24	1994	Deborah Compagnoni, ITA	2:30.97
1968	Nancy Greene, CAN	1:51.97	1998	Deborah Compagnoni, ITA	2:50.59
1972	Marie-Theres Nadig, SWI	1:29.90	2002	Janica Kostelic, CRO	2:30.01
1976	Kathy Kreiner, CAN	1:29.13	2006	Julia Mancuso, USA	2:09.19
1980	Hanni Wenzel, LIE	2:41.66			

Super G

Year		Time	Year		Time
1988	Sigrid Wolf, AUT	1:19.03	1998	Picabo Street, USA	1:18.02
1992	Deborah Compagnoni, ITA	1:21.22	2002	Daniela Ceccarelli, ITA	1:13.59
1994	Diann Roffe-Steinrotter, USA	1:22.15	2006	Michaela Dorfmeister, AUT	1:32.47

Alpine Combined

Year		Points	Year		Time
1936	Christl Cranz, GER	97.06	1994	Pernilla Wiberg, SWE	3:05.16
1948	Trude Beiser, AUT	6.58	1998	Katja Seizinger, GER	2:40.74
1952-84	Not held		2002	Janica Kostelic, CRO	2:43.28
1988	Anita Wachter, AUT	29.25	2006	Janica Kostelic, CRO	2:51.08
1992	Petra Kronberger, AUT	2.55			

BIATHLON

MEN

Multiple gold medals (including relays): Ole Einar Bjoerndalen (5); Aleksandr Tikhonov (4); Mark Kirchner, Michael Greis and Ricco Gross (3); Anatoly Alyabyev, Ivan Biakov, Sergei Chepikov, Sven Fischer, Halvard Hanevold, Frank Luck, Viktor Mamatov, Frank-Peter Roetsch, Magnar Solberg and Dmitri Vasilyev (2).

10 kilometers

Year		Time	Year		Time
1980	Frank Ulrich, E. Ger	32:10.69	1994	Sergei Chepikov, RUS	28:07.0
1984	Erik Kvalfoss, NOR	30:53.8	1998	Ole Einar Bjoerndalen, NOR	27:16.2
1988	Frank-Peter Roetsch, E. Ger	25:08.1	2002	Ole Einar Bjoerndalen, NOR	24:51.3
1992	Mark Kirchner, GER	26:02.3	2006	Sven Fischer, GER	26:11.6

12.5 kilometers

Year		Time	Year		Time
2002	Ole Einar Bjoerndalen, NOR	32:34.6	2006	Vincent Defrasne, FRA	35:20.2

15 kilometers

Year		Time
2006	Michael Greis, GER	47:20.0

20 kilometers

Year		Time	Year		Time
1960	Klas Lestander, SWE	1:33:21.6	1988	Frank-Peter Roetsch, E. Ger	56:33.3
1964	Vladimir Melanin, USSR	1:20:26.8	1992	Yevgeny Redkine, UT	57:34.4
1968	Magnar Solberg, NOR	1:13:45.9	1994	Sergei Tarasov, RUS	57:25.3
1972	Magnar Solberg, NOR	1:15:55.50	1998	Halvard Hanevold, NOR	56:16.4
1976	Nikolai Kruglov, USSR	1:14:12.26	2002	Ole Einar Bjoerndalen, NOR	51:03.3
1980	Anatoly Alyabyev, USSR	1:08:16.31	2006	Michael Greis, GER	54:23.0
1984	Peter Angerer, W. Ger	1:11:52.7			

4x7.5-kilometer Relay

Year		Time	Year		Time	Year		Time
1968	Soviet Union	2:13:02.4	1984	Soviet Union	1:38:51.7	1998	Germany	1:21:36.2
1972	Soviet Union	1:51:44.92	1988	Soviet Union	1:22:30.0	2002	Norway	1:23:42.3
1976	Soviet Union	1:57:55.64	1992	Germany	1:24:43.5	2006	Germany	1:21:51.5
1980	Soviet Union	1:34:03.27	1994	Germany	1:30:22.1			

WOMEN

Multiple gold medals (including relays): Myriam Bedard, Andrea Henkel, Svetlana Ishmouratova, Anfisa Reztsova and Kati Wilhelm (2). Note that Reztsova won a third gold medal in 1988 in the cross country 4x5-kilometer relay.

7.5 kilometers

Year		Time	Year		Time
1992	Anfisa Reztsova, UT	24:29.2	2002	Kati Wilhelm, GER	20:41.4
1994	Myriam Bedard, CAN	26:08.8	2006	Florence Baverel-Robert, FRA	22:31.4
1998	Galina Koukleva, RUS	23:08.0			

10 kilometers

Year		Time	Year		Time
2002	Olga Pyleva, RUS	31:07.7	2006	Kati Wilhelm, GER	36:43.6

12.5 kilometers

Year		Time
2006	Anna Carin Olofsson, SWE	40:36.5

15 kilometers

Year		Time	Year		Time
1992	Antje Misersky, GER	51:47.2	2002	Andrea Henkel, GER	47:29.1
1994	Myriam Bedard, CAN	52:06.6	2006	Svetlana Ishmouratova, RUS	49:24.1
1998	Ekaterina Dafovska, BUL	54:52.0			

4x7.5-kilometer Relay

Year		Time	Year		Time
1992	France	1:15:55.6	2002	Germany	1:27:55.0
1994	Russia	1:47:19.5	2006	Russia	1:16:12.5
1998	Germany	1:40:13.6	**Note:** Event featured three skiers per team in 1992.		

BOBSLED

A two-woman bobsled event was added in 2002. Only drivers are listed in parentheses.

Multiple gold medals: DRIVERS–Andre Lange and Meinhard Nehmer (3); Billy Fiske, Wolfgang Hoppe, Christoph Langen, Eugenio Monti, Andreas Ostler and Gustav Weder (2). CREW–Bernard Germeshausen (3); Donat Acklin, Luciano De Paolis, Cliff Gray, Lorenz Nieberl and Dietmar Schauerhammer (2).

Two-Man

Year		Time	Year		Time
1932	United States (Hubert Stevens)	8:14.74	1980	Switzerland (Erich Schärer)	4:09.36
1936	United States (Ivan Brown)	5:29.29	1984	East Germany (Wolfgang Hoppe)	3:25.56
1948	Switzerland (Felix Endrich)	5:29.2	1988	Soviet Union (Janis Kipurs)	3:54.19
1952	Germany (Andreas Ostler)	5:24.54	1992	Switzerland I (Gustav Weder)	4:03.26
1956	Italy (Lamberto Dalla Costa)	5:30.14	1994	Switzerland I (Gustav Weder)	3:30.81
1960	Not held		1998	(TIE) Italy I (Guenther Huber)	3:37.24
1964	Great Britain (Anthony Nash)	4:21.90		& Canada I (Pierre Lueders)	3:37.24
1968	Italy (Eugenio Monti)	4:41.54	2002	Germany I (Christoph Langen)	3:10.11
1972	West Germany (Wolfgang Zimmerer)	4:57.07	2006	Germany I (Andre Lange)	3:43.38
1976	East Germany (Meinhard Nehmer)	3:44.42			

Two-Woman

Year		Time	Year		Time
2002	United States II (Jill Bakken)	1:37.76	2006	Germany I (Sandra Kiriasis)	3:49.98

Four-Man

Year		Time	Year		Time
1924	Switzerland (Eduard Scherrer)	5:45.54	1972	Switzerland (Jean Wicki)	4:43.07
1928	United States (Billy Fiske)	3:20.5	1976	East Germany (Meinhard Nehmer)	3:40.43
1932	United States (Billy Fiske)	7:53.68	1980	East Germany (Meinhard Nehmer)	3:59.92
1936	Switzerland (Pierre Musy)	5:19.85	1984	East Germany (Wolfgang Hoppe)	3:20.22
1948	United States (Francis Tyler)	5:20.1	1988	Switzerland (Ekkehard Fasser)	3:47.51
1952	Germany (Andreas Ostler)	5:07.84	1992	Austria I (Ingo Appelt)	3:53.90
1956	Switzerland (Franz Kapus)	5:10.44	1994	Germany II (Harald Czudaj)	3:27.78
1960	Not held		1998	Germany II (Christoph Langen)	2:39.41
1964	Canada (Vic Emery)	4:14.46	2002	Germany II (Andre Lange)	3:07.51
1968	Italy (Eugenio Monti)	2:17.39	2006	Germany I (Andre Lange)	3:40.42

Note: Five-man sleds were used in 1928.

CROSS COUNTRY SKIING

Starting with the 1988 Winter Games in Calgary, the classical and freestyle (i.e., skating) techniques were designated for specific events. The Pursuit race was introduced in 1992 and revamped after the 1998 Nagano Games. The Sprint was added in 2002 and the distances have differed slightly (1.5k in 2002 and 1.4k in 2006). The Team Sprint was added in 2006

MEN

Multiple gold medals (including relays): Bjorn Dählie (8); Thomas Alsgaard, Sixten Jernberg, Gunde Svan, Thomas Wassberg and Nikolai Zimyatov (4); Veikko Hakulinen, Eero Mäntyranta and Vegard Ulvang (3); Hallgeir Brenden, Harald Grönningen, Thorleif Haug, Bjoern Lind, Johann Muehlegg, Jan Ottoson, Kristen Skjeldal, Pål Tyldum, Andrus Veerpalu and Vyacheslav Vedenine (2).

Multiple gold medals (including Nordic Combined): Johan Gröttumsbråten and Thorleif Haug (3).

Sprint

Held as a freestyle event.

Year		Time	Year		Time
2002	Tor Arne Hetland, NOR	2:56.9	2006	Bjoern Lind, SWE	2:26.5

Team Sprint (3x1.4 km)

Held as a classical event.

Year		Time
2006	Sweden	17:02.9

10 kilometers

Held as a classical event.

Year		Time	Year		Time
1992	Vegard Ulvang, NOR	27:36.0	1998	Bjorn Dählie, NOR	27:24.5
1994	Bjorn Dählie, NOR	24:20.1	2002	discontinued	

Combined Pursuit

From 1992-98 the pursuit included a 10-km classical race and a 15-km freestyle race contested on separate days. In 2002, the pursuit was shortened to two 10-km races held on the same day. In 2006, the Combined Pursuit was comprised of back-to-back 15-km classical and freestyle races.

Year		Time	Year		Time
1992	Bjorn Dählie, NOR	1:05:37.9	2002	Johann Muehllegg, SPA	49:20.4
1994	Bjorn Dählie, NOR	1:00:08.8	2006	Eugeni Dementiev, RUS	1:17:00.8
1998	Thomas Alsgaard, NOR	1:07:01.7			

15 kilometers

Held over 18 kilometers from 1924-52. Held as a classical event from 1956-88, and since 2002. Replaced by the 15-km combined pursuit (1992-98).

Year		Time	Year		Time
1924	Thorleif Haug, NOR	1:14:31.0	1968	Harald Grönningen, NOR	47:54.2
1928	Johan Gröttumsbräten, NOR	1:37:01.0	1972	Sven-Ake Lundback, SWE	45:28.24
1932	Sven Utterström, SWE	1:23:07.0	1976	Nikolai Bazhukov, USSR	43:58.47
1936	Erik-August Larsson, SWE	1:14:38.0	1980	Thomas Wassberg, SWE	41:57.63
1948	Martin Lundström, SWE	1:13:50.0	1984	Gunde Svan, SWE	41:25.6
1952	Hallgeir Brenden, NOR	1:01:34.0	1988	Mikhail Devyatyarov, USSR	41:18.9
1956	Hallgeir Brenden, NOR	49:39.0		1992-98 Not held	
1960	Hakon Brusveen, NOR	51:55.5	2002	Andrus Veerpalu, EST	37:07.4
1964	Eero Mäntyranta, FIN	50:54.1	2006	Andrus Veerpalu, EST	38:01.3

30 kilometers

Held as a freestyle event from 1956-94, and in 2002. Held as a classical event in 1998.

Year		Time	Year		Time
1956	Veikko Hakulinen, FIN	1:44:06.0	1984	Nikolai Zimyatov, USSR	1:28:56.3
1960	Sixten Jernberg, SWE	1:51:03.9	1988	Alexei Prokurorov, USSR	1:24:26.3
1964	Eero Mäntyranta, FIN	1:30:50.7	1992	Vegard Ulvang, NOR	1:22:27.8
1968	Franco Nones, ITA	1:35:39.2	1994	Thomas Alsgaard, NOR	1:12:26.4
1972	Vyacheslav Vedenine, USSR	1:36:31.15	1998	Mika Myllylae, FIN	1:33:55.8
1976	Sergei Saveliev, USSR	1:30:29.38	2002	Johann Muehllegg, SPA	1:09:28.9
1980	Nikolai Zimyatov, USSR	1:27:02.80	2006	discontinued	

50 kilometers

Held as a classical event from 1924-94, and since 2002. Held as a freestyle event in 1998.

Year		Time	Year		Time
1924	Thorleif Haug, NOR	3:44:32.0	1972	Päl Tyldum, NOR	2:43:14.75
1928	Per Erik Hedlund, SWE	4:52:03.0	1976	Ivar Formo, NOR	2:37:30.05
1932	Veli Saarinen, FIN	4:28:00.0	1980	Nikolai Zimyatov, USSR	2:27:24.60
1936	Elis Wiklund, SWE	3:30:11.0	1984	Thomas Wassberg, SWE	2:15:55.8
1948	Nils Karlsson, SWE	3:47:48.0	1988	Gunde Svan, SWE	2:04:30.9
1952	Veikko Hakulinen, FIN	3:33:33.0	1992	Bjorn Dählie, NOR	2:03:41.5
1956	Sixten Jernberg, SWE	2:50:27.0	1994	Vladimir Smirnov, KAZ	2:07:20.3
1960	Kalevi Hämäläinen, FIN	2:59:06.3	1998	Bjorn Dählie, NOR	2:05:08.2
1964	Sixten Jernberg, SWE	2:43:52.6	2002	Mikhail Ivanov, RUS*	2:06:20.8
1968	Ole Ellefsaeter, NOR	2:28:45.8	2006	Giorgio Di Centa, ITA	2:06:11.8

*Ivanov finished second to Johann Muehllegg of Spain, who was disqualified for failing a drug test.

4x10-kilometer Mixed Relay

Two classical and two freestyle legs.

Year		Time	Year		Time	Year		Time
1936	Finland	2:41:33.0	1968	Norway	2:08:33.5	1992	Norway	1:39:26.0
1948	Sweden	2:32:08.0	1972	Soviet Union	2:04:47.94	1994	Italy	1:41:15.0
1952	Finland	2:20:16.0	1976	Finland	2:07:59.72	1998	Norway	1:40:55.7
1956	Soviet Union	2:15:30.0	1980	Soviet Union	1:57:03.46	2002	Norway	1:32:45.5
1960	Finland	2:18:45.6	1984	Sweden	1:55:06.3	2006	Italy	1:43:45.7
1964	Sweden	2:18:34.6	1988	Sweden	1:43:58.6			

WOMEN

Multiple gold medals (including relays): Lyubov Egorova (6); Larissa Lazutina (5); Galina Kulakova and Raisa Smetanina (4); Claudia Boyarskikh, Olga Danilova and Marja-Liisa Hämäläinen and Elena Valbe (3); Stefania Belmondo, Manuela Di Centa, Nina Gavriluk, Toini Gustafsson, Barbara Petzold, Kristina Smigun and Julija Tchepalova (2).

Multiple gold medals (including relays and Biathlon): Anfisa Reztsova (2).

Cross Country (Cont.)

Sprint

The Sprint was added in 2002 and the distances have differed slightly (1.5km in 2002 and 1.2km in 2006). The Team Sprint was added in 2006

Year	Time	Year	Time
2002 Julija Tchepalova, RUS	3:10.6	2006 Chandra Crawford, CAN	2:12.3

Team Sprint (3x1.2km)

Year	Time
2006 Sweden	16:36.9

5 kilometers

Held as a classical event from 1964-98. From 1992-98 it was half of the combined pursuit event. Discontinued after 1998.

Year	Time	Year	Time
1964 Claudia Boyarskikh, USSR	17:50.5	1984 Marja-Liisa Hämäläinen, FIN	17:04.0
1968 Toini Gustafsson, SWE	16:45.2	1988 Marjo Matikainen, FIN	15:04.0
1972 Galina Kulakova, USSR	17:00.50	1992 Marjut Lukkarinen, FIN	14:13.8
1976 Helena Takalo, FIN	15:48.69	1994 Lyubov Egorova, RUS	14:08.8
1980 Raisa Smetanina, USSR	15:06.92	1998 Larissa Lazutina, RUS	17:37.9

Combined Pursuit

From 1992-98 the pursuit consisted of a 10-km freestyle race in which the starting order was determined by order of finish in the 5-km classical race contested on separate days. In 2002, the pursuit was shortened to a 5-km classical race followed by a 5-km freestyle race contested on the same day. The 5-km classical is no longer a separate medal event. In 2006, the Combined Pursuit was comprised of back-to-back 7½-km classical and freestyle races.

Year	Time	Year	Time
1992 Lyubov Egorova, UT	40:07.7	2002 Olga Danilova, RUS	24:52.1
1994 Lyubov Egorova, RUS	41:38.1	2006 Kristina Smigun, EST	42:48.7
1998 Larissa Lazutina, RUS	46:06.9		

10 kilometers

Held as a classical event from 1952-88, and since 2002. Replaced by 10-km combined pursuit from 1992-98.

Year	Time	Year	Time
1952 Lydia Wideman, FIN	41:40.0	1980 Barbara Petzold, E. Ger	30:31.54
1956 Lyubov Kosyreva, USSR	38:11.0	1984 Marja-Liisa Hämäläinen, FIN	31:44.2
1960 Maria Gusakova, USSR	39:46.6	1988 Vida Venciene, USSR	30:08.3
1964 Claudia Boyarskikh, USSR	40:24.3	1992-98 Not held	
1968 Toini Gustafsson, SWE	36:46.5	2002 Bente Skari, NOR	28:05.6
1972 Galina Kulakova, USSR	34:17.82	2006 Kristina Smigun, EST	27:51.4
1976 Raisa Smetanina, USSR	30:13.41		

15 kilometers

Held as a freestyle event from 1992-94, and 2002. Held as a classical event in 1998.

Year	Time	Year	Time
1992 Lyubov Egorova, UT	42:20.8	1998 Olga Danilova, RUS	46:55.4
1994 Manuela Di Centa, ITA	39:44.5	2002 Stefania Belmondo, ITA	39:54.4

20 kilometers

Held as a classical event from 1984-88. Discontinued in 1992 and replaced by the 30-kilometer freestyle.

Year	Time	Year	Time
1984 Marja-Liisa Hämäläinen, FIN	1:01:45.0	1988 Tamara Tikhonova, USSR	55:53.6

30 kilometers

Replaced 20-km classical event in 1992. Held as a freestyle event 1992-98 and 2006. Held as a classical event in 2002.

Year	Time	Year	Time
1992 Stefania Belmondo, ITA	1:22:30.1	2002 Gabriella Paruzzi, ITA*	1:30:57.1
1994 Manuela Di Centa, ITA	1:25:41.6	2006 Katerina Neumannova, CZE	1:22:25.4
1998 Julija Tchepalova, RUS	1:22:01.5		

*Paruzzi finished second to Larissa Lazutina of Russia, who was disqualified after failing a drug test.

4x5-kilometer Relay

Two classical and two freestyle legs since 1992. Event featured three skiers per team from 1956-72.

Year	Time	Year	Time	Year	Time
1956 Finland	1:09:01.0	1976 Soviet Union	1:07:49.75	1994 Russia	57:12.5
1960 Sweden	1:04:21.4	1980 East Germany	1:02:11.10	1998 Russia	55:13.5
1964 Soviet Union	59:20.2	1984 Norway	1:06:49.7	2002 Germany	49:30.6
1968 Norway	57:30.0	1988 Soviet Union	59:51.1	2006 Russia	54:47.7
1972 Soviet Union	48:46.15	1992 Unified Team	59:34.8		

CURLING

MEN		WOMEN	
Year		**Year**	
1998	**Switzerland**, Canada, Norway	1998	**Canada**, Denmark, Sweden
2002	**Norway**, Canada, Switzerland	2002	**Great Britain**, Switzerland, Canada
2006	**Canada**, Finland, United States	2006	**Sweden**, Switzerland, Canada

FIGURE SKATING

MEN

Multiple gold medals: Gillis Grafström (3); Dick Button and Karl Schäfer (2).

Year		Year		Year	
1908	Ulrich Salchow ....SWE	1952	Dick Button ....USA	1984	Scott Hamilton ....USA
1912	Not held	1956	Hayes Alan Jenkins .....USA	1988	Brian Boitano ....USA
1920	Gillis Grafström ....SWE	1960	David Jenkins ....USA	1992	Victor Petrenko ....UT
1924	Gillis Grafström ....SWE	1964	Manfred Schnelldorfer ....GER	1994	Alexei Urmanov ....RUS
1928	Gillis Grafström ....SWE	1968	Wolfgang Schwarz ....AUT	1998	Ilia Kulik ....RUS
1932	Karl Schäfer ....AUT	1972	Ondrej Nepela ....CZE	2002	Alexei Yagudin ....RUS
1936	Karl Schäfer ....AUT	1976	John Curry ....GBR	2006	Yevgeny Plushenko ....RUS
1948	Dick Button ....USA	1980	Robin Cousins ....GBR		

WOMEN

Multiple gold medals: Sonja Henie (3); Katarina Witt (2).

Year		Year		Year	
1908	Madge Syers ....GBR	1952	Jeanette Altwegg ....GBR	1984	Katarina Witt ....E. Ger
1912	Not held	1956	Tenley Albright ....USA	1988	Katarina Witt ....E. Ger
1920	Magda Julin-Mauroy .....SWE	1960	Carol Heiss ....USA	1992	Kristi Yamaguchi ....USA
1924	Herma Planck-Szabó .....AUT	1964	Sjoukje Dijkstra ....NED	1994	Oksana Baiul ....UKR
1928	Sonja Henie ....NOR	1968	Peggy Fleming ....USA	1998	Tara Lipinski ....USA
1932	Sonja Henie ....NOR	1972	Beatrix Schuba ....AUT	2002	Sarah Hughes ....USA
1936	Sonja Henie ....NOR	1976	Dorothy Hamill ....USA	2006	Shizuka Arakawa ....JPN
1948	Barbara Ann Scott ......CAN	1980	Anett Poetzsch ....E. Ger		

Pairs

Multiple gold medals: MEN–Pierre Brunet, Artur Dmitriev, Sergei Grinkov, Oleg Protopopov and Aleksandr Zaitsev (2). WOMEN–Irina Rodnina (3); Ludmila Belousova, Ekaterina Gordeeva and Andree Joly Brunet (2).

Year		Year	
1908	Anna Hübler & Heinrich Burger Germany	1968	Ludmila Belousova & Oleg Protopopov .....USSR
1912	Not held	1972	Irina Rodnina & Aleksei Ulanov ....USSR
1920	Ludovika & Walter Jakobsson ....Finland	1976	Irina Rodnina & Aleksandr Zaitsev ....USSR
1924	Helene Engelmann & Alfred Berger ....Austria	1980	Irina Rodnina & Aleksandr Zaitsev ....USSR
1928	Andrée Joly & Pierre Brunet ....France	1984	Elena Valova & Oleg Vasiliev ....USSR
1932	Andrée & Pierre Brunet ....France	1988	Ekaterina Gordeeva & Sergei Grinkov .....USSR
1936	Maxi Herber & Ernst Baier ....Germany	1992	Natalia Mishkutienok & Arthur Dmitriev .....UT
1948	Micheline Lannoy & Pierre Baugniet .....Belgium	1994	Ekaterina Gordeeva & Sergei Grinkov ....RUS
1952	Ria & Paul Falk ....Germany	1998	Oksana Kazakova & Artur Dmitriev ....RUS
1956	Elisabeth Schwartz & Kurt Oppelt ....Austria	2002	Elena Berezhnaya & Anton Sikharulidze .....RUS
1960	Barbara Wagner & Robert Paul ....Canada		Jamie Sale & David Pelletier* ....CAN
1964	Ludmila Belousova & Oleg Protopopov ......USSR	2006	Tatyana Totmiyanina & Maxim Marinin ....RUS

*Originally awarded silver medals, Sale & Pelletier later had them upgraded to gold after an investigation by the International Olympic Committee and the International Skating Union concluded that a judge was guilty of misconduct.

Ice Dancing

Multiple gold medals: Oksana Grishuk & Yevgeny Platov (2).

Year		Year	
1976	Lyudmila Pakhomova & Aleksandr Gorshkov ..USSR	1994	Oksana Grishuk & Yevgeny Platov ....RUS
1980	Natalia Linichuk & Gennady Karponosov ....USSR	1998	Oksana Grishuk & Yevgeny Platov ....RUS
1984	Jayne Torvill & Christopher Dean .....Great Britain	2002	Marina Anissina & Gwendal Peizerat ....FRA
1988	Natalia Bestemianova & Andrei Bukin ......USSR	2006	Tatyana Navka & Roman Kostomarov ....RUS
1992	Marina Klimova & Sergei Ponomarenko ....UT		

FREESTYLE SKIING

MEN

Aerials

Year		Points
1994	Andreas Schoebaechler, SWI	.234.67
1998	Eric Bergoust, USA	.255.64
2002	Ales Valenta, CZR	.257.02
2006	Xiaopeng Han, CHN	.250.77

Moguls

Year		Points
1994	Jean-Luc Brassard, CAN	.27.24
1998	Jonny Moseley, USA	.26.93
2002	Janne Lahtela, FIN	.27.97
2006	Dale Begg-Smith, AUS	.26.77

WOMEN

Aerials

Year		Points
1994	Lina Cherjazova, UZB	.166.84
1998	Nikki Stone, USA	.193.00
2002	Alisa Camplin, AUS	.193.47
2006	Evelyne Leu, SWI	.202.55

Moguls

Year		Points
1994	Stine Lise Hattestad, NOR	.25.97
1998	Tae Satoya, JPN	.25.06
2002	Kari Traa, NOR	.25.94
2006	Jennifer Heil, CAN	.26.50

ICE HOCKEY

MEN

Multiple gold medals: Soviet Union/Unified Team (8); Canada (7); Sweden and United States (2).

Year	
1920	**Canada**, United States Czechoslovakia
1924	**Canada**, United States, Great Britain
1928	**Canada**, Sweden, Switzerland
1932	**Canada**, United States, Germany
1936	**Great Britain**, Canada, United States
1948	**Canada**, Czechoslovakia, Switzerland
1952	**Canada**, United States, Sweden
1956	**Soviet Union**, United States, Canada
1960	**United States**, Canada, Soviet Union
1964	**Soviet Union**, Sweden, Czechoslovakia
1968	**Soviet Union**, Czechoslovakia, Canada
1972	**Soviet Union**, United States, Czechoslovakia
1976	**Soviet Union**, Czechoslovakia, West Germany

Year	
1980	**United States**, Soviet Union, Sweden
1984	**Soviet Union**, Czechoslovakia, Sweden
1988	**Soviet Union**, Finland, Sweden
1992	**Unified Team**, Canada, Czechoslovakia
1994	**Sweden**, Canada, Finland
1998	**Czech Republic**, Russia, Finland
2002	**Canada**, United States, Russia
2006	**Sweden**, Finland, Czech Republic

WOMEN

Year	
1998	**United States**, Canada, Finland
2002	**Canada**, United States, Sweden
2006	**Canada**, Sweden, United States

U.S. Gold Medal Hockey Teams

MEN

1960

Forwards: Billy Christian, Roger Christian, Billy Cleary, Gene Grazia, Paul Johnson, Bob McVey, Dick Meredith, Weldy Olson, Dick Rodenheiser and Tom Williams. **Defensemen:** Bob Cleary, Jack Kirrane (captain), John Mayasich, Bob Owen and Rod Paavola. **Goaltenders:** Jack McCartan and Larry Palmer. **Coach:** Jack Riley.

1980

Forwards: Neal Broten, Steve Christoff, Mike Eruzione (captain), John Harrington, Mark Johnson, Rob McClanahan, Mark Pavelich, Buzz Schneider, Dave Silk, Eric Strobel, Phil Verchota and Mark Wells. **Defensemen:** Bill Baker, Dave Christian, Ken Morrow, Jack O'Callahan, Mike Ramsey and Bob Suter. **Goaltenders:** Jim Craig and Steve Janaszak. **Coach:** Herb Brooks.

WOMEN

1998

Forwards: Laurie Baker, Alana Blahoski, Lisa Brown-Miller, Karen Bye, Tricia Dunn, Cammi Granato, Katie King, Shelley Looney, A.J. Mleczko, Jenny Schmidgall, Gretchen Ulion, Sandra Whyte. **Defensemen:** Chris Bailey, Colleen Coyne, Sue Mertz, Tara Mounsey, Vicki Movessian, Angela Ruggiero. **Goaltenders:** Sarah DeCosta and Sarah Tueting. **Coach:** Ben Smith.

LUGE

MEN

Multiple gold medals: (including doubles): Georg Hackl (3); Jan Behrendt, Norbert Hahn, Paul Hildgartner, Thomas Köhler, Stefan Krausse, Hans Rinn and Armin Zoeggeler (2).

Singles

Year		Time	Year		Time
1964	Thomas Köhler, GER	3:26.77	1988	Jens Müller, E. Ger	3:05.548
1968	Manfred Schmid, AUT	2:52.48	1992	Georg Hackl, GER	3:02.363
1972	Wolfgang Scheidel, E. Ger	3:27.58	1994	Georg Hackl, GER	3:21.571
1976	Dettlef Günther, E. Ger	3:27.688	1998	Georg Hackl, GER	3:18.436
1980	Bernhard Glass, E. Ger	2:54.796	2002	Armin Zoeggeler, ITA	2:57.941
1984	Paul Hildgartner, ITA	3:04.258	2006	Armin Zoeggeler, ITA	3:26.088

Doubles

Year		Time	Year		Time
1964	Josef Feistmantl & Manfred Stengl, AUT	1:41.62	1988	Joerg Hoffmann & Jochen Pietzsch, E. Ger.	1:31.940
1968	Klaus Bonsack & Thomas Köhler, E. Ger.	1:35.85	1992	Jan Behrendt & Stefan Krausse, GER	1:32.053
1972	(TIE) Paul Hildgartner/Walter Plaikner, ITA	1:28.35	1994	Kurt Brugger & Wilfred Huber, ITA	1:36.720
	& Richard Bredow/Horst Hornlein, E. Ger.	1:28.35	1998	Jan Behrendt & Stefan Krausse, GER	1:41.105
1976	Norbert Hahn & Hans Rinn, E. Ger.	1:25.604	2002	Patric-Fritz Leitner & Alexander Resch, GER	1:26.082
1980	Norbert Hahn & Hans Rinn, E. Ger.	1:19.331	2006	Andreas Linger & Wolfgang Linger, AUT	1:34.497
1984	Hans Stangassinger & Franz Wembacher, W. Ger.	1:23.620			

WOMEN

Multiple gold medals: Sylke Otto and Steffi Martin Walter (2).

Singles

Year		Time	Year		Time
1964	Ortrun Enderlein, GER	3:24.67	1988	Steffi Martin Walter, E. Ger	3:03.973
1968	Erica Lechner, ITA	2:28.66	1992	Doris Neuner, AUT	3:06.696
1972	Anna-Maria Müller, E. Ger	2:59.18	1994	Gerda Weissensteiner, ITA	3:15.517
1976	Margit Schumann, E. Ger	2:50.621	1998	Silke Kraushaar, GER	3:23.779
1980	Vera Zozulya, USSR	2:36.537	2002	Sylke Otto, GER	2:52.464
1984	Steffi Martin, E. Ger	2:46.570	2006	Sylke Otto, GER	3:07.979

NORDIC COMBINED

Ski jumping followed by a cross country race. Judges stopped converting cross country times into points after the 1994 Games. The times listed are final cross country times adjusted to include the competitors' staggered start time. The staggered start is determined by the Gundersen Method, which is a table that converts final ski jumping point differentials into time intervals.

Multiple gold medals: Samppa Lajunen and Ulrich Wehling (3); Bjarte Engen Vik, Felix Gottwald, Johan Gröttumsbråten, Fred Boerre Lundberg, Takanori Kono and Kenji Ogiwara (2).

Individual

Year		Points	Year		Points
1924	Thorleif Haug, NOR	18.906	1976	Ulrich Wehling, E. Ger	423.39
1928	Johan Gröttumsbråten, NOR	17.833	1980	Ulrich Wehling, E. Ger	432.200
1932	Johan Gröttumsbråten, NOR	446.00	1984	Tom Sandberg, NOR	422.595
1936	Oddbjörn Hagen, NOR	430.3	1988	Hippolyt Kempf, SWI	432.230
1948	Heikki Hasu, FIN	448.80	1992	Fabrice Guy, FRA	426.470
1952	Simon Slattvik, NOR	451.621	1994	Fred Boerre Lundberg, NOR	457.970
1956	Sverre Stenersen, NOR	455.000			Time
1960	Georg Thoma, GER	457.952	1998	Bjarte Engen Vik, NOR	41:21.1
1964	Tormod Knutsen, NOR	469.28	2002	Samppa Lajunen, FIN	39:11.7
1968	Franz Keller, W. Ger	449.04	2006	Georg Hettich, GER	39:44.6
1972	Ulrich Wehling, E. Ger	413.340			

Sprint

New event in 2002.

Year		Time	Year		Time
2002	Samppa Lajunen, FIN	16:40.1	2006	Felix Gottwald, AUT	18:29.0

Team

Year		Points	Year		Time
1988	West Germany	792.08	1998	Norway	54:11.5
1992	Japan	1247.180	2002	Finland	48:42.2
1994	Japan	1368.860	2006	Austria	49:52.6

SKELETON

MEN		
Singles		

Year		Time
1928	Jennison Heaton, USA	3:01.8
1932-36	Not held	
1948	Nino Bibbia, ITA	5:23.2
1952-98	Not held	
2002	Jim Shea, USA	1:41.96
2006	Duff Gibson, CAN	1:55.88

WOMEN		
Singles		

Year		Time
2002	Tristan Gale, USA	1:45.11
2006	Maya Pedersen, SWI	1:59.83

Note: This event was called Cresta when it was held in 1928 and 1948.

SKI JUMPING

Multiple gold medals (including team jumping): Matti Nykänen (4); Jens Weissflog (3); Simon Ammann, Birger Ruud, Thomas Morgenstern and Toni Nieminen (2).

Normal Hill (90 Meters)

Year		Points	Year		Points
1924-60	Not held		1988	Matti Nykänen, FIN	229.1
1964	Veikko Kankkonen, FIN	229.9	1992	Ernst Vettori, AUT	222.8
1968	Jiri Raska, CZE	216.5	1994	Espen Bredesen, NOR	282.0
1972	Yukio Kasaya, JPN	244.2	1998	Jani Soininen, FIN	234.5
1976	Hans-Georg Aschenbach, E. Ger	252.0	2002	Simon Ammann, SWI	269.0
1980	Anton Innauer, AUT	266.3	2006	Lars Bystoel, NOR	266.5
1984	Jens Weissflog, E. Ger	215.2			

Note: Jump held at 70 meters from 1964-92.

Large Hill (120 Meters)

Year		Points	Year		Points
1924	Jacob Tullin Thams, NOR	18.960	1972	Wojciech Fortuna, POL	219.9
1928	Alf Andersen, NOR	19.208	1976	Karl Schäabl, AUT	234.8
1932	Birger Ruud, NOR	228.1	1980	Jouko Törmänen, FIN	271.0
1936	Birger Ruud, NOR	232.0	1984	Matti Nykänen, FIN	231.2
1948	Petter Hugsted, NOR	228.1	1988	Matti Nykänen, FIN	224.0
1952	Arnfinn Bergmann, NOR	226.0	1992	Toni Nieminen, FIN	239.5
1956	Antti Hyvärinen, FIN	227.0	1994	Jens Weissflog, GER	274.5
1960	Helmut Recknagel, GER	227.2	1998	Kazuyoshi Funaki, JPN	272.3
1964	Toralf Engan, NOR	230.7	2002	Simon Ammann, SWI	281.4
1968	Vladimir Beloussov, USSR	231.3	2006	Thomas Morgenstern, AUT	276.9

Note: Jump held at various lengths from 1924-56; at 80 meters from 1960-64; and at 90 meters from 1968-88.

Team (Large Hill)

Year		Points	Year		Points
1988	Finland	634.4	1998	Japan	933.0
1992	Finland	644.4	2002	Germany	974.1
1994	Germany	970.1	2006	Austria	984.0

Women Jumping at Chance for Olympic Debut

With the recent addition of women's bobsled to the slate, ski jumping, and by extension nordic combined, remain the only Winter Olympic sports that do not have events for women. That could change for the next Winter Games set for Vancouver, Canada in 2010. The International Olympic Committee will ultimately make a determination if there is enough international interest to stage a legitimate competition.

The female ski jumpers and Olympic hopefuls got some good news in August 2006 when the International Ski Federation voted to add an individual event for women (Normal Hill) at the 2009 World Championships to be held in Liberec, Czech Republic. Holding a world championships is a requirement to the sport attaining Olympic status.

For women jumpers to compete at the 2010 Games, the sport still must be accepted by the Vancouver Organizing Committee and get endorsed by the IOC at its meeting in July 2007 in Guatemala City where it will also announce the host city for the 2014 Winter Games. The finalists are Sochi, Russia, Salzburg, Austria and PyeongChang, South Korea.

SNOWBOARDING

Multiple gold medals: Philipp Schoch (2).

MEN

Halfpipe

Year		Points
1998	Gian Simmen, SWI	.85.2
2002	Ross Powers, USA	.46.1
2006	Shaun White, USA	.46.8

Giant Slalom

Discontinued after 1998, replaced by Parallel Giant Slalom.

Year		Time
1998	Ross Rebagliati, CAN	.2:03.96

Parallel Giant Slalom

Year		
2002	Philipp Schoch	.SWI
2006	Philipp Schoch	.SWI

Snowboard Cross

Added in 2006.

Year		
2006	Seth Wescott	.USA

WOMEN

Halfpipe

Year		Points
1998	Nicola Thost, GER	.74.6
2002	Kelly Clark, USA	.47.9
2006	Hannah Teter, USA	.46.4

Giant Slalom

Discontinued after 1998, replaced by Parallel Giant Slalom.

Year		Time
1998	Karine Ruby, FRA	.2:17.34

Parallel Giant Slalom

Year		
2002	Isabelle Blanc	.FRA
2006	Daniela Meuli	.SWI

Snowboard Cross

Added in 2006.

Year		
2006	Tanja Frieden	.SWI

SPEED SKATING

MEN

Multiple gold medals: Eric Heiden and Clas Thunberg (5); Ivar Ballangrud, Yevgeny Grishin and Johann Olav Koss (4); Hjalmar Andersen, Tomas Gustafson, Irving Jaffee and Ard Schenk (3); Gaétan Boucher, Enrico Fabris, Knut Johannesen, Erhard Keller, Uwe-Jens Mey, Gianni Romme, Jack Shea and Jochem Uytdehaage (2). Note that Thunberg's total includes the All-Around, which was contested for the only time in 1924.

500 meters

Year		Time		Year		Time	
1924	Charles Jewtraw, USA	.44.0		1972	Erhard Keller, W. Ger	.39.44	**OR**
1928	(TIE) Bernt Evensen, NOR	.43.4	**OR**	1976	Yevgeny Kulikov, USSR	.39.17	**OR**
	& Clas Thunberg, FIN	.43.4	**OR**	1980	Eric Heiden, USA	.38.03	**OR**
1932	Jack Shea, USA	.43.4	**=OR**	1984	Sergei Fokichev, USSR	.38.19	
1936	Ivar Ballangrud, NOR	.43.4	**=OR**	1988	Uwe-Jens Mey, E. Ger	.36.45	**WR**
1948	Finn Helgesen, NOR	.43.1	**OR**	1992	Uwe-Jens Mey, GER	.37.14	
1952	Ken Henry, USA	.43.2		1994	Aleksandr Golubev, RUS	.36.33	**OR**
1956	Yevgeny Grishin, USSR	.40.2	**=WR**	1998	Hiroyashu Shimizu, JPN	.71.35*	**OR**
1960	Yevgeny Grishin, USSR	.40.2	**=WR**	2002	Casey FitzRandolph, USA	.69.23	**OR**
1964	Terry McDermott, USA	.40.1	**OR**	2006	Joey Cheek, USA	.69.76	
1968	Erhard Keller, W. Ger	.40.3					

*The two-race final was introduced; skater with the lowest combined time wins gold.

1000 meters

Year		Time		Year		Time	
1924-72 Not held				1992	Olaf Zinke, GER	.1:14.85	
1976	Peter Mueller, USA	.1:19.32		1994	Dan Jansen, USA	.1:12.43	**WR**
1980	Eric Heiden, USA	.1:15.18	**OR**	1998	Ids Postma, NED	.1:10.64	**OR**
1984	Gaétan Boucher, CAN	.1:15.80		2002	Gerard van Velde, NED	.1:07.18	**WR**
1988	Nikolai Gulyaev, USSR	.1:13.03	**OR**	2006	Shani Davis, USA	.1:08.89	

1500 meters

Year		Time		Year		Time	
1924	Clas Thunberg, FIN	.2:20.8		1968	Kees Verkerk, NED	.2:03.4	**OR**
1928	Clas Thunberg, FIN	.2:21.1		1972	Ard Schenk, NED	.2:02.96	**OR**
1932	Jack Shea, USA	.2:57.5		1976	Jan Egil Storholt, NOR	.1:59.38	**OR**
1936	Charles Mathisen, NOR	.2:19.2	**OR**	1980	Eric Heiden, USA	.1:55.44	**OR**
1948	Sverre Farstad, NOR	.2:17.6	**OR**	1984	Gaétan Boucher, CAN	.1:58.36	
1952	Hjalmar Andersen, NOR	.2:20.4		1988	Andre Hoffman, E. Ger	.1:52.06	**WR**
1956	(TIE) Yevgeny Grishin, USSR	.2:08.6	**WR**	1992	Johann Olav Koss, NOR	.1:54.81	
	& Yuri Mikhailov, USSR	.2:08.6	**WR**	1994	Johann Olav Koss, NOR	.1:51.29	**WR**
1960	(TIE) Roald Aas, NOR	.2:10.4		1998	Aadne Sondral, NOR	.1:47.87	**WR**
	& Yevgeny Grishin, USSR	.2:10.4		2002	Derek Parra, USA	.1:43.95	**WR**
1964	Ants Antson, USSR	.2:10.3		2006	Enrico Fabris, ITA	.1:45.97	

5000 meters

Year		Time		Year		Time	
1924	Clas Thunberg, FIN	8:39.0		1972	Ard Schenk, NED	7:23.61	
1928	Ivar Ballangrud, NOR	8:50.5		1976	Sten Stensen, NOR	7:24.48	
1932	Irving Jaffee, USA	9:40.8		1980	Eric Heiden, USA	7:02.29	OR
1936	Ivar Ballangrud, NOR	8:19.6	OR	1984	Tomas Gustafson, SWE	7:12.28	
1948	Reidar Liaklev, NOR	8:29.4		1988	Tomas Gustafson, SWE	6:44.63	WR
1952	Hjalmar Andersen, NOR	8:10.6	OR	1992	Geir Karlstad, NOR	6:59.97	
1956	Boris Shilkov, USSR	7:48.7	OR	1994	Johann Olav Koss, NOR	6:34.96	WR
1960	Viktor Kosichkin, USSR	7:51.3		1998	Gianni Romme, NED	6:22.20	WR
1964	Knut Johannesen, NOR	7:38.4	OR	2002	Jochem Uytdehaage, NED	6:14.66	WR
1968	Fred Anton Maier, NOR	7:22.4	WR	2006	Chad Hedrick, USA	6:14.68	

10,000 meters

Year		Time		Year		Time	
1924	Julius Skutnabb, FIN	18:04.8		1972	Ard Schenk, NED	15:01.35	OR
1928	Irving Jaffee, USA*	18:36.5		1976	Piet Kleine, NED	14:50.59	OR
1932	Irving Jaffee, USA	19:13.6		1980	Eric Heiden, USA	14:28.13	WR
1936	Ivar Ballangrud, NOR	17:24.3	OR	1984	Igor Malkov, USSR	14:39.90	
1948	Ake Seyffarth, SWE	17:26.3		1988	Tomas Gustafson, SWE	13:48.20	WR
1952	Hjalmar Andersen, NOR	16:45.8	OR	1992	Bart Veldkamp, NED	14:12.12	
1956	Sigvard Ericsson, SWE	16:35.9	OR	1994	Johann Olav Koss, NOR	13:30.55	WR
1960	Knut Johannesen, NOR	15:46.6	WR	1998	Gianni Romme, NED	13:15.33	WR
1964	Jonny Nilsson, SWE	15:50.1		2002	Jochem Uytdehaage, NED	12:58.92	WR
1968	Johnny Höglin, SWE	15:23.6	OR	2006	Bob De Jong, NED	13:01.57	

*Unofficial, according to the IOC. Jaffee recorded the fastest time, but the event was called off in progress due to thawing ice.

Team Pursuit

Added in 2006.

Year	
2006	**Italy**, Canada, Netherlands

WOMEN

Multiple gold medals: Lydia Skoblikova (6); Bonnie Blair (5); Claudia Pechstein (4); Karin Enke, Gunda Niemann-Stirnemann and Yvonne van Gennip (3); Tatiana Averina, Catriona Lemay-Doan, Christa Rothenburger and Marianne Timmer (2).

500 meters

Year		Time		Year		Time	
1960	Helga Haase, GER	45.9		1988	Bonnie Blair, USA	39.10	WR
1964	Lydia Skoblikova, USSR	45.0	OR	1992	Bonnie Blair, USA	40.33	
1968	Lyudmila Titova, USSR	46.1		1994	Bonnie Blair, USA	39.25	
1972	Anne Henning, USA	43.33	OR	1998	Catriona Lemay-Doan, CAN	76.60*	OR
1976	Sheila Young, USA	42.76	OR	2002	Catriona Lemay-Doan, CAN	74.75	OR
1980	Karin Enke, E. Ger	41.78	OR	2006	Svetlana Zhurova, RUS	76.57	
1984	Christa Rothenburger, E. Ger	41.02	OR				

*The two-race final was introduced; skater with the lowest combined time wins gold.

1000 meters

Year		Time		Year		Time	
1960	Klara Guseva, USSR	1:34.1		1988	Christa Rothenburger, E. Ger	1:17.65	WR
1964	Lydia Skoblikova, USSR	1:33.2	OR	1992	Bonnie Blair, USA	1:21.90	
1968	Carolina Geijssen, NED	1:32.6	OR	1994	Bonnie Blair, USA	1:18.74	
1972	Monika Pflug, W. Ger	1:31.40	OR	1998	Marianne Timmer, NED	1:16.51	OR
1976	Tatiana Averina, USSR	1:28.43	OR	2002	Chris Witty, USA	1:13.83	WR
1980	Natalia Petruseva, USSR	1:24.10	OR	2006	Marianne Timmer, NED	1:16.05	
1984	Karin Enke, E. Ger	1:21.61	OR				

1500 meters

Year		Time		Year		Time	
1960	Lydia Skoblikova, USSR	2:25.2	WR	1988	Yvonne van Gennip, NED	2:00.68	OR
1964	Lydia Skoblikova, USSR	2:22.6	OR	1992	Jacqueline Börner, GER	2:05.87	
1968	Kaija Mustonen, FIN	2:22.4	OR	1994	Emese Hunyady, AUT	2:02.19	
1972	Dianne Holum, USA	2:20.85	OR	1998	Marianne Timmer, NED	1:57.58	WR
1976	Galina Stepanskaya, USSR	2:16.58	OR	2002	Anni Friesinger, GER	1:54.02	WR
1980	Annie Borckink, NED	2:10.95	OR	2006	Cindy Klassen, CAN	1:55.27	
1984	Karin Enke, E. Ger	2:03.42	WR				

Speed Skating (Cont.)

3000 meters

Year		Time	
1960	Lydia Skoblikova, USSR	5:14.3	
1964	Lydia Skoblikova, USSR	5:14.9	
1968	Johanna Schut, NED	4:56.2	OR
1972	Christina Baas-Kaiser, NED	4:52.14	OR
1976	Tatiana Averina, USSR	4:45.19	OR
1980	Bjorg Eva Jensen, NOR	4:32.13	OR
1984	Andrea Schöne, E. Ger	4:24.79	OR
1988	Yvonne van Gennip, NED	4:11.94	WR
1992	Gunda Niemann, GER	4:19.90	
1994	Svetlana Bazhanova, RUS	4:17.43	
1998	Gunda Niemann-Stirnemann, GER	4:07.29	OR
2002	Claudia Pechstein, GER	3:57.70	WR
2006	Ireen Wust, NED	4:02.43	

5000 meters

Year		Time	
1960-84 Not held			
1988	Yvonne van Gennip, NED	7:14.13	WR
1992	Gunda Niemann, GER	7:31.57	
1994	Claudia Pechstein, GER	7:14.37	
1998	Claudia Pechstein, GER	6:59.61	WR
2002	Claudia Pechstein, GER	6:46.91	WR
2006	Clara Hughes, CAN	6:59.07	

Team Pursuit
Added in 2006.

Year	
2006	**Germany**, Canada, Russia

SHORT TRACK SPEED SKATING

MEN

Multiple gold medals (including relays): Hyun-Soo Ahn, Marc Gagnon and Kim Ki-Hoon (3); Apolo Anton Ohno (2).

500 meters
added in 1994.

Year		Time	
1994	Chae Ji-Hoon, S. Kor.	43.45	
1998	Takafumi Nishitani, JPN	42.862	
2002	Marc Gagnon, CAN	41.802	OR
2006	Apolo Anton Ohno, USA	41.935	

1000 meters

Year		Time	
1992	Kim Ki-Hoon, S. Kor.	1:30.76	WR
1994	Kim Ki-Hoon, S. Kor.	1:34.57	
1998	Kim Dong-Sung, S. Kor.	1:32.375	
2002	Steven Bradbury, AUS	1:29.109	
2006	Hyun-Soo Ahn, S. Kor.	1:26.739	

1500 meters
added in 2002.

Year		Time	
2002	Apolo Anton Ohno, USA*	2:18.541	
2006	Hyun-Soo Ahn, S. Kor.	2:25.341	

*Ohno finished second to South Korea's Kim Dong-Sung, who was disqualifed for cross-tracking.

5000-m Relay

Year		Time	
1992	South Korea	7:14.02	WR
1994	Italy	7:11.74	OR
1998	Canada	7:06.075	
2002	Canada	6:51.579	
2006	South Korea	6:43.376	

WOMEN

Multiple gold medals (including relays): Chun Lee-Kyung (4); Sun-Yu Jin (3); Kim Yun-Mi, Annie Perrault, Cathy Turner, Won Hye-Kyung and Yang Yang (A) (2)

500 meters

Year		Time	
1992	Cathy Turner, USA	47.04	
1994	Cathy Turner, USA	45.98	OR
1998	Annie Perrault, CAN	46.568	
2002	Yang Yang (A), CHN	44.187	
2006	Meng Wang, CHN	44.345	

1000 meters
added in 1994.

Year		Time	
1994	Chun Lee-Kyung, S. Kor.	1:36.87	
1998	Chun Lee-Kyung, S. Kor.	1:42.776	
2002	Yang Yang (A), CHN	1:36.391	
2006	Sun-Yu Jin, S. Kor.	1:32.859	

1500 meters
added in 2002.

Year		Time	
2002	Ko Gi-Hyun, S. Kor.	2:31.581	
2006	Sun-Yu Jin, S. Kor.	2:23.494	

3000-m Relay

Year		Time	
1992	Canada	4:36.62	
1994	South Korea	4:26.64	WR
1998	South Korea	4:16.260	WR
2002	South Korea	4:12.793	WR
2006	South Korea	4:17.040	

All-Time Leading Medal Winners
MEN

No		Sport	G-S-B	No		Sport	G-S-B
12	Bjørn Dählie, NOR	Cross Country	8-4-0	5	**Eric Heiden, USA**	Speed Skating	5-0-0
9	Sixten Jernberg, SWE	Cross Country	4-3-2	5	Yevgeny Grishin, USSR	Speed Skating	4-1-0
8	Kjetil Andre Aamodt, NOR	Alpine	4-2-2	5	Johann Olav Koss, NOR	Speed Skating	4-1-0
7	Clas Thunberg, FIN	Speed Skating	5-1-1	5	Matti Nykänen, FIN	Ski Jumping	4-1-0
7	Ivar Ballangrud, NOR	Speed Skating	4-2-1	5	Aleksandr Tikhonov, USSR	Biathlon	4-1-0
7	Ricco Gross, GER	Biathlon	3-3-1	5	Nikolai Zimyatov, USSR	Cross Country	4-1-0
7	Veikko Hakulinen, FIN	Cross Country	3-3-1	5	Georg Hackl, GER	Luge	3-2-0
7	Eero Mäntyranta, FIN	Cross Country	3-2-2	5	Samppa Lajunen, FIN	Cross Country	3-2-0
6	Bogdan Musiol, E. Ger/GER	Bobsled	1-5-1	5	Alberto Tomba, ITA	Alpine	3-2-0
6	Ole Einar Bjoerndalen, NOR	Biathlon	5-1-0	5	Marc Gagnon, CAN	ST Sp. Skating	3-0-2
6	Thomas Alsgaard, NOR	Cross Country	4-2-0	5	Harald Grönningen, NOR	Cross Country	2-3-0
6	Gunde Svan, SWE	Cross Country	4-1-1	5	Frank Luck, GER	Biathlon	2-3-0
6	Vegard Ulvang, NOR	Cross Country	3-2-1	5	Pål Tyldum, NOR	Cross Country	2-3-0
6	Johan Gröttumsbråten, NOR	Nordic	3-1-2	5	Sven Fischer, GER	Biathlon	2-2-1
6	Wolfgang Hoppe, E. Ger/GER	Bobsled	2-3-1	5	Knut Johannesen, NOR	Speed Skating	2-2-1
6	Eugenio Monti, ITA	Bobsled	2-2-2	5	Lasse Kjus, NOR	Alpine	1-3-1
6	Felix Gottwald, AUT	Nordic	2-1-3	5	Peter Angerer, W. Ger/GER	Biathlon	1-2-2
6	Vladimir Smirnov, USSR/UT/KAZ	X-country	1-4-1	5	Juha Mieto, FIN	Cross Country	1-2-2
6	Mika Myllylae, FIN	Cross Country	1-1-4	5	Fritz Feierabend, SWI	Bobsled	0-3-2
6	Roald Larsen, NOR	Speed Skating	0-2-4	5	Rintje Ritsma, NED	Speed Skating	0-2-3
6	Harri Kirvesniemi, FIN	Cross Country	0-0-6				

WOMEN

No		Sport	G-S-B	No		Sport	G-S-B
10	Raisa Smetanina, USSR/UT	Cross Country	4-5-1	6	**Bonnie Blair, USA**	Speed Skating	5-0-1
9	Lyubov Egorova, UT/RUS	Cross Country	6-3-0	6	Janica Kostelic, CRO	Alpine	4-2-0
9	Larissa Lazutina, UT/RUS	Cross Country	5-3-1	6	Manuela Di Centa, ITA	Cross Country	2-2-2
9	Stefania Belmondo, ITA	Cross Country	2-3-4	6	Cindy Klassen, CAN	Speed Skating	1-2-3
8	Galina Kulakova, USSR	Cross Country	4-2-0	5	Lee-Kyung Chun, S. Kor	ST Sp. Skating	4-0-1
8	Karin (Enke) Kania, E. Ger	Speed Skating	3-4-1	5	Olga Danilova, RUS	Cross Country	3-2-0
8	Gunda Neimann- Stirnemann, GER	Speed Skating	3-4-1	5	Anfisa Reztsova, USSR/UT	CC/Biathlon	3-1-1
8	Ursula Disl, GER	Biathlon	2-4-2	5	Vreni Schneider, SWI	Alpine	3-1-1
7	Claudia Pechstein, GER	Speed Skating	4-1-2	5	Katja Seizinger, GER	Alpine	3-0-2
7	Marja-Liisa (Hämäläinen) Kirvesniemi, FIN	Cross Country	3-0-4	5	Kati Wilhelm, GER	Biathlon	2-3-0
7	Elena Valbe, UT/RUS	Cross Country	3-0-4	5	Helena Takalo, FIN	Cross Country	1-3-1
7	Andrea (Mitscherlich, Schöne) Ehrig, E. Ger	Speed Skating	1-5-1	5	Bente (Martinsen) Skari, NOR	Cross Country	1-2-2
6	Lydia Skoblikova, USSR	Speed Skating	6-0-0	5	Alevtina Kolchina, USSR	Cross Country	1-1-3
				5	Anja Paerson, SWE	Alpine	1-1-3
				5	Yang Yang (S), CHN	ST Sp. Skating	0-4-1
				5	Anita Moen, NOR	Cross Country	0-3-2

Games Medaled In

MEN–**Aamodt** (1992,94,2002,2006); **Alsgaard** (1994,98,2002); **Angerer** (1980,84,88); **Ballangrud** (1928,32,36); **Bjoerndalen** (1998,2002); **Dählie** (1992,94,98); **Feierabend** (1936,48,52); **Fischer** (1994,98,2002); **Gagnon** (1994,98,2002); **Gottwald** (2002,06); **Grishin** (1956,60,64); **Gross** (1992,94,98,2002); **Gröttumsbråten** (1924,28,32); **Grönningen** (1960,64,68); **Hackl** (1988,92,94,98,2002); **Hakulinen** (1952,56,60); **Heiden** (1980); **Hoppe** (1984,88,92,94); **Jernberg** (1956,60,64); **Johannesen** (1956,60,64); **Kirvesniemi** (1980,84,92,94,98); **Kjus** (1994,98,2002); **Koss** (1992,94); **Lajunen** (1998,2002); **Larsen** (1924,28); **Luck** (1994,98,2002); **Mäntyranta** (1960,64,68); **Mieto** (1976,80,84); **Monti** (1956,60,64,68); **Musiol** (1980,84,88,92); **Myllylae** (1994,98); **Nykänen** (1984,88); **Ritsma** (1994,98); **Smirnov** (1988,92,94,98); **Svan** (1984,88); **Thunberg** (1924,28); **Tikhonov** (1968,72,76,80); **Tomba** (1988,92,94); **Tyldum** (1968,72,76); **Ulvang** (1988,92,94); **Zimyatov** (1980,84).

WOMEN–**Belmondo** (1992,94,98,2002); **Blair** (1988,92,94); **Chun** (1994,98); **Danilova** (1998,2002); **Di Centa** (1992,94); **Disl** (1992,94,98,2002); **Egorova** (1992,94); **Ehrig** (1976,80,84,88); **Kania** (1980,84,88); **Kirvesniemi** (1984,88,94); **Klassen** (2002,06); **Kolchina** (1956,64,68); **Kulakova** (1968,72,76,80); **Lazutina** (1992,94,98,2002); **Moen** (1994,98,2002); **Niemann-Stirnemann** (1992,94,98); **Paerson** (2002,06); **Pechstein** (1992,94,98,2002); **Reztsova** (1988,92,94); **Schneider** (1988,92,94); **Seizinger** (1992,94,98); **Skari** (1998,2002); **Skoblikova** (1960,64); **Smetanina** (1976,80,84,88,92); **Takalo** (1972,76,80); **Valbe** (1992,94,98); **Wilhelm** (2002,06); **Yang** (1998,2002).

All-Time Leading USA Medalists
MEN

No		Sport	G-S-B	No		Sport	G-S-B
5	Eric Heiden	Speed Skating	5-0-0	2	Terry McDermott	Speed Skating	1-1-0
5	Apolo Anton Ohno	ST Sp. Skating	2-1-2	2	Dick Meredith	Ice Hockey	1-1-0
3*	Irving Jaffee	Speed Skating	3-0-0	2	Tommy Moe	Alpine	1-1-0
3	Pat Martin	Bobsled	1-2-0	2	Weldy Olson	Ice Hockey	1-1-0
3	Joey Cheek	Speed Skating	1-1-1	2	Derek Parra	Speed Skating	1-1-0
3	Chad Hendrick	Speed Skatng	1-1-1	2	Dick Rodenheiser	Ice Hockey	1-1-0
3	John Heaton	Bobsled/Skeleton	0-2-1	2	Shani Davis	Speed Skating	1-1-0
2	Dick Button	Figure Skating	2-0-0	2	Ross Powers	Snowboarding	1-0-1
2†	Eddie Eagan	Boxing/Bobsled	2-0-0	2	Stan Benham	Bobsled	0-2-0
2	Billy Fiske	Bobsled	2-0-0	2	Herb Drury	Ice Hockey	0-2-0
2	Cliff Gray	Bobsled	2-0-0	2	Eric Flaim	Sp. Skate/ST Sp. Skate	0-2-0
2	Jack Shea	Speed Skating	2-0-0	2	Bode Miller	Alpine	0-2-0
2	Billy Cleary	Ice Hockey	1-1-0	2	Frank Synott	Ice Hockey	0-2-0
2	Jennison Heaton	Bobsled/Skeleton	1-1-0	2	Danny Kass	Snowboarding	0-2-0
2	David Jenkins	Figure Skating	1-1-0	2	John Garrison	Ice Hockey	0-1-1
2	John Mayasich	Ice Hockey	1-1-0	2	Rusty Smith	ST Sp. Skating	0-0-2

*Jaffee is generally given credit for a third gold medal in the 10,000-meter Speed Skating race of 1928. He had the fastest time before the race was cancelled due to thawing ice. The IOC considers the race unofficial.

†Eagan won the light heavyweight boxing title at the 1920 Summer Games in Antwerp and the four-man Bobsled at the 1932 Winter Games in Lake Placid. He is the only athlete ever to win gold medals in both the Winter and Summer Olympics.

WOMEN

No		Sport	G-S-B	No		Sport	G-S-B
6	Bonnie Blair	Speed Skating	5-0-1	2	Cammi Granato	Ice Hockey	1-1-0
4	Cathy Turner	ST Sp. Skating	2-1-1	2	Carol Heiss	Figure Skating	1-1-0
4	Dianne Holum	Speed Skating	1-2-1	2	Shelley Looney	Ice Hockey	1-1-0
3	Chris Witty	Speed Skating	1-1-1	2	Sue Merz	Ice Hockey	1-1-0
3	Sheila Young	Speed Skating	1-1-1	2	A.J. Mleczko	Ice Hockey	1-1-0
3	Angela Ruggiero	Ice Hockey	1-1-1	2	Tara Mounsey	Ice Hockey	1-1-0
3	Katie King	Ice Hockey	1-1-1	2	Diann Roffe-Steinrotter	Alpine	1-1-0
3	Tricia Dunn	Ice Hockey	1-1-1	2	Picabo Street	Alpine	1-1-0
3	Jenny Potter	Ice Hockey	1-1-1	2	Sarah Teuting	Ice Hockey	1-1-0
3	Leah Poulos Mueller	Speed Skating	0-3-0	2	Anne Henning	Speed Skating	1-0-1
3	Beatrix Loughran	Figure Skating	0-2-1	2	Penny Pitou	Alpine	0-2-0
3	Amy Peterson	ST Sp. Skating	0-2-1	2	Nancy Kerrigan	Figure Skating	0-1-1
2	Andrea Mead Lawrence	Alpine	2-0-0	2	Michelle Kwan	Figure Skating	0-1-1
2	Tenley Albright	Figure Skating	1-1-0	2	Jean Saubert	Alpine	0-1-1
2	Chris Bailey	Ice Hockey	1-1-0	2	Nikki Ziegelmeyer	ST Sp. Skating	0-1-1
2	Laurie Baker	Ice Hockey	1-1-0	2	Jennifer Rodriguez	Speed Skating	0-0-2
2	Karyn Bye	Ice Hockey	1-1-0				
2	Sara DeCosta	Ice Hockey	1-1-0				
2	Gretchen Fraser	Alpine	1-1-0				

Note: The term ST Sp. Skating refers to Short Track (or pack) Speed Skating.

Most Gold Medals

MEN

No		Sport	G-S-B
8	Bjorn Dählie, NOR	Cross Country	8-4-0
5	Clas Thunberg, FIN	Speed Skating	5-1-1
5	Ole Einar Bjoerndalen, NOR	Biathlon	5-1-0
5	**Eric Heiden, USA**	Speed Skating	5-0-0
4	Sixten Jernberg, SWE	Cross Country	4-3-2
4	Kjetil Andre Aamodt, NOR	Alpine	4-2-2
4	Ivar Ballangrud, NOR	Speed Skating	4-2-1
4	Thomas Alsgaard, NOR	Cross Country	4-2-0
4	Gunde Svan, SWE	Cross Country	4-1-1
4	Yevgeny Grishin, USSR	Speed Skating	4-1-0
4	Johann Olav Koss, NOR	Speed Skating	4-1-0
4	Matti Nykänen, FIN	Ski Jumping	4-1-0
4	Aleksandr Tikhonov, USSR	Biathlon	4-1-0
4	Nikolai Zimyatov, USSR	Cross Country	4-1-0
4	Thomas Wassberg, SWE	Cross Country	4-0-0

WOMEN

No		Sport	G-S-B
6	Lyubov Egorova, UT/RUS	Cross Country	6-3-0
6	Lydia Skoblikova, USSR	Speed Skating	6-0-0
5	Larissa Lanina, USSR/UT	Cross Country	4-5-1
4	Galina Kulakova, USSR	Cross Country	4-2-2
4	Janica Kostelic, CRO	Alpine	4-2-0
4	Claudia Pechstein, GER	ST Sp. Skating	4-1-2
4	Lee-Kyung Chun, S. Kor.	ST Sp. Skating	4-0-1

All-Time Medal Standings, 1924-2006

All-time Winter Games medal standings, according to *The Golden Book of the Olympic Games*. Medal counts include figure skating medals (1908 and '20) and hockey medals (1920) awarded at the Summer Games. National medal standings for the Winter and Summer Games are not recognized by the IOC.

		G	S	B	Total
1	Norway	96	102	84	282
2	**United States**	78	81	59	218
3	Soviet Union (1956-88)	78	57	59	194
4	Austria	50	64	71	185
5	Germany (1928-36, 52-64, 1992–)	58	58	38	154
6	Finland	42	57	52	151
7	Sweden	46	32	44	122
8	Canada	38	38	44	120
9	East Germany (1968-88)	43	39	36	118
10	Switzerland	37	37	43	117
11	Italy	36	31	33	100
12	France	25	24	32	81
13	Russia (1994–)	33	26	19	80
14	Netherlands	25	30	23	78
15	West Germany (1968-88)	18	20	19	57
16	China	4	16	13	33
17	Japan	9	10	13	32
18	South Korea	17	8	6	31
19	Great Britain	8	5	14	27
20	Czechoslovakia (1924-92)	2	8	16	26
21	Unified Team (1992)	9	6	8	23
22	Czech Republic (1998–)	3	3	3	9
23	Liechtenstein	2	2	5	9
24	Poland	1	3	4	8
25	Estonia	4	1	1	6
	Hungary	0	2	4	6
	Bulgaria	1	2	3	6
	Belarus (1994–)	0	3	3	6
	Australia	3	0	3	6
30	Kazakhstan (1994–)	1	2	2	5
	Belgium	1	1	3	5
	Ukraine (1994–)	1	1	3	5
33	Croatia	3	1	0	4
	Spain	3	0	1	4
	Yugoslavia (1924-88)	0	3	1	4
	Slovenia	0	0	4	4
	Slovenia (1992–)	0	0	3	3
38	Luxembourg	0	2	0	2
	North Korea	0	1	1	2
40	Uzbekistan (1994–)	1	0	0	1
	Slovakia	0	1	0	1
	Denmark	0	1	0	1
	New Zealand	0	1	0	1
	Romania	0	0	1	1
	Latvia	0	0	1	1

Combined totals	G	S	B	Total
Germany/East Germany/West Germany	119	117	93	329
USSR/Unified Team/Russia	122	89	86	297

Notes: Athletes from the USSR participated in the Winter Games from 1956-88, returned as the Unified Team in 1992 after the breakup of the Soviet Union (in 1991) and then competed for the independent republics of Belarus, Kazakhstan, Russia, Ukraine, Uzbekistan and three others in 1994. Yugoslavia divided into Croatia and Bosnia-Herzegovina in 1992, while Czechoslovakia split into Slovakia and the Czech Republic in 1993.

Germany was barred from the Olympics in 1924 and 1948 as an aggressor nation in both World Wars I and II. Divided into East and West Germany after WWII, both countries competed under one flag from 1952-64, then as separate teams from 1968-88. Germany was reunified in 1990.

1896-2004
Through the Years

SPORTS ALMANAC

Modern Olympic Games

The original Olympic Games were celebrated as a religious festival from 776 B.C. until 393 A.D., when Roman emperor Theodosius I banned all pagan festivals (the Olympics celebrated the Greek god Zeus). On June 23, 1894, French educator Baron Pierre de Coubertin, speaking at the Sorbonne in Paris to a gathering of international sports leaders, proposed that the ancient games be revived on an international scale. The idea was enthusiastically received and the Modern Olympics were born. The first Olympics were held two years later in Athens, where 245 athletes from 14 nations competed in the ancient Panathenaic stadium to large and ardent crowds. Americans captured nine out of 12 track and field events, but Greece won the most medals with 47.

The Summer Olympics

Year	No	Location	Dates	Nations	Most medals	USA medals	
1896	I	Athens, GRE	Apr. 6-15	14	Greece (10-19-18—47)	11- 6- 2— 19	(2nd)
1900	II	Paris, FRA	May 20-Oct. 28	26	France (26-37-32—95)	18-14-15— 47	(2nd)
1904	III	St. Louis, USA. . . .	July 1-Nov. 23	13	USA (78-84-82—244)	78-84-82—244	(1st)
1906-a	—	Athens, GRE	Apr. 22-May 2	20	France (15-9-16—40)	12-6- 6— 24	(3rd)
1908	IV	London, GBR	Apr. 27-Oct. 31	22	Britain (54-46-38—138)	23-12-12— 47	(2nd)
1912	V	Stockholm, SWE .	May 5-July 22	28	Sweden (23-24-17—64)	25-18-20— 63	(2nd)
1916	VI	Berlin, GER	Cancelled (WWI)				
1920	VII	Antwerp, BEL	Apr. 20-Sept. 12	29	USA (41-27-27—95)	41-27-27— 95	(1st)
1924	VIII	Paris, FRA	May 4-July 27	44	USA (45-27-27—99)	45-27-27— 99	(1st)
1928	IX	Amsterdam, NED .	May 17-Aug. 12	46	USA (22-18-16—56)	22-18-16— 56	(1st)
1932	X	Los Angeles, USA.	July 30-Aug. 14	37	USA (41-32-30—103)	41-32-30—103	(1st)
1936	XI	Berlin, GER	Aug. 1-16	49	Germany (33-26-30—89)	24-20-12— 56	(2nd)
1940-b	XII	Tokyo, JPN	Cancelled (WWII)				
1944	XIII	London, GBR	Cancelled (WWII)				
1948	XIV	London, GBR	July 29-Aug. 14	59	USA (38-27-19—84)	38-27-19— 84	(1st)
1952-cd	XV	Helsinki, FIN	July 19-Aug. 3	69	USA (40-19-17—76)	40-19-17— 76	(1st)
1956-e	XVI	Melbourne, AUS . .	Nov. 22-Dec. 8	72	USSR (37-29-32—98)	32-25-17— 74	(2nd)
1960	XVII	Rome, ITA	Aug. 25-Sept. 11	83	USSR (43-29-31—103)	34-21-16— 71	(2nd)
1964	XVIII	Tokyo, JPN	Oct. 10-24	93	USSR (30-31-35—96)	36-26-28— 90	(2nd)
1968-f	XIX	Mexico City, MEX .	Oct. 12-27	112	USA (45-28-34—107)	45-28-34—107	(1st)
1972	XX	Munich, W. GER . .	Aug. 26-Sept. 10	121	USSR (50-27-22—99)	33-31-30— 94	(2nd)
1976-g	XXI	Montreal, CAN . . .	July 17-Aug. 1	92	USSR (49-41-35—125)	34-35-25— 94	(3rd)
1980-h	XXII	Moscow, USSR . . .	July 19-Aug. 3	80	USSR (80-69-46—195)	Boycotted games	
1984-i	XXIII	Los Angeles, USA .	July 28-Aug. 12	140	USA (83-61-30—174)	83-61-30—174	(1st)
1988	XXIV	Seoul, S. KOR . . .	Sept. 17-Oct. 2	159	USSR (55-31-46—132)	36-31-27— 94	(3rd)
1992-j	XXV	Barcelona, SPA . . .	July 25-Aug. 9	169	UT (45-38-29—112)	37-34-37—108	(2nd)
1996	XXVI	Atlanta, USA	July 20-Aug. 4	197	USA (44-32-25—101)	44-32-25—101	(1st)
2000	XXVII	Sydney, AUS	Sept. 15-Oct. 1	199	USA (40-24-33—97)	40-24-33— 97	(1st)
2004	XXVIII	Athens, GRE	Aug. 13-29	202	USA (35-39-29—103)	35-39-29—103	(1st)
2008	XXIX	Beijing, CHN	Aug. 8-24				
2012	XXX	London, ENG	July 27-Aug. 12				

a—The 1906 Intercalated Games in Athens are considered unofficial by the IOC because they did not take place in the four-year cycle established in 1896. However, most record books include these interim games with the others.

b—The 1940 Summer Games are originally scheduled for Tokyo, but Japan resigns as host after the outbreak of the Sino-Japanese War in 1937. Helsinki is the next choice, but the IOC cancels the Games after Soviet troops invade Finland in 1939.

c—Germany and Japan are allowed to rejoin the Olympic community for the first Summer Games since 1936. Though a divided country, the Germans send a joint East-West team until 1964.

d—The Soviet Union (USSR) participates in its first Olympics, Winter or Summer, since the Russian revolution in 1917 and takes home the second most medals (22-30-19—71).

e—Due to Australian quarantine laws, the equestrian events for the 1956 Games are held in Stockholm, June 10-17.

f—East Germany and West Germany send separate teams for the first time and will continue to do so through 1988.

g—The 1976 Games are boycotted by 32 nations, most of them from black Africa, because the IOC will not ban New Zealand. Earlier that year, a rugby team from New Zealand had toured racially segregated South Africa.

h—The 1980 Games are boycotted by 64 nations, led by the USA, to protest the Soviet invasion of Afghanistan on Dec. 27, 1979.

i—The 1984 Games are boycotted by 14 Eastern Bloc nations, led by the USSR, to protest America's overcommercialization of the Games, inadequate security and an anti-Soviet attitude by the U.S. government. Most believe, however, the communist walkout is simply revenge for 1980.

j—Germany sends a single team after East and West German reunification in 1990 and the USSR competes as the Unified Team after the breakup of the Soviet Union in 1991.

Event-by-Event

Gold medal winners from 1896-2004 in the following events: Baseball, Basketball, Boxing, Diving, Field Hockey, Gymnastics, Soccer, Softball, Swimming, Tennis and Track & Field.

BASEBALL

Multiple gold medals: Cuba (3).

Year		Year	
1992	**Cuba**, Taiwan, Japan	2000	**United States**, Cuba, South Korea
1996	**Cuba**, Japan, United States	2004	**Cuba**, Australia, Japan

U.S. Medal-Winning Baseball Teams

1996 (bronze medal): P–Kris Benson, R.A. Dickey, Seth Greisinger, Billy Koch, Braden Looper, Jim Parque and Jeff Weaver; C–A.J. Hinch, Matt LeCroy and Brian Lloyd; INF–Troy Glaus, Kip Harkrider, Travis Lee, Warren Morris, Augie Ojeda and Jason Williams; OF–Chad Allen, Chad Green, Jacque Jones and Mark Kotsay; Manager–Skip Bertman. Final: Cuba over Japan, 13-9

2000 (gold medal): P–Kurt Ainsworth, Ryan Franklin, Chris George, Shane Heams, Rick Krivda, Roy Oswalt, Jon Rauch, Bobby Seay, Ben Sheets, Todd Williams and Tim Young; C–Pat Borders, Marcus Jensen and Mike Kinkade; INF–Brent Abernathy, Sean Burroughs, John Cotton, Gookie Dawkins, Adam Everett and Doug Mientkiewicz; OF–Mike Neill, Anthony Sanders, Brad Wilkerson and Ernie Young; Manager–Tommy Lasorda. Final: USA over Cuba, 4-0.

BASKETBALL

MEN

Multiple gold medals: USA (12), USSR (2).

Year		Year	
1936	**United States**, Canada, Mexico	1976	**United States**, Yugoslavia, Soviet Union
1948	**United States**, France, Brazil	1980	**Yugoslavia**, Italy, Soviet Union
1952	**United States**, Soviet Union, Uruguay	1984	**United States**, Spain, Yugoslavia
1956	**United States**, Soviet Union, Uruguay	1988	**Soviet Union**, Yugoslavia, United States
1960	**United States**, Soviet Union, Brazil	1992	**United States**, Croatia, Lithuania
1964	**United States**, Soviet Union, Brazil	1996	**United States**, Yugoslavia, Lithuania
1968	**United States**, Yugoslavia, Soviet Union	2000	**United States**, France, Lithuania
1972	**Soviet Union**, United States, Cuba	2004	**Argentina**, Italy, United States

U.S. Medal-Winning Men's Basketball Teams

1936 (gold medal): Sam Balter, Ralph Bishop, Joe Fortenberry, Tex Gibbons, Francis Johnson, Carl Knowles, Frank Lubin, Art Mollner, Don Piper, Jack Ragland, Carl Shy, Willard Schmidt, Duane Swanson and William Wheatley. Coach–Jim Needles; Assistant–Gene Johnson. Final: USA over Canada, 19-8.

1948 (gold medal): Cliff Barker, Don Barksdale, Ralph Beard, Louis Beck, Vince Boryla, Gordon Carpenter, Alex Groza, Wallace Jones, Bob Kurland, Ray Lumpp, R.C. Pitts, Jesse Renick, Robert (Jackie) Robinson and Ken Rollins. Coach–Omar Browning; Assistant–Adolph Rupp. Final: USA over France, 65-21.

1952 (gold medal): Ron Bontemps, Mark Freiberger, Wayne Glasgow, Charlie Hoag, Bill Hougland, John Keller, Dean Kelley, Bob Kenney, Bob Kurland, Bill Lienhard, Clyde Lovellette, Frank McCabe, Dan Pippin and Howie Williams. Coach–Warren Womble; Assistant–Forrest (Phog) Allen. Final: USA over USSR, 36-25.

1956 (gold medal): Dick Boushka, Carl Cain, Chuck Darling, Bill Evans, Gib Ford, Burdy Haldorson, Bill Hougland, Bob Jeangerard, K.C. Jones, Bill Russell, Ron Tomsic and Jim Walsh. Coach–Gerald Tucker; Assistant–Bruce Drake. Final: USA over USSR, 89-55.

1960 (gold medal): Jay Arnette, Walt Bellamy, Bob Boozer, Terry Dischinger, Jerry Lucas, Oscar Robertson, Adrian Smith, Burdy Haldorson, Darrall Imhoff, Allen Kelley, Lester Lane and Jerry West. Coach–Pete Newell; Assistant–Warren Womble. Final round: USA defeated USSR (81-57), Italy (112-81) and Brazil (90-63) in round robin.

1964 (gold medal): Jim (Bad News) Barnes, Bill Bradley, Larry Brown, Joe Caldwell, Mel Counts, Dick Davies, Walt Hazzard, Lucious Jackson, Pete McCaffrey, Jeff Mullins, Jerry Shipp and George Wilson. Coach–Hank Iba; Assistant–Henry Vaughn. Final: USA over USSR, 73-59.

1968 (gold medal): Mike Barrett, John Clawson, Don Dee, Cal Fowler, Spencer Haywood, Bill Hosket, Jim King, Glynn Saulters, Charlie Scott, Mike Silliman, Ken Spain, and Jo Jo White. Coach–Hank Iba; Assistant–Henry Vaughn. Final: USA over Yugoslavia, 65-50.

1972 (silver medal refused): Mike Bantom, Jim Brewer, Tom Burleson, Doug Collins, Kenny Davis, Jim Forbes, Tom Henderson, Bobby Jones, Dwight Jones, Kevin Joyce, Tom McMillen and Ed Ratleff. Coach–Hank Iba; Assistants– John Bach and Don Haskins. Final: USSR over USA, 51-50.

1976 (gold medal): Tate Armstrong, Quinn Buckner, Kenny Carr, Adrian Dantley, Walter Davis, Phil Ford, Ernie Grunfeld, Phil Hubbard, Mitch Kupchak, Tommy LaGarde, Scott May and Steve Sheppard. Coach–Dean Smith; Assistants–Bill Guthridge and John Thompson. Final: USA over Yugoslavia, 95-74.

1980 (no medal): USA boycotted Moscow Games. Final: Yugoslavia over Italy, 86-77.

1984 (gold medal): Steve Alford, Patrick Ewing, Vern Fleming, Michael Jordan, Joe Kleine, Jon Koncak, Chris Mullin, Sam Perkins, Alvin Robertson, Wayman Tisdale, Jeff Turner and Leon Wood. Coach–Bobby Knight; Assistants– Don Donoher and George Raveling. Final: USA over Spain, 96-65.

1988 (bronze medal): Stacey Augmon, Willie Anderson, Bimbo Coles, Jeff Grayer, Hersey Hawkins, Dan Majerle, Danny Manning, Mitch Richmond, J.R. Reid, David Robinson, Charles D. Smith and Charles E. Smith. Coach–John Thompson; Assistants–George Raveling and Mary Fenlon. Final: USSR over Yugoslavia, 76-63.

1992 (gold medal): Charles Barkley, Larry Bird, Clyde Drexler, Patrick Ewing, Magic Johnson, Michael Jordan, Christian Laettner, Karl Malone, Chris Mullin, Scottie Pippen, David Robinson and John Stockton. Coach–Chuck Daly; Assistants–Lenny Wilkens, Mike Krzyzewski and P.J. Carlesimo. Final: USA over Croatia, 117-85.

1996 (gold medal): Charles Barkley, Anfernee Hardaway, Grant Hill, Karl Malone, Reggie Miller, Hakeem Olajuwon, Shaquille O'Neal, Gary Payton, Scottie Pippen, David Robinson and John Stockton. Coach–Lenny Wilkens; Assistants–Bobby Cremins, Clem Haskins and Jerry Sloan. Final: USA over Yugoslavia, 95-69.

2000 (gold medal): Shareef Abdur-Rahim, Ray Allen, Vin Baker, Vince Carter, Kevin Garnett, Tim Hardaway, Allan Houston, Jason Kidd, Antonio McDyess, Alonzo Mourning, Gary Payton and Steve Smith. Coach–Rudy Tomjanovich; Assistants–Larry Brown, Gene Keady and Tubby Smith. Final: USA over France, 85-75.

2004 (bronze medal): Carmelo Anthony, Carlos Boozer, Tim Duncan, Allen Iverson, LeBron James, Richard Jefferson, Stephon Marbury, Shawn Marion, Lamar Odom, Emeka Okafor, Amare Stoudemire, Dwyane Wade. Coach—Larry Brown; Assistants—Gregg Popovich, Roy Williams, Oliver Purnell, Dr. Sheldon Burns. Final—USA over Lithuania, 104-96.

WOMEN

Multiple gold medals: USA (4), USSR/UT (3).

Year			Year		
1976	**Soviet Union**, United States, Bulgaria		1992	**Unified Team**, China, United States	
1980	**Soviet Union**, Bulgaria, Yugoslavia		1996	**United States**, Brazil, Australia	
1984	**United States**, South Korea, China		2000	**United States**, Australia, Brazil	
1988	**United States**, Yugoslavia, Soviet Union		2004	**United States**, Australia, Russia	

U.S. Gold Medal-Winning Women's Basketball Teams

1984 (gold medal): Cathy Boswell, Denise Curry, Anne Donovan, Teresa Edwards, Lea Henry, Janice Lawrence, Pamela McGee, Carol Menken-Schaudt, Cheryl Miller, Kim Mulkey, Cindy Noble and Lynette Woodard. Coach—Pat Summitt; Assistant—Kay Yow. Final: USA over South Korea, 85-55.

1988 (gold medal): Cindy Brown, Vicky Bullett, Cynthia Cooper, Anne Donovan, Teresa Edwards, Kamie Ethridge, Jennifer Gillom, Bridgette Gordon, Andrea Lloyd, Katrina McClain, Suzie McConnell and Teresa Weatherspoon. Coach—Kay Yow; Assistants—Sylvia Hatchell and Susan Yow. Final: USA over Yugoslavia, 77-70.

1996 (gold medal): Jennifer Azzi, Ruthie Bolton, Teresa Edwards, Venus Lacy, Lisa Leslie, Rebecca Lobo, Katrina McClain, Nikki McCray, Carla McGee, Dawn Staley, Katy Steding and Sheryl Swoopes. Coach—Tara VanDerveer; Assistants—Ceal Barry, Nancy Darsch and Marian Washington. Final: USA over Brazil, 111-87.

2000 (gold medal): Ruthie Bolton-Holyfield, Teresa Edwards, Yolanda Griffith, Chamique Holdsclaw, Lisa Leslie, Nikki McCray, DeLisha Milton, Katie Smith, Dawn Staley, Sheryl Swoopes, Natalie Williams and Kara Wolters. Coach—Nell Fortner; Assistants—Geno Auriemma and Peggie Gillom. Final: USA over Australia, 76-54.

2004 (gold medal): Sue Bird, Swin Cash, Tamika Catchings, Yolanda Griffith, Shannon Johnson, Lisa Leslie, Ruth Riley, Katie Smith, Dawn Staley, Sheryl Swoopes, Diana Taurasi, Tina Thompson. Coach—Van Chancellor; Assistants—Anne Donovan, Gail Goestenkors, C. Vivian Stringer. Final: USA over Australia, 74-63.

BOXING

Multiple gold medals: László Papp, Felix Savon and Teófilo Stevenson (3); Ariel Hernandez, Angel Herrera, Mario Kindelan, Oliver Kirk, Jerzy Kulej, Boris Lagutin, Harry Mallin, Guillermo Rigondeaux, Oleg Saitov and Hector Vinent (2). All fighters won titles in consecutive Olympics, except Kirk, who won both the bantamweight and featherweight titles in 1904 (he only had to fight once in each division).

Light Flyweight (106 lbs)

Year		Final Match	Year		Final Match
1968	Francisco Rodriguez, VEN	Decision, 3-2	1988	Ivailo Hristov, BUL	Decision, 5-0
1972	György Gedó, HUN	Decision, 5-0	1992	Rogelio Marcelo, CUB	Decision, 24-10
1976	Jorge Hernandez, CUB	Decision, 4-1	1996	Daniel Petrov Bojilov, BUL	Decision, 19-6
1980	Shamil Sabyrov, USSR	Decision, 3-2	2000	Brahim Asloum, FRA	Decision, 23-10
1984	Paul Gonzales, USA	Default	2004	Yan Bhartelemy, CUB	Decision, 21-16

Flyweight (112 lbs)

Year		Final Match	Year		Final Match
1904	George Finnegan, USA	Stopped, 1st	1968	Ricardo Delgado, MEX	Decision, 5-0
1920	Frank Di Gennara, USA	Decision	1972	Georgi Kostadinov, BUL	Decision, 5-0
1924	Fidel LaBarba, USA	Decision	1976	Leo Randolph, USA	Decision, 3-2
1928	Antal Kocsis, HUN	Decision	1980	Peter Lessov, BUL	Stopped, 2nd
1932	István Énekes, HUN	Decision	1984	Steve McCrory, USA	Decision, 4-1
1936	Willi Kaiser, GER	Decision	1988	Kim Kwang-Sun, S. Kor	Decision, 4-1
1948	Pascual Perez, ARG	Decision	1992	Su Choi-Chol, N. Kor	Decision, 12-2
1952	Nate Brooks, USA	Decision, 3-0	1996	Maikro Romero, CUB	Decision, 12-11
1956	Terence Spinks, GBR	Decision	2000	Wijan Ponlid, THA	Decision, 19-12
1960	Gyula Török, HUN	Decision, 3-2	2004	Yuriorkis Gamboa, CUB	Decision, 38-23
1964	Fernando Atzori, ITA	Decision, 4-1			

Bantamweight (119 lbs)

Year		Final Match	Year		Final Match
1904	Oliver Kirk, USA	Stopped, 3rd	1964	Takao Sakurai, JPN	Stopped, 2nd
1908	Henry Thomas, GBR	Decision	1968	Valery Sokolov, USSR	Stopped, 2nd
1920	Clarence Walker, RSA	Decision	1972	Orlando Martinez, CUB	Decision, 5-0
1924	William Smith, RSA	Decision	1976	Gu Yong-Ju, N. Kor	Decision, 5-0
1928	Vittorio Tamagnini, ITA	Decision	1980	Juan Hernandez, CUB	Decision, 5-0
1932	Horace Gwynne, CAN	Decision	1984	Maurizio Stecca, ITA	Decision, 4-1
1936	Ulderico Sergo, ITA	Decision	1988	Kennedy McKinney, USA	Decision, 5-0
1948	Tibor Csik, HUN	Decision	1992	Joel Casamayor, CUB	Decision, 14-8
1952	Pentti Hämäläinen, FIN	Decision, 2-1	1996	Istvan Kovacs, HUN	Decision, 14-7
1956	Wolfgang Behrendt, GER	Decision	2000	Guillermo Rigondeaux, CUB	Decision, 18-12
1960	Oleg Grigoryev, USSR	Decision	2004	Guillermo Rigondeaux, CUB	Decision, 22-13

Boxing (Cont.)

Featherweight (125 lbs)

Year		Final Match	Year		Final Match
1904	Oliver Kirk, USA	Decision	1964	Stanislav Stepashkin, USSR	Decision, 3-2
1908	Richard Gunn, GBR	Decision	1968	Antonio Roldan, MEX	Won on Disq.
1920	Paul Fritsch, FRA	Decision	1972	Boris Kousnetsov, USSR	Decision, 3-2
1924	John Fields, USA	Decision	1976	Angel Herrera, CUB	KO, 2nd
1928	Lambertus van Klaveren, NED	Decision	1980	Rudi Fink, E. Ger	Decision, 4-1
1932	Carmelo Robledo, ARG	Decision	1984	Meldrick Taylor, USA	Decision, 5-0
1936	Oscar Casanovas, ARG	Decision	1988	Giovanni Parisi, ITA	Stopped, 1st
1948	Ernesto Formenti, ITA	Decision	1992	Andreas Tews, GER	Decision, 16-7
1952	Jan Zachara, CZE	Decision, 2-1	1996	Somluck Kamsing, THA	Decision, 8-5
1956	Vladimir Safronov, USSR	Decision	2000	Bekzat Sattarkhanov, KAZ	Decision, 22-14
1960	Francesco Musso, ITA	Decision, 4-1	2004	Alexei Tichtchenko, RUS	Decision, 39-17

Lightweight (132 lbs)

Year		Final Match	Year		Final Match
1904	Harry Spanger, USA	Decision	1964	Józef Grudzien, POL	Decision
1908	Frederick Grace, GBR	Decision	1968	Ronnie Harris, USA	Decision, 5-0
1920	Samuel Mosberg, USA	Decision	1972	Jan Szczepanski, POL	Decision, 5-0
1924	Hans Nielsen, DEN	Decision	1976	Howard Davis, USA	Decision, 5-0
1928	Carlo Orlandi, ITA	Decision	1980	Angel Herrera, CUB	Stopped, 3rd
1932	Lawrence Stevens, S. Afr	Decision	1984	Pernell Whitaker, USA	Foe quit, 2nd
1936	Imre Harangi, HUN	Decision	1988	Andreas Zuelow, E. Ger	Decision, 5-0
1948	Gerald Dreyer, S. Afr	Decision	1992	Oscar De La Hoya, USA	Decision, 7-2
1952	Aureliano Bolognesi, ITA	Decision, 2-1	1996	Hocine Soltani, ALG	Tiebreak, 3-3
1956	Richard McTaggart, GBR	Decision	2000	Mario Kindelan, CUB	Decision, 14-4
1960	Kazimierz Pazdzior, POL	Decision, 4-1	2004	Mario Kindelan, CUB	Decision, 30-22

Light Welterweight (141 lbs)

Year		Final Match	Year		Final Match
1952	Charles Adkins, USA	Decision, 2-1	1980	Patrizio Oliva, ITA	Decision, 4-1
1956	Vladimir Yengibaryan, USSR	Decision	1984	Jerry Page, USA	Decision, 5-0
1960	Bohumil Nemecek, CZE	Decision, 5-0	1988	Vyacheslav Yanovsky, USSR	Decision, 5-0
1964	Jerzy Kulej, POL	Decision, 5-0	1992	Hector Vinent, CUB	Decision, 11-1
1968	Jerzy Kulej, POL	Decision, 3-2	1996	Hector Vinent, CUB	Decision, 20-13
1972	Ray Seales, USA	Decision, 3-2	2000	Mahamadkadyz Abdullaev, UZB	Decision, 27-20
1976	Ray Leonard, USA	Decision, 5-0	2004	Manus Boonjumnong, THA	Decision, 17-11

Welterweight (152 lbs)

Year		Final Match	Year		Final Match
1904	Albert Young, USA	Decision	1968	Manfred Wolke, E. Ger	Decision, 4-1
1920	Bert Schneider, CAN	Decision	1972	Emilio Correa, CUB	Decision, 5-0
1924	Jean Delarge, BEL	Decision	1976	Jochen Bachfeld, E. Ger	Decision, 3-2
1928	Edward Morgan, NZE	Decision	1980	Andrés Aldama, CUB	Decision, 4-1
1932	Edward Flynn, USA	Decision	1984	Mark Breland, USA	Decision, 5-0
1936	Sten Suvio, FIN	Decision	1988	Robert Wangila, KEN	KO, 2nd
1948	Julius Torma, CZE	Decision	1992	Michael Carruth, IRE	Decision, 13-10
1952	Zygmunt Chychla, POL	Decision, 3-0	1996	Oleg Saitov, RUS	Decision, 14-9
1956	Nicolae Linca, ROM	Decision, 3-2	2000	Oleg Saitov, RUS	Decision, 24-16
1960	Nino Benvenuti, ITA	Decision, 4-1	2004	Bakhtiyar Artayev, KAZ	Decision, 36-26
1964	Marian Kasprzyk, POL	Decision, 4-1			

Light Middleweight (156 lbs)

Year		Final Match	Year		Final Match
1952	László Papp, HUN	Decision, 3-0	1980	Armando Martinez, CUB	Decision, 4-1
1956	László Papp, HUN	Decision	1984	Frank Tate, USA	Decision, 5-0
1960	Skeeter McClure, USA	Decision, 4-1	1988	Park Si-Hun, S. Kor	Decision, 3-2
1964	Boris Lagutin, USSR	Decision, 4-1	1992	Juan Lemus, CUB	Decision, 6-1
1968	Boris Lagutin, USSR	Decision, 5-0	1996	David Reid, USA	KO, 3rd
1972	Dieter Kottysch, W. Ger	Decision, 3-2	2000	Yermakhan Ibraimov, KAZ	Decision, 25-23
1976	Jerzy Rybicki, POL	Decision, 5-0	2004	weight class eliminated.	

Middleweight (165 lbs)

Year		Final Match	Year		Final Match
1904	Charles Mayer, USA	Stopped, 3rd	1964	Valery Popenchenko, USSR	Stopped, 1st
1908	John Douglas, GBR	Decision	1968	Christopher Finnegan, GBR	Decision, 3-2
1920	Harry Mallin, GBR	Decision	1972	Vyacheslav Lemechev, USSR	KO, 1st
1924	Harry Mallin, GBR	Decision	1976	Michael Spinks, USA	Stopped, 3rd
1928	Piero Toscani, ITA	Decision	1980	José Gomez, CUB	Decision, 4-1
1932	Carmen Barth, USA	Decision	1984	Shin Joon-Sup, S. Kor	Decision, 3-2
1936	Jean Despeaux, FRA	Decision	1988	Henry Maske, E. Ger	Decision, 5-0
1948	László Papp, HUN	Decision	1992	Ariel Hernandez, CUB	Decision, 12-7
1952	Floyd Patterson, USA	KO, 1st	1996	Ariel Hernandez, CUB	Decision, 11-3
1956	Gennady Schatkov, USSR	KO, 1st	2000	Jorge Gutierrez, CUB	Decision, 17-15
1960	Eddie Crook, USA	Decision, 3-2	2004	Gaydarbek Gaydarbekov, RUS	Decision, 28-18

Light Heavyweight (178 lbs)

Year		Final Match	Year		Final Match
1920	Eddie Eagan, USA	Decision	1968	Dan Poznjak, USSR	Default
1924	Harry Mitchell, GBR	Decision	1972	Mate Parlov, YUG	Stopped, 2nd
1928	Victor Avendaño, ARG	Decision	1976	Leon Spinks, USA	Stopped, 3rd
1932	David Carstens, S. Afr	Decision	1980	Slobodan Kacar, YUG	Decision, 4-1
1936	Roger Michelot, FRA	Decision	1984	Anton Josipovic, YUG	Default
1948	George Hunter, S. Afr	Decision	1988	Andrew Maynard, USA	Decision, 5-0
1952	Norvel Lee, USA	Decision, 3-0	1992	Torsten May, GER	Decision, 8-3
1956	Jim Boyd, USA	Decision	1996	Vasilii Jirov, KAZ	Decision, 17-4
1960	Cassius Clay, USA	Decision, 5-0	2000	Alexander Lebziak, RUS	Decision, 20-6
1964	Cosimo Pinto, ITA	Decision, 3-2	2004	Andre Ward, USA	Decision, 20-13

Note: Cassius Clay changed his name to Muhammad Ali after winning the world heavyweight championship in 1964.

Heavyweight (201 lbs)

Year		Final Match	Year		Final Match
1984	Henry Tillman, USA	Decision, 5-0	1996	Felix Savon, CUB	Decision, 20-2
1988	Ray Mercer, USA	KO, 1st	2000	Felix Savon, CUB	Decision, 21-13
1992	Felix Savon, CUB	Decision, 14-1	2004	Odlanier Solis, CUB	Decision, 22-13

Super Heavyweight (Unlimited)

Year		Final Match	Year		Final Match
1904	Samuel Berger, USA	Decision	1964	Joe Frazier, USA	Decision, 3-2
1908	Albert Oldham, GBR	KO, 1st	1968	George Foreman, USA	Stopped, 2nd
1920	Ronald Rawson, GBR	Decision	1972	Teófilo Stevenson, CUB	Default
1924	Otto von Porat, NOR	Decision	1976	Teófilo Stevenson, CUB	KO, 3rd
1928	Arturo Rodriguez Jurado, ARG	Stopped, 1st	1980	Teófilo Stevenson, CUB	Decision, 4-1
1932	Santiago Lovell, ARG	Decision	1984	Tyrell Biggs, USA	Decision, 4-1
1936	Herbert Runge, GER	Decision	1988	Lennox Lewis, CAN	Stopped, 2nd
1948	Rafael Iglesias, ARG	KO, 2nd	1992	Roberto Balado, CUB	Decision, 13-2
1952	Ed Sanders, USA	Won on Disq.*	1996	Vladimir Klichko, UKR	Decision, 7-3
1956	Pete Rademacher, USA	Stopped, 1st	2000	Audley Harrison, GBR	Decision, 30-16
1960	Franco De Piccoli, ITA	KO, 1st	2004	Alexander Povetkin, RUS	walkover†

*Sanders' opponent, Ingemar Johansson, was disqualified in 2nd round for not trying.
†Povetkin was awarded the gold when his opponet Mohamed Aly failed a pre-fight physical due to a shoulder injury.
Note: Super Heavyweight was called heavyweight through 1980.

DIVING

MEN

Multiple gold medals: Greg Louganis (4); Klaus Dibiasi and Xiong Ni (3); Pete Desjardins, Sammy Lee, Tian Liang, Bob Webster and Albert White (2).

Springboard

Year		Points	Year		Points
1908	Albert Zürner, GER	85.5	1964	Ken Sitzberger, USA	159.90
1912	Paul Günther, GER	79.23	1968	Bernie Wrightson, USA	170.15
1920	Louis Kuehn, USA	675.4	1972	Vladimir Vasin, USSR	594.09
1924	Albert White, USA	696.4	1976	Phil Boggs, USA	619.05
1928	Pete Desjardins, USA	185.04	1980	Aleksandr Portnov, USSR	905.03
1932	Michael Galitzen, USA	161.38	1984	Greg Louganis, USA	754.41
1936	Richard Degener, USA	163.57	1988	Greg Louganis, USA	730.80
1948	Bruce Harlan, USA	163.64	1992	Mark Lenzi, USA	676.53
1952	David Browning, USA	205.29	1996	Xiong Ni, CHN	701.46
1956	Bob Clotworthy, USA	159.56	2000	Xiong Ni, CHN	708.72
1960	Gary Tobian, USA	170.00	2004	Peng Bo, CHN	787.38

Platform

Year		Points	Year		Points
1904	George Sheldon, USA	12.66	1960	Bob Webster, USA	165.56
1906	Gottlob Walz, GER	156.0	1964	Bob Webster, USA	148.58
1908	Hjalmar Johansson, SWE	83.75	1968	Klaus Dibiasi, ITA	164.18
1912	Erik Adlerz, SWE	73.94	1972	Klaus Dibiasi, ITA	504.12
1920	Clarence Pinkston, USA	100.67	1976	Klaus Dibiasi, ITA	600.51
1924	Albert White, USA	97.46	1980	Falk Hoffmann, E. Ger	835.65
1928	Pete Desjardins, USA	98.74	1984	Greg Louganis, USA	710.91
1932	Harold Smith, USA	124.80	1988	Greg Louganis, USA	638.61
1936	Marshall Wayne, USA	113.58	1992	Sun Shuwei, CHN	677.31
1948	Sammy Lee, USA	130.05	1996	Dmitri Sautin, RUS	692.34
1952	Sammy Lee, USA	156.28	2000	Tian Liang, CHN	724.53
1956	Joaquin Capilla, MEX	152.44	2004	Hu Jia, CHN	748.08

Diving (Cont.)

Synchronized Platform

Year		Points	Year		Points
2000	Igor Louckachine & Dmitri Sautin, RUS	365.04	2004	Tian Liang & Yang Jinghui, CHN	383.88

Synchronized Springboard

Year		Points	Year		Points
2000	Xiao Hailiang & Xiong Ni, CHN	365.58	2004	Nikolaos Siranidis & Thomas Bimis, GRE	353.34

WOMEN

Multiple gold medals: Pat McCormick and Fu Mingxia (4); Ingrid Engel-Krämer (3); Vicki Draves, Dorothy Poynton Hill, Guo Jingjing and Gao Min (2).

Springboard

Year		Points	Year		Points
1920	Aileen Riggin, USA	539.9	1968	Sue Gossick, USA	150.77
1924	Elizabeth Becker, USA	474.5	1972	Micki King, USA	450.03
1928	Helen Meany, USA	78.62	1976	Jennifer Chandler, USA	506.19
1932	Georgia Coleman, USA	87.52	1980	Irina Kalinina, USSR	725.91
1936	Marjorie Gestring, USA	89.27	1984	Sylvie Bernier, CAN	530.70
1948	Vicki Draves, USA	108.74	1988	Gao Min, CHN	580.23
1952	Pat McCormick, USA	147.30	1992	Gao Min, CHN	572.40
1956	Pat McCormick, USA	142.36	1996	Fu Mingxia, CHN	547.68
1960	Ingrid Krämer, GER	155.81	2000	Fu Mingxia, CHN	609.42
1964	Ingrid Engel-Krämer, GER	145.00	2004	Guo Jingjing, CHN	633.15

Platform

Year		Points	Year		Points
1912	Greta Johansson, SWE	39.9	1968	Milena Duchková, CZE	109.59
1920	Stefani Fryland-Clausen, DEN	34.6	1972	Ulrika Knape, SWE	390.00
1924	Caroline Smith, USA	33.2	1976	Elena Vaytsekhovskaya, USSR	406.59
1928	Elizabeth Becker Pinkston, USA	31.6	1980	Martina Jäschke, E. Ger	596.25
1932	Dorothy Poynton, USA	40.26	1984	Zhou Jihong, CHN	435.51
1936	Dorothy Poynton Hill, USA	33.93	1988	Xu Yanmei, CHN	445.20
1948	Vicki Draves, USA	68.87	1992	Fu Mingxia, CHN	461.43
1952	Pat McCormick, USA	79.37	1996	Fu Mingxia, CHN	521.58
1956	Pat McCormick, USA	84.85	2000	Laura Wilkinson, USA	543.75
1960	Ingrid Krämer, GER	91.28	2004	Chantelle Newberry, AUS	590.31
1964	Lesley Bush, USA	99.80			

Synchronized Platform

Year		Points	Year		Points
2000	Li Na & Sang Xue, CHN	345.12	2004	Lao Lishi & Li Ting, CHN	53.40

Synchronized Springboard

Year		Points	Year		Points
2000	Vera Ilyina & Yulia Pakhalina, RUS	332.64	2004	Wu Minxia & Guo Jingjing, CHN	336.90

FIELD HOCKEY

MEN

Multiple gold medals: India (8); Great Britain and Pakistan (3); West Germany/Germany and Netherlands (2).

Year		Year	
1908	**Great Britain**, Ireland, Scotland	1968	**Pakistan**, Australia, India
1920	**Great Britain**, Denmark, Belgium	1972	**West Germany**, Pakistan, India
1928	**India**, Netherlands, Germany	1976	**New Zealand**, Australia, Pakistan
1932	**India**, Japan, United States	1980	**India**, Spain, Soviet Union
1936	**India**, Germany, Netherlands	1984	**Pakistan**, West Germany, Great Britain
1948	**India**, Great Britain, Netherlands	1988	**Great Britain**, West Germany, Netherlands
1952	**India**, Netherlands, Great Britain	1992	**Germany**, Australia, Pakistan
1956	**India**, Pakistan, Germany	1996	**Netherlands**, Spain, Australia
1960	**Pakistan**, India, Spain	2000	**Netherlands**, South Korea, Australia
1964	**India**, Pakistan, Australia	2004	**Australia**, Netherlands, Germany

WOMEN

Multiple gold medals: Australia (3).

Year		Year	
1980	**Zimbabwe**, Czechoslovakia, Soviet Union	1996	**Australia**, South Korea, Netherlands
1984	**Netherlands**, West Germany, United States	2000	**Australia**, Argentina, Netherlands
1988	**Australia**, South Korea, Netherlands	2004	**Germany**, Netherlands, Argentina
1992	**Spain**, Germany, Great Britain		

GYMNASTICS

MEN

At least 4 gold medals (including team events): Sawao Kato (8); Nikolai Andrianov, Viktor Chukarin and Boris Shakhlin (7); Akinori Nakayama and Vitaly Scherbo (6); Yukio Endo, Anton Heida, Mitsuo Tsukahara and Takashi Ono (5); Vladimir Artemov, Georges Miez, Valentin Muratov and Alexei Nemov (4).

All-Around

Year		Points	Year		Points
1900	Gustave Sandras, FRA	302	1960	Boris Shakhlin, USSR	115.95
1904	Julius Lenhart, AUT	69.80	1964	Yukio Endo, JPN	115.95
1906	Pierre Payssé, FRA	97.0	1968	Sawao Kato, JPN	115.9
1908	Alberto Braglia, ITA	317.0	1972	Sawao Kato, JPN	114.650
1912	Alberto Braglia, ITA	135.0	1976	Nikolai Andrianov, USSR	116.65
1920	Giorgio Zampori, ITA	88.35	1980	Aleksandr Dityatin, USSR	118.65
1924	Leon Stukelj, YUG	110.340	1984	Koji Gushiken, JPN	118.7
1928	Georges Miez, SWI	247.500	1988	Vladimir Artemov, USSR	119.125
1932	Romeo Neri, ITA	140.625	1992	Vitaly Scherbo, UT	59.025
1936	Alfred Schwarzmann, GER	113.100	1996	Li Xiaoshuang, CHN	58.423
1948	Veikko Huhtanen, FIN	229.7	2000	Alexei Nemov, RUS	58.474
1952	Viktor Chukarin, USSR	115.7	2004	Paul Hamm, USA	57.823
1956	Viktor Chukarin, USSR	114.25			

High Bar

Year		Points	Year		Points
1896	Hermann Weingärtner, GER	–	1968	(TIE) Akinori Nakayama, JPN	19.55
1904	(TIE) Anton Heida, USA	40		& Mikhail Voronin, USSR	19.55
	& Edward Hennig, USA	40	1972	Mitsuo Tsukahara, JPN	19.725
1924	Leon Stukelj, YUG	19.73	1976	Mitsuo Tsukahara, JPN	19.675
1928	Georges Miez, SWI	19.17	1980	Stoyan Deltchev, BUL	19.825
1932	Dallas Bixler, USA	18.33	1984	Shinji Morisue, JPN	20.00
1936	Aleksanteri Saarvala, FIN	19.367	1988	(TIE) Vladimir Artemov, USSR	19.900
1948	Josef Stalder, SWI	19.85		& Valeri Lyukin, USSR	19.900
1952	Jack Günthard, SWI	19.55	1992	Trent Dimas, USA	9.875
1956	Takashi Ono, JPN	19.60	1996	Andreas Wecker, GER	9.850
1960	Takashi Ono, JPN	19.60	2000	Alexei Nemov, RUS	9.787
1964	Boris Shakhlin, USSR	19.625	2004	Igor Cassina, ITA	9.812

Parallel Bars

Year		Points	Year		Points
1896	Alfred Flatow, GER	–	1968	Akinori Nakayama, JPN	19.475
1904	George Eyser, USA	44	1972	Sawao Kato, JPN	19.475
1924	August Güttinger, SWI	21.63	1976	Sawao Kato, JPN	19.675
1928	Ladislav Vácha, CZE	18.83	1980	Aleksandr Tkachyov, USSR	19.775
1932	Romeo Neri, ITA	18.97	1984	Bart Conner, USA	19.95
1936	Konrad Frey, GER	19.067	1988	Vladimir Artemov, USSR	19.925
1948	Michael Reusch, SWI	19.75	1992	Vitaly Scherbo, UT	9.900
1952	Hans Eugster, SWI	19.65	1996	Rustam Sharipov, UKR	9.837
1956	Viktor Chukarin, USSR	19.20	2000	Li Xiaopeng, CHN	9.825
1960	Boris Shakhlin, USSR	19.40	2004	Valeri Goncharov, UKR	9.787
1964	Yukio Endo, JPN	19.675			

Vault

Year		Points	Year		Points
1896	Karl Schumann, GER	–	1964	Haruhiro Yamashita, JPN	19.60
1904	(TIE) George Eyser, USA	36	1968	Mikhail Voronin, USSR	19.00
	& Anton Heida, USA	36	1972	Klaus Köste, E. Ger	18.85
1924	Frank Kriz, USA	9.98	1976	Nikolai Andrianov, USSR	19.45
1928	Eugen Mack, SWI	9.58	1980	Nikolai Andrianov, USSR	19.825
1932	Savino Guglielmetti, ITA	18.03	1984	Lou Yun, CHN	19.95
1936	Alfred Schwarzmann, GER	19.20	1988	Lou Yun, CHN	19.875
1948	Paavo Aaltonen, FIN	19.55	1992	Vitaly Scherbo, UT	9.856
1952	Viktor Chukarin, USSR	19.20	1996	Alexei Nemov, RUS	9.787
1956	(TIE) Helmut Bantz, GER	18.85	2000	Gervasio Deferr, SPA	9.712
	& Valentin Muratov, USSR	18.85	2004	Gervasio Deferr, SPA	9.737
1960	(TIE) Takashi Ono, JPN	19.35			
	& Boris Shakhlin, USSR	19.35			

Gymnastics (Cont.)

Pommel Horse

Year		Points	Year		Points
1896	Louis Zutter, SWI	.–	1968	Miroslav Cerar, YUG	.19.325
1904	Anton Heida, USA	.42	1972	Viktor Klimenko, SOV	.19.125
1924	Josef Wilhelm, SWI	.21.23	1976	Zoltán Magyar, HUN	.19.70
1928	Hermann Hänggi, SWI	.19.75	1980	Zoltán Magyar, HUN	.19.925
1932	Istvän Pelle, HUN	.19.07	1984	(TIE) Li Ning, CHN	.19.95
1936	Konrad Frey, GER	.19.333		& Peter Vidmar, USA	.19.95
1948	(TIE) Paavo Aaltonen, FIN	.19.35	1988	(TIE) Dmitri Bilozerchev, USSR,	.19.95
	Veikko Huhtanen, FIN	.19.35		Zsolt Borkai, HUN	.19.95
	& Heikki Savolainen, FIN	.19.35		& Lyubomir Geraskov, BUL	.19.95
1952	Viktor Chukarin, USSR	.19.50	1992	(TIE) Pae Gil-Su, N. Kor	.9.925
1956	Boris Shakhlin, USSR	.19.25		& Vitaly Scherbo, UT	.9.925
1960	(TIE) Eugen Ekman, FIN	.19.375	1996	Li Donghua, SWI	.9.875
	& Boris Shakhlin, USSR	.19.375	2000	Marius Urzica, ROM	.9.862
1964	Miroslav Cerar, YUG	.19.525	2004	Teng Haibin, CHN	.9.837

Rings

Year		Points	Year		Points
1896	Ioannis Mitropoulos, GRE	.–	1972	Akinori Nakayama, JPN	.19.35
1904	Hermann Glass, USA	.45	1976	Nikolai Andrianov, USSR	.19.65
1924	Francesco Martino, ITA	.21.553	1980	Aleksandr Dityatin, USSR	.19.875
1928	Leon Stukelj, YUG	.19.25	1984	(TIE) Koji Gushiken, JPN	.19.85
1932	George Gulack, USA	.18.97		& Li Ning, CHN	.19.85
1936	Alois Hudec, CZE	.19.433	1988	(TIE) Holger Behrendt, E. Ger	.19.925
1948	Karl Frei, SWI	.19.80		& Dmitri Bilozerchev, USSR	.19.925
1952	Grant Shaginyan, USSR	.19.75	1992	Vitaly Scherbo, UT	.9.937
1956	Albert Azaryan, USSR	.19.35	1996	Yuri Chechi, ITA	.9.887
1960	Albert Azaryan, USSR	.19.725	2000	Szilveszter Csollany, HUN	.9.850
1964	Takuji Haytta, JPN	.19.475	2004	Dimonsthenis Tampakos, GRE	.9.862
1968	Akinori Nakayama, JPN	.19.45			

Floor Exercise

Year		Points	Year		Points
1932	Istvan Pelle, HUN	.9.60	1976	Nikolai Andrianov, USSR	.19.45
1936	Georges Miez, SWI	.18.666	1980	Roland Brückner, E. Ger	.19.75
1948	Ferenc Pataki, HUN	.19.35	1984	Li Ning, CHN	.19.925
1952	William Thoresson, SWE	.19.25	1988	Sergei Kharkov, USSR	.19.925
1956	Valentin Muratov, USSR	.19.20	1992	Li Xiaoshuang, CHN	.9.925
1960	Nobuyuki Aihara, JPN	.19.45	1996	Ioannis Melissanidis, GRE	.9.850
1964	Franco Menichelli, ITA	.19.45	2000	Igors Vihrovs, LAT	.9.812
1968	Sawao Kato, JPN	.19.475	2004	Kyle Shewfelt, CAN	.9.787
1972	Nikolai Andrianov, USSR	.19.175			

Team Combined Exercises

Year		Points	Year		Points
1904	United States	.374.43	1960	Japan	.575.20
1906	Norway	.19.00	1964	Japan	.577.95
1908	Sweden	.438	1968	Japan	.575.90
1912	Italy	.265.75	1972	Japan	.571.25
1920	Italy	.359.855	1976	Japan	.576.85
1924	Italy	.839.058	1980	Soviet Union	.598.60
1928	Switzerland	.1718.625	1984	United States	.591.40
1932	Italy	.541.850	1988	Soviet Union	.593.35
1936	Germany	.657.430	1992	Unified Team	.585.45
1948	Finland	.1358.30	1996	Russia	.576.728
1952	Soviet Union	.574.40	2000	China	.231.919
1956	Soviet Union	.568.25	2004	Japan	.173.821

WOMEN

At least 4 gold medals (including team events): Larissa Latynina (9); Vera Cáslavská (7); Polina Astakhova, Nadia Comaneci, Agnes Keleti and Nelli Kim (5); Olga Korbut, Ecaterina Szabó and Lyudmila Tourischeva (4).

All-Around

Year		Points	Year		Points
1952	Maria Gorokhovskaya, USSR	.76.78	1980	Yelena Davydova, USSR	.79.15
1956	Larissa Latynina, USSR	.74.933	1984	Mary Lou Retton, USA	.79.175
1960	Larissa Latynina, USSR	.77.031	1988	Yelena Shushunova, USSR	.79.662
1964	Vera Cáslavská, CZE	.77.564	1992	Tatiana Gutsu, UT	.39.737
1968	Vera Cáslavská, CZE	.78.25	1996	Lilia Podkopayeva, UKR	.39.255
1972	Lyudmila Tourischeva, USSR	.77.025	2000	Simona Amanar, ROM*	.38.642
1976	Nadia Comaneci, ROM	.79.275	2004	Carly Patterson, USA	.38.387

*Amanar finished second to **Andreea Raducan**, Romania, who was disqualified for testing positive for pseudo-ephedrine, a drug banned by the IOC and found in Nurofen—an over-the-counter medicine she purportedly took to treat a cold.

Vault

Year		Points	Year		Points
1952	Yekaterina Kalinchuk, USSR	.19.20	1984	Ecaterina Szabó, ROM	.19.875
1956	Larissa Latynina, USSR	.18.833	1988	Svetlana Boginskaya, USSR	.19.905
1960	Margarita Nikolayeva, USSR	.19.316	1992	(TIE) Henrietta Onodi, HUN	.9.925
1964	Vera Cáslavská, CZE	.19.483		& Lavinia Milosovici, ROM	.9.925
1968	Vera Cáslavská, CZE	.19.775	1996	Simona Amanar, ROM	.9.775
1972	Karin Janz, E. Ger	.19.525	2000	Elena Zamolodtchikova, RUS	.9.731
1976	Nelli Kim, USSR	.19.80	2004	Monica Rosu, ROM	.9.656
1980	Natalia Shaposhnikova, USSR	.19.725			

Uneven Bars

Year		Points	Year		Points
1952	Margit Korondi, HUN	.19.40	1984	(TIE) Julianne McNamara, USA	.19.95
1956	Agnes Keleti, HUN	.18.966		& Ma Yanhong, CHN	.19.95
1960	Polina Astakhova, USSR	.19.616	1988	Daniela Silivas, ROM	.20.00
1964	Polina Astakhova, USSR	.19.332	1992	Lu Li, CHN	.10.00
1968	Vera Cáslavská, CZE	.19.65	1996	Svetlana Khorkina, RUS	.9.850
1972	Karin Janz, E. Ger	.19.675	2000	Svetlana Khorkina, RUS	.9.862
1976	Nadia Comaneci, ROM	.20.00	2004	Emilie Lepennec, FRA	.9.687
1980	Maxi Gnauck, E. Ger	.19.875			

Balance Beam

Year		Points	Year		Points
1952	Nina Bocharova, USSR	.19.22	1984	(TIE) Simona Pauca, ROM	.19.80
1956	Agnes Keleti, HUN	.18.80		& Ecaterina Szabó, ROM	.19.80
1960	Eva Bosakova, CZE	.19.283	1988	Daniela Silivas, ROM	.19.924
1964	Vera Cáslavská, CZE	.19.449	1992	Tatiana Lyssenko, UT	.9.975
1968	Natalya Kuchinskaya, USSR	.19.65	1996	Shannon Miller, USA	.9.862
1972	Olga Korbut, USSR	.19.40	2000	Liu Xuan, CHN	.9.825
1976	Nadia Comaneci, ROM	.19.95	2004	Catalina Ponor, ROM	.9.787
1980	Nadia Comaneci, ROM	.19.80			

Floor Exercise

Year		Points	Year		Points
1952	Agnes Keleti, HUN	.19.36	1980	(TIE) Nadia Comaneci, ROM	.19.875
1956	(TIE) Agnes Keleti, HUN	.18.733		& Nelli Kim, USSR	.19.875
	& Larissa Latynina, USSR	.18.733	1984	Ecaterina Szabó, ROM	.19.975
1960	Larissa Latynina, USSR	.19.583	1988	Daniela Silivas, ROM	.19.937
1964	Larissa Latynina, USSR	.19.599	1992	Lavinia Milosovici, ROM	.10.000
1968	(TIE) Vera Cáslavská, CZE	.19.675	1996	Lilia Podkopayeva, UKR	.9.887
	& Larissa Petrik, USSR	.19.675	2000	Elena Zamolodtchikova, RUS	.9.850
1972	Olga Korbut, USSR	.19.575	2004	Catalina Ponor, ROM	.9.750
1976	Nelli Kim, USSR	.19.85			

Team Combined Exercises

Year		Points	Year		Points
1928	Netherlands	.316.75	1976	Soviet Union	.466.00
1936	Germany	.506.50	1980	Soviet Union	.394.90
1948	Czechoslovakia	.445.45	1984	Romania	.392.02
1952	Soviet Union	.527.03	1988	Soviet Union	.395.475
1956	Soviet Union	.444.800	1992	Unified Team	.395.666
1960	Soviet Union	.382.320	1996	United States	.389.225
1964	Soviet Union	.280.890	2000	Romania	.154.608
1968	Soviet Union	.382.85	2004	Romania	.114.283
1972	Soviet Union	.380.50			

SOCCER
MEN

Multiple gold medals: Great Britain and Hungary (3); Uruguay and USSR (2).

Year		Year	
1900	**Great Britain**, France, Belgium	1960	**Yugoslavia**, Denmark, Hungary
1904	**Canada**, USA I, USA II	1964	**Hungary**, Czechoslovakia, Germany
1906	**Denmark**, Smyrna (Int'l entry), Greece	1968	**Hungary**, Bulgaria, Japan
1908	**Great Britain**, Denmark, Netherlands	1972	**Poland**, Hungary, East Germany & Soviet Union
1912	**Great Britain**, Denmark, Netherlands	1976	**East Germany**, Poland, Soviet Union
1920	**Belgium**, Spain, Netherlands	1980	**Czechoslovakia**, East Germany, Soviet Union
1924	**Uruguay**, Switzerland, Sweden	1984	**France**, Brazil, Yugoslavia
1928	**Uruguay**, Argentina, Italy	1988	**Soviet Union**, Brazil, West Germany
1936	**Italy**, Austria, Norway	1992	**Spain**, Poland, Ghana
1948	**Sweden**, Yugoslavia, Denmark	1996	**Nigeria**, Argentina, Brazil
1952	**Hungary**, Yugoslavia, Sweden	2000	**Cameroon**, Spain, Chile
1956	**Soviet Union**, Yugoslavia, Bulgaria	2004	**Argentina**, Paraguay, Italy

WOMEN

Multiple gold medals: United States (2).

Year		Year	
1996	**United States**, China, Norway	2004	**United States**, Brazil, Germany
2000	**Norway**, United States, Germany		

SOFTBALL

Multiple gold medals: United States (3).

Year		Year	
1996	**United States**, China, Australia	2004	**United States**, Australia, Japan
2000	**United States**, Japan, Australia		

U.S. Medal-Winning Softball Teams

1996 (gold medal): P–Lisa Fernandez, Michele Granger, Lori Harrigan and Michele Smith; C–Gillian Boxx and Shelly Stokes; INF–Sheila Cornell, Kim Maher, Leah O'Brien, Dot Richardson, Julie Smith and Dani Tyler; OF–Laura Berg, Dionna Harris; Manager–Ralph Raymond. Final: USA over China, 3-1.

2000 (gold medal): P–Lisa Fernandez, Lori Harrigan, Danielle Henderson, Michele Smith and Christa Williams; C–Stacey Nuveman and Michelle Venturella; INF–Jennifer Brundage, Crystl Bustos, Sheila Douty, Jennifer McFalls and Dot Richardson; OF–Christie Ambrosi, Laura Berg, Leah O'Brien-Amico; Manager–Ralph Raymond. Final: USA over Japan, 2-1.

2004 (gold medal): P–Lisa Fernandez, Jennie Finch, Lori Harrigan and Catherine Osterman; C–Stacey Nuveman and Jenny Topping; INF–Crystl Bustos, Jaime Clark, Lovieanne Jung and Natasha Watley; OF–Laura Berg, Nicole Giordano, Kelly Kretschman, Jessica Mendoza and Leah O'Brien-Amico; UT–Tairia Flowers, Amanda Freed and Lauren Lappin ; Manager–Mike Candrea. Final: USA over Australia, 5-1.

SWIMMING

World and Olympic records below that appear to be broken or equaled by winning times in subsequent years, but are not so indicated, were all broken in preliminary heats leading up to the finals. Some events were not held at every Olympics.

MEN

At least 4 gold medals (including relays): Mark Spitz (9); Matt Biondi (8); Gary Hall Jr. and Michael Phelps (6); Charles Daniels, Tom Jager, Don Schollander, Ian Thorpe and Johnny Weissmuller (5); Tamás Darnyi, Roland Matthes, John Naber, Aleksandr Popov, Murray Rose, Vladimir Salnikov and Henry Taylor (4).

50-meter Freestyle

Year	Time		Year	Time	
1904 Zoltán Halmay, HUN (50 yds)	28.0		1996 Aleksandr Popov, RUS	22.13	
1906-84 Not held			2000 (TIE) Anthony Ervin, USA	21.98	
1988 Matt Biondi, USA	22.14	**WR**	& Gary Hall Jr., USA	21.98	
1992 Aleksandr Popov, UT	21.91	**OR**	2004 Gary Hall Jr., USA	21.93	

100-meter Freestyle

Year	Time		Year	Time	
1896 Alfréd Hajós, HUN	1:22.2	**OR**	1936 Ferenc Csik, HUN	57.6	
1904 Zoltán Halmay, HUN (100 yds)	1:02.8		1948 Wally Ris, USA	57.3	**OR**
1906 Charles Daniels, USA	1:13.4		1952 Clarke Scholes, USA	57.4	
1908 Charles Daniels, USA	1:05.6	**WR**	1956 Jon Henricks, AUS	55.4	**OR**
1912 Duke Kahanamoku, USA	1:03.4		1960 John Devitt, AUS	55.2	**OR**
1920 Duke Kahanamoku, USA	1:00.4	**WR**	1964 Don Schollander, USA	53.4	**OR**
1924 Johnny Weissmuller, USA	59.0	**OR**	1968 Michael Wenden, AUS	52.2	**WR**
1928 Johnny Weissmuller, USA	58.6	**OR**	1972 Mark Spitz, USA	51.22	**WR**
1932 Yasuji Miyazaki, JPN	58.2		1976 Jim Montgomery, USA	49.99	**WR**

Year		Time		Year		Time	
1980	Jorg Woithe, E. Ger	.50.40		1996	Aleksandr Popov, RUS	.48.74	
1984	Rowdy Gaines, USA	.49.80	**OR**	2000	Pieter van den Hoogenband, NED	.48.30	
1988	Matt Biondi, USA	.48.63	**OR**	2004	Pieter van den Hoogenband, NED	.48.17	
1992	Aleksandr Popov, UT	.49.02					

200-meter Freestyle

Year		Time		Year		Time	
1900	Frederick Lane, AUS (220 yds)	2:25.2	**OR**	1984	Michael Gross, W. Ger	1:47.44	**WR**
1904	Charles Daniels, USA (220 yds)	2:44.2		1988	Duncan Armstrong, AUS	1:47.25	**WR**
1968	Michael Wenden, AUS	1:55.2	**OR**	1992	Yevgeny Sadovyi, UT	1:46.70	**OR**
1972	Mark Spitz, USA	1:52.78	**WR**	1996	Danyon Loader, NZE	1:47.63	
1976	Bruce Furniss, USA	1:50.29	**WR**	2000	Pieter van den Hoogenband, NED	1:45.35	**WR**
1980	Sergei Kopliakov, USSR	1:49.81	**OR**	2004	Ian Thorpe, AUS	1:44.71	**OR**

400-meter Freestyle

Year		Time		Year		Time	
1896	Paul Neumann, AUT (550m)	8:12.6		1960	Murray Rose, AUS	4:18.3	**OR**
1904	Charles Daniels, USA (440 yds)	6:16.2		1964	Don Schollander, USA	4:12.2	**WR**
1906	Otto Scheff, AUT	6:23.8		1968	Mike Burton, USA	4:09.0	**OR**
1908	Henry Taylor, GBR	5:36.8		1972	Bradford Cooper, AUS*	4:00.27	**OR**
1912	George Hodgson, CAN	5:24.4		1976	Brian Goodell, USA	3:51.93	**WR**
1920	Norman Ross, USA	5:26.8		1980	Vladimir Salnikov, USSR	3:51.31	**OR**
1924	Johnny Weissmuller, USA	5:04.2	**OR**	1984	George DiCarlo, USA	3:51.23	**OR**
1928	Alberto Zorilla, ARG	5:01.6	**OR**	1988	Uwe Dassler, E. Ger	3:46.95	**WR**
1932	Buster Crabbe, USA	4:48.4	**OR**	1992	Yevgeny Sadovyi, UT	3:45.00	**WR**
1936	Jack Medica, USA	4:44.5	**OR**	1996	Danyon Loader, NZE	3:47.97	
1948	Bill Smith, USA	4:41.0	**OR**	2000	Ian Thorpe, AUS	3:40.59	**WR**
1952	Jean Boiteux, FRA	4:30.7	**OR**	2004	Ian Thorpe, AUS	3:43.10	
1956	Murray Rose, AUS	4:27.3	**OR**				

*Cooper finished second to Rick DeMont of the U.S., who was disqualified when he flunked the post-race drug test (his asthma medication was on the IOC's banned list).

1500-meter Freestyle

Year		Time		Year		Time	
1896	Alfréd Hajós, HUN (1200m)	18:22.2	**OR**	1956	Murray Rose, AUS	17:58.9	
1900	John Arthur Jarvis, GBR (1000m)	13:40.2		1960	Jon Konrads, AUS	17:19.6	**OR**
1904	Emil Rausch, GER (1 mile)	27:18.2		1964	Robert Windle, AUS	17:01.7	**OR**
1906	Henry Taylor, GBR (1 mile)	28:28.0		1968	Mike Burton, USA	16:38.9	**OR**
1908	Henry Taylor, GBR	22:48.4	**WR**	1972	Mike Burton, USA	15:52.58	**WR**
1912	George Hodgson, CAN	22:00.0	**WR**	1976	Brian Goodell, USA	15:02.40	**WR**
1920	Norman Ross, USA	22:23.2		1980	Vladimir Salnikov, USSR	14:58.27	**WR**
1924	Andrew (Boy) Charlton, AUS	20:06.6	**WR**	1984	Mike O'Brien, USA	15:05.20	
1928	Arne Borge, SWE	19:51.8	**OR**	1988	Vladimir Salnikov, USSR	15:00.40	
1932	Kusuo Kitamura, JPN	19:12.4	**OR**	1992	Kieren Perkins, AUS	14:43.48	**WR**
1936	Noboru Terada, JPN	19:13.7		1996	Kieren Perkins, AUS	14:56.40	
1948	James McLane, USA	19:18.5		2000	Grant Hackett, AUS	14:48.33	
1952	Ford Konno, USA	18:30.3	**OR**	2004	Grant Hackett, AUS	14:43.40	**OR**

100-meter Backstroke

Year		Time		Year		Time	
1904	Walter Brack, GER (100 yds)	1:16.8		1960	David Theile, AUS	1:01.9	**OR**
1908	Arno Bieberstein, GER	1:24.6	**WR**	1968	Roland Matthes, E. Ger	.58.7	**OR**
1912	Harry Hebner, USA	1:21.2		1972	Roland Matthes, E. Ger	.56.58	**OR**
1920	Warren Kealoha, USA	1:15.2		1976	John Naber, USA	.55.49	**WR**
1924	Warren Kealoha, USA	1:13.2	**OR**	1980	Bengt Baron, SWE	.56.33	
1928	George Kojac, USA	1:08.2	**WR**	1984	Rick Carey, USA	.55.79	
1932	Masaji Kiyokawa, JPN	1:08.6		1988	Daichi Suzuki, JPN	.55.05	
1936	Adolf Kiefer, USA	1:05.9	**OR**	1992	Mark Tewksbury, CAN	.53.98	**OR**
1948	Allen Stack, USA	1:06.4		1996	Jeff Rouse, USA	.54.10	
1952	Yoshinobu Oyakawa, USA	1:05.4	**OR**	2000	Lenny Krayzelburg, USA	.53.72	**OR**
1956	David Theile, AUS	1:02.2	**OR**	2004	Aaron Peirsol, USA	.54.06	

200-meter Backstroke

Year		Time		Year		Time	
1900	Ernst Hoppenberg, GER	2:47.0		1984	Rick Carey, USA	2:00.23	
1964	Jed Graef, USA	2:10.3	**WR**	1988	Igor Poliansky, USSR	1:59.37	
1968	Roland Matthes, E. Ger	2:09.6	**OR**	1992	Martin Lopez-Zubero, SPA	1:58.47	**OR**
1972	Roland Matthes, E. Ger	2:02.82	**=WR**	1996	Brad Bridgewater, USA	1:58.54	
1976	John Naber, USA	1:59.19	**WR**	2000	Lenny Krayzelburg, USA	1:56.76	**OR**
1980	Sándor Wládár, HUN	2:01.93		2004	Aaron Peirsol, USA	1:54.95	**OR**

100-meter Breaststroke

Year		Time		Year		Time	
1968	Don McKenzie, USA	1:07.7	OR	1988	Adrian Moorhouse, GBR	1:02.04	
1972	Nobutaka Taguchi, JPN	1:04.94	WR	1992	Nelson Diebel, USA	1:01.50	OR
1976	John Hencken, USA	1:03.11	WR	1996	Fred deBurghgraeve, BEL	1:00.60	
1980	Duncan Goodhew, GBR	1:03.44		2000	Domenico Fioravanti, ITA	1:00.46	OR
1984	Steve Lundquist, USA	1:01.65	WR	2004	Kosuke Kitajima, JPN	1:00.08	

200-meter Breaststroke

Year		Time		Year		Time	
1908	Frederick Holman, GBR	3:09.2		1964	Ian O'Brien, AUS	2:27.8	WR
1912	Walter Bathe, GER	3:01.8	OR	1968	Felipe Muñoz, MEX	2:28.7	
1920	Hakan Malmroth, SWE	3:04.4		1972	John Hencken, USA	2:21.55	WR
1924	Robert Skelton, USA	2:56.6		1976	David Wilkie, GBR	2:15.11	WR
1928	Yoshiyuki Tsuruta, JPN	2:48.8	OR	1980	Robertas Zhulpa, USSR	2:15.85	
1932	Yoshiyuki Tsuruta, JPN	2:45.4		1984	Victor Davis, CAN	2:13.34	WR
1936	Tetsuo Hamuro, JPN	2:41.5	OR	1988	József Szabó, HUN	2:13.52	
1948	Joseph Verdeur, USA	2:39.3	OR	1992	Mike Barrowman, USA	2:10.16	WR
1952	John Davies, AUS	2:34.4	OR	1996	Norbert Rozsa, HUN	2:12.57	
1956	Masaru Furukawa, JPN	2:34.7*	OR	2000	Domenico Fioravanti, ITA	2:10.87	
1960	Bill Mulliken, USA	2:37.4		2004	Kosuke Kitajima, JPN	2:09.44	OR

*In 1956, the butterfly stroke and breaststroke were separated into two different events.

100-meter Butterfly

Year		Time		Year		Time	
1968	Doug Russell, USA	55.9	OR	1988	Anthony Nesty, SUR	53.0	OR
1972	Mark Spitz, USA	54.27	WR	1992	Pablo Morales, USA	53.32	
1976	Matt Vogel, USA	54.35		1996	Dennis Pankratov, RUS	52.27	
1980	Pär Arvidsson, SWE	54.92		2000	Lars Frolander, SWE	52.00	
1984	Michael Gross, W. Ger	53.08	WR	2004	Michael Phelps, USA	51.25	OR

200-meter Butterfly

Year		Time		Year		Time	
1956	Bill Yorzyk, USA	2:19.3	OR	1980	Sergei Fesenko, USSR	1:59.76	
1960	Mike Troy, USA	2:12.8	WR	1984	Jon Sieben, AUS	1:57.04	WR
1964	Kevin Berry, AUS	2:06.6	WR	1988	Michael Gross, W. Ger	1:56.94	OR
1968	Carl Robie, USA	2:08.7		1992	Melvin Stewart, USA	1:56.26	OR
1972	Mark Spitz, USA	2:00.70	WR	1996	Dennis Pankratov, RUS	1:56.51	
1976	Mike Bruner, USA	1:59.23	WR	2000	Tom Malchow, USA	1:55.35	OR
				2004	Michael Phelps, USA	1:54.04	OR

200-meter Individual Medley

Year		Time		Year		Time	
1968	Charles Hickcox, USA	2:12.0	OR	1992	Tamás Darnyi, HUN	2:00.76	
1972	Gunnar Larsson, SWE	2:07.17	WR	1996	Attila Czene, HUN	1:59.91	
1984	Alex Baumann, CAN	2:01.42	WR	2000	Massimiliano Rosolino, ITA	1:58.98	OR
1988	Tamás Darnyi, HUN	2:00.17	WR	2004	Michael Phelps, USA	1:57.14	OR

400-meter Individual Medley

Year		Time		Year		Time	
1964	Richard Roth, USA	4:45.4	WR	1988	Tamás Darnyi, HUN	4:14.75	WR
1968	Charles Hickcox, USA	4:48.4		1992	Tamás Darnyi, HUN	4:14.23	OR
1972	Gunnar Larsson, SWE	4:31.98	OR	1996	Tom Dolan, USA	4:14.90	
1976	Rod Strachan, USA	4:23.68	WR	2000	Tom Dolan, USA	4:11.76	WR
1980	Aleksandr Sidorenko, USSR	4:22.89	OR	2004	Michael Phelps, USA	4:08.26	WR
1984	Alex Baumann, CAN	4:17.41	WR				

4x100-meter Freestyle Relay

Year		Time		Year		Time	
1964	United States	3:32.2	WR	1988	United States	3:16.53	WR
1968	United States	3:31.7	WR	1992	United States	3:16.74	
1972	United States	3:26.42	WR	1996	United States	3:15.41	
1976-80	Not held			2000	Australia	3:13.67	WR
1984	United States	3:19.03	WR	2004	South Africa	3:13.17	WR

4x200-meter Freestyle Relay

Year		Time		Year		Time	
1906	Hungary (x250m)	16:52.4		1948	United States	8:46.0	WR
1908	Great Britain	10:55.6	WR	1952	United States	8:31.1	OR
1912	Australia/New Zealand	10:11.6	WR	1956	Australia	8:23.6	WR
1920	United States	10:04.4	WR	1960	United States	8:10.2	WR
1924	United States	9:53.4	WR	1964	United States	7:52.1	WR
1928	United States	9:36.2	WR	1968	United States	7:52.33	
1932	Japan	8:58.4	WR	1972	United States	7:35.78	WR
1936	Japan	8:51.5	WR	1976	United States	7:23.22	WR

Year		Time		Year		Time	
1980	Soviet Union	.7:23.50		1996	United States	.7:14.84	
1984	United States	.7:15.69	WR	2000	Australia	.7:07.05	WR
1988	United States	.7:12.51	WR	2004	United States	.7:07.33	
1992	Unified Team	.7:11.95	WR				

4x100-meter Medley Relay

Year		Time		Year		Time	
1960	United States	.4:05.4	WR	1984	United States	.3:39.30	WR
1964	United States	.3:58.4	WR	1988	United States	.3:36.93	WR
1968	United States	.3:54.9	WR	1992	United States	.3:36.93	=WR
1972	United States	.3:48.16	WR	1996	United States	.3:34.84	
1976	United States	.3:42.22	WR	2000	United States	.3:33.73	WR
1980	Australia	.3:45.70		2004	United States	.3:30.68	WR

WOMEN

At least 4 gold medals (including relays): Jenny Thompson (8); Kristin Otto and Amy Van Dyken (6); Krisztina Egerszegi (5), Kornelia Ender, Janet Evans, Dawn Fraser and Dara Torres (4).

50-meter Freestyle

Year		Time		Year		Time	
1988	Kristin Otto, E. Ger	.25.49	OR	2000	Inge de Bruijn, NED	.24.32	
1992	Yang Wenyi, CHN	.24.79	WR	2004	Inge de Bruijn, NED	.24.58	
1996	Amy Van Dyken, USA	.24.87					

100-meter Freestyle

Year		Time		Year		Time	
1912	Fanny Durack, AUS	.1:22.2		1968	Jan Henne, USA	.1:00.0	
1920	Ethelda Bleibtrey, USA	.1:13.6	WR	1972	Sandra Neilson, USA	.58.59	OR
1924	Ethel Lackie, USA	.1:12.4		1976	Kornelia Ender, E. Ger	.55.65	WR
1928	Albina Osipowich, USA	.1:11.0	OR	1980	Barbara Krause, E. Ger	.54.79	WR
1932	Helene Madison, USA	.1:06.8	OR	1984	(TIE) Nancy Hogshead, USA	.55.92	
1936	Rie Mastenbroek, NED	.1:05.9	OR		& Carrie Steinseifer, USA	.55.92	
1948	Greta Andersen, DEN	.1:06.3		1988	Kristin Otto, E. Ger	.54.93	
1952	Katalin Szöke, HUN	.1:06.8		1992	Zhuang Yong, CHN	.54.65	OR
1956	Dawn Fraser, AUS	.1:02.0	WR	1996	Le Jingyi, CHN	.54.50	
1960	Dawn Fraser, AUS	.1:01.2	OR	2000	Inge de Bruijn, NED	.53.83	
1964	Dawn Fraser, AUS	.59.5	OR	2004	Jodie Henry, AUS	.53.84	

200-meter Freestyle

Year		Time		Year		Time	
1968	Debbie Meyer, USA	.2:10.5	OR	1988	Heike Friedrich, E. Ger	.1:57.65	OR
1972	Shane Gould, AUS	.2:03.56	WR	1992	Nicole Haislett, USA	.1:57.90	
1976	Kornelia Ender, E. Ger	.1:59.26	WR	1996	Claudia Poll, CRC	.1:58.16	
1980	Barbara Krause, E. Ger	.1:58.33	OR	2000	Susie O'Neill, AUS	.1:58.24	
1984	Mary Wayte, USA	.1:59.23		2004	Camelia Potec, ROM	.1:58.03	

400-meter Freestyle

Year		Time		Year		Time	
1920	Ethelda Bleibtrey, USA (300m)	.4:34.0	WR	1968	Debbie Meyer, USA	.4:31.8	OR
1924	Martha Norelius, USA	.6:02.2	OR	1972	Shane Gould, AUS	.4:19.44	WR
1928	Martha Norelius, USA	.5:42.8	WR	1976	Petra Thümer, E. Ger	.4:09.89	WR
1932	Helene Madison, USA	.5:28.5	WR	1980	Ines Diers, E. Ger	.4:08.76	OR
1936	Rie Mastenbroek, NED	.5:26.4	OR	1984	Tiffany Cohen, USA	.4:07.10	OR
1948	Ann Curtis, USA	.5:17.8	OR	1988	Janet Evans, USA	.4:03.85	WR
1952	Valéria Gyenge, HUN	.5:12.1	OR	1992	Dagmar Hase, GER	.4:07.18	
1956	Lorraine Crapp, AUS	.4:54.6	OR	1996	Michelle Smith, IRE	.4:07.25	
1960	Chris von Saltza, USA	.4:50.6	OR	2000	Brooke Bennett, USA	.4:05.80	
1964	Ginny Duenkel, USA	.4:43.3	OR	2004	Laure Manaudou, FRA	.4:05.34	

800-meter Freestyle

Year		Time		Year		Time	
1968	Debbie Meyer, USA	.9:24.0	OR	1988	Janet Evans, USA	.8:20.20	OR
1972	Keena Rothhammer, USA	.8:53.68	WR	1992	Janet Evans, USA	.8:25.52	
1976	Petra Thümer, E. Ger	.8:37.14	WR	1996	Brooke Bennett, USA	.8:27.89	
1980	Michelle Ford, AUS	.8:28.90	OR	2000	Brooke Bennett, USA	.8:19.67	OR
1984	Tiffany Cohen, USA	.8:24.95	OR	2004	Ai Shibata, JPN	.8:24.54	

100-meter Backstroke

Year		Time		Year		Time	
1924	Sybil Bauer, USA	.1:23.2	OR	1972	Melissa Belote, USA	.1:05.78	OR
1928	Maria Braun, NED	.1:22.0		1976	Ulrike Richter, E. Ger	.1:01.83	OR
1932	Eleanor Holm, USA	.1:19.4		1980	Rica Reinisch, E. Ger	.1:00.86	WR
1936	Dina Senff, NED	.1:18.9		1984	Theresa Andrews, USA	.1:02.55	
1948	Karen-Margrete Harup, DEN	.1:14.4	OR	1988	Kristin Otto, E. Ger	.1:00.89	
1952	Joan Harrison, S. Afr.	.1:14.3		1992	Krisztina Egerszegi, HUN	.1:00.68	OR
1956	Judy Grinham, GBR	.1:12.9	OR	1996	Beth Botsford, USA	.1:01.19	
1960	Lynn Burke, USA	.1:09.3	OR	2000	Diana Mocanu, ROM	.1:00.21	OR
1964	Cathy Ferguson, USA	.1:07.7	WR	2004	Natalie Coughlin, USA	.1:03.37	
1968	Kaye Hall, USA	.1:06.2	WR				

200-meter Backstroke

Year		Time		Year		Time	
1968	Pokey Watson, USA	2:24.8	OR	1988	Krisztina Egerszegi, HUN	2:09.29	OR
1972	Melissa Belote, USA	2:19.19	WR	1992	Krisztina Egerszegi, HUN	2:07.06	OR
1976	Ulrike Richter, E. Ger	2:13.43	OR	1996	Krisztina Egerszegi, HUN	2:07.83	
1980	Rica Reinisch, E. Ger	2:11.77	WR	2000	Diana Mocanu, ROM	2:08.16	
1984	Jolanda de Rover, NED	2:12.38		2004	Kirsty Coventry, ZIM	2:09.19	

100-meter Breaststroke

Year		Time		Year		Time	
1968	Djurdjica Bjedov, YUG	1:15.8	OR	1988	Tania Dangalakova, BUL	1:07.95	OR
1972	Cathy Carr, USA	1:13.58	WR	1992	Yelena Rudkovskaya, UT	1:08.00	
1976	Hannelore Anke, E. Ger	1:11.16		1996	Penny Heyns, RSA.	1:07.73	
1980	Ute Geweniger, E. Ger	1:10.22		2000	Megan Quann, USA	1:07.05	
1984	Petra van Staveren, NED	1:09.88	OR	2004	Luo Xuejuan, CHN	1:06.64	OR

200-meter Breaststroke

Year		Time		Year		Time	
1924	Lucy Morton, GBR	3:33.2	OR	1972	Beverley Whitfield, AUS	2:41.71	OR
1928	Hilde Schrader, GER	3:12.6		1976	Marina Koshevaya, USSR	2:33.35	WR
1932	Clare Dennis, AUS	3:06.3	OR	1980	Lina Kaciusyte, USSR	2:29.54	OR
1936	Hideko Maehata, JPN	3:03.6		1984	Anne Ottenbrite, CAN	2:30.38	
1948	Petronella van Vliet, NED	2:57.2		1988	Silke Hörner, E. Ger	2:26.71	WR
1952	éva Székely, HUN	2:51.7	OR	1992	Kyoko Iwasaki, JPN	2:26.65	OR
1956	Ursula Happe, GER	2:53.1	OR	1996	Penny Heyns, RSA	2:25.41	
1960	Anita Lonsbrough, GBR	2:49.5	WR	2000	Agnes Kovacs, HUN	2:24.35	
1964	Galina Prozumenshikova, USSR	2:46.4	OR	2004	Amanda Beard, USA	2:23.37	OR
1968	Sharon Wichman, USA	2:44.4	OR				

100-meter Butterfly

Year		Time		Year		Time	
1956	Shelley Mann, USA	1:11.0	OR	1984	Mary T. Meagher, USA	.59.26	
1960	Carolyn Schuler, USA	1:09.5	OR	1988	Kristin Otto, E. Ger	.59.00	OR
1964	Sharon Stouder, USA	1:04.7	WR	1992	Qian Hong, CHN	.58.62	OR
1968	Lynn McClements, AUS	1:05.5		1996	Amy Van Dyken, USA	.59.13	
1972	Mayumi Aoki, JPN	1:03.34	WR	2000	Inge de Bruijn, NED	.56.61	WR
1976	Kornelia Ender, E. Ger	1:00.13	=WR	2004	Petria Thomas, AUS	.57.72	
1980	Caren Metschuck, E. Ger	1:00.42					

200-meter Butterfly

Year		Time		Year		Time	
1968	Ada Kok, NED	2:24.7	OR	1988	Kathleen Nord, E. Ger	2:09.51	
1972	Karen Moe, USA	2:15.57	WR	1992	Summer Sanders, USA	2:08.67	
1976	Andrea Pollack, E. Ger	2:11.41	OR	1996	Susie O'Neill, AUS	2:07.76	
1980	Ines Geissler, E. Ger	2:10.44	OR	2000	Misty Hyman, USA	2:05.88	OR
1984	Mary T. Meagher, USA	2:06.90	OR	2004	Otylia Jedrzejczak, POL	2:06.05	

200-meter Individual Medley

Year		Time		Year		Time	
1968	Claudia Kolb, USA	2:24.7	OR	1992	Lin Li, CHN	2:11.65	WR
1972	Shane Gould, AUS	2:23.07	WR	1996	Michelle Smith, IRE	2:13.93	
1984	Tracy Caulkins, USA	2:12.64	OR	2000	Yana Klochkova, UKR	2:10.68	OR
1988	Daniela Hunger, E. Ger	2:12.59	OR	2004	Yana Klochkova, UKR	2:11.14	

400-meter Individual Medley

Year		Time		Year		Time	
1964	Donna de Varona, USA	5:18.7	OR	1988	Janet Evans, USA	4:37.76	
1968	Claudia Kolb, USA	5:08.5	OR	1992	Krisztina Egerszegi, HUN	4:36.54	
1972	Gail Neall, AUS	5:02.97	WR	1996	Michelle Smith, IRE	4:39.18	
1976	Ulrike Tauber, E. Ger	4:42.77	WR	2000	Yana Klochkova, UKR	4:33.59	WR
1980	Petra Schneider, E. Ger	4:36.29	WR	2004	Yana Klochkova, UKR	4:34.83	
1984	Tracy Caulkins, USA	4:39.24					

4x100-meter Freestyle Relay

Year		Time		Year		Time	
1912	Great Britain	5:52.8	WR	1968	United States	4:02.5	OR
1920	United States	5:11.6	WR	1972	United States	3:55.19	WR
1924	United States	4:58.8	WR	1976	United States	3:44.82	WR
1928	United States	4:47.6	WR	1980	East Germany	3:42.71	WR
1932	United States	4:38.0	WR	1984	United States	3:43.43	
1936	Netherlands	4:36.0	WR	1988	East Germany	3:40.63	OR
1948	United States	4:29.2	WR	1992	United States	3:39.46	WR
1952	Hungary	4:24.4	WR	1996	United States	3:39.29	
1956	Australia	4:17.1	WR	2000	United States	3:36.61	WR
1960	United States	4:08.9	WR	2004	Australia	3:35.94	WR
1964	United States	4:03.8	WR				

4x200-meter Freestyle Relay

Year		Time		Year		Time	
1996	United States	7:59.87		2004	United States	7:53.42	**WR**
2000	United States	7:57.80	**OR**				

4x100-meter Medley Relay

Year		Time		Year		Time	
1960	United States	4:41.1	**WR**	1984	United States	4:08.34	
1964	United States	4:33.9	**WR**	1988	East Germany	4:03.74	**OR**
1968	United States	4:28.3	**OR**	1992	United States	4:02.54	**WR**
1972	United States	4:20.75	**WR**	1996	United States	4:02.88	
1976	East Germany	4:07.95	**WR**	2000	United States	3:58.30	**WR**
1980	East Germany	4:06.67	**WR**	2004	Australia	3:57.32	**WR**

TENNIS

MEN

Multiple gold medals (including men's doubles): John Boland, Max Decugis, Laurie Doherty, Reggie Doherty, Arthur Gore, Andre Grobert, Nicolas Massu, Vincent Richards, Charles Winslow and Beals Wright (2).

Singles

Year			Year		
1896	John Boland	Great Britain/Ireland	1920	Louis Raymond	South Africa
1900	Laurie Doherty,	Great Britain	1924	Vincent Richards	United States
1904	Beals Wright	United States	1928-84	Not held	
1906	Max Decugis	France	1988	Miloslav Mecir	Czechoslovakia
1908	Josiah Ritchie	Great Britain	1992	Marc Rosset	Switzerland
	(Indoor) Arthur Gore	Great Britain	1996	Andre Agassi	United States
1912	Charles Winslow	South Africa	2000	Yevgeny Kafelnikov	Russia
	(Indoor) André Gobert	France	2004	Nicolas Massu	Chile

Doubles

Year		Year	
1896	John Boland, IRE & Fritz Traun, GER	1920	Noel Turnbull & Max Woosnam, GBR
1900	Laurie and Reggie Doherty, GBR	1924	Vincent Richards & Frank Hunter, USA
1904	Edgar Leonard & Beals Wright, USA	1928-84	Not held
1906	Max Decugis & Maurice Germot, FRA	1988	Ken Flach & Robert Seguso, USA
1908	George Hillyard & Reggie Doherty, GBR	1992	Boris Becker & Michael Stich, GER
	(Indoor) Arthur Gore & Herbert Barrett, GBR	1996	Todd Woodbridge & Mark Woodforde, AUS
1912	Charles Winslow & Harold Kitson, S. Afr.	2000	Sebastien Lareau & Daniel Nestor, CAN
	(Indoor) Andre Gobert & Maurice Germot, FRA	2004	Fernando Gonzalez & Nicolas Massu, CHI

WOMEN

Multiple gold medals (including women's doubles): Helen Wills, Gigi Fernandez, Mary Joe Fernandez and Venus Williams (2).

Singles

Year			Year		
1900	Charlotte Cooper	Great Britain	1924	Helen Wills	United States
1906	Esmee Simiriotou	Greece	1928-84	Not held	
1908	Dorothea Chambers	Great Britain	1988	Steffi Graf	West Germany
	(Indoor) Gwen Eastlake-Smith	Great Britain	1992	Jennifer Capriati	United States
1912	Marguerite Broquedis	France	1996	Lindsay Davenport	United States
	(Indoor) Edith Hannam	Great Britain	2000	Venus Williams	United States
1920	Suzanne Lenglen	France	2004	Justine Henin-Hardenne	Belgium

Doubles

Year		Year	
1920	Winifred McNair & Kitty McKane, GBR	1992	Gigi Fernandez & Mary Joe Fernandez, USA
1924	Hazel Wightman & Helen Wills, USA	1996	Gigi Fernandez & Mary Joe Fernandez, USA
1928-84	Not held	2000	Serena Williams & Venus Williams, USA
1988	Pam Shriver & Zina Garrison, USA	2004	Li Ting & Sun Tian Tian, CHN

TRACK & FIELD

World and Olympic records below that appear to be broken or equaled by winning times, heights and distances in subsequent years, but are not so indicated, were all broken in preliminary races and field events leading up to the finals.

MEN

At least 4 gold medals (including relays and discontinued events): Ray Ewry (10); Carl Lewis and Paavo Nurmi (9); Ville Ritola and Martin Sheridan (5); Harrison Dillard, Archie Hahn, Michael Johnson, Hannes Kolehmainen, Alvin Kraenzlein, Eric Lemming, Jim Lightbody, Al Oerter, Jesse Owens, Meyer Prinstein, Mel Sheppard, Lasse Viren and Emil Zátopek (4). Note that all of Ewry's gold medals came before 1912, in the Standing High Jump, Standing Long Jump and Standing Triple Jump.

100 meters

Year	Time		Year	Time	
1896 Tom Burke, USA	12.0		1960 Armin Hary, GER	10.2	**OR**
1900 Frank Jarvis, USA	11.0		1964 Bob Hayes, USA	10.0	**=WR**
1904 Archie Hahn, USA	11.0		1968 Jim Hines, USA	9.95	**WR**
1906 Archie Hahn, USA	11.2		1972 Valery Borzov, USSR	10.14	
1908 Reggie Walker, S. Afr.	10.8	**=OR**	1976 Hasely Crawford, TRI	10.06	
1912 Ralph Craig, USA	10.8		1980 Allan Wells, GBR	10.25	
1920 Charley Paddock, USA	10.8		1984 Carl Lewis, USA	9.99	
1924 Harold Abrahams, GBR	10.6	**=OR**	1988 Carl Lewis, USA*	9.92	**WR**
1928 Percy Williams, CAN	10.8		1992 Linford Christie, GBR	9.96	
1932 Eddie Tolan, USA	10.3	**OR**	1996 Donovan Bailey, CAN	9.84	**WR**
1936 Jesse Owens, USA	10.3w		2000 Maurice Greene, USA	9.87	
1948 Harrison Dillard, USA	10.3	**=OR**	2004 Justin Gatlin, USA	9.85	
1952 Lindy Remigino, USA	10.4				
1956 Bobby Morrow, USA	10.5				

ʷindicates wind-aided.

*Lewis finished second to Ben Johnson of Canada, who set a world record of 9.79 seconds. Two days later, Johnson was stripped of his gold medal and his record when he tested positive for steroid use in a post-race drug test.

200 meters

Year	Time		Year	Time	
1900 Walter Tewksbury, USA	22.2		1960 Livio Berruti, ITA	20.5	**=WR**
1904 Archie Hahn, USA	21.6	**OR**	1964 Henry Carr, USA	20.3	**OR**
1908 Bobby Kerr, CAN	22.6		1968 Tommie Smith, USA	19.83	**WR**
1912 Ralph Craig, USA	21.7		1972 Valery Borzov, USSR	20.00	
1920 Allen Woodring, USA	22.0		1976 Donald Quarrie, JAM	20.23	
1924 Jackson Scholz, USA	21.6		1980 Pietro Mennea, ITA	20.19	
1928 Percy Williams, CAN	21.8		1984 Carl Lewis, USA	19.80	
1932 Eddie Tolan, USA	21.2	**OR**	1988 Joe DeLoach, USA	19.75	**OR**
1936 Jesse Owens, USA	20.7	**OR**	1992 Mike Marsh, USA	20.01	
1948 Mel Patton, USA	21.1		1996 Michael Johnson, USA	19.32	**WR**
1952 Andy Stanfield, USA	20.7		2000 Konstantinos Kenteris, GRE	20.09	
1956 Bobby Morrow, USA	20.6	**OR**	2004 Shawn Crawford, USA	19.79	

400 meters

Year	Time		Year	Time	
1896 Tom Burke, USA	54.2		1956 Charley Jenkins, USA	46.7	
1900 Maxey Long, USA	49.4	**OR**	1960 Otis Davis, USA	44.9	**WR**
1904 Harry Hillman, USA	49.2	**OR**	1964 Mike Larrabee, USA	45.1	
1906 Paul Pilgrim, USA	53.2		1968 Lee Evans, USA	43.86	**WR**
1908 Wyndham Halswelle, GBR	50.0		1972 Vince Matthews, USA	44.66	
1912 Charlie Reidpath, USA	48.2	**OR**	1976 Alberto Juantorena, CUB	44.26	
1920 Bevil Rudd, S. Afr.	49.6		1980 Viktor Markin, USSR	44.60	
1924 Eric Liddell, GBR	47.6	**OR**	1984 Alonzo Babers, USA	44.27	
1928 Ray Barbuti, USA	47.8		1988 Steve Lewis, USA	43.87	
1932 Bill Carr, USA	46.2	**WR**	1992 Quincy Watts, USA	43.50	**OR**
1936 Archie Williams, USA	46.5		1996 Michael Johnson, USA	43.49	**OR**
1948 Arthur Wint, JAM	46.2		2000 Michael Johnson, USA	43.84	
1952 George Rhoden, JAM	45.9	**OR**	2004 Jeremy Wariner, USA	44.00	

800 meters

Year	Time		Year	Time	
1896 Teddy Flack, AUS	2:11.0		1956 Tom Courtney, USA	1:47.7	**OR**
1900 Alfred Tysoe, GBR	2:01.2		1960 Peter Snell, NZE	1:46.3	**OR**
1904 Jim Lightbody, USA	1:56.0	**OR**	1964 Peter Snell, NZE	1:45.1	**OR**
1906 Paul Pilgrim, USA	2:01.5		1968 Ralph Doubell, AUS	1:44.3	**=WR**
1908 Mel Sheppard, USA	1:52.8	**WR**	1972 Dave Wottle, USA	1:45.9	
1912 Ted Meredith, USA	1:51.9	**WR**	1976 Alberto Juantorena, CUB	1:43.50	**WR**
1920 Albert Hill, GBR	1:53.4		1980 Steve Ovett, GBR	1:45.4	
1924 Douglas Lowe, GBR	1:52.4		1984 Joaquim Cruz, BRA	1:43.00	**OR**
1928 Douglas Lowe, GBR	1:51.8	**OR**	1988 Paul Ereng, KEN	1:43.45	
1932 Tommy Hampson, GBR	1:49.7	**WR**	1992 William Tanui, KEN	1:43.66	
1936 John Woodruff, USA	1:52.9		1996 Vebjoern Rodal, NOR	1:42.58	**OR**
1948 Mal Whitfield, USA	1:49.2	**OR**	2000 Nils Schumann, GER	1:45.08	
1952 Mal Whitfield, USA	1:49.2	**=OR**	2004 Yuriy Borzakovskiy, RUS	1:44.45	

1500 meters

Year		Time		Year		Time	
1896	Teddy Flack, AUS	4:33.2		1956	Ron Delany, IRE	3:41.2	OR
1900	Charles Bennett, GBR	4:06.2	WR	1960	Herb Elliott, AUS	3:35.6	WR
1904	Jim Lightbody, USA	4:05.4	WR	1964	Peter Snell, NZE	3:38.1	
1906	Jim Lightbody, USA	4:12.0		1968	Kip Keino, KEN	3:34.9	OR
1908	Mel Sheppard, USA	4:03.4	OR	1972	Pekka Vasala, FIN	3:36.3	
1912	Arnold Jackson, GBR	3:56.8	OR	1976	John Walker, NZE	3:39.17	
1920	Albert Hill, GBR	4:01.8		1980	Sebastian Coe, GBR	3:38.4	
1924	Paavo Nurmi, FIN	3:53.6	OR	1984	Sebastian Coe, GBR	3:32.53	OR
1928	Harry Larva, FIN	3:53.2	OR	1988	Peter Rono, KEN	3:35.96	
1932	Luigi Beccali, ITA	3:51.2	OR	1992	Fermin Cacho, SPA	3:40.12	
1936	John Lovelock, NZE	3:47.8	WR	1996	Noureddine Morceli, ALG	3:35.78	
1948	Henry Eriksson, SWE	3:49.8		2000	Noah Ngeny, KEN	3:32.07	OR
1952	Josy Barthel, LUX	3:45.1	OR	2004	Hicham El Guerrouj, MOR	3:34.18	

5000 meters

Year		Time		Year		Time	
1912	Hannes Kolehmainen, FIN	14:36.6	WR	1968	Mohamed Gammoudi, TUN	14:05.0	
1920	Joseph Guillemot, FRA	14:55.6		1972	Lasse Viren, FIN	13:26.4	OR
1924	Paavo Nurmi, FIN	14:31.2	OR	1976	Lasse Viren, FIN	13:24.76	
1928	Ville Ritola, FIN	14:38.0		1980	Miruts Yifter, ETH	13:21.0	
1932	Lauri Lehtinen, FIN	14:30.0	OR	1984	Said Aouita, MOR	13:05.59	OR
1936	Gunnar Höckert, FIN	14:22.2	OR	1988	John Ngugi, KEN	13:11.70	
1948	Gaston Reiff, BEL	14:17.6	OR	1992	Dieter Baumann, GER	13:12.52	
1952	Emil Zátopek, CZE	14:06.6	OR	1996	Venuste Niyongabo, BUR	13:07.96	
1956	Vladimir Kuts, USSR	13:39.6	OR	2000	Millon Wolde, ETH	13:35.49	
1960	Murray Halberg, NZE	13:43.4		2004	Hicham El Guerrouj, MOR	13:14.39	
1964	Bob Schul, USA	13:48.8					

10,000 meters

Year		Time		Year		Time	
1912	Hannes Kolehmainen, FIN	31:20.8		1968	Naftali Temu, KEN	29:27.4	
1920	Paavo Nurmi, FIN	31:45.8		1972	Lasse Viren, FIN	27:38.4	WR
1924	Ville Ritola, FIN	30:23.2	WR	1976	Lasse Viren, FIN	27:40.38	
1928	Paavo Nurmi, FIN	30:18.8	OR	1980	Miruts Yifter, ETH	27:42.7	
1932	Janusz Kusocinski, POL	30:11.4	OR	1984	Alberto Cova, ITA	27:47.54	
1936	Ilmari Salminen, FIN	30:15.4		1988	Brahim Boutaib, MOR	27:21.46	OR
1948	Emil Zátopek, CZE	29:59.6	OR	1992	Khalid Skah, MOR	27:46.70	
1952	Emil Zátopek, CZE	29:17.0	OR	1996	Haile Gebrselassie, ETH	27:07.34	OR
1956	Vladimir Kuts, USSR	28:45.6	OR	2000	Haile Gebrselassie, ETH	27:18.20	
1960	Pyotr Bolotnikov, USSR	28:32.2	OR	2004	Kenenisa Bekele, ETH	27:05.10	OR
1964	Billy Mills, USA	28:24.4	OR				

Marathon

Year		Time		Year		Time	
1896	Spiridon Louis, GRE	2:58:50		1956	Alain Mimoun, FRA	2:25:00.0	
1900	Michel Théato, FRA	2:59:45		1960	Abebe Bikila, ETH	2:15:16.2	WB
1904	Thomas Hicks, USA	3:28:53		1964	Abebe Bikila, ETH	2:12:11.2	WB
1906	Billy Sherring, CAN	2:51:23.6		1968	Mamo Wolde, ETH	2:20:26.4	
1908	Johnny Hayes, USA*	2:55:18.4	OR	1972	Frank Shorter, USA	2:12:19.8	
1912	Kenneth McArthur, S. Afr.	2:36:54.8		1976	Waldemar Cierpinski, E. Ger	2:09:55.0	OR
1920	Hannes Kolehmainen, FIN	2:32:35.8	WB	1980	Waldemar Cierpinski, E. Ger	2:11:03.0	
1924	Albin Stenroos, FIN	2:41:22.6		1984	Carlos Lopes, POR	2:09:21.0	OR
1928	Boughéra El Ouafi, FRA	2:32:57.0		1988	Gelindo Bordin, ITA	2:10:32	
1932	Juan Carlos Zabala, ARG	2:31:36.0	OR	1992	Hwang Young-Cho, S. Kor	2:13:23	
1936	Sohn Kee-Chung, JPN†	2:29:19.2	OR	1996	Josia Thugwane, RSA	2:12:36	
1948	Delfo Cabrera, ARG	2:34:51.6		2000	Gezahenge Abera, ETH	2:10:11	
1952	Emil Zátopek, CZE	2:23:03.2	OR	2004	Stefano Baldini, ITA	2:10:55	

*Dorando Pietri of Italy placed first, but was disqualified for being helped across the finish line.
†Sohn was a Korean, but he was forced to compete under the name Kitei Son by Japan, which occupied Korea at the time.
Note: Marathon distances—40,000 meters (1896,1904); 40,260 meters (1900); 41,860 meters (1906); 42,195 meters (1908 and since 1924); 40,200 meters (1912); 42,750 meters (1920). Current distance of 42,195 meters measures 26 miles, 385 yards.

110-meter Hurdles

Year		Time		Year		Time	
1896	Tom Curtis, USA	17.6		1956	Lee Calhoun, USA	13.5	OR
1900	Alvin Kraenzlein, USA	15.4	OR	1960	Lee Calhoun, USA	13.8	
1904	Frederick Schule, USA	16.0		1964	Hayes Jones, USA	13.6	
1906	Robert Leavitt, USA	16.2		1968	Willie Davenport, USA	13.3	OR
1908	Forrest Smithson, USA	15.0	WR	1972	Rod Milburn, USA	13.24	=WR
1912	Frederick Kelly, USA	15.1		1976	Guy Drut, FRA	13.30	
1920	Earl Thomson, CAN	14.8	WR	1980	Thomas Munkelt, E. Ger	13.39	
1924	Daniel Kinsey, USA	15.0		1984	Roger Kingdom, USA	13.20	OR
1928	Syd Atkinson, S. Afr.	14.8		1988	Roger Kingdom, USA	12.98	OR
1932	George Saling, USA	14.6		1992	Mark McKoy, CAN	13.12	
1936	Forrest (Spec) Towns, USA	14.2		1996	Allen Johnson, USA	12.95	OR
1948	William Porter, USA	13.9	OR	2000	Anier Garcia, CUB	13.00	
1952	Harrison Dillard, USA	13.7	OR	2004	Liu Xiang, CHN	12.91	OR

400-meter Hurdles

Year		Time		Year		Time	
1900	Walter Tewksbury, USA	.57.6		1964	Rex Cawley, USA	.49.6	
1904	Harry Hillman, USA	.53.0		1968	David Hemery, GBR	.48.12	**WR**
1908	Charley Bacon, USA	.55.0	**WR**	1972	John Akii-Bua, UGA	.47.82	**WR**
1920	Frank Loomis, USA	.54.0	**WR**	1976	Edwin Moses, USA	.47.64	**WR**
1924	Morgan Taylor, USA	.52.6		1980	Volker Beck, E. Ger	.48.70	
1928	David Burghley, GBR	.53.4	**OR**	1984	Edwin Moses, USA	.47.75	
1932	Bob Tisdall, IRE	.51.7		1988	Andre Phillips, USA	.47.19	**OR**
1936	Glenn Hardin, USA	.52.4		1992	Kevin Young, USA	.46.78	**WR**
1948	Roy Cochran, USA	.51.1	**OR**	1996	Derrick Adkins, USA	.47.54	
1952	Charley Moore, USA	.50.8	**OR**	2000	Angelo Taylor, USA	.47.50	
1956	Glenn Davis, USA	.50.1	**=OR**	2004	Felix Sanchez, DOM	.47.63	
1960	Glenn Davis, USA	.49.3	**OR**				

3000-meter Steeplechase

Year		Time		Year		Time	
1900	George Orton, CAN	.7:34.4		1964	Gaston Roelants, BEL	.8:30.8	**OR**
1904	Jim Lightbody, USA	.7:39.6		1968	Amos Biwott, KEN	.8:51.0	
1908	Arthur Russell, GBR	.10:47.8		1972	Kip Keino, KEN	.8:23.6	**OR**
1920	Percy Hodge, GBR	.10:00.4	**OR**	1976	Anders Gärderud, SWE	.8:08.2	**WR**
1924	Ville Ritola, FIN	.9:33.6	**OR**	1980	Bronislaw Malinowski, POL	.8:09.7	
1928	Toivo Loukola, FIN	.9:21.8	**WR**	1984	Julius Korir, KEN	.8:11.80	
1932	Volmari Iso-Hollo, FIN	.10:33.4*		1988	Julius Kariuki, KEN	.8:05.51	**OR**
1936	Volmari Iso-Hollo, FIN	.9:03.8	**WR**	1992	Matthew Birir, KEN	.8:08.84	
1948	Thore Sjöstrand, SWE	.9:04.6		1996	Joseph Keter,KEN	.8:07.12	
1952	Horace Ashenfelter, USA	.8:45.4	**WR**	2000	Reuben Kosgei, KEN	.8:21.43	
1956	Chris Brasher, GBR	.8:41.2	**OR**	2004	Ezekiel Kemboi, KEN	.8:05.81	
1960	Zdzislaw Krzyszkowiak, POL	.8:34.2	**OR**				

*Iso-Hollo ran one extra lap due to lap counter's mistake.

Note: Other steeplechase distances– 2500 meters (1900); 2590 meters (1904); 3200 meters (1908) and 3460 meters (1932).

4x100-meter Relay

Year		Time		Year		Time	
1912	Great Britain	.42.4		1968	United States	.38.23	**WR**
1920	United States	.42.2	**WR**	1972	United States	.38.19	**WR**
1924	United States	.41.0	**=WR**	1976	United States	.38.33	
1928	United States	.41.0	**=WR**	1980	Soviet Union	.38.26	
1932	United States	.40.0	**WR**	1984	United States	.37.83	**WR**
1936	United States	.39.8	**WR**	1988	Soviet Union	.38.19	
1948	United States	.40.6		1992	United States	.37.40	**WR**
1952	United States	.40.1		1996	Canada	.37.69	
1956	United States	.39.5	**WR**	2000	United States	.37.61	
1960	Germany	.39.5	**=WR**	2004	Great Britain	.38.07	
1964	United States	.39.0	**WR**				

4x400-meter Relay

Year		Time		Year		Time	
1908	United States	.3:29.4		1964	United States	.3:00.7	**WR**
1912	United States	.3:16.6	**WR**	1968	United States	.2:56.16	**WR**
1920	Great Britain	.3:22.2		1972	Kenya	.2:59.8	
1924	United States	.3:16.0	**WR**	1976	United States	.2:58.65	
1928	United States	.3:14.2	**WR**	1980	Soviet Union	.3:01.1	
1932	United States	.3:08.2	**WR**	1984	United States	.2:57.91	
1936	Great Britain	.3:09.0		1988	United States	.2:56.16	**=WR**
1948	United States	.3:10.4		1992	United States	.2:55.74	**WR**
1952	Jamaica	.3:03.9	**WR**	1996	United States	.2:55.99	
1956	United States	.3:04.8		2000	United States	.2:56.35	
1960	United States	.3:02.2	**WR**	2004	United States	.2:55.91	

20-kilometer Walk

Year		Time		Year		Time	
1956	Leonid Spirin, USSR	.1:31:27.4		1984	Ernesto Canto, MEX	.1:23:13	**OR**
1960	Vladimir Golubnichiy, USSR	.1:34:07.2		1988	Jozef Pribilinec, CZE	.1:19:57	**OR**
1964	Ken Matthews, GBR	.1:29:34.0		1992	Daniel Plaza Montero, SPA	.1:21:45	
1968	Vladimir Golubnichiy, USSR	.1:33:58.4		1996	Jefferson Perez, ECU	.1:20:07	
1972	Peter Frenkel, E. Ger	.1:26:42.4	**OR**	2000	Robert Korzeniowski, POL	.1:18:59	**OR**
1976	Daniel Bautista, MEX	.1:24:40.6	**OR**	2004	Ivano Brugnetti, ITA	.1:19:40	
1980	Maurizio Damilano, ITA	.1:23:35.5	**OR**				

50-kilometer Walk

Year		Time		Year		Time	
1932	Thomas Green, GBR	4:50:10		1976	Not held		
1936	Harold Whitlock, GBR	4:30:41.4	OR	1980	Hartwig Gauder, E. Ger	3:49:24.0	OR
1948	John Ljunggren, SWE	4:41:52		1984	Raul Gonzalez, MEX	3:47:26	OR
1952	Giuseppe Dordoni, ITA	4:28:07.8	OR	1988	Vyacheslav Ivanenko, USSR	3:38:29	OR
1956	Norman Read, NZE	4:30:42.8		1992	Andrei Perlov, UT	3:50:13	
1960	Don Thompson, GBR	4:25:30.0	OR	1996	Robert Korzeniowski, POL	3:43:30	
1964	Abdon Pamich, ITA	4:11:12.4	OR	2000	Robert Korzeniowski, POL	3:42:22	
1968	Christoph Höhne, E. Ger	4:20:13.6		2004	Robert Korzeniowski, POL	3:38:46	
1972	Bernd Kannenberg, W. Ger	3:56:11.6	OR				

High Jump

Year		Height		Year		Height	
1896	Ellery Clark, USA	5-11¼		1956	Charley Dumas, USA	6-11½	OR
1900	Irving Baxter, USA	6-2¾	OR	1960	Robert Shavlakadze, USSR	7-1	OR
1904	Sam Jones, USA	5-11		1964	Valery Brumel, USSR	7-1¾	OR
1906	Cornelius Leahy, GBR/IRE	5-10		1968	Dick Fosbury, USA	7-4¼	OR
1908	Harry Porter, USA	6-3	OR	1972	Yuri Tarmak, USSR	7-3¾	
1912	Alma Richards, USA	6-4	OR	1976	Jacek Wszola, POL	7-4½	OR
1920	Richmond Landon, USA	6-4	=OR	1980	Gerd Wessig, E. Ger	7-8¾	WR
1924	Harold Osborn, USA	6-6		1984	Dietmar Mögenburg, W. Ger	7-8½	
1928	Bob King, USA	6-4½		1988	Gennady Avdeyenko, USSR	7-9¾	OR
1932	Duncan McNaughton, CAN	6-5½		1992	Javier Sotomayor, CUB	7-8	
1936	Cornelius Johnson, USA	6-8	OR	1996	Charles Austin, USA	7-10	OR
1948	John Winter, AUS	6-6		2000	Sergey Klugin, RUS	7-8½	
1952	Walt Davis, USA	6-8½	OR	2004	Stefan Holm, SWE	7-8¾	

Pole Vault

Year		Height		Year		Height	
1896	William Hoyt, USA	10-10		1956	Bob Richards, USA	14-11½	OR
1900	Irving Baxter, USA	10-10		1960	Don Bragg, USA	15-5	OR
1904	Charles Dvorak, USA	11-5¾		1964	Fred Hansen, USA	16-8¾	OR
1906	Fernand Gonder, FRA	11-5¾		1968	Bob Seagren, USA	17-8½	OR
1908	(TIE) Edward Cooke, USA	12-2		1972	Wolfgang Nordwig, E. Ger	18-0½	OR
	& Alfred Gilbert, USA	12-2	OR	1976	Tadeusz Slusarski, POL	18-0½	=OR
1912	Harry Babcock, USA	12-11½	OR	1980	Wladyslaw Kozakiewicz, POL	18-11½	WR
1920	Frank Foss, USA	13-5	WR	1984	Pierre Quinon, FRA	18-10¼	
1924	Lee Barnes, USA	12-11½		1988	Sergey Bubka, USSR	19-4¼	OR
1928	Sabin Carr, USA	13-9¼	OR	1992	Maksim Tarasov, UT	19-0¼	
1932	Bill Miller, USA	14-1¾	OR	1996	Jean Galfione, FRA	19-5¼	OR
1936	Earle Meadows, USA	14-3¼	OR	2000	Nick Hysong, USA	19-4¼	
1948	Guinn Smith, USA	14-1¼		2004	Timothy Mack, USA	19-6¼	OR
1952	Bob Richards, USA	14-11	OR				

Long Jump

Year		Distance		Year		Distance	
1896	Ellery Clark, USA	20-10		1956	Greg Bell, USA	25-8¼	
1900	Alvin Kraenzlein, USA	23-6¾	OR	1960	Ralph Boston, USA	26-7¾	OR
1904	Meyer Prinstein, USA	24-1		1964	Lynn Davies, GBR	26-5¾	
1906	Meyer Prinstein, USA	23-7½		1968	Bob Beamon, USA	29-2½	WR
1908	Frank Irons, USA	24-6½	OR	1972	Randy Williams, USA	27-0½	
1912	Albert Gutterson, USA	24-11¼	OR	1976	Arnie Robinson, USA	27-4¾	
1920	William Petersson, SWE	23-5½		1980	Lutz Dombrowski, E. Ger	28-0¼	
1924	De Hart Hubbard, USA	24-5		1984	Carl Lewis, USA	28-0¼	
1928	Ed Hamm, USA	25-4½	OR	1988	Carl Lewis, USA	28-7¼	
1932	Ed Gordon, USA	25-0¾		1992	Carl Lewis, USA	28-5½	
1936	Jesse Owens, USA	26-5½	OR	1996	Carl Lewis, USA	27-10¾	
1948	Willie Steele, USA	25-8		2000	Ivan Pedroso, CUB	28-0¾	
1952	Jerome Biffle, USA	24-10		2004	Dwight Phillips, USA	28-2¼	

Triple Jump

Year		Distance		Year		Distance	
1896	James Connolly, USA	44-11¾		1960	Józef Schmidt, POL	55-2	
1900	Meyer Prinstein, USA	47-5¾	OR	1964	Józef Schmidt, POL	55-3½	OR
1904	Meyer Prinstein, USA	47-1		1968	Viktor Saneyev, USSR	57-0¾	WR
1906	Peter O'Connor, GBR/IRE	46-2¼		1972	Viktor Saneyev, USSR	56-11¼	
1908	Timothy Ahearne, GBR/IRE	48-11¼	OR	1976	Viktor Saneyev, USSR	56-8¾	
1912	Gustaf Lindblom, SWE	48-5¼		1980	Jack Uudmäe, USSR	56-11¼	
1920	Vilho Tuulos, FIN	47-7		1984	Al Joyner, USA	56-7½	
1924	Nick Winter, AUS	50-11¼	WR	1988	Khristo Markov, BUL	57-9¼	OR
1928	Mikio Oda, JPN	49-11		1992	Mike Conley, USA	59-7½ᵂ	OR
1932	Chuhei Nambu, JPN	51-7	WR	1996	Kenny Harrison, USA	59-4¼	OR
1936	Naoto Tajima, JPN	52-6	WR	2000	Jonathan Edwards, GBR	58-1¼	
1948	Arne Ahman, SWE	50-6¼		2004	Christian Olsson, SWE	58-4½	
1952	Adhemar da Silva, BRA	53-2¾	WR				
1956	Adhemar da Silva, BRA	53-7¾	OR				

ᵂindicates wind-aided.

Shot Put

Year		Distance		Year		Distance	
1896	Bob Garrett, USA	36-9¾		1956	Parry O'Brien, USA	60-11¼	OR
1900	Richard Sheldon, USA	46-3¼	OR	1960	Bill Nieder, USA	64-6¾	OR
1904	Ralph Rose, USA	48-7	WR	1964	Dallas Long, USA	66-8½	OR
1906	Martin Sheridan, USA	40-5¼		1968	Randy Matson, USA	67-4¾	
1908	Ralph Rose, USA	46-7½		1972	Wladyslaw Komar, POL	69-6	OR
1912	Patrick McDonald, USA	50-4	OR	1976	Udo Beyer, E. Ger	69-0¾	
1920	Ville Pörhölä, FIN	48-7¼		1980	Vladimir Kiselyov, USSR	70-0½	
1924	Bud Houser, USA	49-2¼		1984	Alessandro Andrei, ITA	69-9	
1928	John Kuck, USA	52-0¾	WR	1988	Ulf Timmermann, E. Ger	73-8¾	OR
1932	Leo Sexton, USA	52-6	OR	1992	Mike Stulce, USA	71-2½	
1936	Hans Woellke, GER	53-1¾	OR	1996	Randy Barnes, USA	70-11¼	
1948	Wilbur Thompson, USA	56-2	OR	2000	Arsi Harju, FIN	69-10¼	
1952	Parry O'Brien, USA	57-1½	OR	2004	Yuriy Bilonog, UKR	69-5¼	

Discus Throw

Year		Distance		Year		Distance	
1896	Bob Garrett, USA	95-7½		1956	Al Oerter, USA	184-11	OR
1900	Rudolf Bauer, HUN	118-3		1960	Al Oerter, USA	194-2	OR
1904	Martin Sheridan, USA	128-10½	OR	1964	Al Oerter, USA	200-1	OR
1906	Martin Sheridan, USA	136-0		1968	Al Oerter, USA	212-6	OR
1908	Martin Sheridan, USA	134-2	OR	1972	Ludvik Danek, CZE	211-3	
1912	Armas Taipale, FIN	148-3	OR	1976	Mac Wilkins, USA	221-5	
1920	Elmer Niklander, FIN	146-7		1980	Viktor Rashchupkin, USSR	218-8	
1924	Bud Houser, USA	151-4	OR	1984	Rolf Danneberg, W. Ger	218-6	
1928	Bud Houser, USA	155-3	OR	1988	Jürgen Schult, E. Ger	225-9	OR
1932	John Anderson, USA	162-4	OR	1992	Romas Ubartas, LIT	213-8	
1936	Ken Carpenter, USA	165-7	OR	1996	Lars Riedel, GER	227-8	
1948	Adolfo Consolini, ITA	173-2	OR	2000	Virgilijus Alekna, LIT	227-4	
1952	Sim Iness, USA	180-6	OR	2004	Virgilijus Alekna, LIT*	229-3	OR

*Hungary's **Robert Fazekas** had a throw of 232 feet, 8 inches, and was initially declared the winner, but he was disqualified for failing to submit to a drug test following the competition.

Hammer Throw

Year		Distance		Year		Distance	
1900	John Flanagan, USA	163-1		1960	Vasily Rudenkov, USSR	220-2	OR
1904	John Flanagan, USA	168-1	OR	1964	Romuald Klim, USSR	228-10	OR
1908	John Flanagan, USA	170-4	OR	1968	Gyula Zsivótzky, HUN	240-8	OR
1912	Matt McGrath, USA	179-7	OR	1972	Anatoly Bondarchuk, USSR	247-8	OR
1920	Pat Ryan, USA	173-5		1976	Yuri Sedykh, USSR	254-4	OR
1924	Fred Tootell, USA	174-10		1980	Yuri Sedykh, USSR	268-4	WR
1928	Pat O'Callaghan, IRE	168-7		1984	Juha Tiainen, FIN	256-2	
1932	Pat O'Callaghan, IRE	176-11		1988	Sergey Litvinov, USSR	278-2	OR
1936	Karl Hein, GER	185-4	OR	1992	Andrei Abduvaliyev, UT	270-9	
1948	Imre Németh, HUN	183-11		1996	Balazs Kiss, HUN	266-6	
1952	József Csérmák, HUN	197-11	WR	2000	Szymon Ziolkowski, POL	262-6	
1956	Harold Connolly, USA	207-3	OR	2004	Koji Murofushi, JPN*	272-0	

Hungary's **Adrian Annus** was initially awarded the gold medal for his throw of 272-11, but after questions were raised about the legitimacy of his post-competition drug test, and he failed to submit to a follow-up test, he was disqualified and stripped of the gold.

Javelin Throw

Year		Distance		Year		Distance	
1908	Eric Lemming, SWE	179-10	WR	1964	Pauli Nevala, FIN	271- 2	
1912	Eric Lemming, SWE	198-11	WR	1968	Jänis Lüsis, USSR	295- 7	OR
1920	Jonni Myyrä, FIN	215-10	OR	1972	Klaus Wolfermann, W. Ger	296-10	OR
1924	Jonni Myyrä, FIN	206- 7		1976	Miklos Németh, HUN	310- 4	WR
1928	Erik Lundkvist, SWE	218- 6	OR	1980	Dainis Kula, USSR	299- 2	
1932	Matti Järvinen, FIN	238- 6	OR	1984	Arto Härkönen, FIN	284- 8	
1936	Gerhard Stöck, GER	235- 8		1988	Tapio Korjus, FIN	276- 6	
1948	Kai Tapio Rautavaara, FIN	228-10		1992	Jan Zelezny, CZE	294- 2*	OR
1952	Cy Young, USA	242- 1	OR	1996	Jan Zelezny, CZR	289- 3	
1956	Egil Danielson, NOR	281- 2	WR	2000	Jan Zelezny, CZR	295- 10	OR
1960	Viktor Tsibulenko, USSR	277- 8		2004	Andreas Thorkildsen, NOR	283- 9	

*In 1986 the balance point of the javelin was modified and new records have been kept since.

Decathlon

Year		Points		Year		Points	
1904	Thomas Kiely, IRE	6036		1964	Willi Holdorf, GER	7887	
1906-08	Not held			1968	Bill Toomey, USA	8193	OR
1912	Jim Thorpe, USA	8412	WR	1972	Nikolai Avilov, USSR	8454	WR
1920	Helge Lövland, NOR	6803		1976	Bruce Jenner, USA	8617	WR
1924	Harold Osborn, USA	7711	WR	1980	Daley Thompson, GBR	8495	
1928	Paavo Yrjölä, FIN	8053	WR	1984	Daley Thompson, GBR	8798	=WR
1932	Jim Bausch, USA	8462	WR	1988	Christian Schenk, E. Ger	8488	
1936	Glenn Morris, USA	7900	WR	1992	Robert Zmelik, CZE	8611	
1948	Bob Mathias, USA	7139		1996	Dan O'Brien, USA	8824	
1952	Bob Mathias, USA	7887	WR	2000	Erki Nool, EST	8641	
1956	Milt Campbell, USA	7937	OR	2004	Roman Sebrle, CZE	8893	OR
1960	Rafer Johnson, USA	8392	OR				

WOMEN

At least 4 gold medals (including relays): Evelyn Ashford, Fanny Blankers-Koen, Betty Cuthbert and Bärbel Eckert Wöckel (4).

100 meters

Year		Time		Year		Time	
1928	Betty Robinson, USA	12.2	=WR	1972	Renate Stecher, E. Ger	11.07	
1932	Stella Walsh, POL*	11.9	=WR	1976	Annegret Richter, W. Ger	11.08	
1936	Helen Stephens, USA	11.5W		1980	Lyudmila Kondratyeva, USSR	11.06	
1948	Fanny Blankers-Koen, NED	11.9		1984	Evelyn Ashford, USA	10.97	OR
1952	Marjorie Jackson, AUS	11.5	=WR	1988	Florence Griffith Joyner, USA	10.54W	
1956	Betty Cuthbert, AUS	11.5		1992	Gail Devers, USA	10.82	OR
1960	Wilma Rudolph, USA	11.0W		1996	Gail Devers, USA	10.94	
1964	Wyomia Tyus, USA	11.4		2000	Marion Jones, USA	10.75	
1968	Wyomia Tyus, USA	11.08	WR	2004	Yuliya Nesterenko, BLR	10.93	

*An autopsy performed after Walsh's death in 1980 revealed that she was a man.
Windicates wind-aided.

200 meters

Year		Time		Year		Time	
1948	Fanny Blankers-Koen, NED	24.4		1980	Bärbel Eckert Wockel, E. Ger	22.03	OR
1952	Marjorie Jackson, AUS	23.7	OR	1984	Valerie Brisco-Hooks, USA	21.81	OR
1956	Betty Cuthbert, AUS	23.4	=OR	1988	Florence Griffith Joyner, USA	21.34	WR
1960	Wilma Rudolph, USA	24.0		1992	Gwen Torrence, USA	21.81	
1964	Edith McGuire, USA	23.0	OR	1996	Marie-Jose Perec, FRA	22.12	
1968	Irena Szewinska, POL	22.5	WR	2000	Marion Jones, USA	21.84	
1972	Renate Stecher, E. Ger	22.40	=WR	2004	Veronica Campbell, JAM	22.05	
1976	Bärbel Eckert, E. Ger	22.37	OR				

400 meters

Year		Time		Year		Time	
1964	Betty Cuthbert, AUS	52.0		1988	Olga Bryzgina, USSR	48.65	OR
1968	Colette Besson, FRA	52.03	=OR	1992	Marie-Jose Perec, FRA	48.83	
1972	Monika Zehrt, E. Ger	51.08	OR	1996	Marie-Jose Perec, FRA	48.25	OR
1976	Irena Szewinska, POL	49.29	WR	2000	Cathy Freeman, AUS	49.11	
1980	Marita Koch, E. Ger	48.88	OR	2004	Tonique Williams-Darling, BAH	49.41	
1984	Valerie Brisco-Hooks, USA	48.83	OR				

800 meters

Year		Time		Year		Time	
1928	Lina Radke, GER	2:16.8	WR	1980	Nadezhda Olizarenko, USSR	1:53.42	WR
1932-56	Not held			1984	Doina Melinte, ROM	1:57.60	
1960	Lyudmila Shevtsova, USSR	2:04.3	=WR	1988	Sigrun Wodars, E. Ger	1:56.10	
1964	Ann Packer, GBR	2:01.1	OR	1992	Ellen van-Langen, NED	1:55.54	
1968	Madeline Manning, USA	2:00.9	OR	1996	Svetlana Masterkova, RUS	1:57.73	
1972	Hildegard Falck, W. Ger	1:58.55	OR	2000	Maria Mutola, MOZ	1:56.15	
1976	Tatyana Kazankina, USSR	1:54.94	WR	2004	Kelly Holmes, GBR	1:56.38	

1500 meters

Year		Time		Year		Time	
1972	Lyudmila Bragina, USSR	4:01.4	**WR**	1992	Hassiba Boulmerka, ALG	3:55.30	
1976	Tatyana Kazankina, USSR	4:05.48		1996	Svetlana Masterkova, RUS	4:00.83	
1980	Tatyana Kazankina, USSR	3:56.6	**OR**	2000	Nouria Merah-Benida, ALG	4:05.10	
1984	Gabriella Dorio, ITA	4:03.25		2004	Kelly Holmes, GBR	3:57.90	
1988	Paula Ivan, ROM	3:53.96	**OR**				

5000 meters

Year		Time		Year		Time	
1984	Maricica Puica, ROM	8:35.96		1996	Wang Junxia, CHN	14:59.88	
1988	Tatyana Samolenko, USSR	8:26.53	**OR**	2000	Gabriela Szabo, ROM	14:40.79	**OR**
1992	Elena Romanova, UT	8:46.04		2004	Meseret Defar, ETH	14:45.65	

Note: Event held over 3000 meters from 1984-92.

10,000 meters

Year		Time		Year		Time	
1988	Olga Bondarenko, USSR	31:05.21	**OR**	2000	Derartu Tulu, ETH	30:17.49	**OR**
1992	Derartu Tulu, ETH	31:06.02		2004	Xing Huina, CHN	30:24.36	
1996	Fernanda Ribeiro, POR	31:01.63	**OR**				

Marathon

Year		Time	Year		Time
1984	Joan Benoit, USA	2:24:52	1996	Fatuma Roba, ETH	2:26:05
1988	Rosa Mota, POR	2:25:40	2000	Naoko Takahashi, JPN	2:23:14
1992	Valentina Yegorova, UT	2:32:41	2004	Mizuki Noguchi, JPN	2:26:20

100-meter Hurdles

Year		Time		Year		Time	
1932	Babe Didrikson, USA	11.7	**WR**	1980	Vera Komisova, USSR	12.56	**OR**
1936	Trebisonda Valla, ITA	11.7		1984	Benita Fitzgerald-Brown, USA	12.84	
1948	Fanny Blankers-Koen, NED	11.2	**OR**	1988	Yordanka Donkova, BUL	12.38	**OR**
1952	Shirley Strickland, AUS	10.9	**WR**	1992	Paraskevi Patoulidou, GRE	12.64	
1956	Shirley Strickland, AUS	10.7	**OR**	1996	Ludmila Enquist, SWE	12.58	
1960	Irina Press, USSR	10.8		2000	Olga Shishigina, KAZ	12.65	
1964	Karin Balzer, GER	10.5ᵂ		2004	Joanna Hayes, USA	12.37	**OR**
1968	Maureen Caird, AUS	10.3	**OR**				
1972	Annelie Ehrhardt, E. Ger	12.59	**WR**				
1976	Johanna Schaller, E. Ger	12.77					

ᵂindicates wind-aided.

Note: Event held over 80 meters from 1932-68.

400-meter Hurdles

Year		Time		Year		Time	
1984	Nawal El Moutawakel, MOR	54.61	**OR**	1996	Deon Hemmings, JAM	52.82	**OR**
1988	Debra Flintoff-King, AUS	53.17	**OR**	2000	Irina Privalova, RUS	53.02	
1992	Sally Gunnell, GBR	53.23		2004	Fani Halkia, GRE	52.82	

4x100-meter Relay

Year		Time		Year		Time	
1928	Canada	48.4	**WR**	1972	West Germany	42.81	**WR**
1932	United States	46.9	**WR**	1976	East Germany	42.55	**OR**
1936	United States	46.9		1980	East Germany	41.60	**WR**
1948	Holland	47.5		1984	United States	41.65	
1952	United States	45.9	**WR**	1988	United States	41.98	
1956	Australia	44.5	**WR**	1992	United States	42.11	
1960	United States	44.5		1996	United States	41.95	
1964	Poland	43.6		2000	Bahamas	42.20	
1968	United States	42.87	**WR**	2004	Jamaica	41.73	

4x400-meter Relay

Year		Time		Year		Time	
1972	East Germany	3:23.0	**WR**	1992	Unified Team	3:20.20	
1976	East Germany	3:19.23	**WR**	1996	United States	3:20.91	
1980	Soviet Union	3:20.2		2000	United States	3:22.62	
1984	United States	3:18.29	**OR**	2004	United States	3:19.01	
1988	Soviet Union	3:15.18	**WR**				

20-kilometer Walk

Year		Time	Year		Time
1992	Chen Yueling, CHN	44:32	2000	Wang Liping, CHN	1:29:05
1996	Yelena Ninikolayeva, RUS	41:49	2004	Athanasia Tsoumeleka, GRE	1:29:12

Note: Event was held over 10 kilometers from 1992-96.

Pole Vault

Year		Height		Year		Height	
2000	Stacy Dragila, USA	15-1	**OR**	2004	Yelena Isinbayeva, RUS	16-1¼	**WR**

High Jump

Year	Athlete	Height		Year	Athlete	Height	
1928	Ethel Catherwood, CAN	5-2½		1972	Ulrike Meyfarth, W. Ger	6-3½	=WR
1932	Jean Shiley, USA	5-5¼	WR	1976	Rosemarie Ackermann, E. Ger	6-4	OR
1936	Ibolya Csák, HUN	5-3		1980	Sara Simeoni, ITA	6-5½	OR
1948	Alice Coachman, USA	5-6	OR	1984	Ulrike Meyfarth, W. Ger	6-7½	OR
1952	Esther Brand, RSA	5-5¾		1988	Louise Ritter, USA	6-8	OR
1956	Mildred McDaniel, USA	5-9¼	WR	1992	Heike Henkel, GER	6-7½	
1960	Iolanda Balas, ROM	6-0¾	OR	1996	Stefka Kostadinova, BUL	6-8¾	
1964	Iolanda Balas, ROM	6-2¾	OR	2000	Yelena Yelesina, RUS	6-7	
1968	Miloslava Rezkova, CZE	5-11½		2004	Yelena Slesarenko, RUS	6-9	OR

Long Jump

Year	Athlete	Distance		Year	Athlete	Distance	
1948	Olga Gyarmati, HUN	18-8¼		1980	Tatyana Kolpakova, USSR	23-2	OR
1952	Yvette Williams, NZE	20-5¾	OR	1984	Anisoara Cusmir-Stanciu, ROM	22-10	
1956	Elzbieta Krzesinska, POL	20-10	=WR	1988	Jackie Joyner-Kersee, USA	24-3¼	OR
1960	Vyera Krepkina, USSR	20-10¾		1992	Heike Drechsler, GER	23-5¼	
1964	Mary Rand, GBR	22-2¼	WR	1996	Chioma Ajunwa, NGR	23-4½	
1968	Viorica Viscopoleanu, ROM	22-4½	WR	2000	Heike Drechsler, GER	22-11¼	
1972	Heidemarie Rosendahl, W. Ger	22-3		2004	Tatyana Lebedeva, RUS	23-2½	
1976	Angela Voigt, E. Ger	22-0¾					

Triple Jump

Year	Athlete	Distance		Year	Athlete	Distance
1996	Inessa Kravets, UKR	50-3½		2004	Francoise Mbango Etone, CMR	50-2½
2000	Tereza Marinova, BUL	49-10½				

Shot Put

Year	Athlete	Distance		Year	Athlete	Distance	
1948	Micheline Ostermeyer, FRA	45-1½		1980	Ilona Slupianek, E. Ger	73-6¼	OR
1952	Galina Zybina, USSR	50-1¾	WR	1984	Claudia Losch, W. Ger	67-2¼	
1956	Tamara Tyshkevich, USSR	54-5	OR	1988	Natalia Lisovskaya, USSR	72-11¾	
1960	Tamara Press, USSR	56-10	OR	1992	Svetlana Krivaleva, UT	69-1¼	
1964	Tamara Press, USSR	59-6¼	OR	1996	Astrid Kumbernuss, GER	67-5½	
1968	Margitta Gummel, E. Ger	64-4	WR	2000	Yanina Korolchik, BLR	67-5½	
1972	Nadezhda Chizhova, USSR	69-0	WR	2004	Yumileidi Cumba, CUB*	64-3¼	
1976	Ivanka Hristova, BUL	69-5¼	OR				

*Russia's Irina Korzhanenko (69-1¼) was stripped of the gold for failing a post-competition drug test.

Discus Throw

Year	Athlete	Distance		Year	Athlete	Distance	
1928	Halina Konopacka, POL	129-11¾	WR	1972	Faina Melnik, USSR	218-7	OR
1932	Lillian Copeland, USA	133-2	OR	1976	Evelin Schlaak, E. Ger	226-4	OR
1936	Gisela Mauermayer, GER	156-3	OR	1980	Evelin Schlaak Jahl, E. Ger	229-6	OR
1948	Micheline Ostermeyer, FRA	137-6		1984	Ria Stalman, NED	214-5	
1952	Nina Romaschkova, USSR	168-8	OR	1988	Martina Hellmann, E. Ger	237-2½	OR
1956	Olga Fikotová, CZE	176-1	OR	1992	Maritza Marten, CUB	229-10	
1960	Nina Ponomaryeva, USSR	180-9	OR	1996	Ilke Wyludda, GER	228-6	
1964	Tamara Press, USSR	187-10	OR	2000	Ellina Zvereva, BLR	224-5	
1968	Lia Manoliu, ROM	191-2	OR	2004	Natalya Sadova, RUS	219-10	

Hammer Throw

Year	Athlete	Distance		Year	Athlete	Distance	
2000	Kamila Skolimowska, POL	233-5¾		2004	Olga Kuzenkova, RUS	246-1	OR

Javelin Throw

Year	Athlete	Distance		Year	Athlete	Distance	
1932	Babe Didrikson, USA	143-4		1976	Ruth Fuchs, E. Ger	216-4	OR
1936	Tilly Fleischer, GER	148-3	OR	1980	Maria Colon Rueñes, CUB	224-5	OR
1948	Herma Bauma, AUT	149-6	OR	1984	Tessa Sanderson, GBR	228-2	OR
1952	Dana Zátopková, CZE	165-7	OR	1988	Petra Felke, E. Ger	245-0	OR
1956	Ineze Jaunzeme, USSR	176-8	OR	1992	Silke Renk, GER	224-2	
1960	Elvira Ozolina, USSR	183-8	OR	1996	Heli Rantanen, FIN	222-11	
1964	Mihaela Penes, ROM	198-7	OR	2000	Trine Hattestad, NOR	226-1	OR
1968	Angéla Németh, HUN	198-0	OR	2004	Osleidys Menendez, CUB	234-8	OR
1972	Ruth Fuchs, E. Ger	209-7	OR				

Heptathlon

Year	Athlete	Points		Year	Athlete	Points	
1964	Irina Press, USSR	5246	WR	1988	Jackie Joyner-Kersee, USA	7291	WR
1968	Ingrid Becker, W. Ger	5098		1992	Jackie Joyner-Kersee, USA	7044	
1972	Mary Peters, GBR	4801	WR	1996	Ghada Shouaa, SYR	6780	
1976	Siegrun Siegl, E. Ger	4745		2000	Denise Lewis, GBR	6584	
1980	Nadezhda Tkachenko, USSR	5083	WR	2004	Carolina Kluft, SWE	6952	
1984	Glynis Nunn, AUS	6390	OR				

Note: Seven-event Heptathlon replaced five-event Pentathlon in 1984.

All-Time Leading Medal Winners – Single Games

Athletes who have won the most medals in a single Summer Olympics. Totals include individual, relay and team medals. U.S. athletes are in **bold** type.

MEN

No		Sport	G-S-B	No		Sport	G-S-B
8†	**Michael Phelps**, USA (2004)	Swim	6-0-2	6	Takashi Ono, JPN (1960)	Gym	3-1-2
8	Aleksandr Dityatin, USSR (1980)	Gym	3-4-1	6	Viktor Chukarin, USSR (1956)	Gym	4-2-0
7	**Mark Spitz**, USA (1972)	Swim	7-0-0	6	Konrad Frey, GER (1936)	Gym	3-1-2
7	**Willis Lee**, USA (1920)	Shoot	5-1-1	6	Ville Ritola, FIN (1924)	Track	4-2-0
7	**Matt Biondi**, USA (1988)	Swim	5-1-1	6	Hubert Van Innis, BEL (1920)	Arch	4-2-0
7	Boris Shakhlin, USSR (1960)	Gym	4-2-1	6	**Carl Osburn**, USA (1920)	Shoot	4-1-1
7	**Lloyd Spooner**, USA (1920)	Shoot	4-1-2	6	Louis Richardet, SWI (1906)	Shoot	3-3-0
7	Mikhail Voronin, USSR (1968)	Gym	2-4-1	6	**Anton Heida**, USA (1904)	Gym	5-1-0
7	Nikolai Andrianov, USSR (1976)	Gym	2-4-1	6	**George Eyser**, USA (1904)	Gym	3-2-1
6	Vitaly Scherbo, UT (1992)	Gym	6-0-0	6	**Burton Downing**, USA (1904)	Cycle	2-3-1
6	Li Ning, CHN (1984)	Gym	3-2-1	6	Alexei Nemov, RUS (1996)	Gym	2-1-3
6	Akinori Nakayama, JPN (1968)	Gym	4-1-1	6	Alexei Nemov, RUS (2000)	Gym	2-1-3

†Includes gold medal as preliminary member of 1st-place relay team.

WOMEN

No		Sport	G-S-B	No		Sport	G-S-B
7	Maria Gorokhovskaya, USSR (1952)	Gym	2-5-0	5	Shane Gould, AUS (1972)	Swim	3-1-1
6	Kristin Otto, E. Ger (1988)	Swim	6-0-0	5	Nadia Comaneci, ROM (1976)	Gym	3-1-1
6	Agnes Keleti, HUN (1956)	Gym	4-2-0	5	Karin Janz, E. Ger (1972)	Gym	2-2-1
6	Vera Cáslavská, CZE (1968)	Gym	4-2-0	5	Ines Diers, E. Ger (1980)	Swim	2-2-1
6	Larisa Latynina, USSR (1956)	Gym	4-1-1	5	**Shirley Babashoff**, USA (1976)	Swim	1-4-0
6	Larisa Latynina, USSR (1960)	Gym	3-2-1	5	**Mary Lou Retton**, USA (1984)	Gym	1-2-2
6	Daniela Silivas, ROM (1988)	Gym	3-2-1	5	**Shannon Miller**, USA (1992)	Gym	0-2-3
6	Larisa Latynina, USSR (1964)	Gym	2-2-2	5	**Marion Jones**, USA (2000)	Track	3-0-2
6	Margit Korondi, HUN (1956)	Gym	1-1-4	5	**Dara Torres**, USA (2000)	Swim	2-0-3
5	Kornelia Ender, E. Ger (1976)	Swim	4-1-0	5	**Natalie Coughlin**, USA (2004)	Swim	2-2-1
5	Ecaterina Szabó, ROM (1984)	Gym	4-1-0				

All-Time Leading Medal Winners – Career

MEN

No		Sport	G-S-B	No		Sport	G-S-B
15	Nikolai Andrianov, USSR	Gymnastics	7-5-3	10	**Carl Lewis**, USA	Track/Field	9-1-0
13	Boris Shakhlin, USSR	Gymnastics	7-4-2	10	Aladár Gerevich, HUN	Fencing	7-1-2
13	Edoardo Mangiarotti, ITA	Fencing	6-5-2	10	Akinori Nakayama, JPN	Gymnastics	6-2-2
13	Takashi Ono, JPN	Gymnastics	5-4-4	10	Aleksandr Dityatin, USSR	Gymnastics	3-6-1
12	Paavo Nurmi, FIN	Track/Field	9-3-0	9	Vitaly Scherbo, BLR	Gymnastics	6-0-3
12	Sawao Kato, JPN	Gymnastics	8-3-1	9	**Gary Hall Jr.**, USA	Swimming	5-3-1
12	Alexei Nemov, RUS	Gymnastics	4-2-6	9*	**Martin Sheridan**, USA	Track/Field	5-3-1
11	**Mark Spitz**, USA	Swimming	9-1-1	9*	Zoltán Halmay, HUN	Swimming	3-5-1
11†	**Matt Biondi**, USA	Swimming	8-2-1	9	Giulio Gaudini, ITA	Fencing	3-4-2
11	Viktor Chukarin, USSR	Gymnastics	7-3-1	9	Mikhail Voronin, USSR	Gymnastics	2-6-1
11	**Carl Osburn**, USA	Shooting	5-4-2	9	Heikki Savolainen, FIN	Gymnastics	2-1-6
10*	**Ray Ewry**, USA	Track/Field	10-0-0	9	Yuri Titov, USSR	Gymnastics	1-5-3

†Includes gold medal as preliminary member of 1st-place relay team.
*Medals won by Ewry (2-0-0), Sheridan (2-3-0) and Halmay (1-1-0) at the 1906 Intercalated games are not officially recognized by the IOC.

Games Participated In

Andrianov (1972,76,80); **Biondi** (1984,88,92); **Chukarin** (1952,56); **Dityatin** (1976,80); **Ewry** (1900,04,06,08); **Gerevich** (1932,36,48,52,56,60); **Gaudini** (1928,32,36); **Hall Jr.** (1996,2000,04); **Halmay** (1900,04,06,08); **Kato** (1968,72,76); **Lewis** (1984,88,92,96); **Mangiarotti** (1936,48,52,56,60); **Nakayama** (1968,72); **Nemov** (1996,2000) **Nurmi** (1920,24,28); **Ono** (1952,56,60,64); **Osburn** (1912,20, 24); **Savolainen** (1928,32,36,48,52); **Scherbo** (1992,96): **Shakhlin** (1956,60,64); **Sheridan** (1904,06,08); **Spitz** (1968,72); **Titov** (1956,60,64); **Voronin** (1968,72).

Most Individual Medals

Not including team competition.

		Sport	G-S-B
Men:	12-Nikolai Andrianov, USSR	Gym	6-3-3
Women:	15-Larissa Latynina, USSR	Gym	7-5-3

WOMEN

No		Sport	G-S-B	No		Sport	G-S-B
18	Larissa Latynina, USSR	Gymnastics	9-5-4	8	**Shirley Babashoff**, USA	Swimming	2-6-0
12	**Jenny Thompson**, USA	Swimming	8-3-1	8	Sofia Muratova, USSR	Gymnastics	2-2-4
11	Vera Cáslavská, CZE	Gymnastics	7-4-0	8	Inge de Bruijn, NED	Swimming	4-2-2
10	Birgit Fischer, GER	Canoe/Kayak	7-3-0	7	Krisztina Egerszegi, HUN	Swimming	5-1-1
10	Agnes Keleti, HUN	Gymnastics	5-3-2	7	Irena Kirszenstein Szewinska, POL	Track/Field	3-2-2
10	Polina Astakhova, USSR	Gymnastics	5-2-3	7	Shirley Strickland, AUS	Track/Field	3-1-3
9	Nadia Comaneci, ROM	Gymnastics	5-3-1	7	Maria Gorokhovskaya, USSR	Gymnastics	2-5-0
9	Lyudmila Tourischeva, USSR	Gymnastics	4-3-2	7	Ildiko Sagine-Ujlaki-Rejto, HUN	Fencing	2-3-2
9	**Dara Torres**, USA	Swimming	4-1-4	7	**Shannon Miller**, USA	Gymnastics	2-2-3
8	Kornelia Ender, E. Ger	Swimming	4-4-0	7	Susie O'Neill, AUS	Swimming	2-4-1
8	Dawn Fraser, AUS	Swimming	4-4-0	7	Merlene Ottey, JAM	Track/Field	0-2-5

Games Participated In

Astakhova (1956,60,64); **Babashoff** (1972,76); **Cáslavská** (1960,64,68); **Comaneci** (1976,80); **de Bruijn** (2000,04); **Egerszegi** (1988,92,96); **Ender** (1972,76); **Fischer** (1980,92,96,2000); **Fraser** (1956,60,64); **Gorokhovskaya** (1952); **Keleti** (1952,56); **Latynina** (1956,60,64); **Miller** (1992,96); **Muratova** (1956,60); **O'Neill** (1996,2000) **Ottey** (1980,84,88,92,96) **Sagine-Ujlaki-Rejto** (1960,64,68,72,76); **Strickland** (1948,52,56); **Szewinska** (1964,68,72,76,80); **Thompson** (1992,96,2000,04); **Torres** (1984,88,92,2000) **Tourischeva** (1968, 72,76).

Most Gold Medals

MEN

No		Sport	G-S-B	No		Sport	G-S-B
10*	**Ray Ewry**, USA	Track/Field	10-0-0	7	Boris Shakhlin, USSR	Gymnastics	7-4-2
9	Paavo Nurmi, FIN	Track/Field	9-3-0	7	Viktor Chukarin, USSR	Gymnastics	7-3-1
9	**Mark Spitz**, USA	Swimming	9-1-1	7	Aladar Gerevich, HUN	Fencing	7-1-2
9	**Carl Lewis**, USA	Track/Field	9-1-0				
8	Sawao Kato, JPN	Gymnastics	8-3-1				
8†	**Matt Biondi**, USA	Swimming	8-2-1				
7	Nikolai Andrianov, USSR	Gymnastics	7-5-3				

*Medals won by Ewry (2-0-0) at the 1906 Intercalated games are not officially recognized by the IOC.
†Includes gold medal as preliminary member of 1st-place relay team.

WOMEN

No		Sport	G-S-B	No		Sport	G-S-B
9	Larissa Latynina, USSR	Gymnastics	9-5-4	4	Lyudmila Tourischeva, USSR	Gymnastics	4-3-2
8	**Jenny Thompson**, USA	Swimming	8-3-1	4	**Dara Torres**, USA	Swimming	4-1-4
7	Vera Cáslavská, CZE	Gymnastics	7-4-0	4	**Evelyn Ashford**, USA	Track/Field	4-1-0
7	Birgit Fischer, GER	Canoe/Kayak	7-3-0	4	**Janet Evans**, USA	Swimming	4-1-0
6†	Kristin Otto, E. Ger	Swimming	6-0-0	4	Fu Mingxia, CHN	Diving	4-1-0
6†	**Amy Van Dyken**, USA	Swimming	6-0-0	4	Fanny Blankers-Koen, NED	Track/Field	4-0-0
5	Agnes Keleti, HUN	Gymnastics	5-3-2	4	Betty Cuthbert, AUS	Track/Field	4-0-0
5	Nadia Comaneci, ROM	Gymnastics	5-3-1	4	**Pat McCormick**, USA	Diving	4-0-0
5	Polina Astakhova, USSR	Gymnastics	5-2-3	4	Bärbel Eckert Wäckel, E. Ger	Track/Field	4-0-0
5	Krisztina Egerszegi, HUN	Swimming	5-1-1	4	Inge de Bruijn, NED	Swimming	4-2-2
4	Kornelia Ender, E. Ger	Swimming	4-4-0				
4	Dawn Fraser, AUS	Swimming	4-4-0				

†Includes gold medal as preliminary member of 1st-place relay team.

All-Time Leading Medal Winners – Career (Cont.)
Most Silver Medals

MEN				WOMEN			
No		**Sport**	**G-S-B**	**No**		**Sport**	**G-S-B**
6	Alexandr Dityatin, USSR	Gymnastics	3-6-1	6	**Shirley Babashoff**, USA	Swimming	2-6-0
6	Mikhail Voronin, USSR	Gymnastics	2-6-1	5	Larissa Latynina, USSR	Gymnastics	9-5-4
5	Nikolai Andrianov, USSR	Gymnastics	7-5-3	5	Maria Gorokhovskaya, USSR	Gymnastics	2-5-0
5	Edoardo Mangiarotti, ITA	Fencing	6-5-2	4	Vera Cáslavská, CZE	Gymnastics	7-4-0
5	Zoltán Halmay, HUN	Swimming	3-5-1	4	Kornelia Ender, E. Ger	Swimming	4-4-0
5	Gustavo Marzi, ITA	Fencing	2-5-0	4	Dawn Fraser, AUS	Swimming	4-4-0
5	Yuri Titov, USSR	Gymnastics	1-5-3	4	Erica Zuchold, E. Ger	Gymnastics	0-4-1
5	Viktor Lisitsky, USSR	Gymnastics	0-5-0				

Most Bronze Medals

MEN				WOMEN			
No		**Sport**	**G-S-B**	**No**		**Sport**	**G-S-B**
6	Alexei Nemov, RUS	Gymnastics	4-2-6	5	Merlene Ottey, JAM	Track/Field	0-2-5
6	Heikki Savolainen, FIN	Gymnastics	2-1-6	4	Larissa Latynina, USSR	Gymnastics	9-5-4
5	Daniel Revenu, FRA	Fencing	1-0-5	4	**Dara Torres**, USA	Swimming	4-1-4
5	Philip Edwards, CAN	Track/Field	0-0-5	4	Sofia Muratova, USSR	Gymnastics	2-2-4
5	Adrianus Jong, NED	Fencing	0-0-5				

All-Time Leading USA Medal Winners
Most Overall Medals
MEN

No		**Sport**	**G-S-B**	**No**		**Sport**	**G-S-B**
11	Mark Spitz	Swimming	9-1-1	6	Anton Heida	Gymnastics	5-1-0
11†	Matt Biondi	Swimming	8-2-1	6	Don Schollander	Swimming	5-1-0
11	Carl Osburn	Shooting	5-4-2	6	Johnny Weissmuller	Swim/Water Polo	5-0-1
10*	Ray Ewry	Track/Field	10-0-0	6	Alfred Lane	Shooting	5-0-1
10	Carl Lewis	Track/Field	9-1-0	6	Jim Lightbody	Track/Field	4-2-0
9	Gary Hall Jr.	Swimming	5-3-1	6	George Eyser	Gymnastics	3-2-1
9*	Martin Sheridan	Track/Field	5-3-1	6	Ralph Rose	Track/Field	3-2-1
8†	Michael Phelps	Swimming	6-0-2	6	Michael Plumb	Equestrian	2-4-0
8	Charles Daniels	Swimming	5-1-2	6	Burton Downing	Cycling	2-3-1
7‡	Tom Jager	Swimming	5-1-1	6	Bob Garrett	Track/Field	2-2-2
7	Willis Lee	Shooting	5-1-1				
7	Lloyd Spooner	Shooting	4-1-2				

†Includes gold medal as prelim. member of 1st-place relay team.
*Medals won by Ewry (2-0-0) and Sheridan (2-3-0) at the 1906 Intercalated games are not officially recognized by the IOC.
‡Includes 3 gold medals as prelim. member of 1st-place relay teams.

Games Participated In

Biondi (1984,88,92); **Daniels** (1904,06,08); **Downing** (1904); **Ewry** (1900,04,06,08); **Eyser** (1904); **Garrett** (1896,1900); **Hall Jr.** (1996,2000,04) **Heida** (1904); **Jager** (1984,88,92); **Lane** (1912,20); **Lee** (1920); **Lewis** (1984,88,92,96); **Lightbody** (1904,06); **Osburn** (1912,20,24); **Phelps** (2004), **Plumb** (1960, 64,68,72,76,84); **Rose** (1904,08,12); **Schollander** (1964, 68); **Sheridan** (1904,06,08); **Spitz** (1968,72); **Spooner** (1920); **Weissmuller** (1924,28).

WOMEN

No		**Sport**	**G-S-B**	**No**		**Sport**	**G-S-B**
12	Jenny Thompson	Swimming	8-3-1	5	Evelyn Ashford	Track/Field	4-1-0
9	Dara Torres	Swimming	4-1-4	5	Janet Evans	Swimming	4-1-0
8	Shirley Babashoff	Swimming	2-6-0	5	Florence Griffith Joyner	Track/Field	3-2-0
7	Shannon Miller	Gymnastics	2-2-3	5†	Mary T. Meagher	Swimming	3-1-1
7	Amanda Beard	Swimming	2-4-1	5	Gwen Torrence	Track/Field	3-2-0
6†	Amy Van Dyken	Swimming	6-0-0	5	Marion Jones	Track/Field	3-0-2
6	Jackie Joyner-Kersee	Track/Field	3-1-2	5	Mary Lou Retton	Gymnastics	1-2-2
6	Angel Martino	Swimming	3-0-3	5	Natalie Coughlin	Swimming	2-2-1

†Includes gold medal as prelim. member of 1st-place relay team.

Games Participated In

Ashford (1976,84,88,92); **Babashoff** (1972,76); **Beard** (1996,2000,04); **Coughlin** (2004), **Evans** (1988,92,96); **Griffith Joyner** (1984,88); **Jones** (2000); **Joyner-Kersee** (1984,88,92,96); **Martino** (1992,96); **McCormick** (1952,56); **Meagher** (1984,88); **Miller** (1992, 96); **Retton** (1984); **Thompson** (1988,92,96,2000,04); **Torrence** (1988,92,96); **Torres** (1984,88,92,2000); **Van Dyken** (1996,2000).

Most Gold Medals

MEN

No		Sport	G-S-B
10*	Raymond Ewry	Track/Field	10-0-0
9	Mark Spitz	Swimming	9-1-1
9	Carl Lewis	Track/Field	9-1-0
8†	Matt Biondi	Swimming	8-2-1
6†	Michael Phelps	Swimming	6-0-2
5	Carl Osburn	Shooting	5-4-2
5*	Martin Sheridan	Track/Field	5-3-1
5	Charles Daniels	Swimming	5-1-2
5‡	Tom Jager	Swimming	5-1-1
5	Willis Lee	Shooting	5-1-1
5	Anton Heida	Gymnastics	5-1-0
5	Don Schollander	Swimming	5-1-0
5	Johnny Weissmuller	Swim/Water Polo	5-0-1
5	Alfred Lane	Shooting	5-0-1
5	Morris Fisher	Shooting	5-0-0
5	Gary Hall Jr.	Swimming	5-3-1
4	Jim Lightbody	Track/Field	4-2-0
4	Lloyd Spooner	Shooting	4-1-2
4	Greg Louganis	Diving	4-1-0
4	John Naber	Swimming	4-1-0
4	Meyer Prinstein	Track/Field	4-1-0
4	Mel Sheppard	Track/Field	4-1-0
4	Marcus Hurley	Cycling	4-0-1
4†	Jon Olsen	Swimming	4-0-1
4	Archie Hahn	Track/Field	4-0-0
4	Alvin Kraenzlein	Track/Field	4-0-0
4	Al Oerter	Track/Field	4-0-0
4	Jesse Owens	Track/Field	4-0-0

*Medals won by Ewry (2-0-0) and Sheridan (2-3-0) at the 1906 Intercalated games are not officially recognized by the IOC.
†Includes gold medal as preliminary member of 1st-place relay team.
‡Includes 3 gold medals as preliminary member of 1st-place relay teams.

WOMEN

No		Sport	G-S-B
8	Jenny Thompson	Swimming	8-3-1
6†	Amy Van Dyken	Swimming	6-0-0
4	Dara Torres	Swimming	4-1-4
4	Evelyn Ashford	Track/Field	4-1-0
4	Janet Evans	Swimming	4-1-0
4	Pat McCormick	Diving	4-0-0
3	Florence Griffith Joyner	Track/Field	3-2-0
3	Jackie Joyner-Kersee	Track/Field	3-1-2
3†	Mary T. Meagher	Swimming	3-1-1
3	Gwen Torrence	Track/Field	3-1-1
3	Marion Jones	Track/Field	3-0-2
3	Valerie Brisco-Hooks	Track/Field	3-1-0
3	Nancy Hogshead	Swimming	3-1-0
3	Sharon Stouder	Swimming	3-1-0
3	Wyomia Tyus	Track/Field	3-1-0
3	Chris von Saltza	Swimming	3-1-0
3	Wilma Rudolph	Track/Field	3-0-1
3	Melissa Belote	Swimming	3-0-0
3	Ethelda Bleibtrey	Swimming	3-0-0
3	Tracy Caulkins	Swimming	3-0-0
3†	Nicole Haislett	Swimming	3-0-0
3	Helen Madison	Swimming	3-0-0
3	Debbie Meyer	Swimming	3-0-0
3	Sandra Neilson	Swimming	3-0-0
3	Martha Norelius	Swimming	3-0-0
3†	Carrie Steinseifer	Swimming	3-0-0
3‡	Ashley Tappin	Swimming	3-0-0

†Includes gold medal as preliminary member of 1st-place relay team.
‡Includes 3 gold medals as preliminary member of 1st-place relay teams

Most Silver Medals

MEN

No		Sport	G-S-B		No		Sport	G-S-B
4	Carl Osburn	Shooting	5-4-2		3	Earl Thomson	Equestrian	2-3-0
4	Michael Plumb	Equestrian	2-4-0		3	Alexander McKee	Swimming	0-3-0
3	Martin Sheridan	Track/Field	5-3-1					
3	Burton Downing	Cycling	2-3-1			**WOMEN**		
3	Irving Baxter	Track/Field	2-3-0		**No**		**Sport**	**G-S-B**
					6	Shirley Babashoff	Swimming	2-6-0

All-Time Medal Standings, 1896-2004

All-time Summer Games medal standings, based on *The Golden Book of the Olympic Games*. Medal counts include the 1906 Intercalated Games, which are not recognized by the IOC.

		G	S	B	Total			G	S	B	Total
1	**United States**	907	697	615	2219	19	Netherlands	65	76	94	234
2	USSR (1952-88)	395	319	296	1010	20	Bulgaria	50	83	74	207
3	Great Britain	189	242	237	668	21	Switzerland	48	76	64	188
4	France	199	202	230	631	22	South Korea	55	64	65	184
5	Italy	189	154	168	511	23	Denmark	42	63	64	169
6	Germany (1896-64,92–) ..	151	154	178	483	24	Cuba	64	51	49	164
7	Sweden	140	157	179	476	25	Belgium	38	51	54	143
8	Hungary	158	141	161	460	26	Czechoslovakia (1924-92)	49	49	44	142
9	East Germany (1968-88) ..	159	150	136	445		Greece	38	54	50	142
10	Australia	119	126	154	399	28	Norway	54	44	42	140
11	Japan	113	106	114	333	29	Unified Team (1992)	45	38	29	112
12	West Germany (1968-88) ..	77	104	120	301	30	Spain	28	39	27	94
13	Finland	101	83	114	298	31	Yugoslavia (1924-88,96-2000)	28	32	33	93
14	China	112	96	78	286		Austria	22	36	35	93
15	Romania	82	88	114	284	33	New Zealand	33	14	32	79
16	Poland	59	74	118	251	34	Brazil	16	22	38	76
17	Russia (1896-1912, 96–) ..	85	79	84	248	35	Turkey	36	19	19	74
18	Canada	54	87	101	242	36	Rep. of S. Africa (1904-60, 92–)	20	23	26	69

All-Time Medal Standings, 1896-2004 (Cont.)

		G	S	B	Total
37	Kenya	17	24	20	61
38	Argentina	15	23	22	60
39	Mexico	10	18	23	51
40	Iran	10	15	21	46
	Ukraine	12	15	19	46
42	Jamaica	7	21	14	42
43	North Korea	8	11	16	35
44	Belarus	5	9	18	32
45	Ethiopia	14	5	12	31
46	Estonia	8	7	14	29
47	Czech Republic	7	9	11	27
48	Ireland	9	6	6	21
	Egypt	7	6	8	21
50	Great Britain/Ireland	6	11	3	20
	Portugal	3	6	11	20
	Indonesia	5	8	7	20
53	Nigeria	2	8	9	19
	Morocco	6	4	9	19
55	India	8	4	5	17
	Thailand	5	2	10	17
57	Mongolia	0	5	10	15
	Chinese Taipei	2	6	7	15
	Kazakhstan	4	8	3	15
60	Latvia	1	10	3	14
	Slovakia	4	6	4	14
62	Algeria	4	1	7	12
	Trinidad & Tobago	1	3	8	12
	Lithuania	4	2	6	12
	Chile	2	6	4	12
	Georgia	2	2	8	12
	Croatia	3	4	5	12
68	Uzbekistan	3	3	5	11
69	Pakistan	3	3	4	10
	Uruguay	2	2	6	10
	Venezuela	1	2	7	10
	Slovenia	2	3	5	10
73	Azerbaijan	3	1	5	9
	Philippines	0	2	7	9
75	Bahamas	3	2	3	8
	Colombia	1	2	5	8
77	Uganda	1	3	2	6
	Tunisia	1	2	3	6
	Bohemia	0	1	5	6
	Puerto Rico	0	1	5	6
	Israel	1	1	4	6
82	Cameroon	2	1	1	4
	Zimbabwe	2	1	1	4
	Peru	1	3	0	4
	Costa Rica	1	1	2	4
	Namibia	0	4	0	4
	Lebanon	0	2	2	4
	Moldova	0	2	2	4
	Ghana	0	1	3	4
90	Luxembourg	2	1	0	3
	Armenia	1	1	1	3
	Iceland	0	1	2	3
	Malaysia	0	1	2	3
	Syria	1	1	1	3
95	Hong Kong	1	1	0	2
	Dominican Republic	1	0	1	2
	Japan/Korea	1	0	1	2
	Mozambique	1	0	1	2
	Surinam	1	0	1	2
	Serbia & Montenegro	0	2	0	2
	Tanzania	0	2	0	2
	Great Britain/USA	0	1	1	2
	Haiti	0	1	1	2
	Russia/Estonia	0	1	1	2
	Saudi Arabia	0	1	1	2
	United Arab Republic	0	1	1	2
	Zambia	0	1	1	2
	The Antilles	0	0	2	2
	Panama	0	0	2	2
	Qatar	0	0	2	2
111	Australia/New Zealand	1	0	0	1
	Burkina Faso	1	0	0	1
	Cuba/USA	1	0	0	1
	Denmark/Sweden	1	0	0	1
	Ecuador	1	0	0	1
	Gr. Britain/Ireland/Germany	1	0	0	1
	Gr. Britain/Ireland/USA	1	0	0	1
	Ireland/USA	1	0	0	1
	United Arab Emirates	1	0	0	1
	Belgium/Greece	0	1	0	1
	Ceylon	0	1	0	1
	France/USA	0	1	0	1
	France/Gr. Britain/Ireland	0	1	0	1
	Ivory Coast	0	1	0	1
	Netherlands Antilles	0	1	0	1
	Paraguay	0	1	0	1
	Senegal	0	1	0	1
	Singapore	0	1	0	1
	Smyrna	0	1	0	1
	Tonga	0	1	0	1
	Vietnam	0	1	0	1
	Virgin Islands	0	1	0	1
	Australia/Great Britain	0	0	1	1
	Barbados	0	0	1	1
	Bermuda	0	0	1	1
	Bohemia/Great Britain	0	0	1	1
	Djibouti	0	0	1	1
	Eritrea	0	0	1	1
	France/Great Britain	0	0	1	1
	Guyana	0	0	1	1
	Iraq	0	0	1	1
	Kuwait	0	0	1	1
	Kyrgyzstan	0	0	1	1
	Macedonia	0	0	1	1
	Mexico/Spain	0	0	1	1
	Niger	0	0	1	1
	Scotland	0	0	1	1
	Sri Lanka	0	0	1	1
	Thessalonika	0	0	1	1
	Wales	0	0	1	1

Combined totals:	G	S	B	Total
USSR/UT/Russia	525	436	409	1370
Germany/E. Ger/W. Ger	388	408	434	1230

Notes: Athletes from the USSR participated in the Summer Games from 1952-88, returned as the Unified Team in 1992 after the breakup of the Soviet Union (in 1991) and have competed as independent republics since the 1994 Winter Games. Germany was barred from the Olympics in 1924 and 1948 following World Wars I and II. Divided into East and West Germany after WWII, both countries competed together from 1952-64, then separately from 1968-88. Germany was reunified in 1990. Czechoslovakia split into Slovakia and the Czech Republic in 1993. Croatia and Bosnia-Herzegovina gained independence from Yugoslavia in 1991. Yugoslavia was not invited to the 1992 games (though Serbian and Montenegrin athletes were allowed to compete as independent athletes) but returned in 1996 and competed under the name Serbia & Montenegro starting in 2004. South Africa was banned from 1964-88 for using the apartheid policy in the selection of its teams. It returned in 1992 as the Republic of South Africa (RSA).

SOCCER

The **World Cup** came to **Germany** in 2006 and the flag-waving fans came out to celebrate a nation.

DAS BOOT

Behind a nearly impregnable defense Italy ruled in Germany, bringing a fourth World Cup back to "The Boot" while Zinedine Zidane ended his career with a troubling on-field outburst.

THE VIDEO CLIP THAT WILL ENDURE forever from the 2006 World Cup is Zinedine Zidane viciously head-butting Italian defender Marco Materazzi in extra time of the final.

In an instant, an entire world was distracted from what had been a month-long struggle for the most coveted trophy in sports. That is what happens when one of the game's all-time greats, playing in his final international game, momentarily loses his mind and gets sent off the pitch with only minutes remaining until penalty kicks.

Would Zidane have been a difference-maker in the penalty shootout, which ultimately went to Italy by a 5-3 score?

No one will ever know.

Just as no one will ever know for sure what Materazzi said to set Zidane off (Zidane said Materazzi called his family terrorists, Materazzi says he said only he'd rather have Zidane's sister's shirt than Zizou's).

What the world does know, for sure, is that it was the most bizarre ending ever to a Cup final.

Perhaps it was fitting, in a way, that the 2006 FIFA World Cup, which was expertly hosted by Germany, ended in such an odd way. From start to finish, it was hard to decide whether this was a thrilling tournament, a boring one, or just a weird one.

For every sizzler in the opening round, like Germany's opening 4-2 victory over Costa Rica and Holland's 2-1 triumph over Ivory Coast, you had a snoozer like England's 1-0 victory over Paraguay or France's inexplicable goalless draw with Switzerland. "The ball is round," as they say, so anything can happen. And so it did.

Just ask a U.S. squad that came to Germany with high—perahps

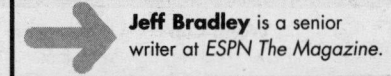
Jeff Bradley is a senior writer at *ESPN The Magazine*.

AP / Wide World Photos

Italy's **Marco Materazzi** said something, that's for sure. Whatever it was, he felt the wrath and forehead of France's Zinedine.

too high—hopes of improving upon its quarterfinal showing in 2002. Five minutes into their opening match with the Czech Republic, the U.S. players and coaches realized they weren't in South Korea anymore. That's when six-foot-seven Czech striker Jan Koller headed a ball past goalkeeper Kasey Keller. The Czechs continued the onslaught and won the game 3-0. It wouldn't get much better either. In fact, the U.S. seemed to be playing catch-up for the rest of the opening round.

Even after a hardfought 1-1 draw with Italy, in a match that saw the Americans play nine against 10 for the entire second half, the U.S. could not muster the attack necessary to beat Ghana and advance to the second round, losing their third and final match, 2-1.

The three-and-out showing marked the end of coach Bruce Arena's eight-year reign as head coach and left American soccer fans wondering who'd be put in charge next.

Host Germany, coached by energetic former player Juergen Klinsmann, rewarded its hard partying fans with some brilliant attacking play. Argentina, thanks to the goal of the tournament, a rocket-volley off the left foot of Maxi Rodriguez in extra time against Mexico, provided hope

Italy and Fabio Cannavaro got a close look at the **World Cup trophy** after beating France 5-3 on penalty kicks following a hard-hitting 1-1 draw in the World Cup final.

shutout of Ukraine. The semifinal vs. Germany looked to be headed for penalties when the Italians scored two goals late into extra time to stun the hosts. Waiting for the Italians in the final was France, the 1998 champions who were trying to recapture glory after their famous collapse of 2002 in which they failed to score a single goal. They were well on their way after their 1-0 win over tournament favorite Brazil in the quarterfinals.

And it was the French, in fact, Zidane, who would score the first goal in the final on a penalty kick in the seventh minute, to force Italy to attack. Italy was up to the challenge of changing tactics, however, and equalized the match through Materazzi just 12 minutes later. Defense took over from there, with Buffon turning himself into a human wall in front of Italy's net.

When Buffon turned back a Zidane header in extra time, penalties seemed inevitable, though no one could foresee the French having to go without their greatest play-maker and captain. Then came the moment of madness. And a red card.

And the video clip that will forever mark the 2006 World Cup.

that this would be a World Cup remembered for goals and excitement. However, lurking in the background was Italy and a defense that was impenetrable.

In the first round, the only goal Italy and goalkeeper Gianluigi Buffon allowed was an own goal in their draw with the U.S. In the second round, they clamped down even tighter. A 1-0 triumph over Australia was followed by a 3-0

AP/Wide World Photos

JEFF BRADLEY'S

10

Greatest Stories of the Year in Soccer.

10 Portland women capture second NCAA crown. With a 4-0 destruction of UCLA in the Women's College Cup final, the University of Portland becomes just the second school to go undefeated and win the title. The only other school to pull the feat, North Carolina, did it 10 times.

09 Donovan Leads LA to Double. They seemed to be sleep-walking through much of the regular season, but when tournament time came, the Los Angeles Galaxy and Landon Donovan knew how to push the right buttons, claiming both the U.S. Open Cup and MLS Cup titles in 2005. For Donovan, who returned to MLS after a brief spell with Leverkusen in Germany, it was his third MLS Cup title in five seasons.

08 Brazil's European Curse Continues. They seemingly always enter the World Cup as favorites, and with players like Ronaldinho and Adriano, 2006

was no different. But when Brazil was defeated in the quarterfinals, 1-0 by France, their streak of having not won a World Cup in Europe since 1958 remained intact.

07 Chelsea Defends Premiership Crown. The big-spending Blues, led by captain John Terry and midfielder Frank Lampard, equal their record-setting total of 29 victories and become just the fifth club since World War II to win back-to-back championships in England's top division.

06 Red Bull buys MetroStars. Just weeks before the start of Major League Soccer's 11th season, Red Bull, the Austrian energy drink company, shocked the American game by purchasing the MetroStars and a piece of their new stadium in Harrison, N.J., for $100 million, and promptly re-named the team Red Bull New York. After the World Cup the club hired new unemployed coach Bruce Arena and rumors began to circulate that they were trying to lure a world star like Ronaldo, Luis Figo or David Beckham.

05 Barcelona wins Champions League. Trailing Chelsea 1-0, in a crazy final that saw Arsenal's goalkeeper Jens Lehmann sent off in the 18th minute, Barca roars back with two late goals, both set up by 60th minute substitute Henrik

Larsson, to claim the UEFA Champions League title at Stade de France in Paris.

04 Arena Era Ends. Coming off a quarterfinal showing in the 2002 World Cup, perhaps expectations were too high for the U.S. national team, who were drawn into a group that included the Czech Republic, Italy and Ghana. Following a 3-0 drubbing at the hands of the Czechs, coach Bruce Arena's squad showed its pride, earning a hardfought 1-1 draw with Italy, despite having to play nine against 10 for nearly the entire second half. At the conclusion of the tournament, Arena's contract is not renewed, bringing an end to a highly-successful eight-year run.

03 Scandal Rocks Italy. In May of 2000, Italian police uncovered a match-fixing scandal, implicating league champions Juventus, and other major teams including A.C. Milan, Fiorentina, Lazio, and Reggina. A number of telephone interceptions showed a thick network of relations between team managers and the referees organization. Juventus were the champions of Serie A at the time. The teams have been accused of rigging games by selecting favorable referees. In the end, Juventus, Lazio and A.C. Milan were all dealt penalties, the most severe being a 30-point penalty on Juve that forced the champions down into Serie B.

02 Zidane Ejected. With but 10 minutes remaining in extra-time and penalties looming, Zinedine Zidane, one of the greatest footballers of all-time, loses his mind. Triggered by some trash talk from Marco Materazzi, Zidane drives his forehead into the Italian defender's chest, earning a straight red card that leaves the French without their greatest star heading into a fatal shootout.

01 Italy wins World Cup. Scandal? What scandal? As much as people want to believe the match-fixing allegations in Italy will drag down the national team, coach Marcelo Lippi's squad plays lock-down defense (allowing only one goal in group play) in front of goalkeeper Gianluigi Buffon and gets enough timely goals to win its fourth World Cup. In the final, the Italians, notorious for losing in penalty kicks, best France 5-3 in the tiebreaker to claim the title.

Italian goalkeeper **Gianluigi Buffon** was a huge part of Italy's 2006 World Cup run. The last Italian keeper to win a World Cup was the legendary Dino Zoff. **>> Did you know** that Zoff, who captained Italy to victory at the 1982 World Cup at age 40 holds the record for the oldest player to win the World Cup?

DID YOU KNOW?

2005-2006
Season in Review

ESPN
SPORTS ALMANAC

2006 FIFA World Cup Tournament

The FIFA World Cup is held every four years to determine the best national team in the world. In 2006 it was contested for the 18th time since its inception in 1930. Held June 9-July 9, 2006 in Germany.

First Round

Round robin; each team played the other three teams in its group once. Note that three points were awarded for a win and one point for a tie. (*) indicates team advanced to second round.

Group A	W	L	T	Pts	GF	GA
*Germany	3	0	0	9	8	2
*Ecuador	2	1	0	6	5	3
Poland	1	2	0	3	2	4
Costa Rica	0	3	0	0	3	9

Results

Date	Site	Result
June 9	Munich	Germany 4, Costa Rica 2
June 9	Gelsenkirchen	Ecuador 2, Poland 0
June 14	Dortmund	Germany 1, Poland 0
June 15	Hamburg	Ecuador 3, Costa Rica 0
June 20	Berlin	Germany 3, Ecuador 0
June 20	Hanover	Poland 2, Costa Rica 1

Group B	W	L	T	Pts	GF	GA
*England	2	0	1	7	5	2
*Sweden	1	0	2	5	3	2
Paraguay	1	2	0	3	2	2
Trinidad & Tobago	0	2	1	1	0	4

Results

Date	Site	Result
June 10	Frankfurt	England 1, Paraguay 0
June 10	Dortmund	Trinidad & Tobago 0, Sweden 0
June 15	Nuremberg	England 2, Trinidad & Tobago 0
June 15	Berlin	Sweden 1, Paraguay 0
June 20	Cologne	Sweden 2, England 2
June 20	Kaiserslautern	Paraguay 2, Trinidad & Tobago 0

Group C	W	L	T	Pts	GF	GA
*Argentina	2	0	1	7	8	1
*Netherlands	2	0	1	7	3	1
Ivory Coast	1	2	0	3	5	6
Serbia & Montenegro	0	3	0	0	2	10

Results

Date	Site	Result
June 10	Hamburg	Argentina 2, Ivory Coast 1
June 11	Leipzig	Netherlands 1, Serbia & Mont. 0
June 16	Gelsenkirchen	Argentina 6, Serbia & Mont. 0
June 16	Stuttgart	Netherlands 2, Ivory Coast 1
June 21	Frankfurt	Netherlands 0, Argentina 0
June 22	Munich	Ivory Coast 3, Serbia & Mont. 2

Group D	W	L	T	Pts	GF	GA
*Portugal	3	0	0	9	5	1
*Mexico	1	1	1	4	4	3
Angola	0	1	2	2	1	2
Iran	0	2	1	1	2	6

Results

Date	Site	Result
June 11	Nuremberg	Mexico 3, Iran 1
June 11	Cologne	Portugal 1, Angola 0
June 16	Hanover	Mexico 0, Angola 0
June 17	Frankfurt	Portugal 2, Iran 0
June 21	Gelsenkirchen	Portugal 2, Mexico 1
June 21	Leipzig	Iran 1, Angola 1

Group E	W	L	T	Pts	GF	GA
*Italy	2	0	1	7	5	1
*Ghana	2	1	0	6	4	3
Czech Republic	1	2	0	3	3	4
USA	0	2	1	1	2	6

Results

Date	Site	Result
June 12	Hanover	Italy 2, Ghana 0
June 12	Gelsenkirchen	Czech Republic 3, USA 0
June 17	Kaiserslautern	Italy 1, USA 1
June 17	Cologne	Ghana 2, Czech Republic 0
June 22	Hamburg	Italy 2, Czech Republic 0
June 22	Nuremberg	Ghana 2, USA 1

Group F	W	L	T	Pts	GF	GA
*Brazil	3	0	0	9	7	1
*Australia	1	1	1	4	5	5
Croatia	0	1	2	2	2	3
Japan	0	2	1	1	2	7

Results

Date	Site	Result
June 12	Kaiserslautern	Australia 3, Japan 1
June 13	Berlin	Brazil 1, Croatia 0
June 18	Munich	Brazil 2, Australia 0
June 18	Nuremberg	Japan 0, Croatia 0
June 22	Dortmund	Brazil 4, Japan 1
June 22	Stuttgart	Croatia 2, Australia 2

Group G	W	L	T	Pts	GF	GA
*Switzerland	2	0	1	7	4	0
*France	1	0	2	5	3	1
South Korea	1	1	1	4	3	4
Togo	0	3	0	0	1	6

Results

Date	Site	Result
June 13	Stuttgart	France 0, Switzerland 0
June 13	Frankfurt	South Korea 2, Togo 1
June 18	Leipzig	France 1, South Korea 1
June 19	Dortmund	Switzerland 2, Togo 0
June 23	Cologne	France 2, Togo 0
June 23	Hanover	Switzerland 2, South Korea 0

Group H	W	L	T	Pts	GF	GA
*Spain	3	0	0	9	8	1
*Ukraine	2	1	0	6	5	4
Tunisia	0	2	1	1	3	6
Saudi Arabia	0	2	1	1	2	7

Results

Date	Site	Result
June 14	Leipzig	Spain 4, Ukraine 0
June 14	Munich	Tunisia 2, Saudi Arabia 2
June 19	Stuttgart	Spain 1, Tunisia 0
June 19	Hamburg	Ukraine 3, Saudi Arabia 0
June 23	Kaiserslautern	Spain 1, Saudi Arabia 0
June 23	Berlin	Ukraine 1, Tunisia 0

2006 FIFA World Cup

| ROUND of 16 | QUARTERS | SEMIS | | SEMIS | QUARTERS | ROUND of 16 |

```
Germany      2
              Germany 1 (4)                                            England      1
Sweden       0                                      England  0 (1)
              Germany 0                                               Ecuador      0
Argentina    2                      Portugal   0
              Argentina 1 (2)                                          Portugal     1
Mexico       1                                      Portugal 0 (3)
                                                                      Netherlands  0
Italy        1
              Italy      3          Italy    1 (5)                     Brazil       3
Australia    0                      France   1 (3)    Brazil   0
              Italy      2                                            Ghana        0
Switzerland 0 (0)                              France   1
              Ukraine    0          THIRD PLACE GAME                   Spain        1
Ukraine     0 (3)                   Germany    3      France   1
                                    Portugal   1                      France       3
```

Round of 16
single elimination

Date	Site	Result
June 24	Munich	Germany 2, Sweden 0
June 24	Leipzig	Argentina 2, Mexico 1 OT
June 25	Stuttgart	England 1, Ecuador 0
June 25	Nuremberg	Portugal 1, Netherlands 0
June 26	Kaiserslautern	Italy 1, Australia 0
June 26	Cologne	Switzerland 0, Ukraine 0
	Ukraine advances on shoot-out, 3-0	
June 27	Dortmund	Brazil 3, Ghana 0
June 27	Hanover	France 3, Spain 1

Quarterfinals

Date	Site	Result
June 30	Berlin	Germany 1, Argentina 1
	Germany advances on shoot-out, 4-2	
June 30	Hamburg	Italy 3, Ukraine 0
July 1	Gelsenkirchen	England 0, Portugal 0
	Portugal advances on shoot-out, 3-1	
July 1	Frankfurt	France 1, Brazil 0

Semifinals

Date	Site	Result
July 4	Dortmund	Italy 2, Germany 0 OT
July 5	Munich	France 1, Portgual 0

Third Place

Date	Site	Result
July 8	Stuttgart	Germany 3, Portugal 1

Tournament Leaders

Leading Goal Scorers	Gms	Goals
Miroslav Klose, Germany	.7	5
Hernan Crespo, Argentina	.4	3
Ronaldo, Brazil	.5	3
Zinedine Zidane, France	.6	3
David Villa, Spain	.4	3
Fernando Torres, Spain	.4	3
Maxi Rodriguez, Argentina	.5	3
Thierry Henry, France	.7	3
Lukas Podolski, Germany	.7	3

Most Valuable Player Voting	Points
Zinedine Zidane, France	.2012
Fabio Cannavaro, Italy	.1977
Andrea Pirlo, Italy	.715

World Cup Final
Italy 1, France 1

Final played July 9 at Olympic Stadium in Berlin, Germany. **Attendance:** 69,000. **Coaches:** Marcello Lippi, Italy; Raymond Domenech, France. **Referee:** Horacio Elizondo (Argentina); **Assistants:** Dario Garcia (Argentina), Rodolfo Otero (Argentina).

	1	2	1OT	2OT		F
Italy	1	0	0	0	—	1
France	1	0	0	0	—	1

Scoring
FRANCE—Zinedine Zidane (7th, penalty kick); ITALY—Marco Materazzi (19th).

Penalty Shoot-out

Italy		France	
Andrea Pirlo	Goal	Sylvian Wiltord	Goal
Marco Materazzi	Goal	David Trezeguet	Crossbar
Daniele De Rossi	Goal	Eric Abidal	Goal
Alessandro Del Piero	Goal	Willy Sagnol	Goal
Fabio Grosso	Goal		

Italy wins World Cup on shoot-out, 5-3

Italy		France	
1	Gianluigi Buffon GK	16	Fabien Barthez GK
3	Fabio Gross	3	Eric Abidal
5	Fabio Cannavaro*	4	Patrick Vieira
8	Gennaro Gattuso	18	Alou Diarra (56')
9	Luca Toni	5	William Gallas
10	Francesco Totti	6	Claude Makelele
	4 Daniele De Rossi (61')	7	Florent Malouda
16	Mauro Camoranesi	10	Zinedine Zidane*
	7 Alessandro Del Piero (86')	12	Thierry Henry
19	Gianluca Zambrotta	11	S. Wiltord (107')
20	Simone Perrotta	15	Lilian Thuram
	15 Vincenzo Iaquinta	19	Willy Sagnol
21	Andrea Pirlo	22	Frank Ribery
23	Marco Materazzi		20 D. Trezeguet (100')

*team captain

Yellow Cards	Yellow Cards
Gianluca Zambrotta (5')	Willy Sagnol (12')
	Claude Makelele (76')
	Florent Malouda (111')

Red Cards
Zinedine Zidane (110')

FIFA Top 50 World Rankings

FIFA announced a new monthly world ranking system on Aug. 13, 1993 designed to "provide a constant international comparison of national team performances." The rankings are based on a mathematical formula that weighs strength of schedule, importance of matches and goals scored for and against. Games considered include World Cup qualifying and final rounds, Continental championship qualifying and final rounds, and friendly matches.

The formula was altered slightly in January 1999. Now the rankings annually take into account a team's seven best matches of the last eight years, thereby favoring some teams that have been consistent over a long period of time but that may have stumbled just recently. At the end of the year, FIFA designates a Team of the Year. Teams of the Year so far have been Germany (1993), Brazil (1994-2000, 2002-05) and France (2001). The USA reached their highest-ever ranking (6th) in July 2005.

2005

#	Team	Points	2004 Rank	#	Team	Points	2004 Rank	#	Team	Points	2004 Rank
1	Brazil	840	1	18	Uruguay	706	16	35	Switzerland	656	51
2	Czech Republic	796	4	19	Iran	703	20	36	Morocco	655	33
3	Netherlands	791	6	20	Croatia	701	23	37	Ecuador	651	39
4	Argentina	772	3	21	Costa Rica	699	27	38	Norway	649	35
5	Mexico	768	7	22	Poland	696	25	39	Bulgaria	638	37
	Spain	768	5	23	Cameroon	695	23	40	Ukraine	630	57
	France	768	2	24	Colombia	692	26	41	Honduras	628	59
8	USA	767	11		Nigeria	692	21	42	Jamaica	626	50
9	England	757	8		Ireland	692	12		Ivory Coast	626	40
10	Portugal	754	9	27	Romania	686	29	44	Israel	622	48
11	Turkey	748	14	28	Tunisia	685	35	45	Slovakia	621	53
12	Italy	741	10	29	South Korea	680	22	46	Finland	614	43
13	Denmark	733	14	30	Senegal	672	31	47	Serbia & Montenegro	612	46
14	Sweden	732	13		Paraguay	672	30	48	Australia	610	58
15	Japan	715	17	32	Egypt	665	34	49	South Africa	609	38
16	Germany	708	19	33	Saudi Arabia	663	28	50	Ghana	608	77
	Greece	708	18	34	Russia	662	32		Trinidad & Tobago	608	63

2006 (as of Sept. 13)

#	Team	Points	2005 Rank	#	Team	Points	2005 Rank	#	Team	Points	2005 Rank
1	Brazil	1574	1	18	Sweden	888	14	35	Poland	737	22
2	France	1534	5	19	Ivory Coast	879	42	36	Israel	731	36
3	Argentina	1492	4	20	Colombia	867	24	37	Bulgaria	728	39
4	England	1477	9	21	Paraguay	854	30	38	Australia	727	48
5	Italy	1474	12	22	Greece	833	16	39	Russia	702	34
6	Netherlands	1327	3	23	Ghana	830	50	40	Norway	698	38
7	Czech Republic	1312	2	24	Croatia	825	20	41	Morocco	694	36
8	Germany	1291	19	25	Romania	817	27	42	Slovakia	685	45
9	Portugal	1272	10	26	Guinea	815	79	43	Ireland	658	24
10	Spain	1255	5	27	Egypt	814	32	44	Iran	658	19
11	Nigeria	1166	24	28	Turkey	810	11	45	Chile	637	64
12	Cameroon	1062	23	29	USA	805	8	46	Peru	611	66
13	Ukraine	1029	40	30	Ecuador	785	37	47	Japan	594	15
14	Switzerland	1016	35	31	Tunisia	780	28	48	Togo	589	56
15	Uruguay	960	18	32	Serbia	759	47	49	South Korea	580	29
16	Denmark	940	13	33	Senegal	756	30	50	Belgium	572	55
17	Mexico	891	5	34	Scotland	746	60				

FIFA Women's World Rankings

As part of its growing recognition of women's soccer FIFA began ranking the women's national teams in 2002 following the inaugural FIFA Women's U19 World Championship in Canada. The rankings are currently released four times a year and are calculated in a similar manner to the men's rankings. The first women's international was held on April 17, 1971 (France vs. the Netherlands). The Top 30 teams are listed below.

2006 (as of Sept. 15)

#	Team	Points	2005 Rank	#	Team	Points	2005 Rank	#	Team	Points	2005 Rank
1	Germany	2233	1		Canada	1932	13	21	Iceland	1773	19
2	USA	2200	2	12	England	1921	12	22	South Korea	1757	23
3	Norway	2062	3	13	Japan	1916	11	23	New Zealand	1751	22
4	Brazil	2053	4	14	Russia	1911	14	24	Nigeria	1736	24
5	Sweden	2032	5	15	Australia	1892	15	25	Mexico	1724	26
6	France	2007	7	16	Finland	1876	16	26	Chinese Taipei	1690	25
7	North Korea	1999	6	17	Ukraine	1834	18	27	Scotland	1688	29
8	China	1989	9	18	Netherlands	1815	17	28	Switzerland	1658	27
9	Denmark	1955	8	19	Czech Republic	1805	21		Poland	1658	27
10	Italy	1932	10	20	Spain	1793	20	30	Serbia	1650	30

U.S. Men's National Team
2006 Schedule and Results
Through June 22, 2006. Games in **bold** type are 2006 World Cup matches.

Date		Result	USA Goals	Site
Jan. 22	Canada	T, 0-0	—	San Diego, Calif.
Jan. 29	Norway	W, 5-0	Twellman (3), Pope, Klein	Carson, Calif.
Feb. 10	Japan	W, 3-2	Pope, Dempsey, Twellman	San Francisco, Calif.
Feb. 19	Guatemala	W, 4-0	Olsen, Ching, Johnson, Klein	Frisco, Texas
Mar. 1	Poland	W, 1-0	Dempsey	Kaiserslautern, Germany
Mar. 22	Germany	L, 1-4	Cherundolo	Dortmund, Germany
Apr. 11	Jamaica	T, 1-1	Olsen	Cary, N.C.
May 23	Morocco	L, 0-1	—	Nashville, Tenn.
May 26	Venezuela	W, 2-0	Ching, Dempsey	Cleveland, Ohio
May 28	Latvia	W, 1-0	McBride	E. Hartford, Conn.
June 12	**Czech Republic**	L, 0-3	—	Gelsenkirchen, Germany
June 17	**Italy**	T, 1-1	own goal	Kaiserslautern, Germany
June 22	**Ghana**	L, 1-2	Dempsey	Nuremberg, Germany

Overall record: 6-4-3. **Team scoring: Goals For**–19; **Goals Against**–14.

2006 U.S. Men's National Team Statistics
Individual statistics through June 22, 2006. Note that the column labeled "Career C/G" refers to career caps and goals.

Forwards	GP	GS	Mins	G	A	Pts	Career C/G
Brian Ching	9	5	421	2	0	4	20/4
Landon Donavan	11	10	925	0	3	3	84/25
Nate Jaqua	1	0	24	0	0		1/0
Eddie Johnson	11	4	586	0	1	1	96/0
Brian McBride	5	4	428	1	0	2	95/30
Chris Rolfe	3	1	101	0	1	1	4/0
Taylor Twellman	6	5	370	4	3	11	19/5
josh Wolff	10	8	451	0	0	0	48/9

Defenders	GP	GS	Mins	G	A	Pts	Career C/G
Gregg Berhalter	2	2	135	0	0	0	44/0
Carlos Bocanegra	4	3	306	0	0	0	42/6
Bobby Boswell	1	0	15	0	0	0	1/0
Steve Cherundolo	7	7	555	1	1	3	38/1
Jimmy Conrad	9	8	759	0	0	0	17/0
Bobby Convey	6	3	306	0	1	1	33/1
Todd Dunivant	2	2	179	0	2	2	2/0
Cory Gibbs	2	2	166	0	0	0	19/0
Frankie Hejduk	4	4	300	0	0	0	72/5
Ugo Ihemelu	1	0	8	0	0	0	1/0
Eddie Lewis	5	4	351	0	0	0	72/8
Oguchi Onyewu	6	6	523	0	0	0	17/1
Heath Pearce	4	2	195	0	0	0	5/0
Eddie Pope	9	9	758	2	0	4	82/8

Midfielders	GP	GS	Mins	G	A	Pts	Career C/G
Freddy Adu	1	0	10	0	0	0	1/0
Chris Albright	2	2	180	0	0	0	20/1
DaMarcus Beasley	7	5	485	0	1	1	61/12
Michael Bradley	2	0	10	0	0	0	2/0
Brian Caroll	2	0	10	0	0	0	4/0
Bobby Convey	8	4	402	0	1	1	42/1
Clint Dempsey	9	7	609	4	1	9	23/6
Chris Klein	6	2	303	2	2	6	22/5
Kyle Martino	1	0	11	0	0	0	8/1
Pablo Mastroeni	7	5	445	0	0	0	50/0
Pat Noonan	3	3	228	0	1	1	13/1
John O'Brien	4	2	179	0	0	0	32/3
Ben Olsen	8	4	395	2	0	4	35/6
Santino Quaranta	2	0	41	0	0	0	11/0
Steve Ralston	1	1	54	0	0	0	33/4
Claudio Reyna	4	4	234	0	0	0	112/8
Kerry Zavagnin	6	5	419	0	0	0	21/0

Goalkeepers	GP	GS	Mins	W-L-T	SO	GAA	Career Caps
Brad Guzan	1	1	79	1-0-0	0	0.00	1
Kevin Hartman	2	2	180	2-0-0	1	1.00	5
Tim Howard	2	1	135	2-0-0	1	0.00	16
Kasey Keller	7	7	585	1-4-1	1	1.69	96
Tony Meola	1	1	90	0-0-1	0	0.00	100
Matt Reis	1	1	90	0-0-1	1	0.00	1
Zach Wells	1	0	11	0-0-0	0	0.00	1
Totals	13	13	1170	6-4-3	6	1.08	

2006 FIFA World Cup — USA in Group E

Czech Republic 3, USA 0
at Gelsenkirchen; Att: 52,000

	1	2	F
USA	0	0	0
Czech Republic	2	1	3

CZE—Jan Koller (Zdenek Grygera) 5'
CZE—Tomas Rosicky (unassisted) 36'
CZE—Rosicky (Pavel Nedved) 76'

USA/CZE	
Shots	6/10
Corner Kicks	2/5
Fouls	15/19
Offside	0/9

USA 1, Italy 1
at Kaiserslautern; Att: 46,000

	1	2	F
USA	1	0	1
Italy	1	0	1

ITA—Al Giardino (Andrea Pirlo) 22'
USA—own goal (Christian Zaccardo) 27'

USA/ITA	
Shots	10/8
Corner Kicks	3/7
Fouls	13/24
Offside	1/11

Ghana 2, USA 1
at Nuremberg; Att: 41,000

	1	2	F
USA	1	0	1
Ghana	2	0	2

GHA—Haminu Draman (unassisted) 22'
USA—Clint Dempsey (D. Beasley) 43'
GHA—Stephen Appiah (PK) 47'

USA/GHA	
Shots	7/9
Corner Kicks	7/2
Fouls	16/32
Offside	6/8

U.S. Women's National Team
2006 Schedule and Results

Date		Result	USA Goals	Site
Jan. 18	Norway	W, 3-1	Lilly, Boxx, Wambach	Guangzhou, China
Jan. 20	France	T, 0-0	—	Guangzhou, China
Jan. 22	China	W, 2-0	Lilly (2)	Guangzhou, China
Mar. 9	China	T, 0-0	—	Faro, Portugal
Mar. 11	Denmark	W, 5-0	Wambach, O'Reilly (2), Lilly, Kai	Quarteira, Portugal
Mar. 13	France	W, 4-1	Lilly, Wagner, Tarpley, Kai	Faro, Portugal
Mar. 15	Germany	T, 0-0 (3-4 PKs)	—	Faro, Portugal
May 7	Japan	W, 3-1	Wambach (3)	Kumamoto, Japan
May 9	Japan	W, 1-0	Kai	Osaka, Japan
July 15	Sweden	W, 3-2	Wambach, Whitehill, Lilly	Blaine, Minn.
July 23	Ireland	W, 5-0	Whitehill (2), O'Reilly, Wambach, Kai	San Diego, Calif.
July 30	Canada	W, 2-0	Wambach, Kai	Cary, N.C.
Aug. 27	China	W, 4-1	Whitehill, Wagner, Lilly (2)	Bridgeview, Ill.
Sept. 13	Mexico	W, 3-1	Wambach (2), Tarpley	Rochester, N.Y.
Oct. 1	Chinese Taipei	W, 10-0	Osborne, Wambach (3), Tarpley (2), Lilly, Lloyd, Rapinoe (2)	Carson, Calif.
Oct. 8	Iceland	W, 2-1	Wambach (2)	Richmond, Va.

Overall record: 13-0-3. **Team Scoring:** Goals for–47; Goals against–8.

2006 U.S. Women's National Team Statistics

Individual statistics through Oct. 8, 2006. Note that the column labeled "Career C/G" refers to career caps and goals.

Forwards	GP	GS	Mins	G	A	Pts	Career C/G
Danesha Adams	1	0	16	0	1	1	1/0
Natasha Kai	11	0	346	5	0	10	11/5
Kristine Lilly	14	14	1218	9	6	24	313/113
Heather O'Reilly	13	11	782	3	2	8	50/8
Megan Rapinoe	4	0	72	2	0	4	4/2
Amy Rodriguez	3	0	40	0	0	0	5/0
India Trotter	1	0	1	0	0	0	1/0
Abby Wambach	16	16	1418	15	6	36	79/64
Christie Welsh	7	4	307	0	2	2	39/20

Defenders	GP	GS	Mins	G	A	Pts	Career C/G
Lori Chalupny	9	7	677	0	1	1	24/2
Tina Frimpong	12	9	736	0	1	1	15/0
Amy LePeilbet	13	9	815	0	0	0	23/0
Stephanie Lopez	7	1	334	0	1	1	8/0
Kate Markgraf	2	2	107	0	0	0	148/0
Heather Mitts	16	15	1298	0	0	0	57/2
Christie Rampone	14	12	1028	0	0	0	150/4
Cat Whitehill	10	9	885	4	1	9	94/10

Midfielders	GP	GS	Mins	G	A	Pts	Career C/G
Shannon Boxx	9	9	793	1	1	3	59/14
Angela Hucles	3	1	137	0	0	0	55/5
Carli Lloyd	14	9	773	1	1	3	16/1
Joanna Lohman	1	0	1	0	0	0	5/0
Marci Miller	6	1	234	0	0	0	8/0
Leslie Osborne	14	7	656	1	1	3	25/1
Lindsay Tarpley	15	10	818	4	2	10	53/12
Aly Wagner	16	15	1208	2	5	9	104/21

Goalkeepers	GP	GS	Mins	W-L-T	SO	GAA	Career Caps
Briana Scurry	2	2	180	2-0-0	1	0.50	157
Hope Solo	13	13	1200	10-0-3	7	0.53	32
Jenni Branam	1	1	90	1-0-0	1	0.00	6
Totals	16	16	1470	13-0-3	9	0.49	

Countdown to China 2007

As of Oct. 1, 2006, eight teams had qualified for the 16-team 2007 Women's World Cup to be held Sept. 10-30, 2007 in China.

Qualified Teams

Asia (2.5 slots*)
Australia
North Korea

Africa (2 slots)
TBD

Oceania (1 slot)
TBD

South America (2 slots)
TBD

Europe (5 slots)
Norway
Sweden
Germany
Denmark
England

North/Central America (2.5 slots*)
TBD

Host Nation (1 slot)
China

*Japan, the third-placed team from Asia, and the third place team from North/Central America (TBD) will play home and away matches, with the winner qualifying for the final competition.

Club Team Competition

2005 FIFA Club World Championship

The FIFA Club World Championship (now officially the FIFA Club World Championship TOYOTA Cup Japan) merged with the Toyota Cup (a.k.a European/South American Cup) in 2005 and is now open to the champions from the African, Asian, Oceanic and North/Central American soccer federations as well as Europe and South America. The four newcomers will play-off for the right to face the seeded European and South American sides in the semi-finals. Like the Toyota Cup, the new six-team knockout tournament will still be held each December in Japan. The previous edition of the FIFA Club World Championship was played once (held in 2000 and won by Brazil's Corinthians) but it fell apart while the Toyota Cup continued uninterrupted.

The 2005 FIFA Club World Championship TOYOTA Cup took place December 11-18. The teams representing their continents were as follows: EUROPE—**Liverpool** (England), NORTH/CENTRAL AMERICA—**Deportivo Saprissa** (Costa Rica), SOUTH AMERICA—**São Paulo** (Brazil), OCEANIA—**Sydney FC** (Australia), ASIA—**Al Ittihad** (Saudi Arabia), AFRICA—**Al Ahly** (Egypt). As the European and South American teams, respectively, Liverpool and Sao Paulo received byes into the semifinals.

Quarterfinals

Al Ittihad 1 . . . . .Al Ahly 0
Deportivo Saprissa 1 . . . . .Sydney FC 0

Semifinals

São Paulo 3 . . . . .Al Ittihad 2
Liverpool 3 . . . . .Deportivo Saprissa 0

5th Place Match

Sydney FC 2 . . . . .Al Ahly 1

3rd Place Match

Deportivo Saprissa 3 . . . . .Al Ittihad 2

Final

Dec. 18 at Yokohama, Japan.
Attendance: 66,821

São Paulo 1 . . . . .Liverpool 0

Scoring

SÃO PAULO—Mineiro 27'
Referee: Benito Armando Archundia, Mexico

SOUTH AMERICA

2006 Libertadores Cup

Contested by the league champions of South America's football union. Two-leg Semifinals and two-leg Final; home teams listed first. Winners Internacional of Brazil qualified for the 2006 FIFA Club World Championship in Japan in December.

Final Four: Internacional (Brazil), Chivas de Guadalajara (Mexico), Libertad (Paraguay) and São Paulo (Brazil).

Semifinals

Internacional vs. Libertad

Libertad 0 . . . . .Internacional 0
Internacional 2 . . . . .Libertad 0
Internacional won 2-0 on aggregate

São Paulo vs. Chivas Guadalajara

Chivas Guadalajara 0 . . . . .São Paulo 1
São Paulo 3 . . . . .Chivas Guadalajara 0
São Paulo won 4-0 on aggregate

Final

Matches played August 9 in in San Paulo, Brazil and August 16 in Porto Alegre, Brazil.

São Paulo 1 . . . . .Internacional 2
Internacional 2 . . . . .São Paulo 2
Internacional won 4-3 on aggregate

2006 Lamar Hunt U.S. Open Cup

Dating back to 1914, the U.S. Open Cup is the oldest soccer competition in the United States and is among the oldest in the world. The U.S. Open Cup is a single-elimination tournament open to all amateur and professional teams in the United States. Forty-two teams competed in the 2006 Lamar Hunt U.S. Open Cup. The tournament was renamed for the U.S. Soccer pioneer and MLS Team owner in 1999. All teams listed below are from the MLS unless otherwise noted.

Fourth Round

D.C. United def. Columbus Crew, 2-1
NY Red Bulls def. Wilmington Hammerheads (USL 2), 2-1
Chicago Fire def. Kansas City Wizards, 2-0
NE Revolution def. Rochester Raging Rhinos (USL 1) on PKs
Los Angeles Galaxy def. Dallas Roma FC (USASA), 2-0
Colorado Rapids def. Real Salt Lake, 1-0
Houston Dynamo def. Carolina Dynamo (USL Dev.), 4-2
FC Dallas def. Charleston Battery (USL 1) on PKs

Quarterfinals

D.C. United def. New York Red Bulls, 3-1
Houston Dynamo def. FC Dallas, 3-0
Chicago Fire def. New England Revolution, 2-1
Los Angeles Galaxy def. Colorado Rapids, 3-1

Semifinals

Los Angeles Galaxy def. Houston Dynamo, 3-1
Chicago Fire def. D.C. United, 3-0

Final (Sept. 27, 2006)

Chicago Fire def. Los Angeles Galaxy, 3-1

EUROPE

There are two major European club competitions sanctioned by the Union of European Football Associations (UEFA). The constantly evolving **Champions League** is currently a 74-team tournament made up from UEFA member countries. The teams are ranked 1-74 depending on how they finish in their own domestic leagues. UEFA ranks the quality of the 52 European national football associations (from number one Spain to number 52 San Marino) and assigns each association a number weighted by their respective ranking (UEFA calls this number a coefficient). Each team's domestic league finish is then multiplied by the coefficient and the teams are finally ranked (countries can enter a maximum of four teams).

The defending champions and the other 15 highest-ranked teams form Group 1 and are given a direct entry into the League but the remaining 16 teams are determined by dividing teams 17-74 into three groups—Group 2 (teams 17-34), Group 3 (35-50) and Group 4 (51-74). The 24 teams in the lowest Group (Group 4) play two-leg, total goal elimination series. The 12 survivors advance to the Second Qualifying Phase and join the 16 teams from Group 3 to play 14 two-leg, total goal elimination series. The 14 clubs that survive this phase join the 18 teams from Group 2 to play in the Third Qualifying Phase. The winning clubs from the 16 two-leg, total goal elimination series advance to the Champions League for the right to play against the top-ranked 16 teams in Europe.

The 32 teams are separated into eight groups of four and play a round-robin series of home-and-home matches. Starting for the 2003-04 Champions League, the eight group winners and eight group runners-up advance to the next round where they are paired and play two home-and-home matches. The home-and-home series are played through the semifinals until ultimately ah single championship match for the European club championship is held.

The updated **UEFA Cup**, which is basically a combination of the what was known as the Cup Winners' Cup (played between national cup champions) and the old UEFA Cup (sort of a "best of the rest" tournament), is single-elimination throughout and features 121 additional teams plus teams that have been already eliminated from the Champions League.

2005-06 Champions League

Following the first three qualifying phases, the first group phase starts with six-game double round-robin format in eight four-team groups (Sept. 14-Dec. 7); top two teams in each group advance to round of 16 (Feb. 21-Mar. 7). While the third-place team from each of the eight groups moves to the third round of the UEFA Cup tournament. (*) indicates team advanced to the next round (of the Champions League). Note that in results listing under each table the home team is listed first.

Group Phase

Group A	W	L	T	GF	GA	Pts
*Juventus (Italy)	5	1	0	12	5	15
*Bayern Munich (Germany)	4	1	1	10	4	13
Club Brugge (Belgium)	2	3	1	6	7	7
Rapid Vienna (Austria)	0	6	0	3	15	0

Group B	W	L	T	GF	GA	Pts
*Arsenal (England)	5	0	1	10	2	16
*Ajax (Netherlands)	3	1	2	10	6	11
FC Thun (Swtizerland)	1	4	1	4	9	4
Sparta Prague (Czech Rep.)	0	4	2	2	9	2

Group C	W	L	T	GF	GA	Pts
*Barcelona (Spain)	5	0	1	16	2	16
*Werder Bremen (Germany)	2	3	1	12	12	7
Udinese (Italy)	2	3	1	10	12	7
Panathinaikos (Greece)	1	4	1	4	16	4

Group D	W	L	T	GF	GA	Pts
*Villarreal (Spain)	2	0	4	3	1	10
*Benfica (Portugal)	2	2	2	5	5	8
Lille (France)	1	2	3	1	2	6
Manchester United (England)	1	2	3	3	4	6

Group E	W	L	T	GF	GA	Pts
*AC Milan (Italy)	3	1	2	12	6	11
*PSV Eindhoven (Germany)	3	2	1	4	6	10
Schalke 04 (Germany)	2	2	2	12	9	8
Fenerbahce (Turkey)	1	4	1	7	14	4

Group F	W	L	T	GF	GA	Pts
*Lyon (France)	5	0	1	13	4	16
*Real Madrid (Spain)	3	2	1	10	8	10
Rosenborg (Norway)	1	4	1	6	11	4
Olympiakos (Greece)	1	4	1	7	13	4

Group G	W	L	T	GF	GA	Pts
*Liverpool (England)	3	0	3	6	1	12
*Chelsea (England)	3	1	2	7	1	11
Real Betis (Spain)	2	3	1	3	7	7
Anderlecht (Belgium)	1	5	0	1	8	3

Group H	W	L	T	GF	GA	Pts
*Inter Milan (Italy)	4	1	1	9	4	13
*Glasgow Rangers (Scotland)	1	1	4	7	7	7
Artmedia Petrzalka (Slovakia)	1	2	3	5	9	6
FC Porto (Portugal)	1	3	2	8	9	5

Round of 16
Two legs, total goals; home team listed first.

Bayern Munich vs. AC Milan
Feb. 21 Bayern Munich 1 . . . . AC Milan 1
Mar. 8 AC Milan 4 . . . . .Bayern Munich 1
AC Milan wins 5-2 on aggregate

Benfica vs. Liverpool
Feb. 21 Benfica 1 . . . . .Liverpool 0
Mar. 8 Liverpool 0 . . . . .Benfica 2
Benfica wins 3-0 on aggregate

PSV Eindhoven vs. Lyon
Feb. 21 PSV Eindhoven 0 . . . . .Lyon 1
Mar. 8 Lyon 4 . . . . .PSV Eindhoven 0
Lyon wins 5-0 on aggregate

Real Madrid vs. Arsenal
Feb. 21 Real Madrid 0 . . . . .Arsenal 1
Mar. 8 Arsenal 0 . . . . .Real Madrid 0
Arsenal wins 1-0 on aggregate

Ajax Amsterdam vs. Inter Milan
Feb. 22 Ajax Amsterdam 2 . . . . .Inter Milan 2
Mar. 14 Inter Milan 1 . . . . .Ajax Amsterdam 0
Inter Milan wins 3-2 on aggregate

Chelsea vs. Barcelona
Feb. 22 Chelsea 1 . . . . .Barcelona 2
Mar. 7 Barcelona 1 . . . . .Chelsea 1
Barcelona wins 3-2 on aggregate

Rangers vs. Villarreal
Feb. 22 Rangers 2 . . . . .Villarreal 2
Mar. 7 Villarreal 1 . . . . .Rangers 1
Aggregate tied 3-3, Villarreal wins on away goals

Werder Bremen vs. Juventus
Feb. 22 Werder Bremen 3 . . . . Juventus 2
Mar. 7 Juventus 2 . . . . .Werder Bremen 1
Aggregate tied 4-4, Juventus wins on away goals

Quarterfinals
Two legs, total goals; home team listed first.

Arsenal vs. Juventus
Mar. 28 Arsenal 2 . . . . .Juventus 0
Apr. 5   Juventus 0 .Arsenal 0
Arsenal wins 2-0 on aggregate

Lyon vs. AC Milan
Mar. 29 Lyon 0 . . . . .AC Milan 0
Apr. 4   AC Milan 3 . . . . .Lyon 1
AC Milan wins 3-1 on aggregate

Benfica vs. Barcelona
Mar. 28 Benfica 0 . . . . .Barcelona 0
Apr. 5   Barcelona 2 . . . . .Benfica 0
Barcelona wins 2-0 on aggregate

Inter Milan vs. Villarreal
Mar. 29 Inter Milan 2 . . . . .Villarreal 1
Apr. 4   Villarreal 1 . . . . .Inter Milan 0
Aggregate tied 2-2, Villarreal wins on away goals

Semifinals
Two legs, total goals; home team listed first.

AC Milan vs. Barcelona
Apr. 18 AC Milan 0 . . . . .Barcelona 1
Apr. 26 Barcelona 0 . . . . .AC Milan 0
Barcelon win 1-0 on aggregate

Arsenal vs. Villarreal
Apr. 19 Arsenal 1 .Villarreal 0
Apr. 25 Villarreal 0 . . . . .Arsenal 0
Arsenal wins 1-0 on aggregate

Final

Barcelona vs. Arsenal
May 17, 2006 at Stade de France in Paris.
Attendance: 79,500

Barcelona 2 . . . . .Arsenal 1

Scoring:

ARSENAL—Sol Campbell (37'); BARCELONA—Samuel Eto'o (76'), Juliano Belletti (80')

2006 UEFA Cup
Two-leg Quarterfinals and Semifinals, one-game Final; home team listed first.

Final Eight: Sevilla (Spain), Schalke 04 (Germany), Basel (Switzerland), Middlesbrough (England), Levski Sofia (Bulgaria), Steaua Bucharest (Romania), Rapid Bucharest (Romania), Zenit St. Petersburg (Russia).

Quarterfinals

Middlesbrough vs. Basel
Mar. 30 Basel 2 . . . . .Middlesbrough 0
Apr. 6   Middlesbrough 4 . . . . .Basel 1
Middlesbrough wins 4-3 on aggregate

Rapid Bucharest vs. Steaua Bucharest
Mar. 30 Rapid Bucharest 1 . . . . .Steaua Bucharest 1
Apr. 6   Steaua Bucharest 0 . . . . .Rapid Bucharest 0
Aggregate tied 1-1, Steaua wins on away goals

Levski Sofia vs. Schalke 04
Mar. 30 Levski Sofia 1 . . . . .Schalke 3
Apr. 6   Schalke 1 . . . . .Levski Sofia 1
Schalke wins 4-2 on aggregate

Sevilla vs. Zenit St. Petersburg
Mar. 30 Sevilla 4 . . . . .Zenit St. Petersburg 1
Apr. 6   Zenit St. Petersburg 1 . . . . .Sevilla 1
Sevilla wins 5-2 on aggregate

Semifinals

Schalke 04 vs. Sevilla
Apr 20 Schalke 0 . . . . .Sevilla 0
Apr. 27 Sevilla 1 . . . . .Schalke 0
Sevilla wins 1-0 on aggregate

Steaua Bucharest vs. Middlesbrough
Apr. 20 Steaua Bucharest 1 . . . . .Middlesbrough 0
Apr. 27 Middlesbrough 4 . . . . .Steaua Bucharest 2
Middlesbrough wins 4-3 on aggregate

Final

Sevilla vs. Middlesbrough
May 10 in Eindhoven, Netherlands.

Sevilla 4 . . . . .Middlesbrough 0

2006 FA Cup
May 13, 2006 at Millenium Stadium, Cardiff, Wales. **Attendance:** 71,140
Liverpool 3 .West Ham Untied 3
Liverpool wins 2006 FA Cup, 3-1, on penalty kicks

Scoring:

WEST HAM UNITED—own goal (Jamie Carragher) 21', Dean Ashton 28', Paul Konchesky 64'; LIVERPOOL—Djibril Cisse 32', Steven Gerrard 54', 91'

Major League Soccer
2006 Final Regular Season Standings

Conference champions (*) and playoff qualifiers (†) are noted. Teams receive three points for a win and one for a tie. The GF and GA columns refer to Goals For and Goals Against in regulation play. Number of seasons listed after each head coach refers to current tenure with club through the 2006 season.

Eastern Conference

Team	W	L	T	Pts	GF	GA
*D.C. United	15	7	10	55	52	38
†N.E. Revolution	12	8	12	48	39	35
†Chicago Fire	13	11	8	47	43	41
†New York Red Bulls	9	11	12	39	41	41
Kansas City Wizards	10	14	8	38	43	45
Columbus Crew	8	15	9	33	30	42

Head Coaches: DC—Peter Nowak (3rd season); **NE**—Steve Nicol (6th); **Chi**—Dave Sarachan (4th); **NY**—Mo Johnston (2nd, 2-3-7) was fired June 27, 2006 and replaced on an interim basis by Richie Williams (1-3-1) then Bruce Arena on July 18 (6-5-4); **KC**—Bob Gansler (8th, 6-10-2) was fired on July 19, 2006 and replaced on an interim basis by asst. Brian Bliss (4-4-6); **Clb**—Sigi Schmid (1st).

Western Conference

Team	W	L	T	Pts	GF	GA
*FC Dallas	16	12	4	52	48	44
†Houston Dynamo	11	8	13	46	44	40
†Chivas USA	10	9	13	43	45	42
†Colorado Rapids	11	13	8	41	36	49
Los Angeles Galaxy	11	15	6	39	37	37
Real Salt Lake	10	13	9	39	45	49

Head Coaches: Dal—Colin Clarke (4th); **Hou**—Dominic Kinnear (2nd); **Chv**—Bob Bradley (1st); **Colo**—Fernando Clavijo (2nd); **LA**—Steve Sampson (3rd, 2-8-1) was fired on June 6, 2006 and replaced by Frank Yallop (9-7-5); **RSL**—John Ellinger (2nd).

Note: The San Jose Earthquakes relocated to Houston and were renamed the Dynamo prior to the 2006 season.

Leading Scorers

Goals

	Gm	No
Jeff Cunningham, RSL	31	16
Christian Gomez, DC	30	14
Ante Razov, Chv	28	14
Carlos Ruiz, Dal	27	13
Landon Donovan, LA	24	12
Brian Ching, Hou	21	11
Kenny Cooper, Dal	31	11
Dwayne De Rosario, Hou	30	11
Jaime Moreno, DC	32	11
Taylor Twellman, NE	32	11

Assists

	Gm	No
Terry Cooke, Col	23	12
Jeff Cunningham, RSL	31	11
Brad Davis, Hou	28	11
Christian Gomez, DC	30	11
Ronnie O'Brien, Dal	27	11
Andy Dorman, NE	32	10
Jaime Moreno, DC	32	10
Ivan Guerrero, Chi	29	9
Richard Mulrooney, Dal	25	9
Seven players tied with 8 each.		

Shots

	Gm	No
Ante Razov, Chv	28	98
Taylor Twellman, NE	32	86
Jeff Cunningham, RSL	31	83
Chris Klein, RSL	32	70
Ronnie O'Brien, Dal	27	69
Clint Dempsey, NE	21	67
Edson Buddle, NY	28	65
Kenny Cooper, Dal	31	65
Brian Ching, Hou	21	64
Christian Gomez, DC	30	63

Shots on Goal

	Gm	No
Jeff Cunningham, RSL	31	45
Taylor Twellman, NE	32	42
Ante Razov, Chv	28	40
Christian Gomez, DC	30	35
Andy Dorman, NE	32	33
Clint Dempsey, NE	21	31
Jaime Moreno, DC	32	31
Brian Ching, Hou	21	30
Kenny Cooper, Dal	31	30
Alecko Eskandarian, DC	22	30

Game-Winning Goals

	Gm	GWG
Kenny Cooper, Dal	31	6
Nicolas Hernandez, Col	30	6
Landon Donovan, LA	24	5
Andy Herron, Chi	20	5
Jaime Moreno, DC	32	5
Ante Razov, Chv	28	5
Jose Burciaga Jr., KC	30	4
Brian Ching, Hou	21	4
Jeff Cunningham, RSL	31	4
Taylor Twellman, NE	32	4

Multi-Goal Games

	Gm	MGG
Jeff Cunningham, RSL	31	4
Ante Razov, Chv	28	4
Landon Donovan, LA	24	3
Dwayne De Rosario, Hou	30	2
Christian Gomez, DC	30	2
Amado Guevara, NY	28	2
Jaime Moreno, DC	32	2
Carlos Ruiz	27	2

MLS All-Star Game
MLS 1, Chelsea 0

Played Saturday, Aug. 5, 2006 at Toyota Park between a team of MLS All-Stars and English Premier League team Fulham FC.

Attendance: 21,210; **MVP:** Dwayne De Rosario, Houston Dynamo, M.

	1	2	Final
Chelsea	0	0	—0
MLS All-Stars	0	1	—1

Scoring
2nd Half: MLS—Dwayne De Rosario (Ronnie O'Brien) 70th.

Misconduct Summary
MLS—Jimmy Conrad (yellow; reckless foul), 31st
CHL—Michael Essien (yellow; tackle from behind), 82nd

Major League Soccer (Cont.)

Fouls Committed

	Gm	No
Simo Valakari, Dal	.31	81
Amado Guevara, NY	.28	64
Ugo Ihemelu, LA	.29	64
Brian Mullan, Hou	.31	60
Danny O'Rourke, NY	.28	59
Eddie Robinson, Hou	.25	58
Ricardo Clark, Hou	.31	57
Seth Stammler, NY	.29	56
Carlos Ruiz, Dal	.27	54
Tyrone Marshall, LA	.25	53
Carey Talley, RSL	.30	53

Fouls Suffered

	Gm	No
Alejandro Moreno, SJ	.30	112
Davy Arnaud, KC	.32	76
Carlos Ruiz, Dal	.27	72
Jose Cancela, NE	.21	67
Clint Dempsey, NE	.21	62
Eddie Gaven, Clb	.30	62
Jaime Moreno, DC	.32	62
Juan Francisco Palencia, Chv	.23	61
Taylor Twellman, NE	.32	60
Kenny Cooper, Dal	.31	59

Offsides

	Gm	Offs
Ante Razov, Chv	.28	43
Juan Francisco Palencia, Chv	.23	36
Jeff Cunningham, RSL	.31	35
Andy Herron, Chi	.20	35
Edson Buddle, NY	.28	32
Carlos Ruiz, Dal	.27	32
Taylor Twellman, NE	.32	32
Nicolas Henandez, Col	.30	29
Joseph Ngwenya, Clb	.22	29

Cautions

	Gm	No
Eddie Robinson, Hou	.25	11
Mike Petke, Col	.26	10
Joe Franchino, NE	.21	9
Five tied with 8 each.		

Ejections

	Gm	No
Dwayne De Rosario, Hou	.30	2
Joshua Gros, DC	.29	2
Joseph Ngwenya, Clb	.22	2
Mike Petke, Col	.26	2

Corner Kicks

	Gm	CKs
Juan Pablo Garcia, Chv	.29	106
Landon Donovan, LA	.24	97
Terry Cooke, Col	.23	91
Jose Burciaga Jr., KC	.30	88
Chris Klein, RSL	.32	75
Jose Cancela, NE	.21	71
Brad Davis, Hou	.28	70

Minutes Played

	Mins
Pat Onstad, Hou	.2880
Matt Reis, NE	.2880
Jonathan Bornstein, Chv	.2878
Taylor Twellman, NE	.2856
Chris Klein, RSL	.2842
Andy Dorman, NE	.2834

2006 MLS Attendance

Number in parentheses indicates last year's rank.

	Gm	Total	Avg
Los Angeles (1)	16	333,016	20,814
CD Chivas USA (4)	16	317,432	19,840
Houston (8*)	16	302,957	18,935
D.C. United (5)	16	291,442	18,215
Real Salt Lake (2)	16	261,855	16,366
Dallas (11)	16	239,714	14,982
New York (6)	16	233,112	14,570
Chicago (3)	16	225,775	14,111
Columbus (9)	16	212,699	13,294
Colorado (7)	16	192,894	12,056
New England (10)	16	188,569	11,786
Kansas City (12)	16	177,322	11,083
TOTALS	192	2,976,787	15,504

*The Houston Dynamo were located in San Jose, Calif. and named the Earthquakes prior to 2006.

Leading Goaltenders

Goals Against Average

	Gm	Min	Shts	Svs	GAA	W-L-T
Jon Conway, NY	12	1080	66	54	**1.00**	7-2-3
Matt Reis, NE	32	2880	176	141	**1.09**	12-8-12
Troy Perkins, DC	30	2700	134	100	**1.13**	15-6-9
Kevin Hartman, LA	28	2520	120	88	**1.14**	10-12-6
Preston Burpo, Chv	19	1710	81	58	**1.21**	7-3-9
Dario Sala, Dal	28	2475	127	93	**1.24**	14-10-4
Pat Onstad, Hou	32	2880	125	85	**1.25**	11-8-13
Zach Thornton, Chi	24	2160	116	86	**1.25**	8-8-8
Scott Garlick, RSL	31	2745	151	108	**1.41**	10-12-9
Bo Oshoniyi, KC	29	2610	136	95	**1.41**	9-12-8
Tony Meola, NY	20	1800	120	91	**1.45**	2-9-9
Brad Guzan, Chv	13	1170	68	49	**1.46**	3-6-4

Save Percentage

	Svs	SOG	SV Pct
Matt Pickens, Chi	.47	57	82.5
Jon Conway, NY	.54	67	80.6
Matt Reis, NE	.141	182	77.5
Tony Meola, NY	.91	120	75.8
Bill Gaudette, Clb	.45	60	75.0
Kevin Hartman, LA	.88	120	73.3
Zach Thornton, Chi	.86	118	72.9

Saves

	Gm	No
Matt Reis, NE	.32	141
Scott Garlick, RSL	.31	108
Troy Perkins, DC	.30	100
Joe Cannon, Col	.28	99
Bo Oshoniyi, KC	.29	95

Shutouts

	Gm	No
Matt Reis, NE	.32	10
Kevin Hartman, LA	.28	9
Troy Perkins, DC	.30	8
Joe Cannon, Col	.28	7
Zach Thornton, Chi	.24	7

Wins

	Gm	No
Troy Perkins, DC	.30	15
Dario Sala, Dal	.28	14
Matt Reis, NE	.32	12
Pat Onstad, Nou	.32	11
Scott Garlick, RSL	.31	10
Kevin Hartman, LA	.28	10
Two tied with 9 each.		

Team-by-Team Statistics
Players who played with more than one club during the season are listed with final team.

Eastern Conference

Chicago Fire

(min. 10 Gms)	Pos	Gm	Min	G	A	Sht
Andy Herron	F	20	1449	9	1	37
Nate Jaqua	F	28	2037	8	2	48
Chris Rolfe	F	21	1636	7	1	39
Chad Barrett	F	16	780	5	1	26
Thiago	M	27	2229	3	2	39
Diego Gutierrez	M	25	1879	2	3	18
Justin Mapp	M	26	1866	2	8	36
Chris Armas	M	27	2366	1	5	20
C.J. Brown	D	28	2429	1	2	7
Calen Carr	F	22	500	1	1	12
Jim Curtin	D	11	660	1	0	1
Brian Plotkin	M	14	529	1	1	14
Dasan Robinson	D	23	2054	1	0	8
Gonzalo Segares	M	25	1984	1	1	7
Ivan Guerrero	M	29	2526	0	9	20
Logan Pause	M/D	25	1782	0	1	4
Tonny Sanneh	D/M	19	1296	0	1	1

Top Goalkeepers	Gm	Min	W-L-T	Shts	Svs	GAA
Zach Thornton	24	2160	8-8-8	118	86	1.25
Matt Pickens	8	720	5-3-0	57	47	1.38

Columbus Crew

(min. 10 Gms)	Pos	Gm	Min	G	A	Sht
Jason Garey	F	25	1712	5	2	31
Joseph Ngwenya	F	20	1398	5	2	27
Eddie Gaven	M	30	2560	4	4	57
Kei Kamara	F	19	930	3	0	26
Sebastian Rozental	F	20	1231	3	1	29
Ned Grabavoy	M	10	388	1	1	7
Ezra Hendrickson	D	24	1869	1	2	15
Ritchie Kotschau	D	26	2109	1	2	6
Chad Marshall	D	26	2255	1	1	11
Jose Reitz	M	22	1732	1	1	22
Jacob Thomas	M	19	1074	1	2	21
Eric Vasquez	M	12	504	1	0	9
Ricardo Virtuso	M	10	571	1	0	15
Knox Cameron	F	10	355	0	0	3
Marcos Gonzalez	D	21	1660	0	0	12
Chris Leitch	D	24	1662	0	1	4
Brandon Moss	M	20	1610	0	0	8
Rusty Pierce	D	18	1524	0	0	8
Tim Ward	D	11	605	0	0	2

Top Goalkeepers	Gm	Min	W-L-T	Shts	Svs	GAA
Bill Gaudette	11	990	3-5-3	60	45	1.18
Noah Palmer	10	900	1-5-4	56	40	1.30
Jon Busch	8	715	3-3-2	45	34	1.13

D.C. United

(min. 10 Gms)	Pos	Gm	Min	G	A	Sht
Christian Gomez	M	30	2367	14	11	63
Jaime Moreno	F	32	2700	11	10	51
Alecko Eskandarian	F	22	1478	7	2	57
Facundo Erpen	D	30	2626	3	2	29
Joshua Gros	D/M	29	2576	3	5	33
Freddy Adu	M	32	2521	2	8	55
Ben Olsen	M	20	1535	2	3	21
Bobby Boswell	D	32	2700	1	1	5
Brian Carroll	M	31	2779	1	3	12
Lucio Filomeno	F	11	437	1	1	11
Clyde Simms	M	24	1351	1	1	8
Jamil Walker	M/F	19	412	1	1	7
Bryan Namoff	D/M	26	2241	0	1	5
John Wilson	D	11	407	0	0	1

Top Goalkeepers	Gm	Min	W-L-T	Shts	Svs	GAA
Troy Perkins	30	2700	15-6-9	140	100	1.13

Kansas City Wizards

(min. 10 Gms)	Pos	Gm	Min	G	A	Sht
Scott Sealy	F	29	1762	10	1	41
Jose Burciaga Jr.	D	30	2590	8	8	50
Josh Wolff	F	19	1587	5	2	41
Davy Arnaud	F/M	32	2785	4	4	57
Dave van den Bergh	F	13	991	3	2	22
Sasha Victorine	M	31	2701	3	8	31
Jimmy Conrad	D	15	1252	2	0	7
Eddie Johnson	F	19	1480	2	1	47
Ryan Pore	F	19	563	2	0	14
Nick Garcia	D	29	2519	1	0	4
Jack Jewsbury	M/F	28	1817	1	3	28
Shavar Thomas	D	24	2147	1	1	7
Alex Zotinca	M/D	24	1303	1	1	23
Matt Groenwald	D	19	1221	0	2	1
Yura Movsisyan	F	10	221	0	0	15
Tyson Wahl	D	10	607	0	0	5
Lance Watson	M	11	450	0	0	4
Kerry Zavagnin	M	25	2069	0	1	8

Top Goalkeeper	Gm	Min	W-L-T	Shts	Svs	GAA
Bo Oshoniyi	29	2610	9-12-8	138	95	1.41

New England Revolution

(min. 10 Gms)	Pos	Gm	Min	G	A	Sht
Taylor Twellman	F	32	2856	11	5	86
Clint Dempsey	F	21	1865	8	4	60
Andy Dorman	M	32	2834	6	10	60
Steve Ralston	M	30	2683	6	5	23
Shalrie Joseph	M	26	2331	3	1	27
Jeff Larentowicz	M/D	26	1974	1	1	20
Pat Noonan	F	14	851	1	3	16
Khano Smith	F	10	342	1	0	10
Kyle Brown	F	12	291	0	1	3
Jose Cancela	F	21	1387	0	5	28
Joe Franchino	M	21	1521	0	1	18
Jay Heaps	D	31	2790	0	4	11
Avery John	D	10	893	0	0	0
Tony Lochhead	M/D	16	797	0	2	0
Michael Parkhurst	D	30	2700	0	0	0
James Riley	D/M	20	1706	0	0	3

Goalkeeper	Gm	Min	W-L-T	Shts	Svs	GAA
Matt Reis	32	2880	12-8-12	182	141	1.09

New York Red Bulls

(min. 9 Gms)	Pos	Gm	Min	G	A	Sht
Amado Guevara	M	28	2346	8	5	56
Edson Buddle	F	28	2112	6	3	65
Jean Phillippe Peguero	F	12	1080	6	2	24
Chris Henderson	M	32	2188	3	1	30
Mike Magee	F/M	17	938	3	1	23
Seth Stammler	M	29	2374	3	5	32
John Wolyniec	F	11	747	3	2	19
Youri Djorkaeff	F/M	21	1824	2	4	59
Todd Dunivant	D	9	725	2	1	8
Peter Canero	M	9	278	0	0	2
Taylor Graham	D	10	568	0	0	2
Steve Jolley	D	16	851	0	1	2
Dema Kovalenko	F	12	1080	0	1	19
Mark Lisi	M	9	506	0	4	3
Carlos Mendes	D	31	2751	0	1	0
Danny O'Rourke	M	28	2400	0	2	7
Jeff Parke	D	31	2771	0	0	6
Marvell Wynne	D	28	2170	0	3	10

Goalkeepers	Gm	Min	W-L-T	Shts	Svs	GAA
Tony Meola	20	1800	2-9-9	120	91	1.45
Jon Conway	12	1080	7-2-3	67	54	1.00

Major League Soccer (Cont.)
Western Conference

Club Deportivo Chivas USA

(min. 9 Gms)	Pos	Gm	Min	G	A	Sht
Ante Razov	F	28	2485	14	8	98
Juan Pablo Garcia	M	29	2438	8	6	51
Jonathan Bornstein	D	32	2878	6	4	38
Claudio Suarez	D	20	1778	6	1	10
Juan Francisco Palencia	F	23	1914	4	4	46
Francisco Mendoza	M	31	2652	3	6	40
Jesse Marsch	M	30	2604	2	3	13
Brent Whitfield	M	11	363	1	1	4
Jason Hernandez	D	29	2243	0	0	3
Sacha Kljestan	M	32	2676	0	7	22
Carlos Llamosa	D	13	921	0	1	2
Orlando Perez	D	23	1173	0	0	3
Tim Regan	D	30	2618	0	0	10
Matt Taylor	F	15	323	0	1	6
Lawson Vaughn	D	17	1046	0	1	0

Goalkeepers	Gm	Min	W-L-T	Shts	Svs	GAA
Preston Burpo	19	1710	7-3-9	87	58	1.21
Brad Guzan	13	1170	3-6-4	70	49	1.46

Colorado Rapids

(min. 9 Gms)	Pos	Gm	Min	G	A	Sht
Kyle Beckerman	M	31	2790	7	2	57
Nicolas Hernandez	F	30	2524	7	6	37
Jovan Kirovski	F/M	26	1865	5	2	40
Dedie Ben Dayan	M/D	16	927	4	2	26
Jacob Peterson	F	28	1548	4	3	16
Thiago Martins	F	25	1393	3	4	46
Clint Mathis	M/F	25	1346	2	1	31
Fabrice Noel	F	9	371	1	0	11
Daniel Wasson	D	17	714	1	0	12
Terry Cooke	M	23	1997	0	12	31
Eric Denton	D	22	1890	0	2	10
Hunter Freeman	D/M	27	2131	0	1	8
Dan Gargan	D	22	1482	0	1	7
Aitor Karanka	D	27	2414	0	1	11
Pablo Mastroeni	M/D	20	1779	0	0	2
Mike Petke	D	26	2256	0	0	7
Chris Wingert	D	10	446	0	0	0

Goalkeepers	Gm	Min	W-L-T	Shts	Svs	GAA
Joe Cannon	28	2440	9-11-7	146	99	1.55

FC Dallas

(min. 9 Gms)	Pos	Gm	Min	G	A	Sht
Carlos Ruiz	F	27	2113	13	5	54
Kenny Cooper	F	31	2453	11	4	65
Ramon Nunez	M	25	1661	6	4	51
Arturo Alvarez	M	19	578	3	1	17
Roberto Mina	F	16	883	3	1	26
Bobby Rhine	D	30	2593	2	2	13
Abe Thompson	F	14	674	2	6	10
Drew Moor	D	27	2280	1	1	12
Richard Mulrooney	M	25	2075	1	9	12
Ronnie O'Brien	M	27	2331	1	11	69
Dominic Oduro	F	16	413	1	0	9
Aaron Pitchkolan	M	10	94	1	0	2
Greg Vanney	D	28	2510	1	2	9
David Wagenfuhr	D	13	495	1	0	6
Mark Wilson	M	12	582	1	1	7
Chris Gbandi	D	28	2393	0	2	14
Clarence Goodson	D	13	886	0	0	8
Simo Valakari	M	31	2608	0	1	10
Alex Yi	D	11	667	0	0	2

Goalkeepers	Gm	Min	W-L-T	Shts	Svs	GAA
Dario Sala	28	2475	14-10-4	129	93	1.24

Houston Dynamo

(min. 9 Gms)	Pos	Gm	Min	G	A	Sht
Brian Ching	F	21	1822	11	2	64
Dwayne De Rosario	M	30	2534	11	5	55
Craig Waibel	D	28	2401	5	1	12
Alejandro Moreno	F	30	2620	3	6	36
Ricardo Clark	M	31	2728	2	1	13
Brian Mullan	M	31	2744	2	4	27
Eddie Robinson	D	25	2084	2	3	8
Ryan Cochrane	D	27	2172	1	0	3
Brad Davis	M	28	2036	1	11	42
Stuart Holden	M	13	344	1	0	6
Adrian Serioux	M/D	20	1412	1	0	6
Wade Barrett	D	31	2756	0	3	14
Ronald Cerritos	F	15	654	0	1	10
Kevin Goldthwaite	D	20	821	0	1	5
Kelly Gray	D	18	868	0	0	4

Goalkeeper	Gm	Min	W-L-T	Shts	Svs	GAA
Pat Onstad	32	2880	11-8-13	132	85	1.25

Los Angeles Galaxy

(min. 10 Gms)	Pos	Gm	Min	G	A	Sht
Landon Donovan	F	24	2147	12	7	44
Herculez Gomez	F	30	1802	5	3	55
Alan Gordon	F	17	1021	4	2	38
Cobi Jones	M	27	1710	4	4	14
Santino Quaranta	F	12	772	3	0	14
Chris Albright	D/M	23	2036	2	5	18
Peter Vagenas	M	25	2046	2	5	15
Josh Gardner	M	18	1058	1	3	13
John Wolyniec	F	10	651	1	0	17
Todd Dunivant	D	13	1133	0	1	6
Ugo Ihemelu	D	29	2610	0	0	0
Ante Jazic	D/M	11	990	0	0	3
Quavas Kirk	M	22	993	0	2	10
Tyrone Marshall	D	25	2149	0	0	13
Paulo Nagamura	M	29	2372	0	4	30
Troy Roberts	D	14	892	0	1	3
Marcelo Saragosa	M	10	822	0	0	5
Nathan Sturgis	D/M	15	1247	0	0	1
Kyle Veris	D	10	732	0	0	7

Top Goalkeeper	Gm	Min	W-L-T	Shts	Svs	GAA
Kevin Hartman	28	2520	10-12-6	120	88	1.14

Real Salt Lake

(min. 9 Gms)	Pos	Gm	Min	G	A	Sht
Jeff Cunningham	F	31	2404	16	11	83
Jason Kreis	M	30	2434	8	5	56
Chris Klein	M	32	2842	7	8	70
Atiba Harris	F	22	1146	4	1	24
Mehdi Ballouchy	M	32	2162	2	2	19
Carey Talley	M/D	30	2618	2	8	19
Andy Williams	M/F	29	1943	2	6	37
Chris Brown	F	9	297	1	0	1
Douglas Sequeira	M	18	1246	1	0	16
Nelson Akwari	D	18	1308	0	0	4
Kenny Cutler	M	15	918	0	0	5
Willis Forko	D	26	2254	0	1	0
Kevin Novak	D	26	2029	0	0	3
Eddie Pope	D	22	1926	0	0	05
Jack Stewart	D	12	987	0	0	4
Daniel Torres	D	16	1363	0	0	1
Jamie Watson	F	10	104	0	0	4

Top Goalkeeper	Gm	Min	W-L-T	Shts	Svs	GAA
Scott Garlick	31	2745	10-12-9	158	108	1.41

MLS Expands to Canada in 2007!
The **Toronto FC** will join the MLS as the league's 13th team and play their home games at the new BMO Field.

United Soccer Leagues
First Division

In November of 2004, as part of the newly reformed United Soccer Leagues, the A-League was renamed the USL First Division. The USL First Division is the second level of soccer (behind only Major League Soccer) in the United States and Division I in Canada. Playoff qualifiers (*) are noted. Top two teams receive a bye into the semifinals.

2006 Final Standings

Team	W	L	T	Pts
*Montreal Impact	14	5	9	51
*Rochester Raging Rhinos	13	4	11	50
*Charleston Battery	13	8	7	46
*Vancouver Whitecaps	12	6	10	46
*Miami FC	11	11	6	39
*Puerto Rico Islanders	10	10	8	38
Seattle Sounders	11	13	4	37
Atlanta Silverbacks	10	13	5	35
Virginia Beach Mariners	8	12	8	32
Toronto Lynx	8	12	8	32
Portland Timbers	7	15	6	27
Minnesota Thunder	7	15	6	27

Leaders

Goals

	Gms	Goals
Romario De Souza-Farias, Miami	23	18
Williams Weaver, Seattle	27	18
Alen Marcina, Puerto Rico	27	13
Joseph Gjertsen, Vancouver	28	12
Gavin Glinton, Charleston	23	11
Kevin Jeffrey, Toronto	22	9
Gregory Simmonds, Virginia Beach	23	9
Ben Hollingsworth, Charleston	25	9
Mauricio Salles, Montreal	26	9
Matthew Delicate, Rochester	28	8

Points

	Gms	Pts
Romario De Souza-Farias, Miami	23	39
Williams Weaver, Seattle	27	39
Joseph Gjertsen, Vancouver	28	31
Alen Marcina, Puerto Rico	27	26
Gavin Glinton, Charleston	23	22
Gregory Simmonds, Virginia Beach	23	22
Ben Hollingsworth, Charleston	25	22

Playoffs

First Round (Total Goals)

Puerto Rico vs. Charleston

Sept. 15	Puerto Rico 2, Charleston 2	at Charleston
Sept. 17	Charleston 1, Puerto Rico 0	at Puerto Rico
	Charleston win 3-2 on aggregate	

Miami FC vs. Vancouver

Sept. 15	Vancouver 4, Miami FC 1	at Vancouver
Sept. 17	Vancouver 2, Miami FC 0	at Seattle
	Vancouver wins 6-1 on aggregate	

Semifinals (Total Goals)

Rochester vs. Charleston

Sept. 22	Rochester 1, Charleston 0	at Rochester
Sept. 24	Charleston 0, Rochester 0	at Charleston
	Rochester wins 1-0 on aggregate	

Vancouver vs. Montreal

Sept. 22	Montreal 0, Vancouver 0	at Vancouver
Sept. 24	Vancouver 2, Montreal 0	at Montreal
	Vancouver wins 2-0 on aggregate	

Final

Sept. 30 at PAETEC Park, Rochester, N.Y.
Attendance: 9,547

Vancouver 3 . . . . Rochester 0

Scoring

1st Half: VAN—own goal 45'.

2nd Half: VAN—Tony Donatelli (Joseph Gjertsen) 55'; Sita-Taty Matondo (David Testo) 86'.

Game MVP: Jeff Clark, Vancouver, M

Awards
2005 FIFA World Players of the Year

As determined by a global vote of 302 national team coaches and captains from 157 FIFA member associations. First-place votes listed and total points. Players receive five points for 1st place votes, three points for 2nd place votes and one point for third place votes. Top 10 vote-getters listed below. USA national team players in **bold** type.

MEN

		1st	Pts
1	Ronaldinho, Brazil	159	956
2	Frank Lampar, England	25	306
3	Samuel Eto'o, Cameroon	15	190
4	Thierry Henry, France	11	172
5	Adriano, Brazil	17	170
6	Andriy Shevchenko, Ukraine	16	153
7	Steven Gerrard, England	11	131
8	Kaká, Brazil	10	101
9	Paolo Maldini, Italy	7	76
10	Didier Drogba, Ivory Coast	3	65

WOMEN

		1st	Pts
1	Birgit Prinz, Germany	75	513
2	Marta, Brazil	55	429
3	**Shannon Boxx**, USA	25	235
4	Hanna Ljungberg, Sweden	20	206
5	Renate Lingor, Germany	19	170
6	Maribel Dominguez, Mexico	13	115
7	Solveig Gulbrandsen, Norway	15	97
	Sandra Minnert, Germany	11	97
9	**Christie Welsh**, USA	4	78
10	Kelly Smith, England	5	60

Colleges

MEN
2005 Final *Soccer America* Top 25

Final 2005 regular season poll including games through Nov. 13. Conducted by the national weekly *Soccer America* and released on Nov. 14. Listing includes records through conference playoffs as well as NCAA tournament record and team lost to. Teams in **bold** type went on to reach College Cup. All tournament games decided by penalty kicks are considered ties. SMU, the fourth team in the College Cup, was not ranked in the top 25.

	Nov. 13 Record	NCAA Recap		Nov. 13 Record	NCAA Recap
1 Akron	17-1-2	2-1 (Maryland)	14 Virginia Tech	10-5-4	0-0-1 (NC-Gr'nsboro)
2 Connecticut	15-3-1	1-0-1 (Akron)	15 NC-Greensboro	15-5-0	1-1-1 (SMU)
3 **New Mexico**	15-1-2	4-1 (Maryland)	16 Creighton	12-4-3	3-1 (Clemson)
4 Duke	12-4-3	0-1 (Creighton)	17 South Carolina	12-6-2	0-1 (Wake Forest)
5 Penn St.	12-6-2	1-1 (Creighton)	18 N.C. State	11-6-1	0-1 (Clemson)
6 **Maryland**	15-4-1	4-0-1	19 South Florida	12-6-1	0-0-1 (Virginia)
7 Indiana	13-2-6	0-1 (Notre Dame)	20 CS-Northridge	14-3-3	1-1 (New Mexico)
8 UCLA	12-4-3	0-1 (SMU)	21 San Francisco	11-5-4	0-1 (SMU)
9 Old Dominion	15-3-2	0-1 (Wake Forest)	22 San Diego St.	9-3-6	0-1 (UC-SB)
10 North Carolina	15-3-3	2-1 (SMU)	23 Wake Forest	11-7-2	2-1 (California)
11 California	13-3-2	1-1-1 (New Mexico)	24 Hartwick	13-5-1	0-1 (Seton Hall)
12 **Clemson**	11-5-3	4-1 (New Mexico)	25 St. John's	9-5-5	2-1 (Maryland)
13 Virginia	12-4-2	0-1-1 (N. Carolina)			

NCAA Division I Tournament

First Round (Nov. 18 or 19)

at Brown 2	Rhode Island 1
at St. John's 3	Marist 1
at West Virginia 1	Robert Morris 0
Stony Brook 2	OT	at Yale 1
at SMU 2	San Francisco 1
at NC-Greensboro 3	James Madison 2
at South Florida 3	Stetson 0
Providence 1	OT	at Hofstra 0
at Notre Dame 2	Western Illinois 0
at Clemson 2	Coastal Carolina 0
at Seton Hall 2	Hartwick 1
at Creighton 3	Lafayette 0
at Santa Clara 1	Ohio St. 0
at Wake Forest 2	South Carolina 0
at UC-Santa Barbara 2	San Diego St. 0
Wisc-Milwaukee 2	Bradley 0

Second Round (Nov. 22)

at Maryland 1	Brown 0
at St. John's 1	Dartmouth 0
at Akron 5	West Virginia 0
at Connecticut 2	Stony Brook 0
SMU 3	at UCLA 0
NC-Greensboro 0	2 OT	at Virginia Tech 0

NC-Greensboro advanced on PKs

at Virginia 4	South Florida 4

Virginia advanced on PKs

at North Carolina 2	Providence 0
Notre Dame 2	at Indiana 0
Clemson 3	at N.C. State 0
at Penn St. 1	Seton Hall 0
Creighton 3	Duke 1
at California 0	2 OT	Santa Clara 0

California advanced on PKs

Wake Forest 2	at Old Dominion 1
CS-Northridge 3	UC-Santa Barbara 2
at New Mexico 2	2 OT	Wisc-Milwaukee 2

New Mexico advanced on PKs

Third Round (Nov. 26 or 27)

at Maryland 3	St. John's 1
Akron 3	2 OT	at Connecticut 3

Akron advanced on PKs

at SMU 3	NC-Greensboro 1
at North Carolina 2	Virginia 1
at Clemson 1	Notre Dame 0
Creighton 3	Penn St. 1
at California 3	2 OT	Wake Forest 2
at New Mexico 1	OT	CS-Northridge 0

Quarterfinals (Dec. 2, 3 or 4)

at Maryland 1	2OT	Akron 1

Maryland advanced on PKs

SMU 3	OT	North Carolina 2
at Clemson 1	Creighton 0
at New Mexico 1	California 0

2005 College Cup
at Cary, North Carolina (Dec. 9 & 11)

Semifinals

Maryland 4	SMU 1
New Mexico 2	Clemson 1

Championship

Maryland 1	New Mexico 0

Scoring
1st Half: MD—Marc Burch (unassisted), 30:33

Attendance: 6,922

Final records: New Mexico (18-2-3); Maryland (19-4-2).
Offensive MVP: Jason Garey, Maryland, F
Defensive MVP: Chris Seitz, Maryland, GK

WOMEN
2005 Final *Soccer America* Top 25

Final 2005 regular season poll including games through Nov. 6. Conducted by the national weekly *Soccer America* and released on Nov. 7. Listing includes records through conference playoffs as well as NCAA tournament record and team lost to. Teams in **bold** type went on to reach College Cup. All tournament games decided by penalty kicks are considered ties.

	Nov. 6 Record	NCAA Recap		Nov. 6 Record	NCAA Recap
1 **Portland**	18-0-1	5-0-1	14 Tennessee	14-5-2	1-1 (Virginia)
2 North Carolina	20-1-0	3-0-1 (Florida St.)	15 Pepperdine	13-3-3	2-1 (North Carolina)
3 **Penn St.**	19-0-1	4-0-1 (Portland)	16 USC	12-5-2	1-1 (CS-Fullerton)
4 **UCLA**	17-1-2	5-1 (Portland)	17 CS-Fullerton	17-3-0	2-1 (Virginia)
5 Notre Dame	19-2-0	3-1 (Portland)	18 Stanford	10-6-3	0-1 (St. Louis)
6 Virginia	15-5-1	3-1 (UCLA)	19 Gonzaga	12-3-4	0-1 (USC)
7 **Florida St.**	17-3-0	4-1-1 (UCLA)	20 BYU	15-2-3	0-0-1 (Weber St.)
8 California	14-3-2	2-1 (Florida St.)	21 Boston College	11-5-2	2-1 (Santa Clara)
9 Texas A&M	16-3-2	2-1 (Penn St.)	22 West Virginia	11-5-3	1-1 (Penn St.)
10 Santa Clara	14-4-2	3-1 (Penn St.)	23 Vanderbilt	16-3-2	0-1 (Samford)
11 Duke	13-5-1	1-1 (Yale)	24 Wisconsin	13-8-2	0-1 (Marquette)
12 Connecticut	15-4-2	0-1 (Boston Univ.)	25 Yale	13-3-1	2-1 (Notre Dame)
13 Marquette	17-3-1	2-1 (UCLA)			

NCAA Division I Tournament

First Round (Nov. 10 or 11)

at Penn St. 6 . . . . Bucknell 0
West Virginia 3 . . . . Hofstra 0
SMU 3 . . . . North Texas 0
at Texas A&M 7 . . . . .Northwestern St. 0
Boston University 1 . . . . . . .2 OT . . . . . . .at Connecticut 0
Boston College 2 . . . . .Dartmouth 1
St. Louis 2 . . . . .Stanford 0
at Santa Clara 5 . . . . .Fresno St. 0
at Notre Dame 6 . . . . .Valparaiso 0
Michigan St. 4 . . . . .Bowling Green 0
at Yale 3 . . . . .Cent. Conn. St. 0
Duke 4 . . . . .Fairfield 0
Weber St. 1 . . . . .2 OT . . . . .BYU 1
Weber St. advanced on PKs
Arizona 1 . . . . .at Utah 0
at Nebraska 1 . . . . .Creighton 0
Portland 5 . . . . .Iowa St. 0
at UCLA 9 .Mississippi Valley St. 0
Colorado 0 . . . . .2 OT . . . . .UC-Riverside 0
Colorado advanced on PKs
WI-Milwaukee 0 . . . . .2 OT . . . . .Purdue 0
WI-Milwaukee advanced on PKs
at CS-Fullerton 1 . . . . .OT . . . . .UNLV 0
UTEP 3 . . . . .OT . . . . .at Texas 2
Illinois 1 . . . . .2 OT . . . . .at Florida 0
Tennessee 5 . . . . .Wake Forest 2
Florida St. 3 . . . . .Florida Atlantic 0
Pepperdine 1 . . . . .Mississippi 0
California 2 . . . . .Rice 0
Samford 1 . . . . .2 OT . . . . .at Vanderbilt 1
Samford advanced on PKs
at North Carolina 2 . . . . .Western Carolina 0
Virginia Commonwealth 3 . . . . .Clemson 1
USC 1 . . . .¦. . . . . . .Gonzaga 0
at Marquette 1 . . . . .Wisconsin 0
at Virginia 4 . . . . .Liberty 0

Second Round (Nov. 12 or 13)

at Penn St. 5 . . . . .West Virginia 2
at Texas A&M 4 . . . . .SMU 2
Boston College 1 . . . . .Boston University 0
at Santa Clara 2 . . . . .St. Louis 0
at Notre Dame 3 . . . . .Michigan St. 0
at Yale 2 . . . . .Duke 1
Arizona 1 . . . . .Weber St. 0
at Portland 3 . . . . .Nebraska 2
at UCLA 3 . . . . .Colorado 0
Marquette 1 . . . . .Wisc-Milwaukee 0
at CS-Fullerton 3 . . . . .USC 1

Third Round (Nov. 18 or 20)

at Virginia 3 . . . . .Tennessee 0
at Florida St. 2 . . . . .Illinois 1
California 2 . . . . .UTEP 1
Pepperdine 2 . . . . .Samford 1
at North Carolina 6 . . . . .Virginia Commonwealth 2

Third Round (Nov. 18 or 20)

at Penn St. 4 . . . . .Texas A&M 1
at Santa Clara 2 . . . . .Boston College 1
at Notre Dame 5 . . . . .Yale 2
at Portland 4 . . . . .Arizona 0
at UCLA 4 . . . . .Marquette 0
at Virginia 2 . . . . .CS-Fullerton 1
at Florida St. 2 . . . . .California 1
at North Carolina 6 . . . . .Pepperdine 0

Quarterfinals (Nov. 25 or 27)

at Penn St. 2 . . . . .Santa Clara 1
at Portland 3 . . . . .Notre Dame 1
at UCLA 5 . . . . .Virginia 0
Florida St. 1 . . . . .at North Carolina 1
Florida St. advanced on PKs

2005 College Cup
at College Station, Texas (Dec. 2 & 4)

Semifinals

UCLA 4 . . . . .Florida St. 0
Portland 0 . . . . .2 OT . . . . .Penn St. 0
Portland advanced on PKs

Championship

Portland 4 . . . . .UCLA 0

Scoring

1st Half: PORT—Angie Woznuk (Megan Rapinoe) 1:32; PORT—Christine Sinclair (Woznuk) 21:21; PORT—Sinclair (Natalie Budge) 41:03.

2nd Half: PORT—Rapinoe (Woznuk) 76:13.

Attendance: 6,578
Final records: Portland (23-0-2), UCLA (22-2-2).
Offensive MVP: Christine Sinclair, Portland, F
Defensive MVP: Cori Alexander, Portland, GK

2005 Annual Awards

Men's Players of the Year

M.A.C. Hermann Trophy . . . . . Jason Garey, Maryland, F
Soccer America . . . . Jason Garey, Maryland, F
NCAA Div. II . . . . Christopher Joyce, Franklin Pierce
NCAA Div. III . . . . .David McClellan, Messiah
NAIA . . . . .Hjortur Hjartarson, Auburn-Montgomery
JuCo Div. I . . . . .Luis Campo, Georgia Perimeter
JuCo Div. III . . . . .Dwight Barnett, Herkimer

Women's Players of the Year

M.A.C. Hermann Trophy . . . .Christine Sinclair, Portland, F
Soccer America . . . . .Christine Sinclair, Portland, F
NCAA Div. II . . . . .Shannon Lovejoy, Seattle Pacific
NCAA Div. III . . . . .Cortney Kjar, Puget Sound
NAIA . . . . .Clare Sykes, Martin Methodist
JuCo Div. I . . . . .Melissa Hornfeck, Monroe
JuCo Div. III . . . . .Andrea Salvador, Solano

NSCAA Coaches of the Year

Women's Div. I . . . . .Paula Wilkins, Penn St.
Men's Div. I . . . . .Sasho Cirovski, Marylnd
Women's Div. II . . . . .Jeremy Gunn, Ft. Lewis
Men's Div. II . . . . .Don Klosterman, Nebraska-Omaha
Women's Div. III . . . . .Scott Frey, Messiah
Men's Div. III . . . . .Larry Zelentz, Gustavus Adolphus
Women's NAIA . . . . .Gerry Cleary, Martin Methodist
Men's NAIA . . . . .Phil Wolf, Azusa Pacific
Men's NCCAA Div. I . . . . .Joe Zackowicz, Mid-Continent
Women's NCCAA Div. I . . . . . Josh Lenarz, Trinity Christian
Men's NCCAA Div. II . .Sam Koleduk, Cincinnati Christian
Women's NCCAA Div. II . Joy Moyer, Philadelphia Biblical
Men's Juco Div. I . . . . .Marc Zagara, Georgia Perimeter
Men's JuCo Div. III . . . .Pepe Aragon, Herkimer County CC
Women's JuCo Div. I . . . . .Tracey Britton, Monroe CC
Women's JuCo Div. III . . . . .Robert Fuqua, Springfield Tech

Division I All-America Teams

MEN

The 2005 first team All-America selections of the National Soccer Coaches Association of America (NSCAA). Holdover from the 2004 NSCAA All-America first team are in **bold** type.

GOALKEEPER—Chris Dunsheath, Bradley.

DEFENDERS—Gregory Dalby, Notre Dame; Tyson Wahl, California; Marvel Wynne, UCLA.

MIDFIELDERS—Medi Ballouchy, Santa Clara; Scott Jones, NC-Greensboro; Yohann Mauger, Akron; Brian Plotkin, Indiana

FORWARDS—**Jeff Rowland**, New Mexico; Jason Garey, Maryland; Ross McKenzie, Akron; Willie Sims, CS-Northridge.

WOMEN

The 2005 first team All-America selections of the National Soccer Coaches Association of America (NSCAA). Holdovers from the 2004 NSCAA All-America first team are in **bold** type.

GOALKEEPER—Erin McLeod, Penn St.

DEFENDERS—Melanie Booth, Florida; Stephanie Lopez, Portland; Jill Oakes, UCLA.

MIDFIELDERS—**Lori Chalupny**, North Carolina; **Lindsey Huie**, Portland; Ali Christoph, Tennessee; Ali Krieger, Penn St.; Megan Rapinoe, Portland.

FORWARDS—**Tiffany Weimer**, Penn St.; Katie Thorlakson, Notre Dame; **Christine Sinclair**, Portland.

Small College Final Fours

MEN

NCAA Division II
at Wichita Falls, Texas. (Dec. 2-4)

Semifinals: Fort Lewis def. Lynn, 6-4; Franklin Pierce 1, Southern Illinois-Edwardsville, 1-0.
Championship: Fort Lewis 3, Franklin Pierce 1. Final records: Fort Lewis (22-0-1), Southern Illinois-Edwardsville (14-6-4).

NCAA Division III
at Greensboro, N.C. (Nov. 25-26)

Semifinals: Messiah def. Plattsburgh, 4-0; Gustavus Adolphus def. Whitworth, 2-1.
Championship: Messiah def. Gustavus Adolphus, 1-0; Final records: Messiah (24-0-0), Gustavus Adolphus (17-3-5).

NAIA
at Daytona Beach, Fla.

Semifinals: Lindsey Wilson (Ky.) def. Southern Nazarene, 2-0 OT; Azusa Pacific (Calif.) def. Hastings, 4-0.
Championship: Lindsey Wilson def. Azusa Pacific, 4-1.

WOMEN

NCAA Division II
at Wichita Falls, Texas (Dec. 1-3)

Semifinals: Nebraska-Omaha def. Franklin Pierce, 2-1; Seattle Pacific def. Carson-Newman, 3-2.
Championship: Nebraska-Omaha def. Seattle Pacific, 2-1 OT. Final records: Nebraksa-Omaha (20-2-0), Seattle Pacific (20-1-4).

NCAA Division III
at Greensboro, N.C. (Nov. 25-26)

Semifinals: Chicago def. Messiah, 2-1 OT; The College of New Jersey def. Tufts, 3-0.
Championship: TCNJ def. Messiah, 1-0. Final records: TCNJ (22-1), Messiah (22-0-1).

NAIA
at Olathe, Kan.

Semifinals: Martin Methodist (Tenn.) def. Westmont, 1-1 (4-3 PKs); Lee (Tenn.) def. Simon Fraser, 1-0.
Championship: Martin Methodist def. Lee, 1-0.

1900-2006
Through the Years

SPORTS ALMANAC

The World Cup

The Federation Internationale de Football Association (FIFA) began the World Cup championship tournament in 1930 with a 13-team field in Uruguay. Sixty-four years later, 138 countries competed in qualifying rounds to fill 24 berths in the 1994 World Cup finals. FIFA increased the World Cup '98 tournament field from 24 to 32 teams, and it remained at 32 in 2006 including automatic berths for defending champion Brazil and host Germany. The other 30 slots were allotted by region: Europe (12), Africa (5), South America (4), CONCACAF (3), Asia (4), the two remaining positions were determined via two home-and-away playoff series. One was between the #4 CONCACAF team (Trinidad & Tobago) and the #5 Asian team (Bahrain) and the other was between the #5 South American team (Uruguay) and the champion of Oceania (Australia).

Tournaments have been played once in Asia (Japan/South Korea), three times in North America (Mexico 2 and U.S.), four times in South America (Argentina, Chile, Brazil and Uruguay) and nine times in Europe (France 2, Italy 2, England, Spain, Sweden, Switzerland and West Germany). Following an outcry when Germany was awarded the 2006 World Cup over South Africa, FIFA announced that, starting in 2010, the World Cup will be rotated among six continents.

Brazil retired the first World Cup (called the Jules Rimet Trophy after FIFA's first president) in 1970 after winning it for the third time. The new trophy, first presented in 1974, is known as simply the World Cup.

Multiple winners: Brazil (5); Italy (4); West Germany (3); Argentina and Uruguay (2).

Year	Champion	Manager	Score	Runner-up	Host Country	Third Place
1930	Uruguay	Alberto Suppici	4-2	Argentina	Uruguay	No game
1934	Italy	Vittório Pozzo	2-1*	Czechoslovakia	Italy	Germany 3, Austria 2
1938	Italy	Vittório Pozzo	4-2	Hungary	France	Brazil 4, Sweden 2
1942-46 Not held						
1950	Uruguay	Juan Lopez	2-1	Brazil	Brazil	No game
1954	West Germany	Sepp Herberger	3-2	Hungary	Switzerland	Austria 3, Uruguay 1
1958	Brazil	Vicente Feola	5-2	Sweden	Sweden	France 6, W. Ger. 3
1962	Brazil	Aimoré Moreira	3-1	Czechoslovakia	Chile	Chile 1, Yugoslavia 0
1966	England	Alf Ramsey	4-2*	W. Germany	England	Portugal 2, USSR 1
1970	Brazil	Mario Zagalo	4-1	Italy	Mexico	W. Ger. 1, Uruguay 0
1974	West Germany	Helmut Schoen	2-1	Netherlands	W. Germany	Poland 1, Brazil 0
1978	Argentina	Cesar Menotti	3-1*	Netherlands	Argentina	Brazil 2, Italy 1
1982	Italy	Enzo Bearzot	3-1	W. Germany	Spain	Poland 3, France 2
1986	Argentina	Carlos Bilardo	3-2	W. Germany	Mexico	France 4, Belgium 2*
1990	West Germany	Franz Beckenbauer	1-0	Argentina	Italy	Italy 2, England 1
1994	Brazil	Carlos Parreira	0-0†	Italy	USA	Sweden 4, Bulgaria 0
1998	France	Aimé Jacquet	3-0	Brazil	France	Croatia 2, Netherlands 1
2002	Brazil	Luiz Felipe Scolari	2-0	Germany	Japan/S. Korea	Turkey 3, S. Korea 2
2006	Italy	Marcelo Lippi	1-1‡	France	Germany	Germany 3, Portugal 1
2010	at South Africa (TBD)					

*Winning goals scored in overtime (no sudden death); †Brazil def. Italy in shootout (3-2); ‡Italy def. France in shootout (5-3).

All-Time World Cup Leaders

Career Goals

World Cup scoring leaders through 2006. Years listed are years played in World Cup.

	No
Ronaldo, Brazil (1994, 98, 2002, 06)	15
Gerd Müller, West Germany (1970, 74)	14
Just Fontaine, France (1958)	13
Pelé, Brazil (1958, 62, 66, 70)	12
Sandor Kocsis, Hungary (1954)	11
Juergen Klinsmann, Germany (1990, 94, 98)	11
Six Players tied with 10 each.	

Most Valuable Player

Officially, the Golden Ball Award, the Most Valuable Player of the World Cup tournament has been selected since 1982 by a panel of international soccer journalists.

Year		Year	
1982	Paolo Rossi, Italy	1998	Ronaldo, Brazil
1986	Diego Maradona, Arg.	2002	Oliver Kahn, Germany
1990	Toto Schillaci, Italy	2006	Zinedine Zidane, France
1994	Romario, Brazil		

Single Tournament Goals

Year		Gm	No
1930	Guillermo Stabile, Argentina	4	8
1934	Angelo Schiavio, Italy	3	4
	Oldrich Nejedly, Czechoslovakia	4	4
	Edmund Conen, Germany	4	4
1938	Leônidas, Brazil	3	8
1950	Ademir, Brazil	6	7
1954	Sandor Kocsis, Hungary	5	11
1958	Just Fontaine, France	6	13
1962	Drazen Jerkovic, Yugoslavia	6	5
1966	Eusébio, Portugal	6	9
1970	Gerd Müller, West Germany	6	10
1974	Grzegorz Lato, Poland	7	7
1978	Mario Kempes, Argentina	7	6
1982	Paolo Rossi, Italy	7	6
1986	Gary Lineker, England	5	6
1990	Toto Schillaci, Italy	7	6
1994	Oleg Salenko, Russia	3	6
	Hristo Stoitchkov, Bulgaria	7	6
1998	Davor Suker, Croatia	7	6
2002	Ronaldo, Brazil	7	8
2006	Miroslav Klose, Germany	7	5

All-Time World Cup Ranking Table

Since the first World Cup in 1930, Brazil is the only country to play in all 17 final tournaments. The FIFA all-time table below ranks all nations that have ever qualified for a World Cup final tournament by points earned through 2006. Victories, which earned two points from 1930-90, were awarded three points starting in 1994. Note that Germany's appearances include 10 made by West Germany from 1954-90. Participants in the 2006 World Cup final are in **bold** type.

		App	Gm	W	L	T	Pts	GF	GA
1	**Brazil**	18	92	64	14	14	153	201	84
2	**Germany**	16	92	56	18	19	142	190	110
3	**Italy**	16	76	56	17	19	115	122	68
4	**Argentina**	14	64	33	20	12	83	113	74
5	**England**	12	55	27	14	16	71	74	47
6	**Spain**	12	49	23	16	10	63	80	57
	France	12	51	25	17	9	63	95	64
8	**Sweden**	11	46	16	17	12	47	74	69
9	**Netherlands**	8	34	16	10	10	44	59	38
10	Russia	9	37	14	14	6	41	64	44
11	Yugoslavia	9	37	16	13	8	40	60	46
	Uruguay	10	40	15	15	10	40	65	57
13	**Poland**	7	31	15	11	5	37	44	40
	Mexico	13	44	11	22	12	37	48	85
15	Hungary	9	32	15	14	3	33	87	57
16	Belgium	11	36	10	17	9	30	46	63
	Czech Republic	9	33	12	16	5	30	47	49
18	Austria	7	29	12	13	4	28	43	47
19	**Portugal**	4	19	12	7	0	27	31	19
20	**Switzerland**	8	26	8	14	4	22	37	51
21	Romania	7	21	8	8	5	21	30	32
	Paraguay	7	22	6	10	6	21	27	36
	South Korea	7	24	5	13	6	21	22	53
24	Chile	7	25	7	12	6	20	31	40
25	Denmark	3	13	7	4	2	18	24	18
26	**USA**	8	25	6	16	3	17	27	51
27	Cameroon	5	17	4	6	7	16	15	29
28	Scotland	8	23	4	12	7	15	25	41
	Turkey	2	10	4	4	1	15	20	17
	Croatia	3	13	6	5	2	15	15	11
31	Bulgaria	7	26	3	15	8	14	22	53
32	Ireland	3	13	2	4	7	12	10	10
33	Peru	4	15	4	8	3	11	19	31
	No. Ireland	3	13	3	5	5	11	13	23
35	Nigeria	3	11	4	6	1	9	14	16
	Ukraine	1	5	3	2	0	9	5	7
37	Morocco	4	13	2	7	4	8	12	18
	Colombia	4	13	3	8	2	8	14	23
	Costa Rica	3	10	3	6	1	8	12	21
	Senegal	1	5	2	1	2	8	7	6
	Japan	3	10	2	6	2	8	8	14
	Ecuador	2	7	3	4	0	8	7	8

		App	Gm	W	L	T	Pts	GF	GA
43	Norway	2	8	2	3	3	7	7	8
44	East Germany	1	6	2	2	2	6	5	5
	South Africa	2	6	1	2	3	6	8	11
	Saudi Arabia	4	13	2	9	2	6	9	32
	Tunisia	4	12	1	7	4	6	8	17
	Ghana	1	3	2	0	1	6	4	3
49	Algeria	2	6	2	3	1	5	6	10
	Wales	1	5	1	1	3	5	4	4
	Australia	2	6	1	4	2	5	5	11
52	**Iran**	3	9	1	6	2	4	6	18
53	North Korea	1	4	1	2	1	3	5	9
	Cuba	1	3	1	1	1	3	5	12
	Jamaica	1	3	1	2	0	3	3	9
	Ivory Coast	1	3	1	2	0	3	5	6
57	Egypt	2	4	0	2	2	2	3	6
	Honduras	1	3	0	1	2	2	2	3
	Israel	1	3	0	1	2	2	1	3
	Angola	1	3	0	1	2	2	1	2
61	**Bolivia**	3	6	0	5	1	1	1	20
	Kuwait	1	3	0	2	1	1	2	6
	Trinidad & Tobago	1	3	0	2	1	1	0	4
64	El Salvador	2	6	0	6	0	0	1	22
	Canada	1	3	0	3	0	0	0	5
	East Indies	1	1	0	1	0	0	0	6
	Greece	1	3	0	3	0	0	0	10
	Haiti	1	3	0	3	0	0	2	14
	Iraq	1	3	0	3	0	0	1	4
	Slovenia	1	3	0	3	0	0	2	7
	New Zealand	1	3	0	2	1	0	2	12
	UAE	1	3	0	3	0	0	2	11
	China	1	3	0	3	0	0	0	9
	Zaire	1	3	0	3	0	0	0	14
	Serbia & Montenegro	1	3	0	3	0	0	2	10
	Togo	1	3	0	3	0	0	1	6

The United States in the World Cup

While the United States has fielded a national team every year of the World Cup, only seven of those teams have been able to make it past the preliminary competition and qualify for the final World Cup tournament. The 1994 national team automatically qualified because the U.S. served as host of the event for the first time. The U.S. played in three of the first four World Cups (1930, '34 and '50) and each of the last five (1990, '94, '98, 2002 and 2006). The Americans have a record of 6-16-3 in 25 World Cup matches.

1930
1st Round Matches
United States 3 . . . . .Belgium 0
United States 3 . . . . .Paraguay 0

Semifinals
Argentina 6 . . . . .United States 1

U.S. Scoring—Bert Patenaude (3), Bart McGhee (2), James Brown and Thomas Florie.

1934
1st Round Match
Italy 7 . . . . .United States 1

U.S. Scoring—Buff Donelli (who later became a noted college and NFL football coach).

1950
1st Round Matches
Spain 3 . . . . .United States 1
United States 1 . . . . .England 0
Chile 5 . . . . .United States 2

U.S. Scoring—Joe Gaetjens, Joe Maca, John Souza and Frank Wallace.

1990
1st Round Matches
Czechoslovakia 5 . . . . .United States 1
Italy 1 . . . . .United States 0
Austria 2 . . . . .United States 1

U.S. Scoring—Paul Caligiuri and Bruce Murray.

1994
1st Round Matches

United States 1 . . . . .Switzerland 1
United States 2 . . . . .Colombia 1
Romania 1 . . . . .United States 0

Round of 16

Brazil 1 . . . . .United States 0
U.S. Scoring–Eric Wynalda, Earnie Stewart and own goal (Colombia defender Andres Escobar).

1998
1st Round Matches

Germany 2 . . . . .United States 0
Iran 2 . . . . .United States 1
Yugoslavia 1 .United States 0
U.S. Scoring–Brian McBride.

2002
1st Round Matches

United States 3 . . . . .Portugal 2
United States 1 . . . . .So. Korea 1
Poland 3 . . . . .United States 1

Round of 16

United States 2 . . . . .Mexico 0

Round of 8

Germany 1 . . . . .United States 0
U.S. Scoring– Landon Donovan (2), Brian McBride (2), John O'Brien, own goal (Portugal defender Jorge Costa) and Clint Mathis.

2006
1st Round Matches

Czech Republic 3 . . . . .United States 0
Italy 1 . . . . .United States 1
Ghana 2 . . . . .United States 1

U.S. Scoring–own goal (Italian defender Christian Zaccardo), Clint Dempsey.

World Cup Finals

Brazil and Germany (formerly West Germany) have played in the most Cup finals with seven but faced each other for the first time in a final in 2002. Note that a four-team round robin determined the 1950 championship–the deciding game turned out to be the last one of the tournament between Uruguay and Brazil.

1930
Uruguay 4, Argentina 2
(at Montevideo, Uruguay)

		1	2–T
July 30	Uruguay (4-0)	1	3–4
	Argentina (4-1)	2	0–2

Goals: Uruguay–Pablo Dorado (12th minute), Pedro Cea (54th), Santos Iriarte (68th), Castro (89th); Argentina–Carlos Peucelle (20th), Guillermo Stabile (37th).
Uruguay–Ballesteros, Nasazzi, Mascheroni, Andrade, Fernandez, Gestido, Dorado, Scarone, Castro, Cea, Iriarte.
Argentina–Botasso, Della Torre, Paternoster, J. Evaristo, Monti, Suarez, Peucelle, Varallo, Stabile, Ferreira, M. Evaristo.
Attendance: 90,000. **Referee:** Langenus (Belgium).

1934
Italy 2, Czechoslovakia 1 (OT)
(at Rome)

		1	2	OT–T
June 10	Italy (4-0-1)	0	1	1–2
	Czechoslovakia (3-1)	0	1	0–1

Goals: Italy–Raimondo Orsi (80th minute), Angelo Schiavio (95th); Czechoslovakia–Puc (70th).
Italy–Combi, Monzeglio, Allemandi, Ferraris IV, Monti, Bertolini, Guaita, Meazza, Schiavio, Ferrari, Orsi.
Czechoslovakia–Planicka, Zenisek, Ctyroky, Kostalek, Cambal, Krcil, Junek, Svoboda, Sobotka, Nejedly, Puc.
Attendance: 55,000. **Referee:** Eklind (Sweden).

1938
Italy 4, Hungary 2
(at Paris)

		1	2–T
June 19	Italy (4-0)	3	1–4
	Hungary (3-1)	1	1–2

Goals: Italy–Gino Colaussi (5th minute), Silvio Piola (16th), Colaussi (35th), Piola (82nd); Hungary–Titkos (7th), Georges Sarosi (70th).
Italy–Olivieri, Foni, Rava, Serantoni, Andreolo, Locatelli, Biavati, Meazza, Piola, Ferrari, Colaussi.
Hungary–Szabo, Polgar, Biro, Szalay, Szucs, Lazar, Sas, Vincze, G. Sarosi, Szengeller, Titkos.
Attendance: 65,000. **Referee:** Capdeville (France).

1950
Uruguay 2, Brazil 1
(at Rio de Janeiro)

		1	2–T
July 16	Uruguay (3-0-1)	0	2–2
	Brazil (4-1-1)	0	1–1

Goals: Uruguay–Juan Schiaffino (66th minute), Chico Ghiggia (79th); Brazil–Friaca (47th).
Uruguay–Maspoli, M. Gonzales, Tejera, Gambetta, Varela, Andrade, Ghiggia, Perez, Miguez, Schiaffino, Moran.
Brazil–Barbosa, Augusto, Juvenal, Bauer, Danilo, Bigode, Friaça, Zizinho, Ademir, Jair, Chico.
Attendance: 199,854. **Referee:** Reader (England).

*Italy won the last **World Cup** (in 1938) before World War II and held the trophy until the return of the tournament in 1950. **Did you know** that during the war Dr. Ottorino Barassi, the Italian Vice President of FIFA, actually hid the World Cup trophy in a shoe box under his bed to save it from falling into the hands of occupying troops?*

World Cup Finals (Cont.)

1954
West Germany 3, Hungary 2
(at Berne, Switzerland)

		1	2–T
July 4	West Germany (4-1) 2		1–3
	Hungary (4-1) 2		0–2

Goals: West Germany—Max Morlock (10th minute), Helmut Rahn (18th), Rahn (84th); Hungary—Ferenc Puskas (4th), Zoltan Czibor (9th).

West Germany—Turek, Posipal, Liebrich, Kohlmeyer, Eckel, Mai, Rahn, Morlock, O. Walter, F. Walter, Schaefer.

Hungary—Grosics, Buzansky, Lorant, Lantos, Bozsik, Zakarias, Czibor, Kocsis, Hidegkuti, Puskas, J. Toth.

Attendance: 60,000. **Referee:** Ling (England).

1958
Brazil 5, Sweden 2
(at Stockholm)

		1	2–T
June 29	Brazil (5-0-1) 2		3–5
	Sweden (4-1-1) 1		1–2

Goals: Brazil—Vava (9th minute), Vava (32nd), Pelé (55th), Mario Zagalo (68th), Pelé (90th); Sweden—Nils Liedholm (3rd), Agne Simonsson (80th).

Brazil—Gilmar, D. Santos, N. Santos, Zito, Bellini, Orlando, Garrincha, Didi, Vava, Pelé, Zagalo.

Sweden—Svensson, Bergmark, Axbom, Boerjesson, Gustavsson, Parling, Hamrin, Gren, Simonsson, Liedholm, Skoglund.

Attendance: 49,737. **Referee:** Guigue (France).

1962
Brazil 3, Czechoslovakia 1
(at Santiago, Chile)

		1	2–T
June 17	Brazil (5-0-1) 1		2–3
	Czechoslovakia (3-2-1) 1		0–1

Goals: Brazil—Amarildo (17th minute), Zito (68th), Vava (77th); Czechoslovakia—Josef Masopust (15th).

Brazil—Gilmar, D. Santos, N. Santos, Zito, Mauro, Zozimo, Garrincha, Didi, Vava, Amarildo, Zagalo.

Czechoslovakia—Schroiff, Tichy, Novak, Pluskal, Popluhar, Masopust, Pospichal, Scherer, Kvasniak, Kadraba, Jelinek.

Attendance: 68,679. **Referee:** Latishev (USSR).

1966
England 4, West Germany 2 (OT)
(at London)

		1	2	OT–T
July 30	England (5-0-1) 1	1		2–4
	West Germany (4-1-1) 1	1		0–2

Goals: England—Geoff Hurst (18th. minute), Martin Peters (78th), Hurst (101st), Hurst (120th); West Germany—Helmut Haller (12th), Wolfgang Weber (90th).

England—Banks, Cohen, Wilson, Stiles, J. Charlton, Moore, Ball, Hurst, B. Charlton, Hunt, Peters.

West Germany—Tilkowski, Hottges, Schnellinger, Beckenbauer, Schulz, Weber, Haller, Seeler, Held, Overath, Emmerich.

Attendance: 93,802. **Referee:** Dienst (Switzerland).

1970
Brazil 4, Italy 1
(at Mexico City)

		1	2–T
June 21	Brazil (6-0) 1		3–4
	Italy (3-1-2) 1		0–1

Goals: Brazil—Pelé (18th minute), Gerson (65th), Jairzinho (70th), Carlos Alberto (86th); Italy—Roberto Boninsegna (37th).

Brazil—Felix, C. Alberto, Everaldo, Clodoaldo, Brito, Piazza, Jairzinho, Gerson, Tostão, Pelé, Rivelino.

Italy—Albertosi, Burgnich, Facchetti, Bertini (Juliano, 73rd), Rosato, Cera, Domenghini, Mazzola, Boninsegna (Rivera, 84th), De Sisti, Riva.

Attendance: 107,412. **Referee:** Glockner (E. Germany).

1974
West Germany 2, Netherlands 1
(at Munich)

		1	2–T
July 7	West Germany (6-1) 2		0–2
	Netherlands (5-1-1) 1		0–1

Goals: West Germany—Paul Breitner (25th minute, penalty kick), Gerd Müller (43rd); Netherlands—Johan Neeskens (1st, penalty kick).

West Germany—Maier, Beckenbauer, Vogts, Breitner, Schwarzenbeck, Overath, Bonhof, Hoeness, Grabowski, Muller, Holzenbein.

Netherlands—Jongbloed, Suurbier, Rijsbergen (De Jong, 58th), Krol, Haan, Jansen, Van Hanegem, Neeskens, Rep, Cruyff, Rensenbrink (R. Van de Kerkhof, 46th).

Attendance: 77,833. **Referee:** Taylor (England).

1978
Argentina 3, Netherlands 1 (OT)
(at Buenos Aires)

		1	2	OT–T
June 25	Argentina (5-1-1) 1	0		2–3
	Netherlands (3-2-2) 0	1		0–1

Goals: Argentina—Mario Kempes (37th minute), Kempes (104th), Daniel Bertoni (114th); Netherlands—Dirk Nanninga (81st).

Argentina—Fillol, Olguin, L. Galvan, Passarella, Tarantini, Ardiles (Larrosa, 65th), Gallego, Kempes, Luque, Bertoni, Ortiz (Houseman, 77th).

Netherlands—Jongbloed, Jansen (Suurbier, 72nd), Brandts, Krol, Poortvliet, Haan, Neeskens, W. Van de Kerkhof, R. Van de Kerkhof, Rep (Nanninga, 58th), Rensenbrink.

Attendance: 77,260. **Referee:** Gonella (Italy).

1982
Italy 3, West Germany 1
(at Madrid)

		1	2–T
July 11	Italy (4-0-3) 0		3–3
	West Germany (4-2-1) 0		1–1

Goals: Italy—Paolo Rossi (57th minute), Marco Tardelli (68th), Alessandro Altobelli (81st); West Germany—Paul Breitner (83rd).

Italy—Zoff, Scirea, Gentile, Cabrini, Collovati, Bergomi, Tardelli, Oriali, Conti, Rossi, Graziani (Altobelli, 8th, and Causio, 89th).

West Germany—Schumacher, Stielike, Kaltz, Briegel, K.H. Forster, B. Forster, Breitner, Dremmler (Hrubesch, 61st), Littbarski, Fischer, Rummenigge (Muller, 69th).

Attendance: 90,080. **Referee:** Coelho (Brazil).

1986
Argentina 3, West Germany 2
(at Mexico City)

		1	2-T
June 29	Argentina (6-0-1) 1		2–3
	West Germany (4-2-1) 0		2–2

Goals: Argentina–Jose Brown (22nd minute), Jorge Valdano (55th), Jorge Burruchaga (83rd); West Germany–Karl-Heinz Rummenigge (73rd), Rudi Voller (81st).

Argentina–Pumpido, Cuciuffo, Olarticoechea, Ruggeri, Brown, Batista, Burruchaga (Trobbiani, 89th), Giusti, Enrique, Maradona, Valdano.

West Germany–Schumacher, Jakobs, B. Forster, Berthold, Briegel, Eder, Brehme, Matthaus, Rummenigge, Magath (Hoeness, 61st), Allofs (Voller, 46th).

Attendance: 114,590. **Referee:** Filho (Brazil).

1990
West Germany 1, Argentina 0
(at Rome)

		1	2-T
July 8	West Germany (6-0-1) 0		1–1
	Argentina (4-2-1) 0		0–0

Goals: West Germany–Andreas Brehme (85th minute, penalty kick).

West Germany–Illgner, Berthold (Reuter, 73rd), Kohler, Augenthaler, Buchwald, Brehme, Haessler, Matthaus, Littbarski, Klinsmann, Voller.

Argentina–Goycoechea, Ruggeri (Monzon, 46th), Simon, Serrizuela, Lorenzo, Basualdo, Troglio, Burruchaga (Calderon, 53rd), Sensini, Dezotti, Maradona.

Attendance: 73,603. **Referee:** Codesal (Mexico).

1994
Brazil 0, Italy 0 (Shoot-out)
(at Pasadena, Calif.)

		1	2	OT–T
July 17	Brazil (6-0-1) 0		0	0– 0*
	Italy (4-2-1) 0		0	0– 0

*Brazil wins shootout, 3-2.

Shootout (five shots each, alternating): ITA–Baresi (miss, 0-0); BRA–Santos (blocked, 0-0); ITA– Albertini (goal, 1-0); BRA–Romario (goal, 1-1); ITA–Evani (goal, 2-1); BRA–Branco (goal, 2-2); ITA–Massaro (blocked, 2-2); BRA–Dunga (goal, 2-3); ITA–R. Baggio (miss, 2-3).

Brazil–Taffarel, Jorginho (Cafu, 21st minute), Branco, Aldair, Santos, Mazinho, Silva, Dunga, Zinho (Viola, 106th), Bebeto, Romario.

Italy–Pagliuca, Mussi (Apolloni, 35th minute), Baresi, Benarrivo, Maldini, Albertini, D. Baggio (Evani, 95th), Berti, Donadoni, R. Baggio, Massaro.

Attendance: 94,194. **Referee:** Puhl (Hungary).

1998
France 3, Brazil 0
(at Paris)

		1	2–	T
July 12	Brazil (6-1) 0		0–	0
	France (7-0) 2		1–	3

Goals: France–Zinedine Zidane (27th and 46th minutes), Petit (92).

Brazil–Taffarel, Cafu, Aldair, Baiano, Carlos, Sampaio (Edmundo, 74th minute), Dunga, Rivaldo, Leonardo (Denilson, 46th minute), Bebeto, Ronaldo.

France–Barthez, Lizarazu, Desailly, Thuram, Leboeuf, Djorkaeff (Viera, 75th minute), Deschamps, Zidane, Petit, Karembeu (Boghossian, 57th minute), Guivarc'h, Dugarry.

Attendance: 75,000. **Referee:** Belqola (Morocco).

2002
Brazil 2, Germany 0
(at Yokohama, Japan)

		1	2–	T
June 30	Germany (5-2) 0		0–	0
	Brazil (7-0) 0		2–	2

Goals: Brazil–Ronaldo (67th and 79th minutes).

Germany–Kahn, Linke, Ramelow, Neuville, Hamann, Klose (Bierhoff, 74th minute), Jeremies (Asamoah, 77th minute), Bode (Ziege, 84th minute), Schneider, Metzelder, Frings.

Brazil–Marcos, Cafu, Lucio, Junior, Edmilson, Carlos, Silva, Ronaldo (Denilson, 90th minute), Rivaldo, Ronaldinho (Paulista, 85th minute), Kleberson.

Attendance: 69,029. **Referee:** Collina (Italy).

2006
Italy 1, France 1 (Shoot-out)
(at Berlin)

		1	2	OT–	T
July 9	Italy (5-2) 1		0	0–	1*
	France (7-0) 1		0	0–	1

*Italy wins shootout, 5-4.

Goals: France–Zinedine Zidane (7th minute); Italy—Marco Materazzi (19th).

Shootout (five shots each, alternating): ITA–Pirlo (goal, 1-0); FRA–Wiltord (goal, 1-1); ITA– Materazzi (goal, 2-1); FRA–Trezeguet miss, 1-2); ITA– De Rossi (goal, 3-1); FRA–Abidal (goal, 2-3); ITA– Del Piero (goal, 4-2); FRA–Sagnol (goal, 3-4); ITA–Grosso (goal, 5-3).

Italy–Buffon, Gross, Cannavaro, Gattuso, Toni, Totti (De Rossi, 61st minute), Camoranesi (Del Piero, 86th), Zambrotta, Perrotta (Iaquinta), Pirlo, Materazzi.

France–Barthez, Abidal, Vieira (Diarra, 56th minute), Gallas, Makelele, Malouda, Zidane, Henry (Wiltord 107th), Thuram, Sagnol, Ribery (Trezeguet 100th).

Attendance: 69,000. **Referee:** Elizondo (Argentina).

World Cup Shoot-outs
Introduced in 1982; winning sides in **bold** type.

Year	Round		Final	SO	Year	Round		Final	SO
1982	Semi	**W. Germany** vs. France	3-3	(5-4)	1998	Second	**Argentina** vs. England	2-2	(4-3)
1986	Quarter	**Belgium** vs. Spain	1-1	(5-4)		Quarter	**France** vs. Italy	0-0	(4-3)
	Quarter	**France** vs. Brazil	1-1	(4-3)	2002	Second	**Spain** vs. Ireland	1-1	(3-2)
	Quarter	**W. Germany** vs. Mexico	0-0	(4-1)		Quarter	**So. Korea** vs. Spain	0-0	(5-3)
1990	Second	**Ireland** vs. Romania	0-0	(5-4)	2006	Second	**Ukraine** vs. Switzerland	0-0	(3-0)
	Quarter	**Argentina** vs.Yugoslavia	0-0	(3-2)		Quarter	**Germany** vs. Argentina	1-1	(4-2)
	Semi	**Argentina** vs. Italy	1-1	(4-3)		Quarter	**Portugal** vs. England	0-0	(3-1)
	Semi	**W. Germany** vs. England	1-1	(4-3)		Final	**Italy** vs. France	1-1	(5-3)
1994	Second	**Bulgaria** vs. Mexico	1-1	(3-1)					
	Quarter	**Sweden** vs. Romania	2-2	(5-4)					
	Final	**Brazil** vs. Italy	0-0	(3-2)					

World Cup (Cont.)
Year-by-Year Comparisons

How the 18 World Cup tournaments have compared in nations qualifying, matches played, players participating, goals scored, average goals per game, overall attendance and attendance per game.

Year	Host	Continent	Nations	Matches	Players	Goals Scored	Goals Per Game	Attendance Overall	Attendance Per Game
1930	Uruguay	So. America	13	18	189	70	3.8	589,300	32,739
1934	Italy	Europe	16	17	208	70	4.1	361,000	21,235
1938	France	Europe	15	18	210	84	4.7	376,000	20,889
1942-46	Not held								
1950	Brazil	So. America	13	22	192	88	4.0	1,044,763	47,489
1954	Switzerland	Europe	16	26	233	140	5.3	872,000	33,538
1958	Sweden	Europe	16	35	241	126	3.6	819,402	23,411
1962	Chile	So. America	16	32	252	89	2.8	892,812	27,900
1966	England	Europe	16	32	254	89	2.8	1,464,944	45,780
1970	Mexico	No. America	16	32	270	95	3.0	1,690,890	52,840
1974	West Germany	Europe	16	38	264	97	2.6	1,809,953	47,630
1978	Argentina	So. America	16	38	277	102	2.7	1,685,602	44,358
1982	Spain	Europe	24	52	396	146	2.8	2,108,723	40,552
1986	Mexico	No. America	24	52	414	132	2.5	2,393,031	46,020
1990	Italy	Europe	24	52	413	115	2.2	2,516,354	48,391
1994	United States	No. America	24	52	437	140	2.7	3,587,088	68,982
1998	France	Europe	32	64	704	171	2.7	2,775,400	43,366
2002	Japan/So. Korea	Asia	32	64	736	161	2.5	2,705,197	42,269
2006	Germany	Europe	32	64	736	147	2.3	3,353,655	52,401

OTHER WORLDWIDE COMPETITION

The Olympic Games

Held every four years since 1896, except during World War I (1916) and World War II (1940-44). Soccer was not a medal sport in 1896 at Athens or in 1932 at Los Angeles. By agreement between FIFA and the IOC, Olympic soccer competition is currently limited to players 23 years old and under with a few exceptions.

Multiple winners: England and Hungary (3); Soviet Union and Uruguay (2).

MEN

Year		Year	
1900	**England**, France, Belgium	1964	**Hungary**, Czechoslovakia, Germany
1904	**Canada**, USA I, USA II	1968	**Hungary**, Bulgaria, Japan
1906	**Denmark**, Smyrna (Int'l entry), Greece	1972	**Poland**, Hungary, East Germany & Soviet Union
1908	**England**, Denmark, Netherlands	1976	**East Germany**, Poland, Soviet Union
1912	**England**, Denmark, Netherlands	1980	**Czechoslovakia**, East Germany, Soviet Union
1920	**Belgium**, Spain, Netherlands	1984	**France**, Brazil, Yugoslavia
1924	**Uruguay**, Switzerland, Sweden	1988	**Soviet Union**, Brazil, West Germany
1928	**Uruguay**, Argentina, Italy	1992	**Spain**, Poland, Ghana
1936	**Italy**, Austria, Norway	1996	**Nigeria**, Argentina, Brazil
1948	**Sweden**, Yugoslavia, Denmark	2000	**Cameroon**, Spain, Chile
1952	**Hungary**, Yugoslavia, Sweden	2004	**Argentina**, Paraguay, Italy
1956	**Soviet Union**, Yugoslavia, Bulgaria	2008	(at Beijing, China)
1960	**Yugoslavia**, Denmark, Hungary		

WOMEN

Multiple winners: United States (2).

Year		Year	
1996	**USA**, China, Norway	2004	**USA**, Brazil, Germany
2000	**Norway**, USA, Germany	2008	(at Beijing, China)

The Under-20 World Cup

Held every two years since 1977. Officially, the FIFA World Youth Championship.

Multiple winners: Argentina (5); Brazil (3); Portugal (2).

Year		Year		Year		Year	
1977	Soviet Union	1985	Brazil	1993	Brazil	2001	Argentina
1979	Argentina	1987	Yugoslavia	1995	Argentina	2003	Brazil
1981	West Germany	1989	Portugal	1997	Argentina	2005	Argentina
1983	Brazil	1991	Portugal	1999	Spain	2007	(at Canada)

The Under-17 World Cup

Held every two years since 1985. Officially, the FIFA U-17 World Championship.

Multiple winners: Brazil (3); Ghana and Nigeria (2).

Year		Year	
1985	Nigeria	1997	Brazil
1987	Soviet Union	1999	Brazil
1989	Saudi Arabia	2001	France
1991	Ghana	2003	Brazil
1993	Nigeria	2005	Mexico
1995	Ghana	2007	(at S. Korea)

Indoor World Championship

First held in 1989. Officially. the FIFA Futsal World Championship.

Multiple winners: Brazil (3), Spain (2).

Year		Year	
1989	Brazil	2000	Spain
1992	Brazil	2004	Spain
1996	Brazil		

Women's World Cup

First held in 1991. Officially, the FIFA Women's World Championship.

Multiple winner: United States (2).

Year		Year	
1991	United States	2003	Germany
1995	Norway	2007	(at China)
1999	United States		

Confederations Cup

First held in 1992. Contested by the Continental champions of Africa, Asia, Europe, North America and South America and originally called the Intercontinental Championship for the King Fahd Cup until it was redubbed the FIFA/Confederations Cup for the King Fahd Trophy in 1997.

Multiple winners: Brazil and France (2).

Year		Year	
1992	Argentina	2001	France
1995	Denmark	2003	France
1997	Brazil	2005	Brazil
1999	Mexico		

CONTINENTAL COMPETITION

European Championship

Held every four years since 1960. Officially, the European Football Championship. Winners receive the Henri Delaunay trophy, named for the Frenchman who first proposed the idea of a European Soccer Championship in 1927. The first one would not be played until five years after his death in 1955.

Multiple winners: Germany/West Germany (3); France (2).

Year		Year		Year		Year	
1960	Soviet Union	1972	West Germany	1984	France	1996	Germany
1964	Spain	1976	Czechoslovakia	1988	Netherlands	2000	France
1968	Italy	1980	West Germany	1992	Denmark	2004	Greece

Copa America

Held irregularly since 1916. Unofficially, the Championship of South America.

Multiple winners: Argentina and Uruguay (14); Brazil (6); Paraguay and Peru (2).

Year		Year		Year		Year		Year	
1916	Uruguay	1926	Uruguay	1946	Argentina	1963	Bolivia	1995	Uruguay
1917	Uruguay	1927	Argentina	1947	Argentina	1967	Uruguay	1997	Brazil
1919	Brazil	1929	Argentina	1949	Brazil	1975	Peru	1999	Brazil
1920	Uruguay	1935	Uruguay	1953	Paraguay	1979	Paraguay	2001	Colombia
1921	Argentina	1937	Argentina	1955	Argentina	1983	Uruguay	2004	Brazil
1922	Brazil	1939	Peru	1956	Uruguay	1987	Uruguay		
1923	Uruguay	1941	Argentina	1957	Argentina	1989	Brazil		
1924	Uruguay	1942	Uruguay	1958	Argentina	1991	Argentina		
1925	Argentina	1945	Argentina	1959	Uruguay	1993	Argentina		

African Nations Cup

Contested since 1957 and held every two years since 1968.

Multiple winners: Egypt (5); Cameroon and Ghana (4); Congo/Zaire (3); Nigeria (2).

Year		Year		Year		Year		Year	
1957	Egypt	1968	Zaire	1978	Ghana	1988	Cameroon	1998	Egypt
1959	Egypt	1970	Sudan	1980	Nigeria	1990	Algeria	2000	Cameroon
1962	Ethiopia	1972	Congo	1982	Ghana	1992	Ivory Coast	2002	Cameroon
1963	Ghana	1974	Zaire	1984	Cameroon	1994	Nigeria	2004	Tunisia
1965	Ghana	1976	Morocco	1986	Egypt	1996	South Africa	2006	Egypt

CONCACAF Gold Cup

The Confederation of North, Central American and Caribbean Football Championship. Contested irregularly from 1963-81 and revived as CONCACAF Gold Cup in 1991.

Multiple winners: Mexico (7); Costa Rica and United States (2).

Year		Year		Year		Year		Year	
1963	Costa Rica	1969	Costa Rica	1977	Mexico	1993	Mexico	2000	Canada
1965	Mexico	1971	Mexico	1981	Honduras	1996	Mexico	2003	Mexico
1967	Guatemala	1973	Haiti	1991	United States	1998	Mexico	2005	United States

FIFA Club World Championship

The FIFA Club World Championship merged with the Toyota Cup in 2005. The Toyota Cup held each December in Japan had previously served as the unofficial world club championship and was played between the champions of Europe and South America. But FIFA took over the tournament starting in 2005 and is now open to the champions from the African, Asian, Oceanic and North/Central American federations as well as Europe and South America. From now on the new six-team tournament will be played each December in Japan. Note that FIFA held an eight-team world club championship tournament in 2000 but the tournament was not held again until late 2005 when it officially merged with the Toyota Cup.

Year		Year	
2000	Corinthians (Brazil)	2005	São Paulo (Brazil)

Toyota Cup

Also known as the **European/South American Cup** and Intercontinental Cup. Until 2005, it was contested annually in December between the winners of the European Champions League (formerly European Cup) and South America's Copa Libertadores for the unofficial World Club Championship. Four European Cup winners refused to participate in the championship match in the 1970s and were replaced each time by the European Cup runner-up: Panathinaikos (Greece) for Ajax Amsterdam (Netherlands) in 1971; Juventus (Italy) for Ajax in 1973; Atlético Madrid (Spain) for Bayern Munich (West Germany) in 1974; and Malmo (Sweden) for Nottingham Forest (England) in 1979. Another European Cup winner, Marseille of France, was prohibited by the Union of European Football Associations (UEFA) from playing for the 1993 Toyota Cup because of its involvement in a match-rigging scandal. Best-of-three game format from 1960-68, then a two-game/total goals format from 1969-79. Toyota became Cup sponsor in 1980, changed the format to a one-game championship and moved it to Toyko.

Multiple winners: AC Milan, Boca Juniors, Nacional, Penarol and Real Madrid (3); Ajax Amsterdam, Bayern Munich, FC Porto, Independiente, Inter Milan, Juventus, Santos and Sao Paulo (2):

Year		Year		Year	
1960	Real Madrid (Spain)	1975	Not held	1990	AC Milan (Italy)
1961	Penarol (Uruguay)	1976	Bayern Munich (W. Germany)	1991	Red Star (Yugoslavia)
1962	Santos (Brazil)	1977	Boca Juniors (Argentina)	1992	Sao Paulo (Brazil)
1963	Santos (Brazil)	1978	Not held	1993	Sao Paulo (Brazil)
1964	Inter Milan (Italy)	1979	Olimpia (Paraguay)	1994	Velez Sarsfield (Argentina)
1965	Inter Milan (Italy)	1980	Nacional (Uruguay)	1995	Ajax Amsterdam (Netherlands)
1966	Penarol (Uruguay)	1981	Flamengo (Brazil)	1996	Juventus (Italy)
1967	Racing Club (Argentina)	1982	Penarol (Uruguay)	1997	Borussia Dortmund (Germany)
1968	Estudiantes (Argentina)	1983	Gremio (Brazil)	1998	Real Madrid (Spain)
1969	AC Milan (Italy)	1984	Independiente (Argentina)	1999	Manchester United (England)
1970	Feyenoord (Netherlands)	1985	Juventus (Italy)	2000	Boca Juniors (Argentina)
1971	Nacional (Uruguay)	1986	River Plate (Argentina)	2001	Bayern Munich (Germany)
1972	Ajax Amsterdam (Netherlands)	1987	FC Porto (Portugal)	2002	Real Madrid (Spain)
1973	Independiente (Argentina)	1988	Nacional (Uruguay)	2003	Boca Juniors (Argentina)
1974	Atlético Madrid (Spain)	1989	AC Milan (Italy)	2004	FC Porto (Portugal)

European Cup/UEFA Champions League

Contested annually since the 1955-56 season by the league champions of the member countries of the Union of European Football Associations (UEFA). In 1999, UEFA announced the formation of a new competition called the UEFA Champions League to take the place of the Cup competition.

Multiple winners: Real Madrid (9); AC Milan (6); Ajax Amsterdam, Bayern Munich and Liverpool (4); Barcelona, Benfica, FC Porto, Inter Milan, Juventus and Nottingham Forest (2).

Year		Year		Year	
1956	Real Madrid (Spain)	1974	Bayern Munich (W. Germany)	1992	Barcelona (Spain)
1957	Real Madrid (Spain)	1975	Bayern Munich (W. Germany)	1993	Marseille (France)*
1958	Real Madrid (Spain)	1976	Bayern Munich (W. Germany)	1994	AC Milan (Italy)
1959	Real Madrid (Spain)	1977	Liverpool (England)	1995	Ajax Amsterdam (Netherlands)
1960	Real Madrid (Spain)	1978	Liverpool (England)	1996	Juventus (Italy)
1961	Benfica (Portugal)	1979	Nottingham Forest (England)	1997	Borussia Dortmund (Germany)
1962	Benfica (Portugal)	1980	Nottingham Forest (England)	1998	Real Madrid (Spain)
1963	AC Milan (Italy)	1981	Liverpool (England)	1999	Manchester United (England)
1964	Inter Milan (Italy)	1982	Aston Villa (England)	2000	Real Madrid (Spain)
1965	Inter Milan (Italy)	1983	SV Hamburg (W. Germany)	2001	Bayern Munich (Germany)
1966	Real Madrid (Spain)	1984	Liverpool (England)	2002	Real Madrid (Spain)
1967	Glasgow Celtic (Scotland)	1985	Juventus (Italy)	2003	AC Milan (Italy)
1968	Manchester United (England)	1986	Steaua Bucharest (Romania)	2004	FC Porto (Portugal)
1969	AC Milan (Italy)	1987	FC Porto (Portugal)	2005	Liverpool (England)
1970	Feyenoord (Netherlands)	1988	PSV Eindhoven (Netherlands)	2006	Barcelona (Spain)
1971	Ajax Amsterdam (Netherlands)	1989	AC Milan (Italy)	*title vacated	
1972	Ajax Amsterdam (Netherlands)	1990	AC Milan (Italy)		
1973	Ajax Amsterdam (Netherlands)	1991	Red Star Belgrade (Yugo.)		

European Cup Winner's Cup

Contested annually from the 1960-61 season through the 1999-2000 season by the cup winners of the member countries of the Union of European Football Associations (UEFA). The Cup Winner's Cup was absorbed by the UEFA Cup in 2000.

Multiple winners: Barcelona (4); AC Milan, RSC Anderlecht, Chelsea and Dinamo Kiev (2).

Year	Year	Year
1961 Fiorentina (Italy)	1974 FC Magdeburg (E. Germany)	1987 Ajax Amsterdam (Netherlands)
1962 Atletico Madrid (Spain)	1975 Dinamo Kiev (USSR)	1988 Mechelen (Belgium)
1963 Tottenham Hotspur (England)	1976 RSC Anderlecht (Belgium)	1989 Barcelona (Spain)
1964 Sporting Lisbon (Portugal)	1977 SV Hamburg (W. Germany)	1990 Sampdoria (Italy)
1965 West Ham United (England)	1978 RSC Anderlecht (Belgium)	1991 Manchester United (England)
1966 Borussia Dortmund (W.Germany)	1979 Barcelona (Spain)	1992 Werder Bremen (Germany)
1967 Bayern Munich (W. Germany)	1980 Valencia (Spain)	1993 Parma (Italy)
1968 AC Milan (Italy)	1981 Dinamo Tbilisi (USSR)	1994 Arsenal (England)
1969 Slovan Bratislava (Czech.)	1982 Barcelona (Spain)	1995 Real Zaragoza (Spain)
1970 Manchester City (England)	1983 Aberdeen (Scotland)	1996 Paris St. Germain (France)
1971 Chelsea (England)	1984 Juventus (Italy)	1997 Barcelona (Spain)
1972 Glasgow Rangers (Scotland)	1985 Everton (England)	1998 Chelsea (England)
1973 AC Milan (Italy)	1986 Dinamo Kiev (USSR)	1999 Lazio (Italy)

UEFA Cup

Contested annually since the 1957-58 season by teams other than league champions and cup winners of the Union of European Football Associations (UEFA). Teams selected by UEFA based on each country's previous performance in the tournament. Teams from England were banned from UEFA Cup play from 1985-90 for the criminal behavior of their supporters. In 1999, with the formation of the new Champions League, UEFA announced that the UEFA Cup would be expanded and include any teams that would have normally played in the Cup Winner's Cup.

Multiple winners: Barcelona, Inter Milan, Juventus, Liverpool and Valencia (3); Borussia Mönchengladbach, Feyenoord, IFK Göteborg, Leeds United, Parma, Real Madrid and Tottenham Hotspur (2).

Year	Year	Year
1958 Barcelona (Spain)	1975 Borussia Mönchengladbach (W. Germany)	1990 Juventus (Italy)
1959 Not held	1976 Liverpool (England)	1991 Inter Milan (Italy)
1960 Barcelona (Spain)	1977 Juventus (Italy)	1992 Ajax Amsterdam (Netherlands)
1961 AS Roma (Italy)	1978 PSV Eindhoven (Netherlands)	1993 Juventus (Italy)
1962 Valencia (Spain)	1979 Borussia Mönchengladbach (W. Germany)	1994 Inter Milan (Italy)
1963 Valencia (Spain)	1980 Eintracht Frankfurt (W. Germany)	1995 Parma (Italy)
1964 Real Zaragoza (Spain)	1981 Ipswich Town (England)	1996 Bayern Munich (Germany)
1965 Ferencvaros (Hungary)	1982 IFK Göteborg (Sweden)	1997 Schalke 04 (Germany)
1966 Barcelona (Spain)	1983 RSC Anderlecht (Belgium)	1998 Inter Milan (Italy)
1967 Dinamo Zagreb (Yugoslavia)	1984 Tottenham Hotspur (England)	1999 Parma (Italy)
1968 Leeds United (England)	1985 Real Madrid (Spain)	2000 Galatasaray (Turkey)
1969 Newcastle United (England)	1986 Real Madrid (Spain)	2001 Liverpool (England)
1970 Arsenal (England)	1987 IFK Göteborg (Sweden)	2002 Feyenoord (Netherlands)
1971 Leeds United (England)	1988 Bayer Leverkusen (W. Germany)	2003 FC Porto (Portugal)
1972 Tottenham Hotspur (England)	1989 Napoli (Italy)	2004 Valencia (Spain)
1973 Liverpool (England)		2005 CSKA Moscow (Russia)
1974 Feyenoord (Netherlands)		2006 Sevilla (Spain)

Copa Libertadores

Contested annually since the 1955-56 season by the league champions of South America's football union.

Multiple winners: Independiente (7); Boca Juniors and Peñarol (5); Estudiantes, Nacional-Uruguay, Olimpia and São Paulo (3); Cruzeiro, Gremio, River Plate and Santos (2).

Year	Year	Year
1960 Peñarol (Uruguay)	1976 Cruzeiro (Brazil)	1992 São Paulo (Brazil)
1961 Peñarol (Uruguay)	1977 Boca Juniors (Argentina)	1993 São Paulo (Brazil)
1962 Santos (Brazil)	1978 Boca Juniors (Argentina)	1994 Velez Sarsfield (Argentina)
1963 Santos (Brazil)	1979 Olimpia (Paraguay)	1995 Gremio (Brazil)
1964 Independiente (Argentina)	1980 Nacional (Uruguay)	1996 River Plate (Argentina)
1965 Independiente (Argentina)	1981 Flamengo (Brazil)	1997 Cruzeiro (Brazil)
1966 Peñarol (Uruguay)	1982 Peñarol (Uruguay)	1998 Vasco da Gama (Brazil)
1967 Racing Club (Argentina)	1983 Gremio (Brazil)	1999 Palmeiras (Brazil)
1968 Estudiantes de la Plata (Argentina)	1984 Independiente (Argentina)	2000 Boca Juniors (Argentina)
1969 Estudiantes de la Plata (Argentina)	1985 Argentinos Jrs. (Argentina)	2001 Boca Juniors (Argentina)
1970 Estudiantes de la Plata (Argentina)	1986 River Plate (Argentina)	2002 Olimpia (Paraguay)
1971 Nacional (Uruguay)	1987 Peñarol (Uruguay)	2003 Boca Juniors (Argentina)
1972 Independiente (Argentina)	1988 Nacional (Uruguay)	2004 Once Caldas (Colombia)
1973 Independiente (Argentina)	1989 Nacional Medellin (Colombia)	2005 São Paulo (Brazil)
1974 Independiente (Argentina)	1990 Olimpia (Paraguay)	2006 Internacional (Brazil)
1975 Independiente (Argentina)	1991 Colo Colo (Chile)	

Annual Awards
World Player of the Year

Presented by FIFA, the European Sports Magazine Association (ESM) and Adidas, the sports equipment manufacturer, since 1991. Winners are selected by national team coaches and captains from around the world.

Multiple winners: Ronaldo and Zinedine Zidane (3); Ronaldinho (2).

Year		Nat'l Team	Year		Nat'l Team
1991	Lothar Matthäus, Inter Milan	Germany	1999	Rivaldo, Barcelona	Brazil
1992	Marco Van Basten, AC Milan	Netherlands	2000	Zinedine Zidane, Juventus	France
1993	Roberto Baggio, Juventus	Italy	2001	Luis Figo, Real Madrid	Portugal
1994	Romario, Barcelona	Brazil	2002	Ronaldo, Real Madrid	Brazil
1995	George Weah, AC Milan	Liberia	2003	Zinedine Zidane, Real Madrid	France
1996	Ronaldo, Barcelona	Brazil	2004	Ronaldinho, Barcelona	Brazil
1997	Ronaldo, Inter Milan	Brazil	2005	Ronaldinho, Barcelona	Brazil
1998	Zinedine Zidane, Juventus	France			

Women's World Player of the Year

Presented by FIFA since 2001. Winners are selected by national team coaches from around the world.

Multiple winners: Birgit Prinz (3), Mia Hamm (2).

Year		Nat'l Team	Year		Nat'l Team
2001	Mia Hamm, Washington Freedom	USA	2004	Birgit Prinz, FFC Frankfurt	Germany
2002	Mia Hamm, Washington Freedom	USA	2005	Birgit Prinz, FFC Frankfurt	Germany
2003	Birgit Prinz, FFC Frankfurt	Germany			

European Player of the Year

Officially, the "Ballon d'Or," or "Golden Ball," and presented by *France Football* magazine since 1956. Candidates are limited to European players in European leagues and winners are selected by a poll of European soccer journalists.

Multiple winners: Johan Cruyff, Michel Platini and Marco Van Basten (3); Franz Beckenbauer, Alfredo di Stéfano, Kevin Keegan, Ronaldo and Karl-Heinz Rummenigge (2).

Year		Nat'l Team	Year		Nat'l Team
1956	Stanley Matthews, Blackpool	England	1981	K.H. Rummenigge, Bayern Munich	W. Ger.
1957	Alfredo di Stéfano, Real Madrid	Arg./Spain	1982	Paolo Rossi, Juventus	Italy
1958	Raymond Kopa, Real Madrid	France	1983	Michel Platini, Juventus	France
1959	Alfredo di Stéfano, Real Madrid	Arg./Spain	1984	Michel Platini, Juventus	France
1960	Luis Suarez, Barcelona	Spain	1985	Michel Platini, Juventus	France
1961	Enrique Sivori, Juventus	Arg./Italy	1986	Igor Belanov, Dinamo Kiev	Soviet Union
1962	Josef Masopust, Dukla Prague	Czech.	1987	Ruud Gullit, AC Milan	Netherlands
1963	Lev Yashin, Dinamo Moscow	Soviet Union	1988	Marco Van Basten, AC Milan	Netherlands
1964	Denis Law, Manchester United	Scotland	1989	Marco Van Basten, AC Milan	Netherlands
1965	Eusébio, Benfica	Portugal	1990	Lothar Matthäus, Inter Milan	W. Ger.
1966	Bobby Charlton, Manchester United	England	1991	Jean-Pierre Papin, Marseille	France
1967	Florian Albert, Ferencvaros	Hungary	1992	Marco Van Basten, AC Milan	Netherlands
1968	George Best, Manchester United	No. Ireland	1993	Roberto Baggio, Juventus	Italy
1969	Gianni Rivera, AC Milan	Italy	1994	Hristo Stoitchkov, Barcelona	Bulgaria
1970	Gerd Müller, Bayern Munich	W. Ger.	1995	George Weah, AC Milan	Liberia
1971	Johan Cruyff, Ajax Amsterdam	Netherlands	1996	Matthias Sammer, Bor. Dortmund	Germany
1972	Franz Beckenbauer, Bayern Munich	W. Ger.	1997	Ronaldo, Inter Milan	Brazil
1973	Johan Cruyff, Barcelona	Netherlands	1998	Zinedine Zidane, Juventus	France
1974	Johan Cruyff, Barcelona	Netherlands	1999	Rivaldo, Barcelona	Brazil
1975	Oleg Blokhin, Dinamo Kiev	Soviet Union	2000	Luis Figo, Real Madrid	Portugal
1976	Franz Beckenbauer, Bayern Munich	W. Ger.	2001	Michael Owen, Liverpool	England
1977	Allan Simonsen, B. Mönchengladbach	Denmark	2002	Ronaldo, Real Madrid	Brazil
1978	Kevin Keegan, SV Hamburg	England	2003	Pavel Nedved, Juventus	Czech Republic
1979	Kevin Keegan, SV Hamburg	England	2004	Andriy Schevchenko, AC Milan	Ukraine
1980	K.H. Rummenigge, Bayern Munich	W. Ger.	2005	Ronaldinho, Barcelona	Brazil

U.S. Player of the Year

Presented by Honda and the Spanish-speaking radio show "Futbol de Primera" since 1991. Candidates are limited to American players who have played with the U.S. National Team and winners are selected by a panel of U.S. soccer journalists.

Multiple winners: Landon Donovan (3); Eric Wynalda (2).

Year		Year		Year		Year	
1991	Hugo Perez	1995	Alexi Lalas	1999	Kasey Keller	2003	Landon Donovan
1992	Eric Wynalda	1996	Eric Wynalda	2000	Claudio Reyna	2004	Landon Donovan
1993	Thomas Dooley	1997	Eddie Pope	2001	Earnie Stewart	2005	Clint Dempsey
1994	Marcelo Balboa	1998	Cobi Jones	2002	Landon Donovan		

South American Player of the Year

Presented by *El Mundo* of Venezuela from 1971-1985 and *El Pais* of Uruguay since 1986. Candidates are limited to South American players in South American leagues and winners are selected by a poll of South American sports editors.

Multiple winners: Elias Figueroa, Carlos Tevez and Zico (3); Enzo Francescoli, Diego Maradona and Carlos Valderrama (2).

Year		Nat'l Team	Year		Nat'l Team
1971	Tostao, Cruzeiro	Brazil	1989	Bebeto, Vasco da Gama	Brazil
1972	Teofilo Cubillas, Alianza Lima	Peru	1990	Raul Amarilla, Olimpia	Paraguay
1973	Pelé, Santos	Brazil	1991	Oscar Ruggeri, Velez Sarsfield	Argentina
1974	Elias Figueroa, Internacional	Chile	1992	Rai, Sao Paulo	Brazil
1975	Elias Figueroa, Internacional	Chile	1993	Carlos Valderrama, Atl. Junior	Colombia
1976	Elias Figueroa, Internacional	Chile	1994	Cafu, Sao Paulo	Brazil
1977	Zico, Flamengo	Brazil	1995	Enzo Francescoli, River Plate	Uruguay
1978	Mario Kempes, Valencia	Argentina	1996	Jose Luis Chilavert, Velez Sarsfield	Paraguay
1979	Diego Maradona, Argentinos Juniors	Argentina	1997	Marcelo Salas, River Plate	Chile
1980	Diego Maradona, Boca Juniors	Argentina	1998	Martin Palermo, Boca Juniors	Argentina
1981	Zico, Flamengo	Brazil	1999	Javier Saviola, River Plate	Argentina
1982	Zico, Flamengo	Brazil	2000	Romario, Vasco da Gama	Brazil
1983	Socrates, Corinthians	Brazil	2001	Juan Roman Riquelme, Boca Juniors	Argentina
1984	Enzo Francescoli, River Plate	Uruguay	2002	Jose Cardozo, Toluca	Paraguay
1985	Julio Cesar Romero, Fluminense	Paraguay	2003	Carlos Tevez, Boca Juniors	Argentina
1986	Antonio Alzamendi, River Plate	Uruguay	2004	Carlos Tevez, Boca Juniors	Argentina
1987	Carlos Valderrama, Deportivo Cali	Colombia	2005	Carlos Tevez, Corinthians	Argentina
1988	Ruben Paz, Racing Buenos Aires	Uruguay			

Asian Player of the Year

Presented by the Asian Football Confederation since 1994. Prior to 1994 it was awarded unoffically.

Multiple winners: Kim Joo-Sung (3); Hidetoshi Nakata (2).

Year		Year		Year	
1988	Ahmed Radhi, Iraq	1995	Masami Ihara, Japan	2002	Shinji Ono, Japan
1989	Kim Joo-Sung, South Korea	1996	Khodadad Azizi, Iran	2003	Mehdi Mahdavikia, Iran
1990	Kim Joo-Sung, South Korea	1997	Hidetoshi Nakata, Japan	2004	Ali Karimi, Iran
1991	Kim Joo-Sung, South Korea	1998	Hidetoshi Nakata, Japan	2005	Hamad Al-Montashari, S. Arabia
1992	no award	1999	Ali Daei, Iran		
1993	Kazuyoshi Miura, Japan	2000	Nawaf Al-Temyat, S. Arabia		
1994	Saeed Al-Owairan, S. Arabia	2001	Fan Zhiyi, China		

African Player of the Year

Officially, the African "Ballon d'Or" and presented by *France Football* magazine from 1970-96. The Arican Player of the Year award has been presented by the CAF (African Football Confederation) since 1997. All African players are eligible for the award.

Multiple winners: George Weah and Abedi Pelé (3); El Hadji Diouf, Samuel Eto'o, Nwankwo Kanu, Roger Milla and Thomas N'Kono (2).

Year		Year		Year	
1970	Salif Keita, Mali	1982	Thomas N'Kono, Cameroon	1994	George Weah, Liberia
1971	Ibrahim Sunday, Ghana	1983	Mahmoud Al-Khatib, Egypt	1995	George Weah, Liberia
1972	Cherif Souleymane, Guinea	1984	Theophile Abega, Cameroon	1996	Nwankwo Kanu, Nigeria
1973	Tshimimu Bwanga, Zaire	1985	Mohamed Timoumi, Morocco	1997	Victor Ikpeba, Nigeria
1974	Paul Moukila, Congo	1986	Badou Zaki, Morocco	1998	Mustapha Hadji, Morocco
1975	Ahmed Faras, Morocco	1987	Rabah Madjer, Algeria	1999	Nwankwo Kanu, Nigeria
1976	Roger Milla, Cameroon	1988	Kalusha Bwalya, Zambia	2000	Patrick Mboma, Cameroon
1977	Dhiab Tarak, Tunisia	1989	George Weah, Liberia	2001	El Hadji Diouf, Senegal
1978	Abdul Razak, Ghana	1990	Roger Milla, Cameroon	2002	El Hadji Diouf, Senegal
1979	Thomas N'Kono, Cameroon	1991	Abedi Pelé, Ghana	2003	Samuel Eto'o, Cameroon
1980	Jean Manga Onguene, Cameroon	1992	Abedi Pelé, Ghana	2004	Samuel Eto'o, Cameroon
1981	Lakhdar Belloumi, Algeria	1993	Abedi Pelé, Ghana	2005	Samuel Eto'o, Cameroon

U.S. PRO LEAGUES

OUTDOOR
Major League Soccer

Sanctioned by U.S. Soccer and FIFA, the international soccer federation. MLS was founded on the heels of the successful 1994 World Cup tournament hosted by the United States and it remains the only FIFA-sanctioned division I outdoor league in the United States. The annual MLS title game is known as the MLS Cup.

Multiple winners: D.C. United (4); Los Angeles and San Jose (2).

MLS Cup

Year	Winner	Head Coach	Score	Loser	Head Coach	Site
1996	D.C. United	Bruce Arena	3-2 OT	Los Angeles Galaxy	Lothar Osiander	Foxboro, Mass.
1997	D.C. United	Bruce Arena	2-1	Colorado Rapids	Glen Myernick	Washington, D.C.
1998	Chicago Fire	Bob Bradley	2-0	D.C. United	Bruce Arena	Pasadena, Calif.
1999	D.C. United	Thomas Rongen	2-0	Los Angeles Galaxy	Sigi Schmid	Foxboro, Mass.
2000	Kansas City Wizards	Bob Gansler	1-0	Chicago Fire	Bob Bradley	Washington, D.C.
2001	San Jose Earthquakes	Frank Yallop	2-1 OT	Los Angeles Galaxy	Sigi Schmid	Columbus, Ohio
2002	Los Angeles Galaxy	Sigi Schmid	1-0 2OT	N.E. Revolution	Steve Nicol	Foxboro, Mass.
2003	San Jose Earthquakes	Frank Yallop	4-2	Chicago Fire	Dave Sarachan	Carson, Calif.
2004	D.C. United	Peter Nowak	3-2	Kansas City Wizards	Bob Gansler	Carson, Calif.
2005	Los Angeles Galaxy	Steve Sampson	1-0 OT	N.E. Revolution	Steve Nicol	Frisco, Texas

MLS Cup '96
D.C. United, 3-2 (OT)
Oct. 20 at Foxboro Stadium, Foxboro, Mass.
Attendance: 34,643

	1	2	OT	
Los Angeles Galaxy	1	1	0	—2
D.C. United	0	2	1	—3

First Half: LA—Eduardo Hurtado (Mauricio Cienfuegos), 5th minute.
Second Half: LA—Chris Armas (unassisted), 56th; DC—Tony Sanneh (Marco Etcheverry), 73rd; DC—Shawn Medved (unassisted), 82nd.
Overtime: DC—Eddie Pope (Etcheverry), 94th.
MVP: Marco Etcheverry, D.C. United, Midfielder

MLS Cup '97
D.C. United, 2-1
Oct. 26 at RFK Stadium, Washington, D.C.
Attendance: 57,431

	1	2	
Colorado Rapids	0	1	—1
D.C. United	1	1	—2

First Half: DC—Jaime Moreno (Tony Sanneh, David Vaudreuil), 37th minute.
Second Half: DC—Sanneh (John Harkes, Richie Williams), 68th; COL—Adrian Paz (David Patino, Matt Kmosko), 75th.
MVP: Jaime Moreno, D.C. United, Forward

MLS Cup '98
Chicago Fire, 2-0
Oct. 25 at the Rose Bowl, Pasadena, Calif.
Attendance: 51,350

	1	2	
D.C. United	0	0	—0
Chicago	2	0	—2

First Half: CHI—Jerzy Podbrozny (Peter Nowak, Ante Razov), 29th minute; CHI—Diego Gutierrez (Nowak), 45th.
MVP: Nowak, Chicago, Midfielder

MLS Cup '99
D.C. United, 2-0
Nov. 21 at Foxboro Stadium, Foxboro, Mass.
Attendance: 44,910

	1	2	
D.C. United	2	0	—2
Los Angeles	0	0	—0

First Half: DC—Jaime Moreno (Roy Lassiter), 19th minute; DC—Ben Olsen (unassisted), 48th.
MVP: Olsen, D.C. United, Midfielder

MLS Cup 2000
Kansas City Wizards, 1-0
Oct. 15 at RFK Stadium, Washington, D.C.
Attendance: 39,159

	1	2	
Chicago	0	0	—0
Kansas City	1	0	—1

First Half: DC— Miklos Molnar (Chris Klein), 11th minute.
MVP: Tony Meola, Kansas City, Goalkeeper

MLS Cup 2001
San Jose Earthquakes, 2-1 (OT)
Oct. 21 at Crew Stadium, Columbus, Ohio
Attendance: 21,626

	1	2	OT	
San Jose	1	0	1	—2
Los Angeles	1	0	0	—1

First Half: LA—Luis Hernandez (Greg Vanney, Kevin Hartman), 21st minute; SJ—Landon Donovan (Ian Russell, Richard Mulrooney), 43rd. **Overtime:** SJ—Dwayne DeRosario (Ronnie Ekelund, Zak Ibsen), 96th.
MVP: Dwayne DeRosario, San Jose, Forward

MLS Cup 2002
Los Angeles Galaxy, 1-0 (2 OT)
Oct. 20 at Gillette Stadium, Foxboro, Mass.
Attendance: 61,316

	1	2	1OT	2OT	
Los Angeles	0	0	0	1	—1
New England	0	0	0	0	—0

2nd OT: LA—Carlos Ruiz, (Tyrone Marshall, Chris Albright), 113th minute.
MVP: Carlos Ruiz, Los Angeles, F

MLS Cup 2003
San Jose Earthquakes, 4-2
Nov. 23 at Home Depot Center, Carson, Calif.
Attendance: 27,000

	1	2	
San Jose	2	2	—4
Chicago	0	2	—2

First Half: SJ— Ronnie Ekelund (unassisted), 5th minute; SJ–Landon Donovan (Jamil Walker), 38th.

Second Half: CHI–DaMarcus Beasley (Andy Williams), 49th; SJ–Richard Mulrooney (Craig Waibel), 50th; CHI–own goal (Chris Roner), 54th; SJ–Donovan (Dwayne De Rosario, Brian Mullan), 71st.

MVP: Landon Donovan, San Jose, F

MLS Cup 2004
D.C. United, 3-2
Nov. 14 at Home Depot Center, Carson, Calif.
Attendance: 25,797

	1	2	
D.C. United	3	0	—3
Kansas City	1	1	—2

First Half: KC— Jose Burciaga Jr. (unassisted), 6th minute; DC–Alecko Eskandarian (Brian Carroll), 19th. DC–Alecko Eskandarian (unassisted), 23rd. DC–own goal (Alex Zotinca), 26th.

Second Half: KC–Josh Wolff (penalty kick), 58th.
MVP: Alecko Eskandarian, D.C. United, F

MLS Cup 2005
Los Angeles Galaxy, 1-0 (OT)
Nov. 13 at Pizza Hut Park, Frisco, Texas
Attendance: 21,193

	1	2	OT	
Los Angeles	0	0	1	—1
New England	0	0	0	—0

Overtime: LA–Guillermo Ramirez (unassisted), 107th.
MVP: Guillermo "Pando" Ramirez, Los Angeles, F

MLS Cup 2006

The 2006 MLS Cup was scheduled for Nov. 12, 2006 at Pizza Hut Park in Frisco, Texas.

Regular Season

Most Valuable Player

Multiple winner: Preki (2).
1996 Carlos Valderrama, Tampa Bay
1997 Preki, Kansas City
1998 Marco Etcheverry, D.C.
1999 Jason Kreis, Dallas
2000 Tony Meola, Kansas City
2001 Alex Pineda Chacón, Miami
2002 Carlos Ruiz, LA
2003 Preki, Kansas City
2004 Amado Guevara, MetroStars
2005 Taylor Twellman, New England

Rookie of the Year

1996 Steve Ralston, Tampa Bay
1997 Mike Duhaney, Tampa Bay
1998 Ben Olsen, D.C.
1999 Jay Heaps, Miami
2000 Carlos Bocanegra, Chicago
2001 Rodrigo Faria, MetroStars
2002 Kyle Martino, Columbus
2003 Damani Ralph, Chicago
2004 Clint Dempsey, New England
2005 Michael Parkhurst, New England

Defender of the Year

Multiple winners: Carlos Bocanegra (2).
1996 John Doyle, San Jose
1997 Eddie Pope, D.C.
1998 Lubos Kubik, Chicago
1999 Robin Fraser, Los Angeles
2000 Peter Vermes, Kansas City
2001 Jeff Agoos, San Jose
2002 Carlos Bocanegra, Chicago
2003 Carlos Bocanegra, Chicago
2004 Robin Fraser, Columbus
2005 Jimmy Conrad, Kansas City

Leading Scorer

Multiple winners: Preki and Taylor Twellman (2).

		G	A	Pts
1996	Roy Lassiter, Tampa Bay	27	4	58
1997	Preki, Kansas City	12	17	41
1998	Stern John, Columbus	26	5	57
1999	Jason Kreis, Dallas	18	15	51
2000	Mamadou Diallo, Tampa Bay	26	4	56
2001	Alex Pineda Chacón, Miami	19	9	47
2002	Taylor Twellman, New England	23	6	52
2003	Preki, Kansas City	12	17	41
2004	Pat Noonan, New England	11	8	30
	& Amado Guevara, MetroStars	10	10	30
2005	Taylor Twellman, New England	17	7	41
2006	Jeff Cunningham, Real Salt Lake	16	11	43

Goalkeeper of the Year

Multiple winners: Joe Cannon and Pat Onstad (2).
1996 Mark Dodd, Dallas
1997 Brad Friedel, Columbus
1998 Zach Thornton, Chicago
1999 Kevin Hartman, Los Angeles
2000 Tony Meola, Kansas City
2001 Tim Howard, MetroStars
2002 Joe Cannon, San Jose
2003 Pat Onstad, San Jose
2004 Joe Cannon, Colorado
2005 Pat Onstad, San Jose

Coach of the Year

1996 Thomas Rongen, Tampa Bay
1997 Bruce Arena, D.C.
1998 Bob Bradley, Chicago
1999 Sigi Schmid, Los Angeles
2000 Bob Gansler, Kansas City
2001 Frank Yallop, San Jose
2002 Steve Nicol, New England
2003 Dave Sarachan, Chicago
2004 Greg Andrulis, Columbus
2005 Dominic Kinnear, San Jose

Other U.S. Pro Leagues (Cont.)
National Professional Soccer League (1967)

Not sanctioned by FIFA, the international soccer federation. The NPSL recruited individual players to fill the rosters of its 10 teams. The league lasted only one season.

	Playoff Final			Regular Season			
Year	Winner	Scores	Loser	Leading Scorer	G	A	Pts
1967	Oakland Clippers	0-1, 4-1	Baltimore Bays	Yanko Daucik, Toronto 20		8	48

United Soccer Association (1967)

Sanctioned by FIFA. Originally called the North American Soccer League, it became the USA to avoid being confused with the National Professional Soccer League (see above). Instead of recruiting individual players, the USA imported 12 entire teams from Europe to represent its 12 franchises. It, too, only lasted a season. The league champion Los Angeles Wolves were actually Wolverhampton of England and the runner-up Washington Whips were Aberdeen of Scotland.

	Playoff Final			Regular Season			
Year	Winner	Score	Loser	Leading Scorer	G	A	Pts
1967	Los Angeles Wolves	6-5 (OT)	Washington Whips	Roberto Boninsegna, Chicago 10		1	21

North American Soccer League (1968-84)

The NPSL and USA merged to form the NASL in 1968 and the new league lasted through 1984. The NASL championship was known as the Soccer Bowl from 1975-84. One game decided the NASL title every year but five. There were no playoffs in 1969; a two-game/aggregate goals format was used in 1968 and '70; and a best-of-three games format was used in 1971 and '84; (*) indicates overtime and (†) indicates game decided by shootout.

Multiple winners: NY Cosmos (5); Chicago (2).

	Playoff Final			Regular Season			
Year	Winner	Score(s)	Loser	Leading Scorer	G	A	Pts
1968	Atlanta Chiefs	0-0,3-0	San Diego Toros	John Kowalik, Chicago 30		9	69
1969	Kansas City Spurs	No game	Atlanta Chiefs	Kaiser Motaung, Atlanta 16		4	36
1970	Rochester Lancers	3-0,1-3	Washington Darts	Kirk Apostolidis, Dallas 16		3	35
1971	Dallas Tornado	1-2*,4-1,2-0	Atlanta Chiefs	Carlos Metidieri, Rochester 19		8	46
1972	New York Cosmos	2-1	St. Louis Stars	Randy Horton, New York 9		4	22
1973	Philadelphia Atoms	2-0	Dallas Tornado	Kyle Rote Jr., Dallas 10		10	30
1974	Los Angeles Aztecs	3-3†	Miami Toros	Paul Child, San Jose 15		6	36
1975	Tampa Bay Rowdies	2-0	Portland Timbers	Steve David, Miami 23		6	52
1976	Toronto Metros	3-0	Minnesota Kicks	Giorgio Chinaglia, New York 19		11	49
1977	New York Cosmos	2-1	Seattle Sounders	Steve David, Los Angeles 26		6	58
1978	New York Cosmos	3-1	Tampa Bay Rowdies	Giorgio Chinaglia, New York 34		11	79
1979	Vancouver Whitecaps	2-1	Tampa Bay Rowdies	Oscar Fabbiani, Tampa Bay 25		8	58
1980	New York Cosmos	3-0	Ft. Laud. Strikers	Giorgio Chinaglia, New York 32		13	77
1981	Chicago Sting	0-0†	New York Cosmos	Giorgio Chinaglia, New York 29		16	74
1982	New York Cosmos	1-0	Seattle Sounders	Giorgio Chinaglia, New York 20		15	55
1983	Tulsa Roughnecks	2-0	Toronto Blizzard	Roberto Cabanas, New York 25		16	66
1984	Chicago Sting	2-1,3-2	Toronto Blizzard	Steve Zungul, Golden Bay 20		10	50

Note: In 1969, Kansas City won the NASL regular season championship with 110 points to 109 for Atlanta. There were no playoffs.

Regular Season MVP
Regular season Most Valuable Player as designated by the NASL.

Multiple winner: Carlos Metidieri (2).

Year		Year		Year	
1967	Rueben Navarro, Phila (NPSL)	1973	Warren Archibald, Miami	1979	Johan Cruyff, Los Angeles
1968	John Kowalik, Chicago	1974	Peter Silvester, Baltimore	1980	Roger Davies, Seattle
1969	Cirilio Fernandez, KC	1975	Steve David, Miami	1981	Giorgio Chinaglia, New York
1970	Carlos Metidieri, Rochester	1976	Pelé, New York	1982	Peter Ward, Seattle
1971	Carlos Metidieri, Rochester	1977	Franz Beckenbauer, New York	1983	Roberto Cabanas, New York
1972	Randy Horton, New York	1978	Mike Flanagan, New England	1984	Steve Zungul, Golden Bay

USL First Division/A-League

The American Professional Soccer League was formed in 1990 with the merger of the Western Soccer League and the New American Soccer League. The APSL was officially sanctioned as an outdoor pro league in 1992 and changed its name to the A-League in 1995. The league was reorganized under the umbrella of the United Soccer Leagues and renamed the USL First Division in 2005.

Multiple winners: Rochester and Seattle (3); Colorado, Milwaukee and Montreal (2).

Year		Year		Year	
1990	Maryland Bays	1996	Seattle Sounders	2002	Milwaukee Rampage
1991	SF Bay Blackhawks	1997	Milwaukee Rampage	2003	Charleston Battery
1992	Colorado Foxes	1998	Rochester Rhinos	2004	Montreal Impact
1993	Colorado Foxes	1999	Minnesota Thunder	2005	Seattle Sounders
1994	Montreal Impact	2000	Rochester Rhinos	2006	Vancouver Whitecaps
1995	Seattle Sounders	2001	Rochester Rhinos		

Women's United Soccer Association (2001-03)

The eight-team WUSA was formed in 2000 as the top women's outdoor professional league and play began in 2001. The league championship game is known as the Founders Cup. The league folded following the 2003 season.

Founders Cup

Year	Winner	Score	Loser	Site
2001	Bay Area CyberRays	3-3*	Atlanta Beat	Foxboro, Mass.
2002	Carolina Courage	3-2	Washington Freedom	Atlanta, Ga.
2003	Washington Freedom	2-1 OT	Atlanta Beat	San Diego, Calif.

*Bay Area won shoot-out, 4-2.

Regular Season

WUSA Most Valuable Player

2001 Tiffeny Milbrett, New York
2002 Marinette Pichon, Philadelphia
2003 Maren Meinert, Boston

WUSA Leading Scorer

		G	A	Pts
2001	Tiffeny Milbrett, New York	16	3	35
2002	Katia, San Jose	15	5	35
2003	Mia Hamm, Washington	11	11	33
	& Abby Wambach, Washington	13	7	33

INDOOR

Major Soccer League (1978-92)

Originally the Major Indoor Soccer League from 1978-79 season through 1989-90. The MISL championship was decided by one game in 1980 and 1981; a best-of-three games series in 1979, best-of-five games in 1982 and 1983; and best-of-seven games since 1984. The MSL folded after the 1991-92 season.

Multiple winners: San Diego (8); New York (4).

Playoff Final

Year	Winner	Series	Loser
1979	New York Arrows	2-0	Philadelphia
1980	New York Arrows	7-4 (1 game)	Houston
1981	New York Arrows	6-5 (1 game)	St. Louis
1982	New York Arrows	3-2 (LWWLW)	St. Louis
1983	San Diego Sockers	3-2 (WWLLW)	Baltimore
1984	Baltimore Blast	4-1 (LWWWW)	St. Louis
1985	San Diego Sockers	4-1 (WWLWW)	Baltimore
1986	San Diego Sockers	4-3 (WLLLWWW)	Minnesota
1987	Dallas Sidekicks	4-3 (LLWWLWW)	Tacoma
1988	San Diego Sockers	4-0	Cleveland
1989	San Diego Sockers	4-3 (LWWWLLW)	Baltimore
1990	San Diego Sockers	4-2 (LWWWLW)	Baltimore
1991	San Diego Sockers	4-2 (WLWLWW)	Cleveland
1992	San Diego Sockers	4-2 (WWWLLW)	Dallas

Regular Season

Leading Scorer		G	A	Pts
1979	Fred Grgurev, Philadelphia	46	28	74
1980	Steve Zungul, New York	90	46	136
1981	Steve Zungul, New York	108	44	152
1982	Steve Zungul, New York	103	60	163
1983	Steve Zungul, NY/Golden Bay	75	47	122
1984	Stan Stamenkovic, Baltimore	34	63	97
1985	Steve Zungul, San Diego	68	68	136
1986	Steve Zungul, Tacoma	55	60	115
1987	Tatu, Dallas	73	38	111
1988	Eric Rasmussen, Wichita	55	57	112
1989	Preki, Tacoma	51	53	104
1990	Tatu, Dallas	64	49	113
1991	Tatu, Dallas	78	66	144
1992	Zoran Karic, Cleveland	39	63	102

Playoff MVPs

MSL playoff Most Valuable Players, selected by a panel of soccer media covering the playoffs.

Multiple winners: Steve Zungul (4); Brian Quinn (2).

Year		Year	
1979	Shep Messing, NY	1986	Brian Quinn, SD
1980	Steve Zungul, NY	1987	Tatu, Dallas
1981	Steve Zungul, NY	1988	Hugo Perez, SD
1982	Steve Zungul, NY	1989	Victor Nogueira, SD
1983	Juli Veee, SD	1990	Brian Quinn, SD
1984	Scott Manning, Bal.	1991	Ben Collins, SD
1985	Steve Zungul, SD	1992	Thompson Usiyan, SD

Regular Season MVPs

MSL regular season Most Valuable Players, selected by a panel of soccer media from every city in the league.

Multiple winners: Steve Zungul (6); Victor Nogueira and Tatu (2).

Year		Year	
1979	Steve Zungul, NY	1986	Steve Zungul, SD/Tac.
1980	Steve Zungul, NY	1987	Tatu, Dallas
1981	Steve Zungul, NY	1988	Erik Rasmussen, Wich.
1982	Steve Zungul, NY	1989	Preki, Tacoma
	& Stan Terlecki, Pit.	1990	Tatu, Dallas
1983	Alan Mayer, SD	1991	Victor Nogueira, SD
1984	Stan Stamenkovic, Bal.	1992	Victor Nogueira, SD
1985	Steve Zungul, SD		

NASL Indoor Champions (1980-84)

The North American Soccer League started an indoor league in the fall of 1979. The indoor NASL, which featured many of the same teams and players who played in the outdoor NASL, crowned champions from 1980-82 before suspending play. It was revived for the 1983-84 indoor season but folded for good in 1984. The NASL held indoor tournaments in 1975 (San Jose Earthquakes won) and 1976 (Tampa Bay Rowdies won) before the indoor league was started.

Multiple winner: San Diego (2).

Year		Year		Year		Year	
1980	Tampa Bay Rowdies	1982	San Diego Sockers	1983	Play suspended	1984	San Diego Sockers
1981	Edmonton Drillers						

Major Indoor Soccer League

The winter indoor MISL began as the American Indoor Soccer Association in 1984-85, then changed its name to the National Professional Soccer League in 1989-90 and was known as the NPSL until 2001 when the name was changed again and the league was relaunched as the MISL.

Multiple winners: Canton (5); Milwaukee (4); Baltimore and Cleveland (3); Kansas City (2).

Year		Year		Year		Year	
1985	Canton (OH) Invaders	1991	Chicago Power	1997	Kansas City Attack	2003	Baltimore Blast
1986	Canton Invaders	1992	Detroit Rockers	1998	Milwaukee Wave	2004	Baltimore Blast
1987	Louisville Thunder	1993	Kansas City Attack	1999	Cleveland Crunch	2005	Milwaukee Wave
1988	Canton Invaders	1994	Cleveland Crunch	2000	Milwaukee Wave	2006	Baltimore Blast
1989	Canton Invaders	1995	St. Louis Ambush	2001	Milwaukee Wave		
1990	Canton Invaders	1996	Cleveland Crunch	2002	Philadelphia Kixx		

Continental Indoor Soccer League (1993-97)

The summer indoor CISL played its first season in 1993 and folded following the 1997 season.

Multiple winner: Monterrey (2).

Year		Year		Year	
1993	Dallas Sidekicks	1995	Monterrey La Raza	1997	Seattle Seadogs
1994	Las Vegas Dustdevils	1996	Monterrey La Raza		

U.S. COLLEGES

NCAA Men's Division I Champions

NCAA Division I champions since the first title was contested in 1959. The championship has been shared three times–in 1967, 1968 and 1989. There was a playoff for third place from 1974-81.

Multiple winners: Saint Louis (10); Indiana (7); San Francisco and Virginia (5); UCLA (4); Clemson, Connecticut, Howard and Michigan St. (2).

Year	Winner	Head Coach	Score	Runner-up	Host/Site	Semifinalists
1959	Saint Louis	Bob Guelker	5-2	Bridgeport	Connecticut	West Chester, CCNY
1960	Saint Louis	Bob Guelker	3-2	Maryland	Brooklyn	West Chester, Connecticut
1961	West Chester	Mel Lorback	2-0	Saint Louis	Saint Louis	Bridgeport, Rutgers
1962	Saint Louis	Bob Guelker	4-3	Maryland	Saint Louis	Mich. St., Springfield
1963	Saint Louis	Bob Guelker	3-0	Navy	Rutgers	Army, Maryland
1964	Navy	F.H. Warner	1-0	Michigan St.	Brown	Army, Saint Louis
1965	Saint Louis	Bob Guelker	1-0	Michigan St.	Saint Louis	Army, Navy
1966	San Francisco	Steve Negoesco	5-2	LIU-Brooklyn	California	Army, Mich. St.
1967-a	Michigan St. & Saint Louis	Gene Kenney Harry Keough	0-0	–	Saint Louis	LIU-Bklyn, Navy
1968-b	Michigan St. & Maryland	Gene Kenney Doyle Royal	2-2 (2 OT)	–	Ga. Tech	Brown, San Jose St.
1969	Saint Louis	Harry Keough	4-0	San Francisco	San Jose St.	Harvard, Maryland
1970	Saint Louis	Harry Keough	1-0	UCLA	SIU-Ed'sville	Hartwick, Howard
1971-c	Howard	Lincoln Phillips	3-2	Saint Louis	Miami	Harvard, San Fran.
1972	Saint Louis	Harry Keough	4-2	UCLA	Miami	Cornell, Howard
1973	Saint Louis	Harry Keough	2-1 (OT)	UCLA	Miami	Brown, Clemson
Year	**Winner**	**Head Coach**	**Score**	**Runner-up**	**Host/Site**	**Third Place**
1974	Howard	Lincoln Phillips	2-1 (4OT)	Saint Louis	Saint Louis	Hartwick 3, UCLA 1
1975	San Francisco	Steve Negoesco	4-0	SIU-Ed'sville	SIU-Ed'sville	Brown 2, Howard 0
1976	San Francisco	Steve Negoesco	1-0	Indiana	Penn	Hartwick 4, Clemson 3
1977	Hartwick	Jim Lennox	2-1	San Francisco	California	SIU-Ed'sville 3, Brown 2
1978-d	San Francisco	Steve Negoesco	4-3 (OT)	Indiana	Tampa	Clemson 6, Phi. Textile 2
1979	SIU-Ed'sville	Bob Guelker	3-2	Clemson	Tampa	Penn St. 2, Columbia 1
1980	San Francisco	Steve Negoesco	4-3 (OT)	Indiana	Indiana	Ala. A&M 1, Hartwick 0
1981	Connecticut	Joe Morrone	2-1 (OT)	Alabama A&M	Stanford	East. Ill. 4, Phi. Textile 2
Year	**Winner**	**Head Coach**	**Score**	**Runner-up**	**Host/Site**	**Semifinalists**
1982	Indiana	Jerry Yeagley	2-1 (8 OT)	Duke	Ft. Lauderdale	Connecticut, SIU-Ed'sville
1983	Indiana	Jerry Yeagley	1-0 (2 OT)	Columbia	Ft. Lauderdale	Connecticut, Virginia
1984	Clemson	I.M. Ibrahim	2-1	Indiana	Seattle	Hartwick, UCLA
1985	UCLA	Sigi Schmid	1-0 (8 OT)	American	Seattle	Evansville, Hartwick
1986	Duke	John Rennie	1-0	Akron	Tacoma	Fresno St., Harvard
1987	Clemson	I.M. Ibrahim	2-0	San Diego St.	Clemson	Harvard, N. Carolina
1988	Indiana	Jerry Yeagley	1-0	Howard	Indiana	Portland, S. Carolina
1989-e	Santa Clara & Virginia	Steve Sampson Bruce Arena	1-1 (2 OT)	–	Rutgers	Indiana, Rutgers
1990-f	UCLA	Sigi Schmid	0-0 (PKs)	Rutgers	South Fla.	Evansville, N.C. State
1991-g	Virginia	Bruce Arena	0-0 (PKs)	Santa Clara	Tampa	Indiana, Saint Louis

Year	Winner	Head Coach	Score	Runner-up	Host/Site	Semifinalists
1992	Virginia	Bruce Arena	2-0	San Diego	Davidson	Davidson, Duke
1993	Virginia	Bruce Arena	2-0	South Carolina	Davidson	CS-Fullerton, Princeton
1994	Virginia	Bruce Arena	1-0	Indiana	Davidson	Rutgers, UCLA
1995	Wisconsin	Jim Launder	2-0	Duke	Richmond	Portland, Virginia
1996	St. John's	Dave Masur	4-1	Fla. International	Richmond	Creighton, NC-Charlotte
1997	UCLA	Sigi Schmid	2-0	Virginia	Richmond	Indiana, Saint Louis
1998	Indiana	Jerry Yeagley	3-1	Stanford	Richmond	Maryland, Santa Clara
1999	Indiana	Jerry Yeagley	1-0	Santa Clara	Charlotte	Connecticut, UCLA
2000	Connecticut	Ray Reid	2-0	Creighton	Charlotte	Indiana, Southern Methodist
2001	North Carolina	Elmar Bolowich	2-0	Indiana	Columbus	St. John's, Stanford
2002	UCLA	Tom Fitzgerald	1-0	Stanford	Dallas	Creighton, Maryland
2003	Indiana	Jerry Yeagley	2-1	St. John's	Columbus	Maryland, Santa Clara
2004-h	Indiana	Mike Freitag	1-1 (PKs)	UCSB	Carson, Calif.	Duke, Maryland
2005	Maryland	Sasho Cirovski	1-0	New Mexico	Cary, N.C.	Clemson, SMU

a—game declared a draw due to inclement weather after regulation time; b—game declared a draw after two overtimes; c—Howard vacated title for using ineligible player; d—San Francisco vacated title for using ineligible player; e—game declared a draw due to inclement weather after two overtimes. f—UCLA wins on penalty kicks (4-3) after four overtimes; g—Virginia wins on penalty kicks (3-1) after four overtimes; h—Indiana wins on penalty kicks (3-2) after two overtimes.

Women's NCAA Division I Champions

NCAA Division I women's champions since the first tournament was contested in 1982.

Multiple winner: North Carolina (17).

Year	Winner	Coach	Score	Runner-up	Host/Site
1982	North Carolina	Anson Dorrance	2-0	Central Florida	Central Florida
1983	North Carolina	Anson Dorrance	4-0	George Mason	Central Florida
1984	North Carolina	Anson Dorrance	2-0	Connecticut	North Carolina
1985	George Mason	Hank Leung	2-0	North Carolina	George Mason
1986	North Carolina	Anson Dorrance	2-0	Colorado College	George Mason
1987	North Carolina	Anson Dorrance	1-0	Massachusetts	Massachusetts
1988	North Carolina	Anson Dorrance	4-1	N.C. State	North Carolina
1989	North Carolina	Anson Dorrance	2-0	Colorado College	N.C. State
1990	North Carolina	Anson Dorrance	6-0	Connecticut	North Carolina
1991	North Carolina	Anson Dorrance	3-1	Wisconsin	North Carolina
1992	North Carolina	Anson Dorrance	9-1	Duke	North Carolina
1993	North Carolina	Anson Dorrance	6-0	George Mason	North Carolina
1994	North Carolina	Anson Dorrance	5-0	Notre Dame	Portland
1995	Notre Dame	Chris Petrucelli	1-0 (3OT)	Portland	North Carolina
1996	North Carolina	Anson Dorrance	1-0 (2OT)	Notre Dame	Santa Clara
1997	North Carolina	Anson Dorrance	2-0	Connecticut	NC-Greensboro
1998	Florida	Becky Burleigh	1-0	North Carolina	NC-Greensboro
1999	North Carolina	Anson Dorrance	2-0	Notre Dame	San Jose, Calif.
2000	North Carolina	Anson Dorrance	2-1	UCLA	San Jose, Calif.
2001	Santa Clara	Jerry Smith	1-0	North Carolina	Dallas
2002	Portland	Clive Charles	2-1 (2OT)	Santa Clara	Austin
2003	North Carolina	Anson Dorrance	6-0	Connecticut	Cary, N.C.
2004-a	Notre Dame	Randy Waldrum	1-1 (PKs)	UCLA	Cary, N.C.
2005	Portland	Bill Irwin	4-0	UCLA	College Station, Tex.

a—Notre Dame wins on penalty kicks (4-3) after two overtimes.

Annual Awards
MEN
Hermann Trophy

College Player of the Year. Voted on by Division I college coaches and selected sportswriters and first presented in 1967 in the name of Robert Hermann, one of the founders of the North American Soccer League.

Multiple winners: Mike Fisher, Mike Seerey, Ken Snow and Al Trost (2).

Year		Year		Year	
1967	Dov Markus, LIU	1980	Joe Morrone, Jr. Connecticut	1993	Claudio Reyna, Virginia
1968	Manuel Hernandez, San Jose St.	1981	Armando Betancourt, Indiana	1994	Brian Maisonneuve, Indiana
1969	Al Trost, Saint Louis	1982	Joe Ulrich, Duke	1995	Mike Fisher, Virginia
1970	Al Trost, Saint Louis	1983	Mike Jeffries, Duke	1996	Mike Fisher, Virginia
1971	Mike Seerey, Saint Louis	1984	Amr Aly, Columbia	1997	Johnny Torres, Creighton
1972	Mike Seerey, Saint Louis	1985	Tom Kain, Duke	1998	Wojtek Krakowiak, Clemson
1973	Dan Counce, Saint Louis	1986	John Kerr, Duke	1999	Ali Curtis, Duke
1974	Farrukh Quraishi, Oneonta St.	1987	Bruce Murray, Clemson	2000	Chris Gbandi, Connecticut
1975	Steve Ralbovsky, Brown	1988	Ken Snow, Indiana	2001	Luchi Gonzalez, SMU
1976	Glenn Myernick, Hartwick	1989	Tony Meola, Virginia	2002	Alecko Eskandarian, Virginia
1977	Billy Gazonas, Hartwick	1990	Ken Snow, Indiana	2003	Chris Wingert, St. John's
1978	Angelo DiBernardo, Indiana	1991	Alexi Lalas, Rutgers	2004	Danny O'Rourke, Indiana
1979	Jim Stamatis, Penn St.	1992	Brad Friedel, UCLA	2005	Jason Garey, Maryland

Missouri Athletic Club Award

College Player of the Year. Voted on by men's team coaches around the country from Division I to junior college level and first presented in 1986 by the Missouri Athletic Club of St. Louis.

Multiple winners: Claudio Reyna and Ken Snow (2).

Year		Year		Year	
1986	John Kerr, Duke	1992	Claudio Reyna, Virginia	1998	Jay Heaps, Duke
1987	John Harkes, Virginia	1993	Claudio Reyna, Virginia	1999	Sasha Victorine, UCLA
1988	Ken Snow, Indiana	1994	Todd Yeagley, Indiana	2000	Ali Curtis, Duke
1989	Tony Meola, Virginia	1995	Matt McKeon, St. Louis	2001	Luchi Gonzalez, SMU
1990	Ken Snow, Indiana	1996	Mike Fisher, Virginia	2002	merged with Hermann Trophy.
1991	Alexi Lalas, Rutgers	1997	Johnny Torres, Creighton		

Coach of the Year

Men's Coach of the Year. Voted on by the National Soccer Coaches Association of America. From 1973-81 all Senior College coaches were eligible. In 1982, the award was split into several divisions. The Division I Coach of the Year is listed since 1982.

Multiple winner: Jerry Yeagley (6).

Year		Year		Year	
1973	Robert Guelker, SIU-Edwardsville	1984	James Lennox, Hartwick	1995	Jim Launder, Wisconsin
1974	Jack MacKenzie, Quincy College	1985	Peter Mehlert, American	1996	Dave Masur, St. John's
1975	Paul Reinhardt, Vermont	1986	Steve Parker, Akron	1997	Sigi Schmid, UCLA
1976	Jerry Yeagley, Indiana	1987	Anson Dorrance, N. Carolina	1998	Jerry Yeagley, Indiana
1977	Klass Deboer, Cleveland St.	1988	Keith Tucker, Howard	1999	Jerry Yeagley, Indiana
1978	Cliff McCrath, Seattle Pacific	1989	Steve Sampson, Santa Clara	2000	Ray Reid, Connecticut
1979	Walter Bahr, Penn St.	1990	Bob Reasso, Rutgers	2001	Elmar Bolowich, North Carolina
1980	Jerry Yeagley, Indiana	1991	Mitch Murray, Santa Clara	2002	Tom Fitzgerald, UCLA
1981	Schellas Hyndman, E. Illinois	1992	Charles Slagle, Davidson	2003	Jerry Yeagley, Indiana
1982	John Rennie, Duke	1993	Bob Bradley, Princeton	2004	Tim Vom Steeg, UCSB
1983	Dieter Ficken, Columbia	1994	Jerry Yeagley, Indiana	2005	Sasho Cirovski, Maryland

WOMEN
Hermann Trophy

Women's College Player of the year. Voted on by Division I college coaches and selected sportswriters and first presented in 1988 in the name of Robert Hermann, one of the founders of the North American Soccer League.

Multiple winners: Mia Hamm, Cindy Parlow and Christine Sinclair (2).

Year		Year		Year	
1988	Michelle Akers, Central Fla.	1994	Tisha Venturini, N. Carolina	2000	Anne Makinen, Notre Dame
1989	Shannon Higgins, N. Carolina	1995	Shannon McMillan, Portland	2001	Christie Welsh, Penn St.
1990	April Kater, Massachusetts	1996	Cindy Daws, Notre Dame	2002	Aly Wagner, Santa Clara
1991	Kristine Lilly, N. Carolina	1997	Cindy Parlow, N. Carolina	2003	Catherine Reddick, N. Carolina
1992	Mia Hamm, N. Carolina	1998	Cindy Parlow, N. Carolina	2004	Christine Sinclair, Portland
1993	Mia Hamm, N. Carolina	1999	Mandy Clemens, Santa Clara	2005	Christine Sinclair, Portland

Missouri Athletic Club Award

Women's College Player of the Year. Voted on by women's team coaches around the country from Division I to junior college level and first presented in 1991 by the Missouri Athletic Club of St. Louis.

Multiple winners: Mia Hamm and Cindy Parlow (2).

Year		Year		Year	
1991	Kristine Lilly, N. Carolina	1995	Shannon McMillan, Portland	1999	Mandy Clemens, Santa Clara
1992	Mia Hamm, N. Carolina	1996	Cindy Daws, Notre Dame	2000	Anne Makinen, Notre Dame
1993	Mia Hamm, N. Carolina	1997	Cindy Parlow, N. Carolina	2001	Christie Welsh, Penn St.
1994	Tisha Venturini, N. Carolina	1998	Cindy Parlow, N. Carolina	2002	merged with Hermann Trophy.

Coach of the Year

Women's Coach of the Year. Voted on by the National Soccer Coaches Association of America. From 1982-87 all Senior College coaches were eligible. In 1988, the award was split into several divisions. The Division I Coach of the Year is listed since 1988.

Multiple winners: Anson Dorrance (3); Kalenkeni M. Banda and Chris Petrucelli (2).

Year		Year		Year	
1982	Anson Dorrance, N. Carolina	1990	Lauren Gregg, Virginia	1998	Becky Burleigh, Florida
1983	David Lombardo, Keene St.	1991	Greg Ryan, Wisc-Madison	1999	Patrick Farmer, Penn St.
1984	Phillip Picince, Brown	1992	Bell Hempen, Duke	2000	Jillian Ellis, UCLA
1985	Kalenkeni M. Banda, UMass	1993	Jac Cicala, George Mason	2001	Jerry Smith, Santa Clara
1986	Anson Dorrance, N. Carolina	1994	Chris Petrucelli, Norte Dame	2002	Clive Charles, Portland
1987	Kalenkeni M. Banda, UMass	1995	Chris Petrucelli, Norte Dame	2003	Anson Dorrance, N. Carolina
1988	Larry Gross, N.C. State	1996	John Walker, Nebraska	2004	Julie Shackford, Princeton
1989	Austin Daniels, Hartford	1997	Len Tsantiris, Connecticut	2005	Paula Wilkins, Penn St.

ACTION
SPORTS

2005 / 2006 YEAR IN REVIEW

Pre-teen skateboarder **Nyjah Huston**, 11, became the youngest competitor in X Games history.

TRICKED OUT

Another year in the ever-growing field of Action Sports features new faces, some old favorites and one sick trick at the Summer X Games by motocross monster Travis Pastrana.

WITH FAN-PACKED ARENAS, superstar-sized paychecks and career-managing agents, it seems the action sports world is growing up. But don't tell it that.

The under-21 crowd has kicked the training wheels. Ryan Sheckler, 16, dominated the street skateboarding contest circuit, beating guys twice his age, while 11-year-old Nyjah Huston, in his first year skating pro contests, often accompanied him on the podium.

On the fluffy white, wunderkind Shaun White, now a 20-year-old vet, followed up a flawless winter (12 consecutive wins, including Olympic and Winter X gold) with a July Dew Tour win in skateboard vert.

On the Olympic frontlines, snowboard cross sweetheart and previously undefeated 21-year-old World Cup champ Lindsey Jacobellis had a gold medal bagged. But she crashed after throwing a showboat air on the final jump before the finish and landed in second, behind 30-year-old Swiss miss Tanja Frieden.

The kids may be coming up, but their elders are holding ground. In January, 31-year-old Blair Morgan became the oldest snowmobile rider to win a Winter X. After a rigorous series of Olympic snowboard qualifiers, key competitors, Hannah Teter and Gretchen Bleiler among them, put Winter X on the backburner in favor of February's Winter Olympics.

Showing up paid off for some, as the four-peat curse was broken twice in one day. Janna Meyen, 29, and Shaun White both won their snowboard slopestyle events, making them the first athletes to win an X Games event four years in a row.

Days before Winter X, 33-year-old skier Jamie Pierre set a world record in Utah for the biggest cliff

Mary Fenton is a senior writer at ESPN.com

AP/Wide World Photos

Action sports poster boy **Shaun White** had a year to remember, highlighted by gold medals at the Winter X Games, Turin Winter Olympics and **U.S. Open**.

huck (255 feet), and in December, freeski prodigy C.R. Johnson suffered a serious head injury while filming at Brighton.

After last year's Great Wall feat, 32-year-old skateboarder Danny Way spent this year doing rocket air backflips and record breaking 28-foot bomb drops off the guitar at Las Vegas's Hard Rock Café and Casino. Bob Burnquist, 30, attempted the first frontflip on the mega ramp and skateboarded/ B.A.S.E. jumped into the Grand Canyon in March.

Thirty-four-year-old Kelly Slater became surfing's oldest world champ in November when he won his seventh title, and then he start-ed the 2006 season with double wins. Through September's Trestles contest, with four events left to surf, Slater led the World Tour, sitting in a sweet spot to score number eight.

On the girls' side of the waves, 31-year-old Melanie Redman-Carr—who had only won three contests in eight years on tour—opened the WCT season with three consecutive wins over six-time world champ Layne Beachley. As of early October, it was any girl's game, with Mel, Layne and defending champ Chelsea Georgeson in the 1-2-3 spots with three events still left to surf.

In other hydro-news, wakeboarding, courted by ESPN since 1996's

In the Action Sports moment of the year, **Travis Pastrana** pulled off a double back flip to win an X Games gold medal in the Moto X Best Trick.

when they passed rally legend Colin McRae and co-driver Nicky Grist down the final stretch after McRae's car rolled over at the Home Depot Center. McRae and Grist recovered to win silver.

Pastrana won every other motorized event at the X Games, save Supermoto, where an early crash forced Pastrana into ninth place.

But the high point of Pastrana's 2006 season took place the previous day at the Moto X Best Trick competition. Not since 1999 and Tony Hawk's historic 900 have X Games fans had such a thrill. Despite a pledge that he'd never attempt such a dangerous trick in competition, Pastrana, facing fierce competition, did the unthinkable and brought out his double backflip. His mother Debbie couldn't watch and closed her eyes while her son made the historic attempt. He landed with another gold medal and a roar from the crowd.

X Games II, was cut from the 2006 roster to make room for the newest X-sport—rally car racing.

The addition of rally brought out the oldest competitors X has seen since 1997's downhill snow mountain biking event, and it complemented the burgeoning medal totals of two-wheel titan Travis Pastrana.

Pastrana and co-driver Christian Edstrom, took the rally car gold

BMX firsts materialized at X, too. To celebrate their first vert best trick 1-2 finish (where they landed BMX vert's first double flair and double tailwhip flatspin, respectively), riding buddies Kevin Robinson, 34, and Chad Kagy, 27, headed to the mega ramp. They did doubles runs off the big hits to wave hello to BMX Big Air, another new X-sport, and goodbye to the 12th edition of summer X.

AP/Wide World Photos

Greatest Stories of the Year in **Action Sports**

10 *First Descent* **debut.** Most action sports have had their Hollywood moment on the big screen, but before December 2005, real snowboarding could only be seen at ski resorts, with rare contest sightings on TV and stunts depicted in movies. The premiere of *First Descent* marks the debut of the sport's first major motion picture. It is released in theaters nationwide and makes nearly half a million dollars at the box office during its opening weekend.

09 **Man vs. Nature.** Landmarks are proof of millenniums of handiwork by Mother Nature and mankind, but not since the days of Evel Knievel has their presence marked a frontier for bravery in action sports. Within the last year, the action sports world saw Danny Way jump the Great Wall of China on a skateboard, Bob Burnquist railslide to BASE jump into the Grand Canyon, and Mike Metzger backflip the fountain at Caesar's Palace in Las Vegas – an homage to Evel's disastrous 1967 attempt.

08 **Old School Bikers.** BMX vert fields the oldest crew of X Games participants. Seven out of nine competitors at X12 were over 30, but these old dogs keep the new tricks coming. During the summer of 2006, Kevin Robinson pulls off BMX vert's first double flair (later bringing it to the mega ramp) and his first X golds, Chad Kagy pulls a double tailwhip flatspin, and Keith McElhinney pulls a frontflip flair—all competition firsts.

07 **Pre-teen power.** With less than a year of professional competition under his belt, 11-year old skateboarder Nyjah Huston came to X Games 12 as the youngest participant the Games has ever seen. Though he finished street finals at X in eighth place, he won 2005's Tampa Am, earned the second highest score for the winning team at the Goofy versus Regular contest and finished the '05 WCS season second overall in street. And he's barely old enough for middle school.

06 **Aussie BMX** rider Ryan Guettler, after four years of competing professionally, dominated the pro circuit during the '05 season. He took a first place win on every stop of the Dew Tour (the World Series of action sports), along with two overall wins, two top five X Games 11 finishes, a Vans Triple Crown win, a CFB win, and a Rebel Jam win to shame the competition and elevate his tax bracket.

05 X Games Fourpeat. In eleven years of X Games, there wasn't one person who won the same event four consecutive times. A total of seven athletes held past X Games three-peats, but at January 2006's Winter X 10, the curse of the elusive four-peat ended—twice in one day. Snowboarders Janna Meyen and Shaun White made X Games history as they both won Slopestyle gold for the fourth year in a row.

04 Record-breaker. January 2005 saw freeskier Jamie Pierre launch a world record-breaking cliff jump off Fred's Mountain near Wyoming's Grand Targhee Resort. The 255-foot drop, which left him submerged, head first in six feet of snow for over a minute, surpassed both the North American height record of 165 feet that Pierre set in 2002 and New Zealander Paul Ahern's 225-foot world record.

03 Slater becomes world champ. Again. Kelly Slater made surfing history by winning an unprecedented seventh world title (breaking his previous record of six) at the penultimate WCT event, November 2005's Nova Schin Pro Brazil. At 33 years and nine months, this makes him both the oldest and youngest pro (at age 20 in 1992) to win a world title.

02 Best Trick. X Games 12 was motocross prodigy Travis Pastrana's time to shine. He took home gold in three of the four events he entered (Freestyle, SuperMoto, Best Trick and Rally Car Racing), but his greatest feat at the Games was landing a trick he said he'd never bring to competition—the double backflip. The FMX bar has been raised, but with a score of 98.6 out of 100, some think it can go higher still.

01 White dominates the field. Nineteen-year old snowboard god Shaun White finishes the 2005-06 season undefeated. Starting with five Grand Prix wins and double golds at Winter X Games 10, White soon took wins at the Turin Winter Olympics and The Session at Vail before finishing it off by winning both the halfpipe and slopestyle events at the U.S. Open—a feat never before seen. Shaun rallied 12 combined wins in halfpipe and slopestyle for the season, tying with mentor Terje Haakonsen as the only snowboarder to win all season.

2005-2006
Season in Review

SPORTS ALMANAC

Summer X Games 12

The annual action sports showcase originally founded by ESPN in 1995. The 12th edition of the Summer X Games was held Aug. 3-6, 2006 at the Staples Center and Home Depot Center in Los Angeles, Calif. Medal winners from each event listed below. **Multiple Medal Winners:** THREE—Travis Pastrana (three gold), Chad Kagy (one gold, two silver), Bob Burnquist (one silver, two bronze); TWO—Bucky Lasek (one gold, one bronze).

Skateboarding

Men's Street

		Score
1	Chris Cole	.90.68
2	Ryan Sheckler	.85.31
3	Andrew Reynolds	.85.06

Women's Street

1 Elissa Streamer
2 Lauren Perkins
3 Lacey Baker

Men's Vert

1 Sandro Dias
2 Bob Burnquist
3 Bucky Lasek

Women's Vert

1 Cara-Beth Burnside
2 Mimi Knoop
3 Karen Jones

Vert Best Trick

		Trick
1	Bucky Lasek	.F/S cab varial heel flip
2	Max Dufour	.B/S kickflip 360 tall grind
3	Bob Burnquist	.F/S tail slide 360 out

Big Air

		Score
1	Danny Way	.95.00
2	Jake Brown	.93.00
3	Bob Burnquist	.91.25

Rally Car Racing

		Time
1	Travis Pastrana & Christian Edstrom	.12:02.19
2	Colin McRae & Nicky Grist	.12:02.71
3	Ken Block & Alex Gelsomino	.12:21.32

Surfing

The Game

Held at Zicatela Beach
in Puerto Escondido, Mexico

West Coast def. East Coast, 103.3-73.85

BMX

Vert

		Score
1	Chad Kagy	.93.00
2	Jamie Bestwick	.91.66
3	Simon Tabron	.90.00

Vert Best Trick

		Trick
1	Kevin Robinson	.Double Flair
2	Chad Kagy	.Double tail whip flat spin
3	Simon Tabron	.Alley oop n/h to t/d 540

Freestyle Park

		Score
1	Scotty Cranmer	.91.66
2	Morgan Wade	.90.00
3	Daniel Dhers	.89.66

Dirt

		Score
1	Corey Bohan	.91.66
2	Ryan Nyquist	.91.33
3	Anthony Napolitan	.90.33

Big Air

		Score
1	Kevin Robinson	.95.00
2	Chad Kagy	.93.66
3	Allan Cooke	.86.00

Moto X

Freestyle

		Score
1	Travis Pastrana	.94.20
2	Adam Jones	.91.40
3	Mike Mason	.90.00

Step Up

		Elimination Height
1	Matt Buyten	.—
2	Jeremy McGrath	.23-0
	Brian Deegan	.23-0

Best Trick

		Score
1	Travis Pastrana	.98.60
2	Mat Rebeaud	.93.80
3	Blake Williams	.91.80

SuperMoto

		Time Behind
1	Jeff Ward	.—
2	Mark Burkhart	.0.572
3	Doug Henry	.24.161

Winter X Games 10

Held January 28-31, 2006 at Aspen, Colorado. Medal winners from each event listed below.
Multiple Medal Winners: TWO—Shaun White (two golds),

Snowboarding

Men's Snowboarder X

1 Nate Holland, USA
2 Marco Huser, SUI
3 Jayson Hale, USA

Women's Snowboarder X

1 Maelle Ricker, CAN
2 Joanie Anderson, USA
3 Claudia Haeusermann, SUI

Men's Slopestyle

	Score
1 Shaun White, USA	95.00
2 Andreas Wiig, NOR	89.00
3 Danny Kass, USA	86.66

Women's Slopestyle

	Score
1 Janna Meyen, USA	91.33
2 Hana Beaman, USA	83.33
3 Jamie Anderson, USA	77.33

Men's SuperPipe

	Score
1 Shaun White, USA	91.00
2 Mason Aguirre, USA	88.66
3 Scotty Lago, USA	82.66

Women's SuperPipe

	Score
1 Kelly Clark, USA	93.33
2 Torah Bright, AUS	90.00
3 Soko Yamaoka, JPN	88.00

Skiing

Men's Skier X

1 Lars Lewen, SWE
2 Reggie Crist, USA
3 Chris del Bosco, USA

Women's Skier X

1 Karin Huttary, AUT
2 Gro Kvinlog, NOR
3 Ophelie David, FRA

Skiing Best Trick

	Score
1 T.J. Schiller, CAN	91.33
2 Charles Gagnier, CAN	89.33
3 Andreas Hatveit, NOR	87.66

Men's SuperPipe

	Score
1 Tanner Hall, USA	92.66
2 Laurent Favre, FRA	91.00
3 Simon Dumont, USA	90.00

Women's SuperPipe

	Score
1 Grete Eliassen, NOR	10.00
2 Sarah Burke, CAN	9.00
3 Marie Martinod-Routin, FRA	8.00

Moto X Best Trick

	Score
1 Jeremy Stenberg, USA	93.00
2 Mat Rebeaud, SUI	92.40
3 Ronnie Faisst, USA	90.60

SnoCross

	Time
1 Blair Morgan, USA	827.891
2 Levi LaVallee, USA	833.469
3 Ross Martin, USA	836.534

2006 U.S. Open of Snowboarding

Held March 14-19 at Stratton Mountain, Vermont

Men's Halfpipe

1 Shaun White
2 Danny Davis
3 Mason Aguirre

Men's Quarterpipe

1 Danny Davis
2 Risto Matilla
3 Kevin Pearce

Women's Halfpipe

1 Torah Bright
2 Gretchen Bleiler
3 Elena Hight

Women's Quarterpipe

1 Hana Beaman
2 Junko Asazuma
3 Molly Aguirre

Men's Slopestyle

1 Shaun White
2 Chas Guidemond
3 Jussi Oksanen

Boy's Junior Jam

1 Broc Waring
2 Ben Watts
3 Brett Esser

Women's Slopestyle

1 Hana Beaman
2 Spencer O'Brien
3 Jaime Anderson

Girl's Junior Jam

1 Palmer Taylor
2 Jennifer Cohen
3 Jessi Huege

Mountain Dew Action Sports Tour

2006 Dew Tour Locations: Panasonic Open, Louisville, Ky. (June 22-25); Right Guard Open, Denver, Colo. (July 13-16); Vans Invitational, Portland, Ore. (Aug. 17-20); Toyota Challenge, San Jose, Calif. (Sept. 7-10); Playstation Pro, Orlando, Fla. (Oct. 12-15).

Panasonic Open
June 22-25 at Louisville, Ky.

Skate Vert

		Score
1	Bob Burnquist	92.00
2	Bucky Lasek	91.00
3	Andy Macdonald	88.25

Skate Park

		Score
1	Ryan Sheckler	92.67
2	Nyjah Huston	88.33
3	Jereme Rogers	83.92

BMX Vert

		Score
1	Simon Tabron	94.75
2	Jamie Bestwick	93.50
3	Kevin Robinson	93.00

BMX Park

		Score
1	Scotty Cranmer	94.50
2	Ryan Guettler	93.75
3	Daniel Dhers	92.00

BMX Dirt

		Score
1	Anthony Napolitan	94.50
2	Luke Parslow	94.50
3	Corey Bohan	93.75

FMX

		Score
1	Nate Adams	93.00
2	Travis Pastrana	92.23
3	Ailo Gaup	90.67

Right Guard Open
July 13-16 at Denver, Colo.

Skate Vert

		Score
1	Shaun White	89.75
2	Sandro Dias	89.25
3	Bucky Lasek	87.00

Skate Park

		Score
1	Jereme Rogers	91.58
2	Nyjah Huston	88.92
3	Rodolfo Ramos	86.25

BMX Vert

		Score
1	Jamie Bestwick	94.00
2	Chad Kagy	92.50
3	Kevin Robinson	92.25

BMX Park

		Score
1	Daniel Dhers	93.00
2	Ryan Nyquist	91.00
3	Alistair Whitton	90.25

BMX Dirt

		Score
1	Ryan Nyquist	96.25
2	Anthony Napolitan	94.50
2	Luke Parslow	93.25

FMX

		Score
1	Travis Pastrana	96.83
2	Nate Adams	96.17
3	Kenny Bartram	95.67

Vans Invitational
Aug. 17-20 at Portland, Ore.

Skate Vert

		Score
1	Sandro Dias	90.75
2	Bucky Lasek	89.25
3	Jean Postec	85.25

BMX Park

		Score
1	Ryan Nyquist	90.25
2	Scotty Cranmer	89.00
3	Daniel Dhers	88.75

Skate Park

		Score
1	Ryan Sheckler	90.17
2	Jereme Rogers	89.50
3	Greg Lutzka	87.17

FMX

		Score
1	Travis Pastrana	97.50
2	Nate Adams	96.17
3	Adam Jones	94.33

BMX Vert

		Score
1	Jamie Bestwick	94.25
2	Chad Kagy	92.25
3	Kevin Robinson	91.00

BMX Dirt

		Score
1	Cameron White	93.75
2	Luke Parslow	92.50
2	Anthony Napolitan	91.75

Special Event
Snowboard Rail Jam

1. Michael Casanova
2. Chris Rotax
3. Colin Langlois

Mountain Dew Action Sports Tour (Cont.)

Toyota Challenge
Sept. 7-10 at San Jose, Calif.

Skate Vert
		Score
1	Bucky Lasek	91.75
2	Sandro Dias	90.75
3	Bob Burnquist	89.25

Skate Park
		Score
1	Ryan Sheckler	91.08
2	Greg Lutzka	88.50
3	Jereme Rogers	87.50

BMX Vert
		Score
1	Jamie Bestwick	95.75
2	Chad Kagy	92.75
3	Simon Tabron	92.75

BMX Dirt
		Score
1	Ryan Guettler	93.25
2	Luke Parslow	91.75
2	Corey Bohan	90.50

BMX Park
		Score
1	Scotty Cranmer	93.75
2	Ryan Nyquist	93.50
3	Daniel Dhers	92.00

FMX
		Score
1	Nate Adams	93.50
2	Mike Mason	91.83
3	Jeremy Lusk	88.67

Special Event

BMX SX

1 Michal Prokop
2 Donny Robinson
3 Arnaud Dubois

PlayStation Pro
Oct. 12-15 at Orlando, Fla.

Skate Vert
		Score
1	Bucky Lasek	92.00
2	Tas Pappas	88.00
3	Pierre-Luc Gagnon	86.50

BMX Vert
		Score
1	Jamie Bestwick	95.75
2	Chad Kagy	94.00
3	Kevin Robinson	92.25

BMX Dirt
		Score
1	Anthony Napolitan	94.25
2	Corey Bohan	94.00
3	Luke Parslow	93.25

Skate Park
		Score
1	Jereme Rogers	91.58
2	Ryan Sheckler	89.75
3	Paul Rodriguez	85.75

BMX Park
		Score
1	Daniel Dhers	96.75
2	Marcus Tooker	90.75
3	Alistair Whitton	90.75

FMX
		Score
1	Mike Mason	95.67
2	Jeremy Lusk	93.00
3	Nate Adams	92.67

2006 Mountain Dew Tour Final Points Standings

In each discipline (SKATE, BMX and FMX), athletes who qualify into each event (Vert, Park, Dirt or FMX) receive points based on the Final results from that event. Riders are awarded points corresponding to their final placing.

Skate Vert
		Pts
1	Bucky Lasek	413
2	Sandro Dias	300
3	Bob Burnquist	273
4	Andy Macdonald	256
5	Jean Postec	218

Skate Park
		Pts
1	Ryan Sheckler	430
2	Jereme Rogers	401
3	Rodolfo Ramos	243
4	Nyjah Huston	205
5	Chad Bartie	203

BMX Vert
		Pts
1	Jamie Bestwick	475
2	Chad Kagy	355
3	Kevin Robinson	307
4	Simon Tabron	267
5	Jimmy Walker	230

BMX Park
		Pts
1	Daniel Dhers	389
2	Scotty Cranmer	330
3	Ryan Nyquist	319
4	Alistair Whitton	256
5	Gary Young	221

BMX Dirt
		Pts
1	Anthony Napolitan	376
2	Luke Parslow	351
3	Corey Bohan	286
4	Ryan Nyquist	277
5	Ryan Guettler	246

FMX
		Pts
1	Nate Adams	413
2	Mike Mason	287
3	Travis Pastrana	275
4	Jeremy Lusk	257
5	Adam Jones	201

Surfing
2006 ASP World Championship Tour
Men

Quiksilver Pro at Gold Coast
1. Kelly Slater
2. Taj Burrow

Rip Curl Pro at Bells Beach
1. Kelly Slater
2. Joel Parkinson

Billabong Pro Teahupoo
1. Bobby Martinez
2. Fredrick Patacchia

Globe WCT Fiji at Tavarua/Namotu
1. Damien Hobgood
2. Shaun Cansdell

Rip Curl Search Mexico
1. Andy Irons
2. Taylor Knox

Billabong Pro at Jeffreys Bay
1. Mick Fanning
2. Taj Burrow

Boost Mobile Pro at Trestles
1. Bede Durbidge
2. Kelly Slater

Quiksilver Pro France
1. Joel Parkinson
2. Mick Fanning

Remaining Men's Events: Billabong Pro at Mundaka, Oct. 2-14; Nova Schin Festival at Florianopolis, Oct. 30-Nov. 8; Rip Curl Pipeline Masters at Oahu, Dec. 8-20

Men's standings
through Quiksilver Pro France (Oct. 1)
1. Kelly Slater (7017 pts.)
2. Taj Burrow (5968 pts.)
3. Andy Irons (5841 pts.)

Women

Roxy Pro at Gold Coast
1. Melanie Redman-Carr
2. Layne Beachley

Roxy Pro at Tavarua/Namotu
1. Melanie Redman-Carr
2. Layne Beachley

Billabong Pro Teahupoo
1. Melanie Redman-Carr
2. Chelsea Georgeson

Billabong Girls at Praia da Tiririca
1. Layne Beachley
2. Jessi Miley-Dyer

Rip Curl Mademoiselle Pro France
1. Chelsea Georgeson
2. Melanie Redman-Carr

Remaining Women's Events: Havaianas Beachley Classic at Northern Beaches, Oct. 9-15; Roxy Pro at Sunset Beach, Nov. 24-Dec. 6; Billabong Pro at Honolua Bay, Dec. 8-20.

Women's standings
through Rip Curl Mademoiselle Pro France (Sept. 5)
1. Melanie Redman-Carr (4752 pts)
2. Layne Beachley (4452 pts)
3. Chelsea Georgeson (4044 pts)

Snowboarding
Chevrolet Grand Prix Series

Breckenridge, Colo. (Dec. 13-17, 2005); Mt. Bachelor, Ore. (Jan. 5-8, 2006); Mountain Creek, N.J. (Jan. 20-21, 2006)

Breckenridge

Men's Pipe Finals #1
1 Shaun White
2 Ross Powers
3 Scotty Lago

Women's Pipe Finals #1
1 Hannah Teter
2 Gretchen Bleiler
3 Elena Hight

Men's Pipe Finals #2
1 Shaun White
2 Mason Aguirre
3 Danny Davis

Men's Pipe Finals #2
1 Gretchen Bleiler
2 Elena Hight
3 Tricia Byrnes

Mt. Bachelor

Men's Pipe Finals
1 Shaun White
2 Mason Aguirre
3 Danny Davis

Women's Pipe Finals
1 Gretchen Bleiler
2 Hannah Teter
3 Elena Hight

Mountain Creek

Men's Pipe Finals #1
1 Shaun White
2 Danny Kass
3 Keir Dillon

Women's Pipe Finals #1
1 Gretchen Bleiler
2 Elena Hight
3 Hannah Teter

Men's Pipe Finals #2
1 Shaun White
2 Andy Finch
3 Steve Fisher

Women's Pipe Finals #2
1 Gretchen Bleiler
2 Kelly Clark
3 Elena Hight

For snowboarding results from the 2006 Winter Olympics in Turin, Italy see the Olympics chapter starting on page 663.

1995-2006
Through the Years

SPORTS ALMANAC

X GAMES

The ESPN Extreme Games, originally envisioned as a biannual showcase for "alternative" sports, were first held June 24-July 1, 1995 in Newport and Providence, R.I. and Mt. Snow, Vt. The success of the inaugural event prompted organizers to make it an annual competition. Newport would again serve as host for the redubbed X Games in 1996. The X Games has evolved rapidly since its inception and have been held in several cities since. New sports and events have been added while others have been dropped.

SUMMER X GAMES

Summer X Games sites: 1995–Newport/Providence, R.I. (and Mt. Snow, Vt.); 1996–Newport/Providence, R.I.; 1997–San Diego; 1998–San Diego; 1999–San Francisco; 2000–San Francisco; 2001–Phiadelphia; 2002–Philadelphia; 2003–Los Angeles; 2004–Los Angeles; 2005–Los Angeles; 2006–Los Angeles.

BMX

Multiple winners: Dave Mirra (13); Ryan Nyquist (4); Jamie Bestwick, Corey Bohan, Martti Kuoppa and Trevor Meyer (3); Matt Hoffman, T.J. Lavin, Brandon Meadows and Kevin Robinson (2)

Year	Vert	Year	Street/Stunt Park	Year	Dirt
1995	Matt Hoffman	1996	Dave Mirra	1995	Jay Miron
1996	Matt Hoffman	1997	Dave Mirra	1996	Joey Garcia
1997	Dave Mirra	1998	Dave Mirra	1997	T.J. Lavin
1998	Dave Mirra	1999	Dave Mirra	1998	Brian Foster
1999	Dave Mirra	2000	Dave Mirra	1999	T.J. Lavin
2000	Jamie Bestwick	2001	Bruce Crisman	2000	Ryan Nyquist
2001	Dave Mirra	2002	Ryan Nyquist	2001	Stephen Murray
2002	Dave Mirra	2003	Ryan Nyquist	2002	Allan Cooke
2003	Jamie Bestwick	2004	Dave Mirra	2003	Ryan Nyquist
2004	Dave Mirra	2005	Dave Mirra	2004	Corey Bohan
2005	Jamie Bestwick	**Year**	**Big Air**	2005	Corey Bohan
2006	Chad Kagy	2006	Kevin Robinson	2006	Corey Bohan
Year	**Vert Best Trick**	**Year**	**Downhill**	**Year**	**Flatland**
2005	Jamie Bestwick	2001	Brandon Meadows	1997	Trevor Meyer
2006	Kevin Robinson	2002	Robbie Miranda	1998	Trevor Meyer
		2003	Brandon Meadows	1999	Trevor Meyer
		2004	event discontinued	2000	Martti Kuoppa
				2001	Martti Kuoppa
				2002	Martti Kuoppa
				2003	Simon O'Brien
				2004	event discontinued

Moto X

Year	Freestyle	Year	Step Up	Year	Big Air
1999	Travis Pastrana	2001	Tommy Clowers	2001	Kenny Bartman
2000	Travis Pastrana	2002	Tommy Clowers	2002	Mike Metzger
2001	Travis Pastrana	2003	Matt Buyten	2003	Brian Deegan
2002	Mike Metzger	2004	Jeremy McGrath	**Year**	**Super Moto**
2003	Travis Pastrana	2005	Tommy Clowers	2004	Ben Bostrom
2004	Nate Adams	2006	Matt Buyten	2005	Doug Henry
2005	Travis Pastrana			2006	Jeff Ward
2006	Jeremy Stenberg			**Year**	**Best Trick**
				2004	Chuck Carothers
				2005	not held
				2006	Travis Pastrana

Rally Car Racing

Year	
2006	Travis Pastrana/Christian Edstrom

Skateboarding

Multiple winners: Tony Hawk (9); Andy Macdonald (8); Bucky Lasek (6); Bob Burnquist (4); Rodil de Araujo Jr., Pierre-Luc Gagnon and Danny Way (3); Cara-Beth Burnside, Sandro Dias, Paul Rodriguez and Chris Senn (2).

Year	Vert Singles
1995	Tony Hawk
1996	Andy Macdonald
1997	Tony Hawk
1998	Andy Macdonald
1999	Bucky Lasek
2000	Bucky Lasek
2001	Bob Burnquist
2002	Pierre-Luc Gagnon
2003	Bucky Lasek
2004	Bucky Lasek
2005	Pierre-Luc Gagnon
2006	Sandro Dias

Year	Women's Vert
2004	L. Adams Hawkins
2005	Cara-Beth Burnside
2006	Cara-Beth Burnside

Year	Street Best Trick
2001	Kerry Getz
2002	Rodil de Araujo Jr.
2003	Chad Muska
2004	event discontinued

Year	Vert Doubles
1997	Hawk/Macdonald
1998	Hawk/Macdonald
1999	Hawk/Macdonald
2000	Hawk/Macdonald
2001	Hawk/Macdonald
2002	Hawk/Macdonald
2003	Lasek/Burnquist
2004	event discontinued

Year	Vert Best Trick
2000	Bob Burnquist
2001	Matt Dove
2002	Pierre-Luc Gagnon
2003	Tony Hawk
2004	Sandro Dias
2005	Bob Burnquist
2006	Bucky Lasek

Year	Park
2003	Ryan Sheckler

Year	Women's Park
2003	Vanessa Torres
2004	event discontinued

Year	Women's Street
2004	Elissa Steamer
2005	Elissa Steamer
2006	Elissa Steamer

Year	Big Air
2004	Danny Way
2005	Danny Way
2006	Danny Way

Year	Street/Park
1995	Chris Senn
1996	Rodil de Araujo Jr.
1997	Chris Senn
1998	Rodil de Araujo Jr.
1999	Chris Senn
2000	Eric Koston
2001	Kerry Getz
2002	Rodil de Araujo Jr.
2003	event discontinued

Year	Street
2003	Eric Koston
2004	Paul Rodriguez
2005	Paul Rodriguez
2006	Chris Cole

Street Luge

Multiple winners: Biker Sherlock (5); Dennis Derammelaere and Rat Sult (2)

Year	Dual
1995	Bob Pereyra
1996	Shawn Goular
1997	Biker Sherlock
1998	Biker Sherlock
1999	Dennis Derammelaere
2000	Bob Ozman
2001	event discontinued

Year	Mass
1995	Shawn Gilbert
1996	Biker Sherlock
1997	Biker Sherlock
1998	Rat Sult
1999	event discontinued

Year	King of the Hill
2001	Dennis Derammelaere
2002	event discontinued

Year	Super Mass
1997	Biker Sherlock
1998	Rat Sult
1999	David Rogers
2000	Bob Pereyra
2001	Brent DeKeyser
2002	event discontinued

Sportclimbing

Multiple winners: Katie Brown, Hans Florine and Elena Ovtchinnikova (3); Maxim Stenkovoy (2).

Year	Men's Difficulty
1995	Ian Vickers
1996	Arnaud Petit
1997	Francois Legrand
1998	Christian Core
1999	Chris Sharma
2000	event discontinued

Year	Women's Difficulty
1995	Robyn Erbersfield
1996	Katie Brown
1997	Katie Brown
1998	Katie Brown
1999	Stephanie Bodet
2000	event discontinued

Year	Men's Speed
1995	Hans Florine
1996	Hans Florine
1997	Hans Florine
1998	Vladimir Netsvetaev
1999	Aaron Shamy
2000	Vladimir Zakharov
2001	Maxim Stenkovoy
2002	Maxim Stenkovoy
2003	event discontinued

Year	Women's Speed
1995	Elena Ovtchinnikova
1996	Cecile Le Flem
1997	Elena Ovtchinnikova
1998	Elena Ovtchinnikova
1999	Renata Piszczek
2000	Etti Hendrawati
2001	Elena Repko
2002	Tori Allen
2003	event discontinued

Having competed in every Summer X Games in history until 2006 when he was forced to withdraw after suffering a Grade 2 lacerated liver in practice >> BMX rider **Dave Mirra** is the most decorated athlete in X Games history with 14 golds in BMX Vert and BMX.

DID YOU KNOW?

Summer X Games (Cont.)

In-Line Skating

Multiple winners: Fabiola da Silva (7); Eito Yasutoko (3), Derek Downing, Jaren Grob, Martina Svobodova, Gypsy Tidwell (2).

Year	Men's Vert
1995	Tom Fry
1996	Rene Hulgreen
1997	Tim Ward
1998	Cesar Mora
1999	Eito Yasutoko
2000	Eito Yasutoko
2001	Taig Khris

Year	Women's Vert
1995	Tash Hodgeson
1996	Fabiola da Silva
1997	Fabiola da Silva
1998	Fabiola da Silva
1999	Ayumi Kawasaki
2000	Fabiola da Silva
2001	Fabiola da Silva

Year	Combined Vert
2002	Takeshi Yasutoko
2003	Eito Yasutoko
2004	Takeshi Yasutoko
2005	event discontinued

Note: In 2002 the men's and women's vert events were combined.

Year	Men's Park
1995	Matt Salerno
1996	Arlo Eisenberg
1997	Arron Feinberg
1998	Jonathan Bergeron
1999	Nicky Adams
2000	Sven Boekhorst
2001	Jaren Grob
2002	Jaren Grob
2003	Bruno Lowe
2004	event discontinued

Year	Women's Park
1997	Sayaka Yabe
1998	Jenny Curry
1999	Sayaka Yabe
2000	Fabiola da Silva
2001	Martina Svobodova
2002	Martina Svobodova
2003	Fabiola da Silva
2004	event discontinued

Year	Vert Triples
1998	Malina/Fogarty/Popa
1999	Khris/Bujanda/Boekhorst
2000	event discontinued

Year	Men's Downhill
1995	Derek Downing
1996	Dante Muse
1997	Derek Downing
1998	Patrick Naylor
1999	event discontinued

Year	Women's Downhill
1995	Julie Brandt
1996	Gypsy Tidwell
1997	Gypsy Tidwell
1998	Julie Brandt
1999	event discontinued

Watersports

Multiple winners: Dallas Friday and Danny Harf (4); Parks Bonifay, Peter Fleck, Tara Hamilton and Darin Shapiro (2).

Year	Barefoot Waterski Jumping
1995	Justin Seers
1996	Ron Scarpa
1997	Peter Fleck
1998	Peter Fleck
1999	event discontinued

Year	Men's Wakeboarding
1996	Parks Bonifay
1997	Jeremy Kovak
1998	Darin Shapiro
1999	Parks Bonifay
2000	Darin Shapiro
2001	Danny Harf
2002	Danny Harf
2003	Danny Harf
2004	Phillip Soven
2005	Danny Harf
2006	event discontinued

Year	Women's Wakeboarding
1997	Tara Hamilton
1998	Andrea Gaytan
1999	Meaghan Major
2000	Tara Hamilton
2001	Dallas Friday
2002	Emily Copeland
2003	Dallas Friday
2004	Dallas Friday
2005	Dallas Friday
2006	event discontinued

X-Venture Race

Year	
1995	Team Threadbo
1996	Team Kobeer
1997	Team Presidio
1998	event discontinued

Bungee Jumping

Year	
1995	Doug Anderson
1996	Peter Bihun
1997	event discontinued

Big-Air Snowboarding

Year	Men
1997	Peter Line
1998	Kevin Jones
1999	Peter Line

Year	Women
1997	Tina Dixon
1998	Janet Matthews
1999	Barrett Christy

Note: Snowboarding was held at the Summer X Games from 1997-99.

Skysurfing

Year	
1995	Fradet/Zipser
1996	Furrer/Scmid
1997	Hartman/Pappadato
1998	Rozov/Burch
1999	Fradet/Iodice
2000	Klaus/Rogers
2001	event discontinued

Surfing

Year	
2003	East Coast
2004	East Coast
2005	East Coast
2006	West Coast

Note: The X Games surfing event is contested by teams of surfers from the East Coast and the West Coast.

Winter X Games

Winter X Games sites: 1997–Snow Summit Mountain Resort, Big Bear Lake, Calif.; 1998–Crested Butte, Colo.; 1999–Crested Butte, Colo.; 2000– Mt. Snow, Vt.; 2001–Mt. Snow, Vt.; 2002–Aspen, Colo.; 2003–Aspen, Colo.; 2004–Aspen, Colo.; 2005–Aspen, Colo; 2006–Aspen, Colo.

Snowboarding

Multiple winners: Tara Dakides and Shaun White (5); Janna Meyen (4); Lindsey Jacobellis and Shaun Palmer (3); Gretchen Bleiler, Barrett Christy, Kelly Clark, Kevin Jones, Ueli Kestenholz, Todd Richards and Maelle Ricker (2).

Year	Men's Big Air	Year	Women's Big Air	Year	Men's Slopestyle	Year	Women's Slopestyle
1997	Jimmy Halopoff	1997	Barrett Christy	1997	Daniel Franck	1997	Barrett Christy
1998	Jason Borgstede	1998	Tina Basich	1998	Ross Powers	1998	Jennie Waara
1999	Kevin Sansalone	1999	Barrett Christy	1999	Peter Line	1999	Tara Dakides
2000	Peter Line	2000	Tara Dakides	2000	Kevin Jones	2000	Tara Dakides
2001	Jussi Oksanen	2001	Tara Dakides	2001	Kevin Jones	2001	Jaime MacLeod
				2002	Travis Rice	2002	Tara Dakides

Year	Men's Boarder X	Year	Women's Boarder X	Year		Year	
1997	Shaun Palmer	1997	Jennie Waara	2003	Shaun White	2003	Janna Meyen
1998	Shaun Palmer	1998	Tina Dixon	2004	Shaun White	2004	Janna Meyen
1999	Shaun Palmer	1999	Maelle Ricker	2005	Shaun White	2005	Janna Meyen
2000	Drew Neilson	2000	Leslee Olson	2006	Shaun White	2006	Janna Meyen
2001	Scott Gaffney	2001	Line Oestvold	**Year**	**Men's Halfpipe**	**Year**	**Women's Halfpipe**
2002	Philippe Conte	2002	Ine Poetzl	1997	Todd Richards	1997	Shannon Dunn
2003	Ueli Kestenholz	2003	Lindsey Jacobellis	1998	Ross Powers	1998	Cara-Beth Burnside
2004	Ueli Kestenholz	2004	Lindsey Jacobellis	1999	Jimi Scott	1999	Michele Taggart
2005	Xavier de le Rue	2005	Lindsey Jacobellis	2000	Todd Richards	2000	S. Brun Kjeldaas
2006	Nate Holland	2006	Maelle Ricker				

Year	Men's Superpipe	Year	Women's Superpipe
2001	Dan Kass	2001	Shannon Dunn
2002	J.J. Thomas	2002	Kelly Clark
2003	Shaun White	2003	Gretchen Bleiler
2004	Steve Fisher	2004	Hannah Teter
2005	Antti Autti	2005	Gretchen Bleiler
2006	Shaun White	2006	Kelly Clark

Skiing

Multiple winners: Aleisha Cline (4); Simon Dumont (3); Reggie Crist, Grete Eliassen, Tanner Hall, Lars Lewen (2).

Year	Men's Big Air	Year	Women's Skier X	Year	Men's Speed
1999	J.F. Cusson	1999	Aleisha Cline	1997	Phil Tintsman
2000	Candide Thovex	2000	Anik Demers	1998	Jurgen Beneke
2001	Tanner Hall	2001	Aleisha Cline	1999	event discontinued
2002	event discontinued	2002	Aleisha Cline	**Year**	**Men's Slopestyle**
Year	**Men's Skier X**	2003	Aleisha Cline	2002	Tanner Hall
1998	Dennis Rey	2004	Karin Huttary	2003	Not held
1999	Enak Gavaggio	2005	Sanna Tidstrand	2004	Simon Dumont
2000	Shaun Palmer	2006	Karin Huttary	2005	Charles Gagnier
2001	Zach Crist	**Year**	**SuperPipe**	2006	event discontinued
2002	Reggie Crist	2002	Jon Olsson	**Year**	**Women's Speed**
2003	Lars Lewen	2003	Candide Thovex	1997	Cheri Elliott
2004	Casey Puckett	2004	Simon Dumont	1998	Elke Brutsaert
2005	Reggie Crist	**Year**	**Men's SuperPipe**	1999	event discontinued
2006	Lars Lewen	2005	Simon Dumont		
		2006	Tanner Hall		
		Year	**Women's SuperPipe**		
		2005	Grete Eliassen		
		2006	Grete Eliassen		

Snomobiling

Year	Snocross	Year	Hillcross
1998	Toni Haikonen	2001	Carl Kuster
1999	Chris Vincent	2002	Carl Kuster
2000	Tucker Hibbert	2003	T.J. Kullas
2001	Blair Morgan	2003	Mike Metzger
2002	Blair Morgan	2004	Levi LaVallee
2003	Not held	2005	event discontinued
2004	Michael Island		
2005	Blair Morgan		
2006	Blair Morgan		

WINTER X GAMES

Winter X Games (Cont.)

Ice Climbing

Year	Men's Difficulty
1997	Jaren Ogden
1998	Will Gadd
1999	Will Gadd
2000	event discontinued

Year	Women's Difficulty
1997	Bird Lew
1998	Kim Csizmazia
1999	Kim Csizmazia
2000	event discontinued

Year	Men's Speed
1997	Jared Ogden
1998	Will Gadd
1999	event discontinued

Year	Women's Speed
1997	Bird Lew
1998	Kim Csizmazia
1999	event discontinued

Super-modified Shovel Racing

Year	
1997	Don Adkins
1999	event discontinued

CrossOver

Year	
1997	Brian Patch
1998	event discontinued

Skiboarding

Year	
1998	Mike Nick
1999	Chris Hawks
2000	Neal Lyons

Moto X

Year	Big Air
2001	Mike Jones
2002	Brian Deegan

Year	Best Trick
2004	Caleb Wyatt
2005	Jeremy Stenberg
2006	Jeremy Stenberg

Ultracross

Year	
2000	McLain/Lind
2001	Palmer/Takizawa
2002	Wescott/Lind

Snow Mountain Bike Racing

Year	Men's Downhill
1997	Shaun Palmer
1998	Andrew Shandro
1999	event discontinued

Year	Women's Downhill
1997	Missy Giove
1998	Marla Streb
1999	event discontinued

Year	Men's Biker X
1999	Steve Peat
2000	Myles Rockwell
2001	event discontinued

Year	Women's Biker X
1999	Tara Llanes
2000	Katrina Miller
2001	event discontinued
2003	Delerue/Zackrisson
2004	Holland/Crist
2005	Huser/Andersson

Mountain Dew Action Sports Tour
All-Time Winners

Panasonic Open (Louisville)

	Skate Vert		
2005	Bucky Lasek	2006	Bob Burnquist
	Skate Park		
2005	Ryan Sheckler	2006	Ryan Sheckler
	BMX Vert		
2005	Jamie Bestwick	2006	Simon Tabron
	BMX Park		
2005	Ryan Guettler	2006	Scotty Cranmer
	BMX Dirt		
2005	Ryan Guettler	2006	Anthony Napolitan
	FMX		
2005	Kenny Batram	2006	Nate Adams

Righ Guard Open (Denver)

	Skate Vert		
2005	Bucky Lasek	2006	Shaun White
	Skate Park		
2005	Ryan Sheckler	2006	Jereme Rogers
	BMX Vert		
2005	Jamie Bestwick	2006	Jamie Bestwick
	BMX Park		
2005	Ryan Guettler	2006	Daniel Dhers
	BMX Dirt		
2005	Ryan Guettler	2006	Ryan Nyquist
	FMX		
2005	Kenny Batram	2006	Travis Pastrana

Vans Invitational (Portland)

	Skate Vert		
2005	Bucky Lasek	2006	Sandro Dias
	Skate Park		
2005	Greg Lutzka	2006	Ryan Sheckler
	BMX Vert		
2005	Jamie Bestwick	2006	Jamie Bestwick
	BMX Park		
2005	Ryan Nyquist	2006	Ryan Nyquist
	BMX Dirt		
2005	Ryan Guettler	2006	Cameron White
	FMX		
2005	Kenny Batram	2006	Travis Pastrana

Toyota Challenge (San Jose)

	Skate Vert		
2005	Pierre-Luc Gagnon	2006	Bucky Lasek
	Skate Park		
2005	Ryan Sheckler	2006	Ryan Sheckler
	BMX Vert		
2005	Jamie Bestwick	2006	Jamie Bestwick
	BMX Park		
2005	Dave Mirra	2006	Scotty Cranmer
	BMX Dirt		
2005	Ryan Guettler	2006	Ryan Guettler
	FMX		
2005	Jeremy Stenberg	2006	Nate Adams

Playstation Pro (Orlando)

	Skate Vert		
2005	Pierre-Luc Gagnon	2006	Bucky Lasek
	Skate Park		
2005	Jereme Rogers	2006	Jereme Rogers
	BMX Vert		
2005	Jamie Bestwick	2006	Jamie Bestwick

	BMX Park		
2005	Scotty Cranmer	2006	Daniel Dhers
	BMX Dirt		
2005	Ryan Nyquist	2006	Anthony Napolitan
	FMX		
2005	Kenny Bartram	2006	Mike Mason

HORSE RACING

2005 / 2006 YEAR IN REVIEW

Jockey Edgar Prado guides **Barbaro** to a runaway win at the 2006 Kentucky Derby.

BEATING THE ODDS

Barbaro romps to a 6½-length win in the Kentucky Derby, then fights for his life after a devastating injury in the Preakness.

JOCKEY EDGAR PRADO HEARD AN AWFUL NOISE AND KNEW SOMETHING HAD GONE HORRIBLY WRONG.

He had guided Preakness-favorite Barbaro out of the starting gate at Pimlico, and was just 100 yards into the race when it happened. The noise he heard was Barbaro's right hind leg shattering into 20 pieces.

Prado immediately pulled up Barbaro, dismounted and could only do his best to comfort the injured bay colt. Moments later, trainer Michael Matz joined Prado, now with tears in his eyes, as the focus turned away from the race and onto to the survival of their horse.

Just two weeks earlier at Churchill Downs, things couldn't have looked more promising for the Lael Stables bay colt.

At the 132nd Kentucky Derby, Barbaro stumbled out of the gate, then stalked the leaders for the first half of the race as he bided his time and navigated his way through traffic. At the behest of Prado, he turned on the jets at the ¾-mile mark, and

then powered his way to the front of the pack as he entered the stretch. And it was all over.

He stormed to the finish for an inspiring 6½-length romp over runner-up Bluegrass Cat and third-place Steppenwolfer, for the largest margin of victory at the Derby since 1946, when Assault won by eight lengths.

It was the sixth race of his career – and the sixth win of his career, as he became just the sixth undefeated horse in the Derby's 132-year history to enter the Run for the Roses and emerge with a win.

After his dominant Derby win, a confident Prado knew his horse had the chance to do something special.

"I got the feeling that we have [the] potential that maybe we can win the Triple Crown this year," he said.

Barbaro was trained by Matz, an Olympic silver medalist in Equestrian and six-time U.S. national show jumping champion. He was the U.S. flag

 Michael Morrison is Co-Editor of the ESPN Sports Almanac.

AP/Wide World Photos

A concerned **Edgar Prado** looks for help after his horse, **Barbaro**, took a bad step 100 yards into the Preakness and pulled up lame.

bearer at the closing ceremonies of the 1996 games, awarded the honor for his heroic actions on the ill-fated United Airlines Flight 232 in June 1989.

The plane, en route from Denver to Chicago, suffered a failure in its hydraulic system and crashed into an Iowa cornfield, killing 111 people. Matz and his fiancé (now wife) were two of the lucky survivors. As he escaped the wreckage, Matz carried three young siblings to safety, before heading back into the burning fuselage to rescue an 11-month-old girl. He was named "Person of the Week" by ABC News.

The siblings, Jody, Melissa and Travis Roth were three of the 157,536 spectators at Churchill Downs.

"It's like we almost expect amazing things from him," Jody, now 31, said.

"No matter what he does. He's just a winner. We can't wait to see him in two weeks."

Barbaro was the heavy favorite to win the 131st Preakness, going off at even odds. He was feeling good moments before the race — possibly a little too good, as he broke through the gate prematurely and had to be reloaded. But 100 yards in, one bad step destroyed hopes of the first Triple

Thoroughbred racing's top trainer **Todd Pletcher** broke his own single-season earnings record in 2006, but came up short in the Triple Crown races.

he got stronger as the race went on and bolted to a 5¼-length win. It was a spectacular performance that was unfortunately tempered with sadness.

Barbaro was taken immediately to the barn at Pimlico for x-rays, then rushed via police escort to the University of Pennsylvania's New Bolton Center, where he underwent six hours of surgery and had a metal plate and 27 screws inserted into his leg to keep it all together.

An astounding show of support flooded into the Bolton Center in the form of banners, flowers, donations and plenty of apples and carrots. Daily (sometimes hourly) news updates became commonplace. The surgery was a success, but Barbaro was far from out of the woods.

Several weeks later, he developed an acute case of laminitis in his left leg, a painful and often fatal condition that caused Secretariat to be euthanized in 1989. Due to the damage to his right leg, Barbaro had shifted his weight to his uninjured left leg and the unbearable strain brought on the laminitis.

Doctors called it "as bad a case as you can get" and labeled his chance for recovery "poor." But again he persevered. By early October, he was still at the Bolton Center, and though he didn't look a whole lot like the horse that crushed the rest of the Derby field five months before, he was walking, grazing...and once again, exceeding expectations.

Crown champion since 1978, and left Barbaro's life in jeopardy.

The race was won by Bernardini, the lightly raced son of A.P. Indy who went off at 12-1 odds and had his name misspelled (Bernadini) on his saddle towel. Trained by Tom Albertrani and ridden by Javier Castellano, Bernardini deftly moved past tiring early leader Like Now and eventual runner-up Sweetnorthernsaint, and surged to the lead down the stretch. Like Barbaro two weeks prior,

AP/Wide World Photos

THE TOP

10 ⬇

Stories of the Year in Horse Racing

10 Yummy!

For the first time in its 132-year history, the Kentucky Derby has an official sponsor. In February, Yum Brands, Inc. – the parent company of Taco Bell, KFC and Pizza Hut – agreed to a 5-year deal to display its logo under the twin spires at Churchill Downs and place various other signage around the venerable track. The race is now officially called the Kentucky Derby Presented by Yum Brands.

09 Head Games

Zinedine Zidane wasn't the only person to deliver a vicious headbutt in 2006. After being thrown from his horse, City Affair, at the start of a July race in Stratford, England, jockey Paul O'Neill (no relation to the Gatorade-smashing ex-Yankee) took matters into his own head. He stood up, grabbed the reins and jammed the front of his helmet into his horse's head. An apologetic O'Neill was later given a 1-day ban by the Horseracing Regulatory Authority. City Affair was uninjured and finished the race in fourth place.

08 Lost...too soon.

Three stellar horses die way before their time in 2006. In August, the 2005 Horse of the Year and Breeders' Cup Classic winner Saint Liam was euthanized after a freak fall during his first year at stud. Less than three weeks later, 2006 Dubai World Cup winner Electrocutionist dies of an apparent heart attack. Then less than two weeks after that, sprinter Lost in the Fog, winner of ten straight races during 2004-05, dies of cancer.

07 Glidemaster wins.

Glidemaster wins the 81st running of the $1.5 million Hambletonian, harness racing's most prestigious event, in a record time of 1:51⅕. He also takes the Kentucky Futurity in early October and only needed a win at the Yonkers Trot on November 28 to become the ninth horse to win trotting's Triple Crown.

06 Legends retire.

Hall of Fame jockeys Jerry Bailey and Gary Stevens announce their retirements. The duo combined for 10,781 wins including 14 Triple Crown events, and over a half billion dollars in earnings in 58 years of service in the saddle.

05 Pletcher's at it again.

After smashing the all-time single-season earnings record for trainers in 2005 with over $20 million, Todd Pletcher breaks his own record in 2006 with over $21 million through early October. He runs his mark to 0-21, however, in Triple Crown races.

04 Jazil takes Belmont.

Jazil, trained by Kiaran McGlaughlin and ridden by 18-year-old Fernando Jara, wins the Belmont Stakes by 1¼ lengths over pre-race favorite Bluegrass Cat and third place finisher Sunriver (both Todd Pletcher entrants). Panama native Jara becomes the youngest jockey to win a Triple Crown event since 18-year-old Steve Cauthen in 1978.

03 Lava's in the air.

Five-year-old gelding and leading Horse of the Year candidate Lava Man is a perfect seven-for-seven in 2006 (through early October) and sets his sights squarely on the $5 million Breeders' Cup Classic in November. His top wins of the year include the Sunshine Millions in January, Santa Anita Handicap in March and the Hollywood Gold Cup in July.

02 Bittersweet victory for Bernardini.

Jockey Javier Castellano guides Bernardini to an impressive 5¼-length win at the Preakness. The celebration is tempered, however, due to the life-threatening injury to Kentucky Derby winner Barbaro. Bernardini, the son of 1992 Horse of the Year A.P. Indy, also wins the Jim Dandy, Travers and Jockey Club Gold Cup to make him a candidate for Horse of the Year.

01 Barbaro captures hearts.

Barbaro surges to a surprising 6½-length win at the Kentucky Derby, the largest margin of victory since 1946. Two weeks later, he suffers a devastating, life-threatening injury 100 yards into the Preakness when a bad step shatters his right hind leg into 20 pieces. Through early October he was recovering and in stable condition.

All three of the 2006 Triple Crown winners — Barbaro, Bernardini and Jazil — won their races from the No. 8 post position.

The last time each of the three race winners started from the same post position was in 1974, when Cannonade (Kentucky Derby) and Little Current (Preakness and Belmont) started and won from the No. 2 post.

2005-2006
Season in Review

SPORTS ALMANAC

Thoroughbred Racing
Major Stakes Races

Winners of major stakes races from Nov. 25, 2005 through Sept. 23, 2006; (T) indicates turf race course; F indicates furlongs.

Late 2005

Date	Race	Track	Miles	Winner	Jockey	Purse
Nov. 25	Clark Handicap	Churchill Downs	1⅛	Magna Graduate	John Velazquez	$573,500
Nov. 28	Japan Cup*	Tokyo	1½ (T)	Alkaased	Frankie Dettori	3,966,667
Dec. 12	Hong Kong Cup*	Sha Tin	1¼ (T)	Vengeance of Rain	Anthony Delpech	2,321,308

*World Series Racing Championship series race (series canceled for 2006).

2006 (through Sept. 23)

Date	Race	Track	Miles	Winner	Jockey	Purse
Jan. 29	Sunshine Millions Classic	Santa Anita	1⅛	Lava Man	Corey Nakatani	$1,000,000
Feb. 4	Charles H. Strub Stakes	Santa Anita	1⅛	High Limit	Patrick Valenzuela	300,000
Feb. 4	Donn Handicap	Gulfstream	1⅛	Brass Hat	Willie Martinez	500,000
Feb. 4	Hutcheson Stakes	Gulfstream	7½ F	Keyed Entry	John Velazquez	150,000
Feb. 4	Holy Bull Stakes	Gulfstream	1⅛	Barbaro	Edgar Prado	150,000
Feb. 11	Santa Maria Handicap	Santa Anita	1 1/16	Star Parade	Martin Pedroza	250,000
Mar. 4	Fountain of Youth Stakes	Gulfstream	1⅛	First Samurai	Edgar Prado	300,000
Mar. 4	Santa Anita Handicap	Santa Anita	1¼	Lava Man	Corey Nakatani	1,000,000
Mar. 11	Santa Margarita Handicap	Santa Anita	1⅛	Healthy Addiction	Jon Court	300,000
Mar. 12	Santa Anita Oaks	Santa Anita	1 1/16	Balance	Victor Espinoza	300,000
Mar. 18	San Felipe Stakes	Santa Anita	1 1/16	A.P. Warrior	Corey Nakatani	250,000
Mar. 18	Rebel Stakes	Oaklawn	1 1/16	Lawyer Ron	John McKee	300,000
Mar. 18	Tampa Bay Derby	Tampa Bay	1 1/16	Deputy Glitters	Jose Lezcano	250,000
Mar. 25	Lane's End Stakes	Turfway	1⅛	With a City	Brice Blanc	500,000
Mar. 25	Dubai World Cup	Nad al-Sheba	1¼	Electrocutionist	Frankie Dettori	6,000,000
Mar. 25	Dubai Golden Shaheen	Nad al-Sheba	¾	Proud Tower Too	David Cohen	2,000,000
Mar. 25	Dubai Duty Free	Nad al-Sheba	1⅛	David Junior	Jamie Spencer	5,000,000
Mar. 25	Dubai Sheema Classic	Nad al-Sheba	1½	Heart's Cry	Christophe Lemaire	5,000,000
Mar. 25	UAE Derby	Nad al-Sheba	1⅛	Discreet Cat	Frankie Dettori	2,000,000
Apr. 1	Florida Derby	Gulfstream	1⅛	Barbaro	Edgar Prado	1,000,000
Apr. 1	WinStar Derby	Sunland	1⅛	Wanna Runner	Victor Espinoza	600,000
Apr. 8	Santa Anita Derby	Santa Anita	1⅛	Brother Derek	Alex Solis	750,000
Apr. 8	Ashland Stakes	Keeneland	1 1/16	Bushfire	Cornelio Velasquez	500,000
Apr. 8	Oaklawn Handicap	Oaklawn	1⅛	Buzzards Bay	Jose Valdivia Jr.	500,000
Apr. 8	Apple Blossom Handicap	Oaklawn	1 1/16	Spun Sugar	Mike Luzzi	500,000
Apr. 8	Illinois Derby	Hawthorne	1⅛	Sweetnorthernsaint	Kent Desormeaux	500,000
Apr. 8	Wood Memorial	Aqueduct	1⅛	Bob and John	Garrett Gomez	750,000
Apr. 15	Blue Grass Stakes	Keeneland	1⅛	Sinister Minister	Garrett Gomez	750,000
Apr. 15	Arkansas Derby	Oaklawn	1⅛	Lawyer Ron	John McKee	1,000,000
Apr. 22	Coolmore Lexington Stakes	Keeneland	1 1/16	Showing Up	Cornelio Velasquez	325,000
Apr. 23	Queen Elizabeth II Cup	Sha Tin	1¼ (T)	Irridescence	Weichong Marwing	1,805,468
May 5	Kentucky Oaks	Churchill Downs	1⅛	Lemons Forever	Mark Guidry	685,900
May 6	**Kentucky Derby**	Churchill Downs	1¼	Barbaro	Edgar Prado	2,213,200
May 6	Woodford Reserve Classic	Churchill Downs	1⅛ (T)	English Channel	Garrett Gomez	454,900
May 19	Pimlico Special	Pimlico	1 3/16	Invasor (ARG)	Ramon Dominguez	500,000
May 19	Black-Eyed Susan Stakes	Pimlico	1⅛	Regal Engagement	Ramon Dominguez	250,000
May 20	**Preakness Stakes**	Pimlico	1 3/16	Bernardini	Javier Castellano	1,000,000
May 29	Gamely BC Handicap	Hollywood Park	1⅛ (T)	Shining Energy	Victor Espinoza	349,500
May 29	Shoemaker BC Mile	Hollywood Park	1 (T)	Aragorn (IRE)	Corey Nakatani	321,000
May 29	Metropolitan Handicap	Belmont	1	Silver Train	Edgar Prado	750,000
June 3	Epsom Derby	Epsom Downs	1½ (T)	Sir Percy	Martin Dwyer	2,457,287
June 10	**Belmont Stakes**	Belmont	1½	Jazil	Fernando Jara	1,000,000
June 10	Manhattan Handicap	Belmont	1¼ (T)	Cacique (IRE)	Edgar Prado	400,000
June 10	Acorn Stakes	Belmont	1	Bushfire	Alex Solis	250,000
June 10	Charles Whittingham H	Hollywood Park	1¼ (T)	Lava Man	Corey Nakatani	$300,000
June 11	Woodbine Oaks	Woodbine	1¼ (T)	Kimchi	Patrick Husbands	454,010

Major Stakes Races (Cont.)

Date	Race	Track	Miles	Winner	Jockey	Purse
June 17	Stephen Foster Handicap	Churchill Downs	1⅛	Seek Gold	Calvin Borel	844,500
June 17	Ogden Phipps Handicap	Belmont	1¹⁄₁₆	Take D'Tour	Cornelio Velasquez	300,000
June 23	Colonial Turf Cup Stakes	Colonial Downs	1³⁄₁₆ (T)	Showing Up	Cornelio Velasquez	1,000,000
June 25	Queen's Plate	Woodbine	1¼	Edenwold	Emile Ramsammy	892,848
July 1	Suburban Handicap	Belmont	1¼	Invasor (ARG)	Fernando Jara	400,000
July 1	Mother Goose Stakes	Belmont	1⅛	Bushfire	Edgar Prado	250,000
July 1	CashCall Mile	Hollywood Park	1 (T)	Dance in the Mood	Victor Espinoza	750,000
July 2	Irish Derby	Curragh	1½ (T)	Dylan Thomas	Kieren Fallon	1,918,800
July 2	American Oaks	Hollywood Park	1¼ (T)	Wait a While	Garrett Gomez	750,000
July 8	United Nations Stakes	Monmouth Park	1⅜ (T)	English Channel	John Velazquez	750,000
July 8	Hollywood Gold Cup	Hollywood Park	1¼	Lava Man	Corey Nakatani	750,000
July 8	Swaps BC Stakes	Hollywood Park	1⅛	Arson Squad	Alex Solis	354,515
July 15	Princess Rooney Handicap	Calder	6 F	Malibu Mint	Josue' Arce	500,000
July 15	Smile Sprint Handicap	Calder	6 F	Nightmare Affair	Jeffrey Sanchez	500,000
July 15	Virginia Derby	Colonial Downs	1¼ (T)	Go Between	Garrett Gomez	1,000,000
July 15	Delaware Oaks	Delaware	1¹⁄₁₆	Adieu	John Velazquez	500,900
July 16	Delaware Handicap	Delaware	1¼	Fleet Indian	Jose Santos	1,001,200
July 22	Coaching Club Am. Oaks	Belmont	1¼	Wonder Lady Anne L	Edgar Prado	300,000
July 22	John C. Mabee Handicap	Del Mar	1⅛ (T)	Dancing Edie	Corey Nakatani	400,000
July 23	Eddie Read Handicap	Del Mar	1⅛ (T)	Aragorn (IRE)	Corey Nakatani	400,000
July 29	K. George VI and Q. Elizabeth Diamond Stakes	Ascot	1½ (T)	Hurricane Run	Christophe Soumillon	1,375,268
July 29	Diana Handicap	Saratoga	1⅛ (T)	Angara (GB)	Fernando Jara	500,000
July 29	Jim Dandy Stakes	Saratoga	1⅛	Bernardini	Javier Castellano	500,000
July 30	Go for Wand Handicap	Saratoga	1⅛	Spun Sugar	Mike Luzzi	250,000
Aug. 5	Test Stakes	Saratoga	7 F	Swap Fliparoo	Eibar Coa	250,000
Aug. 5	Whitney Handicap	Saratoga	1⅛	Invasor (ARG)	Fernando Jara	750,000
Aug. 6	Haskell Invitational	Monmouth	1⅛	Bluegrass Cat	John Velazquez	1,030,000
Aug. 6	West Virginia Derby	Mountaineer Park	1⅛	Bright One	Mark Guidry	750,000
Aug. 12	Sword Dancer Invitational	Saratoga	1½ (T)	Go Deputy	Eibar Coa	500,000
Aug. 12	Arlington Million	Arlington	1¼ (T)	The Tin Man	Victor Espinoza	1,000,000
Aug. 12	Beverly D. Stakes	Arlington	1³⁄₁₆ (T)	Gorella	Julien Leparoux	750,000
Aug. 12	Secretariat Stakes	Arlington	1¼ (T)	Showing Up	Cornelio Velasquez	400,000
Aug. 19	Alabama Stakes	Saratoga	1¼	Pine Island	Javier Castellano	600,000
Aug. 20	Pacific Classic	Del Mar	1¼	Lava Man	Corey Nakatani	1,000,000
Aug. 25	Personal Ensign Handicap	Saratoga	1¼	Fleet Indian	Jose Santos	392,000
Aug. 26	Travers Stakes	Saratoga	1¼	Bernardini	Javier Castellano	1,000,000
Sept. 2	The Woodward Stakes	Saratoga	1⅛	Premium Tap	Kent Desormeaux	500,000
Sept. 3	Grosser Preis von Baden	Baden-Baden	1½ (T)	Prince Flori	Filip Minarik	962,925
Sept. 9	Man o' War Stakes	Belmont	1⅜ (T)	Cacique (IRE)	Edgar Prado	500,000
Sept. 9	Irish Champion Stakes	Leopardstown	1¼ (T)	Dylan Thomas	Kieren Fallon	1,267,100
Sept. 10	Ruffian Handicap	Belmont	1¹⁄₁₆	Pool Land	John Velazquez	294,000
Sept. 17	Woodbine Mile	Woodbine	1 (T)	Becrux (ITA)	Pat Valenzuela	896,460
Sept. 23	Futurity Stakes	Belmont	7 F	King of the Roxy	John Velazquez	250,000
Sept. 23	Matron Stakes	Belmont	1	Meadow Breeze	Kent Desormeaux	250,000
Sept. 23	Super Derby	Louisiana Downs	1⅛	Strong Contender	Robby Albarado	500,000

NTRA National Thoroughbred Poll

The NTRA Thoroughbred Poll conducted by National Thoroughbred Racing Association, covering races through Sept. 24, 2006. Rankings are based on the votes of horse racing media representatives on a 10-9-8-7-6-5-4-3-2-1 basis. First place votes are in parentheses.

		Pts	Age	Sex	'06 Record Sts—1-2-3	Owner	Trainer
1	Lava Man (12)	155	5	Gelding	6—6-0-0	STD Racing Stable & Jason Wood	Doug O'Neill
2	Bernardini (3)	144	3	Colt	6—5-0-0	Darley Stable	Thomas Albertrani
3	Invasor (1)	126	4	Colt	4—3-0-0	Shadwell Stable	Kiaran McLaughlin
4	Silver Train	70	4	Colt	4—2-1-0	Four Roses Thoroughbreds	Richard Dutrow Jr.
5	Gorella	64	4	Filly	4—3-0-0	Martin S. Schwartz	Patrick Biancone
6	Aragorn	61	4	Colt	5—3-2-0	Ballygallon Stud, Ltd.	Neil Drysdale
7	Cacique	51	5	Horse	6—2-3-0	Juddmonte Farms, Inc.	Robert Frankel
8	Henny Hughes	37	3	Colt	2—2-0-0	Sheik Rashid bin Mohammed al Maktoum	Kiaran McLaughlin
9	Barbaro	33	3	Colt	5—4-0-0	Lael Stables	Michael Matz
10	Pine Island	30	3	Filly	6—4-2-0	Phipps Stable	Claude R. McGaughey III

Others receiving votes: 11. Fleet Indian (29 points); **12.** The Tin Man (24); **13.** Wait A While (11); **14.** Circular Quay and Jazil (7); **16.** English Channel (6); **17.** Discreet Cat (5); **18.** Dubai Escapade, Strong Contender and T.H. Approval (4); **21.** Bushfire and Sun King (3); **23.** Go Deputy and Siren Lure (1).

The 2006 Triple Crown

132ND KENTUCKY DERBY

Grade I for three-year-olds; 10th race at Churchill Downs in Louisville. **Date**—May 6, 2006; **Distance**—1¼ miles; **Stakes Purse**—$2,213,200 ($1,453,200 to winner; $400,000 for 2nd; $200,000 for 3rd; $80,000 for each 4th - dead heat); **Track**—Fast; **Off**—6:15 p.m. EDT; **Favorite**—Brother Derek (3-1 odds). **Winner**—Barbaro; **Field**—20 horses; **Time**—2:01.36; **Start**—Good for all except Barbaro (8); **Won**—Driving; **Sire**—Dynaformer (Roberto); **Dam**—La Ville Rouge (Carson City); **Record** (going into race)—5 starts, 5 wins, 0 seconds, 0 thirds; **Last start**—1st in Florida Derby (Apr. 1); **Breeder**—Mr. & Mrs. M. Roy Jackson.

Order of Finish	Jockey	PP	1/4	1/2	3/4	Mile	Stretch	Finish	To $1
Barbaro	Edgar Prado	8	5-½	4-1½	4-½	1-3	1-4	1-6½	6.10
Blue Grass Cat	Ramon Dominguez	13	8-½	5-½	6-½	5-5	2-½	2-2	30.00
Steppenwolfer	Robby Albarado	2	18-½	13-hd	11-½	7-hd	5-1	3-1	16.30
Jazil (dead heat)	Fernando Jara	1	20	20	19-½	17-2	6-1	4-½	24.20
Brother Derek (dead heat)	Alex Solis	18	9-1½	9-½	14-½	10-hd	7-½	4-½	7.70
Showing Up	Cornelio Velasquez	6	4-hd	3-hd	3-hd	4-½	3-1½	6-3	26.20
Sweetnorthernsaint	Kent Desormeaux	11	12-1	11-1	5-½	3-hd	4-hd	7-1	5.50
Deputy Glitters	Jose Lezcano	14	13-1	15-½	16-½	9-1	10-1	8-1¼	60.60
Point Determined	Rafael Bejarano	5	11-½	10-hd	7-1	6-½	8-½	9-hd	9.40
Seaside Retreat	Patrick Husbands	15	7-hd	7-1½	10-½	15-hd	9-hd	10-4½	52.50
Storm Treasure	David Flores	19	19-2½	18-2	13-hd	12-hd	11-½	11-1¾	51.90
Lawyer Ron	John McKee	17	6-½	8-½	9-hd	8-½	12-1½	12-ns	10.20
Cause to Believe	Russell Baze	16	15-½	19-2	20	18-4	17-2	13-3	25.90
Flashy Bull	Mike Smith	20	16-1	17-hd	17-1	14-½	15-1	14-2½	43.00
Private Vow	Shaun Bridgmohan	12	17-½	16-½	12-½	11-½	14-1½	15-2¾	40.50
Sinister Minister	Victor Espinoza	4	2-1½	2-2	2-1½	2-hd	13-1½	16-1½	9.70
Bob and John	Garrett Gomez	7	14-½	12-1	8-hd	16-½	16-½	17-nk	12.90
A.P. Warrior	Corey Nakatani	10	10-½	14-1	18-½	19-5	19-5	18-1½	14.10
Sharp Humor	Mark Guidry	9	3-1½	6-hd	15-1½	20	20	19-7½	30.10
Keyed Entry	Patrick Valenzuela	3	1-hd	1-2	1-1½	13-hd	18-2½	20	28.80

Times—22.63; 46.07; 1:10.88; 1:37.02; 2:01.36.

$2 Mutuel Prices—#8 Barbaro ($14.20, $8.00, $6.00); #13 Bluegrass Cat ($28.40, $15.40); #2 Steppenwolfer ($7.80). **Exacta**—(8-13) for $587.00; **Trifecta**—(8-13-2) for $11,418.40; **$2 Superfecta**—(8-13-2-1) for $84,860.40 and (8-13-2-18) for $59,839.00; **Scratched**—none; **Overweights**—none. **Attendance**—157,536; **TV Rating**—8.4/20 share (NBC).

Trainers & Owners (by finish): **1**—Michael Matz & Lael Stables; **2**—Todd Pletcher & WinStar Farm LLC; **3**—Daniel Peitz & Lawana and Robert Low; **4**—Kiaran McLaughlin & Shadwell Farm LLC; **5**—Dan Hendricks & Cecil N. Peacock; **6**—Barclay Tagg & Lael Stables; **7**—Michael Trombetta & Joseph Balsamo and Ted Theos; **8**—Thomas Albertrani & Joseph Lacombe Stable, Inc.; **9**—Bob Baffert & Robert and Beverly Lewis Trust; **10**—Mark Casse & William S. Farish Jr.; **11**—Steven Asmussen & Mike McCarty; **12**—Robert Holthus & Estate of James T. Hines Jr.; **13**—Jerry Hollendorfer & Peter Abruzzo and Peter Redekop; **14**—Kiaran McLaughlin & West Point Thoroughbreds, LLC; **15**—Steven Asmussen & Mike McCarty; **16**—Bob Baffert & Lanni Family Trust, Mercedes Stable, LLC and Bernard Schiappa; **17**—Bob Baffert & Stonerside Stable; **18**—John Shirreffs & Stan Fulton; **19**—Dale Romans & Purdedel Stable and WinStar Farm, LLC; **20**—Todd Pletcher & Starlight Stable, LLC, Jack Wolf, Paul Saylor and Donald Lucarelli.

131ST PREAKNESS STAKES

Grade I for three-year-olds; 12th race at Pimlico in Baltimore. **Date**—May 20, 2006; **Distance**—1³⁄₁₆ miles; **Stakes Purse**—$1,000,000 ($600,000 to winner; $200,000 for 2nd; $110,000 for 3rd; $60,000 for 4th; $30,000 for 5th); **Track**—Fast; **Off**—6:19 p.m. EDT; **Favorite**—Barbaro (even odds). **Winner**—Bernardini; **Field**—9 horses; **Time**—1:54.65; **Start**—Good; **Won**—Driving; **Sire**—A.P. Indy (Seattle Slew); **Dam**—Cara Rafaela (Quiet American); **Record** (going into race)—3 starts, 2 wins, 0 seconds, 0 thirds; **Last start**—1st in Withers Stakes (Apr. 29); **Breeder**—Darley Stable (Ky.).

Order of Finish	Jockey	PP	1/4	1/2	3/4	Stretch	Finish	To $1
Bernardini	Javier Castellano	8	3-1	4-2	4-4	1-3½	1-5¼	12.90
Sweetnorthernsaint	Kent Desormeaux	7	2-1½	3-½	2-1½	2-6	2-6	8.40
Hemingway's Key	Jeremy Rose	3	7-1½	7-½	7-½	4-4	3-4	29.40
Brother Derek	Alex Solis	5	5-4	2-hd	3-2	3-1½	4-7	3.20
Greeley's Legacy	Richard Migliore	4	8	8	6-1	6-1	5-nk	34.90
Platinum Couple	Jose Espinoza	2	6-3	6-2½	8	8	6-3½	33.20
Like Now	Garrett Gomez	1	1-½	1-1	1-½	5-2	7-2¼	17.40
Diabolical	Ramon Dominguez	9	4-1½	5-5	5-4	7-1	8	26.00
Barbaro	Edgar Prado	6	—	—	—	—	—	0.50

Times—23.21; 46.69; 1:10.24; 1:35.73; 1:54.65.

$2 Mutuel Prices—#8 Bernardini ($27.80, $9.40, $5.80); #7 Sweetnorthernsaint ($7.80, $5.00); #3 Hemingway's Key ($8.00). **Exacta**—(8-7) for $171.60; **Trifecta**—(8-7-3) for $3,912.80; **$1 Superfecta**—(8-7-3-5) for $11,151.20; **Scratched**—none; **Overweights**—none. **Attendance**—118,402; **TV Rating**—6.6/16 share (NBC).

Trainers & Owners (by finish): **1**—Thomas Albertrani & Darley Stable; **2**—Michael Trombetta & Joseph Balsamo and Ted Theos; **3**—Nick Zito & Kinsman Stable; **4**—Dan Hendricks & Cecil Peacock; **5**—George Weaver & Donald Flanagan; **6**—Joseph Lostritto & Team Tristar Stable; **7**—Kiaran McLaughlin & John Dillon; **8**—Steve Klesaris & Puglisi Stables and Steve Klesaris; **9**—Michael Matz & Lael Stables.

The 2006 Triple Crown (Cont.)

138TH BELMONT STAKES

Grade I for three-year-olds; 11th race at Belmont Park in Elmont, N.Y. **Date**—June 10, 2006; **Distance**—1½ miles; **Stakes Purse**—$1,000,000 ($600,000 to winner; $200,000 for 2nd; $110,000 for 3rd; $60,000 for 4th; $30,000 for 5th); **Track**—Fast; **Off**—6:35 p.m. EDT; **Favorite**—Bluegrass Cat (3-1 odds). **Winner**—Jazil; **Field**—12 horses; **Time**—2:27.86; **Start**—Good for all; **Won**—Driving; **Sire**—Seeking the Gold (Mr. Prospector); **Dam**—Better Than Honour (Deputy Minister); **Record** (going into race)—7 starts, 1 win, 3 seconds, 0 thirds; **Last Start**—4th in Kentucky Derby (May 6); **Breeder**—Skara Glen Stables (Ky.).

Order of Finish	Jockey	PP	1/4	1/2	Mile	1-1/4	Stretch	Finish	To $1
Jazil	Fernando Jara	8	12	12	7-½	1-hd	1-½	1-1¼	6.20
Bluegrass Cat	John Velazquez	9	5-½	5-1½	3-½	2-1½	2-1½	2-2¼	4.90
Sunriver	Rafael Bejarano	2	6-1½	6-½	6-hd	3-½	3-½	3-1¼	6.00
Steppenwolfer	Robby Albarado	11	8-½	7-½	11-½	4-hd	4-6	4-5	4.80
Oh So Awesome	Mike Smith	6	11-½	11-½	12	7-½	5-hd	5-2	12.00
Hemingway's Key	Jeremy Rose	3	10-4½	10-1	10-½	8-5	7-1½	6-4½	15.10
Platinum Couple	Jose Espinoza	1	7-hd	9-4½	5-½	6-1	8-6	7-2½	38.00
Bob and John	Garrett Gomez	4	1-½	1-½	1-hd	5-1	6-hd	8-4¼	4.70
Sacred Light	Victor Espinoza	12	9-2½	8-hd	8-½	9-½	9-3½	9-6½	26.50
High Finance	Eibar Coa	5	2-hd	3-½	2-½	10-4	10-6	10-11¼	10.40
Deputy Glitters	Edgar Prado	7	3-1	2-½	4-½	11-8	11	11	12.20
Double Galore	Mike Luzzi	10	4-hd	4-½	9-hd	12	—	—	45.75

Times—23.02; 47.36; 1:12.14; 1:37.53; 2:02.69; 2:27.86.

$2 Mutuel Prices—#8 Jazil ($14.40, $6.70, $4.70); #9 Bluegrass Cat ($6.40, $4.70); #2 Sunriver ($6.10). **Exacta**—(8-9) for $92.00; **Trifecta**—(8-9-2) for $436.00; **Superfecta**—(8-9-2-11) for $1,085.00; **Scratched**—none; **Overweights**—none; **Attendance**—61,168; **TV Rating**—3.8/9 share (ABC).

Trainers & Owners (by finish): **1**—Kiaran McLaughlin & Shadwell Stable; **2**—Todd Pletcher & WinStar Farm LLC; **3**—Todd Pletcher & Aaron and Marie Jones; **4**—Daniel Peitz & Lawana and Robert Low; **5**—James Jerkens & Team Valor Stables LLC; **6**—Nick Zito & Kinsman Stable; **7**—Joseph Lostritto & Team Tristar Stable; **8**—Bob Baffert & Stonerside Stable; **9**—David Hofmans & Amerman Racing Stables LLC; **10**—Richard Violette & West Point Stable; **11**—Thomas Albertrani & Joseph Lacombe Stable Inc.; **12**—Myung Kwon Cho & Myung Kwon Cho.

2005-06 Money Leaders

Official Top 10 standings for 2005 and unofficial Top 10 standings for 2006, through Sept. 30. Results are based on North American races plus select international races. Source: *Equibase Company.*

FINAL 2005

HORSES	Age	Sts	1-2-3	Earnings
Saint Liam	5	6	4-1-0	$3,696,960
Roses in May	5	2	1-1-0	3,695,000
Flower Alley	3	9	4-3-0	2,435,200
Afleet Alex	3	6	4-0-1	2,085,000
Giacomo	3	6	1-1-2	1,846,876
Borrego	4	8	3-1-2	1,536,600
Ouija Board (GB)	4	5	2-1-0	1,491,358
Artie Schiller	4	6	3-2-1	1,448,000
Relaxed Gesture (IRE)	4	7	3-3-1	1,326,186
Pleasant Home	4	8	3-2-2	1,316,420

JOCKEYS	Mts	1st	Earnings
John Velazquez	1148	251	$24,459,923
Edgar Prado	1460	299	18,615,366
Jerry Bailey	654	169	18,297,384
Rafael Bejarano	1346	263	14,427,541
Garrett Gomez	1295	245	14,221,321
Javier Castellano	1158	206	12,507,012
Victor Espinoza	1107	192	12,054,776
Patrick Valenzuela	1012	202	11,794,244
Cornelio Velasquez	1456	216	11,430,591
Ramon Dominguez	1222	312	10,767,955

TRAINERS	Sts	1st	Earnings
Todd Pletcher	1039	257	$20,867,842
Bobby Frankel	583	128	14,122,807
Steven Asmussen	2227	474	13,302,283
Richard Dutrow Jr.	575	151	9,797,126
Doug O'Neill	893	158	9,476,801
Bill Mott	631	108	9,355,603
Scott Lake	1796	417	8,983,267
Nick Zito	462	86	8,199,368
Dale Romans	524	96	8,021,833
Jeff Mullins	497	118	6,279,989

2006 (Through Sept. 30)

HORSES	Age	Sts	1-2-3	Earnings
Lava Man	5	6	6-0-0	$2,470,000
Barbaro	3	5	4-0-0	2,203,200
Bernardini	3	6	5-0-0	1,610,480
Bluegrass Cat	3	7	2-4-0	1,547,500
Lawyer Ron	3	7	5-1-0	1,340,800
Showing Up	3	5	5-0-1	1,130,500
Wait a While	3	8	5-1-2	1,120,807
Fleet Indian	5	5	5-0-0	1,113,720
Cacique (IRE)	5	6	2-3-0	994,432
The Tin Man	8	4	4-0-0	990,000

JOCKEYS	Mts	1st	Earnings
Edgar Prado	1077	215	$14,485,004
Garrett Gomez	968	191	13,935,610
Victor Espinoza	935	203	12,916,032
Ramon Dominguez	1088	297	10,523,738
John Velazquez	728	172	10,496,814
Cornelio Velasquez	1267	200	9,710,802
Julien Leparoux	1390	341	9,188,659
Corey Nakatani	517	101	9,089,847
Javier Castellano	859	144	9,080,793
Eibar Coa	1186	224	8,920,471

TRAINERS	Sts	1st	Earnings
Todd Pletcher	934	244	$19,857,585
Scott Lake	1778	452	7,987,794
Steven Asmussen	1141	241	7,715,373
Doug O'Neill	716	120	7,378,332
Bobby Frankel	444	111	7,216,057
Bob Baffert	314	76	6,844,793
Bill Mott	489	101	6,705,234
Richard Dutrow Jr.	536	131	6,127,628
Kiaran McLaughlin	309	57	4,794,589
Gary Contessa	709	118	4,587,437

Harness Racing
2005-06 Major Stakes Races

Winners of major stakes races from Oct. 2, 2005 through Sept. 23, 2006; all paces and trots cover one mile; (BC) indicates year-end Breeders' Crown series.

Late 2005

Date	Race	Raceway	Winner	Time	Driver	Purse
Oct. 17	**Messenger Stakes**	Harrington	Gryffindor	1:52⁴/₅	David Miller	$364,125
Oct. 22	Governor's Cup	Woodbine	Jereme's Jet	1:53³/₅	Paul MacDonell	593,032
Nov. 26	BC 3-Yr-Old Colt Pace	Meadowlands	Rocknroll Hanover	1:49⁴/₅	Brian Sears	555,000
Nov. 26	BC 3-Yr-Old Filly Pace	Meadowlands	Belovedangel	1:52¹/₅	Ron Pierce	500,000
Nov. 26	BC 3-Yr-Old Colt Trot	Meadowlands	Strong Yankee	1:53⁴/₅	Brian Sears	610,000
Nov. 26	BC 3-Yr-Old Filly Trot	Meadowlands	Blur	1:56¹/₅	Brian Sears	500,000
Nov. 26	BC 2-Yr-Old Colt Pace	Meadowlands	Jereme's Jet	1:52¹/₅	Paul MacDonell	575,400
Nov. 26	BC 2-Yr-Old Filly Pace	Meadowlands	My Little Dragon	1:52¹/₅	Ron Pierce	500,000
Nov. 26	BC 2-Yr-Old Colt Trot	Meadowlands	Chocolatier	1:56¹/₅	Doug Ackerman	507,600
Nov. 26	BC 2-Yr-Old Filly Trot	Meadowlands	Passionate Glide	1:55⁴/₅	Ron Pierce	516,800

2006 (through Sept. 23)

Date	Race	Raceway	Winner	Time	Driver	Purse
May 27	New Jersey Classic	Meadowlands	Feelin Friskie	1:49¹/₅	John Campbell	$500,000
June 17	North America Cup	Woodbine	Total Truth	1:49¹/₅	Ron Pierce	1,336,184
June 24	Canadian Pacing Derby	Mohawk	Lis Mara	1:48⁴/₅	Brian Sears	829,997
June 24	Hoosier Cup	Hoosier Park	Total Truth	1:50¹/₅	Yannick Gingras	450,000
July 15	William Haughton Open Pace	Meadowlands	Leading X Ample	1:48²/₅	David Miller	650,000
July 15	Meadowlands Pace	Meadowlands	Artistic Fella	1:48⁴/₅	Cat Manzi	1,000,000
July 29	BC Open Pace	Meadowlands	Lis Mara	1:47³/₅	Brian Sears	500,000
July 29	BC Mare Trot	Meadowlands	Mystical Sunshne	1:53³/₅	Ron Pierce	250,000
July 29	BC Open Trot	Meadowlands	Sand Vic	1:52³/₅	Brian Sears	800,000
July 29	BC Mare Pace	Meadowlands	Burning Point	1:49²/₅	Ron Pierce	331,500
Aug. 3	Peter Haughton Memorial	Meadowlands	Donato Hanover	1:55	Ron Pierce	456,000
Aug. 3	Merrie Annabelle Final	Meadowlands	Gerri's Joy	1:57	John Campbell	537,000
Aug. 4	Sweetheart Pace	Meadowlands	Isabella Blue Chip	1:52²/₅	David Miller	435,000
Aug. 4	Woodrow Wilson Pace	Meadowlands	Fox Valley Barzgar	1:50²/₅	Tony Morgan	410,000
Aug. 5	**Hambletonian**	Meadowlands	Glidemaster	1:51¹/₅	John Campbell	1,500,000
Aug. 5	Hambletonian Oaks	Meadowlands	Passionate Glide	1:54³/₅	Ron Pierce	750,000
Aug. 5	Mistletoe Shalee	Meadowlands	Armbro Dancer	1:49³/₅	Ron Pierce	325,000
Aug. 5	Nat Ray	Meadowlands	Sand Vic	1:51³/₅	Brian Sears	300,000
Aug. 5	U.S. Pacing Championship	Meadowlands	Holborn Hanover	1:46⁴/₅	George Brennan	195,000
			Ponder	1:48¹/₅	John Campbell	195,000
Aug. 12	Coors Del Miller Adios	The Meadows	Cactus Creek	1:50²/₅	Mike Lachance	450,000
Sept. 2	World Trotting Derby	DuQuoin	Chocolatier	1:53	Doug Ackerman	530,000
Sept. 2	Metro Pace	Mohawk	Yankee Skyscraper	1:54³/₅	Jody Jamieson	900,000
Sept. 4	**Cane Pace**	Freehold	Total Truth	1:51³/₅	Ron Pierce	301,587
Sept. 9	Maple Leaf Trot	Mohawk	Peaceful Way	1:53³/₅	Trevor Ritchie	789,750
Sept. 21	**Little Brown Jug**	Delaware	Mr. Feelgood	1:50³/₅	Mark McDonald	541,000
Sept. 23	Canadian Trotting Classic	Mohawk	Majestic Son	1:52²/₅	Trevor Ritchie	900,000

2005-06 Money Leaders

Official Top 10 standings for 2005 and unofficial Top 10 standings for 2006 through Sept. 30.

FINAL 2005 / 2006 (through Sept. 30)

HORSES	Age	Sts	1-2-3	Earnings	HORSES	Age	Sts	1-2-3	Earnings
Rocknroll Hanover	3ph	18	12-4-2	$2,223,257	Total Truth	3ph	12	5-3-2	$1,214,936
Vivid Photo	3tg	25	16-5-1	1,481,020	Gildemaster	3th	10	4-6-0	1,160,311
Classic Photo	3th	16	10-3-3	1,376,829	Sand Vic	5th	13	9-2-0	985,180
Mr. Muscleman	5tg	14	12-1-0	1,364,220	Lis Mara	4ph	16	10-4-1	945,485
Strong Yankee	3th	20	8-6-1	1,197,307	Artistic Fella	3ph	15	10-1-0	934,135
Jereme's Jet	2ph	7	6-1-0	1,039,376	Majestic Son	3tr	15	11-0-2	887,886
Boulder Creek	5pg	25	6-6-3	978,645	Passionate Glide	3tm	10	10-0-0	883,400
Cabrini Hanover	3pm	18	8-5-5	917,440	Chocolatier	3th	12	6-3-0	816,550
Blur	3tm	12	7-2-0	867,453	Feelin Frisky	3ph	9	3-3-2	696,862
Ponder	4ph	27	8-11-3	804,702	Peaceful Way	5tm	8	4-1-1	665,763

DRIVERS	Mts	1st	Earnings	DRIVERS	Mts	1st	Earnings
Brian Sears	2267	406	$15,085,992	Ron Pierce	2125	350	$10,566,091
Ron Pierce	2459	421	13,538,851	Brian Sears	1871	362	9,279,846
David Miller	2667	418	11,134,706	John Campbell	1370	270	7,949,812
Cat Manzi	3609	727	8,653,808	Mark MacDonald	2665	568	7,916,015
George Brennan	2147	327	7,547,999	David Miller	2219	270	7,081,337
Mark MacDonald	4237	695	7,199,600	Jody Jamieson	2285	444	6,590,225
Paul MacDonell	1846	263	6,725,041	Anthony Morgan	3051	787	6,501,833
Luc Ouellette	2170	312	6,309,393	George Brennan	1775	302	6,496,620
Eric Ledford	1269	194	5,526,285	Cat Manzi	2679	501	6,273,633
Chris Christoforou	2111	321	5,212,878	Yannick Gingras	1951	278	5,400,713

1867-2006
Through the Years

ESPN
SPORTS ALMANAC

Thoroughbred Racing

The Triple Crown

The term "Triple Crown" was coined by sportswriter Charles Hatton while covering the 1930 victories of Gallant Fox in the Kentucky Derby, Preakness Stakes and Belmont Stakes. Before then, only Sir Barton (1919) had won all three races in the same year. Since then, nine horses have won the Triple Crown. Two trainers, James (Sunny Jim) Fitzsimmons and Ben A. Jones, have saddled two Triple Crown champions, while Eddie Arcaro is the only jockey to ride two champions.

Year		Jockey	Trainer	Owner	Sire/Dam
1919	**Sir Barton**	Johnny Loftus	H. Guy Bedwell	J.K.L. Ross	Star Shoot/Lady Sterling
1930	**Gallant Fox**	Earl Sande	J.E. Fitzsimmons	Belair Stud	Sir Gallahad III/Marguerite
1935	**Omaha**	Willie Saunders	J.E. Fitzsimmons	Belair Stud	Gallant Fox/Flambino
1937	**War Admiral**	Charley Kurtsinger	George Conway	Samuel Riddle	Man o' War/Brushup
1941	**Whirlaway**	Eddie Arcaro	Ben A. Jones	Calumet Farm	Blenheim II/Dustwhirl
1943	**Count Fleet**	Johnny Longden	Don Cameron	Mrs. J.D. Hertz	Reigh Count/Quickly
1946	**Assault**	Warren Mehrtens	Max Hirsch	King Ranch	Bold Venture/Igual
1948	**Citation**	Eddie Arcaro	Ben A. Jones	Calumet Farm	Bull Lea/Hydroplane II
1973	**Secretariat**	Ron Turcotte	Lucien Laurin	Meadow Stable	Bold Ruler/Somethingroyal
1977	**Seattle Slew**	Jean Cruguet	Billy Turner	Karen Taylor	Bold Reasoning/My Charmer
1978	**Affirmed**	Steve Cauthen	Laz Barrera	Harbor View Farm	Exclusive Native/Won't Tell You

Note: Gallant Fox (1930) is the only Triple Crown winner to sire another Triple Crown winner, Omaha (1935). Wm. Woodward Sr., owner of Belair Stud, was breeder-owner of both horses and both were trained by Sunny Jim Fitzsimmons.

Triple Crown Near Misses

Forty-nine horses have won two legs of the Triple Crown. Of those, eighteen won the Kentucky Derby (KD) and Preakness Stakes (PS) only to be beaten in the Belmont Stakes (BS). Two others, Burgoo King (1932) and Bold Venture (1936), won the Derby and Preakness, but were forced out of the Belmont with the same injury—a bowed tendon—that effectively ended their racing careers. In 1978, Alydar finished second to Affirmed in all three races, the only time that has happened. Note that the Preakness preceded the Kentucky Derby in 1922, '23 and '31; (*) indicates won on disqualification.

Year		KD	PS	BS	Year		KD	PS	BS
1877	**Cloverbrook**	DNS	won	won	1966	**Kauai King**	won	won	4th
1878	**Duke of Magenta**	DNS	won	won	1967	**Damascus**	3rd	won	won
1880	**Grenada**	DNS	won	won	1968	**Forward Pass**	won*	won	2nd
1881	**Saunterer**	DNS	won	won	1969	**Majestic Prince**	won	won	2nd
1895	**Belmar**	DNS	won	won	1971	**Canonero II**	won	won	4th
1920	**Man o' War**	DNS	won	won	1972	**Riva Ridge**	won	4th	won
1922	**Pillory**	DNS	won	won	1974	**Little Current**	5th	won	won
1923	**Zev**	won	12th	won	1976	**Bold Forbes**	won	3rd	won
1931	**Twenty Grand**	won	2nd	won	1979	**Spectacular Bid**	won	won	3rd
1932	**Burgoo King**	won	won	DNS	1981	**Pleasant Colony**	won	won	3rd
1936	**Bold Venture**	won	won	DNS	1984	**Swale**	won	7th	won
1939	**Johnstown**	won	5th	won	1987	**Alysheba**	won	won	4th
1940	**Bimelech**	2nd	won	won	1988	**Risen Star**	3rd	won	won
1942	**Shut Out**	won	5th	won	1989	**Sunday Silence**	won	won	2nd
1944	**Pensive**	won	won	2nd	1991	**Hansel**	10th	won	won
1949	**Capot**	2nd	won	won	1994	**Tabasco Cat**	6th	won	won
1950	**Middleground**	won	2nd	won	1995	**Thunder Gulch**	won	3rd	won
1953	**Native Dancer**	2nd	won	won	1997	**Silver Charm**	won	won	2nd
1955	**Nashua**	2nd	won	won	1998	**Real Quiet**	won	won	2nd
1956	**Needles**	won	2nd	won	1999	**Charismatic**	won	won	3rd
1958	**Tim Tam**	won	won	2nd	2001	**Point Given**	5th	won	won
1961	**Carry Back**	won	won	7th	2002	**War Emblem**	won	won	8th
1963	**Chateaugay**	won	2nd	won	2003	**Funny Cide**	won	won	3rd
1964	**Northern Dancer**	won	won	3rd	2004	**Smarty Jones**	won	won	2nd
					2005	**Afleet Alex**	3rd	won	won

The Triple Crown Challenge (1987-93)

Seeking to make the Triple Crown more than just a media event and to insure that owners would not be attracted to more lucrative races, officials at Churchill Downs, the Maryland Jockey Club and the New York Racing Association created Triple Crown Productions in 1985 and announced that a $1 million bonus would be given to the horse that performs best in the Kentucky Derby, Preakness Stakes and Belmont Stakes. Furthermore, a bonus of $5 million would be presented to any horse winning all three races.

Revised in 1991, the rules stated that the winning horse must: 1. finish all three races; 2. earn points by finishing first, second, third or fourth in at least one of the three races; and 3. earn the highest number of points based on the following system—10 points to win, five to place, three to show and one to finish fourth. In the event of a tie, the $1 million is distributed equally among the top point-getters. From 1987-90, the system was five points to win, three to place and one to show. The Triple Crown Challenge was discontinued in 1994.

Year		KD	PS	BS	Pts
1987	1 **Bet Twice** 2nd	2nd	1st—	11
	2 Alysheba 1st	1st	4th—	10
	3 Cryptoclearance 4th	3rd	2nd—	4
1988	1 **Risen Star** 3rd	1st	1st—	11
	2 Winning Colors 1st	3rd	6th—	6
	3 Brian's Time 6th	2nd	3rd—	4
1989	1 **Sunday Silence** 1st	1st	2nd—	13
	2 Easy Goer 2nd	2nd	1st—	11
	3 Hawkster 5th	5th	5th—	0
1990	1 **Unbridled** 1st	2nd	4th—	8
	2 Summer Squall 2nd	1st	DNR—	8
	3 Go and Go ....DNR	DNR	1st—	5
	(Unbridled was only horse to run all three races.)			

Year		KD	PS	BS	Pts
1991	1 **Hansel** 10th	1st	1st—	20
	2 Strike the Gold 1st	6th	2nd—	15
	3 Mane Minister 3rd	3rd	3rd—	9
1992	1 **Pine Bluff** 5th	1st	3rd—	13
	2 Casual Lies 2nd	3rd	5th—	8
	(No other horses ran all three races.)			
1993	1 **Sea Hero** 1st	5th	7th—	10
	2 Wild Gale 3rd	8th	3rd—	6
	(No other horses ran all three races.)			

Kentucky Derby

For three-year-olds. Held the first Saturday in May at Churchill Downs in Louisville, Ky. Inaugurated in 1875.

Originally run at 1½ miles (1875-95), shortened to present 1¼ miles in 1896.

Trainers with most wins: Ben Jones (6); D. Wayne Lukas and Dick Thompson (4); Bob Baffert, Sunny Jim Fitzsimmons and Max Hirsch (3).

Jockeys with most wins: Eddie Arcaro and Bill Hartack (5); Bill Shoemaker (4); Angel Cordero Jr., Issac Murphy, Earl Sande and Gary Stevens (3).

Winning fillies: Regret (1915), Genuine Risk (1980) and Winning Colors (1988).

Year	Winner (Margin)	Time	Jockey	Trainer	2nd place	3rd place
1875	**Aristides** (1) 2:37¾		Oliver Lewis	Ansel Anderson	Volcano	Verdigris
1876	**Vagrant** (2) 2:38¼		Bobby Swim	James Williams	Creedmore	Harry Hill
1877	**Baden-Baden** (2) 2:38		Billy Walker	Ed Brown	Leonard	King William
1878	**Day Star** (2) 2:37¼		Jimmy Carter	Lee Paul	Himyar	Leveler
1879	**Lord Murphy** (1) 2:37		Charlie Shauer	George Rice	Falsetto	Strathmore
1880	**Fonso** (1) 2:37½		George Lewis	Tice Hutsell	Kimball	Bancroft
1881	**Hindoo** (4) 2:40		Jim McLaughlin	James Rowe Sr.	Lelex	Alfambra
1882	**Apollo** (½) 2:40¼		Babe Hurd	Green Morris	Runnymede	Bengal
1883	**Leonatus** (3) 2:43		Billy Donohue	John McGinty	Drake Carter	Lord Raglan
1884	**Buchanan** (2) 2:40¼		Isaac Murphy	William Bird	Loftin	Audrain
1885	**Joe Cotton** (nk) 2:37¼		Babe Henderson	Alex Perry	Bersan	Ten Booker
1886	**Ben Ali** (½) 2:36½		Paul Duffy	Jim Murphy	Blue Wing	Free Knight
1887	**Montrose** (2) 2:39¼		Isaac Lewis	John McGinty	Jim Gore	Jacobin
1888	**MacBeth II** (1) 2:38¼		George Covington	John Campbell	Gallifet	White
1889	**Spokane** (ns) 2:34½		Thomas Kiley	John Rodegap	Proctor Knott	Once Again
1890	**Riley** (2) 2:45		Isaac Murphy	Edward Corrigan	Bill Letcher	Robespierre
1891	**Kingman** (1) 2:52¼		Isaac Murphy	Dud Allen	Balgowan	High Tariff
1892	**Azra** (ns) 2:41½		Lonnie Clayton	John Morris	Huron	Phil Dwyer
1893	**Lookout** (5) 2:39¼		Eddie Kunze	Wm. McDaniel	Plutus	Boundless
1894	**Chant** (2) 2:41		Frank Goodale	Eugene Leigh	Pearl Song	Sigurd
1895	**Halma** (3) 2:37½		Soup Perkins	Byron McClelland	Basso	Laureate
1896	**Ben Brush** (ns) 2:07¾		Willie Simms	Hardy Campbell	Ben Eder	Semper Ego
1897	**Typhoon II** (hd) 2:12½		Buttons Garner	J.C. Cahn	Ornament	Dr. Catlett
1898	**Plaudit** (nk) 2:09		Willie Simms	John E. Madden	Lieber Karl	Isabey
1899	**Manuel** (2) 2:12		Fred Taral	Robert Walden	Corsini	Mazo
1900	**Lieut. Gibson** (4) 2:06¼		Jimmy Boland	Charles Hughes	Florizar	Thrive
1901	**His Eminence** (2) 2:07¾		Jimmy Winkfield	F.B. Van Meter	Sannazarro	Driscoll
1902	**Alan-a-Dale** (ns) 2:08¾		Jimmy Winkfield	T.C. McDowell	Inventor	The Rival
1903	**Judge Himes** (¾) 2:09		Hal Booker	J.P. Mayberry	Early	Bourbon
1904	**Elwood** (½) 2:08½		Shorty Prior	C.E. Durnell	Ed Tierney	Brancas
1905	**Agile** (3) 2:10¾		Jack Martin	Robert Tucker	Ram's Horn	Layson
1906	**Sir Huon** (2) 2:08⅘		Roscoe Troxler	Pete Coyne	Lady Navarre	James Reddick
1907	**Pink Star** (2) 2:12⅗		Andy Minder	W.H. Fizer	Zal	Ovelando
1908	**Stone Street** (1) 2:15⅕		Arthur Pickens	J.W. Hall	Sir Cleges	Dunvegan
1909	**Wintergreen** (4) 2:08⅕		Vincent Powers	Charles Mack	Miami	Dr. Barkley

Kentucky Derby (Cont.)

Year	Winner (Margin)	Time	Jockey	Trainer	2nd place	3rd place
1910	**Donau** (½)	2:06⅖	Fred Herbert	George Ham	Joe Morris	Fighting Bob
1911	**Meridian** (¾)	2:05	George Archibald	Albert Ewing	Governor Gray	Colston
1912	**Worth** (nk)	2:09⅖	C.H. Shilling	Frank Taylor	Duval	Flamma
1913	**Donerail** (½)	2:04⅘	Roscoe Goose	Thomas Hayes	Ten Point	Gowell
1914	**Old Rosebud** (8)	2:03⅖	John McCabe	F.D. Weir	Hodge	Bronzewing
1915	**Regret** (2)	2:05⅖	Joe Notter	James Rowe Sr.	Pebbles	Sharpshooter
1916	**George Smith** (nk)	2:04	Johnny Loftus	Hollie Hughes	Star Hawk	Franklin
1917	**Omar Khayyam** (2)	2:04⅗	Charles Borel	C.T. Patterson	Ticket	Midway
1918	**Exterminator** (1)	2:10⅘	William Knapp	Henry McDaniel	Escoba	Viva America
1919	**SIR BARTON** (5)	2:09⅘	Johnny Loftus	H. Guy Bedwell	Billy Kelly	Under Fire
1920	**Paul Jones** (hd)	2:09	Ted Rice	Billy Garth	Upset	On Watch
1921	**Behave Yourself** (hd)	2:04⅕	Charles Thompson	Dick Thompson	Black Servant	Prudery
1922	**Morvich** (1½)	2:04⅗	Albert Johnson	Fred Burlew	Bet Mosie	John Finn
1923	**Zev** (1½)	2:05⅖	Earl Sande	David Leary	Martingale	Vigil
1924	**Black Gold** (½)	2:05⅕	John Mooney	Hanly Webb	Chilhowee	Beau Butler
1925	**Flying Ebony** (1½)	2:07⅗	Earl Sande	William Duke	Captain Hal	Son of John
1926	**Bubbling Over** (5)	2:03⅘	Albert Johnson	Dick Thompson	Bagenbaggage	Rock Man
1927	**Whiskery** (hd)	2:06	Linus McAtee	Fred Hopkins	Osmand	Jock
1928	**Reigh Count** (3)	2:10⅖	Chick Lang	Bert Michell	Misstep	Toro
1929	**Clyde Van Dusen** (2)	2:10⅘	Linus McAtee	Clyde Van Dusen	Naishapur	Panchio
1930	**GALLANT FOX** (2)	2:07⅗	Earl Sande	Jim Fitzsimmons	Gallant Knight	Ned O.
1931	**Twenty Grand** (4)	2:01⅘	Charley Kurtsinger	James Rowe Jr.	Sweep All	Mate
1932	**Burgoo King** (5)	2:05⅕	Eugene James	Dick Thompson	Economic	Stepenfetchit
1933	**Brokers Tip** (ns)	2:06⅘	Don Meade	Dick Thompson	Head Play	Charley O.
1934	**Cavalcade** (2½)	2:04	Mack Garner	Bob Smith	Discovery	Agrarian
1935	**OMAHA** (1½)	2:05	Willie Saunders	Jim Fitzsimmons	Roman Soldier	Whiskolo
1936	**Bold Venture** (hd)	2:03⅗	Ira Hanford	Max Hirsch	Brevity	Indian Broom
1937	**WAR ADMIRAL** (1¾)	2:03⅕	Charley Kurtsinger	George Conway	Pompoon	Reaping Reward
1938	**Lawrin** (1)	2:04⅘	Eddie Arcaro	Ben Jones	Dauber	Can't Wait
1939	**Johnstown** (8)	2:03⅖	James Stout	Jim Fitzsimmons	Challedon	Heather Broom
1940	**Gallahadion** (1½)	2:05	Carroll Bierman	Roy Waldron	Bimelech	Dit
1941	**WHIRLAWAY** (8)	2:01⅖	Eddie Arcaro	Ben Jones	Staretor	Market Wise
1942	**Shut Out** (2½)	2:04⅖	Wayne Wright	John Gaver	Alsab	Valdina Orphan
1943	**COUNT FLEET** (3)	2:04	Johnny Longden	Don Cameron	Blue Swords	Slide Rule
1944	**Pensive** (4½)	2:04⅕	Conn McCreary	Ben Jones	Broadcloth	Stir Up
1945	**Hoop Jr** (6)	2:07	Eddie Arcaro	Ivan Parke	Pot O'Luck	Darby Dieppe
1946	**ASSAULT** (8)	2:06⅗	Warren Mehrtens	Max Hirsch	Spy Song	Hampden
1947	**Jet Pilot** (hd)	2:06⅘	Eric Guerin	Tom Smith	Phalanx	Faultless
1948	**CITATION** (3½)	2:05⅖	Eddie Arcaro	Ben Jones	Coaltown	My Request
1949	**Ponder** (3)	2:04⅕	Steve Brooks	Ben Jones	Capot	Palestinian
1950	**Middleground** (1¼)	2:01⅗	William Boland	Max Hirsch	Hill Prince	Mr. Trouble
1951	**Count Turf** (4)	2:02⅗	Conn McCreary	Sol Rutchick	Royal Mustang	Ruhe
1952	**Hill Gail** (2)	2:01⅗	Eddie Arcaro	Ben Jones	Sub Fleet	Blue Man
1953	**Dark Star** (hd)	2:02	Hank Moreno	Eddie Hayward	Native Dancer	Invigorator
1954	**Determine** (1½)	2:03	Raymond York	Willie Molter	Hasty Road	Hasseyampa
1955	**Swaps** (1½)	2:01⅘	Bill Shoemaker	Mesh Tenney	Nashua	Summer Tan
1956	**Needles** (¾)	2:03⅖	David Erb	Hugh Fontaine	Fabius	Come On Red
1957	**Iron Liege** (ns)	2:02⅕	Bill Hartack	Jimmy Jones	Gallant Man	Round Table
1958	**Tim Tam** (½)	2:05	Ismael Valenzuela	Jimmy Jones	Lincoln Road	Noureddin
1959	**Tomy Lee** (ns)	2:02⅕	Bill Shoemaker	Frank Childs	Sword Dancer	First Landing
1960	**Venetian Way** (3½)	2:02⅖	Bill Hartack	Victor Sovinski	Bally Ache	Victoria Park
1961	**Carry Back** (¾)	2:04	John Sellers	Jack Price	Crozier	Bass Clef
1962	**Decidedly** (2¼)	2:00⅖	Bill Hartack	Horatio Luro	Roman Line	Ridan
1963	**Chateaugay** (1¼)	2:01⅘	Braulio Baeza	James Conway	Never Bend	Candy Spots
1964	**Northern Dancer** (nk)	2:00	Bill Hartack	Horatio Luro	Hill Rise	The Scoundrel
1965	**Lucky Debonair** (nk)	2:01⅕	Bill Shoemaker	Frank Catrone	Dapper Dan	Tom Rolfe
1966	**Kauai King** (½)	2:02	Don Brumfield	Henry Forrest	Advocator	Blue Skyer
1967	**Proud Clarion** (1)	2:00⅗	Bobby Ussery	Loyd Gentry	Barbs Delight	Damascus
1968	**Forward Pass*** (nk)	—	Ismael Valenzuela	Henry Forrest	Francie's Hat	T.V. Commercial
1969	**Majestic Prince** (nk)	2:01⅘	Bill Hartack	Johnny Longden	Arts and Letters	Dike
1970	**Dust Commander** (5)	2:03⅖	Mike Manganello	Don Combs	My Dad George	High Echelon
1971	**Canonero II** (3¼)	2:03⅕	Gustavo Avila	Juan Arias	Jim French	Bold Reason
1972	**Riva Ridge** (3¼)	2:01⅘	Ron Turcotte	Lucien Laurin	No Le Hace	Hold Your Peace
1973	**SECRETARIAT** (2½)	1:59⅖	Ron Turcotte	Lucien Laurin	Sham	Our Native
1974	**Cannonade** (2¼)	2:04	Angel Cordero Jr.	Woody Stephens	Hudson County	Agitate
1975	**Foolish Pleasure** (1¾)	2:02	Jacinto Vasquez	LeRoy Jolley	Avatar	Diabolo
1976	**Bold Forbes** (1)	2:01⅗	Angel Cordero Jr.	Laz Barrera	Honest Pleasure	Elocutionist
1977	**SEATTLE SLEW** (1¾)	2:02⅕	Jean Cruguet	Billy Turner	Run Dusty Run	Sanhedrin
1978	**AFFIRMED** (1½)	2:01⅕	Steve Cauthen	Laz Barrera	Alydar	Believe It

Year	Winner (Margin)	Time	Jockey	Trainer	2nd place	3rd place
1979	**Spectacular Bid** (2¾)	2:02⅖	Ron Franklin	Bud Delp	General Assembly	Golden Act
1980	**Genuine Risk** (1)	2:02	Jacinto Vasquez	LeRoy Jolley	Rumbo	Jaklin Klugman
1981	**Pleasant Colony** (¾)	2:02	Jorge Velasquez	John Campo	Woodchopper	Partez
1982	**Gato Del Sol** (2½)	2:02⅖	E. Delahoussaye	Eddie Gregson	Laser Light	Reinvested
1983	**Sunny's Halo** (2)	2:02⅕	E. Delahoussaye	David Cross Jr.	Desert Wine	Caveat
1984	**Swale** (3¼)	2:02⅖	Laffit Pincay Jr.	Woody Stephens	Coax Me Chad	At The Threshold
1985	**Spend A Buck** (5¼)	2:00⅕	Angel Cordero Jr.	Cam Gambolati	Stephan's Odyssey	Chief's Crown
1986	**Ferdinand** (2¼)	2:02⅘	Bill Shoemaker	Chas. Whittingham	Bold Arrangement	Broad Brush
1987	**Alysheba** (¾)	2:03⅖	Chris McCarron	Jack Van Berg	Bet Twice	Avies Copy
1988	**Winning Colors** (nk)	2:02⅕	Gary Stevens	D. Wayne Lukas	Forty Niner	Risen Star
1989	**Sunday Silence** (2½)	2:05	Pat Valenzuela	Chas. Whittingham	Easy Goer	Awe Inspiring
1990	**Unbridled** (3½)	2:02	Craig Perret	Carl Nafzger	Summer Squall	Pleasant Tap
1991	**Strike the Gold** (1¾)	2:03	Chris Antley	Nick Zito	Best Pal	Mane Minister
1992	**Lil E. Tee** (1)	2:03	Pat Day	Lynn Whiting	Casual Lies	Dance Floor
1993	**Sea Hero** (2½)	2:02⅖	Jerry Bailey	Mack Miller	Prairie Bayou	Wild Gale
1994	**Go For Gin** (2)	2:03⅗	Chris McCarron	Nick Zito	Strodes Creek	Blumin Affair
1995	**Thunder Gulch** (2¼)	2:01⅕	Gary Stevens	D. Wayne Lukas	Tejano Run	Timber Country
1996	**Grindstone** (ns)	2:01	Jerry Bailey	D. Wayne Lukas	Cavonnier	Prince of Thieves
1997	**Silver Charm** (hd)	2:02⅖	Gary Stevens	Bob Baffert	Captain Bodgit	Free House
1998	**Real Quiet** (½)	2:02⅕	Kent Desormeaux	Bob Baffert	Victory Gallop	Indian Charlie
1999	**Charismatic** (nk)	2:03⅕	Chris Antley	D. Wayne Lukas	Menifee	Cat Thief
2000	**Fusaichi Pegasus** (1½)	2:01⅕	Kent Desormeaux	Neil Drysdale	Aptitude	Impeachment
2001	**Monarchos** (4¾)	1:59⅘	Jorge Chavez	John Ward Jr.	Invisible Ink	Congaree
2002	**War Emblem** (4)	2:01	Victor Espinoza	Bob Baffert	Proud Citizen	Perfect Drift
2003	**Funny Cide** (1¾)	2:01	Jose Santos	Barclay Tagg	Empire Maker	Peace Rules
2004	**Smarty Jones** (2¾)	2:04	Stewart Elliott	John Servis	Lion Heart	Imperialism
2005	**Giacomo** (½)	2:02¾	Mike Smith	John Shirreffs	Closing Argument	Afleet Alex
2006	**Barbaro** (6½)	2:01⅖	Edgar Prado	Michael Matz	Blue Grass Cat	Steppenwolfer

*Dancer's Image finished first (in 2:02½), but was disqualified after traces of prohibited medication were found in his system.

Preakness Stakes

For three-year-olds. Held two weeks after the Kentucky Derby at Pimlico Race Course in Baltimore. Inaugurated 1873. Note that the 1918 race was held over two divisions. Originally run at 1½ miles (1873-88), then at 1¼ miles (1889), 1½ miles (1890), 1¹⁄₁₆ miles (1894-1900), 1 mile & 70 yards (1901-07), 1¹⁄₁₆ miles (1908), 1 mile (1909-1910), 1⅛ miles (1911-24), and the present 1³⁄₁₆ miles since 1925.

Trainers with most wins: Robert W. Walden (7); T.J. Healey and D. Wayne Lukas (5); Bob Baffert, Sunny Jim Fitzsimmons and Jimmy Jones (4); J. Whalen (3).

Jockeys with most wins: Eddie Arcaro (6); Pat Day (5); G. Barbee, Bill Hartack and Lloyd Hughes (3).

Winning fillies: Flocarline (1903), Whimsical (1906), Rhine Maiden (1915) and Nellie Morse (1924).

Year	Winner (Margin)	Time	Jockey	Trainer	2nd place	3rd place
1873	**Survivor** (10)	2:43	G. Barbee	A.D. Pryor	John Boulger	Artist
1874	**Culpepper** (¾)	2:56½	W. Donohue	H. Gaffney	King Amadeus	Scratch
1875	**Tom Ochiltree** (2)	2:43½	L. Hughes	R.W. Walden	Viator	Bay Final
1876	**Shirley** (4)	2:44¾	G. Barbee	W. Brown	Rappahannock	Compliment
1877	**Cloverbrook** (2)	2:45½	C. Holloway	J. Walden	Bombast	Lucifer
1878	**Duke of Magenta** (2)	2:41¾	C. Holloway	R.W. Walden	Bayard	Albert
1879	**Harold** (1)	2:40½	L. Hughes	R.W. Walden	Jericho	Rochester
1880	**Grenada** (¾)	2:40½	L. Hughes	R.W. Walden	Oden	Emily F.
1881	**Saunterer** (½)	2:40½	T. Costello	R.W. Walden	Compensation	Baltic
1882	**Vanguard** (nk)	2:44½	T. Costello	R.W. Walden	Heck	Col. Watson
1883	**Jacobus** (4)	2:42½	G. Barbee	R. Dwyer	Parnell	(2-horse race)
1884	**Knight of Ellerslie** (2)	2:39½	S. Fisher	T.B. Doswell	Welcher	(2-horse race)
1885	**Tecumseh** (2)	2:49	Jim McLaughlin	C. Littlefield	Wickham	John C.
1886	**The Bard** (3)	2:45	S. Fisher	J. Huggins	Eurus	Elkwood
1887	**Dunboyne** (1)	2:39½	W. Donohue	W. Jennings	Mahoney	Raymond
1888	**Refund** (3)	2:49	F. Littlefield	R.W. Walden	Bertha B.*	Glendale
1889	**Buddhist** (8)	2:17½	W. Anderson	J. Rogers	Japhet	(2-horse race)
1890	**Montague** (3)	2:36¾	W. Martin	E. Feakes	Philosophy	Barrister
1891-93	Not held					
1894	**Assignee** (3)	1:49¼	F. Taral	W. Lakeland	Potentate	Ed Kearney
1895	**Belmar** (1)	1:50½	F. Taral	E. Feakes	April Fool	Sue Kittie
1896	**Margrave** (1)	1:51	H. Griffin	Byron McClelland	Hamilton II	Intermission
1897	**Paul Kauvar** (1½)	1:51¼	T. Thorpe	T.P. Hayes	Elkins	On Deck
1898	**Sly Fox** (2)	1:49¾	W. Simms	H. Campbell	The Huguenot	Nuto
1899	**Half Time** (1)	1:47	R. Clawson	F. McCabe	Filigrane	Lackland
1900	**Hindus** (hd)	1:48⅖	H. Spencer	J.H. Morris	Sarmatian	Ten Candles
1901	**The Parader** (2)	1:47⅕	F. Landry	T.J. Healey	Sadie S.	Dr. Barlow
1902	**Old England** (ns)	1:45⅘	L. Jackson	G.B. Morris	Maj. Daingerfield	Namtor
1903	**Flocarline** (½)	1:44⅘	W. Gannon	H.C. Riddle	Mackey Dwyer	Rightful
1904	**Bryn Mawr** (1)	1:44⅕	E. Hildebrand	W.F. Presgrave	Wotan	Dolly Spanker

Preakness Stakes (Cont.)

Year	Winner (Margin)	Time	Jockey	Trainer	2nd place	3rd place
1905	**Cairngorm** (hd)	1:45⅘	W. Davis	A.J. Joyner	Kiamesha	Coy Maid
1906	**Whimsical** (4)	1:45	Walter Miller	T.J. Gaynor	Content	Larabie
1907	**Don Enrique** (1)	1:45⅖	G. Mountain	J. Whalen	Ethon	Zambesi
1908	**Royal Tourist** (4)	1:46⅖	Eddie Dugan	A.J. Joyner	Live Wire	Robert Cooper
1909	**Effendi** (1)	1:39⅘	Willie Doyle	F.C. Frisbie	Fashion Plate	Hill Top
1910	**Layminster** (½)	1:40⅗	R. Estep	J.S. Healy	Dalhousie	Sager
1911	**Watervale** (1)	1:51	Eddie Dugan	J. Whalen	Zeus	The Nigger
1912	**Colonel Holloway** (5)	1:56⅗	C. Turner	D. Woodford	Bwana Tumbo	Tipsand
1913	**Buskin** (nk)	1:53⅖	James Butwell	J. Whalen	Kleburne	Barnegat
1914	**Holiday** (¾)	1:53⅘	A. Schuttinger	J.S. Healy	Brave Cunarder	Defendum
1915	**Rhine Maiden** (1½)	1:58	Douglas Hoffman	F. Devers	Half Rock	Runes
1916	**Damrosch** (1½)	1:54⅘	Linus McAtee	A.G. Weston	Greenwood	Achievement
1917	**Kalitan** (2)	1:54⅖	E. Haynes	Bill Hurley	Al M. Dick	Kentucky Boy
1918	**War Cloud** (¾)	1:53⅗	Johnny Loftus	W.B. Jennings	Sunny Slope	Lanius
1918	**Jack Hare Jr** (2)	1:53⅖	Charles Peak	F.D. Weir	The Porter	Kate Bright
1919	**SIR BARTON** (4)	1:53	Johnny Loftus	H. Guy Bedwell	Eternal	Sweep On
1920	**Man o' War** (1½)	1:51⅗	Clarence Kummer	L. Feustel	Upset	Wildair
1921	**Broomspun** (¾)	1:54⅕	F. Coltiletti	James Rowe Sr.	Polly Ann	Jeg
1922	**Pillory** (hd)	1:51⅗	L. Morris	Thomas Healey	Hea	June Grass
1923	**Vigil** (1¼)	1:53⅗	B. Marinelli	Thomas Healey	General Thatcher	Rialto
1924	**Nellie Morse** (1½)	1:57⅕	John Merimee	A.B. Gordon	Transmute	Mad Play
1925	**Coventry** (4)	1:59	Clarence Kummer	William Duke	Backbone	Almadel
1926	**Display** (hd)	1:59⅘	John Maiben	Thomas Healey	Blondin	Mars
1927	**Bostonian** (½)	2:01⅗	Whitey Abel	Fred Hopkins	Sir Harry	Whiskery
1928	**Victorian** (ns)	2:00⅕	Sonny Workman	James Rowe Jr.	Toro	Solace
1929	**Dr. Freeland** (1)	2:01⅗	Louis Schaefer	Thomas Healey	Minotaur	African
1930	**GALLANT FOX** (¾)	2:00⅗	Earl Sande	Jim Fitzsimmons	Crack Brigade	Snowflake
1931	**Mate** (1½)	1:59	George Ellis	J.W. Healy	Twenty Grand	Ladder
1932	**Burgoo King** (hd)	1:59⅘	Eugene James	Dick Thompson	Tick On	Boatswain
1933	**Head Play** (4)	2:02	Charley Kurtsinger	Thomas Hayes	Ladysman	Utopian
1934	**High Quest** (ns)	1:58⅕	Robert Jones	Bob Smith	Cavalcade	Discovery
1935	**OMAHA** (6)	1:58⅖	Willie Saunders	Jim Fitzsimmons	Firethorn	Psychic Bid
1936	**Bold Venture** (ns)	1:59	George Woolf	Max Hirsch	Granville	Jean Bart
1937	**WAR ADMIRAL** (hd)	1:58⅖	Charley Kurtsinger	George Conway	Pompoon	Flying Scot
1938	**Dauber** (7)	1:59⅘	Maurice Peters	Dick Handlen	Cravat	Menow
1939	**Challedon** (1¼)	1:59⅘	George Seabo	Louis Schaefer	Gilded Knight	Volitant
1940	**Bimelech** (3)	1:58⅗	F.A. Smith	Bill Hurley	Mioland	Gallahadion
1941	**WHIRLAWAY** (5½)	1:58⅘	Eddie Arcaro	Ben Jones	King Cole	Our Boots
1942	**Alsab** (1)	1:57	Basil James	Sarge Swenke	Requested & Sun Again (dead heat)	
1943	**COUNT FLEET** (8)	1:57⅖	Johnny Longden	Don Cameron	Blue Swords	Vincentive
1944	**Pensive** (¾)	1:59⅕	Conn McCreary	Ben Jones	Platter	Stir Up
1945	**Polynesian** (2½)	1:58⅘	W.D. Wright	Morris Dixon	Hoop Jr.	Darby Dieppe
1946	**ASSAULT** (nk)	2:01⅖	Warren Mehrtens	Max Hirsch	Lord Boswell	Hampden
1947	**Faultless** (1¼)	1:59	Doug Dodson	Jimmy Jones	On Trust	Phalanx
1948	**CITATION** (5½)	2:02⅖	Eddie Arcaro	Jimmy Jones	Vulcan's Forge	Bovard
1949	**Capot** (hd)	1:56	Ted Atkinson	J.M. Gaver	Palestinian	Noble Impulse
1950	**Hill Prince** (5)	1:59⅕	Eddie Arcaro	Casey Hayes	Middleground	Dooly
1951	**Bold** (7)	1:56⅖	Eddie Arcaro	Preston Burch	Counterpoint	Alerted
1952	**Blue Man** (3½)	1:57⅖	Conn McCreary	Woody Stephens	Jampol	One Count
1953	**Native Dancer** (nk)	1:57⅘	Eric Guerin	Bill Winfrey	Jamie K.	Royal Bay Gem
1954	**Hasty Road** (nk)	1:57⅖	Johnny Adams	Harry Trotsek	Correlation	Hasseyampa
1955	**Nashua** (1)	1:54⅗	Eddie Arcaro	Jim Fitzsimmons	Saratoga	Traffic Judge
1956	**Fabius** (¾)	1:58⅖	Bill Hartack	Jimmy Jones	Needles	No Regrets
1957	**Bold Ruler** (2)	1:56⅕	Eddie Arcaro	Jim Fitzsimmons	Iron Liege	Inside Tract
1958	**Tim Tam** (1½)	1:57⅕	Ismael Valenzuela	Jimmy Jones	Lincoln Road	Gone Fishin'
1959	**Royal Orbit** (4)	1:57	William Harmatz	R. Cornell	Sword Dancer	Dunce
1960	**Bally Ache** (4)	1:57⅗	Bobby Ussery	Jimmy Pitt	Victoria Park	Celtic Ash
1961	**Carry Back** (¾)	1:57⅗	Johnny Sellers	Jack Price	Globemaster	Crozier
1962	**Greek Money** (ns)	1:56⅕	John Rotz	V.W. Raines	Ridan	Roman Line
1963	**Candy Spots** (3½)	1:56⅕	Bill Shoemaker	Mesh Tenney	Chateaugay	Never Bend
1964	**Northern Dancer** (2¼)	1:56⅘	Bill Hartack	Horatio Luro	The Scoundrel	Hill Rise
1965	**Tom Rolfe** (nk)	1:56⅕	Ron Turcotte	Frank Whiteley	Dapper Dan	Hail To All
1966	**Kauai King** (1¾)	1:55⅖	Don Brumfield	Henry Forrest	Stupendous	Amberoid
1967	**Damascus** (2¼)	1:55⅕	Bill Shoemaker	Frank Whiteley	In Reality	Proud Clarion
1968	**Forward Pass** (6)	1:56⅘	Ismael Valenzuela	Henry Forrest	Out Of the Way	Nodouble
1969	**Majestic Prince** (hd)	1:55⅗	Bill Hartack	Johnny Longden	Arts and Letters	Jay Ray
1970	**Personality** (nk)	1:56⅕	Eddie Belmonte	John Jacobs	My Dad George	Silent Screen
1971	**Canonero II** (1½)	1:54	Gustavo Avila	Juan Arias	Eastern Fleet	Jim French
1972	**Bee Bee Bee** (1¼)	1:55⅗	Eldon Nelson	Red Carroll	No Le Hace	Key To The Mint

Year	Winner (Margin)	Time	Jockey	Trainer	2nd place	3rd place
1973	**SECRETARIAT** (2½)	1:54⅖	Ron Turcotte	Lucien Laurin	Sham	Our Native
1974	**Little Current** (7)	1:54⅗	Miguel Rivera	Lou Rondinello	Neapolitan Way	Cannonade
1975	**Master Derby** (1)	1:56⅖	Darrel McHargue	Smiley Adams	Foolish Pleasure	Diabolo
1976	**Elocutionist** (3½)	1:55	John Lively	Paul Adwell	Play The Red	Bold Forbes
1977	**SEATTLE SLEW** (1½)	1:54⅖	Jean Cruguet	Billy Turner	Iron Constitution	Run Dusty Run
1978	**AFFIRMED** (nk)	1:54⅖	Steve Cauthen	Laz Barrera	Alydar	Believe It
1979	**Spectacular Bid** (3½)	1:54⅕	Ron Franklin	Bud Delp	Golden Act	Screen King
1980	**Codex** (4¾)	1:54⅕	Angel Cordero Jr.	D. Wayne Lukas	Genuine Risk	Colonel Moran
1981	**Pleasant Colony** (1)	1:54⅗	Jorge Velasquez	John Campo	Bold Ego	Paristo
1982	**Aloma's Ruler** (½)	1:55⅖	Jack Kaenel	John Lenzini Jr.	Linkage	Cut Away
1983	**Deputed Testamony** (2¾)	1:55⅖	Donald Miller Jr.	Bill Boniface	Desert Wine	High Honors
1984	**Gate Dancer** (1½)	1:53⅗	Angel Cordero Jr.	Jack Van Berg	Play On	Fight Over
1985	**Tank's Prospect** (hd)	1:53⅖	Pat Day	D. Wayne Lukas	Chief's Crown	Eternal Prince
1986	**Snow Chief** (4)	1:54⅘	Alex Solis	Melvin Stute	Ferdinand	Broad Brush
1987	**Alysheba** (½)	1:55⅘	Chris McCarron	Jack Van Berg	Bet Twice	Cryptoclearance
1988	**Risen Star** (1¼)	1:56⅕	E. Delahoussaye	Louie Roussel III	Brian's Time	Winning Colors
1989	**Sunday Silence** (ns)	1:53⅘	Pat Valenzuela	Chas. Whittingham	Easy Goer	Rock Point
1990	**Summer Squall** (2¼)	1:53⅗	Pat Day	Neil Howard	Unbridled	Mister Frisky
1991	**Hansel** (7)	1:54	Jerry Bailey	Frank Brothers	Corporate Report	Mane Minister
1992	**Pine Bluff** (¾)	1:55⅗	Chris McCarron	Tom Bohannan	Alydeed	Casual Lies
1993	**Prairie Bayou** (½)	1:56⅗	Mike Smith	Tom Bohannan	Cherokee Run	El Bakan
1994	**Tabasco Cat** (¾)	1:56⅖	Pat Day	D. Wayne Lukas	Go For Gin	Concern
1995	**Timber Country** (½)	1:54⅖	Pat Day	D. Wayne Lukas	Oliver's Twist	Thunder Gulch
1996	**Louis Quatorze** (3¼)	1:53⅖	Pat Day	Nick Zito	Skip Away	Editor's Note
1997	**Silver Charm** (hd)	1:54⅖	Gary Stevens	Bob Baffert	Free House	Captain Bodgit
1998	**Real Quiet** (2¼)	1:54⅘	Kent Desormeaux	Bob Baffert	Victory Gallop	Classic Cat
1999	**Charismatic** (1½)	1:55⅕	Chris Antley	D. Wayne Lukas	Menifee	Badge
2000	**Red Bullet** (3¾)	1:56	Jerry Bailey	Joe Orseno	Fusaichi Pegasus	Impeachment
2001	**Point Given** (2¼)	1:55⅖	Gary Stevens	Bob Baffert	A P Valentine	Congaree
2002	**War Emblem** (¾)	1:56⅕	Victor Espinoza	Bob Baffert	Magic Weisner	Proud Citizen
2003	**Funny Cide** (9¾)	1:55⅗	Jose Santos	Barclay Tagg	Midway Road	Scrimshaw
2004	**Smarty Jones** (11½)	1:55⅖	Stewart Elliott	John Servis	Rock Hard Ten	Eddington
2005	**Afleet Alex** (4¾)	1:55	Jeremy Rose	Tim Ritchey	Scrappy T	Giacomo
2006	**Bernardini** (5¼)	1:54⅗	Javier Castellano	Thomas Albertrani	Sweetnorthernsaint	Hemingway's Key

* Later named Judge Murray.

AP/Wide World Photos

*Jockey Eddie Arcaro waves from atop **Citation** after his 5½-length victory in the Preakness on May 15, 1948. From left are owner Warren Wright, trainer Jimmy Jones and an unidentified groom.*

Belmont Stakes

For three-year-olds. Held three weeks after Preakness Stakes at Belmont Park in Elmont, N.Y. Inaugurated in 1867 at Jerome Park, moved to Morris Park in 1890 and then to Belmont Park in 1905.

Originally run at 1 mile and 5 furlongs (1867-89), then 1¼ miles (1890-1905), 1⅜ miles (1906-25), and the present 1½ miles since 1926.

Trainers with most wins: James Rowe Sr. (8); Sam Hildreth (7); Sunny Jim Fitzsimmons (6); Woody Stephens (5); Max Hirsch, D. Wayne Lukas and Robert W. Walden (4); Elliott Burch, Lucien Laurin, F. McCabe and D. McDaniel (3).

Jockeys with most wins: Eddie Arcaro and Jim McLaughlin (6); Earl Sande and Bill Shoemaker (5); Braulio Baeza, Pat Day, Laffit Pincay Jr., Gary Stevens and James Stout (3).

Winning fillies: Ruthless (1867) and Tanya (1905).

Year	Winner (Margin)	Time	Jockey	Trainer	2nd place	3rd place
1867	**Ruthless** (½)	3:05	J, Gilpatrick	A.J. Minor	DeCourcey	Rivoli
1868	**General Duke** (2)	3:02	Bobby Swim	A. Thompson	Northumberland	Fanny Ludlow
1869	**Fenian** (6)	3:04¼	C. Miller	J. Pincus	Glenelg	Invercauld
1870	**Kingfisher** (nk)	2:59½	W. Dick	R. Colston	Foster	Midday
1871	**Harry Bassett** (3)	2:56	W. Miller	D. McDaniel	Stockwood	By the Sea
1872	**Joe Daniels** (¾)	2:58¼	James Roe	D. McDaniel	Meteor	Shylock
1873	**Springbok** (¾)	3:01¾	James Roe	D. McDaniel	Count d'Orsay	Strachino
1874	**Saxon** (nk)	2:39½	G. Barbee	W. Prior	Grinstead	Aaron Pennington
1875	**Calvin** (2)	2:42¼	Bobby Swim	A. Williams	Aristides	Milner
1876	**Algerine** (½)	2:40½	Billy Donohue	Major Doswell	Fiddlesticks	Barricade
1877	**Cloverbrook** (1)	2:46	C. Holloway	J. Walden	Loiterer	Baden-Baden
1878	**Duke of Magenta** (2)	2:43½	L. Hughes	R.W. Walden	Bramble	Sparta
1879	**Spendthrift** (6)	2:42¾	George Evans	T. Puryear	Monitor	Jericho
1880	**Grenada** (nk)	2:47	L. Hughes	R.W. Walden	Ferncliffe	Turenne
1881	**Saunterer** (nk)	2:47	T. Costello	R.W. Walden	Eole	Baltic
1882	**Forester** (5)	2:43	Jim McLaughlin	L. Stuart	Babcock	Wyoming
1883	**George Kinney** (3)	2:42½	Jim McLaughlin	James Rowe Sr.	Trombone	Renegade
1884	**Panique** (nk)	2:42	Jim McLaughlin	James Rowe Sr.	Knight of Ellerslie	Himalaya
1885	**Tyrant** (3)	2:43	Paul Duffy	W. Claypool	St. Augustine	Tecumseh
1886	**Inspector B** (1)	2:41	Jim McLaughlin	F. McCabe	The Bard	Linden
1887	**Hanover** (15)	2:43½	Jim McLaughlin	F. McCabe	Oneko	(2-horse race)
1888	**Sir Dixon** (15)	2:40¼	Jim McLaughlin	F. McCabe	Prince Royal	(2-horse race)
1889	**Eric** (½)	2:47¼	W. Hayward	J. Huggins	Diablo	Zephyrus
1890	**Burlington** (2)	2:07¾	Pike Barnes	A. Cooper	Devotee	Padishah
1891	**Foxford** (nk)	2:08¾	Ed Garrison	M. Donavan	Montana	Laurestan
1892	**Patron** (6)	2:12	W. Hayward	L. Stuart	Shellbark	(2-horse race)
1893	**Commanche** (hd)	1:53¼	Willie Simms	G. Hannon	Dr. Rice	Rainbow
1894	**Henry of Navarre** (1½)	1:56½	Willie Simms	B. McClelland	Prig	Assignee
1895	**Belmar** (hd)	2:11½	Fred Taral	E. Feakes	Counter Tenor	Nanki Poo
1896	**Hastings** (hd)	2:24½	H. Griffin	J.J. Hyland	Handspring	Hamilton II
1897	**Scottish Chieftain** (1)	2:23¼	J. Scherrer	M. Byrnes	On Deck	Octagon
1898	**Bowling Brook** (6)	2:32	F. Littlefield	R.W. Walden	Previous	Hamburg
1899	**Jean Beraud** (hd)	2:23	R. Clawson	Sam Hildreth	Half Time	Glengar
1900	**Ildrim** (ns)	2:21¼	Nash Turner	H.E. Leigh	Petruchio	Missionary
1901	**Commando** (2)	2:21	H. Spencer	James Rowe Sr.	The Parader	All Green
1902	**Masterman** (2)	2:22⅗	John Bullman	J.J. Hyland	Renald	King Hanover
1903	**Africander** (2)	2:21¾	John Bullman	R. Miller	Whorler	Red Knight
1904	**Delhi** (4)	2:06⅗	George Odom	James Rowe Sr.	Graziallo	Rapid Water
1905	**Tanya** (½)	2:08	E. Hildebrand	J.W. Rogers	Blandy	Hot Shot
1906	**Burgomaster** (4)	2:20	Lucien Lyne	J.W. Rogers	The Quail	Accountant
1907	**Peter Pan** (1)	N/A	G. Mountain	James Rowe Sr.	Superman	Frank Gill
1908	**Colin** (hd)	N/A	Joe Notter	James Rowe Sr.	Fair Play	King James
1909	**Joe Madden** (8)	2:21⅗	E. Dugan	Sam Hildreth	Wise Mason	Donald MacDonald
1910	**Sweep** (6)	2:22	James Butwell	James Rowe Sr.	Duke of Ormonde	(2-horse race)
1911-12	Not held					
1913	**Prince Eugene** (½)	2:18	Roscoe Troxler	James Rowe Sr.	Rock View	Flying Fairy
1914	**Luke McLuke** (8)	2:20	Merritt Buxton	J.F. Schorr	Gainer	Charlestonian
1915	**The Finn** (4)	2:18⅖	George Byrne	E.W. Heffner	Half Rock	Pebbles
1916	**Friar Rock** (3)	2:22	E. Haynes	Sam Hildreth	Spur	Churchill
1917	**Hourless** (10)	2:17⅘	James Butwell	Sam Hildreth	Skeptic	Wonderful
1918	**Johren** (2)	2:20⅖	Frank Robinson	A. Simons	War Cloud	Cum Sah
1919	**SIR BARTON** (5)	2:17⅖	John Loftus	H. Guy Bedwell	Sweep On	Natural Bridge
1920	**Man o' War** (20)	2:14⅕	Clarence Kummer	L. Feustel	Donnacona	(2-horse race)
1921	**Grey Lag** (3)	2:16⅘	Earl Sande	Sam Hildreth	Sporting Blood	Leonardo II
1922	**Pillory** (2)	2:18⅘	C.H. Miller	T.J. Healey	Snob II	Hea
1923	**Zev** (1½)	2:19	Earl Sande	Sam Hildreth	Chickvale	Rialto
1924	**Mad Play** (2)	2:18⅘	Earl Sande	Sam Hildreth	Mr. Mutt	Modest
1925	**American Flag** (8)	2:16⅘	Albert Johnson	G.R. Tompkins	Dangerous	Swope
1926	**Crusader** (1)	2:32⅕	Albert Johnson	George Conway	Espino	Haste

Year	Winner (Margin)	Time	Jockey	Trainer	2nd place	3rd place
1927	**Chance Shot** (1½)	2:32⅖	Earl Sande	Pete Coyne	Bois de Rose	Flambino
1928	**Vito** (3)	2:33⅕	Clarence Kummer	Max Hirsch	Genie	Diavolo
1929	**Blue Larkspur** (¾)	2:32⅘	Mack Garner	C. Hastings	African	Jack High
1930	**GALLANT FOX** (3)	2:31⅗	Earl Sande	Jim Fitzsimmons	Whichone	Questionnaire
1931	**Twenty Grand** (10)	2:29⅗	Charley Kurtsinger	James Rowe Jr.	Sun Meadow	Jamestown
1932	**Faireno** (1½)	2:32⅘	Tom Malley	Jim Fitzsimmons	Osculator	Flag Pole
1933	**Hurryoff** (1½)	2:32⅗	Mack Garner	H. McDaniel	Nimbus	Union
1934	**Peace Chance** (6)	2:29⅕	W.D. Wright	Pete Coyne	High Quest	Good Goods
1935	**OMAHA** (1½)	2:30⅗	Willie Saunders	Jim Fitzsimmons	Firethorn	Rosemont
1936	**Granville** (ns)	2:30	James Stout	Jim Fitzsimmons	Mr. Bones	Hollyrood
1937	**WAR ADMIRAL** (3)	2:28⅗	Charley Kurtsinger	George Conway	Sceneshifter	Vamoose
1938	**Pasteurized** (nk)	2:29⅖	James Stout	George Odom	Dauber	Cravat
1939	**Johnstown** (5)	2:29⅗	James Stout	Jim Fitzsimmons	Belay	Gilded Knight
1940	**Bimelech** (¾)	2:29⅗	Fred Smith	Bill Hurley	Your Chance	Andy K.
1941	**WHIRLAWAY** (2½)	2:31	Eddie Arcaro	Ben Jones	Robert Morris	Yankee Chance
1942	**Shut Out** (2)	2:29⅕	Eddie Arcaro	John Gaver	Alsab	Lochinvar
1943	**COUNT FLEET** (25)	2:28⅕	Johnny Longden	Don Cameron	Fairy Manhurst	Deseronto
1944	**Bounding Home** (½)	2:32⅕	G.L. Smith	Matt Brady	Pensive	Bull Dandy
1945	**Pavot** (5)	2:30⅕	Eddie Arcaro	Oscar White	Wildlife	Jeep
1946	**ASSAULT** (3)	2:30⅘	Warren Mehrtens	Max Hirsch	Natchez	Cable
1947	**Phalanx** (5)	2:29⅖	R. Donoso	Syl Veitch	Tide Rips	Tailspin
1948	**CITATION** (8)	2:28⅕	Eddie Arcaro	Jimmy Jones	Better Self	Escadru
1949	**Capot** (½)	2:30⅕	Ted Atkinson	John Gaver	Ponder	Palestinian
1950	**Middleground** (1)	2:28⅗	William Boland	Max Hirsch	Lights Up	Mr. Trouble
1951	**Counterpoint** (4)	2:29	David Gorman	Syl Veitch	Battlefield	Battle Morn
1952	**One Count** (2½)	2:30⅕	Eddie Arcaro	Oscar White	Blue Man	Armageddon
1953	**Native Dancer** (nk)	2:28⅗	Eric Guerin	Bill Winfrey	Jamie K.	Royal Bay Gem
1954	**High Gun** (nk)	2:30⅘	Eric Guerin	Max Hirsch	Fisherman	Limelight
1955	**Nashua** (9)	2:29	Eddie Arcaro	Jim Fitzsimmons	Blazing Count	Portersville
1956	**Needles** (nk)	2:29⅘	David Erb	Hugh Fontaine	Career Boy	Fabius
1957	**Gallant Man** (8)	2:26⅗	Bill Shoemaker	John Nerud	Inside Tract	Bold Ruler
1958	**Cavan** (6)	2:30⅕	Pete Anderson	Tom Barry	Tim Tam	Flamingo
1959	**Sword Dancer** (¾)	2:28⅖	Bill Shoemaker	Elliott Burch	Bagdad	Royal Orbit
1960	**Celtic Ash** (5½)	2:29⅕	Bill Hartack	Tom Barry	Venetian Way	Disperse
1961	**Sherluck** (2¼)	2:29⅕	Braulio Baeza	Harold Young	Globemaster	Guadalcanal
1962	**Jaipur** (ns)	2:28⅘	Bill Shoemaker	B. Mulholland	Admiral's Voyage	Crimson Satan
1963	**Chateaugay** (2½)	2:30⅕	Braulio Baeza	James Conway	Candy Spots	Choker
1964	**Quadrangle** (2)	2:28⅖	Manuel Ycaza	Elliott Burch	Roman Brother	Northern Dancer
1965	**Hail to All** (nk)	2:28⅖	John Sellers	Eddie Yowell	Tom Rolfe	First Family
1966	**Amberoid** (2½)	2:29⅗	William Boland	Lucien Laurin	Buffle	Advocator
1967	**Damascus** (2½)	2:28⅘	Bill Shoemaker	F.Y. Whiteley Jr.	Cool Reception	Gentleman James
1968	**Stage Door Johnny** (1¼)	2:27⅕	Gus Gustines	John Gaver	Forward Pass	Call Me Prince
1969	**Arts and Letters** (5½)	2:28⅘	Braulio Baeza	Elliott Burch	Majestic Prince	Dike
1970	**High Echelon** (¾)	2:34	John Rotz	John Jacobs	Needles N Pens	Naskra
1971	**Pass Catcher** (¾)	2:30⅖	Walter Blum	Eddie Yowell	Jim French	Bold Reason
1972	**Riva Ridge** (7)	2:28	Ron Turcotte	Lucien Laurin	Ruritania	Cloudy Dawn
1973	**SECRETARIAT** (31)	2:24	Ron Turcotte	Lucien Laurin	Twice A Prince	My Gallant
1974	**Little Current** (7)	2:29⅕	Miguel Rivera	Lou Rondinello	Jolly Johu	Cannonade
1975	**Avatar** (nk)	2:28⅕	Bill Shoemaker	Tommy Doyle	Foolish Pleasure	Master Derby
1976	**Bold Forbes** (nk)	2:29	Angel Cordero Jr.	Laz Barrera	McKenzie Bridge	Great Contractor
1977	**SEATTLE SLEW** (4)	2:29⅗	Jean Cruguet	Billy Turner	Run Dusty Run	Sanhedrin
1978	**AFFIRMED** (hd)	2:26⅘	Steve Cauthen	Laz Barrera	Alydar	Darby Creek Road
1979	**Coastal** (3¼)	2:28⅗	Ruben Hernandez	David Whiteley	Golden Act	Spectacular Bid
1980	**Temperence Hill** (2)	2:29⅘	Eddie Maple	Joseph Cantey	Genuine Risk	Rockhill Native
1981	**Summing** (nk)	2:29	George Martens	Luis Barerra	Highland Blade	Pleasant Colony
1982	**Conquistador Cielo** (14)	2:28⅕	Laffit Pincay Jr.	Woody Stephens	Gato Del Sol	Illuminate
1983	**Caveat** (3½)	2:27⅘	Laffit Pincay Jr.	Woody Stephens	Slew o' Gold	Barberstown
1984	**Swale** (4)	2:27⅕	Laffit Pincay Jr.	Woody Stephens	Pine Circle	Morning Bob
1985	**Creme Fraiche** (½)	2:27	Eddie Maple	Woody Stephens	Stephan's Odyssey	Chief's Crown
1986	**Danzig Connection** (1¼)	2:29⅘	Chris McCarron	Woody Stephens	Johns Treasure	Ferdinand
1987	**Bet Twice** (14)	2:28⅕	Craig Perret	Jimmy Croll	Cryptoclearance	Gulch
1988	**Risen Star** (14¾)	2:26⅖	E. Delahoussaye	Louie Roussel III	Kingpost	Brian's Time
1989	**Easy Goer** (8)	2:26	Pat Day	Shug McGaughey	Sunday Silence	Le Voyageur
1990	**Go And Go** (8¼)	2:27⅕	Michael Kinane	Dermot Weld	Thirty Six Red	Baron de Vaux
1991	**Hansel** (hd)	2:28	Jerry Bailey	Frank Brothers	Strike the Gold	Mane Minister
1992	**A.P. Indy** (¾)	2:26	E. Delahoussaye	Neil Drysdale	My Memoirs	Pine Bluff
1993	**Colonial Affair** (2)	2:29⅘	Julie Krone	Scotty Schulhofer	Kissin Kris	Wild Gale
1994	**Tabasco Cat** (2)	2:26⅘	Pat Day	D. Wayne Lukas	Go For Gin	Strodes Creek
1995	**Thunder Gulch** (2)	2:32	Gary Stevens	D. Wayne Lukas	Star Standard	Citadeed
1996	**Editor's Note** (1)	2:28⅘	Rene Douglas	D. Wayne Lukas	Skip Away	My Flag

Belmont Stakes (Cont.)

Year	Winner (Margin)	Time	Jockey	Trainer	2nd place	3rd place
1997	**Touch Gold** (¾)	2:28⅘	Chris McCarron	David Hofmans	Silver Charm	Free House
1998	**Victory Gallop** (ns)	2:29	Gary Stevens	Elliott Walden	Real Quiet	Thomas Jo
1999	**Lemon Drop Kid** (hd)	2:27⅘	Jose Santos	Scotty Schulhofer	Vision and Verse	Charismatic
2000	**Commendable** (1½)	2:31⅕	Pat Day	D. Wayne Lukas	Aptitude	Unshaded
2001	**Point Given** (12¼)	2:26⅖	Gary Stevens	Bob Baffert	A P Valentine	Monarchos
2002	**Sarava** (½)	2:29⅗	Edgar Prado	Ken McPeek	Medaglia d'Oro	Sunday Break
2003	**Empire Maker** (¾)	2:28⅕	Jerry Bailey	Bobby Frankel	Ten Most Wanted	Funny Cide
2004	**Birdstone** (1)	2:27⅖	Edgar Prado	Nick Zito	Smarty Jones	Royal Assault
2005	**Afleet Alex** (7)	2:28⅗	Jeremy Rose	Tim Ritchey	Andromeda's Hero	Nolan's Cat
2006	**Jazil** (1¼)	2:27⅘	Fernando Jara	Kiaran McLaughlin	Bluegrass Cat	Sunriver

Breeders' Cup World Championships

Inaugurated on Nov. 10, 1984, the Breeders' Cup World Championships consists of eight races on one track on one day late in the year to determine thoroughbred racing's principle champions.

The Breeders' Cup has been (will be) held at the following tracks (in alphabetical order): Aqueduct Racetrack (N.Y.) in 1985; Arlington Park (Ill.) in 2002; Belmont Park (N.Y.) in 1990, '95, 2001 and '05; Churchill Downs (Ky.) in 1988, '91, '94, '98, 2000 and '06; Gulfstream Park (Fla.) in 1989, '92 and '99; Hollywood Park (Calif.) in 1984, '87 and '97; Lone Star Park (Texas) in 2004; Monmouth Park (N.J.) in 2007; Santa Anita Park (Calif.) in 1986, '93 and 2003 and Woodbine (Toronto) in 1996.

Horses with most wins: Bayakoa, Da Hoss, High Chaparral, Lure, Miesque and Tiznow (2).

Trainers with most wins: D. Wayne Lukas (18); Shug McGaughey (9); Neil Drysdale and Richard Mandella (6); Bill Mott (5); Andre Fabre, Bobby Frankel, Ron McAnally (4); Bob Baffert, Pascal Bary, Francois Boutin, Patrick Byrne, Julio Canani, Aidan O'Brien and Sir Michael Stoute (3).

Jockeys with most wins: Jerry Bailey (15); Pat Day (12); Mike Smith (10); Chris McCarron (9); Gary Stevens (8); Eddie Delahoussaye, Laffit Pincay Jr., Jose Santos and Pat Valenzuela (7); Corey Nakatani and John Velazquez (6); Angel Cordero Jr., Frankie Dettori and Craig Perret (4); David Flores, Michael Kinane, Randy Romero and Alex Solis (3).

Juvenile

Distances: one mile (1984-85, 87); 1 1/16 miles (1986, 1988-2001, 2003–), 1⅛ miles (2002).

Year	Winner (Margin)	Time	Jockey	Trainer	2nd place	3rd place
1984	**Chief's Crown** (¾)	1:36⅕	Don MacBeth	Roger Laurin	Tank's Prospect	Spend A Buck
1985	**Tasso** (ns)	1:36⅕	Laffit Pincay Jr.	Neil Drysdale	Storm Cat	Scat Dancer
1986	**Capote** (1¼)	1:43⅘	Laffit Pincay Jr.	D. Wayne Lukas	Qualify	Alysheba
1987	**Success Express** (1¾)	1:35⅕	Jose Santos	D. Wayne Lukas	Regal Classic	Tejano
1988	**Is It True** (1¼)	1:46⅗	Laffit Pincay Jr.	D. Wayne Lukas	Easy Goer	Tagel
1989	**Rhythm** (2)	1:43⅗	Craig Perret	Shug McGaughey	Grand Canyon	Slavic
1990	**Fly So Free** (3)	1:43⅖	Jose Santos	Scotty Schulhofer	Take Me Out	Lost Mountain
1991	**Arazi** (4¾)	1:44⅗	Pat Valenzuela	Francois Boutin	Bertrando	Snappy Landing
1992	**Gilded Time** (¾)	1:43⅖	Chris McCarron	Darrell Vienna	It'sali'lknownfact	River Special
1993	**Brocco** (5)	1:42⅘	Gary Stevens	Randy Winick	Blumin Affair	Tabasco Cat
1994	**Timber Country** (½)	1:44⅖	Pat Day	D. Wayne Lukas	Eltish	Tejano Run
1995	**Unbridled's Song** (nk)	1:41⅗	Mike Smith	James Ryerson	Hennessy	Editor's Note
1996	**Boston Harbor** (nk)	1:43⅖	Jerry Bailey	D. Wayne Lukas	Acceptable	Ordway
1997	**Favorite Trick** (5½)	1:41⅖	Pat Day	Patrick Byrne	Dawson's Legacy	Nationalore
1998	**Answer Lively** (hd)	1:44	Jerry Bailey	Bobby Barnett	Aly's Alley	Cat Thief
1999	**Anees** (2½)	1:42⅕	Gary Stevens	Alex Hassinger Jr.	Chief Seattle	High Yield
2000	**Macho Uno** (ns)	1:42	Jerry Bailey	Joe Orseno	Point Given	Street Cry
2001	**Johannesburg** (2¼)	1:42⅕	Michael Kinane	Aidan O'Brien	Repent	Siphonic
2002	**Vindication** (2¾)	1:49⅗	Mike Smith	Bob Baffert	Kafwain	Hold That Tiger
2003	**Action This Day** (2¼)	1:43⅗	David Flores	Richard Mandella	Minister Eric	Chapel Royal
2004	**Wilko** (¾)	1:42	Frankie Dettori	Jeremy Noseda	Afleet Alex	Sun King
2005	**Stevie Wonderboy** (1¼)	1:41⅗	Garrett Gomez	Doug O'Neill	Henny Hughes	First Samurai

Breeders' Cup Leaders

The all-time money-winning horses and jockeys in the history of the Breeders' Cup through 2005.

Top 10 Horses

		Sts	1-2-3	Earnings
1	Tiznow	2	2-0-0	$4,560,400
2	Awesome Again	1	1-0-0	2,662,400
3	Pleasantly Perfect	2	1-0-1	2,520,000
4	Saint Liam	1	1-0-0	2,433,600
5	Skip Away	2	1-0-0	2,288,000
6	Cat Thief	3	1-0-1	2,200,000
7	Alysheba	3	1-1-1	2,133,000
8	Alphabet Soup	1	1-0-0	2,080,000
	Volponi	2	1-0-0	2,080,000
	Ghostzapper	1	1-0-0	2,080,000

Top 10 Jockeys

		Sts	1-2-3	Earnings
1	Pat Day	117	12-17-11	$23,033,360
2	Jerry Bailey	102	15-12-14	22,006,440
3	Chris McCarron	101	9-12-7	17,669,600
4	Gary Stevens	99	8-15-11	13,723,910
5	Mike Smith	52	10-6-3	10,505,760
6	John Velazquez	55	6-6-6	8,107,800
7	Jose Santos	62	7-2-4	8,008,800
8	Corey Nakatani	58	6-7-7	7,905,280
9	Eddie Delahoussaye	68	7-3-6	7,775,000
10	Alex Solis	52	3-8-4	7,130,290

Juvenile Fillies

Distances: one mile (1984-85, 87); 1 1/16 miles (1986, 1988-2001, 2003–); 1 1/8 miles (2002).

Year	Winner (Margin)	Time	Jockey	Trainer	2nd place	3rd place
1984	**Outstandingly***	1:37 4/5	Walter Guerra	Pancho Martin	Dusty Heart	Fine Spirit
1985	**Twilight Ridge** (1)	1:35 4/5	Jorge Velasquez	D. Wayne Lukas	Family Style	Steal A Kiss
1986	**Brave Raj** (5½)	1:43 1/5	Pat Valenzuela	Melvin Stute	Tappiano	Saros Brig
1987	**Epitome** (ns)	1:36 2/5	Pat Day	Phil Hauswald	Jeanne Jones	Dream Team
1988	**Open Mind** (1¾)	1:46 3/5	Angel Cordero Jr.	D. Wayne Lukas	Darby Shuffle	Lea Lucinda
1989	**Go for Wand** (2¾)	1:44 1/5	Randy Romero	Wm. Badgett Jr.	Sweet Roberta	Stella Madrid
1990	**Meadow Star** (5)	1:44	Jose Santos	LeRoy Jolley	Private Treasure	Dance Smartly
1991	**Pleasant Stage** (nk)	1:46 2/5	E. Delahoussaye	Chris Speckert	La Spia	Cadillac Women
1992	**Eliza** (nk)	1:42 4/5	Pat Valenzuela	Alex Hassinger	Educated Risk	Boots 'n Jackie
1993	**Phone Chatter** (hd)	1:43	Laffit Pincay Jr.	Richard Mandella	Sardula	Heavenly Prize
1994	**Flanders** (hd)	1:45 1/5	Pat Day	D. Wayne Lukas	Serena's Song	Stormy Blues
1995	**My Flag** (½)	1:42 2/5	Jerry Bailey	Shug McGaughey	Cara Rafaela	Golden Attraction
1996	**Storm Song** (4½)	1:43 3/5	Craig Perret	Nick Zito	Love That Jazz	Critical Factor
1997	**Countess Diana** (8½)	1:42 1/5	Shane Sellers	Patrick Byrne	Career Collection	Primaly
1998	**Silverbulletday** (½)	1:43 3/5	Gary Stevens	Bob Baffert	Excellent Meeting	Three Ring
1999	**Cash Run** (1¼)	1:43 1/5	Jerry Bailey	D. Wayne Lukas	Chilukki	Surfside
2000	**Caressing** (½)	1:42 3/5	John Velazquez	David Vance	Platinum Tiara	She's a Devil Due
2001	**Tempera** (1½)	1:41 2/5	David Flores	Eoin Harty	Imperial Gesture	Bella Bellucci
2002	**Storm Flag Flying** (½)	1:49 3/5	John Velazquez	Shug McGaughey	Composure	Santa Catarina
2003	**Halfbridled** (2½)	1:42 3/5	Julie Krone	Richard Mandella	Ashado	Victory U.S.A.
2004	**Sweet Catomine** (3¾)	1:41 3/5	Corey Nakatani	Julio Canani	Balletto	Runway Model
2005	**Folklore** (1¼)	1:43 4/5	Edgar Prado	D. Wayne Lukas	Wild Fit	Original Spin

*In 1984, winner Fran's Valentine was disqualified for interference in the stretch and placed 10th.

Sprint

Distance: six furlongs (since 1984).

Year	Winner (Margin)	Time	Jockey	Trainer	2nd place	3rd place
1984	**Eillo** (ns)	1:10 1/5	Craig Perret	Budd Lepman	Commemorate	Fighting Fit
1985	**Precisionist** (¾)	1:08 2/5	Chris McCarron	L.R. Fenstermaker	Smile	Mt. Livermore
1986	**Smile** (1¼)	1:08 2/5	Jacinto Vasquez	Scotty Schulhofer	Pine Tree Lane	Bedside Promise
1987	**Very Subtle** (4)	1:08 4/5	Pat Valenzuela	Melvin Stute	Groovy	Exclusive Enough
1988	**Gulch** (¾)	1:10 2/5	Angel Cordero Jr.	D. Wayne Lukas	Play The King	Afleet
1989	**Dancing Spree** (nk)	1:09	Angel Cordero Jr.	Shug McGaughey	Safely Kept	Dispersal
1990	**Safely Kept** (nk)	1:09 3/5	Craig Perret	Alan Goldberg	Dayjur	Black Tie Affair
1991	**Sheikh Albadou** (nk)	1:09 1/5	Pat Eddery	Alexander Scott	Pleasant Tap	Robyn Dancer
1992	**Thirty Slews** (nk)	1:08 1/5	Eddie Delahoussaye	Bob Baffert	Meafara	Rubiano
1993	**Cardmania** (nk)	1:08 3/5	Eddie Delahoussaye	Derek Meredith	Meafara	Gilded Time
1994	**Cherokee Run** (nk)	1:09 2/5	Mike Smith	Frank Alexander	Soviet Problem	Cardmania
1995	**Desert Stormer** (nk)	1:09	Kent Desormeaux	Frank Lyons	Mr. Greeley	Lit de Justice
1996	**Lit de Justice** (1¼)	1:08 3/5	Corey Nakatani	Jenine Sahadi	Paying Dues	Honour and Glory
1997	**Elmhurst** ½)	1:08 1/5	Corey Nakatani	Jenine Sahadi	Hesabull	Bet On Sunshine
1998	**Reraise** (2)	1:09	Corey Nakatani	Craig Dollase	Grand Slam	Kona Gold
1999	**Artax** (½)	1:07 4/5	Jorge Chavez	Louis Albertrani	Kona Gold	Big Jag
2000	**Kona Gold** (½)	1:07 3/5	Alex Solis	Bruce Headley	Honest Lady	Bet On Sunshine
2001	**Squirtle Squirt** (½)	1:08 2/5	Jerry Bailey	Bobby Frankel	Xtra Heat	Caller One
2002	**Orientate** (½)	1:08 4/5	Jerry Bailey	D. Wayne Lukas	Thunderello	Crafty C.T.
2003	**Cajun Beat** (2¼)	1:07 3/5	Cornelio Velasquez	Stephen Margolis	Bluesthestandard	Shake You Down
2004	**Speightstown** (1¼)	1:08	John Velazquez	Todd Pletcher	Kela	My Cousin Matt
2005	**Silver Train** (hd)	1:08 4/5	Edgar Prado	Richard Dutrow Jr.	Taste of Paradise	Lion Tamer

Mile

Year	Winner (Margin)	Time	Jockey	Trainer	2nd place	3rd place
1984	**Royal Heroine** (1½)	1:32 3/5	Fernando Toro	John Gosden	Star Choice	Cozzene
1985	**Cozzene** (2¼)	1:35	Walter Guerra	Jan Nerud	Al Mamoon*	Shadeed
1986	**Last Tycoon** (hd)	1:35 1/5	Yves St.-Martin	Robert Collet	Palace Music	Fred Astaire
1987	**Miesque** (3½)	1:32 4/5	Freddie Head	Francois Boutin	Show Dancer	Sonic Lady
1988	**Miesque** (4)	1:38 3/5	Freddie Head	Francois Boutin	Steinlen	Simply Majestic
1989	**Steinlen** (¾)	1:37 1/5	Jose Santos	D. Wayne Lukas	Sabona	Most Welcome
1990	**Royal Academy** (nk)	1:35 1/5	Lester Piggott	M.V. O'Brien	Itsallgreektome	Priolo
1991	**Opening Verse** (2¼)	1:37 2/5	Pat Valenzuela	Dick Lundy	Val des Bois	Star of Cozzene
1992	**Lure** (3)	1:32 4/5	Mike Smith	Shug McGaughey	Paradise Creek	Brief Truce
1993	**Lure** (2¼)	1:33 2/5	Mike Smith	Shug McGaughey	Ski Paradise	Fourstars Allstar
1994	**Barathea** (hd)	1:34 2/5	Frankie Dettori	Luca Cumani	Johann Quatz	Unfinished Symph
1995	**Ridgewood Pearl** (2)	1:43 3/5	John Murtagh	John Oxx	Fastness	Sayyedati
1996	**Da Hoss** (1½)	1:35 4/5	Gary Stevens	Michael Dickinson	Spinning World	Same Old Wish
1997	**Spinning World** (2)	1:32 3/5	Cash Asmussen	Jonathan Pease	Geri	Decorated Hero
1998	**Da Hoss** (hd)	1:35 1/5	John Velazquez	Michael Dickinson	Hawksley Hill	Labeeb
1999	**Silic** (nk)	1:34 1/5	Corey Nakatani	Julio Canani	Tuzla	Docksider

Breeders' Cup Championship (Cont.)

Mile (Cont.)

Year	Winner (Margin)	Time	Jockey	Trainer	2nd place	3rd place
2000	**War Chant** (nk)	1:34⅗	Gary Stevens	Neil Drysdale	North East Bound	Dansili
2001	**Val Royal** (1¾)	1:32	Jose Valdivia	Julio Canani	Forbidden Apple	Bach
2002	**Domedriver** (¾)	1:36⅘	Thierry Thulliez	Pascal Bary	Rock of Gibraltar	Good Journey
2003	**Six Perfections** (¾)	1:33⅘	Jerry Bailey	Pascal Bary	Touch of the Blues	Century City
2004	**Singletary** (½)	1:36⅘	David Flores	Donald Chatlos Jr.	Antonius Pius	Six Perfections
2005	**Artie Schiller** (¾)	1:36⅕	Garrett Gomez	James Jerkens	Leroidesanimaux	Gorella

*In 1985, 2nd place finisher Palace Music was disqualified for interference and placed 9th.

Distaff

Distances: 1¼ miles (1984-87); 1⅛ miles (since 1988).

Year	Winner (Margin)	Time	Jockey	Trainer	2nd place	3rd place
1984	**Princess Rooney** (7)	2:02⅖	Eddie Delahoussaye	Neil Drysdale	Life's Magic	Adored
1985	**Life's Magic** (6¼)	2:02	Angel Cordero Jr.	D. Wayne Lukas	Lady's Secret	DontstopThemusic
1986	**Lady's Secret** (2½)	2:01⅕	Pat Day	D. Wayne Lukas	Fran's Valentine	Outstandingly
1987	**Sacahuista** (2¼)	2:02⅘	Randy Romero	D. Wayne Lukas	Clabber Girl	Oueee Bebe
1988	**Personal Ensign** (ns)	1:52	Randy Romero	Shug McGaughey	Winning Colors	Goodbye Halo
1989	**Bayakoa** (1½)	1:47⅖	Laffit Pincay Jr.	Ron McAnally	Gorgeous	Open Mind
1990	**Bayakoa** (6¾)	1:49⅕	Laffit Pincay Jr.	Ron McAnally	Colonial Waters	Valay Maid
1991	**Dance Smartly** (½)	1:50⅘	Pat Day	Jim Day	Versailles Treaty	Brought to Mind
1992	**Paseana** (4)	1:48	Chris McCarron	Ron McAnally	Versailles Treaty	Magical Maiden
1993	**Hollywood Wildcat** (ns)	1:48⅕	Eddie Delahoussaye	Neil Drysdale	Paseana	Re Toss
1994	**One Dreamer** (nk)	1:50⅗	Gary Stevens	Thomas Proctor	Heavenly Prize	Miss Dominique
1995	**Inside Information** (13½)	1:46	Mike Smith	Shug McGaughey	Heavenly Prize	Lakeway
1996	**Jewel Princess** (1½)	1:48⅕	Corey Nakatani	Wallace Dollase	Serena's Song	Different
1997	**Ajina** (2)	1:47⅕	Mike Smith	Bill Mott	Sharp Cat	Escena
1998	**Escena** (ns)	1:49⅘	Gary Stevens	Bill Mott	Banshee Breeze	Keeper Hill
1999	**Beautiful Pleasure** (¾)	1:47⅖	Jorge Chavez	John Ward Jr.	Banshee Breeze	Heritage of Gold
2000	**Spain** (1½)	1:47⅗	Victor Espinoza	D. Wayne Lukas	Surfside	Heritage of Gold
2001	**Unbridled Elaine** (hd)	1:49⅕	Pat Day	Dallas Stewart	Spain	Two Item Limit
2002	**Azeri** (5)	1:48⅗	Mike Smith	Laura de Seroux	Farda Amiga	Imperial Gesture
2003	**Adoration** (4½)	1:49⅕	Pat Valenzuela	David Hofmans	Elloluv	Got Koko
2004	**Ashado** (1¼)	1:48⅕	John Velazquez	Todd Pletcher	Storm Flag Flying	Stellar Jayne
2005	**Pleasant Home** (9¼)	1:48⅖	Cornelio Velasquez	Shug McGaughey	Society Selection	Ashado

Turf

Distance: 1½ miles (since 1984).

Year	Winner (Margin)	Time	Jockey	Trainer	2nd place	3rd place
1984	**Lashkari** (nk)	2:25⅕	Yves St.-Martin	de Royer-Dupre	All Along	Raami
1985	**Pebbles** (nk)	2:27	Pat Eddery	Clive Brittain	StrawberryRoad II	Mourjane
1986	**Manila** (nk)	2:25⅖	Jose Santos	Leroy Jolley	Theatrical	Estrapade
1987	**Theatrical** (½)	2:24⅖	Pat Day	Bill Mott	Trempolino	Village Star II
1988	**Gt. Communicator** (½)	2:35⅕	Ray Sibille	Thad Ackel	Sunshine Forever	Indian Skimmer
1989	**Prized** (hd)	2:28	Eddie Delahoussaye	Neil Drysdale	Sierra Roberta	Star Lift
1990	**In The Wings** (½)	2:29⅗	Gary Stevens	Andre Fabre	With Approval	El Senor
1991	**Miss Alleged** (2)	2:30⅘	Eric Legrix	Pascal Bary	Itsallgreektome	Quest for Fame
1992	**Fraise** (ns)	2:24	Pat Valenzuela	Bill Mott	Sky Classic	Quest for Fame
1993	**Kotashaan** (½)	2:25	Kent Desormeaux	Richard Mandella	Bien Bien	Luazur
1994	**Tikkanen** (1½)	2:26⅖	Mike Smith	Jonathan Pease	Hatoof	Paradise Creek
1995	**Northern Spur** (nk)	2:42	Chris McCarron	Ron McAnally	Freedom Cry	Carnegie
1996	**Pilsudski** (1¼)	2:30⅕	Walter Swinburn	Sir Michael Stoute	Singspiel	Swain
1997	**Chief Bearhart** (¾)	2:24	Jose Santos	Mark Frostad	Borgia	Flag Down
1998	**Buck's Boy** (1¼)	2:28⅗	Shane Sellers	Noel Hickey	Yagli	Dushyantor
1999	**Daylami** (2½)	2:24⅗	Frankie Dettori	Saeed bin Suroor	Royal Anthem	Buck's Boy
2000	**Kalanisi** (½)	2:26⅘	John Murtagh	Sir Michael Stoute	Quiet Resolve	John's Call
2001	**Fantastic Light** (¾)	2:24⅕	Frankie Dettori	Saeed bin Suroor	Milan	Timboroa
2002	**High Chaparral** (1¼)	2:30⅕	Michael Kinane	Aidan O'Brien	With Anticipation	Falcon Flight
2003	**High Chaparral***	2:24⅕	Michael Kinane	Aidan O'Brien	—	Falbrav
	& Johar*	2:24⅕	Alex Solis	Richard Mandella		
2004	**Better Talk Now** (1¾)	2:29⅗	Ramon Dominguez	H. Graham Motion	Kitten's Joy	Powerscourt
2005	**Shirocco** (1¾)	2:29⅖	Christophe Soumillon	Andre Fabre	Ace	Azamour

*in 2003, High Chaparral and Johar finished in a dead heat, the first in Breeders' Cup history.

Filly & Mare Turf

Distance: 1⅜ miles (1999-2000, 2004–); 1¼ miles (2001-03).

Year	Winner (Margin)	Time	Jockey	Trainer	2nd place	3rd place
1999	**Soaring Softly** (¾)	2:13⅘	Jerry Bailey	James J. Toner	Coretta	Zomarradah
2000	**Perfect Sting** (¾)	2:13	Jerry Bailey	Joe Orseno	Tout Charmant	Catella
2001	**Banks Hill** (5½)	2:00⅕	Olivier Peslier	Andre Fabre	Spook Express	Spring Oak
2002	**Starine** (1½)	2:03⅗	John Velazquez	Bobby Frankel	Banks Hill	Islington
2003	**Islington** (nk)	1:59	Kieren Fallon	Sir Michael Stoute	L'Ancresse	Yesterday
2004	**Ouija Board** (1½)	2:18⅕	Kieren Fallon	Edward Dunlop	Film Maker	Wonder Again
2005	**Intercontinental** (1¼)	2:02⅖	Rafael Bejarano	Bobby Frankel	Ouija Board	Film Maker

Classic

Distance: 1¼ miles (since 1984).

Year	Winner (Margin)	Time	Jockey	Trainer	2nd place	3rd place
1984	**Wild Again** (hd)	2:03⅖	Pat Day	Vincent Timphony	Slew o' Gold	Gate Dancer*
1985	**Proud Truth** (hd)	2:00⅘	Jorge Velasquez	John Veitch	Gate Dancer	Turkoman
1986	**Skywalker** (1¼)	2:00⅖	Laffit Pincay Jr.	M. Whittingham	Turkoman	Precisionist
1987	**Ferdinand** (ns)	2:01⅖	Bill Shoemaker	C. Whittingham	Alysheba	Judge Angelucci
1988	**Alysheba** (ns)	2:04⅘	Chris McCarron	Jack Van Berg	Seeking the Gold	Waquoit
1989	**Sunday Silence** (½)	2:00⅕	Chris McCarron	C. Whittingham	Easy Goer	Blushing John
1990	**Unbridled** (1)	2:02⅕	Pat Day	Carl Nafzger	Ibn Bey	Thirty Six Red
1991	**Black Tie Affair** (1¼)	2:02⅘	Jerry Bailey	Ernie Poulos	Twilight Agenda	Unbridled
1992	**A.P. Indy** (2)	2:00⅕	Eddie Delahoussaye	Neil Drysdale	Pleasant Tap	Jolypha
1993	**Arcangues** (2)	2:00⅘	Jerry Bailey	Andre Fabre	Bertrando	Kissin Kris
1994	**Concern** (nk)	2:02⅖	Jerry Bailey	Richard Small	Tabasco Cat	Dramatic Gold
1995	**Cigar** (2½)	1:59⅖	Jerry Bailey	Bill Mott	L'Carriere	Unaccounted For
1996	**Alphabet Soup** (ns)	2:01	Chris McCarron	David Hofmans	Louis Quatorze	Cigar
1997	**Skip Away** (6)	1:59⅕	Mike Smith	Hubert Hine	Deputy Commander	Dowty
1998	**Awesome Again** (¾)	2:02	Pat Day	Patrick Byrne	Silver Charm	Swain
1999	**Cat Thief** (1¼)	1:59⅖	Pat Day	D. Wayne Lukas	Budroyale	Golden Missile
2000	**Tiznow** (nk)	2:00⅗	Chris McCarron	Jay Robbins	Giant's Causeway	Captain Steve
2001	**Tiznow** (ns)	2:00⅗	Chris McCarron	Jay Robbins	Sakhee	Albert the Great
2002	**Volponi** (6½)	2:01⅖	Jose Santos	Philip Johnson	Medaglia d'Oro	Milwaukee Brew
2003	**Pleasantly Perfect** (1½)	1:59⅘	Alex Solis	Richard Mandella	Medaglia d'Oro	Dynever
2004	**Ghostzapper** (3)	1:59	Javier Castellano	Bobby Frankel	Roses in May	Pleasantly Perfect
2005	**Saint Liam** (1)	2:01⅖	Jerry Bailey	Richard Dutrow Jr.	Flower Alley	Perfect Drift

*In 1984, 2nd place finisher Gate Dancer was disqualified for interference and placed 3rd.

Annual Money Leaders

Horses

Annual money-leading horses since 1910, according to *The American Racing Manual.*

Multiple leaders: Round Table, Buckpasser, Alysheba and Cigar (2).

Year		Age	Sts	1-2-3	Earnings
1910	Novelty	2	16	11–	$72,630
1911	Worth	2	13	10–	16,645
1912	Star Charter	4	17	6–	14,655
1913	Old Rosebud	2	14	12–	19,057
1914	Roamer	3	16	12–	29,105
1915	Borrow	7	9	4–	20,195
1916	Campfire	2	9	6–	49,735
1917	Sun Briar	2	9	5–	59,505
1918	Eternal	2	8	6–	56,173
1919	Sir Barton	3	13	8-3-2	88,250
1920	Man o' War	3	11	11-0-0	166,140
1921	Morvich	2	11	11-0-0	115,234
1922	Pillory	3	7	4-1-1	95,654
1923	Zev	3	14	12-1-0	272,008
1924	Sarzen	3	12	8-1-1	95,640
1925	Pompey	2	10	7-2-0	121,630
1926	Crusader	3	15	9-4-0	166,033
1927	Anita Peabody	2	7	6-0-1	111,905
1928	High Strung	2	6	5-0-0	153,590
1929	Blue Larkspur	3	6	4-1-0	153,450
1930	Gallant Fox	3	10	9-1-0	308,275
1931	Gallant Flight	2	7	7-0-0	219,000
1932	Gusto	3	16	4-3-2	145,940
1933	Singing Wood	2	9	3-2-2	88,050
1934	Cavalcade	3	7	6-1-0	111,235
1935	Omaha	3	9	6-1-2	142,255
1936	Granville	3	11	7-3-0	$110,295
1937	Seabiscuit	4	15	11-2-2	168,580
1938	Stagehand	3	15	8-2-3	189,710
1939	Challedon	3	15	9-2-3	184,535
1940	Bimelech	3	7	4-2-1	110,005
1941	Whirlaway	3	20	13-5-2	272,386
1942	Shut Out	3	12	8-2-0	238,872
1943	Count Fleet	3	6	6-0-0	174,055
1944	Pavot	2	8	8-0-0	179,040
1945	Busher	3	13	10-2-1	273,735
1946	Assault	3	15	8-2-3	424,195
1947	Armed	6	17	11-4-1	376,325
1948	Citation	3	20	19-1-0	709,470
1949	Ponder	3	21	9-5-2	321,825
1950	Noor	5	12	7-4-1	346,940
1951	Counterpoint	3	15	7-2-1	250,525
1952	Crafty Admiral	4	16	9-4-1	277,225
1953	Native Dancer	3	10	9-1-0	513,425
1954	Determine	3	15	10-3-2	328,700
1955	Nashua	3	12	10-1-1	752,550
1956	Needles	3	8	4-2-0	440,850
1957	Round Table	3	22	15-1-3	600,383
1958	Round Table	4	20	14-4-0	662,780
1959	Sword Dancer	3	13	8-4-0	537,004
1960	Bally Ache	3	15	10-3-1	445,045
1961	Carry Back	3	16	9-1-3	565,349

Annual Money Leaders (Cont.)

Horses (Cont.)

Year		Age	Sts	1-2-3	Earnings
1962	Never Bend	2	10	7-1-2	$402,969
1963	Candy Spots	3	12	7-2-1	604,481
1964	Gun Bow	4	16	8-4-2	580,100
1965	Buckpasser	2	11	9-1-0	568,096
1966	Buckpasser	3	14	13-1-0	669,078
1967	Damascus	3	16	12-3-1	817,941
1968	Forward Pass	3	13	7-2-0	546,674
1969	Arts and Letters	3	14	8-5-1	555,604
1970	Personality	3	18	8-2-1	444,049
1971	Riva Ridge	2	9	7-0-0	503,263
1972	Droll Role	4	19	7-3-4	471,633
1973	Secretariat	3	12	9-2-1	860,404
1974	Chris Evert	3	8	5-1-2	551,063
1975	Foolish Pleasure	3	11	5-4-1	716,278
1976	Forego	6	8	6-1-1	401,701
1977	Seattle Slew	3	7	6-1-1	641,370
1978	Affirmed	3	11	8-2-0	901,541
1979	Spectacular Bid	3	12	10-1-1	1,279,334
1980	Temperence Hill	3	17	8-3-1	1,130,452
1981	John Henry	6	10	8-0-0	1,798,030
1982	Perrault (GBR)	5	8	4-1-2	1,197,400
1983	All Along (FRA)	4	7	4-1-1	2,138,963
1984	Slew o' Gold	4	6	5-1-0	$2,627,944
1985	Spend A Buck	3	7	5-1-1	3,552,704
1986	Snow Chief	3	9	6-1-1	1,875,200
1987	Alysheba	3	10	3-3-1	2,511,156
1988	Alysheba	4	9	7-1-0	3,808,600
1989	Sunday Silence	3	9	7-2-0	4,578,454
1990	Unbridled	3	11	4-3-2	3,718,149
1991	Dance Smartly	3	8	8-0-0	2,876,821
1992	A.P. Indy	3	7	5-0-1	2,622,560
1993	Kotashaan (FRA)	5	10	6-3-0	2,619,014
1994	Paradise Creek	5	11	8-2-1	2,610,187
1995	Cigar	5	10	10-0-0	4,819,800
1996	Cigar	6	8	5-2-1	4,910,000
1997	Skip Away	4	11	4-5-2	4,089,000
1998	Silver Charm	4	9	6-2-0	4,696,506
1999	Almutawakel	4	4	1-1-1	3,290,000
2000	Dubai Millennium (GBR)	4	1	1-0-0	3,600,000
2001	Captain Steve	4	6	2-1-1	4,201,200
2002	Street Cry (IRE)	4	3	2-1-0	4,266,615
2003	Moon Ballad (IRE)	4	3	1-0-0	3,651,101
2004	Smarty Jones	3	7	6-1-0	7,563,535
2005	Saint Liam	5	6	4-1-0	3,696,960

Jockeys

Annual money-leading jockeys since 1910, according to *The American Racing Manual.*

Multiple leaders: Bill Shoemaker (10); Laffit Pincay Jr. (7); Eddie Arcaro and Jerry Bailey (6); Braulio Baeza (5); Chris McCarron and Jose Santos (4); Angel Cordero Jr. and Earl Sande (3); Ted Atkinson, Pat Day, Laverne Fator, Mack Garner, Bill Hartack, Charley Kurtsinger, Johnny Longden, Mike Smith, Gary Stevens, John Velazquez, Sonny Workman and Wayne Wright (2).

Year		Mts	Wins	Earnings
1910	Carroll Shilling	506	172	$176,030
1911	Ted Koerner	813	162	88,308
1912	Jimmy Butwell	684	144	79,843
1913	Merritt Buxton	887	146	82,552
1914	J. McCahey	824	155	121,845
1915	Mack Garner	775	151	96,628
1916	John McTaggart	832	150	155,055
1917	Frank Robinson	731	147	148,057
1918	Lucien Luke	756	178	201,864
1919	John Loftus	177	65	252,707
1920	Clarence Kummer	353	87	292,376
1921	Earl Sande	340	112	263,043
1922	Albert Johnson	297	43	345,054
1923	Earl Sande	430	122	569,394
1924	Ivan Parke	844	205	290,395
1925	Laverne Fator	315	81	305,775
1926	Laverne Fator	511	143	361,435
1927	Earl Sande	179	49	277,877
1928	Linus McAtee	235	55	301,295
1929	Mack Garner	274	57	314,975
1930	Sonny Workman	571	152	420,438
1931	Charley Kurtsinger	519	93	392,095
1932	Sonny Workman	378	87	385,070
1933	Robert Jones	471	63	226,285
1934	Wayne Wright	919	174	287,185
1935	Silvio Coucci	749	141	319,760
1936	Wayne Wright	670	100	264,000
1937	Charley Kurtsinger	765	120	384,202
1938	Nick Wall	658	97	385,161
1939	Basil James	904	191	353,333
1940	Eddie Arcaro	783	132	343,661
1941	Don Meade	1164	210	398,627
1942	Eddie Arcaro	687	123	481,949
1943	Johnny Longden	871	173	573,276
1944	Ted Atkinson	1539	287	899,101
1945	Johnny Longden	778	180	981,977
1946	Ted Atkinson	1377	233	1,036,825
1947	Douglas Dodson	646	141	$1,429,949
1948	Eddie Arcaro	726	188	1,686,230
1949	Steve Brooks	906	209	1,316,817
1950	Eddie Arcaro	888	195	1,410,160
1951	Bill Shoemaker	1161	257	1,329,890
1952	Eddie Arcaro	807	188	1,859,591
1953	Bill Shoemaker	1683	485	1,784,187
1954	Bill Shoemaker	1251	380	1,876,760
1955	Eddie Arcaro	820	158	1,864,796
1956	Bill Hartack	1387	347	2,343,955
1957	Bill Hartack	1238	341	3,060,501
1958	Bill Shoemaker	1133	300	2,961,693
1959	Bill Shoemaker	1285	347	2,843,133
1960	Bill Shoemaker	1227	274	2,123,961
1961	Bill Shoemaker	1256	304	2,690,819
1962	Bill Shoemaker	1126	311	2,916,844
1963	Bill Shoemaker	1203	271	2,526,925
1964	Bill Shoemaker	1056	246	2,649,553
1965	Braulio Baeza	1245	270	2,582,702
1966	Braulio Baeza	1341	298	2,951,022
1967	Braulio Baeza	1064	256	3,088,888
1968	Braulio Baeza	1089	201	2,835,108
1969	Jorge Velasquez	1442	258	2,542,315
1970	Laffit Pincay Jr.	1328	269	2,626,526
1971	Laffit Pincay Jr.	1627	380	3,784,377
1972	Laffit Pincay Jr.	1388	289	3,225,827
1973	Laffit Pincay Jr.	1444	350	4,093,492
1974	Laffit Pincay Jr.	1278	341	4,251,060
1975	Braulio Baeza	1190	196	3,674,398
1976	Angel Cordero Jr.	1534	274	4,709,500
1977	Steve Cauthen	2075	487	6,151,750
1978	Darrel McHargue	1762	375	6,188,353
1979	Laffit Pincay Jr.	1708	420	8,183,535
1980	Chris McCarron	1964	405	7,666,100
1981	Chris McCarron	1494	326	8,397,604
1982	Angel Cordero Jr.	1838	397	9,702,520

Year		Mts	Wins	Earnings	Year		Mts	Wins	Earnings
1983	Angel Cordero Jr.	1792	362	$10,116,807	1995	Jerry Bailey	1367	287	$16,311,876
1984	Chris McCarron	1565	356	12,038,213	1996	Jerry Bailey	1187	298	19,465,376
1985	Laffit Pincay Jr.	1409	289	13,415,049	1997	Jerry Bailey	1136	269	18,206,013
1986	Jose Santos	1636	329	11,329,297	1998	Gary Stevens	869	178	19,358,840
1987	Jose Santos	1639	305	12,407,355	1999	Pat Day	1265	254	18,092,845
1988	Jose Santos	1867	370	14,877,298	2000	Pat Day	1219	267	17,479,838
1989	Jose Santos	1459	285	13,847,003	2001	Jerry Bailey	912	227	22,597,720
1990	Gary Stevens	1504	283	13,881,198	2002	Jerry Bailey	833	214	22,871,814
1991	Chris McCarron	1440	265	14,456,073	2003	Jerry Bailey	776	206	23,354,960
1992	Kent Desormeaux	1568	361	14,193,006	2004	John Velazquez	1327	335	22,248,661
1993	Mike Smith	1510	343	14,024,815	2005	John Velazquez	1148	251	24,459,923
1994	Mike Smith	1484	317	15,979,820					

Trainers

Annual money-leading trainers since 1908, according to *The American Racing Manual*.

Multiple Leaders: D. Wayne Lukas (14); Sam Hildreth (9); Charlie Whittingham (7); Sunny Jim Fitzsimmons and Jimmy Jones (5); Bob Baffert, Laz Barrera, Ben Jones and Willie Molter (4); Hirsch Jacobs, Eddie Neloy and James Rowe Sr. (3); H. Guy Bedwell, Bobby Frankel, Jack Gaver, Todd Pletcher, John Schorr, Humming Bob Smith, Silent Tom Smith and Mesh Tenney (2).

Year		Wins	Earnings
1908	James Rowe Sr.	50	$284,335
1909	Sam Hildreth	73	123,942
1910	Sam Hildreth	84	148,010
1911	Sam Hildreth	67	49,418
1912	John Schorr	63	58,110
1913	James Rowe Sr.	18	45,936
1914	R.C. Benson	45	59,315
1915	James Rowe Sr.	19	75,596
1916	Sam Hildreth	39	70,950
1917	Sam Hildreth	23	61,698
1918	H. Guy Bedwell	53	80,296
1919	H. Guy Bedwell	63	208,728
1920	Louis Feustel	22	186,087
1921	Sam Hildreth	85	262,768
1922	Sam Hildreth	74	247,014
1923	Sam Hildreth	75	392,124
1924	Sam Hildreth	77	255,608
1925	G.R. Tompkins	30	199,245
1926	Scott Harlan	21	205,681
1927	W.H. Bringloe	63	216,563
1928	John Schorr	65	258,425
1929	James Rowe Jr.	25	314,881
1930	Sunny Jim Fitzsimmons	47	397,355
1931	Big Jim Healy	33	297,300
1932	Sunny Jim Fitzsimmons	68	266,650
1933	Humming Bob Smith	53	135,720
1934	Humming Bob Smith	43	249,938
1935	Bud Stotler	87	303,005
1936	Sunny Jim Fitzsimmons	42	193,415
1937	Robert McGarvey	46	209,925
1938	Earl Sande	15	226,495
1939	Sunny Jim Fitzsimmons	45	266,205
1940	Silent Tom Smith	14	269,200
1941	Ben Jones	70	475,318
1942	Jack Gaver	48	406,547
1943	Ben Jones	73	267,915
1944	Ben Jones	60	601,660
1945	Silent Tom Smith	52	510,655
1946	Hirsch Jacobs	99	560,077
1947	Jimmy Jones	85	1,334,805
1948	Jimmy Jones	81	1,118,670
1949	Jimmy Jones	76	978,587
1950	Preston Burch	96	637,754
1951	Jack Gaver	42	616,392
1952	Ben Jones	29	662,137
1953	Harry Trotsek	54	1,028,873
1954	Willie Molter	136	1,107,860
1955	Sunny Jim Fitzsimmons	66	1,270,055
1956	Willie Molter	142	1,227,402
1957	Jimmy Jones	70	1,150,910

Year		Wins	Earnings
1958	Willie Molter	69	$1,116,544
1959	Willie Molter	71	847,290
1960	Hirsch Jacobs	97	748,349
1961	Jimmy Jones	62	759,856
1962	Mesh Tenney	58	1,099,474

Year		Sts	Wins	Earnings
1963	Mesh Tenney	192	40	$860,703
1964	Bill Winfrey	287	61	1,350,534
1965	Hirsch Jacobs	610	91	1,331,628
1966	Eddie Neloy	282	93	2,456,250
1967	Eddie Neloy	262	72	1,776,089
1968	Eddie Neloy	212	52	1,233,101
1969	Elliott Burch	156	26	1,067,936
1970	Charlie Whittingham	551	82	1,302,354
1971	Charlie Whittingham	393	77	1,737,115
1972	Charlie Whittingham	429	79	1,734,020
1973	Charlie Whittingham	423	85	1,865,385
1974	Pancho Martin	846	166	2,408,419
1975	Charlie Whittingham	487	3	2,437,244
1976	Jack Van Berg	2362	496	2,976,196
1977	Laz Barrera	781	127	2,715,848
1978	Laz Barrera	592	100	3,307,164
1979	Laz Barrera	492	98	3,608,517
1980	Laz Barrera	559	99	2,969,151
1981	Charlie Whittingham	376	74	3,993,302
1982	Charlie Whittingham	410	63	4,587,457
1983	D. Wayne Lukas	595	78	4,267,261
1984	D. Wayne Lukas	805	131	5,835,921
1985	D. Wayne Lukas	1140	218	11,155,188
1986	D. Wayne Lukas	1510	259	12,345,180
1987	D. Wayne Lukas	1735	343	17,502,110
1988	D. Wayne Lukas	1500	318	17,842,358
1989	D. Wayne Lukas	1398	305	16,103,998
1990	D. Wayne Lukas	1396	267	14,508,871
1991	D. Wayne Lukas	1497	289	15,942,223
1992	D. Wayne Lukas	1349	230	9,806,436
1993	Bobby Frankel	345	79	8,933,252
1994	D. Wayne Lukas	693	147	9,247,457
1995	D. Wayne Lukas	837	194	12,834,483
1996	D. Wayne Lukas	1006	192	15,966,344
1997	D. Wayne Lukas	824	169	9,993,569
1998	Bob Baffert	538	139	15,000,870
1999	Bob Baffert	735	169	16,934,607
2000	Bob Baffert	678	146	11,831,605
2001	Bob Baffert	660	138	16,354,996
2002	Bobby Frankel	480	117	17,748,340
2003	Bobby Frankel	413	114	19,143,289
2004	Todd Pletcher	948	240	17,511,923
2005	Todd Pletcher	1039	257	20,867,842

All-Time Leaders

The all-time leading horses, trainers and jockeys of North America. Records are courtesy of the *Equibase Company* and include all available earnings from races in foreign countries. Horses must have had at least one start in the United States or Canada. Note that horses, jockeys and trainers who were active in 2006 are in **bold** type.

Records are through Sept. 30, 2006.

Top 20 Horses—Earnings

		Sts	1st	2nd	3rd	Earnings			Sts	1st	2nd	3rd	Earnings
1	Cigar	.33	19	4	5	$9,999,815	11	Singspiel (IRE)	.20	9	8	0	$5,952,825
2	Skip Away	.38	18	10	6	9,616,360	12	Falbrav (IRE)	.26	13	5	5	5,825,517
3	Fantastic Light	.25	12	5	3	8,486,957	13	Medaglia d'Oro	.17	8	7	0	5,754,720
4	Pleasantly Perfect	.18	9	3	2	7,789,880	14	Best Pal	.47	18	11	4	5,668,245
5	Smarty Jones	.9	8	1	0	7,613,155	15	Taiki Blizzard	.23	6	8	2	5,523,549
6	Silver Charm	.24	12	7	2	6,944,369	16	Roses in May	.13	8	4	0	5,490,187
7	Captain Steve	.25	9	3	7	6,828,356	17	High Chaparral (IRE)	.13	10	1	2	5,331,231
8	Alysheba	.26	11	8	2	6,679,242	18	Sulamani (IRE)	.17	9	3	1	5,252,368
9	John Henry	.83	39	15	9	6,591,860	19	Street Cry (IRE)	.12	5	6	1	5,150,837
10	Tiznow	.15	8	4	2	6,427,830	20	Preeminence (JPN)	.50	13	9	7	5,042,956

Top 10 Jockeys—Races Won

		Yrs	Wins	Earnings
1	Laffit Pincay Jr.	.37	9530	$237,120,625
2	**Russell Baze**	.33	9466	143,619,776
3	Bill Shoemaker	.42	8833	123,375,524
4	Pat Day	.33	8803	297,912,019
5	David Gall	.43	7396	24,972,821
6	Chris McCarron	.29	7141	263,985,505
7	Angel Cordero Jr.	.35	7057	164,570,227
8	Jorge Velasquez	.33	6795	125,544,379
9	Sandy Hawley	.31	6449	88,681,292
10	**Earlie Fires**	.32	6397	84,248,671

Top 10 Jockeys—Earnings

		Yrs	Wins	Earnings
1	Pat Day	.33	8803	$297,912,019
2	Jerry Bailey	.31	5893	296,104,129
3	Chris McCarron	.29	7141	263,985,505
4	Laffit Pincay Jr.	.37	9530	237,120,625
5	Gary Stevens	.27	4888	221,207,064
6	**Alex Solis**	.26	4430	197,426,079
7	Eddie Delahoussaye	.36	6384	195,884,940
8	**Kent Desormeaux**	.21	4660	185,843,115
8	**Jose Santos**	.23	4061	185,723,772
10	**Edgar Prado**	.20	5738	181,974,452

Top 10 Trainers—Races Won

		Wins	Earnings
1	**Dale Baird**	.9287	$32,893,697
2	**Jack Van Berg**	.6370	81,297,278
3	**King Leatherbury**	.6165	54,794,902
4	**Jerry Hollendorfer**	.4691	84,787,284
5	**Richard Hazelton**	.4651	38,358,525
6	**D. Wayne Lukas**	.4405	246,757,366
7	Frank Merrill Jr.	.3974	16,980,632
8	**H. Allen Jerkens**	.3678	93,438,360
9	**Grover Delp**	.3667	40,847,664
10	Richard Dutrow Sr.	.3665	36,189,085

Top 10 Trainers—Earnings

		Wins	Earnings
1	**D. Wayne Lukas**	.4405	$246,757,366
2	**Bobby Frankel**	.3367	194,900,691
3	**Bill Mott**	.3522	150,797,893
4	**Bob Baffert**	.1618	119,234,982
5	**Ron McAnally**	.2486	117,620,100
6	Charles Whittingham	.2534	109,215,527
7	**Todd Pletcher**	.1650	107,677,380
8	**Richard Mandella**	.1719	104,655,769
9	**H. Allen Jerkens**	.3678	93,438,360
10	**Claude McGaughey III**	.1477	93,001,773

Horse of the Year (1936-70)

In 1971, the *Daily Racing Form*, the Thoroughbred Racing Associations, and the National Turf Writers Assn. joined forces to create the Eclipse Awards. Before then, however, the *Racing Form* (1936-70) and the TRA (1950-70) issued separate selections for Horse of the Year. Their picks differed only four times from 1950-70 and are so noted. Horses listed in CAPITAL letters are Triple Crown winners; (f) indicates female.

Multiple winners: Kelso (5); Challedon, Native Dancer and Whirlaway (2).

Year		Year		Year		Year	
1936	Granville	1946	ASSAULT	1955	Nashua	1964	Kelso
1937	WAR ADMIRAL	1947	Armed	1956	Swaps	1965	Roman Brother (DRF)
1938	Seabiscuit	1948	CITATION	1957	Bold Ruler (DRF)		Moccasin (TRA)
1939	Challedon	1949	Capot		Dedicate (TRA)	1966	Buckpasser
1940	Challedon	1950	Hill Prince	1958	Round Table	1967	Damascus
1941	WHIRLAWAY	1951	Counterpoint	1959	Sword Dancer	1968	Dr. Fager
1942	Whirlaway	1952	One Count (DRF)	1960	Kelso	1969	Arts and Letters
1943	COUNT FLEET		Native Dancer (TRA)	1961	Kelso	1970	Fort Marcy (DRF)
1944	Twilight Tear (f)	1953	Tom Fool	1962	Kelso		Personality (TRA)
1945	Busher (f)	1954	Native Dancer	1963	Kelso		

Eclipse Awards

The Eclipse Awards, honoring the Horse of the Year and other champions of the sport, are sponsored by the National Thoroughbred Racing Association (NTRA), *Daily Racing Form* and the National Turf Writers Assn. In 1998, the NTRA replaced the Thoroughbred Racing Associations of North America as co-sponsor.

The awards are named after the 18th century racehorse and sire, Eclipse, who began racing at age five and was unbeaten in 18 starts (eight wins were walkovers). As a stallion, Eclipse sired winners of 344 races, including three Epsom Derby champions.

Horses listed in CAPITAL letters won the Triple Crown that year. Age of horse in parentheses where necessary.

Multiple winners: (horses): Forego (8); John Henry (7); Affirmed, Lonesome Glory and Secretariat (5); Azeri, Cigar, Flatterer, Seattle Slew, Skip Away and Spectacular Bid (4); Ack Ack, Susan's Girl, Tiznow and Zaccio (3); All Along, Alysheba, Ashado, Bayakoa, Black Tie Affair, Cafe Prince, Charismatic, Conquistador Cielo, Desert Vixen, Favorite Trick, Ferdinand, Flawlessly, Flat Top, Ghostzapper, Go for Wand, High Chaparral, Holy Bull, Housebuster, Kotashaan, Lady's Secret, Life's Magic, McDynamo, Miesque, Mineshaft, Morley Street, Open Mind, Paseana, Point Given, Riva Ridge, Saint Liam, Silverbulletday, Slew o' Gold and Spend A Buck (2).

Multiple winners: (people): Jerry Bailey (7); Juddmonte Farms and Laffit Pincay Jr. (6); Bobby Frankel (5); Laz Barrera, Pat Day, John Franks, D. Wayne Lukas, Allen Paulson, Ogden Phipps and Frank Stronach (4); Bob Baffert, Steve Cauthen, Harbor View Farm, Fred W. Hooper, Nelson Bunker Hunt, Mr. & Mrs. Gene Klein, Dan Lasater, John & Betty Mabee, Paul Mellon, Bill Shoemaker, Edward Taylor and Charlie Whittingham (3); Adena Springs, Braulio Baeza, C.T. Chenery, Claiborne Farm, Angel Cordero Jr., Kent Desormeaux, Richard Englander, William S. Farish, John W. Galbreath, Chris McCarron, Bill Mott, Todd Pletcher, Mike Smith and John Velazquez (2).

Horse of the Year

Year		Year		Year		Year	
1971	Ack Ack (5)	1980	Spectacular Bid (4)	1989	Sunday Silence (3)	1998	Skip Away (5)
1972	Secretariat (2)	1981	John Henry (6)	1990	Criminal Type (5)	1999	Charismatic (3)
1973	SECRETARIAT (3)	1982	Conquistador Cielo (3)	1991	Black Tie Affair (5)	2000	Tiznow (3)
1974	Forego (4)	1983	All Along (4)	1992	A.P. Indy (3)	2001	Point Given (3)
1975	Forego (5)	1984	John Henry (9)	1993	Kotashaan (5)	2002	Azeri (4)
1976	Forego (6)	1985	Spend A Buck (3)	1994	Holy Bull (3)	2003	Mineshaft (4)
1977	SEATTLE SLEW (3)	1986	Lady's Secret (4)	1995	Cigar (5)	2004	Ghostzapper (4)
1978	AFFIRMED (3)	1987	Ferdinand (4)	1996	Cigar (6)	2005	Saint Liam (5)
1979	Affirmed (4)	1988	Alysheba (4)	1997	Favorite Trick (2)		

Older Male

Year		Year		Year		Year	
1971	Ack Ack (5)	1980	Spectacular Bid (4)	1989	Blushing John (4)	1998	Skip Away (5)
1972	Autobiography (4)	1981	John Henry (6)	1990	Criminal Type (5)	1999	Victory Gallop (4)
1973	Riva Ridge (4)	1982	Lemhi Gold (4)	1991	Black Tie Affair (5)	2000	Lemon Drop Kid (4)
1974	Forego (4)	1983	Bates Motel (4)	1992	Pleasant Tap (5)	2001	Tiznow (4)
1975	Forego (5)	1984	Slew o' Gold (4)	1993	Bertrando (4)	2002	Left Bank (5)
1976	Forego (6)	1985	Vanlandingham (4)	1994	The Wicked North (4)	2003	Mineshaft (4)
1977	Forego (7)	1986	Turkoman (4)	1995	Cigar (5)	2004	Ghostzapper (4)
1978	Seattle Slew (4)	1987	Ferdinand (4)	1996	Cigar (6)	2005	Saint Liam (5)
1979	Affirmed (4)	1988	Alysheba (4)	1997	Skip Away (4)		

Older Female

Year		Year		Year		Year	
1971	Shuvee (5)	1980	Glorious Song (4)	1989	Bayakoa (5)	1998	Escena (5)
1972	Typecast (6)	1981	Relaxing (5)	1990	Bayakoa (6)	1999	Beautiful Pleasure (4)
1973	Susan's Girl (4)	1982	Track Robbery (6)	1991	Queena (5)	2000	Riboletta (5)
1974	Desert Vixen (4)	1983	Amb. of Luck (4)	1992	Paseana (5)	2001	Gourmet Girl (6)
1975	Susan's Girl (6)	1984	Princess Rooney (4)	1993	Paseana (6)	2002	Azeri (4)
1976	Proud Delta (4)	1985	Life's Magic (4)	1994	Sky Beauty (4)	2003	Azeri (5)
1977	Cascapedia (4)	1986	Lady's Secret (4)	1995	Inside Information (4)	2004	Azeri (6)
1978	Late Bloomer (4)	1987	North Sider (5)	1996	Jewel Princess (4)	2005	Ashado (4)
1979	Waya (5)	1988	Personal Ensign (4)	1997	Hidden Lake (4)		

3-Year-Old Male

Year		Year		Year		Year	
1971	Canonero II	1980	Temperence Hill	1989	Sunday Silence	1998	Real Quiet
1972	Key to the Mint	1981	Pleasant Colony	1990	Unbridled	1999	Charismatic
1973	SECRETARIAT	1982	Conquistador Cielo	1991	Hansel	2000	Tiznow
1974	Little Current	1983	Slew o' Gold	1992	A.P. Indy	2001	Point Given
1975	Wajima	1984	Swale	1993	Prairie Bayou	2002	War Emblem
1976	Bold Forbes	1985	Spend A Buck	1994	Holy Bull	2003	Funny Cide
1977	SEATTLE SLEW	1986	Snow Chief	1995	Thunder Gulch	2004	Smarty Jones
1978	AFFIRMED	1987	Alysheba	1996	Skip Away	2005	Afleet Alex
1979	Spectacular Bid	1988	Risen Star	1997	Silver Charm		

Eclipse Awards (Cont.)

3-Year-Old Filly

Year		Year		Year		Year	
1971	Turkish Trousers	1980	Genuine Risk	1989	Open Mind	1998	Banshee Breeze
1972	Susan's Girl	1981	Wayward Lass	1990	Go for Wand	1999	Silverbulletday
1973	Desert Vixen	1982	Christmas Past	1991	Dance Smartly	2000	Surfside
1974	Chris Evert	1983	Heartlight No. One	1992	Saratoga Dew	2001	Xtra Heat
1975	Ruffian	1984	Life's Magic	1993	Hollywood Wildcat	2002	Farda Amiga
1976	Revidere	1985	Mom's Command	1994	Heavenly Prize	2003	Bird Town
1977	Our Mims	1986	Tiffany Lass	1995	Serena's Song	2004	Ashado
1978	Tempest Queen	1987	Sacahuista	1996	Yanks Music	2005	Smuggler
1979	Davona Dale	1988	Winning Colors	1997	Ajina		

2-Year-Old Male

Year		Year		Year		Year	
1971	Riva Ridge	1980	Lord Avie	1989	Rhythm	1998	Answer Lively
1972	Secretariat	1981	Deputy Minister	1990	Fly So Free	1999	Anees
1973	Protagonist	1982	Roving Boy	1991	Arazi	2000	Macho Uno
1974	Foolish Pleasure	1983	Devil's Bag	1992	Gilded Time	2001	Johannesburg
1975	Honest Pleasure	1984	Chief's Crown	1993	Dehere	2002	Vindication
1976	Seattle Slew	1985	Tasso	1994	Timber Country	2003	Action This Day
1977	Affirmed	1986	Capote	1995	Maria's Mon	2004	Declan's Moon
1978	Spectacular Bid	1987	Forty Niner	1996	Boston Harbor	2005	Stevie Wonderboy
1979	Rockhill Native	1988	Easy Goer	1997	Favorite Trick		

2-Year-Old Filly

Year		Year		Year		Year	
1971	Numbered Account	1979	Smart Angle	1988	Open Mind	1997	Countess Diana
1972	La Prevoyante	1980	Heavenly Cause	1989	Go for Wand	1998	Silverbulletday
1973	Talking Picture	1981	Before Dawn	1990	Meadow Star	1999	Chilukki
1974	Ruffian	1982	Landaluce	1991	Pleasant Stage	2000	Caressing
1975	Dearly Precious	1983	Althea	1992	Eliza	2001	Tempera
1976	Sensational	1984	Outstandingly	1993	Phone Chatter	2002	Storm Flag Flying
1977	Lakeville Miss	1985	Family Style	1994	Flanders	2003	Halfbridled
1978	(TIE) Candy Eclair	1986	Brave Raj	1995	Golden Attraction	2004	Sweet Catomine
	& It's in the Air	1987	Epitome	1996	Storm Song	2005	Folklore

Champion Turf Horse

Year		Year		Year		Year	
1971	Run the Gantlet (3)	1973	SECRETARIAT (3)	1975	Snow Knight (4)	1977	Johnny D (3)
1972	Cougar II (6)	1974	Dahlia (4)	1976	Youth (3)	1978	Mac Diarmida (3)

Champion Male Turf Horse

Year		Year		Year		Year	
1979	Bowl Game (5)	1986	Manila (3)	1993	Kotashaan (5)	2000	Kalanisi (4)
1980	John Henry (5)	1987	Theatrical (5)	1994	Paradise Creek (5)	2001	Fantastic Light (5)
1981	John Henry (6)	1988	Sunshine Forever (3)	1995	Northern Spur (4)	2002	High Chaparral (3)
1982	Perrault (5)	1989	Steinlen (6)	1996	Singspiel (4)	2003	High Chaparral (4)
1983	John Henry (8)	1990	Itsallgreektome (3)	1997	Chief Bearhart (4)	2004	Kitten's Joy (3)
1984	John Henry (9)	1991	Tight Spot (4)	1998	Buck's Boy (5)	2005	Leroidesanimaux (5)
1985	Cozzene (4)	1992	Sky Classic (5)	1999	Daylami (5)		

Champion Female Turf Horse

Year		Year		Year		Year	
1979	Trillion (5)	1986	Estrapade (6)	1993	Flawlessly (5)	2000	Perfect Sting (4)
1980	Just A Game II (4)	1987	Miesque (3)	1994	Hatoof (5)	2001	Banks Hill (3)
1981	De La Rose (4)	1988	Miesque (4)	1995	Possibly Perfect (5)	2002	Golden Apples (4)
1982	April Run (4)	1989	Brown Bess (7)	1996	Wandesta (5)	2003	Islington (5)
1983	All Along (4)	1990	Laugh and Be Merry (5)	1997	Ryafan (3)	2004	Ouija Board (3)
1984	Royal Heroine (4)	1991	Miss Alleged (4)	1998	Fiji (4)	2005	Intercontinental (5)
1985	Pebbles (4)	1992	Flawlessly (4)	1999	Soaring Softly (4)		

Sprinter

Year		Year		Year		Year	
1971	Ack Ack (5)	1979	Star de Naskra (4)	1988	Gulch (4)	1997	Smoke Glacken (3)
1972	Chou Croute (4)	1980	Plugged Nickle (3)	1989	Safely Kept (3)	1998	Reraise (3)
1973	Shecky Greene (3)	1981	Guilty Conscience (5)	1990	Housebuster (3)	1999	Artax (4)
1974	Forego (4)	1982	Gold Beauty (3)	1991	Housebuster (4)	2000	Kona Gold (6)
1975	Gallant Bob (3)	1983	Chinook Pass (4)	1992	Rubiano (5)	2001	Squirtle Squirt (3)
1976	My Juliet (4)	1984	Eillo (4)	1993	Cardmania (7)	2002	Orientate (4)
1977	What a Summer (4)	1985	Precisionist (4)	1994	Cherokee Run (4)	2003	Aldebaran (5)
1978	(TIE) Dr. Patches (4)	1986	Smile (4)	1995	Not Surprising (4)	2004	Speightstown (6)
	& J.O. Tobin (4)	1987	Groovy (4)	1996	Lit de Justice (6)	2005	Lost in the Fog (3)

Steeplechase or Hurdle Horse

Year		Year		Year		Year	
1971	Shadow Brook (7)	1980	Zaccio (4)	1989	Highland Bud (4)	1998	Flat Top (5)
1972	Soothsayer (5)	1981	Zaccio (5)	1990	Morley Street (6)	1999	Lonesome Glory (11)
1973	Athenian Idol (5)	1982	Zaccio (6)	1991	Morley Street (7)	2000	All Gong (6)
1974	Gran Kan (8)	1983	Flatterer (4)	1992	Lonesome Glory (4)	2001	Pompeyo (8)
1975	Life's Illusion (4)	1984	Flatterer (5)	1993	Lonesome Glory (5)	2002	Flat Top (8)
1976	Straight and True (6)	1985	Flatterer (6)	1994	Warm Spell (6)	2003	McDynamo (6)
1977	Cafe Prince (7)	1986	Flatterer (7)	1995	Lonesome Glory (7)	2004	Hirapour (8)
1978	Cafe Prince (8)	1987	Inlander (6)	1996	Correggio (5)	2005	McDynamo (8)
1979	Martie's Anger (4)	1988	Jimmy Lorenzo (6)	1997	Lonesome Glory (9)		

Outstanding Jockey

Year		Year		Year		Year	
1971	Laffit Pincay Jr.	1980	Chris McCarron	1989	Kent Desormeaux	1998	Gary Stevens
1972	Braulio Baeza	1981	Bill Shoemaker	1990	Craig Perret	1999	Jorge Chavez
1973	Laffit Pincay Jr.	1982	Angel Cordero Jr.	1991	Pat Day	2000	Jerry Bailey
1974	Laffit Pincay Jr.	1983	Angel Cordero Jr.	1992	Kent Desormeaux	2001	Jerry Bailey
1975	Braulio Baeza	1984	Pat Day	1993	Mike Smith	2002	Jerry Bailey
1976	Sandy Hawley	1985	Laffit Pincay Jr.	1994	Mike Smith	2003	Jerry Bailey
1977	Steve Cauthen	1986	Pat Day	1995	Jerry Bailey	2004	John Velazquez
1978	Darrel McHargue	1987	Pat Day	1996	Jerry Bailey	2005	John Velazquez
1979	Laffit Pincay Jr.	1988	Jose Santos	1997	Jerry Bailey		

Outstanding Apprentice Jockey

Year		Year		Year		Year	
1971	Gene St. Leon	1981	Richard Migliore	1991	Mickey Walls	2000	Tyler Baze
1972	Thomas Wallis	1982	Alberto Delgado	1992	Rosemary Homeister	2001	Jeremy Rose
1973	Steve Valdez	1983	Declan Murphy	1993	Juan Umana	2002	Ryan Fogelsonger
1974	Chris McCarron	1984	Wesley Ward	1994	Dale Beckner	2003	Eddie Castro
1975	Jimmy Edwards	1985	Art Madrid Jr.	1995	Ramon B. Perez	2004	Brian Hernandez Jr.
1976	George Martens	1986	Allen Stacy	1996	Neil Poznansky	2005	Emma-Jayne Wilson
1977	Steve Cauthen	1987	Kent Desormeaux	1997	Roberto Rosado		
1978	Ron Franklin	1988	Steve Capanas		& Philip Teator		
1979	Cash Asmussen	1989	Michael Luzzi	1998	Shaun Bridgmohan		
1980	Frank Lovato Jr.	1990	Mark Johnston	1999	Ariel Smith		

Outstanding Trainer

Year		Year		Year		Year	
1971	Charlie Whittingham	1980	Bud Delp	1989	Charlie Whittingham	1998	Bob Baffert
1972	Lucien Laurin	1981	Ron McAnally	1990	Carl Nafzger	1999	Bob Baffert
1973	H. Allen Jerkens	1982	Charlie Whittingham	1991	Ron McAnally	2000	Bobby Frankel
1974	Sherill Ward	1983	Woody Stephens	1992	Ron McAnally	2001	Bobby Frankel
1975	Steve DiMauro	1984	Jack Van Berg	1993	Bobby Frankel	2002	Bobby Frankel
1976	Laz Barrera	1985	D. Wayne Lukas	1994	D. Wayne Lukas	2003	Bobby Frankel
1977	Laz Barrera	1986	D. Wayne Lukas	1995	Bill Mott	2004	Todd Pletcher
1978	Laz Barrera	1987	D. Wayne Lukas	1996	Bill Mott	2005	Todd Pletcher
1979	Laz Barrera	1988	Shug McGaughey	1997	Bob Baffert		

Outstanding Owner

Year		Year		Year		Year	
1971	Mr. & Mrs. E.E. Fogleson	1980	Mr. & Mrs. Bertram Firestone	1988	Ogden Phipps	1997	Carolyn Hine
1972-73	No award	1981	Dotsam Stable	1989	Ogden Phipps	1998	Frank Stronach
1974	Dan Lasater	1982	Viola Sommer	1990	Frances Genter	1999	Frank Stronach
1975	Dan Lasater	1983	John Franks	1991	Sam-Son Farms	2000	Frank Stronach
1976	Dan Lasater	1984	John Franks	1992	Juddmonte Farms	2001	Richard Englander
1977	Maxwell Gluck	1985	Mr. & Mrs. Gene Klein	1993	John Franks	2002	Richard Englander
1978	Harbor View Farm	1986	Mr. & Mrs. Gene Klein	1994	John Franks	2003	Juddmonte Farms
1979	Harbor View Farm	1987	Mr. & Mrs. Gene Klein	1995	Allen Paulson	2004	Ken & Sarah Ramsey
				1996	Allen Paulson	2005	Michael Gill

Eclipse Awards (Cont.)

Outstanding Breeder

Year		Year		Year		Year	
1971	Paul Mellon	1980	Mrs. Henry Paxson	1989	North Ridge Farm	1998	John & Betty Mabee
1972	C.T. Chenery	1981	Golden Chance Farm	1990	Calumet Farm	1999	William S. Farish
1973	C.T. Chenery	1982	Fred W. Hooper	1991	John & Betty Mabee	2000	Frank Stronach
1974	John W. Galbreath	1983	Edward P. Taylor	1992	William S. Farish	2001	Juddmonte Farms
1975	Fred W. Hooper	1984	Claiborne Farm	1993	Allan Paulson	2002	Juddmonte Farms
1976	Nelson Bunker Hunt	1985	Nelson Bunker Hunt	1994	William T. Young	2003	Juddmonte Farms
1977	Edward P. Taylor	1986	Paul Mellon	1995	Juddmonte Farms	2004	Adena Springs
1978	Harbor View Farm	1987	Nelson Bunker Hunt	1996	Farnsworth Farms	2005	Adena Springs
1979	Claiborne Farm	1988	Ogden Phipps	1997	John & Betty Mabee		

Award of Merit

Year		Year		Year		Year	
1976	Jack J. Dreyfus	1986	Herman Cohen	1993	Paul Mellon	2001	Pete Pederson
1977	Steve Cauthen	1987	J.B. Faulconer	1994	Alfred G. Vanderbilt		& Harry T. Mangurian
1978	Dinny Phipps	1988	John Forsythe	1995	Ted Bassett III	2002	Ogden Phipps
1979	Jimmy Kilroe	1989	Michael Sandler	1996	Allen Paulson		& Howard Battle
1980	John D. Shapiro	1990	Warner L. Jones	1997	Bob & Beverly Lewis	2003	Richard Duchossois
1981	Bill Shoemaker	1991	Fred W. Hooper	1998	D.G. Van Clief Jr.	2004	Oaklawn Park &
1984	John Gaines	1992	Joe Hirsch	2000	Jim McKay		the Cella family
1985	Keene Daingerfield		& Robert P. Strub			2005	Penny Chenery

Special Award

Year		Year		Year		Year	
1971	Robert J. Kleberg	1985	Arlington Park	1995	Russell Baze	2001	Sheikh Mohammed
1974	Charles Hatton	1987	Anheuser-Busch	1998	Oak Tree Racing		al-Maktoum
1976	Bill Shoemaker	1988	Edward J. DeBartolo Sr.		Assoc.	2002	Keeneland Library
1980	John T. Landry	1989	Richard Duchossois	1999	Laffit Pincay Jr.	2004	Dale Baird
	& Pierre E. Bellocq	1994	Eddie Arcaro	2000	John Hettinger	2005	Cash is King Stable
1984	C.V. Whitney		& John Longden				

HARNESS RACING

Triple Crown Winners
PACERS

Ten three-year-olds have won the Cane Pace, Little Brown Jug and Messenger Stakes in the same year since the Pacing Triple Crown was established in 1956. No trainer or driver has won it more than once.

Year		Driver	Trainer	Owner
1959	**Adios Butler**	Clint Hodgins	Paige West	Paige West & Angelo Pellillo
1965	**Bret Hanover**	Frank Ervin	Frank Ervin	Richard Downing
1966	**Romeo Hanover**	Bill Myer & George Sholty*	Jerry Silverman	Lucky Star Stables & Morton Finder
1968	**Rum Customer**	Billy Haughton	Billy Haughton	Kennilworth Farms & L.C. Mancuso
1970	**Most Happy Fella**	Stanley Dancer	Stanley Dancer	Egyptian Acres Stable
1980	**Niatross**	Clint Galbraith	Clint Galbraith	Niagara Acres, Niatross Stables & Clint Galbraith
1983	**Ralph Hanover**	Ron Waples	Stew Firlotte	Waples Stable, Pointsetta Stable, Grant's Direct Stable & P.J. Baugh
1997	**Western Dreamer**	Mike Lachance	Bill Robinson Stable	Matthew, Daniel and Patrick Daly
1999	**Blissful Hall**	Ron Pierce	Benn Wallace	Daniel Plouffe
2003	**No Pan Intended**	David Miller	Ivan Sugg	Bob Glazer

*Myer drove Romeo Hanover in the Cane, Sholty in the other two races.

TROTTERS

Seven three-year-olds have won the Yonkers Trot, Hambletonian and Kentucky Futurity in the same year since the Trotting Triple Crown was established in 1955. Stanley Dancer is the only driver/trainer to win it twice.

Year		Driver/Trainer	Owner
1955	**Scott Frost**	Joe O'Brien	S.A. Camp Farms
1963	**Speedy Scot**	Ralph Baldwin	Castleton Farms
1964	**Ayres**	John Simpson Sr.	Charlotte Sheppard
1968	**Nevele Pride**	Stanley Dancer	Nevele Acres & Lou Resnick
1969	**Lindy's Pride**	Howard Beissinger	Lindy Farms
1972	**Super Bowl**	Stanley Dancer	Rachel Dancer & Rose Hild Breeding Farm
2004	**Windsong's Legacy**	Trond Smedshammer	Fredrick Lindegaard

Triple Crown Near Misses
PACERS

Nine horses have won the first two legs of the Triple Crown, but not the third. The Cane Pace (CP), Little Brown Jug (LBJ), and Messenger Stakes (MS) have not always been run in the same order so numbers after races won indicate sequence for that year.

Year		CP	LBJ	MS	Year		CP	LBJ	MS
1957	**Torpid**	won, 1	won, 2	DNF*	1990	**Jake and Elwood**	won, 1	NE	won, 2
1960	**Countess Adios**	won, 2	NE	won, 1	1992	**Western Hanover**	won, 1	2nd*	won, 2
1971	**Albatross**	won, 2	2nd*	won, 1	1993	**Rijadh**	won, 1	2nd*	won, 2
1976	**Keystone Ore**	won, 1	won, 2	2nd*	1998	**Shady Character**	won, 1	won, 2	6th*
1986	**Barberry Spur**	won, 1	won, 2	2nd*					

*Winning horses:** Meadow Lands (1957), Nansemond (1971), Windshield Wiper (1976), Amity Chef (1986), Fake Left (1992), Life Sign (1993), Fit for Life (1998).

Note: Torpid (1957) scratched before the final heat; Countess Adios (1960) and Jake and Elwood (1990) not eligible for Little Brown Jug.

TROTTERS

Eight horses have won the first two legs of the Triple Crown— the Yonkers Trot (YT) and the Hambletonian (Ham)—but not the third. The winner of the Kentucky Futurity (KF) is listed.

Year		YT	Ham	KF	Year		YT	Ham	KF
1962	**A.C.'s Viking**	won	won	Safe Mission	1987	**Mack Lobell**	won	won	Napoletano
1976	**Steve Lobell**	won	won	Quick Pay	1993	**American Winner**	won	won	Pine Chip
1977	**Green Speed**	won	won	Texas	1996	**Continentalvictory**	won	won	Running Sea
1978	**Speedy Somolli**	won	won	Doublemint	1998	**Muscles Yankee**	won	won	Trade Balance

Note: Green Speed (1977) was not eligible for the Kentucky Futurity; Continentalvictory (1996) was withdrawn from the Kentucky Futurity due to a leg injury.

The Hambletonian

For three-year-old trotters. Inaugurated in 1926 and has been held in Syracuse, N.Y.; Lexington, Ky.; Goshen, N.Y.; Yonkers, N.Y.; Du Quoin, Ill.; and since 1981 at The Meadowlands in East Rutherford, N.J.

Run at one mile since 1947. Winning horse must win two heats.

Drivers with most wins: John Campbell (6); Stanley Dancer, Billy Haughton, Mike Lachance and Ben White (4); Howard Beissinger, Del Cameron and Henry Thomas (3).

Year	Horse	Driver	Fastest Heat	Year	Horse	Driver	Fastest Heat
1926	**Guy McKinney**	Nat Ray	2:04¾	1960	**Blaze Hanover**	Joe O'Brien	1:59⅗
1927	**Iosola's Worthy**	Marvin Childs	2:03¾	1961	**Harlan Dean**	James Arthur	1:58⅖
1928	**Spencer**	W.H. Lessee	2:02½	1962	**A.C.'s Viking**	Sanders Russell	1:59⅗
1929	**Walter Dear**	Walter Cox	2:02¾	1963	**Speedy Scot**	Ralph Baldwin	1:57⅗
				1964	**Ayres**	John Simpson Sr.	1:56⅘
1930	**Hanover's Bertha**	Tom Berry	2:03	1965	**Egyptian Candor**	Del Cameron	2:03⅘
1931	**Calumet Butler**	R.D. McMahon	2:03¼	1966	**Kerry Way**	Frank Ervin	1:58⅘
1932	**The Marchioness**	Will Caton	2:01¼	1967	**Speedy Streak**	Del Cameron	2:00
1933	**Mary Reynolds**	Ben White	2:03¾	1968	**Nevele Pride**	Stanley Dancer	1:59⅖
1934	**Lord Jim**	Doc Parshall	2:02¾	1969	**Lindy's Pride**	Howard Beissinger	1:57⅗
1935	**Greyhound**	Sep Palin	2:02¼				
1936	**Rosalind**	Ben White	2:01¾	1970	**Timothy T**	John Simpson Jr.	1:58⅖
1937	**Shirley Hanover**	Henry Thomas	2:01½	1971	**Speedy Crown**	Howard Beissinger	1:57⅖
1938	**McLin Hanover**	Henry Tomas	2:01¼	1972	**Super Bowl**	Stanley Dancer	1:56⅖
1939	**Peter Astra**	Doc Parshall	2:04¼	1973	**Flirth**	Ralph Baldwin	1:57⅕
				1974	**Christopher T**	Billy Haughton	1:58⅗
1940	**Spencer Scott**	Fred Egan	2:02	1975	**Bonefish**	Stanley Dancer	1:59
1941	**Bill Gallon**	Lee Smith	2:05	1976	**Steve Lobell**	Billy Haughton	1:56⅖
1942	**The Ambassador**	Ben White	2:04	1977	**Green Speed**	Billy Haughton	1:55⅗
1943	**Volo Song**	Ben White	2:02½	1978	**Speedy Somolli**	Howard Beissinger	1:55
1944	**Yankee Maid**	Henry Thomas	2:04	1979	**Legend Hanover**	George Sholty	1:56⅕
1945	**Titan Hanover**	Harry Pownall Sr.	2:04				
1946	**Chestertown**	Thomas Berry	2:02½	1980	**Burgomeister**	Billy Haughton	1:56⅗
1947	**Hoot Mon**	Sep Palin	2:00	1981	**Shiaway St. Pat**	Ray Remmen	2:01½
1948	**Demon Hanover**	Harrison Hoyt	2:02	1982	**Speed Bowl**	Tommy Haughton	1:56⅘
1949	**Miss Tilly**	Fred Egan	2:01⅖	1983	**Duenna**	Stanley Dancer	1:57⅖
				1984	**Historic Freight**	Ben Webster	1:56⅖
1950	**Lusty Song**	Del Miller	2:02	1985	**Prakas**	Bill O'Donnell	1:54⅘
1951	**Mainliner**	Guy Crippen	2:02⅗	1986	**Nuclear Kosmos**	Ulf Thoresen	1:55⅖
1952	**Sharp Note**	Bion Shively	2:02⅗	1987	**Mack Lobell**	John Campbell	1:53⅗
1953	**Helicopter**	Harry Harvey	2:01⅗	1988	**Armbro Goal**	John Campbell	1:54⅗
1954	**Newport Dream**	Del Cameron	2:02⅘	1989	**Park Avenue Joe**	Ron Waples	1:54⅗
1955	**Scott Frost**	Joe O'Brien	2:00⅗		**& Probe ***	Bill Fahy	
1956	**The Intruder**	Ned Bower	2:01⅖				
1957	**Hickory Smoke**	John Simpson Sr.	2:00⅕	1990	**Harmonious**	John Campbell	1:54⅕
1958	**Emily's Pride**	Flave Nipe	1:59⅘	1991	**Giant Victory**	Jack Moiseyev	1:54⅖
1959	**Diller Hanover**	Frank Ervin	2:01⅕	1992	**Alf Palema**	Mickey McNichol	1:56⅖

*In 1989, Park Avenue Joe and Probe finished in a dead heat in the race-off. They were later declared co-winners, but Park Avenue Joe was awarded 1st place money because his three-race summary (2-1-1) was better than Probe's (1-9-1).

The Hambletonian (Cont.)

Year		Driver	Fastest Heat	Year		Driver	Fastest Heat
1993	**American Winner**	Ron Pierce	1:53⅕	2000	**Yankee Paco**	Trevor Ritchie	1:53⅖
1994	**Victory Dream**	Mike Lachance	1:54⅕	2001	**Scarlet Knight**	Stefan Melander	1:53⅘
1995	**Tagliabue**	John Campbell	1:54⅘	2002	**Chip Chip Hooray**	Eric Ledford	1:53⅗
1996	**Continentalvictory**	Mike Lachance	1:52⅘	2003	**Amigo Hall**	Mike Lachance	1:54
1997	**Malabar Man**	Mal Burroughs	1:55	2004	**Windsong's Legacy**	T. Smedshammer	1:54⅕
1998	**Muscles Yankee**	John Campbell	1:52⅖	2005	**Vivid Photo**	Roger Hammer	1:52⅖
1999	**Self Possessed**	Mike Lachance	1:51⅗	2006	**Glidemaster**	John Campbell	1:51⅕

The Little Brown Jug

Harness racing's most prestigious race for three-year-old pacers. Inaugurated in 1946 and held annually at the Delaware, Ohio County Fairgrounds. Winning horse must win two heats.

Year	Year	Year	Year
1946 Ensign Hanover	1962 Lehigh Hanover	1978 Happy Escort	1994 Magical Mike
1947 Forbes Chief	1963 Overtrick	1979 Hot Hitter	1995 Nick's Fantasy
1948 Knight Dream	1964 Vicar Hanover	1980 Niatross	1996 Armbro Operative
1949 Good Time	1965 Bret Hanover	1981 Fan Hanover	1997 Western Dreamer
1950 Dudley Hanover	1966 Romeo Hanover	1982 Merger	1998 Shady Character
1951 Tar Heel	1967 Best Of All	1983 Ralph Hanover	1999 Blissful Hall
1952 Meadow Rice	1968 Rum Customer	1984 Colt Fortysix	2000 Astreos
1953 Keystoner	1969 Laverne Hanover	1985 Nihilator	2001 Bettor's Delight
1954 Adios Harry	1970 Most Happy Fella	1986 Barberry Spur	2002 Million Dollar Cam
1955 Quick Chief	1971 Nansemond	1987 Jaguar Spur	2003 No Pan Intended
1956 Noble Adios	1972 Strike Out	1988 B.J. Scoot	2004 Timesarechanging
1957 Torpid	1973 Melvin's Woe	1989 Goalie Jeff	2005 P-Forty-Seven
1958 Shadow Wave	1974 Armbro Omaha	1990 Beach Towel	2006 Mr. Feelgood
1959 Adios Butler	1975 Seatrain	1991 Precious Bunny	
1960 Bullet Hanover	1976 Keystone Ore	1992 Fake Left	
1961 Henry T. Adios	1977 Governor Skipper	1993 Life Sign	

Annual Awards
Harness Horse of the Year

Selected since 1947 by U.S. Trotting Association and the U.S. Harness Writers Association; age of winning horse is noted; (t) indicates trotter and (p) indicates pacer. **Multiple winners:** Bret Hanover and Nevele Pride (3); Adios Butler, Albatross, Cam Fella, Good Time, Mack Lobell, Moni Maker, Niatross and Scott Frost (2).

Year	Year	Year	Year
1947 Victory Song (4t)	1962 Su Mac Lad (8t)	1977 Green Speed (3t)	1992 Artsplace (4p)
1948 Rodney (4t)	1963 Speedy Scot (3t)	1978 Abercrombie (3p)	1993 Staying Together (4p)
1949 Good Time (3p)	1964 Bret Hanover (2p)	1979 Niatross (2p)	1994 Cam's Card Shark (3p)
1950 Proximity (8t)	1965 Bret Hanover (3p)	1980 Niatross (3p)	1995 CR Kay Suzie (3t)
1951 Pronto Don (6t)	1966 Bret Hanover (4p)	1981 Fan Hanover (3p)	1996 Continentalvictory (3t)
1952 Good Time (6p)	1967 Nevele Pride (2t)	1982 Cam Fella (3p)	1997 Malabar Man (3t)
1953 Hi Lo's Forbes (5p)	1968 Nevele Pride (3t)	1983 Cam Fella (4p)	1998 Moni Maker (5t)
1954 Stenographer (3t)	1969 Nevele Pride (4t)	1984 Fancy Crown (3t)	1999 Moni Maker (6t)
1955 Scott Frost (3t)	1970 Fresh Yankee (7t)	1985 Nihilator (3p)	2000 Gallo Blue Chip (3p)
1956 Scott Frost (4t)	1971 Albatross (3p)	1986 Forrest Skipper (4p)	2001 Bunny Lake (3p)
1957 Torpid (3p)	1972 Albatross (4p)	1987 Mack Lobell (3t)	2002 Real Desire (4p)
1958 Emily's Pride (3t)	1973 Sir Dalrae (4p)	1988 Mack Lobell (4t)	2003 No Pan Intended (3p)
1959 Bye Bye Byrd (4p)	1974 Delmonica Hanover (5t)	1989 Matt's Scooter (4p)	2004 Rainbow Blue (3p)
1960 Adios Butler (4p)	1975 Savoir (7t)	1990 Beach Towel (3p)	2005 Rocknroll Hanover (3p)
1961 Adios Butler (5p)	1976 Keystone Ore (3p)	1991 Precious Bunny (3p)	

Driver of the Year

Determined by Universal Driving Rating System (UDR) and presented by the Harness Tracks of America since 1968. Eligible drivers must have at least 1,000 starts for the season. **Multiple winners:** Herve Filion (10); Dave Palone (4); John Campbell, Walter Case Jr. and Mike Lachance (3); Tony Morgan, Bill O'Donnell, Luc Ouellette and Ron Waples (2).

Year	Year	Year	Year
1968 Stanley Dancer	1979 Ron Waples	1991 Walter Case Jr.	2002 Tony Morgan
1969 Herve Filion	1980 Ron Waples	1992 Walter Case Jr.	2003 Dave Palone
1970 Herve Filion	1981 Herve Filion	1993 Jack Moiseyev	2004 Dave Palone
1971 Herve Filion	1982 Bill O'Donnell	1994 Dave Magee	2005 Cat Manzi
1972 Herve Filion	1983 John Campbell	1995 Luc Ouellette	
1973 Herve Filion	1984 Bill O'Donnell	1996 Tony Morgan	
1974 Herve Filion	1985 Mike Lachance	& Luc Ouellette	
1975 Joe O'Brien	1986 Mike Lachance	1997 Tony Morgan	
1976 Herve Filion	1987 Mike Lachance	1998 Walter Case Jr.	
1977 Donald Dancer	1988 John Campbell	1999 Dave Palone	
1978 Carmine Abbatiello	1989 Herve Filion	2000 Dave Palone	
& Herve Filion	1990 John Campbell	2001 Stephane Bouchard	

TENNIS

2005 / 2006 YEAR IN REVIEW

Andre Agassi said an emotional goodbye after his third-round loss at the U.S. Open.

ROGER RULES

Federer grabs three more Grand Slam singles titles in 2006, but can't solve rival Nadal at the French Open.

THE LIST IS A SHORT ONE.

Really short. Andy Murray and Rafael Nadal. That's it.

Through early October, those are the only two men to have beaten Swiss sensation and world No. 1 Roger Federer in 2006.

Murray, the 19-year-old Scot, played David to Federer's Goliath in mid-August, taking a straight-set shocker in the second round of the Cincinnati Masters, and in the process, ended Federer's run of 55 consecutive wins on the hard court. It was the first time in 18 tournaments that Federer was ousted before the finals.

When it comes to Federer vs. Nadal, it isn't so much a case of David and Goliath, but rather Superman and Kryptonite. Between March 5 and June 11, the duo faced off against each other in a tournament finals four times...and Nadal won them all.

Three of those tournaments were on clay, the only surface Federer has yet to truly master. On the hard court, grass, carpet, wood, tile, or pretty much any surface you can play tennis on, Federer is the top dog. But clay neutralizes Federer's power, speed and aggressiveness, as it did to 14-time Grand Slam champion Pete Sampras. From the start of the 2005 season through early October, 2006, Federer boasted a record of 158-9. Five of those nine losses were on clay, and four of those five were to Nadal.

The 20-year-old Nadal is the only player who consistently looks the world's top player in the eyes without flinching. He's brash, strong-willed and supremely confident, and those attributes only intensify when he steps onto the clay surface. With an early-round win at the 2006 French Open, Nadal broke Guillermo Villas' 29-year-old record for consecutive clay-court wins with his 54th, and when he was done putting the finishing touches on his 1-6, 6-1, 6-4, 7-6 victory over Federer in the finals, the streak was at an even 60.

 Michael Morrison is Co-Editor of the ESPN Sports Almanac.

AP/Wide World Photos

> **Rafael Nadal**, right, got the better of **Roger Federer** at the 2006 French Open, but Federer returned the favor a month later at Wimbledon.

As he did in 2004, Federer won tennis' other three Grand Slam events with relative ease. He barely broke a sweat while rolling through the Australian Open in January, culminating in a four-set win over 21-year-old up-and-comer Marcos Baghdatis. He exacted a measure of revenge at Wimbledon with a four-set finals win over his rival Nadal for his fourth consecutive Wimbledon title. And he cruised to his third straight U.S. Open title with a finals win over the resurgent Andy Roddick.

He lost just two sets during the entire tournament en route to his ninth overall Grand Slam title in the past four years.

But as dominant as his performance was, Federer once again failed to grab the headlines at Flushing Meadows. Even camera-friendly Maria Sharapova, who won her second career Grand Slam title with a 6-4, 6-4 thrashing of Justine Henin-Hardenne, had to settle for second fiddle.

For the second year in a row, it was the Andre Agassi show.

In 2005 Agassi energized the New York faithful by becoming the oldest Grand Slam finalist in over 30 years, ultimately losing to Federer in four sets. In 2006 the 36-year-old fan favorite stole the spotlight again, this time with his emotional retirement.

Frenchwoman **Amelie Mauresmo** sat atop the women's rankings for much of the year and broke through with her first two Grand Slam singles titles

Over his 21-year hall of fame career, Agassi recorded 60 wins (good for seventh on the all-time list). He won eight Grand Slam titles, including the career Grand Slam (Australian, Wimbledon, French and U.S. Open titles), something only five men in the history of the sport have accomplished...and something both Sampras and Federer (thus far) failed to do. And he even added an Olympic gold medal in 1996.

He also grew up, physically, mentally and emotionally. He was married, divorced then married again, all in the public eye, and he transformed himself from a cocky, rebellious teenager with pink spandex, jean shorts and flowing blonde hair to a mature adult and a classy ambassador of the sport.

He thanked the crowd at Arthur Ashe Stadium one last time, and the crowd responded with a four-minute standing ovation.

"Over the last 21 years, I have found you and I will take you and the memory of you with me for the rest of my life. Thank you."

AP/Wide World Photos

THE TOP 10

Stories of the Year in **Tennis**

10 Baghdatis arrives.

Twenty-one-year-old Greek Cypriot Marcos Baghdatis bursts onto the men's tennis scene in 2006, as he enters the top-10 rankings and saves his best tennis for the year's biggest tournaments. Unseeded at the Australian Open, he advances to the finals, and takes the first set off of Roger Federer before eventually losing in four sets. He then reaches the semis at Wimbledon before falling to Rafael Nadal.

09 Jimmy Connors to the rescue!

Former top-ranked player Andy Roddick, without a win through the first half of the year, hires hall of famer Jimmy Connors as his coach in July, with the hopes of reviving his suddenly struggling career. The decision pays immediate dividends as Roddick regains his swagger and just one month after the hire, wins his first tournament of the year in Cincinnati. He follows that up by reaching the finals of the U.S. Open a month later.

08 Hingis returns.

Swiss Miss Martina Hingis, forced to retire in 2002 after multiple foot and ankle injuries, returns to the WTA Tour in 2006. It doesn't take long for her to return to the form that made her the No. 1 women's player in the world as she reaches the quarter-finals of the Australian Open in January, and wins the mixed doubles title with Mahesh Bhupathi.

07 Final Destination.

Justine Henin-Hardenne wins five tournaments through early October and reaches the finals in all four Grand Slam events. She successfully defends her title at the French Open with a win over Svetlana Kuznetsova for the fifth Grand Slam title of her career.

06 Maria Wins No. 2.

Six-foot-two Russian beauty Maria Sharapova loses just one set in seven matches in winning the U.S. Open for her second Grand Slam singles title. She cruises into the finals, where she wins, 6-4, 6-4 over...well, see Item No. 7.

05 Martina says goodbye.

Living legend Martina Navratilova retires a month shy of her 50th birthday, but not before adding one more Grand Slam title to her illustrious resume. She teams with Bob Bryan to win the mixed doubles championship at the U.S. Open for her 59th major title. Only Margaret Smith Court has more (62).

04 Nadal Repeats.
Second-ranked Rafael Nadal cements his position as the player to beat on clay with his second straight win at the French Open. He defeats top-ranked Roger Federer in the finals at Roland Garros, and goes 4-1 against Federer throughout the year, his only loss coming in the finals at Wimbledon.

03 Amelie.
Top-ranked Amelie Mauresmo earns four wins through early October, including the Australian Open and Wimbledon — the first two Grand Slam titles of her career. She is the first French women's singles champion at Wimbledon since Suzanne Lenglen in 1925.

02 Andre retires.
After bowing out of the U.S. Open with a third-round loss to 112th-ranked Benjamin Becker, 36-year-old Andre Agassi retires from tennis. He delivers a tearful speech to the crowd at Arthur Ashe Stadium, who shower him with applause and a four-minute standing ovation. He leaves the game with 60 wins and eight Grand Slam titles.

01 Roger the great.
He's only 25, but talk of him being the best men's tennis player of all-time has already begun. Roger Federer adds three more Grand Slam titles in 2006 (Australian, Wimbledon and U.S.) to make it nine overall. He reaches the finals in 13 of the 14 tournaments he enters through early October, and wins nine of those.

Roger That

As of Oct. 9, Roger Federer's season-long record of 77-5 was the fourth-best winning percentage in the ATP Tour's modern era.

		Record	Pct.
1	John McEnroe (1984)	82-3	.965
2	Jimmy Connors (1974)	89-4	.957
3	Roger Federer (2005)	81-4	.953
4	Roger Federer (2006)	77-5	.939
5	Roger Federer (2004)	74-6	.925
	Ivan Lendl (1986)	74-6	.925

Source: *ATP Tennis Weekly*

Number 1 Runs

Current top-ranked player Amelie Mauresmo has held her lofty position for a total of 35 weeks, good for tenth on the all-time list. She has a ways to go before reaching the top 5.

	Weeks	Years
Steffi Graf	377	1987-1997
M. Navratilova	331	1978-1987
Chris Evert	262	1975-1985
Martina Hingis	209	1997-2001
Monica Seles	178	1991-1996

Source: WTA Tour

2005-2006
Season in Review

SPORTS ALMANAC

Tournament Results

Winners of men's and women's pro singles championships from Nov. 6, 2005 through Oct. 8, 2006.

Men's ATP Tour

Late 2005

Finals	Tournament	Winner	Earnings	Runner-Up	Score
Nov. 6	TMS—Paris	Tomas Berdych	$447,000	I. Ljubicic	63 64 36 46 64
Nov. 20	Tennis Masters Cup (Shanghai)	David Nalbandian	1,400,000	R. Federer	67 67 62 61 76
Dec. 4	Davis Cup Final (Slovakia)	Croatia	—	Slovakia	3-2

2006 (through Oct. 8)

Finals	Tournament	Winner	Earnings	Runner-Up	Score
Jan. 8	Qatar ExxonMobil Open (Doha)	Roger Federer	$142,000	G. Monfils	63 76
Jan. 8	Next Generation Hardcourts (Adelaide)	Florent Serra	57,750	X. Malisse	63 64
Jan. 8	Chennai Open	Carlos Moya	52,000	P. Srichaphan	36 64 76
Jan. 14	Medibank International (Sydney)	James Blake	57,750	I. Andreev	62 36 76
Jan. 14	Heineken Open (Auckland)	Jarkko Nieminen	59,350	M. Ancic	62 62
Jan. 29	**Australian Open** (Melbourne)	Roger Federer	922,560	M. Baghdatis	57 75 60 62
Feb. 5	PBZ Zagreb Indoors	Ivan Ljubicic	52,877	S. Koubek	63 64
Feb. 5	Delray Beach Int'l Champs	Tommy Haas	52,000	X. Malisse	63 36 76
Feb. 5	Movistar Open (Vina Del Mar)	Jose Acasuso	52,000	N. Massu	64 63
Feb. 19	SAP Open (San Jose)	Andy Murray	52,000	L. Hewitt	26 61 76
Feb. 19	Copa Telmex (Buenos Aires)	Carlos Moya	52,000	F. Volandri	76 64
Feb. 19	Open 13 (Marseille)	Arnaud Clement	85,300	M. Ancic	64 62
Feb. 26	Regions Morgan Keegan Champs (Memphis)	Tommy Haas	128,000	R. Soderling	63 62
Feb. 26	ABN/AMRO World Tennis Tournament (Rotterdam)	Radek Stepanek	174,000	C. Rochus	60 63
Feb. 26	Brasil Open (Costa Do Sauipe)	Nicolas Massu	52,000	A. Martin	63 64
Mar. 5	Mexican Open (Acapulco)	Luis Horna	128,000	J.I. Chela	76 64
Mar. 5	Dubai Tennis Championships	Rafael Nadal	187,500	R. Federer	26 64 64
Mar. 5	Tennis Channel Open (Las Vegas)	James Blake	52,000	L. Hewitt	75 26 63
Mar. 19	TMS—Pacific Life Open (Indian Wells)	Roger Federer	455,000	J. Blake	75 63 60
Apr. 2	TMS—Nasdaq 100 Open (Miami)	Roger Federer	533,350	I. Ljubicic	76 76 76
Apr. 16	Valencia Open	Nicolas Almagro	56,544	G. Simon	62 63
Apr. 16	U.S. Clay Court Championships (Houston)	Mardy Fish	52,000	J. Melzer	36 64 63
Apr. 23	TMS—Monte Carlo Open	Rafael Nadal	418,778	R. Federer	62 67 63 76
Apr. 30	Grand Prix Hassan II (Casablanca)	Daniele Bracciali	55,700	N. Massu	61 64
Apr. 30	Open Seat Godo (Barcelona)	Rafael Nadal	164,000	T. Robredo	64 64 60
May 7	Estoril Open	David Nalbandian	95,500	N. Davydenko	63 64
May 7	BMW Open (Munich)	Olivier Rochus	56,100	K. Vliegen	64 62
May 14	TMS—Campionati Internazionali d'Italia (Rome)	Rafael Nadal	340,000	R. Federer	67 76 64 26 76
May 21	TMS—Hamburg	Tommy Robredo	340,000	R. Stepanek	61 63 63
May 27	Hypo Group Tennis Int'l (Portschach)	Nikolay Davydenko	56,200	A. Pavel	60 63
May 27	ARAG World Team Cup (Dusseldorf)	Croatia	—	Germany	2-1
June 11	**French Open** (Roland Garros)	Rafael Nadal	1,180,000	R. Federer	16 61 64 76
June 18	Gerry Weber Open (Halle)	Roger Federer	120,000	T. Berdych	60 67 62
June 18	Stella Artois Championships (London)	Lleyton Hewitt	100,000	J. Blake	64 64
June 24	Red Letter Days Open (Nottingham)	Richard Gasquet	55,000	J. Bjorkman	64 63
June 24	Ordina Open ('s-Hertogenbosch)	Mario Ancic	55,319	J. Hernych	60 57 75
July 9	**Wimbledon** (London)	Roger Federer	1,212,244	R. Nadal	60 76 67 63
July 16	Allianz Swiss Open (Gstaad)	Richard Gasquet	74,200	F. Lopez	76 67 63 63
July 16	Hall of Fame Championships (Newport)	Mark Philipoussis	52,000	J. Gimelstob	63 75
July 16	Synsam Swedish Open (Bastad)	Tommy Robredo	55,750	N. Davydenko	62 61
July 23	Dutch Open (Amersfoort)	Novak Djokovic	56,000	N. Massu	76 64
July 23	Mercedes Cup (Stuttgart)	David Ferrer	127,000	J. Acasuso	64 36 67 75 64
July 23	RCA Championships (Indianapolis)	James Blake	74,250	A. Roddick	46 64 76
July 30	Countrywide Classic (Los Angeles)	Tommy Haas	52,000	D. Tursunov	46 75 63
July 30	Croatia Open (Umag)	Stanislas Wawrinka	59,580	N. Djokovic	66 (ret.)
July 30	Generali Open (Kitzbuhel)	Agustin Calleri	110,000	J.I. Chela	76 62 63

Tournament Results (Cont.)

Finals	Tournament	Winner	Earnings	Runner-Up	Score
Aug. 6	Orange Prokom Open (Sopot)	Nikolay Davydenko	$75,391	F. Mayer	76 57 64
Aug. 6	Legg Mason Classic (Washington D.C.)	Arnaud Clement	74,250	A. Murray	76 62
Aug. 13	TMS—Rogers Masters (Toronto)	Roger Federer	95,500	R. Gasquet	26 63 62
Aug. 20	TMS—Western & Southern Financial Group Masters (Cincinnati)	Andy Roddick	400,000	J.C. Ferrero	63 64
Aug. 27	Pilot Pen (New Haven)	Nikolai Davydenko	84,000	A. Calleri	64 63
Sept. 10	**U.S. Open** (Flushing)	Roger Federer	1,200,000	A. Roddick	62 46 75 61
Sept. 17	China Open (Beijing)	Marcos Baghdatis	69,200	M. Ancic	64 60
Sept. 17	BCR Romanian Open (Bucharest)	Jurgen Melzer	56,107	F. Volandri	61 75
Oct. 1	Campionati Internazionali di Sicilia (Palermo)	Filippo Volandri	56,107	N. Lapentti	57 61 63
Oct. 1	Thailand Open (Bangkok)	James Blake	76,500	I. Ljubicic	63 61
Oct. 2	Kingfisher Airlines Open (Mumbai)	Dmitry Tursunov	52,000	T. Berdych	63 46 76
Oct. 8	Open de Moselle (Metz)	Novak Djokovic	55,500	J. Melzer	46 63 62
Oct. 8	AIG Japan Open (Tokyo)	Roger Federer	118,000	T. Henman	63 63

Note: TMS indicates tournament is part of the ATP Tennis Masters Series.

Women's WTA Tour

Late 2005

Finals	Tournament	Winner	Earnings	Runner-Up	Score
Nov. 6	Advanta Championships (Philadelphia)	Amelie Mauresmo	$93,000	E. Dementieva	75 26 75
Nov. 6	Bell Challenge (Quebec)	Amy Frazier	27,000	S. Arvidsson	61 75
Nov. 13	WTA Championships (Los Angeles)	Amelie Mauresmo	1,000,000	M. Pierce	57 76 64

2006 (through Oct. 8)

Finals	Tournament	Winner	Earnings	Runner-Up	Score
Jan. 7	Mondial Australian Hardcourts (Gold Coast) .	Lucie Safarova	$28,000	F. Pennetta	63 64
Jan. 7	ASB Bank Classic (Auckland)	Marion Bartoli	22,000	V. Zvonareva	62 62
Jan. 13	Moorilla International (Hobart)	Michaella Krajicek	22,900	I. Benesova	62 61
Jan. 13	Canberra Women's Classic	A. Medina Garrigues	22,900	Y. Jeong Cho	64 06 64
Jan. 13	Medibank International (Sydney)	Justine Henin-Hardenne	95,500	F. Schiavone	46 75 75
Jan. 29	**Australian Open** (Melbourne)	Amelie Mauresmo	847,500	J. Henin-Hardenne	61 20 (ret.)
Feb. 5	Toray Pan Pacific Open (Tokyo)	Elena Dementieva	196,900	M. Hingis	62 60
Feb. 12	Pattaya Open (Pattaya City)	Shahar Peer	25,650	J. Kostanic	63 61
Feb. 12	Open Gaz de France (Paris)	Amelie Mauresmo	95,500	M. Pierce	61 76
Feb. 19	Proximus Diamond Games (Antwerp)	Amelie Mauresmo	95,500	K. Clijsters	36 63 63
Feb. 19	Bangalore Open	Mara Santangelo	28,000	J. Kostanic	36 76 63
Feb. 25	Dubai Women's Duty Free Open	Justine Henin-Hardenne	159,000	M. Sharapova	75 62
Feb. 25	Regions Morgan Keegan Championships and Cellular South Cup (Memphis)	Sofia Arvidsson	28,000	M. Domachowska	62 26 63
Feb. 26	Copa Colsanitas (Bogota)	L. Dominguez Lino	28,000	F. Pennetta	76 64
Mar. 5	Qatar Total Open (Doha)	Nadia Petrova	95,500	A. Mauresmo	63 75
Mar. 5	Abierto Mexicano de Tenis (Acapulco)	Anna-Lena Groenefeld	27,970	F. Pennetta	61 46 62
Mar. 19	Pacific Life Open (Indian Wells)	Maria Sharapova	332,000	E. Dementieva	61 62
Apr. 1	Nasdaq 100 Open (Miami)	Svetlana Kuznetsova	533,350	M. Sharapova	64 63
Apr. 9	Bausch & Lomb Championships (Amelia Island)	Nadia Petrova	95,500	F. Schiavone	64 64
Apr. 16	Family Circle Cup (Charleston)	Nadia Petrova	196,900	P. Schnyder	63 46 61
May 7	J&S Cup (Warsaw)	Kim Clijsters	95,500	S. Kuznetsova	75 62
May 7	Estoril Open	Zheng Jie	22,900	Na Li	67 75 (ret.)
May 14	Qatar Total German Open (Berlin)	Nadia Petrova	196,900	J. Henin-Hardenne	46 64 75
May 14	ECM Prague Open	Shahar Peer	22,900	S. Stosur	46 62 61
May 21	Grand Prix De S.A.R. (Rabat)	Meghann Shaughnessy	22,900	M. Sucha	62 36 63
May 21	Internazionali d'Italia (Rome)	Martina Hingis	196,000	D. Safina	62 75
May 27	Strasbourg International	Nicole Vaidisova	28,000	Peng Shuai	76 63
May 27	Istanbul Cup	Shahar Peer	30,500	A. Myskina	16 63 76
June 5	**French Open** (Roland Garros)	Justine Henin-Hardenne	940,000	S. Kuznetsova	64 64
June 18	DFS Classic (Birmingham)	Vera Zvonareva	31,000	J. Jackson	76 76
June 24	Ordina Open ('s-Hertogenbosch)	Michaella Krajicek	28,000	D. Safina	63 64
June 24	Hastings Direct Int'l Champs (Eastbourne) . .	Justine Henin-Hardenne	95,500	A. Myskina	46 61 76
July 8	**Wimbledon** (London)	Amelie Mauresmo	1,156,721	J. Henin-Hardenne	26 63 64
July 23	Western & Southern Open (Cincinnati)	Vera Zvonareva	28,000	K. Srebotnik	62 64
July 23	Palermo International	A. Medina Garrigues	22,900	T. Garbin	64 64
July 30	Bank of the West Classic (Stanford)	Kim Clijsters	95,500	P. Schnyder	64 62
July 30	Tippmix Budapest Grand Prix	Anna Smashnova	22,900	L. Dominguez Lino	61 63
Aug. 6	Acura Classic (San Diego)	Maria Sharapova	196,600	K. Clijsters	75 75

Finals	Tournament	Winner	Earnings	Runner-Up	Score
Aug. 13	Nordea Nordic Light Open (Stockholm)	Zheng Jie	$22,900	A. Myskina	64 61
Aug. 13	JP Morgan Chase Open (Los Angeles)	Elena Dementieva	95,500	J. Jankovic	63 46 64
Aug. 20	Rogers Cup (Toronto)	Ana Ivanovic	196,900	M. Hingis	62 63
Aug. 27	Pilot Pen Tennis (New Haven)	Justine Henin-Hardenne	95,500	L. Davenport	60 10 (ret.)
Aug. 27	Forest Hills Women's Tennis Classic	Meghann Shaughnessy	22,000	A. Smashnova	16 60 64
Sept. 10	**U.S. Open** (Flushing)	Maria Sharapova	1,700,000	J. Henin-Hardenne	64 64
Sept. 17	2006 Fed Cup Final (Charleroi)	Italy	—	Belgium	3-2
Sept. 17	Wismilak International (Bali)	Svetlana Kuznetsova	35,000	M. Bartoli	75 62
Sept. 24	Banka Koper Slovenia Open (Portoroz)	Tamira Paszek	22,900	M.E. Camerin	75 61
Sept. 24	Sunfeast Open (Kolkata)	Martina Hingis	28,000	O. Poutchkova	60 64
Sept. 24	China Open (Beijing)	Svetlana Kuznetsova	95,500	A. Mauresmo	64 60
Oct. 1	Fortis Championships (Luxembourg)	Alona Bondarenko	95,500	F. Schiavone	63 62
Oct. 1	Guangzhou International	Anna Chakvetadze	28,000	A. Medina Garrigues	61 64
Oct. 1	Hansol Korea Open (Seoul)	Eleni Daniilidou	22,900	A. Sugiyama	63 26 76
Oct. 8	Porsche Grand Prix (Stuttgart)	Nadia Petrova	100,000	T. Golovin	63 76
Oct. 8	AIG Japan Open (Tokyo)	Marion Bartoli	28,000	A. Nakamura	26 62 62
Oct. 8	Tashkent Open	Sun Tiantian	22,925	I. Tulyaganova	62 64

2006 Grand Slam Tournaments
Australian Open

MEN'S SINGLES

FINAL EIGHT—# 1 Roger Federer; #4 David Nalbandian; #5 Nikolay Davydenko; #7 Ivan Ljubicic; Niclas Kiefer (21); Sebastien Grosjean (25); plus unseeded Marcos Baghdatis; and Fabrice Santoro.

Quarterfinals

Federer def. Davydenko		64 36 76(7) 76(5)
Kiefer def. Grosjean		63 06 64 67(1) 86
Baghdatis def. Ljubicic		64 62 46 36 63
Nalbandian def. Santoro		75 60 60

Semifinals

Federer def. Kiefer		63 57 60 62
Baghdatis def. Nalbandian		36 57 63 64 64

Final

Federer def. Baghdatis		57 75 60 62

WOMEN'S SINGLES

FINAL EIGHT—#1 Lindsay Davenport; #2 Kim Clijsters; #3 Amelie Mauresmo; #4 Maria Sharapova; #6 Nadia Petrova; #7 Patty Schnyder; #8 Justine Henin-Hardenne; plus unseeded Martina Hingis.

Quarterfinals

Mauresmo def. Schnyder		63 60
Henin-Hardenne def. Davenport		26 62 63
Clijsters def. Hingis		63 26 64
Sharapova def. Petrova		76(6) 64

Semifinals

Mauresmo def. Clijsters		57 62 32 (ret.)
Henin-Hardenne def. Sharapova		46 61 64

Final

Mauresmo def. Henin-Hardenne		61 20 (ret.)

DOUBLES FINALS

Men—#1 Bob Bryan & Mike Bryan def. #7 Martin Damm & Leander Paes, 4-6, 6-3, 6-4.

Women—#12 Yan Zi & Zheng Jie def. #1 Lisa Raymond & Samantha Stosur, 2-6, 7-6 (9-7), 6-3.

Mixed—Martina Hingis & Mahesh Bhupathi def. #6 Elena Likhovtseva & Daniel Nestor, 6-3, 6-3.

French Open

MEN'S SINGLES

FINAL EIGHT—#1 Roger Federer; #2 Rafael Nadal; #3 David Nalbandian; #4 Ivan Ljubicic; #6 Nikolay Davydenko; #12 Mario Ancic; plus unseeded Julien Benneteau and Novak Djokovic.

Quarterfinals

Federer def. Ancic		64 63 64
Nadal def. Djokovic		64 64
Nalbandian def. Davydenko		63 63 26 64
Ljubicic def. Benneteau		62 62 63

Semifinals

Federer def. Nalbandian		36 64 52
Nadal def. Ljubicic		64 62 76(7)

Final

Nadal def. Federer		16 61 64 76(4)

WOMEN'S SINGLES

FINAL EIGHT—#2 Kim Clijsters; #5 Justine Henin-Hardenne; #8 Svetlana Kuznetsova; #11 Venus Williams; #12 Martina Hingis; #13 Anna-Lena Groenefeld; #14 Dinara Safina; #16 Nicole Vaidisova.

Quarterfinals

Clijsters def. Hingis		76(5) 61
Henin-Hardenne def. Groenefeld		75 62
Kuznetsova def. Safina		76(5) 60
Vaidisova def. Williams		67(5) 61 63

Semifinals

Henin-Hardenne def. Clijsters		63 62
Kuznetsova def. Vaidisova		57 76(5) 62

Final

Henin-Hardenne def. Kuznetsova		64 64

DOUBLES FINALS

Men—#2 Jonas Bjorkman & Max Mirnyi def. #1 Bob Bryan & Mike Bryan, 6-7 (7-5), 6-4, 7-5.

Women—#1 Lisa Raymond & Samantha Stosur def. #5 Daniela Hantuchova & Ai Sugiyama, 6-3, 6-2.

Mixed—#8 Katarina Srebotnik & Nenad Zimonjic def. #7 Elena Likhovtseva & Daniel Nestor, 6-3, 6-4.

2006 Grand Slam Tournaments (Cont.)

Wimbledon

MEN'S SINGLES

FINAL EIGHT—#1 Roger Federer; #2 Rafael Nadal; #6 Lleyton Hewitt; #7 Mario Ancic; #14 Radek Stepanek; #18 Marcos Baghdatis; #22 Jarkko Nieminen; plus unseeded Jonas Bjorkman.

Quarterfinals

Federer def. Ancic 64 64 64
Nadal def. Nieminen 63 64 64
Baghdatis def. Hewitt . . . . .61 57 76(5) 62
Bjorkman def. Stepanek . . . . . .76(3) 46 67(5) 76(7) 64

Semifinals

Federer def. Bjorkman 64 60 62
Nadal def. Baghdatis 61 75 63

Final

Federer def. Nadal . . . . .60 76(5) 67(2) 63

WOMEN'S SINGLES

FINAL EIGHT—#1 Amelie Mauresmo; #2 Kim Clijsters; #3 Justine Henin-Hardenne; #4 Maria Sharapova; #7 Elena Dementieva; #9 Anastasia Myskina; #27 Na Li; plus unseeded Severine Bremond.

Quarterfinals

Mauresmo def. Myskina 61 36 63
Clijsters def. Na 64 75
Henin-Hardenne def. Bremond 64 64
Sharapova def. Dementieva 61 64

Semifinals

Mauresmo def. Sharapova 63 36 62
Henin-Hardenne def. Clijsters . . . . .64 76(4)

Final

Mauresmo def. Henin-Hardenne 26 63 64

DOUBLES FINALS

Men—#1 Bob Bryan & Mike Bryan def. #6 Fabrice Santoro & Nenad Zimonjic, 6-3, 4-6, 6-4, 6-2.

Women—#4 Yan Zi & Zheng Jie def. Virginia Ruano Pascual & Paola Suarez, 6-3, 3-6, 6-2.

Mixed—#9 Vera Zvonareva & Andy Ram def. Venus Williams & Bob Bryan, 6-3, 6-2.

U.S. Open

MEN'S SINGLES

FINAL EIGHT—#1 Roger Federer; #2 Rafael Nadal; #5 James Blake; #7 Nikolay Davydeno; #9 Andy Roddick; #14 Tommy Haas; #15 Lleyton Hewitt; plus unseeded Mikhail Youzhny.

Quarterfinals

Federer def. Blake . . . . .76(7) 60 67(9) 64
Davydenko def. Haas . . . . . . .46 67(3) 63 64 64
Roddick def. Hewitt 63 75 64
Youzhny def. Nadal . . . . .63 57 76(5) 61

Semifinals

Federer def. Davydenko 61 75 64
Roddick def. Youzhny . . . . .67(5) 60 76(3) 63

Final

Federer def. Roddick 62 46 75 61

WOMEN'S SINGLES

FINAL EIGHT—#1 Amelie Mauresmo; #2 Justine Henin-Hardenne; #3 Maria Sharapova; #4 Elena Dementieva; #10 Lindsay Davenport; #12 Dinara Safina; #19 Jelena Jankovic; #27 Tatiana Golovin.

Quarterfinals

Mauresmo def. Safina .62 63
Sharapova def. Golovin . . . . .76(4) 76(0)
Jankovic def. Dementieva 62 61
Henin-Hardenne def. Davenport 64 64

Semifinals

Sharapova def. Mauresmo 60 46 60
Henin-Hardenne def. Jankovic 46 64 60

Final

Sharapova def. Henin-Hardenne 64 64

DOUBLES FINALS

Men—#6 Martin Damm & Leander Paes def. #2 Jonas Bjorkman & Max Mirnyi, 6-7 (5-7), 6-4, 6-3.

Women—Nathalie Dechy & Vera Zvonareva def. #8 Dinara Safina & Katarina Srebotnik, 7-6 (7-5), 7-5.

Mixed—#5 Martina Navratilova & Bob Bryan def. Kveta Peschke & Martin Damm, 6-2, 6-3.

2006 Fed Cup

Originally the Federation Cup and started in 1963 by the International Tennis Federation as the Davis Cup of women's tennis.

Quarterfinals (April 22-23)

Winner	Loser
Italy 4	.at France 1
at Spain 5	Austria 0
United States 3	.at Germany 2
at Belgium 3	.Russia 2

Semifinals (July 15-16)

Winner	Loser
Italy 3	.at Spain 1
at Belgium 4	United States 1

Finals

(in Charleroi, Belgium, Sept. 16-17)

Italy 3, Belgium 2

Singles—Francesca Schiavone (ITA) def. Kirsten Flipkens (BEL) 6-1, 6-3; Justine Henin-Hardenne (BEL) def. Flavia Pennetta (ITA) 6-4, 7-5; Henin-Hardenne (BEL) def. Schiavone (ITA) 6-4, 7-5; Mara Santangelo (ITA) def. Flipkens (BEL) 6-7 (3), 6-3, 6-0.

Doubles—Schiavone & Roberta Vinci (ITA) def. Flipkens & Henin-Hardenne (BEL) 3-6, 6-2, 2-0 (ret.).

Singles Leaders

Official Top 20 rankings and money leaders of men's and women's tours for 2005 and unofficial rankings for 2006 (through Oct. 8), as compiled by the ATP Tour (Association of Tennis Professionals) and WTA (Women's Tennis Association). Note that money lists include doubles earnings.

Final 2005 Rankings and Money Won

Listed are events won and times a finalist and semifinalist (Finish, 1-2-SF), match record (W-L), and earnings for the year.

MEN

Rank		Finish 1-2-SF	W-L	Earnings
1	Roger Federer	11-1-2	81-4	$6,137,018
2	Rafael Nadal	11-1-0	79-10	3,874,751
3	Andy Roddick	5-3-3	59-14	1,798,635
4	Lleyton Hewitt	1-2-3	37-9	1,459,437
5	Nikolay Davydenko	1-0-7	56-30	1,628,299
6	David Nalbandian	2-0-2	44-19	2,183,486
7	Andre Agassi	1-2-3	38-12	1,629,596
8	Guillermo Coria	1-3-1	55-27	1,285,726
9	Ivan Ljubicic	2-6-1	62-24	1,491,474
10	Gaston Gaudio	5-1-1	55-21	1,358,024
11	Fernando Gonzalez	3-1-0	49-23	1,187,015
12	Marat Safin	1-1-0	27-11	1,288,115
13	Mariano Puerta	1-3-2	47-30	1,075,903
14	Thomas Johansson	1-0-5	48-25	1,026,266
15	David Ferrer	0-1-4	43-29	951,772
16	Robby Ginepri	1-0-3	37-25	812,626
17	Juan Carlos Ferrero	0-2-2	48-27	727,673
18	Tommy Robredo	0-1-3	44-24	811,883
19	Radek Stepanek	0-2-5	45-26	798,710
20	Dominik Hrbaty	1-0-3	49-28	831,766

WOMEN

Rank		Finish 1-2-SF	W-L	Earnings
1	Lindsay Davenport	6-4-1	60-10	$2,684,490
2	Kim Clijsters	9-0-1	67-9	3,983,654
3	Amelie Mauresmo	4-3-4	56-17	2,843,708
4	Maria Sharapova	3-1-7	53-12	1,921,283
5	Mary Pierce	2-3-0	43-13	2,525,403
6	Justine Henin-Hardenne	4-1-0	34-5	1,705,173
7	Patty Schnyder	2-3-5	58-25	1,101,693
8	Elena Dementieva	0-2-6	45-22	1,524,461
9	Nadia Petrova	1-2-4	56-22	1,305,000
10	Venus Williams	2-2-1	37-10	1,509,065
11	Serena Williams	1-0-1	21-7	1,076,226
12	Nathalie Dechy	0-0-4	41-27	640,306
13	Francesca Schiavone	0-3-1	41-23	528,587
14	Anastasia Myskina	1-1-2	31-18	873,199
15	Nicole Vaidisova	3-1-2	48-15	391,316
16	Ana Ivanovic	1-0-3	40-14	472,547
17	Elena Likhovtseva	0-0-2	30-22	806,796
18	Svetlana Kuznetsova	0-1-2	29-17	1,246,818
19	Daniela Hantuchova	0-1-3	37-25	797,787
20	Dinara Safina	2-0-4	36-20	478,417

2006 Tour Rankings (through Oct. 8)

Listed are tournaments won and times a finalist and semifinalist (Finish, 1-2-SF), match record (W-L), and points earned (Pts). The **Indesit ATP Race** replaced the men's pro tennis tour's 27-year-old computer ranking system in 2000. Under the new system players start from zero on Jan. 1 and accumulate points during the calendar year with the player accumulating the most points becoming the World No. 1. Points are awarded in 18 tournaments: nine Tennis Masters Series events, four Grand Slams and five other International Series events. The Tennis Master Cup will count as a 19th tournament for those that qualify.

MEN

Final ATP Tour singles rankings will be based on points earned from 18 tournaments played in 2006. Tournaments, titles and match won-lost records are for 2006 only.

Rank 06	(05)		Finish 1-2-SF	W-L	Pts
1	1	Roger Federer	9-4-0	77-5	1374
2	2	Rafael Nadal	5-1-2	54-8	825
3	9	Ivan Ljubicic	2-2-1	55-17	436
4	3	Andy Roddick	1-2-2	44-16	434
5	5	Nikolay Davydenko	3-2-3	56-24	418
6	25	James Blake	4-2-0	50-21	396
7	18	Tommy Robredo	2-1-2	44-24	395
8	6	David Nalbandian	1-0-4	34-13	370
9	73	Marcos Baghdatis	1-1-2	36-14	369
10	22	Mario Ancic	1-3-1	48-16	348
11	44	Tommy Haas	3-0-3	43-17	318
12	15	David Ferrer	1-0-1	38-22	285
13	11	Fernando Gonzalez	0-0-5	38-18	280
14	19	Radek Stepanek	1-1-1	30-15	268
15	24	Tomas Berdych	0-2-2	41-21	265
16	4	Lleyton Hewitt	1-2-0	33-15	263
17	32	Jarkko Nieminen	1-0-3	48-23	250
18	83	Novak Djokovic	2-1-1	37-15	248
19	84	Andy Murray	1-1-2	37-23	244
20	17	Juan Carlos Ferrero	0-1-1	28-21	215

WOMEN

WTA Tour singles ranking system based on total Round and Quality Points for each tournament played during the last 12 months (capped at 17 tournaments). Tournaments, titles and match won-lost records, however, are for 2006 only.

Rank 06	(05)		Finish 1-2-SF	W-L	Pts
1	3	Amelie Mauresmo	4-2-3	46-11	3593
2	6	Justine Henin-Hardenne	5-4-2	56-7	3473
3	4	Maria Sharapova	3-2-5	47-8	3037
4	18	Svetlana Kuznetsova	3-2-6	57-16	2408
5	9	Nadia Petrova	5-0-2	40-15	2161
6	2	Kim Clijsters	2-2-4	36-10	2110
7	8	Elena Dementieva	2-1-3	45-16	1983
8	—	Martina Hingis	2-2-3	50-16	1850
9	7	Patty Schnyder	0-2-4	41-21	1843
10	20	Dinara Safina	0-2-2	44-20	1502
11	15	Nicole Vaidisova	1-0-4	34-13	1376
12	13	Francesca Schiavone	0-3-0	34-21	1288
13	1	Lindsay Davenport	0-1-2	21-8	1280
14	14	Anastasia Myskina	0-3-1	31-17	1208
15	16	Ana Ivanovic	1-0-0	31-16	1197
16	22	Jelena Jankovic	0-1-4	40-24	1187
17	5	Mary Pierce	0-0-0	8-6	983
18	21	Anna-Lena Groenefeld	1-0-2	31-24	948
19	37	Marion Bartoli	2-1-1	40-26	923
20	56	Na Li	0-1-1	43-20	876

2006 Money Winners

Amounts include singles and doubles earnings through Oct. 8, 2006.

MEN

		Earnings				Earnings				Earnings
1	Roger Federer	$6,231,885	11	Mario Ancic	$1,007,065		21	Mikhai Youzhny	$666,867
2	Rafael Nadal	3,344,510	12	Max Mirnyi	936,065		22	Lleyton Hewitt	646,680
3	Andy Roddick	1,940,960	13	Radek Stepanek	820,460		23	Dmitry Tursunov	636,959
4	Ivan Ljubicic	1,360,167	14	David Ferrer	804,360		24	Fabrice Santoro	623,940
5	Nikolay Davydenko	1,192,845	15	Tommy Haas	779,305		25	Andy Murray	620,942
6	Marcos Baghdatis	1,122,745	16	Tomas Berdych	777,535		26	Richard Gasquet	602,330
7	Tommy Robredo	1,091,995	17	Jarkko Nieminen	738,065		27	Novak Djokovic	560,290
8	Jonas Bjorkman	1,045,450	18	Fernando Gonzalez	729,030		28	Juan Carlos Ferrero	559,590
9	David Nalbandian	1,039,840	19	Bob Bryan	697,330		29	Olivier Rochus	523,560
10	James Blake	1,035,115		Mike Bryan	697,330		30	Gaston Gaudio	516,685

WOMEN

		Earnings				Earnings				Earnings
1	J. Henin-Hardenne	$3,204,810	11	Jie Zheng	$751,661		21	Katarina Srebotnik	$583,952
2	Maria Sharapova	3,101,616	12	Patty Schnyder	685,860		22	Daniela Hantuchova	572,415
3	Amelie Mauresmo	2,777,507	13	Jelena Jankovic	660,494		23	Zi Yan	569,202
4	Svetlana Kuznetsova	1,768,109	14	Lisa Raymond	640,920		24	Ai Sugiyama	550,387
5	Kim Clijsters	1,122,992	15	Nicole Vaidosova	625,073		25	Tatiana Golovin	491,672
6	Nadia Petrova	1,118,139	16	Ana Ivanovic	617,966		26	Nathalie Dechy	477,587
7	Elena Dementieva	1,043,335	17	Francesca Schiavone	612,037		27	Na Li	447,074
8	Martina Hingis	999,052	18	Anna-Lena Groenefeld	608,750		28	Anna Chakvetadze	435,229
9	Dinara Safina	837,316	19	Vera Zvonareva	601,705		29	Shahar Peer	421,140
10	Samantha Stosur	777,617	20	Anastasia Myskina	593,351		30	V. Ruano Pascual	403,991

Davis Cup

Mario Ancic defeated Mical Mertinak in straight sets in the deciding fifth match of the 2005 final to lift Croatia to its first Davis Cup title, 3-2, over Slovakia. Each country was making its first finals appearance, and Croatia became the 12th champion in the 105-year history of the Davis Cup.

2005 FINAL
Croatia 3, Slovakia 2

at Bratislava, Slovakia (Dec. 2-4)

Day One—Ivan Ljubicic (CRO) def. Karol Kucera (SLO) 6-3, 6-4, 6-3; Dominic Hrbaty (SLO) def. Mario Ancic (CRO) 7-6 (7-4), 6-3, 6-7 (4-7), 6-4.

Day Two—Ancic & Ljubicic (CRO) def. Hrbaty & Michal Mertinak (SLO) 7-6 (7-5), 6-3, 7-6 (7-5).

Day Three—Hrbaty (SLO) def. Ljubicic (CRO) 4-6, 6-3, 6-4, 3-6, 6-4; Ancic (CRO) def. Mertinak (SLO) 7-6 (7-1), 6-3, 6-4.

2006 Early Rounds
FIRST ROUND
(February 10-12)

Winner	Loser
Croatia 3	at Austria 2
at Argentina 5	Sweden 0
at Belarus 4	Spain 1
Australia 3	at Switzerland 2
France 3	at Germany 2
Russia 5	at Netherlands 0
at United States 4	Romania 1
at Chile 3	Slovakia 0

QUARTERFINALS
(April 7-9)

Winner	Loser
Argentina 3	at Croatia 2
at Australia 5	Belarus 0
Russia 4	at France 1
at United States 3	Chile 2

SEMIFINALS
Russia 3, United States 2

at Moscow, Russia (Sept. 22-24)

Day One—Marat Safin (RUS) def. Andy Roddick (USA) 6-4, 6-3, 7-6 (7-5); Mikhail Youzhny (RUS) def. James Blake (USA) 7-5, 1-6, 6-1, 7-5.

Day Two—Bob Bryan & Mike Bryan (USA) def. Dmitry Tursunov & Youzhny (RUS) 6-3, 6-4, 6-2.

Day Three—Tursunov (RUS) def. Roddick (USA) 6-3, 6-4, 5-7, 3-6, 17-15; Blake (USA) def. Safin (RUS) 7-5, 7-6 (7-4).

Argentina 5, Australia 0

at Buenos Aires Argentina (Sept. 22-24)

Day One—David Nalbandian (ARG) def. Mark Philippoussis (AUS) 6-4, 6-3, 6-3; Jose Acasuso (ARG) def. Lleyton Hewitt (AUS) 1-6, 6-4, 4-6, 6-2, 6-1.

Day Two—Agustin Calleri & Nalbandian (ARG) def. Wayne Arthurs & Paul Hanley (AUS) 6-4, 6-4, 7-5.

Day Three—Calleri (ARG) def. Hanley (AUS) 6-0, 6-3; Juan Ignacio Chela (ARG) def. Arthurs (AUS) walkover.

2006 FINAL

The 2006 Davis Cup Final between Russia and Argentina is scheduled for Dec. 1-3 in Moscow. The two countries have never faced each other in a Davis Cup.

1877-2006
Through the Years

SPORTS ALMANAC

Grand Slam Championships
Australian Open
MEN

Became an Open Championship in 1969. Two tournaments were held in 1977; the first in January, the second in December. Tournament moved back to January in 1987, so no championship was decided in 1986. **Surface:** Synpave Rebound Ace (hardcourt surface composed of polyurethane and synthetic rubber).

Multiple winners: Roy Emerson (6); Andre Agassi, Jack Crawford and Ken Rosewall (4); James Anderson, Rod Laver, Adrian Quist, Mats Wilander and Pat Wood (3); Boris Becker, Jack Bromwich, Ashley Cooper, Jim Courier, Stefan Edberg, Roger Federer, Rodney Heath, Johan Kriek, Ivan Lendl, John Newcombe, Pete Sampras, Frank Sedgman, Guillermo Vilas and Tony Wilding (2).

Year	Winner	Loser	Score	Year	Winner	Loser	Score
1905	Rodney Heath	A. Curtis	46 63 64 64	1960	Rod Laver	N. Fraser	57 36 63 86 86
1906	Tony Wilding	H. Parker	60 64 64	1961	Roy Emerson	R. Laver	16 63 75 64
1907	Horace Rice	H. Parker	63 64 64	1962	Rod Laver	R. Emerson	86 06 64 64
1908	Fred Alexander	A. Dunlop	36 36 60 62 63	1963	Roy Emerson	K. Fletcher	63 63 61
1909	Tony Wilding	E. Parker	61 75 62	1964	Roy Emerson	F. Stolle	63 64 62
1910	Rodney Heath	H. Rice	64 63 62	1965	Roy Emerson	F. Stolle	79 26 64 75 61
1911	Norman Brookes	H. Rice	61 62 63	1966	Roy Emerson	A. Ashe	64 68 62 63
1912	J. Cecil Parke	A. Beamish	36 63 16 61 75	1967	Roy Emerson	A. Ashe	64 61 61
1913	Ernie Parker	H. Parker	26 61 62 63	1968	Bill Bowrey	J. Gisbert	75 26 97 64
1914	Pat Wood	G. Patterson	64 63 57 61	1969	Rod Laver	A. Gimeno	63 64 75
1915	Gordon Lowe	H. Rice	46 61 61 64	1970	Arthur Ashe	D. Crealy	64 97 62
1916-18	Not held World War I			1971	Ken Rosewall	A. Ashe	61 75 63
1919	A.R.F. Kingscote	E. Pockley	64 60 63	1972	Ken Rosewall	M. Anderson	76 63 75
1920	Pat Wood	R. Thomas	63 46 68 61 63	1973	John Newcombe	O. Parun	63 67 75 61
1921	Rhys Gemmell	A. Hedeman	75 61 64	1974	Jimmy Connors	P. Dent	76 64 46 63
1922	James Anderson	G. Patterson	60 36 36 63 62	1975	John Newcombe	J. Connors	75 36 64 75
1923	Pat Wood	C.B. St. John	61 61 63	1976	Mark Edmondson	J. Newcombe	67 63 76 61
1924	James Anderson	R. Schlesinger	63 64 36 57 63	1977	Roscoe Tanner	G. Vilas	63 63 63
1925	James Anderson	G. Patterson	11-9 26 62 63		Vitas Gerulaitis	J. Lloyd	63 76 57 36 62
1926	John Hawkes	J. Willard	61 63 61	1978	Guillermo Vilas	J. Marks	64 64 36 63
1927	Gerald Patterson	J. Hawkes	36 64 36 18-16 63	1979	Guillermo Vilas	J. Sadri	76 63 62
1928	Jean Borotra	R.O. Cummings	64 61 46 57 63	1980	Brian Teacher	K. Warwick	75 76 63
1929	John Gregory	R. Schlesinger	62 62 57 75	1981	Johan Kriek	S. Denton	62 76 67 64
1930	Gar Moon	H. Hopman	63 61 63	1982	Johan Kriek	S. Denton	63 63 62
1931	Jack Crawford	H. Hopman	64 62 26 61	1983	Mats Wilander	I. Lendl	61 64 64
1932	Jack Crawford	H. Hopman	46 63 36 63 61	1984	Mats Wilander	K. Curren	67 64 76 62
1933	Jack Crawford	K. Gledhill	26 75 63 62	1985	Stefan Edberg	M. Wilander	64 63 63
1934	Fred Perry	J. Crawford	63 75 61	1986	Not held		
1935	Jack Crawford	F. Perry	26 64 64 64	1987	Stefan Edberg	P. Cash	63 64 36 57 63
1936	Adrian Quist	J. Crawford	62 63 46 36 97	1988	Mats Wilander	P. Cash	63 67 36 61 86
1937	Viv McGrath	J. Bromwich	63 16 60 26 61	1989	Ivan Lendl	M. Mecir	62 62 62
1938	Don Budge	J. Bromwich	64 62 61	1990	Ivan Lendl	S. Edberg	46 76 52 (ret.)
1939	Jack Bromwich	A. Quist	64 61 63	1991	Boris Becker	I. Lendl	16 64 64 64
1940	Adrian Quist	J. Crawford	63 61 62	1992	Jim Courier	S. Edberg	63 36 64 62
1941-45	Not held World War II			1993	Jim Courier	S. Edberg	62 61 26 75
1946	Jack Bromwich	D. Pails	57 63 75 36 62	1994	Pete Sampras	T. Martin	76 64 64
1947	Dinny Pails	J. Bromwich	46 64 36 75 86	1995	Andre Agassi	P. Sampras	46 61 76 64
1948	Adrian Quist	J. Bromwich	64 36 63 26 63	1996	Boris Becker	M. Chang	62 64 26 62
1949	Frank Sedgman	J. Bromwich	63 63 62	1997	Pete Sampras	C. Moya	62 63 63
1950	Frank Sedgman	K. McGregor	63 64 46 61	1998	Petr Korda	M. Rios	62 62 62
1951	Dick Savitt	K. McGregor	63 26 63 61	1999	Yevgeny Kafelnikov	T. Enqvist	46 60 63 76
1952	Ken McGregor	F. Sedgman	75 12-10 26 62	2000	Andre Agassi	Y. Kafelnikov	36 63 62 64
1953	Ken Rosewall	M. Rose	60 63 64	2001	Andre Agassi	A. Clement	64 62 62
1954	Mervyn Rose	R. Hartwig	62 06 64 62	2002	Thomas Johansson	M. Safin	36 64 64 76
1955	Ken Rosewall	L. Hoad	97 64 64	2003	Andre Agassi	R. Schuettler	62 62 61
1956	Lew Hoad	K. Rosewall	64 36 64 75	2004	Roger Federer	M. Safin	76 64 62
1957	Ashley Cooper	N. Fraser	63 9-11 64 62	2005	Marat Safin	L. Hewitt	16 63 64 64
1958	Ashley Cooper	M. Anderson	75 63 64	2006	Roger Federer	M. Baghdatis	57 75 60 62
1959	Alex Olmedo	N. Fraser	61 62 36 63				

WOMEN

Became an Open Championship in 1969. Two tournaments were held in 1977, the first in January, the second in December. Tournament moved back to January in 1987, so no championship was decided in 1986.

Multiple winners: Margaret Smith Court (11); Nancye Wynne Bolton (6); Daphne Akhurst (5); Evonne Goolagong Cawley, Steffi Graf and Monica Seles (4); Joan Hartigan, Martina Hingis and Martina Navratilova (3); Coral Buttsworth, Jennifer Capriati, Chris Evert Lloyd, Thelma Long, Hana Mandlikova, Mall Molesworth, Mary Carter Reitano and Serena Williams (2).

Year	Winner	Loser	Score	Year	Winner	Loser	Score
1922	Mall Molesworth	E. Boyd	63 10-8	1967	Nancy Richey	L. Turner	61 64
1923	Mall Molesworth	E. Boyd	61 75	1968	Billie Jean King	M. Smith	61 62
1924	Sylvia Lance	E. Boyd	63 36 64	1969	Margaret Court	B.J. King	64 61
1925	Daphne Akhurst	E. Boyd	16 86 64	1970	Margaret Court	K. Melville	61 63
1926	Daphne Akhurst	E. Boyd	61 63	1971	Margaret Court	E. Goolagong	26 76 75
1927	Esna Boyd	S. Harper	57 61 62	1972	Virginia Wade	E. Goolagong	64 64
1928	Daphne Akhurst	E. Boyd	75 62	1973	Margaret Court	E. Goolagong	64 75
1929	Daphne Akhurst	L. Bickerton	61 57 62	1974	Evonne Goolagong	C. Evert	76 46 60
1930	Daphne Akhurst	S. Harper	10-8 26 75	1975	Evonne Goolagong	M. Navratilova	63 62
1931	Coral Buttsworth	M. Crawford	16 63 64	1976	Evonne Cawley	R. Tomanova	62 62
1932	Coral Buttsworth	K. Le Messurier	97 64	1977	Kerry Reid	D. Balestrat	75 62
1933	Joan Hartigan	C. Buttsworth	64 63		Evonne Cawley	H. Gourlay	63 60
1934	Joan Hartigan	M. Molesworth	61 64	1978	Chris O'Neil	B. Nagelsen	63 76
1935	Dorothy Round	N. Lyle	16 61 63	1979	Barbara Jordan	S. Walsh	63 63
1936	Joan Hartigan	N. Wynne	64 64	1980	Hana Mandlikova	W. Turnbull	60 75
1937	Nancye Wynne	E. Westacott	63 57 64	1981	Martina Navratilova	C. Evert Lloyd	67 64 75
1938	Dorothy Bundy	D. Stevenson	63 62	1982	Chris Evert Lloyd	M. Navratilova	63 26 63
1939	Emily Westacott	N. Hopman	61 62	1983	Martina Navratilova	K. Jordan	62 76
1940	Nancye Wynne	T. Coyne	57 64 60	1984	Chris Evert Lloyd	H. Sukova	67 61 63
1941-45	Not held World War II			1985	Martina Navratilova	C. Evert Lloyd	62 46 62
1946	Nancye Bolton	J. Fitch	64 64	1986	Not held		
1947	Nancye Bolton	N. Hopman	63 62	1987	Hana Mandlikova	M. Navratilova	75 76
1948	Nancye Bolton	M. Toomey	63 61	1988	Steffi Graf	C. Evert	61 76
1949	Doris Hart	N. Bolton	63 64	1989	Steffi Graf	H. Sukova	64 64
1950	Louise Brough	D. Hart	64 36 64	1990	Steffi Graf	M.J. Fernandez	63 64
1951	Nancye Bolton	T. Long	61 75	1991	Monica Seles	J. Novotna	57 63 61
1952	Thelma Long	H. Angwin	62 63	1992	Monica Seles	M.J. Fernandez	62 63
1953	Maureen Connolly	J. Sampson	63 62	1993	Monica Seles	S. Graf	46 63 62
1954	Thelma Long	J. Staley	63 64	1994	Steffi Graf	A.S. Vicario	60 62
1955	Beryl Penrose	T. Long	64 63	1995	Mary Pierce	A.S. Vicario	63 62
1956	Mary Carter	T. Long	36 62 97	1996	Monica Seles	A. Huber	64 61
1957	Shirley Fry	A. Gibson	63 64	1997	Martina Hingis	M. Pierce	62 62
1958	Angela Mortimer	L. Coghlan	63 64	1998	Martina Hingis	C. Martinez	63 63
1959	Mary Reitano	R. Schuurman	62 63	1999	Martina Hingis	A. Mauresmo	62 63
1960	Margaret Smith	J. Lehane	75 62	2000	Lindsay Davenport	M. Hingis	61 75
1961	Margaret Smith	J. Lehane	61 64	2001	Jennifer Capriati	M. Hingis	64 63
1962	Margaret Smith	J. Lehane	60 62	2002	Jennifer Capriati	M. Hingis	46 76 62
1963	Margaret Smith	J. Lehane	62 62	2003	Serena Williams	V. Williams	76 36 64
1964	Margaret Smith	L. Turner	63 62	2004	J. Henin-Hardenne	K. Clijsters	63 46 63
1965	Margaret Smith	M. Bueno	57 64 52 (ret)	2005	Serena Williams	L. Davenport	26 63 60
1966	Margaret Smith	N. Richey	walkover	2006	Amelie Mauresmo	J. Henin-Hardenne	61 20 (ret)

French Open
MEN

From 1891 to 1925, entry was restricted to members of French clubs. Became an Open Championship in 1968, but closed to contract pros in 1972. Note that Max Decugis won eight tournaments before 1925 (1903-04, 1907-09, 1912-14) to lead all men. **Surface:** Red clay.

Multiple winners (since 1925): Bjorn Borg (6); Henri Cochet (4); Gustavo Kuerten, Rene Lacoste, Ivan Lendl and Mats Wilander (3); Sergi Bruguera, Jim Courier, Jaroslav Drobny, Roy Emerson, Jan Kodes, Rod Laver, Rafael Nadal, Frank Parker, Nicola Pietrangeli, Ken Rosewall, Manuel Santana, Tony Trabert and Gottfried von Cramm (2).

Year	Winner	Loser	Score	Year	Winner	Loser	Score
1925	Rene Lacoste	J. Borotra	75 61 64	1939	Don McNeill	B. Riggs	75 60 63
1926	Henri Cochet	R. Lacoste	62 64 63	1940-45	Not held World War II		
1927	Rene Lacoste	B. Tilden	64 46 57 63 11-9	1946	Marcel Bernard	J. Drobny	36 26 61 64 63
1928	Henri Cochet	R. Lacoste	57 63 61 63	1947	Joseph Asboth	E. Sturgess	86 75 64
1929	Rene Lacoste	J. Borotra	63 26 60 26 86	1948	Frank Parker	J. Drobny	64 75 57 86
1930	Henri Cochet	B. Tilden	36 86 63 61	1949	Frank Parker	B. Patty	63 16 61 64
1931	Jean Borotra	C. Boussus	26 64 75 64	1950	Budge Patty	J. Drobny	61 62 36 57 75
1932	Henri Cochet	G. de Stefani	60 64 46 63	1951	Jaroslav Drobny	E. Sturgess	63 63 63
1933	Jack Crawford	H. Cochet	86 64 63	1952	Jaroslav Drobny	F. Sedgman	62 60 36 64
1934	Gottfried von Cramm	J. Crawford	64 79 36 75 63	1953	Ken Rosewall	V. Seixas	63 64 16 62
1935	Fred Perry	G. von Cramm	63 36 61 63	1954	Tony Trabert	A. Larsen	64 75 61
1936	Gottfried von Cramm	F. Perry	60 26 62 26 60	1955	Tony Trabert	S. Davidson	26 61 64 62
1937	Henner Henkel	H. Austin	61 64 63	1956	Lew Hoad	S. Davidson	64 86 63
1938	Don Budge	R. Menzel	63 62 64	1957	Sven Davidson	H. Flam	63 64 64

Year	Winner	Loser	Score
1958	Mervyn Rose	L. Ayala	63 64 64
1959	Nicola Pietrangeli	I. Vermaak	36 63 64 61
1960	Nicola Pietrangeli	L. Ayala	36 63 64 46 63
1961	Manuel Santana	N. Pietrangeli	46 61 36 60 62
1962	Rod Laver	R. Emerson	36 26 63 97 62
1963	Roy Emerson	P. Darmon	36 61 64 64
1964	Manuel Santana	N. Pietrangeli	63 61 46 75
1965	Fred Stolle	T. Roche	36 60 62 63
1966	Tony Roche	I. Gulyas	61 64 75
1967	Roy Emerson	T. Roche	61 64 26 62
1968	Ken Rosewall	R. Laver	63 61 26 62
1969	Rod Laver	K. Rosewall	64 63 64
1970	Jan Kodes	Z. Franulovic	62 64 60
1971	Jan Kodes	I. Nastase	86 62 26 75
1972	Andres Gimeno	P. Proisy	46 63 61 61
1973	Ilie Nastase	N. Pilic	63 63 60
1974	Bjorn Borg	M. Orantes	26 67 60 61 61
1975	Bjorn Borg	G. Vilas	62 63 64
1976	Adriano Panatta	H. Solomon	61 64 46 76
1977	Guillermo Vilas	B. Gottfried	60 63 60
1978	Bjorn Borg	G. Vilas	61 61 63
1979	Bjorn Borg	V. Pecci	63 61 67 64
1980	Bjorn Borg	V. Gerulaitis	64 61 62
1981	Bjorn Borg	I. Lendl	61 46 62 36 61
1982	Mats Wilander	G. Vilas	16 76 60 64
1983	Yannick Noah	M. Wilander	62 75 76
1984	Ivan Lendl	J. McEnroe	36 26 64 75 75
1985	Mats Wilander	I. Lendl	36 64 62 62
1986	Ivan Lendl	M. Pernfors	63 62 64
1987	Ivan Lendl	M. Wilander	75 62 36 76
1988	Mats Wilander	H. Leconte	75 62 61
1989	Michael Chang	S. Edberg	61 36 46 64 62
1990	Andres Gomez	A. Agassi	63 26 64 64
1991	Jim Courier	A. Agassi	36 64 26 61 64
1992	Jim Courier	P. Korda	75 62 61
1993	Sergi Bruguera	J. Courier	64 26 62 36 63
1994	Sergi Bruguera	A. Berasategui	63 75 26 61
1995	Thomas Muster	M. Chang	75 62 64
1996	Yevgeny Kafelnikov	M. Stich	76 75 76
1997	Gustavo Kuerten	S. Bruguera	63 64 62
1998	Carlos Moya	A. Corretja	63 75 63
1999	Andre Agassi	A. Medvedev	16 26 64 63 64
2000	Gustavo Kuerten	M. Norman	62 63 26 76
2001	Gustavo Kuerten	A. Corretja	67 75 62 60
2002	Albert Costa	J. C. Ferrero	61 60 46 63
2003	Juan Carlos Ferrero	M. Verkerk	61 63 62
2004	Gaston Gaudio	G. Coria	06 36 64 61 86
2005	Rafael Nadal	M. Puerta	67 63 61 75
2006	Rafael Nadal	R. Federer	16 61 64 76

WOMEN

From 1897 to 1925, entry was restricted to members of French clubs. Became an Open Championship in 1968, but closed to contract pros in 1972. Note that Suzanne Lenglen won two titles prior to 1925, giving her six total.

Multiple winners (since 1925): Chris Evert Lloyd (7); Steffi Graf (6); Margaret Smith Court (5); Helen Wills Moody (4); Justine Henin-Hardenne, Arantxa Sanchez Vicario, Monica Seles and Hilde Sperling (3); Maureen Connolly, Margaret Osborne du Pont, Doris Hart, Ann Haydon Jones, Suzanne Lenglen, Simone Mathieu, Margaret Scriven, Martina Navratilova and Lesley Turner (2).

Year	Winner	Loser	Score
1925	Suzanne Lenglen	K. McKane	61 62
1926	Suzanne Lenglen	M. Browne	61 60
1927	Kea Bouman	I. Peacock	62 64
1928	Helen Wills	E. Bennett	61 62
1929	Helen Wills	S. Mathieu	63 64
1930	Helen Moody	H. Jacobs	62 61
1931	Cilly Aussem	B. Nuthall	86 61
1932	Helen Moody	S. Mathieu	75 61
1933	Margaret Scriven	S. Mathieu	62 46 64
1934	Margaret Scriven	H. Jacobs	75 46 61
1935	Hilde Sperling	S. Mathieu	62 61
1936	Hilde Sperling	S. Mathieu	63 64
1937	Hilde Sperling	S. Mathieu	62 64
1938	Simone Mathieu	N. Landry	60 63
1939	Simone Mathieu	J. Jedrzejowska	63 86
1940-45	Not held World War II		
1946	Margaret Osborne	P. Betz	16 86 75
1947	Patricia Todd	D. Hart	63 36 64
1948	Nelly Landry	S. Fry	62 06 60
1949	Margaret du Pont	N. Adamson	75 62
1950	Doris Hart	P. Todd	64 46 62
1951	Shirley Fry	D. Hart	63 36 63
1952	Doris Hart	S. Fry	64 64
1953	Maureen Connolly	D. Hart	62 64
1954	Maureen Connolly	G. Bucaille	64 61
1955	Angela Mortimer	D. Knode	26 75 10-8
1956	Althea Gibson	A. Mortimer	60 12-10
1957	Shirley Bloomer	D. Knode	61 63
1958	Suzi Kormoczi	S. Bloomer	64 16 62
1959	Christine Truman	S. Kormoczi	64 75
1960	Darlene Hard	Y. Ramirez	63 64
1961	Ann Haydon	Y. Ramirez	62 61
1962	Margaret Smith	L. Turner	63 36 75
1963	Lesley Turner	A. Jones	26 63 75
1964	Margaret Smith	M. Bueno	57 61 62
1965	Lesley Turner	M. Smith	63 64
1966	Ann Jones	N. Richey	63 61
1967	Francoise Durr	L. Turner	46 63 64
1968	Nancy Richey	A. Jones	57 64 61
1969	Margaret Court	A. Jones	61 46 63
1970	Margaret Court	H. Niessen	62 64
1971	Evonne Goolagong	H. Gourlay	63 75
1972	Billie Jean King	E. Goolagong	63 63
1973	Margaret Court	C. Evert	67 76 64
1974	Chris Evert	O. Morozova	61 62
1975	Chris Evert	M. Navratilova	26 62 61
1976	Sue Barker	R. Tomanova	62 06 62
1977	Mima Jausovec	F. Mihai	62 67 61
1978	Virginia Ruzici	M. Jausovec	62 62
1979	Chris Evert Lloyd	W. Turnbull	62 60
1980	Chris Evert Lloyd	V. Ruzici	60 63
1981	Hana Mandlikova	S. Hanika	62 64
1982	Martina Navratilova	A. Jaeger	76 61
1983	Chris Evert Lloyd	M. Jausovec	61 62
1984	Martina Navratilova	C. Evert Lloyd	63 61
1985	Chris Evert Lloyd	M. Navratilova	63 67 75
1986	Chris Evert Lloyd	M. Navratilova	26 63 63
1987	Steffi Graf	M. Navratilova	64 46 86
1988	Steffi Graf	N. Zvereva	60 60
1989	A. Sanchez Vicario	S. Graf	76 36 75
1990	Monica Seles	S. Graf	76 64
1991	Monica Seles	A.S. Vicario	63 64
1992	Monica Seles	S. Graf	62 36 10-8
1993	Steffi Graf	M.J. Fernandez	46 62 64
1994	A. Sanchez Vicario	M. Pierce	64 64
1995	Steffi Graf	A.S. Vicario	76 46 60
1996	Steffi Graf	A.S. Vicario	63 67 10-8
1997	Iva Majoli	M. Hingis	64 62
1998	A. Sanchez Vicario	M. Seles	76 06 62
1999	Steffi Graf	M. Hingis	46 75 62
2000	Mary Pierce	C. Martinez	62 75
2001	Jennifer Capriati	K. Clijsters	16 64 1210
2002	Serena Williams	V. Williams	75 63
2003	J. Henin-Hardenne	K. Clijsters	60 64
2004	Anastasia Myskina	E. Dementieva	61 62
2005	J. Henin-Hardenne	M. Pierce	61 61
2006	J. Henin-Hardenne	S. Kuznetsova	64 64

Wimbledon
MEN

Officially called "The Lawn Tennis Championships" at the All England Club, Wimbledon. Challenge round system (defending champion qualified for following year's final) used from 1877-1921. Became an Open Championship in 1968, but closed to contract pros in 1972. **Surface:** Grass.

Multiple winners: Willie Renshaw and Pete Sampras (7); Bjorn Borg and Laurie Doherty (5); Reggie Doherty, Roger Federer, Rod Laver and Tony Wilding (4); Wilfred Baddeley, Boris Becker, Arthur Gore, John McEnroe, John Newcombe, Fred Perry and Bill Tilden (3); Jean Borotra, Norman Brookes, Don Budge, Henri Cochet, Jimmy Connors, Stefan Edberg, Roy Emerson, John Hartley, Lew Hoad, Rene Lacoste, Gerald Patterson and Joshua Pim (2).

Year	Winner	Loser	Score	Year	Winner	Loser	Score
1877	Spencer Gore	W. Marshall	61 62 64	1946	Yvon Petra	G. Brown	62 64 79 57 64
1878	Frank Hadow	S. Gore	75 61 97	1947	Jack Kramer	T. Brown	61 63 62
1879	John Hartley	V. St. L. Goold	62 64 62	1948	Bob Falkenburg	J. Bromwich	75 06 62 36 75
1880	John Hartley	H. Lawford	60 62 26 63	1949	Ted Schroeder	J. Drobny	36 60 63 46 64
1881	Willie Renshaw	J. Hartley	60 61 61	1950	Budge Patty	F. Sedgman	61 8-10 62 63
1882	Willie Renshaw	E. Renshaw	61 26 46 62 62	1951	Dick Savitt	K. McGregor	64 64 64
1883	Willie Renshaw	E. Renshaw	26 63 46 46 63	1952	Frank Sedgman	J. Drobny	46 62 63 62
1884	Willie Renshaw	H. Lawford	60 64 97	1953	Vic Seixas	K. Nielsen	97 63 64
1885	Willie Renshaw	H. Lawford	75 62 46 75	1954	Jaroslav Drobny	K. Rosewall	13-11 46 62 97
1886	Willie Renshaw	H. Lawford	60 57 63 64	1955	Tony Trabert	K. Nielsen	63 75 61
1887	Herbert Lawford	E. Renshaw	16 63 36 64 64	1956	Lew Hoad	K. Rosewall	62 46 75 64
1888	Ernest Renshaw	H. Lawford	63 75 60	1957	Lew Hoad	A. Cooper	62 61 62
1889	Willie Renshaw	E. Renshaw	64 61 36 60	1958	Ashley Cooper	N. Fraser	36 63 64 13-11
1890	Willoughby Hamilton	W. Renshaw	68 62 36 61 61	1959	Alex Olmedo	R. Laver	64 63 64
1891	Wilfred Baddeley	J. Pim	64 16 75 60	1960	Neale Fraser	R. Laver	64 36 97 75
1892	Wilfred Baddeley	J. Pim	46 63 63 62	1961	Rod Laver	C. McKinley	63 61 64
1893	Joshua Pim	W. Baddeley	36 61 63 62	1962	Rod Laver	M. Mulligan	62 62 61
1894	Joshua Pim	W. Baddeley	10-8 62 86	1963	Chuck McKinley	F. Stolle	97 61 64
1895	Wilfred Baddeley	W. Eaves	46 26 86 62 63	1964	Roy Emerson	F. Stolle	64 12-10 46 63
1896	Harold Mahony	W. Baddeley	62 68 57 86 63	1965	Roy Emerson	F. Stolle	62 64 64
1897	Reggie Doherty	H. Mahony	64 64 63	1966	Manuel Santana	D. Ralston	64 11-9 64
1898	Reggie Doherty	L. Doherty	63 63 26 57 61	1967	John Newcombe	W. Bungert	63 61 61
1899	Reggie Doherty	A. Gore	16 46 62 63 63	1968	Rod Laver	T. Roche	63 64 62
1900	Reggie Doherty	S. Smith	68 63 61 62	1969	Rod Laver	J. Newcombe	64 57 64 64
1901	Arthur Gore	R. Doherty	46 75 64 64	1970	John Newcombe	K. Rosewall	57 63 62 36 61
1902	Laurie Doherty	A. Gore	64 63 36 60	1971	John Newcombe	S. Smith	63 57 26 64 64
1903	Laurie Doherty	F. Riseley	75 63 60	1972	Stan Smith	I. Nastase	46 63 63 46 75
1904	Laurie Doherty	F. Riseley	61 75 86	1973	Jan Kodes	A. Metreveli	61 98 63
1905	Laurie Doherty	N. Brookes	86 62 64	1974	Jimmy Connors	K. Rosewall	61 61 64
1906	Laurie Doherty	F. Riseley	64 46 62 63	1975	Arthur Ashe	J. Connors	61 61 57 64
1907	Norman Brookes	A. Gore	64 62 62	1976	Bjorn Borg	I. Nastase	64 62 97
1908	Arthur Gore	R. Barrett	63 62 46 36 64	1977	Bjorn Borg	J. Connors	36 62 61 57 64
1909	Arthur Gore	M. Ritchie	68 16 62 62 62	1978	Bjorn Borg	J. Connors	62 62 63
1910	Tony Wilding	A. Gore	64 75 46 62	1979	Bjorn Borg	R. Tanner	67 61 36 63 64
1911	Tony Wilding	R. Barrett	64 46 26 62 (ret)	1980	Bjorn Borg	J. McEnroe	16 75 63 67 86
1912	Tony Wilding	A. Gore	64 64 46 64	1981	John McEnroe	B. Borg	46 76 76 64
1913	Tony Wilding	M. McLoughlin	86 63 10-8	1982	Jimmy Connors	J. McEnroe	36 63 67 76 64
1914	Norman Brookes	T. Wilding	64 64 75	1983	John McEnroe	C. Lewis	62 62 62
1915-18	Not held World War I			1984	John McEnroe	J. Connors	61 61 62
1919	Gerald Patterson	N. Brookes	63 75 62	1985	Boris Becker	K. Curren	63 67 76 64
1920	Bill Tilden	G. Patterson	26 63 62 64	1986	Boris Becker	I. Lendl	64 63 75
1921	Bill Tilden	B. Norton	46 26 61 60 75	1987	Pat Cash	I. Lendl	76 62 75
1922	Gerald Patterson	R. Lycett	63 64 62	1988	Stefan Edberg	B. Becker	46 76 64 62
1923	Bill Johnston	F. Hunter	60 63 61	1989	Boris Becker	S. Edberg	60 76 64
1924	Jean Borotra	R. Lacoste	61 36 61 36 64	1990	Stefan Edberg	B. Becker	62 62 36 36 64
1925	Rene Lacoste	J. Borotra	63 63 46 86	1991	Michael Stich	B. Becker	64 76 64
1926	Jean Borotra	H. Kinsey	86 61 63	1992	Andre Agassi	G. Ivanisevic	67 64 64 16 64
1927	Henri Cochet	J. Borotra	46 46 63 64 75	1993	Pete Sampras	J. Courier	76 76 36 63
1928	Rene Lacoste	H. Cochet	61 46 64 62	1994	Pete Sampras	G. Ivanisevic	76 76 60
1929	Henri Cochet	J. Borotra	64 63 64	1995	Pete Sampras	B. Becker	67 62 64 62
1930	Bill Tilden	W. Allison	63 97 64	1996	Richard Krajicek	M. Washington	63 64 63
1931	Sidney Wood	F. Shields	walkover	1997	Pete Sampras	C. Pioline	64 62 64
1932	Ellsworth Vines	H. Austin	64 62 60	1998	Pete Sampras	G. Ivanisevic	67 76 64 36 62
1933	Jack Crawford	E. Vines	46 11-9 62 26 64	1999	Pete Sampras	A. Agassi	63 64 75
1934	Fred Perry	J. Crawford	63 60 75	2000	Pete Sampras	P. Rafter	67 76 64 62
1935	Fred Perry	G. von Cramm	62 64 64	2001	Goran Ivanisevic	P. Rafter	63 36 63 26 97
1936	Fred Perry	G. von Cramm	61 61 60	2002	Lleyton Hewitt	D. Nalbandian	61 63 62
1937	Don Budge	G. von Cramm	63 64 62	2003	Roger Federer	M. Philippoussis	76 62 76
1938	Don Budge	H. Austin	61 60 63	2004	Roger Federer	A. Roddick	46 75 76 64
1939	Bobby Riggs	E. Cooke	26 86 36 63 62	2005	Roger Federer	A. Roddick	62 76 64
1940-45	Not held World War II			2006	Roger Federer	R. Nadal	60 76 67 63

WOMEN

Officially called "The Lawn Tennis Championships" at the All England Club, Wimbledon. Challenge round system (defending champion qualified for following year's final) used from 1877-1921. Became an Open Championship in 1968, but closed to contract pros in 1972.

Multiple winners: Martina Navratilova (9); Helen Wills Moody (8); Dorothea Douglass Chambers and Steffi Graf (7); Blanche Bingley Hillyard, Billie Jean King and Suzanne Lenglen (6); Lottie Dod and Charlotte Cooper Sterry (5); Louise Brough (4); Maria Bueno, Maureen Connolly, Margaret Smith Court, Chris Evert Lloyd and Venus Williams (3); Evonne Goolagong Cawley, Althea Gibson, Kitty McKane Godfree, Dorothy Round, May Sutton, Maud Watson and Serena Williams (2).

Year	Winner	Loser	Score	Year	Winner	Loser	Score
1884	Maud Watson	L. Watson	68 63 63	1950	Louise Brough	M. du Pont	61 36 61
1885	Maud Watson	B. Bingley	61 75	1951	Doris Hart	S. Fry	61 60
1886	Blanche Bingley	M. Watson	63 63	1952	Maureen Connolly	L. Brough	75 63
1887	Lottie Dod	B. Bingley	62 60	1953	Maureen Connolly	D. Hart	86 75
1888	Lottie Dod	B. Hillyard	63 63	1954	Maureen Connolly	L. Brough	62 75
1889	Blanche Hillyard	L. Rice	46 86 64	1955	Louise Brough	B. Fleitz	75 86
1890	Lena Rice	M. Jacks	64 61	1956	Shirley Fry	A. Buxton	63 61
1891	Lottie Dod	B. Hillyard	62 61	1957	Althea Gibson	D. Hard	63 62
1892	Lottie Dod	B. Hillyard	61 61	1958	Althea Gibson	A. Mortimer	86 62
1893	Lottie Dod	B. Hillyard	68 61 64	1959	Maria Bueno	D. Hard	64 63
1894	Blanche Hillyard	E. Austin	61 61	1960	Maria Bueno	S. Reynolds	86 60
1895	Charlotte Cooper	H. Jackson	75 86	1961	Angela Mortimer	C. Truman	46 64 75
1896	Charlotte Cooper	A. Pickering	62 63	1962	Karen Susman	V. Sukova	64 64
1897	Blanche Hillyard	C. Cooper	57 75 62	1963	Margaret Smith	B.J. Moffitt	63 64
1898	Charlotte Cooper	L. Martin	64 64	1964	Maria Bueno	M. Smith	64 79 63
1899	Blanche Hillyard	C. Cooper	62 63	1965	Margaret Smith	M. Bueno	64 75
1900	Blanche Hillyard	C. Cooper	46 64 64	1966	Billie Jean King	M. Bueno	63 36 61
1901	Charlotte Sterry	B. Hillyard	62 62	1967	Billie Jean King	A. Jones	63 64
1902	Muriel Robb	C. Sterry	75 61	1968	Billie Jean King	J. Tegart	97 75
1903	Dorothea Douglass	E. Thomson	46 64 62	1969	Ann Jones	B.J. King	36 63 62
1904	Dorothea Douglass	C. Sterry	60 63	1970	Margaret Court	B.J. King	14-12 11-9
1905	May Sutton	D. Douglass	63 64	1971	Evonne Goolagong	M. Court	64 61
1906	Dorothea Douglass	M. Sutton	63 97	1972	Billie Jean King	E. Goolagong	63 63
1907	May Sutton	D. Chambers	61 64	1973	Billie Jean King	C. Evert	60 75
1908	Charlotte Sterry	A. Morton	64 64	1974	Chris Evert	O. Morozova	60 64
1909	Dora Boothby	A. Morton	64 46 86	1975	Billie Jean King	E. Cawley	60 61
1910	Dorothea Chambers	D. Boothby	62 62	1976	Chris Evert	E. Cawley	63 46 86
1911	Dorothea Chambers	D. Boothby	60 60	1977	Virginia Wade	B. Stove	46 63 61
1912	Ethel Larcombe	C. Sterry	63 61	1978	Martina Navratilova	C. Evert	26 64 75
1913	Dorothea Chambers	R. McNair	60 64	1979	Martina Navratilova	C. Evert Lloyd	64 64
1914	Dorothea Chambers	E. Larcombe	75 64	1980	Evonne Cawley	C. Evert Lloyd	61 76
1915-18	Not held World War I			1981	Chris Evert Lloyd	H. Mandlikova	62 62
1919	Suzanne Lenglen	D. Chambers	10-8 46 97	1982	Martina Navratilova	C. Evert Lloyd	61 36 62
1920	Suzanne Lenglen	D. Chambers	63 60	1983	Martina Navratilova	A. Jaeger	60 63
1921	Suzanne Lenglen	E. Ryan	62 60	1984	Martina Navratilova	C. Evert Lloyd	76 62
1922	Suzanne Lenglen	M. Mallory	62 60	1985	Martina Navratilova	C. Evert Lloyd	46 63 62
1923	Suzanne Lenglen	K. McKane	62 62	1986	Martina Navratilova	H. Mandlikova	76 63
1924	Kitty McKane	H. Wills	46 64 64	1987	Martina Navratilova	S. Graf	75 63
1925	Suzanne Lenglen	J. Fry	62 60	1988	Steffi Graf	M. Navratilova	57 62 61
1926	Kitty Godfree	L. de Alvarez	62 46 63	1989	Steffi Graf	M. Navratilova	62 67 61
1927	Helen Wills	L. de Alvarez	62 64	1990	Martina Navratilova	Z. Garrison	64 61
1928	Helen Wills	L. de Alvarez	62 63	1991	Steffi Graf	G. Sabatini	64 36 86
1929	Helen Wills	H. Jacobs	61 62	1992	Steffi Graf	M. Seles	62 61
1930	Helen Moody	E. Ryan	62 62	1993	Steffi Graf	J. Novotna	76 16 64
1931	Cilly Aussem	H. Krahwinkel	62 75	1994	Conchita Martinez	M. Navratilova	64 36 63
1932	Helen Moody	H. Jacobs	63 61	1995	Steffi Graf	A.S. Vicario	46 61 75
1933	Helen Moody	D. Round	64 68 63	1996	Steffi Graf	A.S. Vicario	63 75
1934	Dorothy Round	H. Jacobs	62 57 63	1997	Martina Hingis	J. Novotna	26 63 63
1935	Helen Moody	H. Jacobs	63 36 75	1998	Jana Novotna	N. Tauziat	64 76
1936	Helen Jacobs	H.K. Sperling	62 46 75	1999	Lindsay Davenport	S. Graf	64 75
1937	Dorothy Round	J. Jedrzejowska	62 26 75	2000	Venus Williams	L. Davenport	63 76
1938	Helen Moody	H. Jacobs	64 60	2001	Venus Williams	J. Henin	61 36 60
1939	Alice Marble	K. Stammers	62 60	2002	Serena Williams	V. Williams	76 63
1940-45	Not held World War II			2003	Serena Williams	V. Williams	46 64 62
1946	Pauline Betz	L. Brough	62 64	2004	Maria Sharapova	S. Williams	61 64
1947	Margaret Osborne	D. Hart	62 64	2005	Venus Williams	L. Davenport	46 76 97
1948	Louise Brough	D. Hart	63 86	2006	Amelie Mauresmo	J. Henin-Hardenne	26 63 64
1949	Louise Brough	M. du Pont	10-8 16 10-8				

U.S. Open
MEN

Challenge round system (defending champion qualified for following year's final) used from 1884 to 1911. Known as the Patriotic Tournament in 1917 during World War I. Amateur and Open Championships held in 1968 and '69. Became an exclusively Open Championship in 1970. **Surface:** Decoturf II (acrylic cement).

Multiple winners: Bill Larned, Richard Sears and Bill Tilden (7); Jimmy Connors and Pete Sampras (5); John McEnroe and Robert Wrenn (4); Oliver Campbell, Roger Federer, Ivan Lendl, Fred Perry and Malcolm Whitman (3); Andre Agassi, Don Budge, Stefan Edberg, Roy Emerson, Neale Fraser, Pancho Gonzales, Bill Johnston, Jack Kramer, Rene Lacoste, Rod Laver, Maurice McLoughlin, Lindley Murray, John Newcombe, Frank Parker, Patrick Rafter, Bobby Riggs, Ken Rosewall, Frank Sedgman, Henry Slocum Jr., Tony Trabert, Ellsworth Vines and Dick Williams (2).

Year	Winner	Loser	Score	Year	Winner	Loser	Score
1881	Richard Sears	W. Glyn	60 63 62	1945	Frank Parker	B. Talbert	14-12 61 62
1882	Richard Sears	C. Clark	61 64 60	1946	Jack Kramer	T. Brown, Jr.	97 63 60
1883	Richard Sears	J. Dwight	62 60 97	1947	Jack Kramer	F. Parker	46 26 61 60 63
1884	Richard Sears	H. Taylor	60 16 60 62	1948	Pancho Gonzales	E. Sturgess	62 63 14-12
1885	Richard Sears	G. Brinley	63 46 60 63	1949	Pancho Gonzales	F. Schroeder	16-18 26 61 62 64
1886	Richard Sears	R. Beeckman	46 61 63 64	1950	Arthur Larsen	H. Flam	63 46 57 64 63
1887	Richard Sears	H. Slocum Jr.	61 63 62	1951	Frank Sedgman	V. Seixas	64 61 61
1888	Henry Slocum Jr.	H. Taylor	64 61 60	1952	Frank Sedgman	G. Mulloy	61 62 63
1889	Henry Slocum Jr.	Q. Shaw	63 61 46 62	1953	Tony Trabert	V. Seixas	63 62 63
1890	Oliver Campbell	H. Slocum Jr.	62 46 63 61	1954	Vic Seixas	R. Hartwig	36 62 64 64
1891	Oliver Campbell	C. Hobart	26 75 79 61 62	1955	Tony Trabert	K. Rosewall	97 63 63
1892	Oliver Campbell	F. Hovey	75 36 63 75	1956	Ken Rosewall	L. Hoad	46 62 63 63
1893	Robert Wrenn	F. Hovey	64 36 64 64	1957	Mal Anderson	A. Cooper	10-8 75 64
1894	Robert Wrenn	M. Goodbody	68 61 64 64	1958	Ashley Cooper	M. Anderson	62 36 46 10-8 86
1895	Fred Hovey	R. Wrenn	63 62 64	1959	Neale Fraser	A. Olmedo	63 57 62 64
1896	Robert Wrenn	F. Hovey	75 36 60 16 61	1960	Neale Fraser	R. Laver	64 64 97
1897	Robert Wrenn	W. Eaves	46 86 63 26 62	1961	Roy Emerson	R. Laver	75 63 62
1898	Malcolm Whitman	D. Davis	36 62 62 61	1962	Rod Laver	R. Emerson	62 64 57 64
1899	Malcolm Whitman	P. Paret	61 62 36 75	1963	Rafael Osuna	F. Froehling	75 64 62
1900	Malcolm Whitman	B. Larned	64 16 62 62	1964	Roy Emerson	F. Stolle	64 62 64
1901	Bill Larned	B. Wright	62 68 64 64	1965	Manuel Santana	C. Drysdale	62 79 75 61
1902	Bill Larned	R. Doherty	46 62 64 86	1966	Fred Stolle	J. Newcombe	46 12-10 63 64
1903	Laurie Doherty	B. Larned	60 63 10-8	1967	John Newcombe	C. Graebner	64 64 86
1904	Holcombe Ward	B. Clothier	10-8 64 97	1968	Am-Arthur Ashe	B. Lutz	46 63 8-10 60 64
1905	Beals Wright	H. Ward	62 61 11-9		Op-Arthur Ashe	T. Okker	14-12 57 63 36 63
1906	Bill Clothier	B. Wright	63 60 64	1969	Am-Stan Smith	B. Lutz	97 63 61
1907	Bill Larned	R. LeRoy	62 62 64		Op-Rod Laver	T. Roche	79 61 63 62
1908	Bill Larned	B. Wright	61 62 86	1970	Ken Rosewall	T. Roche	26 64 76 63
1909	Bill Larned	B. Clothier	61 62 57 16 61	1971	Stan Smith	J. Kodes	36 63 62 76
1910	Bill Larned	T. Bundy	61 57 60 68 61	1972	Ilie Nastase	A. Ashe	36 63 67 64 63
1911	Bill Larned	M. McLoughlin	64 64 62	1973	John Newcombe	J. Kodes	64 16 46 62 63
1912	Maurice McLoughlin	W.F. Johnson	36 26 62 64 62	1974	Jimmy Connors	K. Rosewall	61 60 61
1913	Maurice McLoughlin	R. Williams	64 57 63 61	1975	Manuel Orantes	J. Connors	64 63 63
1914	Dick Williams	M. McLoughlin	63 86 10-8	1976	Jimmy Connors	B. Borg	64 36 76 64
1915	Bill Johnston	M. McLoughlin	16 60 75 10-8	1977	Guillermo Vilas	J. Connors	26 63 76 60
1916	Dick Williams	B. Johnston	46 64 06 62 64	1978	Jimmy Connors	B. Borg	64 62 62
1917	Lindley Murray	N. Niles	57 86 63 63	1979	John McEnroe	V. Gerulaitis	75 63 63
1918	Lindley Murray	B. Tilden	63 61 75	1980	John McEnroe	B. Borg	76 61 67 57 64
1919	Bill Johnston	B. Tilden	64 64 63	1981	John McEnroe	B. Borg	46 62 64 63
1920	Bill Tilden	B. Johnston	61 16 75 57 63	1982	Jimmy Connors	I. Lendl	63 62 46 64
1921	Bill Tilden	W. Johnson	61 63 61	1983	Jimmy Connors	I. Lendl	63 67 75 60
1922	Bill Tilden	B. Johnston	46 36 62 63 64	1984	John McEnroe	I. Lendl	63 64 61
1923	Bill Tilden	B. Johnston	64 61 64	1985	Ivan Lendl	J. McEnroe	76 63 64
1924	Bill Tilden	B. Johnston	61 97 62	1986	Ivan Lendl	M. Mecir	64 62 60
1925	Bill Tilden	B. Johnston	46 11-9 63 46 63	1987	Ivan Lendl	M. Wilander	67 60 76 64
1926	Rene Lacoste	J. Borotra	64 60 64	1988	Mats Wilander	I. Lendl	64 46 63 57 64
1927	Rene Lacoste	B. Tilden	11-9 63 11-9	1989	Boris Becker	I. Lendl	76 16 63 76
1928	Henri Cochet	F. Hunter	46 64 36 75 63	1990	Pete Sampras	A. Agassi	64 63 62
1929	Bill Tilden	F. Hunter	36 63 46 62 64	1991	Stefan Edberg	J. Courier	62 64 60
1930	John Doeg	F. Shields	10-8 16 64 16-14	1992	Stefan Edberg	P. Sampras	36 64 76 62
1931	Ellsworth Vines	G. Lott Jr.	79 63 97 75	1993	Pete Sampras	C. Pioline	64 64 63
1932	Ellsworth Vines	H. Cochet	64 64 64	1994	Andre Agassi	M. Stich	61 76 75
1933	Fred Perry	J. Crawford	63 11-13 46 60 61	1995	Pete Sampras	A. Agassi	64 63 46 75
1934	Fred Perry	W. Allison	64 63 16 86	1996	Pete Sampras	M. Chang	61 64 76
1935	Wilmer Allison	S. Wood	62 62 63	1997	Patrick Rafter	G. Rusedski	63 62 46 75
1936	Fred Perry	D. Budge	26 62 86 16 10-8	1998	Patrick Rafter	M. Philippoussis	63 36 62 60
1937	Don Budge	G. von Cramm	61 79 61 36 61	1999	Andre Agassi	T. Martin	64 67 67 63 62
1938	Don Budge	G. Mako	63 68 62 61	2000	Marat Safin	P. Sampras	64 63 63
1939	Bobby Riggs	S.W. van Horn	64 62 64	2001	Lleyton Hewitt	P. Sampras	76 61 61
1940	Don McNeill	B. Riggs	46 68 63 63 75	2002	Pete Sampras	A. Agassi	63 64 57 64
1941	Bobby Riggs	F. Kovacs	57 61 63 63	2003	Andy Roddick	J.C. Ferrero	63 76 63
1942	Fred Schroeder	F. Parker	86 75 36 46 62	2004	Roger Federer	L. Hewitt	60 76 60
1943	Joe Hunt	J. Kramer	63 68 10-8 60	2005	Roger Federer	A. Agassi	63 26 76 61
1944	Frank Parker	B. Talbert	64 36 63 63	2006	Roger Federer	A. Roddick	62 46 75 61

WOMEN

Challenge round system used from 1887-1918. Five set final played from 1887 to 1901. Amateur and Open Championships held in 1968 and '69. Became an exclusively Open Championship in 1970.

Multiple winners: Molla Bjurstedt Mallory (8); Helen Wills Moody (7); Chris Evert Lloyd (6); Margaret Smith Court and Steffi Graf (5); Pauline Betz, Maria Bueno, Helen Jacobs, Billie Jean King, Alice Marble, Elisabeth Moore, Martina Navratilova and Hazel Hotchkiss Wightman (4); Juliette Atkinson, Mary Browne, Maureen Connolly and Margaret Osborne du Pont (3); Tracy Austin, Mabel Cahill, Sarah Palfrey Cooke, Althea Gibson, Darlene Hard, Doris Hart, Marion Jones, Monica Seles, Bertha Townsend, Serena Williams and Venus Williams (2).

Year	Winner	Loser	Score
1887	Ellen Hansell	L. Knight	61 60
1888	Bertha Townsend	E. Hansell	63 65
1889	Bertha Townsend	L. Voorhes	75 62
1890	Ellen Roosevelt	B. Townsend	62 62
1891	Mabel Cahill	E. Roosevelt	64 61 46 63
1892	Mabel Cahill	E. Moore	57 63 64 46 62
1893	Aline Terry	A. Schultz	61 63
1894	Helen Hellwig	A. Terry	75 36 60 36 63
1895	Juliette Atkinson	H. Hellwig	64 62 61
1896	Elisabeth Moore	J. Atkinson	64 46 62 62
1897	Juliette Atkinson	E. Moore	63 63 46 36 63
1898	Juliette Atkinson	M. Jones	63 57 64 26 75
1899	Marion Jones	M. Banks	61 61 75
1900	Myrtle McAteer	E. Parker	62 62 60
1901	Elisabeth Moore	M. McAteer	64 36 75 26 62
1902	Marion Jones	E. Moore	61 10(ret)
1903	Elisabeth Moore	M. Jones	75 86
1904	May Sutton	E. Moore	61 62
1905	Elisabeth Moore	H. Homans	64 57 61
1906	Helen Homans	M. Barger-Wallach	64 63
1907	Evelyn Sears	C. Neely	63 62
1908	Maud B. Wallach	Ev. Sears	63 16 63
1909	Hazel Hotchkiss	M. Barger-Wallach	60 61
1910	Hazel Hotchkiss	L. Hammond	64 62
1911	Hazel Hotchkiss	F. Sutton	8-10 61 97
1912	Mary Browne	E. Sears	64 62
1913	Mary Browne	D. Green	62 75
1914	Mary Browne	M. Wagner	62 16 61
1915	Molla Bjurstedt	H. Wightman	46 62 60
1916	Molla Bjurstedt	L. Raymond	60 61
1917	Molla Bjurstedt	M. Vanderhoef	46 60 62
1918	Molla Bjurstedt	E. Goss	64 63
1919	Hazel Wightman	M. Zinderstein	61 62
1920	Molla Mallory	M. Zinderstein	63 61
1921	Molla Mallory	M. Browne	46 64 62
1922	Molla Mallory	H. Wills	63 61
1923	Helen Wills	M. Mallory	62 61
1924	Helen Wills	M. Mallory	61 63
1925	Helen Wills	K. McKane	36 60 62
1926	Molla Mallory	E. Ryan	46 64 97
1927	Helen Wills	B. Nuthall	61 64
1928	Helen Wills	H. Jacobs	62 61
1929	Helen Wills	P. Watson	64 62
1930	Betty Nuthall	A. Harper	61 64
1931	Helen Moody	E. Whittingstall	64 61
1932	Helen Jacobs	C. Babcock	62 62
1933	Helen Jacobs	H. Moody	86 36 30(ret)
1934	Helen Jacobs	S. Palfrey	61 64
1935	Helen Jacobs	S. Fabyan	62 64
1936	Alice Marble	H. Jacobs	46 63 62
1937	Anita Lizana	J. Jedrzejowska	64 62
1938	Alice Marble	N. Wynne	60 63
1939	Alice Marble	H. Jacobs	60 8-10 64
1940	Alice Marble	H. Jacobs	62 63
1941	Sarah Cooke	P. Betz	75 62
1942	Pauline Betz	L. Brough	46 61 64
1943	Pauline Betz	L. Brough	63 57 63
1944	Pauline Betz	M. Osborne	63 86
1945	Sarah Cooke	P. Betz	36 86 64
1946	Pauline Betz	P. Canning	11-9 63
1947	Louise Brough	M. Osborne	86 46 61

Year	Winner	Loser	Score
1948	Margaret du Pont	L. Brough	46 64 15-13
1949	Margaret du Pont	D. Hart	64 61
1950	Margaret du Pont	D. Hart	64 63
1951	Maureen Connolly	S. Fry	63 16 64
1952	Maureen Connolly	D. Hart	63 75
1953	Maureen Connolly	D. Hart	62 64
1954	Doris Hart	L. Brough	68 61 86
1955	Doris Hart	P. Ward	64 62
1956	Shirley Fry	A. Gibson	63 64
1957	Althea Gibson	L. Brough	63 62
1958	Althea Gibson	D. Hard	36 61 62
1959	Maria Bueno	C. Truman	61 64
1960	Darlene Hard	M. Bueno	64 10-12 64
1961	Darlene Hard	A. Haydon	63 64
1962	Margaret Smith	D. Hard	97 64
1963	Maria Bueno	M. Smith	75 64
1964	Maria Bueno	C. Graebner	61 60
1965	Margaret Smith	B.J. Moffitt	86 75
1966	Maria Bueno	N. Richey	63 61
1967	Billie Jean King	A. Jones	11-9 64
1968	Am-Margaret Court	M. Bueno	62 62
	Op-Virginia Wade	B.J. King	64 62
1969	Am-Margaret Court	V. Wade	46 63 60
	Op-Margaret Court	N. Richey	62 62
1970	Margaret Court	R. Casals	62 26 61
1971	Billie Jean King	R. Casals	64 76
1972	Billie Jean King	K. Melville	63 75
1973	Margaret Court	E. Goolagong	76 57 62
1974	Billie Jean King	E. Goolagong	36 63 75
1975	Chris Evert	E. Cawley	57 64 62
1976	Chris Evert	E. Cawley	63 60
1977	Chris Evert	W. Turnbull	76 62
1978	Chris Evert	P. Shriver	75 64
1979	Tracy Austin	C. Evert Lloyd	64 63
1980	Chris Evert Lloyd	H. Mandlikova	57 61 61
1981	Tracy Austin	M. Navratilova	16 76 76
1982	Chris Evert Lloyd	H. Mandlikova	63 61
1983	Martina Navratilova	C. Evert Lloyd	61 63
1984	Martina Navratilova	C. Evert Lloyd	46 64 64
1985	Hana Mandlikova	M. Navratilova	76 16 76
1986	Martina Navratilova	H. Sukova	63 62
1987	Martina Navratilova	S. Graf	76 61
1988	Steffi Graf	G. Sabatini	63 36 61
1989	Steffi Graf	M. Navratilova	36 75 61
1990	Gabriela Sabatini	S. Graf	62 76
1991	Monica Seles	M. Navratilova	76 61
1992	Monica Seles	A.S. Vicario	63 63
1993	Steffi Graf	H. Sukova	63 63
1994	A. Sanchez Vicario	S. Graf	16 76 64
1995	Steffi Graf	M. Seles	76 06 63
1996	Steffi Graf	M. Seles	75 64
1997	Martina Hingis	V. Williams	60 64
1998	Lindsay Davenport	M. Hingis	63 75
1999	Serena Williams	M. Hingis	63 76
2000	Venus Williams	L. Davenport	64 75
2001	Venus Williams	S. Williams	62 64
2002	Serena Williams	V. Williams	64 63
2003	J. Henin-Hardenne	K. Clijsters	75 61
2004	Svetlana Kuznetsova	E. Dementieva	63 75
2005	Kim Clijsters	M. Pierce	63 61
2006	Maria Sharapova	J. Henin-Hardenne	64 64

Grand Slam Summary

Singles winners of the four Grand Slam tournaments–Australian, French, Wimbledon and United States–since the French was opened to all comers in 1925. Note that there were two Australian Opens in 1977 and none in 1986.

MEN

Three wins in one year: Jack Crawford (1933); Fred Perry (1934); Tony Trabert (1955); Lew Hoad (1956); Ashley Cooper (1958); Roy Emerson (1964); Jimmy Connors (1974); Mats Wilander (1988); Roger Federer (2004, 2006).

Two wins in one year: Roy Emerson and Pete Sampras (4 times); Bjorn Borg (3 times); Rene Lacoste, Ivan Lendl, John Newcombe and Fred Perry (twice); Andre Agassi, Boris Becker, Don Budge, Henri Cochet, Jimmy Connors, Jim Courier, Roger Federer, Neale Fraser, Jack Kramer, John McEnroe, Alex Olmedo, Budge Patty, Bobby Riggs, Ken Rosewall, Dick Savitt, Frank Sedgman and Guillermo Vilas (once).

Year	Australian	French	Wimbledon	U.S.
1925	Anderson	Lacoste	Lacoste	Tilden
1926	Hawkes	Cochet	Borotra	Lacoste
1927	Patterson	Lacoste	Cochet	Lacoste
1928	Borotra	Cochet	Lacoste	Cochet
1929	Gregory	Lacoste	Cochet	Tilden
1930	Moon	Cochet	Tilden	Doeg
1931	Crawford	Borotra	Wood	Vines
1932	Crawford	Cochet	Vines	Vines
1933	Crawford	Crawford	Crawford	Perry
1934	Perry	von Cramm	Perry	Perry
1935	Crawford	Perry	Perry	Allison
1936	Quist	von Cramm	Perry	Perry
1937	McGrath	Henkel	Budge	Budge
1938	**Budge**	**Budge**	**Budge**	**Budge**
1939	Bromwich	McNeill	Riggs	Riggs
1940	Quist	—	—	McNeill
1941	—	—	—	Riggs
1942	—	—	—	Schroeder
1943	—	—	—	Hunt
1944	—	—	—	Parker
1945	—	—	—	Parker
1946	Bromwich	Bernard	Petra	Kramer
1947	Pails	Asboth	Kramer	Kramer
1948	Quist	Parker	Falkenburg	Gonzales
1949	Sedgman	Parker	Schroeder	Gonzales
1950	Sedgman	Patty	Patty	Larsen
1951	Savitt	Drobny	Savitt	Sedgman
1952	McGregor	Drobny	Sedgman	Sedgman
1953	Rosewall	Rosewall	Seixas	Trabert
1954	Rose	Trabert	Drobny	Seixas
1955	Rosewall	Trabert	Trabert	Trabert
1956	Hoad	Hoad	Hoad	Rosewall
1957	Cooper	Davidson	Hoad	Anderson
1958	Cooper	Rose	Cooper	Cooper
1959	Olmedo	Pietrangeli	Olmedo	Fraser
1960	Laver	Pietrangeli	Fraser	Fraser
1961	Emerson	Santana	Laver	Emerson
1962	**Laver**	**Laver**	**Laver**	**Laver**
1963	Emerson	Emerson	McKinley	Osuna
1964	Emerson	Santana	Emerson	Emerson
1965	Emerson	Stolle	Emerson	Santana
1966	Emerson	Roche	Santana	Stolle
1967	Emerson	Emerson	Newcombe	Newcombe
1968	Bowrey	Rosewall	Laver	Ashe
1969	**Laver**	**Laver**	**Laver**	**Laver**
1970	Ashe	Kodes	Newcombe	Rosewall
1971	Rosewall	Kodes	Newcombe	Smith
1972	Rosewall	Gimeno	Smith	Nastase
1973	Newcombe	Nastase	Kodes	Newcombe
1974	Connors	Borg	Connors	Connors
1975	Newcombe	Borg	Ashe	Orantes
1976	Edmondson	Panatta	Borg	Connors
1977	Tanner & Gerulaitis	Vilas	Borg	Vilas
1978	Vilas	Borg	Borg	Connors
1979	Vilas	Borg	Borg	McEnroe
1980	Teacher	Borg	Borg	McEnroe
1981	Kriek	Borg	McEnroe	McEnroe
1982	Kriek	Wilander	Connors	Connors
1983	Wilander	Noah	McEnroe	Connors
1984	Wilander	Lendl	McEnroe	McEnroe
1985	Edberg	Wilander	Becker	Lendl
1986	—	Lendl	Becker	Lendl
1987	Edberg	Lendl	Cash	Lendl
1988	Wilander	Wilander	Edberg	Wilander
1989	Lendl	Chang	Becker	Becker
1990	Lendl	Gomez	Edberg	Sampras
1991	Becker	Courier	Stich	Edberg
1992	Courier	Courier	Agassi	Edberg
1993	Courier	Bruguera	Sampras	Sampras
1994	Sampras	Bruguera	Sampras	Agassi
1995	Agassi	Muster	Sampras	Sampras
1996	Becker	Kafelnikov	Krajicek	Sampras
1997	Sampras	Kuerten	Sampras	Rafter
1998	Korda	Moya	Sampras	Rafter
1999	Kafelnikov	Agassi	Sampras	Agassi
2000	Agassi	Kuerten	Sampras	Safin
2001	Agassi	Kuerten	Ivanisevic	Hewitt
2002	Johansson	Costa	Hewitt	Sampras
2003	Agassi	Ferrero	Federer	Roddick
2004	Federer	Gaudio	Federer	Federer
2005	Safin	Nadal	Federer	Federer
2006	Federer	Nadal	Federer	Federer

Men's, Women's & Mixed Doubles Grand Slam

The tennis Grand Slam has only been accomplished in doubles competition six times in the same calendar year. Here are the doubles teams to accomplish the feat. The two men and three women to win the singles Grand Slam are noted in the Grand Slam Summary tables.

Men's Doubles

1951 . . . . .Frank Sedgman, Australia
& Ken McGregor, Australia

Mixed Doubles

1963 . . . . .Ken Fletcher, Australia
& Margaret Smith, Australia
1967 . . . . .Owen Davidson and two partners*.

*Davidson's partners: AUS–Lesley Turner; FR, WIM, U.S.–Billie Jean King.

Women's Doubles

1960 . . . . .Maria Bueno, Brazil & two partners†
1984 . . . . .Martina Navratilova, USA
& Pam Shriver, USA
1998 . . . .Martina Hingis, Switzerland & two partners#

†Bueno's partners: AUS–Christine Truman; FR, WIM, U.S.–Darlene Hard.

#Hingis' partners: AUS–Mirjana Lucic; FR, WIM, U.S.–Jana Novotna.

WOMEN

Three in one year: Helen Wills Moody (1928 and '29); Margaret Smith Court (1962, '65, '69 and '73); Billie Jean King (1972); Martina Navratilova (1983 and '84); Steffi Graf (1989, '93, '95 and '96); Monica Seles (1991 and '92); Martina Hingis (1997) and Serena Williams (2002).

Two in one year: Chris Evert Lloyd (5 times); Helen Wills Moody and Martina Navratilova (3 times); Maria Bueno, Maureen Connolly, Margaret Smith Court, Althea Gibson, Billie Jean King and Venus Williams (twice); Cilly Aussem, Pauline Betz, Louise Brough, Jennifer Capriati, Evonne Goolagong Cawley, Margaret Osborne du Pont, Shirley Fry, Darlene Hard, Justine Henin-Hardenne, Suzanne Lenglen, Alice Marble, Amelie Mauresmo, Arantxa Sanchez Vicario and Serena Williams (once).

Year	Australian	French	Wimbledon	U.S.
1925	Akhurst	Lenglen	Lenglen	Wills
1926	Akhurst	Lenglen	Godfree	Mallory
1927	Boyd	Bouman	Wills	Wills
1928	Akhurst	Wills	Wills	Wills
1929	Akhurst	Wills	Wills	Wills
1930	Akhurst	Moody	Moody	Nuthall
1931	Buttsworth	Aussem	Aussem	Moody
1932	Buttsworth	Moody	Moody	Jacobs
1933	Hartigan	Scriven	Moody	Jacobs
1934	Hartigan	Scriven	Round	Jacobs
1935	Round	Sperling	Moody	Jacobs
1936	Hartigan	Sperling	Jacobs	Marble
1937	Wynne	Sperling	Round	Lizana
1938	Bundy	Mathieu	Moody	Marble
1939	Westacott	Mathieu	Marble	Marble
1940	Wynne	—	—	Marble
1941	—	—	—	Cooke
1942	—	—	—	Betz
1943	—	—	—	Betz
1944	—	—	—	Betz
1945	—	—	—	Cooke
1946	Bolton	Osborne	Betz	Betz
1947	Bolton	Todd	Osborne	Brough
1948	Bolton	Landry	Brough	du Pont
1949	Hart	du Pont	Brough	du Pont
1950	Brough	Hart	Brough	du Pont
1951	Bolton	Fry	Hart	Connolly
1952	Long	Hart	Connolly	Connolly
1953	**Connolly**	**Connolly**	**Connolly**	**Connolly**
1954	Long	Connolly	Connolly	Hart
1955	Penrose	Mortimer	Brough	Hart
1956	Carter	Gibson	Fry	Fry
1957	Fry	Bloomer	Gibson	Gibson
1958	Mortimer	Kormoczi	Gibson	Gibson
1959	Reitano	Truman	Bueno	Bueno
1960	Smith	Hard	Bueno	Hard
1961	Smith	Haydon	Mortimer	Hard
1962	Smith	Smith	Susman	Smith
1963	Smith	Turner	Smith	Bueno
1964	Smith	Smith	Bueno	Bueno
1965	Smith	Turner	Smith	Smith
1966	Smith	Jones	King	Bueno
1967	Richey	Durr	King	King
1968	King	Richey	King	Wade
1969	Court	Court	Jones	Court
1970	**Court**	**Court**	**Court**	**Court**
1971	Court	Goolagong	Goolagong	King
1972	Wade	King	King	King
1973	Court	Court	King	Court
1974	Goolagong	Evert	Evert	King
1975	Goolagong	Evert	King	Evert
1976	Cawley	Barker	Evert	Evert
1977	Reid & Cawley	Jausovec	Wade	Evert
1978	O'Neil	Ruzici	Navratilova	Evert
1979	Jordan	Evert Lloyd	Navratilova	Austin
1980	Mandlikova	Evert Lloyd	Cawley	Evert Lloyd
1981	Navratilova	Mandlikova	Evert Lloyd	Austin
1982	Evert Lloyd	Navratilova	Navratilova	Evert Lloyd
1983	Navratilova	Evert Lloyd	Navratilova	Navratilova
1984	Evert Lloyd	Navratilova	Navratilova	Navratilova
1985	Navratilova	Evert Lloyd	Navratilova	Mandlikova
1986	—	Evert Lloyd	Navratilova	Navratilova
1987	Mandlikova	Graf	Navratilova	Navratilova
1988	**Graf**	**Graf**	**Graf**	**Graf**
1989	Graf	Vicario	Graf	Graf
1990	Graf	Seles	Navratilova	Sabatini
1991	Seles	Seles	Graf	Seles
1992	Seles	Seles	Graf	Seles
1993	Seles	Graf	Graf	Graf
1994	Graf	Vicario	Martinez	Vicario
1995	Pierce	Graf	Graf	Graf
1996	Seles	Graf	Graf	Graf
1997	Hingis	Majoli	Hingis	Hingis
1998	Hingis	Vicario	Novotna	Davenport
1999	Hingis	Graf	Davenport	S. Williams
2000	Davenport	Pierce	V. Williams	V. Williams
2001	Capriati	Capriati	V. Williams	V. Williams
2002	Capriati	S. Williams	S. Williams	S. Williams
2003	S. Williams	H-Hardenne	S. Williams	H-Hardenne
2004	H-Hardenne	Myskina	Sharapova	Kuznetsova
2005	S. Williams	H-Hardenne	V. Williams	Clijsters
2006	Mauresmo	H-Hardenne	Mauresmo	Sharapova

Overall Leaders

All-Time Grand Slam titleists including all singles and doubles championships at the four major tournaments. Titles listed under each heading are singles, doubles and mixed doubles. Players active in 2006 are in **bold** type.

			MEN					Total
		Career	Australian	French	Wimbledon	U.S.	S-D-M	Titles
1	Roy Emerson	1959-71	6-3-0	2-6-0	2-3-0	2-4-0	12-16-0	28
2	John Newcombe	1965-76	2-5-0	0-3-0	3-6-0	2-3-1	7-17-1	25
3	Frank Sedgman	1949-52	2-2-2	0-2-2	1-3-2	2-2-2	5-9-8	22
	Todd Woodbridge	1988-2005	0-3-1	0-1-1	0-9-1	0-3-3	0-16-6	22
5	Bill Tilden	1913-30	* *	0-0-1	3-1-0	7-5-4	10-6-5	21
6	Rod Laver	1959-71	3-4-0	2-1-1	4-1-2	2-0-0	11-6-3	20
7	Jack Bromwich	1938-50	2-8-1	0-0-0	0-2-2	0-3-1	2-13-4	19
	Neale Fraser	1957-62	0-3-1	0-3-0	1-2-1	2-3-3	3-11-5	19
9	Ken Rosewall	1953-72	4-3-0	2-2-0	0-2-0	2-2-1	8-9-1	18
	Jean Borotra	1925-36	1-1-1	1-5-2	2-3-1	0-0-1	4-9-5	18
	Fred Stolle	1962-69	0-3-1	1-2-0	0-2-3	1-3-2	2-10-6	18
12	Four tied with 17 total titles each.							

Grand Slam Overall Leaders (Cont.)
WOMEN

		Career	Australian	French	Wimbledon	U.S.	S-D-M	Total Titles
1	Margaret Smith Court	1960-75	11-8-2	5-4-4	3-2-5	5-5-8	24-19-19	62
2	**Martina Navratilova**	1974-95, 2000-06	3-8-1	2-7-2	9-7-4	4-9-3	18-31-10	59
3	Billie Jean King	1961-81	1-0-1	1-1-2	6-10-4	4-5-4	12-16-11	39
4	Margaret du Pont	1941-62	*	2-3-0	1-5-1	3-13-9	6-21-10	37
5	Louise Brough	1942-57	1-1-0	0-3-0	4-5-4	1-12-4	6-21-8	35
	Doris Hart	1948-55	1-1-2	2-5-3	1-4-5	2-4-5	6-14-15	35
7	Helen Wills Moody	1923-38	*	4-2-0	8-3-1	7-4-2	19-9-3	31
8	Elizabeth Ryan	1914-34	*	0-4-0	0-12-7	0-1-2	0-17-9	26
9	Suzanne Lenglen	1919-26	*	6-2-2	6-6-3	0-0-0	12-8-5	25
10	Steffi Graf	1982-99	4-0-0	6-0-0	7-1-0	5-0-0	22-1-0	23
11	Pam Shriver	1981-97	0-7-0	0-4-1	0-5-0	0-5-0	0-21-1	22
12	Chris Evert	1974-89	2-0-0	7-2-0	3-1-0	6-0-0	18-3-0	21
	Darlene Hard	1958-69	*	1-3-2	0-4-3	2-6-0	3-13-5	21
14	Natasha Zvereva	1989-2002	0-3-2	0-6-0	0-5-0	0-4-0	0-18-2	20
	Nancye Wynne Bolton	1935-52	6-10-4	0-0-0	0-0-0	0-0-0	6-10-4	20
	Maria Bueno	1958-68	0-1-0	0-1-1	3-5-0	4-5-0	7-12-1	20

All-Time Grand Slam Singles Titles

Men and women with the most singles championships in the Australian, French, Wimbledon and U.S. championships, through 2006. Note that (*) indicates player never played in that particular Grand Slam event; and players active in singles play in 2006 are in **bold** type.

Top 10 Men

		Aus	Fre	Wim	US	Total
1	Pete Sampras	2	0	7	5	14
2	Roy Emerson	6	2	2	2	12
3	Bjorn Borg	0	6	5	0	11
	Rod Laver	3	2	4	2	11
5	Bill Tilden	*	0	3	7	10
6	**Roger Federer**	2	0	4	3	9
7	**Andre Agassi**	4	1	1	2	8
	Jimmy Connors	1	0	2	5	8
	Ivan Lendl	2	3	0	3	8
	Fred Perry	1	1	3	3	8
	Ken Rosewall	4	2	0	2	8

Top 10 Women

		Aus	Fre	Wim	US	Total
1	Margaret Smith Court	11	5	3	5	24
2	Steffi Graf	4	6	7	5	22
3	Helen Wills Moody	*	4	8	7	19
4	Chris Evert	2	7	3	6	18
	Martina Navratilova	3	2	9	4	18
6	Billie Jean King	1	†	6	4	12
	Suzanne Lenglen	*	6	6	0	12
8	Maureen Connolly	1	2	3	3	9
	Monica Seles	4	3	0	2	9
10	Molla Bjurstedt Mallory	*	*	0	8	8

Annual Number One Players

Unofficial world rankings for men and women determined by the *London Daily Telegraph* from 1914-72. Since then, official world rankings computed by men's and women's tours. Rankings included only amateur players from 1914 until the arrival of open (professional) tennis in 1968. No rankings were released during World Wars I and II.

MEN

Multiple winners: Pete Sampras and Bill Tilden (6); Jimmy Connors (5); Henri Cochet, Rod Laver, Ivan Lendl and John McEnroe (4); John Newcombe and Fred Perry (3); Bjorn Borg, Don Budge, Ashley Cooper, Stefan Edberg, Roy Emerson, Roger Federer, Neale Fraser, Lleyton Hewitt, Jack Kramer, Rene Lacoste, Ilie Nastase, Frank Sedgman and Tony Trabert (2).

Year		Year		Year		Year	
1914	Maurice McLoughlin	1938	Don Budge	1964	Roy Emerson	1985	Ivan Lendl
1915-18	No rankings	1939	Bobby Riggs	1965	Roy Emerson	1986	Ivan Lendl
1919	Gerald Patterson	1940-45	No rankings	1966	Manuel Santana	1987	Ivan Lendl
1920	Bill Tilden	1946	Jack Kramer	1967	John Newcombe	1988	Mats Wilander
1921	Bill Tilden	1947	Jack Kramer	1968	Rod Laver	1989	Ivan Lendl
1922	Bill Tilden	1948	Frank Parker	1969	Rod Laver		
1923	Bill Tilden	1949	Pancho Gonzales	1970	John Newcombe	1990	Stefan Edberg
1924	Bill Tilden	1950	Budge Patty	1971	John Newcombe	1991	Stefan Edberg
1925	Bill Tilden	1951	Frank Sedgman	1972	Ilie Nastase	1992	Jim Courier
1926	Rene Lacoste	1952	Frank Sedgman	1973	Ilie Nastase	1993	Pete Sampras
1927	Rene Lacoste	1953	Tony Trabert	1974	Jimmy Connors	1994	Pete Sampras
1928	Henri Cochet	1954	Jaroslav Drobny	1975	Jimmy Connors	1995	Pete Sampras
1929	Henri Cochet	1955	Tony Trabert	1976	Jimmy Connors	1996	Pete Sampras
1930	Henri Cochet	1956	Lew Hoad	1977	Jimmy Connors	1997	Pete Sampras
1931	Henri Cochet	1957	Ashley Cooper	1978	Jimmy Connors	1998	Pete Sampras
1932	Ellsworth Vines	1958	Ashley Cooper	1979	Bjorn Borg	1999	Andre Agassi
1933	Jack Crawford	1959	Neale Fraser	1980	Bjorn Borg	2000	Gustavo Kuerten
1934	Fred Perry	1960	Neale Fraser	1981	John McEnroe	2001	Lleyton Hewitt
1935	Fred Perry	1961	Rod Laver	1982	John McEnroe	2002	Lleyton Hewitt
1936	Fred Perry	1962	Rod Laver	1983	John McEnroe	2003	Andy Roddick
1937	Don Budge	1963	Rafael Osuna	1984	John McEnroe	2004	Roger Federer
						2005	Roger Federer

WOMEN

Multiple winners: Helen Wills Moody (9); Steffi Graf (8); Margaret Smith Court and Martina Navratilova (7); Chris Evert Lloyd and Billie Jean King (5); Lindsay Davenport and Margaret Osborne du Pont (4); Maureen Connolly, Martina Hingis and Monica Seles (3); Maria Bueno, Althea Gibson and Suzanne Lenglen (2).

Year		Year		Year		Year	
1925	Suzanne Lenglen	1950	Margaret du Pont	1970	Margaret Court	1990	Steffi Graf
1926	Suzanne Lenglen	1951	Doris Hart	1971	Evonne Goolagong	1991	Monica Seles
1927	Helen Wills	1952	Maureen Connolly	1972	Billie Jean King	1992	Monica Seles
1928	Helen Wills	1953	Maureen Connolly	1973	Margaret Court	1993	Steffi Graf
1929	Helen Wills Moody	1954	Maureen Connolly	1974	Billie Jean King	1994	Steffi Graf
1930	Helen Wills Moody	1955	Louise Brough	1975	Chris Evert	1995	Steffi Graf
1931	Helen Wills Moody	1956	Shirley Fry	1976	Chris Evert		& Monica Seles*
1932	Helen Wills Moody	1957	Althea Gibson	1977	Chris Evert	1996	Steffi Graf
1933	Helen Wills Moody	1958	Althea Gibson	1978	Martina Navratilova	1997	Martina Hingis
1934	Dorothy Round	1959	Maria Bueno	1979	Martina Navratilova	1998	Lindsay Davenport
1935	Helen Wills Moody					1999	Martina Hingis
1936	Helen Jacobs	1960	Maria Bueno	1980	Chris Evert Lloyd		
1937	Anita Lizana	1961	Angela Mortimer	1981	Chris Evert Lloyd	2000	Martina Hingis
1938	Helen Wills Moody	1962	Margaret Smith	1982	Martina Navratilova	2001	Lindsay Davenport
1939	Alice Marble	1963	Margaret Smith	1983	Martina Navratilova	2002	Serena Williams
		1964	Margaret Smith	1984	Martina Navratilova	2003	Justine Henin-Hardenne
1940-45	No rankings	1965	Margaret Smith	1985	Martina Navratilova	2004	Lindsay Davenport
1946	Pauline Betz	1966	Billie Jean King	1986	Martina Navratilova	2005	Lindsay Davenport
1947	Margaret Osborne	1967	Billie Jean King	1987	Steffi Graf		
1948	Margaret du Pont	1968	Billie Jean King	1988	Steffi Graf		
1949	Margaret du Pont	1969	Margaret Court	1989	Steffi Graf		

*Upon her return to the WTA Tour on Aug. 15, 1995, Seles retained her #1 ranking and was co-ranked at #1 through her first six tournaments (August '95–May '96). Seles was on leave since April 1993 when she was stabbed by a fan during a match.

Annual Top 10 World Rankings (since 1968)

Year by year Top 10 world computer rankings for men (ATP Tour) and women (WTA Tour) since the arrival of open tennis in 1968. Rankings from 1968-72 made by Lance Tingay of the London Daily Telegraph. Since 1973 the WTA Tour and ATP tour had compiled its own computer rankings. Since 2000, the men's rankings reflect the final standings of the ATP Champions Race.

MEN

	1968		**1971**		**1974**		**1977**		**1980**
1	Rod Laver	1	John Newcombe	1	Jimmy Connors	1	Jimmy Connors	1	Bjorn Borg
2	Arthur Ashe	2	Stan Smith	2	John Newcombe	2	Guillermo Vilas	2	John McEnroe
3	Ken Rosewall	3	Rod Laver	3	Bjorn Borg	3	Bjorn Borg	3	Jimmy Connors
4	Tom Okker	4	Ken Rosewall	4	Rod Laver	4	Vitas Gerulaitis	4	Gene Mayer
5	Tony Roche	5	Jan Kodes	5	Guillermo Vilas	5	Brian Gottfried	5	Guillermo Vilas
6	John Newcombe	6	Arthur Ashe	6	Tom Okker	6	Eddie Dibbs	6	Ivan Lendl
7	Clark Graebner	7	Tom Okker	7	Arthur Ashe	7	Manuel Orantes	7	Harold Solomon
8	Dennis Ralston	8	Marty Riessen	8	Ken Rosewall	8	Raul Ramirez	8	Jose-Luis Clerc
9	Cliff Drysdale	9	Cliff Drysdale	9	Stan Smith	9	Ilie Nastase	9	Vitas Gerulaitis
10	Pancho Gonzales	10	Ilie Nastase	10	Ilie Nastase	10	Dick Stockton	10	Eliot Teltscher

	1969		**1972**		**1975**		**1978**		**1981**
1	Rod Laver	1	Stan Smith	1	Jimmy Connors	1	Jimmy Connors	1	John McEnroe
2	Tony Roche	2	Ken Rosewall	2	Guillermo Vilas	2	Bjorn Borg	2	Ivan Lendl
3	John Newcombe	3	Ilie Nastase	3	Bjorn Borg	3	Guillermo Vilas	3	Jimmy Connors
4	Tom Okker	4	Rod Laver	4	Arthur Ashe	4	John McEnroe	4	Bjorn Borg
5	Ken Rosewall	5	Arthur Ashe	5	Manuel Orantes	5	Vitas Gerulaitis	5	Jose-Luis Clerc
6	Arthur Ashe	6	John Newcombe	6	Ken Rosewall	6	Eddie Dibbs	6	Guillermo Vilas
7	Cliff Drysdale	7	Bob Lutz	7	Ilie Nastase	7	Brian Gottfried	7	Gene Mayer
8	Pancho Gonzales	8	Tom Okker	8	John Alexander	8	Raul Ramirez	8	Eliot Teltscher
9	Andres Gimeno	9	Marty Riessen	9	Roscoe Tanner	9	Harold Solomon	9	Vitas Gerulaitis
10	Fred Stolle	10	Andres Gimeno	10	Rod Laver	10	Corrado Barazzutti	10	Peter McNamara

	1970		**1973**		**1976**		**1979**		**1982**
1	John Newcombe	1	Ilie Nastase	1	Jimmy Connors	1	Bjorn Borg	1	John McEnroe
2	Ken Rosewall	2	John Newcombe	2	Bjorn Borg	2	Jimmy Connors	2	Jimmy Connors
3	Tony Roche	3	Jimmy Connors	3	Ilie Nastase	3	John McEnroe	3	Ivan Lendl
4	Rod Laver	4	Tom Okker	4	Manuel Orantes	4	Vitas Gerulaitis	4	Guillermo Vilas
5	Arthur Ashe	5	Stan Smith	5	Raul Ramirez	5	Roscoe Tanner	5	Vitas Gerulaitis
6	Ilie Nastase	6	Ken Rosewall	6	Guillermo Vilas	6	Guillermo Vilas	6	Jose-Luis Clerc
7	Tom Okker	7	Manuel Orantes	7	Adriano Panatta	7	Arthur Ashe	7	Mats Wilander
8	Roger Taylor	8	Rod Laver	8	Harold Solomon	8	Harold Solomon	8	Gene Mayer
9	Jan Kodes	9	Jan Kodes	9	Eddie Dibbs	9	Jose Higueras	9	Yannick Noah
10	Cliff Richey	10	Arthur Ashe	10	Brian Gottfried	10	Eddie Dibbs	10	Peter McNamara

Annual Top 10 World Rankings (since 1968) (Cont.)

MEN

1983
1 John McEnroe
2 Ivan Lendl
3 Jimmy Connors
4 Mats Wilander
5 Yannick Noah
6 Jimmy Arias
7 Jose Higueras
8 Jose-Luis Clerc
9 Kevin Curren
10 Gene Mayer

1984
1 John McEnroe
2 Jimmy Connors
3 Ivan Lendl
4 Mats Wilander
5 Andres Gomez
6 Anders Jarryd
7 Henrik Sundstrom
8 Pat Cash
9 Eliot Teltscher
10 Yannick Noah

1985
1 Ivan Lendl
2 John McEnroe
3 Mats Wilander
4 Jimmy Connors
5 Stefan Edberg
6 Boris Becker
7 Yannick Noah
8 Anders Jarryd
9 Miloslav Mecir
10 Kevin Curren

1986
1 Ivan Lendl
2 Boris Becker
3 Mats Wilander
4 Yannick Noah
5 Stefan Edberg
6 Henri Leconte
7 Joakim Nystrom
8 Jimmy Connors
9 Miloslav Mecir
10 Andres Gomez

1987
1 Ivan Lendl
2 Stefan Edberg
3 Mats Wilander
4 Jimmy Connors
5 Boris Becker
6 Miloslav Mecir
7 Pat Cash
8 Yannick Noah
9 Tim Mayotte
10 John McEnroe

1988
1 Mats Wilander
2 Ivan Lendl
3 Andre Agassi
4 Boris Becker
5 Stefan Edberg
6 Kent Carlsson
7 Jimmy Connors
8 Jakob Hlasek
9 Henri Leconte
10 Tim Mayotte

1989
1 Ivan Lendl
2 Boris Becker
3 Stefan Edberg
4 John McEnroe
5 Michael Chang
6 Brad Gilbert
7 Andre Agassi
8 Aaron Krickstein
9 Alberto Mancini
10 Jay Berger

1990
1 Stefan Edberg
2 Boris Becker
3 Ivan Lendl
4 Andre Agassi
5 Pete Sampras
6 Andres Gomez
7 Thomas Muster
8 Emilio Sanchez
9 Goran Ivanisevic
10 Brad Gilbert

1991
1 Stefan Edberg
2 Jim Courier
3 Boris Becker
4 Michael Stich
5 Ivan Lendl
6 Pete Sampras
7 Guy Forget
8 Karel Novacek
9 Petr Korda
10 Andre Agassi

1992
1 Jim Courier
2 Stefan Edberg
3 Pete Sampras
4 Goran Ivanisevic
5 Boris Becker
6 Michael Chang
7 Petr Korda
8 Ivan Lendl
9 Andre Agassi
10 Richard Krajicek

1993
1 Pete Sampras
2 Michael Stich
3 Jim Courier
4 Sergi Bruguera
5 Stefan Edberg
6 Andrei Medvedev
7 Goran Ivanisevic
8 Michael Chang
9 Thomas Muster
10 Cedric Pioline

1994
1 Pete Sampras
2 Andre Agassi
3 Boris Becker
4 Sergi Bruguera
5 Goran Ivanisevic
6 Michael Chang
7 Stefan Edberg
8 Alberto Berasategui
9 Michael Stich
10 Todd Martin

1995
1 Pete Sampras
2 Andre Agassi
3 Thomas Muster
4 Boris Becker
5 Michael Chang
6 Yevgeny Kafelnikov
7 Thomas Enqvist
8 Jim Courier
9 Wayne Ferreira
10 Goran Ivanisevic

1996
1 Pete Sampras
2 Michael Chang
3 Yevgeny Kafelnikov
4 Goran Ivanisevic
5 Thomas Muster
6 Boris Becker
7 Richard Krajicek
8 Andre Agassi
9 Thomas Enqvist
10 Wayne Ferreira

1997
1 Pete Sampras
2 Patrick Rafter
3 Michael Chang
4 Jonas Bjorkman
5 Yevgeny Kafelnikov
6 Greg Rusedski
7 Carlos Moya
8 Sergi Bruguera
9 Thomas Muster
10 Marcelo Rios

1998
1 Pete Sampras
2 Marcelo Rios
3 Alex Corretja
4 Patrick Rafter
5 Carlos Moya
6 Andre Agassi
7 Tim Henman
8 Karol Kucera
9 Greg Rusedski
10 Richard Krajicek

1999
1 Andre Agassi
2 Yevgeny Kafelnikov
3 Pete Sampras
4 Thomas Enqvist
5 Gustavo Kuerten
6 Nicolas Kiefer
7 Todd Martin
8 Nicolas Lapentti
9 Marcelo Rios
10 Richard Krajicek

2000
1 Gustavo Kuerten
2 Marat Safin
3 Pete Sampras
4 Magnus Norman
5 Yevgeny Kafelnikov
6 Andre Agassi
7 Lleyton Hewitt
8 Alex Corretja
9 Thomas Enqvist
10 Tim Henman

2001
1 Lleyton Hewitt
2 Gustavo Kuerten
3 Andre Agassi
4 Yevgeny Kafelnikov
5 Juan Carlos Ferrero
6 Sebastien Grosjean
7 Patrick Rafter
8 Tommy Haas
9 Tim Henman
10 Pete Sampras

2002
1 Lleyton Hewitt
2 Andre Agassi
3 Marat Safin
4 Juan Carlos Ferrero
5 Carlos Moya
6 Roger Federer
7 Jiri Novak
8 Tim Henman
9 Albert Costa
10 Andy Roddick

2003
1 Andy Roddick
2 Roger Federer
3 Juan Carlos Ferrero
4 Andre Agassi
5 Guillermo Coria
6 Rainer Schuettler
7 Carlos Moya
8 David Nalbandian
9 Mark Philippoussis
10 Sebastien Grosjean

2004
1 Roger Federer
2 Andy Roddick
3 Lleyton Hewitt
4 Marat Safin
5 Carlos Moya
6 Tim Henman
7 Guillermo Coria
8 Andre Agassi
9 David Nalbandian
10 Gaston Gaudio

2005
1 Roger Federer
2 Rafael Nadal
3 Andy Roddick
4 Lleyton Hewitt
5 Nikolay Davydenko
6 David Nalbandian
7 Andre Agassi
8 Guillermo Coria
9 Ivan Ljubicic
10 Gaston Gaudio

WOMEN

1968
1 Billie Jean King
2 Virginia Wade
3 Nancy Richey
4 Maria Bueno
5 Margaret Court
6 Ann Jones
7 Judy Tegart
8 Annette du Plooy
9 Leslie Bowrey
10 Rosie Casals

1969
1 Margaret Court
2 Ann Jones
3 Billie Jean King
4 Nancy Richey
5 Julie Heldman
6 Rosie Casals
7 Kerry Melville
8 Peaches Bartkowicz
9 Virginia Wade
10 Leslie Bowrey

1970
1 Margaret Court
2 Billie Jean King
3 Rosie Casals
4 Virginia Wade
5 Helga Niessen
6 Kerry Melville
7 Julie Heldman
8 Karen Krantczke
9 Francoise Durr
10 Nancy R. Gunter

1971
1 Evonne Goolagong
2 Billie Jean King
3 Margaret Court
4 Rosie Casals
5 Kerry Melville
6 Virginia Wade
7 Judy Tegart
8 Francoise Durr
9 Helga N. Masthoff
10 Chris Evert

1972
1 Billie Jean King
2 Evonne Goolagong
3 Chris Evert
4 Margaret Court
5 Kerry Melville
6 Virginia Wade
7 Rosie Casals
8 Nancy R. Gunter
9 Francoise Durr
10 Linda Tuero

1973
1 Margaret S. Court
2 Billie Jean King
3 Evonne G. Cawley
4 Chris Evert
5 Rosie Casals
6 Virginia Wade
7 Kerry Reid
8 Nancy Richey
9 Julie Heldman
10 Helga Masthoff

1974
1 Billie Jean King
2 Evonne G. Cawley
3 Chris Evert
4 Virginia Wade
5 Julie Heldman
6 Rosie Casals
7 Kerry Reid
8 Olga Morozova
9 Lesley Hunt
10 Francoise Durr

1975
1 Chris Evert
2 Billie Jean King
3 Evonne G. Cawley
4 Martina Navratilova
5 Virginia Wade
6 Margaret S. Court
7 Olga Morozova
8 Nancy Richey
9 Francoise Durr
10 Rosie Casals

1976
1 Chris Evert
2 Evonne G. Cawley
3 Virginia Wade
4 Martina Navratilova
5 Sue Barker
6 Betty Stove
7 Dianne Balestrat
8 Mima Jausovec
9 Rosie Casals
10 Francoise Durr

1977
1 Chris Evert
2 Billie Jean King
3 Martina Navratilova
4 Virginia Wade
5 Sue Barker
6 Rosie Casals
7 Betty Stove
8 Dianne Balestrat
9 Wendy Turnbull
10 Kerry Reid

1978
1 Martina Navratilova
2 Chris Evert Lloyd
3 Evonne G. Cawley
4 Virginia Wade
5 Billie Jean King
6 Tracy Austin
7 Wendy Turnbull
8 Kerry Reid
9 Betty Stove
10 Dianne Balestrat

1979
1 Martina Navratilova
2 Chris Evert Lloyd
3 Tracy Austin
4 Evonne G. Cawley
5 Billie Jean King
6 Dianne Balestrat
7 Wendy Turnbull
8 Virginia Wade
9 Kerry Reid
10 Sue Barker

1980
1 Chris Evert Lloyd
2 Tracy Austin
3 Martina Navratilova
4 Hana Mandlikova
5 Evonne G. Cawley
6 Billie Jean King
7 Andrea Jaeger
8 Wendy Turnbull
9 Pam Shriver
10 Greer Stevens

1981
1 Chris Evert Lloyd
2 Tracy Austin
3 Martina Navratilova
4 Andrea Jaeger
5 Hana Mandlikova
6 Sylvia Hanika
7 Pam Shriver
8 Wendy Turnbull
9 Bettina Bunge
10 Barbara Potter

1982
1 Martina Navratilova
2 Chris Evert Lloyd
3 Andrea Jaeger
4 Tracy Austin
5 Wendy Turnbull
6 Pam Shriver
7 Hana Mandlikova
8 Barbara Potter
9 Bettina Bunge
10 Sylvia Hanika

1983
1 Martina Navratilova
2 Chris Evert Lloyd
3 Andrea Jaeger
4 Pam Shriver
5 Sylvia Hanika
6 Jo Durie
7 Bettina Bunge
8 Wendy Turnbull
9 Tracy Austin
10 Zina Garrison

1984
1 Martina Navratilova
2 Chris Evert Lloyd
3 Hana Mandlikova
4 Pam Shriver
5 Wendy Turnbull
6 Manuela Maleeva
7 Helena Sukova
8 Claudia Kohde-Kilsch
9 Zina Garrison
10 Kathy Jordan

1985
1 Martina Navratilova
2 Chris Evert Lloyd
3 Hana Mandlikova
4 Pam Shriver
5 Claudia Kohde-Kilsch
6 Steffi Graf
7 Manuela Maleeva
8 Zina Garrison
9 Helena Sukova
10 Bonnie Gadusek

1986
1 Martina Navratilova
2 Chris Evert Lloyd
3 Steffi Graf
4 Hana Mandlikova
5 Helena Sukova
6 Pam Shriver
7 Claudia Kohde-Kilsch
8 M. Maleeva-Fragniere
9 Zina Garrison
10 Gabriela Sabatini

1987
1 Steffi Graf
2 Martina Navratilova
3 Chris Evert
4 Pam Shriver
5 Hana Mandlikova
6 Gabriela Sabatini
7 Helena Sukova
8 M. Maleeva-Fragniere
9 Zina Garrison
10 Claudia Kohde-Kilsch

1988
1 Steffi Graf
2 Martina Navratilova
3 Chris Evert
4 Gabriela Sabatini
5 Pam Shriver
6 M. Maleeva-Fragniere
7 Natalia Zvereva
8 Helena Sukova
9 Zina Garrison
10 Barbara Potter

1989
1 Steffi Graf
2 Martina Navratilova
3 Gabriela Sabatini
4 Z. Garrison-Jackson
5 A. Sanchez Vicario
6 Monica Seles
7 Conchita Martinez
8 Helena Sukova
9 M. Maleeva-Fragniere
10 Chris Evert

1990
1 Steffi Graf
2 Monica Seles
3 Martina Navratilova
4 Mary Joe Fernandez
5 Gabriela Sabatini
6 Katerina Maleeva
7 A. Sanchez Vicario
8 Jennifer Capriati
9 M. Maleeva-Fragniere
10 Z. Garrison-Jackson

1991
1 Monica Seles
2 Steffi Graf
3 Gabriela Sabatini
4 Martina Navratilova
5 A. Sanchez Vicario
6 Jennifer Capriati
7 Jana Novotna
8 Mary Joe Fernandez
9 Conchita Martinez
10 M. Maleeva-Fragniere

1992
1 Monica Seles
2 Steffi Graf
3 Gabriela Sabatini
4 A. Sanchez Vicario
5 Martina Navratilova
6 Mary Joe Fernandez
7 Jennifer Capriati
8 Conchita Martinez
9 M. Maleeva-Fragniere
10 Jana Novotna

1993
1 Steffi Graf
2 A. Sanchez Vicario
3 Martina Navratilova
4 Conchita Martinez
5 Gabriela Sabatini
6 Jana Novotna
7 Mary Joe Fernandez
8 Monica Seles
9 Jennifer Capriati
10 Anke Huber

1994
1 Steffi Graf
2 A. Sanchez Vicario
3 Conchita Martinez
4 Jana Novotna
5 Mary Pierce
6 Lindsay Davenport
7 Gabriela Sabatini
8 Martina Navratilova
9 Kimiko Date
10 Natasha Zvereva

1995
1 Steffi Graf
  Monica Seles*
2 Conchita Martinez
3 A. Sanchez Vicario
4 Kimiko Date
5 Mary Pierce
6 Magdalena
  Maleeva
7 Gabriela
  Sabatini
8 Mary Joe Fernandez
9 Iva Majoli
10 Anke Huber

1996
1 Steffi Graf
2 Monica Seles†
  A. Sanchez Vicario
3 Jana Novotna
4 Martina Hingis
5 Conchita Martinez
6 Anke Huber
7 Iva Majoli
8 Kimiko Date
9 Lindsay Davenport
10 Barbara Paulus

Annual Top 10 World Rankings (since 1968) (Cont.)

WOMEN

	1997		1999		2001		2003		2005
1	Martina Hingis	1	Martina Hingis	1	Lindsay Davenport	1	J. Henin-Hardenne	1	Lindsay Davenport
2	Jana Novotna	2	Lindsay Davenport	2	Jennifer Capriati	2	Kim Clijsters	2	Kim Clijsters
3	Lindsay Davenport	3	Venus Williams	3	Venus Williams	3	Serena Williams	3	Amelie Mauresmo
4	Amanda Coetzer	4	Serena Williams	4	Martina Hingis	4	Amelie Mauresmo	4	Maria Sharapova
5	Monica Seles	5	Mary Pierce	5	Kim Clijsters	5	Lindsay Davenport	5	Mary Pierce
6	Iva Majoli	6	Monica Seles	6	Serena Williams	6	Jennifer Capriati	6	J. Henin-Hardenne
7	Mary Pierce	7	Nathalie Tauziat	7	Justine Henin	7	Anastasia Myskina	7	Patty Schnyder
8	Irina Spirlea	8	Barbara Schett	8	Jelena Dokic	8	Elena Dementieva	8	Elena Dementieva
9	A. Sanchez Vicario	9	Julie Halard-Decugis	9	Amelie Mauresmo	9	Chanda Rubin	9	Nadia Petrova
10	Mary Joe Fernandez	10	Amelie Mauresmo	10	Monica Seles	10	Ai Sugiyama	10	Venus Williams

	1998		2000		2002		2004		
1	Lindsay Davenport	1	Martina Hingis	1	Serena Williams	1	Lindsay Davenport		
2	Martina Hingis	2	Lindsay Davenport	2	Venus Williams	2	Amelie Mauresmo		
3	Jana Novotna	3	Venus Williams	3	Jennifer Capriati	3	Anastasia Myskina		
4	A. Sanchez Vicario	4	Monica Seles	4	Kim Clijsters	4	Maria Sharapova		
5	Venus Williams	5	Conchita Martinez	5	J. Henin-Hardenne	5	Svetlana Kuznetsova		
6	Monica Seles	6	Serena Williams	6	Amelie Mauresmo	6	Elena Dementieva		
7	Mary Pierce	7	Mary Pierce	7	Monica Seles	7	Serena Williams		
8	Conchita Martinez	8	Anna Kournikova	8	Daniela Hantuchova	8	J. Henin-Hardenne		
9	Steffi Graf	9	A. Sanchez Vicario	9	Jelena Dokic	9	Venus Williams		
10	Nathalie Tauziat	10	Nathalie Tauziat	10	Martina Hingis	10	Jennifer Capriati		

*Returning to the WTA Tour on Aug. 15, 1995, Seles was co-ranked #1 for her first six tournaments. Seles had been absent from the Tour since April 1993 when she was stabbed by a fan during a match. She was ranked #1 at the time of the stabbing.
†Seles' ranking was revised in May 1996. The revision stipulated that her new modified ranking would be calculated using a divisor of the actual number of tournaments she had played (13), and she would be co-ranked with the player whose average is immediately below her average (Sanchez Vicario).

All-Time Leaders

Tournaments Won (singles)

All-time tournament wins from the arrival of open tennis in 1968 through 2006 (through Oct. 8). Men's totals include ATP Tour, Grand Prix and WCT tournaments. Players active in singles play in 2006 are in **bold** type.

MEN

		Total			Total			Total
1	Jimmy Connors	109	12	**Roger Federer**	42	23	Yevgeny Kafelnikov	26
2	Ivan Lendl	94	13	Stefan Edberg	41	24	Jose-Luis Clerc	25
3	John McEnroe	77	14	Stan Smith	39		Brian Gottfried	25
4	Pete Sampras	64	15	Michael Chang	34		**Lleyton Hewitt**	25
5	Bjorn Borg	62	16	Arthur Ashe	33	27	Jim Courier	23
	Guillermo Vilas	62		Mats Wilander	33		Yannick Noah	23
7	**Andre Agassi**	60	18	John Newcombe	32	29	Eddie Dibbs	22
8	Ilie Nastase	57		Manuel Orantes	32		Goran Ivanisevic	22
9	Boris Becker	49		Ken Rosewall	32		Harold Solomon	22
10	Rod Laver	47	21	Tom Okker	31			
11	Thomas Muster	44	22	Vitas Gerulaitis	27			

WOMEN

		Total			Total			Total
1	Martina Navratilova	167	11	**Conchita Martinez**	33	21	Nancy Richey	25
2	Chris Evert	154		**Venus Williams**	33	22	Jana Novotna	24
3	Steffi Graf	107	13	**Kim Clijsters**	32	23	**Amelie Mauresmo**	23
4	Margaret Smith Court	92	14	Olga Morozova	31	24	Kerry Melville Reid	22
5	E. Goolagong Cawley	68	15	Tracy Austin	30	25	Pam Shriver	21
6	Billie Jean King	67	16	Arantxa Sanchez-Vicario	29	26	Julie Heldman	20
7	Virginia Wade	55	17	**J. Henin-Hardenne**	28	27	M. Maleeva-Fragniere	19
8	Monica Seles	53	18	Hana Mandlikova	27		Nancy Richey	19
9	**Lindsay Davenport**	51		Gabriela Sabatini	27	29	**Mary Pierce**	18
10	**Martina Hingis**	42	20	**Serena Williams**	26	30	Virginia Ruzici	17
							Regina Marsikova	17

Money Won

All-time money winners from the arrival of open tennis in 1968 through 2006 (through Oct. 8). Totals include doubles earnings.

MEN

		Earnings				Earnings				Earnings
1	Pete Sampras	$43,280,489	8	Goran Ivanisevic	$19,876,579	15	Marat Safin	$12,571,075
2	Andre Agassi	31,152,975	9	Michael Chang	19,145,632	16	John McEnroe	12,547,797
3	Roger Federer	26,464,458	10	Lleyton Hewitt	16,609,137	17	Thomas Muster	12,225,910
4	Boris Becker	25,080,956	11	Gustavo Kuerten	14,705,818	18	Carlos Moya	11,983,764
5	Yevgeny Kafelnikov	23,883,797	12	Jim Courier	14,034,132	19	Sergi Bruguera	11,632,199
6	Ivan Lendl	21,262,417	13	Jonas Bjorkman	13,156,784	20	Andy Roddick	11,486,476
7	Stefan Edberg	20,630,941	14	Michael Stich	12,592,483			

WOMEN

		Earnings				Earnings				Earnings
1	Steffi Graf	$21,895,277	8	Monica Seles	$14,891,762	15	Mary Pierce	$9,774,059
2	Lindsay Davenport	21,763,653	9	Kim Clijsters	14,009,637	16	Chris Evert	8,896,195
3	Mart. Navratilova	21,626,089	10	J. Henin-Hardenne	12,573,319	17	Gabriela Sabatini	8,785,850
4	Martina Hingis	19,344,877	11	Amelie Mauresmo	12,310,262	18	Natasha Zvereva	7,792,503
5	A. Sanchez-Vicario	16,942,640	12	Conchita Martinez	11,527,977	19	Maria Sharapova	7,774,967
6	Venus Williams	16,295,594	13	Jana Novotna	11,249,284	20	Elena Dementieva	7,427,051
7	Serena Williams	16,006,592	14	Jennifer Capriati	10,206,639			

Year-end Tournaments

MEN

Tennis Masters Cup

The year-end championship featuring the top eight players in the Tennis Masters Series rankings. Two groups of four players square off in a round-robin tournament followed by a single-elimination semifinals and finals. Originally called the Masters in 1970, the tournament followed a round-robin format, but was revised in 1972 to include a round-robin to decide the four semifinalists then a single elimination format after that. Replaced by ATP Tour World Championship from 1990 through 1999.

Multiple Winners: Ivan Lendl and Pete Sampras (5); Ilie Nastase (4); Boris Becker and John McEnroe (3); Bjorn Borg, Roger Federer and Lleyton Hewitt (2).

Year	Winner	Runner-Up	Year	Winner	Loser	Score
1970	Stan Smith (4-1) *	Rod Laver (4-1)	1988	Boris Becker	I. Lendl	57 76 36 62 76
1971	Ilie Nastase (6-0)	Stan Smith (4-2)	1989	Stefan Edberg	B. Becker	46 76 63 61

Year	Winner	Loser	Score	1990	Andre Agassi	S. Edberg	57 76 75 62
1972	Ilie Nastase	S. Smith	63 62 36 26 63	1991	Pete Sampras	J. Courier	36 76 63 64
1973	Ilie Nastase	T. Okker	63 75 46 63	1992	Boris Becker	J. Courier	64 63 75
1974	Guillermo Vilas	I. Nastase	76 62 36 36 64	1993	Michael Stich	P. Sampras	76 26 76 62
1975	Ilie Nastase	B. Borg	62 62 61	1994	Pete Sampras	B. Becker	46 63 75 64
1976	Manuel Orantes	W. Fibak	57 62 06 76 61	1995	Boris Becker	M. Chang	76 60 76
1978	Jimmy Connors	B. Borg	64 16 64	1996	Pete Sampras	B. Becker	36 76 76 67 64
1979	John McEnroe	A. Ashe	67 63 75	1997	Pete Sampras	Y. Kafelnikov	63 62 62
1980	Bjorn Borg	V. Gerulaitis	62 62	1998	Alex Corretja	C. Moya	36 36 75 63 75
1981	Bjorn Borg	I. Lendl	64 62 62	1999	Pete Sampras	A. Agassi	61 75 64
1982	Ivan Lendl	V. Gerulaitis	67 26 76 62 64	2000	Gustavo Kuerten	A. Agassi	64 64 64
1983	Ivan Lendl	J. McEnroe	64 64 62	2001	Lleyton Hewitt	S. Grosjean	63 63 64
1984	John McEnroe	I. Lendl	63 64 64	2002	Lleyton Hewitt	J.C. Ferrero	75 75 26 26 64
1985	John McEnroe	I. Lendl	75 60 64	2003	Roger Federer	A. Agassi	63 60 64
1986	Ivan Lendl	B. Becker	62 76 63	2004	Roger Federer	L. Hewitt	63 62 (rain)
1986	Ivan Lendl	B. Becker	64 64 64	2005	David Nalbandian	R. Federer	67 67 62 61 76
1987	Ivan Lendl	M. Wilander	62 62 63				

*Smith was declared the winner because he beat Laver in their round-robin match (4-6, 6-3, 6-4).
Note: The tournament switched from December to January in 1977-78, then back to December in 1986.

Playing Sites

1970—Tokyo; **1971**—Paris; **1972**—Barcelona; **1973**—Boston; **1974**—Melbourne; **1975**—Stockholm; **1976, 2003-04**—Houston; **1977-89**—New York City; **1990-95**—Frankfurt, GER; **1996-99**—Hannover, GER; **2000**—Lisbon, POR; **2001**—Sydney, AUS; **2002, 2005-08**—Shanghai, CHN.

WCT Championship (1971-89)

World Championship Tennis was established in 1967 to promote professional tennis and led the way into the open era. Its major singles and doubles championships were held every May among the top eight regular season finishers on the circuit from 1971 until the WCT folded in 1989.

Multiple winners: John McEnroe (5), Jimmy Connors, Ivan Lendl and Ken Rosewall (2).

Year	Winner	Loser	Score	Year	Winner	Loser	Score
1971	Ken Rosewall	R. Laver	64 16 76 76	1976	Bjorn Borg	G. Vilas	16 61 75 61
1972	Ken Rosewall	R. Laver	46 60 63 67 76	1977	Jimmy Connors	D. Stockton	67 61 64 63
1973	Stan Smith	A. Ashe	63 63 46 64	1978	Vitas Gerulaitis	E. Dibbs	63 62 61
1974	John Newcombe	B. Borg	46 63 63 62	1979	John McEnroe	B. Borg	75 46 62 76
1975	Arthur Ashe	B. Borg	36 64 64 60	1980	Jimmy Connors	J. McEnroe	26 76 61 62

Year-end Tournaments (Cont.)

Year	Winner	Loser	Score	Year	Winner	Loser	Score
1981	John McEnroe	J. Kriek	61 62 64	1986	Anders Jarryd	B. Becker	67 61 61 64
1982	Ivan Lendl	J. McEnroe	62 36 63 63	1987	Miloslav Mecir	J. McEnroe	60 36 62 62
1983	John McEnroe	I. Lendl	62 46 63 67 76	1988	Boris Becker	S. Edberg	64 16 75 62
1984	John McEnroe	J. Connors	61 62 63	1989	John McEnroe	B. Gilbert	63 63 76
1985	Ivan Lendl	T. Mayotte	76 64 61				

WOMEN
WTA Championships

The WTA Tour's year-end tournament took place in March from 1972 until 1986 when the WTA decided to adopt a January-to-November playing season. Given the changeover, two championships were held in 1986. Held in Boca Raton (1972-73), Los Angeles (1974-76, 2002-05), New York (1977, 1979-2000), Oakland (1978), Munich (2001), Madrid (2006).

Multiple winners: Martina Navratilova (8); Steffi Graf (5); Chris Evert (4); Monica Seles (3); Kim Clijsters, Evonne Goolagong, Martina Hingis and Gabriela Sabatini (2).

Year	Winner	Loser	Score	Year	Winner	Loser	Score
1972	Chris Evert	K. Reid	75 64	1989	Steffi Graf	M. Navratilova	64 75 26 62
1973	Chris Evert	N. Richey	63 63	1990	Monica Seles	G. Sabatini	64 57 36 64 62
1974	Evonne Goolagong	C. Evert	63 64	1991	Monica Seles	M. Navratilova	64 36 75 60
1975	Chris Evert	M. Navratilova	64 62	1992	Monica Seles	M. Navratilova	75 63 61
1976	Evonne Goolagong	C. Evert	63 57 63	1993	Steffi Graf	A. S. Vicario	61 64 36 61
1977	Chris Evert	S. Barker	26 61 61	1994	Gabriela Sabatini	L. Davenport	63 62 64
1978	M. Navratilova	E. Goolagong	76 64	1995	Steffi Graf	A. Huber	61 26 61 46 63
1979	M. Navratilova	T. Austin	63 36 62	1996	Steffi Graf	M. Hingis	63 46 60 40 60
1980	Tracy Austin	M. Navratilova	62 26 62	1997	Jana Novotna	M. Pierce	76 62 63
1981	M. Navratilova	A. Jaeger	63 76	1998	Martina Hingis	L. Davenport	75 64 46 62
1982	Sylvia Hanika	M. Navratilova	16 63 64	1999	Lindsay Davenport	M. Hingis	64 62
1983	M. Navratilova	C. Evert	62 60	2000	Martina Hingis	M. Seles	67 64 64
1984	M. Navratilova	C. Evert	63 75 61	2001	Serena Williams	L. Davenport	walkover
1985	M. Navratilova	H. Sukova	63 75 64	2002	Kim Clijsters	S. Williams	75 63
1986	M. Navratilova	H. Mandlikova	62 60 36 61	2003	Kim Clijsters	A. Mauresmo	62 60
1986	M. Navratilova	S. Graf	76 63 62	2004	Maria Sharapova	S. Williams	46 62 64
1987	Steffi Graf	G. Sabatini	46 64 60 64	2005	Amelie Mauresmo	M. Pierce	57 76 64
1988	Gabriela Sabatini	P. Shriver	75 62 62				

Note: The final was best-of-five sets from 1984-98 and best-of-three sets from 1972-83 and since 1999.

National Team Tournaments
Davis Cup

Established in 1900 as an annual international tournament by American player Dwight Davis. Originally called the International Lawn Tennis Challenge Trophy. Challenge round system until 1972. Since 1981, the top 16 nations in the world have played a straight knockout tournament over the course of a year. The format is a best-of-five match of two singles, one doubles and two singles over three days. Note that from 1900-24 Australia and New Zealand competed together as Australasia.

Multiple winners: USA (31); Australia (22); France (9); Sweden (7); Australasia (6); British Isles (5); Britain (4); Germany (3); Spain (2).

Challenge Rounds

Year	Winner	Loser	Score	Site	Year	Winner	Loser	Score	Site
1900	USA	British Isles	3-0	Boston	1928	France	USA	4-1	Paris
1901	Not held				1929	France	USA	3-2	Paris
1902	USA	British Isles	3-2	New York	1930	France	USA	4-1	Paris
1903	British Isles	USA	4-1	Boston	1931	France	Britain	3-2	Paris
1904	British Isles	Belgium	5-0	Wimbledon	1932	France	USA	3-2	Paris
1905	British Isles	USA	5-0	Wimbledon	1933	Britain	France	3-2	Paris
1906	British Isles	USA	5-0	Wimbledon	1934	Britain	USA	4-1	Wimbledon
1907	Australasia	British Isles	3-2	Wimbledon	1935	Britain	USA	5-0	Wimbledon
1908	Australasia	USA	3-2	Melbourne	1936	Britain	Australia	3-2	Wimbledon
1909	Australasia	USA	5-0	Sydney	1937	USA	Britain	4-1	Wimbledon
1910	Not held				1938	USA	Australia	3-2	Philadelphia
1911	Australasia	USA	5-0	Christchurch, NZ	1939	Australia	USA	3-2	Philadelphia
1912	British Isles	Australasia	3-2	Melbourne	1940-45	Not held World War II			
1913	USA	British Isles	3-2	Wimbledon	1946	USA	Australia	5-0	Melbourne
1914	Australasia	USA	3-2	New York	1947	USA	Australia	4-1	New York
1915-18	Not held World War I				1948	USA	Australia	5-0	New York
1919	Australasia	British Isles	4-1	Sydney	1949	USA	Australia	4-1	New York
1920	USA	Australasia	5-0	Auckland, NZ	1950	Australia	USA	4-1	New York
1921	USA	Japan	5-0	New York	1951	Australia	USA	3-2	Sydney
1922	USA	Australasia	4-1	New York	1952	Australia	USA	4-1	Adelaide
1923	USA	Australasia	4-1	New York	1953	Australia	USA	3-2	Melbourne
1924	USA	Australia	5-0	Philadelphia	1954	USA	Australia	3-2	Sydney
1925	USA	France	5-0	Philadelphia	1955	Australia	USA	5-0	New York
1926	USA	France	4-1	Philadelphia	1956	Australia	USA	5-0	Adelaide
1927	France	USA	3-2	Philadelphia	1957	Australia	USA	3-2	Melbourne

Year	Winner	Loser	Score	Site	Year	Winner	Loser	Score	Site
1958	USA	Australia	3-2	Brisbane	1963	USA	Australia	3-2	Adelaide
1959	Australia	USA	3-2	New York	1964	USA	Australia	3-2	Cleveland
1960	Australia	Italy	4-1	Sydney	1965	Australia	Spain	4-1	Sydney
1961	Australia	Italy	5-0	Melbourne	1966	Australia	India	4-1	Melbourne
1962	Australia	Mexico	5-0	Brisbane	1967	Australia	Spain	4-1	Brisbane

Final Rounds

Year	Winner	Loser	Score	Site	Year	Winner	Loser	Score	Site
1968	USA	Australia	4-1	Adelaide	1987	Sweden	India	5-0	Göteborg
1969	USA	Romania	5-0	Cleveland	1988	W. Germany	Sweden	4-1	Göteborg
1970	USA	W. Germany	5-0	Cleveland	1989	W. Germany	Sweden	3-2	Stuttgart
1971	USA	Romania	3-2	Charlotte	1990	USA	Australia	3-2	St. Petersburg
1972	USA	Romania	3-2	Bucharest	1991	France	USA	3-1	Lyon
1973	Australia	USA	5-0	Cleveland	1992	USA	Switzerland	3-1	Ft. Worth
1974	So. Africa	India	walkover	Not held	1993	Germany	Australia	4-1	Dusseldorf
1975	Sweden	Czech.	3-2	Stockholm	1994	Sweden	Russia	4-1	Moscow
1976	Italy	Chile	4-1	Santiago	1995	USA	Russia	3-2	Moscow
1977	Australia	Italy	3-1	Sydney	1996	France	Sweden	3-2	Malmo
1978	USA	Britain	4-1	Palm Springs	1997	Sweden	USA	5-0	Göteborg
1979	USA	Italy	5-0	San Francisco	1998	Sweden	Italy	4-1	Milan
1980	Czech.	Italy	4-1	Prague	1999	Australia	France	3-2	Nice
1981	USA	Argentina	3-1	Cincinnati	2000	Spain	Australia	3-1	Barcelona
1982	USA	France	4-1	Grenoble	2001	France	Australia	3-2	Melbourne
1983	Australia	Sweden	3-2	Melbourne	2002	Russia	France	3-2	Paris
1984	Sweden	USA	4-1	Göteborg	2003	Australia	Spain	3-1	Melbourne
1985	Sweden	W. Germany	3-2	Munich	2004	Spain	USA	3-2	Seville
1986	Australia	Sweden	3-2	Melbourne	2005	Croatia	Slovakia	3-2	Bratislava

Note: In 1974, India refused to play the final as a protest against the South African government's policies of apartheid.

Fed Cup

Originally the Federation Cup started by the International Tennis Federation as the Davis Cup of women's tennis. Played by 32 teams over one week at one site from 1963-94. Tournament changed to Davis Cup-style format of four rounds and home site in 1995. Currently 16 teams compete in a knockout format, with winners advancing to the quarterfinals, semifinals and finals.

Multiple winners: USA (17); Australia (7); Czechoslovakia and Spain (5); France, Germany and Russia (2).

Year	Winner	Loser	Score	Site	Year	Winner	Loser	Score	Site
1963	USA	Australia	2-1	London	1985	Czech.	USA	2-1	Japan
1964	Australia	USA	2-1	Philadelphia	1986	USA	Czech.	3-0	Prague
1965	Australia	USA	2-1	Melbourne	1987	W. Germany	USA	2-1	Vancouver
1966	USA	W. Germany	3-0	Italy	1988	Czech.	USSR	2-1	Melbourne
1967	USA	Britain	2-0	W. Germany	1989	USA	Spain	3-0	Tokyo
1968	Australia	Holland	3-0	Paris	1990	USA	USSR	2-1	Atlanta
1969	USA	Australia	2-1	Athens	1991	Spain	USA	2-1	Nottingham
1970	Australia	Britain	3-0	W. Germany	1992	Germany	Spain	2-1	Frankfurt
1971	Australia	Britain	3-0	Perth	1993	Spain	Australia	3-0	Frankfurt
1972	So. Africa	Britain	2-1	So. Africa	1994	Spain	USA	3-0	Frankfurt
1973	Australia	So. Africa	3-0	W. Germany	1995	Spain	USA	3-2	Valencia
1974	Australia	USA	2-1	Italy	1996	USA	Spain	5-0	Atlantic City
1975	Czech.	Australia	3-0	France	1997	France	Netherlands	4-1	Netherlands
1976	USA	Australia	2-1	Philadelphia	1998	Spain	Switzerland	3-2	Geneva
1977	USA	Australia	2-1	Eastbourne	1999	USA	Russia	4-1	Palo Alto
1978	USA	Australia	2-1	Melbourne	2000	USA	Spain	5-0	Las Vegas
1979	USA	Australia	3-0	Spain	2001	Belgium	Russia	2-1	Madrid
1980	USA	Australia	3-0	W. Germany	2002	Slovakia	Spain	3-1	Canary Islands
1981	USA	Britain	3-0	Tokyo	2003	France	USA	4-1	Moscow
1982	USA	W. Germany	3-0	Santa Clara	2004	Russia	France	3-2	Moscow
1983	Czech.	W. Germany	2-1	Zurich	2005	Russia	France	3-2	Paris
1984	Czech.	Australia	2-1	Brazil	2006	Italy	Belgium	3-2	Charleroi

COLLEGES

NCAA team titles were not sanctioned until 1946. NCAA women's individual and team championships started in 1982.

Men's NCAA Individual Champions (1883-1945)

Multiple winners: Malcolm Chace and Pancho Segura (3); Edward Chandler, George Church, E.B. Dewhurst, Fred Hovey, Frank Guernsey, W.P. Knapp, Robert LeRoy, P.S. Sears, Cliff Sutter, Ernest Sutter and Richard Williams (2).

Year		Year		Year	
1883	J. Clark, Harvard (spring)	1888	P.S. Sears, Harvard	1894	Malcolm Chace, Yale
	H. Taylor, Harvard (fall)	1889	R.P. Huntington Jr., Yale	1895	Malcolm Chace, Yale
1884	W.P. Knapp, Yale	1890	Fred Hovey, Harvard	1896	Malcolm Whitman, Harvard
1885	W.P. Knapp, Yale	1891	Fred Hovey, Harvard	1897	S.G. Thompson, Princeton
1886	G.M. Brinley, Trinity, CT	1892	William Larned, Cornell	1898	Leo Ware, Harvard
1887	P.S. Sears, Harvard	1893	Malcolm Chace, Brown	1899	Dwight Davis, Harvard

Colleges (Cont.)

Year		Year		Year	
1900	Ray Little, Princeton	1915	Richard Williams, Harv.	1931	Keith Gledhill, Stanford
1901	Fred Alexander, Princeton	1916	G.C. Caner, Harvard	1932	Cliff Sutter, Tulane
1902	William Clothier, Harvard	1917-1918	Not held	1933	Jack Tidball, UCLA
1903	E.B. Dewhurst, Penn	1919	Charles Garland, Yale	1934	Gene Mako, USC
1904	Robert LeRoy, Columbia	1920	Lascelles Banks, Yale	1935	Wilbur Hess, Rice
1905	E.B. Dewhurst, Penn	1921	Philip Neer, Stanford	1936	Ernest Sutter, Tulane
1906	Robert LeRoy, Columbia	1922	Lucien Williams, Yale	1937	Ernest Sutter, Tulane
1907	G.P. Gardner Jr., Harvard	1923	Carl Fischer, Phi. Osteo.	1938	Frank Guernsey, Rice
1908	Nat Niles, Harvard	1924	Wallace Scott, Wash.	1939	Frank Guernsey, Rice
1909	Wallace Johnson, Penn	1925	Edward Chandler, Calif.	1940	Don McNeill, Kenyon
1910	R.A. Holden Jr., Yale	1926	Edward Chandler, Calif.	1941	Joseph Hunt, Navy
1911	E.H. Whitney, Harvard	1927	Wilmer Allison, Texas	1942	Ted Schroeder, Stanford
1912	George Church, Princeton	1928	Julius Seligson, Lehigh	1943	Pancho Segura, Miami-FL
1913	Richard Williams, Harv.	1929	Berkeley Bell, Texas	1944	Pancho Segura, Miami-FL
1914	George Church, Princeton	1930	Cliff Sutter, Tulane	1945	Pancho Segura, Miami-FL

NCAA Men's Division I Champions

Multiple winners (Teams): Stanford (17); UCLA and USC (16); Georgia (4); William & Mary (2). (Players): Matias Boeker, Alex Olmedo, Mikael Pernfors, Dennis Ralston and Ham Richardson (2).

Year	Team winner	Individual Champion	Year	Team winner	Individual Champion
1946	USC	Bob Falkenburg, USC	1977	Stanford	Matt Mitchell, Stanford
1947	Wm. & Mary	Gardner Larned, Wm.& Mary	1978	Stanford	John McEnroe, Stanford
1948	Wm. & Mary	Harry Likas, San Francisco	1979	UCLA	Kevin Curren, Texas
1949	San Francisco	Jack Tuero, Tulane	1980	Stanford	Robert Van't Hof, USC
1950	UCLA	Herbert Flam, UCLA	1981	Stanford	Tim Mayotte, Stanford
1951	USC	Tony Trabert, Cincinnati	1982	UCLA	Mike Leach, Michigan
1952	USC	Hugh Stewart, USC	1983	Stanford	Greg Holmes, Utah
1953	UCLA	Ham Richardson, Tulane	1984	UCLA	Mikael Pernfors, Georgia
1954	UCLA	Ham Richardson, Tulane	1985	Georgia	Mikael Pernfors, Georgia
1955	USC	Jose Aguero, Tulane	1986	Georgia	Dan Goldie, Stanford
1956	UCLA	Alex Olmedo, USC	1987	Georgia	Andrew Burrow, Miami-FL
1957	Michigan	Barry MacKay, Michigan	1988	Stanford	Robby Weiss, Pepperdine
1958	USC	Alex Olmedo, USC	1989	Stanford	Donni Leaycraft, LSU
1959	Tulane & Notre Dame	Whitney Reed, San Jose St.	1990	Stanford	Steve Bryan, Texas
1960	UCLA	Larry Nagler, UCLA	1991	USC	Jared Palmer, Stanford
1961	UCLA	Allen Fox, UCLA	1992	Stanford	Alex O'Brien Stanford
1962	USC	Rafael Osuna, USC	1993	USC	Chris Woodruff, Tennessee
1963	USC	Dennis Ralston, USC	1994	USC	Mark Merklein, Florida
1964	USC	Dennis Ralston, USC	1995	Stanford	Sargis Sargsian, Ariz. St.
1965	UCLA	Arthur Ashe, UCLA	1996	Stanford	Cecil Mamiit, USC
1966	USC	Charlie Pasarell, UCLA	1997	Stanford	Luke Smith, UNLV
1967	USC	Bob Lutz, USC	1998	Stanford	Bob Bryan, Stanford
1968	USC	Stan Smith, USC	1999	Georgia	Jeff Morrison, Florida
1969	USC	Joaquin Loyo-Mayo, USC	2000	Stanford	Alex Kim, Stanford
1970	UCLA	Jeff Borowiak, UCLA	2001	Georgia	Matias Boeker, Georgia
1971	UCLA	Jimmy Connors, UCLA	2002	USC	Matias Boeker, Georgia
1972	Trinity-TX	Dick Stockton, Trinity-TX	2003	Illinois	Amer Delic, Illinois
1973	Stanford	Alex Mayer, Stanford	2004	Baylor	Benjamin Becker, Baylor
1974	Stanford	John Whitlinger, Stanford	2005	UCLA	Benedikt Dorsch, Baylor
1975	UCLA	Bill Martin, UCLA	2006	Pepperdine	Benjamin Kohlleoffel, UCLA
1976	USC & UCLA	Bill Scanlon, Trinity-TX			

NCAA Women's Division I Champions

Multiple winners (Teams): Stanford (15); Florida (4); Georgia, Texas and USC (2). (Players): Sandra Birch, Patty Fendick, Laura Granville, Amber Liu and Lisa Raymond (2).

Year	Team winner	Individual Champion	Year	Team winner	Individual Champion
1982	Stanford	Alycia Moulton, Stanford	1995	Texas	Keri Phoebus, UCLA
1983	USC	Beth Herr, USC	1996	Florida	Jill Craybas, Florida
1984	Stanford	Lisa Spain, Georgia	1997	Stanford	Lilia Osterloh, Stanford
1985	USC	Linda Gates, Stanford	1998	Florida	Vanessa Webb, Duke
1986	Stanford	Patty Fendick, Stanford	1999	Stanford	Zuzana Lesenarova, S. Diego
1987	Stanford	Patty Fendick, Stanford	2000	Georgia	Laura Granville, Stanford
1988	Stanford	Shaun Stafford, Florida	2001	Stanford	Laura Granville, Stanford
1989	Stanford	Sandra Birch, Stanford	2002	Stanford	Bea Bielik, Wake Forest
1990	Stanford	Debbie Graham, Stanford	2003	Florida	Amber Liu, Stanford
1991	Stanford	Sandra Birch, Stanford	2004	Stanford	Amber Liu, Stanford
1992	Florida	Lisa Raymond, Florida	2005	Stanford	Zuzana Zemenova, Baylor
1993	Texas	Lisa Raymond, Florida	2006	Stanford	Suzi Babos, California
1994	Georgia	Angela Lettiere, Georgia			

GOLF

Tiger Woods lifts the Claret Jug after winning the third British Open of his illustrious career.

MAJOR MELTDOWN

It was Phil's year until he hit a major bump in the road at the U.S. Open. Then Tiger took advantage.

CALL IT WHATEVER YOU WANT:

"The Wreck At Mamaroneck," the "Phil Phailure," or simply, "The Shot Heard 'Round The Hospitality Tent."

But in the end, the definitive moment of a bizarre, emotional and goose-bumpish 2006 golf season will forever be Phil Mickelson's spectacular folding-chair routine on the 72nd and final hole of the U.S. Open at Winged Foot.

In about 20 minutes' time, which is how long it took Mickelson to thoroughly botch a major, the balance of golf power moved from Lefty to a righty—Tiger Woods.

"I am such an idiot," said Mickelson that June day in suburban New York.

He was talking about his Sunday tee shot on Winged Foot's 450-yard, par-4 18th hole, which sliced high, hard and far before caroming off a white hospitality tent and back into the matted down rough.

Then he tried massaging a 3-iron out of the gunk, but instead hit a tree about 25 yards in front of him. Then he hit his third shot into a greenside bunker. And then...well, does it really matter? Mickelson made a double bogey six, blew a one-shot lead to Geoff Ogilvy, and really never challenged again for the rest of the 2006 season.

Pity, since he had won the PGA Championship in 2005, the Masters in 2006, and was on his way to a third consecutive major when he suffered the massive brain cramp. He ruled the PGA Tour. And then, just like that, he didn't.

"It was right there and I let it go," Mickelson said of the Open. "I just cannot believe I did that."

Mickelson ended up tying for second with Colin Montgomerie and Jim Furyk, and the trickle-down effect of his second-place finish was immediate. Instead of strengthening his hold on the 2006 season, Mickelson created an opening for the aforementioned Eldrick Woods.

 Gene Wojciechowski is a senior writer for ESPN.com.

AP/Wide World Photos

→ "Uh, there's the fairway over there, Phil." **Geoff Ogilvy** and **Phil Mickelson** chat after Mickelson's collapse let Ogilvy win his first major at the U.S. Open.

Woods, who was grieving over the death of his father Earl and missed his first-ever majors cut at Winged Foot, returned to Tour play about three weeks later and finished second at the Cialis Western Open. Then he won the British Open (and cried like a newborn after the victory), the Buick Open, the PGA Championship (paired with Mickelson and Ogilvy during the first two rounds), the WGC-Bridgestone Invitational, the Deutsche Bank Championship and the American Express Championship.

And then he rested.

If you're keeping count (and Mickelson was), that's six PGA victories in a row and eight in just 15 events. Woods also earned almost $10 million in prize money through early October, surpassed the 50-career win total, and moved into second place on the list of career major wins (he now trails only Jack Nicklaus, who leads, 18-12— for now). Is that any good when you're 30?

"When you first come out on Tour you just hope to win one," said Woods.

Woods doesn't just win, he dominates. The only drama at the British Open was how many tear stains Woods would leave on caddy Steve Williams' shoulder. Sunday's round at the PGA Championship was more like a 9-hole victory parade. Just ask Vijay Singh what it felt like to have Woods zoom by on the leaderboard

Tiger Woods' third British Open title was bittersweet, as it was his first major win since the death of his father and mentor, Earl Woods, in early May.

AP/Wide World Photos

at the Deutsche Bank tourney. And perhaps his most dominant performance came at the American Express Championship in early October, which he won by a ridiculous eight strokes.

Four of the last eight majors have been won by Woods. He's missed exactly four cuts in his career. He's 12-0 when he enters the final round of a major tied or in the lead. He owns the lowest 72-hole scores in relation to par in the Masters, the U.S. Open, the British Open, and is tied for the PGA record.

"I mean, we all smirk and laugh when he says he's got his 'B' game, but that's better than most of our 'A' games," said Shaun Micheel, who finished second to Woods at the 2006 PGA. "He's just that good."

He's more than that. Woods somehow continues to clear a bar set to his own high standards. He leads the world in hoisting trophies, claret jugs, and those really large fake winner's checks. Everybody waits for a decline, but Woods' game appears to defy failure.

"I mean, he's not going to be 68 years old and in the final round of a major and tied for the lead and he wins," said Sergio Garcia, one Woods' many would-be challengers.

Hmmm. Is Garcia sure about that?

GENE WOJCIECHOWSKI'S

10

Biggest Stories of the Year in **Golf**

10 World Wide Webb.

Karrie Webb, who seemingly hadn't won a major since the Paleozic Era, re-establishes herself as an LPGA force by winning the Kraft Nabisco Championship, as well as three other tournaments. It's her first victory in a major since 2002. Through Oct. 8, the Hall of Famer had amassed more than $1.7 million in earnings, good enough for second on the money list and first on any Comeback Player of the Year ballots.

09 Changes in store.

PGA Tour Commissioner Tim Finchem makes two decisions that could have profound effects on the success of his golf kingdom. First, he chooses the Golf Channel as the Tour's exclusive cable broadcasting partner; second, he introduces the FedEx Cup, a season-long bonus points system (think NASCAR) that eventually concludes with a four-event Championship Series. Not so significant, however, is the Tour's unveiling of an exclusive line of premium wines (can't make this stuff up).

08 Annika answers.

Annika Sorenstam begins her season with a win at the MasterCard Classic and then isn't seen hoisting a trophy for almost four months—unfathomable by Annika standards (she won 10 times on tour in 2005). No worries. She ends the winless streak with a victory at the U.S. Open in July, and in September, wins the State Farm Classic by shooting a final-round 62—the fourth LPGA winner to do so in the last round.

07 Ogilvy delivers.

Geoff Ogilvy wins the U.S. Open and, despite the series of galactically questionable decisions by then-leader Phil Mickelson on the final hole, nobody considers the Aussie's victory a total fluke. After all, Ogilvy played top drawer pressure golf during the latter stages of Sunday's final round, including a chip-in par save on No. 17 and an equally impressive up-and-down par on No. 18 at Winged Foot. This is the same guy who won the Match Play Championship earlier in the season, recorded five top 10 finishes, and earned $4 million plus.

06 Wie's World.

Michelle Wie still doesn't win an LPGA tournament, still doesn't make a PGA Tour cut, and. . . it still doesn't matter. The teenage phenom, who turned 17 in October 2006, continues to mesmerize the golf world not because of her pro victory total (zero, so far), but because of her tantalizing potential and knack for making headlines on and off the course. The golf stuff:

top-five finishes in the Kraft Nabisco Championship, LPGA Championship and U.S. Open; the youngest woman ever to make the cut in a men's professional event (the SK Telecom Open on the Asian Tour); the first female to record the lowest score in a men's U.S. Open local qualifier; the first female pro to leave the John Deere Classic via ambulance after heat exhaustion forces her to withdraw from the tournament after nine holes in the second round (she was going to miss the cut anyway). The off-course stuff: Wie (or Team Wie) fires another caddy, the sixth since 2004.

05 Hootie steps down

The 8-year reign of William "Hootie" Johnson comes to an end at Augusta National Golf Club, as the stubborn (no women members on his watch) and yet oddly progressive (lengthens the course, seriously considers implementing a uniform "Masters" tournament golf ball) 75-year-old chairman calls it quits. Billy Payne, 58, who brought the 1996 Olympics to Atlanta, succeeds Johnson.

04 Earl Woods dies.

Earl Woods, the charismatic golf prophet who predicted greatness for his son Tiger, dies on May 3, 2006, of cancer. Woods' life was full and meaningful. He was the first African-American baseball player in the then-Big Eight Conference, and later served as a Green Beret in the Vietnam War.

03 U.S. team schooled

The U.S. Ryder Cup team once again is given a group golf lesson by the Europeans, who rout the Americans at The K Club by the same 18½-9½ blowout score they recorded at Oakland Hills in 2004. For the first time in the history of the event, the Europeans have won the Cup three consecutive times and eight out of the last 11.

02 Phil's flop.

The once-promising "Year of Lefty" cartwheels into oblivion as Phil Mickelson wins the Masters, but then, with the U.S. Open seemingly his for the taking, suffers one of the great collapses during the 72nd hole at Winged Foot. His double bogey costs him the tournament. Mickelson never truly recovers from his heartbreaking performance.

01 Year of the Tiger...again

Numbed by the recent death of his father, Tiger Woods misses the cut at the U.S. Open (his first-ever at a major), forces himself to watch the weekend action, and vows to return stronger than ever. This is bad news for the rest of the Tour, as Woods eventually wins 1...2...3...4...5...6! PGA tournaments in a row, including the British Open and the PGA Championship (a combined 36-under at the two majors). His heartfelt sobbing session after the July win at Hoylake makes it clear just how much he misses his father Earl—and how much better he is than the rest of the world's best golfers.

2005-2006
Season In Review

SPORTS ALMANAC

Tournament Results

Schedules and results of PGA, LPGA, Champions and European PGA tournaments from Nov. 6, 2005 through Oct. 8, 2006.

PGA Tour
Late 2005

Last Rd	Tournament	Winner	Earnings	Runner-Up
Nov. 6	The Tour Championship	Bart Bryant (263)	$1,170,000	T. Woods (269)
Nov. 6	Southern Farm Bureau Classic	Heath Slocum (267)	540,000	C. Petterson & L. Roberts (269)
Nov. 8@	Tommy Bahama Challenge†	International stars (2½-1½)	400,000	American stars
Nov. 13@	Franklin Templeton Shootout	Kenny Perry/	315,000	Fred Couples/
		John Huston (186)	(each)	Adam Scott (187)
Nov. 20@	WGC: World Cup	Wales—Bradley Dredge/	700,000	England & Sweden (191)
		Stephen Dodge (189)%	(each)	
Nov. 27@	Merrill Lynch Skins Game	Fred Funk (15 skins)	925,000	T. Woods (1 skin)
Dec. 11@	Target World Challenge	Luke Donald (272)	1,300,000	D. Clarke (274)

@ Unofficial PGA Tour money event.
† Four young American stars (under 30) in match play vs. four young international stars.
% Weather-shortened

2006 (through Oct. 8)

Last Rd	Tournament	Winner	Earnings	Runner-Up
Jan. 8	Mercedes Championships	Stuart Appleby (284)*	$1,080,000	V. Singh (284)
Jan. 15	Sony Open in Hawaii	David Toms (261)	918,000	R. Sabbatini & C. Campbell (266)
Jan 22	Bob Hope Chrysler Classic	Chad Campbell (335)+	900,000	J. Parnevik & S. Verplank (338)
Jan. 29	Buick Invitational	Tiger Woods (278)*	918,000	N. Green & J.M. Olazabal (278)
Feb. 5	FBR Open	J.B. Holmes (263)	936,000	5-way tie (270)#
Feb. 12	AT&T Pebble Beach Pro-Am	Arron Oberholser (271)	972,000	R. Sabbatini (276)
Feb. 19	Nissan Open	Rory Sabbatini (271)	918,000	A. Scott (272)
Feb. 26	WGC: Accenture Match Play			
	Championship	Geoff Ogilvy (3&2)	1,300,000	D. Love III
Feb. 26	Chrysler Classic of Tucson	Kirk Triplett (266)	540,000	J. Kelly (267)
Mar. 5	Ford Championship at Doral	Tiger Woods (268)	990,000	D. Toms & C. Villegas (269)
Mar. 12	Honda Classic	Luke Donald (276)	990,000	G. Ogilvy (278)
Mar. 19	Bay Hill Invitational	Rod Pampling (274)	990,000	G. Owen (275)
Mar. 26	The Players Championship	Stephen Ames (274)	1,440,000	R. Goosen (280)
Apr. 2	BellSouth Classic	Phil Mickelson (260)	954,000	Z. Johnson & J.M. Olazabal (273)
Apr. 9	**The Masters** (Augusta, Ga.)	Phil Mickelson (281)	1,260,000	T. Clark (283)
Apr. 16	Verizon Heritage	Aaron Baddeley (269)	954,000	J. Furyk (270)
Apr. 23	Shell Houston Open	Stuart Appleby (269)	990,000	B. Estes (275)
April 30	Zurich Classic of New Orleans	Chris Couch (269)	1,080,000	F. Funk & C. Howell III (270)
May 7	Wachovia Championship	Jim Furyk (276)*	1,134,000	T. Immelman (276)
May 14	EDS Byron Nelson Championship	Brett Wetterich (268)	1,116,000	T. Immelman (269)
May 21	Bank of America Colonial	Tim Herron (268)*	1,080,000	R. Johnson (268)
May 28	FedEx St. Jude Classic	Jeff Maggert (271)	936,000	T. Pernice Jr. (274)
June 4	The Memorial Tournament	Carl Pettersson (276)	1,035,000	Z. Johnson & B. Wetterich (278)
June 11	Barclays Classic	Vijay Singh (274)	1,035,000	A. Scott (275)
June 18	**U.S. Open** (Mamaroneck, N.Y.)	Geoff Ogilvy (285)	1,225,000	3-way tie (286)#
June 27	Booz Allen Classic	Ben Curtis (264)	900,000	4-way tie (269)#
July 2	Buick Championship	J.J. Henry (266)	792,000	H. Mahan & R. Moore (269)
July 9	Gialis Western Open	Trevor Immelman (271)	900,000	M. Goggin & T. Woods (273)
July 16	John Deere Classic	John Senden (265)	720,000	J.P. Hayes (266)
July 23	B.C. Open	John Rollins (269)	540,000	B. May (270)
July 23	**British Open** (Royal Liverpool)	Tiger Woods (270)	1,338,480	C. DiMarco (272)
July 30	U.S. Bank Championship	Corey Pavin (260)	720,000	J. Kelly (262)
Aug. 6	Buick Open	Tiger Woods (264)	864,000	J. Furyk (267)
Aug. 13	The International†	Dean Wilson (+34)*	990,000	T. Lehman (+34)
Aug. 20	**PGA Championship** (Medinah, Ill.) . . .	Tiger Woods (270)	1,224,000	S. Micheel (275)
Aug. 27	WGC: Bridgestone Invitational	Tiger Woods (270)*	1,300,000	S. Cink (270)
Aug. 27	Reno-Tahoe Open	Will MacKenzie (268)	540,000	B. Estes (269)

PGA Tour Results (Cont.)

Last Rd	Tournament	Winner	Earnings	Runner-Up
Sept. 4	Deutsche Bank Championship	Tiger Woods (26)	$990,000	V. Singh (270)
Sept. 10	Canadian Open	Jim Furyk (266)	900,000	B. Bryant (267)
Sept. 17	84 Lumber Classic	Ben Curtis (274)	828,000	C. Howell III (276)
Sept. 24	The Ryder Cup (Kildare, Ire.)	Europe (18½)	—	United States (9½)
Sept. 24	Valero Texas Open	Eric Axley (265)	720,000	3-way tie (268)#
Oct. 1	WGC: American Express Championship	Tiger Woods (261)	1,300,000	I. Poulter & A. Scott (269)
Oct. 1	Southern Farm Bureau Classic	D.J. Trahan (275)*	540,000	J. Durant (275)
Oct. 8	Chrysler Classic of Greensboro	Davis Love III (272)	900,000	J. Bohn (274)

% Weather-shortened.

+ Bob Hope Chrysler Classic is a five-round, 90-hole event played over five days.

† The scoring for The International is based on a modified Stableford system (8 points for a double eagle, 5 for an eagle, 2 for a birdie, 0 for a par, –1 for a bogey, –3 for double bogey or worse).

*Playoffs: Mercedes—Appleby won on 1st hole; **Buick Invit.**—Woods won on 2nd hole; **Wachovia**—Furyk won on 1st hole; **Colonial**—Herron won on 2nd hole; **International**—Wilson won on 2nd hole; **Bridgestone**—Woods won on 4th hole; **Southern Farm Bureau**—Trahan won on 3rd hole.

#Second place ties (3 players or more): 5-WAY—**FBR** (J.J. Henry, S. Lowery, R. Palmer, S. Verplank, C. Villegas); 4-WAY—**Booz Allen** (B. Andrade, P. Harrington, N. O'Hern, S. Stricker); 3-WAY—**U.S. Open** (J. Furyk, C. Montgomerie, P. Mickelson); **Valero Texas** (A. Kim, D. Wilson, J. Rose).

PGA Majors

The Masters

Edition: 70th   **Dates:** April 6–9
Site: Augusta National GC, Augusta, Ga.
Par: 36-36—72 (7445 yards)   **Purse:** $7,000,000

		1 2 3 4	Tot	Earnings
1	Phil Mickelson	70-72-70-69—	281	$1,260,000
2	Tim Clark	70-72-72-69—	283	756,000
3	Jose Maria Olazabal	76-71-71-66—	284	315,700
	Retief Goosen	70-73-72-69—	284	315,700
	Tiger Woods	72-71-71-70—	284	315,700
	Fred Couples	71-70-72-71—	284	315,700
	Chad Campbell	71-67-75-71—	284	315,700
8	Angel Cabrera	73-74-70-68—	285	210,000
	Vijay Singh	67-74-73-71—	285	210,000
10	Stewart Cink	72-73-71-70—	286	189,000

Early round leaders: 1st—Singh (67); 2nd—Campbell (138); 3rd—Mickelson (212).

Top amateur: none made the cut.

U.S. Open

Edition: 106th   **Dates:** June 15–18
Site: Winged Foot Golf Club, Mamaroneck, N.Y.
Par: 35-35—70 (7264 yards)   **Purse:** $6,800,000

		1 2 3 4	Tot	Earnings
1	Geoff Ogilvy	71-70-72-72—	285	$1,225,000
2	Jim Furyk	70-72-74-70—	286	501,249
	Colin Montgomerie . .	69-71-75-71—	286	501,249
	Phil Mickelson	70-73-69-74—	286	501,249
5	Padraig Harrington . .	73-69-74-71—	287	255,642
6	Nick O'Hern	75-70-74-69—	288	183,255
	Jeff Sluman	74-73-72-69—	288	183,255
	Mike Weir	71-74-71-72—	288	183,255
	Steve Stricker	70-69-76-73—	288	183,255
	Vijay Singh	71-74-70-73—	288	183,255
	Kenneth Ferrie	71-70-71-76—	288	183,255

Early round leaders: 1st—Montgomerie (69); 2nd—Stricker (139); 3rd—Mickelson & Ferrie (212).

Top amateur: none made the cut.

British Open

Edition: 135th   **Dates:** July 20–23
Site: Royal Liverpool Golf Club, Hoylake, England
Par: 36-36—72 (7258 yards)   **Purse:** $7,490,400

		1 2 3 4	Tot	Earnings
1	Tiger Woods	67-65-71-67—	270	$1,338,480
2	Chris DiMarco	70-65-69-68—	272	799,370
3	Ernie Els	68-65-71-71—	275	511,225
4	Jim Furyk	68-71-66-71—	276	390,390
5	Sergio Garcia	68-71-65-73—	277	296,510
	Hideto Tanihara . . .	72-68-66-71—	277	296,510
7	Angel Cabrera	71-68-66-73—	278	237,952
8	Adam Scott	68-69-70-72—	279	177,225
	Carl Pettersson	68-72-70-69—	279	177,225
	Andres Romero . . .	70-70-68-71—	279	177,225

Early round leaders: 1st—Graeme McDowell (66); 2nd—Woods (132); 3rd—Woods (203).

Top amateur: Marius Thorp (288, tied for 48th).

PGA Championship

Edition: 88th   **Dates:** Aug. 17–20
Site: Medinah Country Club, Medinah, Ill.
Par: 36-36—72 (7561 yards)   **Purse:** $6,500,000

		1 2 3 4	Tot	Earnings
1	Tiger Woods	69-68-65-68—	270	$1,224,000
2	Shaun Micheel	69-70-67-69—	275	734,400
3	Adam Scott	71-69-69-67—	276	353,600
	Sergio Garcia	69-70-69-68—	276	353,600
	Luke Donald	68-68-66-74—	276	353,600
6	Mike Weir	72-67-65-73—	277	244,800
7	Steve Stricker	72-67-70-69—	278	207,788
	K.J. Choi	73-67-67-71—	278	207,788
9	Ryan Moore	71-72-67-69—	279	165,000
	Ian Poulter	70-70-68-71—	279	165,000
	Geoff Ogilvy	69-68-68-74—	279	165,000

Early round leaders: 1st—Lucas Glover and Chris Riley (66); 2nd—Donald, Henrik Stenson, Billy Andrade & Tim Herron (136); 3rd—Woods & Donald (202).

Top amateur: none.

LPGA Tour
Late 2005

Last Rd	Tournament	Winner	Earnings	Runner-Up
Nov. 6	Mizuno Classic	Annika Sorenstam (195)	$150,000	J. Rosales (198)
Nov. 13	The Mitchell Company TOC	Christina Kim (273)	138,000	R. Hetherington (274)
Nov. 20	ADT Tour Championship	Annika Sorenstam (282)*	215,000	3-way tie (284)
Dec. 11	Lexus Cup	Team International (16)	960,000	Team Asia (6)

#Second place ties (3 players or more): 3-WAY—**ADT** (M. Redman, S-Y Yang, L. Neumann).

2006 (through Oct. 8)

Last Rd	Tournament	Winner	Earnings	Runner-Up
Jan 22	Women's World Cup of Golf	Sweden (281)	$220,000	Scotland (284)
Feb. 18	SBS Open at Turtle Bay	Joo Mi Kim (206)*	150,000	S.Y. Moon & L. Ochoa (206)
Feb. 25	Fields Open in Hawaii	Meena Lee (202)*	165,000	S.H. Lee (202)
Mar. 12	MasterCard Classic	Annika Sorenstam (208)	180,000	H. Alfredsson & S.H. Lee (209)
Mar. 19	Safeway International	Juli Inkster (273)	210,000	Sa. Lee (275)
Apr. 2	**Kraft Nabisco Championship** (Rancho Mirage, Calif.)	Karrie Webb (279)*	270,000	L. Ochoa (279)
Apr. 15	Takefuji Classic	Lorena Ochoa (197)	165,000	S.H. Lee (200)
Apr. 23	Florida's Natural Charity Championship	Sung Ah Kim (272)	210,000	3-way tie (274)#
April 30	Ginn Clubs & Resorts Open	Mi Hyun Kim (276)	375,000	L. Ochoa & K. Webb (278)
May 7	Franklin American Mortgage Champ.	Cristie Kerr (269)	165,000	3-way tie (271)
May 14	Michelob Ultra Open	Karrie Webb (270)	330,000	H-W Han & L. Ochoa (277)
May 21	Sybase Classic	Lorena Ochoa (208)	195,000	K. Bae & H-W Han (210)
May 28	Corning Classic	Hee Won Han (273)*	180,000	M. Lee (273)
June 4	ShopRite Classic	Seon Hwa Lee (197)	225,000	3-way tie (200)#
June 11	**McDonald's LPGA Championship** (Havre de Grace, Md.)	Se Ri Pak (280)*	270,000	K. Webb (280)
June 25	Wegmen's Rochester	Jeong Jang (275)	270,000	J. Granada (276)
July 2	**U.S. Women's Open** (Newport, R.I.)	Annika Sorenstam (284)*	560,000	P. Hurst (284)
July 9	HSBC Women's World Match Play	Brittany Lincicome (3&2)	500,000	J. Inkster
July 16	Jamie Farr Owens Corning Classic	Mi Hyun Kim (266)*	180,000	N. Gulbis (266)
July 29	Evian Masters	Karrie Webb (272)	450,000	L. Davies & M. Wie (273)
Aug. 6	**Weetabix Women's British Open** (Lancashire, England)	Sherri Steinhauer (281)	305,440	C. Kerr & S. Gustafson (284)
Aug 13	CN Canadian Women's Open	Cristie Kerr (276)	255,000	A. Stanford (277)
Aug. 20	Safeway Classic	Pat Hurst (206)	210,000	K. Saiki & J. Jang (207)
Aug. 27	Wendy's Championship for Children	Lorena Ochoa (264)	165,000	S. Prammanasudh & J. Lee (267)
Sept. 3	State Farm Classic	Annika Sorenstam (269)	195,000	C. Kerr (271)
Sept. 10	John Q. Hammons Hotel Classic	Cristie Kerr (199)	150,000	A. Sorenstam (201)
Sept. 24	Longs Drugs Challenge	Karrie Webb (273)	165,000	A. Sorenstam (274)
Oct. 8	Corona Morelia Championship	Lorena Ochoa (272)	150,000	J. Granada (277)

*Playoffs: SBS—Kim won on 2nd hole; **Fields**—Lee won on 3rd hole; **Kraft Nabisco**—Webb won on 1st hole; **Corning**—Han won on 4th hole; **LPGA Championship**—Pak won on 1st hole; **U.S. Open**—Sorenstam won on an 18-hole playoff round; **Jamie Farr**—Kim won on 3rd hole.

#Second place ties (3 players or more): 3-WAY—**Natural Charity** (C. Kerr, K. Webb, A. Sorenstam); **Franklin American** (L. Ochoa, P. Hurst, A. Stanford); **ShopRite** (J. Jang, S. Steinhauer, A. Sorenstam).

LPGA Majors

Kraft Nabisco Championship

Edition: 35th   **Dates:** March 20-April 2
Site: Mission Hills CC, Rancho Mirage, Calif.
Par: 36-36—72 (6569 yards)   **Purse:** $1,800,000

		1 2 3 4	Tot	Earnings
1	Karrie Webb*	70-68-76-65—	279	$270,000
2	Lorena Ochoa	62-71-74-72—	279	168,226
3	Natalie Gulbis	73-71-68-68—	280	108,222
	Michelle Wie	66-71-73-70—	280	108,222
5	Juli Inkster	69-73-74-68—	284	75,985
6	Annika Sorenstam	71-72-73-70—	286	57,104
	Hee-Won Han	75-72-68-71—	286	57,104
8	Brittany Lang	70-74-72-71—	287	41,293
	Helen Alfredsson	70-72-72-73—	287	41,293
	Shi Hyun Ahn	70-71-71-75—	287	41,293

* Webb (4) defeated Ochoa (5) on the first playoff hole.
Early round leaders: 1st—Ochoa (62); 2nd—Ochoa (133); 3rd—Ochoa (207).
Top amateur: Angela Park (290, tied for 15th).

McDonald's LPGA Championship

Edition: 52nd   **Dates:** June 8-11
Site: Bulle Rock Golf Course, Havre de Grace, Md.
Par: 36-36—72 (6596 yards)   **Purse:** $1,800,000

		1 2 3 4	Tot	Earnings
1	Se Ri Pak*	71-69-71-69—	280	$270,000
2	Karrie Webb	70-70-72-68—	280	163,998
3	Mi Hyun Kim	68-71-71-71—	281	105,501
	Ai Miyazato	68-72-69-72—	281	105,501
5	Cristie Kerr	66-74-74-68—	282	57,464
	Michelle Wie	71-68-71-72—	282	57,464
	Shi Hyun Ahn	69-70-71-72—	282	57,464
	Pat Hurst	66-71-72-73—	282	57,464
9	Five tied at 283			34,174

* Pak (3) defeated Webb (DNF) on the first playoff hole.
Early round leaders: 1st—Nicole Castrale (64); 2nd—Hurst (137); 3rd—Miyazato & Hurst (209).
Top amateur: none.

LPGA Majors (Cont.)

U.S. Women's Open

Edition: 61st   **Dates:** June 29-July 3
Site: Newport Country Club, Newport, R.I.
Par: 36-35—71 (6616 yds)   **Purse:** $3,100,000

	1 2 3 4	Tot	Earnings
1 Annika Sorenstam*	.69-71-73-71—	284	$560,000
2 Pat Hurst	.69-71-75-69—	284	335,000
3 Se Ri Pak	.69-74-74-69—	286	156,038
Stacy Prammanasudh	72-71-71-72—	286	156,038
Michelle Wie	.70-72-71-73—	286	156,038
6 Juli Inkster	.73-70-71-73—	287	103,575
7 Brittany Lincicome	.72-72-69-78—	291	93,026
8 Rachel Hetherington	.74-72-73-73—	292	82,460
Shi Hyun Ahn	.71-71-74-76—	292	82,460
10 Six tied at 293			66,174

* Sorenstam (70) defeated Hurst (74) in an 18-hole playoff.

Early round leaders: 1st—Sorenstam, Hurst, Pak & Jane Park (69); 2nd—Sorenstam and Hurst (140); 3rd—Sorenstam, Wie & Lincicome (213).

Top amateur: Amanda Blumenherst and Jane Park (293, tied for 10th).

Weetabix Women's British Open

Edition: 13th   **Dates:** Aug. 3-6
Site: Royal Lytham & St. Annes, Lancashire, England
Par: 35-37—72 (6480 yards)   **Purse:** $1,800,000

	1 2 3 4	Tot	Earnings
1 Sherri Steinhauer	....73-70-66-72—	281	$305,440
2 Cristie Kerr	.71-76-66-71—	284	162,265
Sophie Gustafson	...76-67-69-72—	284	162,265
4 Lorena Ochoa	.74-73-65-73—	285	95,450
Juli Inkster	.66-72-74-73—	285	95,450
6 Lorie Kane	.73-69-74-70—	286	70,633
Beth Daniel	.73-71-70-72—	286	70,633
8 Julieta Granada	.71-73-70-73—	287	61,088
9 Ai Miyazato	.71-75-75-67—	288	55,361
10 Six tied at 290			40,566

Early round leaders: 1st—Inkster (66); 2nd—Inkster (138); 3rd—Steinhauer (209).

Top amateur: Amy Yang (301, 60th place)

Champions Tour
(formerly Senior PGA Tour)

Late 2005

Last Rd	Tournament	Winner	Earnings	Runner-Up
Dec. 4@	MBNA WorldPoints Father/Son Challenge	Bernhard/Stefan Langher (120)	$100,000 (each)	Raymond/Robert Floyd (121)

2006 (through Oct. 8)

Last Rd	Tournament	Winner	Earnings	Runner-Up
Jan. 22	MasterCard Championship	Loren Roberts (191)	$290,000	D. Pooley (192)
Jan. 29	Turtle Bay Championship	Loren Roberts (204)	225,000	S. Simpson (206)
Feb. 6@	Wendy's Champions Skins Game	Raymond Floyd & Dana Quigley (10 skins)	510,000	J. Nicklaus & T. Watson (8 skins)
Feb. 19	ACE Group Classic	Loren Roberts (202)	240,000	B. Bryant & R.W. Eaks (203)
Feb. 26	Outback Steakhouse Pro-Am	Jerry Pate (202)	240,000	3-way tie (203)#
Mar. 12	AT&T Classic	Tom Kite (204)	240,000	G. Morgan (209)
Mar. 19	Toshiba Classic	Brad Bryant (204)	247,500	3-way tie (205)#
Apr. 2	Puerto Vallarta Blue Agave Classic	Morris Hatalsky (207)	240,000	S. Simpson (208)
Apr. 23	Liberty Mutual Legends of Golf	Jay Haas (201)	395,000	P. Jacobsen & C. Stadler (206)
Apr. 30	FedEx Kinko's Classic	Jay Haas (205)	240,000	M. James & T. Kite (207)
May 7	Regions Charity Classic	Brad Bryant (199)	240,000	M. McNulty (201)
May 14	Boeing Championship	Bobby Wadkins (203)	240,000	R. Floyd (204)
May 28	**Senior PGA Championship** (Edmond, Okla.)	Jay Haas (279)*	360,000	B. Bryant (279)
June 4	Allianz Championship	Gil Morgan (197)	225,000	L. Roberts (198)
June 11	Bank of America Championship	Canceled due to inclement weather		
June 25	Commerce Bank Championship	John Harris (202)*	225,000	T. Jenkins (202)
July 2	Greater Kansas City Golf Classic	Dana Quigley (198)	248,000	D. Edwards (201)
July 9	**U.S. Senior Open** (Hutchinson, Kan.)	Allen Doyle (272)	470,000	T. Watson (274)
July 16	**Ford Senior Players Championship** (Dearborn, Mich.)	Bobby Wadkins (274)	375,000	J. Thorpe (275)
July 30	**Senior British Open** (Ayrshire, Scotland)	Loren Roberts (274)*	293,981	E. Romero (274)
Aug. 6	3M Championship	David Edwards (204)	262,500	B. Bryant & C. Stadler (206)
Aug. 20	Boeing Greater Seattle Classic	Tom Kite (201)*	240,000	K. Fergus (201)
Aug. 27	**JELD-WEN Tradition** (Aloha, Ore.)	Eduardo Romero (275)*	375,000	L. Nielsen (275)
Sept. 3	Wal-Mart First Tee Open	Scott Simpson (204)	300,000	D. Edwards & J. Haas (205)
Sept. 9	Georgia-Pacific Grand Champions	Jay Sigel (134)	85,000	Mike McCullough (136)
Sept. 17	Constellation Energy Classic	Bob Gilder (202)	255,000	3-way tie (204)#
Oct. 1	Greater Hickory Classic	Andy Bean (201)*	240,000	R.W. Eaks (201)
Oct. 8	SAS Championship	Tom Jenkins (134)%	300,000	C. Beck & L. Roberts (135)

%Weather-shortened.

@Unofficial Champions Tour money event.

*Playoffs: **Sr. PGA Championship**—Haas won on 3rd hole; **Commerce Bank**—Harris won on 1st hole; **Sr. British**—Roberts won on 1st hole; **Boeing Seattle**—Kite won on 1st hole; **JELD-WEN**—Romero won on 1st hole; **Greater Hickory**—Bean won on 1st hole.

#Second place tie (3 players or more): 3-WAY—**Outback** (M. Hatalsky, M. James, H. Irwin); **Toshiba** (J. Harris, M. Johnson, B. Wadkins); **Constellation Energy** (B. Bryant, J. Haas, D. Pooley).

Champions Tour Majors

Senior PGA Championship

Edition: 67th **Dates:** May 25-28
Site: Oak Tree Golf Club, Edmond, Okla.
Par: 36-35—71 (7102 yards) **Purse:** $2,000,000

	1 2 3 4	Tot	Earnings
1 Jay Haas*	.68-70-73-68—	279	$360,000
2 Brad Bryant	.69-67-72-71—	279	216,000
3 Gil Morgan	.66-70-71-74—	281	136,000
4 Dana Quigley	.69-70-72-71—	282	96,000
5 Loren Roberts	.68-71-71-73—	283	76,000
6 T Nakajima	.71-70-74-69—	284	66,000
7 K Tomori	.69-76-73-67—	285	60,000
Peter Jacobsen	.67-68-75-75—	285	60,000
9 Doug Tewell	.71-75-71-70—	287	54,000
10 D.A. Weibring	.71-71-70-76—	288	50,000

Early round leaders: 1st—Morgan (66); 2nd—Jacobsen (135); 3rd—Morgan (207).

Top amateur: none.

*Haas (4-4-4) defeated Bryant (4-4-DNF) on the 3rd hole of a sudden-death playoff.

U.S. Senior Open

Edition: 27th **Dates:** July 6-9
Site: Prairie Dunes Country Club, Hutchinson, Kan.
Par: 35-35—70 (6646 yards) **Purse:** $2,600,000

	1 2 3 4	Tot	Earnings
1 Allen Doyle	.69-68-67-68—	272	$470,000
2 Tom Watson	.70-66-66-72—	274	280,000
3 Bruce Lietzke	.69-70-70-66—	275	148,567
Peter Jacobsen	.72-66-68-69—	275	148,567
5 Scott Simpson	.72-70-66-68—	276	93,205
Andy Bean	.71-72-64-69—	276	93,205
7 Bob Gilder	.71-66-70-70—	277	78,682
8 D.A. Weibring	.68-71-71-68—	278	67,001
Jay Haas	.67-75-67-69—	278	67,001
Loren Roberts	.72-71-62-73—	278	67,001

Early round leaders: 1st—Haas & Dave Barr (67); 2nd—Watson (136); 3rd—Watson (202).

Top amateur: Randy Reifers (292, tied for 47th).

Ford Sr. Players Championship

Edition: 24th **Dates:** July 13-16
Site: TPC of Michigan, Dearborn, Mich.
Par: 36-36—72 (7069 yards) **Purse:** $2,500,000

	1 2 3 4	Tot	Earnings
1 Bobby Wadkins	.69-72-65-68—	274	$375,000
2 Jim Thorpe	.67-70-69-69—	275	220,000
3 Jay Haas	.68-70-70-68—	276	137,500
Gil Morgan	.70-66-71-69—	276	137,500
Loren Roberts	.71-67-64-74—	276	137,500
Des Smyth	.71-67-68-70—	276	137,500
7 Brad Bryant	.68-69-68-72—	277	85,000
Tom Purtzer	.69-67-72-69—	277	85,000
9 Tom Kite	.68-70-70-70—	278	67,500
Fuzzy Zoeller	.65-72-73-68—	278	67,500

Early round leaders: 1st—Zoeller & Ron Streck (65); 2nd—Morgan, Don Pooley, Joe Ozaki, Jerry Pate, Tom Watson, David Edwards & Mike Reid (136); 3rd—Roberts (202).

Top amateur: none.

Senior British Open

Edition: 20th (4th as major) **Dates:** July 27-30
Site: The Westin Turnberry Resort, Ayrshire, Scotland
Par: 35-35—70 (7012 yards) **Purse:** $1,700,000

	1 2 3 4	Tot	Earnings
1 Loren Roberts*	.65-65-69-75—	274	$293,981
2 Eduardo Romero	.67-63-73-71—	274	196,081
3 Dick Mast	.71-67-70-67—	275	110,383
4 Craig Stadler	.65-66-77-70—	278	88,213
5 Tim Simpson	.66-67-72-74—	279	74,744
6 Jay Haas	.72-68-73-68—	281	57,325
D.A. Weibring	.72-70-71-68—	281	57,325
8 David Edwards	.67-65-76-75—	283	41,796
Gil Morgan	.68-65-75-75—	283	41,796
10 Tom Kite	.69-69-74-72—	284	32,640
Gordon J. Brand	.67-73-75-69—	284	32,640
John Harris	.73-68-72-71—	284	32,640

Early round leaders: 1st—Roberts. Stadler & Peter Jacobsen (65); 2nd—Roberts & Romero (130); 3rd—Roberts (199).

Top amateur: none.

*Roberts (4) defeated Romero (5) on the 1st hole of a sudden-death playoff.

JELD-WEN Tradition

Edition: 18th **Dates:** Aug. 24-27
Site: The Reserve Vineyards & Golf Club, Aloha, Ore.
Par: 35-37—72 (7150 yards) **Purse:** $2,500,000

	1 2 3 4	Tot	Earnings			1 2 3 4	Tot	Earnings
1 Eduardo Romero*	.72-70-68-65—	275	$375,000		8 Andy Bean	.70-69-73-68—	280	$80,000
2 Lonnie Nielsen*	.69-68-68-70—	275	219,000		9 Keith Fergus	.68-70-72-71—	281	60,000
3 Bobby Wadkins	.67-67-71-71—	276	180,000		Bruce Lietzke	.72-70-70-69—	281	60,000
4 Mark James	.72-72-68-67—	279	115,000		Hajime Meshiai	.71-69-71-70—	281	60,000
Tom Kite	.68-70-70-71—	279	115,000		Don Pooley	.73-69-71-68—	281	60,000
Larry Nelson	.71-67-70-70—	279	115,000		Doug Tewell	.76-68-69-68—	281	60,000
Tom Purtzer	.73-68-71-70—	279	115,000					

Early round leaders: 1st—Wadkins, Wayne Levi & Loren Roberts (67); 2nd—Wadkins (134); 3rd—Nielsen & Wadkins (205).

Top amateur: none.

*Romero (4) defeated Nielsen (6) on the 1st hole of a sudden-death playoff.

European PGA Tour

Official money won on the European Tour is presented in euros (E).

Late 2005

Last Rd	Tournament	Winner	Earnings	Runner-Up
Nov. 13	HSBC Champions Tournament	David Howell (268)	E704,517	T. Woods (271)
Nov. 20	WGC: World Cup	Wales—Bradley Dredge/ Stephen Dodge (189)%	E594,581 (each)	England & Sweden (191)
Nov. 27	Volvo China Open	Paul Casey (275)*	184,533	O. Wilson (275)
Dec. 4	UBS Hong Kong Open	Colin Montgomerie (271)	170,591	5-way tie (272)#
Dec. 11	dunhill Championship	Ernie Els (274)	158,579	L. Oosthuizen & C. Schwartzel (277)
Dec. 18	South African Airways Open	Retief Goosen (282)	158,579	E. Els (273)

% Weather-shortened.

*Playoffs: Volvo China—Casey won on 1st hole.

#Second place ties (3 players or more): 5-WAY—**UBS Hong Kong** (K.J. Choi, J. Kingston, K-C Lin, E. Loar, T. Srirot).

2006 (through Oct. 8)

Last Rd	Tournament	Winner	Earnings	Runner-Up
Jan. 8	The Royal Trophy	Europe (9)	$125,000 (each)	Asia (7)
Jan. 22	Abu Dhabi Championship	Chris DiMarco (268)	E275,412	H. Stenson (269)
Jan. 30	Commercialbank Qatar Masters	Henrik Stenson (273)	275,456	P. Broadhurst (276)
Feb. 5	Dubai Desert Classic	Tiger Woods (269)*	329,760	E. Els (269)
Feb. 12	Johnnie Walker Classic	Kevin Stadler (268)	305,468	N. O'Hern (270)
Feb. 19	Maybank Malaysian Open	Charlie Wi (197)%	174,773	T. Jaidee (198)
Feb. 26	WGC: Accenture Match Play Championship	Geoff Ogilvy (3&2)	1,091,886	D. Love III
Mar. 5	Enjoy Jakarta HSBC Indonesia Open	Simon Dyson (268)	140,263	A. Buckle (270)
Mar. 12	OSIM Singapore Masters	Mardan Mamat (276)	138,560	N. Dougherty (277)
Mar. 19	TCL Classic	Johan Edfors (263)	140,215	A. Buckle (264)
Mar. 26	Madeira Island Open	Jean Van de Velde (273)	116,660	L. Slattery (274)
Apr. 2	Portugal Open	Paul Broadhurst (271)	208,330	A. Wall (272)
Apr. 9	The Masters Tournament	Phil Mickelson (281)	1,037,977	T. Clark (283)
Apr. 16	Volvo China Open	Jeev Milkha Singh (278)	247,749	G. Fernandez-Castano (279)
Apr. 23	BMW Asian Open	G. Fernandez-Castano (281)*	247,811	H. Stenson (281)
Apr. 30	Spanish Open	Niclas Fasth (270)*	275,000	J. Bickerton (270)
May 7	Telecom Italia Open	Francesco Molinari (265)	233,330	A. Hansen & J. Sandelin (269)
May 14	Quinn Direct British Masters	Johan Edfors (277)	437,949	3-way tie (278)#
May 21	Nissan Irish Open	Thomas Bjorn (283)	366,660	P. Casey (284)
May 28	BMW Championship	David Howell (271)	708,330	S. Khan (276)
June 4	Celtic Manor Wales Open	Robert Karlsson (260)	364,352	P. Broadhurst (263)
June 11	BA-CA Golf Open	Markus Brier (266)	216,660	S. Hansen (269)
June 18	U.S. Open	Geoff Ogilvy (285)	969,456	3-way tie (286)#
June 18	Aa St. Omer Open	Cesar Monasterio (274)	66,660	M. Maritz & H. Nystrom (275)
June 25	Johnnie Walker Championship	Paul Casey (276)	341,667	S. Hansen & A. Marshall (277)
July 2	French Open	John Bickerton (273)	666,660	P. Harrington (274)
July 9	Smurfit Kappa European Open	Stephen Dodd (279)	578,792	J.M. Lara & A. Wall (281)
July 16	The Barclays Scottish Open	Johan Edfors (271)	577,540	3-way tie (273)#
July 23	British Open (Royal Liverpool)	Tiger Woods (270)	1,045,966	C. DiMarco (272)
July 30	Deutsche Bank TPC	Robert Karlsson (263)	600,000	C. Schwartzel & L. Westwood (267)
Aug. 6	EnterCard Scandinavian Masters	Marc Warren (278)*	266,660	R. Karlsson (278)
Aug. 13	The KLM Open	Simon Dyson (270)*	266,660	R. Green (270)
Aug. 20	PGA Championship	Tiger Woods (270)	959,470	S. Micheel (275)
Aug. 20	Imperial Collection Russian Open	Alejandro Canizares (266)	130,642	D. Drysdale (270)
Aug. 27	WGC: Bridgestone Invitational	Tiger Woods (270)*	1,014,833	S. Cink (270)
Sept. 3	BMW International Open	Henrik Stenson (273)*	333,330	R. Goosen & P. Harrington (273)
Sept. 10	Omega European Masters	Bradley Dredge (267)	333,330	F. Molinari & M. Siem (275)
Sept. 17	Madrid Masters	Ian Poulter (266)	166,660	I. Garrido (271)
Sept. 17	HSBC World Match Play	Paul Casey (10&8)	597,884	S. Micheel
Sept. 24	The Ryder Cup	Europe (18½)	—	United States (9½)
Oct. 1	WGC: AMEX Championship	Tiger Woods (261)	1,015,945	I. Poulter & A. Scott (269)
Oct. 8	dunhill Links Championship	Padraig Harrington (271)	630,566	3-way tie (276)#

% Weather-shortened.

*Playoffs: Dubai Desert—Woods won on 1st hole; **BMW Asian**—Fernandez-Castano won on 1st hole; **Spanish**—Fasth won on 4th hole; **Scandinavian**—Warren won on 2nd hole; **KLM**—Dyson won on 1st hole; **Bridgestone**—Woods won on 4th hole; **BMW**—Stenson won on 1st hole.

#Second place ties (3 players or more): 3-WAY—**Quinn Direct** (G. Emerson, S. Gallacher, J. Sandelin); **U.S. Open** (J. Furyk, P. Mickelson, C. Montgomerie); **Barclay's Scottish** (L. Donald, A. Romero, C. Schwartzel); **dunhill Links** (A. Wall, E. Loar, B. Dredge).

The Official World Golf Ranking

Begun in 1986, the Official World Golf Ranking (formerly the Sony World Ranking) combines the best golfers on the world's six leading professional tours (U.S. PGA Tour, European Tour, Japan Golf Tour, South African PGA Tour, Asian PGA Tour and the PGA Tour of Australasia) in conjunction with the Canadian, Nationwide and Challenge Tours. Rankings are based on a rolling two-year period and weighted in favor of more recent results. Points are awarded after each worldwide tournament according to finish. Final points-per-tournament averages are determined by dividing a player's total points by the number of tournaments played over that two-year period (through Oct. 8, 2006).

		Avg			Avg			Avg
1	Tiger Woods, USA	23.46	6	Ernie Els, RSA	6.26	11	Henrik Stenson, SWE	4.83
2	Jim Furyk, USA	8.77	7	Retief Goosen, RSA	6.14	12	Padraig Harrington, IRE	4.74
3	Phil Mickelson, USA	8.17	8	Luke Donald, ENG	5.67	13	Trevor Immelman, RSA	4.56
4	Adam Scott, AUS	7.20	9	Sergio Garcia, ESP	5.52	14	David Howell, ENG	4.45
5	Vijay Singh, FIJ	6.69	10	Geoff Ogilvy, AUS	5.34	15	Chris DiMarco, USA	4.34

2006 Tour Statistics (through Oct. 8)

Statistical leaders on the PGA, LPGA, Champions and European PGA tours.

PGA

	Scoring	Avg		Putting	Avg		Driving Distance	Avg
1	Tiger Woods	68.11	1	Daniel Chopra	1.717	1	J.B. Holmes	317.8
2	Jim Furyk	68.88	2	Brian Gay	1.723	2	Bubba Watson	317.4
3	Adam Scott	69.03	3	Vaughn Taylor	1.729	3	Robert Garrigus	309.6
4	Luke Donald	69.21	4	Phil Mickelson	1.731	4	Brett Wetterich	307.8
5	Steve Stricker	69.37	5	Steve Stricker	1.734	5	John Daly	306.8
6	Trevor Immelman	69.46	6	David Howell	1.735	6	Tiger Woods	306.4
7	Phil Mickelson	69.50	7	Robert Allenby	1.741	7	Ryan Hietala	305.8
8	Stewart Cink	69.54	8	Jim Furyk	1.741	8	Tag Ridings	304.5
9	Vijay Singh	69.67	9	Michael Allen	1.742	9	Charley Hoffman	304.3
10	Arron Oberholser	69.77	10	Todd Fischer	1.742	10	Scott Gutschewski	303.3

LPGA

	Scoring	Avg		Putting	Avg		Driving Distance	Avg
1	Lorena Ochoa	69.36	1	Cristie Kerr	1.726	1	Karin Sjodin	284.5
2	Annika Sorenstam	69.84	2	Karrie Webb	1.739	2	Brittany Linciome	280.4
3	Cristie Kerr	69.91	3	Seon Hwa Lee	1.740	3	Jee Young Lee	276.8
4	Karrie Webb	70.10	4	Hee-Won Han	1.752	4	Sophie Gustafson	276.2
5	Juli Inkster	70.48	5	Shi Hyun Ahn	1.753	5	Lorena Ochoa	270.9
6	Paula Creamer	70.65	6	Mi Hyun Kim	1.755	6	Kelly Robbins	270.3
7	Hee-Won Han	70.73	7	Lorena Ochoa	1.757	7	Brittany Lang	269.7
8	Jeong Jang	70.75	8	Jee Young Lee	1.758	8	Laura Davies	267.6
9	Mi Hyun Kim	70.79	9	Annika Sorenstam	1.761	9	Alena Sharp	267.4
10	Pat Hurst	70.85	10	Natalie Gulbis	1.765	10	Louise Stahle	266.5

Champions

	Scoring	Avg		Putting	Avg		Driving Distance	Avg
1	Loren Roberts	69.03	1	Loren Roberts	1.721	1	Dan Pohl	292.5
2	Jay Haas	69.26	2	Bob Gilder	1.732	2	Tom Purtzer	288.7
3	Brad Bryant	69.61	3	Gil Morgan	1.743	3	R.W. Eaks	288.4
4	Tom Watson	69.71	4	Brad Bryant	1.746	4	Hajime Meshiai	287.7
5	David Edwards	69.76	5	Jay Haas	1.750	5	Keith Fergus	285.3

European PGA

	Scoring	Avg		Putting	Avg		Driving Distance	Avg
1	Ernie Els	70.02	1	Thaworn Wiratchant	1.718	1	Christian Nilsson	313.9
2	Luke Donald	70.03	2	David Howell	1.723	2	Titch Moore	312.2
3	Sergio Garcia	70.03	3	Darren Clarke	1.727	3	Tuomas Tuovinen	306.8
4	Mikko Ilonen	70.29	4	David Higgins	1.728	4	Angel Cabrera	305.1
5	Padraig Harrington	70.30	5	Henrik Stenson	1.731	5	Johan Edfors	305.0

Key: Scoring—average strokes per round adjusted to the average score of the field each week. If the field is under par, each player's score is adjusted upward a corresponding amount and vice-versa if the field is over par. This keeps a player from receiving an advantage for playing easier-than-average courses. **Putting**—average number of putts taken on greens hit in regulation; **Driving Distance**—average computed by charting exact distances of two tee shots on the most open par-4 or par-5 holes on both front and back nine.

Money Leaders

Official money leaders of PGA, LPGA, Champions and European PGA tours for 2005 and unofficial money leaders for 2006, through Oct. 8, as compiled by the PGA, LPGA and European PGA. Listed are tournaments played (TP), cuts made (CM), 1st, 2nd and 3rd place finishes and earnings for the year.

PGA

Arnold Palmer Award standings

	FINAL 2005	TP	CM	Finish 1-2-3	Earnings		**2006** (through Oct. 8)	TP	CM	Finish 1-2-3	Earnings
1	Tiger Woods	21	19	6-4-2	$10,628,024	1	Tiger Woods	15	14	8-1-1	$9,941,563
2	Vijay Singh	30	26	4-2-3	8,017,336	2	Jim Furyk	22	20	2-3-3	6,429,016
3	Phil Mickelson	21	20	4-1-0	5,699,605	3	Phil Mickelson	19	18	2-1-0	4,256,505
4	Jim Furyk	26	23	1-4-0	4,255,369	4	Geoff Ogilvy	19	16	2-1-0	4,228,869
5	David Toms	25	19	1-1-1	3,962,013	5	Vijay Singh	24	22	1-2-0	4,163,831
6	Kenny Perry	23	19	2-0-1	3,607,155	6	Adam Scott	17	16	0-3-3	3,808,858
7	Chris DiMarco	24	17	0-3-1	3,562,548	7	Trevor Immelman	21	16	1-2-0	3,479,746
8	Retief Goosen	18	17	1-0-2	3,494,106	8	Stuart Appleby	20	17	2-0-0	3,230,297
9	Bart Bryant	26	19	2-0-0	3,249,136	9	Luke Donald	17	15	1-0-1	2,911,408
10	Sergio Garcia	20	17	1-1-2	3,213,375	10	David Toms	21	16	1-1-1	2,764,287

LPGA

	FINAL 2005	TP	CM	Finish 1-2-3	Earnings		**2006** (through Oct. 8)	TP	CM	Finish 1-2-3	Earnings
1	Annika Sorenstam	20	20	10-2-0	$2,588,240	1	Lorena Ochoa	22	22	4-5-2	$2,124,122
2	Paula Creamer	25	23	2-4-2	1,531,780	2	Karrie Webb	18	17	4-3-0	1,873,753
3	Cristie Kerr	22	20	2-2-4	1,360,941	3	Annika Sorenstam	17	16	3-4-0	1,769,408
4	Lorena Ochoa	23	20	1-4-0	1,201,786	4	Cristie Kerr	22	22	3-3-0	1,472,112
5	Jeong Jang	27	26	1-2-0	1,131,986	5	Mi Hyun Kim	24	22	2-0-1	1,272,318
6	Natalie Gulbis	27	26	0-0-2	1,010,154	6	Juli Inkster	18	18	1-1-0	1,190,187
7	Meena Lee	28	19	1-0-0	870,182	7	Pat Hurst	21	16	1-2-1	1,090,498
8	Hee-Won Han	27	25	1-1-2	856,364	8	Jeong Jang	22	21	1-2-0	953,548
9	Gloria Hee Jung Park	28	26	0-2-2	842,349	9	Hee-Won Han	23	22	1-2-0	902,339
10	Catriona Matthew	26	25	0-0-6	776,924	10	Paula Creamer	23	23	0-0-3	881,278

Champions Tour

	FINAL 2005	TP	CM	Finish 1-2-3	Earnings		**2006** (through Oct. 8)	TP	CM	Finish 1-2-3	Earnings
1	Dana Quigley	27	27	2-5-0	$2,170,258	1	Loren Roberts	18	18	4-2-2	$2,105,764
2	Hale Irwin	22	22	4-2-2	1,983,596	2	Jay Haas	18	18	3-2-3	2,026,427
3	Mark McNulty	23	23	2-2-0	1,791,452	3	Brad Bryant	18	18	2-4-1	1,640,625
4	D.A. Weibring	25	25	1-3-0	1,550,030	4	Gil Morgan	24	24	1-1-4	1,458,005
5	Tom Watson	13	13	2-2-2	1,532,482	5	Tom Kite	22	22	2-1-0	1,360,285
6	Tom Jenkins	27	27	1-3-1	1,484,315	6	Scott Simpson	24	24	1-2-2	1,185,809
7	Gil Morgan	25	25	0-3-2	1,364,170	7	Tom Jenkins	24	23	1-1-2	1,179,986
8	Morris Hatalsky	25	25	0-4-0	1,355,336	8	Bobby Wadkins	22	21	2-1-1	1,148,640
9	Craig Stadler	21	20	0-2-1	1,274,719	9	David Edwards	17	17	1-2-2	1,139,273
10	Des Smyth	21	21	2-1-0	1,238,876	10	Allen Doyle	22	22	1-0-0	1,038,238

European PGA

Order of Merit standings. All amounts are listed in Euros (E).

	FINAL 2005	TP	CM	Finish 1-2-3	Earnings		**2006** (through Oct. 8)	TP	CM	Finish 1-2-3	Earnings
1	Colin Montgomerie	25	21	1-3-2	E2,794,223	1	Paul Casey	24	21	3-1-0	E2,409,242
2	Michael Campbell	22	16	2-0-1	2,496,269	2	Padraig Harrington	18	16	1-2-0	2,191,057
3	Paul McGinley	23	21	1-3-1	2,296,423	3	David Howell	20	16	2-0-0	2,166,366
4	Retief Goosen	13	12	1-1-2	2,261,211	4	Robert Karlsson	28	24	2-1-1	1,964,043
5	Angel Cabrera	17	15	1-1-2	1,866,277	5	Ernie Els	15	15	1-2-1	1,716,208
6	Sergio Garcia	11	10	1-2-2	1,828,545	6	Henrik Stenson	22	19	2-2-0	1,641,237
7	David Howell	19	17	1-2-0	1,798,308	7	Ian Poulter	21	18	1-1-1	1,520,952
8	Henrik Stenson	24	21	0-3-4	1,585,750	8	Colin Montgomerie	25	18	1-1-2	1,496,648
9	Thomas Bjorn	23	20	1-2-2	1,561,190	9	Johan Edfors	24	17	3-0-0	1,460,740
10	Jose Maria Olazabal	17	14	1-1-2	1,489,016	10	Retief Goosen	16	14	1-1-1	1,367,399

National Team Competition
2006 Ryder Cup

The 36th Ryder Cup tournament, Sept. 22-24, at Kildare Golf and Country Club, Kildare, Ireland.

Rosters

The 2006 U.S. Team was chosen on the basis of points accumulated at official PGA events from Jan. 9, 2005 through the 2006 PGA Championship, which concluded on Aug. 20. The top 10 finishers on the points list automatically qualified for the 12-member team, and U.S. Captain Tom Lehman selected the final two players.

The 2006 European Team was chosen as follows: the top five players on The Ryder Cup World Points list as of Sept. 3, 2006, as well as the top five players on the European Ryder Cup points list as of Sept. 3, 2006 were automatic qualifiers for the 12-member team. European Team captain Ian Woosnam selected the final two players.

United States: Qualifiers—Tiger Woods, Phil Mickelson, Jim Furyk, Chad Campbell, David Toms, Chris DiMarco, Vaughn Taylor, J.J. Henry, Zach Johnson and Brett Wetterich; Captain's selections—Stewart Cink and Scott Verplank.

Europe: Qualifiers—Paul Casey (England), Luke Donald (England), Sergio Garcia (Spain), Padraig Harrington (Ireland), David Howell (England), Robert Karlsson (Sweden), Paul McGinley (Ireland), Colin Montgomerie (Scotland), Jose Maria Olazabal (Spain) and Henrik Stenson (Sweden); Captain's selections—Darren Clarke (N. Ireland) and Lee Westwood (England).

First Day

Four-Ball Match Results

Winner	Score	Loser
Woods/Furyk	1-up	Harrington/Montgomerie
Casey/Karlsson	halved	Cink/Henry
Garcia/Olazabal	3&2	Toms/Wetterich
Clarke/Westwood	1-up	Mickelson/DiMarco

Europe wins morning, 2½-1½

Foursome Match Results

Winner	Score	Loser
Harrington/McGinley	halved	Campbell/Johnson
Howell/Stenson	halved	Cink/Toms
Westwood/Montgomerie	halved	Mickelson/DiMarco
Donald/Garcia	2-up	Woods/Furyk

Europe wins afternoon, 2½-1½; (Europe leads, 5-3)

Second Day

Four-Ball Match Results

Winner	Score	Loser
Casey/Karlsson	halved	Cink/Henry
Garcia/Olazabal	3&2	Mickelson/DiMarco
Clarke/Westwood	3&2	Woods/Furyk
Verplank/Johnson	2&1	Stenson/Harrington

Europe wins morning, 2½-1½; (Europe leads, 7½-4½)

Foursome Match Results

Winner	Score	Loser
Garcia/Donald	2&1	Mickelson/Toms
Montgomerie/Westwood	halved	Campbell/Taylor
Casey/Howell	5&4	Cink/Johnson
Woods/Furyk	3&2	Harrington/McGinley

Europe wins afternoon, 2½-1½; (Europe leads, 10-6)

Third Day
Singles Match Results

Winner	Score	Loser
Montgomerie	1-up	Toms
Cink	4&3	Garcia
Casey	2&1	Furyk
Woods	3&2	Karlsson
Donald	2&1	Campbell
McGinley	halved	Henry

Winner	Score	Loser
Clarke	3&2	Johnson
Stenson	4&3	Taylor
Howell	5&4	Wetterich
Olazabal	2&1	Mickelson
Westwood	2-up	DiMarco
Verplank	4&3	Harrington

Europe wins day, 8½-3½

Europe wins Ryder Cup, 18½-9½

Overall Records

One point is awarded for a win. One-half point is awarded for a half.

Europe	W	L	H	Pts	United States	W	L	H	Pts
Sergio Garcia	4	1	0	4	Tiger Woods	3	2	0	3
Lee Westwood	3	0	2	4	Stewart Cink	1	1	3	2½
Darren Clarke	3	0	0	3	Scott Verplank	2	0	0	2
Luke Donald	3	0	0	3	Jim Furyk	2	3	0	2
Jose Maria Olazabal	3	0	0	3	Zach Johnson	1	2	1	1½
Paul Casey	2	0	2	3	J.J. Henry	0	0	3	1½
David Howell	2	0	1	2½	Chad Campbell	0	1	2	1
Colin Montgomerie	1	1	2	2	Vaughn Taylor	0	1	1	½
Henrik Stenson	1	1	1	1½	David Toms	0	3	1	½
Robert Karlsson	0	1	2	1	Chris DiMarco	0	3	1	½
Paul McGinley	0	1	2	1	Phil Mickelson	0	4	1	½
Padraig Harrington	0	4	1	½	Brett Wetterich	0	2	0	0

1860-2006
Through the Years

ESPN SPORTS ALMANAC

Major Golf Championships
MEN
The Masters

The Masters has been played every year (except during World War II) since 1934 at the Augusta National Golf Club in Augusta, Ga. Both the course and the tournament were created by Bobby Jones; (*) indicates playoff winner.

Multiple winners: Jack Nicklaus (6); Arnold Palmer and Tiger Woods (4); Jimmy Demaret, Nick Faldo, Gary Player and Sam Snead (3); Seve Ballesteros, Ben Crenshaw, Ben Hogan, Bernhard Langer, Phil Mickelson, Byron Nelson, Jose Maria Olazabal, Horton Smith and Tom Watson (2).

Year	Winner	Score	Runner-up
1934	Horton Smith	.284	Craig Wood (285)
1935	Gene Sarazen*	.282	Craig Wood (282)
1936	Horton Smith	.285	Harry Cooper (286)
1937	Byron Nelson	.283	Ralph Guldahl (285)
1938	Henry Picard	.285	Ralph Guldahl & Harry Cooper (287)
1939	Ralph Guldahl	.279	Sam Snead (280)
1940	Jimmy Demaret	.280	Lloyd Mangrum (284)
1941	Craig Wood	.280	Byron Nelson (283)
1942	Byron Nelson*	.280	Ben Hogan (280)
1943-45	Not held		World War II
1946	Herman Keiser	.282	Ben Hogan (283)
1947	Jimmy Demaret	.281	Frank Stranahan & Byron Nelson (283)
1948	Claude Harmon	.279	Cary Middlecoff (284)
1949	Sam Snead	.282	Lloyd Mangrum & Johnny Bulla (285)
1950	Jimmy Demaret	.283	Jim Ferrier (285)
1951	Ben Hogan	.280	Skee Riegel (282)
1952	Sam Snead	.286	Jack Burke Jr. (290)
1953	Ben Hogan	.274	Porky Oliver (279)
1954	Sam Snead*	.289	Ben Hogan (289)
1955	Cary Middlecoff	.279	Ben Hogan (286)
1956	Jack Burke Jr.	.289	Ken Venturi (290)
1957	Doug Ford	.283	Sam Snead (286)
1958	Arnold Palmer	.284	Doug Ford & Fred Hawkins (285)
1959	Art Wall Jr.	.284	Cary Middlecoff (285)
1960	Arnold Palmer	.282	Ken Venturi (283)
1961	Gary Player	.280	Arnold Palmer & Charles R. Coe (281)
1962	Arnold Palmer*	.280	Dow Finsterwald & Gary Player (280)
1963	Jack Nicklaus	.286	Tony Lema (287)
1964	Arnold Palmer	.276	Jack Nicklaus & Dave Marr (282)
1965	Jack Nicklaus	.271	Arnold Palmer & Gary Player (280)
1966	Jack Nicklaus*	.288	Gay Brewer Jr. & Tommy Jacobs (288)
1967	Gay Brewer Jr.	.280	Bobby Nichols (281)
1968	Bob Goalby	.277	Roberto DeVicenzo (278)
1969	George Archer	.281	Billy Casper, George Knudson & Tom Weiskopf (282)
1970	Billy Casper*	.279	Gene Littler (279)
1971	Charles Coody	.279	Jack Nicklaus & Johnny Miller (281)

Year	Winner	Score	Runner-up
1972	Jack Nicklaus	.286	Bruce Crampton, Bobby Mitchell & Tom Weiskopf (289)
1973	Tommy Aaron	.283	J.C. Snead (284)
1974	Gary Player	.278	Tom Weiskopf, & Dave Stockton (280)
1975	Jack Nicklaus	.276	Johnny Miller & Tom Weiskopf (277)
1976	Ray Floyd	.271	Ben Crenshaw (279)
1977	Tom Watson	.276	Jack Nicklaus (278)
1978	Gary Player	.277	Hubert Green, Rod Funseth & Tom Watson (278)
1979	Fuzzy Zoeller*	.280	Ed Sneed & Tom Watson (280)
1980	Seve Ballesteros	.275	Gibby Gilbert & Jack Newton (279)
1981	Tom Watson	.280	Jack Nicklaus & Johnny Miller (282)
1982	Craig Stadler*	.284	Dan Pohl (284)
1983	Seve Ballesteros	.280	Ben Crenshaw & Tom Kite (284)
1984	Ben Crenshaw	.277	Tom Watson (279)
1985	Bernhard Langer	.282	Curtis Strange, Seve Ballesteros & Ray Floyd (284)
1986	Jack Nicklaus	.279	Greg Norman & Tom Kite (280)
1987	Larry Mize*	.285	Seve Ballesteros & Greg Norman (285)
1988	Sandy Lyle	.281	Mark Calcavecchia (282)
1989	Nick Faldo*	.283	Scott Hoch (283)
1990	Nick Faldo*	.278	Ray Floyd (278)
1991	Ian Woosnam	.277	J.M. Olazabal (278)
1992	Fred Couples	.275	Ray Floyd (277)
1993	Bernhard Langer	.277	Chip Beck (281)
1994	J.M. Olazabal	.279	Tom Lehman (281)
1995	Ben Crenshaw	.274	Davis Love III (275)
1996	Nick Faldo	.276	Greg Norman (281)
1997	Tiger Woods	.270	Tom Kite (282)
1998	Mark O'Meara	.279	Fred Couples & David Duval (280)
1999	J.M. Olazabal	.280	Davis Love III (282)
2000	Vijay Singh	.278	Ernie Els (281)
2001	Tiger Woods	.272	David Duval (274)
2002	Tiger Woods	.276	Retief Goosen (279)
2003	Mike Weir*	.281	Len Mattiace (281)
2004	Phil Mickelson	.279	Ernie Els (280)
2005	Tiger Woods*	.276	Chris DiMarco (276)
2006	Phil Mickelson	.281	Tim Clark (283)

*PLAYOFFS:

1935: Gene Sarazen (144) def. Craig Wood (149) in 36 holes. **1942:** Byron Nelson (69) def. Ben Hogan (70) in 18 holes. **1954:** Sam Snead (70) def. Ben Hogan (71) in 18 holes. **1962:** Arnold Palmer (68) def. Gary Player (71) and Dow Finsterwald (77) in 18 holes. **1966:** Jack Nicklaus (70) def. Tommy Jacobs (72) and Gay Brewer Jr. (78) in 18 holes. **1970:** Billy Casper (69) def. Gene Littler (74) in 18 holes. **1979:** Fuzzy Zoeller (4-3) def. Ed Sneed (4-4) and Tom Watson (4-4) on 2nd hole of sudden death. **1982:** Craig Stadler (4) def. Dan Pohl (5) on 1st hole of sudden death. **1987:** Larry Mize (4-3) def. Greg Norman (4-4) and Seve Ballesteros (5) on 2nd hole of sudden death. **1989:** Nick Faldo (5-3) def. Scott Hoch (5-4) on 2nd hole of sudden death. **1990:** Nick Faldo (4-4) def. Raymond Floyd (4) on 2nd hole of sudden death. **2003:** Mike Weir (5) def. Len Mattiace (6) on 1st hole of sudden death. **2005:** Tiger Woods (3) def. Chris DiMarco (4) on 1st hole of sudden death.

U.S. Open

Played at a different course each year, the U.S. Open was launched by the new U.S. Golf Association in 1895. The Open was a 36-hole event from 1895-97 and has been 72 holes since then. It switched from a 3-day, 36-hole Saturday finish to 4 days of play in 1965. Note that (*) indicates playoff winner and (a) indicates amateur.

Multiple winners: Willie Anderson, Ben Hogan, Bobby Jones and Jack Nicklaus (4); Hale Irwin (3); Julius Boros, Billy Casper, Ernie Els, Retief Goosen, Ralph Guldahl, Walter Hagen, Lee Janzen, John McDermott, Cary Middlecoff, Andy North, Gene Sarazen, Alex Smith, Payne Stewart, Curtis Strange, Lee Trevino and Tiger Woods (2).

Year	Winner	Score	Runner-up	Course	Location
1895	Horace Rawlins	173	Willie Dunn (175)	Newport GC	Newport, R.I.
1896	James Foulis	152	Horace Rawlins (155)	Shinnecock Hills GC	Southampton, N.Y.
1897	Joe Lloyd	162	Willie Anderson (163)	Chicago GC	Wheaton, Ill.
1898	Fred Herd	328	Alex Smith (335)	Myopia Hunt Club	Hamilton, Mass.
1899	Willie Smith	315	George Low, W.H. Way & Val Fitzjohn (326)	Baltimore CC	Baltimore
1900	Harry Vardon	313	J.H. Taylor (315)	Chicago GC	Wheaton, Ill.
1901	Willie Anderson*	331	Alex Smith (331)	Myopia Hunt Club	Hamilton, Mass.
1902	Laurie Auchterlonie	307	Stewart Gardner (313)	Garden City GC	Garden City, N.Y.
1903	Willie Anderson*	307	David Brown (307)	Baltusrol GC	Springfield, N.J.
1904	Willie Anderson	303	Gil Nicholls (308)	Glen View Club	Golf, Ill.
1905	Willie Anderson	314	Alex Smith (316)	Myopia Hunt Club	Hamilton, Mass.
1906	Alex Smith	295	Willie Smith (302)	Onwentsia Club	Lake Forest, Ill.
1907	Alec Ross	302	Gil Nicholls (304)	Phila. Cricket Club	Chestnut Hill, Pa.
1908	Fred McLeod*	322	Willie Smith (322)	Myopia Hunt Club	Hamilton, Mass.
1909	George Sargent	290	Tom McNamara (294)	Englewood GC	Englewood, N.J.
1910	Alex Smith*	298	Macdonald Smith & John McDermott (298)	Phila. Cricket Club	Chestnut Hill, Pa.
1911	John McDermott*	307	George Simpson & Mike Brady (307)	Chicago GC	Wheaton, Ill.
1912	John McDermott	294	Tom McNamara (296)	CC of Buffalo	Buffalo
1913	a-Francis Ouimet*	304	Harry Vardon & Ted Ray (304)	The Country Club	Brookline, Mass.
1914	Walter Hagen	290	a-Chick Evans (291)	Midlothian CC	Blue Island, Ill.
1915	a-John Travers	297	Tom McNamara (298)	Baltusrol GC	Springfield, N.J.
1916	a-Chick Evans	286	Jock Hutchinson (288)	Minikahda Club	Minneapolis
1917-18 Not held			World War I		
1919	Walter Hagen*	301	Mike Brady (301)	Brae Burn CC	West Newton, Mass.
1920	Ted Ray	295	Jock Hutchison, Jack Burke, Leo Diegel & Harry Vardon (296)	Inverness Club	Toledo, Ohio
1921	Jim Barnes	289	Walter Hagen & Fred McLeod (298)	Columbia CC	Chevy Chase, Md.
1922	Gene Sarazen	288	a-Bobby Jones & John Black (289)	Skokie CC	Glencoe, Ill.
1923	a-Bobby Jones*	296	Bobby Cruickshank (296)	Inwood CC	Inwood, N.Y.
1924	Cyril Walker	297	a-Bobby Jones (300)	Oakland Hills CC	Birmingham, Mich.
1925	Willie Macfarlane*	291	a-Bobby Jones (291)	Worcester CC	Worcester, Mass.
1926	a-Bobby Jones	293	Joe Turnesa (294)	Scioto CC	Columbus, Ohio
1927	Tommy Armour*	301	Harry Cooper (301)	Oakmont CC	Oakmont, Pa.
1928	Johnny Farrell*	294	a-Bobby Jones (294)	Olympia Fields CC	Matteson, Ill.
1929	a-Bobby Jones*	294	Al Espinosa (294)	Winged Foot CC	Mamaroneck, N.Y.
1930	a-Bobby Jones	287	Macdonald Smith (289)	Interlachen CC	Hopkins, Minn.
1931	Billy Burke*	292	George Von Elm (292)	Inverness Club	Toledo, Ohio
1932	Gene Sarazen	286	Bobby Cruickshank & Phil Perkins (289)	Fresh Meadow CC	Flushing, N.Y.
1933	a-Johnny Goodman	287	Ralph Guldahl (288)	North Shore GC	Glenview, Ill.
1934	Olin Dutra	293	Gene Sarazen (294)	Merion Cricket Club	Ardmore, Pa.
1935	Sam Parks Jr.	299	Jimmy Thomson (301)	Oakmont CC	Oakmont, Pa.
1936	Tony Manero	282	Harry E. Cooper (284)	Baltusrol GC	Springfield, N.J.
1937	Ralph Guldahl	281	Sam Snead (283)	Oakland Hills CC	Birmingham, Mich.
1938	Ralph Guldahl	284	Dick Metz (290)	Cherry Hills CC	Denver
1939	Byron Nelson*	284	Craig Wood & Denny Shute (284)	Philadelphia CC	Philadelphia

U.S. Open (Cont.)

Year	Winner	Score	Runner-up	Course	Location
1940	Lawson Little*	287	Gene Sarazen (287)	Canterbury GC	Cleveland
1941	Craig Wood	284	Denny Shute (287)	Colonial Club	Ft. Worth
1942-45	Not held		World War II		
1946	Lloyd Mangrum*	284	Byron Nelson & Vic Ghezzi (284)	Canterbury GC	Cleveland
1947	Lew Worsham*	282	Sam Snead (282)	St. Louis CC	Clayton, Mo.
1948	Ben Hogan	276	Jimmy Demaret (278)	Riviera CC	Los Angeles
1949	Cary Middlecoff	286	Clayton Heafner & Sam Snead (287)	Medinah CC	Medinah, Ill.
1950	Ben Hogan*	287	Lloyd Mangrum & George Fazio (287)	Merion Golf Club	Ardmore, Pa.
1951	Ben Hogan	287	Clayton Heafner (289)	Oakland Hills CC	Birmingham, Mich.
1952	Julius Boros	281	Porky Oliver (285)	Northwood Club	Dallas
1953	Ben Hogan	283	Sam Snead (289)	Oakmont CC	Oakmont, Pa.
1954	Ed Furgol	284	Gene Littler (285)	Baltusrol GC	Springfield, N.J.
1955	Jack Fleck*	287	Ben Hogan (287)	Olympic CC	San Francisco
1956	Cary Middlecoff	281	Ben Hogan & Julius Boros (282)	Oak Hill CC	Rochester, N.Y.
1957	Dick Mayer*	282	Cary Middlecoff (282)	Inverness Club	Toledo, Ohio
1958	Tommy Bolt	283	Gary Player (287)	Southern Hills CC	Tulsa
1959	Billy Casper	282	Bob Rosburg (283)	Winged Foot GC	Mamaroneck, N.Y.
1960	Arnold Palmer	280	Jack Nicklaus (282)	Cherry Hills CC	Denver
1961	Gene Littler	281	Doug Sanders & Bob Goalby (282)	Oakland Hills CC	Birmingham, Mich.
1962	Jack Nicklaus*	283	Arnold Palmer (283)	Oakmont CC	Oakmont, Pa.
1963	Julius Boros*	293	Arnold Palmer & Jacky Cupit (293)	The Country Club	Brookline, Mass.
1964	Ken Venturi	278	Tommy Jacobs (282)	Congressional CC	Bethesda, Md.
1965	Gary Player*	282	Kel Nagle (282)	Bellerive CC	St. Louis
1966	Billy Casper*	278	Arnold Palmer (278)	Olympic CC	San Francisco
1967	Jack Nicklaus	275	Arnold Palmer (279)	Baltusrol GC	Springfield, N.J.
1968	Lee Trevino	275	Jack Nicklaus (279)	Oak Hill CC	Rochester, N.Y.
1969	Orville Moody	281	Al Geiberger, Deane Beman & Bob Rosburg (282)	Champions GC	Houston
1970	Tony Jacklin	281	Dave Hill (288)	Hazeltine National GC	Chaska, Minn.
1971	Lee Trevino*	280	Jack Nicklaus (280)	Merion GC	Ardmore, Pa.
1972	Jack Nicklaus	290	Bruce Crampton (293)	Pebble Beach GL	Pebble Beach, Calif.
1973	Johnny Miller	279	John Schlee (280)	Oakmont CC	Oakmont, Pa.
1974	Hale Irwin	287	Forest Fezler (289)	Winged Foot GC	Mamaroneck, N.Y.
1975	Lou Graham*	287	John Mahaffey (287)	Medinah CC	Medinah, Ill.
1976	Jerry Pate	277	Al Geiberger & Tom Weiskopf (279)	Atlanta AC	Duluth, Ga.
1977	Hubert Green	278	Lou Graham (279)	Southern Hills CC	Tulsa
1978	Andy North	285	Dave Stockton & J.C. Snead (286)	Cherry Hills CC	Denver
1979	Hale Irwin	284	Gary Player & Jerry Pate (286)	Inverness Club	Toledo, Ohio
1980	Jack Nicklaus	272	Isao Aoki (274)	Baltusrol GC	Springfield, N.J.
1981	David Graham	273	George Burns & Bill Rogers (276)	Merion GC	Ardmore, Pa.
1982	Tom Watson	282	Jack Nicklaus (284)	Pebble Beach GL	Pebble Beach, Calif.
1983	Larry Nelson	280	Tom Watson (281)	Oakmont CC	Oakmont, Pa.
1984	Fuzzy Zoeller*	276	Greg Norman (276)	Winged Foot GC	Mamaroneck, N.Y.
1985	Andy North	279	Dave Barr, T.C. Chen & Denis Watson (280)	Oakland Hills CC	Birmingham, Mich.
1986	Ray Floyd	279	Lanny Wadkins & Chip Beck (281)	Shinnecock Hills GC	Southampton, N.Y.
1987	Scott Simpson	277	Tom Watson (278)	Olympic Club	San Francisco
1988	Curtis Strange*	278	Nick Faldo (278)	The Country Club	Brookline, Mass.
1989	Curtis Strange	278	Chip Beck, Ian Woosnam & Mark McCumber (279)	Oak Hill CC	Rochester, N.Y.
1990	Hale Irwin*	280	Mike Donald (280)	Medinah CC	Medinah, Ill.
1991	Payne Stewart*	282	Scott Simpson (282)	Hazeltine National GC	Chaska, Minn.
1992	Tom Kite	285	Jeff Sluman (287)	Pebble Beach GL	Pebble Beach, Calif.
1993	Lee Janzen	272	Payne Stewart (274)	Baltusrol GC	Springfield, N.J.
1994	Ernie Els*	279	Colin Montgomerie (279) & Loren Roberts (279)	Oakmont CC	Oakmont, Pa.
1995	Corey Pavin	280	Greg Norman (282)	Shinnecock Hills GC	Southampton, N.Y.

Year	Winner	Score	Runner-up	Course	Location
1996	Steve Jones	278	Davis Love III & Tom Lehman (279)	Oakland Hills CC	Bloomfield Hills, Mich.
1997	Ernie Els	276	Colin Montgomerie (277)	Congressional CC	Bethesda, Md.
1998	Lee Janzen	280	Payne Stewart (281)	Olympic Club	San Francisco
1999	Payne Stewart	279	Phil Mickelson (280)	Pinehurst CC	Pinehurst, N.C.
2000	Tiger Woods	272	Miguel Angel Jimenez & Ernie Els (287)	Pebble Beach GL	Pebble Beach, Calif.
2001	Retief Goosen*	276	Mark Brooks (276)	Southern Hills CC	Tulsa
2002	Tiger Woods	277	Phil Mickelson (280)	Bethpage Black	Farmingdale, N.Y.
2003	Jim Furyk	272	Stephen Leaney (275)	Olympia Fields CC	Olympia Fields, Ill.
2004	Retief Goosen	276	Phil Mickelson (278)	Shinnecock Hills GC	Southampton, N.Y.
2005	Michael Campbell	280	Tiger Woods (282)	Pinehurst CC	Pinehurst, N.C.
2006	Geoff Ogilvy	285	Jim Furyk, Colin Montgomerie & Phil Mickelson (286)	Winged Foot GC	Mamaroneck, N.Y.

*PLAYOFFS:

1901: Willie Anderson (85) def. Alex Smith (86) in 18 holes. **1903:** Willie Anderson (82) def. David Brown (84) in 18 holes. **1908:** Fred McLeod (77) def. Willie Smith (83) in 18 holes. **1910:** Alex Smith (71) def. John McDermott (75) & Macdonald Smith (77) in 18 holes. **1911:** John McDermott (80) def. Mike Brady (82) & George Simpson (85) in 18 holes. **1913:** Francis Ouimet (72) def. Harry Vardon (77) & Edward Ray (78) in 18 holes. **1919:** Walter Hagen (77) def. Mike Brady (78) in 18 holes. **1923:** Bobby Jones (76) def. Bobby Cruickshank (78) in 18 holes. **1925:** Willie Macfarlane (75-72—147) def. Bobby Jones (75-73—148) in 36 holes. **1927:** Tommy Armour (76) def. Harry Cooper (79) in 18 holes. **1928:** Johnny Farrell (70-73—143) def. Bobby Jones (73-71—144) in 36 holes. **1929:** Bobby Jones (141) def. Al Espinosa (164) in 36 holes. **1931:** Billy Burke (149-148) def. George Von Elm (149-149) in 72 holes. **1939:** Byron Nelson (68-70) def. Craig Wood (68-73) and Denny Shute (76) in 36 holes. **1940:** Lawson Little (70) def. Gene Sarazen (73) in 18 holes. **1946:** Lloyd Mangrum (72-72—144) def. Byron Nelson (72-73—145) and Vic Ghezzi (72-73—145) in 36 holes. **1947:** Lew Worsham (69) def. Sam Snead (70) in 18 holes.

1950: Ben Hogan (69) def. Lloyd Mangrum (73) & George Fazio (75) in 18 holes. **1955:** Jack Fleck (69) def. Ben Hogan (72) in 18 holes. **1957:** Dick Mayer (72) def. Cary Middlecoff (79) in 18 holes. **1962:** Jack Nicklaus (71) def. Arnold Palmer (74) in 18 holes. **1963:** Julius Boros (70) def. Jacky Cupit (73) & Arnold Palmer (76) in 18 holes. **1965:** Gary Player (71) def. Kel Nagle (74) in 18 holes. **1966:** Billy Casper (69) def. Arnold Palmer (73) in 18 holes. **1971:** Lee Trevino (68) def. Jack Nicklaus (71) in 18 holes. **1975:** Lou Graham (71) def. John Mahaffey (73) in 18 holes. **1984:** Fuzzy Zoeller (67) def. Greg Norman (75) in 18 holes. **1988:** Curtis Strange (71) def. Nick Faldo (75) in 18 holes. **1990:** Hale Irwin (74-3) def. Mike Donald (74-4) on 1st hole of sudden death after 18 holes. **1991:** Payne Stewart (75) def. Scott Simpson (77) in 18 holes. **1994:** Ernie Els (74-4-4) def. Loren Roberts (74-4-5) and Colin Montgomerie (78) on 2nd hole of sudden death after 18 holes; **2001:** Goosen (70) def. Brooks (72) in 18 holes.

Vardon Trophy

Awarded since 1937 by the PGA of America to the PGA Tour regular with the lowest adjusted scoring average, based on a minimum of 60 rounds. The award is named after Harry Vardon, the six-time British Open champion who also won the U.S. Open in 1900. A point system was used from 1937-41.

Multiple winners: Tiger Woods (6); Billy Casper and Lee Trevino (5); Arnold Palmer and Sam Snead (4); Ben Hogan, Greg Norman and Tom Watson (3); Fred Couples, Bruce Crampton, Tom Kite, Lloyd Mangrum and Nick Price (2).

Year		Pts	Year		Avg	Year		Avg
1937	Harry Cooper	500	1962	Arnold Palmer	70.27	1984	Calvin Peete	70.56
1938	Sam Snead	520	1963	Billy Casper	70.58	1985	Don Pooley	70.36
1939	Byron Nelson	473	1964	Arnold Palmer	70.01	1986	Scott Hoch	70.08
1940	Ben Hogan	423	1965	Billy Casper	70.85	1987	Dan Pohl	70.25
1941	Ben Hogan	494	1966	Billy Casper	70.27	1988	Chip Beck	69.46
1942-46	No award		1967	Arnold Palmer	70.18	1989	Greg Norman	69.49
Year		**Avg**	1968	Billy Casper	69.82	1990	Greg Norman	69.10
1947	Jimmy Demaret	69.90	1969	Dave Hill	70.34	1991	Fred Couples	69.59
1948	Ben Hogan	69.30	1970	Lee Trevino	70.64	1992	Fred Couples	69.38
1949	Sam Snead	69.37	1971	Lee Trevino	70.27	1993	Nick Price	69.11
1950	Sam Snead	69.23	1972	Lee Trevino	70.89	1994	Greg Norman	68.81
1951	Lloyd Mangrum	70.05	1973	Bruce Crampton	70.57	1995	Steve Elkington	69.62
1952	Jack Burke	70.54	1974	Lee Trevino	70.53	1996	Tom Lehman	69.32
1953	Lloyd Mangrum	70.22	1975	Bruce Crampton	70.51	1997	Nick Price	68.98
1954	E.J. Harrison	70.41	1976	Don January	70.56	1998	David Duval	69.13
1955	Sam Snead	69.86	1977	Tom Watson	70.32	1999	Tiger Woods	68.43
1956	Cary Middlecoff	70.35	1978	Tom Watson	70.16	2000	Tiger Woods	67.79
1957	Dow Finsterwald	70.30	1979	Tom Watson	70.27	2001	Tiger Woods	68.81
1958	Bob Rosburg	70.11	1980	Lee Trevino	69.73	2002	Tiger Woods	68.56
1959	Art Wall	70.35	1981	Tom Kite	69.80	2003	Tiger Woods	68.41
1960	Billy Casper	69.95	1982	Tom Kite	70.21	2004	Vijay Singh	68.84
1961	Arnold Palmer	69.85	1983	Ray Floyd	70.61	2005	Tiger Woods	68.66

British Open

The oldest of the Majors, the Open began in 1860 to determine "the champion golfer of the world." While only professional golfers participated in the first year of the tournament, amateurs have been invited ever since. Competition was extended from 36 to 72 holes in 1892. Conducted by the Royal and Ancient Golf Club of St. Andrews, the Open is rotated among select golf courses in England and Scotland. Note that (*) indicates playoff winner and (a) indicates amateur winner.

Multiple winners: Harry Vardon (6); James Braid, J.H. Taylor, Peter Thomson and Tom Watson (5); Walter Hagen, Bobby Locke, Tom Morris Sr., Tom Morris Jr. and Willie Park (4); Jamie Anderson, Seve Ballesteros, Henry Cotton, Nick Faldo, Bob Ferguson, Bobby Jones, Jack Nicklaus, Gary Player and Tiger Woods (3); Harold Hilton, Bob Martin, Greg Norman, Arnold Palmer, Willie Park Jr. and Lee Trevino (2).

Year	Winner	Score	Runner-up	Course	Location
1860	Willie Park	174	Tom Morris Sr. (176)	Prestwick Club	Ayrshire, Scotland
1861	Tom Morris Sr.	163	Willie Park (167)	Prestwick Club	Ayrshire, Scotland
1862	Tom Morris Sr.	163	Willie Park (176)	Prestwick Club	Ayrshire, Scotland
1863	Willie Park	168	Tom Morris Sr. (170)	Prestwick Club	Ayrshire, Scotland
1864	Tom Morris Sr.	167	Andrew Strath (169)	Prestwick Club	Ayrshire, Scotland
1865	Andrew Strath	162	Willie Park (164)	Prestwick Club	Ayrshire, Scotland
1866	Willie Park	169	David Park (171)	Prestwick Club	Ayrshire, Scotland
1867	Tom Morris Sr.	170	Willie Park (172)	Prestwick Club	Ayrshire, Scotland
1868	Tom Morris Jr.	157	Robert Andrew (159)	Prestwick Club	Ayrshire, Scotland
1869	Tom Morris Jr.	154	Tom Morris Sr. (157)	Prestwick Club	Ayrshire, Scotland
1870	Tom Morris Jr.	149	Bob Kirk (161)	Prestwick Club	Ayrshire, Scotland
1871	Not held				
1872	Tom Morris Jr.	166	David Strath (169)	Prestwick Club	Ayrshire, Scotland
1873	Tom Kidd	179	Jamie Anderson (180)	St. Andrews	St. Andrews, Scotland
1874	Mungo Park	159	Tom Morris Jr. (161)	Musselburgh	Musselburgh, Scotland
1875	Willie Park	166	Bob Martin (168)	Prestwick Club	Ayrshire, Scotland
1876	Bob Martin*	176	David Strath (176)	St. Andrews	St. Andrews, Scotland
1877	Jamie Anderson	160	Bob Pringle (162)	Musselburgh	Musselburgh, Scotland
1878	Jamie Anderson	157	Bob Kirk (159)	Prestwick Club	Ayrshire, Scotland
1879	Jamie Anderson	169	Andrew Kirkaldy & James Allan (172)	St. Andrews	St. Andrews, Scotland
1880	Bob Ferguson	162	Peter Paxton (167)	Musselburgh	Musselburgh, Scotland
1881	Bob Ferguson	170	Jamie Anderson (173)	Prestwick Club	Ayrshire, Scotland
1882	Bob Ferguson	171	Willie Fernie (174)	St. Andrews	St. Andrews, Scotland
1883	Willie Fernie*	159	Bob Ferguson (159)	Musselburgh	Musselburgh, Scotland
1884	Jack Simpson	160	Douglas Rolland & Willie Fernie (164)	Prestwick Club	Ayrshire, Scotland
1885	Bob Martin	171	Archie Simpson (172)	St. Andrews	St. Andrews, Scotland
1886	David Brown	157	Willie Campbell (159)	Musselburgh	Musselburgh, Scotland
1887	Willie Park Jr.	161	Bob Martin (162)	Prestwick Club	Ayrshire, Scotland
1888	Jack Burns	171	David Anderson & Ben Sayers (172)	St. Andrews	St. Andrews, Scotland
1889	Willie Park Jr.*	155	Andrew Kirkaldy (155)	Musselburgh	Musselburgh, Scotland
1890	a-John Ball	164	Willie Fernie (167) & A. Simpson (167)	Prestwick Club	Ayrshire, Scotland
1891	Hugh Kirkaldy	166	Andrew Kirkaldy & Willie Fernie (168)	St. Andrews	St. Andrews, Scotland
1892	a-Harold Hilton	305	John Ball, Sandy Herd & Hugh Kirkaldy (308)	Muirfield	Gullane, Scotland
1893	Willie Auchterlonie	322	Johnny Laidley (324)	Prestwick Club	Ayrshire, Scotland
1894	J.H. Taylor	326	Douglas Rolland (331)	Royal St. George's	Sandwich, England
1895	J.H. Taylor	322	Sandy Herd (326)	St. Andrews	St. Andrews, Scotland
1896	Harry Vardon*	316	J.H. Taylor (316)	Muirfield	Gullane, Scotland
1897	a-Harold Hilton	314	James Braid (315)	Hoylake	Hoylake, England
1898	Harry Vardon	307	Willie Park Jr. (308)	Prestwick Club	Ayrshire, Scotland
1899	Harry Vardon	310	Jack White (315)	Royal St. George's	Sandwich, England
1900	J.H. Taylor	309	Harry Vardon (317)	St. Andrews	St. Andrews, Scotland
1901	James Braid	309	Harry Vardon (312)	Muirfield	Gullane, Scotland
1902	Sandy Herd	307	Harry Vardon (308)	Hoylake	Hoylake, England
1903	Harry Vardon	300	Tom Vardon (306)	Prestwick Club	Ayrshire, Scotland
1904	Jack White	296	James Braid (297)	Royal St. George's	Sandwich, England
1905	James Braid	318	J.H. Taylor (323) & Rowland Jones (323)	St. Andrews	St. Andrews, Scotland
1906	James Braid	300	J.H. Taylor (304)	Muirfield	Gullane, Scotland
1907	Arnaud Massy	312	J.H. Taylor (314)	Hoylake	Hoylake, England
1908	James Braid	291	Tom Ball (299)	Prestwick Club	Ayrshire, Scotland
1909	J.H. Taylor	295	James Braid (299)	Deal	Deal, England
1910	James Braid	299	Sandy Herd (303)	St. Andrews	St. Andrews, Scotland
1911	Harry Vardon*	303	Arnaud Massy (303)	Royal St. George's	Sandwich, England
1912	Ted Ray	295	Harry Vardon (299)	Muirfield	Gullane, Scotland

Year	Winner	Score	Runner-up	Course	Location
1913	J.H. Taylor	304	Ted Ray (312)	Hoylake	Hoylake, England
1914	Harry Vardon	306	J.H. Taylor (309)	Prestwick Club	Ayrshire, Scotland
1915-19	Not held		World War I		
1920	George Duncan	303	Sandy Herd (305)	Deal	Deal, England
1921	Jock Hutchison*	296	Roger Wethered (296)	St. Andrews	St. Andrews, Scotland
1922	Walter Hagen	300	George Duncan & Jim Barnes (301)	Royal St. George's	Sandwich, England
1923	Arthur Havers	295	Walter Hagen (296)	Royal Troon	Troon, Scotland
1924	Walter Hagen	301	Ernest Whitcombe (302)	Hoylake	Hoylake, England
1925	Jim Barnes	300	Archie Compston & Ted Ray (301)	Prestwick Club	Ayrshire, Scotland
1926	a-Bobby Jones	291	Al Watrous (293)	Royal Lytham	Lytham, England
1927	a-Bobby Jones	285	Aubrey Boomer (291)	St. Andrews	St. Andrews, Scotland
1928	Walter Hagen	292	Gene Sarazen (294)	Royal St. George's	Sandwich, England
1929	Walter Hagen	292	Johnny Farrell (298)	Muirfield	Gullane, Scotland
1930	a-Bobby Jones	291	Macdonald Smith & Leo Diegel (293)	Hoylake	Hoylake, England
1931	Tommy Armour	296	Jose Jurado (297)	Carnoustie	Carnoustie, Scotland
1932	Gene Sarazen	283	Macdonald Smith (288)	Prince's	Prince's, England
1933	Denny Shute*	292	Craig Wood (292)	St. Andrews	St. Andrews, Scotland
1934	Henry Cotton	283	Sid Brews (288)	Royal St. George's	Sandwich, England
1935	Alf Perry	283	Alf Padgham (287)	Muirfield	Gullane, Scotland
1936	Alf Padgham	287	Jimmy Adams (288)	Hoylake	Hoylake, England
1937	Henry Cotton	290	Reg Whitcombe (292)	Carnoustie	Carnoustie, Scotland
1938	Reg Whitcombe	295	Jimmy Adams (297)	Royal St. George's	Sandwich, England
1939	Dick Burton	290	Johnny Bulla (292)	St. Andrews	St. Andrews, Scotland
1940-45	Not held		World War II		
1946	Sam Snead	290	Bobby Locke (294) & Johnny Bulla (294)	St. Andrews	St. Andrews, Scotland
1947	Fred Daly	293	Frank Stranahan & Reg Horne (294)	Hoylake	Hoylake, England
1948	Henry Cotton	284	Fred Daly (289)	Muirfield	Gullane, Scotland
1949	Bobby Locke*	283	Harry Bradshaw (283)	Royal St. George's	Sandwich, England
1950	Bobby Locke	279	Roberto de Vicenzo (281)	Royal Troon	Troon, Scotland
1951	Max Faulkner	285	Tony Cerda (287)	Royal Portrush	Portrush, Ireland
1952	Bobby Locke	287	Peter Thomson (288)	Royal Lytham	Lytham, England
1953	Ben Hogan	282	Frank Stranahan, Dai Rees, Tony Cerda & Peter Thomson (286)	Carnoustie	Carnoustie, Scotland
1954	Peter Thomson	283	Sid Scott, Dai Rees & Bobby Locke (284)	Royal Birkdale	Southport, England
1955	Peter Thomson	281	Johny Fallon (283)	St. Andrews	St. Andrews, Scotland
1956	Peter Thomson	286	Flory Van Donck (289)	Hoylake	Hoylake, England
1957	Bobby Locke	279	Peter Thomson (282)	St. Andrews	St. Andrews, Scotland
1958	Peter Thomson*	278	Dave Thomas (278)	Royal Lytham	Lytham, England
1959	Gary Player	284	Flory Van Donck & Fred Bullock (286)	Muirfield	Gullane, Scotland
1960	Kel Nagle	278	Arnold Palmer (279)	St. Andrews	St. Andrews, Scotland
1961	Arnold Palmer	284	Dai Rees (285)	Royal Birkdale	Southport, England
1962	Arnold Palmer	276	Kel Nagle (282)	Royal Troon	Troon, Scotland
1963	Bob Charles*	277	Phil Rodgers (277)	Royal Lytham	Lytham, England
1964	Tony Lema	279	Jack Nicklaus (284)	St. Andrews	St. Andrews, Scotland
1965	Peter Thomson	285	Christy O'Connor & Brian Huggett (287)	Royal Birkdale	Southport, England
1966	Jack Nicklaus	282	Doug Sanders & Dave Thomas (283)	Muirfield	Gullane, Scotland
1967	Roberto de Vicenzo	278	Jack Nicklaus (280)	Hoylake	Hoylake, England
1968	Gary Player	289	Jack Nicklaus & Bob Charles (291)	Carnoustie	Carnoustie, Scotland
1969	Tony Jacklin	280	Bob Charles (282)	Royal Lytham	Lytham, England
1970	Jack Nicklaus*	283	Doug Sanders (283)	St. Andrews	St. Andrews, Scotland
1971	Lee Trevino	278	Lu Liang Huan (279)	Royal Birkdale	Southport, England
1972	Lee Trevino	278	Jack Nicklaus (279)	Muirfield	Gullane, Scotland
1973	Tom Weiskopf	276	Johnny Miller & Neil Coles (279)	Royal Troon	Troon, Scotland
1974	Gary Player	282	Peter Oosterhuis (286)	Royal Lytham	Lytham, England
1975	Tom Watson*	279	Jack Newton (279)	Carnoustie	Carnoustie, Scotland
1976	Johnny Miller	279	Seve Ballesteros & Jack Nicklaus (285)	Royal Birkdale	Southport, England
1977	Tom Watson	268	Jack Nicklaus (269)	Turnberry	Turnberry, Scotland

British Open (Cont.)

Year	Winner	Score	Runner-up	Course	Location
1978	Jack Nicklaus	281	Tom Kite, Ray Floyd, Ben Crenshaw & Simon Owen (283)	St. Andrews	St. Andrews, Scotland
1979	Seve Ballesteros	283	Jack Nicklaus & Ben Crenshaw (286)	Royal Lytham	Lytham, England
1980	Tom Watson	271	Lee Trevino (275)	Muirfield	Gullane, Scotland
1981	Bill Rogers	276	Bernhard Langer (280)	Royal St. George's	Sandwich, England
1982	Tom Watson	284	Peter Oosterhuis & Nick Price (285)	Royal Troon	Troon, Scotland
1983	Tom Watson	275	Hale Irwin & Andy Bean (276)	Royal Birkdale	Southport, England
1984	Seve Ballesteros	276	Bernhard Langer & Tom Watson (278)	St. Andrews	St. Andrews, Scotland
1985	Sandy Lyle	282	Payne Stewart (283)	Royal St. George's	Sandwich, England
1986	Greg Norman	280	Gordon J. Brand (285)	Turnberry	Turnberry, Scotland
1987	Nick Faldo	279	Paul Azinger & Rodger Davis (280)	Muirfield	Gullane, Scotland
1988	Seve Ballesteros	273	Nick Price (275)	Royal Lytham	Lytham, England
1989	Mark Calcavecchia*	275	Greg Norman & Wayne Grady (275)	Royal Troon	Troon, Scotland
1990	Nick Faldo	270	Payne Stewart & Mark McNulty (275)	St. Andrews	St. Andrews, Scotland
1991	Ian Baker-Finch	272	Mike Harwood (274)	Royal Birkdale	Southport, England
1992	Nick Faldo	272	John Cook (273)	Muirfield	Gullane, Scotland
1993	Greg Norman	267	Nick Faldo (269)	Royal St. George's	Sandwich, England
1994	Nick Price	268	Jesper Parnevik (269)	Turnberry	Turnberry, Scotland
1995	John Daly*	282	Costantino Rocca (282)	St. Andrews	St. Andrews, Scotland
1996	Tom Lehman	271	Mark McCumber & Ernie Els (273)	Royal Lytham	Lytham, England
1997	Justin Leonard	272	Jesper Parnevik & Darren Clarke (275)	Royal Troon	Troon, Scotland
1998	Mark O'Meara*	280	Brian Watts (280)	Royal Birkdale	Southport, England
1999	Paul Lawrie*	290	Justin Leonard & Jean Van de Velde (290)	Carnoustie	Carnoustie, Scotland
2000	Tiger Woods	269	Thomas Bjorn & Ernie Els (277)	St. Andrews	St. Andrews, Scotland
2001	David Duval	274	Niclas Fasth (277)	Royal Lytham	Lytham, England
2002	Ernie Els*	278	Thomas Levet, Stuart Appleby & Steve Elkington (278)	Muirfield	Gullane, Scotland
2003	Ben Curtis	283	Vijay Singh & Thomas Bjorn (284)	Royal St. George's	Sandwich, England
2004	Todd Hamilton*	274	Ernie Els (274)	Royal Troon	Troon, Scotland
2005	Tiger Woods	274	Colin Montgomerie (279)	St. Andrews	St. Andrews, Scotland
2006	Tiger Woods	270	Chris DiMarco (272)	Royal Liverpool	Hoylake, England

*PLAYOFFS:

1876: Bob Martin awarded title when David Strath refused playoff. **1883:** Willie Fernie (158) def. Robert Ferguson (159) in 36 holes. **1889:** Willie Park Jr. (158) def. Andrew Kirkaldy (163) in 36 holes. **1896:** Harry Vardon (157) def. John H. Taylor (161) in 36 holes. **1911:** Harry Vardon won when Arnaud Massy conceded at 35th hole. **1921:** Jock Hutchison (150) def. Roger Wethered (159) in 36 holes. **1933:** Denny Shute (149) def. Craig Wood (154) in 36 holes. **1949:** Bobby Locke (135) def. Harry Bradshaw (147) in 36 holes. **1958:** Peter Thomson (139) def. Dave Thomas (143) in 36 holes. **1963:** Bob Charles (140) def. Phil Rodgers (148) in 36 holes. **1970:** Jack Nicklaus (72) def. Doug Sanders (73) in 18 holes. **1975:** Tom Watson (71) def. Jack Newton (72) in 18 holes. **1989:** Mark Calcavecchia (4-3-3-3—13) def. Wayne Grady (4-4-4-4—16) and Greg Norman (3-3-4) in 4 holes. **1995:** John Daly (3-4-4-4—15) def. Costantino Rocca (4-5-7-3—19) in 4 holes. **1998:** Mark O'Meara (4-4-5-4—17) def. Brian Watts (5-4-5-5—19) in 4 holes. **1999:** Paul Lawrie (5-4-3-3—15) def. Justin Leonard (5-4-4-5—18) and Jean Van de Velde (6-4-3-5—18) in 4 holes. **2002:** Els (4-3-5-4—16) and Levet (4-2-5-5—16) remained tied after a four-hole playoff that also included Appleby (4-4-4-5—17) and Elkington (5-3-4-5—17). The pair moved on to sudden death, where Els (4) def. Levet (5) on the 1st hole. **2004:** Todd Hamilton (4-4-3-4—15) def. Ernie Els (4-4-4-4—16) in 4 holes.

PGA Championship

The PGA Championship began in 1916 as a professional golfers match play tournament, but switched to stroke play in 1958. Conducted by the PGA of America, the tournament is played on a different course each year.

Multiple winners: Walter Hagen and Jack Nicklaus (5); Gene Sarazen, Sam Snead and Tiger Woods (3); Jim Barnes, Leo Diegel, Ray Floyd, Ben Hogan, Byron Nelson, Larry Nelson, Gary Player, Nick Price, Paul Runyan, Denny Shute, Vijay Singh, Dave Stockton and Lee Trevino (2).

Year	Winner	Score	Runner-up	Course	Location
1916	Jim Barnes	1-up	Jock Hutchison	Siwanoy CC	Bronxville, N.Y.
1917-18 Not held			World War I		
1919	Jim Barnes	6 & 5	Fred McLeod	Engineers CC	Roslyn, N.Y.
1920	Jock Hutchison	1-up	J. Douglas Edgar	Flossmoor CC	Flossmoor, Ill.

Year	Winner	Score	Runner-up	Course	Location
1921	Walter Hagen	3 & 2	Jim Barnes	Inwood CC	Inwood, N.Y.
1922	Gene Sarazen	4 & 3	Emmet French	Oakmont CC	Oakmont, Pa.
1923	Gene Sarazen*	1-up/38	Walter Hagen	Pelham CC	Pelham, N.Y.
1924	Walter Hagen	2-up	Jim Barnes	French Lick CC	French Lick, Ind.
1925	Walter Hagen	6 & 5	Bill Mehlhorn	Olympia Fields CC	Matteson, Ill.
1926	Walter Hagen	5 & 3	Leo Diegel	Salisbury GC	Westbury, N.Y.
1927	Walter Hagen	1-up	Joe Turnesa	Cedar Crest CC	Dallas
1928	Leo Diegel	6 & 5	Al Espinosa	Five Farms CC	Baltimore
1929	Leo Diegel	6 & 4	John Farrell	Hillcrest CC	Los Angeles
1930	Tommy Armour	1-up	Gene Sarazen	Fresh Meadow CC	Flushing, N.Y.
1931	Tom Creavy	2 & 1	Denny Shute	Wannamoisett CC	Rumford, R.I.
1932	Olin Dutra	4 & 3	Frank Walsh	Keller GC	St. Paul, Minn.
1933	Gene Sarazen	5 & 4	Willie Goggin	Blue Mound CC	Milwaukee
1934	Paul Runyan*	1-up/38	Craig Wood	Park CC	Williamsville, N.Y.
1935	Johnny Revolta	5 & 4	Tommy Armour	Twin Hills CC	Oklahoma City
1936	Denny Shute	3 & 2	Jimmy Thomson	Pinehurst CC	Pinehurst, N.C.
1937	Denny Shute*	1-up/37	Harold McSpaden	Pittsburgh FC	Aspinwall, Pa.
1938	Paul Runyan	8 & 7	Sam Snead	Shawnee CC	Shawnee-on-Del, Pa.
1939	Henry Picard*	1-up/37	Byron Nelson	Pomonok CC	Flushing, N.Y.
1940	Byron Nelson	1-up	Sam Snead	Hershey CC	Hershey, Pa.
1941	Vic Ghezzi*	1-up/38	Byron Nelson	Cherry Hills CC	Denver
1942	Sam Snead	2 & 1	Jim Turnesa	Seaview CC	Atlantic City, N.J.
1943	Not held		World War II		
1944	Bob Hamilton	1-up	Byron Nelson	Manito G & CC	Spokane, Wash.
1945	Byron Nelson	4 & 3	Sam Byrd	Morraine CC	Dayton, Ohio
1946	Ben Hogan	6 & 4	Porky Oliver	Portland GC	Portland, Ore.
1947	Jim Ferrier	2 & 1	Chick Harbert	Plum Hollow CC	Detroit
1948	Ben Hogan	7 & 6	Mike Turnesa	Norwood Hills CC	St. Louis
1949	Sam Snead	3 & 2	John Palmer	Hermitage CC	Richmond, Va.
1950	Chandler Harper	4 & 3	Henry Williams Jr.	Scioto CC	Columbus, Ohio
1951	Sam Snead	7 & 6	Walter Burkemo	Oakmont CC	Oakmont, Pa.
1952	Jim Turnesa	1-up	Chick Harbert	Big Spring CC	Louisville
1953	Walter Burkemo	2 & 1	Felice Torza	Birmingham CC	Birmingham, Mich.
1954	Chick Harbert	4 & 3	Walter Burkemo	Keller GC	St. Paul, Minn.
1955	Doug Ford	4 & 3	Cary Middlecoff	Meadowbrook CC	Detroit
1956	Jack Burke	3 & 2	Ted Kroll	Blue Hill CC	Boston
1957	Lionel Hebert	2 & 1	Dow Finsterwald	Miami Valley GC	Dayton, Ohio
1958	Dow Finsterwald	276	Billy Casper (278)	Llanerch CC	Havertown, Pa.
1959	Bob Rosburg	277	Jerry Barber & Doug Sanders (278)	Minneapolis GC	St. Louis Park, Minn.
1960	Jay Hebert	281	Jim Ferrier (282)	Firestone CC	Akron, Ohio
1961	Jerry Barber**	277	Don January (277)	Olympia Fields CC	Matteson, Ill.
1962	Gary Player	278	Bob Goalby (279)	Aronimink GC	Newtown Square, Pa.
1963	Jack Nicklaus	279	Dave Ragan (281)	Dallas AC	Dallas
1964	Bobby Nichols	271	Jack Nicklaus & Arnold Palmer (274)	Columbus CC	Columbus, Ohio
1965	Dave Marr	280	Jack Nicklaus & Billy Casper (282)	Laurel Valley GC	Ligonier, Pa.
1966	Al Geiberger	280	Dudley Wysong (284)	Firestone CC	Akron, Ohio
1967	Don January**	281	Don Massengale (281)	Columbine CC	Littleton, Colo.
1968	Julius Boros	281	Arnold Palmer & Bob Charles (282)	Pecan Valley CC	San Antonio
1969	Ray Floyd	276	Gary Player (277)	NCR GC	Dayton, Ohio
1970	Dave Stockton	279	Arnold Palmer & Bob Murphy (281)	Southern Hills CC	Tulsa
1971	Jack Nicklaus	281	Billy Casper (283)	PGA National GC	Palm Beach Gardens, Fla.
1972	Gary Player	281	Jim Jamieson & Tommy Aaron (283)	Oakland Hills GC	Birmingham, Mich.
1973	Jack Nicklaus	277	Bruce Crampton (281)	Canterbury GC	Cleveland
1974	Lee Trevino	276	Jack Nicklaus (277)	Tanglewood GC	Winston-Salem, N.C.
1975	Jack Nicklaus	276	Bruce Crampton (278)	Firestone CC	Akron, Ohio
1976	Dave Stockton	281	Don January & Ray Floyd (282)	Congressional CC	Bethesda, Md.
1977	Lanny Wadkins**	282	Gene Littler (282)	Pebble Beach GL	Pebble Beach, Calif.
1978	John Mahaffey**	276	Jerry Pate & Tom Watson (276)	Oakmont CC	Oakmont, Pa.
1979	David Graham**	272	Ben Crenshaw (272)	Oakland Hills CC	Birmingham, Mich.
1980	Jack Nicklaus	274	Andy Bean (281)	Oak Hill CC	Rochester, N.Y.
1981	Larry Nelson	273	Fuzzy Zoeller (277)	Atlanta AC	Duluth, Ga.
1982	Ray Floyd	272	Lanny Wadkins (275)	Southern Hills CC	Tulsa
1983	Hal Sutton	274	Jack Nicklaus (275)	Riviera CC	Los Angeles

PGA Championship (Cont.)

Year	Winner	Score	Runner-up	Course	Location
1984	Lee Trevino	273	Lanny Wadkins & Gary Player (277)	Shoal Creek	Birmingham, Ala.
1985	Hubert Green	278	Lee Trevino (280)	Cherry Hills CC	Denver
1986	Bob Tway	276	Greg Norman (278)	Inverness Club	Toledo, Ohio
1987	Larry Nelson**	287	Lanny Wadkins (287)	PGA National	Palm Beach Gardens, Fla.
1988	Jeff Sluman	272	Paul Azinger 275)	Oak Tree GC	Edmond, Okla.
1989	Payne Stewart	276	Andy Bean, Mike Reid & Curtis Strange (277)	Kemper Lakes GC	Hawthorn Woods, Ill.
1990	Wayne Grady	282	Fred Couples (285)	Shoal Creek	Birmingham, Ala.
1991	John Daly	276	Bruce Lietzke (279)	Crooked Stick GC	Carmel, Ind.
1992	Nick Price	278	Nick Faldo, John Cook, Jim Gallagher & Gene Sauers (281)	Bellerive CC	St. Louis
1993	Paul Azinger**	272	Greg Norman (272)	Inverness Club	Toledo, Ohio
1994	Nick Price	269	Corey Pavin (275)	Southern Hills CC	Tulsa
1995	Steve Elkington**	267	Colin Montgomerie (267)	Riviera CC	Pacific Palisades, Calif.
1996	Mark Brooks**	277	Kenny Perry (277)	Valhalla GC	Louisville, Ky.
1997	Davis Love III	269	Justin Leonard (274)	Winged Foot GC	Mamaroneck, N.Y.
1998	Vijay Singh	271	Steve Stricker (273)	Sahalee CC	Redmond, Wash.
1999	Tiger Woods	277	Sergio Garcia (278)	Medinah CC	Medinah, Ill.
2000	Tiger Woods**	270	Bob May (270)	Valhalla GC	Louisville, Ky.
2001	David Toms	265	Phil Mickelson (266)	Atlanta AC	Duluth, Ga.
2002	Rich Beem	278	Tiger Woods (279)	Hazeltine National GC	Chaska, Minn.
2003	Shaun Micheel	276	Chad Campbell (278)	Oak Hill CC	Rochester, N.Y.
2004	Vijay Singh**	280	Chris DiMarco & Justin Leonard (280)	Whistling Straits	Kohler, Wis.
2005	Phil Mickelson	276	Steve Elkington & Thomas Bjorn (277)	Baltusrol GC	Springfield, N.J.
2006	Tiger Woods	270	Shaun Micheel (275)	Medinah CC	Medinah, Ill.

*While the PGA Championship was a match play tournament from 1916-57, the two finalists played 36 holes for the title. In the five years that a playoff was necessary, the match was decided on the 37th or 38th hole.

PLAYOFFS:

1961: Jerry Barber (67) def. Don January (68) in 18 holes. **1967:** Don January (69) def. Don Massengale (71) in 18 holes. **1977:** Lanny Wadkins (4-4-4) def. Gene Littler (4-4-5) on 3rd hole of sudden death. **1978:** John Mahaffey (4-3) def. Jerry Pate (4-4) and Tom Watson (4-5) on 2nd hole of sudden death. **1979:** David Graham (4-4-2) def. Ben Crenshaw (4-4-4) on 3rd hole of sudden death. **1987:** Larry Nelson (4) def. Lanny Wadkins (5) on 1st hole of sudden death. **1993:** Paul Azinger (4-4) def. Greg Norman (4-5) on 2nd hole of sudden death. **1995:** Steve Elkington (3) def. Colin Montgomerie (4) on 1st hole of sudden death. **1996:** Mark Brooks (4) def. Kenny Perry (5) on 1st hole of sudden death. **2000:** Tiger Woods (3-4-5–12) won a three-hole playoff over Bob May (4-4-5–13). **2004:** Vijay Singh (3-3-4–10) won a three-hole playoff over Chris DiMarco (4-3-DNF) and Justin Leonard (4-3-DNF).

Grand Slam Summary

The only golfer ever to win a recognized Grand Slam—four major championships in a single season—was Bobby Jones in 1930. That year, Jones won the U.S. and British Opens as well as the U.S. and British Amateurs.

The men's professional Grand Slam—the Masters, U.S. Open, British Open and PGA Championship—did not gain acceptance until 30 years later when Arnold Palmer won the 1960 Masters and U.S. Open. The media wrote that the popular Palmer was chasing the "new" Grand Slam and would have to win the British Open and the PGA to claim it. He did not, but then nobody has before or since.

Three wins in one year (2): Ben Hogan (1953) and Tiger Woods (2000). **Two wins in one year** (21): Jack Nicklaus (5 times); Tiger Woods (4 times); Ben Hogan, Arnold Palmer and Tom Watson (twice); Nick Faldo, Mark O'Meara, Gary Player, Nick Price, Sam Snead, Lee Trevino and Craig Wood (once).

Year	Masters	US Open	Brit. Open	PGA	Year	Masters	US Open	Brit. Open	PGA
1934	H. Smith	Dutra	Cotton	Runyan	1951	Hogan	Hogan	Faulkner	Snead
1935	Sarazen	Parks	Perry	Revolta	1952	Snead	Boros	Locke	Turnesa
1936	H. Smith	Manero	Padgham	Shute	1953	Hogan	Hogan	Hogan	Burkemo
1937	B. Nelson	Guldahl	Cotton	Shute	1954	Snead	Furgol	Thomson	Harbert
1938	Picard	Guldahl	Whitcombe	Runyan	1955	Middlecoff	Fleck	Thomson	Ford
1939	Guldahl	B. Nelson	Burton	Picard	1956	Burke	Middlecoff	Thomson	Burke
1940	Demaret	Little	—	B. Nelson	1957	Ford	Mayer	Locke	L. Hebert
1941	Wood	Wood	—	Ghezzi	1958	Palmer	Bolt	Thomson	Finsterwald
1942	B. Nelson	—	—	Snead	1959	Wall	Casper	Player	Rosburg
1943	—	—	—	—	1960	Palmer	Palmer	Nagle	J. Hebert
1944	—	—	—	Hamilton	1961	Player	Littler	Palmer	J. Barber
1945	—	—	—	B. Nelson	1962	Palmer	Nicklaus	Palmer	Player
1946	Keiser	Mangrum	Snead	Hogan	1963	Nicklaus	Boros	Charles	Nicklaus
1947	Demaret	Worsham	F. Daly	Ferrier	1964	Palmer	Venturi	Lema	Nichols
1948	Harmon	Hogan	Cotton	Hogan	1965	Nicklaus	Player	Thomson	Marr
1949	Snead	Middlecoff	Locke	Snead	1966	Nicklaus	Casper	Nicklaus	Geiberger
1950	Demaret	Hogan	Locke	Harper	1967	Brewer Jr.	Nicklaus	De Vicenzo	January

Year	Masters	US Open	Brit. Open	PGA	Year	Masters	US Open	Brit. Open	PGA
1968	Goalby	Trevino	Player	Boros	1988	Lyle	Strange	Ballesteros	Sluman
1969	Archer	Moody	Jacklin	Floyd	1989	Faldo	Strange	Calcavecchia	Stewart
1970	Casper	Jacklin	Nicklaus	Stockton	1990	Faldo	Irwin	Faldo	Grady
1971	Coody	Trevino	Trevino	Nicklaus	1991	Woosnam	Stewart	Baker-Finch	J. Daly
1972	Nicklaus	Nicklaus	Trevino	Player	1992	Couples	Kite	Faldo	Price
1973	Aaron	J. Miller	Weiskopf	Nicklaus	1993	Langer	Janzen	Norman	Azinger
1974	Player	Irwin	Player	Trevino	1994	Olazabal	Els	Price	Price
1975	Nicklaus	L. Graham	T. Watson	Nicklaus	1995	Crenshaw	Pavin	Daly	Elkington
1976	Floyd	J. Pate	Miller	Stockton	1996	Faldo	S. Jones	Lehman	Brooks
1977	T. Watson	H. Green	T. Watson	L. Wadkins	1997	Woods	Els	Leonard	Love
1978	Player	North	Nicklaus	Mahaffey	1998	O'Meara	Janzen	O'Meara	Singh
1979	Zoeller	Irwin	Ballesteros	D. Graham	1999	Olazabal	Stewart	Lawrie	Woods
1980	Ballesteros	Nicklaus	T. Watson	Nicklaus	2000	Singh	Woods	Woods	Woods
1981	T. Watson	D. Graham	Rogers	L. Nelson	2001	Woods	Goosen	Duval	Toms
1982	Stadler	T. Watson	T. Watson	Floyd	2002	Woods	Woods	Els	Beem
1983	Ballesteros	L. Nelson	T. Watson	Sutton	2003	Weir	Furyk	Curtis	Micheel
1984	Crenshaw	Zoeller	Ballesteros	Trevino	2004	Mickelson	Goosen	Hamilton	Singh
1985	Langer	North	Lyle	H. Green	2005	Woods	Campbell	Woods	Mickelson
1986	Nicklaus	Floyd	Norman	Tway	2006	Mickelson	Ogilvy	Woods	Woods
1987	Mize	S. Simpson	Faldo	L. Nelson					

U.S. Amateur

Match play from 1895-64, stroke play from 1965-72, match play 1973-79, 36-hole stroke-play qualifying before match play since 1979.

Multiple winners: Bobby Jones (5); Jerry Travers (4); Walter Travis and Tiger Woods (3); Deane Beman, Charles Coe, Gary Cowan, H. Chandler Egan, Chick Evans, Lawson Little, Jack Nicklaus, Francis Ouimet, Jay Sigel, William Turnesa, Bud Ward, Harvie Ward, and H.J. Whigham (2).

Year		Year		Year		Year	
1895	Charles Macdonald	1923	Max Marston	1953	Gene Littler	1980	Hal Sutton
1896	H.J. Whigham	1924	Bobby Jones	1954	Arnold Palmer	1981	Nathaniel Crosby
1897	H.J. Whigham	1925	Bobby Jones	1955	Harvie Ward	1982	Jay Sigel
1898	Findlay Douglas	1926	George Von Elm	1956	Harvie Ward	1983	Jay Sigel
1899	H.M. Harriman	1927	Bobby Jones	1957	Hillman Robbins	1984	Scott Verplank
1900	Walter Travis	1928	Bobby Jones	1958	Charles Coe	1985	Sam Randolph
1901	Walter Travis	1929	Harrison Johnston	1959	Jack Nicklaus	1986	Buddy Alexander
1902	Louis James	1930	Bobby Jones	1960	Deane Beman	1987	Billy Mayfair
1903	Walter Travis	1931	Francis Ouimet	1961	Jack Nicklaus	1988	Eric Meeks
1904	H. Chandler Egan	1932	Ross Somerville	1962	Labron Harris	1989	Chris Patton
1905	H. Chandler Egan	1933	George Dunlap	1963	Deane Beman	1990	Phil Mickelson
1906	Eben Byers	1934	Lawson Little	1964	Bill Campbell	1991	Mitch Voges
1907	Jerry Travers	1935	Lawson Little	1965	Bob Murphy	1992	Justin Leonard
1908	Jerry Travers	1936	John Fischer	1966	Gary Cowan	1993	John Harris
1909	Robert Gardner	1937	John Goodman	1967	Bob Dickson	1994	Tiger Woods
1910	W.C. Fownes Jr.	1938	William Turnesa	1968	Bruce Fleisher	1995	Tiger Woods
1911	Harold Hilton	1939	Bud Ward	1969	Steve Melnyk	1996	Tiger Woods
1912	Jerry Travers	1940	Richard Chapman	1970	Lanny Wadkins	1997	Matt Kuchar
1913	Jerry Travers	1941	Bud Ward	1971	Gary Cowan	1998	Hank Kuehne
1914	Francis Ouimet	1942-45	Not held	1972	Vinny Giles	1999	David Gossett
1915	Robert Gardner	1946	Ted Bishop	1973	Craig Stadler	2000	Jeff Quinney
1916	Chick Evans	1947	Skee Riegel	1974	Jerry Pate	2001	Bubba Dickerson
1917-18	Not held	1948	William Turnesa	1975	Fred Ridley	2002	Ricky Barnes
1919	Davidson Herron	1949	Charles Coe	1976	Bill Sander	2003	Nick Flanagan
1920	Chick Evans	1950	Sam Urzetta	1977	John Fought	2004	Ryan Moore
1921	Jesse Guilford	1951	Billy Maxwell	1978	John Cook	2005	Edoardo Molinari
1922	Jess Sweetser	1952	Jack Westland	1979	Mark O'Meara	2006	Richie Ramsay

Major Championship Leaders

Through 2006; active PGA players in **bold** type.

	US Open	British Open	PGA	Masters	US Am	British Am	Total
Jack Nicklaus	4	3	5	6	2	0	20
Tiger Woods	2	3	3	4	3	0	15
Bobby Jones	4	3	0	0	5	1	13
Walter Hagen	2	4	5	0	0	0	11
Ben Hogan	4	1	2	2	0	0	9
Gary Player	1	3	2	3	0	0	9
John Ball	0	1	0	0	0	8	9
Arnold Palmer	1	2	0	4	1	0	8
Tom Watson	1	5	0	2	0	0	8

Four tied with 7 wins each.

British Amateur

Match play since 1885. **Multiple winners:** John Ball (8); Michael Bonallack (5); Harold Hilton (4); Joe Carr (3); Horace Hutchinson, Ernest Holderness, Trevor Homer, Johnny Laidley, Lawson Little, Peter McEvoy, Dick Siderowf, Frank Stranahan, Freddie Tait, Cyril Tolley and Gary Wolstenholme (2).

Year		Year		Year		Year	
1885	Allen MacFie	1914	J.L.C. Jenkins	1952	Harvie Ward	1981	Phillipe Ploujoux
1886	Horace Hutchinson	1915-19	Not held	1953	Joe Carr	1982	Martin Thompson
1887	Horace Hutchinson	1920	Cyril Tolley	1954	Douglas Bachli	1983	Philip Parkin
1888	John Ball	1921	William Hunter	1955	Joe Conrad	1984	Jose-Maria Olazabal
1889	Johnny Laidley	1922	Ernest Holderness	1956	John Beharrell	1985	Garth McGimpsey
1890	John Ball	1923	Roger Wethered	1957	Reid Jack	1986	David Curry
1891	Johnny Laidley	1924	Ernest Holderness	1958	Joe Carr	1987	Paul Mayo
1892	John Ball	1925	Robert Harris	1959	Deane Beman	1988	Christian Hardin
1893	Peter Anderson	1926	Jess Sweetser	1960	Joe Carr	1989	Stephen Dodd
1894	John Ball	1927	William Tweddell	1961	Michael Bonallack	1990	Rolf Muntz
1895	Leslie Balfour-Melville	1928	Thomas Perkins	1962	Richard Davies	1991	Gary Wolstenholme
1896	Freddie Tait	1929	Cyril Tolley	1963	Michael Lunt	1992	Stephen Dundas
1897	Jack Allan	1930	Bobby Jones	1964	Gordon Clark	1993	Ian Pyman
1898	Freddie Tait	1931	Eric Smith	1965	Michael Bonallack	1994	Lee James
1899	John Ball	1932	John deForest	1966	Bobby Cole	1995	Gordon Sherry
1900	Harold Hilton	1933	Michael Scott	1967	Bob Dickson	1996	Warren Bledon
1901	Harold Hilton	1934	Lawson Little	1968	Michael Bonallack	1997	Craig Watson
1902	Charles Hutchings	1935	Lawson Little	1969	Michael Bonallack	1998	Sergio Garcia
1903	Robert Maxwell	1936	Hector Thomson	1970	Michael Bonallack	1999	Graeme Storm
1904	Walter Travis	1937	Robert Sweeny Jr.	1971	Steve Melnyk	2000	Mikko Ilonen
1905	Arthur Barry	1938	Charles Yates	1972	Trevor Homer	2001	Michael Hoey
1906	James Robb	1939	Alexander Kyle	1973	Dick Siderowf	2002	Alejandro Larrazabal
1907	John Ball	1940-45	Not held	1974	Trevor Homer	2003	Gary Wolstenholme
1908	E.A. Lassen	1946	James Bruen	1975	Vinny Giles	2004	Stuart Wilson
1909	Robert Maxwell	1947	William Turnesa	1976	Dick Siderowf	2005	Brian McElhinney
1910	John Ball	1948	Frank Stranahan	1977	Peter McEvoy	2006	Julien Guerrier
1911	Harold Hilton	1949	Samuel McCready	1978	Peter McEvoy		
1912	John Ball	1950	Frank Stranahan	1979	Jay Sigel		
1913	Harold Hilton	1951	Richard Chapman	1980	Duncan Evans		

WOMEN
Kraft Nabisco Championship

Formerly known as the Colgate Dinah Shore (1972-81) and the Nabisco Dinah Shore (1982-99), the tournament became the LPGA's fourth designated major championship in 1983. Shore's name, which was dropped from the tournament in 2000, is preserved with the Nabisco Dinah Shore Trophy, which is awarded to the winner. The tourney has been played at Mission Hills CC in Rancho Mirage, Calif., since it began; (*) indicates playoff winner.

Multiple winners: (as a major): Amy Alcott, Betsy King and Annika Sorenstam (3); Juli Inkster, Dottie Pepper and Karrie Webb (2).

Year	Winner	Score	Runner-up	Year	Winner	Score	Runner-up
1972	Jane Blalock	213	Carol Mann & Judy Rankin (216)	1990	Betsy King	283	Kathy Postlewait & Shirley Furlong (285)
1973	Mickey Wright	284	Joyce Kazmierski (286)	1991	Amy Alcott	273	Dottie Pepper (281)
1974	Jo Anne Prentice*	289	Jane Blalock & Sandra Haynie (289)	1992	Dottie Pepper*	279	Juli Inkster (279)
1975	Sandra Palmer	283	Kathy McMullen (284)	1993	Helen Alfredsson	284	Amy Benz & Tina Barrett (286)
1976	Judy Rankin	285	Betty Burfeindt (288)	1994	Donna Andrews	276	Laura Davies (277)
1977	Kathy Whitworth	289	JoAnne Carner & Sally Little (290)	1995	Nanci Bowen	285	Susie Redman (286)
1978	Sandra Post*	283	Penny Pulz (283)	1996	Patty Sheehan	281	Kelly Robbins, Meg Mallon & Annika Sorenstam (276)
1979	Sandra Post	276	Nancy Lopez (277)	1997	Betsy King	276	Kris Tschetter (278)
1980	Donna Caponi	275	Amy Alcott (277)	1998	Pat Hurst	281	Helen Dobson (282)
1981	Nancy Lopez	277	Carolyn Hill (279)	1999	Dottie Pepper	269	Meg Mallon (275)
1982	Sally Little	278	Hollis Stacy & Sandra Haynie (281)	2000	Karrie Webb	274	Dottie Pepper (284)
1983	Amy Alcott	282	Beth Daniel & Kathy Whitworth (284)	2001	Annika Sorenstam	281	Akiko Fukushima, Janice Moodie, Dottie Pepper, Rachel Teske & Karrie Webb (284)
1984	Juli Inkster*	280	Pat Bradley (280)				
1985	Alice Miller	275	Jan Stephenson (278)	2002	Annika Sorenstam	280	Liselotte Neumann (281)
1986	Pat Bradley	280	Val Skinner (282)	2003	P. Meunier-Lebouc	281	Annika Sorenstam (282)
1987	Betsy King*	283	Patty Sheehan (283)	2004	Grace Park	277	Aree Song (278)
1988	Amy Alcott	274	Colleen Walker (276)	2005	Annika Sorenstam	273	Rosie Jones (281)
1989	Juli Inkster	279	Tammie Green & JoAnne Carner (284)	2006	Karrie Webb*	279	Lorena Ochoa (279)

PLAYOFFS: 1974: Jo Ann Prentice def. Jane Blalock in sudden death. **1978:** Sandra Post def. Penny Pulz in sudden death. **1984:** Juli Inkster def. Pat Bradley in sudden death. **1987:** Betsy King def. Patty Sheehan in sudden death. **1992:** Dottie Pepper def. Juli Inkster in sudden death. **2006:** Karrie Webb def. Lorena Ochoa in sudden death.

U.S. Women's Open

The U.S. Women's Open began under the direction of the defunct Women's Professional Golfers Assn. in 1946, passed to the LPGA in 1949 and to the USGA in 1953. The tournament used a match play format its first year then switched to stroke play; (*) indicates playoff winner and (a) indicates amateur.

Multiple winners: Betsy Rawls and Mickey Wright (4); Susie Maxwell Berning, Annika Sorenstam, Hollis Stacy and Babe Zaharias (3); JoAnne Carner, Donna Caponi, Juli Inkster, Betsy King, Meg Mallon, Patty Sheehan, Louise Suggs and Karrie Webb (2).

Year	Winner	Score	Runner-up	Course	Location
1946	Patty Berg	5&4	Betty Jameson	Spokane CC	Spokane, Wash.
1947	Betty Jameson	295	a-Sally Sessions & a-Polly Riley (301)	Starmount Forest CC	Greensboro, N.C.
1948	Babe Zaharias	300	Betty Hicks (308)	Atlantic City CC	Northfield, N.J.
1949	Louise Suggs	291	Babe Zaharias (305)	Prince Georges CC	Landover, Md.
1950	Babe Zaharias	291	a-Betsy Rawls (300)	Rolling Hills CC	Wichita, Kan.
1951	Betsy Rawls	293	Louise Suggs (298)	Druid Hills GC	Atlanta, Ga.
1952	Louise Suggs	284	Marlene Hagge (291)	Bala GC	Philadelphia, Penn.
1953	Betsy Rawls*	302	Jackie Pung (302)	CC of Rochester	Rochester, N.Y.
1954	Babe Zaharias	291	Betty Hicks (303)	Salem CC	Peabody, Mass.
1955	Fay Crocker	299	Mary Lena Faulk (303)	Wichita CC	Wichita, Kan.
1956	Kathy Cornelius*	302	Barbara McIntire (302)	Northland CC	Duluth, Minn.
1957	Betsy Rawls	299	Patty Berg (305)	Winged Foot GC	Mamaroneck, N.Y.
1958	Mickey Wright	290	Louise Suggs (295)	Forest Lake CC	Detroit, Mich.
1959	Mickey Wright	287	Louise Suggs (289)	Churchill Valley CC	Pittsburgh, Penn.
1960	Betsy Rawls	292	Joyce Ziske (293)	Worcester CC	Worcester, Mass.
1961	Mickey Wright	293	Betsy Rawls (299)	Baltusrol GC	Springfield, N.J.
1962	Murle Breer	301	Jo Anne Prentice & Ruth Jessen (303)	Dunes GC	Myrtle Beach, S.C.
1963	Mary Mills	289	Sandra Haynie & Louise Suggs (292)	Kenwood CC	Cincinnati, Ohio
1964	Mickey Wright*	290	Ruth Jessen (290)	San Diego CC	Chula Vista, Calif.
1965	Carol Mann	290	Kathy Cornelius (292)	Atlantic City CC	Northfield, N.J.
1966	Sandra Spuzich	297	Carol Mann (298)	Hazeltine National GC	Chaska, Minn.
1967	a-Catherine LaCoste	294	Susie Berning & Beth Stone (296)	Hot Springs GC	Hot Springs, Va.
1968	Susie Berning	289	Mickey Wright (292)	Moselem Springs GC	Fleetwood, Penn.
1969	Donna Caponi	294	Peggy Wilson (295)	Scenic Hills CC	Pensacola, Fla.
1970	Donna Caponi	287	Sandra Haynie (288)	Muskogee CC	Muskogee, Okla.
1971	JoAnne Carner	288	Kathy Whitworth (295)	Kahkwa CC	Erie, Penn.
1972	Susie Berning	299	Kathy Ahern, Pam Barnett & Judy Rankin (300)	Winged Foot GC	Mamaroneck, N.Y.
1973	Susie Berning	290	Gloria Ehret (295)	CC of Rochester	Rochester, N.Y.
1974	Sandra Haynie	295	Carol Mann & Beth Stone (296)	La Grange CC	La Grange, Ill.
1975	Sandra Palmer	295	JoAnne Carner, a-Nancy Lopez & Sandra Post (299)	Atlantic City CC	Northfield, N.J.
1976	JoAnne Carner*	292	Sandra Palmer (292)	Rolling Green CC	Springfield, Penn.
1977	Hollis Stacy	292	Nancy Lopez (294)	Hazeltine National GC	Chaska, Minn.
1978	Hollis Stacy	289	JoAnne Carner & Sally Little (290)	CC of Indianapolis	Indianapolis, Ind.
1979	Jerilyn Britz	284	Debbie Massey & Sandra Palmer (286)	Brooklawn CC	Fairfield, Conn.
1980	Amy Alcott	280	Hollis Stacy (289)	Richland CC	Nashville, Tenn.
1981	Pat Bradley	279	Beth Daniel (280)	La Grange CC	La Grange, Ill.
1982	Janet Anderson	283	Beth Daniel, Sandra Haynie & Donna White (289)	Del Paso CC	Sacramento, Calif.
1983	Jan Stephenson	290	JoAnne Carner (291)	Cedar Ridge CC	Tulsa, Okla.
1984	Hollis Stacy	290	Rosie Jones (291)	Salem CC	Peabody, Mass.
1985	Kathy Baker	280	Judy Dickenson (283)	Baltusrol GC	Springfield, N.J.
1986	Jane Geddes*	287	Sally Little (287)	NCR GC	Dayton, Ohio
1987	Laura Davies*	285	Ayako Okamoto & JoAnne Carner (285)	Plainfield CC	Plainfield, N.J.
1988	Liselotte Neumann	277	Patty Sheehan (280)	Baltimore CC	Baltimore, Md.
1989	Betsy King	278	Nancy Lopez (282)	Indianwood GC	Lake Orion, Mich.
1990	Betsy King	284	Patty Sheehan (285)	Atlanta Athletic Club	Duluth, Ga.
1991	Meg Mallon	283	Pat Bradley (285)	Colonial CC	Ft. Worth, Texas
1992	Patty Sheehan*	280	Juli Inkster (280)	Oakmont CC	Oakmont, Penn.
1993	Lauri Merten	280	Donna Andrews & Helen Alfredsson (281)	Crooked Stick GC	Carmel, Ind.
1994	Patty Sheehan	277	Tammie Green (278)	Indianwood CC	Lake Orion, Mich.
1995	Annika Sorenstam	278	Meg Mallon (279)	The Broadmoor	Colorado Springs, Colo.
1996	Annika Sorenstam	272	Kris Tschetter (278)	Pine Needles Lodge & GC	Southern Pines, N.C.
1997	Alison Nicholas	274	Nancy Lopez (275)	Pumpkin Ridge GC	Cornelius, Ore.

U.S. Women's Open (Cont.)

Year	Winner	Score	Runner-up	Course	Location
1998	Se Ri Pak*	290	a-Jenny Chuasiriporn (290)	Blackwolf Run GC	Kohler, Wis.
1999	Juli Inkster	272	Sherri Turner (277)	Old Waverly GC	West Point, Miss.
2000	Karrie Webb	282	Cristie Kerr & Meg Mallon (287)	Merit Club	Libertyville, Ill.
2001	Karrie Webb	273	Se Ri Pak (281)	Pine Needles Lodge & GC	Southern Pines, N.C.
2002	Juli Inkster	276	Annika Sorenstam (278)	Prairie Dunes CC	Hutchinson, Kan.
2003	Hilary Lunke*	283	Angela Stanford & Kelly Robbins (283)	Pumpkin Ridge GC	North Plains, Ore.
2004	Meg Mallon	274	Annika Sorenstam (276)	Orchards GC	South Hadley, Mass.
2005	Birdie Kim	287	a-Brittany Lang & a-Morgan Pressel (289)	Cherry Hills CC	Cherry Hills Vill., Colo.
2006	Annika Sorenstam*	284	Pat Hurst (284)	Newport CC	Newport, R.I.

*PLAYOFFS:

1953: Betsy Rawls (70) def. Jackie Pung (77) in 18 holes. **1956:** Kathy Cornelius (75) def. Barbara McIntire (82) in 18 holes. **1964:** Mickey Wright (70) def. Ruth Jessen (72) in 18 holes. **1976:** JoAnne Carner (76) def. Sandra Palmer (78) in 18 holes. **1986:** Jane Geddes (71) def. Sally Little (73) in 18 holes. **1987:** Laura Davies (71) def. Ayako Okamoto (73) and JoAnne Carner (74) in 18 holes. **1992:** Patty Sheehan (72) def. Juli Inkster (74) in 18 holes. **1998:** Se Ri Pak def. Jenny Chuasiriporn on the second sudden death hole after both players were tied after an 18-hole playoff. **2003:** Hilary Lunke (70) def. Angela Stanford (71) and Kelly Robbins (73) in 18 holes. **2006:** Annika Sorenstam (70) def. Pat Hurst (74) in 18 holes.

LPGA Championship

Officially the McDonald's LPGA Championship since 1994 (Mazda was the title sponsor from 1987-93), the tournament began in 1955 and has had extended stays at the Stardust CC in Las Vegas (1961-66), Pleasant Valley CC in Sutton, Mass. (1967-68, 70-74), the Jack Nicklaus Sports Center at Kings Island, Ohio (1978-89), Bethesda CC in Maryland (1990-93), DuPont CC in Wilmington, Del. (1994-2004) and Bulle Rock GC in Havre de Grace, Md. (2005–); (*) indicates playoff winner, (a) amateur and (#) weather-shortened.

Multiple winners: Mickey Wright (4); Nancy Lopez, Se Ri Pak, Patty Sheehan, Annika Sorenstam and Kathy Whitworth (3); Donna Caponi, Laura Davies, Sandra Haynie, Juli Inkster, Mary Mills and Betsy Rawls (2).

Year	Winner	Score	Runner-up
1955	Beverly Hanson	220	Louise Suggs (223)
1956	Marlene Hagge*	291	Patty Berg (291)
1957	Louise Suggs	285	Wiffi Smith (288)
1958	Mickey Wright	288	Fay Crocker (294)
1959	Betsy Rawls	288	Patty Berg (289)
1960	Mickey Wright	292	Louise Suggs (295)
1961	Mickey Wright	287	Louise Suggs (296)
1962	Judy Kimball	282	Shirley Spork (286)
1963	Mickey Wright	294	Mary Lena Faulk & Mary Mills (296)
1964	Mary Mills	278	Mickey Wright (280)
1965	Sandra Haynie	279	Clifford A. Creed (280)
1966	Gloria Ehret	282	Mickey Wright (285)
1967	Kathy Whitworth	284	Shirley Englehorn (285)
1968	Sandra Post	294	Kathy Whitworth (294)
1969	Betsy Rawls	293	Susie Berning & Carol Mann (297)
1970	Shirley Englehorn	285	Kathy Whitworth (285)
1971	Kathy Whitworth	288	Kathy Ahern (292)
1972	Kathy Ahern	293	Jane Blalock (299)
1973	Mary Mills	288	Betty Burfeindt (289)
1974	Sandra Haynie	288	JoAnne Carner (290)
1975	Kathy Whitworth	288	Sandra Haynie (289)
1976	Betty Burfeindt	287	Judy Rankin (288)
1977	Chako Higuchi	279	Pat Bradley, Sandra Post & Judy Rankin (282)
1978	Nancy Lopez	275	Amy Alcott (281)
1979	Donna Caponi	279	Jerilyn Britz (282)
1980	Sally Little	285	Jane Blalock (288)
1981	Donna Caponi	280	Jerilyn Britz & Pat Meyers (281)
1982	Jan Stephenson	279	JoAnne Carner (281)
1983	Patty Sheehan	279	Sandra Haynie (281)
1984	Patty Sheehan	272	Beth Daniel & Pat Bradley (282)
1985	Nancy Lopez	273	Alice Miller (281)
1986	Pat Bradley	277	Patty Sheehan (278)
1987	Jane Geddes	275	Betsy King (275)
1988	Sherri Turner	281	Amy Alcott (282)
1989	Nancy Lopez	274	Ayako Okamoto (277)
1990	Beth Daniel	280	Rosie Jones (281)
1991	Meg Mallon	274	Pat Bradley & Ayako Okamoto (275)
1992	Betsy King	267	JoAnne Carner, Karen Noble & Liselotte Neumann (278)
1993	Patty Sheehan	275	Lauri Merten (276)
1994	Laura Davies	279	Alice Ritzman (280)
1995	Kelly Robbins	274	Laura Davies (275)
1996	Laura Davies#	213	Julie Piers (214)
1997	Chris Johnson*	281	Leta Lindley (281)
1998	Se Ri Pak	273	Donna Andrews & Lisa Hackney (276)
1999	Juli Inkster	268	Liselotte Neumann (272)
2000	Juli Inkster*	281	Stefania Croce (281)
2001	Karrie Webb	270	Laura Diaz (272)
2002	Se Ri Pak	279	Beth Daniel (282)
2003	Annika Sorenstam*	278	Grace Park (278)
2004	Annika Sorenstam	271	Shi Hyun Ahn (274)
2005	Annika Sorenstam	277	a-Michelle Wie (280)
2006	Se Ri Pak*	280	Karrie Webb (280)

*PLAYOFFS:

1956: Marlene Hagge def. Patti Berg in sudden death. **1968:** Sandra Post (68) def. Kathy Whitworth (75) in 18 holes. **1970:** Shirley Englehorn def. Kathy Whitworth in sudden death. **1997:** Chris Johnson def. Leta Lindley in sudden death. **2000:** Juli Inkster def. Stefania Croce in sudden death. **2003:** Annika Sorenstam def. Grace Park in sudden death. **2006:** Se Ri Pak def. Karrie Webb in sudden death.

Women's British Open

Sponsored by Weetabix, this has been an official stop on the LPGA Tour since 1994, and it became the fourth designated major championship in 2001 when it replaced the du Maurier Classic.

Multiple winners Karrie Webb and Sherri Steinhauer (3); (as a major): none.

Year	Winner	Score	Runner-up	Course	Location
1994	Liselotte Neumann	.280	Dottie Mochrie & Annika Sorenstam (283)	Woburn G&CC	Milton Keynes, England
1995	Karrie Webb	.278	Annika Sorenstam & Jill McGill (284)	Woburn G&CC	Milton Keynes, England
1996	Emilee Klein	.277	Penny Hammel & Amy Alcott (284)	Woburn G&CC	Milton Keynes, England
1997	Karrie Webb	.269	Rosie Jones (277)	Sunningdale GC	Berkshire, England
1998	Sherri Steinhauer	.292	Sophie Gustafson & Brandie Burton (293)	Royal Lytham	Lytham, England
1999	Sherri Steinhauer	.283	Annika Sorenstam (284)	Woburn G&CC	Milton Keynes, England
2000	Sophie Gustafson	.282	Kirsty Taylor, Liselotte Neumann, Becky Iverson & Meg Mallon (284)	Royal Birkdale	Southport, England
2001	Se Ri Pak	.277	Mi Hyun Kim (279)	Sunningdale GC	Berkshire, England
2002	Karrie Webb	.273	Michelle Ellis & Paula Marti (275)	Turnberry GC	Turnberry, Scotland
2003	Annika Sorenstam	.278	Se Ri Pak (279)	Royal Lytham	Lytham, England
2004	Karen Stupples	.269	Rachel Teske (274)	Sunningdale GC	Berkshire, England
2005	Jeong Jang	.272	Sophie Gustafson (276)	Royal Birkdale GC	Merseyside, England
2006	Sherri Steinhauer	.281	Cristie Kerr & Sophie Gustafson (284)	Royal Lytham	Lytham, England

du Maurier Classic (1979-2000)

The du Maurier Classic was considered a major title on the women's tour from 1979 until it was discontinued in 2000; (*) indicates playoff winner.

Multiple winners (as a major): Pat Bradley (3); Brandie Burton (2).

Year		Year		Year		Year	
1973	Jocelyne Bourassa	1980	Pat Bradley	1987	Jody Rosenthal	1994	Martha Nause
1974	Carole Jo Skala	1981	Jan Stephenson	1988	Sally Little	1995	Jenny Lidback
1975	JoAnne Carner	1982	Sandra Haynie	1989	Tammie Green	1996	Laura Davies
1976	Donna Caponi	1983	Hollis Stacy	1990	Cathy Johnston	1997	Colleen Walker
1977	Judy Rankin	1984	Juli Inkster	1991	Nancy Scranton	1998	Brandie Burton
1978	JoAnne Carner	1985	Pat Bradley	1992	Sherri Steinhauer	1999	Karrie Webb
1979	Amy Alcott	1986	Pat Bradley*	1993	Brandie Burton*	2000	Meg Mallon

Titleholders Championship (1937-72)

The Titleholders was considered a major title on the women's tour until it was discontinued after the 1972 tournament.

Multiple winners: Patty Berg (7); Louise Suggs (4); Babe Zaharias (3); Dorothy Kirby, Marilynn Smith, Kathy Whitworth and Mickey Wright (2).

Year		Year		Year		Year	
1937	Patty Berg	1947	Babe Zaharias	1955	Patty Berg	1963	Marilynn Smith
1938	Patty Berg	1948	Patty Berg	1956	Louise Suggs	1964	Marilynn Smith
1939	Patty Berg	1949	Peggy Kirk	1957	Patty Berg	1965	Kathy Whitworth
1940	Betty Hicks	1950	Babe Zaharias	1958	Beverly Hanson	1966	Kathy Whitworth
1941	Dorothy Kirby	1951	Pat O'Sullivan	1959	Louise Suggs	1967-71	Not held
1942	Dorothy Kirby	1952	Babe Zaharias	1960	Fay Crocker	1972	Sandra Palmer
1943-45	Not held	1953	Patty Berg	1961	Mickey Wright		
1946	Louise Suggs	1954	Louise Suggs	1962	Mickey Wright		

Western Open (1930-67)

The Western Open was considered a major title on the women's tour until it was discontinued after the 1967 tournament.

Multiple winners: Patty Berg (7); Louise Suggs and Babe Zaharias (4); Mickey Wright (3); June Beebe, Opal Hill, Betty Jameson and Betsy Rawls (2).

Year		Year		Year		Year	
1930	Mrs. Lee Mida	1940	Babe Zaharias	1950	Babe Zaharias	1960	Joyce Ziske
1931	June Beebe	1941	Patty Berg	1951	Patty Berg	1961	Mary Lena Faulk
1932	Jane Weiller	1942	Betty Jameson	1952	Betsy Rawls	1962	Mickey Wright
1933	June Beebe	1943	Patty Berg	1953	Louise Suggs	1963	Mickey Wright
1934	Marian McDougall	1944	Babe Zaharias	1954	Betty Jameson	1964	Carol Mann
1935	Opal Hill	1945	Babe Zaharias	1955	Patty Berg	1965	Susie Maxwell
1936	Opal Hill	1946	Louise Suggs	1956	Beverly Hanson	1966	Mickey Wright
1937	Betty Hicks	1947	Louise Suggs	1957	Patty Berg	1967	Kathy Whitworth
1938	Bea Barrett	1948	Patty Berg	1958	Patty Berg		
1939	Helen Dettweiler	1949	Louise Suggs	1959	Betsy Rawls		

Grand Slam Summary

From 1955-66, the U.S. Open, LPGA Championship, Western Open and Titleholders tournaments served as the Women's Grand Slam. From 1983-2000 the U.S. Open, LPGA, du Maurier Classic and Nabisco Championship were the major events. In 2001, the Weetabix Women's British Open replaced the du Maurier Classic as the tour's fourth major. No one has won a four-event Grand Slam on the women's tour.

Three wins in one year (3): Babe Zaharias (1950), Mickey Wright (1961) and Pat Bradley (1986).

Two wins in one year (19): Patty Berg and Mickey Wright (3 times); Juli Inkster, Annika Sorenstam, Louise Suggs and Karrie Webb (twice); Laura Davies, Sandra Haynie, Betsy King, Meg Mallon, Se Ri Pak, Betsy Rawls and Kathy Whitworth (once).

Year	LPGA	US Open	T'holders	Western
1937	—	—	Berg	Hicks
1938	—	—	Berg	Barrett
1939	—	—	Berg	Dettweiler
1940	—	—	Hicks	Zaharias
1941	—	—	Kirby	Berg
1942	—	—	Kirby	Jameson
1943	—	—	—	Berg
1944	—	—	—	Zaharias
1945	—	—	—	Zaharias
1946	—	Berg	Suggs	Suggs
1947	—	Jameson	Zaharias	Suggs
1948	—	Zaharias	Berg	Berg
1949	—	Suggs	Kirk	Suggs
1950	—	Zaharias	Zaharias	Zaharias
1951	—	Rawls	O'Sullivan	Berg
1952	—	Suggs	Zaharias	Rawls
1953	—	Rawls	Berg	Suggs
1954	—	Zaharias	Suggs	Jameson
1955	Hanson	Crocker	Berg	Berg
1956	Hagge	Cornelius	Suggs	Hanson
1957	Suggs	Rawls	Berg	Berg
1958	Wright	Wright	Hanson	Berg
1959	Rawls	Wright	Suggs	Rawls
1960	Wright	Rawls	Crocker	Ziske
1961	Wright	Wright	Wright	Faulk
1962	Kimball	Lindstrom	Wright	Wright
1963	Wright	Mills	M. Smith	Wright
1964	Mills	Wright	M. Smith	Mann
1965	Haynie	Mann	Whitworth	Maxwell
1966	Ehret	Spuzich	Whitworth	Wright
1967	Whitworth	a-LaCoste	—	Whitworth
1968	Post	Berning	—	—
1969	Rawls	Caponi	—	—
1970	Englehorn	Caponi	—	—
1971	Whitworth	Carner	—	—
1972	Ahern	Berning	Palmer	—
1973	Mills	Berning	—	—

Year	LPGA	US Open	T'holders	Western
1974	Haynie	Haynie	—	—
1975	Whitworth	Palmer	—	—
1976	Burfeindt	Carner	—	—
1977	Higuchi	Stacy	—	—
1978	Lopez	Stacy	—	—

Year	LPGA	US Open	duMaurier	Nabisco
1979	Caponi	Britz	Alcott	—
1980	Little	Alcott	Bradley	—
1981	Caponi	Bradley	Stephenson	—
1982	Stephenson	Anderson	Haynie	—
1983	Sheehan	Stephenson	Stacy	Alcott
1984	Sheehan	Stacy	Inkster	Inkster
1985	Lopez	Baker	Bradley	Miller
1986	Bradley	Geddes	Bradley	Bradley
1987	Geddes	Davies	Rosenthal	King
1988	Turner	Neumann	Little	Alcott
1989	Lopez	King	Green	Inkster
1990	Daniel	King	Johnston	King
1991	Mallon	Mallon	Scranton	Alcott
1992	King	Sheehan	Steinhauer	Pepper
1993	Sheehan	Merten	Burton	Alfredsson
1994	Davies	Sheehan	Nause	Andrews
1995	Robbins	Sorenstam	Lidback	Bowen
1996	Davies	Sorenstam	Davies	Sheehan
1997	Johnson	Nicholas	Walker	King
1998	Pak	Pak	Burton	Hurst
1999	Inkster	Inkster	Webb	Pepper
2000	Inkster	Webb	Mallon	Webb

Year	LPGA	US Open	Brit. Open	Nabisco
2001	Webb	Webb	Pak	Sorenstam
2002	Pak	Inkster	Webb	Sorenstam
2003	Sorenstam	Lunke	Sorenstam	Meunier-Lebouc
2004	Sorenstam	Mallon	Stupples	Park
2005	Sorenstam	Kim	Jang	Sorenstam
2006	Pak	Sorenstam	Steinhauer	Webb

Major Championship Leaders

Through 2006; active LPGA players in **bold** type.

	US Open	LPGA	Nabisco	British Open	duM	Title	Western	US Am	Brit Am	Total
Patty Berg	1	0	0	0	0	7	7	1	0	16
Mickey Wright	4	4	0	0	0	2	3	0	0	13
Louise Suggs	2	1	0	0	0	4	4	1	1	13
Babe Didrikson Zaharias	3	0	0	0	0	3	4	1	1	12
Juli Inkster	2	2	2	0	1	0	0	3	0	10
Annika Sorenstam	3	3	3	1	0	0	0	0	0	10
Betsy Rawls	4	2	0	0	0	0	2	0	0	8
JoAnne Carner	2	0	0	0	0	0	0	5	0	7
Karrie Webb	2	1	2	1	1	0	0	0	0	7
Kathy Whitworth	0	3	0	0	0	2	1	0	0	6
Pat Bradley	1	1	1	0	3	0	0	0	0	6
Betsy King	2	1	3	0	0	0	0	0	0	6
Patty Sheehan	2	3	1	0	0	0	0	0	0	6
Glenna C. Vare	0	0	0	0	0	0	0	6	0	6

Tournaments: U.S. Open, LPGA Championship, Nabisco Championship, British Open, du Maurier Classic (1979-2000), Titleholders (1930-72), Western Open (1937-67), U.S. Amateur and British Amateur.

U.S. Women's Amateur

Stroke play in 1895, match play since 1896.

Multiple winners: Glenna Collett Vare (6); JoAnne Gunderson Carner (5); Margaret Curtis, Beatrix Hoyt, Dorothy Campbell Hurd, Juli Inkster, Alexa Stirling, Virginia Van Wie, Anne Quast Decker Welts (3); Kay Cockerill, Beth Daniel, Vicki Goetze, Katherine Harley, Genevieve Hecker, Betty Jameson, Kelli Kuehne and Barbara McIntire (2).

Year		Year		Year		Year	
1895	Mrs. C.S. Brown	1924	Dorothy C. Hurd	1955	Patricia Lesser	1983	Joanne Pacillo
1896	Beatrix Hoyt	1925	Glenna Collett	1956	Marlene Stewart	1984	Deb Richard
1897	Beatrix Hoyt	1926	Helen Stetson	1957	JoAnne Gunderson	1985	Michiko Hattori
1898	Beatrix Hoyt	1927	Miriam Burns Horn	1958	Anne Quast	1986	Kay Cockerill
1899	Ruth Underhill	1928	Glenna Collett	1959	Barbara McIntire	1987	Kay Cockerill
		1929	Glenna Collett			1988	Pearl Sinn
1900	Frances Griscom			1960	JoAnne Gunderson	1989	Vicki Goetze
1901	Genevieve Hecker	1930	Glenna Collett	1961	Anne Quast Decker		
1902	Genevieve Hecker	1931	Helen Hicks	1962	JoAnne Gunderson	1990	Pat Hurst
1903	Bessie Anthony	1932	Virginia Van Wie	1963	Anne Quast Welts	1991	Amy Fruhwirth
1904	Georgianna Bishop	1933	Virginia Van Wie	1964	Barbara McIntire	1992	Vicki Goetze
1905	Pauline Mackay	1934	Virginia Van Wie	1965	Jean Ashley	1993	Jill McGill
1906	Harriot Curtis	1935	Glenna Collett Vare	1966	JoAnne G. Carner	1994	Wendy Ward
1907	Margaret Curtis	1936	Pamela Barton	1967	Mary Lou Dill	1995	Kelli Kuehne
1908	Katherine Harley	1937	Estelle Lawson	1968	JoAnne G. Carner	1996	Kelli Kuehne
1909	Dorothy Campbell	1938	Patty Berg	1969	Catherine Lacoste	1997	Silvia Cavalleri
		1939	Betty Jameson			1998	Grace Park
1910	Dorothy Campbell	1940	Betty Jameson	1970	Martha Wilkinson	1999	Dorothy Delasin
1911	Margaret Curtis	1941	Elizabeth Hicks	1971	Laura Baugh		
1912	Margaret Curtis	1942-45	Not held	1972	Mary Budke	2000	Marcy Newton
1913	Gladys Ravenscroft	1946	Babe D. Zaharias	1973	Carol Semple	2001	Meredith Duncan
1914	Katherine Harley	1947	Louise Suggs	1974	Cynthia Hill	2002	Becky Lucidi
1915	Florence Vanderbeck	1948	Grace Lenczyk	1975	Beth Daniel	2003	V. Nirapathpongporn
1916	Alexa Stirling	1949	Dorothy Porter	1976	Donna Horton	2004	Jane Park
1917-18	Not held			1977	Beth Daniel	2005	Morgan Pressel
1919	Alexa Stirling	1950	Beverly Hanson	1978	Cathy Sherk	2006	Kimberley Kim
		1951	Dorothy Kirby	1979	Carolyn Hill		
1920	Alexa Stirling	1952	Jacqueline Pung	1980	Juli Inkster		
1921	Marion Hollins	1953	Mary Lena Faulk	1981	Juli Inkster		
1922	Glenna Collett	1954	Barbara Romack	1982	Juli Inkster		
1923	Edith Cummings						

British Women's Amateur

Match play since 1893.

Multiple winners: Cecil Leitch and Joyce Wethered (4); May Hezlet, Lady Margaret Scott, Jessie Anderson Valentine, Brigitte Varangot and Enid Wilson (3); Rhona Adair, Pam Barton, Dorothy Campbell, Elizabeth Chadwick, Helen Holm, Rebecca Hudson, Marley Spearman, Louise Stahle, Frances Stephens and Michelle Walker (2).

Year		Year		Year		Year	
1893	Lady Margaret Scott	1924	Joyce Wethered	1956	Wiffi Smith	1983	Jill Thornhill
1894	Lady Margaret Scott	1925	Joyce Wethered	1957	Philomena Garvey	1984	Jody Rosenthal
1895	Lady Margaret Scott	1926	Cecil Leitch	1958	Jessie Valentine	1985	Lillian Behan
1896	Amy Pascoe	1927	Simone de la Chaume	1959	Elizabeth Price	1986	Marnie McGuire
1897	Edith Orr	1928	Nanette le Blan			1987	Janet Collingham
1898	Lena Thomson	1929	Joyce Wethered	1960	Barbara McIntire	1988	Joanne Furby
1899	May Hezlet			1961	Marley Spearman	1989	Helen Dobson
		1930	Diana Fishwick	1962	Marley Spearman		
1900	Rhona Adair	1931	Enid Wilson	1963	Brigitte Varangot	1990	Julie Wade Hall
1901	Mary Graham	1932	Enid Wilson	1964	Carol Sorenson	1991	Valerie Michaud
1902	May Hezlet	1933	Enid Wilson	1965	Brigitte Varangot	1992	Bernille Pedersen
1903	Rhona Adair	1934	Helen Holm	1966	Elizabeth Chadwick	1993	Catriona Lambert
1904	Lottie Dod	1935	Wanda Morgan	1967	Elizabeth Chadwick	1994	Emma Duggleby
1905	Bertha Thompson	1936	Pam Barton	1968	Brigitte Varangot	1995	Julie Wade Hall
1906	Mrs. W. Kennion	1937	Jessie Anderson	1969	Catherine Lacoste	1996	Kelli Kuehne
1907	May Hezlet	1938	Helen Holm			1997	Alison Rose
1908	Maud Titterton	1939	Pam Barton	1970	Dinah Oxley	1998	Kim Rostron
1909	Dorothy Campbell			1971	Michelle Walker	1999	Marine Monnet
		1940-45	Not held	1972	Michelle Walker		
1910	Elsie Grant-Suttie	1946	Jean Hetherington	1973	Ann Irvin	2000	Rebecca Hudson
1911	Dorothy Campbell	1947	Babe Zaharias	1974	Carol Semple	2001	Marta Prieto
1912	Gladys Ravenscroft	1948	Louise Suggs	1975	Nancy Roth Syms	2002	Rebecca Hudson
1913	Muriel Dodd	1949	Frances Stephens	1976	Cathy Panton	2003	Elisa Serramia
1914	Cecil Leitch			1977	Angela Uzielli	2004	Louise Stahle
1915-19	Not held	1950	Lally de St. Sauveur	1978	Edwina Kennedy	2005	Louise Stahle
		1951	Catherine MacCann	1979	Maureen Madill	2006	Belen Mozo
1920	Cecil Leitch	1952	Moira Paterson	1980	Anne Quast Sander		
1921	Cecil Leitch	1953	Marlene Stewart	1981	Belle Robertson		
1922	Joyce Wethered	1954	Frances Stephens	1982	Kitrina Douglas		
1923	Doris Chambers	1955	Jessie Valentine				

Vare Trophy

The Vare Trophy for best scoring average by a player on the LPGA Tour has been awarded since 1953 by the LPGA. The award is named after Glenna Collett Vare, winner of six U.S. women's amateur titles from 1922-35.

Multiple winners: Kathy Whitworth (7); Annika Sorenstam (6); JoAnne Carner and Mickey Wright (5); Patty Berg, Beth Daniel, Nancy Lopez, Judy Rankin and Karrie Webb (3); Pat Bradley and Betsy King (2).

Year		Avg	Year		Avg	Year		Avg
1953	Patty Berg	75.00	1971	Kathy Whitworth	72.88	1989	Beth Daniel	70.38
1954	Babe Zaharias	75.48	1972	Kathy Whitworth	72.38	1990	Beth Daniel	70.54
1955	Patty Berg	74.47	1973	Judy Rankin	73.08	1991	Pat Bradley	70.66
1956	Patty Berg	74.57	1974	JoAnne Carner	72.87	1992	Dottie Pepper	70.80
1957	Louise Suggs	74.64	1975	JoAnne Carner	72.40	1993	Betsy King	70.85
1958	Beverly Hanson	74.92	1976	Judy Rankin	72.25	1994	Beth Daniel	70.90
1959	Betsy Rawls	74.03	1977	Judy Rankin	72.16	1995	Annika Sorenstam	71.00
1960	Mickey Wright	73.25	1978	Nancy Lopez	71.76	1996	Annika Sorenstam	70.47
1961	Mickey Wright	73.55	1979	Nancy Lopez	71.20	1997	Karrie Webb	70.00
1962	Mickey Wright	73.67	1980	Amy Alcott	71.51	1998	Annika Sorenstam	69.99
1963	Mickey Wright	72.81	1981	JoAnne Carner	71.75	1999	Karrie Webb	69.43
1964	Mickey Wright	72.46	1982	JoAnne Carner	71.49	2000	Karrie Webb	70.05
1965	Kathy Whitworth	72.61	1983	JoAnne Carner	71.41	2001	Annika Sorenstam	69.42
1966	Kathy Whitworth	72.60	1984	Patty Sheehan	71.40	2002	Annika Sorenstam	68.70
1967	Kathy Whitworth	72.74	1985	Nancy Lopez	70.73	2003	Se Ri Pak	70.03
1968	Carol Mann	72.04	1986	Pat Bradley	71.10	2004	Grace Park	69.99
1969	Kathy Whitworth	72.38	1987	Betsy King	71.14	2005	Annika Sorenstam	69.25
1970	Kathy Whitworth	72.26	1988	Colleen Walker	71.26			

Champions Tour
(formerly Senior PGA Tour)

Senior PGA Championship
First played in 1937. Two championships played in 1979 and 1984.

Multiple winners: Sam Snead (6); Hale Irwin (4); Gary Player, Al Watrous and Eddie Williams (3); Julius Boros, Jock Hutchison, Don January, Arnold Palmer, Paul Runyan, Gene Sarazen and Lee Trevino (2).

Year		Year		Year		Year	
1937	Jock Hutchison	1956	Pete Burke	1974	Roberto De Vicenzo	1990	Gary Player
1938	Fred McLeod*	1957	Al Watrous	1975	Charlie Sifford*	1991	Jack Nicklaus
1939	Not held	1958	Gene Sarazen	1976	Pete Cooper	1992	Lee Trevino
1940	Otto Hackbarth*	1959	Willie Goggin	1977	Julius Boros	1993	Tom Wargo*
1941	Jack Burke	1960	Dick Metz	1978	Joe Jiminez*	1994	Lee Trevino
1942	Eddie Williams	1961	Paul Runyan	1979	Jack Fleck*	1995	Ray Floyd
1943-44	Not held	1962	Paul Runyan	1979	Don January	1996	Hale Irwin
1945	Eddie Williams	1963	Herman Barron	1980	Arnold Palmer*	1997	Hale Irwin
1946	Eddie Williams*	1964	Sam Snead	1981	Miller Barber	1998	Hale Irwin
1947	Jock Hutchison	1965	Sam Snead	1982	Don January	1999	Allen Doyle
1948	Charles McKenna	1966	Fred Haas	1983	Not held	2000	Doug Tewell
1949	Marshall Crichton	1967	Sam Snead	1984	Arnold Palmer	2001	Tom Watson
1950	Al Watrous	1968	Chandler Harper	1984	Peter Thomson	2002	Fuzzy Zoeller
1951	Al Watrous*	1969	Tommy Bolt	1985	Not held	2003	John Jacobs
1952	Ernest Newnham	1970	Sam Snead	1986	Gary Player	2004	Hale Irwin
1953	Harry Schwab	1971	Julius Boros	1987	Chi Chi Rodriguez	2005	Mike Reid*
1954	Gene Sarazen	1972	Sam Snead	1988	Gary Player	2006	Jay Haas*
1955	Mortie Dutra	1973	Sam Snead	1989	Larry Mowry		

*PLAYOFFS:

1938: Fred McLeod def. Otto Hackbarth in 18 holes. **1940:** Otto Hackbarth def. Jock Hutchison in 36 holes. **1946:** Eddie Williams def. Jock Hutchison in 18 holes. **1951:** Al Watrous def. Jock Hutchison in 18 holes. **1975:** Charlie Sifford def. Fred Wampler on 1st extra hole **1978:** Joe Jiminez def. Paul Harney on 1st extra hole. **1979:** Jack Fleck def. Bill Johnston on 1st extra hole. **1980:** Arnold Palmer def. Paul Harney on 1st extra hole. **1993:** Tom Wargo def. Bruce Crampton on 2nd extra hole. **2005:** Mike Reid def. Dana Quigley and Jerry Pate on 1st extra hole. **2006:** Jay Haas def. Brad Bryant on 3rd extra hole.

Major Senior Championship Leaders

Through 2006. All players are still active. **Note:** The Senior British Open became the Champions Tour's fifth major in 2003.

		Sr. PGA	US Open	Sr. Play	Trad	Br. Open	Tot			Sr. PGA	US Open	Sr. Play	Trad	Br. Open	Tot
1	Jack Nicklaus	1	2	1	4	0	8	4	Allen Doyle	1	2	1	0	0	4
2	Hale Irwin	4	2	1	0	0	7		Ray Floyd	1	0	2	1	0	4
3	Gary Player	3	2	1	0	0	6		Lee Trevino	2	1	0	1	0	4
									Tom Watson	1	0	0	1	2	4

U.S. Senior Open

Established in 1980 for senior players 55 years old and over, the minimum age was dropped to 50 (the Champions Tour entry age) in 1981. Arnold Palmer, Billy Casper, Hale Irwin, Orville Moody, Jack Nicklaus and Lee Trevino are the only golfers who have won both the U.S. Open and U.S. Senior Open.

Multiple winners: Miller Barber (3); Allen Doyle, Hale Irwin, Jack Nicklaus and Gary Player (2).

Year		Year		Year		Year	
1980	Roberto De Vicenzo	1987	Gary Player	1994	Simon Hobday	2001	Bruce Fleisher
1981	Arnold Palmer*	1988	Gary Player*	1995	Tom Weiskopf	2002	Don Pooley*
1982	Miller Barber	1989	Orville Moody	1996	Dave Stockton	2003	Bruce Lietzke
1983	Bill Casper*	1990	Lee Trevino	1997	Graham Marsh	2004	Peter Jacobsen
1984	Miller Barber	1991	Jack Nicklaus*	1998	Hale Irwin	2005	Allen Doyle
1985	Miller Barber	1992	Larry Laoretti	1999	Dave Eichelberger	2006	Allen Doyle
1986	Dale Douglass	1993	Jack Nicklaus	2000	Hale Irwin		

*PLAYOFFS:

1981: Arnold Palmer (70) def. Bob Stone (74) and Billy Casper (77) in 18 holes. **1983:** Tied at 75 after 18-hole playoff, Casper def. Rod Funseth with a birdie on the 1st extra hole. **1988:** Gary Player (68) def. Bob Charles (70) in 18 holes. **1991:** Jack Nicklaus (65) def. Chi Chi Rodriguez (69) in 18 holes. **2002:** Don Pooley and Tom Watson remained tied after a three hole playoff and Pooley won on the second hole of sudden death.

Senior Players Championship

Sponsored by Ford since 1993. First played in 1983 and contested in Cleveland (1983-86), Ponte Vedra, Fla. (1987-89) and Dearborn, Mich. (since 1990).

Multiple winners: Ray Floyd, Arnold Palmer and Dave Stockton (2).

Year		Year		Year		Year	
1983	Miller Barber	1989	Orville Moody	1995	J.C. Snead*	2001	Allen Doyle*
1984	Arnold Palmer	1990	Jack Nicklaus	1996	Ray Floyd	2002	Stewart Ginn
1985	Arnold Palmer	1991	Jim Albus	1997	Larry Gilbert	2003	Craig Stadler
1986	Chi Chi Rodriguez	1992	Dave Stockton	1998	Gil Morgan	2004	Mark James
1987	Gary Player	1993	Jim Colbert	1999	Hale Irwin	2005	Peter Jacobsen
1988	Billy Casper	1994	Dave Stockton	2000	Ray Floyd	2006	Bobby Wadkins

*PLAYOFFS:

1995: J.C. Snead def. Jack Nicklaus on 1st extra hole. **2001:** Allen Doyle def. Doug Tewell on 1st extra hole.

The Tradition

Sponsored by window and door manufacturer JELD-WEN since 2003, it was formerly called The Tradition at Desert Mountain (1989-91), The Tradition (1992-99) and The Countrywide Tradition (2000-02). Held at GC at Desert Mountain in Scottsdale, Ariz. (1989-2001), Superstition Mountain (Ariz.) G & CC (2002) and The Reserve Vineyards & GC in Aloha, Ore. (2003—).

Multiple winners: Jack Nicklaus (4); Gil Morgan (2).

Year		Year		Year		Year	
1989	Don Bies	1994	Ray Floyd*	1999	Graham Marsh	2004	Craig Stadler
1990	Jack Nicklaus	1995	Jack Nicklaus*	2000	Tom Kite	2005	Loren Roberts*
1991	Jack Nicklaus	1996	Jack Nicklaus	2001	Doug Tewell	2006	Eduardo Romero*
1992	Lee Trevino	1997	Gil Morgan	2002	Jim Thorpe*		
1993	Tom Shaw	1998	Gil Morgan	2003	Tom Watson		

*PLAYOFFS:

1994: Ray Floyd def. Dale Douglass on 1st extra hole. **1995:** Jack Nicklaus def. Isao Aoki on 3rd extra hole. **2002:** Jim Thorpe def. John Jacobs on 1st extra hole. **2005:** Loren Roberts def. Dana Quigley on 2nd extra hole. **2006:** Eduardo Romero def. Lonnie Nielsen on 1st extra hole.

Senior British Open

First played in 1987 and contested in Turnberry, Scotland (1987-90, 2003), Lytham, England (1991-94), Portrush, Ireland (1995-99, 2004), Newcastle, Ireland (2000-02) and Royal Aberdeen, Scotland (2005). In 2003 it became the fifth designated major championship on the Champions Tour.

Multiple winners: Gary Player (3); Brian Barnes, Bob Charles, Christy O'Connor Jr. and Tom Watson (2). (as a major): Watson (2).

Year		Year		Year		Year	
1987	Neil Coles	1992	John Fourie	1997	Gary Player	2002	Noboru Sugai
1988	Gary Player	1993	Bob Charles	1998	Brian Huggett	2003	Tom Watson*
1989	Bob Charles	1994	Tom Wargo	1999	Christy O'Connor Jr.	2004	Pete Oakley
1990	Gary Player	1995	Brian Barnes	2000	Christy O'Connor Jr.	2005	Tom Watson*
1991	Bobby Verwey	1996	Brian Barnes	2001	Ian Stanley	2006	Loren Roberts

*PLAYOFFS (as a Major):

2003: Tom Watson def. Carl Mason on 2nd extra hole. **2005:** Tom Watson def. Des Smyth on 3rd extra hole.

Champions Tour (Cont.)

Grand Slam Summary

The Senior Grand Slam had officially consisted of The Tradition, the Senior PGA Championship, the Senior Players Championship and the U.S. Senior Open from 1990-2002. In 2003, the Senior British Open was added. Jack Nicklaus won three of the four events in 1991, but no one has won all four (or now five) in one season.

Three wins in one year: Jack Nicklaus (1991). **Two wins in one year** (8): Gary Player (twice); Hale Irwin, Gil Morgan, Orville Moody, Jack Nicklaus, Arnold Palmer, Lee Trevino and Tom Watson (once).

Year	Tradition	Sr. PGA	Players	US Open	Year	Tradition	Sr. PGA	Players	US Open
1983	—	—	M. Barber	Casper	1993	Shaw	Wargo	Colbert	Nicklaus
1984	—	Palmer	Palmer	M. Barber	1994	Floyd	Trevino	Stockton	Hobday
1985	—	Thomson	Palmer	M. Barber	1995	Nicklaus	Floyd	Snead	Weiskopf
1986	—	Player	Rodriguez	Douglass	1996	Nicklaus	Irwin	Floyd	Stockton
1987	—	Rodriguez	Player	Player	1997	Morgan	Irwin	Gilbert	Marsh
1988	—	Player	Casper	Player	1998	Morgan	Irwin	Morgan	Irwin
1989	Bies	Mowry	Moody	Moody	1999	Marsh	Doyle	Irwin	Eichelberger
1990	Nicklaus	Player	Nicklaus	Trevino	2000	Kite	Tewell	Floyd	Irwin
1991	Nicklaus	Nicklaus	Albus	Nicklaus	2001	Tewell	Watson	Doyle	Fleisher
1992	Trevino	Trevino	Stockton	Laoretti	2002	Thorpe	Zoeller	Ginn	Pooley

Year	Tradition	Sr. PGA	Players	US Open	Sr. Brit. Open
2003	Watson	Jacobs	Stadler	Lietzke	Watson
2004	Stadler	Irwin	James	Jacobsen	Oakley
2005	Roberts	Reid	Jacobsen	Doyle	Watson
2006	Romero	Haas	Wadkins	Doyle	Roberts

Annual Money Leaders

Official annual money leaders on the PGA, European PGA, Champions and LPGA tours.

PGA

Multiple leaders: Jack Nicklaus (8); Tiger Woods (6); Ben Hogan and Tom Watson (5); Arnold Palmer (4); Greg Norman, Sam Snead and Curtis Strange (3); Julius Boros, Billy Casper, Tom Kite, Byron Nelson, Nick Price and Vijay Singh (2).

Year		Earnings	Year		Earnings	Year		Earnings
1934	Paul Runyan	$6,767	1958	Arnold Palmer	$42,608	1982	Craig Stadler	$446,462
1935	Johnny Revolta	9,543	1959	Art Wall	53,168	1983	Hal Sutton	426,668
1936	Horton Smith	7,682	1960	Arnold Palmer	75,263	1984	Tom Watson	476,260
1937	Harry Cooper	14,139	1961	Gary Player	64,540	1985	Curtis Strange	542,321
1938	Sam Snead	19,534	1962	Arnold Palmer	81,448	1986	Greg Norman	653,296
1939	Henry Picard	10,303	1963	Arnold Palmer	128,230	1987	Curtis Strange	925,941
1940	Ben Hogan	10,655	1964	Jack Nicklaus	113,285	1988	Curtis Strange	1,147,644
1941	Ben Hogan	18,358	1965	Jack Nicklaus	140,752	1989	Tom Kite	1,395,278
1942	Ben Hogan	13,143	1966	Billy Casper	121,945	1990	Greg Norman	1,165,477
1943	No records kept		1967	Jack Nicklaus	188,998	1991	Corey Pavin	979,430
1944	Byron Nelson	37,968	1968	Billy Casper	205,169	1992	Fred Couples	1,344,188
1945	Byron Nelson	63,336	1969	Frank Beard	164,707	1993	Nick Price	1,478,557
1946	Ben Hogan	42,556	1970	Lee Trevino	157,037	1994	Nick Price	1,499,927
1947	Jimmy Demaret	27,937	1971	Jack Nicklaus	244,491	1995	Greg Norman	1,654,959
1948	Ben Hogan	32,112	1972	Jack Nicklaus	320,542	1996	Tom Lehman	1,780,159
1949	Sam Snead	31,594	1973	Jack Nicklaus	308,362	1997	Tiger Woods	2,066,833
1950	Sam Snead	35,759	1974	Johnny Miller	353,022	1998	David Duval	2,591,031
1951	Lloyd Mangrum	26,089	1975	Jack Nicklaus	298,149	1999	Tiger Woods	6,616,585
1952	Julius Boros	37,033	1976	Jack Nicklaus	266,439	2000	Tiger Woods	9,188,321
1953	Lew Worsham	34,002	1977	Tom Watson	310,653	2001	Tiger Woods	5,687,777
1954	Bob Toski	65,820	1978	Tom Watson	362,429	2002	Tiger Woods	6,912,625
1955	Julius Boros	63,122	1979	Tom Watson	462,636	2003	Vijay Singh	7,573,907
1956	Ted Kroll	72,836	1980	Tom Watson	530,808	2004	Vijay Singh	10,905,166
1957	Dick Mayer	65,835	1981	Tom Kite	375,699	2005	Tiger Woods	10,628,024

Note: In 1944-45, Nelson's winnings were in War Bonds.

Champions Tour

Multiple leaders: Hale Irwin and Don January (3); Miller Barber, Bob Charles, Jim Colbert, Dave Stockton and Lee Trevino (2).

Year		Earnings	Year		Earnings	Year		Earnings
1980	Don January	$44,100	1989	Bob Charles	$725,887	1998	Hale Irwin	$2,861,945
1981	Miller Barber	83,136	1990	Lee Trevino	1,190,518	1999	Bruce Fleisher	2,515,705
1982	Miller Barber	106,890	1991	Mike Hill	1,065,657	2000	Larry Nelson	2,708,005
1983	Don January	237,571	1992	Lee Trevino	1,027,002	2001	Allen Doyle	2,553,582
1984	Don January	328,597	1993	Dave Stockton	1,175,944	2002	Hale Irwin	3,028,304
1985	Peter Thomson	386,724	1994	Dave Stockton	1,402,519	2003	Tom Watson	1,853,108
1986	Bruce Crampton	454,299	1995	Jim Colbert	1,444,386	2004	Craig Stadler	2,306,066
1987	Chi Chi Rodriguez	509,145	1996	Jim Colbert	1,627,890	2005	Dana Quigley	2,170,258
1988	Bob Charles	533,929	1997	Hale Irwin	2,343,364			

European PGA

Official money in the Volvo Order of Merit was awarded in British pounds from 1961-98 and euros (E) since 1999.

Multiple leaders: Colin Montgomerie (8); Seve Ballesteros (6); Sandy Lyle (3); Gay Brewer Jr., Ernie Els, Nick Faldo, Retief Goosen, Bernard Hunt, Bernhard Langer, Peter Thomson and Ian Woosnam (2).

Year		Earnings	Year		Earnings	Year		Earnings
1961	Bernard Hunt	£4,492	1976	Seve Ballesteros	£39,504	1991	Seve Ballesteros	£790,811
1962	Peter Thomson	5,764	1977	Seve Ballesteros	46,436	1992	Nick Faldo	1,220,540
1963	Bernard Hunt	7,209	1978	Seve Ballesteros	54,348	1993	Colin Montgomerie	798,145
1964	Neil Coles	7,890	1979	Sandy Lyle	49,233	1994	Colin Montgomerie	920,647
1965	Peter Thomson	7,011	1980	Greg Norman	74,829	1995	Colin Montgomerie	1,038,718
1966	Bruce Devlin	13,205	1981	Bernhard Langer	95,991	1996	Colin Montgomerie	1,034,752
1967	Gay Brewer Jr.	20,235	1982	Sandy Lyle	86,141	1997	Colin Montgomerie	1,583,904
1968	Gay Brewer Jr.	23,107	1983	Nick Faldo	140,761	1998	Colin Montgomerie	1,082,833
1969	Billy Casper	23,483	1984	Bernhard Langer	160,883	1999	C. Montgomerie	E2,066,885
1970	Christy O'Connor	31,532	1985	Sandy Lyle	254,711	2000	Lee Westwood	3,125,147
1971	Gary Player	11,281	1986	Seve Ballesteros	259,275	2001	Retief Goosen	2,862,806
1972	Bob Charles	18,538	1987	Ian Woosnam	439,075	2002	Retief Goosen	2,360,128
1973	Tony Jacklin	24,839	1988	Seve Ballesteros	502,000	2003	Ernie Els	2,975,374
1974	Peter Oosterhuis	32,127	1989	Ronan Rafferty	465,981	2004	Ernie Els	4,061,905
1975	Dale Hayes	20,507	1990	Ian Woosnam	737,977	2005	Colin Montgomerie	2,794,223

LPGA

Multiple leaders: Annika Sorenstam and Kathy Whitworth (8); Mickey Wright (4); Patty Berg, JoAnne Carner, Beth Daniel, Betsy King, Nancy Lopez and Karrie Webb (3); Pat Bradley, Judy Rankin, Betsy Rawls, Louise Suggs and Babe Zaharias (2).

Year		Earnings	Year		Earnings	Year		Earnings
1950	Babe Zaharias	$14,800	1969	Carol Mann	$49,152	1988	Sherri Turner	$350,851
1951	Babe Zaharias	15,087	1970	Kathy Whitworth	30,235	1989	Betsy King	654,132
1952	Betsy Rawls	14,505	1971	Kathy Whitworth	41,181	1990	Beth Daniel	863,578
1953	Louise Suggs	19,816	1972	Kathy Whitworth	65,063	1991	Pat Bradley	763,118
1954	Patty Berg	16,011	1973	Kathy Whitworth	82,864	1992	Dottie Pepper	693,335
1955	Patty Berg	16,492	1974	JoAnne Carner	87,094	1993	Betsy King	595,992
1956	Marlene Hagge	20,235	1975	Sandra Palmer	76,374	1994	Laura Davies	687,201
1957	Patty Berg	16,272	1976	Judy Rankin	150,734	1995	Annika Sorenstam	666,533
1958	Beverly Hanson	12,639	1977	Judy Rankin	122,890	1996	Karrie Webb	1,002,000
1959	Betsy Rawls	26,774	1978	Nancy Lopez	189,814	1997	Annika Sorenstam	1,236,789
1960	Louise Suggs	16,892	1979	Nancy Lopez	197,489	1998	Annika Sorenstam	1,092,748
1961	Mickey Wright	22,236	1980	Beth Daniel	231,000	1999	Karrie Webb	1,591,959
1962	Mickey Wright	21,641	1981	Beth Daniel	206,998	2000	Karrie Webb	1,876,853
1963	Mickey Wright	31,269	1982	JoAnne Carner	310,400	2001	Annika Sorenstam	2,105,868
1964	Mickey Wright	29,800	1983	JoAnne Carner	291,404	2002	Annika Sorenstam	2,863,904
1965	Kathy Whitworth	28,658	1984	Betsy King	266,771	2003	Annika Sorenstam	2,029,506
1966	Kathy Whitworth	33,517	1985	Nancy Lopez	416,472	2004	Annika Sorenstam	2,544,707
1967	Kathy Whitworth	32,937	1986	Pat Bradley	492,021	2005	Annika Sorenstam	2,588,240
1968	Kathy Whitworth	48,379	1987	Ayako Okamoto	466,034			

All-Time Leaders

PGA, Champions Tour and LPGA leaders through Oct. 8, 2006.

Tournaments Won

PGA	No	Champions	No	LPGA	No
1 Sam Snead	82	1 Hale Irwin	44	1 Kathy Whitworth	88
2 Jack Nicklaus	73	2 Lee Trevino	29	2 Mickey Wright	82
3 Ben Hogan	64	3 Miller Barber	24	3 Annika Sorenstam	69
4 Arnold Palmer	62	Gil Morgan	24	4 Patty Berg	60
5 Tiger Woods	54	5 Bob Charles	23	5 Louise Suggs	58
6 Byron Nelson	52	6 Don January	22	6 Betsy Rawls	55
7 Billy Casper	51	Chi Chi Rodriguez	22	7 Nancy Lopez	48
8 Walter Hagen	44	8 Bruce Crampton	20	8 JoAnne Carner	43
9 Cary Middlecoff	40	Jim Colbert	20	9 Sandra Haynie	42
10 Gene Sarazen	39	10 George Archer	19	10 Babe Zaharias	41
Tom Watson	39	Larry Nelson	19	11 Carol Mann	38
12 Lloyd Mangrum	36	Gary Player	19	12 Patty Sheehan	35
13 Horton Smith	32	13 Mike Hill	18	13 Betsy King	34
14 Harry Cooper	31	Bruce Fleisher	18	Karrie Webb	34
Jimmy Demaret	31	15 Dave Stockton	14	15 Beth Daniel	33
16 Leo Diegel	30	Raymond Floyd	14	16 Pat Bradley	31
17 Gene Littler	29	17 Jim Dent	12	Juli Inkster	31
Paul Runyan	29	18 Seven tied with 11 wins.		18 Amy Alcott	29
Lee Trevino	29			19 Jane Blalock	27
Vijay Singh	29			20 Judy Rankin	26
Phil Mickelson	29			Marlene Hagge	26

All-Time Leaders (Cont.)
Money Won
All-time earnings through Oct. 8, 2006.

PGA

	Earnings			Earnings			Earnings
1 Tiger Woods	$65,712,324	10 Kenny Perry	$20,335,031	19 Stewart Cink	$18,419,738
2 Vijay Singh	48,941,256	11 Fred Funk	19,400,149	20 Scott Verplank	17,916,494
3 Phil Mickelson	39,514,038	12 Fred Couples	19,129,114	21 Jeff Sluman	17,829,033
4 Davis Love III	34,344,348	13 Mark Calcavecchia	19,126,077	22 Brad Faxon	17,571,909
5 Jim Furyk	30,415,766	14 Tom Lehman	18,810,332	23 Retief Goosen	16,886,017
6 Ernie Els	28,060,045	15 Mike Weir	18,785,533	24 David Duval	16,682,256
7 David Toms	25,669,215	16 Chris DiMarco	18,686,371	25 Sergio Garcia	15,819,592
8 Justin Leonard	21,038,732	17 Stuart Appleby	18,666,310		
9 Nick Price	20,551,208	18 Scott Hoch	18,487,114		

European PGA
Official earnings in Euros (£).

	Earnings			Earnings			Earnings
1 C. Montgomerie	£21,300,883	10 Vijay Singh	£11,031,506	19 Ian Poulter	£7,551,068
2 Ernie Els	18,627,884	11 M. Angel Jimenez	10,984,333	20 Eduardo Romero	7,467,752
3 Retief Goosen	15,862,172	12 Michael Campbell	10,364,292	21 Robert Karlsson	7,154,808
4 Darren Clarke	15,372,334	13 Ian Woosnam	9,584,347	22 Paul Casey	6,793,450
5 Padraig Harrington	14,194,422	14 Angel Cabrera	9,340,682	23 Paul Lawrie	6,459,835
6 Lee Westwood	12,491,924	15 David Howell	8,964,940	24 Adam Scott	6,260,597
7 Bernhard Langer	12,231,109	16 Paul McGinley	8,770,512	25 Barry Lane	6,243,181
8 Thomas Bjorn	11,537,524	17 Sergio Garcia	8,746,302		
9 J. Maria Olazabal	11,162,476	18 Nick Faldo	7,988,365		

Champions Tour

	Earnings			Earnings			Earnings
1 Hale Irwin	$29,280,096	10 Craig Stadler	$15,586,816	19 Allen Doyle	$12,340,167
2 Gil Morgan	22,400,590	11 Bruce Fleisher	14,954,358	20 Dave Stockton	12,136,472
3 Tom Kite	20,899,948	11 Raymond Floyd	14,558,734	21 Bob Gilder	11,122,749
4 Fred Funk	19,504,271	13 Greg Norman	14,188,469	22 Tom Jenkins	10,986,746
5 Scott Hoch	18,556,224	14 Lee Trevino	13,300,105	23 Doug Tewell	10,436,296
6 Tom Watson	18,521,067	15 Dana Quigley	13,193,289	24 Isao Aoki	10,197,639
7 Loren Roberts	18,156,496	16 Jim Colbert	13,126,676	25 Peter Jacobsen	10,167,627
8 Jay Haas	18,007,317	17 Jim Thorpe	12,831,402		
9 Larry Nelson	16,666,496	18 Bruce Lietzke	12,780,085		

LPGA

	Earnings			Earnings			Earnings
1 Annika Sorenstam	$20,102,172	10 Dottie Pepper	$6,827,284	19 Lorena Ochoa	$5,450,451
2 Karrie Webb	12,610,624	11 Cristie Kerr	6,624,880	20 Nancy Lopez	5,320,877
3 Juli Inkster	11,119,414	12 Mi Hyun Kim	6,513,149	21 Sherri Steinhauer	5,197,418
4 Se Ri Pak	8,835,147	13 Lorie Kane	6,462,659	22 Grace Park	5,110,854
5 Meg Mallon	8,818,462	14 Pat Bradley	5,755,951	23 Rachel Hetherington	4,950,520
6 Beth Daniel	8,755,733	15 Kelly Robbins	5,725,742	24 Michele Redman	4,829,982
7 Rosie Jones	8,355,068	16 Liselotte Neumann	5,659,857	25 Catriona Matthew	4,544,053
8 Laura Davies	7,689,035	17 Patty Sheehan	5,513,409		
9 Betsy King	7,637,622	18 Pat Hurst	5,481,336		

Official World Golf Ranking

Begun in 1986, the Official World Golf Ranking (formerly the Sony World Ranking) combines the best golfers on the six pro men's tours which make up the International Federation of PGA Tours. Rankings are based on a rolling two-year period and weighed in favor of more recent results. While annual winners are not announced, certain players reaching No. 1 have dominated each year.

Multiple winners (at year's end): Tiger Woods (8); Greg Norman (6); Nick Faldo (3); Seve Ballesteros (2).

Year		Year		Year		Year	
1986	Seve Ballesteros	1990	Nick Faldo	1994	Nick Price	2000	Tiger Woods
1987	Greg Norman		& Greg Norman	1995	Greg Norman	2001	Tiger Woods
1988	Greg Norman	1991	Ian Woosnam	1996	Greg Norman	2002	Tiger Woods
1989	Seve Ballesteros	1992	Fred Couples	1997	Tiger Woods	2003	Tiger Woods
	& Greg Norman		& Nick Faldo	1998	Tiger Woods	2004	Vijay Singh
		1993	Nick Faldo	1999	Tiger Woods	2005	Tiger Woods

Annual Awards

PGA of America Player of the Year

Awarded by the PGA of America; based on points scale that weighs performance in major tournaments, regular events, money earned and scoring average. **Note:** As of Oct. 8, Tiger Woods had already clinched the award for 2006.

Multiple winners: Tiger Woods (8); Tom Watson (6); Jack Nicklaus (5); Ben Hogan (4); Julius Boros, Billy Casper, Arnold Palmer and Nick Price.

Year		Year		Year		Year	
1948	Ben Hogan	1963	Julius Boros	1978	Tom Watson	1993	Nick Price
1949	Sam Snead	1964	Ken Venturi	1979	Tom Watson	1994	Nick Price
1950	Ben Hogan	1965	Dave Marr	1980	Tom Watson	1995	Greg Norman
1951	Ben Hogan	1966	Billy Casper	1981	Bill Rogers	1996	Tom Lehman
1952	Julius Boros	1967	Jack Nicklaus	1982	Tom Watson	1997	Tiger Woods
1953	Ben Hogan	1968	No award	1983	Hal Sutton	1998	Mark O'Meara
1954	Ed Furgol	1969	Orville Moody	1984	Tom Watson	1999	Tiger Woods
1955	Doug Ford	1970	Billy Casper	1985	Lanny Wadkins	2000	Tiger Woods
1956	Jack Burke	1971	Lee Trevino	1986	Bob Tway	2001	Tiger Woods
1957	Dick Mayer	1972	Jack Nicklaus	1987	Paul Azinger	2002	Tiger Woods
1958	Dow Finsterwald	1973	Jack Nicklaus	1988	Curtis Strange	2003	Tiger Woods
1959	Art Wall Jr.	1974	Johnny Miller	1989	Tom Kite	2004	Vijay Singh
1960	Arnold Palmer	1975	Jack Nicklaus	1990	Nick Faldo	2005	Tiger Woods
1961	Jerry Barber	1976	Jack Nicklaus	1991	Corey Pavin	2006	Tiger Woods
1962	Arnold Palmer	1977	Tom Watson	1992	Fred Couples		

PGA Tour Player of the Year

Award by the PGA Tour starting in 1990. Winner voted on by tour members from list of nominees. Winner receives the Jack Nicklaus Trophy, which originated in 1997.

Multiple winners: Tiger Woods (7); Fred Couples and Nick Price (2).

Year		Year		Year		Year	
1990	Wayne Levi	1994	Nick Price	1998	Mark O'Meara	2002	Tiger Woods
1991	Fred Couples	1995	Greg Norman	1999	Tiger Woods	2003	Tiger Woods
1992	Fred Couples	1996	Tom Lehman	2000	Tiger Woods	2004	Vijay Singh
1993	Nick Price	1997	Tiger Woods	2001	Tiger Woods	2005	Tiger Woods

PGA Tour Rookie of the Year

Awarded by the PGA Tour in 1990. Winner voted on by tour members from list of first-year nominees.

Year		Year		Year		Year	
1990	Robert Gamez	1994	Ernie Els	1998	Steve Flesch	2002	Jonathan Byrd
1991	John Daly	1995	Woody Austin	1999	Carlos Franco	2003	Ben Curtis
1992	Mark Carnevale	1996	Tiger Woods	2000	Michael Clark II	2004	Todd Hamilton
1993	Vijay Singh	1997	Stewart Cink	2001	Charles Howell III	2005	Sean O'Hair

Champions Tour Player of the Year

Awarded by the Champions Tour starting in 1990. Winner voted on by tour members from list of nominees.

Multiple winner: Hale Irwin and Lee Trevino (3); Jim Colbert (2).

Year		Year		Year		Year	
1990	Lee Trevino	1994	Lee Trevino	1999	Bruce Fleisher	2004	Craig Stadler
1991	George Archer & Mike Hill	1995	Jim Colbert	2000	Larry Nelson	2005	Dana Quigley
1992	Lee Trevino	1996	Jim Colbert	2001	Allen Doyle		
1993	Dave Stockton	1997	Hale Irwin	2002	Hale Irwin		
		1998	Hale Irwin	2003	Tom Watson		

European Tour Golfer of the Year

Formerly the Ritz Club Trophy (1985-92), Johnnie Walker Trophy (1993-97) and Asprey Golfer of the Year (1998-2004); voting done by panel of European golf writers and tour members.

Multiple winners: Colin Montgomerie (4); Seve Ballesteros, Ernie Els, and Nick Faldo (3); Bernhard Langer and Lee Westwood (2).

Year		Year		Year		Year	
1985	Bernhard Langer	1991	Seve Ballesteros	1997	Colin Montgomerie	2003	Ernie Els
1986	Seve Ballesteros	1992	Nick Faldo	1998	Lee Westwood	2004	Vijay Singh
1987	Ian Woosnam	1993	Bernhard Langer	1999	Colin Montgomerie	2005	Michael Campbell
1988	Seve Ballesteros	1994	Ernie Els	2000	Lee Westwood		
1989	Nick Faldo	1995	Colin Montgomerie	2001	Retief Goosen		
1990	Nick Faldo	1996	Colin Montgomerie	2002	Ernie Els		

Annual Awards (Cont.)
LPGA Player of the Year

Sponsored by Rolex and awarded by the LPGA; based on performance points accumulated during the year.

Multiple winners: Annika Sorenstam (8); Kathy Whitworth (7); Nancy Lopez (4); JoAnne Carner, Beth Daniel and Betsy King (3); Pat Bradley, Judy Rankin and Karrie Webb (2).

Year		Year		Year		Year	
1966	Kathy Whitworth	1976	Judy Rankin	1986	Pat Bradley	1996	Laura Davies
1967	Kathy Whitworth	1977	Judy Rankin	1987	Ayako Okamoto	1997	Annika Sorenstam
1968	Kathy Whitworth	1978	Nancy Lopez	1988	Nancy Lopez	1998	Annika Sorenstam
1969	Kathy Whitworth	1979	Nancy Lopez	1989	Betsy King	1999	Karrie Webb
1970	Sandra Haynie	1980	Beth Daniel	1990	Beth Daniel	2000	Karrie Webb
1971	Kathy Whitworth	1981	JoAnne Carner	1991	Pat Bradley	2001	Annika Sorenstam
1972	Kathy Whitworth	1982	JoAnne Carner	1992	Dottie Mochrie	2002	Annika Sorenstam
1973	Kathy Whitworth	1983	Patty Sheehan	1993	Betsy King	2003	Annika Sorenstam
1974	JoAnne Carner	1984	Betsy King	1994	Beth Daniel	2004	Annika Sorenstam
1975	Sandra Palmer	1985	Nancy Lopez	1995	Annika Sorenstam	2005	Annika Sorenstam

LPGA Rookie of the Year

Sponsored by Rolex and awarded by the LPGA; based on performance points accumulated during the year. Winner receives Louise Suggs Trophy, which originated in 2000. Officially the Louise Suggs Rolex Rookie of the Year.

Year		Year		Year		Year	
1962	Mary Mills	1973	Laura Baugh	1984	Juli Inkster	1995	Pat Hurst
1963	Clifford Ann Creed	1974	Jan Stephenson	1985	Penny Hammel	1996	Karrie Webb
1964	Susie Berning	1975	Amy Alcott	1986	Jody Rosenthal	1997	Lisa Hackney
1965	Margie Masters	1976	Bonnie Lauer	1987	Tammie Green	1998	Se Ri Pak
1966	Jan Ferraris	1977	Debbie Massey	1988	Liselotte Neumann	1999	Mi Hyun Kim
1967	Sharron Moran	1978	Nancy Lopez	1989	Pamela Wright	2000	Dorothy Delasin
1968	Sandra Post	1979	Beth Daniel	1990	Hiromi Kobayashi	2001	Hee-Won Han
1969	Jane Blalock	1980	Myra Van Hoose	1991	Brandie Burton	2002	Beth Bauer
1970	JoAnne Carner	1981	Patty Sheehan	1992	Helen Alfredsson	2003	Lorena Ochoa
1971	Sally Little	1982	Patti Rizzo	1993	Suzanne Strudwick	2004	Shi Hyun Ahn
1972	Jocelyne Bourassa	1983	Stephanie Farwig	1994	Annika Sorenstam	2005	Paula Creamer

National Team Competition
MEN
Ryder Cup

The Ryder Cup was presented by British seed merchant and businessman Samuel Ryder in 1927 for competition between professional golfers from Great Britain and the United States. The British team was expanded to include Irish players in 1973 and the rest of Europe in 1979. The 2001 event was postponed due to the attacks on America, causing the event to switch from an odd- to even-year schedule. The United States leads the series 24-10-2 after 36 matches.

Year		Year		Year		Year	
1927	USA, 9½-2½	1953	USA, 6½-5½	1973	USA, 19-13	1993	USA, 15-13
1929	Britain-Ireland, 7-5	1955	USA, 8-4	1975	USA, 21-11	1995	Europe, 14½-13½
1931	USA, 9-3	1957	Britain-Ireland, 7½-4½	1977	USA, 12½-13½	1997	Europe, 14½-13½
1933	Great Britain, 6½-5½	1959	USA, 8½-3½	1979	USA, 17-11	1999	USA, 14½-13½
1935	USA, 9-3	1961	USA, 14½-9½	1981	USA, 18½-9½	2002	Europe, 15½-12½
1937	USA, 8-4	1963	USA, 23-9	1983	USA, 14½-13½	2004	Europe, 18½-9½
1939-45	Not held	1965	USA, 19½-12½	1985	Europe, 16½-11½	2006	Europe, 18½-9½
1947	USA, 11-1	1967	USA, 23½-8½	1987	Europe, 15-13		
1949	USA, 7-5	1969	Draw, 16-16	1989	Draw, 14-14		
1951	USA, 9½-2½	1971	USA, 18½-13½	1991	USA, 14½-13½		

Playing Sites

1927—Worcester CC (Mass.); **1929**—Moortown, England; **1931**—Scioto CC (Ohio); **1933**—Southport & Ainsdale, England; **1935**—Ridgewood CC (N.J.); **1937**—Southport & Ainsdale, England; **1939-45**—Not held. **1947**—Portland CC (Ore.); **1949**—Ganton GC, England; **1951**—Pinehurst CC (N.C.); **1953**—Wentworth, England; **1955**—Thunderbird Ranch & CC (Calif.); **1957**—Lindrick GC, England; **1959**—Eldorado CC (Calif.); **1961**—Royal Lytham & St. Annes, England; **1963**—East Lake CC (Ga.); **1965**—Royal Birkdale, England; **1967**—Champions GC (Tex.); **1969**—Royal Birkdale, England; **1971**—Old Warson CC (Mo.); **1973**—Muirfield, Scotland; **1975**—Laurel Valley GC (Pa.); **1977**—Royal Lytham & St. Annes, England; **1979**—The Greenbrier (W.Va.); **1981**—Walton Heath GC, England; **1983**—PGA National GC (Fla.); **1985**—The Belfry, England; **1987**—Muirfield Village GC (Ohio); **1989**—The Belfry, England; **1991**—Ocean Course (S.C.); **1993**—The Belfry, England; **1995**—Oak Hill CC (N.Y.); **1997**—Valderrama, Costa del Sol, Spain; **1999**—The Country Club (Mass.); **2002**— The Belfry, England; **2004**— Oakland Hills CC (Mich.); **2006**— Kildare Hotel & CC, Ireland; **2008**—Valhalla GC (Ky.); **2010**— Celtic Manor, Wales; **2012**— Medinah CC (III.); **2014**— Gleneagles, Scotland; **2016**—Hazeltine National GC (Minn) **2018**—TBA (Europe); **2020**—Whistling Straits (Wisc.).

Presidents Cup

The Presidents Cup is a biennial event played in non-Ryder Cup years in which the world's best non-European players compete against players from the United States. The U.S. leads the series, 4-1-1. In 2003 the match was called off due to darkness after three sudden-death playoff holes. It was deemed a tie with both teams sharing the Cup until 2005.

Year		Year		Year	
1994	USA, 20-12	1998	International, 20½-11½	2003	Tie, 17-17
1996	USA, 16½-15½	2000	USA, 21½-10½	2005	USA, 18½-15½

Walker Cup

The Walker Cup was presented by American businessman George Herbert Walker in 1922 for competition between amateur golfers from Great Britain, Ireland and the United States. The U.S. leads the series against the combined Great Britain-Ireland team, 32-7-1, after 40 matches.

Year	Year	Year	Year
1922 USA, 8-4	1949 USA, 10-2	1973 USA, 14-10	1995 Britain-Ireland, 14-10
1923 USA, 6½-5½	1951 USA, 7½-4½	1975 USA, 15½-8½	1997 USA, 18-6
1924 USA, 9-3	1953 USA, 9-3	1977 USA, 16-8	1999 Britain-Ireland, 15-9
1926 USA, 6½-5½	1955 USA, 10-2	1979 USA, 15½-8½	2001 Britain-Ireland, 15-9
1928 USA, 11-1	1957 USA, 8½-3½	1981 USA, 15-9	2003 Britain-Ireland,
1930 USA, 10-2	1959 USA, 9-3	1983 USA, 13½-10½	12½-11½
1932 USA, 9½-2½	1961 USA, 11-1	1985 USA, 13-11	2005 USA, 12½-11½
1934 USA, 9½-2½	1963 USA, 14-10	1987 USA, 16½-7½	
1936 USA, 10½-1½	1965 Draw, 12-12	1989 Britain-Ireland,	
1938 Britain-Ireland, 7½-4½	1967 USA, 15-9	12½-11½	
1940-46 Not held	1969 USA, 13-11	1991 USA, 14-10	
1947 USA, 8-4	1971 Britain-Ireland, 13-11	1993 USA, 19-5	

WOMEN

Solheim Cup

The Solheim Cup was presented by the Karsten Manufacturing Co. in 1990 for competition between women professional golfers from Europe and the United States. The event was switched from even- to odd-numbered years after 2002 so it would not conflict with the men's Ryder Cup event. The U.S. leads the series, 6-3.

Year	Year	Year
1990 USA, 11½-4½	1996 USA, 17-11	2002 USA, 15½-12½
1992 Europe, 11½-6½	1998 USA, 16-12	2003 Europe, 17½-10½
1994 USA, 13-7	2000 Europe, 14½-11½	2005 USA, 15½-12½

Playing Sites

1990—Lake Nona CC (Fla.); **1992**—Dalmahoy CC, Scotland; **1994**—The Greenbrier (W. Va.); **1996**—Marriott St. Pierre Hotel G&CC, Wales; **1998**—Muirfield Village GC (Ohio); **2000**—Loch Lomond GC, Scotland; **2002**—Interlachen CC (Minn.); **2003**—Barseback G&CC, Sweden; **2005**—Crooked Stick GC (Ind.); **2007**—Halmstad GC (Sweden); **2009**—Rich Harvest Farms (Ill.).

Curtis Cup

Named after British golfing sisters Harriot and Margaret Curtis, the Curtis Cup was first contested in 1932 between teams of women amateurs from the United States and the British Isles.

Competed for every other year since 1932 (except during WWII). The U.S. leads the series, 25-6-3, after 34 matches.

Year	Year	Year	Year
1932 USA, 5½-3½	1956 USA, 5½-3½	1974 USA, 13-5	1992 British Isles, 10-8
1934 USA, 6½-2½	1958 Draw, 4½-4½	1976 USA, 11½-6½	1994 Draw, 9-9
1936 Draw, 4½-4½	1960 USA, 6½-2½	1978 USA, 12-6	1996 British Isles, 11½-6½
1938 USA, 5½-3½	1962 USA, 8-1	1980 USA, 13-5	1998 USA, 10-8
1940-46 Not held	1964 USA, 10½-7½	1982 USA, 14½-3½	2000 USA, 10-8
1948 USA, 6½-2½	1966 USA, 13-5	1984 USA, 9½-8½	2002 USA, 11-7
1950 USA, 7½-1½	1968 USA, 10½-7½	1986 British Isles, 13-5	2004 USA, 10-8
1952 British Isles, 5-4	1970 USA, 11½-6½	1988 British Isles, 11-7	2006 USA, 11½-6½
1954 USA, 6-3	1972 USA, 10-8	1990 USA, 14-4	

COLLEGES

Men's NCAA Division I Champions

College championships decided by match play from 1897-1964 and stroke play since 1965.

Multiple winners (Teams): Yale (21); Houston (16); Oklahoma St. (10); Stanford (7); Harvard (6); Florida, LSU and North Texas (4); Wake Forest (3); Arizona St., Georgia, Michigan, Ohio St. and Texas (2).

Multiple winners (Individuals): Ben Crenshaw and Phil Mickelson (3); Dick Crawford, Dexter Cummings, G.T. Dunlop, Fred Lamprecht and Scott Simpson (2).

Year	Team winner	Individual champion	Year	Team winner	Individual champion
1897	Yale	Louis Bayard, Princeton	1905	Yale	Robert Abbott, Yale
1898	Harvard (spring)	John Reid, Yale	1906	Yale	W.E. Clow Jr., Yale
1898	Yale (fall)	James Curtis, Harvard	1907	Yale	Ellis Knowles, Yale
1899	Harvard	Percy Pyne, Princeton	1908	Yale	H.H. Wilder, Harvard
			1909	Yale	Albert Seckel, Princeton
1900	Not held		1910	Yale	Robert Hunter, Yale
1901	Harvard	H. Lindsley, Harvard	1911	Yale	George Stanley, Yale
1902	Yale (spring)	Chas. Hitchcock Jr., Yale	1912	Yale	F.C. Davison, Harvard
1902	Harvard (fall)	Chandler Egan, Harvard	1913	Yale	Nathaniel Wheeler, Yale
1903	Harvard	F.O. Reinhart, Princeton	1914	Princeton	Edward Allis, Harvard
1904	Harvard	A.L. White, Harvard			

Colleges (Cont.)

Year	Team winner	Individual champion	Year	Team winner	Individual champion
1915	Yale	Francis Blossom, Yale	1962	Houston	Kermit Zarley, Houston
1916	Princeton	J.W. Hubbell, Harvard	1963	Oklahoma St.	R.H. Sikes, Arkansas
1917-18	Not held		1964	Houston	Terry Small, San Jose St.
1919	Princeton	A.L. Walker Jr., Columbia	1965	Houston	Marty Fleckman, Houston
1920	Princeton	Jess Sweetser, Yale	1966	Houston	Bob Murphy, Florida
1921	Dartmouth	Simpson Dean, Princeton	1967	Houston	Hale Irwin, Colorado
1922	Princeton	Pollack Boyd, Dartmouth	1968	Florida	Grier Jones, Oklahoma St.
1923	Princeton	Dexter Cummings, Yale	1969	Houston	Bob Clark, Cal St.-LA
1924	Yale	Dexter Cummings, Yale	1970	Houston	John Mahaffey, Houston
1925	Yale	Fred Lamprecht, Tulane	1971	Texas	Ben Crenshaw, Texas
1926	Yale	Fred Lamprecht, Tulane	1972	Texas	Ben Crenshaw, Texas
1927	Princeton	Watts Gunn, Georgia Tech			& Tom Kite, Texas
1928	Princeton	Maurice McCarthy, G'town	1973	Florida	Ben Crenshaw, Texas
1929	Princeton	Tom Aycock, Yale	1974	Wake Forest	Curtis Strange, W.Forest
1930	Princeton	G.T. Dunlap Jr., Princeton	1975	Wake Forest	Jay Haas, Wake Forest
1931	Yale	G.T. Dunlap Jr., Princeton	1976	Oklahoma St.	Scott Simpson, USC
1932	Yale	J.W. Fischer, Michigan	1977	Houston	Scott Simpson, USC
1933	Yale	Walter Emery, Oklahoma	1978	Oklahoma St.	David Edwards, Okla. St.
1934	Michigan	Charles Yates, Ga.Tech	1979	Ohio St.	Gary Hallberg, Wake Forest
1935	Michigan	Ed White, Texas	1980	Oklahoma St.	Jay Don Blake, Utah St.
1936	Yale	Charles Kocsis, Michigan	1981	Brigham Young	Ron Commans, USC
1937	Princeton	Fred Haas Jr., LSU	1982	Houston	Billy Ray Brown, Houston
1938	Stanford	John Burke, Georgetown	1983	Oklahoma St.	Jim Carter, Arizona St.
1939	Stanford	Vincent D'Antoni, Tulane	1984	Houston	John Inman, N.Carolina
1940	Princeton & LSU	Dixon Brooke, Virginia	1985	Houston	Clark Burroughs, Ohio St.
1941	Stanford	Earl Stewart, LSU	1986	Wake Forest	Scott Verplank, Okla. St.
1942	LSU & Stanford	Frank Tatum Jr., Stanford	1987	Oklahoma St.	Brian Watts, Oklahoma St.
1943	Yale	Wallace Ulrich, Carleton	1988	UCLA	E.J. Pfister, Oklahoma St.
1944	Notre Dame	Louis Lick, Minnesota	1989	Oklahoma	Phil Mickelson, Ariz. St.
1945	Ohio State	John Lorms, Ohio St.	1990	Arizona St.	Phil Mickelson, Ariz. St.
1946	Stanford	George Hamer, Georgia	1991	Oklahoma St.	Warren Schuette, UNLV
1947	LSU	Dave Barclay, Michigan	1992	Arizona	Phil Mickelson, Ariz. St.
1948	San Jose St.	Bob Harris, San Jose St.	1993	Florida	Todd Demsey, Ariz. St.
1949	North Texas	Harvie Ward, N.Carolina	1994	Stanford	Justin Leonard, Texas
1950	North Texas	Fred Wampler, Purdue	1995	Oklahoma St.	Chip Spratlin, Auburn
1951	North Texas	Tom Nieporte, Ohio St.	1996	Arizona St.	Tiger Woods, Stanford
1952	North Texas	Jim Vickers, Oklahoma	1997	Pepperdine	Charles Warren, Clemson
1953	Stanford	Earl Moeller, Oklahoma St.	1998	UNLV	James McLean, Minnesota
1954	SMU	Hillman Robbins, Memphis St.	1999	Georgia	Luke Donald, Northwestern
1955	LSU	Joe Campbell, Purdue	2000	Oklahoma St.	Charles Howell, Oklahoma St.
1956	Houston	Rick Jones, Ohio St.	2001	Florida	Nick Gilliam, Florida
1957	Houston	Rex Baxter Jr., Houston	2002	Minnesota	Troy Matteson, Georgia Tech
1958	Houston	Phil Rodgers, Houston	2003	Clemson	Alejandro Canizares, Ariz. St.
1959	Houston	Dick Crawford, Houston	2004	California	Ryan Moore, UNLV
1960	Houston	Dick Crawford, Houston	2005	Georgia	James Lepp, Washington
1961	Purdue	Jack Nicklaus, Ohio St.	2006	Oklahoma St.	Jonathan Moore, Oklahoma St.

Women's NCAA Division I Champions

College championships decided by stroke play since 1982.

Multiple winners (teams): Arizona St. (6); Duke (4); Arizona, Florida, San Jose St., Tulsa and UCLA (2).

Year	Team winner	Individual champion	Year	Team winner	Individual champion
1982	Tulsa	Kathy Baker, Tulsa	1995	Arizona St.	K. Mourgue d'Algue, Ariz. St.
1983	TCU	Penny Hammel, Miami	1996	Arizona	Marisa Baena, Arizona
1984	Miami-FL	Cindy Schreyer, Georgia	1997	Arizona St.	Heather Bowie, Texas
1985	Florida	Danielle Ammaccapane, Ariz.St.	1998	Arizona St.	Jennifer Rosales, USC
1986	Florida	Page Dunlap, Florida	1999	Duke	Grace Park, Arizona St.
1987	San Jose St.	Caroline Keggi, New Mexico	2000	Arizona	Jenna Daniels, Arizona
1988	Tulsa	Melissa McNamara, Tulsa	2001	Georgia	Candy Hannemann, Duke
1989	San Jose St.	Pat Hurst, San Jose St.	2002	Duke	Virada Nirapathpongporn, Duke
1990	Arizona St.	Susan Slaughter, Arizona	2003	USC	Mikaela Parmlid, USC
1991	UCLA	Annika Sorenstam, Arizona	2004	UCLA	Sarah Huarte, California
1992	San Jose St.	Vicki Goetze, Georgia	2005	Duke	Anna Grzebien, Duke
1993	Arizona St.	Charlotta Sorenstam, Ariz. St.	2006	Duke	Dewi Schreefel, USC
1994	Arizona St.	Emilee Klein, Ariz. St.			

MOTOR SPORTS

2005 / 2006 YEAR IN REVIEW

Rivals **Jeff Gordon** and **Dale Earnhardt Jr.** had their squabbles in 2006, but found time here for a laugh.

CHANGES
AT THE TOP

The Chase is jam-packed with first-timers, and Formula 1 legend Michael Schumacher turns over his keys to the Ferrari.

ONE OF THE BIGGEST STORIES IN RACING THIS YEAR, IN MY OPINION, WAS YOUNG MARCO ANDRETTI'S COMING OF AGE.

At just 19 years old, the Indy Racing League rookie won his first title and came so close to winning the Indianapolis 500. Veteran Sam Hornish Jr. beat him right at the line in what was one of the best Indy 500s in history.

The IRL has seen its share of drivers that are inconsistent – one day they're here and the next day they're gone. But Marco Andretti is different and it was plain to see. He was fast all year long. After his Indy 500 runner-up finish, he went to Infineon Raceway in August and won. I don't think anybody thought he would be as fast on a road course as he was. And it sure wasn't just luck either – he really ran strong throughout the day.

Another big story in Indy Car racing that blew me away was how the Penske Racing cars and the Chip Ganassi Racing cars ran bumper-to-bumper in almost every race. You expected maybe Andretti Green Racing to get up there and mix it up in between them, but it very seldom happened.

To go into the very last race at Chicago and have those teams run bumper-to-bumper for the entire race was amazing. They lapped the rest of the field.

Unfortunately it was a really disappointing year for Danica Patrick. Early in the year, the death of her teammate Paul Dana right off the bat at Homestead, caused her to pull out of the race and fall behind in the points race. It was just too hard catching up.

Her team could never really get their Panoz chassis running. They lost total confidence in it and eventually switched to Dallara. Since they were

Rusty Wallace is the 1989 NASCAR Winston Cup Series champion and winner of 55 career races. He is the lead auto racing analyst for ABC and ESPN.

AP/Wide World Photos

Richard Childress Racing teammates **Jeff Burton** (31, left) and **Kevin Harvick** (29) were just two of the drivers making their Chase debuts in 2006.

already behind, that was no time to figure out a brand-new chassis, especially with limited testing. To compound that, team owner Bobby Rahal felt he had a really good support staff – which he does – but he was putting a lot of effort into his own son, Graham, chasing his racing around the country.

With my own son, Stephen, racing, I can understand. I tend to pay more attention to Stephen than I do to Jamie McMurray when Jamie's driving my Busch Series car. I've already got confidence in Jamie. Stephen's the one I'm nurturing, trying to get along. So I can understand why Bobby would think that. Unfortunately for Bobby though, it backfired

because Danica was struggling and she needed Bobby at the race track as a shoulder to lean on and Bobby wasn't there. Eventually she started working a deal with Andretti Green, and now she's moving on.

In NASCAR this year, one of the most confusing things I saw all year long was the champion of 2005, Tony Stewart, not even making it in the Chase. His year was so sporadic that he just couldn't build any rhythm and got bumped from the top 10 standings.

On the other hand, I was totally surprised to see rookie Denny Hamlin be successful every week – week after week after week. Not only did he win at Pocono, he absolutely dominated,

Seven-time world driving champion **Michael Schumacher** retires after the 2006 season as the all-time Formula 1 leader in wins, poles and podiums.

AP/Wide World Photos

then came back and dominated again to win another race at the same track six weeks later. He's the strongest team at Joe Gibbs Racing right now. I don't know how that happened...I never predicted he would make it to the Chase only because he's a rookie.

One thing that hasn't surprised me, but has given me a real comforting feeling is seeing young Kasey Kahne not only run well but look dominant in many, many races.

Another great story is the year that Richard Childress Racing had. After the death of Dale Earnhardt, Richard Childress could never seem to get any rhythm going, never could seem to get the respect that the organization always had in the past. And to be quite honest, when Kevin Harvick was waffling whether he was going to come back or not, that was a distraction. When Harvick decided to sign a contract extension and put a full effort into it, you could tell that's when the whole organization got focused, including Richard.

And they absolutely hit it out the ballpark when they got veteran Jeff Burton in there (in 2004) to bring some stability to their organization. It became quite evident it wasn't all about Harvick then, it was all about Burton and Harvick.

THE TOP

10 ↓

Stories of the Year in **Motor Sports**

10 Juan Pablo Montoya moves to NASCAR.

Montoya's move might not be earth-shattering in Formula 1 circles, but it's a huge step for NASCAR, a sanctioning body anxious to build a more diverse fan base. The charismatic Montoya can't hurt those efforts, especially if he finds success with Chip Ganassi Racing.

09 Mark Martin moves to MB2 Motorsports

The veteran thought 2005 would be his last full-time Nextel Cup season, but agrees to run one more year with Roush Racing. He initially planned on moving to the Craftsman Truck Series full time with Roush in '07, but changed his mind when the opportunity arose to run 20 points races and two all-star events with MB2 Motorsports.

08 Toyota to Nextel Cup.

Toyota executives make public NASCAR's worst-kept secret in January when it announces it will enter Nextel Cup and Busch Series competition after its third season in the Craftsman Truck Series. Bill Davis Racing, Michael Waltrip Racing and Team Red Bull will field Toyotas in the Nextel Cup in 2007.

07 Richard Childress Racing returns to form.

After struggling since Dale Earnhardt's death in 2001, RCR is back on its game in 2006. Not only does Kevin Harvick dominate on the way to the Busch Series title, but Jeff Burton and Harvick each make the Chase.

06 Penske and Chip Ganassi dominate

Sam Hornish wins the IndyCar championship with Penske teammate Helio Castroneves taking third. Hornish and Castroneves win four races each, while runner-up Dan Wheldon and fourth-place Scott Dixon win twice each. All four drivers have nine top-fives apiece in 14 races.

05 Danica Mania subsides

Danica Patrick doesn't post her breakthrough win in 2006, finishing ninth in points with two top-five and eight top-10 finishes on the season. She makes the most noise off the track, announcing she'd drive for Andretti Green Racing in 2007.

04 Fernando Alonso dominates early.

The defending Formula 1 champion opens the year with a win at Bahrain and claims six of the first nine races, including four straight through June's Canadian Grand Prix. He cools off after that, though, and doesn't win again until Japan in October. Alonso's seventh win ties him with Michael Schumacher (through early October) as the two wage a close battle for the world championship.

03 **Stars miss the Chase**
Not only does defending Nextel Cup Series champion Tony Stewart miss the field for the Chase For The Nextel Cup, but so does Greg Biffle and Carl Edwards, who finished second and third in points in 2005, respectively. They aren't alone, either, as Ryan Newman, Kurt Busch, Jeremy Mayfield and the retired Rusty Wallace were in the field a year ago. Only Mark Martin, Jimmie Johnson and Matt Kenseth make the field in both '05 and '06.

02 **Michael Schumacher retires.**
The winningest driver in Formula 1 history, Schumacher steps out of his Ferrari for the final time after Sao Paulo. Entering the year's last race, he had 91 victories and 154 podiums finishes. A seven-time champion entering the season, how he fared at Sao Paulo would determine whether he added an eighth crown to his collection or would watch Fernando Alonso take the title for a second straight year.

01 **Stars make the Chase**
Jeff Gordon and Dale Earnhardt Jr. return to the Chase a year after their absence had many predicting the demise of the sport. In addition, Jeff Burton, Kevin Harvick, Denny Hamlin, Kasey Kahne and Kyle Busch each make the Chase for the first time.

NASCAR drivers who switched teams prior to 2006

Driver	2006 Team	2005 Team
Kurt Busch	Penske Racing South	Roush Racing
Jamie McMurray	Roush Racing	Chip Ganassi Racing
Bobby Labonte	Petty Enterprises	Joe Gibbs Racing
Ken Schrader	Wood Brothers Racing	BAM Racing
Sterling Marlin	MB2 Motorsports	Chip Ganassi Racing
Michael Waltrip	Waltrip-Jasper Racing	Dale Earnhardt Inc.
Jeff Green	Gene Haas	Petty Enterprises
Dave Blaney	Bill Davis Racing	Richard Childress Racing
Travis Kvapil	PPI Motorsports	Penske-Jasper Racing
Scott Wimmer	Morgan-McClure Motorsports	Bill Davis Racing
Scott Riggs	Evernham Motorsports	MB2 Motorsports

2005-2006
Season in Review

SPORTS ALMANAC

NASCAR RESULTS

Nextel Cup Series

Results of NASCAR Nextel Cup races from Nov. 6, 2005 through Oct. 22, 2006. **Note**: Earnings include bonus money. See *Updates* chapter (pages 969-972) for later results.

Late 2005

Date	Event	Location	Winner (Pos.)	Avg.mph	Earnings	Pole	Qual.mph
Nov. 6	Dickies 500	Ft. Worth	Carl Edwards (30)	151.055	$440,550	R. Newman	192.947
Nov. 13	Checker Auto Parts 500	Phoenix	Kyle Busch (15)	102.641	199,225	D. Hamlin	134.173
Nov. 20	Ford 400	Homestead	Greg Biffle (7)	131.431	308,675	C. Edwards	176.051

Winning cars (entire 2005 season): CHEVROLET (17)—Stewart 5, Johnson and Gordon 4, Ky. Busch 2, Earnhardt Jr. and Harvick; FORD (16)—Biffle 6, Edwards 4, Ku. Busch 3, Kenseth, Jarrett and Martin; DODGE (3)—Kahne, Mayfield and Newman.

2006 Season (through Oct. 22)

Date	Event	Location	Winner (Pos.)	Avg.mph	Earnings	Pole	Qual.mph
Feb. 19	**Daytona 500**	Daytona	Jimmie Johnson (9)	142.667	$1,505,120	J. Burton	189.151
Feb. 26	Auto Club 500	Los Angeles	Matt Kenseth (31)	147.852	324,991	Ku. Busch	187.086
Mar. 12	UAW-DaimlerChrysler 400	Las Vegas	Jimmie Johnson (3)	133.358	386,936	G. Biffle	172.403
Mar. 20	Golden Corral 500	Atlanta	Kasey Kahne (1)	144.098	197,664	K. Kahne	192.553
Mar. 26	Food City 500	Bristol	Kurt Busch (9)	79.427	175,858	T. Stewart	—**
Apr. 2	DirecTV 500	Martinsville	Tony Stewart (3)	72.741	220,786	J. Johnson	96.736
Apr. 9	Samsung/Radio Shack 500	Ft. Worth	Kasey Kahne (1)	137.943	530,164	K. Kahne	190.315
Apr. 22	Subway Fresh 500	Phoenix	Kevin Harvick (15)	107.063	228,486	Ky. Busch	133.745
Apr. 30	Aaron's 499	Talladega	Jimmie Johnson (16)	142.880	326,061	E. Sadler	188.511
May 6	Crown Royal 400	Richmond	Dale Earnhardt Jr. (10)	97.061	239,166	G. Biffle	127.395
May 13	Dodge Charger 500	Darlington	Greg Biffle (9)	135.127	290,175	K. Kahne	169.013
May 20@	Nextel All-Star Challenge	Charlotte	Jimmie Johnson (2)	103.294	1,055,007	K. Kahne	132.465
May 28	**Coca-Cola 600**	Charlotte	Kasey Kahne (9)	128.840	428,114	Scott Riggs	187.865
June 4	Neighborhood Excellence 400	Dover	Matt Kenseth (19)	109.865	323,591	R. Newman	154.633
June 11	Pocono 500	Pocono	Denny Hamlin (1)	131.656	220,100	D. Hamlin	169.639
June 18	3M Performance 400	Michigan	Kasey Kahne (1)	118.788	205,364	K. Kahne	185.644
June 25	Dodge/Save Mart 350	Sonoma	Jeff Gordon (11)	73.953	325,661	No. Busch	93.055
July 1	Pepsi 400	Daytona	Tony Stewart (2)	153.143	369,586	B. Said	186.143
July 9	USG Sheetrock 400	Chicago	Jeff Gordon (13)	132.077	327,761	J. Burton	181.647
July 16	Lenox Industrial Tools 300	Loudon	Kyle Busch (4)	101.384	242,175	R. Newman	129.683
July 23	Pennsylvania 500	Pocono	Denny Hamlin (1)	132.626	230,100	D. Hamlin	169.827
Aug. 6	**Allstate 400/Brickyard**	Indianapolis	Jimmie Johnson (5)	137.182	452,861	J. Burton	182.778
Aug. 13	AMD at The Glen	Watkins Glen	Kevin Harvick (7)	76.718	223,161	Ku. Busch	122.966
Aug. 20	GFS Marketplace 400	Michigan	Matt Kenseth (3)	135.097	221,091	J. Burton	187.936
Aug. 26	Sharpie 500	Bristol	Matt Kenseth (4)	90.025	336,516	Ku. Busch	124.906
Sept. 3	Sony HD 500	Los Angeles	Kasey Kahne (9)	144.462	279,214	Ku. Busch	184.540
Sept. 9	Chevy Rock & Roll 400	Richmond	Kevin Harvick (5)	101.342	234,136	D. Hamlin	127.986

— Chase for the Nextel Cup —

Date	Event	Location	Winner (Pos.)	Avg.mph	Earnings	Pole	Qual.mph
Sept. 17	Sylvania 300	Loudon	Kevin Harvick (1)	102.195	266,461	K. Harvick	132.282
Sept. 24	Dover 400	Dover	Jeff Burton (19)	111.966	230,370	J. Gordon	156.162
Oct. 1	Banquet 400	Kansas City	Tony Stewart (21)	121.753	346,361	K. Kahne	178.377
Oct. 8	**UAW-Ford 500**	Talladega	Brian Vickers (9)	157.602	228,850	D. Gilliland	191.712
Oct. 14	Bank of America 500	Charlotte	Kasey Kahne (9)	132.142	305,889	S. Riggs	191.469
Oct. 22	Subway 500	Martinsville	Jimmie Johnson (9)	70.446	191,886	Ku. Busch	97.568

@ A non-points exhibition event, formerly known as The Winston.

**Qualifying was canceled due to weather and the pole was awarded based on Owner points.

Winning Cars: CHEVROLET (20)—Johnson 5, Harvick 4, Stewart 3, J. Gordon and Hamlin 2, Burton, Ky. Busch, Earnhardt Jr., Vickers; DODGE (7)—Kahne 6, Ku. Busch; FORD (5)—Kenseth 4, Biffle.

Remaining Races (4): Bass Pro Shops MBNA 500 in Atlanta (Oct. 29); Dickies 500 in Fort Worth (Nov. 5); Checker Auto Parts 500 in Phoenix (Nov. 12); Ford 400 in Homestead (Nov. 19).

2006 Daytona 500

Date—Sunday, Feb. 19, 2006, at Daytona International Speedway.
Distance—500 miles; **Course**—2.5 miles; **Field**—43 cars; **Average speed**—142.667 mph; **Margin of victory**—under caution; **Time of race**—3 hours, 33 minutes, 26 seconds; **Caution flags**—11 for 39 laps; **Lead changes**—32 among 18 drivers; **Lap leaders**—Earnhardt Jr. (32), Kenseth (28), Johnson (24), Newman (23), Vickers (21), Stewart (20), Martin (19), Burton (18), Ky. Busch and E. Sadler (5), Biffle, Ku. Busch, Elliott, Harvick, J. Gordon, Kvapil, Lepage and McMurray (1). **Pole sitter**—Jeff Burton at 189.151 mph.

Attendance—200,000 (estimated). **Rating**—11.3/23 share (NBC). (r) indicates rookie driver.

	Driver	Start	Sponsor	Car	Laps	Ended	Earnings
1	Jimmie Johnson	9	Lowe's	Chevrolet	203	Running	$1,505,120
2	Casey Mears	14	Texaco/Halvoline	Dodge	203	Running	1,095,770
3	Ryan Newman	18	ALLTEL	Dodge	203	Running	796,116
4	Elliott Sadler	3	M&M's	Ford	203	Running	684,076
5	Tony Stewart	15	The Home Depot	Chevrolet	203	Running	537,944
6	r-Clint Bowyer	37	Jack Daniel's	Chevrolet	203	Running	411,683
7	Brian Vickers	35	GMAC	Chevrolet	203	Running	347,583
8	Dale Earnhardt Jr.	7	Budweiser	Chevrolet	203	Running	377,694
9	Ken Schrader	23	Little Debbie	Ford	203	Running	328,897
10	Dale Jarrett	25	UPS	Ford	203	Running	326,983
11	Kasey Kahne	27	Dodge Dealers/UAW	Dodge	203	Running	307,347
12	Mark Martin	10	AAA	Ford	203	Running	292,383
13	Robby Gordon	20	Jim Beam	Chevrolet	203	Running	269,558
14	Kevin Harvick	28	GM Goodwrench	Chevrolet	203	Running	302,244
15	Matt Kenseth	11	DeWalt Power Tools	Ford	203	Running	302,549
16	r-Martin Truex Jr.	19	Bass Pro Shops/Tracker	Chevrolet	203	Running	297,816
17	Terry Labonte	43	DLP HDTV/Tweeter	Chevrolet	203	Running	268,558
18	Michael Waltrip	30	NAPA Auto Parts	Dodge	203	Running	274,241
19	Bill Elliott	33	Ginn Clubs & Resorts	Chevrolet	203	Running	257,758
20	Kirk Shelmerdine	42	Apex Electric	Chevrolet	203	Running	272,008
21	r-Brent Sherman	29	Serta	Dodge	203	Running	274,766
22	Dave Blaney	34	Caterpillar	Dodge	203	Running	271,241
23	Kyle Busch	4	Kellogg's	Chevrolet	203	Running	281,833
24	Mike Wallace	24	Miccosukee Gaming & Resorts	Dodge	203	Running	266,533
25	Kevin Lepage	31	Amp Energy Drink	Ford	203	Running	254,683
26	Jeff Gordon	2	DuPont	Chevrolet	203	Running	334,879
27	Travis Kvapil	40	Tide	Chevrolet	203	Running	265,455
28	r-David Stremme	32	Lone Star Steakhouse/Saloon	Dodge	203	Running	263,358
29	r-Reed Sorenson	22	Target	Dodge	203	Running	262,908
30	r-Denny Hamlin	17	FedEx Express	Dodge	203	Running	254,833
31	Greg Biffle	16	National Guard	Ford	203	Running	258,758
32	Jeff Burton	1	Cingular Wireless	Chevrolet	202	Running	302,603
33	Joe Nemechek	38	U.S. Army	Chevrolet	200	Running	279,453
34	Sterling Marlin	39	Waste Management	Chevrolet	200	Running	248,713
35	Bobby Labonte	8	Cheerios/Betty Crocker	Dodge	197	Accident	294,674
36	Jeremy Mayfield	26	Dodge Dealers/UAW	Dodge	197	Running	278,049
37	Jamie McMurray	6	Crown Royal	Ford	196	Accident	287,183
38	Kurt Busch	13	Miller Lite	Dodge	187	Accident	280,366
39	Kyle Petty	12	Wells Fargo	Dodge	173	Running	256,833
40	Hermie Sadler	41	Aaron's	Ford	169	Engine	245,633
41	r-J.J. Yeley	36	Interstate Batteries	Chevrolet	157	Running	279,833
42	Jeff Green	21	Best Buy	Chevrolet	156	Running	253,153
43	Carl Edwards	5	Office Depot	Ford	78	Accident	269,882

Top 5 Finishing Order + Pole

2006 NEXTEL CUP SEASON (through Oct. 22)

No.	Event	Winner	2nd	3rd	4th	5th	Pole
1	Daytona 500	J. Johnson	C. Mears	R. Newman	E. Sadler	T. Stewart	J. Burton
2	Auto Club 500	M. Kenseth	J. Johnson	C. Edwards	K. Kahne	J. Burton	Ku. Busch
3	UAW-DaimerChrysler 400	J. Johnson	M. Kenseth	Ky. Busch	K. Kahne	J. Gordon	G. Biffle
4	Golden Corral 500	K. Kahne	M. Martin	D. Earnhardt Jr.	J. Gordon	T. Stewart	K. Kahne
5	Food City 500	Ku. Busch	K. Harvick	M. Kenseth	C. Edwards	B. Labonte	T. Stewart
6	DirecTV 500	T. Stewart	J. Gordon	J. Johnson	D. Earnhardt Jr.	Ky. Busch	J. Johnson
7	Samsung/RadioShack 500	K. Kahne	M. Kenseth	T. Stewart	D. Hamlin	K. Harvick	K. Kahne
8	Subway Fresh 500	K. Harvick	T. Stewart	M. Kenseth	C. Edwards	C. Bowyer	Ky. Busch

No.	Event	Winner	2nd	3rd	4th	5th	Pole
9	Aaron's 499	J. Johnson	T. Stewart	B. Vickers	J. Burton	J. McMurray	E. Sadler
10	Crown Royal 400	D. Earnhardt Jr.	D. Hamlin	K. Harvick	G. Biffle	Ky. Busch	G. Biffle
11	Dodge Charger 500	G. Biffle	J. Gordon	M. Kenseth	J. Johnson	D. Earnhardt Jr.	K. Kahne
12	Coca-Cola 600	K. Kahne	J. Johnson	C. Edwards	M. Martin	M. Kenseth	S. Riggs
13	Neighbor. Excellence 400	M. Kenseth	J. McMurray	K. Harvick	J. Burton	Ky. Busch	R. Newman
14	Pocono 500	D. Hamlin	Ku. Busch	T. Stewart	B. Vickers	M. Kenseth	D. Hamlin
15	3M Performance 400	K. Kahne	C. Edwards	D. Earnhardt Jr.	G. Biffle	R. Sorenson	K. Kahne
16	Dodge/Save Mart 350	J. Gordon	R. Newman	T. Labonte	G. Biffle	Ku. Busch	Ku. Busch
17	Pepsi 400	T. Stewart	Ky. Busch	Ku. Busch	B. Said	M. Kenseth	B. Said
18	USG Sheetrock 400	J. Gordon	J. Burton	Ky. Busch	K. Harvick	D. Earnhardt Jr.	J. Burton
19	Lenox Industrial Tools 300	Ky. Busch	C. Edwards	G. Biffle	M. Martin	K. Harvick	R. Newman
20	Pennsylvania 500	D. Hamlin	Ku. Busch	J. Gordon	B. Vickers	K. Harvick	D. Hamlin
21	Allstate 400 @ Brickyard	J. Johnson	M. Kenseth	K. Harvick	C. Bowyer	M. Martin	J. Burton
22	AMD at The Glen	K. Harvick	T. Stewart	J. McMurray	R. Gordon	C. Edwards	Ku. Busch
23	GFS Marketplace 400	M. Kenseth	J. Gordon	T. Stewart	K. Kahne	M. Martin	J. Burton
24	Sharpie 500	M. Kenseth	Ky. Busch	D. Earnhardt Jr.	S. Riggs	J. Gordon	Ku. Busch
25	Sony HD 500	K. Kahne	D. Earnhardt Jr.	C. Bowyer	C. Edwards	J. Gordon	Ku. Busch
26	Chevy Rock & Roll 400	K. Harvick	Ky. Busch	K. Kahne	D. Blaney	M. Martin	D. Hamlin

— Chase for the Nextel Cup —

No.	Event	Winner	2nd	3rd	4th	5th	Pole
27	Sylvania 300	K. Harvick	T. Stewart	J. Gordon	D. Hamlin	B. Vickers	K. Harvick
28	Dover 400	J. Burton	C. Edwards	J. Gordon	Ku. Busch	G. Biffle	J. Gordon
29	Banquet 400	T. Stewart	C. Mears	M. Martin	D. Jarrett	J. Burton	K. Kahne
30	UAW-Ford 500	B. Vickers	K. Kahne	Ku. Busch	M. Kenseth	M. Truex Jr.	D. Gilliland
31	Bank of America 500	K. Kahne	J. Johnson	J. Burton	D. Earnhardt Jr.	B. Labonte	S. Riggs
32	Subway 500	J. Johnson	D. Hamlin	B. Labonte	T. Stewart	J. Gordon	Ku. Busch

Chase for the Nextel Cup Standings

Official Top 10 NASCAR Nextel Cup point leaders for 2005 and unofficial leaders for 2006 as of Oct. 22 (with four races remaining). Points are awarded for all qualifying drivers (winner received 180) and lap leaders. Earnings include in-season bonuses. Listed are starts (Sts), top-5 finishes (1-2-3-4-5), poles won (PW) and points (Pts).

NASCAR conducted its first playoff system in 2004, known as the "Chase for the Nextel Cup." After the first 26 official races, the top 10 drivers in the point standings (plus anyone within 400 pts. of the leader) are eligible for the "chase" over the final ten races of the season. All drivers in the "chase" have their point totals adjusted, with the first-place driver beginning with 5,050 points, the second with 5,045 and so on in five-point increments. Drivers not in the top 10 still participate in the final ten races, but are not eligible for the championship.

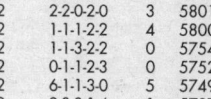

FINAL 2005

		Finishes		
	Sts	1-2-3-4-5	PW	Pts
1 Tony Stewart	36	5-6-1-2-3	3*	6533
2 Greg Biffle	36	6-3-4-1-1	0	6498
Carl Edwards	36	4-0-2-4-3	2	6498
4 Mark Martin	36	1-2-5-3-1	0	6428
5 Jimmie Johnson	36	4-2-3-1-3	1*	6406
6 Ryan Newman	36	1-0-1-2-4	8	6359
7 Matt Kenseth	36	1-2-5-1-3	2	6352
8 Rusty Wallace	36	0-1-1-2-4	0	6140
9 Jeremy Mayfield	36	1-0-0-3-0	0	6073
10 Kurt Busch	34	3-3-3-0-0	0	5974

2006 (through Race 32, Oct. 22)

		Finishes		
	Sts	1-2-3-4-5	PW	Pts
1 Matt Kenseth	32	4-3-3-1-3	0	5848
2 Kevin Harvick	32	4-1-3-1-3	1	5812
3 Jimmie Johnson	32	5-3-1-1-0	1	5807
4 Denny Hamlin	32	2-2-0-2-0	3	5801
5 Jeff Burton	32	1-1-1-2-2	4	5800
6 Dale Earnhardt Jr.	32	1-1-3-2-2	0	5754
7 Mark Martin	32	0-1-1-2-3	0	5752
8 Kasey Kahne	32	6-1-1-3-0	5	5749
9 Jeff Gordon	32	2-3-3-1-4	1	5707
10 Kyle Busch	32	1-3-2-0-3	1	5677

*Does not include poles awarded for being points leader when qualification was canceled.

Matt Kenseth

Kevin Harvick

Jimmie Johnson

Denny Hamlin

Nextel Cup Series (Cont.)

Money Leaders

	FINAL 2005	Earnings		2006 (through Oct. 22)	Earnings
1	Tony Stewart	$13,578,168	1	Jimmie Johnson	$7,961,020
2	Greg Biffle	8,354,052	2	Tony Stewart	6,149,740
3	Jimmie Johnson	8,336,712	3	Matt Kenseth	6,016,150
4	Jeff Gordon	7,930,830	4	Kasey Kahne	5,648,020
5	Mark Martin	7,731,468	5	Kevin Harvick	5,420,510
6	Kurt Busch	7,667,861	6	Jeff Gordon	5,372,880
7	Ryan Newman	7,259,518	7	Casey Mears	4,928,480
8	Matt Kenseth	7,034,134	8	Ryan Newman	4,881,160
9	Carl Edwards	6,893,157	9	Dale Earnhardt Jr.	4,834,710
10	Dale Earnhardt Jr.	6,284,577	10	Jeff Burton	4,562,950

Manufacturer's Standings

	FINAL 2005				2006 (through Oct. 22)		
	Make	Wins	Points		Make	Wins	Points
1	Chevrolet	17	259	1	Chevrolet	20	246
2	Ford	16	246	2	Dodge	7	185
3	Dodge	3	179	3	Ford	5	177

Busch Series

Results of NASCAR Busch Series races through Oct. 13, 2006. **Note**: Earnings include bonus money. See *Updates* chapter (pages 969-972) for later results.

2006 Season (through Oct. 13)

Date	Event	Location	Winner (Pos.)	Avg.mph	Earnings	Pole	Qual.mph
Feb. 18	Hershey's Kissables 300	Daytona	Tony Stewart (16)	125.159	$112,650	J.J. Yeley	183.094
Feb. 25	Stater Bros. 300	Los Angeles	Greg Biffle (3)	147.501	76,500	C. Edwards	182.588
Mar. 5	Telcel-Motorola 200	Mexico	Denny Hamlin (2)	67.528	132,400	B. Said	102.665
Mar. 11	Sam's Town 300	Las Vegas	Kasey Kahne (10)	125.158	94,050	M. Kenseth	169.827
Mar. 18	Nicorette 300	Atlanta	Jeff Burton (8)	127.984	48,540	Ky. Busch	189.707
Mar. 25	Sharpie Mini 300	Bristol	Kyle Busch (20)	71.606	51,625	K. Harvick	—**
Apr. 8	O'Reilly 300	Ft. Worth	Kurt Busch (7)	129.984	61,150	D. Hamlin	187.904
Apr. 15	Pepsi 300	Nashville	Kevin Harvick (7)	111.820	43,875	D. Hamlin	165.282
Apr. 21	Bashas' Supermarkets 200	Phoenix	Kevin Harvick (14)	92.250	67,450	J. Leffler	130.171
Apr. 29	Aaron's 312	Talladega	Martin Truex Jr. (12)	149.785	47,600	J.J. Yeley	184.751
May 5	Circuit City 250	Richmond	Kevin Harvick (10)	79.068	38,725	J. Leffler	126.334
May 12	Diamond Hill Plywood 200	Darlington	Denny Hamlin (1)	106.999	48,075	D. Hamlin	167.670
May 27	Carquest Auto Parts 300	Charlotte	Carl Edwards (9)	110.735	59,700	M. Kenseth	184.011
June 3	StonebridgeRacing.com 200	Dover	Jeff Burton (36)	103.791	40,750	K. Harvick	—**
June 10	Federated Auto Parts 300	Nashville	Carl Edwards (13)	123.511	48,425	T. Kluever	161.930
June 17	Meijer 300	Kentucky	David Gilliland (4)	116.004	106,800	D. Hamlin	177.772
June 24	AT&T 250	Milwaukee	Paul Menard (3)	82.042	60,977	A. Almirola%	122.320
June 30	Winn-Dixie 250	Daytona	Dale Earnhardt Jr. (9)	133.343	84,200	J.J. Yeley	183.509
July 8	USG Durock 300	Chicago	Casey Mears (7)	125.421	79,300	C. Edwards	176.528
July 15	New England 200	Loudon	Carl Edwards (9)	105.624	45,450	Ky. Busch	128.204
July 22	Goody's 250	Martinsville	Kevin Harvick (6)	61.139	74,925	C. Bowyer	95.951
July 29	Busch Silver Celebration 250	Gateway	Carl Edwards (2)	119.142	59,950	D. Hamlin	134.852
Aug. 5	Kroger 200	Indianapolis	Kevin Harvick (6)	81.478	42,075	D. Hamlin	110.442
Aug. 12	Zippo 200	Watkins Glen	Kurt Busch (1)	89.221	37,425	Ku. Busch	121.526
Aug. 19	Carfax 250	Michigan	Dale Earnhardt Jr. (20)	124.524	40,675	M. Martin	183.664
Aug. 25	Food City 250	Bristol	Matt Kenseth (4)	64.458	51,675	R. Newman	124.436
Sept. 2	Ameriquest 300	Los Angeles	Kasey Kahne (4)	137.160	90,825	C. Bowyer	179.399
Sept. 8	Emerson Radio 250	Richmond	Kevin Harvick (5)	85.627	39,025	J. Burton	126.357
Sept. 23	Dover 200	Dover	Clint Bowyer (16)	96.908	41,150	S. Riggs	154.799
Sept. 30	Yellow Transportation 300	Kansas City	Kevin Harvick (7)	111.559	78,800	M. Kenseth	173.723
Oct. 13	Dollar General 300	Charlotte	Dave Blaney (23)	106.999	72,125	C. Edwards	186.245

**Qualifying was canceled due to weather and the pole was awarded based on Owner points.
% Qualifying for Denny Hamlin.

Winning Cars: CHEVROLET (20)—Harvick 7, Burton, Earnhardt Jr. and Hamlin 2, Blaney, Bowyer, Ky. Busch, Gilliland, Menard, Stewart and Truex Jr.; FORD (6)—Edwards 4, Biffle and Kenseth; DODGE (5)—Ku. Busch and Kahne 2, Mears.
Remaining Races (4): Sam's Town 250 in Memphis (Oct. 28); O'Reilly Challenge in Fort Worth (Nov. 4); Arizona.Travel 200 in Phoenix (Nov. 11); Ford 300 in Homestead (Nov. 18).

Top 5 Finishing Order + Pole

2006 BUSCH SERIES SEASON (through Oct. 13)

No.	Event	Winner	2nd	3rd	4th	5th	Pole
1	Hershey's Kissables 300	T. Stewart	B. Lamar	C. Bowyer	J. Wood	K. Harvick	J.J. Yeley
2	Stater Bros. 300	G. Biffle	R. Newman	C. Edwards	J. Burton	J. McMurray	C. Edwards
3	Telcel-Motorola 200	D. Hamlin	B. Said	K. Harvick	J.J. Yeley	P. Menard	B. Said
4	Sam's Town 300	K. Kahne	M. Kenseth	K. Harvick	G. Biffle	C. Edwards	M. Kenseth
5	Nicorette 300	J. Burton	K. Kahne	G. Biffle	M. Kenseth	J.J. Yeley	Ky. Busch
6	Sharpie Mini 300	Ky. Busch	K. Harvick	M. Kenseth	D. Hamlin	C. Edwards	K. Harvick
7	O'Reilly 300	Ku. Busch	G. Biffle	C. Mears	Ky. Busch	M. Kenseth	D. Hamlin
8	Pepsi 300	K. Harvick	C. Bowyer	D. Hamlin	J.J. Yeley	C. Edwards	D. Hamlin
9	Bashas' Supermarkets 200	K. Harvick	R. Sorenson	C. Edwards	Ku. Busch	M. Martin	J. Leffler
10	Aaron's 312	M. Truex Jr.	K. Harvick	Ky. Busch	B. Vickers	C. Bowyer	J.J. Yeley
11	Circuit City 250	K. Harvick	J. Burton	M. Kenseth	G. Biffle	R. Newman	J. Leffler
12	Diamon Hill Plywood 200	D. Hamlin	M. Kenseth	J. McMurray	M. Martin	G. Biffle	D. Hamlin
13	Carquest Auto Parts 300	C. Edwards	Ku. Busch	J.J. Yeley	C. Mears	M. Truex Jr.	M. Kenseth
14	StonebridgeRacing.com 200	J. Burton	C. Edwards	Ku. Busch	C. Bowyer	R. Hornaday	K. Harvick
15	Federated Auto Parts 300	C. Edwards	C. Bowyer	K. Harvick	D. Hamlin	P. Menard	T. Kluever
16	Meijer 300	D. Gilliland	J.J. Yeley	D. Hamlin	M. Wallace	A. Lewis	D. Hamlin
17	AT&T 250	P. Menard	D. Hamlin	J.J. Yeley	J. Leffler	M. Wallace	D. Hamlin
18	Winn-Dixie 250	C. Earnhardt Jr.	B. Vickers	K. Harvick	J.J. Yeley	C. Edwards	J.J. Yeley
19	USG Durock 300	C. Mears	C. Edwards	J. Burton	K. Harvick	M. Kenseth	C. Edwards
20	New England 200	C. Edwards	K. Harvick	D. Hamlin	P. Menard	C. Bowyer	Ky. Busch
21	Goody's 250	K. Harvick	C. Bowyer	D. Hamlin	R. Sorenson	J. Sauter	C. Bowyer
22	Silver Celebration 250	C. Edwards	C. Bowyer	D. Hamlin	R. Sorenson	K. Harvick	D. Hamlin
23	Kroger 200	K. Harvick	R. Sorenson	J.J. Yeley	G. Biffle	J. Burton	D. Hamlin
24	Zippo 200	Ku. Busch	R. Gordon	J. McMurray	G. Biffle	J. Andretti	Ku. Busch
25	Carfax 250	D. Earnhardt Jr.	C. Mears	R. Gordon	M. Kenseth	M. Martin	M. Martin
26	Food City 250	M. Kenseth	K. Harvick	R. Hornaday	K. Kahne	J. Leffler	R. Newman
27	Ameriquest 300	K. Kahne	K. Harvick	M. Martin	P. Menard	A. Lewis	C. Bowyer
28	Emerson Radio 250	K. Harvick	G. Biffle	M. Kenseth	P. Menard	R. Sorenson	J. Burton
29	Dover 200	C. Bowyer	M. Kenseth	K. Harvick	J. McMurray	J. Leffler	S. Riggs
30	Yellow Transportation 300	K. Harvick	M. Kenseth	Ky. Busch	T. Stewart	C. Bowyer	M. Kenseth
31	Dollar General 300	D. Blaney	M. Waltrip	S. Compton	M. Kenseth	D. O'Quinn	C. Edwards

Busch Series Standings

Official Top 10 NASCAR Busch Series point leaders for 2005 and unofficial leaders for 2006 as of Oct. 13 (with five races remaining). Points are awarded for all qualifying drivers (winner received 180) and lap leaders. Earnings include in-season bonuses. Listed are starts (Sts), top-5 finishes (1-2-3-4-5), poles won (PW) and points (Pts). **Note:** as of Oct. 13, Kevin Harvick had already accumulated enough points to clinch the 2006 Busch Series championship.

FINAL 2005

		Sts	Finishes 1-2-3-4-5	PW	Pts
1	Martin Truex Jr.	35	6-2-2-3-2	3	4937
2	Clint Bowyer	35	2-4-2-2-2	2	4869
3	Carl Edwards	34	5-1-5-3-1	4	4601
4	Reed Sorenson	35	2-1-5-2-2	0	4453
5	Denny Hamlin	35	0-0-1-0-0	0	4143
6	Paul Menard	35	0-1-2-0-3	1	4101
7	Kenny Wallace	35	0-3-1-1-0	0	4068
8	David Green	35	1-0-0-2-0	0	3908
9	Jason Keller	35	0-0-0-1-0	0	3866
10	Greg Biffle	27	1-8-1-2-4	0	3865

2006 (through Oct. 13)

		Sts	Finishes 1-2-3-4-5	PW	Pts
1	Kevin Harvick	31	7-5-5-1-2	0	4948
2	Carl Edwards	31	4-2-2-0-4	3	4173
3	Clint Bowyer	31	1-4-1-1-3	2	4101
4	Denny Hamlin	31	2-1-5-2-0	6	4050
5	J.J. Yeley	31	0-1-3-3-1	3	3893
6	Kyle Busch	31	1-0-2-1-0	2	3680
7	Paul Menard	31	1-0-0-3-2	0	3672
8	Greg Biffle	27	1-2-1-4-1	0	3519
9	Johnny Sauter	31	0-0-0-0-1	0	3302
10	Reed Sorenson	30	0-2-0-2-1	0	3286

Money Leaders

FINAL 2005

		Earnings
1	Martin Truex Jr.	$3,143,692
2	Clint Bowyer	2,114,592
3	Reed Sorenson	1,800,178
4	Carl Edwards	1,759,782
5	Denny Hamlin	1,494,198
6	Paul Menard	1,310,560
7	Kenny Wallace	1,275,584
8	Johnny Sauter	1,260,880
9	David Green	1,252,051
10	Greg Biffle	1,212,275

2006 (through Oct. 13)

		Earnings
1	Kevin Harvick	$1,153,050
2	Johnny Sauter	1,065,410
3	Paul Menard	1,039,890
4	Denny Hamlin	973,789
5	Carl Edwards	943,685
6	Clint Bowyer	900,262
7	Burney Lamar	898,682
8	Jason Leffler	893,779
9	David Green	854,639
10	J.J. Yeley	846,329

Craftsman Truck Series

Results of NASCAR Craftsman Truck Series races through Oct. 21, 2006. **Note**: Earnings include bonus money. See *Updates* chapter (pages 969-972) for later results.

Date	Event	Location	Winner (Pos.)	Avg.mph	Earnings	Pole	Qual.mph
Feb. 17	GM Flex Fuel 250	Daytona	Mark Martin (1)	146.622	$88,850	M. Martin	178.628
Feb. 24	racetickets.com 200	Los Angeles	Mark Martin (7)	121.529	57,210	D. Reutimann	178.980
Mar. 17	John Deere 200	Atlanta	Todd Bodine (1)	133.388	59,425	T. Bodine	181.360
Apr. 1	Kroger 250	Martinsville	David Starr (15)	59.219	50,650	B. Hamilton Jr.	95.180
Apr. 29	Dodge Dealers Ram Tough 200	Gateway	Todd Bodine (3)	94.966	63,925	D. Ragan	—**
May 19	Quaker Steak & Lube 200	Charlotte	Kyle Busch (20)	124.845	54,200	M. Skinner	179.378
May 27	City of Mansfield 250	Mansfield	Ron Hornaday (17)	62.999	50,250	T. Bodine	—**
June 2	AAA Insurance 200	Dover	Mark Martin (13)	120.200	56,575	D. Reutimann	153.905
June 9	Sam's Town 400	Ft. Worth	Todd Bodine (6)	132.129	71,600	M. Skinner	183.206
June 17	Con-way Freight 200	Michigan	Johnny Benson (5)	116.534	56,600	M. Skinner	178.758
June 23	Toyota Tundra Milw. 200	Milwaukee	Johnny Benson (5)	85.673	55,500	R. Hornaday	122.021
July 1	O'Reilly Auto Parts 250	Kansas City	Terry Cook (5)	111.581	55,450	M. Skinner	171.772
July 8	Built Ford Tough 225	Kentucky	Ron Hornaday (22)	118.110	84,875	M. Ambrose	176.922
July 15	O'Reilly 200	Memphis	Jack Sprague (1)	88.367	59,175	J. Sprague	117.973
Aug. 4	Power Stroke Diesel 200	Indianapolis	Rick Crawford (3)	75.789	57,900	D. Ragan	109.838
Aug. 12	Toyota Tundra 200	Nashville	Johnny Benson (22)	108.704	55,675	E. Darnell	162.116
Aug. 23	O'Reilly 200	Bristol	Mark Martin (1)	72.081	47,350	M. Martin	125.248
Sept. 16	New Hampshire 200	Loudon	Johnny Benson (2)	92.323	59,375	M. Skinner	129.626
Sept. 23	Smith's Las Vegas 350	Las Vegas	Mike Skinner (1)	117.812	54,675	M. Skinner	178.065
Oct. 7	John Deere 250	Talladega	Mark Martin (5)	138.207	71,650	M. Martin	182.320
Oct. 21	Kroger 200	Martinsville	Jack Sprague (1)	60.172	50,900	J. Sprague	95.675

**Qualifying was canceled due to weather and the pole was awarded based on Owner points.

Winning Cars: TOYOTA (11)—Benson 4, Bodine 3, Sprague 2, Skinner and Starr; FORD (7)—Martin 5, Cook and Crawford; CHEVROLET (3)—Hornaday 2 and Ky. Busch.

Remaining Races (4): EasyCare Vehicle Service Contracts 200 in Atlanta (Oct. 28); Silverado 350 in Ft. Worth (Nov. 3); Phoenix 150 in Phoenix (Nov. 10); Ford 200 in Homestead (Nov. 17).

Top 5 Finishing Order + Pole

2006 CRAFTSMAN TRUCK SERIES SEASON (through Oct. 21)

No. Event	Winner	2nd	3rd	4th	5th	Pole
1 GM Flex Fuel 250	M. Martin	T. Bodine	T. Musgrave	M. Skinner	J. Sprague	M. Martin
2 racetickets.com 200	M. Martin	T. Bodine	T. Musgrave	D. Reutimann	J. Sprague	D. Reutimann
3 John Deere 200	T. Bodine	M. Martin	J. Benson	T. Musgrave	D. Reutimann	T. Bodine
4 Kroger 250	D. Starr	T. Musgrave	M. Crafton	M. Martin	M. Bliss	B. Hamilton Jr.
5 Ram Tough 200	T. Bodine	T. Musgrave	D. Reutimann	J. Sprague	J. Benson	D. Ragan
6 Quaker Steak & Lube 200	Ky. Busch	T. Cook	T. Bodine	T. Musgrave	R. Hornaday	M. Skinner
7 City of Mansfield 250	R. Hornaday	J. Sprague	D. Starr	J. Benson	J. Miller	T. Bodine
8 AAA Insurance 200	M. Martin	C. Edwards	T. Bodine	M. Bliss	D. Reutimann	D. Reutimann
9 Sam's Town 400	T. Bodine	M. Skinner	R. Crawford	D. Reutimann	J. Benson	M. Skinner
10 Con-way Freight 200	J. Benson	M. Martin	B. Labonte	T. Bodine	M. Crafton	M. Skinner
11 Toyota Tundra Milw. 200	J. Benson	M. Bliss	R. Hornaday	J. Sprague	D. Reutimann	R. Hornaday
12 O'Reilly Auto Parts 250	T. Cook	R. Crawford	M. Ambrose	B. Gaughan	M. Skinner	M. Skinner
13 Built Ford Tough 225	R. Hornaday	R. Crawford	B. Gaughan	J. Benson	D. Ragan	M. Ambrose
14 O'Reilly 200, Memphis	J. Sprague	E. Darnell	M. Crafton	R. Hornaday	M. Bliss	J. Sprague
15 Power Stroke Diesel 200	R. Crawford	D. Setzer	R. Hornaday	D. Starr	M. Bliss	D. Ragan
16 Toyota Tundra 200	J. Benson	J. Sprague	M. Ambrose	T. Musgrave	B. Gaughan	E. Darnell
17 O'Reilly 200, Bristol	M. Martin	T. Bodine	T. Musgrave	J. Benson	D. Starr	M. Martin
18 New Hampshire 200	J. Benson	M. Skinner	Ky. Busch	T. Bodine	D. Starr	M. Skinner
19 Smith's Las Vegas 350	M. Skinner	T. Musgrave	M. Bliss	J. Benson	R. Hornaday	M. Skinner
20 John Deere 250	M. Martin	M. Skinner	T. Musgrave	T. Bodine	A. Allmendinger	M. Martin
21 Kroger 200	J. Sprague	D. Starr	E. Darnell	M. Martin		

NASCAR veteran **Todd Bodine** recorded three Craftsman Truck Series wins through late October.

Doug Benc, Getty Images

Craftsman Truck Series Standings

Official Top 10 NASCAR Craftsman Truck Series point leaders for 2005 and unofficial leaders for 2006 as of Oct. 21 (with four races remaining). Points are awarded for all qualifying drivers (winner received 180) and lap leaders. Earnings include in-season bonuses. Listed are starts (Sts), top-5 finishes (1-2-3-4-5), poles won (PW) and points (Pts).

FINAL 2005

		Sts	Finishes 1-2-3-4-5	PW	Pts
1	Ted Musgrave	.25	1-2-3-2-3	1	3535
2	Dennis Setzer	.25	4-2-1-2-1	0	3480
3	Todd Bodine	.25	5-4-2-1-0	0	3462
4	Ron Hornaday	.25	1-1-2-2-1	1	3369
5	Mike Skinner	.25	2-1-0-5-1	7	3273
6	Bobby Hamilton	.25	2-1-2-0-1	1	3164
7	David Starr	.25	0-0-1-1-2	2	3148
8	Jack Sprague	.25	1-3-1-2-0	0	3137
9	Matt Crafton	.25	0-0-0-1-1	1	3095
10	Johnny Benson	.25	0-1-3-2-0	0	3076

2006 (through Oct. 21)

		Sts	Finishes 1-2-3-4-5	PW	Pts
1	Todd Bodine	.21	3-3-2-3-0	1	3197
2	Johnny Benson	.21	4-0-1-4-3	0	3118
3	David Reutimann	.21	0-0-1-2-3	2	2930
4	Ted Musgrave	.21	0-3-4-3-0	0	2923
5	Rick Crawford	.21	1-2-1-0-0	0	2846
6	David Starr	.21	1-1-1-1-2	0	2814
7	Ron Hornaday	.21	2-0-2-1-2	1	2789
8	Jack Sprague	.21	2-2-0-2-2	2	2728
9	Terry Cook	.21	1-1-0-0-0	0	2693
10	Mike Bliss	.21	0-1-1-1-3	0	2671

Money Leaders

FINAL 2005

		Earnings
1	Ted Musgrave	$880,553
2	Todd Bodine	805,908
3	Dennis Setzer	780,312
4	Mike Skinner	579,918
5	Bobby Hamilton	554,378
6	Ron Hornaday	527,787
7	Jack Sprague	459,350
8	Todd Kluever	443,641
9	Johnny Benson	399,499
10	David Starr	398,163

2006 (through Oct. 21)

		Earnings
1	Todd Bodine	$555,740
2	Johnny Benson	492,990
3	Mark Martin	426,800
4	Ted Musgrave	417,205
5	Mike Skinner	416,490
6	Jack Sprague	397,690
7	Rick Crawford	397,070
8	Ron Hornaday	393,820
9	David Starr	334,275
10	Terry Cook	325,905

INDY RACING LEAGUE RESULTS

IndyCar Series

Schedule and results of IndyCar Series events during the 2006 season.

2006 Season

Date	Event	Location	Winner (Pos.)	Time	Avg.mph	Pole	Qual.mph
Mar. 26	Toyota 300	Homestead	Dan Wheldon (6)	1:46:14.5286	167.730	S. Hornish Jr.	218.539
Apr. 2	Honda GP	St. Petersburg	Helio Castroneves (5)	1:56:57.5172	92.340	D. Franchitti	104.054
Apr. 22	Japan 300	Motegi	Helio Castroneves (1)	1:59:01.3704	153.248	H. Castroneves	—**
May 28	**Indianapolis 500**	Indianapolis	Sam Hornish Jr. (1)	3:10:58.7590	157.085	S. Hornish Jr.	228.985
June 4	Watkins Glen GP	Watkins Glen	Scott Dixon (4)	2:00:20.0224	92.418	H. Castroneves	—#
June 10	Bombardier Learjet 500	Ft. Worth	Helio Castroneves (3)	1:34:01.0482	185.710	S. Hornish Jr.	213.624
June 24	SunTrust Challenge	Richmond	Sam Hornish Jr. (3)	1:26:49.4669	129.572	H. Castroneves	—#
July 2	Kansas Lottery 300	Kansas City	Sam Hornish Jr. (2)	1:49:00.3423	167.331	D. Wheldon	213.536
July 15	Firestone 200	Nashville	Scott Dixon (3)	1:36:46.2751	161.205	D. Wheldon	203.293
July 23	A.J. Foyt 225	Milwaukee	Tony Kanaan (4)	1:42:37.8319	133.513	H. Castroneves	172.477
July 30	Firestone 400	Michigan	Helio Castroneves (1)	2:03:43.7441	193.972	H. Castroneves	216.777
Aug. 13	Meijer 300	Kentucky	Sam Hornish Jr. (2)	1:44:03.4120	170.676	H. Castroneves	218.328
Aug. 27	GP of Sonoma	Infineon	Marco Andretti (2)	1:58:05.5416	93.486	S. Dixon	107.484
Sept. 10	Peak Antifreeze 300	Chicago	Dan Wheldon (3)	1:33:37.2662	194.828	S. Hornish Jr.	215.319

**Qualifying was canceled due to inclement weather and the pole was awarded based on entrant points.
Qualifying was canceled due to inclement weather and the pole was awarded based on practice times.

Winning cars (Chassis/Engine): DALLARA/HONDA (12)—Castroneves and Hornish Jr. 4, Wheldon 2, Ma. Andretti, Dixon and Kanaan; PANOZ/HONDA (1)—Dixon.

Indy Racing League Results (Cont.)
90th Indianapolis 500

Date—Sunday, May 28, 2006, at Indianapolis Motor Speedway. **Distance**—500 miles; **Course**—2.5 mile oval; **Field**—33 cars; **Winner's average speed**—157.085 mph; **Margin of victory**—.0635 of a second; **Time of race**—3 hours, 10 minutes, 58.7590 seconds; **Caution flags**—5 for 44 laps; **Lead changes**—14 by 7 drivers; **Lap leaders**—Wheldon (148), Hornish Jr. (19), Kanaan (12), Castroneves (9), Dixon (6), Mi. Andretti (4), Ma. Andretti (2); **Pole Sitter**—Sam Hornish Jr. at 228.985 mph; **Attendance**—400,000 (est.); **TV Rating**—5.0/14 (ABC). Note that (r) indicates rookie driver.

	Driver	Start	Country	Car	Laps	Ended	Earnings
1	Sam Hornish Jr.	1	United States	D/H/F	200	Running	$1,744,855
2	r-Marco Andretti	9	United States	D/H/F	200	Running	688,505
3	Michael Andretti	13	United States	D/H/F	200	Running	455,105
4	Dan Wheldon	3	England	D/H/F	200	Running	571,405
5	Tony Kanaan	5	Brazil	D/H/F	200	Running	340,405
6	Scott Dixon	4	New Zealand	D/H/F	200	Running	361,005
7	Dario Franchitti	17	Scotland	D/H/F	200	Running	307,905
8	Danica Patrick	10	United States	P/H/F	200	Running	285,805
9	Scott Sharp	8	United States	D/H/F	200	Running	283,805
10	Vitor Meira	6	Brazil	D/H/F	200	Running	267,705
11	Ed Carpenter	12	United States	D/H/F	199	Running	264,805
12	Buddy Lazier	25	United States	D/H/F	199	Running	274,805
13	Eddie Cheever Jr.	19	United States	D/H/F	198	Running	255,805
14	Max Papis	18	Italy	D/H/F	197	Running	229,305
15	Kosuke Matsuura	7	Japan	D/H/F	196	Running	247,805
16	Roger Yasukawa	28	United States	P/H/F	194	Running	228,805
17	Jaques Lazier	24	United States	P/H/F	193	Running	219,305
18	Airton Dare	29	Brazil	P/H/F	193	Running	216,805
19	P.J. Jones	32	United States	P/H/F	189	Running	214,305
20	Bryan Herta	16	United States	D/H/F	188	Running	234,805
21	Felipe Giaffone	21	United States	D/H/F	177	Accident	227,305
22	r-Townsend Bell	15	United States	D/H/F	161	Suspension	204,555
23	Jeff Simmons	26	United States	D/H/F	152	Accident	222,305
24	Al Unser Jr.	27	United States	D/H/F	145	Accident	200,305
25	Helio Castroneves	2	Brazil	D/H/F	109	Accident	290,355
26	Buddy Rice	14	United States	P/H/F	108	Accident	224,805
27	Tomas Scheckter	11	South Africa	D/H/F	65	Accident	215,305
28	r-Arie Luyendyk Jr.	31	Netherlands	P/H/F	54	Handling	196,055
29	Stephan Gregoire	30	France	P/H/F	49	Handling	193,305
30	Larry Foyt	23	United States	D/H/F	43	Handling	192,305
31	r-Thiago Medeiros	33	Brazil	P/H/F	24	Electrical	227,555
32	Jeff Bucknum	22	United States	D/H/F	1	Accident	193,805
33	r-P.J. Chesson	20	United States	D/H/F	1	Accident	211,555

Car Legend: Chassis/Engine/Tires. D—Dallara, P—Panoz (chassis); H—Honda (engine); F—Firestone (tires).

Top 5 Finishing Order + Pole

2006 Season

No.	Event	Winner	2nd	3rd	4th	5th	Pole
1	Toyota 300	D. Wheldon	H. Castroneves	S. Hornish Jr.	D. Franchitti	S. Dixon	S. Hornish Jr.
2	Honda GP of St. Pete	H. Castroneves	S. Dixon	T. Kanaan	B. Herta	V. Meira	D. Franchitti
3	Japan 300	H. Castroneves	D. Wheldon	T. Kanaan	S. Hornish Jr.	B. Rice	H. Castroneves
4	Indianapolis 500	S. Hornish Jr.	Ma. Andretti	Mi. Andretti	D. Wheldon	T. Kanaan	S. Hornish Jr.
5	Watkins Glen GP	S. Dixon	V. Meira	R. Briscoe	B. Rice	F. Giaffone	H. Castroneves
6	Bombardier Learjet 500	H. Castroneves	S. Dixon	D. Wheldon	S. Hornish Jr.	S. Sharp	S. Hornish Jr.
7	SunTrust Challenge	S. Hornish Jr.	V. Meira	D. Franchitti	Ma. Andretti	S. Sharp	H. Castroneves
8	Kansas Lottery 300	S. Hornish Jr.	D. Wheldon	V. Meira	S. Dixon	T. Kanaan	D. Wheldon
9	Firestone 200	S. Dixon	D. Wheldon	V. Meira	D. Patrick	H. Castroneves	D. Wheldon
10	AJ Foyt 225	T. Kanaan	S. Hornish Jr.	T. Scheckter	D. Patrick	Ma. Andretti	H. Castroneves
11	Firestone 400	H. Castroneves	V. Meira	D. Wheldon	T. Kanaan	T. Scheckter	H. Castroneves
12	Meijer 300	S. Hornish Jr.	S. Dixon	H. Castroneves	D. Wheldon	T. Kanaan	H. Castroneves
13	GP of Sonoma	Ma. Andretti	D. Franchitti	V. Meira	S. Dixon	H. Castroneves	S. Dixon
14	Peak Antifreeze 300	D. Wheldon	S. Dixon	S. Hornish Jr.	H. Castroneves	E. Carpenter	S. Hornish Jr.

2006 Indy Racing League Point Standings & Money Leaders

Final top-10 Indy Racing League driver points leaders and money leaders for 2006. Points are awarded for places 1 to 33 (winner receives 50) and overall lap leader. Listed are starts (Sts), top-5 finishes, poles won (PW) and points (Pts).

Points

		Sts	Finishes 1-2-3-4-5	PW	Pts
1	Sam Hornish Jr.	14	4-1-2-2-0	4	475
2	Dan Wheldon	14	2-3-2-2-0	2	475
3	Helio Castroneves	14	4-1-1-1-2	6	473
4	Scott Dixon	14	2-4-0-2-1	1	460
5	Vitor Meira	14	0-3-3-0-1	0	411
6	Tony Kanaan	14	1-0-2-1-3	0	384
7	Marco Andretti	14	1-1-0-1-1	0	325
8	Dario Franchitti	13	0-1-1-1-0	1	311
9	Danica Patrick	14	0-0-0-2-0	0	302
10	Tomas Scheckter	14	0-0-1-0-1	0	298

Note: Hornish Jr. wins title with more wins than Wheldon.

Earnings

		Earnings
1	Sam Hornish Jr.	$2,775,205
2	Dan Wheldon	1,625,155
3	Helio Castroneves	1,401,455
4	Marco Andretti	1,377,705
5	Scott Dixon	1,369,605
6	Vitor Meira	1,160,305
7	Tony Kanaan	1,142,805
8	Dario Franchitti	987,105
9	Danica Patrick	923,005
10	Scott Sharp	895,705

CHAMP CAR RESULTS

Schedule and results of Champ Car World Series races from Nov. 6, 2005 through Oct. 22, 2006. Officially the "Bridgestone Presents The Champ Car World Series Powered By Ford" since the 2003 season.

Champ Car World Series

Late 2005

Date	Event	Location	Winner (Pos.)	Time	Avg.mph	Pole	Qual.mph
Nov. 6	Gran Premio Telmex-Tecate	Mexico City	Justin Wilson (1)	1:58:23.479	98.835	J. Wilson	115.813

Winning cars (entire 2005 season): FORD-COSWORTH/LOLA (13)—Bourdais 6, Tracy and Wilson 2, da Matta, Junqueira and Servia.

2006 Season (through Oct. 22)

Date	Event	Location	Winner (Pos.)	Time	Avg.mph	Pole	Qual.mph
Apr. 9	Toyota GP	Long Beach	Sebastien Bourdais (1)	1:40:07.670	87.268	S. Bourdais	105.924
May 13	GP of Houston	Houston	Sebastien Bourdais (5)	1:59.57.021	81.154	M. Dominguez	104.850
May 21	Tecate GP	Monterrey	Sebastien Bourdais (1)	1:39:50.252	96.099	S. Bourdais	103.401
June 4	Time Warner Cable Road Runner 225	Milwaukee	Sebastien Bourdais (1)	1:45:03.946	116.101	S. Bourdais	175.394
June 18	GP of Portland	Portland	A.J. Allmendinger (2)	1:48:32.853	113.989	B. Junqueira	122.684
June 25	GP of Cleveland pres. by U.S. Bank	Cleveland	A.J. Allmendinger (1)	2:00:22.619	99.722	A.J. Allmendinger	134.705
July 9	Molson GP of Toronto	Toronto	A.J. Allmendinger (2)	1:38:01.286	92.386	J. Wilson	108.590
July 23	West Edmonton Mall GP	Edmonton	Justin Wilson (3)	1:40:30.635	100.112	S. Bourdais	121.291
July 30	San Jose GP	San Jose	Sebastien Bourdais (1)	1:38:00.168	85.694	S. Bourdais	106.040
Aug. 13	GP of Denver	Denver	A.J. Allmendinger (2)	1:44:59.557	91.852	S. Bourdais	100.941
Aug. 28	GP de Montreal	Montreal	Sebastien Bourdais (1)	2:01:09.290	89.886	S. Bourdais	121.897
Sept. 24	GP of Road America	Elkhart Lake	A.J. Allmendinger (2)	1:54:43.700	107.967	D. Clarke	126.585
Oct. 22	Lexmark Indy 300	Queensland	Nelson Philippe (5)	1:50:50.985	89.259	W. Power	110.084

Winning cars (Engine/Chassis): FORD-COSWORTH XFE/LOLA (13)—Bourdais 6, Allmendinger 5, Philippe, Wilson.
Remaining Races (1): Grand Premio de Mexico in Mexico City (Nov. 12).

Top 5 Finishing Order + Pole

2006 SEASON (through Oct. 22)

No.	Event	Winner	2nd	3rd	4th	5th	Pole
1	GP of Long Beach	S. Bourdais	J. Wilson	A. Tagliani	M. Dominguez	C. da Matta	S. Bourdais
2	GP of Houston	S. Bourdais	P. Tracy	M. Dominguez	N. Philippe	J. Wilson	M. Dominguez
3	Tecate GP of Monterrey	S. Bourdais	J. Wilson	A. Allmendinger	P. Tracy	A. Tagliani	S. Bourdais
4	Road Runner 225	S. Bourdais	J. Wilson	N. Philippe	A. Allmendinger	O. Servia	S. Bourdais
5	GP of Portland	A. Allmendinger	J. Wilson	S. Bourdais	B. Junqueira	C. da Matta	B. Junqueira
6	GP of Cleveland	A. Allmendinger	B. Junqueira	O. Servia	A. Tagliani	J. Heylen	A. Allmendinger
7	Molson GP of Toronto	A. Allmendinger	N. Philippe	S. Bourdais	J. Wilson	C. da Matta	J. Wilson
8	GP of Edmonton	J. Wilson	S. Bourdais	A. Allmendinger	O. Servia	P. Tracy	S. Bourdais
9	GP of San Jose	S. Bourdais	C. da Matta	J. Wilson	N. Philippe	M. Dominguez	S. Bourdais
10	GP of Denver	A. Allmendinger	B. Junqueira	D. Clarke	W. Power	N. Philippe	S. Bourdais
11	GP de Montreal	S. Bourdais	P. Tracy	N. Philippe	D. Clarke	W. Power	S. Bourdais
12	GP of Road America	A. Allmendinger	B. Junqueira	S. Bourdais	O. Servia	J. Wilson	D. Clarke
13	Indy 300	N. Philippe	M. Dominguez	A. Tagliani	P. Tracy	A. Ranger	W. Power

Champ Car Results (Cont.)

Champ Car Point Standings

Official Top 10 Champ Car World Series point leaders for 2005 and unofficial leaders for 2006 (through Oct. 22). Points are awarded for places 1 to 20, for the pole winner at oval events, fastest driver on each day of qualifying at road/street events, lap leaders and most positions gained. Listed are starts (Sts), top-5 finishes, poles won (PW) and points (Pts). (r) indicates rookie driver. **Note:** With one race remaining in 2006, Sebastien Bourdais had already accumulated enough points to clinch his third straight Champ Car World Series title.

FINAL 2005

		Sts	Finishes 1-2-3-4-5	PW	Pts
1	Sebastien Bourdais	13	6-1-0-1-3	5	348
2	Oriol Servia	13	1-3-3-2-1	1	288
3	Justin Wilson	13	2-0-1-5-0	2	265
4	Paul Tracy	13	2-2-3-0-0	3	246
5	A.J. Allmendinger	13	0-4-1-0-1	1	227
6	Jimmy Vasser	13	0-0-2-1-1		217
7	Alex Tagliani	13	0-0-2-2-1	0	207
8	r-Timo Glock	13	0-1-0-0-1	0	202
9	Mario Dominguez	13	0-1-0-2-3		198
10	r-Andrew Ranger	13	0-1-0-0-0	0	140

2006 (through Oct. 22)

		Sts	Finishes 1-2-3-4-5	PW	Pts
1	Sebastien Bourdais	13	6-1-3-0-0	7	353
2	A.J. Allmendinger	13	5-4-2-1-0	1	285
3	Justin Wilson	12	1-0-1-1-2	1	269
4	Nelson Philippe	13	1-0-2-2-1	0	214
5	Paul Tracy	13	0-2-0-2-1	0	208
6	Mario Dominguez	13	0-1-1-1-1	1	197
7	Bruno Junqueira	13	0-3-0-1-0	1	196
8	r-Will Power	13	0-0-0-1-1	1	187
9	Andrew Ranger	13	0-0-0-0-1	0	184
10	Alex Tagliani	12	0-0-2-1-1	0	183

Money Leaders

FINAL 2005

		Earnings
1	Sebastien Bourdais	$668,500
2	Oriol Servia	500,000
3	Paul Tracy	473,500
4	Justin Wilson	466,000
5	A.J. Allmendinger	400,500
6	Jimmy Vasser	344,500
7	Alex Tagliani	340,500
8	Mario Dominguez	339,000
9	r-Timo Glock	323,000
10	Cristiano da Matta	300,000

2006 (through Oct. 22)

		Earnings
1	Sebastien Bourdais	$682,500
2	A.J. Allmendinger	585,500
3	Justin Wilson	467,500
4	Paul Tracy	386,500
5	Nelson Philippe	382,500
6	Bruno Junqueira	358,000
7	Mario Dominguez	340,500
8	Oriol Servia	306,000
9	Alex Tagliani	305,500
10	r-Will Power	299,000

FORMULA ONE RESULTS

Results of Formula One Grand Prix races in 2006

2006 Season

Date	Grand Prix	Location	Winner (Pos.)	Time	Avg.mph	Pole
Mar. 12	Bahrain	Bahrain	Fernando Alonso (4)	1:29:46.205	128.014	M. Schumacher
Mar. 19	Malaysian	Kuala Lumpur	Giancarlo Fisichella (1)	1:30:40.529	127.628	G. Fisichella
Apr. 2	Australian	Melbourne	Fernando Alonso (3)	1:34:27.870	119.297	J. Button
Apr. 23	San Marino	Imola	Michael Schumacher (1)	1:31:06.486	125.439	M. Schumacher
May 7	European	Nurburgring	Michael Schumacher (2)	1:35:58.765	119.975	F. Alonso
May 14	Spanish	Barcelona	Fernando Alonso (1)	1:26:21.759	131.777	F. Alonso
May 28	Monaco	Monte Carlo	Fernando Alonso (1)	1:43:43.116	93.645	F. Alonso
June 11	British	Silverstone	Fernando Alonso (1)	1:25:51.927	133.886	F. Alonso
June 25	Canadian	Montreal	Fernando Alonso (1)	1:34:37.308	120.280	F. Alonso
July 2	U.S.	Indianapolis	Michael Schumacher (1)	1:34:35.199	120.619	M. Schumacher
July 16	French	Magny-Cours	Michael Schumacher (1)	1:32:07.803	121.870	M. Schumacher
July 30	German	Hockenheim	Michael Schumacher (2)	1:27:51.693	130.039	K. Raikkonen
Aug. 6	Hungarian	Budapest	Jenson Button (14)	1:52:20.941	101.764	K. Raikkonen
Aug. 27	Turkish	Istanbul	Felipe Massa (1)	1:28:51.082	129.823	F. Massa
Sept. 10	Italian	Monza	Michael Schumacher (2)	1:14:51.975	152.742	K. Raikkonen
Oct. 1	Chinese	Shanghai	Michael Schumacher (6)	1:37:32.747	116.597	F. Alonso
Oct. 8	Japanese	Suzuka	Fernando Alonso (5)	1:23:53.413	136.690	F. Massa
Oct. 22	Brazil	Sao Paolo	Felipe Massa (1)	1:31:53.751	124.107	F. Massa

Winning Constructors: FERRARI (9)—M. Schumacher 7, Massa 2; RENAULT (8)—Alonso 7, Fisichella; HONDA (1)—Button.

Top 5 Finishing Order + Pole
2006 Season

No.	Event	Winner	2nd	3rd	4th	5th	Pole
1	Bahrain	F. Alonso	M. Schumacher	K. Raikkonen	J. Button	J. Montoya	M. Schumacher
2	Malaysian	G. Fisichella	F. Alonso	J. Button	J. Montoya	F. Massa	G. Fisichella
3	Australian	F. Alonso	K. Raikkonen	R. Schumacher	N. Heidfeld	G. Fisichella	J. Button
4	San Marino	M. Schumacher	F. Alonso	J. Montoya	F. Massa	K. Raikkonen	M. Schumacher
5	European	M. Schumacher	F. Alonso	F. Massa	K. Raikkonen	R. Barrichello	F. Alonso
6	Spanish	F. Alonso	M. Schumacher	G. Fisichella	F. Massa	K. Raikkonen	F. Alonso
7	Monaco	F. Alonso	J. Montoya	D. Coulthard	R. Barrichello	M. Schumacher	F. Alonso
8	British	F. Alonso	M. Schumacher	K. Raikkonen	G. Fisichella	F. Massa	F. Alonso
9	Canadian	F. Alonso	M. Schumacher	K. Raikkonen	G. Fisichella	F. Massa	F. Alonso
10	U.S.	M. Schumacher	F. Massa	G. Fisichella	J. Trulli	F. Alonso	M. Schumacher
11	French	M. Schumacher	F. Alonso	F. Massa	R. Schumacher	K. Raikkonen	M. Schumacher
12	German	M. Schumacher	F. Massa	K. Raikkonen	J. Button	F. Alonso	K. Raikkonen
13	Hungarian	J. Button	P. de la Rosa	N. Heidfeld	R. Barrichello	D. Coulthard	K. Raikkonen
14	Turkish	F. Massa	F. Alonso	M. Schumacher	J. Button	P. de la Rosa	F. Massa
15	Italian	M. Schumacher	K. Raikkonen	R. Kubica	G. Fisichella	J. Button	K. Raikkonen
16	Chinese	M. Schumacher	F. Alonso	G. Fisichella	J. Button	P. De La Rosa	F. Alonso
17	Japanese	F. Alonso	F. Massa	G. Fisichella	J. Button	K. Raikkonen	F. Massa
18	Brazil	F. Massa	F. Alonso	J. Button	M. Schumacher	K. Raikkonen	F. Massa

2006 Formula One Point Standings

Final top-10 Formula One World Drivers and Constructors Championship point leaders for 2006. Points are awarded for places 1 through 8 only (i.e., 10-8-6-5-4-3-2-1). Listed are starts (Sts), top-8 finishes, poles won (PW) and points (Pts). **Note:** Formula One does not keep money leader standings.

Drivers

		Sts	Finishes 1-2-3-4-5-6-7-8	PW	Pts
1	Fernando Alonso	18	7-7-0-0-2-0-0-0	6	134
2	Michael Schumacher	18	7-4-1-1-1-1-0-1	4	121
3	Felipe Massa	18	2-3-2-2-3-0-1-0	3	80
4	Giancarlo Fisichella	18	1-0-4-3-1-6-0-1	1	72
5	Kimi Raikkonen	18	0-2-4-1-5-0-0-0	3	65
6	Jenson Button	18	1-0-2-5-1-1-1-0	1	56
7	Rubens Barrichello	18	0-0-0-2-1-3-3-1	0	30
8	Juan Pablo Montoya	10	0-1-1-1-1-1-0-0	0	26
9	Nick Heidfeld	18	0-0-1-1-0-0-4-4	0	23
10	Ralf Schumacher	18	0-0-1-0-1-2-2-2	0	20

Constructors

		Pts
1	Renault	206
2	Ferrari	201
3	McLaren-Mercedes	110
4	Honda	86
5	Sauber-BMW	36
6	Toyota	35
7	RBR-Ferrari	16
8	Williams-Cosworth	11
9	STR-Cosworth	1

Major 2006 Endurance Races

24 Hours of Daytona
Jan. 28-29, at Daytona Beach, Fla.

Officially the Rolex 24 at Daytona and first held in 1962 (as a 3-hour race). An IMSA Camel GT race for exotic prototype sports cars and contested over a 3.56-mile road course at Daytona International Speedway. Listed are qualifying position, drivers, chassis and laps completed.

1 (2) Scott Dixon, Dan Wheldon and Casey Mears; LEXUS RILEY; 734 laps (2,613.0 miles) at 108.826 mph; margin of victory—1 lap.

2 (5) Oswaldo Negri, Mark Patterson and A.J. Allmendinger; LEXUS RILEY, 733 laps.

3 (1) Lucas Luhr, Patrick Long and Mike Rockenfeller; PORSCHE CRAWFORD, 731 laps.

4 (29) David Donohue, Darren Law and Sascha Maassen; PORSCHE FABCAR, 730 laps.

5 (30) Tracy Krohn, Nic Jonsson and Jorg Bergmeister; PONTIAC RILEY; 717 laps.

Top qualifier: Lucas Luhr, PORSCHE CRAWFORD, 123.220 mph.

24 Hours of Le Mans
June 17-18, at Le Mans, France

Officially the Le Mans Grand Prix d'Endurance and first held in 1923. Contested over the 8.48-mile Circuit de la Sarthe in Le Mans, France. Listed are qualifying position, drivers, car, and laps completed.

1 (2) Frank Biela, Emanuele Pirro and Marco Werner; AUDI R10; 380 laps (3,222.4 miles) at 133.849 mph.

2 (4) Eric Helary, Franck Montagny and Sebastien Loeb; PESCAROLO C60; 376 laps.

3 (1) Rinaldo Capello, Tom Kristensen and Allan McNish; AUDI R10; 367 laps.

4 (25) Oliver Gavin, Olivier Beretta and Jan Magnussen; CORVETTE C6-R; 355 laps.

5 (3) Nicolas Minassian, Emmanuel Collard and Erik Comas; PESCAROLO C60; 352 laps.

Top qualifier: Rinaldo Capello, AUDI R10, 3:30.466 (145.050 mph).

NHRA RESULTS

Winners of National Hot Rod Association's POWERade Drag Racing events in the Top Fuel, Funny Car, Pro Stock and Pro Stock Motorcycle divisions through Oct. 8, 2006. All times are based on two cars/motorcycles racing head-to-head from a standing start over a straight line, quarter-mile course. Differences in reaction time account for apparently faster losing times.

2006 Season (through Oct. 8)

Top Fuel

Date	Event	Winner	Time	MPH	2nd Place	Time	MPH
Feb. 12	Carquest Winternationals	Melanie Troxel	4.582	321.65	D. Baca	8.677	91.43
Feb. 26	Kragen Nationals	Rod Fuller	4.563	321.42	M. Troxel	4.589	318.92
Mar. 19	ACDelco Gatornationals	David Grubnic	4.943	317.90	M. Troxel	7.995	93.59
Apr. 2	O'Reilly Spring Nationals	Brandon Bernstein	4.534	329.83	M. Troxel	4.580	323.35
Apr. 9	SummitRacing.com Nationals	Melanie Troxel	4.837	285.65	D. Grubnic	4.987	319.60
Apr. 30	Thunder Valley Nationals	Doug Kalitta	4.537	331.53	R. Fuller	13.077	73.32
May 7	Southern Nationals	Doug Kalitta	4.469	327.59	M. Troxel	7.234	133.55
May 21	Pontiac Performance Nationals	Brandon Bernstein	4.531	329.58	C. McClenathan	5.784	147.47
May 28	O'Reilly Summer Nationals	Doug Kalitta*	4.675	310.98	B. Bernstein	4.691	307.09
June 11	Carquest Auto Parts Nationals	Doug Kalitta	4.503	330.23	M. Troxel	crossed centerline	
June 18	K&N Filters SuperNationals	Rod Fuller	4.692	314.24	L. Dixon	4.825	299.73
June 25	O'Reilly Midwest Nationals	Tony Schumacher	4.565	327.59	B. Bernstein	7.447	102.72
July 16	Mopar Mile-High Nationals	J.R. Todd	4.906	291.63	T. Schumacher	4.966	306.33
July 23	Schuck's Auto Supply Nationals	Tony Schumacher	4.690	321.96	D. Grubnic	4.761	316.75
July 30	Fram-Autolite Nationals	J.R. Todd	4.619	309.27	T. Schumacher	4.679	316.01
Aug. 13	Lucas Oil Nationals	Brandon Bernstein	4.510	329.34	T. Schumacher	7.098	126.52
Aug. 20	O'Reilly Mid-South Nationals	Doug Kalitta	4.604	313.95	H. Will	4.644	312.13
Sept. 4	Mac Tools U.S. Nationals	Tony Schumacher	4.505	325.22	B. Bernstein	4.602	274.00
Sept. 24	O'Reilly Fall Nationals	Brandon Bernstein	4.612	323.19	R. Fuller	6.611	122.60
Oct. 1	Toyo Tires Nationals	J.R. Todd	4.494	324.12	M. Troxel	4.538	324.28
Oct. 8	Torco Racing Fuels Nationals	Cory McClenathan	4.644	304.74	R. Fuller	5.926	262.49

Funny Car

Date	Event	Winner	Time	MPH	2nd Place	Time	MPH
Feb. 12	Carquest Winternationals	Robert Hight	4.763	317.94	R. Capps	4.775	323.50
Feb. 26	Kragen Nationals	Tommy Johnson Jr.	5.225	249.76	J. Force	5.705	294.69
Mar. 19	ACDelco Gatornationals	Ron Capps	4.860	316.78	J. Force	crossed centerline	
Apr. 2	O'Reilly Spring Nationals	Ron Capps	5.005	293.47	B. Gilbertson	22.001	72.65
Apr. 9	SummitRacing.com Nationals	Cruz Pedregon	5.417	266.16	R. Capps	6.474	229.31
Apr. 30	Thunder Valley Nationals	Ron Capps	4.793	319.52	J. Force	4.788	310.13
May 7	Southern Nationals	Tony Pedregon	4.740	325.69	R. Hight	4.738	321.81
May 21	Pontiac Performance Nationals	Tony Pedregon	4.923	313.66	W. Bazemore	6.368	146.34
May 28	O'Reilly Summer Nationals	Ron Capps	4.992	293.54	J. Force	6.162	150.53
June 11	Carquest Auto Parts Nationals	John Force	4.930	233.60	R. Hight	4.890	244.56
June 18	K&N Filters SuperNationals	Ron Capps	5.025	299.46*	G. Scelzi	5.012	301.81
June 25	O'Reilly Midwest Nationals	Tony Pedregon	4.859	320.43	J. Force	4.904	269.35
July 16	Mopar Mile-High Nationals	Gary Scelzi	5.132	301.94	C. Pedregon	5.820	202.82
July 23	Schuck's Auto Supply Nationals	Whit Bazemore	5.036	309.42	R. Capps	5.108	293.15
July 30	Fram-Autolite Nationals	Eric Medlen	4.854	316.30	T. Pedregon	5.021	271.62
Aug. 13	Lucas Oil Nationals	Tommy Johnson Jr.	4.741	321.73	G. Scelzi	7.387	112.75
Aug. 20	O'Reilly Mid-South Nationals	John Force	4.786	318.24	T. Pedregon	5.048	238.72
Sept. 4	Mac Tools U.S. Nationals	Robert Hight	4.737	328.38	W. Bazemore	4.756	327.82
Sept. 24	O'Reilly Fall Nationals	Robert Hight	4.796	322.73	M. Ashley	6.024	159.08
Oct. 1	Toyo Tires Nationals	Phil Burkhart	7.528	203.92	R. Hight		broke
Oct. 8	Torco Racing Fuels Nationals	Eric Medlen	4.814	301.00	C. Pedregon	4.873	297.02

Pro Stock Car

Date	Event	Winner	Time	MPH	2nd Place	Time	MPH
Feb. 12	Carquest Winternationals	Greg Anderson	6.665	207.75	M. Edwards	6.726	206.48
Feb. 26	Kragen Nationals	Warren Johnson	6.770	206.13	G. Anderson	13.881	61.48
Mar. 19	ACDelco Gatornationals	Tom Martino	6.677	205.80	E. Enders	18.482	41.77
Apr. 2	O'Reilly Spring Nationals	Mike Edwards	6.731	206.01	J. Yates	6.726	205.63
Apr. 9	SummitRacing.com Nationals	Kurt Johnson	6.842	202.42	D. Connolly	6.874	202.00
Apr. 30	Thunder Valley Nationals	Jason Line	6.716	205.35	G. Anderson	6.752	204.70
May 7	Southern Nationals	Dave Connolly	6.695	205.69	G. Stanfield	7.531	127.34
May 21	Pontiac Performance Nationals	Jim Yates	6.726	205.72	V. Gaines	6.687	206.23
May 28	O'Reilly Summer Nationals	Dave Connolly	6.844	201.34	K. Johnson	6.836	201.70
June 11	Carquest Auto Parts Nationals	Kurt Johnson	6.646	207.46	G. Anderson	6.641	208.10
June 18	K&N Filters SuperNationals	Jason Line	6.729	205.98	D. Connolly	6.739	206.45
June 25	O'Reilly Midwest Nationals	Mike Edwards	6.717	205.76	L. Morgan	6.715	205.82
July 16	Mopar Mile-High Nationals	Dave Connolly	7.173	193.07	J. Line	7.141	194.13
July 23	Schuck's Auto Supply Nationals	Allen Johnson	6.767	204.63	T. Martino	7.368	146.45

Date	Event	Winner	Time	MPH	2nd Place	Time	MPH
July 30	Fram-Autolite Nationals	Jason Line	6.672	207.15	V. Gaines	6.668	207.05
Aug. 13	Lucas Oil Nationals	Dave Connolly	6.743	204.17	J. Line	6.737	205.22
Aug. 20	O'Reilly Mid-South Nationals	Kurt Johnson	6.718	204.42	J. Line	6.703	205.38
Sept. 4	Mac Tools U.S. Nationals	Greg Anderson	6.687	206.83	D. Connolly		red-lighted
Sept. 24	O'Reilly Fall Nationals	Richie Stevens	6.693	204.60	M. Edwards	6.718	206.39
Oct. 1	Toyo Tires Nationals	Greg Anderson	6.656	208.36	G. Stanfield	7.742	120.23
Oct. 8	Torco Racing Fuels Nationals . . .	Jason Line	6.597	208.42	T. Martino	6.645	207.78

Pro Stock Motorcycles

Date	Event	Winner	Time	MPH	2nd Place	Time	MPH
Mar. 19	ACDelco Gatornationals	Angelle Sampey	7.138	187.73	A. Brown	7.134	186.72
Apr. 2	O'Reilly Spring Nationals	Angelle Sampey	7.144	190.11	A. Hines	7.200	188.04
May 7	Southern Nationals	Antron Brown	7.098	187.44	A. Hines	7.089	187.94
May 21	Pontiac Performance Nationals . . .	Angelle Sampey	7.046	188.52	M. Smith	7.122	185.31
June 11	Carquest Auto Parts Nationals	Ryan Schnitz	7.064	182.03	M. Guidera	7.105	185.08
June 18	K&N Filters SuperNationals	Matt Smith	7.111	185.38	K. Stoffer	7.234	186.12
June 25	O'Reilly Midwest Nationals	Chip Ellis	7.153	183.84	M. Phillips	7.298	184.83
July 16	Mopar Mile-High Nationals	Andrew Hines	7.435	179.97	M. Guidera	7.566	176.63
July 30	Fram-Autolite Nationals	Chip Ellis	8.863	88.41	A. Brown	7.067	188.04
Aug. 13	Lucas Oil Nationals	Antron Brown	7.108	186.85	S. Johnson	7.159	187.60
Aug. 20	O'Reilly Mid-South Nationals	Andrew Hines	9.085	96.61	A. Brown		red-lighted
Sept. 4	Mac Tools U.S. Nationals	Matt Smith	7.222	176.95	A. Sampey		red-lighted
Oct. 1	Toyo Tires Nationals	Karen Stoffer	7.097	187.94	G. Scali	8.105	121.86

Remaining Races (2): ACDelco Las Vegas Nationals (Oct. 29); Automobile Club of Southern California Finals in Pomona (Nov. 12).

2006 NHRA POWERade Point Standings (through Oct. 8)

Top Fuel

		Points
1	Doug Kalitta	1515
2	Brandon Bernstein	1432
3	Tony Schumacher	1426
4	Melanie Troxel	1343
5	Rod Fuller	1259
6	David Grubnic	1199
7	Larry Dixon	1066
8	Morgan Lucas	979
9	Cory McClenathan	970
10	J.R. Todd	956

Funny Car

		Points
1	John Force	1463
2	Ron Capps	1417
3	Robert Hight	1409
4	Eric Medlen	1297
5	Tony Pedregon	1265
6	Tommy Johnson	1176
7	Gary Scelzi	1140
8	Whit Bazemore	956
9	Cruz Pedregon	936
10	Phil Burkhart	930

Pro Stock Car

		Points
1	Jason Line	1591
2	Greg Anderson	1472
3	Dave Connolly	1323
4	Mike Edwards	1180
5	Kurt Johnson	1163
6	Allen Johnson	1105
7	Jim Yates	1074
8	Greg Stanfield	1009
9	Larry Morgan	959
10	V. Gaines	947

Pro Stock Motorcycle

		Points			Points
1	Antron Brown	971	6	Matt Smith	731
2	Andrew Hines	944	7	Ryan Schnitz	666
3	Angelle Sampey	907	8	Tom Bradford	599
4	Chip Ellis	825	9	Geno Scali	581
5	Karen Stoffer	752	10	Matt Guidera	557

2006 AMA Motocross/Supercross
Final Championship Point Standings

Motocross

		Points
1	Ricky Carmichael	539
2	Kevin Windham	407
3	David Millsaps	400
4	James Stewart	381
5	Travis Preston	334
6	Chad Reed	333
7	David Vuillemin	314
8	Nick Wey	303
9	Timmy Ferry	265
10	Joshua Summey	181

Motocross Lites

		Points
1	Ryan Villopoto	483
2	Mike Alessi	448
3	Joshua Grant	372
4	Andrew Short	359
5	Brett Metcalfe	335
6	Broc Hepler	293
7	Andrew McFarlane	281
8	Nathan Ramsey	195
	Matthew Goerke	195
10	Troy Adams	191

Supercross

		Points
1	Ricky Carmichael	338
2	James Stewart	336
	Chad Reed	336
4	Ivan Tedesco	255
5	Nick Wey	249
6	Michael Byrne	228
7	Travis Preston	207
8	Ernesto Fonseca	125
9	Ryan Clark	118
10	Mike LaRocco	108
	Timmy Ferry	108

1909-2006
Through the Years

SPORTS ALMANAC

NASCAR CIRCUIT

Daytona 500

Held over 200 laps on 2.5-mile oval at Daytona International Speedway in Daytona Beach, Fla. First race in 1959, although stock car racing at Daytona dates back to 1936. Winners who started from pole position are in **bold** type.

Multiple winners: Richard Petty (7); Cale Yarborough (4); Bobby Allison, Jeff Gordon and Dale Jarrett (3); Bill Elliott, Sterling Marlin and Michael Waltrip (2). **Multiple poles:** Buddy Baker and Cale Yarborough (4); Bill Elliott, Dale Jarrett, Fireball Roberts and Ken Schrader (3); Donnie Allison (2).

Year	Winner	Car	Owner	MPH	Pole Sitter	MPH
1959	Lee Petty	Oldsmobile	Petty Enterprises	135.521	Bob Welborn	140.121
1960	Junior Johnson	Chevrolet	Ray Fox	124.740	Cotton Owens	149.892
1961	Marvin Panch	Pontiac	Smokey Yunick	149.601	Fireball Roberts	155.709
1962	**Fireball Roberts**	Pontiac	Smokey Yunick	152.529	Fireball Roberts	156.999
1963	Tiny Lund	Ford	Wood Brothers	151.566	Fireball Roberts	160.943
1964	Richard Petty	Plymouth	Petty Enterprises	154.334	Paul Goldsmith	174.910
1965-a	Fred Lorenzen	Ford	Holman-Moody	141.539	Darel Dieringer	171.151
1966-b	**Richard Petty**	Plymouth	Petty Enterprises	160.627	Richard Petty	175.165
1967	Mario Andretti	Ford	Holman-Moody	149.926	Curtis Turner	180.831
1968	**Cale Yarborough**	Mercury	Wood Brothers	143.251	Cale Yarborough	189.222
1969	Lee Roy Yarbrough	Ford	Junior Johnson	157.950	Buddy Baker	188.901
1970	Pete Hamilton	Plymouth	Petty Enterprises	149.601	Cale Yarborough	194.015
1971	Richard Petty	Plymouth	Petty Enterprises	144.462	A.J. Foyt	182.744
1972	A.J. Foyt	Mercury	Wood Brothers	161.550	Bobby Isaac	186.632
1973	Richard Petty	Dodge	Petty Enterprises	157.205	Buddy Baker	185.662
1974-c	Richard Petty	Dodge	Petty Enterprises	140.894	David Pearson	185.017
1975	Benny Parsons	Chevrolet	L.G. DeWitt	153.649	Donnie Allison	185.827
1976	David Pearson	Mercury	Wood Brothers	152.181	Ramo Stott	183.456
1977	Cale Yarborough	Chevrolet	Junior Johnson	153.218	Donnie Allison	188.048
1978	Bobby Allison	Ford	Bud Moore	159.730	Cale Yarborough	187.536
1979	Richard Petty	Oldsmobile	Petty Enterprises	143.977	Buddy Baker	196.049
1980	**Buddy Baker**	Oldsmobile	Ranier Racing	177.602*	Buddy Baker	194.099
1981	Richard Petty	Buick	Petty Enterprises	169.651	Bobby Allison	194.624
1982	Bobby Allison	Buick	DiGard Racing	153.991	Benny Parsons	196.317
1983	Cale Yarborough	Pontiac	Ranier Racing	155.979	Ricky Rudd	198.864
1984	**Cale Yarborough**	Chevrolet	Ranier Racing	150.994	Cale Yarborough	201.848
1985	**Bill Elliott**	Ford	Melling Racing	172.265	Bill Elliott	205.114
1986	Geoff Bodine	Chevrolet	Hendrick Motorsports	148.124	Bill Elliott	205.039
1987	**Bill Elliott**	Ford	Melling Racing	176.263	Bill Elliott	210.364†
1988	Bobby Allison	Buick	Stavola Brothers	137.531	Ken Schrader	198.823
1989	Darrell Waltrip	Chevrolet	Hendrick Motorsports	148.466	Ken Schrader	196.996
1990	Derrike Cope	Chevrolet	Bob Whitcomb	165.761	Ken Schrader	196.515
1991	Ernie Irvan	Chevrolet	Morgan-McClure	148.148	Davey Allison	195.955
1992	Davey Allison	Ford	Robert Yates	160.256	Sterling Martin	192.213
1993	Dale Jarrett	Chevrolet	Joe Gibbs Racing	154.972	Kyle Petty	189.426
1994	Sterling Marlin	Chevrolet	Morgan-McClure	156.931	Loy Allen	190.158
1995	Sterling Marlin	Chevrolet	Morgan-McClure	141.710	Dale Jarrett	193.498
1996	Dale Jarrett	Ford	Robert Yates	154.308	Dale Earnhardt	189.510
1997	Jeff Gordon	Chevrolet	Hendrick Motorsports	148.295	Mike Skinner	189.813
1998	Dale Earnhardt	Chevrolet	Richard Childress	172.712	Bobby Labonte	192.415
1999	**Jeff Gordon**	Chevrolet	Hendrick Motorsports	161.551	Jeff Gordon	195.067
2000	**Dale Jarrett**	Ford	Robert Yates	155.669	Dale Jarrett	191.091
2001	Michael Waltrip	Chevrolet	Dale Earnhardt, Inc.	161.783	Bill Elliott	183.565
2002	Ward Burton	Dodge	Bill Davis	142.971	Jimmie Johnson	185.831
2003-d	Michael Waltrip	Chevrolet	Dale Earnhardt, Inc.	133.870	Jeff Green	186.606
2004	Dale Earnhardt Jr.	Chevrolet	Dale Earnhardt, Inc.	156.345	Greg Biffle	188.387
2005	Jeff Gordon	Chevrolet	Hendrick Motorsports	135.173	Dale Jarrett	188.312
2006	Jimmie Johnson	Chevrolet	Hendrick Motorsports	142.667	Jeff Burton	189.151

*Track and race record for winning speed. †Track and race record for qualifying speed.

Notes: a—rain shortened 1965 race to 332.5 miles; **b**—rain shortened 1966 race to 495 miles; **c**—in 1974, race shortened 50 miles due to energy crisis; **d**—rain shortened 2003 race to 272.5 miles. **Also:** Pole sitters determined by pole qualifying race (1959-65); by two-lap average (1966-68); by fastest single lap (since 1969).

UAW-Ford 500

Held over 188 laps on 2.66-mile tri-oval at Talladega Superspeedway in Talladega, Ala.

Previously known as Winston 500 (1970-93, 1997-2000), Winston Select 500 (1994-96) and EA Sports 500 (2001-04). It became the UAW-Ford 500 in 2005. Winners who started from pole position are in **bold** type.

Multiple winners: Dale Earnhardt (4); Bobby Allison, Davey Allison, Buddy Baker, Dale Earnhardt Jr. and David Pearson (3); Dale Jarrett, Mark Martin, Darrell Waltrip and Cale Yarborough (2).

Year		Year		Year		Year	
1970	Pete Hamilton	1980	Buddy Baker	1990	**Dale Earnhardt**	2000	Dale Earnhardt
1971	**Donnie Allison**	1981	**Bobby Allison**	1991	Harry Gant	2001	Dale Earnhardt Jr.
1972	David Pearson	1982	Darrell Waltrip	1992	Davey Allison	2002	Dale Earnhardt Jr.
1973	David Pearson	1983	Richard Petty	1993	Ernie Irvan	2003	Michael Waltrip
1974	**David Pearson**	1984	**Cale Yarborough**	1994	Dale Earnhardt	2004	Dale Earnhardt Jr.
1975	**Buddy Baker**	1985	**Bill Elliott**	1995	**Mark Martin**	2005	Dale Jarrett
1976	Buddy Baker	1986	Bobby Allison	1996	Sterling Marlin	2006	Brian Vickers
1977	Darrell Waltrip	1987	Davey Allison	1997	Mark Martin		
1978	**Cale Yarborough**	1988	Phil Parsons	1998	Dale Jarrett		
1979	Bobby Allison	1989	Davey Allison	1999	Dale Earnhardt		

Coca-Cola 600

Held over 400 laps on 1.5-mile oval at Lowe's Motor Speedway in Concord, N.C.

Previously known as World 600 (1960-85). It has been Coca-Cola 600 since 1986 (in 2002, sponsors announced a one-time-only name change to The Coca-Cola Racing Family 600). Winners who started from pole position are in **bold** type.

Multiple winners: Darrell Waltrip (5); Bobby Allison, Buddy Baker, Dale Earnhardt, Jeff Gordon, Jimmie Johnson and David Pearson (3); Neil Bonnett, Jeff Burton, Fred Lorenzen, Jim Paschal and Richard Petty (2).

Year		Year		Year		Year	
1960	Joe Lee Johnson	1972	Buddy Baker	1984	Bobby Allison	1996	Dale Jarrett
1961	David Pearson	1973	**Buddy Baker**	1985	Darrell Waltrip	1997	**Jeff Gordon***
1962	Nelson Stacy	1974	**David Pearson**	1986	Dale Earnhardt	1998	**Jeff Gordon**
1963	Fred Lorenzen	1975	Richard Petty	1987	Kyle Petty	1999	Jeff Burton
1964	Jim Paschal	1976	**David Pearson**	1988	Darrell Waltrip	2000	Matt Kenseth
1965	**Fred Lorenzen**	1977	Richard Petty	1989	Darrell Waltrip	2001	Jeff Burton
1966	Marvin Panch	1978	Darrell Waltrip	1990	Rusty Wallace	2002	Mark Martin
1967	Jim Paschal	1979	Darrell Waltrip	1991	Davey Allison	2003	Jimmie Johnson*
1968	Buddy Baker*	1980	Benny Parsons	1992	Dale Earnhardt	2004	**Jimmie Johnson**
1969	Lee Roy Yarbrough	1981	Bobby Allison	1993	Dale Earnhardt	2005	Jimmie Johnson
1970	Donnie Allison	1982	Neil Bonnett	1994	**Jeff Gordon**	2006	Kasey Kahne
1971	Bobby Allison	1983	Neil Bonnett	1995	Bobby Labonte		

* rain-shortened.

Allstate 400 at the Brickyard

Held over 160 laps at 2.5-mile Indianapolis Motor Speedway in Indianapolis, Ind.

Previously known as Brickyard 400 (1994-2004). Winners who started from pole position are in **bold** type.

Multiple winners: Jeff Gordon (4); Dale Jarrett (2).

Year		Year		Year		Year		Year	
1994	Jeff Gordon	1997	Ricky Rudd	2000	Bobby Labonte	2003	**Kevin Harvick**	2006	Jimmie Johnson
1995	Dale Earnhardt	1998	Jeff Gordon	2001	Jeff Gordon	2004	Jeff Gordon		
1996	Dale Jarrett	1999	Dale Jarrett	2002	Bill Elliott	2005	Tony Stewart		

Mountain Dew Southern 500

Final race held in 2004. Held over 367 laps on 1.366-mile oval at Darlington International Raceway in Darlington, S.C.

Previously known as Southern 500 (1950-88); Heinz 500 (1989-91); and Pepsi Southern 500 (1998-2000). It was the Mountain Dew Southern 500 from 1992-97, and 2001-04. Winners who started from pole position are in **bold** type.

Multiple winners: Jeff Gordon and Cale Yarborough (5); Bobby Allison (4); Buck Baker, Dale Earnhardt, Bill Elliott, David Pearson and Herb Thomas (3); Harry Gant and Fireball Roberts (2).

Year		Year		Year		Year	
1950	Johnny Mantz	1964	Buck Baker	1978	Cale Yarborough	1992	Darrell Waltrip*
1951	Herb Thomas	1965	Ned Jarrett	1979	David Pearson	1993	Mark Martin*
1952	**Fonty Flock**	1966	Darel Dieringer	1980	Terry Labonte	1994	Bill Elliott
1953	Buck Baker	1967	**Richard Petty**	1981	Neil Bonnett	1995	Jeff Gordon
1954	Herb Thomas	1968	Cale Yarborough	1982	Cale Yarborough	1996	Jeff Gordon
1955	Herb Thomas	1969	Lee Roy Yarbrough*	1983	Bobby Allison	1997	Jeff Gordon*
1956	Curtis Turner	1970	Buddy Baker	1984	**Harry Gant**	1998	Jeff Gordon
1957	Speedy Thompson	1971	**Bobby Allison**	1985	**Bill Elliott**	1999	Jeff Burton*
1958	Fireball Roberts	1972	**Bobby Allison**	1986	**Tim Richmond**	2000	Bobby Labonte*
1959	Jim Reed	1973	Cale Yarborough	1987	Dale Earnhardt*	2001	Ward Burton
1960	Buck Baker	1974	Cale Yarborough	1988	**Bill Elliott**	2002	Jeff Gordon
1961	Nelson Stacy	1975	Bobby Allison	1989	Dale Earnhardt	2003	Terry Labonte
1962	Larry Frank	1976	**David Pearson**	1990	**Dale Earnhardt**	2004	Jimmie Johnson
1963	Fireball Roberts	1977	David Pearson	1991	Harry Gant		* rain-shortened.

NASCAR Circuit (Cont.)
Nextel Cup Series Champions

Originally the Grand National Championship, 1949-70, then the Winston Cup Series Championship, 1971-2003, and based on official NASCAR records. Drivers listed since 2004 are winners of the Chase for the Nextel Cup, NASCAR's first playoff series run over the final ten races of the season. Note that earnings totals include bonus awards.

Multiple winners: (drivers) Dale Earnhardt and Richard Petty (7); Jeff Gordon (4); David Pearson, Lee Petty, Darrell Waltrip and Cale Yarborough (3); Buck Baker, Tim Flock, Ned Jarrett, Terry Labonte, Tony Stewart, Herb Thomas and Joe Weatherly (2).

Multiple winners: (cars) Chevrolet (23); Ford (7); Plymouth (5); Dodge, Oldsmobile and Pontiac (4); Buick and Hudson (3); and Chrysler (2).

Year	Car #	Driver	Car	Owner	Sts	Wins	Poles	Earnings
1949	22	Red Byron	Oldsmobile	Raymond Parks	5	2	1	$5,800
1950	60	Bill Rexford	Oldsmobile	Julian Buesink	17	1	0	6,175
1951	92	Herb Thomas	Hudson	Herb Thomas	34	7	4	18,200
1952	91	Tim Flock	Hudson	Ted Chester	33	8	4	20,210
1953	92	Herb Thomas	Hudson	Herb Thomas	37	11	10	27,300
1954	42	Lee Petty	Chrysler	Herb Thomas	34	7	3	26,706
1955	300	Tim Flock	Chrysler	Carl Kiekhaefer	38	18	19	33,750
1956	300B	Buck Baker	Chevrolet	Carl Kiekhaefer	48	14	12	29,790
1957	87	Buck Baker	Chevrolet	Buck Baker	40	10	5	24,712
1958	42	Lee Petty	Oldsmobile	Petty Enterprises	49	7	4	20,600
1959	42	Lee Petty	Plymouth	Petty Enterprises	42	10	2	45,570
1960	4	Rex White	Chevrolet	White-Clements	40	6	3	45,260
1961	11	Ned Jarrett	Chevrolet	W.G. Holloway Jr.	46	1	4	27,285
1962	8	Joe Weatherly	Pontiac	Bud Moore	52	9	6	56,110
1963	8	Joe Weatherly	Mercury	Wood Brothers	53	3	6	58,110
1964	43	Richard Petty	Plymouth	Petty Enterprises	61	9	8	98,810
1965	11	Ned Jarrett	Ford	Bondy Long	54	13	9	77,960
1966	6	David Pearson	Dodge	Cotton Owens	42	14	7	59,205
1967	43	Richard Petty	Plymouth	Petty Enterprises	48	27	18	130,275
1968	17	David Pearson	Ford	Holman-Moody	48	16	12	118,842
1969	17	David Pearson	Ford	Holman-Moody	51	11	14	183,700
1970	71	Bobby Isaac	Dodge	Nord Krauskopf	47	11	13	121,470
1971	43	Richard Petty	Plymouth	Petty Enterprises	46	21	9	309,225
1972	43	Richard Petty	Plymouth	Petty Enterprises	31	8	3	227,015
1973	72	Benny Parsons	Chevrolet	L.G. DeWitt	28	1	0	114,345
1974	43	Richard Petty	Dodge	Petty Enterprises	30	10	7	299,175
1975	43	Richard Petty	Dodge	Petty Enterprises	30	13	3	378,865
1976	11	Cale Yarborough	Chevrolet	Junior Johnson	30	9	2	387,173
1977	11	Cale Yarborough	Chevrolet	Junior Johnson	30	9	3	477,499
1978	11	Cale Yarborough	Oldsmobile	Junior Johnson	30	10	8	530,751
1979	43	Richard Petty	Chevrolet	Petty Enterprises	31	5	1	531,292
1980	2	Dale Earnhardt	Chevrolet	Rod Osterlund	31	5	0	588,926
1981	11	Darrell Waltrip	Buick	Junior Johnson	31	12	11	693,342
1982	11	Darrell Waltrip	Buick	Junior Johnson	30	12	7	873,118
1983	22	Bobby Allison	Buick	Bill Gardner	30	6	0	828,355
1984	44	Terry Labonte	Chevrolet	Billy Hagan	30	2	2	713,010
1985	11	Darrell Waltrip	Chevrolet	Junior Johnson	28	3	4	1,318,735
1986	3	Dale Earnhardt	Chevrolet	Richard Childress	29	5	1	1,783,880
1987	3	Dale Earnhardt	Chevrolet	Richard Childress	29	11	1	2,099,243
1988	9	Bill Elliott	Ford	Harry Meling	29	6	6	1,574,639
1989	27	Rusty Wallace	Pontiac	Raymond Beadle	29	6	4	2,247,950
1990	3	Dale Earnhardt	Chevrolet	Richard Childress	29	9	4	3,083,056
1991	3	Dale Earnhardt	Chevrolet	Richard Childress	29	4	0	2,396,685
1992	7	Alan Kulwicki	Ford	Alan Kulwicki	29	2	6	2,322,561
1993	3	Dale Earnhardt	Chevrolet	Richard Childress	30	6	2	3,353,789
1994	3	Dale Earnhardt	Chevrolet	Richard Childress	31	4	2	3,400,733
1995	24	Jeff Gordon	Chevrolet	Rick Hendrick	31	7	8	4,347,343
1996	5	Terry Labonte	Chevrolet	Rick Hendrick	31	2	4	4,030,648
1997	24	Jeff Gordon	Chevrolet	Rick Hendrick	32	10	1	6,375,658
1998	24	Jeff Gordon	Chevrolet	Rick Hendrick	33	13	7	9,306,584
1999	88	Dale Jarrett	Ford	Robert Yates	34	4	0	6,649,596
2000	18	Bobby Labonte	Pontiac	Joe Gibbs	34	4	3	7,361,387
2001	24	Jeff Gordon	Chevrolet	Rick Hendrick	36	6	6	10,879,757
2002	20	Tony Stewart	Pontiac	Joe Gibbs	36	3	2	9,163,761
2003	17	Matt Kenseth	Ford	Mark Martin	36	1	0	9,422,764
2004	97	Kurt Busch	Ford	Roush Racing	36	3	1	9,661,513
2005	20	Tony Stewart	Chevrolet	Joe Gibbs	36	5	3	13,578,168

Nextel Cup Rookie of the Year

Sponsored by Raybestos, the official brake of NASCAR, and presented to rookie driver who accumulates the most Nextel Cup Series Raybestos Rookie of the Year points based on their best 17 finishes.

Year		Year		Year		Year	
1957	Ken Rush	1970	Bill Dennis	1983	Sterling Marlin	1996	Johnny Benson
1958	Shorty Rollins	1971	Walter Ballard	1984	Rusty Wallace	1997	Mike Skinner
1959	Richard Petty	1972	Larry Smith	1985	Ken Schrader	1998	Kenny Irwin
1960	David Pearson	1973	Lennie Pond	1986	Alan Kulwicki	1999	Tony Stewart
1961	Woodie Wilson	1974	Earl Ross	1987	Davey Allison	2000	Matt Kenseth
1962	Tom Cox	1975	Bruce Hill	1988	Ken Bouchard	2001	Kevin Harvick
1963	Billy Wade	1976	Skip Manning	1989	Dick Trickle	2002	Ryan Newman
1964	Doug Cooper	1977	Ricky Rudd	1990	Rob Moroso	2003	Jamie McMurray
1965	Sam McQuagg	1978	Ronnie Thomas	1991	Bobby Hamilton	2004	Kasey Kahne
1966	James Hylton	1979	Dale Earnhardt	1992	Jimmy Hensley	2005	Kyle Busch
1967	Donnie Allison	1980	Jody Ridley	1993	Jeff Gordon		
1968	Pete Hamilton	1981	Ron Bouchard	1994	Jeff Burton		
1969	Dick Brooks	1982	Geoff Bodine	1995	Ricky Craven		

Manufacturers' Championship

Awarded to the most successful car manufacturer in the Nextel Cup Series since 1949. Manufacturers whose cars finish in the top six in each race are awarded points based on the following format: 9-6-4-3-2-1. **Note:** By early October, Chevrolet had already clinched the 2006 Manufacturers' Championship.

Multiple winners: Chevrolet (29); Ford (16); Oldsmobile (4); Dodge and Hudson (3); Buick and Pontiac (2).

Year		Year		Year		Year		Year	
1949	Oldsmobile	1961	Chevrolet	1973	Chevrolet	1985	Chevrolet	1996	Chevrolet
1950	Oldsmobile	1962	Pontiac	1974	Chevrolet	1986	Chevrolet	1997	Ford
1951	Oldsmobile	1963	Ford	1975	Dodge	1987	Chevrolet	1998	Chevrolet
1952	Hudson	1964	Ford	1976	Chevrolet	1988	Pontiac	1999	Ford
1953	Hudson	1965	Ford	1977	Chevrolet	1989	Chevrolet	2000	Ford
1954	Hudson	1966	Ford	1978	Chevrolet	1990	Chevrolet	2001	Chevrolet
1955	Oldsmobile	1967	Ford	1979	Chevrolet		& Ford	2002	Ford
1956	Ford	1968	Ford	1980	Chevrolet	1991	Chevrolet	2003	Chevrolet
1957	Ford	1969	Ford	1981	Buick	1992	Ford	2004	Chevrolet
1958	Chevrolet	1970	Dodge	1982	Buick	1993	Chevrolet	2005	Chevrolet
1959	Chevrolet	1971	Dodge	1983	Chevrolet	1994	Ford	2006	Chevrolet
1960	Chevrolet	1972	Chevrolet	1984	Chevrolet	1995	Chevrolet		

Champion Crew Chiefs

Crew chiefs of Nextel Cup Series champions since 1949.

Multiple winners: Dale Inman (8); Kirk Shelmerdine (4); Ray Evernham and Lee Petty (3); Tim Brewer, Travis Carter, Jake Elder, Jeff Hammond, Bud Moore, Herb Nab, Andy Petree, Smokey Yunick and Greg Zipadelli (2).

Year		Year		Year		Year	
1949	Red Vogt	1964	Dale Inman	1979	Dale Inman	1994	Andy Petree
1950	Julian Buesink	1965	John Ervin	1980	Doug Richert	1995	Ray Evernham
1951	Smokey Yunick	1966	Cotton Owens	1981	Tim Brewer	1996	Gary DeHart
1952	B.B. Blackburn	1967	Dale Inman	1982	Jeff Hammond	1997	Ray Evernham
1953	Smokey Yunick	1968	Jake Elder	1983	Gary Nelson	1998	Ray Evernham
1954	Lee Petty	1969	Jake Elder	1984	Dale Inman	1999	Todd Parrott
1955	Carl Kiekhafer	1970	Harry Hyde	1985	Jeff Hammond	2000	Jimmy Makar
1956	Carl Kiekhafer	1971	Dale Inman	1986	Kirk Shelmerdine	2001	Robbie Loomis
1957	Bud Moore	1972	Dale Inman	1987	Kirk Shelmerdine	2002	Greg Zipadelli
1958	Lee Petty	1973	Travis Carter	1988	Ernie Elliott	2003	Robbie Reiser
1959	Lee Petty	1974	Dale Inman	1989	Barry Dodson	2004	Jimmy Fennig
1960	Louis Clements	1975	Dale Inman	1990	Kirk Shelmerdine	2005	Greg Zipadelli
1961	Bud Allman	1976	Herb Nab	1991	Kirk Shelmerdine		
1962	Bud Moore	1977	Herb Nab	1992	Paul Andrews		
1963	Bud Moore	1978	T Brewer/T. Carter	1993	Andy Petree		

Nextel All-Star Challenge

The NASCAR Nextel All-Star Challenge is a non-points event held each May at Lowe's Motor Speedway in Concord, N.C. It is open to race winners from the previous and current season, the winner of the Nextel Open qualifying race, former All-Star winners, former Nextel Cup champions and one driver chosen by fan vote. The Challenge winner earns $1 million.

Multiple winners: Dale Earnhardt and Jeff Gordon (3); Davey Allison, Jimmie Johnson, Terry Labonte and Mark Martin (2).

Year		Year		Year		Year	
1985	Darrell Waltrip	1991	Davey Allison	1997	Jeff Gordon	2003	Jimmie Johnson
1986	Bill Elliott	1992	Davey Allison	1998	Mark Martin	2004	Matt Kenseth
1987	Dale Earnhardt	1993	Dale Earnhardt	1999	Terry Labonte	2005	Mark Martin
1988	Terry Labonte	1994	Geoff Bodine	2000	Dale Earnhardt Jr.	2006	Jimmie Johnson
1989	Rusty Wallace	1995	Jeff Gordon	2001	Jeff Gordon		
1990	Dale Earnhardt	1996	Michael Waltrip	2002	Ryan Newman		

NASCAR Circuit (Cont.)

Nextel Cup All-Time Leaders

NASCAR Nextel Cup's all-time Top 20 drivers in victories, pole positions and earnings based on records through Oct. 22, 2006. Drivers active in 2006 are in **bold** type.

Career

	Victories			Pole Positions			Earnings	
1	Richard Petty	.200	1	Richard Petty	.126	1	**Jeff Gordon**	.$80,259,959
2	David Pearson	.105	2	David Pearson	.113	2	**Mark Martin**	.57,744,547
3	Bobby Allison	.84	3	Cale Yarborough	.70	3	**Dale Jarrett**	.56,287,148
	Darrell Waltrip	.84	4	Darrell Waltrip	.59	4	**Tony Stewart**	.54,617,189
5	Cale Yarborough	.83	5	Bobby Allison	.57	5	**Bobby Labonte**	.49,869,341
6	Dale Earnhardt	.76	6	**Bill Elliott**	.55	6	Rusty Wallace	.49,741,326
7	**Jeff Gordon**	.75		**Jeff Gordon**	.55	7	**Jeff Burton**	.45,021,291
8	Lee Petty	.55	8	Bobby Isaac	.51	8	Dale Earnhardt	.41,742,384
	Rusty Wallace	.55	9	Junior Johnson	.47	9	Ricky Rudd	.40,696,133
10	Ned Jarrett	.50	10	Buck Baker	.44	10	**Dale Earnhardt Jr.**	40,668,506
	Junior Johnson	.50	11	**Mark Martin**	.41	11	**Terry Labonte**	.40,467,029
12	Herb Thomas	.48	12	Buddy Baker	.40	12	**Sterling Marlin**	.39,978,560
13	Buck Baker	.46	13	Tim Flock	.39	13	**Matt Kenseth**	.39,547,838
14	**Bill Elliott**	.44		Herb Thomas	.39	14	**Bill Elliott**	.38,655,942
15	Tim Flock	.40	15	Geoff Bodine	.37	15	**Jimmy Johnson**	.36,220,611
16	Bobby Isaac	.37		**Ryan Newman**	.37	16	**Kurt Busch**	.35,026,005
17	**Mark Martin**	.35	17	Rusty Wallace	.36	17	**Michael Waltrip**	.34,960,494
18	Fireball Roberts	.32	18	Ned Jarrett	.35	18	**Ken Schrader**	.32,003,840
	Dale Jarrett	.32		Fireball Roberts	.35	19	**Jeremy Mayfield**	.30,834,667
20	Rex White	.28		Rex White	.35	20	**Kevin Harvick**	.30,760,742

Single Season (through 2005)

	Victories			Pole Positions			Earnings	
1	Richard Petty, '67	.27	1	Bobby Isaac, '69	.20	1	Tony Stewart, '05	.$13,578,168
2	Richard Petty, '71	.21	2	Richard Petty, '67	.19	2	Jeff Gordon, '01	.10,879,757
3	Tim Flock, '55	.18	3	Tim Flock, '55	.18	3	Kurt Busch, '04	.9,677,543
	Richard Petty, '70	.18	4	Richard Petty, '66	.16	4	Matt Kenseth, '03	.9,422,764
5	Bobby Isaac, '69	.17	5	Cale Yarborough, '80	.14	5	Jeff Gordon, '98	.9,306,584
6	David Pearson, '68	.16	6	David Pearson, '69	.13	6	Tony Stewart, '02	.9,163,761
	Richard Petty, '68	.16		Bobby Isaac, '70	.13	7	D. Earnhardt Jr., '04	.8,913,510
8	Ned Jarrett, '64	.15	8	Fonty Flock, '51	.12	8	Jeff Gordon, '04	.8,439,382
	David Pearson, '66	.15		David Pearson, '64	.12	9	Greg Biffle, '05	.8,354,052
10	Buck Baker, '56	.14		David Pearson, '68	.12	10	Jimmie Johnson, '05	.8,336,712
	Richard Petty, '63	.14		Richard Petty, '68	.12	11	Jimmie Johnson, '04	.8,275,721
						12	Jeff Gordon, '05	.7,930,830
						13	Tony Stewart, '04	.7,830,807

Modern Era (since 1972)

	Victories			Pole Positions			Earnings	
1	Richard Petty, '75	.13	1	Cale Yarborough, '80	.14	14	Jimmie Johnson, '03	.7,745,530
	Jeff Gordon, '98	.13	2	Bobby Allison, '72	.11	15	Mark Martin, '05	.7,731,468
3	Darrell Waltrip, '81	.12		David Pearson, '74	.11	16	Kurt Busch, '05	.7,667,861
	Darrell Waltrip, '82	.12		Darrell Waltrip, '81	.11	17	Matt Kenseth, '04	.7,405,309
5	David Pearson, '73	.11		Bill Elliott, 85	.11	18	Bobby Labonte, '00	.7,361,387
	Bill Elliott, '85	.11		Ryan Newman, '03	.11	19	Ryan Newman, '05	.7,259,518
	Dale Earnhardt, '87	.11	7	Geoff Bodine, '86	.9	20	Matt Kenseth, '05	.7,034,134
8	Eight tied with 10 wins each, including twice by Cale Yarborough and Jeff Gordon.			Rusty Wallace, '00	.9			
				Ryan Newman, '04	.9			
			10	Eight tied with 8 poles each.				

Richard Petty *speeds through qualifying at the 1968 Daytona 500. Petty won 16 races in 1968, tied for 6th on the all-time single-season list and 11 behind his record of 27 set in 1967.*

AP/Wide World Photos

Busch Series Champions

The Busch Series was founded in 1982 as the Budweiser Late Model Sportsman Series, and has since grown into the No. 2 motorsports series in the United States. The series emerged from NASCAR's old Sportsman Division, which was formed in 1950 as NASCAR's short track race division. The series switched sponsorship to the Busch brand in 1984 and became the Busch Grand National Series. Grand National was dumped from the series' title in 2003. Busch Series cars are slightly smaller versions of their Nextel Cup counterparts. Note that earnings totals include bonus awards.

Multiple winners: (drivers) Sam Ard, Dale Earnhardt Jr., Jack Ingram, Randy LaJoie, Larry Pearson and Martin Truex Jr. (2).
Multiple winners: (cars) Chevrolet (14); Oldsmobile (5); Pontiac (4).

Year	Car #	Driver	Car	Owner	Sts	Wins	Poles	Earnings
1982	11	Jack Ingram	Olds/Pontiac	Aline Ingram	29	7	1	$122,100
1983	00	Sam Ard	Oldsmobile	Howard Thomas	35	10	10	192,362
1984	00	Sam Ard	Oldsmobile	Howard Thomas	28	8	7	217,531
1985	11	Jack Ingram	Pontiac	Aline Ingram	27	5	2	164,710
1986	21	Larry Pearson	Pontiac	David Pearson	31	1	1	184,344
1987	21	Larry Pearson	Chevrolet	David Pearson	27	6	3	256,372
1988	99	Tommy Ellis	Buick	John Jackson	30	3	5	200,003
1989	25	Rob Moroso	Oldsmobile	Dick Moroso	29	4	6	346,739
1990	63	Chuck Brown	Pontiac	Hubert Hensley	31	6	4	323,399
1991	44	Bobby Labonte	Oldsmobile	Bobby Labonte	31	2	2	246,368
1992	87	Joe Nemechek	Chevrolet	Joe Nemechek	31	2	1	285,008
1993	31	Steve Grissom	Chevrolet	Wayne Grissom	28	2	0	336,432
1994	44	David Green	Chevrolet	Bobby Labonte	28	1	9	391,670
1995	74	Johnny Benson	Chevrolet	William Baumgardner	26	2	0	469,129
1996	74	Randy LaJoie	Chevrolet	William Baumgardner	26	5	2	532,823
1997	74	Randy LaJoie	Chevrolet	William Baumgardner	30	5	2	1,105,201
1998	3	Dale Earnhardt Jr.	Chevrolet	Dale Earnhardt	31	5	3	1,332,701
1999	3	Dale Earnhardt Jr.	Chevrolet	Dale Earnhardt	32	6	3	1,680,549
2000	10	Jeff Green	Chevrolet	Greg Pollex	32	6	7	1,929,937
2001	2	Kevin Harvick	Chevrolet	Richard Childress	33	5	5	1,833,570
2002	60	Greg Biffle	Ford	Jack Roush	34	4	5	2,337,255
2003	5	Brian Vickers	Chevrolet	Ricky Hendrick	34	3	1	1,987,255
2004	8	Martin Truex Jr.	Chevrolet	T. Earnhardt/D. Earnhardt. Jr.	34	6	7	2,537,171
2005	8	Martin Truex Jr.	Chevrolet	T. Earnhardt/D. Earnhardt. Jr.	35	6	3	3,143,692

Busch Series Rookie of the Year

Sponsored by Raybestos, the official brake of NASCAR, and presented to rookie driver who accumulates the most Busch Series Raybestos Rookie of the Year points based on their best 16 finishes.

Year		Year		Year		Year	
1989	Kenny Wallace	1994	Johnny Benson	1999	Tony Raines	2004	Kyle Busch
1990	Joe Nemechek	1995	Jeff Fuller	2000	Kevin Harvick	2005	Carl Edwards
1991	Jeff Gordon	1996	Glenn Allen	2001	Greg Biffle		
1992	Ricky Craven	1997	Steve Park	2002	Scott Riggs		
1993	Hermie Sadler	1998	Andy Santerre	2003	David Stremme		

Manufacturers' Championship

Officially the Bill France Performance Cup and awarded each year to the most successful car manufacturer in the Busch Series. Manufacturers whose cars finish in the top four in each race are awarded points based on the following format: 9-6-4-3.
Multiple winners: Chevrolet (12); Ford (2).

Year		Year		Year		Year		Year	
1991	Oldsmobile	1994	Chevrolet	1997	Chevrolet	2000	Chevrolet	2003	Chevrolet
1992	Chevrolet	1995	Ford	1998	Chevrolet	2001	Chevrolet	2004	Chevrolet
1993	Chevrolet	1996	Chevrolet	1999	Chevrolet	2002	Ford	2005	Chevrolet

Busch Series All-Time Leaders

NASCAR Busch Series all-time Top 10 drivers in victories, pole positions and earnings based on records through Oct. 13, 2006.

Victories

1	Mark Martin	47
2	Jack Ingram	31
3	Tommy Houston	24
	Kevin Harvick	24
5	Sam Ard	22
	Jeff Burton	22
	Dale Earnhardt Jr.	22
	Tommy Ellis	22
9	Dale Earnhardt	21
	Harry Gant	21

Pole Positions

1	Tommy Ellis	28
	Mark Martin	28
3	Sam Ard	24
4	Jeff Green	23
5	David Green	22
6	Tommy Houston	18
	Joe Nemechek	18
8	Brett Bodine	16
9	Jimmy Hensley	15
	Michael Waltrip	15

Earnings

1	Jason Keller	$10,789,897
2	David Green	8,840,706
3	Greg Biffle	7,837,233
4	Randy LaJoie	7,688,093
5	Kevin Harvick	6,913,609
6	Jeff Green	6,851,548
7	Mike McLaughlin	6,257,873
8	Martin Truex Jr.	6,066,410
9	Kenny Wallace	6,388,551
10	Matt Kenseth	5,835,619

NASCAR Circuit (Cont.)

Craftsman Truck Series Champions

The NASCAR Craftsman Truck Series features modified pickup trucks. The idea for the Series originated in 1993, when a group of off-road racers created a prototype for a NASCAR-style pickup truck. The trucks proved extremely popular and were first displayed during the 1994 Daytona 500. NASCAR created the series, first called the "SuperTruck Series," in 1995. The series became known as the Craftsman Truck Series in 1996. Note that earnings totals include bonus awards.

Multiple winners: (drivers) Jack Sprague (3); Ron Hornaday Jr. (2).
Multiple winners: (cars) Chevrolet (8); Dodge (2).

Year	Truck #	Driver	Car	Owner	Sts	Wins	Poles	Earnings
1995	3	**Mike Skinner**	Chevrolet	Richard Childress	20	8	10	$428,096
1996	16	**Ron Hornaday Jr.**	Chevrolet	Teresa Earnhardt	24	4	2	625,634
1997	24	**Jack Sprague**	Chevrolet	Rick Hendrick	26	3	5	880,835
1998	16	**Ron Hornaday Jr.**	Chevrolet	Teresa Earnhardt	27	6	2	915,407
1999	24	**Jack Sprague**	Chevrolet	Rick Hendrick	25	3	1	834,016
2000	50	**Greg Biffle**	Ford	Jack Roush	24	5	4	1,002,510
2001	24	**Jack Sprague**	Chevrolet	Rick Hendrick	24	4	7	967,493
2002	16	**Mike Bliss**	Chevrolet	Steve Coulter	22	5	4	894,388
2003	16	**Travis Kvapil**	Chevrolet	Steve Coulter	25	1	0	872,395
2004	4	**Bobby Hamilton**	Dodge	Debbie Hamilton	25	4	0	973,428
2005	1	**Ted Musgrave**	Dodge	Jim Smith	25	1	1	880,553

Craftsman Truck Series Rookie of the Year

Sponsored by Raybestos, the official brake of NASCAR, and presented to rookie driver who accumulates the most Craftsman Truck Series Raybestos Rookie of the Year points based on their best 14 finishes.

Year		Year		Year		Year	
1996	Bryan Reffner	1999	Mike Stefanik	2002	Brendan Gaughan	2005	Todd Kluever
1997	Kenny Irwin	2000	Kurt Busch	2003	Carl Edwards		
1998	Greg Biffle	2001	Travis Kvapil	2004	David Reutimann		

Manufacturers' Championship

Awarded each year to the most successful car manufacturer in the Craftsman Truck Series. Manufacturers whose cars finish in the top four in each race are awarded points based on the following format: 9-6-4-3.

Multiple winners: Chevrolet (6); Dodge (3); Ford (2).

Year		Year		Year		Year	
1995	Chevrolet	1998	Chevrolet	2001	Dodge	2004	Dodge
1996	Chevrolet	1999	Ford	2002	Chevrolet	2005	Chevrolet
1997	Chevrolet	2000	Ford	2003	Dodge		

Craftsman Truck Series All-Time Leaders

NASCAR Craftsman Truck Series all-time Top 10 drivers in victories, pole positions and earnings based on records through Oct. 21, 2006.

Victories

1	Ron Hornaday Jr.	29
2	Jack Sprague	27
3	Mike Skinner	19
4	Greg Biffle	16
	Ted Musgrave	16
	Dennis Setzer	16
7	Joe Ruttman	13
8	Mike Bliss	12
9	Bobby Hamilton	10
	Todd Bodine	10

Pole Positions

1	Jack Sprague	29
	Mike Skinner	29
3	Mike Bliss	18
4	Joe Ruttman	17
5	Ron Hornaday Jr.	13
6	Greg Biffle	12
	Ted Musgrave	12
8	Jason Leffler	10
9	Stacy Compton	9
10	Terry Cook	8

Earnings

1	Jack Sprague	$6,107,695
2	Dennis Setzer	4,561,651
3	Ted Musgrave	4,190,089
4	Ron Hornaday Jr.	4,009,375
5	Rick Crawford	3,795,375
6	Terry Cook	3,177,729
7	Joe Ruttman	3,135,757
8	Mike Bliss	3,024,956
9	Mike Skinner	2,486,787
10	David Starr	2,446,999

Auto Racing Royalty

There must be something about auto racing that gets into a family's bloodstream. Generations of racers follow in each other's footsteps, working their way up the rungs of the ladder, starting in go-karts and graduating to the big time circuits. Is the need for speed in the genes? It certainly looks like it when you check out these fast-driving families, considered auto racing royalty in NASCAR and open-wheel racing.

The Allisons

Bobby (b. 12/3/1937): Collected 84 wins in 718 starts; won only Winston Cup title in 1983 at age 45; inducted into IMHOF in 1993; raced 1961-1988.

Donnie, Bobby's brother (b. 9/7/1939): Won 10 Grand National/Winston Cup races in 239 starts; raced from 1966 to 1988 on part-time basis.

Davey, Bobby's son (b. 2/25/1961, d. 7/13/1993): Won 19 Winston Cup races; killed in a 1993 helicopter accident at Talladega Superspeedway at age 32; inducted into IMHOF in 1998; raced from 1985-93.

Clifford, Bobby's son (b. 10/20/1964, d. 8/13/1992): Ran Busch Series from 1990-1992; killed in practice for a Busch Series race at Michigan in 1992 at age 27.

The Andrettis

Mario (b. 2/28/1940): Accumulated 111 career wins racing from 1961-2000; won four Champ Car titles, the 1978 Formula 1 title and the 1979 IROC crown; A.P. named his "Driver of the Century" along with A.J. Foyt.

Aldo, Mario's twin brother (b. 2/28/1940): After his second severe car crash, he retired from racing in 1969.

Michael, Mario's son (b. 10/5/1962): Raced from 1980-2003, won first Champ Car race in 1986 and joined his father's team in 1989; won only Champ Car crown in 1991; totaled 42 Champ Car wins.

Jeff, Mario's son (b. 4/14/1964): Joined father and brother in Champ Car in 1990; was 1991 Indy 500 and CART Rookie of the Year; raced from 1990-2000.

John, Aldo's son (b. 3/12/1963): Started racing in Champ Car in 1987, transitioned into NASCAR in 90's; won two Winston Cup races; currently racing in Busch Series.

Marco, Michael's son (b. 3/13/1987) Third-generation racer debuted as rookie in Indy in 2006; surprised watchers with second place finish at Indy 500; raced Indy 500 with father, who came out of retirement to join son.

The Earnhardts

Ralph (b. 2/23/1928, d. 9/26/1973): "Mr. Consistency" in Grand National; was inducted into IMHOF in 1997; raced from 1956-1964.

Dale, Ralph's son (b. 4/29/1951, d. 2/18/2001): "The Intimidator" won ROY in 1979, seven Winston Cup titles and 76 races; more than $27 million; career was cut short by fatal crash at the 2001 Daytona 500; raced from 1975-2001.

Dale Jr., Dale's son (b. 10/10/1974): "Little E" had won 17 races and won more than $33 million midway through his seventh full season. First full season in Nextel Cup was 2000.

The Jarretts

Ned (b. 10/12/1932): won two Grand National titles; won 50 races in 352 starts; nicknamed "Gentleman Ned"; inducted into IMHOF in 1991; raced from 1953-1966.

Dale, Ned's son (b. 11/26/1956): Started full-time in Winston Cup in 1987; won title in 1999; has 32 wins; with his Cup title, the Jarretts became the second father/son duo after the Pettys to grab titles; began racing in 1984.

The Labontes

Terry (b. 11/16/1956): First NASCAR start came in 1978; won Winston Cup crowns in 1984, 1996; broke Richard Petty's streak of 513 straight starts in 1996 (his eventual record of 655 consecutive starts was broken by Ricky Rudd in 2002).

Bobby, Terry's brother (b. 5/8/1964): Won the 2000 Winston Cup title; win gave the brothers the honor of being the first sibling tandem to win the title. He is the only driver to win both a Busch Series and Cup Series championship; began racing in 1991.

The Pettys

Lee (b. 3/14/1914, d. 4/5/2000): Won 54 strictly Stock/Grand National races, three titles; photo-finish winner of the first Daytona 500 in 1959; inducted into IMHOF in 1990; raced from 1953-1966.

Richard, Lee's son (b. 7/2/1937): "The King" was a seven-time Grand National/Winston Cup champ; 200 wins; seven-time winner of the Daytona 500; won single-season record 27 races in 1967; inducted into IMHOF in 1997; raced from 1958-1992.

Kyle, Richard's son (b. 6/2/1960): More than $24M in career earnings; more than 170 top-10 finishes; began racing in 1979.

Adam, Kyle's son (b. 7/10/1980, d. 5/12/2000): Killed at New Hampshire International Speedway in preparation for only his second Winston Cup start.

The Unsers

The Unser family tree continues to sprout branches of racing addicts. Eight Unsers (Jerry Jr., Louie, Bobby Sr., Al Sr., Johnny, Bobby Jr., Robby and Al Jr.) have spent time in the pits, while third-generation motorsports converts Jason Tanner and Al Unser III are trying their hand at advancing the Unser legacy.

Bobby (b. 2/20/1934): Three-time winner of the Indy 500 (1968, 1975, 1981); 1981 win was controversial, as Mario Andretti was declared winner because Unser passed cars during yellow flag, but Unser appealed and victory was restored; 35 CART wins; raced from 1949-1982.

Al Sr., Bobby's brother (b. 5/29/1939) "Big Al" won Indy 500 four times (1970, 1971, 1978, 1987); won 1987 Indy 500 at 47 years old, the oldest winner in history; posted 39 Indy wins; raced from 1957-1994.

Al Jr., Al's son (b. 4/19/1962): "Little Al" won the Indy 500 in 1992 and 1994; lost CART points title to his father by a single point in 1985; raced from 1982 to 2004.

The Waltrips

Darrell (b. 2/5/1947): Three-time Winston Cup champ, won 1989 Daytona 500; accumulated 84 Cup victories and 59 poles; inducted into IMHOF in 2005; raced 1972-2000.

Michael, Darrell's brother (b. 4/30/1963): two-time Daytona 500 winner; has earned more than $31 million; began racing in 1985.

INDY RACING LEAGUE CIRCUIT
Indianapolis 500

Held every Memorial Day weekend; 200 laps around a 2.5-mile oval at Indianapolis Motor Speedway. First race was held in 1911. The Indy Racing League began in 1996 and made the Indianapolis 500 its cornerstone event. Winning drivers are listed with starting positions. Winners who started from pole position are in **bold** type.

Multiple wins: A.J. Foyt, Rick Mears and Al Unser (4); Louis Meyer, Mauri Rose, Johnny Rutherford, Wilbur Shaw and Bobby Unser (3); Helio Castroneves, Emerson Fittipaldi, Gordon Johncock, Arie Luyendyk, Tommy Milton, Al Unser Jr., Bill Vukovich and Rodger Ward (2).

Multiple poles: Rick Mears (6); A.J. Foyt and Rex Mays (4); Mario Andretti, Arie Luyendyk, Johnny Rutherford and Tom Sneva (3); Scott Brayton, Bill Cummings, Ralph DePalma, Leon Duray, Parnelli Jones, Jimmy Murphy, Duke Nalon, Eddie Sachs and Bobby Unser (2).

Year	Winner (Pos.)	Car	MPH	Pole Sitter	MPH
1911	Ray Harroun (28)	Marmon Wasp	74.602	Lewis Strang	–
1912	Joe Dawson (7)	National	78.719	Gil Anderson	–
1913	Jules Goux (7)	Peugeot	75.933	Caleb Bragg	–
1914	Rene Thomas (15)	Delage	82.474	Jean Chassagne	–
1915	Ralph DePalma (2)	Mercedes	89.840	Howard Wilcox	98.90
1916-a	Dario Resta (4)	Peugeot	84.001	John Aitken	96.69
1917-18	Not held	World War I			
1919	Howdy Wilcox (2)	Peugeot	88.050	Rene Thomas	104.78
1920	Gaston Chevrolet (6)	Monroe	88.618	Ralph DePalma	99.15
1921	Tommy Milton (20)	Frontenac	89.621	Ralph DePalma	100.75
1922	**Jimmy Murphy** (1)	Murphy Special	94.484	Jimmy Murphy	100.50
1923	**Tommy Milton** (1)	H.C.S. Special	90.954	Tommy Milton	108.17
1924	L.L. Corum & Joe Boyer (21)	Duesenberg Special	98.234	Jimmy Murphy	108.037
1925	Peter DePaolo (2)	Duesenberg Special	101.127	Leon Duray	113.196
1926-b	Frank Lockhart (20)	Miller Special	95.904	Earl Cooper	111.735
1927	George Souders (22)	Duesenberg	97.545	Frank Lockhart	120.100
1928	Louie Meyer (13)	Miller Special	99.482	Leon Duray	122.391
1929	Ray Keech (6)	Simplex Piston Ring Special	97.585	Cliff Woodbury	120.599
1930	**Billy Arnold** (1)	Miller-Hartz Special	100.448	Billy Arnold	113.268
1931	Louis Schneider (13)	Bowes Seal Fast Special	96.629	Russ Snowberger	112.796
1932	Fred Frame (27)	Miller-Hartz Special	104.144	Lou Moore	117.363
1933	Louie Meyer (6)	Tydol Special	104.162	Bill Cummings	118.530
1934	Bill Cummings (10)	Boyle Products Special	104.863	Kelly Petillo	119.329
1935	Kelly Petillo (22)	Gilmore Speedway Special	106.240	Rex Mays	120.736
1936	Louie Meyer (28)	Ring Free Special	109.069	Rex Mays	119.644
1937	Wilbur Shaw (2)	Shaw-Gilmore Special	113.580	Bill Cummings	123.343
1938	**Floyd Roberts** (1)	Burd Piston Ring Special	117.200	Floyd Roberts	125.681
1939	Wilbur Shaw (3)	Boyle Special	115.035	Jimmy Snyder	130.138
1940	Wilbur Shaw (2)	Boyle Special	114.277	Rex Mays	127.850
1941	Floyd Davis & Mauri Rose (17)	Noc-Out Hose Clamp Special	115.117	Mauri Rose	128.691
1942-45	Not held	World War II			
1946	George Robson (15)	Thorne Engineering Special	114.820	Cliff Bergere	126.471
1947	Mauri Rose (3)	Blue Crown Spark Plug Special	116.338	Ted Horn	126.564
1948	Mauri Rose (3)	Blue Crown Spark Plug Special	119.814	Rex Mays	130.577
1949	Bill Holland (4)	Blue Crown Spark Plug Special	121.327	Duke Nalon	132.939
1950-c	Johnnie Parsons (5)	Wynn's Friction Proofing	124.002	Walt Faulkner	134.343
1951	Lee Wallard (2)	Belanger Special	126.244	Duke Nalon	136.498
1952	Troy Ruttman (7)	Agajanian Special	128.922	Fred Agabashian	138.010
1953	**Bill Vukovich** (1)	Fuel Injection Special	128.740	Bill Vukovich	138.392
1954	Bill Vukovich (19)	Fuel Injection Special	130.840	Jack McGrath	141.033
1955	Bob Sweikert (14)	John Zink Special	128.213	Jerry Hoyt	140.045
1956	**Pat Flaherty** (1)	John Zink Special	128.490	Pat Flaherty	145.596
1957	Sam Hanks (13)	Belond Exhaust Special	135.601	Pat O'Connor	143.948
1958	Jimmy Bryan (7)	Belond AP Parts Special	133.791	Dick Rathmann	145.974
1959	Rodger Ward (6)	Leader Card 500 Roadster	135.857	Johnny Thomson	145.908
1960	Jim Rathmann (2)	Ken-Paul Special	138.767	Eddie Sachs	146.592
1961	A.J. Foyt (7)	Bowes Seal Fast Special	139.130	Eddie Sachs	147.481
1962	Rodger Ward (2)	Leader Card 500 Roadster	140.293	Parnelli Jones	150.370
1963	**Parnelli Jones** (1)	Agajanian-Willard Special	143.137	Parnelli Jones	151.153
1964	A.J. Foyt (5)	Sheraton-Thompson Special	147.350	Jim Clark	158.828
1965	Jim Clark (2)	Lotus Ford	150.686	A.J. Foyt	161.233
1966	Graham Hill (15)	American Red Ball Special	144.317	Mario Andretti	165.899
1967-d	A.J. Foyt (4)	Sheraton-Thompson Special	151.207	Mario Andretti	168.982
1968	Bobby Unser (3)	Rislone Special	152.882	Joe Leonard	171.559
1969	Mario Andretti (2)	STP Oil Treatment Special	156.867	A.J. Foyt	170.568
1970	**Al Unser** (1)	Johnny Lightning Special	155.749	Al Unser	170.221

Year	Winner (Pos.)	Car	MPH	Pole Sitter	MPH
1971	Al Unser (5)	Johnny Lightning Special	157.735	Peter Revson	178.696
1972	Mark Donohue (3)	Sunoco McLaren	162.962	Bobby Unser	195.940
1973-e	Gordon Johncock (11)	STP Double Oil Filters	159.036	Johnny Rutherford	198.413
1974	Johnny Rutherford (25)	McLaren	158.589	A.J. Foyt	191.632
1975-f	Bobby Unser (3)	Jorgensen Eagle	149.213	A.J. Foyt	193.976
1976-g	**Johnny Rutherford** (1)	Hy-Gain McLaren/Goodyear	148.725	Johnny Rutherford	188.957
1977	A.J. Foyt (4)	Gilmore Racing Team	161.331	Tom Sneva	198.884
1978	Al Unser (5)	FNCTC Chaparral Lola	161.363	Tom Sneva	202.156
1979	**Rick Mears** (1)	The Gould Charge	158.899	Rick Mears	193.736
1980	**Johnny Rutherford** (1)	Pennzoil Chaparral	142.862	Johnny Rutherford	192.256
1981-h	**Bobby Unser** (1)	Norton Spirit Penske PC-9B	139.084	Bobby Unser	200.546
1982	Gordon Johncock (5)	STP Oil Treatment	162.029	Rick Mears	207.004
1983	Tom Sneva (4)	Texaco Star	162.117	Teo Fabi	207.395
1984	Rick Mears (3)	Pennzoil Z-7	163.612	Tom Sneva	210.029
1985	Danny Sullivan (8)	Miller American Special	152.982	Pancho Carter	212.583
1986	Bobby Rahal (4)	Budweiser/Truesports/March	170.722	Rick Mears	216.828
1987	Al Unser (20)	Cummins Holset Turbo	162.175	Mario Andretti	215.390
1988	**Rick Mears** (1)	Pennzoil Z-7/Penske Chevy V-8	144.809	Rick Mears	219.198
1989	Emerson Fittipaldi (3)	Marlboro/Penske Chevy V-8	167.581	Rick Mears	223.885
1990	Arie Luyendyk (3)	Domino's Pizza Chevrolet	185.981*	Emerson Fittipaldi	225.301
1991	**Rick Mears** (1)	Marlboro Penske Chevy	176.457	Rick Mears	224.113
1992	Al Unser Jr. (12)	Valvoline Galmer '92	134.477	Roberto Guerrero	232.482
1993	Emerson Fittipaldi (9)	Marlboro Penske Chevy	157.207	Arie Luyendyk	223.967
1994	**Al Unser Jr.** (1)	Marlboro Penske Mercedes	160.872	Al Unser Jr.	228.011
1995	Jacques Villeneuve (5)	Player's Ltd. Reynard Ford	153.616	Scott Brayton	231.604
1996	Buddy Lazier (5)	Reynard Ford	147.956	Tony Stewart	233.100&
1997	**Arie Luyendyk** (1)	G-Force Olds Aurora	145.827	Arie Luyendyk	218.263
1998	Eddie Cheever Jr. (17)	Dallara Olds Aurora	145.155	Billy Boat	223.503
1999	Kenny Brack (8)	Dallara Olds Aurora	153.176	Arie Luyendyk	225.179
2000	Juan Montoya (2)	G-Force Olds Aurora	167.607	Greg Ray	223.471
2001	Helio Castroneves (11)	Dallara Olds Aurora	153.601	Scott Sharp	226.037
2002-i	Helio Castroneves (13)	Dallara Chevrolet	166.499	Bruno Junqueira	231.342
2003	Gil de Ferran (10)	G-Force Toyota	156.291	Helio Castroneves	231.725
2004-j	**Buddy Rice** (1)	G-Force Honda	138.518	Buddy Rice	222.024
2005	Dan Wheldon (16)	Dallara Honda	157.603	Tony Kanaan	227.566
2006	**Sam Hornish Jr.** (1)	Dallara Honda	157.085	Sam Hornish Jr.	228.985

*Track record for winning time.

& Scott Brayton won the pole position with an avg. mph of 233.718 but was killed in a practice run. Stewart was awarded pole position with the next fastest speed.

Notes: a—1916 race scheduled for 300 miles; **b**—rain shortened 1926 race to 400 miles; **c**—rain shortened 1950 race to 345 miles; **d**—1967 race postponed due to rain after 18 laps (May 30), resumed next day (May 31); **e**—rain shortened 1973 race to 332.5 miles; **f**—rain shortened 1975 race to 435 miles; **g**—rain shortened 1976 race to 255 miles; **h**—in 1981, runner-up Mario Andretti was awarded 1st place when winner Bobby Unser was penalized a lap after the race was completed for passing cars illegally under the caution flag. Unser and car-owner Roger Penske appealed the race stewards' decision to the U.S. Auto Club. Four months later, USAC overturned the ruling, saying that the penalty was too harsh and Unser should be fined $40,000 rather than stripped of his championship; **i**—Team Green, runner-up Paul Tracy's team, appealed Castroneves' victory, citing video evidence and driver testimonials that proved Tracy passed Castroneves moments before the caution flag on lap 199. The IRL denied the appeal the following day; **j**—rain shortened 2004 race to 450 miles.

Indy 500 Rookie of the Year

Officially the JP Morgan Chase Rookie of the Year Award and voted on by a panel of auto racing media. Award does not necessarily go to highest-finishing first-year driver. Graham Hill won the race on his first try in 1966, but the rookie award went to Jackie Stewart, who led with 10 laps to go only to lose oil pressure and finish 6th.

Father and son winners: Mario and Michael Andretti (1965 and 1984); Michael and Marco Andretti (1984 and 2006); Bill and Billy Vukovich III (1968 and 1988).

Year		Year		Year		Year	
1952	Art Cross	1966	Jackie Stewart	1980	Tim Richmond	1993	Nigel Mansell
1953	Jimmy Daywalt	1967	Denis Hulme	1981	Josele Garza	1994	Jacques Villeneuve
1954	Larry Crockett	1968	Bill Vukovich	1982	Jim Hickman	1995	Christian Fittipaldi
1955	Al Herman	1969	Mark Donohue	1983	Teo Fabi	1996	Tony Stewart
1956	Bob Veith	1970	Donnie Allison	1984	Michael Andretti	1997	Jeff Ward
1957	Don Edmunds	1971	Denny Zimmerman		& Roberto Guerrero	1998	Steve Knapp
1958	George Amick	1972	Mike Hiss	1985	Arie Luyendyk	1999	Robby McGehee
1959	Bobby Grim	1973	Graham McRae	1986	Randy Lanier	2000	Juan Montoya
1960	Jim Hurtubise	1974	Pancho Carter	1987	Fabrizio Barbazza	2001	Helio Castroneves
1961	Parnelli Jones	1975	Bill Puterbaugh	1988	Billy Vukovich III	2002	Alex Barron
	& Bobby Marshman	1976	Vern Schuppan	1989	Bernard Jourdain		& Tomas Scheckter
1962	Jimmy McElreath	1977	Jerry Sneva		& Scott Pruett	2003	Tora Takagi
1963	Jim Clark	1978	Rick Mears	1990	Eddie Cheever	2004	Kosuke Matsuura
1964	Johnny White		& Larry Rice	1991	Jeff Andretti	2005	Danica Patrick
1965	Mario Andretti	1979	Howdy Holmes	1992	Lyn St. James	2006	Marco Andretti

Indy Racing League Circuit (Cont.)

IRL IndyCar Series Champions

The Indy Racing League (IRL) split from the open-wheel CART series in 1994. Led by Indianapolis Motor Speedway President Tony George, the league's inaugural three-race series began in January 1996 and ended with the league's keystone event—the Indianapolis 500. Past series' sponsors include Pep Boys (1998-99) and Northern Light Technology, Inc., an Internet search engine (2000-01). **Multiple winner:** Sam Hornish Jr. (3).

Year	Driver	Car	Team	Sts	Wins	Poles	Earnings
1996	**Buzz Calkins**	Reynard Ford	A.J. Foyt Enterprises	3	1	0	$345,553
	Scott Sharp	Lola Ford	A.J. Foyt Enterprises	3	0	0	330,303
1997	**Tony Stewart**	Dallara Oldsmobile	Team Menard	10	1	4	1,142,450
1998	**Kenny Brack**	Dallara Oldsmobile	A.J. Foyt Enterprises	11	3	0	2,106,700
1999	**Greg Ray**	Dallara Oldsmobile	Team Menard	10	3	4	2,061,800
2000	**Buddy Lazier**	Dallara Oldsmobile	Hemelgarn Racing	9	2	1	2,176,200
2001	**Sam Hornish Jr.**	Dallara Oldsmobile	Panther Racing	13	3	0	2,477,025
2002	**Sam Hornish Jr.**	Dallara Oldsmobile	Panther Racing	15	5	2	2,470,615
2003	**Scott Dixon**	G-Force Toyota	Target Chip Ganassi	16	3	5	1,481,265
2004	**Tony Kanaan**	Dallara Honda	Andretti Green Racing	16	3	2	1,912,990
2005	**Dan Wheldon**	Dallara Honda	Andretti Green Racing	17	6	0	2,711,005
2006	**Sam Hornish Jr.**	Dallara Honda	Marlboro Team Penske	14	4	4	2,775,205

Note: In 1996, Calkins and Sharp were named co-champions after finishing the series tied in drivers' points (246).

IRL Rookie of the Year

Officially the Bombardier Rookie of the Year Award, presented to rookie driver who accumulates the most points in the IRL standings.

Year		Year		Year		Year	
1996	None	1999	Scott Harrington	2002	Laurent Redon	2005	Danica Patrick
1997	Jim Guthrie	2000	Airton Dare	2003	Dan Wheldon	2006	Marco Andretti
1998	Robby Unser	2001	Felipe Giaffone	2004	Kosuke Matsuura		

All-Time IRL Leaders

IRL IndyCar Series all-time Top 10 drivers in victories, pole positions and earnings, based on records through the 2006 season. Earnings totals include season-ending contingency awards. Drivers active in 2006 are in **bold** type. (*) Denotes driver is active, but in NASCAR Nextel Cup Series.

Victories

1	**Sam Hornish Jr.**	18
2	**Dan Wheldon**	11
	Helio Castroneves	11
4	**Scott Sharp**	9
5	**Buddy Lazier**	8
6	**Tony Kanaan**	7
7	**Scott Dixon**	6
8	**Eddie Cheever Jr.**	5
	Greg Ray	5
	Gil de Ferran	5

Pole Positions

1	**Helio Castroneves**	17
2	Greg Ray	13
3	**Sam Hornish Jr.**	12
4	Billy Boat	9
5	**Tomas Scheckter**	8
6	Tony Stewart*	7
7	**Tony Kanaan**	6
	Scott Dixon	6
9	**Scott Sharp**	5
	Gil de Ferran	5
	Buddy Rice	5

Earnings

1	**Sam Hornish Jr.**	$13,142,305
2	**Buddy Lazier**	10,188,509
3	**Helio Castroneves**	9,449,505
4	**Scott Sharp**	9,109,058
5	**Dan Wheldon**	7,896,565
6	**Tony Kanaan**	7,397,050
7	**Eddie Cheever Jr.**	6,763,298
8	Greg Ray	6,250,690
9	Kenny Brack	5,983,575
10	**Scott Dixon**	5,796,565

CHAMP CAR CIRCUIT

Champ Car Series Champions

Officially the "Bridgestone Presents The Champ Car World Series Powered by Ford" since 2003. Formerly, AAA (American Automobile Assn., 1909-55), USAC (U.S. Auto Club, 1956-78), CART (Championship Auto Racing Teams, 1979-91). CART was renamed IndyCar in 1992 and then lost use of the name in 1997. It was known as the FedEx Championship Series from 1998-2002.

Multiple titles: A.J. Foyt (7); Mario Andretti (4); Jimmy Bryan, Earl Cooper, Ted Horn, Rick Mears, Louie Meyer, Bobby Rahal, Al Unser (3); Tony Bettenhausen, Sebastien Bourdais, Gil de Ferran, Ralph DePalma, Peter DePaolo, Joe Leonard, Rex Mays, Tommy Milton, Ralph Mulford, Jimmy Murphy, Wilbur Shaw, Al Unser Jr., Bobby Unser, Rodger Ward and Alex Zanardi (2).

AAA

Year		Year		Year		Year	
1909	George Robertson	1920	Tommy Milton	1931	Louis Schneider	1942-45	No racing
1910	Ray Harroun	1921	Tommy Milton	1932	Bob Carey	1946	Ted Horn
1911	Ralph Mulford	1922	Jimmy Murphy	1933	Louie Meyer	1947	Ted Horn
1912	Ralph DePalma	1923	Eddie Hearne	1934	Bill Cummings	1948	Ted Horn
1913	Earl Cooper	1924	Jimmy Murphy	1935	Kelly Petillo	1949	Johnnie Parsons
1914	Ralph DePalma	1925	Peter DePaolo	1936	Mauri Rose	1950	Henry Banks
1915	Earl Cooper	1926	Harry Hartz	1937	Wilbur Shaw	1951	Tony Bettenhausen
1916	Dario Resta	1927	Peter DePaolo	1938	Floyd Roberts	1952	Chuck Stevenson
1917	Earl Cooper	1928	Louie Meyer	1939	Wilbur Shaw	1953	Sam Hanks
1918	Ralph Mulford	1929	Louie Meyer	1940	Rex Mays	1954	Jimmy Bryan
1919	Howard Wilcox	1930	Billy Arnold	1941	Rex Mays	1955	Bob Sweikert

USAC

Year		Year		Year		Year	
1956	Jimmy Bryan	1962	Rodger Ward	1968	Bobby Unser	1974	Bobby Unser
1957	Jimmy Bryan	1963	A.J. Foyt	1969	Mario Andretti	1975	A.J. Foyt
1958	Tony Bettenhausen	1964	A.J. Foyt	1970	Al Unser	1976	Gordon Johncock
1959	Rodger Ward	1965	Mario Andretti	1971	Joe Leonard	1977	Tom Sneva
1960	A.J. Foyt	1966	Mario Andretti	1972	Joe Leonard	1978	A.J. Foyt
1961	A.J. Foyt	1967	A.J. Foyt	1973	Roger McCluskey		

Champ Car World Series (formerly CART)

Year	Driver	Car	Team	Sts	Wins	Poles	Earnings
1979	**Rick Mears**	Penske Ford	Penske	14	3	2	$408,078
1980	**Johnny Rutherford**	Chaparral Ford	Chaparral	12	5	3	503,595
1981	**Rick Mears**	Penske Ford	Penske	11	6	2	323,670
1982	**Rick Mears**	Penske Ford	Penske	11	4	8	306,454
1983	**Al Unser**	Penske Ford	Penske	13	1	0	500,109
1984	**Mario Andretti**	Lola Ford	Newman/Haas	16	6	8	931,929
1985	**Al Unser**	March Ford	Penske	14	1	1	843,885
1986	**Bobby Rahal**	March Ford	TrueSports	17	6	2	1,488,049
1987	**Bobby Rahal**	Lola Ford	TrueSports	15	3	1	1,261,098
1988	**Danny Sullivan**	Penske Chevrolet	Penske	15	4	9	1,222,791
1989	**Emerson Fittipaldi**	Penske Chevrolet	Patrick	15	5	4	2,166,078
1990	**Al Unser Jr.**	Lola Chevrolet	Galles-Kraco	16	6	1	1,946,833
1991	**Michael Andretti**	Lola Chevrolet	Newman/Haas	17	8	8	2,461,734
1992	**Bobby Rahal**	Lola Chevrolet	Rahal-Hogan	16	4	3	2,235,298
1993	**Nigel Mansell**	Lola Ford	Newman/Haas	15	5	7	2,526,953
1994	**Al Unser Jr.**	Penske Ilmor	Marlboro Team Penske	16	8	4	3,535,813
1995	**Jacques Villeneuve**	Reynard Ford	Team Green	17	4	6	2,996,269
1996	**Jimmy Vasser**	Reynard Honda	Target Chip Ganassi	16	4	4	3,071,500
1997	**Alex Zanardi**	Reynard Honda	Target Chip Ganassi	16	5	4	2,096,250
1998	**Alex Zanardi**	Reynard Honda	Target Chip Ganassi	19	7	0	2,229,250
1999	**Juan Montoya**	Reynard Honda	Target Chip Ganassi	20	7	7	1,973,000
2000	**Gil de Ferran**	Reynard Honda	Marlboro Team Penske	20	2	5	1,677,000
2001	**Gil de Ferran**	Reynard Honda	Marlboro Team Penske	20	2	5	1,761,500
2002	**Cristiano da Matta**	Lola Toyota	Newman/Haas	19	7	7	2,053,000
2003	**Paul Tracy**	Lola Ford-Cosworth	Player's/Forsythe	18	7	6	1,007,000
2004	**Sebastien Bourdais**	Lola Ford-Cosworth	Newman/Haas	14	7	8	843,500
2005	**Sebastien Bourdais**	Lola Ford-Cosworth	Newman/Haas	13	6	5	668,500

Champ Car Rookie of the Year

Officially the Roshfrans Rookie of the Year Award and presented to the rookie who accumulates the most Champ Car Series points among first year drivers. Roshfrans is the official lubricant of Champ Car.

Year		Year		Year		Year	
1979	Bill Alsup	1986	Dominic Dobson	1993	Nigel Mansell	2000	Kenny Brack
1980	Dennis Firestone	1987	Fabrizio Barbazza	1994	Jacques Villeneuve	2001	Scott Dixon
1981	Bob Lazier	1988	John Jones	1995	Gil de Ferran	2002	Mario Dominguez
1982	Bobby Rahal	1989	Bernard Jourdain	1996	Alex Zanardi	2003	Sebastien Bourdais
1983	Teo Fabi	1990	Eddie Cheever	1997	Patrick Carpentier	2004	A.J. Allmendinger
1984	Roberto Guerrero	1991	Jeff Andretti	1998	Tony Kanaan	2005	Timo Glock
1985	Arie Luyendyk	1992	Stefan Johansson	1999	Juan Montoya		

All-Time Champ Car Leaders

Champ Car's all-time Top 10 drivers in victories, pole positions and earnings, based on records through Oct. 22, 2006. Drivers active in 2006 are in **bold** type. Totals include victories, poles and earnings before Champ Car (then CART) was established in 1979. Earnings totals include year-end performance awards.

Victories

1	A.J. Foyt	67
2	Mario Andretti	52
3	Michael Andretti	42
4	Al Unser	39
5	Bobby Unser	35
6	Al Unser Jr.	31
7	**Paul Tracy**	30
8	Rick Mears	29
9	Johnny Rutherford	27
10	Rodger Ward	26

Pole Positions

1	Mario Andretti	67
2	A.J. Foyt	53
3	Bobby Unser	49
4	Rick Mears	40
5	Michael Andretti	32
6	Al Unser	27
7	**Paul Tracy**	25
	Sebastien Bourdais	25
9	Johnny Rutherford	23
10	Gordon Johncock	20

Earnings (unofficial)

1	Al Unser Jr.	$18,828,406
2	Michael Andretti	18,228,119
3	Bobby Rahal	16,344,008
4	Emerson Fittipaldi	14,293,625
5	**Jimmy Vasser**	11,726,249
6	Mario Andretti	11,552,154
7	**Paul Tracy**	11,207,270
8	Rick Mears	11,050,807
9	Danny Sullivan	8,884,126
10	Arie Luyendyk	7,732,188

FORMULA ONE CIRCUIT
United States Grand Prix

Federation Internationale Sportive Automobile (FISA) sanctioned two annual U.S. Grand Prix–USA/East and USA/West–from 1976-80 and 1983-84. Phoenix was the site of the U.S. Grand Prix from 1989-91. Indianapolis Motor Speedway has hosted the U.S. Grand Prix since 2000.

Indianapolis 500
Officially sanctioned as Grand Prix race from 1950-60 only. See page 902 for details.

U.S. Grand Prix—East

Held from 1959-80 and 1981-88 at the following locations: Sebring, Fla. (1959); Riverside, Calif. (1960); Watkins Glen, N.Y. (1961-80); and Detroit (1982-88). There was no race in 1981. Race discontinued in 1989.

Multiple winners: Jim Clark, Graham Hill and Ayrton Senna (3); James Hunt, Carlos Reutemann and Jackie Stewart (2).

Year	Driver / Car		Year	Driver / Car	
1959	Bruce McLaren, NZE	Cooper Climax	1974	Carlos Reutemann, ARG	Brabham Ford
1960	Stirling Moss, GBR	Lotus Climax	1975	Niki Lauda, AUT	Ferrari
1961	Innes Ireland, GBR	Lotus Climax	1976	James Hunt, GBR	McLaren Ford
1962	Jim Clark, GBR	Lotus Climax	1977	James Hunt, GBR	McLaren Ford
1963	Graham Hill, GBR	BRM	1978	Carlos Reutemann, ARG	Ferrari
1964	Graham Hill, GBR	BRM	1979	Gilles Villeneuve, CAN	Ferrari
1965	Graham Hill, GBR	BRM	1980	Alan Jones, AUS	Williams Ford
1966	Jim Clark, GBR	Lotus BRM	1981	Not held	
1967	Jim Clark, GBR	Lotus Ford	1982	John Watson, GBR	McLaren Ford
1968	Jackie Stewart, GBR	Matra Ford	1983	Michele Alboreto, ITA	Tyrrell Ford
1969	Jochen Rindt, AUT	Lotus Ford	1984	Nelson Piquet, BRA	Brabham BMW Turbo
1970	Emerson Fittipaldi, BRA	Lotus Ford	1985	Keke Rosberg, FIN	Williams Honda Turbo
1971	Francois Cevert, FRA	Tyrrell Ford	1986	Ayrton Senna, BRA	Lotus Renault Turbo
1972	Jackie Stewart, GBR	Tyrrell Ford	1987	Ayrton Senna, BRA	Lotus Honda Turbo
1973	Ronnie Peterson, SWE	Lotus Ford	1988	Ayrton Senna, BRA	McLaren Honda Turbo

U.S. Grand Prix—West

Held from 1976-83 at Long Beach, Calif. Races also held in Las Vegas (1981-82), Dallas (1984) and Phoenix (1989-91). Race discontinued in 1992.

Multiple winners: Alan Jones and Ayrton Senna (2).

Year	Driver / Car		Year	Driver / Car	
1976	Clay Regazzoni, SWI	Ferrari	1983	John Watson, GBR	McLaren Ford
1977	Mario Andretti, USA	Lotus Ford	1984	Keke Rosberg, FIN	Williams Honda Turbo
1978	Carlos Reutemann, ARG	Ferrari	1985-88	Not held	
1979	Gilles Villeneuve, CAN	Ferrari	1989	Alain Prost, FRA	McLaren Honda
1980	Nelson Piquet, BRA	Brabham Ford	1990	Ayrton Senna, BRA	McLaren Honda
1981	Alan Jones, AUS	Williams Ford	1991	Ayrton Senna, BRA	McLaren Honda
1982	Niki Lauda, AUT	McLaren Ford			

U.S. Grand Prix
Held since 2000 at Indianapolis Motor Speedway.

Multiple winner: Michael Schumacher (4).

Year	Driver / Car		Year	Driver / Car	
2000	Michael Schumacher, GER	Ferrari	2004	Michael Schumacher, GER	Ferrari
2001	Mika Hakkinen, FIN	McLaren Mercedes	2005	Michael Schumacher, GER	Ferrari
2002	Rubens Barrichello, BRA	Ferrari	2006	Michael Schumacher, GER	Ferrari
2003	Michael Schumacher, GER	Ferrari			

World Champions

Officially called the World Championship of Drivers and based on Formula One (Grand Prix) records through the 2006 season.

Multiple winners: Michael Schumacher (7); Juan-Manuel Fangio (5); Alain Prost (4); Jack Brabham, Niki Lauda, Nelson Piquet, Ayrton Senna and Jackie Stewart (3); Fernando Alonso, Alberto Ascari, Jim Clark, Emerson Fittipaldi, Mika Hakkinen and Graham Hill (2).

Year	Driver	Country	Car	Sts	Wins	Poles	Runner(s)-up
1950	**Guiseppe Farina**	Italy	Alfa Romeo	7	3	2	J.M. Fangio, ARG
1951	**Juan-Manuel Fangio**	Argentina	Alfa Romeo	8	3	4	A. Ascari, ITA
1952	**Alberto Ascari**	Italy	Ferrari	8	6	5	G. Farina, ITA
1953	**Alberto Ascari**	Italy	Ferrari	9	5	6	J.M. Fangio, ARG
1954	**Juan-Manuel Fangio**	Argentina	Maserati/Mercedes	9	6	5	F. Gonzalez, ARG
1955	**Juan-Manuel Fangio**	Argentina	Mercedes	7	4	3	S. Moss, GBR
1956	**Juan-Manuel Fangio**	Argentina	Lancia/Ferrari	8	3	5	S. Moss, GBR
1957	**Juan-Manuel Fangio**	Argentina	Maserati	8	4	4	S. Moss, GBR
1958	**Mike Hawthorn**	Great Britain	Ferrari	11	1	4	S. Moss, GBR
1959	**Jack Brabham**	Australia	Cooper Climax	9	2	1	T. Brooks, GBR
1960	**Jack Brabham**	Australia	Cooper Climax	10	5	3	B. McLaren, NZE

Year	Driver	Country	Car	Sts	Wins	Poles	Runner(s)-up
1961	**Phil Hill**	United States	Ferrari	8	2	5	W. von Trips, GER
1962	**Graham Hill**	Great Britain	BRM	9	4	1	J. Clark, GBR
1963	**Jim Clark**	Great Britain	Lotus Climax	10	7	7	G. Hill, GBR
							& R. Ginther, USA
1964	**John Surtees**	Great Britain	Ferrari	10	2	2	G. Hill, GBR
1965	**Jim Clark**	Great Britain	Lotus Climax	10	6	6	G. Hill, GBR
1966	**Jack Brabham**	Australia	Brabham Repco	9	4	3	J. Surtees, GBR
1967	**Denis Hulme**	New Zealand	Brabham Repco	11	2	0	J. Brabham, AUS
1968	**Graham Hill**	Great Britain	Lotus Ford	12	3	2	J. Stewart, GBR
1969	**Jackie Stewart**	Great Britain	Matra Ford	11	6	2	J. Ickx, BEL
1970	**Jochen Rindt**	Austria	Lotus Ford	13	5	3	J. Ickx, BEL
1971	**Jackie Stewart**	Great Britain	Tyrrell Ford	11	6	6	R. Peterson, SWE
1972	**Emerson Fittipaldi**	Brazil	Lotus Ford	12	5	3	J. Stewart, GBR
1973	**Jackie Stewart**	Great Britain	Tyrrell Ford	15	5	3	E. Fittipaldi, BRA
1974	**Emerson Fittipaldi**	Brazil	McLaren Ford	15	3	2	C. Regazzoni, SWI
1975	**Niki Lauda**	Austria	Ferrari	14	5	9	E. Fittipaldi, BRA
1976	**James Hunt**	Great Britain	McLaren Ford	16	6	8	N. Lauda, AUT
1977	**Niki Lauda**	Austria	Ferrari	17	3	2	J. Scheckter, RSA
1978	**Mario Andretti**	United States	Lotus Ford	16	6	8	R. Peterson, SWE
1979	**Jody Scheckter**	South Africa	Ferrari	15	3	1	G. Villeneuve, CAN
1980	**Alan Jones**	Australia	Williams Ford	14	5	3	N. Piquet, BRA
1981	**Nelson Piquet**	Brazil	Brabham Ford	15	3	4	C. Reutemann, ARG
1982	**Keke Rosberg**	Finland	Williams Ford	16	1	1	D. Pironi, FRA
							& J. Watson, GBR
1983	**Nelson Piquet**	Brazil	Brabham BMW Turbo	15	3	1	A. Prost, FRA
1984	**Niki Lauda**	Austria	McL. TAG Turbo	16	5	0	A. Prost, FRA
1985	**Alain Prost**	France	McL. TAG Turbo	16	5	2	M. Alboreto, ITA
1986	**Alain Prost**	France	McL. TAG Turbo	16	4	1	N. Mansell, GBR
1987	**Nelson Piquet**	Brazil	Williams Honda Turbo	16	3	4	N. Mansell, GBR
1988	**Ayrton Senna**	Brazil	McLaren Honda Turbo	16	8	13	A. Prost, FRA
1989	**Alain Prost**	France	McLaren Honda	16	4	2	A. Senna, BRA
1990	**Ayrton Senna**	Brazil	McLaren Honda	16	6	10	A. Prost, FRA
1991	**Ayrton Senna**	Brazil	McLaren Honda	16	7	8	N. Mansell, GBR
1992	**Nigel Mansell**	Great Britain	Williams Renault	16	9	14	R. Patrese, ITA
1993	**Alain Prost**	France	Williams Renault	16	7	13	A. Senna, BRA
1994	**Michael Schumacher**	Germany	Benetton Ford	14	8	6	D. Hill, GBR
1995	**Michael Schumacher**	Germany	Benetton Renault	17	9	4	D. Hill, GBR
1996	**Damon Hill**	Great Britain	Williams Renault	16	8	9	J. Villeneuve, CAN
1997	**Jacques Villeneuve**	Canada	Williams Renault	17	7	10	H.H. Frentzen, GER
1998	**Mika Hakkinen**	Finland	McLaren Mercedes	16	8	9	M. Schumacher, GER
1999	**Mika Hakkinen**	Finland	McLaren Mercedes	16	5	11	E. Irvine, GBR
2000	**Michael Schumacher**	Germany	Ferrari	17	9	9	M. Hakkinen, FIN
2001	**Michael Schumacher**	Germany	Ferrari	17	9	11	D. Coulthard, GBR
2002	**Michael Schumacher**	Germany	Ferrari	17	11	7	R. Barrichello, BRA
2003	**Michael Schumacher**	Germany	Ferrari	16	6	5	K. Raikkonen, FIN
2004	**Michael Schumacher**	Germany	Ferrari	18	13	8	R. Barrichello, BRA
2005	**Fernando Alonso**	Spain	Renault	19	7	6	K. Raikkonen, FIN
2006	**Fernando Alonso**	Spain	Renault	18	7	6	M. Schumacher, GER

All-Time Leaders

The all-time Top 15 Grand Prix winning drivers, based on records through 2006. Listed are starts (Sts), poles won (Pole), wins (1st), second place finishes (2nd), and third (3rd). Drivers active in 2006 and career victories in **bold** type.

		Sts	Pole	1st	2nd	3rd			Sts	Pole	1st	2nd	3rd
1	**M. Schumacher**	249	68	**91**	43	20	9	Nelson Piquet	207	24	**23**	20	17
2	Alain Prost	199	33	**51**	35	20	10	Damon Hill	99	20	**22**	15	5
3	Ayrton Senna	161	65	**41**	23	16	11	Mika Hakkinen	163	27	**20**	14	17
4	Nigel Mansell	187	32	**31**	17	11	12	Stirling Moss	66	16	**16**	5	3
5	Jackie Stewart	99	17	**27**	11	5	13	**Fernando Alonso**	88	15	**15**	14	8
6	Jim Clark	72	33	**25**	1	6	14	Jack Brabham	126	13	**14**	10	7
	Niki Lauda	171	24	**25**	20	9		Emerson Fittipaldi	144	6	**14**	13	8
8	Juan-Manuel Fangio	51	28	**24**	10	1		Graham Hill	176	13	**14**	15	7

ENDURANCE RACES

The 24 Hours of Le Mans

Officially, the Le Mans Grand Prix. First run May 22-23, 1923. All subsequent races have been held in June, except in 1956 (July) and 1968 (September). Originally contested on a 10.73-mile track, the circuit was shortened to 8.383 miles in 1932 and has fluxuated around 8.5 miles ever since.

Multiple winners: Tom Kristensen (7); Jacky Ickx (6); Derek Bell (5); Frank Biela, Yannick Dalmas, Oliver Gendebien, Henri Pescarolo and Emanuele Pirro (4); Woolf Barnato, Luigi Chinetti, Hurley Haywood, Phil Hill, Al Holbert and Klaus Ludwig (3); Sir Henry Birkin, Ivoe Bueb, Rinaldo Capello, Ron Flockhart, Jean-Pierre Jaussaud, Gerard Larrousse, JJ Lehto, Andre Rossignol, Raymond Sommer, Hans Stuck, Gijs van Lennep, Marco Werner and Jean-Pierre Wimille (2).

Year	Drivers	Car	MPH
1923	Andre Lagache & Rene Leonard	Chenard & Walcker	57.21
1924	John Duff & Francis Clement	Bentley	53.78
1925	Gerard de Courcelles & Andre Rossignol	La Lorraine	57.84
1926	Robert Bloch & Andre Rossignol	La Lorraine	66.08
1927	J.D. Benjafield & Sammy Davis	Bentley	61.35
1928	Woolf Barnato & Bernard Rubin	Bentley	69.11
1929	Woolf Barnato & Sir Henry Birkin	Bentley Speed 6	73.63
1930	Woolf Barnato & Glen Kidston	Bentley Speed 6	75.88
1931	Earl Howe & Sir Henry Birkin	Alfa Romeo	78.13
1932	Raymond Sommer & Luigi Chinetti	Alfa Romeo	76.48
1933	Raymond Sommer & Tazio Nuvolari	Alfa Romeo	81.40
1934	Luigi Chinetti & Philippe Etancelin	Alfa Romeo	74.74
1935	John Hindmarsh & Louis Fontes	Lagonda	77.85
1936	Not held		
1937	Jean-Pierre Wimille & Robert Benoist	Bugatti 57G	85.13
1938	Eugene Chaboud & Jean Tremoulet	Delahaye	82.36
1939	Jean-Pierre Wimille & Pierre Veyron	Bugatti 57G	86.86
1940-48	Not held		
1949	Luigi Chinetti & Lord Selsdon	Ferrari	82.28
1950	Louis Rosier & Jean-Louis Rosier	Talbot-Lago	89.71
1951	Peter Walker & Peter Whitehead	Jaguar C	93.50
1952	Hermann Lang & Fritz Reiss	Mercedes-Benz	96.67
1953	Tony Rolt & Duncan Hamilton	Jaguar C	98.65
1954	Froilan Gonzalez & Maurice Trintignant	Ferrari 375	105.13
1955	Mike Hawthorn & Ivor Bueb	Jaguar D	107.05
1956	Ron Flockhart & Ninian Sanderson	Jaguar D	104.47
1957	Ron Flockhart & Ivor Bueb	Jaguar D	113.83
1958	Oliver Gendebien & Phil Hill	Ferrari 250	106.18
1959	Roy Salvadori & Carroll Shelby	Aston Martin	112.55
1960	Oliver Gendebien & Paul Fräre	Ferrari 250	109.17
1961	Oliver Gendebien & Phil Hill	Ferrari 250	115.88
1962	Oliver Gendebien & Phil Hill	Ferrari 250	115.22
1963	Lodovico Scarfiotti & Lorenzo Bandini	Ferrari 250	118.08
1964	Jean Guichet & Nino Vaccarella	Ferrari 275	121.54
1965	Masten Gregory & Jochen Rindt	Ferrari 250	121.07
1966	Bruce McLaren & Chris Amon	Ford Mk. II	125.37
1967	A.J. Foyt & Dan Gurney	Ford Mk. IV	135.46
1968	Pedro Rodriguez & Lucien Bianchi	Ford GT40	115.27
1969	Jacky Ickx & Jackie Oliver	Ford GT40	129.38
1970	Hans Herrmann & Richard Attwood	Porsche 917	119.28
1971	Gijs van Lennep & Helmut Marko	Porsche 917	138.13
1972	Graham Hill & Henri Pescarolo	Matra-Simca	121.45
1973	Henri Pescarolo & Gerard Larrousse	Matra-Simca	125.67
1974	Henri Pescarolo & Gerard Larrousse	Matra-Simca	119.27
1975	Derek Bell & Jacky Ickx	Mirage-Ford	118.98
1976	Jacky Ickx & Gijs van Lennep	Porsche 936	123.49
1977	Jacky Ickx, Jurgen Barth & Hurley Haywood	Porsche 936	120.95
1978	Jean-Pierre Jaussaud & Didier Pironi	Renault-Alpine	130.60
1979	Klaus Ludwig, Bill Wittington & Don Whittington	Porsche 935	108.10
1980	Jean-Pierre Jaussaud & Jean Rondeau	Rondeau-Cosworth	119.23
1981	Jacky Ickx & Derek Bell	Porsche 936	124.94
1982	Jacky Ickx & Derek Bell	Porsche 956	126.85
1983	Vern Schuppan, Hurley Haywood & Al Holbert	Porsche 956	130.70
1984	Klaus Ludwig & Henri Pescarolo	Porsche 956	126.88
1985	Klaus Ludwig, Paolo Barilla & John Winter	Porsche 956	131.75
1986	Derek Bell, Hans Stuck & Al Holbert	Porsche 962	128.75
1987	Derek Bell, Hans Stuck & Al Holbert	Porsche 962	124.06
1988	Jan Lammers, Johnny Dumfries & Andy Wallace	Jaguar XJR	137.75
1989	Jochen Mass, Manuel Reuter & Stanley Dickens	Sauber-Mercedes	136.39
1990	John Nielsen, Price Cobb & Martin Brundle	Jaguar XJR-12	126.71
1991	Volker Weider, Johnny Herbert & Bertrand Gachof	Mazda 787B	127.31

Year	Drivers	Car	MPH
1992	Derek Warwick, Yannick Dalmas & Mark Blundell	Peugeot 905B	123.89
1993	Geoff Brabham, Christophe Bouchut & Eric Helary	Peugeot 905	132.58
1994	Yannick Dalmas, Hurley Haywood & Mauro Baldi	Porsche 962LM	129.82
1995	Yannick Dalmas, JJ Lehto & Masanori Sekiya	McLaren BMW	105.00
1996	Davy Jones, Manuel Reuter & Alexander Wurz	TWR Porsche	124.65
1997	Michele Alberto, Stefan Johansson & Tom Kristensen	TWR Porsche	126.88
1998	Laurent Aiello, Allan McNish & Stephane Ortelli	Porsche 911 GT1	123.86
1999	Yannick Dalmas, Joachim Winkelhock & Pierluigi Martini	BMW V-12 LMR	129.38

Year	Drivers	Car	MPH
2000	Frank Biela, Tom Kristensen & Emanuele Pirro	Audi R8	128.34
2001	Frank Biela, Tom Kristensen & Emanuele Pirro	Audi R8	129.66
2002	Frank Biela, Tom Kristensen & Emanuele Pirro	Audi R8	131.89
2003	Tom Kristensen, Rinaldo Capello & Guy Smith	Bentley Speed 8	143.43
2004	Tom Kristensen, Rinaldo Capello & Seiji Ara	Audi R8	133.86
2005	Tom Kristensen, JJ Lehto & Marco Werner	Audi R8	130.73
2006	Frank Biela, Emanuele Pirro & Marco Werner	Audi R10	133.85

The 24 Hours of Daytona

Officially, the Rolex 24 at Daytona. First run in 1962 as a three-hour race and won by Dan Gurney in a Lotus 19 Ford. Contested over a 3.56-mile course at Daytona (Fla.) International Speedway. There have been several distance changes since 1962: the event was a three-hour race (1962-63); a 2,000-kilometer race (1964-65); a 24-hour race (1966-71); a six-hour race (1972) and a 24-hour race again since 1973. The race was canceled in 1974 due to a national energy crisis.

Multiple winners: Hurley Haywood (5); Peter Gregg, Pedro Rodriguez and Bob Wollek (4); Derek Bell, Butch Leitzinger, Rolf Stommelen and Andy Wallace (3); Mauro Baldi, A.J. Foyt, Al Holbert, Ken Miles, John Paul Jr., Brian Redman, Elliott Forbes-Robinson, Lloyd Ruby, Wayne Taylor, Didier Theys and Al Unser Jr. (2).

Year	Drivers	Car	MPH
1962	Dan Gurney	Lotus 19 Ford	104.101
1963	Pedro Rodriguez	Ferrari GTO	102.074
1964	Pedro Rodriguez & Phil Hill	Ferrari GTO	98.230
1965	Ken Miles & Lloyd Ruby	Ford GT	99.944
1966	Ken Miles & Lloyd Ruby	Ford Mk. II	108.020
1967	Lorenzo Bandini & Chris Amon	Ferrari 330	105.688
1968	Vic Elford & Jochen Neerpasch	Porsche 907	106.697
1969	Mark Donohue & Chuck Parsons	Lola Chevrolet	99.268
1970	Pedro Rodriguez & Leo Kinnunen	Porsche 917	114.866
1971	Pedro Rodriguez & Jackie Oliver	Porsche 917K	109.203
1972	Mario Andretti & Jacky Ickx	Ferrari 312P	122.573
1973	Peter Gregg & Hurley Haywood	Porsche Carrera	106.225
1974	Not held		
1975	Peter Gregg & Hurley Haywood	Porsche Carrera	108.531
1976	Peter Gregg, Brian Redman & John Fitzpatrick	BMW CSL	104.040
1977	Hurley Haywood, John Graves & Dave Helmick	Porsche Carrera	108.801
1978	Peter Gregg, Rolf Stommelen & Antoine Hezemans	Porsche Turbo	108.743
1979	Hurley Haywood, Ted Field & Danny Ongais	Porsche Turbo	109.249
1980	Rolf Stommelen, Volkert Merl & Reinhold Joest	Porsche Turbo	114.303
1981	Bobby Rahal, Brian Redman & Bob Garretson	Porsche Turbo	113.153
1982	John Paul Sr., John Paul Jr. & Rolf Stommelen	Porsche Turbo	114.794
1983	A.J. Foyt, Preston Henn, Bob Wollek & Claude Ballot-Lena	Porsche Turbo	98.781
1984	Sarel van der Merwe, Tony Martin & Graham Duxbury	March Porsche	103.119

Year	Drivers	Car	MPH
1985	A.J. Foyt, Bob Wollek, Al Unser Sr. & Thierry Boutsen	Porsche 962	104.162
1986	Al Holbert, Derek Bell & Al Unser Jr.	Porsche 962	105.484
1987	Al Holbert, Derek Bell, Chip Robinson & Al Unser Jr.	Porsche 962	111.599
1988	Raul Boesel, Martin Brundle & John Nielsen	Jaguar XJR-9	107.943
1989	John Andretti, Derek Bell & Bob Wollek	Porsche 962	92.009
1990	Davy Jones, Jan Lammers & Andy Wallace	Jaguar XJR-12	112.857
1991	Hurley Haywood, John Winter, Frank Jelinski, Henri Pescarolo & Bob Wollek	Porsche 962-C	106.633
1992	Masahiro Hasemi, Kazuyoshi Hoshino & Toshio Suzuki	Nissan R-91	112.897
1993	P.J. Jones, Mark Dismore & Rocky Moran	Toyota Eagle	103.537
1994	Paul Gentilozzi, Scott Pruett, Butch Leitzinger & Steve Millen	Nissan 300 ZXT	104.80
1995	Jurgen Lassig, Christophe Bouchut, Giovanni Lavaggi & Marco Werner	Porsche Spyder	102.280
1996	Wayne Taylor, Scott Sharp & Jim Pace	Olds Arness MK-III	103.32
1997	Rob Dyson, James Weaver, Butch Leitzinger, Andy Wallace, John Paul Jr., Eliot Forbes-Robinson & John Schneider	Ford R&S MK-III	102.29
1998	Mauro Baldi, Arie Luyendyk, Gianpiero Moretti & Didier Theys	Ferrari 333	105.40
1999	Elliot Forbes-Robinson, Butch Leitzinger & Andy Wallace	Riley & Scott Ford	104.957
2000	Olivier Beretta, Dominique Dupuy & Karl Wendlinger	Dodge Viper	107.207
2001	Ron Fellows, Franck Freon, Chris Kneifel & Johnny O'Connell	Chevy Corvette	97.293

The 24 Hours of Daytona (Cont.)

Year	Drivers	Car	MPH	Year	Drivers	Car	MPH
2002	Mauro Baldi, Fredy Lienhard, Max Papis & Didier Theys	Dallara LMP900	106.143	2005	Wayne Taylor, Max Angelelli & Emmanuel Collard	Pontiac Riley	105.204
2003	Kevin Buckler, Michael Schrom, Timo Bernhard & Jorg Bergmeister	Porsche GT3 RS	115.969	2006	Scott Dixon, Dan Wheldon & Casey Mears	Lexus Riley	108.826
2004	Terry Borcheller, Forest Barber, Andy Pilgrim & Christian Fittipaldi	Pontiac Doran	77.927				

NHRA DRAG RACING

NHRA Champions

Based on points earned during the NHRA POWERade Drag Racing series. The series, originally sponsored by the R.J. Reynolds Tobacco Company's Winston brand, began for Top Fuel, Funny Car and Pro Stock in 1975. The Coca-Cola Company's POWERade brand soft drink began a five-year sponsorship deal with the series in 2002.

Top Fuel

Multiple winners: Joe Amato (5); Don Garlits, Shirley Muldowney, Gary Scelzi and Tony Schumacher (3); Kenny Bernstein, Larry Dixon and Scott Kalitta (2).

Year		Year		Year		Year	
1975	Don Garlits	1983	Gary Beck	1991	Joe Amato	1999	Tony Schumacher
1976	Richard Tharp	1984	Joe Amato	1992	Joe Amato	2000	Gary Scelzi
1977	Shirley Muldowney	1985	Don Garlits	1993	Eddie Hill	2001	Kenny Bernstein
1978	Kelly Brown	1986	Don Garlits	1994	Scott Kalitta	2002	Larry Dixon
1979	Rob Bruins	1987	Dick LaHaie	1995	Scott Kalitta	2003	Larry Dixon
1980	Shirley Muldowney	1988	Joe Amato	1996	Kenny Bernstein	2004	Tony Schumacher
1981	Jeb Allen	1989	Gary Ormsby	1997	Gary Scelzi	2005	Tony Schumacher
1982	Shirley Muldowney	1990	Joe Amato	1998	Gary Scelzi		

Funny Car

Multiple winners: John Force (13); Don Prudhomme, Kenny Bernstein (4); Raymond Beadle (3); Frank Hawley (2).

Year		Year		Year		Year	
1975	Don Prudhomme	1983	Frank Hawley	1991	John Force	1999	John Force
1976	Don Prudhomme	1984	Mark Oswald	1992	Cruz Pedregon	2000	John Force
1977	Don Prudhomme	1985	Kenny Bernstein	1993	John Force	2001	John Force
1978	Don Prudhomme	1986	Kenny Bernstein	1994	John Force	2002	John Force
1979	Raymond Beadle	1987	Kenny Bernstein	1995	John Force	2003	Tony Pedregon
1980	Raymond Beadle	1988	Kenny Bernstein	1996	John Force	2004	John Force
1981	Raymond Beadle	1989	Bruce Larson	1997	John Force	2005	Gary Scelzi
1982	Frank Hawley	1990	John Force	1998	John Force		

Pro Stock

Multiple winners: Bob Glidden (9); Warren Johnson (6); Lee Shepherd (4); Greg Anderson (3); Darrell Alderman, Jeg Coughlin Jr. and Jim Yates (2).

Year		Year		Year		Year	
1975	Bob Glidden	1983	Lee Shepherd	1991	Darrell Alderman	1999	Warren Johnson
1976	Larry Lombardo	1984	Lee Shepherd	1992	Warren Johnson	2000	Jeg Coughlin Jr.
1977	Don Nicholson	1985	Bob Glidden	1993	Warren Johnson	2001	Warren Johnson
1978	Bob Glidden	1986	Bob Glidden	1994	Darrell Alderman	2002	Jeg Coughlin Jr.
1979	Bob Glidden	1987	Bob Glidden	1995	Warren Johnson	2003	Greg Anderson
1980	Bob Glidden	1988	Bob Glidden	1996	Jim Yates	2004	Greg Anderson
1981	Lee Shepherd	1989	Bob Glidden	1997	Jim Yates	2005	Greg Anderson
1982	Lee Shepherd	1990	John Myers	1998	Warren Johnson		

All-Time Leaders
Career Victories
All-time leaders through Oct. 8, 2006. Drivers active in 2006 are in **bold**.

	Top Fuel			Funny Car			Pro Stock	
1	Joe Amato	52	1	**John Force**	121	1	**Warren Johnson**	96
2	Kenny Bernstein	39	2	Don Prudhomme	35	2	Bob Glidden	85
3	**Larry Dixon**	38	3	**Tony Pedregon**	32	3	**Greg Anderson**	42
4	Don Garlits	35	4	Kenny Bernstein	30	4	**Kurt Johnson**	35
5	**Tony Schumacher**	33	5	**Cruz Pedregon**	23	5	**Jeg Coughlin**	34

BOXING

Just when you think he was done for good following his dominating win over Antonio Tarver in 2006, rumors began to swirl that **Bernard Hopkins** could be back in 2007.

RED DAWN

Don't look now but America has lost its long standing grip on the heavyweight division which is now firmly in the grasp of three fighters from the former Soviet Republic.

THAT RED YOU SEE IN THE HEAVYWEIGHT DIVISION ISN'T JUST BLOOD DRIPPING FROM A CUT. It's the invasion of fighters from the former Soviet Union.

This is not your father's heavyweight division, the one where the heavyweight championship was once viewed as a virtual American birthright.

Joe Louis, Rocky Marciano, Muhammad Ali, Joe Frazier, George Foreman, Larry Holmes, Mike Tyson, Riddick Bowe, Evander Holyfield.

All heavyweight champions.

All American heroes.

Those days are gone. The first inkling came in 1999, when England's Lennox Lewis defeated Holyfield for the undisputed championship. But once Lewis retired in early 2004, the division was left without a dominant force, and one by one, the fractured titles slipped away from American champions.

As 2005 came to a close, Nikolai Valuev of Russia, the so-called "Beast from East," became the biggest heavyweight champion in history, outpointing John Ruiz to win the WBA crown in a tightly contested decision victory.

An astonishing seven-feet tall and weighing 320-plus pounds, Valuev is a stunning mountain of a man. Once viewed as nothing more than a freak show, he is now taken far more seriously.

He has made two title defenses—knockouts of Owen Beck and Monte Barrett—to move to 45-0 and within four wins of Marciano's hallowed 49-0 mark.

Although Valuev is based in Germany, promoter extraordinaire Don King, with a share of Valuev's promotional contract, brought him to the United States to defend

 **Dan Rafael** covers boxing for ESPN.com.

AP/Wide World Photos

The biggest of the big Russians was **Nikolai Valuev** who took the title from a distinctly outsized John Ruiz and then successfully defended his title twice in 2006.

against Barrett in suburban Chicago while using the Sears Tower as a promotional backdrop for the tallest champion in history.

Next up was little-known Sergei Liakhovich, a former amateur standout from Belarus. Thought to be fodder for emerging WBO title holder Lamon Brewster, Liakhovich was given a shot at the title.

Brewster and Liakhovich went to war and waged the year's most exciting heavyweight fight. It was a brawl from the opening bell, and Brewster bravely fought through a detached retina suffered early in the bout.

When the rock 'em, sock 'em slugfest was over, Liakhovich had claimed a close unanimous decision and the belt.

Three weeks later, Wladimir Klitschko of Ukraine, the 1996 Olympic super heavyweight gold medalist and the best-known of the foreign heavyweights, bludgeoned IBF champion Chris Byrd for a seventh-round TKO. It was all Klitschko, whose power shots were too much for Byrd to handle. It was an even more ferocious display than Klitschko's overwhelming points win against Byrd in 2000.

American Hasim Rahman had ascended to the WBC championship when Vitali Klitschko, the older brother of Wladimir Klitschko, abruptly retired days before his title

Ukrainian heavyweight **Wladimir Klitschko** beat up American champion Chris Byrd and took his IBF belt in 2006.

Although Maskaev had become a U.S. citizen two years ago, Top Rank promoter Bob Arum couldn't resist the time-honored tradition of promoting a fight with a nationalistic theme.

Dubbed "America's Last Line of Defense," the fight was draped in the red, white and blue and Rahman seemingly took his responsibility to keep a title in American hands quite seriously.

But as the rounds wore on, Rahman was getting more and more tired and Maskaev, who owned a 1999 knockout of Rahman, started landing blows at an alarming rate.

Finally, in the 12th round, Maskaev dropped a weary Rahman. Moments later Maskaev stopped him to claim the title and give the former Soviet fighters the last piece of the puzzle.

The unheard of sweep had Arum pondering the plight of the American heavyweight when he finally found the words.

"Everybody in boxing says white guys can't fight," Arum said. "White guys can fight. White American guys can't fight. White Russian guys can fight."

defense against Rahman at the end of 2005.

Vitali Klitschko, who had already put the mandatory fight with Rahman off several times, could not overcome a knee injury.

In his initial defense, Rahman retained the belt with a draw against flabby James Toney. Then, in another WBC mandatory defense, Rahman faced challenger Oleg Maskaev of Kazakhstan.

AP/Wide World Photos

DAN RAFAEL'S

10

Greatest Stories of the Year in **Boxing**

10 **Middleweight champion Jermain Taylor** can't seem to escape controversy. The 2000 U.S. Olympic bronze medalist, already with a pair of tight, disputed decisions against long-reigning champ Bernard Hopkins in his previous two bouts, makes the second defense of his unified titles against No. 1 contender Winky Wright. They wage an exciting fight, and when it's over Taylor escapes with an unpopular title-retaining draw.

09 **British superstar Ricky Hatton's** invasion of America doesn't exactly remind anyone of the Beatles. The junior welterweight champ, who had stopped fearsome Kostya Tszyu in 2005, signs a lucrative deal with cable giant HBO and there are great expectations. Instead, Hatton struggles to a controversial decision win against WBA welterweight titlist Luis Collazo, sits out the rest of the year and decides to move back to junior welterweight in 2007.

08 **Out of the ring for 16 months** since losing to Kevin McBride and announcing his retirement, former heavyweight champ Mike Tyson returns. Sort of. A Las Vegas resort hires the broke and out of shape Tyson to put on daily open workouts in the hopes that he will draw a crowd. That leads to the launch of "Mike Tyson's World Tour," a series of four-round exhibitions designed to help him out of bankruptcy. The first outing against former sparring partner Corey Sanders is such a critical flop that the future of the tour is in doubt after just one night.

07 **Filipino icon Manny Pacquiao exacts** revenge for his close decision loss to junior lightweight star Erik Morales. In their exciting rematch, Morales dominates the first half of the fight until he runs out of gas and Pacquiao pours it on to score a dominant 10th-round knockout. It sets the stage for a much-anticipated rubber match.

06 **Oscar De La Hoya triumphantly returns** from a 20-month layoff to batter Ricardo Mayorga into a sixth-round TKO and win the WBC super welterweight title. The victory earns De La Hoya his 10th world title covering six divisions. The fight also generates a shockingly high 925,000 pay-per-view subscriptions, reinforcing De La Hoya's status as boxing's most bankable attraction.

05 **Carlos Baldomir**, an obscure fighter from Argentina, pulls off a pair of monumental upsets. First, he stuns undisputed welterweight champion Zab Judah in Judah's hometown of New York to win the title. Baldomir follows with a ninth-round beatdown of New Jersey hero Arturo Gatti in Atlantic City. The wins set Baldomir up for a showdown with pound-for-pound king Floyd Mayweather Jr.

04 **Oscar De La Hoya's Golden Boy Promotions** emerges as the dominant promotional force in the sport with a host of high-profile signings and an increasingly cozy relationship with cable giant HBO. With company boss De La Hoya and partners Bernard Hopkins, Shane Mosley and Marco Antonio Barrera already fighting under its banner, Golden Boy adds several champions, contenders and prospects to its stable, including stars Manny Pacquiao, Juan Manuel Marquez and Diego Corrales.

03 **When former two-time lightweight champion Jose Luis Castillo** fails to make the 135-pound limit the day before his rubber match with WBC champion Diego Corrales, the fight is canceled in a stunning turn of events. It is the second time in a row that Castillo fails to make weight for a title bout with his rival. Then it is Corrales' turn. He is stripped of the title for failing to make weight for a rubber match with Joel Casamayor. The next day, Casamayor wins the vacant belt via split decision.

02 **Former undisputed middleweight champion Bernard Hopkins** moves up to light heavyweight to face division king Antonio Tarver in what Hopkins insists will be his farewell fight. Hopkins, under the tutelage of renowned fitness guru Mackie Shilstone, bulks up to 175 pounds and puts on a clinic. He knocks Tarver down and easily outpoints him before officially announcing his retirement. How long will it last? A few months later, Hopkins talks about his desire to unretire to move up in weight again, this time to challenge WBC heavyweight champion Oleg Maskaev.

01 **Fighters from the former Soviet Republic complete** an unprecedented sweep of the four major heavyweight titles. All of them defeat reigning Americans to win belts. Nikolai Valuev of Russia unseats John Ruiz in December 2005 for the WBA belt. Sergei Liakhovich outpoints Lamon Brewster for the WBO title in April. Three weeks later, Wladimir Klitschko crushes Chris Byrd in seven rounds to claim the IBF championship. In August, Kazakhstan's Oleg Maskaev scores a 12th-round knockout of Hasim Rahman.

2005-2006
Season in Review

SPORTS ALMANAC

Current Champions
WBA, WBC, and IBF Titleholders (through Oct. 29, 2006)

The champions of professional boxing's 17 principal weight divisions, as recognized by the Word Boxing Association (WBA), World Boxing Council (WBC) and International Boxing Federation (IBF). Where applicable, records listed below fighters' names indicate wins-losses-draws-no contest.

	Weight Limit	WBA Champion	WBC Champion	IBF Champion
Heavyweight	—	Nikolai Valuev 45-0-0, 33 KOs	Oleg Maskaev 33-5-0, 26 KOs	Wladimir Klitschko 46-3-0, 41 KOs
Cruiserweight	190 lbs	Virgil Hill 50-5-0, 23 KOs	O'Neil Bell 26-1-0, 24 KOs	vacant
Light Heavyweight	175 lbs	vacant	Tomasz Adamek 31-0-0, 21 KOs	Clinton Woods 40-3-1, 24 KOs
Super Middleweight	168 lbs	Mikkel Kessler 38-0-0, 29 KOs	Mikkel Kessler 38-0-0, 29 KOs	Joe Calzaghe 42-0-0, 31 KOs
Middleweight	160 lbs	Jermain Taylor* 25-0-1, 17 KOs	Jermain Taylor 25-0-1, 17 KOs	Arthur Abraham 22-0-0, 17 KOs
Jr. Middleweight	154 lbs	Jose Antonio Rivera 38-4-1, 24 KOs	Oscar De La Hoya 38-4-0, 30 KOs	Cory Spinks 35-3-0, 21 KOs
Welterweight	147 lbs	vacant	Carlos Baldomir 43-9-6, 13 KOs	Kermit Cintron 27-1-0, 25 KOs
Jr. Welterweight	140 lbs	Souleymane M'baye 35-1-0, 20 KOs	Junior Witter 34-1-2, 19 KOs	Juan Urango 17-0-1, 13 KOs
Lightweight	135 lbs	Juan Diaz 30-0-0, 15 KOs	Joel Casamayor 34-3-1, 21 KOs	Jesus Chavez 42-3-0, 29 KOs
Jr. Lightweight	130 lbs	Edwin Valero 20-0-0, 20 KOs	Marco Antonio Barrera 63-4-0, 42 KOs	Gairy St. Clair 38-3-2, 17 KOs
Featherweight	126 lbs	Juan Manuel Marquez* 44-2-1, 33 KOs	Rudy Lopez 19-2-0, 13 KOs	Robert Guerrero 19-1-0, 12 KOs
Jr. Featherweight	122 lbs	Celestino Caballero 25-2-0, 18 KOs	Israel Vazquez 41-3-0, 29 KOs	vacant
Bantamweight	118 lbs	Wladimir Sidorenko 19-0-10, 6 KOs	Hozumi Hasegawa 20-2-0, 7 KOs	Rafael Marquez 36-3-0, 32 KOs
Jr. Bantamweight	115 lbs	Nobuo Nashiro 8-0-0, 5 KOs	Masamori Tokuyama 321-3-1, 8 KOs	Luis Perez 24-1-0, 15 KOs
Flyweight	112 lbs	Lorenzo Parra 27-0-0, 17 KOs	Pongsaklek Wonjongkam 62-2-0, 32 KOs	Vic Darchinyan 27-0-0, 21 KOs
Jr. Flyweight	108 lbs	Koki Kameda 12-0-0, 10 KOs	Omar Nino Romero 24-2-1, 10 KOs	Ulises Solis 21-1-2, 16 KOs
Minimumweight	105 lbs	Yutaka Niida 20-1-3, 8 KOs	Eagle Kyowa 16-1-0, 6 KOs	Muhammad Rachman 51-7-4, 23 KOs

*Jermain Taylor is the WBA middleweight "super world champion;" Juan Manuel Marquez is the WBA featherweight "super world champion."

Note: The following weight divisions are also known by these names—**Cruiserweight** as Jr. Heavyweight; **Jr. Middleweight** as Super Welterweight; **Jr. Welterweight** as Super Lightweight; **Jr. Lightweight** as Super Featherweight; **Jr. Featherweight** as Super Bantamweight; **Jr. Bantamweight** as Super Flyweight; **Jr. Flyweight** as Light Flyweight; and **Minimumweight** as Strawweight or Mini-Flyweights.

Major Bouts, 2005-06

Division by division, from Nov. 1, 2005 through Oct. 29, 2006.

WBA, WBC and IBF champions are listed in **bold** type. Note the following Result columm abbreviations (in alphabetical order): **Disq.** (won by disqualification); **KO** (knockout); **MDraw** (majority draw); **NC** (no contest); **SDraw** (split draw); **TDraw** (technical draw); **TKO** (technical knockout); **TWm** (won by technical majority decision); **TWs** (won by technical split decision); **TWu** (won by technical unanimous decision); **Wm** (won by majority decision); **Ws** (won by split decision) and **Wu** (won by unanimous decision).

Heavyweights

Date	Winner	Loser	Result	Title	Site
Nov. 19	Calvin Brock	David Bostice	Wu 12	—	Charlotte, N.C.
Dec. 17	Nikolai Valuev	**John Ruiz**	Wm 12	**WBA**	Berlin
Feb. 25	Calvin Brock	Zuri Lawrence	TKO 6	—	Las Vegas
Mar. 18	**Hasim Rahman**	James Toney	MDraw 12	**WBC**	Atlantic City
Apr. 1	Sergei Liakhovich	Lamon Brewster	Wu 12	WBO	Cleveland, Ohio
Apr. 22	Wladimir Klitschko	**Chris Byrd**	TKO 7	**IBF**	Mannheim, Germany
June 3	**Nikolai Valuev**	Owen Beck	TKO 3	**WBA**	Hannover, Germany
June 24	Calvin Brock	Timur Ibragimov	Wu 12	—	Las Vegas
Aug. 12	Oleg Maskaev	**Hasim Rahman**	TKO 12	**WBC**	Las Vegas
Sept. 2	Samuel Peter	James Toney	Ws 12	—	Los Angeles
Oct. 7	**Nikolai Valuev**	Monte Barrett	TKO 11	**WBA**	Rosemont, Ill.

Cruiserweights (190 lbs)
(Jr. Heavyweights)

Date	Winner	Loser	Result	Title	Site
Jan. 7	**O'Neill Bell**	**Jean-Marc Mormeck**	KO 10	**IBF/WBA/WBC***	New York City
Jan. 27	Virgil Hill	Valery Brudov	Wu 10	WBA†	Atlantic City

*Bell retained his IBF belt and won Mormeck's WBA and WBC belts to become the first undisputed cruiserweight champion since Evander Holyfield in 1988.
†Hill won the WBA belt but note that O'Neil Bell is the WBA "super" world champion.

Light Heavyweights (175 lbs)

Date	Winner	Loser	Result	Title	Site
May 13	**Clinton Woods**	Jason Delisle	TKO 6	**IBF**	Sheffield, England
June 2	Chad Dawson	Eric Harding	Wu 12	—	Santa Ynez, Calif.
June 10	Bernard Hopkins	Antonio Tarver	Wu 12	—	Atlantic City
July 27	Silvio Branco	Manny Siaca	Wu 12	WBA*	Milan, Italy
Sept. 2	**Clinton Woods**	Glen Johnson	Ws 12	**IBF**	Lancashire, England
Oct. 7	**Tomasz Adamek**	Paul Briggs	Wm 12	**WBC**	Rosemont, Ill.

*Branco won the vacant interim WBA title.

Super Middleweights (168 lbs)

Date	Winner	Loser	Result	Title	Site
Nov. 5	**Jeff Lacy**	Scott Pemberton	KO 2	**IBF**	Stateline, Nev.
Nov. 18	Chad Dawson	Ian Gardner	TKO 11	—	New Haven, Conn.
Jan. 14	**Mikkel Kessler**	Eric Lucas	TKO 10	**WBA**	Copenhagen
Jan. 28	**Markus Beyer**	Alberto Colajanni	TKO 12	**WBC**	Berlin
Mar. 4	Joe Calzaghe	**Jeff Lacy**	Wu 12	**IBF**/WBO*	Manchester, England
May 13	**Markus Beyer**	Sakio Bika	TDraw 4†	**WBC**	Zwickau, Germany
Oct. 14	**Joe Calzaghe**	Sakio Bika	Wu 12	**IBF**/WBO	Manchester, England
Oct. 14	**Mikkel Kessler**	**Markus Beyer**	TKO 3	**WBA/WBC**	Copenhagen, Denmark

*Calzaghe retained his WBO belt and captured Lacy's IBF belt with the victory.
†Beyer retained his belt and the fight was ruled a technical draw when the fight was stopped in the fourth round afer Beyer suffered a cut under his right eye caused by an accidental headbutt.

Major Bouts Scheduled for Fall 2006

Date	Division	Match-up	Title	Location
Nov. 4	welterweight	Carlos Baldomir-Floyd Mayweather	WBC	Las Vegas
Nov. 4	heavyweight	Sergei Liakhovich-Shannon Briggs	WBO	Phoenix
Nov. 4	lightweight	Juan Diaz-Fernando Angulo	WBA	Phoenix
Nov. 10	heavyweight	Evander Holyfield-Fres Oquendo	—	San Antonio
Nov. 11	heavyweight	Wladimir Klitschko-Calvin Brock	IBF	New York
Nov. 18	junior lightweight	Manny Pacquiao-Erik Morales	—	Las Vegas
Dec. 2	welterweight	Miguel Cotto-Carlos Quintana	WBA	Atlantic City, N.J.
Dec. 2	welterweight	Antonio Margarito-Joshua Clottey	WBO	Atlantic City, N.J.
Dec. 2	middleweight	Winky Wright-Ike Quartey	—	Tampa, Fla.
Dec. 9	middleweight	Jermain Taylor-Kassim Ouma	WBC/WBO	Little Rock, Ark.
Dec. 10	heavyweight	Oleg Maskaev-Peter Okhello	WBC	Moscow
Dec. 20	junior flyweight	Koki Kameda-Juan Landaeta	WBA	Tokyo

Middleweights (160 lbs)

Date	Winner	Loser	Result	Title	Site
Dec. 3	**Jermain Taylor**	Bernard Hopkins	Wu 12	**WBA/WBC**	Las Vegas
Dec. 10	Winky Wright	Sam Soliman	Tu 12	—	Uncasville, Conn.
Dec. 10	Arthur Abraham	Kinglsey Ikeke	TKO 5	**IBF***	Leipzig, Germany
Mar. 4	**Arthur Abraham**	Shannon Taylor	Wu 12	**IBF**	Oldenburg, Germany
Mar. 11	Felix Sturm	**Maselino Masoe**	Wu 12	WBA†	Hamburg, Germany
Apr. 29	Andre Ward	Andy Kolle	TKO 6	—	Mashantucket, Conn.
May 13	**Arthur Abraham**	Kofi Jantuah	Wu 12	**IBF**	Zwickau, Germany
June 17	**Jermain Taylor**	Winky Wright	Draw 12	**WBA/WBC**	Memphis, Tenn.
July 15	Javier Castillejo	**Felix Sturm**	TKO 3	WBA†	Hamburg, Germany
Sept. 23	**Arthur Abraham**	Edison Miranda	Wu 12	**IBF**	Wetzlar, Germany

*Abraham won the vacant IBF title that Taylor gave up in order to give Bernand Hopkins a rematch.
†Sturm won (then later lost) the WBA belt but note that Jermain Taylor is the WBA "super" world champion.

Junior Middleweights (154 lbs)
(Super Welterweights)

Date	Winner	Loser	Result	Title	Site
Jan. 21	Manny Pacquiao	Erik Morales	TKO 10		Las Vegas
Feb. 25	Shane Mosley	Fernando Vargas	TKO 10	—	Las Vegas
May 6	Jose Antonio Rivera	**Alejandro Garcia**	Wu 12	**WBA**	Worcester, Mass.
May 6	Oscar De La Hoya	**Ricardo Mayorga**	TKO 6	**WBC**	Las Vegas
July 8	Cory Spinks	**Roman Karmazin**	Wm 12	**IBF**	St. Louis
July 15	Shane Mosley	Fernando Vargas	TKO 6		Las Vegas
Aug. 5	Vernon Forrest	Ike Quartey	Wu 10	—	New York City
Aug. 5	Kasim Ouma	Sechew Powell	Wu 10	—	New York City
Sept. 26	Grady Brewer	Steve Forbes	Ws 12	—	Los Angeles

Note: The Grady Brewer-Steve Forbes bout (on Sept. 26) was the championship match of the ESPN reality series, "The Contender."

Welterweights (147 lbs)

Date	Winner	Loser	Result	Title	Site
Jan. 7	Carlos Baldomir	**Zab Judah**	Wu 12	**WBC**	New York City
Jan. 28	Arturo Gatti	Thomas Damgaard	TKO 11		Atlantic City
Apr. 8	Floyd Mayweather	**Zab Judah**	Wu 12	**IBF**	Las Vegas
May 13	Ricky Hatton	**Luis Collazo**	Wu 12	**WBA**	Boston, Mass.
July 22	**Carlos Baldomir**	Arturo Gatti	TKO 9	**WBC**	Atlantic City
July 29	Joshua Clottey	Richard Gutierrez	Wm 12	—	Santa Ynez, Calif.
Aug. 18	Paul Williams	Sharmba Mitchell	TKO 4	—	Augusta, Georgia
Oct. 28	Kermit Cintron	Mark Suarez	TKO 5	**IBF***	West Palm Beach, Fla.

*Cintron won the IBF title that was left vacant when Floyd Mayweather renounced the belt to fight for more money against WBC champion Carlos Baldomir.
Note: Judah's IBF title was not at risk for his January 7 fight with Carlos Baldomir. So despite the loss, he retained the belt until officially losing it to Floyd Mayweather in April.

Junior Welterweights (140 lbs)
(Super Lightweights)

Date	Winner	Loser	Result	Title	Site
Nov. 19	**Floyd Mayweather**	Sharmba Mitchell	TKO 6	**WBC**	Portland, Ore.
Nov. 26	**Ricky Hatton**	**Carlos Maussa**	KO 9	**IBF/WBA**	Sheffield, England
Mar. 3	Rustam Nugaev	Anthony Mora	TKO 5	—	Santa Ynez, Calif.
Mar. 4	Miguel Cotto	Gianluca Branco	TKO 8	—	Bayamon, Puerto Rico
June 30	Juan Urango	Naoufel Ben Rabah	Wu 12	**IBF***	Hollywood, Florida
July 29	Vivian Harris	Stevie Johnston	TKO 7	—	Santa Ynez, Calif.√
Sept. 2	Souleymane M'baye	Raul Balbi	TKO 4	**WBA***	Lancashire, England
Sept. 15	Junior Witter	DeMarcus Corley	Wu 12	**WBC†**	London
Oct. 21	Juan Lazcano	Manuel Garnica	Wu 10	—	El Paso, Texas

*Urango won the IBF belt that was vacated by Ricky Hatton when he moved up to the welterweight division.
*M'baye won the WBA belt that was vacated by Ricky Hatton when he moved up to the welterweight division.
†Witter won the WBC belt that was vacated by Floyd Mayweather when he moved up to the welterweight division.

Major Bouts, 2005-06 (Cont.)

Lightweights (135 lbs)

Date	Winner	Loser	Result	Title	Site
Feb. 4	Jose Luis Castillo	Rolando Reyes	Wu 12	—	El Paso, Tex.
Feb. 4	Jose Armando Santa Cruz	Edner Cherry	Wu 12	—	El Paso, Tex.
Apr. 8	**Juan Diaz**	Jose Miguel Cotto	Wu 12	**WBA**	Las Vegas
Apr. 29	Acelino Freitas	Zahir Raheem	Ws 12	—	Mashantucket, Conn.
May 18	Julio Diaz	Ricky Quiles	Wu 12	IBF*	Hollywood, Florida
May 20	Jose Armando Santa Cruz	Chikashi Inada	TKO 6	WBC**	Los Angeles
Aug. 12	David Diaz	J.A. Santa Cruz	TKO 10	WBC**	Las Vegas
Oct. 6	Joel Casamayor	Diego Corrales	Ws 12	**WBC†**	Las Vegas
Oct. 7	Nate Campbell	Matt Zegan	Wu 12	—	Rosemont, Ill.

*Diaz won the interim IBF belt.
**Santa Cruz won (then lost) the interim WBC belt
†Casamayor won the title that became vacant when titleholder Diego Corrales could not make the 135-pound weight limit for their scheduled title bout.

Junior Lightweights (130 lbs)
(Super Featherweights)

Date	Winner	Loser	Result	Title	Site
May 12	**Vicente Mosquera**	Jose Pablo Estrella	Ws 12	**WBA**	Cordoba, Argentina
May 20	**Marco Antonio Barrera**	Rocky Juarez	Ws 12	**WBC**	Los Angeles
May 31	Cassius Baloyi	Manuel Medina	KO 11	**IBF**	Airway Heights, Wash.
July 29	Gairy St. Clair	**Cassius Baloyi**	Wu 12	**IBF**	Johannesburg, S. Africa
Aug. 5	Edwin Valero	**Vicente Mosquera**	TKO 10	**WBA**	Panama City
Sept. 16	**Marco Antonio Barrera**	Rocky Juarez	Wu 12	**WBC**	Las Vegas
Sept. 16	Joan Guzman	Jorge Barrios	Ws 12	WBO*	Las Vegas

*Guzman won the WBO belt that was vacated by Jorge Barrios when he failed to make the 130-pound weight limit for their junior lightweight fight.

Featherweights (126 lbs)

Date	Winner	Loser	Result	Title	Site
Dec. 2	Gamaliel Diaz	Robert Guerrero	Ws 12	—	Lemoore, Calif.
Jan. 20	Valdemir Pereira	Phafrakorb Rakkietgym	Wu 12	IBF*	Mashantucket, Conn.
Jan. 29	Takashi Koshimoto	**In Jin Chi**	Ws 12	**WBC**	Fukuoka, Japan
Feb. 17	Humberto Soto	Oscar Leon	KO 9	WBC**	Los Mochis, Mexico
Mar. 4	**Chris John**	Juan Manuel Marquez	Wu 12	**WBA**	Tenggarong City, Indonesia
May 13	Eric Aiken	**Valdemir Pereira**	Disq. 8^	IBF	Boston, Mass.
June 23	Robert Guerrero	Gamaliel Diaz	KO 6	—	Oakland, Calif.
July 30	Rudy Lopez	**Takashi Koshimoto**	TKO 7	**WBC**	Fukuoka, Japan
Aug. 5	Juan Manuel Marquez	Terdsak Jandaeng	TKO 7	WBO†	Stateline, Nev.
Sept. 2	Robert Guerrero	**Eric Aiken**	TKO 8‡	IBF	Los Angeles
Sept. 9	**Chris John**	Renan Acosta	Wu 12	**WBA**	Jakarta, Indonesia

*Pereira won the vacant IBF title.
**Soto retained his interim WBC title.
^Pereira was disqualified at 1:37 of the eighth round due to repeated low blows.
†Marquez won the interim WBO title.
‡Aiken's corner stopped the fight following the eighth round.

Junior Featherweights (122 lbs)
(Super Bantamweights)

Date	Winner	Loser	Result	Title	Site
Dec. 3	**Israel Vazquez**	**Oscar Larios**	TKO 3	**IBF/WBC**	Las Vegas
Feb. 4	Celestino Caballero	Roberto Bonilla	TKO 7	WBA*	Panama City, Panama
Mar. 18	Somsak Sithchatchawal	**Mahyar Monshipour**	TKO 10	**WBA**	Levallois, France
June 10	**Israel Vazquez**	Ivan Hernandez	TKO 8	**WBC**	Atlantic City
Sept. 16	**Israel Vazquez**	Johnny Gonzalez	TKO 10	**WBC**	Las Vegas
Oct. 4	Celestino Caballero	**S. Sithchatchawal**	TKO 3	**WBA**	Ban Rai, Thailand
Oct. 21	Daniel Ponce De Leon	Al Seeger	TKO 8	—	El Paso, Texas

*Caballero retained his interim WBA title.

Bantamweights (118 lbs)

Date	Winner	Loser	Result	Title	Site
Nov. 5	**Rafael Marquez**	Silence Mabuza	TKO 4	**IBF**	Stateline, Nev.
Nov. 26	**Wladimir Sidorenko**	Jose de Jesus Lopez	Wu 12	**WBA**	Leverkusen, Germany
Feb. 25	Jhonny Gonzalez	Mark Johnson	KO 8	**WBO**	Las Vegas
Mar. 11	**Wladimir Sidorenko**	Ricardo Cordoba	MDraw 12	**WBA**	Hamburg, Germany
Mar. 25	**Hozumi Hasegawa**	Veerapol Sahaprom	KO 9	**WBC**	Kobe, Japan
May 27	Jhonny Gonzalez	Fernando Montiel	Ws 12	**WBO**	Carson, Calif.
July 15	**Wladimir Sidorenko**	P. Kratingdaenggym	Wu 112	**WBA**	Hamburg, Germany
Aug. 5	**Rafael Marquez**	Silence Mabuza	TKO 9	**IBF**	Stateline, Nev.
Oct. 21	Gerry Penalosa	Mauricio Martinez	TKO 9	—	El Paso, Texas
Oct. 21	Irene Pacheco	Leon Moore	Ws 12	—	Barranquilla, Colombia

Junior Bantamweights (115 lbs)
(Super Flyweights)

Date	Winner	Loser	Result	Title	Site
Jan. 20	Nonito Donaire	Kahren Harutyunyan	Ws 10	—	Temecula, Calif.
Jan. 21	**Martin Castillo**	Alexander Munoz	Ws 12	**WBA**	Las Vegas
Feb. 27	**Masamori Tokuyama**	Jose Navarro	Wu 12	**WBC**	Osaka, Japan
May 6	**Luis Perez**	Dimitri Kirilov	Ws 12	**IBF**	Worcester, Mass.
July 22	Nobuo Nashiro	**Martin Castillo**	TKO 10	**WBA**	Osaka, Japan
Sept. 18	Cristian Mijares	Katsushige Kawashima	Ws 12	WBC*	Yokohama, Japan
Sept. 23	Jorge Arce	Hawk Makepula	KO 4	—	Hidalgo, Texas

*interim title.

Flyweights (112 lbs)

Date	Winner	Loser	Result	Title	Site
Dec. 5	**Lorenzo Parra**	Brahim Asloum	Wu 12	**WBA**	Paris
Jan. 28	Jorge Arce	Adonis Rivas	TKO 10	WBC†	Cancun, Mexico
Feb. 16	**P. Wonjongkam**	Gilberto Keb Baas	Wu 12	**WBC**	Chainart, Thailand
Mar. 3	**Vic Darchinyan**	Diosdado Gabi	TKO 8	**IBF**	Santa Ynez, Calif.
May 1	**P. Wonjongkam**	Daigo Nakahiro	Wu 12	**WBC**	Bangkok, Thailand
June 3	**Vic Darchinyan**	Luis Maldonado	TKO 8	**IBF**	Las Vegas
June 30	**P. Wonjongkam**	Everardo Morales	TKO 4	**WBC**	Bangkok
Oct. 7	**Vic Darchinyan**	Glenn Donaire	TWu 6*	**IBF**	Las Vegas

*Darchinyan won by technical decision when the fight was stopped at 1:27 of the sixth round after his opponent suffered a broken jaw following what was ruled an accidental clash of heads.
†Arce retained the interim WBC belt

Junior Flyweights (108 lbs)
(Light Flyweights)

Date	Winner	Loser	Result	Title	Site
Nov. 19	**Roberto Vasquez**	Nerys Espinoza	Wu 12	**WBA**	Panama City
Jan. 7	Ulises Solis	**Will Grigsby**	Wu 12	**IBF**	New York City
Feb. 18	**Brian Viloria**	Jose Antonio Aguirre	Wu 12	**WBC**	Las Vegas
Mar. 25	**Ulises Solis**	Erik Ortiz	TKO 9	**IBF**	Guadalajara, Mexico
May 20	**Roberto Vasquez**	Noel Arambulet	Wu 12	**WBA**	Panama City
July 18	Wandee Singwangcha . .	Juanito Rubillar	Wu 12	WBC*	Bangkok
Aug. 2	Koki Kameda	Juan Landaeta	Ws 12	**WBA****	Yokohama, Japan
Aug. 4	**Ulises Solis**	Omar Salado	Draw 12	**IBF**	Tijuana, Mexico
Aug. 10	Omar Nino				
Sept. 29	Eric Ortiz	Benji Garcia	Wu 10	—	Camp Pendleton, Calif.
Oct. 1	Hugo Cazares	Nelson Dieppa	TKO 10	**WBO**	Caguas, Puerto Rico
Oct. 9	Wandee Singwangcha†	Munetsugu Kayo	Wu 12	—	Tokyo

*interim title.
**Kameda captured the WBA title that was left vacant by Roberto Vasquez when he announced plans to move up to the flyweight division.
†Singwangcha was the interim WBC titleholder but was stripped of the belt before the bout because he failed to make the weight.

Minimumweights (105 lbs)
(Strawweights or Mini-Flyweights)

Date	Winner	Loser	Result	Title	Site
Oct. 21	Ivan Calderon	Jose Luis Varela	Wu 12	—	Barranquilla, Colombia
Jan. 9	**Eagle Kyowa**	Ken Nakajima	TKO 7	**WBC**	Yokohama, Japan
Mar. 4	**Yutaka Niida**	Ronaldo Barrera	Wu 12	**WBA**	Tokyo
May 6	**Eagle Kyowa**	Rodel Mayol	Wu 12	**WBC**	Tokyo
May 6	**Muhammad Rachman**	Omar Soto	KO 6	**IBF**	Jakarta, Indonesia

†Eagle Kyowa was formerly known as Eagle Akakura.
*Rachman retained his IBF belt when the fight was stopped in round three following an unintentional head butt.

1892-2006
Through the Years

SPORTS ALMANAC

World Heavyweight Championship Fights

Widely accepted world champions in **bold** type. Note following result abbreviations: KO (knockout), TKO (technical knockout), Wu (unanimous decision), Wm (majority decision), Ws (split decision), Ref (referee's decision), ND (no decision), Disq. (won on disqualification).

Year Date	Winner	Age	Wgt	Loser	Wgt	Result	Location
1892 Sept. 7	James J. Corbett	26	178	John L. Sullivan	212	KO 21	New Orleans
1894 Jan. 25	**James J. Corbett**	27	184	Charley Mitchell	158	KO 3	Jacksonville, Fla.
1897 Mar. 17	Bob Fitzsimmons	34	167	**James J. Corbett**	183	KO 14	Carson City, Nev.
1899 June 9	James J. Jeffries	24	206	**Bob Fitzsimmons**	167	KO 11	Coney Island, N.Y.
1899 Nov. 3	**James J. Jeffries**	24	215	Tom Sharkey	183	Ref 25	Coney Island, N.Y.
1900 Apr. 6	**James J. Jeffries**	24	NA	Jack Finnegan	NA	KO 1	Detroit
1900 May 11	**James J. Jeffries**	25	218	James J. Corbett	188	KO 23	Coney Island, N.Y.
1901 Nov. 15	**James J. Jeffries**	26	211	Gus Ruhlin	194	TKO 6	San Francisco
1902 July 25	**James J. Jeffries**	27	219	Bob Fitzsimmons	172	KO 8	San Francisco
1903 Aug. 14	**James J. Jeffries**	28	220	James J. Corbett	190	KO 10	San Francisco
1904 Aug. 25	**James J. Jeffries***	29	219	Jack Munroe	186	TKO 2	San Francisco
1905 July 3	Marvin Hart	28	190	Jack Root	171	KO 12	Reno, Nev.
1906 Feb. 23	Tommy Burns	24	180	**Marvin Hart**	188	Ref 20	Los Angeles
1906 Oct. 2	**Tommy Burns**	25	NA	Jim Flynn	NA	KO 15	Los Angeles
1906 Nov. 28	**Tommy Burns**	25	172	Phila. Jack O'Brien	163½	Draw 20	Los Angeles
1907 May 8	**Tommy Burns**	25	180	Phila. Jack O'Brien	167	Ref 20	Los Angeles
1907 July 4	**Tommy Burns**	26	181	Bill Squires	180	KO 1	Colma, Calif.
1907 Dec. 2	**Tommy Burns**	26	177	Gunner Moir	204	KO 10	London
1908 Feb. 10	**Tommy Burns**	26	NA	Jack Palmer	NA	KO 4	London
1908 Mar. 17	**Tommy Burns**	26	NA	Jem Roche	NA	KO 1	Dublin
1908 Apr. 18	**Tommy Burns**	26	NA	Jewey Smith	NA	KO 5	Paris
1908 June 13	**Tommy Burns**	26	184	Bill Squires	183	KO 8	Paris
1908 Aug. 24	**Tommy Burns**	27	181	Bill Squires	184	KO 13	Sydney
1908 Sept. 2	**Tommy Burns**	27	183	Bill Lang	187	KO 6	Melbourne
1908 Dec. 26	Jack Johnson	30	192	**Tommy Burns**	168	TKO 14	Sydney
1909 Mar. 10	**Jack Johnson**	30	NA	Victor McLaglen	NA	ND 6	Vancouver
1909 May 19	**Jack Johnson**	31	205	Phila. Jack O'Brien	161	ND 6	Philadelphia
1909 June 30	**Jack Johnson**	31	207	Tony Ross	214	ND 6	Pittsburgh
1909 Sept. 9	**Jack Johnson**	31	209	Al Kaufman	191	ND 10	San Francisco
1909 Oct. 16	**Jack Johnson**	31	205½	Stanley Ketchel	170¼	KO 12	Colma, Calif.
1910 July 4	**Jack Johnson**	32	208	James J. Jeffries	227	KO 15	Reno, Nev.
1912 July 4	**Jack Johnson**	34	195½	Jim Flynn	175	TKO 9	Las Vegas, Nev.
1913 Dec. 19	**Jack Johnson**	35	NA	Jim Johnson	NA	Draw 10	Paris
1914 June 27	**Jack Johnson**	36	221	Frank Moran	203	Ref 20	Paris
1915 Apr. 5	Jess Willard	33	230	**Jack Johnson**	205½	KO 26	Havana
1916 Mar. 25	**Jess Willard**	34	225	Frank Moran	203	ND 10	NYC (Mad.Sq. Garden)
1919 July 4	Jack Dempsey	24	187	**Jess Willard**	245	TKO 4	Toledo, Ohio
1920 Sept. 6	**Jack Dempsey**	25	185	Billy Miske	187	KO 3	Benton Harbor, Mich.
1920 Dec. 14	**Jack Dempsey**	25	188¼	Bill Brennan	197	KO 12	NYC (Mad. Sq. Garden)
1921 July 2	**Jack Dempsey**	26	188	Georges Carpentier	172	KO 4	Jersey City, N.J.
1923 July 4	**Jack Dempsey**	28	188	Tommy Gibbons	175½	Ref 15	Shelby, Mont.
1923 Sept. 14	**Jack Dempsey**	28	192½	Luis Firpo	216½	KO 2	NYC (Polo Grounds)
1926 Sept. 23	Gene Tunney	29	189½	**Jack Dempsey**	190	Wu 10	Philadelphia
1927 Sept. 22	**Gene Tunney**	30	189½	Jack Dempsey	192½	Wu 10	Chicago
1928 July 26	**Gene Tunney****	31	192	Tom Heeney	203	TKO 11	NYC (Yankee Stadium)
1930 June 12	Max Schmeling	24	188	Jack Sharkey	197	Disq. 4	NYC (Yankee Stadium)
1931 July 3	**Max Schmeling**	25	189	Young Stribling	186½	TKO 15	Cleveland

*James J. Jeffries retired as champion on May 13, 1905, then came out of retirement to fight Jack Johnson for the title in 1910.
**Gene Tunney retired as champion in 1928.

Year	Date	Winner	Age	Wgt	Loser	Wgt	Result	Location
1932	June 21	Jack Sharkey	29	205	**Max Schmeling**	188	Ws 15	Long Island City, N.Y.
1933	June 29	Primo Carnera	26	260½	**Jack Sharkey**	201	KO 6	Long Island City, N.Y.
1933	Oct. 22	**Primo Carnera**	26	259½	Paulino Uzcudun	229¼	Wu 15	Rome
1934	Mar. 1	**Primo Carnera**	27	270	Tommy Loughran	184	Wu 15	Miami
1934	June 14	Max Baer	25	209½	**Primo Carnera**	263¼	TKO 11	Long Island City, N.Y.
1935	June 13	James J. Braddock	29	193¾	**Max Baer**	209	Wu 15	Long Island City, N.Y.
1937	June 22	Joe Louis	23	197¼	**James J. Braddock**	197	KO 8	Chicago
1937	Aug. 30	**Joe Louis**	23	197	Tommy Farr	204¼	Wu 15	NYC (Yankee Stadium)
1938	Feb. 23	**Joe Louis**	23	200	Nathan Mann	193½	KO 3	NYC (Mad. Sq. Garden)
1938	Apr. 1	**Joe Louis**	23	202½	Harry Thomas	196	KO 5	Chicago
1938	June 22	**Joe Louis**	24	198¾	Max Schmeling	193	KO 1	NYC (Yankee Stadium)
1939	Jan. 25	**Joe Louis**	24	200¼	John Henry Lewis	180¾	KO 1	NYC (Mad. Sq. Garden)
1939	Apr. 17	**Joe Louis**	24	201¼	Jack Roper	204¾	KO 1	Los Angeles
1939	June 28	**Joe Louis**	25	200¾	Tony Galento	233¾	TKO 4	NYC (Yankee Stadium)
1939	Sept. 20	**Joe Louis**	25	200	Bob Pastor	183	KO 11	Detroit
1940	Feb. 9	**Joe Louis**	25	203	Arturo Godoy	202	Ws 15	NYC (Mad. Sq. Garden)
1940	Mar. 29	**Joe Louis**	25	201½	Johnny Paychek	187½	KO 2	NYC (Mad. Sq. Garden)
1940	June 20	**Joe Louis**	26	199	Arturo Godoy	201¼	TKO 8	NYC (Yankee Stadium)
1940	Dec. 16	**Joe Louis**	26	202¼	Al McCoy	180¾	TKO 6	Boston
1941	Jan. 31	**Joe Louis**	26	202½	Red Burman	188	KO 5	NYC (Mad. Sq. Garden)
1941	Feb. 17	**Joe Louis**	26	203½	Gus Dorazio	193½	KO 2	Philadelphia
1941	Mar. 21	**Joe Louis**	26	202	Abe Simon	254½	TKO 13	Detroit
1941	Apr. 8	**Joe Louis**	26	203½	Tony Musto	199½	TKO 9	St. Louis
1941	May 23	**Joe Louis**	27	201½	Buddy Baer	237½	Disq. 7	Washington, D.C.
1941	June 18	**Joe Louis**	27	199½	Billy Conn	174	KO 13	NYC (Polo Grounds)
1941	Sept. 29	**Joe Louis**	27	202¼	Lou Nova	202½	TKO 6	NYC (Polo Grounds)
1942	Jan. 9	**Joe Louis**	27	206¾	Buddy Baer	250	KO 1	NYC (Mad. Sq. Garden)
1942	Mar. 27	**Joe Louis**	27	207½	Abe Simon	255½	KO 6	NYC (Mad. Sq. Garden)
1942-45 World War II								
1946	June 9	**Joe Louis**	32	207	Billy Conn	187	KO 8	NYC (Yankee Stadium)
1946	Sept. 18	**Joe Louis**	32	211	Tami Mauriello	198½	KO 1	NYC (Yankee Stadium)
1947	Dec. 5	**Joe Louis**	33	211½	Jersey Joe Walcott	194½	Ws 15	NYC (Mad. Sq. Garden)
1948	June 25	**Joe Louis***	34	213½	Jersey Joe Walcott	194¾	KO 11	NYC (Yankee Stadium)
1949	June 22	**Ezzard Charles**	27	181¾	Jersey Joe Walcott	195½	Wu 15	Chicago
1949	Aug. 10	**Ezzard Charles**	28	180	Gus Lesnevich	182	TKO 8	NYC (Yankee Stadium)
1949	Oct. 14	**Ezzard Charles**	28	182	Pat Valentino	188½	KO 8	San Francisco
1950	Aug. 15	**Ezzard Charles**	29	183¼	Freddie Beshore	184½	TKO 14	Buffalo
1950	Sept. 27	**Ezzard Charles**	29	184½	Joe Louis	218	Wu 15	NYC (Yankee Stadium)
1950	Dec. 5	**Ezzard Charles**	29	185	Nick Barone	178½	KO 11	Cincinnati
1951	Jan. 12	**Ezzard Charles**	29	185	Lee Oma	193	TKO 10	NYC (Mad. Sq. Garden)
1951	Mar. 7	**Ezzard Charles**	29	186	Jersey Joe Walcott	193	Wu 15	Detroit
1951	May 30	**Ezzard Charles**	29	182	Joey Maxim	181½	Wu 15	Chicago
1951	July 18	Jersey Joe Walcott	37	194	**Ezzard Charles**	182	KO 7	Pittsburgh
1952	June 5	**Jersey Joe Walcott**	38	196	Ezzard Charles	191½	Wu 15	Philadelphia
1952	Sept. 23	Rocky Marciano	29	184	**Jersey Joe Walcott**	196	KO 13	Philadelphia
1953	May 15	**Rocky Marciano**	29	184½	Jersey Joe Walcott	197¾	KO 1	Chicago
1953	Sept. 24	**Rocky Marciano**	30	185	Roland LaStarza	184¾	TKO 11	NYC (Polo Grounds)
1954	June 17	**Rocky Marciano**	30	187½	Ezzard Charles	185½	Wu 15	NYC (Yankee Stadium)
1954	Sept. 17	**Rocky Marciano**	31	187	Ezzard Charles	192½	KO 8	NYC (Yankee Stadium)
1955	May 16	**Rocky Marciano**	31	189	Don Cockell	205	TKO 9	San Francisco
1955	Sept. 21	**Rocky Marciano****	32	188¼	Archie Moore	188	KO 9	NYC (Yankee Stadium)
1956	Nov. 30	Floyd Patterson	21	182¼	Archie Moore	187¾	KO 5	Chicago
1957	July 29	**Floyd Patterson**	22	184	Tommy Jackson	192½	TKO 10	NYC (Polo Grounds)
1957	Aug. 22	**Floyd Patterson**	22	187¼	Pete Rademacher	202	KO 6	Seattle
1958	Aug. 18	**Floyd Patterson**	23	184½	Roy Harris	194	TKO 13	Los Angeles
1959	May 1	**Floyd Patterson**	24	182½	Brian London	206	KO 11	Indianapolis
1959	June 26	Ingemar Johansson	26	196	**Floyd Patterson**	182	TKO 3	NYC (Yankee Stadium)
1960	June 20	Floyd Patterson	25	190	**Ingemar Johansson**	194¾	KO 5	NYC (Polo Grounds)
1961	Mar. 13	**Floyd Patterson**	26	194¾	Ingemar Johansson	206½	KO 6	Miami Beach
1961	Dec. 4	**Floyd Patterson**	26	188½	Tom McNeeley	197	KO 4	Toronto
1962	Sept. 25	Sonny Liston	30	214	**Floyd Patterson**	189	KO 1	Chicago
1963	July 22	**Sonny Liston**	31	215	Floyd Patterson	194½	KO 1	Las Vegas
1964	Feb. 25	Cassius Clay**	22	210½	**Sonny Liston**	218	TKO 7	Miami Beach

*Joe Louis retired as champion on Mar. 1, 1949, then came out of retirement to fight Ezzard Charles for the title in 1950.

**Rocky Marciano retired as undefeated champion on Apr. 27, 1956.

World Heavyweight Championship Fights (Cont.)

Year	Date	Winner	Age	Wgt	Loser	Wgt	Result	Location
1965	Mar. 5	Ernie Terrell WBA	25	199	Eddie Machen	192	Wu 15	Chicago
1965	May 25	**Muhammad Ali**	23	206	Sonny Liston	215¼	KO 1	Lewiston, Maine
1965	Nov. 1	Ernie Terrell WBA	26	206	George Chuvalo	209	Wu 15	Toronto
1965	Nov. 22	**Muhammad Ali**	23	210	Floyd Patterson	196¾	TKO 12	Las Vegas
1966	Mar. 29	**Muhammad Ali**	24	214½	George Chuvalo	216	Wu 15	Toronto
1966	May 21	**Muhammad Ali**	24	201½	Henry Cooper	188	TKO 6	London
1966	June 28	Ernie Terrell WBA	27	209½	Doug Jones	187½	Wu 15	Houston
1966	Aug. 6	**Muhammad Ali**	24	209½	Brian London	201½	KO 3	London
1966	Sept. 10	**Muhammad Ali**	24	203½	Karl Mildenberger	194¼	TKO 12	Frankfurt, W. Ger.
1966	Nov. 14	**Muhammad Ali**	24	212¾	Cleveland Williams	210½	TKO 3	Houston
1967	Feb. 6	**Muhammad Ali**	25	212¼	Ernie Terrell WBA	212¼	Wu 15	Houston
1967	Mar. 22	**Muhammad Ali**	25	211½	Zora Folley	202½	KO 7	NYC (Mad. Sq. Garden)
1968	Mar. 4	Joe Frazier	24	204½	Buster Mathis	243½	TKO 11	NYC (Mad. Sq. Garden)
1968	Apr. 27	Jimmy Ellis	28	197	Jerry Quarry	195	Wm 15	Oakland
1968	June 24	Joe Frazier NY	24	203½	Manuel Ramos	208	TKO 2	NYC (Mad. Sq. Garden)
1968	Aug. 14	Jimmy Ellis WBA	28	198	Floyd Patterson	188	Ref 15	Stockholm
1968	Dec. 10	Joe Frazier NY	24	203	Oscar Bonavena	207	Wu 15	Philadelphia
1969	Apr. 22	Joe Frazier NY	25	204½	Dave Zyglewicz	190½	KO 1	Houston
1969	June 23	Joe Frazier NY	25	203½	Jerry Quarry	198½	TKO 8	NYC (Mad. Sq. Garden)
1970	Feb. 16	Joe Frazier NY	26	205	Jimmy Ellis WBA	201	TKO 5	NYC (Mad. Sq. Garden)
1970	Nov. 18	**Joe Frazier**	26	209	Bob Foster	188	KO 2	Detroit
1971	Mar. 8	**Joe Frazier**	27	205½	Muhammad Ali	215	Wu 15	NYC (Mad. Sq. Garden)
1972	Jan. 15	**Joe Frazier**	28	215½	Terry Daniels	195	TKO 4	New Orleans
1972	May 26	**Joe Frazier**	28	217½	Ron Stander	218	TKO 5	Omaha, Neb.
1973	Jan. 22	George Foreman	24	217½	**Joe Frazier**	214	TKO 2	Kingston, Jamaica
1973	Sept. 1	**George Foreman**	24	219½	Jose (King) Roman	196½	KO 1	Tokyo
1974	Mar. 26	George Foreman	25	224¾	Ken Norton	212¾	TKO 2	Caracas, Venezuela
1974	Oct. 30	Muhammad Ali	32	216½	**George Foreman**	220	KO 8	Kinshasa, Zaire
1975	Mar. 24	**Muhammad Ali**	33	223½	Chuck Wepner	225	TKO 15	Cleveland
1975	May 16	**Muhammad Ali**	33	224½	Ron Lyle	219	TKO 11	Las Vegas
1975	June 30	**Muhammad Ali**	33	224½	Joe Bugner	230	Wu 15	Kuala Lumpur, Malaysia
1975	Oct. 1	**Muhammad Ali**	33	224½	Joe Frazier	215	TKO 14	Manila, Philippines
1976	Feb. 20	**Muhammad Ali**	34	226	Jean Pierre Coopman	206	KO 5	San Juan, P.R.
1976	Apr. 30	**Muhammad Ali**	34	230	Jimmy Young	209	Wu 15	Landover, Md.
1976	May 24	**Muhammad Ali**	34	220	Richard Dunn	206½	TKO 5	Munich, W. Ger.
1976	Sept. 28	**Muhammad Ali**	34	221	Ken Norton	217½	Wu 15	NYC (Yankee Stadium)
1977	May 16	**Muhammad Ali**	35	221¼	Alfredo Evangelista	209¼	Wu 15	Landover, Md.
1977	Sept. 29	**Muhammad Ali**	35	225	Earnie Shavers	211¼	Wu 15	NYC (Mad. Sq. Garden)
1978	Feb. 15	Leon Spinks	24	197¼	**Muhammad Ali**	224¼	Ws 15	Las Vegas
1978	June 9	Larry Holmes	28	209	Ken Norton WBC††	220	Ws 15	Las Vegas
1978	Sept. 15	Muhammad Ali†	36	221	**Leon Spinks**	201	Wu 15	New Orleans
1978	Nov. 10	Larry Holmes WBC	29	214	Alfredo Evangelista	208¼	KO 7	Las Vegas
1979	Mar. 23	Larry Holmes WBC	29	214	Osvaldo Ocasio	207	TKO 7	Las Vegas
1979	June 22	Larry Holmes WBC	29	215	Mike Weaver	202	TKO 12	NYC (Mad. Sq. Garden)
1979	Sept. 28	Larry Holmes WBC	29	210	Earnie Shavers	211	TKO 11	Las Vegas
1979	Oct. 20	John Tate	24	240	Gerrie Coetzee	222	Wu 15	Pretoria, S. Africa
1980	Feb. 3	Larry Holmes WBC	30	213½	Lorenzo Zanon	215	TKO 6	Las Vegas
1980	Mar. 31	Mike Weaver	27	232	John Tate WBA	232	KO 15	Knoxville, Tenn.
1980	Mar. 31	Larry Holmes WBC	30	211	Leroy Jones	254½	TKO 8	Las Vegas
1980	July 7	Larry Holmes WBC	30	214¼	Scott LeDoux	226	TKO 7	Minneapolis
1980	Oct. 2	Larry Holmes WBC	30	211½	Muhammad Ali	217½	TKO 11	Las Vegas
1980	Oct. 25	Mike Weaver WBA	28	210	Gerrie Coetzee	226½	KO 13	Sun City, S. Africa
1981	Apr. 11	**Larry Holmes**	31	215	Trevor Berbick	215½	Wu 15	Las Vegas
1981	June 12	**Larry Holmes**	31	212½	Leon Spinks	200¼	TKO 3	Detroit
1981	Oct. 3	Mike Weaver WBA	29	215	James (Quick) Tillis	209	Wu 15	Rosemont, Ill.
1981	Nov. 6	**Larry Holmes**	32	213¼	Renaldo Snipes	215¾	TKO 11	Pittsburgh
1982	June 11	**Larry Holmes**	32	212½	Gerry Cooney	225½	TKO 13	Las Vegas
1982	Nov. 26	**Larry Holmes**	33	217½	Randall (Tex) Cobb	234¼	Wu 15	Houston
1982	Dec. 10	Michael Dokes	24	216	Mike Weaver WBA	209¾	TKO 1	Las Vegas

**After defeating Liston, Cassius Clay announced that he had changed his name to Muhammad Ali. He was later stripped of his title by the WBA and most state boxing commissions after refusing induction into the U.S. Army on Apr. 28, 1967.

† Muhammad Ali retired as champion on June 27, 1979, then came out of retirement to fight Larry Holmes for the title in 1980.

†† WBC recognized Ken Norton as world champion when Leon Spinks refused to meet Norton before Spinks' rematch with Muhammad Ali. Norton had scored a 15-round split decision over Jimmy Young on Nov. 5, 1977 in Las Vegas.

Year	Date	Winner	Age	Wgt	Loser	Wgt	Result	Location
1983	Mar. 27	**Larry Holmes**	33	221	Lucien Rodriguez	209	Wu 12	Scranton, Pa.
1983	May 20	Michael Dokes WBA	24	223	Mike Weaver	218½	Draw 15	Las Vegas
1983	May 20	**Larry Holmes**	33	213	Tim Witherspoon	219½	Ws 12	Las Vegas
1983	Sept. 10	**Larry Holmes**	33	223	Scott Frank	211¼	TKO 5	Atlantic City
1983	Sept. 23	Gerrie Coetzee	28	215	Michael Dokes WBA	217	KO 10	Richfield, Ohio
1983	Nov. 25	**Larry Holmes**	34	219	Marvis Frazier	200	TKO 1	Las Vegas
1984	Mar. 9	Tim Witherspoon*	26	220¼	Greg Page	239½	Wm 12	Las Vegas
1984	Aug. 31	Pinklon Thomas	26	216	Tim Witherspoon	217	Wm 12	Las Vegas
1984	Nov. 9	**Larry Holmes** IBF	35	221½	Bonecrusher Smith	227	TKO 12	Las Vegas
1984	Dec. 1	Greg Page	26	236½	Gerrie Coetzee WBA	218	KO 8	Sun City, S. Africa
1985	Mar. 15	**Larry Holmes** IBF	35	223½	David Bey	233¼	TKO 10	Las Vegas
1985	Apr. 29	Tony Tubbs	26	229	Greg Page WBA	239½	Wu 15	Buffalo
1985	May 20	**Larry Holmes** IBF	35	224¼	Carl Williams	215	Wu 15	Las Vegas
1985	June 15	Pinklon Thomas WBC	27	220¼	Mike Weaver	221¼	KO 8	Las Vegas
1985	Sept. 21	Michael Spinks	29	200	**Larry Holmes** IBF	221½	Wu 15	Las Vegas
1986	Jan. 17	Tim Witherspoon	28	227	Tony Tubbs WBA	229	Wm 15	Atlanta
1986	Mar. 22	Trevor Berbick	33	218½	Pinklon Thomas WBC	222¾	Wu 15	Las Vegas
1986	Apr. 19	**Michael Spinks** IBF	29	205	Larry Holmes	223	Ws 15	Las Vegas
1986	July 19	Tim Witherspoon WBA	28	234¾	Frank Bruno	228	TKO 11	Wembley, England
1986	Sept. 6	**Michael Spinks** IBF	30	201	Steffen Tangstad	214¾	TKO 4	Las Vegas
1986	Nov. 22	Mike Tyson	20	221¼	Trevor Berbick WBC	218½	TKO 2	Las Vegas
1986	Dec. 12	Bonecrusher Smith	33	228½	Tim Witherspoon WBA	233½	TKO 1	NYC (Mad. Sq. Garden)
1987	Mar. 7	Mike Tyson WBC	20	219	Bonecrusher Smith WBA	233	Wu 12	Las Vegas
1987	May 30	Mike Tyson	20	218¾	Pinklon Thomas	217¾	TKO 6	Las Vegas
1987	May 30	Tony Tucker**	28	222¼	Buster Douglas	227¼	TKO 10	Las Vegas
1987	June 15	**Michael Spinks**†	30	208¾	Gerry Cooney	238	TKO 5	Atlantic City
1987	Aug. 1	Mike Tyson	21	221	Tony Tucker IBF	221	Wu 12	Las Vegas
1987	Oct. 16	Mike Tyson	21	216	Tyrell Biggs	228¾	TKO 7	Atlantic City
1988	Jan. 22	Mike Tyson	21	215¾	Larry Holmes	225¾	TKO 4	Atlantic City
1988	Mar. 20	Mike Tyson	21	216¼	Tony Tubbs	238¼	KO 2	Tokyo
1988	June 27	Mike Tyson	21	218¼	**Michael Spinks**	212¼	KO 1	Atlantic City
1989	Feb. 25	**Mike Tyson**	22	218	Frank Bruno	228	TKO 5	Las Vegas
1989	July 21	**Mike Tyson**	23	219¼	Carl Williams	218	TKO 1	Atlantic City
1990	Feb. 10	Buster Douglas	29	231½	**Mike Tyson**	220½	KO 10	Tokyo
1990	Oct. 25	Evander Holyfield	28	208	**Buster Douglas**	246	KO 3	Las Vegas
1991	Apr. 19	**Evander Holyfield**	28	208	George Foreman	257	Wu 12	Atlantic City
1991	Nov. 23	**Evander Holyfield**	29	210	Bert Cooper	215	TKO 7	Atlanta
1992	June 19	**Evander Holyfield**	29	210	Larry Holmes	233	Wu 12	Las Vegas
1992	Nov. 13	Riddick Bowe	25	235	**Evander Holyfield**	205	Wu 12	Las Vegas
1993	Feb. 6	**Riddick Bowe**	25	243	Michael Dokes	244	TKO 1	NYC (Mad. Sq. Garden)
1993	May 8	Lennox Lewis WBC‡	27	235	Tony Tucker	235	Wu 12	Las Vegas
1993	May 22	**Riddick Bowe**	25	244	Jesse Ferguson	224	TKO 2	Washington, D.C.
1993	Oct. 1	Lennox Lewis WBC	28	233	Frank Bruno	238	TKO 7	Cardiff, Wales
1993	Nov. 6	Evander Holyfield	31	217	**Riddick Bowe** WBA/IBF	246	Wm 12	Las Vegas
1994	Apr. 22	Michael Moorer	26	214	**Evander Holyfield**	214	Wm 12	Las Vegas
1994	May 6	Lennox Lewis WBC	28	235	Phil Jackson	218	TKO 8	Atlantic City
1994	Sept. 25	Oliver McCall	29	231¼	**Lennox Lewis** WBC	238	TKO 2	London
1994	Nov. 5	George Foreman!	45	250	**Michael Moorer**	222	KO 10	Las Vegas
1995	Apr. 8	Oliver McCall WBC	29	231	Larry Holmes	236	Wu 12	Las Vegas
1995	Apr. 8	Bruce Seldon!	28	236	Tony Tucker	240	TKO 7	Las Vegas
1995	Apr. 22	**George Foreman**!	46	256	Axel Schulz	221	Ws 12	Las Vegas
1995	Aug. 19	Bruce Seldon WBA	28	234	Joe Hipp	223	TKO 10	Las Vegas
1995	Sept. 2	Frank Bruno	33	248	Oliver McCall WBC	235	Wu 12	London
1995	Dec. 9	Frans Botha*	27	237	Axel Schulz	222	Wu 12	Stuttgart, GER
1996	Mar. 16	Mike Tyson	29	220	Frank Bruno WBC	247	TKO 3	Las Vegas

*WBC recognized winner of Mar. 9, 1984 fight between Tim Witherspoon and Greg Page as world champion after Larry Holmes relinquished title in dispute. IBF then recognized Holmes.

**IBF recognized winner of May 30, 1987 fight between Tony Tucker and James (Buster) Douglas as world champion after Michael Spinks relinquished title in dispute.

†The July 15, 1987 Spinks-Cooney fight was not an official championship bout because it was not sanctioned by any boxing associations, councils or federations.

‡WBC recognized Lennox Lewis as world champion when Riddick Bowe gave up that portion of his title on Dec. 14, 1992, rather than fight Lewis, the WBC's mandatory challenger.

!George Foreman won WBA and IBF championships when he beat Michael Moorer on Nov. 5, 1994. He was stripped of WBA title on Mar. 4, 1995, when he refused to fight No. 1 contender Tony Tucker, and he relinquished IBF title on June 29, 1995, rather than give Axel Schulz a rematch. Tucker lost to Bruce Seldon in their April 8, 2001 fight for vacant WBA title.

World Heavyweight Championship Fights (Cont.)

Year	Date	Winner	Age	Wgt	Loser	Wgt	Result	Location
1996	June 22	Michael Moorer*	28	222	Axel Schulz	223	Ws 12	Dortmund, GER
1996	Sept. 7	Mike Tyson WBC†	30	219	Bruce Seldon WBA	229	TKO 1	Las Vegas
1996	Nov. 9	Evander Holyfield	34	215	**Mike Tyson** WBA	222	TKO 11	Las Vegas
1997	Feb. 7	Lennox Lewis†	31	251	Oliver McCall	237	TKO 5	Las Vegas
1997	Mar. 29	Michael Moorer IBF	29	212	Vaughn Bean	212	Wm 12	Las Vegas
1997	June 28	**Evander Holyfield** WBA‡	34	218	Mike Tyson	218	Disq. 3	Las Vegas
1997	July 12	Lennox Lewis WBC	31	242	Henry Akinwande	237½	Disq. 5	Stateline, Nev.
1997	Oct. 4	Lennox Lewis WBC	32	244	Andrew Golota	244	TKO 1	Atlantic City
1997	Nov. 8	Evander Holyfield WBA	35	214	Michael Moorer IBF	223	TKO 8	Las Vegas
1998	Mar. 28	Lennox Lewis WBC	32	243	Shannon Briggs	228	TKO 5	Atlantic City
1998	Sept. 19	**Evander Holyfield** WBA/IBF	35	217	Vaughn Bean	231	Wu 12	Atlanta
1998	Sept. 26	Lennox Lewis WBC	33	250	Zeljko Mavrovic	220	Wu 12	Uncasville, Conn.
1999	Mar. 13	Lennox Lewis WBC	33	246	**Evander Holyfield** WBA/IBF	215	Draw 12	NYC (Mad. Sq. Garden)
1999	Nov. 13	Lennox Lewis WBC	34	240	**Evander Holyfield** WBA/IBF	218	Wu 12	Las Vegas
2000	Apr. 29	**Lennox Lewis** WBC/IBF!	34	247	Michael Grant	250	KO 2	NYC (Mad. Sq. Garden)
2000	July 15	**Lennox Lewis** WBC/IBF·	34	250	Frans Botha	237	TKO 2	London
2000	Aug. 12	Evander Holyfield	37	221	John Ruiz	224	Wu 12	Las Vegas
2000	Nov. 11	**Lennox Lewis** WBC/IBF	35	249	David Tua	245	Wu 12	Las Vegas
2001	Mar. 3	John Ruiz	29	227	Evander Holyfield	217	Wu 12	Las Vegas
2001	Apr. 22	Hasim Rahman	28	237	**Lennox Lewis** WBC/IBF	253	KO 5	Johannesburg, S. Africa
2001	Nov. 17	Lennox Lewis	36	247	**Hasim Rahman** WBC/IBF	236	KO 4	Las Vegas
2001	Dec. 15	**John Ruiz** WBA	29	232	Evander Holyfield	219	Draw 12	Mashantucket, Conn.
2002	June 8	**Lennox Lewis** WBC/IBF@	36	249	Mike Tyson	235	KO 8	Memphis, Tenn.
2002	July 27	**John Ruiz** WBA	30	233	Kirk Johnson	238	Disq. 10	Las Vegas
2002	Dec. 14	Chris Byrd	32	214	Evander Holyfield	220	Wu 12	Atlantic City
2003	Mar. 1	Roy Jones Jr.	34	193	**John Ruiz** WBA	226	Wu 12	Las Vegas
2003	June 21	**Lennox Lewis** WBC	37	257	Vitali Klitschko	248	TKO 6	Los Angeles
2003	Sept. 20	**Chris Byrd** IBF	33	212	Fres Oquendo	224	Wu 12	Uncasville, Conn.
2003	Dec. 13	John Ruiz WBA%	31	241	Hasim Rahman	246	Wu 12	Atlantic City
2004	Apr. 17	**John Ruiz** WBA	32	240	Fres Oquendo	222	TKO 11	NYC (Mad. Sq. Garden)
2004	Apr. 17	**Chris Byrd** IBF	33	210	Andrew Golota	237	Draw 12	NYC (Mad. Sq. Garden)
2004	Apr. 24	Vitali Klitschko WBC^	32	245	Corrie Sanders	236	TKO 8	Los Angeles
2004	Nov. 13	**John Ruiz** WBA	32	226	Andrew Golota	240	Wu 12	NYC (Mad. Sq. Garden)
2004	Nov. 13	**Chris Byrd** IBF	34	214	Jameel McCline	270	Wu 12	NYC (Mad. Sq. Garden)
2004	Dec. 11	**Vitali Klitschko** WBC	33	250	Danny Williams	270	TKO 8	Las Vegas
2005	Apr. 30	James Toney$	36	233	**John Ruiz** WBA	241	NC	NYC (Mad. Sq. Garden)
2005	Oct. 1	**Chris Byrd** IBF	35	213	DaVarryl Williamson	225	Wu 12	Reno, Nev.

*Frans Botha won the vacant IBF title with a controversial 12-round decision over Axel Schulz on Dec. 9, 1995, but after legal sparring, was eventually stripped of the IBF belt for using anabolic steroids. Moorer then claimed the revacated title with his June 22, 1996 win over Schulz.

†Mike Tyson won the WBC belt from Frank Bruno on Mar. 16, 1996 and still held it at the time of his Sept. 7, 1996 win over Bruce Seldon (although it was not at risk for that fight) but was forced to relinquish the title after the bout for not fighting mandatory challenge Lennox Lewis. Tyson also paid Lewis $4 million to step aside and allow the Tyson-Seldon bout to take place. Lewis then fought Oliver McCall for the vacant WBC belt. The fight was stopped 55 seconds into round 5 because, inexplicably, McCall was visibly distraught and stopped throwing punches.

‡Holyfield won the bout by disqualification and retained the WBA belt after Tyson spit out his mouthpiece and bit off a piece of Holyfield's ear. Tyson had received a two-point deduction from referee Mills Lane and after a stern warning and a short delay the fight was allowed to continue. Later in round 3, he bit Holyfield's other ear and Tyson was disqualified.

!Lewis was stripped of the WBA title for choosing to fight Michael Grant instead of John Ruiz, the WBA's #1 challenger. The WBA sanctioned the Evander Holyfield-John Ruiz August 12 bout for its vacant heavyweight belt.

@Lewis effectively sold his IBF title to promoter Don King for $1 million and a Range Rover in September 2002. Lewis stepped aside (in exchange for the car and substantial fee), relinquishing his IBF belt by declining to fight Chris Byrd the mandatory challenger. The IBF sanctioned the Dec. 14, 2002 fight between Byrd and Holyfield for its vacant heavyweight belt.

%Ruiz won the interim WBA title after Roy Jones Jr. declined to defend the title he won from Ruiz on Mar. 1, 2003. The interim tag was later dropped when Jones returned to the light heavyweight division.

^Klitschko won the WBC title vacated by the retirement of Lennox Lewis.

$Toney won a uaninmous 12-round decision but tested positive for steroids in a post-fight drug test.

Year	Date	Winner	Age	Wgt	Loser	Wgt	Result	Location
2005	Dec. 17	Nikolai Valuev	32	324	**John Ruiz** WBA	238	Wm 12	Berlin
2006	Mar. 18	**Hasim Rahman** WBC*33		238	James Toney	237	MDraw 12	Atlantic City
2006	Apr. 22	Wladimir Klitschko	30	241	**Chris Byrd** IBF	231	TKO 7	Mannheim, Germany
2006	June 3	**Nikolai Valuev** WBA	32	321	Owen Beck	243	TKO 3	Hannover, Germany
2006	Aug. 12	Oleg Maskaev	37	238	**Hasim Rahman** WBC	235	TKO 12	Las Vegas
2006	Oct. 7	**Nikolai Valuev** WBA	33	330	Monte Barrett	229	TKO 11	Rosemont, Ill.

*The WBC voted to award interim champ Rahman its heavyweight belt on Nov. 10, 2005 in the wake of the retirement of titleholder Vitali Klitschko who had previously postponed his scheduled rematch with Rahman four times.

AP/Wide World Photos

All-Time Heavyweight Upsets

Buster Douglas was a 42-1 underdog when he defeated previously unbeaten heavyweight champion Mike Tyson on Feb. 10, 1990. That 10th-round knockout ranks as the biggest upset in boxing history. By comparison, 45-year-old George Foreman was only a 3-1 underdog before he unexpectedly won the title from Michael Moorer on Nov. 5, 1994.

Here are the best-known upsets in the annals of the heavyweight division. All fights were for the world championship except the Max Schmeling-Joe Louis bout.

Date	Winner	Loser	Result	KO Time	Location
9/7/1892	James J. Corbett	John L. Sullivan	KO 21	1:30	Olympic Club, New Orleans
4/5/1915	Jess Willard	Jack Johnson	KO 26	1:26	Mariano Race Track, Havana
9/23/26	Gene Tunney	Jack Dempsey	Wu 10	–	Sesquicentennial Stadium, Phila.
6/13/35	James J. Braddock	Max Baer	Wu 15	–	Mad. Sq.Garden Bowl, L.I. City
6/19/36	Max Schmeling	Joe Louis	KO 12	2:29	Yankee Stadium, New York
7/18/51	Jersey Joe Walcott	Ezzard Charles	KO 7	0:55	Forbes Field, Pittsburgh
6/26/59	Ingemar Johansson	Floyd Patterson	TKO 3	2:03	Yankee Stadium, New York
2/25/64	Cassius Clay	Sonny Liston	TKO 7	*	Convention Hall, Miami Beach
10/30/74	Muhammad Ali	George Foreman	KO 8	2:58	20th of May Stadium, Zaire
2/15/78	Leon Spinks	Muhammad Ali	Ws 15	–	Hilton Pavilion, Las Vegas
9/21/85	Michael Spinks	Larry Holmes	Wu 15	–	Riviera Hotel, Las Vegas
2/10/90	Buster Douglas	Mike Tyson	KO 10	1:23	Tokyo Dome, Tokyo
11/5/94	George Foreman	Michael Moorer	KO 10	2:03	MGM Grand, Las Vegas
11/9/96	Evander Holyfield	Mike Tyson	TKO 11	0:37	MGM Grand, Las Vegas
4/22/2001	Hasim Rahman	Lennox Lewis	KO 5	2:32	Johannesburg, South Africa

*Liston failed to answer bell for Round 7.

Major Titleholders

Note the following sanctioning body abbreviations: NBA (National Boxing Association), WBA (World Boxing Association), WBC (World Boxing Council), GBR (Great Britain), IBF (International Boxing Federation), plus other national and state commissions. Fighters who retired as champion are indicated by (*) and champions who abandoned or relinquished their titles are indicated by (†).

Heavyweights

Widely accepted champions in CAPITAL letters. Current champions in **bold** type (as of Oct. 31, 2005).

Note: Muhammad Ali was stripped of his world title in 1967 after refusing induction into the Army (see Muhammad Ali's Career Pro Record). George Foreman was stripped of his WBA and IBF titles in 1995, but remained active as linear champion.

Champion	Held Title
JOHN L. SULLIVAN	1885–92
JAMES J. CORBETT	1892–97
BOB FITZSIMMONS	1897–99
JAMES J. JEFFRIES	1899–1905*
MARVIN HART	1905–06
TOMMY BURNS	1906–08
JACK JOHNSON	1908–15
JESS WILLARD	1915–19
JACK DEMPSEY	1919–26
GENE TUNNEY	1926–28*
MAX SCHMELING	1930–32
JACK SHARKEY	1932–33
PRIMO CARNERA	1933–34
MAX BAER	1934–35
JAMES J. BRADDOCK	1935–37
JOE LOUIS	1937–49*
EZZARD CHARLES	1949–51
JERSEY JOE WALCOTT	1951–52
ROCKY MARCIANO	1952–56*
FLOYD PATTERSON	1956–59
INGEMAR JOHANSSON	1959–60
FLOYD PATTERSON	1960–62
SONNY LISTON	1962–64
CASSIUS CLAY (MUHAMMAD ALI)	1964–67
Ernie Terrell (WBA)	1965–67
Joe Frazier (NY)	1968–70
Jimmy Ellis (WBA)	1968–70
JOE FRAZIER	1970–73
GEORGE FOREMAN	1973–74
MUHAMMAD ALI	1974–78
LEON SPINKS	1978
Ken Norton (WBC)	1978
Larry Holmes (WBC)	1978–80
MUHAMMAD ALI	1978–79*
John Tate (WBA)	1979–80
Mike Weaver (WBA)	1980–82
LARRY HOLMES	1980–85
Michael Dokes (WBA)	1982–83
Gerrie Coetzee (WBA)	1983–84
Tim Witherspoon (WBC)	1984
Pinklon Thomas (WBC)	1984–86
Greg Page (WBA)	1984–85
MICHAEL SPINKS	1985–87
Tim Witherspoon (WBA)	1986
Trevor Berbick (WBC)	1986
Mike Tyson (WBC)	1986–87
James (Bonecrusher) Smith (WBA)	1986–87
Tony Tucker (IBF)	1987
MIKE TYSON (WBC, WBA, IBF)	1987–90
BUSTER DOUGLAS (WBC, WBA, IBF)	1990
EVANDER HOLYFIELD (WBC, WBA, IBF)	1990–92
RIDDICK BOWE (WBA, IBF)	1992–93
Lennox Lewis (WBC)	1992–94
EVANDER HOLYFIELD (WBA, IBF)	1993–94
MICHAEL MOORER (WBA, IBF)	1994
Oliver McCall (WBC)	1994–95
GEORGE FOREMAN (WBA, IBF)	1994–95
Bruce Seldon (WBA)	1995–96
GEORGE FOREMAN	1995–96
Frank Bruno (WBC)	1995–96
Mike Tyson (WBC)	1996†
Mike Tyson (WBA)	1996
Michael Moorer (IBF)	1996–1997
Evander Holyfield (WBA, IBF)	1996–2000
Lennox Lewis (WBC)	1997–2000
LENNOX LEWIS (WBA, WBC, IBF)	2000
Evander Holyfield (WBA)	2000–01
LENNOX LEWIS (WBC, IBF)	2000–01
John Ruiz (WBA)	2001-03
Hasim Rahman (WBC, IBF)	2001
LENNOX LEWIS (WBC, IBF)	2001–02†
LENNOX LEWIS (WBC)	2001–04*
Roy Jones Jr. (WBA)	2003–04
Chris Byrd (IBF)	2003–06
John Ruiz (WBA)	2004–05
Vitali Klitschko (WBC)	2004–05*
Hasim Rahman (WBC)	2005–06
Nikolai Valuev (WBA)	2005—
Wladimir Klitschko (IBF)	2006—
Oleg Maskaev (WBC)	2006—

Note: John L. Sullivan held the Bare Knuckle championship from 1882-85.

Cruiserweights

Current champions in **bold** type.

Champion	Held Title
Marvin Camel (WBC)	1980
Carlos De Leon (WBC)	1980–82
Ossie Ocasio (WBA)	1982–84
S.T. Gordon (WBC)	1982–83
Carlos De Leon (WBC)	1983–85
Marvin Camel (IBF)	1983–84
Lee Roy Murphy (IBF)	1984–86
Piet Crous (WBA)	1984–85
Alfonso Ratliff (WBC)	1985
Dwight Braxton (WBA)	1985–86
Bernard Benton (WBC)	1985–86
Carlos De Leon (WBC)	1986–88
Evander Holyfield (WBA)	1986–88
Ricky Parkey (IBF)	1986–87
Evander Holyfield (WBA/IBF)	1987–88
Evander Holyfield	1988†
Toufik Belbouli (WBA)	1989
Robert Daniels (WBA)	1989–91
Carlos De Leon (WBC)	1989–90
Glenn McCrory (IBF)	1989–90
Jeff Lampkin (IBF)	1990
Massimiliano Duran (WBC)	1990–91
Bobby Czyz (WBA)	1991–92†
Anaclet Wamba (WBC)	1991–95
James Pritchard (IBF)	1991
James Warring (IBF)	1991–92
Alfred Cole (IBF)	1992–96
Orlin Norris (WBA)	1993–95
Nate Miller (WBA)	1995–97
Marcelo Dominguez (WBC)	1996–98
Adolpho Washington (IBF)	1996–97
Uriah Grant (IBF)	1997

Champion	Held Title
Imamu Mayfield (IBF)	1997–98
Arthur Williams (IBF)	1998–99
Fabrice Tiozzo (WBA)	1997–2000
Juan Carlos Gomez (WBC)	1998–2002†
Vassiliy Jirov (IBF)	1999–2003
Virgil Hill (WBA)	2000–02
Jean-Marc Mormeck (WBA)	2002–06

Champion	Held Title
Wayne Braithwaite (WBC)	2002–05
James Toney (IBF)	2003†
Kelvin Davis (IBF)	2004–05
Jean-Marc Mormeck (WBA/WBC)	2005–06
O'Neil Bell (IBF)	2005–
O'NEIL BELL (IBF/WBA/WBC)	2006–

Light Heavyweights

Widely accepted champions in CAPITAL letters. Current champions in **bold** type.

Champion	Held Title
JACK ROOT	1903
GEORGE GARDNER	1903
BOB FITZSIMMONS	1903–05
PHILADELPHIA JACK O'BRIEN	1905–12*
JACK DILLON	1914–16
BATTLING LEVINSKY	1916–20
GEORGES CARPENTIER	1920–22
BATTLING SIKI	1922–23
MIKE McTIGUE	1923–25
PAUL BERLENBACH	1925–26
JACK DELANEY	1926–27†
Jimmy Slattery (NBA)	1927
TOMMY LOUGHRAN	1927-29
JIMMY SLATTERY	1930
MAXIE ROSENBLOOM	1930–34
George Nichols (NBA)	1932
Bob Godwin (NBA)	1933
BOB OLIN	1934–35
JOHN HENRY LEWIS	1935–38
MELIO BETTINA (NY)	1939
Len Harvey (GBR)	1939–42
BILLY CONN	1939–40†
ANTON CHRISTOFORIDIS (NBA)	1941
GUS LESNEVICH	1941–48
Freddie Mills (GBR)	1942–46
FREDDIE MILLS	1948–50
JOEY MAXIM	1950–52
ARCHIE MOORE	1952–62
Harold Johnson (NBA)	1961
HAROLD JOHNSON	1962–63
WILLIE PASTRANO	1963–65
Eddie Cotton (Mich.)	1963–64
JOSE TORRES	1965–66
DICK TIGER	1966–68
BOB FOSTER	1968–74*
Vicente Rondon (WBA)	1971–72
John Conteh (WBC)	1974–77
Victor Galindez (WBA)	1974–78
Miguel A. Cuello (WBC)	1977–78
Mate Parlov (WBC)	1978
Mike Rossman (WBA)	1978–79
Marvin Johnson (WBC)	1978–79
Matthew (Franklin) Saad Muhammad (WBC)	1979–81
Marvin Johnson (WBA)	1979–80

Champion	Held Title
Eddie (Gregory) Mustapha Muhammad (WBA)	1980–81
Michael Spinks (WBA)	1981–83
Dwight (Braxton) Muhammad Qawi (WBC)	1981–83
MICHAEL SPINKS	1983–85†
J.B.Williamson (WBC)	1985–86
Slobodan Kacar (IBF)	1985–86
Marvin Johnson (WBA)	1986–87
Dennis Andries (WBC)	1986–87
Bobby Czyz (IBF)	1986–87
Leslie Stewart (WBA)	1987
Virgil Hill (WBA)	1987–91
Prince Charles Williams (IBF)	1987–93
Thomas Hearns (WBC)	1987
Donny Lalonde (WBC)	1987–88
Sugar Ray Leonard (WBC)	1988
Dennis Andries (WBC)	1989
Jeff Harding (WBC)	1989–90
Dennis Andries (WBC)	1990–91
Jeff Harding (WBC)	1991–94
Thomas Hearns (WBA)	1991–92
Iran Barkley (WBA)	1992†
Virgil Hill (WBA)	1992–97
Henry Maske (IBF)	1993–96
Virgil Hill (WBA/IBF)	1996–97
Mike McCallum (WBC)	1994–95
Fabrice Tiozzo (WBC)	1995–96
Roy Jones Jr. (WBC)	1996
Montell Griffin (WBC)	1996
D. Michaelczewski (WBA/IBF)	1997†
William Guthrie (IBF)	1997–98
Lou Del Valle (WBA)	1997–98
ROY JONES JR. (WBA/WBC)	1997–2003†
Reggie Johnson (IBF)	1998–99
ROY JONES JR. (WBA/WBC/IBF)	1999–2003†
Antonio Tarver (WBC/IBF)	2003
Mehdi Sahnoune (WBA)	2003
ROY JONES JR. (WBC)	2003–04
Silvio Branco (WBA)	2003–04
Antonio Tarver (WBC)	2003–04†
Glen Johnson (IBF)	2004†
Fabrice Tiozzo (WBA)	2004–06*
ANTONIO TARVER	2005–06†
Clinton Woods (IBF)	2006—
Tomasz Adamek (WBC)	2006—

Super Middleweights

Current champions in **bold** type.

Champion	Held Title
Murray Sutherland (IBF)	1984
Chong-Pal Park (IBF)	1984–87
Chong-Pal Park (WBA)	1987–88
Graziano Rocchigiani (IBF)	1988–89
Fulgencio Obelmejias (WBA)	1988–89
Ray Leonard (WBC)	1988–90†
In-Chut Baek (WBA)	1989–90
Lindell Holmes (IBF)	1990–91
Christophe Tiozzo (WBA)	1990–91
Mauro Galvano (WBC)	1990–92
Victor Cordova (WBA)	1991

Champion	Held Title
Darrin Van Horn (IBF)	1991–92
Iran Barkley (WBA)	1992
Nigel Benn (WBC)	1992–96
James Toney (IBF)	1992–94
Michael Nunn (WBA)	1992–94
Steve Little (WBA)	1994
Frank Liles (WBA)	1994–99
Roy Jones (IBF)	1994–96
Thulane Malinga (WBC)	1996
Vincenzo Nardiello (WBC)	1996
Robin Reid (WBC)	1996–97

Major Titleholders (Cont.)
Super Middleweights (Cont.)

Champion	Held Title
Charles Brewer (IBF)	1997–98
Sven Ottke (IBF)	1998–2004*
Thulane Malinga (WBC)	1997–98
Richie Woodhall (WBC)	1998–99
Byron Mitchell (WBA)	1999–2000
Markus Beyer (WBC)	1999–2000
Glenn Gatley (WBC)	2000
Dingaan Thobela (WBC)	2000
Bruno Girard (WBA)	2000–01†
Dave Hilton (WBC)	2000†
Byron Mitchell (WBA)	2001–03

Champion	Held Title
Eric Lucas (WBC)	2001–03
Sven Ottke (IBF/WBA)	2003–04*
Markus Beyer (WBC)	2003–04
Anthony Mundine (WBA)	2004
Manny Siaca (WBA)	2004
Cristian Sanavia (WBC)	2004
Jeff Lacy (IBF)	2004–06
Markus Beyer (WBC)	2004–06
Mikkel Kessler (WBA)	2004–
Joe Calzaghe (IBF)	2006–
Mikkel Kessler (WBA/WBC)	2006–

Middleweights

Widely accepted champions in CAPITAL letters. Current champions in **bold** type.

Champion	Held Title
JACK (NONPAREIL) DEMPSEY	1884–91
BOB FITZSIMMONS	1891–97
CHARLES (KID) McCOY	1897–98
TOMMY RYAN	1898–1907
STANLEY KETCHEL	1908
BILLY PAPKE	1908
STANLEY KETCHEL	1908–10
FRANK KLAUS	1913
GEORGE CHIP	1913–14
AL McCOY	1914–17
Jeff Smith (AUS)	1914
Mick King (AUS)	1914
Jeff Smith (AUS)	1914–15
Lee Darcy (AUS)	1915–17
MIKE O'DOWD	1917–20
JOHNNY WILSON	1920–23
Wm. Bryan Downey (Ohio)	1921–22
Dave Rosenberg (NY)	1922
Jock Malone (Ohio)	1922–23
Mike O'Dowd (NY)	1922
Lou Bogash (NY)	1923
HARRY GREB	1923–26
TIGER FLOWERS	1926
MICKEY WALKER	1926–31†
GORILLA JONES	1931–32
MARCEL THIL	1932–37
Ben Jeby (NY)	1932–33
Lou Brouillard (NBA, NY)	1933
Vince Dundee (NBA, NY)	1933–34
Teddy Yarosz (NBA, NY)	1934–35
Babe Risko (NBA, NY)	1935–36
Freddie Steele (NBA, NY)	1936–38
FRED APOSTOLI	1937–39
Al Hostak (NBA)	1938
Solly Krieger (NBA)	1938–39
Al Hostak (NBA)	1939–40
CEFERINO GARCIA	1939–40
KEN OVERLIN	1940–41
Tony Zale (NBA)	1940–41
BILLY SOOSE	1941
TONY ZALE	1941–47
ROCKY GRAZIANO	1947–48
TONY ZALE	1948
MARCEL CERDAN	1948–49
JAKE La MOTTA	1949–51
SUGAR RAY ROBINSON	1951
RANDY TURPIN	1951
SUGAR RAY ROBINSON	1951–52*
CARL (BOBO) OLSON	1953–55
SUGAR RAY ROBINSON	1955–57
GENE FULLMER	1957
SUGAR RAY ROBINSON	1957

Champion	Held Title
CARMEN BASILIO	1957–58
SUGAR RAY ROBINSON	1958–60
Gene Fullmer (NBA)	1959–62
PAUL PENDER	1960–61
TERRY DOWNES	1961–62
PAUL PENDER	1962–63
Dick Tiger (WBA)	1962–63
DICK TIGER	1963
JOEY GIARDELLO	1963–65
DICK TIGER	1965–66
EMILE GRIFFITH	1966–67
NINO BENVENUTI	1967
EMILE GRIFFITH	1967–68
NINO BENVENUTI	1968–70
CARLOS MONZON	1970–77*
Rodrigo Valdez (WBC)	1974–76
RODRIGO VALDEZ	1977–78
HUGO CORRO	1978–79
VITO ANTUOFERMO	1979–80
ALAN MINTER	1980
MARVELOUS MARVIN HAGLER	1980–87
SUGAR RAY LEONARD	1987
Frank Tate (IBF)	1987–88
Sumbu Kalambay (WBA)	1987–89
Thomas Hearns (WBC)	1987–88
Iran Barkley (WBC)	1988–89
Michael Nunn (IBF)	1988–91
Roberto Duran (WBC)	1989–90*
Mike McCallum (WBA)	1989–91
Julian Jackson (WBC)	1990–93
James Toney (IBF)	1991–93†
Reggie Johnson (WBA)	1992–93
Roy Jones Jr. (IBF)	1993–94†
Gerald McClellan (WBC)	1993–95†
John David Jackson (WBA)	1993–94
Jorge Castro (WBA)	1994–97
Julian Jackson (WBC)	1995
Bernard Hopkins (IBF)	1995–
Quincy Taylor (WBC)	1995–96
Shinji Takehara (WBA)	1995–96
William Joppy (WBA)	1996–97
Keith Holmes (WBC)	1996–98
Julio Cesar Green (WBA)	1997–98
William Joppy (WBA)	1998–2001
Hassine Cherifi (WBC)	1998–99
Keith Holmes (WBC)	1999–2001
Bernard Hopkins (IBF/WBC)	2001–
Felix Trinidad (WBA)	2001
BERNARD HOPKINS (IBF/WBA/WBC)	2001–05
JERMAIN TAYLOR (IBF/WBA/WBC)	2005–06†
JERMAIN TAYLOR (WBA/WBC)	2005–
Arthur Abraham (IBF)	2006–

Junior Middleweights

Widely accepted champions in CAPITAL letters. Current champions in **bold** type.

Champion	Held Title
ERNILE GRIFFITH (EBU)	1962–63
DENNIS MOYER	1962–63
RALPH DUPAS	1963
SANDRO MAZZINGHI	1963–65
NINO BENVENUTI	1965–66
KI-SOO KIM	1966–68
SANDRO MAZZINGHI	1968
FREDDIE LITTLE	1969–70
CARMELO BOSSI	1970–71
KOICHI WAJIMA	1971–74
OSCAR ALBARADO	1974–75
KOICHI WAJIMA	1975
Miguel de Oliveira (WBC)	1975–76
JAE-DO YUH	1975–76
Elisha Obed (WBC)	1975–76
KOICHI WAJIMA	1976
JOSE DURAN	1976
Eckhard Dagge (WBC)	1976–77
MIGUEL ANGEL CASTELLINI	1976–77
EDDIE GAZO	1977–78
Rocky Mattioli (WBC)	1977–79
MASASHI KUDO	1978–79
Maurice Hope (WBC)	1979–81
AYUB KALULE	1979–81
Wilfred Benitez (WBC)	1981–82
SUGAR RAY LEONARD	1981–82
Tadashi Mihara (WBA)	1981–82
Davey Moore (WBA)	1982–83
Thomas Hearns (WBC)	1982–84
Roberto Duran (WBA)	1983–84
Mark Medal (IBF)	1984
THOMAS HEARNS	1984–86
Mike McCallum (WBA)	1984–87
Carlos Santos (IBF)	1984–86
Buster Drayton (IBF)	1986–87
Duane Thomas (WBC)	1986–87
Matthew Hilton (IBF)	1987–88
Lupe Aquino (WBC)	1987
Gianfranco Rosi (WBC)	1987–88
Julian Jackson (WBA)	1987–90
Donald Curry (WBC)	1988–89
Robert Hines (IBF)	1988–89
Darrin Van Horn (IBF)	1989
Rene Jacquote (WBC)	1989
John Mugabi (WBC)	1989–90
Gianfranco Rosi (IBF)	1989–94
Terry Norris (WBC)	1990–94
Gilbert Dele (WBA)	1991
Vinny Pazienza (WBA)	1991–92
Julio Cesar Vasquez (WBA)	1992–95
Simon Brown (WBC)	1994
Terry Norris (WBC)	1994–
Vincent Pettway (IBF)	1994–95
Paul Vaden (IBF)	1995
Carl Daniels (WBA)	1995
Terry Norris (WBC)	1995–97
Terry Norris (IBF)	1995–96
Laurent Boudouani (WBA)	1996–99
Raul Marquez (IBF)	1997
Keith Mullings (WBC)	1997–99
Yori Boy Campas (IBF)	1997–98
Fernando Vargas (IBF)	1998–2000
Javier Castillejo (WBC)	1999–2001
David Reid (WBA)	1999–00
Felix Trinidad (WBA/IBF)	2000–01†
Oscar De La Hoya (WBC)	2001–03
Fernando Vargas (WBA)	2001–02
Winky Wright (IBF)	2001–
Oscar De La Hoya (WBA/WBC)	2002-03
Shane Mosley (WBA/WBC)	2003–04
WINKY WRIGHT (IBF/WBA/WBC)	2004
WINKY WRIGHT (WBA/WBC)	2004–05†
Kassim Ouma (IBF)	2004–05
Javier Castillejo (WBC)	2005
Roman Karmazin (IBF)	2005–06
Alejandro Garcia (WBA)	2005–06
Ricardo Mayorga (WBC)	2005–06
Jose Antonio Rivera (WBA)	2006–
Oscar De La Hoya (WBC)	2006–
Cory Spinks (IBF)	2006–

Welterweights

Widely accepted champions in CAPITAL letters. Current champions in **bold** type.

Champion	Held Title
PADDY DUFFY	1888–90
MYSTERIOUS BILLY SMITH	1892–94
TOMMY RYAN	1894–98
MYSTERIOUS BILLY SMITH	1898–1900
MATTY MATTHEWS	1900
EDDIE CONNOLLY	1900
JAMES (RUBE) FERNS	1900
MATTY MATHEWS	1900–01
JAMES (RUBE) FERNS	1901
JOE WALCOTT	1901–04
THE DIXIE KID	1904–05
HONEY MELLODY	1906–07
Mike (Twin) Sullivan	1907–08†
Harry Lewis	1908–11
Jimmy Gardner	1908
Jimmy Clabby	1910–11
WALDEMAR HOLBERG	1914
TOM McCORMICK	1914
MATT WELLS	1914–15
MIKE GLOVER	1915
JACK BRITTON	1915
TED (KID) LEWIS	1915–16
JACK BRITTON	1916–17
TED (KID) LEWIS	1917–19
JACK BRITTON	1919–22
MICKEY WALKER	1922–26
PETE LATZO	1926–27
JOE DUNDEE	1927–29
JACKIE FIELDS	1929–30
YOUNG JACK THOMPSON	1930
TOMMY FREEMAN	1930–31
YOUNG JACK THOMPSON	1931
LOU BROUILLARD	1931–32
JACKIE FIELDS	1932–33
YOUNG CORBETT III	1933
JIMMY McLARNIN	1933–34
BARNEY ROSS	1934
JIMMY McLARNIN	1934–35
BARNEY ROSS	1935–38
HENRY ARMSTRONG	1938–40
FRITZIE ZIVIC	1940–41
Izzy Jannazzo (Md.)	1940–41
Freddie (Red) Cochrane	1941–46
MARTY SERVO	1946*
SUGAR RAY ROBINSON	1946–51†
Johnny Bratton	1951
KID GAVILAN	1951–54
JOHNNY SAXTON	1954–55
TONY DeMARCO	1955
CARMEN BASILIO	1955–56
JOHNNY SAXTON	1956
CARMEN BASILIO	1956–57†

Major Titleholders (Cont.)
Welterweights (Cont.)

Champion	Held Title	Champion	Held Title
VIRGIL AKINS	1958	Mark Breland (WBA)	1989–90
DON JORDAN	1958–60	MARLON STARLING (WBC)	1989–90
BENNY (KID) PARET	1960–61	Aaron Davis (WBA)	1990–91
EMILE GRIFFITH	1961	Maurice Blocker (WBC)	1990–91
BENNY (KID) PARET	1961–62	Meldrick Taylor (WBA)	1991–92
EMILE GRIFFITH	1962–63	Simon Brown (WBA)	1991
LUIS RODRIGUEZ	1963	Maurice Blocker (IBF)	1991–93
EMILE GRIFFITH	1963–66†	Buddy McGirt (WBC)	1991–93
Charlie Shipes (Calif.)	1966–67	Crisanto Espana (WBA)	1992–94
CURTIS COKES	1966–69	Pernell Whitaker (WBC)	1993–97
JOSE NAPOLES	1969–70	Felix Trinidad (IBF)	1993–99
BILLY BACKUS	1970–71	Ike Quartey (WBA)	1994–98†
JOSE NAPOLES	1971–75	James Page (WBA)	1998–2000†
Hedgemon Lewis (NY)	1972–73	Oscar De La Hoya (WBC)	1997–99
Angel Espada (WBA)	1975–76	Felix Trinidad (WBC/IBF)	1999–2000†
JOHN H. STRACEY	1975–76	Oscar De La Hoya (WBC)	2000
CARLOS PALOMINO	1976–79	Shane Mosley (WBC)	2000–00
Pipino Cuevas (WBA)	1976–80	Andrew Lewis (WBA)	2001–02
WILFREDO BENITEZ	1979	Vernon Forrest (IBF)	2001–02†
SUGAR RAY LEONARD	1979–80	Vernon Forrest (WBC)	2002–03
ROBERTO DURAN	1980	Richard Mayorga (WBA)	2002–03
Thomas Hearns (WBA)	1980–81	Michele Piccirillo (IBF)	2002–03
SUGAR RAY LEONARD	1980–82	Richard Mayorga (WBA/WBC)	2003
Donald Curry (WBA)	1983–85	Cory Spinks (IBF)	2003–05
Milton McCrory (WBC)	1983–85	CORY SPINKS (IBF/WBA/WBC)	2003–05
DONALD CURRY	1985–86	ZAB JUDAH (IBF/WBA/WBC)	2005–06
LLOYD HONEYGHAN	1986–87	Zab Judah (IBF)	2006
JORGE VACA (WBC)	1987–88	**Carlos Baldomir** (WBC)	2006–
LLOYD HONEYGHAN (WBC)	1988–89	**Floyd Mayweather** (IBF)	2006–
Mark Breland (WBA)	1987	**Ricky Hatton** (WBA)	2006–
Marlon Starling (WBA)	1987–88		
Tomas Molinares (WBA)	1988–89		
Simon Brown (IBF)	1988–91		

Junior Welterweights

Widely accepted champions in CAPITAL letters. Current champions in **bold** type.

Champion	Held Title	Champion	Held Title
PINKEY MITCHELL	1922–25	Antonio Cervantes (WBA)	1977–80
RED HERRING	1925	Sang-Hyun Kim (WBC)	1978–80
MUSHY CALLAHAN	1926–30	Saoul Mamby (WBC)	1980–82
JACK (KID) BERG	1930–31	Aaron Pryor (WBA)	1980–83
TONY CANZONERI	1931–32	Leroy Haley (WBC)	1982–83
JOHNNY JADICK	1932–33	Aaron Pryor (IBF)	1983–85
Sammy Fuller	1932–33	Bruce Curry (WBC)	1983–84
BATTLING SHAW	1933	Johnny Bumphus (WBA)	1984
TONY CANZONERI	1933	Bill Costello (WBC)	1984–85
BARNEY ROSS	1933–35	Gene Hatcher (WBA)	1984–85
TIPPY LARKIN	1946	Ubaldo Sacco (WBA)	1985–86
CARLOS ORTIZ	1959–60	Lonnie Smith (WBC)	1985–86
DUILIO LOI	1960–62	Patrizio Oliva (WBA)	1986–87
EDDIE PERKINS	1962	Gary Hinton (IBF)	1986
DUILIO LOI	1962–63	Rene Arredondo (WBC)	1986
Roberto Cruz	1963	Tsuyoshi Hamada (WBC)	1986–87
EDDIE PERKINS	1963–65	Joe Louis Manley (IBF)	1986–87
CARLOS HERNANDEZ	1965–66	Terry Marsh (IBF)	1987
SANDRO LOPOPOLO	1966–67	Juan Coggi (WBA)	1987–90
PAUL FUJII	1967–68	Rene Arredondo (WBC)	1987
NICOLINO LOCHE	1968–72	Roger Mayweather (WBC)	1987–89
Pedro Adigue (WBC)	1968–70	James McGirt (IBF)	1988
Bruno Arcari (WBC)	1970–74	Meldrick Taylor (IBF)	1988–90
ALFONSO FRAZER	1972	Julio Cesar Chavez (WBC)	1989–94
ANTONIO CERVANTES	1972–76	Julio Cesar Chavez (IBF)	1990–91
Perico Fernandez (WBC)	1974–75	Loreto Garza (WBA)	1990–91
Saensak Muangsurin (WBC)	1975–76	Juan Coggi (WBA)	1991
WILFRED BENITEZ	1976–79	Edwin Rosario (WBA)	1991–92
Miguel Velasquez (WBC)	1976	Rafael Pineda (IBF)	1991–92
Saensak Muangsurin (WBC)	1976–78	Akinobu Hiranaka (WBA)	1992

Champion	Held Title
Pernell Whitaker (IBF)	1992–93†
Charles Murray (IBF)	1993–94
Jake Rodriguez (IBF)	1994–95
Juan Coggi (WBA)	1993–94
Frankie Randall (WBC)	1994
Frankie Randall (WBA)	1994–96
Juan Coggi (WBA)	1996
Julio Cesar Chavez (WBC)	1994–96
Kostya Tszyu (IBF)	1995–97
Frankie Randall (WBA)	1996–97
Oscar De La Hoya (WBC)	1996–97†
Khalid Rahilou (WBA)	1997–98
Sharmba Mitchell (WBA)	1998–2001

Champion	Held Title
Vincent Phillips (IBF)	1997–99
Terronn Millet (IBF)	1999–00†
Kostya Tszyu (WBC)	1999–2005
Zab Judah (IBF)	2000–01
Kostya Tszyu (WBA/WBC)	2001–04†
KOSTYA TSZYU (IBF/WBA/WBC)	2001–04†
KOSTYA TSZYU (IBF/WBC)	2004–05
Vivian Harris (WBA)	2004–05
Arturo Gatti (WBC)	2005
Ricky Hatton (IBF)	2005–
Ricky Hatton (IBF/WBA)	2005–
Carlos Maussa (WBA)	2005–06
Floyd Mayweather (WBC)	2005–

Lightweights

Widely accepted champions in CAPITAL letters. Current champions in **bold** type.

Champion	Held Title
JACK McAULIFFE	1886–94
GEORGE (KID) LAVIGNE	1896–99
FRANK ERNE	1899–02
JOE GANS	1902–04
JIMMY BRITT	1904–05
BATTLING NELSON	1905–06
JOE GANS	1906–08
BATTLING NELSON	1908–10
AD WOLGAST	1910–12
WILLIE RITCHIE	1912–14
FREDDIE WELSH	1915–17
BENNY LEONARD	1917–25*
JIMMY GOODRICH	1925
ROCKY KANSAS	1925–26
SAMMY MANDELL	1926–30
AL SINGER	1930
TONY CANZONERI	1930–33
BARNEY ROSS	1933–35†
TONY CANZONERI	1935–36
LOU AMBERS	1936–38
HENRY ARMSTRONG	1938–39
LOU AMBERS	1939–40
Sammy Angott (NBA)	1940–41
LEW JENKINS	1940–41
SAMMY ANGOTT	1941–42
Beau Jack (NY)	1942–43
Slugger White (Md.)	1943
Bob Montgomery (NY)	1943
Sammy Angott (NBA)	1943–44
Beau Jack (NY)	1943–44
Bob Montgomery (NY)	1944–47
Juan Zurita (NBA)	1944–45
IKE WILLIAMS	1947–51
JAMES CARTER	1951–52
LAURO SALAS	1952
JAMES CARTER	1952–54
PADDY DeMARCO	1954
JAMES CARTER	1954–55
WALLACE (BUD) SMITH	1955–56
JOE BROWN	1956–62
CARLOS ORTIZ	1962–65
Kenny Lane (Mich.)	1963–64
ISMAEL LAGUNA	1965
CARLOS ORTIZ	1965–68
CARLOS TEO CRUZ	1968–69
MANDO RAMOS	1969–70
ISMAEL LAGUNA	1970
KEN BUCHANAN	1970–72
Pedro Carrasco (WBC)	1971–72
Mando Ramos (WBC)	1972
ROBERTO DURAN	1972–79†
Chango Carmona (WBC)	1972
Rodolfo Gonzalez (WBC)	1972–74
Ishimatsu Suzuki (WBC)	1974–76
Esteban De Jesus (WBC)	1976–78

Champion	Held Title
Jim Watt (WBC)	1979–81
Ernesto Espana (WBA)	1979–80
Hilmer Kenty (WBA)	1980–81
Sean O'Grady (WBA, WAA)	1981
Alexis Arguello (WBC)	1981–82
Claude Noel (WBA)	1981
Andrew Ganigan (WAA)	1981–82
Arturo Frias (WBA)	1981–82
Ray Mancini (WBA)	1982–84
ALEXIS ARGUELLO	1982–83
Edwin Rosario (WBC)	1983–84
Choo Choo Brown (IBF)	1984
Livingstone Bramble (WBA)	1984–86
Harry Arroyo (IBF)	1984–85
Jose Luis Ramirez (WBC)	1984–85
Jimmy Paul (IBF)	1985–86
Hector Camacho (WBC)	1985–86
Edwin Rosario (WBA)	1986–87
Greg Haugen (IBF)	1986–87
Julio Cesar Chavez (WBA)	1987–88
Jose Luis Ramirez (WBC)	1987–88
JULIO CESAR CHAVEZ (WBC, WBA)	1988–89
Vinny Pazienza (IBF)	1987–88
Greg Haugen (IBF)	1988–89
Pernell Whitaker (IBF, WBC)	1989–90
Edwin Rosario (WBA)	1989–90
Juan Nazario (WBA)	1990
PERNELL WHITAKER (IBF, WBC, WBA)	1990–92†
Joey Gamache (WBA)	1992
Miguel A. Gonzalez (WBC)	1992–96
Tony Lopez (WBA)	1992–93
Dingaan Thobela (WBA)	1993
Fred Pendleton (IBF)	1993–94
Orzubek Nazarov (WBA)	1993–98
Rafael Ruelas (IBF)	1994–95
Oscar De La Hoya (IBF)	1995†
Phillip Holiday (IBF)	1995–97
Jean-Baptiste Mendy (WBC)	1996–97
Stevie Johnston (WBC)	1997–98
Shane Mosley (IBF)	1997–99†
Cesar Bazan (WBC)	1998–99
Jean-Baptiste Mendy (WBA)	1998–99
Julien Lorcy (WBA)	1999
Stevie Johnston (WBC)	1999–00
Stefano Zoff (WBA)	1999
Israel Cardona (IBF)	1999
Paul Spadafora (IBF)	1999–2004†
Gilberto Serrano (WBA)	1999–00
Takanori Hatakeyama (WBA)	2000–01
Jose Luis Castillo (WBC)	2000–02
Julien Lorcy (WBA)	2001
Raul Balbi (WBA)	2001–02
Leonard Dorin (WBA)	2002–03
Floyd Mayweather (WBC)	2002–04†
Javier Jauregui (IBF)	2003–04

Major Titleholders (Cont.)
Lightweights (Cont.)

Champion	Held Title	Champion	Held Title
Lakva Sim (WBA)	2004	Leavander Johnson (IBF)	2005
Juan Diaz (WBA)	2004–	**Jesus Chavez** (IBF)	2005–
Jose Luis Castillo (WBC)	2004–05	**Joel Casamayor** (WBC)	2006–
Julio Diaz (IBF)	2004–05		
Diego Corrales (WBC)	2005–		

Junior Lightweights

Widely accepted champions in CAPITAL letters. Current champions in **bold** type.

Champion	Held Title	Champion	Held Title
JOHNNY DUNDEE	1921–23	ALFREDO LAYNE	1986
JACK BERNSTEIN	1923	BRIAN MITCHELL	1986–91
JOHNNY DUNDEE	1923–24	Rocky Lockridge (IBF)	1987–88
STEVE (KID) SULLIVAN	1924–25	Azumah Nelson (WBC)	1988–94
MIKE BALLERINO	1925	Tony Lopez (IBF)	1988–89
TOD MORGAN	1925–29	Juan Molina (IBF)	1989–90
BENNY BASS	1929–31	Tony Lopez (IBF)	1990–91
KID CHOCOLATE	1931–33	Joey Gamache (WBA)	1991
FRANKIE KLICK	1933–34	Brian Mitchell (IBF)	1991
SANDY SADDLER	1949–50	Genaro Hernandez (WBA)	1991–95
HAROLD GOMES	1959–60	James Leija (WBC)	1994
GABRIEL (FLASH) ELORDE	1960–67	Juan Molina (IBF)	1991–95
YOSHIAKI NUMATA	1967	Gabriel Ruelas (WBC)	1994–95
HIROSHI KOBAYASHI	1967–71	Eddie Hopson (IBF)	1995
Rene Barrientos (WBC)	1969–70	Tracy Patterson (IBF)	1995
Yoshiaki Numata (WBC)	1970–71	Azumah Nelson (WBC)	1995–97
ALFREDO MARCANO	1971–72	Choi Yong-Soo (WBA)	1995–98
Ricardo Arredondo (WBC)	1971–74	Arturo Gatti (IBF)	1995–98†
BEN VILLAFLOR	1972–73	Genaro Hernandez (WBC)	1997–98
KUNIAKI SHIBATA	1973	Floyd Mayweather Jr. (WBC)	1998–2002†
BEN VILLAFLOR	1973–76	Takanori Hatakeyama (WBA)	1998–99
Kuniaki Shibata (WBC)	1974–75	Roberto Garcia (IBF)	1998–99
Alfredo Escalera (WBC)	1975–78	Lavka Sim (WBA)	1999
SAMUEL SERRANO	1976–80	Diego Corrales (IBF)	1999–2001
Alexis Arguello (WBC)	1978–80	Baek Jong-Kwon (WBA)	1999–2000
YASUTSUNE UEHARA	1980–81	Joel Casamayor (WBA)	2000–02
Rafael Limon (WBC)	1980–81	Steve Forbes (IBF)	2001-02†
Cornelius Boza-Edwards (WBC)	1981	Acelino Freitas (WBA)	2002–04†
SAMUEL SERRANO	1981–83	Sirimongkol Singmanassak (WBC)	2002–03
Rolando Navarrete (WBC)	1981–82	Jesus Chavez (WBC)	2003–04
Rafael Limon (WBC)	1982	Carlos Hernandez (IBF)	2003–04
Bobby Chacon (WBC)	1982–83	Erik Morales (WBC)	2004
ROGER MAYWEATHER (WBC)	1983–84	Erik Morales (IBF/WBC)	2004
Hector Camacho (WBC)	1983–84	**Marco Antonio Barrera** (WBC)	2004–
ROCKY LOCKRIDGE	1984–85	Marco Antonio Barrera (IBF/WBC)	2005–06
Hwan-Kil Yuh (IBF)	1984–85	Vicente Mosquera (WBA)	2005–06
Julio Cesar Chavez (WBC)	1984–87	Cassius Baloyi (IBF)	2006
Lester Ellis (IBF)	1985	**Gairy St. Clair** (IBF)	2006–
WILFREDO GOMEZ	1985–86	**Edwin Valero** (WBA)	2006–
Barry Michael (IBF)	1985–87		

Featherweights

Widely accepted champions in CAPITAL letters. Current champions in **bold** type.

Champion	Held Title	Champion	Held Title
TORPEDO BILLY MURPHY	1890	JOHNNY KILBANE	1912–23
YOUNG GRIFFO	1890–92	Jem Driscoll (GBR)	1912–13
GEORGE DIXON	1892–97	EUGENE CRIQUI	1923
SOLLY SMITH	1897–98	JOHNNY DUNDEE	1923–24†
Ben Jordan (GBR)	1898–99	LOUIS (KID) KAPLAN	1925–26†
Eddie Santry (GBR)	1899–1900	Dick Finnegan (Mass.)	1926–27
DAVE SULLIVAN	1898	BENNY BASS	1927–28
GEORGE DIXON	1898–1900	TONY CANZONERI	1928
TERRY McGOVERN	1900–01	ANDRE ROUTIS	1928–29
YOUNG CORBETT II	1901–04	BATTLING BATTALINO	1929–32†
JIMMY BRITT	1904	Tommy Paul (NBA)	1932–33
ABE ATTELL	1904	Kid Chocolate (NY)	1932–33
BROOKLYN TOMMY SULLIVAN	1904–05	Freddie Miller (NBA)	1933–36
ABE ATTELL	1906–12	Baby Arizmendi (MEX)	1935–36

Champion	Held Title
Mike Belloise (NY)	1936–37
Petey Sarron (NBA)	1936–37
HENRY ARMSTRONG	1937–38†
Joey Archibald (NY)	1938–39
Leo Rodak (NBA)	1938–39
JOEY ARCHIBALD	1939–40
Petey Scalzo (NBA)	1940–41
Jimmy Perrin (La.)	1940–41
HARRY JEFFRA	1940–41
JOEY ARCHIBALD	1941
Richie Lemos (NBA)	1941
CHALKY WRIGHT	1941–42
Jackie Wilson (NBA)	1941–43
WILLIE PEP	1942–48
Jackie Callura (NBA)	1943
Phil Terranova (NBA)	1943–44
Sal Bartolo (NBA)	1944–46
SANDY SADDLER	1948–49
WILLIE PEP	1949–50
SANDY SADDLER	1950–57*
HOGAN (KID) BASSEY	1957–59
DAVEY MOORE	1959–63
ULTIMINIO (SUGAR) RAMOS	1963–64
VICENTE SALDIVAR	1964–67*
Howard Winstone (GBR)	1968
Raul Rojas (WBA)	1968
Jose Legra (WBC)	1968–69
Shozo Saijyo (WBA)	1968–71
JOHNNY FAMECHON (WBC)	1969–70
VICENTE SALDIVAR (WBC)	1970
KUNIAKI SHIBATA (WBC)	1970–72
Antonio Gomez (WBA)	1971–72
CLEMENTE SANCHEZ (WBC)	1972
Ernesto Marcel (WBA)	1972–74
JOSE LEGRA (WBC)	1972–73
EDER JOFRE (WBC)	1973–74
Ruben Olivares (WBA)	1974
Bobby Chacon (WBC)	1974–75
ALEXIS ARGUELLO (WBA)	1974–76†
Ruben Olivares (WBC)	1975
David (Poison) Kotey (WBC)	1975–76
DANNY (LITTLE RED) LOPEZ (WBC)	1976–80
Rafael Ortega (WBA)	1977
Cecilio Lastra (WBA)	1977–78
Eusebio Pedroza (WBA)	1978–85
SALVADOR SANCHEZ (WBC)	1980–82
Juan LaPorte (WBC)	1982–84
Wilfredo Gomez (WBC)	1984

Champion	Held Title
Min-Keun Oh (IBF)	1984–85
Azumah Nelson (WBC)	1984–88
Barry McGuigan (WBA)	1985–86
Ki-Young Chung (IBF)	1985–86
Steve Cruz (WBA)	1986–87
Antonio Rivera (IBF)	1986–88
Antonio Esparragoza (WBA)	1987–91
Calvin Grove (IBF)	1988
Jorge Paez (IBF)	1988–91†
Jeff Fenech (WBC)	1988–90†
Marcos Villasana (WBC)	1990–91
Yung-Kyun Park (WBA)	1991–93
Troy Dorsey (IBF)	1991
Manuel Medina (IBF)	1991–93
Paul Hodkinson (WBC)	1991–93
Tom Johnson (IBF)	1993–97
Goyo Vargas (WBC)	1993
Kevin Kelley (WBC)	1993–95
Eloy Rojas (WBA)	1993–96
Alejandro Gonzalez (WBC)	1995
Manuel Medina (WBC)	1995–96
Wilfredo Vasquez (WBA)	1996–98†
Luisito Espinosa (WBC)	1995–99
Naseem Hamed (IBF)	1997†
Hector Lizarraga (IBF)	1997–98
Freddie Norwood (WBA)	1998
Manuel Medina (IBF)	1998–99
Antonio Cermeno (WBA)	1998–99
Cesar Soto (WBC)	1999–00
Paul Ingle (IBF)	1999–2000
Mbuelo Botile (IBF)	2000–01
Guty Espadas (WBC)	2000–01
Freddie Norwood (WBA)	1999–00
Derrick Gainer (WBA)	2000–03
Erik Morales (WBC)	2001–02
Frankie Toledo (IBF)	2001
Manuel Medina (IBF)	2001–02
Johnny Tapia (IBF)	2002†
Erik Morales (WBC)	2002–03†
Juan Manuel Marquez (IBF)	2003–05†
Juan Manuel Marquez (WBA)	2003–06†
Chi In-jin (WBC)	2004–06
Chris John (WBA)	2006–
Takashi Koshimoto (WBC)	2006
Rudy Lopez (WBC)	2006–
Robert Guerrero (IBF)	2006–

Junior Featherweights

Current champions in **bold** type.

Champion	Held Title
Jack (Kid) Wolfe	1922–23
Carl Duane	1923–24
Rigoberto Riasco (WBC)	1976
Royal Kobayashi (WBC)	1976
Dong-Kyun Yum (WBC)	1976–77
Wilfredo Gomez (WBC)	1977–83
Soo-Hwan Hong (WBA)	1977–78
Ricardo Cardona (WBA)	1978–80
Leo Randolph (WBA)	1980
Sergio Palma (WBA)	1980–82
Leonardo Cruz (WBA)	1982–84
Jaime Garza (WBC)	1983
Bobby Berna (IBF)	1983–84
Loris Stecca (WBA)	1984
Seung-Il Suh (IBF)	1984–85
Victor Callejas (WBA)	1984–85
Juan (Kid) Meza (WBC)	1984–85
Ji-Woo Kim (IBF)	1985–86
Lupe Pintor (WBC)	1985–86
Samart Payakaroon (WBC)	1986–87

Champion	Held Title
Seung-Hoon Lee (IBF)	1987–88
Louie Espinoza (WBA)	1987
Jeff French (WBC)	1987
Julio Gervacio (WBA)	1987–88
Daniel Zaragoza (WBC)	1988–90
Jose Sanabria (IBF)	1988–90
Bernardo Pinango (WBA)	1988
Juan Jose Estrada (WBA)	1988–89
Fabrice Benichou (IBF)	1989–90
Jesus Salud (WBA)	1989–90
Welcome Ncita (IBF)	1990–92
Paul Banke (WBC)	1990
Luis Mendoza (WBA)	1990–91
Raul Perez (WBA)	1992
Pedro Decima (WBC)	1990–91
Kiyoshi Hatanaka (WBC)	1991
Daniel Zaragoza (WBC)	1991–92
Tracy Patterson (WBC)	1992–94
Kennedy McKinney (IBF)	1993–94
Wilfredo Vasquez (WBA)	1992–95

Major Titleholders (Cont.)
Junior Featherweights (Cont.)

Champion	Held Title	Champion	Held Title
Vuyani Bungu (IBF)	1994–99†	Yorber Ortega (WBA)	2001–02
Hector Acero Sanchez (WBC)	1994–95	Yoddamrong Sithyodthong (WBA)	2002
Antonio Cermeno (WBA)	1995–98†	Osamu Sato (WBA)	2002
Daniel Zaragoza (WBC)	1995–97	Salim Medjkoune (WBA)	2002–03
Erik Morales (WBC)	1997–00†	Oscar Larios (WBC)	2002–05
Enrique Sanchez (WBA)	1998	Mahyar Monshipour (WBA)	2003–06
Nestor Garza (WBA)	1998–00	Israel Vazquez (IBF)	2004–06
Lehlohonolo Ledwaba (IBF)	1999–2001	Israel Vazquez (IBF/WBC)	2005†
Clarence Adams (WBA)	2000–01†	**Israel Vazquez** (WBC)	2005–
Willie Jorrin (WBC)	2000–02	Somsak Sithchatchawal (WBA)	2006
Manny Pacquiao (IBF)	2001–04†	**Celestino Caballero** (WBA)	2006–

Bantamweights

Widely accepted champions in CAPITAL letters. Current champions in **bold** type.

Champion	Held Title	Champion	Held Title
TOMMY (SPIDER) KELLY	1887	JIMMY CARRUTHERS	1952–54*
HUGHEY BOYLE	1887–88	ROBERT COHEN	1954–56
TOMMY (SPIDER) KELLY	1889	Raul Macias (NBA)	1955–57
CHAPPIE MORAN	1889–90	MARIO D'AGATA	1956–57
Tommy (Spider) Kelly	1890–92	ALPHONSE HALIMI	1957–59
GEORGE DIXON	1890–91	JOE BECERRA	1959–60*
Billy Plummer	1892–95	Johnny Caldwell (EBU)	1961–62
JIMMY BARRY	1894–99	EDER JOFRE	1961–65
Pedlar Palmer	1895–99	MASAHIKO FIGHTING HARADA	1965–68
TERRY McGOVERN	1899–1900	LIONEL ROSE	1968–69
HARRY HARRIS	1901–02	RUBEN OLIVARES	1969–70
DANNY DOUGHERTY	1900–01	CHUCHO CASTILLO	1970–71
HARRY FORBES	1901–03	RUBEN OLIVARES	1971–72
FRANKIE NEIL	1903–04	RAFAEL HERRERA	1972
JOE BOWKER	1904–05	ENRIQUE PINDER	1972–73
JIMMY WALSH	1905–06†	ROMEO ANAYA	1973
OWEN MORAN	1907–08	Rafael Herrera (WBC)	1973–74
MONTE ATTELL	1909–10	ARNOLD TAYLOR	1973–74
FRANKIE CONLEY	1910–11	SOO-HWAN HONG	1974–75
JOHNNY COULON	1911–14	Rodolfo Martinez (WBC)	1974–76
Digger Stanley (GBR)	1910–12	ALFONSO ZAMORA	1975–77
Charles Ledoux (GBR)	1912–13	Carlos Zarate (WBC)	1976–79
Eddie Campi (GBR)	1913–14	JORGE LUJAN	1977–80
KID WILLIAMS	1914–17	Lupe Pintor (WBC)	1979–83
Johnny Ertle	1915–18	JULIAN SOLIS	1980
PETE HERMAN	1917–20	JEFF CHANDLER	1980–84
Memphis Pal Moore	1918–19	Albert Davila (WBC)	1983–85
JOE LYNCH	1920–21	RICHARD SANDOVAL	1984–86
PETE HERMAN	1921	Satoshi Shingaki (IBF)	1984–85
JOHNNY BUFF	1921–22	Jeff Fenech (IBF)	1985
JOE LYNCH	1922–24	Daniel Zaragoza (WBC)	1985
ABE GOLDSTEIN	1924	Miguel (Happy) Lora (WBC)	1985–88
CANNONBALL EDDIE MARTIN	1924–25	GABY CANIZALES	1986
PHIL ROSENBERG	1925–27	BERNARDO PINANGO	1986–87
Teddy Baldock (GBR)	1927	Wilfredo Vasquez (WBA)	1987–88
BUD TAYLOR (NBA)	1927–28†	Kevin Seabrooks (IBF)	1987–88
Willie Smith (GBR)	1927–28	Kaokor Galaxy (WBA)	1988
Bushy Graham (NY)	1928–29	Moon Sung-Kil (WBA)	1988–89
PANAMA AL BROWN	1929–35	Kaokor Galaxy (WBA)	1989
Sixto Escobar (NBA)	1934–35	Raul Perez (WBC)	1988–91
BALTAZAR SANGCHILLI	1935–36	Orlando Canizales (IBF)	1988–94†
Lou Salica (NBA)	1935	Luisito Espinosa (WBA)	1989–91
Sixto Escobar (NBA)	1935–36	Greg Richardson	1991
TONY MARINO	1936	Joichiro Tatsuyoshi (WBC)	1991–92
SIXTO ESCOBAR	1936–37	Israel Contreras (WBA)	1991–92
HARRY JEFFRA	1937–38	Eddie Cook (WBA)	1992
SIXTO ESCOBAR	1938–39*	Victor Rabanales (WBC)	1992–93
Georgie Pace (NBA)	1939–40	Jorge Julio (WBA)	1992–93
LOU SALICA	1940–42	Jung-Il Byun (WBC)	1993
MANUEL ORTIZ	1942–47	Junior Jones (WBA)	1993–94
HAROLD DADE	1947	Yasuei Yakushiji (WBC)	1993–95
MANUEL ORTIZ	1947–50	John M. Johnson (WBA)	1994
VIC TOWEEL	1950–52	Daorung Chuvatana (WBA)	1994–95

Champion	Held Title
Harold Mestre (IBF)	1995
Mbuelo Botile (IBF)	1995–97
Wayne McCullough (WBC)	1995–96
Veerapol Sahaprom (WBA)	1995–96
Nana Yaw Konadu (WBA)	1996
Daorung Chuvatana (WBA)	1996–97
Nana Yaw Konadu (WBA)	1997–98
Sirimongkol Singmanassak (WBC)	1996–97
Tim Austin (IBF)	1997–2003

Champion	Held Title
Joichiro Tatsuyoshi (WBC)	1997–98
Johnny Tapia (WBA)	1998–99
Veerapol Sahaprom (WBC)	1998–2005
Paulie Ayala (WBA)	1999–2001
Eidy Moya (WBA)	2001–02
Johnny Bredahl (WBA)	2002–04†
Rafael Marquez (IBF)	2003–
Wladimir Sidorenko (WBA)	2005–
Hozumi Hasegawa (WBC)	2005–

Junior Bantamweights

Widely accepted champions in CAPITAL letters. Current champions in **bold** type.

Champion	Held Title
Rafael Orono (WBC)	1980–81
Chul-Ho Kim (WBC)	1981–82
Gustavo Ballas (WBA)	1981
Rafael Pedroza (WBA)	1981–82
Jiro Watanabe (WBA)	1982–84
Rafael Orono (WBC)	1982–83
Payao Poontarat (WBC)	1983–84
Joo-Do Chun (IBF)	1983–85
JIRO WATANABE (IBF)	1984–86
Kaosai Galaxy (WBA)	1984
Ellyas Pical (IBF)	1985–86
Cesar Polanco (IBF)	1986
GILBERTO ROMAN	1986–87
Ellyas Pical (IBF)	1986
Santos Laciar (WBC)	1987
Tae-Il Chang (IBF)	1987
Sugar Rojas (WBC)	1987–88
Ellyas Pical (IBF)	1987–89
Gilberto Roman (WBC)	1988–89
Juan Polo Perez (IBF)	1989–90
Nana Konadu (WBC)	1989–90
Sung-Kil Moon (WBC)	1990–93
Robert Quiroga (IBF)	1990–93
Julio Borboa (IBF)	1993–94
Katsuya Onizuka (WBA)	1993–94
Lee Hyung-Chul (WBA)	1994–96

Champion	Held Title
Jose Luis Bueno (WBC)	1993–94
Hiroshi Kawashima (WBC)	1994–97
Harold Grey (IBF)	1994–95
Alimi Goitia (WBA)	1995–96
Yokthai Sith-Oar (WBA)	1996–97
Carlos Salazar (IBF)	1995–96
Harold Grey (IBF)	1996
Danny Romero (IBF)	1996–97
Gerry Penalosa (WBC)	1997–98
Johnny Tapia (IBF)	1997–98†
Satoshi Iida (WBA)	1997–98
Cho In-Joo (WBC)	1998–00
Jesus Rojas (WBA)	1998–99
Mark Johnson (IBF)	1999–00†
Hideki Todaka (WBA)	1999–2000
Masanori Tokuyama (WBC)	2000–04
Felix Machado (IBF)	2000–03
Leo Gamez (WBA)	2000–01
Celes Kobayashi (WBA)	2001–02
Alexander Munoz (WBA)	2002–04
Luis Perez (IBF)	2003–
Katsushige Kawashima (WBC)	2004–05
Martin Castillo (WBA)	2004–06
Masmori Tokuyama (WBC)	2005–
Nobuo Nashiro (WBA)	2006–

Flyweights

Widely accepted champions in CAPITAL letters. Current champions in **bold** type.

Champion	Held Title
Sid Smith (GBR)	1913
Bill Ladbury (GBR)	1913–14
Percy Jones (GBR)	1914
Joe Symonds (GBR)	1914–16
JIMMY WILDE	1916–23
PANCHO VILLA	1923–25
FIDEL LaBARBA	1925–27*
FRENCHY BELANGER (NBA,IBU)	1927–28
Izzy Schwartz (NY)	1927–29
Johnny McCoy (Calif.)	1927–28
Newsboy Brown (Calif.)	1928
FRANKIE GENARO (NBA,IBU)	1928–29
Johnny Hill (GBR)	1928–29
SPIDER PLADNER (NBA,IBU)	1929
FRANKIE GENARO (NBA,IBU)	1929–31
Willie LaMorte (NY)	1929–30
Midget Wolgast (NY)	1930–35
YOUNG PEREZ (NBA,IBU)	1931–32
JACKIE BROWN (NBA,IBU)	1932–35
BENNY LYNCH	1935–38†
Small Montana (NY,Calif.)	1935–37
PETER KANE	1938–43
Little Dado (NBA,Calif.)	1938–40
JACKIE PATERSON	1943–48
RINTY MONAGHAN	1948–50*
TERRY ALLEN	1950
SALVADOR (DADO) MARINO	1950–52

Champion	Held Title
YOSHIO SHIRAI	1953–54
PASCUAL PEREZ	1954–60
PONE KINGPETCH	1960–62
MASAHIKO (FIGHTING) HARADA	1962–63
PONE KINGPETCH	1963
HIROYUKI EBIHARA	1963–64
PONE KINGPETCH	1964–65
SALVATORE BURRINI	1965–66
Horacio Accavallo (WBA)	1966–68
WALTER McGOWAN	1966
CHARTCHAI CHIONOI	1966–69
EFREN TORRES	1969–70
Hiroyuki Ebihara (WBA)	1969
Bernabe Villacampo (WBA)	1969–70
CHARTCHAI CHIONOI	1970
Berkrerk Chartvanchai (WBA)	1970
Masao Ohba (WBA)	1970–73
ERBITO SALAVARRIA	1970–73
Betulio Gonzalez (WBC)	1972
Venice Borkorsor (WBC)	1972–73
VENICE BORKORSOR	1973
Chartchai Chionoi (WBA)	1973–74
Betulio Gonzalez (WBA)	1973–74
Shoji Oguma (WBC)	1974–75
Susumu Hanagata (WBA)	1974–75
Miguel Canto (WBC)	1975–79
Erbito Salavarria (WBA)	1975–76

Major Titleholders (Cont.)
Flyweights (Cont.)

Champion	Held Title	Champion	Held Title
Alfonso Lopez (WBA)	1976	Duke McKenzie (IBF)	1988–89
Guty Espadas (WBA)	1976–78	Dave McAuley (IBF)	1989–92
Betulio Gonzalez (WBA)	1978–79	Sot Chitalada (WBC)	1989–91
Chan-Hee Park (WBC)	1979–80	Jesus Rojas (WBA)	1989–90
Luis Ibarra (WBA)	1979–80	Yul-Woo Lee (WBA)	1990
Tae-Shik Kim (WBA)	1980	Leopard Tamakuma (WBA)	1990–91
Shoji Oguma (WBC)	1980–81	Muangchai Kittikasem (WBC)	1991–92
Peter Mathebula (WBA)	1980–81	Yong-Kang Kim (WBA)	1991–92
Santos Laciar (WBA)	1981	Rodolfo Blanco (IBF)	1992
Antonio Avelar (WBC)	1981–82	Yuri Arbachakov (WBC)	1992–97
Luis Ibarra (WBA)	1981	Aquiles Guzman (WBA)	1992
Juan Herrera (WBA)	1981–82	Phichit Sithbangprachan (IBF)	1992–94†
Prudencio Cardona (WBC)	1982	David Griman (WBA)	1992–94
Santos Laciar (WBA)	1982–85	Saen Sor Ploenchit (WBA)	1994–96
Freddie Castillo (WBC)	1982	Francisco Tejedor (IBF)	1995
Eleoncio Mercedes (WBC)	1982–83	Danny Romero (IBF)	1995–96
Charlie Magri (WBC)	1983	Mark Johnson (IBF)	1996–99†
Frank Cedeno (WBC)	1983–84	Jose Bonilla (WBA)	1996–97
Soon-Chun Kwon (IBF)	1983–85	Chatchai Sasakul (WBC)	1997–98
Koji Kobayashi (WBC)	1984	Hugo Soto (WBA)	1998–99
Gabriel Bernal (WBC)	1984	Manny Pacquiao (WBC)	1998–99
Sot Chitalada (WBC)	1984–88	Irene Pacheco (IBF)	1999–2005
Hilario Zapate (WBA)	1985–87	Leo Gamez (WBA)	1999
Chong-Kwan Chung (IBF)	1985–86	Medgoen Lukchaopormasak (WBC)	1999–00
Bi-Won Chung (IBF)	1986	Sornpichai Kratindaenggym (WBA)	1999–00
Hi-Sup Shin (IBF)	1986–87	Eric Morel (WBA)	2000–03
Dodie Penalosa (IBF)	1987	Malcolm Tunacao (WBC)	2000–01
Fidel Bassa (WBA)	1987–89	**Pongsaklek Wonjongkam** (WBC)	2001–
Choi Chang-Ho (IBF)	1987–88	**Lorenzo Parra** (WBA)	2003–
Rolando Bohol (IBF)	1988	**Vic Darchinyan** (IBF)	2004–
Yong-Kang Kim (WBC)	1988–89		

Junior Flyweights
Current champions in **bold** type.

Champion	Held Title	Champion	Held Title
Franco Udella (WBC)	1975	Rolando Pascua (WBC)	1990
Jaime Rios (WBA)	1975–76	Melchor Cob Castro (WBC)	1991
Luis Estaba (WBC)	1975–78	Humberto Gonzalez (WBC)	1991–93
Juan Guzman (WBA)	1976	Hirokia Ioka (WBA)	1991–92
Yoko Gushiken (WBA)	1976–81	Michael Carbajal (WBC)	1993–94
Freddy Castillo (WBC)	1978	Myung-Woo Yuh (WBA)	1993
Netrnoi Vorasingh (WBC)	1978	Leo Gamez (WBA)	1993–95
Sung-Jun Kim (WBC)	1978–80	Humberto Gonzalez (WBC/IBF)	1994–95
Shigeo Nakajima (WBC)	1980	Choi Hi-Yong (WBA)	1995–96
Hilario Zapata (WBC)	1980–82	Saman Sor Jaturong (WBC/IBF)	1995–96
Pedro Flores (WBA)	1981	Carlos Murillo (WBA)	1996
Hwan-Jin Kim (WBA)	1981	Keiji Yamaguchi (WBA)	1996
Katsuo Tokashiki (WBA)	1981–83	Michael Carbajal (IBF)	1996–97
Amado Urzua (WBC)	1982	Saman Sor Jaturong (WBC)	1995–99
Tadashi Tomori (WBC)	1982	Phichit Chor Siriwat (WBA)	1996–00†
Hilario Zapata (WBC)	1982–83	Mauricio Pastrana (IBF)	1997–98†
Jung-Koo Chang (WBC)	1983–88	Will Grigsby (IBF)	1999
Lupe Madera (WBA)	1983–84	Choi Yo-Sam (WBC)	1999–2002
Dodie Penalosa (IBF)	1983–86	Ricardo Lopez (IBF)	1999–2003*
Francisco Quiroz (WBA)	1984–85	Beibis Mendoza (WBA)	2000–01
Joey Olivo (WBA)	1985	Rosendo Alvarez (WBA)	2001–04†
Myung-Woo Yuh (WBA)	1985–91	Jorge Arce (WBC)	2002–05†
Jum-Hwan Choi (IBF)	1986–88	Jose Victor Burgos (IBF)	2003–05
Tacy Macalos (IBF)	1988–89	Eric Ortiz (WBC)	2005
German Torres (WBC)	1988–89	**Roberto Vasquez** (WBA)	2005–
Yul-Woo Lee (WBC)	1989	**Brian Viloria** (WBC)	2005–
Muangchai Kittikasem (IBF)	1989–90	Will Grigsby (IBF)	2005–06
Humberto Gonzalez (WBC)	1989–90	**Ulises Solis** (IBF)	2006–
Michael Carbajal (IBF)	1990–94		

Strawweights
Current champions in **bold** type.

Champion	Held Title
Franco Udella (WBC)	1975
Jaime Rios (WBA)	1975–76
Luis Estraba (WBC)	1975–78
Juan Guzman (WBA)	1976
Yoko Gushiken (WBA)	1976–81
Freddy Castillo (WBC)	1978
Netrnoi Vorasingh (WBC)	1978
Sung-Jun Kim (WBA)	1978–80
Shigeo Nakajima (WBC)	1980
Hilario Zapata (WBC)	1980–82
Pedro Flores (WBA)	1981
Hwan-Jin Kim (WBA)	1981
Katsuo Tokashiki (WBA)	1981–83
Amado Urzua (WBC)	1982
Tadashi Tomori (WBC)	1982
Hilario Zapata (WBC)	1982–83
Jung-Koo Chang (WBC)	1983–88
Lupe Madera (WBA)	1983–84
Dodie Penalosa (IBF)	1983–86
Francisco Quiroz (WBA)	1984–85
Joey Olivo (WBA)	1985
Myung-Woo Yuh (WBA)	1985–93
Jum-Hwan Choi (IBF)	1986–88
Tacy Macalos (IBF)	1988–89
German Torres (WBC)	1988–89
Yul-Woo Lee (WBC)	1989
Muangchai Kittikasem (IBF)	1989–90
Humberto Gonzalez (WBC)	1989–90

Champion	Held Title
Michael Carbajal (IBF)	1990
Rolando Pascua (WBC)	1990
Melchor Cob Castro (WBC)	1991
Ricardo Lopez (WBC)	1990–98
Ratanapol Voraphin (IBF)	1992–97
Chana Porpaoin (WBA)	1993–95
Rosendo Alvarez (WBA)	1995–98
Ricardo Lopez (WBA/WBC)	1998–99†
Zolani Petelo (IBF)	1997–2001†
Wandee Chor Chareon (WBC)	1999–00
Noel Arambulet (WBA)	1999–00†
Joma Gamboa (WBA)	2000
Keitaro Hoshino (WBA)	2000–01
Jose Antonio Aguirre (WBC)	2000–04
Chana Porpaoin (WBA)	2001
Robert Leyva (IBF)	2001–02
Yutaka Niida (WBA)	2001*
Keitaro Hoshino (WBA)	2002
Noel Arambulent (WBA)	2002–04
Miguel Barrera (IBF)	2002–03
Edgar Cardenas (IBF)	2003
Daniel Reyes (IBF)	2003–04
Eagle Kyowa (WBC)	2004
Yutaka Niida (WBA)	2004–
Muhammad Rachman (IBF)	2004–
Isaac Bustos (WBC)	2004–05
Katsunari Takayama (WBC)	2005
Eagle Kyowa (WBC)	2005–

Annual Awards

Ring Magazine Fight of the Year
First presented in 1945 by Nat Fleischer, who started *The Ring* magazine in 1922.

Multiple matchups: Muhammad Ali vs. Joe Frazier, Marco Antonio Barrera vs. Erik Morales; Carmen Basilio vs. Sugar Ray Robinson, Arturo Gatti vs. Micky Ward and Rocky Graziano vs. Tony Zale (2).

Multiple fights: Muhammad Ali (6); Carmen Basilio (5); George Foreman, Arturo Gatti and Joe Frazier (4); Rocky Graziano, Rocky Marciano, Micky Ward and Tony Zale (3); Marco Antonio Barrera, Nino Benvenuti, Bobby Chacon, Ezzard Charles, Marvin Hagler, Thomas Hearns, Evander Holyfield, Sugar Ray Leonard, Erik Morales, Floyd Patterson, Sugar Ray Robinson, Jersey Joe Walcott (2).

Year	Winner	Loser	Result		Year	Winner	Loser	Result
1945	Rocky Graziano	Red Cochrane	KO 10		1972	Bob Foster	Chris Finnegan	KO 14
1946	Tony Zale	Rocky Graziano	KO 6		1973	George Foreman	Joe Frazier	KO 2
1947	Rocky Graziano	Tony Zale	KO 6		1974	Muhammad Ali	George Foreman	KO 8
1948	Marcel Cerdan	Tony Zale	KO 12		1975	Muhammad Ali	Joe Frazier	KO 14
1949	Willie Pep	Sandy Saddler	W 15		1976	George Foreman	Ron Lyle	KO 4
1950	Jake LaMotta	Laurent Dauthuille	KO 15		1977	Jimmy Young	George Foreman	W 12
1951	Jersey Joe Walcott	Ezzard Charles	KO 7		1978	Leon Spinks	Muhammad Ali	W 15
1952	Rocky Marciano	Jersey Joe Walcott	KO 13		1979	Danny Lopez	Mike Ayala	KO 15
1953	Rocky Marciano	Roland LaStarza	KO 11		1980	Saad Muhammad	Yaqui Lopez	KO 14
1954	Rocky Marciano	Ezzard Charles	KO 8		1981	Sugar Ray Leonard	Thomas Hearns	KO 14
1955	Carmen Basilio	Tony DeMarco	KO 12		1982	Bobby Chacon	Rafael Limon	W 15
1956	Carmen Basilio	Johnny Saxton	KO 9		1983	Bobby Chacon	C. Boza-Edwards	W 12
1957	Carmen Basilio	Sugar Ray Robinson	W 15		1984	Jose Luis Ramirez	Edwin Rosario	KO 4
1958	Sugar Ray Robinson	Carmen Basilio	W 15		1985	Marvin Hagler	Thomas Hearns	KO 3
1959	Gene Fullmer	Carmen Basilio	KO 14		1986	Stevie Cruz	Barry McGuigan	W 15
1960	Floyd Patterson	Ingemar Johansson	KO 5		1987	Sugar Ray Leonard	Marvin Hagler	W 12
1961	Joe Brown	Dave Charnley	W 15		1988	Tony Lopez	Rocky Lockridge	W 12
1962	Joey Giardello	Henry Hank	W 10		1989	Roberto Duran	Iran Barkley	W 12
1963	Cassius Clay	Doug Jones	W 10		1990	Julio Cesar Chavez	Meldrick Taylor	KO 12
1964	Cassius Clay	Sonny Liston	KO 7		1991	Robert Quiroga	Akeem Anifowoshe	W 12
1965	Floyd Patterson	George Chuvalo	W 12		1992	Riddick Bowe	Evander Holyfield	W 12
1966	Jose Torres	Eddie Cotton	W 15		1993	Michael Carbajal	Humberto Gonzalez	KO 7
1967	Nino Benvenuti	Emile Griffith	W 15		1994	Jorge Castro	John David Jackson	TKO 9
1968	Dick Tiger	Frank DePaula	W 10		1995	Saman Sorjaturong	Chiquita Gonzalez	KO 7
1969	Joe Frazier	Jerry Quarry	KO 7		1996	Evander Holyfield	Mike Tyson	TKO 11
1970	Carlos Monzon	Nino Benvenuti	KO 12		1997	Arturo Gatti	Gabriel Ruelas	KO 5
1971	Joe Frazier	Muhammad Ali	W 15		1998	Ivan Robinson	Arturo Gatti	W 10

Annual Awards (Cont.)

Ring Magazine Fight of the Year (Cont.)

Year	Winner	Loser	Result	Year	Winner	Loser	Result
1999	Paulie Ayala	Johnny Tapia	W 12	2003	Arturo Gatti	Micky Ward	W 10
2000	Erik Morales	Marco Antonio Barrera	W 12	2004	Marco Antonio Barrera	Erik Morales	W 12
2001	Micky Ward	Emanuel Burton	W 10				
2002	Micky Ward	Arturo Gatti	W 10	2005	Diego Corralles	Jose Luis Castillo	KO 10

Ring Magazine Fighter of the Year

First presented in 1928 by Nat Fleischer, who started *The Ring* magazine in 1922.

Multiple winners: Muhammad Ali (5); Joe Louis (4); Joe Frazier, Evander Holyfield and Rocky Marciano (3); Ezzard Charles, George Foreman, Marvin Hagler, Thomas Hearns, Ingemar Johansson, Sugar Ray Leonard, Tommy Loughran, Floyd Patterson, Sugar Ray Robinson, Barney Ross, Dick Tiger, James Toney and Mike Tyson (2).

Year		Year		Year	
1928	Gene Tunney	1955	Rocky Marciano	1981	Sugar Ray Leonard & Salvador Sanchez
1929	Tommy Loughran	1956	Floyd Patterson	1982	Larry Holmes
1930	Max Schmeling	1957	Carmen Basilio	1983	Marvin Hagler
1931	Tommy Loughran	1958	Ingemar Johansson	1984	Thomas Hearns
1932	Jack Sharkey	1959	Ingemar Johansson	1985	Donald Curry & Marvin Hagler
1933	No award	1960	Floyd Patterson	1986	Mike Tyson
1934	Tony Canzoneri & Barney Ross	1961	Joe Brown	1987	Evander Holyfield
1935	Barney Ross	1962	Dick Tiger	1988	Mike Tyson
1936	Joe Louis	1963	Cassius Clay	1989	Pernell Whitaker
1937	Henry Armstrong	1964	Emile Griffith	1990	Julio Cesar Chavez
1938	Joe Louis	1965	Dick Tiger	1991	James Toney
1939	Joe Louis	1966	No award	1992	Riddick Bowe
1940	Billy Conn	1967	Joe Frazier	1993	Michael Carbajal
1941	Joe Louis	1968	Nino Benvenuti	1994	Roy Jones Jr.
1942	Sugar Ray Robinson	1969	Jose Napoles	1995	Oscar De La Hoya
1943	Fred Apostoli	1970	Joe Frazier	1996	Evander Holyfield
1944	Beau Jack	1971	Joe Frazier	1997	Evander Holyfield
1945	Willie Pep	1972	Muhammad Ali & Carlos Monzon	1998	Floyd Mayweather Jr.
1946	Tony Zale	1973	George Foreman	1999	Paulie Ayala
1947	Gus Lesnevich	1974	Muhammad Ali	2000	Felix Trinidad
1948	Ike Williams	1975	Muhammad Ali	2001	Bernard Hopkins
1949	Ezzard Charles	1976	George Foreman	2002	Vernon Forrest
1950	Ezzard Charles	1977	Carlos Zarate	2003	James Toney
1951	Sugar Ray Robinson	1978	Muhammad Ali	2004	Glen Johnson
1952	Rocky Marciano	1979	Sugar Ray Leonard	2005	Ricky Hatton
1953	Carl (Bobo) Olson	1980	Thomas Hearns		
1954	Rocky Marciano				

Note: Cassius Clay changed his name to Muhammad Ali after winning the heavyweight title in 1964.

Dan Rafael's Annual Awards

ESPN.com's resident boxing expert Dan Rafael has been his handing out his annual awards since 2000.

Fighter of the Year

Year		Year		Year	
2000	Felix Trinidad	2002	Vernon Forrest	2004	Glen Johnson
2001	Bernard Hopkins	2003	James Toney	2005	Ricky Hatton

Fight of the Year

Year	Winner	Loser	Result	Year	Winner	Loser	Result
2000	Felix Trinidad	Fernando Vargas	TKO 12	2004	Marco Antonio Barrera	Erik Morales	W 12
2001	Micky Ward	Emanuel Burton	W 10				
2002	Micky Ward	Arturo Gatti	W 10	2005	Diego Corralles	Jose Luis Castillo	KO 10
2003	Arturo Gatti	Micky Ward	W 10				

Round of the Year

Year	Winner	Loser	Round	Year	Winner	Loser	Round
2000	Erik Morales	Marco Antonio Barrera	5th	2004	Marco Antonio Barrera	Erik Morales	11th
2001	Micky Ward	Emanuel Burton	9th				
2002	Micky Ward	Arturo Gatti	9th	2005	Diego Corrales	Jose Luis Castillo	10th
2003	Acelino Freitas	Jorge Barrios	11th				

Knockout of the Year

Year	Winner	Loser	Result		Year	Winner	Loser	Result
2000	Lennox Lewis	Frans Botha	TKO 2		2003	Rocky Juarez	Antonio "Chelo" Diaz	KO 10
2001	Lennox Lewis	Hasim Rahman	KO 4		2004	Antonio Tarver	Roy Jones Jr.	KO 2
2002	Roy Jones	Glenn Kelly	KO 7		2005	Allan Green	Jaidon Codrington	KO 1

Prospect of the Year

Year		Year		Year	
2000	Julio Diaz	2002	Miguel Cotto	2004	Samuel Peter
2001	Francisco Bojado	2003	Jermain Taylor	2005	Joel Julio

All-Time Leaders

Based on rankings compiled by *The Ring Record Book and Encyclopedia.*

Knockouts

		Division	Career	No
1	Archie Moore	Lt. Heavy	1936–63	130
2	Young Stribling	Heavy	1921–33	126
3	Billy Bird	Welter	1920–48	125
4	George Odwel	Welter	1930–45	114
5	Sugar Ray Robinson	Middle	1940–65	110
6	Sandy Saddler	Feather	1944–56	103
7	Sam Langford	Middle	1902–26	102
8	Henry Armstrong	Welter	1931–45	100
9	Jimmy Wilde	Fly	1911–23	98
10	Len Wickwar	Lt. Heavy	1928–47	93

Total Bouts

		Division	Career	No
1	Len Wickwar	Lt. Heavy	1928–47	463
2	Reggie Strickland	Lt. Heavy	1987–05	363
3	Jack Britton	Welter	1905–30	350
4	Johnny Dundee	Feather	1910–32	333
5	Billy Bird	Welter	1920–48	318
6	George Marsden	n/a	1928–46	311
7	Maxie Rosenbloom	Lt. Heavy	1923–39	299
8	Harry Greb	Middle	1913–26	298
9	Young Stribling	Lt. Heavy	1921–33	286
10	Battling Levinsky	Lt. Heavy	1910–29	282

Triple Champions

Fighters who have won widely-accepted world titles in more than two divisions. Henry Armstrong is the only fighter listed to hold three titles simultaneously. Note that (*) indicates title claimant.

Sugar Ray Leonard (5) WBC Welterweight (1979-80,80-82); WBA Jr. Middleweight (1981); WBC Middleweight (1987); WBC Super Middleweight (1988-90); WBC Light Heavyweight (1988).

Roy Jones Jr. (4) IBF Middleweight (1993-94); IBF Super Middleweight (1994-96); WBC Light Heavyweight (1996, 1997-2003); WBA Light Heavyweight (1998–); IBF Light Heavyweight (1999-2003); WBA Heavyweight (2003-04).

Oscar De La Hoya (4) IBF Lightweight (1995-96); WBC Super Lightweight (1996-97); WBC Welterweight (1997-99); WBC Jr. Middleweight (2001-03); WBA Jr. Middleweight (2002-03); WBC Jr. Middleweight (2006).

Roberto Duran (4) Lightweight (1972-79); WBC Welterweight (1980); WBA Jr. Middleweight (1983-84); WBC Middleweight (1989-90).

Leo Gamez (4) WBA Strawweight (1988-90); WBA Jr. Flyweight (1993-95); WBA Flyweight (1999); WBA Junior Bantamweight (2000-01).

Thomas Hearns (4) WBA Welterweight (1980-81); WBC Jr. Middleweight (1982-84); WBC Light Heavyweight (1987); WBC Middleweight (1987-88); WBA Light Heavyweight (1991).

Floyd Mayweather (4) Jr. Lighweight (1998-2002); Lightweight (2002-04); Jr. Welterweight (2005-06); Welterweight (2006–)

James Toney (4) IBF Middleweight (1991-93); IBF Super Middlweight (1992-94); IBF Cruiserweight (2003); WBA Heavyweight† (2005).

Pernell Whitaker (4) IBF/WBC/WBA Lightweight (1989-92); IBF Jr. Welterweight (1992-93); WBC Welterweight (1993-97); WBC Jr. Middleweight (1995).

Alexis Arguello (3) WBA Featherweight (1974-77); WBC Jr. Lightweight (1978-80); WBC Lightweight (1981-83).

Henry Armstrong (3) Featherweight (1937-38); Welterweight (1938-40); Lightweight (1938-39).

†Toney won a uninimous 12-round decision over WBA champion John Ruiz but tested positive for steroids in a post-fight drug test and the fight was ruled a no-contest.

Iran Barkley (3) WBC Middleweight (1988-89); IBF Super Middleweight (1992-93); WBA Light Heavyweight (1992).

Wilfredo Benitez (3) Jr. Welterweight (1976-79); Welterweight (1979); WBC Jr. Middleweight (1981-82).

Tony Canzoneri (3) Featherweight (1928); Lightweight (1930-33); Jr. Welterweight (1931-32,33).

Julio Cesar Chavez (3) WBC Jr. Lightweight (1984-87); WBA/WBC Lightweight (1987-89); WBC/IBF Jr. Welterweight (1989-91); WBC Jr. Welterweight (1991-94, 1994).

Jeff Fenech (3) IBF Bantamweight (1985); WBC Jr. Featherweight (1986-88); WBC Featherweight (1988-90).

Bob Fitzsimmons (3) Middleweight (1891-97); Light Heavyweight (1903-05); Heavyweight (1897-99).

Wilfredo Gomez (3) WBC Super Bantamweight (1977-83); WBC Featherweight (1984); WBA Jr. Lightweight (1985-86).

Emile Griffith (3) Welterweight (1961,62-63,63-66); Jr. Middleweight (1962-63); Middleweight (1966-67,67-68).

Mike McCallum (3) WBA Jr. Middleweight (1984-88); WBA Middleweight (1989-91); WBC Light Heavyweight (1994-95).

Terry McGovern (3) Bantamweight (1899-1900); Featherweight (1900-01); Lightweight* (1900-01).

Erik Morales (3) WBC Jr. Featherweight (1997-2000); WBC Featherweight (2001-02); IBF/WBC Jr. Lightweight (2004)

Barney Ross (3) Lightweight (1933-35); Jr. Welterweight (1933-35); Welterweight (1934, 35-38).

Johnny Tapia (3) IBF Jr. Bantamweight (1997-98); WBA Bantamweight (1998-99); IBF Featherweight (2002).

Felix Trinidad (3) IBF/WBC Welterweight (1993-2000); WBA/IBF Jr. Middleweight (2000-01); WBA Middleweight (2001).

Wilfredo Vazquez (3) WBA Bantamweight (1987-88); WBA Jr. Featherweight (1992-95); WBA Featherweight (1996-98).

Muhammad Ali's Career Pro Record

Born Cassius Marcellus Clay, Jr. on Jan. 17, 1942, in Louisville; Amateur record of 100-5; won light-heavyweight gold medal at 1960 Olympic Games; Pro record of 56-5 with 37 KOs in 61 fights.

1960

Date	Opponent (location)	Result
Oct. 29	Tunney Hunsaker, Louisville	Wu 6
Dec. 27	Herb Siler, Miami Beach	TKO 4

1961

Date	Opponent (location)	Result
Jan. 17	Tony Esperti, Miami Beach	TKO 3
Feb. 7	Jim Robinson, Miami Beach	TKO 1
Feb. 21	Donnie Fleeman, Miami Beach	TKO 7
Apr. 19	Lamar Clark, Louisville	KO 2
June 26	Duke Sabedong, Las Vegas	Wu 10
July 22	Alonzo Johnson, Louisville	Wu 10
Oct. 7	Alex Miteff, Louisville	TKO 6
Nov. 29	Willi Besmanoff, Louisville	TKO 7

1962

Date	Opponent (location)	Result
Feb. 10	Sonny Banks, New York	TKO 4
Feb. 28	Don Warner, Miami Beach	TKO 4
Apr. 23	George Logan, Los Angeles	TKO 4
May 19	Billy Daniels, Los Angeles	TKO 7
July 20	Alejandro Lavorante, Los Angeles	KO 5
Nov. 15	Archie Moore, Los Angeles	KO 4

1963

Date	Opponent (location)	Result
Jan. 24	Charlie Powell, Pittsburgh	KO 3
Mar. 13	Doug Jones, New York	Wu 10
June 18	Henry Cooper, London	TKO 5

1964

Date	Opponent (location)	Result
Feb. 25	Sonny Liston, Miami Beach	TKO 7

(won World Heavyweight title)

After the fight, Clay announces he is a member of the Black Muslim religious sect and has changed his name to Muhammad Ali.

1965

Date	Opponent (location)	Result
May 25	Sonny Liston, Lewiston, Me	KO 1
Nov. 22	Floyd Patterson, Las Vegas	TKO 12

1966

Date	Opponent (location)	Result
Mar. 29	George Chuvalo, Toronto	Wu 15
May 21	Henry Cooper, London	TKO 6
Aug. 6	Brian London, London	KO 3
Sept. 10	Karl Mildenberger, Frankfurt	TKO 12
Nov. 14	Cleveland Williams, Houston	TKO 3

1967

Date	Opponent (location)	Result
Feb. 6	Ernie Terrell, Houston	Wu 15
Mar. 22	Zora Folley, New York	KO 7
Apr. 28	Refuses induction into U.S. Army and is stripped of world title by WBA and most state commissions the next day.	
June 20	Found guilty of draft evasion in Houston; fined $10,000 and sentenced to 5 years; remains free pending appeals, but is barred from the ring.	

1968-69 (Inactive)

1970

Date	Opponent (location)	Result
Feb. 3	Announces retirement.	
Oct. 26	Jerry Quarry, Atlanta	TKO 3
Dec. 7	Oscar Bonavena, New York	TKO 15

1971

Date	Opponent (location)	Result
Mar. 8	Joe Frazier, New York	Lu 15

(for World Heavyweight title)

June 28	U.S. Supreme Court reverses Ali's 1967 conviction saying he had been drafted improperly.	
July 26	Jimmy Ellis, Houston	TKO 12

(won vacant NABF Heavyweight title)

Nov. 17	Buster Mathis, Houston	Wu 12
Dec. 26	Jurgen Blin, Zurich	KO 7

1972

Date	Opponent (location)	Result
Apr. 1	Mac Foster, Tokyo	Wu 15
May 1	George Chuvalo, Vancouver	Wu 12
June 27	Jerry Quarry, Las Vegas	TKO 7
July 19	Al (Blue) Lewis, Dublin, Ire	TKO 11
Sept. 20	Floyd Patterson, New York	TKO 7
Nov. 21	Bob Foster, Stateline, Nev	TKO 8

1973

Date	Opponent (location)	Result
Feb. 14	Joe Bugner, Las Vegas	Wu 12
Mar. 31	Ken Norton, San Diego	Ls 12

(lost NABF Heavyweight title)

Sept. 10	Ken Norton, Inglewood, Calif	Ws 12

(regained NABF Heavyweight title)

Oct. 20	Rudi Lubbers, Jakarta, Indonesia	Wu 12

1974

Date	Opponent (location)	Result
Jan. 28	Joe Frazier, New York	Wu 12
Oct. 30	George Foreman, Kinshasa, Zaire	KO 8

(regained World Heavyweight title)

1975

Date	Opponent (location)	Result
Mar. 24	Chuck Wepner, Cleveland	TKO 15
May 16	Ron Lyle, Las Vegas	TKO 11
June 30	Joe Bugner, Kuala Lumpur, Malaysia	Wu 15
Oct. 1	Joe Frazier, Manila, Philippines	TKO 14

1976

Date	Opponent (location)	Result
Feb. 20	Jean Pierre Coopman, San Juan	KO 5
Apr. 30	Jimmy Young, Landover, Md	Wu 15
May 24	Richard Dunn, Munich	TKO 5
Sept. 28	Ken Norton, New York	Wu 15

1977

Date	Opponent (location)	Result
May 16	Alfredo Evangelista, Landover	Wu 15
Sept. 29	Earnie Shavers, New York	Wu 15

1978

Date	Opponent (location)	Result
Feb. 15	Leon Spinks, Las Vegas	Ls 15

(lost World Heavyweight title)

Sept. 15	Leon Spinks, New Orleans	Wu 15

(regained World Heavyweight title)

1979

Date		
June 27	Announces retirement.	

1980

Date	Opponent (location)	Result
Oct. 2	Larry Holmes, Las Vegas	TKO by 11

1981

Date	Opponent (location)	Result
Dec. 11	Trevor Berbick, Nassau	Lu 10

(retires after fight)

MISCELLANEOUS SPORTS

2005 / 2006 YEAR IN REVIEW

Rufus, a Colored Bull Terrier, was named Best in Show at the 130th Westminster Dog Show.

BOWLING

Major Championships
MEN
U.S. Open

Started in 1941 by the Bowling Proprietors' Association of America, 18 years before the founding of the Professional Bowlers Association. Originally the BPAA All-Star Tournament, it became the U.S. Open in 1971.

Multiple winners: Don Carter and Dick Weber (4); Dave Husted and Pete Weber (3); Del Ballard Jr., Marshall Holman, Junie McMahon, Connie Schwoegler, Andy Varipapa and Walter Ray Williams Jr. (2).

Year		Year		Year		Year	
1942	John Crimmins	1958	Don Carter	1974	Larry Laub	1990	Ron Palombi Jr.
1943	Connie Schwoegler	1959	Billy Welu	1975	Steve Neff	1991	Pete Weber
1944	Ned Day	1960	Harry Smith	1976	Paul Moser	1992	Robert Lawrence
1945	Buddy Bomar	1961	Bill Tucker	1977	Johnny Petraglia	1993	Del Ballard Jr.
1946	Joe Wilman	1962	Dick Weber	1978	Nelson Burton Jr.	1994	Justin Hromek
1947	Andy Varipapa	1963	Dick Weber	1979	Joe Berardi	1995	Dave Husted
1948	Andy Varipapa	1964	Bob Strampe	1980	Steve Martin	1996	Dave Husted
1949	Connie Schwoegler	1965	Dick Weber	1981	Marshall Holman	1997	Not held
1950	Junie McMahon	1966	Dick Weber	1982	Dave Husted	1998	Walter Ray Williams Jr.
1951	Dick Hoover	1967	Les Schissler	1983	Gary Dickinson	1999	Bob Learn Jr.
1952	Junie McMahon	1968	Jim Stefanich	1984	Mark Roth	2000	Robert Smith
1953	Don Carter	1969	Billy Hardwick	1985	Marshall Holman	2001	Miko Koivuniemi
1954	Don Carter	1970	Bobby Cooper	1986	Steve Cook	2003	Walter Ray Williams Jr.
1955	Steve Nagy	1971	Mike Limongello	1987	Del Ballard Jr.	2004	Pete Weber
1956	Bill Lillard	1972	Don Johnson	1988	Pete Weber	2005	Chris Barnes
1957	Don Carter	1973	Mike McGrath	1989	Mike Aulby	2006	Tommy Jones

PBA World Championship

The Professional Bowlers Association was formed in 1958 and its first national championship tournament was held in Memphis in 1960. Formerly known as the PBA National Championship, the name was changed in 2002. The tournament was held in various locations (1960-80), Toledo, Ohio (1981-2002) and Taylor, Mich. (2003-).

Multiple winners: Earl Anthony (6); Walter Ray Williams Jr. (3); Mike Aulby, Dave Davis, Mike McGrath, Pete Weber and Wayne Zahn (2).

Year		Year		Year		Year	
1960	Don Carter	1972	Johnny Guenther	1984	Bob Chamberlain	1996	Butch Soper
1961	Dave Soutar	1973	Earl Anthony	1985	Mike Aulby	1997	Rick Steelsmith
1962	Carmen Salvino	1974	Earl Anthony	1986	Tom Crites	1998	Pete Weber
1963	Billy Hardwick	1975	Earl Anthony	1987	Randy Pedersen	1999	Tim Criss
1964	Bob Strampe	1976	Paul Colwell	1988	Brian Voss	2000	Norm Duke
1965	Dave Davis	1977	Tommy Hudson	1989	Pete Weber	2001	Walter Ray Williams Jr.
1966	Wayne Zahn	1978	Warren Nelson	1990	Jim Pencak	2002	Doug Kent
1967	Dave Davis	1979	Mike Aulby	1991	Mike Miller	2003	Walter Ray Williams Jr.
1968	Wayne Zahn	1980	Johnny Petraglia	1992	Eric Forkel	2004	Tom Baker
1969	Mike McGrath	1981	Earl Anthony	1993	Ron Palombi Jr.	2005	Patrick Allen
1970	Mike McGrath	1982	Earl Anthony	1994	David Traber	2006	Walter Ray Williams Jr.
1971	Mike Limongello	1983	Earl Anthony	1995	Scott Alexander		

Tournament of Champions

Originally the Firestone Tournament of Champions (1965-93), the tournament has also been sponsored by General Tire (1994), Brunswick Corp. (1995-2000) and Dexter (2002-). Held in Akron, Ohio in 1965, then Fairlawn, Ohio (1966-94), Lake Zurich, Ill. (1995-96, 2000), Reno, N.V. (1997), Overland Park, Kan. (1998-99) and Uncasville, Conn. (2002-).

Multiple winners: Jason Couch and Mike Durbin (3); Earl Anthony, Dave Davis, Jim Godman, Marshall Holman and Mark Williams (2).

Year		Year		Year		Year	
1965	Billy Hardwick	1976	Marshall Holman	1987	Pete Weber	1998	Bryan Goebel
1966	Wayne Zahn	1977	Mike Berlin	1988	Mark Williams	1999	Jason Couch
1967	Jim Stefanich	1978	Earl Anthony	1989	Del Ballard Jr.	2000	Jason Couch
1968	Dave Davis	1979	George Pappas	1990	Dave Ferraro	2001	Not held
1969	Jim Godman	1980	Wayne Webb	1991	David Ozio	2002	Jason Couch
1970	Don Johnson	1981	Steve Cook	1992	Marc McDowell	2003	Patrick Healey Jr.
1971	Johnny Petraglia	1982	Mike Durbin	1993	George Branham III	2005	Steve Jaros
1972	Mike Durbin	1983	Joe Berardi	1994	Norm Duke	2006	Chris Barnes
1973	Jim Godman	1984	Mike Durbin	1995	Mike Aulby		
1974	Earl Anthony	1985	Mark Williams	1996	Dave D'Entremont		
1975	Dave Davis	1986	Marshall Holman	1997	John Gant		

USBC Masters Tournament

Sponsored by the United States Bowling Congress, the Masters became an official PBA Tour title event in 1998. It is open to qualified pros and amateurs. The tournament was formerly known as the American Bowling Congress Masters.

Multiple winners: Mike Aulby (3); Earl Anthony, Billy Golembiewski, Dick Hoover and Billy Welu (2).

Year		Year		Year		Year	
1951	Lee Jouglard	1965	Billy Welu	1979	Doug Myers	1993	Norm Duke
1952	Willard Taylor	1966	Bob Strampe	1980	Neil Burton	1994	Steve Fehr
1953	Rudy Habetler	1967	Lou Scalia	1981	Randy Lightfoot	1995	Mike Aulby
1954	Red Elkins	1968	Pete Tountas	1982	Joe Berardi	1996	Ernie Schlegel
1955	Buzz Fazio	1969	Jim Chestney	1983	Mike Lastowski	1997	Jason Queen
1956	Dick Hoover	1970	Don Glover	1984	Earl Anthony	1998	Mike Aulby
1957	Dick Hoover	1971	Jim Godman	1985	Steve Wunderlich	1999	Brian Boghosian
1958	Tom Hennessey	1972	Bill Beach	1986	Mark Fahy	2000	Mika Koivuniemi
1959	Ray Bluth	1973	Dave Soutar	1987	Rick Steelsmith	2001	Parker Bohn III
1960	Billy Golembiewski	1974	Paul Colwell	1988	Del Ballard Jr.	2002	Brett Wolfe
1961	Don Carter	1975	Eddie Ressler Jr.	1989	Mike Aulby	2003	Bryon Smith
1962	Billy Golembiewski	1976	Nelson Burton Jr.	1990	Chris Warren	2004*	Walter Ray Williams Jr.
1963	Harry Smith	1977	Earl Anthony	1991	Doug Kent	2004*	Danny Wiseman
1964	Billy Welu	1978	Frank Ellenburg	1992	Ken Johnson	2005	Mike Scroggins

*held Jan. and Oct., 2004

WOMEN
U.S. Open

Started by the Bowling Proprietors' Association of America in 1949. Originally the BPAA Women's All-Star Tournament (1949-70); and U.S. Open from 1971-2003. There were two BPAA All-Star tournaments in 1955, in January and December.

Multiple winners: Marion Ladewig (8); Donna Adamek, Paula Sperber Carter, Pat Costello, Dotty Fothergill, Dana Miller-Mackie, Aleta Sill and Sylvia Wene (2).

Year		Year		Year		Year	
1949	Marion Ladewig	1963	Marion Ladewig	1977	Betty Morris1978	1991	Anne Marie Duggan
1950	Marion Ladewig	1964	LaVerne Carter		Donna Adamek	1992	Tish Johnson
1951	Marion Ladewig	1965	Ann Slattery	1979	Diana Silva	1993	Dede Davidson
1952	Marion Ladewig	1966	Joy Abel	1980	Patty Costello	1994	Aleta Sill
1953	Not held	1967	Gloria Simon	1981	Donna Adamek	1995	Cheryl Daniels
1954	Marion Ladewig	1968	Dotty Fothergill	1982	Shinobu Saitoh	1996	Liz Johnson
1955	Sylvia Wene	1969	Dotty Fothergill	1983	Dana Miller	1997	Not held
1955	Anita Cantaline	1970	Mary Baker	1984	Karen Ellingsworth	1998	Aleta Sill
1956	Marion Ladewig	1971	Paula Sperber	1985	Pat Mercatanti	1999	Kim Adler
1957	Not held	1972	Lorrie Koch	1986	Wendy Macpherson	2000	Tennelle Grijalva
1958	Merle Matthews	1973	Millie Martorella	1987	Carol Norman	2001	Kim Terrell
1959	Marion Ladewig	1974	Patty Costello	1988	Lisa Wagner	2002	Not held
1960	Sylvia Wene	1975	Paula Sperber Carter	1989	Robin Romeo	2003	Kelly Kulick
1961	Phyllis Notaro	1976	Patty Costello	1990	Dana Miller-Mackie	2004	discontinued
1962	Shirley Garms						

WIBC Queens

Sponsored by the Women's International Bowling Congress, the Queens is open to qualified pros and amateurs. **Note**: Beginning in 2006, the tournament will be known as the USBC Queens, sponsored by the United States Bowling Congress.

Multiple winners: Wendy Macpherson and Millie Martorella (3); Donna Adamek, Dotty Fothergill, Aleta Sill and Katsuko Sugimoto (2).

Year		Year		Year		Year	
1961	Janet Harman	1973	Dotty Fothergill	1985	Aleta Sill	1997	Sandra Jo Odom
1962	Dorothy Wilkinson	1974	Judy Soutar	1986	Cora Fiebig	1998	Lynda Norry
1963	Irene Monterosso	1975	Cindy Powell	1987	Cathy Almeida	1999	Leanne Barrette
1964	D.D. Jacobson	1976	Pam Rutherford	1988	Wendy Macpherson	2000	Wendy Macpherson
1965	Betty Kuczynski	1977	Dana Stewart	1989	Carol Gianotti	2001	Carolyn Dorin-Ballard
1966	Judy Lee	1978	Loa Boxberger	1990	Patty Ann	2002	Kim Terrell
1967	Millie Martorella	1979	Donna Adamek	1991	Dede Davidson	2003	Wendy Macpherson
1968	Phyllis Massey	1980	Donna Adamek	1992	Cindy Coburn-Carroll	2004	Marianne DiRupo
1969	Ann Feigel	1981	Katsuko Sugimoto	1993	Jan Schmidt	2005	Tennelle Milligan
1970	Millie Martorella	1982	Katsuko Sugimoto	1994	Anne Marie Duggan	2006	Shannon Pluhowsky
1971	Millie Martorella	1983	Aleta Sill	1995	Sandra Postma		
1972	Dotty Fothergill	1984	Kazue Inahashi	1996	Lisa Wagner		

Annual Leaders
Average
PBA Tour

The George Young Memorial Award, named after the late ABC Hall of Fame bowler. Based on at least 16 national PBA tournaments from 1959-78, and at least 400 games of tour competition since 1979.

Multiple winners: Mark Roth and Walter Ray Williams Jr. (6); Earl Anthony (5); Marshall Holman (3); Parker Bohn III, Norm Duke, Billy Hardwick, Don Johnson and Wayne Zahn (2).

Year		Avg	Year		Avg	Year		Avg
1962	Don Carter	212.84	1977	Mark Roth	218.17	1992	Dave Ferraro	219.70
1963	Billy Hardwick	210.35	1978	Mark Roth	219.83	1993	Walter Ray Williams Jr.	222.98
1964	Ray Bluth	210.51	1979	Mark Roth	221.66	1994	Norm Duke	222.83
1965	Dick Weber	211.90	1980	Earl Anthony	218.54	1995	Mike Aulby	225.49
1966	Wayne Zahn	208.63	1981	Mark Roth	216.70	1996	Walter Ray Williams Jr.	225.37
1967	Wayne Zahn	212.14	1982	Marshall Holman	216.15	1997	Walter Ray Williams Jr.	222.00
1968	Jim Stefanich	211.90	1983	Earl Anthony	216.65	1998	Walter Ray Williams Jr.	226.13
1969	Billy Hardwick	212.96	1984	Marshall Holman	213.91	1999	Parker Bohn III	228.04
1970	Nelson Burton Jr.	214.91	1985	Mark Baker	213.72	2000	Chris Barnes	220.93
1971	Don Johnson	213.98	1986	John Gant	214.38	2002	Parker Bohn III	221.54
1972	Don Johnson	215.29	1987	Marshall Holman	216.80	2003	Walter Ray Williams Jr.	224.94
1973	Earl Anthony	215.80	1988	Mark Roth	218.04	2004	Mika Koivuniemi	222.73
1974	Earl Anthony	219.34	1989	Pete Weber	215.43	2005	Walter Ray Williams Jr.	227.07
1975	Earl Anthony	219.06	1990	Amleto Monacelli	218.16			
1976	Mark Roth	215.97	1991	Norm Duke	218.21			

Note: After its first nine events of 2001, the PBA instituted a new September-to-March schedule with the statistics for those first nine tournaments rolled over into players' final 2001-02 statistics.

PWBA Tour

The Professional Women's Bowling Association (PWBA) went by the name Ladies Professional Bowling Tour (LPBT) from 1981-97 and the Women's Professional Bowling Association prior to that. This table is based on at least 282 games of tour competition, with the expection of 2003 when the minimum was 122 games. In 2003 the fall season was unexpectedly cancelled, shortening the year to eight tournaments. There was no PWBA Tour in 2004, 2005 or 2006.

Multiple winners: Leanne Barrette (4); Nikki Gianulias, Wendy Macpherson and Lisa Rathgeber Wagner (3); Carolyn Dorin-Ballard, Anne Marie Duggan and Aleta Sill (2).

Year		Avg	Year		Avg	Year		Avg
1981	Nikki Gianulias	213.71	1989	Lisa Wagner	211.87	1997	Wendy Macpherson	214.68
1982	Nikki Gianulias	210.63	1990	Leanne Barrette	211.53	1998	Dede Davidson	217.25
1983	Lisa Rathgeber	208.50	1991	Leanne Barrette	211.48	1999	Wendy Macpherson	218.85
1984	Aleta Sill	210.68	1992	Leanne Barrette	211.36	2000	Cara Honeychurch	215.18
1985	Aleta Sill	211.10	1993	Tish Johnson	215.39	2001	Carolyn Dorin-Ballard	214.73
1986	Nikki Gianulias	213.89	1994	Anne Marie Duggan	213.47	2002	Leanne Barrette	216.45
1987	Wendy Macpherson	211.11	1995	Anne Marie Duggan	215.79	2003	Carolyn Dorin-Ballard	215.22
1988	Lisa Wagner	213.02	1996	Tammy Turner	215.23			

Money Won
PBA Tour

Multiple winners: Earl Anthony and Walter Ray Williams Jr. (6); Mark Roth and Dick Weber (4); Mike Aulby (3); Parker Bohn III, Don Carter and Norm Duke (2).

Year		Earnings	Year		Earnings	Year		Earnings
1959	Dick Weber	$7,672	1975	Earl Anthony	$107,585	1991	David Ozio	$225,585
1960	Don Carter	22,525	1976	Earl Anthony	110,833	1992	Marc McDowell	176,215
1961	Dick Weber	26,280	1977	Mark Roth	105,583	1993	Walter Ray Williams Jr.	296,370
1962	Don Carter	49,972	1978	Mark Roth	134,500	1994	Norm Duke	273,752
1963	Dick Weber	46,333	1979	Mark Roth	124,517	1995	Mike Aulby	219,792
1964	Bob Strampe	33,592	1980	Wayne Webb	116,700	1996	Walter Ray Williams Jr.	244,630
1965	Dick Weber	47,675	1981	Earl Anthony	164,735	1997	Walter Ray Williams Jr.	240,544
1966	Wayne Zahn	54,720	1982	Earl Anthony	134,760	1998	Walter Ray Williams Jr.	238,225
1967	Dave Davis	54,165	1983	Earl Anthony	135,605	1999	Parker Bohn III	232,595
1968	Jim Stefanich	67,375	1984	Mark Roth	158,712	2000	Norm Duke	136,900
1969	Billy Hardwick	64,160	1985	Mike Aulby	201,200	2002	Parker Bohn III	245,200
1970	Mike McGrath	52,049	1986	Walter Ray Williams Jr.	145,550	2003	Walter Ray Williams Jr.	419,700
1971	Johnny Petraglia	85,065	1987	Pete Weber	179,516	2004	Mika Koivuniemi	238,590
1972	Don Johnson	56,648	1988	Brian Voss	225,485	2005	Patrick Allen	350,740
1973	Don McCune	69,000	1989	Mike Aulby	298,237			
1974	Earl Anthony	99,585	1990	Amleto Monacelli	204,775			

Note: After its first nine events of 2001, the PBA instituted a new September-to-March schedule with the statistics for those first nine tournaments rolled over into players' final 2001-02 statistics.

All-Time Leaders

All-time leading tournament winners on the PBA Tour, through Oct. 22, 2006. PBA figures date back to 1959.

PBA Top 20 Tournaments Won

		Titles			Titles
1	Walter Ray Williams Jr.	42	11	Marshall Holman	22
2	Earl Anthony	41	12	Dick Ritger	20
3	Mark Roth	34		Wayne Webb	20
4	Pete Weber	32	14	Amleto Monacellia	19
5	Parker Bohn III	30	15	Dave Davis	18
6	Mike Aulby	27	16	Nelson Burton Jr.	17
7	Don Johnson	26		Billy Hardwick	17
	Dick Weber	26		Carmen Salvino	17
9	Brian Voss	24		Dave Soutar	17
10	Norm Duke	23	20	Steve Cook	15

Annual Awards

MEN

BWAA Bowler of the Year

Winners selected by Bowling Writers Association of America.

Multiple winners: Walter Ray Williams Jr. (8); Earl Anthony and Don Carter (6); Mark Roth (4); Mike Aulby and Dick Weber (3); Parker Bohn III, Buddy Bomar, Ned Day, Norm Duke, Billy Hardwick, Don Johnson and Steve Nagy (2).

Year		Year		Year		Year	
1942	John Crimmins	1958	Don Carter	1974	Earl Anthony	1990	Amleto Monacelli
1943	Ned Day	1959	Ed Lubanski	1975	Earl Anthony	1991	David Ozio
1944	Ned Day	1960	Don Carter	1976	Earl Anthony	1992	Marc McDowell
1945	Buddy Bomar	1961	Dick Weber	1977	Mark Roth	1993	Walter Ray Williams Jr.
1946	Joe Wilman	1962	Don Carter	1978	Mark Roth	1994	Norm Duke
1947	Buddy Bomar	1963	Dick Weber	1979	Mark Roth	1995	Mike Aulby
1948	Andy Varipapa	1964	Billy Hardwick	1980	Wayne Webb	1996	Walter Ray Williams Jr.
1949	Connie Schwoegler	1965	Dick Weber	1981	Earl Anthony	1997	Walter Ray Williams Jr.
1950	Junie McMahon	1966	Wayne Zahn	1982	Earl Anthony	1998	Walter Ray Williams Jr.
1951	Lee Jouglard	1967	Dave Davis	1983	Earl Anthony	1999	Parker Bohn III
1952	Steve Nagy	1968	Jim Stefanich	1984	Mark Roth	2000	Norm Duke
1953	Don Carter	1969	Billy Hardwick	1985	Mike Aulby	2001	Parker Bohn III
1954	Don Carter	1970	Nelson Burton Jr.	1986	Walter Ray Williams Jr.	2002	Walter Ray Williams Jr.
1955	Steve Nagy	1971	Don Johnson	1987	Marshall Holman	2003	Walter Ray Williams Jr.
1956	Bill Lillard	1972	Don Johnson	1988	Brian Voss	2004	Walter Ray Williams Jr.
1957	Don Carter	1973	Don McCune	1989	Mike Aulby	2005	Patrick Allen

PBA Player of the Year

Named after longtime broadcaster Chris Schenkel, winners are selected by members of Professional Bowlers Association. The PBA Player of the Year has differed from the BWAA Bowler of the Year four times—in 1963, '64, '89 and '92.

Multiple winners: Earl Anthony and Walter Ray Williams Jr. (6); Mark Roth (4); Mike Aulby, Parker Bohn III, Norm Duke, Billy Hardwick, Don Johnson and Amleto Monacelli (2).

Year		Year		Year		Year	
1963	Billy Hardwick	1974	Earl Anthony	1985	Mike Aulby	1996	Walter Ray Williams Jr.
1964	Bob Strampe	1975	Earl Anthony	1986	Walter Ray Williams Jr.	1997	Walter Ray Williams Jr.
1965	Dick Weber	1976	Earl Anthony	1987	Marshall Holman	1998	Walter Ray Williams Jr.
1966	Wayne Zahn	1977	Mark Roth	1988	Brian Voss	1999	Parker Bohn III
1967	Dave Davis	1978	Mark Roth	1989	Amleto Monacelli	2000	Norm Duke
1968	Jim Stefanich	1979	Mark Roth	1990	Amleto Monacelli	2002	Parker Bohn III
1969	Billy Hardwick	1980	Wayne Webb	1991	David Ozio	2003	Walter Ray Williams Jr.
1970	Nelson Burton Jr.	1981	Earl Anthony	1992	Dave Ferraro	2004	Mika Koivuniemi
1971	Don Johnson	1982	Earl Anthony	1993	Walter Ray Williams Jr.	2005	Patrick Allen
1972	Don Johnson	1983	Earl Anthony	1994	Norm Duke	2006	Tommy Jones
1973	Don McCune	1984	Mark Roth	1995	Mike Aulby		

Note: After its first nine events of 2001, the PBA instituted a new September-to-March schedule with the statistics for those first nine tournaments rolled over into players' final 2001-02 statistics. Individual awards were handed out in 2002.

CHESS

World Champions

Garry Kasparov became the youngest man to win the world chess championship when he beat fellow Russian Anatoly Karpov in 1985 at age 22. In 1993, Kasparov and then-#1 challenger Nigel Short of England broke away from the established International Chess Federation (FIDE) to form the Professional Chess Association (the PCA was disbanded in 1998). FIDE retaliated by stripping Kasparov of the world title and arranging a playoff that was won by Karpov, the former title-holder. Karpov successfully defended the FIDE title several times before failing to show up for the 1999 FIDE World Championship Tournament that was won by Alexander Khalifman. Indian Viswanathan Anand won the 2000 FIDE World Championship.

In his first title defense in five years, Kasparov faced world #2 Vladimir Kramnik for 16 matches in the unofficial (though more widely recognized) world championship from Oct. 8-Nov. 4, 2000 in London. The 25-year-old Kramnik defeated the longtime world champion 8½-6½ in a stunning result. Kasparov failed to win a single game, but despite the loss was still the top-ranked player in the world. Ruslan Ponomariov of Ukraine won the 2002 FIDE title and a plan, known as the Prague Agreement, to unify the world chess championship was hatched. FIDE hosted a knockout tournament in 2003 which was won by the 18-year-old Ponomariov. Ponomariov was supposed to then play world No. 1 Kasparov. But Ponomariov could not agree to the terms set for his match with Kasparov and was stripped of his title.

Uzbekistan's Rustam Kasimdzhanov won the FIDE title in 2004 (however many of the world's top players didn't compete) and was scheduled to play Kasparov in 2005. The winner of that match was supposed to play the winner of the Kramnik-Peter Leko match (Kramnik retained his title in a 7-7 draw) but Kasparov withdrew from the Kasimdzhanov match in a financial dispute, effectively ending the Prague Agreement. In 2005, the FIDE championship was won by 30-year-old Bulgarian Veselin Topalov. The tournament included eight of the world's top players; each played two games against the others in a round-robin format. However, Kramnik, the linear world champion, did not compete.

Meanwhile, Kasparov stunned many when he announced his retirement from professional chess in March 2005 after winning the prestigious Linares tournament in Spain, claiming there are no real challenges on the horizon.

The 2006 FIDE Championship took place in Russia from Sept. 23-Oct. 13. Linear champ Vladimir Kramnik defeated the world's top-rated player, Veselin Topalov, 2½-1½ in a series of rapid tie-break games following a disputed 6-6 tie in the 12 games series. In a strange twist, the bathroom arrangements had an impact on the match when Topalov complained about Kramnik's frequent in-match bathroom breaks, seeming to imply Kramnik may be getting help from outside sources. Outraged at the accusations, Kramnik balked at playing game 5 and FIDE ruled it a forfeit. Despite that Kramnik prevailed in the tie-break.

Years		Years		Years	
1866-94	Wilhelm Steinitz, Austria	1957-58	Vassily Smyslov, USSR	1975-85	Anatoly Karpov, USSR
1894-1921	Emanuel Lasker, Germany	1958-59	Mikhail Botvinnik, USSR	1985-2000	Garry Kasparov, RUS
1921-27	Jose Capablanca, Cuba	1960-61	Mikhail Tal, USSR	2000–	**Vladimir Kramnik**, RUS
1927-35	Alexander Alekhine, France	1961-63	Mikhail Botvinnik, USSR	2002-03	Ruslan Ponomariov, UKR
1935-37	Max Euwe, Holland	1963-69	Tigran Petrosian, USSR	2004-05	Rustam Kasimdzhanov, UZB
1937-46	Alexander Alekhine, France	1969-72	Boris Spassky, USSR	2005-06	Veselin Topalov, BUL
1948-57	Mikhail Botvinnik, USSR	1972-75	Bobby Fischer, USA*		

*Fischer defaulted the championship in 1975.

DOGS

Iditarod Trail Sled Dog Race

Fifty-year-old musher Jeff King became the oldest ever winner of the Iditarod, crossing under the burled arch in Nome, Alaska to win the 34th edition of the annual race for the fourth time. King, of Denali, Alaska, called his 2006 dog team the greatest he's ever had and won $69,000 and a new pickup truck. Fellow four-time race winner Doug Swingley finished in second place about three hours behind King.

In even-numbered years the trail follows the 1,151-mile Northern Route, while in odd-numbered years, it takes a slightly different 1,161-mile Southern Route. The Iditarod, the longest sled dog race in the world, commemorates a 674-mile relay race from Nenana to Nome in 1925 when mushers and dog teams successfully delivered serum to stave off an outbreak of diphtheria among children.

Multiple winners: Rick Swenson (5); Martin Buser, Susan Butcher, Jeff King and Doug Swingley (4); Robert Sorlie (2).

Year		Elapsed Time	Year		Elapsed Time
1973	Dick Wilmarth	20 days, 00:49:41	1991	Rick Swenson	12 days, 16:34:39
1974	Carl Huntington	20 days, 15:02:07	1992	Martin Buser	10 days, 19:17:00
1975	Emmitt Peters	14 days, 14:43:45	1993	Jeff King	10 days, 15:38:15
1976	Gerald Riley	18 days, 22:58:17	1994	Martin Buser	10 days, 13:02:39
1977	Rick Swenson	16 days, 16:27:13	1995	Doug Swingley	9 days, 02:42:19
1978	Dick Mackey	14 days, 18:52:24	1996	Jeff King	9 days, 05:43:13
1979	Rick Swenson	15 days, 10:37:47	1997	Martin Buser	9 days, 08:31:45
1980	Joe May	14 days, 07:11:51	1998	Jeff King	9 days, 05:52:26
1981	Rick Swenson	12 days, 08:45:02	1999	Doug Swingley	9 days, 14:31:07
1982	Rick Swenson	16 days, 04:40:10	2000	Doug Swingley	9 days, 00:58:06
1983	Rick Mackey	12 days, 14:10:44	2001	Doug Swingley	9 days, 19:55:50
1984	Dean Osmar	12 days, 15:07:33	2002	Martin Buser	8 days, 22:46:02*
1985	Libby Riddles	18 days, 00:20:17	2003	Robert Sorlie	9 days, 15:47:36
1986	Susan Butcher	11 days, 15:06:00	2004	Mitch Seavey	9 days, 12:20:22
1987	Susan Butcher	11 days, 02:05:13	2005	Robert Sorlie	9 days, 18:39:31
1988	Susan Butcher	11 days, 11:41:40	2006	Jeff King	9 days, 11:11:36
1989	Joe Runyan	11 days, 05:24:34			
1990	Susan Butcher	11 days, 01:53:23			

*Race record.

Westminster Kennel Club

Best in Show

The Best in Show prize at the 130th annual All-Breed Dog Show of the Westminster Kennel Club, held Feb. 13-14, 2006 at Madison Square Garden, went to Ch. Rocky Top's Sundance Kid ROM, a Colored Bull Terrier. The 5-year-old, 70-pound dog, who answers to the name Rufus, was selected from more than 2,500 dogs in 166 breeds and varieties. Rufus, who became the first Colored Bull Terrier ever to win the title at Westminster was handled by Kathy Kirk. A White Bull Terrier previously won the top prize in 1918. The Westminster show is the most prestigious dog show in the country, and one of America's oldest annual sporting events.

Multiple winners: Ch. Warren Remedy (3); Ch. Chinoe's Adamant James, Ch. Comejo Wycollar Boy, Ch. Flornell Spicy Piece of Halleston; Ch. Matford Vic, Ch. My Own Brucie, Ch. Pendley Calling of Blarney, Ch. Rancho Dobe's Storm (2).

Year	Breed	Year	Breed
1907 Warren Remedy	Fox Terrier	1960 Chick T'Sun of Caversham	Pekingese
1908 Warren Remedy	Fox Terrier	1961 Cappoquin Little Sister	Toy Poodle
1909 Warren Remedy	Fox Terrier	1962 Elfinbrook Simon	W. Highland Terrier
1910 Sabine Rarebit	Fox Terrier	1963 Wakefield's Black Knight	English Springer Spaniel
1911 Tickle Em Jock	Scottish Terrier	1964 Courtenay Fleetfoot of Pennyworth	Whippet
1912 Kenmore Sorceress	Airedale	1965 Carmichaels Fanfare	Scottish Terrier
1913 Strathway Prince Albert	Bulldog	1966 Zeloy Mooremaides Magic	Fox Terrier
1914 Brentwood Hero	Old English Sheepdog	1967 Bardene Bingo	Scottish Terrier
1915 Matford Vic	Old English Sheepdog	1968 Stingray of Derryabah	Lakeland Terrier
1916 Matford Vic	Old English Sheepdog	1969 Glamoor Good News	Skye Terrier
1917 Comejo Wycollar Boy	Fox Terrier	1970 Arriba's Prima Donna	Boxer
1918 Haymarket Faultless	Bull Terrier	1971 Chinoe's Adamant James	E.S. Spaniel
1919 Briergate Bright Beauty	Airedale	1972 Chinoe's Adamant James	E.S. Spaniel
1920 Comejo Wycollar Boy	Fox Terrier	1973 Acadia Command Performance	Standard Poodle
1921 Midkiff Seductive	Cocker Spaniel	1974 Gretchenhof Columbia River	German SH Pointer
1922 Boxwood Barkentine	Airedale	1975 Sir Lancelot of Barvan	Old Eng. Sheepdog
1923 No best-in-show award		1976 Jo Ni's Red Baron of Crofton	Lakeland Terrier
1924 Barberryhill Bootlegger	Sealyham	1977 Dersade Bobby's Girl	Sealyham
1925 Governor Moscow	Pointer	1978 Cede Higgens	Yorkshire Terrier
1926 Signal Circuit	Fox Terrier	1979 Oak Tree's Irishtocrat	Irish Water Spaniel
1927 Pinegrade Perfection	Sealyham	1980 Sierra Cinnar	Siberian Husky
1928 Talavera Margaret	Fox Terrier	1981 Dhandy Favorite Woodchuck	Pug
1929 Land Loyalty of Bellhaven	Collie	1982 St. Aubrey Dragonora of Elsdon	Pekingese
1930 Pendley Calling of Blarney	Fox Terrier	1983 Kabik's The Challenger	Afghan Hound
1931 Pendley Calling of Blarney	Fox Terrier	1984 Seaward's Blackbeard	Newfoundland
1932 Nancolleth Markable	Pointer	1985 Braeburn's Close Encounter	Scottish Terrier
1933 Warland Protector of Shelterock	Airedale	1986 Marjetta National Acclaim	Pointer
1934 Flornell Spicy Bit of Halleston	Fox Terrier	1987 Covy Tucker Hill's Manhattan	German Shepherd
1935 Nunsoe Duc de la Terrace of Blakeen	Stan. Poodle	1988 Great Elms Prince Charming II	Pomeranian
1936 St. Margaret Magnificent of Clairedale	Sealyham	1989 Royal Tudor's Wild As The Wind	Doberman
1937 Flornell Spicy Bit of Halleston	Fox Terrier	1990 Wendessa Crown Prince	Pekingese
1938 Daro of Maridor	English Setter	1991 Whisperwind on a Carousel	Stan. Poodle
1939 Ferry v.Rauhfelsen of Giralda	Doberman	1992 Lonesome Dove	Fox Terrier
1940 My Own Brucie	Cocker Spaniel	1993 Salilyn's Condor	E.S. Spaniel
1941 My Own Brucie	Cocker Spaniel	1994 Chidley Willum	Norwich Terrier
1942 Wolvey Pattern of Edgerstoune	W. Highland Terrier	1995 Gaelforce Post Script	Scottish Terrier
1943 Pitter Patter of Piperscroft	Miniature Poodle	1996 Clussex Country Sunrise	Clumber Spaniel
1944 Flornell Rarebit of Twin Ponds	Welsh Terrier	1997 Parsifal di Casa Netzer	Standard Schnauzer
1945 Shieling's Signature	Scottish Terrier	1998 Fairewood Frolic	Norwich Terrier
1946 Hetherington Model Rhythm	Fox Terrier	1999 Loteki's Supernatural Being	Papillon
1947 Warlord of Mazelaine	Boxer	2000 Salilyn 'N Erin's Shameless	E.S. Spaniel
1948 Rock Ridge Night Rocket	Bedling. Terrier	2001 Special Times Just Right	Bichon Frise
1949 Mazelaine's Zazarac Brandy	Boxer	2002 Surrey Spice Girl	Miniature Poodle
1950 Walsing Winning Trick of Edgerstoune	Scot. Terrier	2003 Torums Scarf Michael	Kerry Blue Terrier
1951 Bang Away of Sirrah Crest	Boxer	2004 Darbydale's All Rise Pouchcove	Newfoundland
1952 Rancho Dobe's Storm	Doberman	2005 Kan-Point's VJK Autumn Roses	German SH Pointer
1953 Rancho Dobe's Storm	Doberman	2006 Rocky Top's Sundance Kid ROM	Colored Bull Terrier
1954 Carmor's Rise and Shine	Cocker Spaniel		
1955 Kippax Fearnought	Bulldog		
1956 Wilber White Swan	Toy Poodle		
1957 Shirkhan of Grandeur	Afghan Hound		
1958 Puttencove Promise	Standard Poodle		
1959 Fontclair Festoon	Miniature Poodle		

FISHING

IGFA All-Tackle World Records

All-tackle records are maintained for the heaviest fish of any species caught on any line up to 130-lb (60 kg) class and certified by the International Game Fish Association. Records logged through Dec. 31, 2004. **Address:** 300 Gulf Stream Way, Dania Beach, Fla. 33004. **Telephone:** (954) 927-2628. **Web:** www.igfa.org

FRESHWATER FISH

Species	Lbs-Oz	Where Caught	Date	Angler
Barramundi	83-7	N. Queensland, Australia	Sept. 23, 1999	David Powell
Bass, Guadalupe	3-11	Lake Travis, TX	Sept. 25, 1983	Allen Christenson Jr.
Bass, largemouth	22-4	Montgomery Lake, GA	June 2, 1932	George W. Perry
Bass, Roanoke	1-5	Nottoway River, VA	Nov. 11, 1991	Tom Elkins
Bass, rock	3-0	York River, Ontario	Aug. 1, 1974	Peter Gulgin
	3-0	Lake Erie, PA	June 18, 1998	Herbert G. Ratner Jr.
Bass, shoal	8-12	Apalachicola River, FL	Jan. 28, 1995	Carl W. Davis
Bass, smallmouth	10-14	Dale Hollow, TN	Apr. 24, 1969	John T. Gorman
Bass, spotted	10-4	Pine Flat Lake, CA	Apr. 21, 2001	Bryan Shishido
Bass, striped (landlocked)	67-8	O'Neill Forebay, San Luis, CA	May 7, 1992	Hank Ferguson
Bass, Suwannee	3-14	Suwannee River, FL	Mar. 2, 1985	Ronnie Everett
Bass, white	6-13	Lake Orange, VA	July 31, 1989	Ronald L. Sprouse
Bass, whiterock	27-5	Greers Ferry Lake, AR	Apr. 24, 1997	Jerald C. Shaum
Bass, yellow	2-9	Duck River, TN	Feb. 27, 1998	John T. Chappell
Bass, yellow (hybrid)	3-5	Big Cypress Bayou, TX	Mar. 27, 1991	Patrick Collin Myers
Bluegill	4-12	Ketona Lake, AL	Apr. 9, 1950	T.S. Hudson
Bowfin	21-8	Florence, SC	Jan. 29, 1980	Robert L. Harmon
Buffalo, bigmouth	70-5	Bussey Brake, Bastrop, LA	Apr. 21, 1980	Delbert Sisk
Buffalo, black	63-6	Mississippi River, IA	Aug. 14, 1999	Jim Winters
Buffalo, smallmouth	82-3	Athens Lake, AL	June 6, 1993	Randy Collins
Bullhead, black	7-7	Mill Pond, NY	Aug. 25, 1993	Kevin Kelly
Bullhead, brown	6-1	Waterford, NY	Apr. 26, 1998	Bobby Triplett
Bullhead, yellow	4-4	Mormon Lake, AZ	May 11, 1984	Emily Williams
Burbot	18-11	Angenmanelren, Sweden	Oct. 22, 1996	Margit Agren
Carp, bighead	61-15	Old Hickory Lake, TN	Mar. 27, 2002	Rick Richard
Carp, black	40-12	Chiba, Japan	Apr. 1, 2000	Kenichi Hosoi
Carp, common	75-11	St. Cassien, France	May 21, 1987	Leo van der Gugten
Carp, crucian	5-1	Kalterersee, Italy	July 16, 1997	Jorg Marquand
Catfish, blue	124-0	Mississippi River, IL	May 21, 2005	Tim Pruitt
Catfish, channel	58-0	Santee-Cooper Res., SC	July 7, 1964	W.B. Whaley
Catfish, flathead	123-0	Elk City Reservoir, KS	Mar. 14, 1998	Ken Paulie
Catfish, flatwhiskered	16-15	Xingu River, Brazil	Aug. 7, 2001	Ian-Arthur de Sulocki
Catfish, gilded	85-8	Amazon River, Brazil	Nov. 15, 1986	Gilberto Fernandes
Catfish, redtail	97-7	Amazon River, Brazil	July 16, 1988	Gilberto Fernandes
Catfish, sharptoothed	79-5	Orange River, South Africa	Dec. 5, 1992	Hennie Moller
Catfish, white	21-8	East Lyme, CT	Apr. 22, 2001	Thomas Urquahart
Char, Arctic	32-9	Tree River, Canada	July 30, 1981	Jeffery Ward
Crappie, black	4-8	Kerr Lake, VA	Mar. 1, 1981	L. Carl Herring Jr.
Crappie, white	5-3	Enid Dam, MS	July 31, 1957	Fred L. Bright
Dolly Varden	20-14	Wulik River, AK	July 7, 2001	Raz Reid
Dorado	51-5	Corrientes, Argentina	Sept. 27, 1984	Armando Giudice
Drum, freshwater	54-8	Nickajack Lake, TN	Apr. 20, 1972	Benny E. Hull
Gar, alligator	279-0	Rio Grande, TX	Dec. 2, 1951	Bill Valverde
Gar, Florida	10-0	The Everglades, FL	Jan. 28, 2002	Herbert G. Ratner Jr.
Gar, longnose	50-5	Trinity River, TX	July 30, 1954	Townsend Miller
Gar, shortnose	5-12	Rend Lake, IL	July 16, 1995	Donna K. Willmart
Gar, spotted	9-12	Lake Mexia, TX	Apr. 7, 1994	Rick Rivard
Goldfish	6-10	Lake Hodges, CA	Apr. 17, 1996	Florentino M. Abena
Grayling, Arctic	5-15	Katseyedie River, N.W.T.	Aug. 16, 1967	Jeanne P. Branson
Inconnu	53-0	Pah River, AK	Aug. 20, 1986	Lawrence E. Hudnall
Kokanee	9-6	Okanagan Lake, Brit. Columbia	June 18, 1988	Norm Kuhn
Muskellunge	67-8	Hayward, WI	July 24, 1949	Cal Johnson
Muskellunge, tiger	51-3	Lac Vieux-Desert, WI-MI	July 16, 1919	John A. Knobla
Peacock, butterfly	12-9	Chiguao River, Venezuela	Jan. 6, 2000	Antonio Campa G.
Peacock, speckled	27-0	Rio Negro, Brazil	Dec. 4, 1994	Gerald (Doc) Lawson
Perch, Nile	230-0	Lake Nasser, Egypt	Dec. 20, 2000	William Toth
Perch, white	3-1	Forest Hill Park, NJ	May 6, 1989	Edward Tango
Perch, yellow	4-3	Bordentown, NJ	May, 1865	Dr. C.C. Abbot
Pickerel, chain	9-6	Homerville, GA	Feb. 17, 1961	Baxley McQuaig Jr.
Pickerel, grass	1-0	Dewart Lake, IN	June 9, 1990	Mike Berg
Pickerel, redfin	2-4	Gall Berry Swamp, NC	June 27, 1997	Edward C. Davis
Pike, northern	55-1	Lake of Grefeern, Germany	Oct. 16, 1986	Lothar Louis
Redhorse, greater	9-3	Salmon River, Pulaski, NY	May 11, 1985	Jason Wilson

Species	Lbs-Oz	Where Caught	Date	Angler
Redhorse, silver	.11-7	Plum Creek, WI	May 29, 1985	Neal D.G. Long
Salmon, Atlantic	.79-2	Tana River, Norway	1928	Henrik Henriksen
Salmon, chinook	.97-4	Kenai River, AK	May 17, 1985	Les Anderson
Salmon, chum	.35-0	Edye Pass, Brit. Columbia	July 11, 1995	Todd Johansson
Salmon, coho	.33-4	Salmon River, Pulaski, NY	Sept. 27, 1989	Jerry Lifton
Salmon, pink	.14-13	Monroe, WA	Sept. 30, 2001	Alexander Minerich
Salmon, sockeye	.15-3	Kenai River, AK	Aug. 9, 1987	Stan Roach
Sauger	.8-12	Lake Sakakawea, ND	Oct. 6, 1971	Mike Fischer
Shad, American	.11-4	Conn. River, S. Hadley, MA	May 19, 1986	Bob Thibodo
Shad, gizzard	.4-6	Lake Michigan, IN	Mar. 2, 1996	Mike Berg
Sturgeon, lake	.168-0	Georgian Bay, Canada	May 29, 1982	Edward Paszkowski
Sturgeon, white	.468-0	Benicia, CA	July 9, 1983	Joey Pallotta 3rd
Tigerfish, giant	.97-0	Zaire River, Kinshasa, Zaire	July 9, 1988	Raymond Houtmans
Tilapia, spotted	.3-0	Pembroke Pines, FL	Mar. 20, 1999	Jay Wright Jr.
Trout, Apache	.5-3	White Mountain, AZ	May 29, 1991	John Baldwin
Trout, brook	.14-8	Nipigon River, Ontario	July, 1916	Dr. W.J. Cook
Trout, brown	.40-4	Little Red River, AR	May 9, 1992	Rip Collins
Trout, bull	.32-0	Lake Pend Orielle, ID	Oct. 27, 1949	N.L. Higgins
Trout, cutthroat	.41-0	Pyramid Lake, NV	Dec., 1925	John Skimmerhorn
Trout, golden	.11-0	Cooks Lake, WY	Aug. 5, 1948	Charles S. Reed
Trout, lake	.72-0	Great Bear Lake, N.W.T.	Aug. 19, 1995	Lloyd E. Bull
Trout, rainbow	.42-2	Bell Island, AK	June 22, 1970	David Robert White
Trout, tiger	.20-13	Lake Michigan, WI	Aug. 12, 1978	Peter M. Friedland
Walleye	.25-0	Old Hickory Lake, TN	Aug. 2, 1960	Mabry Harper
Warmouth	.2-7	Guess Lake, Holt, FL	Oct. 19, 1985	Tony D. Dempsey
Whitefish, lake	.14-6	Meaford, Ontario	May 21, 1984	Dennis M. Laycock
Whitefish, mountain	.5-8	Elbow River, Manitoba	Aug. 1, 1995	Randy G. Woo
Whitefish, round	.6-0	Putahow River, Manitoba	June 14, 1984	Allan J. Ristori
Zander	.25-2	Trosa, Sweden	June 12, 1986	Harry Lee Tennison

SALTWATER FISH

Species	Lbs-Oz	Where Caught	Date	Angler
Albacore	.88-2	Gran Canaria, Canary Islands	Nov. 19, 1977	Siegfried Dickemann
Amberjack, greater	.155-12	Challenger Bank, Bermuda	Aug. 16, 1992	Larry Trott
Angelfish, gray	.4-0	S.Beach Jetty, Miami, FL	July 12, 1999	Rene G. de Dios
Barracuda, great	.85-0	Christmas Is., Rep. of Kiribati	Apr. 11, 1992	John W. Helfrich
Barracuda, Mexican	.21-0	Phantom Island, Costa Rica	Mar. 27, 1987	E. Greg Kent
Barracuda, pickhandle	.25-5	Scottburgh, South Africa	July 3, 1996	Demetrios Stamatis
Bass, barred sand	.13-3	Huntington Beach, CA	Aug. 29, 1988	Robert Halal
Bass, black sea	.10-4	Virginia Beach, VA	Jan. 1, 2000	Allan P. Paschall
Bass, European	.20-14	Cap d'Agde, France	Sept. 8, 1999	Robert Mari
Bass, giant sea	.563-8	Anacapa Island, CA	Aug. 20, 1968	J.D. McAdam Jr.
Bass, striped	.78-8	Atlantic City, NJ	Sept. 21, 1982	Albert R. McReynolds
Bluefish	.31-12	Hatteras, NC	Jan. 30, 1972	James M. Hussey
Bonefish	.19-0	Zululand, South Africa	May 26, 1962	Brian W. Batchelor
Bonito, Atlantic	.18-4	Faial Island, Azores	July 8, 1953	D. Gama Higgs
Bonito, Pacific	.21-3	Malibu, CA	July 30, 1978	Gino M. Picciolo
Cabezon	.23-0	Juan de Fuca Strait, WA	Aug. 4, 1990	Wesley Hunter
Cobia	.135-9	Shark Bay, W. Australia	July 9, 1985	Peter W. Goulding
Cod, Atlantic	.98-12	Isle of Shoals, NH	June 8, 1969	Alphonse Bielevich
Cod, Pacific	.35-0	Unalaska Bay, AK	June 16, 1999	Jim Johnson
Conger	.133-4	South Devon, England	June 5, 1995	Vic Evans
Dolphinfish	.88-0	Highbourne Cay, Bahamas	May 5, 1998	Richard D. Evans
Drum, black	.113-1	Lewes, DE	Sept. 15, 1975	Gerald M. Townsend
Drum, red	.94-2	Avon, NC	Nov. 7, 1984	David G. Deuel
Eel, American	.9-4	Cape May, NJ	Nov. 9, 1995	Jeff Pennick
Eel, marbled	.36-1	Durban, South Africa	June 10, 1984	Ferdie van Nooten
Flounder, southern	.20-9	Nassau Sound, FL	Dec. 23, 1983	Larenza Mungin
Flounder, summer	.22-7	Montauk, NY	Sept. 15, 1975	Charles Nappi
Grouper, goliath	.680-0	Fernandina Beach, FL	May 20, 1961	Lynn Joyner
Grouper, Warsaw	.436-12	Gulf of Mexico, Destin, FL	Dec. 22, 1985	Steve Haeusler
Haddock	.14-15	Saltraumen, Germany	Aug. 15, 1997	Heike Neblinger
Halibut, Atlantic	.355-6	Valevag, Norway	Oct. 20, 1997	Odd Arve Gunderstad
Halibut, California	.58-9	Santa Rosa Island, CA	June 26, 1999	Roger W. Borrell
Halibut, Pacific	.459-0	Dutch Harbor, AK	June 11, 1996	Jack Tragis
Jack, almaco (Pacific)	.132-0	La Paz, Baja Calif., Mexico	July 21, 1964	Howard H. Hahn
Jack, crevalle	.58-6	Barra do Kwanza, Angola	Dec. 10, 2000	Nuno A.P. da Silva
Jack, horse-eye	.29-8	Ascencion Island, South Atlantic	May 28, 1993	Mike Hanson
Kawakawa	.29-0	Clarion Island, Mexico	Dec. 17, 1986	Ronald Nakamura
Lingcod	.76-9	Gulf of Alaska	Aug. 11, 2001	Antwan D. Tinsley
Mackerel, cero	.17-2	Islamorada, FL	Apr. 5, 1986	G. Michael Mills

FISHING (Cont.)

Species	Lbs-Oz	Where Caught	Date	Angler
Mackerel, king	93-0	San Juan, Puerto Rico	Apr. 18, 1999	Steve Perez Graulau
Mackerel, Spanish	13-0	Ocracoke Inlet, NC	Nov. 4, 1987	Robert Cranton
Marlin, Atlantic blue	1402-2	Vitoria, Brazil	Feb. 29, 1992	Paulo R.A. Amorim
Marlin, black	1560-0	Cabo Blanco, Peru	Aug. 4, 1953	A.C. Glassell Jr.
Marlin, Pacific blue	1376-0	Kaaiwi Point, Kona, HI	May 31, 1982	Jay W. deBeaubien
Marlin, striped	494-0	Tutakaka, New Zealand	Jan. 16, 1986	Bill Boniface
Marlin, white	181-14	Vitoria, Brazil	Dec. 8, 1979	Evandro Luiz Coser
Permit	56-2	Ft. Lauderdale, FL	June 30, 1997	Thomas Sebestyen
Pollack, European	27-6	Salcombe, Devon, England	Jan. 16, 1986	Robert S. Milkins
Pollock	50-0	Salstraumen, Norway	Nov. 30, 1996	Thor-Magnus Lekang
Pompano, African	50-8	Daytona Beach, FL	Apr. 21, 1990	Tom Sargent
Roosterfish	114-0	La Paz, Baja Calif., Mexico	June 1, 1960	Abe Sackheim
Runner, blue	11-2	Dauphin Island, AL	June 28, 1997	Stacey M. Moiren
Runner, rainbow	37-9	Clarion Island, Mexico	Nov. 21, 1991	Tom Pfleger
Sailfish, Atlantic	141-1	Luanda, Angola	Feb. 19, 1994	Alfredo de Sousa Neves
Sailfish, Pacific	221-0	Santa Cruz Is., Ecuador	Feb. 12, 1947	C.W. Stewart
Seabass, white	83-12	San Felipe, Mexico	Mar. 31, 1953	L.C. Baumgardner
Seatrout, spotted	17-7	Ft. Pierce, FL	May 11, 1995	Craig F. Carson
Shark, blue	528-0	Montauk Point, NY	Aug. 9, 2001	Joe Seidel
Shark, great white	2664-0	Ceduna, S. Australia	Apr. 21, 1959	Alfred Dean
Shark, Greenland	1708-9	Trondheimsfjord, Norway	Oct. 18, 1987	Terje Nordtvedt
Shark, hammerhead	991-0	Sarasota, FL	May 30, 1982	Allen Ogle
Shark, shortfin mako	1221-0	Chatham, MA	July 21, 2001	Luke Sweeney
Shark, porbeagle	507-0	Pentland Firth, Scotland	Mar. 9, 1993	Christopher Bennet
Shark, bigeye thresher	802-0	Tutukaka, New Zealand	Feb. 8, 1981	Dianne North
Shark, tiger	1780-0	Cherry Grove, SC	June 14, 1964	Walter Maxwell
Snapper, cubera	121-8	Cameron, LA	July 5, 1982	Mike Hebert
Snapper, red	50-4	Gulf of Mexico, LA	June 23, 1996	Capt. Doc Kennedy
Snook, Pacific black	57-12	Rio Naranjo, Quepos, Costa Rica	Aug. 23, 1991	George Beck
Spearfish, Mediterranean	90-13	Madeira Island, Portugal	June 2, 1980	Joseph Larkin
Swordfish	1182-0	Iquique, Chile	May 7, 1953	Louis Marron
Tarpon	283-4	Sherbro Is., Sierra Leone	Apr. 16, 1991	Yvon Victor Sebag
Tautog	25-0	Ocean City, NJ	Jan. 20, 1998	Anthony R. Monica
Tuna, Atlantic bigeye	392-6	Gran Canaria, Puerto Rico	July 25, 1996	Dieter Vogel
Tuna, blackfin	45-8	Key West, FL	May 4, 1996	Sam J. Burnett
Tuna, bluefin	1496-0	Aulds Cove, Nova Scotia	Oct. 26, 1979	Ken Fraser
Tuna, longtail	79-2	Montague Is., NSW, Australia	Apr. 12, 1982	Tim Simpson
Tuna, Pacific bigeye	435-0	Cabo Blanco, Peru	Apr. 17, 1957	Dr. Russell Lee
Tuna, skipjack	45-4	Flathead Bank, Mexico	Nov. 16, 1996	Brian Evans
Tuna, southern bluefin	348-5	Whakatane, New Zealand	Jan. 16, 1981	Rex Wood
Tuna, yellowfin	388-12	San Benedicto Island, Mexico	Apr. 1, 1977	Curt Wiesenhutter
Tunny, little	35-2	Cap de Garde, Algeria	Dec. 14, 1988	Jean Yves Chatard
Wahoo	158-8	Loreto, Baja Calif., Mexico	June 10, 1996	Keith Winter
Weakfish	19-2	Jones Beach, Long Island, NY	Oct. 11, 1984	Dennis R. Rooney
	19-2	Delaware Bay, DE	May 20, 1989	William E. Thomas

Bassmasters Classic

Luke Clausen led wire-to-wire and landed a three-day total of 56 pounds, two ounces in bass to set a tournament record at the 36th annual CITGO Bassmasters Classic on Florida's Lake Tohopekaliga. The Spokane Valley, Washington angler also landed the $500,000 check that goes to the winner. Rick Morris of Virginia took second place at an even 51 pounds of bass.

Clausen threw a Mann's hard-nosed, six-inch junebug worm to land his lunkers and fished along the shoreline. The worm produced four of his five fish on the tournament's final day. His three-day haul broke the previous record of 55-10 set by Davy Hite in 1999. Higher totals have been recorded (see 1984) but that was before the current five-fish limit was instituted.

The CITGO Bassmasters Classic, hosted by B.A.S.S. (Bass Anglers Sportsman Society), is professional bass fishing's world championship. Qualifiers for the three-day event include the 40 top pros on the CITGO Bassmaster Tour and the five top-ranked anglers from each of three CITGO Bassmasters Open circuits. Anglers may weigh only five bass per day and each bass must be at least 12 inches long. Only artificial lures are permitted. The first Classic, held at Lake Mead, Nev. in 1971, was a $10,000 winner-take-all event.

Multiple winners: Rick Clunn (4); George Cochran, Bobby Murray, Hank Parker and Kevin VanDam (2).

Year		Weight	Year		Weight
1971	Bobby Murray, Hot Springs, Ark	43-11	1979	Hank Parker, Clover, S.C	31-0
1972	Don Butler, Tulsa, Okla	38-11	1980	Bo Dowden, Natchitoches, La	54-10
1973	Rayo Breckenridge, Paragould, Ark	52-8	1981	Stanley Mitchell, Fitzgerald, Ga	35-2
1974	Tommy Martin, Hemphill, Tex	33-7	1982	Paul Elias, Laurel, Miss	32-8
1975	Jack Hains, Rayne, La	45-4	1983	Larry Nixon, Hemphill, Tex	18-1
1976	Rick Clunn, Montgomery, Tex	59-15	1984	Rick Clunn, Montgomery, Tex	75-9
1977	Rick Clunn, Montgomery, Tex	27-7	1985	Jack Chancellor, Phenix City, Ala	45-0
1978	Bobby Murray, Nashville, Tenn	37-9	1986	Charlie Reed, Broken Bow, Okla	23-9

Year		Weight	Year		Weight
1987	George Cochran, N. Little Rock, Ark	15-5	1997	Dion Hibdon, Stover, Mo.	34-13
1988	Guido Hibdon, Gravois Mills, Mo	28-8	1998	Denny Brauer, Camdenton, Mo.	46-3
1989	Hank Parker, Denver, N.C.	31-6	1999	Davy Hite, Prosperity, S.C.	55-10
1990	Rick Clunn, Montgomery, Tex	34-5	2000	Woo Daves, Spring Grove, Va.	27-13
1991	Ken Cook, Meers, Okla	33-2	2001	Kevin VanDam, Kalamazoo, Mich.	32-5
1992	Robert Hamilton Jr., Brandon, Miss	59-6	2002	Jay Yelas, Tyler, Texas	45-13
1993	David Fritts, Lexington, N.C.	48-6	2003	Michael Iaconelli, Woodbury Heights, N.J.	37-14
1994	Bryan Kerchal, Newtown, Conn	36-7	2004	Takahiro Omori, Emory, Texas	39-2
1995	Mark Davis, Mount Ida, Ark.	47-14	2005	Kevin VanDam, Kalamazoo, Mich.	12-15
1996	George Cochran, Hot Springs, Ark.	31-14	2006	Luke Clausen, Spokane Valley, Wash.	56-2

LITTLE LEAGUE BASEBALL

World Series

Columbus, Ga. won the 2006 Little League World Series to give the United States its first back-to-back win at the LLWS since Long Beach, Calif. repeated as champs in 1993. Behind a two-run home run by Cody Walker and 11 strikeouts from Kyle Carter, Columbus beat Japan's Kawaguchi City, 2-1.

The Long Beach repeat only became possible when Zamboanga City of the Philippines was disqualified (see note at bottom of the page). An American team hadn't won back-to-back Little League titles with different teams since 1982-83 when Kirkland, Wash., and Marietta, Ga., won in consecutive seasons.

The third-place game between Beaverton, Ore., and Matamoros, Mexico, was rained out.

Played annually in late August in Williamsport, Penn. at Original Field in Williamsport, Penn. from 1947-1958 and at Howard J. Lamade Stadium since 1959 and also at newly constructed Volunteer Stadium starting in 2001.

In order to be invited to the World Series, teams must first win their regional tournaments. There are eight regions from the U.S. (Great Lakes, Midwest, Mid-Atlantic, New England, Northwest, Southeast, Southwest and West) and eight outside of the U.S. (Asia, Canada, Caribbean, European, Latin America, Mexico, Pacific and Trans-Atlantic). The eight U.S. regions then play each other and the the eight international regions play each other and the two winners from each meet in the championship game. This insures that a team from the U.S. will always participate in the final game.

Multiple winners: Taiwan (16); Japan (6); California (5); Connecticut, New Jersey and Pennsylvania (4); Mexico (3); Georgia, New York, South Korea, Texas and Venezuela (2).

Year	Winner	Score	Loser	Year	Winner	Score	Loser
1947	Williamsport, PA	16-7	Lock Haven, PA	1978	Pin-Tung, Taiwan	11-1	Danville, CA
1948	Lock Haven, PA	6-5	St. Petersburg, FL	1979	Hsien, Taiwan	2-1	Campbell, CA
1949	Hammonton, NJ	5-0	Pensacola, FL				
				1980	Hua Lian, Taiwan	4-3	Tampa, FL
1950	Houston, TX	2-1	Bridgeport, CT	1981	Tai-Chung, Taiwan	4-2	Tampa, FL
1951	Stamford, CT	3-0	Austin, TX	1982	Kirkland, WA	6-0	Hsien, Taiwan
1952	Norwalk, CT	4-3	Monongahela, PA	1983	Marietta, GA	3-1	Barahona, D. Rep.
1953	Birmingham, AL	1-0	Schenectady, NY	1984	Seoul, S. Korea	6-2	Altamonte, FL
1954	Schenectady, NY	7-5	Colton, CA	1985	Seoul, S. Korea	7-1	Mexicali, Mex.
1955	Morrisville, PA	4-3	Merchantville, NJ	1986	Tainan Park, Taiwan	12-0	Tucson, AZ
1956	Roswell, NM	3-1	Merchantville, NJ	1987	Hua Lian, Taiwan	21-1	Irvine, CA
1957	Monterrey, Mexico	4-0	La Mesa, CA	1988	Tai Ping, Taiwan	10-0	Pearl City, HI
1958	Monterrey, Mexico	10-1	Kankakee, IL	1989	Trumbull, CT	5-2	Kaohsiung, Taiwan
1959	Hamtramck, MI	12-0	Auburn, CA				
				1990	Taipei, Taiwan	9-0	Shippensburg, PA
1960	Levittown, PA	5-0	Ft. Worth, TX	1991	Taichung, Taiwan	11-0	Danville, CA
1961	El Cajon, CA	4-2	El Campo, TX	1992	Long Beach, CA	6-0	Zamboanga, Phil.
1962	San Jose, CA	3-0	Kankakee, IL	1993	Long Beach, CA	3-2	Panama
1963	Granada Hills, CA	2-1	Stratford, CT	1994	Maracaibo, Venezuela	4-3	Northridge, CA
1964	Staten Island, NY	4-0	Monterrey, Mex.	1995	Tainan, Taiwan	17-3	Spring, TX
1965	Windsor Locks, CT	3-1	Stoney Creek, Can.	1996	Taipei, Taiwan	13-3	Cranston, RI
1966	Houston, TX	8-2	W. New York, NJ				(called after 5th inn.)
1967	West Tokyo, Japan	4-1	Chicago, IL	1997	Guadalupe, Mexico	5-4	Mission Viejo, CA
1968	Osaka, Japan	1-0	Richmond, VA	1998	Toms River, NJ	12-9	Kashima, Japan
1969	Taipei, Taiwan	5-0	Santa Clara, CA	1999	Osaka, Japan	5-0	Phenix City, AL
1970	Wayne, NJ	2-0	Campbell, CA	2000	Maracaibo, Venezuela	3-2	Bellaire, TX
1971	Tainan, Taiwan	12-3	Gary, IN	2001	Tokyo, Japan	2-1	Apopka, FL
1972	Taipei, Taiwan	6-0	Hammond, IN	2002	Louisville, KY	1-0	Sendai, Japan
1973	Tainan City, Taiwan	12-0	Tucson, AZ	2003	Tokyo, Japan	10-1	Boynton Beach, FL
1974	Kao Hsiung, Taiwan	12-1	Red Bluff, CA	2004	Willemstad, Curacao	5-2	Thousand Oaks, CA
1975	Lakewood, NJ	4-3*	Tampa, FL	2005	West Oahu, HI	7-6	Willemstad, Curacao
1976	Tokyo, Japan	10-3	Campbell, CA	2006	Columbus, GA	2-1	Kawaguchi City, Jap.
1977	Li-Teh, Taiwan	7-2	El Cajon, CA				

* Foreign teams were banned from the tournament in 1975, but allowed back in the following year.

Note: In 1992, Zamboanga City of the Philippines beat Long Beach, 15-4, but was stripped of the title a month later when it was discovered that the team had used several players from outside the city limits. Long Beach was then awarded the title by forfeit, 6-0 (one run for each inning of the game).

AP/Wide World Photos

→ Former Hollywood talent agent **Jamie Gold**, no relation to Ari, won a huge pile of money at the 2006 World Series of Poker in Las Vegas.

POKER

World Series of Poker

Created by Benny Binion in 1970, the World Series of Poker is held each year at Binion's Horseshoe Casino in Las Vegas, Nev. and brings together the world's greatest poker players. The marquee event is the no-limit Texas hold-'em tournament. The first World Series was a seven-player tournament in which the champion Johnny Moss was chosen by a vote of his peers.

The 2006 World Champion was former Hollywood agent Jamie Gold, who beat out 8,773 entrants over 12 days and won a first prize of $12 million—a larger payday than the winner of the Kentucky Derby, Wimbledon, Indianapolis 500 and the Masters combined. The 36-year-old bluffed early and often and then went all in when he paired his pocket Queen on the flop of what would turn out to be the 236th and final hand, head's up against Paul Wasicka who showed pocket 10s. Golds Queens held up on the turn and the river and he took the gold winner's bracelet.

Anyone that's over 21 years old and can pay the $10,000 entry fee can compete.

No-Limit Texas Hold-'em Champions

Multiple winners: Johnny Moss and Stu Ungar (3); Doyle Brunson and Johnny Chan (2).

Year	Champion	Prize Money	Year	Champion	Prize Money
1970	Johnny Moss	n/a	1989	Phil Hellmuth Jr.	$ 755,000
1971	Johnny Moss	$ 30,000	1990	Mansour Matloubi	895,000
1972	"Amarillo Slim" Preston	80,000	1991	Brad Daugherty	1,000,000
1973	Puggy Pearson	130,000	1992	Hamid Datsmalchi	1,000,000
1974	Johnny Moss	160,000	1993	Jim Bechtel	1,000,000
1975	Sailor Roberts	210,000	1994	Russ Hamilton	1,000,000
1976	Doyle Brunson	220,000	1995	Dan Harrington	1,000,000
1977	Doyle Brunson	340,000	1996	Huck Seed	1,000,000
1978	Bobby Baldwin	210,000	1997	Stu Ungar	1,000,000
1979	Hal Fowler	270,000	1998	Scotty Nguyen	1,000,000
1980	Stu Ungar	385,000	1999	Noel Furlong	1,000,000
1981	Stu Ungar	375,000	2000	Chris Ferguson	1,500,000
1982	Jack Strauss	520,000	2001	Carlos Mortensen	1,500,000
1983	Tom McEvoy	580,000	2002	Robert Varkyoni	2,000,000
1984	Jack Keller	660,000	2003	Chris Moneymaker	2,500,000
1985	Bill Smith	700,000	2004	Greg Raymer	5,000,000
1986	Berry Johnston	570,000	2005	Joseph Hachem	7,500,000
1987	Johnny Chan	625,000	2006	Jamie Gold	12,000,000
1988	Johnny Chan	700,000			

POWER BOAT RACING

APBA Gold Cup

The American Power Boat Association Challenge Cup, better knwn as the Gold Cup, for unlimited hydroplane racing is the oldest active motorsports trophy in North America. The first Gold Cup was competed for on the Hudson River in New York in June and September 1904. Since then several cities have hosted the race, led by Detroit (36 times) and Seattle (14).

The current format of 52½ miles on a 2½-mile course was introduced in 1991 at Detroit. The race is run over a two-day period with two heats on Saturday and three heats on Sunday. The Saturday heats are 7½ miles while the Sunday heats are 12½ miles.

Note that (*) indicates driver was also owner of the winning boat.

Drivers with multiple wins: Chip Hanauer (11); Bill Muncey (8); Dave Villwock and Gar Wood (5); Dean Chenoweth (4); Caleb Bragg, Tom D'Eath, Lou Fageol, Ron Musson, George Reis and J.M. Wainwright (3); Danny Foster, George Henley, Vic Kliesrath, E.J. Schroeder, Bill Schumacher, Zalmon G. Simmons Jr., Joe Taggart, Mark Tate and George Townsend (2).

Year	Boat	Driver	Avg. MPH	Year	Boat	Driver	Avg. MPH
1904	Standard (June)	Carl Riotte*	23.160	1958	Hawaii Kai III	Jack Regas	103.000
1904	Vingt-Et-Un II (Sept.)	W. Sharpe Kilmer*	24.900	1959	Maverick	Bill Stead	104.481
1905	Chip I	J.M. Wainwright*	15.000	1960	Not held		
1906	Chip II	J.M. Wainwright*	25.000	1961	Miss Century 21	Bill Muncey	99.678
1907	Chip II	J.M. Wainwright*	23.903	1962	Miss Century 21	Bill Muncey	100.710
1908	Dixie II	E.J. Schroeder*	29.938	1963	Miss Bardahl	Ron Musson	105.124
1909	Dixie II	E.J. Schroeder*	29.590	1964	Miss Bardahl	Ron Musson	103.433
1910	Dixie III	F.K. Burnham*	32.473	1965	Miss Bardahl	Ron Musson	103.132
1911	MIT II	J.H. Hayden*	37.000	1966	Tahoe Miss	Mira Slovak	93.019
1912	P.D.Q. II	A.G. Miles*	39.462	1967	Miss Bardahl	Bill Shumacher	101.484
1913	Ankle Deep	C.S. Mankowski*	42.779	1968	Miss Bardahl	Bill Shumacher	108.173
1914	Baby Speed Demon II	Jim Blackton & Bob Edgren	48.458	1969	Miss Budweiser	Bill Sterett	98.504
1915	Miss Detroit	Johnny Milot & Jack Beebe	37.656	1970	Miss Budweiser	Dean Chenoweth	99.562
				1971	Miss Madison	Jim McCormick	98.043
1916	Miss Minneapolis	Bernard Smith	48.860	1972	Atlas Van Lines	Bill Muncey	104.277
1917	Miss Detroit II	Gar Wood*	54.410	1973	Miss Budweiser	Dean Chenoweth	99.043
1918	Miss Detroit II	Gar Wood	51.619	1974	Pay 'n Pak	George Henley	104.428
1919	Miss Detroit III	Gar Wood*	42.748	1975	Pay 'n Pak	George Henley	108.921
1920	Miss America I	Gar Wood*	62.022	1976	Miss U.S.	Tom D'Eath	100.412
1921	Miss America I	Gar Wood*	52.825	1977	Atlas Van Lines	Bill Muncey*	111.822
1922	Packard Chriscraft	J.G. Vincent*	40.253	1978	Atlas Van Lines	Bill Muncey*	100.412
1923	Packard Chriscraft	Caleb Bragg	43.867	1979	Atlas Van Lines	Bill Muncey*	100.765
1924	Baby Bootlegger	Caleb Bragg	45.302	1980	Miss Budweiser	Dean Chenoweth	106.932
1925	Baby Bootlegger	Caleb Bragg*	47.240	1981	Miss Budweiser	Dean Chenoweth	116.387
1926	Greenwich Folly	George Townsend*	47.984	1982	Atlas Van Lines	Chip Hanauer	120.050
1927	Greenwich Folly	George Townsend*	47.662	1983	Atlas Van Lines	Chip Hanauer	118.507
				1984	Atlas Van Lines	Chip Hanauer	130.175
1928	Not held			1985	Miller American	Chip Hanauer	120.643
1929	Imp	Richard Hoyt*	48.662	1986	Miller American	Chip Hanauer	116.523
1930	Hotsy Totsy	Vic Kliesrath*	52.673	1987	Miller American	Chip Hanauer	127.620
1931	Hotsy Totsy	Vic Kliesrath*	53.602	1988	Miss Circus Circus	Chip Hanauer & Jim Prevost	123.756
1932	Delphine IV	Bill Horn	57.775				
1933	El Lagarto	George Reis*	56.260	1989	Miss Budweiser	Tom D'Eath	131.209
1934	El Lagarto	George Reis*	55.000	1990	Miss Budweiser	Tom D'Eath	143.176
1935	El Lagarto	George Reis*	55.056	1991	Winston Eagle	Mark Tate	137.771
1936	Impshi	Kaye Don	45.735	1992	Miss Budweiser	Chip Hanauer	136.282
1937	Notre Dame	Clell Perry	63.675	1993	Miss Budweiser	Chip Hanauer	141.296
1938	Alagi	Theo Rossi*	64.340	1994	Smokin' Joe's	Mark Tate	145.532
1939	My Sin	Z.G. Simmons Jr.*	66.133	1995	Miss Budweiser	Chip Hanauer	149.160
1940	Hotsy Totsy III	Sidney Allen*	48.295	1996	Pico/American Dream	Dave Villwock	149.328
1941	My Sin	Z.G. Simmons Jr.*	52.509				
1942-45	Not held			1997	Miss Budweiser	Dave Villwock	129.366
1946	Tempo VI	Guy Lombardo*	68.132	1998	Miss Budweiser	Dave Villwock	140.704
1947	Miss Peps V	Danny Foster	57.000	1999	Miss Pico	Chip Hanauer	152.591
1948	Miss Great Lakes	Danny Foster	46.845	2000	Miss Budweiser	Dave Villwock	139.416
1949	My Sweetie	Bill Cantrell	73.612	2001	Tubby's Subs	Mike Hanson	140.519
1950	Slo-Mo-Shun IV	Ted Jones	78.216	2002	Miss Budweiser	Dave Villwock	143.093
1951	Slo-Mo-Shun V	Lou Fageol	90.871	2003	Miss Fox Hills Chrysler Jeep-Sun Coatings	Mitch Evans	144.152
1952	Slo-Mo-Shun IV	Stan Dollar	79.923				
1953	Slo-Mo-Shun IV	Joe Taggart & Lou Fageol	99.108	2004	Miss Detroit Yacht Club	Nate Brown	141.195
1954	Slo-Mo-Shun V	Lou Fageol	92.613	2005	Miss Al Deeby Dodge	Terry Troxell	142.345
1955	Gale V	Lee Schoeneith	99.552	2006	Miss Beacon Plumbing	Jean Theoret	142.289
1956	Miss Thriftway	Bill Muncey	96.552				
1957	Miss Thriftway	Bill Muncey	101.787				

PRO RODEO

All-Around Champion Cowboy

Ryan Jarrett of Summerville, Georgia, in only his second full season in the PRCA, won his first All-Around Champion Cowboy belt buckle at the 47th National Finals Rodeo held Dec. 2-11, 2005 at the Thomas & Mack Center in Las Vegas. Jarrett became the second-youngest champion in history behind only the legendary Ty Murray when he won his first title in 1989.

The Professional Rodeo Cowboys Association (PRCA) title of all-around world champion cowboy goes to the rodeo athlete who wins the most prize money in a single year in two or more events, earning a minimum of $3,000 in each event. Only prize money earned in sanctioned PRCA rodeos is counted. From 1929-44, all-around champions were named by the Rodeo Association of America (earnings for those years are not available).

Multiple winners: Ty Murray (7); Tom Ferguson and Larry Mahan (6); Jim Shoulders (5); Joe Beaver, Trevor Brazile, Lewis Feild and Dean Oliver (3); Everett Bowman, Louis Brooks, Clay Carr, Bill Linderman, Phil Lyne, Gerald Roberts, Casey Tibbs and Harry Tompkins (2).

Year		Year		Year		Year	
1929	Earl Thode	1934	Leonard Ward	1939	Paul Carney	1944	Louis Brooks
1930	Clay Carr	1935	Everett Bowman	1940	Fritz Truan	1945	No award
1931	John Schneider	1936	John Bowman	1941	Homer Pettigrew	1946	No award
1932	Donald Nesbit	1937	Everett Bowman	1942	Gerald Roberts		
1933	Clay Carr	1938	Burel Mulkey	1943	Louis Brooks		

Year		Earnings	Year		Earnings	Year		Earnings
1947	Todd Whatley	$18,642	1967	Larry Mahan	$ 51,996	1987	Lewis Feild	$144,335
1948	Gerald Roberts	21,766	1968	Larry Mahan	49,129	1988	Dave Appleton	121,546
1949	Jim Shoulders	21,495	1969	Larry Mahan	57,726	1989	Ty Murray	134,806
1950	Bill Linderman	30,715	1970	Larry Mahan	41,493	1990	Ty Murray	213,772
1951	Casey Tibbs	29,104	1971	Phil Lyne	49,245	1991	Ty Murray	244,231
1952	Harry Tompkins	30,934	1972	Phil Lyne	60,852	1992	Ty Murray	225,992
1953	Bill Linderman	33,674	1973	Larry Mahan	64,447	1993	Ty Murray	297,896
1954	Buck Rutherford	40,404	1974	Tom Ferguson	66,929	1994	Ty Murray	246,170
1955	Casey Tibbs	42,065	1975	Tom Ferguson	50,300	1995	Joe Beaver	141,753
1956	Jim Shoulders	43,381	1976	Tom Ferguson	87,908	1996	Joe Beaver	166,103
1957	Jim Shoulders	33,299	1977	Tom Ferguson	65,981	1997	Dan Mortensen	184,559
1958	Jim Shoulders	32,212	1978	Tom Ferguson	83,734	1998	Ty Murray	264,673
1959	Jim Shoulders	32,905	1979	Tom Ferguson	96,272	1999	Fred Whitfield	217,819
1960	Harry Tompkins	32,522	1980	Paul Tierney	105,568	2000	Joe Beaver	225,396
1961	Benny Reynolds	31,309	1981	Jimmie Cooper	105,861	2001	Cody Ohl	296,419
1962	Tom Nesmith	32,611	1982	Chris Lybbert	123,709	2002	Trevor Brazile	273,998
1963	Dean Oliver	31,329	1983	Roy Cooper	153,391	2003	Trevor Brazile	294,839
1964	Dean Oliver	31,150	1984	Dee Pickett	122,618	2004	Trevor Brazile	253,170
1965	Dean Oliver	33,163	1985	Lewis Feild	130,347	2005	Ryan Jarrett	263,665
1966	Larry Mahan	40,358	1986	Lewis Feild	166,042			

SOAP BOX DERBY

All-American Soap Box Derby

The 69th annual All-American Soap Box Derby was held on July 22, 2006 in Akron, Ohio. A record number of boys and girls competed.

The AASBD is a coasting race for small gravity-powered cars built by their drivers and assembled within strict guidelines on size, weight and cost. The Derby was started by Dayton, Ohio newsman Myron Scott after he witnessed several boys racing handmade carts down a hill while on a photographic assignment in 1933. Scott decided to start an organized race for kids and the first All-American Soap Box Derby was held in Dayton in 1934. The race got its name because early on most cars were built from wooden soap boxes. The following year, the race was moved to Akron because of its central location and hilly terrain. In 1936, town leaders saw the need for a permanent site for the growing event and with the help of the Works Progress Administration, Derby Downs was constructed.

Held every summer at Derby Downs in Akron, Ohio, the Soap Box Derby is open to all boys and girls from 8 to 17 years old who qualify. There are three competitive divisions: 1. Stock (ages 8-17)— made up of generic, prefab racers that come from Derby-approved kits, can be assembled in four hours and don't exceed 200 pounds when driver, car and wheels are weighed together; 2. Super Stock (ages 10-17)— the same as Stock only with a weight limit of 220 pounds; 3. Masters (ages 11-17)— made up of racers designed by the drivers, but constructed with Derby-approved hardware. The racing ramp at Derby Downs is 989 feet, four inches with an 11 percent grade.

One champion reigned at the All-American Soap Box Derby each year from 1934-75; Junior and Senior division champions from 1976-87; Kit and Masters champions from 1988-91; Stock, Kit and Masters champions from 1992-94; Stock, Super Stock and Masters champions starting in 1995.

Year		Hometown	Age	Year		Hometown	Age
1934	Robert Turner	Muncie, IN	11	1942-45	Not held		
1935	Maurice Bale Jr.	Anderson, IN	13	1946	Gilbert Klecan	San Diego	14
1936	Herbert Muench Jr.	St. Louis	14	1947	Kenneth Holmboe	Charleston, WV	14
1937	Robert Ballard	White Plains, NY	12	1948	Donald Strub	Akron, OH	13
1938	Robert Berger	Omaha, NE	14	1949	Fred Derks	Akron, OH	15
1939	Clifton Hardesty	White Plains, NY	11	1950	Harold Williamson	Charleston, WV	15
1940	Thomas Fisher	Detroit	12	1951	Darwin Cooper	Williamsport, PA	15
1941	Claude Smith	Akron, OH	14	1952	Joe Lunn	Columbus, GA	11

Year	Hometown Age		Year	Hometown Age	
1953 Fred Mohler	Muncie, IN	14	1989 KIT: David Schiller	Dayton, OH	12
1954 Richard Kemp	Los Angeles	14	MAS: Faith Chavarria	Ventura, CA	12
1955 Richard Rohrer	Rochester, NY	14	1990 MAS: Sami Jones	Salem, OR	13
1956 Norman Westfall	Rochester, NY	14	KIT: Mark Mihal	Valparaiso, IN	12
1957 Terry Townsend	Anderson, IN	14	1991 MAS: Danny Garland	San Diego, CA	14
1958 James Miley	Muncie, IN	15	KIT: Paul Greenwald	Saginaw, MI	13
1959 Barney Townsend	Anderson, IN	13	1992 MAS: Bonnie Thornton	Redding, CA	12
1960 Fredric Lake	South Bend, IN	11	KIT: Carolyn Fox	Sublimity, OR	11
1961 Dick Dawson	Wichita, KS	13	STK: Loren Hurst	Hudson, OH	10
1962 David Mann	Gary, IN	14	1993 MAS: Dean Lutton	Delta, OH	14
1963 Harold Conrad	Duluth, MN	12	KIT: D.M. Del Ferraro	Stow, OH	12
1964 Gregory Schumacher	Tacoma, WA	14	STK: Owen Yuda	Boiling Springs, PA	14
1965 Robert Logan	Santa Ana, CA	12	1994 MAS: D.M. Del Ferraro	Akron, OH	13
1966 David Krussow	Tacoma, WA	12	KIT: Joel Endres	Akron, OH	14
1967 Kenneth Cline	Lincoln, NE	13	STK: Kristina Damond	Jamestown, NY	13
1968 Branch Lew	Muncie, IN	11	1995 MAS: J. Fensterbush	Kingman, AZ	11
1969 Steve Souter	Midland, TX	12	SS: Darcie Davisson	Kingman, AZ	11
1970 Samuel Gupton	Durham, NC	13	STK: Karen Thomas	Jamestown, NY	11
1971 Larry Blair	Oroville, CA	13	1996 MAS: Tim Scrofano	Conneaut, OH	12
1972 Robert Lange Jr.	Boulder, CO	14	SS: Jeremy Phillips	Charlestown, WV	14
1973 Bret Yarborough	Elk Grove, CA	11	STK: Matt Perez	No. Canton, OH	12
1974 Curt Yarborough	Elk Grove, CA	11	1997 MAS: Wade Wallace	Elk Hart, IN	11
1975 Karren Stead	Lower Bucks, PA	11	SS: Dolline Vance	Salem, OR	13
1976 JR: Phil Raber	Sugarcreek, OH	11	STK: Mark Stephens	Waynesboro, VA	13
SR: Joan Ferdinand	Canton, OH	14	1998 MAS: James Marsh	Cleveland, OH	12
1977 JR: Mark Ferdinand	Canton, OH	10	SS: Stacy Sharp	Kingman, AZ	14
SR: Steve Washburn	Bristol, CT	15	STK: Hailey Simpson	Salem, OR	10
1978 JR: Darren Hart	Salem, OR	11	1999 MAS: Allan Endres	Barberton, OH	14
SR: Greg Cardinal	Flint, MI	13	SS: Alisha Ebner	Salem, OR	15
1979 JR: Russell Yurk	Flint, MI	10	STK: Justin Pillow	Deland, FL	12
SR: Craig Kitchen	Akron, OH	14	2000 MAS: Cody Butler	Anderson, IN	12
1980 JR: Chris Fulton	Indianapolis	11	SS: Derek Etherington	Anderson, IN	11
SR: Dan Porul	Sherman Oaks, CA	12	STK: Rachel Curran	Medina, OH	13
1981 JR: Howie Fraley	Portsmouth, OH	11	2001 MAS: Michael Flynn	Harrison Township, MI	12
SR: Tonia Schlegel	Hamilton, OH	13	SS: James Rogers	Hilton, NY	15
1982 JR: Carol A. Sullivan	Rochester, NH	10	STK: Chad Eyerly	Alta Loma, CA	11
SR: Matt Wolfgang	Lehigh Val., PA	12	2002 MAS: Evan Griffin	Winter Park, FL	15
1983 JR: Tony Carlini	Del Mar, CA	10	SS: Roger Youmans Jr.	Spencerport, NY	13
SR: Mike Burdgick	Flint, MI	14	STK: Cameron Vannatta	Anderson, IN	12
1984 JR: Chris Hess	Hamilton, OH	11	2003 MAS: Anthony Marulli	Rochester, NY	14
SR: Anita Jackson	St. Louis	15	SS: Corey Harkins	Chicago	14
1985 JR: Michael Gallo	Danbury, CT	12	STK: Nicholas Sibeto	New Castle, PA	12
SR: Matt Sheffer	York, PA	14	2004 MAS: Hilary Pearson	Kansas City, MO	14
1986 JR: Marc Behan	Dover, NH	9	SS: RickiLea Murphy	Mantua, OH	12
SR: Tami Jo Sullivan	Lancaster, OH	13	STK: Perrin Norris	Tullahoma, TN	10
1987 JR: Matt Margules	Danbury, CT	11	2005 MAS: Stephanie Inglezakis	Stow, OH	16
SR: Brian Drinkwater	Bristol, CT	14	SS: Tyler Gallagher	Mantua, OH	14
1988 KIT: Jason Lamb	Des Moines, IA	10	STK: Nick Hoffaman	Lancaster, OH	9
MAS: David Duffield	Kansas City	13	2006 MAS: Garrett Kysar	Martinsburg, WV	14
			SS: Sally Sue Thornton	Vallejo, CA	14
			STK: Michael Neely	North Canton, OH	14

SOFTBALL

Men's and women's national champions since 1933 in Major Fast Pitch, Major Slow Pitch and Super Slow Pitch (men only). Sanctioned by the Amateur Softball Association of America.

MEN
Major Fast Pitch

Multiple winners: Clearwater Bombers (10); Raybestos Cardinals (5); Sealmasters (4); Briggs Beautyware, Decatur Pride, Pay'n Pak and Zollner Pistons (3); Billard Barbell, Farm Tavern, Frontier Players Casino, Hammer Air Field, Kodak Park, Meierhoffer, National Health Care, Penn Corp, Peterbilt Western and Tampa Bay Smokers (2).

Year	Year	Year
1933 J.L. Gill Boosters, Chicago	1943 Hammer Air Field, Fresno, CA	1953 Briggs Beautyware
1934 Ke-Nash-A, Kenosha, WI	1944 Hammer Air Field	1954 Clearwater Bombers
1935 Crimson Coaches, Toledo, OH	1945 Zollner Pistons, Ft. Wayne, IN	1955 Raybestos Cardinals,
1936 Kodak Park, Rochester, NY	1946 Zollner Pistons	1956 Clearwater Bombers
1937 Briggs Body Team, Detroit	1947 Zollner Pistons	1957 Clearwater Bombers
1938 The Pohlers, Cincinnati	1948 Briggs Beautyware, Detroit	1958 Raybestos Cardinals
1939 Carr's Boosters, Covington, KY	1949 Tip Top Tailors, Toronto	1959 Sealmasters, Aurora, IL
1940 Kodak Park	1950 Clearwater (FL) Bombers	1960 Clearwater Bombers
1941 Bendix Brakes, South Bend, IN	1951 Dow Chemical, Midland, MI	1961 Sealmasters
1942 Deep Rock Oilers, Tulsa, OK	1952 Briggs Beautyware	1962 Clearwater Bombers

Softball (Cont.)

Year		
1963 Clearwater Bombers	1980 Peterbilt Western, Seattle	1994 Decatur (IL) Pride
1964 Burch Tool, Detroit	1981 Archer Daniels Midland,	1995 Decatur Pride
1965 Sealmasters	Decatur, IL	1996 Green Bay All-Car,
1966 Clearwater Bombers	1982 Peterbilt Western	Green Bay, WI
1967 Sealmasters	1983 Franklin Cardinals,	1997 Tampa Bay Smokers,
1968 Clearwater Bombers	Stratford, CA	Tampa Bay, FL
1969 Raybestos Cardinals	1984 California Kings, Merced, CA	1998 Meierhoffer-Fleeman,
	1985 Pay'n Pak, Seattle	St. Joseph, MO
1970 Raybestos Cardinals	1986 Pay'n Pak	1999 Decatur Pride
1971 Welty Way, Cedar Rapids, IA	1987 Pay'n Pak	
1972 Raybestos Cardinals	1988 TransAire, Elkhart, IN	2000 Meierhoffer
1973 Clearwater Bombers	1989 Penn Corp, Sioux City, IA	2001 Frontier Players Casino,
1974 Gianella Bros., Santa Rosa, CA		St. Joseph, MO
1975 Rising Sun Hotel, Reading, PA	1990 Penn Corp	2002 Frontier Players Casino
1976 Raybestos Cardinals	1991 Gianella Bros., Rohnert Park, CA	2003 Farm Tavern, Madison, WI
1977 Billard Barbell, Reading, PA	1992 National Health Care,	2004 Farm Tavern
1978 Billard Barbell	Sioux City, IA	2005 Tampa Bay Smokers,
1979 McArdle Pontiac/Cadillac,	1993 National Health Care	Tampa Bay, FL
Midland, MI		2006 Circle Tap, Denmark, WI

Super Slow Pitch

Multiple winners: Ritch's/Superior (4); Howard's/Western Steer and Steele's Sports (3); Lighthouse/Worth and Long Haul (2).

Year		
1981 Howard's/Western Steer,	1989 Ritch's Salvage, Harrisburg, NC	1996 Ritch's/Superior
Denver, NC	1990 Steele's Silver Bullets	1997 Ritch's/Superior
1982 Jerry's Catering, Miami	1991 Sun Belt/Worth, Atlanta	1998 Lighthouse/Worth
1983 Howard's/Western Steer	1992 Ritch's/Superior,	1999 Team Easton, California
1984 Howard's/Western Steer	Windsor Locks, CT	2000 Team TPS, Louisville, KY
1985 Steele's Sports, Grafton, OH	1993 Ritch's/Superior	2001 Long Haul, Albertville, MN
1986 Steele's Sports	1994 Bellcorp., Tampa	2002 Long Haul
1987 Steele's Sports	1995 Lighthouse/Worth, Stone Mt., GA	2003 Resmondo/Hagae,
1988 Starpath, Monticello, KY		Canal Winchester, OH

Major Slow Pitch

Multiple winners: Gatliff Auto Sales, Riverside Paving and Skip Hogan A.C. (3); Campbell Carpets, Hamilton Tailoring, Howard's Furniture, Long Haul TPS and New Construction (2).

Year		
1953 Shields Construction, Newport, KY	1973 Howard's Furniture, Denver, NC	1992 Vernon's, Jacksonville, FL
1954 Waldneck's Tavern, Cincinnati	1974 Howard's Furniture	1993 Back Porch/Destin (FL) Roofing
1955 Lang Pet Shop, Covington, KY	1975 Pyramid Cafe, Lakewood, OH	1994 Riverside Paving, Louisville
1956 Gatliff Auto Sales, Newport, KY	1976 Warren Motors, J'ville, FL	1995 Riverside Paving
1957 Gatliff Auto Sales	1977 Nelson Painting, Okla. City	1996 Bell II, Orlando, FL
1958 East Side Sports, Detroit	1978 Campbell Carpets, Concord, CA	1997 Long Haul TPS, Albertville, MN
1959 Yorkshire Restaurant, Newport, KY	1979 Nelco Mfg. Co., Okla. City	1998 Chase Mortgage/Easton,
1960 Hamilton Tailoring, Cincinnati	1980 Campbell Carpets	Wilmington, NC
1961 Hamilton Tailoring	1981 Elite Coating, Gordon, CA	1999 Gasoline Heaven/Worth,
1962 Skip Hogan A.C., Pittsburgh	1982 Triangle Sports, Minneapolis	Commack, NY
1963 Gatliff Auto Sales	1983 No.1 Electric & Heating,	2000 Long Haul TPS
1964 Skip Hogan A.C.	Gastonia, NC	2001 New Construction
1965 Skip Hogan A.C.	1984 Lilly Air Systems, Chicago	2002 Twin States/Worth,
1966 Michael's Lounge, Detroit	1985 Blanton's Fayetteville, NC	Montgomery, AL
1967 Jim's Sport Shop, Pittsburgh	1986 Non-Ferrous Metals, Cleveland	2003 New Construction/B&J/Snap-On,
1968 County Sports, Levittown, NY	1987 Stapath, Monticello, KY	Metamora, IL
1969 Copper Hearth, Milwaukee	1988 Bell Corp/FAF, Tampa, FL	2004 U.S. Vinyl, Houston, TX
1970 Little Caesar's, Southgate, MI	1989 Ritch's Salvage, Harrisburg, NC	2005 AM/Las Vegas/Benfield,
1971 Pile Drivers, Va. Beach, VA	1990 New Construction, Shelbyville, IN	Bowling Green, KY
1972 Jiffy Club, Louisville, KY	1991 Riverside Paving, Louisville	

WOMEN
Major Fast Pitch

Multiple winners: Raybestos/Stratford Brakettes (25); Orange Lionettes (9); Jax Maids (5); California Commotion (4); Arizona Ramblers and Redding Rebels (3); Hi-Ho Brakettes, J.J. Krieg's, National Screw & Manufacturing and Phoenix Storm (2).

Year	Year	Year
1933 Great Northerns, Chicago	1958 Raybestos Brakettes,	1982 Raybestos Brakettes
1934 Hart Motors, Chicago	Stratford, CT	1983 Raybestos Brakettes
1935 Bloomer Girls, Cleveland	1959 Raybestos Brakettes	1984 Los Angeles Diamonds
1936 Nat'l Screw & Mfg., Cleveland	1960 Raybestos Brakettes	1985 Hi-Ho Brakettes, Stratford, CT
1937 Nat'l Screw & Mfg.	1961 Gold Sox, Whittier, CA	1986 So. California Invasion
1938 J.J. Krieg's, Alameda, CA	1962 Orange Lionettes	1987 Orange County Majestics,
1939 J.J. Krieg's	1963 Raybestos Brakettes	Anaheim, CA
1940 Arizona Ramblers, Phoenix	1964 Erv Lind Florists, Portland, OR	1988 Hi-Ho Brakettes
1941 Higgins Midgets, Tulsa, OK	1965 Orange Lionettes	1989 Whittier (CA) Raiders
1942 Jax Maids, New Orleans	1966 Raybestos Brakettes	1990 Raybestos Brakettes
1943 Jax Maids	1967 Raybestos Brakettes	1991 Raybestos Brakettes
1944 Lind & Pomeroy, Portland, OR	1968 Raybestos Brakettes	1992 Raybestos Brakettes
1945 Jax Maids	1969 Orange Lionettes	1993 Redding (CA) Rebels
1946 Jax Maids	1970 Orange Lionettes	1994 Redding Rebels
1947 Jax Maids	1971 Raybestos Brakettes	1995 Redding Rebels
1948 Arizona Ramblers	1972 Raybestos Brakettes	1996 California Commotion,
1949 Arizona Ramblers	1973 Raybestos Brakettes	Woodland Hills
1950 Orange (CA) Lionettes	1974 Raybestos Brakettes	1997 California Commotion
1951 Orange Lionettes	1975 Raybestos Brakettes	1998 California Commotion
1952 Orange Lionettes	1976 Raybestos Brakettes	1999 California Commotion
1953 Betsy Ross Rockets, Fresno, CA	1977 Raybestos Brakettes	2000 Phoenix Storm, Phoenix, AZ
1954 Leach Motor Rockets, Fresno, CA	1978 Raybestos Brakettes	2001 Phoenix Storm
1955 Orange Lionettes	1979 Sun City (AZ) Saints	2002 Stratford Brakettes, Stratford, CT
1956 Orange Lionettes	1980 Raybestos Brakettes	2003 Stratford Brakettes
1957 Hacienda Rockets, Fresno, CA	1981 Orlando (FL) Rebels	2004 Stratford Brakettes
		2005 Stratford Brakettes

TRIATHLON

World Championship

Contested since 1989, the Triathlon World Championship consists of a 1.5-kilometer swim, a 40-kilometer bike ride and a 10-kilometer run. The 2006 championship was held Sept. 6 in Lausanne, Switzerland.
Multiple winners: MEN—Simon Lessing (4); Peter Robertson (3); Spencer Smith (2). WOMEN—Emma Snowsill (3); Emma Carney, Michellie Jones and Karen Smyers (2).

MEN

Year		Time	Year		Time
1989	Mark Allen, United States	1:58:46	1998	Simon Lessing, Great Britain	1:55:31
1990	Greg Welch, Australia	1:51:37	1999	Dimitry Gaag, Kazahkstan	1:45:25
1991	Miles Stewart, Australia	1:48:20	2000	Oliver Marceau, France	1:51:41
1992	Simon Lessing, Great Britain	1:49:04	2001	Peter Robertson, Australia	1:48:01
1993	Spencer Smith, Great Britain	1:51:20	2002	Iván Raña, Spain	1:50:41
1994	Spencer Smith, Great Britain	1:51:04	2003	Peter Robertson, Australia	1:54:13
1995	Simon Lessing, Great Britain	1:48:29	2004	Bevan Docherty, New Zealand	1:41:04
1996	Simon Lessing, Great Britain	1:39:50	2005	Peter Robertston, Austrlia	1:49:31
1997	Chris McCormack, Australia	1:48:29	2006	Tim Don, Great Britain	1:51:32

WOMEN

Year		Time	Year		Time
1989	Erin Baker, New Zealand	2:10:01	1998	Joanne King, Australia	2:07:25
1990	Karen Smyers, United States	2:03:33	1999	Loretta Harrop, Australia	1:55:28
1991	Joanne Ritchie, Canada	2:02:04	2000	Nicole Hackett, Australia	1:54:43
1992	Michellie Jones, Australia	2:02:08	2001	Siri Lindley, United States	1:58:51
1993	Michellie Jones, Australia	2:07:41	2002	Leanda Cave, Wales	2:01:31
1994	Emma Carney, Australia	2:03:19	2003	Emma Snowsill, Australia	2:06:40
1995	Karen Smyers, USA	2:04:58	2004	Sheila Taormina, United States	1:52:17
1996	Jackie Gallagher, Australia	1:50:52	2005	Emma Snowsill, Australia	1:58:03
1997	Emma Carney, Australia	1:59:22	2006	Emma Snowsill, Australia	2:04:03

Ironman Championship

Contested in Hawaii since 1978, the Ironman Triathlon Championship consists of a 2.4-mile swim, a 112-mile bike ride and 26.2-mile run. The race begins at 7 A.M. and continues all day until the course is closed at midnight.

MEN

Multiple winners: Mark Allen and Dave Scott (6); Peter Reid (3); Tim DeBoom, Luc Van Lierde, Normann Stadler and Scott Tinley (2).

Year	Date	Winner	Time	Runner-up	Margin	Start	Finish	Location
I	2/18/78	Gordon Haller	11:46	John Dunbar	34:00	15	12	Waikiki Beach
II	1/14/79	Tom Warren	11:15:56	John Dunbar	48:00	15	12	Waikiki Beach
III	1/10/80	Dave Scott	9:24:33	Chuck Neumann	1:08	108	95	Ala Moana Park
IV	2/14/81	John Howard	9:38:29	Tom Warren	26:00	326	299	Kailua-Kona
V	2/6/82	Scott Tinley	9:19:41	Dave Scott	17:16	580	541	Kailua-Kona
VI	10/9/82	Dave Scott	9:08:23	Scott Tinley	20:05	850	775	Kailua-Kona
VII	10/22/83	Dave Scott	9:05:57	Scott Tinley	0:33	964	835	Kailua-Kona
VIII	10/6/84	Dave Scott	8:54:20	Scott Tinley	24:25	1036	903	Kailua-Kona
IX	10/25/85	Scott Tinley	8:50:54	Chris Hinshaw	25:46	1018	965	Kailua-Kona
X	10/18/86	Dave Scott	8:28:37	Mark Allen	9:47	1039	951	Kailua-Kona
XI	10/10/87	Dave Scott	8:34:13	Mark Allen	11:06	1380	1284	Kailua-Kona
XII	10/22/88	Scott Molina	8:31:00	Mike Pigg	2:11	1277	1189	Kailua-Kona
XIII	10/15/89	Mark Allen	8:09:15	Dave Scott	0:58	1285	1231	Kailua-Kona
XIV	10/6/90	Mark Allen	8:28:17	Scott Tinley	9:23	1386	1255	Kailua-Kona
XV	10/19/91	Mark Allen	8:18:32	Greg Welch	6:01	1386	1235	Kailua-Kona
XVI	10/10/92	Mark Allen	8:09:08	Cristian Bustos	7:21	1364	1298	Kailua-Kona
XVII	10/30/93	Mark Allen	8:07:45	Paulli Kiuru	6:37	1438	1353	Kailua-Kona
XVIII	10/15/94	Greg Welch	8:20:27	Dave Scott	4:05	1405	1290	Kailua-Kona
XIX	10/7/95	Mark Allen	8:20:34	Thomas Hellriegel	2:25	1487	1323	Kailua-Kona
XX	10/26/96	Luc Van Lierde	8:04:08	Thomas Hellriegel	1:59	1420	1288	Kailua-Kona
XXI	10/18/97	Thomas Hellriegel	8:33:01	Jurgen Zack	6:17	1534	1365	Kailua-Kona
XXII	10/3/98	Peter Reid	8:24:20	Luc Van Lierde	7:37	1487	1379	Kailua-Kona
XXIII	10/23/99	Luc Van Lierde	8:17:17	Peter Reid	5:37	1471	1419	Kailua-Kona
XXIV	10/14/00	Peter Reid	8:21:01	Tim DeBoom	2:09	1525	1426	Kailua-Kona
XXV	10/6/01	Tim DeBoom	8:31:18	Cameron Brown	14:52	1558	1364	Kailua-Kona
XXVI	10/19/02	Tim DeBoom	8:29:56	Peter Reid	3:10	1540	1457	Kailua-Kona
XXVII	10/18/03	Peter Reid	8:22:35	Rutger Beke	5:51	1647	1569	Kailua-Kona
XXVIII	10/16/04	Normann Stadler	8:33:29	Peter Reid	10:11	1728	1579	Kailua-Kona
XXIX	10/15/05	Faris Al-Sultan	8:14:17	Cameron Brown	5:19	1743	1688	Kailua-Kona
XXX	10/21/06	Normann Stadler	8:11:56	Chris McCormack	1:11	1627	1689	Kailua-Kona

WOMEN

Multiple winners: Paula Newby-Fraser (8); Natascha Badmann (6); Erin Baker, Lori Bowden and Sylviane Puntous (2).

Year	Winner	Time	Runner-up	Year	Winner	Time	Runner-up
1978	No finishers			1992	Paula Newby-Fraser	8:55:28	Julie Anne White
1979	Lyn Lemaire	12:55.00	None	1993	Paula Newby-Fraser	8:58:23	Erin Baker
1980	Robin Beck	11:21:24	Eve Anderson	1994	Paula Newby-Fraser	9:20:14	Karen Smyers
1981	Linda Sweeney	12:00:32	Sally Edwards	1995	Karen Smyers	9:16:46	Isabelle Mouthon
1982	Kathleen McCartney	11:09:40	Julie Moss	1996	Paula Newby-Fraser	9:06:49	Natascha Badmann
1982	Julie Leach	10:54:08	Joann Dahlkoetter	1997	Heather Fuhr	9:31:43	Lori Bowden
1983	Sylviane Puntous	10:43:36	Patricia Puntous	1998	Natascha Badmann	9:24:16	Lori Bowden
1984	Sylviane Puntous	10:25:13	Patricia Puntous	1999	Lori Bowden	9:13:02	Karen Smyers
1985	Joanne Ernst	10:25:22	Liz Bulman	2000	Natascha Badmann	9:26:17	Lori Bowden
1986	Paula Newby-Fraser	9:49:14	Sylviane Puntous	2001	Natascha Badmann	9:28:37	Lori Bowden
1987	Erin Baker	9:35:25	Sylviane Puntous	2002	Natascha Badmann	9:07:54	Nina Kraft
1988	Paula Newby-Fraser	9:01:01	Erin Baker	2003	Lori Bowden	9:11:55	Natascha Badmann
1989	Paula Newby-Fraser	9:00:56	Sylviane Puntous	2004	Natascha Badmann*	9:50:04	Heather Fuhr
1990	Erin Baker	9:13:42	P. Newby-Fraser	2005	Natascha Badmann	9:09:30	Michellie Jones
1991	Paula Newby-Fraser	9:07:52	Erin Baker	2006	Michellie Jones	9:18:31	Desiree Ficker

Great Outdoor Games

Sites: Lake Placid, N.Y. (2000-02); Reno-Tahoe, Nev. (2003); Madison, Wis. (2004); Orlando, Fla. (2005). Note that the Great Outdoors Games was not held in 2006 but there are plans to bring it back in 2007.

Sporting Dogs

Year	Retriever Trials
2000	Barry Lyons & Skeet
2001	Jerry Day & Super Sue
2002	A. Washburn & Ticket
2003	Chris Akin & Boomer
2004	J.P. Jackson & Achilles

Year	Big Air
2000	Beth Gutteridge & Heidi
2001	Mike Wallace & Jerry
2002	Mike Jackson & Little Morgan
2003	Terry Casey & Skeeter
2004	Mike Jackson & Little Morgan
2005	Chris Piacun & Beau

Year	Agility (large dogs)
2000	D. Bommarito & Lacey
2001	Julie Daniels & Spring
2002	Olga Chaiko & Luz
2003	S. Kluever & Ransom
2004	Marcus Topps & Juice
2005	Marcus Topps & Juice

Year	Superweave (large)
2003	Ken Fairchild & Echo
2004	S. Kluever & Ransom
2005	Marcus Topps & Juice

Year	Agility (small dogs)
2001	Jean LaValley & Taz
2002	Erin Schaefer & Jag
2003	C. Frank & Kimie
2004	Renee King & Hamlet
2005	Susan Garrett & DeCaff

Year	Superweave (small)
2003	Jean LaValley & Taz
2004	Not held

Year	Disc Drive
2004	Tim Gelb & Lock-Eye Razzle

Year	Launch
2005	Angela Jones & Nestle

Year	Hot Zone
2005	Ron Watson & Split

ATV

Year	Terracross
2005	Marty Hart

Year	Four Wheel Frenzy
2005	John Natalie

Fishing

Year	Flyfishing
2000	Tom Rowland
2001	Chuck Farneth
2002	Peter Erickson
2003	Lance Egan
2004	Lance Egan

Year	Flycasting
2002	Carter Andrews
2003	Mike McFarland
2004	John Wilson

Year	Bass Fishing
2000	Peter Thliveros
2001	Peter Thliveros
2002	Shaw Grigsby
2003	S. Grigsby & G. Klein
2004	M. Gofron & D. Brauer

Target Sports

Year	Rifle
2000	Bob Mastroianni
2001	Jerry Miculek
2002	Jerry Miculek
2003	Doug Koenig
2004	Mike Cumming

Year	Shotgun
2000	Doug Fuller
2001	Dustin Long
2002	Robbie Purser
2003	Scott Robertson
2004	Travis Mears

Year	Archery
2000	Jackie Caudle
2001	Randy Hendrix
2002	Randy Hendrix
2003	Darren Collins
2004	Randy Hendrix
2005	Keith Brown

Timber Events

Year	Endurance (women)
2000	Sheree Taylor
2001	Penny Halvorson
2002	Sheree Taylor
2003	Peg Engasser
2004	Sheree Taylor
2005	Sheree Taylor

Year	Endurance (men)
2000	Jason Wynyard
2001	Jason Wynyard
2002	Matt Bush
2003	Jason Wynyard
2004	Jason Wynyard
2005	Dion Lane

Year	Hot Saw
2000	Harry Burnsworth
2001	Mel Lentz
2002	Mike Sullivan
2003	Mike Sullivan
2004	Matt Bush
2005	Harry Burnsworth

Year	Springboard
2000	Mitch Hewitt
2001	Mitch Hewitt
2002	Mitch Hewitt
2003	Dave Bolstad
2004	Dale Ryan

Year	Boom Run (men)
2000	J.R. Salzman
2001	J.R. Salzman
2002	Jamie Fischer
2003	Jamie Fischer
2004	J.R. Salzman
2005	Jamie Fischer

Year	Boom Run (women)
2000	Tina Salzman
2001	Mandy Erdmann
2002	Mandy Erdmann
2003	Abby Hosechler
2004	Mandy Erdmann
2005	Mandy Erdmann

Year	Boom Run (mixed)
2003	Jamie Fischer & Tanya Fischer
2004	J.R. Salzman & Shana Martin

Year	Log Rolling (men)
2000	J.R. Salzman
2001	J.R. Salzman
2002	Darren Hudson
2003	Jamie Fischer
2004	J.R. Salzman
2005	J.R. Salzman

Year	Log Rolling (women)
2000	Tina Salzman
2001	Tina Salzman
2002	Tina Bosworth
2003	Tina Bosworth
2004	Tina Bosworth
2005	Lizzie Hoeschler

Year	Speed Climbing
2000	Wade Stewart
2001	Brian Bartow
2002	Brian Bartow
2003	Brian Bartow
2004	Wade Stewart
2005	Brian Bartow

Year	Tree Topping
2000	Mick Lee
2001	Gregg Hart
2002	Wade Stewart
2003	Greg Hart
2004	Brian Bartow

Year	Team Relay
2001	Team Halvorson
2002	Team Clarke
2003	Team Wynard
2004	Team Zalewski
2005	Team USA East

Year	SuperJack
2005	Cassidy Scheer

YACHTING

The America's Cup

International yacht racing was launched in 1851 when England's Royal Yacht Squadron staged a 60-mile regatta around the Isle of Wight and offered a silver trophy to the winner. The 101-foot schooner *America*, sent over by the New York Yacht Club, won the race and the prize. Originally called the Hundred-Guinea Cup, the trophy was renamed The America's Cup after the winning boat's owners deeded it to the NYYC with instructions to defend it whenever challenged.

From 1870-1980, the NYYC successfully defended the Cup 25 straight times; first in large schooners and J-class boats that measured up to 140 feet in overall length, then in 12-meter boats. A foreign yacht finally won the Cup in 1983 when *Australia II* beat defender *Liberty* in the seventh and deciding race off Newport, R.I. Four years later, the San Diego Yacht Club's *Stars & Stripes* won the Cup back, sweeping the four races of the final series off Fremantle, Australia.

Then in 1988, New Zealand's Mercury Bay Boating Club, unwilling to wait the usual three- to four-year period between Cup defenses, challenged the SDYC to a match race, citing the Cup's 102-year-old Deed of Gift, which clearly stated that every challenge had to be honored. Mercury Bay announced it would race a 133-foot monohull. San Diego countered with a 60-foot catamaran. The resulting best-of-three series (Sept. 7-8) was a mismatch as the SDYC's catamaran *Stars & Stripes* won two straight by margins of better than 18 and 21 minutes. Mercury Bay syndicate leader Michael Fay protested the outcome and took the SDYC to court in New York State (where the Deed of Gift was first filed) claiming San Diego had violated the spirit of the deed by racing a catamaran instead of a monohull. N.Y. State Supreme Court judge Carmen Ciparick agreed and on March 28, 1989, ordered the SDYC to hand the Cup over to Mercury Bay. The SDYC refused, but did consent to the court's appointment of the New York Yacht Club as custodian of the Cup until an appeal was ruled on.

On Sept. 19, 1989, the Appellate Division of the N.Y. Supreme Court overturned Ciparick's decision and awarded the Cup back to the SDYC. An appeal by Mercury Bay was denied by the N.Y. Court of Appeals on April 26, 1990, ending three years of legal wrangling. To avoid the chaos of 1988-90, a new class of boat—75-foot monohulls with 110-foot masts—has been used by all competing countries since 1992. Note that (*) indicates skipper was also owner of the boat.

The America's Cup moved to Europe for the first time when the Swiss Alinghi Team beat Team New Zealand, 5-0, in the best-of-nine series in February and March 2003.

The Swiss Team will defend the cup in Valencia, Spain in June-July 2007.

Schooners And J-Class Boats

Year	Winner	Skipper	Series	Loser	Skipper
1851	*America*	Richard Brown	—	—	
1870	*Magic*	Andrew Comstock	1-0	*Cambria*, GBR	J. Tannock
1871	*Columbia* (2-1)	Nelson Comstock	4-0	*Livonia*, GBR	J.R. Woods
	& *Sappho* (2-0)	Sam Greenwood			
1876	*Madeleine*	Josephus Williams	2-0	*Countess of Dufferin*, CAN	J.E. Ellsworth
1881	*Mischief*	Nathanael Clock	2-0	*Atalanta*, CAN	Alexander Cuthbert*
1885	*Puritan*	Aubrey Crocker	2-0	*Genesta*, GBR	John Carter
1886	*Mayflower*	Martin Stone	2-0	*Galatea*, GBR	Dan Bradford
1887	*Volunteer*	Henry Haff	2-0	*Thistle*, GBR	John Barr
1893	*Vigilant*	William Hansen	3-0	*Valkyrie II*, GBR	Wm. Granfield
1895	*Defender*	Henry Haff	3-0	*Valkyrie III*, GBR	Wm. Granfield
1899	*Columbia*	Charles Barr	3-0	*Shamrock I*, GBR	Archie Hogarth
1901	*Columbia*	Charles Barr	3-0	*Shamrock II*, GBR	E.A. Sycamore
1903	*Reliance*	Charles Barr	3-0	*Shamrock III*, GBR	Bob Wringe
1920	*Resolute*	Charles F. Adams	3-2	*Shamrock IV*, GBR	William Burton
1930	*Enterprise*	Harold Vanderbilt*	4-0	*Shamrock V*, GBR	Ned Heard
1934	*Rainbow*	Harold Vanderbilt*	4-2	*Endeavour*, GBR	T.O.M. Sopwith
1937	*Ranger*	Harold Vanderbilt*	4-0	*Endeavour II*, GBR	T.O.M. Sopwith

12-Meter Boats

Year	Winner	Skipper	Series	Loser	Skipper
1958	*Columbia*	Briggs Cunningham	4-0	*Sceptre*, GBR	Graham Mann
1962	*Weatherly*	Bus Mosbacher	4-1	*Gretel*, AUS	Jock Sturrock
1964	*Constellation*	Bob Bavier & Eric Ridder	4-0	*Sovereign*, AUS	Peter Scott
1967	*Intrepid*	Bus Mosbacher	4-0	*Dame Pattie*, AUS	Jock Sturrock
1970	*Intrepid*	Bill Ficker	4-1	*Gretel II*, AUS	Jim Hardy
1974	*Courageous*	Ted Hood	4-0	*Southern Cross*, AUS	John Cuneo
1977	*Courageous*	Ted Turner	4-0	*Australia*	Noel Robins
1980	*Freedom*	Dennis Conner	4-1	*Australia*	Jim Hardy
1983	*Australia II*	John Bertrand	4-3	*Liberty*, USA	Dennis Conner
1987	*Stars & Stripes*	Dennis Conner	4-0	*Kookaburra III*, AUS	Iain Murray

60-ft Catamaran vs 133-ft Monohull

Year	Winner	Skipper	Series	Loser	Skipper
1988	*Stars & Stripes*	Dennis Conner	2-0	*New Zealand*, NZE	David Barnes

75-ft International America's Cup Class

Year	Winner	Skipper	Series	Loser	Skipper
1992	*America [3]*	Bill Koch* & Buddy Melges	4-1	*Il Moro di Venezia*, ITA	Paul Cayard
1995	*Black Magic*, NZE	Russell Coutts	5-0	*Young America*, USA	Dennis Conner & Paul Cayard
2000	*Black Magic*, NZE	Russell Coutts & Dean Barker	5-0	*Luna Rossa*, ITA	Francesco de Angelis
2003	*Alinghi*, SWI	Russell Coutts	5-0	*New Zealand*, NZE	Dean Barker

2005 / 2006 YEAR IN REVIEW

Australian **Peter Norman** was the other guy in this famous Tommie Smith-John Carlos photo from the 1968

Notable deaths in the world of sports from Nov. 1, 2005-Oct. 30, 2006.

Oscar Acosta, 49; manager of the Rookie League's Gulf Coast Yankees; led the team to the league championship in the last two seasons; former major league pitching coach with the Chicago Cubs and Texas Rangers; in a car accident; in Santo Domingo, Dominican Republic, Apr. 19.

Arnold "Red" Auerbach, 89; Hall of Fame coach and executive with the Boston Celtics, retired as the all-time winnigest coach in NBA history after building the greatest dynasty in pro basketball history; won nine NBA titles as a coach and seven more as an executive; became famous also for his lighting his victory cigar courtside; of a heart attack; in Washington, D.C.; Oct. 28.

Elden Auker, 95; former major league pitcher who was known as the last living man to strike out Babe Ruth; also was a golfing buddy of the Babe and a friend to Ted Williams; the submarine style right-hander won a World Series in 1935 with the Detroit Tigers; retired with a career record of 130-101 and 126 complete games; three-sport All-American (baseball, football and basketball) at Kansas State; in Vero Beach, Fla.; Aug. 4.

Steve Belichick, 86; longtime assistant football coach at the U.S. Naval Academy from 1956-89; father of New England Patriots head coach Bill Belichick; of heart failure; in Annapolis, Md.; Nov. 19.

Trevor Berbick, 52; former heavyweight champion who lost his title to a 20-year-old Mike Tyson and was the last man to fight Muhammad Ali; career ring record of 50-11-1 with 33 KOs; apparently murdered; in Kingston, Jamaica; Oct. 27.

Patty Berg, 88; pioneer of women's golf who helped found the LPGA Tour in 1950 and served as the Tour's first president; won a Tour record 15 majors; named the Associated Press Female Athlete of the Year in 1938, 1943 and 1955; ended her career with 60 tournament wins; named to the LPGA Tour and World Golf Halls of Fame; also served in the U.S. Marine Corps during World War II; of complications from Alzheimer's disease; in Fort Myers, Fla.; Sept. 10.

George Best, 59; hard-playing and hard-partying soccer star in England during the 1960s and 1970s with Manchester United; widely considered one of the best players of all-time; battled alcoholism and was charged with drunk driving twice; of liver disease; Nov. 25, 2005.

Susan Butcher, 51; the four-time winner of the Iditarod Trail Sled Dog Race becoming the second ever female champion in 1986 and then adding wins in three of the next four years (1987-88, 1990); of leukemia; in Seattle, Wash.; Aug. 5.

John Campo Sr., 67; longtime horse trainer, whose most famous pupil was Pleasant Colony, the winner of the 1981 Kentucky Derby and Preakness Stakes; Pleasant Colony lost to Summing by less than two lengths to miss out on the Triple Crown; saddled three Eclipse Award winners (Pleasant Colony, Protagonist, and Talking Picture) and 1,431 winners in 12,826 starts and his horses earned almost $26 million in prize money; following a long illness; in Ozone Park, N.Y.; Nov. 15, 2005.

Bud Carson, 75; defensive coordinator who devised Pittsburgh's famous "Steel Curtain" defense in the 1970s; working under head coach Chuck Noll, Carson and the Steelers won three Super Bowls thanks in large part to their dominating defense; he was defensive coordinator of the Los Angeles Rams when they were defeated by his old team in Super Bowl XIV, giving Pittsburgh its fourth championship; later served as head coach of the Cleveland Browns from 1989-90 and his team won the AFC Central but lost to Denver in the 1989 AFC championship game; fired during the 1990 season after a 2-7 start; of emphysema; in Sarasota, Fla.; Dec. 7, 2005.

Jack Concannon, 62; former NFL quarterback who played with four teams: Philadelphia Eagles (1964-66), Chicago Bears (1967-71), Green Bay Packers (1974), Detroit Lions (1975); threw for 6,270 yards, 36 touchdowns, and 63 interceptions in 90 career games; was a football, basketball and baseball star at Boston College; of a heart attack; in Boston, Mass.; Nov. 30, 2005.

James E. Collie, 84; former head basketball coach at Illinois State from 1957-1970; finished with a coaching record of 329-222, retiring when he discovered he suffered from multiple sclerosis; in Normal, Ill.; May. 3.

Steve Courson, 50; former offensive lineman with the Pittsburgh Steelers and Tampa Bay Buccaneers from 1978-85 who became one of the first NFL players to admit to steroid use and later testified before Congress on the issue; won two Super Bowl rings with the Steelers in 1978 and 1979; died when a tree he was cutting down fell on him; in Henry Clay Township, Penn.; Nov. 10, 2005.

Floyd Curry, 81; four-time Stanley Cup winner with the Montreal Canadiens, scoring 105 goals and 204 points over 601 NHL games and 11 seasons; recorded his one career hat trick at

AP/Wide World Photos
Patty Berg

AP/Wide World Photos
Curt Gowdy

AP/Wide World Photos
Ray Meyer

the Montreal Forum on Oct. 29, 1951 in front of Queen Elizabeth; moved into the Canadiens front office following his playing days; in Montreal; Sept. 18.

Paul Dana, 30; Indy Racing League rookie driver who died after a two-car crash during warmups at the season-opening Toyota Indy 300 at Homestead-Miami Speedway; his car hit Ed Carpenter's stalled car at an estimated speed of 200 m.p.h.; a former auto racing journalist who graduated from Northwestern; Mar. 26.

Nelson de la Rosa, 38; diminutive actor who played a small role in ending the Curse of the Bambino in 2004 when he became Boston Red Sox pitcher Pedro Martinez's lucky charm; The 2-foot-4 Dominican Republic native appeared alongside Marlon Brando in the 1996 film "The Island of Dr. Moreau" and was once listed by the *Guinness Book of World Records* as the shortest known adult; of unknown causes; in New York, N.Y.; Oct. 22.

Jim Delsing, 80; former St. Louis Browns outfielder whose claim to fame was pinch-running for Eddie Gaedel after the midget infamously drew a four-ball walk on team owner Bill Veeck's publicity stunt in the second game of a doubleheader against the Detroit Tigers; of cancer; in Chesterfield, Mo.; May 10.

Maggie Dixon, 28; rookie women's basketball coach at Army who led the team to its first NCAA Tournament; led Army to its first Patriot League championship in 2006; former assistant at DePaul; after suffering heart arrhythmia; in Valhalla, N.Y.; Apr. 6.

Bob Dove, 85; college hall of fame end at Notre Dame from 1940-42 who played eight seasons in the NFL with the Chicago Cardinals and Detroit Lions, winning championships with the Lions in 1953 and 1954; was later a long-time assistant coach at Youngstown St.; following a long illness; in Austintown, Ohio; Apr. 19.

Frank Gatski, 86; Hall of Fame offensive lineman who played in 10 straight championship games for the Cleveland Browns from 1946-56; said to have never missed a game or practice in high school, college or the pros; Nov. 22, 2005.

Bernie "Boom Boom" Geoffrion, 75; High-scoring Hockey Hall of Famer who is widely credited with inventing the slap shot; won six Stanley Cups with the Montreal Canadiens in the 1950s and 1960s; won the Hart Trophy as NHL MVP for 1960-61 season after becoming the second player in league history to score 50 goals in a season; finished with career totals of 393 goals and 429 assists in 883 regular season games over 16 seasons, 14 of which were with the Canadiens; of stomach cancer, in Atlanta, Ga.; Mar. 11.

Marshall Goldberg, 88; hall of fame running back at Pittsburgh in the 1930s who finished second to Davey O'Brien in the 1938 Heisman Trophy vote; compiled 1,957 yard for the Panthers from 1936-38; twice named to the All-America team (1937 and 1938); went on to play pro football with the Chicago Cardinals in an All-Pro career interrupted by a stint with the Navy Seals during World War II; in Chicago, Ill.; Apr. 3

Curt Gowdy, 86; legendary broadcaster with a resume of big events that may never be matched; he described the action at numerous Final Fours, 13 World Series, 16 baseball All-Star Games and several Super Bowls; also made the call of Ted Williams' final home run as the main play-by-play announcer for the Boston Red Sox from 1951-65; hosted the popular TV program the "American Sportsman" on ABC from the from the 1960s to the 1980s; of leukemia; in Palm Beach, Fla.; Feb. 20.

Eric Gregg, 55; former major league umpire who lost his job along with 21 other umps in 1999 when their plan to resign en masse to negotiate a more favorable contract backfired; he worked his first game in 1975 and became a full-time NL ump starting in 1978; worked the 1989 World Series; known for his large strike zone; following a massive stroke; in Philadelphia; June. 5.

George F. Haines, 82; hall of fame coach of three U.S. Olympic swim teams; founded the Santa Clara Swim Club in 1950 and produced 53 Olympians that would go on to win 44 Olympic gold medals, 14 silver and 10 bronze; in his sleep; Carmichael, Calif.; May 2.

Barry Halper, 66; baseball memorabilia collector who amassed a collection of 80,000 items including the jersey Lou Gehrig wore during his farewell speech at Yankee Stadium, an original ticket from the first World Series and the contract that sent Babe Ruth from the Boston Red Sox to the N.Y. Yankees; also became a limited partner in the Yankees; from complications of diabetes; Livingston, N.J.; Dec. 19, 2005.

Craig "Ironhead" Heyward, 39; bruising NFL fullback who played with five teams; played 149 games scoring 30 touchdowns on 1,031 carries and 4,301 yards; made the Pro Bowl after rushing for 1,083 yards and six touchdowns with Atlanta Falcons in 1995; following a long battle with brain cancer; in Atlanta, Ga.; May 27.

Dick Hickox, 68; All-American basketball guard at the University of Miami who led the team to a 23-3 record and a No. 8 ranking in 1960, which remains the highest ranking in school history; of cancer; Aug. 23.

Wilbert "Dutch" Hiller, 90; speedy left-winger for the N.Y. Rangers 1940 Stanley Cup winning team; scored 91 goals and 113 assists in 383 games; in Glendale, Calif.; Nov. 12.

Billy Hitchcock, 89; major league infielder and then later manager with the Detroit Tigers, Baltimore Orioles and Atlanta Braves in the 1960s; in 1951 he hit .306 in 77 games for the Philadelphia Athletics; also played running back at Auburn where he scored the Tigers' only touchdown at the 1937 Bacardi Bowl in Havana; of undisclosed causes; in Opelika, Ala.; Apr. 10.

Steve Howe, 48; left-handed relief pitcher with four major-league teams (Los Angeles, Minnesota, Texas and N.Y. Yankees) who fought an addiction to cocaine and was suspended by MLB seven times; the fireballing lefty won the 1980 NL Rookie of the Year award with the Dodgers and won a World Series with the team in 1981; recorded a career W-L mark of 47-41 and 91 saves; in a one-car accident; in Coachella, Calif.; Apr. 28.

Dick Hutcherson, 73; NASCAR driver who won 14 races in 103 starts in the 1960s; also served as David Pearson's crew chief in 1968 and 1969; of a heart attack; in Columbia, S.C.; Nov. 6, 2005.

John Kimbrough, 87; college football star at Texas A&M; nicknamed the "Haskell Hurricane," the speedy fullback played on A&M's 1939 national championship team, finishing second in the Heisman Trophy voting a year later; following a bout of pneumonia; in Haskell, Texas; May 9.

Dale Lloyd, 19; freshman defensive back at Rice University who died a day after collapsing on the field during a workout; in Houston, Tex.; Sept. 25.

Cory Lidle, 34; New York Yankees pitcher and amateur pilot who died when the small plane he was flying crashed into a high-rise Manhattan apartment building; the right-hander played nine seasons with seven different teams and compiled a career record of 82-72 and an ERA of 4.57; in New York City; Oct. 11.

Sheikh Maktoum, 62; prime minister of the United Arab Emirates and ruler of Dubai who was also well known around the world as a prominent horse breeder and owner; Maktoum owned four stud farms including a large farm in central Kentucky; in Queensland, Australia; June 4.

Brad Martin, 30; two-time football captain at BYU, who battled an addiction to pain killers after sustaining injuries in a car accident during his senior year; he filed a lawsuit against BYU claiming that the university contributed to his addiction by offering a ready supply of painkillers so he could play football; in Salt Lake City; June 3.

Bob Mathias, 75; two-time Olympic decathlon champion and four-term Republican U.S. congressman from California; became the youngest Olympic gold medalist in a track and field event when, at age 17, he won the decathlon at the 1948 Summer Olympics in London; four years later he became the first repeat-winner at the Olympic decathlon when he won gold at the 1952 Helsinki Summer Games; cause of death not released; in Fresno, Calif.; Sept. 2.

Ray Meyer, 92; legendary DePaul basketball coach who built the program into a powerhouse, taking the Blue Demons to the NCAA Final Four twice and an NIT title in his 42 years on campus; he mentored hall of fame center and two-time college player of the year George Mikan just after starting his coaching career at DePaul; either coached or broadcasted 1,467 consecutive DePaul games over 55 years; retired from coaching in 1984 with a record of 724-354; of natural causes; in Chicago, Ill.; Mar. 17.

AP/Wide World Photos
Byron Nelson

AP/Wide World Photos
Floyd Patterson

AP/Wide World Photos
Kirby Puckett

Glenn "Mooch" Myernick, 51; former head coach of the MLS's Colorado Rapids from 1997-2000; recording a 63-61-4 win-loss mark; also served as an assistant to U.S. National Team coach Bruce Arena at the 2002 and 2006 World Cups; played professionally in the NASL and won the 1976 Hermann Trophy while at Hartwick College; of a heart attack; in Thornton, Colo.; Oct. 9.

Eric Namesnik, 35; two-time Olympic silver medal-winning swimmer, taking second in the 400-meter individual medley at the 1992 Barcelona Summer Olympics and 1996 Atlanta Summer Games; of injuries sustained in a car accident; in Ypsilanti, Mich.; Jan. 11.

Byron Nelson, 94; golfing legend who in 1945, had perhaps the greatest year in golf history, winning 18 tournaments, including a record 11 in a row; won five majors in his career (2 Masters–1937, 1942; 1 U.S. Open–1939; 2 PGA Championships–1940, 1945); won 52 PGA Tour events, currently sixth all-time; once had a streak of 113 consecutive cuts made; elected to the PGA Hall of Fame in 1953; cause of death not released; in Irving, Texas; Sept. 26.

Joe Niekro, 61; former All-Star pitcher who won 20 games twice (1979 and 1980) and 221 games in his long career; brother of 300-game winner Phil and father of current Giants first baseman Lance; of a brain aneurysm; in Tampa, Fla.; Oct. 27.

Peter Norman, 64; Australian sprinter who won a silver medal and then shared the podium with Americans Tommie Smith and John Carlos when they gave their famous black power salute at the 1968 Summer Olympics in Mexico City following the 200 meters; of a heart attack; in Melbourne, Australia; Oct. 3.

Tom Nugent, 92; hall of fame college football coach who devised the I formation while at Virginia Military Institute from 1949-52; later coached at Florida State from 1953-58 where he mentored ESPN analyst Lee Corso and actor Burt Reynolds; also coached at Maryland; of congestive heart failure; in Tallahassee, Fla.; Jan. 19.

Buck O'Neil, 94; slick-hitting Negro leagues first baseman with the Kansas City Monarchs; became known in recent years as a Negro leagues historian when he was featured prominently in Ken Burns' PBS documentary series *Baseball*; also served as a long-time coach and scout in the Chicago Cubs organization; in Kansas City, Mo.; Oct. 6.

Peter Osgood, 59; star soccer forward with England's Chelsea club during the 1970s helping the Blues win the European Cup Winners' Cup; also played in the United States with the NASL's Philadelphia Fury; of undisclosed causes; in Slough, England; Mar. 1.

Floyd Patterson, 71; hall of fame boxer who became the youngest heavyweight champ in history when, at 21 years old, he won the vacant title (against Archie Moore) in 1956 following the retirement of Rocky Marciano; surprisingly lost his title to Ingemar Johansson in 1959 but then beat him a year later to become the first man to regain the heavyweight belt; an undersized heavyweight, he was known for getting knocked down—and getting back up—frequently; lost his title for good on a first-round knockout to Sonny Liston in 1962; lost rematch in same fashion a year later; won middleweight gold medal at 1952 Summer Olympics; finished his pro career with a 55-8-1 ring record with 40 knockouts; following a long illness; in New Paltz, N.Y.; May 11.

Vic Power, 78; Gold Glove first baseman who once stole home twice in one game with Cleveland in 1958; from cancer; in Bayamon, Puerto Rico; Nov. 29, 2005.

Kirby Puckett, 45; Hall of Fame outfielder and fan favorite who won two World Series (1987 and 1991) in his 12-year playing career with the Minnesota Twins; the 10-time All-Star known for his quick bat and quicker smile was forced to retire from baseball due to glaucoma in his right eye; a career .318 hitter who won six Gold Gloves; following a stroke; in Scottsdale, Ariz.; Mar. 6.

Darrell Russell, 29; former Pro Bowl defensive tackle who was suspended from the NFL seven times for violating the league's substance abuse policy; taken second overall by the Raiders in 1997 NFL draft and played in the 1998 and 1999 Pro Bowls; in a speed-related car accident; in Los Angeles, Dec. 15, 2005.

Clint Sampson, 44; former wide receiver for the Denver Broncos who played with John Elway and caught three balls on Elway's first fourth-quarter game-winning drive in the NFL; third-round pick in the 1983 draft and went on to play 59 games with Denver, finishing his career with 66 receptions for 1014 yards and eight touchdowns; in a car accident; in Los Angeles; Dec. 29, 2005.

Agapito Sanchez, 35; former WBO junior featherweight boxing champion who compiled a pro record of 36-11-3 (18 KOs) but suffered from cataracts and vacated his title in 2002; of gun shot wounds; in Santo Domingo, Dominican Republic; Nov. 15.

John Sandusky, 80; successful former NFL assistant coach under Don Shula most notably with the Baltimore Colts and Miami Dolphins; he coached five Hall of Fame lineman including Art Donovan and Gino Marchetti; also served as head coach of the Colts for nine games in 1972; of complications from internal bleeding; in Coral Springs, Fla.; Mar. 5.

Ron Schipper, 77; hall of fame college football coach at Div. III Central College in Iowa; compiled an impressive 287-67-3 record from 1961-96, including an NCAA record 36 consecutive winning seasons; won the Div. III national championship in 1974; served as president of the American Football Coaches Association in 1994; cause of death not disclosed; in Holland, Mich.; Mar. 26.

Ted Schroeder, 84; American tennis player who, despite winning the men's singles title at Wimbledon (1949) and the U.S. Open (1942), decided not to turn professional; also won three U.S. Open doubles titles (with Jack Kramer); was inducted into the International Tennis Hall of Fame in 1996; of cancer; in La Jolla, Calif.; May 26.

Louise Smith, 89; pioneering female auto racer who ran on the NASCAR circuit from 1945-56, winning 38 modified events; she became the first woman inducted into the International Motorsports Hall of Fame in 1999; in Greenville, S.C.; Apr. 15.

Jack Snow, 62; sure-handed and speedy wide receiver for the Los Angeles Rams; had 340 catches and 6,012 yards in 11 seasons with the Rams; named to the 1967 Pro Bowl after scoring eight touchdowns on 28 receptions; drafted eighth overall by Minnesota in 1965 after a collegiate career at Notre Dame; father of Gold Glove first baseman J.T. Snow; following a staph infection; in St. Louis, Mo.; Jan. 10.

Ernie Stautner, 80; Hall of Fame defensive lineman with the Pittsburgh Steelers; named to the Pro Bowl nine times; was also a longtime assistant of Tom Landry with the Dallas Cowboys serving as the defensive coordinator from 1973-88; of complications from Alzheimer's disease; in Carbondale, Colo.; Feb. 16.

Syd Thrift, 77; longtime baseball executive who spent time in the front offices of the Baltimore Orioles, Chicago Cubs, New York Yankees, Pittsburgh Pirates, Oakland Athletics and Kansas City Royals; also pitched in the minor leagues; served as a scout with the Yankees and Pirates; following knee replacement surgery; in Milford, Del.; Sept. 18.

Robert Tisch, 79; co-owner of the NFL's New York Giants died just weeks after the team's other co-owner Wellington Mara; served as U.S. postmaster general from 1986-88; bought 50 percent of the Giants in 1991 just after the team's win in Super Bowl XXV; of brain cancer; in New York; Nov. 16.

Fermin Vialpando, 17; senior football player at Harrison High School who collapsed during a game and died shortly thereafter; in Colorado Springs, Colo.; Oct. 7.

Randy Walker, 52; head football coach at Northwestern University from 1999-2005 who compiled a seven-season record of 37-46; his tenure at Northwestern was characterized by onfield success and an exemplary graduation rate of at, or near, 100 percent; he became the first coach to lead the Wildcats to three bowl games, the first NU coach to beat all 10 Big Ten Conference opponents and the first coach in more than 100 years to guide the school to four seasons with at least six wins; of a heart attack; in Evanston, Ill.; June 29.

Mervyn Wood, 89; four-time Olympic sculler (1936,48,52,56) from Australia who won three medals (a gold, silver and bronze); of cancer; Aug. 19.

Earl Woods, 74; father and first coach to Tiger Woods who forged the dazzling skills and stunning career of the game's greatest player; after a long battle with prostate cancer; at his home; May 3.

UPDATES

2005 / 2006 YEAR IN REVIEW

Pro basketball giant **Red Auerbach** died Oct. 28, 2006 at age 89. He won 9 NBA titles as Celtics coach.

AP/Wide World Photos

AUTO RACING

Late 2006 Results
NASCAR
Chase for the Nextel Cup

Date	Event	Location	Winner (Pos)	Avg.mph	Earnings	Pole	Qual.mph
Oct. 29	Bass Pro Shops 500 . . . . . . Atlanta		Tony Stewart (11)	143.421	$373,286	M. Kenseth	—**

**Qualifiying was canceled due to weather and the pole was awarded based on Owner points.
Winning Cars: CHEVROLET (1)—Stewart.
Remaining Races (3): Dickies 500 in Texas (Nov. 5); Checker Auto Parts 500 in Phoenix (Nov. 12); Ford 400 in Homestead-Miami (Nov. 19).

Busch Series

Date	Event	Location	Winner (Pos)	Avg.mph	Earnings	Pole	Qual.mph
Oct. 28	Sam's Town 250 . . . . . Memphis		Kevin Harvick (5)	74.336	$53,150	Johnny Sauter	118.614

Winning Cars: CHEVROLET (1)—Harvick.
Remaining Races: (3) O'Reilly Challenge in Fort Worth (Nov. 4); Arizona.Travel 200 in Phoenix (Nov. 11); Ford 300 in Homestead (Nov. 18).

Craftsman Truck Series

Date	Event	Location	Winner (Pos)	Avg.mph	Earnings	Pole	Qual.mph
Oct. 28	EasyCare 200 . . . . Memphis		Mike Bliss (16)	123.200	$60,175	Mike Skinner	180.993

Winning Cars: CHEVROLET (1)—Bliss.
Remaining Races: (3) Silverado 350 in Fort Worth (Nov. 3); Casino Arizona in Phoenix (Nov. 10); Ford 200 in Homestead (Nov. 17).

GYMNASTICS

2006 World Championships
Held Oct. 14-21 in Aarhus, Denmark.

MEN

All-Around

		Points
1	Wei Yang, CHN	94.400
2	Hiroyuki Tomita, JPN	93.175
3	Fabian Hambuechen, GER	92.975

Top USA: 18th—Guillermo Alvarez (88.175).

Floor Exercise

		Points
1	Marian Dragulescu, ROM	16.250
2	Diego Hypolito, BRA	16.150
3	Kyle Shewfelt, CAN	15.700

Top 8 USA: none.

Horizontal Bar

		Points
1	Philippe Rizzo, AUS	16.125
2	Aljaz Pegan, SLO	15.900
3	Vlasios Maras, GRE	15.800

Top 8 USA: none.

Parallel Bars

		Points
1	Wei Yang, CHN	16.075
2	Hiroyuki Tomita, JPN	15.950
	Won Chul Yoo, KOR	15.950

Top 8 USA: none.

Pommel Horse

		Points
1	Qin Xiao, CHN	16.025
2	Prashanth Sellathurai, AUS	15.750
3	Alexander Artemev, USA	15.500

Other Top 8 USA: none.

Rings

		Points
1	Yibing Chen, CHN	16.525
2	Jordan Jovtchev, BUL	16.325
3	Yuri Van Gelder, NED	16.300

Top 8 USA: none.

Vault

		Points
1	Marian Dragulescu, ROM	16.487
2	Dimitri Kaspoarovich, BLR	16.312
3	Fabian Hambuechen, GER	15.825

Top 8 USA: none.

Team

		Points
1	China	277.775
2	Russia	275.400
3	Japan	274.800

WOMEN

All-Around

		Points
1	Vanessa Ferrari, ITA	61.025
2	Jana Bieger, USA	60.750
3	Sandra Raluca Izbasa, ROM	60.250

Vault

		Points
1	Fei Cheng, CHN	15.712
2	Alicia Sacramone, USA	15.325
3	Oksana Chusovitina, GER	15.100

Top 8 USA: none.

Floor Exercise

		Points
1	Fei Cheng, CHN	15.875
2	Jana Bieger, USA	15.550
3	Vanessa Ferrari, ITA	15.450

Top 8 USA: 7th—Natasha Kelley (15.300).

Uneven Bars

		Points
1	Elizabeth Tweddle, GBR	16.200
2	Anastasia Liukin, USA	16.050
3	Vanessa Ferrari, ITA	15.775

Other Top 8 USA: 5th—Jana Bieger (14.550).

WOMEN (Cont.)

Balance Beam

		Points
1	Iryna Krasnianska, UKR	15.575
2	Sandra Raluca Izbasa, ROM	15.500
3	Elyse Hopfner-Hibbs, CAN	15.475

Top 8 USA: none.

Team

		Points
1	China	182.200
2	United States	181.350
3	Russia	177.325

TENNIS

Late 2006 Tournament Results
Men's Tour

Finals	Tournament	Winner	Earnings	Loser	Score
Oct. 15	Kremlin Cup (Moscow)	Nikolay Davydenko	$142,000	M. Safin	64 57 64
Oct. 15	BA-CA Tennis Trophy (Vienna)	Ivan Ljubicic	135,767	F. Gonzalez	63 64 75
Oct. 15	Stockholm Open	James Blake	120,015	J. Nieminin	64 62
Oct. 22	TMS—Madrid	Roger Federer	476,980	F. Gonzalez	75 61 60
Oct. 29	St. Petersburg Open	Mario Ancic	1,000,000	T. Johansson	75 76 (2)
Oct. 29	Swiss Indoors (Basel)	Roger Federer	153,648	F. Gonzalez	63 62 76 (3)
Oct. 29	Grand Prix of Tennis (Lyon)	Richard Gasquet	96,000	M. Gicquei	63 61

Remaining Events (3): BNP Paribas Paris Masters (Nov. 5); Tennis Masters Cup Shanghai (Nov. 20); Davis Cup Final (Dec. 3).

Women's Tour

Finals	Tournament	Winner	Earnings	Loser	Score
Oct. 15	Kremlin Cup (Moscow)	Anna Chakvetadze	$196,900	N. Petrova	64 64
Oct. 15	Thailand Open (Bangkok)	Vania King	30,500	T. Tanasugarn	26 64 64
Oct. 22	Zurich Open	Maria Sharapova	196,900	D. Hantuchova	61 46 63
Oct. 29	Generali Open (Linz)	Maria Sharapova	93,000	N. Petrova	75 62

Remaining Events (3): Gaz De France Stars (Nov. 5), Bell Challenge (Nov. 6); WTA Tour Championships (Nov. 12).

THOROUGHBRED RACING

Late 2006 Major Stakes Races

Date	Race	Location	Miles	Winner	Jockey	Purse
Sept. 30	Yellow Ribbon Stakes	Santa Anita	1¼ (T)	Wait a While	Garrett K. Gomez	$ 400,000
Sept. 30	Clement L. Hirsch Turf Championship Stakes	Santa Anita	1¼ (T)	Tin Man	Victor Espinoza	250,000
Sept. 30	Kelso Handicap	Belmont	1 (T)	Ashkal	Mike Luzzi	250,000
Sept. 30	Oak Leaf Stakes	Santa Anita	1¹⁄₁₆	Cash Included	Corey Nakatani	250,000
Oct. 7	Vosburgh Stakes	Belmont	6 F	Henny Hughes	John Velazquez	400,000
Oct. 7	Beldame Stakes	Belmont	1⅛	Fleet Indian	Jose A. Santos	600,000
Oct. 7	Flower Bowl Invitational	Belmont	1¼ (T)	Honey Ryder	John R. Velazquez	600,000
Oct. 7	Joe Hirsch Turf Classic Invit.	Belmont	1½ (T)	English Channel	John R. Velazquez	600,000
Oct. 7	Jockey Club Gold Cup	Belmont	1¼	Bernardini	Javier Castellano	750,000
Oct. 7	Goodwood B.C. Handicap	Santa Anita	1⅛	Lava Man	Corey Nakatani	500,000
Oct. 7	Oak Tree B.C. Mile	Santa Anita	1 (T)	Aragorn	Corey Nakatani	250,000
Oct. 7	Lane's End Futurity Stakes	Keeneland	1¹⁄₁₆	Great Hunter	Victor Espinoza	500,000
Oct. 7	Shadwell Turf Mile	Keeneland	1 (T)	Aussie Rules	Garrett K. Gomez	600,000
Oct. 8	Juddmonte Spinster Stakes	Keeneland	1⅛	Asi Siempre	Julien R. Leparoux	500,000
Oct. 8	Norfolk Stakes	Santa Anita	1¹⁄₁₆	Stormello	Kent Desormeaux	250,000
Oct. 14	First Lady Stakes	Keeneland	8 F	Gorella	Julien R. Leparoux	400,000
Oct. 14	Frizette Stakes	Belmont	1¹⁄₁₆	Sutra	Michael J. Luzzi	400,000
Oct. 14	Champagne Stakes	Belmont	1¹⁄₁₆	Scat Daddy	John R. Velazquez	400,000
Oct. 14	QE II Challenge Cup	Keeneland	1⅛ (T)	Vacare	Carlos H. Marquez Jr.	500,000
Oct. 22	Empire Classic Handicap	Belmont	1⅛	Organizer	Eibar Coa	250,000
Oct. 22	Canadian International*	Woodbine	1½ (T)	Collier Hill	Dean McKeown	2,000,000

*World Series Racing Championship race.

Tony Stewart was the hottest driver but not part of the 2006 Chase for the Cup. Meanwhile Dale Earnardt Jr. and the others were trying to catch Chase leader Matt Kenseth.

HARNESS RACING

Late 2006 Major Stakes Races

Date	Race	Raceway	Winner	Driver	Purse
Oct. 7	Kentucky Futurity	Lexington	Glidemaster	John Campbell	$526,000

SOCCER

2006 Major League Soccer Playoffs

Eastern Conference

Semifinals (Total Goals)

New England Revolution vs. Chicago Fire
Oct. 21　at Chicago 1 . . . . .New England 0
Oct. 28　at New England 2 . . . . .Chicago 1
Aggregate tied, 2-2 Revolution advances, 4-2, on PKs

D.C. United vs. New York Red Bulls
Oct. 21　at New York 0 . . . . .D.C. United 1
Oct. 29　at D.C. United 1 . . . . .New York 1
D.C. United advances on aggregate, 2-1

Finals (Single Elimination)
Nov. 4
New England at D.C. United

Western Conference

Semifinals (Total Goals)

FC Dallas vs. Colorado Rapids
Oct. 21　at Colorado 1 . . . . .Dallas 2
Oct. 28　at Dallas 2 . . . . .Colorado 3
Aggregate tied, 4-4. Colorado advances, 5-4, on PKs

Houston Dynamo vs. Chivas USA
Oct. 22　at Chivas USA 2 . . . . .Houston 1
Oct. 29　at Houston 2 . . . . .Chivas USA 0
Houston advances on aggregate, 3-2

Finals (Single Elimination)
Nov. 5
Colorado at Houston

MLS Cup 2006
Nov. 12 at Pizza Hut Park
Frisco, Texas

PIZZA HUT PARK & PITCHER'S IS

RESEARCH MATERIAL

Many sources were used in the gathering of information for this almanac. Day-to-day material was almost always found in copies of USA Today, The Boston Globe, and The South Florida Sun-Sentinel or online at various World Wide Web addresses (see below).

Several weekly and bi-weekly periodicals were also used in the past year's pursuit of facts and figures, among them— Baseball America, ESPN the Magazine, The NCAA News, Soccer America, Sports Illustrated, The Sporting News, Street & Smith's Sports Business Journal, Track & Field News and USA Today Baseball Weekly.

In addition, the following books provided background material for one or more chapters of the almanac.

Arenas & Ballparks

The Ballparks, by Bill Shannon and George Kalinsky; Hawthorn Books, Inc. (1975); New York.

Diamonds, by Michael Gershman; Houghton Mifflin Co. (1993); Boston.

Green Cathedrals (Revised Edition), by Philip Lowry; Addison-Wesley Publishing Co. (1992); Reading, Mass.

The NFL's Encyclopedic History of Professional Football, Macmillan Publishing Co. (1977); New York.

Take Me Out to the Ballpark, by Lowell Reidenbaugh; The Sporting News Publishing Co. (1983); St. Louis.

24 Seconds to Shoot (An Informal History of the NBA), by Leonard Koppett; Macmillan Publishing Co. (1968); New York.

Auto Racing

Indy: 75 Years of Racing's Greatest Spectacle, by Rich Taylor; St. Martin's Press (1991); New York.

2003 CART FedEx Championship Series Media Guide; Championship Auto Racing Teams; Troy, Mich.

2003 Indy Racing League Media Guide, by IMS Publications; Indianapolis.

2003 NASCAR Winston Cup Series Media Guide, compiled and edited by Sports Marketing Enterprises; NASCAR Winston Cup Series; Winston-Salem, N.C.

Marlboro Grand Prix Guide, 1950-1998 (1999 Edition), compiled by Jacques Deschenaux and Claude Michele Deschenaux; Charles Stewart & Company Ltd; Brentford, England.

NASCAR Online, produced by Turner Sports Interactive, http://www.nascar.com

CART Online, maintained by CART and VFX Digital Solutions, http://www.cart.com

Indy Racing Online, maintained by IRL, http://www.indyracingleague.com

NHRA Online, maintained by NHRA, http://www.nhra.com

Baseball

The All-Star Game (A Pictorial History, 1933 to Present), by Donald Honig; The Sporting News Publishing Co. (1987); St. Louis.

The Baseball Chronology, edited by James Charlton; Macmillan Publishing Co. (1991); New York.

The Baseball Encyclopedia (Ninth Edition), editorial director, Rick Wolff; Macmillan Publishing Co. (1993); New York.

The Complete 2002 Baseball Record Book, edited by Craig Carter; The Sporting News Publishing Co.; St. Louis.

The Scrapbook History of Baseball by Jordan Deutsch, Richard Cohen, Roland Johnson and David Neft; Bobbs-Merrill Company, Inc. (1975); Indianapolis/New York.

2002 Sporting News Official Baseball Guide, edited by Craig Carter and Dave Sloan; The Sporting News Publishing Co.; St. Louis.

2002 Sporting News Official Baseball Register, edited by Jeff Paur, David Walton, John Duxbury; The Sporting News Publishing Co.; St. Louis.

The Sports Encyclopedia: Baseball (1996 Edition), edited by David Neft and Richard Cohen; St. Martin's Press; New York.

Total Baseball (Seventh Edition), edited by John Thorn, Pete Palmer and Michael Gershman; Total Sports Publishing (2001); Kingston, N.Y.

The Official Site of Major League Baseball, produced by Major League Baseball Properties, Inc., http://www.mlb.com

College Basketball

All the Moves (A History of College Basketball), by Neil D. Isaacs; J.B. Lippincott Company (1975); New York.

College Basketball, U.S.A. (Since 1892), by John D. McCallum; Stein and Day (1978); New York.

Collegiate Basketball: Facts and Figures on the Cage Sport, by Edwin C. Caudle; The Paragon Press (1960); Montgomery, Ala.

The Encyclopedia of the NCAA Basketball Tournament, written and compiled by Jim Savage; Dell Publishing (1990); New York.

The Final Four (Reliving America's Basketball Classic), compiled by Billy Reed; Host Communications, Inc. (1988); Lexington, Ky.

2000 NCAA Final Four Records Book, compiled by Gary Johnson; edited by Marty Benson; NCAA Books; Indianapolis.

The Modern Encyclopedia of Basketball (Second Revised Edition), edited by Zander Hollander; Dolphins Books (1979); Doubleday & Company, Inc.; Garden City, N.Y.

2000 NCAA Men's Records Book, compiled by Gary Johnson and Sean Straziscar; edited by Marty Benson; NCAA Books; Indianapolis.

2000 NCAA Women's Records Book, compiled by Richard M. Campbell and Jenifer L. Scheibler; edited by Vanessa L. Abell; NCAA Books; Indianapolis.

NCAA Online, produced by National Collegiate Athletic Association, http://www.ncaa.org

Plus many 2004-2005 NCAA Division I conference guides from America East to the WAC.

Pro Basketball

The Official NBA Basketball Encyclopedia (Third Edition), edited by Jan Hubbard; Doubleday (2000); New York.

2002-03 Sporting News Official NBA Guide; edited by Craig Carter and Rob Reheuser; The Sporting News Publishing Co.; St. Louis.

2002-03 Sporting News Official NBA Register, edited by David Walton, John Gardella; The Sporting News Publishing Co.; St. Louis.

NBA Online, produced by NBA Media Ventures, LLC, ESPN Internet Ventures, http://www.nba.com

Bowling

1995 Bowlers Journal Annual & Almanac; Luby Publishing; Chicago.

2001 PWBA Guide, Professional Women's Bowling Association; Rockford, Ill.

2002-03 PBA Tour Media Guide; Professional Bowlers Association; Seattle, Wash.

PBA Online, produced by the Pro Bowlers Association, http://www.pba.com

Boxing

The Boxing Record Book (1996 Edition), edited by Phill Marder; Fight Fax Inc.; Sicklerville, N.J.

The Ring 1985 Record Book & Boxing Encyclopedia, edited by Herbert G. Goldman; The Ring Publishing Corp.; New York.

The Ring: Boxing, The 20th Century, Steven Farhood, editor-in-chief; BDD Illustrated Books (1993); New York.

College Sports

1994-95 National Collegiate Championships, edited by Ted Breidenthal; NCAA Books; Overland Park, Kan.

1999-2000 National Directory of College Athletics, edited by Kevin Cleary; Collegiate Directories, Inc.; Cleveland.

NCAA Online, produced by National Collegiate Athletic Association, http://www.ncaa.org

NAIA.org, produced by National Association of Intercollegiate Athletics, http://www.naia.org

College Football

Football: A College History, by Tom Perrin; McFarland & Company, Inc. (1987); Jefferson, N.C.

Football: Facts & Figures, by Dr. L.H. Baker; Farrar & Rinehart, Inc. (1945); New York.

Great College Football Coaches of the Twenties and Thirties, by Tim Cohane; Arlington House (1973); New Rochelle, N.Y.

2000 NCAA College Football Records Book, compiled by Richard M. Campbell, John Painter and Sean Straziscar; edited by Scott Deitch; NCAA Books; Indianapolis.

Saturday Afternoon, by Richard Whittingham; Workman Publishing Co., Inc. (1985); New York.

Saturday's America, by Dan Jenkins; Sports Illustrated Books; Little, Brown & Company (1970); Boston.

Tournament of Roses, The First 100 Years, by Joe Hendrickson; Knapp Press (1989); Los Angeles.

NCAA Online, produced by National Collegiate Athletic Association, http://www.ncaa.org

Plus numerous college football team and conference guides, especially the 2001 guides compiled by the Atlantic Coast Conference, Big Ten, Big 12 and Southeastern Conference.

Pro Football

2002 Canadian Football League Guide, compiled by the CFL Communications Dept.; Toronto.

The Football Encyclopedia (The Complete History of NFL Football from 1892 to the Present), compiled by David Neft and Richard Cohen; St. Martin's Press (1994); New York.

The Official NFL Encyclopedia, by Beau Riffenburgh; New American Library (1986); New York.

Official NFL 1999 Record and Fact Book, compiled by the NFL Communications Dept. and Seymour Siwoff, Elias Sports Bureau; edited by Chris McCloskey and Matt Marini; produced by NFL Properties, Inc.; Los Angeles.

The Scrapbook History of Pro Football, by Richard Cohen, Jordan Deutsch, Roland Johnson and David Neft; Bobbs-Merrill Company, Inc. (1976); Indianapolis/New York.

2003 Sporting News Football Guide, edited by Craig Carter, Terry Shea and Christen Sager; The Sporting News Publishing Co.; St. Louis.

2003 Sporting News Football Register, edited Brendan Roberts; The Sporting News Publishing Co.; St. Louis.

1995 Sporting News Super Bowl Book, edited by Tom Dienhart, Joe Hoppel and Dave Sloan; The Sporting News Publishing Co.; St. Louis.

Total Football II, edited by Bob Carroll, Michael Gershman, David Neft and John Thorn; HarperCollins; New York.

NFL Online, produced by NFL Enterprises http://www.nfl.com

CFL Online, produced by SLAM! Sports, http://www.cfl.ca

Golf

The Encyclopedia of Golf (Revised Edition), compiled by Nevin H. Gibson; A.S. Barnes and Company (1964); New York.

Guinness Golf Records: Facts and Champions, by Donald Steel; Guinness Superlatives Ltd. (1987); Middlesex, England.

The History of the PGA Tour, by Al Barkow; Doubleday (1989); New York.

The Illustrated History of Women's Golf, by Rhonda Glenn, Taylor Publishing Co. (1991); Dallas.

2003 LPGA Player Guide, produced by LPGA Communications Dept.; Ladies Professional Golf Assn. Tour; Daytona Beach, Fla.

2003 PGA Tour Guide, written and edited by Chuck Adams, James Cramer, Nelson Luis and Lee Patterson; Professional Golfers Assn. Tour; Ponte Vedra, Fla.

Official Guide of the PGA Championships; Triumph Books (1994); Chicago.

The PGA World Golf Hall of Fame Book, by Gerald Astor, Prentice Hall Press (1991); New York.

2003 Champions Tour Guide, written and edited by Dave Senko, Phil Stambaugh and Joan Von Thron-Alexander; Professional Golfers Assn. Tour; Ponte Vedra, Fla.

Pro-Golf 2003, PGA European Tour Media Guide, Virginia Water, Surrey, England.

The Random House International Encyclopedia of Golf, by Malcolm Campbell; Random House (1991); New York.

USGA Record Books (1895-1959, 1960-80 and 1981-90); U.S. Golf Association; Far Hills, N.J.

LPGA Online, produced by the LPGA and Ignite Sports Media LLC., http://www.lpga.com

PGA Online, produced by the PGA of America, http://www.pgaonline.com

PGATour Online, produced by PGA Tour Inc., http://www.pgatour.com

Hockey

Canada Cup '87: The Official History, No.1 Publications Ltd.; Toronto.

The Complete Encyclopedia of Hockey; edited by Zander Hollander; Visible Ink Press (1993); Detroit.

The Hockey Encyclopedia, by Stan Fischler and Shirley Walton Fischler; research editor, Bob Duff; Macmillan Publishing Co. (1983); New York.

Hockey Hall of Fame (The Official History of the Game and Its Greatest Stars), by Dan Diamond and Joseph Romain; Doubleday (1988); New York.

The National Hockey League, by Edward F. Dolan Jr.; W H Smith Publishers Inc. (1986); New York.

The Official National Hockey League 75th Anniversary Commemorative Book, edited by Dan Diamond; McClelland & Stewart, Inc. (1991); Toronto.

2003 Official NHL Guide & Record Book, compiled by the NHL Public Relations Dept.; New York/Montreal/Toronto.

2003 Sporting News Hockey Guide, edited by Craig Carter; The Sporting News Publishing Co.; St. Louis.

2003 Sporting News Hockey Register, edited by David Walton; The Sporting News Publishing Co.; St. Louis.

The Stanley Cup, by Joseph Romain and James Duplacey; Gallery Books (1989); New York.

The Trail of the Stanley Cup (Volumes I-III), by Charles L. Coleman; Progressive Publications Inc. (1969); Sherbrooke, Quebec.

Total Hockey (Second Edition), edited by Dan Diamond, et al.; Total Sports Publishing; Kingston, N.Y.

NHL Online, produced by the NHL Interactive Cyber Enterprises, http://www.nhl.com

Horse Racing

1999 NTRA Media Guide, compiled by the National Thoroughbred Racing Association; New York.

1997 American Racing Manual, compiled by the Daily Racing Form; Hightstown, N.J.

1997 Breeders' Cup Statistics; Breeders' Cup Limited; Lexington, Ky.

1996 Directory and Record Book, Thoroughbred Racing Associations of North America Inc.; Elkton, Md.

2001 Trotting and Pacing Guide, compiled and edited by John Pawlak; United States Trotting Association; Columbus, Ohio.

USTA Online, produced by the USTA, http://www.ustrotting.com

NTRA Online, hosted by Equibase Company LLC, http://www.ntra.com

Equibase.com, hosted by Equibase Company LLC, http://www.equibase.com

International Sports

Athletics: A History of Modern Track and Field (1860-1990, Men and Women), by Roberto Quercetani; Vallardi & Associati (1990); Milan, Italy.

1999 International Track & Field Annual, Association of Track & Field Statisticians; edited by Peter Matthews; SportsBooks Ltd.; Surrey, England.

Track & Field News' Little Blue Book; Metric conversion tables; From the editors of Track & Field News (1989); Los Altos, Calif.

US Ski Team Online, produced by US Ski Team and SportsLine USA, http://www.usskiteam.com

Miscellaneous

The America's Cup 1851-1987 (Sailing for Supremacy), by Gary Lester and Richard Sleeman; Lester-Townsend Publishing (1986); Sydney, Australia.

The Encyclopedia of Sports (Fifth Revised Edition), by Frank G. Menke; revisions by Suzanne Treat; A.S. Barnes and Co., Inc. (1975); Cranbury, N.J.

ESPN SportsCentury, edited by Michael MacCambridge; Hyperion (1999); New York.

The Great American Sports Book, by George Gipe; Doubleday & Company, Inc. (1978); Garden City, N.Y.

1999 Official PRCA Media Guide, edited by Steve Fleming; Professional Rodeo Cowboys Association; Colorado Springs.

The Sail Magazine Book of Sailing, by Peter Johnson; Alfred A. Knopf (1989); New York.

Ten Years of the Ironman, Triathlete magazine; October, 1988; Santa Monica, Calif.

The Ultimate Book of Sports Lists, by Mike Meserole; DK Publishing (1999); New York.

Iditarod Online, produced by the Iditarod Trail Committee and GCI, http://www.iditarod.com

PRCA Online, produced by the Pro Rodeo Cowboys Association, http://www.prorodeo.com

Olympics

All That Glitters Is Not Gold (An Irreverent Look at the Olympic Games); by William O. Johnson, Jr.; G.P. Putnam's Sons (1972); New York.

Barcelona/Albertville 1992; edited by Lisa H. Albertson; for U.S. Olympic Committee by Commemorative Publications; Salt Lake City.

Chamonix to Lillehammer (The Glory of the Olympic Winter Games); edited by Lisa H. Albertson; for U.S. Olympic Committee by Commemorative Publication (1994); Salt Lake City.

The Complete Book of the Olympics (1992 Edition); by David Wallechinsky; Little, Brown and Co.; Boston.

The Games Must Go On (Avery Brundage and the Olympic Movement), by Allen Guttmann; Columbia University Press (1984); New York.

The Golden Book of the Olympic Games, edited by Erich Kamper and Bill Mallon; Vallardi & Associati (1992); Milan, Italy.

Hitler's Games (The 1936 Olympics), by Duff Hart-Davis; Harper & Row (1986); New York/London.

An Illustrated History of the Olympics (Third Edition); by Dick Schaap; Alfred A. Knopf (1975); New York.

The Nazi Olympics, by Richard D. Mandell; Souvenir Press (1972); London.

The Official USOC Book of the 1984 Olympic Games (1984), by Dick Schaap; Random House/ABC Sports; New York.

The Olympics: A History of the Games, by William Oscar Johnson; Oxmoor House (1992); Birmingham, Ala.

Pursuit of Excellence (The Olympic Story), by The Associated Press and Grolier; Grolier Enterprises Inc. (1979); Danbury, Conn.

The Story of the Olympic Games (776 B.C. to 1948 A.D.), by John Kieran and Arthur Daley; J.B. Lippincott Company (1948); Philadelphia/New York.

United States Olympic Books (Seven Editions): 1936 and 1948-88; U.S. Olympic Association; New York.

The USA and the Olympic Movement, produced by the USOC Information Dept.; edited by Gayle Plant; U.S. Olympic Committee (1988); Colorado Springs.

Soccer

The American Encyclopedia of Soccer, edited by Zander Hollander; Everest House Publishers (1980); New York.

The European Football Yearbook (1994-95 Edition), edited by Mike Hammond; Sports Projects Ltd; West Midlands, England.

The Guinness Book of Soccer Facts & Feats, by Jack Rollin; Guinness Superlatives Ltd. (1978); Middlesex, England.

History of Soccer's World Cup, by Michael Archer; Chartwell Books, Inc. (1978); Secaucus, N.J.

The Simplest Game, by Paul Gardner; Collier Books (1994); New York.

The Story of the World Cup, by Brian Glanville; Faber and Faber Limited (1993); London/Boston.

2001 MLS Official Media Guide, edited by the MLS Communications staff; Los Angeles.

1991-92 MSL Official Guide, Major (Indoor) Soccer League; Overland Park, Kan.

FIFA Online, produced by FIFA, http://www.fifa.com

MLSnet, produced by Major League Soccer, http://mlsnet.com

Tennis

Bud Collins' Modern Encyclopedia of Tennis, edited by Bud Collins and Zander Hollander; Visible Ink Press (1994); Detroit.

The Illustrated Encyclopedia of World Tennis, by John Haylett and Richard Evans; Exeter Books (1989); New York.

Official Encyclopedia of Tennis, edited by the staff of the U.S. Lawn Tennis Assn.; Harper & Row (1972); New York.

2004 ATP Tour Player Guide, edited by Greg Sharko; Association of Tennis Professionals Tour Publications; Ponte Vedra Beach, Fla.

2004 WTA Tour Media Guide, compiled by Sanex WTA Public Relations staff; St. Petersburg, Fla.

ATP TourOnline, produced by ATP Tour, Inc., http://www.atptour.com

WTA Tour Online, produced by the WTA Tour, http://www.wtatour.com

Who's Who

The Guinness International Who's Who of Sport, edited by Peter Mathews, Ian Buchanan and Bill Mallon; Guinness Publishing (1993); Middlesex, England.

101 Greatest Athletes of the Century, by Will Grimsley and the Associated Press Sports Staff; Bonanza Books (1987); Crown Publishers, Inc.; New York.

The New York Times Book of Sports Legends, edited by Joseph Vecchione; Simon & Schuster (1991); New York.

Superstars, by Frank Litsky; Vineyard Books, Inc. (1975); Secaucus, N.J.

A Who's Who of Sports Champions (Their Stories and Records), by Ralph Hickok, Houghton Mifflin Co. (1995); Boston.

Other Reference Books/Sites

Facts & Dates of American Sports, by Gorton Carruth & Eugene Ehrlich; Harper & Row, Publishers, Inc. (1988); New York.

Sports Market Place 1997 (January Edition), edited by Kevin J. Myers; Franklin Quest Sports; Phoenix, Ariz.

The World Book Encyclopedia (1988 Edition); World Book, Inc.; Chicago.

The World Book Yearbook (Annual Supplements, 1954-95); World Book, Inc.; Chicago.

ESPN.com, produced by ESPN Internet Ventures., http://espn.com

CBS SportsLine, produced by CBS and SportsLine USA, http://cbs.sportsline.com

BALLPARKS & ARENAS

BUSINESS

INTER- NATIONAL SPORTS

OLYMPIC GAMES

SOCCER

ACTION SPORTS

HORSE RACING

TENNIS

GOLF

MOTOR SPORTS

BOXING

MISC.

Insider gets you access to predictive analysis, exclusive fantasy content, and RealTime scores. Subscribe now and receive a 30-day free trial.

VISIT ESPN.COM

SEARCH: INSIDERAL

FANTASY CONTENT
Analysis from leading experts

ESPN ANALYSTS
Expert insight from Mel Kiper Jr., Len Pasquarelli, Dick Vitale, and others

RUMORS
Find out the scoop on trades before they happen

REALTIME SCORING
Automatic updates, no refreshing

ESPN LOCAL
News about your favorite teams every day, all in one place

insider | One Step Ahead of the Game